Introduction

Chambers Biographical Dictionary has long been a valued reference book on the shelves of all good libraries. In this two-volume paperback form it is now readily available to a much wider reading public.

It sets out in an eminently readable way the main facts about people of importance through the ages. To do this within the limits of a concise reference book is no easy task, but we have tried to include the prominent men and women of all centuries, all nationalities and all fields of interest.

The readability of the book is due to the fact that the information is not presented as mere catalogues of facts. It has been editorial policy to clothe these facts with human interest and critical observation—and to provide in most cases useful suggestions for further reading.

It is obviously helpful if the basic details for each entry are capable of being read at a glance. We have therefore placed at the beginning of each article the names, with pronunciation where necessary, and dates of birth and death, designation and birthplace.

Such a book as this can never be completely up to date but this latest revision takes account of major events to the end of 1973. Some additions, which could not be incorporated in the main text, are included in the Supplement at the beginning of Volume One.

A guide to the pronunciation symbols is given on page vi and a subject index for easy reference at the end of Volume Two.

Key to Pronunciation

Vowel Sounds

ay	=	a in fate	*oo*	=	oo in moon
a	=	a in lad	*u*	=	u in but
ah	=	a in father	*ü*	=	Ger. ü, Fr. u, etc. (nearly *ee*)
e	=	e in led	*œ*	=	Ger. ö, Fr. œu, etc. (nearly as *u* in fur)
ee	=	e in we			
ė	=	e in other	Diphthongs		
i	=	i in lid	*yoo*	=	u in tube
ī	=	i in mine	*aw*	=	aw in saw
o	=	o in lot	*ow*	=	ow in cow
ō	=	o in vote	*oy*	=	oy in boy

The *tilde* sign (˜) over a vowel denotes that it is nasalized, i.e. pronounced partly through the nose. The nasalized -ai and e after i is represented by *ĩ*, e.g., Pétain. Bastien-Lepage (*pay-tĩ, bas-tyĩ-lė-pazh*).

Consonant Sounds

The consonants b, d, f, h, j, k, l, m, n, p, r, t, v, w, y (not used as vowel), z, have in English unambiguous values, and are used for these values.

g	=	g in get	*y'*	=	final y sound as in Fr. Ligne (*leen'y'*) or y sound after palatalized consonants, as in Russ. Lifar (*li-far'y'*)
s	=	s in set			
ch	=	ch in church			
sh	=	sh in shore	*r'*	=	unvoiced consonant as in Fr. Delambre (*dė-lã'br'*)
zh	=	z in azure			
th	=	th in thin			
TH	=	th in this			
KH	=	ch in Scots loch			

Accentuation

The sign ' is used to denote that the preceding syllable is stressed. Stress is not generally indicated in French names, where the correct effect is better obtained by slightly raising the pitch of the voice on the final syllable.

JEWETT, Sara Orne (1849–1909), American novelist, born at South Berwick, Maine, wrote *The Country of the Pointed Firs* (1896) and other novels and stories based on the provincial life of her state. See Life by F. O. Matthiessen (1929).

JEWSBURY, Geraldine Endsor (1812–80), English novelist, was born at Measham, Derbyshire, and from 1854 lived at Chelsea, to be near the Carlyles. See her *Letters to Mrs Carlyle*, edited by Mrs Ireland (1892).—Her sister, **Maria Jane** (1800–33), wrote poetry.

JEX-BLAKE, Sophia (1840–1912), English pioneer of medical education for women, sister of **Thomas William** (1832–1915), headmaster of Rugby and dean of Wells, was born at Hastings, studied at Queen's College for Women, London, and became a tutor in mathematics there (1859–61). From 1865 she studied medicine in New York under Elizabeth Blackwell (q.v.), but since English medical schools were closed to women, could not continue her studies on return. She fought her way into Edinburgh University, however, where with five other women she was allowed to matriculate in 1869, but the university authorities reversed their decision in 1873. She waged a public campaign in London, opened the London School of Medicine for Women in 1874 and in 1876 won her campaign when medical examiners were permitted by law to examine women students. In 1886 she founded a medical school in Edinburgh, where from 1894 women were finally allowed to graduate in medicine. See Life by M. Todd (1918).

JEZREEL, James Jershom, the name assumed by an ex-private, **James White** (1840–85), founder of the Southcottian subsect of 'Jezreelites', their headquarters Gillingham near Chatham, who believed that Christ redeemed by his death only souls and that the body can only be saved by the law.

JHERING, Rudolf von, *yayr'ing* (1818–92), German jurist who founded a school of jurisprudence based on teleological principles rather than precedent, was born at Aurich, and died at Göttingen. See Life by Merkel (Jena 1893).

JIMÉNEZ, *hee-may'neth,* **(1) Francisco.** See XIMENES.

(2) **Juan Ramón** (1881–1958) Spanish lyric poet, born at Moguer, Huelva, which he made famous by his delightful story of the young poet and his donkey, *Platero y Yo* (1914; trans. 1956), one of the classics of modern Spanish literature, abandoned his law studies and settled in Madrid. His early poetry, impressionistic and rich in evocative imagery and sound, echoed that of Verlaine. *Almas de Violeta* (1901), *Arias Tristes* (1903) and *Jardines Lefanos* (1905) belong to this period. With *El Silencio de Oro* (1922) there came a mood of optimism and a zest for experimentation with styles and rhythms. In 1936 he left Spain because of the Civil War and settled in Florida. In his last period he emerges as a major poet, treating the major themes of life in novel sounds, illusions and styles in a subtly spun *vers libre.* In 1956, the year he was awarded the Nobel prize, a pilgrimage of poets riding on donkeys went to a small village near Moguer as a gesture of homage. See the anthology of his poems, trans. J. B. Trend (1957).

JINNAH, Mohammed Ali (1876–1948), Pakistani statesman, born December 25 in Karachi, studied at Bombay and Lincoln's Inn, London, and was called to the bar in 1897. He obtained a large practice in Bombay, in 1910 was elected to the Viceroy's Legislative Council and, already a member of the Indian National Congress, in 1913 joined the Indian Muslim League and as its president brought about peaceful coexistence between it and the Congress party through the 'Lucknow Pact' (1916). Although he supported the efforts of Congress to boycott the Simon Commission (1928), he opposed Gandhi's civil disobedience policy and, resigning from the Congress party, which he believed to be exclusively fostering Hindu interests, continued to advocate his 'fourteen points' safeguarding Moslem minorities at the London Round Table Conference (1931). By 1940 he was strongly advocating separate statehood for the Moslems and he stubbornly resisted all British efforts, such as the Cripps mission (1942) and Gandhi's statesmanlike overtures (1944), to save Indian unity. Thus on August 15, 1947, the Dominion of Pakistan came into existence and Jinnah, *Quaid-i-Azam* 'Great Leader', became its first governor-general and had to contend with the consequences of the new political division, the refugee problem, the communal riots in Punjab and the fighting in Kashmir. See Life by H. Bolitho (1954).

JOACHIM, Joseph, *yō'aKH-im* (1831–1907), Hungarian violinist and composer, born at Kittsee near Pressburg, first appeared in London in 1844. In 1869 he became director of the Berlin Conservatorium, composed three violin concertos and overtures to *Hamlet* and *Henry IV.* See Life by Moser (1910) and his *Letters.*

JOACHIM OF FLORIS, *jō'ē-kim* (*c.* 1135–1202), Italian mystic, born in Calabria, became in 1177 abbot of the Cistercian monastery of Corazzo and later founded a stricter order, Ordo Florensis, at San Giovanni in Fiore, which was absorbed by the Cistercians in 1505. His mystical interpretation of history, based on historical parallels or 'concordances' between the history of the Jewish people and that of the church, was grouped into three ages, each corresponding to a member of the Trinity, the last, that of the Spirit, which was to usher in perfect liberty to commence in 1260. This mystical historicism was widely accepted although condemned by the Lateran council in 1215, but lost influence, unlike the modern historicisms of Hegel and Marx, when its prophecies did not come to pass. See studies by J. Huck (1938), H. Grundmann (1950) and L. Tondelli, *Il Libro delle figure* (1940).

JOAD, Cyril Edwin Mitchinson (1891–1953), English controversialist and popularizer of philosophy, educated at Blundell's School and Balliol College, Oxford, was a civil servant from 1914 to 1930, when he became reader and head of the philosophy department at Birkbeck College, London. *Guide to Philosophy* (1936) and *Guide to the Philo-*

sophy of Morals and Politics (1938) are possibly the best of his 47 highly personal books, written in the manner of Shavian prefaces, revealing the great talent for exposition of this Bohemian, Fabian reformer, 'anti-ugly' lover of the countryside, pacifist, anti-Victorian and until his last work, *Recovery of Belief* (1952), fashionable atheist. He upset academic circles by using the title of professor in journalism, by going up a lone alley resurrecting a version of philosophical realism in *Matter, Life and Value* (1929) and by throwing only quasi-philosophical stones at Professor Ayer in his *Critique of Logical Positivism* (1950). But his one concession to linguistic philosophy was his highly successful B.B.C. Brains Trust gimmick, 'It all depends what you mean by . . .' which prompted Max Beerbohm's reference to 'the agile, mellifluous and quodlibetarian Joad'. See his *The Testament of Joad* (1937) and *The Book of Joad* (1942).

JOAN. See EDWARD THE BLACK PRINCE.

JOAN, or Joanna, of Navarre (*c.* 1370–1437), married in 1386 the Duke of Brittany, and in 1403 Henry IV of England.

JOAN OF ARC, St, Fr. Jeanne d'Arc (*c.* 1412–1431), French patriot and martyr, one of the most remarkable women of all time, was born the daughter of well-off peasants at Domrémy, a hamlet on the borders of Lorraine and Champagne, January 6. The English over-ran the area in 1421 and in 1424 withdrew. Joan received no formal education but was richly endowed with an argumentative nature and shrewd common sense. At the age of thirteen she thought she heard the voices of St Michael, St Catherine and St Margaret bidding her rescue the Paris region from English domination. She presented herself before the local commander, Robert de Baudricourt, and persuaded him, after he had had her exorcised, to take her across English-occupied territory to the dauphin at Chinon, which they reached March 6, 1429. She, according to legend, was called into a gathering of courtiers, among them the dauphin in disguise, and her success in identifying him at once was interpreted as divine confirmation of his previously doubted legitimacy and claims to the throne. She was equally successful in an ecclesiastical examination to which she was subjected at Poitiers and was consequently allowed to join the army assembled at Blois for the relief of Orleans. Clad in a suit of white armour and flying her own standard, she entered Orleans with an advance guard on April 29 and by May 8 forced the English to raise the siege and retire in June from the principal strongholds on the Loire. To put further heart into the French resistance, she took the dauphin with an army of 12,000 through English-held territory to be crowned Charles VII in Rheims cathedral on July 17, 1429. She then found it extremely difficult to persuade him to undertake further military exploits, especially the relief of Paris. At last she set out on her own to relieve Compiègne from the Burgundians, was captured in a sortie and sold to the English by John of Luxembourg for 10,000 crowns. She was put on trial (February 21–May 17 1431) for heresy and sorcery by an ecclesiastical court of the Inquisition, presided over by Pierre Cauchon, Bishop of Beauvais. Considering the political and religious implications, the trial was fair if judged by such modern equivalents as the Russian purge trials of the '30s and McCarthy's un-American activities investigations. Most of the available facts concerning Joan's life are those preserved in the records of the trial. She was found guilty, taken out to the churchyard of St Ouen on May 24 to be burnt, but at the last moment broke down and made a wild recantation. This she later abjured and suffered her martyrdom at the stake in the market-place of Rouen on May 30, faithful to her 'voices'. In 1456, in order to strengthen the validity of Charles VII's coronation, the trial was declared irregular. In 1904 she was designated Venerable, declared Blessed in 1908 and finally canonized in 1920. She was neither beautiful nor cultivated. Belief in her divine mission made her flout military advice—in the end disastrously, but she rallied her countrymen, halted the English ascendancy in France for ever and was one of the first in history to die for a Christian-inspired concept of nationalism. See Life by Anatole France (trans. 1909) and studies by A. Lang (1908), J. M. Robertson (1926), account of the trial by W. P. Barrett (1931) and preface and plays by Bernard Shaw (1924) and E. Garnett (1931).

JOAN, pope, a fictitious personage long believed to have been, as John VII, pope (855–58). One legend has it that she was born at Mainz, the daughter of English parents, and so well educated by her lover that she in due time became cardinal and pope. Her reign was said to have ended abruptly when she died on giving birth to a child during a papal procession between St Peter's and the Lateran, a route since avoided on such occasions.

JOASH. See ATHALIAH.

JOB. The Book of Job was regarded by the Jews as strictly historical. In the Christian Church the view gradually obtained currency either that it contained history poetically treated, or was simply a religious poem. Elihu's speeches (xxxii–xxxvii) are believed to be a later insertion. Job is assumed to have lived in the Patriarchal period, but the internal evidence points to the exile as the date of the book. See studies by C. J. Ball (1922) and W. B. Stevenson (1947).

JOCELIN DE BRAKELOND (*c.* 1155–1215), a Benedictine monk at Bury St Edmunds, wrote a domestic chronicle of his abbey from 1173 to 1202. The *Chronica* inspired Carlyle's *Past and Present.*

JODELLE, Étienne, *zhō-del* (1532–73), French poet and dramatist, the only Parisian member of the *Pléiade*, wrote the first French tragedy *Cléopatre captive* (1552), also two comedies. See H. Chamard, *Histoire de la Pléiade* (1940).

JODL, Alfred, *yō'dl'* (1890–1946), German soldier, nephew of the philosopher Friedrich Jodl (1849–1914), born at Aachen, was an artillery subaltern in World War I and rose to the rank of General of Artillery in 1940.

For the remainder of World War II he was the planning genius of the German High Command and Hitler's chief adviser. He condemned the anti-Hitler plot (1944), counselled terror bombing of English cities and signed orders to shoot commandos and prisoners of war. From January 1945 he was Chief of the Operations Staff. He was found guilty of war crimes on all four counts at Nuremberg (1946) and executed. A Munich denazification court posthumously exonerated him on charges of being a 'major offender' in 1953.

JOFFRE, Joseph Jacques Césaire, *zhof'r'* (1852–1931), French general, was born at Rivesaltes, entered the army in 1870, and rose to be French chief of staff (1914) and commander-in-chief (1915). Silent, patient, mathematical, he carried out a policy of attrition or 'nibbling' against the German invaders of France. He was promoted marshal of France in 1916, in 1917 became president of the Allied War Council, in 1918 was elected to the Académie française, and awarded the O.M. in 1919. See study by C. Dawburn (1916) and Life by G. Hanotaux and J. G. A. Fabry (1921).

JOHANNES SECUNDUS, Jan Everts, or **Everaerts** (1511–36), Latin poet, born at The Hague, studied law at Bourges, and was secretary to the archbishop of Toledo, the bishop of Utrecht, and the Emperor Charles V. His famous work is *Basia.*

JOHANNES VON SAAZ (*c.* 1350–1415), German author, born at Schüttwa, wrote *Der Ackermann aus Böhmen* (*c.* 1400), a classic piece of German prose in which the author arraigns Death for the loss of his wife, Margarete, before the heavenly Judge.

JOHANNSEN, Wilhelm Ludwig (1857–1927), Danish botanist and geneticist, pioneered experimental genetics by his experiments with Princess beans which led to the pure line theory.

JOHN, St, one of the twelve apostles, son of Zebedee and younger brother of James, was a Galilean fisherman, probably a native of Bethsaida. Some have thought that his mother was Salome, who may have been the sister of the mother of Jesus. Early tradition represents him as having been slain by the Jews, like his brother James. But from the time of Justin (*c.* 150) he has been identified with the author of the Apocalypse, and from that of Irenaeus (*c.* 175) he has been represented as spending his closing years at Ephesus, and dying there at an advanced age, after having written the Apocalypse, the Gospel and the three Epistles which bear his name. There are various theories of the authorship of these works. There are expository works on the Johannine writings by J. E. Carpenter (1927), W. F. Howard (1943 and 1945) and C. H. Dodd (1946).

JOHN THE BAPTIST, St (fl. *c.* 27), the forerunner of Christ, was the son of the priest Zacharias and Elizabeth, the cousin of Mary, the mother of Jesus. He baptized and preached repentance and forgiveness of sins, denounced Herod Antipas for taking Herodias, his brother Philip's wife, and was imprisoned and executed at the request of Salome, daughter of Herodias. See Life by J. Steinmann tr. M. Boyes (1958).

JOHN OF BEVERLEY, St (d. 721), born at Cherry Burton near Beverley, in 687 became Bishop of Hexham, in 705 of York, and died at Beverley.

JOHN, St, Chrysostom. See CHRYSOSTOM.

JOHN OF THE CROSS, St (1542–91), founder with St Teresa of the Discalced Carmelites, was born Juan de Yepes y Álvarez at Fontiveros, Ávila, accompanied St Teresa to Valladolid, where he lived an extremely ascetic life in a hovel until she appointed him to a convent in Ávila, where he was arrested (1577), imprisoned at Toledo, escaped (1578) and lived in illness at the monastery of Úbeda. He was canonized in 1726. See his Works, tr. Allison Peers (1934), who also wrote a Life (1954), study by McNabb (1955) and Life by Crisogóno de Jesus, tr. K. Pond (1959).

JOHN OF DAMASCUS, St, or **Chrysorrhoas** (*c.* 676–*c.* 754), Greek theologian and hymn writer of the Eastern Church, was born at Damascus, and carefully educated by the learned Italian monk Cosmas. He replied to the iconoclastic measures of Leo the Isaurian with two addresses in which he vigorously defended image worship. His later years were spent in a monastery near Jerusalem. There, ordained a priest, he wrote his hymns, an encyclopaedia of Christian theology, treatises against superstitions, Jacobite and Monophysite heretics, homilies, and *Barlaam and Joasaph,* now known to be a disguised version of the life of Buddha. His works are included in Migne's *Patrologia* (1864). See Neale, *Hymns of the Eastern Church* (1870) and Lives by J. Langen (1879), J. H. Lupton (1882), E. Gilson, *La Philosophie au moyen âge* (1944).

JOHN OF NEPOMUK, St (*c.* 1330–93), patron saint of Bohemia, was born at Pomuk near Pilsen, studied at Prague, and became confessor to Sophia, wife of Wenceslaus IV. For refusing to betray to this monarch the confession of the queen John was put to the torture, then flung into the Moldau. In 1729 he was canonized. By some historians two personages of the same name are enumerated —one, the martyr of the confessional; the other, a victim to the simoniacal tyranny of Wenceslaus. See Wratislaw's *Life of St John Nepomucen* (1873), and works by A. L. Frind (Prague rev. ed. 1929), J. Weisskopf (Vienna 1931).

JOHN, the name of twenty-one popes and two antipopes XVI or XVII (997–8) and XXIII. the former included in the papal numbering, which erroneously contained a fictitious John XV who was thought to have ruled for a few weeks immediately prior to the true John XV (985–96). The following are noteworthy:

John XII, pope (955–64), the grandson of Marozia, was elected pope by the dominant party when only eighteen. The Emperor Otto in 963 in a synod of the clergy caused sentence of deposition for scandalous life to be pronounced against him, and Leo VIII to be elected in his stead. John drove out Leo next year; but he died prematurely in debauchery.

John XXII, pope (1316–34), one of the most celebrated of the popes of Avignon, was born at Cahors in 1244, and elected in 1316. Attempting to carry out the policy of Gregory VII, he interposed his authority in the contest for the imperial crown between Louis of Bavaria and Frederick of Austria, supporting the latter and excommunicating his rival. A long contest ensued both in Germany and Italy, where the Guelph or papal party was represented by Robert, king of Naples, and the Ghibelline by Frederick of Sicily. The latter was also excommunicated by John; but in 1327 Louis entered Italy, and, crowned at Milan with the crown of Lombardy, advanced upon Rome, expelled the papal legate, and was crowned emperor by two Lombard bishops. He now caused the pope to be deposed on a charge of heresy and breach of fealty, When Louis returned to Germany, Guelphic predominance at Rome was restored; but John died at Avignon in 1334, having accumulated a vast treasure.

John XXIII, antipope (1410–15), a Neapolitan noble, born *c.* 1370, a cardinal who was recognized throughout most of Europe as the successor of Alexander V, having been elected by the Alexandrian faction in 1410. He convened the council of Constance, but was deposed in 1415 for his excesses, yet re-appointed cardinal.

John XXIII, pope (1958–63), born Angelo Giuseppe Roncalli, the son of a peasant at Sotto il Monte near Bergamo in northern Italy, in 1881. Ordained in 1904, he served as sergeant in the medical corps and as chaplain in World War I, and subsequently as apostolic delegate to Bulgaria, Turkey and Greece. In 1944 he became the first Papal Nuncio to liberated France and championed the controversial system of worker-priests. Patriarch of Venice in 1953, he was elected pope in October 1958 on the twelfth ballot. He convened the 21st oecumenical council in order to seek unity between the various Christian sects and broke with tradition by leaving the Vatican for short visits to hospitals and prisons in Rome. See Lives by A. Lazzarini (trans. 1959) and Leone (1963).

JOHN, surnamed Lackland (1167–1216), king of England, youngest son of Henry II, was born at Oxford, December 24. His father sent him to Ireland as governor in 1185, but his misconduct soon compelled his recall. He attempted to seize the crown during King Richard's captivity in Austria; but he was pardoned and nominated his successor by his brother on his deathbed. John was crowned at Westminster, May 27, 1199, although Arthur (q.v.), son of John's elder brother Geoffrey, was the rightful heir. On the Continent Arthur was acknowledged and his claims were supported by Philip of France, whom, however, in May 1200 John succeeded in buying off. In the same year he obtained a divorce from his cousin Hawisa of Gloucester, and married Isabel of Angoulême. In the war in France Arthur was taken prisoner, and before Easter 1203 was murdered by John's orders. Philip at once marched against John, and captured city after city, until by March 1204 only a portion of Aquitaine was left to John. In 1205 John entered on his quarrel with the church, the occasion being a disputed election to the archbishopric of Canterbury. In 1207 Innocent III consecrated Stephen Langton, an English cardinal, and John declined to receive him. In 1208 the kingdom was placed under an interdict. John retaliated by confiscating the property of the clergy who obeyed the interdict, and banished the bishops. He compelled the Scots king, William the Lion, who had joined his enemies, to do him homage (1209), put down a rebellion in Ireland (1210), and subdued Llewellyn, the independent prince of Wales (1212). Meanwhile he had been excommunicated (1209), and, in 1212, the pope issued a bull deposing him, Philip being charged with the execution of the sentence. John, finding his position untenable, was compelled to make abject submission to Rome, agreeing (May 1213) to hold his kingdom as a fief of the papacy, and to pay a thousand marks yearly as tribute. Philip, disappointed, turned his forces against Flanders; but the French fleet was surprised at Damme by the English, 300 vessels being captured, and 100 burned. In 1214 John made a campaign in Poitou, but it turned out ill, and he returned to enter on the struggle with his subjects. A demand by the barons, clergy, and people that John should keep his oath and restore the laws of Henry I was scornfully rejected. Preparations for war began on both sides. The army of the barons assembled at Stamford and marched to London; they met the king at Runnymede, and on June 15, 1215, was signed the Great Charter (Magna Carta), the basis of the English constitution. In August the pope annulled the charter, and the war broke out again. The first successes were all on the side of John, until the barons called over the French dauphin to be their leader. Louis landed in May 1216, and John's fortunes had become desperate, when he died at Newark, October 19. His reign, however, saw improvements in the civil administration, the exchequer and the law courts. Royal charters were granted to towns and English local government introduced into Ireland. See Life by K. Norgate (1902) and study of his reign by Painter (1949).

JOHN II (1319–64), king of France, succeeded his father, Philip VI, in 1350. In 1356 he was taken prisoner by Edward the Black Prince at Poitiers and carried to England. After the treaty of Bretigny (1360) he returned home, leaving his second son, the Duke of Anjou, as a hostage; and when the duke broke his parole, and escaped (1363), John chivalrously returned to London, and died there.

JOHN (1296–1346), the blind king of Bohemia, son of Count Henry III of Luxemburg (afterwards the Emperor Henry VII). Having married (1310) the heiress of Bohemia, he was crowned king in 1311. In the struggle between Austria and Bavaria for the imperial crown he contributed to the Bavarian victory at Mühldorf in 1322. In 1333–35 he was warring in Italy for the Guelph party. In 1334 he married a Bourbon, became an ally of the French king, and fell at Crécy August 26, 1346, and his motto *Ich Dien*, 'I serve', was adopted by the Black Prince, in respect for his father, Edward III, who commanded the English army in the battle. John had been blind since 1337.

JOHN III (1624–96), king of Poland, was the son of James Sobieski, castellan of Cracow. After the defeat of the Poles by the Russians at Pilawiecz, John took up arms. On November 11, 1673, he defeated the Turks at Choczim, and was elected king of Poland, May 21, 1674. He raised the Turkish siege of Vienna in 1683 by a famous victory which, however, did not benefit Poland, but his later undertakings against the Turks were not equally successful. Troubles in Poland also clouded the last years of his reign. See German Life by Battaglia (1946).

JOHN, (1) **Augustus** (1878–1961), British painter, born at Tenby, studied at the Slade (1896–99) with his sister Gwen (see below), and in Paris, and made an early reputation for himself by his etchings (1900–14). Although a considerable draughtsman, John had no special predilection for pure design; Wyndham Lewis had described him as 'a great man of action into whose hands the fairies stuck a brush instead of a sword'. John's favourite themes were gipsies, fishing folk and wild, lovely, yet naturally regal women, as in *Lyric Fantasy* (1913, private). In his portraits of women, including many of his wife Dorelia, he is concerned more with unique items of individual beauty or dignity than with portrayal of character, as for example the beautifully caught posture of the scarlet-gowned cellist *Madame Suggia* (1923, Tate). But character he could portray, as the studies of Shaw (*c.* 1914), Thomas Hardy (1923, both Fitzwilliam, Cambridge) and Dylan Thomas (Cardiff) amply testify. His best purely formal portrait is *Judge Dowdall as Lord Mayor of Liverpool* (1908–09, Melbourne). He also had a Jimsonlike passion for murals. His study for a Canadian War Memorial was never translated into full size reality, but there is the magnificent *Galway* (1916) in the Tate. He was elected R.A. in 1928, resigned in 1938 and was re-elected in 1940. He was awarded the O.M. in 1942. See his autobiography *Chiaroscuro* (1952) and studies by A. Bertram (1923), J. Rothenstein (1944) and *Fifty-Two Drawings*, intro. Lord David Cecil (1957). His sister, **Gwen** (1876–1939), settled at Meudon, France, where, with intimate friendships with Rodin, Rilke and the philosopher Maritain, she became a Catholic and painted striking, sad-faced pictures of nuns, orphan children, cats and her sister-in-law, Dorelia. *Young Woman holding a Black Cat* is in the Tate, London.

(2) **Otto,** *yōn* (1909–), West German ex-security chief and defendant in the most curious postwar treason case, was chief legal adviser to the German civil aviation company *Lufthansa*. In 1944 he played, with his brother Hans, a prominent rôle in the abortive anti-Hitler plot of July 20, after which he made good his escape to Britain via Spain and worked for the British Psychological Warfare Executive. At the end of the war, he joined a London legal firm and appeared as a prosecution witness in the Nuremberg and von Manstein trials. In 1950 he was appointed to the newly formed West German Office for the protection of the constitution. His sensitivity against former Nazi influence in postwar German political life earned him the enmity of Adenauer and Schröder. Attending the annual commemorative ceremony of July 20 in West Berlin in 1954, he mysteriously disappeared and later broadcast for the East German Communists. In 1956 he returned to the West, was arrested, tried, and sentenced to four years' hard labour for treasonable falsification and conspiracy. John's case was that he was drugged by a friend, a wealthy Communist-sympathizing doctor in West Berlin, Wohlgemuth, and driven to the Communist sector where he was held a prisoner and forced to make broadcasts until he managed to escape. Released in 1958, he still protests his innocence. See W. Frischauer, *The Man Who Came Back* (1958).

JOHN OF AUSTRIA (1547–78), Spanish soldier, natural son of the Emperor Charles V and Barbara Blomberg of Ratisbon, was born at Ratisbon. He was early brought to Spain, and after the death of his father was acknowledged by his half-brother Philip II. In 1570 he was sent with an army against the Moors in Granada, whom he completely rooted out of the country. On October 7, 1571, with the fleets of Spain, the pope and Venice, he defeated the Turks in the great sea fight of Lepanto. In 1573 he took Tunis, and conceived the scheme of forming a kingdom for himself. But Philip, jealous of this design, sent him to Milan, and in 1576 as viceroy to the Netherlands. He sought to win the favour of the people by mildness; hard pressed for a time by William the Silent, he with the help of Parma's troops won the victory of Gembloux in 1577. Don John died at Namur, perhaps poisoned. See monographs by Sir W. Stirling-Maxwell (1883) and L. Coloma (1912).

JOHN OF GAUNT (1340–99), Duke of Lancaster, fourth son of Edward III, was born at Ghent (Fr. *Gand*). In 1359 he married his cousin, Blanche of Lancaster, and was created duke in 1362. She died in 1369, and in 1372 he married Constance, daughter of Pedro the Cruel of Castile, and assumed the title of King of Castile, though he failed by his expeditions to oust his rival, Henry of Trastamare. Before his father's death John became the most influential personage in the realm, and was thought to be aiming at the crown. He opposed the clergy and protected Wycliffe. Young King Richard, distrusting him, sent him in 1386 on another attempt to secure the crown of Castile; and this time he secured a treaty for the marriage of his daughter Catharine to the future king of Castile. After his return to England (1389) he reconciled Richard to his (John's) brother, the Duke of Gloucester, and by Richard was made Duke of Aquitaine, and sent on several embassies to France. On his second wife's death he had married in 1396 his mistress, Catharine Swynford, by whom he had three sons, legitimated in 1397; from the eldest descended Henry VIII. See work by Armitage-Smith (1904).

JOHN OF LEYDEN (1509–36), Dutch Anabaptist, born Beuckelszoon, Beuckels or Bockhold at Leyden, wandered about for some time as a journeyman tailor, then settled in his native city as merchant and innkeeper, and became noted as an orator. Turning Anabaptist, he in 1534 came to Münster, and, succeeding Matthiesen as head of the Anabaptists, set up a 'kingdom of Zion', with polygamy and community of goods. In June 1535 the city was taken by the Bishop of Münster, and John and his accomplices tortured to death. See Baring-Gould's *Historic Oddities* (2nd series, 1890).

JOHN OF SALISBURY (*c.* 1115–80), English scholar and divine, born at Salisbury, studied at Paris, was clerk of Pope Eugenius III, and in 1176 became bishop of Chartres. A learned classical writer, he wrote lives of Becket and Anselm, *Polycraticus* (ed. Webb 1909), on church and state diplomacy, *Metalogicon* (ed. Webb 1929), on logic and Aristotelian philosophy, *Entheticus*, *Historia Pontificalis* (ed. Poole 1927), and Letters. See studies by Schaarschmidt (1869) and Webb (1929).

JOHN OF TREVISA (1326–1412), Cornish translator of Higden, Glanville and Bartholomaeus Anglicus, was a fellow of Exeter and Queen's Colleges, Oxford, and vicar of Berkeley and canon of Westbury (probably Westbury-on-Trym).

JOHNS HOPKINS. See HOPKINS (6).

JOHNSON, (1) **Amy** (1903–41), English airwoman, born at Hull, flew solo from England to Australia (1930), to Japan via Siberia (1931), and to Cape Town (1932), making new records in each case. A pilot in Air Transport Auxilary in World War II, she was drowned after baling out over the Thames estuary. See MOLLISON; and Life by C. B. Smith (1967).

(2) **Andrew** (1808–75), 17th president of the United States, was born of humble parentage at Raleigh, N.C., December 29. In 1824 he went to Laurens, S.C., to work as a journeyman tailor, and in 1826 emigrated to Greenville, Tennessee. He served as alderman and mayor; in 1835 and 1839 became a member of the legislature; in 1841 was elected to the state senate, and in 1843 to congress. In 1853 and 1855 he was chosen governor of Tennessee, and in 1857 U.S. senator. After the Civil War broke out he became a leader of the Southern Union men, was made military governor of Tennessee (1862), and elected to the vice-presidency (March 1865). On Lincoln's assassination (April 14, 1865) he became president. He sought to carry out the conciliatory policy of his predecessor, but the assassination had provoked a revulsion of public feeling, and Johnson's policy was denounced as evincing disloyal sympathies. Soon a majority of congress were opposing his policy, and while he urged the readmission of Southern representatives, the majority insisted that the Southern states should be kept for a period under military government. Johnson vetoed the congressional measures; and congress passed them over his veto. Finally, his removal of secretary Stanton from the war department precipitated a crisis. Johnson claimed the right to change his 'constitutional advisers', and in return he was charged with violation of the 'Tenure of Office Act', in doing so without the consent of the senate. He was impeached and brought to trial, but acquitted. He retired from office in March 1869, and was elected to the senate in January 1875. See works by Dewitt (1903) and L. P. Stryker (1929).

(3) **Esther.** See SWIFT.

(4) **Hewlett,** the 'Red Dean' (1874–1966), English ecclesiastic, born of a capitalist family at Macclesfield, studied at Manchester and Oxford Universities. He began life as a 13-shillings-a-week engineering apprentice, did welfare work in the Manchester slums, joined the I.L.P. and, resolving to become 'a missionary engineer', was ordained in 1905. In 1924 he became dean of Manchester and from 1931 to 1963 was dean of Canterbury. In 1938 he visited Russia; with the publication of *The Socialist Sixth of the World* began his years of praise for Sovietism. In 1951 he received the Stalin peace prize. Though he was not a member of the Communist party, his untiring championship of Communist states and Marxist policies involved him in continuous and vigorous controversy in Britain. His sobriquet was a self-bestowed title when, during the Spanish War, he said 'I saw red—you can call me red'. Other publications include *Christians and Communism* (1956) and the autobiographical *Searching for Light* (1968).

(5) **Jack** (1878–1946), American Negro boxer, born at Galveston, knocked out Bob Fitzsimmons (1907) and won the world's heavyweight championship by beating Tommy Burns at Sydney (1908). He defeated Jeffries (1910) and lost his title to Jess Willard at Havana (1915). His arrogance and cruelty made him an unpopular champion. He served a prison sentence in 1919, and died in a car accident in N. Carolina.

(6) **James Weldon** (1871–1938), American Negro author, born in Jacksonville, Florida, where he practised at the bar (1897–1901). In 1906 he was U.S. consul at Puerto Cabello, Venezuela, and at Corinto, Nicaragua (1909–12). He was secretary of the National Association of Colored People (1916–30) and was awarded the Spingarn medal (1925). From 1930 he was professor of Creative Literature at Fisk University.

(7) **Lionel Pigot** (1867–1902), English poet and critic, born at Broadstairs, Kent. His *Poems* (1895) and *Ireland and Other Poems* (1897) draw their inspiration from his conversion to Roman Catholicism and his passion for the Irish Renaissance. 'By the Statue of King Charles at Charing Cross' is his best known piece. See also his *Reviews and Critical Papers* (1921).

(8) **Lyndon Baines** (1908–73), 36th President of the U.S.A., born at Stonewall, Texas, worked his way through college to become a teacher, then a congressman's secretary before being elected a strong 'New Deal' Democrat representative in 1937. He joined the U.S. Navy immediately after Pearl Harbour, and was decorated. 'L.B.J.' was elected senator

in 1948 and became vice president under Kennedy in 1960. A professional politician, he was majority leader in the senate. In Kennedy's motorcade at the latter's assassination in Dallas, Texas, in 1963, he was immediately sworn in as president. He was returned as president in the 1964 election with a huge majority. Under his administration the Civil Rights Act (1964), introduced by Kennedy the previous year, and the Voting Rights Act (1965) were passed, making effective, if limited, improvements to the Negro position in American society. The continuation and ever-increasing escalation of the war in Vietnam led to active protest and growing unpopularity for Johnson, however, and in 1968 he announced his decision not to stand for another presidential term of office and to retire from active politics. See works by P. L. Geyelin (1966) and R. Evans and R. Novak (1967).

(9) **Pamela Hansford.** See SNOW.

(10) **Richard Mentor** (1781–1850), vice president of the United States, was a member of congress in 1807–19, of the U.S. senate till 1829, and of congress till 1837. He was elected vice president (1837–41) by the senate, after the elections had not thrown up a majority in the electoral college for any one candidate.

(11) **Samuel** (1709–84), English lexicographer, critic and poet, was born at Lichfield, son of a bookseller. He was educated at Lichfield Grammar School and Pembroke College, Oxford, where he spent little over a year before poverty and perhaps insult drove him into the career of petty schoolmastering, first as an usher at Market Bosworth, later in a private venture at Edial, where Garrick was one of his pupils and where he wrote his frigid play *Irene*. In 1737 he came up to London. The struggle for a living there is reflected in his first poem, *London* (1738), an adaptation of Juvenal's third satire, contributed to the *Gentleman's Magazine*, which gave him a start in journalism. From 1740 to 1743 he wrote for it debates in Parliament, largely concocted by himself, in which 'the Whig dogs' got the worst of it. His famous *Dictionary* occupied him for eight years from 1747, but even this heroic labour did not exhaust his energies. To this period belongs his splendid adaptation of another satire of Juvenal, the tenth, 1749; and also the periodical *The Rambler*, afterwards published in three volumes compact of morality and keen observation of life, but now unreadable Poverty and bereavement oppressed him in those years—the former Garrick partly relieved by producing *Irene* in 1749, from which Johnson gained £300; the latter, viz., the death of his wife in 1752 and of his mother in 1759, permanently depressed him. The prose tale of Abyssinia, *Rasselas*, is said to have been written in a week to defray the burial expenses of the latter. Its theme is that the pursuit of happiness is vain, a theme congenial to him and made supportable by his strong religious faith. In 1762 he was relieved of the drudgery of hack work by the bestowal of a crown pension of £300 a year and was thereafter enabled to figure as the arbiter of letters and the great social personality whose every recorded word and gesture have been treasured by posterity. The Literary Club, of which he was a founder member (1764), was the chief place where his genius shone amid a galaxy of other talent, but private society, especially that of the Thrales, husband and wife, did much to make him occupied and happy. The Thrales indeed are woven into the texture of his social life in this middle period and it was only when Mrs Thrale, now a widow, married Piozzi, an Italian singer (1784), that Johnson deprived himself of her sprightly acquaintance. As if to bear out his favourite theme of the vanity of human hopes, his social circle was narrowed by the death of Goldsmith, Beauclerk, Garrick and Mr Thrale within a few years of each other, but not before he had undertaken with Boswell in 1773 what is surely the most instructive and entertaining tour in literary history of which we have happily the two complementary records, Johnson's *Journey to the Western Isles* (1775) and Boswell's *Tour to the Hebrides*. *The Lives of the Poets* (1779–81) is the only other important contribution to letters in this late period; it includes *The Life of Mr Richard Savage* which had appeared more than thirty years before, in 1747, and which recorded with manly emotion the trials the friends had shared. Johnson died in 1784 and was buried in Westminster Abbey. Johnson's literary career then falls into four periods. The first includes much hack work for Cave's *Gentleman's Magazine*, but also *London* and the biography of Savage. The second (1748–60), the most fertile, contains the *Dictionary*, with its fine and discriminating *Preface*, the splendid *Vanity of Human Wishes*, and *Rasselas*. Despite the heavy moralizing and the style of his periodical essays in *The Rambler*, *The Idler*, &c., there is much in them for the student. The third period, besides his unrivalled conversations recorded by Boswell (which are after all part of his 'works'), includes his edition of Shakespeare (1765), with its masterly Preface. In his last period, from 1772 onwards, political pamphleteering employed his pen—the full-blooded Tory appears in the *Patriot* and *Taxation no Tyranny* (1775). His *Journey to the Western Isles* is treasure trove, but *The Lives of the Most Eminent English Poets* (1779–81) is his enduring monument, and this despite his cantankerous treatment of Milton and Gray and his failure to appreciate metaphysical poetry. His reputation as man and conversationalist outweighs his literary reputation. For the picture of Johnson in society we are indebted above all to Boswell, who has painted him with all his hard sense and unreasonableness, his peremptory conclusion to argument, his humility and piety, his loveableness. The English see themselves in this picture, but foreigners have never understood the national homage. For one thing his ideas were circumscribed, he had no touch in him of the philosopher, and this no doubt makes for the fun of his verbal tussles with Boswell, who had imbibed something of philosophism but who wisely allowed himself usually to be 'corrected' by his

friend. See the Yale edition of his works (vol. I, 1959), Lives by J. Boswell (q.v.) (new ed. L. F. Powell, 1934), Sir John Hawkins (1787), Mrs Piozzi's *Anecdotes* (1786), and studies by W. Raleigh (1910), S. C. Roberts (1935), Elton, *Survey of English Literature, 1780–1830* and H. Pearson, *Johnson and Boswell* (1958).

(12) **Sir William** (1715–74), Irish merchant and administrator, born in County Down, in 1738 went to America, and as a fur-trader acquired great influence with the Red Indians, whom he led often against the French. His third wife (or mistress) was a Mohawk girl. In 1755 he was created a baronet. See Griffis's *Sir William Johnson and the Six Nations* (1891) and Life by A. Pound (1930).

(13) **William Eugene,** nicknamed **Pussyfoot** (1862–1945), American temperance propagandist, born in Coventry, N.Y. He became a journalist and a special officer in the U.S. Indian Service, where he received his nickname from his methods in raiding gambling saloons in Indian Territory. He was prominent during the prohibitionist movement in America and lectured for the cause all over Europe. In 1919 he lost an eye when he was struck and dragged from a lecture platform in London by medical students.

JOHNSTON, (1) **Albert Sidney** (1803–62), American soldier, born in Kentucky, served in the U.S. army until 1834. In 1836 he joined the army of Texas, and became its head, and in 1838 war secretary of Texas. He served in the Mexican war under General Taylor, who in 1849 appointed him paymaster in the U.S. army. In 1858 he brought the Mormon rebellion to an end. As brigadier-general he commanded in Utah and on the Pacific until 1861, when he passed over to the South. Appointed to the command of Kentucky and Tennessee, he fortified Bowling Green, and held the Northern army in check until February 1862, when he retreated to Nashville and later to Corinth, Mississippi. Here he concentrated 50,000 men, with which force he attacked Grant at Shiloh, April 6, 1862. The Union army was surprised, and the advantage lay with the Confederates till Johnston was mortally wounded. Next day Grant's supports came up and the Confederates, now under Beauregard, were driven back to Corinth. See Life by W. P. Johnston (1878).

(2) **Alexander Keith** (1804–71), Scottish cartographer, was born near Penicuik, and died at Ben Rhydding. His *National Atlas* (1843) procured him the appointment of geographer royal for Scotland. Other works are a *Physical Atlas* (1848) and the famous *Royal Atlas* (1861), besides atlases of astronomy, &c., a physical globe, and a gazetteer.

(3) **Alexander Keith** (1844–79), son of (2), born in Edinburgh, also wrote geographical works. He joined an exploring expedition to Paraguay in 1874, and in 1879 was appointed leader of the Royal Geographical Society's expedition to East Africa. He died between the Coast and Lake Nyasa, June 28, 1879, and his work was taken up by Joseph Thomson.

(4) or **Jonston, Arthur** (1587–1641), Scottish physician and humanist, born at Caskieben, Aberdeenshire, graduated M.D. at Padua in 1610, and visited many seats of learning. He practised medicine in France, whence his fame as a Latin poet spread over Europe. About 1625 he was appointed physician to King Charles I. His famous translation of the Psalms of David into Latin verse was published at Aberdeen in 1637. He helped to bring out the *Deliciae Poetarum Scotorum hujus Aevi* (1637), to which he also contributed notable poems. In 1637 he became rector of King's College, Aberdeen. He died suddenly at Oxford. See works ed. by Sir W. D. Geddes (1892–95).

(5) **Sir Harry Hamilton** (1858–1927), British explorer and novelist, born at Kennington, London, from 1879 travelled in Africa, led the Royal Society's expedition to Kilimanjaro in 1884, and as commissioner for South Central Africa made possible British acquisition of Northern Rhodesia and Nyasaland. G.C.M.G., K.C.B., he wrote on the Congo, zoology, five novels and *The Story of My Life* (1923). See Life by his brother (1929), study by R. Oliver (1957).

(6) **Herrick Lee** (1898–), American chemist, born at North Jackson, Ohio, professor of Chemistry at Ohio and director of the Manhattan Project Research (1942–46), achieved with Giauque a temperature of less than one degree from absolute zero in gases.

(7) **Joseph Eggleston** (1807–91), American soldier, born in Virginia, graduated at West Point, fought in the Seminole war, became captain of engineers in 1846, served in the war with Mexico, and in 1860 was quartermaster-general. He resigned in 1861 to enter the Confederate service, and as brigadier-general took command of the army of the Shenandoah. He supported Beauregard at the first battle of Bull Run, in 1862 was disabled by a wound, in 1863 failed to relieve Vicksburg, and in 1864 stubbornly contested Sherman's progress towards Atlanta, but, being steadily driven back, was relieved of his command. In February 1865 Lee ordered him to 'drive back Sherman'; but he had only a fourth of the Northern general's strength. On Lee's surrender he accepted the same terms, afterwards engaged in railway and insurance business, was elected to congress in 1877, was a U.S. commissioner of railroads and died at Washington. See his *Narrative* (1874). Lives by Johnson (1891), Hughes (1893) and D. S. Freeman, *Lee's Lieutenants* (1942-44).

JOHNSTONE, name of a Scottish noble family taken from the lordship of Johnstone in Annandale, Dumfriesshire. In former days it was one of the most powerful and turbulent clans of the west Borders, and was at constant feud with its neighbours, especially the Maxwells. Of three branches, Johnstone of Annandale, Johnstone of Westerhall, and Johnston of Hilton and Caskieben in Aberdeenshire, the first, which retained the ancient patrimony, was ennobled by Charles I, and became successively Lords Johnstone of Lochwood, Earls of Hartfell, and Earls and Marquises of Annandale.

These titles, being limited to heirs-male, became dormant in 1792. Both the Houses of Westerhall and Caskieben had the rank of baronet, and a branch of the former was in 1881 raised to the peerage as Baron Derwent. See works by C. L. Johnstone (1889) and G. H. Johnstone (1909).

JOHNSTONE, James, Chevalier de (1719–*c.* 1800), Scottish soldier, the son of an Edinburgh merchant, as Prince Charles Edward's aide-de-camp fought at Culloden, and, then taking service with the French, was present at the capture of Louisbourg and the capitulation of Quebec. See his Memoirs (tr. from French, 3 vols. 1870–71).

JOINVILLE, *zhwī-veel,* (1) **François Ferdinand d'Orléans, Prince de** (1818–1900), French sailor and author, born at Neuilly, the third son of Louis Philippe, served in the French navy from 1834 to 1848, and was on McClellan's staff during the Virginian campaign in the American Civil War (1862); exiled from France in 1870, returned incognito and served in war against Prussia; in 1871-75 he sat in the National Assembly. He died in Paris. See his *Vieux Souvenirs* (1894; Eng. trans. 1896).

(2) **Jean, Sire de** (*c.* 1224–1319), French historian, born in Champagne, became seneschal to the count of Champagne and king of Navarre. He took part in the unfortunate crusade of Louis IX (1248–54), returned with him to France, and lived partly at court, partly on his estates. At Acre in 1250 he composed a Christian manual, his *Credo*; and throughout the crusade he took notes of events and wrote down his impressions. When almost eighty he undertook his delightful *Vie de Saint Louis* (1309). His style conforms closely to his character: it is veracious, flowing, naïve, often singularly expressive. See edition by de Wailly (1874) and trans. with intro. by Evans (1938).

JÓKAI, Maurus, or **Mór,** *yō'koy* (1825–1904), Hungarian novelist, born at Komaróm, was an active partisan of the Hungarian struggle in 1848. Besides dramas, humorous essays, poems, &c., he wrote many novels and romances, good examples of which are *The Turks in Hungary* (1852), *The Magyar Nabob* (1853) and its continuation *Zoltan Karpathy* (1854), *The New Landlord* (1862), *Black Diamonds* (1870), *The Romance of the Coming Century* (1873), *The Modern Midas* (1875), *The Comedians of Life* (1876), *God is One* (1877), *The White Woman of Leutschau* (1884) and *The Gipsy Baron* (1885); several have appeared in English. A jubilee edition in 100 volumes was published in 1894. Jókai was editor of several newspapers and conspicuous as a Liberal parliamentarian.

JOLIOT-CURIE, *zho-lyō-küree,* name of a French couple, both nuclear physicists:

(1) **Irène,** *née* **Curie** (1897–1956), wife (1926) of (2) and daughter of Pierre and Marie Curie (qq.v.), born in Paris, worked as her mother's assistant at the Radium Institute, taking charge of the work in 1932. In that year she discovered, with her mother, the projection of atomic nuclei by neutrons, and in 1934 she and her husband (2) succeeded in producing radioactive elements artificially, for which they received the 1935 Nobel prize for chemistry. She died of cancer, caused by lifelong exposure to radioactivity.

(2) **Jean Frédéric,** original surname Joliot (1900–58), husband (1926) of (1), born in Paris, studied under Langevin at the Sorbonne where in 1925 he became assistant to Madame Curie, mother of Irène. In 1935 he shared with his wife the Nobel prize for their discovery of artificial radioactivity. Professor at the Collège de France (1937), he became a strong supporter of the Resistance movement during World War II, and a membe of the Communist party. After the liberation he became director of scientific research and (1946–50) high commissioner for atomic energy, a position from which he was dismissed when the hitherto exclusively peaceful objectives were subordinated to defence requirements. President of the Communist-sponsored World Peace Council, he was awarded the Stalin peace prize (1951). Commander of the *Légion d'honneur*, he was given a state funeral by the Gaullist government when he died from cancer, caused by lifelong exposure to radioactivity.

JOLSON, Al, stage-name of **Asa Yoelson** (1886–1950), Russian-born American actor and singer, born in St Petersburg, son of a rabbi, emigrated to the United States in 1893 and made his stage début in *The Children of the Ghetto* (1899). He toured with circus and minstrel shows and became famous for his characteristic imitations of Negro singers in such hits as ' Mammy ' (1909), ' Sonny Boy ', &c. His recorded voice featured in the commemorative films *The Jolson Story* and *Jolson Sings Again.*

JOLY, John (1857–1933), Irish geologist and physicist, born in Offaly, Ireland, studied at Trinity College, Dublin, where he became professor of Geology and Mineralogy in 1897. He invented a photometer in 1888, calculated the age of the earth by measuring the sodium content of the sea (1899) and formulated the theory of thermal cycles based on the radioactive elements in the earth's crust. With Stevenson he evolved the ' Dublin method ' in radiotherapy, pioneered colour photography and the radium treatment of cancer. He was elected F.R.S. in 1892.

JOMINI, Henri, Baron, *zho-mee-nee* (1779–1869), Swiss soldier and strategist, born at Payerne in Vaud, after commanding a Swiss battalion attached himself to Ney, to whom he became chief of staff; he was created baron after the peace of Tilsit. He attracted Napoleon's notice by his *Traité des grandes opérations militaires* (1804). He distinguished himself at Jena, in the Spanish campaigns and during the retreat from Russia; but, offended at his treatment by Napoleon, he entered the Russian service (1814), and fought against Turkey (1828). He wrote a great history of the wars of the Revolution (1806), a Life of Napoleon (1827) and a *Précis de l'art de guerre* (1830). See E. M. Earle, *Makers of Modern Strategy* (1944).

JOMMELLI, Niccoló, *yo-mel'li* (1714–74), Italian composer of more than fifty operas, born at Aversa, germanized his style and lost his popularity after a spell as *kapellmeister* to the Duke of Württemberg.

JONAS, Justus, *yō-nās* (1493–1555), German professor at Wittenberg, sided with Luther in the Reformation. See monograph by Pressel (1863).

JONES, (1) **Daniel** (1881–1967), English phonetician, was called to the bar in 1907, when he was also appointed lecturer in Phonetics (professor 1921–49) at London. He collaborated with others in compiling Cantonese (1912), Sechuana (1916) and Sinhalese (1919) phonetic readers, compiled an *English Pronouncing Dictionary* (1917; new ed. 1956) and wrote *The Phoneme* (1950), *Cardinal Vowels* (1956), &c. He was secretary (1928–49) and president of the International Phonetic Association.

(2) **Ebenezer** (1820–60), English minor poet, born at Islington, was brought up a strict Calvinist and despite long hours as a clerk completed *Studies of Sensation and Event* (1843), which were admired by Browning and Rossetti. In his *Land Monopoly* (1849) he anticipated the economic theory of Henry George (q.v.) by thirty years.

(3) **Edward** (1777–1837), founder in 1800 of the Welsh Wesleyan Methodists, was born near Ruthin, and died at Leek.

(4) **Edward Burne.** See BURNE-JONES.

(5) **Ernest** (1819–69), English Chartist poet and leader, the son of Major Jones, equerry to the Duke of Cumberland, afterwards king of Hanover, was born at Berlin, and came to England in 1838. In 1841 he published his romance, *The Wood Spirit*, was called to the bar in 1844, and next year became leader of the Chartist movement, issuing *The Labourer*, *Notes of the People* and *The People's Paper*, and resigning nearly £2000 per annum, left to him on condition that he should abandon the Chartist cause. For his part in the Chartist proceedings at Manchester in 1848 he got two years' solitary confinement, and in prison composed an epic, *The Revolt of Hindostan*. After his release he wrote *The Battleday* (1855), *The Painter of Florence* and *The Emperor's Vigil* (1856), and *Beldagon Church* and *Corayda* (1860). He made several vain efforts to enter parliament. See G. D. H. Cole, *Chartist Portraits* (1941), and studies, ed. Saville (1952).

(6) **Ernest** (1879–1958), Welsh psychoanalyst, born at Llwchwr, Glamorgan, studied at Cardiff University College and qualified with gold medals as physician in London. Medical journalism and neurological research brought him into contact with the work of Freud and his new approach to neurosis. Jones learnt German in order to study this more closely and in 1908 became a lifelong disciple and personal friend of the founder of psychoanalysis, introduced it into Britain and in 1912 formed a committee of Freud's closest collaborators of which he was the only Gentile, pledged to uphold the Freudian theory in the face of detractors and deviationists. He introduced psychoanalysis into America and Britain, founding the British Psycho-Analytical Society in 1913, also in 1920 the *International Journal of Psycho-Analysis* which he edited (1920–33). He was professor of Psychiatry at Toronto and director of the London Clinic for Psycho-Analysis. Among his numerous works and translations is a psychoanalytical study of *Hamlet* and the authoritative biography of Freud (1953–57). See his autobiography, *Free Associations* (1959).

(7) **Henry** (1831–99), English physician who as 'Cavendish' published many books on whist and other games.

(8) **Henry Arthur** (1851–1929), English dramatist, together with Pinero the founder of the 'realist problem' drama in Britain, born at Grandborough, Bucks, was in business till 1878, when *Only Round the Corner* was produced at Exeter. His first great hit was a melodrama, *The Silver King* (1882). This was followed by *Saints and Sinners* (1884), *Rebellious Susan* (1894), *The Philistines* (1895), *The Liars* (1897), *The Manoeuvres of Jane* (1898), *Mrs Dane's Defence* (1900), *Mary Goes First* (1913) and other social comedies. See *Life and Letters* by his daughter (1930), and study by R. A. Cordell (1932).

(9) **Sir Henry Stuart** (1867–1939), British classical scholar, born at Hunslet, Leeds, studied at Balliol College, Oxford, and in Greece and Italy, became Camden professor of Ancient History at Oxford and principal of University College, Aberystwyth, in 1927, and was knighted in 1933. He contributed to archaeological studies and ancient history, edited Thucydides (1898–1900) and edited the Greek lexicon of Liddell and Scott (9th ed. 1925–40).

(10) **Inigo** (1573–1652), the first of the great English architects, born in London July 15, studied landscape painting in Italy, and from Venice introduced the Palladian style into England. In Denmark, he is said to have designed the palaces of Rosenborg and Frederiksborg. In 1606 James I employed him in arranging the masques of Ben Jonson. He introduced the proscenium arch and movable scenery to the English stage. In 1613–14 he revisited Italy and on his return in 1615 was appointed surveyor-general of the royal buildings. In 1616 he designed the queen's house at Greenwich, completed in the 1630s. Other commissions included the rebuilding of the Whitehall banqueting hall, the nave and transepts and a large Corinthian portico of old St Paul's, Marlborough Chapel, the Double-Cube room at Wilton and possibly the York Water Gate. He laid out Covent Garden and Lincoln's Inn Fields. See Life by Cunningham (1848) and studies by J. A. Gotch (1928), R. Blomfield (1935), S. Sitwell, *British Architects and Craftsmen* (1945) and J. L. Milne (1953).

(11) **Owen** (1741–1814), Welsh antiquary, was all his life a London furrier, but early developed a taste for Welsh poetry. His *Myvyrian Archaeology of Wales* (1801–07; new ed. 1870) is a collection of poetic pieces dating from the 6th to the 14th century.—His son, **Owen Jones** (1809–74), art decorator, was superintendent of works for the London Exhibition of 1851, and director of decoration for the Crystal Palace.

(12) **Paul** (1747–92), Scottish-born American sailor, was born at Kirkbean, Kirkcud-

brightshire, July 6, the son of a gardener, John Paul. Apprenticed as sailor boy, he made several voyages to America, and in 1773 inherited a property in Virginia, having meanwhile for five years been mate on a slaver; about the same date he assumed the name of Paul Jones. When the American congress in 1775 resolved to fit out a naval force he offered his services. In April 1778, visiting the British coast in a brig of eighteen guns, he performed some daring exploits, including a descent on the Solway. The year after, as commodore of a small French squadron displaying American colours, he threatened Leith, and on September 23, fought off Flamborough Head a desperate engagement, in which he captured two British men-of-war. Louis XVI created him a Chevalier of the Order of Military Merit. In 1788 he entered the Russian service, and as rear-admiral of the Black Sea fleet served against Turkey. He died in Paris. See Lives by Sherburne (1825), Mackenzie (1841), Brady (1900), Buell (1900); *Life and Letters*, by Mrs de Koven (1914); also Sir J. K. Laughton's *Studies in Naval History* (1887).

(13) **Robert** (fl. 1600), English lutenist and composer, graduated at Oxford (1597), composed madrigals, including a six-part one in Morley's *The Triumphes of Oriana* as well as five books of 'ayres', with lute accompaniments.

(14) **Robert Tyre (Bobby)** (1902–71), American golfer, born in Atlanta. He studied law and was called to the Georgia bar in 1928. He won the National Amateur Championship in 1924, 1925, 1927 and 1928, the National Open Championship in 1923, 1926 and 1929, and both Championships in 1930, in which year he also won the Amateur and Open Championships of Great Britain. He wrote *Down the Fairway* (1927), and in 1958 received the freedom of St Andrews.

(15) **Sir William** (1746–94), British Orientalist, born in London, was educated at Harrow and University College, Oxford, where his remarkable attainments attracted attention. In 1765 he became tutor to the son of Earl Spencer; in 1774 was called to the bar; and in 1776 became commissioner of bankrupts, publishing meanwhile a *Persian Grammar* (1772), Latin Commentaries on Asiatic Poetry (1774), and a translation of seven ancient Arabic poems (1780). In 1783 he obtained a judgeship in the Supreme Court of Judicature in Bengal, and was knighted. He devoted himself to Sanskrit, whose startling resemblance to Latin and Greek he was the first to point out in 1787. He established the Asiatic Society of Bengal (1784), and was its first president. He completed a translation of *Sakuntala*, the *Hitopadesa*, parts of the Vedas, and Manu, before his death. See Memoirs by Lord Teignmouth appended to his works (9 vols. 1799–1804), and appreciation by A. J. Arberry (1946).

JONGEN, *yong'ėn*, (1) **Joseph** (1873–1953), Belgian composer, won the Belgian *Prix de Rome* and was professor at Liège Conservatoir until the outbreak of World War I when he went to England. He became director of the Brussels Conservatoire (1920–39). He composed piano, violin and organ works, the symphonic poem *Lalla Roukh*, an opera and a ballet.

(2) **Leon** (1885–), brother of (1), followed him in 1939 as director of the Brussels Conservatoire. He has written works for the piano, operas, and *Rhapsodia Belgia* for violin and orchestra.

JONSON, Ben (1572–1637), English dramatist, born at Westminster, probably of Border descent. He was educated at Westminster School under Camden, to whom he paid the tribute 'Camden most reverend head to whom I owe/All that I am in arts, all that I know'. After working for a while with his stepfather, a bricklayer, he volunteered for military service in Flanders before joining Henslowe's company of players. He killed a fellow player in a duel, became a Catholic in prison, but later recanted. His *Every Man in his Humour* with Shakespeare in the cast, was performed at the Curtain in 1598 to be followed not so successfully by *Every Man Out of His Humour* in 1599. The equally tiresome *Cynthia's Revels*, largely allegorical, was succeeded by *The Poetaster* which at least was salted by a personal attack on Dekker and Marston. He now tried Roman tragedy, but his *Sejanus* (1603) and his later venture, *Catiline* (1611), are so larded with classical references as to be merely closet plays. If he was trying to show Shakespeare how to write a Roman tragedy he failed badly, but his larger intent of discarding romantic comedy and writing realistically (though his theory of 'humours' was hardly comparable with genuine realism) helped to produce his four masterpieces—*Volpone* (1606), *The Silent Woman* (1609), *The Alchemist* (1610) and *Bartholomew Fair* (1614). *Volpone* is an unpleasant satire on senile sensuality and greedy legacy hunters. *The Silent Woman* is farcical comedy involving a heartless hoax. Dryden praised it for its construction, but *The Alchemist* is better with its single plot and strict adherence to the unities. *Bartholomew Fair* has indeed all the fun of the fair, salted by Ben's anti-Puritan prejudices, though the plot gets lost in the motley of eccentrics. After the much poorer *The Devil is an Ass* (1616), Jonson turned or rather returned to the masque—he had collaborated with Inigo Jones in *The Masque of Blacknesse*, 1605—and produced a number of those glittering displays down to 1625 when James's death terminated his period of Court favour. His renewed attempt to attract theatre audiences left him in the angry mood of the ode 'Come leave the loathed stage' (1632). Only his unfinished pastoral play *The Sad Shepherd* survives of his declining years. Ben attracted the learned and courtly, to several of whom his superb verse letters are addressed. Perhaps we should not wonder at the success of *The Sad Shepherd*, for his lyric genius was second only to Shakespeare's. 'Drink to me only with thine Eyes' in *Volpone* (of all places) and 'Queen and Huntress chaste and fair' and 'Slow, slow fresh Fount' in the dreary stretches of *Cynthia's Revels* are but a few of these gemlike lyrics. His *Timber; or*

Discoveries, printed in the folio of 1640, prove him a considerable critic with a bent towards the neoclassicism which Cowley and Dryden inaugurated. His works were edited by William Gifford in 1816 and by Colonel Cunningham in 1875. These were superseded by Herford's splendid edition. There have been numerous studies, the best perhaps by J. A. Symonds (1886), Swinburne (1889) and G. Gregory Smith (1919), G. B. Johnston (1945), G. E. Bentley (1945), Partridge (1958) and Thayer (1963).

JÓNSSON, (1) Einar (1874–1954), Icelandic sculptor, studied at Rome and Copenhagen, and created a reputation for himself by the independence, realism and grandeur of his works (*The Outlaw*, *Evolution*, *New Life*, &c.).

(2) **Finnur** (1858–1934), Icelandic scholar, born at Akureyri, studied, lectured and became professor in 1898 at Copenhagen. He published *Den oldnorske og oldislandske litteraturs historie* (1894–1902), a history of the mediaeval literatures of Norway and Iceland.

JOOS VAN CLEVE. See CLEVE.

JOPLIN, Thomas (*c.* 1790–1847), English economist, born at Newcastle-on-Tyne, wrote a number of works on joint-stock banking in Scotland, advocated a merger of small provincial banks and became a director of such a scheme with the founding of the National Provincial Bank (1833) and opposed the monopoly of the Bank of England.

JORDAENS, Jakob, *yor'dahns* (1593–1678), Flemish painter, who was born and died at Antwerp, ranks next to Rubens amongst Flemish painters. He became a member of an Antwerp Guild in 1616 and from 1630 came under the influence of Rubens, who obtained for him the patronage of the kings of Spain and Sweden. His early paintings such as the *Four Evangelists* (1632, Louvre) show him to be deficient in the handling of chiaroscuro effects and colour generally, but he improved vastly in such later canvases as *The Triumph of Frederick Henry* (1652, House in the Wood, The Hague) although he never achieved the delicacy of Rubens. He also designed tapestries, and painted portraits. See monograph by M. Rooses (tr. 1908).

JORDAN, (1) Camille, *zhor-dã* (1771–1821), French Liberal politician, born at Lyons, supported the royalists during the Revolution and fled (1793). He subsequently became a member of the council of The Five Hundred (1797), opposed Napoleon and became a deputy in 1816.

(2) **Dorothea,** *née* **Bland,** *jor'dėn* (1762–1816), Irish actress, born near Waterford, made her début in Dublin (1777), soon became popular and in 1782 obtained an engagement from Tate Wilkinson at Leeds. She appeared with phenomenal success at Drury Lane in *The Country Girl* in October 1785. For nearly thirty years it was in the rôles of romps and boys that she mainly kept her hold on the public. In 1790 commenced her connection with the Duke of Clarence, afterwards William IV, which endured until 1811. After playing in London and in the provinces until 1814, she is said to have been compelled to retire to France for a debt of £2000. She certainly lived in apparent poverty at St Cloud, where she died, though there is a legend that she returned to live in England for some years after her supposed death. In 1831 King William made their eldest son Earl of Munster. See books by Sergeant (1913), Jerrold (1914).

(3) **Marie Ennemond Camille,** *zhor-dã* (1838–1922), French mathematician, born at Lyons, became professor at the École Polytechnique and at the Collège de France. He applied group theory to geometry, wrote on the theory of linear differential equations and on the theory of functions, which he applied to the curve which bears his name.

(4) **Rudolf,** *yor-dahn* (1810–87), German painter of fisher folk, was born at Berlin, and died at Düsseldorf.

JORDANES, *-dah'neez* (fl. 530), historian, was first a notary at the Ostrogoth court in Italy, but became a monk, and finally Bishop of Crotona. He wrote two historical works in Latin—*De Regnorum ac Temporum Successione*, a compendium of history from the creation to 552 A.D., and *De Getarum Origine et Rebus Gestis* (Eng. trans. with introd. by Mierow, 1915), which, based on the earlier work (now lost) of the Roman Cassiodorus, is an important source of information about the Goths.

JÖRGENSEN, *yœr'gen-sen*, **(1) Johannes** (1866–1956), Danish novelist and poet, lived most of his life in Assisi, Italy, became a Roman Catholic (1896) but returned to Svendborg, his birth-place, shortly before his death. His works include *Frans af Assisi* (1907), *Den hellige Katharina af Siena* (1915) and *Mit Livs Legende* (1916–28).

(2) **Jörgen,** 'King of Iceland' (1779–*c.* 1845), Danish adventurer, the son of a Copenhagen watchmaker, was born in 1779. On June 21, 1809, having previously visited Iceland as interpreter, he arrived at Reykjavik in an armed London merchantman. But all trade being prohibited by the laws of the island, a few days afterwards he landed and seized the governor. He then proclaimed the independence of Iceland, 'under English protection', and appropriated all he could lay his hands on for the 'state chest'. On August 9 a British sloop of war arrived, and he was carried to England. He lived in London for some years, but was convicted of robbery in 1820, and transported to Tasmania.

JOSEPH, the name of many biblical personages. The most important are:

Joseph, the elder of the two sons of Jacob by Rachel. His being sold into Egypt and his ultimate rise to power there are recorded in Genesis.

Joseph, husband of the Virgin, a carpenter at Nazareth, appears last in the gospel history when Jesus is twelve years old (Luke, ii. 43); he is never mentioned during his ministry, and may be assumed to have been already dead.

Joseph, one of the two persons chosen as worthy to fill the vacant place of Judas among the Twelve.

Joseph of Arimathea, a rich Israelite who went to Pilate and begged the body of Jesus, burying it in his own rock-hewn tomb.

JOSEPH, the name of two Holy Roman emperors:

Joseph I (1678–1711), succeeded his father Leopold I as emperor of Germany in 1705. He granted privileges to the Protestants, and, in alliance with Britain, prosecuted successfully the war of the Spanish succession against France.

Joseph II (1741–90), emperor of Germany, son of Francis I and Maria Theresa, was born March 13. In 1764 he was elected king of the Romans, and after his father's death (1765) emperor of Germany; but until his mother's death (1780) his power was limited to the command of the army and the direction of foreign affairs. Although he failed to add Bavaria to the Austrian dominions (1777–79 and again in 1785), he acquired Galicia, Lodomeria, and Zips, at the first partition of Poland in 1772; and in 1780 he appropriated a great part of Passau and Salzburg. As soon as he found himself in full possession of the government of Austria he declared himself independent of the pope, and prohibited the publication of any new papal bulls without his *placet*. He suppressed 700 convents, reduced the number of the regular clergy from 63,000 to 27,000, prohibited papal dispensations as to marriage, and in 1781 published the Edict of Toleration for Protestants and Greeks. He also abolished serfdom, reorganized taxation, and curtailed the feudal privileges of the nobles. In 1788 he engaged in an unsuccessful war with Turkey. See study by S. K. Padover (1934).

JOSEPH, king of Naples. See BONAPARTE.

JOSEPH, Père (1577–1638), French diplomat, Richelieu's *alter ego*, the 'Grey Eminence', born François le Clerc du Tremblay in Paris, from a soldier turned Capuchin in 1599, and went on several important diplomatic missions for Richelieu. See books by Fagniez (Paris 1893–94) and Huxley (1941).

JOSÉPHINE, *née* **Marie Joséphine Rose Tascher de la Pagerie** (1763–1814), wife of Napoleon and French empress, was born in Martinique, June 23, and in 1779 married there the Vicomte de Beauharnais (q.v.). In 1796, two years after his execution, she married Napoleon Bonaparte, and accompanied him in his Italian campaign, but soon returned to Paris. At Malmaison, and afterwards at the Luxembourg and the Tuileries, she attracted round her the most brilliant society of France, and contributed not a little to the establishment of her husband's power. But the marriage, being childless, was dissolved December 16, 1809. Joséphine retained the title of empress, and, if allowed, would have rejoined Bonaparte after his fall. See works by Aubenas (1859), Sergeant(1908), Méneval (trans. 1912), Turquan (trans. 1913), Geer (1925), Wilson (1930) and Knapton (1964).

JOSEPHUS, Flavius, *jō-see'fus* (37–?100), Jewish historian and soldier, was born at Jerusalem, the son of a priest, while his mother was descended from the Asmonean princes. His acquirements in Hebrew and Greek literature soon drew public attention upon him, and he became conspicuous amongst the Pharisees, the national party, at twenty-six being chosen delegate to Nero. When the Jews rose in their last and fatal insurrection against the Romans, Josephus, as governor of Galilee, displayed great valour and prudence; but the advance of Vespasian (67) made resistance hopeless, and Jotapata, the city into which he had thrown himself, was taken after holding out for 47 days. Josephus was kept in a sort of easy imprisonment for three years, and was present in the Roman army at the siege of Jerusalem by Titus (70). After this he appears to have resided at Rome. He survived Agrippa II, who died in 100. His works are *History of the Jewish War*, written both in Hebrew and Greek (the Hebrew version is no longer extant); *Jewish Antiquities*, containing the history of his countrymen from the earliest times to the end of the reign of Nero; a treatise on the *Antiquity of the Jews*, against Apion; and an *Autobiography* (A.D. 37–90). The *editio princeps* of the Greek text appeared at Basel in 1544. See trans. by H. St J. Thackeray (with text; 1926 *et seq.*). Lion Feuchtwanger's historical romance *Der jüdische Krieg* was translated as *Josephus* (1932). See studies by N. Bentwich (1926) and F. Jackson (1930).

JOSHUA, son of Nun, of the tribe of Ephraim, was one of the twelve spies sent to collect information about the Canaanites, and during the forty years' wanderings acted as 'minister' or personal attendant of Moses. After 'the Lord was angry with Moses' Joshua was expressly designated to lead the people into Canaan. The Book of Joshua is a narrative of the conquest and settlement of Canaan under his leadership.

JOSIAH (649–609 B.C.), king of Judah, succeeded his father Amon at eight. He re-established the worship of Jehovah, and instituted the rites in the newly-discovered 'Book of the Law'. He fell at Megiddo attempting to check Pharaoh-Necho's advance against the Assyrians.

JOSIKA, Baron Miklós von, *yō'shee-kė* (1794–1865), Hungarian novelist in the romantic tradition of Sir Walter Scott, was involved in the revolution of 1848, and had to live an exile in Brussels and Dresden. See Magyar Life by Szaak (1891).

JOUBERT, *zhoo-bayr*, (1) **Joseph** (1754–1824), French writer and moralist, was born at Montignac in Périgord, and studied and taught at the college of Toulouse. He then went to Paris, and lived through all the fever of the Revolution. In 1809 he was nominated by Napoleon to the council of the new university. Fourteen years later, his friend Chateaubriand edited a small volume from his papers, and Joubert's fame was from that moment assured; his *Pensées* are worthy of their place beside those of La Rochefoucauld, Pascal, La Bruyère and Vauvenargues. There are translations by Calvert (1867), Attwell (1877), and Lyttelton (1899). See Sainte-Beuve's *Causeries du lundi* (vol. i), *Portraits littéraires* (vol. ii), and *Chateaubriand et son groupe*; also Matthew Arnold's *Essays in Criticism* (1865) and study by A. Beaunier (1918).

(2) **Petrus Jacobus** (1834–1900), Boer soldier and statesman, born at Cango,

Cape Colony, was conqueror of Colley in 1881 and of Jameson in 1896, organized the first Boer successes in the South African war of 1899–1902, but died after a short illness.

JOUFFROY, Théodore Simon, *zhoo-frwah* (1796–1842), French philosopher, born at Pontets in the Jura, professor of Philosophy at Paris (1817), in 1838 became university librarian. He wrote lucid commentaries on Reid and Dugald Stewart, translated their works and wrote *Mélanges philosophiques* (1833), *Cours de droit naturel* (1835), &c. See Life by Tissot (1876).

JOUFFROY D'ABBANS, Claude, Marquis de, *zhoo-frwah dab-ã* (1751–1832), French inventor of steam-navigation, served in the army, and in 1783 made a small paddle-wheel steamboat. Compelled to emigrate and ruined by the Revolution, he failed to float a company till after Fulton had made his successful experiments on the Seine in 1803. See monograph by Prost (Paris 1889).

JOULE, James Prescott, *jool* (1818–89), English physicist, famous for his experiments in heat, born December 24 at Salford, studied chemistry under Dalton and in a series of notable researches (1843–78) showed experimentally that heat is a form of energy, determined quantitatively the amount of mechanical, and later electrical, energy to be expended in the propagation of heat energy and established the mechanical equivalent of heat. This became the basis of the theory of the conservation of energy. With Lord Kelvin, he measured the fall in temperature when a gas expands without doing external work and formulated the absolute scale of temperature. He also showed that the molecular heat of a compound solid is equal to the sum of the atomic heats of its components, and was the first to describe the phenomenon of magnetostriction. He was elected F.R.S. in 1850 and awarded the Copley (1860) and Royal medals. His collected papers were published by the Physical Society (1884–87). See J. G. Crowther, *British Scientists of the Nineteenth Century* (1935).

JOURDAN, Jean-Baptiste, Comte, *zhoor-dã* (1762–1833), French marshal, born at Limoges, defeated the Austrians at Wattignies (October 16, 1793), gained the victory of Fleurus (June 26, 1794), and then drove the Austrians across the Rhine, took Luxemburg, and besieged Mainz. But on October 11, 1795, he was defeated at Höchst, and four times in 1796–99 by the Archduke Charles. Napoleon employed him in 1800 in Piedmont; in 1804 he was made marshal, and in 1806 governor of Naples. In 1813 he was defeated by Wellington at Vitoria, and in 1814 transferred his allegiance to the Bourbons, who made him a count. He supported the Revolution of 1830.

JOUVENEL, Henri de (1876–1935), French politician and journalist, husband (1910–1935) of the authoress Colette, born in Paris, attained a high position in the ministry of justice before editing *Le Matin*. Elected senator in 1921, he was delegate to the League of Nations (1922 and 1924) and was high commissioner in Syria (1925–26).

JOUVET, Louis, *zhoo-vay* (1887–1951), French theatre and film director and actor, born in Finistère, graduated as a pharmacist but took to the stage. He fought in the first World War and toured the United States with Jacques Copeau's company (1918–19). He became stage-manager (1922) and director (1924) of the Comédie des Champs Élysées. Equally at home in modern as in classical French drama, he was the first to recognize Giraudoux, all but one of whose plays (1928–46) he produced, as well as Cocteau's *La Machine infernale* (1931). In 1934 his company transferred to the Théâtre de l'Athénée and he was honoured by being the first director to be appointed professor at the Paris Conservatoire, outside the Comédie Française. At the latter, however, he directed (1936–37) outstanding productions of Molière's *L'École des femmes* and Corneille's *L'Illusion*. He was equally outstanding as an actor in such films as *Topaze*, *Carnival in Flanders* (1935), and directed *Carnet de bal* (1937), *La Fin du jour* (1939), *Volpone* (1940) and *Retour à la vie* (1949), &c. He was awarded the Legion of Honour (1926) and in 1949 was chosen best French film actor of the year. See study by B. L. Knapp (1958).

JOUY, Victor Joseph Étienne de, *zhwee* (1764–1846), French playwright, librettist, and author of *L'Hermite de la Chaussée d'Antin* (1812–14) and other prose works, was born at Jouy near Versailles; till 1797 served as a soldier in India and at home; and in 1815 was elected to the Academy.

JOWETT, Benjamin (1817–93), English Greek scholar, born at Camberwell, was educated at St Paul's School and Balliol, Oxford, where he won the Hertford in 1837, a classical first in 1839, and the Latin essay in 1841. Already a fellow in 1838, he was tutor from 1840 till his election as master in 1870; from 1855 to 1893 he was regius professor of Greek, from 1882 till 1886 vice-chancellor. As master of Balliol his Liberal influence permeated the college to a degree almost unexampled. Jowett belonged to the Broad Church party. For his article 'On the Interpretation of Scripture' in *Essays and Reviews* (1860) he was tried but acquitted by the vice-chancellor's court. He is best known for his beautiful translation, marred somewhat for philosophers by lack of exact scholarship, of the *Dialogues* of Plato (1871; 3rd ed. 1892) and his (less happy) versions of Thucydides (1881) and the *Politics* of Aristotle (1885). See his *Life and Letters* ed. by Evelyn Abbott and Lewis Campbell (1897), and *Portrait* by G. Faber (1957).

JOWITT, William Allen, (1885–1957), 1st Earl Jowitt, Viscount Stevenage, British politician, born at Stevenage, Herts, and educated at Marlborough and Oxford. He was called to the bar in 1909 and took silk in 1922. He was Liberal M.P. for the Hartlepools (1922–24) and for five months for a Preston constituency (1929), which seat he resigned on joining the Labour party and becoming attorney-general; he was returned with an increased majority as a Socialist. In 1931 he joined the National Government, was expelled from the Labour party, returned to it in 1936, becoming M.P. for Ashton-under-Lyne in 1939. In 1945 he became lord chancellor, and piloted through the Conservative House of Lords a mass of Socialist legislation. His publications include *The Strange Case of Alger Hiss* (1953) and *Some Were Spies* (1954).

JOYCE, (1) James Augustine Aloysius (1882–1941), Irish writer, born at Dublin, was educated at the National University of Ireland, went in 1903 to Paris to study medicine and subsequently took up voice training for a concert platform career. Back in Dublin, he published a few stories, but, unable to make a living by his pen, he left for Trieste to tutor in English. Dublin saw him for the last time in 1912, when he started the short-lived Volta Cinema Theatre; and at the outbreak of World War I he was again in Trieste. He went to Zürich in 1915, where he formed a company of Irish players to perform his *Exiles* (an Ibsenite drama). He settled in Paris in 1920, remaining there until 1940 when he returned to Zürich, where he shortly afterwards died. His first publication was a collection of lyrics, *Chamber Music* (1907). *Dubliners*, short stories, appeared in 1914, to be followed by *Portrait of the Artist as a Young Man* (1917), originally serialized by Ezra Pound in the *Egoist* during 1914–15. His best-known book, *Ulysses*, appeared in Paris in 1922, but was banned in Britain and America for some years. *Work in Progress* began to appear in 1927, in sections and under different titles, and finally emerged as *Finnegans Wake* (1939). These novels flout the accepted conventions of the novel form prior to Joyce. The time factor becomes elastic and consciousness takes over and dictates the sequence of events. Plot and character emerge in a stream of association that carries on its ripples all the mental flotsam and jetsam that in the ordinary novel never rise to the surface. In addition, Joyce, particularly in the second novel, employs language like a musical notation, that is, the sound superficially supersedes the sense (to the average mind), but in reality communicates (like music) profundities which conventionalized words cannot express. That, at any rate, is what Joyce intends, but not many readers can go along with him all the way. Of the value of his experiment with his elaborate system of analogy there can be no doubt, and he conducts the experiment brilliantly, but it is self-evident that further analogy must turn back, in convolutions, on itself; there can, therefore, be no development after a certain point is reached and that point is reached in *Finnegans Wake*. Joyce's peculiar achievement has been to translate to the art of writing the conception and technique of the art of musical composition. See also the *Critical Writings of James Joyce*, ed. E. Mason and R. Ellman (1959), biographical studies by Kenner (1956), his brother, S. Joyce, with a preface by T. S. Eliot (1958), K. Sullivan (1958), M. and P. Colum (1958) and C. P. Curran (1968), and studies by H. S. Gorman (1941), ed. T. S. Eliot (1942), L. A. G. Strong (1949), W. Y. Tindall (1950), Smidt (1955), Ussher (1955), L. Gillet (trans. 1958), R. Ellmann (1959).

(2) William (1906–46), British traitor, was born in Brooklyn, U.S.A., of Irish parentage. As a child he lived in Ireland and in 1922 his family emigrated to England. In 1933 he joined Sir Oswald Mosley's British Union of Fascists and secured a British passport by falsely claiming to have been born in Galway. Expelled from Mosley's party in 1937, he founded his own fanatical, Hitler-worshipping, British National Socialist Party. He fled to Germany before war broke out and from September 1939 to April 1945 broadcast from Radio Hamburg Goebbelasian propaganda of falsehood, abuse and threats against Britain. Each broadcast was heralded by the characteristic 'Chairmanny Calling', in a pretentious voice which earned him the title 'Lord Haw-Haw'. He was captured by the British at Flensburg, was tried at the Old Bailey, London, in September 1945, convicted and executed. His defence was his American birth, but his British passport, valid until July 1940, established nine months of treason. See Rebecca West, *The Meaning of Treason* (1949) and Life by Cole (1964).

JOYNSON-HICKS, William, 1st Viscount Brentford (1865–1932), British Conservative politician, entered parliament in 1908 and was successively postmaster-general, minister of health and home secretary (1924–29). He played a leading part in defeating the Prayer Book Measure (1927). His second son, **Lancelot William, 3rd Viscount** (1902–), was also a Conservative politician.

JUAN DE LA CRUZ. See JOHN OF THE CROSS.

JUAN, Don. See JOHN OF AUSTRIA.

JUÁREZ, Benito Pablo, *hwah'res* (1806–72), president of Mexico, was born of Indian parents near Oaxaca. Exiled in 1853 for two years, in 1857 he was elected president of the supreme court. In 1858 he was compelled to retire to Vera Cruz, whence he issued decrees abolishing religious orders and confiscating church property. In 1861 he entered the capital, and was elected president for four years. In 1866 the French emperor declared war against him. But on the withdrawal of the French. he re-entered Mexico City in July 1867, the Emperor Maximilian (q.v.) having meanwhile been shot. Juárez was then elected president, and again in 1871. See Lives by U. R. Burke (1894), Zo Enníquez (1906), P. Martinez (1933), and C. Smart (1964).

JUBA, king of Numidia, having supported Pompey against Caesar, committed suicide, 46 B.C.

JUDAH, fourth son of Jacob and Leah, was founder of the greatest of the twelve tribes.

JUDAS, the betrayer of Jesus, surnamed Iscariot, was probably a native of Kerioth in the tribe of Judah. See the essay by De Quincey.

JUDAS MACCABAEUS. See MACCABEES.

JUDD, (1) John Wesley (1840–1916), British geologist, was born at Portsmouth, and entered the Royal School of Mines. In 1867 he joined the Geological Survey; in 1876 became professor at the School of Mines, in 1881 at the Royal College of Science. *Volcanoes* (1881) is by him.

(2) Sylvester (1813–53), American writer,

born at Westhampton, Mass., from 1840 a Unitarian pastor at Augusta, Me., wrote against slavery, war, intemperance, &c.

JUDE, St, was probably the Judas who was one of the 'brethren of the Lord' (Matt. xiii. 55; Mark vi. 3). His epistle was placed among the *Antilegomena*, or disputed books, by the primitive church. Many critics hold that it is directed against the Gnostics of the 2nd century.

JUDITH, a Jewish heroine, who, in the Apocryphal book named after her, is said to have made her way into the tent of Holofernes, general of Nebuchadnezzar, cut off his head, and so saved her native town of Bethulia.

JUDSON, Adoniram (1788–1850), American missionary, born in Malden, Mass., thought of turning playwright, but in 1812, having married, went to Burma as a Baptist missionary, and was a prisoner during the Burmese war. His Burmese translation of the Bible (1833) was followed by a Burmese-English dictionary. He died at sea. See Lives by Wayland (1853), E. Judson (his son) (1883), Mathieson (1929).

JUGURTHA (d. 104 B.C.), king of Numidia, by the murder of one cousin secured a part of the kingdom of his grandfather Masinissa, and bribed the Roman senate to support him (116 B.C.). But he soon invaded his surviving cousin Adherbal's part of the kingdom, in spite of Roman warnings, besieged him in Cirta (112), and put him and the Romans who were with him to death. Thereupon war was declared by the Romans; but, by bribery, Jugurtha contrived to baffle their power, until in 106 he had to flee to the king of Mauritania, whom Marius compelled to deliver him up. He was left to die in prison at Rome. See Sallust's history of the Jugurthine war, ed. Coleridge (1894).

JUIN, Alphonse Pierre, *zhwī* (1888–1967), French general, born at Bône, Algeria, passed out top of his class, which included de Gaulle, at the St Cyr Military Academy, fought in the Moroccan campaigns (1912–14) and World War I, and in 1938 became chief of staff in North Africa. As divisional commander in the First French Army he fought and was captured by the Germans in 1940, but was released in June 1941. Became military governor of Morocco, having declined the post of Vichy minister of war. After the Allied invasion of Tunisia, he changed sides, helped to defeat von Arnim's Afrika Corps remnants and distinguished himself in the subsequent Italian campaign. He became chief of staff of the National Defence Committee in Liberated France (1944–47), was resident-general in Morocco (1947–51) and served in senior N.A.T.O. commands (1953–56). He was made an honorary G.C.B. (1944), awarded the *Grand Croix de la Légion d'honneur*, promoted field-marshal (1952) and elected French Academician (1953). Publications include *Mémoires* (1959–60), and *La France en Algérie* (1963).

JUKES, Joseph Beete, (1811–69), British geologist, born near Birmingham, in 1839 became geological surveyor of Newfoundland, and in 1842 helped to explore the coasts of Australia. He next surveyed part of North Wales for the Geological Survey (1846–50), and in 1850 became local director of the survey in Ireland. He lectured on geology in Dublin. His chief works are *Excursions in and about Newfoundland* (1842), *Surveying Voyage of H.M.S. 'Fly', in Torres Strait, &c.* (1847), and *Student's Manual of Geology* (1858), &c. See his Letters (1871).

JULIA (39 B.C.–A.D. 14), daughter of the Emperor Augustus, was married at fourteen to her cousin Marcellus, a nephew of Augustus, and after his death in 23 B.C. to Marcus Vipsanius Agrippa, to whom she bore three sons and two daughters. He died in 12 B.C., whereupon Julia was married to Tiberius. The marriage was unhappy and her conduct far from irreproachable; but it was chiefly the jealous hatred of Livia, Tiberius's mother, that procured Julia's banishment first to the isle of Pandataria, and then to Reggio, where she died voluntarily of starvation. See novel by R. Graves, *I, Claudius*.

JULIAN (Flavius Claudius Julianus), 'the Apostate' (*c.* 331–63), Roman emperor (361–63), born at Constantinople, was the youngest son of Constantius, half-brother of Constantine the Great. On Constantine's death in 337, and the accession of his three sons, there was a general massacre of the males of the younger line of the Flavian family. Julian and his elder half-brother Gallus were alone spared as too young to be dangerous, when their father, brother, uncle and cousins perished. His youth was embittered by this tragedy, which stripped him of all belief in the Christian religion now established. In 355 he spent a few happy months at Athens in the study of Greek philosophy, and the same year was summoned to Milan to assume the rank of Caesar, and marry the emperor's sister, Helena. The next five years he served as soldier, overthrowing the Alemanni neas Strasbourg, and subduing the Frankish triber along the Rhine. He endeared himself to the soldiers by his personal courage, his success in war, and the severe simplicity of his life. In April 360 the emperor, alarmed at his growing popularity, demanded that he should send some of his best troops to serve against the Persians, but his soldiers rose in insurrection and proclaimed him Augustus. Next, he set out with his army for Constantinople. At Sirmium on the Danube he openly declared himself a pagan. There he learnt of the opportune death of his cousin (361), which opened up to him the government of the world. The first winter he spent at Constantinople in a course of public reforms. Towards Christians and Jews he adopted a policy of toleration, but none the less he devoted himself to restoring the dignity of the old religion. He stripped the church of its privileges by every means short of persecution. He spent 362–363 at Antioch, and made himself somewhat unpopular by fixing an arbitrary price on corn in order to stave off a threatened famine. In 363 he set out against the Persians. He crossed the Tigris, advanced to Ctesiphon, was enticed farther by a Persian traitor, and was at length forced to retreat through barren country, harassed by swarms of Persian cavalry. The enemy were repeatedly beaten off, but in one of the attacks the emperor was mortally wounded by a spearthrust. Julian's extant writings are a series of *Epistles*; nine *Orations*; *Caesares*, satires on past Caesars; and the *Misopōgōn*. His chief work, *Kata Christianōn* is lost. See Life by J. Bidez (1930).

JULIANA, Louise Emma Marie Wilhelmina (1909–), queen of the Netherlands (1948–), born at The Hague and educated at Leyden University. In 1930 she passed her final examination in international law. She married in 1937 Prince Bernhard zur Lippe-Biesterfeld (q.v.), and they have four daughters: Princess Beatrix Wilhelmina Armgard (b. 1938), heiress to the throne, married West German diplomat Claus-Georg Wilhelm Otto Friedrich Gerd von Amsberg (b. 1926) in 1966; their son (b. 1967) is the first male Dutch heir in over a century; Princess Irene Emma Elizabeth (b. 1939), married Prince Hugo of Bourbon-Parma (b. 1939), son of the Carlist pretender to the Spanish throne, Prince Xavier, in 1964 (against her parents' wishes, and forfeiting her right of succession); Princess Margriet Francisca (b. 1943), married a commoner, Pieter van Vollenhoven, in 1967; and Princess Maria Christina (b. 1947). On the German invasion of Holland in 1940 Juliana escaped to Britain and later resided in Canada. She returned to Holland in 1945, and in 1948, on the abdication of her mother Queen Wilhelmina, became queen.

JULIUS, the name of three popes, of whom the following are noteworthy:

Julius II (1443–1513), pope from 1503, born Giuliano della Rovere at Albizuola, forced, after his election, Cesare Borgia to yield his conquests in Romagna. Julius's public career was mainly devoted to political and military enterprises for the re-establishment of papal sovereignty in its ancient territory, and for the extinction of foreign domination in Italy. To compel Venice to restore the papal provinces on the Adriatic, Julius entered into the league of Cambrai with the Emperor Maximilian, Ferdinand of Aragon and Louis XII of France, and placed the republic under the ban of the church. On the submission of Venice, suspecting the designs of Louis, he entered into a 'Holy League' with Spain and England. Louis XII ineffectually attempted to enlist the church against the pope. The Council of Pisa, convened under Louis's influence, was a failure; and the fifth Lateran Council, assembled by Julius, completely frustrated the designs of the French king. A Liberal patron of the arts, he employed Bramante for the design of St Peter's begun in 1506, had Raphael brought to Rome to decorate his private apartments and commissioned Michelangelo for the frescoes on the roof of the Sistine chapel and for his own tomb. His military exploits inspired Erasmus' satire *Julius Excluus*.

Julius III (1487–1555), pope from 1550, born Gianmaria del Monte in Rome, was one of the three delegates to the Council of Trent, which he reopened after his election. He sent Cardinal Pole to organize with Mary Tudor the reunion of England with the Church of Rome.

JULLIEN, Louis Antoine, *zhü-lyī* (1812–60), French musician, born in the Basses Alpes, became conductor of concerts at Paris in 1836, but in 1838 made London his headquarters, and did much to popularize music and helped to establish the promenade concerts. Bankrupt in 1857, he retired to Paris, was imprisoned for debt, and died in a lunatic asylum. See Life by Carse (1951).

JUMIÈGES. See ROBERT and WILLIAM OF.

JUNG, *yoong*, **Carl Gustav** (1875-1961), Swiss psychiatrist, studied medicine at Basel, worked under Eugen Bleuler at the Burghölzli mental clinic at Zürich (1900-09). His early *Studies in Word Association* (1904-09; in them he coined the term 'complex') and *The Psychology of Dementia Praecox* (1906-07) led to his meeting Freud in Vienna in 1907. He became Freud's leading collaborator and was elected President of the International Psychoanalytical Association (1910-14). His independent researches, making him increasingly critical of Freud's exclusively sexual definition of libido and incest, and published in *The Psychology of the Unconscious* (1911-12), caused a break in 1913. From then onwards he steadily developed his own theories ('analytical psychology') foremost among which are: a description of psychological types ('extraversion/introversion', 1921); a theory of psychic energy (1928), emphasizing a final point of view as against a purely causal one; a dynamic concept of the symbol as 'transformer of energy' (1928); the discovery and exploration of the 'collective unconscious' with its 'archetypes', an impersonal substratum underlying the 'personal unconscious'; the concept of the psyche as a 'self-regulating system' expressing itself in the process of 'individuation'. To this latter process Jung devoted most of his later work, constantly enlarging the scope of his researches to include dreams and drawings of patients, the symbolism of religions, myths, historical antecedents as e.g. alchemy, and even modern physics ('synchronicity'). Jung's work has proved of great importance not only for psychology but also for anthropology, religion, art and literature, history, etc. Jung held professorships at Zürich and Basel, receiving many honorary degrees. Other main works: *On Psychic Energy* (1928), *Psychology and Religion* (1937), *Psychology and Alchemy* (1944), *Aion* (1951), *The Undiscovered Self* (1957). See *Collected Works* (19 vols., 1953ff.); also Jung, *Memories, Dreams, Reflections*, recorded and ed. by A Jaffé; F. Fordham, *An Introduction to Jung's Psychology* (1953), J. Jacobi, *The Psychology of C. G. Jung* (1962), G. Adler, *Studies in Analytical Psychology* (1966).

(2) **Johann Heinrich**, known as 'Jung Stilling' (1740–1817), German mystic and writer. Though qualified in medicine, he became Professor of Political Economy at Marburg (1787–1804), then at Heidelberg, and wrote semi-mystical, semipietistic romances and works on political economy, as well as a charming autobiography including *Heinrich Stillings Jugend*, ed. Goethe (1777–1804).

JUNG BAHADUR, Sir (1816–77), prime-minister of Nepal, assisted the British with a body of Gurkhas during the Indian Mutiny.

JUNGE, *yoong'ĕ*, also **Jung** or **Jungius, Joachim** (1587–1657), German scientist, born at Lübeck, studied at Rostock and Giessen, where he became professor of Mathematics, a position he resigned in 1614 to study medicine at Padua. He returned to Rostock and founded the Societas Ereunetica in 1622, but accused of heresy, he passed the rest of his life in the minor post of rector of the Hamburg High School. An early champion of the atomic theory, he anticipated the botanical classification of Ray and Linnaeus.

JUNIUS, Franciscus (1589–1677), German-born philologist, born at Heidelberg, and brought up in Holland by his brother-in-law Vossius, from 1621 to 1651 lived in England in the Earl of Arundel's family, returned in 1674, and died near Windsor. He studied Anglo-Saxon and Gothic, and wrote also on ancient art.

JUNKER, Wilhelm, *yoong'kėr* (1840–92), German traveller, was born of German parents in Moscow, and studied medicine in Germany. In 1876–78 he travelled amongst the western tributaries of the Upper Nile; in 1879 he set off to explore the Welle. After four years among the Monbuttu and Niam-Niam, and some time with Emin Pasha, he returned in 1887. See his Travels (1889; trans. 1890).

JUNKERS, Hugo, *yoong'kėrs* (1859–1935), German aircraft engineer, born at Rheydt, was professor of Mechanical Engineering at Aachen (1897–1912). After the 1914–18 war he founded aircraft factories at Dessau, Magdeburg and Stassfurt, which produced many famous planes, both civil and military.

JUNOT, Andoche, *zhü-nō* (1771–1813), French general, born at Bussy-le-Grand, distinguished himself in the early wars of the republic. He was adjutant under Napoleon in Egypt. In 1806 he was made governor of Paris, and in 1807 was appointed to the command of the army for Portugal. He quickly made himself master of all the strong places in the kingdom, was created Duc d'Abrantès, and appointed governor of Portugal; but, defeated by Wellington at Vimeiro, was obliged to conclude the Convention of Cintra and retire from Portugal. He served in Germany and Russia, and, made one of the scapegoats for the Russian disaster, was sent to govern Illyria. Mentally deranged, he threw himself from a window of his father's house near Dijon and died a week later. His wife, the extravagant Duchesse d'Abrantès (1784–1838), gained a reputation by her *Mémoires* (1831–1835).

JUNQUEIRO, Abilio Guerra, *zhoong-kay'-ee-roo* (1850–1923), Portuguese lyric poet and satirist, born at Freixo, became a deputy in 1872, opposed the Braganzas and was tried for *lèse majesté* in 1907. After the revolution he was minister to Switzerland. His poetry shows the influence of Victor Hugo.

JUSSERAND, Jean Adrien Antoine Jules, *zhüs-rã* (1855–1932), French writer and diplomat, born at Lyons, served in the French embassy in London in 1887–90, and in 1902–25 was ambassador to the United States. He wrote (in French and in English) on English wayfaring life, on the literary history of the English people (new ed. 1926), on Shakespeare in France, &c.

JUSSIEU, *zhü-syœ,* name of a family of French botanists:

(1) **Antoine Laurent de** (1748–1836), nephew of (2), studied at Paris and became professor at the Jardin des Plantes. He elaborated in his *Genera Plantarum* (1778–89) his uncle's system of classification. His son **Adrien** (1797–1853) wrote a botanical textbook and memoirs.

(2) **Bernard** (*c.* 1699–1777), uncle of (1), demonstrated at the Jardin des Plantes (1722), created a botanical garden at Trianon for Louis XV and adopted a system which has become the basis of modern natural botanical classification. He first suggested that polyps were animals. His brother **Antoine** (1686–1758), a physician and professor of the Jardin des Plantes, edited Tournefort's *Institutiones Rei Herbariae* (1719).

JUSTIN, St, surnamed the **Martyr** (*c.* 100–*c.* 165), one of the Fathers of the Church, was born at Sichem in Samaria, and was successively a Stoic and a Platonist; and after his conversion to Christianity travelled about on foot defending its truths. At Rome between 150 and 160 he wrote the *Apologia* of Christianity addressed to the Emperor, followed by a second one. He is said to have been martyred about A.D. 165. There is an edition by Otto of his works, including numerous treatises falsely attributed to him (1876–81). There are two English translations. See works by Semisch (1842), Aubé (1874), Stählin (1880), Freppel (1885), Huth (1894), Veil (1895), Goodenough (1923) and A. Lukyn Williams (1930).

JUSTIN, name of two rulers of the Eastern Roman empire:

Justin I (450–527), born in Illyria, became commander in the imperial bodyguard, and in 518 was raised to the Byzantine throne by the army. Owing to his total want of learning he wisely resigned the civil administration to the quaestor Proclus. In 519 he entered into an arrangement with the pope; in 523 resigned to Theodoric, king of Italy, the right of appointing 'consuls' in Rome; and in the same year became involved in a war with the Persians. He was succeeded by his nephew Justinian.

Justin II (d. 578), succeeded his uncle, Justinian I, in 565, and married and was ruled by Sophia, the unscrupulous niece of the Empress Theodora. He yielded part of Italy to the Lombards, was unsuccessful against the Persians and Avars, and became insane. See study by Vasiliev (1950).

JUSTINIAN, name of two rulers of the Eastern Roman empire:

Justinian I (Flavius Anicius Justinianus) (*c.* 482–565), emperor from 527, nephew of Justin I, was born at Tauresium in Illyria, the son of a Slavonic peasant, and was originally called Sabbatius. Through his uncle he was educated at Constantinople, in 521 was named consul, and in 527 was proclaimed by Justin his colleague in the empire. Justin died the same year, and Justinian, proclaimed sole emperor, was crowned along with his wife Theodora, once an actress. His reign is the most brilliant in the history of the late empire. He had the good fortune or the skill to select the ablest generals; and under Narses (q.v.) and Belisarius (q.v.) his reign may be said to have restored the Roman empire to its ancient limits, and to have reunited the East and West. His first war—that with Persia—ended in a favourable treaty. But the conflict of the Blue and Green factions in 532 was an outburst of political discontent, which went so far as to elect a rival emperor. Justinian had thought of flight, when Narses, Belisarius and Theodora repressed the tumults relentlessly; 35,000 victims fell in a single day. Through Belisarius's generalship, the Vandal kingdom of Africa was reannexed to the empire; and Belisarius and Narses restored the imperial authority in Rome, Northern Italy and Spain. Justinian constructed or renewed a vast line of fortifications along the eastern and south-eastern frontier of his empire, which, with his great public buildings, involved a burdensome expenditure. It was as legislator that Justinian gained his most enduring renown. He set himself to collect and codify the principal imperial *constitutiones* or statutes in force at his accession. The *Codex*, by which all previous imperial enactments were repealed, was published in 529. The writings of the jurists or commentators were next harmonized, and published under the title *Digesta* or *Pandectae* in 533. The direction of this work was entrusted to Tribonian, with a committee of professors and advocates, who also prepared a systematic and elementary treatise on the law—the *Institutiones* (533), based on the *Institutiones* of Gaius. A new edition of the *Codex* was issued in 534. During the subsequent years of his reign Justinian promulgated from time to time several new laws or constitutions, known as *Novellae*. The Institutes, Digest, Code and Novels together make up what is known as the *Corpus Juris Civilis*. An able ruler, Justinian died November 14, 565. See Lives by Isambert (1856), Body (6th ed. 1889); Roby, *Introduction to the Digest* (1884); Diehl, *Justinien et la Civilisation Byzantine* (1901); Holmes, *The Age of Justinian* (1905–07), and Ure (Penguin).

JUVENAL, Decimus Junius Juvenalis (*c.* 55–*c.* 140), Roman lawyer and satirist, born at Aquinum in the Volscian country, received the usual rhetorical education, and served as tribune in the army, fulfilled some local functions at Aquinum, was in Britain, and returned home in safety. He was also for a time in Egypt. His 16 brilliant satires in verse of Roman times (*c.* 100–*c.* 128) and vices, written from his viewpoint of an angry Stoic moralist, range from exposures of unnatural vices, the misery of poverty, the extravagance of the ruling classes and the precarious makeshift life of their hangers-on, to his hatred of Jews and women. The last was the subject of his sixth satire, of which a part was not discovered until 1899. Dryden's versions of five of Juvenal's satires are amongst the best things he ever did. Johnson imitated two of the most famous in his *London* and *Vanity of Human Wishes*. See edition by A. E. Housman (1931), and H. E. Butler, *Post-Augustan Poetry* (1909), and study by Highet (1954).

JUXON, William (1582–1663), English divine, born at Chichester, was educated at Merchant Taylors' School and St John's College, Oxford, succeeded Laud as its president in 1621, and became a prebendary of Chichester and dean of Worcester (1627), Bishop of London (1633), and lord high treasurer (1635). In Charles I's vacillation about the fate of Strafford, Juxon advised him to refuse his assent to the bill. He ministered to the king in his last moments and the king gave him his insignia of the Order of the Garter with the word 'Remember' before putting his head on the execution block. During the Commonwealth Juxon retired to his Gloucestershire seat, and after the Restoration was appointed Archbishop of Canterbury. See Life by W. H. Marah (1869).

K

KADAR, Janos, *kah'dahr* (1912–), Hungarian politician, was born at Kapoly in S.W. Hungary, began life as an instrument-maker and was early attracted to the Communist party. During the second World War he was a member of the Central Committee of the underground party, escaping from capture by the Gestapo. He emerged after the war as first party secretary and one of the leading figures of the Communist régime. In 1950, as minister of the interior, he was arrested for 'Titoist' sympathies. He was freed in 1953, was rehabilitated in 1954 and became secretary of the Party Committee for Budapest in 1955. When the Hungarian anti-Soviet revolution broke out in October 1956 he was a member of the 'national', anti-Stalinist government of Imre Nagy. On November 1 he declared that the Communist party had been dissolved as it had 'degenerated into perpetuating despotism and national slavery'. But as Soviet tanks crushed the revolution, he formed a puppet government which in the closing months of 1956 held Hungary in a ruthless reign of terror. The majority of his countrymen regarded him as betrayer, but a few as a helpless victim of forces beyond his control. He resigned in 1958, but became premier and first secretary of the central committee in 1961. In 1965 he lost the premiership, but remained first secretary. See Fryer, *Hungarian Tragedy* (1956).

KAFKA, Franz (1883–1924), Austrian novelist, born of Jewish parentage in Prague, where he graduated in Law, and although overwhelmed by a desire to write, found employment (1907–23) as an official in the accident prevention department of the government-sponsored Worker's Accident Insurance

Institution. A hypersensitive, almost exclusively introspective person with an extraordinary attachment for his father, he eventually moved to Berlin to live with Dora Dymant in 1923, his only brief spell of happiness before succumbing to a lung disease of long standing. His short stories and essays, including *Der Heizer* 'The Boilerman' (1913) *Betrachtungen* 'Meditations' (1913), *Die Verwandlung* 'The Metamorphosis' (1916), &c., were published in his lifetime, but he refused the same for his three unfinished novels, which, through his friend Max Brod (q.v.), were published posthumously and translated by Edwin and Willa Muir. They are *Ein Prozess* (1925) 'The Trial' (1937), *Das Schloss* (1926) 'The Castle' (1937) and *Amerika* (1927; trans. 1938). Literary critics have interpreted the second variously, as a modern *Pilgrim's Progress* (but there is literally no progress), as a literary exercise in Kierkegaardian existentialist theology, as an allegory of the Jew in a Gentile world, or psychoanalytically as a monstrous expression of Kafka's Oedipus complex, but his solipsism primarily portrays society as a pointless schizophrenically rational organization into which the bewildered but unshocked individual has strayed. Kafka has exerted a tremendous influence on Western literature, not least on such writers as Albert Camus, Rex Warner and Samuel Beckett. See *Collected Works* (1935–37) and *Diaries, 1914-1923* (1949), both edited by M. Brod, who has written a definitive life (trans. 1947), also *Letters*, ed. W. Haas (trans. 1953), *Conversations*, by G. Janouch (trans. 1953), and studies by A. Camus (1942), Magny and Flores (N.Y. 1946), C. Neider (1949), E. Heller, *The Disinherited Mind* (1952), and R. Gray (1956).

KAGANOVICH, Lazar Moiseyevich, *-nō'-* (1893–), Russian politician, was born at Gomel, joined the Communist party in 1911 and after the Revolution became secretary of the Ukrainian central committee. In 1928 he became Moscow party secretary. From 1934 to 1942 and from 1943 to 1944 he was commissar for railways. In 1947 he became deputy chairman of the Council of Ministers. He survived the death of his brother-in-law, Stalin, in 1953, but he was dismissed in 1957. He was last heard of in August 1957, in 'a position of considerable responsibility'—a Siberian cement works.

KAGAWA, Toyohiko (1888–1960), Japanese missionary and writer, studied at Princeton University, then returned to Japan, where his work in the fields of social reform and evangelism made him one of the great figures of modern Christianity. See studies by W. Axling (1947), E. O. Bradshaw (Minnesota 1952) and C. J. Davey (1960).

KAISER, *kī'zėr*, (1) **Georg** (1878–1945), German dramatist, born at Magdeburg, lived at Buenos Aires and in Germany, and wrote plays, mostly expressionist. See study by M. J. Fruchter (Philadelphia 1933).

(2) **Henry John** (1882–1967), American industrialist, born in New York State. From 1914 to 1933 he worked on various civil engineering projects in the United States, Canada and the West Indies. As manager of seven highly productive shipyards on the Pacific coast of the United States during World War II, he developed revolutionary methods of prefabrication and assembly in shipbuilding—enabling his ships to be constructed and launched within six days. His vast industrial empire included a motor, a steel, and an aluminium and chemical corporation.

KÁLIDÁSA (fl. A.D. 450), India's greatest dramatist, is best known through his drama *Sákuntala*. See studies by B. S. Upadhyaya (India 1947) and G. C. Jhala (1949).

KALININ, Mikhail Ivanovich, *kah-lee'-nin* (1875–1946), Russian politician, born at Tver (which was renamed after him in 1932), was in early life a peasant and a metal-worker. Entering politics as a champion of the peasant class, he won great popularity, becoming president of the Soviet central executive committee (1919–38), and of the Presidium of the Supreme Soviet (1938–46). He died in Moscow.

KÁLNOKY VON KÖRÖSPATAK, Gustav Sigismund, Count (1832–98), Austrian statesman, born at Lettowitz in Moravia, entered the diplomatic service in 1850. He was sent as ambassador to Copenhagen in 1870, to St Petersburg in 1880, and in 1881 became minister of foreign affairs. He resigned in 1895.

KALTENBRUNNER, Ernst (1902–46), Austrian Nazi leader, head of the S.S. at the time of the Anschluss, became head of the security police in 1943, sent millions of Jews and political suspects to their death in concentration camps, and was responsible for orders sanctioning the murder of prisoners of war and baled-out airmen. He was condemned by the Nuremberg Tribunal and hanged.

KAMENEV, orig. **Rosenfeld, Lev Borisovich** (1883–1936), Russian politician, born of Jewish parentage in Moscow, was an active revolutionary from 1901 and was exiled to Siberia in 1915. Liberated during the revolution in 1917, he became a member of the Communist central committee. Expelled as a Trotskyist in 1927, he was readmitted next year but again expelled in 1932. He was shot after being arrested with Zinoviev (q.v.) for conspiring against Stalin.

KAMERLINGH ONNES. See ONNES.

KAMES, Henry Home, Lord (1696–1782), Scottish philosopher, born at Kames in Berwickshire, was called to the bar in 1723 and raised to the bench as Lord Kames in 1752. Besides books on Scots law he published *Essays on Morality* (1751), *An Introduction to the Art of Thinking* (1761), *Elements of Criticism* (his best-known work, 1762), and *Sketches of the History of Man* (1774). See critical study by H. W. Randall (Northampton, Mass., 1944).

KÄMPFER, Engelbert, *kemp'fėr* (1651–1716), German traveller, after visiting India, Java and Siam, spent two years in Japan (1692–94). His *History of Japan and Siam* appeared in English in 1727 and in 1906.

KANARIS, Constantine, *ka-nah'rees* (1790–1877), a Greek merchant-captain, born in the Isle of Ipsara, who blew up the Turkish admiral's ship in the Strait of Chios (1822), repeated a like feat in the harbour of Tenedos, and in 1824 burnt a Turkish frigate and some transport ships. He was appointed to important commands, was made senator in 1847, and was repeatedly at the head of ministries. He died at Athens.

KANDINSKY, Vasily (1866–1944), Russian painter, was born in Moscow. He spent his childhood in Italy, and his early work was done in Paris. After a stay (1914–21) in Russia, where he founded the Russian Academy and became head of the Museum of Modern Art, he spent a few years in charge of the Weimar Bauhaus. From 1923 on he lived in Paris. An individual painter, who developed his own abstract theories, he exercised great influence on young European artists and was a leader of the 'Blaue Reiter' group. Studies by W. Grohmann (1959) and H. Rebay von Chrenwiesen (N.Y. 1945).

KANE, (1) Elisha Kent (1820–57), Arctic explorer, born in Philadephia. Entering the U.S. navy as surgeon, he visited China, the East Indies, Arabia, Egypt, Europe, the west coast of Africa and Mexico. In 1850 he sailed as surgeon and naturalist with the first Grinnell (q.v.) expedition. His account of it appeared in 1854. In 1853 he again set out as commander of an expedition (see his *Second Grinnell Expedition*, 1856). See Life by Elder (1858), the briefer one by Jones (1890), and J. Mirsky (Canada 1954).

(2) **Sir Robert** (1809–90), Irish chemist, born in Dublin, studied medicine, and became a professor of Chemistry there (1831), next year starting the *Dublin Journal of Medical Science*. In 1846 he originated the Museum of Industry in Ireland, was appointed its first director, and was knighted. He was president of Queen's College, Cork (1845–73), and in 1877 was elected president of the Royal Irish Academy. His chief books are *Elements of Chemistry* (1842) and *Industrial Resources of Ireland* (1844). Life by D. O'Raghallaigh (Cork 1942).

KANT, Immanuel, *kahnt* (1724–1804), German philosopher, the greatest of the idealist school, born April 22, in Königsberg, where he spent his entire life, the son of a saddler, reputedly of Scottish origin. Brought up in relative poverty and the puritanical strictness of Pietism, Kant studied at the university and after some years as private tutor in 1755 obtained his doctorate and was appointed *privatdozent*. His lectures, unlike his written works, were often witty, humorous and full of interesting red herrings. The same year he published an essay in Newtonian cosmology in which he anticipated the nebular theory of Laplace and predicted the existence of the planet Uranus, before its actual discovery by Herschel in 1781. At first a rationalist, he became more sceptical of metaphysics in his 'pre-critical' works as in *Träume eines Geistersehers* (1766) 'Dreams of a Ghost-seer' against Swedenborg's mysticism. But Kant was dissatisfied with Hume's reduction of knowledge of things and causation to mere habitual associations of sense-impressions. How for example was it possible for mathematics to apply to the objects of our sense-impressions? From 1775 he laboured on an answer to Hume, which materialized in his *Kritik der reinen Vernunft* (1781; 2nd ed., in parts re-written, 1786) 'Critique of Pure Reason' (2nd edn., including the sections omitted from the 1st, trans. N. Kemp Smith 1933), a philosophical classic, in which he shows that the immediate objects of perception are due not only to the evidence provided by our sensations but also to our own perceptual apparatus which orders our sense-impressions into intelligible unities. Whereas the former are rightly empirical and *synthetic*, the ordering is not dependent upon experience, i.e., *a priori*. Hence Kant's famous claim that 'though our knowledge begins with experience, it does not follow that it arises out of experience'. This has the corollary which Kant likened to a Copernican revolution in philosophy, that instead of presuming that all our knowledge must conform to objects, it is more profitable to suppose the reverse. Knowledge of objects as such, 'things in themselves' (*noumena*), is impossible since we can only know our ordered sense-impressions (*phenomena*). Space and time are subjective particulars, *a priori* intuitions. All ordering of sense-impressions takes place in time, with the appropriate application of general concepts. Antinomies arise when general concepts (categories) are misapplied to non-experiential data or space and time are treated as if they were categories. Hence we cannot prove the existence of God, but Kant recognizes three principal ideas of reason, God, freedom and immortality, which pure reason leads us to form for practical, i.e., moral, considerations. These are developed in *Prolegomena* (1783, trans. P. G. Lucas 1953), *Grundlagen zur Metaphysik der Sitten* (1785) 'Groundwork to a Metaphysics of Morals' (trans. H. J. Paton 1948), and *Kritik der praktischen Vernunft* (1788) 'Critique of Practical Reason'. The *Groundwork* contains his ethical theory based on the good will, enshrined in the famous Categorical Imperative: 'Act only on that maxim through which you can at the same time will that it should become a universal law.' This important if over-formal rendering of moral obligation was criticized by Jacobi as 'the good will that wills nothing'. *Kritik der Urteilskraft* (1790) 'Critique of Judgment' (trans. J. H. Bernard 1892) completes the Kantian system. It comprises a remarkable treatment of the basic philosophical problems in aesthetics, not least the claim that the aesthetic judgment is independent of personal, psychological and moral considerations, yet singular and universally valid. Kant lived an extremely orderly life, possibly because of his delicate constitution, and many people are supposed to have set their watches by his daily walk. He was very friendly with two English businessmen, Green and Motherby, an admirer of Rousseau, the French Revolution but not the reign of terror, Liberal in his politics and theological lectures, which, interpreted as anti-Lutheran, he was asked by the Prussian government to cease giving. At the death of Frederick William II he considered himself absolved and published his lectures together with the acrimonious correspondence with the authorities. In *Zum ewigen Frieden* (1795) 'Perpetual Peace' he advocated a world federation of free states. Kant's system is greater than any of the idealist schools to which it gave rise, although Fichte, Hegel, and Schopenhauer have been more widely influential. The philosophical questions he raised and his treatment of them will remain of permanent interest. See Life by E. Paulsen (trans. 1902), *Gesammelte Schriften*, Royal Prussian Academy (1902–38 ff.), of his critical philosophy, commentaries by A. C. Ewing (1938), T. D. Weldon (1945), S. Körner (Pelican, 1953), studies by E. Caird (1877), M. Heidegger (1929) N. Kemp Smith (1933), H. J. Paton (1935), A. H. Smith (1947), *Kantstudien* (1896–1936, 1942–44, 1953 ff.), of his theology, by A. Schweitzer (1899), science by G. Martin (trans. 1955), aesthetics, E. Cassirer (1938) and ethics, H. J. Paton (1947), A. E. Teale (1951).

KAPITZA, Peter, Russ. Pëtr Leonidovich Kapitsa (1894–), Russian physicist, born at Kronstadt, studied at Petrograd and under Rutherford at Cambridge, where he became assistant director of magnetic research at the Cavendish laboratory (1924–32). In 1934 he returned to Russia. He is known for his work on high-intensity magnetism, on low temperature, and on the liquefaction of hydrogen and helium.

KAPP, (1) **Friedrich** (1824–84), German politician, went to New York after the 1848 revolution, returned to Berlin in 1870, wrote a number of histories, including *Aus und über Amerika* (1876), and was a member of the Reichstag in 1871–78 and 1881–84.

(2) **Wolfgang** (1858–1922), son of (1), born in New York, in 1920 contrived a putsch against the Weimar republic in Berlin, which was baulked of success by a general strike. In 1922, on returning from Sweden, whence he had fled, he was arrested, but died while awaiting trial.

KAPTEYN, Jacobus Cornelius, *kap-tīn'* (1851–1922), Dutch astronomer, born at Barnevelt, professor at Groningen from 1878, plotted the stars of the southern hemisphere from the photographic survey of Sir David Gill (q.v.), and is celebrated for his discovery that all stars whose proper motion can be detected are part of one of two streams moving in different directions at different speeds. See Life by A. van Maenen (U.S. 1925).

KARADJORDJE. See CZERNY, GEORGE.

KARADŽIĆ, Vuk Stefanović, *ka'ra-jich* (1787–1864), Serbian poet and philologist, born at Tršić, published collections of national songs and tales, and evolved the simplified Cyrillic alphabet in order to produce literature in the vernacular. He translated the New Testament into Serbian.

KARAMZIN, Nikolai Mikhailovich, *ka-ram-zyeen'* (1766–1826), Russian historian and novelist, born at Mikhailovka in Orenburg. Among his writings are *Letters of a Russian Traveller* (1790–92), an account of his travels in Western Europe, several novels, including *Poor Lisa* (1792) and *Natalia, The Boyar's Daughter* (1792), and a great unfinished *History of Russia* (1816–29) down to 1613. His influence on the literature of Russia and its development was considerable. He modernized the literary language by his introduction of western idioms and his writing as a whole reflected western thought. See D. S. Mirsky, *History of Russian Literature* (1927).

KARL. See CHARLES.

KARLFELDT, Erik Axel, *karl'felt* (1864–1931), Swedish poet, born in Folkärna, in the historic province of Dalarna. His poetry is highly individual, mainly reflecting, in a language and style which is often deliberately archaic, the traditional life and customs of his native province. He declined the Nobel prize for literature in 1918, and was awarded it posthumously in 1931.

KARP, David (1922–), American author, born in New York of Russian-Jewish descent, served in U.S. army, worked as journalist, as radio, TV and paperback writer, and emerged as a serious novelist with *One* (1953), an Orwellian condemnation of totalitarianism. Other works include *The Day of the Monkey* (1955), on British colonialism, *All Honourable Men* (1956) and *The Sleepwalkers* (1960).

KARR, (Jean Baptiste) Alphonse (1808–90), French writer, born in Paris. His *Sous les tilleuls* (1832) by its originality and wit found its author an audience for a long series of novels, of which *Geneviève* (1838) only need be mentioned. In 1839 he became editor of *Figaro*, and started the issue of the bitterly satirical *Les Guêpes*. His *Voyage autour de mon jardin* (1845) is his best-known book. See his reminiscences, *Livre de bord* (4 vols. 1879–80).—His daughter, **Thérèse** (1835–87) published tales and historical books.

KARRER, Paul (1889–), Swiss chemist, born in Moscow, was educated at Zürich, where he became professor of Organic Chemistry (1919). He was the first to isolate vitamins A and K, and he produced synthetically vitamins B_2 and E. He shared the Nobel chemistry prize with Haworth in 1937.

KASTLER, Alfred (1902–), French scientist, of the Ecole Normale Supérieure in Paris, was awarded the Nobel prize for Physics in 1966 for his work on the development of lasers.

KÄSTNER, Erich (1899–), German writer, born in Dresden, is best known for his books for children. His writing career, however, began with two volumes of verse, *Herz auf Taille* (1928) and *Lärm im Spiegel* (1929), both cleverly satirical. His novels include *Fabian* (1931, trans. 1932), and *Three Men in the Snow* (1934, trans. 1935). His delightful children's books, which include *Emil and the Detectives* (1928), *Annaluise and Anton* (1929), and *The Flying Classroom* (1933), gained him worldwide fame. Among his later writings is the autobiographical *When I was a Little Boy* (1957, trans. 1959).

KATE, Jan Jacob Lodewijk ten, *ka'tė* (1819–1889), Dutch poet, celebrated for his parodies, born at The Hague, and died at Amsterdam.

KATER, Henry (1777–1835), English physicist of German descent, inventor of Kater's pendulum, became F.R.S. in 1815, and in 1817 won the Copley medal for his work on measuring instruments, which he brought to high standards of accuracy.

KATHARINE. See CATHARINE.

KATKOV, Mikhail Nikiforovich (1818–87), Russian journalist, was professor of Philosophy at Moscow, and after 1861 editor of the *Moscow Gazette*, was at first an advocate of reform, but was converted by the Polish rising of 1863 into a Panslavist leader and a supporter of reactionary government.

KAUFFMANN, Angelica, *kowf'-man* (1741–1807), Swiss painter, born at Chur in the Grisons, at eleven was painting portraits of notabilities in Italy, and in 1766 was persuaded to go to London. There she soon became famous as a painter of classic and mythological pictures, and as a portrait-painter, and was nominated one of the first batch of Royal Academicians (1769). After an unhappy marriage (*c.* 1767) with an adventurer, the 'Count de Horn', in 1781 she married the Venetian painter, Antonio Zucchi (q.v.), and returned to Italy. Her rather pretty paintings are well known from engravings by Bartolozzi. Her story furnishd the theme for Lady Ritchie's *Miss Angel* (1875). See Lives by Gerard (1892), Manners and Williamson (1924) and Hartcup (1954).

KAUFMAN, George Simon (1889–1961), American playwright, born in Pittsburgh. In collaboration with Moss Hart wrote *You Can't Take it with You* (Pulitzer prize 1936) and *The Man Who Came to Dinner* (1939). Other works include *The Solid Gold Cadillac* (with Howard Teichmann, 1953) and many musicals, some of which have been filmed.

KAUFMANN, Constantine Petrovich von (1818–82), Russian general, distinguished himself at Kars (1855) and in 1867 became governor of Turkestan. In 1868 he occupied Samarkand, and in 1873 conducted the campaign against Khiva. Died at Tashkent. See Boulger's *Central Asian Portraits* (1880).

KAULBACH, Wilhelm von, *kowl'bakh* (1805–1874), German painter, born at Arolsen, from 1849 director of the Munich Academy of Painting, painted grandiose historical subjects. See Life by H. Müller (Berlin 1892). His son **Hermann** (1846–1909), nephew **Friedrich** (1822–1903), and the latter's son **Friedrich August** (1850–1920) were also painters.

KAUNDA, Kenneth David, *kah-oon'da* (1924–), Zambian politician, born at Lubwa, became a teacher, founded the Zambian African National Congress (1958), subsequently was imprisoned and the movement banned. In 1960 elected president of the United National Independent Party, he played a leading part in his country's independence negotiations, and became premier in January 1964, the country obtaining independence in October that year. See his *Zambia Shall Be Free* (1962), *A Humanist in Africa* (1966).

KAUNITZ-RIETBERG, Wenzel Anton, Prince von, *kow'nits* (1711–94), Austrian statesman, distinguished himself in 1748 at the congress of Aix-la-Chapelle, and as Austrian ambassador at the French court in 1750–52 converted old enmity into friendship. In 1753 he was appointed chancellor, and for almost 40 years directed Austrian politics. Active in the ecclesiastical reforms of Joseph II, he was a liberal patron of arts and sciences. See Life by Beer (1872), and G. Küntzel, *Fürst Kaunitz-Rietberg als Staatsmann* (1923).

KAUTSKY, Karl Johann, *kowt'ski* (1854–1938), German Socialist leader, born at Prague, founded (1883) and edited *Die Neue Zeit*. A disciple of Marx, he wrote against Bolshevism (trans. 1918, 1931), against William II, on Sir Thomas More, &c. See Lenin's *The Proletarian Revolution and Kautsky the Renegade* (trans. 1920).

KAVANAGH, Arthur Macmorrough, *kav'ä-nah* (1831–89), of Borris House, Co. Carlow, an Irish Conservative M.P. from 1866 to 1880, who, though all but armless and legless, rode, shot, yachted, painted, and in 1849–51 travelled overland to India.

KAY, (1) John. See ARKWRIGHT.

(2) **John** (1742–1826), born near Dalkeith, prosperous Edinburgh barber until (1785) he opened a print shop for caricatures of local celebrities etched by himself. They have little merit beyond humour and likeness. His *Original Portraits, with Biographical Sketches* is an invaluable record of Edinburgh social life.

KAY-SHUTTLEWORTH, Sir James Phillips, D.C.L. (1804–77), English educationist, born at Rochdale, studied and practised medicine. As secretary to the Committee of the Privy Council on Education he was instrumental in establishing a system of government school inspection. The pupil teacher system originated with him and he founded his own training college which later became St John's College, Battersea. On his retirement in 1849 he was created a baronet. In 1842 he married the heiress of the Shuttleworths of Gawthorpe, and assumed her surname.

KAYE, (1) Danny, professional name of **Daniel Kominski** (1913–), American stage, radio and film actor, born in New York. He intended to be a doctor, but soon began a stage career. In 1943 he made his first film, *Up in Arms*, following it with *Wonder Man* (1944), which made his reputation as a film comedian, together with international success in *The Secret Life of Walter Mitty* (1946). Other films include *The Inspector General* (1950), *Hans Christian Andersen* (1952) and *Knock on Wood* (1954). He does a great deal of work for UNICEF.

(2) **Sir John William** (1814–76), historian, served from 1832 in the Bengal Artillery, but in 1841 devoted himself to literature. A secretary from 1858 in the India Office, he wrote books on Indian history, and *Essays of an Optimist* (1870).

KAYE-SMITH, Sheila (1887–1956), born at St Leonards, wrote novels mainly of fate and Sussex soil. In 1924 she married T. P. Fry, a clergyman and heir to a baronetcy, and in 1929 became a Roman Catholic. Her writings include *Sussex Gorse* (1916), *Tamarisk Town* (1919), *Joanna Godden* (1921), *The End of the House of Alard* (1923).

KAZAN, Elia (1909–), American stage and film director, born in Constantinople, studied at Williams College and Yale. He acted in minor rôles on Broadway and in Hollywood before becoming director of plays and films influenced by 'The Method'. His Broadway productions include the works of Wilder, Miller, and Williams. Many of his films have a social or political theme, e.g., *Gentleman's Agreement* (Oscar winner, 1948), on anti-Semitism, *Pinky* (1949), on the colour problem, *Viva Zapata* (1952), *On the Waterfront* (Oscar winner, 1954), and *Face in the Crowd* (1957). The latter three deal with kinds of megalomania, the revolutionary figure without statecraft, the trades union boss turned gangster, and the TV demagogue. Other notable films include Williams' *Streetcar Named Desire* (1951) and *Baby Doll* (1956), Steinbeck's *East of Eden* (1954), Inge's *Splendour in the Grass* (1962), and *America, America* (1964), based on his autobiographical novel (1963).

KAZINCZY, Ferenc, *ko'zin-tsi* (1759–1831), Hungarian writer, born at Érsemlyén, was a leading figure in the Hungarian literary revival and a strong advocate of the reform of the language. He translated many European classics, wrote poetry, and there are 22 volumes of letters. Died of cholera.

KEAN, (1) **Charles John** (1809 or 1811–68), actor, born at Waterford, son of (2), educated at Eton, to support his mother and himself became an actor. He appeared at Drury Lane in 1827 as Young Norval, with ill success, but worked assiduously in the provinces until he attained a air position. In 1850 he became joint-lessee of the Princess's Theatre, and produced a long series of gorgeous 'revivals'. In 1859 he virtually retired, though he played in America and the provinces to within seven months of his death. In 1842 he married the actress, **Ellen Tree** (1805–80). See Life by J. W. Cole (1860), *Letters of Mr and Mrs Charles Kean* (Washington University, 1945).

(2) **Edmund** (*c.* 1789–1833), English actor, was born in London the son of Nance Carey (Henry Carey's granddaughter), hawker and stroller. A stage Cupid and a cabin-boy to Madeira, he himself about sixteen turned a stroller, and after ten years in the provinces, made his first appearance at Drury Lane as Shylock (January 26, 1814), and at once took rank as the first actor of the day. A period of wonderful success followed, but by his irregularities he gradually forfeited public approval, his reputation being finally ruined by the 'criminal conversation' *cause célèbre* of Cox *v.* Kean (1825). He was cordially received in 1827 following a twelvemonth visit to America, but both mind and body gave way, and breaking down hopelessly in March, 1833, he died at Richmond on May 15th. See Lives by Barry Cornwall (1835), Hawkins (1869), Molloy (1888), Hillebrand (1933), G. Playfair (1939) and M. W. Disher (1950).

KEANE, Augustus Henry (1833–1912), ethnologist, born at Cork. He taught languages at Hameln and Southampton, and was Hindustani professor at University College, London, 1882–85.

KEATE, John (1773–1852), headmaster of Eton 1809–34, was born at Wells, and died at his Hampshire rectory of Hartley Westpall. A diminutive man, he was a stern disciplinarian and once flogged eighty boys together.

KEATS, John (1795–1821), English poet, was born in London, the son of a livery-stable keeper, and went to school at Enfield. In 1811 he was apprenticed to a surgeon at Edmonton and later (1815–17), he was a medical student in the London hospitals. Though he did creditably there his mind was set on the arts. His friends were painters, he appreciated 'divine' Mozart, but above all, poetry claimed him. Leigh Hunt, his neighbour in Hampstead, introduced him to other young romantics, including Shelley, and published his first sonnets in his *Examiner* (1816). His first volume of poems (1817), is 'sicklied o'er' with Hunt's sentimentality and the long mythological poem *Endymion* (1818) combines Hunt's influence with Elizabethan lusciousness in word and image. Nevertheless, it contains some felicitous descriptions and the 'Hymn to Pan' and the 'Bacchic procession' anticipate the great odes to come. Keats returned from a walking tour in Scotland (1818), which exhausted him, to find the savage reviews of *Endymion* in *Blackwood's Magazine* and the *Quarterly*. To add to his troubles his younger brother Tom was dying of consumption and his love affair with Fanny Brawne seems to have brought him more vexation than comfort. It was in these circumstances that he braced himself for the supreme effort which makes the volume of 1820, *Lamia and Other Poems*, a landmark in English poetry. Except for the romantic poem 'Isabella or The Pot of Basil', a romance based on Boccaccio's *Decameron*, and the first version of his epical poem, 'Hyperion', all the significant verse in this famous volume is the work of 1819, viz., the two splendid romances 'The Eve of St Agnes' and 'Lamia' and the great odes—'On a Grecian Urn', 'To a Nightingale', 'To Autumn', 'On Melancholy' and 'To Psyche'. Jeffrey, who had not joined in the denigration of *Endymion* praised the volume in the *Edinburgh Review* and Shelley, who had been somewhat critical of his earlier poetry, hailed 'Hyperion' as a noble work. That this poem in its two versions is only a magnificent fragment is due partly to the allegory and partly to the Miltonic cast of the diction, which he had come to regard as inimical to his art. The romances and odes better suited his genius, which he now perceived was more Shakespearian or Elizabethan than Miltonic. The former, particularly 'The Eve of St Agnes', display a wealth of sensuous imagery almost unequalled in English poetry. In 'Lamia', the best told of the tales, he turns from stanza form to the couplet as used by Dryden in his romantic *Fables*. The odes are the perfect expression of his genius. Critics have toyed with the notion that had he lived he would have gone on to something truly dramatic and tragical as Shakespeare did after his decorative 'first fruits'. The 'Grecian Urn' and 'Psyche' are the full expression of the charm exercised on him by the Greek myths. 'Autumn' may be hardly an ode, rather a seasonal vignette, but has any poet, Shakespeare apart, so invoked the sensuous beauty of the season? And to show the variety of his genius in different modes, the fragmentary 'Ode to Maia', written in 1818, instinct with the feeling for the Greek, vies with 'La Belle Dame Sans Merci' which is as pre-Raphaelite as 'The Eve of St Mark' is in another way. Keats's letters are regarded in some quarters as equally important with his poems (see Lionel Trilling, *The Opposing Self*), and they certainly throw a valuable light on his poetical development no less than on his unhappy love affair with Fanny Brawne. It is clear that he was both attracted and repelled by the notion of the poet as teacher or prophet. Though profoundly aware of the suffering in life, he preferred to think of himself as of Shakespeare, that is as the 'chameleon poet' who enters with equal delight into all states, good and evil. He distrusted the utopianism of his liberal friends, but 'the burden of the mystery' oppressed him. Like Wordsworth and Coleridge he made imagination the supreme gift so that 'what the Imagination seizes as beauty must be truth'. In other words, 'Beauty is truth, truth beauty.' Valid or not for the philosopher, this was valid for Keats's poetry. Having prepared the 1820 volume for the press, Keats, now seriously ill with consumption, sailed for Italy in September 1820, reached Rome and died there attended only by his artist friend Severn. Shelley lamented him in *Adonais* and his grave in the Protestant cemetery is a place of pilgrimage to this day. Except for his sister Fanny, the family, his loyalty to which is witnessed in the letters, was extinct in England, his brother George, to whom some of the most important letters are addressed, having emigrated to America in 1818. Modern editions are by E. de Selincourt (1921), M. B. Forman (1931), Garrod (1956), and H. E. Rollins, 2 vols. (1959). See Lives by Houghton (1848), Colvin (1886, 1917), Amy Lowell (1925), Dorothy Hewlett (1937), Murchie (1955), Middleton Murry (4th ed. 1955), Bate (1964), Gittings (1968), and essays ed. by K. Muir (1959).

KEBLE, John (1792–1866), English churchman, was born at Fairford, Gloucestershire, near his father's living of Coln St Aldwins. At fifteen he was elected a scholar at Corpus, Oxford, and in 1810 took a double first. In 1811 he was elected a fellow of Oriel and in 1812 won the Latin and English prize essays. In 1815 he was ordained deacon, beginning active work as curate of East Leach, while still continuing to reside in Oxford, where he was college tutor 1818–23. In 1827 he published *The Christian Year*. His theory of poetry, explained in the *British Critic* in 1838, was worked out at length in his Latin lectures delivered as Oxford professor of Poetry (1831–41). Meanwhile Keble had gathered round him a small band of pupils of whom the most striking was Hurrell Froude, and in this circle originated the Tractarian movement. In his sermon on National Apostasy (1833) Keble gave the signal for action, and for the next eight years was engaged with Newman, Pusey, I. Williams and others in the issue of *Tracts for the Times*, brought to an end by Tract No. 90 in 1841. Keble had in 1835 married, and had removed to the Hampshire living of Hursley, where he remained until his death. With Dr Pusey he was the steadying influence which supported the party under the shock caused by Newman's secession to Rome. Other works are a Life of Bishop Wilson, an edition of Hooker, the *Lyra Innocentium* (1846), a poetical translation of the Psalter, *Letters of Spiritual Counsel*, twelve volumes of parochial sermons, *Studia Sacra*, &c. Keble College, Oxford, was erected as a memorial of him (1870). See *Memoir* by Sir J. Coleridge (1869), J. C. Shairp's *Essay* and *Studies* (1872), a collection of memorials by J. F. Moor (1866), Lives by Locke (1893), Wood (1909), and study by Battiscombe (1963).

KEELER, James Edward (1857–1900), American astronomer, born at La Salle, Ill., and educated at The Johns Hopkins University, Heidelberg and Berlin. Director of the Lick Observatory from 1898, he discovered the composition of Saturn's rings, and carried out important spectroscopic work on nebulae, discovering 120,000 of them.

KEELEY, Robert (1793–1869), English comedian, was born and died in London. He married Miss Mary Goward (1806–99), who, born at Ipswich, made her début at the Lyceum in 1825. Their daughters were both actresses. See W. Goodman's *The Keeleys on the Stage and at Home* (1895).

KEENE, Charles Samuel (1823–91), English illustrator, born at Hornsey, having tried both law and architecture, was apprenticed to a wood engraver. He worked for the *Illustrated London News* and for *Punch* from 1851 to within five months of his death at Hammersmith. He also illustrated books, including *Robinson Crusoe* and *The Cloister and the Hearth*. See Lives by Layard (1893) and D. Hudson (1947), and work by Pennell and Chesson (1897).

KEIGHTLEY, Thomas, *kīt'li* (1789–1872), Irish writer, born in Dublin, in 1824 settled in London. His histories of Rome, Greece, and England long held their place as school manuals and his *Fairy Mythology* (1850) and his Life and annotated edition of Milton (1855–59) are still remembered.

KEITEL, Wilhelm, *kī'tĕl* (1882–1946), German field-marshal, joined the army in 1901 and was an artillery staff officer in World War I. In the 'thirties he became an ardent Nazi, his faith being rewarded in 1938 by the post of chief of the supreme command of the armed forces. In 1940 he signed the Compiègne armistice with France and in 1945 he was one of the German signatories of unconditional surrender to Russia and the Allies in Berlin. He was executed in October 1946 for war crimes.

KEITH, (1) Viscount. See ELPHINSTONE (1).

(2) **Sir Arthur** (1866–1955), Scottish anthropologist, born at Aberdeen, wrote *Introduction to the Study of Anthropoid Apes* (1896), *Human Embryology and Morphology* (1901) and works on ancient man, including *Concerning Man's Origin* (1927) and *New Theory of Human Evolution* (1948). He was knighted in 1921.

(3) **Arthur Berriedale** (1879–1944), professor of Sanskrit at Edinburgh University from 1914, wrote on Sanskrit literature, and Dominion constitutions.

(4) **James** (1696–1758), Scottish soldier and Prussian field-marshal, was born at the castle of Inverugie near Peterhead. He came of a family, represented now by the Earl of Kintore, which from the 12th century had held the hereditary office of Great Marischal of Scotland. Sir William Keith was created Earl Marischal in 1458; and George, the fifth Earl (*c.* 1553–1623), in 1593 founded Marischal College in Aberdeen. William, ninth Earl (d. 1712), was the father of Marshal Keith and of his elder brother,

George, tenth Earl Marischal (1693–1778). James was destined for the law, but in 1715 he engaged with his brother in the Jacobite rising, and in 1719 in Alberoni's expedition to the West Highlands, which ended in the 'battle' of Glenshiel. Both times the brothers escaped to the Continent. James held for nine years a Spanish colonelcy and took part in the siege of Gibraltar (1726–27). But his creed, the Episcopal, was against him and in 1728 he entered the Russian service as a major-general. He distinguished himself in the wars with Turkey and Sweden, particularly at the siege of Otchakoff (1737) and the reduction of the Åland Islands (1743). He next visited Paris and London, where he made his peace with the Hanoverian government. In 1747, finding the Russian service disagreeable, he exchanged it for that of Prussia, and Frederick the Great gave him at once the rank of field-marshal. From this time his name is associated with that of Frederick, who relied as much on Keith's military genius as he did on the diplomatic ability of his brother, the Earl Marischal. Keith's talents became still more conspicuous upon the breaking out of the Seven Years' War (1756). He shared Frederick's doubtful fortunes before Prague, was present at the victories of Lobositz and Rossbach, and conducted the masterly retreat from Olmütz. At Hochkirch he was shot dead while for the third time charging the enemy. Keith died poor and unmarried, but he left children by his mistress, the Swede, Eva Merthens (d. 1811). See his own *Memoir*, 1714–34 (Spalding Club, 1843); *Memoir of Marshal Keith* (Peterhead 1869); Carlyle's *Frederick*; Cuthell's *Last Earl Marischall* (1915); German Lives by Varnhagen von Ense (1844; new ed. 1888) and Lieut. von Paczynski-Tenczyn (1889).

(5) **Robert** (1681–1757), from 1727 an Episcopal bishop, was born at Uras, Kincardineshire, and lived in Edinburgh and Leith. His *History of the Scottish Reformation* (1734) was republished by the Spottiswoode Society in 1844–45.

KEITH-FALCONER. See FALCONER (2).

KEKULÉ VON STRADONITZ, Friedrich August, *kay'koo-lay* (1829–96), German chemist, born at Darmstadt, became professor at Ghent and at Bonn (1867). He made a major contribution to organic chemistry by developing structural theories, including the cyclic structure of benzene.

KELLER, (1) **Gottfried** (1819–90), Swiss poet and novelist, born near Zürich, studied landscape painting at Munich 1840–42, but took to literature. From 1861 to 1876 he was state secretary of his native canton. His chief works are *Der grüne Heinrich* (1854), *Die Leute von Seldwyla* (1856; includes *A Village Romeo and Juliet*), *Sieben Legenden* (1872), *Züricher Novellen* (1878), and *Martin Salander* (1886). It was as a writer of short stories rather than as a poet or novelist that he excelled and his powers of characterization and description and his sense of humour are best illustrated in his volumes of *Novellen*. See studies by Huch (1904), Maync (1925), Hauch (1916), M Hay (1920) and H. W. Reichert (1949).

(2) **Helen Adams** (1880–1968), born at Tuscumbia, Ala., became deaf and blind at nineteen months, but, educated by Miss Anne M. Sullivan (Mrs Macy), she later learnt to speak, graduated B.A. 1904, and attained high distinction as a lecturer, writer and scholar. See *Autobiography and Letters* (1946), and study by Tibble (1957).

KELLERMANN, François Étienne Christophe, Duke of Valmy (1735–1820), born at Wolfsbuchweiler in Alsace, entered the French army and was major-general at the Revolution. In 1792 he repelled the Duke of Brunswick, and delivered France by the famous 'cannonade of Valmy'. Yet on allegation of treason he was imprisoned by Robespierre. He afterwards served in Italy, and under the Empire was made a marshal and duke. In 1809 and 1812 he commanded the reserves on the Rhine. At the Restoration he attached himself to the Bourbons. His son, **François Étienne** (1770–1835), by a charge turned Marengo into a victory.

KELLGREN, Johan Henrik (1751–95), Swedish poet, born at Floby. From satire and didactic poems he turned to pure lyrics, in which he excelled. He was first director of the Swedish Academy. See studies by Atterbom (1863) and O. Sylwan (1912).

KELLOGG, Frank Billings (1856–1937), American statesman, born at Potsdam, N.Y., was senator (1917–23), ambassador in London (1923–25), secretary of state (1925–1929). He drew up the Briand-Kellogg Pact (1928) outlawing war, which became the legal basis for the Nuremberg trials (1945–46), and was a judge of the Permanent Court of Justice at the Hague (1930–35). In 1929 he was awarded the Nobel peace prize.

KELLY, or Kelley, Edward. See DEE, JOHN.

KELLY, (1) **Sir Gerald Festus** (1879–1972), English painter, born in London. He was educated at Eton and Trinity Hall, Cambridge, and studied art in Paris. He was elected an A.R.A. in 1922, an R.A. in 1930 and was P.R.A. (1949–54). In 1945 he painted state portraits of King George VI and Queen Elizabeth. He was knighted in 1945 and made a K.C.V.O. in 1955.

(2) **Ned** (1855–80), horse-thief and from 1878 bushranger in Victoria and New South Wales, was hanged at Melbourne. See Life by M. Brown (1948).

KELVIN, William Thomson, 1st Baron (1824–1907), Scottish mathematician and physicist, was born in Belfast, and at eleven entered Glasgow University, where his father had become professor of Mathematics. At Cambridge he highly distinguished himself as an original thinker even in his undergraduate days. He was second wrangler and first Smith's prizeman of 1845, and was elected a fellow of Peterhouse. In 1846 he became professor of Natural Philosophy in the University of Glasgow. In an early paper (1842) he solved important problems in electrostatics. It was largely owing to his refined researches in the transmission of electric currents in submarine cables that the Atlantic cable was successful (for which in 1866 he was knighted). In 1892 he was created a peer with the title of Lord Kelvin. His electrometers of various design—absolute, portable, quadrant, &c.—embody the perfection of mechanical and geometrical adjustment. He constructed ampère-meters, voltmeters and watt-meters, suitable alike for the electrical workshop and laboratory. His sounding apparatus and compass were adopted by the Admiralty and the principal mercantile lines. In pure science Lord Kelvin did incomparable work. Specially may be mentioned his thermodynamic researches from 1848 onwards, including the doctrine of the dissipation or degradation of energy; his magnetic and electric discoveries, including general theorems of great value and the beautiful method of electric images; and his work in hydrodynamics, more especially in wave-motion and in vortex-motion. Basing upon the phenomena of gyrostatic motion, he imagined a kinetic theory of inertia of high interest; and his dynamical theory of dispersion, and indeed all his views on the nature of the ether, are full of significance. In 1872 his electrostatic and magnetic papers were reprinted in collected form (2nd ed. 1884); and his other papers have been similarly published under the title *Mathematical and Physical Papers* (6 vols. 1882–1911), besides *Popular Lectures* (3 vols. 1889–94), *Molecular Tactics of a Crystal* (1894), &c. He was joint-author with Professor Tait of *A Treatise on Natural Philosophy* (vol. i 1867; 2nd ed. 1879). He was president of the British Association (1871), repeatedly president of the Royal Society of Edinburgh, and (1890) president of the Royal Society of London. He died December 17. See the Life by Silvanus Thompson (1910), and books by Mrs King (1910), Miss A. G. King (1925) and A. Russell (1938).

KEMAL PASHA. See MUSTAFA KEMAL.

KEMBLE, family of actors:

(1) **Adelaide** (1816–79), daughter of (2), operatic singer, retired in 1842 on her marriage with F. Sartoris. Author of *A Week in a French Country House* (1867), *Medusa and Other Tales* (1868), and *Past Hours* (1880).

(2) **Charles** (1775–1854), actor, brother of (5), born at Brecon, made his first appearance at Sheffield in 1792 and in 1794 played Malcolm to John Kemble's Macbeth. He retired from the stage in 1840, when he was appointed examiner of plays. He chiefly excelled in characters of the second rank, and in comedy he specially distinguished himself.

(3) **Frances Anne,** 'Fanny Kemble' (1809–1893), daughter of (2), made her début at Covent Garden on October 5, 1829, when her 'Juliet' created a great sensation. For three years she played leading parts in London, then in 1832 went with her father to America, where in 1834 she married Pierce Butler, a Southern planter. They were divorced in 1848 and, resuming her maiden name, she gave Shakespearian readings for twenty years. She published dramas, poems, eight volumes of autobiography, &c. See Lives by Bobbé (1932) and L. S. Driver (1933).

(4) **John Mitchell** (1807–57), Anglo-Saxon scholar, son of (2), attended Trinity, Cambridge, and studied at Göttingen under Jakob Grimm. His edition of *Beowulf* (1833–37) and *Codex Diplomaticus Aevi Saxonici* (1839–48) were valuable, but less important than his unfinished *History of the Saxons in England* (1849; new ed. by Birch, 1876). He edited the *British and Foreign Review* (1835–1844) and in 1840 succeeded his father as examiner of plays. See Study by B. Dickens (1940).

(5) **John Philip** (1757–1823), eldest son of (6), was born at Prescot. His father intended him for the Catholic priesthood, and sent him to a seminary at Sedgley Park, Staffordshire, and to the English college at Douai. But the stage mania was on him, and he became an actor. His first appearance was at Wolverhampton, January 8, 1776. He joined the York circuit under Tate Wilkinson and he played in Ireland. The success of his sister, Mrs Siddons, gave him his opportunity, and on September 30, 1783, he played Hamlet at Drury Lane, and aroused the keenest interest. He continued to play leading tragic characters at Drury Lane for many years, and in 1788 became Sheridan's manager. In 1802 he purchased a share in Covent Garden Theatre, became manager, and made his first appearance there in 1803 as Hamlet. In 1808 the theatre was burned, and on the opening of the new building (1809) the notorious O. P. (i.e., 'Old Price') Riots broke out. Kemble retired in 1817, and afterwards settled at Lausanne, where he died. Handsome, stately, and of remarkable intellectual power, he probably has had no superior as a tragedian. See Life by Borden (1925).

(6) **Roger** (1721–1802), a travelling manager, father of (2), (5) and (7).

(7) **Stephen** (1758–1822), brother of (5), born at Kington, Herefordshire, was chiefly remarkable for his enormous bulk, which enabled him to play Falstaff without stuffing. He was (1792–1800) manager of the Edinburgh theatre, where he was in continual hot water through lawsuits and other troubles.

KEMP, (1) **George Mickle (or Meikle)** (1795–1844), Scottish draughtsman, born at Hillriggs near Biggar, until fourteen assisted his shepherd father. Becoming a carpenter and millwright, he sought work in England and France, settling where he could study Gothic architecture. He returned to Scotland in 1826, and became a draughtsman in Edinburgh. In 1838 his second design for the Scott Monument at Edinburgh was accepted, but before its completion he was accidentally drowned in the canal at Edinburgh. See Life by T. Bonnar (1892).

(2) **John** (*c.* 1380–1454), born at Olantigh near Ashford, Kent, became a fellow of Merton College, Oxford, Bishop of Rochester (1419), and of Chichester and London (1421), chancellor and Archbishop of York (1426), a cardinal (1439), and Archbishop of Canterbury (1452). See Hook's *Lives of the Archbishops*, vol. v.

(3) **William** (d. 1603), a comedian who in 1599 danced from London to Norwich. See his *Nine Daies Wonder* (ed. by Dyce, Camden Society).

KEMPE, Margery (b. 1364), mystic, daughter of a mayor of Lynn, wife of a burgess there, mother of fourteen children. Her spiritual autobiography, *The Book of Margery Kempe* (printed in part by Wynkyn de Worde, *c.* 1501), recounts her persecution by devils and men, repeated accusations of Lollardy, her copious weepings, her journeys to Jerusalem and to Germany, and has been hailed as a classic. See *The Book of Margery Kempe* (modernized text) by W. Butler-Bowdon (1936), the original text ed. by Neech and Hope Allen (1940), and study by K. Cholmely (1947).

KEMPIS, Thomas à (1379–1471), German religious writer, so called from his birthplace, Kempen. In 1400 entered the Augustinian convent of Agnetenberg near Zwolle, took Holy Orders in 1413, was chosen subprior in 1429, and died as superior. Wrote sermons, ascetical treatises, pious biographies, letters and hymns, the only one of special note the treatise *On the Following* (*or Imitation*) *of Christ*. In its pages, says Dean Milman, 'is gathered and concentred all that is elevating, passionate, profoundly pious in all the older mystics'. Translated into English about 1440 and again (by Atkinson and the Lady Margaret) about 1502, the *Imitation* has been ascribed to the celebrated Jean Gerson (q.v.), and, from the 17th century, to Gersen, abbot of Vercelli, whose very existence has not been proved. Most authorities, however, assign it to Kempis. Its theology is almost purely ascetical, and (excepting the 4th book, which is based on the doctrine of the real presence) the work has been used by Christians of all denominations. Probably completed between 1415 and 1424, the first edition (Augsburg 1471 or 1472) was reprinted by Dr Adrian Fortescue. See study by S. Kettlewell (1883).

KEMSLEY, James Gomer Berry, 1st Viscount (1883–1968), British newspaper proprietor, born at Merthyr Tydfil, became chairman of Kemsley Newspapers Ltd in 1937, controlling the *Sunday Times* and other newspapers. Created a baronet in 1928, raised to the peerage in 1936, he received a viscountcy in 1945. In 1950 published *The Kemsley Manual of Journalism*. His brothers, **Henry Seymour, Lord Buckland** (1877–1928), and **William Ewert, 1st Viscount Camrose** (q.v.), also owned newspapers. See Camrose's *British Newspapers and Their Controllers* (1947).

KEN, Thomas (1637–1711), born at Little Berkhampstead, Herts, held several livings and in 1666 was elected a fellow of Winchester where he prepared his *Manual of Prayers for Scholars of Winchester College* (1674), and wrote his morning, evening, and midnight hymns, the first two of which, 'Awake, my soul', and 'Glory to Thee, my God, this night', are among the best-known hymns. In 1679 he was appointed by Charles II chaplain to Princess Mary, wife of William of Orange, but offended William, and returned home in 1680, when he became a royal chaplain. In 1683, on the king's visit to Winchester, Ken refused to give up his house for the accommodation of Nell Gwynne. In 1683 too he went to Tangiers as a chaplain, and in 1685 was consecrated Bishop of Bath and Wells. The chief event of his bishopric was his trial and acquittal among the 'Seven Bishops' in 1688, for refusing to read the *Declaration of Indulgence*. At the Revolution he refused to take the oath to William, and was deprived of his bishopric in 1691. See Lives by Bowles (1831), Anderdon (1851–54), Plumptre (2 vols. 1888), and Clarke (1896).

KENDAL, Madge, stage name of **Margaret Brunton Grimston**, *née* Margaret Shafto Robertson (1849–1935), English actress, born at Cleethorpes, sister of T. W. Robertson (q.v.). Appeared in Shakespearean rôles and by the 1870s was leading lady at the Haymarket Theatre. In 1869 she married **William Hunter Kendal**, properly **Grimston** (1843–1917), actor, with whom she appeared in many productions, particularly Shakespearean. She was created a D.B.E. in 1926.

KENDALL, Edward Calvin (1886–1972), American chemist, born at S. Norwalk, Conn., known for his isolation of thyroxin (1915), and for his research on adrenal hormones, for which, with P. S. Hench and T. Reichstein (qq.v.), he won the Nobel prize for medicine in 1950. See his autobiography (1971).

KENDREW, John Cowdery (1917–), British scientist, born at Oxford, educated at Clifton and Trinity College, Cambridge. With Perutz (q.v.) he carried out researches in the chemistry of the blood and discovered the structure of myoglobin, and shared the Nobel chemistry prize for 1962.

KENNEDY, (1) **Benjamin Hall** (1804–89), English classical scholar, born at Summerhill, Birmingham. After teaching at Harrow (1830–36), and Shrewsbury (1836–67), he became professor of Greek at Cambridge. The most celebrated of his many classical writings is *Sabrinae Corolla* (1850).

(2) **James** (*c.* 1408–65), Scottish bishop, grandson of Robert III and nephew of James I, was a graduate of St Andrews University, becoming Bishop of Dunkeld in 1437. Later, as Bishop of St Andrews and advisor to James II, he opposed the growing dominance of the Douglases in Scotland. During the minority of James III, he led the 'old lords' party in support of the Lancastrians. He founded St Salvator's College at St Andrews. See book by Dowden (1912).

(3) **John Fitzgerald** (1917–63), 35th president of the U.S., son of (4), born at Brookline, Mass., studied at Harvard and under Laski (q.v.) in London, and after service at the embassy there (1938), wrote a thesis on Britain's unpreparedness for war. His *Profiles of Courage* (1956) won the Pulitzer prize. As a torpedo boat commander in the Pacific, he was awarded the Navy medal and the Purple Heart. Elected Democrat representative (1947) and senator (1952) for Massachusetts, in 1960 he was the first Catholic, and the youngest person, to be elected president, on the smallest majority of the popular vote. The conservatism of Congress stalled his bid for a 'new frontier' in social legislation. Through his brother (6) he supported federal desegregation policy in schools and universities, and prepared further civil rights legislation. He displayed firmness and moderation in foreign policy, and in October 1962 at the risk of nuclear war induced Russia to withdraw its missiles from Cuba, and achieved a partial nuclear test ban treaty with Russia in 1963. On Nov. 22, 1963, he was assassinated by rifle fire while

being driven in an open car through Dallas, Texas. The alleged assassin, **Lee Oswald**, was himself shot and killed at point blank range two days later while under heavy police escort on a jail transfer. See Schlesinger, *A Thousand Days* (1965), Sorensen, *Kennedy* (1965), W. Manchester, *The Death of a President* (1967), *The Official Warren Commission Report* (1964) on the assassination, and M. Lane, *Rush to Judgement* (1966), criticizing the latter.—In 1953 Kennedy had married **Jacqueline Lee Bouvier** (b. 1929), who in 1968 married Aristotle Onassis (q.v.).

(4) **Joseph Patrick** (1888–1969), American multi-millionaire, born in Boston, grandson of an Irish Catholic immigrant, son of a Boston publican, educated at Harvard, made a large fortune in the 1920s, and during the 1930s was a strong supporter of Roosevelt and the 'New Deal', being rewarded with minor administrative posts, and the ambassadorship to Britain (1938–40). After World War II he concentrated on fulfilling his ambitions of a political dynasty through his sons. He had married in 1914 **Rose Fitzgerald**, daughter of a local politician, John F. Fitzgerald, also of Irish immigrant descent. They had nine children, including four sons, at whose political disposal he placed his fortune. The eldest, **Joseph Patrick** (1915–44), was killed in a flying accident while on naval service in World War II. For the careers of **John** and **Robert**, see (3) and (6). The youngest and only surviving son, **Edward Moore** (1932–), was born at Brookline, Mass., educated at Harvard and Virginia University Law School, admitted to the Massachusetts bar in 1959, and was elected as Democratic senator for his brother John's Massachusetts seat in 1962. In 1969 he became the youngest-ever majority whip in the U.S. senate. See McCarthy, *The Remarkable Kennedys* (1962), and R. J. Whalen, *The Founding Father* (1965).

(5) **Margaret** (1896–1967), English novelist, journalist, and playwright, born in London. Her many light novels all gained a fair measure of success, particularly her second, *The Constant Nymph* (1924). In 1934 her play, *Escape Me Never*, was published. In 1925 she married David Davies, knighted 1952, died 1964.

(6) **Robert Francis** (1925–68), American politician, third son of (4), born at Brookline, Mass., educated at Harvard and Virginia University Law School, served at sea (1944–1946) in World War II, was admitted to the Massachusetts bar (1951) and served on the Select Committee on Improper Activities (1957–59), when he prosecuted several top union leaders. An efficient manager of his brother's (3) presidential campaign, he was an energetic attorney-general (1961–64) under the latter's administration, notable in his dealings with civil rights problems. Senator for New York from 1965, his tardy decision to stand as a Democratic presidential candidate in 1968 branded him as an opportunist to some, as an idealistic reformer, closely identified with the struggles of America's underprivileged minorities, to others. On June 5, 1968, after winning the Californian primary election, he was shot, and died the following day. His assassin, **Sirhan Bishara Sirhan**, a 24-year-old Jordanian-born immigrant, was sentenced to the gas chamber in 1969. See his *To Seek a Newer World* (1968), and Life by M. Laing (1968).

KENNELLY, Arthur Edwin (1861–1939), American engineer, born in Bombay, became a professor at Harvard in 1902, and in the same year discovered, almost simultaneously with Oliver Heaviside (q.v.), the ionized layer in the atmosphere known sometimes as the Kennelly-Heaviside layer, more often as the Heaviside layer.

KENNETH I, called **Macalpine**, seems to have succeeded his father Alpin as king of the remnant of the Dalriada Scots in 834, and to have repelled a Danish invasion and completely conquered the Picts in 846. He was connected by blood with the Pictish royal family. He became king of a united Alban extending to the Firths of Clyde and Forth.

KENNICOTT, Benjamin (1718–83), biblical scholar, born at Totnes, educated at Wadham College, Oxford, known for his edition of the Hebrew Old Testament (1776–80), for which 615 Hebrew MSS and 16 MSS of the Samaritan Pentateuch were collated.

KENNINGTON, Eric Henri, A.R.A. (1888–1960), English painter and sculptor, born in London. He was an official war artist in both world wars, and in the field of sculpture, designed many memorials, etc., e.g., his head of T. E. Lawrence in St. Paul's Cathedral. His books include *Drawing the R.A.F.* (1942) and *The British Home Guard* (1945).

KENNY, Elizabeth (1886–1954) Australian nursing sister, renowned for her method of treating poliomyelitis.

KENT, Dukes of:

(1) **Edward** (1767–1820), 4th son of George III, born at Buckingham Palace. At Gibraltar, first (1790–91) as colonel, and then (1802) as governor, his martinet discipline caused continual mutinies. These culminated in an encounter in which blood was shed, after which he was recalled. In 1818 he married Victoria Mary Louisa (1786–1861), daughter of the Duke of Saxe-Saalfeld-Coburg, and widow of the Prince of Leiningen. For the sake of economy they lived at Leiningen, and came to England for the birth (May 24, 1819) of their child the Princess Victoria. The duke died 8 months later. Owing to the deaths of his three elder brothers, George IV, the Duke of York, and William IV, without issue, the crown came to the Princess Victoria.

(2) **George Edward Alexander Edmund** (1902–42), 4th son of King George V and Queen Mary, passed out of Dartmouth Naval College in 1920, but because of delicate health, served in the Foreign Office and inspected factories for the Home Office, the first member of the royal family to work in the Civil Service. In 1934 he was created duke and married **Princess Marina** of Greece and Denmark (1906–68), a first cousin of King George I of Greece and a great-niece of Queen Alexandra. He was killed on active service, as chief welfare officer of the R.A.F. Home Command, when his Sunderland flying-boat on its way to Iceland crashed in the north of Scotland. Their three children are: (1) **Edward** (b. 1935), Duke of Kent, who

married in 1961 Katharine Worsley (b. 1933); their son is George Philip Nicholas (b. 1962), Earl of St Andrews, and daughter Helen Marina Lucy (b. 1964).—(2) **Alexandra** (b. 1936), who married in 1963 the Hon. Angus James Bruce Ogilvy (b. 1928); their son is James Robert Bruce (b. 1964), and daughter Marina Victoria Alexandra (b. 1966).—(3) **Michael** (b. 1942).

KENT, (1) **James** (1763–1847), American lawyer, born at Fredericksburgh, N.Y., after serving in the New York legislature was professor of Law in Columbia College 1794–98, and then a justice of the supreme court of New York. In 1804 he became chief justice, and in 1814–23 was state chancellor. Kent's *Commentaries on American Law* (1826–30) is a standard work.

(2) **William** (1684–1748), painter, landscape gardener, and Palladian architect, was a native of Yorkshire, and died at Burlington House. His best-known work is the Horse Guards block in Whitehall. See Life by M. Jourdain (1948).

KENTIGERN, St (*c.* 518–603), the apostle of Cumbria, according to legend son of a Princess Thenew, who was cast from Traprain Law, then exposed on the Firth of Forth in a coracle. It carried her to Culross, where she bore a son (about 518). Mother and child were baptized by St Serf (an anachronism), who reared the boy in his monastery, where he was so beloved that his name Kentigern (' chief lord ') was often exchanged for Mungo (' dear friend '). He founded a monastery at Cathures (now Glasgow), and in 543 was consecrated Bishop of Cumbria. In 553 he was driven to seek refuge in Wales, where he visited St David, and where he founded another monastery and a bishopric, which still bears the name of his disciple, St Asaph. In 573 he was recalled by a new king, Rederech Hael, and about 584 was visited by Columba. He was buried in Glasgow Cathedral. A fragment of a Life and the *Vita Kentigerni* by Joceline of Furness both belong to the 12th century. See Bishop Forbes's *Lives of SS. Ninian and Kentigern* (1874), Skene's *Celtic Scotland* (vol. ii, 1877), and Beveridge's *Culross* and *Tulliallan* (1885).

KENYATTA, Jomo (*c.* 1889–), Kenyan politician, born an orphan at Mitumi, Kenya, educated at a Scots mission school and began as a herd boy. Joined the Kikuyu Central Association (1922), and became its president. Visited Britain in 1929 and from 1931 to 1944. Studied for a year at London University under Malinowski, who wrote the preface to his book *Facing Mount Kenya* (1938). Visited Russia thrice, and was president of the Pan African Federation with Nkrumah (q.v.) as secretary. Worked on the land during the war and married an Englishwoman in 1942. On returning to Kenya in 1946 his Kenya African Union advocated extreme nationalism, and he led the *Mau Mau* terrorist society. Sentenced to 7 years' hard labour in 1952, he was released in 1958, but exiled first to a remote northern area, then to his native village. Elected president of the dominant K.A.N.U. party, and M.P. in 1961, he became prime minister in June 1963, retaining the post after Kenya's independence in Dec. 1963, and president of the republic of Kenya in Dec. 1964. See Life by G. Delf (1961).

KENYON, (1) **Sir Frederic George** (1863–1952), English classical scholar, born in London, director and chief librarian of the British Museum (1909–30). He edited Bacchylides' poems and was responsible for a number of editions of classical and biblical texts.

(2) **John** (1784–1856), British philanthropist, the wealthy acquaintance of Coleridge, Lamb, Landor, Crabb Robinson, Ticknor, &c., was born in Jamaica, and died at Cowes. A lifelong friend of Browning, he was responsible for introducing the poet to Elizabeth Barrett. He published some poetry.

KEPLER, or **Keppler, Johann** (1571–1630), German astronomer, was born at Weil der Stadt in Württemberg. He studied at Tübingen, in 1593 was appointed professor of Mathematics at Graz, about 1596 commenced a correspondence with Tycho Brahe, and in 1600 went to Prague to aid him in his work. After Tycho's death (1601) Kepler was astronomer, often unpaid, to the Emperor Rudolf II. In 1612 he became a mathematics teacher at Linz, and in 1628 astrologer to Wallenstein. In his *Mysterium* (1596), he proclaimed that 5 kinds of regular polyhedral bodies govern the 5 planetary orbits; and in his *Harmonice Mundi*, 1619, Kepler's Third Law, that the ' square of a planet's periodic time is proportional to the cube of its mean distance from the sun ', appeared. He tried to find a law for the movements of Mars, and in 1609 published his First and Second Laws, which formed the groundwork of Newton's discoveries, and are the starting-point of modern astronomy. He also made many discoveries in optics, general physics, and geometry. See studies by Donsky (1880), Herz (1895), Bryant (1921), C. Baumgardt (1952), M. Caspar (trans. 1960), and an opera on his life by Hindemith, *Die Harmonie der Welt* (1957).

KEPPEL, (1) **Augustus, 1st Viscount** (1725–1786), admiral, son of the second Earl of Albemarle, served under Hawke in 1757, captured Goree in 1758, took part in the battle of Quiberon Bay in 1759, and in the capture of Belleisle in 1761, and commanded at the capture of Havana in 1762. In 1778 he encountered the French fleet off Ushant on July 27. Owing to a disagreement with Palliser, his second in command, the French escaped. Both admirals were tried by court martial, but acquitted. In 1782 created Viscount Keppel, he became first lord of the Admiralty. See Life by T. Keppel (1842).

(2) **Sir Henry** (1809–1904), successively vice-admiral (1867), admiral (1869), and admiral of the fleet (1877), was a son of the fourth Earl of Albemarle. He saw service during the war against China in 1842, and in a campaign against pirates, and commanded the naval brigade before Sebastopol. In 1857 he took part in the destruction of the Chinese fleet. G.C.B. (1871), O.M. (1902), he wrote on Borneo, &c. See his *A Sailor's Life under Four Sovereigns* (3 vols. 1899), and memoir by West (1905).

KER, (1) **John** (1673–1726), of Kersland, Dalry parish, Ayrshire, a Cameronian who intrigued with the Jacobites, but was really a government spy. See his shameless Memoirs (1726).

(2) **William Paton** (1855–1923), Scottish scholar, born in Glasgow, educated there and at Balliol, was professor of English at Cardiff (1883), London (1889), and of Poetry at Oxford (1920). Talker, lecturer, and writer of prodigious learning and vitality, he wrote *Epic and Romance* (1897), *The Art of Poetry* (1923), &c.

KERENSKY, Alexander (1881–1970), Russian revolutionary, born at Simbirsk (now Ulyanovsk), son of a high school principal, studied law in Leningrad. He took a leading part in the revolution of 1917, becoming minister of justice (March), for war (May), and premier (July). He crushed Kornilov's military revolt (September), but was deposed (November) by the Bolsheviks and fled to France. In 1940 he went to Australia and in 1946 to America. His writings include *The Prelude to Bolshevism* (1919), *The Catastrophe* (1927), *The Road to Tragedy* (1935), and *The Kerensky Memoirs* (1966).

KERGUÉLEN-TRÉMAREC, Yves (1745–97), a French naval officer, born at Quimper in Brittany, who in 1772 discovered Kerguelen's Land.

KERN, Jerome (1885–1945), American composer, born in New York, wrote a vast quantity of music for musical comedy and films. His scores include *The Red Petticoat*, which first brought a 'western' setting to Broadway in 1912, *Sally*, *Roberta*, and *Very Warm for May*, and contain such evergreen songs as 'Look for the Silver Lining' and 'Smoke Gets in your Eyes'. His greatest success came with the operetta *Show Boat* (1927), a work which has had a lasting influence upon American light entertainment.

KERNER, Andreas Justinus (1786–1862), German poet, born in Ludwigsburg in Württemberg, became a physician at Wildbad, and settled finally at Weinsberg in 1818. He published several volumes of poetry between 1811 and 1852, studied animal magnetism, believed in occultism, and wrote *Die Seherin von Prevorst* (1829). See A. Watts, *Life and works of Kerner* (1884); English Goethe Society, *Letters of J. Kerner to Graf A. von Württemberg* (1938).

KEROUAC, Jack (officially **John**) (1922–69), American author born in Lowell, Mass., won a scholarship to Columbia University, the while wandering through the country doing odd jobs. His first novel *The Town and the City* (1950) was written in the orthodox manner which he abandoned in *On the Road* (1957), a spontaneous work in 'beatnik' idiom, expressing the youthful discontent of the 'beat' generation. Later works include *The Dharma Bums*, *The Subterraneans* (1958) and *Big Sur* (1962).

KERR, or **Ker,** an Anglo-Norman family, found in Scotland at the end of the 12th century. Sir Andrew Ker of Cessford (d. 1526), whose younger brother, George, was ancestor of the Kers of Faudonside, had two sons—Sir Walter, whose grandson, Robert Ker, was created Earl of Roxburghe 1616, and Mark, commendator of Newbattle, whose son, Mark Kerr, was created Earl of Lothian 1606. The second Earl of Roxburghe was only a Ker by his mother. His grandson, fifth Earl, was created duke in 1707. John, third Duke (1740–1804), was the famous book-collector. Robert Carre (see OVERBURY) belonged to the Fernihirst line.

KERR, John (1824–1907), Scottish physicist, born at Ardrossan, educated at Glasgow in theology, became a lecturer in mathematics and was later elected F.R.S. In 1876 he discovered the magneto-optic effect which was then named after him. He was the author of *An Elementary Treatise on Rational Mechanics* (1867).

KERVYN DE LETTENHOVE, Joseph, *let-en-hō'vė* (1817–91), Belgian historian, died at Brussels. Works include *Froissart* (1857), and series of chronicles.

KESSELRING, Albert (1885–1960), German air commander in World War II, led the Luftwaffe attacks on France and (unsuccessfully) on Britain. In 1943 he was made c.-in-c. in Italy and in 1945 in the West. Condemned to death as a war criminal in 1947, he had his sentence commuted to life imprisonment but was released in 1952. See his Memoirs (1953).

KETCH, Jack (d. 1686), hangman and headsman from about 1663.

KETT, Robert (d. 1549), a landowner of Wymondham in Norfolk, who in July 1549 headed 16,000 insurgents, enclosures being their principal grievance. Norwich was twice captured by the rebels; on the second occasion they held it until they were driven out by the Earl of Warwick, Kett being captured and hanged, December 7. See books by F. W. Russell (1860), Joseph Clayton (1912), and S. T. Bindoff (1949).

KETTELER, Wilhelm (1811–77), German ecclesiastic, from 1850 Ultramontane bishop of Mainz. He was principal opponent of Bismarck's *Kulturkampf*.

KEULEN, L. van. See CEULEN, L. VAN.

KEY, (1) Ellen (1849–1926), Swedish author, born at Sundsholm, Småland, took to teaching (1880) when her father lost his fortune, and made her name as a writer and lecturer on the feminist movement, child welfare, &c. See Life by Hamilton (1913).

(2) **Francis Scott** (1780–1843), American lawyer, attorney for the District of Columbia, during the British attack on Baltimore (1814), which he witnessed from a British man-of-war, wrote 'The Star-spangled Banner'. See O. G. T. Sonneck, *The Star-spangled Banner* (1914).

(3) **Thomas Hewitt** (1799–1875), English scholar, headmaster of University College School, professor of Comparative Grammar in University College London, author of a *Latin Grammar* and of a *Latin-English Dictionary*. See Life by J. P. Hicks (1893).

KEYES, (1) Roger John Brownlow, 1st Baron Keyes (1872–1945), British admiral, entered the Royal Navy in 1885, served at Witu (1890) and in the Boxer Rebellion (1900), in World War I was chief of staff Eastern Mediterranean (1915) and in 1918 commanded the Dover Patrol, leading the raid on Zeebrugge. He was created K.C.B. in 1918. Recalled in 1940, he was appointed director of amphibious warfare, subsequently becoming liaison officer to the

Belgians. See his *Naval Memoirs* (2 vols. 1934–35), *Adventures Ashore and Afloat* (1939) and *Amphibious Warfare and Combined Operations* (1943). His son, **Lieut-Col. Geoffrey Keyes**, M.C. and posthumous V.C., was killed in the historic commando raid on Rommel's H.Q. in 1941.

(2) **Sydney** (1922–43), English poet, born at Dartford, Kent, was killed in Tunisia in April 1943. His first book of poems, *The Iron Laurel*, was published in 1942, and his second, *The Cruel Solstice*, in 1944, in which year he was posthumously awarded the Hawthornden prize. See his *Collected Poems*, edited with memoir and notes by M. Meyer (1945).

KEYNES, John Maynard, 1st Baron (1883–1946), English economist, pioneer of the theory of full employment, son of **John Neville** (1852–1949) the Cambridge logician and political economist, born at Cambridge and educated at Eton and King's College, Cambridge, where he became one of the 'Bloomsbury group' and where off and on from 1908 he lectured in economics. He was at the India Office (1906–08) and in 1913 as a member of the Royal Commission on Indian finance and currency, published his first book on this subject. In both world wars he was an adviser to the Treasury, which he represented at the Versailles Peace Conference but resigned in strong opposition to the terms of the draft treaty, set out in his *Economic Consequences of the Peace* (1919) written with the encouragement of Smuts. In 1921 *Treatise of Probability* appeared, in which he explored the logical relationships between calling something 'highly probable' and a 'justifiable induction'. In 1923 he became chairman of the Liberal periodical, *Nation*, and pamphleteered his controversial views on European reconstruction, strongly attacking Churchill's restoration of the gold standard (1925). The unemployment crises inspired his two great works, *A Treatise on Money* (1930) and the revolutionary *General Theory of Employment, Interest and Money* (1936). He argued that full employment was not an automatic condition, expounded a new theory of the rate of interest, and set out the principles underlying the flows of income and expenditure, and fought the Treasury view that unemployment was incurable. His views on a planned economy influenced Roosevelt's 'New Deal' administration. He married a Diaghilev ballerina, **Lydia Lopokova** and with her helped to found the Vic-Wells ballet. He financed the establishment of the Arts Theatre, Cambridge. In 1943 he proposed the international clearing union, played a leading part (1944–46) in the formulation of the Bretton Woods agreements, the establishment of the International Monetary Fund, and the troublesome, abortive negotiations for a continuation of American *Lend-lease*. Created C.B. (1917), elected F.B.A. (1929), he died just prior to being awarded the O.M. See his *Essays in Persuasion* (1931), *Essays in Biography* (1933), studies by Dillard (1948), Pigou (1950), Memoirs, ed. at Cambridge (1949), F. A. Keynes (1950), and Life by Harrod (1951).

KEYSERLING, Hermann Graf, *kī'ser-ling* (1880–1946), German philosopher, born at Koenno in Livonia, travelled widely, founded a 'School of Wisdom' at Darmstadt and attempted a synthesis of western and eastern thought. See his *Travel Diary of a Philosopher* (1919; trans. 1925), and M. G. Parks, *Introduction to Keyserling* (1934).

KHAMA, (1) (1835–1923), a reforming chief of the Bamangwato in the Bechuanaland Protectorate. See Life by J. Mockford (1931).

(2) **Sir Seretse** (1921–), African politician, born at Serowe, Bechuanaland (now Botswana), nephew of Tshekedi Khama (1905–59), who was chief regent of the Bamangwato from 1925. Seretse was educated in Africa and Balliol College, Oxford. While a student at the Inner Temple in 1948 he married an English woman, and in 1950, with his uncle, was banned from the chieftainship and the territory of the Bamangwato. Allowed to return in 1956, he became active in politics, and was restored to the chieftainship in 1963. He became first prime minister of Bechuanaland in 1965 and president of Botswana in 1966, having received a knighthood.

KHAN, (Mohammed) Ayub (?–), Pakistani statesman, born Abbottabad, educated Aligarh Moslem University and Sandhurst, served in World War II, became first C.-in-C. of Pakistan's army (1951) and field-marshal (1959). He became president of Pakistan in 1958 after a bloodless army *coup*, and established a stable economy and political autocracy. In March 1969, after widespread civil disorder and violent opposition from both right and left wings, Ayub Khan relinquished power and martial law was re-established. See his *Friends, Not Masters* (1967).

KHATCHATURIAN, Aram (1903–), Russian composer, student of folksongs, and authority on oriental music, born at Tiflis in 1903. His compositions include two symphonies, concertos, ballets, film and instrumental music. See Lives by Martinov (Moscow 1947) and Shneerson (trans. 1960).

KHAYYÁM, Omar. See OMAR.

KHRUSHCHEV, Nikita Sergeyevich, *kroosh'-chof* (1894–1971), Soviet politician, born at Kalinovka near Kursk, was a shepherd boy and a locksmith and is said to have been almost illiterate until the age of 25. Joining the Communist Party in 1918, he fought in the Civil War and rose rapidly in the party organization. In 1939 he was made a full member of the Politburo and of the Presidium of the Supreme Soviet. In World War II he organized guerrilla warfare against the invading Germans and took charge of the reconstruction of devastated territory. In 1949 he launched a drastic reorganization of Soviet agriculture. In 1953 on the death of Stalin he became first secretary of the All Union Party and three years later, at the 20th Congress of the Communist Party, denounced Stalinism and the 'personality cult'. The following year he demoted Molotov, Kaganovich and Malenkov—all possible rivals. Khrushchev, who did much to enhance the ambitions and status of the Soviet Union abroad, was nevertheless deposed in 1964 and forced into retirement. He was at his peak the greatest power behind the Iron Curtain, and a decisive voice in world politics and strategy. See Lives by V. Alexandrov (1957), and G. Paloczi-Horvath (1960), and studies by E. Crankshaw (1966) and M. Frankland (1966).

KIDD, (1) **John** (1775–1851), English chemist and physician, born in London, studied medicine at Guy's Hospital, and became professor of Chemistry at Oxford (1803), and fellow of the Royal Society. In 1819, with Garden, he discovered naphthalene in coal tar.

(2) **William** (*c.* 1645–1701), Scottish privateer and pirate, born probably at Greenock, son, it is thought, of a Covenanting minister who died in 1679, went early to sea, saw much privateering service, and gained a high reputation for courage, and in 1691 a reward of £150 from New York City. In 1696 he was given a ship of 30 guns to act against the French and to seize pirates. In 1697 he reached Madagascar, the pirates' chief rendezvous, but turned pirate himself. After a two years' cruise he returned to the West Indies, and venturing to Boston, was arrested, sent to England and hanged May 23, 1701. See the *Trial* (ed. Brooks, 1930), C. N. Dalton, *The real Captain Kidd: a vindication* (1911); H. T. Wilkins, *Captain Kidd and his Skeleton Island* (1935).

KIELLAND, Alexander, *kel'ahn* (1849–1906), Norwegian novelist, was born at Stavanger, where in 1891 he became burgomaster. His works include *Garman and Worse* (1884), *Skipper Worse* (1885), *Tales of Two Countries* (1891).

KIENZL, Wilhelm, *keen'tsl'* (1857–1941), Austrian composer, born at Waizenkirchen, Austria, became *kapellmeister* at Amsterdam, Krefeld, Graz, Hamburg and Munich. His third opera, *Der Evangelimann* (Berlin 1895; London 1897), was his first success. See his *Richard Wagner* (Munich 1904).

KIEPERT, Heinrich, *kee'pert* (1818–99), German geographer, born at Berlin, conducted the Geographical Institute at Weimar (1845–52), in 1859 became professor of Geography at Berlin, and wrote on ancient geography. Published works include *Atlas antiquus, 12 maps of the ancient world* (7th ed. 1882).

KIERKEGAARD, Sören Aaby, *keer'kė-gawr* (1813–55), Danish philosopher and theologian, progenitor of modern existentialism, was born deformed at Copenhagen, where he read theology (in which he graduated in 1840 but without taking orders), philosophy and literature. Obsessed by some mysterious guilt of his father's, he broke off, after much heart-searching, his engagement to Regine Olsen. Such deliberate, significant choosing of one's future self became the basis of his philosophizing. It is something that has to be lived through and experienced, purely speculative systems of thought such as Hegel's being irrelevant to existence-making choices, because existence on account of its multiplicity can never be incorporated into a system. For Hegel's synthesis, Kierkegaard substituted the disjunction *Either/Or* (1843), the basis of choice. In *Philosophical Fragments* (1844; tr. Princeton 1936) and especially in *Concluding Unscientific Postscript* (1846; tr. Princeton 1941) he attacked all philosophical system building and formulated the thesis that subjectivity is truth. He also attacked organized dogmatic Christianity in nine issues of the journal, *The Instant*, because it failed to make sufficiently clear the absolute moral isolation of the individual, the necessity for really choosing Christ, instead of just adhering to prescribed dogma and ritual. Forerunner of the existentialism of Sartre, Heidegger, Jaspers, Barth and Buber. See his *Samlede Voerker* (1920–31; tr. W. Lowrie 1938 ff.), biographical *Glimpses and Impressions*, ed. T. H. Croxall (1959) and studies by E. Hirsch (1933), T. Haecker (tr. A. Dru 1936), L. Shestov (1936), R. Jolivet (1951), J. D. Collins (1954) and H. Diem (1959).

KILIAN, St. See CILIAN.

KILLIGREW, (1) **Thomas** (1612–83), English dramatist, brother of (2), page in the household of Charles I, and afterwards a companion of Charles II in exile and his groom of the bedchamber after the Restoration. He published in 1664 nine indifferent plays, written, he tells us, in nine different cities. He was for some time manager of the king's company, and obtained permission to give female parts to women.

(2) **Sir William** (1606–95), English dramatist, brother of (1), fought in the Civil War, and wrote a comedy, *Pandora*, and tragicomedies, *Selindra*, *Ormasdes*, and *The Siege of Urbin*. See book by Harbage (Philadelphia 1930).

KILMUIR, 1st Earl of (1900–67), formerly **Sir David Patrick Maxwell Fyfe,** British lawyer and Conservative politician, born in Aberdeen and educated at George Watson's College, Edinburgh, and at Balliol College, Oxford. He took silk in 1934, the youngest K.C. since the time of Charles II. He was M.P. for West Derby (Liverpool) (1935–54) when he became lord high chancellor. He was deputy chief prosecutor at the Nuremberg trial of the principal Nazi war criminals. Home secretary and minister for Welsh affairs in the 1951 Government, he advised on a heavy programme of controversial legislation. Knighted 1942, created Viscount 1954, and Earl and Baron Fyfe of Dornoch in 1962. He wrote *Monopoly* (1948) and *Political Adventure* (1964).

KILVERT, Francis (1840-79), English clergyman, whose *Diary* (*1870-79*) (discovered 1937, ed. by W. Plomer in 3 vols. 1938, 1939, 1940, n.e. 1961; in 1 vol. 1944) describing his life as curate and vicar, is an important social historical document of his period, if not quite on a par with Pepys and Evelyn.

KILWARDBY, Robert (d. 1279), a Dominican, was in 1273 made Archbishop of Canterbury, and in 1278 a cardinal. He died at Viterbo. See study by E. Sommer-Seckendorff (Rome 1937).

KIMBERLEY, John Wodehouse, 1st Earl of (1826–1902), Liberal statesman, was lord privy-seal 1868–70, colonial secretary 1870–74 and 1880–82, secretary for India 1882–85 and 1886, secretary for India and lord president of the Council 1892–94, and then foreign secretary till 1895. Kimberley in South Africa was named after him.

KIMHI, or Kimchi, David, *kim'KHi* (*c.* 1160–1235), Jewish grammarian, lived and died at Narbonne. Subsequent Hebrew grammars and lexicons are based on his. See his *Hebrew grammar systematically presented and critically annotated* by W. Chomsky (New York 1952).

KINCK, Hans Ernst (1865–1926), Norwegian novelist and dramatist, born at Öksfjord. His works illustrate his deep love of nature and his interest in the lives of peasants and include *Sneskaulenbrast* (1918–19) and *Driftekaren* (1908), a verse play. He died at Oslo.

KING, (1) Edward (1612–37), Milton's fellow-student, whose drowning off the Welsh coast is commemorated in *Lycidas*.

(2) **Edward** (1829–1910), English bishop, son of the Archdeacon of Rochester, graduated from Oriel College, Oxford in 1851, and was principal of Cuddesdon 1863–73, and regius professor of Pastoral Theology 1873–1885, and then bishop of Lincoln. Tried in 1890 for ritualistic practices, he was condemned on only two charges. See his *Sermons and addresses* (1911), and study by Randolph and Townroe (1918).

(3) **Martin Luther** (1929–68), American Negro minister, born at Atlanta, Ga., son of a Baptist pastor, studied systematic theology at Boston University, and set up first ministry at Montgomery, Ala. Became a leader of a civil rights movement, based on principle of non-violence. In 1964 he received an honorary doctorate from Yale, the Kennedy peace prize, and the Nobel peace prize. He was assassinated in Memphis, Tenn., while on a civil rights mission. His white assassin, **James Earl Ray**, was apprehended in London, and in 1969 was sentenced in Memphis to 99 years.

(4) **William Lyon Mackenzie** (1874–1950), Canadian Liberal statesman, born at Kitchener, Ontario, studied law at Toronto, won a fellowship in political science at Ontario and accepted the newly created post of deputy minister of labour (1900–08), when he left the civil service and became an M.P., being appointed minister of labour (1909–14). In 1914 he became director of industrial relations in the Rockefeller Foundation for industrial problems, publishing an important study on the subject, *Industry and Humanity* in 1918. In 1919 he became Liberal leader and was prime minister 1921–26, 1926–30, and 1935–48. His view that the dominions should be autonomous communities within the British Empire and not form a single entity as Smuts advocated, materialized in the famous Statute of Westminster (1931). He opposed sanctions against Italy over Ethiopia and on the eve of World War II wrote to Hitler, Mussolini and President Mosicki of Poland urging them to preserve the peace, but promptly declared war on Germany with the other dominions once Poland was attacked. He opposed conscription, except eventually for overseas service, and signed agreements with Roosevelt (1940–41) integrating the economies of the two countries and represented Canada at the London and San Francisco foundation conferences of the United Nations (1945). He was awarded the O.M. in 1947. See study by Ferns and Ostry (1955) and Lives by Hutchison (1952), Dawson, Vol. I (1958) and Neatby, Vol. II (1963).

(5) **William Rufus** (1786–1853), American statesman, born in N. Carolina, member of the state legislature for 3 years, entered congress in 1810, senator for Alabama 1820–1844, minister to France 1844–46, senator again 1846–53, and, just before his death, vice president of the U.S.

KINGDON-WARD, Frank (1885–1958), English botanist, plant explorer and writer, son of the botanist **Harry Marshall Ward** (1854–1906), made important botanical journeys in China, Tibet, Burma, Thailand, &c., and wrote on his travels and on his associated plant discoveries. His publications include *The Land of the Blue Poppy* (1913), *In Farthest Burma* (1921), &c.

KINGLAKE, Alexander William (1809–91), English historian, born at Wilton House, near Taunton, from Eton passed in 1828 to Trinity College, Cambridge. He was called to the bar in 1837, and made a fair practice, but retired in 1856 to devote himself to literature and politics. A tour about 1835 had already given birth to *Eōthen* (1844), one of the most brilliant and popular books of Eastern travel. In 1854 he went out to the Crimea. He was returned for Bridgwater as a Liberal in 1857, took a prominent part against Lord Palmerston's Conspiracy Bill, and denounced the French annexation of Savoy. His *History of the War in the Crimea* (8 vols. 1863–87) is on the literary side one of the finest historical works of its century. See a study by Tuckwell (1902).

KINGO, Thomas Hansen, *keeng'ō* (1634–1703), Danish religious poet, born in Slangerup. He was of Scottish descent, and became Bishop of Fyn in 1677. He wrote several collections of hymns and much religious and secular poetry.

KINGSFORD, Anna, *née* **Bonus** (1846–88), English doctor and writer, born at Stratford, Essex. In 1867 she married a Shropshire clergyman, and thereafter became a convert to Catholicism (1870), an antivivisectionist, M.D. of Paris (1880), a vegetarian, a Theosophist, &c. See Life by E. Maitland (1895).

KINGSLEY, (1) Charles (1819–75), English author, born at Holne vicarage, Dartmoor. In 1838 entered Magdalene College, Cambridge, and took a classical first in 1842. As curate and then (1844) rector, he spent the rest of his life at Eversley in Hampshire. His dramatic poem, *The Saint's Tragedy, or The True Story of Elizabeth of Hungary* (1848), was followed by *Alton Locke* (1850) and *Yeast* (1851), brilliant social novels which had enormous influence at the time. He had thrown himself into various schemes for the improvement of the working classes, and like Maurice was a 'Christian Socialist'. As 'Parson Lot' he published an immense number of articles on current topics, especially in the *Christian Socialist* and *Politics for the People*. *Hypatia* (1853) is a brilliant picture of early Christianity in conflict with Greek philosophy at Alexandria. *Westward Ho!* (1855) is a lifelike presentment of Elizabethan England and the Spanish Main. *Two Years Ago* (1857) and *Hereward the Wake* (1866) were his later novels. In 1860 he was appointed professor of Modern History at Cambridge, *The Roman and the Teuton* (1864) being based on his Cambridge lectures. In

1869 he resigned his professorship and was appointed canon of Chester. In 1869–70 he made a voyage to the West Indies, and on his return issued the charming record *At Last*. In 1873 he was appointed canon of Westminster and chaplain to the Queen. The collected works of this combative, enthusiastic and sympathetic apostle of what was called (*not* by him) 'muscular Christianity' fill 28 volumes (1879–81), and include *Glaucus* (1855), *The Heroes* (1856), *The Water Babies* (1863), *Town Geology* (1872), *Prose Idylls* (1873) and *Health and Education* (1874). See Life by his widow (2 vols. 1877), G. Kendall, *Charles Kingsley and his Ideas* (1947), U. Pope-Hennessy, *Canon Charles Kingsley* (1948).

(2) **George Henry** (1827–92), brother of (1), studied medicine, travelled much, and wrote many books of sport and travel, including *South Sea Bubbles* (1872).

(3) **Henry** (1830–76), brother of (1), was educated at King's College School, London, and Worcester College, Oxford. From 1853 to 1858 he resided in Australia, and on his return published a vigorous picture of colonial life in *Geoffry Hamlyn* (1859). To this succeeded *Ravenshoe* (1861), his masterpiece; *Austin Elliot* (1863); *The Hillyars and the Burtons*, another novel of Australian life (1865), &c. In 1869–70 he edited the *Edinburgh Daily Review*. See S. M. Ellis, *Henry Kingsley*.

(4) **Mary** (1862–1900), daughter of (2), was an enterprising traveller in West Africa, wrote admirably, and died a nurse in a South African hospital during the Boer war. See Lives by Gwynne (1932), C. Howard (1957) and Olwen Campbell (1957). H. Simpson, *A Woman Among Wild Men* (1938), I. M. Holmes, *In Africa's Service* (1949) and R. Glynn, *Mary Kingsley in Africa* (1956).

(5) **Mary St Leger** (1852–1931), daughter of (1), married in 1876 the Rev. W. Harrison, rector of Clovelly, and as 'Lucas Malet' completed her father's *Tutor's Story* (1916) and wrote powerful novels—*Mrs Lorimer* (1882), *Colonel Enderby's Wife* (1885), *The Wages of Sin* (1890), *The Carissima* (1896), *Sir Richard Calmady* (1901), &c. She became a Roman Catholic in 1899.

KINGSTON, William Henry Giles (1814–80), English author, son of a merchant in Oporto, where he spent much of his youth. He wrote over 150 boys' adventure stories including such favourites as *Peter the Whaler* (1851) and *The Three Midshipmen* (1862).

KINKEL, (1) **Gottfried** (1815–82), German poet, born at Oberkassel near Bonn, lectured at Bonn on theology, poetry and the history of art. Involved in the revolutionary movement of 1848, he was imprisoned in Spandau (1850), from where he escaped. He taught German in London until 1866, when he was appointed professor of Archaeology and Art at Zürich. As a poet his fame rests upon *Otto der Schütz* (1846; 73rd ed. 1894), *Der Grobschmied von Antwerpen* (1872), *Tanagra* (1883), *Gedichte* (1843–68), and a drama, *Nimrod* (1857). He also wrote a history of art (1845) and monographs on Freiligrath (1867), Rubens (1874), &c. See Lives by Strodtmann (1850), Henne-Am Rhyn (1883), and Lübke (1893), also E. Bebler, *Conrad F. Meyer und Gottfried Kinkel* (Zürich 1949). His first wife, **Johanna** (1810–58), a distinguished musician, wrote a novel, *Hans Ibeles in London* (1860), and, with her husband, *Erzählungen* (1849), a collection of tales.

KINMONT WILLIE. See ARMSTRONG (8).

KIPLING, Rudyard (1865–1936), English writer, was born at Bombay, the son of John Lockwood Kipling, C.I.E. (1837–1911), principal in 1875–93 of the School of Art at Lahore, and author of *Beast and Man in India* (1891). Rudyard was educated in England, but returned in 1880 to India, where he worked as a journalist on the Lahore *Civil and Military Gazette*. His mildly satirical verses *Departmental Ditties* (1886), and the short stories *Plain Tales from the Hills* (1888) and *Soldiers Three* (1889), won him a reputation in England, whither he returned in 1889 and settled in London, where *The Light that Failed* (1890), his first attempt at a full-length novel—a genre in which he was never too happy—was not altogether successful. In London he met Wolcott Balestier the American author-publisher, with whom he collaborated in *The Naulakha* (1892), and whose sister Caroline he married (1892). A spell of residence in his wife's native state of Vermont ended abruptly in 1899 through incompatibility with in-laws and locals, and the remainder of Kipling's career was spent in England. Meanwhile he had written the brilliantly successful *Barrack Room Ballads* (1892) and *The Seven Seas* (1896), both collections of verse, and further short stories published as *Many Inventions* (1893) and *The Day's Work* (1899). The two *Jungle Books* (1894–95) have won a place among the classic animal stories, and *Stalky and Co* (1899) presents semi-autobiographical but delightfully uninhibited episodes based on the author's schooldays at the United Services College at Westward Ho!. *Kim* appeared in 1901, and the children's classic *Just So Stories* in 1902. The verse collection *The Five Nations* (1903) included the highly successful, though now somewhat *démodé*, 'Recessional' written for Queen Victoria's diamond jubilee. Later works include *Puck of Pook's Hill* (1906), *Rewards and Fairies* (1910), *Debits and Credits* (1926), and the autobiographical *Something of Myself* (1937). Kipling's real merit as a writer has tended to become obscured in recent years by the decline in his popularity brought about by the current fashion of denigrating Britain's period of colonial greatness; but those who condemn his forthright patriotism as 'jingoistic' and 'imperialistic' ignore not only the great body of his work which was far removed from this sphere, but also his own criticisms and satire on some of the less admirable aspects of colonialism. It must not be forgotten that he was awarded the Nobel prize for literature in 1907. See bibliography by F. V. Livingston (N.Y. 1927) with Supplement (Cambridge, Mass. 1938); also Lives by B. Dobrée (1951) and C. E. Carrington (1955), and study by J. M. S. Tompkins (1959).

KIPP, Petrus Jacobus (1808–64), Dutch chemist, was born in Utrecht, Holland, and started a business in laboratory apparatus in Delft in 1830. He invented the apparatus called after him for the continuous and automatic production of gases such as carbon dioxide, hydrogen and hydrogen sulphide. A representation of it appears in the arms of the Dutch Chemical Society. He also invested a method of fixing carbon and pastel drawings.

KIPPING, Frederick Stanley (1863–1949), British chemist, F.R.S. (1897), professor of Chemistry at Nottingham, investigated silicon compounds and was responsible for their development and use in the production of plastics capable of resisting higher temperatures. See Perkin and Kipping: *Organic Chemistry* (1894; new edition 1949).

KIRBY, William (1759–1850), English entomologist, born at Witnesham Hall, Suffolk, author of *Monographia Apum Angliae* (1802), *Introduction to Entomology* (1815–26), written with James Spence, and *Habits and Instincts of Animals* (Bridgewater Treatise, 1835). See Life by Freeman (1852).

KIRCHHOFF, Gustav Robert, *keer*KH*'hōf* (1824–87), German physicist, born at Königsberg, became professor at Berlin in 1874. He distinguished himself in elasticity, heat, optics and especially spectrum analysis. See Life by Boltzmann (1888).

KIRCHNER, Ernst Ludwig, *kir*HK*-nêr* (1880–1938), German artist, born at Aschaffenburg. He studied architecture at Dresden, but he became the leading spirit in the formation, with Erich Heckel and Karl Schmidt-Rottluff, of ' Die Brücke ' (1905–13), the first group of German expressionists, whose work was much influenced by primitive German woodcuts. Many of his works were confiscated as degenerate in 1937, and he committed suicide in 1938. See monograph by W. Grohmann (1926).

KIRK, Robert (*c.* 1641–92), Scottish author, turned the metrical Psalms into Gaelic, and was the author of *The Secret Commonwealth of Elves, Fauns, and Fairies* (1691), latest ed. (1933) with introduction by R. B. Cunninghame Graham.

KIRKCALDY, Sir William, of Grange (*c.* 1520–73), Scottish politician, as one of Beaton's murderers (1546) was imprisoned at Mont St Michel (1547–50). He took service with France, but in 1559 was opposing the French cause in Scotland. He figured at Carberry Hill, was made governor of Edinburgh Castle, and did much to win Langside; but going over to Queen Mary's party, held Edinburgh Castle for her till May 1573. He was hanged on August 3. See Lives by James Grant (1849) and Barbé (1897).

KIRKE, (1) **Edward** (1553–1613), Spenser's friend, author of the preface and commentary of his *Shepheardes Calender* (1579), and from 1580 rector of Risby, Bury St Edmunds.

(2) **Percy** (*c.* 1646–91), English Army colonel who had served 1681–84 in Tangiers, and whose men (' Kirke's Lambs ') committed after Sedgemoor (1685) fearful atrocities. He early deserted to William, and helped to raise the siege of Londonderry.

KIRKUP, Seymour Stocker (1788–1880), English artist, Dante scholar, and spiritualist, the friend of Haydon, Landor, Trelawny, the Brownings, &c., was born in London, and from 1816 lived in Italy, chiefly at Florence, where in 1840 he discovered Giotto's portrait of Dante.

KIRKWOOD, Daniel (1814–95), American astronomer, born at Harford, Maryland, became professor of Mathematics at Delaware (1851) and at Indiana (1856). He explained the unequal distribution of asteroids in the ring system of Saturn in terms of the ' Kirkwood gaps ' and subjected La Place's theories to penetrating criticism. His works include *Comets and Meteors* (1873) and *The Asteroids* (1887).

KIRWAN, Richard (1733–1812), Irish chemist, born in Galway, published (1784) the first systematic English treatise on mineralogy, and was a leading exponent of the phlogiston theory.

KISFALUDY, *kish'fê-loo-di,* (1) **Karoly** (1788–1830), Hungarian dramatist, brother of (2), regenerator of the national drama, became famous by his *Tartars in Hungary* (1819).

(2) **Sandor** (1772–1844), Hungarian poet, brother of (1), served in the Austrian army, 1793–1801, and again in 1809. The rest of his life was devoted to literature and farming.

KITAIBEL, Paul (1757–1817), Hungarian chemist, in 1789 discovered tellurium independently of Müller, and in 1794 became professor of Botany and Chemistry at Pest.

KITASATO, Shibasaburo (1856–1931), Japanese bacteriologist, studied in Germany under Koch and later founded in Japan an Institute for Infectious Diseases. He discovered the bacillus of bubonic plague (1894), isolated the bacilli of symptomatic anthrax, dysentery and tetanus, and prepared a diphtheria antitoxin.

KITCHENER, Horatio Herbert, 1st Earl, Kitchener of Khartoum (1850–1916), English soldier and statesman, was born near Ballylongford, Kerry, and entered the Engineers in 1871. On the Palestine survey, 1874–78, and then on that of Cyprus till 1882, he served in the Sudan campaign 1883–85. Sirdar of the Egyptian army from 1890, he by the final rout of the Khalifa at Omdurman, September 2, 1898, won back the Sudan for Egypt, and was made a peer. Successively chief of the staff and commander-in-chief in South Africa (1900–02), he finished the Boer war, received a grant of £50,000, was made viscount, O.M., commander-in-chief in India (1092–09), and agent and consul-general in Egypt (1911). Made secretary for war August 7, 1914, he organized a great army before he was lost with H.M.S. *Hampshire* (mined off Orkney), June 5, 1916. See Life by Arthur (1920); R. B. Esher, *The Tragedy of Lord Kitchener* (1921); V. W. Germains, *The Truth about Kitchener* (1925); C. R. Ballard, *Kitchener* (1930); P. Magnus, *Kitchener: Portrait of an Imperialist* (1958).

KITTO, John (1804–54), English biblical scholar, born at Plymouth, author of *The Pictorial Bible* (1838; new ed. 1855), *Pictorial History of Palestine* (1839–40), *Daily Bible Illustrations* (1849–53; new ed. by Dr Porter, 1867), &c. See Lives by Ryland (1856) and Eadie (1857).

KIVI, Aleksis, real name **Steuvall** (1834–72), Finnish dramatist and novelist, born at Nurmijärvi, wrote penetratingly of Finnish peasant life, and is now recognized as one of his country's greatest writers, but died insane, poverty-stricken and unrecognized. See Life by Tarkainen (1916).

KJELDAHL, Johan Gustav Christoffer Thorsager, *kel'dahl* (1849–1900), Danish chemist, was noted for his analytical methods of determination, and specially so for the method of nitrogen determination named after him.

KJELLAND. See KIELLAND.

KJERULF, Halfdan, *ke'roolf* (1815–68), Norwegian composer, best known for his charming songs, was born and died in Christiania.

KLAPKA, George (1820–92), Hungarian soldier and patriot, born at Temesvár, became lieut.-gen. in the Austrian army, but in the revolution fought valiantly against the Austrians, holding Komorn for eight weeks after the rest of Hungary had submitted. The amnesty of 1867 let him return from exile, and he died at Budapest. He wrote a history of the war (1851) and *Memoirs* (1850–87).

KLAPROTH, *klap'rōt,* **(1) Heinrich Julius von** (1783–1835), German orientalist, son of (2), born at Berlin, in 1805 was appointed interpreter to a Russian embassy to China. It was stopped on the frontier, when Klaproth explored Siberia, as afterwards (in 1807–08) the Caucasus and Georgia. In 1816 he was appointed professor of Asiatic Languages by the king of Prussia, with permission to work in Paris.

(2) **Martin Heinrich** (1743–1817), German chemist, born at Wernigerode, father of (1), became the first professor of Chemistry at Berlin University, devised new analytical methods, discovered zirconium and uranium, and named tellurium.

KLÉBER, Jean Baptiste (1753–1800), French soldier, born at Strasbourg, in 1776 obtained a commission in the Austrian army. Inspector for a time of public buildings at Belfort, in 1792 he enlisted as a volunteer, and by 1793 had risen to a general of brigade. As such he commanded in the Vendean war, but was recalled for leniency. In 1794 he led the left wing at Fleurus, and captured Maastricht; in June 1796 he gained the victory of Altenkirchen. He accompanied Bonaparte to Egypt, was wounded at Alexandria, and won the battle of Mount Tabor (1799). When Bonaparte left Egypt he entrusted the chief command to Kléber, who concluded a convention with Sir Sidney Smith for its evacuation; but on Admiral Keith's refusal to ratify it Kléber resolved to reconquer Egypt, and destroyed the Turkish army at Heliopolis. In the course of an attempt to conclude a treaty with the Turks, he was assassinated by a Turkish fanatic at Cairo in 1800. See G. Lecomte, *Au chant de la Marseillaise . . . Merceau et Kléber* (Paris 1929).

KLEE, Paul, *klay* (1879–1940), Swiss artist, born at Münchenbuchsee near Bern. He studied at Munich and settled there, being associated with Marc and Kandinsky in the Blaue Reiter group (1911–12). From 1920 to 1932 he taught at the Bauhaus, his *Pädagogisches Skizzenbuch* being published in 1925. After he had returned to Bern in 1933, many of his works were confiscated in Germany as degenerate. Klee's work has been called surrealist, but in his fantastic, small-scale, mainly abstract pictures he created, with supreme technical skill in many media, a very personal world of free fancy, expressed with a sly wit and subtle colouring and giving the effect of inspired doodling, e.g., the well-known *Twittering Machine* in the Museum of Modern Art, New York. See the monographs by D. Cooper (1949), W. Grohmann (1954), and Schmidt (1958), and study by G. di San Lazzaro (1957).

KLEIBER, Erich, *klī'-ber* (1890–1956), Austrian conductor, born in Vienna, at the age of 33 became director of the Berlin State Opera, which post he held for 12 years until forced by the Nazis to leave Germany. In 1938 he became a citizen of the Argentine. After the war he was again appointed director of the Berlin State Opera until his resignation in 1955. He gave the first performance of Berg's *Wozzeck.*

KLEIST, *klīst,* **(1) Ewald Christian von** (1715–1759), German poet, born at Zeblin, Pomerania. He was killed at the battle of Kunersdorf. See Life by Einbeck (1861).

(2) **Heinrich von** (1777–1811), German dramatist and poet, born at Frankfurt-on-Oder, October 18, left the army in 1799 to study, and soon devoted himself to literature. His best plays are still popular, notably *Prinz Friedrich von Homburg* (1811). His finest tale is *Michael Kohlhaas.* He shot himself November 21, 1811. See Lives by E. and G. Romien (1931), R. March (1954), and E. L. Stahl, *H. von Kleist's Dramas* (1949).

KLEMPERER, Otto (1885–1973), German conductor, born in Breslau, studied at Frankfurt and Berlin and first appeared as a conductor in 1907. He made a name as a champion of modern music and in 1927 he was appointed director of the Kroll Opera in Berlin until it was closed down in 1931. Naziism drove him to the United States (in 1933) where he was director of the Los Angeles Symphony Orchestra till 1939. In spite of continuing ill-health, he was musical director of Budapest opera from 1947 to 1950. In his later years he concentrated mainly on the German classical and romantic composers, and was particularly known for his interpretation of Beethoven. He has composed a mass and lieder.

KLINGER, (1) Friedrich Maximilian von (1752–1831), German playwright and romance writer, was born at Frankfurt-am-Main, died at Dorpat. The 'Sturm-und-Drang' school was named after one of his tragedies. See works by Erdmann (1877) and Rieger (1880).

(2) **Max** (1857–1920), German artist, born at Leipzig, studied at Karlsruhe, Brussels and Paris, and excited hostility as well as admiration by his pen drawings and etchings, which were audaciously original in concept and often imbued with macabre realism. Later, he turned to painting, and did much work in coloured sculpture, including Beethoven (1902). See study by M. Schmid (1926).

KLOPSTOCK, Friedrich Gottlieb (1724–1803), German poet, was born at Quedlinburg. Inspired by Virgil and Milton, he began *The Messiah* as a student at Jena (1745), continued it at Leipzig (1748), and completed it in 1773. He settled in Hamburg in 1771 with a sinecure appointment, and pensions from Frederick V of Denmark (from 1751) and the Margrave of Baden. Regarded in his own time as a great religious poet, he helped to inaugurate the golden age of German literature, especially by his lyrics and odes. See Life by Muncker (1888).

KLUCK, Alexander von (1846–1934), Prussian general, born at Münster, in August 1914 drove the Anglo-French forces almost to Paris, but, defeated at the Marne (September 6), had to retreat. Wounded 1915, he retired in 1916. See his *Der Marsch auf Paris* . . . (1920).

KLUGE, Günther von, *kloo'gė* (1882–1944), German general who carried out the Nazi occupation (1939) of the Polish corridor, commanded the German armies on the Central Russian front (1942) and in July 1944 replaced Rundstedt as commander-in-chief of the Nazi armies in France confronting the Allied invasion, but was himself replaced after the Falaise gap débâcle.

KNELLER, Sir Godfrey (1646–1723), portrait painter, born at Lübeck, studied at Amsterdam and in Italy, in 1676 came to London, and in 1680 was appointed court painter. In 1691 William III knighted him, and in 1715 George I made him a baronet. He died at Twickenham. His best-known works are the *Beauties of Hampton Court* (painted for William III), his forty-eight portraits of the 'Kit-Cat Club,' and of nine sovereigns (Charles II to George I, Louis XIV, Peter the Great, and the Emperor Charles VI). See C. H. C. Baker, *Lely and Kneller* (1922); M. M. Killanin, *Sir Godfrey Kneller and his Times* (1948). His brother, **John Zacharias** (1644–1702), architectural and portrait painter, also settled in England.

KNICKERBOCKER, Harmen Jansen (*c.* 1650–*c.* 1716), of Friesland, was one of the earliest settlers of New Amsterdam (New York). A descendant, Johannes (1749–1827), was a friend of Washington Irving, who immortalized the name through his *History of New York* by 'Diedrich Knickerbocker' (1809).

KNIGHT, (1) Charles (1791–1873), English author and publisher, born in Windsor. From journalism, as proprietor of the *Windsor and Eton Express* (1811–21) he turned to publishing popular editions of serious literature (*Pictorial Shakespeare*, 1838–41, *Popular History of England*, 1862, &c.) and reference books (*Penny Cyclopaedia*, 1838, &c.). From 1860 he published the *London Gazette*. See his *Passages of a Working Life* (1863–65), and Life by A. Clowes (1892).

(2) **Harold** (1874–1961), English portrait painter, husband of (3). He studied at Nottingham and in Paris, and worked in Yorkshire, Cornwall and Holland. Knight painted a large number of commissioned portraits, including those of *Sir Laurence Olivier* and *Lord Iliffe*. He was elected R.A. in 1937.

(3) **Dame Laura** (1877–1970), English artist, wife of (2), born at Long Eaton. She studied at Nottingham, married her fellow-student, Harold Knight, in 1903, and travelled in many parts of the world. She produced a long series of oil paintings of the ballet, the circus and gipsy life, in a lively and forceful style, and also executed a number of watercolour landscapes. She was created D.B.E. in 1929 and elected R.A. in 1936. See her autobiography *Oil Paint and Grease Paint* (1936).

(4) **Richard Payne** (1750–1824), English numismatist, a London connoisseur, who left his coins, bronzes, gems, &c. to the British Museum. He was M.P. for Leominster (1780), and Ludlow (1784–1806).

KNIPPERDOLLING, Bernhard (*c.* 1490–1536), German reformer, a noted leader (1527–36) of the fanatical Münster Anabaptists. See E. B. Bax, *Rise and Fall of the Anabaptists* (1903).

KNOBLOCK, Edward (1874–1945), British playwright and novelist, born in New York. Educated at Harvard, he came to Britain to write a series of successful plays, Among these are *The Faun* (1911), *My Lady's Dress* (1914) which some consider to be his best, *Tiger, Tiger* (1918), *The Mulberry Bush* (1930). He collaborated with Arnold Bennett in two plays, *Milestones* (1912), *London Life* (1924). He also produced stage versions of Vicki Baum's *Grand Hotel* (1931) and J. B. Priestley's *Good Companions* (1931) with the author. *The Ant Heap* (1929), *The Man with Two Mirrors* (1931) *Love Lady* (1933) and *Inexperience* (1941) are some of his novels. He became a naturalized British subject in 1916.

KNOLLES, *nōlz,* **(1) Richard** (*c.* 1550–1610), English historian, a schoolmaster at Sandwich, wrote a *Generall Historie of the Turkes* (1603).

(2) **Sir Robert** (*c.* 1317–1407), English soldier, a leader of free companies in France, who some time followed the Black Prince and opposed Du Guesclin. He died at his Norfolk seat, Sculthorpe.

KNOLLYS, Sir Francis, *nōlz* (*c.* 1514–96), English statesman, from 1572 treasurer of Queen Elizabeth's household. In 1568–69 he had charge of Mary, Queen of Scots.

KNOWLES, (1) Herbert (1798–1817), English poet, born at Gomersal, Leeds, and remembered by his 'Stanzas in Richmond Churchyard'.

(2) **Sir James** (1831–1908), English architect and editor, born in London, educated at University College, designed many important churches and edifices. Early a contributor to literature, he in 1869 founded the Metaphysical Society, became editor of the *Contemporary Review* in 1870, and in 1877 founded the *Nineteenth Century*.

(3) **James Sheridan** (1784–1862), Irish dramatist, born at Cork, was a cousin of Richard Brinsley Sheridan (q.v.). After serving in the militia and studying medicine, he appeared on the stage first at Bath and then at Dublin. But he never attained much eminence, and subsequently he became a teacher in Belfast and (1816–28) in Glasgow. His *Caius Gracchus* (1815) was first performed at Belfast. *Virginius*, his most effective play, had been a success in Glasgow before Macready in 1820 produced it at Covent Garden. Besides *William Tell*, in which Macready achieved one of his greatest triumphs.

Knowles's other best plays are *Love*, *The Hunchback*, *The Love Chase*, and *The Wife*. Knowles appeared with fair success in many of his own pieces. About 1844 he became a Baptist preacher, drew large audiences to Exeter Hall, and published two anti-Roman Catholic works. From 1849 he had a civil list pension of £200 a year. He died at Torquay. Of a Life (1872) by his son only twenty-five copies were printed. See L. H. Meeks, *Sheridan Knowles and the Theatre of his Time* (1933).

KNOX, (1) **Edmund George Valpy,** pen-name 'Evoe' (1881–1971), English humorous writer and parodist, brother of (4), who joined the staff of *Punch* in 1921 and became editor from 1932 to 1949, contributing articles under his pen-name. His best work was republished in book form and includes *Parodies Regained, Fiction as She is Wrote, It Occurs to Me, Awful Occasions, Here's Misery* and *Folly Calling*.

(2) **John** (*c.* 1513–72), Scottish reformer, born at or near Haddington, was educated there and probably at the University of Glasgow. From 1540 to 1543 he acted as notary in Haddington, and must till the latter year have been in Catholic orders. In 1544 he was acting as tutor to the sons of two families, by whom he was brought into contact with George Wishart (q.v.), now full of zeal for the Lutheran reformation; and with him Knox thenceforward identified himself. Wishart was burned in March 1546, and Beaton was murdered in May. The cardinal's murderers held the castle of St Andrews; and here Knox joined them with his pupils (1547). Here he was formally called to the ministry, and preached with acceptance. A few months later the castle surrendered to the French and for eighteen months Knox remained a prisoner on the French galleys. In February 1549, on the intercession of Edward VI, Knox regained his liberty, and for four years made his home in England. In 1551 he was appointed one of six chaplains to Edward VI, and in 1552 was offered but refused the bishopric of Rochester. Knox, with five others, was consulted by Cranmer regarding his forty-two articles, and largely on Knox's representation the thirty-eighth article was so couched as to commit the Church of England to the Genevan doctrine of the eucharist. On Mary's accession Knox fled to Dieppe, and thence early in 1554 went to Geneva. In the autumn he accepted a call from the English congregation at Frankfurt-am-Main, where he remained only a few months. At Geneva he found a congregation of his own way of thinking, but ventured into Scotland in September 1555, making preaching journeys to Kyle, Castle Campbell, &c., and returned to Geneva in July 1556. For the next two years he remained chiefly in Geneva, and was much influenced by Calvin. To 1558 belongs his *First Blast of the Trumpet against the Monstrous Regiment of Women*. In 1557 the advocates of reform in Scotland bound themselves to religous revolution by the *First Covenant*; and by 1558 they felt themselves strong enough to summon Knox to their aid. From May 1559 Knox, again in Scotland, was preaching at Perth and St Andrews. He gained these important towns to his cause, and by his labours in Edinburgh he also won a strong party. But the Reformers could not hold their ground against the regent, Mary of Guise, subsidized by France with money and soldiers. Mainly through the efforts of Knox, the assistance of England was obtained against the French invasion; and by the treaty of Leith and the death of the regent (1560) the insurgent party became masters of the country. Parliament ordered the ministers to draw up a Confession of Faith and Protestantism was established. Now the ministers drew up the first *Book of Discipline*, with its suggestions for the religious and educational organization of the country. The return of the young queen to Scotland (August 1561) introduced new elements into the strife of parties; and during the six years of her reign Knox's attitude towards her was that of uncompromising antagonism. The celebration of mass in Holyrood Chapel first roused his wrath; and a sermon delivered by him in St Giles led to the first of his famous interviews with Mary. He went so far as to alienate the most powerful noble of his own party—Lord James Stuart, afterwards the Regent Moray; but the marriage of Mary with Darnley (1565) brought them together again. After the murder of Rizzio he withdrew to Ayrshire, where he wrote part of his *History of the Reformation in Scotland*. The murder of Darnley, Mary's marriage with Bothwell, and her flight into England again threw the management of affairs into the hands of the Protestant party; and under Moray as regent the acts of 1560 in favour of the Reformed religion were duly ratified by the Estates. The assassination of Moray in 1570, and the formation of a strong party in favour of Mary, once more endangered the cause, and Knox removed to St Andrews for safety. On November 9, 1572, at the induction of his successor, he made his last public appearance at St Giles. He died on the 24th, and was buried in the churchyard then attached to St Giles. His first wife, Marjory Bowes, died in 1560, leaving him two sons. By his second wife, Margaret Stewart, daughter of Lord Ochiltree, whom (then not above sixteen) he married in 1564, he had three daughters. Knox is the pre-eminent type of the religious Reformer—dominated by his one transcendent idea, indifferent or hostile to every interest of life that did not subserve its realization. The term fanatic is hardly applicable to one who combined in such degree the shrewdest worldly sense with ever-ready wit and native humour. The impress of his individuality, stamped on every page of his *History of the Reformation in Scotland*, renders his work unique. See E. Muir, *John Knox, Portrait of a Calvinist* (1929); Lord E. Percy, *John Knox* (1937); H. Watt, *John Knox in Controversy* (1950); G. MacGregor, *The Thundering Scot* (1958); A new edition of *The History of the Reformation in Scotland* appeared in 1950.

(3) **Robert** (1791–1862), Scottish anatomist, born in Edinburgh, became conservator of the newly-established museum of Edinburgh

College of Surgeons in 1824, and from 1826–1840 ran an anatomy school. He won fame as a teacher but attracted considerable odium through having obtained subjects for dissection from Burke (q.v.) and Hare. He is the subject of Bridie's play *The Anatomist*.

(4) **Ronald Arbuthnott** (1888–1957), English theologian and essayist, brother of (1), was born in Birmingham. Educated at Eton and Balliol College, Oxford, he became a fellow and lecturer at Trinity College, Oxford, in 1910, but resigned in 1917 on his reception into the Church of Rome. From 1926 to 1939 he was Catholic chaplain at the University. Author of numerous works of apologetics, his translation of the Bible, widely used by Roman Catholics, is specially noteworthy. His essays are distinguished by their satirical wit and trenchant criticism of some contemporary modes and manners. See Life by E. Waugh (1959).

KNUT. See CANUTE.

KOCH, *koKH*, (1) **Karl** (1809–79), German botanist, born near Weimar, in 1836 visited southern Russia, and in 1843–44 Armenia, Transcaucasia, &c. He became extraordinary professor of Botany at Jena in 1836, and in 1848 at Berlin. His chief work is *Dendrologie* (1869–72); with books of travel, *Flora des Orients* (1848–54), &c.

(2) **Ludwig** (1881–), German naturalist, author, and lecturer. He followed a musical career in Paris and Milan, first as a violinist, then as a lieder and oratorio singer. He organized the 'Music in the Life of the Nations' exhibition (1927), and in 1928 joined the staff of a recording company. He made the first out-door recordings of songs of wild birds, and, coming to England in 1936, became known, particularly through his broadcasts, for his unique collection of bird and animal sounds. His joint publications include *Songs of Wild Birds* (1936) and *Animal Language* (1938): see also his *Memoirs of a Birdman* (1955). Became an M.B.E. (1960).

(3) **Robert** (1843–1910), German bacteriologist, born at Klausthal in the Harz, practised medicine at Hanover and elsewhere. His work on wounds, septicaemia and splenic fever gained him a seat on the imperial board of health in 1880. Further researches in microscopy and bacteriology led to his discovery in 1882 of the *Bacillus tuberculosis*. In 1883 he was leader of the German expedition sent to Egypt and India in quest of the cholera germ. For his discovery of the cholera bacillus he received a gift of £5000 from the government. His discovery in 1890 of the phthisis bacillus and his lymph-inoculation cure (tuberculin) raised higher hopes than were realized. Professor at Berlin (1885), and director of the hygienic institute, in 1891 he became director of the new institute for infectious diseases. In 1896 and 1903 he was summoned to S. Africa to study rinderpest and other cattle plagues. He won a Nobel prize in 1905. See Lives by C. Wezel (Berlin 1912), Heymann (Leipzig 1932).

KOCHANOWSKI, Jan, *koKH-an-of'ski* (1530–1584), Polish poet, knew Ronsard in Paris, and was secretary to King Sigismund Augustus. He wrote elegies, epigrams, Latin poems, and translated the Psalms. See his poems trans. by D. P. Radin (California 1928).

KOCHBAS. See BAR COCHBA.

KÖCHEL, Ludwig Ritter von, *kœ-KHėl* (1800–1877), Austrian musicologist, born at Stein, compiler of the famous catalogue of Mozart's works, which he arranged in chronological order, giving them the numbers commonly used to identify them today.

KOCHER, Emil Theodor, *koKH'ėr* (1841–1917), Swiss surgeon, born and educated in Berne where he became a professor in 1872, was noted for his work on the physiology, pathology and surgery of the thyroid gland. In 1909 he was awarded the Nobel prize for physiology and medicine. See R. A. Leonard *History of Surgery* (1943).

KOCK, Paul de (1794–1871), French novelist, born at Passy, produced an endless series of novels, vivacious, piquant and very readable. His son, **Henri** (1819–92), followed with a far weaker series of works.

KODÁLY, Zoltán, *kō'dal-y'* (1882–1967), Hungarian composer, born at Kecskemét, studied in Budapest Conservatoire where he became professor. Among his best known works are his *Háry János* suite, *Dances of Galanta* and his many choral compositions, especially his *Psalmus Hungaricus* and *Te Deum*. In 1913 he and Bartok drafted a plan for a Hungarian folk-music collection, but the first volume was not published until 1951. For bibliography see Janos Bartok's article in *Magyar Zenei Szemle* (Budapest 1943).

KOENIG, Karl Rudolph, *kœ'neeg* (1832–1901), German physicist who settled in Paris and became an authority on acoustics. One of his inventions was a clock fork for the determination of absolute pitch.

KOESTLER, Arthur (1905–), Hungarian-born author and journalist, the best known political refugee and prisoner of his time, born in Budapest, studied pure science at Vienna and embracing the cause of Zionism as described in *Promise and Fulfilment* (1949) worked on a collective farm in Palestine (1926), but his idealism modified by his experiences, he became a political correspondent and later scientific editor for a German newspaper group. Dismissed as a Communist, he travelled in Russia (1932–33), but became disillusioned, breaking with the party finally in 1938 as described in *The Gods that Failed* (1950). He reported the Spanish Civil War (1936–37) for the London *News Chronicle*, was imprisoned under death-sentence by Franco, as retold in *Spanish Testament* (1938) and *Dialogue with Death* (1942) and again by the French (1940), escaped from German-occupied France via the French Foreign Legion, and, after a short imprisonment in London, joined the Pioneer Corps. These experiences, described in *Scum of the Earth* (1941), provided the background of his first novel in English, *Arrival and Departure* (1943). The degeneration of revolutionary idealism in Roman times under Spartacus he portrayed in *The Gladiators* (1939) which was followed in 1940 by the striking modern equivalent, *Darkness at Noon*, Koestler's masterpiece and one of the great political novels of the century. Intelligent humanism and anti-Communism provide the themes for such essays as *The Yogi and the Commissar* (1945), *The Trail of the Dinosaur* (1955), *Reflections on Hanging* (1956) and *The Sleepwalkers*, intro. H. Butterfield (1959), on the theories, lives and struggles with religious orthodoxy of Copernicus, Kepler and Galileo. *The Act of Creation* (1964) and *The Ghost in the Machine* (1967) are among his recent works. See his autobiography (1954) and *Arthur Koestler* by J. Atkins (1956).

KOFFKA, Kurt (1886–1941), German psychologist, held posts in U.S.A. and at Oxford. With Wertheimer and Köhler he founded the *Gestalt* school of psychology. See his *Principles of Gestalt Psychology* (1935).

KÖHLER, Wolfgang, *kœ'lėr* (1887–1967), German psychologist, born in Estonia, an authority on *Gestalt* psychology, specially noted also for research in animal psychology.

KOHLRAUSCH, Friedrich Wilhelm Georg, *kōl-rowsh* (1840–1910), German physicist, professor of physics at Berlin, noted for his researches on magnetism and electricity. See his handbook, *Leitfaden der praktischen Physik* (1870).

KOKOSCHKA, Oskar, *-kosh'-* (1886–), British artist, born at Pöchlarn, Austria. He studied from 1904–08 at Vienna and taught at the Dresden Academy of Art (1919–24); from this time he travelled widely, and painted many Expressionist landscapes in Spain, France, England, &c. In 1938 he fled to England for political reasons, becoming naturalized in 1947, and painted a number of politically symbolic works, as well as portraits and landscapes. In the 'twenties he also wrote a number of Expressionist dramas, including *Orpheus und Eurydike*. In 1959 he was awarded the C.B.E. See biography by E. Hoffmann (1947) and monograph by H. M. Wingler (1958).

KOLBE, Hermann (1818–84), German scientist, born near Göttingen, was professor at Leipzig (1865). He did much in the development of chemical theory.

KOLCHAK, Aleksandr Vasilievich (1874–1920), Russian admiral (1916), who rose in World War I to command the Black Sea Fleet. After the revolution of November 1917, he became the chief hope of the anti-Bolsheviks, and till 1919 had much military success, but in 1920 yielded place to Denikin, and coming into the hands of the Bolsheviks, was shot (February 7).

KOLLÁR, Jan (1793–1852), Czech poet and Slavonic scholar, a Hungarian Slovak, Protestant pastor at Pest, and then, from 1849, professor of Archaeology at Vienna. See Autobiography in his *Collected Works* (2nd ed. 1868).

KÖLLIKER, Rudolph Albert von (1817–1905), Swiss anatomist and embryologist, famous for his microscopic work, was born at Zürich, and became professor there (1845) and at Würzburg (1847). His chief works include: *Manual of Human Histology* (1852; trans. 1854) and *Entwicklungsgeschichte des Menschen* (1861). See his *Erinnerungen* (1899).

KOLTSOV, Alexei Vasilievich (1809–42), Russian lyric poet, was born and died at Voronezh.

KOMENSKÝ. See COMENIUS.

KOMOROWSKI, Tadeusz Bór, *kom-or-ov'-skee* (1895–1966), Polish soldier, born at Lwów, as 'General Bór' led the heroic but unsuccessful Warsaw rising against the occupying Germans (1944), and settled in England after World War II.

KÖNIG, Friedrich (1774–1833), German printer, inventor of the steam-press, born at Eisleben, obtained in 1810 through the support of Bensley, a printer in London, a patent for a press. A second patent was obtained in 1811 for a cylinder-press, improved and in 1814 adopted by *The Times*. He also made steam printing-presses near Würzburg. See Goebel's monograph (1883).

KÖNIGSMARK, (1) Marie Aurora, Countess of Königsmark (1668?–1728), sister of (2), became in 1694 mistress of Augustus II of Saxony, and by him mother of Marshal Saxe; she died prioress at Quedlinburg. See German books by Corvin-Wiersbitzky (2nd ed. 1890), Burg (1925).

(2) **Count Philipp Christoph von** (1665–*c.* 1694), a Swede, entered the service of Hanover, was accused of an intrigue with Sophia Dorothea (1666–1726), wife of the future George I (q.v.) of England, and suddenly disappeared (probably murdered) in 1694. See Wilkins, *The Love of an Uncrowned Queen* (1900).

KONRAD. See CONRAD.

KOO, Vi Kyuin Wellington (1888–), Chinese statesman, was educated at Columbia University, U.S.A. He was Chinese ambassador to Britain 1941–46, to U.S. 1946–56. In 1964 he became vice president of the international court of justice.

KOPP, Hermann Franz Moritz (1817–92), German chemist, professor of Chemistry at Giessen and Heidelberg, was one of the founders of physical chemistry and a historian of the subject.

KORDA, Sir Alexander (1893–1956), Hungarian film producer, born at Turkeÿe, Hungary. First a newspaperman in Budapest, he became a film producer there, then in Vienna, Berlin, Hollywood, where he was director of United Artists Corporations of America and Paris. He came to Britain and in 1932 founded London Film Productions and Denham studios. His films include *The Private Life of Henry VIII*, *Rembrandt*, *The Third Man* and *The Red Shoes*. He was knighted in 1942. See Life by Tabori (1959).

KORNBERG, Arthur (1918–), American biochemist, born in Brooklyn, became professor of Biochemistry at Stanford in 1959, the year in which he was awarded, with Ochoa (q.v.), the Nobel prize for medicine for his work on the biological synthesis of nucleic acids.

KÖRNER, Karl Theodor (1791–1813), German lyric poet, born at Dresden, wrote fiery patriotic songs (*Leier und Schwert*, 1814). The *Schwert-Lied* was written shortly before his death in battle. See Life by his father Christian G. Körner, a friend of Schiller and correspondent of Goethe.

KORNILOV, Lavr Georgyevich (1870–1918), Russian commander-in-chief (August 1917), a Cossack born in W. Siberia, marched on St Petersburg, 8 September, to set up a military directory, but was forced to surrender by Kerensky. Next year he fell in battle.

KOROLENKO, Vladimir (1853–1921), Russian novelist, was born at Zhitomir. Returning from exile in Siberia (1885), he published *Makar's Dream*, and made a name by stories and articles.

KOSCIUSKO (Kosciuszko), Tadeusz, *kosh-chyoosh'ko* (1746–1817), Polish patriot, born near Slonim in Lithuania, chose the career of arms, and was trained in France. In 1777 he went to the United States, where he fought for the colonists and became brigadier-general. When Russia attacked his country in 1792, with 4000 men he held Dubienka for five days against 18,000. In 1794, after the second partition of Poland, he headed the national movement in Cracow, and was appointed dictator and commander-in-chief. His defeat of a greatly superior force of Russians at Raclawice was followed by a rising in Warsaw. He established a provisional government and took the field, but, defeated, fell back upon Warsaw and maintained himself there, until overpowered by superior numbers in the battle of Maciejowice, October 10, 1794, and wounded, he was taken prisoner. Two years later the Emperor Paul restored him to liberty. He went first to England, then in 1797 to America, and finally in 1798 to France, where he farmed near Fontainebleau. In 1806 he refused to support Napoleon's plan for the restoration of Poland. He settled at Soleure in Switzerland in 1816, and died by the fall of his horse over a precipice. See Lives by Michelet (1863), Cholonievski (1902) and Gardner (1920).

KOSSEL, (1) Albrecht (1853–1927), German physiological chemist, father of (2), professor at Heidelberg (1901–23), Nobel prize-winner for medicine (1910), investigated the chemistry of cells and of proteins.

(2) **Walther** (1888–1956), physicist, son of (1), professor of Physics at Kiel (1921) and Danzig (1932), did much research on atomic physics, especially on Röntgen spectra, and was known for his physical theory of chemical valency.

KOSSUTH, Louis, *kos'ooth* (1802–94), leader of the Hungarian revolution, was born at Monok near Zemplin of poor but noble family. He practised law for a time, in 1832 was a deputy at the diet of Pressburg, and edited a journal which, owing to the law, was not printed, but transcribed. The issue of a lithographed paper led, in 1837, to imprisonment. Liberated in 1840, he became editor of the *Pesti Hirlap*, advocating extreme Liberal views. In 1847, sent by Pest to the diet, he became leader of the opposition; and after the French Revolution of 1848 he demanded an independent government for Hungary. In September 1848, at the head of the Committee of National Defence, he prosecuted with extraordinary energy the measures necessary for carrying on war; and in April 1849 he induced the National Assembly at Debrecen to declare that the Hapsburg dynasty had forfeited the throne. Appointed provisional governor of Hungary, he sought in vain to secure the intervention of the Western Powers; and finding that the dissensions between himself and Görgei (q.v.) were damaging the national cause, he resigned his dictatorship in favour of Görgei. After the defeat at Temesvár on August 9, 1849 he fled to Turkey, where he was made a prisoner, but not extradited. In September 1851, liberated by British and American influence, he came to England, where, as subsequently in the United States, he was received with respect and sympathy. From 1852 he resided mainly in England till, on the Franco-Italian war with Austria in 1859, he proposed to Napoleon to arrange a Hungarian rising against Austria. The peace of Villafranca bitterly disappointed Kossuth; and in 1861 and in 1866 he tried in vain to bring about a rising against Austria. When in 1867 Deák effected the reconciliation of Hungary with the dynasty, Kossuth retired from active political life, and afterwards lived mostly in Turin. In 1867 he refused to avail himself of the general amnesty. In 1880–82 he published three volumes of *Memories of my Exile* (Eng. ed. vol. i, 1880); others followed in 1890; and at his death he had completed a work on Hungarian history.

KOSTER. See JANSZOON.

KOSYGIN, Alexei Nikolayevich (1904–), Russian politician, born and educated in Leningrad. Elected to the Supreme Soviet (1938), he held a variety of industrial posts, being a member of the Central Committee (1939–60) and of the *Politburo* (1946–52). Chairman of state economic planning commission (1959–60) and first deputy prime minister (with Mikoyan) from 1960 he in 1964 succeeded Khruschev as chairman of the Council of Ministers.

KOTELAWALA, Sir John, *kot-ė-lah'wė-la* (1896–), Sinhalese statesman, educated at Colombo and Cambridge University, became leader of the House of Representatives in 1952, and was prime minister of Ceylon (1953–56). He was created K.B.E. in 1948.

KOTZEBUE, *kot'-*, **(1) August Friedrich Ferdinand von** (1761–1819), German dramatist, born at Weimar, filled various offices in the service of Russia, and was a facile writer of plays, tales, satires, historical works, &c.; he was stabbed, March 23, 1819, by Sand, a Jena student, because he had ridiculed the *Burschenschaft* movement. Besides quarrelling with Goethe, Kotzebue satirized the leaders of the Romantic school. Among his two hundred lively but superficial dramas are *Menschenhass und Reue* (known on the English stage as *The Stranger*), *Die Hussiten vor Naumburg*, *Die beiden Klingsberge*, &c. See French Life by Rabany (1893).

(2) **Otto** (1787–1846), son of (1), born at Reval, accompanied Krusenstern round the world in 1803–06, and afterwards made two voyages of exploration in the Pacific. He died at Reval. His two books on his voyages were translated into English (1821 and 1830).

KOVALEVSKY, (1) Alexander (1840–1901), Russian embryologist, was born at Dünaburg, and became professor at St Petersburg. He is known for his researches on the embryology of invertebrates, which led to Haeckel's Gastraea theory; for his discovery of the life history and true position of the Ascidians; and for investigations of the development of the Amphioxus, Balanoglossus, Sagitta, and Brachiopods.

(2) **Sonia or Sophie** (1850–91), sister-in-law of (1), daughter of a Moscow artillery officer, made a distinguished name for herself throughout Europe as a mathematician. In 1884 she became professor of Mathematics at Stockholm, and left a brilliant series of novels, of which *Vera Barantzova* was translated in 1895. See Leffler's monograph (trans. 1895).

KOZLOV, (1) **Ivan Ivanovich** (1779–1840), Russian poet, translated Byron and Moore. He turned to poetry after going blind at the age of thirty.

(2) **Peter** (1863–1935), Russian traveller and archaeologist, explored the Altai, the Gobi desert, and the head-waters of the great Chinese rivers. In 1909 he discovered the ancient city of Khara Khoto in the Gobi, with library, &c.

KRAEPELIN, Emil (1856–1926), German psychiatrist, professor at Munich, a pioneer in the psychological study of mental diseases, which he divided into two groups, manic-depressive and dementia-praecox. He did research on brain fatigue and on the mental effects of alcohol.

KRAFFT-EBING, Richard, Freiherr von (1840–1902), German specialist in nervous diseases, born at Mannheim, in 1889 accepted a chair at Vienna.

KRAPOTKIN. See KROPOTKIN.

KRASIŃSKI, Zygmunt, Count (1812–59), Polish poet, was born and died in Paris. One of his principal works is the strange poem *Nieboska Komedya* ('The Undivine Comedy,' 1834). See M. Gardner's *The Anonymous Poet of Poland* (1919).

KRASZEWSKI, Józef Ignacy, *krash-ef'skee* (1812–87), Polish historical novelist and poet, born in Warsaw, was one of the most prolific of all Polish authors, his works exceeding 300. His best-known novel is *Jermola the Potter* (1857). In 1884 he was imprisoned at Magdeburg for treason.

KRAUSE, Karl Christian Friedrich, *krow'zė* (1781–1832), German philosopher, born at Eisenberg, studied at Jena, lived at Dresden 1805–13, lectured at Göttingen 1823–30, and died at Munich. His *Ideal of Humanity* was translated in 1890.

KREBS, Sir Hans Adolf (1900–), German-British physiologist, born at Hildesheim, winner (with Lipmann) of the Nobel prize for physiology and medicine in 1953 for researches into metabolic processes. He was knighted in 1958.

KREISLER, Fritz, *krīs'-* (1875–1962), Austrian violinist, born in Vienna, studied medicine and was an Uhlan officer. He composed violin pieces, a string quartet and an operetta, *Apple Blossoms* (1919), which was a Broadway success. He became a U.S. citizen in 1943 and died in New York.

KŘENEK, Ernst, *kėr-zhe'-nek* (1900–), Czech-Jewish composer born in Vienna, became eventually professor at Vassar College, New York. He has written operas and symphonies, and his style ranges from austere counterpoint to jazz (as in his famous opera *Jonny spielt auf*, Leipzig 1927). He has written *Über neue Musik* (1937), &c.

KRETZER, Marx, *kret'sėr* (1854–1941), German novelist, born at Posen. Essentially a writer on social problems and working people, he has, on account of his realism, been called the German Zola. His books include *Die Betrogenen* (1882), on poverty and prostitution, *Die Verkommenen* (1883), *Meister Timpe* (1888), and *Das Gesicht Christi* (1897).

KREUGER, Ivar, *krü'gėr* (1880–1932), Swedish financier, was born at Kalmar. Trained as a civil engineer, he emigrated to America where he worked as real-estate salesman and building contractor. He went to South Africa before returning to Sweden in 1907. In 1913 he founded the United Swedish Match Company and began the series of acquisitions and combinations which brought him control of three-quarters of the world's match trade. He lent large sums to governments in return for monopolistic concessions. In 1931 he was in difficulties and in March 1932, unable to meet a bank demand, he committed suicide. Irregularities over seven years were revealed after his death.

KRILOF. See KRYLOV.

KRISHNA MENON, Vengalil Krishnan (1896–), Indian politician, born at Calicut, Malabar, and educated at the Presidency College, Madras, and at London University. He came to Britain in 1924 and became a history teacher and a London barrister. In 1929 he became secretary of the India League and the mouthpiece of Indian nationalism in Britain. When India became a Dominion in 1947 he became India's high commissioner in London. In 1952 he became leader of the Indian delegation to the United Nations, bringing Pandit Nehru's influence to bear on international problems as leader of the Asian 'uncommitted' and 'neutralist' bloc. During the first 1956 Suez crisis on the nationalization of the Canal he formulated a plan to deal with it. As defence minister (1957–62), he came into conflict at the United Nations with Britain over Kashmir. He was minister of defence production for a short time in 1962.

KRISHNAMURTI (1891–), Indian theosophist, born in Madras, was educated in England by Dr Annie Besant, who in 1925 proclaimed him the Messiah. Later he dissolved *The Order of the Star in the East* (founded by Dr Besant), and retired.

KROGH, (Schack) August (Steenberg), *krawg* (1874–1949), Danish physiologist, professor at Copenhagen. He was Nobel prizewinner for medicine (1920) for his discovery of the regulation of the motor mechanism of capillaries.

KROPOTKIN, Prince Peter (1842–1921), Russian geographer, savant, revolutionary, Nihilist, was born at Moscow, and in 1857 entered the Corps of Pages. After five years' service and exploration in Siberia, he returned to the capital in 1867 to study mathematics, whilst acting as secretary to the Geographical Society. In 1871 he explored the glacial deposits of Finland and Sweden; in 1872 he associated himself with the extremest section of the International. Arrested (March 1874) and imprisoned in Russia, in July 1876 he effected his escape to England. At Lyons he was condemned in 1883 to five years' imprisonment for anarchism. Released in 1886, he settled in England till the Revolution of 1917 took him back to Russia. He wrote on anarchism, the French Revolution, Russian literature, Asia, mutual aid in evolution; and *Memoirs of a Revolutionist* (1900). See *The Anarchic Prince* by S. Woodcock and Avakumovic (1950).

KRÜDENER, Barbara Juliana von (1764–1824), religious enthusiast, daughter of Baron von Vietinghoff, was born at Riga. Married in 1782 to Baron von Krüdener, Russian ambassador at Venice, she from 1789 lived mostly apart from him, in Riga, St Petersburg and Paris. In 1803 she published a remarkable novel, *Valérie*, supposed to be autobiographical, and presently gave herself up to an exaggerated mysticism. Expelled in 1817–18 from Switzerland and Germany, and repulsed by her former worshipper, the Emperor Alexander, she retired to her paternal estates near Riga, where she entered into relations with the Moravian Brethren. She died at Karasu-Bazar in the Crimea. See Krug's *Conversations with Mme von Krüdener* (1818), and books by Eynard (1849) and Knapton (1939).

KRUGER, Stephanus Johannes Paulus (1825–1904), born at Colesberg in Cape Colony, with his fellow-Boers trekked to Natal, the Orange Free State, and the Transvaal, and won such a reputation for cleverness, coolness, and courage that in the war against Britain (1881), he was appointed head of the provisional government. In 1883 he was elected president of the Transvaal or South African Republic, and again in 1888, 1893 and 1898. 'Oom Paul' was the soul of the policy that issued in the war of 1899–1902, showed consummate 'slimness', resolution, and energy, but after the tide had fairly turned against the Boers, came to Europe to seek (in vain) alliances against Britain. He made his headquarters at Utrecht, and thence issued *The Memoirs of Paul Kruger, told by Himself* (1902). See M. Nathan's *Paul Kruger, his Life and Times* (3rd ed. 1942).

KRUPP, *kroop*, name of a German family of armament manufacturers and industrialists, of whom the most noteworthy in chronological order were:—

(1) **Alfred** (1812–87), born at Essen, succeeded his father **Friedrich** (1787–1826), who had founded a small iron forge there in 1810. At the Crystal Palace Great Exhibition (1851) he exhibited a solid flawless ingot of cast steel weighing 4000 kg, established the first Bessemer steel plant and became the foremost arms supplier not only to Germany but to any country in the world, his first steel gun being manufactured in 1847. He acquired large mines, collieries, docks, and became a dominating force in the development of the Ruhr territories. See Life by W. Berdow (1926).

(2) **Friedrich Alfred** (1854–1902), son of (1), incorporated shipbuilding, armour-plate manufacture (1890) and chrome nickel steel production into the Krupp empire and became a personal friend of the Prussian emperor. See Life by W. Berdow (1915).

(3) **Bertha** (1886–1957), daughter of (2), married in 1906 **Gustav von Bohlen und Halbach**. By special imperial edict he was allowed to adopt the name 'Krupp' (inserted before the 'von'). He took over the firm, gained the monopoly of German arms manufacture during World War I and manufactured the long range gun for the shelling of Paris, nicknamed 'Big Bertha'. He turned to agricultural machinery and steam engines after the war, backed first Hindenburg against Hitler, but then supported the latter's party financially and connived in secret rearmament, contrary to the Versailles Treaty, after the latter's rise to power in 1933. Hitler's *Lex-Krupp* (1943) confirmed exclusive family ownership for the firm. After World War II, the Krupp empire was split up by the Allies, but Gustav was too senile to stand trial as war criminal at Nuremberg.

(4) **Alfred Alwin Felix** (1907–67), son of (3), graduated at Aachen Technical College, became deputy director (1934), an honorary member of Hitler's S.S., and in 1943 succeeded his father to the Krupp empire. He was arrested (1945) and convicted (1947) with eleven fellow-directors by an American Military Tribunal for plunder in Nazi-occupied territories and for employment under inhuman conditions of concentration camp victims and non-German slave labour. He was sentenced to 12 years' imprisonment and his property was to be confiscated. By an amnesty (1951) he was released, his property restored with the proviso under the Mehlem agreement (1953) negotiated with the three allied powers and incorporated in the Federal German Constitution, that he should sell for a reasonable offer within five years his iron and steel assets, this period being extended yearly from 1958 with diminishing prospect of fulfilment. Meanwhile he actually increased these assets by the acquisition of the Bochumer Verein (1958). Krupps played a prominent part in the West German 'economic miracle', building entire factories in Turkey, Pakistan, India and the Soviet Union. In 1959 he belatedly agreed to pay some compensation to former forced labour, but of Jewish origin only. His son **Arndt** succeeded him. See Life by G. Young (1960), family study by B. Menn (1939) and of the firm by G. von Klass (trans. 1954).

KRUSENSTERN, Adam Johann, Baron von (1770–1846), Russian admiral, born at Haggud in Estonia, served (1793–99) in the British navy, and was put in command of a Russian exploring expedition in the North Pacific, which ultimately became a voyage round the world (1803–06).

KRYLOV, Ivan Andreevich, *kree'lof* (1768–1844), Russian fabulist, born in Moscow, was a writer from his twentieth year. Secretary to a prince, and then aimless traveller through Russia, he obtained a government post in 1806, and, settling down, wrote the fables for which he is famous. Collections appeared in 1809 and 1811. See also translation into English verse by B. Pares (1927).

KUBELIK, (1) Jan (1880–1940), Czech violin virtuoso and composer, born near Prague, studied there, and becoming a Hungarian citizen took the name of Polgar.

(2) **Jeronym Rafael** (1914–), Czech conductor, son of (1), born at Bychory, studied at Prague Conservatory, and first conducted the Czech Philharmonic Orchestra before he was twenty. By 1939 he had established an international reputation, and in 1948 settled in England. He was conductor of the Chicago Symphony Orchestra (1950–1953), at Covent Garden (1955–58) and from 1961 with the Bavarian Radio Orchestra. He has composed an opera, *Veronika*, 2 symphonies, concertos, and other works.

KUBIN, Alfred, *koo'bin* (1877–1959), Austrian painter and engraver, born at Leitmeritz. He exhibited in Munich with the Blaue Reiter group in 1911. He was also influenced by Goya and Odilon Redon in his drawings and engravings of dreamlike subjects, and he illustrated many books in this vein.

KUBLAI KHAN, *koo'blī kahn* (1214–94), Mongol khan, emperor of China, grandson of Genghis Khan, completed the conquest of northern China. An energetic prince, he suppressed his rivals, adopted the Chinese mode of civilization, encouraged men of letters, and made Buddhism the state religion. An attempt to invade Japan ended in disaster. He established himself at Cambaluc (the modern Peking), the first foreigner ever to rule in China. His dominions extended from the Arctic Ocean to the Strait of Malacca, and from Korea to Asia Minor and the confines of Hungary. The splendour of his court inspired the graphic pages of Marco Polo, who spent seventeen years in the service of Kublai—and at a later date fired the imagination of Coleridge. See Yule's *Marco Polo* (1875), and Cordier's (1920); Howorth's *History of the Mongols* (part i, 1876).

KUENEN, Abraham, *kü'nen* (1828–91), Dutch theologian, was born at Haarlem, and became, in 1855, professor at Leyden. His *Historisch-Critisch Onderzoek* (1861–65) embodied modern theories on the history of Israel, developed further in *De Godsdienst van Israel* (1869–70; trans. 1873–75), and in the 2nd edition of his *Onderzoek* (1885–1889).

KUGLER, Franz, *koog'ler* (1808–58), born at Stettin, in 1833 became professor in the Academy of Art and *docent* at the University of Berlin. Part of his history of painting from the time of Constantine the Great (1837) was translated by the Eastlakes (6th ed. 1891) and others.

KUHLAU, Friedrich, *koo'low* (1786–1832), German composer of operas, chamber music, and piano sonatinas much used as teaching pieces, was born at Ülzen.

KUHN, *kün,* (1) **Franz Felix Adalbert** (1812–1881), German philologist and folklorist, born at Königsberg, died in Berlin.

(2) **Richard** (1900–67), Austrian chemist, known for his work on the structure and synthesis of vitamins and carotenoids. He refused the Nobel prize under Nazi pressure in 1938.

KÜHNE, Wilhelm, *kü'nė* (1837–1900), German physiologist, professor at Heidelberg from 1871, noted for his study of the chemistry of digestive processes. He introduced the term *enzyme* to describe organic substances which activate chemical changes.

KUN, Béla (1886–*c.* 1937), communist leader, born in Transylvania, was a journalist, soldier and prisoner in Russia, and in March 1919 set up in Hungary a Soviet republic which lasted till August. He then returned to Russia.

KUNIGUNDE, St (d. 1030), who vindicated her chastity by walking barefoot over hot ploughshares, was the daughter of Count Siegfried of Luxemburg, and wife of Duke Henry of Bavaria, chosen emperor in 1014. After his death in 1024 she retired into the convent of Kaufungen near Cassel, and died there. She was canonized in 1200.

KUPRIN, Alexander (1870–1938), Russian novelist, gave up the army for literature. As a teller of short tales he ranks next to Chekhov. *The Duel, The River of Life, A Slav Soul, The Bracelet of Garnets, Sasha,* &c., have been translated.

KURCHATOV, Igor Vasilevich (1903–60), Russian physicist, born in Eastern Russia, was appointed director of nuclear physics at the Leningrad Institute (1938) and, before the end of World War II, of the Soviet Atomic Energy Institute. He carried out important studies of neutron reactions and was the leading figure in the building of Russia's first atomic (1949) and thermonuclear (1953) bombs. He became a member of the Supreme Soviet in 1949 and was awarded the Stalin prize and the Order of Lenin.

KUROKI, Tamasada, Count (1844–1923), Japanese general, born in Satsuma, defeated the Russians in Manchuria, at Yalu, Kiu-lien-ling, &c. (1904–05).

KUROPATKIN, Alexei Nikolaievich (1848–1925), born a noble of Pskov, was Russian chief of staff under Skobeleff in the Turkish war 1877–78, commander-in-chief in Caucasia 1897, minister of war 1898, commander-in-chief in Manchuria (1904–05) against the victorious Japanese. He commanded the Russian armies on the northern front Feb.–Aug. 1916, and then was governor of Turkestan till the Revolution in 1917.

KUROSAWA, Akira (1910–), Japanese film director who brilliantly adapted the techniques of the *No* theatre to film-making in such films as *Rashomon* (1951), which won the Venice Film Festival prize, *The Seven Samurai* and *Living*. Also characteristic are his adaptations of Shakespeare's *Macbeth* and Dostoevsky's *The Idiot*.

KUSCH, Polykarp (1911–), American physicist, born at Blankenburg, Germany, professor of Physics at Columbia (1949), shared the 1955 Nobel award for physics for his precision determination of the magnetic movement of the electron.

KUTS, Vladimir, *koots* (1927–), Russian and world champion athlete. He broke the 10,000 metre record in Moscow in 1956 in 28 minutes 30·4 seconds, and the 5000 metre record at Rome in 1957 in 13 minutes 35 seconds. He was voted the best athlete at the 1956 Olympic Games.

KUTUZOV, Mikhail Ilarionovich, Prince of Smolensk, *koo-too'zof* (1745–1813), Russian field-marshal, distinguished himself in the

Turkish war, and in 1805 commanded against the French. In 1812, as commander-in-chief, he fought Napoleon obstinately at Borodino, obtained a great victory over Davout and Ney at Smolensk.

KUYP. See CUYP.

KUZNETSOV, Pavel, *koos-nyi-tsof'* (1878–), Russian artist, born at Saratov. He studied in Moscow and produced mainly realistic landscapes and scenes of Kirghiz life, his work being represented in the Tretiakov Gallery in Moscow.

KYAN, John Howard (1774–1850), inventor 1812–36 of the 'kyanizing' process for preserving wood. Born in Dublin, he died in New York.

KYD, Thomas (1558–94), English dramatist, born in London and probably educated at Merchant Taylors' School, was most likely brought up as a scrivener under his father. His tragedies early brought him reputation, specially *The Spanish Tragedy.* Kyd translated from the French (1594) a tedious tragedy on Pompey's daughter Cornelia, perhaps produced *Solyman and Perseda* (1592) and *Arden of Feversham.* He has been credited with a share in other plays, and probably wrote the lost original *Hamlet.* In 1590–93 he was in the service of an unknown lord. Imprisoned in 1593 on a charge of atheism (Unitarianism), which he tried to shift on to Marlowe's shoulders, Jonson's 'sporting Kyd' died in poverty. An edition of his plays by Boas was published in 1901.

KYNEWULF. See CYNEWULF.

KYRLE, John (1637–1724), English philanthropist, styled the 'Man of Ross' by Pope, having passed most of his life at Ross in Herefordshire. He spent his time and fortune in building churches and hospitals on an income of £600 a year. Pope sang his praises in his third *Moral Epistle,* and Warton said that he deserved to be celebrated beyond any of the heroes of Pindar.

L

LAAR, Pieter van, known as Il Bamboccio, (*c.* 1590–*c.* 1658), Dutch painter of pastoral scenes, fairs, &c., was born and died at Haarlem, but worked much in Rome.

LABADIE, Jean de (1610–74), French ex-Jesuit Protestant pietist, was born at Bourg near Bordeaux, and died at Altona.

LA BALUE, Jean de (1421–91), French cardinal, Bishop of Evreux and Angers, a minister of Louis XI, who imprisoned him, but not in an iron cage, 1469–80. He was born in Poitou, and died in Rome.

LABANOFF, Prince Alexander (1788–1866), a Russian general, the chivalrous defender of Mary, Queen of Scots, whose Letters he edited (7 vols. London 1844).

LABÉ, or Charlieu, Louise (*c.* 1520–66), a beautiful French poetess, born at Parcieux, Ain, who in 1542 fought disguised as a knight at the siege of Perpignan, and afterwards married a wealthy rope manufacturer, Perrin, at Lyons; hence she was called 'la Belle Cordière'. See works by Gonon (1844) and Laur (1873).

LABÉDOYÈRE, Charles, Comte de, *la-bed-wah-yayr* (1786–1815), a Napoleonic field-marshal, born in Paris, was shot after the second Bourbon restoration.

LABICHE, Eugène, *la-beesh* (1815–88), French author of over a hundred comedies, farces and vaudevilles, was born and died in Paris, and in 1880 was elected to the Academy. His *Frisette* (1846) was the original of Morton's 'Box and Cox' and *Le Voyage de M. Perrichon* (1860) is a perennial classroom favourite. See Augier's introduction to the *Théâtre de Labiche* (10 vols. 1879), P. Soupault, *Eugène Labiche, sa vie, son œuvre* (1945).

LABLACHE, Luigi (1794–1858), operatic singer, was born and died in Naples. His father was a French émigré, his mother an Irishwoman. He sang at La Scala, Milan (1817), and elsewhere. He taught singing to Queen Victoria. His voice was a magnificent deep bass and his acting was almost as remarkable as his singing.

LABOUCHÈRE, *la-boo-shayr,* **(1) Henry, Baron Taunton** (1798–1869), English statesman, of Huguenot ancestry, was educated at Winchester and Christ Church, Oxford. In 1826 he became a Whig M.P., from 1830 for Taunton; and, having been president of the Board of Trade and colonial secretary, was in 1859 raised to the peerage.

(2) **Henry** (1831–1912), nephew of (1), was educated at Eton, and from 1854 to 1864 was attaché or secretary at Washington, Munich, Stockholm, St Petersburg, Dresden, Constantinople, &c. A Liberal M.P. 1866–1906, he founded (1877), edited, and till 1910 owned *Truth.* See Lives by Thorold (1913), Pearson (1936).

LABOULAYE, Edouard René de, *la-boo-lay* (1811–83), French jurist and politician, was born and died in Paris, and in 1849 became professor of Comparative Jurisprudence in the Collège de France. His chief works are on French law, and a *Histoire politique des États-Unis* (1855–66). He edited a historical review and some of his tales, including *Paris en Amérique,* have been translated. He entered the National Assembly in 1871, and in 1876 became a life senator. See Life by Wallon (1889).

LA BOURDONNAIS, Bertrand François Mahé de, *la boor-don-nay* (1699–1753), French sailor, born at St-Malo, by 1723 had distinguished himself as captain in the naval service of the French Indies. In 1734 he became governor of Île de France and Bourbon and as such he lives for ever in *Paul et Virginie* by J. H. Bernardin de Saint-Pierre. In 1740 he inflicted great loss upon England; in 1746 compelled Madras to capitulate, but granted terms on payment of 9,000,000 livres. Accused by Dupleix of betraying the company's interests, he returned to Paris in 1748, and he languished in the Bastille until 1752, when he was declared guiltless.

LA BRUYÈRE, Jean de, *brü-yayr* (1645–96), French writer, born at Paris, and educated by the Oratorians, was chosen to aid Bossuet in educating the dauphin. For a time he was treasurer at Caen. He became tutor to the Duc de Bourbon, grandson of the Great Condé, and received a pension from the Condés until his death. His *Caractères* (1688), which gained him a host of implacable enemies as well as an immense reputation, consists of two parts, the one a translation of Theophrastus, the other a collection of maxims, reflections and character portraits of men and women of the time. He found a powerful protectress in the Duchesse de Bourbon, a daughter of Louis XIV. In 1693 he was elected to the Academy. His *Dialogues sur le quiétisme* (1699) were directed against Fénelon. A great writer rather than a great thinker, his insight into character is shrewd rather than profound. See the edition by Servois (3 vols. 1864–82); the translation of the *Caractères* by Helen Stott (1890); Sainte-Beuve's *Portraits littéraires*; and works by Morillot (1904), Lange (1909) and Magne (1914).

LACAILLE, Nicolas Louis de, *la-kah'y'* (1713–62), a French astronomer, who in 1751 visited the Cape. He was the first to measure a South African arc of the meridian.

LA CALPRENÈDE. See CALPRENÈDE.

LACÉPÈDE, Bernard de Laville, Comte de, *la-se-ped* (1756–1825), French writer and naturalist, born at Agen, became curator in the Royal Gardens at Paris in 1785, and at the Revolution professor of Natural History in the Jardin des Plantes. He was made senator in 1799, minister of state in 1809, and in 1814 peer of France. Besides continuing Buffon's *Natural History*, he wrote *Histoire naturelle des poissons* (1803), *Les Âges de la nature* (1830), &c. An edition of his works appeared in 1876.

LACHAISE, François d'Aix (1624–1709), French Jesuit, born at the castle of Aix in Forez. Louis XIV selected him for his confessor in 1675—a post he retained till his death in spite of the difficulties of his position. The cemetery *Père Lachaise* was called after him. See Life by Chantelauze (1859).

LA CHAUSSÉE, Pierre Claude Nivelle de, *la shō-say* (1692–1754), French playwright, born in Paris, began writing plays after he was forty and produced several of a sentimental nature, which enjoyed great popularity. *La Comédie larmoyante*, as his work was named by critics, did however have a certain influence on later writers, including Voltaire. Among his plays were *Préjuge à la mode* (1735), *Mélanide* (1741), and *L'École des mères* (1744). See G. Lanson, *Nivelle de la Chaussée* (1887).

LACHMANN, Karl Konrad Friedrich Wilhelm, *lakh'man* (1793–1851), German critic and philologist, born at Brunswick, was professor successively at Königsberg and Berlin, and a member of the Academy. He edited the *Nibelungenlied*, Walter von der Vogelweide, Propertius, Lucretius, &c. In his *Betrachtungen* he maintained that the *Iliad* consisted of sixteen independent lays enlarged and interpolated. The smaller edition of his New Testament appeared in 1831; the larger in 1842–50—both based mainly on uncial MSS. See Life by Hertz (1851).

LACLOS, Pierre Ambroise François Choderlos de, *-klō* (1741–1803), French novelist and politician, born in Amiens. Romantic and frustrated, he spent nearly all his life in the army but saw no active service until he was sixty and ended his career as a general. He is remembered by his one masterpiece, *Les Liaisons dangereuses* (1782). This novel in letters reveals the influence of Rousseau and Richardson and is a cynical, detached analysis of personal and sexual relationships. A translation by R. Aldington, under the title of *Dangerous Acquaintances*, appeared in 1924, and a modern film version by R. Vadim in 1960.

LACOMBE, Louis Trouillon, *-kõb* (1818–84), French composer, born at Bourges. His best-known work is the cantata *Sappho* (1878). His opera *Winkelried* was produced at Geneva in 1892. See Life by Boyer (Paris 1888).

LACONDAMINE, Charles Marie de (1701–1774), French geographer, was born and died in Paris, served in the army, travelled extensively, and was sent to Peru (1735–43) to measure a degree of the meridian. He explored the Amazon, brought back curare and definite information as to india rubber, and wrote in favour of inoculation.

LACORDAIRE, Jean Baptiste Henri (1802–1861), French theologian, born at Recey-sur-Ource, studied law in Paris. A convert from Deism, he was ordained in 1827. He attracted attention by his *Conférences* at Notre Dame (1835–36) but withdrew to Rome at the height of his fame, entering the Dominican order in 1839. Next year he reappeared at Notre Dame, where he renewed his success, and in 1854 he delivered his last and most eloquent *Conférences* at Toulouse, thereafter becoming director of the Collège de Sorèze. He was a member of the Academy. See his letters, his *Testament* (1870), and Lives by Montalembert (trans. 1863), Chocarne (trans. 1867), De Broglie (1889), Honnef (1924).

LACOSTE, Robert (1898–), French Socialist politician, was born at Azerat, S.W. France, and began his career as a tax-collector. Later he became editor of the civil servants' journal and a member of the administrative committee of the C.G.T. In World War II, he began the first trade union Resistance group. In 1944 he was minister of industrial production and minister for industry and commerce in 1946–47 and again in 1948. In 1956–57 he was resident minister in Algeria, and his at times ruthless campaign against the rebels there served to underline one controversial aspect of French postwar politics.

LACRETELLE, (1) Jean Charles Dominique de (1766–1855), French journalist and historian, born at Metz, was attracted to

Paris on the outbreak of the Revolution. He helped to edit the *Débats* and the *Journal de Paris*, was a member of the French Academy from 1811 and its president in 1816. Of his works the best-known are *Histoire du dix-huitième siècle* (1808), *Précis historique de la Révolution* (1801–06), and *Histoire de France pendant les guerres de religion* (1814–16). See Life by Alden (1959).

(2) **Pierre Louis** (1751–1824), brother of (1), was an advocate and journalist, and wrote on law. He was a member of the Paris Commune and was elected to the States-General and Legislative Assembly.

LACROIX, *la-krwah,* (1) **Paul** (1806–84), French scholar, better known as **P. L. Jacob, Bibliophile,** was born and died in Paris. While still at school he began to edit the old French classics, as Marot, Rabelais, &c. He wrote an immense number of romances, plays, histories, biographies, and a great series on the manners, customs, costumes, arts and sciences of France from the middle ages. He also wrote two elaborate works on the *History of Prostitution* under the name 'Pierre Dufour'. From 1855 he was keeper of the Arsenal library.

(2) **Silvestre François** (1765–1843), French mathematician, was born and died in Paris. His works on the Calculus (1797–1800) are famous. They were translated into English in 1816.

LACTANTIUS, Lucius Caelius (or **Caecilius**) **Firmianus** (4th cent.), Christian apologist, was brought up in Africa, and settled as a teacher of rhetoric in Nicomedia in Bithynia, where he was converted probably by witnessing the constancy of the Christian martyrs under the persecution of Diocletian. About 313 he was invited to Gaul by Constantine, to act as tutor to his son Crispus. His principal work is his *Divinarum Institutionum libri vii.* See editions by Migne (vol. vi, 1844) and Brandt and Laubmann (Vienna 1890–97).

LACY, Peter, Count (1678–1751), Russian field-marshal, was born in Limerick, and had fought as an Irish Jacobite and in the French service, when about 1698 he entered that of Russia.

LAËNNEC, René Théophile Hyacinthe (1781–1826), French physician, born at Quimper in Brittany, from 1799 an army doctor, in 1814 became editor of the *Journal de Médecine* and physician to the Salpêtrière and in 1816 chief physician to the Hôpital Necker, where he invented the stethoscope. His work on tuberculosis, peritonitis and chest diseases was valuable. In 1819 he published his *Traité de l'auscultation médiate.* See Lives by Lallour (1868), Du Chatellier (1885), Webb (1928).

LA FARGE, John (1835–1910), American landscape and ecclesiastical painter, born in New York, is best known by his mural and stained-glass work. He wrote *Lectures on Art, Letters from Japan,* &c.

LA FARINA, Giuseppe (1815–63), Italian historian and statesman, was born at Messina. He died in Turin. He was an early advocate of Italian unity and wrote a history of Italy.

LAFAYETTE, Marie Joseph Paul Yves Roch Gilbert Motier, Marquis de (1757–1834), French reformer, was born in the castle of Chavagnac in Auvergne. He entered the army, sailed for America in 1777 to aid the colonist, and by Washington was given a division. He was home for a few months in 1779, crossed the Atlantic again, was charged with the defence of Virginia, and shared in the battle of Yorktown. On a third visit to America in 1784, he had an enthusiastic reception. Now a pronounced reformer, he was called to the Assembly of Notables in 1787, sat in the States-General, and in the National Assembly of 1789. He laid on its table a declaration of rights based on the American Declaration of Independence and, appointed to command the armed citizens, formed the National Guard. He struggled incessantly for order and humanity, but the Jacobins hated his moderation, the court abhorred his reforming zeal. He supported the abolition of title and all class privileges. He won the first victories at Philippeville, Maubeuge and Florennes, but the hatred of the Jacobins increased, and at length he rode over the frontier to Liège and was imprisoned by the Austrians till Bonaparte obtained his liberation in 1797. He sat in the Chamber of Deputies in 1818–24 as one of the extreme Left, and in 1825–30 was again a leader of the Opposition. In 1830 he took part in the Revolution, and commanded the National Guards. In 1824 he revisited America, by invitation of Congress, who voted him 200,000 dollars and a township. He died at Paris. See *Mémoires, Correspondance, et Manuscrits* (1837–40); studies by Warin (1824), Sarrans (1832), Tuckerman (1889), Bardoux (1892–93), Tower (1895), Crow (1916), Delteil (1928), Kayser (1928), Whitlock (1929), De la Bedoyère (1933), Gottschalk (1942).

LA FAYETTE, Marie Madeleine Pioche de Lavergne, Comtesse de (1634–93). French novelist and reformer of French romance-writing, was born in Paris, her father being marshal and governor of Le Havre. She married the Comte de La Fayette in 1655, and in her thirty-third year formed a liaison with La Rochefoucauld, which lasted until his death in 1680. Down to her own death she still played a leading part at the French court, as was proved by her *Lettere inedite* (Turin 1880); prior to their publication it was believed that her last years were given to devotion. Her novels are *Zaïde* (1670) and *La Princesse de Clèves* (1678) which is a vivid picture of the court-life of her day and led to a reaction against the long-winded romances of Calprenède and Scudéry. See *Mémoires* (ed. by Asse 1890), books by Ashton (1922), Magne (1922), Styger (1944), and Sainte-Beuve's *Portraits de Femmes.*

LAFERTÉ, Victor. See DOLGORUKOVA.

LAFFITTE, (1) **Jacques** (1767–1844), French financier and statesman, born at Bayonne, acquired great wealth as a Paris banker, and in 1814 became governor of the Bank of France. He was elected to the Chamber of Deputies in 1817. In 1830 his house was the headquarters of the Revolution, and he supplied a great part of the funds needed. In November he formed a cabinet, but he only held power until March. From the ruins of his fortune he founded a Discount Bank in 1837. In 1843 he was elected president of the Chamber of Deputies. See his *Souvenirs* (1844), as recorded by Marchal.

(2) **Pierre** (1823–1903), French philosopher, born at Beguey (Gironde), was friend and disciple of Comte.

LA FOLLETTE, Robert Marion (1855–1925), American politician, born at Primrose, Wis., was a senator from 1905, and as 'Progressive' candidate for the presidency was defeated in 1924, having gained nearly 5 million votes.

LA FONTAINE, Jean de (1621–95), French poet, born at Château-Thierry in Champagne, assisted his father, a superintendent of woods and forests. He early devoted himself to the study of the old writers and to verse writing. In 1654 he published a verse translation of the *Eunuchus* of Terence, and then went to Paris, where Fouquet became his patron. His *Contes et nouvelles en vers* appeared in 1665, his *Fables choises mises en vers* in 1668, and his *Amours de Psyché et de Cupidon* in 1669. For nearly twenty years he was maintained in the household of Mme de la Sablière. In 1684 he read an admirable *Discours en vers* on his reception by the Academy. He was one of the most frivolous and dissipated of men, but he was likewise one of the most charming and gifted. La Fontaine was a great and brilliant writer and his verse, especially as found in the *Contes* and *Fables*, lively and original. The best edition is by Regnier (11 vols. 1883–92). See Sainte-Beuve's *Portraits*, vol. i; works by Girardin (2nd ed. 1876), Taine (1882), Faguet (1900), F. Hamel (1912), Gohin (1931); English verse translation by E. Marsh (1933).

LAGERKVIST, Pär (1891–), Swedish writer, studied at Uppsala, began his literary career as an expressionist poet with *Angest* (1916) and *Kaos* (1918), emphasizing the catastrophe of war, but later, in the face of extremist creeds and slogans, adopted a critical humanism in such plays as *Bödeln* (1934) and *Dvärgen* (1944), which expose the political and social destroyer. He was awarded the Nobel prize in 1951 for the novel *Barabbas* (1951), the thief in whose place Christ was crucified. The ideological play *Lat människan Leva*, 'Let Man Live' (1949), is a study of political terrorism in which Christ, Socrates, Bruno, Joan of Arc and an American negro appear as victims. He was elected a Swedish Academician in 1940.

LAGERLÖF, Selma (1858–1940), Swedish novelist, born in Värmland, became a schoolteacher, and sprang to fame with *Gösta Berling's Saga* (1891). Her fairy tales and romances earned her a Nobel prize (1909), and a seat in the Swedish Academy (1914).

LAGRANGE, Joseph Louis, Comte, *-grãzh* (1736–1813), mathematician, was born of French ancestry at Turin. In 1766 he was appointed director of the Berlin Academy, having gained a European reputation by his completion of the Calculus of Variations, investigations of sound, harmonics, &c. While in Prussia (1766–87), Lagrange read before the Berlin Academy about sixty dissertations on the application of the higher analysis to mechanics and dynamics; one of these was his principal work, the *Mécanique analytique* (1788), its central theory the principle of virtual velocities, which he had established in 1764. In Paris he was welcomed by the court and lodged in the Louvre with a pension of 6000 francs. After the Revolution he was appointed professor in the Normal and Polytechnic Schools and a member of the Bureau des longitudes. Napoleon made him a member of the senate and a Count, and gave him the Grand Cross of the Legion of Honour. Other important works are *Théorie des fonctions*, *Leçons sur le calcul des fonctions*, and *Résolution des équations numériques*. Lagrange died at Paris, and was buried in the Panthéon. His works have been edited by Serret and Darboux (14 vols. 1866–92).

LA GUARDIA, Fiorello Henry (1882–1947), American lawyer and politician, born in New York of Italian-Jewish origin, became deputy attorney-general of New York (1915–17), served with the American air force in Italy and sat in congress (1917–21, 1923–33) as a Republican. As a popular mayor of New York (thrice re-elected, 1933–45) he initiated housing and labour safeguards schemes, was one of the early opponents of Hitler's anti-Semitic policies—he had his ears boxed in public by enraged American fascists—and was civil defence director (1941–42). He became civil administrator of allied-occupied Italy, and in 1946 was appointed director-general of U.N.R.R.A. New York's airport is named after him. See his autobiography (1948), and Life by E. Cuneo (1955).

LAGUERRE, Louis (1663–1721), French artist, born in Paris. In 1683 he came to London, where he carried out schemes of elaborate, allegorical decoration at Chatsworth, Petworth, Blenheim, &c.

LAHARPE, Frédéric César (1754–1838), Swiss politician, born at Rolle in Vaud, president of the Helvetic Republic in 1798–1800, lived a good deal in Russia as tutor and as guest of Alexander I. He died at Lausanne.

LA HARPE, Jean François de (1739–1803), French poet and critic, born at Paris, in 1763 produced a successful tragedy, *Warwick*. His best-known works are, however, his critical lectures, *Lycée, ou Cours de littérature* (1799–1805). His *Correspondance littéraire* (1801) by the bitterness of its criticisms rekindled fierce controversies. He supported the Revolution at first, but after five months' imprisonment (1794) became a firm supporter of church and crown.

LAIDLAW, William (1780–1845), Scottish friend and amanuensis of Sir Walter Scott, and himself a writer of lyrics, was born at Blackhouse in Selkirkshire. After farming with little success at Traquair and Liberton, he settled in 1817 as a kind of factor on the Abbotsford estate, and was Scott's trusted counsellor in all his schemes of improvement. Here, with the exception of three years after the disaster in Scott's affairs, he lived till Scott's death in 1832. Afterwards he was factor successively on two Ross-shire estates.

LAING, (1) Alexander Gordon (1793–1826), Scottish explorer, born at Edinburgh, served seven years as an officer in the West Indies. He was sent to explore the Niger's source which he found, but was murdered after leaving Timbuktu.

(2) **David** (1793–1878), Scottish antiquary, the son of an Edinburgh bookseller, for thirty years followed his father's trade, and from 1837 till his death was librarian of the Signet Library. He was honorary secretary of the Bannatyne Club, and edited many of its issues. An LL.D. of Edinburgh, he left behind him a private library of unusual value, and bequeathed many rare MSS. to Edinburgh University. His more important works were his editions of Baillie's *Letters and Journals* (1841–42), of John Knox (1846–64), Sir David Lyndsay, Dunbar and Henryson. See Life by G. Goudie (1914).

(3) **John.** See HALKETT, SAMUEL.

(4) **Malcolm** (1762–1818), Scottish historian, was born in Orkney, educated at Kirkwall and Edinburgh University, and called to the bar in 1785, but never became a successful advocate. He completed Henry's *History of Great Britain* (1793), and in 1802 published his own *History of Scotland, 1603–1707*. His *Poems of Ossian* is an onslaught on Macpherson.

(5) **Samuel** (1780–1868), brother of (4), travelled and wrote on Norway, Sweden, Russia, France, &c., and translated the *Heimskringla*.

(6) **Samuel** (1812–97), son of (5), chairman of the Brighton railway, Liberal M.P. for Wick, wrote on the conflict of scince with religion.

LAIRD, (1) **John** (1805–74), a Birkenhead shipbuilder and M.P., born at Greenock, one of the earliest constructors of iron vessels.

(2) **John** (1887–1946), Scottish philosopher, born at Durris, Kincardineshire, studied at Edinburgh, Heidelberg and Cambridge, and was professor at Dalhousie, Nova Scotia (1912), Belfast (1913–24) and at Aberdeen (1924–46). His *Study in Realism* (1920) defined his own metaphysical standpoint. He is best known, however, for his studies of Hume (1932) and Hobbes (1934) and his edition of Samuel Alexander's works (1939). He was Gifford lecturer at Glasgow (1939) and was elected F.B.A. in 1933.

(3) **Macgregor** (1808–61), brother of (1), also born at Greenock, shared Lander's last expedition to the Niger.

LAIRESSE, Gérard de (1641–1711), Dutch painter and etcher, the author, after he became blind in 1690, of *Art of Painting* (trans. 1738).

LAÏS, the name of two Corinthian courtesans, famous for their beauty. The elder flourished during the Peloponnesian war; the younger, born in Sicily, came as a child to Corinth, and sat as a model to Apelles.

LAKE, Gerard, Viscount (1744–1808), British general, served in Germany 1760–62, America 1781, and the Low Countries 1793–94, his most brilliant exploit being the capture of some forts near Lille. In 1798 he routed the rebels at Vinegar Hill, and received the surrender of the French near Cloone. In N.W. India (1801–07), against Sindia and Holkar he won several battles and took Aligarh, Delhi and Agra. See Memoir by Pearce (1908).

LALANDE, Joseph Jérôme Le Français de (1732–1807), French astronomer, born at Bourg-en-Bresse, was sent to Berlin in 1751 to determine the moon's parallax. He was from 1762 professor of Astronomy in the Collège de France, from 1795 director of the Paris Observatory. His chief work is *Traité d'astronomie* (1764; 3rd ed. 1792).

LALIQUE, René, *la-leek* (1860–1945), French jeweller, born at Ay. He was also an artist-craftsman in glass which he decorated with relief figures, animals and flowers.

LALLY, (1) **Thomas Arthur, Comte de, Baron de Tollendal** (1702–66), French general, born at Romans in Dauphiné, son of Sir Gerard O'Lally, an Irish Jacobite in the French service. Lally distinguished himself in Flanders, accompanied Prince Charles Edward to Scotland in 1745, and in 1756 became commander-in-chief in the French East Indies. He commenced vigorous hostilities against the British, and besieged Madras; but being defeated, retreated to Pondicherry, which was attacked in March 1760 by a superior British force. Lally capitulated in January 1761, and was conveyed to England. Accused of cowardice, he returned to France, and was thrown into the Bastille. The parliament of Paris at last condemned him, and he was executed May 7, 1766. But his son, supported by Voltaire, procured a royal decree in 1778, declaring the condemnation unjust, and restoring all the forfeited honours. See Malleson's *French in India*.

(2) **Trophime Gérard, Marquis de Lally-Tollendal** (1751–1830), son of (1), was one of those nobles who acted in the States-General in 1789 with the Third Estate, but soon allied himself with the court. He advocated a constitution with two chambers, and sought to protect the king, but had to flee to England. Louis XVIII made him a peer. He wrote *Defence of the French Emigrants* (1794), and *Life of Wentworth, Earl of Strafford* (2nd ed. 1814).

LALO, (Victor Antoine) Édouard (1823–92), French composer and viola player, born at Lille of a military family. His musical compositions include *Symphonie espagnole* and other violin works, and operas, the best known being *Le Roi d'Ys*, and the ballet *Namouna*.

LAMARCK, Jean Baptiste Pierre Antoine de Monet, Chevalier de (1744–1829), French naturalist and pre-Darwinian evolutionist, was born at Bazentin, and at seventeen joined the French army in Germany. Stationed as an officer at Toulon and Monaco, he became interested in the Mediterranean flora; and resigning after an injury, he held a post in a Paris bank, and meanwhile worked at botany. In 1773 he published a *Flore française*. In 1774 he became a member of the French Academy and keeper of the royal garden (afterwards the nucleus of *Jardin des plantes*), and here he lectured for twenty-five years on Invertebrate Zoology. About 1801 he had begun to think about the relations and origin of species, expressing his conclusions in his famous *Philosophie zoologique* (1809). His *Histoire des animaux sans vertèbres* appeared in 1815–22. Hard work and illness enfeebled his sight and left him blind and poor. Lamarck broke with the old notion of species, expressly denied the unchangeableness of species, sought to explain their transformation and the evolution of the animal world, and prepared the way for the now accepted theory of descent. See Cuvier's *Éloge* of him (1832); C. Claus, *Lamarck als Begründer der Descendenztheorie* (1888); Haeckel, *Darwin, Goethe, und Lamarck* (1882), Packard, *Lamarck the Founder of Evolution* (1902), E. Perrier, *Lamarck* (1925), and H. G. Cannon, *Lamarck and Modern Genetics* (1960).

LA MARMORA, Alfonso Ferrero, Marquis de (1804–78), Italian soldier, born at Turin, distinguished himself in the national war of 1848, and in 1849 was appointed minister of war. He commanded the Sardinian troops in the Crimea (1855), took part in the war of 1859, was commander-in-chief in 1861, and in 1864 prime minister. In the campaign against Austria in 1866 he lost the battle of Custozza. His publication (1873) of the secret negotiations between Prussia and Italy incurred the censure of Bismarck. See monograph by Massari (1880).

LAMARTINE, Alphonse Marie Louis de (1790–1869), French poet, statesman and historian, born at Mâcon, was brought up on ultraroyalist principles, spent much of his youth in Italy, and on the fall of Napoleon entered the garde royale. His first volume of poems, probably his best known and most successful, the *Méditations*, was published in 1820. He was successively secretary of legation at Naples and *chargé d'affaires* at Florence. In 1829 he declined the post of foreign secretary in the Polignac ministry, and by another series of poems, *Harmonies poétiques et religieuses*, achieved his unanimous election to the Academy. Lamartine, still a royalist, disapproved of the Revolution of 1830. A tour to the East produced his *Souvenirs d'Orient*. Recalled to France in 1833, he became deputy for Mâcon. Between 1834 and 1848 he published his poems, *Jocelyn* and *La Chute d'un ange*, and the celebrated *Histoire des Girondins*. The Orleanist *régime* was repugnant to him; and he became a member of the Provisional Government (1848), and, as minister of foreign affairs, the ruling spirit. After two risings of the extreme party of Louis Blanc and Ledru Rollin, the executive committee resigned, and conferred the command of the forces on Cavaignac. After a terrible conflict the insurrection was suppressed. When Napoleon came to power Lamartine devoted himself to literature, publishing *Confidences*, *Raphaël* (both autobiographical), *Geneviève*, the *Tailleur de pierres de St-Point* (a prose tale), and *Histoire de la restauration*. He wrote on Joan of Arc, Cromwell, Madame de Sévigné, &c., and issued monthly *Entretiens familiers*. He died at Passy, February 28. See monographs by Lady M. Domville (1888), Reyssié (1892), Rod (1892), Deschanel (1893), Quentin-Bauchart (1903–07), Doumic (1912), Lanson (1915), Barthou (1916), Whitehouse (1919); and Baillon and Harris: *L'État présent des études lamartiniennes* (1933).

LAMB, (1) Lady Caroline. See MELBOURNE.

(2) **Charles** (1775–1834), English essayist, was born in the Temple, London, where his father was clerk to Samuel Salt, a wealthy bencher. At Christ's Hospital 1782–89, he soon afterwards obtained a situation in the South Sea House, but in 1792 procured promotion to the India House, where he remained for more than thirty years. In 1792 also, Samuel Salt died, and with a legacy from him, Charles's salary, and whatever his elder sister Mary (1764–1847) could earn by needlework, the family retired to humble lodgings. In 1796 the terrible disaster occurred which was destined to mould the future life of Charles Lamb. The strain of insanity inherited from the mother, began to show itself in Mary and in an attack of mania she stabbed her mother. Her brother's guardianship was accepted by the authorities and to this trust Charles Lamb from that moment devoted his life. In the meantime Charles had fallen in love, but renounced all hope of marriage when the duty of tending his sister appeared to him paramount. Lamb's earliest poems (1795), first printed with Coleridge's in 1796–97, were prompted by this deep attachment. In 1798 Lamb and Charles Lloyd made a venture in a slight volume of their own (*Blank Verse*); and here for the first time Lamb's individuality made itself felt in the 'Old Familiar Faces'. In 1797 he also published his little prose romance, *The Tale of Rosamund Gray and Old Blind Margaret*; and in 1801 *John Woodvil*—the fruit of that study of the dramatic poetry of the Elizabethan period, in whose revival he was to bear so large a part. Meantime, Lamb and his sister were wandering from lodging to lodging, and in 1801 they removed to Lamb's old familiar neighbourhood, where they continued for sixteen years. Charles's experiments in literature had as yet brought him neither money nor reputation and, to raise a few pounds, he wrote a farce, *Mr H.*, produced at Drury Lane in December 1806, and famous only for its failure. For William Godwin's 'Juvenile Library', Charles and Mary wrote in 1807 their *Tales from Shakespeare*—Mary Lamb taking the comedies, Charles the tragedies. This was Lamb's first success. The brother and sister next composed jointly *Mrs Leicester's School* (1807) and *Poetry for Children* (1809). Charles also made a prose version of the *Adventures of Ulysses*; and a volume of selections from the Elizabethan dramatists exhibited him as one of the most subtle and original of poetical critics. Three years later his unsigned articles in Leigh Hunt's *Reflector* on Hogarth and the tragedies of Shakespeare proved him a prose writer of new and unique quality. In 1818 Lamb collected his scattered verse and prose in two volumes as the *Works of Charles Lamb*, and this paved the way for his being invited to join the staff of the new *London Magazine*. His first essay, in August 1820, 'Recollections of the old South Sea House', was signed *Elia*, the name of a foreigner who had been a fellow-clerk. *The Last Essays of Elia* were collected in 1833. In 1825 Lamb, who had been failing in health, resigned his

post in the India House, with a pension of £441. The brother and sister were now free to wander; finally they removed to Edmonton. The absence of settled occupation had not brought Lamb the comfort he had looked for: the separation from his friends and the now almost continuous mental alienation of his sister left him companionless, and with the death of Coleridge in 1834 the chief attractions of his life were gone. In December of that year, he too died. He was buried in Edmonton churchyard. His sister survived him nearly thirteen years, and was buried by his side. Lamb's place in literature is unique and unchallengeable. As a personality he is more intimately known to us than any other figure in literature, unless it be Samuel Johnson. He is familiar to us through his works, which are composed in the form of personal confidences; through his many friends who have made known his every mood and trait; and through his letters, the most fascinating correspondence in our language. The profound and imaginative character of his criticism, and with it the reckless humour of the Bohemian and the *farceur*; his loyalty and generosity to his friends; his wild fun alternating with tenderness or profound philosophic musings —it is this wonderful blending of opposites that has made Lamb the most dearly loved of English men of letters. The chief authorities for Lamb are his own writings, and the *Life and Letters* (1837) and *Final Memorials* (1848) by Talfourd. See monographs by B. W. Procter (1866), Ainger (1882), Derocquigny (Paris 1904); Life of Mary Lamb by Mrs Gilchrist (1883); *The Lambs* by Hazlitt (1897); Edmund Blunden, *Charles Lamb and his Contemporaries* (1933), and *Charles Lamb: His Life Recorded by his Contemporaries* (1934); the editions by Ainger (1883–88), W. Macdonald (12 vols. 1903), and E. V. Lucas (in 7 vols., together with the Life in 2 vols., 1903–05; revised 1921; Letters, 3 vols., 1935).

(3) **William.** See MELBOURNE.

(4) **Willis Eugene** (1913–), American physicist, professor of Physics at Columbia (1948), Stanford (1951), Oxford (1956), Yale (1962). In 1955 he shared with Kusch the Nobel prize for physics for his researches into the hydrogen spectrum.

LAMBALLE, Marie Thérèse Louise de Savoie-Carignan, Princess de (1749–92), born at Turin, daughter of the Prince of Carignan, in 1767 married Louis of Bourbon, Prince of Lamballe, but next year was left a widow. Beautiful and charming, she was made by Marie Antoinette superintendent of the household (1774), and her own intimate companion. She escaped to England in 1791, but returned to share the queen's imprisonment in the Temple, and refused the oath of detestation of the king, queen and monarchy (September 3, 1792). As she stepped out of the courtroom she was cut down, amid barbarities that have since been exaggerated. See Lives by Lescure (1865), Bertin (2nd ed. 1894), Sir F. Montefiore (1896) and B. C. Hardy (1908).

LAMBE, John (d. 1628), an astrologer, patronized by Buckingham, and mobbed to death.

LAMBERT, (1) Constant (1905–51), English composer, conductor and critic, the son of George Washington Lambert, A.R.A. (1873–1930), portrait painter, was born in London. His first success came when, as a student at the Royal College of Music, he was commissioned by Diaghilev to write a ballet, *Romeo and Juliet*, first performed in 1926. For several years Lambert worked as conductor for the Camargo Society and later of Sadler's Wells Ballet, upon which company his outstanding musicianship and understanding of the problems of ballet had a lasting influence; he was also active as a concert conductor and music critic. His book *Music Ho!* (1934) is enlivened by his understanding of painting, his appreciation of jazz, his devotion to Elizabethan music and the works of such debatable composers as Liszt and Berlioz, and by its acidly witty, polished style. Of his compositions, *The Rio Grande* (1929), one of the most successful concert works in jazz idiom, is perhaps the most famous, but his lyrical gifts show themselves in the ballets *Pomona* (1927) and *Horoscope* (1938) as well as the cantata *Summer's Last Will and Testament* (1936). His concerto for piano and chamber orchestra was composed in memory of Philip Heseltine.

(2) **Johann Heinrich** (1728–77), German mathematician, was born at Mülhausen in Alsace, and died in Berlin. From 1764 he was a member of the Academy of Sciences. He first showed how to measure scientifically the intensity of light, in his *Photometria* (1760). A work of his on analytical logic (1764) was greatly valued by Kant. Among his other works are *Kosmologische Briefe* (1761) and *Anlage zur Architektonik* (1771). See Life by Huber (1829) and Baensch's monograph on his philosophy (1902).

(3) **John** (1619–84), English soldier, born at Calton near Settle, Yorkshire, studied at the Inns of Court, but on the outbreak of the Great Rebellion became a captain under Fairfax, and at Marston Moor led Fairfax's cavalry. Commissary-general of the army in the north (1645), and major-general of the northern counties (1647), he helped Cromwell to crush Hamilton at Preston, and captured Pontefract Castle in March 1649. In 1650 he went with Cromwell to Scotland as major-general, led the van at Dunbar, won the victory of Inverkeithing, followed Charles to Worcester, and at the battle commanded the troops on the eastern bank of the Severn. He helped to instal Oliver as protector, but opposed the proposition to declare him king. He headed the cabal which overthrew Richard Cromwell; was now looked upon as the leader of the Fifth Monarchy or extreme republican party; suppressed the royalist insurrection in Cheshire, August 1659 and virtually governed the country with his officers as the 'committee of safety'. Monk's counter-plot frustrated his designs. He was sent to the Tower, tried in 1662, and kept prisoner on Drake's Island till his death. See W. H. Dawson, *Cromwell's Understudy* (1938).

LAMBTON, John George. See DURHAM.

LAMÉ, Gabriel (1795–1870), French mathematician and engineer worked in Russia as an engineer before becoming professor of Physics at the École polytechnique in Paris. He investigated problems of elasticity and heat.

LAMENNAIS, Félicité Robert de, *la-mê-nay* (1782–1854), French writer, born at St-Malo, retired with his brother, a priest, to their estate at La Chesnaie near Dinan, where he wrote *Réflexions sur l'état de l'église* (1808) which was suppressed by Napoleon. On returning from London, whither he had fled during the Hundred Days, he was ordained priest, and began in 1816 his famous *Essai sur l'indifférence en matière de religion* (1818–24), a magnificent, if paradoxical denunciation of private judgment and toleration, which was favourably received at Rome. But notions of popular liberty, fanned by the revolution of 1830, began to change his outlook, and *L'Avenir*, a journal founded by him in 1830 with Montalembert and others, was suspended in 1831 and officially condemned by the pope in 1832. The *Paroles d'un croyant* (1834) brought about complete rupture with the church, and revolutionary doctrines in his later work got him a year's imprisonment. Active in the 1848 revolution, he sat in the Assembly until the *coup d'état*. At his death he refused to make peace with the church. His works include the remarkable *Esquisse d'une philosophie* (1840–46). See works by Roussel (1892), Gibson (1896), Marechal (1907–13) and Duine (1922).

LAMETTRIE, Julien Offray de (1709–51), French philosopher, born at St-Malo, became a French army surgeon in 1742; but the publication in 1745 of a materialistic work, *L'Histoire naturelle de l'âme*, roused such odium that he sought refuge in Leyden (1746). He published *L'Homme machine* (1748), and escaped arrest by accepting an invitation from Frederick the Great. In Berlin he continued his materialistic studies in *L'Homme plante* (1748), *L'Art de jouir* (1751), *La Volupté*, &c. He also wrote satirical books against doctors. See a memoir by Frederick prefixed to his works (1774), and monographs by Quépat (1873), Du Bois-Reymond (1875) and Poritzky (1900).

LAMOND, Frederic (1868–1948), Scottish pianist and composer, born in Glasgow. A pupil of Bülow and Liszt, he made his début at Berlin in 1885. He excelled in playing Beethoven. Among his compositions are an overture *Aus dem schottischen Hochlande*, a symphony and several piano works.

LAMONT, Johann von (1805–79), Scottish-German astronomer, born in Braemar, went in 1817 to the Scottish seminary at Ratisbon, and became in 1835 director of Bogenhausen Observatory. In 1852 he became professor of Astronomy at Munich. He wrote *Handbuch des Erdmagnetismus*.

LAMORICIÈRE, Christophe Léon Louis Juchault de, *la-mor-ees-yayr* (1806–65), French general, born at Nantes, entered the army in 1826, and served in Algeria 1833–47. Through his energy chiefly the war was brought to an end by the capture of Abd-el-Kader in 1847. In June 1848 he carried the Paris barricades and quelled the Socialists. He was war minister under Cavaignac, but was banished at the *coup d'état* of 1851. He went to Rome in 1860, commanded the papal troops, but, defeated by Cialdini (September 18), capitulated at Ancona. He died near Amiens. See Lives by Keller (3rd ed. 1891) and Rastoul (1894).

LA MOTTE, (1) Antoine Houdar de (1672–1731), French poet and playwright, was born and died in Paris. He was translator of the *Iliad* into French verse. Of his other writings, perhaps the best known is the play *Inès de Castro*.

(2) **Jeanne de Valois, Comtesse de** (1756–1791), French adventuress who duped the Cardinal de Rohan over the Diamond Necklace, and was branded and imprisoned (1786), but escaped (1787) to London, where she was killed by falling drunk from a three-story window. See her autobiography (1793), and Carlyle's *Essays* (1837).

LA MOTTE FOUQUÉ. See FOUQUÉ.

LANCASTER, (1) Sir James (1554 or 1555–1618), English navigator, was a soldier and merchant in Portugal, visited the East Indies in 1591–94, and in 1595 captured Pernambuco. In 1600–03 he commanded the first fleet of the East India Company that visited the East Indies, and on his return was knighted. He promoted the voyages of Hudson, Baffin, &c., in search of the Northwest Passage. See Markham's *Voyages of Sir James Lancaster* (1877), and *The Voyages of Sir James Lancaster*, ed. Sir W. Foster (1940).

(2) **Joseph** (1778–1838), English educationist, opened a school in London in 1798 based on a monitorial system which was taken up by the Nonconformists, Andrew Bell and his rival system being supported by the Church of England. The Lancasterian schools were undenominational, and the Bible formed a large part of the teaching. The Royal Lancasterian Society, afterwards known as the British and Foreign School Society, was formed in 1808. Thriftless and unmethodical, Lancaster quitted the Society in anger, emigrated in 1818 to the U.S., and died at New York. See Life by Salmon (1904).

LANCRET, Nicolas, *lã-kray* (1690–1743), French painter, born in Paris, who imitated the style of Watteau. His fête-galante paintings have charm, are cleverly executed but fall short of Watteau's in depth.

LAND, Edwin Herbert (1909–), American inventor and physicist, born at Bridgeport, Conn., known especially for his discoveries relating to light polarization, for his invention of the 'Polaroid' camera, which takes and processes photographs on the spot, and for research on the nature of colour vision.

LANDAU, Lev Davidovich (1908–68), Russian scientist, born at Baku, graduated at Leningrad, became professor of Physics at Moscow. Known for his important quantum theory researches, he received the Nobel prize for physics in 1962 for work on theories of condensed matter, particularly helium.

LANDELLS, (1) Ebenezer (1808–60), English wood-engraver, born at Newcastle-on-Tyne, the originator in 1841 of *Punch*, worked under Bewick, and in 1829 settled in London. He contributed wood engravings to both *Punch* and the *Illustrated London News*.

(2) **Robert Thomas** (1833–77), eldest son

of (1), was a war artist for the *Illustrated London News* in the Crimean and Franco-Prussian wars.

LANDER, Richard (1804–34), British traveller, born at Truro, in 1825 accompanied Clapperton as his servant to Sokoto. There Clapperton died, and Lander published an account of the expedition. The British government sent him and his brother John (1807–39) to make further researches along the lower Niger. In 1830 they proved that the Niger falls by many mouths into the Bight of Benin, as described in their *Journal* (1832). During a third expedition, Richard Lander was wounded by Niger natives, and died at Fernando Pó. See Laird and Oldfield's *Narrative* of this journey (1837).

LANDESMANN, Heinrich, pseud. **Hieronymus Lorm** (1821–1902), German deaf and blind poet and prose-writer, born at Nikolsburg in Moravia.

LANDOR, Walter Savage (1775–1864), English writer, was born at Warwick, the son of an ex-doctor. At ten he was sent to Rugby, but was removed for insubordination; and from Trinity College, Oxford, which he entered in 1793, he was rusticated next year. Soon after publishing *Poems* in 1795, he quarrelled with his father, but was reconciled, and retired to South Wales on an allowance of £150 a year. *Gebir* (1798), a poem showing the influence of Milton and Pindar, was the occasion of his lifelong friendship with Southey; but it was a failure. On his father's death in 1805 Landor had a considerable income, but much of it went in equipping volunteers to fight Napoleon in Spain (1808). Next year he purchased Llanthony Abbey, but soon quarrelled with neighbours and tenantry alike, and had ruin staring him in the face. In 1811 he married unhappily Miss Julia Thuillier, and in 1814 he left her in Jersey and crossed to France. Rejoined by his wife at Tours, he went in 1815 to Italy, where he remained at Como, Pisa and Florence till 1835, with the exception of a short visit to England. *Count Julian*, lacking in all the qualities of a successful tragedy, had appeared in 1812; and to this period belongs his best-known work, *Imaginary Conversations* (i and ii, 1824–29). A second quarrel with his wife in 1835 led to his return to Bath till 1858. During these years he wrote the *Examination of Shakespeare* (1834), *Pericles and Aspasia* (1836), *Pentameron* (1837), *Hellenics* (1847), and *Poemata et Inscriptiones* (1847). In 1858 an unhappy scandal (see his *Dry Sticks Fagoted*), which involved him in an action for libel, again drove him to Italy; and at Florence he lived till his death. Physically imposing, strong-willed, and intelligent, Landor is ranked, by a narrow circle of admirers, with the great names of English literature. But many readers find his work artificial. See Forster, *Life and Works* (2 vols, 1869; new ed. 1895); Sidney Colvin, *Landor* (1881); S. Wheeler's *Letters of Landor* (1897–99); Minch in *Last Days, Letters, and Conversation* (1934); M. Elwin, *Savage Landor* (1942) and *Landor, a Replevin* (1958); the *Complete Works*, ed. Welby and Wheeler (1927–33); the *Letters* (1897) and the *Poetical Works* (1937), ed. Wheeler.

LANDOWSKA, Wanda, *lan-dof'ska* (1879–1959), Polish pianist, harpsichordist, and musical scholar, born in Warsaw. In 1900 went to Paris, and in 1912 became professor of the Harpsichord at the Berlin Hochschule. After World War I, in which she was detained, she undertook many extensive concert tours. At Saint-Leu-la-Forêt near Paris she established in 1927 her École de musique ancienne, where she gave specialized training in the performance of old works. In 1940 she had to flee first to the south of France, then to Switzerland, and finally in 1941 to the U.S. She excelled as a player in the music of Bach and Handel. She renewed interest in the harpsichord and Falla wrote for her his concerto for this instrument. She herself composed songs and piano and orchestral pieces. She made a profound study of old music and on this subject wrote *La Musique ancienne* (1908, trans. 1927). Among her other writings were *Bach et ses Interprètes* (1906) and many articles.

LANDRU, Henri Desiré, *lã-drü* (1869–1922), French murderer, born in Paris, served in the army, then worked in garages or was employed in the furniture trade. Between 1904 and 1915 he was imprisoned four times for swindling, &c. His career as a mass murderer began in 1915 and lasted for four years, and he was convicted of the murders of ten women and a boy. He was arrested in 1919, tried in 1921 and executed.

LANDSEER, Sir Edwin Henry (1802–73), English animal painter, born in London, son of the engraver, John Landseer, A.E.R.A. (1769–1852). Trained by his father to sketch animals from life, he began exhibiting at the Royal Academy when only thirteen. His animal pieces were generally made subservient to some sentiment or idea, without, however, losing their correctness and force of draughtsmanship. Dogs and deer were his favourite and best subjects; the scene of several fine pictures is laid in the highlands of Scotland, which he first visited in 1824. In 1826 he was elected an A.R.A., in 1830 an R.A., and in 1850 was knighted. His *Monarch of the Glen*, which in 1892 fetched 6900 guineas, was exhibited in 1851; the bronze lions at the foot of Nelson's Monument in Trafalgar Square were modelled by him (1859–66). Elected P.R.A. in 1866, he declined the honour. He was buried in St Paul's. Most of Landseer's pictures are well known from the excellent engravings of them by his elder brother **Thomas** (1796–1880). See works by Stephens (1880), Loftie (1891), Manson (1902).

LANDSTEINER, Karl (1868–1943), Austrian pathologist, born in Vienna, was professor of Pathological Anatomy there from 1909. In the United States he was a member of the Rockefeller Institute for Medical Research (1922–39) and won the Nobel prize in 1930 for physiology and medicine, especially for his valuable discovery of the four different types of human blood and of the Rh factor.

LANE, (1) **(William) Arbuthnot** (1856–1943), Scottish surgeon, born at Fort George, Inverness-shire. He was one of the most outstanding surgeons of his day, being the first to join fractures with metal plates instead of wires. Other important contributions to medicine were his treatment of the cleft palate and of 'chronic intestinal stasis'. In 1925 he founded the New Health Society.

(2) **Edward William** (1801–76), English Arabic scholar, born at Hereford, began life as an engraver; but the need of a warmer climate took him to Egypt (1825–28, 1833–1835), and with Egypt the whole of his subsequent work was connected. The result was his *Manners and Customs of the Modern Egyptians* (1836). This was followed by the annotated translation of the *Thousand and One Nights* (1838–40), which was the first accurate rendering, and by *Selections from the Koran* (1843). Lane's third visit to Egypt (1842–49) was devoted to laborious preparation for the great work of his life, the *Arabic Lexicon* (5 vols. 1863–74), completed (1876–90) by his grand-nephew, Stanley Lane-Poole (q.v.), who also wrote his Life (1877). See also POOLE.

(3) **Sir Hugh Percy** (1875–1915), Irish art collector, was born at Ballybrack, Cork. He was responsible for founding a gallery of modern art in Dublin at the beginning of the 20th century by his encouragement of contemporary artists, such as John B. Yeats and William Orpen, and by his own gifts of pictures. Director of the National Gallery of Ireland in 1914, he was drowned the following year when the *Lusitania*, on which he was a passenger, was torpedoed. He bequeathed to Dublin in a codicil to his will, his collection of thirty-nine French impressionist pictures; but as this was not witnessed they were held by the National Gallery in London until in 1959 a compromise was arranged whereby each half of the collection was to go to Dublin's municipal art gallery for five years successively over a period of twenty years.

(4) **Richard James** (1800–72), brother of (2), born at Berkeley Castle, associate-engraver of the R.A. (1827), turned to lithography, reproducing with unsurpassed delicacy and precision works by Lawrence, Gainsborough, Leslie, Landseer and G. Richmond. He was also no mean sculptor.

LANE-POOLE, (1) **Reginald** (1857–1939), English historian, born in London, was keeper of the Bodleian (1914–26) and an authority on Wyclif. His many and scholarly writings include *The Huguenots of the Dispersion* (1880), *Illustrations of Medieval Thought* (1884) and *The Exchequer in the Twelfth Century* (1912).

(2) **Stanley** (1854–1931), English archaeologist, brother of (1), was born in London and graduated from Corpus Christi College, Oxford, in 1878. He went, for the government, as archaeologist to Egypt and Russia and wrote on Mohammedan history, Oriental numismatics, Egyptian life, &c. He was the author of a Life of his grand-uncle Edward William Lane (q.v.), whose *Arabic Lexicon* he also completed. He was professor of Arabic at Trinity College, Dublin (1898–1904).

LANFRANC (*c.* 1005–89), Archbishop of Canterbury, was born at Pavia, and educated for the law. About 1039 he founded a school at Avranches, in 1041 became a Benedictine at Bec, and in 1046 was chosen prior. He contended against Berengarius in the controversy as to the real presence. He at first condemned the marriage of William of Normandy with his cousin, but in 1059 went to Rome to procure the papal dispensation; and in 1062 William made him prior of St Stephen's Abbey at Caen, and in 1070 Archbishop of Canterbury. His chief writings are Commentaries on the Epistles of St Paul, a Treatise against Berengar. and Sermons. See Life by A. J. Macdonald (1926), Hook's *Lives of the Archbishops of Canterbury*, vol. ii, Freeman's *Norman Conquest*, vols. ii-v, and Z. N. Brooke, *The English Church and the Papacy* (1935).

LANFRANCO, Giovanni (*c.* 1581–1647), religious painter, born at Parma, was one of the first Italian baroque painters. His work, the best of which can be seen on the dome of S. Andrea della Valle in Rome and in his paintings for the cathedral at Naples, was widely copied by later painters. He died in Rome. See E. K. Waterhouse, *Baroque Painting in Rome* (1937).

LANFREY, Pierre, *lä-fray* (1828–77), French historian and republican politician, was born at Chambéry, and died at Pau. His great work was his (hostile) *Histoire de Napoléon I* (5 vols. 1867–75).

LANG, (1) **Andrew** (1844–1912), Scottish man of letters, born at Selkirk, was educated at Edinburgh Academy, St Andrews University and Balliol College, Oxford. He was elected a fellow of Merton in 1868. Soon he became one of the busiest and most versatile writers in the world of London journalism. He took a leading part in the controversy with Max Müller and his school about the interpretation of mythology and folk tales. LL.D. of St Andrews (1885), in 1888 he was first Gifford lecturer there. *Ballads and Lyrics of Old France* (1872), *Ballades in Blue China* (1880), *Helen of Troy* (1882), *Rhymes à la Mode* (1884), *Grass of Parnassus* (1888), and *Ballades of Books* (1888) are volumes of graceful verse. *Custom and Myth* (1884), *Myth, Ritual, and Religion* (1887; 2nd ed. 1899), *Modern Mythology* (1897), and *The Making of Religion* (1898) are solid contributions to the study of the philosophy and religion of primitive man. Other works are *The Library* (1881), *Books and Bookmen* (1886), *Letters to Dead Authors* (1886), *Lost Leaders* (1889), a history of St Andrews (1894), a novel, *The Monk of Fife* (1895), a *History of Scotland* (3 vols. 1899–1904), a *History of English Literature* (1912), *Magic and Religion* (1901), many fairy books, and volumes on Homer, Joan of Arc, Scott, Lockhart, Mary Stuart, John Knox, Prince Charlie, Pickle the Spy, Tennyson, Gowrie Conspiracy, &c. He translated Theocritus and Homer (*Iliad* with W. Leaf and E. Myers; *Odyssey* with S. H. Butcher). See M. Beerbohm's *Andrew Lang* (1929) and studies by Green (1946 and 1962).

(2) **Cosmo Gordon** (1864–1945), Anglican prelate, born at Fyvie, Aberdeenshire, third son of **John Marshall Lang** (1834–1909), principal of Aberdeen University. Entering the Church of England in 1890, he was a curate at Leeds, became Dean of Divinity at Magdalen

College, Oxford, Bishop of Stepney (1901–08) and Canon of St Paul's. In 1908 he was appointed Archbishop of York and in 1928 Archbishop of Canterbury until he retired in 1942. He was created Baron Lang of Lambeth in 1942. A man of wide interests, he was accepted by all parties in the Church of England and was both counsellor and friend to the royal family. See Charles Herbert's *Twenty Years as Archbishop of York* (1928) and J. G. Lockhart's *Cosmo Gordon Lang* (1949).

LANGE, (1) **Carl Georg** (1834–1900), Danish physician and psychologist, with William James advanced the James-Lange theory of emotion. He also wrote a history of materialism, but his main work was *Über Gemütsbewegungen* (1887).

(2) **Johann Peter** (1802–84), German theologian, born at Sonnborn near Elberfeld, in 1841 became professor of Theology at Zürich, and in 1854 at Bonn. His best-known works are a *Life of Jesus Christ* (1839; Eng. trans. by Marcus Dods), and his great *Bibelwerk* (1857 *et seq.*).

LANGER, Susanne (1895–), American aesthetic philosopher, disciple of Ernst Cassirer, whose influence permeates her first work, *Philosophy in a New Key* (1942). Her formalist theory of art is set out in *Feeling and Form* (1953) and *Problems of Art* (1957), and her edited *Reflections on Art* (1958) examine the considerations, facts and views which form the basis of her theory. She is the leading aesthetic philosopher of her time.

LANGEVIN, *lãzh-vĩ,* (1) **Sir Hector Louis** (1826–1906), Canadian statesman, born in Quebec, was called to the bar in 1850 and became mayor of Quebec (1858–60). Thereafter he held many government posts, including solicitor-general (1864–66), postmaster-general (1860–67) and secretary of state (1867–69).

(2) **Paul** (1872–1946), French physicist, professor at the Sorbonne (1909), noted for his work on the molecular structure of gases, and for his theory of magnetism. Imprisoned by the Nazis after the occupation of France, he was later released, and though kept under surveillance at Troyes managed to escape to Switzerland. After the liberation he returned to Paris, where he died.

LANGHAM, Simon (d. 1376), born at Langham in Rutland, became prior and abbot of Westminster (1349), treasurer of England (1360), Bishop of Ely (1362), chancellor (1363), Archbishop of Canterbury (1366) and a cardinal (1368). He died at Avignon. See vol. iv of Hook's *Lives of the Archbishops of Canterbury.*

LANGHORNE, John (1735–79), English poet, born at Winton, Kirkby Stephen, from 1766 was rector of Blagdon, Somerset. He wrote poems and, with his brother, the Rev. **William Langhorne** (1721–72), translated Plutarch's Lives (6 vols. 1770).

LANGLAND, or Langley, **William** (*c.* 1332–*c.* 1400), English poet, born probably at Ledbury in Herefordshire; became a clerk, but, having married early, could not take more than minor orders, and possibly earned a poor living by singing in a chantry and by copying legal documents. He lived many years in London in poverty. His famous *Vision of William concerning Piers the Plowman* has great defects as a work of art, but the moral earnestness and energy of the author sometimes glow into really noble poetry brightened by vivid glimpses of the life of the poorer classes. The conception of the Plowman grows as the poem proceeds from a mere honest labourer into Christ. The verse is alliterative. The earlier editions were superseded by Prof. Skeat's for the Early English Text Society (1867–84). See Jusserand, *La Poésie mystique de William Langland* (1893; trans. 1894), a book by Bright (1929), and modern versions by K. E. Warren (1895) and H. W. Wells (1895). A theory of multiple authorship was advanced by Prof. Manly in the *Cambridge English Literature*, vol. ii (1908); see also R. W. Chambers, *Man's Unconquerable Mind* (1939).

LANGLEY, (1) **John Newport** (1852–1925), British physiologist, professor at Cambridge from 1903, was noted for his research on the sympathetic nervous system. He owned and edited the *Journal of Physiology*.

(2) **Samuel Pierpont** (1834–1906), American astronomer and aeronautics pioneer, born at Roxbury, Mass., was in 1867 appointed professor of Astronomy at Western University of Pennsylvania and director of the Allegheny Observatory. He became from 1887 secretary of the Smithsonian Institution. He greatly advanced solar physics, invented the bolometer for measuring radiant heat, and built an aeroplane that failed to launch in 1903 but flew well in 1914. He is recognized as a pioneer of flying machines. See F. Cajori, *History of Physics* (1899) and M. J. B. Davy, *Interpretive History of Flight* (1937).

LANGMUIR, Irving (1881–1957), American chemist, born in Brooklyn, N.Y., educated at Columbia and Göttingen, was associated with the General Electric Company (1909–1950), being from 1932 associate director of the research laboratory. He won the Nobel prize in 1932 for work on surface chemistry. His many inventions include the gas-filled tungsten lamp, and atomic hydrogen welding.

LANGTON, (1) **Bennet** (1737–1801), a Lincolnshire gentleman and militia officer, one of Johnson's greatest friends. Also a scholar, he was professor of Ancient Literature at the Academy. See Birkbeck Hill, *Dr Johnson, his Friends and his Critics* (1878).

(2) **Stephen** (*c.* 1150–1228), English theologian, whose birthplace is unknown, educated at the University of Paris. His friend and fellow-student Pope Innocent III in 1206 gave him a post in his household and made him a cardinal. On the disputed election to the see of Canterbury in 1205–07, Langton was recommended by the pope, and, having been elected, was consecrated by Innocent himself at Viterbo, June 27, 1207. His appointment was resisted by King John, and Langton was kept out of the see until 1213, living mostly at Pontigny. He sided warmly with the barons against John, and his name is the first of the subscribing witnesses of Magna Carta. Although the pope excommunicated the barons, Langton refused to publish the excommunication, and was

suspended from his functions in 1215. He was reinstated in 1218. See Hook's *Archbishops* (1861), and studies by Leeming (1915), Powicke (1928).

LANGTRY, Lillie, properly **Emilie Charlotte,** *née* **Le Breton** (1853–1929), British actress, born in Jersey, daughter of the dean of the island, one of the most noted beauties of her time. She married Edward Langtry in 1874, and made her first important stage appearance in 1881. Her sobriquet, *The Jersey Lily*, originated in the title of Millais's portrait of her. She managed the Imperial theatre which was never successful and which had to be taken down. Widowed in 1897, she married in 1899 (later Sir) Hugo Gerald de Bathe (Bt.), and became well-known as a racehorse owner. She died in Monte Carlo. She wrote *All at Sea* (as Lillie de Bathe) in 1909, and her reminiscences *The Days I Knew* (1925). See Life by E. Dudley (1958), and novel by P. Sichel (1958).

LANIER, Sidney, *lan-eer'* (1842–81), American poet, born at Macon, Ga., Confederate private in Virginia, advocate at Macon, flute player at Baltimore, and lecturer in English Literature at Johns Hopkins University. Among his writings are a novel, *Tiger Lilies* (1867), *The Science of English Verse* (1880), *The English Novel* (1883), as well as poetry. He believed in a scientific approach towards poetry-writing, breaking away from the traditional metrical techniques and making it more akin to musical composition, illustrated in later poems, such as 'Corn' and 'The Symphony'. See Works (Centennial Edition in 10 volumes in 1945) and Life by Starke (1933).

LANJUINAIS, Jean Denis, *lã-zhwee-nay* (1753–1827), French statesman, born at Rennes, a Girondist, made a count by Napoleon, and a peer by Louis XVIII. See Life by his son, prefixed to his *Oeuvres complètes* (4 vols. 1832).

LANKESTER, Sir Edwin Ray (1847–1929), English zoologist, born in London, the son of Dr Edwin Lankester (1814–74), scientific writer. Was fellow and tutor of Exeter College, professor in London and in Oxford, and 1898–1907 director of the British Museum (Natural History). His contributions to zoology were many and varied and included important work in embryology and protozoology. Largely responsible for the founding of the Marine Biological Association in 1884, he became president of it in 1892. Among his many books are *Comparative Longevity* (1871), *Degeneration* (1880), *Advancement of Science* (1890), *Science from an Easy Chair* (1910–12), and he edited a great *Treatise on Zoology* (1900–09).

LANNES, Jean, Duke de Montebello, *lan* (1769–1809), French marshal, born at Lectoure (Gers), son of a livery stable keeper, entered the army in 1792, and by his conspicuous bravery in the Italian campaign fought his way up to be general of brigade by 1796. He rendered Napoleon important service on the 18th Brumaire. In 1800, he won the battle of Montebello, and had a distinguished share at Marengo, Austerlitz, Jena, Eylau and Friedland, and took Saragossa. In 1809 he commanded the centre at Aspern, where he was mortally wounded and died at Vienna. See Life by Thoumas (Paris 1891).

LANSBURY, George (1859–1940), British politician, born near Lowestoft, for many years before entering parliament worked for the reform of the conditions of the poor. He was first elected Labour member of parliament for Bow and Bromely in 1910, resigning in 1912 to stand again as a supporter of women's suffrage. He was defeated and was not re-elected until 1922. Meanwhile he founded the *Daily Herald*, which he edited until 1922, when it became the official paper of the Labour Party. In 1929 he became first commissioner of works and a very able leader of the Labour party (1931–35). Besides his help to the poor, he opened up London's parks for games and provided a bathing place on the Serpentine. See his *My Life* (1928) and Life by Postgate (1951).

LANSDOWNE, (1) Henry Petty-Fitzmaurice, 3rd Marquis of (1780–1863), son of the first marquis, better known as the Earl of Shelburne (q.v.). Graduated at Cambridge in 1801, and was returned for Calne next year. He led in the attack on Lord Melville (1805), and succeeded Pitt as member for Cambridge University (1806), and also as chancellor of the Exchequer in the Grenville administration. In 1809, by the death of his half-brother, he became marquis. A cautious Liberal, he in 1826 entered the Canning cabinet, and in the Goderich administration (1827–28) presided at the Foreign Office. Under Lord Grey (1830) Lansdowne became president of the council, and helped to pass the Reform Bill of 1832. He held office, with a short interval, till 1841. In 1846, under Russell, he resumed his post, taking with it the leadership of the Lords. Requested to form an administration in 1852, he preferred to serve without office in the Aberdeen coalition and in 1855 again declined the premiership. He formed a great library and art collection. See A. Aspinall, *Formation of Canning's Ministry* (1937); *Greville Memoirs*, ed. P. W. Wilson (1927) and G. P. Gooch, *Later Correspondence of Lord John Russell* (1925).

(2) **Henry Charles Keith Petty-Fitzmaurice, 5th Marquis of** (1845–1927), became marquis in 1866, from 1868 held minor offices in the Liberal administration. In 1872–74 under-secretary for war, in 1880 for India, joining the Liberal Unionists. Governor-general of Canada (1883–88), of India (1888–94), war secretary in 1895–1900. In 1900–05 as foreign secretary promoted arbitration treaties (with U.S.A., &c.), the *Entente Cordiale*, and the Japanese alliance. Unionist leader in the Lords from 1903, he sat (without portfolio) in Asquith's coalition cabinet 1915–16, advocating peace by negotiation in 1917. See Life by Newton (1929).

LANSING, Robert (1864–1928), American lawyer and statesman, born at Watertown, N.Y., became a barrister 1889, and made a name as U.S. counsel in arbitration cases (Behring Sea, N. Atlantic coast fisheries, &c.). An authority on international law, he became counsellor for the department of state in 1914, succeeded Bryan as Woodrow Wilson's secretary of state in June 1915, supported the

President during the Great War, attended the Peace Conference in Paris, 1919, and resigned in 1920. He was author of *The Peace Negotiations* (1921) and *The Big Four and others of the Peace Conference* (1921).

LANSON, Gustave, *lā-sõ* (1857–1934), French critic and historian, born at Orleans, became professor of French Literature at the Sorbonne in 1900, and director of the École normale supérieure 1919–27. Among his scholarly works are a standard history of French literature (1894), *Manuel bibliographique de la littérature française moderne* (1913), and critical studies of French authors and their works, including Voltaire, Corneille and Lamartine.

LANSTON, Tolbert (1844–1913), American inventor, born in Troy, Ohio, patented his Monotype, 'a type-forming and composing machine', in 1887. It was first used commercially in 1897 and revolutionized printing processes.

LANZI, Luigi, *lan'tzee* (1732–1810), Italian antiquary, held Etruscan to be akin to Latin, Oscan, Umbrian and Greek. His *History of Painting in Italy* (1792–1806) was translated by Roscoe (1828). See Life by Cappi (1840).

LÂO-TSZE (' Old Philosopher ') (*c.* 604 B.C.–?), is said to have been the founder of Tâoism, which shares the allegiance of the Chinese with Confucianism and Buddhism. He was for some time a curator of the royal library at Loh in Ho-nan. The treatise called the *Tâo Teh King* is our sole record of his teaching of the way in which things came into being, and in which the phenomena of nature go on quietly without striving. The secret of good government is to let men alone. Tâoism as a religion is dated much later.

LA PÉROUSE, Jean François de Galaup, Comte de, *pay-rooz* (1741–88), French navigator, born at Guo near Albi, distinguished himself in the naval war against Britain (1778–83), by destroying the forts of the Hudson's Bay Company. In 1785, in command of an expedition of discovery, he visited the north-west coast of America, explored the north-eastern coasts of Asia, and sailed through La Pérouse Strait between Sakhalin and Yezo. In 1788 he sailed from Botany Bay, and his two ships were wrecked north of the New Hebrides. Part of his journals had been sent home and was published as *Voyage autour du monde* (1797). See Life by Marcel (1888).

LAPLACE, Pierre Simon, Marquis de (1749–1827), French mathematician and astronomer born at Beaumont-en-Auge, near Trouville, the son of a poor farmer. He studied at Caen, and, after teaching mathematics, went to Paris and, as professor in the Royal Military School, became famous for his mastery of the whole range of mathematical science and its application to practical astronomy. He was chosen an associate of the Academy of Sciences in 1773 and member in 1785. His great generalization that our planetary system is stable bestowed upon astronomy the 'Three Laws of Laplace'. He explained the 'secular inequalities' in the motions of Jupiter and Saturn. He was the first to construct a complete theory of the satellites of Jupiter, and his investigation of the tidal theory was one of his greatest achievements. He helped to establish the Polytechnic and Normal Schools in Paris, and was president of the Bureau des Longitudes. Bonaparte made him minister of the interior, but superseded him in six weeks. In 1799 Laplace entered the senate; in 1803 he was appointed its chancellor. A count under the empire, he was created in 1815 a peer, in 1817 a marquis, by Louis XVIII. Elected to the Academy in 1816, he was next year appointed president. He published many treatises on lunar and planetary problems, molecular physics, electricity and magnetism. *Mécanique céleste* (1799–1825) stands alone amongst works on mathematical astronomy. The *Système du monde* (1796), written for non-mathematicians, is a clear statement of all the leading astronomical facts and theories. In a note at the end of the later editions occurs the famous Nebular Hypothesis. In 1784 Laplace issued his *Théorie des planètes*, and in 1812–14–20 his *Théorie analytique des probabilités*. The last remains a classic to algebraists. His *Oeuvres complètes* were issued by the Academy (14 vols. 1878–1912).

LAPPENBERG, Johann Martin (1794–1865), German historian, born in Hamburg, was keeper of the archives there for forty years, wrote histories of England, the Hanse towns, Heligoland, the Steelyard in London, &c. See Memoir by Meyer (1867).

LAPWORTH, Charles (1842–1920), British geologist, born at Farringdon, was a schoolteacher at Galashiels and did important work in elucidating the geology of the south of Scotland and also of the northwest Highlands. He was professor of Geology at Birmingham 1881–1913 and wrote especially on graptolites. The term Ordovician was introduced by him. He became a fellow of the Royal Society in 1888.

LA RAMÉE. See OUIDA.

LARDNER, (1) Dionysius (1793–1859), Irish scientific writer, born in Dublin, attracted attention by works on algebraic geometry (1823) and the calculus (1825), but is best known as the originator and editor of *Lardner's Cyclopaedia* (132 vols. 1830–44), followed by the historical *Cabinet Library* (12 vols. 1830–32), and *Museum of Science and Art* (12 vols. 1854–56). In 1840 he went to the United States and gave lectures there until in 1845 he went to Paris. He died in Naples.

(2) **Nathaniel** (1684–1768), English Nonconformist (ultimately Unitarian) divine and biblical scholar, was born and died at Hawkhurst in Kent. See Life by Kippis prefixed to his works (11 vols. 1788).

LARGILLIÈRE, Nicolas, *lar-zheel-yer* (1656–1746), French portrait painter, was born and died in Paris, having lived for some years in England where he was Lely's assistant. He was one of the most popular portraitists of his day.

LARIVEY, Pierre (*c.* 1550–1612), French dramatist of Italian descent, as the introducer of Italian-style comedy to the French stage foreshadowed Molière and Regnard. His licentious *Comédies facétieuses* (2 vols.;

1579, 1611) were adaptations of existing Italian pieces.

LARKIN, (1) **James** (1876–1947), Irish Labour leader, born in Liverpool, was organizer of the Irish Transport and General Workers' Union. Deported from U.S.A. in 1923 for his anarchistic activities, he continued at the head of the I.T. and G.W.U., organizing strikes and fostering strife until expelled in 1924. He was Ireland's representative at the Third International, but later gave up Communism, continuing as an extreme Labour leader.

(2) **Philip** (1922–), English poet and novelist, librarian of Hull University. His collections of poems include *The North Ship* (1945), *The Less Deceived* (1955), *The Whitsun Weddings* (1964). In 1965 he won the Queen's Gold Medal for Poetry.

LA ROCHEFOUCAULD, François, 6th Duc de, *rosh-foo-kō* (1613–80), French writer, born at Paris, devoted himself to the cause of the queen in opposition to Richelieu, and became entangled in a series of love adventures and political intrigues, the result being that he was forced to live in exile from 1639 to 1642. About 1645 he formed a liaison with Mme de Longueville. He then joined the Frondeurs and was wounded at the siege of Paris. In 1652, wounded again, he retired to the country. On Mazarin's death in 1661 he repaired to the court of Louis XIV, and about the same time began his liaison with Mme de Sablé. A surreptitious edition of his *Mémoires*, written in retirement, was published in 1662; as it gave wide offence he disavowed its authorship. His *Réflexions, ou sentences et maximes morales*, appeared in 1665. His last years were brightened by his friendship with Mme de La Fayette, which lasted until he died. For brevity, clearness and finish of style the *Maxims* could hardly be excelled. Their author was a remorseless analyst of man's character, tracks out self-love in its most elusive forms and under its cunningest disguises, and forgets that self-love is not the sole motive by which men are impelled. The best edition of La Rochefoucauld's works is that by D. L. Gilbert and J. Gourdault (1868–84). See work in German by Rahstede (Brunswick 1888) and French by Bourdeau (1895), and *Les Maximes*, ed. F. C. Green (1945).

LAROCHEJAQUELEIN, Du Verger de, *la-rosh-zhak-lī*, an old noble family named from a place in Poitou:

(1) **Henri, Comte de** (1772–94), after August 10, 1792, headed the insurgent royalists in La Vendée. He for a time successfully repelled the republican forces, but was defeated on December 21, 1793. He raised a new body of troops, but was killed at Nouaillé.

(2) **Louis du Verger, Marquis de** (1777–1815), brother of (1), emigrated at the Revolution, returned to France in 1801, and in 1813 headed the royalists in La Vendée. Louis XVIII gave him in 1814 the command of the army of La Vendée, where, during the Hundred Days, he maintained the royalist cause, supported by the British. He fell at Pont-des-Mathis.

(3) **Marie Louise Victoire** (1772–1857), wife of (2), published valuable *Mémoires* of the war (1815). See her Life by Mrs Maxwell Scott (1911).

LAROUSSE, Pierre Athanase (1817–75), French lexicographer, born at Toucy in Yonne, edited the *Grand dictionnaire universel* (15 vols. 1864–76).

LARRA, Mariano José de (1809–37), Spanish poet, satirist and political writer, was born at Madrid. As a journalist he was unequalled and he published two periodicals between 1828 and 1833, but it was as a satirist that he became well known. His prose writings are masterly and include *El Doncel de Don Enrique el Doliente* (1834), a novel, *Macías* (1834), a play and adaptations of French plays. See Life by I. S. Estevan (1934).

LARREY, Jean Dominique, Baron, *la-ray* (1766–1842), French surgeon, born at Beaudéan near Bagnères-de-Bigorre, served as a naval surgeon, and in 1793 joining the army, introduced the 'flying ambulance' service. From 1797 he accompanied Napoleon in his campaigns, became head of the army medical department, and a baron. He wrote on army surgery and the treatment of wounds. See German memoir by Werner (1885).

LARSSON, Lars Erik (1908–), Swedish composer, he was a student in Stockholm and in Vienna, where Alban Berg was his master. He has written three symphonies, an opera *The Princess of Cyprus*, a cantata *The Disguised God*, a saxophone concerto and music for the stage and films.

LA SALLE, (1) **Antoine de** (*c.* 1398–1470), French writer, born in Burgundy or Touraine, lived at the courts of Provence and Flanders, and wrote *Chronique du petit Jehan de Saintré*, a knightly romance *Quinze joyes de mariage*, and was the reputed author of *Cent nouvelles nouvelles*.

(2) **Jean Baptiste, Abbé de** (1651–1719), French educational reformer, born at Rheims, set up schools for the poor, training colleges for teachers, and reformatories, and was the founder in 1684 of the Brothers of Christian Schools. He was canonized in 1900. See W. J. Battersby, *De la Salle Education* (1948).

(3) **Robert Cavelier, Sieur de** (1643–87), French explorer was born at Rouen, and, having settled in Canada at twenty-three, descended the Ohio and Mississippi to the sea (1682). Two years later an expedition was fitted out to establish a French settlement on the Gulf of Mexico. But La Salle spent two years in fruitless journeys, while his harshness embittered his followers, and he was assassinated. See works by Parkman (q.v.), and Life by R. Syme (1953).

LASCARIS, (1) **Constantine** (d. 1493 or 1501), Greek grammarian who, after the capture of Constantinople by the Turks, fled to Italy, and revived the study of Greek at Rome, Naples and Messina, where he died. His Greek grammar (1476) was the first Greek book printed in Italy. His library is now in the Escorial. See A. F. Villemain, *Lascaris ou les Grecs du 15e siècle* (1825).

(2) **John** or **Janus,** called **Rhyndacenus** (*c.* 1445–1535) collected MSS. for Lorenzo dei Medici, taught Greek, and on Lorenzo's

death went to Paris, and finally was employed in literary work and diplomatic missions to France and Venice by Leo X. He died at Rome. He edited Greek classics, and wrote grammars, letters and epigrams. See works by Villemain (1825), Vast (1878) and P. de Nolhac (1886), and J. E. Sandys, *History of Classical Scholarship* (1902–08).

LAS CASAS, Bartolomé de (1474–1566), the 'Apostle of the Indians', was born at Seville. He sailed in the third voyage of Columbus, and in 1502 went to Hispaniola. Eight years later he was ordained to the priesthood. In 1511 he accompanied Diego Velázquez to Cuba, assisted in the pacification of the island, and was rewarded by a commandery of Indians. But soon love for, and a desire to protect and defend the natives, made him give up his own slaves, and he went to Spain, where he prevailed on Cardinal Ximenes to send a commission of inquiry to the West Indies. He revisited Spain to secure stronger measures; and finally, to prevent the extirpation of the natives, he proposed that the colonists should be permitted to import negro slaves—a proposal only too readily acceded to. He also attempted to carry out Castilian peasants as colonists, but failed, and spent eight years (1522–30) in a convent in Hispaniola. In 1530 he again visited Spain, and, after missionary travels in Mexico, Nicaragua, Peru and Guatemala, returned to devote four years to the cause of the Indians, writing his *Veynte Razones* and *Brevísima Relación*. Appointed Bishop of Chiapa, he was received (1544) with hostility by the colonists, returned to Spain, and resigned his see (1547). He still contended with the authorities in favour of the Indians until his death in Madrid. His most important work is the unfinished *Historia de las Indias* (1875–76). See Life by Sir A. Helps (1868) and study by F. A. MacNutt (1909).

LAS CASES, Emmanuel Dieudonné, Comte de, *kahz* (1766–1842), French historian, born at Las Cases, Haute Garonne, was a lieutenant in the navy, but fled to England at the Revolution. His *Atlas historique* (1803–04) gave him a European reputation. Though a royalist by birth, he was so fascinated by Napoleon's genius that he insisted on sharing his exile. Deported to the Cape by Sir Hudson Lowe in 1816, he returned to Europe, and published (1821–23) the *Mémorial de Sainte-Hélène*, which caused an immense sensation.

LASCO, Johannes a, or Jan Łaski (*c.* 1499–1560), Polish reformer, was highly born at Lask, Piotrkow. He was ordained priest in 1521, and in 1523 at Basel came in contact with Erasmus and Farel. Caught in the current of the Reformation, he left home in 1538 and about 1540 moved to East Friesland, where he established a presbyterian form of church government as superintendent at Emden. In 1550, on Cranmer's invitation, he became head of a congregation of Protestant refugees in London. Mary's accession in 1553 drove him back to Emden, and he finally returned to Poland in 1556. See Dalton's unfinished *John a Lasco* (Eng. trans. from the German, 1886), and Pascal's *Jean de Lasco* (Paris 1894).

LASHLEY, Karl Spencer (1890–1958), American psychologist, born at Davis, Virginia, research professor of neuropsychology at Harvard (1937). In 1942 he became director of Yerkes laboratories of primate biology at Orange Park, Florida. A specialist in genetic psychology, he made valuable contributions to the study of localization of brain function. His writings include *Brain Mechanisms and Intelligence* (1929).

LASKER, (1) Eduard (1829–84), Prussian Liberal politician, was born of Jewish parentage in Posen. He was one of the founders of the National Liberal party and is important chiefly for the codification of the laws of Germany, for which he was largely responsible. He died at New York on a visit to America.

(2) **Emanuel** (1868–1941), German chess-player and mathematician, born at Berlinchen, Prussia, held the world's championship 1894–1921, 1924–25. See Life by Hannak (1959).

LASKI, (1) Harold Joseph (1893–1950), English political scientist and socialist, born, a Jew, at Manchester. He was educated at Manchester Grammar School and New College, Oxford, and lectured at McGill University (1914–16), Harvard (1916–20), Amherst (1917) and Yale (1919–20, 1931). In 1920 he joined the staff of the London School of Economics, and became professor of Political Science in 1926. He was chairman of the Labour party (1945–46). Laski was a brilliant talker and as lecturer at the London School of Economics had a great influence over his students, who revered him. His political philosophy was a modified Marxism. He had a strong belief in individual freedom, but the downfall of the Labour government in 1931 forced him to feel that some revolution in Britain was necessary. His works include *Authority in the Modern State* (1919), *A Grammar of Politics* (1925), *Liberty in the Modern State* (1930) and *The American Presidency* (1940). See *Holmes-Laski Letters*, ed. M. de Wolfe Howe (2 vols. 1953) and Life by Kingsley Martin (1953).

(2) **Jan.** See LASCO.

(3) **Marghanita** (1915–), English-Jewish novelist and critic, born in Manchester and educated at Oxford. Her first novel, *Love on the Supertax*, appeared in 1944, and she has written extensively for newspapers and reviews. Her later novels include *Little Boy Lost* (1949) and *The Victorian Chaise-longue* (1953). In 1959 she wrote a play *The Offshore Island*. She married John E. Howard in 1937.

LASSALLE, Ferdinand (1825–64), German social democrat, was born, the son of a rich Jewish merchant, at Breslau. A disciple of Hegel, he wrote a work on Heraclitus (published 1858), and in Paris made the acquaintance of Heine. On his return to Berlin he met in 1844–45 the Countess Sophie Hatzfeld (1805–81), a lady at variance with her husband, prosecuted her cause before thirty-six tribunals, and after eight years of litigation forced the husband to a compromise favourable to the countess. He took part in the revolution of 1848, and for an inflammatory speech got six months in prison. He lived in the Rhine country till 1857, when he returned to Berlin, and wrote his *System der erworbenen Rechte* (1861). At Leipzig he founded the Universal German Workingmen's Association to agitate for universal suffrage. In 1863–64 he tried to win the Rhineland and Berlin to his cause; in his *Bastiat-Schulze, or Capital and Labour*, he attacked Schulze-Delitzsch, the representative of Liberalism. In 1864 Lassalle met Helene von Dönniges, and they resolved to marry in spite of the strongest opposition from her parents. Under pressure from them she renounced Lassalle in favour of the Wallachian Count Racowitza. Lassalle sent to both father and lover a challenge, which was accepted by the latter and at Geneva he fell mortally wounded, and died two days afterwards. He taught that Europe's historical development is to culminate in a democracy of labour, in which political interests shall be subservient to social—the social democracy. See the Memoirs (1879) and *Autobiography* (trans. 1910) of Helene von Racowitza (who committed suicide in 1911); works by Brandes (trans. 1911), W. H. Dawson (1888), Bernstein (trans. 1893), Seillière (1897), Oncken (1904), Rosenbaum (1911), Mayer (1921–25), Footman (1946); Meredith's *Tragic Comedians* (ed. with Lassalle bibliography by C. K. Shorter, 1891); Lassalle's Diary (Breslau 1891).

LASSELL, William (1799–1880), British astronomer, born at Bolton, built an observatory at Starfield near Liverpool, where he constructed and mounted equatorial reflecting telescopes. He discovered several planetary satellites, including Triton and Hyperion (at the same time as W. C. Bond of Harvard). At Malta with a larger reflecting telescope he made observations (1861–65); and then settled near Maidenhead.

LASSEN, Christian (1800–76), Norwegian orientalist, born at Bergen, assisted Schlegel and Eugène Burnouf, and was professor of Ancient Indian Languages at Bonn from 1830 till he became blind in 1864. Amongst his most important books are works on Persian cuneiforms (1836–45), the Greek Kings in Bactria (1838), Prakrit (1837), and Indian civilization (1844–61).

LASSUS, Orlandus, or **Orlando di Lasso** (*c.* 1532–94), Netherlands musician, born at Mons, composer of many masses, motets, &c. He died at Munich, having visited Italy, England and France, and been ennobled by Maximilian II in 1570. Unlike Palestrina, his contemporary, he wrote not only church music but also a vast number of secular works, and ranks as one of the greatest composers of early times. See Lives by Declève (Mons 1894), Destouches (Munich 1894), Schnitz (1915) and Van den Borren (3rd ed. 1930).

LÁSZLÓ, Sir Philip, properly **Philip Alexius László de Lombos,** *lahs'lō* (1869–1937), portrait painter, born at Budapest. He studied at Budapest, Munich and Paris, and came to England in 1907, being naturalized in 1914. During his lifetime he gained an international reputation as a painter of royalty and heads of states, e.g., Edward VII, Theodore Roosevelt and Lord Roberts.

LATHAM, (1) **John,** M.D. (1740–1837), English ornithologist, one of the founders of the Linnaean Society, born at Eltham, lived from 1796 at Romsey.

(2) **Robert Gordon** (1812–88), English ethnologist and philologist, was born at Billingborough vicarage, Lincolnshire. From Eton he passed in 1829 to King's College, Cambridge, of which he was elected fellow. From 1842 (when he took his M.D.) to 1849 he held appointments in London hospitals; in 1839 he became professor of English in University College London, a tour six years before in Denmark and Norway having directed his attention to Scandinavian philology. The author of textbooks on English language, philology and etymology, he revised Johnson's Dictionary (1870), and wrote also on the ethnology of the British Isles and Europe. In *Elements of Comparative Philology* (1862) he advanced the view that the Aryan race originated in Europe. In 1863 he received a government pension of £100. He died at Putney.

LATIMER, Hugh (*c.* 1485–1555), English Protestant martyr, was born, a yeoman's son, at Thurcaston, near Leicester. He was sent to Cambridge, in 1510 was elected a fellow of Clare, and was in 1522 appointed a university preacher. In 1524 for his B.D. thesis he delivered a philippic against Melanchthon, for he was, in his own words, 'as obstinate a papist as any in England'. Next year, however, through Bilney (q.v.), he 'began to smell the Word of God, forsaking the school doctors and such fooleries', and soon becoming noted as a zealous preacher of the reformed doctrines. One of the Cambridge divines appointed to examine the lawfulness of Henry's marriage, he declared on the king's side; and he was made chaplain to Anne Boleyn and rector of West Kington in Wiltshire. In 1535 he was consecrated Bishop of Worcester and at the opening of Convocation in June 1536 he preached two powerful sermons urging on the Reformation. As that work rather retrograded him, out of favour at court he retired to his diocese, and laboured there in a continual round of 'teaching, preaching, exhorting, writing, correcting and reforming'. Twice during Henry's reign he was sent to the Tower, in 1539 and 1546, on the former occasion resigning his bishopric. At Edward VI's accession he declined to resume his episcopal functions, but devoted himself to preaching and practical works of benevolence. Under Mary he was (1554) examined at Oxford, and committed to jail. In September 1555, with Ridley and Cranmer, he was found guilty of heresy, and on October 16 was burned with Ridley opposite Balliol College. His powerful, homely, humorous sermons, letters, &c., were edited, with a memoir, by Corrie (2 vols. 1844–45). See Lives by Gilpin (1755), Demaus (1869; new ed. 1922), R. M. and A. J. Carlyle (1899), and works by Darby (1953) and Chester (1954).

LATINI, Brunetto, *la-tee'nee* (*c.* 1210–*c.* 1295), a Florentine statesman, author during his banishment to France of the encyclopaedic *Livres dou Trésor,* as also of an Italian poem.

LA TOUCHE, Gaston, *la-toosh* (1854–1913), French painter and engraver, born at St Cloud, was a pupil of Manet.

LATOUR, Maurice Quentin de, *la-toor* (1704–1788), French pastellist and portrait painter, was born and died at St Quentin. His best works include portraits of Madame de Pompadour, Voltaire and Rousseau.

LA TOUR, Georges de, *la toor* (1593–1652), French artist, born at Vic-sur-Seille. He was identified about 1915, some of his works having been previously attributed to Le Nain and followers of Caravaggio. His works are mainly dramatically-lighted religious paintings, for example, the *St Jerome* and *St Joseph* in the Louvre. Only fourteen of his works are known. See study by P. Jamot (Paris 1942).

LA TOUR D'AUVERGNE, Théophile Malo Corret de, *la toor dō-vern'y'* (1743–1800), French soldier, born at Carhaix in Finistère, enlisted in 1767, distinguished himself at Port Mahon in 1782, steadily refused advancement and was killed, a simple captain, at Oberhausen in Bavaria. His remains were interred in the Panthéon in 1889. French biographies are full of instances of his valour, Spartan simplicity and chivalrous affection. He was known as the 'First Grenadier of France'. He wrote a book on the Breton language and antiquities.

LATREILLE, Pierre André, *la-tray* (1762–1833), French entomologist, was born at Brives in Corrèze, and died professor of Natural History at Paris. He is best known for his work on the classification of insects and crustaceans.

LATTRE DE TASSIGNY, Jean de, *tas-seen-yee* (1889–1952), French general, was born at Mouilleron-en-Pareds, was educated at the Jesuit College at Poitiers and St Cyr, and commanded an infantry battalion during World War I, was wounded four times and decorated with the Croix de Guerre. By 1940 he commanded the 14th division in rearguard actions against the advancing Germans, was sent by the Vichy government to command in Tunisia, recalled for sympathy with the Allies and arrested in 1942 for resisting the German occupation of the neutral zone. He escaped from Rion prison in 1943, was secretly flown by an R.A.F. plane to London, and later he took a brilliant part in the Allied liberation of France 1944–45, signing the German surrender. He was responsible for the reorganization of the French army and was appointed c.-in-c. of Western Union Land Forces under Montgomery in 1948. In 1950 he successfully turned the tide against the Vietminh rebels, by introducing novel tactics as c.-in-c. in French Indo-China. He was posthumously made a Marshal of France in 1952.

LATUDE, Henri Masers de (1725–1805), French artillery officer who sought to secure Madame de Pompadour's favour by revealing a plot to poison her. The plot was of his own contriving, and he was sent without trial to the Bastille in 1749. He made three daring but futile escapes from prison, and was at last released in 1777, on condition that he lived in his native village of Montagnac in Languedoc. Lingering in Paris, he was reimprisoned till 1784. At the Revolution he was treated as a victim of despotism and voted a pension. See monograph by Thiéry (1792; re-edited by Bertin 1889).

LAUBE, Heinrich, *low'bė* (1806–84), German playwright and manager, was born at Sprottau in Silesia and died in Vienna. He was one of the leaders of the 'Young Germany' movement and editor of *Die elegante Welt*, its literary organ. He was director of Vienna's Burgtheater, 1850–67, and among his writings are works on the theatre, on historical themes, novels such as *Das junge Europa* (1833–37), *Die Karlsschüler* (1847), a drama of the young Schiller, and a biography of Grillparzer. See *Gesammelte Werke*, ed. H. H. Houben (50 vols., 1908–10), J. Proelss, *Das junge Deutschland* (1892), H. H. Houben, *Laubes Leben und Schriften* (1906), M. Krammer, *H. Laube* (1926).

LAUD, William (1573–1645), Archbishop of Canterbury, was born at Reading, a well-to-do clothier's son. From Reading free school he passed at sixteen to St John's College, Oxford, of which four years later he became a fellow. Ordained in 1601, he made himself obnoxious to the university authorities by his open antipathy to the dominant Puritanism; but his solid learning, his amazing industry, his administrative capacity, his sincere and unselfish churchmanship, soon won him friends and patrons. One of these was Charles Blount, Earl of Devonshire, whom in 1605 Laud married to the divorced Lady Rich (an offence that always was heavy on his conscience); another was Buckingham, to whom he became confessor in 1622, having a month previously disputed before him and the countess his mother with Fisher the Jesuit. Meanwhile he rose steadily from preferment to preferment—incumbent of five livings (1607–10), D.D. (1608), president of his old college and king's chaplain (1611), prebendary of Lincoln (1614), Archdeacon of Huntingdon (1615), Dean of Gloucester (1616), prebendary of Westminster and Bishop of St Davids (1621), Bishop of Bath and Wells, Dean of the Chapel Royal, and a privy councillor (1626), Bishop of London (1628), Chancellor of Oxford (1630), and finally Archbishop of Canterbury (1633), in the very week that he received two offers of a cardinal's hat. Already, after Buckingham's assassination, he had virtually become the first minister of the crown, one with Strafford and Charles I in the triumvirate whose aim was absolutism in church and state. Laud's task was to raise the Church of England to its rightful position of a branch of the Church Catholic, to root out Calvinism in England and Presbyterianism in Scotland. In the former country he drew up a list of 'Orthodox' and 'Puritan' ministers, whom he proceeded to separate by scolding, suspending, depriving. Freedom of worship was withdrawn from Walloon and French refugees; Englishmen abroad were forbidden to attend Calvinistic services; and at home 'gospel preaching', justification by faith, and Sabbatarianism were to be superseded by an elaborate ritual, by the doctrine of the real presence, celibacy and confession, and by the Book of Sports—changes rigorously enforced by the court of High Commission and the Star Chamber. In Scotland Laud's attempt (1635–37) to Anglicize the Scottish Church gave birth to the riot in St Giles', Edinburgh, that riot to the Covenant, the Covenant to the 'Bishops' war', and this to the meeting of the Long Parliament, which on December 18, 1640, impeached the archbishop of treason, and ten weeks later sent him to the Tower. He would not escape (Grotius urged him to do so); and at last, after a tedious and complicated trial before a handful of peers, on December 17, 1644, he was voted 'guilty of endeavouring to subvert the laws, to overthrow the Protestant religion, and to act as an enemy to Parliament'. The judges declared that this was not treason; but under an unconstitutional ordinance of attainder, he was beheaded on Tower Hill. Of Laud's works (7 vols. Anglo-Catholic Library, 1847–60) the most interesting is his Diary, published in 1694. Peter Heylin, Laud's chaplain, first wrote his biography, *Cyprianus Anglicanus* (1668); and there are also Lives by Le Bas (1836), Mozley (1845; republished in *Essays*, 1878), Hook (*Archbishops*, 1875), A. C. Benson (1887), Simpkinson (1894), W. H. Hutton (1895), Duncan-Jones (1927) and H. R. Trevor-Roper (1940).

LAUDER, (1) Sir Harry (1870–1950), Scottish comic singer, born at Portobello, started his career on the music hall stage as an Irish comedian, but made his name as a singer of Scots songs, many of which were of his own composition, e.g., *Roamin' in the Gloamin'*. He was knighted in 1919 for his work in organizing entertainments for the troops during the 1914–18 war. His appeal was by no means confined to Scottish audiences; almost his biggest successes were on the stages of London's famous music halls and his popularity abroad was immense, especially in the United States and the Commonwealth countries, which he toured almost every year after 1907. He wrote volumes of memoirs, the best known of which is *Roamin' in the Gloamin'* (1928).

(2) **Robert Scott** (1803–69), Scottish painter, born at Silvermills, Edinburgh, in 1829 became R.S.A. He lived in Italy and at Munich in 1833–38, then in London till 1849, when he returned to Edinburgh. Sir Walter Scott's novels provided him with subjects for his most successful paintings.

(3) **Sir Thomas Dick** (1784–1848), Scottish writer, eldest son of Sir Andrew Lauder of Fountainhall, served in the Cameron Highlanders, married in 1808 the heiress of Relugas in Morayshire, succeeded to the baronetcy in 1820, and lived at the Grange, Edinburgh, from 1832 until his death. He was secretary to the Board of Scottish Manufactures (1839–1848). Lauder wrote two romances, *Lochandhu* (1825) and *The Wolfe of Badenoch* (1827), but his best works are his *Morayshire Floods* (1830) and unfinished *Scottish Rivers*, which appeared in *Tait's Magazine*, 1847–49. His *Legendary Tales of the Highlands* (1841) may also be mentioned. He was a Liberal, and of unwearying public spirit. See Dr John Brown's preface to the reprint of *Scottish Rivers* (1874).

(4) **William** (*c.* 1680–1771), Scottish one-legged scholar, who sought in 1747–50 by impudent forgeries to prove Milton a plagiarist. He died poor in Barbados.

LAUDERDALE, John Maitland, Duke of (1616–82), Scottish statesman, was born at Lethington (now Lennoxlove) near Haddington. He displayed ardent zeal for the Covenant, and in 1643 was a Scottish commissioner at the Westminster Assembly. He succeeded his father as second Earl of Lauderdale in 1645, was taken prisoner at Worcester in 1651, and lay nine years in the Tower, at Windsor and at Portland. At the Restoration he became Scottish secretary of state, and for the first seven years he was engaged in an incessant struggle to maintain his place against rivals. His main object was to bring about the absolute power of the crown in church and state, and for this end he laboured with unceasing persistence. He formed a militia of 20,000 men, and drilled the Episcopal Church into complete subservience. A member of the privy council, he had a seat in the Cabal ministry, and was created duke in 1672. Fresh intrigues against him (1674) were foiled by his own ability and the king's regard for him. In May 1678 a vote was carried in the Commons praying for Lauderdale's removal from the royal presence for ever; but through corrupt practices, it was thrown out by a single vote. Another short struggle with Hamilton in the Convention of Estates left him again triumphant for two years more. It seems probable that many of Lauderdale's harsher measures, especially towards Scotland, were due not so much to personal ambition but to his inability to suffer gladly the follies and indiscretions of his much less astute contemporaries. His dukedom died with him in 1682, while the earldom passed to his brother. See Airy's selection (Camden Society 1884–85) from Lauderdale MSS., and Life (1923) by Mackenzie.

LAUE, Max von, *low'ė* (1879–1960), German physicist, born near Koblenz, was professor at Zürich, Frankfurt and Berlin. He did good work in relativity and X-rays, and was a Nobel prizeman in physics (1914). He was later appointed director of the Kaiser Wilhelm Institute for Theoretical Physics.

LAUGHTON, *law'tėn,* (1) **Charles** (1899–1962), English actor, born at Scarborough, became U.S. citizen in 1950. He first appeared on the stage in 1926 and his parts included Ephikhodov in *The Cherry Orchard*, Mr Crispin in *A Man with Red Hair*, Poirot in *Alibi* and William Marble in *Payment Deferred*. He appeared with the Old Vic Company, played in and produced Shaw's *Don Juan in Hell* and *Major Barbara*, and as a Shakespearean actor gave fine performances in, among others, *Macbeth*, *Measure for Measure* and *King Lear*. He began to act in films in 1932 and his great dramatic sense and technique made memorable such rôles as Henry VIII in *The Private Life of Henry VIII*, Mr Barrett in *The Barretts of Wimpole Street* and Bligh in *Mutiny on the Bounty*.

(2) **Sir John Knox** (1830–1915), English naval historian, born in Liverpool, became professor of Modern History at King's

College in 1883. His books include *Studies in Naval History* (1887), *Defeat of the Spanish Armada* (1894) and *Nelson* (1895).

LAURENCIN, Marie, *lō-rā-sī* (1885–1957), French artist, born in Paris. She exhibited in the Salon des Indépendents in 1907. Best known for her portraits of women in misty pastel colours, she also illustrated many books with water colours and lithographs.

LAURENS, *lō-rās,* (1) **Henri** (1885–1954), French painter and sculptor, born in Paris, a leading exponent of three-dimensional Cubism.

(2) **Jean Paul** (1838–1921), French historical painter, was born at Fourquevaux. A painter of scenes and subjects from church history, he was called the Benedictine.

LAURENT, Auguste (1807–53), French chemist, born at La Folie, Haute Marne, spent most of his life in poverty and died of tuberculosis. After eight years as professor in Bordeaux he went to Paris to work with Gerhardt (q.v.). Ignored by his fellow-scientists, he was forced by financial difficulties to become assayer at the Mint. He propounded the nucleus theory of organic radicals, discovered anthracine, worked on the classification of organic compounds and gave his name to ' Laurent's Acid '. His very valuable *Méthode de chimie* was published posthumously in 1854.

LAURIER, Sir Wilfrid (1841–1919), Canadian statesman, born at St Lin, Quebec, shone at the Canadian bar and in 1877 was minister of inland revenue in the Liberal ministry. In 1891 he became leader of the Liberal party and prime minister in 1896. He was the first French-Canadian and also the first Roman Catholic to be premier of Canada. In 1911 his government was defeated on the question of commercial reciprocity with the United States, but he remained Liberal leader. Though he had a strong feeling for Empire, Laurier was a firm supporter of self-government for Canada. During World War I his party was divided on the conscription question, Laurier being against conscription though entirely in agreement with Canada's entering the war. In his home policy he was an advocate of free trade, passed many reforms to benefit the working classes and helped to plan a transcontinental railway, the Grand Trunk. See O. D. Skelton, *Life and Letters of Sir Wilfrid Laurier* (2 vols. 1921).

LAURISTON, Alexandre Jacques Bernard Law, Marquis de, *lō-rees-tō* (1768–1828), French soldier, born at Pondicherry, was a grand-nephew of John Law (q.v.), the financier. He was Napoleon's comrade at the Artillery School, filled diplomatic appointments at Copenhagen and London, held high commands at Wagram (1809) and in the retreat from Moscow (1812), fought at Bautzen (1813) and Katzbach, and was taken prisoner at Leipzig. Already ennobled, he was made a peer by Louis XVIII, became marquis in 1817 and marshal in 1821.

LAUZUN, Antonin Nompar de Caumont, Duc de, *lō-zœ̃* (1633–1723), Gascon soldier, who in 1688 conducted Mary of Modena on her flight from London to Paris. He was imprisoned by Louis XIV for his affair with Mme de Montpensier, whom he may have wed secretly. See Lives by Duc de la Force (1913) and M. F. Sandars (1908), and V. Sackville-West, *Daughter of France* (1959). Armand Louis de Gontaut, Duc de Biron (q.v.), also bore the title of Duc de Lauzun.

LAVAL, (1) **Carl Gustaf Patrik de** (1845–1913), Swedish engineer, born at Orsa, invented a steam turbine and a centrifugal cream separator. He died at Stockholm.

(2) **Pierre** (1883–1945), French politician, born at Châteldon (Puy-de-Dôme), became an advocate, deputy (1914), senator (1926), premier (1931–32, 1935–36). From Socialism he moved to the Right, and in the Vichy government was Pétain's deputy (1940), rival and prime minister (1942–44), when he openly collaborated with the Germans. Fleeing after the liberation, from France to Germany and Spain, he was brought back, condemned to death as a collaborationist and executed in 1945. See study by Thomson (1951).

LAVALETTE, Antoine Marie Chamans, Comte de (1769–1830), French politician and Napoleonic general, who served in the Alps, was aide-de-camp to Napoleon and, after the war, French minister to Saxony, postmaster general and a councillor of state. After the second Bourbon restoration (1815) he was condemned to death, but escaped by changing clothes with his wife, a niece of the Empress Josephine.

LA VALLIÈRE, Louise Françoise de Labaume Leblanc, Duchesse de, *la val-yayr* (1644–1710), born at Tours, was brought to court by her mother, became Louis XIV's mistress in 1661 and bore him four children. When Madame de Montespan superseded her she retired to a Carmelite nunnery in Paris (1674). *Réflexions sur la miséricorde de Dieu par une dame pénitente* (1680) is attributed to her. See her Letters; Lives by Lair (trans. 1908), Trouncer (1936), and J. Sanders, *The Devoted Mistress* (1959).

LAVAL-MONTMORENCY, François Xavier, *-mō-mō-rā-see* (1622–1708), French missionary, was sent as Vicar Apostolic to Quebec in 1659. Laval University was named after him.

LAVATER, Johann Kaspar (1741–1801), Swiss physiognomist, theologian and poet, born at Zürich, in 1769 received Protestant orders. He made himself known by a volume of poems, *Schweizerlieder* (1767). His *Aussichten in die Ewigkeit* (1768–78) is characterized by religious enthusiasm and mysticism. He attempted to elevate physiognomy into a science in his *Physiognomische Fragmente* (1775–78; trans. by Holcroft 1793). Whilst tending the wounded at the capture of Zürich by Masséna (September 1799) he received a wound, of which he later died.

LAVELEYE, Émile Louis Victor de, *lav-lay* (1822–92), Belgian economist, born at Bruges, in 1864 became professor of Political Economy at Liège. His works include *De la propriété* (1874; trans. 1878); *Le Socialisme contemporain* (1881; trans. 1885); *Éléments d'économie politique* (1882); &c. He was made a baron just before his death. See Life by Count Goblet d'Alviella (1894).

LAVER, James (1899–), English writer and art critic, born in Liverpool, in 1921 was awarded the Newdigate prize for verse at Oxford, and later books of verse include *His Last Sebastian* (1922) and *Ladies' Mistakes* (1933). In 1922 he was appointed an assistant keeper at the Victoria and Albert Museum and in 1927 a keeper, retiring in 1959. He has written several books of art criticism, e.g., *French Painting and the 19th century* (1937) and *Fragonard* (1956), and has made a substantial contribution to the history of English costume with such books as *Taste and Fashion* (1937), *Fashions and Fashion Plates* (1943), *Children's Costume in the 19th Century* (1951), &c.

LAVERAN, Charles Louis Alphonse, *lav-rã* (1845–1922), French physician and parasitologist, born and educated at Paris, became professor of Military Medicine and Epidemic Diseases at the military college of Val de Grâce (1874–78) and again (1884–94). He studied malaria in Algeria (1878–83), discovering in 1880 the blood parasite which caused the disease. He also did important work on other diseases including sleeping-sickness and kala-azar. From 1896 until his death he was at the Pasteur Institute at Paris. In 1907 he was awarded the Nobel prize for physiology and medicine.

LAVERY, Sir John (1856–1941), Irish painter, born at Belfast, studied in Glasgow, London and Paris. He was a portrait painter of the Glasgow school and his work enjoyed great popularity, especially his paintings of women. Elected R.S.A. in 1896, R.A. in 1921, he was knighted in 1918. He wrote a lively autobiography, *The Life of a Painter* (1940). See W. Shaw-Sparrow, *John Lavery and his Work* (1912).

LAVIGERIE, Charles Martial Allemand, Cardinal, *la-veezh-ree* (1825–92), born at Bayonne, in 1863 was made Bishop of Nancy, in 1867 Archbishop of Algiers. He became well-known for his missionary work in Africa and he founded the order of the White Fathers. See Clarke's *Cardinal Lavigerie and the African Slave-trade* (1890), and French Lives by Préville (1894) and Lavigerie (1896).

LAVISSE, Ernest, *la-vees* (1842–1922), French historian, born at Nouvion-en-Thiérache, Aisne. He taught history to the son of Napoleon III and was professor of History at the Sorbonne, where he completely changed the teaching methods. In 1892 he was elected to the Academy, edited the *Revue de Paris* (1894) and became director of the École normale supérieure (1902–20). He wrote works on Prussian history after visiting Germany, but is perhaps best known for the immense history which he published in collaboration with Rambaud, *Histoire générale du IVe siècle à nos jours* (1893–1900). Then came *Histoire de France depuis les origines jusqu'à la Revolution* (9 vols. 1903–11) and *Histoire contemporaine* (10 vols. completed 1922).

LAVOISIER, Antoine Laurent, *la-vwaz-yay* (1743–94), French chemist, born at Paris. To obtain means for his investigations, he accepted in 1768 the office of farmer general of taxes and in that year was also made an Academician. As director of the government powder mills, he (1775) greatly improved gunpowder, its supply and manufacture, and successfully applied chemistry to agriculture. Regarded as the founder of modern chemistry, he discovered oxygen, by rightly interpreting Priestley's facts, its importance in respiration, combustion and as a compound with metals. His *Traité elémentaire de chimie* (1789) was a masterpiece. Politically Liberal, he saw the great necessity for reform in France but was against revolutionary methods. But despite a lifetime of work for the state, inquiring into the problems of taxation, which he helped to reform, hospitals and prisons, he was guillotined as a farmer of taxes. See Lives by Grimaux (1888), Berthelot (1890), Cochrane (1931) and McKie (1952).

LA VOISIN, *vwa-zĩ* (?–1680), French poisoner, whose real name was **Catherine Monvoison.** She amassed riches by concocting potions and selling them to the ladies at the court of Louis XIV. When the poison plots were discovered in 1679 involving such well-known figures as the Duchess Mancini and Mme de Montespan, La Voisin was found to be responsible after an examination by a secret tribunal. She was burned in 1680.

LAW, (1) Andrew Bonar (1858–1923), British statesman, born in New Brunswick, was an iron merchant in Glasgow. Unionist M.P. from 1900, in 1911 he succeeded Balfour as Unionist leader in the House of Commons, was colonial secretary in 1915–16, then a member of the War Cabinet, chancellor of the exchequer (1916–18), lord privy seal (1919), and from 1916 leader of the House of Commons. He retired in March 1921, but despite ill-health was premier October 1922 to May 1923.

(2) **Edward.** See ELLENBOROUGH.

(3) **John** (1671–1729), Scottish financier, born at Edinburgh, son of a goldsmith and banker, who was proprietor of the estate of Lauriston. In 1694 he had to flee from London for having killed 'Beau' Wilson in a duel. At Amsterdam he made a study of the credit operations of the bank. In 1700 he returned to Edinburgh, a zealous advocate of a paper currency; but his proposals to the Scottish parliament on this subject were unfavourably received. Back on the Continent, he won and lost vast sums in gambling and speculation, but at last settling in Paris, he and his brother William (1675–1752) set up in 1716 a private bank. This prospered so that the Regent Orleans adopted in 1718 Law's plan of a national bank. In 1719 Law originated a joint-stock company for reclaiming and settling lands in the Mississippi valley, called the *Mississippi scheme*, and next year he was made comptroller-general of finances. When the bubble burst he became an object of popular hatred, quitted France, and spent four years in England. He finally settled in Venice, where he died poor and forgotten. See Lives by Levasseur (1854), Alexi (Berlin 1885), Wiston-Glynn (1908), Oudard (1927), H. M. Hyde (1948).

(4) **William** (1686–1761), English divine, born at Kingscliffe, Northamptonshire, son of a grocer, entered Emmanuel College,

Cambridge, in 1705, becoming a fellow in 1711. He was unable to subscribe the oath of allegiance to George I, and forfeited his fellowship. About 1727 he became tutor to the father of Edward Gibbon, and for ten years was 'the much-honoured friend and spiritual director of the whole family'. The elder Gibbon died in 1737, and three years later Law retired to Kingscliffe, and was joined by his disciples, Miss Hester Gibbon, sister of his pupil, and Mrs Hutcheson. The two ladies had a united income of about £3000 a year, and most of this they spent in works of charity. About 1733 Law had begun to study Jacob Boehme, and most of his later books are expositions of his mysticism. Law won his first triumphs against Bishop Hoadly in the famous Bangorian controversy with his *Three Letters* (1717). His *Remarks on Mandeville's Fable of the Bees* (1723) is a masterpiece of caustic wit and vigorous English. Only less admirable is the *Case of Reason* (1732), in answer to Tindal the Deist. But his most famous work remains the *Serious Call to a Devout and Holy Life* (1729), which profoundly influenced Dr Johnson and the Wesleys. See Walton's *Notes and Materials for a Complete Biography* (1854), Overton's *William Law, Nonjuror and Mystic* (1881), and books by A. Whyte (1892), S. Hobhouse (1927) and Talon (1948).

LAWES, (1) **Henry** (1596–1662), English composer, born at Dinton, Wiltshire, set Milton's *Comus* to music and also the verses of Herrick. Highly regarded by Milton, who sang his praises in a sonnet, his adaptation of music to verse and rhythm was masterly. His half-brother, **William** (d. 1645), was also a composer, one of Charles I's court musicians; he was killed at Chester during the Civil War. See Life by Lefkowitz (1960).

(2) **Sir John Bennet** (1814–1900), English agriculturist, born at Rothamsted, St Albans, carried out a long series of experiments with plants and then with crops on his estate there and from these grew the artificial fertilizer industry. For the manufacture of his superphosphates he set up a factory at Deptford Creek in 1842. Even more important than this commercial enterprise were his purely scientific researches into agriculture. With him, aided by his partner J. H. Gilbert (q.v.), agriculture became a science and the Rothamsted Experimental Station which he founded in 1843, now controlled largely by the government, has become famous throughout the world. Elected F.R.S. in 1854 he received with Gilbert the gold medal of the Society in 1867.

LAWLER, **Ray** (1911–), Australian playwright, born in Melbourne, was a factory-hand at the age of thirteen but soon gravitated to the stage. His *Summer of the Seventeenth Doll*, a play of the 'outback', with its down-to-earth realism and with Lawler himself in a leading rôle, brought him fame outside Australia.

LAWRENCE, **St** (martyred 258), said to have been born at Huesca in Spain, became a deacon at Rome. In the persecution of Valerian he was condemned to be broiled.

LAWRENCE, (1) **David Herbert** (1885–1930), English poet and novelist, born in Eastwood, Notts, the son of a miner. With tuberculous tendencies, of which he eventually died, he became, through his mother's devotion, a schoolmaster and began to write, encouraged by the notice taken of his work by Ford Madox Hueffer and Edward Garnett. In 1911, after the success of his first novel, *The White Peacock*, he decided to live by writing. He travelled in Germany, Austria and Italy during 1912 and 1913, and in 1914, after her divorce from Professor Ernest Weekley, married Frieda von Richthofen, a cousin of the German air ace, Baron von Richthofen (q.v.). They returned to England at the outbreak of war and lived in an atmosphere of suspicion and persecution in a cottage in Cornwall. In 1915 he published *The Rainbow* and was horrified to find himself prosecuted for obscenity. He left England in 1919, and after three years' residence in Italy, left for America, settling in Mexico until the progress of his disease drove him in 1921 back to Italy where his last years were spent. His sensitive spirit was again shocked by his further prosecutions for obscenity over the publication in Florence of *Lady Chatterley's Lover* in 1928 and over an exhibition of his paintings in London the same year. Opinion is still divided over Lawrence's worth as a writer; but there can be no doubt about his effect on the younger intellectuals of his period. He challenged them by his attempt to interpret human emotion on a deeper level of consciousness than that handled by his contemporaries. This provoked either sharp criticism or an almost idolatrous respect. Now that his strong but ambiguous personality is removed, it is possible to agree with T. S. Eliot, who said that he was 'a writer who had to write often badly in order to write sometimes well'. His descriptive passages are sometimes superb, but he had little humour, and this occasionally produced unintentionally comic effects. His burning idealism—and it is entirely wrong to imagine that Lawrence was ever deliberately erotic—glows through all his work. His finest writing occurs in his poems, where all but essentials have been pared away; but the larger proportion of his novels have an enduring strength. These include: *Sons and Lovers* (1913), *Women in Love* (1921), *Aaron's Rod* (1922), *Kangaroo* (1923) and *The Plumed Serpent* (1926). His collected poems were published in 1928. See J. Middleton Murry, *Son of Woman* (1931), R. Aldington, *Portrait of a Genius, But . . .* (1950), a composite biography (ed. by Nehls in 3 vols., 1957–59), his *Collected Letters* (ed. by Moore in 2 vols., 1962), and studies by Leavis (1955), Rees (1958), and Moore and Roberts (1966).

(2) **Ernest Orlando** (1901–58), American physicist, born at Canton, South Dakota, studied there, at Minnesota and at Yale, became assistant professor at Berkeley, California, in 1927, where in 1936 he was appointed director of the radiation laboratory, having constructed the first cyclotron for the production of artificial radioactivity, fundamental to the development of the atomic bomb. He was awarded the Hughes Medal of the Royal Society (1937), the Comstock Prize (1937), and the Nobel prize (1939),

becoming an officer of the Légion d'Honneur in 1948.

(3) **Geoffrey, 3rd Baron Trevithin and 1st Baron Oaksey** (1880–), English lawyer, a son of Lord Trevithin (succeeding his brother to the title in 1959), lord chief justice of England, graduated at Oxford and was called to the bar in 1906. He became a judge of the high court of justice (King's Bench Division) in 1932, a lord justice of appeal in 1944 and was a lord of appeal in ordinary between 1947 and 1957. He was president of the International Tribunal for the trial of war criminals at Nuremberg in 1945 and was distinguished for his fair and impartial conduct of the proceedings. He was knighted in 1932, created baron in 1947.

(4) **Sir Henry Montgomery** (1806–57), British soldier and administrator, born at Matara, Ceylon, was educated at Derry, Bristol and Addiscombe, and in 1823 joined the Bengal Artillery. He took part in the first Burmese war (1828), in the first Afghan war (1838), and in the Sikh wars (1845 and 1848). In 1856 he pointed out the danger of reducing the British army, and the latent germs of rebellion. In 1857 he was appointed to Lucknow, and did all he could to restore contentment there, but the mutiny broke out in May. It was owing to his foresight that it was made possible for a thousand Europeans and eight hundred Indians to defend the Residency for nearly four months against 7000 rebels. He was mortally injured by a shell. ' Here lies Henry Lawrence, who tried to do his duty ', is his self-chosen epitaph. See Lives by Edwardes and Merivale (1872–1873), Innes (1898), Morison (1934).

(5) **John Laird Mair, 1st Baron** (1811–79), British administrator, brother of (4), was born at Richmond, Yorkshire. In 1827 he obtained a presentation to Haileybury College. His first years in the Indian civil service were spent at Delhi. Successively commissioner and lieutenant-governor of the Punjab, he used every effort to curb the oppression of the people by their chiefs, devised a system of land tenure, and devoted his whole energy to restoring peace and prosperity. The once restless Sikhs had become so attached to his rule that Lawrence was enabled to disarm the mutineers in the Punjab, to raise an army of 59,000 men, and to capture Delhi from the rebels after a siege of over three months. In 1863 he succeeded Lord Elgin as governor-general of India. He did not believe in British interference in Asia beyond the frontier of India, and was especially opposed to intriguing in Afghanistan. Created Baron Lawrence on his return home in 1869, he was chairman of the London School-board 1870–73. He devoted the last days of his life in parliament (1878) to an exposure of the policy which led up to the disastrous Afghan war. See Lives by Bosworth Smith (1883), Temple (1889) and Aitchison (1892) and study by Pal (1952).

(6) **Sir Thomas** (1769–1830), English painter, son of a Bristol innkeeper, was famed as a child for his portraits. At twelve he had his studio at Bath, at eighteen he entered as a student of the Royal Academy, having a year before given up crayons for oils. His full-length portrait of Queen Charlotte, now in the National Gallery, which he painted at the age of twenty, was remarkable for its maturity and is one of his best works. In 1791 he was elected A.R.A., and in 1794 R.A., in 1792 was appointed limner to the king, in 1815 was knighted by the Prince Regent, and in 1820 succeeded West as P.R.A. He died in London, and was buried in St Paul's. Lawrence was the favourite portrait painter of his time, and had an immense practice, but many of his paintings are now deemed over-facile, lacking in dignity, and his colouring blatant. He was perhaps most sincere in his fine portraits of Frederick William III of Prussia and Archduke Charles of Austria. See Life by Goldring (1951).

(7) **Thomas Edward** (1888–1935), British soldier, was a junior member of the British Museum archaeological team at Carchemish, on the Euphrates, and thus made his first intimate acquaintance with the desert dwellers. With the war of 1914–18 his ability to penetrate the ' closed shop ' of nomadic tribal life enabled him to reanimate the wilting Arab revolt against the Turk. Operating in command of the Emir Feisal's levies, his co-operation with General Allenby's triumphal advance demonstrated his outstanding abilities as a partisan leader. As a delegate to the Peace Conference and, later, as adviser on Arab affairs to the Colonial Office, his inability to secure all he had set out to achieve for the Arab cause he had espoused led to his withdrawal from what he termed ' the shallow grave of public duty ', and to his obscure but valuable service, under the name of Aircraftsman Shaw, in the R.A.F. He was killed in a motor-cycling accident in May 1935. Publications: *The Seven Pillars of Wisdom* (for private circulation, 1926), *Revolt in the Desert* (1927), *Crusader Castles* (1936), *Oriental Assembly* (ed. A. W. Lawrence, 1929) and *The Mint* (1955). See Lives by R. Graves (1927), Lowell Thomas (1958), Aldington (1955) and Villars (1958), his *Letters* (ed. by Garnett, 1964), and Rattigan's play *Ross* (1960).

LAWSON, (1) Cecil Gordon (1851–82), English landscape painter, was born at Wellington, Shropshire, but brought up in London. He exhibited at the Academy in 1870, but remained obscure, many of his pictures being rejected, till 1878, when his *Minister's Garden* at the Grosvenor made him famous. The short remainder of his life was a brilliant success. See Memoir by Gosse (1883).

(2) **Henry Hertzberg** (1867–1922), Australian writer, born in New South Wales of Scandinavian ancestry, published short stories and narrative verse of the Australian scene, collected in *Short Stories in Prose and Verse* (1894), *While the Billy Boils* (1896), &c.

LAXNESS, Haldór Kiljan, *lahks'-* (1902–), Icelandic writer, born in Reykjavik, travelled in Europe and America after the first World War and became a Catholic. A Christian communism is a favourite theme in his works, which include *Salka Valka* (1934), a story of Icelandic fishing folk, the epic *Sjalfstaet folk* (1934–35), *Islands Klukkan* (1943), which describes 18th-century Iceland under Danish rule, *Gerpla* (1952), &c. A master of the narrative, he rejuvenated his native tongue and was awarded the Nobel prize in 1955.

LAYAMON (fl. early 13th cent.), English priest at Ernley (now Areley), on the Severn near Bewdley. He produced an amplified imitation of Wace's *Brut d'Angleterre*, important in the history of English versification as the first poem written in Middle English. See Madden's edition (1847); *Layamon's Brut Selections*, ed. Hall (1924); E. K. Chambers's *Arthur of Britain* (1927).

LAYARD, Sir Austin Henry (1817–94), English archaeologist and politician, was born in Paris, a son of a Dean of Bristol, and passed his boyhood in Italy. In 1845–47 he carried on excavations at the ruins of Nimrud, the supposed site of Nineveh, finding the remains of four palaces. He published *Nineveh and its Remains* (1848), *Monuments of Nineveh* (1850), &c. He was appointed M.P. for Aylesbury 1852–57, for Southwark 1860–69, foreign under-secretary 1861–66, chief commissioner of Works 1868–69. In 1869 he went as British ambassador to Spain, in 1877 to Constantinople (where he showed strong philo-Turkish sympathies). See his *Early Adventures* (1878) and his *Autobiography and Letters* (ed. Bruce, 1903).

LAZARUS, Emma (1849–87), a New York Jewess who from 1866 published five striking volumes of poems and translations. See her *Poems* (2 vols. 1888).

LEACOCK, Stephen Butler (1869–1944), Canadian economist and humorist, educated at the University of Toronto, became first a teacher, later a lecturer at McGill University, and in 1908 head of the Economics department there. He wrote several books on his subject, including *Elements of Political Science* (1906), *Practical Political Economy* (1910) and *The Economic Prosperity of the British Empire* (1931). It is, however, as a humorist that he became widely known. Among his popular short stories, essays and parodies are *Literary Lapses* (1910), *Nonsense Novels* (1911), *Behind the Beyond* (1913), *Winsome Winnie* (1920) and *The Garden of Folly* (1924). He wrote also biographies of Twain (1932) and Dickens (1933). *The Boy I Left Behind Me*, an autobiography, appeared in 1946. See P. McArthur, *Stephen Leacock* (1923).

LEADE, Jane, *née* **Ward**. See BOEHME.

LEAKE, William Martin (1777–1860), English topographer of Greece and antiquarian, born in London. In the army from 1794, he served in Turkey and other parts of the Levant. He helped in the survey of the valley of the Nile and retired from the army with the rank of lieutenant-colonel in 1823. He wrote learned works on Greece and Greek antiquities, including *Topography of Athens* (1821) and *Numismata Hellenica* (1854). See *Memoir* by Marsden (1864).

LEAKEY, Louis Seymour Bazett (1903–72). British anthropologist, born at Kabete, Kenya, educated at Weymouth College and St. John's College, Cambridge, took part in several archaeological expeditions in East Africa, made a study of the Kikuyu and wrote much on African anthropology. He was curator of the Coryndon Memorial Museum at Nairobi (1945–61). His great discoveries took place in East Africa, where in 1959 he unearthed the skull of *Zinjanthropus*, nicknamed 'nutcracker man', a primitive species 1¾ million years old; in 1964 remains of *Homo habilis*, a smaller species some 2 million years old (postulating the simultaneous evolution of two different species, of which *Homo habilis* was the true ancestor of man, while *Zinjanthropus* became extinct); and in 1967 *Kenyapithecus Africanus*, fossilized remains of 'pre-man', *c.* 14 million years old.

LEAR, Edward (1812–88), English artist and author, born in London, had a passion for painting, and was sent by the Earl of Derby to Italy and Greece, where he painted many landscapes. He exhibited at the Royal Academy from 1850 to 1873. His later years were spent in Italy, and he died at San Remo. Lear is less known by his paintings than by his illustrated books of travels—*Sketches of Rome* (1842) *Illustrated Excursions in Italy* (1846), &c. But it is by his *Book of Nonsense* (1846), written for the Earl of Derby's grandchildren, that he is now remembered. *Nonsense Songs, Stories and Botany* followed in 1870, *More Nonsense Rhymes* in 1871, *Laughable Lyrics* in 1876. See Life by A. Davidson (1938).

LEARMONT. See THOMAS THE RHYMER.

LEAVIS, Frank Raymond (1895–), English critic, from 1936 to 1962 fellow of Downing College, Cambridge, fought against mere literary dilettantism in the quarterly, *Scrutiny* (1932–53), which he edited, as well as in *New Bearings in English Poetry* (1932). His sociological study, *Culture and Environment* (1933; with D. Thomson), deploring their separation in modern times and stressing the importance of inculcating critical standards in the young, has become a classic. Other works include *Revaluation* (1936), *The Great Tradition* (1948), *The Common Pursuit* (1952), *D. H. Lawrence* (1955), *Two Cultures?* (1962), in which he challenged the theories of C. P. Snow (q.v.) on literature and science, and *Anna Karenina and Other Essays* (1967).

LEBEDEV, Pëtr Nikolajevich (1866–1912), Russian physicist, born in Moscow, studied at Strasbourg under Kundt and became professor of Physics at Moscow (1912). He proved that light exerts a pressure on bodies, and investigated the earth's magnetism.

LEBRUN, Albert, *lè-brœ̃* (1871–1950), French statesman, was born at Mercy-le-Haut (Meurthe-et-Moselle), studied mining engineering, became a deputy (Left Republican) in 1900, was minister for the colonies 1911–14, for blockade and liberated regions 1917–19, senator 1920, and president of the Senate 1931. The last president of the Third Republic, he surrendered his powers to Pétain in 1940, and went into retirement from which he did not re-emerge, although consulted by General de Gaulle in 1944. His health was affected by a period of internment after arrest by the Gestapo in 1943.

LE BRUN, (1) Charles (1619–90), French historical painter, born in Paris, studied four years in Rome, and for nearly forty years (1647–83) exercised a despotic influence over French art and artists, being usually considered the founder of the French school of painting. He helped to found the Academy of Painting and Sculpture in 1648 and was the first director of the Gobelins tapestry works (1662). From 1668 to 1683 he was employed by Louis XIV in the decoration of Versailles. See works by Genevay (1885), Jouin (1889) and Marcel (1909).

(2) **Marie Élisabeth Louise** (1755–1842), French painter, born in Paris, a daughter of one Vigée, a painter, in 1776 married J. B. P. Le Brun, picture dealer and grand-nephew of Charles Le Brun. Her great beauty and the charm of her painting speedily made her work fashionable. Her portrait of Marie Antoinette (1779) led to a lasting friendship with the queen and she painted numerous portraits of the royal family. She left Paris for Italy at the outbreak of the Revolution, and after a kind of triumphal progress through Europe, arrived in London in 1802. There she painted portraits of the Prince of Wales, Lord Byron, &c. In 1805 she returned to Paris. See her *Souvenirs* (1837; trans. 1904), *Memoirs* (1926) and a study by Helm (1915).

LE CARON, Major Henri, *ka-rõ* (1840–94), assumed name of **Thomas Beach,** of Colchester, whose spying on Irish-American Fenians is described in his *Twenty-five Years in the Secret Service* (1892).

LE CHATELIER. See CHATELIER.

LECKY, William Edward Hartpole (1838–1903), Irish historian and philosopher, born near Dublin, graduated B.A. in 1859 at Trinity College. In 1861 he published anonymously *The Leaders of Public Opinion in Ireland*, four brilliant essays on Swift, Flood, Grattan and O'Connell. One of the greatest and most unbiased historians, his works include *History of England in the 18th Century* (1878–90). A decided Unionist but having a real sympathy with Irish problems, he became M.P. for Dublin University in 1895, a privy councillor in 1897 and O.M. (1902). See Life by his wife (1909), and *A Victorian Historian* (Private Letters 1859–78), ed. Hyde (1947).

LECLAIR, Jean Marie (1697–1764), French composer and violinist, wrote many fine sonatas for the instrument, also the opera *Scylla et Glaucis* (1746).

LECLANCHÉ, Georges, *le-klã-shay* (1839–82), French chemist, born in Paris, remembered for the galvanic cell invented by him and given his name.

LE CLERC, Jean, *lė-kler*, or **Johannes Clericus** (1657–1736), Arminian theologian and Biblical scholar, born at Geneva, became in 1684 professor of Philosophy in the Remonstrant seminary at Amsterdam. His works number over seventy, and revealed what were then startling opinions on the authorship of the Pentateuch and on inspiration generally. His Bible commentaries were completed in 1731. Serial publications were *Bibliothèque universelle et historique* (25 vols. 1686–93), *Bibliothèque choisie* (28 vols. 1703–13), and *Bibliothèque ancienne et moderne* (29 vols. 1714–26).

LÉCLUSE, Charles de, *lay-klüz* (1525–1609), the botanist 'Clusius', was born at Arras, travelled in Spain, England, Hungary, &c., and from 1593 was a professor at Leyden.

LECOCQ, Alexandre Charles (1832–1918), French composer of comic operas, was born at Paris. His many Offenbachian operettas include *Le Docteur Miracle* (1857), *Giroflé-Girofla* (1874) and *L'Égyptienne* (1890).

LECONTE DE LISLE, Charles Marie, *lė-kõt dė leel* (1818–94), French poet, was born in Réunion, and after some years of travel settled to a literary life in Paris. He exercised a profound influence on all the younger poets, headed the school called *Parnassiens*, and succeeded to Victor Hugo's chair at the Academy in 1886. His early poems appeared as *Poésies complètes* (1858). Other volumes are *Poèmes barbares* (1862) and *Poèmes tragiques* (1884); and he translated many classics. His verse is marked by regularity and faultlessness of form. See monographs, Dornis (1895), Leblond (1906), Flottes (1939) and A. Fairlie, *Leconte de Lisle's Poems on the Barbarian Races* (1947).

LE CORBUSIER. See CORBUSIER.

LECOUVREUR, Adrienne, *le-koov-rœr* (1692–1730), French actress, born near Chalons, made her début at the Comédie Française in 1717, and soon became famous for her acting, her fascinations, and her admirers, amongst whom were Marshal Saxe, Voltaire and Lord Peterborough. Her death was by some ascribed to poisoning by a rival, the Duchesse de Bouillon. This is the plot of the play by Scribe and Legouvé. See Monval's *Lettres d'Adrienne Lecouvreur* (1892), and study by Rivollet (1925).

LEDRU-ROLLIN, Alexandre Auguste, *-lĩ* (1807–74), French politician, was born at Fontenay. Admitted to the bar in 1830, he made a name as defender of Republicans and as a democratic agitator. In 1841 he was elected deputy for Le Mans, and visited Ireland during O'Connell's agitation. His *Appel aux travailleurs* (1846) declared universal suffrage the panacea for the miseries of the working classes. At the Revolution of 1848 he became minister of the interior in the Provisional Government, and in May was elected one of the interim government. But he gave offence by his arbitrary conduct, and resigned June 28. As candidate for the presidency against Louis Napoleon he was beaten and an unsuccessful attempt to provoke an insurrection in June 1849 drove him to England. He was amnestied in 1870, and after his return was elected to the Assembly. See his *Discours politiques et écrits divers* (1879), and Calman's *Ledru-Rollin and the Second French Republic* (1922).

LEE, (1) **Ann** (1736–84), English mystic, the illiterate daughter of a Manchester blacksmith, married in 1762 Abraham Stanley, also a blacksmith. Imprisoned in 1770 for street-preaching, she emigrated to America in 1774, and in 1776 founded at Niskayuna, 7 miles northwest of Albany, N.Y., the parent Shaker settlement. See *The Shakers*, by F. W. Evans (N.Y. 1859), and short Life by Axon (1876).

(2) **Charles** (1731–82), a cantankerous American general in the War of Independence, was born in Cheshire, and had served several years as a British officer in America. *Junius's Letters* have been ascribed to him.

(3) **Harriet** (1757–1851), English novelist, born in London, wrote with her sister *The Canterbury Tales*, one of which was dramatized by Byron and called *Werner, or, The Inheritance*.

(4) **James Paris** (1831–1904), American inventor, born at Hawick, Scotland. He emigrated with his parents to Canada, later going from Ontario to Hartford, Connecticut. The Lee-Enfield and Lee-Metford rifles are based in part on his designs. See METFORD, W. E.

(5) **Nathaniel** (1649–92), English dramatist, from Westminster passed to Trinity College, Cambridge, failed as an actor through nervousness (1672), produced nine or ten tragedies between 1675 and 1682, spent five years in Bedlam (1684–89). His best play is *The Rival Queens* (1677). He wrote with Dryden two plays, *Oedipus* and *The Duke of Guise*. See Hann, *Otway and Lee* (1931).

(6) **Richard Henry.** See LEE, ROBERT EDWARD.

(7) **Robert**, D.D. (1804–68), Scots divine, was born at Tweedmouth, and educated at Berwick (where he was also for a time a boat-builder) and St Andrews. In 1843 he became minister at Old Greyfriars, Edinburgh, and in 1846 he was appointed professor of Biblical Criticism in Edinburgh University and a Queen's chaplain. In 1857 he began his reform of the Presbyterian church-service. He restored the reading of prayers, kneeling at prayer and standing during the singing and in 1863 he introduced a harmonium, in 1865 an organ, into his church. These ' innovations ' brought down upon him bitter attacks. His works include a *Handbook of Devotion* (1845), *Prayers for Public Worship* (1857), &c. See Life by R. H. Story (1870).

(8) **Robert Edward** (1807–70), American soldier, was fifth in descent from Richard Lee of Shropshire, who emigrated to Virginia in the reign of Charles I, received large grants of land between the Potomac and Rappahannock rivers, and built the original Stratford House. In a later house, erected by his grandson, Thomas Lee, were born the distinguished brothers, **Richard Henry** (1732–1794), mover of the resolution in favour of American Independence and a signer of the Declaration; **Francis Lightfoot** (1734–1797), a signer of the Declaration; and **William** (1737–95) and **Arthur** (1740–92), diplomatists. There also was born Robert Edward, the son of General Henry Lee. At eighteen he entered West Point, graduated second in his class in 1829, and received a commission in the engineers. In the Mexican war (1846) he was chief engineer of the central army in Mexico, and at the storming of Chapultepec was severely wounded. In 1852–55 he commanded the U.S. Military Academy, and greatly improved its efficiency. His next service was as a cavalry officer on the Texan border 1855–59. At the John Brown raid he was ordered to Harper's Ferry to capture the insurgents. He was in command in Texas in 1860, but was recalled to Washington in March 1861 when seven states had formed the Southern Confederacy. Virginia seceded on April 17, and Colonel Lee, believing that his allegiance was due to his state, sent in his resignation. Within two days he was made commander-in-chief of the forces of Virginia. At Richmond he superintended the defences of the city till the autumn, when he was sent to oppose General Rosecrans in West Virginia. In the spring of 1862 he was working at the coast defences of Georgia and South Carolina, but on McClellan's advance was summoned to the capital. General J. E. Johnston, chief in command, was wounded at Seven Pines in May, and Lee was put in command of the army around Richmond. His masterly strategy in the seven days' battles around Richmond defeated McClellan's purpose; his battles and strategy in opposing General Pope, his invasion of Maryland and Pennsylvania, and other achievements are cardinal to the history of the war. The increasing resources of the North and the decreasing resources of the South could only result in the final success of the former. On April 9, 1865, Lee surrendered his army of 28,231 men to General Grant at Appomattox Courthouse, Virginia, and the war was practically ended. After the close of the war he frankly accepted the result, and although deprived of his former property at Arlington on the Potomac, and the White House on the Pamunky, he declined offers of pecuniary aid, and accepted the presidency of what came to be called the Washington and Lee University at Lexington, Virginia. He married in 1832 Mary Randolph Custis (1806–73). Their eldest son, George Washington Custis Lee, resigned as first-lieutenant in the U.S. army in 1861, was aide-de-camp to Jefferson Davis 1861–63, major-general of a division in 1864, and successor of his father as president of the Washington and Lee University. William Henry Fitzhugh Lee, second son, was major-general of Confederate cavalry, and was elected to congress. Captain Robert E. Lee of the Confederate cavalry was the third son. See *Lee's Dispatches* (1915); studies by Long (1886), F. Lee (1894), White (1897), Trent (1899), R. E. Lee (1904), Bradford (1912), Freeman (1934), Burne (1939).

(9) **Samuel** (1783–1852), English orientalist, born at Longnor, Shropshire, was the author of *Hebrew, Chaldaic and English Lexicon* (1840).

(10) **Sir Sidney** (1859–1926), English critic, born in London, became assistant editor of the *Dictionary of National Biography* in 1883, editor in 1891, and professor of English, East London College, 1913. He wrote a standard *Life of Shakespeare* (1898; new ed. 1915); Lives of Queen Victoria (1902), Edward VII (1925–27), &c. He was knighted in 1911. See Life by C. H. Firth (1931).

(11) **Sophia** (1750–1824), English writer, sister of (3), wrote plays and novels, including *The Chapter of Accidents* (1780), the success of which enabled her to open a girls' school at Bath.

(12) **Tsung-Dao** (1926–), Chinese physicist, born in Shanghai, educated at Kiangsi and at Chekiang University, won a scholarship to Chicago in 1946, became a lecturer at the University of California, and from 1956 was professor at Columbia University, as well as a member of the Institute for Advanced Study (1960–63). With Yang

(q.v.) he disproved the parity principle, till then considered a fundamental physical law, and they were awarded the Nobel prize for 1957.

(13) **Vernon**, pen-name of **Violet Paget** (1856–1935), English aesthetic philosopher, critic and novelist, born in Boulogne of English parentage, travelled widely in her youth and settled in Florence. Her studies of Italian and Renaissance art, *Euphorion* (1884), and *Renaissance Fancies and Studies* (1895), were followed by her philosophical study, *The Beautiful* (1913), one of the best expositions of the empathy theory of art. She also wrote two novels and a dramatic trilogy *Satan the Waster* (1920) giving full rein to her pacifism. See study by P. Gunn (1964).

LEECH, John (1817–64), English artist of Irish descent, born in London, the son of a coffee-house proprietor, went to the Charterhouse with Thackeray, studied medicine, but at eighteen published *Etchings and Sketchings, by A. Pen, Esq.* In 1836 he was contributing to *Bell's Life* and sent his first contribution to *Punch* in 1841. His *Punch* cartoons are full of high qualities; but even more delightful are the smaller woodcuts. In the intervals of work for *Punch* Leech contributed much to other journals and publications, including woodcuts in *Once a Week* (1859–62) and the *Illustrated London News* (1856), in *The Comic English* and *Latin Grammars* (1840), Hood's *Comic Annual* (1842), Smith's *Wassail Bowl* (1843), and *A Little Tour in Ireland* (1859); etchings in *Bentley's Miscellany, Jerrold's Magazine*, the Christmas books of Dickens, the *Comic History of England* (1847–48), *Comic History of Rome* (1852), and the *Handley Cross* sporting novels. He also drew several lithographed series, of which *Portraits of the Children of the Mobility* (1841) is the most important. Leech was buried close to Thackeray at Kensal Green. See Brown's *John Leech* (1882), Kitton's *Biographical Sketch* (1883) and Life by Frith (1891).

LEEDS, Thomas Osborne, Duke of (1632–1712), English statesman, better known as Earl of Danby, was the son of a Yorkshire baronet. He entered parliament for York in 1661, and in 1667 became a treasury auditor, in 1671 treasurer of the Navy, in 1673 Viscount Latimer and Baron Danby, and in 1674 lord high treasurer and Earl of Danby. He sought to enforce the laws against Roman Catholics and Dissenters, used his influence to get Princess Mary married to William of Orange in 1677, and negotiated with Louis XIV for bribes to Charles. Louis, however, intrigued for Danby's downfall, and the Commons impeached him in 1678 for treating with foreign powers, aiming at the introduction of arbitrary power and squandering public money. He was kept in the Tower until 1684, although Charles at once gave him a full pardon, as the Commons persisted in the impeachment. When James began to threaten the Established Church Danby signed the invitation to William of Orange. His reward was the marquisate of Carmarthen and the presidency of the council, and he resumed his old methods of government. He was created Duke of Leeds in 1694. In 1695, again impeached for accepting 5000 guineas from the East India Company, he staved off condemnation. But his power was gone, and in 1699 he retired, though he spoke in defence of Sacheverell in 1710. He died at Easton, Northants. See books by Courtenay (1838), A. Browning (1913, 1945, &c.).

LEESE, Sir Oliver William Hargreaves, Bart. (1894–   ), English general, won the D.S.O. in World War I and in 1939 became deputy chief of staff of the British Expeditionary Force in France. In 1942 he was promoted lieutenant-general and commanded an army corps from El Alamein to Sicily, where he succeeded Montgomery to the command of the Eighth Army during the Italian campaign. In November 1944 he commanded an army group in Burma. He was created K.C.B. in 1943 and was appointed lieutenant of the Tower of London in 1954.

LEEUWENHOEK, Anton van, *lay'ven-hook* (1632–1723), Dutch scientist, born at Delft, was a clerk in an Amsterdam cloth warehouse till 1654, and after that became at Delft the most famous microscopist, conducting a series of epoch-making discoveries in support of the circulation of the blood, and in connection with blood corpuscles, spermatozoa, &c. He first detected the fibres of the crystalline lens, the fibrils and striping of muscle, the structure of ivory and hair, the scales of the epidermis, and the distinctive characters of rotifers. His *Opera* appeared at Leyden in 1719–22; an English selection at London in 1798–1801. See a monograph by C. Dobell (1932).

LE FANU, Joseph Sheridan, *lef'ė-nyoo* (1814–1873), Irish novelist, was born and died in Dublin. He was a grand-nephew of Richard Sheridan. He began writing for the *Dublin University Magazine*, of which he was editor and later, proprietor. His novels include *The House by the Churchyard* (1863), *Uncle Silas* (1864), probably his best known, *In a Glass Darkly* (1872), and fourteen other works. A leading feature in them is their weird uncanniness. His *Poems* were edited by A. P. Graves (1896). See Memoir prefixed to his *Purcell Papers* (1880), *Seventy Years of Irish Life*, by his brother, W. R. Le Fanu (1893), S. M. Ellis, *Wilkie Collins, Le Fanu and others* (1931), and N. Browne, *Le Fanu* (1951).

LEFEBVRE, François Joseph, Duke of Danzig, *lė-fay'vr'* (1755–1820), marshal of France, was born at Ruffach in Alsace, and was a sergeant in the Guards at the Revolution. He fought at Fleurus, Altenkirchen and Stockach, in 1799 took part with Bonaparte in the overthrow of the Directory, and in 1804 was made a marshal. He took Danzig, and was created Duke of Danzig (1807), distinguished himself in the early part of the Peninsular war, and suppressed the insurrection in the Tyrol. During the Russian campaign he had the command of the Imperial Guard, and in 1814 of the left wing of the French army. Submitting to the Bourbons, he was made a peer, a dignity restored to him in 1819, though he had sided with his old master during the Hundred Days.

LEFORT, François Jacob, *lė-for* (1653–99), Swiss diplomat, born at Geneva of Scottish extraction, served in the Swiss Guard at

Paris, but entered the Russian service in 1675. Heading the intrigues which made Peter sole ruler, he became his first favourite. An able diplomat and administrator, he backed up the tsar's reforms, and in 1694 was made admiral and generalissimo. See German Lives by Posselt (1866) and Blum (1867).

LEFROY, Sir John Henry (1817–90), British soldier, born at Ashe, Hants, he became an artillery officer, director-general of ordnance and governor of Bermuda (1870–77). He was made K.C.M.G. in 1877 and was appointed governor of Tasmania in 1880. He wrote on the Bermudas, antiquities and on ordnance, his *Handbook of Field Ordnance* (1854) being the first of this type of text-book.

LE GALLIENNE, (1) **Eva** (1899–), English actress on American stage, daughter of (2), founder (1926) and director of the Civic Repertory Theater of New York.

(2) **Richard** (1866–1947), English writer, born of Guernsey ancestry at Liverpool, in 1891 became a London journalist but later lived in New York. He published many volumes of prose and verse from 1887. His style, that of the later 19th century, is outmoded and mannered, but his best books are *Quest of the Golden Girl* (1896), *The Romantic Nineties* (1926) and *From a Paris Garret* (1936). See study by Egan and Smerdon (1960).

LEGENDRE, Adrien Marie, *lė-zhã'dr'* (1752–1833), French mathematician, was born at Toulouse, studied at Paris, and became professor of Mathematics at the Military School, and (1783) member of the Academy of Sciences. Appointed in 1787 one of the commissioners to connect Greenwich and Paris by triangulation, he was elected an F.R.S. In his report Legendre first enunciated the 'proposition of spherical excess', just as in 1806 he made the first proposal to use the 'method of least squares'. In 1827 appeared his famous *Traité des fonctions elliptiques*; in 1830 his *Théorie des nombres.* Carlyle translated his *Éléments de géométrie* (1794).

LÉGER, Fernand, *lay-zhay* (1881–1955), French painter, born in Argentan, helped to form the cubist movement, but later developed his own 'aesthetic of the machine'. He worked in New York and Paris. See monograph by D. Cooper (1950).

LEGGE, James (1815–97), Scottish Chinese scholar, born at Huntly, graduated at Aberdeen in 1835. He took charge of the Anglo-Chinese college in Malacca; next worked for thirty years at Hong Kong, and in 1876 became professor of Chinese at Oxford. His greatest work was the *Chinese Classics*, with text, translation, notes, &c. (1861–86).

LEGOUIS, Émile, *lė-gwee* (1861–1937), French scholar, born at Honfleur, became professor of English at the Sorbonne, 1904–1932. He wrote books on Wordsworth, Chaucer and Spenser, and *Histoire de la littérature anglaise* (1924) (trans. 1926).

LEGOUVÉ, Ernest, *lė-goo-vay* (1807–1903), French playwright and prose writer, born in Paris. He was Scribe's collaborateur in *Adrienne Lecouvreur* (1849). He was elected to the Academy in 1855. See his *Soixante Ans de souvenirs* (1886–87).

LEGRENZI, Giovanni (1625–90), Venetian composer, born at Clusone near Bergamo, wrote church music for St Mark's, much chamber music, and 18 operas.

LEGROS, *lė-grō,* (1) **Alphonse** (1837–1911), French painter and etcher, born at Dijon, was apprenticed to a house painter. Attracting attention in the Salon between 1859 and 1866, he settled in London, and, becoming naturalized, was in 1876 appointed Slade Professor in University College, London.

(2) **Pierre** (1656–1719), French sculptor, born in Paris, lived and died in Rome.

LEHÁR, Franz (1870–1948), Hungarian composer, born at Komárom, was a conductor in Vienna and wrote a violin concerto. He is best known for his operettas which include his most popular *The Merry Widow* (1905), *The Count of Luxembourg*, *Frederica* and *The Land of Smiles.* See Life by Pope and Murray (1953).

LEHMANN, (1) **Beatrix** (1903–), English actress, daughter of (6) and sister of (2) and (4), was born at Bourne End, Bucks. She first appeared on the stage in 1924 at the Lyric, Hammersmith, and since then has appeared in many successful plays, including, in recent years, *Family Reunion,* Ustinov's *No Sign of the Dove*, and *Waltz of the Toreadors.* In 1946 she became director-producer of the Arts Council Midland Theatre company. She has also appeared in films and written two novels and several short stories.

(2) **John Frederick** (1907–), English poet and man-of-letters, born at Bourne End, Buckinghamshire, was educated at Eton and Trinity College, Cambridge, founded the periodical in book format, *New Writing*, in 1936. He was managing director of the Hogarth Press (1938–46), and ran his own firm with his sister, Rosamond, as codirector from 1946 to 1953. In 1954 he inaugurated *The London Magazine*, which he edited until 1961. He has published, among many works, a *Garden Revisited* (1931), *Forty Poems* (1942), and a study *Edith Sitwell* (1952), and has conducted a literary radio-magazine on the B.B.C. See his autobiography (3 vols., 1955, 1960 and 1966), and *Ancestors and Friends* (1962). He was made C.B.E. in 1964.

(3) **Liza,** properly **Elizabeth Nina Mary Frederika** (1862–1918), English soprano and composer, daughter of (5), was born in London. Very popular as a concert singer, she also composed ballads, a light opera *The Vicar of Wakefield* (1906) and a song-cycle *In a Persian Garden* (1896).

(4) **Rosamond Nina** (1903–), English novelist, sister of (1) and (2), born in London, educated at Cambridge. Her novels show a fine sensitive insight into character and her women especially are brilliantly drawn. Among her books are *Dusty Answer* (1927), *A Note in Music* (1930), and *The Echoing Grove* (1953). She has also written a play *No More Music* (1939), and a volume of short stories *The Gypsy's Baby* (1946). See her *The Swan in the Evening* (1967).

(5) **Rudolf** (1819–1905), German painter, born near Hamburg, in 1866 settled in London and became a naturalized British subject. He married a daughter of Dr Robert Chambers. See his *An Artist's Reminiscences* (1894).

(6) **Rudolph Chambers** (1856–1929), English journalist, nephew of (5) and father of (1), (2) and (4), was born at Sheffield. He was a journalist on *Punch* (1890–1919), editor of the *Daily News* (1901), Liberal M.P. for Harborough (1906–10). A well-known oarsman and coach, he published *The Complete Oarsman* in 1908.

LEHMBRUCK, Wilhelm, *laym-brook* (1881–1919), German sculptor and illustrator, was born in Meidensich near Duisberg, and committed suicide in Berlin. He was early influenced by Maillol, and later produced expressionist sculpture, specializing in elongated and exaggerated female torsos.

LEIBL, Wilhelm, *lī'bl'* (1844–1900), German artist, born at Cologne. He studied in Paris, being much influenced by Courbet's realism, and later worked in Munich. Most of his paintings are genre scenes of Bavaria and the lower Alps, although he painted a number of portraits. See the monograph by W. L. Waldmann (1921).

LEIBNIZ, Gottfried Wilhelm, *līb'nits* (1646–1716), German philosopher and mathematician, one of the world's great intellects, born July 6 in Leipzig, where his father was professor of Moral Philosophy. Refused a doctorate there in 1666 on account of his youth, he was granted one by the University of Altdorf and, preferring a less secluded life, turned down the accompanying offer of a professorship. Through a fellow-member of a Rosicrucian circle in Nuremberg, the diplomat Baron von Boineburg, he obtained a position at the court of the powerful Elector of Mainz, partly on the strength of an essay on legal education. To divert Louis XIV from his designs on Germany, Leibniz was dispatched by the German princes to Paris with a master plan, devised by him for a French invasion of Egypt, said to have been consulted more than a century later by Napoleon. In Paris Leibniz met Malebranche, Arnauld and Huygens, studied Cartesianism and mathematics and invented a calculating machine, for which he was elected F.R.S. on his visit to London in 1673. There he met English mathematicians acquainted with Newton's work and this led to the undignified controversy later as to whether he or Newton was the inventor of the infinitesimal calculus. Leibniz certainly invented a system, the basis of that employed today, with a more advanced notation than that of Newton, in Paris in 1675–76, which he published in 1684, whereas Newton did not publish until 1687, although his system of 'fluxions' dates back to 1665. Clarke defended Newton's claims, but Leibniz was forced to conduct his own defence through an imaginary protagonist author of his *Historia et Origo Calculi Differentialis.* The controversy was never really settled, despite the Royal Society's formal declaration for Newton in 1711. On his way to take up his last post as librarian to the duke of Brunswick at Hanover in 1676, Leibniz met Spinoza in Amsterdam and discussed parts of the latter's *Ethics* with him. He improved the drainage of mines and the coinage, arranged the library at Wolfenbüttel, and in Austria and Italy gathered materials for a history of the house of Brunswick. He worked for a reconciliation of Protestant and Roman Catholic churches and induced Frederick I to found (1700) the Academy of Sciences in Berlin, of which he became first president. Unpopular with George of Hanover, he was left behind when the court moved to London and was allowed to die without recognition, November 14, 1716. Leibniz left a vast corpus of writings, only a fraction of which was published in his lifetime. Bertrand Russell, in his brilliant study of Leibniz's philosophy (1900), distinguished between the popular works, written with an eye to popular and princely favour (such as the *Théodicée* (1710; trans. E. M. Huggard 1952), a perversion of which, summed up by its optimistic doctrine of 'all is for the best in this best of all possible worlds', Voltaire brilliantly satirized in *Candide*) and the *Monadologie* (1714; trans. R. Latta 1898) the esoteric philosophical doctrines of which seem less so when read in conjunction with the profoundly logical, but theologically controversial arguments, prudently left unpublished, such as the *Discours de metaphysique* (1846; trans. P. Lucas and L. Grant 1953) and the correspondence with Arnauld (trans. G. R. Montgomery, Chicago 1902) and Clarke (trans. H. G. Alexander 1956). Leibniz defined substance as an infinite number of indivisible, therefore nonmaterial mutually isolated *monads,* each one reflecting the world from its own point of view. These monads form a hierarchy, the very highest of which is God, and they constitute a dualism with material phenomena, synchronized, as when a human being lifts his arm, by a pre-established harmony. Each monad is the sum of its predicates throughout its existence. Human choice is still subject in a special way to this determinism, for by the principle of sufficient reason there are always 'inclining reasons' for one action rather than another, although 'not necessitating'. Leibniz's mathematical preoccupations led him to conceive of a universal linguistic calculus, incorporating all existing knowledge, which would render argument obsolete and displace it by a process of calculation. His great influence, not least upon Russell, was primarily as a mathematician and as a pioneer of modern symbolic logic. The complete edition of his works was published by the Berlin Academy (1923 ff.). See also his *Nouveaux Essais* (1765) criticizing Locke, Lives in German by G. E. Guhrauer (1846), K. Fischer (1920), and in English by J. T. Herz (1884), also W. H. Barber, *Leibniz in France* (1953), studies by B. Russell (1900, n.e. 1937), confirmed by L. Couturat's (Paris 1901) comprising freshly discovered logical fragments, H. W. B. Joseph, *Lectures,* ed. J. L. Austin (1949) and R. L. Saw (1954).

LEICESTER, Robert Dudley, Earl of, *les'ter* (*c.* 1532–88), was fifth son of John Dudley, Duke of Northumberland, and grandson of the notorious Edmund Dudley (q.v.) beheaded by Henry VIII. His father was executed for his support of Lady Jane Grey (q.v.). He too was sentenced to death, but, liberated in 1554, was by Elizabeth made master of the horse, Knight of the Garter, a privy councillor, high steward of the

University of Cambridge, Baron Dudley, and finally in 1564, Earl of Leicester. In 1550 he had married Amy, daughter of Sir John Robsart. On September 8, 1560, at Cumnor Place, Berkshire, the house of Anthony Forster, a creature of her husband's, she was found dead, as some think by suicide; but it was generally believed that she was murdered, and that Dudley, if not Elizabeth herself, was an accessory to the crime; and the archives at Simancas indicate that there had been a plot to poison her. Elizabeth continued to favour Leicester in spite of his unpopularity and of his secret marriage in 1573 to the Dowager Lady Sheffield. In 1563 she had suggested him as a husband for Mary, Queen of Scots, and in 1575 she was magnificently entertained by him at his castle of Kenilworth. In 1578 he bigamously married the widow of Walter, Earl of Essex; yet Elizabeth was only temporarily greatly offended. In 1585 he commanded the expedition to the Low Countries in which Sir Philip Sidney, his nephew, met with his death at Zutphen. In 1587 he again showed his military incapacity in the same field, and had to be recalled. In 1588 he was appointed to command the forces assembled at Tilbury against the Spanish Armada. He died suddenly on September 4 of the same year at Cornbury, in Oxfordshire, of poison, said rumour, intended for his wife. See Milton Waldman, *Elizabeth and Leicester* (1944).

LEICESTER OF HOLKHAM, Thomas William Coke, Earl of, *les'ter of hōk'ėm* (1752–1842), was a descendant of the famous lawyer Coke. He was one of the first agriculturists of England; by his efforts northwest Norfolk was converted from a rye-growing into a wheat-growing district, and more stock and better breeds were kept on the farms. Coke represented Norfolk as a Whig most of the period 1776–1833, and in 1837 he was created Earl of Leicester of Holkham, to distinguish the title from the Townshend earldom of Leicester. He died at Longford Hall, Derbyshire.

LEICHHARDT, Ludwig, *līKH'-hart* (1813–48), German explorer, born at Trebatsch near Frankfurt-on-Oder, in 1841 went to Australia, and led an expedition (1843–48) from Moreton Bay to the Gulf of Carpentaria. In 1846 he failed to cross Cape York Peninsula. In December 1847 he again started from Moreton Bay to cross the continent, but was last heard of on April 3, 1848. See *Journal of an Overland Expedition in Australia* (1847) and Life by Mrs C. D. Cotton (1938).

LEIF ERIKSSON, *layv*, born in Iceland, the son of Eric the Red, christianized Greenland and discovered land (*c.* 1000), which he named Vinland after the vines he found growing there. It is still uncertain where Vinland actually is, some saying Labrador or Newfoundland, others Massachusetts. See E. Haughen, *Voyages to Vinland* (1942).

LEIGHTON, *lay'tėn*, (1) **Frederic, 1st Baron Leighton** (1830–96), English painter, was born at Scarborough, a doctor's son. He early showed a gift for painting, visited Rome, Florence, Frankfurt, Berlin, Paris and Brussels, and everywhere received instruction from the most distinguished masters. He exhibited at the Royal Academy in 1855 his *Cimabue's Madonna carried in Procession through Florence*—a picture purchased by Queen Victoria. Among his later works were *Paolo and Francesca* (1861), *The Daphnephoria* (1876; sold in 1893 for £3700), and *The Bath of Psyche* (1890). Lord Leighton also won distinction as a sculptor, and in 1877 his *Athlete struggling with a Python* was purchased out of the Chantrey Bequest. Several of his paintings, as for example *Wedded* (1882), became mass bestsellers in photogravure reproduction. In 1864 he was elected A.R.A., in 1869 R.A., and in 1878 president and knighted. His *Addresses* were published in 1896. He was created a baronet in 1886, and Lord Leighton of Stretton in January 1896. He died unmarried, and was buried in St Paul's. His *Academy Addresses* appeared in 1897. See a study by Ernest Rhys (new ed. 1900), and his *Life and Letters* by Mrs Russell Barrington (1906).

(2) **Robert** (1611–84), Scottish archbishop, born probably in London, was the second son of Alexander Leighton, M.D. (*c.* 1568–*c.* 1649), Presbyterian minister in London and Utrecht, author of *Sion's Plea against the Prelacie* (1628), which earned him from Laud scourging, the pillory, branding and mutilation, heavy fine and imprisonment. Robert studied at Edinburgh University and spent some years in France. He was ordained minister of Newbattle in 1641, signed the Covenant two years later, and took part in all the Presbyterian policy of the time; most of the *Sermons* and the *Commentary on the First Epistle of Peter* were the work of the Newbattle period. In 1653 he was appointed principal of Edinburgh University. Soon after the Restoration Leighton was induced by the king himself to become one of the new bishops, chose Dunblane, the poorest of all the dioceses, and for the next ten years he laboured to build up the shattered walls of the church. His aim was to preserve what was best in Episcopacy and Presbytery as a basis for comprehensive union; but he succeeded only in being misunderstood by both sides. The continued persecution of the Covenanters drove him to London in 1665 to resign his see, but Charles persuaded him to return. Again in 1669 he went to London to advocate his scheme of 'accommodation' and became Archbishop of Glasgow in the same year. Next followed his fruitless conferences at Edinburgh (1670–71) with leading Presbyterians. In despair of success he was allowed to retire in 1674. His last ten years he spent at Broadhurst Manor, Sussex often preaching in the church of Horsted Keynes, where he lies. He died in a London inn. There have been several editions of his works—all of which reveal a deep spirituality, a heavenly exaltation and devotion—since that by his friend Fall (1692–1708). There are *Selections* (1883) by Blair; *Life and Letters* by Rev. D. Butler (1903); a Life by Bp. E. A. Knox (1930).

LEININGEN. See KENT, DUKE OF.

LEISHMAN, Sir William Boog (1865–1926), Scottish bacteriologist, born in Glasgow, became professor of Pathology in the Army Medical College, and director-general,

Army Medical Service (1923). He discovered an effective vaccine for inoculation against typhoid and was first to discover the parasite of the disease kala-azar. He was knighted in 1909. See H. H. Scott's *History of Tropical Medicine* (ii) (1939).

LELAND, (1) Charles Godfrey, pseud. Hans Breitmann (1825–1903), American author, born in Philadelphia, graduated at Princeton in 1845, and afterwards studied at Heidelberg, Munich and Paris. He was admitted to the Philadelphia bar in 1851, but turned to journalism. From 1869 he resided chiefly in England and Italy, and investigated the Gypsies, a subject on which between 1873 and 1891 he published four valuable works. He is best known for his poems in 'Pennsylvania Dutch', the famous *Hans Breitmann Ballads* (1871; continued in 1895). Other similar volumes gained him great popularity during his lifetime. He also translated the works of Heine. See his *Memoirs* (1893), and his *Life and Letters* by Mrs Pennell (1906).

(2) **John** (*c.* 1506–52), English antiquary, born in London, was educated at St Paul's School under William Lily, then at Christ's College, Cambridge, and All Souls, Oxford. After a residence in Paris he became chaplain to Henry VIII, who in 1533 made him 'king's antiquary', with power to search for records of antiquity in the cathedrals, colleges, abbeys and priories of England. In six years he collected 'a whole world of things very memorable'. His church preferments were the rectories of Peuplingues near Calais and Haseley in Oxfordshire, a canonry of King's College (now Christ Church), Oxford, and a prebend of Salisbury. Most of his papers are in the Bodleian and British Museum. Besides his *Commentarii de Scriptoribus Britannicis* (ed. by Hall, 1709), his chief works are *The Itinerary* (ed. by L. T. Smith, 1905–10) and *De Rebus Britannicis Collectanea* (ed. by Hearne, 1715). See Huddesford's *Lives of Leland, Hearne, and Wood* (1772).

(3) **John** (1691–1766), English Presbyterian minister, born at Wigan, was educated at Dublin, where from 1716 he was minister. He wrote against Tindal (1733) and Morgan (1739–40). His chief work is *A View of the Principal Deistical Writers* (1754–56). See Life prefixed to his *Discourses* (1768–89).

LELY, Sir Peter (1618–80), Dutch painter, originally Pieter van der Faes, was born probably at Soest, Westphalia. He settled in London in 1641 as a portrait painter. He was employed by Charles I, Cromwell, and Charles II, for whom he changed his style of painting. The last nominated him court-painter, and in 1679 knighted him. His *Beauties* are collected at Hampton Court. The 13 Greenwich portraits are among his best works; these, the English admirals who fought in the second Dutch war, are outstanding for depth and sincerity of characterization. They present a marked contrast to his very popular and often highly sensuous court portraits which have often a hasty, superficial appearance. See C. H. Collins Baker, *Lely and the Stuart Portrait Painters* (1912).

LEMAIRE, Philippe Honoré (1798–1880), French sculptor, was born at Valenciennes, and died in Paris. Among his works is a statue of Hoche at Versailles and one of Napoleon at Lille.

LE MAIRE DE BELGES, Jean (*c.* 1473–1524), the first French humanist poet, served the Duc de Bourbon, Margaret of Austria, to whom he dedicated his *Épîtres de l'amant vert*, and Louis XII. See studies by P. Spaax (1926) and K. M. Munn (1936).

LEMAÎTRE, (1) François Élie Jules (1853–1914), French playwright and critic, was born at Vennecy, Loiret, and in 1895 was elected to the Academy. His articles written first for the *Journal des débats* were issued in book form as *Impressions de théâtre* (1888–1898), and those written for *Revue bleue* on modern French literature became *Les Contemporains* (1886–99). A masterly critic with a charming, lucid style, he wrote also *Rousseau* (1907), *Racine* (1908), *Fenélon* (1910) and *Chateaubriand* (1912). See works by Morice (1924), Durrière (1934) and Seillière (1935).

(2) **Frédérick** (1800–76), French actor, born at Le Havre. His first success was in *Richard Darlington*, a play based on Scott's *The Surgeon's Daughter*, and this was followed by a succession of triumphs including *Hamlet*, *Kean ou Désordre et Genie*, *Ruy Blas*, and the greatest of all, *L'Auberge des Adrets*. This last was in reality Lemaître's own play. Based on an inferior melodrama, he made the character Robert Macaire a villain of genius. Writers of the day acclaimed him; Dumas called him the French Kean, Flaubert called his Macaire the greatest symbol of the age and Hugo wrote *Ruy Blas* for him. He visited London four times and on one occasion shocked Queen Victoria by his Ruy Blas. He suffered ill health in his later years and died in great poverty. See Lives by Lecomte (2 vols. 1888) and Baldick (1959).

(3) **Georges Henri** (1894–1966), Belgian astrophysicist, professor of the Theory of Relativity at Louvain, internationally known for his work on that subject and on its application to the theory of the expanding universe.

LEMAN, Gérard Mathieu, *lè-mã* (1851–1920), Belgian general, born at Liège, was also a director of studies, engineer and mathematician. He was wounded and captured at Liège, whose forts, as military governor, he gallantly held against the Germans, August 4–7, 1914.

LEMNIUS (*c.* 1505–50), German humanist and Latin poet, was a student of Melanchthon at Wittenberg. Antagonistic to Luther and his teaching, he wrote against him in two books of epigrams (1538). His other works included *Monachopornomachia*, a satirical poem, love poems, *Amores* (1542) and a Latin translation of the Odyssey (1549). He died at Chur.

LEMOINE, Sir James MacPherson, *lè-mwan* (1825–1912), born in Quebec, became superintendent of inland revenue at Quebec in 1858. He studied archaeology, ornithology and other sciences, wrote on Canadian history and was the first Canadian author to receive a knighthood.

LEMON, Mark (1809–70), English author and journalist, born in London, in 1835 wrote a farce, followed by melodramas, operettas, novels (the best, perhaps, *Falkner Lyle*, 1866), children's stories, a *Jest Book* (1864) and essays. In 1841 he helped to establish *Punch*, becoming first joint editor, then sole editor from 1843 to his death. See J. Hatton, *Reminiscences of Mark Lemon* (1871).

LEMONNIER, *lė-mon-yay*, (1) **Antoine Louis Camille** (1844–1913), Belgian writer, born at Ixelles near Brussels, took to art criticism in 1863, and by his novels *Un Mâle* (1881), *Happe-Chair* (1888) and other works, in French, but full of strong Flemish realism and mysticism, won fame as one of Belgium's leading prose writers. He wrote books on art, including *Gustave Courbet* (1878), *Alfred Stevens et son œuvre* (1906) and *L'École Belge de la peinture* (1906).

(2) **Pierre Charles** (1715–99), French astronomer, born in Paris, was a member of the Academy of Sciences at the age of twenty because of his lunar map. He greatly advanced astronomical measurement in France, and made twelve observations of Uranus before it was recognized as a planet.

LE MOYNE, *lė-mwan*, (1) **Charles** (1626–83), French pioneer, born at Dieppe, sailed for Canada in 1641, lived among the Hurons, and fought with the Iroquois. In 1668 Louis XIV made him Seigneur de Longueuil. He was long captain of Montreal.

(2) **Charles** (1656–1729), eldest son of (1), served in the French army, was governor of Montreal and commandant-general of the colony, and was made a baron in 1700. His descendant, Charles Colmor Grant, had his Canadian title of seventh Baron de Longueuil recognized by Queen Victoria in 1880.

(3) **François** (1688–1737), French painter of mythological subjects, e.g., the Salon d'Hercule at Versailles, was born and committed suicide at Paris. Boucher was his pupil. See examples in the Wallace Collection.

(4) **Joseph** (1668–1734), son of (1), served in the French navy, and in 1719 captured Pensacola. In 1723 he became governor of Rochefort.

LEMPRIÈRE, John, *lã-pryayr* (*c.* 1765–1824), British scholar, born in Jersey, was headmaster of Abingdon and Exeter grammar schools, and rector of Meeth and Newton-Petrock in Devon. His *Classical Dictionary* (1788) was long a standard work. Another book was *Universal Biography* (1808).

LENARD, Philipp Eduard Anton (1862–1947), German physicist, born at Pozsony (Bratislava), professor of Physics at Heidelberg (1896–98 and 1907–31), was awarded the Nobel prize in 1905. His main research concerned cathode rays, upon which subject he wrote several books. He was an enthusiastic believer in Nazi doctrines.

LENAU, Nikolaus (Nikolaus Niembsch von Strehlenau), *lay'nau* (1802–50), German poet, born at Czatad in Hungary, studied law and medicine at Vienna. His life was rendered unhappy by his morbid poetic discontent; and in 1844 he became insane, dying in an asylum near Vienna. His poetic power is best shown in his short lyrics; his longer pieces include *Faust* (1836), *Savonarola* (1837) and *Die Albigenser* (1842). See Lives by Schurz (1855), Frankl (1885–92) and Roustan (1899).

LENBACH, Franz, *len-bakh* (1836–1904), German portrait painter, born at Schrobenhausen, Bavaria, worked mostly in Munich. For some time he copied the great masters, including Titian, Rubens and Velasquez, before becoming one of the greatest 19th-century German portrait painters. His portraits of Bismarck are specially famous.

LENCLOS, Anne, called **Ninon de**, *lã-klõ* (1616–1706), born of good family at Paris, commenced at sixteen her long career of gallantry. Among her lovers were two marquises, two marshals, the great Condé, the Duc de Larochefoucauld, and an abbé or two. She had two sons, but never showed the slightest maternal feeling. One of them, brought up in ignorance of his mother, conceived a passion for her. Informed of their relationship, he blew out his brains. Ninon was nearly as celebrated for her manners as for her beauty. The most respectable women sent their children to her to acquire taste, style, politeness. Mirecourt's *Mémoires* is a romance; the letters attributed to her are mostly spurious. See books by Hayes (1908), Rowsell, Magne 1925), Day (1958).

LENGLEN, Suzanne, *lã-lã* (1899–1938), French lawn tennis player, born at Compiègne. Trained by her father, she became famous in 1914 by winning the women's world hard-court singles championship at Paris. She was the woman champion of France (1919–1923, 1925–26), and her Wimbledon championships were the women's singles and doubles (1919–23, 1925), and the mixed doubles (1920, 1922, 1925). In 1921 she was Olympic champion. She became a professional in 1926, toured the U.S., and retired in 1927 to found the Lenglen School of Tennis in Paris. Perhaps the greatest woman player of all time, she set a new fashion in female tennis dress. She published *Lawn Tennis, the Game of Nations* (1925) and a novel, *The Love-Game* (1925). See Olliff's *The Romance of Wimbledon* (1949).

LENIN (formerly **Ulyanov**), **Vladimir Ilyich** (1870–1924), Russian revolutionary, was born into a family of the minor intelligentsia at Simbirsk (Ulyanov). He was educated at Kazan University and in 1892 began to practise law in Samara (Kuibyshev). In 1894, after five years' intensive study of Marx, he moved to St Petersburg (Leningrad), organizing the illegal 'Union for the Liberation of the Working Class'. Arrested for his opinions, he was exiled to Siberia for three years. His Western exile began in 1900 in Switzerland, where with Plekhanov he developed an underground Social Democratic Party, to assume leadership of the working classes in a revolution against Tsarism. In 1903 he became leader of the Bolshevik wing whose Marxism was opposed to the 'bourgeois reformism' of the Mensheviks. Lenin returned to Russia in 1905, ascribing the failure of the rising of that year to lack of support for his own programme. He determined that when the time came Soviets (councils of workers, soldiers and peasants) should be the instruments of total revolution.

Lenin left Russia in 1907 and spent the next decade strengthening the Bolsheviks against the Mensheviks, interpreting the gospel of Marx and Engels and organizing underground work in Russia. In April 1917, a few days after the deposition of the tsar Nicholas II, Lenin made with German connivance his fateful journey in a sealed train from Switzerland to Petrograd. He told his followers to prepare for the overthrow of the shaky Provisional Government and the remaking of Russia on a Soviet basis. In the October Revolution the Provisional Government collapsed and the dominating Bolshevik 'rump' in the second Congress of Soviets declared that supreme power rested in them. Lenin inaugurated the 'dictatorship of the proletariat' with the formal dissolution of the Constituent Assembly. For three years he grappled with war and anarchy. In 1922 he began his 'new economic policy' of limited free enterprise to give Russia a breathing space before entering the era of giant state planning. He died on January 21, 1924, and his body was embalmed for veneration in a crystal casket in a mausoleum in the Red Square, Moscow. He left a testament in which he proposed the removal of the ambitious Stalin as secretary of the Communist Party. Shrewd, dynamic, implacable, pedantic, opportunist, as ice-cold in his economic reasoning as in his impersonal political hatreds that could encompass millions, Lenin lived only for the furtherance of Marxism. He inspired in the name of democracy a despotism boundless in the power of its ambition and sense of destiny. For years after his death Lenin was looked upon in the Soviet Union as a demi-god. Publications include: *Workers of the World Unite* (Geneva 1897) and *Imperialism the Last Stage of Capitalism* (1917). See Selected Works (English trans. 1936–39), and Lives and studies of Lenin by L. Trotsky (1925), V. Marcu (1928), D. S. Mirsky (1931), G. Vernadsky (1931), R. Fox (1933), P. Kerzhensev (1937), C. Hill (1947), D. Shrub (1948).

LENNEP, Jacob van (1802–62), Dutch writer and lawyer, born at Amsterdam, achieved a great reputation for legal knowledge. He has been called the Walter Scott of Holland. His most popular works were comedies, *Het Dorp aan die Grenzen* and *Het Dorp over die Grenzen*. Of his novels, several (e.g., *The Rose of Dekama* and *The Adopted Son*) have been translated.

LENO, Dan, *lee'nō*, stage name of **George Galvin** (1860–1904), English comedian. He began his career at the age of four, singing and dancing in public houses, and by eighteen became a champion clog-dancer and was invited to appear in the Surrey pantomime. Ten years later he joined the Augustus Harris management at Drury Lane, where he appeared for many years in the annual pantomime. Leno was a thin, small man and his foil was the huge, bulky Herbert Campbell. When Campbell died in 1904 as the result of an accident, Leno pined and died six months later, insane from overwork and loneliness. He will be remembered for his realistic 'dames' with their inimitable blend of Cockney humour and sentiment. See Hickory Wood, *Dan Leno* (1905) and M. W. Disher, *Winkles and Champagne* (1938).

LENOIR, Jean Joseph Étienne (1822–1900), French inventor who constructed an internal combustion engine (*c.* 1859) and later a small car (1860).

LENORMAND, Henri René, *lė-nor-mã* (1882–1951), French dramatist, born in Paris, the author of *Les Possédés* (1909), *Le Mangeur de rêves* (1922), a modern equivalent of *Oedipus Rex*, *L'Homme et ses fantômes* (1924), and other plays in which Freud's theory of subconscious motivation is adapted to dramatic purposes. See study by P. Blanchard (1947).

LENORMANT, François, *lė-nor-mã* (1837–1883), French archaeologist, was born in Paris, the son of Charles Lenormant (1802–1859), himself profoundly learned in Egyptology, numismatics and archaeology generally. At twenty he carried off the prize in numismatics of the Académie des Inscriptions, at twenty-three was digging at Eleusis; and he continued his explorations, in the intervals of his work as sub-librarian at the Institute (1862–72), and professor of Archaeology at the Bibliothèque Nationale (1874–83), until his health broke down from overwork and a wound received during the siege of Paris. Just before his death he was converted to Catholicism from scepticism. His chief work was *Les Origines de l'histoire d'après la Bible* (1880–84).

LENÔTRE, André (1613–1700), the creator of French landscape-gardening, was born and died in Paris. He designed the gardens at Versailles, and laid out St James's Park in London. See monograph by J. Guiffrey (1912).

LENTHALL, William (1591–1662), English barrister, born at Henley, was Speaker of the Long Parliament 1640–53, and master of the Rolls from 1643. He was again made Speaker in 1654, and in 1657 became one of Cromwell's peers.

LENZ, (1) Heinrich Friedrich Emil (1804–65), German physicist, was born at Dorpat and died at Rome. He first studied theology, but became professor of Physics at St Petersburg and a member of the Russian Academy of Sciences. He was the first to state Lenz's law governing induced current, and is credited with discovering the dependence of electrical resistance on temperature (Joule's law).

(2) **Jakob Michael Reinhold** (1751–92), German author, born in Livonia, was one of the young authors who surrounded Goethe in Strasbourg. He first wrote two plays which were well received, *Der Hofmeister* (1774) and *Die Soldaten* (1776). Like all the 'Sturm und Drang' poets he was a fervent admirer of Shakespeare, and this was expressed in his *Anmerkungen übers Theater* (1774). He was a gifted writer of lyrics, some of them being at first attributed to Goethe. He suffered a mental breakdown while still young and died in poverty at Moscow. See studies by Waldmann (1894), Rosanow (1909).

LEO, the name of thirteen popes, whose tenures of the papacy were as follows: I

(440–61); II (682–83); III (795–816); IV (847–55); V (903); VI (928–29); VII (936–39); VIII (963–65); IX (1049–54); X (1513–21); XI (1605); XII (1823–29); XIII (1878–1903).

Leo I (*c.* 390–461), 'the Great', a saint, and one of the most eminent of the Latin Fathers, was of good Roman family. In a council held at Rome in 449 he set aside the proceedings of the Council of Ephesus, which had pronounced in favour of Eutyches, and summoned a new council at Chalcedon, in which Leo's celebrated 'Dogmatical Letter' was accepted 'as the voice of Peter'. He interposed with Attila (q.v.) in defence of Rome, and with Gaiseric (q.v.). See the Rev. C. L. Feltoe (Library of Fathers, vol. xii 1896) and T. G. Jalland's *Life of St Leo the Great* (1941).

Leo III (*c.* 750–816), saw during his pontificate the formal establishment of the Empire of the West. In the 8th century the popes, through the practical withdrawal of the Eastern emperors, had exercised a temporal supremacy in Rome, under the protectorate of the Frankish sovereigns. Leo was in 799 obliged to flee to Spoleto, whence he repaired to Paderborn to confer with Charlemagne. On his return to Rome he was received with honour. In 800 Charlemagne, having come to Rome, was crowned emperor by the pope, and the temporal sovereignty of the pope over the Roman city and state was formally established, under the suzerainty of the emperor.

Leo X, Giovanni de' Medici (1475–1521), second son of Lorenzo the Magnificent, was created cardinal at the age of thirteen. In the expulsion of the Medici from Florence the young cardinal was included. He was employed as legate by Julius II, at whose death in 1513 he was chosen pope as Leo X. He brought to a successful conclusion the fifth Lateran Council. He concluded a concordat with Francis I of France; he consolidated and extended the reconquests of his warlike predecessor, Julius II. His desertion of Francis I for Charles V was dictated by the interests of Italy. But it is as a patron of learning and art that the reputation of Leo has lived. He founded a Greek college in Rome and established a Greek press. His vast project for the rebuilding of St Peter's, and his permitting the preaching of an indulgence in order to raise funds, provoked Luther's Reformation. He regarded the movement as of little importance; and though he condemned the propositions of Luther, his measures were not marked by severity. In his moral conduct he maintained a strict propriety, and, although not free from nepotism, he was an enlightened prince. See works on him by Ranke; Creighton; Vaughan's *Medici Popes* (1908); Symonds's *Renaissance* (1875–86) and G. B. Picotti, *La Giovinezza di Leone X* (1928).

Leo XIII (1810–1903), 258th Roman pontiff, was born at Carpineto, son of Count Ludovico Pecci. Having become Doctor of Laws, he was appointed by Gregory XVI a domestic prelate in 1837, received the title of prothonotary apostolic, and was a vigorous apostolic delegate at Benevento, Perugia and Spoleto. He was made Archbishop of Damietta *in partibus* and sent to Belgium as nuncio in 1843, nominated Archbishop of Perugia in 1846, and in 1853 created a cardinal by Pius IX, soon holding the important office of camerlengo. Upon the death of Pius IX in 1878 Vincenzo Gioacchino Cardinal Pecci was elected to the papacy under the title of Leo XIII. He restored the hierarchy in Scotland and composed the difficulty with Germany. In 1888 he denounced the Irish Plan of Campaign. He manifested enlightened views, but on questions affecting the church and his own status held staunchly to his rights. He regarded himself as the despoiled sovereign of Rome, and as a prisoner at the Vatican; and persistently declined to recognize the law of guarantees. He protested against heresy and 'godless' schools, and in his encyclicals affirmed that the only solution to the socialistic problem is the influence of the papacy. In 1894 he constrained the French clergy and the monarchists to accept the republic. In 1883 he opened the archives of the Vatican for historical investigations, and he made himself known as a poet, chiefly in the Latin tongue. The jubilee of his episcopate in 1893 was marked by pilgrimages, addresses and gifts, as was that of his priesthood in 1887. In 1896 he issued an encyclical pronouncing Anglican orders invalid. See Lives by O'Reilly (1887), T'serclaes (Paris 1894, 1907), Boyer d'Agen (*Jeunesse de Léon XIII*, 1896), McCarthy (1896), and in German by W. Goetz (1923), Walterbay (6th ed. 1931), also his addresses, &c., in *The Pope and the People* (new ed. 1913).

LEO III (*c.* 680–741), called **the Isaurian** from being born in Isauria in Asia Minor, raised the Byzantine Empire from a very low condition, having, as a general in the East, seized the crown in 716. He reorganized the army and financial system, and in 718 repelled a formidable attack of the Saracens. In 726 he by an edict prohibited the use of images (i.e., pictures or mosaics; statues were hardly known as yet in churches) in public worship. In Italy, however, the appearance of the Image-breakers or Iconoclasts roused an enthusiastic resistance on the part of the people, and the controversy raised by the edict rent the empire for over a century. In 728 the exarchate of Ravenna was lost, and the eastern provinces became the prey of the Saracens, over whom, however, Leo won a great victory in Phrygia. See J. B. Bury, *The Later Roman Empire* (vol. 2, 1889) and *Histoire du moyen âge*, ed. Glotz (vol. 3 1944).

LEO AFRICANUS (properly **Alhassan ibn Mohammed Alwazzan** or **Alwezaz**) (1494–1552), a Cordovan Moor, who from *c.* 1512 travelled in northern Africa and Asia Minor. Falling into the hands of Venetian corsairs, he was sent to Leo X at Rome, where he lived twenty years, and accepted Christianity, but returned to Africa and (perhaps) his old faith, and died at Tunis. He wrote *Africae Descriptio* (1526) an account of his African travels in Italian (first printed 1550), long the chief source of information about the Sudan. Dr R. Brown re-edited John Pory's translation of 1600 (Hakluyt Society 1896).

LEOCHARES, *lee-ok'a-reez* (*c.* 370 B.C.), an Athenian sculptor who, with his master Scopas (q.v.), decorated the Mausoleum of Halicarnassus.

LEÓN, Ponce de. See PONCE DE LEÓN.

LEONARDO DA VINCI (1452–1519), Italian painter, sculptor, architect and engineer, was born at Vinci, between Pisa and Florence, the natural son of a Florentine notary. About 1470 he entered the studio of Andrea del Verrocchio. In 1482 he settled in Milan, and attached himself to Lodovico Sforza. His famous *Last Supper* (1498), commissioned jointly by Lodovico and the monks of Santa Maria delle Grazie, was painted on a wall of the refectory of the convent. Owing to dampness, and to the method of tempera painting—not oil, nor fresco—upon plaster, it soon showed signs of deterioration, and it has been often 'restored'; yet still it is one of the world's masterpieces. Among other paintings in Milan were portraits of two mistresses of the duke—one of them perhaps *La Belle Ferronnière* of the Louvre. Leonardo also devised a system of hydraulic irrigation of the plains of Lombardy and directed the court pageants. After the fall of Duke Lodovico in 1500 Leonardo retired to Florence, and entered the service of Cesare Borgia, then Duke of Romagna, as architect and engineer. In 1503 he returned to Florence, and commenced a *Madonna and Child with St Anne*, of which only the cartoon now in the Royal Academy, London, was completed. Both he and Michelangelo received commissions to decorate the Sala del Consiglio in the Palazzo della Signoria with historical compositions. Leonardo dealt with *The Battle of Anghiari*, a Florentine victory over Milan, and finished his cartoon; but, having employed a method of painting upon the plaster which proved a failure, he in 1506 abandoned the work. About 1504 he completed his most celebrated easel picture, *Mona Lisa* (stolen from the Louvre 1911; recovered 1913). Another work, now lost, portrayed the celebrated beauty Ginevra Benci; and Pacioli's *De divina Proportione* (1509) contained sixty geometrical figures from Leonardo's hand. In 1506 he was employed by Louis XII of France. Francis I bestowed on him in 1516 a yearly allowance, and assigned to his use the Château Cloux, near Amboise; hither he came that same year, and here he died May 2, 1519. Among his later works are *The Virgin of the Rocks*, now in the National Gallery, London (a replica in the Louvre), a figure of *St John the Baptist*, and a *Saint Anne*. There is in existence no sculpture which can positively be attributed to him, but he may well have designed or been closely associated with three works—the three figures over the north door of the Baptistery at Florence, a bronze statuette of horse and rider in the Budapest Museum and the wax bust of Flora. In his art Leonardo was hardly at all influenced by the antique; his practice was founded upon the most patient and searching study of nature and in particular the study of light and shade. He occupies a supreme place as an artist, but so few in number are the works by his hand that have reached us that he may be most fully studied in his drawings, of which there are rich collections at Milan, Paris, Florence and Vienna, as well as in the British Museum and at Windsor. His celebrated *Trattato della Pittura* was published in 1651; but a more complete manuscript, discovered by Manzi in the Vatican, was published in 1817. Voluminous MSS by him in Milan (*Codice-Atlantico*), Paris, Windsor, &c. have been reproduced in facsimile (1881–1901). Leonardo had a wide knowledge and understanding far beyond his times of most of the sciences, including biology, physiology, hydrodynamics, aeronautics, and his notebooks contain original remarks on all of these. See his *Literary Works*, ed. by Richter (1883; rev. and enl. 1939); his *Note-books*, trans. by MacCurdy (1938); monographs by Richter (1880), Séailles (new ed. 1906), Müntz (trans. 1899), MacCurdy (1904, 1933), Von Seidlitz (1909), Thiis (1913), Sirén (trans. 1916), Mrs Annand Taylor (1927), C. Bax (1932), Uzielli (2nd ed. 1896), Merezhkovsky (1931), K. M. Clark (1939), Goldscheider (1959); A. E. Popham, *The Drawings of Leonardo da Vinci* (1946).

LEONCAVALLO, Ruggiero (1858–1919), Italian composer, born at Naples, produced *I Pagliacci* (1892), followed by other less successful operas including *La Bohème* which failed where Puccini's on the same theme was a success.

LEONI, Leone, *lay-ō'nee* (1509–90), Italian goldsmith, medallist and sculptor, was born at Arezzo, worked at Milan, Genoa, Brussels and Madrid, and was the rival of Benvenuto Cellini in talent, vice and violence. His fine medals often depicted well-known artists, as Titian and Michelangelo, and his sculpture which was mostly in bronze included busts of Charles V and Philip II, both of whom he served for some time. See French monograph by Plon (1887).

LEONIDAS, *-on'-* (d. 480 B.C.), king of Sparta, succeeded his half-brother, Cleomenes, 491 B.C. When the Persian king Xerxes approached with an immense army Leonidas opposed him at the narrow pass of Thermopylae (480 B.C.) with his 300 Spartans; there all of them found a heroic death.

LEOPARDI, Giacomo, *lay-ō-pahr'dee* (1798–1837), Italian poet, was born of poor but noble parentage at Recanati. At sixteen he had read all the Latin and Greek classics, could write with accuracy French, Spanish, English and Hebrew, and wrote a commentary on Plotinus. After a short sojourn in Rome, he devoted himself at home to literature, but finding his home increasingly unbearable he began to travel and now a confirmed invalid, he lived successively in Bologna, Florence, Milan and Pisa. In 1833 he accompanied his friend Ranieri to Naples, and there in constant bodily anguish and hopeless despondency he lived till his death. His pessimism was unquestionably the genuine expression of Leopardi's deepest nature as well as of his reasoned conviction. Ranieri edited his works (1845). He was specially gifted as a writer of lyrics, which were collected under the title *I Canti* and are among the most beautiful in Italian literature. His prose works include the Dialogues and

Essays classed as *Operette Morali*, and his *Pensieri* and letters. His Essays and Dialogues were trans. by Edwardes (1882), his Poems by G. Bickersteth (with critical introduction and bibliography, 1923). See Gladstone's *Gleanings*, vol. ii; and works by Carducci (1898), De Sanctis (1921), Origo (1953) and J. H. Whitfield (1954).

LEOPOLD, name of two Holy Roman emperors:

Leopold I (1640–1705), in 1658 succeeded his father, the Emperor Ferdinand III. He provoked the Hungarians to rebellion by his severity. Tekeli received aid from the Porte, and Kara Mustapha besieged Vienna (1683), which was rescued only by an army of Poles and Germans under John Sobieski. The power of the Turks now declined. In 1686 they lost Buda, after occupying it for nearly 150 years; and by the treaty of Carlowitz (1699) they were almost entirely cleared out of Hungary. The struggle between Leopold and Louis XIV of France for the heirship to the king of Spain led to the war of the Spanish Succession. Leopold was of sluggish and phlegmatic character, wholly under Jesuit influences. See German Life of him by Baumstark (1873).

Leopold II (1747–92), third son of Francis I and Maria Theresa, succeeded his father as Grand-duke of Tuscany in 1765, and his brother, Joseph I, as emperor in 1790. He succeeded in pacifying the Netherlands and Hungary; was led by the downfall of his sister, Marie Antoinette, to form an alliance with Prussia against France; but died before the war broke out.

LEOPOLD, name of three kings of Belgium:

Leopold I (1790–1865), king of the Belgians, son of Francis, Duke of Saxe-Coburg, and uncle of Queen Victoria, was a general in the Russian army, and served at Lützen, Bautzen and Leipzig. He married in 1816 the Princess Charlotte (q.v.); in 1829 (morganatically and unhappily) Caroline Bauer (q.v.); in 1832 Louise, daughter of Louis-Philippe. After hesitation he declined the crown of Greece (1830) and in June 1831 he was elected king of the Belgians. He conducted himself with prudence and moderation, with constant regard to the principles of the Belgian constitution and by his policy did much to prevent Belgium becoming too involved in the revolutions which were raging in other European countries in 1848. See L. de Lichtervilde, *Leopold I et la formation de la Belgique contemporaine* (1928).

Leopold II (1835–1909), born in Brussels, son of Leopold I, his chief interest was the expansion of Belgium abroad. He became king in 1885 of the independent state of the Congo, which was annexed to Belgium in 1908. At home he strengthened his country by military reforms and established a system of fortifications. He was not popular as a king, but under him Belgium flourished, developing commercially and industrially, especially during the later part of his reign. He was succeeded by his nephew, Albert (q.v). See N. Ascherson's *The King Incorporated* (1963).

Leopold III (1901–), son of Albert, king from 1934, on his own authority ordered the capitulation of the army to the Nazis (May 28, 1940), thus opening the way to Dunkirk, and remained a prisoner in his own palace at Laeken. He refused to abdicate until July 16, 1951, in favour of his son Baudouin (q.v.).

LEOPOLD V (1157–94), Duke of Austria, crusader in 1182 and 1190–92, and the captor of Richard I (q.v.) of England.

LEOPOLD, Prince. See ALBANY (DUKE OF).

LEPAGE. See BASTIEN-LEPAGE.

LEPIDUS, Marcus Aemilius (d. 13 B.C.), Roman politician, declared for Caesar against Pompey (49 B.C.), and was by Caesar made dictator of Rome and his colleague in the consulate (46 B.C.). He supported Anthony, and became one of the triumvirate with Octavian and Antony, with Africa for his province (40–39 B.C.). He thought he could maintain himself in Sicily against Octavian, but his soldiers deserted him.

LE PLAY, Pierre Guillaume Frédéric (1806–1882), French political economist and engineer, was born at Honfleur, and lived in Paris, where he was professor in the School of Mines. He was one of the first to realize the importance of sociology and its effect on economics; he stressed the need for cooperation between employer and employee without intervention from government. See his *Les Œuvriers européens* (1855) and *Reforme sociale en France* (1864).

LEPSIUS, Karl Richard (1810–84), German Egyptologist, was born at Naumburg. His first work on palaeography as an instrument of philology (1834) obtained the Volney prize of the French Institute. In 1836 at Rome he studied Egyptology, Nubian, Etruscan, and Oscan, writing numerous treatises. In 1842–45 he was at the head of an antiquarian expedition sent to Egypt by the king of Prussia, and in 1846 was appointed professor in Berlin. His *Denkmäler aus Aegypten und Aethiopien* (12 vols. 1849–60) remains a masterpiece; his *Chronologie der Aegypter* laid the foundation for a scientific treatment of early Egyptian history. Other works are his letters from Egypt, Ethiopia and Sinai (1852), the *Königsbuch* (1858), the *Todtenbuch* (1867), the Egyptian Book of the Dead. He wrote on Chinese, Arabic and Assyrian philology; and was a member of the Royal Academy, director of the Egyptian section of the Royal Museum, and chief-librarian of the Royal Library at Berlin. See Life by Ebers (1885, trans. New York 1887).

LERINS, Vincent of. See VINCENTIUS.

LERMONTOV, Mikhail Yurevich (1814–41), Russian poet, was born, of Scottish extraction (Learmont), in Moscow. He attended the Moscow University for a short time and then the military cavalry school of St Petersburg, where he received a commission in the Guards. A poem which he wrote in 1837 on the death of Pushkin caused his arrest and he was sent to the Caucasus. Reinstated, he was again banished following a duel with the son of the French ambassador. Another duel was the cause of his death in 1841. He started writing at an early age, but much of his work was not published until the last years of his short life and his fame was posthumous. The sublime scenery of the Caucasus inspired his best poetic pieces, such as 'The Novice', 'The Demon', 'Ismail

Bey', &c. His novel, *A Hero of our Time* (1839; trans. 1912, 1928, 1940), was a masterpiece of prose writing. He wrote also a romantic verse play, *Masquerade*. See *Poems*, ed. by E. N. Steinhart, with trans., biography, &c. (1917), and *Lermontov in English* by Heifetz (N.Y. 1942), and studies by Laurin (1959) and Mersereau (1962).

LEROUX, Pierre, *lè-roo* (1797–1871), French Humanitarian, born near Paris, influenced George Sand and with her founded *Revue Indépendente* (1841). A member of the Constituent Assembly and the Legislative Assembly he was exiled from 1851 to 1869 after opposing Louis Napoleon's *coup d'état*. He wrote *De l'Humanité* (1840) and *De l'Egalité* (1848).

LE SAGE, Alain René, *lè-sazh* (1668–1747), French novelist and dramatist, born at Sarzeau in Brittany, in 1692 went to Paris to study law, but an early marriage drove him to seek a less tardy livelihood in literature. The Abbé de Lionne, who had a good Spanish library, made Le Sage free of it, with a pension of 600 livres. The first fruit was a volume (1700) containing two plays imitated from Rojas and Lope de Vega. In 1702 *Le Point d'honneur*, from Rojas, failed on the stage. His next venture (1704) was a rifacimento of Avellaneda's *Don Quixote*. In 1707 *Don César Ursin*, from Calderón, was played with success at court, and *Crispin rival de son maître* in the city; more successful was the *Diable boiteux* (largely from Luis Velez de Guevara). In 1708 the Théâtre-Français accepted but shelved one play and rejected another, afterwards altered into his famous *Turcaret*. In 1715 *Gil Blas* (vols. i and ii) came out, followed in 1717–21 by an attempt at an Orlando. In 1724 came vol. iii of *Gil Blas*; in 1726 a largely extended *Diable boiteux*; in 1732 *Guzman de Alfarache* and *Robert Chevalier de Beauchêne*; in 1734 *Estebanillo Gonzalez*; in 1735 vol. iv of *Gil Blas* and the *Journée des Parques*; in 1736–38 the *Bachelier de Salamanque*; in 1739 his plays, in two vols.; in 1740 *La Valise trouvée*, a volume of letters; and in 1743 the *Mélange amusant*, a collection of facetiae. The death of his son (1743), a promising actor, and his own increasing infirmities, made him abandon Paris and literary life, and retreat with his wife and daughter to Boulogne, where his second son held a canonry; and there he died in his eightieth year. Le Sage's reputation as a dramatist and as a novelist rests in each case on one work. The author of *Turcaret* might have become, but did not, almost a second Molière; the author of *Gil Blas* stands in the front rank of the novelists. Some deny originality to one who borrowed ideas, incidents and tales from others as Le Sage did; but he was the first to perceive the capabilities of the picaresque novel. His delightful style makes him the prince of raconteurs, and the final effect of his work is all his own. See works by Barberet (1887), Claretie (1890–94) and Lintilhac (1893), and F. C. Green, *French Novels, Manners and Ideas* (1928).

LESCOT, Pierre, *les-kō* (*c.* 1510–78), French Renaissance architect, born in Paris. One of the greatest architects of his time, among his works are the screen of St Germain l'Auxerrois, the Fontaine des Innocents and the Hôtel de Ligneris. His masterpiece was the Louvre, one wing of which he completely rebuilt.

LESKIEN, August, *les-keen'* (1840–1916), German Slavonic philologist, born at Kiel, became one of the 'Young Grammarians' at Leipzig, where he was a professor from 1870. Of his writings on Slavonic language, most important are his *Handbuch des Altbulgarischen* (1871) and *Deklination im Slavisch-Litauischen und Germanischen* (1876).

LESLIE, Lesly, or Lesley, the Family of, is first found between 1171 and 1199 in possession of the pastoral parish of Lesslyn or Leslie in Aberdeenshire, and was ennobled in 1457, when George Leslie of Rothes was made Earl of Rothes and Lord Leslie. The fourth earl was father of Norman Leslie, Master of Rothes, chief actor in the murder of Cardinal Beaton. John, sixth earl (1600–41), was one of the ablest of the Covenanting leaders. His son John (1630–81) became lord chancellor of Scotland in 1667, and in 1680 was created Duke of Rothes, &c. These honours became extinct upon his death without male issue in 1681. The earldom of Rothes went to his elder daughter, in whose family the title has continued. The Balquhain branch gave birth to several men of mark, such as the learned John Leslie (q.v.), Bishop of Ross, the champion of Mary, Queen of Scots; Sir Alexander Leslie of Auchintoul, a general in the Muscovite service (died 1663); and Charles Leslie. Other distinguished members of the family were:

(1) **Alexander** (*c.* 1580–1661), who became field-marshal of Sweden under Gustavus Adolphus. Recalled to Scotland in 1639, he took command of the Covenanting army, and in 1641 was made Earl of Leven and Lord Balgony. His honours and lands eventually passed to his great-grandson, David Melville, third Earl of Leven and second Earl of Melville. See *Life and Campaigns*, by Sanford Terry (1899).

(2) **David** (1601–82), fifth son of the first Lord Lindores (a son of the fifth Earl of Rothes), served under Gustavus Adolphus, and, returning to Scotland in 1640, acted as lieutenant-general to the Earl of Leven. He was present at Marston Moor, and defeated Montrose at Philiphaugh. Routed by Cromwell at Dunbar in 1650, and taken prisoner by him at Worcester in 1651, he was imprisoned in the Tower till the Restoration. He was made Lord Newark in 1661.

(3) **Walter** (1606–67), a cadet of the Balquhain line, distinguished himself in the Austrian army, and in 1637 was created a count, as a reward for his services in the murder of Wallenstein. He was succeeded (1667) by his nephew, James, Austrian field-marshal. The title became extinct in 1844.

LESLIE, (1) **Charles** (1650–1722), nonjuror, born at Dublin, became chancellor of the cathedral of Connor in 1687. Deprived at the Revolution for declining the oath of allegiance, he retired to England and wrote against Papists, Deists, Socinians, Jews and Quakers, as well as in support of the non-juring interests. He was mostly with the

Pretender in France and Italy (1713–21), and then returning to Ireland, died at Glaslough. His *Short and Easy Method with the Jews* appeared in 1684; his *Short and Easy Method with the Deists* in 1697; he issued a collected edition of his *Theological Works* in 1721 (new ed. 1832). See Life by R. J. Leslie (1885).

(2) **Charles Robert** (1794–1859), genre painter, was born in London of American parentage. Educated from 1800 at Philadelphia, in 1811 he returned to England and entered as a student in the Royal Academy. His paintings were mostly scenes from famous plays and novels. He was elected R.A. in 1824. In 1833 he was for one year professor of Drawing at West Point, New York, and from 1848 to 1852 he was professor of Painting at the Royal Academy. His lectures were published in the *Handbook for Young Painters* (1855). He wrote a Life of Constable (1843), and began one of Reynolds, completed by Tom Taylor, who edited his *Autobiographical Recollections* (1860). His son, **George Dunlop** (1835–1921), born in London, aimed ' to paint pictures from the sunny side of English domestic life ', was elected R.A. in 1876. He wrote *Letters to Marco* (1893), *Riverside Letters*, and *Inner Life of the Royal Academy* (1914).

(3) **Frank**, the name adopted by **Henry Carter** (1821–80), English illustrator and journalist, who was born at Ipswich. At seventeen he entered a London mercantile house and the success of sketches sent by him to the *Illustrated London News* led him to join its staff. In 1848 he went to the United States, assumed the name Frank Leslie, and in 1854 founded the *Gazette of Fashion* and the *New York Journal*. *Frank Leslie's Illustrated Newspaper* began in 1855 (German and Spanish editions later), the *Chimney Corner* in 1865; he also started the *Boys' and Girls' Weekly*, the *Lady's Journal*, &c.

(4) **John** (1527–96), Scottish prelate, son of the rector of Kingussie, studied at King's College, Aberdeen, at Paris, and at Poitiers, and in 1566 became Bishop of Ross. A zealous partisan of Queen Mary, he joined her at Tutbury in 1569, suffered imprisonment, and in 1574 went to France. He died in a monastery near Brussels. His Latin history of Scotland *De Origine, Moribus, et Rebus Gestis Scotorum* (Rome, 1578) was rendered into Scots in 1596 by a Scottish Benedictine of Ratisbon, Father James Dalrymple (ed. by Father Cody, Scottish Text Society 1884–91).

(5) **Sir John** (1766–1832), Scottish natural philosopher, born at Largo, studied at St Andrews and Edinburgh, and travelled as tutor in America and on the Continent, meanwhile engaging in experimental research. The fruits of his labours were a translation of Buffon's *Birds* (1793), the invention of a differential thermometer, a hygrometer and a photometer, and *Inquiry into Heat* (1804). In 1805 he obtained the chair of Mathematics at Edinburgh, though keenly opposed by the ministers as a follower of Hume. In 1810 he succeeded in freezing water under the air pump. Transferred to the chair of Natural Philosophy (1819), he invented the pyroscope, atmometer and aethrioscope. He was knighted in 1832. See Memoir by Macvey Napier (1838).

(6) **Thomas Edward Cliffe** (1827–82), Irish political economist, born in Co. Wexford, qualified for the bar, but in 1853 became professor of Economics and Jurisprudence at Belfast. His writings were published as *The Land Systems* (1870), studies on the land question in Ireland, Belgium, and France, and *Essaysin Political and Moral Philosophy* (1879). He was one of the founders of the historic method of political economy.

(7) **Walter, Count.** See LESLIE Family (3).

LESPINASSE, Claire Françoise, or Jeanne Julie Eléonore de (1732–76), was born at Lyons, an illegitimate daughter of the Countess d'Albon. At first a teacher, she became in 1754 companion to Madame du Deffand, whose friends, especially d'Alembert, she quickly attached to herself, and after the inevitable rupture, she was enabled to maintain a salon of her own which became a centre for the literary figures of her day. The charm she exercised was in no way due to beauty. Her passion for the Marquis de Mora, and later for M. de Guibert, cost her the deepest pangs, when the first died and the second married. Many of her letters (aglow with fire and passion) to her two lovers have been published since 1809. See also her *Lettres inédites* (1887; mostly to Condorcet); *Letters* (trans. 1902); *Love Letters to and from the Comte de Guibert* (1929); books by C. Jebb (1908), Marquis de Ségur (new Eng. ed. 1913), and N. Royde-Smith (1931).

LESSEPS, Ferdinand, Vicomte de (1805–94), French engineer, born at Versailles, a cousin of the Empress Eugénie, from 1825 held diplomatic posts at Lisbon, Tunis, Cairo, &c. In 1854 he conceived his scheme for a Suez Canal, and in 1856 obtained a concession from the viceroy. The works were begun in 1860, and completed in August 1869. He received the Grand Cross of the Legion of Honour, an English knighthood, election to the Academy, &c. In 1881 work began on his stupendous scheme for a Panamá Canal; but in 1892–93 the management was charged with breach of trust, and five directors were condemned—Lesseps, now a broken old man, to five years' imprisonment and a fine, as was also his son Charles. Charles was released in June 1893; his father, who had been too ill to be taken from his house, died December 7, 1894. Lesseps wrote an *Histoire du canal de Suez* (1875–79; trans. 1876) and *Souvenirs de quarante ans* (1887; trans. 1887). See Lives by Bertrand and Ferrier (Paris 1887), Barnett Smith (2nd ed. 1895) and C. Beatty (1956).

LESSING, Gotthold Ephraim (1729–81), German man of letters, was born, a pastor's son, at Kamenz in Saxony, and in 1746 entered as a theological student at Leipzig. Soon he was writing plays in the French style, and leaving Leipzig in debt, at Berlin joined the unorthodox Mylius in publishing *Beiträge zur Historie des Theaters* (1750), and independently wrote plays, translated and did literary hack-work; his chief support was the *Vossische Zeitung*, to which he contributed criticisms. In 1751 he withdrew to Wittenberg, took his master's degree, and produced a series of *Vindications* of unjustly maligned or forgotten writers, such as Cardan, Lemnius, &c. Again at Berlin he in *Ein Vademecum für Herrn S. G. Lange* (1754) displayed unrelenting hostility to pretentious ignorance; with Moses Mendelssohn he wrote an essay on *Pope, ein Metaphysiker* (1755). His successful tragedy *Miss Sara Sampson* (1755) is after English models. In 1758 he was assisting Mendelssohn and Nicolai with a new critical Berlin journal, in which he revolted from the dictatorship of French taste, combated the inflated pedantry of the Gottsched school, and extolled Shakespeare. While secretary to the governor of Breslau he wrote his famous *Laokoon* (1766), a critical treatise defining the limits of poetry and the plastic arts. The comedy *Minna von Barnhelm* (1767) is the first German comedy on the grand scale. Appointed playwright to a new theatre at Hamburg in 1767, he wrote the *Hamburgische Dramaturgie* (1769), in which he finally overthrew the dictatorship of the French drama. The Hamburg theatre failed, and Lessing was soon in the thick of a controversy, this time with Klotz, a Halle professor, producing the *Briefe antiquarischen Inhalts* (1769) and *Wie die Alten den Tod gebildet* (1769). In 1769 the Duke of Brunswick appointed Lessing Wolfenbüttel librarian; and he at once began to publish some of the less-known treasures of the library in *Zur Geschichte und Litteratur* (1773–81). In 1772 he wrote the great tragedy *Emilia Galotti.* Shortly before his marriage he spent eight months in Italy as companion to the young Prince Leopold of Brunswick. In 1774–78 he published the *Wolfenbüttelsche Fragmente*, a rationalist attack on orthodox Christianity from the pen of Reimarus (q.v.), which, universally attributed to Lessing, provoked a storm of refutations. The best of Lessing's counter-attacks were *Anti-Goeze* (1778) and the fine dramatic poem, *Nathan der Weise* (1779), one of the noblest pleas for toleration ever penned. Later works were *Erziehung des Menschengeschlechts* (1780) and *Ernst und Falk* (1778–80), five dialogues on free-masonry. Lessing died at Brunswick. His *Sämmtliche Schriften*, ed. by Lachmann, were reissued by Muncker in 1886–1907. His chief works have been translated into English. See Lives by Danzel and Guhrauer (2nd ed. 1880), Düntzer (1882), Stahr (10th ed. 1900), Erich Schmidt (4th ed. 1923), Borinski (1900), Sime (1877), Helen Zimmern (1878), and Rolleston (1889)—the last three in English. See also J. G. Robertson, *Lessing's Dramatic Theory* (1939).

L'ESTRANGE, Sir Roger (1616–1704), English journalist, born at Hunstanton, narrowly escaped hanging as a royalist spy for a plot to seize Lynn in 1644, and was imprisoned in Newgate, whence he escaped after four years. Pardoned by Cromwell in 1653, he lived quietly till the Restoration made him licenser of the press. He fought in all the quarrels of the time with a shower of pamphlets, vigorous and not coarser than those of his antagonists; and he holds a place in the history of journalism by his papers, *The Public Intelligencer* (1663–66) and *The Observator* (1681–87). He translated Aesop's *Fables*, Seneca's *Morals*, Cicero's *Offices*, the *Colloquies* of Erasmus, Quevedo's *Visions*, and Josephus. He was knighted in 1685. See Life by G. Kitchin (1913).

LE SUEUR, *lė sü-œr*, (1) **Eustache** (1617–55), French painter, pupil of Vouet, whose style he imitated until, about 1645, he came under the influence of Nicolas Poussin's classical style. In his early style his most important work was the decoration of two rooms in the Hôtel Lambert in Paris and in his later manner paintings of the life of St Bruno for the Charterhouse of Paris. The Louvre possesses 36 religious pictures by him, and 13 mythological.

(2) **Hubert** (*c.* 1580–*c.* 1670), French sculptor, born in Paris, came to England about 1628. His most important work was the equestrian statue of Charles I at Charing Cross (1633).

LESZCZYŃSKI. See STANISLAUS.

LETHINGTON. See MAITLAND.

LETTS, Thomas (1803–73), English bookbinder, born at Stockwell, London, began after his father's death in 1803 to manufacture diaries and by 1839 was producing twenty-eight varieties.

LEUCHTENBERG. See BEAUHARNAIS.

LEUCIPPUS (fl. *c.* 400 B.C.), Greek philosopher, born at Miletus (not Abdera), was the founder of the Atomic school of Greek philosophy and forerunner of Democritus. He wrote *The Great World System* and *On Mind.*

LEUCKART, Karl Georg Friedrich Rudolf, *loy'-kart* (1822–98), German zoologist, born at Helmstedt, studied at Göttingen, and in 1850 became professor of Zoology at Giessen, in 1869 at Leipzig. His work on classification is important and especially noteworthy was his division of the Radiata into Coelenterata and Echinodermata. He distinguished himself by his study of the Entozoa, writing his great work *Parasites of Man* from 1879–94 (trans. 1886).

LEUTZE, Emanuel, *loy'tzė* (1816–68), German painter, born at Gmünd in Württemberg, was brought up in America, studied in Europe 1841–59, then settled in New York in 1859. His paintings were mainly scenes from American history, the best known of which was *Washington crossing the Delaware.*

LEVAILLANT, François, *lė-vī-yã* (1753–1824), French traveller and ornithologist, was born at Paramaribo, Dutch Guiana, and studied in Paris. He explored in South Africa 1781–84, and wrote of his expeditions in *Voyage dans l'intérieur de l'Afrique* (1790), &c., and published books on birds.

LEVEN, Earl of. See LESLIE.

LEVER, (1) **Charles** (1806–72), Irish novelist, was born of purely English parentage in Dublin, graduated at Trinity College in 1827, and then went to Göttingen to study medicine. His most popular work, *Charles O'Malley*, is a reflex of his own college life in Dublin. About 1829 he spent some time in the backwoods of Canada and North America, and embodied his experiences in *Con Cregan* and *Arthur O'Leary.* He practised medicine at various Irish country towns, and in 1840 at Brussels. Returning to Dublin, he published *Jack Hinton* in 1843, and from 1842 to 1845 acted as editor of the *Dublin University Magazine*, and wrote further novels. In 1845 he again went to Brussels, Bonn, Karlsruhe, where he published the *Knight of Gwynne*, and to Florence, where he wrote *Roland Cashel*. At Spezia *Luttrel of Arran* and three other novels were produced in rapid succession. Then, completely changing his style, he wrote the *Fortunes of Glencore*, followed by *The Martins of Cro-Martin* and *The Daltons*. Lever was in 1858 appointed British vice-consul at Spezia, and continued to write, his work including some racy essays in *Blackwood's* by ' Cornelius O'Dowd '. In 1867 he was promoted to the consulship at Trieste, where he died. Lever's work contained brilliant, rollicking sketches of a phase of Irish life which was passing away, though no doubt his caricatures created a false idea of Irish society and character. His daughter edited his novels (37 vols. 1897–99). See *Life and Letters* by Downey (1906), and L. Stevenson, *Dr Quicksilver* (1939).

(2) **William Hesketh, 1st Viscount Leverhulme** (1851–1925), British soapmaker and philanthropist, born at Bolton. Beginning in his father's grocery business, he opened new shops and in 1886 with his brother, James, started the manufacture of soap from vegetable oils instead of tallow and the new town of Port Sunlight was founded. Among his many benefits, he endowed at Liverpool University a school of tropical medicine and gave Lancaster House to the nation. He was made a Baron in 1917 and a Viscount in 1922. See W. H. L. Leverhulme, *Viscount Leverhulme, by his Son* (1927).

LEVERRIER, Urbain Jean Joseph, *lė-ver-yay* (1811–77), French astronomer, born at St Lô, Normandy, in 1836 became teacher of astronomy at the Polytechnique. His *Tables de Mercure* and several memoirs gained him admission to the Academy in 1846. From disturbances in the motions of planets he inferred the existence of an undiscovered planet, and calculated the point in the heavens where, a few days afterwards, Neptune was actually discovered by Galle at Berlin. For this he received the Grand Cross of the Legion of Honour and a chair of Astronomy in the Faculty of Sciences. Elected in 1849 to the Legislative Assembly, he became counter-revolutionary. In 1852 Louis Napoleon made him a senator and in 1854 he succeeded Arago as director of the Observatory of Paris. See ADAMS (JOHN COUCH).

LEVESON-GOWER, George, 2nd Earl Granville, *loo'sėn gōr'* (1815–91), English statesman, was educated at Eton and Oxford, in 1836 became M.P. for Morpeth, in 1840 for Lichfield, and was for a brief period under-secretary for foreign affairs. He was a consistent Liberal and a freetrader. He succeeded to the peerage in 1846, and became foreign secretary in 1851, president of the council in 1853, and leader of the House of Lords in 1855. Having failed to form a ministry in 1859, he joined Lord Palmerston's second administration. He retired with Earl Russell in 1866, having been made lord warden of the Cinque Ports in 1865. In December, 1868 he became colonial secretary in Gladstone's first ministry, and in 1870 foreign secretary, as again in 1880–85, when he had to face the troubles in Egypt and the Sudan, differences with Germany and France, and the threatened rupture with Russia over the Afghan boundary question. He returned once more for a few months to office as colonial secretary in 1886 and supported Gladstone's home-rule policy. See Life by E. Fitzmaurice (1905).

LEVI. See MATTHEW, SAINT.

LEVI CIVITA, Tullio, *lay'vee chee-vee'ta* (1873–1942), Italian mathematician, noteworthy for his studies on differential geometry and relativity. Professor of Mechanics at Padua and at Rome from 1918 to 1938, he was a member of the Royal Society in 1930. Among his works are *Lezioni di meccanica rationali* (1922) in collaboration with U. Amaldi, *Questioni di meccanica classica et relativisti* (1924) and *The Absolute Differential Calculus* (1937).

LEVITA, Elias, *lė-vee'ta* (1465–1549), Jewish grammarian and exegete, was born at Neustadt near Nuremberg. An expulsion of Jews forced him to Italy, where he taught successively in Padua (1504), Venice, Rome (1514), and finally (1527) Venice again. He wrote on Job, the Psalms, Proverbs, Amos, and the vowel points; a Hebrew grammar; and a Talmudic and Targumic Dictionary. See Life by J. Leir (Breslau 1888).

LEWALD, Fanny, *lay'valt* (1811–89), German novelist, born at Königsberg, in 1855 married Adolf Stahr (1805–76), a Berlin critic. She was an enthusiastic champion of women's rights. Her best book is perhaps *Von Geschlecht zu Geschlecht* (1863–65). An English translation of *Stella* (1884) appeared in the same year. She wrote records of travel in Italy (1847) and Great Britain (1852), and published an autobiography, *Meine Lebensgeschichte* (1861–63). See K. Frenzel, *Erinnerungen und Strömungen* (1890).

LEWES, George Henry (1817–78), English littérateur, was born in London, a grandson of the comedian, **Charles Lee Lewes** (1740–1803). Educated partly at Greenwich under Dr Burney, and partly in Jersey and Brittany, he left school early to enter first a notary's office, and then the house of a Russian merchant. He next tried walking the hospitals, but could not stand the operating room. In 1838 he went to Germany for nearly two years, studying the life, language and literature of the country. On his return to London he fell to work writing about anything and everything as a Penny Encyclopaedist and Morning Chronicler, as a contributor afterwards to a dozen more journals, reviews and magazines, and as editor of the *Leader* (1851–54), and of the *Fortnightly* (1865–66), which he himself founded. He was unhappily married and had children when his connection with George Eliot (q.v.) began in July 1854; it ended only with his death at their house in Regent's Park. His works, besides a tragedy and two novels (1841–48), include *The Spanish Drama* (1846); a *Life of Robespierre* (1848); *Comte's Philosophy of the Sciences* (1853), which is more than a translation; the admirable *Life and Works of Goethe* (1855);

Studies in Animal Life (1862); *Aristotle* (1864); *On Actors and the Art of Acting* (1875); and *Problems of Life and Mind* (1874–79). See A. T. Kitahel, *George Lewes and George Eliot* (1934).

LEWIS, (1) **Alun** (1915–44), Welsh poet, born in S. Wales, was killed in Arakan. His poetry is contained in *Raiders' Dawn* (1942) and *Ha! Ha! the Trumpets* (1944).

(2) **Clive Staples** (1898–1963), British medievalist and Christian apologist, born at Belfast, professor of Medieval and Renaissance English at Cambridge from 1954, published his first book *Dymer* (1926) under the name of Clive Hamilton. It is a narrative poem in rhyme royal, at once satirical and idealistic, a flavour which characterizes most of his work. His *Allegory of Love* was awarded the Hawthornden Prize (1936). His widest-known book is *The Screwtape Letters* (1942). Other titles include *The Problem of Pain* (1940), *Beyond Personality* (1944), works of scientific fiction including *Out of the Silent Planet* (1938) and *Perelandra* (1943), and books for children of which *The Last Battle* was awarded the Carnegie Prize in 1957. See Life by C. Walsh (1949).

(3) **Sir George Cornewall** (1806–63), English statesman and author, born in London, was educated at Eton and Christ Church, Oxford. Called to the bar in 1831, he became a Poor-Law commissioner in 1839. Liberal M.P. for Herefordshire 1847–52, for the Radnor Boroughs from 1855, he was chancellor of the exchequer 1855–58, home secretary 1859–61, and then war secretary. He edited the *Edinburgh Review* from 1852 to 1855 and succeeded to a baronetcy in 1855. He wrote *Origin of the Romance Languages* (1835), *Inquiry into the Credibility of Ancient Roman History* (1855–against Niebuhr), *Astronomy of the Ancients* (1859), *Dialogue on the Best Form of Government* (1859), &c. See his *Letters* (1870) and Bagehot's *Literary Studies* (1879).

(4) **Sir George Henry** (1833–1911), English criminal solicitor, was born at Holborn. His cases included the Hatton Garden diamond robbery, and he was solicitor for Parnell and other Irish nationalists (1888–89). He was knighted in 1893 and made a baronet in 1902.

(5) **John Llewellyn** (1880–1969), American labour leader, born in Iowa, was president of the United Mine Workers' Union from 1920 to 1960. In 1935 he formed a combination of unions, the Congress of Industrial Organizations, of which he was president till 1940. A skilful negotiator, he has made the miners' union one of the most powerful in the United States.

(6) **Matthew Gregory,** nicknamed **Monk** (1775–1818), English novelist, born in London, was educated at Westminster, Christ Church, Oxford, and Weimar, where he was introduced to Goethe. In 1794 he went as an attaché to The Hague, and there, inspired by Glanvill and the *Mysteries of Udolpho*, wrote *Ambrosio, or the Monk* (1795), the gruesome, unclean romance which made him so famous that in 1798 his invitation to dine at an Edinburgh hotel could elate Scott as nothing before or afterwards. A musical drama, *The Castle Spectre* (1798), *The Bravo of Venice* (1804) and a host more of blood-and-thunder plays, novels and tales are mostly forgotten. In 1796 he entered parliament as a silent member, and in 1812 he inherited from his father two large estates in Jamaica. So, to better the condition of his slaves there, he made the two voyages, in 1815–17, which furnished materials for his one really valuable work, the posthumous *Journal of a West India Proprietor* (1834; ed. by M. Wilson, 1929). On his way home he died of yellow fever. See his *Life and Correspondence* (1839), Birkhead's *The Tale of Terror* (1921) and A. M. Killen, *Le Roman terrifiant* (1923).

(7) **(Harry) Sinclair** (1885–1951), American novelist, born in Sauk Center, Minnesota. The son of a doctor, educated at Yale, he became a journalist and wrote several minor works before *Main Street* (1920), the first of a series of best-selling novels satirizing the arid materialism and intolerance of American small-town life. *Babbitt* (1922) still lends its title as a synonym for middle-class American philistinism. Other titles of this period are *Martin Arrowsmith* (1925), *Elmer Gantry* (1927) and *Dodsworth* (1929). Thereafter he tended to exonerate the ideologies and self-sufficiency he had previously pilloried, though he continued to be eagerly read. His later novels include *Cass Timberlane* (1945) and *Kingsblood Royal* (1947). He refused the Pulitzer prize for *Arrowsmith*, but accepted the Nobel prize for literature in 1930, being the first American writer to receive it. See Lives by C. Van Doren (N.Y., 1933) and M. Schorer (1963).

(8) **(Percy) Wyndham** (1884–1957), English artist, writer and critic, born in Bay of Fundy, Maine. He studied at the Slade School of Art, and with Ezra Pound founded *Blast*, the magazine of the Vorticist school. His writings are satirical, and include the novels *Tarr* (1918), *Childermass* (1928), *Men Without Art* (1934), and two autobiographical books *Blasting and Bombardiering* (1937) and *Rude Assignment* (1950). His paintings include works of abstract art, a series of war pictures, imaginative works and portraits, notably those of Eliot and Edith Sitwell. Five works of his are in the Tate Gallery, London. See studies by Porteous (1933), Kenner (1954), Tomlin (1955), *The Art of Wyndham Lewis* (ed. Read, 1951), and his *Letters* (ed. by Rose, 1963).

LEYDEN, John (1775–1811), Scottish poet and orientalist, was born, a shepherd's son, at Denholm, Roxburghshire. He studied medicine, &c., at Edinburgh University, and was licensed as a preacher in 1798. He helped Scott to gather materials for his *Border Minstrelsy*, and his translations and poems in the *Edinburgh Magazine* attracted attention. In 1803 he sailed for India as assistant surgeon at Madras. travelled widely in the East, acquired 34 languages, and translated the gospels into five of them. He accompanied Lord Minto as interpreter to Java, and died of fever at Batavia. His ballads have taken a higher place than his longer poems, especially *Scenes of Infancy* (1803); his dissertation on Indo-Chinese languages is also well known. See Lives by Scott (1811), Reith (1908) and Seshadri (1913).

L'HÔPITAL, Michel de, *lō-pee-tal* (1507–73), French statesman, born at Aigueperse in Auvergne, studied law at Toulouse and Padua and settled as an advocate in Paris at thirty. In 1547–48 he represented Henry II at the Council of Trent, and then was in the household of the Duchess of Berri. In 1554 he became superintendent of finances, in 1560 chancellor of France. He strove to pacify the religious quarrel by staying the hand of the Catholic persecutors. After 1563 he lost ground and in 1568 resigned and retired to his estate near Étampes. His Latin poems, speeches, &c., appeared in 1824–25. See Lives by C. T. Atkinson (1900), A. E. Shaw (1905), R. Anchel (1937).

LHOTE, André, *lōt* (1885–1962), French artist, teacher, and writer on art, born at Bordeaux. He associated with the Cubists and in his painting he combined classic precision of composition and a free, sensitive use of colour, but his greatest influence was exerted through his writings, e.g., *Treatise on Landscape* (1939) and *Treatise on the Figure* (1950), and his teaching in Paris. See the monograph by P. Courthion (Paris 1936).

LIADOV, Anatol Konstantinovich, *lya'dof* (1855–1914), Russian composer, born at St Petersburg, where he studied under Rimsky-Korsakov. His works include music for the piano and the vivid nationalist symphonic poems *Baba-Yaga*, *Kikimora* and *The Enchanted Lake*. He also made collections of Russian folksongs, conducted and was professor at St Petersburg.

LIAQUAT ALI KHAN (1895–1951), Pakistani statesman, after leaving Oxford became a member of the Inner Temple. He joined the Moslem League in 1923, and became prime minister of Pakistan in 1947. He was assassinated in 1951.

LIBANIUS (A.D. 314–393), Greek sophist, born at Antioch, taught at Athens, Constantinople and Antioch. A pagan, he yet was the instructor and friend of St Chrysostom and St Basil. See Lives by Petit (1866) and Sievers (1868).

LIBBY, Willard Frank (1908–), American scientist, born at Grand Valley, Colorado, studied and lectured at Berkeley, Cal., where he became associate professor in 1945. He did atom-bomb research (1941–45) on the separation of the isotopes of uranium at Columbia, and from 1945–54 was professor of Chemistry at Chicago. From 1954–59 he served on the U.S. Atomic Energy Commission. He was awarded the Nobel prize in chemistry (1960) for his part in the invention of the Carbon-14 method of determining the age of an object. From 1959 he has been professor of Chemistry at California University, and from 1962 director of the Institute of Geophysics.

LIBERIUS (d. 366), born in Rome, became pope in 352, but was banished in 355 for refusing to confirm the decree against Athanasius (q.v.). In 358 he regained the papal throne.

LICHTENBERG, Georg Christoph (1742–99), German physicist and satirist, born near Darmstadt, in 1770 became professor of Mathematics at Göttingen. He visited England, admired Garrick, and wrote a witty Commentary on Hogarth's plates (1794). See works by Grisebach (1871), Meyer (1886), Lauchert (1893), Bouillier (1915).

LICK, James (1796–1876), a Californian millionaire, born at Fredericksburg, Pa., the founder of the Lick Observatory on Mount Hamilton.

LIDDELL, Henry George (1811–98), English scholar, from Charterhouse passed to Christ Church, Oxford, and took a double first in 1833. He became tutor of his college, and in 1845 professor of Moral Philosophy. Headmaster of Westminster 1846–55, he returned to Christ Church as dean, was vice-chancellor 1870–74, and resigned the deanship in 1891. The great *Greek Lexicon* (1843), based on Passow, was a joint work by him and Robert Scott, D.D. (1811–87), master of Balliol (1854–70), and then Dean of Rochester. Liddell also wrote a *History of Rome* (1855; abridged as *The Student's Rome*). See Life by Thompson (1899).

LIDDELL HART, Basil Henry (1895–1970), English military journalist and historian, born in Paris, educated at St Paul's and Cambridge, served in the 1914–18 war and retired from the army in 1927. He was responsible for various tactical developments during the war, and wrote the postwar official manual of Infantry Training (1920). He was military correspondent to the *Daily Telegraph* (1925–1935) and to *The Times* (1935–39). In 1937 he relinquished his position as personal adviser to the minister of war to publicize the need for immediate development of air power and mechanized warfare. He wrote more than thirty books on warfare, as well as biographies of Scipio, T. E. Lawrence, &c. See his *Memoirs* (2 vols., 1965).

LIDDON, Henry Parry (1829–90), English divine, born at North Stoneham, Hampshire, graduated at Oxford in 1850. Ordained in 1852, from 1854 to 1859 he was vice-principal of Cuddesdon Theological College, and in 1864 became a prebendary of Salisbury, in 1870 a canon of St Paul's, and Ireland professor of Exegesis at Oxford (till 1882). In 1866 he delivered his Bampton Lectures on the *Divinity of Our Lord*. He strongly opposed the Church Discipline Act of 1874, and as warmly supported Mr Gladstone's crusade against the Bulgarian atrocities in 1876. Canon Liddon was the most able and eloquent exponent of Liberal High Church principles. He died suddenly at Weston-super-Mare. An *Analysis of the Epistle to the Romans* was published in 1893; his Life of Pusey was edited by Johnston and Wilson. See his own Life by Johnston (1904).

LIE, *lee*, (1) **Jonas** (1833–1908), Norwegian novelist and poet, was born at Eker near Drammen and abandoned law for literature. His novels, which give realistic pictures of fisher-life in Norway, include *The Visionary* (1870; trans. 1894), *One of Life's Slaves* (1883; trans. 1896), &c. He also wrote *Weird Tales* (trans. 1893) and comedies.

(2) **Marius Sophus** (1842–99), Norwegian mathematician, was educated at Christiania (Oslo) University, where he became an assistant tutor and in 1872 professor of Mathematics. In 1886 he was appointed professor at Leipzig but returned to Christiania in 1898. He is specially noted for his

theory of tangential transformations. See his *Theorie der Transformationsgruppen* (1893).

(3) **Trygve Halvdan** (1896–1968), Norwegian lawyer, born in Oslo, was a Labour member of the Norwegian parliament and held several posts, including minister of justice and minister of supply and shipping, before having to flee in 1940 with the government to Britain, where he acted as its foreign minister until 1945. He was elected secretary-general of the U.N. in 1946, but resigned in 1952. He was minister of industry (1963–1964) and of commerce and shipping from 1964. See his *In the Cause of Peace* (1954).

LIEBER, Francis, *lee'ber* (1800–72), German writer on law, government, &c., was born in Berlin, but in 1827 went to America for political reasons and became a naturalized American and professor of History and Political Economy at South Carolina College, Columbia and Columbia Law School. See Life by T. Sergeant Perry (Boston 1882).

LIEBERMANN, Max, *lee'ber-man* (1847–1935), German painter and etcher, born in Berlin, studied at Weimar and in Paris, where he first won fame. In Germany from 1878 he painted open-air studies and scenes of humble life which were often sentimental. Later, however, his work became more colourful and romantic, and, influenced by the French impressionists, he became the leading painter of that school in his own country.

LIEBIG, Justus, Freiherr von, *lee'bi*KH (1803–1873), German chemist, born at Darmstadt, studied at Bonn and Erlangen, and in 1822 went to Paris, where Gay-Lussac took him into his laboratory. In 1824 he became professor of Chemistry at Giessen, and in 1852 at Munich. In 1845 he was created Baron. Liebig was one of the most illustrious chemists of his age; equally great in method and in practical application, he made his mark in organic chemistry, animal chemistry, the doctrine of alcohols, &c. He was the founder of agricultural chemistry, a discoverer of chloroform and chloral and with Wohler (q.v.) of the benzoyl radical. By him an admirable chemical laboratory, practically the first, was established at Giessen. He vastly extended the method of organic analysis, and invented appliances for analysis by combustion and Liebig's condenser. His most important treatises were on the analysis of organic bodies (1837), *Animal Chemistry* (1842), *Organic Chemistry* (1843), and *Agricultural Chemistry* (1855), &c., and numerous papers in scientific journals (317 in the Royal Society's *Transactions*). See four volumes of his Correspondence (1884–92), and books by A. W. Hofmann (1876), W. A. Shenstone (1895), Vollhard (1909) and Benrath (1921).

LIEBKNECHT, *leeb'kne*KH*t*, (1) **Karl** (1871–1919), German barrister and politician, son of (2), was a member of the Reichstag from 1912 to 1916. During the 1914–18 war he was imprisoned as an independent, anti-militarist, social democrat. He took part in the Revolution (1918) and was murdered.

(2) **Wilhelm** (1826–1900), German social democrat, born at Giessen, for his part in the Baden insurrection of 1848–49 had to take refuge in Switzerland and England. He returned to Germany in 1862 and during a two-years' imprisonment was elected to the Reichstag (1874). With Bebel (q.v.) he edited *Vorwärts*.

LIEBRECHT, Felix, *leeb're*KH*t* (1812–90), German writer, born at Namslau in Silesia, was professor of German at Liège 1849–67. He early made himself known by articles on the origin and diffusion of folk tales, and by translations enriched with annotations. Among these are *Basile's Pentamerone* (1846), *Barlaam und Josaphat* (1847), and Dunlop's *Geschichte der Prosadichtungen* (1851).

LIEVEN, Dorothea, Princess, ***née*** **von Benkendorf** (1784–1857), early married the Russian diplomatist Prince Lieven (1774–1857), and from 1837 lived mostly in Paris, where her salon was much visited by diplomats. See her Correspondence with Earl Grey (1891), letters from London (1902), *Unpublished Diary* (1925), and Parry's *The Correspondence of Lord Aberdeen and Princess Lieven* (1939).

LIEVENSZ (Lievens), Jan (1607–74), Dutch historical painter and etcher, born at Leyden. A friend of Rembrandt, he shared a studio with him in Leyden. He visited England and lived in Antwerp before returning to Holland, where his paintings of allegorical subjects and his portraits became very successful.

LIFAR, Serge, *li-far'y'* (1905–), Russian dancer and choreographer, born in Kiev, became a student and friend of Diaghilev, whose company he joined at the age of eighteen. Since his first important appearance in *La Boutique fantasque*, he has danced with Pavlova, Karsavina and Spessirtzeva, and his many successes include *Le Pas d'Acier*, *Apollon* and *L'Après-Midi d'un faune*. He scored his first triumph as a choreographer in Paris in 1929 with *Créatures de Promethée* and since then he has been the force and the genius behind the Paris Opéra. He has written a biography of Diaghilev (1940) and *The Three Graces* (trans. 1959).

LIGHTFOOT, (1) Hannah. See GEORGE III.

(2) **John** (1602–75), Hebraist, born at Stoke-upon-Trent, studied at Christ's College, Cambridge, and in 1630 became rector of Ashley, Staffordshire, in 1643 of St Bartholomew's, London, and in 1644 of Great Munden, Herts. He was one of the most influential members of the Westminster Assembly, but, as an 'Erastian', often stood alone. In 1650 he was appointed master of Catharine Hall, Cambridge, in 1654–55 vice-chancellor, and in 1668 a prebendary of Ely, where he died. Lightfoot's works include the unfinished *Harmony of the Four Evangelists* (1644–50), *Commentary upon the Acts of the Apostles* (1645), and *Horae Hebraicae et Talmudicae* (1658–74), the great labour of his life. The best edition of his works is by Pitman, with Life (1822–25).

(3) **Joseph Barber** (1828–89), Bishop of Durham, was born at Liverpool, and from King Edward's School, Birmingham, passed in 1847 to Trinity College, Cambridge, where he graduated in 1851. Elected fellow in 1852, and ordained in 1854, he became tutor of Trinity in 1857, Hulsean professor of divinity in 1861, canon of St Paul's in 1871, Lady Margaret professor of Divinity at Cambridge

in 1875, and Bishop of Durham in 1879. A supreme grammarian and textual critic, he wrote admirable commentaries on the Pauline epistles, *Galatians* (1860), *Philippians* (1868), *Colossians and Philemon* (1875). His many other works include *On a Fresh Revision of the English New Testament* (1871), *Biblical Essays* (1893), and several volumes of sermons. The work of the Church Temperance Society and the White Cross Army was furthered by his exertions. He died at Bournemouth, and was buried at Durham. See short Life by Westcott (1894) and *Lightfoot of Durham*, by Eden and Macdonald (1932).

LIGNE, Charles Joseph, Prince de, *leen'y'* (1735–1814), Austrian soldier, born at Brussels, son of an imperial field-marshal whose seat was at Ligne near Tournai. He served at Kolin, Leuthen, Hochkirch and the siege of Belgrade (1789). A skilful diplomatist, the favourite of Maria Theresa and Catharine of Russia, and the friend of Frederick the Great, Voltaire and Rousseau, he wrote *Mélanges* (34 vols. 1795–1811), *Oeuvres posthumes* (1817), a Life of Prince Eugene (1809), and *Lettres et Pensées* (1809).

LIGONIER, John, 1st Earl, *lig-ō-neer'* (1680–1770), British soldier, born at Castres of Huguenot parentage, escaped to Dublin in 1697, and from 1702 served with high distinction under Marlborough. Colonel from 1720 of a splendid Irish regiment of dragoons, he commanded the foot at Fontenoy (1745), was taken prisoner at Val (1747), was made commander-in-chief and a viscount (1757), an earl and field-marshal (1766). He was buried in Westminster Abbey. See Life by R. Whitworth (1958).

LIGUORI, St Alfonso Maria de, *lee-gwō'ree* (1696–1787), Italian bishop, born at Naples, forsook law to take orders, and in 1732 with twelve companions founded the order of Liguorians or Redemptorists. In 1762 he became Bishop of Sant' Agata de' Goti, and proved an ideal bishop; but he resigned in 1775, and returned to his order. He was canonized in 1839. His works, edited by Monza in 70 vols., embrace divinity, casuistry, exegesis, history, canon law, hagiography, asceticism, even poetry. See Lives by Berthe (trans. 1906) and Baron Angot des Rotours (trans. 1916).

LI HUNG-CHANG, *lee-hoong-jang* (1823–1901), Chinese statesman, born at Hofei in Nganhui, took the Hanlin degree in 1849. In 1853, in the Taiping rebellion, he joined the Imperial army as secretary, was appointed a provincial judge, and in 1862 governor of Kiangsu, out of which, in conjunction with 'Chinese Gordon', he drove the rebels in 1863. Made an hereditary noble of the third class, in 1864 he was appointed governor-general of the Kiang provinces, and in 1872 of Chih-li and senior grand secretary. He founded the Chinese navy and promoted a native mercantile marine. On the outbreak of the war with Japan (1894), Li, in supreme command in Korea, was thwarted by the incompetence, dishonesty and cowardice of inferior officers. The Chinese were swept out of Korea, and Li, whose policy was that of peace, was deprived of his honours and summoned to Peking. He refused to comply, and the disastrous course of events soon compelled the emperor to restore him to honour. Through his efforts the war was brought to a termination in 1895, China ceding Formosa and paying a war indemnity of £35,000,000. Well aware of the value of Western culture and industry, he visited Europe and America in 1896. Intriguing with Russia, he fell in 1898. See his *Memoirs* (1913) and Life by J. O. P. Bland (1917).

LILBURNE, John (*c.* 1614–57), English Leveller or ultra-republican, born at Greenwich, and whipped and imprisoned by the Star Chamber in 1638, rose in the Parliamentary army to the rank of lieutenant-colonel. He became an indefatigable agitator, thought Cromwell's republic too aristocratic, and demanded greater liberty of conscience and numerous reforms. Repeatedly imprisoned for his treasonable pamphlets, he died at Eltham. See Life by P. Gregg (1961).

LILIENCRON, Detlev von, *lee'lee-en-krōn* (1844–1909), German poet and novelist, born at Kiel, fought in the Prussian army 1866 and 1870. He went to America but returned to Holstein in 1882, where for a time he held a civil service post. He is best known for his lyrics, which are fresh, lively and musical; his first volume *Adjutantenritte* appeared in 1883. Other volumes of verse were *Der Heidegänger* (1890), *Neue Gedichte* (1893) and *Gute Nacht* (1909). He also wrote, but not so successfully, novels and an epic poem *Poggfred* (1896). See Life by H. Spiero (Berlin 1913).

LILIENTHAL, Otto, *leel'yen-tahl* (1849–96), German aeronautical inventor, born at Anklam, studied bird-flight in order to build heavier-than-air flying machines resembling the birdman designs of Leonardo da Vinci. He made many short flights in his machines, but crashed to his death near Berlin in 1896. His brother, **Gustav** (1849–1933), continued his experiments and also invented a weather-proofing material. See Otto's *Der Vogelflug als Grundlage der Fliegerkunst* (1889) on the theory of flying machines.

LILLIE, Beatrice, by marriage **Lady Peel** (1898–), Canadian revue singer, born in Toronto, after an unsuccessful start as a drawing-room ballad singer found her true bent in 1914 in music hall and the new vogue of 'intimate revue' which Charlot had brought over from Paris. An unrivalled comic singer, she made famous Noel Coward's 'Mad Dogs and Englishmen'. During World War II she played to the troops and was decorated by General de Gaulle. She married Sir Robert Peel, 5th Bart., in 1920.

LILLO, George (1693–1739), English dramatist and jeweller, born in London of mixed Dutch and English Dissenting parentage, wrote seven plays, including *George Barnwell* (1731) and *Fatal Curiosity* (1736), both tragedies edited by Sir A. W. Ward (1906). His *Arden of Feversham* (brought out 1759) is a weak version of the anonymous play of that title (1592). Among the first to put middle-class characters on the English stage he had a considerable influence on European drama. See Life by T. Davies prefixed to his

Dramatic Works (1810) and W. H. Hudson, *A Quiet Corner in a Library* (1915).

LILLY, William (1602–81), English astrologer, born at Diseworth, Leicestershire, in 1620 went to London, where for seven years he served an ancient citizen, married his widow, and on her death in 1633 inherited £1000. He took up astrology, and soon acquired a considerable fame and large profits. In 1634 he obtained permission to search for hidden treasure in the cloisters of Westminster, but was driven from his midnight work by a storm, which he ascribed to demons. From 1644 till his death he annually issued his *Merlinus Anglicus, Junior*, containing vaticinations. In the Civil War he attached himself to the Parliamentary party as soon as it promised to be successful, and was rewarded with a pension. After the Restoration he was imprisoned for a little, and was reapprehended on suspicion of knowing something about the great fire of London in 1666. He died at Hersham. He wrote nearly a score of works on astrology. See his *History of his Life and Times* (1715).

LILLYWHITE, Frederick (1792–1854), English cricketer, was born near Goodwood, and started as a bricklayer. Famous as a round-arm bowler, he did not become a professional cricketer until middle age. 'Me bowling, Pilch batting, and Box keeping wicket' was his definition of cricket.

LILY, John. See LYLY.

LILYE, or Lily, William (*c.* 1466–1522), English classical grammarian, was born at Odiham, Hampshire, studied at Magdalen College, Oxford. He visited Jerusalem, Rhodes and Italy, and learned Greek from refugees from Constantinople. After teaching for a while in London he was appointed (1512) by Dean Colet first headmaster of his new school of St Paul's; this post he held till he was carried off by the plague. Lilye, who has good claims to be considered the first who taught Greek in London, had a hand in Colet's *Brevissima Institutio*, which, as corrected by Erasmus, and redacted by Lilye himself, was known as the *Eton Latin Grammar*. Besides this he wrote Latin poems (Basel 1518) and a volume of Latin verse against a rival schoolmaster (1521).

LIMBORCH, Philip van, *lim'bor*KH (1633–1712), Dutch theologian, was preacher at Gouda and Amsterdam, and became in 1668 professor in the Remonstrant or Arminian college at Amsterdam. Of his numerous works the most valuable are *Institutiones Theologiae Christianae* (1686, trans. 1702) and *History of the Inquisition* (trans. 1731).

LIMBURG, Pol, Henneguin and **Hermann de,** *lim'-bœr*KH (fl. early 15th cent.), three brothers, Flemish miniaturists, of whom comparatively little is known. Taken prisoner as youths in Brussels in time of war, on their way home from Paris they were released by the Duke of Burgundy and attached to his household as painters. In 1411 they became court painters to the Duke of Berry and produced 39 illustrations for his celebrated manuscript *Très Riches Heures du Duc de Berri*. Other works have been attributed to Pol de Limbourg, including *Heures d'Ailly*, two pages of the Turin-Milan Hours and several in a book of Terence. It is now believed that the three brothers were all dead by 1416. See P. Durieu, *Les Très Riches Heures de Jean, Duc de Berry* (1904).

LIMOUSIN, or Limosin, Léonard, *lim-oo-zi* (*c.* 1505–77), French painter in enamel, flourished from 1532 to 1574 at the French court and was appointed by Francis I head of the royal factory at Limoges.

LINACRE, Thomas (*c.* 1460–1524), English humanist and physician, born at Canterbury, studied at Oxford, was elected fellow of All Souls in 1484, and went to Italy, where he learned Greek, and took his M.D. at Padua. Erasmus and Sir Thomas More were both taught Greek by him. About 1501 Henry VII made him tutor to Prince Arthur. As king's physician to Henry VII and Henry VIII he practised in London; he also founded the Royal College of Physicians. Late in life he took orders. Linacre was one of the earliest champions of the New Learning. He translated several of Galen's works into Latin, and wrote grammatical treatises. See Lives by Johnson (1835) and Osler (1908).

LINCOLN, (1) Abraham (1809–65), sixteenth president of the United States, was born near Hodgenville, Ky., the son of a restless pioneer. After several moves, the family settled in southwest Indiana in 1816. In 1818 Abraham's mother died and his father remarried shortly. His stepmother encouraged Abraham's education although there was little schooling in that backwoods country. In 1830 the Lincolns moved on to Illinois and Abraham went to work as a clerk in a store at New Salem, Illinois. Defeated as a candidate for the legislature, he purchased a small store, whose failure left him in debt; but, being made village postmaster and deputy county surveyor, he studied law and grammar. Elected to the legislature in 1834, he served until 1842, being leader of the Whigs. He began the practice of law in 1836. At Springfield, in 1842, he married Mary Todd (1818–82). In 1846 he sat in congress; but professional work was drawing him from politics when in 1854 Stephen A. Douglas repealed the Missouri Compromise of 1820, and reopened the question of slavery in the territories. The bill roused intense feeling throughout the North, and Douglas defended his position in a speech at Springfield in October. Lincoln delivered in reply a speech which first fully revealed his power as a debater. He was then elected to the legislature. When the Republican party was organized in 1856 to oppose the extension of slavery Lincoln was its most prominent leader in Illinois, and the delegates of his state presented him for the vice-presidency. In 1858 Douglas, seeking re-election to the senate, began a canvass of Illinois in advocacy of his views of 'popular sovereignty'. Lincoln was also a candidate, and the contest, which gave Douglas the election, attracted the attention of the whole country. In May 1860 the Republican convention on the third ballot nominated Lincoln for the presidency. The Democratic party was divided between Douglas and Breckinridge. After an exciting campaign Lincoln received a popular vote of 1,866,462; Douglas, 1,375,157; Breckinridge, 847,953; and Bell, 590,631. Of the electors Lincoln had 180; Breckinridge, 72; Bell, 39; and Douglas, 12. South Carolina now seceded from the Union, and with the six Gulf states formed, in February 1861, the Confederate States of America. Lincoln, at his inaugural address on March 4, declared the Union perpetual, argued the futility of secession, and expressed his determination that the laws should be faithfully executed in all the states. On April 12, 1861, the Confederates began the Civil War by attacking Fort Sumter in Charleston harbour. Lincoln called a special session of congress, summoned 75,000 militia, ordered the enlistment of 65,000 regulars, and proclaimed a blockade of the southern ports. The Confederacy soon had control of eleven states, and put in the field 100,000 men. The first important battle was fought at Bull Run, Virginia, July 21, 1861, and resulted in the rout of the Union army. On September 22, 1862, just after McClellan's victory at Antietam, Lincoln proclaimed that on and after January 1, 1863, all slaves in states or parts of states then in rebellion should be free. On the following New Year's Day the final proclamation of emancipation was made. This greatest achievement of his administration, wrung from him by the exigencies of Civil War, was completed by the passage (1865) of the Thirteenth Amendment of the Constitution, which he planned and urged. In July 1863 Grant's capture of Vicksburg restored to the Union full control of the Mississippi River, while Meade's defeat of Lee at Gettysburg destroyed the last hope of the Confederates to transfer the seat of war north of the Potomac. General Grant, called to the chief command in March 1864, entered upon that policy of persistent attrition of the Confederate forces which finally brought peace. In the Republican Convention in June Lincoln was unanimously nominated for a second term. The Democrats nominated General McClellan. In November Lincoln received of the popular vote 2,216,000, and McClellan 1,800,000; of the electoral votes Lincoln had 212, McClellan 21. In his second inaugural address, in March 1865, Lincoln set forth the profound moral significance of the war. On Good Friday, April 14, at Ford's Theatre, Washington, he was shot by J. Wilkes Booth, an actor, and died next morning. Lincoln was fair and direct in speech and action, steadfast in principle, sympathetic and charitable, a man of strict morality, abstemious and familiar with the Bible, though not a professed member of any church. His fame is established as the saviour of his country and the liberator of a race. His *Collected Works* are to be found in several editions. These include his eloquent speeches—*Emancipation Proclamation* of 1862, the *Gettysburg Address* of 1863 when first were heard these words, 'government of the people, by the people, for the people', and the *Inaugural Address* of 1865. See Lives by Arnold (1885), Herndon and Weik (1889), Nicolay and Hay (10 vols. 1890), Morse (1893), Binns (1907), Strunsky (1914), Charnwood (1916), Barton (1925), Sandburg (1926, 1939), Beveridge (1928), Ludwig (trans. 1932), and the synthetic autobiography compiled by Stephenson (1927).

(2) **Benjamin** (1733–1810), American soldier, born at Hingham, Mass., in 1776 reinforced Washington after the defeat on Long Island and in 1777 was appointed major-general, in August receiving command of the southern department. In 1780 besieged by Clinton in Charleston, he was compelled to capitulate. He took part in the siege of Yorktown, and was secretary of war 1781–84.

LIND, (1) **James** (1716–94), Scottish physician, born in Edinburgh, first served in the Navy as a surgeon's mate, then, after qualifying in medicine at Edinburgh, became physician to the naval hospital at Haslar. His work towards the cure and prevention of scurvy induced the Admiralty in 1795 at last to issue the order that the Navy should be supplied with lemon juice. His *A Treatise of the Scurvy* (1753) was and is a classic of medical literature and won him an international reputation. See R. S. Allison, *Sea Diseases* (1943), M. E. M. Walker, *Pioneers of Public Health* (1930) and *Lind's Treatise on Scurvy* contained in a 'Bicentenary Volume with Additional Notes' issued by the Edinburgh University Press (1953).

(2) **Jenny** (1820–87), Swedish soprano, born of humble family at Stockholm, at nine entered the court theatre school of singing, and after lessons in Paris attained great popularity everywhere. Her earnings were largely devoted to founding and endowing musical scholarships and charities in Sweden and England. In 1852 the 'Swedish Nightingale' married Otto Goldschmidt (1829–1907). In 1883–86 she was professor of Singing at the Royal College of Music. See Life by Bulman (1956).

(3) **Samuel Colville** (1879–1965), American chemist, director of the School of Chemistry, Minnesota (1926), and dean of the Institute of Technology there (1935), invented an electroscope for radium measurements and advanced the ionization theory of the chemical effects of radium rays.

LINDAU, *lin'dow*, (1) **Paul** (1839–1919), German writer, born at Magdeburg, founded *Die Gegenwart* and *Nord und Süd*, and wrote books of travel and works of criticism. He is better known as a writer of plays and novels; the most successful of the former was perhaps *Maria und Magdalena*. The novels include *Herr und Frau Bewer* (1882), and *Berlin* (1886–87).

(2) **Rudolf** (1829–1910), brother of (1), author and diplomatist, wrote travel books, novels, &c., and was an editor of *Revue des deux mondes* and *Journal des débats*.

LINDBERGH, Charles Augustus (1902–), American aviator, born in Detroit, made the first solo nonstop transatlantic flight (New York-Paris, 1927), in the monoplane *The Spirit of St Louis*. His book of that name (1953) gained the Pulitzer prize (1954). See Life by K. S. Davis (1960). His wife, **Anne Morrow Lindbergh** (1906–), has written *North to the Orient* (1935), *Listen, the Wind* (1938), &c.

LINDEMANN. See CHERWELL.

LINDLEY, John (1799–1865), English botanist, was born at Catton near Norwich, the son of a nursery-gardener, author of *Orchard and Kitchen Gardens*. Appointed assistant-secretary to the Horticultural Society in 1822, he from 1829 to 1860 was professor of Botany in University College, London. Of his writings, *The Vegetable Kingdom* (1846) was the most important.

LINDSAY, (1) see CRAWFORD.

(2) **Alexander Dunlop, 1st Baron Lindsay of Birker** (1879–1952), Scottish scholar, born in Glasgow and educated at Glasgow University and University College, Oxford. A lecturer at Victoria University, he became in 1906 fellow of Balliol and Jowett lecturer in 1911. From 1922 to 1924 he was professor of Moral Philosophy at Glasgow, becoming in the latter year Master of Balliol. In 1949 he was appointed head of the new University College of North Staffordshire. His philosophical writings include *The Essentials of Democracy* (1929), &c., but he is best known for his excellent translation of Plato's *Republic* (1907).

(3) **Sir David.** See LYNDSAY.

(4) **Nicholas Vachel** (1879–1931), American poet, born at Springfield, Ill., tramped in America, trading and reciting his very popular ragtime rhymes for hospitality. His irrepressible spirits appear in *General Booth enters Heaven* (1913) and *The Congo* (1914). His later volumes of verse were less successful, and having lost his zest for life he returned to Springfield and committed suicide.

(5) **Robert.** See PITSCOTTIE.

LINGARD, John (1771–1851), English historian, born at Winchester of Catholic parents, was sent in 1782 to the English College of Douai, where he remained till the Revolution. In 1795 he received priest's orders, and in 1811 accepted the mission of Hornby, near Lancaster, declining the offer of a chair at Maynooth, as fourteen years later of a cardinal's hat. In 1821 he obtained his doctorate from Pius VII and in 1839 received a crown pension of £300. His *Antiquity of the Anglo-Saxon Church* (1806) was the pioneer of what became the labour of his life—a *History of England to 1688* (1819–30). This was fiercely assailed in the *Edinburgh Review*, but Lingard increased his reputation as a candid Catholic scholar. See his *Life and Letters* by Haile and Bonney (1911).

LINKLATER, Eric (1899–), Scottish novelist, born at Dounby in Orkney, was educated at Aberdeen, where he studied first medicine, then English. After serving in World War I he became a journalist in Bombay, an assistant lecturer in English at Aberdeen University and while in the United States (1928–30) wrote *Poet's Pub* (1929), the first of a series of clever satirical novels. His books include *Laxdale Hall* (1951), filmed in 1953, *Juan in America* (1931), *Private Angelo* (1946), filmed in 1949, and *The Merry Muse* (1959). *The Man on my Back* (1941) is autobiographical.

LINLEY, Thomas (1732–95), English composer, born at Wells, taught singing and conducted concerts at Bath. In 1775 his son-in-law Sheridan induced him to set his comic opera *The Duenna* to music. In 1776 they and Ford bought Garrick's share of Drury Lane Theatre. During the next fifteen years Linley was its musical director, composing songs, operas, &c. Of his sons, **Thomas** (1756–78), a friend of Mozart, possessed real musical genius, and **William** (1767–1835) composed glees, songs, &c. Of his gifted daughters, **Elizabeth Ann** (1754–92), singer, married Sheridan (q.v.). See C. Black's *Linleys of Bath* (1911; new ed. 1926).

LINNAEUS, or **Linné, Carl** (1707–78), Swedish botanist, founder of modern botany, was born the son of the parish clergyman of Råshult in South Sweden, and studied at Lund and Uppsala. In 1730 he was appointed assistant to the professor of Botany in Uppsala. An exploring trip through Swedish Lapland produced his *Flora Lapponica* (1737). Then followed a journey of scientific exploration through Dalecarlia; and in 1735–38 he was in Holland, mainly at Leyden, working at botany and arranging gardens. Meanwhile he had visited England and Paris, and published *Systema Naturae Fundamenta Botanica*, *Genera Plantarum*, *Critica Botanica*, in which he expounded his system of classification, based on sexual characteristics, long the dominant system. He practised as a physician in Stockholm, and in 1742 became professor of Botany at Uppsala. In 1745–46 he published *Flora Suecica* and *Fauna Suecica*; in 1751 *Philosophia Botanica*; and in 1753 *Species Plantarum*. He was ennobled in 1757. See Life by Fries (Eng. adaptation by Jackson, 1923), who also edited his Correspondence, and N. Gourlie, *Prince of Botanists* (1953).

LINNELL, John (1792–1882), English artist, a disciple and patron of Blake, was born in London, and studied at the Royal Academy. He painted portraits of Blake, Malthus, Whately, Peel, Carlyle, &c. His landscapes were mostly Surrey scenes. He is also known for his sculpture and engraving. See Life by A. T. Story (1892).

LIN PIAO (1908–), Chinese soldier and politician, son of a factory owner, educated at Whampoo military academy, joined the Communists against the Kuomintang in 1927, and was commander of the Northeast People's Liberation Army in 1945. He became defence minister and a vice chairman in 1959, and emerged from the 'cultural revolution' of 1966 as second-in-command to Mao Tse Tung, whose most likely successor he is at present.

LINSCHOTEN, Jan Huygen van (*c.* 1563–1611), Dutch traveller, born at Haarlem, wrote *Voyages into the East and West Indies* (trans. 1598).

LINTON, (1) **Sir James Dromgole** (1840–1916), English painter, born in London, laboured with success to elevate the status of painting in watercolours and reorganized the Royal Institute of Painters in Watercolours. Its first president in 1884–99, he was re-appointed in 1909. In 1885 he was knighted.

(2) **William James** (1812–98), English wood-engraver born in London, did some of his finest work for the *Illustrated London News*. In 1867 he went to the United States, and settled at New Haven, Conn. A zealous Chartist, he wrote *The Plaint of Free-*

dom (1852), *Life of Thomas Paine* (1879), &c. See his *Memories* (1895). His wife, **Eliza Lynn** (1822–98), born at Keswick, was also a writer, first as a novelist and later as a journalist. With her husband she prepared a volume on *The Lake Country* (1864), he furnishing the illustrations. In 1867 they separated. Her ' Girl of the Period ' articles in the *Saturday* were collected in 1883. See her *My Literary Life* (1899) and Life by Layard (1901).

LINTOT, Barnaby Bernard (1675–1736), English publisher, born at Horsham in Sussex, was associated with many of the celebrated writers of his day. Among the works which he published were Pope's translation of the *Iliad* in 6 volumes (1715–1720), and his *Odyssey* (1725–56), the first complete edition of Steele's *Dramatic Works* in collaboration with his rival publisher Jacob Tonson, and works by Gay, Cibber, Parnell and Rowe.

LIN YUTANG, *lin'yü-* (1895–), Chinese author, born at Changchow, Amoy, studied at Shanghai, Harvard and Leipzig, became professor of English at Peking (1923–26), secretary of the Ministry of Foreign Affairs (1927) and was chancellor of Singapore University (1954–55). He is best known for his numerous essays on, and anthologies of, Chinese wisdom and culture, and as co-author of the official romanization plan for the Chinese alphabet. See A. A. Lin, *Our Family* (1941).

LIPCHITZ, Jacques (1891–), Lithuanian-born sculptor, worked in Paris and, from 1941, in the U.S.A. At first an exponent of Cubism, he developed in the 'thirties a more dynamic style which he applied with telling effect to bronze figure and animal compositions.

LIPMANN, Fritz Albert (1899–), German-American biochemist, born at Königsberg, professor of Biochemistry at Harvard 1949–1957. He has done notable work on the vitamin-B complex. His discovery of ' coenzyme A ' brought him a Nobel prize for physiology and medicine (jointly with Krebs) in 1953.

LI PO, *lee-pō* (*c.* 700–762), Chinese poet, born in the province of Szechwan, led a gay dissipated life at the Emperor's court and later, as one of a wandering band calling themselves ' The Eight Immortals of the Wine Cup '. Regarded as the greatest poet of China, he wrote colourful verse of wine, women and nature. It is believed that he was drowned while attempting to kiss the moon's reflection. See Waley, *Poetry and Career of Li Po* (1951).

LIPPI, (1) **Filippino** (*c.* 1458–1504), Italian painter, son of (2), was a contemporary and associate of Botticelli, who almost certainly was a pupil of his father. He completed *c.* 1484 the frescoes in the Brancacci Chapel in the Carmine, Florence, left unfinished by Masaccio. Other celebrated series of frescoes were painted by him between 1487 and 1502, one in the Strozzi Chapel in Sta Maria Novella and one in the Caraffa Chapel, S. Maria sopra Minerva in Rome. Easel pictures painted by him are *The Virgin and Saints*, *The Adoration of the Magi* and *The Vision of St Bernard.* His predilection for antiquity led him to over-introduce it into his later works. See works by Konody (1911), and J. B. Supino's *Les Deux Lippi* (2nd ed. 1904).

(2) **Fra Filippo,** called **Lippo** (*c.* 1406–69), Italian religious painter, was born in Florence. An orphan, he was sent to the Carmine in Florence, where the Brancacci Chapel was painted by Masaccio whose pupil Lippi became. The style of his master can be seen in his early work, for example in the frescoes, *The Relaxation of the Carmelite Rule* (*c.* 1432). Of his stay in Padua, *c.* 1434, no artistic record has survived. The *Tarquinia Madonna* (1437), his first dated painting, shows the Flemish influence. His greatest work was on the choir walls of Prato cathedral begun in 1452. Between 1452 and 1464 he abducted and later was allowed to marry the nun Lucrezia, who was the model for many of his fine Madonnas. She was the mother of his son Filippino (1). His later works are deeply religious and include the series of *Nativities*. He was working in the cathedral at Spoleto when he died. See books by Strutt (1901), Konody (1911), Oertel (1942).

LIPPINCOTT, Joshua Ballinger (1813–86), American publisher, born in Burlington, N.J., had charge of a bookseller's business in Philadelphia 1834–36, and then founded his well-known publishing firm. *Lippincott's Magazine* dates from 1868.

LIPPMANN, (1) **Gabriel** (1845–1921), French physicist, professor of Mathematical and Experimental Physics at the Sorbonne (1886), was a Nobel prizewinner in 1908, when he was also elected F.R.S. He invented a capillary electrometer, and produced the first coloured photograph of the spectrum.

(2) **Walter** (1889–), American journalist, born in New York, educated at Harvard, on the editorial staff of the *New York World* until 1931, then a special writer for the *Herald Tribune*. His daily columns became internationally famous, and he won many awards, including the Pulitzer prize for International Reporting (1962). Among his best known books are *The Cold War* (1947), *Western Unity and the Common Market* (1962), &c.

LIPPS, Theodor (1851–1914), German aesthetic philosopher and psychologist, born at Wallhaben, was professor at Bonn, Breslau and Munich, and is best known as an early exponent of the psychological and aesthetic theory of empathy, i.e., self-projection into an experienced object, especially in his book *Ästhetik* (1903–06), which influenced Vernon Lee (q.v.).

LIPSIUS, (1) **Justus,** or **Joest Lips** (1547–1606), Flemish humanist, born at Issche, near Brussels, a great classical scholar of Louvain, who was successively Catholic, Lutheran, Calvinist and once more Catholic. Professor at Louvain, Jena and Leyden, his writings include editions of Tacitus and Seneca. See French Lives of him by Galesloot (1877) and Amiel (1884), and J. E. Sandys, *History of Classical Scholarship* (1903–08).

(2) **Richard Adelbert** (1830–92), German theologian, born at Gera, became professor at Vienna in 1861, at Kiel in 1865, and at Jena in 1871. A pioneer of the evangelical

movement, he wrote on dogmatics. His brother, **Justus Hermann** (1834–1920), in 1869 became professor of Classical Philology at Leipzig, and edited the *De Corona* of Demosthenes (1876), &c. Their sister **Marie** (1837–1927) made valuable contributions to music and its history.

LIPTON, Sir Thomas Johnstone (1850–1931), Scottish business man and philanthropist, born in Glasgow. When nine years old he began work as an errand-boy, and in 1865 went to America, where he worked successively on a tobacco plantation, in the rice-fields and in a grocer's shop. Returning to Glasgow, in 1871 he opened there his first grocer's shop, which was rapidly followed by many others. They prospered, due to high-quality goods at low prices and astute advertising, to the extent of making him a millionaire at the age of thirty. His munificent gifts to various charities brought him a knighthood in 1898 and a baronetcy in 1902. In 1899 he made his first challenge for the America's Cup with his yacht *Shamrock I*, this being followed at intervals by four other attempts, all of them unsuccessful. See *The Lipton Story* by A. Waugh (1951).

LISLE, *līl*, (1) **Alicia** (*c.* 1614–85), the widow of one of Cromwell's lords, was beheaded at Winchester by order of Judge Jeffreys for sheltering a rebel fugitive from Sedgemoor. At Charles I's execution she had said that her 'blood leaped within her to see the tyrant fall'.

(2) See ROUGET DE LISLE.

LISSAJOUS, Jules Antoine, *lee-sa-zhoo* (1822–80), French physicist, professor at the Collège St Louis, Paris, in 1857 invented the vibration microscope which showed visually the 'Lissajous figures' obtained as the resultant of two simple harmonic motions at right angles to one another. His researches extended to acoustics and optics. His system of optical telegraphy was used during the siege of Paris (1871).

LISSAUER, Ernst, *lis'ow-er* (1882–1937), German poet and dramatist, born in Berlin, much of whose writings had a strong nationalist flavour. *1813* (1913), a poem cycle, is a eulogy on the Prussian people in their fight to remove Napoleon from their land, as is the successful drama *Yorck* (1921) about the Prussian general. The poem *Hassgesang gegen England* (1914) achieved tremendous popularity in wartime Germany with its well-known refrain 'Gott strafe England'. Other works include a play about Goethe called *Eckermann* (1921), poems on Bruckner, *Gloria Anton Bruckners* (1921) a critical work, *Von der Sendung des Dichters* (1922), and some volumes of verse.

LIST, Friedrich (1789–1846), German political economist, born at Reutlingen, Württemberg, was a disciple of Adam Smith. Charged with sedition in 1824, he went to the U.S.A. and became a naturalized citizen. He was U.S. consul at Baden, Leipzig and Stuttgart successively. A strong advocate of protection for new industries, he did much by his writings to form German economic practice. His main work was *National System of Political Economy*, published in Germany in 1841. See Lives by Goldschmidt (Berlin 1878), Jentsch (1901), M. E. Hirst (1909).

LISTER, Joseph, Lord (1827–1912), English surgeon, was the second son of the microscopist, Joseph Jackson Lister, F.R.S. (1786–1869), of Upton, Essex. He graduated at London University in arts (1847) and medicine (1852), and became F.R.C.S. (1852) and F.R.C.S.E. (1855), after being house surgeon to James Syme (q.v.), whose daughter he married in 1856. He was successively lecturer on Surgery, Edinburgh; regius professor of Surgery, Glasgow; professor of Clinical Surgery, Edinburgh (1869), of Clinical Surgery, King's College Hospital, London (1877–93); president of the Royal Society (1895–1900). In addition to important observations on the coagulation of the blood, inflammation, &c., his great work was the introduction (1860) of the antiseptic system, which revolutionized modern surgery. He was president of the British Association in 1896. He was made a baronet in 1883, a baron in 1897, O.M. in 1902. See Lives by R. J. Godlee (1917; rev. 1924), Thompson (1934), H. C. Cameron (1948), K. Walker (1956).

LISTON, (1) **John** (1776–1846), English low comedian, born in London, played from 1805 to 1837 at the Haymarket, Drury Lane, and the Olympic. 'Paul Pry' (1825) was his best creation.

(2) **Robert** (1794–1847), Scottish surgeon, born at Ecclesmachan manse, Linlithgow, studied at Edinburgh and London, and settled in Edinburgh in 1818 as lecturer on Surgery and Anatomy. His surgical skill soon won him a European reputation. In 1835 he became professor of Clinical Surgery at University College, London. It was he who first used a general anaesthetic in a public operation at University College Hospital on December 21, 1846. His chief works are *Elements of Surgery* (1831) and *Practical Surgery* (1837).

LISZT, Franz (1811–86), Hungarian composer and pianist, was born at Raiding near Oedenburg. At nine he played in public, and was sent to study at Vienna. He afterwards went to Paris, studied and played there. He next made a tour to Vienna, Munich, Stuttgart and Strasburg; visited England thrice (1824–1827); in 1831 heard Paganini, and was fired by the resolve to become the Paganini of the piano. He became intimate with most of the great *littérateurs* then in Paris, and from 1835 to 1839 lived with the Comtesse d'Agoult (q.v.), by whom he had three children, one of whom, Cosima, married Wagner. Between 1839 and 1847 he was at the height of his brilliance, giving concerts throughout Europe. He met Princess Carolyne zu Sayn-Wittgenstein in 1847 with whom he lived till his death. In 1849, at the height of popularity, he retired to Weimar to direct the opera and concerts, to compose and teach. Here he brought out Wagner's *Lohengrin* and Berlioz's *Benvenuto Cellini*, and Weimar became the musical centre of Germany. In 1861 he resigned his appointment, and his life was subsequently divided mainly between Weimar, Rome and Budapest. In 1865 he received minor orders in the Church of Rome, and was known as Abbé. His visit to London in 1886 was a triumphal progress. He died at Bayreuth, where he is buried. As a pianist Liszt was unapproachable. His supreme command of technique was forgotten by hearers in admiration of the poetic qualities of his playing. His literary works on music include monographs on Chopin and Franz, and the music of the Gypsies. All his original compositions have a very distinct, sometimes a very strange, individuality. In his twelve symphonic poems he created a new form of orchestral music. One or two masses, the *Legend of St Elizabeth*, and a few other works, embody his religious aspirations. See his *Letters* (trans. 1894); Lives by Ramann (1880–94; trans. 1882), Nohl (trans. 1884), Martin (1886), Beaufort (1886), Göllerich (1888), Vogel (1888), Kapp (1909), Huneker (N.Y. 1911); Janka Wohl, *Recollections* (1888); and books by Hervey (1911), by his daughter, Cosima Wagner (1911), F. Corder (1925), S. Sitwell (1955), W. Beckett (1956).

LI T'AI PO. See LI PO.

LITHGOW, William (1582–*c.* 1645), Scottish traveller, born at Lanark, had already visited the Shetlands, Bohemia, Switzerland, &c., when, in 1610, he set out on foot from Paris to Palestine and Egypt. His second tramp led him through North Africa from Tunis to Fez, and home by way of Hungary and Poland. In his last journey (1619–21) to Spain via Ireland he was seized as a spy at Malaga and tortured. At London Gondomar, the Spanish ambassador, promised him reparation, but contented himself with promising. So Lithgow assaulted, or by another account was assaulted by, him in the king's ante-room, for which he was placed in the Marshalsea. He died at Lanark. His interesting *Rare Adventures and Paineful Peregrinations* was published in a complete form in 1632, incompletely in 1614. Besides he wrote *The Siege of Breda* (1637), *Siege of Newcastle* (1645), *Poems* (ed. by Maidment, 1863), &c.

LITTLETON, or Lyttleton, Sir Thomas (1402–81), English jurist, born at Frankley House, Bromsgrove, was recorder of Coventry in 1450, king's sergeant in 1455, in 1466 judge of common pleas, and in 1475 a knight of the Bath. His reputation rests on his treatise on *Tenures*, written in law French, first printed at London (? 1481), translated into English about 1500. It was the text that E. Coke (q.v.) commented on in his *Coke upon Littleton* (1826).

LITTRÉ, Maximilien Paul Émile, *lee-tray* (1801–81), French lexicographer and philosopher, born in Paris, from medicine turned to philology. His translation of Hippocrates (q.v.) procured his election in 1839 to the Academy of Inscriptions. He fought on the barricades in 1830, was one of the principal editors of the *National* down to 1851, and became an enthusiastic Comtist. *La Poésie homérique et l'Ancienne Poésie française* (1847) was an attempt to render book i of the *Iliad* in the style of the trouvères. In 1854 Littré became editor of the *Journal des savants*. His splendid *Dictionnaire de la langue française* (1863–72; supplement, 1878) did not prevent the Academy in 1863 from rejecting its author, whom Bishop Dupanloup denounced as holding impious doctrines. In 1871 Gambetta appointed him professor of History and Geography at the École polytechnique; he was chosen representative of the Seine department in the National Assembly; and in December 1871 the Academy at last admitted him. See Sainte-Beuve's *Notice* (1863), and *Nouveaux Lundis* (vol. v); Caro, *Littré et le Positivisme* (1883); and Pasteur's discourse (1882).

LITVINOV, Maxim (1876–1951), Soviet politician born, a Polish Jew, at Bielostok, in Russian Poland. He early joined in revolutionary activities and was exiled to Siberia, but escaped. In 1917–18 he was Bolshevist ambassador in London. He became in 1921 deputy people's commissar for foreign affairs and commissar from 1930 to 1939. From 1941 to 1942 he was ambassador to the U.S.A., and from 1942 to 1946 vice-minister of foreign affairs. By his efforts at international conferences, &c., he furthered acceptance of the Soviet Union abroad, and his skill in diplomacy was recognized more by America and Britain than in his own country.

LIUTPRAND, or Luitprand, *lyoot-prant* (*c.* 922–72), Italian prelate and historian, was born of a Longobard family in Pavia, passed from the service of Berengar, king of Italy, to that of the Emperor Otto I. Otto made him Bishop of Cremona, and sent him on an embassy to Constantinople. His *Antapodosis* treats of history from 886 to 950. *De Rebus Gestis Ottonis* covers 960–964, and *De Legatione Constantinopolitanâ* is a satire on the Greek court. See his works, ed. Becker (1915); trans. Wright (1930), and books by Köpke (1842) and Baldeschi (1889).

LIVENS. See LIEVENSZ.

LIVERPOOL, Robert Banks Jenkinson, Earl of (1770–1828), British statesman, son of the first Earl (1727–1808), was educated at the Charterhouse and Christ Church, Oxford, and entered parliament in 1791 as member for Rye. A Tory with Liberal ideas on trade and finance, in 1794 he became a member of the India Board, and in 1801 as foreign secretary negotiated the unpopular Treaty of Amiens. In 1803 he was created Lord Hawkesbury, and on Pitt's return to power he went to the Home Office. On the death of Pitt he declined to form an administration. In 1807 he again took the Home Office, and next year succeeded his father as Earl of Liverpool. In Perceval's ministry of 1809 he was secretary for war and the colonies. In 1812 he formed an administration which lasted for nearly fifteen years. The attitude of the government to Poland, Austria, Italy and Naples, coercive measures at home, and an increase in the duty on corn were regarded as reactionary. Lord Liverpool himself was a Free Trader, and ultimately sought to liberalize the tariff. Notwithstanding the blunder of the sinking fund, his financial policy generally was sound, enlightened and economical. He united the old and the new Tories at a critical period. In February 1827 he was struck with apoplexy, and died the following year. See Life by C. D. Yonge (3 vols. 1868), and studies by W. R. Brock (1941) and Petrie (1954).

LIVINGSTON, an American family, descended from the fifth Lord Livingstone, guardian of Mary, Queen of Scots, and from his grandson, John Livingstone (1603–72), minister of Ancrum, banished for refusing the oath of allegiance to Charles II, and from 1663 pastor of the Scots kirk at Rotterdam. His son Robert (1654–1728) went to America in 1673, settled at Albany, and received land. See Life by L. H. Ledler (1961). Of his grandsons, Philip (1716–78) signed the Declaration of Independence; and William (1723–90), was the first and able governor of New Jersey 1776–90. **Robert R. Livingston** (1746–1813), great-grandson of the first Robert, was born in New York, and admitted to the bar in 1773. Sent to congress in 1775, he was one of the five charged with drawing up the Declaration of Independence, and till 1801 was chancellor of New York state. As minister plenipotentiary at Paris he negotiated the cession of Louisiana. He enabled Fulton to construct his first steamer, and introduced in America the use of sulphate of lime as a manure, and the merino sheep. See Life by F. De Peyster (1876). **Edward Livingston** (1764–1836), also a great-grandson of the first Robert, was born at Clermont, N.Y., and called to the bar in 1785. He sat in congress from 1795 to 1801, when he became U.S. district attorney for New York, and mayor of New York; but in 1803, owing to a subordinate's misappropriations, he found himself in debt to the federal government. He handed over his property to his creditors, and in 1804 settled in New Orleans, where he obtained lucrative practice at the bar. During the second war with England he was aide-de-camp to General Jackson; and 1822–29 he represented New Orleans in congress. In 1823–24 he systematized the civil code of Louisiana. His criminal code was completed, but not directly adopted. Livingston was elected in 1829 to the senate, and in 1831 appointed secretary of state. In 1833 he went to France as plenipotentiary. He died at Rhinebeck, N.Y. See Life by C. H. Hunt (1864).

LIVINGSTONE, David (1813–73), Scottish missionary and traveller, was born at Low Blantyre, Lanarkshire, and from ten till twenty-four years of age was a worker in a cotton factory there. A pamphlet by Karl Gutzlaff kindled the desire to become a missionary; and he resolved to apply himself to medicine. Having completed his studies in London, prevented by war from carrying out his wish to work in China, he was attracted to Africa by Dr Moffat, and, ordained under the London Missionary Society in November 1840, reached Simon's Bay March 11, 1841, Kuruman July 31, and for several years laboured in Bechuanaland. Repulsed by the Boers in an effort to plant native missionaries in the Transvaal, he travelled northward, discovered Lake Ngami, and determined to open trade routes east and west. The journey occupied from June 1852 to May 1856, when he arrived at Quilimane. It was accomplished with a mere handful of followers, amid sicknesses, perils and difficulties without number. But a vast amount of valuable information was gathered respecting the country, its products and the native tribes. Not the least among his discoveries was the Victoria Falls of the Zambezi. He was welcomed home with extraordinary enthusiasm. During the fifteen months spent in England and Scotland he published his *Missionary Travels* (1857), and having severed his connection with the London Missionary Society in order to be free to undertake future explorations, was appointed by the government chief of an expedition for exploring the Zambezi. Setting out in March 1858, he explored the Zambezi, Shiré and Rovuma; discovered Lakes Shirwa and Nyasa, and came to the conclusion that Lake Nyasa and its neighbourhood was the best field for commercial and missionary operations, though he was hampered by the Portuguese authorities, and by the discovery that the slave trade was extending in the district. His wife Mary, Moffat's daughter, whom he had married in 1844, died in 1862, and was buried at Shupanga. The expedition was recalled in July 1863. At his own cost he now journeyed a hundred miles westward from Lake Nyasa; then himself navigated his little steamer to Bombay; and returned to England in 1864. His second book, *The Zambesi and its Tributaries* (1865), was designed to expose the Portuguese slave traders, and to find means of establishing a settlement for missions and commerce near the head of the Rovuma. A proposal was made to him by the Royal Geographical Society to return to Africa and settle a disputed question regarding the watershed of central Africa and the sources of the Nile. In March 1866 he started from Zanzibar, pressed westward amid innumerable hardships, and in 1867–68 discovered Lakes Mweru and Bangweulu. Obliged to return for rest to Ujiji, he struck westward again as far as the river Lualaba, thinking it might be the Nile, but far from certain that it was not, what it proved afterwards to be, the Congo. On his return after severe illness to Ujiji, Livingstone was found there by Stanley (q.v.), sent to look for him by the *New York Herald*. Determined to solve the problem, he returned to Bangweulu, but fell into wretched health, and in Old Chitambo (now in Zambia), on the morning of May 1, 1873, he was found by his attendants, dead. His faithful people embalmed his body, and carried it to the coast. It was conveyed to England, and was buried in Westminster Abbey. Livingstone's *Last Journals*, brought down to within a few days of his death, were published in 1874; the family letters in 1959; the *Private Journals* (1851–53) in 1960. See Blaikie's *Personal Life of David Livingstone* (1880), Lives by Thomas Hughes (1889), R. J. Campbell (1929), Macnair (1940), Seaver (1957), Sir H. H. Johnston's *Livingstone and the Exploration of Central Africa* (1891), and Sir R. Coupland's *Livingstone's Last Journey* (1945).

LIVIUS. See Livy.

LIVIUS ANDRONICUS (fl. 3rd cent. B.C.), the father of Roman dramatic and epic poetry, was a Greek by birth, probably a native of Tarentum, was carried as a slave to Rome in 272 B.C., but was afterwards freed by his master. He translated the *Odyssey* into Latin Saturnian verse, and wrote tragedies, comedies, and hymns after Greek models. Only fragments are extant (ed. by L. Müller, 1885).

LIVY, properly **Titus Livius** (59 B.C.–A.D. 17), Roman historian, was born at Padua, of a noble and wealthy family, and on coming to Rome was admitted to the court of Augustus. He never flattered the emperor, but avowed his preference for a republic. He praised Brutus and Cassius, sympathized with Pompey, and stigmatized Cicero, an accessory to the murder of Caesar, as having got from Antony's bravoes only his deserts. Of the great Caesar himself he doubted whether he was more of a curse or a blessing to the commonwealth. Such friendship as they had for each other Livy and Augustus never lost. Livy died at his native Patavium. His history of Rome from her foundation to the death of Drusus, 9 B.C., comprised 142 books, of which those from the 11th to the 20th, and from the 46th to the 142nd, have been lost. Of the 35 that remain, the 41st and 43rd are imperfect. The 'periochae', or summaries of the contents of each book, composed in the wane of Roman literature, to catalogue names and events for rhetorical purposes, have all, however, come down to us, except those of books 136 and 137. But what has been spared is more than enough to confirm in modern days the judgment of antiquity which places Livy in the forefront of Latin writers. His impartiality is not less a note of his work than his veneration for the good, the generous, the heroic in man. His style is as nearly perfect as is compatible with his ideal of the historian. For investigation of facts he did not go far afield. Accepting history as fine art rather than as science, he was content to take his authorities as he found them, and where they differed was guided by taste or predilection. Gronovius, Drakenborch, Ruddiman, Madvig, Alschefski, Weissenborn, Luchs, Müller, and Zingerle purified Livy's text, also critically edited by Conway and Walters (1914 *et seq.*). See edition with trans. by Foster (1919 *et seq.*), and Philemon Holland's fine Elizabethan English trans. (1600).

LLEWELLYN, Richard, *hloo-el'lin*, pseud. of **Richard Doyle Vivian Llewellyn Lloyd** (1907–), Welsh author, born at St David's, Pembrokeshire, established himself, after service with the regular army and a short spell as a film director, as a best-selling novelist with *How Green was my Valley* (1939), a good example of the Welsh genius for blending realism and humour with sympathetic understanding of the human condition. Later works include *None but the Lonely Heart* (1943), and *The Flame of Hercules* (1957).

LLORENTE, Juan Antonio, *lyō-rayn'tay* (1756–1823), Spanish priest and historian, born at Rincón del Soto, rose to be secretary to the Inquisition in 1789 and was made canon of Toledo in 1806. In 1809, when the Inquisition was suppressed, Joseph Bonaparte placed all its archives in his hands and he went to Paris, where the *Histoire critique de l'inquisition d'Espagne* came out in 1817–18. Its value was recognized at once, but it provoked bitter feeling, and Llorente was ordered to quit France. See his *Autobiography*.

LLOYD, (1) **Charles** (1775–1839), English poet, the friend of Coleridge and Lamb, born of Quaker parentage at Birmingham, about 1811 began to become deranged, and died in an asylum near Versailles.

(2) **Edward** (d. *c.* 1730), the London coffee-house keeper in 1688–1726, after whom is named 'Lloyd's', the London society of underwriters. The coffee house became a haunt of merchants and shipowners and for them Lloyd started his *Lloyd's News*, later to become *Lloyd's List*.

(3) **Humphrey** (1800–81), Irish scientist, born and educated in Dublin, where he became provost of Trinity College, was president of the British Association in 1857. He is best known for his researches in optics and his experiments on internal conical refraction

(4) **(John) Selwyn Brooke** (1904–), English politician, born in Liverpool of Anglo-Welsh parentage, was educated at Fettes and Cambridge. He studied law and became a barrister in 1930 with a practice in Liverpool. He stood unsuccessfully as Liberal candidate for Macclesfield and in 1931 transferred his allegiance to the Conservative party. Meantime he entered local government, becoming in 1936 chairman of the Hoylake Urban District Council. During World War II, he was a staff officer rising to the rank of colonel general staff, Second Army. In parliament in 1945 as Conservative member for Wirral, he continued to practise law, becoming a K.C. in 1947. In 1951 he was appointed minister of state, and in 1954 became successively minister of supply and minister of defence. As foreign secretary in 1955, he defended Eden's policy on Suez, and was retained in this post until 1960 when he became chancellor of the Exchequer, resigning in Macmillan's 'purge' in 1962. Refusing a peerage, he was given the task of investigating the Conservative Party organization. He was lord privy seal and leader of the House (1963–64).

LLOYD-GEORGE OF DWYFOR, (1) **David Lloyd George, 1st Earl** (1863–1945), Liberal statesman of Welsh parentage, was born in Manchester. At the age of two when his father died his family were taken to Wales to Llanystumdwy near Criccieth, the home of his uncle Richard Lloyd, and it was he who, seeing the latent brilliance in the young Lloyd George, took his education in hand. It was from his uncle that he acquired his religion, his industry, his vivid oratory, his radical views and his Welsh nationalism. He became a solicitor and in 1890 his career as a politician began when he was elected as an advanced Liberal for Carnarvon Boroughs. From 1905 to 1908 he was president of the Board of Trade and was responsible for the passing of three important Acts—the Merchant Shipping Act and the Census of Production Act in 1906, and the Patents Act of 1907. As chancellor of the Exchequer from 1908 to 1915, he reached the heights as a social reformer with his Old Age Pensions Act in 1908, the National Insurance Act in 1911, and the momentous budget of 1909–10, whose rejection by the Lords led to the constitutional crisis and the Parliament Act of 1911. Up to the outbreak of the war in 1914 he had been regarded as a pacifist. As a strong upholder of the national rights of a smaller country he saw the parallel between the Welsh and the Boers and his condemnation of the Boer War had been loud. The threat of invasion of Belgium by Germany dispelled all pacifist tendencies. In 1915 he was appointed minister of munitions, and in 1916 became war secretary and superseded Asquith as coalition prime minister, holding office from 1916 to 1922. By his forceful policy he was, as Hitler later said of him, 'the man who won the war'. He was one of the 'big three' at the peace negotiations, which he handled brilliantly although he was inclined to pay too much attention to the demands of the small countries. This later, as with Greece, led Britain into difficulties. At home there was a split in the Liberal party which never completely healed. In 1921 he treated with the Sinn Feiners and conceded the Irish Free State. This was very unpopular with the Conservatives in the government and led to his downfall and the downfall of the Liberals as a party at the election of 1922. He retained his seat until the year of his death, in which year he was made an earl. He wrote his *War Memoirs* (1933–36) and *The Truth about the Peace Treaties* (1938). See Lives by A. J. Sylvester (1947), M. Thomson (1949), Earl Lloyd George (1960), and W. George, *My Brother and I* (1958).

(2) **Gwilym, 1st Viscount Tenby** (1894–1967), politician, second son of (1), was born at Criccieth and entered parliament as Liberal member for Pembrokeshire in 1922, again from 1929 to 1950 during which term he was parliamentary secretary to the Board of Trade (1939–41) and minister of fuel and power (1942–45). In 1951 he was returned as Liberal-Conservative member for Newcastle North and was minister of food until 1954. He was minister for Welsh affairs until 1957, when he was created Viscount Tenby of Bulford.

(3) **Lady Megan** (1902–66), politician, born at Criccieth, younger daughter of (1), was elected Liberal member of parliament for Anglesey in 1929 and Independent Liberal between 1931 and 1945. Defeated in the election of 1951, she in 1955 joined the Labour party and was M.P. for Carmarthen from 1957. She was awarded the C.H. posthumously.

LLYWARCH HÊN, Welsh poet, flourished about 700.

LLYWELYN, the name of two Welsh princes, *hloo-el'in*, (1) **ab Iorwerth,** called **the Great** (d. 1240), successfully maintained his independence against King John and Henry III. He died, a Cistercian, at Aberconway.

(2) **ab Gruffydd** (d. 1282), grandson of (1), the opponent of Edward I, was slain near Builth and with him Wales lost her political independence.

LOBACHEVSKI, Nikolai (1793–1856), Russian mathematician, born at Makariev, founder of non-Euclidean geometry. He became professor at Kazan in 1814. His ideas were published in *Über die Principien der Geometrie* (1829–30).

L'OBEL or **Lobel, Matthias de** (1538–1616), Flemish naturalist, born at Lille, became botanist and physician to James VI and I, and gave his name to the *Lobelia*. He died at Highgate.

LÔBO, (1) **Francisco Rodrigues** (*c.* 1580–1622), Portuguese writer, born at Leiria, wrote *Primavera* (1601) and other remarkable prose pastorals and verse. He was drowned in the Tagus. His lyrics are of great beauty and his work holds a valuable place in the literature of his country. See A. F. G. Bell, *Portuguese Literature* (1922).

(2) **Jeronimo** (1593–1678), Portuguese Jesuit traveller, born at Lisbon, went to India in 1621, and was superintendent of missions in Abyssinia, 1625–34. He wrote of his travels in *Voyage historique d'Abissinie*, translated and published in French in 1728.

LOCHIEL. See CAMERON OF LOCHIEL.

LOCHNER, Stefan, *loKH'ner* (*c.* 1400–51), German painter, born at Meersburg on Lake Constance, and the principal master of the Cologne school, marking the transition from the Gothic style to naturalism. His best-known work is the great triptych in Cologne Cathedral. His use of a varnish medium, as in his *Three Saints* in the National Gallery, London, gives him an important place in the early development of oil painting.

LOCKE, (1) **Alain LeRoy** (1886–1954), American Negro educationist, born at Philadelphia, was a Rhodes scholar at Oxford (1907–10), and from 1917 professor of Philosophy at Howard University. He wrote *The New Negro* (1925), *Negro Art* (1937), &c.

(2) **John** (1632–1704), English philosopher, the principal founder of philosophical Liberalism and with Bacon, of English Empiricism, born August 29 at Wrington, Somerset, was educated at Westminster School under Richard Busby (q.v.) and at Christ Church, Oxford, where he found the prevailing Aristotelianism 'perplexed with obscure terms and useless questions'. He was elected to a life studentship there, which was withdrawn in 1684 by order of the king. His dislike of the Puritan intolerance of the College divines prevented him from taking orders. Instead, he dabbled in medicine and scientific experimentation and discussion and became known as 'Doctor Locke'. In 1667 he entered as physician the household of Anthony Ashley Cooper, later first Earl of Shaftesbury (q.v.). After successfully operating upon the latter for an abscess in the chest (1668) he became Ashley's close confidential adviser in political and scientific matters and was elected F.R.S. The latter directed Locke's interests towards philosophy. A small club for discussion of theological and philosophical questions was founded by Locke, and at such a gathering in the winter (1670–1671) the group welcomed Locke's suggestion, which was to be key to his famous *Essay*, that before attempting to solve any such questions, they should first of all discover what the human understanding was fitted to deal with. In 1672, Ashley became first Earl of Shaftesbury and lord chancellor, and Locke secretary of the Board of Trade. For health reasons he spent the politically

troublesome years (1675–79) in Montpelier and Paris, where he made contact with the brilliant circle of Gassendi and Arnauld. Shaftesbury, after a short spell in the Tower, was restored to favour and Locke re-entered his service. In 1683, however, he found it prudent to follow his late master to Holland. How far Locke was involved in Shaftesbury's secret plotting for Monmouth is not certain. But Locke settled under the name of Dr Van der Linden in Amsterdam, where he struck up an intimate friendship with the liberal theologians Limborch and Le Clerc. In 1687 he removed to Rotterdam and joined the English supporters of William of Orange. His famous *Treatises on Government* (1689), published anonymously, were not, as is commonly supposed, written to justify the 'Glorious Revolution' (1688). There is evidence that they may have been written as early as 1681 and they constitute Locke's reply to the patriarchal Divine Right Theory of Sir Robert Filmer and *a fortiori* the political philosophy of Hobbes. Locke also built up his political theory from the shortcomings of an imagined pre-civil society, which for Hobbes was simply war of everyman with everyman. Locke, however, insisted on the natural morality of pre-social man. Hence, contracting into civil society by surrendering personal power to a ruler and magistrates is for Locke a method of securing natural morality more efficiently. The ruling body if it offends against natural law must be deposed. This sanctioning of rebellion, together with Locke's curious doctrine of property, became for the American colonists and the French revolutionaries in the next century, in the words of Oakeshott, 'a brilliant abridgement of the political habits of Englishmen'. It was enshrined in the American Constitution. On his return to England, he declined an ambassadorship and became a commissioner of appeals. His last years were spent at Oates, Essex, at the home of Sir Francis and Lady Masham, an admirer, the daughter of Cudworth (q.v.). His *Essay Concerning Human Understanding* (1690), in its acceptance of the possibility of rational demonstration of moral principles and the existence of God, its scholastic doctrine of substance, is still caught up in Cartesian rationalism, but its denial of innate ideas, its demonstration that 'all knowledge is founded on and ultimately derives itself from sense . . . or sensation' was the real starting-point of British empiricist epistemology. Locke's *Thoughts on Education* (1693), the four *Letters on Toleration* (1689, 1690, 1692, and posthumous fragment), his *Reasonableness of Christianity* (1695) in which he aimed at a reunion of the churches, as well as his several defences of his doctrines against Norris, Stillingfleet, Leibniz, Proast, are also important. He died October 28, 1704, and was buried in the churchyard of High Laver. As a philosopher Locke had his betters. But as a champion and codifier of liberal principles in an intolerant age and as a pioneer of new ways of thought, he has few equals. See Life by M. Cranston (1957), *Correspondence with Clarke*, ed. B. Rand (1927), Leibniz's criticisms in the latter's *Nouveaux Essais* (1765), and studies by S. Alexander (1908), J. Gibson (1917), R. I. Aaron (1937), D. J. O'Connor (1952), J. W. Yolton (1956), M. Salvadori (1960).

(3) **Matthew** (*c.* 1630–77), English composer, born in Exeter. He collaborated with Shirley on the masque *Cupid and Death*, winning a reputation as a theatre composer. After composing the music for Charles II's coronation procession, Locke became composer-in-ordinary to the king. His works include much incidental music for plays (though that for *Macbeth* long attributed to him is of doubtful authenticity), Latin church music, songs and chamber works. Locke was a champion of the 'modern' French style of composition.

(4) **William John** (1863–1930), English novelist, born at Demerara, British Guiana (Guyana), educated in Trinidad and at Cambridge. He taught between 1890 and 1897 at Clifton and Glenalmond. Disliking teaching, he then became secretary of the Royal Institute of British Architects until 1907. In 1895 appeared the first of a long series of novels and plays which with their charmingly written sentimental themes had such a success during his life in both Britain and America. *The Morals of Marcus Ordeyne* (1905) and *The Beloved Vagabond* (1906) assured his reputation. Others of his popular romances included *Simon the Jester* (1910), *The Joyous Adventures of Aristide Pujol* (1912) and *The Wonderful Fear* (1916). His plays, some of which were dramatized versions of his novels, were all produced with success on the London Stage.

LOCKER-LAMPSON, Frederick (1821–95), English writer, born in London, came of naval ancestry, and from Mincing Lane and Somerset House passed to the Admiralty, where he became the trusted confidant of three first lords. *London Lyrics* (1857) revealed him as a writer of bright and clever *vers de société*; later books were *Lyra Elegantiarum* (1867) and *Patchwork* (1879). In 1850 he married Charlotte (d. 1872), daughter of the seventh Earl of Elgin; and in 1874 Hannah (d. 1915), only daughter of Sir Curtis Lampson, whose name he added to his own. See his *My Confidences* (1896), and Life by A. Birrell (1920).

LOCKHART, (1) **George** (1673–1731), of Carnwath, Lanarkshire, from 1702 a Jacobite M.P., was killed in a duel. See the *Lockhart Papers* (1817).

(2) **John Gibson** (1794–1854), Scottish biographer and critic, born near Wishaw, spent his boyhood in Glasgow, where at eleven he passed from the high school to the college. At thirteen, with a Balliol Snell exhibition, he went up to Oxford. In 1813 he took a first in classics; then, after a visit to the Continent (to Goethe at Weimar), studied law at Edinburgh, and in 1816 was called to the Scottish bar. But he was no speaker; and having while still at Oxford written the article 'Heraldry' for the *Edinburgh Encyclopaedia*, and translated Schlegel's *Lectures on the History of Literature*, from 1817 he took more and more to letters, and with Wilson became the chief mainstay of *Blackwood's*. In its pages he

first exhibited the caustic wit that made him the terror of his Whig opponents. *Peter's Letters to His Kinsfolk* ('2nd ed.' 1819), a clever skit on Scottish society, was followed by four novels—*Valerius* (1821), *Adam Blair* (1822), *Reginald Dalton* (1823) and *Matthew Wald* (1824). *Ancient Spanish Ballads* appeared in 1823; Lives of Burns and Napoleon in 1828 and 1829; and the Life of Scott, Lockhart's masterpiece, in 1837–38. He had met Scott in May 1818, and in April 1820 married his eldest daughter, Sophia. In 1825 he removed to London to become editor until 1853 of the *Quarterly Review*. In 1843 he also became auditor of the duchy of Cornwall. But his closing years were clouded by illness and deep depression; by the secession to Rome of his only daughter, with her husband, J. R. Hope-Scott; and by the loss of his wife in 1837, of his two boys in 1831 and 1853. The elder was the 'Hugh Littlejohn' of Scott's *Tales of a Grandfather*; the younger, Walter, was a scapegrace in the army. Like Scott, Lockhart visited Italy in search of health; like Scott, he came back to Abbotsford to die. He is buried in Dryburgh at Sir Walter's feet. See Life by Andrew Lang (2 vols. 1896), and study by G. Macbeth (1935).

(3) **William Ewart** (1846–1900), Scottish subject painter, born at Annan in Dumfriesshire, was elected an A.R.S.A. in 1870, an R.S.A. in 1878. He painted the Jubilee Celebration in Westminster (1887) and was popular as a portrait painter.

(4) **Sir William Stephen Alexander** (1841–1900), K.C.B. (1887), K.C.S.I. (1895), British officer saw service in Abyssinia, Afghanistan, Burma, &c. In 1897 he commanded the expedition against the Afridis. He was c.-in-c. in India from 1898.

LOCKYER, Sir Joseph Norman (1836–1920), English astronomer, born at Rugby, became a clerk in the War Office (1857) and in the Science and Art Department (1875). In 1868 (26 years before Ramsay) he detected helium in the sun's chromosphere by daylight. In 1869 he was made F.R.S., and in 1870 lecturer on Astronomy at South Kensington. He headed many eclipse expeditions, started (1869) and edited *Nature*, and wrote much on solar chemistry and physics, on the meteoritic hypothesis, and on the orientation of stone circles.

LODGE, (1) Edmund (1756–1839), English biographer and writer on heraldry, is best known by his *Portraits of Illustrious Personages* (1821–34) and *The Genealogy of the Existing British Peerage* (1832, enlarged 1859).

(2) **Henry Cabot** (1850–1924), American Republican senator, historian and biographer, was born in Boston. He was assistant editor of the *North American Review*, but from 1878 his career was mainly political and he became a senator in 1893. See his *Early Memories* (1914). His grandson, **Henry Cabot** (1902–), became a Republican senator in 1936, was American U.N. delegate (1953–60), and ambassador to South Vietnam 1963–64, and from 1965.

(3) **Sir Oliver Joseph** (1851–1940), English physicist, born at Penkhull, studied at the Royal College of Science and at University College, London, and became in 1881 professor of Physics at Liverpool. In 1900 he was appointed first principal of the new university at Birmingham and was knighted in 1902. Specially distinguished in electricity, he was a pioneer of wireless telegraphy. He was made a fellow of the Royal Society in 1887. His scientific writings include *Signalling across Space without Wires* (1897), *Talks about Wireless* (1925) and *Advancing Science* (1931). He gave much time to psychical research and on this subject wrote *Raymond* (1916) and *My Philosophy* (1933). *Past Years: An Autobiography*, appeared in 1931. His brother, **Sir Richard** (1855–1936), was the first professor of Modern History at Glasgow University (1894–99) and thereafter at Edinburgh University (1899–1933). Among his works are *A History of Modern Europe* (1885) and *The Close of the Middle Ages, 1273–1494* (1901).

(4) **Thomas** (*c.* 1558–1625), English dramatist, romance writer, and poet, was born at West Ham. From Merchant Taylors' he passed to Trinity College, Oxford, and thence in 1578 to Lincoln's Inn, but led a wild and rollicking life. About 1588 and in 1591 he took part in two sea expeditions and wrote a euphuistic romance, *Rosalynde* (1590), his best-known work, which supplied Shakespeare with many of the chief incidents in *As You Like It*, besides two second-rate dramas, *The Wounds of the Civil War* (1594) and *A Looking-glass for London and England* (with Greene, 1594). He turned Catholic and is believed to have taken a medical degree at Avignon (1600), and to have written a *History of the Plague* (1603). He died in London. Among his remaining writings are *A Fig for Momus* (1595); translations of Seneca (1614) and Josephus (1602); *Life of William Longbeard* (1593); *Robin the Divell, Wits Miserie*, and *Glaucus and Silla*, a collection of poems (1589). See his *Works* (4 vols. ed. Gosse, 1884); Gosse's *Seventeenth Century Studies* (1883); Life by Paradise (1931), and *Thomas Lodge and Other Elizabethans*, ed. Sisson (1933).

LOEB, *lœb*, **(1) Jacques** (1859–1924), German-American biologist, born in Mayen and educated at Berlin, Munich and Strasbourg, emigrated to U.S.A. (1891) and after various university appointments became head of the general physiology division at the Rockefeller Institute for Medical Research (1910–24). He did pioneer work on artificial parthenogenesis and also carried out research in comparative physiology and psychology. His writings include *Dynamics of Living Matter* (1906) and *Artificial Parthenogenesis and Fertilisation* (1913).

(2) **James** (1867–1933), American banker with the firm of Kuhn Loeb & Co., was born in New York City. With his fortune he founded the Institute of Musical Art in New York, a mental clinic in Munich and, himself a classical scholar, provided funds for the publication of the famous Loeb Classical Library of Latin and Greek texts with English translations.

LOEWE, Johann Karl Gottfried, *lœ'vė* (1796–1869), German composer, was born near Halle, studied music and theology at Halle, and in 1822 became a musical teacher at Stettin. In 1847 he sang and played before the court in London. He composed operas (of which only one, *The Three Wishes*, was performed), oratorios, symphonies, concertos, duets, and other works for piano, but his ballads, his most notable bequest, are (including the *Erlkönig*) remarkable dramatic poems. See A. Bach, *The Art Ballad* (1890); Loewe's Autobiography (1870); and German Lives by Runze (1884–1888), Wellmer (1886) and Wossidlo (1894).

LOEWI, Otto, *lœ'vee* (1873–1961), German pharmacologist, born at Frankfurt-am-Main, educated at Strasbourg and Munich, was professor of Pharmacology at Graz (1909–38) and research professor at New York Univ. College of Medicine from 1940. In 1936 he shared with Sir Henry Hallet Dale (q.v.) the Nobel prize for medicine, for investigations on nerve impulses and their chemical transmission.

LÖFFLER, Friedrich August Johann (1852–1915), German bacteriologist, born at Frankfurt an der Oder, was a military surgeon, professor at Greifswald (1883) and from 1913 director of the Koch Institute in Berlin. He first cultured the diphtheria bacillus (1884) discovered by Klebs and called the 'Klebs-Löffler bacillus', discovered the causal organism of glanders and swine erysipelas (1886), isolated an organism causing food poisoning and prepared a vaccine against foot-and-mouth disease (1899). He wrote an unfinished history of bacteriology (1887).

LOFFT, Capell (1751–1824), English writer and lawyer, born in London, the patron of Bloomfield, was a Whig barrister with a taste for letters, especially poetry. His best work was a translation of Spanish, Italian and other foreign verse under the title of *Laura, an Anthology of Sonnets* (5 vols. 1814). His fourth son, **Capell** (1806–73), who died at Millmead, Va., wrote poetry and an autobiography called *Self-Formation* (1837).

LOFTUS, Cissie. See McCarthy, Justin.

LOGAN, (1) **James** (*c.* 1794–1872), Celtic antiquary, author in 1831 of the *Scottish Gael*, was born in Aberdeen, and lived and died in London.

(2) **John** (1748–88), Scottish poet, was born a farmer's son, at Soutra, Midlothian. In 1773 he was chosen minister of South Leith; but in 1786, owing to intemperance and other matters of scandal, he had to resign his charge, and took to literary work in London. Besides two posthumous volumes of sermons, he wrote a tragedy, *Runnamede* (1783), withdrawn after a single performance at Edinburgh. His *Poems* (1781) included the 'Ode to the Cuckoo' and others that he had already published as the work of Michael Bruce (q.v.). Logan's authorship of the exquisite 'Braes of Yarrow' is not disputed, though its best lines are justifiably reminiscent.

(3) **John Alexander** (1826–86), American soldier and legislator, born in Illinois, served in the Mexican war, was called to the bar in 1852, and was elected to congress as a Democrat in 1858. He raised an Illinois regiment in the civil war, and retired at its close as major-general. Returned to congress as a Republican in 1866, he was repeatedly chosen a U.S. senator. See Life by G. F. Dawson (1887).

(4) **Sir William Edmund** (1798–1875), Scottish geologist, born, a baker's son, at Montreal, was sent over in 1814 to Edinburgh High School and University. After ten years in a London counting house, he became (1828) book-keeper at Swansea to a copper-smelting company. There he made a map of the coal basin, which was incorporated into the geological survey. In 1842–71 he directed the Canadian Geological Survey. Knighted in 1856, he died in Wales. See Life by Harrington (1883).

LOISY, Alfred Firmin, *lwa'zee* (1857–1940), French theologian, born at Ambrières, Haute-Marne, ordained priest in 1879 and in 1881 became professor of Holy Scripture at the Institut Catholique, where by his lectures and writings he incurred the disfavour of the church and was dismissed. In 1900 he was appointed lecturer at the Sorbonne, but resigned after his works on Biblical criticism were condemned by Pope Pius X in 1903 as too advanced. These books, which proved him to be the founder of the modernist movement, were, *L'Évangile et l'Église* (1902), *Quatrième Évangile* (1903) *and Autour d'un petit livre* (1903). For subsequent works of the same kind he was excommunicated in 1908. He was professor of History of Religion in the Collège de France in 1909–32. See his *Choses passées* (1913), and study by Petre (1944).

LOMBARD, Peter (*c.* 1100–64), Italian theologian, born near Novara in Lombardy, studied at Bologna, at Reims, and (under Abelard) at Paris, and, after holding a chair of Theology there, in 1159 became Bishop of Paris. He was generally styled *Magister Sententiarum*, or the 'Master of Sentences', from his collection of sentences from Augustine and other Fathers on points of Christian doctrine, with objections and replies. The theological doctors of Paris in 1300 denounced some of his teachings as heretical; but his work was the standard textbook of Catholic Theology down to the Reformation.

LOMBROSO, Cesare (1836–1909), Italian founder of the science of criminology, was born of Jewish stock at Verona, and after acting as an army surgeon, professor of Mental Diseases at Pavia, and director of an asylum at Pesaro, became professor of Forensic Medicine and Psychiatry at Turin. His theory postulated the existence of a criminal type distinguishable from the normal man. His great work is *L'uomo delinquente* (1875). See Life by H. Kurella (trans. 1911).

LOMONOSOV, Mikhail Vasilievich, *-nō'sof* (1711–65), Russian philologist, poet, writer and scientist, born at Denisovka, near Archangel. The son of a fisherman, he ran away to Moscow in search of education, and later studied at St Petersburg and at Marburg under Christian Wolff; he returned to St Petersburg and became professor of Chemistry there. In his poetry he introduced a new form of versification, and his greatest contribution to Russian culture was his systemization of the grammar and orthography. His writings include works on rhetoric (1748), grammar (1755), and ancient

Russian history (1766). See *History of Russian Literature* by D. S. Mirsky (1927) and study by A. Martel (Paris 1933).

LONDON, Jack (1876–1916), American novelist, born at San Francisco, was successively sailor, tramp and gold miner before he took to writing. He used his knowledge of the Klondyke in the highly successful *Call of the Wild* (1903) and *White Fang* (1907), and of the sea in *Sea-Wolf* (1904) and *The Mutiny of the 'Elsinore'* (1914), and, as well as pure adventure tales, wrote the more serious political novel *The Iron Heel* (1907), and his autobiographical tale of alcoholism *John Barleycorn* (1913). His wife, **Charmian,** wrote his biography (1921), &c. See also *The Bodley Head Jack London* (ed. by Calder-Marshall), *Jack London, American Rebel* (ed. by Foner, 1947), and studies by O'Connor (1965) and Walcutt (1966).

LONDONDERRY. See PITT and CASTLEREAGH.

LONG, (1) **Crawford Williamson** (1815–78), American physician, was born at Danielsville, Ga. In 1842, operating on a neck tumour, he was the first to use ether as an anaesthetic, but did not reveal his discovery until 1849.

(2) **Earl Kemp** (1895–1960), brother of (4), continued his brother's methods of corrupt administration coupled with sound social legislation, as lieutenant-governor (1936–38) and governor (1939–40, 1948–52, 1956–60) of Louisiana. Suffering from paranoiac schizophrenia, he was at his wife's request placed in a mental hospital in May 1959 and forcibly detained there with police help, until, using his powers as governor, he dismissed the mental hospitals superintendent and appointed politically favourable medical officers. See Life by A. J. Liebling (1962).

(3) **George** (1800–79), English scholar, born at Poulton, Lancashire, a fellow (1823) of Trinity College, Cambridge, professor at the universities of Virginia (1824–28) and London (1828–46), a founder of the Royal Geographical Society (1830), published *Decline of the Roman Republic* (1864–74), translated the classics, and edited the *Penny Encyclopaedia* (1833–46).

(4) **Huey Pierce** (1893–1935), American politician, brother of (2), born at Winnfield, La., was a lawyer and became governor of Louisiana (1928–31). Notorious for corruption and demagoguery, he won the support of the poor by his intensive social service and public works programmes. He was murdered.

LONGCHAMP, William de, *lõ-shã* (d. 1197), English prelate, a low-born favourite of Richard I, who in 1189–90 made him chancellor, Bishop of Ely, and joint justiciar of England; in 1191 he was likewise made papal legate, but for his heated arrogance he had to withdraw to Normandy. He regained Richard's favour by raising his ransom, and was made chancellor again. He died at Poitiers. See French monograph by L. Boivin Champeaux (1885).

LONGFELLOW, Henry Wadsworth (1807–1882), American poet, born at Portland, Me., graduated at Bowdoin College in Brunswick, Me. In 1826 the college trustees sent him to Europe to qualify for the chair of Foreign Languages, and he spent three years abroad. He married in 1831, but his wife died in 1835. *Outre Mer*, an account of his first European tour, appeared in 1835; and *Hyperion*, which is a journal of the second, in 1839. In 1836 he became professor of Modern Languages and Literature in Harvard, and held the chair nearly eighteen years. *Voices of the Night* (1839), his first book of verse, made a favourable impression, which was deepened by *Ballads* (1841), including 'The Skeleton in Armour', 'The Wreck of the Hesperus'. 'The Village Blacksmith', and 'Excelsior'. *Poems on Slavery* appeared in 1842. Longfellow made a third visit to Europe in 1842, and next year married his second wife, who was burned to death in 1861. *The Belfry of Bruges and other Poems* appeared in 1846. One of his most popular poems is *Evangeline* (1847), a tale (in hexameters) of the French exiles of Acadia. *The Golden Legend* (1851) is based on *Der arme Heinrich* of Hartmann von Aue; *Hiawatha* (1855), on legends of the Redskins. *The Courtship of Miles Standish* (1858) is a story in hexameters of the early days of the Plymouth colony in Massachusetts. His translation of Dante (1867–70) has added little and his plays less to his reputation. *Flower-de-Luce* (1867) has had its admirers. He paid a last visit to Europe in 1868–69. As a poet he was extremely popular during his lifetime and although his work lacks the real depth of great poetry, his gift of simple, romantic story-telling in verse makes it still read widely and with pleasure. He died in his home at Cambridge, Mass. See Lives by his brother, the Rev. Samuel Longfellow (1891), Higginson (1902) and Gorman (1927).

LONGHI or **Falca, Pietro,** *long'gee* (1702–85), Venetian painter. He was a pupil of Balestra, and excelled in small-scale satiric pictures of Venetian life. Most of his work is in Venetian public collections, but the National Gallery, London, has three, of which the best known is *Rhinoceros in an Arena*. His son **Alessandro** (1733–1813) was a pupil of Nogari. Some of Alessandro's portraits are now attributed to his father. See A. Ravà, *Pietro Longhi* (1923).

LONGINUS, Dionysius Cassius (*c.* A.D. 213–273), Neoplatonic philosopher, taught rhetoric in Athens, but settling at Palmyra, became chief counsellor to Queen Zenobia. For this Aurelian beheaded him. It is now very doubtful that the treatise *On the Sublime* was written by him. This has been edited by (among others) Rhys Roberts (1899), Prickard (1906) and W. Hamilton Fyfe (1932).

LONGLEY, Charles Thomas (1794–1868), English prelate, born near Rochester, from Westminster passed to Christ Church, Oxford; was headmaster of Harrow 1829–1836, and became Bishop of Ripon (1836), Archbishop of York (1860) and Archbishop of Canterbury (1862).

LONGMAN, Thomas (1699–1755), founder of the publishing firm which bears his name, son of a Bristol merchant, bought a bookselling business in Paternoster Row in 1724, and shared in publishing Boyle's *Works*, Ainsworth's *Latin Dictionary*, Ephraim Chambers's *Cyclopaedia*, and Johnson's *Dictionary*. His nephew, Thomas Longman (1730–97), brought out a new edition of Chambers's *Cyclopaedia.* Under Thomas Norton Longman (1771–1842) the firm had relations with Wordsworth, Southey, Coleridge, Scott, Moore, Sydney Smith, &c. After Constable's failure in 1826 the *Edinburgh Review* became the property of the firm, who also published Lardner's *Cabinet Cyclopaedia* (1829–46). Thomas Longman (1804–79), eldest son of T. N. Longman, issued under his special care a beautifully illustrated New Testament. His brother, William (1813–77), wrote *Lectures on the History of England* (1859), *History of Edward III* (1869), &c. The event of this generation was the publication of Macaulay's *Lays* (1842), *Essays* (1843) and *History* (1848–61). See Cox and Chandler *The House of Longman* (1925).

LONGOMONTANUS, Christian Sörensen (1562–1647), Danish astronomer, born at Longberg, Jutland, in 1589 became an assistant of Tycho Brahe (q.v.), whom he accompanied to Germany. Returning to Denmark he became a professor at Copenhagen, where he inaugurated the building of the observatory.

LONGSTREET, James (1821–1904), American general, born in South Carolina, fought in the Mexican war, and, as a Confederate, in both battles of Bull Run, at Williamsburg, Richmond, Fredericksburg, Gettysburg, Chickamauga and the Wilderness. He was minister to Turkey in 1880–81.

LONGUEVILLE, Anne, Duchesse de, *lõ-veel* (1619–79), born at Vincennes, the 'soul of the Fronde', was the only daughter of the Prince of Condé, and in 1639 was married to the Duc de Longueville. She exerted a considerable influence on politics in which she first began to interest herself as the mistress of the Duc de la Rochefoucauld. In the first war of the Fronde (1648) she sought in vain to gain over her brother, the Great Condé. In the second she won over both him and Turenne. After the death of her husband and her desertion by la Rochefoucauld, she entered a convent but continued to have influence at court. See Lives by Cousin (1891–97) and Williams (1907).

LONGUS, wrote the Greek prose romance *Daphnis and Chloe,* possibly in the 3rd century A.D.

LÖNNROT, Elias, *lœn'rot* (1802–84), Finnish scholar, born at Sammatti in Nyland, practised medicine for twenty years in Kajana, and was professor of Finnish at Helsingfors 1853–62. He published collections of Finnish folksongs, notably the *Kalevala* which by his hand became a long, connected epic poem, proverbs, riddles, and a great Finnish-Swedish Dictionary (1866–1880) which helped to further his aim of establishing a literary Finnish language. See Life by Ahlqvist (Helsingfors 1885).

LONSDALE, (1) Frederick (1881–1954), British playwright, born in Jersey, Frederick Leonard, son of a tobacconist, known for his witty and sophisticated society comedies, among them *The Last of Mrs Cheyney* (1925), *On Approval* (1927) and *Canaries Sometimes Sing* (1929). He collaborated in operettas, including *Maid of the Mountains* (1916). See Life by F. Donaldson (1957).

(2) **Hugh Cecil Lowther, 5th Earl of** (1857–1944), was a noted sportsman and Cumberland landowner. He founded the Lonsdale belt for boxing. See *The Yellow Earl* by D. Sutherland (1965).

(3) **William** (1794–1871), English geologist, born at Bath, served in the army but left it in 1815 and took up geology. He made a study of the fossils in north and south Devon, in 1837 placing them between the Silurian and the Carboniferous. This led to the establishment of the Devonian System by Murchison and Sedgwick (1839).

LOOMIS, Elias (1811–89), American writer on mathematics, astronomy, meteorology, &c., born at Willington, Conn., graduated at Yale, was tutor there (1833–36), professor at Cleveland (1837–44), New York (1844–60) and Yale (from 1860).

LOPE (DE VEGA). See VEGA CARPIO.

LOPES, Francisco Higino Craveiro (1894–1964), Portuguese politician, born in Lisbon of a distinguished military family. Educated at the Military School, Lisbon, he fought in the Expeditionary Force in Mozambique in the first World War. As a full colonel in 1942 he entered negotiations for co-operation with the Allies and was responsible for the modernization of the Portuguese air force. In 1944 he entered parliament, in 1949 he was promoted to general, and was president of Portugal from 1951 to 1958.

LÓPEZ, Francisco Solano (1827–70), born in Asunción, a grand-nephew of Francia, succeeded his father as president of Paraguay in 1862. In 1864 he provoked war with Brazil and was faced with an alliance of Brazil, Uruguay and Argentina. The war lasted for five years during which Paraguay was completely devastated and López himself having fled was shot by a soldier.

LÓPEZ DE AYALA. See AYALA.

LOPOKOVA, Lydia. See KEYNES.

LORCA, Federigo García (1899–1936), Spanish poet, was born in Fuente Vaqueros, and was killed, by design or misunderstanding, early in the Spanish Civil War at Granada. His gypsy songs—*Canciones* (1927) and *Romancero Gitano* (1928 and 1935), probably his best and most widely-read work, reveal a classical control of imagery, rhythm and emotion. He wrote, also, several successful plays, including *Bodas de Sangre* (1933); *Yerma* and *La Casa de Bernarda Alba.* See study by R. Campbell (1952).

LORD, Thomas (1755–1832), English sportsman, born in Thirsk, Yorkshire, founder of Lord's Cricket Ground, home of the Marylebone Cricket Club since 1787.

LOREBURN, Robert Threshie Reid, 1st Earl of (1846–1923), lawyer, born of Scottish parents at Corfu, studied at Balliol, was called to the bar in 1871, and became M.P. in 1880, solicitor-general and attorney-general in 1894, and in 1905 lord chancellor and a baron, in 1911 an earl. He resigned in 1912.

LORENTZ, Hendrik Antoon (1853–1928), Dutch physicist, born at Arnhem, studied at Leiden, became professor of Mathematical Physics there in 1878. He also directed research at Haarlem from 1923. He worked out the explanation by the 'Fitzgerald-Lorentz Contraction' of the Michelson-

Morley experiment, and prepared the way for Einstein. In 1902 he was awarded, with Zeeman, the Nobel prize for physics.

LORENZETTI, (1) **Ambrogio** (?1300–?48), Sienese artist, younger brother of (2). He worked at Cortona and Florence, but is best known for his allegorical frescoes in the Palazzo Pubblico at Siena, symbolizing the effects of good and bad government. An *Annunciation* is also at Siena. See studies by G. Sinibaldi (1933) and G. Rowley (1959).

(2) **Pietro,** also called **Pietro Laurati** (?1280–?1348), Sienese artist, elder brother of (1), probably the pupil of Duccio. He was one of the liveliest of the early Sienese painters, and he also worked at Arezzo (the polyptych in S. Maria della Pieve) and Assisi, where he painted dramatic frescoes of the *Passion* in the Lower Church of S. Francis. A *Madonna* (1340) is in the Uffizi Gallery. See studies by E. T. De Wald (Cambridge, Mass., 1930) and G. Sinibaldi (1933).

LORENZO, called **il Monaco** (*c.* 1370–*c.* 1425), Italian painter, born at Siena. He worked in Florence, and was the master of Fra Angelico. His charming pictures, usually on a small scale, are represented in both the Uffizi and the Louvre galleries. See studies by O. Siren (1905) and V. Golzio (1931).

LORIMER, (1) **James** (1818–90), Scottish jurist, born at Aberdalgie, Perthshire, was an eminent authority on international law, and from 1862 professor at Edinburgh. *The Institutes of the Law of Nations* was his best-known book.

(2) **Sir Robert Stodart** (1864–1929), Scottish architect and younger son of (1), by his work in restoring several castles, &c., did much to further the national domestic style. Among the buildings so restored are Earlshall, Balmanno, Dunblane Cathedral and Paisley Abbey. He was the architect of the Scottish War Memorial at Edinburgh Castle and the Thistle Chapel in St Giles', which brought him international recognition. See C. Hussey, *The Architecture of Sir Robert Lorimer* (1931).

LORJOU, Bernard, *-zhoo* (1908–), French artist, born at Blois. He was the founder of L'Homme Témoin group in 1949 and among a number of large satirical paintings is his *Atomic Age* (1951).

LORM. See LANDESMANN.

LORNE, Marquis of. See ARGYLL.

LORRAINE, (1) **Charles, Cardinal de.** See GUISE.

(2) **Claude.** See CLAUDE LORRAINE.

(3) **Ducal House of.** See GUISE.

LORRIS, Guillaume de, *lor-ees* (fl. 13th cent.), French poet, wrote, before 1260, the first part (*c.* 4000 lines) of the *Roman de la Rose,* continued by Jean de Meung.

LORTZING, Gustav Albert (1801–51) German musician, born in Berlin, went early on the stage, sang in opera, conducted and composed *Zar und Zimmermann* (1837) and other operas with librettos by himself.

LOSINGA, Herbert de (*c.* 1054–1119), Bishop of Thetford from 1091, and from 1094 first Bishop of Norwich, was probably a native of Lorraine. See Life by Goulburn and Symonds (1878).

LOTHROP, Amy. See WARNER (4).

LOTI, Pierre. See VIAUD.

LOTTI, Antonio (*c.* 1665–1740), Italian church and operatic composer, was born and died in Venice. He was organist of St Mark's from 1704.

LOTTO, Lorenzo (*c.* 1480–1556), Italian religious painter, was born at Venice. A masterly portrait painter, his subjects are alive and full of character. He worked in Treviso, Bergamo, Venice and Rome, finally becoming a lay brother in the Loreto monastery, where he died. See monograph by Berenson (1956).

LOTZE, Rudolf Hermann (1817–81), German idealist philosopher, born at Bautzen, studied medicine and philosophy at Leipzig, and became professor of Philosophy there in 1842, at Göttingen in 1844. It was as a physiologist that he first attracted notice, combating the then accepted doctrine of vitalism. His *General Physiology of Bodily Life* (1851) led many to rank him with the materialists, though his real views were expressed in his *Metaphysik* (1841). The most comprehensive statement of his teleological idealism is in his *Microcosmus* (1856–1864). Books on *Logic* (1874) and on *Metaphysics* (1879) were part of an unfinished comprehensive system. See works by H. Jones (1895), Falckenberg (1901 *et seq.*), Schoen (1902), E. E. Thomas (1922).

LOUBET, Émile, *loo-bay* (1838–1929), French statesman, born at Marsanne (Drôme), was seventh president of the Republic (1899–1906).

LOUCHEUR, Raymond, *loo-shœr* (1899–), French composer, born at Tourcoing, who studied at the Paris Conservatoire under Gédalge and D'Indy. Winner of the *grand prix de Rome* in 1928 and the Georges Bizet prize in 1935, he has composed two symphonies, songs, chamber music, the *Rapsodie malgache* and the ballet *Hop Frog* based on the tale by Edgar Allan Poe. This was a tremendous success when presented at the Paris Opera House in 1953. In 1956 he became director of the Conservatoire.

LOUDON, (1) **Gideon Ernst, Freiherr von** (1717–90), Austrian generalissimo, born at Tootzen, Livonia, whither his ancestor had migrated from Ayrshire in the 14th century. In 1732 he entered the Russian service, but ten years later exchanged into that of Austria. In the Seven Years' War he won the battle of Kunersdorf (1759); and his loss of the battle of Liegnitz (1760) was due mainly to Lacy and Daun. As field-marshal he commanded in the war of the Bavarian succession (1778), and against the Turks (1788–89), capturing Belgrade and Semendria. See Life by Malleson (1884).

(2) **John Claudius** (1783–1843), Scottish horticulturist, born at Cambuslang, studied landscape gardening from an early age, working in England and travelling in Europe. The results of his studies are to be found in many works on horticulture including his *Encyclopaedia of Gardening* (1822).

LOUGHBOROUGH. See WEDDERBURN.

LOUIS. The name of eighteen French kings.

Louis I (778–840), 'the Debonair' of

France, was also emperor, and was a son of Charlemagne. **Louis II** (846–879), 'the Stammerer', was the son of Charles the Bold. and began to reign over France in 877. **Louis III** (d. 881), was his eldest son. **Louis IV** (921–954), grandson of Louis II, began to reign in 936. **Louis V**, 'le Fainéant' (966–987), son of Lothair III, was the last of the Carolingians. **Louis VI**, 'the Fat' (1078–1137), was son of Philip I, and succeeded in 1108. **Louis VII**, his son (1120–80), came to the crown 1137, launched the disastrous second crusade (1147–49), divorced his wife Eleanor of Aquitaine, who afterwards married Henry II of England, and so gave rise to long wars for the possession of that territory. **Louis VIII** (1187–1226), son of Philip Augustus, came to the throne 1223, led the Albigensian crusade, and acquired Languedoc for the crown.

Louis IX, or **St Louis** (1215–70), king of France, born at Poissy, succeeded his father, Louis VIII, in 1226, and by his victories compelled Henry III of England to acknowledge French suzerainty in Guienne. During a dangerous illness he made a vow to go as a crusader. Having appointed his mother (the pious Blanche of Castile) regent, he landed with 40,000 men in Egypt in 1249. He captured Damietta, but was afterwards defeated, taken prisoner, and ransomed for 100,000 marks in 1250. He proceeded to Acre with the remnant of his army, and remained in Palestine till his mother's death (1252) compelled his return to France. He did much to strengthen loyalty to his house, determined by the Pragmatic Sanction the relation of the French Church to the pope, countenanced the Sorbonne, set up in the provinces royal courts of justice or parliaments, and authorized a new code of laws. He embarked on a new crusade in 1270, and died of plague at Tunis. Pope Boniface VIII canonized him in 1297. See *Vie de St Louis* by his friend Joinville (q.v.), and *Cambridge Medieval History*, VI (1929).

Louis X (1289–1316), 'the Quarrelsome', was the son of Philip IV and reigned for only two years, 1314–16, during which time he was guided in his policy by Charles of Valois.

Louis XI (1423–83), eldest son of Charles VII, born at Bourges, made unsuccessful attempts against his father's throne, and had to flee to Burgundy. In 1461 he succeeded to the crown. The severe measures which he adopted against the great vassals led to a coalition against him, headed by Burgundy and Brittany. Louis owed his success more to cunning than to arms. His agents stirred up Liège to revolt against Charles the Bold, Duke of Burgundy, and Charles seized Louis, and compelled him to assist in the punishment of Liège. Louis now stirred up against Charles the Flemish towns and the Swiss republics; and the Swiss defeated Charles twice, and killed him (1477). Louis then claimed Burgundy as a vacant fief, but failed, as Mary, the rightful heir, was married to Maximilian of Austria. The latter defeated the French at Guinegate (1479), but after a new war and the death of Mary, a treaty (1482) gave Burgundy and Artois to France. Louis also annexed Provence. In order to weaken his feudal vassals he increased the power and number of parliaments. He spent his later years in great misery, in superstitious terrors and excessive horror of death; his chief advisers the barber Olivier le Dain, Tristan l'Hermite and Cardinal Balue. He died at Plessis-lez-Tours. He cherished art and sciences, and founded three universities. See his *Lettres* (1883–1909); Comines's *Mémoires*; works by Legeay (1874), Willert (1876), Buet (2nd ed. 1886), Vaesen and Charavay (1885–90), Sée (1892), Hare (1907), Champion (1927); and *Quentin Durward*.

Louis XII (1462–1515), succeeded Charles VIII in 1498, and by his just and kindly rule became known as the 'Father of the People'. He overran Milan, and helped the Spaniards to conquer Naples. He humbled the Venetians in 1509, was driven out of Italy in 1513, and defeated at the 'Battle of the Spurs' (1513) by the emperor and Henry VIII of England. He was married to a daughter of Louis XI, to Anne of Brittany, and to a sister of Henry VIII, and was succeeded by his son-in-law Francis I. See works by Seyssel (1558), Maulde-La Clavière (1890–95) and Bridge (1929–36).

Louis XIII (1601–43), son of Henry IV and Marie de' Medici, born at Fontainebleau, succeeded on his father's assassination (1610), his mother being regent. She entered into alliance with Spain and the pope, and betrothed the king to Anne of Austria, daughter of Philip III of Spain, upon which the Huguenots took up arms; but peace was concluded in 1614. The king, now declared of age, confirmed the Edict of Nantes, and the French States-General were summoned for the last time till the reign of Louis XVI. The restoration of Catholic church rights in Béarn led to the religious war which ended in 1622. After the death of De Luynes, in 1624, Richelieu became chief minister. He obtained complete control over the weak king, and greatly increased monarchical power. The overthrow of the Huguenots was completed by the capture of Rochelle in 1628. Richelieu now led Louis to take part in the Thirty Years' War, supporting Gustavus Adolphus and the Dutch against the Spaniards and Austrians. His eldest son was Louis XIV; his second, Philip, Duke of Orleans, ancestor of the present House of Orleans. See MARIE DE' MEDICI, RICHELIEU; and works by Bazin (new ed. 1846), Topin (1876), Zeller (1879–92), Batiffol (1907–10), Patmore (1909), Romain (1934), Vaunois (1936), Champigneule (1958).

Louis XIV (1638–1715), born at St Germain-en-Laye, succeeded Louis XIII in 1643. His mother, Anne of Austria, became regent, and Mazarin (q.v.) her minister. In 1648 certain of the nobles, aggrieved at being excluded from high offices, rose in rebellion, and began the civil wars of the *Fronde*, so called from *frondeur*, a slinger; metaphorically, a grumbler. Peace was concluded in 1659; and in the following year Louis married the Infanta Maria Theresa. On Mazarin's death in 1661 Louis assumed the reins of government, and from that time forth exercised with rare energy a pure despotism. He had a cool and clear head, much dignity and amenity of manners, and indomitable perseverance. He was ably supported by his ministers, and manufactures began to flourish. Colbert restored prosperity to the ruined finances, and provided the means for war, while Louvois raised admirably equipped armies. On the death of Philip IV of Spain Louis, as his son-in-law, claimed part of the Spanish Netherlands; in 1667, with Turenne, he crossed the frontier, and made himself master of French Flanders and Franche Comté. The *triple alliance*—between England, Holland and Sweden—arrested his conquests; and the treaty of Aix-la-Chapelle (1668) surrendered Franche Comté. He now made German alliances, purchased the friendship of Charles II of England, seized Lorraine in 1670, and in 1672 again entered the Netherlands with Condé and Turenne, and conquered half the country in six weeks. The States-General formed an alliance with Spain and the emperor, but Louis made himself master of ten cities of the empire in Alsace, in 1674 took the field with three great armies, and, notwithstanding the death of Turenne and the retirement of Condé, continued to extend his conquests in the Netherlands. The peace of Nijmegen in 1678 left him fortresses in the Spanish Netherlands and Franche Comté. He now established in Metz and elsewhere packed courts of law, which confiscated to him territories belonging to the Elector Palatine, the Elector of Trier, and others, and in 1681 made a sudden and successful descent on Strasburg, a free and powerful German city, which he finally secured by treaty in 1684. Louis had now reached the zenith of his career. All Europe feared him; France regarded him with Asiatic humility; all remnants of political independence had been swept away. Even the courts of justice yielded to the absolute sway of the monarch, who interfered at pleasure with the course of law by commissions, or withdrew offenders by *lettres de cachet*, of which he issued about 9000. The court was the heart of the national life of France, and there the utmost splendour was maintained. In 1685 Louis married his mistress, Madame de Maintenon, who was herself governed by the Jesuits—hence the revocation of the Edict of Nantes (1685) and a bloody persecution of Protestants, which drove half a million of the best and most industrious inhabitants of France to other lands. Yet Louis convened a council of French clergy, which declared the papal power to extend only to matters of faith. The Elector Palatine dying in 1685, Louis claimed part of the territory for the Duchess of Orleans. A French army invaded the Palatinate, Baden, Württemberg and Trier in 1688, and in 1689 the Lower Palatinate was laid waste by fire and sword. Success for a time attended the French arms, but reverses ensued, and the war continued for years with varying success. After the French had gained the battle of Neerwinden (1693), the means of waging war were almost exhausted, and Louis concluded the peace of Ryswick (1697) amid universal distress and discontent. Charles II of Spain at his death (1700) left all his dominions to a grandson of his sister, Louis's queen. Louis supported the claim of his grandson (Philip V) while the Emperor Leopold supported that of his son, afterwards the Emperor Charles VI. The 'War of the Spanish Succession' had to be maintained both in the Netherlands and in Italy. One defeat followed another; Marlborough was victorious in the Low Countries, and Prince Eugene in Italy. In April 1713 peace was concluded at Utrecht, the French prince obtaining the Spanish throne, but at a sacrifice to France of valuable colonies. France, indeed, now was almost completely ruined; but the monarch maintained to the last an unbending despotism. He was succeeded by his great-grandson, Louis XV, his son and his eldest grandson having both died in 1711. The reign of Louis XIV, 'le Roi Soleil', is regarded as the Augustan age of French literature and art, producing such writers as Corneille, Racine, Molière and Boileau, and divines like Bossuet, Fénelon, Bourdaloue and Massillon. See Voltaire's *Siècle de Louis XIV* (1740); Saint-Simon (1788); works by Chotard (1890), Gérin (1894), Chérot (1894), Hassall (Eng. 1895), Perkins (Eng. 1897), Lavisse's *Histoire de France* (vii–viii, 1908), the *Cambridge Mod. Hist*. (v, 1908), de St Leger and Sagnac (1935), Gaxotte (1944), Bailly (1946), Lewis (1959).

Louis XV (1710–74), great-grandson of Louis XIV, born at Versailles, succeeded September 1, 1715. The Duke of Orleans was regent, and became infatuated with the financial schemes of the Scotsman, Law. All available capital was pocketed by the financial cliques, the court, and the state. At fifteen Louis married Maria Leszczyńska, daughter of Stanislas, the dethroned king of Poland. At the death of the regent Louis reigned personally, under the advice of his wise teacher, Cardinal Fleury. In the war of the Polish Succession the duchy of Lorraine was obtained for Louis's father-in-law, and for the French crown after him. In 1740 commenced the war of the Austrian Succession, in which France supported the claims of the Elector of Bavaria to the imperial crown, against those of Maria Theresa, Queen of Hungary. After a course of easy conquest in 1741, the French were badly beaten in 1742: regret and worry brought Fleury to the grave next year. But presently France, in alliance with Frederick the Great of Prussia, was repeatedly victorious on land, as at Fontenoy (1745), over English, Austrians and Dutch, though the English put an end to the French navy and sea trade. After the peace of Aix-la-Chapelle the king sank under the control of Madame de Pompadour, to whom he gave notes on the treasury for enormous sums. War broke out again with Britain concerning the boundaries of Nova Scotia. In 1756 began the Seven Years' War, and an alliance was formed between France and Austria against Prussia and Britain. In spite of disaster, financial embarrassment, and the misery of the people, the king, governed by his mistress, obstinately persevered in war, even after the terrible defeat of Minden in 1759; while the British conquered almost all the French colonies both in the East and West Indies, with Canada. A humiliating peace was concluded in 1763. The Paris parliament secured, after a contest, the suppression of the Jesuits in 1764, and now attempted, ineffectively, to limit the power of the crown by refusing to register edicts of taxation. The Duc de Choiseul was dismissed, a new mistress, Madame du Barry, having taken the place of Madame de Pompadour. The councillors of the parliament of Paris were banished, and a dutiful parliament appointed (1771). The gifts to Madame du Barry in five years amounted to 180 millions of livres. Louis, whose constitution was ruined by a life of vice, was seized with smallpox, and 'le bien aimé' died unwept. See Voltaire's *Siècle de Louis XV* (1768–70), and works by Tocqueville (2nd ed. 1847), Bonhomme (1873), Broglie (Eng. trans. 1879), Pajol (1881–92), Vandal (1882), Carré (1891), Soulange-Bodin (1894), Haggard (1906), Imbert de Saint-Amand (1887–95), Gaxotte (1933), Leroy (1938), Mazé (1944).

Louis XVI (1754–93), was the third son of the dauphin, Louis, only son of Louis XV, and became dauphin by the death of his father and his elder brothers. He was married in 1770 to Marie Antoinette, youngest daughter of the Empress Maria Theresa. When he ascended the throne (1774) the public treasury was empty, the state was burdened with a debt of 4000 millions of livres, and the people were crushed under the taxes. By advice of Maurepas the king restored to the Paris and provincial parliaments their semi-political rights. Malesherbes and Turgot proposed thoroughgoing reforms, accepted by the king, but rejected by the court, aristocracy, parliaments, and church. Turgot resigned. Yet Louis remitted some of the most odious taxes, made a few inconsiderable reforms, and was for a time extremely popular, being handsome, healthy, and moral, fond of manly exercises, and of working as a locksmith. In 1777 Necker was made director-general, and succeeded in bringing the finances to a more tolerable condition; but through France's outlay in the American War of Independence he was obliged to propose the taxation of the privileged classes, and their resistance compelled him to resign. The lavish Calonne (1783) renewed for a while the splendour of the court, and advised the calling together of an Assembly of Notables. The noblemen, clergymen, state officials, councillors of parliaments, and municipal officers thus collected compelled him to fly to London. His successor, Brienne, obtained some new taxes, but the parliament of Paris refused to register the edict. The convening of the States-General was universally demanded. The king registered the edicts and banished the councillors of parliament, but had to recall them. In May 1788 he dissolved all the parliaments and established a *Cour plénière*. Matters became still worse when in August appeared the edict that the treasury should cease all cash payments except to the troops. Brienne resigned, and Necker again became minister. An assembly of the States of the kingdom, in abeyance since 1614, was resolved upon; and by the advice of Necker the Third Estate was called in double number. The States-General met in May 1789 at Versailles. The *tiers-état*, taking matters into their own hands, formed themselves into a National Assembly, thereby commencing the Revolution; and undertaking to make a new constitution, they called themselves the Constituent Assembly. The resistance of Louis to the demands of the deputies for political independence, equal rights and universal freedom, led to their declaration of inviolability. The king retaliated by ordering troops under arms, dissolving the ministry, and banishing Necker. The consequence was revolutionary outbreaks in Paris on July 12, 1789. Next day the National Guard of Paris was called out, and on the 14th the people stormed the Bastille. Meanwhile the provinces repeated the acts of Paris. On August 4 feudal and manorial rights were abrogated by the Assembly, which declared the equality of human rights. The royal princes and all the nobles who could escape sought safety in flight. The royal family, having in vain attempted to follow their example, tried to conciliate the people by the feigned assumption of republican sentiments, but on October 5 the rabble attacked Versailles and compelled Louis and his family to return to Paris, whither the Assembly also moved. The next two years witnessed the inauguration and the subsequent withdrawal of various constitutional schemes. Louis alternately made concessions to the republicans, and devised schemes for escaping from their surveillance (in June 1791 the king and queen had got as far as Varennes, whence they were brought back), and each month added to his humiliation and to the audacity of those surrounding him. The Constituent Assembly was succeeded in 1791 by the Legislative Assembly. The king was compelled by the Girondists to a war with Austria in April 1792, and the early defeats of the French were visited on Louis, who was confined, in August, with his family in the Temple. The advance of the Prussians under the Duke of Brunswick into Champagne threw Paris into the wildest excitement. The Assembly dissolved itself in September; the National Convention took its place, and the Republic was proclaimed. In December the king was brought to trial, and called upon to answer for repeated acts of treason against the Republic. On January 20, 1793, sentence of death was passed, and next day he was guillotined in the Place de la Révolution. See MARIE ANTOINETTE, NECKER, TURGOT MIRABEAU; and works by Beaucourt (1892), Souriau (1893), Haggard (1909), Ségur (1909–13), Webster (1936–37), Mazé (1941–1943), de la Fuye (1943), Faÿ (trans. 1968).

Louis XVII, Charles (1785–95), second son of Louis XVI, became dauphin on the death of his brother in 1789. After the death of his father he continued in prison under the charge of a Jacobin shoemaker named Simon. He died, so it was reported, June 8, 1795—rumour said by poison. Several persons subsequently claimed to be the dauphin—one of them a half-caste Indian, another a Potsdam watchmaker, Karl Wilhelm Naundorf, who, with a striking resemblance to the Bourbons, found his way to France in 1833, but was expelled in 1836, lived a while in England, and died at Delft, August 10, 1845. His children in 1851 and 1874 raised fruitless actions against the Comte de Chambord. See books by C. Welch (1908), Turquan (1908), Allen (1912), Buckley (1927), A. Castelot (1948).

Louis XVIII, Stanislas Xavier (1755–1824), younger brother of Louis XVI, in his brother's reign opposed every salutary measure of the government. He fled from Paris to Belgium, and assumed the royal title in 1795. The victories of the republic and Napoleon's enmity compelled him frequently to change his place of abode, till in 1807 he found a refuge in England (at Hartwell, Bucks). On the fall of Napoleon (April 1814) he landed at Calais; and then began the ascendency of the 'legitimist' party. The Napoleonic constitution was set aside, and though a new constitution, with two chambers, was granted, in every essential the king resumed the baneful traditions of the ancient monarchy. The nobles and priests moved him to severe treatment of Imperialists, Republicans and Protestants. This opened the way for Napoleon's return from Elba, when the royal family fled from Paris, and remained at Ghent till after Waterloo. Louis issued from Cambrai a proclamation in which he acknowledged former errors, and promised an amnesty to all but traitors. But the Chamber of Deputies was so reactionary that the king dissolved it; whereupon arose royalist plots for his dethronement. Assassins slew hundreds of adherents of the Revolution and of Protestants. Driven by royalist fanatics, the king dismissed his too moderate prime minister Decazes, and sent an army to Spain to maintain absolutism. See works by Petit (1885), Imbert de Saint-Amand (1891), M. F. Sandars (1910).

LOUIS, Ger. **Ludwig**. Name of three Bavarian kings, of the family of Wittelsbach.

Louis I (1786–1868), born in Strasbourg, came to the throne in 1825, and by his lavish expenditure on pictures, public buildings and favourites, and by taxes and reactionary policy, provoked active discontent in 1830, and again in 1848, when he abdicated in favour of his son, Maximilian II. See MONTEZ (LOLA).

Louis II (1845–86), Maximilian's son, was born in Nymphenburg, and succeeded in 1864. He devoted himself to patronage of Wagner and his music. In 1870 he decidedly threw Bavaria on the side of Prussia, and offered the imperial crown to William I, though he took no part in the war, and lived the life of a recluse. He was almost constantly at feud with his ministers and family, mainly on account of his insensate outlays on superfluous palaces, and was declared insane in 1886. A few days later he accidentally or intentionally drowned himself (and his physician) in the Starnberger Lake near his castle of Berg. See books by Pourtalès (1929) and Mayr-Ofen (trans. 1937).

Louis III (1854–1921), the son of the Prince Regent Luitpold, was born in Munich and reigned for only five years, from 1913 to 1918, when he abdicated. He was the last of the Wittelsbach family to be on the throne.

LOUIS, Joe, *loo'is* (1914–), professional name of **Joseph Louis Barrow**, American Negro boxer, 'the Brown Bomber', born in Lafayette. In 1934 he won the amateur light-heavyweight title and turned professional, becoming world heavyweight champion when he beat Braddock in 1936. He held the title for twelve years, defending it twenty-five times. He retired in 1948, but returned in 1950 and lost his title to Ezzard Charles. He then won eight more fights before being knocked out by Marciano in 1951. In all, he won sixty-eight out of seventy-one fights. See his autobiograph (1947) and study by Diamond (1956).

LOUIS NAPOLEON. See NAPOLEON.

LOUIS-PHILIPPE (1773–1850), king of the French, born in Paris, was the eldest son of the Duke of Orleans, and was brought up by Madame de Genlis. He entered the National Guard, and, along with his father, renounced his titles, and assumed the surname Égalité. He fought in the wars of the republic, but was included in the order for arrest issued against Dumouriez, and escaped with him into Austrian territory. For a time he supported himself as a teacher in Switzerland; he went in 1796 to the United States, and in 1800 took up his abode at Twickenham near London. In 1809 he married Marie Amélie, daughter of Ferdinand I of the Two Sicilies. On the Restoration he recovered his estates, and though disliked by the court, was very popular in Paris. After the Revolution of 1830 he was first appointed lieutenant-general, and then accepted the crown as the elect of the sovereign people. The country prospered under the rule of the 'citizen king', and the middle classes amassed riches. The parliamentary franchise was limited to the aristocracy of wealth and their hangers-on. The political corruption of the *bourgeoisie*, and its wholesale bribery by the king, united all extremists in a cry for electoral reform. A man of great ability but of little character, Louis-Philippe was by fear carried into paths of reactionary violence. The newspapers were muzzled, and trial by jury was tampered with. Prince Louis Napoleon seized this opportunity of acting twice the part of a pretender (1836, 1840). After the Duke of Orleans's death in 1842, republicans, socialists, communists, became more and more threatening. In vain did Louis-Philippe provide, by campaigning in Algeria, an outlet for the military spirit of his subjects. 'Reform banquets' began to be held. Their repression led to violent debates in the Chamber. The Paris mob rose in February 1848, with the complicity of the regulars, national guards, and municipal police. Louis-Philippe dismissed Guizot (q.v.), and promised reforms; but it was too late. He had to abdicate, and escaped to England as 'Mr Smith'. He died at Claremont. See P. de La Gorce, *La Restoration* (1931); J. Lucas-Dubreton, *Louis-Philippe* (1938), an account of his early years in V. Wyndham's *Life of Madame de Genlis* (1958), and Howarth (1961).

LOUISA (1776–1810), queen of Prussia, was born at Hanover, where her father, Duke

Karl of Mecklenburg-Strelitz, was commandant. Married to the Crown Prince of Prussia, afterwards Frederick-William III, in 1793, she was the mother of Frederick-William IV and William I, afterwards emperor. She endeared herself to her people by her spirit and energy during the period of national calamity that followed the battle of Jena, and especially by her patriotic and self-denying efforts to obtain concessions at Tilsit from Napoleon, though he had shamelessly slandered her.

LOUVEL, Pierre Louis. See BERRI.

L'OUVERTURE. See TOUSSAINT L'OUVERTURE.

LOUVOIS, François Michel le Tellier, Marquis de, *loo-vwah* (1641–91), war minister of Louis XIV, born in Paris. His father was chancellor and secretary of state in the war department; the son joined him as assistant secretary in 1662, and became an energetic war minister in 1668, reforming and strengthening the army. His labours bore fruit in the great war that ended with the peace of Nijmegen (1678). He took a leading part in the capture of Strasburg (1681) and in the persecution of Protestants. See Lives by C. Rousset (6th ed. 1879) and L. André (1942).

LOUŸS, Pierre, *lwee* (1870–1925), French poet and novelist, born at Ghent, came to Paris, where in 1891 he founded a review called *La Conque* to which Régnier, Gide and Valéry were contributors. In this were printed his first poems, most of which later appeared in *Astarté* (1891). His lyrics, based on the Greek form which he so much admired, are masterpieces of style. Other volumes are *Poésies de Méléagre de Gédara* (1893), *Scènes de la vie des courtisanes de Lucien* (1894) and *Les Chansons de Bilitis* (1894). In 1896 his novel *Aphrodite* was published with great success and a psychological novel *La Femme et le pantin* appeared in 1898.

LOVAT, Simon Fraser, Lord (*c.* 1667–1747), Scottish chief, was born at Tomich in Ross-shire. In the 14th century his ancestor had migrated from Tweeddale to Inverness-shire, and Hugh, his grandson, had been made Lord Lovat in 1431. Simon took his M.A. at Aberdeen in 1695, having the year before accepted a commission in a regiment raised for King William. In 1696 his father, on the death of his grand-nephew, Lord Lovat, assumed that title, and Simon next year attempted to abduct the late lord's daughter and heiress, a child nine years of age. Baffled in this, he seized and forcibly married her mother, a lady of the Atholl family—a crime for which he was found guilty of high treason and outlawed. After four years of petty rebellion (during which, in 1699, he succeeded his father as twelfth Lord Lovat), in 1702, when the Atholl family became all powerful, he fled to France, but a year later returned to Scotland as a Jacobite agent. He was at the bottom of the 'Queensberry plot', in which he professed to reveal the policy of the exiled court and a plan for a Highland rising; but the discovery of his duplicity obliged him once more to escape to France. He was still the darling of his clan, and in 1714 they called him over. Next year Simon took the government side; his clan at once left the insurgents; and for this service he obtained a full pardon, with possession of the Lovat territory. In the '45 Lovat sent forth the clan under his son to fight for the Pretender, whilst he was protesting his loyalty. Culloden lost, he fled, but was captured and brought up to London, being sketched at St Albans by Hogarth. At his impeachment he defended himself with ability and dignity, and he met death (by beheading) gallantly. A finished courtier, a good scholar, an elegant letter-writer, he was also a ruffian, a liar, a traitor and a hypocrite. During the lifetime of the lady he had ravished he twice more married. See Lives by Hill Burton (1847), Mackenzie (1908); Sir W. Fraser's *Chiefs of Grant* (1883), *Major Fraser's Manuscript* (ed. Fergusson, 1889), the *Fraser Papers* (1924; Scot. Hist. Soc.) and M. McLaren, *Lord Lovat of the '45* (1957).

LOVELACE, Richard (1618–57), Cavalier lyrist, was born at Woolwich, or perhaps in Holland, in 1618, the eldest son of a Kentish knight. He was educated at Charterhouse and Gloucester Hall, Oxford, found his way to court and went on the Scottish expedition in 1639. In 1642 he was imprisoned for presenting to the House of Commons a petition from the royalists of Kent 'for the restoring the king to his rights', and was released on bail. He spent his estate in the king's cause, assisted the French in 1646 to capture Dunkirk from the Spaniards, and was flung into jail on returning to England in 1648. In jail he revised his poems, and in 1649 published *Lucasta*. He was set free at the end of 1649. In 1659 his brother collected his poems. Most of Lovelace's work does not reach the heights he attained in the faultless lyrics, 'To Althea from Prison' and 'To Lucasta on going to the Wars', but many others have been set to music. See C. H. Wilkinson's edition of his Poems (1925; abbrev. 1930).

LOVELL, Sir Alfred Charles Bernard (1913–), English astronomer, a graduate of Bristol University, in 1951 became professor of Radio Astronomy at Manchester University and director of Jodrell Bank experimental station. Elected a fellow of the Royal Society in 1955, he gave the Reith Lectures in 1958, taking for his subject *The Individual and the Universe*. He has written several books on radio astronomy and on its relevance to life and civilization today. His works include *Science and Civilisation* (1939), *World Power Resources and Social Development* (1945) *Radio Astronomy* (1951) *The Story of Jodrell Bank* (1968). He was knighted in 1961.

LOVER, Samuel (1797–1868), Irish artist, novelist, songwriter and dramatist, born in Dublin, in 1818 established himself there as a marine painter and miniaturist. He published *Legends and Stories of Ireland* (1831), *Rory O'More* (1836) and *Handy Andy* (1842), having in 1835 settled in London, where he wrote for the periodicals, and in 1844 started an entertainment, called 'Irish Evenings', which was a hit both at home and in America (1846–48). See Lives by Bernard (1874) and Symington (1880).

LOW, (1) **Sir David** (1891–1963), British political cartoonist, born in Dunedin, N.Z., worked for several newspapers in New Zealand and for the *Bulletin* of Sydney, before coming in 1919 to the *Star* in London. In 1927 he joined the staff of the *Evening Standard*, for which he drew some of his most successful cartoons. His art ridiculed all political parties, and some of his creations will never die, notably Colonel Blimp, who has been incorporated into the English language. From 1953 he worked with *The (Manchester) Guardian*, and was knighted in 1962. He produced volumes of collected cartoons, including *Lloyd George and Co.* (1922), *Low and I* (1923), *A Cartoon History of the War* (1941), *Low's Company* (1952), *Low's Autobiography* (1956) and many more.

(2) **Sampson** (1797–1886), English publisher born in London, began business in 1819 as a bookseller and stationer. In 1848 he opened a publishing office at Red Lion Court, Fleet Street.

LOWE, (1) **Sir Hudson** (1769–1844), British soldier, born at Galway, in 1809 helped to conquer Zante and Cephalonia, and for nearly two years was governor of Santa Maura, Ithaca and Cephalonia. He was afterwards attached to the Prussian army of Blücher. In April 1816 he arrived as governor at St Helena, where his strict guard over Napoleon brought rancorous attacks, especially from O'Meara (q.v.). In 1825–31 he had an appointment in Ceylon.

(2) **Robert.** See SHERBROOKE.

LÖWE, Karl. See LOEWE.

LOWELL, (1) **Amy** (1874–1925), American imagist poet, born at Brookline, Mass. She wrote volumes of vers libre which she named 'unrhymed cadence' and also polyphonic prose. Her works, apart from her own verse, include *Six French Poets* (1915), *Tendencies in Modern American Poetry* (1917) and a biography of Keats (1925).

(2) **James Russell** (1819–91), American poet, essayist and diplomat, was born in Cambridge, Massachusetts, the son of a minister, and graduated at Harvard in 1838. In 1841–44 he published two volumes of poetry, in 1845 *Conversations on the Old Poets*; and in 1843 he helped to edit *The Pioneer*, with Hawthorne, Poe and Whittier for contributors. In 1846, at the outbreak of the war with Mexico, he wrote a satiric poem in the Yankee dialect denouncing the pro-slavery party and the conduct of the government; and out of this grew the *Biglow Papers*. A great many serious poems were written about 1848, and formed a third volume. *A Fable for Critics* (1848) is a series of witty and dashing sketches of American authors. In 1851–52 he visited Europe. In 1855 he was appointed professor of Modern Languages and Literature at Harvard and went to Europe to prosecute his studies. He also edited the *Atlantic Monthly* from 1857, and with C. E. Norton the *North American Review* 1863–67. His prose writings —*My Study Windows* and *Among my Books*— have high qualities. The second series of *Biglow Papers* appeared during the civil war. Lowell was an ardent abolitionist, and from the first gave himself unreservedly to the cause of freedom. Though he had never been a politician, he was appointed in 1877 U.S. minister to Spain, and was transferred in 1880 to Great Britain, where he remained until 1885. His *Collected Writings* were published in 1890–91. See his Letters (1893, 1934), and Lives by Underwood (1893), Scudder (1900), Greenslet (1906).

(3) **Percival** (1855–1916), American astronomer, born at Boston, educated at Harvard, established the Flagstaff Observatory in Arizona (1894). He is best known for his observations of Mars and for his prediction of the existence of the planet Pluto. He was the author of works on astronomy and on Japan.

LOWNDES, William Thomas (*c.* 1798–1843), English bookseller and bibliographer, born in London, to whom we owe *The Bibliographer's Manual of English Literature* (1834) and *The British Librarian* (1839).

LOWRY, (Laurence) Stephen (1887–), English artist, born and trained in Manchester, becoming A.R.A. in 1955, and R.A. in 1962. He has produced many pictures of the Lancashire industrial scene, mainly in brilliant whites and greys, peopled with scurrying antlike men and women. See *Drawings of L. S. Lowry* by M. Levy (1963).

LOWTH, Robert (1710–87), English bishop and scholar, born at Winchester, in 1741 became professor of Poetry at Oxford, in 1766 Bishop of St Davids and of Oxford, and in 1777 of London. He published *De Sacra Poesi Hebraeorum* (1753), *Life of William of Wykeham* (1758) and a new translation of Isaiah. He was one of the first to treat the Bible poetry as literature.

LOWTHER, (1) **Hugh Cecil.** See LONSDALE.

(2) **James William, 1st Viscount Ullswater** (1855–1949), was Conservative M.P. for Penrith 1886–1921, and Speaker of the House of Commons 1905–21.

LOYOLA, Ignatius de, *loy-ō'la* (1491–1556), is the name by which history knows Iñigo López de Recalde, Spanish soldier and ecclesiastic, born at his ancestral castle of Loyola in the Basque province of Guipúzcoa. A page in the court of Ferdinand, he then embraced the profession of arms. In the defence of Pampeluna he was severely wounded in the leg, which he had to have re-broken in order to be re-set. After this operation his convalescence was slow; and, his stock of romances exhausted, he turned to the lives of Christ and of the saints. The result was a spiritual enthusiasm as intense as that by which he had hitherto been drawn to chivalry. Renouncing the pursuit of arms, he resolved to begin his new life by a pilgrimage to Jerusalem. In 1522 he set out on his pilgrimage, the first step of which was a voluntary engagement to serve the poor and sick in the hospital of Manresa. There his zeal and devotion attracted such notice that he withdrew to a cavern in the vicinity, where he pursued alone his course of self-prescribed austerity, until, utterly exhausted, he was carried back to the hospital. From Manresa he repaired to Rome, whence he proceeded on foot to Venice and there embarked for Cyprus and the Holy Land. He returned ot Venice and Barcelona in 1524. He now resolved to prepare himself for the work of religious teaching, and at thirty-three returned to the rudiments of grammar, followed up by a course at Alcalá, Salamanca and Paris. In 1534 he founded with five associates the Society of Jesus. The original aim was limited to a pilgrimage to the Holy Land, and the conversion of the Infidels, but as access to the Holy Land was cut off by war with the Turks, the associates sought to meet the new wants engendered by the Reformation. Loyola went to Rome in 1539, and submitted to Pope Paul III the rule of the proposed order, and the vow by which the members bound themselves to go as missionaries to any country the pope might choose. The rule was approved in 1540, and next year the association elected Loyola as its first general. From this time he resided in Rome. At Manresa he wrote the first draft of the *Spiritual Exercises*, so important for the training of the Jesuits. He died July 31, 1556; was beatified in 1609; and was canonized in 1622. See books by Ribadaneira (1572), Maffei (1585), Bouhours (1679), Denis (1885), Rose (1891), Gothein (1896), Thompson (1909), Sedgwick (1923), Van Dyke (1926), Astrain (trans. 1928) and J. Brodrick (1956).

LOYSON, Charles. See HYACINTHE, PÈRE.

LUBBOCK, (1) Sir John, 1st Baron Avebury (1834–1913), born in London, the son of the astronomer, Sir J. W. Lubbock (1803–65). From Eton he went at fourteen into his father's banking house; in 1856 became a partner; served on several educational and currency commissions; and in 1870 was returned for Maidstone in the Liberal interest, in 1880 for London University—from 1886 till 1900 as a Liberal-Unionist. He succeeded in passing more than a dozen important measures, including the Bank Holidays Act (1871), the Bills of Exchange Act, the Ancient Monuments Act (1882), and the Shop Hours Act (1889). He was vice-chancellor of London University 1872–80, president of the British Association (1881), V.P.R.S., president of the London Chamber of Commerce, chairman of the London County Council 1890–92, &c. Best known for his researches on primitive man and on the habits of bees and ants, he published *Prehistoric Times* (1865; revised 1913), *Origin of Civilisation* (1870) and many books on natural history. See Life by Horace Hutchinson (1914), and *The Life-work of Lord Avebury* by A. Grant Duff (1924).

(2) **Percy** (1879–1965), English critic and essayist, born in London, the grandson of (1). He was librarian of Magdalene College from 1906 to 1908, and among his writings are *The Craft of Fiction* (1921), *Earlham* (1922), a book of personal childhood memories, and studies of Pepys (1909) and Edith Wharton (1947). In 1952 he was made a C.B.E.

LÜBKE, Wilhelm (1826–93), German writer on art, was born at Dortmund, and died at Karlsruhe. His most important work was *Grundriss der Kunstgeschichte* (1860).

LUCA DELLA ROBBIA. See ROBBIA (3).

LUCAN, George Charles Bingham, Earl of (1800–88), British soldier, accompanied the Russians as a volunteer against the Turks in 1828, succeeded as third earl in 1839, and as commander of cavalry in the Crimea fought at the Alma, Balaklava and Inkermann. Made G.C.B. in 1869, he became field-marshal in 1887.

LUCANUS, Marcus Annaeus (A.D. 39–65), Latin poet, was born at Corduba (Córdoba) in Spain. Annaeus Seneca, the rhetorician, had three sons—M. Annaeus Seneca, the Gallio of the Acts of the Apostles; L. Annaeus Seneca, the philosopher; and M. Annaeus Mela, father of Lucan. Rome's attraction had already drawn thither Seneca, the philosopher; and Mela, with his wife, followed, to place their son under his uncle's charge. Young Lucan became proficient in rhetoric and philosophy; and his aptitude for prose and verse was ominous of the fatal fluency which evolved the first three books of the *Pharsalia* while yet in his teens. At first the young emperor and the young poet were friends, and Nero's favour had conferred on Lucan the quaestorship. But when, in a great public contest, the palm went over Nero's head to Lucan, the emperor's marked discourtesies were returned by his successful rival with satire and with redoubled efforts to outshine him, till Nero was stung into forbidding Lucan either to publish poems or to recite them. Lucan became a ringleader of the Pisonian conspiracy; it was discovered and he himself betrayed. He was ordered to die, and, having had his veins opened, bled to death in a bath. Except a few fragments, we now have nothing of Lucan's many writings but the *Pharsalia*, recounting the mighty duel of Pompey and Caesar for the empire of the world. It is frequently bombastic, careless and inaccurate historically, but his descriptions are powerful, his use of language vivid and at its best his rhetoric is brilliant. See editions by Oudendorp (1728), Haskins (1887), Hosius (1905), Francken (1895–98), Housman (1926). There are translations by Marlowe (1st book), Sir F. Gorges, T. May (who continued the poem in Latin verse), Rowe (1718), Ridley (1897), and in prose by Riley (1853), Duff (1928).

LUCARIS, or Lukaris, Cyril (1572–1638), Greek theologian, born in Crete, studied at Venice, Padua and Geneva, where he was influenced by Calvinism. He rose by 1621 to be Patriarch of Constantinople. He opened negotiations with the Calvinists of England and Holland with a view to union and the reform of the Greek Church; he corresponded with Gustavus Adolphus, Archbishop Abbot and Laud; he presented the Alexandrian Codex to Charles I. The *Eastern Confession of the Orthodox Church*, of strong Calvinistic tendency, issued in 1629, it is now thought may not have been written by him. The Jesuits five times brought about his deposition, and are supposed by the Greeks to have instigated his murder by the Turks. In June 1637 he was seized, and believed to have been strangled.

LUCAS, *loo'kas*, (1) **Colin Anderson** (1906–), English architect, born in London. He studied at Cambridge, and in 1930 designed a house at Bourne End which was the first English example of the domestic use of monolithic reinforced concrete. Subsequent designs (1933–39), in partnership with A. D.

Connell and Basil Ward, played an important part in the development in England of the ideas of the European modern movement in architecture. He is a founder member of the MARS group of architects.

(2) **Edward Verrall** (1868–1938), English essayist and biographer, born at Eltham, Kent, became a bookseller's assistant, a reporter, contributor to and assistant editor of *Punch* and finally a publisher. He compiled anthologies, wrote novels, the best of which was *Over Bemerton's* (1908), books of travel and about 30 volumes of essays in a light, charming vein. An authority on Lamb, he wrote a Life in 1905.

(3) **Frank Lawrence** (1894–1967), English critic and poet, born at Hipperholme, Yorkshire. A fellow of and former reader in English at King's Coll., Cambridge, he wrote many scholarly works of criticism, including *Seneca and Elizabethan Tragedy* (1922), and *Eight Victorian Poets* (1930). Among his volumes of poetry are *Time and Memory* (1929) and *Ariadne* (1932). His plays include *Land's End* (1938). He also wrote novels and popular translations of Greek drama and poetry.

(4) **James** (1813–74), Dickens's 'Mr Mopes', from 1849 lived as an unwashed hermit on buns and gin at Elmwood, Hertfordshire.

(5) **John Seymour** (1849–1923), English historical painter, born in London, became A.R.A. in 1886, R.A. in 1897. Among his works is a fresco at the Royal Exchange depicting William the Conqueror's granting of London's first charter.

LUCAS VAN LEYDEN or **Lucas Jacobsz** (1494–1533), Dutch painter and engraver, was born and died at Leyden. He practised almost every branch of painting, and as an engraver ranks but little below Albrecht Dürer, whom he knew and by whom he was much influenced. See French work by Evrard (1883) and German ones by Volbehr (1888) and M. Friedlaender (1924).

LUCE, Henry Robinson (1898–1967), American magazine publisher and editor, born in Shantung, China, founded *Time* (1923), *Fortune* (1930) and *Life* (1936). He also in the 1930s inaugurated the radio programme 'March of Time', which became a film feature. He married in 1935 Clare Boothe (q.v.).

LUCIAN (*c.* A.D. 117–180), Greek writer, was born at Samosata in Syria. Having learned Greek and studied rhetoric, he practised as an advocate in Antioch, and wrote and recited show speeches for a living, travelling through Asia Minor, Greece, Italy and Gaul. Having thus made a fortune and a name, he settled in Athens, and there devoted himself to philosophy. There, too, he produced a new form of literature—humorous dialogue. In his old age he accepted a good appointment in Egypt, where he died. Lucian lived when the old faiths, the old philosophy, the old literature, were all rapidly dissolving. Never was there a fairer field for satire; and Lucian revelled in it. The absurdity of retaining the old deities without the old belief is brought out in the *Dialogues of the Gods*, *Dialogues of the Dead*, *Charon*, &c. Whether philosophy was more disgraced by the shallowness or the vices of those who now professed it, it would be hard to tell from his *Symposium*, *Halieus*, *Biōn Prasis*, *Drapetae* &c. The old literature had been displaced by novels or romances of adventure of the most fantastic kind, which Lucian parodies in his *True Histories*. Apart from the purity of his Greek, his style is simple, sparkling, delightful. See editions by Hemsterhuis and Reitz (1730–45), Lehmann (1822–29), Bekker (1853), Sommerbrodt (1888), Nilén (1906); translations by Fowler and Harmon.

LUCILIUS, Gaius (*c.* 180–102 B.C.), Roman satirist, was born at Suessa Aurunca in Campania, and died at Naples. He wrote thirty books of *Satires*, of which only fragments remain. Written in hexameters, they give a critical insight into his times. See the editions by Lachmann (1876), L. Muller (1872), F. Marx (1904–05), Terzaghi (1934).

LUCRETIA, wife of L. Tarquinius Collatinus, when outraged by Sextus Tarquinius, summoned her husband and friends, and, making them take oath to drive out the Tarquins, plunged a knife into her heart. The tale has formed the basis of several works, notably Shakespeare's *Rape of Lucrece* and the opera *The Rape of Lucretia* by Benjamin Britten. See BRUTUS.

LUCRETIUS (Titus Lucretius Carus) (*c.* 99–55 B.C.), Roman poet, was said to have died mad from the effects of a love potion given to him by his wife Lucilia (so in Tennyson's poem). The great work of Lucretius is his hexameter poem *De Natura Rerum*, in six books. Lucretius aspired to popularize the philosophical theories of Democritus and Epicurus on the origin of the universe, with the special purpose of eradicating anything like religious belief, which he savagely denounces as the one great source of man's wickedness and misery. A calm and tranquil mind was his *summum bonum*, and the only way to it lay through a materialistic philosophy. His poem abounds in strikingly picturesque phrases; up and down are episodes of exquisite pathos and vivid description, perhaps hardly equalled in Latin poetry; and when he allegorizes myths into moral truths, he is one of the sublimest of poets. Lachmann's text (1850) was improved by Munro (1860), who added (1864) a commentary and translation. See Creech's (1714) and Trevelyan's (1937) verse trans., Bailey's (1910) and Jackson's (1929) prose trans.; also Sellar's *Roman Poets* (1863); books by Veitch (1875), Masson (1907–09), Thomson (1915), Sikes (1936).

LUCULLUS, Lucius Licinius (*c.* 110–57 B.C.), Roman general, commanded the fleet in the first Mithridatic war, as consul in 74 defeated Mithridates, and introduced admirable reforms into Asia Minor. He twice defeated Tigranes of Armenia (69 and 68). But his legions became mutinous, and he was superseded by Pompey (66). He attempted to check Pompey's power, and was one of the first triumvirate, but soon withdrew from politics. He had acquired prodigious wealth and spent the rest of his life in luxury. See J. M. Cobban, *Senate and Provinces* 79–49 B.C. (1935).

LUCY, St (d. 303), the patron of the blind

was a virgin martyred under Diocletian at Syracuse. Her feast is kept on December 13.

LUCY, (1) **Sir Henry William** (1845–1924), English journalist, born at Crosby near Liverpool, worked as reporter on the *Shrewsbury Chronicle*, the *Pall Mall Gazette* and the *Exeter Gazette* (of which he became assistant editor), before being appointed *Daily News* parliamentary reporter. The 'Toby, M.P.' of *Punch* from 1881 to 1916, he was also a novelist and a writer of books on parliamentary process. See his autobiography, *Fifty Years in the Wilderness* (1909).

(2) **Sir Thomas** (1532–1600), Warwickshire squire and Justice of the Peace, said to have prosecuted Shakespeare for stealing deer from Charlecote Park, and to have been the original of Justice Shallow.

LUDD, Ned (fl. 1779), a Leicestershire idiot, destroyed some stocking frames about 1782. From him the Luddite rioters (1812–18) took their name.

LUDENDORFF, Erich von (1865–1937), German general, born near Posen, was a staff-officer 1904–13. In 1914 as quartermaster-general in East Prussia he defeated Samsonov at Tannenberg. When Hindenburg superseded Falkenhayn in 1916, Ludendorff as his first quartermaster sent Mackensen to the Dobruja, and, in general, conducted the war to the end, having been transferred to the Western front, where he conducted a series of defensive campaigns. In 1923 he was a leader in the Hitler putsch at Munich, but he was acquitted of treason. As a candidate for the presidency of the Reich in 1925 he polled few votes. Strongly opposed to Jews, Jesuits and freemasons, he was for a time a member of the National Socialist party, but from 1925 led a minority party of his own. See his *War Memories* (trans. 1919) and study by D. J. Goodspeed (1966).

LUDLOW, (1) **Edmund** (*c.* 1617–92), English regicide, born at Maiden Bradley, Wilts, served under Waller and Fairfax, was returned for Wilts in 1646, sat among the king's judges, and was elected to the council of state. In 1651 he was sent to Ireland as lieutenant-general of horse, but refused to recognize Cromwell's protectorate. Member for Hindon in 1659, he urged the restoration of the Rump, commanded again a while in Ireland, was nominated by Lambert to the committee of safety, and strove in vain to reunite the republican party. After the Restoration he made his way to Vevey. In 1689 he came back, but, the House of Commons demanding his arrest, he returned to Vevey. See his valuable *Memoirs* (ed. Firth (1894).

(2) **John Malcolm Forbes** (1821–1911), British social reformer, and founder of the Christian socialists. He was chief registrar of Friendly Societies.

LUDMILLA, St (d. 921), Bohemia's patroness, the wife of its first Christian duke, was murdered by her heathen daughter-in-law, Drahomira.

LUDWIG, *lood'veeKH*, (1) see LOUIS.

(2) originally **Cohn, Emil** (1861–1948), German author, born at Breslau, long resident in Switzerland, wrote some plays, but made his name as a biographer of the intuitive school, with lives of Goethe, Napoleon, William II, Bismarck, Christ, Lincoln, &c.

(3) **Karl Friedrich Wilhelm** (1816–95), German physiologist, born at Witzenhausen, professor at Leipzig (1865–95), did pioneer research on glandular secretions, and his invention of the mercurial blood-gas pump revealed the rôle of oxygen and other gases in the bloodstream.

LU HSUN or **Lu Hsin,** *shoon* (1881–1936), Chinese writer, born at Shaohsin in Chekiang, of a family of scholars, became in 1909 dean of studies at the Shaohsin Middle School and later its principal. By 1913 he was professor of Chinese Literature at the National Peking University and National Normal University for Women. In 1926 he went as professor to Amoy University and later was appointed dean of the College of Arts and Letters at Sun Yat-Sen University, Canton. His career as an author began with a short story, *Diary of a Madman* (1918). In 1921 appeared *The True Story of Ah Q*. Considered his most successful book, it has been translated into many languages. Between 1918 and 1925 he wrote 26 short stories and these appear in two volumes entitled *Cry* and *Hesitation.*

LUINI, or **Lovino, Bernardino,** *loo-ee'nee* (*c.* 1481–1532), Lombard painter, born at Luino on Lago Maggiore, was trained in the school of Leonardo da Vinci, to whom many of his works have been attributed. He painted much at Milan. He is one of the five whose 'supremacy' Ruskin affirmed. See Life by G. C. Williamson (1899) and monograph by L. Beltrami (1911).

LUITPRAND. See LIUTPRAND.

LUKE, (1) (*Loukas*, i.e., *Lucanus*), a companion of St Paul, mentioned in Col. iv. 14 as 'the beloved physician'; his name is suggestive of an Italian origin. Church tradition made him a native of Antioch in Syria, one of 'the seventy' mentioned in Luke x, a painter by profession, and a martyr. He is first named as author of the third gospel in the Muratorian canon (2nd century); and tradition has ever since ascribed to him both that work and the Acts of the Apostles. See A. Harnack, *Luke the Physician* (1907) and *Acts of the Apostles* (1909); J. M. Creed, *Gospel according to St Luke* (1930).

(2) **Sir Samuel.** See BUTLER, SAMUEL.

LULL, Ramón. See LULLY (2).

LULLY, (1) **Giovanni Battista,** *loo'lee* (1632–1687), French composer of Italian parentage, born in Florence, came as a boy to Paris, and was finally, after much ambitious intriguing, made operatic director by Louis XIV (1672). With Quinault as librettist, he composed many operas, in which he made the ballet an essential part; the favourites (till Gluck's time) were *Thésée, Armide, Phaéton, Atys, Isis,* and *Acis et Galatée.* He also wrote church music, dance music and pastorals. See books by Radet (1891), Prunières (1910).

(2) **Raymond** (sometimes **Lull**) (*c.* 1232–1315), Spanish theologian and philosopher, 'the enlightened doctor', born at Palma in Majorca, in his youth served as a soldier and led a dissolute life, but from 1266 gave himself up to asceticism and resolved on a

spiritual crusade for the conversion of the Mussulmans. To this end, after some years of study, he produced his *Ars Magna*, the 'Lullian method'; a mechanical aid to the acquisition of knowledge and the solution of all possible problems by a systematic manipulation of certain fundamental notions (the Aristotelian categories, &c.). He also wrote a book against the Averroists, and in 1291 went to Tunis to confute and convert the Mohammedans, but was imprisoned and banished. After visiting Naples, Rome, Majorca, Cyprus and Armenia, he again sailed (1305) for Bugia (Bougie) in Algeria, and was again banished; at Paris lectured against the principles of Averroes; and once more at Bugia, was stoned and died a few days afterwards. The Lullists combined religious mysticism with alchemy, but it has been disproved that Lully himself ever dabbled in alchemy. Apart from his *Ars Magna*, of his works *Llibre de Contemplació* is masterly and he was the first to use a vernacular language for religious or philosophical writings. He also wrote impressive poetry. See Life by Allison Peers (1929).

LUMIÈRE, *lüm-yayr*, **Auguste Marie Louis Nicolas** (1862–1954), and **Louis Jean** (1864–1948), French chemists, brothers, manufacturers of photographic materials, invented a cine camera (1893) and a process of colour photography.

LUMUMBA, Patrice Emergy (1925–61), Congolese politician, born in Katako Kombe, became leader of the Congolese national movement and when the Congo became an independent republic in 1960 was made premier. Almost immediately the country was plunged into chaos by warring factions, and after being deposed in 1960, Lumumba was assassinated in 1961.

LUNARDI, Vincenzo (1759–1806), Italian aeronaut, born at Lucca, made from Moorfields, on September 15, 1784, the first hydrogen balloon ascent in England.

LUPTON, Thomas Goff (1791–1873), English mezzotint engraver, was born and died in London. He was one of the first to use steel in engraving. Among his works are Turner's *Ports* and *Rivers*.

LUSIGNAN. See GUY DE LUSIGNAN.

LUTHARDT, Christoph Ernst, *loo-tart* (1823–1902), Lutheran theologian, became professor at Marburg (1854) and at Leipzig (1856). He wrote a Commentary on John's Gospel (1852–1853; 2nd ed. 1876), *St John the Author of the Fourth Gospel*, works on ethics, dogmatics, &c. See his *Reminiscences* (2nd ed. 1891).

LUTHER, Martin (1483–1546), German religious reformer, was born at Eisleben, the son of a miner, and went to school at Magdeburg and Eisenach. In 1501 he entered the University of Erfurt, and took his degree in 1505. Before this, however, he was led to the study of the Scriptures, and spent three years in the Augustinian monastery at Erfurt. In 1507 he was ordained a priest, in 1508 lectured on philosophy in the University of Wittenberg, in 1509 on the Scriptures, and as a preacher produced a still more powerful influence. In 1511 he was sent to Rome, and after his return his career as a Reformer commenced. Money was greatly needed at Rome; and its emissaries sought everywhere to raise funds by the sale of indulgences. Luther's indignation at the shameless traffic carried on by the Dominican John Tetzel (1517) became irrepressible. He drew out ninety-five theses on indulgences, denying to the pope all right to forgive sins; and these on October 31 he nailed on the church door at Wittenberg. Tetzel retreated from Saxony to Frankfurt an der Oder, where he published a set of counter-theses and burnt Luther's. The Wittenberg students retaliated by burning Tetzel's. In 1518 Luther was joined by Melanchthon. The pope, Leo X, at first took little heed of the disturbance, but in 1518 summoned Luther to Rome to answer for his theses. His university and the elector interfered, and ineffective negotiations were undertaken by Cardinal Cajetan and by Miltitz, envoy of the pope to the Saxon court. Eck and Luther held a memorable disputation at Leipzig (1519). Luther meantime attacked the papal system as a whole more boldly. Erasmus and Hutten now joined in the conflict. In 1520 the Reformer published his famous address to the 'Christian Nobles of Germany', followed by a treatise *On the Babylonish Captivity of the Church*, which works attacked also the doctrinal system of the Church of Rome. The papal bull, containing forty-one theses, issued against him he burned before a multitude of doctors, students, and citizens in Wittenberg. Germany was convulsed with excitement. Charles V had convened his first diet at Worms in 1521; an order was issued for the destruction of Luther's books, and he was summoned to appear before the diet. Ultimately he was put under the ban of the Empire, on his return from Worms he was seized, at the instigation of the Elector of Saxony, and lodged (really for his protection) in the Wartburg. During the year he spent here he translated the Scriptures and composed various treatises. Disorders recalled Luther to Wittenberg in 1522; he rebuked the unruly spirits, and made a stand against lawlessness on the one hand and tyranny on the other. In this year he published his acrimonious reply to Henry VIII on the seven sacraments. Estrangement had gradually sprung up between Erasmus and Luther, and there was an open breach in 1525, when Erasmus published *De Libero Arbitrio*, and Luther followed with *De Servo Arbitrio*. In that year Luther married Katharina von Bora (q.v.), one of nine nuns who had withdrawn from conventual life. In 1529 he engaged in his famous conference at Marburg with Zwingli and other Swiss divines, obstinately maintaining his views as to the Real (consubstantial) Presence in the Eucharist. The drawing up of the Augsburg Confession, Melanchthon representing Luther, marks the culmination of the German Reformation (1530). Luther died at Eisleben, and was buried at Wittenberg. Endowed with broad human sympathies, massive energy, manly and affectionate simplicity, and rich, if sometimes coarse, humour, he was undoubtedly a spiritual genius. His intuitions of divine truth were bold, vivid and penetrating, if not philosophical and comprehensive; and he possessed the power of kindling other souls with the fire of his own convictions. His voluminous works include *Table-talk*, *Letters* and *Sermons*. His Commentaries on Galatians and the Psalms are still read; and he was one of the great leaders of sacred song, his hymns having an enduring power. The great editions of his works are those of Wittenberg (12 vols. German; 7 vols. Latin, 1539–58); Halle, ed. by Walch (German, 24 vols. 1740–53); Erlangen and Frankfort (67 vols. German; 33 vols. Latin, 1826–73); and Weimar (1883 *et seq.*). See Lives by Köstlin (1875; 5th ed. 1903), Kolde (1884–1893), H. Grisar (trans. 1913–17; Catholic), Boehmer (1925, trans. 1957), and in English by Mackinnon (4 vols. 1925–30), Aubigne (1948), Bainton (1952), and Osborne's play *Luther* (1961).

LUTHULI, Albert John (1899?–1967), African resistance leader, son of a Zulu Christian missionary, was educated at an American mission school near Durban and spent 15 years as a teacher before being elected tribal chief of Groutville, Natal. Deposed for anti-apartheid activities, he became president-general of the African National Congress, in which capacity he dedicated himself to a campaign of non-violent resistance and was a defendant in the notorious Johannesburg treason trial (1956–59). In 1961 he was awarded the Nobel Peace prize for his unswerving opposition to racial violence in the face of repressive measures by the South African government and impatience from extremist Africans. He was elected rector of Glasgow University (1962) but severe restrictions imposed by the South African government (in 1961, and for another five years in 1964), prevented him from leaving Natal. See his *Let My People Go* (1962).

LUTTEREL or **Luttrell, Edward** (fl. 1670–1710), English engraver who probably came from Dublin to London, where he was a student of law. But abandoning this for art he became a crayon painter and one of the first mezzotint engravers. He executed portraits of Samuel Butler, Bishop Morley and Archbishop Sancroft.

LUTYENS, Sir Edwin Landseer (1869–1944), English architect, born in London, has been called the greatest architect since Christopher Wren. His designs ranged from the picturesque of his early country houses, including Marsh Court, Stockbridge and Lindisfarne Castle to those in the Renaissance style as Heathcote, Ilkley and Salutation, Sandwich, and finally he evolved a classical style exhibited in the Cenotaph, Whitehall, and which reached its height in his design for Liverpool R.C. Cathedral. Other prominent works were his magnificent Viceroy's House, New Delhi, a masterpiece in classical design, the British Pavilion at the Rome Exhibition of 1910, &c. He became president of the Royal Academy in 1938 and in 1942 received the Order of Merit. See Life by C. Hussey (1951).

LÜTZOW, Ludwig Adolf Wilhelm, Freiherr von, *lüt'zō* (1782–1834), Prussian soldier, born in Berlin, gave name to a renowned corps of volunteers, 'the Black Jäger', raised by him during the war of liberation in 1813. See work by von Jagwitz (1892).

LUXEMBOURG, Duc de, François Henri de Montmorency-Bouteville (1628–95), born in Paris, was trained by his aunt, mother of the Great Condé, and adhered to Condé through the wars of the Fronde. After 1659 he was pardoned by Louis XIV, who created him Duc de Luxembourg (1661)—he had just married the heiress of Luxembourg-Piney. In 1667 he served under Condé in Franche-Comté; in 1672 he himself successfully invaded the Netherlands, and, driven back in 1673, conducted a masterly retreat. During the war he stormed Valenciennes and twice defeated the Prince of Orange. Made a marshal in 1675, soon after the peace (1678) he quarrelled with Louvois (q.v.), and was not employed for twelve years. In 1690 he commanded in Flanders, and defeated the allies at Fleurus, and later twice more routed his old opponent, now William III, at Steinkirk and Neerwinden. He died in Paris.

LUXEMBURG, Rosa (1871–1919), German revolutionary of the extreme left, born at Zamość in Poland, was with Karl Liebknecht leader of the Spartakusbund, and with him was murdered in Berlin. She wrote *Die Akkumulation des Kapitals* (1913).

LUYNES, Charles d'Albert, Duc de, *lü-een* (1578–1621), the unworthy favourite of Louis XIII of France, became in 1619 a peer of France, and in 1621 chancellor. See Life by Zeller (Paris 1879).

LVOV, Prince Georgi Evgenievich (1861–1925), Russian liberal politician, head of the provisional government in the revolution of 1917. Succeeded by Kerensky, he left Russia.

LWOFF, André (1902–), French scientist, of Russo-Polish origin, born in Allier dept., professor of Microbiology at the Sorbonne. He was awarded Nobel prize for medicine in 1965 with Jacob (3) and Monod.

LYALL, Sir Alfred Comyn (1835–1911), English administrator and author, born at Coulsdon, Surrey, educated at Eton and Haileybury, was lieutenant-governor of the northwest Provinces of India (1882–87). He wrote on India and on literature, &c. See Life by H. M. Durand (1913).

LYAUTEY, Louis Hubert Gonzalve, *lee-ō-tay* (1854–1934), French marshal (1921), born at Nancy, held administrative posts in Algeria, Tongking and Madagascar (under Galliéni); but his most brilliant work was done in Morocco, where he was resident commissary-general in 1912–16, 1917–25. See Life by Maurois (trans. 1931).

LYCURGUS *lī-kur'goos,* (1) traditional, possibly mythological, law-giver of Sparta, assigned to the 9th century B.C.

(2) (*c.* 396–324 B.C.), Attic orator, supported Demosthenes, and as manager of the public revenue distinguished himself by his integrity and love of splendid architecture. One speech and a fragment have survived.

LYDEKKER, Richard, *-dek'-* (1849–1915), English naturalist and geologist, born in London, was an authority on mammals. He studied at Trinity, Cambridge, and worked on the Indian Geological Survey (1874–82). His works include *Phases of Animal Life* (1892), &c.

LYDGATE, John (*c.* 1370–*c.* 1451), an imitator of Chaucer, was born at Lydgate, near Newmarket, and became a Benedictine monk at Bury St Edmunds. He may have studied at Oxford and Cambridge; he travelled in France and perhaps Italy, and became prior of Hatfield Broadoak in 1423. A court poet, he received a pension in 1439, but died in poverty. Lydgate's longer works are the *Troy Book*, the *Siege of Thebes* and the *Fall of Princes*. The *Siege of Thebes* is represented as a new Canterbury tale, and was based on a French verse romance. The versification is rough, and the poem dull and prolix. The *Troy Book* was founded on Colonna's Latin prose *Historia Trojana*, and the *Fall of Princes* on Boccaccio. Other works include the *Daunce of Machabre*, from the French, and *Temple of Glas*, a copy of Chaucer's *House of Fame*. See E.E.T.S. editions (esp. *Temple of Glas* by Schick and *Minor Poems* by H. N. MacCracken, who attempts to establish the Lydgate canon).

LYELL, Sir Charles (1797–1875), Scottish geologist, born at Kinnordy, Forfarshire, the eldest son of the mycologist and Dante student, Charles Lyell (1767–1849). Brought up in the New Forest, and educated at Ringwood, Salisbury, and Midhurst, in 1816 he entered Exeter College, Oxford, and took his B.A. in 1819. At Oxford in 1819 he attended the lectures of Buckland, and acquired his taste for geology. He studied law, and was called to the bar; but devoting himself to geology, made European tours in 1824 and 1828–30, and published the results in the *Transactions of the Geological Society* and elsewhere. His *Principles of Geology* (1830–33) may be ranked next after Darwin's *Origin of Species* among the books which exercised the most powerful influence on scientific thought in the 19th century. It denied the necessity of stupendous convulsions, and taught that the greatest geological changes might have been produced by forces still at work. *The Elements of Geology* (1838) was a supplement. *The Geological Evidences of the Antiquity of Man* (1863) startled the public by its unbiased attitude towards Darwin. Lyell also published *Travels in North America* (1845) and *A Second Visit to the United States* (1849). In 1832–33 he was professor of Geology at King's College, London. Repeatedly president of the Geological Society, and in 1864 president of the British Association, he was knighted in 1848, and created a baron in 1864. See *Life, Letters, and Journals* (1881), a work by Bonney (1895), and Life by Bailey (1963).

LYLY, John, *lil'i* (*c.* 1554–1606), English dramatist and novelist, 'the Euphuist', was born in the Weald of Kent. He took his B.A. from Magdalen College, Oxford, in 1573, and studied also at Cambridge. Lord Burghley gave him some post of trust in his household, and he became vice-master of the St Paul's choristers. Having in 1589 taken part in the Marprelate controversy, he was returned to parliament for Aylesbury and Appleby, 1597–1601. His *Euphues*, a romance in two parts—*Euphues, the Anatomie of Wit* (1579), and *Euphues and his England* (1580)—was received with great applause. One peculiarity of his 'new English' is the constant employment of similes drawn from fabulous stories about the properties of animals, plants and minerals; another is the excessive indulgence in antithesis. Lyly's earliest comedy was *The Woman in the Moone*, produced in or before 1583. *Campaspe* and *Sapho and Phao* were published in 1584, *Endimion* in 1591, *Gallathea* and *Midas* in 1592, *Mother Bombie* in 1594, and *Love's Metamorphosis* in 1601. The delightful songs (of doubtful authorship) were first printed in the edition of 1632. Lyly's *Complete Works* were edited by R. Warwick Bond in 1902. See books by C. G. Child (Leipzig 1894), Feuillerat (1910), V. M. Jeffery (1929), G. K. Hunter (1962).

LYND, Robert (1879–1949), Irish essayist and critic, born in Belfast. He was for many years literary editor of the *News Chronicle* and also contributed to the *New Statesman*, signing himself Y. Y. His essays, of which he wrote numerous volumes, are on a wide variety of topics. Of an intimate, witty and charming nature rather reminiscent of Lamb, some titles are *The Art of Letters* (1920), *The Blue Lion* (1923), and *In Defence of Pink* (1939).

LYNDHURST, John Singleton Copley, Baron (1772–1863), Anglo-American lawyer, son of J. S. Copley, R.A. (q.v.), was born at Boston, Mass. At three, with his mother, he followed the painter to London, and in 1790 entered Trinity College, Cambridge, graduating in 1794. Next year he got a fellowship, and in 1796 paid a visit to the States. On his return he studied for the bar, and was called in 1804. Success was slow till 1812, when he made a hit by his ingenious defence of a Luddite rioter. In 1817 he obtained the acquittal of Thistlewood and Watson on their trial for high treason; but for the next state prosecution the government secured him on their side, and in 1818 he entered parliament as member for Yarmouth. Henceforward he continued a fairly consistent Tory. In 1819, as Sir John Copley, he became solicitor-general, in 1824 attorney-general, and in 1826 master of the rolls. As Baron Lyndhurst he was lord chancellor under three administrations from 1827 to 1830, when his Whig opponents made him chief baron of the Exchequer; that office he exchanged for the woolsack under Peel (1834–35). In 1841–46 he was for the third time lord chancellor. Lyndhurst's judgments have never been excelled for lucidity, method and legal acumen. See Atlay, *Victorian Chancellors* (1906).

LYNDSAY, or Lindsay, Sir David, of the Mount (*c.* 1486–1555), Scottish poet, was born probably at one of his father's seats—the Mount near Cupar, Garmylton (now Garleton), near Haddington. In 1512 he was appointed 'usher' of the newborn prince who became James V. In 1522 or earlier Lyndsay married Janet Douglas, the king's sempstress; in 1524 (probably), under the Douglases, he lost (or changed) his place; in 1538 he seems to have been Lyon King-of-Arms; by 1542 he had been knighted. He went on embassies to the Netherlands, France, England and Denmark. He or another David Lyndsay represented Cupar in the parliaments of 1540–46. For two centuries he was the poet of the Scottish people. His poems, often coarse, are full of humour, good sense and knowledge of the world, and were said to have done more for the Reformation in Scotland than all the sermons of Knox. The earliest and most poetic of his writings is *The Dreme*; the most ambitious, *The Monarche*; the most remarkable, *The Satyre of the Thrie Estaitis* (a dramatic work first performed at Linlithgow in 1540, and revived with great success at the Edinburgh Festivals of 1948 and 1959); the most amusing, *The Historie of Squyer Meldrum*. There are editions by Chalmers (1806), Laing (1879), Small, Hall, and Murray (E.E.T.S. 1865–71), Hamer (S.T.S. 1931–36). See also Murison, *Sir David Lyndsay* (1938).

LYNDSAY OF PITSCOTTIE. See PITSCOTTIE.

LYNEDOCH, Thomas Graham, 1st Baron, *lin'do*KH (1748–1843), son of the laird of Balgowan in Perthshire, raised in 1793 the 99th Regiment of foot, and served at Quiberon and in Minorca (1798). He besieged Valetta in 1800, was at Coruña and in Walcheren (1809), at Barrosa defeated the French (1811), fought at Ciudad Rodrigo (1812), Badajoz, and Salamanca, commanded the left wing at Vitoria (1813), captured Tolosa and San Sebastián and in Holland conquered at Merxem, but failed to storm Bergen-op-Zoom (1814). He was created Baron Lynedoch of Balgowan (1814). He founded the Senior United Service Club (1817). See Lives by Graham (2nd ed. 1877) and Delavoye (1880).

LYNEN, Feodor (1911–), German biochemist, head of Biochemistry at Munich Univ., and director of Max Planck Inst. für Zelichemie. He was awarded the Nobel prize for Medicine with Bloch (5) in 1964 for his work in lipid biochemistry on the formation of the cholesterol molecule, discovering the biochemistry of the vitamin biotin.

LYON, John (d. 1592), English yeoman, in 1571 founded the great public school of Harrow.

LYONS, (1) Edmund, 1st Baron (1790–1858), English admiral, born at Burton, Hants, commanded in the Dutch West Indies (1810–1811) and in Crimean waters, and was made a peer in 1856.

(2) **Sir Joseph** (1848–1917), English business man, born in London, first studied art and invented a stereoscope before joining with three friends, Isidore and Montague Gluckstein and Barnett Salmon, to establish what was to become J. Lyons and Co. Ltd. Starting in Piccadilly with a teashop, he became head of one of the largest catering businesses in Britain. He was knighted in 1911.

(3) **Joseph Aloysius** (1879–1939), Australian statesman, born at Stanley, Tasmania, educated at Tasmania University, became a teacher but entered politics in 1909 as Labour member in the Tasmanian House of Assembly. He held the post of minister of education and railways (1914–16) and was premier (1923–29). In the federal parliament, he was in turn postmaster-general, minister of public works and treasurer. In 1931 he broke away as a protest against the government's financial policy and led an opposition party, the United Australian Party, which he himself founded. In 1932 he became prime minister, which position he held until his death.

(4) **Richard Bickerton Pemell, 1st Earl** (1817–87), born at Lymington, son of (1), English diplomat, was ambassador to the United States, Turkey and France, was made a viscount in 1881, an earl in 1887. See Life by Lord Newton (1913).

LYRA, Nicolaus de (1270?–1340), born at Lyre near Évreux, was a lecturer at Paris, provincial of the Franciscans, and author of very famous *Postillae* or commentaries on scripture, in which he insisted on the literal meanings and protested against the traditional allegorizing method.

LYSANDER (d. 395 B.C.), Spartan admiral, as commander of the fleet defeated the Athenians at Aegospotami (405), and in 404 took Athens, thus ending the Peloponnesian war.

LYSENKO, Trofim Denisovich (1898–), the *enfant terrible* of Soviet genetics, born in Karlovka, Ukraine, gained a considerable reputation as an instiller of good crop husbandry into the Russian peasantry during the famines of the early 'thirties. On the basis of a borrowed discovery that the phases of plant growth can be accelerated by short doses of low temperature, he built up a quasi-scientific creed, compounded of Darwinism and the Michurinian thesis, that heredity can be changed by good husbandry, but otherwise more in line with Marxism than with genuine scientific theorizing. Failing to obtain scientific pre-eminence in the usual manner, he in 1948 with the approval of the Communist Party, declared the accepted Mendelian theory erroneous and banished many outstanding Soviet scientists. With the rise of Khrushchev and his agricultural policies, Lysenko faded from the limelight but was reinstated in 1958. He finally resigned from the presidency of the Academy of Agricultural Sciences, of which he was in charge (1938–56; 1958–62), on grounds of ill-health, and after Khrushchev's downfall was relieved of his post as head of the Institute of Genetics (1965). He was awarded the Order of Lenin in 1949 and the Stalin prize in 1949 for his book *Agrobiology* (1948).

LYSIAS (*c.* 450–380 B.C.), Greek orator, was the son of a rich Syracusan, who settled in Athens about 440. He was educated at Thurii in Italy. The Thirty Tyrants in 404 stripped him and his brother Polemarchus of their wealth, and killed Polemarchus. The first use to which Lysias put his eloquence was, on the fall of the Thirty (403), to prosecute Eratosthenes, the tyrant chiefly to blame for his brother's murder. He then practised with success as a writer of speeches for litigants. From his surviving speeches we see that Lysias is delightfully lucid in thought and expression, and strong in character-drawing.

LYSIMACHUS, *li-sim'a-koos* (d. 281 B.C.), Macedonian general of Alexander, afterwards King of Thrace, to which he later added north-west Asia Minor and Macedonia. He was defeated and killed at Koroupedion by Seleucus.

LYSIPPUS, *-sip'-* (fl. *c.* 360–316 B.C.), of

Sicyon, a prolific Greek sculptor, made several portrait busts of Alexander the Great. See Gardner's *Six Greek Sculptors* (1910).

LYTE, Henry Francis (1793–1847), Scottish hymnwriter, born at Ednam, near Kelso, entered Trinity College, Dublin. He took orders in 1815, and was for twenty-five years incumbent of Lower Brixham. His *Poems, chiefly Religious* (1833; reprinted as *Miscellaneous Poems*, 1868), are nearly forgotten; but 'Abide with me', 'Pleasant are thy courts', and other hymns have endured. See Life prefixed to his *Remains* (1850) and J. Julian, *A Dictionary of Hymnology* (1892).

LYTTLETON, (1) George, 1st Baron (1709–1773), English politician and author son of Sir Thomas Lyttleton of Hagley in Worcestershire, entered parliament in 1730, soon acquired eminence as a speaker, held several high political offices, and was raised to the peerage in 1759. His poetry gained him a place in Johnson's *Lives of the Poets*; his prose works include *The Conversion and Apostleship of St Paul* (1747), *Dialogues of the Dead* (1750), &c. See *Memoirs and Correspondence* (1845), and Rao, *A Minor Augustan* (1934).

(2) **George William, 4th Baron, second creation** (1817–76), as chairman of the Canterbury Association sent Anglican colonists to New Zealand and so founded Canterbury, N.Z., the port of which bears his name. He was under-secretary for the Colonies (1846).

(3) **Oliver.** See CHANDOS.

(4) **Thomas, Lord Lyttelton** (1744–79), son of (1), the 'wicked Lord Lyttelton', died three days after a death-warning dream. The *Poems by a Young Nobleman* (1780) may partly have been his, but the *Letters of the late Lord Lyttelton* (1780–82) were probably by W. Combe. See Lives by Frost (1876), Blunt (1936), Lang, *Valet's Tragedy* (1903).

(5) **Sir Thomas.** See LITTLETON.

LYTTON, (1) Edward George Lytton Bulwer-, 1st Baron (1803–73), English novelist, playwright, essayist, poet and politician, was born in London, youngest son of General Earle Bulwer (1776–1807) by Elizabeth Barbara Lytton (1773–1843), the heiress of Knebworth in Hertfordshire. He took early to poetry and in 1820 he published *Ismael and other Poems*. At Trinity Hall, Cambridge (1822–25), he won the Chancellor's gold medal for a poem upon 'Sculpture', but left with only a pass degree. His unhappy marriage (1827), against his mother's wishes, to the Irish beauty, Rosina Wheeler, ended in separation (1836), but called forth a marvellous literary activity, for the temporary estrangement from his mother threw him almost wholly on his own resources. His enormous output, vastly popular during his lifetime, but now forgotten, includes *Eugene Aram* (1832), *The Last Days of Pompeii* (1834), and *Harold* (1843). Some of his plays are *The Lady of Lyons* (1838), *Richelieu* (1839), *Money* (1840), and his poetry includes an epic, *King Arthur* (1848–49). M.P. for St Ives (1831–41), he was created a baronet in 1838, and in 1843 he succeeded to the Knebworth estate and assumed the surname of Lytton. He re-entered parliament as member for Hertfordshire in 1852, and in the Derby government (1858–59) as colonial secretary he called into existence the colonies of British Columbia and Queensland and in 1866 he was raised to the peerage. See his *Life, Letters, and Literary Remains* (vols. i-ii, 1883) by his son (down to 1832), Memoir (1913) by his grandson, 2nd Earl of Lytton. See also Life by Escott (1910), and the 'panorama' by Sadleir (i, 1931).

(2) **Edward Robert Bulwer, 1st Earl of** (1831–91), poet, diplomatist and statesman, son of (1), was born in London, and educated at Harrow and at Bonn. In 1849 he went to Washington as attaché and private secretary to his uncle, Sir Henry Bulwer (q.v.); and subsequently he was appointed attaché, secretary of legation, consul or *chargé d'affaires* at Florence (1852), Paris (1854), The Hague (1856), St Petersburg and Constantinople (1858), Vienna (1859), Belgrade (1860), Constantinople again (1863), Athens (1864), Lisbon (1865), Madrid (1868), Vienna again (1869) and Paris (1873). In the last year he succeeded his father as second Lord Lytton, and in 1874 became minister at Lisbon, in 1876–80 was Viceroy of India, and in 1880 was made Earl of Lytton; in 1887 he was sent as ambassador to Paris, and there he died. His works, published mostly under the pseudonym of 'Owen Meredith', include novels, poems, and translations from Serbian. See his *Indian Administration* (1899) and his *Letters* (1906), both edited by his daughter, Lady Betty Balfour.

(3) **Sir Henry Alfred** (1867–1936), English actor, born in London, first appeared on the stage in the D'Oyly Carte Opera Company in Glasgow in 1884. Till 1932 he played leading parts in Gilbert and Sullivan opera. He wrote *Secrets of a Savoyard* (1927), *A Wandering Minstrel* (1933).

M

MAARTENS, Maarten, pen-name of **Jost Marius Willem van der Poorten Schwart** (1858–1915), who, born at Amsterdam, spent part of his boyhood in England, went to school in Germany, and studied and taught law at Utrecht University. He wrote powerful novels in nervous English, including *The Sin of Joost Avelingh* (1889), *God's Fool* (1893), &c. See his *Letters*, ed. his daughter (1930), and a study by Maanen (1928).

MABILLON, Jean, *mab-ee-yõ* (1632–1707), French Benedictine monk, born at St

Pierremont in Champagne, from 1664 worked in St Germain-des-Prés at Paris, where he died. He edited St Bernard's works (1667), wrote a history of his order (1668–1702), &c.

MABLY, Gabriel Bonnot de, *ma-blee* (1709–1785), French historian, born at Grenoble, the elder brother of Condillac, for a time was secretary to the minister Cardinal Tencin, his uncle, and wrote *Entretiens de Phocion* (1763), *Parallèle des Romains et des Français* (1740) and *Observations sur l'histoire de la Grèce* (1766). His *De la manière d'écrire l'histoire* (1783) contains severe strictures on Hume, Robertson, Gibbon and Voltaire. See books by Guerrier (1886) and Whitfield (1930).

MABUSE, Jan, real name **Gossart,** *ma-büz* (*c.* 1470–1532), Flemish painter, was born at Maubeuge (Mabuse), in 1503 entered the painters' guild of St Luke at Antwerp, and was influenced by Memlinc and Quentin Matsys. In 1508–09 he accompanied Philip of Burgundy to Italy, and returned with his style greatly modified by the Italian masters. Drunken but sumptuous, he lived latterly at Middelburg, and died at Antwerp.

McADAM, John Loudon (1756–1836), inventor of the 'macadamizing' system of road-making, was born at Ayr, September 21, 1756. He went to New York in 1770, became a successful merchant, and on his return to Scotland in 1783 bought the estate of Sauchrie, Ayrshire. Surveyor (1816) to the Bristol Turnpike Trust, he re-made the roads there cheaply and well. His advice was sought in all directions. Impoverished through his labours, he petitioned parliament in 1820, and in 1825 was voted £2000, in 1827 made surveyor-general of metropolitan roads. He died November 26. He wrote three books on road-making (1819–22). See Life by M. R. R. M. Pember-Devereux (1940).

MACALPINE, John. See MACHABEUS.

MacARTHUR, Douglas (1880–1964), American soldier, born at Little Rock, Arkansas, and educated at West Point. Commissioned in the Corps of Engineers in 1903, he went to Tokyo in 1905 as aide to his father, then chief U.S. observer at the Russo-Japanese war. In the first World War he served with distinction in France, was decorated thirteen times and cited seven additional times for bravery. Promoted brigadier in August 1918, he became in November the youngest divisional commander in France. In 1919 he became the youngest-ever superintendent of West Point and in 1930 was made a general and chief of staff of the U.S. Army. In 1935 he became head of the U.S. military mission to the Philippines and in 1941 commanding general of the U.S. armed forces in the Far East. In March 1942, after a skilful but unsuccessful defence of the Bataan peninsula, he was ordered to evacuate from the Philippines to Australia, where he set up H.Q. as supreme commander of the SW. Pacific Area. As the war developed he carried out a brilliant 'leap-frogging' strategy which enabled him to recapture the Philippine Archipelago from the Japanese. In 1944 he was appointed a general of the Army, and completed the liberation of the Philippines in July 1945. Then, formally accepting as supreme commander of the Allied Powers the surrender of Japan, he exercised in the occupied Empire almost unlimited authority. He gave Japan a new constitution and carried out a programme of sweeping reform. When war broke out in Korea in June 1950 President Truman ordered him to support the South Koreans in accordance with the appeal of the U.N. Security Council. In July he became c.-in-c. of the U.N. forces. After initial setbacks he pressed the war far into North Korea, but after the Chinese entered the war in November, MacArthur demanded powers to blockade the Chinese coast, bomb Manchurian bases and to use Chinese Nationalist troops from Formosa against the Communists. This led to acute differences with the U.S. Democratic Administration and on April 11, 1951, President Truman relieved him of his commands. He failed to be nominated for the presidency in 1952. A brilliant military leader and a ruler of Japan imbued with a deep moral sense, MacArthur was almost a legend in his lifetime. Equally he inspired criticism for his imperious belief in his own mission, his strong sense of self-dramatization. See *The General and the President*, by Rovere and Schlesinger (1952), and his own *Reminiscences* (1965).

MACARTNEY, George, 1st Earl (1737–1806), British diplomat, born at Lissanoure near Belfast, and educated at Trinity College, Dublin, in 1764 was sent as an envoy to Russia, in 1769–72 was chief-secretary of Ireland, and in 1775 was governor of Grenada. There (an Irish baron from 1776) he was taken prisoner by the French in 1779. Governor of Madras 1781–85, in 1792 he was made an earl and headed the first diplomatic mission to China. After a mission to Louis XVIII at Verona (1795–96), he went out as governor to the Cape (1796), but returned in ill health in 1798. See Life by Mrs Robbins (1908), *Private correspondence* ed. by Davies (1950).

MACAULAY, (1) Rose (1889–1958), English novelist, essayist and poet. Her father, G. C. Macaulay, was a Cambridge lecturer and translator of Herodotus and Froissart, and having imbibed from this background a taste for literature she began writing at an early age, her first book, *Abbots Verney*, appearing in 1906, followed by *Views and Vagabonds* (1912) and *The Lee Shore* (1913), which won a publisher's £1000 prize. Among her many witty and erudite subsequent books were *Dangerous Ages* (1921), which was awarded the Femina Vie Heureuse Prize, *Told by an Idiot* (1923), *They were Defeated* (1932), *Fabled Shore* (1949), *The Pleasure of Ruins* (1953), and *The Towers of Trebizond* (1956), which won The Tait Black Memorial Prize. She was renowned for her enormous vigour and zest for life, which she retained even in her old age. Despite her apparent physical frailty she was an indefatigable traveller and an all-the-year-round swimmer. She was made a D.B.E. in 1958.

(2) Thomas Babington, 1st Baron Macaulay (1800–59), British author, son of (3), was born at Rothley Temple, Leics., on October 25. In 1812 young Macaulay was sent to a private school at Little Shelford near Cambridge, moved in 1814 to Aspenden Hall in Hertfordshire, whence, an exceptionally precocious boy, he entered Trinity College, Cambridge, in 1818. He detested mathematics, but twice won the Chancellor's medal for English verse, and obtained a prize for Latin declamation. In 1821 he carried off the Craven, in 1822 took his B.A., and in 1824 was elected to a fellowship. He was one of the most brilliant disputants in the Union. Called to the bar in 1826, he had no liking for his profession—literature had irresistible attractions for him. In 1823 he became a contributor to *Knight's Quarterly Magazine*, in which appeared some of his best verses—*Ivry*, *The Spanish Armada* and *Naseby*. In 1825 he was discovered by Jeffrey, and his famous article on Milton in the August number of the *Edinburgh Review* secured him a position in literature. For nearly twenty years he was one of the most prolific and popular of the writers to the *Edinburgh*. In 1830 he entered parliament for the pocket borough of Calne, and in the Reform Bill debates his great powers as an orator were established. Commissioner, and then secretary, to the Board of Control, he still wrote steadily for the *Edinburgh*, and made a great reputation as a conversationalist in society. Mainly for the sake of his family, impoverished by the father's devotion to philanthropy, he accepted the office of legal adviser to the Supreme Council of India, with a salary of £10,000, and sailed for Bengal in 1834, returning to England in 1838. In 1839 he was elected member of parliament for Edinburgh, and entered Lord Melbourne's Cabinet as secretary at war. The *Lays of Ancient Rome* (1842) won an immense popularity; so too did his collected *Essays* (3 vols. 1843). His connection with the *Edinburgh* ceased in 1845; he had now commenced his *History of England from the Accession of James II*. In 1846 he was re-elected for Edinburgh; but defeated at the general election of 1847. In 1852 he was again returned for Edinburgh; in 1856 he retired. The first two volumes of his *History* appeared in 1848, and at once attained greater popularity than had ever fallen to a purely historical work; the next two followed in 1855, and an unfinished fifth volume was published in 1861. In 1849 he was elected lord rector of Glasgow University. In 1857 he was raised to the peerage as Baron Macaulay of Rothley. He died in his armchair at Holly Lodge, Kensington, December 28, 1859, and was buried in Westminster Abbey. Macaulay's reputation is not what once it was—he has been convicted of historical inaccuracy, of sacrificing truth for the sake of epigram, of allowing personal dislike and Whig bias to distort his views of men and incidents. But as a picturesque narrator he has no rival. See his *Life and Letters* by his nephew, G. O. Trevelyan (1876), Morison's Monograph (1882), an essay by Morley (*Critical Miscellanies*, 1886), and studies by Bryant (1932), Giles St Aubyn (1953) and M. Thomson (1959).

(3) **Zachary** (1768–1838), father of (2), had a somewhat chequered career as a West India merchant, but was best known as an abolitionist and a member of the 'Clapham sect'. See Lives by Knutsford (1900), Booth (1934).

McAULEY, Catherine (1787–1841), Irish religious foundress born in Dublin. She founded the Order of Sisters of Mercy in 1831. See Life by R. B. Savage (1949).

MACBETH (d. 1057), Mormaer of Moray, married Gruoch, granddaughter of Kenneth Dubh, King of Alban, and became commander of the forces of Scotland. In 1040 he slew King Duncan, and succeeded him. He seems to have represented a Celtic reaction against English influence; and his seventeen years' reign is commemorated in the chronicles as a time of plenty. Malcolm Canmore, Duncan's son, ultimately defeated and killed him at Lumphanan, August 15, 1057. Shakespeare got his story from Holinshed, who drew on Boece. See Skene's *Celtic Scotland* (1876).

MacBRIDE, Maud, *née* **Gonne** (1865–1953), Irish nationalist, the daughter of an English colonel, became an agitator for the cause of Irish independence, edited a nationalist newspaper, *L'Irlande libre*, in Paris, and married Major John MacBride, who fought against the British in the Boer War and was executed as a rebel in 1916. After his death she became an active Sinn Feiner in Ireland. W. B. Yeats dedicated poems to her. Her son **Sean** (b. 1904) was foreign minister of the Irish Republic from 1948 to 1951.

MacBRYDE, Robert (1913–), Scottish artist, born in Ayrshire. He worked in industry for five years before studying at the Glasgow School of Art and later worked with Robert Colquhoun, painting brilliantly-coloured cubist still lifes, and later, brooding expressionist figures.

MACCABEES, a celebrated Jewish family. The founder of the dynasty, Mattathias, a priest, was the first to make a stand against the persecutions of the Jewish nation and creed by Antiochus Epiphanes. He was the great-great-grandson of Hasmon and the family is often known as the 'Hasmoneans'. Mattathias and his five sons, Jochanan, Simon, Jehudah, Eleazer and Jonathan, together with a handful of faithful men, rose against the national foe, destroyed heathen worship, and fled into the wilderness of Judah. Their number soon increased; they were able to make descents into the villages and cities, where they restored the ancient worship of Jehovah. At the death of Mattathias (166 B.C.) his son Jehudah or Judas, now called Makkabi (*Makkab*, 'hammerer') or Maccabaeus, took the command of the patriots, and repulsed the enemy, reconquered Jerusalem, purified the Temple, and re-inaugurated the holy service (164). Having concluded an alliance with the Romans, he fell in battle (160). His brother Jonathan renewed the Roman alliance, acquired the dignity of high priest, but was treacherously slain by the Syrians. Simon, the second brother, completely re-established the independence of the nation (141), and 'Judah prospered as of old'. But he was foully murdered (135) by his son-in-law, Ptolemy. See the articles HYRCANUS, HEROD; the Apocryphal books of the Maccabees; and histories of the period by De Saulcy (1880), Ewald, and Schürer.

MacCAIG, Norman Alexander (1910–), Scottish poet, born at Edinburgh, and educated at the University there. His poetry collections include *Far Cry* (1943), *Riding Lights* (1955), *A Common Grace* (1960), *A Round of Applause* (1962), and *Surroundings* (1966). Though he writes in English his topics and temperament are unmistakably Scots. A metaphysical approach to ideas with the speculation subtly expressed, is the hallmark of his work, which is deliberately quiet in tone. He edited *Honour'd Shade* (1959), an anthology of the most modern and significant in Scottish poetry commemorating the bicentenary of Burns.

MacCARTHY, (1) **Denis Florence** (1817-82), Irish author, born in Dublin, was prepared for the priesthood, but wrote poetry, translated Calderón, and published *Shelley's Early Life* (1872).

(2) **Sir Desmond** (1878–1952), writer and critic, born at Plymouth. Educated at Eton and Trinity College, Cambridge, he entered journalism and was successively editor of *New Quarterly* and *Eye Witness* (later *New Witness*). By 1913 he was writing for *The New Statesman*, of which he became literary editor in 1920, and later dramatic critic. He became editor of *Life and Letters*, book reviewer for *The Sunday Times*, and a broadcaster of repute. He was knighted in 1951. His criticism, collected in book form, is represented by *Portraits* (1931), *Experience* (1935), *Drama* (1940), *Humanities* (1954) and *Theatre* (1955). See *A Number of People* by Marsh (1939), the preface to *Humanities* by MacCarthy's son-in-law, David Cecil, and his autobiographical *Memories* (1953).

McCARTHY, (1) **Joseph Raymond** (1909–57), American politician and inquisitor, born at Grand Chute, Wisconsin, studied at Marquette University, Milwaukee, and in 1939 was a state circuit judge. After war services in the Marines and as an air-gunner, he was elected senator in 1945, although as a serving judge his election was contrary to the Constitution. Defying a Supreme Court ruling, he took his seat in the senate and in 1950 was re-elected by a huge majority, having exploited the general uneasiness felt after the treason trials of Nunn May, Fuchs and Alger Hiss, by accusing the State Department of harbouring 205 prominent Communists, a charge that he was later incapable of substantiating, before a special subcommittee on foreign relations. Undaunted, he accused the Truman administration of being 'soft on Communism' and the Democratic party of a record of 'twenty years of treason'. After the Eisenhower victory, McCarthy, in January 1953, became chairman of the powerful Permanent Subcommittee on Investigations and by hectoring cross-examination, damaging innuendo, and 'guilt by association' arraigned a great number of mostly innocent citizens and officials, often with full television publicity, overreaching himself when he came into direct conflict with the army, which he accused of 'coddling Communists'. Formally condemned by the Senate, again controlled by the Democrats in 1954, for financial irregularities, he was stung into attacking President Eisenhower and so lost most of his remaining Republican support. Truman rightly described him as a 'pathological character assassin'. See Life by J. Anderson and R. W. May (1953), and critical study by R. H. Rovere (1960).

(2) **Justin** (1830–1912), Irish politician, novelist and historian, born in Cork, joined the staff of the *Northern Times*, Liverpool, in 1853, and in 1860 entered the reporters' gallery for the *Morning Star*, becoming its chief editor in 1864. He resigned in 1868, and devoted the next three years to a tour of the United States. Soon after his return he became connected with the *Daily News*, and he contributed to the *London*, *Westminster* and *Fortnightly Reviews*. He entered parliament in 1879 for Longford. He is better known, however, as a novelist than as a politician. His novels include *Dear Lady Disdain* (1875) and *Miss Misanthrope* (1877). Other works are *A History of our Own Times* (7 vols. 1879–1905), *The Four Georges and William IV* (4 vols. 1889-1901), &c. See his *Reminiscences* (1899–1911).

(3) **Justin Huntly** (1860–1936), son of (2), was a Nationalist M.P. 1884–92; in 1894 he married the clever impersonator and actress, Cissie Loftus (1876–1943; born in Glasgow), who divorced him in 1899. He wrote stories, plays, verse, *England under Gladstone* (1884), *Ireland since the Union* (1887), *The French Revolution* (4 vols. 1890–97), &c.

(4) **Mary** (1912–), American novelist and critic, born at Seattle. Orphaned in 1918, she was brought up in Minneapolis, and educated at Vassar Coll. She has worked as publisher's editor, theatre critic and teacher, as well as publishing novels, including *The Company She Keeps* (1942), *The Oasis* (1949), *The Groves of Academe* (1952), a book of short stories, and *The Group* (1963). Other works include *Sights and Spectacles* (1956), *Vietnam* (1967), and her autobiographical *Memories of a Catholic Girlhood* (1957).

MACCHABEUS. See MACHABEUS.

MACCHIAEVLLI. See MACHIAVELLI.

McCLELLAN, George Brinton (1826–85), American general, was born at Philadelphia. At the Civil War in 1861, as major-general in the U.S. army, he drove the enemy out of West Virginia, and was called to Washington to reorganize the Army of the Potomac. In November he was made commander-in-chief, but held the honour only five months. His Virginian campaign ended disastrously. He advanced near to Richmond, but was compelled to retreat, fighting the 'seven days' battles' (June 25 to July 1, 1862). After the disastrous second battle of Bull Run (August 29–30), followed by a Confederate invasion of Maryland, he reorganized the army at Washington, marched north, met Lee at Antietam, and compelled him to recross the Potomac. He followed the Confederates into Virginia, but too slow and cautious, he was superseded by Burnside. In 1864 he opposed Lincoln for the presidency, and in 1877 was elected governor of New Jersey. See *McClellan's Own Story* (1886), and vindication by J. H. Campbell (1917).

McCLINTOCK, Admiral Sir Francis Leopold (1819–1907), British polar explorer, born at Dundalk, entered the navy in 1831, and was knighted in 1860 for discovering the fate of the Franklin (q.v.) expedition. In 1891 he was created a K.C.B.

McCLURE, Sir Robert John le Mesurier (1807–73), was born at Wexford, January 28, entered the navy in 1824, and served in Back's Arctic Expedition in 1836, and Ross's Franklin Expedition in 1848. As commander of a ship in another Franklin Expedition (1850–54) he penetrated eastwards to the north coast of Banks Land. Having been icebound there for nearly two years, he was rescued by Captain Kellett, who had come westwards. The rescuing ship was in turn abandoned after another winter. Thus in three ships, with two ice journeys, McClure accomplished the Northwest Passage. After serving in Chinese waters he died, an admiral. See his *Voyages* (2 vols. 1884).

MacCOLL, Dugald Sutherland (1859–1948), Scottish painter and art historian, born in Glasgow, graduated at London University and at Oxford, where he won the Newdigate Prize in 1882. After travelling Europe studying works of art he established a reputation as a critic and brought out his *Nineteenth Century Art* in 1902. As keeper of the Tate Gallery (1906–11) and of the Wallace Collection (1911–24) he instituted many reforms and improvements, and he also published poems and a noteworthy biography of Wilson Steer (1945; Tait Black Memorial Prize). See his *Confessions of a Keeper* (1931).

McCORMACK, John (1884–1945), Irish tenor singer, born in Athlone. He studied in Milan, made his London début in 1905, and was engaged for Covent Garden opera for the 1905–06 season, appearing also in oratorio and as a lieder singer. As an Irish nationalist, he did not appear in England during World War I, but took American citizenship in 1917, and turned to popular sentimental songs. He was raised to the papal peerage as a count in 1928. See Lives by Strong (1949) and Foxall (1963).

McCOSH, James (1811–94), Scottish philosopher, born at Carskeoch, Ayrshire, became a minister of the Church of Scotland and later of the Free Church. In 1851 he became professor of Logic at Belfast and in 1868 president of Princeton. His *Intuitions of the Mind* (1860) brought the natural realism of the Scottish school back from Hamilton's Kantian superstructure to the 'common sense' positions of Reid and Stewart. In his *Examination of Mr J. S. Mill's Philosophy* (1866) he attempted a vindication of the Scottish school against the mortal blow dealt it by Mill. See his *The Scottish Philosophy* (1875). See Life by W. M. Sloane.

McCRACKEN, Esther Helen, *née* **Armstrong** (1901–), English playwright and actress, born in Newcastle-on-Tyne. From 1924 to 1937 she acted with the Newcastle Repertory Company. Her first play, *The Willing Spirit*, was produced in 1936, but it was with *Quiet Wedding* (1938) that her reputation was made as a writer of domestic comedy. Other successes were *Quiet Weekend* (1941) and *No Medals* (1944). Her first husband, Lt.-Col. Angus McCracken, died of wounds in 1943, and the following year she married Mungo Campbell.

McCRIE, Thomas (1772–1835), Scottish historian and divine, born at Duns, author of lives of Knox (1812) and Melville (1819) and of *History of the Reformation in Spain* (1829). See Life (1840) by his son, **Thomas** (1798–1875), professor in the Presbyterian college at London, and himself author of *Sketches of Scottish Church History* (1841) and *Annals of English Presbytery* (1872).

MacCRIMMON, a Skye family, hereditary pipers to Macleod of Dunvegan, the greatest Patrick Mór (fl. 1650). See book by F. T. Macleod (1933).

McCULLERS, Carson, *née* **Smith** (1917–67), American author, born in Columbus, Ga., educated Columbia and New York Universities. Her novels, set in the deep south, are both realistic, often tragic, and symbolic. They include *The Heart is a Lonely Hunter* (1940), *Reflections in a Golden Eye* (1941), a violent melodrama set on a peacetime army camp, *The Member of the Wedding* (1946, which she turned into a play, 1950 (New York Critics Award), filmed 1952), a sympathetic study of unhappy adolescence, and *Clock Without Hands* (1961). She also wrote a novella, *The Ballad of the Sad Café* (1951), another play and short stories.

MACCULLOCH, John (1773–1835), Scottish geologist, born in Guernsey, noted for his geological studies of the Western Isles.

McCULLOCH, John Ramsay (1789–1864), political economist, born at Whithorn, March 1, 1789, edited the *Scotsman* 1818–19, and for twenty years provided most of the articles on economics in the *Edinburgh Review*. He lectured in London; in 1828 became professor of Political Economy in University College, and in 1838 comptroller of H.M. Stationery Office. He wrote books on economics and commerce.

MacCUNN, Hamish (1868–1916), Scottish composer, born in Greenock, March 22, 1868, studied at the Royal College of Music, and in 1888–94 was professor of Harmony at the Royal Academy of Music. His works, largely Scottish in character and subject, include the overtures *Cior Mhor* (1887), *Land of the Mountain and the Flood*, and *The Dowie Dens of Yarrow*, choral works, such as *The Lay of the Last Minstrel*, the operas *Jeanie Deans* (1894) and *Diarmid* (1897), and songs.

MacDIARMID, Hugh, *mak-dir'mid*, pen-name of **Christopher Murray Grieve** (1892–), Scottish poet, pioneer of the Scottish literary renaissance, born at Langholm, Dumfries, served with the medical corps in Greece during World War I and was a munitions worker in World War II. A journalist in Montrose in the 'twenties, he took to poetry, fostering his own work in the *Scottish Chapbook*, a monthly review which he edited. Beginning with such outstanding early lyrical verse as 'Watergaw', he established himself as the new prophetic voice of Scotland by *A Drunk Man Looks at the Thistle* (1926), bursting with political, metaphysical and nationalistic reflections on the Scottish predicament. In his later works, however, this master of polemic, or 'flyting' increasingly allowed his poetical genius to be overburdened by philosophical gleanings, in the service of a highly personal form of Communism. Nevertheless items such as 'The Seamless Garment', 'Cattle Shaw', 'At Lenin's Tomb' raise these later works to a very high level. They are *To Circumjack Cencrastus* (1930), the two *Hymns to Lenin* (1930; 1935), *Scots Unbound* (1932), *Stony Limits* (1934), *A Kist o' Whistles* (1947) and *In Memorian James Joyce* (1955). His numerous essays such as *Albyn* (1927), *The Islands of Scotland* (1939) suffer from the same intellectual scrapbook tendency. Founder-member of the Scottish National Party, off and on an active Communist, he stood against Sir Alec Douglas-Home as a Communist candidate in 1963. He dedicated his life to the regeneration of the Scottish literary language, repudiated by his fellow Scottish poet, Edwin Muir, in 1936. He brilliantly succeeded by employing a vocabulary drawn from all regions and periods, intellectualizing a previously parochial tradition. He received an honorary Edinburgh doctorate in 1957. See his autobiography, *Lucky Poet* (1943), and *The Company I've Kept* (1966), Wittig, *The Scottish Tradition in Literature* (1958), and studies by Buthley (1964) and Glen (1964).

MacDONALD, (1) James Ramsay (1866–1937), British politician, born at Lossiemouth (Morayshire), and educated at a Board school, wrote on Socialism and other problems. He was a leading member of the I.L.P. (1893–1930) and was secretary (1900–11) and leader (1911–14, 1922–31) of the Labour Party. A member of the L.C.C. (1901–04) and of parliament from 1906, he became leader of the Opposition in 1922, and from January to November 1924 was prime minister and foreign secretary of the first Labour government in Britain—a minority government at the mercy of the Liberals. The election of 1924 put him out of office; that of 1929 brought him in again; but he met the financial crisis of 1931 by forming a predominantly Conservative 'National' government, the bulk of his party opposing; and in 1931 reconstructed it after a general election. In 1935–37 he was lord president. See Lives by G. E. Elton (1939), L. M. Weir (1938).

(2) **Malcolm** (1901–), British administrator, son of (1), born at Lossiemouth, studied at Oxford, was National Government M.P. (1936–45) and held several ministerial appointments, including those of colonial secretary (1935; 1938–40) and minister of Health (1940–41). He has held positions as high commissioner in Canada (1941–46), governor-general of Malaya and Borneo (1946–48), commissioner-general in South East Asia (1948–55), high commissioner in India (1955–60), governor-general (1963–64), and high commissioner (1964–65) in Kenya, and special representative in east and central Africa from 1965. His books include *Borneo People* (1956) and *Angkor* (1958), and several on ornithology.

MACDONALD, (1) Fr. *mak-do-nahl*, **Jacques Étienne Joseph Alexandre** (1765–1840), marshal of France, was born at Sedan, the son of a Scottish Jacobite schoolmaster. He entered the army in 1785, distinguished himself in the cause of the Revolution, and rapidly rose to high rank. In 1798 he was made governor of Rome, and subjugated Naples. Suvoroff defeated him after a bloody contest on the Trebbia (1799). In 1805 he lost the favour of Bonaparte; but, restored to command in 1809, he took Laibach, distinguished himself at Wagram, and was created marshal and Duke of Taranto. He held a command in Spain in 1810, and in the Russian campaign; and in 1813 he contributed to the successes of Lützen and Bautzen, but was routed by Blücher at the Katzbach. After Leipzig he helped to cover the French retreat. The Bourbons made him a peer, and from 1816 he was chancellor of the Legion of Honour. See his *Souvenirs* (2nd ed. 1892; Eng. trans. 1892).

(2) **Flora** (1722–90), Scottish heroine, born in South Uist, lost her father, a tacksman, at two; and at thirteen was adopted by Lady Clanranald, wife of the chief of the clan. When the rebellion of the '45 broke down she is said to have conducted the Pretender (June 1746), disguised as 'Betty Burke', from Benbecula to Portree. Flora was not a Jacobite; but those three short perilous days endeared her to more than Jacobites, and she was much fêted during her year's captivity on the troopship in Leith Roads and at London. In 1750 she married the son of Macdonald of Kingsburgh, where in 1773 she entertained Dr Johnson. In 1774 her husband emigrated to North Carolina, and in 1776 in the War of Independence became a brigadier-general. He was made prisoner and Flora returned to Scotland in 1779. After two years she was rejoined by her husband, and they settled again at Kingsburgh. The *Autobiography of Flora Macdonald* (1869) is a forgery; but see works by Macgregor (1882) and Jolly (1886).

(3) **George** (1824–1905), Scottish poet and novelist, born at Huntly, was educated at Aberdeen and the Congregationalist College at Highbury. He became pastor at Arundel and at Manchester, but ill-health drove him to literature. He wrote poetry and novels, but is now best known for his children's books. In 1877 he received a Civil List pension of £100. See a Life by his son (1924).

(4) **Sir George** (1862–1940), born at Elgin, educated at Ayr Academy, Edinburgh University and Balliol, Oxford, became secretary of the Scottish Education Department and a great authority on Roman Britain. See Memoir by A. O. Curle (1940).

(5) **Sir John Alexander** (1815–91), Canadian statesman, born in Glasgow, emigrated with his parents in 1820. He was called to the bar in 1836 and appointed Q.C. Entering politics he became leader of the Conservatives and premier in 1856, and in 1867 formed the first government for the new Dominion, minister of Justice and attorney-general of Canada until 1873, he was again in power from 1878 till his death at Ottawa. He was mainly instrumental in bringing about the confederation of Canada and in securing the construction of the intercolonial and Pacific railways. His widow was made a peeress. See Lives by Collins (1892), Pope (1894), Parkin (1906).

MACDONELL, Alastair Ruadh (*c.* 1724–61), Scottish Jacobite, was a captain in the French Scots brigade, lay in the Tower of London 1745–47, succeeded his father in 1754 as thirteenth chief of Glengarry, and died with the character of 'one of the best men in the Highlands'. Andrew Lang proved him to have been a spy on his fellow Jacobites. See *Pickle the Spy* (1897) and *Companions of Pickle* (1899).

McDOUGALL, William (1871–1938), Anglo-American psychologist, born in Lancashire. After studying at Weimar, Manchester and Cambridge, he trained in medicine at St Thomas's, and in 1898 accompanied an anthropological expedition to the Torres Strait. He held academic posts in both Oxford and Cambridge, served in the R.A.M.C. in World War I, and in 1920 went to Harvard as professor of Psychology. In 1927 he transferred to Duke University, North Carolina. He preached purposive psychology as opposed to behaviourism. His chief works are *Physiological Psychology* (1905), *Body and Mind* (1911), *Outlines of Psychology* (1923) and *The Energies of Man* (1933).

MacDOWELL, Edward Alexander, *mak-dow'ėl* (1861–1908), American composer and pianist, born in New York. He studied in Paris, Wiesbaden and Frankfurt, and in 1881 was appointed head teacher of pianoforte at Darmstadt conservatoire. At the invitation of Liszt, he played his First Piano Concerto in Zürich in 1882. He returned to the United States in 1888, and was head of the newly-organized department of music at Columbia University from 1896 until 1904, when he suffered a mental breakdown. He composed extensively for orchestra, voices and piano, and is best remembered for some of his small-scale piano pieces, as *Woodland Sketches* and *Sea Pieces*. See Life by his wife (1950).

McEVOY, Ambrose, *mak'-* (1878–1927), English painter, known especially for his portraits and genre paintings. His *The Earring* is in the Tate Gallery. He was elected A.R.A. in 1924.

McEWEN, Sir John Blackwood (1868–1948), Scottish composer, born at Hawick, taught music in Glasgow, and was principal of the Royal College of Music in London, 1924–36.

MACFARREN, Sir George Alexander (1813–1887), born in London, studied at the Royal Academy of Music. In 1837 he became a professor there, in 1875 principal, and professor of Music at Cambridge. He was knighted in 1883. In 1865 he became blind. Among his works are operas, cantatas, oratorios and books on musical theory and history. See Life by Banister (1891).

McGILL, James (1744–1813), born in Glasgow, emigrated to Canada, and made a fortune in the northwest fur trade and at Montreal. He bequeathed land and money to found McGill College, Montreal, which became McGill University in 1821.

McGONAGALL, William (b. 1830), Scottish doggerel poet, son of an Irish weaver, came from Dundee to Edinburgh, where he gave readings in public houses, published broadsheets of topical verse, and was lionized by the legal and student fraternity. His poems are uniformly bad, but possess a disarming naïveté and a calypso-like disregard for metre which still never fail to entertain. See *Poetic Gems* (1934) and *More Poetic Gems* (1963).

MacGREGOR, John (1825–92), British writer and traveller, born at Gravesend, graduated at Trinity College, Cambridge, travelled widely in Europe, the Middle East and Russia, but is best remembered as the pioneer and popularizer of canoeing in Britain and designer of the Rob Roy type canoe. His travel books include *A Thousand Miles in a Rob Roy Canoe* (1866), &c.

McGREGOR, Robert. See ROB ROY.

MACGREGOR, Sir William, P.C., G.C.M.G., M.D. (1847–1919), was governor of New Guinea, Lagos, Newfoundland, and (1909–1914) Queensland.

MACH, Ernst, *mah*KH (1838–1916), Austrian physicist and philosopher, born in Turas, Moravia, studied at Vienna University, and became professor of Mathematics at Graz in 1864, of Physics at Prague in 1867, and of Physics also at Vienna in 1895. He carried out much experimental work on supersonic projectiles and on the flow of gases, obtaining some remarkable early photographs of shock waves and gas jets. His findings have proved of great importance in aeronautical design and the science of projectiles, and his name has been given to the ratio of the speed of flow of a gas to the speed of sound (Mach number) and to the angle of a shock wave to the direction of motion (Mach angle). In the field of epistemology he was determined to abolish idle metaphysical speculation. His writings greatly influenced Einstein and laid the foundations of logical positivism. See his *Mechanik in ihrer Entwickelung* (1883, trans. 1902) and *Beiträge zur Analyse der Empfindung*, 'Contributions to the Analysis of Sensation' (1897).

MACHABEUS, Johannes (d. 1557), a Scottish reformer, one of the clan Macalpine, was Dominican Prior at Perth 1532–34, fled then as a heretic to England, married, went on to Germany, and from 1542 was professor of Theology at Copenhagen till his death.

MACHADO, Antonio, *ma-chah'*THō (1875–1939), Spanish writer, born at Seville, wrote lyrics characterized by a nostalgic melancholy, among them *Soledades, Galerias y otros poemas* (1907) and *Campos de Castilla* (1912). See study by Trend (1953). His brother **Manuel** (1874–1947), also a poet, collaborated with him in several plays. See study by Brotherston (1968).

MACHAR, Josef Svatopluk, *ma*KH*'ar* (1864–1942), Czech poet, author of satirical and political verse, known for the trilogy *Confiteor* (1887), the verse romance *Magdalena* (1893), the epic *Warriors of God* (1897), &c. See study by Martinek (1912).

MACHAUT, Guillaume de. See GUILLAUME DE MACHAUT.

MACHIAVELLI, Niccolo di Bernardo dei, *mak-ee-a-vel'lee* (1469–1527), Italian statesman, born at Florence, May 3, 1469, saw the troubles of the French invasion (1493), when the Medici fled, and in 1498 became secretary of the Ten, a post he held until the fall of the republic in 1512. He was employed in a great variety of missions, including one to Cesare Borgia in 1502, of which an account is preserved in fifty-two letters, one to the Emperor Maximilian, and four to France. His dispatches during these journeys, and his treatises on the 'Affairs of France and Germany', are full of a far-reaching insight. On the restoration of the Medici, Machiavelli was involved in the downfall of his patron, the Gonfaloniere Soderini. Arrested on a charge of conspiracy in 1513, and put to the torture, he disclaimed all knowledge of the alleged conspiracy; but although pardoned, he was obliged to withdraw from public life, and devoted himself to literature. It was not till 1519 that he was commissioned by Leo X to draw up his report on a reform of the state of Florence; in 1521–25 he was employed in diplomatic services and as historiographer. After the defeat of the French at Pavia (1525), Italy lay helpless before the advancing forces of the Emperor Charles V, and Machiavelli strove to avert from Flo ence the invading army on its way to Rome. In May 1527 the Florentines again drove out the Medici and proclaimed the republic; but Machiavelli, bitterly disappointed that he was to be allowed no part in the movement for liberty, and already in feeble health, died on June 22. Through misrepresentation and misunderstanding his writings were spoken of as almost diabolical, his most violent assailants being the clergy. The first great edition of his works was not issued until 1782. From that period his fame as the founder of political science has steadily increased. Besides his letters and state papers, Machiavelli's historical writings comprise *Florentine Histories*, *Discourses on the First Decade of Titus Livius*, a *Life of Castruccio Castracani* (unfinished), and *History of the Affairs of Lucca*. His literary works comprise an imitation of the *Golden Ass* of Apuleius, an essay on the Italian language, and several minor compositions. He also wrote *Seven Books on the Art of War*. But the great source of his reputation, for good or for evil, is *De Principatibus* or *Il Principe* (Rome 1532). The main theme of the book is that all means may be resorted to for the establishment and maintenance of authority and that the worst and most treacherous acts of the ruler are justified by the wickedness and treachery of the governed. *The Prince* was condemned by Pope Clement VIII. The comedies of Machiavelli form an epoch in the history of the Italian theatre; *La Mandragola*, full of biting humour and shameless indecency, is a masterpiece of art. See books by Villari (1877–82; 3rd ed. 1912; trans. 1892), Tommasini (1883–1911), Prezzolini (trans. 1928), Macaulay's essay, Ranke's study, Morley's lecture (1897), Butterfield (revised ed. 1955) and Chabod (1956).

MACÍA, Francisco, *ma-thee'a* (1859–1933), leader of the Catalan movement and first president of Catalonia.

MacINDOE, Sir Archibald (1900–60), British plastic surgeon, born in Dunedin, N.Z., was educated at Otago, the Mayo Clinic, and St Bartholomew's Hospital. The most eminent pupil of Sir Harold Gillies (q.v.), he won fame during World War II as surgeon-in-charge at the Queen Victoria Hospital, East Grinstead, where the faces and limbs of injured airmen were remodelled with unsurpassed skill. He was knighted in 1947, and was vice-president of the Royal College of Surgeons (1957–59). See Lives by McLeave (1961) and Mosley (1962).

MACINTOSH, Charles (1766–1843), a Glasgow manufacturing chemist, patented (1823) and gave name to Syme's (q.v.) method of waterproofing.

McINTYRE, Duncan Ban (1724–1812), the Gaelic poet-gamekeeper of Beinndòrain, was born in Glenorchy, fought as a Hanoverian at Falkirk in 1746, and in 1799–1806 was one of the City Guard of Edinburgh. See his *Poems* ed. and trans. by A. Macleod (1952).

MACK, Karl, Freiherr von (1752–1828), Austrian general, born at Nennslingen in Franconia, in 1770 entered the Austrian service, and, after fighting the Turks and the French republicans, was in 1797 created field-marshal. For the king of Naples he occupied Rome, but had to conclude an armistice with the French, and was driven to seek safety with them by riots in Naples. He was carried prisoner to Paris, but escaped in 1800. Having surrendered with his army to the French at Ulm in 1805, he was tried by court martial and condemned to death, but the sentence was commuted to twenty years' imprisonment. In 1808 he was liberated, in 1819 fully pardoned.

MACKAIL, John William (1859–1945), Scottish classical scholar, born at Kingarth, Bute, after a brilliant career at Oxford was elected a fellow of Balliol in 1882, left university life for the civil service and became assistant secretary to the Board of Education, but resigned in 1919 to give his full time to scholarship and criticism. His reputation rests on his studies on Virgil, on his *Latin Literature* (1895), his lectures on classical subjects and on the English poets, and his biographies of William Morris (1899) and George Wyndham (1925). He was elected professor of Poetry at Oxford in 1906 and was awarded the O.M. in 1935. He married the daughter of the artist Burne-Jones (q.v.), and his son **Denis** (1892–1971) and his daughter **Angela Thirkell** (1890–1961) are both well-known as novelists.

MACKAY, *mė-kī',* (1) **Alexander Murdoch** (1849–90), pioneer missionary to Uganda 1878–87, was born at Rhynie in Aberdeenshire, trained as an engineer, but during a residence at Berlin in 1873 was led by the court preacher Baur to turn to missionary work. See Lives by his sister (1891) and A. R. Evans (1956).

(2) **Charles** (1814–89), Scottish songwriter, born at Perth, was editor of the *Glasgow Argus* 1844–47, of the *Illustrated London News* 1848–59 and New York correspondent of the *Times* during the civil war (1862–65). Two of his songs, 'There's a Good Time Coming' and 'Cheer, Boys, Cheer', had an extraordinary vogue. His prose works included *Popular Delusions* (1841), *Forty Years' Recollections* (1877), &c. His daughter was Marie Corelli (q.v.) and his son **Eric** (1851–98) achieved a reputation as a poet.

(3) **Robert** (1714–78), the Reay country Gaelic poet 'Rob Donn' ('brown'), was a Sutherland herd. See Life with his *Poems* (1898).

MACKENSEN, August von (1849–1945),

German field-marshal, born at Leipnitz, swept the Russians from Galicia 1915, the Rumanians from Dobrudja 1916. See Life by M. Luyken (1920).

MACKENZIE, (1) Sir Alexander (*c.* 1755–1820), Canadian fur-trader, born at Stornoway, in 1789 discovered the Mackenzie River, and in 1792–93 crossed the Rockies to the Pacific. See Life by Wade (1927).

(2) **Alexander** (1822–92), Canadian statesman, born at Logierait, Perthshire, removed to Canada in 1842, and was a mason and contractor. In 1852 he became editor of a Reform paper, from 1867 led the opposition in the Dominion parliament, and in 1873–78 was premier. He thrice declined knighthood, and died at Toronto.

(3) **Sir Alexander Campbell** (1847–1935), Scottish composer, born in Edinburgh, studied music at Sondershausen, and from 1862 at the Royal Academy, London. In 1865–79 he was teacher, violinist and conductor in Edinburgh, and in 1887–1924 was principal of the Royal Academy of Music. *The Rose of Sharon* (1884), an oratorio, contains some of his best work. He wrote operas; cantatas; Scottish rhapsodies; a concerto and a *pibroch* for violin; chamber music, songs, &c. See his *A Musician's Narrative* (1927).

(4) **Sir (Edward Montague) Compton** (1883–1972), British writer, born in West Hartlepool. His first novel, *The Passionate Elopement*, was published in 1911. There followed, *Carnival* (1912), *Sinister Street* (two volumes, 1913–14), *Guy and Pauline* (1915). In 1917 he became director of the Aegean Intelligence Service in Syria. Thereafter, from his considerable output, may be mentioned: *Sylvia Scarlett* (1918), *Poor Relations* (1919), *Rich Relatives* (1921), *Vestal Fire* (1927), *The Four Winds of Love* (4 volumes, 1937–45), *Aegean Memories* (1940), *Whisky Galore* (1947), *Eastern Epic*, vol. I (1951), and *Rockets Galore* (1957). He was awarded the O.B.E. in 1919, knighted in 1952 and was made a C.Lit. in 1968. See his monumental autobiography *My Life and Times* (1963–71) in ten *Octaves*, and book by Urquhart (1956).

(5) **Sir George** (1636–91), Scottish lawyer, born at Dundee, studied at St Andrews, Aberdeen and Bourges; in 1656 was called to the bar at Edinburgh; and in 1661 defended the Marquis of Argyll. He was knighted, entered parliament for Ross-shire in 1669, and in 1677 was named king's advocate. His career up to this point had been patriotic; unhappily in the popular mind he lives as 'Bluidy Mackenzie', the criminal prosecutor in the days of the persecution. He cultivated literature, was one of the first Scots to write English with purity, and in 1682 founded the Advocates Library at Edinburgh. He retired at the Revolution to Oxford, and dying in London, May 8, 1691, was buried at Edinburgh in Greyfriars Churchyard. His works were collected by Ruddiman (1716–22). See his *Memoirs of the Affairs of Scotland*, edited by T. Thomson (1821); and Andrew Lang's *Sir George Mackenzie* (1909).

(6) **Henry** (1745–1831), Scottish author, the 'Man of Feeling', born in Edinburgh, became crown attorney in the Scottish Court of Exchequer, and in 1804 comptroller of taxes. For upwards of half a century he was 'one of the most illustrious names connected with polite literature in Edinburgh', where he died. His *Man of Feeling* was published in 1771 (ed. H. Miles 1928); *The Man of the World* followed in 1773, and *Julia de Roubigné* in 1777. He deserves remembrance for his recognition of Burns, and as an early admirer of Lessing and of Schiller. See *A Scottish Man of Feeling* (1931) by H. W. Thompson, who edited his *Anecdotes and Egotisms* (1928).

(7) **Sir James** (1853–1925), British physician, elected F.R.S. (1915), an authority on the heart, invented the polygraph to record graphically the heart's action. See his *Diseases of the Heart* (1908). See Life by R. M. Wilson (1945).

(8) **Sir Morell** (1837–92), British throat specialist, born at Leytonstone, was knighted in 1887 after attending the German Crown Prince (later Frederick III), whose throat condition proved ultimately to be malignant and fatal, contrary to Mackenzie's diagnosis. Mackenzie's apologia provoked much resentment in German medical circles and earned him the censure of the Royal College of Surgeons. See Life by Haweis (1893).

(9) **William Forbie** (1801–62), Scottish politician, born at Portmore, Peeblesshire, M.P. for Peeblesshire 1837–52, introduced a liquor Act for Scotland, passed in 1853, providing for Sunday closing and other controls.

(10) **William Lyon** (1795–1861), Canadian politician, born in Dundee, emigrated to Canada in 1820, and in 1824 established the *Colonial Advocate*. In 1828 he was elected to the provincial parliament for York, but was expelled in 1830 for libel on the Assembly. In 1837 he published in his paper a declaration of independence, headed a band of insurgents, and after a skirmish with a superior force, for a time maintained a camp on an island. Having fled to New York, he was sentenced by the U.S. authorities to twelve months' imprisonment. He returned to Canada in 1849, was a member of parliament 1850–58, and died at Toronto. He was the grandfather of W. L. Mackenzie King (q.v.). See Life by his son-in-law Charles Lindsey (1862), also M. Bellasis, *Rise, Canadians* (1955).

MACKENZIE KING. See KING (3).

McKINLEY, William (1843–1901), twenty-fourth president of the United States, was born January 29, 1843, at Niles in Ohio, and served in the Civil War, retiring in 1867 as major to Canton, where he practised law. He was elected to congress in 1877, and repeatedly re-elected. In 1891 he was made governor of Ohio, his name being identified with the high protective tariff carried in the McKinley Bill of 1890, though subsequently modified by the Democrats in 1894. Chosen Republican candidate for the presidency in 1896 and 1900, he conducted exciting contests with W. J. Bryan, who advocated the cause of free silver, denounced trusts, high tariffs, and imperialism, and was understood to favour labour at the expense of capital. Some Democrats, 'Gold Democrats' or 'Sound Money

Democrats', in spite of their dislike of McKinley's policy on many points, supported him. In November 1900, as in 1896, he secured a large majority in the electoral college, as the representative of a gold standard and of capital. In his first term the war with Spain (1898) took place, with the conquest of Cuba and the Philippines. He was shot by an anarchist September 6, and died September 14, 1901. See studies by M. Leech (1959) and H. Wayne Morgan (1963).

MACKINTOSH (1) Charles Rennie (1868–1928), Scottish architect, was born in Glasgow. He exercised considerable influence on European design, his chief work being Glasgow School of Art. See Pevsner's *Pioneers of the Modern Movement* (1936), and study by Howarth (1952).

(2) **Elizabeth** (? –1952), British novelist and playwright, born in Inverness. Under the pseudonym of **Gordon Daviot** she wrote her best known novel, *Kif* (1929), and her more serious works, including the historical drama, *Richard of Bordeaux* (1932)—the work for which she is most remembered—and a biography of Claverhouse (1937). *The Daughter of Time* (1951), a detective story, was one of several which she wrote as **Josephine Tey**.

(3) **Sir James** (1765–1832), Scottish writer, born at Aldourie in Inverness-shire, studied medicine but settled in London as a journalist. His *Vindiciae Gallicae* (1791) was written in reply to Burke's *Reflections on the French Revolution*; and he became secretary of the 'Friends of the People'. He was called to the bar in 1795. In 1799 he delivered a brilliant series of lectures on the law of nature and of nations at Lincoln's Inn; and his defence of Peltier (1803), charged with a libel on Bonaparte, was a splendid triumph. In 1804 he was knighted, and appointed recorder of Bombay, and in 1806 judge of its Admiralty Court; he spent seven years at Bombay, entering parliament after his return as Whig member for Nairn (1813). He wrote on history and philosophy. See the *Memoirs* by his son (1835), and the essays of Macaulay and De Quincey.

(4) **William** (1662–1743), Scottish Jacobite, of Borlum, Inverness-shire, was 'out' in 1715 and 1719, and the first time escaped from Newgate, but died after long captivity in Edinburgh Castle. He was an early arboriculturist.

MACKLIN, Charles (*c.* 1697–1797), actor, born in the North of Ireland, the son of William McLaughlin, after a wild, unsettled youth, played in Bristol and Bath, and in 1733 was engaged at Drury Lane. He steadily rose in public favour, till in 1741 he appeared in his great character, Shylock. From this time he was accounted one of the best actors whether in tragedy or comedy. His last performance was at Covent Garden in 1789; but he survived, with an annuity of £200, till July 11, 1797. He was generous, high-spirited, but irascible: in 1735 he killed a brother-actor in a quarrel over a wig, and was tried for murder. He wrote a tragedy and several farces and comedies; of these *Love à la Mode* (1759) and *The Man of the World* (1781) were printed. See *Lives* by Congreve (1798) and Parry (1891).

MACLAREN, (1) Charles (1782–1866), Scottish writer and editor, born at Ormiston, East Lothian, was the first editor of *The Scotsman*, editor of *The Encyclopaedia Britannica* (6th edition), and wrote *Geology of Fife and the Lothians* (1839).

(2) **Ian**, pen name of **John Watson** (1850–1907), a Liverpool Presbyterian minister, born of Scottish parentage at Manningtree in Essex, whose amazing success with his *Beside the Bonnie Brier Bush* (1894), &c., gave rise to the name 'Kailyard School'.

MACLAURIN, Colin (1698–1746), Scottish mathematician, born at Kilmodan, Argyll, graduated at Glasgow in 1713, and in 1717 became professor of Mathematics at Aberdeen, in 1725 at Edinburgh. In 1719 he was made F.R.S. and published *Geometrica Organica*. His *Treatise on Fluxions* (1742) was of great importance.

MACLEAN, Sir Fitzroy Hew (1911–), British diplomat and soldier, educated at Eton and Cambridge, served with the Foreign Office from 1933, and in World War II distinguished himself as commander of the British military mission to the Jugoslav partisans (1943–45). M.P. for Lancaster from 1941, and for Bute and N. Ayrshire from 1959, he was under-secretary for war from 1954 to 1957. His *Eastern Approaches* (1949), *Disputed Barricade* (1957), *A Person from England* (1958), and *Back from Bokhara* (1959) have gained for him a considerable reputation. He was created a baronet in 1957.

MACLEHOSE, Agnes, *née* **Craig** (1759–1841), Scottish surgeon's daughter, married in 1776 a Glasgow lawyer, from whom she separated in 1780, and who went to Jamaica in 1784. She met Burns at a party in 1787, and subsequently carried on with him the well-known correspondence under the name 'Clarinda'. A number of Burns's poems and songs were dedicated to her.

MacLEISH, Archibald (1892–), American poet, born at Glencoe, Ill., started out as a lawyer, was librarian of Congress 1939–44, and professor of Rhetoric at Harvard 1949–62. His first volume of poetry *Tower of Ivory* appeared in 1917, and he won Pulitzer prizes for *Conquistador* (1932), a long poem on Cortez, for *Collected Poems 1917-52* (1953), and for one of his several social dramas in modern verse, *J.B.* (1959), based on the story of Job, affirming modern man's nobler qualities.

McLENNAN, John Cunningham (1867–1935), Canadian physicist, professor at Toronto (1907–31), did much research on electricity and the superconductivity of metals. In 1932 he succeeded in liquefying helium.

MacLEOD, George Fielden, *-lowd'* (1895–), Scottish presbyterian divine, second son of Sir John MacLeod, 1st Bart, a Glasgow M.P., was educated at Winchester and Oriel College, Oxford, won the M.C. and Croix de Guerre in World War I, and subsequently studied theology at Edinburgh, becoming a minister of St Cuthbert's there (1926–30) and at Govan (1930–38). He founded the Iona Community, which set about restoring the ruined abbey on that historic island. The original dozen ministers and helpers soon grew in number and, working there every summer, renovated most of the monastic buildings. As moderator of the General Assembly (1957–58) he created controversy by supporting the unpopular scheme to introduce bishops into the kirk in the interests of church unity. Well known as a writer and broadcaster, he is strongly left-wing, as his *Only One Way Left* (1956) testifies. He succeeded to the baronetcy in 1924, but prefers not to use the title. In 1967 he was created a life peer, as Baron MacLeod of Fuinary.

MACLEOD, (1) Fiona. See SHARP (6).

(2) **John James Rickard** (1876–1935), Scottish physiologist, educated at Aberdeen, Leipzig and Cambridge, professor of Physiology at Cleveland, Ohio (1903), Toronto (1918) and Aberdeen (1928), in 1922 along with Banting and Best discovered insulin. He was elected F.R.S. in 1923, in which year also he shared the Nobel prize with Banting.

(3) **Norman** (1812–72), Scottish divine, was born, a minister's son, at Campbeltown, Argyll. He attended Glasgow University, and was minister of Loudon 1838–43, Dalkeith 1843–45 and the Barony Church, Glasgow, from 1851 till his death. He was made a Queen's Chaplain in 1857, and in 1869 was moderator of the General Assembly. From 1860 till 1872 he edited and contributed to *Good Words*, and wrote several books. See *Memoir* by Macleod (1876).

MACLISE, Daniel (1806–70), British painter, son of a Highland soldier named McLeish, born at Cork, entered the school of the Royal Academy, London, in 1828. His frescoes in the Royal Gallery of the House of Lords, *The Meeting of Wellington and Blücher* (1861) and *The Death of Nelson* (1864) are his most notable works. His sketches of contemporaries in *Fraser's Magazine* (1830–38) were republished in 1874 and 1883. See the Memoir by O'Driscoll (1871).

MACMAHON, Marie Edmé Patrice Maurice de, *mèk-mahn'* (1808–93), descended from an Irish Jacobite family, was born at Sully near Autun. Entering the army, he served in Algeria, and distinguished himself at Constantine (1837), commanded at the Malakoff (1855), was again conspicuous in Algeria (1857–58), and for his services in the Italian campaign (1859) was made marshal and Duke of Magenta. He became governor-general of Algeria in 1864. In the Franco-German war (1870–71) he commanded the first army corps, but was defeated at Wörth, and captured at Sedan. After the war, as commander of the army of Versailles, he suppressed the Commune. In 1873 he was elected president of the Republic for seven years, and was suspected, not unjustly, of reactionary and monarchical leanings. He resigned in 1879. See Lives by Grandin (1893) and Montbrillant (1894).

MacMASTER, John Bach (1852–1932), American historian, born at Brooklyn, studied civil engineering, but in 1883–1920 was professor of American History in Pennsylvania University. He wrote a *History of the People of the U.S.* (8 vols. 1883–1913), *Franklin as a Man of Letters* (1887), and other works.

MACMILLAN, (1) Alexander (1818–96). See (2).

(2) **Daniel** (1813–57), Scottish bookseller and publisher, was born at Upper Corrie, Arran. Apprenticed to booksellers in Scotland and Cambridge, in 1843 he and his brother Alexander opened a bookshop in London, and in the same year moved to Cambridge. By 1844 he had branched out into publishing, first educational and religious works and by 1855 English classics such as Kingsley's *Westward Ho!* and *Tom Brown's Schooldays* in 1857. In the year after his death (1858) the firm opened a branch in London and by 1893 had become a limited liability company with Daniel's son, **Frederick** (1851–1936), as chairman. His other son, **Maurice**, father of (3) was also a partner. See a memoir by Hughes (1882), a life of Alexander by C. L. Graves (1910) and Morgan, *House of Macmillan* (1943).

(3) **Maurice Harold** (1894–), British statesman, educated at Eton, took a first class in classical Moderations at Balliol College, Oxford, his studies having been interrupted by service with the Grenadier Guards during World War I, in which he was seriously wounded. In 1919–20 he was in Canada as A.D.C. to the governor-general, the Duke of Devonshire, whose daughter **Lady Dorothy** (d. 1966) he married. Returning to Britain, he partnered his brother Daniel in the family publishing firm, but preserved his interest in politics and stood successfully as Conservative M.P. for Stockton-on-Tees in 1924, was defeated in 1929, but was re-elected in 1931. Partly because he was not always willing to conform with the party line, and partly, no doubt, because his air of intellectual superiority irked his more senior colleagues, he remained a backbencher until 1940, when Churchill made him parliamentary secretary to the Ministry of Supply. After a brief spell as colonial under-secretary in 1942 he was sent to North Africa to fill the new Cabinet post of minister resident at Allied Headquarters where he achieved distinction by his foresight and acumen and by his ability as a mediator in the many clashes of factions and personalities which bedevilled his term of office. Defeated in the Socialist landslide of 1945, he was returned later the same year for Bromley, which he held until his retiral in 1964. He was minister of housing (1951–54), silencing general doubts by achieving his promised target of 300,000 houses in a year. He was minister of defence from autumn to spring 1954–55, and thereafter foreign minister to the end of 1955, when he was appointed chancellor of the Exchequer. On Eden's resignation in 1957 he emerged, in Butler's words, as 'the best prime minister we have', his appointment being received without enthusiasm, for as an intellectual and a dyed-in-the-wool aristocrat he was regarded with suspicion by many. Nevertheless, his economic expansionism at home, his resolution in foreign affairs, his integrity, and his infectious optimism inspired unforeseen confidence, and his popularity soared. Having piloted the Conservatives to victory in the General Election, he embarked upon a

new term as prime minister in 1959. His 'wind of change' speech at Cape Town (1960) acknowledged the inevitability of African independence. In 1962, after some electoral setbacks, he carried out a drastic 'purge' of his government, involving seven cabinet ministers. Further setbacks followed, however, with the Vassall spy case (1962) and the Profumo scandal (1963), and a prostate gland operation brought about his reluctant resignation on October 10, 1963. See his autobiographical *Winds of Change, 1914–39* (1966) and *The Blast of War, 1939–1945* (1967) and study by A. Sampson (1967).

(4) **John** (1670–1753), founder of the Reformed Presbyterians, was born in Minnigaff, Kirkcudbrightshire, and died at Bothwell.

MacMILLAN, Donald Baxter (1874–1970), American Arctic explorer, carried out anthropological research among the Eskimos of Labrador, and important exploration in Greenland (1913–17). He also led expeditions to Baffin Land (1921–22), North Greenland (1923–24), the Pole (1925), &c. See his *Four Years in the White North* (1926) and *Etah and Beyond* (1927).

McMILLAN, (1) Edwin Mattison (1907–), American physical chemist, born in California, professor of Physics at the University of California from 1946, was awarded (with Seaborg) the 1951 Nobel prize for chemistry for his part in the discovery of the transuranic elements.

(2) **Margaret** (1860–1931), British educational reformer, born in New York and brought up near Inverness. She agitated ceaselessly in the industrial north for medical inspection and school clinics, and in 1902 she joined her sister **Rachel** (1859–1917) in London, where they opened the first school clinic in 1908, and the first open-air nursery school in 1914. After Rachel's death, the Rachel McMillan Training College for nursery and infant teachers was established as a memorial. Margaret received the C.B.E. in 1917 and became a C.H. in 1930. See studies by D'Arcy Cresswell (1948), Stevinson (1954), and Life by Lowndes (1960).

McNAUGHTON, Daniel, *mėk-naw'tėn*, was tried in 1843 for the murder of Edward Drummond, private secretary to Sir Robert Peel. The question arose whether he knew the nature of his act. The House of Lords took the opinion of the judges, and the law of England as to the criminal responsibility of the insane is now embodied in the judges' 'answers', known as the McNaughton Rules: (*a*) Every man is presumed sane until the contrary is proved. (*b*) It must be clearly proved that at the time of committing the act, the accused was labouring under such a defect of reason as not to know the nature of the act, or that he was doing wrong.

MACNEE, Sir Daniel (1806–82), Scottish portrait painter, born at Fintry, Stirlingshire, became P.R.S.A. in 1876, knighted in 1877.

MacNEICE, Louis (1907–63), British writer, born in Belfast. Primarily a poet, he was the author of several memorable verse plays for radio, as well as translations of Aeschylus and of Goethe's *Faust*. He also produced several volumes of literary criticism. His *Collected Poems* were published in 1949.

MACPHERSON, James (1736–96), 'translator' of the Ossianic poems, was born at Ruthven in Inverness-shire, where he became a schoolmaster. He published a poem, the *Highlander* (1758), and at Moffat in 1759 showed 'Jupiter' Carlyle and John Home some fragments of Gaelic verse, with 'translations', published in 1760. The Faculty of Advocates now sent Macpherson on a tour through the Highlands to collect more; but his unsatisfactory statements about his originals excited grave suspicions. The result of his labours was the appearance at London in 1762, of *Fingal, an Epic Poem, in Six Books*, and, in 1763, *Temora, an Epic Poem, in Eight Books*. A storm of controversy soon arose in regard to their genuineness. The general verdict is that though Macpherson probably based some of the work on truly Gaelic originals, the poems of Ossian as he published them are largely his own invention. Macpherson was appointed in 1764 surveyor-general of the Floridas, in 1779 agent to the Nabob of Arcot, and sat in parliament for Camelford from 1780. He was buried at his own cost in Westminster Abbey. He wrote a poor prose translation of the *Iliad*, &c. See Lives by Smart (1905), and Thomson, *The Gaelic Sources of Macpherson's 'Ossian'* (1952).

MACQUARIE, Lachlan, *mė-kwor'ee* (1761–1824), Scottish soldier and colonial administrator, born on the isle of Ulva, off Mull, joined the Black Watch, and after service in North America, India and Egypt, was appointed governor of New South Wales following the deposition of Bligh (q.v.). The colony, depressed and demoralized, populated largely by convicts, and exploited by influential land-grabbers and monopolists, was raised by his energetic administration and firm rule to a state of prosperity; its population trebled, extensive surveys were carried out, and many miles of road were built. In 1821 political chicanery by the monopolists and his own ill health compelled him to return to Britain. Known as the 'Father of Australia' he has given name to the Lachlan and Macquarie rivers, and to Macquarie Island. See Life by M. H. Ellis (1947).

MACQUER, Pierre Joseph, *ma-kayr* (1718–1784), French chemist, one of the first to study platinum, discovered the arsenates of potassium and sodium. He was the compiler of a chemical dictionary (1766).

MACREADY, William Charles (1793–1873), English actor, son of W. McCready, actor and provincial manager, was born in London, March 3, 1793, and sent to Rugby. He was intended for the bar, but his father failing, he made his début at Birmingham in 1810; in 1816 he appeared at Covent Garden; but not till 1837 did he take his position as leading English actor. In 1837 he inaugurated his famous Covent Garden management, during which he produced Shakespeare worthily. After two seasons he took Drury Lane (1841–1843), then played in the provinces, Paris and America. His last visit to the U.S. was marked by terrible riots (May 10, 1849) arising out of the ill-feeling borne by the American actor Forrest to Macready. In 1851 Macready took his farewell of the stage at Drury Lane. See his *Reminiscences and Diaries* (1875), *Diaries* (ed. by W. Toynbee, 1912), memoirs by Pollock (2nd ed. 1885), Archer (1890), Price (1895) and Life by Trewin (1955).

MACROBIUS, Ambrosius Theodosius, a 5th-century neo-Platonist who wrote a commentary on Cicero's *Somnium Scipionis*, and *Saturnaliorum Conviviorum Libri Septem*, a series of historical, mythological and critical dialogues. See study by Whittaker (1923).

McTAGGART, John McTaggart Ellis (1866–1925), British philosopher, born in London, was educated at Clifton College and, under Sidgwick and Ward, at Trinity College, Cambridge, where he lectured (1897–1923). His brilliant commentaries and studies on Hegel's dialectic (1896), cosmology (1901) and logic (1910) in which he clarified and consolidated Hegel's system, although rejecting many of the latter's arguments and in particular Hegelian ethics and political philosophy, were preliminaries to his own constructive system-building in *Nature of Existence* (vol. I, 1921; vols II and III, posthumously, 1927). In this he argued for Hegelian conclusions but from novel starting-points which owed more to Leibniz than to Hegel. His arguments for the unreality of time bewitched Russell and drove Moore to philosophizing in protest. An atheist yet a member of the Church of England, he set out his arguments for human immortality in *Some Dogmas of Religion* (1906). He was elected F.B.A. in 1906. See memoir by C. D. Broad in 2nd edition of the above (1930), Life by G. Lowes Dickinson (1931) and an exhaustive *Examination* by C. D. Broad (1933–38). A summary of his system appeared, *Contemporary British Philosophy*, vol. I, ed. J. H. Muirhead (1924).

MacTAGGART, William (1835–1910), Scottish artist, born in Kintyre, studied painting with Macnee and Scott Lauder, and lived in and near Edinburgh, painting genre and landscape with imaginative insight. See Life by Caw (1917). His grandson **Sir William** (1903–), also a painter, is a prominent representative of the modern Scottish school. He was elected R.S.A. in 1948, P.R.S.A. in 1959, was knighted in 1962 and received the *Légion d'honneur* in 1968.

MacWHIRTER, John (1839–1911), Scottish artist, born at Edinburgh, was apprenticed to a bookseller, but turned to painting, specializing in Highland scenery. He was elected R.S.A. in 1867 and R.A. in 1893. See Life by Spielmann.

MADARIAGA, Salvador de, *ma-*THA*-ryah'ga* (1886–), Spanish writer, was born at Coruña, was educated at the Instituto del Cardenal Cisneros, Madrid, and at the École Polytechnique, Paris. He was a London journalist from 1916 to 1921 and director of the disarmament section of the League of Nations Secretariat from 1922 to 1927. From 1928 to 1931 he was professor of Spanish Studies at Oxford and was Spanish ambassador to the U.S.A. in 1931 and to France from 1932 to 1934. A Liberal opponent of the Franco régime, he has lived in exile since. Publications include: *The Genius of Spain* (1923), *Theory and Practice of International Relations* (1938), *Portrait of Europe* (1952) and *Democracy v. Liberty?* (1958), *Latin America between the Eagle and the Bear* (1962).

MADDEN, Sir Frederick (1801–73), English antiquary, born at Portsmouth, and knighted in 1832, was keeper of MSS. in the British Museum (1837–66). He wrote in *Archaeologia*, and edited *Havelok the Dane* (1833), *William and the Werwolf* (1832), the early English versions of the *Gesta Romanorum* (1838), *The Wycliffite Versions of the Bible* (1850), Layamon's *Brut* (1847), and Matthew Paris (1858).

MADERO, Francisco Indalecio, *ma-*THAY*'rō* (1873–1913), Mexican politician, born at San Pedro, Coahuila State, and educated at the university of California. After some years' exile in France, he entered Radical politics in Mexico in 1903 and in 1910 became leader in the successful revolutionary war against the government of Díaz. He was elected president in 1911 and assassinated in 1913. See studies by S. R. Ross (1955) and J. C. Valadés (1959).

MADISON, James (1751–1836), fourth president of the United States, born at Port Conway, Va., March 16, 1751, in 1776 was a member of the Virginia Convention, in 1780 of the Continental Congress, and in 1784 of the legislature of Virginia. In the Convention of 1787, which framed the Federal constitution, he acted with Jay and Hamilton, and with them wrote the *Federalist*. He was the chief author of the ' Virginia plan ', and suggested the compromise by which, for taxation, representation, &c., slaves were regarded as population and not chattels, five being reckoned as three persons, and which secured the adoption of the constitution by South Carolina and the other slave-holding states. Madison was elected to the first national congress, now showed himself anxious to limit the powers of the central government, and became a leader of the Jeffersonian Republican party. In 1801, Jefferson having been elected president, Madison was made secretary of state. In 1809 he was elected president. The European wars of that period, with their blockades, &c., were destructive of American commerce, and brought on a war with Britain (1812). In 1817, at the close of his second term, Madison retired. He died at Montpelier, Va., June 28, 1836. See Lives (1902) by G. Hunt, who edited his *Writings* (9 vols. 1900–10), and I. Brant (5 vols. 1941–56).

MÄDLER, Johann Heinrich von, *may'dler* (1794–1874), astronomer, born at Berlin, became director of Tartu Observatory, produced a map of the moon and carried out research on double stars. He died at Hanover.

MADOC, a Welsh prince, long believed by his countrymen to have discovered America in 1170. The story is in Lloyd and Powell's *Cambria* (1584), and in Southey's poem; the essay by Thomas Stephens written in 1858 for the Eisteddfod, and published in 1893, proves it to be baseless.

MADVIG, Johan Nicolai (1804–86), Danish classical scholar, in 1829 became professor of Latin at Copenhagen, in 1848 inspector of higher schools. He was one of the chief speakers of the national Liberal party, was minister of religion and education (1848–51), and was repeatedly president of the Danish parliament. Among his works were *Opuscula Academica* (1834–42), the great *Latin Grammar* (1841), *Greek Syntax* (1846) and an *Autobiography* (1887).

MAECENAS, Gaius Cilnius (d. 8 B.C.), Roman statesman and trusted counsellor of Augustus, whose name has become a synonym for a patron of letters. See J. W. Duff, *Minor Latin Poets* (1934).

MAELZEL, Johann Nepomuk (1770–1838), German patentee of the metronome. See BEETHOVEN.

MAERLANT, Jacob van (*c.* 1235–*c.* 1300), Flemish didactic poet, author of verse translations of French and Latin originals, including the *Roman de Troie* (*c.* 1264) and de Beauvais' *Speculum Majas* (1284).

MAETERLINCK, Count Maurice, *may'tėr-lingk* (1862–1949), Belgian dramatist, born at Ghent. He studied law at Ghent University, but became a disciple of the Symbolist movement, and in 1889 produced his first volume of poetry, *Les Serres chaudes.* In the same year came his prose play, *La Princesse Maleine,* and in 1892 *Pelléas et Mélisande,* on which Debussy based his opera; other plays include *Joyzelle* (1903) and *Mary Magdalene* (1910). *La Vie des abeilles* (1901) is one of his many popular expositions of scientific subjects, and he also wrote several philosophical works. He was awarded the Nobel prize for literature in 1911, made a count of Belgium in 1932, and a member of the French Academy of Moral and Political Sciences in 1937. See Lives by A. Bailey (1931) and W. Halls (1960).

MAFFEI, Francesco Scipione, Marchese di, *maf-fay'ee* (1675–1755), Italian dramatist, born at Verona, served 1703–04 under his brother Alessandro, a field-marshal. His tragedy *Merope* (1714) ran through seventy editions; the comedy *Le Ceremonie* (1728) was also successful; and *Verona illustrata* (1731–32) was an important work. See Life by N. Ivanoff (Padova 1942).

MAGELLAN, Port. **Magalhães, Ferdinand** (*c.* 1480–1521), Portuguese navigator, born near Villa Real in Tras os Montes, served in the East Indies, and was lamed for life in action in Morocco. Offering his services to Spain, he laid before Charles V a scheme for reaching the Moluccas by the west, and sailed from Seville, August 10, 1519, with five ships of from 130 to 60 tons. Having coasted Patagonia, he threaded the strait which bears his name (October 21–November 28, 1520), and reached the ocean which he named the Pacific. He fell in an expedition in the Philippine Isles; but his ship, brought safely to Spain, September 6, 1522, completed the first circumnavigation of the world. See books by E. F. Benson (1929), S. Zweig (1938), and J. A. Robertson's translation (1906) of Pigafetta's contemporary account.

MAGENDIE, François, *ma-zhã-dee* (1783–1855), French physiologist and physician, was born at Bordeaux, became prosector in Anatomy (1804), physician to the Hôtel-Dieu in Paris, and professor of Anatomy in the Collège de France (1831). He made important additions to our knowledge of nerve physiology, the veins and the physiology of food, and wrote numerous works, including the *Elements of Physiology.* In his *Journal de la physiologie expérimentale* are recorded the experiments on living animals which gained for him the character of an unscrupulous vivisector.

MAGINN, William (1794–1842), Irish writer, born at Cork, and educated at Trinity College, Dublin; took his LL.D. at an early age, taught in Cork for ten years, and in 1823 removed to London. He was a prolific contributor to *Blackwood's Magazine,* the *Standard* and *Fraser's Magazine.* A collection of his tales was edited by Partridge (1933). See study by M. Thrale (N.Y. 1934).

MAGINOT, André, *ma-zhee-nō* (1877–1932), French politician, born in Paris, was first elected to the Chamber in 1910. As minister of war (1922–24; 1926–31) he pursued a policy of military preparedness and began the system of frontier fortifications which was named the 'Maginot Line' after him. See Life by P. Belpenon (Paris 1940).

MAGLIABECHI, Antonio, *mal-ya-bek'ee* (1633–1714), Italian bibliophile, born at Florence, was till his fortieth year a goldsmith, but gradually entombed himself among books. His learning and his memory were prodigious and precise. In 1673 he was appointed court-librarian by the Grand-duke of Tuscany; his vanity and intolerance involved him in bitter literary squabbles. His library of 30,000 vols. he bequeathed to the Grand-duke; it is now a free library, and bears its collector's name. See Hill Burton's *Book-Hunter* (1862).

MAGNUS, St, (1) a Scandinavian Earl of Orkney, assassinated 1114 in Egilsay by his cousin Hakon. See study by J. Mooney.

(2) A monk of St Gall, traditionally brought the gospel to the Allgäu, and founded the monastery of Füssen, where he died *c.* 750.

MAGNUS. The name of seven kings of Norway.

Magnus I, called **The Good** (reigned 1024–47), made a succession treaty (1038) with Hardicanute of Denmark, of which country he became ruler on the latter's death in 1042. He also inherited Hardicanute's title to the English throne but could not enforce it owing to internal strife.

Magnus V, called **Lageböter,** 'improver of the laws' (1238–80), ascended the throne in 1263, gave up the Western Isles and the Isle of Man to Scotland, and evolved a new legal code, introducing the principle that crime was an offence against the state rather than against the individual.

MAGNUS, or **Magni, Olaus** (1490–1558), Swedish historian, became secretary to his brother Johannes, Archbishop of Uppsala. After the Reformation they settled in Rome. On Johannes' death Olaus became titular archbishop. Both wrote on Swedish history; Olaus' famous work is his *Historia de Gentibus Septentrionalibus* (1555).

MAHAN, Alfred Thayer, *ma-han'* (1840–1914), American naval historian, born at West Point, N.Y., served in the U.S. navy (1854–1896), and in 1906 was given the rank of rear-admiral retired. He wrote *Influence of Sea Power upon History, 1660–1812* (3 vols. 1890–92), Lives of Farragut, Nelson, &c. See life by W. D. Puleston (1939) and bibliography (N.Y. 1925).

MAHDI. See MOHAMMED ALI.

MAHLER, Gustav (1860–1911), Czech-Austrian composer, born in Kalist. In 1875 he went to Vienna Conservatory, where he studied composition and conducting. Unsuccessful in an opera composition with the work which he later turned into the cantata *Das klagende Lied*, he turned to conducting, rapidly reaching important positions at Prague, Leipzig, Budapest and Hamburg, and in 1897 he became conductor and artistic director at Vienna State Opera House, where he established the high standards for which that theatre has since become famous. Disliking the intrigues of theatrical life and the frequent personal attacks upon him due to his Jewish birth (though he had become a convert to Roman Catholicism), he resigned after ten years to devote himself to composition and the concert platform, and from 1908 to 1911 he was conductor of the New York Philharmonic Society, spending his summers composing in Austria. His mature works consist entirely of songs and symphonies, in which latter form he composed nine works on a large scale, five of them requiring voices, and he is best known by the song-symphony *Das Lied von der Erde*, which is not included in the nine; he left a Tenth Symphony unfinished. One of the greatest masters of the orchestra, his work, gaining popularity in Britain and already accepted in America and on the Continent, is the bridge between the late romantic 19th-century style and the revolutionary works of Schoenberg and his followers. See *Gustav Mahler, Memories and Letters*, by A. Mahler (trans. B. Creighton, 1946), and biographies by B. Walter (1937) and D. Mitchell (1958).

MAHMUD II (1785–1839), Sultan of Turkey from 1808. His reign was marked by the cession of Bessarabia to Russia (1812), Greece's successful struggle for independence (1820–28), a disastrous war with Russia (1828–29), and by the triumphs of Mehemet Ali (q.v.). He shattered the power of the janissaries by a massacre in 1826. He introduced many domestic reforms such as compulsory primary education and did much to westernize Turkey.

MAHMUD OF GHAZNI (971–1030), sovereign from 997 of Khorasan and Ghazni, repeatedly invaded India, and carried his conquering arms to Kurdistan on the west, to Samarkand on the north. See Life by M. Nāzim (1931).

MAHOMET. See MOHAMMED.

MAHON, Lord. See STANHOPE (5).

MAHONY, Francis (1804–66), Irish priest, known as ' Father Prout ', born at Cork in 1804, became a Jesuit priest, but forsook his calling for journalism and poetry, and is remembered as author of the poems ' The Bells of Shandon ' and ' The Lady of Lee '. See his works ed. Charles Kent (1881).

MAI, Angelo, *mah'ee* (1782–1854), Italian cardinal, born at Schilpario in Lombardy, was educated to be a Jesuit, but became a secular priest at Milan, and keeper of the Ambrosian Library, where he discovered and edited MSS. or fragments of several long-lost works. Transferred to the Vatican, he edited a number of important ancient texts, and left an edition of the *Codex Vaticanus* unfinished at his death. See Life by Prina (1882).

MAIDMENT, James (1794–1879), Scottish lawyer and editor, born in London, was called to the Scottish bar in 1817, and became a great authority on genealogical law cases. His most ambitious work was *The Dramatists of the Restoration* (14 vols. 1872–79), edited with W. H. Logan. See bibliography by T. G. Stevenson (1883).

MAILLOL, Aristide Joseph Bonaventure, *ma-yol* (1861–1944), French sculptor, born at Banyuls-sur-mer. He studied at the École des Beaux-Arts, and spent some years designing tapestries. The latter half of his life was devoted to the representation of the nude female figure (e.g., the *Three Graces* in the Tate Gallery, London) in a style of monumental simplicity and classical serenity. See the monograph by Bouvier (1945).

MAIMBOURG, Louis, *mī-boor* (1610–86), French Jesuit church-historian, born at Nancy, was expelled in 1685 from the order for his defence of Gallicanism, but became a pensioner of Louis XIV. He wrote histories of Arianism, Lutheranism, Calvinism, and the prerogatives of the Church of Rome.

MAIMON, Solomon, *mī'mon* (*c.* 1754–1800), German philosopher, born of Jewish parents in Lithuania, married at the age of twelve and studied medicine in Berlin. He wrote a critical commentary on the philosophy of Maimonides and was one of the earliest critics of the Kantian system in *Versuch über die Transzendentalphilosophie* (1790) which Kant acknowledged.

MAIMONIDES, *mī-mon'i-deez*, or **Rabbi Moses ben Maimon** (1135–1204), Jewish philosopher, was born at Córdoba, March 30, 1135, and studied the Aristotelian philosophy and Greek medicine under the best Arab teachers. His family had to conform to Mohammedanism, and migrated to Egypt, where he became physician to Saladin, and died at Cairo, December 13, 1204. He has been reckoned next to Moses himself for his influence on Jewish thought. Among his works are a commentary on the Mishna, and the *Book of the Precepts*, written first in Arabic; the *Mishne Torah* or ' Second Law ' (in Hebrew); and his greatest achievement, *Guide for the Perplexed* (see edition by Roth 1948). See bibliography by J. I. Gorfinkle (N.Y. 1932) and Lives by S. Zertlin (1935), A. Heschel (1935) and L. Roth (1948).

MAINE, Sir Henry James Sumner (1822–88), English historian, born August 15, 1822, from Christ's Hospital passed in 1840 to Pembroke College, Cambridge. After various teaching posts in England, and administrative appointments in India, he was elected master of Trinity Hall at Cambridge in 1877, and in 1887 Whewell professor of International Law. He died at Cannes, February 3, 1888. It is by his work on the origin and growth of legal and social institutions that Maine will be best remembered. His books include *Ancient Law* (1861), *Early Law and Custom*

(1883), and *International Law* (1888). See Memoir by Sir M. E. Grant Duff (1892).

MAINTENON, Françoise d'Aubigné, Marquise de, *mĩ-tė-nõ* (1635–1719), second wife of Louis XIV, granddaughter of the Huguenot Théodore Agrippa d'Aubigné (q.v.), was born near the conciergerie of Niort where her father was a prisoner, November 27, 1635. At four years old she was carried to Martinique, whence she returned to France after her father's death (1645), and became a Catholic; her mother's death left her at fifteen in penury. She married the crippled poet Scarron (1652), and on his death (1660) again was reduced to poverty; but her husband's pension was continued to her. In 1669 she was given the charge of the king's two sons by Madame de Montespan. By 1674 the king's presents enabled her to purchase the estate of Maintenon, and in 1678 she had it made a marquisate. She had firmly established her ascendency over Louis, who, after the queen's death (1683), married her privately in 1685. Her morals were severe, for her heart was cold. Her political influence was supreme in all but important questions of policy; she was a liberal patroness of letters. Often unhappy, she turned for solace to the home for poor girls of good family she had established at St Cyr. Hither she retired when the king died (1715); and here she died, April 15, 1719. Her pretended *Mémoires* (1755) are spurious, but her delightful *Lettres* (1756; ed. Lavallée, 1856; ed. Geffroy, 1887) are genuine. See works by M. Cruttwell (1930), M. Langlois (1932) and H. C. Barnard (1934).

MAIR, John. See MAJOR.

MAISTRE, *mes'tr'*, (1) **Joseph Marie, Comte de** (1753–1821), French diplomat and political philosopher, born at Chambéry, on the occupation of Savoy in 1792 by the French, went into exile; in 1803–17 he was the king of Sardinia's ambassador to St Petersburg. In his writings de Maistre maintained the pope as the source and centre of all earthly authority, and an ordered theocracy as the only protection from social and religious anarchy. See study by F. Bayle (Paris 1945).

(2) **Xavier, Comte de** (1763–1852), brother of (1), born at Chambéry, joined the Russian army and became a general. He was an accomplished landscape and portrait artist, and wrote several charming novels. He died at St Petersburg. See books by Rey (1865), Maystre and Perrin (1895).

MAITLAND, (1) **Frederick William** (1850–1906), English historian, grandson of the historian **Samuel Roffey Maitland** (1792–1866), educated at Eton and Trinity, Cambridge, was a barrister (1876), reader in English Law at Cambridge (1884) and Downing professor (1888). He wrote a *History of English Law* (1895, with Sir F. Pollock, q.v.), *Domesday Book and Beyond* (1897), and other brilliant works on legal antiquities and history. See A. L. Smith, *F. W. Maitland, two Lectures and a bibliography* (1908), and Life by H. A. L. Fisher (1910).

(2) **Sir Richard** (1496–1586), of Lethington, Scottish lawyer and poet, father of (3), became a lord of session in 1551, lord privy seal in 1562, and was conspicuous for his moderation and integrity. His poems—mostly lamentations for the distracted state of his country—were published in 1830 by the Maitland Club. He made a collection of early Scottish poetry, now forming two MS. vols., which are in the Pepysian collection at Cambridge. He wrote also a *Historie of the Hous of Seytoun.*

(3) **William** (*c.* 1528–73), son of (2), 'Secretary Lethington', who in 1558 became secretary of state to the queen-regent, and in 1559 joined the lords of the congregation, then in arms against her. In August 1560 he acted as speaker in the Convention of Estates, and was sent to the English court to represent the interests of the Protestants. On the arrival of Queen Mary in 1561, Maitland associated himself with Moray in opposing the extreme proposals of Knox. He represented Mary more than once at the court of Elizabeth; but made her his enemy by his connivance at Rizzio's murder (1566), again, however, to become her counsellor. At first he favoured Bothwell, and was privy to the murder of Darnley, yet on Bothwell's marriage with Mary he acted with the insurgents. Nevertheless, after the queen's flight to England, while seeming to side with the new government, he secretly favoured the exiled queen. One of the commissioners who accompanied Moray to present to Elizabeth their indictment against Mary (1568), he was plotting against his colleagues; and the formation of a party in favour of Mary was mainly his work. Shut up in Edinburgh Castle, Maitland and Kirkcaldy of Grange surrendered, May 29, 1573. Maitland died in prison in Leith on June 9. See Buchanan's *Chamaeleon*; studies by J. Skelton (1887–88), E. Russell (1912). See also LAUDERDALE.

MAJOR, or **Mair, John** (*c.* 1470–1550), Scottish theologian and historian, born near North Berwick, studied at Oxford, Cambridge and Paris, lectured on Scholastic Logic and Philosophy. He also wrote commentaries on Peter Lombard, and a history of England and Scotland. He was provost of St Salvator's College, St Andrews, from 1533 until his death. See Arch. Constable's translation of his *History* (Scottish Hist. Soc. 1892).

MAKARIOS III, properly **Mihail Christodoulou Mouskos** (1913–), Archbishop and Primate of the Orthodox Church of Cyprus, born in Ano Panciyia near Paphos. He was ordained priest in 1946, elected Bishop of Kition in 1948 and Archbishop in 1950. He reorganized the Enosis Movement and in so doing revealed himself as a very shrewd politician and publicist. Implicated by the 'Grivas Diaries' in the affairs of Eoka terrorism, he was arrested and detained for a time in the Seychelles, but returned to a tumultuous welcome in March 1959 to become chief Greek-Cypriot minister in the new Greek-Turkish provisional government. In December 1959 he was elected president of Cyprus, an office which he has held ever since.

MAKART, Hans, *mah'kart* (1840–84), Austrian painter, born at Salzburg, studied at Munich and in Italy, settled in Vienna in

1869, and in 1879 became professor at the academy there. He painted spectacular and historical pictures, of bold colour and of gigantic size. See the Life of him by Von Lützow (1886).

MAKEHAM, William Matthew, *mayk'ėm* (d. 1892), British statistician, who formulated about 1860 the law of human mortality which bears his name. It was recognized by the Institute of Actuaries in 1887, but was later superseded in actuarial practice.

MAKKARI, Ahmed el-, *mak'-* (*c.* 1585–1631) Moorish historian, born at Makkara in Algeria. He wrote a *History of the Mohammedan Dynasties of Spain.*

MALACHY, St (*c.* 1094–1148), born at Armagh, became Abbot of Bangor (1121), Bishop of Connor (1125) and Archbishop of Armagh (1134). In 1140 he journeyed to Rome, visiting St Bernard at Clairvaux. On his return (1142) he introduced the Cistercian Order into Ireland. In 1148 he once more went to France, and died at Clairvaux in St Bernard's arms. The curious so-called 'Prophecies of St Malachy' first published in *Lignum Vitae* (1595) by the Flemish Benedictine, Arnold Wion, are erroneously ascribed to him. See St Bernard's *Vita Malachiae* (in Migne's *Patr.* clxxi) and Life by Luddy (1930).

MALAN, Daniel François, *ma-lahn'* (1874–1959), South African politician, born at Riebeek West, Cape Province, and educated at Victoria College, Stellenbosch, and Utrecht University. On his return to South Africa in 1905 he became a predikant of the Dutch Reformed Church and after ten years abandoned his clerical career to become editor of *Die Burger*, the Nationalist newspaper. He became an M.P. in 1918 and in 1924 in the Nationalist-Labour government he held the portfolios of the interior, of education and of public health. He introduced measures strengthening the Nationalist position—in particular, that making Afrikaans an official language. He was leader of the Opposition from 1934 to 1939 and from 1940 to 1948 when, becoming prime minister and minister for external affairs, he embarked on the hotly controversial policies of *apartheid* with the aim of re-aligning South Africa's multi-racial society. He described as the kernel of his segregation policies the Group Areas Act, dividing the country into white, black and coloured zones. The *apartheid* legislation, which involved strongly-contested constitutional changes, was met by non-violent civil disobedience at home and vigorous criticism abroad. Dr Malan resigned from the premiership in 1954. Crusty, austere, a scholar of profound convictions and an uncompromising manner, Dr Malan was a back-veldt Moses to the Boers. He never wavered in his pulpiteering belief in a strict white supremacy, in a Heaven-sent Afrikaner mission and a rigidly hierarchical society. He died at his home at Stellenbosch on Feb. 7, 1959.

MALCOLM, name of four kings of Scotland.

Malcolm I, son of Donald, king of Alban 942-954.

Malcolm II, son of Kenneth, king of Scotia 1005–34.

Malcolm III, called **Canmore** (Gael. *Ceann-mor*, 'great head'), was a child when his father, King Duncan, was slain by Macbeth (1040). He spent his youth in Northumbria with his uncle, Earl Siward, who in 1054 established him in Cumbria and Lothian. In 1057, after Macbeth was slain, he became king of all Scotland. His first wife, Ingibiorg, widow of Thorfinn of Orkney, had died; and in 1069 Malcolm wedded Margaret (q.v.), sister of Edgar the Atheling, whose cause he made his own. Five times he harried Northumbria (1069, 1070, 1079, 1091, 1093); and there were counter invasions by William the Conqueror and Prince Robert, in 1072 and 1080. In 1092 Rufus wrested from Scotland all Cumbria south of the Solway; and next year Malcolm marched into England, but was entrapped and slain at Alnwick, November 13, 1093. He left five sons, of whom four succeeded him, Duncan, Edgar, Alexander and David.

Malcolm IV (1141–65), Malcolm the Maiden, king of Scotland from 1153.

MALCOLM, Sir John (1769–1833), British soldier and diplomat, born at Burnfoot near Langholm, at thirteen entered the Madras army; was thrice ambassador to Persia (1800, 1807, 1810), governor of Bombay (1827–30) and was knighted in 1812. He entered parliament in 1831, opposing the Reform Bill. He published works on India and Persia. See Life by Kaye (1856).

MALEBRANCHE, Nicolas, *mal-brãsh* (1638–1715), French philosopher, born at Paris, joined the Oratorians (1660), and studied theology till Descartes's works drew him to philosophy. His famous *De la recherche de la vérité* (1674; 6th ed. 1712) combines a psychological investigation of the causes of error with a mystic idealism—' the vision of all things in God', the intervention of God being necessary to bridge over the gulf between things so unlike as the human soul and the body. Other works are *Traité de la nature et de la grâce* (1680), *Méditations chrétiennes et métaphysiques* (1683) and *Traité de morale* (1684). He died October 13, 1715. For bibliography see E. A. Blampignon (1882). See studies by R. W. Church (1931), A. A. Luce (1934).

MALENKOV, Georgi Maksimilianovich, *mahl'yen-kof* (1902–), Soviet politician, born at Orenburg, became a deputy prime minister of the U.S.S.R. in 1946, and succeeded Stalin in 1953. In February 1955 Malenkov suddenly resigned, pleading inadequate experience and admitting responsibility for the failure of Soviet agricultural policy. He was succeeded by Marshal Bulganin (q.v.) and relegated to the office of minister for electrical power stations, but in July 1957, having been accused, with Molotov and Kaganovich, of setting up an 'anti-party group', he was dismissed not only from the government but from the party Presidium and Central Committee, and was rusticated to remotest Kazakhstan as manager of a hydroelectric plant.

MALESHERBES, Chrétien Guillaume de Lamoignon de, *mal-zerb* (1721–94), French statesman, born at Paris, December 6, became in 1750 president of the *cour des* *aides*. He was a determined opponent of government rapacity and tyranny; as censor of the press he showed himself tolerant, and to him we may ascribe the publication of the *Encyclopédie*. In 1771 his remonstrances against royal abuses of law led to his banishment to his country-seat of Ste Lucie; at Louis XVI's accession (1774) he was recalled, and took office, but retired on the dismissal of Turgot, and, save a short spell in office in 1787, spent his time in travel or in the improvement of his estates. Under the Convention he came to Paris to defend the king, and from that day himself was doomed. He was arrested in December 1793, and guillotined, April 22, 1794, along with his daughter and her husband. Malesherbes was a member of the Academy, and brought an able pen to the discussion of agriculture and botany as well as political and financial questions. His *Oeuvres choisies* (1809) contains his most interesting writings. See Lives by Boissy d'Anglas (1818), Rozet (1831), Dupin (1841) and Vignaux (1874), and studies by H. Robert (1927) and J. Allison (1938).

MALET, (1) David. See MALLET.

(2) Lucas. See KINGSLEY (5).

MALHERBE, François de (1555–1628), French poet, born at Caen, ingratiated himself with Henry IV, and received a pension. He was an industrious writer, producing odes, songs, epigrams, epistles, translations, criticisms, &c. His own poetry is colourless and insipid, but he founded a literary tradition—'Enfin Malherbe vint'; he led his countrymen to disdain the richly-coloured and full-sounding verses of Ronsard, and to adopt a style clear, correct and refined, but cold and prosaic. See Tilley's *From Montaigne to Molière* (1908); and study by J. de Celles (Paris 1937).

MALIBRAN, Marie Felicita, *mal-ee-brã* (1808–36), Spanish mezzo-soprano singer, born at Paris, March 24, 1808, was the daughter of the Spanish singer Manuel García (q.v.). See Life by A. Flauent (Paris 1937).

MALIK, Jacob Alexandrovich (1906–), Soviet politician, was born in the Ukraine. Said to be one of Stalin's favourite 'juniors', he was ambassador to Japan from 1942 to 1945 and deputy foreign minister in 1946. In 1948 he succeeded Andrei Gromyko as Soviet spokesman at UNO and was ambassador to Britain 1953–60. Since 1960 he has again been deputy foreign minister.

MALINOVSKY, Rodion Yakovlevich, *-nof'-* (1898–1967), Russian general, born in Odessa, was a corporal in the first World War, when, after the Russian collapse, he escaped via Siberia and Singapore to fight in a Russian brigade in France, joined the Red Army after the revolution and was major-general at the time of the Nazi invasion in 1941. He commanded the forces which liberated Rostov, Kharkov and the Dnieper basin and led the Russian advance on Budapest and into Austria (1944–45). When Russia declared war on Japan, he took a leading part in the Manchurian campaign. In October 1957 he succeeded Zhukov as Khrushchev's minister of defence and appeared to be the latter's *éminence grise* at the abortive East-West 'Summit' meeting in Paris in May 1960.

MALINOWSKI, Bronislaw (1884–1942), Polish anthropologist, born in Cracow, professor at London University and Yale, took part in expeditions to New Guinea and Melanesia, after which he wrote *Argonauts of the Western Pacific* (1922), *Sex and Repression in Savage Society* (1927), &c. He died in New Haven, Conn., on May 16, 1942. See H. M. Gluckman, *Analysis of Sociological Theories of Malinowski* (1949).

MALIPIERO, Francesco, *'mal-i-pyav'rō* (1882–), Italian composer born at Venice, studied under Bossi and later went to Paris. He has written much symphonic music in a highly characteristic style and has edited Monteverdi and Vivaldi. He is the author of *Claudio Monteverdi* (Milan 1930), *Igor Stravinsky* (Venice 1945) and the autobiographical *Cosi va lo mondo, 1922-45* (Milan 1946). See also book by M. Bontempelli (Milan 1942).

MALLARMÉ, Stéphane (1842–98), French Symbolistic poet, born at Paris, taught English in various schools in Paris and elsewhere and visited England on several occasions. He translated Poe's 'The Raven' (1875) and other poems. In prose and verse he was a leader of the Symbolist school, revelling in allegory, obscurity, bizarre words and constructions, *vers libre* and word-music. *L'Après-midi d'un faune*, illustrated by Manet (1876) is his best-known poem and made the wilful obscurity of his style famous. His *Les Dieux antiques* (1880), *Poésies* (1899), and *Vers et prose* (1893) were other works admired by the 'decadents'. See works by H. Cooperman (1933) and H. Mondor (Paris 1941–42), and bibliography by M. Mondor and F. Monkel (1927).

MALLET, David (*c.* 1705–65), Scottish poet, was born near Crieff, the son of a farmer. Janitor at Edinburgh High School in 1717–18, he then studied at the university; in 1720 became a tutor, from 1723 to 1731 in the family of the Duke of Montrose, living mostly in London, and changed his name 'from Scots Malloch to English Mallet'. *William and Margaret* gained him a reputation as a poet, which he enhanced by *The Excursion* (1728). He also tried his hand at play-writing. *Mustapha* pleased for a while in 1739; *Eurydice* (1731) and *Elvira* (1763), tragedies, were failures. *Alfred, a Masque* (1740), was written in conjunction with Thomson, and one of its songs, 'Rule Britannia', was claimed for both. See memoir by Dinsdale prefixed to his *Ballads and Songs* (1857).

MALLOCK, William Hurrell (1849–1923), English political philosopher and satirist, a nephew of the Froudes, born at Cockington Court, Devon, won the Newdigate in 1871 while at Balliol, Oxford. He made a hit with *The New Republic* (1877) and *The New Paul and Virginia* (1878).

MALMESBURY, Earls of:

(1) James Harris, 1st Earl (1746–1820), English diplomat, grandfather of (2), son of 'Hermes' Harris (q.v.), held posts at Madrid (1768), Berlin, St Petersburg, The Hague (1784), and was made K.C.B. (1778), baron (1788) and Earl of Malmesbury (1800). In

1793 he had seceded from Fox to Pitt, and in 1795 had married by proxy and conducted to England the Princess Caroline. See *Diaries and Correspondence* (1844) and *Lord Malmesbury and his Friends* (1870).

(2) James Howard Harris, 3rd Earl (1807–1889), English statesman, grandson of (1), who succeeded in 1841, and in 1852 and 1858–59 was foreign secretary; in 1866–68 and 1874–76, privy seal. See his *Memoirs of an Ex-Minister* (1884).

MALMESBURY, William of. See WILLIAM OF MALMESBURY.

MALONE, Edmund (1741–1812), Irish editor of Shakespeare, born in Dublin, graduated at Trinity College, was called to the Irish bar in 1767, but from 1777 devoted himself to literary work in London, his first work being a 'supplement' to Steevens's edition of Shakespeare (1778). Malone's own edition of the great dramatist (1790) was warmly received. He had been one of the first to express his disbelief in Chatterton's Rowley poems, and in 1796 he denounced the Shakespeare forgeries of Ireland (q.v.). He left behind a large mass of materials for 'The Variorum Shakespeare', edited in 1821 by James Boswell the younger. See Life by J. Prior (1860).

MALORY, Sir Thomas (d. 1471), English writer, immortal in his work, the *Morte d'Arthur*. We learn from Caxton's preface that Malory was a knight, that he finished his work in the ninth year of the reign of Edward IV (1469–70), and that he 'reduced' it from some French book. Probably he was the Sir Thomas Malory (d. 1471) of Newbold Revel, Warwickshire, whose quarrels with a neighbouring priory and (probably) Lancastrian politics brought him imprisonment. Of Caxton's black-letter folio but two copies now exist (reprinted by Oskar Sommer with essay by A. Lang, 1889–91). An independent manuscript was discovered at Winchester in 1934. *Morte d'Arthur* 'is indisputably', says Scott, 'the best prose romance the English language can boast of', and was a happy attempt to give epic unity to the whole mass of French Arthurian romance. Tennyson, Swinburne and many others are debtors to Malory. See his Works edited by E. Vinaver (3 vols. 1947), and Lives by E. Hicks (1928), E. Vinaver (1929).

MALPIGHI, Marcello, *mal-pee'gee* (1628–94), Italian physiologist, was born March 10, 1628, near Bologna, where he studied medicine. He was professor at Pisa, Messina and Bologna, and from 1691 chief physician to Pope Innocent XII. A pioneer in microscopic anatomy, animal and vegetable, he wrote a series of works on his discoveries. See Italian essays on him by Virchow, Haeckel, &c. (1897), and bibliography by C. Frati (Milan 1897).

MALRAUX, André, *mal-rō* (1901–), French writer, born in Paris, studied oriental languages and spent much time in China, where he worked for the Kuomintang and was active in the 1927 revolution. He also fought as a pilot in the Spanish Civil War, and in World War II he escaped from a prisoner-of-war camp to join the French resistance movement. He was minister of information in de Gaulle's government (1945-46), minister delegate from 1958 and minister of cultural afairs (1960–69). He is known for his novels, which constitute a dramatic meditation on human destiny and are highly coloured by his personal experience of war, revolution and resistance to tyranny. Among them are *Les Conquérants* (1928), *La Condition humaine* (1933, winner of Goncourt prize) and *L'Espoir* (1937). He also wrote *La Psychologie de l'art* (1947). See studies by Mauriac (Paris 1946), Savane (Paris 1946), Hartmann (1960) and his *Anti-mémoires* (1967).

MALTHUS, Thomas Robert (1766–1834), English economist, was born at The Rookery near Dorking, February 17, 1766. He was ninth wrangler at Cambridge in 1788, was elected fellow of his college (Jesus) in 1793, and in 1797 became curate at Albury, Surrey. In 1798 he published anonymously his *Essay on the Principle of Population*, of which in 1803 he brought out a greatly enlarged and altered edition. In it he maintained that the optimistic hopes of Rousseau and Godwin are rendered baseless by the natural tendency of population to increase faster than the means of subsistence. Malthus gives no sanction to the theories and practices currently known as Malthusianism. An amiable and benevolent man, he suffered much misrepresentation and abuse at the hands of both revolutionaries and conservatives. The problem had been handled by Franklin, Hume and many other writers, but Malthus crystallized the views of those writers, and presented them in systematic form with elaborate proofs derived from history. Darwin saw 'on reading Malthus *On Population* that natural selection was the inevitable result of the rapid increase of all organic beings', for such rapid increase necessarily leads to the struggle for existence. In 1804 Malthus married happily, and next year was appointed professor of Political Economy in the East India College at Haileybury. He wrote *An Inquiry into the Nature and Progress of Rent* (1815), largely anticipating Ricardo, and *Principles of Political Economy* (1820); and died near Bath, December 23, 1834. See Bonar's *Malthus and his Work* (1885).

MALUS, Étienne Louis (1775–1812), French physicist, born in Paris, carried out research in optics and discovered the polarization of light by reflection. His paper explaining the theory of double refraction in crystals won him the Institute's prize in 1810. His death in Paris at an early age was due to the hardships of campaigning—he was an army instructor engineer.

MALVERN. See HUGGINS (1).

MAMAEA, mother of Alexander Severus (q.v.).

MAMELI, Goffredo (1827–49), Italian poet and patriot, born at Genoa, wrote the fine war song *Fratelli d'Italia*, and died in defence of Rome. See Life by M. Marchini (Milan 1928).

MANASSEH (1), eldest son of Joseph, and founder of a tribe.

(2) Son of pious Hezekiah, succeeded him as king of Judah (697–642 B.C.), but earned an evil name for idolatry and wickedness till, a

captive in Babylon, he repented. *The Prayer of Manasseh* is apocryphal.

MANASSEH BEN ISRAEL (1604–57), Jewish scholar, born at Lisbon and taken early to Amsterdam, at eighteen became chief rabbi of the synagogue there. In 1655–57 he was in England, securing from Cromwell the readmission of the Jews. He wrote works in Hebrew, Spanish and Latin, and in English a *Humble Address* to Cromwell, *A Declaration*, and *Vindiciae Judaeorum* (1656). See Life by C. Roth (1934).

MANBY, George William (1765–1854), English inventor, barrack-master at Yarmouth from 1803, showed in 1807 how to save shipwrecked persons by firing a rope to the ship from a mortar on shore. He wrote on this method, on lifeboats, criminal law and other subjects. He was elected F.R.S. in 1831.

MANCHESTER, Edward Montagu, 2nd Earl of (1602–71), after leaving Sidney Sussex College, Cambridge, accompanied Prince Charles to Spain (1623), and in 1626 was raised to the House of Lords as Baron Montagu of Kimbolton, but was better known by his courtesy title of Viscount Mandeville. Siding with the popular party, and an acknowledged leader of the Puritans in the Upper House, he was charged by the king (January 3, 1642) with entertaining traitorous designs, along with the five members of the House of Commons. He succeeded his father as second earl in the same year. On the outbreak of hostilities he of course fought for the parliament. He served under Essex at Edgehill, then held the associated (eastern) counties against Newcastle, took Lincoln (1644), and routed Prince Rupert at Marston Moor—that is to say, he nominally commanded; the real fighting was done by Cromwell and his Ironsides. He then marched to oppose the royalists in the southwest, and defeated them at Newbury (the second battle). But after this battle he again showed slackness in following up the victory, a fault that had been noticed after Marston Moor. In consequence Cromwell accused him of military incompetency in the House of Commons, and the two had a downright quarrel. The Self-denying Ordinance deprived Manchester of his command (1645), and this did not allay his bitterness against Cromwell. He opposed the trial of the king, and protested against the Commonwealth. Afterwards, having been active in promoting the Restoration, he was made lord chamberlain, a step designed to conciliate the Presbyterians.

MANCINI, *man-chee'nee*, a Roman family famous for five sisters, daughters of Michele Lorenzo Mancini and Jeronima, sister of Cardinal Mazarin:

(1) **Hortense, Duchesse de Mazarin** (1646–1699), was married off by Mazarin to Armand Charles de la Porte, who assumed the Mazarin title, but she separated from him and became famous for her beauty at the court of Charles II of England. She died at Chelsea.

(2) **Laura, Duchesse de Mercoeur** (1636–57), came to the French court and was married to Louis de Vendôme. The famous Duc de Vendôme (q.v.) was their son.

(3) **Marie, Princesse de Colonna** (1640–1715), was a favourite of Louis XIV, who was prevented from marrying her only by the machinations of Mazarin. She lived in Spain for most of her life.

(4) **Marie Anne, Duchesse de Bouillon** (1649–1714), became renowned for her literary salon and for her patronage of La Fontaine. She was banished in 1680, having been involved in the *cause celèbre* of the notorious sorceress La Voisin (q.v.).

(5) **Olympe, Comtesse de Soissons** (1639–1708), also a court favourite, was involved with her sister in the La Voisin intrigues and, accused of poisoning her husband and the Queen of Spain, fled to the Netherlands. Her son was Prince Eugene of Savoy.

MANDER, Karel van (1548–1606), Flemish painter of portraits, born at Meulebeke, lived mostly in Haarlem, and is chiefly remembered for his *Schilderbouck* (1604), a collection of biographical profiles of painters, important as a source for the art history of the Low Countries.

MANDEVILLE, (1) Bernard (1670–1733), English satirist, born at Dort in Holland, took his M.D. at Leyden in 1691, immediately settled in London in medical practice, and died there. He is known as the author of a short work in doggerel verse originally entitled *The Grumbling Hive* (1705), and finally *The Fable of the Bees* (1723). Writing in a vein of acute paradox, he affirms that 'private vices are public benefits', and that every species of virtue is at bottom some form of gross selfishness, more or less modified. The book was condemned by the grand jury of Middlesex, and was attacked by Law the nonjuror, by Berkeley, Brown, Warburton, Hutcheson and others. Other works in an unpleasant tone are *The Virgin Unmasked*, *Free Thoughts on Religion*, &c. See J. M. Robertson's *Pioneer Humanists* (1907).

(2) **Geoffrey de, Earl of Essex** (d. 1144), succeeded his father as constable of the Tower about 1130, proved a traitor alternately to King Stephen and the Empress Matilda, and taking finally to open brigandage, was besieged in the Cambridgeshire fens and slain. See monograph by J. H. Round (1892).

(3) **Jehan de, or Sir John,** the name assigned to the compiler of a famous book of travels, published apparently in 1366, and soon translated from the French into all European tongues. It seems to have been written by a physician, Jehan de Bourgogne, otherwise Jehan à la Barbe, who died at Liège in 1372, and who is said to have revealed on his death-bed his real name of Mandeville (or Maundevylle), explaining that he had had to flee from his native England for a homicide. Some scholars, however, attribute it to Jean d'Outremeuse, a Frenchman. Mandeville claims to have travelled through Turkey, Persia, Syria, Arabia, North Africa and India, but much of his book is a compilation from various literary sources. See Hamelius's edition (E.E.T.S. 1919–23) and studies by M. Letts (1949) and J. W. Bennett (1954).

MÁNES, Josef, *mah'-* (1820–71), Czech artist, born in Prague. He was the pupil of his father, the landscape artist **Antonin** (1784–

1843), and he was well known for his genre and historical paintings and portraits, many of which are in the Prague museums. See study by M. Lamač (Prague 1952).

MANET, Édouard, *ma-nay* (1832–83), French painter. Intended for a legal career, he was sent on a voyage to Rio to distract his thoughts from art, but this proved ineffectual, and having studied for a while under Couture he exhibited at the Salon in 1861. His *Déjeuner sur l'herbe* (1863), which scandalized the traditional classicists, was rejected, and, although the equally provocative *Olympia* was accepted in 1865, the Salon remained hostile and Manet's genius was not recognized until after his death. With Monet, Renoir and other rebels against tradition, he exhibited in the *Salon des Refusés* and helped to form the group out of which the Impressionist movement arose. Manet's works are all characterized by a masterly understanding of the effects of light, but it is in his later canvases, such as *Bar at the Folies Bergères* (1882), that he is seen in the more truly Impressionistic vein. See a Life by Tabarant (1947).

MANETHO, Egyptian historian, was high-priest of Heliopolis in the 3rd century B.C. Only epitomes of his history of the 30 dynasties are given by Julius Africanus (A.D. 300), Eusebius, and George Syncellus (A.D. 800).

MANFRED (1232–66), King of Sicily, was a natural son of the Emperor Frederick II, and was made Prince of Tarentum. For his half-brother, Conrad IV, he acted as regent in Italy (especially Apulia), and subsequently for his nephew Conradin (q.v.) bravely defended the interests of the empire against the aggression of Pope Innocent IV, who, however, compelled Manfred to flee for shelter to the Saracens. With their aid he defeated the papal troops, and became, in 1257, master of the whole kingdom of Naples and Sicily. On the (false) rumour of Conradin's death (1258) he was crowned king at Palermo, and, in spite of excommunication by Pope Alexander VI, occupied Tuscany. His brief government was mild and vigorous; but Pope Urban IV renewed the excommunication, and bestowed his dominions on Charles of Anjou, brother of Louis IX of France. Manfred fell in battle at Benevento.

MANGAN, James Clarence (1803–49), Irish poet and attorney's clerk, whose life was a tragedy of hapless love, poverty and intemperance, till his death in a Dublin hospital. There is fine quality in his original verse, as well as in his translations from old Irish and German. See editions of his Poems (1903), Prose Writings (1904), Lives by D. J. O'Donoghue (1897) and J. D. Sheridan (1937). For bibliography see P. S. O'Hegarty (1941).

MANGNALL, Richmal (1769–1820), English teacher, born probably in Manchester, was the headmistress of a ladies' school near Wakefield, where she died. Her redoubtable *Questions*, the pride and terror of generations of schoolgirls, reached an 84th edition in 1857, and was even reprinted in 1892.

MANICHAEUS, or **Mani**, *man-i-kee'us* (*c.* A.D. 215–276), the founder of the heretical Manichaeans, was born at Ecbatana, and about 245 began to proclaim his new religion at the court of the Persian king, Sapor (Shahpur) I. Bahram I abandoned him to his enemies, who crucified him. See study by E. Rochat (Geneva 1897).

MANIN, Daniele (1804–57), Venetian statesman, born of Jewish ancestry at Venice, practised at the bar, and became a leader of liberal opinion; made president of the Venetian republic (1848), he was the soul of the heroic five months' defence against the Austrians. When Venice capitulated (August 24, 1849), Manin, with thirty-nine others, was excluded from the amnesty, but escaped to Paris, where he taught Italian, and died of heart disease. His bones were brought to free Venice in 1868. See Lives by R. Errera (1923) and G. M. Trevelyan (1923).

MANKOWITZ, (Cyril) Wolf, *man'kō-vits* (1924–), British author, playwright and antique dealer, was born at Bethnal Green, London. An authority on Wedgwood, he published *Wedgwood* (1953), *The Portland Vase* (1953), and is an editor of *The Concise Encyclopedia of English Pottery and Porcelain* (1957). Other publications include the novels *Make Me an Offer* (1952) and *A Kid for Two Farthings* (1953), and a collection of short stories, *The Mendelman Fire* (1957). Among his plays is *The Bespoke Overcoat* (1954).

MANLEY, Mary de la Rivière (*c.* 1672–1724), English author of plays, and of the scandalous anti-Whig *New Atalantis* (1709), and Swift's successor as editor of *The Examiner* (1711), was born in Jersey, about 1688 married bigamously a cousin, John Manley of Truro, M.P., and died at Lambeth.

MANN, (1) **Heinrich** (1871–1950), German novelist, brother of (4), born at Lübeck, began to be described as the German Zola for his ruthless exposure of pre-1914 German society in *Im Schlaraffenland* (1901), translated as *Berlin, the Land of Cockaigne* (1925), and the trilogy describing the three classes of Kaiser Wilhelm II's empire, *Die Armen* (1917) the proletariat, *Der Untertan* (1918) the underling or bourgeois, and *Der Kopf* (1929) the head or governing class. He is best known for the macabre, expressionist novel, *Professor Unrat* (1904), describing the moral degradation of a once outwardly respectable schoolmaster, which was translated and filmed as *The Blue Angel* (1932). He lived in France (1933–40) and then escaped to the United States. Other works include *Die kleine Stadt* (1901), set in a small Italian town, and a remarkable autobiography, *Ein Zeitalter wird besichtigt* (1945–46). His influence is noticeable in Wassermann and Feuchtwanger. See studies by W. Schröder (1931), K. Lemke (1946) and H. Thering (1951).

(2) **Sir Horace** (1701–86), Horace Walpole's lifelong correspondent, from 1740 was British plenipotentiary at Florence. See Doran's *Mann and Manners* (1876), and Sieveking's memoir (1912).

(3) **Horace** (1796–1859), American educationist, born at Franklin, Mass., entered the Massachusetts legislature in 1827, and was president of the state senate. He was for eleven years secretary of the Board of

Education. From 1853 he was president of Antioch College in Ohio. See *Life and Works* (1891) and books by G. A. Hubbell (Philadelphia 1910) and E. I. F. Williams (N.Y. 1937).

(4) **Thomas** (1875–1955), the greatest modern German novelist, brother of (1), born June 6 into a patrician family of merchants and senators of the Hanseatic city of Lübeck, his mother being a talented musician of mixed German and Portuguese West Indian blood. The opposition between a conservative business outlook and artistic inclinations, the clash between Nordic and Latin temperaments inherent in his own personality, and the Schopenhauerian doctrine of art, being the self-abnegation of the will as the end product of decay, were to form his subject-matter. At nineteen, without completing school, he settled with his mother in Munich, and after dabbling at the university, he joined his brother in Italy, where he wrote his early masterpiece, *Buddenbrooks* (1901; trans. 1924), the saga of a family like his own, tracing its decline through four generations, as business acumen gives way to artistic sensibilities. At twenty-five Mann thus became a leading German writer. On his return to Munich, he became reader for the satirical literary magazine, *Simplicissimus*, which published many of his early, remarkable short stories. The novelettes *Tonio Kröger* (1902), *Tristan* (1903) and *Der Tod in Venedig*, 'Death in Venice' (1913; trans. 1916), all deal with the problem of the artist's salvation, positively in the case of the first, who resembles Goethe's Werther, negatively in the last in which a successful writer dies on the brink of perverted eroticism. World War I precipitated a quarrel between the two novelist brothers, Thomas's *Betrachtungen eines Unpolitischen*, 'Meditations of an Unpolitical Person' (1918), revealing his militant German patriotism, already a feature of his essay on Frederick the Great (1915) and a distrust of political ideologies, including the radicalism of his brother. *Der Zauberberg*, 'The Magic Mountain' (1924; trans. 1927), won him the Nobel prize in 1929. It was inspired by a visit to his wife at a sanatorium for consumptives at Davos in 1913 and tells the story of such a patient, Hans Castorp, the sanatorium representing Europe in its moral and intellectual disintegration. The same year, Mann delivered a speech against the rising Nazis and in 1930 exposed Italian fascism in *Mario und der Zauberer*, 'Mario and the Magician' (1930; trans. 1934). He left Germany for Switzerland after 1933 and in 1936 delivered an address for Freud's eightieth birthday. Both shared an enthusiasm for Joseph, and Mann wrote a tetralogy on the life of that biblical figure (1933–43; trans. 1934–44). He settled in the United States in 1936 and wrote a novel on a visit to Goethe by an old love, Charlotte Buff, *Lotte in Weimar* (1939). His anti-Hitler broadcasts to Germany were collected under the titles *Achtung Europa!* and *Deutsche Hörer* (1945). In 1947 he returned to Switzerland and was the only returning exile to be fêted by both West and East Germany. His greatest work, a modern version of the medieval legend, *Doktor Faustus* (1947; trans. 1948), runs together art and politics in the simultaneous treatment of the life and catastrophic end of an atonality-pioneering composer, Adrian Leverkühn, and German disintegration in two world wars. His last unfinished work, hailed as Germany's greatest comic novel, *Bekenntnisse des Hochstapler's Felix Krull*, Part I (1954), 'Confessions of the Confidence Trickster Felix Krull' (trans. 1955), written with astonishing wit, irony and humour and without the tortuous stylistic complexities of the *Bildungsroman*, commended itself most to English translators. Mann died August 12, 1955. Essentially a 19th-century German conservative, whose cultural landmarks vanished in the first World War, he was compelled towards a critique of the artistic. Ambivalently the artist and the bourgeois fearer of Bohemianism, the unpolitical man with political duties, he was the brilliant story-teller in the classical German tradition, whose subject-matter was paradoxically the end of that tradition. Other later works include *Der Erwählte* (1951), on the life of the incestuous Pope Gregory, *Die Betrogene* (1953) and *Last Essays* (trans. 1959), on Schiller, Goethe, Nietzsche and Chehov. See bibliography, ed. K. W. Jonas (Minnesota 1955), Mann's *Sketch of My Life* (trans. 1961), biographical studies by J. Cleugh (1933) and J. G. Brennan (1942), and critical studies by H. Hatfield (1952), J. M. Lindsay (1954), R. H. Thomas (1956) and especially E. Heller, *The Ironic German* (1958).

(5) **Tom** (1856–1941), English Labour leader, by profession an engineer, was born in Warwickshire. See his *Memoirs* (1923).

MANNERHEIM, Carl Gustav Emil, Freiherr von, *man'ĕr-hīm* (1867–1951), Finnish soldier and statesman, was born at Villnäs and became an officer in the Russian Army in 1889. He fought in the Russo-Japanese War of 1904–05 and in World War I. When Finland declared her independence in 1918 (after the Russian Revolution), he became supreme commander and regent. Defeated in the presidential election of 1919, he retired into private life, but returned as commander-in-chief against the Russians in the Winter War of 1939–40. He continued to command the Finnish forces until 1944, when he became president of the Finnish Republic until 1946. See book by T. Borenius (1940).

MANNERS. See RUTLAND and GRANBY.

MANNING, (1) **Henry Edward** (1808–92), English Roman Catholic cardinal, born at Totteridge, Hertfordshire, from Harrow passed in 1827 to Balliol College, Oxford, and, after taking a classical first in 1830, was in 1832 elected a fellow of Merton. An eloquent preacher and a High Churchman, in 1833 he became rector of Woollavington and Graffham, Sussex, and in 1840 Archdeacon of Chichester. On April 6, 1851, he joined the Church of Rome, and in 1865 succeeded Cardinal Wiseman as Archbishop of Westminster. At the Oecumenical Council of 1870 Manning was one of the most zealous supporters of the infallibility dogma; and, named cardinal in 1875, he continued a leader of the Ultramontanes. He was a member of the royal commissions on the housing of the poor (1885) and on education (1886), and took a prominent part in temperance and benevolent movements. He died January 14, 1892. See Lives by E. S. Purcell (2 vols. 1896), V. A. McLelland (1962) and E. E. Reynolds, *Three Cardinals* (1958).

(2) **Robert.** See ROBERT DE BRUNNE.

(3) **Thomas** (1772–1840), English traveller, born at Broome rectory, Suffolk, in 1790 entered Caius College, Cambridge; stayed there some years, studying Chinese; in 1799 formed his friendship with Lamb; in 1806 went out as a doctor to Canton; in 1811–12 visited Lhasa in Tibet, the first Englishman ever there; returned in 1817 to England; visited Italy 1827–29; and died at Bath. See Memoir by C. R. Markham (1876).

MANNS, Sir August (1825–1907), German musician, born in Prussia, in 1855 became musical director at the Crystal Palace, and in 1883–1902 conducted the Handel Festivals. He was knighted in 1903. See study by H. S. Wyndham (1909).

MANNY, Sir Walter de (d. 1372), English knight, born in Hainault, followed Queen Philippa to England in 1327, and fought splendidly for Edward III by land and sea against the Scots, Flemings and French. He was knighted and made Lord de Manny, received large grants of land, founded the Charterhouse monastery, and died in London.

MANNYNG, Robert. See ROBERT DE BRUNNE.

MANOEL I. See EMANUEL I.

MANOEL II. See MANUEL II.

MANRIQUE, Jorge, *-ree'kay* (1440–79), Spanish poet, born at Paredes de la Nava, is remembered for his fine elegy on his father's death, *Coplas por la muerte de su padre*.

MANSARD, or **MANSART,** *mã-sahr,* (1) **François** (1598–1666), French architect, brought a simplified adaptation of the Baroque style into use in France, designed Ste Marie de la Visitation (1632) and other Paris churches, the Château de Blois, Château de Maisons-Lafitte, &c., and made fashionable the high pitched type of roof which bears his name. See studies by Sir R. Blomfield (1935) and A. Blunt (1941).

(2) **Jules Hardouin** (1645–1708), French architect, great nephew of (1), born in Paris, became chief architect to Louis XIV and designed part of the palace of Versailles, including the Grand Trianon.

MANSBRIDGE, Albert (1878–1952), C.H. (1931), English educationist, born at Gloucester, founded the Workers' Educational Association (1903). See his *Trodden Road* (1940).

MANSEL, Henry Longueville (1820–71), English philosopher, Dean of St Paul's, was born at Cosgrove rectory, Northamptonshire. Educated at Merchant Taylors' and St John's College, Oxford, he became Waynflete professor in 1859, professor of Ecclesiastical History and Canon of Christ Church in 1867, and Dean of St Paul's in 1869. The pupil and part-editor of Hamilton (q.v.), he went beyond his master in emphasizing the relativity of knowledge—alleging that we have no positive conception of the attributes of God. His works include *Prolegomena Logica* (1851), *Metaphysics* (1860), *The Limits of Religious Thought* (Bampton Lectures, 1858), *The Philosophy of the Conditioned* (1866) and *The Gnostic Heresies* (with Life, 1874). See study by Matthews (1956).

MANSFELD, Counts of, a noble German family (founded *c.* 1060), whose castle stood near the Harz Mountains, 14 miles NW. of Halle.

(1) **Count Peter Ernst I** (1517–1604), afterwards prince, took part in Charles V's expedition against Tunis, and was made governor of Luxembourg. He fought against the French, made a name as one of the most brilliant Spanish generals in the Low Countries, was sent by Alva to the assistance of the French king against the Protestants (1569), and acted as governor of the Spanish Low Countries.

(2) **Count Ernst** (1580–1626), natural son of (1), was a soldier of fortune in the Thirty Years' War. Refused his father's possessions, the promised reward for his brilliant services in Hungary and elsewhere, he went over to the Protestant princes. After defending the Count-Palatine Frederick for a time (1618–20), he was driven by the disaster of the Weissenberg to retreat to the Palatinate, from which he carried on for two years a predatory war on the imperialists, defeating Tilly in 1622. He afterwards took service with the United Netherlands, beating the Spaniards at Fleurus (1622). At Richelieu's solicitation he raised an army of 12,000 men (mostly in England), but in 1626 he was crushed by Wallenstein at Dessau. Later, when marching to join Bethlen Gabor of Transylvania, he died near Sarajevo in Bosnia.

MANSFIELD, Earls of:

(1) **William Murray, 1st Earl** (1705–93), British judge, born at Perth, the fourth son of Viscount Stormont, from Westminster passed to Christ Church, Oxford, graduating B.A. in 1727. Called to the bar, he soon acquired an extensive practice; was appointed solicitor-general in 1742; entered the House of Commons as member for Boroughbridge; was appointed attorney-general in 1754; and became chief-justice of the King's Bench in 1756, a member of the cabinet, and Baron Mansfield. He was impartial as a judge, but his opinions were unpopular; Junius bitterly attacked him, and during the Gordon riots of 1780 his house was burned. Made earl in 1776, he resigned office in 1788. See Lives by Holliday (1797), Fifoot (1936).

(2) **David Murray, 2nd Earl** (1727–96), British statesman, held various diplomatic posts abroad, became a privy councillor in 1763, a secretary of state in 1779–82, and president of the council in 1783 and 1794–96.

MANSFIELD, Katherine, pen name of **Kathleen Middleton Murry,** *née* **Beauchamp** (1888–1923), English short-story writer, born in Wellington, New Zealand, in 1908 settled in Europe. She married John Middleton Murry (q.v.) in 1918, and died of tuberculosis at the Gurdiev settlement at Fontainebleau. Her sensitive style, which owed much to Chehov, has had a powerful influence on subsequent writers in the same genre. Her chief works are: *Bliss* (1920), *The Garden Party* (1922) and *Something Childish* (1924). Other publications are her

Journal (1927), *Letters* (1930), *Collected Short Stories* (1945) and *Letters to John Middleton Murry* (1951). See studies by A. Alpers (1954) and J. Middleton Murry (1959).

MANSON, (1) George (1850–76), Scottish watercolour painter, born in Edinburgh, in 1866 became a wood-engraver with Messrs W. & R. Chambers. In 1871 he devoted himself wholly to painting. See Memoir by J. M. Gray (1880).

(2) **Sir Patrick** (1844–1922), Scottish doctor, known as 'Mosquito Manson'—from his pioneer work with Ross in malaria research—was born in Aberdeenshire, practised medicine in the East, became medical adviser to the Colonial Office, and helped to found the London School of Tropical Medicine. See Life by P. Manson-Bahr (1962).

MANSTEIN, Fritz Erich von, *man'shtīn* (1887–), German general, became at the outset of World War II chief of staff to Rundstedt in the Polish campaign and later in France, where he was architect of Hitler's *Blitzkreig* invasion plan. In 1941 he was given command of an army corps on the eastern front and though not trained in armoured warfare handled his panzers with great resource in the Crimea. Given the unenviable task of pulling the chestnuts out of the fire after the disaster of Stalingrad, he contrived with slender resources to extricate the right wing in sufficient strength to stage a successful counter-attack at Kharkov, though he failed to relieve the sixth army, beleaguered through Paulus's blind obedience to Hitler's imbecilic 'stand fast' orders. After being captured in 1945 he was imprisoned as a war criminal but released in 1953. A strong advocate of fluid defence for preventing the enemy from exploiting an advantage, he embodied his theories and an account of his military career in his *Lost Victories* (Eng. trans. 1959).

MANSUR. See ALMANSUR.

MANTEGAZZA, Paolo, *man-te-gat'za* (1831–1910), Italian physiologist, born at Monza, practised medicine in Argentina and at Milan, and became professor in 1860 of Pathology at Pavia, in 1870 of Anthropology at Florence. He wrote largely on the physiology of pleasure, pain and love, on spontaneous generation, and on physiognomy, as well as books of travel and novels. See Memoir by Raynaudi (Milan 1894).

MANTEGNA, Andrea, *man-tayn'ya* (1431–1506), Italian painter, born in Vicenza in 1431, was the favourite pupil and adopted son of Squarcione, the tailor-painter; a precocious genius, he set up a studio of his own when only seventeen. Having married a sister of the Bellinis and quarrelled with Squarcione, he was in 1460 induced by Lodovico Gonzaga, Duke of Mantua, to settle in his city. There he remained, with the exception of a visit to Rome (1488–90) to paint a series of frescoes (now destroyed) for Pope Innocent VIII's private chapel in the Vatican, until his death. His greatest works at Mantua were nine tempera pictures representing the *Triumph of Caesar* (1482–92), acquired by Charles I, and now at Hampton Court. Mantegna was also engraver, architect, sculptor and poet. He did not aim at grace and beauty in his pictures—some of them are ugly; but his technical excellences greatly influenced Italian art. See books by Julia Cartwright (1881), Maud Cruttwell (1901), Kristeller (trans. Armstrong, 1901), W. G. Constable (1937) and E. Tietze-Conrat (1955).

MANTELL, Gideon Algernon (1790–1852), English palaeontologist, born at Lewes, practised as a doctor there and at Brighton, Clapham and London, wrote popular books, and did important work on Wealden fossils.

MANTEUFFEL, Edwin Hans Karl Freiherr von, *man'toy-fel* (1809–85), Russian field-marshal, born at Dresden of old Pomeranian family, was colonel of the Prussian guards by 1854. As commander of the Prussian troops in Sleswick he began the war with Austria in 1866, helped to reduce the Hanoverians to capitulation, and defeated the Bavarians in four battles. In 1870–71 he first commanded the army of the north, then in command of the army of the south drove Bourbaki and 80,000 men into Switzerland. As viceroy of Alsace-Lorraine (from 1879) he was very unpopular. See Life by Keck (1889).

MANUCCI, A. See ALDUS MANUTIUS.

MANUEL, name of two Byzantine emperors:

Manuel I, Comnenus (*c.* 1120–80), son of John II, during his reign (1143–80), attempted to restore the fortunes of the East Roman Empire, and was successful against the Turks until his defeat at Myriokephalon in 1176, which invalidated all his earlier successes and marked the beginning of the downfall of the empire.

Manuel II, Palaeologus (1350–1423), son of Johannes V, for much of his reign, which extended from 1391 to 1423, was besieged in Constantinople by the Turks. At one point he was relieved by Tamur the Tartar advancing into Asia Minor, but, being a scholar rather than a statesman, he failed to profit from this diversion and was overwhelmed.

MANUEL, *man'yoo-el*, kings of Portugal:

Manuel I, more often known as **Emanuel** (q.v.).

Manuel II, also **Manoel** (1889–1932), King of Portugal, born at Lisbon, on the assassination of his father King Carlos I and the Crown Prince Luis on February 1, 1908, became king, but was forced to abdicate at the revolution of October 3, 1910. He settled in England at Fulwell Park, Twickenham, where he died.

MANUEL, (1) Nikolaus, called Deutsch (1484–1530), Swiss poet, painter and reformer, was born and died at Bern. Beginning as a painter of stained glass, he changed over to orthodox media and produced biblical and mythological pictures in the Renaissance style, often showing the influence of Baldung in his tendency toward the macabre. He held several government offices, was a member of the Great Council, and wrote satirical verse. See works by Handeke (1889) and Mandach and Kögler (1940). His son, **Hans Rudolf** (1525–71), was also a painter.

(2) **Peter** (1931–58), Scottish criminal, perpetrator of at least eight of the most callous murders in the history of crime. Between September 1956 and January 1958,

in addition to committing a number of burglaries, he broke into the house of a Mr William Watt in Rutherglen and shot the three occupants dead, strangled and robbed a girl at Mount Vernon, robbed the house at Uddingston of a family named Smart, all three members of which he killed, and he shot dead a Newcastle taxi driver. He was also accused of battering to death Ann Kneilands at East Kilbride, but was acquitted through lack of evidence. His trial at Glasgow High Court was one of the most sensational in legal history. Having already successfully defended himself against a former charge, he clearly considered himself more than a match for the conventional forces of law and order, and arrogantly dismissed the eminent counsel appearing on his behalf. Conducting his case with considerable skill, he brought in a special defence plea giving alibis and attributing the Rutherglen murders to Watt, who had already suffered 67 days of imprisonment as a suspect. But he overreached himself, was found guilty of seven of the murders, and was hanged on June 19, 1958. The Newcastle shooting was later officially attributed to him by an inquest jury. See J. G. Wilson, *The Trial of Peter Manuel* (1959).

MANUZIO. See ALDUS MANUTIUS.

MANZONI, Alessandro (1785–1873), Italian novelist and poet, was nobly born at Milan, where he died. He published his first poems in 1806, married happily in 1810, and spent the next few years in writing sacred lyrics and a treatise on the religious basis of morality. But the work which gave Manzoni European fame is his historical novel, *I Promessi Sposi*, a Milanese story of the 17th century (1825–27), the most notable novel in Italian literature. Despite his Catholic devoutness, he was a strong advocate for a united Italy. His last years were darkened by the frequent shadow of death within his household. See Hoepli's edition of his complete works, including his letters (Milan 1913), and books on him by Graf (1898), De Sanctis (1922), B. Reynolds (1950) and A. Colquhoun (1954).

MAO TSE-TUNG, *mow'dze-doong'* (1893–), Chinese Communist leader, first chairman (1949) of the People's Republic of China, was born in Hunan, the son of a peasant farmer. Educated at Changsha, he went in 1918 to the university of Peking, where as a library assistant he studied the works of Marx and others and helped to found the Chinese Communist party. Thereafter he set up a Chinese Soviet Republic in S.E. China, defying the attacks of Chiang Kai-shek's forces until 1934, when he and his followers were obliged to uproot themselves and undertake an arduous and circuitous 'long march' to NW. China. From his headquarters in Yenan he resisted the Japanese, and on their collapse issued forth to shatter the Nationalist régime of Chiang Kai-shek and proclaim the People's Republic of China in Peking in September 1949. He resigned the chairmanship of the republic in January 1959, but continued as chairman of the party Politburo. He was conspicuously absent from the Moscow conference of Communist leaders (1960). Ideological differences over Khruschev's policy of peaceful coexistence became apparent. The Chinese were bitter over Khruschev's *volte face* over missiles on Cuba (1962) and Moscow gave no support to the Chinese in their border war (1962) with India. Chinese-Soviet talks in Moscow in 1963 proved in vain, each power canvassing support among other Communist parties. The Communism of Mao Tse-tung, with its emphasis on the peasants, though allied with that of Russia, is neither modelled on it nor dominated by it: it is set forth in his *New Democracy* (1940). His personal power was greatly reinforced by the Red Guard 'cultural revolution' in 1967 which eliminated the more liberal forces. See Life by R. Payne (1951), and studies by Schwartz (1951), J. Ch'ên (1965), and S. Schram (1967 ed.).

MAO-TUN, pseud. of **Shen Yen-ping** (1896–), Chinese author, born in Chekiang province, became a leading literary figure in Peking, where he was a founder member of the Literary Research Society. His military experiences in Chiang Kai-shek's Northern Expedition of 1926 provide colour for his famous trilogy *Shih* (1927–28). In Britain he is better known for his short stories, several of which have appeared in translation.

MAP, or Mapes, Walter (*c.* 1137–1209), Welsh poet and ecclesiastic, was born, of Welsh family, apparently in Herefordshire, studied at Paris, became a clerk of the royal household, went on a mission to Rome, and became canon of St Paul's and archdeacon of Oxford. He was certainly the author of the *De Nugis Curialium* (ed. M. R. James, 1915); probably reduced the Arthurian romances to their existing shape; and may have written some part of the Latin poems (see Wright's edition, 1841), in connection with which his name is best known. The *Confessio Goliae* is also attributed to him. See studies by Foster (1913) and Pauphilet (1921).

MAR, John Erskine, 6th or 11th Earl of (1675–1732), Scottish Jacobite, born at Alloa, began life as a Whig, and by his frequent change of sides earned the nickname of 'Bobbing Joan'. He headed the Jacobite rebellion of 1715, was defeated at Sheriffmuir, and died in exile at Aix-la-Chapelle. See his *Legacy*, published by the Scottish History Society in 1896. See the Earl of Crawford's *Earldom of Mar in Sunshine and Shade* (1882), and study by W. D. Simpson (1949).

MARAIS, Marin, *ma-ray* (1656–1728), French composer and viol player, was born and died in Paris. As a boy he was in the Sainte Chapelle choir, later becoming a bass violist in the Royal Band and in the orchestra of the Opera, of which he later became joint conductor. A pupil of Lully, he wrote several operas, the most famous of which was *Alcyone* (1705), but his posthumous and ever-increasing reputation is based on his music for the viol.

MARAT, Jean Paul, *ma-ra* (1743–93), French revolutionary politician, was born at Boudry near Neuchâtel. He studied medicine at Bordeaux, next went to Paris, Holland and London, and practised there with success. He was made brevet-physician to his guards by the Comte d'Artois, afterwards Charles X—

an office which he held till 1786. Meantime he continued work in optics and electricity, and wrote several scientific works. But now revolution was in the air, and Marat became a member of the Cordelier Club, and established his infamous paper, *L'ami du peuple*. His virulence provoked hatred; but it made him the darling of the scum of Paris, and placed great power in his hands. Twice at least he had to flee to London, and once he was forced to hide in the sewers of Paris. His misadventures increased his hatred of constituted authority, and on his head rests in great measure the guilt of the infamous September massacres. He was elected to the Convention as one of the deputies for Paris, but was one of the least influential and most unpopular men in the House. After the king's death his last energies were spent in a mortal struggle with the Girondins. But he was dying fast of a disease contracted in the sewers, and could only write sitting in his bath. There his destiny reached him through the knife of Charlotte Corday (q.v.), on the evening of July 13, 1793. His body was committed to the Panthéon with the greatest public honours, to be cast out fifteen months later amid popular execration. See Ch. Simond's *Autobiographie de Marat* (1909); his *Correspondance*, ed. by Vellay (1908); Bax's *Marat* (1900), Phipson's (1924); Lives by Chèvremont (1881), Cabanès (1890, 1911), L. Gottschalk (N.Y. 1927) and J. Shearing's *Angel of the Assassination* (1935).

MARATTI, Carlo (1625–1713), Italian painter, was born at Camerano, a leader of the 17th-century Baroque school. His chief works are in Rome, but the British Royal Collection contains a number of his drawings.

MARBECK, or Merbecke, John (d. *c.* 1585), English musician and theologian, organist of St George's Chapel, Windsor, was condemned to the stake in 1544 as a Reformer, but pardoned by Bishop Gardiner. In 1550 he published his famous *Boke of Common Praier Noted*, an adaptation of the plain chant to the first Prayer-book of Edward VI. He prepared the earliest concordance to the whole English Bible, and wrote several theological works.

MARC, Franz (1880–1916), German artist, born at Munich, studied at Munich and in Italy and France; with Kandinsky he founded the Blaue Reiter expressionist group in Munich in 1911. Most of his paintings were of animals (e.g. the famous *Tower of the Blue Horses*) portrayed in forceful colours, with a well-defined pictorial rhythm. He was killed at Verdun. See the monograph by A. J. Schardt (1936).

MARCANTONIO, or in full Marcantonio Raimondi (*c.* 1488–1534), Italian engraver, born at Bologna, was at first a goldsmith. At Rome, where he worked from 1510, he was chiefly engaged in engraving Raphael's works; and he is reckoned the best amongst the engravers of the great painter. The capture of Rome by the Constable Bourbon in 1527 drove him back to Bologna, where he seems to have died. See A. M. Hind's monograph (1912).

MARCEAU, François Séverin Desgraviers, *mar-sō* (1769–96), French general, born at Chartres, helped in 1792 to defend Veraun with a body of volunteers, and for his services with the republican army in La Vendée was made general of division. He commanded the right wing at Fleurus, and in 1796 the first division of Jourdan's army, investing Mainz, Mannheim and Coblenz. But while covering the French retreat at Altenkirchen he was shot, September 19, and died of his wound. His body was brought to the Panthéon in 1889. See Lives by Maze, Parfait, T. G. Johnson (1896), Chuquet's *Quatre Généraux de la Révolution* (1911–12) and study by G. Lecomte (Paris 1929).

MARCEL, Gabriel (1889–), French Christian Existentialist philosopher and author, born in Paris, lectured and taught from 1912, served in the Red Cross during World War I, and in his *Journal metaphysique* (1927; trans. 1947) and in the essay *Existence et Objectivité* (appended 1952) struggled to break from idealism to a closer understanding of actual 'existence'. Even the empiricist explanation of the universe through sensations is to obscure actual existence by treating one's own body as a 'third person'. Philosophical reflection should not abstract but get as close as possible to actual existence. Even God's existence cannot be arrived at intellectually but is bound up with our own ontological nature. *Être et Avoir* (1935), 'Being and Having' (trans. 1950), *The Philosophy of Existence* (trans. 1948), in which he criticizes the more undisciplined ethics of Sartre's Existentialism, and *Le Mystère de l'être* (1951), his Gifford Lectures at Aberdeen (1949–50), take his Existentialism further. In 1929 he became a Roman Catholic. See also his plays, *Un Homme de Dieu* (1929), *Le Chemin de Crête* (1936), *La Soif* (1938), *Croissez et multipliez* (1955), &c. He was awarded the Grand Prix de l'Académie française (1948). See also studies by E. Gilson (1947) and R. Troisfontaines, *De l'Existence à l'Être* (2 vols., Paris 1953).

MARCELLO, Benedetto (1686–1739), Italian composer, was a judge of the Venetian republic, and a member of the Council of Forty, and afterwards held offices at Pola and Brescia. As a composer he is remembered for his *Estro poetico armonico* (1724–27), an 8-volume collection of settings for 50 of the Psalms of David, for his oratorio *Le Quattro Stagioni* (1731), and for his keyboard and instrumental sonatas. He wrote the satirical *Il Teatro alla moda* (1720). See Lives by Busi (1884) and D'Angeli (Milan 1940). His brother **Alessandro** (*c.* 1684–*c.* 1750), philosopher and mathematician as well as composer, published a number of cantatas, sonatas and concertos under the pseudonym 'Eterico Stinfalico'.

MARCELLUS, (1) the name of two popes, the first martyred in 310; the second as Cardinal Marcello Cervini presided over the Council of Trent, was elected pope in 1555, but survived his elevation only three weeks. See study by G. B. Manucci (Siena 1921).

(2) **M. Claudius** (*c.* 268 B.C.–208 B.C.), Roman general, who, in his first consulship (222 B.C.) defeated the Insubrian Gauls, and slew their king, Britomartus or Virido-

marus, whose spoils he dedicated as *spolia opima*—the third and last time in Roman history. In the second Punic war he checked Hannibal at Nola (216). Again consul in 214, he conducted the siege of Syracuse, which yielded only in 212. In his fifth consulship, 208, he fell in a skirmish against Hannibal.

MARCH, *mark*, (1) **Auziàs** (1397–1459), Catalan poet, born in Valencia, was pioneer of the trend away from the lyricism of the troubadours towards a more metaphysical approach. Influenced by Italian models, he wrote chiefly on the themes of love and death. See study by Pagès (Paris 1912).

(2) **Francis Andrew,** LL.D. (1825–1911), American philologist, born at Millbury, Mass., graduated at Amherst 1845, and became known for his historical researches in English grammar. See book by R. N. Hart (Easton, Pa. 1907).

MARCHAND, Jean Baptiste, *mar-shã* (1863–1934), French soldier, joined the army at twenty, explored the White Nile, and caused a Franco-British crisis by hoisting the tricolor at Fashoda in 1898. As a general he distinguished himself in World War I. See Life by J. Delebecque (Paris 1936).

MARCHMONT. See HUME (6).

MARCION (*c.* 100–*c.* 165), early Christian heretic, a wealthy shipowner of Sinope in Pontus, about 140 repaired to Rome, and founded the semi-Gnostic Marcionites (144). See studies by A. Harnack (Leipzig 1924), E. S. Blackman (1948).

MARCONI, Guglielmo, Marchese (1874–1937), Italian inventor, was born at Bologna in 1874, his mother being Irish. He successfully experimented with wireless telegraphy in Italy and England and succeeded in sending signals across the Atlantic in 1901. He was awarded the Nobel prize in 1909 and took some part in Italian foreign affairs. See Lives by O. E. Dunlap (N.Y. 1937), S. Epstein and B. Williams (N.Y. 1943).

MARCO POLO. See POLO.

MARCUS AURELIUS ANTONINUS (121–180). See AURELIUS.

MARCUS AURELIUS ANTONINUS (176–217). See CARACALLA.

MARE, De La. See DE LA MARE.

MARENZIO, Luca (1560–99), Italian composer, born at Coccaglio near Brescia, court musician to Sigismund III of Poland, was a prolific writer of madrigals.

MAREY, Étienne Jules (1830–1903), French physiologist, born at Beaune, pioneered scientific cinematography with his studies (1887–1900) of animal movement. In the course of his researches he invented a number of improvements in camera design and succeeded in reducing exposure time to the region of 1/25,000 of a second for the purpose of photographing the flight of insects.

MARGARET, Saint (*c.* 1045–93), Scottish queen, born in Hungary, later came to England, but after the Norman Conquest with her mother, sister and her boy brother, Edgar the Atheling (q.v.), she fled from Northumberland to Scotland. Young, lovely, learned and pious, she won the heart of the Scottish king, Malcolm Canmore (q.v.), who next year wedded her at Dunfermline. She did much to civilize the northern realm, and still more to assimilate the old Celtic Church to the rest of Christendom. She built, too, a stately church at Dunfermline, and re-founded Iona. Innocent IV canonized her in 1251. See the Latin Life ascribed to her confessor Turgot (trans. by Forbes-Leith, 3rd ed. 1896), Samuel Cowan's *The Princess Margaret* (1911), Lucy Menzies's *St Margaret* (1925), and Life by A. Henderson-Howat (1948).

MARGARET (1353–1412), Queen of Denmark, Norway and Sweden, was the daughter of Waldemar IV of Denmark, and wife of Haakon VI of Norway and on the death of her father without male heirs in 1375, the Danish nobles offered her the crown in trust for her infant son Olaf (who died 1387). By Haakon's death in 1380 Margaret became ruler of Norway; and in 1388 the Swedish nobles, disgusted with their king, Albert of Mecklenburg, offered her his crown, whereupon she invaded Sweden, and took Albert prisoner. She got her grand-nephew Eric of Pomerania crowned king of the three Scandinavian kingdoms (1396), the power remaining in her own hands. In 1397 the Union of Calmar stipulated that the three kingdoms should remain for ever under one king, each retaining its laws. See Life by M. Hill (1899).

MARGARET OF ANJOU (1429–82), Queen of England, daughter of René of Anjou, in 1445 was married to Henry VI (q.v.) of England. Owing to his weak intellect she was the virtual sovereign; and the war of 1449, in which Normandy was lost, was laid by the English to her charge. In the Wars of the Roses, Margaret, after a brave struggle of nearly twenty years, was finally defeated at Tewkesbury (1471), and lay in the Tower four years, till ransomed by Louis XI. She then retired to France, and died at the castle of Dampierre near Saumur. See Lives by Mrs Hookham (1872) and J. J. Bagley (1948).

MARGARET OF AUSTRIA (1480–1530), regent of the Netherlands, daughter of Maximilian I, she married first the Infante Juan, then Philibert II of Savoy. From 1507 she proved a wise regent of the Netherlands. See works by C. Hare (1907), Tremayne (1908), M. Brucher (Lille 1927), H. Carton de Wiart (Paris 1935).

MARGARET OF NAVARRE (1492–1549), Queen of Navarre, in her youth known as Marguerite d'Angoulême, was the sister of Francis I of France. In 1509 she was married to the Duke of Alençon, who died in 1525; and in 1527 to Henri d'Albret, titular King of Navarre, to whom she bore Jeanne d'Albret, mother of the great Henry IV. She encouraged agriculture, the arts and learning, and sheltered religious reformers like Marot. Her writings include Letters (ed. by Génin, 1843), poems entitled *Les Marguerites de la marguerite des princesses* (1547; ed. by Frank, 1873), and especially the famous *Heptaméron* (1558; ed. by Leroux de Lincy, 5 vols. 1855; trans., with critical essay by Saintsbury, 1894) and modelled on Boccaccio. In 1895 were discovered two dramas, letters, dialogues, and *Le Navire* and *Les Prisons*, written in the last four years of her life, many of them in mental anguish (*Les Dernières poésies*, ed. by A. Lefranc, 1896). See the scholarly study by Pierre Jourda (Paris 1931); also *The Pearl of Princesses* by Williams (1916), and works by S. Putnam (1936), L. Febvre (1944) and Iongh (1954).

MARGARET OF PARMA (1522–86), regent of the Netherlands, natural daughter of Charles V, married in 1536 Alessandro de' Medici, and in 1538 Ottavio Farnese, Duke of Parma and Piacenza, to whom she bore Alessandro Farnese. From 1559 to 1567 she was regent of the Netherlands, masterful, able, a staunch Catholic. Her correspondence with Philip II was edited by Reiffenburg (1842) and also by Gachard (1867–1881). See Life by F. Rachfal (Monaco 1898).

MARGARET OF SCOTLAND (1424–44), Queen of France, a poetess, and the eldest daughter of James I, in 1436 married at Tours the Dauphin Louis (Louis XI), who hated and neglected her. See Jusserand's *English Essays* (1895) and a study by Barbé (1917).

MARGARET OF VALOIS (1553–1615), Queen of Navarre, daughter of Henry II and Catharine de' Medici, in 1572 became the first wife of Henry IV (q.v.) of France—a childless marriage, dissolved in 1599. See her *Mémoires* (trans. by Violet Fane, 1892) and Lives by Saint-Poncy (1887), J. H. Mariéjol (Paris 1928; Eng. trans. 1930) and M. Donnay (Paris 1946).

MARGARET ROSE, Princess (1930–), only sister of Queen Elizabeth II, was born at Glamis Castle, Scotland, on August 21, 1930, the second daughter of King George VI and Queen Elizabeth and the first scion of the Royal House in the direct line of succession to be born in Scotland for more than three centuries. A girl of great beauty and charm, her name was often linked in the newspapers with those of possible suitors. In 1955 she denied rumours of her possible marriage to Group-Captain Peter Townsend, whose previous marriage had been dissolved. In April 1958, as the representative of Queen Elizabeth, she officially inaugurated the first Parliament of the West Indian Federation. In May 1960 she married **Antony Armstrong-Jones** (1930–), a photographer, who was created Viscount Linley and Earl of Snowdon in October 1961. The former title devolved upon Princess Margaret's son, David Albert Charles, born on November 3, 1961. A second child, Sarah Frances Elizabeth, was born on May 1, 1964.

MARGARET TUDOR (1489–1541), Queen of Scotland, the eldest daughter of Henry VII, in 1503 married James IV (q.v.) of Scotland, in 1514 Archibald Douglas, Earl of Angus, and, having divorced him, in 1527 Henry Stewart, Lord Methven. She spent most of her life in a series of political intrigues. See vol. iv of Mrs Green's *Princesses of England*, and Life by M. Glenne (1952).

MARGGRAF, Andreas Sigismund (1709–82), German chemist, studied at Berlin, Strasbourg, Halle and Freiberg. In 1747 he discovered the sugar in sugar-beet and so prepared the way for the sugar-beet industry.

MARGUERITE D'ANGOULÊME. See MARGARET OF NAVARRE.

MARGUERITTE, Paul (1860–1918), and his brother **Victor** (1866–1942), born in Algeria, wrote in collaboration or separately novels, histories, &c., many dealing with the Franco-German war period, as the series *Une Époque* (1898–1904). See works by E. Pilon (Paris 1905), J. Guiree (Paris 1927, 1929).

MARHEINEKE, Philipp Konrad, *mahr-hī'nė-kė* (1780–1846), German Protestant theologian, born at Hildesheim, was professor of Theology at Berlin (1811–46) and represented orthodox Hegelianism. He wrote on dogmatics, Christian ethics, and the Reformation. See study by A. Weber (Strasbourg 1857).

MARIA CHRISTINA (1806–78), Queen of Spain, the daughter of Francis I, king of the Two Sicilies, and fourth wife of Ferdinand VII of Spain, was left by Ferdinand at his death regent for their daughter Isabella II. A Carlist war broke out, and in 1836 she was forced to grant a constitution; in 1840 she was driven to France, whence she returned in 1843. Her share in the schemes of Louis-Philippe as to the marriage of her daughters in 1846, and her reactionary policy, made her unpopular. In 1854 a revolution again drove her to France, where, except in 1864–68 (when she was in Spain), she afterwards lived. See E. B. D'Auvergne's *A Queen at Bay* (1910).

MARIA THERESA (1717–80), empress, daughter of the Emperor Charles VI, was born at Vienna, May 13, 1717. By the 'Pragmatic Sanction', for which the principal European powers became sureties, her father appointed her heir to his hereditary thrones. In 1736 she married Francis of Lorraine, afterwards Grand-duke of Tuscany; and at her father's death in 1740 she became Queen of Hungary and of Bohemia, and Archduchess of Austria. At her accession the chief European powers put forward claims to her dominions. The young queen was saved by the chivalrous fidelity of the Hungarians, supported by Britain. The War of the Austrian Succession (1741–48) was terminated by the Peace of Aix-la-Chapelle. She lost Silesia to Prussia, and some lands in Italy, but her rights were admitted and her husband was recognized as emperor. Maria Theresa instituted financial reforms, fostered agriculture, manufactures and commerce, and nearly doubled the national revenues, while decreasing taxation. Marshal Daun reorganized her armies; Kaunitz (q.v.) took charge of foreign affairs. But the loss of Silesia rankled in her mind; and, with France as an ally, she renewed the contest with the Prussian king. But the issue of the Seven Years' War (1756–1763) was to confirm Frederick in the possession of Silesia. After the peace she carried out a series of reforms; her son Joseph, after the death of her husband (1765), being associated with her in the government. She joined with Russia and Prussia in the first partition of Poland (1772), securing Galicia and Lodomeria; while from the Porte she obtained Bukovina (1777), and from Bavaria several districts. She died November 29, 1780. A woman of majestic figure and an undaunted spirit, she combined feminine tact with masculine energy; and not merely won the affection and even enthusiastic admiration of her subjects, but raised Austria from a wretched condition to a position of assured power. Although a zealous Roman Catholic, she sought to correct some of the worst abuses in the church. Of her ten surviving children, the eldest son, Joseph II, succeeded her; Leopold, Grand-duke of Tuscany, succeeded him as Leopold II; Ferdinand became Duke of Modena; and Marie Antoinette was married to Louis XVI of France. See Lives by Arneth (Vienna, 10 vols. 1863–79), J. F. Bright (1910), Mary M. Moffat (1911), C. L. Morris (1938); *Frederick the Great and Maria Theresa*, by the Duc de Broglie (trans. 1883); study by G. P. Gooch (1951); and other works under FREDERICK II.

MARIANA, Juan de (1536–1624), Spanish Jesuit historian, born at Talavera, taught in Jesuit colleges in Rome, Sicily and Paris. His last years of ill-health he spent in literary labour at Toledo. His invaluable *Historiae de Rebus Hispaniae* (1592) he afterwards continued down to the accession of Charles V in 1605; and his own Spanish translation (1601–1609) is a classic. His *Tractatus VII Theologici et Historici* (1609) roused the suspicion of the Inquisition. But his most celebrated work is the *De Rege et Regis Institutione* (1599), which answers affirmatively the question whether it be lawful to overthrow a tyrant, even if he is a lawful king. See study by J. Laurès (N.Y. 1928).

MARIANUS SCOTUS, (1) (*c.* 1028–83), Irish chronicler, was a Benedictine monk at Cologne (1052–58) and then a recluse at Fulda and at Mainz. His *Chronicon Universale*, from the creation to 1082, was printed in 1559, 1601 and 1706, but first correctly by Waitz in *Monumenta Germaniae*.

(2) (d. *c.* 1088), Irish abbot and calligrapher, came to Bamberg in 1067, became a Benedictine, was founder and abbot of the monastery of St Peter's at Ratisbon. He was a great calligraphist, copied the whole Bible repeatedly, and left commentaries on Paul's Epistles and on the Psalms.

MARIE AMÉLIE (1782–1866), queen of Louis-Philippe (q.v.), born at Caserta, the daughter of Ferdinand IV of Naples, she married Louis-Philippe in 1809. After the revolution of 1848 she lived with her husband at Claremont. See books by Imbert de St Amand (1891–94).

MARIE ANTOINETTE, Josephe Jeanne (1755–93), Queen of France, was born November 2, 1755, the fourth daughter of Maria Theresa and the Emperor Francis I; and was married to the Dauphin, afterwards Louis XVI, on May 16, 1770. Young and inexperienced, she aroused criticism by her extravagance and disregard for conventions, and on becoming queen (1774) she soon deepened the dislike of her subjects by her devotion to the interests of Austria, as well as by her opposition to all the measures devised by Turgot and Necker for relieving the financial distress of the country. The miseries of France became identified with her extravagance, and in the affair of the Diamond Necklace (1784–86) her guilt was taken for granted. She made herself a centre of opposition to all new ideas, and prompted the poor vacillating king into a retrograde policy to his own undoing. She was capable of strength rising to the heroic, and she possessed the power of inspiring enthusiasm. Amid the horrors of the march of women on Versailles (1789) she alone maintained her courage. But to the last she failed to understand the troublous times; and the indecision of Louis and his dread of civil war hampered her plans. She had an instinctive abhorrence of the liberal nobles like Lafayette and Mirabeau, but was at length prevailed on to make terms with Mirabeau (July 1790). But she was too independent frankly to follow his advice, and his death in April 1791 removed the last hope of saving the monarchy. Less than three months later occurred the fatal flight to the frontier, intercepted at Varennes. The storming of the Tuileries and slaughter of the brave Swiss guards, the trial and execution of the king (January 21, 1793), quickly followed, and soon she herself was sent to the Conciergerie like a common criminal (August 2, 1793). After eight weeks more of insult and brutality, the 'Widow Capet' was herself arraigned before the Revolutionary Tribunal. She bore herself with dignity and resignation. Her answers were short with the simplicity of truth. After two days and nights of questioning came the inevitable sentence, and on the same day, October 16, 1793, she died by the guillotine. See the Histories of the French Revolution, letters ed. by A. von Arneth and others (Paris 1865–91), Heidenstam (1913), Söderhjolm (1934). Among many lives the following are some of the most recent: S. Zweig (1933), C. Kunstler (Eng. trans. 1940), H. Belloc (7th ed. 1951), F. W. Kenyon (1956), A. Castelot (Eng. trans. 1957).

MARIE DE FRANCE (fl. *c.* 1160–90), French poetess, was born in Normandy but spent much of her life in England, where she wrote her *Lais* sometime before 1167 and her *Fables* sometime after 1170. She translated into French the *Tractatus de Purgatorio Sancti Patricii* (c. 1190) and her works contain many classical allusions. The *Lais*, her most important work, dedicated to 'a noble king', probably Henry II, comprise 14 romantic narratives in octosyllabic verse based on Celtic material. A landmark in French literature, they influenced a number of later writers. See edition with introduction by Ewert (1944), and study by Hoepffner (1935).

MARIE DE' MEDICI (1573–1642), daughter of Francis I, Grand-duke of Tuscany, was married to Henry IV of France in 1600, and gave birth to a son, afterwards Louis XIII, in 1601. She was an obstinate and passionate woman, greatly under the influence of favourites; and the murder of her husband (1610) did not greatly grieve her. She proved as worthless a regent (1610–17) as she had been a wife; and when (1617) young Louis XIII assumed royal power the queen-mother was confined to her own house. She made her submission to her son in 1619. Failing to win over Richelieu, she tried to undermine his influence with the king, failed, was imprisoned, but escaped to Brussels in 1631. Her last years were spent in utter destitution.

MARIE LOUISE (1791–1847), Empress of France, daughter of Francis I of Austria, was married to Napoleon in 1810 (after the divorce of Josephine), and in 1811 bore him a son, who was created King of Rome and who became Napoleon II. On Napoleon's abdication she returned to Austria, and was awarded the Duchy of Parma. In 1822 she contracted a morganatic marriage with Count von Neipperg. See Mrs Cuthell's *An Imperial Victim* (1911); works by Imbert de Saint-Amand (trans. 1886–91), Billard (trans. 1910), Méneval (1911); her *Correspondance* (1887); the *Mémoires* of Mme Durand (1885); Life by E. M. Oddie (1931).

MARIE LOUISE, full name **Francisca Josepha Louise Augusta Marie Helene Christina, Princess** (1872–1956), granddaughter of Queen Victoria, daughter of Prince Christian of Schleswig-Holstein and great-aunt of Queen Elizabeth II. In 1891 she married Prince Aribert of Anhalt, but the marriage was dissolved in 1900 by her father-in-law and the Princess returned to England, where she dedicated herself to social and charitable work. See *My Memories of Six Reigns* (1956).

MARIETTE PASHA, Auguste Édouard (1821–1881), Egyptian explorer, was born at Boulogne, where he was made professor in 1841. In 1849 he entered the Louvre, and in 1850 was dispatched to Egypt, where he brought to light important monuments and inscriptions in Memphis, Sakkara and Gizeh. In 1858 he was appointed keeper of monuments to the Egyptian government, and excavated the Sphinx, the temples of Dendera and Edfu, and made many other discoveries. He wrote various works and his *Itinéraire de la haute Égypte* was translated by his brother (*Monuments of Upper Egypt*, 1877). He was made a pasha in 1879. See his *Oeuvres diverses* (1904) with Life by Maspero.

MARIN, John (1872–1953), American artist, born in New Jersey, trained and worked as an architect before studying art in Pennsylvania, New York and Paris. Famous for his brilliant watercolour sketches of the New York and Maine regions and for his unusual seascapes, he exhibited annually in New York from 1909. His paintings are to be found in many European and American galleries.

MARINETTI, Emilio Filippo Tommaso (1876–1944), Italian poet and writer, born in Alexandria, studied in Paris and Genoa, and published the original Futurist manifesto in *Figaro* in 1909. In his writings he glorified war, the machine age, speed and 'dynamism', and in 1919 he became a Fascist. His publications include *Le Futurisme* (1911), *Teatro sintetico futuristo* (1916) and *Manifesti del Futurismo* (4 vols. 1920). He condemned all traditional forms of literature and art, and his ideas were applied to painting by Boccioni, Balla and others. See *Il Potea Marinetti e il Futurismo* by A. Viviani (Turin 1940).

MARINI, Giambattista (1569–1625), an Italian poet who was born and died at Naples, was ducal secretary at Turin, and wrote his best work, the *Adone* (1622) at the court of France. His florid hyperbole and overstrained imagery were copied by the Marinist school. See study by J. V. Mirollo (1965).

MARIO, Guiseppe (1810–83), Italian tenor, by birth **Don Giovanni de Candia** and son of a general, born at Cagliari, achieved a long series of operatic triumphs in Paris, London, St Petersburg and America. His wife was the famous singer Giulia Grisi. After his retirement he lost his fortune through disastrous speculations. See Pearse and Hird's *Romance of a Great Singer* (1910).

MARIOTTE, Edme (1620–84), French physicist, born in Burgundy, was prior of St Martin-sous-Beaune, and died at Paris. One of the earliest members of the Academy of Sciences, he wrote on percussion, air and its pressure, the movements of fluid bodies and of pendulums, colours, &c. What was for a long time on the Continent called Mariotte's Law was rather Boyle's Law.

MARIS, Dutch family of three brothers, all painters. (1) **Jakob** (1837–99), painter of landscape and genre, was born at The Hague, and studied there, at Antwerp, and 1866–71 in Paris, coming under the influence of Diaz, Corot and Millet. (2) **Matthijs** (1839–1917) and (3) **Willem** (1843–1910), were also famous See D. C. Thomson, *The Brothers Maris* ('Studio', 1907).

MARISCHAL. See KEITH (4).

MARITAIN, Jacques, *ma-ree-tī* (1882–), French Catholic philosopher, was professor at the Institut Catholique in Paris (1913–40) and subsequently at Toronto, and from 1948 at Princeton. He early abandoned Bergsonism for orthodox neo-Thomism and was converted to Roman Catholicism. His most thorough-going philosophical work is *Distinguer pour unir, ou Les degrés du savoir* (1932, trans. 1938), He is best known outside France for his numerous writings on art, politics and history, including *Creative Intuition in Art and Poetry* (1953) and *On the Philosophy of History* (1957), &c. He was French ambassador to the Holy See (1945–1948). See study by C. A. Fecher (1953).

MARIUS, (1) Gaius (157–86 B.C.), Roman general, served at Numantia (134), and in 119 was tribune. He served in Africa during the war against Jugurtha, and as consul ended it in 106. Meanwhile an immense horde of Cimbri and Teutons had burst into Gaul, and repeatedly defeated the Roman forces. Marius, consul for the second, third, fourth and fifth times (104–101), annihilated them after two years' fighting in a terrible two days' battle near Aix, in Provence, where 100,000 Teutons were slain; and turning to the Cimbri in north Italy, crushed them also near Vercellae (101). Marius was declared the saviour of the state, the third founder of Rome, and was made consul for the sixth time in 100. When Sulla as consul was entrusted with the conduct of the Mithridatic war, Marius, insanely jealous of his patrician rival, attempted to deprive him of the command, and a civil war began (88). Marius was soon forced to flee, and after frightful hardships and hairbreadth escapes made his way to Africa. Here he remained until a rising of his friends took place under Cinna. He then hurried back to Italy, and, with Cinna marched against Rome, which had to yield. Marius was delirious in his revenge upon the aristocracy; 4000 slaves carried on the work of murder for five days and nights. Marius and Cinna were elected consuls for the year 86, but Marius died a fortnight afterwards.

(2) (Ger. Mayr), **Simon** (1570–1624), German astronomer, a pupil of Tycho Brahe, in 1609 claimed to have discovered the four satellites of Jupiter independently of Galileo. He named them Io, Europa, Ganymede and Callisto, but other astronomers would not follow his example and merely numbered them, as they did not recognize his claim to discovery. He was one of the earliest users of a telescope and the first to observe by this means the Andromeda nebula (1612).

MARIVAUX, Pierre Carlet de Chamblain de, *ma-ree-vō* (1688–1763), born at Paris of a good Norman family, published *L'Homère travesti*, a burlesque of the *Iliad*, in 1716, and brought out his best comedy, *Le Jeu de l'amour et du hasard* in 1730. His famous romance, *La Vie de Marianne* (1731–41), he never concluded; it is marked by an affected 'precious' style—'Marivaudage'. His numerous comedies are the work of a clever analyst rather than a dramatist. His other romances, *Pharamond* and *Le Paysan parvenu*, are greatly inferior to *Marianne*. See works by Fleury (1881), Deschamps (1897), Green (1928), McKee (1959).

MARK, more fully, 'John, whose surname was Mark' (Acts, xii. 12, 25), is named by the oldest tradition as the author of the second canonical gospel. Mark accompanied Paul and Barnabas on their first missionary journey, but quitted them at Perga, was later reconciled with Paul, and, according to tradition, was the 'disciple and interpreter' of Peter in Rome. He is also said to have gone to Alexandria as preacher. In medieval art Mark is symbolized by the lion.

MARK ANTONY. See ANTONIUS.

MARKHAM, (1) Mrs. See PENROSE.

(2) **Sir Clements Robert** (1830–1916), English geographer, born at Stillingfleet near York, educated at Westminster, was in the navy 1844–51, and served in the Franklin search. He explored (1852–54) Peru, introduced (1860) cinchona culture from South America into India, and was geographer (1867–68) to the Abyssinian expedition. He wrote travel books and biographies, and edited the *Geographical Magazine* (1872–1878). He was made K.C.B. (1896). See Life (1917) by his brother, Sir Albert H. Markham (1841–1918), well-known Arctic voyager.

MARKIEVICZ, Constance Georgine, Countess, *mahr-kyay'vich* (1868–1927), Irish nationalist, daughter of Sir Henry Gore-Booth of County Sligo, married Count Casimir Markievicz, fought in the Easter Rebellion (1916) and was sentenced to death but reprieved. Elected the first British woman M.P. in 1918, she did not take her seat, but was a member of the Dail from 1923. See Life by S. O'Faoláin (1934).

MARKOVA, Dame Alicia, professional name of **Lilian Alivia Marks,** *mar-ko'fa* (1910–), English prima ballerina, born in London, after studying under Seraphine Astafieva, joined the Diaghilev company in 1924, and appeared for the Sadlers Wells Ballet company from 1933 to 1935. There followed a period of partnership with Anton Dolin, after which she joined the Ballet Russe de Monte Carlo and (1941–45) the Opera Ballet of New York Metropolitan Opera; then, after further collaboration with Dolin, she was from 1950 to 1952 prima ballerina of the Festival Ballet Company. She was created C.B.E. in 1958 and D.B.E. in 1963. See biography by H. Fisher (1964).

MARLBOROUGH, John Churchill, 1st Duke of (1650–1722), English general, born either May 26 or June 24 (according to different sources), the son of Sir Winston Churchill, an impoverished Devonshire Royalist. Young Churchill's first post was as page to the Duke of York. Handsome and attractive, the favour of the voluptuous Duchess of Cleveland enriched him with a *douceur* of £5000, and secured him an ensigncy in the Guards. Meritorious service in Tangier and with the British contingent under the Duke of Monmouth and Marshal Turenne in Holland, together with the influence of his cousin Arabella as York's mistress, combined to bring Churchill promotion to colonel. His prospects were even further enhanced by his clandestine marriage, in 1677, to the beautiful termagant, Sarah Jennings. In 1678 his discreet handling of a confidential mission to William of Orange led to his ennoblement as Baron Churchill of Eyemouth in Scotland (1682). In 1685 he faithfully completed the task of quelling the rebellion raised by his old comrade-in-arms, Monmouth; his reward being an English barony. But with the landing of the Prince of Orange his lingering fealty to an obviously moribund cause was not proof against the call of ambition, and he pledged his support to the cause of 'Dutch Billy'. The value of his defection was recognized by his elevation to the earldom of Marlborough. Yet by 1692, despite his brilliant service in William's Irish campaign, the suspicion that he was still sympathetic to the Jacobites brought him into temporary disfavour. It was not until the War of the Spanish Succession that the supreme command of the British forces was conferred on him by Queen Anne, with an annual stipend of £10,000. Marlborough's earlier activities were gravely hampered by the reluctance of the Dutch field deputies to commit their troops to action. But as the British Army gained in strength, the Duke could operate with greater impact and freedom. His splendidly organized march to the Danube brought him the invaluable co-operation of Prince Eugène of Savoy, and led to the victory of Donauworth and the costly but unequivocal triumph of Blenheim. Made a prince of the Holy Roman Empire, additional honours were showered upon the victor—the Garter, a dukedom, the master-generalship of the ordnance, and an estate and palatial residence at Woodstock, while Duchess Sarah flaunted it as groom of the stole, mistress of the robes, keeper of the privy purse, and the Queen's bosom friend. In the campaign of 1706 the military pretensions of Louis XIV were sharply rebuffed at Ramillies; while in 1708 Vendôme's attempt to recover Flanders led to his shattering defeat at Oudenarde and the surrender of Lille and Ghent. With superior man-power to call upon, the French recovered from their failure at Malplaquet of 1709; but in 1711 the manoeuvre by which Marlborough forced Villars' 'impregnable' *ne plus ultra* lines and went on to capture Bouchain, exhibited the hallmark of consummate generalship. But in England Harley and the Tories had been conspiring for a compromise peace—the Treaty of Utrecht, which sacrificed virtually all the objects for which the war had been fought—and for Marlborough's public overthrow. In this design Harley was inadvertently aided by the folly with which Sarah still sought to domineer over a queen who, wearying of being hectored, had transferred her favour to the Duchess's cousin, the subtle intriguante Abigail Masham. Charges were preferred against the Duke of having illicitly received some £63,000 in regular payments from the Army's bread contractors, and a deduction of 2½ per cent. from the pay of the foreign auxiliaries. Despite the fact that Marlborough proved conclusively that this was a perquisite regularly allowed to the commander-in-chief in Flanders to maintain his secret service fund, on December 31, 1711, the Duke was dismissed from all public employment. In appointing the Duke of Ormond as his successor, the Ministry proceeded to confirm him in the very perquisites it had previously declared to be illegal. Publicly reviled in England, for a time Marlborough sojourned in honoured retirement abroad. With the accession of George I the Duke was restored to his honours; his advice being freely sought at the time of the Jacobite uprising of 1715. He died on June 16, 1722; his obsequies in Westminster Abbey being attended by many loyal but humble veterans of his campaigns. Singularly sweet tempered and serene, Marlborough was a devoted husband and fond parent. His concern for the welfare of his troops was deep-rooted and unfailing; and having restored mobility to warfare, he exploited it with a skill amounting to genius. If, on occasion, he employed somewhat dubious means to secure his advancement, that was no more than the common practice of the times in which he lived. See Lives by Coxe (1819), Lord Wolseley (1894), Fortescue (1932), Belloc (1933) and W. S. Churchill (1933). **Sarah Jennings,** who was born in 1660, survived till October 1744. See studies by S. J. Reid (1914), Dobrée (1927), F. Chancellor (1932) and L. Kronenberger (1958).

For 3rd Duke, see SUNDERLAND (3).

MARLOWE, Christopher (1564–93), the greatest of Shakespeare's predecessors in English drama, was born, a shoemaker's son, at Canterbury. From the King's School there he was sent to Benet (now Corpus) College, Cambridge; proceeded B.A. in 1583; and commenced M.A. in 1587. His *Tamburlaine the Great*, in two parts, was first printed in 1590, and probably produced in 1587. In spite of its bombast and violence it is infinitely superior to any tragedy that had yet appeared on the English stage. Earlier dramatists had employed blank verse, but it had been stiff and ungainly, and Marlowe was the first to discover its strength and variety. *The Tragical History of Dr Faustus* was probably produced soon after *Tamburlaine*; the earliest edition is dated 1604. *Faustus* is rather a series of detached scenes than a finished drama; some of these scenes are evidently not by Marlowe; but the nobler scenes are marvellously impressive. *The Jew of Malta*, produced after 1588 and first published in 1633, is a very unequal play. The first two acts are conducted with masterly skill and vigour; but the last three are absurdly extravagant, degenerating into vulgar caricature. *Edward II*, produced about 1590, is the most mature of Marlowe's plays. It has not the magnificent poetry that we find in *Faustus* and in the first two acts of *The Jew of Malta*, but it is planned and executed with more firmness and solidity. The various characters are skilfully discriminated, and the action is never allowed to flag. Many critics have preferred it to Shakespeare's *Richard II*; it is certainly no whit inferior. *The Massacre at Paris*, the weakest of Marlowe's plays, has descended in a mutilated state. It was written after the assassination of Henry III of France (August 2, 1589), and was probably one of the latest plays. *The Tragedy of Dido* (1594), left probably in a fragmentary state by Marlowe and finished by Nash, is of slight value. Marlowe had doubtless a hand in the three parts of *Henry VI*, and probably in *Titus Andronicus*. A wild, shapeless tragedy, *Lust's Dominion* (1657), may have been adapted from one of Marlowe's lost plays. The unfinished poem, *Hero and Leander*, composed in heroic couplets of consummate beauty, was first published in 1598; a second edition, with Chapman's continuation, followed the same year. Shakespeare quoted in *As You Like It* the line, 'Who ever loved that loved not at first sight?' and feelingly apostrophized the poet as 'Dead Shepherd'. Marlowe's translations of Ovid's *Amores* and of the first book of Lucan's *Pharsalia* add nothing to his fame. The pastoral ditty, 'Come, live with me and be my love,' to which Sir Walter Raleigh wrote an Answer, was imitated, but not equalled, by Herrick, Donne and others. It was first printed in *The Passionate Pilgrim* (1599), without the fourth and sixth stanzas, with the author's name, 'C. Marlowe', subscribed. Another anthology, Allot's *England's Parnassus* (1600), preserves a fragment by Marlowe, beginning 'I walked along a stream for pureness rare'. Marlowe led an irregular life, mingled with the *canaille*, and was on the point of being arrested for disseminating atheistic opinions when, in May 1593, at the age of twenty-nine, he was fatally stabbed at Deptford in a tavern brawl. In tragedy he prepared the way for Shakespeare, on whose early work his influence is firmly stamped. See the editions by Dyce (1850 and 1858), Cunningham (1872), Havelock Ellis (best plays; 1887), Bullen (1888), Tucker-Brooke (1910) and Case (1930). See books by Ingram (1904), Hotson (1925), Ellis-Fermor (1927), Boas (1929, 1940), Eccles (1934), Bakeless (1938, 1942), Norman (1948), Steane (1964).

MARMION, (1) of Scrivelsby, the family

which long provided the hereditary champions at English coronations, came in with the Conqueror, but became extinct under Edward I.

(2) **Shackerley** (1603–39), minor dramatist, born at Aynho, Northants, squandered a fortune, and fought in the Low Countries. He left behind an epic, *Cupid and Psyche*, and three comedies, *Holland's Leaguer, A Fine Companion* and *The Antiquary*.

(3) **Simon** (1425–89), French miniaturist, born probably at Amiens, whose illuminations are the finest in 15th-century manuscript art.

MARMONT, Auguste Frédéric Louis Viesse de (1774–1852), Marshal of France, was born at Châtillon-sur-Seine, went with Napoleon to Italy, and fought at Lodi, in Egypt, and at Marengo. He was sent to Dalmatia in 1805, defeated the Russians there, and was made Duke of Ragusa. In 1809 he was entrusted at Wagram with the pursuit of the enemy, won the battle of Znaim, and earned a marshal's baton. He was next governor of the Illyrian provinces, and in 1811 succeeded Massena in Portugal. A severe wound at Salamanca compelled him to retire to France. In 1813 he fought at Lützen, Bautzen and Dresden, and maintained the contest in France in 1814 till further resistance was hopeless, when he concluded a truce with the Russians, which compelled Napoleon to abdicate, and earned Marmont from the Bonapartists the title of the traitor. The Bourbons loaded him with honours. At the Revolution of 1830 he endeavoured to reduce Paris to submission, and finally retreating with a few faithful battalions, conducted Charles X across the frontier. Thenceforward he resided chiefly in Vienna or in Venice, where he died. See his *Esprit des institutions militaires* (1845) and his *Mémoires* (9 vols. 1856–57).

MARMONTEL, Jean François (1723–99), French author, was born at Bort in the Limousin, and studied in a Jesuit college. Settling in Paris in 1745 by advice of Voltaire, he wrote successful tragedies and operas, and in 1753 got a secretaryship at Versailles through Madame de Pompadour. In the official journal, *Le Mercure*, now under his charge, he began his oft-translated *Contes moraux* (1761). Elected to the Academy in 1763, he became its secretary in 1783, as well as historiographer of France. His most celebrated work was *Bélisaire*, a dull and wordy political romance, containing a chapter on toleration which excited furious hostility. His uncritical *Éléments de littérature* (1787) consists of his contributions to the *Encyclopédie*. See his *Mémoires* (1805), Saintsbury's edition of the *Moral Tales* (1895) and study by Knauer (1936).

MARMORA, La. See La Marmora.

MARNIX, Philippe de, Baron de St Aldegonde (1538–98), Flemish statesman, born at Brussels, studied under Calvin and Beza at Geneva, and at home was active in the Reformation, and in 1566 in the revolt against Spain. An intimate friend of William of Orange, he represented him at the first meeting of the Estates of the United Provinces, held at Dort in 1572, and was sent on special missions to the courts of France and England. As burgomaster of Antwerp, he defended the city thirteen months against the Spaniards; but having then capitulated, he incurred so much ill-will that he retired from public life. He wrote the patriotic *Wilhelmus* song; the prose satire, *The Roman Beehive* (1569); a metrical translation of the Psalms (1580); and part of a prose translation of the Bible. See Lives in Dutch by Broes (1840), Frédéricq (1882), von Schelven (1939), and in French by Juste (1858).

MARO. See Virgil.

MAROCHETTI, Carlo, Baron, *ma-ro-ket'tee* (1805–67), sculptor, born at Turin and trained at Paris and in Rome, settled at Paris, and at the revolution of 1848 came to London, where he produced many fine statues (Queen Victoria, Coeur-de-Lion, &c.). He died at Passy.

MAROT, Clément, *ma-rō* (*c.* 1497–1544), French poet, born at Cahors, entered the service of the Princess Margaret, afterwards Queen of Navarre. He was wounded at the battle of Pavia in 1525, and soon after imprisoned on a charge of heresy, but liberated next spring. He made many enemies by his witty satires, and in 1535 fled first to the court of the Queen of Navarre, and later to that of the Duchess of Ferrara. He returned to Paris in 1536, and in 1538 began to translate the Psalms into French, which when sung to secular airs, helped to make the new views fashionable; but the part published in 1541 having been condemned by the Sorbonne, he had again to flee in 1543. He made his way to Geneva, but, finding Calvin's company uncongenial, went on to Turin, where he died. His poems consist of elegies, epistles, rondeaux, ballads, sonnets, madrigals, epigrams, nonsense verses and longer pieces; his special gift lay in badinage and graceful satire. Probably, like many of his friends, he had no very definite theological beliefs. See Life by Vitet (1868); Douen's *Clément Marot et le Psautier Huguenot* (1879), Plattard's *Marot, sa carrière poétique, son oeuvre* (1938), and Kinch, *La Poésie satirique de Clément Marot*.

MAROZIA (d. 938), a Roman lady of noble birth, but of infamous reputation, was thrice married, the mistress of Pope Sergius III, and mother of Pope John XI and grandmother of Pope John XII. She had influence enough to secure the deposition of Pope John X, her mother's lover, and the election of her own son, John XI. She died in prison at Rome.

MARQUAND, John Phillips (1893–1960), American writer, born at Wilmington, Del., known for his detective stories and social satires, some with an oriental background. His *The Late George Apley* (1937) won him the Pulitzer prize. See study by Hamburger (1953).

MARQUET, (Pierre) Albert, *mar-kay* (1875–1947), French artist, born at Bordeaux, studied under Gustave Moreau and was one of the original Fauves. After initial hardships, he became primarily an Impressionist landscape painter and travelled widely, painting many pictures of the Seine (e.g., the *Pont neuf*), Le Havre and Algiers in a cool restrained style. In his swift sketches he showed himself a master of line.

MARQUETTE, Jacques (1637–75), French Jesuit missionary, born at Laon, was sent in 1666 to North America, where he brought Christianity to the Ottawa Indians around Lake Superior and accompanied Jolliet on the expedition which discovered and explored the Mississippi (1673). See his account of the journey, and a Life by A. Repplier (1929).

MARQUIS, Don, properly **Donald Robert** (1878–1937), American writer, was a New York columnist, creator of comic characters (the Old Soak, Archy the cockroach, Mehitabel the cat, &c.) which he used as vehicles for social and political satire.

MARRIOTT, (1) Charles (1811–58), English divine who was associated with the Tractarian and Oxford movements, joint editor of *The Library of the Fathers*. See J. W. Burgon's *Twelve Good Men* (1888); B. C. Boulter's *Anglican Reformers* (1933).

(2) **Sir John Arthur Ransome** (1859–1945), English historian and educationist, was educated at Oxford, where he later administered successfully for twenty-five years the University Extension delegacy. From 1917 to 1929 he was a member of parliament, and was knighted in 1924. He was an expert on the Eastern Question, modern European history and the British Empire, on which subjects he wrote extensively.

MARRYAT, (1) Florence (1838–99), English novelist, daughter of (2), was successively Mrs Ross Church and Mrs Lean, was born at Brighton, and from 1865 published about eighty novels, besides a drama and many articles in periodicals. She edited *London Society* (1872–76). See H. C. Black's *Notable Women Authors* (1893).

(2) **Frederick** (1792–1848), English naval officer and novelist, father of (1), the son of an M.P., in 1806 sailed as midshipman under Lord Cochrane. After service in the West Indies, he had command of a sloop cruising off St Helena to guard against the escape of Napoleon (1820–21); he also did good work in suppressing the Channel smugglers, and some hard fighting in Burmese rivers. On his return to England (1826) he was made C.B., and was given the command of the *Ariadne* (1828). He resigned in 1830, and thenceforth led the life of a man of letters. He was the author of a series of novels on sea life of which the best known are *Frank Mildmay* (1829), *Peter Simple* (1833), *Jacob Faithful* (1834) and *Mr Midshipman Easy* (1834). In 1837 Marryat set out for a tour through the United States, where he wrote *The Phantom Ship* (1839) and a drama, *The Ocean Waif*. He received £1200 for *Mr Midshipman Easy* and £1600 for his *Diary in America* (1839), but was extravagant and unlucky in his speculations, and at last was financially embarrassed. *Poor Jack*, *Masterman Ready*, *The Poacher* and *Percival Keene* appeared before he settled (1843) on his small farm of Langham, Norfolk, where he spent his days in farming and in writing stories for children. He died at Langham, August 9, 1848. For improvements in signalling, &c., he had been made F.R.S. (1819) and a member of the Legion of Honour (1833). As a writer of sea stories Marryat has no superior; his sea fights, his chases and cutting-out expeditions, are told with irresistible gusto. See *Collected Novels* (26 vols. 1929–30), the *Life and Letters* by his daughter (1872) and Lives by D. Hannay (1889), C. Lloyd (1939), O. Warner (1953).

MARS, Anne Françoise Boutet Monvel (1779–1847), was a leading French actress at the Comédie-Française from 1799, excelling in the plays of Molière and Beaumarchais. She retired in 1841. See *Mémoires* (2 vols. 1849) and *Confidences* (3 vols. 1855).

MARSCHNER, Heinrich (1795–1861), German operatic composer, born at Zittau, successively music director at Dresden, Leipzig and Hanover, is remembered mainly for his opera *Hans Heiling*. See Lives by G. Fischer (Hanover 1918) and G. Hausswald (Dresden 1938).

MARSH, (1) George Perkins (1801–82), American diplomatist and philologist, was born in 1801 at Woodstock, Vermont; studied law; was elected to congress in 1842; and was U.S. minister to Turkey (1849–53) and Italy (1861–82). He was made LL.D. of Harvard in 1859. He died at Vallombrosa in Italy, July 23, 1882. He wrote *Lectures on the English Language* (1861), *Origin and History of English* (1862), *Man and Nature* (1864; largely recast, 1874), &c. See Life by his widow (1888).

(2) **James** (1789–1846), English chemist, expert on poisons, worked at the Royal Arsenal, Woolwich, and assisted Faraday at the Military Academy for a payment of thirty shillings a week, thereby leaving his widow and family in straitened circumstances. He invented the standard test for arsenic which has been given his name.

(3) **Othniel Charles** (1831–99), American palaeontologist, born at Lockport, N.Y., October 29, 1831, studied at Yale, at New Haven, and in Germany, and became first professor of Palaeontology at Yale 1866. He discovered (mainly in the Rocky Mountains) over a thousand species of extinct American vertebrates, and described them in monographs (published by government) on *Odontornithes* (1880), *Dinocerata* (1884), *Sauropoda* (1888), &c. He died March 18, 1899. See Life by C. M. Le Vene (1940).

MARSHAL, William, 1st Earl of Pembroke and Strigul (*c.* 1146–1219), English knight, regent of England (1216–19), a nephew of the Earl of Salisbury, won a military reputation fighting the French and in 1170 was appointed tutor to the young prince Henry. After displaying his knightly prowess in Europe, he supported Henry against Richard Coeur de Lion and at his dying behest went on a crusade to the Holy Land. Pardoned by Richard, who recognized his worth, he was given in 1189 the hand of the heiress of Strongbow (q.v.), which brought him his earldom. He was appointed a justiciar and shared the marshalcy of England with his brother John until the latter's death gave him full office. He saw further fighting in Normandy in 1196–99, and after Richard had been mortally wounded he supported the new king, John, but was shabbily treated by him and spent the years 1207–12 in Ireland. When John's troubles with the pope and with his barons began to mount, however, his loyalty asserted itself, and he returned to become the king's chief adviser. After John's death in 1216 he was by common consent appointed regent for the nine-year-old Henry III, and as such concluded a peace treaty with the French. He died at Caversham, having served in the reigns of four monarchs with unswerving fidelity.

MARSHALL, (1) Alfred (1842–1924), English economist, born in London, and educated at Merchant Taylors' and St John's, Cambridge, became a fellow (1865), principal of University College, Bristol (1877), lecturer on Political Economy at Balliol (1883) and professor of Political Economy at Cambridge (1885–1908). Of his works, his *Principles of Economics* (1890) is still a standard text-book, containing his concept of 'time analysis' and other contributions to the science. See Pigou's study (1926), and his wife's autobiography, *What I remember* (1951).

(2) General George Catlett (1880–1959), American soldier and statesman, born at Uniontown, Pa., was educated at the Virginia Military Institute, and commissioned in 1901. He rose to the highest rank and as chief of staff (1939–45) he directed the U.S. Army throughout the second World War. After two years in China as special representative of the president he became secretary of state (1947–49) and originated the Marshall Aid plan for the post-war reconstruction of Europe (E.R.P.). He was awarded the Nobel Peace Prize in 1953. See *Speeches* ed. H. A. De Weerd (1945).

(3) John (1755–1835), American judge, born in Virginia, studied law, but served 1775–79 in the army. He rose in his profession, in 1788 was elected to the state convention and in 1799 to Congress. In 1800–01 he was secretary of state; and from 1801 he was chief-justice of the United States. His decisions are a standard authority on constitutional law; a selection was published at Boston in 1839. He wrote a Life of Washington (1807; new ed. 1892). See monograph by Magruder (1885) and Lives by A. J. Beveridge (1916), D. Loth (1949).

(4) William Calder (1813–94), Scottish sculptor, was born in Edinburgh, and trained under Chantrey. He exhibited at the Royal Academy, becoming A.R.S.A. 1842 and R.A. 1852. As well as memorial statues, busts, &c., he did the group *Agriculture* on the Albert Memorial.

MARSHMAN, Joshua (1768–1837), English missionary and orientalist, born at Westbury, Leigh, Wilts, had been a bookseller's apprentice, a weaver and a schoolmaster, when in 1799 he went as a Baptist missionary to Serampur, where he founded a college and translated the Bible into various dialects.—His son, **John Clark** (1794–1877), assisted his father in his work and later made much by publishing, and spent much on native education, returning to England in 1852. He wrote *History of India* (1842; 5th ed. 1860), *Life and Times of the Serampore Missionaries* (1859), &c.

MARSTON, (1) John (1576–1634), English dramatist and satirist, a son of John Marston of Gayton in Salop, by his wife, daughter of an Italian surgeon, was born at Wardington, Oxfordshire, and studied at Brasenose, Oxford. Except *The Insatiate Countess* (which is of doubtful authorship), all his plays were published between 1602 and 1607. He then gave up play-writing, took orders in 1609, and in 1616–31 held the living of Christ Church, Hampshire. He died in London. His first work was *The Metamorphosis of Pygmalion's Image: and Certain Satires* (1598). The licentious poem was condemned by Archbishop Whitgift. Another series of uncouth and obscure satires, *The Scourge of Villany*, appeared in the same year. Two gloomy and ill-constructed tragedies, *Antonio and Mellida* and *Antonio's Revenge*, were published in 1602; in them passages of striking power stand out above the general mediocrity. *The Malcontent* (1604), more skilfully constructed, was dedicated to Ben Jonson, between whom and Marston there were many quarrels and reconciliations. *Eastward Ho* (1605), written in conjunction with Chapman and Jonson, is far more genial than any comedy that Marston wrote single-handed. For some reflections on the Scots the authors were imprisoned (1604). Other plays include *Parasitaster, or the Fawn* (1606), *Sophonisba* (1606) and *What You Will* (1607). The rich and graceful poetry scattered through *The Insatiate Countess* (1613) is unlike anything that we find in Marston's undoubted works. Probably Marston left the play unfinished when he took orders, and William Barksteed took it in hand. See editions by Halliwell-Phillipps (1856), Bullen (1887) and Harvey Wood (1934 *et seq.*), and works by M. S. Allen (Columbus 1920) and T. S. Eliot (in *Elizabethan Essays* 1934).

(2) John Westland (1819–90), English dramatic poet, father of (3), born at Boston, gave up law for literature; and in 1842 his *Patrician's Daughter* was brought out at Drury Lane by Macready. It was the most successful of more than a dozen plays, all Sheridan-Knowlesian, and all forgotten. He wrote a novel (1860), a good book on *Our Recent Actors* (1888), and a mass of poetic criticism. He died in London, January 5. See his Collected Works (2 vols. 1876).

(3) Philip Bourke (1850–87), English poet, son of (2), was born in London, became blind at the age of three. He was grief-stricken at the death of his fiancée and then of his sisters, and his friends, Oliver Madox Brown and Rossetti. He is remembered for his friendship with Rossetti, Watts-Dunton and Swinburne rather than for his sonnets and lyrics—although a few of these are exquisite. *Songtide, All in All* and *Wind Voices* were the three volumes of poetry he published between 1870 and 1883; to a posthumous collection of his short stories (1887) is prefixed a memoir by W. Sharp. See Life by C. C. Osborne (1926).

MARTEL, (1) Charles. See CHARLES MARTEL.

(2) Sir Giffard Le Quesne (1889–1958), British soldier, during World War I aided in the development of the first tanks, and in 1925 was responsible for the construction of the first one-man tank. In 1940 he commanded the Royal Armoured Corps and in 1943 headed the British military mission in Moscow.

MARTEL DE JANVILLE, Comtesse de. See GYP.

MARTEN, Harry (1602–80), English regicide, elder son of the civilian, Sir Henry Marten (*c.* 1562–1641), was born and educated at Oxford. He was a prominent member of the Long Parliament, but was expelled from it 1643–46 as an extremist, and fought meantime in the great Rebellion. He sat on Charles I's trial, led an immoral life and fell into debt, had his life spared at the Restoration, but died still a prisoner at Chepstow. See Forster's *Lives of British Statesmen* (vol. iv, 1837).

MARTENSEN, Hans Lassen (1808–84), Danish theologian, Metropolitan of Denmark, became professor of Philosophy at Copenhagen, and in 1845 court-preacher also. In 1840 he published a monograph on *Meister Eckhart*, and in 1849 the conservative Lutheran *Christian Dogmatics* (trans. 1866). This gained him in 1854 the primacy, but provoked a powerful attack by Kierkegaard. His *Christian Ethics* (1871–78; trans. 1873–1892) made his influence more dominant than ever. See his *Autobiography* (1883), and Life by S. Arildsen (Copenhagen 1932).

MARTIAL, Marcus Valerius Martialis (*c.* 40–*c.* A.D. 104), Latin poet and epigrammatist, born in Spain, came to Rome in A.D. 64 and became a client of the influential Spanish house of the Senecas, through which he found a patron in L. Calpurnius Piso. The tragic failure of the Pisonian plot lost Martial his warmest friends—Lucan and Seneca. He courted imperial and senatorial patronage by his *vers de circonstance*. When (A.D. 80) Titus dedicated the Colosseum, Martial's epigrams brought him equestrian rank; his flattery of Domitian was gross and venal. Advancing years having bereft him of Domitian and his friends of the palace, in a fit of home-sickness he borrowed from his admirer, the younger Pliny, the means of returning to Bilbilis, where he spent the rest of his life. Much of his best work is his least pure. If, however, we excise 150 epigrams from the 1172 of the first twelve books, his writings are free from licentiousness. His genius and skill in verse are hard to overestimate. See the editions of Martial by Friedländer (1886), Lindsay (1902) and Ker (with trans. 1919–20).

MARTIN, St (*c.* 316–*c.* 400), Bishop of Tours, was born, a military tribune's son, at Sabaria in Pannonia, was educated at Pavia, and served in the army under Constantine and Julian. He became a disciple of Hilary of Poitiers, and, returning to Pannonia, was so persecuted by the Arian party that he removed first to Italy, then to Gaul, where about 360 he founded a monastery near Poitiers; but in 371–72 he was drawn by force from his retreat, and made Bishop of Tours. The fame of his sanctity and his repute as a worker of miracles attracted crowds of visitants; and to avoid distraction he established the monastery of Marmoutier near Tours, in which he himself resided. His Life by his contemporary, Sulpicius Severus, teems with miraculous legends. See Cazenove's *St Hilary and St Martin* (1883), Scullard's *Martin of Tours* (1891); Life by P. Monceaux (Paris 1926, Eng. trans. 1928).

MARTIN, the name of five popes.

St Martin I, a Tuscan, became pope in 649, held the first Lateran Council (against the Monothelites), and was banished by Constans II in 654 to the Crimea, where he died in 655.

Martin II, properly Marinus I, born at Gallese, was pope 883–884.

Martin III, properly Marinus II, was pope in 942–946.

Martin IV, Simon de Brie (*c.* 1210–85), born at Montpensier in Touraine, elected pope in 1281, was a mere tool of Charles of Anjou.

Martin V, Oddone Colonna (1368–1431), the pontiff in whose election the Western Schism was finally extinguished, was elected in 1417 during the Council of Constance, over whose remaining sessions he presided. He died suddenly in 1431, just after the opening of the Council of Basel. See work by K. A. Finke (Berlin 1938).

MARTIN, (1) Archer John Porter (1910–), British biochemist, with R. L. M. Synge developed the technique of paper chromatography now widely used in chemistry for purposes of analysis and shared the Nobel prize for chemistry (1952).

(2) **Bon Louis Henri**, *mar-tī* (1810–83), French historian, was born at St Quentin, February 20, 1810, and educated as a notary. He joined Paul Lacroix, the 'Bibliophile Jacob', in his vast project for a History of France in 48 vols. of extracts from old histories and chronicles, published the first volume in 1833, and henceforward toiled alone at the work, which was completed on a reduced scale in 1836, as the great *Histoire de France* (15 vols.). Martin was chosen deputy for Aisne in 1871, senator in 1876 and a member of the Academy in 1878. See Life by Hanotaux (1885), Mulot's *Souvenirs intimes* (1885), and Jules Simon's *Mignet, Michelet, Henri Martin* (1889).

(3) **Frank**, *mar-tī* (1890–), Swiss composer and pianist, born in Geneva, studied at Geneva Conservatoire and in 1928 was appointed professor at the Jacques-Dalcroze Institute in Geneva. His works are marked by refinement and precision of style, and include the oratorios *Golgotha* and *In Terra Pax*, a Mass and the cantata *Le Vin herbé*, based upon the legend of Tristan and Isolde, as well as incidental music and works for orchestra and chamber combinations.

(4) **John** (1789–1854), English painter, brother of (5), was born at Haydon Bridge near Hexham. After a struggling youth in London (from 1806) as an heraldic and enamel painter, he in 1812 exhibited at the Royal Academy the first of his sixteen 'sublime' works, displaying 'immeasurable spaces, innumerable multitudes, and gorgeous prodigies of architecture and landscape'. Their memory is kept lurid by the coloured engravings of the *Fall of Babylon* (1819), *Belshazzar's Feast* (1821), *The Deluge* (1826), &c. See Lives by M. L. Hendered (1923) and

T. Balston (1948), and study by J. Seznec (1964).

(5) **Jonathan** (1782–1838), brother of (4), after serving in the Navy became mentally deranged, developed extremist religious ideas and eventually fired York Minster in 1829. The rest of his life was spent in an asylum. See his *Autobiography* (1826 and later edns.).

(6) **Martin** (d. 1719), Scottish author and traveller, was a Skye factor, who took his M.D. at Leyden, and died in London in 1719. He wrote *Voyage to St Kilda* (1698) and *A Description of the Western Isles of Scotland* (1703) which aroused Dr Johnson's interest in the country.

(7) **Richard** (1754–1834), Irish lawyer and humanitarian, dubbed 'Humanity Martin' by George IV, who was his friend, was born at Dublin and educated at Harrow and Trinity, Cambridge. As M.P. for Galway (1801–26) he sponsored in 1822 a bill to make illegal the cruel treatment of cattle, the first legislation of its kind. Through his efforts the R.S.P.C.A. was formed. See Life by W. Pain (1925).

(8) **Sir Theodore** (1816–1909), Scottish man of letters, born in Edinburgh and educated there, in 1846 settled in London, and became a parliamentary solicitor. The well-known *Bon Gaultier Ballads* (1855), written in conjunction with Aytoun, were followed by verse translations from Goethe, Horace, Catullus, Dante and Heine. He was requested by Queen Victoria to write the life of Prince Albert (5 vols. 1874–80) and also wrote Lives of Aytoun (1867), and Lord Lyndhurst (1883), and the Princess Alice (1885). His wife, **Helen Faucit** (1820–98), was a well-known actress, noted for her interpretations of Shakespeare's heroines. See Life by her husband (1900).

(9) **Violet Florence**, pseud. **Martin Ross** (1862–1915), Irish writer, born in County Galway, is known chiefly for a series of novels written in collaboration with her cousin **Edith Oenone Somerville** (1858–1949), including *An Irish Cousin* (1889), *Some Experiences of an Irish R.M.* (1908); also travel books about the Irish countryside.

MARTIN DU GARD, Roger, *mar-tī dü gahr* (1881–1958), French novelist, born at Neuilly, known for his eight-novel series *Les Thibault* (1922–40) dealing with family life during the first decades of the present century. Author also of several plays, he was awarded the Nobel prize in 1937. See study by H. C. Rice (1941).

MARTINEAU, (1) Harriet (1802–76), English writer, sister of (2), born at Norwich, June 12, in 1821 wrote her first article for the (Unitarian) *Monthly Repository*, and next produced *Devotional Exercises* and short stories about machinery and wages. In 1829 the failure of the house in which she, her mother and sisters had placed their money obliged her to earn her living. In 1832 she became a successful authoress through *Illustrations of Political Economy* (repeatedly refused by publishers), and settled in London. After a visit to America (1834–36) she published *Society in America* and a novel, *Deerbrook*, in 1839. From 1839 to 1844 she was an invalid at Tynemouth but recovered through mesmerism (her subsequent belief in which alienated many friends), and fixed her abode at Ambleside in 1845, the year of *Forest and Game-law Tales*; after visiting Egypt and Palestine she issued *Eastern Life* (1848). In 1851, in conjunction with Mr H. G. Atkinson, she published *Letters on the Laws of Man's Social Nature* (so agnostic as to give much offence); and in 1853 she translated and condensed Comte's *Philosophie positive*. She also wrote much for the daily and weekly press and the larger reviews. Always delicate, and after 1820 very deaf, she died June 27, 1876, and was buried at Birmingham. See her *Autobiography* (1877), and Lives by T. Bosanquet (1927), J. C. Nevill (1943) and R. K. Webb (1960).

(2) **James** (1805–1900), English theologian, brother of (1), was born at Norwich, April 21. He was educated at the grammar-school there and under Dr Lant Carpenter at Bristol, and had been a Unitarian minister at Dublin and Liverpool, when in 1841 he was appointed professor of Mental and Moral Philosophy at Manchester New College. He removed to London in 1857, after that institution had been transferred thither, becoming also a pastor in Little Portland Street Chapel. He was principal of the college 1869–85. One of the profoundest thinkers and most effective writers of his day, he wrote *Endeavours after the Christian Life* (1843–47), *A Study of Spinoza* (1882), *Types of Ethical Theory* (1885), *A Study of Religion* (1888), *The Seat of Authority in Religion* (1890), &c. He died January 11, 1900. See his *Life and Letters* by Drummond and Upton (1902), and Carpenter's study (1905).

MARTINET, Jean (d. 1672), French officer, won renown as a military engineer and tactician (he devised forms of battle manœuvre, pontoon bridges, and a type of copper assault boat used in Louis XIV's Dutch campaign), but notoriety for his stringent and brutal forms of discipline.

MARTÍNEZ DE CAMPOS, Arsenio, *mar-tee'nayth* (1831–1900), Spanish general, put down one Cuban rebellion in 1877, but failing to end another, was recalled (1896).

MARTÍNEZ RUIZ, José. See AZORÍN.

MARTÍNEZ SIERRA, Gregorio (1881–1947), Spanish novelist and dramatist. A theatre manager and an original and creative producer as well as publisher, he was also a prolific writer. His plays *The Cradle Song* (Eng. trans. 1917), *The Kingdom of God* (Eng. trans. 1923) and *The Romantic Young Lady* (Eng. trans. 1923) were popular in England and America. Much of his writing was done in collaboration with his wife Maria, whose feminist opinions find expression in some of the plays.

MARTINI, (1) Frederick (1832–97), Swiss engineer, a Hungarian by birth and Swiss by adoption, served as engineer officer in the Austrian army in the Italian war of 1859, and establishing machine-works at Frauenfeld in Switzerland, invented the breech-action, which, with the Henry barrel, constituted the Martini-Henry rifle (1871).

(2), or **Memmi, Simone** (*c.* 1284–1344), Italian painter, born at Siena, was a pupil of Duccio and the most important artist of the

14th-century Sienese school, notable for his grace of line and exquisite colour. He worked at Assisi from 1333 to 1339 and at the Papal court at Avignon from then until 1344. His *Annunciation* is in the Uffizi Gallery. See *Simone Martini et les peintures de son école* (1920) by V. R. S. van Marle, and study by G. Paccagnini (trans. 1957).

MARTINU, Bohuslav, *mahr'ti-noo* (1890–1959), Czech composer, born at Polička. The son of a cobbler, Martinu began to compose at the age of ten, and in 1906 he was sent by a group of fellow-townsmen to Prague Conservatoire, where disciplinary regulations and the routine course of studies irritated him. Expelled from the Conservatoire, he played the violin in the Czech Philharmonic Orchestra, and in 1920 attracted attention with his ballet *Ishtar*. Readmitted to the Conservatoire, he studied under Suk until interest in the French Impressionist composers led him to work in Paris until 1941, when he escaped from Occupied France to America, where he produced a number of important works, including his first symphony, commissioned by Koussevitsky for the Boston Symphony Orchestra in 1942. In 1945 he returned to Prague as professor of Composition at the Conservatoire. A prolific composer, he ranges from orchestral works in 18th-century style, including a harpsichord concerto, to modern programme pieces evoked by unusual stimuli such as football (*Half Time*) or aeroplanes (*Thunderbolt P. 47*). His operas include the miniature *Comedy on a Bridge*, written for radio and successfully adapted for television and stage.

MARTIUS, Carl Friedrich Philipp von, *mahr'-tsee-oos* (1794–1868), German naturalist, born at Erlangen, studied medicine there, and in 1817–20 made important researches in Brazil, described in books on the journey and on the plants, aborigines and languages of the country. He was professor of Botany (1826–64) at Munich, where he died. See Lives by Schramm (2 vols. Leipzig 1869) and Meissner (Munich 1869).

MARTYN, Henry (1781–1812), English missionary, born at Truro, February 18, graduated from St John's College, Cambridge, as senior wrangler and first Smith's prizeman in 1801, and in 1802 became a fellow. Through the influence of Charles Simeon he sailed in 1805 for India as a chaplain under the Company. He translated the New Testament into Hindustani, Hindi and Persian, as well as the Prayer-book into Hindustani and the Psalms into Persian. After a missionary journey in Persia, he died of fever at Tokat in Asia Minor, October 16, 1812. See *Journals and Letters* (1837), and Lives by Sargent (1819; new ed. 1885), G. Smith (1892), and C. E. Padwick (1922).

MARTYR, Peter. See PETER.

MARVELL, Andrew (1621–78), English poet, born March 31, 1621, at Winestead rectory, S.E. Yorkshire, and educated at Hull and Trinity College, Cambridge, travelled (1642–1646) in Holland, France, Italy and Spain. After a period as tutor to Lord Fairfax's daughter, when he wrote his pastoral and garden poems, he was appointed tutor to Cromwell's ward, William Dutton; and in 1657 he became Milton's assistant. In January 1659 he took his seat in Richard Cromwell's parliament as member for Hull, for which he was returned again in 1660 and 1661. In 1663–65 he accompanied Lord Carlisle as secretary to the embassy to Muscovy, Sweden and Denmark, but the rest of his life was devoted to his parliamentary duties, doing battle against intolerance and arbitrary government. His republicanism was less the outcome of abstract theory than of experience. He accepted the Restoration without ceasing to praise Cromwell. His writings show him willing to give Charles II a fair chance, but convinced at last that the Stewarts must go. His last satires are a call to arms against monarchy. Though circulated in manuscript only, they were believed to endanger his life. He died in August 1678 through the stubborn ignorance of his physician—a baseless rumour suggested poison. Marvell's works are divided by the Restoration into two very distinct groups. After 1660 his pen was given up to politics, except when his friendship for Milton drew from him the lines prefixed to the second edition of *Paradise Lost*. In 1672–73 he wrote *The Rehearsal Transpros'd* against religious intolerance; and in 1677 his most important tractate, the *Account of the Growth of Popery and Arbitrary Government*, was published anonymously. As a poet Marvell belongs to the pre-Restoration period. 'A witty delicacy', in Lamb's phrase, and a genuine enjoyment of nature and of gardens mark his poetry; Birrell recognizes his 'glorious moments' and 'lovely stanzas'. He is perhaps the greatest master in English of the eight-syllable couplet. See books by Birrell (1905), Pierre Legouis (Paris 1928), Bradbrook and Thomas (1940).

MARX, (1) Julius (Groucho) (1895–), American comedian, born in New York. With his brothers **Leonard (Chico)** (1891–1961), **Arthur (Harpo)** (1893–1964) and **Herbert (Zeppo)** (1901–), he began his stage career in vaudeville in a team called the Six Musical Mascots that included his mother, Minnie (d. 1929), and an aunt. Later, the brothers appeared as The Four Nightingales and finally as the Marx Brothers. They appeared in musical comedy, but their main reputation was made in a series of films including *Animal Crackers*, *Monkey Business* (both 1932), *Horse Feathers* and *Duck Soup* (both 1933). Herbert retired from films in 1935 and the remaining trio scored further successes in *A Night at the Opera*, *A Day at the Races*, *A Day at the Circus*, *Go West* and *The Big Store*. The team then broke up and the brothers led individual careers. Each had a well-defined stencil: Groucho with his wisecracks, Chico, the pianist with his own technique, and Harpo, the dumb clown and harp maestro. Julius Marx is the author of *Many Happy Returns* and a serious study of American Income Tax. See biography by Kyle Crichton (1951) and autobiography, *Groucho and Me* (1959).

(2) **Karl** (1818–83), German founder of modern international Communism, born at Trier, May 5, the son of a Jewish lawyer, studied law at Bonn and Berlin but took up

history, Hegelian philosophy and Feuerbach's materialism. In 1842 he became editor of the democratic *Rheinische Zeitung* but his virulent attacks upon the government brought about its closure. He married, moved to Paris in 1843, and there wrote *Deutsch-französische Jahrbücher* (1843) and edited *Vorwärts* (1844). Expelled from Paris in 1845, he settled in Brussels, where he attacked Proudhon's socialist *Philosophie de la misère* with *Misère de la philosophie* (1847). With Engels (q.v.) as his closest collaborator and disciple, he reorganized the Communist League, which met in London in 1847. Engels having written a first draft, Marx rewrote the famous *Communist Manifesto* (1848), a masterpiece of political propaganda and intellectual brow-beating, ending with the celebrated watchwords: 'The workers have nothing to lose but their chains. They have a world to win. Workers of all lands, unite!' In it the state is attacked as a mere instrument of oppression, religion and culture are mere ideologies of the capitalist class, overproduction the latter's inevitable downfall. Utopian Socialism is dismissed as a feeble *petit-bourgeois* attempt to avoid the crash. The immediate result was Marx's expulsion from Brussels, and after participating in the revolutionary upheavals in the Rhineland, in 1849 he settled with his family in London. Often reduced to poverty, he was supported by Engels and Lassalle, and three of his children died young. At the British Museum reading room, where he was the first to make use of government blue books, he acquired a vast knowledge of economics, supplemented by Engels' first-hand experience of British industry. *Zur Kritik der politischen Oekonomie* (1859) was followed by his *magnum opus*, Vol. I of *Das Kapital* (1867). Here he argues that capitalist expansion depends on surplus value, the difference between the mere subsistence wage paid to labour and the considerably greater value produced by it. Capitalist competition however is only successful at the expense of the worker, who becomes poorer, more desperate and self-conscious. The antagonisms must inevitably lead to revolution. Here we have the Hegelian dialectic, but inverted, not in terms of spiritual abstraction but materialism. The synthesis which results from the extinction of the capitalist class is, after a short dictatorship of the proletariat, the classless society, in which the state has 'withered away'. The rôle of the Communist is to alleviate the birth pangs of the new era, by making the proletariat conscious of its historic rôle. 'Philosophers have previously offered various interpretations of the world. Our business is to change it.' Marx was among the founders of the First International (Working-men's Association) which broke up in 1873 into Marxist and Bakunin's anarchist factions, the former surviving until 1876. With *Das Kapital* unfinished, Marx died March 14, 1883, and was buried in Highgate cemetery. Marx provided an original and compelling analysis of the underlying social tensions of his time, which revolutionized the manner in which economic history and sociology were to be conducted. The defects of his dialectical approach are endemic to all forms of historicism. He failed to provide a political programme because on his thesis politics come to an end with the classless society. He did not foresee the future decisive rôle of the managerial class, which has no place in his system. But as the propounder of a political creed he exerted a powerful influence which a century after the publication of the *Manifesto* showed no signs of abating. See also his *Civil War in France* (1850; trans. Postgate 1921), *Der 18te Brumaire des Louis Bonaparte* (1852), Vols. 2 and 3 of *Das Kapital*, ed. F. Engels (1885–95), their joint work, published posthumously, *German Ideology*, written (1845–46) and Collected Works, ed. Marx-Engels Institute (1927 ff.). See also biographical studies by M. Beer (1925), R. W. Postgate (1933), E. H. Carr (1934), F. Mehring (trans. E. Fitzgerald 1935), S. Hook (1936), H. J. Laski, C. J. Sprigge (1939), I. Berlin (1939), studies by B. Croce (1914), V. I. Lenin (1919), K. Kautsky (1919), A. D. Lindsay (1925), G. D. H. Cole (1934 and 1948), L. Schwarzschild (1948), H. Marcuse (1959), and K. R. Popper, *The Open Society*, Vol. 2 (1945), H. B. Acton, *The Illusion of an Epoch* (1955), and G. A. Wetter, *Dialectical Materialism* (Freiburg 1952, trans. P. Heath 1959).

MARY (Heb. *Miriam*, Gr. *Mariam*), the Blessed Virgin, the mother of Jesus Christ. The genealogy of Jesus in St Matthew is traced through Joseph; and it is assumed that Mary was of the same family. The incidents in her personal history will be found in Matt. i, ii, xii; Luke i, ii; John ii, xix; and Acts i. The date of her death is often given as A.D. 63; the tradition of her having been assumed into heaven is celebrated in the festival of the Assumption. See works by F. M. William (1938), C. C. Martindale (1940).

MARY I (1516–58), Queen of England, daughter of Henry VIII by his first wife, Catharine of Aragon, was born at Greenwich, February 18, 1516. She was well educated, a good linguist, fond of music, devoted to her mother, and devoted to her church. With the divorce of her mother her troubles began. Henry forced her to sign a declaration that her mother's marriage had been unlawful. During the reign of her half-brother Edward she lived in retirement, and no threats could induce her to conform to the new religion. On his death (1553) she became entitled to the crown by her father's testament and the parliamentary settlement. The Duke of Northumberland had, however, induced Edward and his council to set Henry's will aside in favour of his daughter-in-law Lady Jane Grey (q.v.), but the whole country favoured Mary, who without bloodshed entered London on August 3 in triumph. Northumberland and two others were executed, but Lady Jane and her husband were, for the present, spared. The queen proceeded very cautiously to bring back the old religion. She reinstated the Catholic bishops and imprisoned some of the leading Reformers, but dared not restore the pope's supremacy. The question upon which all turned was the queen's marriage; and she, in spite of the protests of the nation, obstinately set her heart on Philip of Spain. The unpopularity of the proposal brought about the rebellion of Wyatt, quelled mainly through the courage and coolness of the queen. Lady Jane was now, with her husband and father, brought to the block; the Princess Elizabeth, suspected of complicity, was committed to the Tower. Injunctions were sent to the bishops to restore ecclesiastical laws to their state under Henry VIII. In July 1554 Philip was married to Mary, remaining in England for over a year. In November Pole entered England as papal legate, parliament petitioned for reconciliation to the Holy See, and the realm was solemnly absolved from the papal censures. Soon after, the persecution which gave the queen the name of 'Bloody Mary' began. In 1555 Ridley and Latimer were brought to the stake; Cranmer followed in March 1556; and Pole, now Archbishop of Canterbury, was left supreme in the councils of the queen. How far Mary herself was responsible for the cruelties practised is doubtful; but during the last three years of her reign 300 victims perished in the flames. Broken down with sickness, with grief at her husband's heartlessness, with disappointment at her childlessness, and with sorrow for the loss of Calais to the French, Mary died November 17, 1558. See *England under Edward VI and Mary*, by Tytler, M. Hume's *Two English Queens and Philip* (1908), a study by J. M. Stone (1901), Life by F. H. M. Prescott (1953).

MARY II (1662–94). See WILLIAM III.

MARY, Queen, formerly Princess of Teck. See GEORGE V.

MARY OF GUELDRES. See JAMES II (Scotland).

MARY OF GUISE. See GUISE (6).

MARY OF MEDICI. See MARIE DE' MEDICI.

MARY OF MODENA (1658–1718), Queen of James II, only daughter of the Duke of Modena, in 1673 became the second wife of the Duke of York, who in 1685 succeeded as James II (q.v.). Five daughters and one son had all died in infancy, when on June 10, 1688, she gave birth to Prince James Francis Edward, and six months later escaped with him to France. She bore a daughter in 1692, and spent her last days at St Germain. See Lives by M. Haile (1905) and C. Oman (1962).

MARY, Queen of Scots (1542–87), was the daughter of James V of Scotland by his second wife, Mary of Guise, and was born at Linlithgow, December 7 or 8, 1542, while her father lay on his deathbed at Falkland. A queen when she was a week old, she was promised in marriage by the regent Arran to Prince Edward of England, but the Scottish parliament declared the promise null. War with England followed, and the disastrous defeat of Pinkie (1547); but Mary was offered in marriage to the eldest son of Henry II of France and Catharine de' Medici. The offer was accepted; and in 1548 Mary sailed from Dumbarton to Roscoff, and was affianced to the Dauphin at St Germain. Her next ten years were passed at the French court, where she was carefully educated; and in 1558 she was married to the Dauphin, who was a year younger than herself. Mary was induced to sign a secret deed, by which, if she died childless, both her Scottish realm and her right of succession to the English crown (she was the great-granddaughter of Henry VII) were conveyed to France. In 1559 the death of the French king called her husband to the throne as Francis II, and the government passed into the hands of the Guises; but the sickly king died in 1560, when the reins of power were grasped by Catharine de' Medici as regent for her next son, Charles IX. The young queen's presence was already urgently needed in Scotland, which the death of her mother had left without a government, while convulsed by the throes of the Reformation; and she sailed from Calais on the 14th, and arrived at Leith on August 19, 1561. Her government began auspiciously. The Reformation claimed to have received the sanction of the Scottish parliament, and Mary was content to leave affairs as she found them, stipulating only for liberty to use her own religion. Her chief minister was a Protestant, her illegitimate brother, James Stuart, whom she created Earl of Moray. Under his guidance, in the autumn of 1562, she made a progress to the north, which ended in the defeat and death of the Earl of Huntly, the powerful chief of the Roman Catholic party in Scotland. Meanwhile the kings of Sweden, Denmark and France, the Archduke Charles of Austria, Don Carlos of Spain, the Dukes of Ferrara, Nemours and Anjou, the Earl of Arran, and the Earl of Leicester were proposed as candidates for her hand. Her own preference was for Don Carlos, and only after all hopes of obtaining him were quenched, her choice fell, somewhat suddenly (1565), on her cousin, Henry Stewart, Lord Darnley, son of the Earl of Lennox, by his marriage with a granddaughter of Henry VII of England. He was thus among the nearest heirs to the English crown; and this and his good looks were his sole recommendation. He was weak, needy, insolent and vicious; he was a Roman Catholic; and he was three years younger than Mary. The marriage was the signal for an easily quelled insurrection by Moray and the Hamiltons. But Mary almost at once was disgusted by Darnley's debauchery, and alarmed by his arrogance. She had given him the title of king, but she hesitated to grant his demand that the crown should be secured to him for life, and that, if she died without issue, it should descend to his heirs. Her chief adviser since Moray's rebellion had been her Italian secretary David Rizzio (q.v.). The king had been his sworn friend, but now suspected in him the real obstacle to his designs upon the crown. In this belief, he entered into a formal compact with Moray, Ruthven, Morton and other Protestant chiefs, and himself led the way into the queen's cabinet and held her while the others killed the Italian in an antechamber (March 9, 1566). Dissembling her indignation, Mary succeeded in detaching her husband from his allies, and escaped with him from Holyrood to Dunbar; Ruthven and Morton fled to England; Moray was received by the queen; and Darnley, who had betrayed both sides, became an object of mingled abhorrence and contempt. A little before the birth (June 19, 1566) of the prince who became James VI, the queen's affection for her husband seemed to revive; but the change was only momentary; and before the boy's baptism, in December, her estrangement was greater than ever. Divorce was openly discussed, and Darnley spoke of leaving the country, but fell ill of the smallpox at Glasgow about January 9, 1567. On the 25th Mary went to see him, and brought him to Edinburgh on the 31st. He was lodged in a small mansion beside the Kirk o' Field, just outside the southern walls. There Mary visited him daily, slept for two nights in a room below his bedchamber, and passed the evening of Sunday, February 9, by his bedside in kindly conversation. She left him between ten and eleven o'clock to take part in a masque at Holyrood, at the marriage of a favourite valet; and about two hours after midnight the house in which the king slept was blown up by gunpowder, and his lifeless body was found in the garden. The chief actor in this tragedy was undoubtedly the Earl of Bothwell (q.v.), who had of late enjoyed the queen's favour; but there were suspicions that the queen herself was not wholly ignorant of the plot. On April 12 Bothwell was brought to a mock-trial, and acquitted; on the 24th he intercepted the queen on her way from Linlithgow to Edinburgh, and carried her, with scarcely a show of resistance, to Dunbar. On May 7 he was divorced from his comely and newly-married wife; on the 12th Mary publicly pardoned his seizure of her person, and created him Duke of Orkney; and on the 15th, three months after her husband's murder, she married the man every one regarded as his murderer. This fatal step at once arrayed her nobles in arms against her. Her army melted away without striking a blow on the field of Carberry (June 15), when nothing was left but to surrender to the confederate lords. They led her to Edinburgh, where the insults of the rabble drove her well-nigh frantic. Hurried next to Lochleven, she was constrained (July 24) to sign an act of abdication in favour of her son, who, five days afterwards, was crowned at Stirling. Escaping from her island-prison (May 2, 1568), she found herself in a few days at the head of an army of 6000 men, which was defeated (May 13) by the regent Moray at Langside near Glasgow. Three days afterwards Mary crossed the Solway, and threw herself on the protection of Queen Elizabeth, only to find herself a prisoner for life—first at Carlisle, then at Bolton, Tutbury, Wingfield, Coventry, Chatsworth, Sheffield, Buxton, Chartley and Fotheringay. The presence of Mary in England was a constant source of uneasiness to Elizabeth and her advisers. A large Catholic minority naturally looked to Mary as the likely restorer of the old faith. Plot followed plot; and that of Antony Babington had for its object the assassination of Elizabeth and the deliverance of Mary. It was discovered; letters from Mary approving the death of Elizabeth fell into Walsingham's hands; and, mainly on the evidence of copies of these letters, Mary was brought to trial in September 1586. Sentence of death was pronounced against her on October 25 but it was not until February 1, 1587, that Elizabeth took courage to sign the warrant of execution. It was carried into effect on the 8th, when Mary laid her head upon the block with the dignity of a queen and the resignation of a martyr, evincing to the last her devotion to the church of her fathers. Her body, buried at Peterborough, was in 1612 removed to Henry VII's Chapel at Westminster, where it still lies in a sumptuous tomb erected by James VI. The statue there and the contemporary portraits by Clouet (q.v.) are the best representations of Mary. Her beauty and accomplishments have never been disputed. The charm of her soft, sweet voice is described as irresistible; and she sang well, accompanying herself on the harp, the virginal and the lute. She spoke three or four languages, conversed admirably, and wrote in both prose and verse. Of six extant pieces of her poetry (less than 300 lines) the best is the poem of eleven stanzas on the death of her first husband. The longest is a *Meditation* of a hundred lines, written in 1572. All are in French, except one sonnet in Italian. The sweet lines beginning 'Adieu, plaisant pays de France', are not hers. A volume of French verse on the *Institution of a Prince* has been lost since 1627, along with a Latin speech in vindication of learned women, delivered in the Louvre. See works by Philippson (1891–92), Skelton (1893), Hay Fleming (1897), S. Cowan (1901, 1907), Stoddart (1908), Shelley (1913), Mumby (1914, 1921), Mahon (1924, 1930), N. B. Morrison (1960); Lang's *Mystery of Mary Stuart* (1901), her *Trial* (ed. Steuart, 1951), and *Papal Negotiations* (Scot. Hist. Soc., 1901); Rait and Cameron, *King James's Secret* (1927); Willcocks (1939); and Tannenbaum's bibliography (3 vols. 1944–46).

MASACCIO, *maz-at'chō*, (1) real name **Tomasso Guidi** (1401–28?), Italian painter, a pioneer of Italian renaissance painting, influenced such great masters as Michelangelo and Raphael. See works by Somaré (1924), H. Lindberg (1931), Salmi (1935).

(2) real name **Maso di Bartolommeo** (1406–1457), Italian sculptor, a Florentine, assisted Donatello and worked in Florence Cathedral and other N. Italian churches.

MASANIELLO, properly **Tommaso Aniello**, *ma-zan-ee-el'lō* (1623–47), Neapolitan patriot, a fisherman of Amalfi, led the successful revolt of the Neapolitans against their Spanish oppressors on July 7, 1647. He was assassinated by agents of the Spanish viceroy on July 16. See Lives by M. Schipa (Bari 1925), A. Rosso (Naples 1952).

MASARYK, *ma-sa-rik'*, (1) **Jan** (1886–1948), Czech diplomat and statesman, son of (2), served in Czech diplomatic service after 1918, being minister in London 1925–38. He became foreign minister in the Czech government set up in London in 1940 and continued in that post after 1945 in Prague. In 1948 the Communists took control of the government and he is thought to have committed suicide. See Life by Lockhart (1956).

(2) **Thomas Garrigue** (1850–1937), first

president of the Czechoslovak Republic (1918–35), father of (1), was born at Hodonin, Moravia. An ardent Slovak, while in exile during World War I he organized the Czechoslovak independence movement. See Lives by Seton-Watson (1943) and Birley (1951).

MASCAGNI, Pietro, *mas-kan'yee* (1863–1945), Italian composer, born a baker's son at Leghorn, produced in 1890 the brilliantly successful one-act opera, *Cavalleria Rusticana*. His many later operas failed to repeat this success, though arias and intermezzi from them are still performed. They include *L'Amico Fritz* (1891), *Guglielmo Ratcliffe* (1895), *Le Maschere* (1901) and *Londoletta* (1917). See the autobiographical *Mascagni parla* (Rome 1945), Lives by C. Cogo (Venice 1931) and E. Mascagni (1936).

MASCALL, Eric Lionel (1905–), Anglo-Catholic theologian, author, and since 1962 professor of Historical Theology at King's College, London. He read mathematics for four years at Cambridge with the intention of making his career as an applied mathematician. An interest in philosophy led to another in theology, however, and he was ordained priest in 1932. After a few years in parish work he became sub-warden of Lincoln Theological College where he remained for eight years. From 1946 to 1962 he was tutor in Theology and university lecturer in the Philosophy of Religion at Christ Church, Oxford. Apart from his academic work, he has shown a considerable interest in the life of the religious communities of the Church of England and in the ecumenical field. See his books *He Who Is* (1943) and *Existence and Analogy* (1949) which have acquired more or less the character of textbooks on Natural Theology, *Christian Theology and Natural Science* (Oxford Bampton Lectures, 1956) on the relations of theology and science, and the ecumenical *The Recovery of Unity* (1958).

MASEFIELD, John (1878–1967), English poet and novelist, was born at Ledbury. Schooled for the merchant service, he served his apprenticeship on a windjammer and acquired that intimate knowledge of the sea which gives atmosphere and authenticity to his work. Ill-health drove him ashore, and after three years in New York he returned to England to become a writer in 1897, first making his mark as a journalist. His earliest poetical work, *Salt Water Ballads*, appeared in 1902; *Dauber* (1913) confirmed his reputation as a poet of the sea. *Nan* (1909) is a tragedy of merit. His ability to tell a story in verse is reminiscent of Chaucer. This is specially noticeable in his finest narrative poem *Reynard the Fox* (1919). Other works are *The Everlasting Mercy* (1911); *The Widow in the Bye-Street* (1912); *Shakespeare* (1911); *Gallipoli* (1916); the novels *Sard Harker* (1924), *Odtaa* (1926) and *The Hawbucks* (1929); and the plays *The Trial of Jesus* (1925) and *The Coming of Christ* (1928). He became poet laureate in 1930 and was awarded the O.M. in 1935. See his autobiographical *In the Mill* (1941) and *So Long to Learn* (1952), and studies by Hamilton (1922) and Thomas (1932).

MASHAM, Abigail, Lady, *née* **Hill** (d. 1734), cousin to the Duchess of Marlborough (q.v.), whom she superseded as Queen Anne's favourite. She married in 1707, and died December 6, 1734.

MASINISSA (*c.* 238–149 B.C.), King of the Eastern Numidians, helped the Carthaginians to subdue the Massylii or Western Numidians, accompanied his allies to Spain, and fought valiantly against the Romans. But going over to them (*c.* 210 B.C.), he received as his reward Western Numidia and large portions of Carthaginian territory.

MASKELYNE, *mas'ke-lin,* (1) **John Nevil** (1839–1917), English illusionist, born in Wiltshire. Of farming stock, he became a watchmaker, which directed his interest towards the automata which he used so effectively in his entertainments. As a young man he joined forces with a Mr Cooke and they appeared together, first at Cheltenham and then at the Crystal Palace, in 1865. In 1873 they leased the Egyptian Hall for three months, but their tenancy lasted for thirty-one years. Maskelyne then moved his 'Home of Magic' to the St George's Hall in 1905, where his particular brand of spectacular conjuring continued to flourish under his son's management. He devoted much energy to exposing spiritualistic frauds. His grandson, **Jasper** (1903–), first appeared in his grandfather's show at the age of eleven, and has continued as a conjuror on his own. He utilized his peculiar knowledge to confound the enemy during World War II and wrote an account of the family in *White Magic* (1936).

(2) **Mervyn Herbert Nevil Story-** (1823–1911), English mineralogist, grandson of (3), advocated the study of natural science at Oxford, where he became Waynflete professor of Mineralogy and also reorganized the mineralogy department of the British Museum. He was also F.R.S. and M.P.

(3) **Nevil** (1732–1811), English astronomer, grandfather of (2), educated at Westminster and Trinity College, Cambridge, in 1758 was elected F.R.S., went to Barbadoes to test the chronometers (1763), and in 1765 was appointed astronomer-royal. During the forty-six years that he held this office he improved methods and instruments of observation, invented the prismatic micrometer, and made important observations. In 1774 he measured the earth's density from the deflection of the plumb-line at Schiehallion in Perthshire. His numerous publications include the *British Mariner's Guide* (1763), the *Nautical Almanac* (1765–67), *Tables for computing the Places of the Fixed Stars &c.*, and the first volume of the Greenwich *Astronomical Observations.* He was rector from 1775 of Shrawardine, Salop, and from 1782 of North Runcton, Norfolk, and died February 9, 1811. See *Royal Observatory Greenwich* (1900) for account of his life and work.

MASOLINO DA PANICALE (1383–1447), Florentine artist, identified with **Tomasso Fini.** A distinguished early Renaissance painter, he was the master of Masaccio (q.v.), with whom he collaborated in the Brancacci chapel. His frescoes in Castiglione d'Olona were only discovered in 1843. He also worked in Hungary and Rome. See works by Layard (1868) and Toesca (1958).

MASON, (1) Alfred Edward Woodley (1865–1948), English novelist, born at Dulwich, educated at Oxford, became a successful actor, subsequently combined writing with politics, being Liberal M.P. for Coventry in 1906–10. His first published novel was *A Romance of Wastdale* (1895). *Four Feathers* (1902) captured the popular imagination and *The Broken Road* (1907) cemented his success. With *At the Villa Rose* (1910) Mason embarked on the novel of detection and introduced his ingenious Inspector Hanaud; thereafter he alternated historical adventure and detective fiction. Several of his books have been filmed. Representative titles are: *The House of the Arrow* (1924); *No other Tiger* (1927); *The Prisoner in the Opal* (1929); *Fire over England* (1936); *Königsmark* (1938); *Life of Francis Drake* (1941).

(2) **Charles** (1730–87), British astronomer, employed at Greenwich, with **Jeremiah Dixon** (of whom little is known except that he is reputed to have been born in a coal-mine) he observed the transit of Venus at the Cape of Good Hope in 1761. From 1763 to 1767 Mason and Dixon were engaged by Lord Baltimore and Mr Penn to survey the boundary between Maryland and Pennsylvania and end an eighty-year-old dispute. They reached a point 224 miles west of the Delaware River, but were prevented from further work by Indians. The survey was completed by others, but the boundary was given the name Mason-Dixon Line.

(3) **Daniel Gregory** (1873–1953), grandson of (5), American composer, born in Brookline, Mass., studied under D'Indy in Paris, and became a leading exponent of neo-classical composition in America. He wrote books on American musical conditions and a study of Beethoven's String Quartets. Mason composed three symphonies, the last of which is a study of Abraham Lincoln, and a considerable amount of chamber music.

(4) **Sir Josiah** (1795–1881), English philanthropist and pen manufacturer, born at Kidderminster, began life as a hawker, after 1822 manufactured split-rings, and in 1829 began to make pens for Perry & Co., and soon became the greatest pen-maker in the world. He was partner with Elkington in electroplating (1842–65), and had smelting-works for copper and nickel. He endowed almshouses and an orphanage at Erdington at a cost of £260,000, and gave £180,000 to found the Mason College (now Birmingham University). See Memoir by Bunce (1890).

(5) **Lowell** (1792–1872), American musician, born in Medfield, Mass., as organist of a Presbyterian church in Savannah, compiled a book of hymns, taking melodies from the works of Handel, Mozart and Beethoven. The success of this work led him to produce similar volumes for school use, and additional hymn books. In 1832 he founded the Boston Academy of Music, to give free instruction to children, and was compelled by its success to organize classes for adults. The most famous of his compositions is probably the hymn tune 'From Greenland's icy mountains'.

(6) **William** (1725–97), English poet, was a friend of Gray, who had been attracted to him by his *Musaeus* (1747), a lament for Pope in imitation of Milton's *Lycidas*. He published two poor tragedies, *Elfrida* and *Caractacus*; the *English Garden* (1772–82), a tedious poem in blank verse; and, as Gray's executor, the *Memoirs of Gray* in 1775. He became vicar of Aston, Yorkshire, in 1754, canon of York in 1762. See his *Correspondence with Walpole* (1851), *with Gray* (1853), and Life by Draper (1929).

(7) **William** (1829–1908), son of (5), studied the piano under Liszt and, in the course of a successful concert career, organized influential chamber music concerts in Boston.

MASPERO, Sir Gaston, Hon. K.C.M.G. (1846–1916), French Egyptologist, born at Paris of Italian parents, in 1874 became professor of Egyptology at the Collège de France, and was in 1881–86, 1899–1914 keeper of the Bulak Museum and director of explorations in Egypt, making valuable discoveries at Sakkara, Dahshûr, Ekhmim, &c. He wrote many works on Egyptology.

MASSÉNA, André, *mas-say'na* (1758–1817), French soldier, the greatest of Napoleon's marshals, served fourteen years in the Sardinian army, and in the French Revolution rose rapidly in rank, becoming in 1793 a general of division. He distinguished himself greatly in the campaigns in Upper Italy, gained his crushing victory over Suvorov's Russians at Zürich (1799), and became marshal of the empire in 1804. In Italy he kept the Archduke Charles in check, crushed him at Caldiero, and overran Naples. In 1807, after Eylau, he commanded the right wing, and was created Duke of Rivoli. In the campaign of 1809 against Austria he covered himself with glory and earned the title of Prince of Essling. In 1810 he compelled Wellington to fall back upon his impregnable lines at Torres Vedras, was forced after five months, by total lack of supplies, to make a masterly retreat, but was recalled with ignominy by his imperious master. At the Restoration he adhered to the Bourbons and on Napoleon's return from Elba Masséna refused to follow him; he died April 4, 1817. See his *Mémoires* (7 vols. 1849–50), and books by Toselli (1869), Gachot (5 vols. 1901–13) and Sabor (1926).

MASSENET, Jules, *mas-è-nay* (1842–1912), French composer, born near St Étienne, studied at the Paris Conservatoire, where in 1878–96 he was professor. He made his fame by the comic opera *Don César de Bazan* in 1872. Other operas are *Hérodiade* (1884), *Manon* (1885), *Le Cid* (1885), *Werther* (1892) and *Thaïs* (1894), and among his works are oratorios, orchestral suites, music for piano and songs. See his autobiographical *Mes Souvenirs* (Paris 1912, Eng. trans. Boston 1919), Life by Bruneau (Paris 1935).

MASSEY, (1) Gerald (1828–1907), English poet and mystic, born near Tring, became a Christian Socialist, edited a journal, lectured, and between 1851 and 1869 published eight or nine volumes of poetry (*Babe Christabel and other Poems*, *Craigcrook Castle*, &c.), mostly collected in *My Lyrical Life* (1890). He wrote also mystical and speculative theological or cosmogonic works, and discovered a 'Secret Drama' in Shakespeare's sonnets. See book by Flower (1895), and Collins's *Studies* (1905).

(2) **Vincent** (1887–1967), Canadian statesman and diplomat, born in Toronto, joined the Canadian cabinet after World War I, became Canadian minister in Washington (1926–30), high commissioner in London (1935–46), and governor-general of Canada (1952–59). His brother **Raymond** (1896–), is a well-known actor of stage (début in 1922 in *In the Zone*, played Lincoln in *Abe Lincoln* (1938–39)), screen (played leading parts in *Things to come*, *49th Parallel*, &c.), and television (in the rôle of 'Dr Gillespie' in the long-running *Dr Kildare* series during the 1960s).

(3) **William Ferguson** (1856–1925), New Zealand statesman, born in Ireland, went to New Zealand and became a farmer. Elected to the house of representatives he became opposition leader and in 1912 prime minister, which office he held until his death. See Life by H. J. Constable (1925).

MASSILLON, Jean Baptiste, *mas-see-yõ* (1663–1742), French preacher, born at Hyères in Provence, was trained for the church in the Oratory. He preached before Louis XIV, became Bishop of Clermont, and next year preached before Louis XV his celebrated *Petit Carême*—a series of ten short Lenten sermons. In 1719 he was elected to the Academy; in 1723 he preached the funeral oration of the Duchess of Orleans, his last public discourse in Paris. From this time he lived almost entirely for his diocese, where his charity and gentleness gained him the love of all. He died of apoplexy. See Blampignon's monograph (1884), Sainte-Beuve's *Causeries du Lundi* (vol. ix) and works by Ingold (1880) and Pauthe (1908).

MASSINE, Léonide, *ma-seen'* (1896–), Russo-American dancer and choreographer, born in Moscow. He was principal dancer and choreographer with Diaghilev and the Ballet Russe de Monte Carlo, and has produced and danced in ballets in Europe and America, among his best known works being *La Boutique fantasque* and *Le Sacré du printemps*. See study by Anthony (1939).

MASSINGER, Philip (1583–1640), English dramatist, baptized at St Thomas's, Salisbury, November 24, was a son of a retainer of the Earl of Pembroke. After leaving Oxford without a degree he became a playwright and was associated with Henslowe, who died in 1616. In later years he wrote many plays single-handed, but much of his work is mixed up with that of other men, particularly Fletcher. Fletcher was buried in St Saviour's Church, Southwark, August 29, 1625; and Massinger was laid in the same grave, March 18, 1640. Probably the earliest of Massinger's extant plays is *The Unnatural Combat*, a repulsive tragedy, printed in 1639. The first in order of publication is *The Virgin Martyr* (1622), partly written by Dekker. In 1623 was published *The Duke of Milan*, a fine tragedy, but too rhetorical. Other plays include *The Bondman*, *The Roman Actor* (1626), *The Great Duke of Florence* (1627), and *The Emperor of the East* (1631), &c. Nathaniel Field joined Massinger in writing the fine tragedy *The Fatal Dowry*, printed in 1632. *The City Madam*, licensed in 1632, and *A New Way to Pay Old Debts*, printed in 1633, are Massinger's most masterly comedies—brilliant satirical studies, though without warmth or geniality. Some of Massinger's plays are (as Coleridge said) as interesting as a novel; others are as solid as a treatise on political philosophy. His verse, though fluent and flexible, lacks the music and magic of Shakespeare's. No writer repeats himself more frequently. It is difficult to say how far Massinger was concerned in the authorship of plays that pass under the name of 'Beaumont and Fletcher'. There are editions (none complete) by Gifford (1805, 1813), Coleridge (1840), Cunningham (1867), and Symons (1887–89, 1904); studies by Cruickshank (1920), Maxwell (1939) and Dunn (1958).

MASSON, David (1822–1907), Scottish scholar and literary critic, the biographer of Milton, was born at Aberdeen, and educated at Marischal College there and the University of Edinburgh. In 1847 he settled in London, writing for reviews, encyclopaedias, &c. In 1852 he became professor of English Literature in University College London, and in 1865 in Edinburgh University; he resigned in 1895. His *Essays, Biographical and Critical* (1856), were extended in 1874–76. His *Life of John Milton* (6 vols. 1859–80) is the most complete biography of any Englishman. Other works include editions of Milton's poems and De Quincey's works (14 vols. 1889–91). See his autobiographical *Memories of London in the Forties* (1908) and *Letters* (1908).

MASSYS. See MATSYS.

MASTERS, Edgar Lee (1869–1950), American author, wrote the satirical *Spoon River Anthology* (1915), dealing with the lives of people in the midwest. See his autobiography *Across Spoon River* (1936).

MASÛDI, Abul Hassan Ali, *ma-soo'dee* (d. 957), Arab traveller, born at Bagdad, visited Egypt, Palestine, the Caspian, India, Ceylon, Madagascar, perhaps even China. His chief works are the *Annals*, *Meadows of Gold* (printed with French trans. 1861–77, and at Boulak in 1867), and *Indicator*.

MATA HARI, stage name of **Margarete Gertrude Zelle** (1876–1917), Dutch spy, born at Leeuwarden, who became a dancer in France and, found guilty of espionage for the Germans, was shot in Paris. See book by Newman (1956).

MATEJKO, Jan Alois, *ma-te'y'-kō* (1838–93), Polish painter, born at Cracow, noted for his paintings of scenes from Polish history.

MATHER, (1) Cotton (1663–1728), American divine, son of (2), after graduating at Harvard became colleague to his father at Boston. He published as many as 382 books, and his *Memorable Providences relating to Witchcraft and Possessions* (1685) did much to fan the cruel fury of the New Englanders. During the Salem witchcraft mania Mather wrote his *Wonders of the Invisible World* (1692), and on his head must rest a heavy burden of bloodguiltiness. His *Magnalia Christi Americana* (1702) is an undigested mass of materials for the church history of New England. The *Essays to do Good* (1710) are feeble. He died February 13, 1728. See his Life by his son (1729); Upham, *The Salem Delusion* (1831); and Lives by Marvin (1892), and R. and L. Boas (1929).

(2) **Increase** (1639–1723), American divine, father of (1), was the eldest son of an English Nonconformist minister who emigrated in 1635. He was born at Dorchester, Mass., June 21, 1639, and graduated at Harvard in 1656, and again at Trinity College, Dublin, in 1658. His first charge was Great Torrington in Devon; but in 1661, finding it impossible to conform, he returned to America, and from 1664 till his death, August 23, 1723, was pastor of the North Church, Boston, and from 1681 also president of Harvard. He published no less than 136 separate works, including *Remarkable Providences* (1684) and a *History of the War with the Indians* (1676). Sent to England in 1689 to lay colonial grievances before the king, he obtained a new charter from William III. He was far less an alarmist about witchcraft than his son, and his *Causes of Conscience concerning Witchcraft* (1693) helped to cool the heated imaginations of the colonists. See Life by K. B. Murdock (1925).

MATHEW, Theobald, called 'Father Mathew' (1790–1856), Irish temperance reformer, was born at Thomastown in Tipperary, October 10, 1790. He took priest's orders in the Capuchin order in 1814; and in his ceaseless labours at Cork, seeing how much of the degradation of his people was due to drink, became (1838) an ardent advocate of total abstinence. His crusade extended to England, Scotland and America. He achieved great success, and everywhere roused enthusiasm and secured warm affection. Ill health followed, and he was only saved from serious pecuniary distresses by a Civil List pension and a private subscription. Worn out by his labours, he died at Queenstown. See Lives by Maguire (1863), Matthew (1890), Tynan (1908) and Rogers (1943).

MATHEWS, (1) Charles (1776–1835), English comedian, father of (2), made his début as an actor at Richmond in 1793, but forsook the legitimate stage in 1818 and achieved great success as an entertainer, visiting America twice. See his Memoirs by his wife (4 vols. 1839).

(2) **Charles James** (1803–78), English comedian, son of (1), was a delightful light comedian of charming grace and delicacy. In 1838 he married Madame Vestris (q.v.). See his *Life*, edited by the younger Dickens (1879).

MATHIAS CORVINUS. See MATTHIAS.

MATHIEU, Georges, *ma-tyœ* (1921–), French painter, born at Boulogne, took a degree in literature, but began to paint in 1942; he settled in Paris in 1947, and exhibited there and in New York. With Bryen and others, he has perfected a form of lyric, nongeometrical abstraction, in close sympathy with the American neo-Expressionists. See his *Au-delà du Tachisme* (1963).

MATHILDA (d. 1115), countess of Tuscany, a daughter of the count of Tuscany, supported (with money and men) Pope Gregory VII in his long struggle with the Empire, and married first Godfrey, Duke of Lorraine, and then the young Welf of Bavaria. In 1077 she made a gift of all her vast possessions to the Church. It was at her castle of Canossa that Henry IV did penance to Gregory. See Lives by N. Duff (1909) and N. Grimaldi (Florence 1928).

MATHIS. See GRÜNEWALD (2).

MATILDA, called 'the Empress Maud,' (1102–67), who carried on the Civil War in England with Stephen (q.v.), was the only daughter of Henry I. In 1114 she was married to the Emperor Henry V, and in 1128 to Geoffrey of Anjou, by whom she became the mother of Henry II. See Life by O. Rössler (Berlin 1897).

MATISSE, Henri, *ma-tees* (1869–1954), French artist, born at Le Cateau, studied at the Académie Julian and at the École des Beaux-Arts under Gustave Moreau. From 1904 he became the leader of the Fauves (Derain, Vlaminck, Dufy, Rouault and others). Although he painted several pictures influenced by the Cubists, the Impressionists and by Cézanne, his most characteristic paintings display a bold use of brilliant, luminous areas of primary colour, organized within a rhythmic two-dimensional design, which has affinities with the art of Gauguin and oriental work. The purity of his line-drawing is seen in his many sketches, book illustrations, and etchings, and in many of his paintings. During the early 1930s he travelled in Europe and the U.S.A., and in 1949 he decorated a Dominican chapel at Venice. He was working right up to his death, his style fundamentally unchanged, producing pictures more sophisticated than his early work, but with exquisite sense of design and balance of colour. His works are represented in the Tate Gallery, London, and the Museums of Modern Art in Paris and New York. See monographs by R. Fry (1935), G. Diehl (1954), J. Lassaigne (trans. 1959) and R. Escholier (trans. 1960).

MATSYS, or **Massys, (1) Jan** (1509–75), son of (2), was an imitator of his father and worked in Antwerp.

(2) **Quentin** (*c.* 1466–*c.* 1531), Flemish painter, father of (1), born at Louvain, was, according to legend, a blacksmith. In 1491 he joined the painters' guild of St Luke in Antwerp. His pictures are mostly religious, treated with a reverent spirit, but with decided touches of realism, and of exquisite finish. He ranks high as a portrait painter. See works by M. J. Friedländer (1929) and study by Sir M. Conway, *The Van Eycks and their followers* (1921).

MATTEOTTI, Giacomo, *-ot'-* (1885–1924), Italian politician. A member of the Italian Chamber of Deputies, in 1921 he began to organize the United Socialist Party on a constitutional basis in opposition to Mussolini's Fascists. Matteotti's protests against Fascist outrages led to his murder in 1924, which caused a crisis and nearly brought the Fascist régime to an end.

MATTHAY, Tobias, *ma-tay* (1858–1945), English pianist and teacher, of German descent, born in London, was professor of Pianoforte at the Royal Academy of Music from 1880 to 1925, when he resigned to devote himself to his own school, which he had founded in 1900. His method of piano playing was enunciated in *The Act of Touch* (1903) and subsequent publications.

MATTHESON, Johann (1681–1764), German composer, born at Hamburg, was a singer and orchestral player before beginning to compose operas and many choral and instrumental pieces, and was also the author of manuals on continuo playing. See study by H. Schmidt (1897).

MATTHEW, Saint (1st cent. A.D.), one of the twelve apostles, was a tax gatherer before becoming a disciple of Jesus, and is identified with **Levi** in Mark (ii, 14) and Luke (v, 27). According to tradition he was the author of the first gospel, was a missionary to the Hebrews, and suffered martyrdom, but nothing is known with certainty about his life.

MATTHEW OF WESTMINSTER, long the supposed author of the *Flores Historiarum* (first printed by Archbishop Parker in 1567; ed. by Luard in 1890; trans. by Yonge, 1853), is of doubtful existence, the work being perhaps merely an abridgment of Matthew Paris (q.v.) or of Roger of Wendover, named from a copy at Westminster.

MATTHEW PARIS. See PARIS (3).

MATTHEWS, (1) Alfred Edward (1869-1960), English actor, born at Bridlington, began his career in 1887, filled innumerable comedy rôles from *Charley's Aunt* to *Quiet Weekend* and was still a popular favourite at ninety. See his *Autobiography* (1952).

(2) **Sir Stanley** (1915–), English footballer, born in Hanley. The son of Jack Matthews, 'the fighting barber of Hanley', a notable pugilist in his day, he started his athletic career as a sprinter. He soon concentrated on football and was picked to play for England at twenty. He played for Blackpool from 1947 to 1961, received fifty-six international caps, and celebrated his silver jubilee in association football in 1956. He was created C.B.E. in 1957, knighted in 1965, and became Port Vale club manager in 1965. See his Autobiography (1960).

MATTHIAS CORVINUS (*c.* 1443–90), king of Hungary, the second son of John Hunyady (q.v.), was elected in 1458. But it cost him a six years' hard struggle against Turks, Bohemians, the Emperor Frederick III and disaffected magnates before he could have himself crowned. He drove the Turks back across the frontiers; made himself master of Bosnia (1462) and of Moldavia and Wallachia (1467); and in 1478 concluded peace with Ladislaus of Bohemia, obtaining Moravia, Silesia, and Lusatia. Out of this war grew another with Frederick III, in which Matthias besieged and captured Vienna (1485), and took possession of a large part of Austria proper. He greatly encouraged arts and letters: he founded the University of Buda, built an observatory, adorned his capital with the works of renowned sculptors, employed literary men in Italy to copy MSS., and so founded a magnificent library. Finances were brought into order, industry and commerce promoted, and justice administered strictly. But his rule was arbitrary and his taxes heavy. See Life by Fraknoi (German trans. 1891).

MATURIN, (1) Basil William (1847–1915), Irish Catholic preacher and writer, son of (3), one of the Cowley brotherhood, and a well-known pulpit orator, when in 1897 he 'went over' to Rome. He was on the torpedoed *Lusitania*. See *Memoir* by M. Ward (1920).

(2) **Charles Robert** (1782–1824), Irish dramatist and romancer, father of (3), a curate of St Peter's, Dublin, made his name with a series of extravagant novels in macabre vein that rivalled those of Mrs Radcliffe. These included *The Fatal Revenge*, *Melmoth* (1820), and *The Albigenses.* His tragedy, *Bertram*, had a success at Drury Lane in 1816; its successors, *Manuel* and *Fredolpho*, were failures. See memoir prefixed to new edition of *Melmoth* (1892) and *Letters* (1927).

(3) **William** (1803–87), Irish divine, son of (2), father of (1), a High Churchman, whose views kept him from preferment. He was perpetual curate of Grangegorman from 1844.

MAUD. See MATILDA.

MAUDE, (1) Cyril (1862–1951), English actor-manager, made his name in *The Second Mrs Tanqueray* and *The Little Minister*, was associate-manager of the Haymarket Theatre (1896–1905) and in 1907–15 directed his own company at the Playhouse. He was famous as Andrew Bullivant in *Grumpy* (1915). His son, **John Cyril** (1901–), an eminent judge and Q.C., sat in parliament for Exeter (1945–51).

(2) **Sir Frederick Stanley** (1864–1917), major-general, served in the Sudan and South Africa. In World War I he took part in the Dardanelles evacuation, and in command in Mesopotamia turned a British failure to a success, but died of cholera. See Life by Callwell (1920).

MAUDLING, Reginald (1917–), British Conservative politician, born in London, was educated at Merchant Taylors' and Merton College, Oxford, was called to the bar, served in the air force during World War II and in 1945 became one of Mr Butler's 'backroom boys' in the Conservative Central Office. He entered parliament in 1950 and after two junior ministerial posts, became minister of supply (1953–57), paymaster-general (1957–1959), president of the Board of Trade (1959–61), colonial secretary (1961), chancellor of the Exchequer (1962–64), and deputy leader of the Opposition in 1964.

MAUDSLAY, Henry (1771–1831), English engineer, learned his job as apprentice to Joseph Bramah (q.v.), set up on his own in 1797 and invented various types of machinery, including a screw-cutting lathe. With **Joshua Field** (1757–1863) he began producing marine engines and started the famous firm of Maudslay, Sons and Field (1810).

MAUDSLEY, Henry (1835–1918), English mental pathologist, born near Giggleswick, was physician to the Manchester Asylum, and professor of Medical Jurisprudence at University College, 1869–79. He was one of the first to consider mental illness as curable in some cases, and the Maudsley Hospital, Denmark Hill, London, is named after him.

MAUGHAM, William Somerset, *mawm* (1874–1965), British writer, a modern master of the short story, born January 25, in Paris, of Irish origin, was educated at King's School, Canterbury, read philosophy and literature at Heidelberg and qualified as a surgeon at St Thomas's Hospital, London. Afflicted by a bad stammer, he turned to writing in his student days and a year's medical practice in the London slums gave him the material for his first novel, the lurid *Liza of Lambeth* (1897), and the magnificent autobiographical novel, *Of Human Bondage*, eventually published in 1915. Attempts to have his plays accepted having failed, he settled in Paris and with Laurence Housman (q.v.) revived a 19th-century annual, *The Venture* (1903–04). With the success of *Lady Frederick* (1907), four of his plays ran in London in 1908. In 1914 he served first with a Red Cross unit in France, then as a secret agent in Geneva and finally in Petrograd, attempting to prevent the outbreak of the Russian Revolution. *Ashenden* (1928) is based on these experiences. He voyaged in the South Seas, visiting Tahiti, which inspired *The Moon and Sixpence* (1919), in which an English Gauguin, Strickland, leaves wife and stockbroking to end his life in a leper's hut. Maugham spent two years in a Scottish tuberculosis sanatorium and this again finds expression in several excellent short stories. He then visited the Far East, writing such plays as *East of Suez* (1922) and *Our Betters* (1923). In 1928 he settled in the South of France, where he wrote his astringent, satirical masterpiece, *Cakes and Ale* (1930). A British agent again in World War II, he fled from France in 1940 with only a suitcase, and lived until 1946 in the U.S., where he ventured into mysticism with *The Razor's Edge* (1945). But Maugham is best known for his short stories, several of which were filmed under the titles *Quartet* (1949), *Trio* (1950) and *Encore* (1951). The best of them, *Rain*, originally published in the collection, *The Trembling of a Leaf* (1921), an early, if unconscious piece of Freudian literature, exposes the tragic flaw of unhealthy asceticism in a devout missionary who falls from divine grace for a fellow-passenger, a prostitute, and commits suicide. His sparse, careful prose has sometimes unjustly been mistaken for superficiality. He refused to do more than tell a story; all else is propaganda, which seriously impairs a work of art. He was made C.H. in 1954. Other works include *Catalina* (1948), *The Complete Short Stories* (3 vols., 1951), *A Writer's Notebook* (1949) and essays on Goethe, Chehov, James, Mansfield in *Points of View* (1958). See bibliography (Mass. 1950) and studies by Aldington (1939), Stott (1950), Brophy (1952), Jonas (1954), Pfeiffer (1959), Cordell (1961), and R. Maugham, *Somerset and All the Maughams* (1966).

MAUNDEVILLE. See MANDEVILLE.

MAUPASSANT, Guy de, *mō-pas-ã* (1850–93), French novelist, born on August 5, at the Norman château of Miromesnil, was educated at Rouen and spent his life in Normandy. After a short spell as a soldier in the Franco-German war he became a government clerk, but encouraged by Flaubert, who was a friend of his mother, he took to writing and mingled with Zola and other disciples of Naturalism. His stories range from the short tale of one or two pages to the full-length novel. Free from sentimentality or idealism, they lay bare with minute and merciless observation the pretentiousness and vulgarity of the middle class of the period and the animal cunning and traditional meanness of the Norman peasant. His first success, *Boule de suif* (1880), which could be called either a short novel or a long short story, exposes the hypocrisy, prudery and ingratitude of the bourgeois in the face of a heroic gesture by a woman of the streets, while *La Maison Tellier* (1881) tells with penetrating satire and humour the tale of an outing for the inmates of a provincial house of ill-fame. At the other end of the scale *Le Horla* and *La Peur* describe madness and fear with a horrifying accuracy which foreshadows the insanity which beset de Maupassant in 1892 and finally caused his death. His short stories number nearly 300, and he wrote several full-length novels, including *Une Vie* (1883) and *Bel Ami* (1885). See Life by R. Dumesnil (1948) and studies by E.D. Sullivan (1954) and A. M. Vial (1954).

MAUPEOU, Nicolas Augustin de, *mō-poo* (1714–92), succeeded his father as chancellor of France in 1768, and incurred great unpopularity by suppressing the *parlements* and establishing new courts. On Louis XV's death (1774) he was banished. See *Remontrances du Parlement de Paris au 18e siècle* by J. G. Flammermont (1888).

MAUPERTUIS, Pierre Louis Moreau de, *mō-per-twee* (1698–1759), mathematician, was born at St Malo, served in the army, and as a strenuous supporter of Newton's physical theories was made a member of the Royal Society of London in 1728. In 1736–37 he was at the head of the French Academicians sent to Lapland to measure a degree of longitude. Frederick the Great made him president of the Berlin Academy. But his temper provoked general dislike and the special enmity of Voltaire, who satirized him in *Micromégas*, &c., driving him to Basel, where he died. See Lives by La Beaumelle (1856) and Lesueur (1897).

MAUREPAS, Jean Frédéric Phélippeux, Comte de, *mō-rè-pah* (1701–81), French statesman, and later minister of marine, rendered services to his department by promoting the French expedition to the North Pole and the Equator in 1736–37, but he displeased the all-powerful Pompadour, and was banished from court in 1749. Recalled and made first minister in 1774, he sought to humiliate England by recognizing the United States. See his *Mémoires* (4 vols. 1792).

MAURIAC, François, *mō-ryak* (1885–1970), French novelist, born at Bordeaux of Roman Catholic parentage, being regarded as the leading novelist of that faith. His treatment of the themes of temptation. sin and redemption, set in the brooding Bordeaux countryside, showed his art as cathartic, exploring the universal problems of sinful, yet aspiring, man. His principal novels, all translated into English, are: *Le Baiser au Lépreux* (1922); *Génitrix* (1923); the *Thérèse* novels; and *Nœud de Vipères* (1932). Also important is his play *Asmodée* (1938). He was awarded the 1952 Nobel prize for literature. See his *Mémoires politiques* (1968); and studies by E. Rideau (Paris 1945; with bibliography) and M. Jarret-Kerr (1954).

MAURICE, Prince of Orange and **Count of Nassau** (1567–1625), son of William the Silent, on whose assassination (1584) he was chosen stadhouder. A great part of the Netherlands was still in the hands of the Spaniards; but Maurice, aided by an English contingent under Leicester and Sidney, rapidly wrested from them the cities and fortresses. In 1597 he defeated the Spaniards at Turnhout, and in 1600 at Nieuwpoort; and for more than three years baffled all the power of Spain by his defence of Ostend. Finally, in 1609, Spain was compelled to acknowledge the United Provinces as a free republic. From this time keen religious dissension grew up between the Orange party, who favoured the orthodox Gomarists, and the liberal Remonstrants or Arminians (see BARNEVELDT, ARMINIUS), and the former triumphed. See Groen van Prinsterer, *Maurice et Barneveldt* (1875).

MAURICE, Prince (1620–52). See RUPERT.

MAURICE, Duke of Saxony. See AUGUSTUS II OF POLAND, CHARLES V, HOLY ROMAN EMPEROR.

MAURICE, (1) **John Frederick Denison** (1805–1872), English theologian, son of a Unitarian minister, was born at Normanston near Lowestoft, and studied at Trinity College and Trinity Hall, Cambridge, but as a Dissenter, left in 1827 without a degree, and commenced a literary career in London. He wrote a novel, *Eustace Conway*, and for a time edited the *Athenaeum*. Influenced by Coleridge, he took orders in the Church of England, became chaplain to Guy's Hospital (1837) and to Lincoln's Inn (1841–60); in 1840 he became professor of Literature at King's College, London, where he was professor of Theology 1846–53, and from 1866 till his death was professor of Moral Philosophy at Cambridge. The publication in 1853 of his *Theological Essays*, dealing with the atonement and eternal life, lost him his professorship of Theology. His books include *Moral and Metaphysical Philosophy*, *The Conscience*, and *Social Morality*. Maurice strenuously controverted Mansel's views on our knowledge of God, and denounced as false any political economy founded on selfishness and not on the universe. He was the mainspring of the movement known as Christian Socialism; and was the founder of the Working Man's College and of the Queen's College for Women, in both of which he taught. See Life by H. G. Wood (1950).

(2) **Sir John Frederick** (1841–1912), son of (1), professor (1885–92) of Military History at the Staff College, was author of *Life of Frederick Denison Maurice* (1884), a *System of Field Manœuvres* (1872), *The Ashantee War* (1874), *War* (1891), &c.

MAURIER. See DU MAURIER.

MAUROIS, André, pseud. of **Emile Herzog,** *mōr-wa* (1885–1967), French novelist and biographer, born in Elbeuf of a family of Jewish industrialists from Alsace who settled in Normandy after 1870. He was a pupil of Alain and took a degree in philosophy. During World War I he was a liaison officer with the British army and began his literary career with two books of shrewd and affectionate observation of British character, *Les Silences du Colonel Bramble* (1918) and *Les Discours du Docteur O'Grady* (1920). His large output includes *Ariel*, a life of Shelley (1923), *Disraeli* (1927), *Voltaire* (1935), *A la recherche de Marcel Proust* (1949), and *The Life of Sir Alexander Fleming* (trans. 1959). See studies by G. Lemaître (1940) and V. Dupin (Lausanne, 1945).

MAURRAS, Charles, *mō-rah* (1868–1952), French journalist and critic, born at Martigues (Bouches-du-Rhône). A student of philosophy at Paris, he was early influenced by the ideas of Auguste Comte, and this influence, combined with discipleship to the *Félibrige* movement, fostered in him a spirit critical of the contemporary scene, but by 1894 he had outgrown the association and was established as an *avant-garde* journalist. A trip to Greece made him a pronounced philhellene, and influenced by the Dreyfus case, he moved away from republicanism to a belief in the efficacy of monarchy. *Trois idées politiques . . .* (1898) and *Enquête sur la monarchie* (1901) state his views with clarity and vigour. From 1908, in *Action française*, his articles wielded a powerful influence on the youth of the country and this was reinforced by such studies as *Les Conditions de la victoire* (1916–18). *Action française* was finally discredited and in 1936 Maurras was imprisoned for violent attacks on the government of the day, the culmination of his bitter campaign in *Figaro*, *Gazette de France*, and other newspapers, against democratic ideals. His election to the Académie Française in 1938 accordingly caused much controversy and feeling ran very high when, at the fall of France in 1940, he supported the Vichy government. When the country was liberated in 1945, he was brought to trial and sentenced to life imprisonment. He was released, on medical grounds, in March 1952, and later that year died, a man whose considerable talent for dialectics and capacity for uninhibited expression of his strongly-held views had finally availed him nothing, since he had sponsored an unworthy cause.

MAURY, *mō-ree*, (1) **Jean Siffrein** (1746–1817), French prelate, was born at Valréas (dep. Vaucluse). Eloquent *éloges* on the dauphin, &c., gained him in 1784 admission to the Academy. In 1789 he was sent to the States General, where as an orator he rivalled Mirabeau and was one of the chief supporters of the crown. At the dissolution of the Constituent Assembly he withdrew to Rome, and was made an archbishop *in partibus*, and cardinal (1794); but he made his submission in 1804 to Napoleon, who appointed him in 1810 Archbishop of Paris. See Lives by his nephew (1827), Poujoulat (1835), and Ricard (1887).

(2) **Matthew Fontaine** (1806–73), American hydrographer, born at Spotsylvania, Va., entered the U.S. navy in 1825, and during a voyage round the world commenced his well-known *Navigation* (1834). Lamed for life in 1839, he was appointed superintendent in 1842 of the Hydrographical Office at Washington, and in 1844 of the Observatory. Here he wrote his *Physical Geography of the Sea* (1856), and his works on the Gulf Stream, Ocean Currents, and Great Circle Sailing. He became an officer of the Confederate navy, and later professor of Physics at Lexington. See Life by his daughter (1888).

MAUSER, Paul von, *mow'zèr*, (1838–1914), German fire-arm inventor, born in Oberndorf, Neckar, with his brother **Wilhelm** (1834–82) was responsible for the improved needle-gun (adopted by the German army in 1871) and for the improved breech-loading cannon. Paul produced the first magazine-rifle in 1897.

MAUSOLUS. See ARTEMISIA.

MAUVE, Anton, *mow'vè* (1838–88), Dutch painter, born at Zaandam, one of the greatest landscapists of his time, was influenced by Corot and Millet and painted country scenes. From 1878 he lived at Laren, gathering other painters round him in a kind of Dutch Barbizon school.

MAVOR, (1) O. H. See BRIDIE.

(2) **William Fordyce** (1758–1837), an Oxfordshire clergyman and schoolmaster, born at New Deer, compiled a commonplace book in his own system of shorthand, *c.* 1810.

MAWSON, Sir Douglas (1882–1958), English explorer and geologist, born at Bradford, Yorks, was educated at Sydney University, and in 1907 was appointed to the scientific staff of Shackleton's Antarctic expedition. In 1911 he was appointed leader of the Australasian Antarctic expedition, which charted 2000 miles of coast; he was knighted on his return. He was awarded the O.B.E. in 1920, and led the joint British-Australian-New Zealand expedition to the Antarctic in 1929–31. See F. Hurley, *Argonauts of the South* (1925).

MAX, Adolphe, *maks* (1869–1939), Belgian politician and patriot, born in Brussels. First a journalist, then an accountant, he became burgomaster of Brussels in 1909. When the German troops approached Brussels in August 1914, he boldly drove to meet them and opened negotiations. He defended the rights of the Belgian population against the invaders, and in September was imprisoned by the Germans, later refusing an offer of freedom on condition that he went to Switzerland and desisted from anti-German agitation. In November 1918 he returned to Belgium, was elected to the house of representatives, and became a minister of state.

MAXIM, Sir Hiram Stevens (1840–1916), born at Sangersville, Maine, U.S., became a coachbuilder. From 1867 he took out patents for gas apparatus, electric lamps, &c. His machine gun was perfected in London in 1883; he also invented a pneumatic gun, a smokeless powder, and a flying machine (1894). He was knighted in 1901. See *My Life* (1915), and Life by Mottelay (1920).

MAXIMILIAN I (1459–1519), German emperor, the son of Frederick III. By his marriage with Mary, heiress of Charles the Bold, he acquired Burgundy and Flanders; but this involved him in war with Louis XI of France, and in 1482 he was forced to give Artois and Burgundy to Louis. In 1486 he was elected King of the Romans. In 1490 he drove out the Hungarians who, under Matthias Corvinus, had seized (1487) much of the Austrian territories. At Villach in 1492 he routed the Turks, and in 1493 he became emperor. Having next married a daughter of the Duke of Milan, he turned his ambition towards Italy. But after years of war he was compelled (1515) to give up Milan to France and Verona to the Venetians; and in 1499 the Swiss completely separated themselves from the German Empire. The hereditary dominions of his house, however, were increased by the peaceful acquisition of Tirol; the marriage of his son Philip with the Infanta Joanna united the Houses of Spain and Hapsburg; while the marriage in 1521 of his grandson Ferdinand with the daughter of Ladislaus of Hungary and Bohemia brought both these kingdoms to Austria. He also improved the administration of justice, greatly encouraged the arts and learning, and caused to be written *Theuerdank* in verse and *Weisskunig* in prose, of both of which he himself is the hero, and probably part-author. He was called 'the foremost knight of the age'. See Lives by Klüpfel (1864) Ulmann (1884–91), 'Christopher Hare' (1913) and study by Waas (1941).

MAXIMILIAN, Ferdinand-Joseph, Emperor of Mexico (1832–67), the younger brother of Francis-Joseph I, became an Austrian admiral. In 1863 the French called together a Mexican assembly, which offered the crown of Mexico to Maximilian; he accepted it, and in June 1864 entered Mexico. But Juarez (q.v.) again raised the standard of independence, and Napoleon III had to withdraw his troops. In vain the Empress Charlotte (1840–1927), a daughter of Leopold I of Belgium, went to Europe to enlist support; her reason gave way under grief and excitement. Maximilian felt bound to remain and share the fate of his followers. With 8000 men he made a brave defence of Querétaro, but in May 1867 was betrayed, and on June 19 shot. He has been called a 'marionette Emperor'. Seven volumes of his sketches of travel, essays, &c. (*Aus meinem Leben*) were published in 1867. See books by Martin (1914), Corti (1928), Blasio (1944) and Hyde (1946).

MAX-MÜLLER. See MÜLLER (3).

MAXTON, James (1885–1946), Scottish politician, born in Glasgow, was educated at the university there and became a teacher. A supporter of the Independent Labour Party, he became its chairman in 1926 and he sat as M.P. for Bridgeton from 1922 until his death. A man of strong convictions, he was a staunch pacificist, and suffered imprisonment for attempting to foment a strike of shipyard workers during World War I, in which he was a conscientious objector. His extreme views claimed few supporters, but his sincerity won the respect of all. See Life by McNair (1955).

MAXWELL, (1) James Clark. See CLERK-MAXWELL.

(2) **Sir William Stirling.** See STIRLING-MAXWELL.

MAY, (1) Phil (1864–1903), English caricaturist, born at Wortley near Leeds, was left an orphan at nine, after years of poverty became poster artist and cartoonist of the *St Stephen's Review*, went to Australia and on his return in 1890 established himself by his *Annual* and contributions to *Punch*, &c. He excelled in depicting East London types. See Life by J. Thorpe (1948).

(2) **Thomas** (1594–1650), English dramatist and historian, was educated at Cambridge, and became a member of Gray's Inn and a courtier. He wrote dramas, comedies, poems and translations of the Georgics and Lucan. As secretary and historiographer to parliament he produced a *History of the Parliament 1640–1643* (1647), and a *Breviary* (1650). See Life by Chester (1932).

(3) **Sir Thomas Erskine, 1st Baron Farnborough** (1815–86), English constitutional jurist, educated at Bedford School, became assistant librarian of the House of Commons in 1831, clerk-assistant in 1856, and clerk of the House in 1871. He was created a baron in 1881 on his retirement. His *Treatise on the Law, Privileges, Proceedings, and Usage of Parliament* (1844) has been translated into various languages and remains a standard work; his *Constitutional History of England 1760–1860* (1861–63; edited and continued by F. Holland, 1912) is a continuation of Hallam.

MAYAKOVSKY, Vladimir (1894–1930), Soviet poet, began writing at an early age, became interested in new techniques, and was regarded as the leader of the futurist school. During the 1917 Revolution he emerged as the propaganda mouthpiece of the Bolsheviks. Among his revolutionary pieces are *150 million* (1920) and *Mystery Bouffe* (1918). He also wrote satirical plays. He died by his own hand. See study with translations by H. Marshall (1945).

MAYER, *mī'er*, **Julius Robert von** (1814–78), German physicist, was born at Heilbronn, and settled as physician there in 1841. In 1842 he announced from physiological considerations, the equivalence of heat and work and the law of the conservation of energy, independently of Joule (q.v.), and his mental health suffered on account of the dispute over priority. See studies by Dühring (1893) and Weyrauch (1889).

MAYHEW, Henry (1812–87), English author and joint editor of *Punch* with Mark Lemon (q.v.), was born in London, ran away from Westminster School and collaborated with his brother **Augustus** (1826–75) in writing numerous successful novels such as *The Good Genius that turns everything to Gold* (1847), *Whom to Marry* (1848), &c. He also wrote on many subjects, his best-known work being the classic social survey, *London Labour and the London Poor* (1851–62). Another brother, **Horace** (1816–72), also collaborated with Henry and was a contributor to *Punch*. See R. G. G. Price, *History of 'Punch'* (1957).

MAYO, (1) Charles Horace (1865–1939), American surgeon, made a special study of goitre, and with his brother organized the Mayo Clinic within what is now St Mary's Hospital, Rochester, Minn.

(2) **Katherine** (1868–1940), American journalist, born at Ridgeway, Pa., is remembered for her books exposing social evils, especially *Isles of Fear* (1925), condemning American administration of the Philippines, and *Mother India* (1927), a forthright indictment of child marriage and other customs.

(3) **Richard Southwell Bourke, Earl of** (1822–72), Indian statesman, was born in Dublin, and was educated at Trinity College, Dublin. He entered the House of Commons as a Conservative in 1847, and was appointed chief-secretary of Ireland by Lord Derby in 1852, 1858, and 1866. Sent out in 1868 to succeed Lord Lawrence, he was eminently successful as viceroy of India, but was fatally stabbed by a convict while inspecting the settlement at Port Blair on the Andaman Islands. See Life by Hunter (2 vols. 1875).

(4) **William James** (1861–1939), American surgeon, brother of (1), specialist in stomach surgery, established the Mayo Clinic and along with (1) set up the Mayo Foundation for Medical Education and Research (1915).

MAYOW, John (1640–79), English chemist, fellow of All Souls, Oxford, and of the Royal Society, preceded Priestley and Lavoisier by a century with his discoveries relating to respiration and the chemistry of combustion.

MAZARIN, *ma-za-rī*, **Jules,** orig. **Giulio Mazarini** (1602–61), cardinal and minister of France, was born July 14 at Pescina in the Abruzzi, studied under the Jesuits at Rome and at Alcalá in Spain. He accompanied a papal legate to the court of France, was papal nuncio there (1634–36), entered the service of Louis XIII as a naturalized Frenchman (1639), and two years later became cardinal through the influence of Richelieu, who before his death in 1642 recommended Mazarin to the king as his successor. Louis died in 1643, but Mazarin knew how to retain his power under the queen-regent, Anne of Austria; she certainly loved him, even if it cannot be proved that there was a private marriage between them (the cardinal had never taken more than the minor orders). He ruled more efficiently than Richelieu, and was almost as powerful. The parliament resisted the registration of edicts of taxation; but Mazarin caused the leaders of the opposition to be arrested (August 1648), upon which the disturbances of the Fronde began. The court retired to St Germain, but at length triumphed by the aid of Condé. The hatred against Mazarin, however, blazed out anew in the provinces, when at his instigation the queen-regent arrested Condé, Conti and Longueville in January 1650. Mazarin triumphed at Réthel, but soon had to succumb and retire to Brühl. Meantime the press teemed with pamphlets and satires against him—the *Mazarinades.* The cardinal used all his influence to form a new royal party, won the support of Turenne, and in February 1653 returned to Paris, regaining all his power and popularity. He acquired the alliance of Cromwell at the price of Dunkirk; and by the marriage of Louis XIV with the Infanta Maria Theresa (1659), brought the succession to the throne of Spain nearer. Mazarin died at Vincennes, March 9, leaving an immense fortune. His magnificent library was bequeathed to the Collège Mazarin, and his name lives in the rare 'Mazarin Bible'. His seven nieces whom he brought from Italy to the French court varied in character and ultimate fate, but all married counts, dukes or princes, though more than one died in poverty or obscurity. See Chéruel's Histories of France (1879–82), his edition of Mazarin's Letters (1879–91) and works by Renée (1856), Masson (1886), Hassall (1903), Roca (1908), Bailly (1935).

MAZEPPA, Ivan Stepanovich, *ma-zyay'pa* (*c.* 1644–1709), hetman of the Cossacks, was born of a noble family, and became a page at the court of Poland. A nobleman, having surprised him in an intrigue with his wife, had him bound naked upon his horse, which, let loose, carried him, torn and bleeding, to its native wilds of the Ukraine—or, in another story, to his own home. Mazeppa now joined the Cossacks, and in 1687 was elected hetman. He won the confidence of Peter the Great, who made him Prince of the Ukraine; but when Peter curtailed the freedom of the Cossacks, Mazeppa entered into negotiations with Charles XII of Sweden. His hopes of an independent crown perished in the disaster of Pultowa (1709), and he fled with Charles to Bender, where he died. His story is the theme of poems, notably that by Byron, plays, novels, opera, paintings, &c., and of a history by Kostomaroff (1882).

MAZZINI, *mat-zee'nee,* **Giuseppe** (1805–72), Italian patriot, was born at Genoa, June 22, studied at the university there, and at nineteen was practising as an advocate. In 1821 his heart was stirred by the sight of refugees from the unsuccessful rising in Piedmont. He wrote in favour of romanticism, became a more and more ardent champion of liberalism, and joining the Carbonari in 1829, was betrayed (1830) to the Sardinian police, and imprisoned in Savona. Released next year, he organized at Marseilles the Young Italy Association, which sought to create a free and united nation of Italians—republican from the nature of the case—and to work for the governance of the world by the moral law of progress. In 1831 he addressed to Charles Albert of Piedmont an appeal, urging him to put himself at the head of the struggle for Italian independence; the answer, under Metternich's influence, was a sentence of perpetual banishment, and in 1832 the French authorities expelled him from France. Henceforward he was the most untiring political agitator in Europe. He wrote incessantly with fervid eloquence and intense conviction. In 1834 he organized an abortive invasion of Savoy. The next two years Mazzini spent in Switzerland scattering, by means of his journal *Young Italy*, the seeds of republican revolt through Europe. Banished from Switzerland, he found a refuge in London in 1837; and, struggling with poverty, contrived to teach and civilize many of his poorer countrymen, the organ-boys of London. In 1844 he proved his charge against the British government of opening his letters and communicating their contents to the rulers in Italy—a charge which raised a storm of indignation throughout the country. He threw himself into the thick of the Lombard revolt in 1848. After Milan capitulated he tried with Garibaldi to keep the war alive in the valleys of the Alps. Leghorn received him with wild enthusiasm in February 1849, just before the republic was proclaimed at Rome, where in March Mazzini, Saffi, and Armellini were appointed a triumvirate with dictatorial powers. In April the French arrived; after a struggle the republic fell; and the triumvirs indignantly resigned (June). From London Mazzini planned the attempted risings at Mantua (1852), Milan (1853), Genoa (1857), and Leghorn (1857). Here also he founded, along with Kossuth and Ledru-Rollin, the republican European Association, and organized the Society of the Friends of Italy. In 1859 Mazzini condemned the alliance between Piedmont and Napoleon III. He supported Garibaldi in his expedition against Sicily and Naples; and when Piedmont defeated and took him prisoner at Aspromonte (1862), Mazzini broke finally with the monarchical party. In 1866–67 Messina in protest elected him its deputy to the Italian parliament four times in succession. Again expelled from Switzerland, he was (1870) arrested at sea and imprisoned for two months at Gaeta. He settled at Lugano, but died at Pisa, March 10, 1872. Utopian idealist, political dreamer, apostle of the democratic evangel, and restless conspirator, Mazzini was also a man of great organizing power; thoroughly sincere and disinterested, he felt only impatience and scorn for moderates and opportunists. It was inevitable that he and Cavour should dislike and distrust one another. Yet it was Mazzini who prepared the ground for Italian unity, Garibaldi who did most of the harvesting, and Cavour who entered into their labours. Mazzini's writings are mostly political. *On the Duties of Man* (new ed. 1955) contains an outline of ethical theory; *Thoughts upon Democracy in Europe* is a discussion of economics and socialism. See the collected edition of his *Scritti, editi ed inediti* (16 vols. 1861); the English *Life and Writings* (1864–70); the *Selected Essays* (edited by Clarke, 1887); the selections by Stubbs (1891); *Memoir* by Venturi (1874); and Lives by B. King (1938), C. O. Griffith (1932), D. Silone (1939), C. Sforza (1926), and G. Salvemini (1956).

MBOYA, Tom (1930–1969), African nationalist leader, born on a sisal estate in the white highlands of Kenya, educated at Holy Ghost College, Mangu, became a sanitary inspector (1951) but soon came under the influence of Kenyatta (q.v.) and joined his Kenya African Union, of which he was P.R.O. and later (1953) treasurer. On the suppression of the party, he turned to trade union activity, becoming secretary of the Kenya Federation of Labour. The unsatisfactory new Constitution of 1954 drove him to passive resistance and campaigning for independence. At the round-table conference in London (1960), he obtained important constitutional concessions for Africans, especially on land reform. After the resurgence of Kenyatta's party as the Kenya African National Union in 1960 he became its general secretary; he was Kenyan minister of labour (1962–63), minister of justice (1963–64), and minister of economic development and planning from 1964. He was assassinated in Nairobi in1969.

MEAD, (1) Margaret (1901–), American anthropologist, born in Philadelphia, was appointed assistant curator of ethnology at the American Museum of Natural History in 1926, associate curator from 1942, and curator from 1964. After expeditions to Samoa and New Guinea she wrote *Coming of Age in Samoa* (1928) and *Growing up in New Guinea* (1930). Her works combine authority with the ability to make anthropology intelligible to the layman. Later publications include *Male and Female* (1949) and *Growth and Culture* (1951).

(2) **Richard** (1673–1754), fashionable London physician, succeeded Radcliffe as leader of his profession and published on poisons and infections. Physician to Queen Anne, he was consulted by the consumptive French painter Watteau, who visited London specially for the purpose. See Memoirs by Maty (1755) and Winslow, *Conquest of Epidemic Disease* (1944).

MEADE, George Gordon (1815–72), American general, born at Cadiz in Spain, graduated at West Point in 1835, and served against the Seminoles and in the Mexican War. In 1861 he distinguished himself at Antietam and Fredericksburg, and in 1863 he commanded the Army of the Potomac and defeated Lee at Gettysburg. See Lives by his son (New York 1913) and Pennypacker (1901); also T. Lyman *Meade's Headquarters, 1863–65* (Boston 1922).

MEADOWS-TAYLOR, Philip. See TAYLOR.

MEAGHER, *mah'ėr*, **Thomas Francis** (1822–1867), Irish patriot, was born in Waterford. He became a prominent member of the Young Ireland party and in 1848 was transported for life to Van Diemen's Land. He made his escape in 1852, studied law in the United States, in 1861 organized the 'Irish brigade' for the Federals, and distinguished himself at Richmond and elsewhere. While secretary of Montana territory, and keeping the Indians in check, he was drowned in the Missouri. See Cavanaugh, *Memoirs of General Thomas Francis Meagher* (1892).

MECHNIKOV, Ilya (1845–1916), Russian biologist, was born at Ivanovka near Kharkov and in 1870 became professor at Odessa. In 1888 he joined Pasteur in Paris and shared the Nobel prize with Ehrlich in 1908 for his work on immunology. He discovered the phagocytes, cells which devour infective organisms. See Life by his widow (1921).

MEDAWAR, Sir Peter Brian (1915–), Brazilian-born British zoologist, professor of Zoology at Birmingham (1947–51), Jodrell professor of Comparative Anatomy at London University (1951–62), director of National Inst. for Medical Research, Mill Hill, from 1962. He shared the Nobel prize in 1960 with Burnet (3) for experiments on immunological intolerance. He gave the brilliant Reith Lectures (1959) on *The Future of Man*, became C.B.E. in 1958, was knighted in 1965, and was created C.H. in 1971.

MEDHURST, George (1759–1827), English engineer who first suggested a pneumatic dispatch (1810), was born at Shoreham.

MEDICI, *may'dee-chee*, a Florentine family which amassed great wealth by the efforts of Giovanni (1360–1429), the banker of Cafaggiolo in the Mugello, and which exerted a great political and cultural influence from the 14th century onwards. See works on the Medici Family by Smeaton (1902), Schevill (1909), G. F. Young (1909), Pieraccini (1925), Neale (1943). Noteworthy members were:

(1) **Catharine.** See CATHARINE DE' MEDICI.

(2) **Cosimo** (1389–1464), 'Pater Patriae', son of the banker Giovanni, and father of (7), began the glorious epoch of the family. He procured for Florence (nominally still republican) security abroad and peace from civil dissensions. He employed his wealth in encouraging art and literature. He made Florence the centre of the revival of learning, and enriched her with splendid buildings and great libraries. See works on him by Armstrong (1900) and Gutkind (1938).

(3) **Cosimo I** (1519–74), 'the great', was descended on his mother's side from (6). He possessed the astuteness of character, the love of art and literature of his greater predecessors, but was cruel and relentless in his enmities, though one of the ablest rulers of his century. He was created grand-duke of Tuscany in 1569 and thus became the founder of a dynasty which lasted until the 18th century. The later Medici grand-dukes were not of outstanding ability but managed to preserve the character of the Florentine state during the years of foreign domination. See Life by Booth (1921).

(4) **Giovanni** (1475–1521), cardinal, son of (6), became Pope Leo X (q.v.).

(5) **Giulio** (1478–1534), grandson of (7), became Pope Clement VII (q.v.).

(6) **Lorenzo** (1449–92), 'the magnificent', son of (7) and father of (4) and (8), became at twenty joint-ruler with his brother **Giuliano** (1453–78). The growing power of the Medici had roused much envy; and in 1478 the malcontents, headed by the Pazzi and in league with the pope, Sixtus IV, formed a plot to overthrow them. Giuliano fell a victim to the assassins; Lorenzo increased his popularity by the courage and judgment that he showed in this crisis. He was a just and magnanimous ruler, one of the most distinguished lyric poets of the day, an enthusiastic member of the Platonic Academy, the friend of artists and scholars, a promoter of the art of printing. His many-sided gifts combined to make the Laurentian Age (1469–1492) the most glorious period in Florentine history. Yet he sapped the existing forms of government, and by seeking the advancement of his family, left Florence a ready prey to her enemies. See Lives by E. Rho (1926), Fiori (1938), and Ady (1955).

(7) **Piero I** (1414–69), 'the gouty', son of (2), father of (6), ruled for five troubled years.

(8) **Piero II** (1471–1503), son of (6), allied himself with the king of Naples against Lodovico Sforza of Milan; and when the latter in 1492 called to his aid Charles VIII of

France, Piero surrendered Pisa and Leghorn to the French. The magistrates and people, incensed at his cowardice, drove him from Florence and declared the Medici traitors and rebels. All efforts of the Medici to regain their power were vain until in 1512 a Spanish papal army invaded Tuscany, Prato was taken and sacked, and the Florentines, helpless and terrified, recalled the Medici, headed by **Giuliano II** (1478–1516). In 1513 the elevation of (4) to the papal chair completed the restoration of the family to all their former splendour and made Florence into a papal dependency.

MEDTNER, Nikolai (1879–1951), Russian composer and pianist of German descent, born in Moscow, lived in the West from 1922. His classical-romantic compositions included two piano concertos and much piano music. See R. Holt, *Nicholas Medtner* (1955).

MEDWALL, Henry (1462–*c.* 1505), English dramatist, wrote *Fulgens and Lucres*, the earliest English secular play extant written before 1500.

MEE, Arthur (1875–1943), English journalist, editor and writer, born at Stapleford, Nottingham, most widely known for his *Children's Encyclopaedia* (1908) and for his *Children's Newspaper*. He also produced a *Self-Educator* (1906), a *History of the World* (1907), both with Sir John Hammerton, a *Popular Science* (1912), a *Children's Shakespeare* (1926), and *The King's England* (1936–1953), a series of topographical books describing the English counties.

MEEGEREN, Van. See VAN MEEGEREN.

MEGASTHENES, *me-gas'the-neez* (fl. 300 B.C.), a Greek ambassador (306–298 B.C.) at the Indian court of Sandrocottus or Chandra Gupta. Here he gathered materials for his *Indica*, from which Arrian, Strabo, &c. borrowed. The fragments were edited by Schwanebeck (1846) and Müller (1848).

MEGERLE, Ulrich. See ABRAHAM-A-SANTA-CLARA.

MEHEMET 'ALI (*c.* 1769–1849), better **Mohammed 'Ali**, viceroy of Egypt, an Albanian officer of militia, was sent to Egypt with a Turkish-Albanian force on the French invasion in 1798. After the departure of the French he, at the head of his Albanians, supported the Egyptian rulers in their struggles with the Mamelukes. Having become the chief power in Egypt, he in 1805 had himself proclaimed viceroy by his Albanians, and was confirmed in this post by the sultan. He secured for Egypt a galvanic prosperity by the massacre of the Mamelukes in the citadel of Cairo (1811), the formation of a regular army, the improvement of irrigation, and the introduction of the elements of European civilization. In 1816 he reduced part of Arabia by the generalship of his adopted son Ibrahim; in 1820 he annexed Nubia and part of the Sudan; and from 1821 to 1828 his troops, under Ibrahim, occupied various points in the Morea and Crete, to aid the Turks in their war with the insurgent Greeks. The Egyptian fleet was annihilated at Navarino, and Ibrahim remained in the Morea till forced to evacuate by the French in 1828. In 1831 Ibrahim began the conquest of Syria, and in 1832 totally routed the Ottoman army at Koniya, after which the Porte ceded Syria to Mehemet Ali on condition of tribute. The victory at Nezib in 1839 might have elevated him to the throne of Constantinople; but the quadruple alliance in 1840, the fall of Acre to the British, and the consequent evacuation of Syria compelled him to limit his ambition to Egypt. In 1848 he became insane and was succeeded by Ibrahim. See works by Mouriez (1857), Sabry (1930), Dodwell (1931).

MEHRING, Franz (1846–1919), German left-wing writer, born in Schlawe, Pomerania, was a founder of the German Communist Party and author of historical studies of the workers' movement, including *Geschichte der deutsche Sozialdemocratie* (1898) and a life of Marx (1919).

MÉHUL, Étienne Nicolas, *may-ül* (1763–1817), French operatic composer, born at Givet, became in 1795 professor of the Paris Conservatoire. Of his numerous operas, *Joseph* (1807) is his masterpiece. See Lives by Pougin (1889) and Brancour (Paris 1912).

MEILHAC, *may-yak*, **Henri** (1831–97), French playwright, born in Paris, from 1855 produced a long series of light comedies—some in conjunction with Halévy, and some, including *La Belle Hélène*, well known through Offenbach's music. His *chef-d'œuvre* is *Frou-Frou* (1869). He also collaborated with Halévy and Gille respectively in the libretti of the operas *Carmen* and *Manon*.

MEILLET, Antoine, *may-yay* (1866–1936), French philologist, born at Moulins, a great authority on Indo-European languages, was professor at the Collège de France from 1906, and wrote standard works on Old Slav, Greek, Armenian, Old Persian, &c.

MEINHOLD, Johann Wilhelm, *mīn-holt* (1797–1815), born on the island of Usedom, Lutheran pastor there and at Krummin and Rehwinkel, published poems and dramas, but is best known for his *Amber Witch* (trans. 1894).

MEINONG, Alexius von, *mī'-* (1853–1930), Austrian philosopher, born at Lemberg, *privatdozent* at Vienna (1878), was appointed professor at Graz (1882). A disciple of Brentano (q.v.), he wrote *Humestudien* (1877–92) and, in his *Untersuchungen zur Gegenstandstheorie und Psychologie*, 'Investigations into the theory of objects and psychology' (1904), attempted to preserve an objectivity for all kinds of entities. Bertrand Russell brilliantly attacked this on the principle of Occam's razor, that entities ought not to be multiplied except of necessity, differentiating sharply between grammatical and logical objects. See study by J. N. Findlay (1933) and RUSSELL.

MEI SHENG (d. 140 B.C.), Chinese poet to whom is given the credit of introducing the five-character line. For this he is sometimes called the father of modern Chinese poetry.

MEISSONIER, Jean Louis Ernest, *may-son-yay* (1813–91), French painter, mostly of genre and military scenes, was born at Lyons. See Lives by Mollet (1882), Gréard (1897) and Formentin (1901).

MEITNER, Lise, *mīt'nėr* (1878–1968), Austrian physicist, born in Vienna, professor in Berlin and member (1917–38) of the Kaiser

Wilhelm Institute for Chemistry, in 1917 shared with Hahn the discovery of the radioactive element protactinium. She is known for her work on nuclear physics. In 1938 she went to Sweden, to the Nobel Physical Institute, and in 1947 to the Royal Swedish Academy of Engineering Sciences, Stockholm, retiring to England in 1960.

MELA, Pomponius (fl. A.D. 40), the first Latin writer who was strictly a geographer, was born in S. Spain, and lived under the Emperor Claudius. His work, an unsystematic compendium, is entitled *De Situ Orbis*. The text is very corrupt. See work by H. Zimmermann (1895).

MELANCHTHON (Gk. for original surname **Schwarzerd**, 'black earth'), **Philip**, *mel-ank'thon* (1497–1560), German religious reformer, born at Bretten in the Palatinate, was appointed professor of Greek at Wittenberg in 1516 and became Luther's fellow-worker. His *Loci Communes* (1521) is the first great Protestant work on dogmatic theology. The Augsburg Confession (1530) was composed by him. After Luther's death he lost the confidence of some Protestants by concessions to the Catholics; while the zealous Lutherans were displeased at his approximation to the doctrine of Calvin on the Lord's Supper. His conditional consent to the introduction of the stringent Augsburg Interim (1549) in Saxony led to painful controversies. See Life by C. J. Manschreck (1957), studies by C. L. Hill (1944) and Hildebrandt (1946), and works by Harnack (1897), Ellinger (1902) and Engelland (1931).

MELBA, Dame Nellie, *née* **Mitchell** (1861–1931), Australian prima donna, born at Melbourne, appeared at Covent Garden in 1888. The wonderful purity of her soprano voice won her worldwide fame. She was created D.B.E. (1927). See her autobiographical *Melodies and Memories* (1925) and P. Colson, *Melba* (1931).

MELBOURNE, William Lamb, 2nd Viscount (1779–1848), English statesman, born in London, March 15, and educated at Eton, Trinity, Cambridge and Glasgow, became Whig M.P. for Leominster in 1805, but accepted in 1827 the chief-secretaryship of Ireland in Canning's government, and retained it under Goderich and Wellington. Succeeding as second viscount (1828), he returned to the Whigs, became home secretary in 1830, for a few months of 1834 was premier, and, premier again in 1835, was still in office at the accession of Queen Victoria (1837), when he showed remarkable tact in introducing her to her duties. In 1841 he passed the seals of office to Peel, and after that took little part in public affairs. His wife (1785–1828), a daughter of the Earl of Bessborough, wrote novels as Lady Caroline Lamb, and was notorious for her nine month's devotion (1812–13) to Lord Byron. The charge brought against Melbourne in 1836 of seducing the Hon. Mrs Norton (q.v.) was thrown out at once. See Lives by Torrens (1878), Dunckley (1880) and Lord David Cecil (1965). See also A Cecil, *Queen Victoria and her Prime Ministers* (1952).

MELCHETT. See MOND (1).

MELCOMBE, Lord. See DODINGTON.

MELEAGER, *mel-ee-ah'jèr* (fl. 80 B.C.), of Gadara, Palestine, was author of 128 exquisite epigrams. See translations by Headlam (1891) and Aldington (1920).

MELÉNDEZ VALDÉS, Juan (1754–1817), Spanish poet, born near Badajoz, became a professor of Classics at the University of Salamanca and fought for Napoleon in the War of Independence. Reckoned the greatest lyric poet of his time, he is known for his odes, ballads and romantic verses. See study by W. E. Colford (1942).

MELLON, (1) **Andrew William** (1855–1937), American politician, born in Pittsburgh, inherited a fortune from his father, which he used to establish himself as a banker and industrial magnate. Entering politics, he became secretary of the treasury in 1921 and made controversial fiscal reforms. He was ambassador to the U.K. in 1932–33. He endowed the National Gallery of Art at Washington.

(2) **Harriot** (*c.* 1777–1837), English actress, born in London, appeared at Drury Lane in 1795. She married her elderly protector, Thomas Coutts (q.v.), who left her all his money, in 1815; and in 1827 the Duke of St Albans. See her Memoirs (2 vols. 1886) and book by Pearce (1915).

MELLONI, Macedonio (1798–1854), Italian physicist, born at Parma, where later he was professor of Physics (1824–31), had to flee to France on account of political activities. Returning to Naples in 1839, he directed the Vesuvius Observatory till 1848. He is specially noted for his work on radiant heat. He introduced the term diathermancy to denote the capacity of transmitting infrared radiation.

MELO, Francisco Manuel de (1608–66), Portuguese writer, born at Lisbon, had an arduous and hazardous life as soldier, political prisoner, and exile in Brazil, whence he returned in 1657. He wrote in both Spanish and Portuguese, and is better remembered for his critical works and his history of the Catalan wars than for his voluminous poetry.

MELVILL, Thomas (1726–53), Scottish scientist, educated at Glasgow for the church, was the first (1752) to study the spectra of luminous gases. His early death at Geneva obscured the importance of his experiments.

MELVILLE, (1) **Andrew** (1545 – *c.* 1622), Scottish Presbyterian theologian, uncle of (6), was born at Baldowie, Montrose, and educated at St Andrews and Paris, became in 1568 professor at Geneva. On his return to Scotland (1574) he rendered eminent service as principal of Glasgow University. He had a very important share in drawing up the Presbyterian Second Book of Discipline. Chosen principal of St Mary's College, St Andrews (1580), besides lecturing on theology, he taught Hebrew, Chaldee and Syriac. In 1582 he preached boldly against absolute authority before the General Assembly; in 1584, to escape imprisonment, he went to London. He was repeatedly moderator of the General Assembly. In 1596 he headed a deputation to 'remonstrate' with James VI; and in 1606, with seven other ministers, was called to England to confer with him.

Having ridiculed the service in the Chapel Royal in a Latin epigram, he was summoned before the English privy council, and sent to the Tower. In 1611 he was released through the intercession of the Duke of Bouillon, who wanted his services as a professor in his university at Sedan. See Lives by McCrie (1819) and Morison (1899).

(2) **George John Whyte.** See WHYTE-MELVILLE.

(3) **Henry Dundas, 1st Viscount.** See DUNDAS Family (1).

(4) **Herman** (1819–91), American novelist, born in New York, became a bank clerk, but in search of adventure, joined a whaling ship bound for the South Seas. He deserted at the Marquesas and spent some weeks with a savage tribe in the Typee valley, an episode which inspired his first book, *Typee* (1846). Having been taken off by an Australian whaler, he was jailed at Tahiti as a member of a mutinous crew, but escaped and spent some time on the island. This adventure was the basis of his second book, *Omoo* (1847). *Mardi* (1849) also dealt with the South Seas, but entered the realm of satire not too successfully, so that Melville returned to adventure fiction with *Redburn* (1849) and *White Jacket* (1850), in which he drew on his experiences as a seaman on the man-of-war which brought him home from Tahiti. In 1847 he had married, and after three years in New York he took a farm near Pittsfield, Mass., where Nathaniel Hawthorne (q.v.) was his neighbour and friend. It was during this period that he wrote his masterpiece, *Moby Dick* (1851), a novel of the whaling industry, whose extraordinary vigour and colour and whose philosophical and allegorical undertones reflecting on the nature of evil have given it a place among the classic sea stories. Later novels include *Pierre* (1852), in a symbolic vein which was not appreciated by his readers, the satirical *Confidence Man* (1857), and *Billy Budd*, published posthumously in 1924 and used as the subject of an opera by Benjamin Britten in 1950. Now regarded as one of America's greatest novelists, Melville was not so successful during his life, even *Moby Dick* being unappreciated. After 1857, disillusioned and now a New York customs official, he wrote only some poetry. Recognition did not come until some thirty years after his death. See his *Letters* (1960), and studies by Weaver (1922), Mumford (1929), Anderson (1939), Sedgwick (1944), Arvin (1940), and Humphreys (1962).

(5) **Sir James,** of Halhill (1535–1617), Scottish soldier and diplomat, went to France as page to the young Queen Mary, and subsequently undertook missions to the courts of England and the Palatinate. See his Memoirs (Bannatyne Club, 1827).

(6) **James** (1556–1614), Scottish Reformer and diarist, nephew of (1), was born near Montrose, professor of Oriental Languages at St Andrews and minister in 1586 of Kilrenny, Fife. He took a leading part with his uncle in ecclesiastical politics and went to London in 1606. He was moderator of the general assembly in 1589. He is best known for his *Diary* (1556–1601), written in a racy, vigorous and idiomatic Scots.

MEMLINC, or Memling, Hans (*c.* 1440–94), Flemish religious painter, was born at Seligenstadt of Dutch parents, and lived mostly at Bruges. A pupil of Roger van der Weyden (q.v.), he repeated the types of his master. The triptych of the *Madonna Enthroned* at Chatsworth (1468), the *Marriage of St Catherine* (1479) and the *Shrine of St Ursula* (1489), both at Bruges, are among his best works. He was also an original and creative portrait painter. See Lives by Weale (1901), and K. Voll (New York 1913), also M. Conway, *The Van Eycks and their Followers* (1921).

MEMMI, Simone. See MARTINI (2).

MENAECHMUS (375–325 B.C.), Greek mathematician, one of the tutors of Alexander the Great, was the first to investigate conics as sections of a cone.

MÉNAGE, *may-nahzh,* **Giles** (1613–92), French lexicographer, born at Angers, gave up the bar for the church, but chiefly spent his time in literary pursuits. He founded, in opposition to the Academy, a salon, the Mercuriales, which gained him European fame and Molière's ridicule as Vadius in *Femmes savantes.* His chief work is his *Dictionnaire étymologique* (1650). See Lives by Baret (1859) and Ashton (Ottawa 1920).

MENANDER (*c.* 343–291 B.C.), the greatest Greek poet of the New Comedy, was born at Athens, and was drowned at the Piraeus. His comedies were more successful with cultured than with popular audiences; but Quintilian praised him without reserve, and Terence imitated him closely. Only a few fragments of his work were known till 1906, when Lefebvre discovered in Egypt a papyrus containing 1328 lines from four different plays. In 1957, however, the complete text of the comedy *Dyskolos* (' The Bad-tempered Man') was brought to light in Geneva. See G. Norwood, *Greek Comedy* (1931), and Webster, *Studies n Menander* (1950).

MENCHIKOV. See MENSHIKOV.

MENCIUS, properly **Meng-tse** (372–289 B.C.), a Chinese sage, born in Shantung, founded a school on the model of that of his great predecessor Confucius. When forty years of age he travelled from one princely court to another for more than twenty years, seeking a ruler who would put into practice his system of social and political order. But, finding none, he retired. After his death his disciples collected his sayings and published them as the *Book of Meng-tse.* The aim of his teaching was practical: how men, especially rulers, shall best regulate their conduct. His system is based on belief in the ethical goodness of man's nature, from which follow the cardinal virtues of benevolence, righteousness, moral wisdom, and propriety of conduct. He advocated free trade, the deposition of bad rulers, division of labour, inspection of work by government, maintenance of good roads and bridges, poor laws, education and the abolition of war. See Legge's Life (1875) and studies by Richards (1932) and Giles (1942).

MENCKEN, Henry Louis (1880–1956), American philologist, editor and satirist, born at Baltimore, became a journalist and literary critic. Satirical, individual and iconoclastic, he greatly influenced the American literary scene in the 'twenties. In 1924 he founded the *American Mercury*, and his great work, *The American Language*, was first published in 1918. See his autobiographical *Days of H. L. Mencken* (3 vols. in 1, N.Y. 1947), Life by Manchester (1952), and studies by Goldberg (1925) and Kemler (Boston 1950).

MENDEL, (1) **Gregor Johann** (1822–84), Austrian biologist, was born, son of a peasant proprietor, near Odrau in Austrian Silesia. Entering an Augustinian cloister in Brünn, he was ordained a priest in 1847. After studying science at Vienna (1851–53) he returned to Brünn, and in 1868 became abbot there. Meanwhile he had been pursuing remarkable researches on hybridity in plants, and eventually established the Mendelian Law of dominant and recessive characters. His principle of factorial inheritance and the quantitative investigation of single characters have become the basis of modern genetics. See works by Bateson (1913), Iltis (trans. 1932) and Ford (1931).

(2) **Lafayette Benedict** (1872–1935), American chemist, professor at Yale, did much original work on nutrition, discovering Vitamin A (1913) and the function of Vitamin C.

MENDELEYEV, Dmitri Ivanovich, *myen-dye-lyay'ef* (1834–1907), Russian chemist, born at Tobolsk, professor of Chemistry at St Petersburg from 1866, formulated the periodic law by which he predicted the existence of several elements which were subsequently discovered. Element No 101 is named mendelevium after him. See *Essays* by Thorpe (1923).

MENDELSOHN, Erich (1887–1953), German architect (from 1933 in England and from 1941 in America), was born in Allenstein. A leading exponent of functionalism, his most famous works include the Einstein Tower at Potsdam and the Hebrew University at Jerusalem. See study by Whittick (1940).

MENDELSSOHN, Moses (1729–86), German philosopher, grandfather of the composer, Mendelssohn-Bartholdy (q.v.), was born at Dessau. His father, whose name was Mendel, was a Jewish schoolmaster and scribe. He went to study in Berlin at thirteen and eventually became the partner of a rich silk manufacturer. He was a diligent student of Locke, Shaftesbury and Pope; and as a zealous defender of enlightened Monotheism, was an apostle of Deism, and the prototype of Lessing's *Nathan*. His principal works are on Pope as a philosopher (conjointly with Lessing, 1755), on the Sensations (1755), on Evidence in Metaphysics (1763); and *Jerusalem* (1783). See Lives by Kayserling (2nd ed. 1887) and F. Bamberger (1923).

MENDELSSOHN - BARTHOLDY, Felix (1809–47), German composer, the grandson of Moses Mendelssohn (q.v.), was born the son of a Hamburg banker who added the name Bartholdy. Felix was carefully educated, especially in music, and at ten made his first public appearance as pianist. Within the next few years he formed the acquaintance of Goethe, Weber and Moscheles, and composed his Symphony in C minor and the B minor Quartet. The August of 1825 saw the completion of his opera, *Camacho's Wedding*. With the *Midsummer Night's Dream* overture (1826) Mendelssohn may be said to have attained his musical majority. In London in 1829 he conducted his *Symphony in C Minor*. A tour of Scotland in the summer inspired him with the *Hebrides* overture and the *Scotch Symphony*. He conducted the Lower Rhine festival at Düsseldorf in 1833 and 1834 and in 1835 the Gewandhaus concerts at Leipzig. He settled in Berlin in 1841 when the king of Prussia asked his assistance in the founding of an Academy of Arts. In 1843 the new music school at Leipzig was opened for him with Schumann and David among his associates. He produced his *Elijah* in Birmingham in 1846. He had scarcely returned from his tenth and last visit to England, in May 1847, when the news of his sister Fanny's death reached him. Periods of illness and depression followed rapidly; and he died at Leipzig on November 4. He was eminent as pianist and organist. His music, however, suffers from lack of emotional range, often deteriorates into fairylike prestos and sugary sentimental andantes. His violin concerto (1844) characterizes this criticism, yet its charm almost defies it. See Lives by Benedict (1850), Moscheles (1873), Stratton (1901), Petitpierre (1948), Radcliffe (1954), his *Letters* (ed. Selden-Gott, 1947) and Jacob's *Mendelssohn and his Times* (1963).

MENDERES, Adnan, *men'de-rez* (1899–1961), Turkish statesman, born near Aydin. Though educated for the law, he became a farmer, entered politics in 1932, at first in opposition, then with the party in power under Kemal Ataturk. In 1945 he became one of the leaders of the new Democratic party and was made prime minister when it came to power in 1950. Re-elected in 1954 and 1957, in May 1960 he was deposed and superseded by General Cemal Gursel after an army *coup*. He appeared as defendant with over 500 officials of his former Democratic Party administration at the Yassiada trials (1960–61), was sentenced to death and hanged on Sept. 17, 1961, at Imrali.

MENDÈS, Catulle, *mã-dez* (1841–1909), French writer, born at Bordeaux of Jewish parentage, passed from the Parnassians to the Romantics, and wrote poems, novels, dramas and libretti as well as journalistic articles and criticisms. See critical biography (French) by A. Bertrand (1908).

MENDÈS-FRANCE, Pierre, *mã-dez-frãs* (1907–), French statesman, entered parliament in 1932 as a Radical. In 1941 he made a daring escape from imprisonment in Vichy France and came to England to join the Free French forces. After a short time as minister for national economy under de Gaulle in 1945, he became prominent on the opposition side, and in June 1954 succeeded M. Laniel as prime minister. At a troubled period he handled France's foreign affairs with firmness and decision, but his government was defeated on its North African policy, and he resigned in 1955. A firm critic of de Gaulle, he lost his seat in the 1958 election. See study by A. Werth (1956).

MENDOZA, distinguished family of Basque origin:

(1) **Diego Hurtado de** (1503–75), great-

grandson of (2). He was entrusted by Charles V with the conduct of his Italian policy and the representation of his views at the Council of Trent. He inherited his ancestor's gifts as a statesman and man of letters. His *War of Granada* is a masterpiece of prose.

(2) **Inigo Lopez de** (fl. 1450), Spanish statesman and poet, father of (3) and great-grandfather of (1), created Marquis of Santillana by John II of Castile in 1445 for his services on the field, was a wise statesman, a sturdy patriot, and an admired poet. He left an excellent account of the Provençal, Catalan and Valencian poets, and was an early folklorist and collector of popular proverbs.

(3) **Pedro Gonzalez de** (1428–95), Spanish prelate and son of (2), was Cardinal Archbishop of Toledo and trusted prime minister of Ferdinand and Isabella.

MENÉNDEZ PIDAL, Ramon, *pee-THahl'* (1869–), Spanish philologist and critic, born at Coruña, a pupil of Menéndez Pelayo (q.v.), became professor at the University of Madrid in 1899, founded the Madrid Centre of Historical Studies, and carried on the tradition of exact scholarship. His *La España del Cid* (1929) is the finest Spanish modern historical study. He published critical works on Spanish ballads and chronicles.

MENÉNDEZ Y PELAYO, Marcelino, *may-nen'dayth ee pay-lah'yō* (1856–1912), Spanish scholar, critic and poet, regarded as the founder of modern Spanish literary history. His writings, all exemplifying his traditionalism and Catholicism, include the *History of Aesthetic Ideas in Spain* (1844–91) and history of Spanish heterodoxies (1880–81). His verse includes *Odes* (1883) and anthologies. See studies by M. Artigas (Madrid 1927) and A. Sandoval (Madrid 1944).

MENGER, Karl (1840–1921), a founder of the 'Austrian school' of economics, was a native of Galicia, and from 1873 professor in Vienna. See J. A. Schumpeter, *Ten Great Economists* (1952).

MENGS, Anton Raphael (1728–79), German painter, was born, the son of a Danish artist, at Aussig in Bohemia. Having eventually settled at Rome, he turned Catholic, married, and directed a school of painting. In Madrid (1761–70 and 1773–76) he decorated the dome of the grand salon in the royal palace with the *Apotheosis of the Emperor Trajan.*

MENG-TSE. See MENCIUS.

MENIER, Émile Justin, *mèn-yay* (1826–81), French industrialist, established at Noisiel a great chocolate factory.

MENKEN, Adah Isaacs, originally (probably) **Adah Bertha Theodore** (1835?–68), Jewish actress, born near New Orleans, appeared as Mazeppa with immense success in London (1864) and elsewhere. She had many husbands (Heenan, the 'Benicia Boy', illegally as she discovered), and many literary friends. Her posthumous poems, *Infelicia*, were dedicated to Dickens. See B. Falk, *The Naked Lady* (1952).

MENNIN, Peter (1923–), American composer, born in Erie, Pennsylvania, studied at the Eastman College of Music and rapidly established himself as a composer of large-scale works. He has composed 7 symphonies, including *The Cycle*, a choral work to his own text, as well as concertos, choral and chamber music.

MENOTTI, Gian-Carlo (1911–), American composer, born in Milan, settled in America at the age of seventeen. Instinctively imbued with the Italian operatic tradition, Menotti has achieved international fame with a series of operas that began with *Amelia goes to the Ball*, produced in 1937 at Philadelphia, where he was a student. Menotti writes his own libretti, and his later works, *The Medium* (1946), *The Consul* (1950; Pulitzer prize), *Amahl and the Night Visitors* (1951) composed for television performance, *The Saint of Bleecker Street* (1954; Pulitzer prize), *Maria Golovin* (1958), &c., have great theatrical effectiveness although their musical style is derived from a wide variety of models.

MENSHIKOV, (1) Alexander Danilovich (*c.* 1660–1729), Russian field-marshal and statesman, was born of poor parents in Moscow, but entering the army, distinguished himself at the siege of Azov, and afterwards accompanied Peter the Great in his travels to Holland and England. During the war with Sweden (1702–13) he played an important part at Pultowa—Peter made him a field-marshal there—Riga, Stettin, &c. At the capture of Marienburg the girl who became Catharine I fell into Menshikov's hands, and was through him introduced to the tsar. Towards the end of Peter's reign Menshikov lost favour owing to extortions and suspected duplicities. But when Peter died he secured the succession of Catharine, and during her reign and that of her young successor, Peter II, he governed Russia with almost absolute authority. He was about to marry his daughter to the young tsar when the jealousy of the old nobility led to his banishment to Siberia and the confiscation of his estates.

(2) **Alexander Sergeievich** (1789–1869), great-grandson of (1), rose to the rank of general in the campaigns of 1812–15, was severely wounded at Varna in the Turkish campaign of 1828, and was made head of the Russian navy. His overbearing behaviour as ambassador at Constantinople brought about the Crimean war. He commanded at Alma and Inkermann, and defended Sebastopol, but in 1855 was recalled because of illness.

MENTEITH, Sir John de, *men-teeth'*, Scottish knight who captured Wallace (q.v.) at Glasgow and took him to London (1305).

MENUHIN, Yehudi, *men'yoo-in* (1916–), American violinist, born in New York, at the age of seven appeared as soloist with the San Francisco Symphony Orchestra. This was followed by appearances all over the world as a prodigy, and after eighteen months' retirement for study, he continued his career as a virtuoso, winning international renown. His sister **Hephzibah** (b. 1920) is a gifted pianist. See Life by Magidoff (1956).

MENZEL, *men'tsel,* **(1) Adolf** (1815–1905), German painter, illustrator and engraver, born at Breslau, is known for his drawings illustrating the times of Frederick the Great and William I. See works by Jordan (1905) and Waldmann (1941).

(2) **Wolfgang** (1798–1873), German critic

and historian, born at Waldenburg in Silesia, studied at Jena and Bonn, but from 1825 lived mainly in Stuttgart. He edited magazines, and wrote poems, novels, histories of German literature, poetry, &c., a history of the world, literary criticism and polemics. See his autobiographical *Denkwürdigkeiten* (1876).

MENZIES, Sir Robert Gordon (1894–), Australian statesman, born at Jeparit, Victoria, practised as a barrister before entering politics, becoming member of the Victoria parliament in 1928. Six years later, in 1934, he went to the Federal House of Representatives, sitting as the member for Kooyang. He was Commonwealth attorney-general for the years 1935 to 1939, prime minister from 1939 to 1941, and leader of the opposition from 1943 to 1949, when he again took office as premier of the coalition government. He had been appointed a privy councillor in 1937; and his qualities of high purpose and warm humanity were displayed during the war and the succeeding years. In 1956 he headed the Five Nations Committee which sought to come to a settlement with Nasser on the question of Suez. He was knighted in 1963 (K.T.) and retired in 1966.

MERCATOR, (1) Gerhardus, Latinized form of **Gerhard Kremer** (1512–94), a Flemish mathematician, geographer and map-maker, of German extraction. The projection which has since borne his name was used in his map of 1568. See L. A. Brown, *The Story of Maps* (Boston 1950).

(2) (Ger. **Kaufmann**), **Nicolaus** (*c.* 1620–87), German mathematician and astronomer, as engineer was responsible for the construction of the fountains at Versailles, as mathematician is credited with the discovery of a series for log $(1+x)$. From 1660 he lived in England.

MERCER, (1) Cecil William. See YATES (1).

(2) **John,** *mœr'sėr* (1791–1866), English dye chemist, born near Blackburn, Lancs., is chiefly known for his invention of mercerization—a process by which cotton is given a silky lustre resembling silk. Almost entirely self-educated, he made many important discoveries connected with dyeing and calico printing, and became F.R.S. in 1852.

MEREDITH, (1) George (1828–1909), English novelist, was born at Portsmouth, the grandson of a famous tailor (the ' great Mel ' of *Evan Harrington*), and was educated privately and in Germany. He was thus able to view the English class system with detachment. In London after being articled to a solicitor he turned to journalism and letters, his first venture appearing in *Chambers's Journal* in 1849, the year in which he married Mary Ellen Nicolls, a widowed daughter of Thomas Love Peacock. No doubt this disastrous marriage gave him an insight into sex relations, which bulk as largely in his work as his other great interest, viz., natural selection as Nature's way of perfecting man. His works did not bring him much financial reward; he had to rely on his articles in *The Fortnightly* and his work as a reader in the publishing house of Chapman and Hall. His prose works started with a burlesque Oriental fantasy, *The Shaving of Shagpat* (1855), to be succeeded in 1859 by *The Ordeal of Richard Feverel*, which turns on parental tyranny and a false system of private education. The mawkish love affairs make it barely readable today. He did not achieve general popularity as a novelist till the delightful *Diana of the Crossways* appeared in 1885. Intermediately we may write off his two novels on the Italian revolt of 1848, *Sandra Belloni* (1864) and *Vittoria* (1866); but not *Evan Harrington* (1860), for the light it throws on Meredith's origins; *Harry Richmond* (1871); and least of all *Beauchamp's Career*, which poses the question of class and party and is well constructed and clearly written. This last cannot be said of Meredith's later major novels, *The Egoist* (1879), a study of refined selfishness, and *The Amazing Marriage* (1895). These two powerful works are marred by the artificiality and forced wit which fatigues in so much of his poetry. His first volume of verse (1851) is quite unremarkable, but *Poems and Lyrics of the Joy of Earth* (1883) displays his new cryptic manner and discusses the two master themes —the ' reading of earth ' and the sex duel. His masterpiece on the latter theme had appeared in 1862 when he consorted with the pre-Raphaelite poets and painters. This is *Modern Love*, a novelette in pseudo-sonnet sequence form in which the novelist in him plays powerfully on incompatibility of temper. His reading of earth is expressed cryptically in the magnificent *Woods of Westermain*, intelligibly in *The Thrush in February* and thrillingly in *The Lark Ascending*. The volume called *A Reading of Life* (1901) adds little to the record. The modern revaluation of the Victorians has enhanced the fame of this very cerebral poet. See studies by G. M. Trevelyan (1906), R. Galland (1923), M. S. Gretton (1926), L. Stevenson (1953), J. Lindsay (1956) and P. Bartlett (1963).

(2) **Owen.** See LYTTON (2).

MEREZHKOVSKI, Dmitri Sergeyevich (1865–1941), Russian novelist, critic and poet, born at St Petersburg, wrote a historical trilogy, *Christ and Antichrist* (*The Death of the Gods, The Forerunner, Peter and Alexis*), books on Tolstoy, Ibsen, &c. His wife, **Zinaida Nikolayevna Hippius** (1870–1945), was also a poet, novelist and critic.

MERGENTHALER, Ottmar, *mer'gen-tahl-ėr* (1854–99), German-American inventor, born at Hachtel in Germany, became an American citizen in 1878 and invented the linotype machine (patented in 1884).

MÉRIMÉE, Prosper, *me-ree-may* (1803–70), French novelist, born at Paris, son of a painter, studied law, visited Spain in 1830, and held posts under the ministries of the navy, commerce and the interior. Admitted to the Academy in 1844, he became a senator in 1853. His last years were clouded by ill-health and melancholy, and the downfall of the empire hastened his death, at Cannes. He wrote novels and short stories, archaeological and historical dissertations, and travels, all of which display exact learning, keen observation, strong intellectual grasp, real humour, and an exquisite style. Among his novels are *Colomba*, *Mateo Falcone*, *Carmen*, *La Vénus d'Ille*, *Lokis*, *Arsène Guillot*, *La Chambre bleue* and *L'Abbé Aubain*. His letters include the famous *Lettres à une inconnue* (1873), the *Lettres à une autre inconnue* (1875) and the Letters to Panizzi (1881). See works by D'Haussonville (1888), Filon (1894–98), W. H. Pater (1900), Pinvert (1906, 1911), Trahard (1925) and Johnstone (1926).

MERIVALE, Charles (1803–93), English historian, son of **John Herman** (1779–1844), Greek scholar, and brother of **Herman** (1806–1874), English economist, was educated at Harrow and St John's College, Cambridge, where he became fellow and tutor. His *History of the Romans under the Empire* (1850–62) is too generous to imperialism. See his autobiography (1899). His son, **Herman Charles** (1839–1906), wrote some successful plays and novels. See his autobiography (1902).

MERLE D'AUBIGNÉ. See D'AUBIGNÉ (1).

MERLIN, an ancient British prophet and magician, supposed to have flourished during the decline of the native British power in its contest with the Saxons, and a hero of the Arthurian legend. There may have been two real Merlins—a 5th-century Welsh Merlin and a Caledonian 6th-century duplicate. See W. E. Mead, *Outline of the History of Merlin* (1889), and E. K. Chambers, *Arthur of Britain* (1927).

MERRICK, orig. Miller, Leonard (1864–1939), English novelist, born in London, wrote a number of sentimental novels, mostly with a Paris setting, such as *The Actor Manager* (1898), *A Chair on the Boulevard* (1908), *While Paris Laughed* (1918), &c.

MERRILL, Stuart (1863–1915), American symbolist poet, born at Hempstead, Long Island, New York, and educated in Paris. His French poems *Les Gammes* (1895), *Les Quatre Saisons* (1900), &c., developed the musical conception of poetry, often with alliteration's artful aid. See study by Henry (1927).

MERRIMAN, (1) Henry Seton, pseud. of Hugh Stowell Scott (1862–1903), English novelist, born at Newcastle-upon-Tyne, wrote *The Sowers* (1896), *The Velvet Glove* (1901) and many other novels in the Dumas tradition.

(2) **John Xavier** (1841–1926), South African statesman, born at Street, Somerset, went early to South Africa—his father was Bishop of Grahamstown—was a member of various Cape ministries from 1875, and premier (South African party) 1908–10. See Life by P. Laurence (1930).

MERSENNE, Marin (1588–1648), French mathematician and musician and a friend of Descartes, took the habit of a Minim Friar in 1611, and spent his life in study, teaching in convent schools, and travel. He stoutly defended the orthodoxy of the Cartesian philosophy.

MERTENS, Eva. See KEITH (4).

MERTON, (1) John Ralph (1913–), English artist, was born in London. He studied at Oxford and in Italy, and painted many portraits in tempera, including a notable one of the Countess of Dalkeith (1958).

(2) **Walter de** (d. 1277), founder in 1264 of Merton College, Oxford, the prototype of the collegiate system in English universities, was probably born at Merton in Surrey, and was Bishop of Rochester from 1274.

MERYON, Charles (1821–68), French etcher, was born in Paris, the son of an Englishman. After serving for a short time as a naval officer, he worked in poverty in Paris, and is known by his sombre and imaginative etchings of Paris streets and buildings. He was colour blind, and became insane. See monographs by Burty (1879), Wedmore (new ed. 1892), L. Delteil (trans. 1928) and C. Dodgson (1921).

MESDAG, Hendrik Willem (1831–1915), Dutch marine painter, born at Groningen, settled at The Hague, where his personal collection is housed in the Mesdag Museum. See H. Zilcken, *Mesdag, Painter of the North Sea* (trans. 1896).

MESMER, Friedrich Anton or Franz (1734–1815), Austrian physician and founder of mesmerism, born near Constance, studied medicine at Vienna, and about 1772 took up the opinion that there exists a power which he called animal magnetism. In 1778 he went to Paris, where he created a sensation. He refused 20,000 livres for his secret; but in 1785, a learned commission reporting unfavourably, he retired into obscurity in Switzerland. See books by Graham (1890) and F. A. Goldsmith (1934); also S. Zweig, *Mental Healers* (1933).

MESSAGER, André Charles Prosper, *-sa-zhay* (1853–1929), French composer, mostly of operettas, was born at Montlugon. *La Basoche* (1890), a comic opera, was his best. See study by M. Auge-Laribe (Paris 1951).

MESSALINA, Valeria (d. A.D. 48), the wife of the emperor Claudius, a woman infamous for avarice, lust and cruelty. Among her victims were the daughters of Germanicus and Drusus, Valerius Asiaticus, and her confederate Polybius. In the emperor's absence she publicly married one of her favourites. The emperor at last had her executed. See study by Stadelmann (1924).

MESSERSCHMITT, Wilhelm (1898–), German aviation designer and production chief, in 1923 established the Messerschmitt aircraft manufacturing works, of which he was the chairman and director. During World War II he supplied the Luftwaffe with its foremost types of combat aircraft. From 1955 he continued his activities with the revived Lufthansa and later also entered the automobile industry.

MESSIAEN, Olivier Eugène Prosper Charles, *mes-i-ã* (1908–), French composer and organist, son of the poetess Cécile Sauvage, was born in Avignon. He studied under Duprès and Dukas, and was appointed professor at the Schola Cantorum. In 1941, he became professor of Harmony at the Paris Conservatoire. Messiaen has composed extensively for organ, orchestra, voice and piano, and made frequent use of new instruments such as the 'Ondes Martenot'. His music, which has evolved intricate mathematical rhythmic systems, is motivated by religious mysticism, and is best known outside France by the two-and-a-half-hour piano work, *Vingt regards sur l'enfant Jésus*, and the mammoth *Turangalila* Symphony, which makes use of Indian themes and rhythms. See the *Technique de mon language musicale* (2 vols. 1944, trans. 1957).

MESTROVIĆ, Ivan, *mesh'tro-vich* (1883–1962), Yugoslav sculptor, was born at Vrpolje in Dalmatia; a shepherd boy, he was taught woodcarving by his father, eventually studying in Vienna and Paris, where he became a friend of Rodin (q.v.). He designed the national temple at Kossovo (1907–12). He lived in England during World War II and executed many portrait busts, including that of Sir Thomas Beecham. After the war he designed several war memorials. His work is naturalistic, emotionally intense and is characterized by an impressive simplicity. See Life by M. Curcin (trans. 1935). His self-portrait bust is in the Tate.

METASTASIO, the Grecized name of **Pietro Trapassi** (1698–1782), Italian poet, who was born at Rome. A precocious gift for improvising verses gained him a patron in Gravina, a lawyer, who educated him, and left him (1718) his fortune. He gained his reputation by his masque, *The Garden of Hesperides* (1722), wrote the libretti for 27 operas, including Mozart's *Clemenza di Tito*, and became court poet at Vienna in 1729. See his Letters, edited by Carducci (1883); Vernon Lee's *Studies* (1886); and Lives by Burney (1796) and L. Russo (1921).

METAXAS, Yanni, *me-taks'as* (1870–1941), Greek politician, born in Ithaka, graduated from the Military College in 1890, fought in the Thessalian campaign against the Turks in 1897, and later studied military science in Germany. He took a leading part in reorganizing the Greek army before the 1912–13 Balkan Wars and in 1913 became chief of the general staff. A Royalist rival of the Republican Venizelos, he opposed Greek intervention in World War I. On King Constantine's fall he fled to Italy, but returned with him in 1921. In 1923 he founded the Party of Free Opinion. In 1935 he became deputy prime minister after the failure of the Venizelist coup, and in April 1936 became prime minister, in August establishing an authoritarian government with a cabinet of specialist and retired service officers. His work of reorganizing Greece economically and militarily bore fruit in the tenacious Greek resistance to the Italian invasion of 1940–41.

METCALF, John, *met'kahf* (1717–1810), 'Blind Jack of Knaresborough', lost his eyesight at six, but, tall and vigorous, fought at Falkirk and Culloden, smuggled, drove a stagecoach, and from 1765 constructed 185 miles of road and numerous bridges in Lancashire and Yorkshire.

METCHNIKOFF. See Mechnikov.

METELLUS, a Roman plebeian family which rose to front rank in the nobility. One member of it twice defeated Jugurtha (109 B.C.); another conquered Crete (97 B.C.).

METFORD, William Ellis (1824–99), English engineer and inventor, born at Taunton. He was appointed in 1857 to the East India Railway, where his experiences during the Mutiny impaired his health, and he returned to England. His work on an explosive rifle bullet was frustrated by the condemnation of the St Petersburg Convention, and he turned to the design of breech-loading rifles. In 1888 the Lee-Metford rifle was adopted by the British War Office. See Lee (4).

METHODIUS. See Cyril.

METHUEN, until 1899 **Stedman, Sir Algernon Methuen Marshall,** Bart., *meth'yoo-in* (1856–1924), English publisher, born in London. He was a teacher of Classics and French (1880–95), and began publishing as a sideline in 1889 to market his own textbooks. His first publishing success was Kipling's *Barrack-Room Ballads* (1892), and, amongst others, he published works of Belloc, Chesterton, Conrad, Masefield, R. L. Stevenson and Oscar Wilde. He was created a baronet in 1916.

METSU, Gabriel, *met-sü'* (1630–67), Dutch genre painter, born at Leyden, settled in Amsterdam.

METTERNICH, Prince Clemens Lothar Wenzel (1773–1859), Austrian statesman, born at Coblenz, May 15, the son of an Austrian diplomat, studied at Strasburg and Mainz, was attached to the Austrian embassy at The Hague, and at twenty-eight was Austrian minister at Dresden, two years later at Berlin, and in 1805 (after Austerlitz) at Paris. In 1807 he concluded the treaty of Fontainebleau; in 1809 was appointed Austrian foreign minister, and as such negotiated the marriage between Napoleon and Marie Louise. In 1812–13 he maintained at first a temporizing policy, but at last declared war against France; the Grand Alliance was signed at Teplitz; and Metternich was made a prince of the empire. He took a very prominent part in the Congress of Vienna, rearranging a German confederation (while disfavouring German unity under Prussian influence), and guarding Austria's interests in Italy. From 1815 he was the most active representative of reaction all over Europe, persistently striving to repress all popular and constitutional aspirations. As the main supporter of autocracy and police despotism at home and abroad he is largely responsible for the tension that led to the upheaval of 1848. The French Revolution of that year, which overturned for a time half the thrones of Europe, was felt at Vienna, and the government fell. Metternich fled to England, and in 1851 retired to his castle of Johannesberg on the Rhine. He died at Vienna, June 11. A brilliant diplomat, a man of iron nerve and will, though personally kind, he had few deep convictions, no warm sympathies, and no deep insight into the lessons of history. See his not too trustworthy *Autobiography* (trans. 1880–83), and works by Sandeman (1911), F. de Reichenberg (1938), A. Cecil (3rd ed., 1947), C. de Grunwald (trans. 1953), G. de Bertier de Sauvigny (1962), and H. A. Kissinger, *A World restored* (1957).

METTRIE. See Lamettrie.

MEULEN, *mœ'len,* **Adam François van der** (1632–90), Flemish painter, born at Brussels, was from 1666 battle painter to Louis XIV.

MEUNG, Jean de, *mœ̃*, or **Jean Clopinel** (*c.* 1250–1305), satirist, flourished at Paris under Philip the Fair. He translated many books into French, and left a witty *Testament*. But his great work is his lengthy continuation (18,000 lines) of the *Roman de la Rose*, which substituted for tender allegorizing satirical pictures of actual life and an encyclopaedic discussion of every aspect of contemporary learning, which inspired many later authors to write in support of or in opposition to his views.

MEURSIUS, Lat. form of **De Meurs**, (1) **Johannes** or **Jan** (1579–1639), Dutch classical scholar, father of (2), born at Loozduinen near The Hague, became in 1610 professor of History, and in 1611 of Greek, at Leyden, historiographer to the States-General, and in 1625 professor of History at Sorö in Denmark, where he died. He edited Cato's *De Re Rustica*, Plato's *Timaeus*, Theophrastus's *Characters*, and a long series of the later Greek writers; he also wrote on Greek antiquities and Dutch and Danish history.

(2) **Johannes** (1613–54), son of (1), also wrote antiquarian works of value, but his name has wrongly been connected with the filthy *Elegantiae linguae Latinae* (probably by Chorier of Vienne, 1609–92).

MEUSNIER, Jean Baptiste Marie, *mœ-nyay* (1754–93), French general and scientist, made ascents in a balloon, stated the theorem which bears his name, relating to the centre of curvature of any plane section, and in the military field defended the fort of Königstein against the Prussians (1793).

MEYER, *mī'ėr*, (1) **Conrad Ferdinand** (1825–1898), Swiss poet and novelist, was born at Zürich. After a period during which he concentrated mainly on ballads and verse romances, he composed the epic poem *Huttens Letzte Tage* (1871) and a number of historical novels such as *Jürg Jenatsch* (1876), *Der Heilige* (1880), &c., in which he excels in subtle and intricate psychological situations and complex characters. See works on him by Mayne (1925), Burkhardt (1932), and Williams (1963).

(2) **Joseph** (1796–1856), German publisher, was born at Gotha, and issued many important serial works, editions of German classics, the encyclopaedia known as *Konversations-lexikon*, historical libraries, &c. His business, the ' Bibliographical Institute ', was in 1828 transferred from Gotha to Hildburghausen, in 1874 (by his son) to Leipzig.

(3) **Julius Lothar von** (1830–95), German chemist, born at Varel, Oldenburg, became the first professor of Chemistry at Tübingen in 1876. He discovered the Periodic Law independently of Mendeleyev (q.v.) in 1869 and showed that atomic volumes were functions of atomic weights.

(4) **Viktor** (1848–97), German chemist who studied under Bunsen in Heidelberg, became professor at Zürich, Göttingen, and finally at Heidelberg (1889). He discovered and investigated thiophene and the oximes. The nature of his work undermined his health and he died by his own hand.

MEYERBEER, Giacomo, *mī'ėr-bayr* (1791–1864), German operatic composer, was born at Berlin. Originally Jakob Beer, son of a Jewish banker, he adopted the name Meyer from a benefactor, and reconstructed and Italianized the whole. At seven he played in public Mozart's D-minor concerto, and at fifteen was received into the house of Abt Vogler at Darmstadt, where Weber was his fellow-pupil. His earlier works were unsuccessful, but in Vienna he obtained fame as a pianist. After three years' study in Italy he produced operas in the new (Rossini's) style, which at once gained a cordial reception. From 1824 to 1831 he lived mostly in Berlin. He next applied himself to a minute study of French opera. The result of this was seen in the production at Paris in 1831 of *Robert le Diable* (libretto by Scribe), whose totally new style secured unparalleled success over all Europe. It was followed in 1836 by the even more successful *Huguenots*. Appointed *kapellmeister* at Berlin, he wrote the opera *Ein Feldlager in Schlesien*. His first comic opera, *L'Étoile du nord* (1854), was a success, as was *L'Africaine*, produced after his death at Paris. Praised extravagantly by Fétis and others, Meyerbeer was severely condemned by Schumann and Wagner on the ground that he made everything subsidiary to theatrical effect. His successive adoption of widely-different styles bears this out. But even opponents concede the power and beauty of some of his pieces. See Lives by Hervey (1913), Dauriac (1930) and Kapp (1932).

MEYERHOF, Otto Fritz, *mī'ėr-hōf* (1884–1951), German physiologist, professor at Kiel (1918–24), director of the physiology department at the Kaiser Wilhelm Institute for Biology (1924–29), professor at Heidelberg (1930–38), is best known for his work on the metabolism of muscles. Forced to leave Germany in 1938, he continued his work in France and later in America. In 1922 he shared with A. V. Hill the Nobel prize for medicine. He died in Philadelphia.

MEYNELL, Alice Christiana Gertrude, *née* **Thompson**, *men'ėl* (1847–1922), English essayist and poet, was born in Surrey. Her volumes of essays include *The Rhythm of Life* (1893), *The Colour of Life* (1896) and *Hearts of Controversy* (1917). She published several collections of her own poems, and anthologies of Patmore, of lyric poetry, and of poems for children. With her husband, **Wilfrid Meynell** (1852–1948), author and journalist, she edited several periodicals. See the memoir by her daughter, V. Meynell (1929).

MEYRINK, Gustav, *mī'-* (1868–1932), German writer, born in Vienna, translated Dickens and wrote satirical novels with a strong element of the fantastic and grotesque. Among the best known are *Der Golem* (1915), *Das grüne Gesicht* (1916) and *Walpurgisnacht* (1917).

MIALL, Edward (1809–81), English divine, born at Portsmouth, was an Independent minister at Ware and Leicester. In 1840 he founded the *Nonconformist* newspaper in which he led the campaign for the disestablishment of the Church of England. He was M.P. from 1852. See Life by Miall (1884).

MICAH (fl. *c.* 700 B.C.), the sixth of the twelve minor Old Testament prophets, was a native of Moresheth Gath in SW. Judah, and prophesied during the reigns of Jotham, Ahaz and Hezekiah, being a younger contemporary of Isaiah, Hosea and Amos. On the book of Micah, see works by Caspar (1852) and Ryssel (1889) in German; and commentaries in English by Robinson (1926) and Wade (1932).

MICHAEL (1921–), king of Rumania 1927–30, 1940–47, son of Carol II, first succeeded to the throne on the death of his grandfather Ferdinand I, his father having renounced his own claims in 1925. In 1930 he was supplanted by Carol, but again made king in 1940 when the Germans gained control of Rumania. In 1944 he played a considerable part in the overthrow of the dictatorship of Antonescu. He announced the acceptance of the Allied peace terms, and declared war on Germany. His attempts after the war to establish a broader system of government were foiled by the progressive Communization of Rumania. In 1947 he was forced to abdicate and has since lived in exile.

MICHAEL VIII PALAEOLOGUS (1234–82), Eastern Roman emperor from 1259, distinguished himself as a soldier and was made regent for John Lascaris, whom he ultimately deposed and banished. His army took Constantinople in 1261 and defeated the Greeks in 1263–64. Involved in hostilities with Charles of Sicily, he was obliged to acknowledge papal supremacy in 1274, a policy which provoked discontent among his subjects, precipitated Charles's unsuccessful attempt on Constantinople (1281), and was a contributory cause of the revolt and massacre known as the Sicilian Vespers (1282). See study by Geanakoplos (1960).

MICHAELIS, Johann David, *mee-kay'lis* (1717–91), German Protestant theologian, was born at Halle, professor of Philosophy (1746) and Oriental Languages (1750) at Göttingen, pioneered historical criticism in biblical interpretation. See his *Introduction to the New Testament* (trans. 1801), &c., and *Autobiography* (1793).

MICHEL, *mee-shel,* **(1) Francisque** (1809–87), French antiquary, born at Lyons, from 1839 a professor at Bordeaux, earned a reputation by researches in Norman history, French *chansons*, argot and the Basques, and wrote *Les Écossais en France et les français en Écosse* (1862) and *A Critical Inquiry into the Scottish Language* (1882).

(2) Louise (1830–1905), French anarchist, born at Vroncourt, spent many years preaching revolution, and suffered imprisonment. She resided for ten years in London. See her *Mémoires* (Paris 1886) and Life by Boyer (Paris 1927).

MICHELANGELO, properly **Michelagniolo di Lodovico Buonarroti** (1475–1564), Italian sculptor, painter and poet, born 6 March at Caprese in Tuscany, where Lodovico his father was mayor. A few weeks after his birth the family returned to Florence. The boy was placed in the care of a stonemason and his wife at Settignano where Lodovico owned a small farm and marble quarry. At school the boy devoted his energies more to drawing than to his studies. Despite his father's opposition, in 1488 Michelangelo was bound to Domenico Ghirlandaio for 3 years. By this master he was recommended to Lorenzo de' Medici and entered the school for which the 'Magnifico' had gathered together a priceless collection of antiques. Lorenzo was not long in noting his talents, and to the beneficence of his patron Michelangelo owed the acquaintanceship of Poliziano, poet and tutor of the Medici children, and many of the most learned men of his time. To this period belong two interesting reliefs. In the *Battle of the Centaurs* the classical influence of Lorenzo's garden is strikingly apparent, though the straining muscles and contorted limbs, which mark the artist's mature work, are already visible. A marvellous contrast to the *Centaurs* is the *Madonna*, conceived and executed in the spirit of Donatello, which though not consciously antique, is far more classical. After Lorenzo's death in 1492, Piero, his son and successor, is said to have treated the artist with scant courtesy; and Michelangelo fled to Bologna for a time, but in 1495 he returned to Florence. During this sojourn to his native city he fashioned the marble *Cupid*. An acquaintance persuaded him to bury the work to give it an antique look and then send it to Rome to be sold. The *Cupid* was bought by Cardinal San Giorgio who discovered the fraud but recognized the talent of the sculptor and summoned him to Rome in 1496. The influence of Rome and the antique is easily discernible in the *Bacchus*, now in the National Museum in Florence. To the same period belongs the exquisite *Cupid* of the South Kensington Museum in London. The *Pieta* (1497), now in St Peter's, shows a realism wholly at variance with the antique ideal. For four years the sculptor remained in Rome and then, returning to Florence, fashioned the *David* out of a colossal block of marble. *David* is the Gothic treatment of a classical theme; in pose and composition there is a stately grandeur, a dignified solemnity. The *Holy Family of the Tribune* and the *Madonna* in the National Gallery in London belong to the same time, and, like a cartoon (now existing only as a copy) for a fresco never completed in the Great Hall of the Council, prove that Michelangelo had not wholly neglected the art of painting. His genius, however, was essentially plastic; he had far more interest in form than in colour. In 1503 Julius II, succeeding to the pontificate, summoned the painter-sculptor back to Rome. Michelangelo could as little brook opposition as the pope, and their dealings were continually interrupted by bitter quarrels and recriminations. The pope commissioned the sculptor to design his tomb, and for forty years Michelangelo clung to the hope that he would yet complete the great monument; but intrigue and spite were too strong for him. Other demands were continually made upon his energy, and the sublime statue of Moses is the best fragment that is left to us of the tomb of Julius. Bramante, if Vasari's account be true, poisoned the pope's mind against the sculptor; instead of being allowed to devote himself to the monument, he was ordered to decorate the ceiling of the Sistine Chapel with paintings. In vain he protested that sculpture was his profession, in vain he urged Raphael's higher qualifications for the task; the pope was obdurate, and in 1508–1512 Michelangelo achieved a masterpiece of decorative design.

Almost superhuman invention, miraculous variety of attitude and gesture, place this marvellous work among the greatest achievements of human energy. No sooner had he finished his work in the Sistine Chapel than he returned with eagerness to the tomb. But in 1513 Pope Julius II died, and the cardinals, his executors, demanded a more modest design. Then Pope Leo X, of the Medici family, commissioned Michelangelo to rebuild the façade of the church of San Lorenzo at Florence and enrich it with sculptured figures. The master reluctantly complied, and set out for Carrara to quarry marble; from 1514 to 1522 his artistic record is a blank, as the elaborate scheme was ultimately given up, though the sculptor remained in Florence. But in 1528 danger to his native city forced him to the science of fortification, and when in 1529 Florence was besieged Michelangelo was foremost in its defence. After the surrender he completed the monuments to Giuliano and Lorenzo de' Medici, which are among the greatest of his works. In 1533 yet another compact was entered into concerning Pope Julius's ill-fated sepulchre; whereupon he was once again commissioned to adorn the Sistine Chapel with frescoes. After some years he began in 1537 to paint *The Last Judgment*, which was his last pictorial achievement. Next year he was appointed architect of St Peter's, and devoted himself to the work with loyalty until his death, on February 18, 1564. Michelangelo is by far the most brilliant representative of the Italian Renaissance. He was not only supreme in the arts of sculpture and painting—in which grandeur and sublimity rather than beauty was his aim—but was versed in all the learning of his age, a poet, architect and military engineer. See bibliography by Steinmann and Wittkower (1927), studies by C. Tolnay (1945–54) and A. Allan (1956) and Milanesi's *Lettere di Michelangelo* (1873).

MICHELET, Jules, *meesh-lay* (1798–1874), French historian, born in Paris, lectured on history at the École Normale, assisted Guizot at the Sorbonne, worked at the Record Office, and was ultimately elected to the Academy in 1838 and appointed professor of History at the Collège de France. The greatest of many historical works are his monumental *Histoire de France* (24 vols. 1833–67) and his *Histoire de la Révolution* (7 vols. 1847–53). By refusing to swear allegiance to Louis Napoleon he lost his appointments, and henceforth worked mostly in Brittany and the Riviera. His second wife, **Adèle Mialaret,** is believed to have collaborated in several nature books, including *L'Oiseau* (1856), *L'Insecte* (1857) and *La Mer* (1861). In his last years he set himself to complete his great *Histoire,* but lived to finish only 3 volumes (1872–75). See books by G. Monod (1875 and 1905), Corréard (1886), J. Simon (1889) and Mme Quinet (1900).

MICHELL, John (1724–93), English geologist, born in Nottinghamshire, fellow of Queen's College, Cambridge, and professor of Geology (1769), described a method of magnetization, founded seismology, and is credited with the invention of the torsion balance. In 1767 he became rector of Thornhill, Yorkshire.

MICHELOZZI, Michelozzo di Bartolommeo, *mee-ke-lot'see* (1396–1472), Italian architect and sculptor, born at Florence, was associated with Ghiberti (q.v.) on his famous bronze doors for the baptistery there, and collaborated with Donatello (q.v.) in several major sculpture groups, including monuments to Pope John XXIII and Cardinal Brancacci (1427). He was court architect to Cosimo de' Medici, with whom he was in exile at Venice, where he designed a number of buildings. One of his finest works is the Ricardi Palace in Florence. See study by Wolff (1900).

MICHELSON, Albert Abraham (1852–1931), American physicist, born at Strelno in Germany, professor of Physics at Chicago from 1892, became in 1907 the first American scientist to win a Nobel prize. He invented an interferometer and an echelon grating, and did important work on the spectrum, but is chiefly remembered for the Michelson-Morley experiment to determine ether drift, the negative result of which set Einstein on the road to the theory of relativity.

MICKIEWICZ, Adam, *mits-kyay'vich* (1798–1855), Polish poet, was born near Novogrodek in Lithuania (Minsk), December 24, and educated at Vilna. He published his first poems in 1822, and as founder of a students' secret society was banished to Russia (1824–1829); there he produced three epic poems, glowing with patriotism. After a journey in Germany, France and Italy appeared (1834) his masterpiece, the epic *Pan Tadeusz* ('Thaddeus'; Eng. trans. 1886)—a brilliant delineation of Lithuanian scenery, manners and beliefs. After teaching at Lausanne, he was appointed Slavonic professor at Paris in 1840, but deprived in 1843 for political utterances. He went to Italy to organize the Polish legion, but in 1852 Louis Napoleon appointed him a librarian in the Paris Arsenal. He died November 28, 1855, at Constantinople, where the emperor had sent him to raise a Polish legion for service against Russia. His body, first buried at Montmorency in France, was in 1890 laid beside Kosciusko's in Cracow cathedral. Mickiewicz, the national poet of the Poles, is after Pushkin the greatest of all Slav poets. See Lives by his son (1888), M. M. Gardner (1911) and M. Jastrun (1949).

MICKLE, William Julius (1735–88), Scottish poet, born in Langholm manse, and educated at Edinburgh High School, failed as a brewer, and turned author in London. In 1765 he published a poem, *The Concubine* (or *Syr Martyn*), and in 1771–75 his version rather than translation of the *Lusiad* of Camoens. In 1779 he went to Lisbon as secretary to Commodore Johnstone, but his last years were spent in London. His ballad of *Cumnor Hall* (which suggested *Kenilworth* to Scott) is poor poetry, but 'There's nae luck aboot the hoose' is assured of immortality. See Life by Sim prefixed to Mickle's *Poems* (1806), and ADAM (4).

MIDDLETON, (1) Conyers (1683–1750), English controversialist, born at Richmond in Yorkshire, became a fellow of Trinity College, Cambridge, librarian to the university, and rector of Hascombe in Surrey. He died at his seat at Hildersham in Cambridgeshire. His *Letter from Rome, showing an exact Conformity between Popery and Paganism* (1729) was an attack on the Catholic ritual. He next assailed the orthodox Waterland, giving up literal inspiration and the historical truth of the Old Testament. He professed to be answering Tindal and other Deists, but it is none too certain that he was not himself a freethinker. In 1747–48 he published his *Introductory Discourse* and the *Free Inquiry* into the miraculous powers claimed for the post-Apostolic church. His famous *Life of Cicero* (1741) was largely borrowed from Bellenden (q.v.).

(2) **Sir Hugh** (*c.* 1560–1631), a London goldsmith, born at Galch Hill near Denbigh, in 1609–13 constructed the New River, a canal bringing water from springs in Hertfordshire to the New River Head at Clerkenwell to augment London's supply. He represented Denbigh from 1603, and was made a baronet in 1622.

(3) **Thomas** (*c.* 1570–1627), English dramatist, is first mentioned in Henslowe's *Diary* in 1602, when he was engaged with Munday, Drayton and Webster on a lost play, *Cæsar's Fall.* First on the list of his printed plays is *Blurt, Master Constable* (1602), a light, fanciful comedy. Two interesting tracts, *Father Hubbard's Tale* and *The Black Book*, exposing London rogues, were published in 1604, to which year belongs the first part of *The Honest Whore* (mainly written by Dekker, partly by Middleton). *The Phœnix* and *Michaelmas Term* (1607) are lively comedies; even more diverting is *A Trick to Catch the Old One* (1608); and *A Mad World, My Masters*, from which Aphra Behn pilfered freely in *The City Heiress*, is singularly adroit. *The Roaring Girl* (1611; written with Dekker) idealizes the character of a noted cutpurse and virago. Middleton was repeatedly employed to write the Lord Mayor's pageant. *A Chaste Maid in Cheapside* was probably produced in 1613, as was *No Wit, No Help like a Woman's. A Fair Quarrel* (1617) and *The World Lost at Tennis* (1620) were written in conjunction with Rowley, as were probably *More Dissemblers Besides Women* (1622?) and *The Mayor of Quinborough.* In 1620 Middleton was appointed city chronologer, and a MS. Chronicle by him was extant in the 18th century. The delightful comedy, *The Old Law*, first published in 1656, is mainly the work of Rowley, with something by Middleton, all revised by Massinger. In the three posthumously-published plays, *The Changeling, The Spanish Gypsy* and *Women Beware Women*, Middleton's genius is seen at its highest. Rowley had a share in the first two and probably in the third. A very curious and skilful play is *A Game at Chess*, acted in 1624. *The Widow*, published in 1652, was mainly by Middleton. *Anything for a Quiet Life* (*c.* 1619) may have been revised by Shirley. Middleton was concerned in the authorship of some of the plays included in the works of Beaumont and Fletcher. See study by R. H. Barker (1959).

MIERIS, Frans van, *meer'ees* **(1635–81), Dutch painter, born at Leyden, excelled in** small-scale, exquisitely finished genre paintings in the style of Dou and Ter Borch. His sons **Jan** (1660–90) and **Willem** (1662–1747) followed his example. Willem's son **Frans** (1689–1773) was less successful as a painter, but made his name as a writer of antiquarian works.

MIES VAN DER ROHE, Ludwig, *mees* (1886–1969), German-born American architect, born at Aachen, was a director of the famous Bauhaus at Dessau (1929–33), then emigrated to the U.S. where he was from 1938–58 professor of Architecture at the Chicago Technical Institute (later called the Illinois) for which he built new premises on characteristically functional lines. Other notable designs include the German pavilion at Barcelona (1929) and flats in Berlin (1926) and Chicago (1948–49). See study by P. C. Johnson (N.Y. 1947).

MIGNE, Jacques Paul, *meen'y'* (1800–75), French theologian, born at St Flour, was ordained in 1824. A difference with his bishop drove him to Paris in 1833, where he started the Catholic *L'Univers.* In 1836 he sold the paper, and soon after set up a great publishing house at Petit Montrouge near Paris, which gave to the world *Scripturae Sacrae Cursus* and *Theologiae Cursus* (each 28 vols. 1840–45), *Collection des orateurs sacrés* (100 vols. 1846–48), *Patrologiae Cursus* (383 vols. 1844 *et seq.*), and *Encyclopédie théologique* (171 vols. 1844–66). None of these possesses critical value. The Archbishop of Paris, thinking that the undertaking had become a commercial speculation, forbade it to be continued, and when Migne resisted, suspended him. A great fire put an end to the work in February 1868.

MIGNET, François Auguste Marie, *meen-yay* (1796–1884), French historian, was born at Aix in Provence, and there studied law with Thiers. In 1821 he went to Paris, wrote for the *Courrier français*, and lectured on Modern History. His *Histoire de la révolution française* (1824) was the first, a sane and luminous summary. With Thiers he signed the famous protest of the journalists in 1830, and after the Revolution became keeper of the archives at the Foreign Office (till 1848). In 1833 he explored the famous Simancas Archives. Elected to the Academy of Moral Sciences at its foundation in 1832, he succeeded Comte as its perpetual secretary in 1837, and was elected to fill Raynouard's chair among the Forty in 1836. His works include *La Succession d'Espagne sous Louis XIV* (1836–42), *Antonio Perez et Philippe II* (1845), *Franklin* (1848), *Marie Stuart* (1851), *Charles-Quint* (1854), *Éloges historiques* (1843–64–77), and *François I et Charles V* (1875). See works by Trefort (Budapest 1885), E. Petit (Paris 1889), J. Simon (1889).

MIGUEL, Maria Evarist (1802–66), king of Portugal, born at Lisbon, the third son of King John VI, plotted (1824) to overthrow the constitutional form of government granted by his father; but with his mother, his chief abettor, was banished. At John's death in 1826 the throne devolved upon Miguel's elder brother, Pedro, emperor of Brazil; he, however, resigned it in favour of his daughter, Maria, making Miguel regent; but Miguel summoned a Cortes, which proclaimed him king in 1828. In 1832 Pedro captured Oporto and Lisbon, and Charles Napier destroyed Miguel's fleet off Cape St Vincent (1833). Next year Maria was restored, and Miguel withdrew to Italy. He died at Bronnbach in Baden.

MIHAILOVICH, Dragoljub or **Drazha**, *me-hīl'o-vich* (1893–1946), Serbian soldier, was a regular officer in World War I, after which he rose to the rank of colonel in the Yugoslav army. In 1941 he remained in Yugoslavia, after the German occupation, and from the mountains organized resistance, forming groups called Chetniks to wage guerrilla warfare. When Tito's Communist Partisans' resistance developed, Mihailovich allied himself with the Germans and then with the Italians in order to fight the Communists. He was executed by the Tito government for collaboration with the occupying powers.

MIKLOSICH, Franz von (1813–91), Slavonic scholar, born at Luttenberg, studied at Graz, worked in the Imperial library at Vienna, and was professor of Slavonic at the University of Vienna (1850–85), being elected to the Academy in 1851, and knighted in 1869. His thirty works include *Lexicon Linguae Palaeoslovenicae* (1850), *Vergleichende slawische Grammatik* (1852–74), works on the Gypsies (1872–80) and the great *Etymologica Slav Dictionary* (1886).

MIKOLAJCIK, Stanislaw, *-lī'chik* (1901–67), Polish politician, born, a miner's son, in Westphalia, became leader of the Peasant Party in Poland in 1937. In 1940–43 he held office in the exiled Polish government in London, and in 1943–44 was prime minister. After the German defeat he became deputy premier in the new coalition government in Warsaw, but fled to the U.S.A. when the Communists seized power in 1947.

MIKOYAN, Anastas Ivanovich (1895–1970), Soviet politician, born in Armenia, of poor parents, studied theology and became a fanatical revolutionary. Taken prisoner in the fighting at Baku, he escaped and made his way to Moscow, where he met Lenin and Stalin. A member of the Central Committee in 1922, he helped Stalin against Trotsky, and in 1926 became minister of trade, in which capacity he did much to improve Soviet standards of living. He showed himself willing to learn from the West, e.g., in the manufacture of canned goods and throughout the food industry generally. While other politicians came and went, Mikoyan's genius for survival enabled him to become a first vice-chairman of the council of ministers (1955–64), and president of the presidium of the Supreme Soviet from 1964.

MILFORD, Robin Humphrey (1903–), English composer, studied under Vaughan Williams, wrote much choral music, a violin concerto and other instrumental works, and the oratorio *A Prophet in the Land* (1931).

MILHAUD, Darius, *mee-yō* (1892–), French composer, born at Aix-en-Provence, studied under Widor and D'Indy, and from 1917 to 1918 was attached to the French Embassy at Rio de Janeiro, where he met the playwright Paul Claudel, with whom he frequently collaborated, e.g., on the opera *Christopher Columbus*. For a time he was a member of *Les Six*. In 1940 he went to the U.S., where he was professor of Music at Mills Coll., Calif. (1940–47), and since then has lived in both France and America. Milhaud is one of the most prolific of modern composers, having written several operas, much incidental music for plays, ballets (including the jazz ballet *La Création du monde*), symphonies and orchestral, choral and chamber works.

MILL, (1) James (1773–1836), Scottish philosopher, father of (3), born, a shoemaker's son, near Montrose, studied for the ministry at Edinburgh, but in 1802 settled in London as a literary man. He edited and wrote for various periodicals, and in 1806 commenced his *History of British India* (1817–18). In 1819 the directors of the East India Company made him (though a Radical) assistant-examiner with charge of the revenue department, and in 1832 head of the examiner's office, where he held control of all the departments of Indian administration. Many of his articles (on government, jurisprudence, colonies, &c.) for the *Encyclopaedia Britannica* were reprinted. In 1821–22 he published *Elements of Political Economy*, in 1829 *Analysis of the Human Mind* and in 1835 the *Fragment on Mackintosh*. He was no mere disciple of Bentham, but a man of profound and original thought, as well as of great learning. His conversation gave a powerful stimulus to many young men like his own son and Grote. He took a leading part in founding University College London. See J. S. Mill's *Autobiography* and A. Bain (1882) and bibliography under (3).

(2) **John** (1645–1707), English New Testament critic, born at Shap in Westmorland, entered Queen's College, Oxford, as servitor in 1661, and was fellow and tutor, rector of Blechingdon, Oxfordshire (1681), principal of St Edmund's Hall (1685), and prebendary of Canterbury (1704). His *Novum Testamentum Graecum*, the labour of thirty years, sponsored by Dr Fell (q.v.), appeared a fortnight before his death.

(3) **John Stuart** (1806–73), English philosopher and radical reformer, born May 20 in London, the son of (1), who made himself responsible for John's unique education. He was taught Greek at the age of three, Latin and arithmetic at eight, logic at twelve, and political economy at thirteen, his only recreation being a daily walk with his father, who conducted all the while oral examinations. In 1820 he visited France, and on his return read history, law and philosophy. His first published writings appeared in the newspaper *The Traveller* (1822). In 1823 he began a career under his father at the India Office, from which he retired in 1858 as head of his department, declining a seat on the new India Council. His father moulded him into a future leader of the Benthamite movement and in 1823 he became a member of a small Utilitarian society which met in Bentham's house, the adjective 'utilitarian' having been taken to describe its doctrines from one of Galt's novels. He also became a frequent orator in

the London Debating Society, met Maurice and Sterling, 'the Coleridge Liberals', corresponded with Carlyle, and often contributed to the *Westminster Review*. A devout Malthusian, he was arrested in 1824 for helping to distribute birth control literature among London's poor. In 1826 he underwent an intellectual crisis which modified his attitude to Benthamism, which stressed reason to the exclusion of emotion. He realized that happiness was best achieved not by making it a direct aim but indirectly by enthusiastically following some ideal or cultural pursuit. His reviews on Tennyson (1835), Carlyle (1837) and particularly on Bentham (1838) indicate his newly-found divergencies from the creed he still professed to serve. In 1830 he met Harriet Taylor, the blue-stocking wife of a wealthy London merchant, and their long romance culminated in marriage in 1851, two years' after her tolerant husband's death, and she prevented Mill's modifications of Utilitarianism from going too far. In 1843 he published his great *System of Logic* with its four celebrated canons of inductive method which function effectively, provided that causality or Mill's 'Law of the Uniformity of Nature' is assumed. His treatment of induction influenced Jevons, Venn, Johnson and Keynes, and its rejection formed the basis of the mathematical logic systems of Frege, Meinong and Russell. In 1848 he published *Principles of Political Economy*, which foreshadowed the marginal utility theory and remained long a standard work. But he is best remembered for his brilliant essay *On Liberty* (1859), revised with great care in collaboration with Harriet, shortly before her death. It argues not only for political freedom but for social freedom, not only against the tyranny of the majority but also against the social tyranny of prevailing conventions and opinions. Essays on *Representative Government* and *Utilitarianism* (both 1861) followed, the latter making explicit Mill's modification of Benthamism, admitting qualitative differences in pleasures and providing proofs of the two chief Utilitarian principles that happiness alone is intrinsically good and that a right action is one which makes for the happiness of the greatest number. In proving the first he commits the celebrated howler of equating 'desired' with 'desirable'. His *Examination of Sir W. Hamilton's Philosophy* (1865) effectively criticized that philosopher's mixture of Scottish school and Kantian philosophy. Standing as a working-man's candidate for Westminster in 1865, he was surprisingly elected and also became lord rector of St Andrews University. His three years in parliament were devoted to women's suffrage, supporting the Advanced Liberals and campaigning against the governor of Jamaica's handling of a mutiny. Inspired by his late wife's views on the marriage contract and the inequalities suffered by women, he wrote *The Subjection of Women* (1869), an essay which provoked great antagonism. In 1872 he became godfather 'in a secular sense' to Lord Amberley's second son, Bertrand Russell, who was later to outrival him in terms of pure philosophical achievement. But Mill, like Locke, changed the intellectual climate and exerted a profound and abiding influence on the political reformers of his day. He died May 8, 1873, and was buried at Avignon. Other works include an important preface to his father's *Analysis of the Phenomena of the Human Mind* (1869), *Auguste Comte and Positivism* (1865), *Three Essays on Religion* (1874), *Dissertations and Discussions* (1859–75), *Letters*, ed. H. S. R. Elliot (1910), *Autobiography* (1873; new ed. H. J. Laski 1924). See Lives by A. Bain (1882), F. A. Hayek (1951), R. Borchard (1957), M. St J. Packe (1957), M. Cranston (1958), and studies by J. McCosh (1866), A. Bain (1884), T. Whittaker (1908), R. Jackson (1941), R. P. Anschotz (1953), K. Britton (1953), B. Russell (1955), J. C. Rees (1956), J. Plamenatz, *The English Utilitarians* (1950) and *British Empirical Philosophers*, ed. A. J. Ayer and P. Winch (1951).

MILLAIS, Sir John Everett, *mil-ay* (1829–96), English painter, born at Southampton, June 8, of an old Jersey family, studied in the schools of the Royal Academy, and at seventeen exhibited his *Pizarro seizing the Inca of Peru*. He now became associated with the pre-Raphaelite Brotherhood, especially with Dante Gabriel Rossetti and Holman Hunt, and was markedly influenced by them and by Ruskin. His first pre-Raphaelite picture, a scene from the *Isabella* of Keats, figured in the Academy in 1849, where it was followed in 1850 by *Christ in the House of His Parents*, which met the full force of the anti-pre-Raphaelite reaction. The pre-Raphaelite style is also apparent in the well-known *Ophelia* and *The Order of Release* (1853), but *Autumn Leaves* and *The Blind Girl* (1856) embody more sincerity and depth of feeling. The exquisite *Gambler's Wife* (1869) and *The Boyhood of Raleigh* (1870) mark the transition of his art into its final phase, displaying brilliant and effective colouring, effortless power of brushwork, and delicacy of flesh-painting. The interest and value of his later works lie mainly in their splendid technical qualities. In great part they are portraits (Bright, Beaconsfield, Newman, Gladstone, &c.), varied by a few such important landscapes as *Chill October* (1871), and by such an occasional figure piece as *The Northwest Passage* (1873). Millais executed a few etchings, and his illustrations in *Good Words*, *Once a Week*, *The Cornhill*, &c. (1857–64) place him in the very first rank of woodcut designers. He became a baronet in 1885, P.R.A. in February 1896; and, dying on August 13, was buried in St Paul's. See Ruskin's Notes on his Grosvenor Exhibition in 1886, Spielmann's *Millais and his Works* (1898), and Lives by Armstrong (new ed. 1896) and (1899) Sir John's fourth son, **John Guille** (1865–1931), animal painter, naturalist and big-game hunter.

MILLAY, Edna St Vincent (1892–1950), American poet, born at Rockland, Me., won the Pulitzer prize with her *The Harp-Weaver* (1922). Her published work includes *A Few Figs from Thistles* (1920), *Conversation at Midnight* (1937) and *The Murder of Lidice* (1942), as well as collections of lyrics and sonnets. See study by E. Atkins (1936).

MILLE, DE. See De Mille.

MILLER, (1) **Arthur** (1915–), American playwright, was born in New York City. His *Death of a Salesman* (1949) won the Pulitzer prize and brought him international recognition, though *All My Sons* (1947) had already placed him in the front rank of American dramatists. *The Crucible* (1953) is probably, to date, his most lasting work, since its theme, the persecution of the Salem witches equated with contemporary political persecution, stands out of time. Other works include *A View from the Bridge* (1955), the filmscript of *The Misfits* (1960) and *After the Fall* (1963). His marriage to Marilyn Monroe (d. 1962), the film actress, from whom he was divorced in 1961, and his brush with the authorities over early Communist sympathies brought him considerable publicity.

(2) **Henry** (1891–), American author, born in New York, is known for his satires and reminiscences coloured by the wanderings of an adventurous early life and by antagonism to various facets of modern society. His early books, published in Paris, were originally banned in Britain and America. His works include *Tropic of Cancer* (1934), *Tropic of Capricorn* (1938), *Air-Conditioned Nightmare* (1945) and *Selected Prose* (2 vols., 1965). See study by Perlès (1956).

(3) **Hugh** (1802–56), Scottish geologist and writer, born at Cromarty, from sixteen to thirty-three worked as a common stonemason, devoting the winter months to writing, reading and natural history. In 1829 he published *Poems written in the Leisure Hours of a Journeyman Mason*, followed by *Scenes and Legends of the North of Scotland* (1835). His *Letter to Lord Brougham* on the 'Auchterarder Case' brought him into notice. In 1834–39 he acted as bank accountant; in 1839 was invited to Edinburgh to edit the Non-intrusion *Witness*; and in 1840 published in its columns the geological articles afterwards collected as *The Old Red Sandstone* (1841). At the British Association of 1840 he was warmly praised by Murchison and Buckland; and Agassiz proposed that a fossil discovered by him in a formation thought to be nonfossiliferous should be named *Pterichthys Milleri*. Miller's editorial labours during the heat of the Disruption struggle were immense; he used the term 'Free Church' before 1843. Worn out by overwork, he shot himself. Miller contributed to Wilson's *Tales of the Borders* (1835) and to *Chambers's Journal*. His *First Impressions of England* (1847) is the record of a journey in 1845; in *Footprints of the Creator* (1850) he combated the evolution theory; *My Schools and Schoolmasters* (1854) is the story of his youth; and *Testimony of the Rocks* (1857) is an attempt to reconcile the 'days' of Genesis with geology. Posthumous works include *The Cruise of the Betsey* (1858), geological investigations among the islands of Scotland, *Sketch Book of Popular Geology* (1859), &c. See Lives by Bayne (1871), Leask (1896), and Geikie's address (1902).

(4) **Joaquin,** pen-name of **Cincinnatus Heine Miller** (1839–1913), American poet. Born in Indiana, he became a miner in California, fought in the Indian wars, was an express messenger, practised law in Oregon, edited a paper suppressed for disloyalty, in 1866–70 was a county judge in Oregon, was a Washington journalist, and in 1887 settled in California as a fruitgrower. His poems include *Songs of the Sierras* (1871); his prose works, *The Danites in the Sierras* (1881). He also wrote a successful play, *The Danites.* See his *My Life among the Modocs* (1873) and *My Own Story* (new ed. 1891), Life by Peterson (1937), and M. M. Marbury's *Splendid Poseur* (1954).

(5) **Patrick** (1731–1815), Scottish inventor of an early experimental steamboat with an engine by William Symington (q.v.), which he launched on the loch at his estate, Dalswinton, near Dumfries, in 1788.

(6) **William** (1781–1849), a New York farmer, founded the religious sect of Second Adventists or Millerites. See Lives by S. Bliss (1853) and J. White (1875).

(7) **William** (1810–72), Scottish poet, born in Glasgow, was a woodturner by profession, having relinquished a medical career through ill-health. He is now remembered only as the author of *Wee Willie Winkie*, one of his numerous dialect poems about children and childhood. A collection, *Scottish Nursery Songs and Other Poems*, appeared in 1863.

MILLERAND, Alexandre, *-rã* (1859–1943) French statesman, born in Paris, edited socialist papers, entered parliament 1885, was minister of commerce 1899–1902, of works 1909–10, of war 1912–13, when he resigned over a personal incident but was reinstated until 1915, when he resigned on complaints of deficiency of supplies. His chief critic, Clemenceau, later appointed him commissaire général in Alsace Lorraine 1919. As prime minister, 1920, he formed a coalition (Bloc National) and gave support to the Poles during the Russian invasion 1920. He became president 1920 and resigned in 1924 in face of opposition from *cartel des gauches* under M. Herriot. He later entered the senate and organized the opposition to the *cartel.*

MILLES, Carl Vilhelm Emil (1875–1955), Swedish sculptor, born near Uppsala, was especially renowned as a designer of fountains. Much of his work is in Sweden and the U.S.A., noteworthy examples being *Wedding of the Rivers* (1940) at St Louis, and *St Martin of Tours* (1955) at Kansas City, his last work. See Life by C. G. Laurin (Stockholm 1936).

MILLET, Jean François, *mee-lay* (1814–75) French painter, born at Grouchy near Gréville, worked on the farm with his father, a peasant, but, showing a talent for art, he was in 1832 placed under a painter at Cherbourg, who induced the municipality to grant his pupil an annuity. In 1837 Millet came to Paris, worked under Delaroche, studied the great masters, and eked out a living by producing fashionable potboilers after Boucher and Watteau. In 1840 and 1842 his entries for the Salon were rejected, but in 1844 his *Milkwomen* and *Riding Lesson* were hung. The 1848 Revolution and dire need drove him from Paris, and he settled with his wife and children at Barbizon, near the forest of Fontainebleau, living much like the peasants around him, and painting the rustic life of France with sympathetic power His famous *Sower* was completed in 1850. His *Peasants Grafting* (1855) was followed by *The Gleaners* (1857), *The Angelus* (1859) and other masterpieces He also produced many charcoal drawings of high quality, and etched a few plates. He received little public notice, and was never well off, but after the Great Exhibition of 1867 at Paris, in which nine of his best works were on show, his merit came to be recognized, and he was awarded the *Légion d'honneur*. After 1870, too late for him to benefit, his pictures began to realize high prices. See works by Roger-Milès (1895), Rolland (1902), Gurney (1954), and D. C. Thomson, *Barbizon School* (1890). Two minor French landscape painters were also named **Jean François Millet**, father (1642–79) and son (1666–1732).

MILLIKAN, Robert Andrews (1868–1954), American physicist, born in Illinois, studied at Oberlin College, Berlin, and Göttingen, taught physics in Chicago University from 1896 (as professor from 1910) till 1921 when he became head of Pasadena Institute of Technology. He determined the charge on the electron, gained a Nobel prize (1923), and discovered cosmic rays (1925) which he explained as due to atom-building. See his *Autobiography* (1951).

MILLS, Percy Herbert, 1st Viscount Mills (1896–1968), English politician and industrialist, born at Thornaby-on-Tees, won recognition in the drive to step up war production in 1939–45, and as one of the leaders of the Allied Control Commission played a leading part in fixing the level of Germany's postwar steel production. He was adviser to the government on housing (1951–52), chairman of the National Research and Development Association (1950–55), from 1957–59 held the newly-created office of minister of power, from 1959–61 was paymaster-general, and from 1961–62 minister without portfolio. He was created baronet in 1953, baron in 1957, and viscount in 1962.

MILMAN, (1) Henry Hart (1791–1868), English poet and church historian, was born in London, son of Sir Francis Milman (1746–1821), physician to George III. He was educated at Eton and Oxford, where he won the Newdigate Prize (1812). In 1816 he became vicar at Reading; in 1821–31 professor of Poetry at Oxford and in 1849 Dean of St Paul's. His *Poems and dramatic works* (3 vols. 1839) are almost forgotten except a few hymns. His principal historical work is *The History of Latin Christianity* (1854–55). See Life by his son (1900).

(2) **Robert** (1816–76), poet and theologian, nephew of (1), became Bishop of Calcutta in 1867. He published poems and theological works. See Life by his sister (1879).

MILN, James (1819–81), Scottish antiquary, made excavations on a Roman site at Carnac, Brittany (1872–80). Miln Museum, Carnac, contains his collection. Results published: *Excavations at Carnac* 1877 and 1881.

MILNE, (1) Alan Alexander (1882–1956), English author, born at St John's Wood, London, educated at Westminster and Trinity College, Cambridge, where he edited the undergraduate magazine *Granta*. He joined the staff of *Punch*, and became well known for his light essays and his comedies, notably *Wurzel-Flummery* (1917), *Mr Pim Passes By* (1919) and *The Dover Road* (1922). In 1924 he achieved world fame with his book of children's verse, *When We were Very Young*, written for his own son, Christopher Robin; further children's classics include *Winnie-the-Pooh* (1926), *Now We are Six* (1927) and *The House at Pooh Corner* (1928). See his autobiographical *It's Too Late Now* (1939).

(2) **Edward Arthur** (1896–1950), British astrophysicist, assistant director of the Cambridge Solar Physics Observatory (1920–1924), professor of Mathematics at Oxford (1928), president of the Royal Astronomical Society (1943–45), made notable contributions to the study of cosmic dynamics. He estimated the age of the universe to be *c.* 2,000,000,000 years.

(3) **John** (1859–1913), British seismologist, was born at Liverpool, worked in Newfoundland as a mining engineer, was for twenty years mining engineer and geologist to the Japanese government, married a Japanese wife, became a supreme authority on earthquakes, travelled widely, and finally established a private seismological observatory at Newport, Isle of Wight. He published important works on earthquakes, seismology and crystallography.

MILNE-EDWARDS, (1) Alphonse (1835–1900), French naturalist, son of (3), whom he assisted in his later work.

(2) **Frederick William** (1777–1842), physiologist, elder brother of (3).

(3) **Henri** (1800–85), naturalist, was born at Bruges, his father being English, studied medicine at Paris, became professor at the Jardin des plantes, and wrote a famous *Cours élémentaire de zoologie* (1834; rewritten 1851; trans. 1863), works on the crustacea, the corals, physiology and anatomy, researches on the natural history of the French coasts (1832–45) and the coasts of Sicily, and on the natural history of the mammalia (1871).

MILNER, (1) Alfred, 1st Viscount Milner (1854–1925), British statesman, born at Bonn, son of the university lecturer on English at Tübingen, had a brilliant career at Oxford, winning a New College fellowship. For a time he was assistant editor of the *Pall Mall Gazette*, and then private secretary to Goschen, who recommended him (1889) for the under-secretaryship of Finance in Egypt, where he wrote *England in Egypt* (1892; 12th ed. 1915). In 1892–97 he was chairman of the Board of Inland Revenue, in 1897–1901 governor of the Cape Colony, governor of the Transvaal and Orange River Colony 1901–05, and high commissioner for S. Africa 1897–1905, receiving a barony (1901) and a viscountcy (1902) for his services before and during the Boer War. In December 1916 he entered the War Cabinet; in 1918–19 he was secretary for war; in 1919–21 colonial secretary. K.G. in 1921, he recommended virtual independence for Egypt. See *Milner Papers, South Africa, 1897–1899* (1931) and *1899–1905* (1933); studies by E. A. Walker (1943), L. Curtis (1951), V. Halperin (1952), and Life by J. E. Wrench (1958).

(2) **Isaac** (1750–1820), English mathematician, Dean of Carlisle and Lucasian professor at Cambridge, wrote the life and edited works of his brother (4), besides works on scientific and theological subjects.

(3) **John** (1752–1826), English divine, called by Newman 'the English Athanasius', was born in London. Catholic priest at Winchester from 1779, in 1803 he was made a bishop *in partibus* and vicar-apostolic of the Midlands. He wrote a great history of Winchester (1798–1801) and much polemical theology. See Life by Husenbeth (1862).

(4) **Joseph** (1744–97), English church historian, born at Leeds and educated at Cambridge, was headmaster of Hull grammar school, and in 1797 vicar of Holy Trinity, Hull. His principal work, *History of the Church of Christ* (1794–1908), was completed by his brother Isaac (2). See Life by his niece (1842).

MILNER-GIBSON. See Gibson (7).

MILNES, Richard Monckton, 1st Baron Houghton (1809–85), English politician, was born in London (not at Pontefract). His father, 'single-speech Milnes' (1784–1858), declined the chancellorship of the Exchequer and a peerage; his mother was a daughter of the fourth Lord Galway. At Cambridge he was a leader in the Union, and one of the famous 'Apostles', and he was M.P. for Pontefract from 1837 until he entered the House of Lords in 1863. A Maecenas of poets, he got Lord Tennyson the laureateship, soothed the dying hours of poor David Gray, and was one of the first to recognize Swinburne's genius. Besides this, Lord Houghton —the 'Mr Vavasour' of Beaconsfield's *Tancred*—was a traveller, a philanthropist, an unrivalled after-dinner speaker, and Rogers' successor in the art of breakfast-giving. He went up in a balloon and down in a diving-bell; he was the first publishing Englishman who gained access to the harems of the East; he championed oppressed nationalities, liberty of conscience, fugitive slaves, the rights of women; and carried a bill for establishing reformatories (1846). As well as his poetry and essays, he published *Life, Letters and Remains of Keats* (1848). See Life by Wemyss-Reid (1890). His son, **Robert Offley Ashburton Crewe Milnes** (1858–1945), viceroy of Ireland 1892–95, Earl of Crewe (1895), marquis (1911), married Lord Rosebery's daughter and wrote his Life (1931), held cabinet rank 1905–16, 1931, was British ambassador in Paris 1922–28.

MILO, of Crotona in Magna Graecia, twelve times victor for wrestling at the Olympic and Pythian games, commanded the army which defeated the Sybarites (511 B.C.). He carried a live ox upon his shoulders through the stadium of Olympia, and afterwards, it was said, ate the whole of it in one day. In old age he attempted to split up a tree, which closed upon his hands, and held him fast until he was devoured by wolves.

MILTIADES, *mil-tī'a-deez* (d. *c.* 488 B.C.), Greek general, won the victory of Marathon against the Persians. He also attacked the island of Paros to gratify a private enmity, but, failing in the attempt, was on his return to Athens condemned to pay a fine of fifty talents, but died in prison of a wound received in Paros before paying it.

MILTON, John (1608–74), English poet, was born at Bread Street, Cheapside, the son of a London scrivener, a composer of some distinction who early discerned the boy's genius. From St Paul's School he went up to Christchurch, Cambridge, where he spent seven not altogether blameless years, followed by six years of studious leisure at Horton which he regarded as preparation for his life's work as a poet. His prentice work at Cambridge—apart from some poems of elegant Latinity written there or at Horton—includes the splendid Nativity Ode, the brilliant epitaph on Shakespeare and 'At a Solemn Music'. The poems he wrote at Horton—*L'Allegro* and *Il Penseroso*, *Comus* and *Lycidas*—he also regarded as preparatory for the great poem or drama which was to be 'doctrinal and exemplary for a nation'. *L'Allegro* and *Il Penseroso* are indeed set studies, but to eye and ear the alternative delights, gay and reflective of country life, are communicated with consummate art. *Comus* (1634) was the libretto of a masque which depends for its effect on the outside setting and on dance and song. The 'Doric delicacy' of the numbers offset the somewhat priggish Puritanism of the dialogue, which, however, is cast in a smooth early Shakespearean blank verse. *Lycidas* (1637) is our finest pastoral elegy, though it was censured for its outburst against the Laudian clergy by critics who were ignorant of the Renaissance pastoral convention. No doubt the acrimony of the outburst is prophetic of the struggle ahead. With this note struck so ominously Milton concluded his formal education with a visit to Italy (1638–39). The fame of his Latin poems had preceded him and he was received in the academies with distinction. His Italian tour was interrupted by news of the imminent outbreak of Civil War. This event, into which he threw himself with revolutionary ardour, silenced his muse for twenty years except for occasional sonnets, most of which were published in the volume of 1645. They range from civilities to friends to trumpet-blasts against his and the Commonwealth's detractors. Two stand out—the noble 'On His Blindness' and 'On the Late Massacre in Piedmont'. The reading of Milton's sonnets made Wordsworth a sonneteer on the Petrarchian model and in the same lofty vein. On his return to London in 1639 Milton undertook the education of his two nephews, but in 1641, the year when 'the dykes gave way', he emerged as the polemical champion of the revolution in a series of pamphlets against episcopacy, including an *Apology for Smectymnuus* (1642), Smectymnuus (q.v.) being an attack on episcopacy by five Presbyterians. He was now launched on his second series of controversial pamphlets—the divorce pamphlets which were occasioned by the refusal of his wife, Mary Powell, daughter of a Royalist, whom he married in 1642, to return to him after a visit to her people. The first of these, *The Doctrine and Discipline of Divorce* (1643), involved him in three supplementary pamphlets against the opponents of his views on divorce, and these occasioned a threat of prosecution by a parliamentary committee dominated by the Presbyterians who were now to be reckoned his chief enemies after episcopacy. *Areopagitica, A Speech for the Liberty of Unlicensed Printing* (1644) was the famous vindication which is still quoted when the press is in danger. The contemporary *Tractate on Education*, a brilliant exposition of the Renaissance ideals of education, has much less appeal to moderns. Meanwhile his wife returned to him in 1645 accompanied by her whole family as refugees after the 'crowning mercy' of Naseby, and two years later, his father having left him a competence, he was able to give up schoolmastering. The execution of King Charles launched him on his third public controversy, now addressed however to the conscience of Europe. As Latin secretary to the new council of state to which he was appointed immediately after his defence of the regicides, *The Tenure of Kings and Magistrates* (1649), he became official apologist for the Commonwealth and as such wrote *Eikonoklastes* and two *Defensiones*, the first *Pro Populo Anglicano Defensio* (1650), addressed to the celebrated humanist Salmasius; the second, also in Latin, *Defensio Secunda* (1654), which contains autobiographical matter and so supplements the personal matter in the *Apology for Smectymnuus*. Meanwhile, his wife having died in 1652, leaving three daughters, he married Catherine Woodcock, whose death two years later is the theme of his beautiful and pathetic sonnet 'Methought I saw my late espoused Saint'. Although blind from 1652 onwards, he retained his Latin secretaryship till the Restoration, which he roused himself to resist in his last despairing effort as pamphleteer. But the fire had gone out of him, and *The Readie and Easie Way*, which pointed to dictatorship, became the target of the Royalist wits. After the Restoration Milton went into hiding for a short period, and then after the Act of Oblivion (August 1660) he devoted himself wholly to poetry with the exception of his prose *De Doctrina Christiana*, which did not see the light till 1823. He married a third wife, Elizabeth Minshull, in 1662 and spent his last days in what is now Bunhill Row. His wife survived him. The theme of *Paradise Lost* had been in Milton's mind since 1641. It was to be a sacred drama then; but when in 1658 his official duties were lightened so as to allow him to write, he chose the epical form. The first three books reflect the triumph of the godly—so soon to be reversed; the last books, written in 1663, are tinged with despair. God's kingdom is not of this world. Man's intractable nature frustrates the planning of the wise. The heterodox theology of the poem which is made clear in his late *De Doctrina Christiana* did not trouble Protestant readers till modern critics examined it with hostile intent; at the same time they made him responsible for that 'dissociation of sensibility' in the language of poetry which had fatal effects on his 18th-century imitators. T. S. Eliot's recantation of the latter charge does not go very far. *Paradise Regained* ought to have appeased these critics, for its manner is quiet and grave, though not without grand rhetorical passages. The theme here is the triumph of reason over passion; Christ is more the elevated stoic than the redeemer. The disparagement of ancient poetry and philosophy may mean that, as Grierson says, 'The Humanist in Milton has succumbed to the Puritan'. Resignation is the note of *Paradise Regained* but *Samson Agonistes*, published along with it in 1674, shows the reviving spirit of rebellion, due no doubt to the rise of Whig opposition about 1670. The parallel of his own fortunes, both in the private and the public sphere, with those of Samson made Milton pour out his great spirit into this Greek play, the only one which in itself or as the libretto of Handel's oratorio has succeeded in English. Samson's reviving powers following on repentance are a sign of God's grace and their exercise in public may herald a new triumph of the 'good old cause' in England. The public cause and the vituperation of woman are the twin themes of this great poem, but it also plumbs the depths of questioning and despair. H. Darbishire's *Early Lives of Milton* (1932) includes the near-contemporary Lives by Milton's nephews, John and Edward Philips, and Toland. See also Lives by Symmons, Mitford, Todd, and Masson's great Life (7 vols. 1859–94) which is a too compendious history of the times. Dr Johnson's Life in *Lives of the Poets* is a fascinating study of honest but often misguided criticism struggling with distaste for Milton and all he stood for. Later and more discriminating studies are by R. Bridges (1893), Sir W. Raleigh (1900), D. Saurat (1924), E. M. Tillyard (1930), T. S. Eliot (1947), D. Daiches (1958) and R. Tuve (1958).

MINDSZENTY, Jozsef, Cardinal (1892–), Roman Catholic primate of Hungary, born at Mindszent, Vas, Hungary, son of Janos Pehm, became internationally known in 1948 when charged with treason by the Communist government in Budapest. He was sentenced to life imprisonment in 1949, but in 1955 was released on condition that he did not leave Hungary. In 1956 he was granted asylum in the American legation at Budapest. See S. K. Swift's *The Cardinal's Story* (1950), and book by Shuster (1956).

MINGHETTI, Marco, *min-get'tee* (1818–86), Italian statesman, Cavour's successor, was born in Bologna, studied there, and travelled in Europe and Britain. Pope Pius IX in 1846 made him, now a journalist, minister of public works. The pope's reforming zeal was short-lived, and Minghetti entered the Sardinian army, and at Custozza earned a knighthood. After Novara he settled at Turin, an ardent student of economics, a free-trader and a devoted friend of Cavour. Premier in 1863, he concluded with the Emperor Napoleon the 'September Convention' in 1864. At Rome in 1873–76 he was prime minister for the second time. He wrote on Raphael and Dante, *Economia pubblica* (1859), and *La Chiesa e lo Stato* (1878). See his *Ricordi* (1888).

MINIÉ, Claude Étienne, *meen-yay* (1804–79), French improver of firearms, born in Paris, from a private became colonel, and in 1849 invented the Minié rifle, and also perfected the expanding bullet. He was for a time at Cairo in the Khedive's service.

MINKOWSKI, Hermann, *min-kof'ski* (1864–1909), Russian-German mathematician, born near Kovno, was professor at Königsberg (1895), Zürich (1896), where he taught Einstein, and Göttingen (1902). He wrote on the theory of numbers and on space and time (1909), preparing the way for Einstein.

MINOT, George Richards (1885–1950), American physician, professor of Medicine at Harvard (1928–48), first suggested, with Murphy (2), the importance of a liver diet in the treatment of pernicious anaemia. In 1934 they shared the Nobel prize for medicine.

MINSHEU, John, *min'shoo* (fl. 1617), English lexicographer, taught languages in London. His dictionary, *Guide into Tongues* (1617), in eleven languages, is of great value for the study of Elizabethan English.

MINTO, Earls of, (1) Sir Gilbert Elliot-Murray-Kynynmound, 1st Earl (1751–1814), British statesman, born in Edinburgh, educated in France, Edinburgh and Oxford, was called to the bar in 1774. Elected M.P. in 1776, he supported Burke against Warren Hastings. He was later viceroy of Corsica (1794–96), and as governor-general of India (1806–13) he established order and security. See Life by his greatniece, Countess of Minto (1874–80).

(2) **Gilbert John Elliot-Murray-Kynynmound, 4th Earl** (1847–1914), colonial administrator, great-grandson of (1), served in many wars 1870–82. He was governor-general of Canada (1898–1904), and as viceroy of India (1905–10) was associated with Morley in the constitutional reforms. See Life by J. Buchan (1924); correspondence in Mary, Countess of Minto's *India, Minto and Morley* (1934), and study by Wasti (1964).

MINTO, William (1845–93), Scottish man of letters and critic, born near Alford, Aberdeenshire, became, after a spell of journalism, professor of Logic and English at Aberdeen. He wrote *Manual of English Prose Literature* (1872) and *Characteristics of English Poets* (1874). See Wright's *Some 19th Century Scotsmen* (1902).

MINTOFF, Dominic (1916–), Malta Labour politician, was educated at Malta and Oxford Universities, afterwards becoming a civil engineer. In 1947 he joined the Malta Labour Party and in the first Malta Labour government that year he became minister of works and deputy prime minister. He became prime minister in 1955 and in 1956–57 undertook negotiations with Britain to integrate Malta more closely with the former. These broke down in 1958, when his demands for independence and irresponsible political agitation over the transfer of the naval dockyard to a commercial concern, led directly to the suspension of Malta's constitution in January 1959. Having resigned in 1958 to lead the Malta Liberation Movement, he became opposition leader in 1962.

MINTON, (1) (Francis) John (1917–57), English artist, born at Cambridge. He studied in London and Paris, and from 1943 to 1956 taught at various London art schools. He was noted for his book illustrations and his brilliant watercolours, and also as a designer of textiles and wallpaper.

(2) **Thomas** (1765–1836), English pottery and china manufacturer, born at Shrewsbury, founded the firm which bears his name. Originally trained as a transfer-print engraver, he worked for Spode for a time, but in 1789 he set up his own business at Stoke-on-Trent, producing copper plates for transfer-printing in blue underglaze. He is reputed to have invented the willow pattern (for which an original copperplate engraved by him is in the British Museum). In 1793 he built a pottery works at Stoke, but he very soon produced a fine bone china (approximating to hard paste) for which the best period is 1798–1810. Much of it was tableware, decorated with finely painted flowers and fruit. His son, **Herbert** (his partner from 1817 to 1836), took over the firm at his death.

MINUCIUS FELIX (*c.* 2nd cent.), early Christian apologist, author of *Octavius*, a dialogue between a pagan and a Christian. See Rendall's edition (Loeb Library, 1931), Kühn's monograph (1882), Freese's trans. (1918) and Account by H. J. Baylis (1928).

MIRABEAU, *mee-ra-bō*, **(1) André Boniface Riqueti, Vicomte de** (1754–92), French soldier and politician, son of (3), brother of (2), fought in the American army (1780–1785) and at the outbreak of the French Revolution was returned to the States General. He raised a legion of *emigrés* against the republic but was accidentally killed at Freiburg-im-Breisgau. Notorious for his thirst and his corpulence, he was nicknamed *tonneau*—i.e., barrel. See Lives by Sarrazin (Leipzig 1893) and E. Berger (1904).

(2) **Honoré Gabriel Riqueti, Comte de** (1749–91), French orator and revolutionary, son of (3), brother of (1), was born at Bignon, in Loiret, March 9, 1749. At seventeen he entered a cavalry regiment, and lived so recklessly that his father imprisoned him in 1768 on the Île de Rhé, and next sent him with the army to Corsica. But his father refusing to purchase him a company, he left the service in 1770. He married (1772), but lived extravagantly and unhappily; and on account of his debts his father confined him (1773–75) at Manosque, the Château d'If, and the castle of Joux near Pontarlier. Hence he fled with the young wife of the grey-haired Marquis de Monnier to Amsterdam, where for eight months he earned his bread by laborious hack work for the booksellers. His *Essai sur le despotisme* made a sensation by its audacity. Meantime the *parlement* of Besançon sentenced him to death; and in May 1777 he was handed over by the States-General and flung into the castle of Vincennes, where, in close imprisonment of three and a half years, he wrote *Erotica*

biblion, *Ma conversion*, and his famous *Essai sur les lettres de cachet* (2 vols. 1782). In 1780 he was released, and in 1782 he got his sentence annulled. Drowned in debt, he made for some years a shifty living by writing. In England he was intimate with the Earl of Minto, Lord Lansdowne and Romilly, and his close observation of English politics taught him the good of moderation, compromise and opportunism. In 1786 he was sent on a secret mission to Berlin, and there obtained the materials for his work, *Sur la monarchie prussienne sous Frédéric le Grand* (4 vols. 1787). Rejected by the nobles of Provence as candidate for the States-General, he turned to the *tiers état*, and was elected by both Marseilles and Aix. When the *tiers état* constituted itself the National Assembly, Mirabeau's political sagacity made him a great force, while his audacity and volcanic eloquence endeared him to the mob. It was he who proposed the establishment of a citizen-guard, but he trembled at the revolutionary legislation of August 4, 1789. In conjunction with the Count de la Marck, a friend of Marie Antoinette, he drew up a memoir, setting forth the necessity for a new constitution, with a responsible ministry after the English pattern. But the queen detested the great tribune, and the Assembly passed a self-denying ordinance that no member should take office under the crown. Mirabeau surrounded himself with a group of friends who provided him with his facts, and even wrote his speeches and articles; he fused the materials so prepared for him in the alembic of his own genius. In the spring of 1790 communication opened anew with the court; Mirabeau was mortified to find himself mistrusted; but the court provided money to pay his debts and promised a monthly allowance. He risked all his popularity by successfully opposing Barnave's motion that the right of peace and war should rest not with the king but the Assembly. The queen gave him an interview in the gardens at Saint-Cloud, and Mirabeau assured her that the monarchy was saved. But as the popular movement progressed his dream of placing the king at the head of the Revolution became hopeless, and he found that the court did not grant him its full confidence, though he showed himself a really great financier in his measures to avert national bankruptcy. His secret aim was now to undermine the Assembly and compel it to dissolve, hoping that he might guide a new Assembly to wise concessions. But the queen would not commit herself to his guidance. In 1790 he was president of the Jacobin Club; on January 30, 1791, he was elected president of the Assembly for the fortnight. He defeated the proposed law against emigration, and successfully resisted Sieyès' motion that in the event of the king's death the regent should be elected by the Assembly. But his health had been sinking, though he refused to abate his giant labours; and he died April 2, 1791. His writings were collected by Blanchard (10 vols. 1822). See *Mémoires de Mirabeau écrits par lui-même, par son père, son oncle, et son fils adoptif* (8 vols. 1834); Loménie, *Les Mirabeau* (5 vols. 1878–91); French books by Rousse (1891) Mézières (2nd ed. 1908), Barthou (1913, 1926), Meunier (1926), Caste (1942), Vallentin (1948, Eng. trans. 1949); German by Stern (1889), Erdmannsdörffer (1900); English by Willert (1898), Warwick (1905), Trowbridge (1907), Fling (1908), Tallentyre (1908).

(3) **Victor Riqueti, Marquis de** (1715–89), French soldier and economist, father of (1) and (2), expounded physiocratic political philosophy in *Ami des hommes* (1756) and *La Philosophie rurale* (1763). See Loménie, *Les Mirabeau* (1879), Oncten (Berne 1886), Ripert (1901).

MIRANDA. See SÁ DE MIRANDA.

MIRANDOLA. See PICO.

MIRBEAU, Octave, *meer-bō* (1850–1917), dramatist, novelist, journalist, was born at Trevières (Calvados). A radical, he attracted attention by the violence of his writings. His *Les Affaires sont les affaires* (1903) was adapted by Sidney Grundy (1905). See *Œuvres complètes* (9 vols. 1934–36), study by M. Renon (Paris 1924).

MIRÓ, Joán, *mee-rō'* (1893–), Spanish artist, born at Montroig, studied in Paris and Barcelona, and exhibited in Paris with the Surrealists. He lived in Spain from 1940 to 1944, but has mainly worked in France. His paintings are predominantly abstract, and his humorous fantasy makes play with a restricted range of pure colours and dancing shapes, for example, *Catalan Landscape* (*The Hunter*) of 1923–24 in the Museum of Modern Art, New York. See monograph by S. Hunter (1959).

MISES, Richard von, *mee'zes* (1883–1953), German mathematician and philosopher, was professor at Dresden (1919), Berlin (1920–33), and from 1933 at Istanbul. An authority in aerodynamics and hydrodynamics, he set out in *Wahrscheinlichkeit, Statistik und Wahrheit*, ' Probability, Statistics and Truth ' (1928), a frequency theory of probability which he claimed to be empirical, although his requirement of ' randomness ' or ' principle of impossibility of gambling systems ' together with his reliance on convergence in an infinite series, raised the question whether his frequency-assertions could be confirmed or falsified by empirical investigations, which are confined to finite series. See W. Kneale, *Probability and Induction* (1949).

MISTINGUETT, stage name of **Jeanne Marie Bourgeois,** *mees-tī-get* (1874–1956), French dancer and actress, born at Pointe de Raquet, made her début in 1895 and became the most popular French music hall artiste of the first three decades of the century, reaching the height of success with Maurice Chevalier at the Folies Bergère. She also distinguished herself as a straight actress in *Madame Sans-Gêne*, *Les Misérables*, &c. See her *Toute ma vie* (1954).

MISTRAL, (1) Frédéric (1830–1914), Provençal poet, was born, lived and died at Maillane near Avignon. After studying law at Avignon, he went home to work on the land and write poetry; and he helped to found the Provençal renaissance movement (Félibrige school). In 1859 his epic *Miréio* (trans. 1890) gained him the poet's prize of the French academy and the *Légion d'honneur*. He was awarded a Nobel prize in 1904. Other works are *Calendau* (epic, 1861), *Lis Isclo d'or* (poems, 1876), *La Reino Jano* (tragedy, 1890), and a Provençal-French dictionary (1878–86). See his *Mémoires* (trans. 1907), and books by Downer (N.Y. 1901), Coulon (1930), Girdlestone (1937) and Leonard (Paris 1945).

(2) **Gabriela**, pseud. of **Lucila Godoy de Alcayaga** (1889–1957), Chilean educationalist, diplomatist and writer, born in Vicuña, as a teacher won a poetry prize with her *Sonetos de la muerte* at Santiago in 1915. She taught at Columbia University, Vassar and in Puerto Rico, and was formerly consul at Madrid and elsewhere. The cost of publication of her first book, *Desolación* (1922), was defrayed by the teachers of New York. Her work is inspired by her vocation as a teacher, by religious sentiments and a romantic preoccupation with sorrow and death, infused with an intense lyricism. She was awarded the Nobel prize for literature in 1945.

MITCHEL, John (1815–75), Irish patriot, born, a Presbyterian minister's son, near Dungiven, Co. Derry, studied at T.C.D., practised as an attorney, and became assistant editor of the *Nation*. Starting the *United Irishman* (1848), he was tried for his articles on a charge of 'treason-felony' and sentenced to fourteen years' transportation; but in 1853 he escaped from Van Diemen's Land to the United States, and published his *Jail Journal* (1854). Returning in 1874 to Ireland, he was next year elected to parliament for Tipperary, declared ineligible and re-elected, but died the same month. He published a *Life of Hugh O'Neill* (1845) and a *History of Ireland from the Treaty of Limerick* (1868). See studies by W. Dillon (1888), E. Montégut (trans. 1915), O'Hegarty (1917).

MITCHELL, (1) Donald Grant, pseud. **Ik Marvel** (1822–1908), American author, born in Norwich, Conn., was in 1853 appointed U.S. consul at Venice. He wrote *Reveries of a Bachelor* and *Dream Life* (1850–51; new eds. 1889); a novel, *Dr Johns* (1866); and *English Lands, Letters, and Kings* (4 vols. 1889–97). See Life by Dunn (N.Y. 1922).

(2) **James Leslie.** See Gibbon, Lewis Grassic.

(3) **Margaret** (1900–49), American novelist, was born at Atlanta, Georgia, and studied for a medical career. She turned to journalism, but after her marriage to J. R. Marsh in 1925, began the ten-year task of writing her only novel, *Gone with the Wind* (1936). This book sold eight million copies, was translated into thirty languages and filmed.

(4) **Sir Peter Chalmers** (1864–1945), Scottish zoologist and journalist, started his career as a lecturer at Oxford and London, and in 1903 was elected secretary of the Zoological Society. He inaugurated a period of prosperity at the London Zoo and was responsible for the Mappin terraces, Whipsnade, the Aquarium and other improvements. He was scientific correspondent to *The Times* from 1922 to 1934, and wrote a number of books on zoological subjects. He retired to Spain, but was forced to return by the Civil War. He was created C.B.E. in 1918, and knighted in 1929. See his autobiographical *My Fill of Days* (1937).

(5) **Reginald Joseph** (1895–1937), English aircraft designer. Trained as an engineer, he was led by his interest in aircraft to join in 1916 an aviation firm, where he soon became chief designer. He designed seaplanes for the Schneider trophy races (1922–1931) and later the famous Spitfire, the triumph of which he did not live to see.

(6) **Silas Weir** (1829–1914), American physician and author, was born at Philadelphia. He specialized in nervous diseases and pioneered in the application of psychology to medicine. As well as historical novels and poems he wrote medical texts, including *Injuries of Nerves* (1872) and *Fat and Blood* (1877). See his *Works* (16 vols., N.Y. 1913–14), and Lives by Burr (N.Y. 1929), Mumey (1934) and Earnest (1950).

(7) **Sir Thomas Livingstone** (1792–1855), Scottish explorer, born at Craigend, Stirlingshire, served in the Peninsular War, and from 1828 was surveyor-general of New South Wales. In four expeditions (1831, 1835, 1836, 1845–47) he did much to explore Eastern Australia ('Australia Felix') and Tropical Australia, especially the Murray, Glenelg and Barcoo rivers. He wrote on his travels, and was knighted in 1839.

(8) **William** (1879–1936), American aviation pioneer, beginning his army career in the signal service, he became an early enthusiast for flying and commanded the American air forces in World War I. He foresaw the development and importance of air power in warfare, but his outspoken criticism of those who did not share his convictions resulted in a court martial which suspended him from duty. His resignation followed and he spent the rest of his life lecturing and writing in support of his ideas. His vindication came with World War II and he was posthumously promoted and decorated. See Lives by E. Garreau (N.Y. 1942), I. D. Levine (N.Y. 1943), R. Mitchell (N.Y. 1953).

MITCHISON, Naomi Margaret (1897–), British writer, born in Edinburgh, daughter of J. S. Haldane (q.v.), won instant attention with her brilliant and personal evocations of Greece and Sparta in a series of novels: *The Conquered* (1923), *When the Bough Breaks* (1924), *Cloud Cuckoo Land* (1925), *Black Sparta* (1928), &c. In 1931 came the erudite *Corn King and Spring Queen*, which brought to life the civilizations of ancient Egypt, Scythia and the Middle East. She married **Gilbert Richard Mitchison** (b. 1890; created life peer, 1964) in 1916. He was a Labour M.P. (1945–64), and joint parliamentary secretary, ministry of land (1964–66).

MITFORD, (1) Diana. See Mosley.

(2) **John** (1781–1859), miscellaneous writer, was born at Richmond, Surrey, ordained and was a pluralist in Suffolk. Much of his time was devoted to literary pursuits, collecting and gardening. He edited the *Gentleman's Magazine* from 1834 to 1850 and also volumes for the *Aldine Poets* including Gray, Cowper and Milton. See his *Letters* by Houstoun (new ed. 1891).

(3) **John Freeman, 1st Baron Redesdale**

(1748–1830), English lawyer, brother of (7), M.P. 1788. He became successively solicitor-general, attorney-general, speaker of the House of Commons and lord chancellor of Ireland. He opposed Catholic emancipation in Ireland, which made him unpopular.

(4) **Mary Russell** (1787–1855), English novelist and dramatist, daughter of a spendthrift physician, at the age of ten drew £20,000 in a lottery and went to school at Chelsea. As the family became more and more impoverished she had to write to earn money. Several plays were produced successfully but failed to keep the stage. Her gift was for charming sketches of country manners, scenery and character, which after appearing in magazines were collected as *Our Village* (5 vols. 1824–32). She received a civil list pension in 1837 which was augmented on her father's death from subscriptions raised to pay his debts. In 1852 she published *Recollections of a Literary Life*. See *Letters* (ed. A. G. L'Estrange, 3 vols. 1870, ed. H. F. Chorley, 2 vols. 1872), *Friendships* (ed. A. G. L'Estrange, 2 vols. 1872), *Correspondence with Boner and Ruskin* (ed. E. Lee, 1914), Lives by W. J. Roberts (1913), C. Hill (1920), M. Astin (1930), V. G. Watson (1949).

(5) **Nancy** (1904–73), English author, sister of (1) and (6), and daughter of the 2nd Baron Redesdale, established a reputation with her witty novels such as *Pursuit of Love* (1945) and *Love in a Cold Climate* (1949). Her biographical books, *Madame de Pompadour* (1953), *Voltaire in Love* (1957), *The Sun King* (1966), are also popular. As one of the essayists in *Noblesse Oblige*, edited by herself (1956), she helped to originate the famous 'U', or upper-class, and 'non-U' classification of linguistic usage and behaviour. Her marriage (1933) to the Hon. Peter Rodd was dissolved in 1958. A fourth sister, **Jessica** (b. 1917), wrote *Hons and Rebels* (1960), her autobiography and story of the unconventional Mitford childhood.

(6) **Unity Valkyrie** (1914–48), sister of (1) and (5), was notorious for her associations with leading Nazis in Germany but returned to Britain during World War II in January 1940, suffering from a gunshot wound.

(7) **William** (1744–1827), English historian, brother of (3), born in London, studied at Queen's College, Oxford, in 1761 succeeded to the family estate of Exbury, and in 1769 became a captain in the South Hampshire Militia, of which Gibbon was major. On Gibbon's advice he undertook his pugnacious anti-democratic *History of Greece* (5 vols. 1784–1818), which, in virtue of careful research, held the highest place in the opinion of scholars until the appearance of Thirlwall and Grote. He sat in parliament 1785–1818. See Memoir prefixed to 7th edition of his *History* (1838), by his brother (3).

MITHRADATES, *mith-ra-day'teez* (Grecized from the Persian, 'gift of Mithras'), the name of several kings of Pontus, Armenia, Commagene and Parthia.

Mithradates VI, surnamed **Eupator**, called **the Great**, king of Pontus, succeeded to the throne about 120 B.C., a boy of barely thirteen, soon subdued the tribes who bordered on the Euxine as far as the Crimea, and made an incursion into Cappadocia and Bithynia, then Roman. In the *First Mithradatic War*, commenced by the Romans (88), Mithradates' generals repeatedly defeated the Asiatic levies of the Romans, and he himself occupied the Roman possessions in Asia Minor. But in 85 he was defeated by Flavius Fimbria, and compelled to make peace with Sulla, relinquishing all his conquests in Asia, giving up 70 war galleys, and paying 2000 talents. The wanton aggressions of the Roman legate gave rise to the *Second Mithradatic War* (83–81), in which Mithradates was wholly successful. In the *Third Mithradatic War* (74) he obtained the services of Roman officers of the Marian party, and at first prospered; but Lucullus compelled him to take refuge with Tigranes of Armenia (72), and defeated both of them at Artaxata (68). In 66 Pompey defeated Mithradates on the Euphrates, and compelled him to flee to his territories on the Cimmerian Bosporus. Here his new schemes of vengeance were frustrated by his son's rebellion, and he killed himself (63 B.C.). He had received a Greek education, spoke twenty-two languages, and made a great collection of pictures and statues. See study by Reinach (Paris 1890) and Life by Duggan (1958).

MITSCHERLICH, Eilhard, *mi'-cher-likh* (1794–1863), German chemist, born at Neuende near Jeve, professor of Chemistry at Berlin from 1822, studied Persian at Heidelberg and Paris, medicine at Göttingen, and geology, mineralogy, chemistry and physics at Berlin and Stockholm. His name is identified with the laws of isomorphism and dimorphism, and with artificial minerals, benzene and ether. His *Lehrbuch der Chemie* (1829) went through several editions. See memoir by his son (1894).

MIVART, St George (1827–1900), English biologist, was educated for the bar, but devoted himself to the biological sciences, and before his death was by Cardinal Vaughan debarred from the sacraments for his liberalism. In 1874–84 he was professor of Zoology and Biology at the Roman Catholic University College in Kensington, and in 1890 accepted a chair of the Philosophy of Natural History at Louvain. An evolutionist save as regards the origin of mind, he was yet an opponent of the 'Natural Selection' theory. Among his works are *The Genesis of Species* (1871), *Nature and Thought* (1883), *The Origin of Human Reason* (1889). See account in Murray's *Science and Scientists* (1925).

MODIGLIANI, Amedeo, *mō-deel-yah'nee* (1884–1920), Italian painter and sculptor of the modern school of Paris, was born in Leghorn. His early work was influenced by the painters of the Italian Renaissance, particularly the primitives, and in 1906 he went to Paris, where he was further influenced by Toulouse-Lautrec and 'les Fauves'. In 1909, impressed by the Rumanian sculptor Brancuşi, he took to sculpture and produced a number of elongated stone heads in African style, a style he continued to use when he later resumed painting, with a series of richly-coloured, elongated portraits—a feature characterizing all his later work. In 1918 in Paris he held virtually his first one-man show, which included some very frank nudes; the exhibition was closed for indecency on the first day. It was only after his death from tuberculosis that Modigliani obtained recognition and the prices of his paintings soared. See study by C. Roy (1958), and Lives by his daughter Jeanne (trans. E. R. Clifford, 1959) and A. Salmon (1961).

MODJESKA, Helena (1844–1909), Polish actress, born in Cracow, began to act in 1861, made a great name at Cracow in 1865, and 1868–76 was the first actress of Warsaw. After learning English, however, she achieved her greatest triumphs in the United States and in Great Britain, in such rôles as Juliet, Rosalind, Beatrice, and in *La Dame aux camélias*. See her *Memories and Impressions* (N.Y. 1910) and Lives by M. Collins (1883) and A. Gronowicz (1959).

MOE, Jörgen (1813–82). See ASBJÖRNSEN.

MOERAN, Edward James (1895–1950), English composer, born in Middlesex, studied at the Royal College of Music and, after service in World War I, under John Ireland. He first emerged as a composer in 1923, but left London to live in Herefordshire, where he worked prolifically in all forms. As well as a large number of songs, Moeran composed a symphony and concertos for violin, piano and cello.

MOFFAT, Robert (1795–1883), Scottish missionary, born at Ormiston, East Lothian, turned from gardening to the mission field in 1815. Arriving at Capetown in January 1817, he began his labours (1818) in Great Namaqualand. He finally settled at Kuruman (1826–70) in Bechuanaland, which soon became, through his efforts, a centre of Christianity and civilization. He printed both New (1840) and Old (1857) Testaments in Sechwana and published *Labours and Scenes in South Africa* (1842). Livingstone married his daughter. See Lives by J. S. Moffat (1885), E. W. Smith (1925), J. C. W. Holt (1955).

MOFFATT, James (1870–1944), Scottish theologian, was born in Glasgow and ordained a minister of the United Free Church of Scotland in 1896. He held professorships at Mansfield College, Oxford (1911–14), at the United Free Church College, Glasgow, (1914–27) and at the Union Theological Seminary New York (1927–39). His most famous work is the translation of the Bible into modern English. His New Testament was published in 1913 and his Old Testament in 1924. He also wrote theological works, including *Presbyterianism* (1928).

MOGRIDGE, George (1787–1854), English miscellaneous writer, born at Ashted near Birmingham, failed in business and took to writing. Author of many children's books, religious tracts and ballads, he wrote under various pseudonyms including 'Old Humphrey' and 'Peter Parley' (also used by other writers). See Life by C. Williams (1856), A. R. Buckland (in *John Strong* 1904).

MOHAMMED or **Mahomet**, western forms of Arabic **Muhammad**, 'praised' (570–632), born at Mecca, the son of Abdallâh, a poor merchant (though of the powerful tribe of the Koreish), who died soon after the child's birth; the mother died when he was six years old, and the boy was brought up by his uncle, Abu Tâlib. For a time he gained a scanty livelihood by tending sheep; but in his twenty-fifth year he entered the service of a rich widow, named Khadîja, who, fifteen years his senior, by-and-by offered him her hand, and, a faithful wife, bore him two sons (who died early) and four daughters. Mohammed continued his merchant's trade at Mecca, but spent most of his time in solitary contemplations. Just beforeMohammed's time some earnest men in the Hedjaz denounced the futility of the ancient pagan creed, and preached the unity of God; and many, roused by their words, turned either to Judaism or to Christianity. Mohammed felt moved to teach a new faith, which should dispense equally with idolatry, narrow Judaism and corrupt Christianity. He was forty years of age when, at the mountain Hirâ near Mecca, Gabriel appeared to him, and in the name of God commanded him to preach the true religion. His poetical mind had been profoundly impressed with the doctrine of the unity of God and the moral teaching of the Old Testament, as well as with the legends of the Midrash. His whole knowledge of Christianity was confined to a few apocryphal books, and with all his deep reverence for Jesus, whom he calls the greatest prophet next to himself, his notions of the Christian religion were vague. His first revelation he communicated to no one but his wife, daughters, stepson and one friend, Abu Bekr. In the fourth year of his mission, however, he had made forty proselytes, chiefly slaves and very humble people; and now some verses were revealed to him, commanding him to come forward publicly as a preacher. He inveighed against the superstition of the Meccans, and exhorted them to a pious and moral life, and to the belief in an all-mighty, all-wise, everlasting, indivisible, all-just but merciful God, who had chosen him as he had chosen the prophets of the Bible before him, so to teach mankind that they should escape the punishments of hell and inherit everlasting life. God's mercy was principally to be obtained by prayer, fasting and almsgiving. The Káaba and the pilgrimage were recognized by the new creed. The prohibition of certain kinds of food belongs to this first period, when Mohammed was under the influence of Judaism; the prohibition of gambling, usury and wine came after the Hegira. His earliest Koranic dicta, written down by amanuenses, consisted of brief, rhymed sentences, and for a time the Meccans considered him a common 'poet' or 'soothsayer', perhaps not in his right senses. Gradually, however, fearing for the sacredness of Mecca, they rose in fierce opposition against the new prophet and his growing adherents. Mohammed's faithful wife Khadîja died, and his uncle and protector, Abu Tâlib; and he was reduced to utter poverty. An emigration to Taïf proved a failure; he barely escaped with his life. About this time he converted some pilgrims from Medina. The next pilgrimage brought twelve, and the third more than seventy adherents to the new faith from Medina; and now he resolved to seek refuge in their friendly city, and about June A.D. 622 (the date of the Mohammedan Era, the Hegira) fled thither. A hundred families of his faithful followers had preceded him. Heretofore a despised 'madman or impostor', he now assumed at once the position of highest judge, lawgiver, and ruler of the city and two powerful tribes. He failed in securing the support of the Jews in the city, and became their bitter adversary. The most important act in the first year of the Hegira was his permission to go to war with the enemies of Islam—especially the Meccans—in the name of God. The first battle, between 314 Moslems and 600 Meccans, was fought at Badr, in December 623; the former gained the victory and made many prisoners. A great number of adventurers now flocked to Mohammed, and he successfully continued his expeditions against the Koreish and the Jewish colonies. In January 625 the Meccans defeated him at Ohod, where he was dangerously wounded. The siege of Medina by the Meccans in 627 was frustrated by Mohammed's ditch and earthworks. In 628 he made peace with the Meccans, and was allowed to send his missionaries all over Arabia. Some Meccans having taken part in a war against a tribe in Mohammed's alliance, he marched at the head of 10,000 men against Mecca; it surrendered, and Mohammed was recognized as chief and prophet. With this the victory of the new religion was secured in Arabia (630). In March 632 he undertook his last pilgrimage to Mecca, and there on Mount Arafat fixed for all time the ceremonies of the pilgrimage (Hajj). He fell ill soon after his return, and when too weak to visit the houses of his nine wives, chose as his last sojourn that of Ayeshah, his best-beloved, the daughter of Abu Bekr. He took part in the public prayers as long as he could, and died in Ayeshah's lap about noon of Monday the 12th (11th) of the third month in the year 11 of the Hegira (June 8, 632). See Sir W. Muir's *Life of Mahomet* (4 vols. 1858–61, new ed. 1912, abr. ed. 1923) and *Mahomet and Islam* (1887); also books by Syed Ameer Ali (1890), A. N. Wollaston (1904), D. S. Margoliouth (N.Y. 1905), J. T. Andrae (Stockholm 1917, Ger. trans. 1932, Eng. trans. 1936 and N.Y. 1957), R. V. C. Bodley (1946), W. M. Watt (1953, 1956), Mohammed Ibn Ishak (Eng. trans. 1955), Emile Dermenghem (trans. J. M. Watt, 1959).

MOHAMMED, the name of six sultans of Turkey, of whom

Mohammed I (*c.* 1387–1421), sultan 1413–1421, led recovery from conquests of Tamburlaine.

Mohammed II (1430–81), born at Adrianople, succeeded his father, Murad II, in 1451, and took Constantinople in 1453—thus extinguishing the Byzantine Empire and giving the Turks their commanding position on the Bosphorus. Checked by Hunyady at Belgrade, he yet annexed most of Serbia, all Greece, and most of the Aegean Islands, threatened Venetian territory, was repelled from Rhodes by the Knights of St John (1479), took Otranto in 1480 and died in a campaign against Persia. See Kritoboulos, *History of Mehmed the Conqueror* (1955).

Mohammed III (1566–1603), sultan 1595–1603, son of Murad III.

Mohammed IV (*c.* 1641–91), sultan 1648–1687, son of Ibrahim; deposed 1687.

Mohammed V (1844–1918), sultan 1909–18.

Mohammed VI (1861–1926), sultan 1918–1922, brother of V, unsuccessful in suppressing the Nationalists led by Mustafa Kemal; died in exile.

MOHAMMED AHMED (1848–85), the Mahdi (or Moslem Messiah), born in Dongola, was for a time in the Egyptian Civil Service, then a slave trader, and finally a relentless and successful rebel against Egyptian rule in the Eastern Sudan. He made El Obeid his capital in 1883, and on November 5 defeated Hicks Pasha and an Egyptian army. On January 26, 1885, Khartum was taken, and General Gordon (q.v.) killed. The Mahdi died June 22, 1885. See books by F. R. Wingate, *Mahdism* (1891), R. Bermann, *Mahdi of Allah* (1931), and A. B. Theobald, *The Mahdīya: history of Anglo-Egyptian Sudan 1881–99* (1951).

MOHAMMED 'ALI. See MEHEMET 'ALI.

MOHAMMED BEN YOUSEF. See SIDI MOHAMMED.

MOHL, (1) Hugo von (1805–72), German botanist, professor of Botany at Tübingen, carried out researches on the anatomy and physiology of vegetable cells. In 1846 he discovered and named protoplasm.

(2) **Julius von** (1800–76), German orientalist, born at Stuttgart, became professor of Persian at the Collège de France in 1847. His great edition of the *Sháh Námeh* was published in 1838–78. The salon of his accomplished wife, *née* Mary Clarke (1793–1883), was a popular centre for Parisian intellectuals. See studies by K. O'Meara (1885), M. C. M. Simpson (1887) and M. E. Smith (Paris 1927).

MÖHLER, Johann Adam (1796–1838), German theologian, born at Igersheim, professor of Roman Catholic theology at Tübingen and Munich, wrote *Symbolik* (1832), on the doctrinal differences of Catholics and Protestants. See J. Friedrich, *J. A. Möhler* (Munich 1894).

MOHN, Henrik (1835–1916), Norwegian meteorologist, was born at Bergen, studied at Oslo, and became keeper of the university observatory and director of the meteorological institute 1866–1913. He superintended a scientific expedition off the northern coasts of Norway in 1876–78, wrote on meteorology, on the climate of Norway, on the Arctic Ocean, and first worked out the theory of Arctic drift and currents that Nansen utilized.

MOHS, Friedrich (1773–1839), German mineralogist, born Gernrode, was successively professor at Graz, Freiburg and Vienna. His scale of hardness is still in use. He died at Agordo in Italy. Author of *The Natural History System of Mineralogy* (1821), and *Treatise on Mineralogy* (3 vols. 1825).

MOHUN, Charles, 4th Baron Mohun, *moon* (*c.* 1675–1712), notorious rake, involved in frequent duels and brawls, was twice tried by House of Lords for murder and acquitted

In 1701 he was involved in lawsuit with James Douglas, 4th Duke of Hamilton, which ended in a duel in which both were killed. This duel figures in Thackeray's *Henry Esmond*. See also R. S. Forsythe, *A Noble Rake: Life of Charles, 4th Lord Mohun* (Mass. 1928).

MOINAUX. See COURTELINE.

MOIR, David Macbeth (1798–1851), Scottish physician and writer, born at Musselburgh, practised there as a physician from 1817 till his death. Under his pen-name of *Delta* (Δ) he contributed verses to *Blackwood's Magazine* (coll. 1852), and is remembered for his humorous *The Life of Mansie Wauch* (1828).

MOISEIWITSCH, Benno, *moy-zay'vich* (1890–1963), Russian-born British pianist, born in Odessa, studied at the Imperial Academy of Music, Odessa, where he won the Rubinstein prize at the age of nine, and subsequently worked in Vienna under Leschetitzky. Rapidly winning recognition as an exponent of the music of the romantic composers, he first appeared in Britain in 1908, and took British nationality in 1937.

MOISSAN, Henri, *mwa-sã* (1852–1907), French chemist, was born in Paris. A noted experimenter and teacher, he held various posts in Paris, including the professorships of Toxicology at the School of Pharmacy (1886) and Inorganic Chemistry at the Sorbonne (1900). He was awarded the Lacase prize (1887) and the Nobel prize for chemistry (1906). He is chiefly known for his work on fluorine and the electric furnace, which he developed to further his researches with the carbides, silicides and borides. He discovered carborundum and was able to produce tiny artificial diamonds in his laboratory. For a bibliography see *Notice sur les travaux scientifiques de M. Henri Moissan* (1891).

MOIVRE, Abraham de. See DEMOIVRE.

MOKANNA, al (Arab. 'The Veiled'), properly **Hakim ben Atta** (d. 780), was the founder of a sect in the Persian province of Khurasan. Ostensibly to protect onlookers from the dazzling rays from his divine countenance, but actually to conceal the loss of an eye, he wore a veil. Setting himself up as a reincarnation of God he gathered enough followers to seize several fortified places, but the khalif Almahdi, after a long siege, took his stronghold of Kash (A.D. 780), when, with the remnant of his army, Mokanna took poison. His story is the subject of one of Thomas Moore's poems in *Lalla Rookh*.

MOLÉ, Louis Matthieu, Comte (1781–1855), French politician, whose father was guillotined during the Terror. In his *Essai de morale et de politique* (1806) he vindicated Napoleon's government on the ground of necessity, and was made a count. Louis XVIII made him a peer and minister for the navy; and Louis-Philippe foreign minister and, in 1836, prime minister, but his régime was unpopular. He left politics after the *coup d'état* of 1851. See Helie de Noailles, *Le Comte Molé, sa vie, ses mémoires* (6 vols. 1922–30).

MOLESWORTH, (1) John Edward Nassau (1790–1877), English clergyman and writer, father of (4), born in London, and educated at Greenwich and Trinity College, Oxford, from 1840 was vicar of Rochdale. He edited *Penny Sunday Reader*, sermons, pamphlets and a novel, *The Rick-Burners*, popular at the time of the Chartist movement.

(2) **Mary Louisa,** *née* **Stewart** (1839–1921), novelist and writer of children's stories, born, of Scottish parentage, at Rotterdam, May 29, passed her childhood in Manchester, Scotland and Switzerland. She began writing as a novelist under the pseudonym 'Ennis Graham', but she is best known as a writer of stories for children, some of which, such as *The Carved Lion* and *Cuckoo Clock*, are still published today. See R. L. Green's *Mrs Molesworth* (1961).

(3) **Sir William, Bt.** (1810–55), English politician, born in London, studied at Edinburgh (1824–27) and Cambridge (1827–1828), and was M.P. for East Cornwall (1832–37), Leeds (1837–41) and Southwark (1845–55). He held office under Aberdeen and Palmerston. Spokesman with Grote for the 'philosophical radicals', he founded the *London Review* (1835) and merged it with the *Westminster Review* (1836), transferring ownership to J. S. Mill (1837). He edited Hobbes (16 vols. 1839–45), denounced transportation, and promoted colonial self-government. See M. G. Fawcett, *Life of Sir William Molesworth* (1903).

(4) **William Nassau** (1816–90), historian, eldest son of (1), born at Millbrook, educated at Canterbury and Cambridge, held a living near Rochdale (1844–89). Friend of Bright and Cobden, he was an early supporter of the Co-operative Movement which he became acquainted with through the Rochdale Pioneers. Works include *History of the Reform Bill of 1832* (1864), *History of England from 1830* (1871–73), *History of the Church of England from 1660* (1882), &c.

MOLIÈRE, stage name of **Jean Baptiste Poquelin** (1622–73), French playwright, was born in Paris, January 15, the son of a well-to-do upholsterer. He studied under the Jesuits at the Collège de Clermont, under Gassendi, the philosopher, and under the regular teachers of law. He may have been called to the bar. His mother, who had some property, died when he was ten years old, and thus when he came of age he received his share of her fortune at once. He declined to follow his father's business, hired a tennis-court, and embarked on a theatrical venture (1643) with the Béjart family and others, under the style of *L'Illustre Théâtre*, which lasted for over three years in Paris and failed. The company then proceeded to the provinces (from Lyons to Rouen), and had sufficient success to keep going from 1646 to 1658. The Prince de Conti took it under his protection for a time; and when he took to Catholic Methodism, Molière obtained the patronage of the king's brother, Philippe d'Orléans, so that his troupe became the servants of Monsieur. He played before the king on October 24, 1658, and organized a regular theatre, first in the Petit Bourbon, then, on its demolition, in the Palais Royal. In the provinces Molière had acquired experience as a comic writer, mostly in the style of the old farces. But he had also written *L'Étourdi* and *Le Dépit amoureux*. As a theatre manager he had to give tragedy as well as comedy. Corneille's *Nicomède*, with which he opened, was not a success; and though the other great tragedian of the day, Racine, was a personal friend of Molière's, their connection as manager and author was brief and unfortunate. But Molière soon realized his own immense resources as a comic writer. *Les Précieuses ridicules* was published in November 1659, and from that time to his death no year passed without at least one of the greatest achievements in their own line that the world has seen. In the spring of 1662 Molière married Armande Béjart, an actress in his own company, probably about nineteen, and the youngest member of the Béjart family, of which two other sisters, Madeleine and Geneviève, and one brother, Joseph, had been members of the Illustre Théâtre. It has been asserted, in the face of such evidence as exists, that Madeleine Béjart and Molière were lovers, that Armande was Madeleine's daughter, even that Molière was the father of his own wife! It is also said that Armande was unfaithful to her husband. In August 1665 the king adopted Molière's troupe as his own servants. In 1667 symptoms of lung disease showed themselves; on February 17, 1673, the night after having acted as the *Malade* in the seventh representation of his last play, Molière died in his own house in the Rue de Richelieu of haemorrhage from the bursting of a blood vessel. His character would appear to have been generous and amiable; and there are insufficient grounds for the accusations of irreligion brought against him. The dates and titles of Molière's plays are: *L'Étourdi, Le Dépit amoureux* (1658; in the provinces 1656); *Les Précieuses ridicules* (1659); *Sganarelle* (1660); *Don Garcie de Navarre* (1661); *L'École des maris, Les Fâcheux, L'École des femmes* (1662); *La Critique de l'école des femmes, Impromptu de Versailles* (1663); *Le Mariage forcé, La Princesse d'Élide, Tartuffe* (partially, 1664); *Le Festin de Pierre* [*Don Juan*], *L'Amour médecin* (1665); *Le Misanthrope, Le Médecin malgré lui, Mélicerte, Le Sicilien* (1666); *Tartuffe* (1667); *Amphitryon, George Dandin, L'Avare* (1668); *Monsieur de Pourceaugnac* (1669); *Les Amants magnifiques, Le Bourgeois gentilhomme* (1671); *Les Fourberies de Scapin* (1671); *La Comtesse d'Escarbagnas, Les Femmes savantes* (1672); *Le Malade imaginaire* (1673). To this must be added part of *Psyché* (1671), in collaboration with Quinault and Corneille, two farces, a few court masques, and some miscellaneous poems. In France he is called a poet; but, though he could manage verse well enough, he is best almost always in prose. It is as a comic dramatist of manners, satirizing folly and vice, yet without sacrificing the art to the purpose, that he is absolutely unrivalled. Romantic or poetical comedy he hardly ever tried. It is instructive to compare *Les Précieuses ridicules*, almost his first play, with *Les Femmes savantes*, almost his last. Amusing as *Les Précieuses ridicules* is, it is not much more than farce of the very best sort; *Les Femmes savantes* is comedy of the highest kind. It is not till *L'École des femmes*, perhaps not till *Le Misanthrope*, that the full genius of the author appears; and these two, with *Tartuffe, Le Festin de Pierre, Les Femmes savantes, Le Malade imaginaire*, and perhaps the admirable *Le Bourgeois gentilhomme* as an example of the lower kind, may be said to be Molière's masterpieces. But from *Le Dépit amoureux* onward no play of his, not even the slightest, is without touches of his admirable wit, his astonishing observation, his supreme power over his own language, his masterly satire. Of all French writers he is the one whose reputation stands highest by the combined suffrage of his own countrymen and of foreigners, and even after three hundred years, his best plays still hold the stage. The first complete edition of Molière's works was that in 1682 by La Grange and Vinot; by far the best as to text, life, lexicon, &c., is that of Despois and Mesnard ('Les Grands Écrivains français'; 13 vols. 1873–1900). Other editions are by Anatole France ('Collection Lemerre'; 7 vols. 1876–91), and with notes by G. Monval ('Librairie des bibliophiles'; 8 vols. 1882). A bibliography which supplements that in vol. xi of the Despois edition is Saintonge and Christ's *Fifty Years of Molière Studies: A Bibliography 1892–1941* (Baltimore 1942). See also M. Turnell, *The Classical Moment* (1947), W. G. Moore, *Molière: A New Criticism* (1949), and Life by D. B. Wyndham Lewis (1959).

MOLINA, Luis (1535–1600), Spanish Jesuit theologian, was born at Cuenca, studied at Coimbra, was professor of Theology at Evora for twenty years, and died at Madrid. His principal writings are a commentary on the *Summa* of Aquinas (1593); a treatise, *De Justitia et Jure* (1592); and the celebrated treatise on grace and free will, *Concordia Liberi Arbitrii cum Gratiae Donis* (1588). Molina asserts that predestination to eternal happiness or punishment is consequent on God's foreknowledge of the free determination of man's will. This view was assailed as a revival of Pelagianism, and hence arose the dispute between Molinists and Thomists. A papal decree in 1607 permitted both opinions; and Molinism has been taught by the Jesuits. For bibliography see *L. R. Molina, antecedentes, titulos y trabajos* (Buenos Aires 1942). See also TÉLLEZ.

MOLINOS, Miguel de (1640–97), Spanish divine, was born, of noble parentage, near Saragossa, December 21. He was arrested for his views, which embodied an exaggerated form of Quietism, and after a public retraction, condemned to life imprisonment. See his *Spiritual Guide*, ed. by K. Lyttelton (6th ed. 1950), and study by Dudon, *Le Quiétiste espagnol Miguel de Molinos* (1921). His ideas are used by Shorthouse in his *John Inglesant*.

MÖLLER, Poul Martin (1794–1838), Danish literary figure, born at Uldum, graduated in theology at Copenhagen and later became a professor of Philosophy, first in Oslo, and then in Copenhagen. His chief work, *A Danish Student's Tale*, which he finished in 1824, but which was published posthumously, is a charming, light-hearted account of student life in Copenhagen. During a journey to China he wrote in verse nostalgically of his homeland. *Leaves from Death's Diary* is a representative work, showing how he eschews the abstract and metaphysical, for his credo was 'all poetry that does not come from life is a lie'. He made the first Danish translation of *The Odyssey*, wrote philosophical essays and coined brilliant aphorisms. His early death was a loss to Danish letters. See study by T. Rönning (1911).

MOLLET, Guy Alcide, *mol-ay* (1905–), French Socialist politician, born at Flers, Normandy, of working-class parentage, joined the Socialist party in 1923 and shortly afterwards became English master at the Arras Grammar School—a post which he occupied till World War II, from which he emerged as a captain in the secret resistance army. In 1946 he became mayor of Arras, an M.P., secretary-general of the Socialist party and a cabinet minister in the Léon Blum government. A keen supporter of a Western European Federation, he became in 1949 a delegate to the Consultative Assembly of the Council of Europe and was its president in 1955. He became prime minister in February 1956. He survived the international crisis over the Anglo-French intervention in Suez in November, but fell from office in May 1957 after staying in power longer than any French premier since the war. In 1959 he was elected a senator of the French Community.

MOLLISON, James Allan (1905–59), Scottish airman, born in Glasgow, a consultant engineer who was commissioned into the R.A.F. in 1923, won fame for his record flight, Australia-England in July-August 1931 in 8 days 19 hours 28 mins. In 1932 he married his female rival, Amy Johnson (q.v.), made the first east-west crossing of the North Atlantic and in February 1933 the first England-South America flight. With his wife, he flew Britain-U.S.A. (1933) and Britain-India (1934). He was awarded the Britannia Trophy (1933). His marriage was dissolved in 1938.

MOLNÁR, Ferenc (1878–1952), Hungarian novelist and dramatist, born in Budapest, is best known for his novel *The Paul Street Boys* (1907), and his plays *The Devil* (1907), *Liliom* (1909) and *The Good Fairy* (1930), all of which have achieved success in English translation.

MOLOTOV, orig. **Skriabin, Vyacheslav Mikhailovich,** *-mol'-* (1890–), Russian politician, born at Kukaida, Vyatka, was educated at Kazan High School and Polytechnic. In the 1905 revolution he joined the Bolshevik section of Lenin's Social Democratic Workers' party and in 1912 became the staunch disciple of Stalin when *Pravda* was launched. During the March 1917 Revolution he headed the Russian bureau of the central committee of the Bolshevik party and in October was a member of the military revolutionary committee which directed the coup against Kerensky. In 1921 he became secretary of the central committee of the Russian Communist party and the youngest candidate-member of the Politburo. In 1928 his appointment to the key position of secretary of the Moscow committee of the all-Union Party marked the launching of the first Five-year Plan. Molotov, who was chairman of the council of people's commissars from 1930 to 1941, became an international figure in May 1939 when he took on the extra post of commissar for foreign affairs, shaping the policy which led to the nonaggression pact with Nazi Germany. In 1942 he signed in London the 20 years' Treaty of Alliance with Britain. He was Marshal Stalin's chief adviser at Teheran and Yalta and represented the Soviet Union at the 1945 founding conference of the United Nations at San Francisco and at the Potsdam Conference. After the war Molotov, who negotiated the pacts binding the satellite states to the Soviet Union, emerged as the uncompromising champion of world Sovietism. His 'no' at meetings of the United Nations and in the councils of foreign ministers became a byword. His attitude led to the prolongation of the 'cold war' and the division of Germany into two conflicting States. In 1949 he was released from his duties as foreign minister but retained his post as deputy prime minister. He was re-appointed foreign minister in the 1953 Malenkov government and switched to the 'peace offensive'. He resigned in 1956 and was appointed minister of state control. In 1957 Mr Khrushchev called him a 'saboteur of peace', accused him of policy failures and appointed him ambassador to Outer Mongolia (until 1960). This prim revolutionary stood at the centre of the Soviet Union's executive machine for quarter of a century. His unwearied diplomacy was backed by a fanatical Slavophilism and an intense devotion to the Revolution and Marshal Stalin. See *Both Sides of the Curtain* by Sir Maurice Peterson (1950), and study by B. Bromage (1956).

MOLTKE, (1) **Helmuth, Count von** (1800–91), Prussian field-marshal, was born October 26. In 1819 he became lieutenant in a Danish regiment, but in 1822 entered the Prussian service. In 1832 he was appointed to the staff, and in 1835 obtained leave to travel. Asked by the sultan to remodel the Turkish army, he did not return to Berlin till 1839. From 1858 to 1888 he was chief of the general staff in Berlin, and reorganized the Prussian army. His wonderful strategical power was displayed in the successful wars with Denmark in 1863–64, with Austria in 1866, and with France in 1870–71. He married in 1841 his stepsister's daughter by an English father, Marie von Burt (1825–68). Known as 'The Silent', he was a man of great modesty and simplicity of character. He died in Berlin. His Military Works were issued (1892 *et seq.*) by the general staff, for whom he prepared histories of the campaigns against Denmark, Austria and France. See his *Letters* (trans. 1878–96), *Essays, Speeches, and Memoirs* (trans. 1893), Life by M. Jähns (1894–1900), *Moltke, His Life and Character* (trans. M. Herms, 1892), F. E. Whitton, *Moltke* (1921), and study by E. Kessel (Stuttgart 1959).

(2) **Helmuth** (1848–1916), nephew of (1), likewise rose to be chief of the general staff in

1906, but was superseded by Falkenhayn early in Great War 1 (December 1914).

MOMMSEN, Theodor (1817–1903), German historian, was born, the son of a pastor, at Garding in Schleswig, November 30. He studied at Kiel for three years, examined Roman inscriptions in France and Italy for the Berlin Academy (1844–47), and in 1848 was appointed to a chair of Law at Leipzig, of which he was deprived two years later for the part he took in politics. In 1852 he became professor of Roman Law at Zürich, and in 1854 at Breslau, in 1858 of Ancient History at Berlin. He edited the monumental *Corpus Inscriptionum Latinarum*, helped to edit the *Monumenta Germaniae Historica*, and from 1873 to 1895 was perpetual secretary of the Academy. In 1882 he was tried and acquitted on a charge of slandering Bismarck in an election speech. His greatest works remain his *History of Rome* (3 vols. 1854–55) and *The Roman Provinces* (1885). He was awarded a Nobel prize for literature in 1902, and died November 1, 1903. Amongst his 920 separate publications were works on the Italic dialects (1845, 1850), Neapolitan inscriptions (1857), Roman coins (1850), Roman constitutional law (1871), and an edition of the Pandects (1866–70). For bibliography see K. Zangemeister, *Theodore Mommsen als Schriftsteller* (Heidelberg 1887), and supplement by E. Jacobs (Berlin 1905). See also studies by C. Bardt (1903), Hartmann (1908) and Heuss (1956).

MOMPESSON, William (1639–1709), rector of Eyam, Derbyshire, when in 1665–66 the plague (brought from London in a box of infected cloths) carried off 267 of his 350 parishioners. He persuaded his people to confine themselves entirely to the parish, and the disease was not spread. In 1669 he became rector of Eakring, Notts, and in 1676 was made a prebendary of Southwell. See Wood's *History of Eyam* (4th ed. 1865) and C. Daniel, *The Plague Village: A History of Eyam* (new ed. 1938).

MONBODDO, James Burnett, Lord (1714–1799), Scottish judge and anthropologist, born at Monboddo House, Kincardineshire, was educated at Aberdeen, Edinburgh and Gröningen, in 1737 was called to the Scottish bar, and in 1767 was raised to the bench as Lord Monboddo. His *Origin and Progress of Language* (6 vols. 1773–92) is a learned but eccentric production, whose theory of human affinity with monkeys seems less laughable now; and in his study of man as one of the animals he anticipated the modern science of anthropology. He further published, also anonymously, *Ancient Metaphysics* (6 vols. 1779–99). See study by W. Knight (1900).

MONCK. See MONK (1).

MONCKTON, (1) Lionel (1861–1924), English composer, was born in London. Prominent as an amateur actor while at Oxford, he turned to composition and contributed songs to many of the shows of George Edwardes, at the Gaiety Theatre and elsewhere in London. He was composer of several musical comedies, of which *The Quaker Girl* and *The Country Girl* remain popular.

(2) Walter Turner, 1st Viscount Monckton of Brenchley (1891–1965), British lawyer and Conservative minister, born at Plaxtol, Kent, was educated at Harrow and Balliol, called to the bar in 1919, and became attorney-general to the Prince of Wales in 1932, in which capacity he was adviser to him (as Edward VIII) in the abdication crisis of 1936. He held many legal offices, and in World War II was director-general of the Ministry of Information; in the 1945 caretaker government he was solicitor-general. M.P. for Bristol West from 1951 until his elevation to the peerage in 1957, he was minister of labour (1951–55), of defence (1955–56) and paymaster-general (1956–57).

MONCRIEFF, *mon-kreef′*, **Colonel Sir Alexander**, K.C.B. (1829–1906), Scottish soldier and engineer, born in Edinburgh, invented the Moncrieff Pits and disappearing carriages for siege and fortress guns.

MOND, (1) Alfred Moritz, 1st Baron Melchett (1868–1930), British industrialist and politician, son of (2), after some years in industry became Liberal M.P. in 1906, was first commissioner of works (1916–21) and minister of health (1922). He helped to form the I.C.I., of which he became chairman and a conference he organized in 1928 with the T.U.C. suggested the formation of a national industrial council. He was raised to the peerage in 1928. See life by H. H. Bolitho (1932).

(2) Ludwig (1839–1909), German-English chemist and industrialist, father of (1), was born at Cassel, and settling in England in 1864, perfected at Widnes his sulphur recovery process. He founded in 1873 great alkali-works at Winnington, Cheshire, made discoveries in nickel manufacture, &c., and in 1896 gave to the Royal Institution for the nation a physico-chemical laboratory costing £100,000. See lives by F. G. Donnan (1939) and J. M. Cohen (1955).

MONDRIAN or **Mondriaan, Piet,** *mon′dree-an* (1872–1944), Dutch artist, born at Amersfoort, was associated with his compatriot, van Doesburg (1883–1931), in founding the De Stijl movement in architecture and painting. From 1919 until 1938 he worked in Paris, subsequently going to London and thence in 1940 to New York. His rectilinear abstracts in black, white and primary colours have had considerable influence and he is considered the leader of neo-Plasticism. See his collected essays, *Plastic Art and Pure Plastic Art* (1951), and the monograph by M. Seuphor (1956).

MONET, Claude, *mon-ay* (1840–1926), French Impressionist painter, born in Paris, spent his youth in Le Havre, where he met Boudin (q.v.), who encouraged him to work in the open air. Moving to Paris, he associated with Renoir, Pissarro and Sisley, and exhibited with them at the first Impressionist Exhibition in 1874: one of his works at this exhibition, *Impression: soleil levant*, gave name to the movement. Later he worked much at Argenteuil. With Pissarro, Monet is recognized as being one of the creators of Impressionism, and he was one of its most consistent exponents. He visited England, Holland and Venice, and he spent his life in expressing his instinctive way of seeing the most subtle nuances of colour, atmosphere and light in landscape. Apart from many sea and river scenes, he also executed several series of paintings of subjects under different aspects of light—e.g., *Haystacks* (1890–91), *Rouen Cathedral* (1892–95) and the almost abstract *Waterlilies* (at the Orangerie, Paris). The last years of his life were spent as a recluse at Giverny. He is represented in the Tate Gallery, the Louvre, and in many other galleries in Europe and in the United States. See the monographs by G. Besson (1951) and D. Rouart (1958).

MONGE, Gaspard, *mõzh* (1746–1818), French mathematician, physicist and inventor of descriptive geometry, born at Beaune, became professor of Mathematics at Mézières in 1768, and in 1780 was elected to the French Academy, in the same year becoming professor of Hydraulics at the Lycée in Paris. While there he discovered (1783), independently of Watt or Cavendish, that water resulted from an electrical explosion of oxygen and hydrogen. During the Revolution he was minister for the navy, but soon took charge of the national manufacture of arms and gunpowder. He helped to found (1794) the École polytechnique, and became professor of Mathematics there. The following year there appeared his *Leçons de géométrie descriptive*, in which he stated his principles regarding the general application of geometry to the arts of construction (descriptive geometry). He was sent by the Directory to Italy, from where he followed Napoleon to Egypt. In 1805 he was made a senator and Count of Pelusium, but lost both dignities on the restoration of the Bourbons. See Lives by L. de Launay (1933), R. Taton (Paris 1951) and P. Aubry (1954).

MONICA. See AUGUSTINE.

MONIER-WILLIAMS. See WILLIAMS (5).

MONIZ, Antonio Egas (1874–1955), Portuguese neurosurgeon and diplomat, introduced the operation of prefrontal lobotomy for relief of schizophrenia. He was awarded the Nobel prize for medicine in 1949. He also led the Portuguese delegation to the Paris Peace conference (1919).

MONK, (1) **George, 1st Duke of Albemarle** (1608–70), English general, the second son of a Devonshire baronet of loyalist sympathies, was a ' volunteer ' in the *Île de Rhé* expedition of 1628. Ten years active campaigning in the Low Countries preceded his service with the Royalists in Scotland. Captured at the battle of Nantwich, after two years' imprisonment in the Tower he was persuaded to support the Commonwealth cause. His successful activities in Ireland brought him to the notice of Cromwell. Conspicuous at Dunbar in 1650, and successful in pacifying Scotland, with the first Dutch War he speedily adapted his talents to sea fighting, playing a major part in the 1653 victory over the Hollanders off the Gabbard. Returning to his command in Scotland, with the Lord Protector's death Monk's intensely practical nature revolted at the turmoil and confusion that characterized Richard Cromwell's faction-torn régime. Convinced that the catalyst required to heal the nation's health was a revival of monarchal rule, he was instrumental in bringing about the restoration of Charles II. He was rewarded with the Dukedom of Albemarle, an annual pension of £7000, and the appointment of lieutenant-general of the forces. In the second Dutch War Monk played a conspicuous and useful part, defeating the Dutch at St James's Fight on July 25, 1666. Throughout the Great Plague he exercised a wise and enheartening rule over stricken London. In 1667, with De Ruyter raiding the Medway virtually unopposed, Monk hastened to Gillingham to take command of the defences. Thereafter canny, taciturn ' Old George ' retired more and more into private life. He died and was buried in Westminster Abbey in 1670. See Lives by Gumble (1671), Skinner (1723), Corbett (1889), O. Warner (1936), and the *Regimental History of Cromwell's Army*, Firth and Davies (1940).

(2) **Maria** (*c.* 1817–50), Canadian impostor who pretended in 1835 to have escaped from a nunnery at Montreal, and published *Awful Disclosures*. See works by W. L. Stone (1836, 1837).

(3) **William Henry** (1823–89), English organist and composer, professor of Music and organist at several London churches, is best known as musical editor of *Hymns Ancient and Modern* and composer of the tune to ' Abide with me ' and to other hymns.

MONKHOUSE, William Cosmo (1840–1901), English poet and art critic, a Board of Trade official by occupation, published several books of poetry and did important work as art critic and historian. See article by Sir E. Gosse in *Art Journal* (1902).

MONMOUTH, James, Duke of (1649–85), natural son of Charles II, was born at Rotterdam, April 9, 1649 the son of Lucy Walter by Charles II (q.v.), she said, but more likely by Colonel Robert Sidney. Charles committed the boy to the care of Lord Crofts; and in 1662 ' Mr James Crofts ' came to England with the queen-dowager. In 1663 he was created Duke of Monmouth, wedded to a rich heiress, Anne, Countess of Buccleuch (1651–1732), and also made Duke of Buccleuch; in 1670 he succeeded Monk as captain-general. A weak, pretty, affable libertine, he became the idol of the populace, thanks to his humanity at Bothwell Bridge (1679), to the Popish Plot and the Exclusion Bill, and to his two semi-royal progresses (1680–82). Shaftesbury pitted the ' Protestant Duke ' against the popish heir-presumptive, and enmeshed him in the Rye House Plot (1683), on whose discovery Monmouth fled to the Low Countries. At Charles's death, in concert with Argyll's Scottish expedition, he landed (June 11, 1685) at Lyme Regis with eighty-two followers, branded James as a popish usurper, and asserted his own legitimacy and right to the crown. At Taunton he was proclaimed King James II; and on July 6 he attempted with 2600 foot and 600 horse (peasants mostly and miners) to surprise the king's forces, 2700 strong, encamped on Sedgemoor near Bridgwater. His men were mowed down by the artillery. Monmouth fled, but on the 8th was taken in a ditch near Ringwood. Brought before James, he wept and crawled, and even offered to turn Catholic; but on July 15 he was beheaded upon Tower Hill. For the 'Bloody Assize', see JEFFREYS. See Lives by Elizabeth D'Oyley (1938), D. J. Porrit (1953), and studies by W. R. Emerson (1951), B. Little (1956).

MONNET, Jean, *mon-ay* (1888–), French statesman, born at Cognac, was educated locally, and in 1914 entered the ministry of commerce. A distinguished economist and expert in financial affairs, he became in 1947 commissioner-general for the 'Plan de modernisation et d'équipement de la France' (Monnet Plan). He was awarded the Prix Wateler de la Paix (1951), and he was president of the European Coal and Steel High Authority (1952–55). In 1956 he became president of the Action Committee for the United States of Europe.

MONNIER, Marc, *mon-yay* (1829–85), French writer of novels, comedies, historical works, &c., was born at Florence and died at Geneva, where he was professor of Comparative Literary History from 1870. See studies by Godet (Paris 1888) and Baridon (1942).

MONOD, *mon-ō*, (1) **Adolphe** (1802–56), French Protestant pastor, brother of (2), born of Swiss parentage at Copenhagen, laboured as a preacher or professor at Naples, Lyons, Montauban and Paris, and published sermons, &c. See his Life and Letters (Eng. trans. 1885), works by Bossuet (1898), F. Dahlbohm (1923).

(2) **Frédéric** (1794–1863), French Protestant pastor, brother of (1), was thirty years a prominent pastor in Paris, and helped (1849) to found the Free Reformed Church of France.

(3) **Jacques** (1910–), French scientist, born in Paris, head of the Cellular Biochemistry department at the Pasteur Institute, Paris, since 1954, professor of Molecular Biology at the Collège de France since 1967. He was awarded the Nobel prize for medicine with Jacob and Lwoff in 1965.

(4) **Théodore** (1902–), French ethnographer and archaeologist, born at Rouen, founded the Institut Français d'Afrique Noire in Dakar (1938), and wrote on the Cameroons and on the archaeology of the Sahara.

MONRO, *mėn-rō'*, (1) **Alexander** (1697–1767), Scottish anatomist, was born in London, and studied at London, Paris, and Leyden under Boerhaave. From 1719 he lectured at Edinburgh on anatomy and surgery, and was professor of these subjects 1725–59. He helped to found the Infirmary, and gave clinical lectures there. He wrote *Osteology* (1726), *Essay on Comparative Anatomy* (1744), *Observations Anatomical and Physiological* (1758), and *Account of the Success of Inoculation of Smallpox in Scotland.* See Life by A. Duncan (1780), D. Monro (in *Works* 1781).

(2) **Alexander** (1733–1817), Scottish anatomist, son of (1), father of (3), studied at Edinburgh, Berlin and Leyden, succeeded to his father's chair, and wrote on the nervous system (1783), the physiology of fishes (1785), and the brain, eye and ear (1797). See Life by A. Duncan (1818), Memoir by A. Monro (Edinburgh 1840).

(3) **Alexander** (1773–1859), Scottish anatomist, son of (2), succeeded his father and wrote on hernia, the stomach and human anatomy.

(4) **Edward** (1815–66), English divine and author, born in London and educated at Harrow and Oriel, from 1842 was incumbent of Harrow Weald, where he established a college for poor boys, and from 1860 of St John's, Leeds. His stories and allegories were popular and influential.

MONROE, (1) **Harriet** (1860–1936), American poet and critic, born in Chicago, founded in 1912 the magazine *Poetry*, which was influential in publicizing the work of Lindsay, Eliot, Pound and Frost, among others. She wrote the 'Columbian Ode' on the 400th anniversary of the discovery of America.

(2) **James** (1758–1831), fifth president of the United States, was born in Westmoreland County, Va., April 28. After serving in the War of Independence he was elected to the assembly of Virginia and in 1783 to congress, where he sat for three years. He was chairman of the committee (1785) that prepared the way for framing the constitution, which, however, as a States' Rights man, he disapproved. As a member of the United States senate 1790–94, he opposed Washington and the Federalists; the government recalled him in 1796 from the post of minister to France. He was governor of Virginia 1799–1802, and in 1803 he helped to negotiate the Louisiana purchase. The next four years were spent in less successful diplomacy at London and Madrid. In 1811 he was again governor of Virginia, in 1811–17 secretary of state, and in 1814–15 also secretary of war. In 1816 he was elected president of the United States, and in 1820 re-elected almost unanimously. His most popular acts were the recognition of the Spanish American republics, and the promulgation in a message to congress (1823) of the 'Monroe Doctrine', embodying the principle 'that the American continents . . . are henceforth not to be considered as subjects for future colonization by any European power', though existing colonies were not to be interfered with. In 1825 Monroe retired to his seat at Oak Hill, Va., till, deep in debt, he found refuge with relatives in New York. See his *Writings* (1898–1903); *Autobiography*, ed. S. G. Brown (1960); Lives by Adams (1850), Cresson (1947); books by Kraus (1913), Hart (1916), Perkins (1927).

(3) **Marilyn.** See MILLER (1).

MONSARRAT, Nicholas John Turney (1910–), English novelist, born at Liverpool, was educated at Winchester and at Trinity College, Cambridge, abandoned law for literature and wrote three novels, passably successful, and a play, *The Visitors*, which reached the London stage. During the war Monsarrat served in the Navy. Out of his experiences emerged his extremely successful, bestselling novel *The Cruel Sea* (1951), which was filmed. *The Story of Esther Costello* (1953) repeated the pattern of success. He settled in Ottawa, Canada, as director of the U.K. Information Office (1953–56) after holding a similar post in South Africa (1946–52). See his autobiography, *Life is a Four-Letter Word* (vol. 1, 1966).

MONSON, Sir William, *mun'sėn* (1569–1643), English admiral, born at South Carlton, Lincs fought the Spaniards (1585–1602), was a prisoner (1591–93) on Spanish galleys, and was admiral of the narrow seas (1604–16). He wrote *Naval Tracts* which are partly autobiographical (5 vols. 1902–14, ed. M. Oppenheim).

MONSTRELET, Enguerrand de, *mõstrê-lay* (*c.* 1390–1453), French chronicler, born near Boulogne, was provost of Cambrai. His Chronicle, 1400–44, written from the Burgundian standpoint, was edited by Douet d'Arcq (1857–62); and a continuation by Mathieu d'Escouchy to 1461 by Beaucourt (1863).

MONTAGNA, Bartolomeo, *mon-ta'nya* (*c.* 1450–1523), Italian painter, a native of Brescia, probably studied at Venice under Giovanni Bellini and Carpaccio. He founded a school of painting at Vicenza and also worked at Verona and other places. See works by A. Foratti (Padua 1908), and *Painters of Vicenza* by T. Borenius (1909).

MONTAGU, (1) *mon'ta-gyoo.* See HALIFAX, MANCHESTER and SANDWICH.

(2) **Elizabeth,** *née* **Robinson** (1720–1800), English writer and society leader, first of the 'blue-stockings', with £10,000 a year, who entertained everyone from king to chimney-sweep, and wrote an *Essay on Shakespeare.* See books by E. J. Climenson (1903), R. Huchon (1907), R. Blunt (1923) and J. Busse (1928).

(3) **Lady Mary Wortley** (1689–1762), English writer, eldest daughter of the Earl (later Duke) of Kingston, who, losing his wife in 1694, made his clever daughter preside at his table at a very early age. She married Edward Wortley Montagu in 1712, and lived in London, where she gained a brilliant reputation, and was the intimate of Addison, Pope and others. In 1716 Montagu was appointed ambassador at Constantinople, and there till 1718 he and his wife remained. There she wrote her entertaining *Letters* describing Eastern life, and thence she introduced inoculation for smallpox into England. For the next twenty years her abode was at Twickenham. In 1739, for reasons unknown, she left England and her husband, parting from him, however, on very good terms, though they never met again. She lived till 1761 in Italy, where Horace Walpole, meeting her in Florence in 1740 referred to her as an 'old, foul, tawdry, painted, plastered personage'. She died August 21. See her works, ed. with Life by her great-grandson, Lord Wharncliffe (3rd ed. 1887); books by I. Barry (1928), V. S. Wortley (1948), L. Gibbs (1949), R. Halsband (1956); and her *Letters,* (2 vols. 1966, ed. Halsband).

(4) **Richard** (1577–1641), English bishop. As an opponent of Puritanism he was the centre of controversy, but with Laud's influence he became successively Bishop of Chichester (1628) and Norwich (1638).

MONTAGUE, Charles Edward (1867–1928), English novelist and essayist, of Irish parentage, was on the staff of the *Manchester Guardian* in 1890–1925. His writings include *A Hind Let Loose, Disenchantment* (1922), *Rough Justice* (1926). See memoir by O. Elton (1929).

MONTAIGNE, Michel Eyquem de, *mõ-ten'y'* (1533–92), French essayist, third son of the Seigneur de Montaigne, was born at the Château de Montaigne in Périgord, February 28. Till the age of six the boy spoke no language but Latin; and at the Collège de Guienne in Bordeaux he remained for seven years, boarding in the rooms of his famous teachers, George Buchanan and Muretus. He subsequently studied law; but from the age of thirteen to twenty-four little is known of him, though it is certain that he was frequently in Paris, knew something of court life, and took his full share of its pleasures. By-and-by he obtained a post in connection with the *parlement* of Bordeaux, and for thirteen years was a city counsellor. He formed a close friendship with Étienne de la Boëtie (1530–63). He married (September 27, 1565) Françoise de la Chassaigne, daughter of a fellow counsellor. A translation (1569) of the *Natural History* of a 15th-century professor at Toulouse was his first effort in literature, and supplied the text for his *Apologie de Raymond Sebond,* in which he exhibited the full scope of his own sceptical philosophy. In 1571, his two elder brothers being dead, Montaigne succeeded to the family estate, and here till his death on September 13, 1592, he lived the life of a country gentleman, varied only by visits to Paris and a tour in Germany, Switzerland and Italy; here, too, he began those *Essais* which were to give him a place among the first names in literary history. The record of his journey (1580–81) in French and Italian was first published in 1774. Unanimously elected mayor of Bordeaux (against his wish), he performed his duties to the satisfaction of the citizens, and was re-elected. Notwithstanding the free expression of scepticism in his writings, he devoutly received the last offices of the church. From the very first, men like Pascal, profoundly separated from him on all the fundamental problems of life (as in his inconclusive philosophy, his easy moral opinions, his imperfect sense of duty), have acknowledged their debt to his fearless and all-questioning criticism, expounded mainly in haphazard remarks, seemingly inspired by the mere caprice of the moment, but showing the highest originality, the very broadest sympathies, and a nature capable of embracing and realizing the largest experience of life. There are translations by Florio (q.v.), by Charles Cotton (q.v.), by G. B. Ives (1926) and D. M. Frame (1958); and of the *Journals* by Waters (1903–04). See books by M. E. Lowndes (1898), G. Norton (1905), F. Strowski (Paris 1906), G. Lanson (Paris 1930), P. Villey (Paris 1933), A. Gide (1948) and A. Thibaudet (1963); bibliography by S. A. Tannenbaum (N.Y. 1942).

MONTALE, Eugenio, *mon-tah'lay* (1896–), Italian poet, was born in Genoa. He is the leading poet of the modern Italian 'Hermetic' school, and his primary concern is with language and meaning. His works include *Ossi di seppia* (1925), *Le occasioni* (1939), *La bufera* (1956). See study by R. Lunardi (1948).

MONTALEMBERT, Charles René Forbes de, *mõ-ta-lã-ber* (1810–70), French historian and politician. He was born in London, May 15, the eldest son of a noble French *émigré* and his English wife, was educated at Fulham and the Collège Ste Barbe. In 1830 he eagerly joined the Abbé Lamennais and Lacordaire in the *Avenir*, a High Church Liberal newspaper. In 1831 Montalembert and Lacordaire opened a free school in Paris, which was immediately closed by the police. Montalembert, who had succeeded to his father's peerage, pleaded with great eloquence the cause of religious liberty, and when the *Avenir*, being condemned by the pope (1831), was given up, Montalembert lived for a time in Germany, where he wrote the *Histoire de Ste Élizabeth*. In 1835 again in Paris, he spoke in the Chamber in defence of the liberty of the press, and a famous protest against tyranny was his great speech in January 1848 upon Switzerland. After the Revolution he was elected a member of the National Assembly; and he supported Louis Napoleon till the confiscation of the Orleans property, when he became a determined opponent of the imperial régime. He was elected to the Academy in 1851, visited England in 1855, and wrote *L'Avenir politique de l'Angleterre*. In 1858 an article in the *Correspondant* made such exasperating allusions to the imperial government that he was sentenced to six months' imprisonment and a fine of 3000 francs—a sentence remitted by the emperor. Besides his great work, *Les Moines d'occident* (7 vols. 1860–77; 5th ed. 1893), he wrote *Une Nation en deuil: la Pologne* (1861), *L'Église libre dans l'état libre* (1863), *Le Pape et la Pologne* (1864), &c. He died in Paris, March 13, 1870, sixteen days after writing a celebrated letter on papal infallibility. See Memoir by Mrs Oliphant (1872), and French works by Foisset (1877), L. R. P. Lecanuet (3 vols. 1897–1901), the Vicomte de Meaux (1897), P. de Lallemand (Paris 1927), A. Trannoy (Paris 1947).

MONTANO. See ARIAS.

MONTCALM, Louis Joseph, Marquis de Montcalm Gezan de Saint Véran, *mõ-kalm* (1712–59), French general, born near Nîmes. A soldier at fifteen, in 1746 he was severely wounded and made prisoner at the battle of Piacenza. In 1756 he assumed command of the French troops in Canada, and captured the British post of Oswego, and also Fort William Henry, where the prisoners (men, women and children) were massacred by the Indian allies. In 1758 he, with a small force, successfully defended Ticonderoga and after the loss to the French of Louisburg and Fort Duquesne, removed to Quebec, and with 16,000 troops prepared to defend it against a British attack. In 1759 General Wolfe (q.v.) ascended the St Lawrence with about 8000 troops and a naval force under Admiral Saunders. After repeated attempts to scale the heights of Montmorency, he, before dawn on September 13, with 5000 men, gained the plateau, and in a battle on the Plains of Abraham drove the French in disorder on the city. Montcalm tried in vain to rally his force, was borne back by the rush, and, mortally wounded, died next morning (September 14). See Parkman's *Montcalm and Wolfe* (1884), H. R. Casgrain's *Wolfe and Montcalm* (1906, rev. 1926), and Life by G. Robitaille (Montreal 1936).

MONTECUCCULI, Raimondo, Count, *-koo'koo-lee* (1608–81), Italo-Austrian general, born near Modena, entered the Austrian service in 1625, and distinguished himself during the Thirty Years' War, against the Turks (1664), and against the French on the Rhine (1672–75). He was made a Prince and Duke of Melfi. See his *Opere Complete* (new ed. 1821), and the Lives by Campori (1876), Grossmann (1878), I. Senesi (Turin 1933).

MONTEFIORE, Sir Moses Haim, *-fyõ'ray* (1784–1885), Anglo-Jewish philanthropist, was born in Leghorn, retired with a fortune from stockbroking in 1824, and from 1829 was prominent in the struggle for removing Jewish disabilities. After long exclusion and repeated re-election, he was admitted sheriff of London in 1837, being knighted the same year, and made a baronet in 1846. Between 1827 and 1875 he made seven journeys in the interests of his oppressed countrymen in Poland, Russia, Rumania and Damascus. He endowed a Jewish college at Ramsgate in 1865. See the *Diaries of Sir Moses and Lady Montefiore* (1890), Lives by L. Wolf (1884), E. Wolbe (1909), P. Goodman (Philadelphia 1925).

MONTELIUS, Oscar (1843–1921), Swedish archaeologist, born at Stockholm, became director of archaeology there, wrote on early Swedish culture and developed the typological method. See *Memoir* (Stockholm 1922).

MONTEMAYOR, Jorge de, *-mah'yor* (*c.* 1515–61), Spanish novelist and poet of Portuguese descent, wrote *Diana* (pastoral romance), &c., in Castilian, and influenced Sir Philip Sidney and others. See Life by G. Schönherr (Halle 1886), and H. A. Rennert, *Spanish Pastoral Romances* (1892).

MONTESI, Wilma, *mon-tay'zee* (1932–53), Italian model, the daughter of a Roman middle-class carpenter. The finding of her body on the beach near Ostia in April 1953 led to prolonged investigations involving sensational allegations of drug and sex orgies in Roman society. After four years of debate, scandal, arrests, re-arrests and libel suits, the Venice trial in 1957 of the son of a former Italian foreign minister, a self-styled marquis and a former Rome police chief for complicity in her death ended in their acquittal after many conflicts of evidence. The trial left the mystery unsolved, but exposed corruption in high public places and helped to bring about the downfall of the Scelba Government in 1955. See W. Young, *The Montesi Scandal*, and M. S. Davis, *All Rome Trembled* (both 1957).

MONTESPAN, Françoise Athénais, Marquise de, *mõ-tês-pã* (1641–1707), French favourite of Louis XIV, daughter of the Duc de Mortemart, married in 1663 the Marquis de Montespan, and became attached to the household of the queen. Her beauty and wit captivated the heart of Louis XIV, and about 1668 she became his mistress. The marquis was flung into the Bastille, and in 1676 his marriage was annulled. Montespan reigned till 1682, and bore the king seven children, who were legitimized, but was supplanted by Madame de Maintenon, the governess of her children. In 1687 she left the court, and retired to a convent. See her *Mémoires* (trans. 1895); studies by H. N. Williams (1903), G. Truc (1936), H. Carré (1939).

MONTESQUIEU, Charles de Secondat, Baron de la Brède et de, *mõ-tès-kyœ* (1689–1755), French philosopher and jurist, was born January 18 at the Château La Brède near Bordeaux, became counsellor of the *parlement* of Bordeaux in 1714, and its president in 1716. He discharged the duties of his office faithfully, but, till defective eyesight hindered him, by preference devoted himself to scientific researches. His first great literary success was the *Lettres persanes* (1721), containing a satirical description, put in the mouths of two Persian visitors to Paris, of French society. Weary of routine work, he sold his office in 1726, and then settled in Paris. He travelled for three years to study political and social institutions, visiting, among other places, England, where he remained for two years (1729–31), mixing with its best society, frequenting the Houses of Parliament, studying the political writings of Locke, and analysing the English constitution. *Causes de la grandeur des Romains et de leur décadence* (1734) is perhaps the ablest of his works. His monumental *De l'esprit des lois* (1748) was published anonymously and put on the Index, but passed through twenty-two editions in less than two years. By the spirit of laws he means their *raison d'être*, and the conditions determining their origin, development and forms; the discussion of the influence of climate was novel. The work, which held up the free English constitution to the admiration of Europe, had an immense influence. In 1750 he published a *Défense de l'esprit des lois*, followed afterwards by *Lysimaque* (1748), a dialogue on despotism, *Arsace et Isménie*, a romance, and an essay on taste in the *Encyclopédie*. A member of the French Academy since 1728, he died, totally blind, at Paris, February 10. See books by Sorel (trans. 1887), C. P. Ilbert (1904), Barckhausen (1907), Churton Collins (1908), J. Dedieu (1913), G. Lanson (1932), F. T. H. Fletcher (1939), P. Barrière (1946).

MONTESSORI, Maria (1870–1952), Italian doctor and educationalist, born at Rome, studied feeble-minded children, and developed (*c.* 1909), a system of education for children of three to six based on spontaneity and freedom from restraint. The system was later worked out for older children. See her *The Montessori Method* (rev. ed. 1919). See Lives by A. M. Maccheroni (Edinburgh 1947), E. M. Standing (1958).

MONTEVERDI, Claudio (1567–1643), Italian composer, born at Cremona, was the eldest son of a doctor. As a pupil of Ingegneri at Cremona cathedral between 1580 and 1590 he became a proficient violist and learnt the art of composition, publishing a set of three-part choral pieces, *Cantiunculae Sacrae*, at the age of fifteen. About 1590 he was appointed court musician to the Duke of Mantua, with whose retinue he travelled in Switzerland and the Netherlands, and whose *maestro di capella* he became in 1602. In 1612 the duke died and his successor dismissed Monteverdi, who returned to Cremona in straitened circumstances with arrears of salary unpaid. Luckily the post of *maestro di capella* at St Mark's, Venice, fell vacant in 1613 and he was appointed, remaining there until his death. By his efforts the musical reputation of that church, sadly declined since the great days of the Gabrielis (q.v.), was restored to its former high position. Monteverdi left no purely instrumental compositions. His 8 books of madrigals, which appeared at regular intervals between 1587 and 1638, embody in the later examples some audaciously experimental harmonies which brought much criticism from academic quarters but underlined the composer's originality and pioneering spirit, while his first opera, *Orfeo* (1607), with its programmatic use of orchestral sonorities, its dramatic continuity and the obbligato character of the accompaniment, marked a considerable advance in the evolution of the *genre*. The two surviving operas of his later period, *Il Ritorno d'Ulisse* (1641) and *L'Incoronazione di Poppea* (1642), both written when he was well past seventy, show further development towards the Baroque style and foreshadow the use of the *leitmotif*. Monteverdi's greatest contribution to church music is the magnificent Mass and Vespers of the Virgin (1610), the excellence of which was a deciding factor in his appointment to St Mark's, and which contained tone colours and harmonies well in advance of its time. Among other new features introduced by Monteverdi were the orchestral ritornello, and the use of tremolo and pizzicato. Monteverdi has been called the 'last madrigalist and first opera composer', an inaccurate designation which, even if it were entirely true, would not be the reason for the immense importance of his rôle, which is that of a great innovator at one of the most formative periods in the history of musical style. See works by H. Prunières (trans. 1926), G. F. Malipiero (Milan 1930), Schrade (1951) and Redlich (1952).

MONTEZ, Lola (1818–61), Irish dancer and adventuress, born at Limerick, after an unsuccessful marriage turned dancer at Her Majesty's Theatre, and while touring Europe, came to Munich (1846), where she soon won an ascendency over the eccentric artist-king, Louis I, who created her Countess of Landsfeld. For a whole year she exercised enormous influence in favour of Liberalism and against the Jesuits; but the revolution of 1848 sent her adrift. She died, a penitent, at Astoria, Long Island. See her *Autobiography* (1858); books by H. Wyndham (1935), I. Goldberg (1936), H. Holdredge (1957).

MONTEZUMA, the name of two Mexican emperors:

Montezuma I (*c.*1390–1464), ascended the throne about 1437, annexed Chalco, and crushed the Tlascalans.

Montezuma II (1466–1520), last Mexican emperor, succeeded in 1502, was a distinguished warrior and legislator and died during the Spanish conquest. (See CORTÉS). One of his descendants was viceroy of Mexico 1697–1701. The last, banished from Spain for Liberalism, died at New Orleans 1836. See study by M. Collis (1954).

MONTFORT, (1) Simon IV de, Earl of

Leicester (*c.* 1160–1218), Norman crusader, father of (2), undertook in 1208 the crusade against the Albigenses and fell at the siege of Toulon. See study by H. J. Warner, *Albigensian Heresy* (1928).

(2) **Simon de, Earl of Leicester** (*c.* 1208–65), English statesman and soldier, son of (1). Young Simon was well received by Henry III of England in 1230, was confirmed in his title and estates in 1232, and in 1238 married the king's youngest sister, Eleanor. In 1239 he quarrelled with the king and crossed to France, but, soon nominally reconciled, was again in England by 1242. In 1248, sent as king's deputy to Gascony, Simon put down disaffection with a heavy hand. But his jealous master listened eagerly to complaints against his rule, and arraigned him. Earl Simon, acquitted, resigned his post in 1253, and returned to England. Bad harvests, famine, fresh exactions of Rome and the rapacity of foreign favourites had exhausted the endurance of the country, and in 1258, at Oxford, the parliament drew up the Provisions of Oxford, which the king swore solemnly to observe. Prince Edward intrigued with the subtenants, and the barons quarrelled among themselves; and in 1261 the king announced that the pope had declared the Provisions null and void. All men now looked to Earl Simon as leader of the barons and the whole nation, and he at once took up arms. After some varying success, both sides sought an arbitrator in Louis IX of France, who decided in the *Mise* of Amiens for surrender to the royal authority. London and the Cinque Ports repudiated the agreement, and Simon, collecting his forces, surprised the king's army at Lewes, and captured Prince Edward (1264). The *Mise* of Lewes arranged that there were to be three electors, Earl Simon, the Earl of Gloucester, and the Bishop of Hereford, who were to appoint nine councillors to nominate the ministers of state. To aid these councillors in their task a parliament was called, in which, together with the barons, bishops and abbots, there sat four chosen knights from each shire, and for the first time two representatives from certain towns. This, the Model Parliament, held the germ of our modern parliament. But the great earl's constitution was premature; the barons soon grew dissatisfied with the rule of Simon the Righteous; and his sons' arrogance injured his influence. Prince Edward, escaping, combined with Gloucester, and defeated Simon at Evesham, August 4, 1265. See Stubbs's *Constitutional History*; and Lives by Pauli (1867; trans. 1876), C. Bémont (1884; trans. 1930), M. Creighton (1876), G. W. Prothero (1877), S. Bateman (1923), B. C. Boulter (1939) and M. W. Labarge (1962).

MONTGOLFIER, Joseph Michel, *mõ-gol-fyay* (1740–1810), and **Jacques Étienne** (1745–99), French aeronauts, sons of a paper manufacturer of Annonay, became intensely interested in the aeronautical theories propounded by the 14th-century Augustine monk, Albert of Saxony, and the 17th-century Jesuit priest, Francesco de Luna. In 1782 they constructed a balloon whose bag was lifted by lighting a cauldron of paper beneath it, thus heating and rarefying the air it contained. A flight of six miles, at 300 feet, was achieved; but additional experiments were frustrated by the outbreak of the French Revolution, Étienne being proscribed, and his brother returning to his paper factory. Joseph was subsequently elected to the Académie des sciences and created a *Chevalier de la légion d'honneur* by Napoleon.

MONTGOMERIE, (1). See EGLINTON.

(2) **Alexander** (*c.* 1545–*c.* 1611), Scottish poet, born probably at Hessilhead Castle near Beith, was 'maister poet' to James VI. He was detained in a Continental prison, and embittered by the failure of a law-suit involving loss of a pension. Implicated in Barclay of Ladyland's Catholic plot, he was denounced as a rebel in 1597. His fame rests on the *Cherrie and the Slae* (ed. Harvey Wood, 1937), which, partly a love-piece, partly didactic, has real descriptive power, with dexterous mastery of rhyme. See his works, ed. by Cranstoun (Scot. Text Soc. 1886–87; supplement by Stevenson, 1910). See works by D. Hoffman (Altenburg 1894), C. M. Maclean (1915).

MONTGOMERY, (1) Bernard Law, 1st Viscount Montgomery of Alamein (1887–), British field-marshal, was born November 17, the son of the late Bishop Montgomery, and educated at St Paul's School and R.M.C. Sandhurst. He served with the Royal Warwickshire Regiment in World War I. Thereafter, a succession of staff and command appointments brought him to the head of the 3rd Division, with which he shared the retreat to Dunkirk. In North Africa in 1941 the 8th Army had only partially recovered from its rough handling by the Axis forces when Montgomery was appointed to its command. His quality of bravura and supreme ability in 'putting himself over' proved invaluable in dealing with 'Hostilities Only' formations, and he speedily restored bruised confidence and the will to win. Conforming to General Alexander's sound strategic plans, Montgomery launched the successful battle of Alamein (October 1942). This was energetically followed up by a series of hard-fought engagements that eventually drove the Axis forces back to Tunis. Montgomery's subsequent activities in Sicily and Italy were solid if somewhat pedestrian. Appointed commander for the ground forces for the Normandy invasion, his strategy was characterized by wariness and unflagging tenacity. By deliberately attracting the main weight of the German counter-offensive to the British flank, he freed the American armoured formations to inaugurate the joint drive across France and Belgium. His attempt to roll up the German right flank by way of Arnhem lacked co-ordination and the deployment of the proper means to ensure success; but his timely intervention helped materially to frustrate Rundstedt's surprise offensive of December 1944. Accepting the German capitulation on Lüneburg Heath, his command of the Occupation Forces was followed by his appointment as deputy supreme commander to the representative contingents serving under NATO. He retired in 1958. Montgomery's forte was the set-battle, launched after careful planning and never willingly undertaken with anything but the most comprehensive resources in men and material. He became field-marshal 1944, K.C.B. 1942, K.G. 1946, viscount 1946. His publications include *Normandy to the Baltic* (1947), his controversial *Memoirs* (1958), *The Path to Leadership* (1961) and *History of Warfare* (1968). See de Guingand, *Operation Victory* (1947), and Lives by Moorhead (1946), Peacock (1951) and Clark (1960).

(2) **Gabriel, Comte de** (*c.* 1530–74), French soldier, an officer in the French king's Scottish Guard, at a tournament in 1559 wounded Henry II, who died eleven days after. He retired to Normandy and England, turned Protestant, and returned to become a leader of the Huguenot cause. Narrowly escaping to Jersey and England from the massacre of St Bartholomew, he later landed in Normandy, but was compelled to surrender, taken to Paris, and beheaded. See Life by L. Marlet (Paris 1890).

(3) **James** (1771–1854), Scottish poet, was born at Irvine. The son of a Moravian pastor, he settled down, after various occupations, as a journalist in Sheffield, where in 1794 he started the *Sheffield Iris*, which he edited till 1825. In 1795 he was fined £20, and got three months in York Castle for printing a 'seditious' ballad; in 1796 it was £30 and six months for describing a riot. Yet by 1832 he had become a moderate Conservative, and in 1835 accepted from Peel a pension of £150. He died at Sheffield. His poems (4 vols. 1849) are 'bland and deeply religious'. See *Memoirs* by J. Holland and J. Everett (1856–58) and W. Odem, *Sheffield Poets* (1929).

(4) **Robert** (1807–55), English preacher and poet, was born at Bath, natural son of Gomery, a clown. He studied at Lincoln College, Oxford; and from 1843, after some years in Glasgow, was minister of Percy Chapel, London. *The Omnipresence of the Deity* (1828; 29th ed. 1855) and *Satan* (1830) are remembered by Macaulay's onslaught in the *Edinburgh Review* for April 1830. See study by E. Clarkson (1830).

MONTHERLANT, Henri Millon de, *mõ-ter-lã* (1896–1972), French novelist and playwright, was born in Neuilly-sur-Seine. He was severely wounded in the first World War, after which he travelled in Spain, Africa and Italy. Himself a man of athletic interests, in his novels, as in his plays, he advocates the overcoming of the conflicts of life by vigorous action, disdaining the consolation of bourgeois sentiment. His novels, all showing his mastery of style, include the largely autobiographical *La Relève du matin* (1920), *Le Songe* (1922), *Les Bestiaires* (trans. 1927, *The Bullfighters*), *Les Jeunes filles* (1935–39) and *L'Histoire d'amour de la rose de sable* (1954). His plays include *La Reine morte* (1942), *Malatesta* (1946), *Don Juan* (1958) and *Le Cardinal d'Espagne* (1960). See studies by M. Saint-Pierre (1949) and Perruchot (1959).

MONTHOLON, Charles Tristan, Marquis de, *mõ-to-lõ* (1783–1853), French general and diplomat, born at Paris, served in the navy and cavalry, was wounded at Wagram, and in 1809 was made Napoleon's chamberlain. He accompanied him to St Helena, and with Gourgaud published *Mémoires pour servir à l'histoire de France sous Napoléon, écrits sous sa dictée* (8 vols. 1822–25). Condemned in 1840 to twenty years' imprisonment as Louis Napoleon's proposed chief of the staff, he was liberated in 1848, having published in 1846 *Récits de la captivité de Napoléon.* See *Letters*, ed. Connard (1906), J. T. Tussaud, *The Chosen Four* (1928).

MONTI, Vincenzo (1754–1828), Italian poet, born at Alfonsine, remarkable for his political tergiversation, was professor at Pavia and historiographer to Napoleon. He wrote epics and tragedies and translated Homer. See *Collected Works* (Milan 1939–42) and books by C. Cantu (Milan 1879), E. Bevilagua (Florence 1928), U. Fraccia (1947), G. Bustico, *Bibliography of M.* (Florence 1924).

MONTICELLI, Adolphe Joseph Thomas (1824–86), French painter, born at Marseilles, studied at Paris, where he lived mainly till 1870, returned to Marseilles, and died there in poverty. His most characteristic paintings are notable for masses of warm and luxurious colour, and vague, almost invisible figures, in Impressionistic style, though he is placed with the Barbizon group. See works by G. Arnaud d'Agnel and E. Isnard (Paris 1926), L. Guinard (1931), L. Venturi in *Burlington Magazine* (1938).

MONTLUC, Blaise de, *mõ-lük* (1502–77), French marshal, fought in Italy, and as governor of Guienne treated the Huguenots with great severity. His *Mémoires* (best ed. 1865–72) were called 'la bible du soldat' by Henry IV. See Lives by J. J. de Broqua (Paris 1924) and J. Le Gras (Paris 1927).

MONTMORENCY, *mõ-mor-ã-see,* (1) **Anne, Duc de** (1493–1567), Marshal and Constable of France, grandfather of (2), distinguished himself at Marignano (1515), Mézières and Bicocca, was taken prisoner along with Francis I at Pavia (1525), defeated Charles V at Susa (1536) and became constable (1538). Suspected by the king of siding with the Dauphin, he was banished from court in 1541. He was restored to his dignities by Henry II (1547), commanded at the disaster of St Quentin (1557), and was taken prisoner by the Spaniards. He opposed the influence of Catharine de' Medici, commanded against the Huguenots at Dreux (1562), and was taken prisoner a third time. In 1563 he drove the English out of Havre. He again engaged Condé at St Denis (1567), but received his death-wound. See Life by Decrue (1885–89).

(2) **Henri, Duc de** (1595–1632), French marshal, grandson of (1), commanded the Catholics of the south in the religious wars (1621–30), took Ré and Oléron (1625), and penetrated into Piedmont (1630). But provoked into rebellion by Richelieu, he was defeated at Castelnaudary and beheaded at Toulouse. See Life by Hartmann (1928).

MONTPENSIER, Anne Marie Louise d'Orleans, Duchesse de, *mõ-pã-syay* (1627–1693), known as 'La Grande Mademoiselle', a niece of Louis XIII, she supported her father and Condé in the Fronde, where she commanded an army and later the Bastille. After a period in disgrace she returned to the court and wished to marry M. de Lauzun, but the king refused his consent for many years. Her marriage in the end was not successful and her last years were spent in religious duties. See her *Mémoires* (1729 and later edns.), Lives by B. N. de C. La Force (Paris 1927), A. Ducasse (1937), F. Steegmüller (1955) and V. Sackville-West (1959).

MONTROSE, James Graham, Marquis of (1612–50), Scottish general, was educated at St Andrews and travelled in Italy, France and the Low Countries. He returned in the very year (1637) of the 'Service-book tumults' in Edinburgh, and he was one of the four noblemen who drew up the National Covenant. In 1638 he was dispatched to Aberdeen, which he occupied for the Covenanters. When Charles invited several Covenanting nobles to meet him at Berwick, Montrose was one of those who went; and the Presbyterians dated his 'apostasy' from that interview. In the General Assembly of 1639 he showed disaffection towards the Covenant. In the second Bishops' War Montrose was the first of the Scottish army to ford the Tweed (August 20, 1640); but that very month he had entered into a secret engagement against Argyll. It leaked out that he had been communicating with the king; he was cited before a committee of the Scottish parliament, and next year was confined five months in Edinburgh Castle. In 1644 he quitted his forced inaction at Oxford, and, disguised, made his way into Perthshire as lieutenant-general and Marquis of Montrose. At Blair Atholl he met 1200 Scoto-Irish auxiliaries under Macdonell ('Colkitto'), and the clans quickly rallied round him. On September 1 he routed the Covenanters under Lord Elcho at Tippermuir near Perth. He next gained a victory at Aberdeen (September 13), and took the city, which was this time abandoned for four days to the horrors of war. The approach of Argyll with 4000 men compelled Montrose to retreat; but he suddenly appeared in Angus, where he laid waste the estates of the Covenanting nobles. Later, receiving large accessions from the clans, he marched into the Campbell country, devastated it, drove Argyll himself from his castle at Inveraray, and then wheeled north towards Inverness. The 'Estates' placed a fresh army under Baillie, who was to take Montrose in front, while Argyll should fall on his rear; but Montrose instead surprised and utterly routed Argyll at Inverlochy, February 2, 1645. He then passed with fire and sword through Moray and Aberdeenshire, eluded Baillie at Brechin, captured and pillaged Dundee (April 3), and escaped into the Grampians. On May 4 he defeated Baillie's lieutenant at Auldearn near Nairn, and on July 2 routed Baillie himself at Alford; towards the end of the month he marched southward with over 5000 men. Baillie, following, was defeated with a loss of 6000 at Kilsyth (August 15); this, the most notable of Montrose's six victories, seemed to lay Scotland at his feet, but the clansmen slipped away home to secure their booty. Still, with 500 horse and 1000 infantry, he had entered the Border country, when, on September 13, he was surprised and routed by 6000 troopers under David Leslie at Philiphaugh near Selkirk. Escaping to Athole, he endeavoured, vainly, to raise the Highlands; on September 3, 1646, he sailed for Norway, and so passed to Paris, Germany and the Low Countries. When news of Charles's execution reached him, he swore to avenge the death of the martyr, and, undertaking a fresh invasion of Scotland, lost most of his little army by shipwreck in the passage from Orkney to Caithness, but pushed on to the borders of Ross-shire, where, at Invercharron, his dispirited remnant was cut to pieces, April 27, 1650. He was nearly starved to death in the wilds of Sutherland, when he fell into the hands of Macleod of Assynt, who delivered him to Leslie, and, conveyed with all contumely to Edinburgh, he was hanged in the High Street, May 21, 1650. Eleven years afterwards his mangled remains were collected from the four airts, and buried in St Giles', where a stately monument was reared to him in 1888. Montrose's few passionately loyal poems are little known, save the one stanza, 'He either fears his fate too much', &c.; even its ascription to Montrose (first made in 1711) is doubtful. See Latin Memoirs by his chaplain, Dr Wishart (Amsterdam 1647; Eng. trans. 1893); Mark Napier's *Memoirs of Montrose* (1838; 4th ed. 1856); Lives by J. Buchan (1913; new ed., 1957), C. V. Wedgwood (1952) and M. Irwin, *Proud Servant* (a novel, 1934).

MONTUCLA, Jean Étienne, *mõ-tük-la* (1725–1799), French mathematician, born at Lyons, wrote the first history of mathematics worthy of the name.

MONTYON, Jean Baptiste Auget, Baron de, *mõ-tyõ* (1733–1820), French lawyer and philanthropist, is best known for the prizes he established for scientific and literary achievements. He also wrote on economics from a philanthropic point of view. See Life by L. Guimbaud (1909).

MOODY, (1) **Dwight Lyman** (1837–99), American evangelist, born at Northfield, Mass., February 5, was a shopman in Boston, and in 1856 went to Chicago, where he engaged in missionary work. In 1870 he was joined by **Ira David Sankey** (1840–1908), who was born at Edinburgh, Pennsylvania. In 1873 and 1883 they visited Great Britain as evangelists, Moody preaching and Sankey singing; afterwards they worked together in America. See Lives by his sons W. R. Moody (1930), P. D. Moody (1938) and by G. Bradford (1927). See also Sankey's *Autobiography* (1906).

(2) **William Vaughn** (1869–1910), American poet and dramatist, wrote *The Mask of Judgment* (1900), *The Death of Eve*, *The Firebringer*, &c., as well as prose plays and dramas, of which the best known were *The Great Divide* (1906) and *The Faith Healer* (1909). See *Collected Works* (1912), *Letters*, ed. D. G. Mason (1913), and Lives by E. H. Lewis (1914), D. C. Henry (Boston 1934).

MOON, William (1818–94), English inventor of type for the blind, was born in Kent. Partially blind from the age of four, Moon became totally blind in 1840 and began to teach blind children. Dissatisfied with existing systems of embossed type, he invented a system based on Roman capitals, and he later invented a stereotype plate for use with his type. Although requiring more space, his type is easier to learn and is still widely used. See Life by J. Rutherford (1898).

MOORE, (1) **Albert Joseph** (1841–93), English painter, son of (14), brother of (8), is best known for his Hellenic decorative paintings. See Life by A. H. Baldry (1894).

(2) **Anne,** *née* **Pegg** (1761–1813), English impostor, from 1807 to 1813 the 'fasting woman of Tutbury', then proved a fraud. See Life by E. Anderson, and various accounts (1809–13).

(3) **Edward** (1712–57), English dramatist, was a London linen-draper, born at Abingdon, who, going bankrupt, took to writing plays. *The Gamester* (1753) is his best-known production. He also edited *The World* (1753–57). See Life by J. H. Caskey (New Haven 1927).

(4) **Francis** (1657–1715), English astrologer, born at Bridgnorth, practised physic in London, and in 1700 started 'Old Moore's' astrological almanac.

(5) **George** (1852–1933), Irish writer, was the son of a landed gentleman in southwest Ireland who was an M.P. and bred horses for racing. Moore's youth was spent partly there and partly in London. He early became an agnostic, abandoned the military career proposed for him by his family, and lived a bohemian life in London before his father's death in 1870 left him free to follow his bent as a dilettante artist and writer in Paris. After ten years of this life Zola's example revealed to him his true métier as a novelist of the realist school. His importance as a writer is that in the years of relative poverty in London, that is from 1880 to 1892, he introduced this type of fiction into England. Arnold Bennett confessed his debt to Moore's *A Mummer's Wife* (1884), and it is not difficult to see the same influence on Somerset Maugham and others. *Esther Waters* (1894), the last of his novels in this vein, was regarded as rather offensive, but these novels of low life, drawn from Moore's own experience of racing touts and shabby lodgings, introduced the public to a wider world than the fashionable novel of the day. The Boer war saw Moore self-exiled to Ireland—such was his hatred of England's wars—and this had the double effect of raising his interests, as in *Evelyn Innes* (1898), and *Sister Teresa* (1901), to love, theology and the arts, and encouraging his preoccupation with the texture of his prose which more and more engaged his attention. The Irish scene also helped to woo him from sordid realism as in *A Drama in Muslin* (1886), and the stories in *An Untilled Field* (1903). Moore returned to England early in the century and eventually occupied the flat in Ebury Street whence emanated dialogues, conversations (*Conversations in Ebury Street*) and confessions—a sure sign that he had exhausted his experience for novel writing. He had already written *Confessions of a Young Man* (1888), but now we have *Memoirs of My Dead Life* (1906) and the belated (and inferior) *In Single Strictness* (1926). The most famous of his works of this sort is *Hail and Farewell* in three parts, *Ave* (1911), *Salve* (1912) and *Vale* (1914). The malicious element in this trilogy in which he wrote about his friends and his associates in setting up the Abbey Theatre in Dublin, particularly W. B. Yeats, does not detract from his claim to be one of the great memoirists. With his prose style now perfected, Moore turned in his last phase to romanticize history, beginning with the masterpiece *The Brook Kerith* (1916), which relates an apocryphal story of Paul and Jesus among the Essenes. The slightly archaic English in this novel enhances the limpid purity of his diction. *Héloïse and Abelard* (1921) tells the famous love-story with distinction and compassion. In the mythical *Aphrodite in Aulis* (1930), the manner begins to pall on us, as all contrived manners must in the end. See studies by John Freeman (1922) and Humbert Wolfe (1931). Also Nancy Cunard, *Memories of George Moore* (1956), and short study in F. Swinnerton's, *The Georgian Literary Scene* (1935).

(6) **George Edward** (1873–1958), English Empiricist philosopher, leader of the philosophical revolution against idealism, brother of (13), born November 4, in London, was educated at Dulwich College and read classics at Trinity College, Cambridge, until he was persuaded by a senior fellow-student, Bertrand Russell, to change over to philosophy. With the latter, he suffered a brief infatuation with Hegelian idealism, brilliantly represented at Cambridge by McTaggart (q.v.), but it was the singularity of such philosophers' claims, as for example, that time is unreal, that drove Moore to philosophizing in protest. Awarded a prize fellowship in 1898, he struck the first blow for philosophical 'common sense' in an article in the periodical *Mind* (1899) entitled 'The Nature of Judgment'. This effected Russell's 'emancipation from idealism' and in 1903, that red letter year in modern British philosophy, three great works appeared by the two friends. Russell's *Principles of Mathematics*, Moore's famous *Mind* article, *The Refutation of Idealism*, and his *Principia Ethica*, a restatement of which appeared as a famous monograph, *Ethics* (1916), written while he was living in Edinburgh and Richmond (1904–11). Moore made the important discovery, overlooked by almost all moral philosophers, particularly the Utilitarians, that the word 'good' cannot be defined in terms of natural qualities, because whichever of them are chosen for this special rôle, it will always make sense to ask whether anything possessing them is good. His further classification of goodness as a simple, non-natural quality is controversial, but nevertheless his teaching and outlook dominated what later became known as the 'Bloomsbury circle', Leonard Woolf, Lowes Dickinson, Keynes and Forster included. In 1911 he returned to Cambridge as university lecturer in Moral Science and became professor of Mental Philosophy and Logic (1925–39). He also followed Stout as editor (1921–47) of the periodical *Mind* and made it the outstanding

philosophical journal of the English-speaking world. In 1925 he published his important essay entitled *A Defence of Common Sense* in *Contemporary British Philosophy*, vol. i (1925), and emerged as a disciple of Reid in his British Academy Lecture, 'The Proof of an External World' (1939). Moore showed that philosophy must not undermine common-sense matters of fact, but rather provide an analysis of them. This Socratic analytical quest, he pursued with supreme honesty. In *Reply to My Critics* in *The Philosophy of G. E. Moore*, ed. P. A. Schilpp (2nd edn. 1952), he characteristically admitted that in the case of the two major problems with which he had wrestled all his life, the objectivity of goodness and the problem of perception, he was still unable to make up his mind between two incompatible views. He also paid a truly self-effacing tribute to a former student and later colleague, Wittgenstein, whose lectures (1930–33) he attended and recorded in *Philosophical Papers* (1959). Moore lectured in America (1940–44), was elected F.B.A. in 1918 and awarded the O.M. in 1951. See also *Philosophical Studies* (1922), *Some More Problems in Philosophy* (1954), study by A. R. White (1958), and G. J. Warnock, *English Philosophy since 1900* (1958).

(7) **Gerald** (1899–), English pianoforte accompanist, born at Watford, studied music at Toronto and established himself as an outstanding accompanist of the world's leading singers and instrumentalists, a constant performer at international music festivals and a notable lecturer and TV broadcaster on music. See his engaging and instructive account of his art and experiences in *The Unashamed Accompanist* (1943; n.e. 1959).

(8) **Henry** (1831–95), English painter, son of (14), brother of (1), starting as a landscape painter, later achieved great success as a sea painter and became A.R.A. (1886) and R.A. (1893).

(9) **Henry Spencer** (1898–), English sculptor, born at Castleford, Yorkshire, the son of a coal miner, studied at Leeds and at the Royal College of Art, London, where he taught sculpture from 1924 to 1931, and from 1931 to 1939 he taught at the Chelsea School of Art. He travelled in France, Italy, Spain, U.S.A. and Greece, and was an official war artist from 1940 to 1942. During this time he produced a famous series of drawings of air-raid shelter scenes. In 1948 he won the International Sculpture Prize at the Venice Biennale. He is recognized as one of the most original and powerful modern sculptors, producing mainly figures and groups in a semi-abstract style based on the organic forms and rhythms found in landscape and natural rocks. His interest lies in the spatial, three-dimensional quality of sculpture, an effect he achieves by the piercing of his figures. His principal commissions include the well-known *Madonna and Child* in St Matthew's Church, Northampton (1943–44), and the decorative frieze (1952) on the Time-Life building, London. Examples of his work may be seen in the Tate Gallery, the Victoria and Albert Museum, the Museum of Modern Art, New York, and in many other public galleries. He was awarded the O.M. in 1963. See the Life by G. C. Argan, the monographs edited by Herbert Read (1949 and 1955), and study by E. Neumann (trans. 1960).

(10) **John** (1729–1802), Scottish physician and writer, father of (11), after studying medicine and practising in Glasgow, travelled with the young Duke of Hamilton 1772–78, and then settled in London. His *View of Society in France, Switzerland, Germany, and Italy* (1779–81) was well received; but it is for the novel *Zeluco* (1789), which suggested Byron's *Childe Harold*, that he is best remembered today. Moore died at Richmond. See Memoir by Anderson prefixed to his Works (7 vols. 1820).

(11) **Sir John** (1761–1809), British general, son of (10), born at Glasgow, distinguished himself in the descent upon Corsica (1794) and served in the West Indies (1796), in Ireland (1798), and in Holland (1799). He was in Egypt in 1801, obtaining the Order of the Bath; and in 1802 served in Sicily and Sweden. In 1808 he was sent with a corps of 10,000 men to strengthen the English army in Spain, and in August assumed the chief command. In October he received instructions to co-operate with the Spanish forces in the expulsion of the French from the Peninsula, and moved his army from Lisbon towards Valladolid. But Spanish apathy, French successes elsewhere, and the intrigues of his own countrymen soon placed him in a critical position. When the news reached him that Madrid had fallen, and that Napoleon was marching to crush him with 70,000 men, Moore, with only 25,000, was forced to retreat. In December he began a disastrous march from Astorga to Coruña, nearly 250 miles, through a mountainous country, made almost impassable by snow and rain, and harassed by the enemy. They reached Coruña in a lamentable state; and Soult was waiting to attack as soon as the embarkation should begin. In a desperate battle on January 16, 1809, the French were defeated with the loss of 2,000 men. Moore was mortally wounded by a grape-shot in the moment of victory, and was buried early next morning (as in Wolfe's poem). See Lives by his brother (1835) and Gen. Maurice (1897), and Maurice's reply in his edition of Moore's *Diary* (1904) to strictures in Oman's *Peninsular War* (1902). See also Lives by B. Brownrigg (1923), C. Oman (1953), and study by J. F. C. Fuller (1925).

(12) **Thomas** (1779–1852), Irish poet, born at Dublin, May 28, the son of a Catholic grocer, was educated at Trinity College, Dublin, and the Middle Temple. His translation of Anacreon (1800) proved a great hit, and, with his musical talent, procured him admission to the best society. In 1803 appointed registrar of the admiralty court at Bermuda, he arranged for a deputy and returned after a tour of the States and Canada. In 1811 he married an actress, Bessy Dyke, and later settled in Wiltshire. Meanwhile Moore had published the earlier of the *Irish Melodies* (1807–34) and *The Twopenny Post-bag* (1812). In 1817 the long-

expected *Lalla Rookh* appeared, dazzling as a firefly, for which Longmans paid him 3000 guineas; the *Irish Melodies* brought in £500 a year. Moore had 'a generous contempt for money', his Bermuda deputy embezzled £6000, and in 1819, to avoid arrest, he went to Italy and then to Paris. He returned in 1822 to Wiltshire, where he passed his last thirty years, during which he wrote lives of Sheridan and Byron and other works. In 1835 he received a pension of £300, but his last days were clouded by the loss of his two sons. Moore in his lifetime was as popular as Byron. His poetry was light, airy, graceful, but soulless. He is best in his lyrics. See his *Memoirs*, 'edited' by Lord John Russell (8 vols. 1852–56), and studies by Stephen Gwynn (1905), L. A. G. Strong (1937), H. M. Jones (N.Y. 1937).

(13) **Thomas Sturge** (1870–1944), English poet, critic and wood-engraver, brother of (6), born in Sussex, is known as the author of polished verse of classical style, works on Dürer and other artists and as a distinguished designer of book-plates. See Life by F. L. Gwynn (1952).

(14) **William** (1790–1851), English painter, father of (1) and (8), a well-known portrait painter in York, he was the father of thirteen sons, several of whom also became well-known artists.

MOR, More or Moro, Anthonis (1519–75), Dutch portrait-painter, born at Utrecht, in 1547 entered the Antwerp guild of St Luke; in 1550–51 visited Italy, in 1552 Spain, and in 1553 England, where he was knighted (Sir Anthony More), and painted Queen Mary. From about 1568 he lived at Antwerp. See Life by V. Hymans (Brussels 1910).

MORAND, Paul, *mo-rã* (1889–), French diplomat and writer, born in Paris. In the French diplomatic service from 1912 until 1944, his early posts included the secretaryship of the French embassies in London—where he was also minister plenipotentiary in 1940—Rome and Madrid. In 1939 he was head of the French mission of economic warfare in England, in 1943 minister at Bucharest and in 1944 ambassador at Berne. He turned to writing in 1920, beginning with poetry, then publishing short stories and novels, with a background of cosmopolitan life in postwar Europe. These include *Ouvert l anuit* (1922), *Fermé la nuit* (1923) and *Lewis et Irène* (1924). He has also written travel books, studies of cities, and political and biographical works. Among his later works are *Vie de Maupassant* (1942), *Journal d'un attaché d'ambassade* (1948), *Fouquet* (1961) and *Tais-toi* (1965).

MORANT, Philip (1700–70), English antiquary and historian, an Essex clergyman, he wrote *The History of Essex* (2 vols. 1760–1768), other historical and theological works, and also edited some of the ancient records of parliament.

MORATA, Olympia (1526–55), Italian scholar and poetess, daughter of the poet Morato, she gave public lectures when fifteen; but, having in 1548 married the German physician Andreas Grundler, she followed him to Germany, became a Protestant, and, reduced to penury, died at Heidelberg, leaving numerous Latin and Greek poems, a treatise on Cicero, dialogues, letters, &c. See the monograph by Bonnet (4th ed. Paris 1865).

MORATIN, Leandro de (1760–1828), Spanish dramatist and poet, born at Madrid, wrote a number of successful comedies influenced by French ideas and especially by Molière. His acceptance of the post of librarian to Joseph Bonaparte resulted in his exile to Paris in 1814. See works by J. M. Rubio (Valencia 1893), F. Venizer (Paris 1909).

MORAY, James Stuart, Earl of (1531–70), regent of Scotland, the natural son of James V of Scotland, by a daughter of Lord Erskine, in 1538 was made prior *in commendam* of St Andrews, in 1556 joined the Reformers. In 1561 he was dispatched to France, to invite his half-sister, Queen Mary, to return to her kingdom; and on her arrival he acted as her prime minister. In 1562 she created him Earl of Moray, and also of Mar; and he put down for her the Border banditti, and defeated Huntly at Corrichie. On her marriage to Darnley (1565) he appealed to arms, but was forced to take refuge in England. He did not return to Edinburgh till the day after Rizzio's murder (in 1566), to which he was privy. In April 1567 he withdrew to France, but next August was recalled by the nobles in arms against Mary, to find her a prisoner at Lochleven, and himself appointed regent of the kingdom. On Mary's escape he defeated her forces at Langside (May 13, 1568), and was one of the commissioners sent to England to conduct the negotiations against her. After his return to Scotland, by his vigour and prudence he succeeded in securing the peace of the realm and settling the affairs of the church. But on January 20, 1570, he was shot at Linlithgow by James Hamilton of Bothwellhaugh. See RANDOLPH, SIR THOMAS, and study by M. Lee (1953).

MORDAUNT. See PETERBOROUGH.

MORE, (1) Hannah (1745–1833), English writer, was born at Stapleton near Bristol, February 2. She wrote verses at an early age, and in 1762 published *The Search after Happiness*, a pastoral drama. In 1774 she was introduced to the best literary society of London. During this period she wrote two tales in verse, and two tragedies, *Percy* and *The Fatal Secret*, both of which were acted. Led by her religious views to withdraw from society, she retired to Cowslip Green near Bristol, where she did much to improve the condition of the poor. Her essays on *The Manners of the Great* and *The Religion of the Fashionable World*, her novel *Coelebs in Search of a Wife* (1809), and a tract called *The Shepherd of Salisbury Plain* were her most popular works. See Lives by Harland (1901), Meakin (1911), M. A. Hopkins (1947), M. G. Jones (1952) and her *Letters*, ed. R. B. Johnson (1925).

(2) **Henry** (1614–87), English philosopher, known as the 'Cambridge Platonist', was educated at Eton and Christ's College, Cambridge, where he became fellow in 1639, and remained all his life. He gave himself entirely to philosophy, especially to Plato and the Neoplatonists; and his earlier

rationality gradually gave place to hopeless mysticism and theosophy. His *Divine Dialogues* (1668) is a work of unusual interest; his *Philosophicall Poems* were edited by Dr Grosart ('Chertsey Library' 1878), and by Bullough (1931). See Lives by Ward (1710; new ed. 1911), P. R. Anderson (N.Y. 1933), and F. J. Powicke, *Cambridge Platonists* (1926).

(3) **Sir Thomas** (1478–1535), English statesman, born in London, February 7, the son of a judge, was educated at Oxford under Colet and Linacre. Having completed his legal studies at New Inn and Lincoln's Inn, he was for three years reader in Furnival's Inn, and spent the next four years in the Charterhouse in 'devotion and prayer'. During the last years of Henry VII he became under-sheriff of London and member of parliament. Introduced to Henry VIII through Wolsey, he became master of requests (1514), treasurer of the exchequer (1521), and chancellor of the Duchy of Lancaster (1525). He was speaker of the House of Commons, and was sent on missions to Francis I and Charles V. On the fall of Wolsey in 1529, More, against his own strongest wish, was appointed lord chancellor. In the discharge of his office he displayed a primitive virtue and simplicity. The one stain on his character as judge is the harshness of his sentences for religious opinions. He sympathized with Colet and Erasmus in their desire for a more rational theology and for radical reform in the manners of the clergy, but like them also he had no promptings to break with the historic church. He saw with displeasure the successive steps which led Henry to the final schism from Rome. In 1532 he resigned the chancellorship. In 1534 Henry was declared head of the English Church; and More's steadfast refusal to recognize any other head of the church than the pope led to his sentence for high treason after a harsh imprisonment of over a year. Still refusing to recant he was beheaded on July 7, 1535. More was twice married; his daughter Margaret, the wife of his biographer William Roper, was distinguished for her high character, her accomplishments, and her pious devotion to her father. By his Latin *Utopia* (1516; Eng. trans. 1556) More takes his place with the most eminent humanists of the Renaissance. His *History of King Richard III* (1513) 'begins modern English historical writing of distinction'. From Erasmus we realize the virtues and attractions of a winning rather than an imposing figure. In 1935 he was canonized. See Lives by Roper (ed. Hitchcock 1935), Harpsfield (ed. with Rastell's fragments, 1932), Bridgett (1891), C. Hollis (1934), A. Cecil (1936), L. Pane (1953), E. E. Reynolds (1953), J. Farrow (1954); also Campbell on *Utopia* (1930), his edition of the *English Works* (1931), Chambers and others, *Fame of Blessed Thomas More* (1930), Routh, *More and his Friends* (1934), and *Correspondence* ed. E. F. Rogers (1947).

MORÉAS, Jean, orig. **Yannis Papadiamantopoulos** (1856–1910), French poet, born at Athens, wrote first in Greek, then settled in Paris (1879) and became a leader of the Symbolist school, to which he gave its name, though his later work shows a return to classical and traditional forms. His works include *Les Syrtes* (1884), *Cantilènes* (1886), *Le Pèlerin passioné* (1891) and *Les Stances* (1905), the masterpiece of his classical period. See studies by M. Barrès (Paris 1910) and R. Niklaus (Paris 1936).

MOREAU, Jean Victor, *mor-ō* (1761–1813), French general, born at Morlaix, August 11, the son of an advocate, he studied law, but at the Revolution commanded the volunteers from Rennes, served under Dumouriez in 1793, and in 1794 was made a general of division; he took part, under Pichegru, in reducing Belgium and Holland. In command on the Rhine and Moselle, he drove the Austrians back to the Danube, was forced to retreat and later deprived of his command. In 1798 he took command in Italy and skilfully conducted the defeated troops to France. The party of Sieyès, which overthrew the Directory, offered him the dictatorship; he declined it, but lent his assistance to Bonaparte on 18th Brumaire. In command of the army of the Rhine, he gained victory after victory over the Austrians in 1800, drove them back behind the Inn, and at last won the decisive battle of Hohenlinden. Napoleon, grown very jealous of Moreau, accused him of sharing in the plot of Cadoudal (q.v.); and, a sentence to two years' imprisonment (1804) being commuted to banishment, Moreau settled in New Jersey. In 1813 he accompanied the Emperor of Russia in the march against Dresden, where (August 27) a French cannon-ball broke both his legs. Amputation was performed, but he died at Laun in Bohemia, September 2. He was buried in St Petersburg. See works by Beauchamp (trans. 1814), E. Picard (Paris 1905) and Daudet (1909).

MORERI, Louis, *mor-ay-ree* (1643–80), French scholar, born in Provence, took orders, and was a noted preacher at Lyons, where he published his *Grand dictionnaire historique* (1674; 20th ed. 1759; Eng. trans. 1694). In 1675 he went to Paris, and laboured at the dictionary's expansion till his death.

MORESBY, John (1830–1922), English admiral and explorer, born at Allerton, Somerset, known for his exploration and survey work in New Guinea, where he discovered the fine natural harbour now fronted by Port Moresby, which was named after him.

MORETTO DA BRESCIA, properly **Alessandro Bonvicino** (1498–1554), Italian painter, was born in Brescia, where he painted for several churches and also became a fine portrait painter. See Pater's *Miscellaneous Studies* (1895), and study by G. Gombosi (Basel 1943).

MORGAGNI, Giovanni Battista, *mor-gan'yee* (1682–1771), Italian physician, born at Forlí, became professor of Medicine at Padua and founded the science of pathological anatomy. See book by G. Bilancioni (Rome 1922), and H. E. Sigerist, *Great Doctors* (1933).

MORGAN, (1) **Augustus De.** See DE MORGAN (1).

(2) **Charles Langbridge** (1894–1958), English author, was born in Kent, son of

Sir Charles Morgan, civil engineer. He served in Atlantic and China waters as a midshipman, 1911–13, but finding the life uncongenial (*vide* his *Gunroom*, 1919), resigned. He rejoined the navy, however, in 1914 and was later interned in Holland until 1917. On repatriation, he went to Oxford University, where he became a well-known personality. In 1921, on leaving Oxford, he joined the editorial staff of *The Times*, and was their principal dramatic critic from 1926 until 1939. Under the pen-name of 'Menander' he also wrote for *The Times Literary Supplement* critical essays of a mellow, meditative sort, called *Reflections in a Mirror*, which were later (1944–45) collected in two series. In *Liberties of the Mind* (1951) the urbanity has disappeared and Morgan reveals himself as deeply disturbed by the age's loss of liberty in mental and moral judgments and choices. His novels and plays show high professional competence, but lack vividness and urgency. *Portrait in a Mirror* (1929), which won the Femina Vie Heureuse prize in 1930, is Morgan's most satisfying novel. Later works show too much preoccupation with values of the heart to the detriment of narrative sweep, and his earnestness seems unduly solemn, pompous and vaguely sentimental. None the less, *The Fountain* (1932) won the Hawthornden prize and *The Voyage* (1940) won the James Tait Black Memorial prize. His plays are *The Flashing Stream* (1938), *The River Line* (1952) and *The Burning Glass* (1953). See study by Duffin (1959) and *Selected Letters*, ed. by E. Lewis, with Memoir (1967).

(3) **Sir Henry** (*c.* 1635–88), British buccaneer, born in Glamorganshire of good family, seems to have been kidnapped at Bristol, and shipped to Barbadoes. Joining the buccaneers, he conducted triumphant, unbridled expeditions against Spanish possessions (Porto Bello, Maracaibo, Panama, &c.). He died lieutenant-governor of Jamaica. See Haring's *Buccaneers in the West Indies* (1910), and Lives by C. Hutcheson (1890) and W. A. Roberts (1933).

(4) **John Pierpont** (1837–1913), American financier, was born at Hartford, Conn., the son of **Junius Spencer Morgan** (1813–90), founder of the international banking firm of J. S. Morgan and Company. His house organized the Steel Trust, formed an Atlantic shipping combine, controlled railways, &c. Philanthropist and art collector, he left over £15,000,000. His like-named only son (1867–1943) placed contracts, raised loans, &c., for the British government during the first World War. See Lives by H. L. Satterlee (1939) and F. L. Allen (1949).

(5) **Lady**, *née* **Sydney Owenson** (1780–1859), Irish novelist, was born in Dublin. Her father, a theatrical manager, falling into difficulties, she supported the family, first as governess, next as author. In 1812 she married Thomas Charles Morgan, M.D. (1783–1843), afterwards knighted. Her works—lively novels, verse, travels, &c.—include *St Clair* (1804), *The Wild Irish Girl* (1806), *O'Donnel* (1814) and *Memoirs* (1862).

(6) **Lewis Henry** (1818–81), American archaeologist, was born at Aurora, N.Y., became a lawyer at Rochester, and served in the state assembly (1861) and senate (1868). An authority on American-Indian tribal culture, he wrote *The League of the Iroquois* (1851), *The American Beaver* (1868), *Consanguinity and Affinity* (1869), *Ancient Society* (1877), *House-life of the American Aborigines* (1881), &c.

(7) **William De.** See DE MORGAN (2).

MORGHEN, Raphael (1758–1833), Italian engraver, born at Naples, known for his plates after Raphael, Leonardo (notably *The Last Supper*) and others, under the patronage of the Grand Duke of Tuscany. See work by Fred. R. Halsey (New York 1885).

MORIER, James Justinian (1780–1849), English novelist, son of the consul at Smyrna, turned to literature after a diplomatic career. His great work is that inimitable picture of Persian life, *The Adventures of Hajji Baba of Ispahan* (1824), with the less brilliant *Hajji Baba in England* (1828).

MÖRIKE, Eduard, *mœ'ri-kė* (1804–75), German poet and novelist, born in Ludwigsburg, entered the theological seminary at Tübingen in 1822 and became vicar of Kleversulzbach in 1834, retiring in 1843. He was weak, hypochondriacal, unhappily married and lazy, yet he produced a minor masterpiece in *Mozart auf der Reise nach Prag* (1856) and many poems of delicacy and beauty with something of the deceptive simplicity of Heine. These were collectively published in 1838. Three volumes of his collected letters, edited by H. Mayne, appeared between 1909 and 1914.

MORIN, or **Morinus, Jean** (1591–1659), French theologian, a founder of biblical criticism, wrote on ecclesiastical antiquities.

MORISON, (1) **James** (1816–93), Scottish divine, a Kilmarnock United Secession minister, born at Bathgate, in 1843, with three other ministers, founded the Evangelical Union, its system a modified Independency.

(2) **Robert** (1620–83), Scottish botanist, a native of Aberdeen, having borne arms as a royalist, retired to France, took his M.D. at Angers (1648), and had charge of the garden of the Duke of Orleans. Charles II made him one of his physicians, 'botanist royal', and professor of Botany at Oxford. His chief work is *Plantarum Historia Universalis Oxoniensis* (1680).

(3) **Stanley** (1889–1967), English typographer, typographical adviser to Cambridge University Press (1923-44 and 1947–59) and to the Monotype Corporation, from 1923 designed the Times New Roman type, introduced in 1932, edited *The Times Literary Supplement* (1945–47) and was the author of many works on typography and calligraphy. He also edited the history of *The Times* (1935–52). In 1961 he was appointed to the editorial board of the *Encylopaedia Britannica*.

MORISOT, Berthe Marie Pauline, *mo-ree-sō* (1841–95), French painter, a great-granddaughter of Fragonard, was the leading female exponent of Impressionism. Her early work shows the influence of Corot, who was her friend and mentor, but her later style owes more to Renoir. She herself exercised an influence on Manet, whose brother

Eugène she married. See her *Correspondance*, ed. Rouart, trans. B. W. Hubbard (1957).

MORITZ, Karl Philipp, *mō-rits'* (1756–93), German writer, born at Hameln, was in turn hat-maker's apprentice, actor, teacher and professor. Self-educated, he travelled in England and Italy and wrote *Reisen eines Deutschen in England* (1783), and *Reisen eines Deutschen in Italien* (1792–93). His autobiographical novel, *Anton Reiser* (1785–90), influenced Goethe. Moritz was a precursor of the German Romantic movement, delved into the past, and wrote *Versuch einer deutschen Prosodie* (1786), which he dedicated to Frederick the Great. See studies by M. Dessoir (Berlin 1889) and H. Henning (1908).

MORLAND, George (1763–1804), English painter, was born in London, June 26, the eldest son of the crayonist Henry Morland (1712–97), who brought him up with extreme rigour. From the time he was his own master, his life was a downward course of drunkenness and debt. Yet in the last eight years of his life he turned out nearly nine hundred paintings and over a thousand drawings, many of them hastily completed to bring in money and inferior in quality. His strength lay in country subjects (pigs, gypsies, and stable interiors). He died of brain-fever in a Holborn sponging-house. See works by Dawe (1807), Ralph Richardson (1895), J. T. Nettleship (1899), G. C. Williamson (1904), Sir W. Gilbey (1907).

MORLEY, (1) Christopher Darlington (1890–1957), American novelist and essayist, born in Haverford, Pa., was a Rhodes scholar at Oxford. His style is distinguished by its whimsical urbanity and an occasional flight into satiric fantasy. His work includes *Parnassus on Wheels* (1917), *Thunder on the Left* (1925), *Swiss Family Manhattan* (1932), *Human Being* (1932), *Streamlines* (1937), *Kitty Foyle* (1939), *The Ironing Board* (1949) and a book of poems, *The Middle Kingdom* (1944).

(2) **Henry** (1822–94), English writer and editor, born in London, became a lecturer (1857–65) and professor of English (1865–89) at London University, wrote biographical and critical works, and edited 'Morley's Universal Library' of English classics. See Life by Solly (1899).

(3) **John, 1st Viscount Morley** (1838–1923), English journalist, biographer, philosophical critic, Radical politician and statesman, was born at Blackburn, December 24. Educated at Cheltenham and Lincoln College, Oxford, he was called to the bar, but chose literature as a profession. His works (collected 1921 *et seq.*) include *Edmund Burke* (1867), *Critical Miscellanies* (1871–77), *Voltaire* (1872), *On Compromise* (1874), *Rousseau* (1876), *Diderot and the Encyclopaedists* (1878), *Richard Cobden* (1881; new ed. 1896) and *Studies in Literature* (1891). From 1867 till 1882 he edited the *Fortnightly Review*; and he was editor of the 'English Men of Letters' series, writing the volume on Burke, while for the 'English Statesmen' he wrote *Walpole* (1889). From 1880 to 1883 he edited the *Pall Mall Gazette*. His articles and speeches in favour of Home Rule made him Gladstone's most conspicuous supporter. In 1886 he was a successful Irish Secretary, and again in 1892–95. He sat for Newcastle 1883–95, for Montrose Burghs from 1896 until his elevation to the peerage in 1908, was secretary for India in 1905–10 (repressing sedition and making the government more representative), and lord president of the council from 1910 till Britain entered the war, August 1914. O.M. (1902), he wrote a great life of Gladstone (4 vols. 1903), and *Recollections* (1917). See studies by Morgan (1924), Ali Khan, Braybrooke (1924), F. W. Hirst (1927).

(4) **Samuel** (1809–86), English woollen manufacturer, politician and philanthropist, born in Homerton, the son of a hosier. By 1860 he had greatly extended his father's business with mills in Nottingham, Leicester and Derbyshire. Deeply religious, he was a conscientious employer, a supporter of the temperance movement and was a Liberal M.P. (1865–85). See Life by E. Hodder (1887). His son, **Arnold** (1849–1916), was chief Liberal whip and P.M.G. (1892–95).

(5) **Thomas** (1557–1603), English composer, was a pupil of William Byrd (q.v.). He became organist at St Paul's cathedral, and from 1592 was a Gentleman of the Chapel Royal. He is best known for his *A Plaine and Easie Introduction to Practicall Musicke* (1597), written in entertaining dialogue with the purpose of encouraging part-singing for pleasure; also for his volumes of madrigals and canzonets, which include such evergreen favourites as 'Now is the month of maying', 'My bonny lass she smileth' and 'It was a lover and his lass'. He was compiler of the collection called, in honour of Queen Elizabeth, *The Triumphes of Oriana* (1603).

MORNAY, Philippe de, Seigneur du Plessis-Marly (1549–1623), a French statesman, converted to Protestantism in 1560, and nicknamed the 'Pope of the Huguenots'. His treatise on Christianity was translated into English in 1589 at the request of his dead friend, Sir Philip Sidney.

MORNY, Charles Auguste Louis Joseph, Duc de (1811–65), was believed to be the son of Queen Hortense and the Comte de Flahault, and so half-brother of Louis Napoleon. Born in Paris, and adopted by the Comte de Morny, he served in Algeria; but soon he left the army, and in 1838 became a manufacturer of beet sugar. From that time he was mixed up in all sorts of speculations. Chosen a deputy in 1842, he quickly became prominent in financial questions. After 1848 he supported his half-brother, took a prominent part in the *coup d'état*, and became minister of the interior. In 1854–65 he was president of the *corps législatif*, and was ambassador to Russia in 1856–57. He is the 'Duc de Mora' in Daudet's *Nabab*. See Loliée's *Frère d'empereur* (1909) and Life by M. Chapman (1931).

MORONI, Giovanni Battista (1525–78), Italian portrait and religious painter, was born at Bondo near Albino. A splendid example of his style is *The Tailor* in the National Gallery, London. See study by Lendorff (Bologna 1939).

MORPHY, Paul (1837–84), American advocate and chess champion, was born at New Orleans.

MORRIS, (1) George Pope (1802–64), American poet, author of 'Woodman, spare that Tree', was born in Philadelphia, founded and edited the *New York Mirror* (1823), and died in New York.

(2) **Gouverneur** (1752–1816), American statesman, born in Morrisania, N.Y., January 31, was admitted to the bar in 1771. In 1780 he lost a leg by an accident. Assistant in the finance department 1781–84, in 1787 he took his seat in the convention that framed the U.S. constitution, and in 1788 sailed for Paris. The greater part of 1791 he spent in England as Washington's agent, and then till 1794 was U.S. minister to France. Returning to America in 1798, he sat in the Senate 1800–03, and died November 6. See *Memoirs* by Jared Sparks (1832), monograph by Roosevelt (1888), and Morris's *Diary and Letters* (1889).

(3) **Sir Lewis** (1833–1907), Welsh poet, born in Carmarthen, January 23, was educated at Sherborne and Jesus College, Oxford. *Songs of Two Worlds* (3 vols. 1871–75) by 'A New Writer' was followed in 1876 by *The Epic of Hades*, which ran into several series, and more verse and drama. In 1895 he was made a knight-bachelor.

(4) **Reginald Owen** (1886–1948), English composer and writer on music, was born in York. He taught at the Royal College of Music, London, and at the Curtis Institute, Philadelphia, and published *Contrapuntal Technique in the 16th Century* (1922).

(5) **Robert** (1734–1806), the 'Financier of the American Revolution', went early from Lancashire to Philadelphia, was a signatory of the Declaration of Independence, and in old age was a prisoner for debt. See Life by W. G. Sumner (1892).

(6) **Tom** (1821–1908), 'the Nestor of golf', was born in St Andrews, and served an apprenticeship as golf-ball maker with the celebrated Allan Robertson. He went to Prestwick as green-keeper in 1851, won the championship belt in 1861–62, 1864, 1866, having returned to St Andrews as green-keeper in 1863. His son 'Tommy' (1851–75) was the best player of his time, and carried off the champion belt by winning it three times in succession (1868–70).

(7) **William** (1834–96), English craftsman and poet, was educated at Marlborough and Exeter College, Oxford. He meant to take orders, but his friendship with members of the pre-Raphaelite brotherhood, particularly Burne-Jones, made him realize that his interest in theology was limited to an ardent love of Gothic architecture. From architecture he turned, on Rossetti's advice, to painting, which he practised professionally from 1857 to 1862, when he discovered his true métier and also his social gospel, the revival of the handicrafts and finally the revolutionizing of the art of house decoration and furnishing in England. To this end he founded, with the help of his pre-Raphaelite associates, the firm of Morris, Marshall, Faulkner and Company. Morris decoration and furnishing have, like other fashions, passed out and even become slightly ridiculous, but his experience as a master-workman added to his enthusiasm for the Gothic persuaded him that the excellence of mediaeval arts and crafts came from the joy of the free craftsman which was destroyed by mass-production and capitalism. In 1883 he joined the Social Democratic Federation and a year later on its disruption he organized the Socialist League. English Socialism has far less to do with Continental Marxism than with the Utopia imagined for it by Morris. His two prose romances, *The Dream of John Ball* (1888) and *News from Nowhere* (1891), were romances of Socialist propaganda, charming but a little fatiguing too, owing to the sense of unreality. His other prose romances being inspired by his late enthusiasm for the Icelandic sagas do not suffer in this way—these include *The House of the Wolfings* (1889), *The Roots of the Mountains* (1890) and *The Story of the Glittering Plain* (1891). These all show that trait which appeared in his first volume of poetry, *The Defence of Guinevere* (1858), that is, a primitivism in which the brutalities of chivalrous life are blended with soft romance. Tennyson had not dared to show that side of the age of chivalry. The long narrative poems, *The Life and Death of Jason* (1867) and *The Earthly Paradise* (1868–70), are perhaps too prolix for modern taste and they suffer from Morris's idea of the epic as anything a 'singer' could extemporize as he wove at the loom. Chaucer is his model in *The Earthly Paradise* and his framework allows for alternate Greek and mediaeval tales with beautiful seasonal intercalations. Norse inspiration, however, gave his muse a decided lift—*Sigurd the Volsung* (1876), with its savagery and sense of doom expressed in something like Homeric dactyllics, is his best narrative poem. Later, as we have seen, the prose romance almost exclusively occupied his leisure, but *Poems by the Way* (1891) praised revolutionary Socialism. His Virgil's *Aeneid* (1875) and Homer's *Odyssey* cannot rank high as translation, for he has gothicized them out of recognition, but passages in them have a bizarre charm. The translation of many of the Icelandic sagas in which he collaborated with Magnusson are more faithful to the text. His exuberant energy and love of beautiful craft caused him in 1890 to set up the Kelmscott Press at Hammersmith, whence issued his own works and reprints of classics. A brief notice of Morris hardly does justice to his influence in the waning Victorian era—his resistance to technology and mass production and to high finance was no doubt vain and perhaps his nostalgic mediaevalism was not the best way of resisting them, but his career was a symbol of the revolt of man against the machine and of the love of beautiful things in the home and in public places. See *Collected Works* (24 vols., edited by May Morris, 1910–15); Lives by J. W. Mackail (1899), May Morris (1936) and E. P. Thomson (1955); also Margaret Grennan, *W. Morris, Mediaevalist and Revolutionary* (1945) and R. Page Arnot, *W. Morris, The Man and the Myth* (1964).

MORRISON, (1) Arthur (1863–1945), English novelist, born in Kent, became a clerk, then a journalist. His reputation rests on his powerfully realistic novels of London life such as *A Child of the Jago* (1896).

(2) **Herbert Stanley, Baron Morrison of Lambeth** (1888–1965), British politician, born at Lambeth, London, was educated at an elementary school and by intensive private reading. After being an errand-boy and a shop-assistant, he helped to found the London Labour Party, and became its secretary in 1915. Mayor of Hackney from 1920 to 1921, he entered the L.C.C. in 1922, becoming its leader in 1934; he grouped together London's passenger transport system, and much of the credit for the 'Green Belt' was due to him. He was M.P. for South Hackney three times between 1923 and 1945, when he was elected for East Lewisham. In Winston Churchill's Cabinet he was home secretary and minister of home security. He was a powerful figure in the postwar social revolution, uniting the positions of deputy prime-minister, lord president of the Council, and leader of a Commons which enacted the most formidable body of legislation ever entrusted to it. For seven months in 1951 he was, less felicitously, foreign secretary. In 1951 he became deputy leader of the opposition and a Companion of Honour, and in 1955 was defeated by Hugh Gaitskell in the contest for the leadership of the labour party. He was created a life peer in 1959. He wrote *How London is Governed* (1949) and *Government and Parliament* (1954). See *Autobiography* (1960).

(3) **Richard James.** See ZADKIEL.

(4) **Robert** (1782–1834), Scottish missionary. He was born near Morpeth or Jedburgh, and after studying theology in his spare time, in 1807 was sent to Canton by the London Missionary Society. In 1809–14 he translated and printed the New Testament. By 1819, with some help, he had done the same with the Old Testament; and in 1823 he completed his great *Chinese Dictionary*. In 1818 he established an Anglo-Chinese College at Malacca. After a visit to Europe (1824–26) he returned to China, where he spent the rest of his life. See Lives by his widow (1839), Townsend (1888), M. Broomhall (1924), L. Ride (Hong Kong 1957).

MORRITT, John Bacon Sawrey (1772–1843), English traveller and scholar, who, after travelling in the East and surveying the site of Troy, returned to England and was an M.P. for many years. He is best remembered as a friend of Sir Walter Scott, who dedicated *Rokeby* to him.

MORROW, Dwight Whitney (1873–1931), American diplomat and finance expert, born at Huntington, W. Va., became a leading member of the banking firm of J. P. Morgan, and in 1927 was appointed ambassador to Mexico. See Life by Nicolson (1935).

MORSE, Samuel Finley Breese (1791–1872), American artist and inventor, the eldest son of Rev. Dr Jedidiah Morse, geographer, was born at Charlestown, Mass. He graduated at Yale in 1810, went to England to study painting, and was a founder and first president of the National Academy of Design at New York. He studied chemistry and electricity, and in 1832 conceived the idea of a magnetic telegraph, which he exhibited to congress in 1837, and vainly attempted to patent in Europe. He struggled on heroically against scanty means until 1843, when congress appropriated 30,000 dollars for a telegraph line between Washington and Baltimore. His system, widely adopted, at last brought him honours and rewards. The well-known Morse code was evolved by him for use with his telegraph. See his *Letters and Journals*, ed. by his son (1915); Lives by Mabee (1943), O. W. Larkin (Boston 1954), J. L. Latham (N.Y. 1954)

MORTARA, Edgar (1852–1940), Italian Jew, principal in the 'Mortara' case, was in 1858 carried off from his parents by the Archbishop of Bologna, on the plea that he had been baptized, when an infant, by a Catholic maid servant. The refusal of the authorities to give him up to his parents excited great indignation in England. He became an Augustinian monk, and retained his Christian faith.

MORTIER, Édouard Adolphe Casimir Joseph, Duke of Treviso, *mor-tyay* (1768–1835), French soldier, marshal of Napoleon, campaigned brilliantly in Germany, Russia and Spain. He held high office under Louis-Philippe, at whose side he was killed by a bomb.

MORTIMER, Favell Lee, ***née*** **Bevan** (1802–1878), English writer, a keen educationalist, wrote many books for children, the most popular being *Peep of Day*. After the death of her husband, a clergyman, she devoted herself to the care of the destitute.

MORTIMER, Earls of March. See EDWARD II and III.

MORTON, Earls of, a branch of the family of Douglas (q.v.):

James Douglas, 4th Earl (*c.* 1525–81), regent of Scotland, the younger son of Sir George Douglas of Pittendriech near Edinburgh, became Earl of Morton in right of his wife, and in 1563 was made lord high chancellor. Conspicuous in Rizzio's assassination (1566), he fled to England, but obtained his pardon from the queen. He was privy to the plan for Darnley's murder, but purposely absented himself from Edinburgh (1567); and, on Bothwell's abduction of Mary, he joined the confederacy of the nobles against them. He figured prominently at Carberry Hill; discovered the 'Casket Letters'; led the van at Langside (1568); and, after the brief regencies of Moray, Lennox, and Mar, in November 1572 was himself elected regent. His policy was in favour of Elizabeth, from whom in 1571 he was receiving bribes; and his high-handed treatment alike of the nobles and of the Presbyterian clergy, his attempts to restore episcopacy, and the rapacity imputed to him swelled the number of his enemies. He seemed to have retrieved his temporary downfall by the seizure two months later of Stirling Castle (May 1578); but Esmé Stuart in 1580 completely supplanted him in young King James's favour; and on June 2, 1581, as 'art and part' in Darnley's murder, he was beheaded by means of the 'Maiden' in the Edinburgh Grassmarket.

MORTON, (1) **Henry Vollam** (1892–   ), English author and journalist who began his career on the staff of the *Birmingham Gazette* in 1910 and became assistant editor in 1912. He is the author of many informative and informal travel books, including *The Heart of London* (1925), *In the Steps of the Master* (1934), *Middle East* (1941), *In Search of London* (1951), others in the *In Search of*... series, and *A Wanderer in Rome* (1957).

(2) **John** (*c.* 1420–1500), English cardinal and statesman, born at Milborne St Andrew in Dorsetshire, practised as an advocate in the Court of Arches. He adhered with great fidelity to Henry VI, but after the battle of Tewkesbury he made his peace with Edward IV and was made master of the rolls and Bishop of Ely. Richard III imprisoned him, but he escaped, and joining Henry VII, was made Archbishop of Canterbury and chancellor (1486). In 1493 he became a cardinal. See Gairdner's *Henry VII* (1889), and a Life of Morton by Woodhouse (1895).

(3) **John Cameron Andrieu Bingham Michael** (1893–), English author and journalist, after serving through World War I he took up writing and has published many books of humour, fantasy and satire, as well as a number of historical works including several on the French Revolution. Since 1924 he has contributed a regular humorous column to the *Daily Express* under the name of ' Beachcomber '.

(4) **John Maddison** (1811–91), English dramatist, son of (6), born at Pangbourne, became a prolific writer of farces (mostly from the French), but is best remembered as the author of *Cox and Box* (1847). The rise of burlesque was his ruin and he became a ' poor brother ' of the Charterhouse. See the memoir by Clement Scott prefixed to *Plays for Home Performance* (1889).

(5) **Levi Parsons** (1824–1920), American banker and politician, born at Shoreham, Vt., began as a country storekeeper's assistant, and in 1863 founded banking-houses in New York and London. In 1878–80 he was returned to congress as a Republican, in 1881–85 was minister to France, vice-president of the U.S. (1889–93), governor of New York State (1895–96). See Life by McElroy (1930).

(6) **Thomas** (1764–1838), English dramatist, father of (4), born in Durham, quitted Lincoln's Inn for play writing, and produced *Speed the Plough* (1798, with its invisible ' Mrs. Grundy '), *The Blind Girl* (1801), *Town and Country* (1807), *School for Grown Children* (1826), and other popular plays. For thirty-five years he lived at Pangbourne near Reading, till in 1828 he removed to London. See study by R. A. L. Mortvedt in *Summaries of Harvard Theses* (Cambridge, Mass., 1935).

(7) **Thomas** (1781–1832), Scottish shipbuilder, inventor about 1822 of the patent slip, which provides a cheap substitute for a dry dock.

(8) **William Thomas Green** (1819–68), American dentist, born at Charlton, Mass., in 1846 was the first to employ in operations anaesthesia produced by sulphuric ether. See Life by R. M. Baker (N.Y. 1946).

MORYSON, Fynes (1566–1630), English traveller, was born at Cadeby, Lincs, and after becoming a fellow of Peterhouse, Cambridge, he travelled over Europe and the Levant, and published his *Itinerary* (1617; complete ed. 4 vols Glasgow 1907–08).

MOSCHELES, Ignaz, *mō'she-les* (1794–1870), Bohemian pianist and composer, born at Prague of Jewish parents, was by 1808 the favourite musician and music-master of Vienna. He taught in London from 1825, and from 1844 in Leipzig. He edited in English Schindler's *Life of Beethoven* (1841). See Life by his wife, his Correspondence with Mendelssohn (trans. 1888) and *Fragments of an Autobiography* (1899).

MOSCHUS, *mos'kus* (fl. 150 B.C.), Greek poet of Syracuse, was author of a short epic *Europa*. His works are generally printed along with those of Theocritus and Bion, and there is a fine prose translation of the three by Andrew Lang (1889).

MOSCICKI, Ignacy, *mosh-cheets'kee* (1867–1946), president of Poland, was born at Mierzanow. An ardent patriot, he spent many years in Switzerland, where he became a chemist. He later returned to Poland, where he was a professor of Chemistry until 1926, when his friend Pilsudski made him president. In 1939 he fled to Rumania and then retired to Switzerland where he died.

MOSELEY, Henry Gwyn Jeffreys (1887–1915), English physicist, a lecturer under Rutherford at Manchester and later at Oxford, began research in radioactivity and determined by means of X-ray spectra the atomic numbers of the elements. His brilliant career was cut short at Gallipoli.

MOSER, (1) **George Michael** (1704–83), Swiss gold chaser and enameller, father of (2), coming early to London, became the head of his profession. A founder member of the Royal Academy, he was elected the first keeper.

(2) **Mary** (?1744–1819), English flower painter, daughter of (1), was one of the founder members of the Royal Academy, and an intimate friend of the royal family.

MOSES (Heb. *Môsheh*) (15th–13th cent. B.C.), Hebrew prophet and lawgiver, according to the Pentateuch led the people of Israel out of Egypt by way of Sinai, Kadesh and Moab (where he died) towards the Holy Land. The Pentateuch used to be regarded as his work; but most modern critics agree that its historical portions, as well as most of the legislative documents, belong to a much later time. See Gressman, *Mose und seine Zeit* (1913), study by M. Buber (1946), and M. Noth, *A History of Israel* (1960).

MOSES, Anna Mary, known as **Grandma Moses** (1860–1961), American primitive artist, born in Washington County, N.Y. She began to paint at about the age of seventy-five, mainly country scenes remembered from her childhood—' old timey things . . . all from memory '. From her first show in New York in 1940, she had great popular success in the United States. See her *My Life's History* (1952).

MOSHEIM, Johann Lorenz von, *mōs'hīm* (1694–1755), German theologian, born at Lübeck, in 1723 became professor of Theology at Helmstedt, and in 1747 at Göttingen. His *Institutiones Historiae Ecclesiasticae* (1726; new ed. 1755) proved him, in Gibbon's phrase, ' full, rational correct, and moderate', and was translated into English. See Life by K. Heussi (1960).

MOSLEY, Sir Oswald Ernald, 6th Bart. (1896–), English politician, successively Conservative, Independent and Labour M.P., was a member of the 1929 Labour government. He later resigned and became leader of the British Union of Fascists. Detained under the Defence Regulations during World War II, he founded a new 'Union' Movement in 1948. His vision of a politically and economically united Europe is embodied in his *Europe: Faith and Plan* (1958). He married **the Hon. Diana Mitford** in 1936. See study by J. Drennan (1934).

MOSSADEGH, Mohammed (1881–1967), Persian statesman, born in Tehran, held office in Persia in the 1920's, returned to politics in 1944, and directed his attack on the Anglo-Iranian Oil Co., which, by his Oil Nationalization Act of 1951 (in which year he became prime minister), he claimed to have expropriated. His government was overthrown by a Royalist uprising in 1953, and he was imprisoned. He was released in 1956.

MÖSSBAUER, Rudolf (1929–), American physicist, born in Munich, discovered the 'Mössbauer effect' concerning gamma radiation in crystals, and shared the 1961 Nobel prize with Hofstadter for research into atomic structure. Mössbauer has been professor of Experimental Physics at the Technische Hochschule, Munich, and visiting professor of physics at the Californian Institute of Technology since 1964.

MOSZKOWSKI, Moritz, *mosh-kof'skee* (1854–1925), Polish composer and pianist, born at Breslau, taught at the Kullak Academy, Berlin, and later lived in Paris. A prolific composer for piano and orchestra, he is now remembered almost solely for his lively *Spanish Dances*.

MOTHERWELL, William (1797–1835), Scottish journalist and poet, a native of Glasgow, from 1819 to 1829 sheriff-clerk depute of Renfrewshire, published *Minstrelsy, Ancient and Modern* (1819) and other verse collections. See Memoir prefixed to his *Poetical Remains* (1848).

MOTLEY, John Lothrop (1814–77), American historian and diplomat, was born in Dorchester, Mass., studied at Harvard and several German universities, and began a diplomatic career. He soon turned to literature, however, and ten years were spent on his *Rise of the Dutch Republic* (1856), which established his fame. This was continued in the *History of the United Netherlands* which appeared in 1860–69. In 1861–67 he was minister to Austria, in 1869–70 to Great Britain. His last work was *The Life and Death of John Barneveld*, a biography which is virtually a part of his main theme. See his Correspondence edited by G. W. Curtis (1888 and 1910); short Life by Prof. Jameson (1897); and study by C. Lynch (Washington, D.C., 1944).

MOTT, John R. (1865–1955), American Y.M.C.A. leader, born at Livingston Manor, New York, became known the world over by his work for the Young Men's Christian Associations, Student Volunteer Movement and World Missionary Conference. See Lives by Matthews (1934) and Fisher (N.Y. 1953).

MOTTE, William de la (1775–1863), English painter, of Huguenot ancestry, was born at Weymouth. He became well-known for his watercolour landscapes and exhibited at the Royal Academy for many years.

MOTTEUX, Peter Anthony, *mo-tœ* (1660–1718), English playwright and translator, left Rouen for London after the revocation of the Edict of Nantes (1685) and after a time took up journalism. He is best known for his translations of Rabelais and *Don Quixote*. See Lives by Van Laun (1880), R. N. Cunningham (1933); bibliography by R. N. Cunningham (1933).

MOTTRAM, Ralph Hale (1883–1971), English novelist, born in Norwich, began his working life as a banker. Galsworthy is the main influence in his work, as is clearly seen in his first book, *Spanish Farm* (1924). See his autobiographical *Window Seat, or Life Observed* (1954).

MOULINS, Master of, *moo-lī* (*c.* 1460–*c.* 1529), French artist whose principal work was the triptych in Moulins Cathedral of the *Virgin and Child*, and he is regarded as the most accomplished French artist of the time. The influence of Hugo van der Goes can be seen in his vividly coloured and realistic paintings, and some authorities identify him with Jean Perreal or Jean de Paris, court painter to Charles VIII.

MOUNTBATTEN, surname assumed in 1917 by (1) and members of the Battenberg family (q.v.) in Britain:

(1) **Prince Louis Alexander** (1854–1921), father of (2), married in 1884 the eldest daughter of the Princess Alice of Hesse and became Marquess of Milford Haven in 1917, having relinquished his German titles and taken the surname, Mountbatten. He was first sea lord (1912–14) and admiral of the Fleet (1921).

(2) **Louis (Francis Albert Victor Nicholas), 1st Earl Mountbatten of Burma** (1900–), British sea lord, the younger son of (1), was educated at Osborne and Cambridge, entering the Royal Navy in 1913. He was commander of the 5th destroyer flotilla in 1939 and in 1942 was made chief of combined operations. Appointed C.-in-C. S.E. Asia, he saw Burma reconquered before presiding over the transfer of power in India as viceroy and governor-general. Service afloat in 1952 was followed by his appointment as first sea lord in 1955 and he was chief of the defence staff from 1959–65, when he became governor of the Isle of Wight. He was created an earl in 1947. See R. Murphy, *The Last Viceroy* (1948). He married in 1922 the **Hon. Edwina Cynthia Annette Ashley** (1901–1960), who rendered distinguished service particularly during the London 'Blitz' (1940–42) to the Red Cross and St John's Ambulance Brigade, of which she became superintendent-in-chief in 1942. As vicereine of India (1947) her work in social welfare brought her the friendship of Gandhi. She died suddenly while on an official tour in Borneo. See M. Masson, *Edwina* (1958).

(3) **Prince Philip.** See EDINBURGH, DUKE OF.

MOUNTEVANS, Edward Ratcliffe Garth

Russell Evans, 1st Baron (1881–1957), British admiral, educated at Merchant Taylors' School, entered the Royal Navy in 1897. In 1900–04 he was second-in-command to Scott's Antarctic expedition. In the 1914–18 war he fought at Jutland, and in command of H.M.S. *Broke*—in company with Commander Peck—he scored an outstanding victory over four German destroyers. In 1929 he was appointed rear admiral commanding the Royal Australian Navy, subsequently serving as C.-in-C. Africa Station. Recalled in 1939, he assumed the post of London regional commissioner. He was made a baron in 1945. See his *Keeping the Seas* (1920) and *South with Scott* (1921).

MOUSSORGSKY, Modest Petrovich (1835–1881), Russian composer, born at Karevo (Pskov), was educated for the army but resigned his commission in 1858 after the onset of a nervous disorder and began the serious study of music under Balakirev. A member of the Glinka-inspired nationalist group in St Petersburg, which included Dargomizhsky and Rimsky-Korsakov, Moussorgsky first made a name with his songs, among them the well-known setting of Goethe's satirical 'Song of the Flea' (1879); but his great masterpiece is the opera *Boris Godunov*, first performed at St Petersburg in 1874; his piano suite *Pictures from an Exhibition* (1874) has also kept a firm place in the concert repertoire. Other operas and large-scale works remained uncompleted as the composer sank into the chronic alcoholism which hastened his early death. His friend Rimsky-Korsakov undertook the task of musical executor, arranged or completed many of his unfinished works and rearranged some of the finished ones, sometimes to the detriment of their robust individuality. See studies by von Riesemann (1935) and Calvacoressi (1946).

MOYNIHAN, (1) Berkeley George Andrew, 1st Baron Moynihan of Leeds (1865–1936), an outstandingly skilful and bold English operating surgeon, was born in Malta. He held various posts at the Leeds General Infirmary, specializing in the techniques of abdominal, gastric and pancreatic operations. The driving impulse of his life was the promotion of scientific surgery, and he set out his doctrine in his *Abdominal Operations* (1905). He formed the Moynihan Chirurgical Club, was active in starting the Association of Surgeons of Great Britain and Ireland, and was also a leader of the movement to found the *British Journal of Surgery*. He was president of the Royal College of Surgeons from 1926 to 1932. Knighted in 1912, he was created a baronet in 1922, and raised to the peerage in 1929.

(2) **Rodrigo** (1910–), English painter, studied at the Slade School, and joined the London Group in 1933. From 1943 to 1944 he was an official war artist, and was professor of Painting at the Royal College of Art 1948–57. Most of his works are of an Impressionist nature, with soft tones (e.g., his portrait of Queen Elizabeth II as *Princess Elizabeth*), but he has now changed to non-figurative painting—of equal sensitivity. Elected R.A. in 1954, he resigned in 1957.

MOZART, Wolfgang Amadeus Chrysostom, *mō'tsahrt* (1756–91), Austrian composer, the younger child of Leopold Mozart, *kapellmeister* to the Archbishop of Salzburg, where he was born. He made his first professional tour through Europe when he was six years old. Other tours followed and a period of study in Italy, and in 1781 Mozart settled in Vienna as *konzertmeister* to the Archbishop, who had moved thither from Salzburg. He was badly treated, however, and resigned when his employer left the city. He married Constanze Weber, cousin of the composer, who was a charming wife but a wretched manager; and debts and difficulties increased. The lively opera *Die Entführung aus dem Serail* paved the way for the *Marriage of Figaro* (1786), which created a furore. The extraordinary success of *Don Giovanni* (1787) made it impossible for the court still to overlook the composer, and he was appointed chamber musician to Joseph II, at a salary of £80 a year. The emperor ordered a new opera, *Così fan tutte*, but owing to his death and the indifference to art of Leopold II, the composer reaped no pecuniary benefit. His carelessness, improvidence, and senseless generosity overwhelmed him with endless embarrassments. In 1791 Schikaneder, a theatre manager, begged of him a new opera on an incoherent subject of his own, *The Magic Flute*, which, at first coldly received, ended by making Schikaneder's fortune. In writing the noble Requiem Mass commissioned for Count Walsegg, he felt he was writing his own requiem; and he caught typhus and died before it was finished. He was buried in the common ground of St Mark's Churchyard. Mozart wrote more than 600 compositions; he left no branch of the art unenriched by his genius. Gifted with an inexhaustible vein of the richest, purest melody, he is at once the glory and the reproach of the Italian school; for, while he surpasses all Italians on their own chosen ground, his strict training in the German school placed at his service wonderful resources of harmony and instrumentation. Of forty-one symphonies three hold pre-eminence—the C major (called the 'Jupiter'), G minor and E flat. The quartets are very beautiful and exceedingly original. His pianoforte sonatas and those for the violin and piano are few of them of great importance except in the development of musical form, but his piano concertos are brilliant. The complete works were indexed in 1862–64 by Ludwig Köchel (q.v.) (3rd ed. 1937) and individual compositions are often referred to by their 'Köchel number' to avoid confusion. See Lives by Otto Jahn (1856–59; trans. 1882), Nohl (trans. 1877), Meinardus (1882), Holmes (2nd ed. 1878), Wyzewa and G. de Saint-Foix (5 vols. Paris 1912–46); books by Dent (2nd ed. 1947), Hussey (1927), W. J. Turner (1938), A. Einstein (1956 ed.); the Correspondence edited by Nohl (2nd ed. 1877), *Letters of Mozart and his Family*, ed. and trans. Emily Anderson (1938).

MOZLEY, (1) James Bowling (1813–78), English theologian, brother of (2), born at Gainsborough, became a fellow of Magdalen. He took an active part in the Oxford Movement and was appointed in 1871 regius professor of Divinity at Oxford. He wrote on predestination, baptism and miracles, and published volumes of sermons. See his *Letters* (1884), and Liddon's *Pusey* (1893–1894).

(2) **Thomas** (1806–93), English divine and journalist brother of (1), an enthusiastic tractarian, wrote much in support of the movement, and later became a leader writer for *The Times*. See his *Reminiscences of Oriel College* (1882) and *Reminiscences Chiefly of Towns* (1885).

MUDIE, Charles Edward (1816–90), English bookseller, was born at Chelsea, and after some experience as a bookseller, established in 1842 his library, which became a well-known institution.

MUFTI OF JERUSALEM. See HUSSEINI.

MUGGLETON, Lodowick (1609–98), English Sectarian, a London Puritan tailor, who, with his cousin, John Reeve (1608–58), founded about 1651 the sect of Muggletonians. See Jessopp's *Coming of the Friars* (1888).

MUIR, (1) Edwin (1887–1959), Scottish poet, was born in Orkney, the son of crofter folk who, when he was fourteen, migrated to Glasgow, where he suffered the period of drab existence described in his *The Story and the Fable* (1940), revised as *An Autobiography* in 1954. He moved from job to job, but spent much time reading Nietzsche, Shaw, Ibsen, Heine and Blatchford, and he interested himself in left-wing politics. In course of time his material circumstances improved; in 1919 he married Willa Anderson, with whom he migrated to Prague, where the couple collaborated in translations of Kafka and Feuchtwanger, and where he published his first volume of verse in 1925. Returning to Scotland on the outbreak of World War II, he joined the staff of the British Council in 1942, and in 1945 returned to Prague as first director of the British Institute there, which was closed after the Communist coup of 1948. He then took over the British Institute in Rome until 1950, when he was appointed warden of the adult education college at Newbattle Abbey, Midlothian. After a year as Eliot Norton Professor of Poetry at Harvard (1955–56), he retired to Swaffham Prior near Cambridge, where he died. His verses appeared in eight slim volumes—*First Poems* (1925), *Chorus of the Newly Dead* (1926, omitted from *Collected Poems*), *Variations on a Time Theme* (1934), *Journeys and Places* (1937), *The Narrow Place* (1943), *The Voyage* (1946), *The Labyrinth* (1949), *New Poems* (1949–51) and finally *Collected Poems* (1952). Other poems appeared in *The Listener* and other periodicals later. Muir's poetry springs organically from the archetypal world, but the landscape of his vision is that of his native Orkney which quickened in his mind the belief that our life is lived on two planes, the actual and the fabulous. Without obvious virtuosity as a poet (his early poetry has no distinction of language or metre) he is able to depict this double vision in a singularly vivid manner. His later poetry shows a considerable advance in virtuosity without ever compromising his native simplicity, so that he was able to employ successfully various lyrical and elegiac forms in such a way as to suggest the 17th rather than the 20th century. Muir's critical work includes a controversial study of John Knox, *Scott and Scotland*, *Essays on Literature and Society* and *Structure of the Novel*. See J. C. Hall's introduction to *Collected Poems* (1952), and *Belonging* (1968), a memoir by Willa Muir.

(2) **John** (1810–82), Scottish Sanskrit scholar, brother of (4), was born in Glasgow, and after spending twenty-five years in the East India Company's Civil Service in Bengal, settled in Edinburgh, where he founded a chair of Sanskrit. His great work was his *Original Sanskrit Texts* (5 vols. 1858–70; 2nd ed. 1868–73). Another book is *Metrical Translations from Sanskrit Writers* (1878).

(3) **Thomas** (1765–99), Scottish politician, born in Glasgow, advocated parliamentary reform, was transported for sedition to Botany Bay, escaped in 1796, but died in France of a wound received (1796) on a Spanish frigate in a fight with British vessels. See Life by G. Pratt-Insh (1949).

(4) **Sir William** (1819–1905), Anglo-Indian administrator and scholar, brother of (2), joined the Bengal Civil Service, and became foreign secretary to the Indian government in 1865. He held other high offices in India and from 1885 to 1902 was principal of Edinburgh University. His works include a *Life of Mahomet* (4 vols. 1858–61), *The Caliphate* (new ed. 1915), *The Corân* (1878).

MUIRHEAD, (1) John Henry (1855–1940), Scottish Idealist philosopher, born in Glasgow, editor of the well-known *Library of Philosophy* from 1890, and professor of Mersey College, Birmingham (1897–1921), wrote *The Platonic Tradition in Anglo-Saxon Philosophy* (1931), a Life and study of Caird, with Sir H. Jones (1921), *Bernard Bosanquet and his Friends* (1935) and other works from a neo-Platonist standpoint. See Autobiography, ed. J. W. Harvey (1942).

(2) **(Litellus) Russell** (1896–   ), British editor and traveller, educated at University College School and Christ's College, Cambridge, in 1930 became editor of the 'Blue Guides' to Europe, his other editorial work including scientific journals and the *Penguin* guides to England and Wales (1938–49). The author of numerous travel books and articles, he has broadcast on topographical subjects.

MUKADDASI (fl. 967–985), Arab geographer, born at Jerusalem, travelled much and described Moslem lands in a work published in A.D. 985. His works were edited by G. S. A Ranking and R. F. Azoo (Calcutta 1897–1901).

MULCASTER, Richard (*c.* 1530–1611), English educationist, a native of Cumberland and a brilliant Greek and Oriental scholar, was one of the great Elizabethan schoolmasters, his ideas on education being well in advance of his time. His *Positions* (1581) was re-edited by Quick in 1888, with a biography. See Life by T. Klahr (1893) and *Educational Writings* ed. J. Oliphant (1903).

MULHALL, Michael George (1836–1900), Irish writer on statistics, was born in Dublin, and went to Buenos Aires, where he founded an English newspaper. His *Dictionary of Statistics* was published in 1883 (4th ed. 1899).

MULLER, Hermann Joseph (1890–1967), American biologist, born in New York, held academic appointments in Moscow (1933–37), Edinburgh (1938–40) and Indiana (from 1945), and was one of the great authorities on genes. He was awarded the Nobel prize for physiology in 1946.

MÜLLER, (1) **Sir Ferdinand** (1825–96), German-Australian botanist, born at Rostock, emigrated to Australia in 1847, and was director of Melbourne Botanic Gardens 1857–73. He introduced the blue gum tree into America, Europe and Africa. See Life by M. Willis (Sydney 1949).

(2) **Franz Joseph, Baron von Reichenstein** (1740–1825), Austrian chemist and mineralogist, in 1783 discovered a new metal which Klaproth (q.v.) named tellurium.

(3) **Friedrich Max** (1823–1900), Anglo-German philologist and orientalist, was born at Dessau, where his father, Wilhelm Müller (1794–1827), lyric poet, was ducal librarian. He studied at Dessau, Leipzig and Berlin, and took up the then novel subject of Sanskrit and its kindred sciences of philology and religion. In Paris he began (1845) to prepare an edition of the Rig-Veda, the sacred hymns of the Hindus, coming to England in 1846 to examine the MSS. and the East India Company commissioned him (1847) to edit it at their expense (1849–74). For a time Taylorian professor of Modern Languages at Oxford, he was in 1866 appointed professor there of Comparative Philology, a study he did more than any one else to promote in England. He became a naturalized British subject. Among his most popular works were *Lectures on the Science of Language* (1861–64), *Auld Lang Syne* (1898), *My Indian Friends* (1898), and he edited the *Sacred Books of the East* (51 vols. 1875 onwards). A foreign member of the French Institute, he was a knight of the *Ordre pour le mérite*, commander of the *Légion d'honneur* (1896), LL.D. of various universities, and P.C. (1896). His widow edited his *Life and Letters* (1902).

(4) **Fritz** (1821–97), German zoologist, brother of (6), Darwin's 'prince of observers', born near Erfurt, went with Blumenau to Brazil, studied butterflies, and advanced Darwinism with his *Für Darwin* (1864). See work by A. Möller (Jena 1915–31).

(5) **Georg** (1805–98), German-English preacher and philanthropist, was born at Kroppenstedt, studied at Halle, and came to London in 1829. Called to a Nonconformist chapel in Teignmouth, he abolished collections and depended on voluntary gifts. In 1836 he founded an Orphan House at Ashleydown, Bristol. See *Autobiography* (1905); *The Lord's Dealings with George Müller* (1837–56); Lives by A. T. Pierson (1899), and K. G. Sabiers (Los Angeles 1943); also his Diary (ed. Short, 1954).

(6) **Hermann** (1829–83), German botanist, brother of (4), born at Mühlberg, studied at Halle and Berlin, and wrote a classical book on insect pollination of flowers (1873).

(7) **Johann.** See REGIOMONTANUS.

(8) **Johannes** (1801–58), German physiologist, the founder of modern physiology, born at Coblenz, was professor of Physiology and Anatomy at Bonn and from 1833 at Berlin. His *Handbuch der Physiologie des Menschen* (1833–40; Eng. trans. 1840–49) exercised a great influence. He studied the nervous system and comparative anatomy. See Life by W. Haberling (Leipzig 1924).

(9) **Johannes von** (1752–1809), Swiss historian, was born at Schaffhausen, and studied at Göttingen. In 1774–80 he taught in Geneva, wrote his *Allgemeine Geschichte* (3 vols. 1810), and commenced his *Geschichte der schweizerischen Eidgenossenschaft* (5 vols. 1786–1808; new ed. 1826). He held posts at Cassel, Mainz and Vienna. At Berlin in 1804 he was installed as royal historiographer; and Napoleon appointed him (1807) secretary of state for Westphalia. See Lives by Monnard (French 1839), Thiersch (1881) and R. Henking (Stuttgart, 2 vols. 1910–18).

(10) **Julius** (1801–78), German theologian, brother of (11), was professor of Theology at Halle from 1839 and wrote *Der christliche Lehre von der Sünde* (1839; 7th ed. 1889; trans. 1868). See Life by Kähler (1878) and study by L. Schültze (Bremen 1879).

(11) **Karl Otfried** (1797–1840), German archaeologist, brother of (10), born at Brieg, in Silesia, became professor of Archaeology at Göttingen in 1819, and made valuable contributions to the scientific study of archaeology and mythology. His great work is *Geschichte hellenischer Stämme und Städte* (new ed. 1844); and other valuable works are *System of Mythology* (1825, trans. 1844), *Ancient Art* (1830; new ed. 1878; trans. 1847), and *History of the Literature of Ancient Greece* (1841; new ed. 1884; trans. 1846). See Memoirs by Lücke (1841), F. Ranke (1870), O. and E. Kern (1908).

(12) **Otto Frederick** (1730–84), Danish biologist, born in Copenhagen, was the first to describe diatoms and bring to notice the animal kingdom of *Infusoria*. He was the inventor of the naturalist's dredge.

(13) **Paul** (1899–1965), Swiss chemist, who in 1939 synthesized D.D.T. and demonstrated its insecticidal properties. He gained the Nobel prize for medicine for 1948.

(14) **William James** (1812–45) English painter, born at Bristol. His early landscapes dealt mainly with Gloucestershire and Wales. He later travelled abroad and produced many masterly sketches. See Life by N. Neal Solly (1875) and study by G. E. Bunt (1948).

MULLIKEN, Robert Sanderson (1896–), U.S. scientist, professor at Chicago University, won the Nobel prize for chemistry, 1966, for work on chemical bonds and the electronic structure of molecules.

MULOCK, Miss. See CRAIK (2).

MULREADY, William (1786–1863), Irish painter, a native of Ennis, studied at the Royal Academy, painting such subjects as *A Roadside Inn*, *Barber's Shop*, *Boys Fishing* (1813), &c. He was elected A.R.A. in 1815, and R.A. in 1816. He also worked at portrait painting and book illustration, and designed the 'Mulready envelope'. See Life by Stephens (1890).

MULTATULI. See DEKKER (1).

MUMFORD, Lewis (1895–), American author, editor and critic, a lecturer on social problems, was born at Flushing, Long Island. He wrote *The Story of Utopias* (1922), *The Brown Decades* (1931), *Faith for Living* (1940), *The Human Prospect* (1955), &c.

MUNCH, Edvard, *moongk* (1863–1944), Norwegian painter, born at Löten, studied at Oslo, travelled in Europe and finally settled in Norway in 1908. While in Paris, he came under the influence of Gauguin. He was obsessed by subjects such as death and love, and illustrated them in his characteristic Expressionist Symbolic style, using bright colours and a tortuously curved design, e.g., *The Scream* (1893). His engraved work was also important and influenced Die Brücke in Germany. See Life by F. B. Deknatel (1950), and studies by Moen (1956) and O. Benesch (1960).

MÜNCHHAUSEN, Karl Friedrich Hieronymus, Baron von (1720–97), German soldier, born at Bodenwerder, a member of an ancient Hanoverian house, proverbial as narrator of ridiculously exaggerated exploits, served in Russian campaigns against the Turks. A collection of marvellous stories attributed to him was first published in English as *Baron Munchausen's Narrative of his Marvellous Travels and Campaigns in Russia* (London 1785; final form, 1792). The best of it was written by **Rudolf Erich Raspe** (1737–94), a scholarly and versatile author who became professor of Archaeology and keeper of the gems and medals at Cassel. Found to be stealing and selling the medals, he fled to England, held a post in a Cornish mine, catalogued Tassie's collections in Edinburgh, as a mining expert swindled Sir John Sinclair (suggesting to Scott his Dousterswivel), and died of fever, skulking in Donegal. *Munchausen* is based partly on 16th-century German jokes, partly on hits at Bruce and other travellers. See Seccombe's edition (1895) and Life of Raspe by Carswell (1950).

MUNDAY, Anthony (1553–1633), English poet and playwright, was born in London. A stationer and actor, he wrote many poems and pamphlets and plays in collaboration. He reported on the activities of English Catholics in France and Italy and was pageant writer for London. See bibliography by S. A. Tannenbaum (N.Y. 1942) and Life by C. Turner (Berkeley, Cal., 1928).

MUNGO, St. See KENTIGERN.

MUNK, Kaj, born **Kaj Petersen,** *moongk* (1898–1944), Danish dramatist, priest and patriot, born in Maribo, Laaland, studied at Copenhagen, and as vicar of a small parish in Jutland, wrote essays, poems and notably plays, displaying his sincere faith and ardent patriotism. His first play was *En Idealist* (1928), and there followed *Ordet* (1932; 'The Word') and *Han sidder ved smeltediglen* (1938; 'He sits by the melting-pot'). He became one of the spiritual leaders of the Danish resistance movement during the German occupation, and, taken away from home by German officers on the night of January 4, 1944, he was found murdered in a ditch near Silkeborg the following morning.

MUNKÁCSY or Lieb, Michael, *moon'kah-chi* (1846–1900), Hungarian painter, born at Munkács, went as apprentice to Vienna, studied painting, and in 1872 settled in Paris. His best known pictures include *Christ before Pilate* (1881) and *Death of Mozart* (1884). See study by Waller (Los Angeles 1947).

MUNNINGS, Sir Alfred (1878–1959), English painter, was born in Suffolk, the son—like Constable—of a miller. A specialist in the painting of horses and sporting pictures, he became president of the Royal Academy (1944–49). His work is in many public galleries and he is well known for forthright criticism of modern art. See his *Autobiography* (3 vols. 1950–52), and studies by L. Lindsay (1942) and R. Pound (1962).

MUNRO, (1) **Sir Hector,** of Novar (1726–1805), Anglo-Indian general, was victor at the decisive battle of Buxar in Bihar, and in other hard-won Indian battles.

(2) **Hector Hugh,** pseud. **Saki** (1870–1916), British novelist and short-story writer, was born in Burma and came to London about 1900, becoming a successful journalist. He is best known for his short stories, humorous and macabre, which are highly individual, full of eccentric wit and unconventional situations. Collections of his stories are *Reginald* (1904), *The Chronicles of Clovis* (1911) and *Beasts and Superbeasts* (1914). His novels *The Unbearable Bassington* (1912) and *When William Came* (1913) show his gifts as a social satirist of his contemporary upper-class Edwardian world. Munro was killed on the French front during the war. See the biography by his sister in his *The Square Egg* (1924).

(3) **Hugh Andrew Johnstone** (1819–85), Scottish classical scholar, a native of Elgin, professor of Latin at Cambridge (1869–1872), his greatest achievement was an edition of Lucretius. See memoir by J. D. Duff in his translation of Lucretius (1908).

(4) **Neil** (1864–1930), Scottish novelist and journalist, was born at Inveraray and wrote *The Lost Pibroch* (1896), *John Splendid* (1898) and other romances, and edited the *Glasgow Evening News*. See his autobiography, *Brave Days* (1931).

(5) **Robert** (1835–1920), Scottish archaeologist, who, after practising as a doctor, retired and founded (1911) at Edinburgh a lectureship in Anthropology and Prehistoric Archaeology. He wrote *Lake-Dwellings of Scotland* (1882), *Lake-Dwellings of Europe* (1890), *Bosnia* (1896), *Prehistoric Problems* (1897), *Prehistoric Britain* (1914). See his *Autobiographic Sketch* (1921).

(6) **Sir Thomas** (1761–1827), Anglo-Indian general, born at Glasgow, served from 1780 as soldier and administrator in Madras and was governor from 1819. He promoted the education of the natives and championed their rights. See Lives by Gleig (1830), Bradshaw (1894) and P. R Krishnaswami (Madras 1947).

MÜNSTER, Sebastian (1489–1552), German theologian and cosmographer, born at Ingelheim, became a Franciscan monk, but after the Reformation taught Hebrew and theology at Heidelberg, and from 1536 mathematics at Basel. He brought out a Hebrew Bible (1534–35), Hebrew and

Chaldee grammars, &c., and wrote a famous *Cosmographia* (1544). See Life by V. Hautsch (Leipzig 1898).

MUNTHE, Axel, *mun'tė* (1857–1949), Swedish physician and writer, was born at Oskarshamn. He practised as a physician and psychiatrist in France and Italy, was Swedish court physician and retired to Capri, where he wrote his best-selling autobiography, *The Story of San Michele* (1929). See Life by G. L. Munthe (1953).

MÜNZER, Thomas, *mün'tsėr* (*c.* 1489–1525), German preacher and Anabaptist, born at Stolberg, studied theology, and in 1520 began to preach at Zwickau. His socialism and mystical doctrines soon brought him into collision with the authorities. After preaching widely he was in 1525 elected pastor of the Anabaptists of Mühlhausen, where his communistic ideas soon roused the whole country. But in May 1525 he was defeated at Frankenhausen, and executed a few days after. See Life and Letters, ed. D. H. Brandt (Jena 1933).

MURASAKI, Shikibu (978–*c.* 1031), Japanese authoress, wrote a remarkable novel, *Genji Monagatari, or The Tale of Genji* (trans. A. Waley, 1925–33). See A. S. Omori and D. Kochi, *Diaries of Court Ladies of Old Japan* (Tokyo 1935).

MURAT, *mü-rah,* (1) **Joachim** (1767–1815), French marshal and king of Naples, father of (2) and (3), born, an innkeeper's son, at La Bastide-Fortunière near Cahors, March 25, at the Revolution entered the army, and soon rose to be colonel. He served under Bonaparte in Italy and in Egypt, rose to be general of division (1799), returned with Bonaparte to France, and on 18th Brumaire dispersed the Council of Five Hundred at St Cloud. Bonaparte gave him his sister, Caroline, in marriage. In command of the cavalry at Marengo he covered himself with glory, and in 1801 was nominated governor of the Cisalpine Republic. He contributed not a little to the victories of Austerlitz (1805), Jena and Eylau. In 1806 the grand-duchy of Berg was bestowed upon him, and in 1808 he was proclaimed king of the Two Sicilies as Joachim Napoleon. He took possession of Naples, though the Bourbons, supported by Britain, retained Sicily, and won the hearts of his subjects. In the Russian expedition he commanded the cavalry, and indeed the army after Napoleon left it. He crushed the Austrians at Dresden (1813), fought at Leipzig, and concluded a treaty with Austria and a truce with the British admiral; but, on Napoleon's escape from Elba, he commenced war against Austria, and was twice defeated. With a few horsemen he fled to Naples, and thence to France. After Napoleon's final overthrow, he proceeded with a few followers to the coast of Calabria, and proclaimed himself king; but was taken, court-martialled, and shot, October 13, 1815. See books by Gallois (1828), Coletta (1821), Helfert (1878), Hilliard-Atteridge (1911), M. Dupont (Paris 1934) and J. Lucas-Dubreton (1944).

(2) **Napoléon Achille** (1801–47), French-American author, son of (1), settled in Florida, married a niece of Washington, and published a work on American government (1833). See Life by A. H. Hanna (Norman Okla., 1946).

(3) **Napoléon Lucien Charles** (1803–78), French senator, son of (1), suffered reverses in fortune, but, returning to France after 1848, attached himself to Louis Napoleon, who in 1849 sent him as ambassador to Turin, and in 1852 made him a senator.

MURATORI, Lodovico Antonio, *moo-ra-tō'ree* (1672–1750), Italian historian, born near Modena, in 1695 was appointed Ambrosian librarian at Milan, and ducal librarian and archivist at Modena in 1700. He published *Rerum Italicarum Scriptores* (29 vols. fol. 1723–51), *Annali d'Italia* (12 vols. 1744–1749), and *Antiquitates Italica* (6 vols. 1738–42, containing the 'Muratorian Fragment', a canon of the New Testament books, apparently written by a contemporary of Irenaeus). In later years he was attacked by the Jesuits for teaching heresies, but found a protector in Pope Benedict XIV. See Lives by his nephew (1756), G. Bertoni (Rome 1926) and G. Cavazzutti (Turin 1939).

MURCHISON, Sir Roderick Impey (1792–1871), Scottish geologist, born at Tarradale, Ross-shire, served in Spain and Portugal, and, quitting the army in 1816, devoted himself to geology. His establishment of the Silurian system won him the Copley Medal and European fame, increased by his exposition of the Devonian, Permian and Laurentian systems. He explored parts of Germany, Poland and the Carpathians; and in 1840–45, with others, carried out a geological survey of the Russian empire. Struck with the resemblance between the Ural Mountains and Australian chains, Murchison in 1844 foreshadowed the discovery of gold in Australia. He was president of the British Association in 1846, and for many years of the Royal Geographical Society. In 1855 he was made director-general of the Geological Survey and director of the Royal School of Mines. His principal works were *The Silurian System* (1839) and *The Geology of Russia in Europe and the Urals* (1845; 2nd ed. 1853). See Life by Geikie (1875).

MURDOCH, Iris, *mœr'dok* (1919–), Irish novelist and philosopher, born in Dublin, was educated at Badminton School, Bristol, and Somerville College, Oxford, was an assistant-principal at the Treasury (1938–42) and served with U.N.R.R.A. (1944–46). In 1948 she was appointed fellow and tutor at St Anne's College, Oxford. A professional philosopher in the Moore-Wittgenstein tradition, which has no point of contact with French existentialism, she yet wrote an excellent study of Sartre (1953) and as a hobby took to novel-writing. *Under the Net* (1954), *Flight from the Enchanter* (1955), *The Sandcastle* (1957) combine philosophical speculations with fanciful, ironical and even shocking situations in which rootless intellectuals, amorous outsiders of postwar disillusionment, are depicted objectively, but with compassion. *The Bell* (1958), describing the tangle of human relationships within a small Anglican lay community, established her as an outstanding novelist, who without disturbing the genuine logical achievements of anti-metaphysical philosophizing, yet learnt to appreciate the value of a metaphysical basis for a self-discovered personal morality. Later works include *An Unofficial Rose* (1962), *The Red and the Green* (1965), *The Time of the Angels* (1966) and *The Nice and the Good* (1968). See her essay 'Metaphysics and Ethics' in *Nature of Metaphysics*, ed. Pears (1957).

MURDOCK, William (1754–1839), Scottish engineer and inventor of coal gas, was born near Auchinleck. He worked with his father, a millwright, and then with Boulton & Watt of Birmingham, by whom he was sent to Cornwall to erect mining engines. At Redruth he constructed in 1784 the model of a high-pressure engine to run on wheels. He introduced labour-saving machinery, a new method of wheel rotation, an oscillating engine (1785), a steam-gun, &c.; and he also improved Watt's engine. His distillation of coal gas began at Redruth in 1792; successful experiments were made at Neath Abbey in 1796; but it was not till 1803 that the premises at Soho were lighted with gas. See Life by A. Murdoch (1892).

MURE, Sir William (1594–1657), Scottish poet, of Rowallan in Ayrshire, was wounded at Marston Moor, and wrote *The True Crucifixe for True Catholikes* (1629), a fine version of the Psalms (1639), &c. See his *Works*, ed. by W. Tough (2 vols. 1898).

MURET, Marc Antoine, *mü-ray* (1526–85), French humanist, born at Muret near Limoges, lectured on civil law in France, but later settled in Italy, edited Latin authors and wrote orations, poems, &c. See monograph by Dejob (Paris 1881).

MURFREE, Mary. See CRADDOCK.

MURGER, Henri, *mür-zhay* (1822–61), French writer, born in Paris, began life as a notary's clerk, and, giving himself to literatrue, led the life of privation and adventure described in his first and best novel, *Scènes de la vie de Bohème* (1845), the basis of Puccini's opera. During his later years he wrote slowly and fitfully in the intervals of dissipation. *Le Manchon de Francine* is one of the saddest short stories ever penned. Other prose works are *La Vie de jeunesse*, *Le Pays Latin*, &c. His poems, *Les Nuits d'hiver*, are graceful and often deeply pathetic; several were translated by Andrew Lang in his *Lays of old France*. See Lives by Montorgueil (1929), Moss and Marvel (1948).

MURILLO, Bartolomé Esteban, *moo-ree'lyō* (1618–82), Spanish painter, was born, of humble parentage, at Seville, where he learned to paint, and produced stiff and rough religious pictures for the fairs of Seville and for exportation to South America. At Madrid (1641), by favour of his townsman Velázquez, he was enabled to study the *chefs d'oeuvre* of Italian and Flemish art in the royal collections. In 1645 he returned to Seville and painted eleven remarkable pictures for the convent of San Francisco, became famous, and was soon the head of the school there. In 1648 he married a lady of fortune, and maintained a handsome establishment. He now passed from his first or 'cold' style—dark with decided outlines—to his second or 'warm' style, in which the drawing is softer and the colour improved. In 1656 he produced the first examples of his third or 'vaporous' manner, the outlines vanishing in a misty blending of light and shade. The Academy of Seville was founded by him in 1660. After this came Murillo's most brilliant period; eight of the eleven pictures painted in 1661–74 for the almshouse of St Jorge are accounted his masterpieces. He executed some twenty pieces for the Capuchin Convent after 1675. He frequently chose the Immaculate Conception orAssumption of the Virgin as a subject, and treated them much alike; the *Conception* in the Louvre was bought (1852) at the sale of Marshal Soult's pictures for £24,000. In 1681 he fell from a scaffold when painting an altarpiece at Cadiz, and died at Seville, April 3. His pictures naturally fall into two great groups—scenes from low life, as gypsies and beggar children (mostly executed early in his life), and religious works. See books by E. E. Minor (1882), C. B. Curtis (1883), G. C. Williamson (1902), P. Lafond (Paris 1930).

MURPHY, (1) Arthur (1727–1805), Irish actor and playwright, born at Clomquin, Roscommon, was educated at St Omer. In 1752–74 he published the weekly *Gray's Inn Journal*, and so got to know Dr Johnson. By going on the stage he paid his debts, and entered Lincoln's Inn in 1757. In 1758 he produced *The Upholsterer*, a successful farce; in 1762 he was called to the bar, but continued to write for the stage. His translation of Tacitus (1793) is excellent; not so his *Essay on Johnson* and *Life of Garrick*. See Lives by Jesse Foot (1811) and H. H. Dunbar (N.Y. 1946).

(2) **William Parry** (1892–), American physician, taught for some years at Harvard and then in 1923 took up private practice in Boston. He made a special study of anaemia and with Minot (q.v.) first suggested the liver diet. They shared the Nobel prize for medicine (1934).

MURRAY, (1) Alexander (1775–1813), Scottish philologist, born, a shepherd's son, in Minnigaff parish, Kirkcudbright, acquired, while a shepherd, a mastery of the classics, the chief European tongues and Hebrew, and after 1794 studied at Edinburgh. In 1806 he became minister of Urr, in 1812 professor of Oriental Languages at Edinburgh. He left a *History of the European Languages* (with Life by Sir H. W. Moncrieff, 1823).

(2) **Charles** (1754–1821), Scottish actor and dramatist, son of (9), father of (13), trained as a surgeon, later took to the stage, where he was commended for the parts of old men. He is credited with one or two poor plays.

(3) **Charles** (1864–1941), Scottish poet, born in Aberdeenshire, trained as an engineer and had a successful career in South Africa, where in 1917 he was director of defence. His poems were written in the Aberdeenshire dialect and admirably portrayed country life and character at the turn of the century. His first collection, *Hamewith* (1900), was his best and most characteristic. It was followed by *A Sough o' War* (1917) and *In Country Places* (1920). See a memoir by C. Christie (Pretoria 1943).

(4) **Sir David** (1849–1933), Scottish painter, was born at Glasgow and educated for commerce, but instead became a painter noted for landscapes of Scotland, the Italian lakes, &c. He was elected R.A. in 1905 and knighted in 1918.

(5) **Lord George** (*c.* 1700–60), Scottish Jacobite general, son of the Duke of Atholl, took part in the Jacobite risings of 1715 and 1719 and was later pardoned. In 1745 he joined the Young Pretender, and was one of his generals. After Culloden he escaped abroad and died in Holland. See books by W. Duke (1927) and K. Tommason (1958).

(6) **George Gilbert Aimé** (1866–1957), classical scholar, author and lifelong Liberal, was born in Sydney, N.S.W. Arriving in England aged eleven, he went to the Merchant Taylors' School and Oxford. He was appointed professor of Greek at Glasgow University (1889) and regius professor of Greek at Oxford (1908). His work as a classical historian and translator of Greek dramatists brought him acclamation as 'the foremost Greek scholar of our time'. His celebrated verse translations of Greek plays, including *The Trojan Women*, *Bacchae*, *Medea* and *Electra*, were performed at London's Court Theatre from 1902. Many works on classics include *History of Ancient Greek Literature* (1897), *The Rise of the Greek Epic* (1907), *Five Stages of Greek Religion* (1913). He stood for parliament, unsuccessfully, six times. President of the League of Nations Union (1923–38), and first president of the United Nations Association General Council, he was awarded the O.M. in 1941. See his *Unfinished Autobiography* (1960), and Life by J. A. K. Thomson (1958).

(7) **Sir James Augustus Henry** (1837–1915), Scottish philologist and lexicographer, born at Denholm, was for many years master at Mill Hill school. His *Dialects of the Southern Counties of Scotland* (1873) established his reputation. The great work of his life, the editing of the Philological Society's New English Dictionary, was begun at Mill Hill (1879), and (barring supplements) completed (1928) at Oxford. Murray himself edited about half the work, but he created the organization and the inspiration for completing it. See Memoir by H. Bradley, *Proc. Brit. Acad.* (viii, 1917–18).

(8) **Sir John** (1841–1914), British marine zoologist, was born at Cobourg, Ontario, studied in Canada and at Edinburgh University, and after a voyage on a whaler, was appointed one of the naturalists to the *Challenger* Expedition (1872–76), and successively assistant editor and editor-in-chief (1882) of the *Reports*. He wrote a *Narrative* of the expedition and a report on deep-sea deposits, and published innumerable papers on oceanography and biology, fresh-water lakes, &c.

(9) **Sir John** (1715–77), Scottish Jacobite, father of (2), of Broughton, Peeblesshire, was Prince Charles Edward's secretary during the '45, but, captured after Culloden, saved his life by betraying his fellow Jacobites. He succeeded as baronet in 1770. See his *Memorials*, edited by Fitzroy Bell (Scot. Hist. Soc. 1898).

(10) **John** (1745–93), British publisher, originally McMurray, was born in Edinburgh, became an officer in the Royal Marines in 1762, but in 1768 bought Sandby's bookselling business in London, and published the *English Review*, Disraeli's *Curiosities of Literature*, &c. His son, **John** (1778–1843), who carried the business from Fleet Street to Albemarle Street, projected the *Quarterly Review* of which the first issue appeared in 1809. Byron received £20,000 for his works, Crabbe, Moore, Campbell and Irving being treated generously. His 'Family Library' was begun in 1829, and he issued the travels of Mungo Park, Belzoni, Parry, Franklin, &c. His son, **John Murray** the third (1808–92), issued the works of Livingstone, Borrow, Darwin, Smiles, Smith's dictionaries, and *Handbooks for Travellers* (begun 1836). See Memoir (1919) by his son and successor, **Sir John Murray** (1851–1928; K.C.V.O. 1926), who absorbed Smith, Elder & Co., 1917, edited Gibbon's *Autobiography* and Byron's letters and began publication of the *Letters of Queen Victoria*. **Sir John** (1884–1967), his son, completed the publication of Queen Victoria's letters. See a history of the firm (1930), book by G. Paston (1932), and Smiles, *A Publisher and his Friends* (1891).

(11) **John** (1741–1815), Anglo-American divine, born in England, went to America and preached the doctrine of universal salvation and became known as the 'Father of American Universalism'. See his Autobiography (1816).

(12) **Lindley** (1745–1826), Anglo-American grammarian, born at Swatara, Pa., practised law, made a fortune during the War of Independence and then, for health reasons, retired to England and bought an estate near York. His *English Grammar*, long a standard (1795), was followed by *English Exercises*, the *English Reader*, and religious works. See his *Memoirs* (1826), and Life by W. H. Egle (N.Y. 1885).

(13) **William Henry** (1790–1852), Scottish actor-manager, son of (2), born at Bath, went to Edinburgh (1809), where he remained for over forty years as actor and manager. He was particularly associated with dramatizations of the Waverley novels.

MURRY, John Middleton (1889–1957), British writer and critic, born in Peckham, wrote some poetry and many volumes of essays and criticism which had a strong influence on the young intellectuals of the 'twenties. He was the husband of Katherine Mansfield and introduced her work in *The Adelphi*, of which he was editor from 1923 to 1948. He also produced posthumous selections from her letters and diaries, and a biography in 1932. He became a pacifist and was editor of *Peace News* from 1940 to 1946. Towards the end of his life he became interested in agriculture, and started a community farm in Norfolk. See Life by F. A. Lea (1959).

MUSAEUS, *moo-zee'us*, (1) Greek poet, reputed author of oracles, hymns, &c., of which we possess but a few doubtful fragments.

(2) (5th–6th cent. A.D.), Greek poet, wrote a beautiful little Greek poem *Hero and Leander*, which has been translated into many lan-

guages. See trans. by E. H. Blakeney (1935), F. L. Lucas (1949).

MUSA IBN NOSAIR (640–717), Arab general, conquered northern Africa in 699–709 and Spain in 712, fell under the displeasure of the Khalif of Damascus, and died in poverty in the Hejaz.

MUSÄUS, Johann Karl August, *moo-zay'oos* (1735–87), German writer, born at Jena, studied theology there, and in 1770 became professor at the Weimar gymnasium. His first book (1760) was a parody of Richardson's *Sir Charles Grandison*; in 1798 he satirized Lavater in *Physiognomische Reisen*. But his fame rests on his German popular tales, which professed, falsely, to be a collection taken down from the lips of old people. Their chief note is artificial naïveté, but they are a blending of satirical humour, quaint fancy and graceful writing. See Life by M. Müller (1867) and study by A. Ohlmer (Munich 1912).

MUSORGSKI. See MOUSSORGSKY.

MUSPRATT, James (1793–1886), British chemist, took part in the Peninsular War and then returned to his trade of druggist. He began manufacturing acids, &c., and greatly improved the methods of so doing. With Josias Gamble he was the founder of the chemical industry in St Helens.

MUSSCHENBROEK, Pieter van, *mœ'sên-brook* (1692–1761), Dutch physicist, born at Leyden, where he studied and later became professor of Physics, invented the pyrometer and in 1746 discovered the principle of the Leyden jar.

MUSSET, Alfred de, *mü-say* (1810–57), French poet and dramatist, was born in Paris, December 11. After tentative study first at the law, then at medicine, he found he had a talent for writing and at eighteen published a translation of De Quincey's *Opium Eater*. His first collection of poems, *Contes d'Espagne et d'Italie* (1830), largely Byronic in outlook, won the approval of Victor Hugo (q.v.) who accepted him into his *Cénacle*, the inner shrine of militant Romanticism. But Musset had no real desire to commit himself to any particular cult; indeed he had already begun to poke gentle fun at the Movement, and had indicated that he wished to ' se déhugotiser '. His first excursion into drama, *La Nuit vénitienne*, failed at the Odéon in 1830, and thenceforward he conceived an ' armchair theatre ' with plays intended for reading only. The first of these, *La Coupe et les lèvres* and *À quoi rêvent les jeunes filles*, together with the narrative poem *Namouna*, were published as *Spectacle dans un fauteuil* in 1832, and next year the tragi-comedies *André del Sarto* and *Les Caprices de Marianne* appeared in the *Revue des deux mondes*. Also among his *Comédies et proverbes*, as these pieces were called, are *Lorenzaccio* (1834), *On ne badine pas avec l'amour* (1836) and *Il ne faut jurer de rien* (1836). *Un Caprice*, published in 1837, and several of his other ' armchair ' plays were staged successfully more than ten years later, and thus reassured he wrote *On ne saurait penser de tout* (1849), *Carmosine* (1850) and *Bettine* (1851) for actual performance. Musset's dramatic work, much of which is devoted to dissecting the anatomy of love between the sexes, is unique for originality, intensity, wit and variety. In 1833 Musset had met George Sand (q.v.), and there began the stormy love affair which coloured much of his work after that date. The pair set out to spend the winter together at Venice, but Musset became ill, George became capricious, and in April the poet returned alone, broken in health and sunk in depression. His *Nuits*, from *Nuit de mai* (1835) through *Nuit de décembre* (1835) and *Nuit d'août* (1836) to *Nuit d'octobre* (1837), trace the emotional upheaval of his love for George Sand from despair to final resignation. His autobiographical poem *Confessions d'un enfant du siècle* (1835) is a study of the prevalent attitude of mind—the *mal du siècle*—resulting from the aftermath of revolution and the unrest of the early years of the century; much of his work is tinged with this outlook, and his heroes, who are often amoral and charming at the same time, portray the consequent blend of hedonism and pessimism as seen in *Namouna*, *Rolla* and elsewhere. *L'Espoir en Dieu*, an expression of the soul's longing for certainty, is perhaps not altogether convincing. In 1838 Musset was appointed Home Office librarian; in 1852 he was elected to the Academy. He died of heart failure, probably exacerbated by high living. See Lives by Oliphant (1890), Séché (1907), Donnay (1915), Villiers (Paris 1939), van Tieghem (1945); for both sides of the love affair with George Sand see her *Elle et lui*, and his brother Paul's *Lui et elle*.

MUSSOLINI, Benito (1883–1945), Italian dictator, born a blacksmith's son, at Predappio, near Forlí, Romagna, edited the Socialist *Avanti*, but after serving in the First World War, founded the *Popolo d'Italia*, and organized the Fascisti as militant nationalists to defeat socialism. In October 1922 his blackshirts marched on Rome; and ' Il Duce ' established himself as dictator by melodramatic means, including murder. He ruled forcefully and intolerantly, not without efficiency. Greece was bullied, the League of Nations flouted. The Vatican State was set up by the Lateran Treaty (1929). The Axis with Germany was formed. Franco was aided in Spain. With the annexation of Abyssinia (1936) and Albania (1939) to the Italian crown Mussolini's dream of a new Roman empire seemed to be coming true. At the most favourable moment (1940) he entered the second World War, and met with disaster everywhere. In 1943 his followers fell away and he resigned (July 25), was arrested, was rescued by German parachutists, and sought to regain what he had lost. On April 28, 1945, he and other Fascists were caught by Italians at Dongo on the Lake of Como, and, after some form of trial, shot, their bodies being exposed to insult in Como and in Milan, the old headquarters of Fascism. See his Autobiography (trans. 1928) and works by M. H. H. Macartney (1944), P. Saporiti (1947), R. Dabrowski (1956); I. Kirkpatrick (1964); and Rachele Mussolini, *My Life with Mussolini* (1959).

MUSSORGSKY. See MOUSSORGSKY.

MUSTAFA KEMAL ATATÜRK (1881–1938), Turkish general and statesman, born in Salonika, led the Turkish nationalist movement from 1909 and was a general in World War I. Elected president (1923–38), he was responsible for many reforms and for the modernization of Turkey. See Lives by H. C. Armstrong (1932), R. Brock (N.Y. 1954) and Kinross (1964).

MYERS, (1) **Ernest James** (1844–1921), English poet and translator, brother of (2), published several volumes of verse, translated Pindar, and collaborated in a translation of the *Iliad*.

(2) **Frederic William Henry** (1843–1901), English poet and essayist, the son of the Rev. Frederic Myers of Keswick (author of four series of *Catholic Thoughts*), was from 1872 a school inspector. He wrote poems (collected 1921), essays, *Wordsworth* (1881), and *Human Personality and its Survival of Bodily Death* (1903). He was one of the founders of the Society for Psychical Research. See memoir by Oliver Lodge and others (1901), A. C. Benson's *The Leaves of the Tree* (1911), and book by G. D. Cummings (1948).

MYLNE, (1) **Robert** (1734–1811), Scottish architect, born in Edinburgh, designed Blackfriars' Bridge (erected in 1769 and pulled down in 1868) and planned the Gloucester and Berkeley Ship Canal and the Eau Brink Cut for fen drainage at King's Lynn. His buildings, for example St Cecilia's Hall, Edinburgh (1763–65), show an elegance typical of the best late 18th-century work. Mylne was elected F.R.S. in 1767. See the monograph by A. E. Richardson (1955).

(2) or **MILN, Walter** (d. 1558), last Scottish Protestant martyr, while on a visit to Germany became imbued with the doctrines of the Reformation, and later as priest of Lunan in Angus was denounced for heresy. Condemned by Cardinal Beaton to be burnt wherever he might be found, he fled the country, but after the cardinal's death he mistakenly thought it safe to return. Taken prisoner at Dysart, he was tried at St Andrews and although by this time over eighty years old was condemned to the stake.

MYRON (fl. 450 B.C.), Greek sculptor. A contemporary of Phidias, he worked in bronze and is known for the celebrated *Discobolos*. See study by P. E. Arias (Florence 1940).

MYTENS, Daniel, *mī'tens* (*c.* 1590–1642), Flemish portrait-painter, born at The Hague, he worked for James I and Charles I, who made him 'King's painter'. He painted portraits of many notable persons of the time. See work by C. H. Collins (1912).

N

NABOKOV, Vladimir (1899–), Russian-born American author, was born and educated in St Petersburg, studied at Trinity College, Cambridge, and in 1940 settled in the United States, where he became a research fellow in entomology at Harvard, and in 1948 professor of Russian Literature at Cornell. A considerable Russian author, he established himself also as a novelist in English with *The Real Life of Sebastian Knight* (1941), *Bend Sinister* (1947), *Pnin* (1957) and a collection of his best short stories, *Nabokov's Dozen* (1959). But he is best known by his controversial novel *Lolita* (1955; in Britain 1959), which concerns the attachment of a middle-aged intellectual for a twelve-year-old girl. Nabokov coined the word 'nymphet' for a fledgling charmer of this type. See his autobiographical *Conclusive Evidence* (1950) and *Speak Memory* (1967); and study by A. Field (1968).

NACHTIGAL, Gustav, *naKH'ti-gahl* (1834–1885), German traveller, was born at Eichstedt, studied medicine, served as army surgeon, and in 1863 went to North Africa. He travelled across the Sahara from Tripoli to Cairo (1869–74) and in 1884 he went to annex Togoland, Cameroons and Angra Pequena for Germany, and died on the return journey off Cape Palmas. See his *Sahara and Sudan* (1879–89), and works by D. Berlin (1887), J. Weise (1914), H. Heuer (1927).

NADIR SHAH, the Conqueror (1688–1747), king of Persia, was born in Khorasan of a Turkish tribe, expelled the Afghan rulers of Persia and restored Tamasp to the throne. He defeated the Turks in 1731, imprisoned Tamasp, and elevated his infant son, Abbas III, to the throne in 1732. The death of this puppet in 1736 opened the way for Nadir himself, who resumed the war with the Turks, and ultimately was victorious. He also conquered Afghanistan and drove back the Uzbegs. Difficulties arose with the Great Mogul, and Nadir ravaged the north-west of India and took Delhi, with rich booty, including the Koh-i-nûr. He next reduced Bokhara and Khiva; but he was assassinated June 20. See Maynard's *Nadir Shah* (1885), and Lives by L. Lockhart (1938) and J. D. Fraser (Calcutta 1954).

NAEVIUS, Gnaeus (*c.* 264–194 B.C.), Roman poet and dramatist, was born, probably in Campania, about 264 B.C., and served in the first Punic war. A plebeian, he for thirty years satirized and lampooned the Roman nobles in his plays, and was compelled to withdraw from Rome, ultimately retiring to Utica in Africa, where he died in 194 B.C. Fragments of an epic, *De Bello Punico*, are extant. See Warmington (ed. and trans.) *Remains of Old Latin* (ii, 1936), and W. Beare, *The Roman Stage* (1950).

NÄGELI, Karl Wilhelm von, *nay'gel-ee* (1817–1891), Swiss botanist and physicist, professor at Munich (1858), was one of the early writers on evolution. He investigated the growth of cells and originated the micellar theory relating to the structure of starch grains, cell walls, &c. He died at Munich.

NAGY, Imre, *nod'y'* (1895–1958), Hungarian politician, born at Kaposvar, Hungary, was captured in the Austrian Army in the first World War, and sent to Siberia. At the Revolution he escaped, joined the Bolshevik forces and became a Soviet citizen in 1918. Back in Hungary in 1919 he had a minor post in the Béla Kun revolutionary government, but later fled to Russia, where he remained throughout the second World War. Returning with the Red Army, he became minister of agriculture in the provisional government, enforcing Communist land reforms. In 1947 he became speaker of the Hungarian Parliament, and in 1953 prime minister, introducing a 'new course' of milder political and economic control. In February 1955 the Rakosi régime removed him from office as a 'right deviationist'. He returned to the premiership in 1956 on Rakosi's downfall. When the revolution broke out in October 1956 he promised free elections and a Russian military withdrawal. When, in November, Soviet forces began to put down the revolution he appealed to the world for help, but was displaced by the Soviet puppet Janos Kadar and was later executed.

NAHUM (7th cent. B.C.), one of the twelve minor Hebrew prophets, who seems to have been an Israelite or Judaean who had been a captive in Nineveh, and wrote his prophecy between 663 and 612 B.C.

NAIDU, Sarojini, *née* **Chattopadhyay,** *nah'i-doo* (1879–1949), Indian poet and feminist, born at Hyderabad, was educated at Madras, London and Cambridge. Her verse (1905–1917) showed her mastery of the lyric form in English and was translated into many Indian languages. She then turned to national and feminist affairs. Associated with Gandhi, she was the first Indian woman to be chairman of the National Congress (1925), and with Gandhi took part in the Round Table Conference (1931). She was imprisoned for her part in the civil disobedience movement and later took part in the negotiations leading to independence. In 1947 she became governor of the United Provinces. As leader of the women's movement in India she did much to remove the barrier of purdah. See Life by R. R. Bhatnagar (Allahabad 1946).

NAIRNE, Carolina Oliphant, Baroness (1766–1845), Scottish song writer, was born at the 'auld hoose' of Gask in Perthshire, third daughter of its Jacobite laird. In 1806 she married her second cousin, Major Nairne (1757–1830), who became sixth Lord Nairne. She lived at Edinburgh and, after her husband's death, in Ireland, then on the Continent. Her eighty-seven songs appeared first in *The Scottish Minstrel* (1821–24), and posthumously as *Lays from Strathearn.* Some of them are mere bowdlerizations of 'indelicate' favourites; but four at least are immortal—the 'Land o' the Leal' (*c.* 1798), 'Caller Herrin',' 'The Laird o' Cockpen', and 'The Auld Hoose'. See Lives by Rogers (1869), G. Henderson (1900); and Kington Oliphant's *Jacobite Lairds of Gask* (1870).

NAMIER, Sir Lewis Bernstein, *nay'mee-ėr* **(1888–1960), British historian, of Russian** origin, was educated at Balliol College, and had a long and distinguished career, crowned with the professorship of Modern History at the University of Manchester from 1931 to 1952. His influence created a Namier School of history, in which the emphasis was on microscopic analysis of events and institutions, particularly Parliament, so as to reveal the entire motivation of the individuals involved in them. He compelled a 're-thinking' of history through his *Structure of Politics at the Accession of George III* (1929) and *England in the Age of the American Revolution*, Vol. I (1930). His followers have been thought by some critics, perhaps unjustly, to be making more ado about the trees than the wood, but there was no detracting from Namier's achievement. For a critical appraisal of the Namier school, see H. Butterfield, *George III and the Historians* (1957); for an appreciation, *Essays*, ed. Pares and Taylor (1956).

NANAK, *na'-* (1469–1538), founder of Sikhism, was born near Lahore. A Hindu by birth and belief, he fell under Moslem influence and denounced many Hindu practices as idolatrous. His doctrine, set out later in the *Adi-Granth*, sought a fusion of Brahmanism and Islam on the grounds that both were monotheistic, although Nanak's own ideas leaned rather towards pantheism.

NANA SAHIB, *nom de guerre* of **Brahmin Dundhu Panth** (*c.* 1820–*c.* 1859), Indian rebel, adopted son of the ex-peshwa of the Mahrattas, became known as the leader of the Indian Mutiny in 1857. He was disappointed that the peshwa's pension was not continued to himself, on the outbreak of the Mutiny was proclaimed peshwa, and perpetrated the massacres at Cawnpore. After the collapse of the rebellion he escaped into Nepal. He died probably after 1859.

NANSEN, Fridtjof (1861–1930), Norwegian explorer, was born near Oslo, and studied at the university there, as well as later at Naples. In 1882 he made a voyage into the Arctic regions in the sealer *Viking*, and on his return was made keeper of the natural history department of the museum at Bergen. In the summer of 1888 he made an adventurous journey across Greenland from east to west. He described it in *The First Crossing of Greenland* (trans. 1890). But his great achievement was the partial accomplishment of his scheme for reaching the North Pole by letting his ship get frozen into the ice north of Siberia and drift with a current setting towards Greenland. He started in the *Fram*, built for the purpose, in August 1893, reached the New Siberian islands in September, made fast to an ice floe, and drifted north to 84° 4′ on March 3, 1895. There, accompanied by Johansen, he left the *Fram* and pushed across the ice, reaching the highest latitude till then attained, 86° 14′ N., on April 7. The two wintered in Franz Josef Land. *Farthest North* (2 vols. 1897) recounts his adventures. Professor of Zoology (1897) and of Oceanography (1908) at Oslo, Nansen furthered the separation of Norway and Sweden, and was Norwegian ambassador in London (1906–08). He published *In Northern Mists* (1911), *Through Siberia* (1914), &c. In 1922 he got a

Nobel peace prize for Russian relief work and he did much for the League of Nations. See books by Sörenson (trans. 1933), Ristelhueber (Montreal 1944), Reynolds (1956) and Höyer (1958).

NAOROJI, Dadhabai, *now-rō'jee* (1825–1917), Indian politician, born at Bombay, became professor of Mathematics in Elphinstone College there, and a member of the Legislative Council; and in 1892–95 represented Finsbury in the House of Commons —the first Indian M.P., and was also president of the Indian National Congress. See Life by R. P. Masani (1939).

NAPIER, (1) **Sir Charles** (1786–1860), British admiral, born at Merchiston Hall near Falkirk, a cousin to the hero of Sind, went to sea at thirteen, received his first command in 1808, and later served as a volunteer in the Peninsular army. Commanding the *Thames* in 1811, he inflicted incredible damage upon the enemy in the Mediterranean. In 1814 he led the way in the ascent of the Potomac, and he took part in the operations against Baltimore. In command of the fleet of the young queen of Portugal, he defeated the Miguelite fleet and placed Donna Maria on the throne. In the war between the Porte and Mehemet Ali he stormed Sidon, defeated Ibrahim Pasha in Lebanon, attacked Acre, blockaded Alexandria, and concluded a convention with Mehemet Ali. A K.C.B., he commanded the Baltic fleet in the Russian war; but the capture of Bomarsund failed to realize expectations, and he was superseded. He twice sat in parliament, and until his death he laboured to reform the naval administration. See Lives by E. Napier (1862), Noel Williams (1917).

(2) **Sir Charles James** (1782–1853), British general, brother of (7), conqueror of Sind, was a descendant of Napier of Merchiston. He was born at Westminster, served in Ireland during the rebellion, in Portugal (1810), against the United States (1813), and in the storming of Cambrai (1815). In 1838 he was made K.C.B., and in 1841 was ordered to India to command in the war with Sind, and at the battle of Meeanee (1843) broke the power of the amirs. After another battle at Hyderabad, Napier was made governor. He gained the respect of the inhabitants, but was soon engaged in an acrimonious war of dispatches with the home authorities. In 1847 he returned to England, but was back in India before the close of the Sikh war. As commander-in-chief of the army in India, he quarrelled with Lord Dalhousie about military reform, and bade a final adieu to the East in 1851. See Lives by his brother (1857), W. Napier Bruce (1885), W. Butler (1890), R. N. Lawrence (1952) and H. T. Lambrick (1952).

(3) **John** (1550–1617), Scottish mathematician, the inventor of logarithms, was born at Merchiston Castle, Edinburgh, matriculated at St Andrews in 1563, travelled on the Continent, and settled down to a life of literary and scientific study. In 1593 he published his *Plaine Discouery of the whole Reuelation of Saint John*, which was translated into Dutch, French and German. He made a contract with Logan of Restalrig for the discovery of treasure in Fast Castle (1594), devised warlike machines for defence against Philip of Spain, and recommended salt as a fertilizer of land. A strict Presbyterian, he was also a believer in astrology and divination. He described his famous invention of logarithms in *Mirifici Logarithmorum Canonis Descriptio* (1614), and the calculating apparatus called ' Napier's Bones ' in *Rabdologiae seu Numerationis per Virgulas libri duo* (1617); and two years later a second work on logarithms was published by his son Robert (new ed. by W. R. Macdonald, 1889). Napier's eldest son was raised to the peerage as Lord Napier in 1627, and the ninth Baron Napier in 1872 became Baron Ettrick also. See Lives by the Earl of Buchan (1787) and Mark Napier (1834), who also edited Napier's *Ars Logistica*, a system of arithmetic and algebra (1839); and the *Tercentenary Memorial Volume* (1916).

(4) **Macvey** (1776–1847), Scottish lawyer and editor, born at Glasgow, in 1799 became a writer to the signet in Edinburgh, in 1805 signet librarian (till 1837), and in 1824 first professor of Conveyancing. He edited the supplement to the fifth edition of the *Encyclopaedia Britannica* (1816–24), the seventh edition (1830–42) and from 1829 the *Edinburgh Review*. See *Correspondence* (1879).

(5) **Robert** (1791–1876), Scottish shipbuilder and engineer, born at Dumbarton, built the first four Cunard steamships and some of the earliest ironclad warships and helped to make the Clyde a great shipbuilding centre. See Life by J. Napier (1904).

(6) **Robert Cornelis, 1st Baron Napier of Magdala** (1810–90), British soldier, born at Colombo, Ceylon, was educated at Addiscombe, and entered the Bengal Engineers in 1826. He served in campaigns in India, and during the Indian Mutiny he distinguished himself at the siege of Lucknow, and was made K.C.B. He received the thanks of parliament for his services in the Chinese war of 1860 and for his brilliant conduct of the expedition in Abyssinia in 1868. In 1870 he became commander-in-chief in India and a member of the Indian Council, and was subsequently governor of Gibraltar, field-marshal, and constable of the Tower. See Life by his son (1927).

(7) **Sir William Francis Patrick,** K.C.B. (1785–1860), British soldier and military historian, brother of (2), served through the Peninsular campaign and retired from the army in 1819. He began writing and published his *History of the War in the Peninsula* (1828–40), *The Conquest of Scinde* (1845) and the Life of his brother (1857). See Lives by H. A. Bruce (1864), W. F. Butler (1890).

NAPOLEON I or **Napoleon Bonaparte** (1769–1821), second son of **Charles Bonaparte** (q.v.), assessor to the royal tribunal of Corsica, was born at Ajaccio, August 15. Granted free military education in France, he studied French at Autun before entering the military schools at Brienne (1779) and Paris (1784). In 1785 he was commissioned second-lieutenant of artillery in the regiment of la Fère, garrisoned at Valence. At Auxonne he saw the beginnings of the French Revolution, but, more concerned with Corsica than France, he went home on leave to organize a revolution and was temporarily struck off the army list for returning to his regiment late (1792). He was given command of the artillery at the siege of Toulon (1793) and was promoted general of brigade. On the fall of Robespierre Napoleon was arrested on a charge of conspiracy because of his friendship with the younger Robespierre, but the charges were not proven and he was released. In 1795 he helped to defeat supporters of the counter-Revolution in Paris and was then appointed commander of the Army of Italy (1796), in which rôle he was able to demonstrate his great military genius. Two days before his departure for Italy he married Joséphine, widow of General Vicomte de Beauharnais, who had been executed during the Reign of Terror. On arrival at Nice he was appalled by the poverty and indiscipline of the French army. Since his army was outnumbered by the combined Piedmontese-Austrian forces he determined to separate them. He finally routed the Piedmontese at Mondovi, after which Sardinia sued for peace, and the Austrians at Lodi, after which he entered Milan. He next broke through the Austrian centre and occupied the line of the Adige, taking Verona and Legnago from the neutral republic of Venice. Austria made attempts to recover Lombardy, but she was defeated at Arcola and Rivoli. When Napoleon's position in Italy was secured he advanced on Vienna, and reached Leoben in April 1797. Negotiations for a peace settlement with Austria commenced but progressed slowly as Austria hoped to benefit from the political crisis in France, where the moderates and royalists were gaining power on the legislative councils. Napoleon, however, despatched General Augerau to assist the Directory in disposing of their opponents by force. In October 1797 Austria signed the Treaty of Campo Formio, by which France obtained Belgium, the Ionian Islands and Lombardy, while Austria got Istria, Dalmatia and Venetia and engaged to try to get the left bank of the Rhine for France. The Directory, fearing Napoleon's power and ambition, hoped to keep him away from Paris by giving him command of the Army of England. But, realizing the folly of invading England while her fleet was supreme, he set out on an expedition to Egypt in the hope of damaging Britain's trade with India. He set sail in May 1798, captured Malta, and, escaping the British fleet, arrived at Alexandria on June 30. He then twice defeated the Mamelukes and entered Cairo on July 24, but his position was endangered by the destruction of the French fleet on August 1 by Nelson at the battle of the Nile. He defeated the Turks at Mount Tabour but failed to capture St Jean d'Acre, defended by the British squadron under Sir Sidney Smith, and was obliged to return to Egypt. He defeated a Turkish army which had landed at Aboukir, but learning of French reverses in Italy and on the Rhine, he secretly embarked for France on August 22, 1799. Sieyès, one of the Directors, realizing the unpopularity and weakness of the government, was considering a *coup d'état* when Napoleon arrived. They coalesced, despite their distrust of each other, and the Revolution of 18th Brumaire followed (November 9, 1799), when Sieyès, Roger Ducos and Napoleon drew up a new constitution. Under it the executive was vested in three consuls, Napoleon, Cambacérès and Lebrun, of whom Napoleon was nominated first consul for ten years. Before embarking on military campaigns Napoleon had to improve the perilous state of the French treasury. He made plans to found the Bank of France, stabilize the franc and regulate the collection of taxes by employing paid officials. He also tried to improve the system of local government and the judicial system which had become very lax. Offers of peace negotiations were made to England and Austria but he was not surprised when these were rejected. While Masséna occupied the attention of the Austrian general Mélas in Piedmont Napoleon secretly collected an army, reached the plains of Italy, and occupied Milan. In June 1800 the Austrians were routed at Marengo. Napoleon returned to Paris to disprove the rumours about his defeat and death. Moreau's victory at Hohenlinden (1800) led to the signing of the Treaty of Luneville (February 1801) by which the French gains of the Campo Formio treaty were reaffirmed and increased. France's power in Europe was further consolidated by the Concordat with Rome by which Pope Pius VII recognized the French Republic and by the peace of Amiens with war-weary England (1802). By this treaty England was allowed to retain Ceylon and Trinidad but relinquished Egypt, Malta and the Cape of Good Hope; France agreed to evacuate Naples; the independence of Portugal and the Ionian Islands was recognized. Napoleon then continued his domestic reforms: he restored the church, realizing that many people, especially the peasants, felt the need of religion; he made an effort to improve secondary education; and he instituted the *Légion d'honneur*. He was elected first consul for life. Peace between England and France did not last long because Napoleon annexed Piedmont, occupied Parma and interfered in Swiss internal affairs and because Britain refused to give up Malta. Napoleon made vast preparations for the invasion of England, at the same time seizing Hanover. England sent help to the royalist conspirators led by Cadoudal, who were plotting against Napoleon's life, but Napoleon arrested the conspirators and rid himself of Moreau, his most dangerous rival, by accusing him of conspiring with the royalists. He also executed the Duc d'Enghien, a young Bourbon prince, although his connection with the conspirators was not proved. He assumed the hereditary title of emperor, May 18, 1804, because France did not want to be left without a rightful leader in the event of his death. In 1805 he found himself at war with Russia and Austria, as well as with England. Forced by England's naval supremacy to abandon the notion of invasion, he suddenly, in August 1805, led his armies from Boulogne to the Danube, leaving Villeneuve to face the English fleet. He succeeded in surprising the Austrians under Mack at Ulm and they surrendered (October 19), leaving him free to enter Vienna on November 13. On December 2 he inflicted a disastrous defeat on the Russians and Austrians at Austerlitz. The Holy Roman Empire came to an end, the Confederation of the Rhine was formed under French protection, and Napoleon then entered into negotiations for peace with Russia and England. Prussia, afraid that an Anglo-French alliance would mean the loss of Hanover to England, mobilized her army in August 1806; but Napoleon crushed her at Jena and Auerstadt on October 14. Russia, who had intervened, was defeated at Friedland, June 14, 1807. By the peace of Tilsit Prussia lost half her territory and Napoleon was now the arbiter of Europe. Knowing England's reliance on her trade he tried to cripple her by the Continental System, by which he ordered the European states under his control to boycott British goods. He sent an army under Junot to Portugal, who refused to adhere to the Continental System, another under Murat to Spain because he was uncertain of her loyalty. When he placed his brother Joseph on the throne many of the nobles and clergy rebelled against the French, while a British army, under Wellesley, landed in Portugal, defeated Junot at Vimeiro (1808) and forced him to evacuate Portugal under the terms of the Convention of Cintra. So began the Peninsular war which was to occupy a large part of the French army until 1813 when Wellington routed the French and forced them out of Spain. Meanwhile the Prussian reformer Stein was trying to rouse the Prussians to rebel against the French domination but Napoleon forced the government to dismiss him (1808). In 1809 Austria took advantage of the French troubles in Spain to declare war on France. Napoleon drove the Austrians out of Ratisbon, and entered Vienna, May 13, and won the battle of Wagram on July 5 and 6. Although resistance was kept up for a time in Tirol by the patriot Hofer, by the treaty of Schönbrunn (October 20, 1809) France obtained from Austria the Illyrian provinces, and a heavy money indemnity. In December Napoleon, desirous of an heir, divorced Joséphine, who was childless, and married, April 1, 1810, the Archduchess Marie Louise of Austria. A son was born on March 20, 1811. Still bent on the humiliation of England, he soon increased the stringency of the Continental System, and he annexed Holland and Westphalia. Russia opened its ports to neutral shipping and convinced Napoleon that the tsar was contemplating alliance with England. He decided to invade Russia and teach her a lesson. He narrowly defeated the Russians at Borodino (September 6) leaving him free to enter Moscow, which he found deserted and which was destroyed by the fires which broke out the next night. He was then forced to retreat from Moscow, his army hungry, encumbered by the sick and wounded and suffering from the effects of the Russian winter which he had underestimated. Only a mere fraction of the Grand Army that had set out for Russia reached Vilna. Napoleon hurried to Paris to raise new levies, stem the rising panic and belie rumours of his death. Meanwhile the Prussian and Austrian contingents withdrew from the Grand Army. Prussia and Saxony allied with Russia, but Austria and the middle states doubted the ability of the allies to defeat Napoleon and disliked the idea of an alliance with Russia. Napoleon left Paris on April 15, 1813, moved on Leipzig, and won the battle of Lützen on May 2. He then followed the allies, beat them at Bautzen, May 20 and 21, and forced them to retire into Silesia. Austria then asked for concessions of territory; but he merely offered to concede Illyria to them and Austria joined the allies. Napoleon inflicted a crushing defeat on the Austrians near Dresden but part of the French army under Vandamme were forced to surrender at Kulm. In October he was defeated at Leipzig and led back the remnant of his army across the Rhine. The invasion of France followed the rejection of peace terms which deprived France of much of her territorial conquests. Napoleon won four battles in four days at Champaubert, Montmirail, Vauchamps and Montereau but benefited little from the battles of Craonne and Laon which followed. On March 30, 1814, the allies attacked Paris, and Marmont signed the capitulation of Paris. Napoleon fell back to Fontainebleau; but his position was desperate and Wellington had now led his army across the Pyrenees into France. The French marshals forced him to abdicate, first in favour of his son, then unconditionally (April 11). By the treaty of Fontainbleau he was given the sovereignty of Elba, allowed to retain the title of emperor, and awarded a revenue from the French government. The Bourbons in the person of Louis XVIII were restored to the throne of France, but their return was unpopular. The army was disgusted at their treatment by the king and also at the appointment to commands of *émigrés* who had fought against France, and alarm was caused by proposals to return national lands to the *émigrés* and the church. The coalition, too, broke up because of quarrels over territorial settlement, especially over Prussia. Napoleon hoped to take advantage of the situation and landed on the French coast on March 1, 1815. On the 20th he entered Paris, having been joined by the army. Europe had declared war against him but only a mixed force under Wellington in Belgium and a Prussian army under Blücher in the Rhine provinces were in the field. Napoleon's aim being to strike suddenly and then defeat each force separately, he occupied Charleroi and on June 16 defeated Blücher at Ligny. But not till next day did he send Grouchy to follow the retreating Prussians, thus enabling Blücher to move on to Wavre to join Wellington who had retired to Mont St Jean, while Grouchy was engaged with the Prussian rearguard only. After his defeat by Wellington and Blücher at Waterloo, Napoleon fled to Paris, abdicated on June 22, decided to throw himself on the mercy of England, and surrendered to Captain Maitland of the *Bellerophon* at Rochefort on July 15. He was banished by the British government to St Helena, where he died on May 5, 1821, of either liver disease or cancer of the stomach. The bibliography falls into three categories: firstly, books dealing with his career by writers more or less contemporary with him, such as Thiers and Jomini, and his generals, such as Masséna; secondly, books concerning his private life by contemporaries, such as Bourrienne (Eng. trans. 4 vols. 1893), Las Cases, and O'Meara; thirdly, modern works in a more critical spirit, such as Lanfrey's *Histoire de Napoléon I* (5 vols. 1867-75), Jung's *Bonaparte et son Temps* (1880-81), and books on him by Seeley (1885), Wolseley (1895), Sloane (1896-1897), Lavisse and Rambaud (1897), Rose (1902 *et seq.*), Fournier (trans. 1911), F. Masson (1893 *et seq.*), H. A. L. Fisher (1913), N. Young (1914-15), W. H. Hudson (1915), Dirault (1910-27, 1928, 1930), Bainville (1932), Lefebvre (1935), Geyl (1949), Savant (1958), Markham (1963). See, too, his *Correspondance* (33 vols. 1858-87); *Lettres inédites* (1898, 1903); and bibliographies by G. Davois (1909-12), F. M. N. Kircheisen (1908 *et seq.*).

NAPOLEON II (1811–32), king of Rome, Duke of Reichstadt, was Napoleon I's son by Marie Louise. See Lives by Bourgoing (Paris 1933), Derville (1934), Bibl (1935).

NAPOLEON III, Charles Louis Napoléon Bonaparte (1808–73), born at Paris, April 20, the third son of Louis Bonaparte (q.v.), King of Holland, was brought up at Geneva, Augsburg, and his mother's residence, the Swiss castle of Arenenberg on the Lake of Constance. He hastened with his elder brother Louis into Italy in 1831 to assist the Romagna in its revolt against pontifical rule, an expedition in which Louis perished of fever. On the death of the Duke of Reichstadt, only son of Napoleon I, in 1832, he became the head of the Napoleonic dynasty. He published in 1832–36 his *Rêveries politiques*, *Projet de constitution*, and *Considérations politiques et militaires sur la Suisse*. In 1836 he put his chances to a premature test by appearing among the military at Strasburg, was easily overpowered, and conveyed to America. He was recalled to Europe by his mother's last illness (1837); and when the French government demanded of Switzerland his expulsion he settled in London. In 1838 he published his *Idées napoléoniennes*. In 1840 he made at Boulogne a second and equally abortive attempt on the throne of France, and was condemned to perpetual imprisonment in the fortress of Ham. Here he continued his Bonapartist propaganda by writing *Aux mânes de l'empereur*, &c., and actually helped to edit the *Dictionnaire de la conversation*. After an imprisonment of more than five years he made his escape (May 25, 1846), and returned to England. The Revolution of February 1848 was a victory of the working-men, to whom some of his political theories were especially addressed; he hurried back to France as a virtual nominee of the *Fourth Estate*, or working-classes. Elected deputy for Paris and three other departments, he took his seat in the Constituent Assembly, June 13, 1848. On the 15th he resigned and left France. His quintuple election recalled him in September, and he commenced his candidature for the presidency; 5,562,834 votes were recorded for him, only 1,469,166 for General Cavaignac, his genuinely Republican competitor. On December 20 he took the oath of allegiance to the Republic. For a few days concord seemed established between the different political parties in the Assembly; but the beginning of 1849 witnessed the commencement of a struggle between the president and the majority of the Assembly. Then he committed the command of the army to those devoted to him, and established his supporters in posts of influence. He paraded as a protector of popular rights and of national prosperity; but, hampered by the National Assembly in his efforts to make his power perpetual, he threw off the mask of a constitutional president. On December 2, 1851, he, with the help of the military, dissolved the Constitution. Imprisonment, deportation, the bloody repression of popular rebellion, marked this black day's work. France appeared to acquiesce; for when the vote was taken on it in December, he was re-elected for ten years by 7,000,000 votes. The imperial title was assumed a year after the *coup d'état*, in accordance with another plebiscite. Political parties were either demoralized or broken. Napoleon III gagged the press, awed the *bourgeoisie*, and courted the clergy to win the peasantry. On January 29, 1853, he married Eugénie de Montijo (1826–1920), a Spanish countess, born at Granada. The Emperor now proclaimed the right of peoples to choose their own masters, availing himself of it in the annexation (1860) of Savoy and Nice to France, in his Mexican intervention, and in his handling of the Italian question. At home the price of bread was regulated, public works enriched the working-men, while others were undertaken to enhance in value the property of the peasantry. The complete remodelling of Paris under the direction of Baron Haussmann raised the value of house property. International exhibitions and treaties of commerce were a further inducement to internal peace. A brilliant foreign policy seemed to dawn on the Crimean war (1854–56); the campaign in Lombardy against Austria (1859), to which Napoleon was somewhat paradoxically encouraged by the murderous attack of Orsini on his person; and the expeditions to China (1857–60). In all those undertakings Napoleon had the support if not the co-operation of Great Britain. With Prussia his relations were very different. At the death of Morny in 1865 the controlling power of Napoleon's measures was almost spent. His *Vie de César*, written to extol his own methods of government, met with loud protests. Forewarned, Napoleon reorganized his army, set himself up more proudly as an arbiter in Europe, and took a more conciliatory attitude to liberalism. In 1869 his prime minister Rouher, an advocate of absolutism, was dismissed, and new men were called into power to liberalize the constitution. By another plebiscite the new parliamentary scheme was sanctioned by 7½ million votes (May 8, 1870). But 50,000 dissentient votes given by the army revealed an unsuspected source of danger. Anxious to rekindle its ardour, and ignorant of the corruption that existed in his ministry of war, he availed himself of a pretext—the scheme to place Leopold of Hohenzollern on the Spanish throne—to declare war against Prussia, July 15, 1870. By July 30, Prussia had 500,000 men in the field, while the French had with great exertion collected 270,000 by the beginning of August. The emperor assumed the command, but never got across the Rhine, and had to fight at a disadvantage within Alsace and Lorraine. The campaign opened with a small success at Saarbrücken (August 2), followed by the defeats of Weissenburg (August 4), Wörth and Spicheren (August 6). Napoleon had retired to Metz, and abandoned the chief command to Marshal Bazaine, whose escape from Metz was prevented by the defeats of Mars-la-Tour (August 16) and Gravelotte (August 18). Metz surrendered on October 27. Meanwhile a hastily organized force of 120,000 men under Marshal Macmahon was moved to the assistance of Bazaine. On reaching Sedan Macmahon found himself surrounded by the Germans, and on September 1 suffered a crushing defeat. Next day the emperor surrendered with 83,000 men. On September 4 the Second Empire was ended. Till the conclusion of peace he was confined at Wilhelmshöhe. In March 1871 he joined the ex-empress at Chislehurst, Kent, and resided there in exile till his death. His son, **Eugène Louis Jean Joseph** (1856–79), Prince Imperial, born March 16, was in the field with his father in 1870, but escaped to England, where he entered Woolwich Academy. He was killed (June 1) in the Zulu campaign of 1879. See Lives and studies of Napoleon III by B. Jerrold (4 vols. 1874–82), F. A. Simpson (1925), Baron d'Ambès (trans. 1912), Aubry (1933), Sencourt (1933), and Zeldin (1958); De la Gorce, *Histoire du Second Empire* (1894–1905); Ollivier, *L'Empire libéral* (1894–1913); Lives of the Prince Imperial by Hérisson (1890), Martinet (1895), Filon (1912), F. A. Simpson (1958); books on the Empress, her son, and the Court by E. Legge (1910–16), and studies by T. Zeldin (1958) and G. P. Gooch (1960).

NAPOLEON, **Prince.** See BONAPARTE.

NARES, **Sir George Strong,** *nayrz* (1831–1915), Scottish vice-admiral and explorer, born at Aberdeen, commanded the *Challenger* (1872–74) and the *Alert-Discovery* expedition (1875–76). See his *Voyage to the Polar Sea* (2 vols. 1878).

NARSES (*c.* A.D. 478–573), Byzantine statesman and Persian general, born in Armenia, rose in the imperial household at Constantinople to be keeper of the privy purse to Justinian. In 538 he was sent to Italy, but recalled the next year. In 552 Belisarius was recalled from Italy and Narses succeeded him, defeated the Ostrogoths, took possession of Rome, and completely extinguished the Gothic power in Italy. Justinian appointed him prefect of Italy in 554, and he administered its affairs with vigour and ability. But he was charged with avarice; and on Justinian's death the Romans complained to Justin, who deprived him in 567 of his office. See Diehl, *Justinian* (1901).

NARVÁEZ, **Ramón María,** *nahr-vah'ayth* (1800–68), Spanish general and statesman, born at Loja, defeated the Carlists in 1836, and took part in the insurrection against Espartero in 1840, but that failing, fled to France, where he was joined by Queen Christina, and set about those plots which overthrew Espartero in 1843. In 1844 he was made president of council and Duke of Valencia. His ministry was reactionary, but was overthrown in 1846. After a brief exile as special ambassador to France he was premier again several times.

NASH, (1) **John** (1752–1835), English architect, born in London or Cardigan, trained as an architect, but after coming into a legacy retired to Wales. Having lost heavily by speculations in 1792, he resumed practice and gained a reputation by his country house designs. He came to the notice of the Prince of Wales, later the Prince Regent, and was engaged (1811–25) to plan the layout of the new Regent's Park and its approaches. He re-created Buckingham Palace from old Buckingham House, designed the Marble Arch which originally stood in front of it, and rebuilt Brighton Pavilion in oriental style. On the strength of a patent (1797) for improvements to the arches and piers of bridges he claimed much of the credit for introducing steel girders. The skilful use of terrain and landscape features in his layouts marks him as one of the greatest town planners. See Life by Summerson (2nd ed. 1950) and study by Davis (1960).

(2) **Paul** (1899–1946), English painter, born in London, was educated at St Paul's and the Slade School. He became an official war artist in 1917, and as such is remembered for his poignant *Menin Road* (1919). Developing a style which reduced form to bare essentials without losing the identity of the subject, he won renown as a landscape painter and also practised scene painting, commercial design, and book illustration. For a while he taught at the Royal College of Art. Experiments in a near abstract manner were followed by a phase of surrealism until, in 1939, he again filled the rôle of war artist, this time for the Air Ministry and the Ministry of Information, producing such pictures as *Battle of Britain* and *Totes Meer*. Shortly before his death he turned to a very individual style of flower painting. See his autobiography, *Outline* (1949), *Memorial Volume* (ed. Eates, 1948), and books by A. Bertram (1955) and G. F. W. Digby (1955).

(3) **Richard** (1674–1762), 'Beau Nash', English dandy, born at Swansea, educated at Carmarthen and Oxford, held a commission in the army, and in 1693 entered the Middle Temple. He then made a shifty living by gambling, but in 1704 became master of the ceremonies at Bath, where he conducted the public balls with a splendour never before witnessed. His reforms in manners, his influence in improving the streets and buildings and his leadership in fashion helped to transform Bath into a fashionable holiday centre. See Life by Goldsmith (1762), Gosse's *Gossip in a Library* (1891), study by L. Melville (1907) and Life by W. Connely (1955).

NASHE, Thomas (1567–1601), English dramatist and satirist, born at Lowestoft, studied for seven years at St John's College, Cambridge, travelled in France and Italy, and then went to London to earn a precarious living by his pen. His first work was the *Anatomie of Absurditie* (1589), perhaps written at Cambridge. He plunged into the Martin Marprelate controversy, giving expression to a talent for vituperation which never left him. *Pierce Penilesse, his Supplication to the Divell* (1592) began the series of attacks on the Harveys (Richard Harvey had criticized Nashe's preface to Greene's *Menaphon*) which culminated in *Have with you to Saffron Walden* (1596), against Gabriel Harvey who had by then assailed Greene's memory in *Foure Letters*. In 1599 the controversy was suppressed by the Archbishop of Canterbury. Nashe's satirical masque *Summer's Last Will and Testament* (1592) contains the well-known song 'Spring the sweet Spring is the year's pleasant king'. *The Unfortunate Traveller* (1594) is a picaresque tale, one of the earliest of its kind. After Marlowe's death, Nashe prepared his unfinished tragedy *Dido* (1596) for the stage. His own play *The Isle of Dogs* (1597), now lost, drew such attention to abuses in the state that it was suppressed, the theatre closed, and the writer himself thrown into the Fleet prison. His last work was *Lenten Stuffe* (1599). See McKerrow's edition of works (1904–07, revised by F. P. Wilson, 1958) and study by E. G. Harman (1923).

NASMITH, David (1799–1839), Scottish philanthropist, born in Glasgow, founded the city missions in various cities in Europe and America, and other benevolent associations. See memoir by J. Campbell.

NASMYTH, *nay'smith*, (1) **Alexander** (1758–1840), Scottish painter, father of (2) and (3), born in Edinburgh, was a pupil of Allan Ramsay and became a well-known portrait painter in Edinburgh, his portrait of Burns in the Scottish National Gallery being particularly famous. He later confined himself to landscape painting.

(2) **James** (1808–90), Scottish engineer, son of (1), born in Edinburgh, from boyhood he evinced a bent for mechanics; and in 1834 he started in business at Manchester, and in 1836 established at Patricroft the Bridgewater Foundry. His steam hammer was devised in 1839 for forging an enormous wrought-iron paddle-shaft, and in 1842 he found it at work at Le Creusot in France; it had been adapted from his own scheme-book. Nasmyth patented his invention, and it was adopted by the Admiralty in 1843. Among other of his inventions was a steam pile-driver. He published *Remarks on Tools and Machinery* (1858) and *The Moon* (1874). He died in London, May 7, 1890. See Autobiography, edited by Smiles (1883).

(3) **Patrick** (1787–1831), Scottish landscape painter, son of (1), born in Edinburgh, settled in England, painted many English scenes and became known as the 'English Hobbema'.

NASO. See Ovid.

NASR-ED-DIN (1829–96), shah of Persia from 1848, visited England in 1873 and 1889, introduced European ideas into Persia, granted trade concessions to Britain and Russia, and was shot near Teheran by an assassin. He was succeeded by his second son, Muzzaffar-ed-Din. See selections from his *Diary*, ed. Hadiqa-i-Fasahar (1905).

NASSER, Gamal Abdel (1918–70), Egyptian political leader, president of the United Arab Republic, born in Alexandria, as an army officer with bitter experience of the mismanaged Palestine campaign of 1948, he became dissatisfied with the inefficiency and corruption of the Farouk régime, and founded the military Junta which encompassed its downfall. Chief power behind the *coup* of 1952, he was mainly responsible for the rise to power of General Neguib (q.v.), but tension between the two, as a result of Neguib's suspected dictatorial ambitions, culminated in Nasser's assumption of the premiership in April 1954 and of presidential powers in November 1954, when Neguib was deposed. Nasser was officially elected president in June 1956, and his almost immediate action in expropriating the Suez Canal led to a state of tension in the Middle East which culminated in Israel's invasion of the Sinai Peninsula. When Anglo-French forces intervened, widespread differences of opinion in Britain and elsewhere, coupled with veiled Russian threats, enabled Nasser to turn an abject military débacle into a political victory. His aim was clearly now to build an Arab empire stretching across North Africa, the first step being the creation, by federation with Syria, of the United Arab Republic in February 1958. In March 1958 the Yemen and the U.A.R. formed the United Arab States. This was followed by a sustained effort to break up the Baghdad Pact and liquidate the remaining sovereign states in the Middle East, a policy which succeeded in Iraq, but was thwarted in Jordan and the Lebanon by the deployment of American and British forces. His plans for unity among the Arab states received a setback when Syria withdrew from the U.A.R. and when the union with the Yemen was dissolved (1961). In 1964, however, the U.A.R. formed joint Presidency Councils with Iraq and the Yemen. After the six-day Arab-Israeli war in June 1967, heavy losses on the Arab side led to Nasser's resignation but he was persuaded to withdraw it almost immediately.

NATION, Mrs Carry (1846–1911), American temperance agitator, after 1890 pursued a career of saloon wrecking (her weapon and emblem a hatchet) in Kansas and elsewhere, and suffered repeated imprisonments. See Asbury's *Life* (1930), Autobiography (1904).

NATTA, Guilio (1903–), Italian chemist, was a professor at Pavia, Rome and Turin, and from 1939 held the chair of Industrial Chemistry at Milan Institute of Technology. With Karl Ziegler, he was awarded the Nobel prize for chemistry in 1963 for his researches on polymers which led to important developments in plastics and other industrial chemicals.

NATTIER, Jean Marc, *nat-yay* (1685–1766), French artist, was born and died in Paris. His father was a portrait painter, his mother the miniaturist Marie Courtois, and as the result of parental tuition he won the Academy prize at the age of fifteen. He executed historical pictures and portraits, including those of Peter the Great and the Empress Catherine, but after losing his money in the John Law (q.v.) financial crisis he took up the fashionable stereotyped style of court portraiture now labelled 'le portrait Nattier'.

NAUNDORF, Karl W. See LOUIS XVII.

NAUNTON, Sir Robert (1563–1635), English statesman and writer, born at Alderton, Suffolk, became public orator at Cambridge in 1594, travelled, entered parliament, and was secretary of state 1618–23. He wrote *Fragmenta Regalia* (1641), a sketch of Elizabeth's courtiers. See Memoirs (1814).

NAVARRO, Mme de. See ANDERSON (8).

NAVILLE, Henri Edouard, *na-veel* (1844–1926), Swiss Egyptologist, born at Geneva, became professor of Egyptology there, excavated in Egypt for many years, edited the Book of the Dead, and wrote a number of books on Egypt.

NAYLER, James (*c.* 1617–60), English Quaker minister, born at Ardsley near Wakefield, served in the parliamentary army. Later he became a Quaker, gathered a band of disciples and was persecuted and imprisoned for blasphemy. See Lives by M. R. Brailsford (1927) and E. Fogelklou (Eng. trans. 1931).

NAZIANZEN. See GREGORY.

NAZIMOVA, Alla, *na-zim'ō-va* (1879–1945), Russian actress, born in the Crimea, she made her début in St Petersburg in 1904, and in 1905 appeared in New York as Hedda Gabler. In 1910 she took the 39th Street Theatre, rechristening it 'The Nazimova', and became one of the most popular emotional actresses of her day. She had a successful period in films, her films including *The Brat*, *Camille*, *A Doll's House*, *The Red Lantern* and her own *Salome*, based on the Beardsley illustrations to Wilde's play. She specialized in the plays of Ibsen, Turgenev, Chehov and O'Neill.

NAZOR, Vladimir, *nas'or* (1876–1949), Croatian poet, born at Postire on the island of Brač, wrote lyrics and ballads as well as epic poems and dramatic works in a style approaching that of the Symbolists. His works include *Slav Legends* (1900), *Lirika* (1910), *Carmen Vitae*, an anthology (1922), and a diary of his experiences with the Yugoslav partisans in World War II.

NEAL, (1) **Daniel** (1678–1743), English clergyman and historian, born in London, in 1706 became an Independent minister there. He wrote a *History of New England* (1720) and the laborious and accurate *History of the Puritans* (1732–38; new ed., with Life by J. Toulmin, 1793).

(2) **John** (1793–1876), American writer, born of Quaker parentage at Falmouth (now Portland, Maine), in 1816 failed in business, and turned to law, supporting himself the while by his pen. He was one of the first Americans to write in the greater English magazines, and lived in England 1823–27. After his return he practised law, edited newspapers and lectured. See his autobiographical *Wandering Recollections of a Somewhat Busy Life* (1869), and Life by W. P. Daggett (1920).

NEALE, (1) **Edward Vansittart** (1810–92), English social reformer, born at Bath, graduated at Oxford, became a barrister, and from 1851 he was a pioneer Christian Socialist and an advocate of co-operation, devoting much time and money to the movement. See *Memorial* by H. Pitman (Manchester 1894).

(2) **John Mason,** D.D. (1818–66), English hymnologist, born in London, January 24, was a scholar of Trinity College, Cambridge, and from 1846 warden of Sackville College, East Grinstead, where he died, August 6. An advanced High Churchman, he was inhibited by his bishop 1849–63. He wrote many books on Church history, &c., but is remembered chiefly for his hymns, and many of his translations are cherished by all English-speaking Christendom. Among his best-known pieces are 'Jerusalem the Golden' and 'O happy band of pilgrims'. See his *Collected Hymns* (1914); Life by E. A. Towle (1906).

NEANDER, Johann August Wilhelm, orig. **David Mendel,** *ne-an'der* (1789–1850), German church historian, born at Göttingen of Jewish parentage, in 1806 he renounced Judaism and changed his name. In 1813 he became professor of Church History at Berlin. Profoundly devotional, sympathetic, glad-hearted, profusely benevolent, he inspired universal reverence, and attracted students from all countries. He probably contributed more than any other to overthrow antihistorical Rationalism and dead Lutheran formalism. He wrote many books on church history, of which the best known is his *General History of the Christian Religion and Church* (Eng. trans. 9 vols. 1847–55). See studies by Schaff (1886), Wiegand (with bibliography, 1889), Schneider (1894).

NEARCHUS, *nee-ar'kus* (4th cent. B.C.), Macedonian general, was a native of Crete, who settled in Amphipolis during the reign of Philip, and became the companion of the young Alexander the Great. In 330 B.C. he was governor of Lycia; in 329 he joined Alexander in Bactria with a body of Greek mercenaries, and took part in the Indian campaigns. Having built a fleet on the Hydaspes (mod. Jhelum), Alexander gave Nearchus the command. He left the Indus in November 325, and, skirting the coast, reached Susa in February 324. His narrative is preserved in the *Indica* of Arrian.

NEBUCHADREZZAR II (d. 562 B.C.), king of Babylon, succeeded his father Nabopolassar in 605 B.C. During his reign of forty-three years he recovered the long-lost provinces of the kingdom, and once more made Babylon queen of nations. He not only restored the empire and rebuilt Babylon, but almost every temple throughout the land underwent restoration at his hands. Not a mound has been opened by explorers which has not contained bricks, cylinders or tablets inscribed with his name. In 597 he captured Jerusalem; and in 586 he destroyed the city, and removed most of the inhabitants to Chaldea.

NECKAM or Nequam, Alexander (1157–1217),

English scholar, born at St Albans on the same night as Richard I, was nursed by his mother along with the future king. Educated at St Albans and Paris (where he lectured), he returned to England to be schoolmaster at Dunstable. In 1213 he became Abbot of Cirencester. In his *De naturis rerum* and *De utensilibus* he was the first in Europe to describe the use of a magnetic needle by sailors.

NECKER, Jacques (1732–1804), French statesman and financier, born at Geneva, at fifteen went to Paris as a banker's clerk, and in 1762 established the London and Paris bank of Thellusson and Necker. In 1776 he was made director of the Treasury, and next year director-general of Finance. Some of his remedial measures were a boon to suffering France, but his most ambitious scheme—the establishment of provincial assemblies, one of whose functions should be the apportionment of taxes—proved a disastrous failure. His retrenchments were hateful to the queen, and his famous *Compte rendu* (1781) occasioned his dismissal. He retired to Geneva, but in 1787 returned to Paris; and when M. de Calonne cast doubt on the *Compte rendu*, he published a justification which drew upon him his banishment from Paris. Recalled to office in September 1788, he quickly made himself the popular hero by recommending the summoning of the States-General. But the successful banker quickly proved himself unfit to steer the ship of state amid the storms of revolution. On July 11 he received the royal command to leave France at once, but the fall of the Bastille three days later frightened the king into recalling him amid the wildest popular enthusiasm. But after spurning the help of Lafayette and Mirabeau, and leading the king to surrender his suspensive veto, he finally resigned, September 1790. He retired to his estate near Geneva where he died. His works were edited by his grandson (with Life prefixed, 1820–21). See also *Manuscrits de M. Necker*, published by his famous daughter, Mme de Staël (q.v.), in 1804; her *Vie privée de M. Necker* (1804); the *Mélanges* from his wife's papers (1798–1802), D'Haussonville's *Salon de Mme Necker* (trans. 1882), and Gambier-Parry's *Mme Necker* (1913); and Lives by E. Lavaquery (Paris 1933) and E. Chapuisat (1938).

NEFERTITI, *-tee'tee* (14th cent. B.C.), Egyptian queen, the consort of Akhnaton (q.v.), immortalized in the beautiful sculptured head found at Amarna in 1912, now in the Berlin museum.

NEGRETTI, Henry (1817–79), Italian-English optician, born at Como, came to London in 1829, and was partner with Joseph Warren Zambra from 1850.

NEGRI, Ada, *nay'gree* (1870–1945), Italian poet, born at Milan, became a teacher, wrote socialistic verse and short stories. See study by N. Podenanzi (Milan 1930).

NEGUIB, Mohammed, *ne-geeb'* (1901–), Egyptian leader, was general of an army division when in July 1952 he carried out a *coup d'état* in Cairo which banished King Farouk and initiated the 'Egyptian Revolution'. Taking first the offices of commander-in-chief and prime minister, he abolished the monarchy in 1953 and became president of the republic, but was deposed in 1954 and succeeded by Colonel Abdel Nasser (q.v.).

NEGUS, Francis (d. 1732), English soldier, a colonel who had served under Marlborough, he is reputed to have invented the drink 'negus' called after him.

NEHEMIAH (5th cent. B.C.), Jewish prophet, cupbearer to Artaxerxes Longimanus, who in 444 B.C. obtained full powers to act as governor-extraordinary of Judaea. He had the walls of Jerusalem rebuilt, and repopulated the city by drafts from the surrounding districts. We read of a second visit of Nehemiah to Jerusalem, twelve years afterwards, on which occasion he either initiated or renewed and completed certain reforms which henceforth were among the most characteristic features of post-exilic Judaism. The canonical Book of Nehemiah originally formed the closing chapters of the undivided work, Chronicles-Ezra-Nehemiah. Compare Sayce, *Introduction to Ezra, Nehemiah, and Esther* (3rd ed. 1889); the commentary of Bertheau-Ryssel (1887), and those of Keil (Eng. trans. 1873), and Rawlinson (*Speaker's Commentary*). See study by L. W. Batten (Edinburgh 1913).

NEHRU, *nay'roo*, family of distinguished Indian political leaders:

(1) **Jawaharlal** (1889–1964), Indian statesman, son of (2), was born at Allahabad. After an undistinguished career at Harrow School and Trinity College, Cambridge, where he took the natural sciences tripos, he read for the bar (Inner Temple 1912), returned home and served in the high court of Allahabad. A persistent vision of himself as an Indian Garibaldi made him become a member of the Indian Congress Committee in 1918 and brought him, if with scientific reservations, under the spell of Mahatma Gandhi. He was imprisoned in 1921 and spent 18 of the next 25 years in gaol. In 1928 he was elected president of the Indian National Congress, an office he often held afterwards. Although sympathetic to the Allied Cause in World War II, he, in common with other Congress Party leaders, did not cooperate and turned down the Cripps offer of dominion status for India made in 1942. But in 1947 when India achieved independence, Nehru became her first prime minister and minister of external affairs. As democratic leader of the first republic within the Commonwealth, he followed a policy of neutralism and peace-making during the Cold War, often acting as a go-between between the Great Powers. He committed India to a policy of industrialization, to a reorganization of its states on a linguistic basis and, although championing his people's claim to Kashmir, acted with restraint to bring this outstanding dispute with Pakistan to a peaceful solution. His many works include *Soviet Russia* (1929), *India and the World* (1936), *Independence and After* (1950) and an *Autobiography* (1936). See also a Life by F. Moraes (1956) and studies by D. E. Smith (1959) and V. Sheean (1960).

(2) **Motilal** (1861–1931), Indian nationalist

leader, lawyer and journalist, father of (1), became a follower of Gandhi in 1919, founded the *Independent* of Allahabad and became the first president of the reconstructed Indian National Congress. See J. Nehru's *Autobiography* (1936).

NEILSON, (1) **James Beaumont** (1792–1865), Scottish inventor, born at Shettleston, invented the hot-blast in iron manufacture and was foreman and manager of Glasgow gasworks 1817–47. See Life by T. B. Mackenzie (1928).

(2) **Julia** (1868–1957), English actress, was born in London. After a brilliant career at the Royal Academy of Music, she made her début at the Lyceum in 1888; her greatest success was as Rosalind in the record-breaking run of *As You Like It* (1896–98). She married Ellen Terry's brother **Fred** (1863–1933), who often appeared with her and who partnered her in management from 1900. Their children **Dennis** (1895–1932) and **Phyllis** (1892–) **Neilson-Terry** also became famous for their acting, the latter especially in the title rôle of *Trilby*, and for their productions.

NEKRASOV, Nikolai Alexeievich (1821–78), Russian lyrical poet of the Realistic school, was born near Vinitza, Podolia, and suffered great poverty before making his name as a singer of the social wrongs of the humble. His epic, *Who can be Happy and Free in Russia?*, was translated in 1917. See studies by N. L. Stepanov (1947), C. Corbet (1948).

NELSON, (1) **Horatio, Viscount Nelson** (1758–1805), born September 29 at Burnham Thorpe rectory, Norfolk, entered the navy in 1770. He made a voyage to the West Indies, served in the Arctic expedition of 1773, and afterwards in the East Indies, whence he returned invalided in September 1776. As lieutenant of the *Lowestoft* frigate (1777) he went to Jamaica, and in 1779 was posted to the *Hinchingbrook* frigate. In January 1780 he commanded the naval force in the expedition against San Juan; on the pestilential river his health again broke down. In 1781 he commissioned the *Albemarle*, and joined the squadron under Lord Hood in America. In 1784 he was appointed to the *Boreas* frigate for service in the West Indies, where he enforced the Navigation Act against the Americans. Here he married the widow of Dr Nisbet of Nevis; and in December 1787 he retired with his wife to Burnham Thorpe for five years. Appointed to the *Agamemnon* in 1793, he accompanied Lord Hood to the Mediterranean. When Toulon was given up to the allies Nelson was ordered to Naples. He was employed in the blockade of Corsica, and next year commanded the naval brigade at the reduction of Bastia and of Calvi; here a blow from a bit of gravel, scattered by a shot, destroyed his right eye. In 1795 he was in Hotham's two victories outside Toulon. During 1796 with a small squadron in the Gulf of Genoa he commanded the road along the shore. When Spain concluded a treaty with France, and sent her fleet into the Mediterranean, Jervis found himself opposed by very superior forces, and retired ultimately to Lisbon. He was determined that the Spanish fleet should not pass, and inflicted a signal defeat on it off Cape St Vincent, February 14, 1797. Nelson, now commodore, was in the rear of the line. In thwarting an attempt to reunite the two divisions of the Spanish fleet, he for nearly half an hour withstood the whole Spanish van. When the Spaniards fled, Nelson let his ship fall foul of the Spanish *San Nicolas*, which he boarded, and, leading his men across her deck to the *San Josef*, took possession of her also. Nelson was rewarded with the Cross of the Bath; and, promoted rear-admiral in July, was sent with an inadequate squadron to seize a richly-laden Spanish ship at Santa Cruz. The attack was made on the night of July 21; but the boats were repulsed with severe loss, and Nelson had his right elbow shattered by a grapeshot, and amputated. In March 1798 he hoisted his flag on the *Vanguard*, and was sent into the Mediterranean with a small squadron to watch the French. But the *Vanguard*, dismasted in a gale, was obliged to put into San Pietro to refit, while the French expedition sailed to Egypt. On June 7 Nelson was reinforced by ten sail of the line; but his frigates had all parted company, and after a fruitless search he put into Syracuse, when he learned at last that they had gone to Egypt. Thither he followed, and on August 1 found them at anchor in Aboukir Bay. His fleet was numerically inferior, but the wind was blowing along the French line, so he concentrated his attack on the weather end. He thus captured or destroyed the whole fleet, with the exception of the two rearmost ships and two of the frigates, which fled. Nelson returned in triumph to Naples, the queen welcomed him with ardour, and Lady Hamilton (q.v.), the wife of the English ambassador, fell on his breast in a paroxysm of rapture. A woman of extreme beauty, winning manners and shady antecedents, she enslaved Nelson by her charms, and the two became bound by a liaison which only death severed. Nelson was raised to the peerage as Baron Nelson of the Nile, parliament voted him a pension of £2000 a year, the East India Company awarded him £10,000 and the king of Naples conferred on him the title of Duke of Bronte, in Sicily. After subduing the Jacobin uprising in Naples, in July 1799 Nelson received an order from Lord Keith, commander-in-chief in the Mediterranean, to bring the greater part of his force to defend Minorca. Nelson refused to obey the order; and when it was repeated, sent Sir John Duckworth, his second in command, while he himself remained at Naples or Palermo, and controlled the blockade of Malta. The Admiralty censured him for his disobedience, and, resigning his command, he made his way home overland with Lady Hamilton and her husband, arriving in November 1800. His meeting with his wife was not a happy one, and after an angry interview they parted for good. In January 1801 Nelson was promoted to be vice-admiral, and was appointed second in command of the expedition to the Baltic, under Sir Hyde Parker. The whole conduct of the attack on Copenhagen and the Danish fleet was entrusted to Nelson. After three to four hours of furious combat, the enemy's ships were subdued. A suspension of hostilities led to an armistice, which the news of the tsar's death converted into a peace. Nelson, created a viscount, succeeded Parker as commander-in-chief; but, his health having given way, he returned to England. He was ordered to undertake the defence of the coast, in prospect of a French invasion; and though he failed in an attempt to destroy the flotilla at Boulogne, his watch was so vigilant that the boats never ventured from under the protection of their batteries. On the renewal of the war Nelson cruised for eighteen months off Toulon. During a temporary absence, in March 1805, the French fleet put to sea under Villeneuve, and got away to Martinique, where they expected to be joined by the fleet from Brest. Nelson, though delayed for six weeks by his ignorance of Villeneuve's movements, was only twenty days behind him; and Villeneuve hastily returned to Europe. Nelson again followed, and arrived off Cadiz some days before the French approached the shores of Europe. Conceiving that Villeneuve's aim might be to overpower the fleet off Brest, he reinforced it with most of his ships, returning himself to England. Within a fortnight it was known that Villeneuve had gone to Cadiz, and Nelson resumed the command in September. Villeneuve was meantime urged by positive orders to put to sea, and on October 20 he reluctantly came out. Of French and Spanish ships there were thirty-three; Nelson had twenty-seven. At daybreak on the 21st the two fleets were in presence of each other off Cape Trafalgar. At noon the lee division of the British fleet, under Collingwood in the *Royal Sovereign*, broke through the rear of the Franco-Spanish line. Nelson, with the other division, threw himself on the centre of the van. As the *Victory* passed astern of Villeneuve's flagship she fell foul of the *Redoutable* of seventy-four guns, and her quarter-deck became exposed to the musketry fire from the *Redoutable*'s tops. Nelson, while speaking to Captain Hardy, fell mortally wounded by a shot on the left shoulder. He was carried below, and died some three hours later, just as the battle ended in victory. The enemy's fleet was annihilated. Nelson's body was brought home and buried in St Paul's. See Lives by Clarke and McArthur (2 vols. 1809; 2nd ed. 1840), Southey (1813), Laughton (1895), Mahan (2 vols. 1897), Wilkinson (1931), Oman (1947), Warner (1958); Nelson's *Dispatches and Letters*, edited by N. H. Nicolas (1844–46); his *Last Diary* (1917); his *Letters to his Wife*, ed. Naish (1958); J. C. Jeaffreson's *Lady Hamilton and Nelson* (1888) and *The Queen of Naples and Nelson* (1889); and E. H. Moorhouse's *Nelson in England* (1913).

(2) **Robert** (1656–1714), born in London, son of a rich Turkish merchant, went with his widowed mother to Dryfield in Gloucestershire, where he was brought up by Dr George Bull. In 1680, elected an F.R.S., he travelled with Halley in France and Italy, returning with Lady Theophila Lucy (1654–7105), a widow and daughter to the Earl of Berkeley, who in 1683 became his wife, and soon after was converted to Catholicism by Cardinal Howard and Bossuet. Her ill-health had taken them again to Italy at the Revolution; but Nelson was from the first a (passive) Jacobite, and on his return in 1691 he joined the Nonjurors. He was received back into the Established Church in 1710, though he still would not pray for Queen Anne. He died at Kensington. One of the earliest members of the S.P.C.K. and S.P.G., Nelson was the author of five devotional works, of which *Festivals and Fasts* (1703) sold 10,000 copies in four and a half years. See Lives by Teale (1840–46) and Secretan (1860).

(3) **Thomas** (1780–1861), an Edinburgh publisher, who left two sons, **William** (1816–1887) and **Thomas** (1822–92), the former the restorer of the old Parliament Hall.

NEMOURS, Duc de, *ne-moor* (1814–96), the second son of Louis Philippe, after the fall of the monarchy played an inconspicuous part. See Life by R. Bazin (1907).

NENNI, Pietro, *nen'nee* (1891–), Italian Socialist politician, born at Faenza, Romagna. An agitator at seventeen, as editor of *Avanti* he was exiled by the Fascists in 1926. In the Spanish War he was political commissar of the Garibaldi Brigade. He became secretary-general of the Italian Socialist party in 1944, vice-premier in the De Gasperi coalition cabinet (1945–46), and foreign minister (1946–47). His pro-Soviet party did not break finally with the Communists till 1956. In 1963 Nenni became deputy prime minister in the new central-left four-party coalition government, including Social Democrats and Socialists. In 1966 he succeeded in his longstanding aim of uniting the two groups as the United Socialist party. In the 1968 elections, the coalition had overall gains, but the Socialists lost ground, mainly to the Communist party, and against Nenni's advice, withdrew from the coalition in June 1968. He was foreign minister in a new coalition government from December 1968 but resigned July 1969.

NENNIUS (fl. 796), Welsh writer, the reputed author of a *Historia Britonum*. His book gives the mythical account of the origin of the Britons, the Roman occupation, the settlement of the Saxons, and closes with King Arthur's twelve victories. See works by W. F. Skene (1868), H. Zimmer (Berlin 1893) and F. Lot (Paris 1934).

NEOT, St, *neet* (d. 877), Saxon hermit, according to legend a monk of Glastonbury, lived in Cornwall. His relics were brought to Crowland about 1003. See work by W. A. Axworthy (1894).

NEPOMUK, St John of. See JOHN OF NEPOMUK, ST.

NEPOS, Cornelius (*c.* 99–25 B.C.), Roman historian, a native of Pavia or Hostilia, he was the contemporary of Cicero, Atticus and Catullus. Of his *De Viris Illustribus* only twenty-five biographies of warriors and statesmen, mostly Greeks, survive—untrustworthy, but written in a clear and elegant style. See Freudenberg, *Quaestiones historicae in C. Nepotis vitas* (1839), and Eng. trans. by Rolfe (*Loeb Library* 1929).

NERI, St Philip (1515–95), Italian founder of the Oratory, was born at Florence. He went to Rome at the age of eighteen, and for many years spent most of his time in works of charity and instruction, and in solitary prayer. In 1551 he became a priest, and gathered around him a following of disciples which in 1564 became the Congregation of the Oratory and later received the approbation of the pope. The community was finally established at Vallicella, where Philip built a new church (Chiesa Nuova) on the site of Sta Maria. He was canonized with Ignatius Loyola and others in 1622. Philip's literary remains consist of a few letters (1751) and some sonnets. The best Life was by Bacci (1622; trans. ed. by F. W. Faber, 1849; new ed. 1902). See also Life by Archbishop Capecelatro (trans. 2nd ed. 1894), and works by L. Ponnelle and L. Bordet (Eng. trans. 1932), V. J. Matthews (1934) and T. Maynard (Milwaukee 1946).

NERNST, Walther Hermann (1864–1941), German physical chemist, was born in Briesen in W. Prussia and died in Berlin. Nernst became professor of Chemistry in Göttingen (1891) and in Berlin (1905). In 1925 he became director of the Berlin Physical Institute. In 1906 he proposed the heat theorem (third law of thermodynamics). He also investigated the specific heat of solids at low temperature in connection with quantum theory, and proposed the atom chain-reaction theory in photochemistry. He won the Nobel prize for chemistry in 1920.

NERO (A.D. 37–68), Roman emperor from A.D. 54 to 68, was born at Antium, son of Cneius Domitius Ahenobarbus and of the younger Agrippina, daughter of Germanicus. His mother became the wife of the Emperor Claudius, who adopted him (50). After the death of Claudius (54) the Praetorian Guards declared him emperor. His reign began with much promise, but owing to the baleful influence of his mother and his own moral weakness and sensuality, he soon plunged headlong into debauchery, extravagance and tyranny. He caused Britannicus, the son of Claudius, to be poisoned, and afterwards murdered his mother and his wife Octavia. In July 64 occurred a great conflagration in Rome, by which two-thirds of the city was burned. Nero is stated to have been the incendiary; and we are told that he admired the spectacle from a distance, reciting verses about the burning of Troy. But he found a scapegoat in the Christians, many of whom were put to death with unheard-of cruelties. He rebuilt the city with great magnificence, and reared on the Palatine Hill a splendid palace; but in order to provide for his expenditure Italy and the provinces were plundered. A conspiracy against Nero in 65 failed, and Seneca and the poet Lucan fell victims to his vengeance. In a fit of passion he murdered his wife Poppaea, by kicking her when she was pregnant. He then offered his hand to Antonia, daughter of Claudius, but was refused; whereupon he caused her to be put to death, and married Statilia Messallina, after murdering her husband. He also executed or banished many persons distinguished for integrity and virtue. His vanity led him to seek distinction as poet, philosopher, actor, musician and charioteer. In 68 the Gallic and Spanish legions, and after them the Praetorian Guards rose against him to make Galba emperor. Nero fled to the house of a freedman, four miles from Rome, and saved himself from execution by suicide, June 11, 68. See W. Wolfe Capes, *Early Roman Empire*, Merivale's *Romans under the Empire*, the Life by B. W. Henderson (1903), and works by M. P. Charlesworth (1939), C. M. Franzero (1954), G. Walter (1957).

NERUDA, (1) Jan (1834–91), Czech writer, born in Prague, began as a disciple of Romanticism but developed into the foremost classical poet in modern Czech literature. He is also known for some excellent prose and drama.

(2) **Madame.** See HALLÉ.

NERVA, M. Cocceius (*c.* 32–98), Roman emperor, was elected in A.D. 96. He introduced liberal reforms and died in 98. See B. W. Henderson, *Five Roman Emperors* (1927).

NERVAL, Gérard de, properly **Gérard Labrunie** (1808–55), French writer, was born at Paris. He published at twenty a translation of *Faust*. Desultory work, a love affair, fits of restless travel, of dissipation, of gloom and of insanity, and death by his own hand, sum up the story of his life. Nerval wrote admirably alike in prose and verse. But his travels, criticism, plays and poems are less interesting than his fantastic short tales, the *Contes et facéties* (1852), the semi-autobiographic series of *Filles du feu* (1856) and *La Bohème galante*. See works by Arvède Barine (1897), Gauthier Ferrières (1906), Aristide Marie (1914), R. Bizet (1928), A. Béguin (1936), L. H. Sébillotte (1948), S. A. Rhodes (1951), and the *Fortnightly*, December 1897.

NERVI, Pier Luigi (1891–), Italian architect, graduated as an engineer and set up as a building contractor. His works include a complex of exhibition halls at Turin (1948–50) and he achieved an international reputation by his designs for the Olympic stadii in Rome (1960), in which a bold and imaginative use is made of concrete in roofing in the large areas. In 1960 he was awarded the gold medal of the R.I.B.A.

NESBIT, Edith, maiden and pen name of **Mrs Hubert Bland**, from 1917 **Mrs Thomas Tucker** (1858–1924), English writer, born in London, educated at a French convent, who began her literary career by writing poetry but is perhaps best remembered for her children's stories, which reacted against the namby-pamby moralizing then prevalent and have remained popular to the present day. Among them are *The Story of the Treasure Seekers* (1899), *The Wouldbegoods* (1901), *Five Children and It* (1902) and *The Railway Children* (1906). See life by D. L. Moore (1933, rev. 1967), study by N. Streatfield (1958) and monograph by A. Bell (1960).

NESSELRODE, Karl Robert, Count, *-rō'dė* (1780–1862), Russian diplomatist, was born at Lisbon, son of the Russian ambassador. He gained the confidence of the Emperor Alexander, took a principal part in the negotiations which ended in the Peace of Paris, and in the Congress of Vienna, and was one of the most active diplomatists of the Holy Alliance. He dealt a deadly blow to the revolutionary cause in Hungary in 1849. He exerted himself to preserve peace with the Western Powers, and in 1854 strove for the re-establishment of peace. See his autobiography (1866), *Lettres et Papiers* (1904–12).

NESTORIUS (d. A.D. 451), Syrian ecclesiastic, was a native of Germanicia in northern Syria, and as priest became so eminent for his zeal, ascetic life, and eloquence that he was selected as patriarch of Constantinople (428). The presbyter Anastasius having denied that the Virgin Mary could be truly called the Mother of God, Nestorius warmly defended him; and so emphasized the distinction of the divine and human natures that antagonists accused him—falsely—of holding that there were two persons in Christ. A controversy ensued, and at a general council at Ephesus in 431 Nestorius was deposed. He was confined in a monastery near Constantinople, was banished to Petra in Arabia, and died (*c.* 451) after confinement in the Greater Oasis in Upper Egypt and elsewhere. There are still a few Nestorians in Kurdistan and Iraq, and a small body of Christians in India are nominally Nestorian. See books by Bethune-Baker (1908) and Loofs (1914).

NESTROY, Johann (1801–62), Austrian dramatist, born in Vienna, began life as an operatic singer, turned playwright and was director of the Vienna Carl-Theater (1854–60). His sixty-odd plays, which include *Der böse Geist lumpazivagabundus* (1833), *Einen Jux will er sich machen* (1842), *Der Unbedeu tende* (1846), *Judith und Holofernes* (1849), are mostly elaborate jibes at theatrical sentimentality characterized by a deft play on words, thoughts and afterthoughts. They revolutionized the Viennese theatre and influenced Wittgenstein (q.v.).

NETTLESHIP, (1) Henry (1839–93), English classical scholar, brother of (2), from 1878 Corpus Latin professor at Oxford, he was born at Kettering, and educated at Lancing, Durham, Charterhouse and Corpus, taking only a second, but winning the Hertford, Gaisford and Craven. He was elected a fellow of Lincoln, was a master at Harrow 1868–73, completed Conington's *Virgil*, and published *Contributions to Latin Lexicography* (1889), &c. See his *Literary Remains* by A. Bradley (1897).

(2) **Richard Lewis** (1846–92), English philosopher, brother of (1), took the place of T. H. Green as a tutor of Balliol. He was lost on Mont Blanc. The Nettleship scholarship at Balliol was founded in his honour. See his *Philosophical Lectures and Remains*, edited, with memoir, by Bradley and Benson (2 vols. 1897).

NEUMANN, *noy'man*, **(1) Balthasar** (1687–1753), German architect, born at Eger, was at first a military engineer in the service of the Archbishop of Würzburg, but soon found his true *métier*, and after visiting Paris and absorbing new ideas, he became professor of Architecture at Würzburg. Many outstanding examples of the Baroque style were designed by him, the finest being probably Würzburg Palace and Schloss Bruchsal. See studies by Sedlmaier and Pfister (1923) and F. Knapp (1937).

(2) **Johann von** (1903–57), Hungarian American mathematician, born in Budapest, escaped from Hungary during the Communist régime (1919), studied chemistry at Berlin, chemical engineering at Zürich, mathematics at Budapest and on a Rockefeller fellowship at Göttingen became acquainted with Oppenheimer (q.v.). In 1931 he became professor at Princeton and in 1933 research professor at the Institute for Advanced Study there. His classic work on quantum mechanics (1932) proved rigorously that cause-and-effect operates for large-scale physical phenomena only and not for subatomic events. He worked on the atomic bomb project at Los Alamos during World War II and his mathematical treatment of shock waves helped to determine the height of the explosions over Hiroshima and Nagasaki in August 1945. He made important contributions to point-set theory, theory of continuous groups, operator theory and mathematical logic, such giant computers as M.A.N.I.A.C. (his own ironical label) having been constructed on the basis of his mathematical work for high-speed calculations for H-bomb development. In *Theory of Games and Economic Behaviour* (1944), written with O. Morgenstern, he distinguishes between the more complex games, requiring strategy, and nonstrategic games. R. B. Braithwaite utilized this theory as *A Tool for the Moral Philosopher* (1955). He differed with Oppenheimer on the advisability of advancing the H-Bomb projects, but testified to the latter's loyalty and integrity (1954). He died of cancer.

NEURATH, Baron Konstantin von, *noy'raht* (1873–1956), Nazi 'Protector of Bohemia and Moravia', was born at Klein-Glattbach, Württemberg, in 1873. After consular service, he joined the German Embassy in Istanbul and in 1921 became ambassador to Italy and in 1930 to Britain. He was foreign minister from 1932 to 1938. From 1939 to 1943 he was the Reich protector of the Czech territories. At the Nuremberg Trial he was sentenced to 15 years' imprisonment for war crimes, but released in 1954.

NEUVILLE, Alphonse Marie de, *nœ-veel* (1836–85), French painter of pictures of French military exploits in the Crimea, Italy and Mexico, and against Germany. He excelled as an illustrator of books.

NEVILLE, Richard. See WARWICK.

NEVINSON, (1) Christopher Richard Wynne (1889–1946), English artist, son of (2), born at Hampstead, studied at the Slade School and in Paris, and painted a number of Futurist pictures about 1912. He achieved fame as an official war artist (1914–15), his war pictures being exhibited in London in 1916. He also achieved note as an etcher and lithographer. See his autobiographical *Paint and Prejudice* (1937).

(2) **Henry Woodd** (1856–1941), English war correspondent and journalist, father of (1), born in Leicester, was correspondent

for various papers in, among many other campaigns, the Boer War, the Balkans and the Dardanelles. In 1904 he exposed the Portuguese slave trade in Angola. His publications include *Lines of Life* (verse, 1920), *Essays in Freedom and Rebellion* (1921) and a study of Goethe (1931). See his autobiographical series, *Changes and Chances* (1925–28).

NEVISON, John (1639–84), English highwayman, born at Pontefract, after a long career of robbery and murder was hanged at York.

NEWALL, (1) Hugh Frank (1857–1944), British astronomer, son of (2), born near Gateshead, educated at Rugby and Trinity College, Cambridge, worked at the Cavendish Laboratory under Thomson, and in 1909 became first professor of Astrophysics. In 1913 he was appointed first director of the Solar Physics Observatory, a position which he held for the rest of his life, carrying out important research on solar phenomena.

(2) **Robert Stirling** (1812–89), British engineer and astronomer, father of (1), was born at Dundee. In 1940 he patented a new type of wire rope and founded a business to manufacture it at Gateshead. Turning his inventive genius to the submarine cable, he devised improvements both to the cable itself and to methods of laying it, and his firm was responsible for many of the early undersea cables in different parts of the world.

NEWBERY, John (1713–67), English publisher and bookseller, born a Berkshire farmer's son, settled about 1744 in London as a vendor of books and patent medicines. He was the first to publish little books for children, and he was himself—perhaps with Goldsmith—part author of some of the best of them, notably *Goody Two-Shoes.* In 1758 he started the *Universal Chronicle, or Weekly Gazette*, in which the *Idler* appeared. In the *Public Ledger* (1760) appeared Goldsmith's *Citizen of the World.* See a book on him by C. Welsh (1885). Since 1922 the Newbery medal has been awarded annually for the best American children's book.

NEWBOLT, Sir Henry John (1862–1938), English poet, born at Bilston, Staffs., studied at Oxford, went to the bar, and in 1895 published *Mordred*, a drama. He is best known, however, for his sea songs—*Admirals All*, *The Island Race*, *Drake's Drum*, &c. He was knighted in 1915. See his autobiography (1932) and *Later Life and Letters*, ed. by his wife (1942).

NEWCASTLE. See CAVENDISH and PELHAM.

NEWCOMB, Simon (1835–1909), American astronomer, born at Wallace, Nova Scotia, graduated at Harvard, in 1861–97 was professor of Mathematics in the U.S. navy, had charge of the naval observatory at Washington, and edited the American *Nautical Almanac*. In 1894–1901 he was professor in the Johns Hopkins University. He made many astronomical discoveries, and wrote, besides innumerable memoirs, a long series of works, including *Elements of Astronomy*, *The Stars*, and his own Reminiscences (1903).

NEWCOMEN, Thomas (1663–1729), English inventor, born at Dartmouth, by 1698 had invented the atmospheric steam engine, an improvement on one by Capt. Savery, with whom he became associated. From 1712 his invention was used for pumping water out of mines. See work by R. Jenkins (1913).

NEWDIGATE, Sir Roger (1719–1806), English antiquary, was born and died at Arbury, Warwickshire, having sat for thirty-six years as member for Middlesex and Oxford University. He built up a famous collection of antiquities and endowed the Newdigate prize poem at Oxford, winners of which have included Heber, Ruskin, M. Arnold, Laurence Binyon and John Buchan. See Lady Newdigate-Newdegate's *Cheverels of Cheverel Manor* (1898), and work by R. Churton (1881).

NEWLANDS, John Alexander Reina (1837–1898), English chemist, worked in a sugar refinery at the Victoria Docks. He was the first to arrange the elements in order of atomic number and to see the connection between every eighth. This 'Law of Octaves' brought him ridicule at the time (1864), but it was the first idea of a periodic law and in 1887 the Royal Society awarded him its Davy medal in recognition of his work. He was the author of a handbook on sugar (1888).

NEWMAN, (1) Ernest (1868–1959), English music critic, born in Liverpool, was successively music critic of the *Manchester Guardian*, the *Birmingham Post* and the *Sunday Times* (from 1920). His writings are noted for their wit and elegance, and for their strict factual accuracy. His works include studies of Gluck and Hugo Wolf, and of opera (e.g., *Opera Nights* and *Wagner Nights*); but it is for his far-reaching studies and deep understanding of Wagner that he is best known—his four-volume biography of that composer (1933–37) is the most complete and authoritative account of the composer in existence. In *A Musical Critic's Holiday* Newman vindicates music criticism as a valuable study.

(2) **Francis William** (1805–97), English scholar, brother of (3), was born in London. In 1826 he obtained a double first at Oxford and resigned a Balliol fellowship. He withdrew from the university in 1830, declining subscription to the Thirty-nine Articles. After a three years' stay in the East, he became classical tutor in Bristol College in 1834, in 1840 professor in Manchester New College, and in 1846–63 professor of Latin in University College, London. In religion he took a part directly opposite to his brother's, being eager for a religion including whatever is best in all the historical religions. *Phases of Faith* (1853), the best known of his works, was preceded by *The Soul* (1849), and other works include a small book on his brother (1891). See *Memoir and Letters*, by I. G. Sieveking (1909).

(3) **John Henry, Cardinal** (1801–90), English theologian, brother of (2), was born in London, February 21, 1801. His father was a banker; his mother, a moderate Calvinist, deeply influenced his early religious views. He went up to Trinity College, Oxford, in 1817, and in 1822, in spite of his second-class, he was elected a fellow of

Oriel, and here he formed his close intimacy with Pusey and Hurrell Froude. In 1824 he was ordained, in 1828 became vicar of St Mary's, in 1830 broke definitely with Evangelicalism. His first book, *The Arians of the Fourth Century* (1833), argued that Arianism was a Judaizing heresy which sprang up in Antioch. In 1832–33 Newman accompanied Hurrell Froude and his father on a Mediterranean tour, when many of the poems in *Lyra Apostolica* (1834) were written and also 'Lead, kindly Light'. He was present at Keble's Oxford assize sermon on National Apostasy (July 1833), which he regarded as the beginning of the Tractarian movement. Into the *Tracts for the Times* Newman threw himself with energy, and he himself composed a number of them. Tract 90 (1841) was the most famous of the tracts. Newman contended that the intention of the Thirty-nine Articles was Catholic in spirit, and that they were aimed at the supremacy of the pope and the popular abuses of Catholic practice, and not at Catholic doctrine. But Tract 90 provoked an explosion which was the end of the Tractarian movement, and brought on the conversion to Rome of those of the Tractarians who were most logical as well as most in earnest. Newman struggled for two years longer to think his position tenable, but in 1843 resigned the vicarage of St Mary's, which he had held since 1828, and retired to Littlemore. The magnificent sermon on 'Development in Christian Doctrine' was the last which he preached in the university pulpit, February 2, 1843. In October 1845 he invited the Passionist Father Dominic to his house at Littlemore in order that he might be received into the Roman Catholic Church. He went to Rome for a year and a half, and on his return in 1848 he established a branch of the brotherhood of St Philip Neri in England at Edgbaston, a suburb of Birmingham; and here he did a great deal of hard work, devoting himself to the sufferers from cholera in 1849 with the utmost zeal. The lectures on *Anglican Difficulties* (1850) drew public attention to Newman's great power of irony and the singular delicacy of his literary style, and were followed by his lectures on *Catholicism in England* (1851). His long series of Oxford sermons contain some of the finest ever preached from an Anglican pulpit, and his Roman Catholic volumes—*Sermons addressed to Mixed Congregations* (1849) and *Sermons on Various Occasions* (1857)—though less remarkable for their pathos, are even fuller of fine rhetoric, and show the rarest finish. In 1864 a casual remark by Canon Kingsley in *Macmillan's Magazine* on the indifference of the Roman Church to the virtue of truthfulness, an indifference which he asserted that Dr Newman approved, led to a correspondence which resulted in the publication of the remarkable *Apologia pro Vita Sua*. In 1865 he wrote a poem of singular beauty, *The Dream of Gerontius*, republished in *Verses on Various Occasions* (1874). In 1870 he published his *Grammar of Assent*, on the philosophy of faith. In the controversies which led to the Vatican Council Newman sided with the Inopportunists. He was at this time in vehement opposition to the Ultramontanes under Manning and William George Ward, and the bitterness between the two parties ran very high. Leo XIII, anxious to show his sympathy with the moderates, in 1879 summoned Newman to Rome to receive the cardinal's hat. He died at Edgbaston, August 11, 1890. See the Life by Wilfred Ward (1912, 3rd ed. 1927); books by Waller and Burrow (1902), Barry (1904), Brémond (1905–12), Whyte (1901), Sarolea (1908), Bellasis (1916), Dark (1934), Houghton (1945), Ward (1948), Harrold (1955), Bouyer (1958) and Trevor (2 vols. 1962); *Newman's Letters*, ed. by Miss Mozley (1891), *Autobiographical Writings*, ed. Tristram (1957) and *Letters and Diaries*, definitive edition by Dessain, from 1961.

NEWNES, Sir George (1851–1910), English publisher, the son of a Matlock Congregational minister, was educated at Shireland Hall, Warwickshire, and the City of London School. He founded *Tit-Bits* (1881), *The Strand Magazine* (1891), *The Wide World Magazine* (1898), &c.; was Gladstonian M.P. for the Newmarket division 1885–95; and then was created a baronet. See Life by H. Friederichs (1911).

NEWTON, (1) **Alfred** (1829–1907), English zoologist, born at Geneva, was in 1866 appointed professor of Zoology at Cambridge, and wrote valuable works on ornithology. See Life by A. F. R. Wollaston (1921).

(2) **Sir Charles Thomas** (1816–94), English archaeologist, born at Bredwardine, held a British Museum post 1840–52, as vice-consul at Mitylene made important finds (*Discoveries in the Levant*, 1865), and was British Museum keeper of antiquities 1861–1885.

(3) **Eric** (1893–1965), English writer and art critic, born at Marple Bridge, near Glossop, Derbyshire, worked as a mosaic designer and craftsman, and was art critic to the *Manchester Guardian* from 1930 to 1947, and to the *Sunday Times* from 1937 to 1951. His publications include *European Painting and Sculpture* (1941), *Tintoretto* (1952) and *The Romantic Rebellion* (1962).

(4) **Sir Isaac** (1642–1727), English scientist and mathematician, was born at Woolsthorpe, Lincolnshire, near Grantham, at whose grammar school he got his education. In 1661 he entered Trinity College, Cambridge. In 1665, when he took his B.A., he committed to writing his first discovery on fluxions; and in 1665 or 1666 the fall of an apple suggested the train of thought that led to the law of gravitation. But on his first attempt so to explain lunar motions, it is commonly said that an erroneous estimate of the radius of the earth produced such discrepancies that he dropped the investigation for the time, though better estimates seem to have been available. Be this as it may, he turned to study the nature of light and the construction of telescopes. By a variety of experiments upon sunlight refracted through a prism, he concluded that rays of light which differ in colour differ also in refrangibility—a discovery which suggested that the indistinctness of the image formed

by the object-glass of telescopes was due to the different coloured rays of light being brought to a focus at different distances. He concluded (rightly for an object-glass consisting of a single lens) that it was impossible to produce a distinct image, and was led to the construction of reflecting telescopes; and the form devised by him is that which reached such perfection in the hands of Herschel and Rosse. Newton became a fellow of Trinity in 1667, and Lucasian professor of Mathematics in 1669, and in 1671–72 he was elected a member of the Royal Society. He resumed his calculations about gravitation, and by 1684 had demonstrated the whole theory, which, on the solicitation of Halley, he expounded first in *De Motu Corporum*, and more completely in *Philosophiae Naturalis Principia Mathematica* (1687). The part he took in defending the rights of the university against the illegal encroachments of James II procured him a seat in the Convention Parliament (1689–90). A crisis of some sort in 1693 seems to have left his suspicious, quarrelsome temper worse than ever. In 1696 he was appointed warden of the Mint, and was master of the Mint from 1699 till the end of his life. He again sat in parliament in 1701 for his university. He solved two celebrated problems proposed in June 1696 by John Bernoulli, as a challenge to the mathematicians of Europe; and performed a similar feat in 1716, by solving a problem proposed by Leibniz. Newton was president of the Royal Society from 1703 till his death. He superintended the publication of Flamsteed's *Greenwich Observations*, which he required for the working out of his lunar theory—not without much disputing between himself and Flamsteed. In the controversy between Newton and Leibniz as to priority of discovery of the differential calculus or the method of fluxions, Newton acted secretly through his friends. The verdict of science is that the methods were invented independently, and that although Newton was the first inventor, a greater debt is owing to Leibniz for the superior facility and completeness of his method. In 1699 Newton was elected foreign associate of the Academy of Sciences, and in 1705 he was knighted by Queen Anne. He died March 20, 1727, and was buried in Westminster Abbey. An admirable reprint of the *Principia* is that by Lord Kelvin and Professor Blackburn (1871). Clarke's Latin translation of the *Optics* appeared in 1706, the *Optical Lectures* in 1728, the *Fluxions* in 1736, and Horsley edited an edition of his Collected Works (1779–85). Newton was a student of alchemy; and he left a remarkable MS. on the prophecies of Daniel and on the Apocalypse, a history of Creation, and some tracts. See Lives by Brewster (1855), de Morgan (1885), More (1934), Sullivan (1938), Andrade (1950), Sootin (N.Y. 1955), and his *Correspondence* (vols. 1–3 ed. by Turnbull, 1959–61, and vol. 4 ed. by Scott, 1967).

(5) **John** (1725–1807), English divine and writer, was born in London, son of a shipmaster, sailed with his father for six years, and for ten years engaged in the African slave trade. In 1748 he was converted, but still went on slave trading; in 1755 he became tide surveyor at Liverpool; and in 1764 he was offered the curacy of Olney in Bucks, and took orders. To Olney the poet Cowper came four years later, and an extraordinary friendship sprang up. In 1779 Newton became rector of St Mary Woolnoth, London. Newton's prose works are little read, save the *Remarkable Particulars in his own Life*. But some of his *Olney Hymns* have been taken to the heart by the English world, including 'Approach, my soul, the mercy-seat', 'How sweet the name of Jesus sounds' and 'One there is above all others'. See Lives by Cecil (1808), R. Bickersteth (1865) and B. Martin (1950); Collected Works (1816); and books cited at COWPER.

NEXÖ, Martin Andersen, *nik'sœ* (1869–1954), Danish novelist, was born in a poor quarter of Copenhagen, and spent his boyhood in Bornholm near Nexö (whence his name). From shoemaking and bricklaying he turned to books and teaching, and in 1906 won European fame with *Pelle the Conqueror* (trans. 1915–17; 4 parts), describing poor life from within and the growth of the labour movement. See his Reminiscences (Copenhagen 4 vols. 1932–39) and work by W. A. Berendsohn (Copenhagen 1948).

NEY, Michel (1769–1815), French marshal, was born, a cooper's son, at Saarlouis, and rose to be adjutant-general (1794) and general of brigade (1796). For the capture of Mannheim he was made general of division in 1799. Under the empire he was made marshal. In 1805 he stormed the entrenchments of Elchingen, and was created Duke of Elchingen. He distinguished himself at Jena and Eylau, and his conduct at Friedland earned him the grand eagle of the *Légion d'honneur*. Serving in Spain, he quarrelled with Masséna and returned to France. In command of the third corps (1813) he covered himself with glory at Smolensk and Borodino, received the title of Prince of the Moskwa, and led the rear-guard in the disastrous retreat. In 1813 he was present at Lützen and Bautzen, but was defeated by Bülow at Dennewitz. He fought heroically at Leipzig, but submitted to Louis XVIII, who loaded him with favours. On Napoleon's return from Elba Ney, sent against him, went over to his old master's side. He opposed Brunswick at Quatrebras, and led the centre at Waterloo. After the capitulation of Paris he was condemned for high treason, and shot. See his *Mémoires* (1833), and books by Bonnal (1910–14), A. H. Atteridge (1913), L. Blythe (1937) and J. B. Morton (1958).

NIARCHOS, Stavros Spyros, *ni-ahr'kos* (1909–), Greek ship-owner, controller of one of the largest independent fleets in the world, served during World War II in the Royal Hellenic Navy, then pioneered the construction of super-tankers, as did his brother-in-law Aristotle Onassis (q.v.).

NICCOLA PISANO. See PISANO (3).

NICCOLO DI FOLIGNO, or Di Liberatore. See ALUNNO.

NICHOL, (1) **John** (1833–94), Scottish writer, son of (2), Glasgow professor of

English Literature 1861–89, he wrote poems and books on Byron, Bacon, Burns, *American Literature* (1882), &c. See Life by Knight (1896).

(2) **John Pringle** (1804–59), Scottish astronomer, father of (1), after several years teaching he became professor of Astronomy at Glasgow and was well known for his public lectures.

NICHOLAS, St (4th cent.), patron saint of Russia, Bishop of Myra in Lycia, was imprisoned under Diocletian and released under Constantine, and his supposed relics were conveyed to Bari in 1087. St Nicholas is the patron of youth, particularly of scholars (*Santa Claus* is an American corruption of the name), merchants, sailors, travellers, thieves. See books by L'Abbé Marin (1917), E. Crozier (1949).

NICHOLAS, the name of five popes and an antipope:

Nicholas I, St (pope, 858–867), asserted the supremacy of the Church and forbade the divorce of Lothair, King of Lorraine. See Life by J. Roy (1899), studies by E. Perels (Berlin 1920) and J. Haller (1937).

Nicholas II (pope, 1058–61), enacted regulations for papal elections. See study by P. Brand and J. Garin (Chambéry 1925).

Nicholas V (1397–1455), pope from 1447, prevailed on the antipope, Felix V, to abdicate and thus restored the peace of the Church. A liberal patron of scholars, he may almost be said to have founded the Vatican Library. He vainly endeavoured to arouse Europe to the duty of succouring the Greek empire. See studies by G. Sforza (Lucca 1884) and K. Pleyer (Stuttgart 1927).

Nicholas V (antipope, 1328–30), set up in opposition to John XXII.

NICHOLAS, the name of two emperors of Russia:

Nicholas I (1796–1855), third son of Paul I, on July 13, 1817, married the daughter of Frederick-William III of Prussia. On the death of his brother, Alexander I (1825), owing to the resignation of Constantine, he succeeded to the throne, and suppressed a military conspiracy with vigour and cruelty. After a brief ebullition of reforming zeal, he reverted to the ancient policy of the tsars—absolute despotism, supported by military power. Wars with Persia and Turkey resulted in giving Russia increase of territory. The movement of 1830 in the west of Europe was followed by a rising of the Poles, which was suppressed after a severe contest of nine months; and Nicholas, converting Poland into a Russian province, strove to extinguish the Polish nationality. In Russia intellectual activity was kept under official guidance. The tsar's Panslavism also prompted him to Russianize all the inhabitants of the empire, and to convert Roman Catholics and Protestants to the Russian Greek Church. During the political storm of 1848–49 he assisted the emperor of Austria in quelling the Hungarian insurrection, and drew closer the alliance with Prussia. The re-establishment of the French empire confirmed these alliances, and led Nicholas to think that the time had come for absorbing Turkey; but the opposition of Britain and France brought on the Crimean war, during which he died, March 2, 1855. See Lacroix, *Histoire de Nicolas I* (1864–73); works by J. Schiemann (Berlin 1904–08), C. de Grunwald (Eng. trans. 1954).

Nicholas II (1868–1918), in 1894 succeeded his father, Alexander III, married a princess of Hesse, and initiated (1898) The Hague Peace Conference. His reign was marked by the alliance with France, *entente* with Britain, disastrous war with Japan (1904–05), and the establishment of the Duma (1906). He took command of the Russian armies against the Central Powers in 1915. Forced to abdicate at the Revolution, he was shot with his family by the Red Guards. See Lives by P. Gilliard (Eng. trans. 1921), C. Radziwill (1931).

NICHOLAS, Grand-Duke (1856–1929), Russian general, a nephew of Alexander II, was Russian commander-in-chief against Germany and Austria, August 1914 to September 1915, and commander-in-chief in the Caucasus 1915–17. After 1919 he lived quietly in France. See Life by J. Daniloff (Berlin 1930).

NICHOLAS OF CUSA. See NICOLAUS.

NICHOLS, (1) John (1745–1826), father of (2), editor of the *Gentleman's Magazine* (1797–1826), edited and published literary and historical works, including *Literary Anecdotes of the Eighteenth Century*. See his Memoirs (1804).

(2) **John Bowyer** (1779–1863), son of (1), father of (3), succeeded his father as editor of the *Gentleman's Magazine* for a time and published many important county histories. See memoir by J. G. Nichols (1864).

(3) **John Gough** (1806–73), son of (2). He too edited the *Gentleman's Magazine* and also made valuable contributions to the materials of English history and genealogy. See memoir by R. C. Nichols (1874).

NICHOLSON, (1) Ben (1894–), English artist, son of (8), born at Denham, exhibited with the Paris Abstraction-Création group in 1933–34 and at the Venice Biennale in 1954, designed a mural panel for the Festival of Britain (1951) and in 1952 executed another for the Time-Life building in London. As one of the leading abstract artists, he has an international reputation and won the first Guggenheim award in 1957 against competition from 13 countries. Although he has produced a number of purely geometrical paintings and reliefs, in general he uses conventional still-life objects as a starting point for his finely drawn and subtly balanced and coloured variations. Three times married, his second wife was Barbara Hepworth (q.v.). See monograph by Read (2 vols. 1948, 1956) and study by Hodin (1958).

(2) **John** (1822–57), British soldier and administrator, was born at Lisburn (or possibly in Dublin), in 1839 joined the East India Company's service, and in 1842 was captured at Ghazni in Afghanistan. During the Sikh rebellion of 1848 he saved the fortress of Attock, and at Chillianwalla and Gujrat earned the special approval of Lord Gough. Nicholson was appointed deputy-commissioner (1851) of the Punjab, and in 1857 he perhaps did more than any other

man to hold the province. As brigadier-general, on September 14 he led the storming party at the siege of Delhi, and was mortally wounded. See Lives by Captain Trotter (1897) and H. Pearson (1939).

(3) **Joseph Shield** (1850–1927), English economist, was born at Wrawby near Brigg, and in 1880–1925 was professor of Political Economy at Edinburgh. He wrote on *Money* (1888), *Principles of Political Economy* (3 vols. 1893–1901), and other works on economics advocating the ideas of Adam Smith. See Life by W. R. Scott (1928).

(4) **Seth Barnes** (1891–1963), American astronomer, born at Springfield, Ill., notable as the discoverer of the 9th, 10th and 11th satellites of Jupiter.

(5) **William** (1753–1815), English physicist, waterworks engineer for Portsmouth and Gosport, invented the hydrometer named after him, and also a machine for printing on linen. With Carlisle he constructed the first voltaic pile in England, and in so doing discovered that water could be dissociated by electricity. He compiled a *Dictionary of Practical and Theoretical Chemistry* (1808).

(6) **William** (1781–1844), Scottish portrait painter and etcher, born in Ovingham-on-Tyne, about 1814 settled in Edinburgh, was the first secretary of the Royal Scottish Academy, and was noted for his portraits of Sir Walter Scott and other famous contemporaries.

(7) **William** (1816–64), Australian statesman, born near Whitehaven, emigrated as a grocer to Melbourne in 1841, became mayor 1850, and premier of Victoria 1859. He had the ballot adopted in 1855.

(8) **Sir William Newzam Prior** (1872–1949), English artist, father of (1), born at Newark, studied in Paris and was influenced by Whistler and Manet. He became a fashionable portrait painter, but is principally remembered for the posters produced (with his brother-in-law, James Pryde) under the name of **J. and W. Beggarstaff**, for his woodcut book illustrations, and for his glowing still-life paintings (e.g., the *Mushrooms* in the Tate Gallery). He was knighted in 1936. See studies by M. Steen (1943) and L. Browse (1956); also a Life of J. Pryde by D. Hudson (1949).

NICIAS (d. 413 B.C.), Athenian statesman and general, belonged to the aristocratic party, and opposed Cleon and Alcibiades. In 427–426 B.C. he defeated the Spartans and the Corinthians. In 424 he ravaged Laconia, but in 421 made peace between Sparta and Athens. In the naval expedition against Sicily (418) he was one of the commanders. In 415 he laid siege to Syracuse, and was at first successful, but subsequently experienced a series of disasters; his troops were forced to surrender, and he was put to death. See Plutarch's *Life of Nikias* (ed. by H. A. Holden, 1887).

NICOL, (1) Erskine (1825–1904), Scottish painter, was born at Leith, lived in Dublin 1843–46, and settled in London in 1862. He was R.S.A. and A.R.A. and painted homely incidents in Irish and Scottish life.

(2) **William** (*c.* 1744–97), Scottish schoolmaster, a classics master in the High School of Edinburgh, was the too convivial intimate of Robert Burns.

NICOLAI, (1) Christoph Friedrich (1733–1811), German author, bookseller and publisher, born at Berlin, early distinguished himself by a series of critical letters (1756) contributed to many literary journals, and for many years edited the *Allgemeine deutsche Bibliothek* (106 vols. 1765–92). He wrote topographical works, satires, anecdotes of Frederick the Great, and an autobiography (recording strange apparitions and hallucinations of his own). See studies by M. Sommerfeld (Halle 1921) and W. Strauss (Stuttgart 1927).

(2) **Otto** (1810–49), German composer, born at Königsberg, in 1847 became *kapellmeister* at Berlin, where his opera *The Merry Wives of Windsor* was produced just before he died. See Life by G. R. Kruse (Berlin 1911).

NICOLAS, Sir Nicholas Harris (1799–1848), English antiquary, born at Dartmouth, served in the navy 1808–16, and was called to the bar in 1825. He devoted himself chiefly to genealogical and historical studies, as in his *History of British Orders of Knighthood* (1841–42), *Synopsis of the Peerage* (1825), &c.

NICOLAUS OF CUSA (1400–64), German cardinal and philosopher, born at Cusa or Cues on the Moselle, studied at Heidelberg and at Padua. As Archdeacon of Liège he took a prominent part in the Council of Basel, insisting in *De Concordantia Catholica* that the pope was subordinate to Councils; but ultimately he sided with the pope, and was made cardinal. As papal legate he visited Constantinople to promote the union of the Eastern and Western churches. He exposed the false Isidorian decretals, was in advance of his time in science, denounced perverted scholasticism in an *Apologia Doctae Ignorantia* and taught that the earth went round the sun. See German monographs by Düx (1848), Scharpff (1871), Glossner (1891) and Jaspers (1964).

NICOLE, Pierre (1625–95), French Jansenist, born at Chartres, was one of the most distinguished of the Port Royalists, the friend of Arnauld and Pascal, and author of *Essais de morale* (1671 *et seq*). See works by E. Thouverex (Paris 1926) and Le Breton-Grandmaison (Paris 1945). See JANSEN.

NICOLINI. See PATTI (1).

NICOLL, Sir William Robertson (1851–1923), Scottish man of letters, was born at Lumsden, studied at Aberdeen, was Free Church minister at Dufftown 1874–77 and Kelso 1877–85. He then addressed himself to literary work in London, becoming editor of the *Expositor*, the *British Weekly* (1886) and the *Bookman*. He wrote books on theology and literature, and was knighted in 1909. See Life by T. H. Darlow (1925).

NICOLLE, Charles Jules Henri (1866–1936), French physician and bacteriologist, a pupil of Pasteur, was director of the Pasteur Institute at Tunis (1903), and professor at the Collège de France (1932). He discovered that the body louse is a transmitter of typhus fever, and in 1928 was awarded the Nobel prize for medicine.

NICOLSON, (1) **Adela Florence.** See HOPE (2).

(2) **Sir Harold George** (1886–1968), English diplomat, author and critic, was born in Teheran, where his father, later 1st Baron Carnock, was British chargé-d'affaires. Educated at Wellington College and Balliol College, Oxford, Nicolson had a distinguished career as a diplomat, entering the service in 1909, and holding posts in Madrid, Constantinople, Tehran and Berlin until his resignation in 1929, when he turned to journalism. From 1935 to 1945 he was National Liberal M.P. for West Leicester. He wrote several biographies, including those of Tennyson, Swinburne and the official one of George V, as well as books on history, politics and, in *Good Behaviour* (1955), manners. He was highly regarded as a literary critic. In 1913 he married Victoria Sackville-West (q.v.), and he was knighted in 1953. See his *Diaries and Letters* (2 vols., ed. by his son, 1966, 1967).

(3) **William** (1655–1727), English divine and antiquary, born at Plumbland, became successively Bishop of Carlisle and Derry, published the *Historical Library* (English, Scottish and Irish) and other important works and collections. See Life by F. G. James (1957) and *Letters*, ed. J. Nichols (1809).

NICOT, Jean, *nee-kō* (1530–1600), French diplomat and scholar, born at Nîmes, became French ambassador at Lisbon, and in 1561 introduced into France the tobacco plant, called after him *Nicotiana*. He compiled one of the first French dictionaries (1606). See his *Correspondance*, ed. E. Falgairolle (Paris 1897).

NIEBUHR, (1) **Barthold Georg** (1776–1831), German historian, son of (2), he was born at Copenhagen, and studied at Kiel, London and Edinburgh (1798–99). In 1800 he entered the Danish state service, and in 1806 the Prussian civil service. The opening of Berlin University in 1810 introduced a new era in his life. He gave (1810–12) a course of lectures on Roman History, which established his position as one of the most original and philosophical of modern historians. In 1816 he was appointed Prussian ambassador at the papal court, and on his return in 1823 he took up his residence at Bonn, where his lectures gave a powerful impetus to historical learning. Niebuhr possessed great intuitive sagacity in sifting true from false historic evidence; and though his scepticism as to the credibility of early history goes too far, the bulk of his contribution to history still stands substantially unshaken. His *Römische Geschichte* and other important works were translated into English. See Madame Hensler's *Lebensnachrichten* (1838; trans. 1852), and studies by Classen (1876), C. Seitz (1909) and F. Schnabel (1931).

(2) **Carsten** (1733–1815), German traveller, father of (1), born at Lauenburg, joined a Danish expedition and travelled in Africa, Arabia and India. He then settled in Denmark and wrote about his travels. See Life by his son (1817).

(3) **Reinhold** (1892–1971), American theologian, born in Wright City, Mo., educated at Yale, professor of Christian Ethics in the Union Theological Seminary, New York, from 1928. He wrote *Nature and Destiny of Man* (1941–43). See study by Davis (1945).

NIEL, Adolphe (1802–69), French marshal, was born at Muret (Upper Garonne), and entered the army as an engineer officer. He took part in the storming of Constantine in Algeria (1836), the siege of Rome (1849), the bombardment of Bomarsund (1854), the fall of Sebastopol (1856), and the battles of Magenta and Solferino (1859) and became minister of war in 1867. See Life by J. J. de la Tour (Paris 1912).

NIELSEN, Carl August, *neel'sėn* (1865–1931), Danish composer, was born at Nørre-Lyndelse, near Odense, Fünen, the son of a house-painter who was also a village fiddler, became a bandsman at Odense, and in 1883 entered Copenhagen Conservatoire. His compositions of this time—including the G minor quartet and oboe fantasias—are not revolutionary, being rather in the tradition of Gade (q.v.), but with his first symphony (1894) his new tendencies of progressive tonality and rhythmic audacity become apparent, though still within a classical structure. In his second symphony (' The Four Temperaments ', 1901–02) polytonality is first used in Danish music, along with the contrapuntal style which was to become characteristic of Nielsen. His other works include four further symphonies (1912, 1916, 1922 and 1925), the tragic opera *Saul and David* (1902), the comic opera *Masquerade* (1906), chamber music, concertos for flute, clarinet and violin, and a huge organ work, *Commotio* (1931). In 1915 he was appointed director of Copenhagen Conservatoire. As Denmark's greatest twentieth-century composer, striving through new harmonies, rhythms and melodic ideas of truly Nordic character to divest Danish music of its prevalent romanticism, and as a conductor of note, Nielsen exerted a tremendous influence on the musical development of Denmark. See Life by R. W. L. Simpson (1952), and his early autobiography, translated as *My Childhood* (1953).

NIEMBSCH. See LENAU.

NIEMÖLLER, Martin, *nee'-* (1892–), German Lutheran pastor and defier of Hitler, born at Lippstadt, Westphalia, rose from midshipman to one of Germany's ace submarine commanders in World War I, studied theology, was ordained in 1924 and became pastor at Berlin-Dahlem in 1931. Summoned with other Protestant church leaders to Hitler, who wished to get their co-operation for the Nazi régime, Niemöller declared that he, like Hitler, had also a responsibility for the German people, given by God, which he could not permit Hitler to take away from him. His house was ransacked by the Gestapo and, continuing openly to preach against the *Führer*, he was arrested and confined from 1937 to 1945 in Sachsenhausen and Dachau concentration camps. Acclaimed by the Allies as one of the few ' good Germans ' at the end of the war, he caused great astonishment when it was discovered that he had in 1941 volunteered in vain to serve again in the German navy, despite his opposition to Hitler. His explanation was that he had a duty to 'give unto Caesar what is Caesar's'. In 1945 he was responsible for the 'Declaration of Guilt' by the German churches for not opposing Hitler more strenuously. On the other hand he loudly condemned the abuses of the de-Nazification courts. He vigorously opposed German rearmament and the nuclear arms race. Federal Germany he described as 'begotten in Rome and born in Washington'. In 1947–64 he was church president of the Evangelical Church in Hesse and Nassau. In 1961 he became president of the World Council of Churches. See his *Vom U-Boot zur Kanzel*, 'From U-Boat to the Pulpit' (Berlin 1934), and collections of his sermons (1935, 1939, 1946, 1956), particularly *Six Dachau Sermons* (Munich 1946), also Life by D. Schmidt (trans. 1959).

NIEPCE, *nee-eps*, (1) **de St Victor, Claude Marie François** (1805–70), French photographer, nephew of (2), further developed photography as invented by his uncle and Daguerre and wrote a treatise on the subject (1856). See Life by R. Colson (Paris 1898).

(2) **Joseph Nicéphore** (1765–1833), French chemist, uncle of (1), one of the inventors of photography, was born at Chalon-sur-Saône, served in the army, and in 1795 became administrator of Nice. At Chalon in 1801 he devoted himself to chemistry, and at length succeeded in producing a photograph on metal. He co-operated with Daguerre in further research. See Life by Fouqué (1867), and H. and A. Gernsheim's *Daguerre* (1956).

NIETZSCHE, Friedrich Wilhelm, *neetz'shė* (1844–1900), German philosopher and critic, born at Röcken, Saxony, the son of a Lutheran pastor, was passionately religious as a boy and so brilliant an undergraduate at Bonn and Leipzig that he was offered and accepted the professorship of Classical Philology at Basel (1869–79) before graduating. A disciple of Schopenhauer, he dedicated his first book, *Die Geburt der Tragödie* (1872), 'The Birth of Tragedy' (trans. 1909), to his friend Wagner, whose operas he regarded as the true successors to Greek tragedy. In four brilliant critical essays, *Unzeitgemässige Betrachtungen*, 'Untimely Contemplations' (1873–76), he first expressed his enthusiasm for the aristocratic ideal and his contempt for the masses in history. Convinced that Christianity was bankrupt, he determined to give his age new values, Schopenhauer's 'will to power' serving as the basic principle, but turned from a pessimistic to a zestful 'Yea-saying' affirmation of life by the warrior-aristocrat. Only the strong ought to survive. Human sympathy only perpetuates the unfit and the mediocre. These egotistical evolutionary ethical doctrines begin to appear in his *Menschliches, Allzumenschliches*, 'Human, all too Human' (1878), *Fröhliche Wissenschaft* (1882), 'Joyous Wisdom' (trans. 1910), of his positivist period beginning with his breach with Wagner (1876) whose *Parsifal* he thought Christian-inspired. His major work, *Also sprach Zarathustra* (1883–1885), 'Thus spake Zarathustra' (trans. 1933), develops the idea of the superman; *Jenseits von Gut und Böse*, 'Beyond Good and Evil' (1886), the twin moralities for the master on the principle 'Nothing is true; everything is allowed' and slaves whose suffering is insignificant for 'almost everything we call higher culture is based upon the spiritualizing and intensifying of cruelty'. Etymological justification for his transformation of moral terms is presented in *Genealogie der Moral* (1887). Much of his esoteric doctrine appealed to the Nazis, but intensely individualistic, he was no nationalist and not anti-Semitic. With Kierkegaard whom he despised, he greatly influenced Existentialism. He died after twelve years of insanity at Weimar. See Collected Works, ed. Nietzsche Archiv (Weimar 1922), Life by his sister, E. Förster-Nietzsche (1895–1904), who also wrote three biographical studies (trans. 1912, 1915, 1924), and *Letters* (1909–26) to Wagner (trans. 1922), Lives by D. Halévy (1909), and C. Andler (1920–31); and studies by K. Jaspers (1936), F. C. Copleston (1942), J. Laurin (1948), W. A. Kaufmann (1950), E. Heller, *The Disinherited Mind* (1952) and F. A. Lea (1957).

NIEUWLAND, Julius Arthur (1878–1936), American chemist, born in Belgium, took holy orders (1903) and became professor of Chemistry at Notre Dame University (1923). His researches led to the production of artificial rubber (duprene) and he played an important part in the discovery of lewisite.

NIGHTINGALE, Florence (1820–1910), English hospital reformer, daughter of William Edward Nightingale of Embly Park, Hants, was born at Florence. She went into training as a nurse at Kaiserswerth (1851) and Paris. In 1854 war was declared with Russia; after the battle of the Alma Miss Nightingale offered to go out and organize a nursing department at Scutari, and in October she departed with thirty-eight nurses. She arrived in time to receive the wounded from Inkermann (November 5) into overcrowded wards; soon she had 10,000 sick men under her care. But she saw in the bad sanitary arrangements of the hospitals the causes of their frightful mortality, and devoted herself to the removal of these causes. She returned to England in 1856 and a fund of £50,000 was subscribed to enable her to form an institution for the training of nurses at St Thomas's and at King's College Hospital. She devoted many years to the question of Army sanitary reform, to the improvement of nursing and to public health in India. Her main work, *Notes on Nursing* (1859), went through many editions. She received the Order of Merit in 1907. See books by E. Cook (1913), D. E. Muir (1946), C. Woodham-Smith (1950) and Z. Pope (1958), and *Selected Writings*, ed. L. R. Seymer (1954).

NIJINSKY, Vaslav, *ni-zhin'ski* (1890–1950), Russian dancer, born in Kiev, was trained at the Imperial School, St Petersburg, and first appeared in ballet at the Maryinski Theatre. As the leading dancer in a company taken to Paris in 1909 by Diaghilev, Nijinsky became enormously popular, and in 1911 he appeared as Petrouchka in the first performance of Stravinsky's ballet. His work as a choreographer, except for the controversial *L'Après-midi d'un faune*, was not successful. Nijinsky was interned in Hungary during the early part of World War I, rejoined Diaghilev for a world tour, but became insane in 1917 in Switzerland. See Life by R. Nijinsky.

NIKISCH, Arthur (1855–1922), Hungarian conductor, was conductor of the Boston Symphony Orchestra 1889–93, Gewandhaus Concerts, Leipzig, from 1895, and Berlin Philharmonic Orchestra. See Life by F. Pfohl (Hamburg 1925).

NILAND, D'Arcy, *nī'-* (? –), Australian writer, contributed over five hundred short stories to magazines and established himself as a leading Australian novelist with his natural and vivid descriptions of life in the 'outback' in *The Shiralee* (1955), which was filmed, *Call me when the Cross turns over* (1958), *Big Smoke* (1959), and *The Ballad of the Fat Bushranger* (1961).

NILSSON, Christine (1843–1921), Swedish operatic singer, born at Wexiö, Sweden, made her début at Paris in 1864, and became a leading prima donna in Europe and the United States. She retired in 1888. See Lives by H. Headland (Rock Island, Ill., 1943) and M. L. Löfgren (Stockholm 1944).

NIMITZ, Chester William, *nim'its* (1885–1966), American admiral, born at Fredericksburg, Texas, graduated from the U.S. Naval Academy in 1905, served mainly in submarines, and by 1938 had risen to the rank of rear-admiral. Chief of the bureau of navigation during 1939–41, in 1941–45 he commanded the U.S. Pacific Fleet and Pacific Ocean areas, contributing largely to the defeat of Japan. He was made a fleet admiral in 1944, and became chief of naval operations in 1945–47, signing the Japanese surrender documents for the U.S. Special assistant to the secretary of the Navy (1947–49), he led the U.N. mediation commission in the Kashmir dispute in 1949. He was created G.C.B. in 1945. See S. E. Morison's *History of U.S. Naval Operations in World War II* (1947–54).

NIMROD. See APPERLEY, C. J.

NINIAN, St, Lowland Scots, **Ringan** (*c.* 360–*c.* 432), the first known missionary in Scotland, was born on the shores of the Solway Firth. He made a pilgrimage to Rome, was consecrated bishop (394) by the pope, visited St Martin at Tours, and he founded the church of Whithorn (397). He laboured successfully for the evangelization of the Britons and Southern Picts. See his Life by St Ailred (1109–66), edited by Bishop Forbes (1874), and studies by A. B. Scott (1916) and W. D. Simpson (1940).

NIPKOW, Paul, *nip'kof* (1860–1940), German engineer, born at Lauenburg, one of the pioneers of television, became interested in the electrical transmission of visual images and invented in 1884 the Nipkow disc, a mechanical scanning device consisting of a revolving disc with a spiral pattern of apertures. In use until 1932, it was superseded by electronic scanning.

NITHARDT, M. See GRÜNEWALD, M.

NITHSDALE, William Maxwell, 5th Earl of (1676–1744), Scottish Jacobite, at seven succeeded his father, in 1699 married Lady Winifred Herbert (*c.* 1679–1749), youngest daughter of the Marquis of Powis, and lived at his Kirkcudbrightshire seat, Terregles. A Catholic in 1715 he joined the English Jacobites and was taken prisoner at Preston. He was tried for high treason in London, and sentenced to death; but on February 23, 1716—the night before the day fixed for his execution—he escaped from the Tower in woman's apparel, through the heroism of his countess. They settled at Rome, where the earl died. See W. Fraser's *Book of Carlaverock* (1873) and H. Taylor, *Lady Nithsdale* (1939).

NITZSCH, (1) **Gregor Wilhelm** (1790–1861), German philologist, son of (3), father of (4), brother of (2), fought as a volunteer at Leipzig and from 1827 devoted himself to defending the unity of the Homeric poems. See study by Lübker (Jena 1864).

(2) **Karl Immanuel** (1787–1868), German Lutheran theologian, son of (3), brother of (1), became professor at Bonn in 1822, and in 1847 at Berlin. He subordinated dogma to ethics, and was one of the leaders of the broad evangelical school. His chief books are *System der christlichen Lehre* (1829; Eng. trans. 1849), *Praktische Theologie* (1847–67), *Christliche Glaubensleh.* (1858), several volumes of sermons and essays. See studies by Beyschlag (2nd ed. 1882) and Hermens (1886).

(3) **Karl Ludwig** (1751–1831), German Protestant theologian, father of (1) and (2), in 1790 became professor at Wittenburg. See study by Hoppe (Halle 1832).

(4) **Karl Wilhelm** (1818–80), German historian, son of (1), a pupil of Niebuhr, he was professor at Kiel, Königsberg and Berlin. His writings embrace historical studies on Polybius (1842) and the Gracchi (1847), *Die römische Annalistik* (1873), *Deutsche Studien* (1879), German history to the peace of Augsburg (1883–85), and a history of the Roman republic (1884–85).

NIVELLE, Robert (1857–1924), French general, born at Tulle, was artillery colonel in August 1914, and made his name when in command of the army of Verdun by recapturing Douaumont and other forts (October–December 1916). He was commander-in-chief, December 1916 to May 1917, when his Aisne offensive failed and he was superseded by Pétain. See study by Hellot (1917).

NIXON, Richard Milhous (1913–), American politician, born in Yorba Linda, California, after five years in practice as a lawyer, he served in the U.S. Navy, prior to his election to the House of Representatives in 1946. He became a senator in 1950, and vice-president in 1952. His swift climb in political circles was a result of fearless outspokenness and brilliant political tactics, and he was particularly prominent as a member of the Committee on Un-American Activities, working on the Alger Hiss (q.v.) case. In May 1958 he and his wife were subjected to violent anti-American demonstrations in Peru and Venezuela, during a goodwill tour of Latin America, and in 1959 on a visit to Moscow he achieved notoriety by his outspoken exchanges with Mr Khruschev. As the Republican candidate, he lost the presidential election (1960) to Kennedy by a tiny margin. Standing for the governorship of California in 1962, he was again defeated. See his autobiography, *Six Crises* (1962). He won the presidential election in 1968 by a small margin, and was re-elected in 1972 by a large majority.

NKRUMAH, Kwame (1909–72), Ghanaian politician, was born at Ankroful and was educated at Achimota College, Lincoln University, Penn., and London School of Economics. He returned to Africa and in 1949 formed the nationalist Convention People's party with the slogan ' self-government now '. In 1950 he was imprisoned for his part in calling strikes and was elected to parliament while still in jail. A year later he was released, elected as first municipal member for Accra and became virtual prime minister with the title of Leader of Business in the Assembly. He was confirmed in power at the 1956 election and in 1957 became the first prime minister of the independent Commonwealth State of Ghana. In the earlier years of his government he aroused criticism for his ' dictatorial ' attitudes, though he was worshipped by West Africans as the ' Gandhi of Africa ' and a significant leader first of the movement against white domination and then of Pan-African feeling. Ghana became a republic in 1960. Nkrumah was the moving spirit behind the Charter of African States (1961), a form of association between Ghana, Guinea and Mali. He pursued a policy of nonalignment in the Cold War. Domestically, drastic economic reforms sparked off political opposition and several attempts on his life. Legal imprisonment of political opponents for five years and more without trial, and interference with the judiciary in the treason trial (1963), when he dismissed the chief justice, heralded the successful referendum for a one-party state in 1964 in which the secrecy of the ballot was called in question. In 1966 his regime was overthrown by military *coup* during his absence in China. He returned to Guinea where he was appointed head of state. Publications include *Towards Colonial Freedom* (1946), his Autobiography (1957), *Consciencism* (1964). See Life by Timothy (1955).

NOAILLES, *nō-ah'y'*, distinguished French family:

(1) **Adrien Maurice, 3rd Duke of** (1678–1766), son of (3), grandfather of (9), won his marshal's baton in Louis XV's wars. See his *Mémoires* (1839).

(2) **Anna-Elisabeth, Comtesse de** (1876–1933), poet and novelist, wrote many poems and novels and was acclaimed ' Princesse des lettres '. See books by J. Larnac (Paris 1931) and C. Fournet (Geneva 1950).

(3) **Anne Jules, 2nd Duke of** (1650–1708), father of (1), brother of (8), commanded against the Huguenots and in Spain and became marshal.

(4) **Antoine de** (1504–62), admiral and ambassador to England 1553–56.

(5) **Emanuel Henri Victurnien de** (1830–1909), diplomat, son of (10), brother of (7), was ambassador in Italy, Constantinople and Berlin, and wrote on Poland.

(6) **Emanuel Marie Louis de** (1743–1822), diplomat, brother of (11), grandfather of (10), was ambassador at Amsterdam, London and Vienna.

(7) **Jules, 7th Duke of** (1826–95), economist and writer, son of (10), brother of (5).

(8) **Louis Antoine de** (1651–1729), ecclesiastic, brother of (3), Archbishop of Paris (1695), he became cardinal in 1700 and was a reformer of clerical practice. See book by E. de Barthelemy (Paris 1886).

(9) **Louis Marie de** (1756–1804), soldier, grandson of (1), served in America under Lafayette, supported the French Revolution for a time, then returned to America and defended San Domingo against the English.

(10) **Paul, 6th duke of** (1802–85), historian, grandson of (6), grandnephew of (11), was a member of the Academy (1849) and ambassador to St Petersburg (1871).

(11) **Paul François, 5th duke of** (1739–1824), chemist, brother of (6), granduncle of (10), was a soldier who later attained eminence as a chemist.

NOBEL, Alfred (1833–96), Swedish inventor and manufacturer, was born at Stockholm, October 21. His father, a manufacturer, settled 1837–59 in St Petersburg, and in 1860 began to manufacture nitro-glycerine. In 1867 Alfred, who assisted him, discovered, by accident, how to make a safe and manageable explosive—dynamite. He also invented blasting-jelly and several kinds of smokeless powder. Ultimately he had manufactories at Brefors in Sweden, and experimented on mild steel for armour-plates, &c. He left a fortune of over £2,000,000, most of which he destined to go for annual prizes in the fields of physics, chemistry, physiology or medicine, literature and peace. See Lives by Pauli (1947), Halasz (1960) and Bergengren (1962).

NOBILE, Umberto, *nō'bee-lay* (1885–), Italian airman, born at Lauro, became an aeronautical engineer and built the airships *Norge* and *Italia*. Wrecked in the airship *Italia* when returning from the North Pole (May 1928), he was adjudged (1929) responsible for the disaster. In the U.S.A. 1939–42, he later returned to Italy and was re-instated. See AMUNDSEN.

NOBILI, Leopoldo (1784–1835), Italian physicist, professor of Physics at Florence, invented the thermopile used in measuring radiant heat, and the astatic galvanometer.

NOCARD, Edmond Isidore Étienne (1850–1903), French biologist, made important discoveries in the field of veterinary science, and demonstrated that meat and milk from tubercular cattle could transmit the disease to man.

NODDACK, Ida Eva (1896–), **and Walter Karl Friedrich** (1893–1960), German chemists, husband and wife, in 1925 discovered the elements *masurium* and *rhenium*.

NODIER, Charles, *nod-yay* (1780–1844), French writer, deeply influenced the Romanticists of 1830, but only his short stories and fairy tales are remembered. See studies by Wey (1844), Magnin (1911), and Henri-Rosier (1931).

NOEL-BAKER, Philip (1889–), British Labour politician, after a brilliant athletic and academic career at Cambridge, captained the British Olympic team (1912), and in the war commanded a Friends' ambulance unit. He served on the secretariat of the peace conference (1919) and of the League of Nations (1919–22), was M.P. for Coventry (1929–31) and for Derby from 1936. He was Cassel professor of International Relations at London (1924–29) and Dodge Lecturer at Yale (1934), where he was awarded the Howland prize. He has written a number of books on international problems, including *Disarmament* (1926), and a standard work, *The Arms Race* (1958). During and after World War II he held several junior ministerial posts and was Labour secretary of state for Air (1946–47), of commonwealth relations (1947–50) and minister of fuel and power (1950–51). He was awarded the Nobel peace prize in 1959. His son, **Francis** (1920–), was a Labour M.P. 1945–50 and from 1955.

NOGUCHI, Hideyo (1876–1928), Japanese bacteriologist, born in Japan, worked in the U.S. from 1899, and made important discoveries in the cause and treatment of syphilis and also of yellow fever from which he died. See Life by G. Eckstein (1931).

NOLDE, Emil, pseud. of **Emil Hansen** (1867–1956), German artist, born at Nolde, was one of the most important Expressionist painters, his powerful style being summed up by the phrase 'blood and soil'. He was a member of Die Brücke (1906–07) and produced a large number of etchings, lithographs and woodcuts. See his *My Own Life* (2 vols. 1931–34).

NOLLEKENS, Joseph, R.A. (1737–1823), English sculptor, born in London, executed likenesses of most of his famous contemporaries—Garrick, Sterne, Goldsmith, Johnson, Fox, Pitt, George III, &c. See J. T. Smith's *Nollekens and his Times* (1828, new ed. 1949) and P. Colson, *Their Ruling Passions* (1950).

NOLLET, Jean Antoine, *nol-ay* (1700–70), French abbé and physicist, discovered osmosis (1748), invented an electroscope, and improved the Leyden jar.

NONIUS MARCELLUS (4th cent. A.D.), Latin grammarian, was the author of a poor treatise, *De Compendiosa Doctrina*, precious as preserving many words in forgotten senses, and passages from ancient Latin authors now lost. See ed. by W. M. Ramey (1903).

NONNUS (5th cent. A.D.), Greek poet of Panopolis (Egypt), wrote a long Bacchus epic (*Dionysiaca*, trans. Rouse, 1940) and a verse paraphrase of St John's Gospel. See study by J. Golega (1930).

NORDAU, Max Simon (1849–1923), Jewish-Hungarian author, born of Jewish descent at Budapest, he studied medicine and established himself as physician, first at his birthplace (1878), and then at Paris (1886). He wrote several books of travel, but became known as the author of works on moral and social questions, including *Conventional Lies of Society* (1883; 15th ed. 1890; Eng. trans. 1895), and as a novelist. He was also an active Zionist leader in Europe. See books by A. and M. Nordau (N.Y. 1943) and M. Ben-Horin (N.Y. 1957).

NORDEN, John (1548–1625?), English cartographer, born in Somerset, became an attorney, but about 1580 began to make surveys of the English counties. He published descriptions of several counties and maps which were the first printed English maps to show roads and a scale. Several of his maps were used for Camden's *Britannia*. He made surveys of Crown lands, and other works include a travel guide (1625).

NORDENSKJÖLD, (1) Baron Nils Adolf Erik, *nor'dėn-shœl* (1832–1901), Swedish Arctic navigator, was born at Helsingfors, November 18, 1832, naturalized himself in Sweden, and made several expeditions to Spitsbergen, mapping the south of the island. After two preliminary trips proving the navigability of the Kara Sea, he accomplished (June 1878–September 1879) the navigation of the North-east Passage, from the Atlantic to the Pacific along the north coast of Asia. He later made two expeditions to Greenland. See his *Voyage of the Vega* (Eng. trans. 1881), *Scientific Results of the Vega Expedition* (1883), &c.; and works by A. Leslie (1879) and S. Hedin (1928).

(2) **Nils Otto Gustav** (1869–1928), Swedish Antarctic explorer, nephew of (1), after travels in S. America led an expedition to the Antarctic (1901–03) and explored the Andes (1920–21). See Life by H. Munthe (Stockholm 1928).

NORFOLK, Dukes of. See HOWARD.

NORMAN, Montagu, 1st Baron (1871–1950), English banker, after serving in the South African war entered banking and became associated with the Bank of England. He was elected governor of the Bank in 1920 and held this post until 1944. During this time he wielded great influence on national and international monetary affairs. See Lives by Clay (1957) and Boyle (1967).

NORRIS, (1) Frank (1870–1902), American novelist, born in Chicago, first studied art but later turned to journalism, and while a reporter was involved in the Jameson raid in South Africa. He was influenced by Zola and was one of the first American naturalist writers, his major novel being *McTeague* (1899). See Life by F. Walker (1932) and study by E. Marchand (1942).

(2) **Kathleen** (1880–1966), American novelist, born in San Francisco, began writing stories and published her first novel, *Mother*, in 1911. After that she wrote many popular novels and short stories, including *Certain People of Importance* (1922) and *Over at the Crowleys* (1946).

NORTH, (1) Brownlow (1810–75), English evangelist, after living a life of pleasure for many years, became an evangelist preaching mainly in Scotland. See Life by K. Moody-Stuart (1929).

(2) **Sir Dudley** (1641–91), economist, brother of (5), (7), (9), a Turkey merchant, lived for a time in Constantinople, became a sheriff of London and a commissioner of customs. He was a keen-eyed observer, and had great mechanical genius, and his *Discourses upon Trade* (1691) anticipated Adam Smith. See Life by R. North (1744).

(3) **Sir Dudley Burton Napier** (1881–1961), British admiral, entered the navy in 1895 and was commander of the cruiser *New Zealand* at Heligoland and Jutland. He was chief of

staff of the home fleet from 1932 to 1933 and commanded the North Atlantic station in 1939–40. He was relieved of his command after six Vichy French warships had been allowed to pass through the Gibraltar Straits to oppose the Dakar landing. In 1957 the prime minister, while exonerating him from charges of negligence, refused to open an inquiry into his case.

(4) **Sir Edward, 1st Baron** (1496–1564), lawyer, father of (10), a privy councillor, held important posts during the reigns of Henry VIII, Edward VI, Mary and Elizabeth. See work by Lady F. Bushby (1911).

(5) **Francis, 1st Baron Guilford** (1637–85), lawyer, brother of (2), (7), (9), educated at Cambridge and called to the bar in 1655, was successively solicitor-general, attorney-general, lord chief-justice of the court of common pleas, privy councillor, lord chancellor (1682), and Baron Guilford (1683). See Life by R. North (1742).

(6) **Frederick, 8th Lord North and 2nd Earl of Guilford** (1732–92), statesman, entered parliament at the age of twenty-two, became a lord of the treasury, chancellor of the exchequer and in 1770 prime minister. He was largely responsible for the measures that brought about the loss of America, being too ready to surrender his judgment to the king's. In 1782 he resigned and later entered into a coalition with Fox, hitherto his opponent, and served with him under the Duke of Portland in 1783. See Lives by R. Lucas (1913), W. B. Pemberton (1938) and study by H. Butterfield (1949).

(7) **John** (1645–83), scholar, brother of (2), (5), (9), a fellow of Jesus College, Cambridge, succeeded Barrow as master of Trinity College in 1677, and became clerk of the closet to Charles II. See Life by R. North (1744).

(8) **Marianne** (1830–90), flower painter, a descendant of (9), painted flowers in many countries and gave her valuable collection to Kew Gardens. See her Autobiography (2 vols. 1892–93).

(9) **Roger** (1653–1734), lawyer and writer, brother of (2), (5), (7), was educated at Jesus College, Cambridge, entered the Middle Temple and rose to a lucrative practice at the bar. A Nonjuror, he retired after the Revolution. His three hypereulogistic biographies, his autobiography (all collected by Jessop in 1890) and his *Examen* (1740) give him a place in English literature.

(10) **Sir Thomas** (?1535–?1601), translator, son of (4), is known for his translation of Plutarch (1579), a noble monument of English from which Shakespeare drew his knowledge of ancient history (ed. by Wyndham 6 vols. 1895 *et seq.*). See work by F. Bushby (1911).

NORTHBROOK. See Baring (4).

NORTHCLIFFE, Lord. See Harmsworth (1).

NORTHCOTE, (1) James (1746–1831), English painter, the son of a Plymouth watchmaker, painted portraits and historical pictures, among them the well-known *Princes in the Tower* and *Prince Arthur and Hubert*, but is also remembered by Hazlitt's *Conversations with Northcote* (ed. by Gosse, 1894) and his own with Ward (1901). He was elected R.A. in 1787. See Life by Gwynn (1898).

(2) **Sir Stafford.** See Iddesleigh.

NORTHROP, John Howard (1891–), American biochemist, born at New York, educated at Columbia University, became professor of Bacteriology at California in 1949. He discovered the fermentation process for the manufacture of acetone, worked on enzymes and published *Crystalline Enzymes* (1939). In 1946 he shared the Nobel prize for chemistry with Stanley and Sumner for their study of ways of producing purified enzymes and virus products.

NORTHUMBERLAND, Dukes of. See Percy.

NORTON, (1) Andrews (1786–1853), American Unitarian theologian, father of (3), studied at Harvard, became professor there, and wrote *Reasons for not believing the Doctrines of Trinitarians* (1833), and two works on *The Genuineness of the Gospels.*

(2) **Caroline Elizabeth Sarah** (1808–77), Irish poet and novelist, was born in London, second of the three beautiful grand-daughters of Richard Brinsley Sheridan. In 1827 she married a barrister, the Hon. George Chapple Norton (1800–75). She bore him three sons, of whom the second succeeded as fourth Lord Grantley; but the marriage proved most unhappy, and her friendship with Lord Melbourne (q.v.) led her husband to institute a groundless and unsuccessful action of divorce (1836). She supported her family by her writings, and her experiences and publications helped to improve the legal status of women. In March 1877 she married Sir William Stirling Maxwell (q.v.), but died June 15. See Lives by J. G. Perkins (1909) and A. Acland (1948).

(3) **Charles Eliot** (1827–1908), American author, son of (1), joint editor with Lowell of the *North American Review*, was professor of Art at Harvard from 1875 and personal friend of Carlyle, Lowell, Emerson, Ruskin and Clough, whose letters he edited. See his *Letters* (N.Y. 1913), study by E. W. Emerson and W. F. Harris (N.Y. 1912), and Life by K. Vanderbilt (1960).

(4) **Thomas** (1532–84), English lawyer, M.P., and poet, with Sackville (q.v.) joint author of *Gorboduc*, was born in London.

NORWAY, N. S. See Shute (2).

NORWICH. See Cooper (2).

NOSTRADAMUS, or Michel de Notredame (1503–66), French astrologer, born at St Remi in Provence, December 14, 1503, became doctor of medicine in 1529, and practised at Agen, Lyons, &c. He set himself up as a prophet about 1547. His *Centuries* of predictions in rhymed quatrains (two collections, 1555–58), expressed generally in obscure and enigmatical terms, brought their author a great reputation. Charles IX on his accession appointed him physician-in-ordinary. See books on him by Jaubert (1656) and C. A. Ward (1891); *Complete prophecies*, ed. H. C. Roberts (1947).

NOTTINGHAM, Earls of. See Finch (2) and Howard Family (6).

NOVÁK, Viteslav (1870–1949), Czech composer, born at Kamenitz, studied then taught at Prague. His many compositions bear the impress of his native folk melody.

NOVALIS, the pen-name of **Friedrich von Hardenberg** (1772–1801), German Romantic poet, who was called the 'Prophet of Romanticism'. At Weissenfels (1795) he fell in love with a beautiful girl, whose early death left a lasting impression upon him. He died of consumption. He left two philosophical romances, both incomplete, *Heinrich von Ofterdingen* and *Lehrlinge zu Sais*. His *Hymnen an die Nacht* and his *Poems* and *Sacred Songs* are completed works. See Carlyle's *Miscellaneous Essays* (vol. ii), the Life published at Gotha (2nd ed. 1883), and the correspondence with the Schlegels (1880).

NOVATIAN (fl. 3rd cent. A.D.), a Roman Stoic, was converted to Christianity and ordained a priest. In A.D. 251, soon after the Decian persecution, a controversy arose about those who fell away during persecution. Pope Cornelius (251–53) defended indulgence towards the lapsed; Novatian was chosen by a small party and ordained bishop in opposition to Cornelius. The Novatians denied the lawfulness of readmitting the lapsed to communion. The sect, in spite of persecution, survived into the 6th century.

NOVELLO, (1) **Ivor**, in full **Ivor Novello Davies** (1893–1951), Welsh actor, composer, songwriter and dramatist, son of the singer Dame Clara Novello Davies, was born in Cardiff and educated at Magdalen College School, Oxford, where he was a chorister. His song 'Keep the Home Fires Burning' was one of the most successful of World War I. He first appeared on the regular stage in London in 1921. He enjoyed great popularity, his most successful and characteristic works being his 'Ruritanian' musical plays such as *Glamorous Night* (1935), *The Dancing Years* (1939), *King's Rhapsody* (1949). See Life by P. Noble (1951).

(2) **Vincent** (1781–1861), English organist, composer and music publisher, born in London of an Italian father and English mother, was a founder of the Philharmonic (1813), and its pianist and conductor. His compositions improved church music, and he was a painstaking editor of unpublished works. His son, **Joseph Vincent** (1810–96), also organist and music publisher, from 1857 lived at Nice and at Genoa with his sister, Mrs Cowden Clarke (q.v.). Another sister, **Clara Anastasia** (1818–1908), vocalist, born in London, won triumphs all over Europe; in 1843 married Count Gigliucci; but returned to the stage 1850–60.

NOYES, (1) **Alfred** (1880–1958), English poet, born in Staffordshire, began writing verse as an undergraduate at Oxford, and on the strength of getting a volume published in his final year he left without taking a degree. This book, *The Loom of Years* (1902), which gained a word of praise from George Meredith, was followed by *The Flower of Old Japan* (1903) and *The Forest of Wild Thyme* (1905), both of which attracted some notice. Noyes now turned to the subject of some of his most successful work—the sea, and in particular the Elizabethan tradition. *Forty Singing Seamen* (1908) and the epic *Drake* (1908) were in this vein. Having married an American, he travelled in the U.S.A. lecturing and receiving many academic honours, culminating in the visiting professorship of Poetry at Princeton (1914). In 1922 appeared *The Torchbearers*, a panegyric in blank verse on the hitherto comparatively unsung men of science. Noyes' verse shows great craftsmanship, and has rhythm, melody and lyric quality; he has however been criticized for conservatism and unwillingness to experiment. That he had no affection whatsoever for modern trends is apparent in his *Some Aspects of Modern Poetry* (1924), which is a defence of traditionalism. He also wrote essays, plays, and studies of William Morris and Voltaire. The latter, published shortly after his conversion to Roman Catholicism, involved him in a mild controversy with the clergy. See his autobiographical *Two Worlds for Memory* (1953).

(2) **John Humphrey** (1811–86), American Perfectionist, born at Brattleboro, Vermont, as a theological student thought that the prevailing theology was wrong. He founded a 'Perfectionist' church at Putney, Vermont, and he and his converts put their property into a common stock. In 1848 the communists removed to Oneida, N.Y. See his several works, Hepworth Dixon's *New America*, &c.; Nordhoff, *Communistic Societies of the United States* (1875).

NUFFIELD, William Richard Morris, 1st Viscount (1877–1963), British motor magnate and philanthropist, started in the cycle business and by 1910 was manufacturing prototypes of Morris Oxford cars. He was the first British manufacturer to develop the mass production of cheap cars. He received a baronetcy in 1929 and was raised to the peerage in 1934. He used part of his vast fortune to benefit hospitals, charities and Oxford University. In 1943 he established the Nuffield Foundation for medical, scientific and social research.

NUNCOMAR. See HASTINGS (4).

NÚÑEZ DE ARCE, Gaspar, *noo'nyeth THay ar'thay* (1834–1903), Spanish poet, dramatist and statesman, born at Valladolid, held office in the government in 1883 and 1888, and in 1894 received a national ovation at Toledo. As a lyric poet he may be styled the 'Spanish Tennyson', and among his poems are *Gritos del Combate* (1875), *Última Lamentación de Lord Byron* (1879), *El Vértigo* (1879), *La Pesca* (1884) and *La Maruja* (1886). His plays include *La Cuenta del Zapatero* (1859) and *El Haz de Leña* (1872).

NUR ED-DIN MAHMÛD, Malek al-Adel (1117–73), born at Damascus, succeeded his father as ruler of Northern Syria in 1145, and from this time his life was one long duel with the Christians. Count Joscelin's great defeat at Edessa gave occasion to the second Crusade; and the Crusaders were foiled by Nur ed-Din before Damascus. The emir next conquered Tripolis, Antioch and Damascus (1153). His nephew, Saladin, completed the conquest of Egypt from the Fatimites. Nur ed-Din, created by the khalif of Baghdad sultan of Syria and Egypt, became jealous of Saladin, and was preparing to march into Egypt when he died.

NUREYEV, Rudolf (1939–), Russian ballet-dancer, born in Siberia, obtained political asylum in Paris in 1961 and became a member of Le Grand Ballet du Marquis de Cuevas. Since then he has played many different rôles in various countries of the world, often appearing with Margot Fonteyn (q.v.), with whom he made his Covent Garden début in 1962. Films in which he has appeared include *Swan Lake* (1966). See his Autobiography (1962).

NURI ES-SA'ID. See Es-Sa'id.

NYERERE, Julius Kambarage, *nī-reer'-ee* (1922?–), Tanzanian politician, born at Butiama village, Lake Victoria, qualified as teacher at Makerere College and, after a spell of teaching, took a degree in history and economics at Edinburgh. On his return, he reorganized the nationalists into the Tanganyika African National Union (1954) of which he became president, entered the Legislative Council (1958) and in 1960 became chief minister. In 1961, Tanganyika was granted internal self-government and Nyerere became premier. During 1962 he retired for a while to reorganize his party, but was elected president in December when Tanganyika became a republic. In 1964 he negotiated the union of Tanganyika and Zanzibar (which became Tanzania in October of the same year).

O

OAKSEY. See Lawrence, Geoffrey.

OASTLER, Richard (1789–1861), English reformer, advocate of a ten-hours' working day and the factory laws, by his opposition to the Poor Law irritated his employer, Thomas Thornhill, who dismissed him from his stewardship of Fixby estate, near Huddersfield, and had him jailed (1840–44) for a debt of £2000, ultimately paid by subscription. See Life by C. Driver (1947).

OATES, (1) Lawrence Edward Grace (1880–1912), English explorer, was born in Putney in 1880, and educated at Eton, which he left to serve in the South African War with the Inniskilling Dragoons. In 1910 he set out with Scott's Antarctic Expedition, and was one of the party of five to reach the South Pole (January 17, 1912). On the return journey the explorers suffered dangerous delay and became weatherbound. Lamed by severe frostbite, Oates, convinced that his crippled condition would fatally handicap his companions' prospect of winning through, walked out into the blizzard, deliberately sacrificing his life to enhance his comrades' chances of survival. See L. C. Bernacchi, *A Very Gallant Gentleman* (1933).

(2) **Titus** (1649–1705), English conspirator and perjurer, born at Oakham, the son of an Anabaptist preacher, attended Cambridge University. Next taking orders, he held curacies and a naval chaplaincy, from all of which he was expelled for infamous practices. With the Rev. Dr Tonge he resolved to concoct the 'narrative of a horrid plot', and, feigning conversion to Catholicism, was admitted to the Jesuit seminaries of Valladolid and St Omer. From both in a few months he was expelled for misconduct, but, returning to London in June 1678, he forthwith communicated to the authorities his pretended plot, the main features of which were a rising of the Catholics, a general massacre of Protestants, the burning of London, and the assassination of the king, his brother James being placed on the throne. He swore to the truth of it before a magistrate, Sir Edmund Berry Godfrey, who on October 17 was found dead in a ditch—murdered possibly by Titus and his confederates. All London straightway went wild with fear and rage, and Oates became the hero of the day. Many other wretches came forward to back or emulate his charges; the queen herself was assailed; and many Catholics were cast into prison. He was directly or indirectly the cause of thirty-five judicial murders; but after two years a reaction set in. In May 1683 Oates was fined £100,000 for calling the Duke of York a traitor, and being unable to pay, was imprisoned; in May 1685 he was found guilty of perjury, and sentenced to be stripped of his canonicals, pilloried, flogged and imprisoned for life. The Revolution of 1688 set him at liberty, and he was even granted a pension. See Seccombe's *Lives of Twelve Bad Men* (1894), and Pollock's *The Popish Plot* (new ed. 1944).

OBEL, Matthias de l'. See L'Obel.

OBERLIN, Johann Friedrich, *ō'bėr-leen* (1740–1826), Alsatian clergyman, was born at Strasburg, and in 1767 became Protestant pastor of Waldbach, in the Ban de la Roche, which had suffered in the Thirty Years' War. Oberlin introduced better methods of cultivation and manufacture, made roads and bridges, founded a library and schools. See Lives by Bodemann (1868) and Butler (1882), and study by Scheuermann (1941).

O'BRIEN, (1) William (1852–1928), Irish journalist and Nationalist, born at Mallow, became a journalist, founded *United Ireland*, sat in parliament as a Nationalist (1883–95), was nine times prosecuted and imprisoned for two years. He retired in 1895 owing to dissensions in the party, headed the Independent Nationalists, but returned to parliament (1900–18) for Cork, and founded the (anti-Redmondite) United Irish League. He wrote *Recollections* (1905), *Evening Memories* (1920), *An Olive Branch* (on 'All-for-Ireland', 1910), *The Irish Revolution* (1923), &c.

(2) **William Smith** (1803–64), Irish insur-

gent, son of Sir Edward O'Brien, born in County Clare, entered parliament in 1826, and though a Protestant, supported the Catholic claims as a Whig. In October 1843 he joined O'Connell's Repeal Association. But O'Connell's aversion to physical force made a wide gulf between him and the fiery 'Young Ireland' party. After many disputes O'Brien in 1846 withdrew from the Association, and the Young Irelanders set up a Repeal League under his leadership. The sentence of John Mitchel for 'treason-felony' in 1848 hastened the projected rising, which ended ludicrously in an almost bloodless battle in a cabbage-garden at Ballingarry. Smith O'Brien was arrested, tried and sentenced to death; but the sentence was commuted to transportation for life. In 1854 he was released on condition of not returning to Ireland, and in 1856 he received a free pardon. He died at Bangor (N. Wales).

O'BRYAN, William (1778–1868), English Nonconformist, son of a Cornish yeoman, quarrelled with the Methodists and founded a new Methodist communion, the (Arminian) Bible Christians or Bryanites.

O'CASEY, Sean (1884–1964), Irish playwright, born in a poor part of Dublin, picked up what education he could and worked as a labourer and for nationalist organizations before beginning his career as a dramatist. His early plays, dealing with low life in Dublin—*Shadow of a Gunman* (1923) and *Juno and the Paycock* (1924)—were written for the Abbey Theatre. Later he became more experimental and impressionistic. Other works include *The Silver Tassie* (1929), *Cockadoodle Dandy* (1949) and *The Bishop's Bonfire* (1955). He also wrote essays, such as *The Flying Wasp* (1936). He was awarded the Hawthornden Prize in 1926. See his autobiography, begun in 1939 with *I Knock at the Door* and continuing through several volumes to *Sunset and Evening Star* (1954). See study by Krause (1960).

OCCAM, William. See OCKHAM.

OCCLEVE, Thomas. See HOCCLEVE.

OCHINO, Bernardino, *ō-kee'nō* (1487–1564), Italian Protestant reformer, born at Siena, joined the Franciscans, but in 1534 changed to the Capuchins. In four years' time he was vicar-general of the order. In 1542 he was summoned to Rome to answer for evangelical tendencies, but fled to Calvin at Geneva. In 1545 he became preacher to the Italians in Augsburg. Cranmer invited him to England, where he was pastor to the Italian exiles and a prebend in Canterbury. At Mary's accession (1553) he fled to Switzerland, and ministered to the Italian exiles in Zürich for ten years. The publication of *Thirty Dialogues*, one of which the Calvinists said contained a defence of polygamy, led to his being banished. Ochino fled to Poland, but was not permitted to stay there and died at Slavkow in Moravia. See Lives by Benrath (Eng. trans. 1876) and Bainton (1940).

OCHOA, Severo (1905–), American biochemist, born in Spain, studied medicine in Madrid and emigrated to the U.S.A. in 1940, joining the staff of the New York College of Medicine two years later. He was awarded, with Kornberg, the 1959 Nobel prize for medicine for work on the biological synthesis of nucleic acids.

OCHTERLONY, Sir David, *-lō'-* (1758–1825), British general, born of Scottish descent at Boston, Mass., went to India as a cadet, and was made lieutenant-colonel in 1803. His greatest services were rendered against the Gurkhas of Nepal in 1814 and 1815, with whom a treaty was made in 1816. The same year Ochterlony was made a baronet. He also held a command in the Pindari and Mahratta wars of 1817 and 1818.

OCKHAM, or **Occam, William of** (*c.* 1300–*c.* 1349), English Nominalist philosopher, was born at Ockham, Surrey. He entered the Franciscan order, studied at Oxford and Paris, and headed the Franciscans' revolt against Pope John XXII's denunciation of Evangelical poverty (1322). After four months' imprisonment at Avignon he fled to Munich, and found there a defender in the Emperor Louis of Bavaria, whom he in his turn defended stoutly against the temporal pretensions of the pope. In 1342 he seems to have become general of the Franciscans. Besides insisting on the independent divine right of temporal rulers, Ockham won fame as the reviver of Nominalism (the doctrine that universal ideas are merely names), for which he won a final victory over the rival Realism. To some of the arguments of theologians he applied the dictum that beings ought not to be multiplied except out of necessity—known as 'Occam's razor'. His views on civil government are expounded in *Super Potestate Papali* and his *Dialogues*, his philosophical views in *Summa Logices* (1488), commentaries on Porphyry and Aristotle, and the commentary on the *Sentences* of Peter the Lombard, and his theological in this last and the *Tractatus de Sacramento Altaris* (1516).

OCKLEY, Simon (1678–1720), English orientalist, in 1711 became Arabic professor at Oxford. His *History of the Saracens* (1708–1718) was long a standard, though not based on the best authorities.

O'CONNELL, Daniel (1775–1847), Irish political leader, called 'the Liberator', was born near Cahirciveen, Co. Kerry, August 6. Called to the Irish bar in 1798 he built up a highly successful practice. Leader of the agitation for the rights of Catholics, he formed in 1823 the Catholic Association, which successfully fought elections against the landlords. Elected M.P. for Clare in 1828, he was prevented as a Catholic from taking his seat, but was re-elected in 1830, the Catholic Emancipation Bill having been passed in the meantime. He formed a new society for Repeal of the union, revived as often as suppressed by others under new names. He denounced the ministry of Wellington and Peel, but in the face of a threatened prosecution (1831) he temporized, saved himself, and was made King's Counsel. In 1830 the potato crop had been very poor, and under O'Connell's advice the people declined to pay tithes, and that winter disorder was rampant everywhere. He had sat last for Kerry, when at the general election of 1832 he was returned for Dublin. At this time he nominated about half of the candidates returned, while three of his sons and two of his sons-in-law composed his 'household brigade'. Of the 105 Irish members 45—his famous 'tail'—were declared Repealers. He fought fiercely against the Coercion Act of 1833. By Feargus O'Connor, the *Freeman's Journal*, and his more ardent followers he was forced to bring the Repeal movement prematurely into parliament; a motion for inquiry was defeated by 523 to 38. For the next five years (1835–40) he gave the Whigs a steady support. Mulgrave and Drummond governed Ireland so mildly that O'Connell was prepared to abandon the Repeal agitation. In 1836 he was unseated on petition for Dublin, and he was returned for Kilkenny. In 1837 the mastership of the rolls was offered to him but declined. In August he founded his 'Precursor Society', and in April 1840 his famous Repeal Association. Yet the agitation languished till the appearance of the *Nation* in 1842 brought him the aid of Dillon, Duffy, Davis, Mangan and Daunt. In 1841 O'Connell lost his seat at Dublin, but found another at Cork, and in November he was elected lord mayor of Dublin. In 1843 he brought up Repeal in the Dublin corporation, and carried it by 41 to 15. The agitation now leaped into prominence, but the Young Ireland party began to grow impatient of the old chief's tactics, and O'Connell allowed himself to outrun his better judgment. Wellington poured 35,000 men into Ireland. A great meeting was fixed at Clontarf for Sunday, October 8, 1843, but it was proclaimed the day before, and O'Connell issued a counter-proclamation abandoning the meeting. Early in 1844, with his son and five of his chief supporters, he was imprisoned and fined for a conspiracy to raise sedition. The House of Lords set aside the verdict on September 4; but for fourteen weeks the Tribune lay in prison. He opposed Peel's provincial 'godless colleges', and it soon came to an open split between him and Young Ireland (1846). Next followed the potato famine. A broken man, he left Ireland for the last time in January 1847, and died at Genoa. Of O'Connell's writings the most characteristic is the *Letter to the Earl of Shrewsbury* (1842). His *Memoir of Ireland* (1843) is poor and inaccurate. There are Lives by his son John (1846), MacDonagh (1903), Gwynn (1929), O'Faolain (1938) and Tierney (1949); also *Correspondence*, ed. Fitzpatrick (1888).

O'CONNOR, (1) **Feargus Edward** (1794–1855), Irish Chartist, studied at Trinity College, Dublin, was called to the Irish bar, and entered parliament for Cork Co. in 1832. Estranged from O'Connell, he devoted himself to the cause of the working classes in England. His eloquence and enthusiasm gave him vast popularity, and his Leeds *Northern Star* (1837) did much to advance Chartism. Elected for Nottingham 1847, he presented the monster petition in April 1848. In 1852 he became hopelessly insane.

(2) **Frank,** pseud. of **Michael O'Donovan** (1903–66), Irish writer, born at Cork. Although he wrote plays and some excellent literary criticism—*Art of the Theatre* (1947), *The Modern Novel* (1956), *The Mirror in the Roadway* (1957)—his best medium was almost exclusively the short story. Yeats said of him that he was 'doing for Ireland what Chehov did for Russia'. Representative titles are: *Guests of the Nation* (1931), *Bones of Contention* (1936), *Crab Apple Jelly* (1944), *Travellers' Samples* (1956), and collections of short stories (1946, 1953, 1954 and 1956). He also wrote a memoir, *An Only Child* (1961), and critical studies, *The Lonely Voice* (1963) and *Shakespeare's Progress* (1960). See his autobiography (1968).

(3) **Thomas Power** (1848–1929), P.C. (1924), born at Athlone, was educated at Queen's College, Galway, became a journalist. Elected M.P. for Galway in 1880, he sat for Liverpool 1885, and was a conspicuous Irish Nationalist. He wrote *Memoirs of an Old Parliamentarian* (1928), &c. See Life by Hamilton Fyfe (1934).

OCTAVIA (d. 11 B.C.), sister of the Emperor Augustus, distinguished for beauty and womanly virtues. On the death of her first husband, Marcellus, she consented in 40 B.C. to marry Antony, to reconcile him and her brother; but in a few years Antony forsook her for Cleopatra.

OCTAVIAN. See AUGUSTUS.

ODESCALCHI. See INNOCENT XI.

ODETS, Clifford, *o-dets'* (1906–63), American playwright and actor, born in Philadelphia, in 1931 joined the Group Theatre, New York, under whose auspices his early plays were produced. The most important American playwright of the 1930s, his works are marked by a strong social conscience and grow largely from the conditions of the Great Depression of that time. They include *Waiting for Lefty*, *Awake and Sing* and *Till the Day I Die*, all produced in 1935, and *Golden Boy* (1937). He was responsible for a number of film scenarios, including *The General Died at Dawn*, *None but the Lonely Heart* (which he directed), *Deadline at Dawn*, *The Big Knife*.

ODLING, William (1829–1921), British chemist, Waynflete professor of Chemistry at Oxford, F.R.S. (1859), classified the silicates and advanced suggestions with regard to atomic weights which made O=16 instead of 8.

ODO (*c.* 1036–97), Bishop of Bayeux and Earl of Kent, was half-brother to William the Conqueror (q.v.), and played under him a conspicuous part in English history. He rebuilt Bayeux cathedral and may have commissioned the Bayeux tapestry.

ODOACER, or **Odovacar,** *ō-dō-ay'sėr* (d. 493), barbarian warrior, son of a Germanic captain in the service of the Western Roman empire, took part in the revolution which (475) drove Julius Nepos from the throne and conferred on Orestes's son Romulus the title of Augustus, scoffingly turned to Augustulus. With the Herulians and other Germanic mercenaries he marched against Pavia, and stormed the city (476). Romulus abdicated, and thus perished the Roman empire. Odoacer was a politic ruler; but his increasing power excited the alarm of the Byzantine Emperor Zeno, who encouraged Theoderic, King of the Ostrogoths, to undertake an expedition against Italy (489). Odoacer, defeated in three great battles, shut himself up in Ravenna, which he defended for three years. Compelled by famine, he capitulated (493); a fortnight later he was assassinated by Theoderic himself. See Hodgkin's *Italy and her Invaders*.

O'DONNELL, (1) **Hugh Roe** (?1571–1602), Lord of Tyrconnel, fought against the English in Ireland, and fled to Spain in 1602, leaving his power to his brother, **Rory** (1575–1608), who kissed the king's hand, and was made Earl of Tyrconnel (1603); but having plotted to seize Dublin Castle (1607), fled, and died at Rome.

(2) **Leopold** (1809–67), marshal of Spain, born at Tenerife, was descended from an Irish family. He supported the infant Isabella against Don Carlos, and emigrated with the queen-mother to France. In 1843 his intrigues against Espartero were successful; and as governor-general of Cuba he amassed a fortune. He returned to Spain in 1846; was made war minister by Espartero in 1854, but in 1856 supplanted him by a *coup d'état*. He was in three months' time succeeded by Narváez, but in 1858 he returned to power; in 1859 he commanded in Morocco, took the Moorish camp, and was made Duke of Tetuan. In 1866 his cabinet was upset by Narváez.

O'DONOVAN, Michael. See O'CONNOR, FRANK.

OECOLAMPADIUS, Joannes, Latinized Greek for Hüssgen or **Hausschein** (1482–1531), was born at Weinsberg in Swabia. He studied at Heidelberg, became tutor to the sons of the Elector Palatine, and subsequently preacher at Basel, where Erasmus employed him. In 1516 he entered a convent at Augsburg, but under Luther's influence commenced reformer at Basel in 1522 as preacher and professor of Theology. On the Lord's Supper he gradually adopted the views of Zwingli, disputed with Luther at Marburg in 1529, and wrote treatises. See Lives by Herzog (1843) and Hagenbach (1859).

OEHLENSCHLÄGER, Adam Gottlob, *œ'lèn-shlay-gèr* (1779–1850), born in Copenhagen, was by 1805 foremost of Danish poets. *Hakon Jarl* was his first tragedy (1807; trans. by Lascelles, 1875); *Correggio* (trans. by Theod. Martin, 1854) dates from 1809. In 1810 he was made professor of Aesthetics in Copenhagen University. His fame rests principally on his twenty-four tragedies. See his Autobiography (1830–31) and Reminiscences (1850).

OERSTED, Hans Christian (1777–1851), Danish physicist, professor at the University of Copenhagen, discovered electromagnetism.

OETINGER, Christoph Friedrich, *œh'-ting-er* (1702–82), German theosophic theologian, leader of the Pietists and a disciple of Swedenborg.

O'FAOLAIN, Sean, *ō-fay'lèn* (1900–), Irish writer, born in Dublin, was educated at the National University of Ireland, and took his M.A. at Harvard. He lectured for a period (1929) at Boston College, then took a post as a teacher at Strawberry Hill, Middlesex. In 1933 he returned to Ireland to teach. His first writing was in the Gaelic, and he produced an edition of translations from the Gaelic—*The Silver Branch*—in 1938. Before this, however, he had attracted attention with a novel, *A Nest of Simple Folk* (1933). He never quite repeated its success with later novels, and thereafter wrote many biographies, including *Daniel O'Connell* (1938), *De Valera* (1939), and *The Great O'Neill* (1942), this last being a life of the 2nd Earl of Tyrone. He edited the autobiography of Wolfe Tone (1937). His *Stories of Sean O'Faolain* (1958) cover thirty years of writing and progress from the lilting 'Irishry' of his youth to the deeper and wider artistry of his maturity, showing him as a master of this most exacting literary form.

OFFA (d. 796), king of Mercia from 757, contended successfully against Wessex and the Welsh, and made Mercia the principal state in England. He was probably the most powerful English monarch before the tenth century, and is reputed to have founded the abbeys of Bath and StputAlbans.

OFFENBACH, Jacques (1819–80), German-Jewish composer of *opéra bouffe*, born at Cologne, came to Paris in 1833, becoming *chef d'orchestre* in the Théâtre-Français in 1848, and manager of the *Bouffes parisiens* in 1855. He composed a vast number of light, lively operettas, *Le Mariage aux lanternes*, &c., but is best known as inventor of modern *opéra bouffe*, represented by *Orphée aux enfers* (1858), *La Belle Hélène*, *La Barbe bleu*, *La Grande Duchesse*, *Geneviève de Brabant*, *Roi Carotte*, and *Madame Favart*. The well-known *Contes d'Hoffmann* was not produced till after his death. See the diary of his American tour, trans. MacClintock (1948) and study by Kracauer (Eng. trans. 1937).

O'FLAHERTY, Liam, *ō-flah'-* (1897–), Irish writer, born in the Aran Islands, Galway. He fought in the British army during World War I and on the Republican side in the Irish civil war. *The Informer* (1926) won the James Tait Black prize and was a popular success. Other books, reflecting the intensity of his feeling and style, include *Spring Sowing* (1926), *The Assassin* (1928), *The Puritan* (1932), *Famine* (1937) and*Land* (1946). See his autobiographical *Two Years* (1930) and *Shame the Devil* (1934).

OFTERDINGEN, Heinrich von (12th–13th cent.), one of the famous minnesinger or lyric poets of Germany, who flourished between the years 1170 and 1250.

OGDEN, Charles Kay (1889–1957), English linguistic reformer, educated at Rossall School, took a first class in classics at Cambridge, where he was first editor of the *Cambridge Magazine* (1912–22) and founder in 1917 of the Orthological Institute. In the 1920s he conceived the idea of Basic English, which he developed, with the help of **Ivor Armstrong Richards** (1893–), another eminent Cambridge scholar, into a practical, easily learnt language with a vocabulary of only 850 words.

OGIER LE DANOIS, a vassal noble of Charlemagne, whose revolt against the emperor is the theme of a *chanson de geste*, written by Raimbert of Paris before 1150.

OGILBY, John (1600–76), Edinburgh-born topographer, printer and map-maker, became a dancing teacher in London and a tutor in Strafford's household, lost all in the Civil War, but after the Restoration obtained court recognition and became a London publisher. The great fire of 1666 destroyed his stock but got him the job, with William Morgan, of surveying the gutted sites in the city. With the proceeds he established a thriving printing house and was appointed 'king's cosmographer and geographic printer'. His early productions include his own translations of Vergil and Homer (sneered at by Pope), but his most important publications were the maps and atlases engraved in the last decade of his life, including Africa (1670), America (1671) and Asia (1673); also a road atlas of Britain (1675) unfinished at his death. His map of London, completed by Morgan (1677), is also important.

OGLETHORPE, James Edward (1696–1785), English general, born in London, the son of Sir Theophilus Oglethorpe, served with Prince Eugene, and in 1722–54 sat in parliament. Meanwhile he projected a colony in America for debtors from English jails and persecuted Austrian Protestants. Parliament contributed £10,000; George II gave a grant of land, after him called Georgia; and in 1732 Oglethorpe went out with 120 persons and founded Savannah. In 1735 he took out 300 more, including the two Wesleys; and in 1738 he was back again with 600 men. War with Spain was declared in 1739; in 1740 Oglethorpe invaded Florida, and in 1742 repulsed a Spanish invasion of Georgia. In 1743 he left the colony to repel malicious charges. He was tried and acquitted after the '45 for failing as major-general to overtake Prince Charles's army. He died at Cranham Hall, Essex. See Lives by Harris (1841), Cooper (1904), Ettinger (1936).

O'HIGGINS, Bernardo (1778–1842), Chilean revolutionary, natural son of Ambrosio O'Higgins (*c.* 1720–1801), the Irish-born viceroy of Chile (1789) and of Peru (1795), was born at Chillán, played a great part in the Chilean revolt of 1810, and in 1817–23 was the new republic's first president.

OHM, Georg Simon (1787–1854), German physicist, became in 1849 professor at Munich. Ohm's Law was a result of his researches in electricity, and the measure of resistance is called the *ohm*.

OHNET, Georges, *ō-nay* (1848–1918), French novelist, was born in Paris. Under the general title of *Les Batailles de la vie*, he published a series of novels, some of which went beyond a hundredth edition.

OHTHERE (9th cent.), a Norse sailor, made two exploring voyages for King Alfred between 880 and 900—one round the North Cape to the White Sea.

OKEGHEM, Joannes, *o'keg-em* (1430–95), Flemish composer, born probably at Termonde, E. Flanders, in 1452 became a court musician to Charles VII of France, and was in 1459 treasurer of the abbey of St Martin at Tours. He was also *kapellmeister* to Louis XI. He played an important part in the stylistic development of church music in the 15th century and was renowned as a teacher; Josquin des Prés (q.v.) was among his pupils. See studies by de Marcy (Termonde 1895) and Brenet (Paris 1911).

O'KELLY, Sean Thomas (1882–1966), Irish statesman, born in Dublin, a pioneer in the Sinn Fein movement and the Gaelic league, fought in the Easter Rising (1916) and was imprisoned. Elected to the first Dail in 1918, he became Speaker (1919–21), minister for local government (1932–39) and for finance and education (1939–45). He was president of the Irish Republic in 1945–52, and again in 1952–59.

OKEN, Lorenz (1779–1851), German naturalist and nature philosopher, became professor of Medicine at Jena in 1807. In 1816 he issued a journal called *Iris*, which led to government interference and his resignation. In 1828 he obtained a professorship at Munich, and in 1832 at Zürich. His theory that the skull is a modified vertebra is exploded.

OLAF, the name of five kings of Norway, of whom the following are noteworthy:

Olaf I Tryggvessön (*c.* 965–1000), grandson of Harald Haarfagr, was an exile in his youth, but took part in Viking expeditions against Britain and came to the throne of Norway after overthrowing King Haakon in 995. Having turned Christian, he attempted the conversion of Norway with limited success. He was killed in a naval battle against the Danes and Swedes.

Olaf II Haraldssön, St (*c.* 995–1030), fought as a young man in England for Ethelred against the Danes, became a Christian and completed successfully the work of conversion which Olaf I had begun, but his reforms provoked internal dissension and he was defeated and killed by a rebel army at the battle of Stiklestad. He was later recognized as the patron saint of Norway.

Olav V (1903–), only child of Haakon VII (q.v.) and Maud, daughter of Edward VII born in England, educated in Norway and, at Balliol College, Oxford, succeeded his father to the Norwegian throne in 1957. An outstanding sportsman in his youth, Olav was appointed head of the Norwegian Armed Forces in 1944, and later that year escaped with his father to England on the Nazi occupation, returning in 1945. In 1929 he married Princess Martha (1901–54) of Sweden, and had two daughters and a son, **Harald** (1937–), heir to the throne.

OLAUS. See MAGNUS and PETRI (2).

OLBERS, Heinrich Wilhelm Matthäus (1758–1840), German physician and astronomer, practised medicine at Bremen. He calculated the orbit of the comet of 1779; discovered the minor planets Pallas (1802) and Vesta (1807); discovered five comets (all but one already observed at Paris); and invented a method for calculating the velocity of falling stars. See the Life prefixed to his works by Schilling (3 vols. 1894–97).

OLCOTT, Colonel Henry Steel (*c.* 1830–1907), American theosophist, was by 1856 distinguished in the United States as an agriculturist, fought in the Civil War, and held posts in the accounts department of the army and navy. After the war he devoted himself to theosophy.

OLDCASTLE, Sir John (*c.* 1378–1417),

Lollard leader and rebel, the 'good Lord Cobham', is first heard of as serving Henry IV on the Welsh marches. He acquired the title of Lord Cobham by marrying the heiress, and presented a remonstrance to the Commons on the corruptions of the church. He had Wycliffe's works transcribed and distributed, and paid preachers to propagate his views. In 1411 he commanded an English army in France, and forced the Duke of Orléans to raise the siege of Paris; but in 1413, after the accession of Henry V, he was examined, and condemned as a heretic. He escaped from the Tower into Wales; a Lollard conspiracy in his favour was stamped out; and after four years' hiding he was captured, brought to London, and was 'hanged and burnt hanging'. Halliwell-Phillipps first proved in 1841 that Shakespeare's Sir John Falstaff was based on a popular tradition of dislike for the heretic Oldcastle. Though he stood high in the favour of Prince Hal, there is no historical ground for representing him as his 'boon companion'.

OLDENBARNEVELDT. See BARNEVELDT.

OLDFIELD, Anne (1683–1730), English actress, was born in London, made her début in 1700, stood high in public favour by 1705, and played till the last year of her life. See Edward Robins, *The Palmy Days of Nance Oldfield* (1898).

OLDHAM, John (1653–83), English poet, born near Tetbury, graduated at Oxford. His Juvenalian satires against the Jesuits won the praise of Dryden.

OLDMIXON, John (1673–1742), English author of dull, partisan histories of England, Scotland, Ireland and America, and of works on logic and rhetoric. He is one of the heroes of Pope's *Dunciad*.

OLD MORTALITY. See PATERSON (3).

OLDYS, William, *olds* (1696–1761), English bibliographer, natural son of Dr Oldys, chancellor of Lincoln, for about ten years was librarian to the Earl of Oxford, whose valuable collections of books and MSS. he arranged and catalogued, and by the Duke of Norfolk he was appointed Norroy king-of-arms. His chief works are a *Life of Sir Walter Raleigh*, prefixed to Raleigh's *History of the World* (1736); *The British Librarian* (1737); *The Harleian Miscellany* (1753), besides many miscellaneous articles.

OLE-LUK-OIE. See SWINTON.

OLGA, St (d. 968), a Russian saint, wife of the Duke of Kiev, who governed during the minority of her son, till 955. Thereafter she was baptized at Constantinople, and returning to Russia, laboured for the new creed.

OLIPHANT, (1) Laurence (1829–88), English travel writer and mystic, was born at Capetown, son of the attorney-general there. His first work, *A Journey to Khatmandu* (1852), was followed by *The Russian Shores of the Black Sea* (1853). As secretary to the Earl of Elgin he travelled to China, thus finding material for further books. In 1861, while acting as *chargé d'affaires* in Japan, he was severely wounded by assassins. From 1865 to 1868 he sat for the Stirling burghs. His *Piccadilly* (1870) was a book of exceptional promise, bright with wit and delicate irony. He joined the religious community of T. L. Harris (q.v.) in America, and later settled at Haifa in Palestine. His mystical views he published in *Sympneumata* (1886) and *Scientific Religion* (1888). See Memoir by M. Oliphant (1891).

(2) **Marcus Laurence Elwin** (1901–), Australian nuclear physicist, born in Adelaide, studied there and at Trinity College and Cavendish Laboratory, Cambridge, where he did valuable work on the nuclear disintegration of lithium. Professor at Birmingham (1937), he designed and built a sixty-inch cyclotron, completed after World War II. He worked on the atomic bomb project at Los Alamos (1943–45), but at the end of hostilities strongly argued against the American monopoly of atomic secrets. In 1946 he became Australian representative of the U.N. Atomic Energy Commission, designed a proton-synchroton for the Australian government and in 1950 became research professor at Canberra. Elected F.R.S. in 1937, he was awarded the Hughes Medal (1943) and was made K.B.E. (1959).

(3) **Margaret,** *née* **Wilson** (1828–97), Scottish novelist, born at Wallyford near Musselburgh, in 1849 her *Passages in the Life of Mrs Margaret Maitland* instantly won approval. This was followed by a rapid succession of novels, including the *Chronicles of Carlingford* with which she made her name. Her contributions to general literature, mostly historical and biographical, were numerous. See her *Autobiography and Letters* (1899).

OLIVARES, Gaspar de Guzmán, Count of (1587–1645), Duke of San Lúcar, born at Rome where his father was ambassador, was the favourite of Philip IV of Spain, and his prime minister for twenty-two years. He wrung money from the country to carry on foreign wars. His attempts to rob the people of their privileges provoked insurrections and roused the Portuguese to shake off the Spanish yoke in 1640, and the king was obliged to dismiss him in 1643.

OLIVE, Princess, assumed title of **Mrs Olivia Serres,** *née* **Wilmot** (1772–1834), English impostor, was born at Warwick, the daughter of a house painter, Robert Wilmot, and married in 1791 John Thomas Serres (1759–1825), a marine painter, from whom she separated in 1804. In 1817 she claimed to be an illegitimate daughter of the Duke of Cumberland, brother of George III, then in 1821 had herself rechristened as Princess Olive, legitimate daughter of the Duke and his first wife, Olive. The same year, arrested for debt, she produced an alleged will of George III, leaving £15,000 to her as his brother's daughter, but in 1823 her claims were found to be baseless, and she died within the rules of the King's Bench. Her elder daughter, **Mrs Lavinia Ryves** (1797–1871), took up her mother's claim of legitimacy, which a jury finally repudiated in 1866.

OLIVER, Isaac (*c.* 1560–1617), miniature painter, probably of Huguenot origin, but usually regarded as English, was the pupil and later the rival of Nicholas Hilliard, and executed portraits of Sir Philip Sidney, Anne of Denmark, &c. His son and pupil,

Peter (1594–1648), continued his work, and was employed by Charles I to copy old master paintings in miniature. See G. Reynolds, *Nicholas Hilliard and Isaac Oliver* (1947).

OLIVIER, (1) Sir Laurence Kerr (1907–), English actor, producer and director, born in Dorking. His first professional appearance was as the Suliot officer in *Byron* in 1924, since when he has played all the great Shakespearean rôles, including a memorable Titus, while his versatility was underlined by his virtuoso display in *The Entertainer* (1957) as a broken-down low comedian. After war service he became in 1944 codirector of the Old Vic Company. He produced, directed and played in films of *Henry V*, *Hamlet* and, notably, *Richard III*. He was knighted in 1947. He was divorced from his first wife, Jill Esmond, in 1940 and in the same year married **Vivien Leigh** (1913–1967), English actress, who first appeared professionally in *The Green Sash*. Her beauty, charm and ability were exhibited in *The Doctor's Dilemma*, *The Skin of our Teeth*, and other plays, and in film rôles such as Scarlett O'Hara in *Gone With the Wind* and Blanche in *A Streetcar Named Desire*. See F. Barker, *The Oliviers* (1953). They were divorced in 1960, and Miss Leigh died of T.B. in 1967. In 1961 Olivier married **Joan Plowright** (b. 1929), the English stage actress. In 1962 he succeeded brilliantly as director of a new venture, the Chichester Theatre Festival and later the same year was appointed director of the National Theatre, where among many successes he directed and acted a controversial but outstanding *Othello* (1964).

(2) **Sidney, 1st Baron Olivier of Ramsden** (1859–1943), British colonial administrator and writer, was governor of Jamaica (1907–1913), secretary to the Board of Agriculture (1913–17) and in the Labour government of 1924 he was secretary for India, being raised to the peerage in the same year. A founder of the Fabian Society, of which he was secretary (1886–90), he contributed to *Fabian Essays* (1889) and wrote several authoritative books on colonial questions.

OLLIVIER, Olivier Émile, *ol-leev-yay* (1825–1913), French politician, born at Marseilles, established a reputation at the Parisian bar, and after 1864 acquired influence as a member of the Legislative Assembly. In 1865 the viceroy of Egypt appointed him to a judicial office. In January 1870 Napoleon III charged him to form a constitutional ministry. But 'with a light heart' he rushed his country into war with Germany. He was overthrown on August 9 and withdrew to Italy for a time. He was the author of numerous works, including *L'Empire libéral*, a defence of his policy (16 vols. 1894–1912). See study by T. Zeldih (1963).

OLMSTED, Frederick Law (1822–1903), American landscape architect and travel writer, born at Hartford, Conn., was co-designer of Central Park, New York, and of other famous parks, and planned the layout of the Chicago World's Fair of 1893.

OLNEY, Richard (1835–1917), American Democratic statesman, was born at Oxford, Mass. He was educated at Harvard, and called to the bar. In 1893 he became attorney-general under Cleveland, in June 1895 secretary of state, and within six months caused a crisis by his interference, in virtue of the Monroe Doctrine, in the boundary question between British Guiana and Venezuela. In 1897 he returned to the bar at Boston. In 1913 he declined the ambassadorship to London.

OLYMPIAS (d. 316 B.C.), wife of Philip of Macedon, and mother of Alexander the Great, was the daughter of the king of Epirus. When Philip left her and married Cleopatra, niece of Attalus, she instigated (337 B.C.) his assassination, and subsequently brought about the murder of Cleopatra. After Alexander's death she secured the death of his half-brother and successor. Cassander besieged her in Pydna, and on its surrender put her to death.

OLYMPIODORUS, name of several Greek authors: (1) (6th cent. A.D.), an Alexandrian Neoplatonist, left a *Life of Plato*, with commentaries on several of his dialogues; (2) (5th cent.), a Peripatetic, also at Alexandria; (3) (5th cent.), from Thebes in Egypt, wrote in Greek a history of the Western empire.

O'MAHONY, *ō-mah'nee*, **(1) Daniel** (d. 1714), Irish soldier, went to France in 1692, held commands under Villeroy and Vendôme, and did prodigies with his Irish dragoons at Almanza in the Spanish service.

(2) **John** (1816–77), Fenian head-centre (leader), was born at Kilbeheny, Co. Limerick, studied at Trinity College, Dublin, translated Keating's *History of Ireland*, joined in 1848 in Smith O'Brien's rebellion, and after Stephens played the most prominent part in organizing Fenianism.

OMAN, Sir Charles William Chadwick (1860–1946), English historian, born at Muzaffarpur in India, was educated at Winchester and New College, Oxford, and was made a fellow of All Souls in 1883, establishing his reputation with brilliant studies on Warwick the Kingmaker (1891), Byzantine history (1892), and the art of war in the Middle Ages (1898). The appearance in 1902 of the first part of his great 7-volume history of the Peninsular war, which took him 28 years to complete, gave an indication of the immense scholarship and meticulous research which became the hallmark of his many authoritative works on mediaeval and modern history. In 1905 he was elected Chichele professor of Modern History, and from 1919 to 1935 sat in parliament for the university. He was knighted in 1920 in recognition of his services to the Foreign Office during the war. See his *Things I have Seen* (1933) and *Memories of Victorian Oxford* (1941).

OMAR, or 'Umar (*c.* 581–64), the second khalif, was father of one of Mohammed's wives, and succeeded Abu-bekr in 634. By his generals he built up an empire comprising Persia, Syria and all North Africa. He was assassinated.

OMAR KHAYYĀM, or 'Umar Khayyám (*c.* 1050–*c.* 1123), the astronomer-poet of Persia, was born (a tent-maker's son) and died at Nishapur. Summoned to Merv by the sultan, he reformed the Moslem calendar.

Of his Arabic mathematical treatises, one on algebra was edited and translated by Woepke (1851); and it was as a mathematician that he was known to the western world, until in 1859 Edward FitzGerald published his 'translation' of seventy-five of his *Rubáiyát* or quatrains. Omar was the poet of Agnosticism, though some see nothing in his poetry save the wine-cup and roses, and others read into it that Sufi mysticism with which it was largely adulterated long after Omar's death. FitzGerald's translation is far finer than the original. The *Rubáiyát* is now regarded as an anthology of which little or nothing may be by Omar. There are editions of the *Rubáiyát* by Nicolas (464 quatrains, 1867), Sadik Ali (nearly 800 quatrains, 1878), Whinfield (1883), Dole (1896), Heron Allen (1912). Other translations are by Whinfield (1882), J. H. McCarthy (prose, 1889), J. Payne (1898), E. Heron Allen (prose, 1898), Pollen (1915). See Life by Shirazi (1905), works cited at FITZGERALD, and Potter's *Bibliography of the Rubáiyát of Omar Khayyám*.

OMAR PASHA, properly **Michael Latas** (1806–71), Ottoman general, was born at Plasky in Croatia, and served in the Austrian army. In 1828 he deserted, fled to Bosnia, and, embracing Mohammedanism, became writing-master to Abdul-Medjid, on whose accession to the Ottoman throne in 1839 Omar Pasha was made colonel, and in 1842 governor of Lebanon. In 1843–47 he suppressed insurrections in Albania, Bosnia and Kurdistan. On the invasion of the Danubian Principalities by the Russians in 1853 he defeated the Russians in two battles. In February 1855 he repulsed the Russians at Eupatoria in the Crimea. He was sent too late to relieve Kars. In 1861 he again pacified Bosnia and Herzegovina, and overran Montenegro in 1862.

O'MEARA, Barry Edward (1786–1836), Irish physician, served as surgeon in the army, but was dismissed in 1808 for his share in a duel. He was on the *Bellerophon* when Napoleon came on board, and accompanied him as private physician to St Helena, took part in his squabbles with Sir Hudson Lowe, and was compelled to resign in 1818. Asserting in a letter to the Admiralty that Sir Hudson Lowe had dark designs against his captive's life, he was dismissed from the service. His *Napoleon in Exile* (1822) made a great sensation.

OMNIUM, Jacob. See HIGGINS (1).

ONASSIS, Aristotle Socrates (1906–), millionaire ship-owner, born in Smyrna, now an Argentinian subject. At sixteen he left Smyrna for Greece as a refugee, and from there went to Buenos Aires where later he was Greek consul for a time. Since the purchase of his first ships (1932–33) he has built up one of the world's largest independent fleets, and is a pioneer in the construction of super-tankers. He married (1) Athina, daughter of Stavros Livanos, a Greek ship-owner, and (2) Jacqueline Kennedy, widow of John F. Kennedy (q.v.).

O'NEILL, (1) **Eugene Gladstone** (1888–1953), American playwright, born in New York, the son of the actor James O'Neill (1847–1920). After a fragmentary education and a year at Princeton, he took various clerical and journalistic jobs and signed on as a sailor on voyages to Australia, South Africa and elsewhere. Then he contracted tuberculosis and spent six months in a sanatorium where he felt the urge to write plays, the first being *The Web*. He joined the Provincetown Players in 1915, for whom *Beyond the Horizon* (1920; Pulitzer prize) was written. This was followed, during the next two years, by *Exorcism*, *Diff'rent*, *The Emperor Jones*, *Anna Christie* (1922; Pulitzer prize) and *The Hairy Ape*. *Desire Under the Elms*, his most mature play to date, appeared in 1924. He then began experimenting in new dramatic techniques. In *The Great God Brown* (1926) he used masks to emphasize the differing relationships between a man, his family and his soul. *Marco Millions* (1931) is a satire on tycoonery. *Strange Interlude* (1928; Pulitzer prize), a marathon nine-acter, lasting five hours, uses asides, soliloquies and 'streams of consciousness'. In the same year he wrote *Lazarus Laughed*, a humanistic affirmation of his belief in the conquest of death. *Mourning Becomes Electra* (1931) is a re-statement of the Orestean tragedy in terms of biological and psychological cause and effect. *Ah, Wilderness*, a nostalgic comedy, appeared in 1933 and *Days Without End* in 1934. Then, for twelve years he released no more plays but worked on *The Iceman Cometh* (New York 1946, London 1958) and *A Moon for the Misbegotten* (1947). The former is a gargantuan, broken-backed, repetitive parable about the dangers of shattering illusions. It is impressive by its sheer weight and redeemed by O'Neill's never-failing sense of the theatre. *Long Day's Journey into Night* (1957; Pulitzer prize), probably his masterpiece, whose tragic Tyrone family is closely based on O'Neill's early life, *Hughie* and *A Touch of the Poet* were published posthumously. He was awarded the Nobel prize for literature in 1936, the first American dramatist to be thus honoured. See Life by A. and B. Gelb (1962), studies by B. H. Clark (rev. ed. 1947), C. Leech (1963) and J. H. Raleigh (1965), and, by his second wife, A. Boulton, *Part of a Long Story* (1958).

(2) **Hugh,** Earl of Tyrone, and 'arch-rebel', was the son of an illegitimate son of Con O'Neill (?1484–?1559), a warlike Irish chieftain who was made Earl of Tyrone on his submission to Henry VIII in 1542. His grandson, Hugh (born about 1540), was invested with the title and estates in 1587, but soon plunged into intrigues with the Irish rebels and the Spaniards against Elizabeth, as 'the O'Neill' spread insurrection in 1597 all over Ulster, Connaught and Leinster, and in spite of Spanish support was defeated by Mountjoy at Kinsale and badly wounded. He made submission, but intrigued with Spain against James I, and in 1607 fled, dying at Rome in 1616. His nephew, **Owen Roe** (?1590–1649), won a distinguished place in the Spanish military service, came to Ireland in 1642, fought for a time with great success against Scots and English for an independent Ireland, but died suddenly when

about to measure himself against Cromwell. See a monograph by J. F. Taylor (1896). A kinsman, **Sir Phelim,** was the leader of the insurrection, not so much against the English government as against the English and Scots settlers in Ulster, in which occurred the massacre of 1641. **Shane** (?1530–67), eldest legitimate son of Con O'Neill, was second Earl of Tyrone, nominally acknowledged Elizabeth, but was always at war with the Scots and the O'Donnells.

(3) **Peggy.** See EATON.

ONKELOS (?2nd cent. A.D.), the reputed author of an Aramaic Targum of the Pentateuch, produced by the scholars of R. Akiba between A.D. 150 and 200 in Palestine. 'Onkelos' is a corruption of Akylas (Greek for Aquila), the name of the actual translator of the Old Testament into Greek, *c.* A.D. 130.

ONNES, Heike Kamerlingh, *ō'nes* (1853–1926), born at Groningen, became professor of Physics at Leyden. He obtained liquid helium, and discovered that the electrical resistance of metals cooled to near absolute zero all but disappears. In 1913 he was awarded the Nobel prize for physics.

ONSLOW, Arthur (1691–1768), son of a commissioner of excise, was trained a barrister, entered parliament in 1720, and for thirty-three years was a dignified and blameless speaker of the House of Commons.

OPIE, (1) Amelia (1769–1853), wife of (2), the daughter of a Norwich physician, Dr Alderson, while very young wrote songs and tragedies. She was married to Opie in 1798. In 1801 her first novel, *Father and Daughter,* appeared; next year a volume of poems. On her husband's death she published his lectures, with a memoir. Mrs Opie became a Quaker in 1825, and afterwards published moral tracts and articles, but no more novels. See *Memoirs* by Miss Brightwell (1854), Lady Richmond Ritchie's *Book of Sibyls* (1883), and works by Macgregor (1933), Menzies-Wilson and Lloyd (1937).

(2) **John** (1761–1807), English portrait and historical painter, was born, a carpenter's son, near St Agnes, Cornwall. His attempts at portrait painting interested Dr Wolcot ('Peter Pindar'), by whom in 1780 he was taken to London to become the 'Cornish Wonder'. His works include the well-known *Murder of Rizzio, Jephtha's Vow* and *Juliet in the Garden.* He wrote a Life of Reynolds and a discourse on Art, and lectured on Art at the Royal Institution.

OPITZ, Martin (1597–1639), German poet, born at Bunzlau in Silesia. He earned an inflated reputation by toadying to the German princes. In 1620 he fled to Holland to escape war and the plague; but of the plague he died in Danzig. His poems have no imagination and little feeling, and are cold, formal, didactic, pedantic. His works include translations from classic authors (Sophocles and Seneca), the Dutchmen Heinsius and Grotius, and from the Bible. See books by Palm (1862), Borinski (1883), Berghöfer (1888), Stössel (1922) and Gundolf (1923).

OPPENHEIM, Edward Phillips (1866–1946), English novelist, born in London, had his first book published in 1887 and went on to become a pioneer of the novel of espionage and diplomatic intrigue. Among his best are *Mr Grex of Monte Carlo* (1915), *Kingdom of the Blind* (1917), *The Great Impersonation* (1920) and *Envoy Extraordinary* (1937). See his autobiography, *The Pool of Memory* (1941).

OPPENHEIMER, (1) Sir Ernest (1880–1957), South African mining magnate, politician and philanthropist, was born at Friedberg, Germany, the son of a Jewish cigar merchant. At the age of seventeen he worked for a London firm of diamond merchants and, sent out to Kimberley as their representative, soon became one of the leaders of the diamond industry. In 1917 he formed the Anglo-American Corporation of South Africa and at the time of his death his interests extended over 95 per cent. of the world's supply of diamonds. He was mayor of Kimberley (1912–15), raised the Kimberley Regiment and, a friend of Smuts, was M.P. for Kimberley (1924–38). He endowed university chairs and slum clearance schemes in Johannesburg. He was knighted in 1921. His son, **Harry Frederick** (b. 1908), succeeded him in 1957 and in 1960 criticized the South African government's *apartheid* policy.

(2) **J. Robert** (1904–67), American nuclear physicist, born in New York, studied at Harvard, Cambridge (England), Göttingen, Leyden and Zürich, became assistant professor of Physics at the California Institute of Technology (1929), studied electron-positron pairs, cosmic ray theory and worked on deuteron reactions. In 1942 he joined the atom bomb project and in 1943 became director of the Los Alamos laboratory, resigning in 1945. He argued for joint control with the Soviet Union of atomic energy. He was chairman of the advisory committee to the U.S. Atomic Energy Commission (1946–1952) and in 1947 became director and professor of Physics at the Institute for Advanced Study, Princeton. In 1953 he was suspended from secret nuclear research by a security review board, although many people disagreed with the charges brought against him. He delivered the B.B.C. Reith Lectures (1953), and received the Enrico Fermi award in 1963.

ORANGE, Princes of. See WILLIAM III, WILLIAM THE SILENT.

ORCAGNA, Andrea, *or-kan'ya* (*c.* 1308–68), a nickname, corrupted from *Arcagnuolo,* 'Archangel', of **Andrea di Cione,** who, the son of a Florentine silversmith, distinguished himself as sculptor, painter, architect and poet. The tabernacle in Or San Michele at Florence is a triumph in sculpture. His greatest paintings are frescoes, an altarpiece in Santa Maria Novella, and *Coronation of the Virgin* in the National Gallery. He is considered by many to be second in the 14th century only to Giotto, who influenced him.

ORCHARDSON, Sir William Quiller (1832–1910), Scottish painter, born in Edinburgh, came to London in 1862, and was elected R.A. in 1877. He painted portraits, but is best known for historical and social subject paintings. Most famous is the scene of Napoleon on board the *Bellerophon* (1880) in the Tate Gallery; among other well-known subjects are *Queen of the Swords* (1877), *Mariage de convenance* (1884) and *Her*

Mother's Voice (1888). He was knighted in 1907. See Life by his daughter, Mrs Gray (1930).

ORCZY, Baroness Emmuska, *or'tsi* (1865–1947), British novelist and playwright, born, the daughter of a musician, in Tarnaörs, Hungary. *The Scarlet Pimpernel* (1905) was the first success in the Baroness's long writing career. It was followed by many popular adventure romances, including *The Elusive Pimpernel* (1908) and *Mam'zelle Guillotine* (1940), which never quite attained the success of her early work. See her autobiographical *Links in the Chain of Life* (1947).

ORDERICUS VITALIS (1075–1143), mediaeval historian, born, the son of a French priest and an Englishwoman, at Atcham near Shrewsbury, and educated in the Norman abbey of St Evroul, where he spent his life, although he visited England to collect materials for his *Historia Ecclesiastica* (1123–41), a history mainly of Normandy and England—a singular mixture of important history and trivial gossip. See Dean Church's *St Anselm* (1870) and Freeman's *Norman Conquest*.

O'REILLY, John Boyle (1844–90), the son of a schoolmaster near Drogheda, was bred a compositor, but becoming a hussar in 1863, was in 1866 sentenced to twenty years' penal servitude for spreading Fenianism in the army. He escaped in 1867 from Western Australia, and settled as a journalist in Boston, U.S., where he became known as an author of songs and novels.

O'RELL, Max. See BLOUET.

ORELLANA, Francisco de (*c.* 1500–*c.* 49), Spanish explorer, born at Trujillo, went with Pizarro to Peru and, crossing the Andes, descended the Amazon to its mouth (1541). See study by F. Markham (Hakluyt Soc. 1859).

ORFF, Carl (1895–), German composer, born in Munich, studied under Kaminski and in 1925 helped to found the Günter School in Munich and subsequently taught there. His aim, to which his didactic composition *Schulwerk* (1930–54) testifies, was to educate in the creative aspects of music. The influence of Stravinsky is apparent in his compositions, which include three realizations of Monteverdi's *Orfeo* (1925, 1931, 1941), an operatic setting of a 13th-century poem entitled *Carmina burana* (1936), *Die Kluge*, 'The Prudent Woman' (1943), an operatic version of Hölderlin's translation of *Antigone* (Salzburg Festival, 1949) and *Astutuli* (1953).

ORFILA, Mathieu Joseph Bonaventure (1787–1853), French chemist, founder of toxicology, born at Mahón in Minorca, studied at Valencia, Barcelona and Paris. In 1811 he lectured on chemistry, botany and anatomy. In 1813 appeared his celebrated *Traité de toxicologie générale*. In 1819 he became professor of Medical Jurisprudence, and in 1823 of Chemistry.

ORFORD. See WALPOLE.

ORIGEN (185–254), the most learned and original of the early church fathers, was born probably at Alexandria, and was the son of the Christian martyr Leonidas. He studied in the catechetical school of Clement, and soon acted as master. He made a thorough study of Plato, the later Platonists and Pythagoreans, and the Stoics, under the Neoplatonist Ammonius Saccas: At Alexandria he taught for twenty-eight years (204–232), composed the chief of his dogmatic treatises, and commenced his great works of textual and exegetical criticism. During his visit to Palestine in 216 the bishops of Jerusalem and Caesarea employed him to lecture in the churches, and in 230 they consecrated him presbyter without referring to his own bishop. An Alexandrian synod deprived him of the office of presbyter. The churches of Palestine, Phoenicia, Arabia and Achaea declined to concur in this sentence; and Origen, settling at Caesarea in Palestine, founded a school of literature, philosophy and theology. In the last twenty years of his life he made many journeys. In the Decian persecution at Tyre he was cruelly tortured, and there he died in 254. His exegetical writings extended over nearly the whole of the old and New Testaments, and included *Scholia*, *Homilies* and *Commentaries*. Of the Homilies only a small part has been preserved in the original, much, however, in the Latin translations by Rufinus and Jerome; but the translators tampered with them. Of the Commentaries a number of books on Matthew and John are extant in Greek. His gigantic *Hexapla*, the foundation of the textual criticism of the Scriptures, is mostly lost. His *Eight Books against Celsus*, preserved entire in Greek, constitute the greatest of early Christian apologies. The speculative theology of the *Peri Archon* is extant mostly in the garbled translation of Rufinus. Two books on *The Resurrection* and ten books of *Stromata* are lost. The eclectic philosophy of Origen bears a Neoplatonist and Stoical stamp. The idea of the proceeding of all spirits from God, their fall, redemption and return to God, is the key to the development of the world, at the centre of which is the incarnation of the Logos. All scripture admits of a threefold interpretation—literal, psychical or ethical, and pneumatic or allegorical. See Harnack's *Dogmengeschichte*, Farrar's *Lives of the Fathers* (1889); German works on Origen by Thomasius (1837), Redepenning (1846) and Lieske (1938); French by Joly (1860), Freppel (1868), Denis (1884), de Faye (3 vols. 1923–28), Cadion (1932); English by J. Patrick (1892), Fairweather (1901).

ORKHAN, Turkish sultan (1326–59), son of Othman, took Brusa in his father's time, and afterwards reduced Nicaea and Mysia. He organized the state and founded the Janissaries.

ORLÉANS (Eng. *Orleans*), a ducal title thrice conferred by French kings on brothers—in 1392 by Charles VI, in 1626 by Louis XIII, and in 1660 by Louis XIV on Philippe (1640–1701). His son was the regent, Philippe (1674–1723), and his great-grandson was 'Égalité' (see 4). Égalité's son was King Louis Philippe (q.v.). His eldest son (1810–1842) took the title, but it was not borne by that duke's son, the Comte de Paris (q.v.), who settled in England in 1883, became head of the Bourbon house, and died in

1894. His son (see (5)) resumed the old ducal title. (Louis Philippe's younger sons were the Dukes of Aumale, Nemours, Montpensier, and the Prince de Joinville.)

(1) **Charles** (1391–1465), married in 1406 his cousin Isabella, widow of Richard II of England. In alliance with the infamous Bernard d'Armagnac, he did his best to avenge on the Duke of Burgundy his father's murder. He commanded at Agincourt (October 1415), and was taken prisoner and carried to England, where he spent over a quarter of a century. composing ballades, rondels, &c., in French and English, conventional, musical and graceful. He was ransomed in 1440, and during the last third of his life he maintained a kind of literary court at Blois. His son became Louis XII. See his *English Poems*, ed. Steele (E.E.T.S. 1941), and R. L. Stevenson, in *Familiar Studies* (1882).

(2) **Jean Baptiste Gaston** (1608–60), third son of Henry IV of France, troubled his country with bloody but fruitless intrigues against Richelieu. He was lieutenant-general of the kingdom during the minority of Louis XIV, was at the head of the Fronde, but soon made terms with Mazarin. See his *Mémoires* (1683).

(3) **Philippe** (1674–1723), regent of France during the minority of Louis XV, son of the first Duke Philippe, and grandson of Louis XIII, possessed excellent talents, but was early demoralized. He showed courage at Steenkirk and Neerwinden, and commanded with success in Italy and Spain. For some years he lived in exile from the court, spending his time by turns in profligacy, the fine arts and chemistry. Louis XIV at his death appointed (1715) the Duke of Orléans sole regent. (Orléans had married Mlle de Blois, daughter of Louis XIV and Mme de Montespan.) He was popular, but his adoption of Law's schemes led to disaster. His alliance with England and Holland (1717) was joined by the emperor, and overthrew Alberoni. He expelled the Pretender from France, debarred the parliament of Paris from meddling with political affairs, and to appease the Jesuits sacrificed the Jansenists. See works by Piossens (1749), Capefigue (1838), Leclerq (1921), Saint-André (1928), Soulié (1933), d'Erlanger (1938).

(4) **Louis Philippe Joseph** (1747–93), the famous Égalité, succeeded to the title on his father's death in 1785. He early fell into debauchery, and was looked upon coldly at court, especially after the accession of Louis XVI (1774). He visited London frequently, became an intimate friend of the Prince of Wales, afterwards George IV, infected young France with Anglomania in the form of horse-racing and hard drinking, and made himself popular by profuse charity. In 1787 he showed his liberalism boldly against the king, and was sent by a *lettre-de-cachet* to his château of Villers-Cotterets. As the States-General drew near he lavished his wealth in disseminating throughout France books and papers by Sieyès and other Liberals. In 1788 he promulgated his *Délibérations*, written by Laclos, to the effect that the *tiers état* was the nation, and in June 1789 he led the forty-seven nobles who seceded from their own order to join it. He dreamed of becoming constitutional king of France, or at least regent. He gradually lost influence, felt hopeless of the Revolution, and thought of going to America. In 1792, all hereditary titles being swept away, he adopted the name of Philippe Égalité, was twentieth deputy for Paris to the Convention, and voted for the death of the king. His eldest son, afterwards King Louis-Philippe, rode with Dumouriez, his commander, into the Austrian camp. Égalité was at once arrested, with all the Bourbons still in France, and, after six months' durance, was found guilty of conspiracy and guillotined. See works by Baschet, by Tournois (1840–43), by Britsch (1926), and Elliot's *Journal* (1859).

(5) **Louis Philippe Robert** (1869–1926), eldest son of the Comte de Paris, went to France in 1890, and was imprisoned for contravening the law banishing the heirs of families that have reigned.

(6) **Jean, Duc de Guise** (1874–1940), his brother-in-law, son of the Duc de Chartres, succeeded as head of the house. His brother, **Prince Henri of Orleans** (1867–1901), traveller (his *Tonkin and Siam* was translated 1893), fought a duel with the Count of Turin in 1897.

ORLEY, Bernard, or **Barend van** (*c.* 1491–1542), Flemish painter, was born and died at Brussels, became court painter to the regent, Margaret of Austria, and was one of the first Flemish painters to adopt the Italian Renaissance style. He executed a number of altarpieces and tryptyches of biblical subjects to be seen in Brussels, at the Louvre, the Prado, the Metropolitan Museum at New York and elsewhere, and in his later years he designed tapestries and stained glass. See Friedlander on Flemish painting (1930).

ORLOV, a Russian family that rose to eminence, when one of its members, Gregory (1734–83), succeeded Poniatowski as the favourite of Catharine II. It was he who planned the murder of Peter III, and his brother Alexis (1737–1808) who committed the deed (1762). The legitimate line of Orlov became extinct; but Feodor, a brother of Gregory and Alexis, left four illegitimate sons, one of whom, Alexis (1787–1862), distinguished himself in the French wars and in Turkey, represented Russia at the London conference of 1832, in 1844 was at the head of the secret police, stood high in favour with the Emperor Nicholas, in 1856 was Russian representative at the congress of Paris, and was made president of the grand council of the empire.

ORM, or **Ormin** (fl. *c.* 1200), versifier and spelling reformer, born probably in Lincolnshire, was an Augustinian monk, author of the 'Ormulum' named after him, a series of homilies in verse on the gospel history.

ORMEROD, Eleanor Anne (1828–1901), LL.D. (Edin. 1900), entomologist, daughter of George Ormerod (1785–1873), the historian of Cheshire, in 1882–92 was consulting entomologist to the Royal Agricultural Society. She was the author of *Manual of Injurious Insects* (1881), *Guide to Methods of Insect Life* (1884), and *Agricultural Entomol-*

ogy (2nd ed. 1892). See her *Autobiography* (1904).

ORMONDE, (1) **James Butler, Duke of** (1610–1688), of the ancient Anglo-Irish family of Butler, was born in London, and in 1632 succeeded to the earldom and estates of Ormonde. During the Strafford administration he greatly distinguished himself, and in the rebellion of 1640 was appointed to the chief command of the army; but when, in 1643, he concluded an armistice, his policy was condemned by both great parties. In the last crisis of the king's fortunes he retired to France, returned again to Ireland with the all but desperate design of restoring the royal authority, but after a gallant struggle was compelled (1650) to return to France. At the Restoration he was rewarded by the ducal title of Ormonde. He twice again returned to the government of Ireland. In 1679 an attempt was made on his life by the notorious Colonel Blood, supposed to have been instigated by the Duke of Buckingham. He escaped uninjured, and lived until 1688. See Lives by Carte (1736) and Lady Burghclere (1912).

(2) **James Butler, 2nd Duke** (1665–1746), grandson of (1), was born in Dublin. As Earl of Ossory he served in the army against Monmouth. After his accession to the dukedom in 1688, he took his share in the Revolution conflict. He headed William's lifeguards at the battle of the Boyne. In 1702 he commanded the troops in Rooke's expedition against Cadiz; in 1703 he was appointed lord-lieutenant of Ireland, and in 1711 commander-in-chief against France and Spain. Under George I he fell into disgrace, and was impeached in 1715 of high treason, his estates being attainted; he retired to France, spent years in the intrigues of the Pretender, and died abroad. Letters written by him in organizing the attempt by Spain to invade England and Scotland in 1719 were in 1890 brought to light, and in 1896 published by the Scottish History Society.

ORNSTEIN, Leo, *orn'stīn* (1895–), American composer, born in Russia, had appeared as a child prodigy at the piano in Russia before his parents settled in the U.S.A. in 1906, and he made his American début at sixteen. In the years following 1915, Ornstein composed much music that placed him among the *avant-garde* and has had considerable influence upon younger American composers, but his later works, which include a symphony and various pieces of piano music, are more traditional in style.

OROSIUS, Paulus (5th cent. A.D.), a Spanish presbyter and historian, visited Augustine in 415, and went to study under Jerome at Bethlehem. His uncritical compilation, *Historiarum adversus Paganos Libri vii* (ed. by Zangemeister, Vienna 1882), from the Creation to A.D. 417, a favourite textbook during the Middle Ages, was translated into English by King Alfred (ed. Sweet, 1883). There is a modern English version by I. W. Raymond (1936).

O'ROURKE, Sir Brian-na-Murtha (d. 1591), Irish chieftain in Galway, Sligo, and the west of Ulster, was in frequent collision with the English authorities, sheltered the Spaniards of the Armada wrecked on Irish coasts, and in 1591 went to Scotland to seek support from James VI, who handed him over to the English. He was tried and executed at Tyburn in 1591.

ORPEN, Sir William (1878–1931), British painter, born at Stillorgan, Co. Dublin, studied at the Metropolitan School of Art at Dublin and at the Slade School. He did many sketches and paintings at the front in World War I, and was present at the Paris peace conference as official painter. The results may be seen at the Imperial War Museum. He is also known for Irish genre subjects, but is most famous for his portraits, whose vitality and feeling for character place them among the finest of the century. He was knighted in 1918 and elected R.A. in 1919.

ORR, Boyd. See BOYD ORR.

ORRERY. See BOYLE.

ORSINI, Felice (1819–58), Italian conspirator, born at Meldola, in the States of the Church, of an ancient and distinguished family, was, as the son of a conspirator, early initiated into secret societies, and in 1844 was sentenced at Rome to the galleys, amnestied, and again imprisoned for political plots. In 1848 he was elected to the Roman Constituent Assembly. He took part in the defence of Rome and Venice, agitated in Genoa and Modena, and in 1853 was shipped by the Sardinian government to England, where he formed close relations with Mazzini. Next year he was at Parma, Milan, Trieste, Vienna, until arrested and confined at Mantua. In 1856 he escaped to England, where he supported himself by public lecturing, and wrote *Austrian Dungeons in Italy* (1856). In 1857 he went to Paris to assassinate Napoleon III as an obstacle to revolution in Italy. Orsini and three others threw three bombs under Napoleon's carriage (January 14, 1858); 10 persons were killed, 156 wounded, but Napoleon and the empress remained unhurt. Orsini and another were guillotined March 13. See his *Memoirs*, written by himself (Eng. trans. 1857), his Letters (1861), and a work by Montazio (1862).

ORTEGA Y GASSET, José, *or-tay'ga ee gah-set'* (1883–1955), Spanish humanist, born in Madrid, was professor there from 1911. His introduction of such writers as Proust and Joyce to Spain and his critical writings made him there the most influential author of his time. *Meditaciones del Quijote* (1914) outlines national symbols in Spanish literature and compares them with those of others. In *Tema de nuestro tiempo* (1923) he argues that great philosophies demarcate the cultural horizons of their epochs. *La Rebelión de Las Masas* (1930) foreshadowed the Civil War. He lived in South America and Portugal (1931–46). *Man of Crisis* (1959) is a collection of lectures, posthumously translated, also *On Love*, trans. T. Talbot (1959).

ORTELIUS (1527–98), the Latinized name of the geographer Abraham Ortel, born of German parents at Antwerp, where he died. His *Theatrum Orbis Terrarum* (1570) was the first great atlas.

ORTON, Arthur. See TICHBORNE.

ORWELL, George, pseud. of **Eric Arthur Blair** (1903–50), English novelist and essayist, born at Motihari in Bengal, was educated at Eton College, served in Burma in the Indian Imperial Police from 1922 until 1927 (later recalled in the novel *Burmese Days* (1935)) and then was literally *Down and Out in Paris and London* (1933), making an occasional living as tutor or bookshop assistant. *Coming Up for Air* (1939) is a plea for the small man against big business. He fought and was wounded in the Spanish Civil War and he developed his own brand of socialism in *The Road to Wigan Pier* (1937), *Homage to Catalonia* (1938) and *The Lion and the Unicorn* (1941). During World War II, he was war correspondent for the B.B.C. and *The Observer* and wrote for *Tribune*. His intellectual honesty motivated his biting satire of Communist ideology in *Animal Farm* (1945) which was made into a cartoon film, and the hair-raising prophecy for mankind in *Nineteen Eighty-Four* (1949), the triumph of the scientifically perfected servile state, the extirpation of political freedom by thought-control and an ideologically delimited basic language or *newspeak* in which 'thought crime is death'. Other penetrating collections of essays include *Inside the Whale* (1940) and *Shooting an Elephant* (1950). See *Collected Essays, Journalism and Letters* (4 vols.) ed. by S. Orwell and I. Angus (1968) and studies by Atkins (1954), Brander (1954), Hopkinson (1955), Hollis (1956), and Thomas (1965).

OSBORN, (1) **Henry Fairfield** (1857–1935), American zoologist, born at Fairfield, Conn., studied at Princeton, was assistant professor there 1881–90, professor of Zoology at Columbia University 1891–1910, and thereafter research professor. His work especially on fossil vertebrates is important, and as director he made the American Museum of Natural History famous. He wrote also on evolution, education, a Life of Cope, &c.

(2) **Sherard** (1822–75), British naval officer, born at Madras, entered the navy in 1837. He took part in the Chinese war of 1841–42, commanded vessels in two expeditions (1849 and 1852–55) in search of Sir John Franklin, was head of the British squadron in the Sea of Azov during the Crimean war, and took a leading share in the Chinese war of 1857–59. He helped to lay a cable between Great Britain and Australia, was made rear-admiral in 1873, and helped to fit out the Arctic expedition of Nares and Markham (1875). He published his *Arctic Journal* (1852), *Journals of McClure* (1856) and *Fate of Sir John Franklin* (1860).

OSBORNE, (1) **Dorothy**. See TEMPLE (3).

(2) **John James** (1929–), British playwright and actor, son of a Welsh commercial artist, left Belmont College, Devon, at sixteen and became a copywriter for trade journals. Hating it, he turned actor (1948) and by 1955 was playing leading rôles in new plays at the Royal Court Theatre. There his fourth play, *Look Back in Anger* (1956; filmed 1958), and *The Entertainer* (1957; filmed 1960), with Sir Laurence Olivier playing Archie Rice, established Osborne as the leading younger exponent of British social drama. The 'hero' of the first, Jimmy Porter, the prototype 'Angry Young Man', as well as the pathetic, mediocre music hall joker of the latter, both echo the author's uncompromising hatred of outworn social and political institutions and attitudes. An earlier play, *Epitaph for George Dillon*, written in collaboration with A. Creighton and exploring the moral problems of a would-be literary genius, was also staged in 1957. Among other works are *Luther* (1960), *Inadmissible Evidence* (1965), *Time Present* and *The Hotel in Amsterdam* (1968), and the filmscript of *Tom Jones*. See his *Credo* in *Declaration*, ed. T. Maschler (1957).

(3) **Thomas**, See LEEDS.

OSBOURNE, Lloyd (1868–1947), American author, stepson and collaborator of R. L. Stevenson (q.v.), born in San Francisco, was U.S. vice-consul in Samoa, and wrote *Love the Fiddler*, stories and dramas.

OSCAR I (1799–1859), king of Sweden and Norway, ascended the throne in 1844, carried out social and economic reforms and pursued a policy of Scandinavian unity and Swedish neutrality.

OSCAR II (1829–1907), king of Sweden (1872–1907), and of Norway (1872–1905), a great-grandson of Charles XIV (q.v.), translated *Faust*, wrote a Life of Charles XII and poems.

O'SHAUGHNESSY, Arthur (1844–81), British poet, born in London, in 1861 entered the British Museum (the natural history department in 1863), and wrote *Epic of Women* (1870), *Lays of France* (1872), *Music and Moonlight* (1874) and *Songs of a Worker* (1881). His best-known poem is *The Music-Makers*. See Life by L. C. Moulton (1894).

OSIANDER, Andreas (1498–1552), German reformer, born at Gunzenhausen, a preacher at Nürnberg (1522), persuaded that city to declare for Luther. Deprived for refusing to agree to the Augsburg Interim (1548), he was made professor of Theology at Königsberg, but soon became entangled in bitter theological strife, disputing the imputation of Christ's righteousness in favour of an infusion doctrine. See Lives by Wilken (1844), Möller (1870) and Hase (1879).

OSLER, Sir William (1849–1919), British physician, born in Canada, became professor of Medicine at McGill (1875–84), Pennsylvania (1884–88), Johns Hopkins (1889–1905), and finally Oxford (1905–11). He became a baronet in 1911. His special study was angina pectoris, and he wrote also on the history of medicine. His *Principles and Practice of Medicine* (1892) became a standard work. See Life by Cushing (1940).

OSMAN. See OTHMAN.

OSMAN DIGNA, *né* **George Nisbet** (1836–1926), born at Rouen, a slave-dealer and from 1881 a Mahdist leader on the Red Sea coast and the Abyssinian frontier, was defeated and taken at Tokar (1900). See Life by H. C. Jackson (1926).

OSMAN NURI PASHA (1837–1900), Turkish general, born at Amasia or at Tokat, held Plevna against the Russians in 1877. See work by Levaux (1891).

OSMUND, St (d. 1099), coming from Normandy with the Conqueror, became chancellor (1072) and Bishop of Salisbury (1078). He established the 'Use of Sarum'.

OSSIAN, heroic poet of the Gael, and son of the 3rd-century hero Fingal or Fionn MacCumhail, whose poems James Macpherson (q.v.) professed to have collected and translated. See *Ossian*, with introduction by W. Sharp (1897).

OSSOLI. See FULLER (4).

OSTADE, Adriaan van, *os-tah'dė* (1610–85), Dutch painter and engraver, born probably at Haarlem, was a pupil of Frans Hals, and his use of chiaroscuro shows the influence of Rembrandt. His subjects are taken mostly from everyday life—tavern scenes, farmyards, markets, village greens, &c. His *Alchemist* is in the National Gallery. His brother **Isaac** (1621–49) treated similar subjects, but excelled at winter scenes and landscapes. See a study by Van der Wiele (Paris 1893) on both brothers, and one by Godefroy (Paris 1930) on Adriaan's engraved work.

OSTROVSKY, Alexander (1823–85), Russian dramatist, born at Moscow, whose best known play is *The Storm* (1860; trans. C. Garnett, 1899).

OSTWALD, Wilhelm, *-valt* (1853–1932), German chemist, born at Riga, was professor at Leipzig 1887–1906, and was awarded a Nobel prize (1909). He discovered the dilution law which bears his name, and invented a process for making nitric acid by the oxidation of ammonia. He also developed a new theory of colour.

OSWALD, St (*c.* 605–642), son of Ethelfrith of Bernicia, fought his way to the Northumbrian crown by the defeat (635) of Caedwalla the Welsh king. He had been converted to Christianity at Iona, and established Christianity in Northumbria with St Aidan's help. He fell in battle with Penda.

OTHMAN, or Osman I (1259–1326), founder of the Ottoman (Turkish) power, was born in Bithynia, and, on the overthrow of the Seljuk sultanate of Iconium in 1299 by the Mongols, gradually subdued a great part of Asia Minor. From his name are derived the terms Ottoman and Osmanli.

OTHMAN (d. 656), third caliph, was Mohammed's secretary and son-in-law, and was chosen in 644. His weak government raised complaints and insurrections on all sides. But Persia was finally subdued, and Herat, Merv and Balkh captured. He was besieged in Medina, and murdered.

OTHO, Marcus Salvius (32–69), joined Galba in his revolt against Nero (68), but, not being proclaimed Galba's successor, rose against the new emperor, who was slain. Otho was recognized as emperor everywhere save in Germany, whence Vitellius marched on Italy, and completely defeated Otho's forces. Next day Otho, who had worn the purple only three months, stabbed himself.

OTIS, James (1725–83), American statesman, born at West Barnstable, Mass., became a leader of the Boston bar. He was advocate-general in 1760, when the revenue officers demanded his assistance in obtaining from the superior court general search warrants allowing them to enter any man's house in quest of smuggled goods. Otis refused, resigned, and appeared in defence of popular rights. In 1761, elected to the Massachusetts assembly, he was prominent in resistance to the revenue acts. In 1769 he was savagely beaten by revenue officers and others, and lost his reason. He was killed by lightning. His fame chiefly rests on *The Rights of the Colonies Asserted* (1764). See Life by W. Tudor (1823).

OTTO, the name of four Holy Roman Emperors:

Otto I (912–973), son of Henry I, in 936 crowned king of the Germans, in 962 emperor, subdued many turbulent tribes, maintained almost supreme power in Italy, and established Christianity in Scandinavian and Slavonic lands. See study by Holtzmann (1936).

Otto II (955–983), son of Otto I, became emperor in 973, successfully fought the Danes and Bohemians, and subdued insurgent Bavaria which he reduced in size by splitting it up. He invaded France, but overreached himself in attempts on the Eastern Empire.

Otto III (980–1002), son of Otto II, came to the throne as a child of three. His mother held the regency until her death (991), despite attempts to seize power by the Duke of Bavaria, and was succeeded by his grandmother Adelaide. Having engineered first his cousin then his tutor into the papacy, he lived most of his short life in Rome, whence he was driven by the hostility of the people to Paterno, where he died.

Otto IV (*c.* 1174–1218), son of Henry the Lion, elected emperor in 1198, was immediately involved in rivalry for the throne with Philip of Swabia, after whose murder in 1208 a new election was held in which Otto's claim was re-established, and he was crowned in 1209. Excommunicated for attacking Tuscany, Apulia and Sicily, he was supplanted on the German throne by Frederick of Sicily. Civil war followed, and he was defeated by Philip of France at Bouvines (1214). He fled to Saxony and Frederick replaced him as emperor (see FREDERICK II) in 1215.

OTTO, Nikolaus August (1832–91), German engineer, born near Schlangenbad, invented in 1876 the four-stroke internal combustion engine, the sequence of operation of which is named the Otto cycle after him.

OTWAY, Thomas (1652–85), English dramatist, was born at Trotton in Sussex, and from Winchester passed in 1669 to Christ Church College, Oxford. He quitted the university without a degree in 1672, failed utterly as an actor, but made a fair hit with his tragedy *Alcibiades* (1675). In it beautiful Mrs Barry made her first appearance, and with her Otway is said to have fallen in love. In 1676 Betterton accepted his *Don Carlos*, a good tragedy in rhyme. In 1677 Otway translated Racine's *Titus and Berenice*, as well as Molière's *Cheats of Scapin.* In 1678–79 he was in Flanders as a soldier; in the May of the former year appeared his coarse but diverting comedy, *Friendship in Fashion.* The year 1680 yielded two tragedies, *The Orphan* and *Caius Marius*, and his one important poem, *The Poet's Complaint of his Muse*; to 1681 belongs *The Soldier's Fortune.* His greatest work, *Venice Preserved, or a Plot Discovered* (1682), is a masterpiece of tragic passion. For a time he sinks out of sight, to reappear again in 1684 with *The Atheist*, a feeble comedy, and in February 1685 with *Windsor Castle*, a poem addressed to the new king, James II. He died in poverty. In 1719 a badly edited tragedy, *Heroick Friendship*, was published as his. The best edition of his works is by Ghosh (1932). See R. G. Ham's *Otway and Lee* (1931).

OUD, Jacobus Johann Pieter, *owd* (1890–), Dutch architect, born at Purmerend, collaborated with Mondrian (q.v.) and others in launching the review *de Stijl* and became a pioneer of the modern architectural style based on simplified forms and pure planes. Appointed city architect at Rotterdam in 1918, he designed a number of striking buildings, including municipal housing blocks. See study by Hitchcock (1931).

OUDINOT, *oo-dee-nō*, (1) **Nicolas Charles** (1767–1847), marshal of France, born at Bar-le-Duc, served in the revolutionary wars. In 1805 he obtained the Grand Cross of the Legion of Honour and the command of ten reserve battalions, the ' grenadiers Oudinot '. He fought at Austerlitz and Jena, gained the battle of Ostrolenka (1807), and helped at Friedland. Conspicuous in the Austrian campaign of 1809, he was created Marshal of France and Duke of Reggio. In 1810 he was charged with the occupation of Holland, and took part in the Russian campaign and in the battles of 1813 with the Russians and Austrians. He was one of the last to abandon Napoleon. At the second restoration he became a minister of state, commander-in-chief of the royal and national guards, peer of France, &c. In 1823 he commanded in Spain. See Lives by Nollet (1850) and Stiegler (1894), and *Memoirs of Marshal Oudinot* (trans. 1896).

(2) **Nicolas Charles Victor,** Duke of Reggio (1791–1863), son of (1), fought in Algeria, and commanded the expedition to Rome in 1849.

OUGHTRED, William, *aw'tred* (1575–1660), English mathematician, educated at Eton (where he was born) and Cambridge, wrote much on mathematics, notably *Clavis Mathematica* (1631), a textbook on arithmetic in which he introduced multiplication and proportion signs. He invented the trigonometric abbreviations *sin*, *cos*, &c. Another invention was a slide rule. He died at Albury, Surrey.

OUIDA, *wee'da*, pseud. of **Louise Ramé or de la Ramée** (1839–1908), English novelist. Born at Bury St Edmunds, she lived long in London, from 1874 made her home in Italy, and died in poverty at Lucca. She wrote *Strathmore* (1865), *Under Two Flags* (her best, 1868), and many other romantic novels as well as children's stories. See Lives by Elizabeth Lee (1914), Y. ffrench (1938).

OUSELEY, (1) **Sir Frederick Arthur Gore, 2nd Bart.** (1825–89), English musician, son of (2), born in London, graduated at Oxford, where he became professor of Music in 1855. He was founder and benefactor of St Michael's College, Tenbury, to which he bequeathed his music library.

(2) **Sir Gore, 1st Bart.** (1770–1844), English diplomat and Orientalist, father of (1), was ambassador in Persia (1810–15).

(3) **Sir William (1767–1842), Orientalist,** brother of (2), wrote on Persian history, language and literature, and on his travels in the East. His son, **Sir William Gore** (1797–1866), held important diplomatic offices in South America.

OUTRAM, Sir James (1803–63), British soldier, the ' Bayard of India ', was born at Butterley Hall, Derbyshire, the residence of his father, Benjamin Outram (1764–1805), engineer, and was educated in Aberdeen. In 1819 he joined the Bombay native infantry, organized a corps of wild Bhils (1825–35), and was political agent in Gujrat (1835–38). In 1839 he attended Sir John Keane as aide-de-camp into Afghanistan, and did good service; and his eight days' ride of 355 miles from Kelat through the Bolan Pass to the sea is famous. Political agent in Sind (1840), he defended the residency at Hyderabad against 8000 Beluchis (1843), and opposed Sir Charles Napier's aggressive policy towards the Amir. He was afterwards resident at Satara and Baroda, and in 1854, on the eve of the annexation of Oudh, was made resident at Lucknow. In 1857 he commanded the brief and brilliant Persian expedition, and he returned to India a G.C.B. when the Mutiny was raging. Lord Canning tendered him the command of the forces advancing to the relief of Lucknow, but he chivalrously waived the honour in favour of his old lieutenant, Havelock, and accompanied him as a volunteer and as chief-commissioner of Oudh. Lucknow was relieved, and Outram took command, only to be in turn himself besieged. He held the Alum-bagh against overwhelming odds, until Sir Colin Campbell relieved him; and his skilful movement up the Gumti led to a complete victory. For his services he was in 1858 made lieutenant-general, thanked by parliament, and created a baronet. He took his seat as a member of the Supreme Council at Calcutta, but in 1860 had to return to England. He spent a winter in Egypt, died at Pau, and was buried in Westminster Abbey. See Lives by Goldsmid (1880) and Trotter (1903).

OVERBECK, Johann Friedrich (1789–1869), German painter, born at Lübeck, studied art at Vienna (1806–10), and settled in Rome, where he allied himself with the like minded Cornelius, Schadow, Schnorr and Veit, who, from the stress they laid on religion and moral significance, were nicknamed the Nazarenes, and scoffed at as Church Romanticists, pre-Raphaelites, &c. A Madonna (1811) brought Overbeck into notice; and Bartholdy, the Prussian consul, employed him to adorn his house with Scripture subjects. He next painted in fresco, in the villa of the Marchese Massimo, five compositions from Tasso's *Jerusalem Delivered*. In 1813 he became a Roman Catholic. His oil pictures are inferior to his frescoes. See Life by Atkinson (1882) and study by Heise (1928).

OVERBURY, Sir Thomas (1581–1613), English courtier and poet, was born at Compton-Scorpion, Warwickshire. After three years at Oxford (1595–98), he studied at the Middle Temple, then travelled on the Continent.

In 1601 at Edinburgh he met Robert Carr, afterwards minion of James I, who in 1611 made him Viscount Rochester. The two became inseparable friends, and Overbury was, through Carr's influence, knighted by James I in 1608. Meanwhile, in 1606, the lovely but profligate Frances Howard (1592–1632) had married the third Earl of Essex, and had intrigued with more than one lover—Carr the most favoured. Overbury had played pander; but when Carr proposed to get Lady Essex divorced, and marry her, he declared she might do for a mistress but not for a wife. Lady Essex offered Sir Davy Wood £1000 to assassinate him. On April 26, 1613, Overbury, on a trivial and illegal pretext—his refusal to go on an embassy—was thrown into the Tower, where on September 15 he was poisoned. Three months later Carr (now Earl of Somerset) and his paramour were married. But in 1615 an inquiry was instituted, and four of the humbler instruments were hanged. In May 1616 the countess pleaded guilty, and the earl was found guilty; but by a stretch of the royal prerogative they were pardoned. In 1622 they were released from the Tower; and Somerset survived till 1645. Overbury's works, posthumous and partly spurious, include *The Wife* (1614), a didactic poem; *Characters* (1614; partly his); and *Crumms fal'n from King James's Table* (1715; doubtful). Rimbault collected them in 1856. See Amos's *The Great Oyer of Poisoning* (1846), Whibley's *Essays in Biography* (1913) and Parry's *Overbury Mystery* (1925).

OVERLAND, Arnulf (1889–), Norwegian lyric poet, born at Kristiansund, wrote patriotic lyrics and from 1940 was prominent in the resistance movement. He was interned in a concentration camp in 1941–45.

OVERSTONE, Samuel Jones Loyd, Baron (1796–1883), English economist, born in London, entered his father's banking house, later merged in the London and Westminster Bank, and established himself as a leading authority on banking and currency by his famous series of tracts (1837–57). Whig M.P. for Hythe in 1819–26, he was made a peer in 1850.

OVID, in full **Publius Ovidius Naso** (43 B.C.–A.D. 17), Latin poet, born at Sulmo (Solmona), in the Abruzzi, son of a well-to-do *eques*, was trained for the bar; but in spite of extraordinary forensic aptitude, he gave his whole energies to poetry, and visited Athens. His first literary success was his tragedy *Medea*. Then came his *Epistolae* or *Heroides*, imaginary love letters from ladies of the heroic days to their lords, and his *Amores*, short poems about his mistress, Corinna. His *Medicamina Faciei* (a practical poem on artificial aids to personal beauty) seems to have been preliminary to his true masterwork, the *Ars Amandi*, or *Ars Amatoria*, in three books, which appeared about 1 B.C., followed by a subsidiary book entitled *Remedia Amoris*. His second period of poetic activity opens with the *Metamorphoses*, in fifteen books, and with the *Fasti*, designed to be in twelve, of which six only were completed. Midway in composition he was banished (A.D. 8), for some reason unknown, to Tomi on the Black Sea. There he died in A.D. 17. On his way from Rome he began his third period with the elegies which he published in five books, the *Tristia*. Similar in tone and theme are the four books of the *Epistolae ex Ponto*. His *Ibis*, written in imitation of Callimachus, and his *Halieutica*, a poem extant only in fragments, complete the list of his remains. A master of metrical form, Ovid is the most voluminous of Latin poets. See the monograph by Zingerle (1869–71), and books by A. Church (1876), Rand (1926), Wright (1938).

OVIEDO Y VALDÉS, Gonzalo Hernández de, *ov-yay'*THō *ee val-days'* (1478–1557), Spanish historian, born at Madrid, was sent to San Domingo in 1514 as inspector-general of goldmines, and, as historiographer of the Indies, wrote after his return a history thereof (1526; trans. by Eden, 1555).

OWEN, (1) **John** (*c.* 1560–1622), Welsh epigrammatist, born at Llanarmon, Pwllheli, became a fellow of New College, Oxford, in 1584, and about 1594 a schoolmaster at Warwick. His Latin *Epigrammata* (1606–13; best ed. by Renouard, Paris 1794) have been five times translated into English since 1619.

(2) **John** (1616–83), English Puritan, born at Stadhampton vicarage, Oxfordshire, took his B.A. in 1632 from Queen's College, Oxford, and in 1637 was driven from Oxford by dislike of Laud's statutes. He spent some years as private chaplain; then in 1642 he removed to London, and published *The Display of Arminianism* (1643), for which he was rewarded with the living of Fordham in Essex. In 1646 he removed to Coggeshall, and showed his preference for Independency over Presbyterianism. Cromwell took him in 1649 as his chaplain to Ireland, where he regulated the affairs of Trinity College. Next year (1650) he went with Cromwell to Scotland. In 1651–52 he became dean of Christ Church and vice-chancellor of Oxford University. Here he wrote a number of theological works. He was one of the Triers appointed to purge the church of scandalous ministers. He opposed the giving the crown to the Protector, and the year after Cromwell's death he was ejected from his deanery. He bought an estate at Stadhampton, and formed a congregation. In 1673 he became pastor in Leadenhall Street. To the end he preached and wrote incessantly. See Orme's *Memoirs* (1820), and *Life* by Thomason, prefixed to Goold's edition of Owen's works (1850–1855).

(3) **Sir Richard** (1804–92), English zoologist, born at Lancaster, studied medicine at Edinburgh and at St Bartholomew's; became curator in the museum of the Royal College of Surgeons, where he produced a marvellous series of descriptive catalogues; and in 1834–55 he lectured as professor of Comparative Anatomy, for two years at Bartholomew's, and afterwards at the College of Surgeons. He was a commissioner of health (1843–46), and for the Great Exhibition of 1851. In 1856 he became superintendent of the natural history department of the British Museum, but continued to teach at the Royal Institution and elsewhere. F.R.S. (1834), president of the British Association

(1857), associate of the French Institute (1859), C.B. (1873), K.C.B. (1883), he also received many scientific medals, degrees and honorary titles from many nations. His essay on *Parthenogenesis* was a pioneer work. A pre-Darwinian, he maintained a cautious attitude to detailed evolutionist theories. See Life by his grandson (1894).

(4) **Robert** (1771–1858), Welsh social reformer, was born, a saddler's son, at Newtown, Montgomeryshire. At ten he was put into a draper's shop at Stamford, and by nineteen had risen to be manager of a cotton-mill. In 1799 he married the daughter of David Dale (q.v.), the philanthropic owner of the New Lanark cotton mills, where next year he settled as manager and part owner. He laboured to teach his workpeople the advantages of thrift, cleanliness, and good order, and established infant education. He began social propagandism in *A New View of Society* (1813), and finally adopted socialism; he lost much of his influence by his utterances on religion. His socialistic theories were put to the test in experimental communities at Orbiston near Bothwell, and later at New Harmony in Indiana, in County Clare, and in Hampshire, but all were unsuccessful. In 1828 his connection with New Lanark ceased; and, his means having been exhausted, the remainder of his days were spent in secularist, socialistic and spiritualistic propagandism. See Holyoake, *Co-operation in England* (1875); Owen's Autobiography (1857–58); also Lives by Booth (1869), Jones (1890), Podmore (1906), Cole (1925).

(5) **Robert Dale** (1801–77), son of (4), born in Glasgow, went to America in 1825 to help in the New Harmony colony. He settled in America in 1827, edited the *Free Inquirer* in New York, was a member of the Indiana legislature, and entered congress in 1843. Later he helped to remodel the constitution of Indiana; acted first as *chargé d'affaires*, next as minister at Naples (1853–58); and was an abolitionist and spiritualist. See his autobiography (1874). Two other sons of (4), **David Dale** (1807–60) and **Richard** (1810–1890), were notable geologists.

(6) **Wilfred** (1893–1918), English poet of World War I, killed in action on the Western Front. His poems were edited by his friend Siegfried Sassoon (1920). They were distinguished by the use of assonance in place of rhyme. See study by Welland (1960) and *Memoirs* by his brother, H. Owen (3 vols. 1963–65).

OWEN AP GRUFFYDD (d. 1169). prince of Gwynedd or North Wales, fiercely resisted Henry II, but ultimately submitted.

OWEN GLENDOWER. See GLENDOWER.

OWENS, (1) **James Cleveland (Jesse)** (1913–), American athlete, born in Decatur, Alabama, won three gold medals, and was a member of a winning U.S. relay team at the 1936 Olympic Games at Berlin. Snubbed on that occasion by Hitler, who refused to shake hands with him as a gold medallist because he was coloured, at the 1956 Games he was President Eisenhower's personal representative.

(2) **John** (1790–1846), a Manchester cotton merchant, who left £96,655 for the foundation of an nonsectarian college there, now a university.

(3) **Robert Bowie** (1870–1940), American chemist and engineer, professor at Nebraska, McGill and Philadelphia, invented a differentiation machine, an electric accelerometer and an electromagnetic system for guiding ships and aeroplanes. He is sometimes credited with the discovery of alpha-rays.

OWENSON, Sydney. See MORGAN (5).

OXENSTJERNA, or **Oxenstern, Count Axel** (1583–1654), Swedish statesman, was trained for the church, but entered the public service in 1602, and from 1612 till his death was chancellor. He negotiated peace with Denmark, with Russia, with Poland; and though he sought to prevent Gustavus Adolphus from plunging into the Thirty Years' War, he supported him in it loyally throughout, and on his death kept the Swedish armies together and sustained the Protestant cause. His eldest son, **Johan** (1611–57), was a diplomatist; another, **Erik** (1624–56), succeeded his father as chancellor.

OXFORD, Earl of. See ASQUITH, HARLEY, VERE.

OYAMA, Iwao, Prince (1842–1916), Japanese field-marshal (Hon. O.M. 1906), born in Satsuma, took Port Arthur and Wei-hei-Wei from China (1894–95), and commanded against Russia (1904–05).

OZANAM, Antoine Frédéric (1813–53), French literary historian, a Neo-Catholic of the school of Lacordaire, and one of the founders of the Society of St Vincent de Paul, born at Milan, became in 1841 professor of Foreign Literature at the Sorbonne. He wrote *Dante et la philosophie catholique* (1839), *Histoire de la civilisation au Ve siècle* (1845; trans. 1868), and *Études germaniques* (1847–49). See Lives by O'Meara (1876), Baunard (1912); and Letters (trans. 1886).

OZENFANT, Amédée, *o-zã-fã* (1886–1966), French artist, born at St Quentin, was the leader of the Purist movement in Paris and published a manifesto of Purism with Le Corbusier in 1919. From 1921 to 1925 they published an *avant-garde* magazine, *Esprit nouveau*, and in 1925 the book *La Peinture moderne*. His still-lifes based on this theory reduce vases and jugs to a static counterpoint of two-dimensional shapes. He founded art schools in London (1935) and New York (1938); his publications include *Art* (1928) and his diaries for the years 1931–34. See the monograph by K. Nierendorf (1931).

P

PAASIKIVI, Juo Kusti, *pah'-* (1870–1956), Finnish statesman, born in Tampere, became conservative prime minister after the civil war in 1918. He recognized the need for friendly relations with Russia, and took part in all Finnish-Soviet negotiations. He sought to avoid war in September 1939, conducted the armistice negotiations and became prime minister again in 1944. He succeeded Mannerheim as president (1946–56).

PACHECO, Francisco, *pa-chay'kō* (1571–1654), Spanish painter, was born and died at Seville. Influenced by Raphael, he painted portraits and historical subjects, and he opened a school of art at Seville, where Velasquez was his pupil and became his son-in-law. He wrote a notable technical treatise *Arte de la pintura* (1639).

PACHELBEL, Johann, *paKH'el-bel* (*c.* 1653–1706), German composer and organist, born in Nuremberg, held a variety of organist's posts before, in 1695, he returned to Nuremberg as organist of St Sebalds' Church. His works profoundly influenced J. S. Bach.

PACHMANN, Vladimir de, *paKH'-* (1848–1933), pianist, born at Odessa, studied at Vienna, and won fame as an interpreter of Chopin.

PACHOMIUS (4th cent.), an Egyptian, superseded the system of solitary recluse life by founding (*c.* A.D. 318), the first monastery on an island in the Nile.

PADEREWSKI, Ignace Jan, *pad-ĕ-ref'skee* (1860–1941), Polish pianist, composer and patriot, born at Kurylowka in Podolia, began to play as an infant of three. He studied at Warsaw, becoming professor in the Conservatoire there in 1878. In 1884 he taught in the Strasbourg Conservatoire, but thereafter became a virtuoso, appearing with prodigious success in Europe and America. He became director of Warsaw Conservatoire in 1909. In 1919 he was one of the first premiers of Poland, for whose freedom he had striven. Very soon, however, he retired from politics and went to live in Switzerland. He resumed concert work for some years, but when Poland's provisional parliament was established in Paris in 1940, he was elected president. He died in Switzerland.

PADILLA, Juan de, *pa-deel'ya* (1490–1521), a Spanish popular hero, was commandant of Saragossa under Charles V, headed an insurrection against the intolerable taxation, and after some successes was defeated (April 23, 1521) and beheaded. His wife held Toledo against the royal forces.

PAGANINI, Nicolo (1782–1840), Italian violin virtuoso, was born, a porter's son, at Genoa. He gave his first concert in 1793 (when his father reduced his age by two years in advertisements); began his professional tours in Italy in 1805; in 1828–31 made a great sensation in Austria and Germany, Paris and London. His dexterity and technical brilliance acquired an almost legendary reputation and it was said that he was in league with the devil. He revolutionized violin technique, among his innovations being the use of stopped harmonics. See study by G. I. C. de Courcy (1958).

PAGE, (1) Sir Frederick Handley (1885–1962), English pioneer aircraft designer and engineer, in 1909 founded the firm of aeronautical engineers which bears his name. His twin-engined 0/400 (1918) was one of the earliest heavy bombers, and his Hampden and Halifax bombers were used in the second World War; his civil aircraft include the Hannibal, Hermes and Herald transports. He was knighted in 1942.

(2) **Thomas Nelson** (1853–1922), American diplomat, born at Oakland, Va., practised law at Richmond, wrote many stories, some in Negro dialect, and became U.S. ambassador to Italy in 1913.

(3) **Walter Hines** (1855–1918), American diplomat, born in N. Carolina, edited the *Forum* (1890–95), *Atlantic Monthly* (1896–99), *World's Work* (1900–13), and became U.S. ambassador in London in 1913. See his *Life and Letters* by Hendrick (1922).

PAGÈS. See GARNIER-PAGÈS.

PAGET, (1) Sir George Edward (1809–92), born at Yarmouth, studied at Cambridge, and in 1872 became regius professor of Physics there. See his *Lectures*, with memoir by C. E. Paget (1893).

(2) **Sir James** (1814–99), brother of (1), born at Yarmouth, wrote standard *Lectures on Surgical Pathology* and *Clinical Lectures.* See *Memoirs* (1901) by his son.

(3) **Violet.** See LEE, VERNON.

PAHLAVI, Mohammad Reza (1919–), Shah of Persia, succeeded on the abdication of his father, Reza Shah, in 1941. His first two marriages, to Princess Fawzia, sister of Farouk, and to Soraya Esfandiari, ended in divorce after the failure of either to produce a male heir. By his third wife Farah Diba, daughter of an army officer, he has had two sons, Crown Prince Reza (1960), Ali Reza (1966), and a daughter, Princess Farahnaz (1963). His reign has been marked by social reforms and a movement away from the old-fashioned despotic concept of the monarchy.

PAIN, Barry Eric Odell (1867–1928), English humorous novelist and parodist, born in Cambridge, wrote *Eliza* (1900), &c.

PAINE, Thomas (1737–1809), English deist and radical, was born at Thetford, the son of an ex-Quaker stay-maker, had by turns been stay-maker and marine, schoolmaster, exciseman, and tobacconist, when in 1774 he sailed for Philadelphia. In 1776 his pamphlet *Common Sense* argued for complete independence; his *Crisis* came a year later; and Paine, then serving with the American army, was made secretary to the committee of foreign affairs. He lost that post in 1779 for divulging state secrets, but was appointed clerk of the Pennsylvania legislature, and in 1785 received from congress $3000 and a farm. In 1787 he returned to England, where in 1791–92 he published *The Rights of Man*, most famous of the replies to Burke's *Reflections*, which involved many in heavy penalties. Paine had slipped off to Paris, having been elected by Pas-de-Calais deputy to the National Convention. He voted with the Girondists, proposed to offer the king an asylum in America, and so offending the Robespierre faction, in 1794 was imprisoned. Just before his arrest he wrote part i of *The Age of Reason*, in favour of Deism. Part ii appeared in 1795, and a portion of part iii in 1807. The book alienated Washington and most of his old friends. After an imprisonment of eleven months he was released and restored to his seat in the Convention, but became disgusted with French politics. In 1802 he returned to America, and he died in New York. There are editions of his works by Mendum (1850) and Moncure Conway (4 vols. 1895–96); among biographies are those by 'Francis Oldys' (i.e., George Chalmers, 1791), Cheetham (1809), Rickman (1819), Sherwin (1819), Vale (1841), Blanchard (1860), Conway (1892), E. Sedgwick (1899), Gould (1925), Best (1927), Pearson (1937), C. Cohen (1945), W. E. Woodward (N.Y. 1945), H. M. Fast (N.Y. 1946).

PAINLEVÉ, Paul, *pĩ-lè-vay* (1863–1933), French mathematician and statesman, born in Paris, was professor at Lille, the Sorbonne, and the École polytechnique, repeatedly minister for war, twice air minister, and twice (1917, 1925) premier.

PAINTER, William (?1540–94), English translator, studied at Cambridge, was master of Sevenoaks school, but in 1561 became clerk of ordnance in the Tower. His *Palace of Pleasure* (1566–67; ed. Miles, 1930), largely composed of stories from Boccaccio, Bandello, and Margaret of Navarre, became popular, and was the main source whence many dramatists drew their plots, Shakespeare among them.

PAISIELLO, Giovanni (1740–1816), Italian composer, born at Taranto, studied at Naples, wrote at first only church music, but turned successfully to opera, and in 1776–84 was court musician to the Empress Catharine at St Petersburg. In 1799 he was appointed director of national music by the republican government of France and later enjoyed the patronage of Napoleon. He returned to Naples in 1804. Paisiello was the most successful Neapolitan opera composer of his time; his *Barbiere di Seviglia* was so popular that Rossini's use of the same libretto met with considerable hostility, but his ninety-odd pieces are seldom if ever staged today, possibly because of their comparative superficiality, though they contain a wealth of delightful tunes, one of which, *Nel cor più non mi sento*, was used by both Beethoven and Paganini as a theme for variations.

PALACIO VALDÉS. See VALDÉS (1).

PALACKÝ, František, *pa'lat-ski* (1798–1876), was a Czech publicist and politician in Prague, and the most distinguished historian of Bohemia.

PALAFOX Y MELZI, José de, *-fokh'* (1780–1847), Spanish patriot, nominally head of the heroic defence of Saragossa (July 1808 to February 1809), was carried prisoner to France, and not released until 1813. He was made Duke of Saragossa (1836) and grandee of Spain (1837).

PALESTRINA, Giovanni Pierluigi da (1525–1594), Italian composer, born at Palestrina, was sent at the age of ten to the choir school of Sta Maria Maggiore at Rome, where he learnt composition and organ playing. In 1544 he became organist and *maestro di canto* at the cathedral of St Agapit in his native town, and at the age of twenty-two married the heiress of a well-to-do citizen. The new pope, Julius III, had been bishop of Palestrina and aware of the talent possessed by his late organist, appointed him master of the Julian choir at St Peter's, for which he composed many fine masses. In 1555 Julius engineered him into the exclusive and highly privileged Pontifical Choir without an entrance examination or the customary election by existing members, but Paul IV, coming to the papal throne in the same year, tightened up the regulations and Palestrina was compulsorily retired. He now became choirmaster at the Lateran, but walked out without notice in 1560, probably owing to his disagreement with economy cuts imposed by the impoverished canons. In 1561 he returned to Sta Maria Maggiore as choirmaster, remaining until 1567, though only on a part-time basis after 1565, when he was appointed music master at the new Roman Seminary set up by the Council of Trent. The years between 1572 and 1580 were tragic ones for Palestrina, who during this time lost his wife and three sons in the terrible epidemics which intermittently ravaged Rome. Eight months after his wife's death he was married again, this time to a wealthy widow who had come into a furrier's business, which he took over, apparently with success. A great task entrusted to him at this time was the revision of the Gradual, ordained in 1577 by the Council of Trent, a monumental labour which was abandoned after a few years. He continued to live in Rome, composing and working at St Peter's, refusing an offer from the Duke of Mantua, an old friend of his, to become his musical director. He died in Rome, February 2, 1594, and was buried in St Peter's. Palestrina's place as the most distinguished composer of the Renaissance is unchallenged, as is his status as one of the greatest figures in musical history, to whom generations of later composers, including Bach, Mozart, Wagner, Liszt and Debussy, have acknowledged their debt. His works include over 90 masses and a large number of motets, hymns and other liturgical pieces as well as some excellent madrigals. Apart from a few organ *ricercari* of doubtful authenticity, no instrumental music has been ascribed to him His compositions, free from sentimentality yet with an extraordinary depth of feeling, are characterized by an uncanny skill in the handling of contrapuntal texture, but also contain examples of homophony and subtle dissonances which are immensely effective chorally. Having in its original form no division into bars, his music is free-flowing and unhampered by rhythmic conventions. See Life by Pyne (1922), and studies by Coates (1938) and Jeppesen (1946); also H. K. Andrews, *An Introduction to the Technique of Palestrina* (1958).

PALEY, William (1743–1805), English theologian, born at Peterborough, fellow and tutor of Christ's College, Cambridge (1768–1776), published *Principles of Moral and Political Philosophy* (1785), expounding a form of utilitarianism. In 1790 appeared his most original work, *Horae Paulinae*, the aim of which is to prove the great improbability of the hypothesis that the New Testament is a cunningly devised fable. It was followed in 1794 by his famous *Evidences of Christianity*. In 1802 he published perhaps the most widely popular of all his works, *Natural Theology, or Evidences of the Existence and Attributes of the Deity*. See the Life by G. W. Meadley (1809).

PALGRAVE, (1) Sir Francis (1788–1861), English historian, was born in London, the son of Meyer Cohen, a Jewish stockbroker, but on his marriage (1823) he assumed his mother-in-law's maiden name. He was called to the bar in 1827; and, knighted in 1832, was in 1838 appointed deputy-keeper of Records. Among his works are *The English Commonwealth* (1832), *The Merchant and the Friar*, and a *History of Normandy and of England* (1851–64 incomplete). He also edited *Parliamentary Writs* (1830–34), *Rotuli Curiae Regis* (1835), *Ancient Kalendars of the Treasury of the Exchequer* (1836), and *Documents illustrating the History of Scotland* (1837). A collected edition of his historical works (1919–22) was started by his third son, **Sir Robert Harry Inglis** (1827–1919), political economist.

(2) **Francis Turner** (1824–97), eldest son of (1), poet and critic, born in London, became scholar of Balliol, Oxford, and fellow of Exeter, was successively vice-principal of a training college, private secretary to Earl Granville, an official in the education department, and professor of Poetry at Oxford (1886–95). His works include *Idylls and Songs* (1854), *Essays on Art* (1866), *Hymns* (1867), *Lyrical Poems* (1871), *Visions of England* (1881), and *Landscape in Poetry* (1897). He is best known as the editor of the *Golden Treasury of English Lyrics* (1861, re-edited 1896; poor 2nd series, 1897); *Children's Treasury of Lyrical Poetry* (1875); *Sonnets and Songs of Shakespeare* (1877); selections from Herrick (1877) and Keats (1885); and *Treasury of Sacred Song* (1889). See Life (1899) by G. F. Palgrave, his daughter.

(3) **Sir Reginald Francis Douce** (1829–1904), K.C.B. (1892), fourth son of (1), was in 1886 appointed clerk to the House of Commons, and wrote on parliamentary practice and history.

(4) **William Gifford** (1826–88), second son of (1), graduated at Oxford in 1846. He joined the Bombay Native Infantry, but becoming a Jesuit, studied at Rome, and was sent as a missionary to Syria. For Napoleon III he went disguised as a physician on a daring expedition through Arabia (1862–63), described in his (untrustworthy) *Narrative of a Year's Journey through Central and Eastern Arabia* (1865). Quitting the Jesuits in 1864, he was sent by the British government in 1865 to treat for the release of the captives in Abyssinia. He became consul at Trebizond, St Thomas and Manila; consul-general in Bulgaria 1878, and Siam 1880; and British minister to Uruguay 1884. There he married, was reconciled to the church, and died.

PALISSY, Bernard (*c.* 1509–89), French potter, was born in Agen, and, after wandering for ten years over France as a glass-painter, about 1538 married and settled at Saintes. Resolved to discover how to make enamels, he neglected all else and experimented for sixteen years, exhausting all his resources, but was at length rewarded with success (1557). His ware bearing in high relief plants and animals coloured to represent nature, soon made him famous; and, though as a Huguenot he was in 1562 imprisoned, he was speedily released and taken into royal favour. In 1564 he established his workshop at the Tuileries, and was specially exempted from the massacre of St Bartholomew (1572). During 1575–84 he lectured on natural history, physics and agriculture. In 1588 he was again arrested as a Huguenot and was thrown into the Bastille of Bucy, where he died. Palissy's writings, with an account of his experiences, were edited by A. France (1880). See Life by H. Morley (1852), and French ones by Audiat (1868), Burty (1886), Dupuy (1902) and Levoux (1928).

PALLADIO, Andrea (1518–80), Italian architect, was born and died at Vicenza. He founded modern Italian architecture, as distinguished from the earlier Italian Renaissance. The Palladian style is modelled on the ancient Roman as apprehended by Vitruvius. His *Quattro Libri dell' Architettura* (1570) greatly influenced his successors, especially Inigo Jones, whose notes are given in Leoni's Eng. trans. (1715), and Christopher Wren. See Lives by B. F. Fletcher (1902), Zanella (1880), Barichella (1880).

PALLADIUS, (1) St, is said to have been sent ' in Scotiam ', in 430, by Pope Celestine; but the Scotia here meant was certainly Ireland. Skene doubts if Palladius was ever in Scotland till after his death, when St Ternan brought his relics to Fordoun in Kincardineshire.

(2) **Rutilius Taurus Aemilianus** (4th cent. A.D.), Roman author, who wrote *De Re Rustica* (On Agriculture), in fourteen books

PALLAS, Peter Simon (1741–1811), born at Berlin, was in 1768 invited to St Petersburg by the Empress Catharine as an eminent naturalist. He spent six years (1768–74) exploring the Urals, the Kirghiz Steppes, the Altai range, part of Siberia, and the steppes of the Volga, returning with an extraordinary treasure of specimens; and he wrote a series of works on the geography, ethnography, flora and fauna of the regions visited. He settled in the Crimea.

PALLAVICINO, Sforza, *-vi-chee'nō* (1607–1667), Italian historian, became in 1638 a Jesuit, and a cardinal in 1659. His best-known work is *Istoria del Concilio di Trento* (1656–57), a reply to the work of Sarpi.

PALMA, Jacopo, called Palma Vecchio (' Old Palma ') (*c.* 1480–1528), stands at the head of the second class of great Venetian artists. His pictures are sacred subjects or portrait groups. See work by Locatelli (1890). His brother's grandson, **Jacopo** (1544–1628), called **Il Giovane** (' the Younger '), painted poorish religious pictures.

PALMER, (1) **Daniel David** (1845–1913), American osteopath and founder of chiropractic, born at Toronto, settled at Davenport, Iowa, where he first practised spinal adjustment and founded the Palmer School of Chiropractic in 1898. Later he established a college of chiropractic at Portland, Oregon.

(2) **Edward Henry** (1840–82), English orientalist, was born at Cambridge, and at the university he devoted himself to oriental studies. In 1871 he was appointed Lord Almoner's professor of Arabic at Cambridge, and in 1874 he was called to the bar. In 1881 he turned journalist, writing principally for the *Standard.* In 1882, on the eve of Arabi's Egyptian rebellion, sent by government to win over the Sinai tribes, he, Capt. Gill, R.E., and Lieut. Charrington, R.N., were murdered in the ravine of Wady Sadr. Among Palmer's works are the *Desert of the Exodus* (1871) and a translation of the *Koran* (1880). See Life by Besant (1883), and Haynes, *Man-hunting in the Desert* (1894).

(3) **Roundell** and **William.** See SELBORNE.

(4) **Samuel** (1805–81), English landscape painter and etcher, born in London, produced chiefly watercolours in a mystical and imaginative style derived from Blake, who was his friend. His work, outmoded during his lifetime by the Victorian demand for realistic sentimentality, is now assessed at its true value.

PALMERSTON, Henry John Temple, 3rd Viscount (1784–1865), was born at 20 Queen Anne's Gate, Westminster, of the Irish branch of the ancient English family of Temple. In 1800 he went to Edinburgh University, in 1802 succeeded his father, and was at Cambridge University (1803–06). As Tory candidate for the university he was rejected in 1806, elected in 1807 for Newport (Wight); but from 1811 he represented his *alma mater* for twenty years, and only lost his seat when he supported the Reform Bill. Afterwards he was returned for South Hampshire, lost his seat in 1835, but found a seat for Tiverton. He was junior lord of the Admiralty and secretary at war under Perceval, the Earl of Liverpool, Canning, Goderich and the Duke of Wellington (1809–28). His official connection with the Tory party ceased in 1828. The Duke's government was swept away in 1830, and Earl Grey offered the seals of the foreign office to Palmerston. For the first time on record England and France acted in concert. Palmerston took a leading part in securing the independence of Belgium, in establishing the thrones of Isabella of Spain and Maria of Portugal, and in endeavouring, in alliance with Austria and Turkey, to check Russian influence in the East. In 1841 Palmerston went out of office with the Whigs on the question of free trade in corn, and under Lord John Russell in 1846 resumed the seals of the Foreign Office. His second term was embarrassed by the Spanish marriages (see GUIZOT), the revolutions in 1848, the rupture between Spain and Great Britain, the affair of Don Pacifico (a Gibraltar Jew living in Athens, who claimed the privileges of a British subject), and the consequent quarrel with Greece. His self-asserting character, his brusque speech, his interferences in foreign affairs, were little calculated to conciliate opponents at home, and secured for ' Firebrand Palmerston ' many enemies abroad. A vote of censure on the foreign policy was in 1850 carried in the House of Lords, but defeated in the Lower House. In December 1851 Palmerston expressed to the French ambassador his approbation of the *coup d'état* of Louis Napoleon, without consulting either the premier or the Queen, and Lord John Russell advised his resignation. Next February he shattered the Russell administration on a Militia Bill. He refused office under the Earl of Derby, but was home secretary in Aberdeen's coalition (1852), whose fall (1855) brought Palmerston the premiership. He vigorously prosecuted the Russian war. Defeated in 1857 on Cobden's motion condemning the Chinese war, he appealed to the country, and met the House of Commons with a largely increased majority, but fell in February 1858, over the Conspiracy Bill. In June 1859 he again became prime minister, remaining in office till his death, the chief events the American Civil War, Napoleon's war with Austria, and the Austro-Prussian war with Denmark. It was his ambition to be the minister of a nation rather than of a political party, and his opponents admitted that he held office with more general acceptance than any minister since Chatham. He is buried in Westminster Abbey. See Lives by Dalling and Ashley (5 vols. 1870–76), Trollope (1882), the Duke of Argyll (1892), Bell (1936), Webster (1951), and Martin (1963); also *Regina v. Palmerston* (ed. Connell, 1962).

PALMIERI, Luigi (1807–96), Italian meteorologist, became in 1847 professor at Naples, and in 1854 director of the Vesuvius observatory. He invented a rain gauge and other meteorological instruments.

PALTOCK, Robert (1697–1767), English writer, born in London, and bred to the law, wrote *Peter Wilkins* (1751); its authorship remained a mystery till 1835. See Bullen's edition (1884) and *Athenaeum* (1884–85).

PALUDAN-MÜLLER, Frederik (1809–76), Danish poet, wrote poems, dramas and romances. But his fame rests on *Adam Homo* (1841–49), a humorous, satiric, didactic poem. See Brandes, *Eminent Authors* (1886), and a study by F. Lange (1899).

PANCRAS, St (d. 304), Christian martyr, son of a heathen noble of Phrygia, was baptised at Rome, but immediately afterwards was slain in the Diocletian persecution, being only fourteen years old.

PANDER, Christian Heinrich (1794–1865), Russian scientist, was born at Riga. At Würzburg he did valuable research on chick development in the egg, with particular regard to the embryonic layers now called by his name. Having published his findings in 1817, in 1820 he accompanied as a naturalist a Russian mission to Bokhara, and was elected a member of the St Petersburg Academy of Sciences in 1826.

PANDULF, Cardinal (d. 1226), Italian prelate, the commissioner sent (1213) by Innocent III to King John, who returned to England as legate (1218–21), and in 1218 was made Bishop of Norwich.

PANHARD, René (1841–1908), French engineer and inventor, born at Paris, a pioneer of the motor industry. With Émile Levassor, his partner from 1886, he was the first to mount an internal combustion engine on a chassis (1891). He founded the Panhard Company.

PANIZZI, Sir Anthony (1797–1879), Italian bibliographer, born at Brescello in Modena, was an advocate, but, sharing in the revolution of 1821, fled to Liverpool, and in 1828 became Italian professor in University College London, in 1831 assistant librarian, and in 1856 chief librarian of the British Museum, where he showed great administrative ability, undertook a new catalogue, and designed the reading room, politically active the while for the Italian cause. See Lives by Brooks (1931), Miller (1967).

PANKHURST, Emmeline (1857–1928), English suffragette, born (**Goulden**) at Manchester, organized (1905) the Women's Social and Political Union, and fought for women's suffrage by violent means. Of her daughters and fellow workers, **Dame Christabel** (1880–1958), turned later to preaching Christ's Second Coming; and **Sylvia** (1882–1960) diverged to pacificism, internationalism and Labour politics, and wrote a Life of her mother (1935). See Christabel's *Unshackled* (1959), and Mitchell, *The Fighting Pankhursts* (1967).

PANZINI, Alfredo (1863–1939), Italian writer of short stories, novels and criticisms, born at Senigallia, educated at Bologna, taught in Milan and Rome, and was an original academician.

PAOLI, Pasquale de (1725–1807), Corsican patriot, born at Stretta in Corsica, son of a patriot driven in exile to Naples in 1739. Thence Pasquale returned to take part in the heroic struggle against the Genoese, and in 1755 was appointed to the chief command. The Genoese sold the island (1768) to France. For a year he held out against a French army, but was overpowered, and escaped to England, where he was welcomed. Boswell, who had visited him in Corsica, introduced him to Dr Johnson. On the French Revolution he became governor of Corsica, but he organized a fresh insurrection against the Convention, favouring union with England. He returned to England in 1796. See Life by Ravenna (Florence 1927).

PAOLO, Fra. See SARPI.

PAPAGOS, Field-Marshal Alexander (1883–1956), Greek statesman, a distinguished soldier who, after a brilliant military career, became in 1952 prime minister of Greece at the head of an exclusively Greek Rally government.

PAPEN, Franz von, *pah'pėn* (1879–), German politician, born at Werl, Westphalia, was military attaché at Mexico and Washington, chief of staff with a Turkish army, and took to Centre party politics. As Hindenburg's chancellor (1932) he suppressed the Prussian Socialist government, as Hitler's vice-chancellor (1933–34) signed a concordat with Rome. He was ambassador to Austria (1936–38) and Turkey (1939–44) and was taken prisoner in 1945. He stood trial at Nuremberg in 1946 but was acquitted.

PAPIAS (2nd cent. A.D.), bishop at Hierapolis in Phrygia, a 'companion of Polycarp'. Irenaeus, Eusebius, &c., preserve fragments of his lost 'Exposition of Oracles of the Lord'.

PAPIN, Denis, *pa-pi* (1647–?1712), French physicist, born at Blois, helped Huygens and Boyle in their experiments, invented the condensing pump and the steam digester (1681), and was made a member of the Royal Society (1680). For four years he was at Venice, was back in London in 1684, in 1687 became professor of Mathematics at Marburg but from 1696 to 1707 worked in Cassel, after which he returned to England.

PAPINEAU, Louis Joseph (1789–1871), French-Canadian party leader, speaker of the House of Assembly for Lower Canada (1815–37), opposed the union with Upper Canada, and agitated against the imperial government. At the rebellion of 1837 a warrant was issued against him for high-treason. He escaped to Paris; but returned to Canada, amnestied, in 1847.

PAPINI, Giovanni, *-pee'nee* (1881–1956), Italian author and philosopher, born at Florence and educated there, wrote *Un Uomo finito* (1913), *Storia di Cristo* (1921), *Sant' Agostino* (1929), &c.

PAPINIANUS, Aemilius (*c.* A.D. 140–212), Roman jurist, held offices at Rome under Septimius Severus, but was put to death by Caracalla. Nearly 600 excerpts from his legal works were incorporated in Justinian's *Pandects*.

PAPPENHEIM, Gottfried Heinrich Graf zu (1594–1632), imperial general in the Thirty Years' War, was born at Pappenheim in Franconia, of an ancient Swabian family. At twenty he went over to the Roman Catholic Church, served the king of Poland, joined the army of the Catholic League, and decided the battle of Prague (1620). In 1625 he became general of the Spanish horse in Lombardy; but in 1626 re-entered the Austrian service, and after suppressing a peasant revolt cooperated with Tilly against Danes, Swedes and Saxons. On his head rests in great measure the guilt of the ferocious massacres at Magdeburg. He involved Tilly in the disastrous battle of Breitenfeld, but made heroic efforts to protect the retreat. After Tilly's death he served under Wallenstein. He arrived at Lützen when Wallenstein's army was on the point of being routed by Gustavus Adolphus, and charged the Swedes' left wing with such fury as to throw it into confusion. He was mortally wounded in the last charge, and died next day.

PAPPUS OF ALEXANDRIA (fl. late 3rd-early 4th cent. A.D.), Greek mathematician, whose 'Mathematical Collection' is extant in an incomplete form. See Hultsch's edition (1876–78).

PARACELSUS, a name coined for himself by **Theophrastus Bombastus von Hohenheim** (1493–1541), son of a physician at Einsiedeln (Schwyz). He went to Basel University at sixteen, studied alchemy and chemistry with Trithemius, Bishop of Würzburg, and then learned the properties of metals and minerals at the mines in Tirol. In subsequent wanderings he amassed a vast store of facts, learned the actual practice of medicine, but lost all faith in scholastic disquisitions and disputations. He acquired fame as a medical practitioner (1526), was made town physician at Basel, and lectured on medicine at the university, but flouted at Galen and Avicenna, and justified the furious enmities that pursued him by his own vanity, arrogance, aggressiveness and intemperate habits. A dispute with the magistrates in 1528 drove him from Basel; he wandered for a dozen years, and settled in 1541 at Salzburg. His works are mainly written in Swiss-German. The earliest printed work was *Practica D. Theophrasti Paracelsi* (1529). Collected German editions appeared at Basel in 1589–1591 and again in 1603–05 (reissued 1618), Latin editions in 1603–05 and 1658. In spite of his attraction to alchemy and mysticism, he made new chemical compounds, and improved pharmacy and therapeutics, encouraged research and experiment, and, in an empirical fashion, revolutionized hidebound medical methods. See books by M. B. Lessing (1839), Marx (1842), Mook (1876), Kahlbaum (1894), Stoddart (1915), Stillman (1920), Gundolf (1928), W. Pagel (Basel 1959) and Browning's poem.

PARDO BAZÁN, Emilia, Condesa de, *ba-*THahn' (1851–1921), Spanish novelist, reckoned the best of her time, born near Coruña, passed from romanticism to naturalism. Her greatest works are *La Cuestión palpante* (1883), *Los Pazos de Ulloa* (1886), *La Madre naturaleza* (1887), *La Piedra Angular* (1891), *Dulce Dueño* (1911). She also wrote plays, and was an ardent feminist.

PARÉ, Ambroise (1517–90), French surgeon, 'the father of modern surgery', was born near Laval, in 1537 as surgeon joined the army starting for Italy, and was surgeon to Henry II, Charles IX and Henry III. He died in Paris. Paré improved the treatment of gunshot wounds, and substituted ligature of the arteries for cauterization with a red-hot iron after amputation. His *Cinq Livres de chirurgie* (1562) and other writings exercised a great influence on surgery. See Lives by Paulmier (1884), Stephen Paget (1898), F. R. Packard (1922), and H. E. Sigerist, *Great Doctors* (1933).

PARES, Sir Bernard (1867–1949), English historian, educated at Harrow and Cambridge, was professor of Russian History, Language and Literature at Liverpool University (1908–17) and at London University (1919–36). Among his many authoritative books on Russian subjects are *A History of Russia* (1926), *Fall of the Russian Monarchy* (1939) and *Russia and the Peace* (1944). He also contributed the chapters on Russia in the *Cambridge Modern History*.

PARETO, Vilfredo (1848–1923), Italian economist and sociologist, born in Paris, was professor of Political Economy at Lausanne, writing well-known textbooks on the subject in which he demonstrated a mathematical approach. In Sociology his *Trattato di sociologica generale* (1916; trans. *The Mind and Society*) anticipated some of the principles of Fascism.

PARINI, Giuseppe (1729–99), Italian poet, born near Milan became a priest in 1754. He made his name as a poet by the sequence of poems called collectively *Il Giorno* (1763–1803).

PARIS, (1) **Gaston** (1839–1903), French scholar, born at Paris, in 1872 became professor of Old French at the Collège de France in succession to his father, Paulin Paris (1800–81). He edited mediaeval poems, wrote a long series of valuable works on mediaeval French literature, founded *Romanio* (1872), a review of Romance Philology, and was in 1896 elected to the Academy.

(2) **Louis Philippe, Comte de** (1834–94), grandson of King Louis-Philippe, served in the American war (of which he wrote a history), lived mainly in England, and on the death of the Comte de Chambord (q.v.) became head of the Bourbon house. See BOURBON, ORLEANS.

(3) **Matthew** (*c.* 1200–59), the best Latin chronicler of the 13th century, was born in England, entered the Benedictine monastery of St Albans in 1217, and later went on a mission to Norway. His principal work is his *Historia Major*, or *Chronica Majora*, a history from the creation down to 1259, the first part compiled from Roger of Wendover and others, from 1235 his own work. It was published in 1571 by Archbishop Parker. The *Historia Anglorum* is abridged from the greater work. Other works are lives of abbots and a book of *Additamenta.* See Jessopp, *Studies by a Recluse* (1892), and study by R. Vaughan (1958).

PARK, Mungo (1771–1806), Scottish explorer of Africa, was born at Foulshiels on the Yarrow, and studied medicine in Edinburgh (1789–91). Through Sir Joseph Banks, he was named assistant surgeon on the *Worcester* bound for Sumatra (1792); and in 1795 his services were accepted by the African Association. He learnt Mandingo at an English factory on the Gambia, started inland in December, was imprisoned by a chief, but escaping, reached the Niger at Sego in July 1796. He pursued his way westward along its banks to Bammaku, and then crossing a mountainous country, fell ill, but was ultimately brought back by a slave trader to the factory again, after an absence of nineteen months. He told his adventures in *Travels in the Interior of Africa* (1799). He married (1799), and settled as a surgeon at Peebles; but the life was repugnant to him, and in 1805 he undertook another journey to Africa at government expense. Again he started from Pisania on the Gambia, with a company of forty-five; but when he reached the Niger he had only seven followers. From Sansanding he sent back his journals and letters in November 1805 and embarked in a canoe with four European companions. Through many perils and difficulties they reached Boussa, where they were attacked by the natives, and drowned in the fight. See Life by Wishaw prefixed to his later *Journal* (1815), and works by Joseph Thomson (1890), Maclachlan (1898) and S. Gwynn (1934).

PARKER, (1) **Dorothy**, *née* **Rothschild** (1893–1967), American writer, noted for her satiric humour as shown in her collections of verse *Enough Rope* (1926), *Not so Deep as a Well* (1936), &c., and of short stories *Laments for the Living* (1930), *Here Lies* (1939), &c.

(2) **Sir Gilbert** (1862–1932), British author, born in Canada, became lecturer in English at a college in Toronto, edited a paper in Sydney, and wrote novels, including *When Valmond came to Pontiac* (1895), *The Battle of the Strong* (1898), &c.. He was M.P. (Unionist) for Gravesend in 1900–18, and was made a knight in 1902, baronet in 1915, P.C. in 1916.

(3) **Sir Hyde** (1739–1807), British admiral, son of vice-admiral Sir Hyde Parker (1714–1782), in 1801 was appointed to command the fleet sent to the Baltic to act against the armed coalition of Russia, Sweden and Denmark. He had no share in the battle of Copenhagen, which was directed by Nelson.

(4) **Joseph** (1830–1902), English Congregationalist preacher and author, the son of a stonecutter, born at Hexham, studied at Moorfields Tabernacle and University College London (1852), and became pastor of Congregational chapels at Banbury, Manchester, and, in 1869, of what became in 1874 the City Temple in London. He was noted as a pulpit orator, and as the author of many religious works. See Life by W. Adamson (1902).

(5) **Matthew** (1504–75), second Protestant Archbishop of Canterbury, born at Norwich, became chaplain to Queen Anne Boleyn (1535), dean of a college at Stoke in Suffolk, a royal chaplain, canon of Ely, master of Corpus Christi (1544), vice-chancellor (1545) and dean of Lincoln. He married, and by Mary was deprived of his preferments. Under Elizabeth he was consecrated Archbishop of Canterbury (1559). The ritual was not the Roman one; but the scandalous fable that he was informally consecrated in an inn called the Nag's Head originated in Catholic circles forty years later. The new primate strove to bring about more general conformity. The Thirty-nine Articles were passed by convocation in 1562; and his 'Advertisements' for the regulation of service, and measures of repression perhaps forced upon him by the queen, provoked great opposition in the growing Puritan party. Parker originated the revised translation of the Scriptures known as the Bishops' Bible. He edited works by Aelfric, Matthew Paris, Walsingham and Giraldus Cambrensis, was an indefatigable collector of books, and maintained printers, transcribers, engravers. *De Antiquitate Britannicae Ecclesiae* (1572) was an original work. His letters fill a volume (Parker Soc. 1853). See Lives by Strype (1824), Kennedy (1908); Hook's *Archbishops*, vol. ix.

(6) **Richard** (*c.* 1767–97), English seaman, born at Exeter, volunteered into the navy in 1797, and from May 10 till June 13 that year was ringleader of the mutiny at the Nore, having for a time thirteen ships of the line, besides frigates, under his orders. He was hanged on June 30.

(7) **Theodore** (1810–60), American preacher, was born at Lexington, Mass., graduated at Harvard in 1836, and settled as Unitarian minister at West Roxbury, now in Boston. The rationalistic views which separated him from conservative Unitarians were expounded in *A Discourse of Matters pertaining to Religion* (1841), followed by *Sermons for the Times*. From then on he wrote incessantly. He lectured throughout the States, and plunged into the antislavery agitation. His health broke down, and he died in Florence. See Lives by Weiss (1864), Dean (1877), Chadwick (1900) and Commager (1936).

PARKES, (1) **Alexander** (1813–90), British chemist and inventor, born in Birmingham, noted for his inventions in connection with electroplating, in the course of which he even electroplated a spider's web. He invented xylonite (celluloid; first patented 1855).

(2) **Sir Harry Smith** (1828–85), British diplomat, born near Walsall, went to China in 1841, served as consul at Canton, Amoy and Foochow, figured prominently in the *Arrow* episode, and in 1858 was appointed a commissioner after the capture of Canton. His treacherous seizure by the Chinese while acting as Lord Elgin's envoy in 1860 led to the burning of the Summer Palace at Pekin. He was British minister in China from 1883.

(3) **Sir Henry** (1815–96), Australian statesman, was born, the son of a yeoman, at Stoneleigh, Warwickshire, emigrated to New South Wales in 1839, and at Sydney became eminent as a journalist. A member of the colonial parliament in 1854, he held various offices, from 1872 was repeatedly prime minister, and was identified with free trade. He was made K.C.M.G. in 1877. See his autobiography (1892) and Lives by Charles E. Lyne (1897) and Sir T. Bavin (1941).

PARKINSON, (1) **Cyril Northcote** (1909–), English political scientist, graduated from Emmanuel College, Cambridge, of which he became a fellow in 1935. Professor of History at the University of Malaya (1950–58), and visiting professor at Harvard and Illinois, he has written many works on historical, political and economic subjects, but achieved wider renown by his seriocomic tilt at bureaucratic malpractices *Parkinson's Law, the Pursuit of Progress* (1958). 'Parkinson's Law'—that work expands to fill the time available for its completion, and subordinates multiply at a fixed rate, regardless of the amount of work produced—has passed into the language.

(2) **James** (1755–1824), British physician, in 1817 gave the first description of paralysis agitans, or Parkinson's disease as it has been called. He had already (1812) described appendicitis and perforation, and was the first to recognize the latter condition as a cause of death.

(3) **John** (1567–1650), a London herbalist, a native probably of Nottinghamshire, was apothecary to James I and author of *Paradisus Terrestris* (1629) and *Theatrum Botanicum* (1640), long the most comprehensive English herbal.

PARKMAN, Francis (1823–93), American historian, graduated at Harvard in 1844, studied law, and became the authoritative writer on the rise and fall of the French dominion in America. His works included *The California and Oregon Trail* (1849), *The Pioneers of France in the New World* (1865), *La Salle and the Great West* (1869), *Frontenac and New France* (1877), *A Half-Century of Conflict* (1893), *Montcalm and Wolfe* (1884). See Lives by Farnham (1900) and Sedgwick (1904), and D. Leon, *History as a Romantic Art* (1960).

PARLEY, Peter. See GOODRICH.

PARMENIDES, *pahr-men'i-dees* (fl. 5th cent. B.C.), with Heraclitus (q.v.), whose doctrines he opposed, the greatest of the Greek Presocratic philosophers, was a native of the Greek settlement of Elea in southern Italy and became the greatest of the Eleatic school, which derived its doctrines from the Pythagoreans. Parmenides held that nothing changes. All that one is logically entitled to do is to affirm existence, say 'it is', since it is impossible to know what is not, for 'it is the same thing that can be thought and can be'. His doctrines are set out in a didactic poem, *On Nature,* divided into two parts 'the way of truth' and 'the way of opinion', foreshadowing Plato's metaphysics. He is not so much the founder of logic, but the pioneer of certain perennial metalogical arguments concerning the category of substance. His great disciple was Zeno (q.v.). See fragments, ed. Diehls (1897), J. Burnet, *Early Greek Philosophy* (4th ed. 1952), and G. S. Kirk and J. E. Raven, *The Presocratic Philosophers* (1957).

PARMIGIANO, or **Parmigianino,** properly **Girolamo Francesco Maria Mazzola,** *-jah'no* (1503–40), Italian painter of the Lombard school, born at Parma, at first painted there, but after 1523 worked at Rome, whence he fled to Bologna when the city was sacked in 1527. At Bologna he painted his famous Madonna altarpiece for the nuns of St Margaret before returning to Parma in 1531. He shows the influence of Correggio and Raphael. His *Vision of St Jerome* is in the National Gallery, London. See monograph by Freedberg (1950).

PARNELL, (1) **Charles Stewart** (1846–91), Irish politician, was born at Avondale, Co. Wicklow. His father belonged to an old Cheshire family which purchased an estate in Ireland under Charles II. His great-grandfather, Sir John Parnell (1744–1801), was chancellor of the Irish Exchequer. Thomas Parnell (q.v.), the poet, belonged to the same family. Charles, whose mother was the daughter of an American admiral, studied four years at Magdalen College, Cambridge, but took no degree. In 1874 he became high sheriff of County Wicklow; that same year he contested County Dublin without success, but in April 1875 was returned as a Home Ruler for County Meath. In 1877–78 he gained great popularity in Ireland by his audacity in the use of deliberate obstruction in parliamentary tactics. In 1878 he threw himself into agrarian agitation, and was elected president of the Irish National Land League. From the United States he brought home £70,000 for the cause. In 1880 he was returned for Meath and Mayo and for the city of Cork, sat for the last, and was chairman of the Irish parliamentary party. In 1880 too he formulated the method of 'boycotting'. Mr Gladstone's government put Parnell and other leading members of the Land League on trial, but the jury failed to agree. In opposing the government's Coercion Bill, Parnell was ejected from the House, with thirty-four of his followers (February 3, 1881). He refused to accept Mr Gladstone's Land Bill as a final settlement. In October Mr Gladstone sent him to Kilmainham jail; he was released on May 2, 1882. Parnell in the House of Commons expressed his detestation of the tragedy of Phoenix Park. The Crimes Act was now hurried through parliament in spite of the Irish party. The Land League, proclaimed illegal after the issue of the 'No Rent' manifesto, was revived in 1884 as the National League, Parnell being president. The year before the sum of £35,000, mostly raised in America, had been presented to him by his admirers. After an unsuccessful attempt to make terms with the Conservatives, Parnell flung his vote—now eighty-six strong—into the Liberal scale, and brought about the fall of the short-lived first Salisbury government. Mr Gladstone's Home Rule Bill was defeated owing to the defection of Liberal members. The consequent appeal to the country (July 1886) gave Lord Salisbury a Unionist majority of over a hundred, and threw Parnell into a close alliance with Mr Gladstone. Now it was that *The Times* published 'Parnellism and Crime'—with letters as by Parnell, expressing approval of Mr Burke's murder. A Special Commission sat 128 days, and, after the flight and suicide at Madrid of Pigott (q.v.), who had imposed upon *The Times* with forgeries, cleared Parnell (November 1889) of the charge of having been personally guilty of organizing outrages; but his party were declared guilty of incitements to intimidation, out of which had grown crimes which they had failed to denounce. Parnell now raised an action against *The Times*, settled by a payment of £5000. The 'uncrowned king' of Ireland was presented with the freedom of Edinburgh in July 1889. His frequent mysterious absences from his parliamentary duties were explained by his appearance as co-respondent in a divorce case brought by Captain O'Shea against his wife, and decree was granted with costs against Parnell (November 17, 1890). The Gladstonian party now demanded his retirement from leadership; and though the Irish members had reappointed him chairman, they met to reconsider the position a week later, and, after five days of wrangling, the majority elected Justin McCarthy chairman. Parnell, with the remnants of his party. carried the warfare into Ireland; but his condemnation by the church and the emphatic defeat of his nominees at by-elections foretokened the collapse of his party at the general election of 1892, when seventy-two anti-Parnellites were returned against nine of his supporters. Before this, Parnell had died suddenly at Brighton, five months after his marriage to Mrs O'Shea; he is buried in

Glasnevin cemetery, Dublin. His sister, **Fanny Parnell** (1854–82), wrote fiery poems and articles in aid of the cause. There are Lives by T. P. O'Connor (1891), R. F. Walsh (N.Y. 1892), Barry O'Brien (1899), his widow (1914), his brother John (1916). See also T. P. O'Connor's *Parnell Movement* (1886), and *Gladstone, Parnell, and the Great Irish Struggle* (1891); Justin McCarthy, *A History of Our Own Times* (vol. v 1897); and studies by St John Ervine (1925), W. O'Brien (1926) and Harrison (1931).

(2) **Thomas** (1679–1718), English poet, born in Dublin, was educated at Trinity College, took orders, and received the archdeaconry of Clogher, a prebend, and the vicarage of Finglass. The head of an English family settled in Ireland, with property both there and in Cheshire, he lived mostly in London, where his wit procured him the friendship of Harley, Swift and Pope. After his wife's death he took to drinking, and died at Chester, while on his way to Ireland. Next year Pope published a selection of his poems, the best-known of which is the *Hermit*. The *Nightpiece* and the *Hymn to Contentment* are better poetry. See Mitford's edition of the poems, with Life, &c., re-edited by G. A. Aitken (1894).

PARR, (1) **Catharine** (1512–48), sixth wife of Henry VIII, daughter of Sir Thomas Parr of Kendal, married first Edward Borough, and next Lord Latimer, and on July 12, 1543, became queen of England by marriage with Henry VIII. She was distinguished for her learning and knowledge of religious subjects, her discussion of which with the king well-nigh brought her to the block. She persuaded Henry to restore the succession to his daughters. Very soon after Henry's death (1547) she married a former lover, Lord Thomas Seymour of Sudeley, and died in childbirth next year at Sudeley Castle near Cheltenham.

(2) **Thomas** ('**Old Parr**') (?1483–1635), was born, according to the tradition, in 1483. He was a Shropshire farm-servant, and when 120 years old married his second wife, and till his 130th year performed all his usual work. In his 152nd year his fame had reached London, and he was induced to journey thither to see Charles I. But he was treated at court so royally that he died, November 14, 1635. Taylor, the Water-poet, wrote his Life, and the great Harvey in his postmortem report repeats the popular hearsay. There is no sound evidence.

PARRHASIUS (4th cent. B.C.), according to tradition the greatest painter of ancient Greece, and reputedly the first to use shading, worked at Athens.

PARRISH, Edward (1822–72), American pharmacist of Philadelphia, introduced 'Parrish's Chemical Food', the *Compound Syrup of Phosphate of Iron*.

PARRY, (1) **Sir Charles Hubert Hastings** (1848–1918), composer, was born at Bournemouth, the son of **Thomas Gambier Parry** (1816–88) of Highnam Court, Gloucester, inventor of the spirit-fresco process. Educated at Eton and Oxford, in 1883 he became professor in the Royal College of Music, and in 1895 its director. He composed the oratorios *Judith, Job* and *King Saul*; an opera on *Lancelot and Guinevere*; symphonies, quartets, cantatas, &c.; and wrote *Evolution of the Art of Music* (1896), a Life of Bach, *The Oxford History of Music*, vol. iii (1907). See Life by C. L. Graves (1926).

(2) **Joseph** (1841–1903), Welsh musician, was born at Merthyr Tydfil, studied at the Royal Academy of Music, and became professor at Cardiff College. He composed oratorios and operas, songs and hymns.

(3) **Sir William Edward** (1790–1855), Arctic navigator, was born at Bath, son of **Caleb Hillier Parry** (1755–1822), an eminent physician. Entering the navy as midshipman, he served against the Danes in 1808, and in 1810 was sent to the Arctic regions to protect the whale fisheries. He took command in five expeditions to the Arctic regions—in 1818 (under Ross), 1819, 1821–23, 1824–25, and 1827—the last an attempt to reach the Pole on sledges from Spitsbergen. In 1829 he was knighted, and in 1837 was made comptroller of a department of the navy. He was subsequently superintendent of Haslar (1846), made rear-admiral (1852), and governor of Greenwich Hospital (1853). See the collected edition of his voyages (1833), and the Life by his son (1857).

PARSONS, (1) **Alfred William** (1847–1920), English painter and book illustrator, known especially for his watercolour landscapes. Elected R.A. in 1911, he was president of the Royal Society of Painters in Watercolour (1914–20).

(2) **Sir Charles Algernon** (1854–1931), British engineer, the fourth son of the third Earl of Rosse, educated at Cambridge, developed the steam turbine, and built the first turbine-driven steamship (1897). He was knighted in 1911.

(3) **Robert** (1546–1610), English Jesuit, born at Nether Stowey, Somerset, passed from Taunton to Oxford, and became a fellow and tutor of Balliol. His enemies secured his forced retirement from Oxford in 1574. He now turned Catholic, and at Rome entered the Society of Jesus (1575), becoming a priest in 1578. With Campion (q.v.), Parsons landed at Dover in 1580, disguised as a merchant of jewels, amazed Catholics and Protestants by his activity and success, and for twelve months baffled all the attempts of government to catch him. In 1581 he escaped to the Continent. In 1582 he was at Paris conferring with the Provincial of the French Jesuits, the Archbishop of Glasgow, the papal nuncio, and the agent of the king of Spain, concerning his own project for the invasion of England; and this plan he himself carried to King Philip at Madrid. Now began his influence with the Spanish king, and the series of political enterprises which culminated in the Armada of 1588. At Rouen in 1582 he had finished his *Christian Directory*; in 1588 he was rector of the college at Rome, and he founded a number of Jesuit seminaries. In *The Conference on the next Succession to the Crown* he insists on the right of the people to set aside, on religious grounds, the natural heir to the throne.

PARTON, James (1822–91), American writer, was born at Canterbury, but taken when a child to America, where he became a journalist, wrote biographies of Greeley, Butler, Franklin, Voltaire and others, and did much miscellaneous work. He married in 1856 Sara, a sister of N. P. Willis (q.v.), who, as ' Fanny Fern ', wrote many children's books.

PARTRIDGE, (1) **Sir Bernard** (1861–1945), English artist, born in London, began as a stained-glass designer but made his name as staff cartoonist for *Punch* (from 1891). He was knighted in 1925.

(2) **Eric Honeywood** (1894–), British lexicographer, born near Gisborne, N.Z., educated at Queensland and Oxford Universities, became, after fighting in World War I, Queensland travelling fellow at Oxford. He was a lecturer at Manchester and London Universities in 1925–27 and wrote on French and English literature, but later, and especially after World War II, in which he served in the R.A.F., he made a specialized study of slang and colloquial language. His works in this field include the standard *Dictionary of Slang and Unconventional English* (1937, 3rd ed. 1949), *Usage and Abusage* (1947), *Dictionary of Forces Slang* (with W. Granville and F. Roberts, 1948), and *A Dictionary of the Underworld, British and American* (1950).

(3) **John** (1644–1715), English astrologer and almanac-maker, was originally a shoe maker at East Sheen, but contrived to learn Latin, Greek, Hebrew, medicine and astrology, and published a number of astrological books. The manifold quackery of his prophetic almanac, *Merlinus Liberatus*, led Swift (under the name of Bickerstaff) to ridicule and expose him.

PASCAL, Blaise, *-kahl* (1623–62), French mathematician, physicist, theologian and man-of-letters, was born June 19 at Clermont-Ferrand, the son of the local president of the court of exchequer. The mother having died, the family in 1630 moved to Paris, where the father, a considerable mathematician, personally undertook his children's education. Unlike John Stuart Mill, Blaise was not allowed to begin a subject until his father thought he could easily master it. Consequently it was discovered that the eleven-year-old boy had worked out for himself in secret the first twenty-three propositions of Euclid, calling straight lines ' bars ' and circles ' rounds '. At sixteen he published a paper on solid geometry which Descartes refused to believe was the handiwork of a youth. Father and son collaborated in experiments to confirm Torricelli's theory, unpalatable to the schoolmen, that nature does, after all, not abhor a vacuum. These experiments carried out by Blaise's brother-in-law, Florin Périer, consisted in carrying up the Puy de Dôme two glass tubes containing mercury, inverted in a bath of mercury and noting the fall of the mercury columns with increased altitude. Again Descartes surprisingly disbelieved the principle, which Blaise fully described in three papers on the void published in 1647, when he also patented a calculating machine, later simplified by Leibniz, which Blaise had built to assist his father in his accounts. The former led on to the invention of the barometer, the hydraulic press and the syringe. In 1648 Richelieu appointed Pascal senior to a post at Rouen, but the latter died in 1651. Pascal's sister, Jacqueline, entered the Jansenist convent at Port-Royal, but Blaise divided his time between mathematics and the social round in Paris until November 23, 1654, approaching midnight when he had the first of two revelations, according to a note found sewn into his clothes, and he came to see that his religious attitude had been too intellectual and remote. Promptly he joined his sister in her retreat at Port-Royal, gave up mathematics and social life almost completely and joined battle for the Jansenists against the Jesuits of the Sorbonne who had publicly denounced Arnauld (q.v.), the Jansenist mathematician, as a heretic. In eighteen brilliant anonymous pamphlets, the *Lettres provinciales* (1656–57), Pascal attacked in superb prose, novel in its directness, the Jesuits' meaningless jargon, casuistry and moral laxity. This early prose masterpiece in the French language, the model for Voltaire, failed to save Arnauld, but undermined for ever Jesuit authority and prestige. Pascal's papers on the area of the cycloid (1661) heralded the invention of the differential calculus. Fragments jotted down for a case book of Christian truths were discovered after his death, August 19, 1662, and published as the *Pensées* in 1669 in order of completeness, but this arbitrariness was exposed by Cousin in 1842. No edition of these fragments is entirely satisfactory. The groundwork for Pascal's intended Christian apology, they contain the most profound insight into religious truths coupled, however, with scepticism of rationalist thought and theology. Their style owes much to Montaigne, Charron and the 13th-century Spaniard, Raimundo Marti. For Jacqueline Pascal, see works by Cousin (1845) and Weizel (New York 1880). See Life by his sister, Mme Périer, prefacing the *Pensées* (1687), biographical studies by C. A. Sainte Beuve, Port-Royal, vols. i-iii, 6th ed. (1901), E. Mortimer (1959), and studies by F. Strowski (1907–13), H. F. Stewart (1915, 1940, 1942 and 1945), J. Chevalier (1922, 1944), L. C. Brunschvicg (1924, 1945), C. C. J. Webb (1929), J. Lhermet (1931), F. Mauriac (1941), D. G. M. Patrick (1947), J. Mesnard, intro. R. A. Knox (trans. 1952).

PASCHAL was the name of two popes (817–824 and 1099–1118), and of an antipope (died 1168).

PASCOLI, Giovanni, *pas'kō-lee* (1855–1912), Italian poet and writer, born at San Mauro di Romagna, was professor of Latin at Bologna from 1907. Much of his poetry set in the background of native Romagna is of a tragic nature and his volumes of verse include *Myricae* (1891), *In Or San Michele* (1903) and *Canti di Castelvecchio* (1903). *Sotto il Velame* (1900) and *La Mirabile Visione* (1902) are critical studies of Dante's *Divine Comedy*. See *Giovanni Pascoli* by Croce (1920).

PAŠIĆ, Nikola, *pash'eet-y'* (*c.* 1846–1926), Serb ' Old Radical ' leader, born at Zaječar, condemned to death 1883 for his part in the ' Revolution of Zaitchar ', a plot against King Milan, but he survived on the accession of King Peter to be prime minister of Serbia and later of Yugoslavia 1891-92, 1906, and from 1908 almost continuously until his death.

PASKEVICH, Ivan Feodorovich, *pus-kyay'vich* (1782-1856), Russian field-marshal, was born at Poltava, served against the French in 1805, and against the Turks, and took a prominent part in the campaign of 1812. In 1826, conquering Persian Armenia and taking Erivan, he was made Count of Erivan; in 1828–29 he made two campaigns against the Turks in Asia, taking Kars and Erzerûm. In 1831 he suppressed the rising in Poland, and was made Prince of Warsaw. Under his governorship Poland was (1832) incorporated with Russia. In 1848, sent to the support of Austria, he defeated the insurgent Hungarians. In 1854 he commanded the Russian army on the Danube, was wounded at Silistria and retired to Warsaw, where later he died. See French Lives by Tolstoi (1835) and Stcherbatoff (1888).

PASMORE, Edwin John Victor (1908–), English artist, born at Chelsham, began painting without academic training. One of the founders of the London 'Euston Road School' (1937), he became an art teacher and after World War II began to paint in a highly abstract style, in which colour is often primarily used to suggest relief. His works include *Rectangular Motif* (1949), *Inland Sea* (1950, Tate, London) and *Relief Construction in White, Black, Red and Maroon* (1957). He was created C.B.E. in 1959.

PASQUIER, Étienne Denis, Duc de, *pa-kyay* (1767–1862), French statesman under Napoleon, the Bourbons and Louis-Philippe, was chancellor of France in 1837–48. See his *History of my Time* (trans. 1894).

PASSAGLIA, Carlo, *pas-sahl'ya* (1812–87), Italian theologian, born at Lucca, in 1827 entered the Society of Jesus, and in 1844 became professor in the Collegio Romano. In 1849–51 he taught in England. In 1855 he wrote on the Immaculate Conception, then, leaving the Jesuits, against the temporal power, *Pro Causo Italica* (1859). He withdrew to Turin, where he was professor of Moral Philosophy.

PASSFIELD, Baron. See WEBB (6).

PASSOW, Franz, *pah'sō* (1786–1833), German scholar, born at Ludwigslust in Mecklenburg, in 1815 became professor of Greek at Weimar gymnasium and of Ancient Literature at Breslau. His *Handwörterbuch der griechischen Sprache* (1819–24; 5th ed. 1841–57) formed the basis of Liddell and Scott's *Greek Lexicon.* Other works include *Grundzüge der griechischen und römischen Literatur—und Kunstgeschichte* (2nd ed. 1829) and editions of classical authors. See Life by Wachler (1839).

PASSY, *pa-see,* (1) **Frederic** (1822–1912), French economist and author, father of (2), born at Paris, became a member (1881–1889) of the Chamber of Deputies, was a founder member of the International Peace League in 1867, and a member of the International Peace Bureau in Bern in 1892. In 1901 he shared the Nobel peace prize with Jean Dunant. His writings include *Mélanges économiques* (1857), *L'Histoire du travail* (1873) and *Vérités et paradoxes* (1894).

(2) **Paul Édouard** (1859–1940), French philologist and phonetician, son of (1), was born at Versailles. An advocate of phonetic selling, he founded the International Phonetic Association in 1894, and was assistant professor of Phonetics at the Sorbonne. His publications include *Le Français parlé* (1886) and *Etudes sur les changements phonétiques* (1890).

PASTERNAK, Boris Leonidovich (1890–1960), Russian lyric poet, novelist and translator of Shakespeare, son of **Leonid** (1862–1945), the painter and illustrator of Tolstoy's works, was born in Moscow, studied law at the university, then musical composition under Scriabin, abandoning both for philosophy at Marburg. A factory worker in the Urals during the first World War, he was employed in the library of the education ministry, Moscow, after the revolution. His early collections of verse written between 1912 and 1916 were published under the title *Above the Barriers* (1931), followed by *My Sister, Life* (1922), *Themes and Variations* (1923). Under the influence of his friend Mayakovsky (q.v.) he wrote the political poems *The Year 1905* (1927), on the Bolshevik uprising, and *Lieutenant Schmidt* (1927), on the *Potemkin* mutiny. *Spectorsky* and *Second Birth* (both 1932) are autobiographical. Among his outstanding short stories are the collection *Aerial Ways* (1933) and particularly *The Childhood of Lyuvers* (1924), a delicate presentation of a girl's first impressions of womanhood, and *A Tale* (1934) translated as 'The Last Summer' (1959), in which Pasternak's imagery is at its freshest and most unexpected. The long years of Stalin turned Pasternak into the official translator into Russian of Shakespeare, Verlaine, Goethe and Kleist, but he did compose incidental verse such as *In Early Trains* (1936–41) and *The Sapper's Death* (1943). With Khrushchev's misleading political 'thaw' Pasternak abortively ventured into verse (1954) and caused a political earthquake with his first novel, *Dr Zhivago* (trans. M. Hayward and M. Harari, 1958), banned in the Soviet Union. A fragmentary, poet's novel, it describes with intense feeling the Russian revolution as it impinged upon one individual, both doctor and poet. But the vast array of characters fail to live, they are creatures of poetic necessity. Yet despite its technical shortcomings, it has a sublime moral grandeur. Its strictures on the post-revolutionary events are those not of an anti-Marxist but of a Communist who is disappointed that history has not conformed to his vision. Expelled by the Soviet Writers' Union in October 1958, Pasternak had to take the unprecedented step of refusing the Nobel prize and in a thoroughly self-critical letter to Khrushchev, echoed Ovid by his plea that exile would for him be the equivalent of death. See the autobiographical *Safe Conduct* (1931; trans. A. Brown and L. Pasternak-Slater, 1959), *Essay in Autobiography* (1954; trans. M. Harari and intro. E. Crankshaw, 1959), *Letters to Georgian Friends* (1968), and *Prose and Poems*, ed. Schimanski, trans. B. Scott and intro. J. M. Cohen (1959).

PASTEUR, Louis, *pas-tœr* (1822–95), French chemist, born at Dôle, studied at Besançon and Paris, and held academic posts at Strasbourg, Lille and Paris, where in 1867 he became professor of Chemistry at the Sorbonne. His work was at first chemical, as on tartrate crystals and 'left-handed' tartrates. He discovered a living ferment, a microorganism comparable in its powers to the yeast plant, which would, in a solution of paratartrate of ammonia, select for food the 'right-handed' tartrates alone, leaving the 'left-handed'. He next showed that other fermentations, lactic, butyric, acetic, are essentially due to organisms, greatly extended Schwann's researches on putrefaction, gave valuable rules for making vinegar and preventing wine disease, and refuted supposed proofs of spontaneous generation. On his findings the modern study of bacteriology was based. After 1865 he tackled, with brilliant success, silkworm disease, injurious growths in beer, splenic fever, and fowl cholera. He showed that it was possible to attenuate the virulence of injurious micro-organisms by exposure to air, by variety of culture, or by transmission through various animals. He thus demonstrated by a memorable experiment that sheep and cows 'vaccinated' with the attenuated bacilli of anthrax were protected from the evil results of subsequent inoculation with the virulent virus; and, by the culture of antitoxic reagents, prophylactic treatment of diphtheria, tubercular disease, cholera, yellow fever and plague has been found effective. His treatment of hydrophobia depends on similar proofs and in 1888 the Institut Pasteur was founded for the treatment by inoculation of this disease. Here Pasteur worked until his death. See studies by Frankland (1898), Vallery-Radot (1919), Descours (1922), Holmes (1925), and Life by Cuny (1965).

PASTON, a Norfolk family, named from the village of Paston, whose letters and papers, published in 1787–1789–1823 as the *Paston Letters*, shed a vivid light on domestic life in the 15th century. Gairdner edited them with more fullness in 1872–75, and again completely in 1904, after the recovery of two long lost volumes. See also a selection edited by N. Davis (1958). The chief members of the family were William Paston (1378–1444), justice of common pleas; his son John (1421–66); Clement (*c.* 1515–97), a sailor; and Sir Robert (1631–83), Earl of Yarmouth. See *The Pastons and their England* by H. S. Bennett (1922).

PATER, (1) **Jean Baptiste Joseph,** *pa-tayr* (1695–1736), French genre painter, born at Valenciennes, was a talented pupil and follower of Watteau.

(2) **Walter,** *pay'tėr* (1839–94), English critic, born in London, was educated at King's School, Canterbury, and Queen's College, Oxford, became a fellow of Brasenose and thenceforth lived the retired life of the scholar. His *Studies in the History of the Renaissance* (1873), which first brought him to the notice of the scholarly public, shows the influence of the pre-Raphaelites with whom he associated. His philosophic romance *Marius the Epicurean* (1885) appealed to a wider audience for it dealt in an extremely seductive manner with the spread of Christianity in the days of the catacombs. His *Imaginary Portraits* (1887) and *Appreciations* (1889), followed by *Plato and Platonism* (1893), established his position as a critic, but already people were beginning to talk of his influence as being unhealthy, in the sense that he advocated a cultivated hedonism. That his neo-Cyrenaism, as it might be called, involved strenuous self-discipline, hardly occurred to his critics, who found in his style alone an enervating quality. His influence on Oxford, however, was profound. He died at Oxford, having left unfinished another romance, *Gaston de Latour* (1896), dealing with the France of Charles IX and containing portraits of Montaigne and Ronsard with whom his philosophy of charm and the cultivation of beauty had much in common. See studies by A. C. Benson (1904), T. Wright (1907), Edward Thomas (1913) and A. Symonds (1932).

PATERCULUS, Marcus Velleius (*c.* 19 B.C.–*c.* A.D. 30), Roman historian, served under Tiberius, was alive in A.D. 30, and may have perished next year as a friend of Sejanus. His *Historiae Romanae*, a compendium of universal, but more particularly of Roman history, is not complete, and is superficial and rhetorical.

PATERSON, (1) **Andrew Barton,** nicknamed 'Banjo' (1864–1941), Australian journalist and poet, was a first World War correspondent and the author of several books of light verse including *The Animals Noah Forgot* (1933). He is best known however as the author of 'Waltzing Matilda', adapted from a traditional ditty, which became Australia's premier national song.

(2) **Helen.** See ALLINGHAM (2).

(3) **Robert** (1715–1801), Scottish stone-cutter, the original 'Old Mortality', born, a farmer's son, near Hawick, was apprenticed to a stone mason, and rented a quarry in Morton parish. From about 1758 he neglected to return to his wife and five children, and for over forty years devoted himself to the task of repairing or erecting headstones to Covenanting martyrs. He died at Bankhill, and was buried at Caerlaverock, where a monument was erected to him by Messrs A. & C. Black in 1869. See Introduction to Scott's *Old Mortality* and Ramage's *Drumlanrig Castle* (1876).

(4) **William** (1658–1719), Scottish financier founder of the Bank of England, was born at Skipmyre farm, in Tinwald parish, Dumfriesshire, and spent some years in the West Indies. Returning to Europe, he promoted his Darien Scheme in London, Hamburg, Amsterdam (where he worked for the Revolution of 1688) and Berlin, made a fortune by commerce in London, founded the Hampstead Water Company in 1690, projected the Bank of England, and was one of its first directors in 1694. At Edinburgh, as a strong advocate of free trade, he talked the whole nation into his Darien Scheme. He sailed with the expedition in a private capacity, shared all its troubles, and returned with its survivors a broken man in December 1699. But his energy remained unabated.

He had a considerable share in promoting the Scottish union, and was elected to the first united parliament by the Dumfries burghs. In 1715 he was awarded £18,000 as indemnity for his Darien losses. See the Life by S. Bannister (1858), editor of his *Works* (1859); and that by J. S. Barbour (1907). See also G. P. Insh, *The Company Scotland* (1932), and J. Clapham, *The Bank of England*, vol. i (1944).

PATHÉ, Charles, *pa-tay* (1863–1957), French film pioneer, the inaugurator of the newsreel in France in 1909 and in America in 1910. In 1911 the company of Pathé Frères was established which gave Britain her first newsreel and the screen magazine Pathé Pictorial. In 1949 the Company became Associated British Pathé Ltd.

PATMORE, Coventry Kersey Dighton (1823–1896), English poet, born at Woodford, was an assistant in the library of the British Museum and was associated with the pre-Raphaelite brotherhood. His magnum opus, *The Angel in the House*, which delighted the respectable Victorian public till Swinburne flaunted his less respectable muse, described with domestic, often ludicrous, detail the intimacies of a rectory courtship. The poem lives not by its narrative part but by its Preludes, which display profound knowledge of a lover's moods and felicitous expression. Only in the Preludes do we have a hint of the Patmore who can be acclaimed as a major poet—the poet of *The Unknown Eros*. We should associate the change from the Victorian domesticity of *The Angel in the House* to the erotic mysticism of *The Unknown Eros* (1877), with the death of his first wife in 1862 and his conversion to the Roman Catholic faith in 1864. Four of the odes which compose the book—'The Azalea', 'Departure', 'The Toys' and 'If I were dead'—are about his dead wife and his motherless children. Others show his rabid Toryism which ascribed the decline of England to 'the disfranchisement (in 1867) of the upper and middle class by the false English nobles and their Jew'. The rest are in a vein of lofty mysticism in which the myth of Eros and Psyche is used to symbolize the marriage of earthly and heavenly love. Apparently the 'Song of Solomon' justified him in applying this erotic language to sacred mysteries, but churchmen—Newman and Hopkins—were offended. Nevertheless, the metaphysical reaction of the last generation finds in them and in less mystical poems like the early *Tamerton Church Tower* and *Amelia* (1878), 'true poetry of the rarest and perhaps highest kind'. Nor is Sir Herbert Read singular in this verdict. On the other hand, his arrogance and Biblical eroticism will always repel average taste. Patmore would not have his odes called Pindarics—they are extremely loose but are not uncontrolled. His prosodic innovation was to discard the metrical foot and substitute the musical 'bar' measured from stress to stress. He explained his metrics in an Appendix to his *Collected Poetical Works* in 1886. See Derek Patmore, *Portrait of My Family* (1933), expanded as *Life and Times of Coventry Patmore* (1949); also *The Memoirs and Correspondence of Coventry Patmore* ed. Basil Champneys (1900); and studies by Burdett (1921) Herbert Read in *The Great Victorians* (1932), F. Page (1933) and E. J. Oliver (1956).

PATON, (1) Alan (1903–), South African writer and educator, National President of the South African Liberal Party, born in Pietermaritzburg, spent ten years as a schoolteacher, first in a native school and later at Pietermaritzburg College. In 1935 he was appointed principal of the Diepkloof Reformatory, where he became known for the success of his enlightened methods. From his deep concern with the racial problem in South Africa sprang the novel *Cry the Beloved Country* (1948). Later books include *Too Late the Phalarope* (1953), *Hope for South Africa* (1958), a political study written from the Liberal standpoint, and *Debbie Go Home* (1961), short stories.

(2) **John** (d. 1684), Scottish Covenanter, was the son of a farmer at Fenwick in Ayrshire, became a captain in the army of Gustavus Adolphus, fought at Rullion Green and Bothwell Brig (1679), and, apprehended in 1684, was hanged May 9.

(3) **John Gibson** (1824–1907), Scottish missionary, the son of a stocking-maker, was born in Kirkmahoe parish, Dumfriesshire. In 1858 he went as a missionary of the Reformed Presbyterian Church to the cannibals of the New Hebrides. His brother published and edited his missionary narratives (1889). See also A. K. Langridge and F. H. L. Paton, *John G. Paton: Later Years* (1910).

(4) **Sir Joseph Noel** (1821–1901), Scottish painter, was born in Dunfermline, and studied at the Royal Academy, London. A painter of historical, fairy, allegorical and religious subjects, notable early pictures are the two on *Oberon and Titania*, both in the National Gallery at Edinburgh. He illustrated Aytoun's *Lays of the Scottish Cavaliers* and the *Ancient Mariner*. R.S.A., Queen's Limner for Scotland from 1865, knighted (1867), he published two volumes of poems. See *Art Journal* for April 1895.

PATRICK, St (*c.* 385–*c.* 461), the Apostle of Ireland, must have been born late in the 4th century, perhaps in South Wales, less probably at Boulogne-sur-Mer, or Kilpatrick near Dumbarton. His father was a deacon named Calpurnius. His own Celtic name or nickname was Succat. In his sixteenth year he was seized by pirates, carried to Ireland and sold to an Antrim chief called Milchu. After six years he escaped, and, probably after a second captivity, went to France, where he became a monk, first at Tours and afterwards at Lérins. He was ordained a bishop at forty-five, and in 432 it is thought went as a missionary to Ireland, Palladius, sent thither by Pope Celestine a short time before, having died. Patrick landed at Wicklow; thence he sailed north to convert his old master Milchu. In Down he converted another chief, Dichu. At Tara in Meath he preached to the king of Tara, Laoghaire. Thence he proceeded to Croagh-Patrick in Mayo, to Ulster, and as far as Cashel in the south. He addressed himself first to the chiefs, and made use of the spirit of clanship. After twenty years spent in missionary labours, he fixed his see at Armagh (454). He died at Saul (Saul-patrick; *Sabhal*, 'barn'), the spot which Dichu had given him on his arrival, and was very probably buried at Armagh. Ussher, followed by Todd, fixes his death at 493—a date that would make Patrick's age quite 120 years; but the true date seems to be *c.* 461. The only certainly authentic literary remains of the Saint (both in very rude Latin) are his 'Confession' and a letter addressed to Coroticus, a British chieftain who had carried off some Irish Christians as slaves. See the Lives by J. H. Todd (1863), Newell (1890), Zimmer (1904, disputing his historical existence), J. B. Bury (1905, reaffirming it), Ardill (1931), E. Macneill (1934), P. Gallico (1958); the *Tripartite Life*, ed. Stokes (1887).

PATTERSON-BONAPARTE. See BONAPARTE (1).

PATTESON, John Coleridge (1827–71), English martyr-bishop, was born in London, the son of Sir John Patteson, judge in the King's Bench, and of a niece of Coleridge. He passed through Eton and Balliol, and was a fellow of Merton, and curate of Alfington in Devonshire. From 1855 he spent sixteen years in missionary work in the New Hebrides, Banks, Solomon and Loyalty Islands; and in 1861 he was consecrated Bishop of Melanesia. He was killed by the natives of the Santa Cruz group. See Life by C. M. Yonge (2 vols. 1874).

PATTI, *paht'tee*, (1) **Adelina** (1843–1919), Italian singer, was born at Madrid, the daughter of a Sicilian tenor. At seven she sang in New York, and there she made her début as 'Lucia' in 1859. In London she appeared in 1861, when her success was as splendid as it afterwards was wherever she sang. Her voice was an unusually high, rich, ringing soprano. She married in 1866 the Marquis de Caux, and, on her divorce in 1886, the Breton tenor Ernesto Nicolini (1834–98), and in 1899 the Swedish Baron Cederström. Her home was Craig-y-nos Castle near Swansea. In 1898 she was naturalized. See Life by Klein (1920).

(2) **Carlotta** (1840–89), sister of (1), also a great soprano, was born at Florence, made her début at New York in 1861 as a concert singer (being debarred by lameness from opera), and married in 1879 the 'cellist Ernst de Munck.

PATTISON, (1) **Dorothy Wyndlow** (1832–78), English philanthropist, sister of (2), was born at Hauxwell. In 1861 she started a life of labour for others as schoolmistress at Little Woolston near Bletchley. In 1864 she joined a sisterhood at Coatham near Redcar, and in 1865 she began as 'Sister Dora' her devoted labours as nurse at Walsall. In 1877 she took charge of the municipal epidemic hospital (mainly for smallpox). She was indefatigable in all good works. See Margaret Lonsdale's *Sister Dora* (1880).

(2) **Mark** (1813–84), English scholar and critic, brother of (1), born at Hornby in Yorkshire, graduated from Oriel, Oxford (1837), and was elected fellow of Lincoln (1839). Under Newman's influence he forsook Evangelicalism and almost followed his master into Catholicism. Then came a reaction towards liberalism, and he soon became a tutor of exceptional influence. An attempt to deprive him of his fellowship failed; but for ten years he took little share in Oxford life. He published an article on education in the *Oxford Essays*, went with a commission on education to Germany, and served for three months of 1858 as *Times* correspondent at Berlin. In 1861, he was elected rector of his college, and in 1862 he married Emilia Frances Strong (afterwards Lady Dilke, q.v.). His standard of perfection in scholarship was so high that his actual achievement is only suggestive of his powers, and the greatest project of his life—the study of Scaliger—remains a fragment, printed by Prof. Nettleship in vol. i of Pattison's collected *Essays* (1889). He did publish *Suggestions on Academical Organisation* (1868); admirably annotated editions of Pope's *Essay on Man* (1869) and *Satires and Epistles* (1872); *Isaac Casaubon* (1875); *Milton*, in the 'Men of Letters' (1879); the *Sonnets* of Milton (1883); and *Sermons* (1885). See his frank posthumous *Memoirs* (1885) and Lionel Tollemache's *Recollections of Pattison* (1895).

PATTON, George Smith (1885–1945), American general, was born at San Gabriel, California, and graduated from West Point in 1909. In the first World War he commanded an armoured brigade on the Western Front. In 1941 he commanded the 1st Armoured Corps and later led the first U.S. troops to fight in North Africa. In 1943 he commanded the 7th Army in the Sicilian campaign. At the head of the 3rd Army he swept across France in 1944 and in the following year reached the Czech frontier. See his *War As I Knew It* (1948), and Ayer, *Before the Colours Fade* (1965).

PAUL, (1) **Charles Kegan** (1828–1902), English author and publisher, born at White Laekington in Somerset, was a graduate of Oxford and entered the Church, becoming in 1852 a chaplain at Eton and in 1862 vicar at Sturminster Hall. During this time he wrote religious works and edited the *New Quarterly Magazine*. In 1874 he left the Church to settle in London, where he wrote *William Godwin, his Friends and Contemporaries* (1876). In 1877 he took over the publishing firm of H. S. King, which became C. Kegan Paul & Co. Among his first publications were the monthly *Nineteenth Century*, and the works of G. W. Cox, Tennyson, Meredith and Stevenson. Joined by Alfred Trench in 1881, the firm became Kegan Paul, Trench & Co., in 1889 a limited company, Kegan Paul, Trench, Trübner & Co. Ltd., and finally incorporated in the publishing house George Routledge & Sons, Ltd. Paul became a Roman Catholic and among his many works were *Biographical Sketches* (1883), *Maria Drummond* (1891), works on religion and translations from Goethe and Pascal.

(2) **Jean.** See RICHTER (4).

(3) **Lewis** (d. 1759), English inventor of French descent, a ward of Lord Shaftesbury, who invented a roller-spinning machine and with the mechanic John Wyatt opened two mills, one at Birmingham and one at Northampton. This machine was a failure commercially, although the idea was later utilized by Arkwright. In 1738 he invented a

carding machine which was used in Lancashire after his death and in 1758 patented another type of spinning machine. He was befriended by Samuel Johnson, who took a lively interest in his enterprises.

(4) **Vincent de.** See VINCENT DE PAUL.

PAUL (fl. 1st cent. A.D.), the Apostle of the Gentiles, was born of Jewish parents at Tarsus in Cilicia. At the age of about fourteen, he trained as a rabbi under Gamaliel at Jerusalem, acquiring also the trade of tent-maker. A strenuous Pharisee, he assisted in persecuting the Christians. He was on his way to Damascus on this mission when a vision of the Crucified converted him into a fervent adherent of the new faith. After three years spent mainly at Damascus, but partly in Arabia, he visited Jerusalem again, and after the apostles had been persuaded by Barnabas of his conversion, he began to preach: but opposition to him was strong and for ten years he lived in retirement at Tarsus. Brought to Antioch by Barnabas, he was there for a year before undertaking with him and John Mark his first mission-tour in Cyprus, Pisidia, Pamphylia and Lycaonia. Returning to Antioch, he found the controversy raised as to the condition under which Gentiles and Jews respectively were to be admitted to the Christian Church, a controversy which led to the first apostolic council in Jerusalem *c.* A.D. 49 or 50. Paul opposed Peter during the debate and when the question was finally settled by a compromise, he addressed himself thereafter mainly to the Gentiles. His second mission-journey led him, with Silas, again to Asia Minor and through Galatia and Phrygia to Macedonia and Achaia, where in Corinth he was especially successful. A year and a half later he was again at Jerusalem and Antioch, and then undertook a third mission-tour—to Galatia and Phrygia. Driven from Ephesus, he visited Achaia and Macedonia again, and by way of Miletus returned by sea to Jerusalem. There the fanaticism of the Jews against him led to disturbances, whereupon he was brought to Caesarea to be tried before Felix the procurator, and after two years' imprisonment, before Felix's successor M. Porcius Festus. Now using his right as a Roman citizen, Paul appealed to Caesar, and in the spring of A.D. 62 arrived in Rome, where he spent two years a prisoner, but in his own hired house. He was executed under Nero—probably at the end of the two years' captivity, though tradition makes him visit Spain and other countries. The ancient church recognized thirteen of the New Testament Epistles as Paul's, but did not unanimously regard Hebrews as his. All but the most destructive modern critics accept unhesitatingly as Paul's the Epistles to the Galatians, Romans and Corinthians (1st and 2nd). But a considerable body of scholars dispute the Pauline authorship of the Pastoral Epistles, 2nd Thessalonians and Ephesians, and some also Colossians and Philippians. The order of the Epistles is certainly not chronological, though it is difficult to fix the succession. See the works on Paul by Deissmann (1912), Schweitzer (1912), Smith (1919), Foakes-Jackson (1927), Scott (1927), Nock (1938), W. Barclay (1959) and C. Tresmontant, trans. D. Attwater (1958).

PAUL, name of six popes:

Paul I (757–67) and **Paul II** (1464–71) were unimportant.

Paul III, named **Alessandro Farnese** (1468–1549), a Tuscan, created cardinal-deacon in 1493, was pope from 1534. One of his first acts was to give cardinal's hats to two of his boy grandsons, and throughout his reign he laboured to advance his bastard sons. Yet he surrounded his throne with good cardinals like Contarini, Pole and Sadolet. He convoked a general council in 1542, but it did not actually assemble (in Trent) until 1545. In 1538 he issued the bull of excommunication and deposition against Henry VIII of England, and also the bull instituting the order of the Jesuits in 1540.

Paul IV, named **Giovanni Pietro Caraffa** (1476–1559), was born in Naples. As Bishop of Chieti he laboured for the reformation of abuses and for the revival of religion and morality. A rigorous enemy of heresy, under his influence Paul III organized the Inquisition in Rome. Elected pope in 1555, he enforced upon the clergy the observance of all the clerical duties, and enacted laws for the maintenance of public morality. He established a censorship, issued a full *Index librorum prohibitorum*, completed the organization of the Roman Inquisition, and helped the poor. He was embroiled with the Emperor Ferdinand, with Philip II of Spain, and with Cosmo, Grand-duke of Tuscany.

Paul V, named **Camillo Borghese** (1552–1621), born in Rome, became nuncio in Spain, and cardinal, and on the death of Leo XI in 1605 was elected pope. In his time took place the great conflict with the republic of Venice, as to the immunity of the clergy from the jurisdiction of civil tribunals, and other questions. Paul issued a denouncing excommunication against the doge and senate, placing the republic under an interdict. By the intervention of Henry IV of France the dispute was settled in 1607, after the pope had abandoned his claims. Paul promoted charities and useful public works.

Paul VI, named **Giovanni Battista Montini** (1897–), born at Concesio, son of the editor of a Catholic daily paper, graduated at the Gregorian University of Rome, was ordained in 1920, and entered the Vatican diplomatic service, where he remained until 1944. He was then appointed Archbishop of Milan, in which important diocese he became known for his liberal views and support of social reform. Made a cardinal in 1958, he was elected pope on the death of John XXIII, many of whose opinions he shared, in 1963.

PAUL (1754–1801), emperor of Russia, second son of Peter III and Catharine II, succeeded his mother in 1796. His father's murder and his mother's neglect had exerted a baneful influence on his character. His earliest measures were the exile of the murderers and the pardon of Polish prisoners, including Kosciusko. But he soon revealed his violent temper and lack of capacity, and irritated all his subjects by vexatious regulations. He suddenly declared for the allies against France, and sent an army of 56,000 men under Suvorov into Italy; sent a second to cooperate with the Austrians, retired from the alliance, quarrelled with England, and entered into close alliance with Bonaparte. After his convention with Sweden and Denmark, England sent a fleet into the Baltic under Nelson to dissolve the coalition (1801). His own officers conspired to compel Paul to abdicate, and in a scuffle he was strangled.

PAUL I, King of the Hellenes (1901–64), was born in Athens and educated at the Naval Academy. In 1922 he served with the Greek Navy in the campaign against the Turks, but in 1924 when a Republic was proclaimed went into exile with his elder brother George II. In 1935 he returned to Greece as crown prince. In World War II he served with the Greek General Staff in the Albanian campaign. In exile in London from 1941 until 1946, he succeeded his brother in 1947.

PAUL OF SAMOSATA (fl. 3rd cent. A.D.), was born at Samosata on the Euphrates, and in 260 became bishop or patriarch of Antioch, and so was practically the viceregent of Queen Zenobia of Palmyra; but in 272 was deposed for monarchianism—the doctrine that the Son is rather an attribute of the Father than a person.

PAULA. See FRANCIS, SAINT (2).

PAULDING, James Kirke, *pol'ding* (1778–1860), American writer, born in Putnam Co., N.Y., was a friend of Washington Irving. He wrote part of *Salmagundi,* and during the 1812 war published the *Diverting History of John Bull and Brother Jonathan.* In 1814 a more serious work, *The United States and England,* gained him an appointment on the Board of Naval Commissioners. He also wrote *The Dutchman's Fireside* (1831), *Westward Ho!* (1832), a *Life of Washington* (1835), and a defence of *Slavery in the United States* (1836). In 1837 he became secretary of the navy. See *Literary Life* by his son (1867) and Life by A. L. Herold (1926).

PAULET, or **Poulet, Sir Amyas,** *paw'let* (*c.* 1536–88), succeeded his father as governor of Jersey, was ambassador to France (1576–1579), and was keeper of Mary, Queen of Scots from 1585 till her death (1587). See his *Letter-book* (ed. Morris, 1874).

PAULI, *pow'lee,* (1) **Reinhold** (1823–82), German historian, was born in Berlin, studied at Bonn and at Oxford, and in 1849–1852 was private secretary to Bunsen. He was successively professor of History at Rostock, Tübingen, Marburg and Göttingen. Pauli's lifelong studies were devoted to English history, on which he wrote several books.

(2) **Wolfgang** (1900–58), Austrian-Swiss theoretical physicist, born in Vienna, the son of the professor of Chemistry, studied under Sommerfeld at Munich and Niels Bohr in Copenhagen. He formulated the 'exclusion principle' (1924), that no two electrons can be in the same energy state, of great importance in the application of the quantum theory to the periodic table of chemical elements, and postulated (1931) the existence of an electrically neutral particle in subatomic physics, later confirmed by Fermi, and in 1957 carried out experiments confirming the nonparity theory of Yang and Lee (qq.v.) in nuclear interactions. He was visiting professor at Princeton in 1935 and at Einstein's invitation again (1939–46). A Nobel prizewinner in 1945, he was a foreign member of the Royal Society.

PAULING, Linus Carl (1901–), American biochemist, born at Portland, Oregon, professor of Chemistry at the California Institute of Technology (1961–63), at the University of California at San Diego from 1967, applied the quantum theory to chemistry and was awarded the Nobel prize (1954) for his contributions to the electrochemical theory of valency, and with Campbell and Pressman, prepared artificial antibodies. An official inspector of defence projects in World War II, he became a controversial figure from 1955, as the leading professionally scientific critic of the American nuclear deterrent policy, forcibly setting out his views in *No More War* (1958). He was elected a foreign member of the Royal Society, and was awarded the Nobel peace prize in 1963.

PAULINUS, (1) St, of Nola (**Pontius Meropius Anicius Paulinus**) (353–431), born in Bordeaux, accepted Christian baptism (*c.* 389) and settled at Nola in Italy, where he became known for his charity and his rigid asceticism. He was consecrated Bishop of Nola (*c.* 409). He is remembered for his *Carmina* and for his epistles to Augustine, Jerome, Sulpicius Severus, and Ausonius.

(2) (d. 644), first Archbishop of York, was a Roman sent with Augustine to Kent by Pope Gregory in 601. Ordained bishop by Justus, fourth archbishop, in 625, he accompanied Ethelburga on her marriage to the heathen Edwin of Northumbria, who was baptized at York in 627. Edwin's death in battle drove him back to Kent, where, having in 633 received the *pallium* as Archbishop of York, he remained till his death.

PAULUS, (1). See AEMILIUS and SCIPIO AFRICANUS.

(2) **Friedrich,** *pow'loos* (1890–1957), German field-marshal and tank specialist, capitulated to the Russians with the remnants of his army at the siege of Stalingrad in 1943. Released from captivity in 1953, he became a lecturer on military affairs under the East German Communist government.

(3) **Heinrich Eberhard Gottlob** (1761–1851), German pioneer of rationalism, was born at Leonberg near Stuttgart, studied at Tübingen and, as professor at Jena (1789–1803), produced a New Testament commentary (1800–04), one on the Psalms (1791), and one on Isaiah (1793). He was afterwards professor at Würzburg and at Heidelberg, where he died. In his theological works he asserted the impossibility of the supernatural, and explained the miracles as due to mistaken opinions and errors. See his Autobiography (1839) and study by Meldegg (1853).

PAULUS AEGINETA (fl. 7th cent.), Greek physician, was born in Aegina. His *Synopsis of the Medical Art* went through many editions and translations.

PAULUS DIACONUS (fl. 8th cent.), 'Paul the Deacon', Lombard historian, was born at Friuli, and probably resided at the court of the Duke of Beneventum. He became a monk about 774, but spent some years at the court of Charlemagne, and retired to Monte Cassino in 787. His *Historia Romana* is based on Eutropius. The *Historia Langobardorum* comes down to 744. Other works are a *Life of Gregory the Great*; *Gesta Episcoporum Mettensium*; a *Book of Homilies*, selected from Augustine, Chrysostom, &c.; and poems and letters.

PAUL VERONESE. See VERONESE.

PAUSANIAS, (1) Spartan regent and general, a nephew of Leonidas, commanded the Greeks at Plataea (479 B.C.), where the Persians were routed. He then compelled the Thebans to give up the chiefs of the Persian party, and haughtily treated the Athenians and other Greeks. Capturing the Cyprian cities and Byzantium, he negotiated with Xerxes in the hope of becoming ruler under him of all Greece and was twice recalled for treachery. He tried to stir up the helots, was betrayed, and fled to a temple of Athena, where he was built up and only taken out to die of hunger.

(2) (fl. 2nd cent. A.D.), Greek geographer and historian, born probably in Lydia, travelled through almost all Greece, Macedonia and Italy, and also through part of Asia and Africa, and composed from his observations and researches an *Itinerary* of Greece, describing the different parts of that country and the monuments of art. His style is unpretentious and easy. and his *Itinerary* possesses the rare merit of being the work of an accurate eye-witness, one of the earliest examples of the antiquary; bare and meagre as it is, it remains one of the most precious records of antiquity. There are translations by Shilleto and Frazer. See M. Verrall's *Ancient Athens* (1890), and books by Kalkmann (1886), Gurlitt (1890), Bencker (1890), Heberdey (1896), Frazer (1900) and Robert (1909).

PAVLOV, Ivan Petrovich (1849–1936), Russian physiologist, born near Ryazan, a village priest's son, studied medicine at St Petersburg, conducted research in Breslau and Leipzig, and returned to St Petersburg, where he became professor (1891) and director of the Institute of Experimental Medicine (1913). He worked at the physiology of circulation and digestion, but is most famous for his study of 'conditioned' or acquired reflexes, associated each with some part of the brain cortex—the brain's only function being in his view the coupling of neurones to produce reflexes. He was awarded the Nobel prize for medicine in 1904. See Life by B. P. Babkin (1951).

PAVLOVA, Anna, *pav'lo-va* (1885–1931), Russian ballerina, born at St Petersburg, became world famous, forming her own company in 1909, and some of her most successful performances were in *Giselle*, *The Dying Swan*, *Don Quixote* and her own ballet *Autumn Leaves*. See Life by her husband, V. Dandré (1932).

PAXTON, Sir Joseph (1801–65), English gardener and architect, born at Milton-Bryant near Woburn, was a working gardener to the Duke of Devonshire, at Chiswick and Chatsworth; he remodelled the gardens, and managed the duke's Derbyshire estates. He designed a building for the Great Exhibition of 1851, which he re-erected as the Crystal Palace (destroyed by fire 1936). He wrote on gardening, and sat as Liberal for Coventry from 1854. See Life by V. Markham (1935).

PAYER, Julius von (1842–1915), born at Teplitz, went with Weyprecht on an Arctic expedition, and discovered and explored Franz-Josef Land (1872). Afterwards he went to Munich and became a painter.

PAYN, James (1830–98), English novelist, was born at Cheltenham, and educated at Eton, Woolwich Academy, and Trinity, Cambridge. In 1855 he published a volume of poems, in 1859–74 was Leitch Ritchie's successor as editor of *Chambers's Journal*, and in 1882–96 edited the *Cornhill*. He wrote a hundred novels. See his *Some Literary Recollections* (1886) and *Gleams of Memory* (1894).

PAYNE, (1) **Henry Neville** (d. *c.* 1710), wrote tragedies and comedies, intrigued in Scotland for James II after the Revolution, was tortured in Edinburgh with 'the boot' in 1690, and was imprisoned till 1700.

(2) **John Howard** (1791–1852), American actor and playwright, born in New York, made his début there in February 1809, and in 1813 appeared in London. For thirty years he had a successful career as actor and author of plays, chiefly adaptations; that called *Clari* contains the song *Home, Sweet Home*, the music being by Sir Henry Bishop. Payne was appointed American consul at Tunis in 1841, and died there.

(3) **Peter** (*c.* 1380–1455), English Wycliffite, was born near Grantham, studied at Oxford, and became in 1410 principal of St Edmund Hall. Charged with heresy, he fled about 1416 to Bohemia, where, till his death in 1455, he played a conspicuous part as a controversialist amongst the Hussites, taking the Taborite or extreme view. See Baker's *A Forgotten Great Englishman* (1894).

(4) **Roger** (1739–97), English bookbinder, born at Windsor, became famous, after 1766, as the most artistic bookbinder in London. See *Roger Payne* by C. J. Davenport (1929).

PAYNE-SMITH, Robert (1819–95), English theologian, was born at Chipping Camden, studied at Pembroke College, Oxford, and, as sub-librarian of the Bodleian (1857–65), began his great *Thesaurus Syriacus* (1870–93). Sermons on *Isaiah* (1862) led to his appointment as regius professor of Theology at Oxford (1865–70), whence he removed to the deanery of Canterbury.

PEABODY, George (1795–1869), American philanthropist, born at South Danvers, Mass., now called Peabody, became a partner in a Baltimore dry-goods store in 1829. He established himself in London in 1837 as a merchant and banker, and in his lifetime gave away a million and a half for philanthropic purposes—Kane's Arctic expedition, education (at Harvard, &c.), industrial homes in London. He died in London. See Life by P. A. Hanaford (1882).

PEACE, Charles (1832–79), English criminal and murderer, born in Sheffield. First imprisoned for robbery at the age of eighteen, he subsequently divided his time between picture-frame making by day and burglary by night. In August 1876 he shot a policeman in Whalley Range, Manchester, and after escaping attended the trial of William and

John Habron for his crime. John was found not guilty, and William was, on account of his youth, sentenced to life imprisonment for the crime. In November 1876 Peace murdered Arthur Dyson, whose wife he had been annoying, in Sheffield, but again escaped. He made his way to London, where he lived a life of seeming respectability, and was, two years later, arrested for attempted murder, having fired upon a policeman while attempting a burglary in Blackheath. In the following January, while serving sentence for the latter crime, he was accused of the murder of Dyson and found guilty. Shortly before his execution, he confessed to the Whalley Range murder. See his *Trials*, ed. N. Teignmouth Shore (1926).

PEACH, Benjamin Neeve (1842–1926), British geologist, born at Gorran Haven, Cornwall, educated at Peterhead and Wick academies and London School of Mines, worked along with Dr John Horne on the Geological Survey. Their brilliant collaboration elucidated the very intricate geology of the northwest Highlands. Their joint works include the *Silurian Rocks of Scotland* (1899) and *Chapters on the Geology of Scotland* (1930).

PEACOCK, Thomas Love (1785–1866), English novelist and poet, born at Weymouth, was the son of a London merchant and friend of Shelley. He entered the service of the East India Company in 1819 after producing three satirical romances, *Headlong Hall* (1816), *Melincourt* (1817) and *Nightmare Abbey* (1818). *Crotchet Castle* (1831) concluded this series of satires, but in 1860 the veteran returned to the stage with *Gryll Grange*, which shows signs of hardening. He also published two romances properly so-called, *Maid Marian* (1822) and *The Misfortunes of Elphin* (1829). The framework of his satirical fictions is always the same—a company of humorists meet in a country house and display their crotchets or prejudices which are the things Peacock, the reasonable man, most disliked, that is, morbid romance, the mechanical sort of political economy, the 'march of science' and transcendental philosophy. The satire is relieved by some excellent songs and the eccentrics by one or two less unbalanced men and some gay natural young women. Otherwise the characters are stock types as in Ben Jonson's comedies. Exception should be made for the mellow divine who first appears as Dr Gaster in *Headlong Hall*, becomes three-dimensional in Dr Folliott in *Crotchet Castle* and reappears as Dr Opimian in *Gryll Grange*. To add to the piquancy of the fictions the poets of the Romantic school, Wordsworth, Coleridge, Shelley, Byron, Southey, are caricatured along with the Edinburgh Reviewers, who offer the extra target of being Scots. His two romances vary in tone from genuine love of romance to boisterous fun or Rabelaisian comedy. Peacock was poised between the Voltairian and the romantic view of life—hence the 'sauce piquant' of his admirable satires. See *The Novels of Thomas Love Peacock*, ed. D. Garnett (1949); the Life by Van Doren (1911); studies by A. M. Freeman (1911) and J. B. Priestley (1927).

PEANO, Giuseppe, *pay-ah'nō* (1858–1932), Italian mathematician, born at Cuneo, taught at the University of Turin, was known for his work on mathematical logic and for his promotion of a universal language based on uninflected Latin.

PEARS, Peter, *peerz* (1910–), English tenor, born in Farnham, after being organ scholar of Hertford College, Oxford, studied singing (1933–34) at the Royal College of Music. He toured the U.S.A. and Europe with Benjamin Britten, and in 1943 joined Sadler's Wells. After the success of *Peter Grimes* (1945) he joined Britten in the English Opera Group, and was co-founder with him, in 1948, of the Aldeburgh Festival. He is noted for his sympathy with and understanding of modern works. He was created C.B.E. in 1957.

PEARSE, Patrick (or **Padraic**) **Henry** (1879–1916), Irish writer and nationalist, was a leader of the Gaelic revival and editor of its journal. Having commanded the insurgents in the Easter rising of 1916 he was proclaimed president of the provisional government, but, after the revolt had been quelled, was arrested, court-martialled and shot. He wrote poems, short stories and plays. See Life by Ryan (1919).

PEARSON, (1) Sir Cyril Arthur (1866–1921), English newspaper and periodical proprietor, born at Wookey, Somerset, educated at Winchester, became a journalist, founded *Pearson's Weekly* in 1890 and various other periodicals. In 1900 he became associated with newspapers, founding the *Daily Express*, and amalgamating the *St James Gazette* with the *Evening Standard*. Turning blind, he founded St Dunstan's home for blinded soldiers and was president of the National Institution for the Blind.

(2) **Hesketh** (1887–1964), English biographer, born at Hawford in Worcestershire, worked in a shipping office before beginning a successful stage career in 1911. In 1931 he emerged as a writer of popular and racy biographies. Among these are *Gilbert and Sullivan* (1935), *Shaw* (1942), *Conan Doyle* (1943), *Oscar Wilde* (1946), whose *Works* and *Essays* he edited, *Dizzy* (1951), *Sir Walter Scott* (1955), and *Charles II* (1960). He also wrote *Common Misquotations* (1937) and a play *Writ for Libel* (1950) with Colin Hurry.

(3) **John** (1613–86), English divine, was born at Great Snoring, Norfolk, son of the Archdeacon of Suffolk. He was educated at Eton and at Queen's and King's Colleges, Cambridge, and in 1640 appointed chaplain to the lord-keeper Finch, and later presented to the rectory of Thorington in Suffolk. In 1659 he published his learned *Exposition of the Creed*, and edited the remains of John Hales of Eton. In 1660 he was presented to the rectory of St Christopher's in London, and made prebendary of Ely, archdeacon of Surrey, and master of Jesus College, Cambridge. In 1661 he was the principal antagonist of Baxter in the Savoy Conference, and became Margaret professor of Divinity; in 1662 he was made master of Trinity, Cambridge, and in 1673 bishop of Chester. He defended the genuineness of the Ignatian epistles (1672), and in 1684 published his *Annales Cyprianici*.

(4) **Karl** (1857–1936), British scientist, born in London, turned from the law to mathematics, becoming professor of Applied Mathematics in University College London, and Galton professor of Eugenics. He published *The Grammar of Science* (1892), and works on eugenics, mathematics, biometrics. In his *Life of Galton* (1914–30) the head of the Eugenics Laboratory applies the methods of his science to the study of its founder. See Life by his son, E. S. Pearson (1938).

(5) **Lester Bowles** (1897–1972), Canadian politician, was born in Newtonbrook, Ontario, educated at Toronto and Oxford Universities. He became successively first secretary at the London office of the Canadian high commissioner (1935–39), assistant under-secretary of state for external affairs (1941), ambassador in Washington (1945–46). He was a senior adviser at the Charter Conference of the U.N. in 1945 and was later leader of Canadian U.N. delegations. In 1952–53 he was president of the U.N. General Assembly, and in 1957 was awarded the Nobel peace prize. Secretary of state for external affairs (1948–57), and leader of the Opposition party from 1958, he became prime minister in 1963, retaining power with a minority government in 1965. He resigned as party leader and as prime minister in 1968. He was awarded the O.M. in 1971.

PEARY, Robert Edwin (1856–1920), American admiral and explorer, born at Cresson Springs, Penn., made eight Arctic voyages by the Greenland coast, in 1891–92 arriving on the east coast by crossing the ice. In 1906 he reached 87° 6′ N. lat., and on April 6, 1909, attained the North Pole. See accounts of his travels by himself in *Northward over the Great Ice* (1898), *The North Pole* (1910), &c., his wife, Heilprin, and Hobbs (1936).

PEASE, (1) **Edward** (1767–1858), English industrialist, born at Darlington, carried on till 1817 his father's woollen mill there. He later promoted railways, and was George Stephenson's supporter in his famous Stockton to Darlington project of 1825. The family were Quakers and worked for the Peace and Antislavery Societies; two of Edward's sons entered zealously into their father's schemes, and were in parliament.

(2) **Francis Gladheim** (1881–1938), American astronomer and designer of optical instruments, was born at Cambridge, Mass. He was observer and optician at Yerkes Observatory, Wis. (1901–04), and instrument-maker (1908–13) at the Mount Wilson Observatory, Pasadena, where he designed the 100-inch telescope, and the 50-foot interferometer telescope by means of which he gained direct measurements of star diameters. He was also associated in the design of the 200-inch Palomar telescope.

PECOCK, Reginald, *pee′kok* (*c.* 1395–*c.* 1460), Welsh theologian, was a fellow of Oriel, Oxford, and received priest's orders in 1422. He was master of Whittington College, London, and rector of its church (1431); bishop of St Asaph's (1444); and of Chichester (1450). He plunged into the Lollard and other controversies, and compiled many treatises including *The Reule of Crysten Religioun* (*c.* 1443; ed. Greet, E.E.T.S., 1927), *The Book of Feith* (ed. Morison, 1909) and *The Repressor of Over Much Blaming of the Clergy* (*c.* 1455; ed. Babington, Rolls Series, 1860). His philosophic breadth and independence of judgment brought upon him the suspicions of the church. In 1457 he was denounced for having written in English, and for making reason paramount to the authority of the old doctors. He was summoned before Archbishop Bourchier, condemned as a heretic, and given the alternative of abjuring or being burned. He elected to abjure, gave up fourteen of his books, resigned his bishopric, and retired to Thorney Abbey. See study by V. H. H. Green (1945).

PECQUET, Jean, *pek-ay* (1622–74), French anatomist, born in Dieppe, worked at Montpellier, where in 1647 he was the first to see clearly the thoracic duct. He described his findings in *Experimenta nova anatomica* (1651). He became a dipsomaniac and died in Paris.

PEDEN, Alexander (*c.* 1626–86), Scottish Covenanter, studied at Glasgow, was ejected in 1662 from his ministry at New Luce in Galloway, and subsequently wandered preaching at conventicles and hiding in caves. He was repeatedly in Ireland, and in 1673–77 was imprisoned on the Bass Rock. Many of his utterances were regarded as prophecies.

PEDERSEN, Christiern (1480–1554), Danish writer, born probably at Elsinore, a leader of the Reformation in Denmark, is remembered for his Danish-Latin dictionary, and his translations of the New Testament (1521) and the Psalms (1531). He also worked on the famous 'Christian III' version of the Bible, which appeared in 1550.

PEDRELL, Felipe (1841–1922), Spanish composer, born at Tortosa, was self-taught. He wrote operas, choral works, songs, &c. He became professor at Madrid, and lived later at Barcelona. He was the author of critical and historical works on music.

PEDRO, name of two emperors of Brazil:

Pedro I (1798–1834), second son of John VI of Portugal, fled to Brazil with his parents on Napoleon's invasion, and became prince-regent of Brazil on his father's return to Portugal (1821). A Liberal in outlook, he declared for Brazilian independence in 1822, and was crowned as Pedro I. The new empire did not start smoothly, and Pedro in 1831 abdicated and withdrew to Portugal. He was Pedro IV of Portugal on the death of his father, but abdicated in favour of his daughter.

Pedro II (1825–91), son of Pedro I, succeeded on his father's abdication, and, distinguished by his love of learning and scholarly tastes, reigned in peace until the 1889 revolution drove him to Europe. He died in Paris. See Life by M. W. Williams (1938).

PEDRO THE CRUEL (1334–69), king of Castile and León, succeeded his father, Alfonso XI, in 1350, and assuming full power in 1353, became exceedingly popular with the people for his justice, but alienated the nobles and clergy. When he had marched to suppress a revolt in Estremadura, he was betrayed by his brother Henry and taken prisoner. Escaping, despite the excommunication of the pope, he speedily crushed the rebels. But now he became suspicious of everyone; and the rest of his reign was devoted to the establishment of his own authority on the ruins of the feudal tyranny of the great vassals, and to long-continued and bloody wars with Aragon and Granada. He owes the epithet Cruel mainly to the murder of his brother Don Fadrique in 1358. The people were in general well and justly governed, but heavy taxes dissipated his popularity. Henry returned from France (1366) at the head of a body of exiles, backed by Du Guesclin, and aided by Aragon, France and the pope. Edward the Black Prince, persuaded to espouse Pedro's cause in 1367, defeated Henry and Du Guesclin at Navarrete (April 13). But, disgusted by his ally's nonfulfilment of his promises, the English prince repassed the Pyrenees and left Pedro to his fate. The whole kingdom groaned under his cruelties; rebellions broke out everywhere; and when, in 1367, Henry returned, Pedro was routed at Montiel (1369), and in single combat with Henry, developing into a mêlée, was slain. See studies by Prosper Mérimée (1848) and Storer (1910).

PEEL, Sir Robert (1788–1850), English statesman, was born near Bury in Lancashire. His father, **Sir Robert Peel** (1750–1830) (M.P. from 1790, created baronet in 1800), was a wealthy cotton manufacturer and calico printer, and from him he inherited a great fortune. He had three years at Harrow, took a double first from Christ Church, Oxford, in 1808, and entered parliament in 1809 as Tory member for Cashel. In 1811 he was appointed under-secretary for the colonies, and in 1812–18 was secretary for Ireland. In this capacity 'Orange Peel' displayed a strong anti-Catholic spirit, and was so fiercely attacked by O'Connell (q.v.) that he challenged him to a duel. From 1818 till 1822 Peel remained out of office, but sat for the University of Oxford. In 1819 he was chairman of the Bank Committee, and moved the resolutions which led to the resumption of cash payments. In 1822 he re-entered the ministry as home secretary, and he and Canning as foreign secretary worked together pretty well, Peel devoting himself to the currency. But on 'Roman Catholic emancipation' Canning was in advance of Peel, and when Canning formed a Whig-Tory ministry, Peel, along with the Duke of Wellington and others, withdrew from office (1827). Yet, when the death of Canning led to the Wellington-Peel government, its great measure was that for the relief of the Roman Catholics (1829). As home secretary he reorganized the London police force ('Peelers' or 'Bobbies'). Peel opposed parliamentary reform, and in 1830 the Wellington-Peel ministry was succeeded by a Whig ministry under Earl Grey, which, in 1832, carried the Reform Bill. Peel shrank from factious obstruction of the measure, but as leader of the 'Conservative' opposition, sought by vigilant criticism of Whig measures to retard the too rapid strides of Liberalism. Rejected by Oxford in 1829, but returned for Westbury, Peel represented Tamworth from 1833 till his death. In November 1834 he accepted office as prime minister but gave place to Lord Melbourne in April 1835. The general election of 1841 was virtually a contest between Free Trade and Protection, and Protection won. The Conservative party, headed by Peel, now came into office. The Whigs were bent upon a fixed but moderate duty on foreign corn; the Anti-Corn-Law League would hear of nothing short of repeal; while Sir Robert carried (1842) a modification of the sliding-scale. The deficit in the revenue led him to impose (1842) an 'income tax' of 7d. in the pound, to be levied for three years. To alleviate the new burden Peel revised the general tariff, and either abolished or lowered the duties on several very important articles of commerce. He resolutely repressed the malcontents of Ireland, and O'Connell's influence was broken. In 1845 the allowance to Maynooth was changed into a permanent endowment, and the Irish unsectarian colleges were founded. But the potato rot in Ireland, followed by a frightful famine, rendered 'cheap corn' a necessity. Cobden and the League redoubled their exertions. Peel again yielded, telling his colleagues that the corn laws were doomed. Lord Stanley (afterwards Earl of Derby) seceded, and, with Lord George Bentinck, Disraeli and others, formed a 'no-surrender' Tory party; but the Duke of Wellington, Graham, Aberdeen, Gladstone and other eminent Conservatives stood by him, and repeal was carried. Defeated on an Irish Protection of Life Bill, he retired in June 1846, giving place to a Whig administration under Lord John Russell to which he gave independent but general support. In the critical times of 1847–48 he was one of the most important props of the government, whose free trade principles he had now accepted. He had a keen English interest in sport, and a cultivated taste in matters literary and artistic. On June 29, 1850, he was thrown from his horse, and was so much injured that he died July 2. See his (non-biographical) *Memoirs*, edited by Earl Stanhope and Viscount Cardwell (1857), *Speeches* (1835 and 1853), his *Private Letters* (ed. G. Peel, 1920), and C. S. Parker's *Peel Papers* (3 vols. 1891–99); his *Life and Times* by Sir T. Lever; books by Guizot (1851), Laurence Peel, Lord Dalling, Barnett Smith, F. C. Montague, Justin McCarthy, J. R. Thursfield, A. A. W. Ramsay (1928), G. K. Clark (1929); Shaw Lefevre, *Peel and O'Connell* (1887). Peel's eldest son, **Sir Robert** (1822–95), and the second, **Sir Frederick** (1823–1906), held office as ministers; **Arthur Wellesley**, the fifth and youngest (1829–1912), was speaker of the House of Commons 1884–95, and then was created Viscount Peel.

PEELE, George (*c.* 1558–98), English Elizabethan dramatist, born in London, went up to Oxford in 1571. He took his bachelor's degree in 1577, his master's in 1579. By 1581 he had removed to London, where for seventeen years he lived a roistering Bohemian life as actor, poet and playwright. He was one of those warned to repentance by Greene in his *Groatsworth of Wit* (1592). *The Arraignment of Paris* (1584), is a dramatic pastoral containing ingenious flatteries of Elizabeth.

Other works include his *Farewell* to Sir John Norris on his expedition to Portugal (1589, eked out by *A Tale of Troy*), *Eclogue Gratulatory* (1589) to the Earl of Essex, *Polyhymnia* (1590), *Speeches* for the reception of Queen Elizabeth (1591), and *Honour of the Garter* (1593). The historical play of *Edward I* (1593) is marred by its slanders against Queen Eleanor. His play, *The Old Wives' Tale* (1595), probably gave Milton the subject for his *Comus*. *David and Bethsabe* was published in 1599. Peele's works were first collected by Dyce (1828–39; reissue, with Greene, in 1861). A later edition is by A. H. Bullen (1888). See Symonds's *Shakspere's Predecessors* (1884).

PÉGUY, Charles Pierre, *pay-gee* (1873–1914), French nationalist, publisher, and neo-Catholic poet, born of peasant stock at Orléans, he was educated at the École Normale and the Sorbonne, after which he opened a bookshop. In 1900 he founded the *Cahiers de la quinzaine* in which were first published his own works as well as those of such writers as Romain Rolland, who later became famous. Deeply patriotic, he combined sincere Catholicism with Socialism and his writings reflect his intense desire for justice and truth. His most important works include *Le Mystère de la charité de Jeanne d'Arc* (1910), *Victor Marie, Comte Hugo* (1910), *L'Argent* (1912) and *La Tapisserie de Notre Dame* (1913). He was killed in World War I. See studies by Halévy (1918; trans. 1947), A. Rousseaux (1947), Dru (1956), and B. Guyon (1961).

PEIRCE, *purse*, (1) **Benjamin** (1809–80), American mathematician, father of (2), in 1833 became professor at Harvard, in 1849 astronomer to the American Nautical Almanac, and in 1867–74 was superintendent of the Coast Survey. His papers on the discovery of Neptune (1848), on Saturn's rings (1851–55) and his *Treatise on Analytic Mechanics* (1857) attracted great attention.

(2) **Charles Sanders** (1839–1914), American philosopher, pioneer of pragmatism, son of (1), born at Cambridge, Mass., through his father became associated with the Coastal and Geodesic Survey (1861–91), but devoted most of his leisure time to philosophy and spent the rest of his life in almost complete seclusion, apart from private tutoring at Milford, subsisting on the generosity of William James, whose version of pragmatism so repelled Peirce, however, that he relabelled himself 'pragmaticist'. For Peirce, truth is the opinion which is fated to be ultimately agreed by all who investigate. A profoundly original mathematical logician, he modified Booleian logical algebra to accommodate De Morgan's logic, distinguished a threefold division of predicates and elaborated a triadic theory of meaning. See his *Studies in Logic* (1883), *Collected Papers*, vols. i-vi, ed. C. Hartshorne and P. Weiss (1931–35), vols. vii-viii, ed. A. W. Burks (1958), and studies by J. Buchler (1940), T. A. Goudge (1950), ed. P. P. Wiener and F. H. Young (1952) and W. B. Gallie (1952).

PEIRSON, Francis (1757–81), major, commanding the troops at St Helier in Jersey, after the governor had been captured by a French force, was killed in victoriously repelling the invaders. His death is the subject of Copley's famous picture in the National Gallery.

PEISISTRATOS. See PISISTRATUS.

PELAGIUS (*c.* 360–*c.* 420), heretic, was born a Briton or an Irishman, his name being a Greek translation of the Celtic *Morgan* ('sea-born'). He was a monk, but never took orders, and settled in Rome about 400. Here he wrote *On the Trinity*, *On Testimonies* and *On the Pauline Epistles*, and attached Celestius, an Irish Scot, to his views. About 409 the two withdrew to Africa, and Pelagius made a pilgrimage to Jerusalem. Celestius having sought ordination at Carthage, his doctrines were examined and condemned; and in 415 Pelagius too was accused of heresy before the synod of Jerusalem. The Pelagian heresy was held to deny original sin; the will is equally free to choose to do good and to do evil. The impeachment failed, but a new synod of Carthage in 416 condemned Pelagius and Celestius; and ultimately Pope Zosimus adopted the canons of the African Council, and Pelagius was banished from Rome in 418. The Pelagian sect was soon extinguished, but Pelagianism and Semi-Pelagianism often troubled the church.

PELAYO (fl. 8th cent.), said to have been the first Christian king in Spain, seems to have made headway against the Arabs in Asturias. His deeds are obscured by legend.

PELHAM, name of an English land-owning family:

(1) **Sir Thomas** (*c.* 1650–1712), in 1706 was created Baron Pelham.

(2) **Thomas Pelham Holles** (1693–1768), son and successor of (1), succeeded in 1711 to the estates of his maternal uncle, John Holles, Duke of Newcastle. George I created him Earl of Clare (1714) and Duke of Newcastle (1715). A Whig and a supporter of Walpole, in 1724 he became secretary of state, and held the office for thirty years. In 1754 he succeeded his brother, Henry Pelham, as premier, but retired in 1756. In July 1757 he was again premier, and compelled to take the first William Pitt into his ministry and to give him the lead in the House of Commons and the supreme direction of the war and of foreign affairs—Newcastle, an incapable minister, but strong in courtcraft and intrigue, being a mere figurehead. On the accession of George III Bute superseded Newcastle (1762). In the Rockingham ministry (1765), he was for a few months lord privy seal.

(3) **Henry Pelham** (*c.* 1695–1754), younger brother of (2), took an active part in suppressing the rebellion of 1715, became secretary for war in 1724, and was a zealous supporter of Walpole. In 1743 he took office. Events during his ministry (reconstructed in 1744 as the 'Broad-bottom administration') were the Austrian Succession war, the '45, the financial bill of 1750, the reform of the calendar, and Hardwicke's Marriage Act.

(4) **Henry Pelham-Clinton** (1811–64), fifth Duke of Newcastle and twelfth Earl of Lincoln, represented South Notts from 1832 to 1846, when he was ousted for supporting Peel's free trade measures. He was a lord

of the treasury in 1834–35, first commissioner of woods and forests in 1841–46, and then Irish secretary. He succeeded to the dukedom in 1851, and returned to office in 1852, being colonial secretary in the Aberdeen government. At the Crimean war he was made secretary of state for war—the first to hold that office. But the sufferings of the British army in the winter of 1854 raised a storm, and he resigned. He was colonial secretary under Palmerston, 1859–64. See Life by Martineau (1908).

PÉLISSIER, Aimable Jean Jacques, Duc de Malakoff, *pay-lees-yay* (1794–1864), French military leader, born near Rouen, served in Spain in 1823, in the Morea in 1828, in Algeria in 1830 and 1839. In 1845 he acquired notoriety by suffocating 500 fugitive Arabs in caves in the Dahna. In the Crimean war (1854) he commanded the first corps, and succeeded Canrobert in the chief command before Sebastopol. For storming the Malakoff he was made Marshal and Duc de Malakoff. In 1858–59 he was French ambassador in London and thereafter governor of Algeria.

PELL, John (1610–85), English mathematician and clergyman, born at Southwick in Sussex, a brilliant student at Cambridge, was appointed professor of Mathematics at Amsterdam in 1643 and lecturer at the New College at Breda in 1646. Employed by Cromwell, first as a mathematician and later in 1654 as his agent, he went to Switzerland in an attempt to persuade Swiss Protestants to join a Continental Protestant league led by England. In 1661 he became rector at Fobbing in Essex and in 1663 vicar of Laindon. His published mathematical writings are relatively few, but a large collection of unpublished papers is in the British Museum. He is remembered chiefly for his equation called the Pell equation and for introducing the division sign ÷ into England. He was one of the early fellows of the Royal Society.

PELLEGRINI, Carlo, *pel-leg-ree'nee* (1839–1889), Italian caricaturist, born at Capua, came to London in 1864, and from 1869 till his death was the cartoonist, 'Ape', of *Vanity Fair*.

PELLETIER, Pierre Joseph, *pel-tyay* (1788–1842), French chemist, born in Paris, professor and later assistant director at the School of Pharmacy there, with J. B. Caventou discovered strychnine, quinine, brucine and other alkaloids. He was responsible for the naming of chlorophyll.

PELLICO, Silvio (1788–1854), Italian writer and patriot, born at Saluzzo in Piedmont, spent four years at Lyons, and at Milan (1810) was French tutor in the military school. His tragedies of *Laodamia* and *Francesca da Rimini* gained him a name, and he translated Byron's *Manfred*. In 1820 he was arrested and imprisoned for two years at Venice. He was then, on a charge of Carbonarism, condemned to death, but had his sentence commuted to fifteen years' imprisonment in the Spielberg near Brünn, and was liberated in 1830. During this time he wrote two other dramas. He published an account of his imprisonment, *Le mie Prigioni* (1833), and subsequently numerous tragedies, poems and a catechism on the duties of man. See Lives by Chiala (Italian, 1852), Bourdon (8th ed. Paris 1885), Rivieri (1899–1901) and Barbiera (1936).

PELLISSON-FONTANIER, Paul, *pel-lee-sõ-fõ-tan-yay* (1624–93), French writer of a history of the French Academy, and was a member of it. Sainte Beuve ranks him as a classic.

PELOPIDAS (d. 364 B.C.), Theban general, in 382 B.C. was driven from Thebes by the oligarchic party, who were supported by the Spartans, and sought refuge at Athens, whence he returned with a few associates in 379, and recovered possession of the citadel. His 'sacred band' of Theban youth largely contributed to Epaminondas's victory at Leuctra (371). In the expedition against Alexander of Pherae (368) he was treacherously taken prisoner, but rescued by Epaminondas next year. He was then ambassador to the Persian court. In 364, in command of a third expedition against Alexander of Pherae, he marched into Thessaly, and won the battle of Cynoscephalae, but was himself slain.

PELTIER, Jean Charles Athanase, *pel-tyay* (1785–1845), French physicist, born at Hain, Somme, originally a watchmaker, discovered the thermoelectric reduction of temperature known as the Peltier effect and later used by Lenz as a method of freezing water. He died in Paris.

PEMBERTON, Sir Max (1863–1950), English reviewer and novelist, born at Birmingham, educated at Merchant Taylors' School and Caius College, Cambridge, made writing his career. He was editor of *Chums* (1892–93) and from 1894 to 1906 editor of *Cassell's Magazine*. He produced a succession of readable novels, many of them historical adventure stories, and also wrote plays. Successful titles were: *Impregnable City* (1895), *Queen of the Jesters* (1897), *The Show Girl* (1909), *Captain Black* (1911), *The Mad King Dies* (1928). He founded the London School of Journalism and in 1920 became a director of Northcliffe newspapers, two years later publishing a biography of Lord Northcliffe. He was knighted in 1928.

PEMBROKE. See HERBERT, MARSHAL, STRONGBOW.

PENDA (*c.* 577–655), heathen king of Mercia, constantly at war with Northumbria, defeated Edwin at Heathfield (633), Oswald at Maserfelth (642), but was himself defeated and slain by Oswy on the Winwaed, either in Lothian or in Yorkshire.

PENDEREL, the name of five Shropshire Catholic yeomen who aided Charles II (q.v.) at Boscobel. See Allan Fea's *Flight of the King* (1897).

PENGELLY, William (1812–94), English geologist, born at Looe, a schoolmaster and tutor at Torquay, was eminent as a geologist, especially in connection with the exploration of the Brixham Cave and Kent's Cavern. See the Life by his daughter (1897).

PENG TEH-HUAI (1899–), Chinese Communist general, born in Hunan, fought in the Sino-Japanese War (1937–45), became second-in-command to Chu Teh (q.v.), and led the Chinese 'volunteer' forces in the Korean war.

PENIAKOFF, Vladimir, nicknamed **Popski** (1897–1951), soldier and author, of Russian parentage, born in Belgium and educated in England, joined the British army and from 1940 to 1942 served with the Long Range Desert Group and the Libyan Arab Force. In October 1942, with the sanction of the army, he formed his own force, the famous Popski's Private Army which carried out spectacular raids behind the German lines. He rose to the rank of lieutenant-colonel and was decorated for bravery by Britain, France and Belgium. His book *Private Army* was published in 1950. See Willett's *Popski* (1954) and Yunnie's *Warriors on Wheels* (1959).

PENN, William (1644–1718), English Quaker and founder of Pennsylvania, the son of Admiral William Penn, was born in London. He was sent down from Christ Church, Oxford, for having become a zealous Quaker; and his father sent him to the Continent, in the hope that the gaiety of French life would alter the bent of his mind. He returned a polished man of the world, having served for a little in the Dutch war. In 1666 the admiral dispatched him to look after his estates in Cork, but he was imprisoned for attending a Quaker meeting in Cork. He returned to England a thoroughgoing Quaker. In 1668 he was thrown into the Tower for his *Sandy Foundation Shaken*, in which he attacked the ordinary doctrines of the Trinity. While in prison he wrote the most popular of his books, *No Cross, no Crown*, and *Innocency with her Open Face*, a vindication of himself that contributed to his liberation, obtained through the intervention of his father's friend, the Duke of York. In September 1670 Admiral Penn died, leaving his son an estate of £1500 a year. In the same month he was again imprisoned for preaching; and in 1671 he was sent to Newgate for six months. He took advantage of the Indulgence for making preaching tours, and he visited Holland and Germany for the advancement of Quakerism. In 1681 he obtained from the crown, in lieu of his father's claim upon it, a grant of territory in North America, called Pensilvania in honour of the old admiral; his desire being to establish a home for his co-religionists. Penn with his emigrants sailed for the Delaware in 1682, and in November held his famous interview with the Indians on the site of Philadelphia. He planned the city of Philadelphia, and for two years governed the colony wisely, with full tolerance for all that was not regarded as wicked by Puritanism (card-playing, play-going, &c., being strictly forbidden as 'evil sports and games'). Penn returned to England to exert himself in favour of his persecuted brethren at home. His influence with James II and his belief in his good intentions were curiously strong. The suspicion that Penn allowed himself to be used as a tool is not justified by any known facts. Through his exertions, in 1686 all persons imprisoned on account of their religious opinions (including 1200 Quakers) were released. After the accession of William III Penn was repeatedly accused of treasonable adherence to the deposed king, but was finally acquitted in 1693. In 1699 he paid a second visit to Pennsylvania, where his constitution had proved unworkable, and had to be much altered. He did something to mitigate the evils of slavery, but held Negro slaves himself. He departed for England in 1701. His last years were embittered by disputes about boundaries, &c.; he was even, in financial embarrassment, thrown for nine months into the Fleet in 1708. He was twice married, and wrote over forty works and pamphlets. See Lives by Dixon (1856), Dobrée (1932), Vulliamy (1934), Monastier (1944) and Peare (1960).

PENNANT, Thomas (1726–98), Welsh traveller, was born at Downing near Holywell, Flintshire. In 1744 he went to Oxford, but left without a degree. His many tours included visits to Ireland (1754), the Continent (1765), Scotland (1769 and 1772), and the Isle of Man (1774), besides rambles through England and Wales. He was F.R.S. and D.C.L. From boyhood a naturalist, for years a correspondent of Linnaeus, Pennant published *British Zoology* (1765–77), *British Quadrupeds* (1771), *Arctic Zoology* (1785), *History of London* (1790), &c. He is remembered by his *Tours* in Scotland (1771–75) and Wales (1778–81). See his *Literary Life* by himself (1793), and the memoir in Rhys's edition of the *Tours in Wales* (1883).

PENNELL, Joseph (1860–1926), American etcher and book illustrator, born at Philadelphia, lived much in England. He wrote on book illustration and produced illustrated tours on the Thames, in Provence, in Hungary and elsewhere, and a Life of Whistler (1908). His wife, **Elizabeth Robins** (1855–1936), an authoress, many of whose books he illustrated, wrote, among others, biographies of *Mary Wollstonecraft* (1884), and *Charles Godfrey Leland* (1906).

PENNEY, Baron William George (1909–), British physicist, born in Gibraltar, became professor of Mathematics at the Imperial College of Science in South Kensington, where he had been a student before going to the Universities of Wisconsin and Cambridge. He became well known for his research work on nuclear weapons and was an observer when the atomic bomb was dropped on Nagasaki. In 1947 he was appointed chief superintendent of armament research at the Ministry of Supply, made a K.B.E. in 1952, and became director of the Atomic Weapons Research Establishment at Aldermaston (1953–59). In 1959 he headed the British team of scientists in the 'technical working group' set up by the Geneva three-power conference, and was deputy chairman (1961), and then chairman (1964–67), of the U.K. Atomic Energy Authority. He was created a life peer in 1967 and became rector of Imperial College.

PENNY, Thomas (d. 1589), English clergyman and botanist, educated at Cambridge, was a prebendary of St Paul's. His interest in botany and entomology was such that he assisted Gesner (q.v.) in his work. After his death his drawings passed into the possession of Moffet, who made use of them in his *Insectorum Theatrum* (1634).

PENRY, John (1559–93), Welsh Puritan pamphleteer, born in Brecknockshire, graduated at both Cambridge and Oxford, and set up (*c.* 1588) a printing press which turned out anti-Episcopal tracts under the name Martin Marprelate. Hounded from place to place, the press was ultimately discovered, but Penry escaped to Edinburgh (1590). Venturing to London in 1592, he was arrested and hanged.

PENTREATH, Dolly (1685–1777), reputed to be the last person to speak Cornish (others say Bernard Victor, d. 1875), an itinerant fishwife and fortune-teller, and wife of a man called Jeffery. She was born and died at Mousehole on Mount's Bay. See Jago's *Ancient Language of Cornwall* (1882).

PÉPIN, or Pippin, *pay-pī* or *pi-pèen*, the name of a Frankish family of which the following became rulers: (1) **of Héristal** (d. 714), was mayor of the palace in Austrasia, to which he added after 687 the similar vice-royalties of Neustria and Burgundy, and called himself 'Duke and Prince of the Franks'. He was their real ruler during several reigns. He was father of Charles Martel. (2) (*c.* 715–68), surnamed 'the Short', king of the Franks, younger son of Charles Martel (q.v.) and father of Charlemagne (q.v.), founded the Frankish dynasty of the Carlovingians. Childeric, the last of the Merovingians, having been deposed, Pépin was chosen king in his stead (751). When Pope Stephen III was hard pressed by the Longobards, Pépin led an army into Italy (754), compelled the Longobard Aistulf to become his vassal, and laid the foundation of the temporal sovereignty of the popes (756). The rest of his life was spent in semicrusading wars against Saxons and Saracens. (3) (777–810), son of Charlemagne, was crowned king of Italy in 781, and fought against the Avars, Slavs, Saxons and Saracens.

PEPLOE, Samuel John (1871–1935), Scottish artist, was born in Edinburgh. As a mature and established painter, he went to Paris in 1911 and returned to Edinburgh to remodel his style in accordance with Fauve colouring and Cézannesque analysis of form. His later still-life paintings brought him fame as a colourist. See the study by S. Cursiter (1947).

PEPPER, John Henry (1821–1900), English inventor, born in Westminster, became in 1848 analytical chemist at the Royal Polytechnic, and wrote several handbooks of popular science. He is best known as the improver and exhibitor of 'Pepper's Ghost' (see DIRCKS). Pepper travelled with this show in America and Australia, and became public analyst at Brisbane.

PEPUSCH, Johann Christoph (John Christopher), *pe'poosh* (1667–1752), German composer and musical theorist, born in Berlin, was appointed to the Prussian court at the age of fourteen, but subsequently emigrated to Holland and settled in London in his early thirties. Best known as the arranger of the music for Gay's *The Beggar's Opera* from popular and traditional sources, Pepusch was a prolific composer of music for the theatre and church as well as of instrumental works.

PEPYS, Samuel (1633–1703), English Admiralty official and diarist, son of a London tailor, was educated at St Paul's School and Magdalene College, Cambridge. In Commonwealth times he lived poorly with his young wife whom he married in 1655, but after the Restoration, through the patronage of the Earl of Sandwich, his father's cousin, he rose rapidly in the naval service and became secretary to the Admiralty in 1672. He lost his office on account of his alleged complicity in the Popish Plot, 1679, but was reappointed in 1684 and in that same year became president of the Royal Society. At the Revolution he was again 'outed'. Probably he did not feather his nest at the Admiralty more than was customary in those times, and his famous Diary attests his punctilious regard for the efficiency of the service. The Diary, which ran from January 1, 1660, to May 31, 1669, the year his wife died and his eyesight failed him, is of extraordinary interest, both as the personal record (and confessions) of a man of abounding love of life, and for the vivid picture it gives of contemporary life, including naval administration and Court intrigue. The highlights are probably the accounts of the three disasters of the decade—the great plague, the burning of London and the sailing up the Thames by the Dutch fleet (1665–67). The veracity of the Diary has been accepted. It was written in cipher, in which form it remained at Magdalene College till 1825, when it was deciphered by John Smith and edited by Lord Braybrooke. The complete edition was edited by Henry B. Wheatley in 4 vols. (1893–99). See, among others, J. B. Tanner, *Mr Pepys: an Introduction to the Diary* (1925), and studies by Arthur Bryant (1947–49).

PERCEVAL, Spencer (1762–1812), British statesman, second son of the second Earl of Egmont, was educated at Harrow and Trinity, Cambridge, and called to the bar in 1786. He soon obtained a reputation as a diligent lawyer, in 1796 entered parliament for Northampton, and became a strong supporter of Pitt. In the Addington administration he became solicitor-general in 1801 and attorney-general in 1802, and in the Portland administration of 1807 chancellor of the Exchequer, and was even then the real head of the government, being trusted by George III for his opposition to Catholic claims. At Portland's death in 1809 Perceval became premier also, and retained office till his tragic death, when he was shot while entering the lobby of the House of Commons by a bankrupt Liverpool broker, John Bellingham, who was later hanged for the murder. See Lives by Spencer Walpole (1874) and P. Treherne (1909).

PERCIER, Charles, *per-syay* (1764–1838), French architect, born in Paris, who, with his friend and partner, Pierre Fontaine (1762–1853), was among the first to create buildings in the Empire style. For Napoleon they remodelled the Malmaison, worked on the Rue de Rivoli, the palace of St Cloud, the Louvre and the Tuileries, and in the gardens there erected the Arc du Carrousel in 1807. See M. Fouché, *Percier et Fontaine* (1905).

PERCIVAL, (1) James Gates (1795–1856), American poet, born at Berlin, Conn., graduated at Yale in 1815, studied botany and medicine. and became professor of Chemistry at West Point in 1824, geologist of Wisconsin in 1854. His poems *Prometheus* and *Clio* appeared in 1822–27; and *The Dream of a Day* in 1843. See Life by J. H. Ward (1866), and a study in M. Rukeyser's *Willard Gibbs* (1942).

(2) John (1834–1918), English schoolmaster, born at Brough, became headmaster of Clifton in 1862, president of Trinity, Oxford, in 1878, headmaster of Rugby in 1887, and Bishop of Hereford in 1895.

PERCY, (1) a noble north of England family, whose founder, **William de Percy** (*c.* 1030–96), came with the Conqueror, and received lands in Yorkshire, Lincolnshire, Hampshire and Essex. **Richard** (*c.* 1170–1244) was one of the barons who extorted Magna Carta. Henry (*c.* 1272–1315) aided Edward I in subduing Scotland, was governor of Galloway; driven out of Turnberry Castle by Robert Bruce, he received from Edward II a grant of Bruce's forfeited earldom of Carrick and the wardenship of Bamburgh and Scarborough Castles. In 1309 he purchased from Bishop Antony Bek the barony of Alnwick, the chief seat of the family ever since. His son defeated and captured David II of Scotland at Neville's Cross (1346); his grandson fought at Crécy; his great-grandson, Henry (1342–1408), fourth Lord Percy of Alnwick, in 1377 was made marshal of England and Earl of Northumberland. His eldest son, **Henry** (1364–1403), was the famous Hotspur whom Douglas defeated at Otterburn (1388), and who himself fell fighting against Henry IV at Shrewsbury, where his uncle, **Sir Thomas, Earl of Worcester** (q.v.), was captured and soon after executed. The father, who had helped Henry of Lancaster to the throne, was dissatisfied with Henry's gratitude, and with his sons plotted the insurrection. Later he joined Archbishop Scrope's plot, and fell at Bramham Moor (1408), when his honours were forfeited, but restored (1414) to his grandson, who became High Constable of England, and fell in the first battle of St Albans (1455). His son, the third earl, fell at Towton (1461). The title and estates were now given to a brother of Warwick, the kingmaker, but in 1469 Henry, son of the third earl, was restored by Edward IV. The sixth earl, who had in youth been the lover of Anne Boleyn, died childless in 1537, and as his brother, Sir Thomas Percy, had been attainted and executed for his share in the Pilgrimage of Grace, the title of Duke of Northumberland was conferred by Edward VI upon John Dudley, Earl of Warwick, who in turn was attainted and executed under Mary in 1553. In 1557 Mary granted the earldom to Thomas Percy (1528–72), son of the attainted Sir Thomas. A devoted Catholic, he took part in the Rising of the North, and was beheaded at York. His brother Henry, eighth earl, became involved in Throgmorton's conspiracy in favour of Mary Stuart, and was committed to the Tower, where he was found dead in bed (1585). His son, ninth earl, was imprisoned for fifteen years in the Tower, and fined £30,000 on a baseless suspicion of being privy to the Gunpowder Plot. His son, tenth earl, fought for parliament in the Civil War; on the death of his son (1670), eleventh earl, the male line of the family became extinct. Charles II created his third bastard by the Duchess of Cleveland Earl, and afterwards Duke of Northumberland, but he died childless in 1716. The eleventh earl's daughter, Baroness Percy, married Charles Seymour, Duke of Somerset; their son was created in 1749 Baron Warkworth and Earl of Northumberland, with remainder to his son-in-law, Sir Hugh Smithson (1715–86), who assumed the name of Percy, and in 1766 was created Duke of Northumberland. See E. B. de Fonblanque's *House of Percy* (privately printed, 1887), and Brenan's *House of Percy* (1902).

(2) **Eustace, 1st Baron of Newcastle** (1887–1958), English statesman, seventh son of the Duke of Northumberland, entered the diplomatic service and was for several years in Washington. Member of parliament for Hastings from 1921 to 1937, he became president of the Board of Education (1924–1929) and minister without portfolio (1935–1936). His books include *The Responsibilities of the League* (1920), *Education at the Crossroads* (1930), *Democracy on Trial* (1931) and *The Heresy of Democracy* (1954). *Some Memories* was published in the year of his death.

(3) and (4) **Reuben** and **Sholto,** were the names under which Thomas Byerley (d. 1826) and Joseph Clinton Robertson (d. 1852) published *The Percy Anecdotes* (1820–23).

(5) **Thomas** (1729–1811), English antiquary, poet and churchman, born, a grocer's son, at Bridgnorth, in 1746 entered Christ Church, Oxford, and in 1753 became vicar of Easton Maudit, Northamptonshire, and in 1756 also rector of Wilby. He produced *Hau Kiou Choaun* (1761), a Chinese novel translated from the Portuguese, and *Miscellaneous Pieces relating to the Chinese* (1762), as well as anonymously *Runic Poetry translated from Icelandic* (1763), prompted by the success of Macpherson, and *A New Translation of the Song of Solomon* (1764). In 1764 his friend Dr Johnson paid him a visit. In 1765 Percy published the *Reliques of Ancient English Poetry*. He had long been engaged in collecting old ballads from every quarter, and a large folio MS. of ballads had fallen accidentally into his hands. Of the 176 pieces in the first edition, only 45 (a good deal touched up) were taken from the MS., which was only printed in full by Dr Furnivall (1867–68), with Introductions by Professor Hales and himself. Made chaplain to the Duke of Northumberland and George III, Percy in 1770 published his translation of the *Northern Antiquities* of Paul Henri Mallet (q.v.). In 1771 Percy wrote the 'Hermit of Warkworth'. In 1778 he was appointed Dean of Carlisle, in 1782 Bishop of Dromore. See the Life by Pickford in Hales and Furnivall, and that by A. C. C. Gaussen (1908).

PERDICCAS (d. 321 B.C.), Macedonian general under Alexander the Great and virtually regent for his successors, was murdered by mutineers from his own army.

PEREDA, José María de, *pay-ray'*THa (1833–1906), Spanish novelist, 'the modern Cervantes', was born at Polanco near Santander.

His novels give a realistic picture of the people and scenery of the region where he was born and where much of his life was spent, an outstanding example being *Sotileza* (1885). Other novels are *Del Tal palo tal astilla* (1880), *Pedro Sanchez* (1883), and perhaps his finest, *Peñas arriba* (1895).

PEREGRINUS, Petrus (Peter the Pilgrim, Peter de Maricourt) (fl. 13th cent.), French scientist and soldier, a native of Picardy, a Crusader, was the first to mark the ends of a round natural magnet and to call them poles. He also invented a compass with a graduated scale.

PEREIRA, Jonathan, *pay-ray'ra* (1804–53), English pharmacologist, born in London, was lecturer on chemistry and physician to the London Hospital (1841), author of *Elements of Materia Medica* (1839–40), *Diet*, and *Polarised Light* (1843).

PEREIRE, orig. **Pereira, Giacobbo Rodriguez,** *pay-rayr'* (1715–80), Spanish-born inventor of a sign language for deaf-mutes, gave up business at Bordeaux to devote himself to his humanitarian work with such success that in 1749 he presented a pupil before the Paris Academy of Sciences and in 1759 was made a member of the Royal Society.

PERETZ, David (1906–), Bulgarian artist, born at Plovdiv, studied in Sofia, and worked in Paris under André Lhote. His paintings, of still life and Provençal landscape, are of thick impasto and vigorous colour.

PÉREZ, Antonio, *pay'rayth* (*c.* 1540–1611), Spanish statesman, secretary to Philip II. Don John of Austria having become an object of suspicion, Pérez procured, with the king's consent, the assassination of Escovedo, Don John's secretary and abettor (1578), who had threatened to tell the king of Pérez's love for the Princess Éboli. The family of Escovedo denounced Pérez, and though the king sought to shield him, he was arrested in July 1579, and ultimately forced to confess. Condemned to imprisonment for embezzlement, he escaped to Aragon, where he put himself under protection of its *fueros*. The king next got the Inquisition to apprehend him, but the people rose in tumult; at last (1591) Philip entered Aragon with an army and abolished the old constitutional privileges. Pérez escaped to Paris and to London, where he was the intimate of Bacon and the Earl of Essex. He spent his later years in Paris, and died there, in great poverty. See his own *Relaciones*, books by Mignet (5th ed. 1881) and J. Fitzmaurice-Kelly (1922).

PÉREZ DE AYALA, Ramón, *a-yah'la* (1881–1962), Spanish novelist, poet and critic, born at Oviedo, first attracted attention with his poetry when *La Paz der sendero* was published in 1904. A sequel volume appeared in 1916 under the title *El Sendero innumerable*. As a novelist he combines realism with beauty, best shown in the philosophical *Belarmino y Apolonio* (1921). Other novels include the humorous and satirical *Troteras y Danzaderas* (1913), the anti-Jesuit *A.M.D.G.* (1910), and perhaps his best, *Tigre Juan* (1924), which with *El Curandero de ru honra* appeared in English as *Tiger Juan* (1933). Among his works of criticism are *Máscaras* and *Politica y Toros*. He was ambassador to London from 1931 to 1936.

PÉREZ DE HITA, Ginés, *ee'ta* (1544–1619), Spanish writer and soldier who fought in the Moorish war in 1569–70 and wrote a semi-romantic history entitled *Historia de los bandos de los Zegries y Abencérajes* in two parts (1595 and 1604). Known as *Las Guerras civiles de Granada*, it was republished in Madrid (1913–15).

PÉREZ GALDÓS, Benito (1843–1920), Spanish novelist and dramatist, born in the Canary Islands, was brought up in Madrid. Regarded as Spain's greatest novelist after Cervantes, he was deeply interested in his own country and its history. His short *Episodios nacionales*, of which there are forty-six, gives a vivid picture of 19th-century Spain from the viewpoint of the people. The longer novels included in the *Novelas españolas contemporáneas* number thirty-one, and in these the conflicts and ideas of the Europe of his day are recorded forcefully but often with humour. Some of these, including *Trafalgar*, *Gloria*, *Doña Perfecta*, *León Roch*, have been translated. His plays, many of them based on his novels, also achieved success. See L. B. Walton, *Pérez Galdós and the Spanish Novel of the 19th Century* (1928), and a study by H. C. Berkowitz (1948).

PERGOLESI, Giovanni Battista, *per-go-lay'zee* (1710–36), Italian musician, was born at Jesi near Ancona, and died at Naples. His first great works were the oratorio *San Guglielmo* (1731) and the operetta *La Serva Padrona* (1732). His last works were the cantata *Orfeo* and his great *Stabat Mater*. He also composed operas, oratorios, &c.

PERI, Jacopo, *pay'ree* (1561–1633), Italian composer, born in Rome, as a student became attached to the Medici family in Florence, and became the leading composer in a group of artists whose aim was to restore what they believed to be the true principles of Greek tragic declamation. Experimenting in instrumentally-accompanied declamatory style, they hit upon the principles of modern opera, a form which Peri exploited in a series of works, beginning with *Dafne* and *Euridice*, with libretti by the poet Rinuccini, historically accepted as the first genuine operas.

PERIANDER, Gr. **Periandros** (*c.* 665–585 B.C.), one of the Seven Wise Men of Greece, succeeded his father Cypselus as tyrant of Corinth (*c.* 625 B.C.). He conquered Epidaurus and Corcyra (Corfu).

PERICLES, *per'i-kleez* (*c.* 490–429 B.C.), Athenian statesman, born of distinguished parents, was carefully educated, and rapidly rose to the highest power as leader of the dominant democracy. About 463 he struck a great blow at the oligarchy by depriving the Areopagus of its most important political powers. His successful expeditions to the Thracian Chersonese and to Sinope, together with his numerous colonies, increased the naval supremacy of Athens. His greatest project was to form a grand Hellenic confederation to put an end to mutually destructive wars; but the Spartan aristocrats brought the scheme to nothing. Athens and Sparta were already in the mood which rendered the Peloponnesian war ineviable; but the first troubles were allayed by a thirty years' peace with Sparta (445). Cimon was now dead, and the next leaders of the aristocratic party sought in vain (in 444 B.C.) to overthrow the supremacy of Pericles by attacking him in the popular assembly for squandering the public money on buildings and in festivals and amusements. Thereafter Pericles reigned undisputed master in the city of Aeschylus, Sophocles, Euripides, Anaxagoras, Zeno, Protagoras, Socrates, as well as Myron and Phidias. In the Samian war (439) Pericles gained high renown as a naval commander. His enemies, who dared not attack himself, struck at him in the persons of his friends—Aspasia, Phidias, Anaxagoras. Greek architecture and sculpture under the patronage of Pericles reached perfection. To him Athens owed the Parthenon, the Erechtheum, the Propylaea, the Odeum and numberless other public and sacred edifices; he liberally encouraged music and the drama; and during his rule industry and commerce flourished. At length in 431 the inevitable Peloponnesian war broke out between Athens and Sparta. The plague ravaged the city in 430, and in the autumn of 429 Pericles himself died after a lingering fever. See Thucydides and Plutarch; the histories of Greece by Thirlwall, Grote, and Curtius; Watkiss Lloyd's *Age of Pericles* (1875); A. J. Grant's *Greece in the Age of Pericles* (1893); *Cambr. Anc. Hist.* v (1927); studies by Abbott (1891), Mackenzie (1937), de Sanctis (1944), Burn (1948).

PÉRIER, Casimir, *payr-yay* (1777–1832), French statesman, born at Grenoble, founded a Paris bank with his brother Antoine Scipion (1776–1821). He secured a seat in the Chamber of Deputies in 1817, was minister of finance in 1828, president of the council in 1830, and premier in 1831. For his son, see CASIMIR-PÉRIER.

PERKIN, Sir William Henry (1838–1907), English chemist, born in London and knighted in 1906, was assistant to Hofmann, and in 1856 made the discovery of mauve, which led to the foundation of the aniline dye industry. His son and namesake (1860–1929) became in 1892 professor of Chemistry at Manchester, in 1912 at Oxford.

PERMEKE, Constant, *per'may-kė* (1886–1951), Belgian painter and sculptor, born at Antwerp, studied at Bruges and Ghent, and later settled in Laethem-Saint-Martin, where he became the leader of the modern Belgian Expressionist school. After 1936, he concentrated on sculpture.

PERÓN, (1) **Juan Domingo** (1895–), Argentine soldier and statesman, born in Lobos, took a leading part in the army revolt of 1943, achieved power and great popularity among the masses (because of social reforms), and became (1946) president of a virtually totalitarian régime. In 1955, having antagonized the Church, the armed forces and many of his former supporters among the labour movements, he was deposed and exiled. See T. Owen, *Perón: His Rise and Fall* (1957).

(2) **Maria Eva Duarte De** (1919–52), wife of (1), born at Los Toldos, Buenos Aires, was an actress before her marriage in 1945. She became a powerful political influence, agitating for women's suffrage, and acquiring control of newspapers and business companies. She founded the Eva Perón Foundation for the promotion of social welfare.

PEROSI, Lorenzo (1872–1956), Italian priest and composer, the son of a musician at Tortona in Piedmont, was ordained priest, and is author of *The Resurrection of Lazarus, The Passion of Christ* and other oratorios.

PÉROUSE. See LA PÉROUSE.

PEROWNE, John James Stewart (1823–1904), English prelate, the son of a missionary in Bengal, educated at Corpus, Cambridge, held office at King's College (London), Lampeter, Trinity College (Cambridge), became Dean of Peterborough in 1878. From 1875 he had been also Hulsean professor of Divinity at Cambridge. In 1891–1901 he was Bishop of Worcester. Perowne sat on the committee for the revision of the Old Testament. His works include a Commentary on the Psalms (1864–68), Hulsean Lectures on *Immortality* (1869) and *Remains* of Thirlwall (1878).

PERRAULT, Charles, *per-ō* (1628–1703), French writer, was born at Paris, studied law, and filled from 1654 till 1664 an easy post under his brother, the receiver-general of Paris. In 1663 he became a secretary or assistant to Colbert, through whom he was admitted to the Academy in 1671. His poem, *Le Siècle de Louis XIV*, read to th Academy, and Boileau's outspoken criticisms of it, opened up the dispute about the relative merits of the ancients and moderns; to the modern cause Perrault contributed his poor *Parallèle des anciens et des modernes* (1688–1696), and his *Hommes illustres du siècle de Louis XIV* (1696–1700). His *Mémoires* appeared in 1769. All his writings would have been forgotten but for his eight inimitable fairy-tales, the *Histoires ou Contes du temps passé* (1697), including 'The Sleeping Beauty', 'Red Riding Hood' and 'Bluebeard'. There are editions by Giraud (1865), Lefèvre (1875), Paul Lacroix (1876) and Andrew Lang (1888). See Deschanel's *Boileau, Perrault* (1888).

PERRET, Auguste, *per-ay* (1874–1954), French architect, born in Brussels, spent most of his life in Paris, where he pioneered the use of reinforced concrete in a number of buildings, mainly in the neo-classical style, including the Théâtre des Champs Élysées and the Musée des travaux publics. He also designed churches at le Raincy and Montmagny. See study by P. Jamot (Paris 1927).

PERRIN, Jean Baptiste, *pe-rī* (1870–1942), French physicist, born at Lille, educated at Paris, was from 1910 professor of Physical Chemistry at the University of Paris. For important researches in molecular physics and radioactivity, and for his discovery of the equilibrium of sedimentation he was awarded the Nobel prize in 1926.

PERRON, General (really **Pierre Aullier**) (1755–1834), French military adventurer, was born in Sarthe, went as a soldier to the Île-de-France, served for a time in the navy, deserted and took service with various native Indian princes. In 1790 he obtained an appointment under his countryman De Boigne. then commanding Sindia's forces.

He succeeded De Boigne, and exercised enormous military and political influence in India, but was crushed in 1803 by Lake at Laswari, and by Wellesley at Assaye. He returned the same year to France. See H. Compton's *European Military Adventurers of Hindustan* (1892).

PERRONNEAU, Jean Baptiste, *per-on-nō* (*c.* 1715–83), French pastellist painter, best known for his *Girl with a Kitten* painted in 1745 and now in the National Gallery, London. He travelled widely in Europe and died in Amsterdam.

PERROT, (1) **Georges,** *per-ō* (1832–1914), French archaeologist, travelled in Greece and Asia Minor, in 1877 became professor of Archaeology in the University of Paris and in 1833 director of the École normale. He wrote on Crete (1866) and archaeology, especially, with Charles Chipiez, a *History of Art in Antiquity* (in Egypt, Chaldaea, Primitive Greece, &c.; 1882 *et seq.*).

(2) **Sir John,** *-ot* (*c.* 1527–92), commonly reputed to be a son of Henry VIII, was lord deputy of Ireland during the troublous time there of Queen Elizabeth, and died in the Tower, under trial for treason with Spain.

PERRY, Oliver Hazard (1785–1819), American sailor, born at South Kingston, Rhode Island, defeated a British squadron on Lake Erie in 1813. See Lives by Mackenzie (1843) and Lyman (1905).

PERSE. See St John Perse.

PERSHING, John Joseph (1860–1948), American soldier, born in Linn County, Mo., was first a schoolteacher, went to West Point, and became military instructor there and at Nebraska University. He served in the Cuban War in 1898, in the Japanese army during the Russo-Japanese War (1904–05) and was in Mexico during World War I. In 1917 he was appointed c.-in-c. of the American Expeditionary Force in Europe and chief of staff, U.S. Army, 1921–24.

PERSIGNY, Jean Gilbert Victor Fialin, Duc de, *per-seen-yee* (1808–72), French politician, born at Saint-Germain Lespinasse, expelled from the army in 1831, secured the favour of Louis Napoleon, and had the chief hand in the affairs of Strasbourg (1836) and Boulogne (1840), where he was captured, and condemned to twenty years' imprisonment. Released in 1848, he strongly supported his patron then and in 1851, in 1852–55 and 1860–63 was minister of the Interior, in 1855–60 ambassador to England, and a senator until the fall of the empire. See his *Mémoires* (1896), and study by Chrétien (1943).

PERSIUS (Aulus Persius Flaccus) (A.D. 34–62), Roman satirist, born of a distinguished equestrian family at Volaterrae in Etruria, was educated in Rome, where he came under Stoic influence. But he died before completing his twenty-eighth year. He wrote fastidiously and sparingly, leaving at his death six admirable satires, the whole not exceeding 650 hexameter lines. These were published by his friend Caesius Bassus after his death. Dryden and others have translated them into verse.

PERTHES, family of German publishers:

(1) **Friedrich Christoph** (1772–1843), nephew of (2), started business in Hamburg in 1796, and soon was in the front rank of publishers. An ardent patriot, he in 1810 started the *National Museum*, and resisted the establishment of French authority in Germany. After the peace, he removed in 1821 to Gotha. See Life (7th ed. 1892; trans. 1878) by his son Clemens Theodor.

(2) **Johann Georg Justus** (1749–1816), established a publishing-house at Gotha in 1785, which acquired, in the hands of his sons, a great reputation as a geographical institute; it issued *Petermann's Mitteilungen*, Stieler's *Atlas*, books of travel and geography, and the *Almanach de Gotha*.

PERTINAX, Publius Helvius (A.D. 126–193), Roman emperor, born at Alba-Pompeia in Liguria. When the assassins of Commodus forced him to accept the purple, his accession was hailed with delight; but he was slain by rebellious praetorians three months after.

PERUGINO ('The Perugian'), *per-oo-jee'nō* (*c.* 1450–1523), the usual name of the painter **Pietro Vannucci,** born at Città della Pieve in Umbria, who established himself in Perugia. He executed works, no longer extant, at Florence, Perugia (1475) and Cerqueto (1478). At Rome, where he went about 1483, Sixtus IV employed him in the Sistine Chapel; his fresco of *Christ giving the Keys to Peter* is the best of those still visible, others being destroyed to make way for Michelangelo's *Last Judgment.* At Florence (1486–1499) he had Raphael for his pupil. At Perugia (1499–1504) he adorned the Hall of the Cambio; after 1500 his art visibly declined. In his second Roman sojourn (1507–12) he also, along with other painters, decorated the Stanze of the Vatican; and one of his works there, the Stanza del Incendio, was the only fresco spared when Raphael was commissioned to repaint the walls and ceilings. He died of the plague near Perugia. See also Bartoli (2) and F. Canuti's *Il Perugino* (2 vols. 1931).

PERUTZ, Max Ferdinand (1914–), Austrian-born British scientist, graduated at Vienna, came to Cambridge in 1936 to carry on research at the Cavendish Laboratory, where he began work on the structure of haemoglobin and became director of the Medical Research Council's unit for Molecular Biology. Twenty-five years' work in this field resulted in the joint award to Perutz and Kendrew (q.v.) of the Nobel chemistry prize for 1962.

PERUZZI, Baldassare Tommaso, *pay-root'see* (1481–1536), Italian architect, was born at Ancajano near Volterra. In 1503 he went to Rome, where he designed the Villa Farnesina, and painted frescoes in the Church of S. Maria della Pace in 1516. After a short period as city architect in Siena, he returned to Rome in 1535 and designed the Palazzo Massimo. He was influenced by Bramante and ancient Italian architecture; drawings and designs by him are in the Uffizi Gallery.

PESTALOZZI, Johann Heinrich, *-lot'see* (1746–1827), Swiss educationalist, born at Zürich, devoted himself to the children of the very poor. Believing in the moralizing virtue of agricultural occupations and rural environment, he chose a farm in the canton Aargau upon which to live with his collected waifs and strays; but owing to faulty domestic organization it had to be abandoned after a five years' struggle (1780). He then for a time withdrew from practical life, to think out the educational problem, and wrote his *Evening Hours of a Hermit* (1780). Then came a social novel, *Leonard and Gertrude* (1781). In 1798 he opened his orphan school at Stanz, but at the end of eight months it was broken up. He next took a post in the people's school at Berthoud (Burgdorf), in canton Bern, only to be ejected from it by the jealous senior master. In partnership with others, and under the patronage of the Swiss government, he opened a school of his own at Berthoud. While there he published *How Gertrude Educates her Children* (1801), the recognized exposition of the Pestalozzian method, setting forth that the development of human nature should be in dependence upon natural laws, with which it is the business of education to comply, observation being the method by which all objects of knowledge are brought home to us. In 1805 Pestalozzi moved his school to Yverdon, and applied his method in a large secondary school. His incapacity in practical affairs brought the school down step by step till it was closed in 1825. Pestalozzi addressed to mankind the *Song of the Swan*, a last educational prayer, and withdrew to Brugg, where he died. See books by Green (1913), Anderson (1932), Reinhart (1945) and Silber (1960).

PÉTAIN, Henri Philippe Omer, *pay-tī* (1856–1951), Marshal of France, born at Cauchy-à-la-Tour, passed through St Cyr to a commission in the *chasseurs alpins.* As a junior officer, his confidential report was marked, 'If this officer rises above the rank of major it will be a disaster for France'; but seniority brought him the military governorship of Paris and appointments on the instructional staff. A temporary brigadier in 1914, by 1916 he was in command of an army corps and entrusted with the defence of Verdun. Succeeding as commander-in-chief in 1917, his measures of appeasement, while 'puttying-up' the widespread mutinies that had followed on General Nivelle's disastrous offensive, ended by virtually removing the French army as a fighting force from the war. Minister for war in 1934, his eager sponsorship of the useless Maginot Line defence system only too faithfully reflected the defeatist spirit of contemporary France. With the French collapse in early 1940, he succeeded M. Reynaud as the head of the government and immediately sought terms from the Germans. Convinced that France could 'only be regenerated through suffering', his administration at Vichy was the tool of such outright collaborationists as Laval and Deat. With the liberation of France Pétain was brought to trial, his death sentence for treason being commuted to life imprisonment on the Île de Yeu. He died in captivity in 1951. See 'Pertinax', *The Gravediggers of France* (1944), and Life by G. Bolton (1957).

PETAVIUS, Dionysius, or **Denys Petau** (1583–1652), French theologian, born at Orleans, became in 1621 professor of Theology in Paris. In 1646 he retired and devoted himself to the completion of about fifty works in philology, history and theology. An ardent Jesuit, among his learned writings are *Rationarium Temporum* (1634) and *De Theologicis Dogmatibus* (1644–50).

PETER, St, apostle, named originally **Symeon** or **Simon,** was of Bethsaida, but during the public ministry of Jesus had his house at Capernaum. Originally a fisherman, he soon became leader amongst the twelve apostles, regarded by Jesus with particular favour and affection. He was the spokesman of the rest on the day of Pentecost, he was the first to baptise a Gentile convert, and he took a prominent part in the council at Jerusalem. At Antioch he for a time worked in harmony with Paul, but ultimately the famous dispute arose (Gal. ii. 11–21) which, with other causes, led to the termination of Paul's ministry in that city. Bauer regarded him as the head of the Judaic party in opposition to the wider Pauline school. Peter's missionary activity seems to have extended to Pontus, Cappadocia, Galatia, Asia and Bithynia. That he suffered martyrdom is clear from John xxi. 18, 19, and is confirmed by ecclesiastical tradition: Eusebius says he was impaled or crucified with his head downward; as to the place, tradition from the end of the 2nd century mentions Rome. But the comparatively late tradition which assigns him a continuous bishopric of twenty-five years in Rome from A.D. 42 to A.D. 67 is unhistorical. Many distinguished scholars (Protestant) deny that Peter ever was in Rome. The first Epistle of Peter is usually accepted as genuine, but not the second. Holtzmann's *Einleitung* (1886), Salmon (*Introduction*) and Weiss defend the genuineness of both. See Littledale's *Petrine Claims* (1889); Lightfoot's *Apostolic Fathers*; Döllinger's *First Age of the Church*; Schmid's *Petrus in Rom*; Lipsius, *Die apokryphen Apostelgeschichten* (1883–90); Foakes-Jackson's monograph (1927); Selwyn's commentary (1946); Beare (1947).

PETER THE CRUEL. See PEDRO.

PETER, the name of 3 emperors of Russia:

Peter I, the Great (1672–1725), emperor of Russia, was the son of the Tzar Alexei, and was born at Moscow. His father died in 1676, leaving the throne to his eldest son, Feodor, Peter's half-brother, who, dying in 1682, named Peter as his successor, to the exclusion of his own full brother, Ivan, who was weak-minded. This step provoked an insurrection of the 'streltzi' or militia, fomented by Ivan's sister, the grand-duchess Sophia, who secured the coronation (July 1682) of Ivan and Peter as joint rulers, and her own appointment as regent; and Peter was put under the charge of a capable tutor, Lefort, a Genevese. In 1689, on his marriage to Eudoxia, Peter called upon his sister to resign. At first worsted in the struggle, he was soon joined by the foreigners in the Russian service, with Patrick Gordon (q.v.) and Lefort at their head; and the streltzi flocking to his standard, Sophia resigned the contest, and was shut up in a convent, where she died in 1704. Peter gave Ivan nominal supremacy and precedence, reserving the power for himself. Ivan died in 1696. Peter's first care was to organize an army on

European principles. He also laboured to create a navy, both armed and mercantile. But at this time Russia had only one port, Archangel being shut out from the Baltic by Sweden and Poland; so, for his fleet's sake, Peter declared war against Turkey, and took (1696) the city of Azov. Peter was eager to see for himself the countries for which civilization had done so much; and, after repressing a revolt of the streltzi, he left Russia in April 1697, in the train of an embassy of which Lefort was the head. He visited the three Baltic provinces, Prussia and Hanover, reaching Amsterdam, where, and at Zaandam, he worked as a common shipwright; he also studied astronomy, natural philosophy, geography, and even anatomy and surgery. For three months at London and Deptford, he amassed information, and from England he carried (1698) English engineers, artificers, surgeons, artisans, artillerymen, &c., to the number of 500. From Vienna a formidable rebellion of the streltzi recalled him to Russia. General Gordon had already crushed the revolt, and Peter finally broke up the institution that had given him so much trouble. The Empress Eudoxia, as associated with the conspiracy, which had been the work of the anti-reform party, was divorced and shut up in a convent. Peter put the press on a proper footing, published translations of famous foreign books, and established naval and other schools. Trade with foreign countries was permitted, or even insisted upon. Many changes in dress, manners and etiquette were introduced and enforced and the national church was reorganized. In 1700 Peter, with Poland and Denmark, attacked Sweden, but was defeated at Narva; yet he quietly appropriated a portion of Ingria, in which he laid the foundation of the new capital, St Petersburg (1703), which soon became the Russian commercial depot for the Baltic. In the long contest with Sweden the Russians were almost always defeated; but at last the Swedish king, Charles XII, was totally routed at Pultowa in 1709. Peter seized the whole of the Baltic provinces and a portion of Finland in 1710. He now prepared for strife with the Turks, who, at the instigation of Charles XII, had declared war against him. In this contest Peter was reduced to great straits, but a treaty was concluded (1711) by which Peter lost only Azov and the territory belonging to it. The war against Sweden in Pomerania was pushed on with the greater vigour. In 1712 he married his mistress, Catharine (see CATHARINE I), and the government was transferred to St Petersburg. In 1716–17, in company with the tsarina, he made another tour of Europe. Soon after this his son Alexis, who had opposed some of his father's reforms, was condemned to death, and died in prison. Many nobles implicated in his plans were punished with savage barbarity. In 1721 peace was made with Sweden, which definitely ceded the Baltic provinces, Ingria and part of Finland. In 1722 Peter commenced a war with Persia, and secured three Caspian provinces. During his last years he was chiefly engaged in beautifying and improving his new capital and carrying out plans for the diffusion of knowledge and education. In the autumn of 1724 he was seized with a serious illness and died soon after. Catharine succeeded him. See Russian Lives by Golikov (1797) and Ustjalov (1858–63), French by Waliszewski (trans. 1897), and English by Graham (1929), Schuyler (1944), Klynchevsky (trans. 1959) and Grey (1962).

Peter II (1715–30), grandson of Peter the Great and son of Alexis, succeeded Catharine I (1727), but died of smallpox.

Peter III (1728–62), grandson of Peter the Great (son of his eldest daughter Anna, wife of the Duke of Holstein-Gottorp), was born at Kiel. In 1742 he was declared by the Tsarina Elizabeth (q.v.) her successor, and married Sophia-Augusta, a princess of Anhalt-Zerbst, who assumed the name of Catharina Alexeievna. Peter succeeded Elizabeth on her death in 1762 and his first act was to restore East Prussia to Frederick the Great, and to send to his aid 15,000 men. In 1762 a formidable conspiracy, headed by his wife, broke out, originating in the general discontent at the tsar's liberal innovations, the preference he showed for Germans, his indifference to the national religion, and his servility to Frederick the Great. He was declared to have forfeited his crown; his wife was proclaimed as Catharine II; and Peter was strangled by Orlov and some of the conspirators.

PETER II, king of Yugoslavia (1923–70). A grandson of Peter I, he succeeded his father, Alexander I, in 1934 with his uncle Prince Paul as regent. He assumed sovereignty in 1941 at the time of the German invasion, and lost his throne in 1945 when his country became a republic. His memoirs, *A King's Heritage*, appeared in 1955.

PETER LOMBARD. See LOMBARD.

PETER THE HERMIT (*c.* 1050–*c.* 1115), French monk, a preacher of the First Crusade, was born about the middle of the 11th century at Amiens. He served some time as a soldier, became a monk, and is said to have made a pilgrimage to Palestine before 1095. Legends have gathered round his name, and his importance has been exaggerated. The scheme of a crusade originated with the pope, Urban II, to whom Alexius Comnenus had appeared. At a council at Clermont in France (1096) it was definitely resolved upon. After Urban's famous sermon there many preachers, of whom Peter was one of the most notable, traversed Europe, preaching everywhere, and producing extraordinary enthusiasm by impassioned descriptions of the cruelties of the Turks towards pilgrims, and their desecration of the holy places. When the feelings of Europe had been sufficiently heated, four armies, amounting to 275,000 disorderly persons, started for Palestine. The first was cut to pieces in Bulgaria. The second, led by Peter in person, reached Asia Minor, but was utterly defeated by the Turks at Nicaea. The other two were exterminated by the Hungarians. A fifth crusading army, 600,000 strong, under renowned leaders, set out in 1096, and was joined by Peter the Hermit. During the siege of Antioch, which lasted seven months, the besiegers' ranks were fearfully thinned by famine and disease. Many lost heart, and among the deserters was Peter, who was several miles on his way home when he was brought back to undergo a public reprimand. He founded a monastery in France or the Low Countries.

PETER MARTYR, (1) (d. 1252), patron saint of the Inquisition, a Dominican of Verona, who, for the severity with which he exercised his inquisitorial functions, was slain at Como by the populace. He was canonized in 1253.

(2) Ital. **Pietro Martire Vermigli (1500–62),** reformer, born in Florence; became a canon of St Augustine and abbot at Spoleto and Naples. As visitor-general of his order in 1541 his rigour made him hateful to the dissolute monks, and he was sent to Lucca as prior, but soon fell under the suspicions of the Inquisition, and fled to Zürich (1542). At Strasbourg he was made Old Testament professor. In 1547 he came to England, and lectured at Oxford. Mary's accession drove him back to Strasbourg, and in 1555 to Zürich, where he died. His *Loci Communes* was printed at London in 1575. See C. Schmidt's *Leben der Väter der reformirten Kirche* (1858).

PETER MARTYR ANGLERIUS (1459–1525), Italian historian, born at Arona on Lago Maggiore, from 1487 rose to high ecclesiastical preferment in Spain, and was named Bishop of Jamaica. He wrote *De Orbe Novo* (1516), giving the first account of the discovery of America, *De Legatione Babylonica* (1516), and *Opus Epistolarum* (1530).

PETER THE WILD BOY (d. 1785), was found in July 1725 in a wood near Hameln in Hanover; ' he was walking on his hands and feet, climbing up trees like a squirrel, and feeding upon grass and moss of trees'. Brought to England in 1726 by George I, he could never be taught to articulate more than a few syllables, and was apparently an idiot. From 1737 till his death he lived on a Hertfordshire farm near Berkhampstead.

PETERBOROUGH, Charles Mordaunt, 3rd Earl of (*c.* 1658–1735), seems to have gone to Oxford in 1674, but by 1680 had been in (perhaps three) naval expeditions to the Barbary coast. In that year he began to take an active part in politics, identifying himself with the extreme Whig party; and on the accession of James II he was one of the earliest intriguers for his overthrow. After the Revolution he rose into high favour with the new king, being made first commissioner of the treasury and Earl of Monmouth. On William's departure for Ireland, he was one of the Queen's council of regency. He became hostile to the king and his measures, and was embroiled in plots that resulted (January 1697) in his committal to the Tower for three months. In 1705, in the war of the Spanish Succession, Monmouth, now Earl of Peterborough (by his uncle's death), was appointed to the command of an army of 4000 Dutch and English soldiers, with which he proceeded to Barcelona, captured the strong fort of Montjuich, and so reduced the city. Gerona, Tarragona, Tolosa and Lérida opened their gates; and he reached Valencia early in February 1706. Meanwhile an army under the Duke of Anjou, the French claimant to the throne, and Marshal Tessé was closely investing Barcelona, which was at the same time blockaded by a fleet under the Count of Toulouse. Hurrying back, Peterborough himself took command of the English squadron, and drove Toulouse and his fleet from before the port. This success was followed by the raising of the siege. Now came a series of disputes with his colleagues and allies, recriminations and futile schemes and expeditions hither and thither. His imperious temper seems to have made him unfit for anything but supreme command, and led to his recall in March 1707. He was an intimate friend of Pope. The famous singer Anastasia Robinson (d. 1755), whom he married secretly, it is said, in 1722, was not publicly acknowledged as his countess till shortly before his death. See Lives by Russell (2 vols. 1887), Stebbing (1890), Ballard (1929).

PETERMANN, August (1822–78), Gotha cartographer and geographer. See PERTHES.

PETERS, (1) Hugh (1598–1660), English Independent divine, born in Cornwall, emigrated to Holland, then to New England, but returning in 1641, became army chaplain, and was active in parliamentarian politics. He published numerous pamphlets, and was executed for assumed complicity in the death of Charles I.

(2) **Karl (1856–1918),** German traveller and administrator, born at Neuhaus in Hanover, helped to establish German East Africa as a colony by his negotiations with native chiefs in 1884. In the same year he had formed the Gesellschaft für deutsche Kolonisation. Without the sanction of Bismarck, he claimed Uganda for Germany, was made commissioner of Kilimanjaro (1891–93), but his harsh treatment of the natives caused his recall. He returned to Africa in 1906 when gold was discovered in the Zambesi district.

PETERSEN, Nis (1897–1943), Danish poet and novelist, cousin of Kaj Munk (q.v.), born in South Jutland, rebelled against a strict upbringing, was a journalist, casual labourer and vagabond until he became famous for his novel of Rome in the time of Marcus Aurelius, *Sandalmagernes Gade* (trans. 1932 as *The Street of the Sandalmakers*). His later poetry has given him a high place among modern Danish writers.

PÉTION DE VILLENEUVE, Jérôme, *pay-tyõ dė veel-nœv* (*c.* 1756–94), French revolutionary, born at Chartres, in 1789 was elected deputy to the *Tiers État*. He was a prominent member of the Jacobin Club, and became a great ally of Robespierre. He was one of those who brought back the royal family from Varennes, advocated the deposition of the king, was elected mayor of Paris, and was the first president of the Convention. On the triumph of the Terrorists, he cast in his lot with the Girondists. He voted at the king's trial for death, but headed the unsuccessful attack on Robespierre. Proscribed on June 2, 1793, he escaped to Caen, and thence, on the failure of the attempt to make armed opposition against the Convention, to the Gironde, where his and Buzot's bodies were found in a cornfield, partly devoured by wolves. His *Oeuvres* fill 3 vols. (1792). See works by Regnault-Warin (1792) and Dauban (1866).

PETIT, *pè-tee,* (1) **Alexis Thérèse** (1791–1820), French physicist, born at Vesoul, H.-S., professor at the Lycée Bonaparte, enunciated with Dulong the 'law of Dulong and Petit' that for all elements the product of the specific heat and the atomic weight is the same. He died in Paris.

(2) **Jean Louis** (1674–1750), French surgeon, gained experience with the army and then lectured in Paris on anatomy and surgery. He was the inventor of the screw tourniquet and the first to operate with success for mastoiditis. He died in Paris.

(3) **Roland** (1924–), French choreographer and dancer, born in Paris, at nine began his studies at the Ballet de l'Opéra under Ricaux and Lifar and was its *premier danseur* (1943–44). Equally ambitious as a choreographer, he founded his own *troupe* in 1945 and in 1948 the world-famous company which bears his name. He has created a whole repertory of new ballet including *Le Rossignol et la Rose* (1944), a story by Oscar Wilde set to Schumann's music ; *Les Forains* (1945) with Cocteau; *Le Jeune Homme et la Mort* (1946) which the latter had rehearsed strictly to jazz until the opening night when Bach was substituted; and Anouilh's *Les Desmoiselles de la Nuit* (1948). He was also responsible for the ballet sequences in the film *Hans Christian Andersen* (1952).

PETIT DE JULLEVILLE, Louis (1841–1900), French critic, born in Paris, became professor at the École normale supérieure and the Sorbonne. He wrote an *Histoire du théâtre en France* and edited a monumental *Histoire de la langue et de la littérature française.*

PETITOT, Jean, *pet-ee-tō* (1607–91), Swiss painter in enamel, born in Geneva, after some years in Italy went to England and obtained the patronage of Charles I. After the king's execution he moved to Paris, where Louis XIV gave him lodgings in the Louvre and a share in his patronage. As a Protestant, he fled back to Geneva after the revocation of the Edict of Nantes (1685). Examples of his work may be seen in the South Kensington Museum.

PETO, Sir Samuel Morton (1809–89), English civil engineer and contractor, born at Woking, Surrey, attained great wealth as a contractor, laying railways in England, Russia, Norway, Algiers and Australia. He was a Liberal M.P. (1847–68), and was created a baronet in 1855. See *Memorial Sketch* (1893).

PETÖFI, Sandor, *pet'œ-fee* (1823–49), Hungarian poet, born at Kiskörös, was successively actor, soldier and literary hack, but by 1844 had secured his fame as a poet. In 1848 he threw himself into the revolutionary cause, writing numerous war-songs. He fell in battle at Segesvár. His poetry broke completely with the old pedantic style, and, warm with human and national feeling, began a new epoch in Hungarian literature. Selections have been translated by Bowring and others. He also wrote a novel, *The Hangman's Rope*, and translated Shakespeare's *Coriolanus*. See Lives by Opitz (1868), Fischer (1888) and Ferenczi (Budapest 1897).

PETRARCH, Francesco Petrarca (1304–74), Italian poet and scholar, one of the earliest and greatest of modern lyric poets, was the son of a Florentine notary, who, exiled (1302) along with Dante, settled in Arezzo, where Francesco was born. In 1312 his father went to Avignon, to the then seat of the papal court; and there and at Bologna the boy devoted himself with enthusiasm to the study of the classics. After his father's death Petrarch returned to Avignon (1326). Being without means, he became a churchman, though perhaps never a priest, and lived on the small benefices conferred by his many patrons. It was at this period (1327) that he first saw Laura (possibly Laure de Noves, married in 1325 to Hugo de Sade; she died, the mother of eleven children, in 1348). She inspired him with a passion which has become proverbial for its constancy and purity. Now began also his friendship with the powerful Roman family of the Colonnas. As the fame of Petrarch's learning and genius grew, his position became one of unprecedented consideration. His presence at their courts was competed for by the most powerful sovereigns of the day. He travelled repeatedly in France, Germany and Flanders, searching for MSS. In Liège he found two new orations of Cicero, in Verona a collection of his letters, in Florence an unknown portion of Quintilian. Invited by the senate of Rome on Easter Sunday, 1341, he ascended the capitol clad in the robes of his friend and admirer, King Robert of Naples, and there, after delivering an oration, he was crowned poet laureate. In 1353, after the death of Laura and his friend Cardinal Colonna, he left Avignon (and his country house at Vaucluse) for ever, disgusted with the corruption of the papal court. His remaining years were passed in various towns of Northern Italy, and at Arquà near Padua he died. Petrarch may be considered as the earliest of the great humanists of the Renaissance. He himself chiefly founded his claim to fame on his epic poem *Africa*, the hero of which is Scipio Africanus, and his historical work in prose, *De Viris Illustribus*, a series of biographies of classical celebrities. Other Latin works are the eclogues and epistles in verse; and in prose the dialogues, *De Contemptu Mundi* (or *Secretum*), the treatises *De Otio Religiosorum* and *De Vita Solitaria*, and his letters—he was in constant correspondence with Boccaccio. Great as were his merits as patriot or student, it is by his lyrics alone that his fame has lasted for over five centuries. His title deeds to fame are in his *Canzoniere*, in the Italian sonnets, madrigals, and songs, almost all inspired by his unrequited passion for Laura. The *Opera Omnia* appeared at Basel in 1554. His Italian lyrics were published in 1470, and have since gone through innumerable editions—a notable one that of Marsand (1819), used by Leopardi for his edition and commentary (1826). See the Abbé de Sade, *Mémoires de Pétrarque* (1764); Mézières, *Pétrarque* (1868; new ed.

1896); Koerting, *Petrarcas Leben* (1878); Eppelsheimer, *Petrarca* (Bonn 1926); works by Henry Reeve (1878), De Sanctis (1869), Zumbini (1878), Nolhac (Paris 1892), Robinson and Rolfe (1894), Hollway-Calthorp (1907), Maud Jerrold (1909), Tatham (1925–26), Tonelli (1930), Whitfield (1943).

PETRE, Edward, *pee'tėr* (1631–99), born in London of an old Catholic house, studied at St Omer, but was not admitted a Jesuit until 1671. His influence as confessor of James II made him extremely unpopular. In 1693 he became rector of St Omer.

PETRI, *pay'tree*, (1) **Laurentius** (1499–1573), Swedish reformer, studied under Luther at Wittenberg, was made professor at Uppsala, and in 1531 first Protestant Archbishop of Uppsala. He and his brother Claus did most to convert Sweden to the Reformed doctrines, and superintended the translation of the Bible into Swedish (1541).

(2) **Olaus** (1493–1552), brother of (1), gained, after his return (1519) from Wittenberg, the ear of Gustavus Vasa, who made him (1531) chancellor of the kingdom—a post he resigned in 1539 to spend the rest of his life as first pastor of Stockholm. His works include memoirs, a mystery-play, hymns and controversial tracts.

PETRIE, *pee'tree*, (1) **George** (1789–1866), Irish archaeologist, born at Dublin, was trained to be a landscape-painter, but was early attracted by the old buildings of Ireland. In 1833–46 he was attached to the Ordnance Survey of Ireland, and from 1832 he contributed much to the *Dublin Penny Journal*. He wrote on Tara, Irish music, &c.; and his famous *Essay on Round Towers* proved that they were Christian ecclesiastical buildings.

(2) **Sir William Matthew Flinders** (1853–1942), English Egyptologist, was born at Charlton, Kent. His earliest studies bore fruit in his *Stonehenge* (1880), and he next turned his attention to the pyramids and temples of Gizeh, to the mounds of Said and Naukratis. Year after year, even in old age, he excavated in Egypt and Palestine, and published a long succession of books mainly on his own diggings and methods, besides occupying (1892–1933) the chair of Egyptology in University College London. See his *Seventy Years of Archaeology* (1931), &c.

PETRONIUS ARBITER (fl. 1st cent. A.D.), Latin writer, supposed to be the Gaius Petronius whom Tacitus calls 'arbiter elegantiae' at the court of Nero, is generally believed to be the author of *Satirae*, the satirical romance in prose and verse, of which the 15th and 16th books have, in a fragmentary state, come down to us. The work depicts with wit, humour and realism the licentious life in Southern Italy of the upper or moneyed class. The favour Petronius enjoyed as aider and abettor of Nero and the *jeunesse dorée* in every form of sensual indulgence aroused the jealousy of another confidant, Tigellinus, who procured his disgrace and banishment. Ordered to commit suicide, he opened his veins.

PETROVITCH. See ALEXEI (2).

PETTENKOFER, Max von (1818–1901), German chemist, born near Neuburg, in 1847–94 was professor of Chemistry at Munich. He made valuable contributions to science on gold refining, gas-making, ventilation, clothing, epidemics and hygiene. He shot himself. Of his works, the best known is his *Handbuch der Hygiene* (1882 *et seq.*).

PETTIE, John (1839–93), Scottish painter, born in Edinburgh, joined Orchardson in London in 1862. He was elected A.R.A. in 1866 and R.A. in 1873. His works, apart from his portraits, were mainly of historical and literary subjects and had considerable popularity. Examples of these are *Juliet and Friar Lawrence* (1874) and *The Vigil* (1884).

PETTIT, Edison (1890–1962), American astronomer, famous for research on the sun and on ultra-violet light with reference to biology, in 1920 was appointed astronomer at the Mount Wilson observatory. See his *Forms and Motions of the Solar Prominences* (1925).

PETTY, Sir William (1623–87), English economist, was born at Romsey, Hants, the son of a clothier. He went to sea, and then studied at a Jesuit college in Caen, at Utrecht, Amsterdam, Leyden, Paris and Oxford, where he taught anatomy. Appointed physician to the army in Ireland (1652), he executed a fresh survey of the Irish lands forfeited in 1641 and started ironworks, lead-mines, sea-fisheries and other industries on estates he bought in southwest Ireland. He was made surveyor-general of Ireland by Charles II, who knighted him. Inventor of a copying machine (1647), and a double-keeled sea-boat (1663), he was one of the first members of the Royal Society. In political economy he was a precursor of Adam Smith, and wrote a *Treatise on Taxes* (1662) and *Political Arithmetic* (1691), the latter a discussion of the value of comparative statistics. He married the Baroness Shelburne, and his sons were successively Lord Shelburne (q.v.). His *Economic Writings* were edited by C. H. Hull (2 vols. 1899). See Life by Lord Edmond Fitzmaurice (1895).

PEUTINGER, Conrad, *poy'ting-ėr* (1465–1547), German scholar, a keeper of the archives of Augsburg, who published a series of Roman inscriptions. His *Tabula Peutingeriana*, now at Vienna, is a copy, made in 1264, of an itinerary or a Roman map of the military roads of the 4th century A.D.

PEVSNER, (1) **Antoine** (1886–1962), French constructivist sculptor, was born in Russia. In Moscow he helped to form the Suprematist Group, with Malevitch, Tatlin and his brother Naum Gabo (q.v.). In 1920 he broke away from the Suprematists and issued the *Realist Manifesto* with his brother: this ultimately caused their exile from Russia, and he migrated to Paris. Several of his completely nonfigurative constructions (mainly in copper and bronze) are in the Museum of Modern Art, New York.

(2) **Nikolaus** (1903–), German art historian, born in Leipzig, lost his post at Göttingen University on the advent of Hitler and came to Britain, where he has become an authority on architecture and especially on English architecture. On the editorial board of *The Architectural Review*, art editor

of Penguin Books, he was from 1949 to 1955 Slade professor of Fine Art at Cambridge and in 1955 gave the Reith lecture on the Englishness of English art. Since the appearance of his *Pioneers of Modern Design* (1936), which made a strong impression in architectural circles, his scholarly but lucid works have stimulated a wide popular interest in art and architecture. Outstanding among these was *An Outline of European Architecture* (1942) in the Pelican series. Of his many other writings the monumental and unique work, as yet unfinished is *The Buildings of England* in 50 volumes for Penguin Books.

PFEFFER, Wilhelm (1845–1920), German botanist, born near Cassel, a specialist in plant physiology, professor successively at Bonn, Basel, Tübingen and Leipzig, was noted particularly for his researches on osmotic pressure. His *Handbuch der Pflanzenphysiologie* (1881) was a standard work.

PFEIFFER, *pfī'fėr*, (1) **Ida,** *née* **Reyer** (1797–1858), Austrian traveller, born at Vienna, made two journeys round the world (1846–1848, 1851–54). In 1856 she went on an expedition to Madagascar, endured terrible hardships, and came home to die. She wrote accounts of all her journeys; that of the last, edited by her son, contains a Life.

(2) **Richard Friedrich Johannes** (1858–?1945), German bacteriologist, was born near Posen (now Poznań, Poland), studied under Koch (q.v.), and became professor at Berlin (1894), Königsberg (1899) and Breslau (1901). He worked on the immunization of man against typhoid, on the influenza bacillus, discovered a serum against cholera, and published books on hygiene and microbiology. He was presumed dead in 1945.

PFITZNER, Hans Erich (1869–1949), German musician, born in Moscow, taught in various German conservatoria, and conducted in Berlin, Munich and Strasbourg. He composed *Palestrina* (1917) and other operas, choral and orchestral music (*Von deutscher Seele*, 1921) and chamber music. A romantic, he went his own way, refusing to follow passing fashions.

PFLEIDERER, *pflī'dėr-ėr*, (1) **Edmund** (1842–1902), German philosopher, became professor of Philosophy at Kiel in 1873, and in 1878 at Tübingen. His writings include studies on Leibniz (1870), Hume (1874), Kantian criticism and English philosophy (1881), &c.

(2) **Otto** (1839–1908), German philosophic theologian, brother of (1), was born at Stetten in Württemberg, studied at Tübingen (1857–61), became pastor at Heilbronn in 1868, in 1870 professor of Theology at Jena, and in 1875 at Berlin. In New Testament criticism Pfleiderer belonged to the critical school which grew out of the impulse given by Baur, and was an independent thinker, suggestive and profoundly learned. His works include *Primitive Christianity* (14 vols. trans. 1906–11), *The Influence of the Apostle Paul on Christianity* (Hibbert Lectures, 1885) and *The Philosophy of Religion* (Gifford Lectures, 1894).

PFLÜGER, Eduard Friedrich Wilhelm (1829–1910), German physiologist, born at Hanau, professor at Bonn (1859), did important work on the sensory function of the spinal cord and on the digestive and metabolic systems. He helped in the construction of the mercurial blood pump. He died at Bonn.

PHAEDRUS, or **Phaeder** (1st cent. A.D.), translator of Aesop's fables into Latin verse, was a Graecized Macedonian, who came young to Italy. From a slave he became the freedman of Augustus or Tiberius. Under Tiberius he published the first two books of his fables, but his biting though veiled allusions to the tyranny of the emperor and his minister Sejanus caused him to be accused and condemned—to what punishment is unknown. On the death of Sejanus he published his third book. The fourth and fifth books belong to his last years. He died probably at an advanced age. Phaedrus was more than a reproducer of Aesop; he invented fables of his own, and it seems certain that the five books contain many fables that are not from his pen. See the editions of Bentley, Dressel, Orelli, Müller, Ramorino (1884), Havet (1895), Postgate (1922).

PHALARIS (6th cent. B.C.), Greek tyrant of Agrigentum in Sicily, was an adventurer from Asia Minor, who greatly embellished the city, and extended his sway over large districts in Sicily. After holding power for sixteen years he was overthrown for his cruelties, and roasted alive in his own invention, the brazen bull. The 148 letters bearing his name were proved by Bentley in 1697 and 1699 to be spurious.

PHELPS, Samuel (1804–78), English actor-manager, born in Devonport, became quite early a reader on the *Globe* and *Sun* newspapers, but by 1826 his interest in acting led him to his stage career. By 1837 he was a success, especially with his performance as Shylock, but his genius did not get full scope until he became manager of Sadler's Wells. For eighteen years with an excellent company of actors he produced legitimate plays, appearing himself equally successfully in comic and tragic rôles. See Life by W. M. Phelps and J. Forbes-Robertson (1886).

PHIDIAS (Gr. *Pheidias*), *fī'di-as* (5th cent. B.C.), the greatest sculptor of Greece, was born at Athens *c.* 500 B.C., and received from Pericles a magnificent commission to execute the chief statues with which he proposed to adorn the city, and was superintendent of all public works. He had under him architects, statuaries, bronze-workers, stone-cutters, &c. He constructed the Propylaea and the Parthenon, and the gold and ivory Athena there and the Zeus at Olympia were accounted the masterpieces of his own chisel. Charged with appropriating gold from the statue and carving his own head on an ornament, he was accused of impiety, and disappeared from Athens.

PHILARET (1782–1867), Russian prelate, the greatest preacher and the most influential Russian churchman of his day, became in 1817 Bishop of Reval, in 1819 Archbishop of Tver, and in 1821 of Moscow.

PHILIDOR, François André Danican (1726–1795), French chess player and operatic composer, was born at Dreux, and died in London.

PHILIP II (382–336 B.C.), king of Macedonia, father of Alexander the Great, was born at Pella, the youngest son of Amyntas II. The assassination of his eldest brother (367), and the death in battle of his second (359), left him guardian to his infant nephew Amyntas, but in a few months he made himself king. Dangers beset him from without and within, but in a year he had secured the safety of his kingdom, and gained for himself a dreaded name; henceforward his policy was one of aggression. The Greek towns on the coast of Macedonia were the first objects of attack. In Thrace he captured Crenides, which as Philippi soon acquired wealth. The gold-mines of the surrounding district supplied him with the means of paying his armies and of bribing traitorous Greeks. He advanced into Thessaly, but Thermopylae he found strongly guarded by the Athenians. He therefore directed his arms against the Thracians, and captured all the towns of Chalcidice, including Olynthus. Requested by the Thebans to interfere in the 'Sacred War' raging between them and the Phocians, he marched into Phocis, destroyed its cities, and sent many of the inhabitants as colonists to Thrace (346). He next secured a footing in the Peloponnese, by espousing the cause of the Argives, Messenians and others against the Spartans. In 339 the Amphictyonic Council declared war against the Locrians of Amphissa, and in 338 appointed Philip commander-in-chief of their forces. The Athenians, alarmed, formed a league with the Thebans against him; but their army was utterly defeated at Chaeronea (338), and all Greece lay at the feet of the conqueror. He was now in a position to enter on the dream of his later years—the invasion of the Persian empire. Preparations for it were in progress when he was assassinated by Pausanias (336). See David G. Hogarth's *Philip and Alexander of Macedon* (1897) and A. Momigliano's *Filippo il Macedone* (1934).

PHILIP. Name of six kings of France:

Philip I (1052–1108), son of Henry I, reigned from 1067 without glory or credit.

Philip II (1165–1223), better known as **Philip-Augustus**, son of Louis VII, was crowned joint king in 1179, succeeded his father in 1180, and married Isabella of Hainault, the last direct descendant of the Carlovingians. His first war, against the Count of Flanders, gave him Amiens. He punished heretics and despoiled the Jews, and reduced the Duke of Burgundy. He supported the sons of Henry II of England against their father. Richard (Coeur de Lion) and he set out on the Third Crusade, but they quarrelled in Sicily. After three months in Syria he returned to France, having sworn not to molest Richard's dominions; but no sooner had he returned than he made a bargain with John for the partition of Richard's French territories. Richard's sudden return occasioned an exhausting war till 1199. On Richard's death Philip supported Arthur against his uncle John in the French domains of the English crown, but was for a while fully occupied by his quarrel with the pope. He had put away his second wife Ingeborg of Denmark, in order to marry Agnes of Meran, but the anger of the Vatican forced him to replace Ingeborg upon her throne. The murder of Arthur again gave him the excuse he sought. The fortress of Château Gaillard surrendered to him in 1204, and that same year he added to his dominions Normandy, Maine, Anjou and Touraine, with part of Poitou, as well as the overlordship of Brittany. The victory of Bouvines (August 29, 1214) over the Flemish, the English, and the Emperor Otho established his throne securely, and the rest of his reign he devoted to reforms of justice and to the building and fortifying of Paris—Notre Dame remaining a lasting monument of this great king. He died at Nantes. See works by Mazabran (1878), Davidsohn (Stuttgart 1888), Luchaire (Paris 2nd ed. 1909), W. H. Hutton (1896), Cambridge Medieval History, vol. 6 (1929).

Philip III, 'le Hardi' (1245–85), was with his father St Louis at his death in Tunis (1270), fought several unlucky campaigns in Spain, the last of which, the attack on Aragon, caused his death. See Life by Langlois (1887).

Philip IV, 'the Fair' (1268–1314), succeeded his father, Philip III, in 1285. By his marriage with Queen Joanna of Navarre he obtained Navarre, Champagne and Brie. He overran Flanders, but a Flemish revolt broke out at Bruges, and at Courtrai on the 'Day of Spurs' he was disastrously defeated. His great struggle with Pope Boniface VIII grew out of his attempt to levy taxes from the clergy. In 1296 Boniface forbade the clergy to pay taxes; Philip replied by forbidding the export of money or valuables. A temporary reconciliation in 1297 was ended by a fresh quarrel in 1300. Philip imprisoned the papal legate, and summoned the Estates. Boniface issued the bull *Unam Sanctam.* Philip publicly burned the bull, and confiscated the property of those prelates who had sided with the pope. Boniface now excommunicated him, and threatened to lay the kingdom under interdict, but the king sent to Rome William de Nogaret, who seized and imprisoned the pope, with the aid of the Colonnas. Boniface soon afterwards died. In 1305 Philip obtained the elevation of one of his own creatures as Clement V, and placed him at Avignon, the beginning of the seventy years' 'captivity'. He compelled the pope to condemn the Templars (1310) and abolish the order (1312); they were condemned and burned by scores, and Philip appropriated their wealth. Under him the taxes were greatly increased, the Jews persecuted and their property confiscated.

Philip V, 'the Tall' (1293–1322), second son of the preceding, succeeded his brother, Louis X, in 1316. He ended the war with Flanders (1320), and tried to unify the coinage.

Philip VI, of Valois (1293–1350), son of Charles of Valois, younger brother of Philip IV, succeeded to the throne of France on the death of Charles IV in 1328. His right was denied by Edward III of England, son of the daughter of Philip IV, who declared that females, though excluded by the Salic law, could transmit their rights to their children.

Marching into Flanders to support the count against his rebellious subjects, he vanquished them at Cassel (August 23, 1328). He gave up Navarre, but retained Champagne and Brie. The Hundred Years' War with England began in 1337. The French fleet was destroyed off Sluys (1340). In 1346 Edward III landed in Normandy, ravaged to the environs of Paris, and defeated Philip at Crécy. A truce was concluded just as destruction threatened France in the 'Black Death'.

PHILIP. Name of five kings of Spain, of whom the following are noteworthy:

Philip I (1478–1506), son of the Emperor Maximilian, reigned only for a few months.

Philip II (1527–98), only son of the Emperor Charles V, was born at Valladolid. In 1543 he married Mary of Portugal, who died in 1546, after bearing the ill-fated Don Carlos. He spent three years with his father at Brussels. In 1554 he made a marriage of policy with Mary Tudor, Queen of England. During his fourteen months' stay in England he laboured unsuccessfully to ingratiate himself with his wife's subjects. In 1555 he became by the abdication of his father the most powerful prince in Europe, having under his sway Spain, the Two Sicilies, the Milanese, the Low Countries, Franche Comté, Mexico and Peru. But the treasury was deficient, drained by the expenditure of his father's wars. His first danger was a league formed between Henry II of France and Pope Paul IV. Alva overran the papal territories, while Philip's troops defeated the French at St Quentin (1557) and Gravelines (1558), and Henry made peace (1559). In January 1558 the French had captured Calais, and Mary Tudor died eleven months later. Philip failed to secure the hand of Elizabeth, and in 1559 married Isabella of France. Seeking to concentrate all power in himself, he laboured to destroy free institutions in all his dominions, while putting himself at the head of the Catholic party in Europe. He found the Inquisition the best engine of his tyranny in Spain, but in the Low Countries it caused a formidable revolt, which ended in 1579 with the independence of the Seven United Provinces. To replenish his treasury Philip exacted enormous contributions. His son, Don Carlos (q.v.), whom he hated, died in prison in 1568. Philip did not disdain the aid of murder in the pursuit of his policy, and the death of William the Silent (1584) and the persecution of Antonio Pérez (q.v.) show how pitiless and persistent was his hatred. He married in 1570 his niece, Anne of Austria, whose son by him became Philip III. His one great triumph was the naval victory of Lepanto (1571), won by his half-brother, Don John of Austria, over the Turks. In 1580, the direct male line of Portugal having become extinct, Philip claimed the throne, and dispatched Alva to occupy the kingdom. His attempt to conquer England resulted in hopeless disaster, as the Armada was swept to destruction (1588). His intrigues against Henry of Navarre were foiled (1592). The stubborn heroism of the Netherlanders and the ravages of the English on the Spanish Main, added to financial distress at home, embittered Philip's last years. He possessed great abilities but little political wisdom, and he engaged in so many vast enterprises at once as to overtask his resources without leading to any profitable result. He dealt a fatal blow to Spain by crushing its chivalrous spirit, and destroyed its commerce by oppressive exactions and by a bitter persecution of the industrious Moriscos. The good points of Philip, who was a tender husband and very affectionate to his daughters, are brought out in Froude's *Spanish Story of the Armada* (1892), Martin Hume's *Philip II of Spain* (1897), and *Two English Queens and Philip* (1908). See also the histories of Prescott, Motley and Froude; Forneron's *Histoire de Philippe II* (3rd ed. 1887); and books by Gachard, Mignet, Rubis, Tomas and Petrie (1963).

Philip V (1683–1746), first Bourbon king of Spain, second son of the Dauphin Louis (son of Louis XIV and Maria Theresa of Spain), was born at Versailles. In 1700, when Duke of Anjou, he was bequeathed the crown of Spain by Charles II. He entered Madrid in February 1701, and after a long struggle against his rival, the Archduke Charles, was left in possession of the throne by the peace of Utrecht in 1713. Next year died the queen, Maria Louisa, daughter of the Duke of Savoy, whom Philip had married in 1702; and soon after he married 'the termagant' Elizabeth Farnese (q.v.). By her influence the government was committed to Alberoni, but Philip was obliged by the Quadruple Alliance to dismiss him in 1719. He abdicated in favour of his son Don Louis in 1724, but resumed the crown on Louis' death eight months later. The queen's dearest wish was to drive the Hapsburgs out of Italy in the interests of her sons by a former marriage, but she only secured the Two Sicilies for Don Carlos. Spain joined the coalition against Maria Theresa, and her younger son Don Philip was at first successful in conquering the Milanese; but as soon as the Silesian war was closed the Austrian queen drove the Spaniards out of Italy. At the crisis Philip died. See Baudrillart's *Philippe V et la cour de France, 1700–15* (1890–91).

PHILIP. Name of two Dukes of Burgundy:

Philip the Bold ('le Hardi') (1342–1404), founder of the second and last ducal House of Burgundy, was the fourth son of John the Good, king of France. At Poitiers (1356) he displayed heroic courage, shared his father's captivity in England, and was made Duke of Burgundy in 1363. He married Margaret, heiress of Flanders, in 1369. In 1372 he commanded with success against the English, and in 1380 helped to suppress the sedition of the Flemish towns against his father-in-law; but the rebels, especially the burghers of Ghent, were finally subdued only after the defeat of Rosbeck (1382), where 26,000 Flemings were slain. Flanders fell to him by the death of the count in 1384, and his wise government won the esteem of his new subjects. He encouraged arts, manufactures and commerce, and his territory was one of the best governed in Europe. For his imbecile nephew, Charles VI of France, he was obliged to take the helm of affairs. See study by R. Vaughan (1963).

Philip the Good (1396–1467), son of John

the Fearless and grandson of Philip the Bold, bent on avenging his father's murder by the dauphin, entered into an alliance with Henry V of England in 1419, recognizing him as heir to the French crown. This agreement was sanctioned by the French king and States-General (1420), but the dauphin (Charles VII after 1422) took to arms, and was twice defeated. Disputes with the English prompted Philip to conclude a treaty with Charles in 1429. But by ceding to him Champagne and paying a large sum, the English regained his alliance. At this time, by falling heir to Brabant, Holland and Zeeland, he was at the head of the most powerful realm in Europe. Smarting under fresh insults of the English viceroy, he made final peace (1435) with Charles. When the English committed great havoc on Flemish ships, Philip declared war against them, and, with the king of France, gradually expelled them from their French possessions. The imposition of taxes excited a rebellion, headed by Ghent; but the duke inflicted a terrible defeat (July 1454) upon the rebels, of whom 20,000 fell. The later part of his reign was troubled by the quarrels between Charles VII and his son (afterwards Louis XI) who sought shelter with Philip. Under him Burgundy was the most wealthy, prosperous and tranquil state in Europe. He was founder of the order of the Golden Fleece.

PHILIP, Prince. See EDINBURGH, DUKE OF.

PHILIP, an American-Indian chief (d. 1676), son of a staunch ally of the Pilgrim settlers of Plymouth, became the leader of a confederation of nearly 10,000 warriors, and in King Philip's War (1675) against the whites thirteen towns were destroyed and 600 colonists slain. After reprisals and retaliations Philip's supporters fell away, and he was surprised and shot by Captain Benjamin Church. See Drake's edition of *King Philip's War* by Church (1825).

PHILIP NERI, St. See NERI.

PHILIPPA OF HAINAULT (*c.* 1314–69), in 1328 married Edward III at York. In 1347 she obtained mercy for the Calais burgesses. See B. C. Hardy's *Philippa and her Times* (1900).

PHILIPS, (1) Ambrose (1674–1749), English poet, born at Shrewsbury, was educated at St John's College, Cambridge. A friend of Addison and Steele, he did hack work for Tonson, and gained a reputation by the *Winter-piece* in the *Tatler* and six Pastorals in Tonson's *Miscellany* (1709). Pope's jealousy started a bitter feud. He was dubbed 'Namby Pamby' by either Carey or Swift for the over-sentimentality of some of his poetry. Of his plays only *The Distrest Mother*, based on Racine's *Andromaque*, found favour with his contemporaries. Philips sat for Armagh, was secretary to the Archbishop of Armagh, purse-bearer to the Irish lord chancellor, and registrar of the Prerogative Court. See *The Poems of Ambrose Philips*, ed. Segar (1937).

(2) **John** (1676–1709), English poet, was born at Bampton, Oxfordshire, the son of the Archdeacon of Shropshire, and educated at Winchester and Christ Church, Oxford. He wrote three very popular poems, *The Splendid Shilling* (1701), a Miltonic burlesque; *Blenheim* (1705), a Tory celebration of Marlborough's great victory; and *Cyder* (1708), an imitation of Virgil's *Georgics*. He died at Hereford of consumption and was buried in the cathedral there. He has a monument in Westminster Abbey. Lloyd Thomas edited his *Poems* (1927).

(3) **Katherine** (1631–64), *née* **Fowler,** English poetess, called 'the matchless Orinda', was born in London, the daughter of a London merchant, and at sixteen married James Philips of Cardigan Priory. Orinda is the earliest English sentimental writer (her first printed poem was an address to Vaughan the Silurist). She received a dedication from Jeremy Taylor (*Discourse on the Nature, Offices and Measures of Friendship*, 1659). On a visit to London she caught smallpox, and died. She translated Corneille's *Pompée* and the greater part of his *Horace*. Her poems, surreptitiously printed in 1663, were issued in 1667. See Saintsbury's *Minor Poets of the Caroline Period* (1905), Gosse's *Seventeenth Century Studies* (2nd ed. 1885), P. W. Souers's study (Harvard 1931) and her own letters, *From Orinda to Poliarchus*.

PHILLIMORE, Sir Robert Joseph (1810–85), English judge, educated at Westminster and Christ Church, after serving in the Board of Control had a brilliant career at the bar. He sat in parliament as a Whig 1853–57; and became advocate-general (1862, when he was knighted), judge advocate-general (1871), judge of the Arches Court (1867–75), and of the High Court of Admiralty (1867–83). He was made a baronet in 1881. He wrote *Commentaries upon International Law* (1854–1861) and *Ecclesiastical Law* (1873–76).

PHILLIP, (1) Arthur (1738–1814), first governor of New South Wales, born in London, trained at Greenwich and joined the navy in 1755. He saw service in the Mediterranean with Byng, was at the taking of Havana, and in 1787 as captain led the 'First Fleet' to Botany Bay. Finding that site unsuitable, he founded his settlement at Sydney (1788). He explored the Hawkesbury River, piloted his colony through difficulties and predicted its future importance. He left in 1792, being made vice-admiral in 1809. See Lives by G. Mackaness (1937) and M. B. Eldershaw (1938).

(2) **John** (1817–67), Scottish painter, was born, an old soldier's son, at Aberdeen. He was apprenticed to a painter and glazier, but in 1836 was sent by Lord Panmure to London, where in 1838 he began to exhibit in the Academy. Most of his early subjects were Scottish, but after a visit to Spain (1851), for health, his main triumphs were in Spanish themes. He became an R.A. in 1859.

PHILLIPPS. See HALLIWELL-PHILLIPPS.

PHILLIPS, (1) Edward (1630–*c.* 1696), English writer, son of Milton's sister Ann, was brought up and educated by his uncle. He went to Oxford in 1650, but left next year without taking a degree. In 1663 he was tutor to the son of John Evelyn, and is mentioned in Evelyn's Diary as 'not at all infected by Milton's principles', yet he not only extolled his uncle in his *Theatrum Poetarum*, but has left us a short Life of the poet. Among his numerous works are a complete edition (the first) of the Poems of Drummond of Hawthornden (1656); *New World of English Words* (1658), a kind of dictionary; the *Continuation* of Baker's *Chronicle of the Kings of England* (1665); *Theatrum Poetarum, or a Complete Collection of the Poets* (1675).

(2) **John** (1631–1706), English writer, brother of (1), also educated by his uncle, replied to Salmasius's attack on him, and acted as his amanuensis. His *Satyr against Hypocrites* (1655) was a bitter attack on the Presbyterian ministers, *Speculum Crape Gownorum* on the High Churchmen. *Maronides* travesties Virgil. An anonymous Life of Milton is attributed to him by Helen Darbishire.

(3) **John** (1800–74), English geologist, born at Marden in Wiltshire, worked with his uncle William Smith, the father of English geology, and was professor of Geology at London, Dublin and Oxford. He was keeper of the Ashmolean Museum (1854–70) and president of the Geological Society of London (1859–60). His writings include *Geology of Yorkshire* (1829–36), and *Life on the Earth: Its Origin and Succession* (1860).

(4) **Stephen** (1868–1915), English poet, was born, son of the precentor of Peterborough Cathedral, at Somertown, near Oxford. For six years he acted in Benson's company, next taught history, then took to literature, and from 1913 edited the *Poetry Review*. He wrote *Christ in Hades* (1896), *Poems* (1897), which enjoyed a transitory success, and blank verse plays, the best *Paolo and Francesca* (1899).

(5) **Wendell** (1811–84), abolitionist, born at Boston, Mass., graduated at Harvard 1831, and was called to the bar 1834. But by 1837 he was the chief orator of the antislavery party. He also championed the causes of temperance and women, and advocated the rights of the Indians. His speeches and letters were collected in 1863. See Life by Austin (1888).

PHILLPOTTS, (1) Eden (1862–1960), English novelist, dramatist and poet, born at Mount Aboo, India, studied for the stage in London, but took to literature instead (1893), and made his name by realistic novels chiefly dealing with Devonshire. Of his plays, *The Farmer's Wife* (1917: staged 1924) and *Yellow Sands* (1926), which he wrote with his daughter Adelaide, were perhaps the most successful. In all he wrote more than 250 books.

(2) **Henry** (1778–1869), Bishop of Exeter, born at Bridgwater, was elected fellow of Magdalen in 1795, and became Dean of Chester in 1828, and Bishop of Exeter in 1831. A zealous Tory, a High Churchman, a keen controversialist, he refused to institute Gorham (q.v.).

PHILO (*c.* 2nd cent. B.C.), Byzantine scientist, wrote a treatise on military engineering of which some fragments remain. He was probably the first to record the contraction of air in a globe over water when a candle is burnt in it.

PHILO JUDAEUS (fl. 1st cent. A.D.), Hellenistic Jewish philosopher, born at Alexandria of a wealthy family, was nurtured in Greek culture but remained faithful to the Jewish religion. When over fifty he went to Rome to plead for certain Alexandrians who had refused to worship the insane Caligula, described in his *De Legatione*. His importance to Jews and Christians alike is his fusion of Platonic philosophy with the doctrines of the Hebrew scriptures. Most of his writings have been lost, but three works on the Pentateuch are still extant. See translations (1929 ff.) and studies by Drummond (1888), H. E. Ryle (1895), Moore (1927) and Woolfson (1947).

PHILO OF BYBLIUS (fl. late 1st and 2nd cents. A.D.), a Hellenized Phoenician grammarian of Byblus in Phoenicia, wrote a distorted and misleading account of the religion and history of the Phoenicians, much of it professedly translated from Sanchoniathon.

PHILOPOEMEN, *fil-ō-pee'men* (*c.* 252–183 B.C.), Greek general, born at Megalopolis, as commander-in-chief of the Achaean League crushed the Spartans at Mantinea (208), sought to unite Greece against the Romans, and was poisoned by the Messenians.

PHILOSTRATUS, *fi-los'-* (*c.* 170–245 A.D.), Greek sophist, studied at Athens, and established himself at Rome, where he wrote an idealized Life of Apollonius of Tyana, the bright *Lives of the Sophists*, and the amatory *Epistles*. The *Heroicon* and the *Imagines*, a description of thirty-four pictures supposed to be hung in a villa near Naples, are now ascribed to his nephew; and further *Imagines* to a third and related Philostratus. See texts by Kayser (1844) and Westermann (1849), and translations by Conybeare (1912) and Phillimore (1912).

PHIPPS, Sir William (1651–95), American colonial governor, born at Pemmaquid (Bristol), Maine, was successively shepherd, carpenter and trader, and in 1687 recovered £300,000 from a wrecked Spanish ship off the Bahamas. This gained him a knighthood and the appointment of provost-marshal of New England. In 1690 he captured Port Royal (now Annapolis) in Nova Scotia, but failed in 1691 in a naval attack upon Quebec. In 1692 he became governor of Massachusetts. He died in London. See Life by Bowen in Sparks's *American Biography* (1834–37), and that by H. O. Thayer (1927).

PHIZ. See BROWNE (5).

PHOCAS (d. 610), emperor of Constantinople, overthrew his predecessor Maurice in 602. Through his monstrous vices, tyranny and incapacity the empire sank into utter anarchy, and he was overthrown in 610 by Heraclius (q.v.).

PHOCION, *fō'shi-on* (*c.* 402–317 B.C.), Athenian general, commanded a division of the Athenian fleet at Naxos in 376, and helped to conquer Cyprus in 351 for Artaxerxes III. In 341 he crushed the Macedonian party in Euboea, and in 340 forced Philip to evacuate the Chersonesus, but advised Athens to make friends with him. The advice was not taken; but the fatal battle of Chaeronea proved its soundness. After the murder of Philip (336) he struggled at Athens to repress the reckless desire for war, and again on the death of Alexander in

323 vainly endeavoured to hinder the Athenians from going to war with Antipater. Ultimately regarded as a traitor, he fled to Phocis, was in the intrigues of Cassander, the rival of Polyperchon, who delivered him up to the Athenians, and was condemned to drink hemlock.

PHOTIUS (*c.* 820–91), ex-soldier and secretary, on the deposition of Ignatius from the patriarchate of Constantinople for correcting the vices of the Emperor Michael, was hurried through all the stages of Holy Orders, and installed in his stead. In 862, however, Pope Nicholas I called a council at Rome, which declared Photius's election invalid, excommunicated him, and reinstated Ignatius. Supported by the emperor, Photius assembled a council at Constantinople in 867, which condemned many points of doctrine and discipline of the Western Church as heretical, excommunicated Nicholas, and withdrew from the communion of Rome. Under the Emperor Basilius in 867 Photius was banished to Cyprus, and Ignatius reinstated. In 869 the eighth general council, at which Pope Adrian II's legates presided, assembled at Constantinople; Photius was again excommunicated, and the intercommunion of the churches restored. Yet, on the death of Ignatius, Photius was reappointed. In 879 he assembled a new council at Constantinople, renewed the charges against the Western Church, and erased the *filioque* from the creed. Photius was finally deprived, and exiled to Armenia by Leo, son of Basilius, in 886. His chief remains are *Myriobiblon* or *Bibliotheca*, a summary review of 280 works which Photius had read, and many of which are lost; a *Lexicon*; the *Nomocanon*, a collection of the acts and decrees of the councils and ecclesiastical laws of the emperors; and a collection of letters. See F. Dvornik's *The Photian Schism* (1948).

PHRYNE, *frī'nee* (4th cent. B.C.), a beautiful Greek courtesan of antiquity, born at Thespiae in Boeotia, became enormously rich through her many lovers. Accused of profaning the Eleusinian mysteries, she was defended by the orator Hyperides (q.v.), who threw off her robe, showing her loveliness and so gained the verdict.

PIAGET, Jean (1896–), Swiss psychologist, born at Neuchâtel, professor of Psychology at Geneva University, director of the Centre d'Epistémologie génétique and a director of the Institut des Sciences de l'Education. He is best known for his research on the development of cognitive functions (perception, intelligence, logic) and for his intensive case study methods of research. His many publications include *La Gènese du nombre chez l'enfant* (1941, trans. 1952), *Le Développement de la notion de temps chez l'enfant* (1946), *La Répresentation de l'espace chez l'enfant* (with Inhelder, 1947, trans. 1956) and *Logic and Psychology* (1957).

PIAZZI, Giuseppe, *pya'tsee* (1746–1826), Italian astronomer, professor of Mathematics in Palermo; he set up an observatory there (1789) and published a catalogue of the stars (1803, 1814).

PICABIA, Francis (1879–1953), French *Dadaist* painter, born in Paris, took part in the Parisian artistic revolutions from neo-Impressionism, Cubism with Marcel Duchamp, whom he met in 1910, to Futurism, and finally to *Dadaism* (see DUCHAMP), which they introduced to New York in 1915. His anti-art productions, often portraying senseless machinery, include *Parade Amoureuse* (1917), *Infant Carburettor*, and many of the cover designs for the American anti-art magazine *291* which he edited. See study by M. Sanouillet (Paris, 1964).

PICARD, *pee-kar*, (1) **Charles Émile** (1856–1941), French mathematician, professor at the Sorbonne (1886–97), president of the French Academy of Science (1910), was specially noted for his work on the theory of functions and on differential equations, published in his *Théorie des fonctions algébriques de deux variables indépendantes* (1897–1906) and *Traité d'analyse* (1891–96).

(2) **Jean** (1620–82), French astronomer, born at La Flèche, Anjou. In 1645 he became professor in the Collège de France and helped to found the Paris observatory. He made the first accurate measurement of a degree of a meridian and thus arrived at an estimate of the radius of the earth. He visited Tycho Brahe's observatory on the island of Hven, and determined its latitude and longitude. He died in Paris.

PICASSO, Pablo, *pee-kas'sō* (1881–1973), Spanish-born painter, the dominating figure of early 20th-century French art and, with Braque, a pioneer of Cubism, was born October 25 at Malaga, Andalusia, of which his mother, Maria Picasso, was a native. His father, José Ruiz Blasco, painter and art teacher, came from the Basque country. At the age of fourteen Pablo entered the academy at Barcelona and painted *Barefoot Girl* (1895) and two years later transferred to Madrid for advanced training. In 1898 he won a gold medal for *Customs of Aragon*, which was exhibited in his native town. In 1901 he set up in a studio at 13 Rue de Ravignon (now Place Émile-Goudeau), Montmartre. By now a master of the traditional forms of art, to which such works as his *Gipsy Girl on the Beach* (1898) abundantly testify, Picasso quickly absorbed the neo-Impressionist influences of the Paris school of Toulouse-Lautrec, Dégas and Vuillard, exemplified by such works as *Longchamp* (1901), *The Blue Room* (1901; Washington), but soon began to develop his own idiom. The blue period (1902–04), a series of striking studies of the poor in haunting attitudes of despair and gloom, gave way to the gay, life-affirming pink period (1904–06), in which Picasso achieved for harlequins, acrobats and the incidents of circus life what Dégas had previously done for the ballet. Pink turned to brown in *La Coiffure* (1905–1906; Modern Art, N.Y.) and the remarkable portrait of Gertrude Stein (1906). His first dabblings in sculpture and his new enthusiasm for Negro art are fully reflected in the transitional *Two Nudes* (1906), which heralded his epoch-making break with tradition in *Les Demoiselles d'Avignon* (1906–07; Modern Art, N.Y.), the first full-blown exemplar of analytical Cubism, an attempt to render the three-dimensional on the flat picture surface without resorting to perspective. Nature was no longer to be copied, decorated or idealized, but exploited for creative ends. Its exclusive emphasis on formal, geometrical criteria contrasted sharply with the cult of colour of the *Fauvists*, to whom Braque for a time belonged, before joining forces with Picasso in 1909 for their exploration of Cubism through its various phases; analytic, synthetic, hermetic and rococo, in which *collage*, i.e., pieces of wood, wire, newspaper and string became mediums side by side with paint. The *Ma Jolie* series of pictures, after the music-hall song score which appears in them (1911–14), are examples of the last phase. Braque broke with Picasso in 1914. From 1917 Picasso, through Jean Cocteau, became associated with Diaghilev's Russian Ballet, designing costumes and sets for *Parade* (1917), *Le Tricorne* (1919), *Pulcinella* (1920), *Le Train bleu* (1924), in both Cubist and neo-Classical styles, and thus made the former acceptable to a wider public. The grotesque facial and bodily distortions of the *Three Dancers* (1925; Modern Art, N.Y.) foreshadows the immense canvas of *Guernica* (1937; Modern Art, N.Y. and filmed 1949), which expressed in synthetic Cubism Picasso's horror of the bombing of this Basque town during the Civil War, of war in general and compassion and hope for its victims. The canvas was exhibited in the Spanish Pavilion in the Paris World Fair (1937) and Picasso became director of the Prado Gallery, Madrid (1936–39). During World War II he was mostly in Paris, and after the liberation joined the Communists. Neither *Guernica* nor his portrait of Stalin (1953) commended him to the party. Only the 'Picasso Peace Dove' had some propagandist value. He designed stage sets for Cocteau and Petit, illustrated translations of classical texts, experimented in sculpture, ceramics and lithography, allowed his canvas to be filmed while at work and wrote a play. He is above all the great innovator. See studies by Gertrude Stein (1938), W. Boeck and J. Sabarté (1955), Elgar (1955), F. Wittgens (1957) and R. Penrose (1958), who also edited the catalogue of the exhibition at the Tate, London (1960).

PICCARD, (1) **Auguste,** *pee-kar* (1884–1962), Swiss physicist, born at Basel, became professor at Brussels in 1922 and held posts at Lausanne, Chicago and Minnesota Universities. He ascended 16–17 km. by balloon (1931–32) into the stratosphere. In 1948 he explored the ocean depths off W. Africa in a bathyscaphe constructed from his own design. His son **Jacques,** together with an American naval officer **Donald Walsh,** established a world record by diving more than seven miles in the U.S. bathyscaphe *Trieste* into the Marianas Trench of the Pacific Ocean in January 1960. See the father's *In Balloon and Bathyscaphe* (1956).

(2) **Jean Felix** (1884–1963), Swiss scientist, twin brother of (1), took a Chemical Engineering degree at the Swiss Institute of Technology in 1907. Subsequently held a chair at New York, and became professor emeritus of Aeronautical Engineering at Minnesota University. His chief interest was in exploration of the stratosphere and he designed and ascended (with his wife) in a balloon from Dearborn, Detroit, in 1934, to a height of 57,579 ft, collecting valuable data concerning cosmic rays.

PICCINNI, Niccola, *pee-chee'nee* (1728–1800), Italian composer, born at Bari, wrote over a hundred operas as well as oratorios and church music. In 1766 he was summoned to Paris, and became the representative of the party opposed to Gluck (q.v.). See E. Demoiresterres, *Gluck et Piccinni* (1872).

PICCOLOMINI, an old Italian family, who obtained possession of the duchy of Amalfi. It produced numerous *littérateurs* and warriors, one pope (**Pius II**), and several cardinals. **Ottavio,** Duke of Amalfi (1599–1656), entered the Spanish service, and, sent to aid the Emperor Ferdinand II, fought against the Bohemians (1620), in the Netherlands, and in Wallenstein's army at Lützen (1632), and contributed to the fall of Wallenstein. He won great distinction at Nördlingen (1634), and next year was sent to aid the Spaniards in the Netherlands to drive out the French. In 1640 he stopped the advance of the Swedes for a time, but he was worsted by them in Silesia. In 1643 he commanded the Spanish armies in the Netherlands, and after the peace of Westphalia (1648) was created field-marshal. His son Max, who figures in Schiller's *Wallenstein,* is a poetical fiction. See German works by Weyhe-Eimke (1870–71), and Elster (1911).

PICHEGRU, Charles, *peesh-grü* (1761–1804), French soldier, born, a labourer's son, at Arbois, enlisted in 1783, and by 1793 was a general of division. With Hoche, he drove back the Austrians and overran the Palatinate; then defeating the Austrians at Fleurus in 1794, he continued the struggle into the winter, and entered Amsterdam in 1795. Recalled by the Thermidorians, Pichegru crushed an insurrection in Paris, and next took Mannheim. But at the height of his fame he sold himself to the Bourbons, and by deliberately remaining inactive, allowed Jourdan to be defeated. The Directory superseded him by Moreau. In 1797 he became president of the council of Five Hundred, and continued his Bourbon intrigues, but was arrested and deported to Cayenne. Escaping next year, he made his way to London, and thereafter lived in Germany and England until the Bourbon conspiracy of Cadoudal (q.v.) for the assassination of the first consul. The pair reached Paris, but were betrayed, and Pichegru was lodged in the Temple, where he was found strangled in bed. See works by Sir John Hall (1915) and Caudrillier (1908).

PICHON, Stéphen Jean Marie, *pee-shõ* (1857–1933), French statesman and journalist, born at Arnay-le-Duc in Burgundy, served on Clemenceau's paper *La Justice* before entering in 1885 the Chamber of Deputies. Sent in turn as minister to Port-au-Prince, San Domingo, Rio de Janeiro, Peking and Tunis, he represented the powers in negotiations with China during the Boxer Rebellion. He became minister of foreign affairs twice, in 1906 and again from 1917 to 1920, when he joined *Le Petit Journal* as its political editor.

PICKEN, (1) **Andrew** (1788–1833), Scottish

author, was born in Paisley and died in London, having published a series of novels, including *The Sectarian* (1829), *The Dominie's Legacy* (1830) and *Waltham* (1833).

(2) **Ebenezer** (1769–1816), Scottish poet, born at Paisley, died a teacher in Edinburgh. He published several volumes of Scots poems and a *Pocket Dictionary of the Scottish Dialect* (1818).

PICKERING, (1) Edward Charles (1846–1919), American astronomer, born at Boston, educated at Harvard, became professor of Physics at the Massachusetts Institute of Technology. In 1876 he was appointed professor of Astronomy and director of the observatory at Harvard, where his work was concerned with stellar photometry and classification of spectra of the stars. He invented the meridian photometer.

(2) **William** (1796–1854), English publisher, set up for himself in 1820, and became known by his 'Diamond Classics' (1821–31), his 'Aldine' edition of the poets, &c.

(3) **William Henry** (1858–1938), American astronomer, brother of (1), born at Boston, discovered Phoebe, the 9th satellite of Saturn. He was in charge of an observation station at Arequipa and from 1900 director of a station at Mandeville, Jamaica.

PICKFORD, Mary, *née* **Gladys Mary Smith** (1893–), American actress, born in Toronto, first appeared on the stage at the age of five, and in 1913 made her first film, *The Violin Maker of Cremona*, directed by D. W. Griffith. Her beauty and ingenuous charm soon won her the title of 'The World's Sweetheart'. Her many successful films included *Rebecca of Sunnybrook Farm*, *Poor Little Rich Girl* and *The Taming of the Shrew*.

PICKLE THE SPY. See MACDONELL.

PICO DELLA MIRANDOLA (1463–94), Italian philosopher, the son of the Count of Mirandola, in his youth visited the chief universities of Italy and France. In 1486 he issued a challenge to all comers to debate on any of nine hundred theses at Rome, but the debate was forbidden by the pope on the score of the heretical tendency of some of the theses, and Pico suffered persecution until Alexander VI in 1493 absolved him of heresy. He was the last of the schoolmen; and his works are a bewildering compound of mysticism and recondite knowledge. A humanist as well as a theologian, he wrote various Latin epistles and elegies and a series of florid Italian sonnets. His philosophical writings include *Heptaplus* and *De Hominis Dignitate*, the theme of which is free will. See the Life by his nephew (trans. by Sir Thomas More; best ed. by J. M. Rigg, 1890) and A. Dulles, *Princeps Concordiae* (1941).

PICTET, *peek-tay.* Name of a Swiss family to which belonged:

(1) **Adolphe** (1799–1875), a native of Geneva, and writer on the Celts and primitive Aryans.

(2) **François Jules** (1809–72), zoologist and palaeontologist.

(3) **Marcus Auguste** (1752–1825), physicist.

(4) **Raoul** (1846–1929), chemist and physicist at Geneva and Berlin, known from his liquefaction of oxygen, hydrogen and carbonic acid.

PICTON, Sir Thomas (1758–1815), British soldier, born at Poyston, Pembrokeshire, entered the army in 1771. In 1794 he went out to the West Indies, took part in the conquest of several of the islands, and was appointed (1797) governor of Trinidad, in 1801 becoming general. In 1803 he was superseded, but immediately after appointed commandant of Tobago. He returned, however, to England to take his trial for having permitted, under the old Spanish laws, a female prisoner to be tortured. He was found technically guilty (1806), but on appeal was acquitted. He saw active service again in the Walcheren expedition (1809), and was made governor of Flushing. In 1810 he went to Spain, and in command of the 'Fighting Division' rendered brilliant service at Busaco, Fuentes de Oñoro, Ciudad Rodrigo, Badajoz, Vitoria, the battles of the Pyrenees, Orthez and Toulouse. Created a G.C.B., he was seriously wounded at Quatre Bras, and fell leading his men to the charge at Waterloo. See Memoirs by H. B. Robinson (1835).

PIERCE, Franklin (1804–69), American politician, fourteenth president of the United States, born at Hillsborough, N.H., studied law, and was admitted to the bar in 1827. From 1829 to 1833 he was a member of the state legislature, and for two years speaker; he was then elected to congress as a Democrat, and in 1837 to the U.S. Senate. As a leader of his party, he advocated the annexation of Texas with or without slavery, and, after his opponents, the Whigs and Freesoilers, had been victorious in 1846, volunteered for the Mexican war and was made brigadier-general. In 1852 Pierce was nominated as a compromise candidate for the presidency against General Scott, the Whig nominee, and elected. He defended slavery and the fugitive slave law. The events of his administration were the treaty for reciprocity of trade with the British American colonies, the treaty with Japan, the filibustering expeditions of Walker to Nicaragua and of others to Cuba, and, especially, the repeal of the Missouri Compromise and the passing of the Kansas-Nebraska Act, which kindled a flame that ultimately led to the Civil War. The unpopularity of this act led to his enforced retirement from politics in 1857.

PIERO DELLA FRANCESCA, *fran-chays'ka* (*c.* 1420–92), a Florentine religious painter, was born and died at Borgo San Sepolcro. He is known especially for his frescoes, long neglected, the *Story of the True Cross* in the choir of San Francesca, Arezzo. He also wrote a treatise on geometry and a manual on perspective. See studies by K. Clark (1951), Venturi (1953) and Berenson (1954).

PIERO DI COSIMO, properly **Piero di Lorenzo** (1462–1521), Florentine painter, took the name of his master, Cosimo Rosselli. His later style was influenced by Signorelli and Leonardo da Vinci and among his best-known works are *Perseus and Andromeda* (Uffizi) and *Death of Procris* (Nat. Gallery, London). See monograph by R. Langton Douglas (1946).

PIERRE, Abbé, properly **Grouès, Henri Antoine** (1912–), French priest, born in Lyon, served with distinction during World War II and became a member of the resistance movement in 1942. Elected deputy in the constituent assembly after the war, he resigned in 1951 to concentrate on helping the homeless of Paris. Forming his band of Companions of Emmaus, he provided, with little monetary assistance, at least a minimum of shelter for hundreds of families and finally secured the aid of the French government in dealing with this problem.

PIERSON, originally **Pearson, Henry Hugo** (1815–73), English composer, born at Oxford, the son of the Dean of Salisbury, was educated at Harrow and Trinity College, Cambridge. In 1844–45 he was Reid professor of Music in Edinburgh, and from 1846 lived in Germany. He composed the music for the second part of Goethe's *Faust*, the operas *Leila* and *Contarini*, the oratorios *Jerusalem* and *Hezekiah*, and many songs.

PIETRO. See PETER.

PIGAFETTA, Francesco Antonio (1491–1535), Italian traveller, born at Vicenza, sailed with Magellan (q.v.), and wrote the account of the voyage (trans. with introd. by Robertson, 1906).

PIGALLE, Jean Baptiste, *pee-gal* (1714–85), French sculptor, born and died in Paris, was extremely popular in his day. His works include a statue of Voltaire and the tomb of Marshal Maurice de Saxe at Strasbourg. His *Vénus, l'Amour et l'Amitié* is in the Louvre.

PIGNON, Edouard, *peen-yõ* (1905–), French painter, born at Marles-les-Mines, was a Sunday painter until 1943. His works are rich in colour, and his treatment of forms was influenced by the Cubists and by Villon. Many of his pictures are studies of miners—e.g., the *Mineur mort* (1952)—and of harvest scenes and peasants.

PIGOTT, Richard (*c.* 1828–89), Irish journalist, born in County Meath, became editor and proprietor of *The Irishman* and two other papers of Fenian or extreme Nationalist type, which he disposed of in 1881 to Parnell and others. Already suspected by his party, he sold in 1886 to a 'Loyal and Patriotic Union' papers incriminating Parnell in the Phoenix Park tragedy, on which were based *The Times* articles 'Parnellism and Crime'. Convicted of falsehood, he confessed that he had forged the more important papers, fled, and shot himself in Madrid. See his *Reminiscences* (2nd ed. 1883).

PIJPER, Willem, *pī'per* (1894–1947), Dutch composer, born at Zeist, one of the foremost of modern composers of the Netherlands, taught at Amsterdam Conservatoire. He wrote symphonies and other orchestral pieces and an opera, *Halewijn*.

PILATE, Pontius, fifth Roman procurator of Judaea and Samaria, from A.D. 26 to 36, in whose time Jesus suffered. Under his rule there were many outbreaks, and at length Vitellius sent him to Rome to answer to Caesar (A.D. 36) on charges of rapacity and cruelty. Eusebius tells us that Pilate made away with himself; others say he was banished to Vienna Allobrogum (*Vienne*), or beheaded under Nero. Tradition makes him (or his wife) accept Christianity, and associates him with Pilatus in Switzerland. The so-called *Acts of Pilate* are utterly unauthentic. See Lipsius, *Die Pilatus-Acten* (1871).

PILE, Sir Frederick Alfred, 2nd Bart. (1884–), British general, won the D.S.O. and the M.C. in the first World War and throughout the second commanded Britain's anti-aircraft defences. In 1945 he was appointed director-general of the Ministry of Works.

PILNYAK, Boris (1894–?1938), Russian author whose real name was Boris Andreyevich Vogau, wrote novels and short stories including *The Naked Year* (1922) and *The Volga Flows Down to the Caspian Sea* (1930; English trans. 1932). His main theme was the effect of the revolution on the middle classes in Russia. He was arrested in 1938 and may now be dead. See G. Struve, *Twenty-five Years of Soviet Russian Literature* (1944).

PILON, Germain, *pee-lõ* (1537–90), French sculptor, born in Paris, is recognized as one of the leading Renaissance artists Among his works are the statues of Henry II and Catherine de' Medici at St Denis, the 'Virgin' in St Paul de Louis in Paris and the bronze Cardinal René de Biraque in the Louvre. In these, in contrast with his earlier more conventional work, such as 'The Three Graces', his keen feeling for and observation of nature have produced figures which are both more realistic and more emotional. He also produced skilful medals, especially of the French royal family. See study by J. Babelon (1927).

PILOTY, Karl von (1826–86), German painter, born at Munich, became head of a new Munich school of painters, in 1856 professor of Painting at the Munich Academy, and in 1874 director. Piloty was a pronounced realist. His finest pictures belong to the class of historical genre. Most have melancholy subjects.

PILPAY. See BIDPAI.

PIŁSUDSKI, Józef (1867–1935), Polish marshal and statesman, born at Zulów (Wilno), suffered frequent imprisonment in the cause of Polish independence. In 1887 he was sent to Siberia for five years, on his return becoming leader of the Polish Socialist party and from 1894 editor of the unauthorized *Workman*. After further terms of imprisonment in Warsaw and St Petersburg, he escaped to Cracow and began to form a band of troops which at the beginning of the 1914–18 war fought on the side of Austria. In 1917, realizing that Poland's situation was not to be bettered by a change from Russian to Austro-German domination, he disbanded his fighting force and was imprisoned in Magdeburg by the Germans. In 1918 a republic was set up in Poland with Piłsudski as its provisional president. In 1919, now a marshal, he led an army in a struggle to establish Poland's frontiers, but was driven back in 1920 by the Bolshevik army. In 1921 he went into retirement owing to disagreement with the government which he returned to overthrow in 1926, becoming minister of war and later premier. His reforms in the constitution produced in Poland a dictatorship which prevailed until his death. Although he had resigned the premiership in 1928, he remained the real ruler of the country in his capacity of minister of war. See Life by R. Landau (English trans. 1931).

PINAY, Antoine, *pee-nay* (1891–), French politician, born in the Rhône department. Primarily an industrialist and very successful mayor of the town of St Chamond, he entered politics in 1936 as deputy, becoming senator in 1938. He has been minister of transport and public works and of tourism; in 1952 became prime minister from March to December; and was minister of foreign affairs (1955–56), and of finance and economic affairs (1958–60).

PINCHBECK, (1) **Christopher** (*c.* 1670–1732), a London clockmaker and constructor of automata, invented the alloy of copper and zinc called by his name.

(2) **Christopher** (*c.* 1710–83), 2nd son of (1), invented astronomical clocks, automatic pneumatic brakes, patent candle snuffers, &c.

PINCKNEY, Charles Cotesworth (1746–1825), American statesman, born at Charleston, S.C., was sent to England and educated at Oxford, read law, and studied at Caen Military Academy. He afterwards settled as barrister at Charleston. He was Washington's aide-de-camp at Brandywine and Germantown, but was taken prisoner at the surrender of Charleston (1780). A member of the convention that framed the U.S. constitution (1787), he introduced the clause forbidding religious tests. In 1796 the Directory refused to receive him as minister to France. In 1804–08 he was twice Federalist candidate for the presidency.

PINDAR, (1) Gr. **Pindaros** (*c.* 522 B.C.–*c.* 440 B.C.), the chief lyric poet of Greece, born of an old and illustrious family, at Cynoscephalae near Thebes, the capital of Boeotia. He commenced his career as a composer of choral odes at twenty with a song of victory still extant (*Pyth.* X, written in 502). He soon reached the highest rank in his profession, and composed odes for persons in all parts of the Greek world—for the tyrants of Syracuse and Macedon, as well as for the free cities of Greece. In his poems he gives advice and reproof as well as praise to his patrons. Pindar was in the prime of life when Salamis and Thermopylae were fought, when Greek poetry and philosophy were at their greatest. He wrote hymns to the gods, paeans, dithyrambs, odes for processions, mimic dancing songs, convivial songs, dirges, and odes in praise of princes. Of all these poems we possess fragments only, but his *Epinikia* or Triumphal Odes have come down to us entire. They are divided into four books, celebrating the victories won in the Olympian, Pythian, Nemean and Isthmian games. They show the intense admiration of the Greeks for bodily prowess and beauty; such gifts come from the gods and are sacred. The groundwork of Pindar's poems consists of those legends which form the Greek religious literature, and his protest against myths dishonouring to the gods shows his pious nature. See works by Tycho Mommsen (1845), L. Schmidt (1862), Friederichs (1863), Norwood (1945) and Bowra (1964).

(2) **Peter.** See WOLCOT.

PINEL, Philippe (1745–1826), French physician, born in Languedoc, graduated at Toulouse, worked in Montpellier and in 1793 became head of the Bicêtre and later worked at the Salpêtrière. His humanitarian methods, emphasizing the psychological approach, reformed the old barbarous treatment of the insane and are contained in his great *Traité médico-philosophique sur l'aliénation mentale* (1801).

PINERO, Sir Arthur Wing, *pi-nay'rō* (1855–1934), English playwright, born in London, studied law, but in 1874 made his début on the stage at Edinburgh, and in 1875 joined the Lyceum company. His first play, *£200 a Year*, appeared in 1877, followed by a series of comedies. In 1893, with *The Second Mrs Tanqueray*, generally reckoned his best, he began a period of realistic tragedies which were received with enthusiastic acclamation and made him the most successful playwright of his day. The author of some fifty plays which included *The Squire* (1881) and *The Profligate* (1889) from his earlier works and from his later *The Gay Lord Quex* (1899), *His House in Order* (1906), and *Mid-Channel* (1909), he was knighted in 1909.

PINKERTON, (1) **Allan** (1819–84), American detective, born in Glasgow, was a cooper and a Chartist who in 1842 settled at Dundee, Ill. He became a detective and deputy-sheriff and in 1861 guarded Abraham Lincoln. He was head of the American secret service, and founder at Chicago of a great detective agency, the first in the U.S.

(2) **John** (1758–1826), Scottish man of letters, born at Edinburgh, in 1780 settled in London, and in 1802 in Paris. His 24 books include *Essay on Medals* (1784), *Origin of the Scythians or Goths* (1787), in which he first fell foul of the Celts against whom he was strongly prejudiced, *Iconographia Scotica* (1795–97) and *Walpoliana* (1799). See his *Literary Correspondence* (1830).

PINTER, Harold (1930–), British dramatist, born the son of a London East End tailor of Portuguese-Jewish ancestry (da Pinta), became a repertory actor and wrote poetry and later plays. His first London production was trounced by the critics unused to his highly personal dramatic idiom. A superb verbal acrobat, he exposes and utilizes the illogical and inconsequential in everyday talk, not to illustrate some general idea (as does Ionesco), but to induce an atmosphere of menace in *The Birthday Party* (1957), or of claustrophobic isolation in *The Caretaker* (1958; filmed 1963). His TV play *The Lover* (1963) won the Italia prize. Other plays include *The Collection* (TV 1961; stage 1962), *The Dwarfs* (radio 1960; stage 1963), and *The Homecoming* (1965). Filmscripts: *The Servant* (1963), *The Pumpkin Eaters* (1964), &c.

PINTO, Fernão Mendez (*c.* 1510–83), Portuguese adventurer, born near Coimbra, at twenty-seven made his way to India, and remained for 21 years in southeast Asia, leading a life of adventure, fighting pirates, trading and going on special missions to Japan or elsewhere. He returned in 1558, and wrote an extravagant account of his adventures, *Peregrinaçam* (1614; Eng. trans. by F. Cogan, 1663; abridged ed. 1891).

PINTURICCHIO, the name given to the painter **Bernardino di Betto Vagio**, *peen-too-reek'yō* (1454–1513), was born at Perugia. An assistant to Perugino, he helped him with the frescoes in the Sistine Chapel at Rome, and he himself painted frescoes in several Roman churches and in the Vatican library, also at Orvieto, Siena, &c. See two works by Schmarsow (1880–82), and one by Ricci (trans. 1902).

PINWELL, George John (1842–75), English artist, born in London, known for his wood engravings and illustrations for Goldsmith, Jean Ingelow, *The Arabian Nights*, &c., and for exquisite watercolour subject paintings, few in number because of his early death.

PINZÓN, Vicente Yáñez, *peen-thon'* (*c.* 1460–*c.* 1524), Spanish discoverer of Brazil, belonged to a wealthy Andalusian family. He commanded the *Nina* in the first expedition of Columbus (1492), and, unlike his brother, Martin, who commanded another vessel, remained loyal to his chief. In 1499 he sailed on his own account, and on January 26, 1500, landed near Pernambuco, on the Brazil coast, which he followed north to the Orinoco. He was made governor of Brazil by Ferdinand and Isabella. See J. R. McClymont's *Vicente Añez Pinçon* (1916).

PIOMBO, Sebastian del, *pyom'bō* (1485–1547), painter, was of the family of Luciani, and was called Del Piombo (' of the Seal ') from his becoming in 1523 sealer of briefs to Pope Clement VII. He studied under Giovanni Bellini and Giorgione; went to Rome about 1510, where he worked in conjunction with Michelangelo. In 1519 he painted his masterpiece, the *Raising of Lazarus* (now in the National Gallery, London); and was an excellent portrait painter. See Milanesi, *Les Correspondants de Michel Ange* (Fr. trans. 1890).

PIOZZI or **THRALE, Mrs**, *née* **Hester Lynch Salusbury**, *pyot'see* (1741–1821), was born at Bodvel in Caernarvonshire, and in 1763 married Henry Thrale, a prosperous Southwark brewer. Dr Samuel Johnson in 1765 conceived an extraordinary affection for her, was domesticated in her house at Streatham Place for over sixteen years, and for her sake learned to soften many of his eccentricities. Thrale also esteemed Johnson, carried him to Brighton, to Wales in 1774, and to France in 1775, and made him one of his four executors. Thrale died in April 1781, after his wife had borne him twelve children, and in 1784 the brewery was sold for £135,000. Dr Johnson began to feel himself slighted as the widow became attached to the Italian musician Piozzi, whom she married in 1784. After extensive travels in Europe, the couple returned to England in 1787, to Streatham in 1790; but soon after Mrs Piozzi built Brynbella on the Clwyd, where Piozzi died in 1809. She wrote poems and published *Anecdotes of Dr Johnson* (1786) and *Letters to and from Dr Johnson* (1788). See her *Autobiography* (reprinted 1861), her *Thraliana* (notebook; ed. by Hughes, 1913), her letters to Penelope Pennington (1913), *French Journals of Mrs Thrale and Dr Johnson* (1932), the *Queeney Letters* (ed. Lord Lansdowne, 1934—Queeney was her eldest daughter), Mangin's *Piozziana* (1833), books by Clifford (1941), and Scott, *The Blue-stocking Ladies* (1947).

PIPER, John (1903–), English artist, born at Epsom. In 1933 he met Braque, and experiments in many media, including collage, led to a representational style which grew naturally from his abstract discipline. He designed sets for the theatre and painted a series of topographical pictures, e.g., the watercolours of *Windsor Castle* commissioned by H.M. the Queen in 1941–42, and dramatic pictures of war damage. His publications include *Brighton Aquatints* (1939) and *Buildings and Prospects* (1949). See the study edited by S. J. Woods (1955).

PIPPI. See GIULIO ROMANO.

PIPPIN. See PÉPIN.

PIRANDELLO, Luigi (1867–1936), Italian dramatist, novelist and short story writer, was born at Girgenti (Agrigento). He studied at Rome and Bonn, becoming a lecturer in literature at Rome (1897–1922). After writing powerful and realistic novels and short stories, including *Il Fu Mattia Pascal* (1903) and *Si Gira* (1916), he turned to the theatre and became a leading exponent of the ' grotesque ' school of contemporary drama. Among his plays are *Six Characters in Search of an Author* (1920), *Enrico IV* (1922) and *Come Tu Mi Vuoi* (1930). In 1925 he established a theatre of his own in Rome and his company took his plays all over Europe. Many of his later plays have been filmed. In 1934 he was awarded the Nobel prize for literature. See study by W. Starkie (1927).

PIRANESI, Giambattista, *pee-ra-nay'zee* (1720–78), Italian architect and copper-engraver of Roman antiquities, was born at Venice. He worked in Rome producing innumerable etchings of the city both in ancient times and in his own day. See studies by Mayor (1952) and H. Thomas (1954).

PIRE, Georges, *peer* (1910–69), Belgian priest, born at Dinant, lectured in moral philosophy at Louvain (1937–47) and was awarded the Croix de Guerre for resistance work as priest and intelligence officer in the second World War and in 1958 the Nobel Peace prize for his scheme of ' European villages ', including ' Anne Frank village ', in Germany, for elderly refugees and destitute children. See his Autobiography (trans. 1960).

PIRON, Alexis, *pee-rõ* (1689–1773), French poet, playwright and wit, born at Dijon, who, according to his own epitaph, ' was nothing, not even an Academician '. See Saintsbury's *Miscellaneous Essays* (1892).

PISANO, (1) **Andrea** (*c.* 1270–1349), Italian sculptor, born at Pontedera, became famous as a worker in bronze and a sculptor in marble, settling in Florence. In 1347 he worked in the cathedral at Orvieto on reliefs and statues.

(2) **Giovanni** (*c.* 1250–*c.* 1320), Italian sculptor, assisted his father (3). He built the fine pulpit in Pisa cathedral and for several years worked on Siena cathedral.

(3) **Niccola** (*c.* 1225–*c.* 1284), Italian

sculptor of Pisa, father of (2), executed three works still admired for their excellence—the pulpit of the baptistery at Pisa (1260), the shrine of St Dominic for a church at Bologna (1267) and the pulpit of Siena cathedral (1268). He was also an architect and engineer.

(4) **Vittore**, or **Antonio Pisanello** (*c.* 1395–*c.* 1455), born at San Visilio, was both fresco-painter and medallist and also was noted for his drawings of animals.

PISISTRATUS, Gr. **Peisistratos**, *pī-sis'trĕ-tus* (*c.* 600–527 B.C.), 'tyrant' of Athens, acted at first with his kinsman Solon, but soon became leader of a people's party in Attica, eager for equality of political privileges. In 560, with a band of personal followers, he seized the Acropolis. The leaders of the aristocratic party fled, but returned in 554 and drove Pisistratus into exile (552). Supported by Thebes and Argos, he in 541 landed at Marathon, and marched on the capital. At Pallene he completely defeated his opponents, and thenceforward lived in undisturbed possession of power, transmitting at his death his supremacy to his sons, Hippias and Hipparchus, the *Pisistratidae*. He enforced obedience to the laws of Solon, emptied the city of its poorest citizens, making them agriculturists, and secured provision for old and disabled soldiers.

PISSARRO, *pee-sa-rō*, (1) **Camille** (1830–1903), French Impressionist artist, born at St Thomas, West Indies, went in 1855 to Paris, where he was much influenced by Corot's landscapes. In 1870 he lived in England for a short time, this being the first of several visits. Most of his works were painted in the countryside round Paris, and he lived at Pontoise from 1872 to 1884. In the next year he met Signac and Seurat and for the next five years adopted their divisionist style. Pissarro was the leader of the original Impressionists, and the only one to exhibit at all eight of the Group exhibitions in Paris from 1874 to 1886. He had considerable influence on Cézanne and Gauguin at the beginning of their artistic careers. His famous painting of the *Boulevard Montmartre* by night (1897) is in the National Gallery, London. See his *Letters to his son Lucien*, edited in 1943 by J. Rewald.

(2) **Lucien** (1863–1944), French painter, designer, wood-engraver and printer, son of (1), came to England in 1890, founded (1894) the Eragny press, designed types, and painted landscapes, showing the divisionist touch.

PISTON, **Walter** (1894–), American composer of Italian descent, born in Rockland, Me., trained as an artist, first took a serious interest in music as a student at Harvard. He later studied in Paris under Nadia Boulanger and returned to Harvard as professor of Music. He has produced books on harmony, counterpoint and orchestration. His compositions are in a modern, neoclassical style that includes elements from jazz and popular music.

PITCAIRN, **Robert** (1793–1855), Scottish writer and antiquary, born in Edinburgh, was editor of *Criminal Trials in Scotland, 1484–1624* (1830–33). He held a post in the Register House at Edinburgh.

PITCAIRNE, **Archibald** (1652–1713), Scottish physician and satirist, born in Edinburgh, practised medicine there before being appointed in 1692 professor at Leyden. Returning to Edinburgh in 1693, he was notorious as a Jacobite, an Episcopalian and satirist of Presbyterianism. He founded the medical faculty at Edinburgh and his medical writings appeared in 1701 under the title of *Dissertationes medicae*. See Life by Webster (1781).

PITMAN, **Sir Isaac** (1813–97), English inventor of a shorthand system, was born at Trowbridge, Wiltshire. First a clerk, he became a schoolmaster at Barton-on-Humber (1832–36) and at Wotton-under-Edge, where he issued his *Stenographic Sound Hand* (1837). Dismissed from Wotton because he had joined the New (Swedenborgian) Church, he conducted a school at Bath (1839–43). Henceforward his career is the history of the development of shorthand and spelling reform. In 1842 he brought out the *Phonetic Journal*, and in 1845 opened premises in London. He was knighted in 1894. See Life by A. Baker (1908).

PITSCOTTIE, **Robert Lindsay of** (*c.* 1500–65), Scottish historian, born at Pitscottie near Cupar, was the author of *The Chronicles of Scotland, 1436–1565*. His style is quaint and graphic, and his facts trustworthy, except where he deals in marvels. The best edition is Mackay's (1899–1911).

PITT, (1) **Thomas** (1653–1726), son of the rector of Blandford, became a wealthy East India merchant, governor of Madras, and purchaser for £20,400 of the Pitt Diamond, which he sold in 1717 to the French regent to become one of the state jewels of France. In 1791 it was valued at £480,000. His eldest son, Robert, was father of the Earl of Chatham (q.v.); his second, Thomas (*c.* 1688–1729), was first Earl of Londonderry.

(2) **William, the Elder.** See CHATHAM.

(3) **William** (1759–1806), English statesman, second son of the Earl of Chatham, was born at Hayes near Bromley. He was never sent to school, but entered Pembroke Hall, Cambridge, at fourteen. From his youth he was trained for political life. He became an excellent classical scholar, but he valued the classical writers mainly as a school of language and of taste. He was called to the bar in June 1780, but in September parliament was dissolved, and he stood for Cambridge University, but was rejected. Sir James Lowther, however, gave him a seat for Appleby, and Pitt entered the House of Commons in January 1781. The Tory ministry of Lord North was then tottering under the disasters in America, and confronted by the Old Whigs who followed Rockingham, among them Fox and Burke, and by a smaller body who had been attached to the fortunes of Chatham, such as Shelburne, Camden, and Barré. Pitt threw himself into the fray, and on several occasions assailed the falling ministry, but refused to cast in his lot with the opposition. Upon North's resignation in March 1782 a ministry was formed under Rockingham, but Pitt declined several offers of position. He gave general support to the new ministers, but brought forward the question of parliamen-

tary reform. On July 1, 1782, Rockingham died, and while Fox insisted on the leadership of the Duke of Portland, the king made Shelburne first lord. Fox resigned, and Pitt became chancellor of the Exchequer. Peace negotiations between England and the United States were signed in November and with France and Spain in January 1783, while a truce was established with Holland, and the first steps were taken towards a liberal commercial treaty with the United States. While Pitt's reputation steadily rose, the Shelburne ministry was weak and divided; but Pitt stood loyally by his chief. Two votes of censure directed against the peace were carried through the Commons, and on February 24, 1783, Shelburne resigned. The king implored Pitt, who had displayed splendid parliamentary talents, to accept the leadership, and gave him an absolute authority to name his colleagues. It was a dazzling offer, but he saw clearly that the hour of triumph had not yet come. After a long struggle the king was obliged to yield, and on April 2 a coalition ministry was formed under the Duke of Portland, with Fox and North as joint secretaries of state. Pitt refused his old post of chancellor of the Excheuqer, and as leader of the Opposition brought forward an elaborate scheme of parliamentary reform. He was defeated by 293 to 149, but he succeeded in bringing Fox and North into direct collision. His other measure for the reform of abuses in the public offices passed the Commons, but was rejected in the Lords. A government bill modifying the charter of the East India Company shared a like fate; the ministry refused to resign, and the Commons supported them by large majorities; but the king dismissed them in December 1783, and Pitt took office as chancellor of the Exchequer and first lord of the Treasury. His position seemed hopeless; there was a majority of more than a hundred against him in the Commons, in which Pitt was the only Cabinet minister, while Dundas was the only considerable debater who supported him against the attacks of North, Fox, Burke and Sheridan. But Pitt fought his battle with a skill and resolution never surpassed in parliamentary history. A long succession of hostile votes was carried, but failed to drive him from office, and soon signs appeared that the country was with him. The magnanimity he showed in refusing a great sinecure office added greatly to his popularity. The majorities against him grew steadily smaller. At last, on March 25, 1784, parliament was dissolved, and the ensuing election made Pitt one of the most powerful ministers in all English history, and prepared the way for a ministry which lasted, almost unbroken, for twenty years. Now the House of Commons acquired a new importance in the constitution, the people a new control over its proceedings, and the first lord of the Treasury complete ascendency in the government. The regency question established parliamentary rights. Direct parliamentary corruption was finally put down. Great numbers of sinecure places were abolished, reforms were introduced into revenue methods, and the whole system of taxation and of trade duties was thoroughly revised. The finances of the country, disorganized by the American war, became once more flourishing. An enlightened commercial treaty was negotiated with France. In foreign politics Pitt was for some years equally successful. His love of peace was sincere, but the influence of England in European councils rose greatly, and he showed much tact in extricating England from the ambitious designs of Prussia. But he cast aside too lightly on the first serious opposition parliamentary reform and the abolition of the slave trade. His attempt to establish free trade between England and Ireland failed through an explosion of manufacturing jealousy in England. More real blame attaches to his opposition to reforming the enormous abuses in the Irish parliament and to his uncertain policy towards the Irish Catholics. He created peerages with extreme lavishness. When the French Revolution broke out his policy was one of absolute neutrality. Reluctantly he drew the sword believing that a struggle with France would be both short and easy. His early military enterprises were badly planned and badly executed but the navy, fostered by him in peace time, was much stronger than that of France. Through fear of the revolutionary spirit, he was led into stern domestic measures. Corn had risen to famine price and great distress prevailed, and the government attempted to meet it by very ill-conceived relaxations of the poor laws. In Ireland Pitt tried first to win the Catholics by measures of conciliation. He then, after the rebellion, suggested a legislative union which, was to be followed by Catholic emancipation, the payment of the priests and a commutation of tithes. The first measure was carried by very corrupt means, but the king declared himself inexorably opposed to Catholic emancipation. Pitt resigned his office into the hands of his follower Addington in February 1801; but a month later he declared that he would abandon Catholic claims and resumed office in May 1804 on this understanding. The war, suspended by the peace of Amiens, had broken out with renewed vehemence. There was danger of invasion, and Pitt desired to combine the most eminent men of all parties in the ministry; but the king's animosity towards Fox lost him Fox's supporters and he was not aided by an alliance with the weak Addington. But with little help from his colleagues Pitt was hailed as the saviour of Europe after the great victory of Trafalgar in 1805. His health was now broken, however, and he died at Putney, and was buried in Westminster Abbey. Pitt was never married, and he never mixed much in general society. Few men possessed to a higher degree the power of commanding, directing and controlling, and he inspired the nation with unbounded confidence. He was one of the first statesmen to adopt the teaching of Adam Smith. His political Life was written by Gifford (1809) and Bishop Tomline (1822); the standard biography is by Lord Stanhope (4th ed. 1879). See Macaulay's essay, books by Sergeant (1882), Walford (1890), Lord

Rosebery (1891), Lord Ashbourne (1899), Whibley (1906), Holland Rose (1911–12, 1926), Sir Charles Petrie (1935).

PITTACUS OF MITYLENE (*c.* 650–570 B.C.), Greek ruler, one of the 'Seven Wise Men' of Greece, whose experience, according to the ancients, was embodied in 'Know thine opportunity' and other aphorisms.

PITTER, Ruth (1897–), English poetess, born at Ilford, Essex, wrote verse from a very early age and later was encouraged by Hilaire Belloc. Her writing belongs to no particular school and for inspiration she has drawn mainly upon the beauty of natural things. In 1955 she was awarded the Queen's Gold Medal for Poetry, having already won the Hawthornden Prize in 1936 with *A Trophy of Arms.* Other volumes include *First and Second Poems* (1927), *A Mad Lady's Garland* (1934), *Urania* (1951) and *The Ermine* (1953).

PITT-RIVERS, Augustus Henry Lane-Fox (1827–1900), English soldier and archaeologist, born in Yorkshire, educated at Sandhurst, worked to improve army small arms training and was a promoter of the Hythe school of musketry, ultimately becoming a lieutenant-general (1882). Having in 1880 inherited Wiltshire estates, rich in Romano-British and Saxon remains, from his great-uncle, Lord Rivers, he devoted himself to archaeology, evolving a new scientific approach to excavation which became a model for later workers. His collections were presented to Oxford museum. He became F.R.S. in 1876, first inspector of ancient monuments in 1882.

PIUS, the name of twelve Roman pontiffs.

Pius I was Bishop of Rome 140–155.

Pius II, named **Enea Silvio de Piccolomini** (1405–64), in youth wrote poems, letters and a novel. At twenty-six he was secretary to the Bishop of Fermo at the Council of Basel, and in 1432–35 was employed on missions to Scotland, England and Germany. He took an office under the Emperor Frederick III, regulated his life, took orders, was made Bishop of Trieste, and after returning to Italy (1456) a cardinal. On the death of Callistus III in 1458 he was elected pope, and took the name of Pius II. His reign is memorable for his efforts to organize an armed confederation of Christian princes to resist the Turkish arms. Aeneas Sylvius was one of the most eminent scholars of his age. His works (Basel 1551) are chiefly historical; his letters throw a vivid light upon their age. See Lives by Voigt (1856–63), Weiss (1897), Boulting (1909), Ady (1913), Creighton's *History of the Papacy* (vol. ii 1882), and Pastor's *History of the Popes* (vol. iii 1895).

Pius IV, named **Giovanni Angelo Medici** (1499–1565), born at Milan, became cardinal in 1549, and pope in 1559. He brought to a close the deliberations of the Council of Trent, and issued (1564) the Creed of Pius IV, or Tridentine Creed.

Pius V, named **Michele Ghislieri** (1504–72), born near Alessandria, became a bishop in 1556, and a cardinal in 1557. As inquisitor-general for Lombardy he rigorously repressed the Reformed doctrines. Pope from 1566, he laboured to restore discipline and morality, and reduced the expenditure of his court. The bull *In Coena Domini* (1568) applies to the 16th century the principles and the legislation of Hildebrand. His bull releasing Queen Elizabeth's subjects from their allegiance (1570) was ineffectual. The most momentous event of his pontificate was the expedition which he organised, with Spain and Venice, against the Turks, resulting in the naval engagement of Lepanto (1571). He was canonized in 1712.

Pius VI, named **Giovanni Angelo Braschi** (1717–99), was born at Cesena, became cardinal in 1773, pope in 1775. To him Rome owes the drainage of the Pontine Marsh, the improvement of the port of Ancona, the completion of St Peter's, the foundation of the New Museum of the Vatican, and the embellishment of the city. The pope repaired to Vienna, but failed to restrain the reforming Emperor Joseph from further curtailing his privileges. Soon after came the French Revolution and the confiscation of church property in France. The pope launched his thunders in vain, and then the murder of the French agent at Rome (1793) gave the Directory an excuse for the attack. Bonaparte took possession of the Legations, and afterwards of the March of Ancona, and extorted (1797) the surrender of these provinces from Pius. The murder of a member of the French embassy in December was avenged by Berthier taking possession of Rome. Pius was called on to renounce his temporal sovereignty, and on his refusal was seized, carried to Siena, the Certosa, Grenoble and finally Valence, where he died.

Pius VII, named **Luigi Barnaba Chiaramonti** (1742–1823), was born at Cesena. He became Bishop of Tivoli, and, already a cardinal, succeeded Pius VI in 1800. Rome was now restored to the papal authority and next year the French troops were withdrawn from most of the papal territory. Pius restored order in his states, and in 1801 concluded a concordat with Napoleon, which the latter altered by autocratic *Articles organiques.* In 1804 Napoleon compelled Pius to come to Paris to consecrate him as emperor. He failed to get any modification of the articles, and soon after his return to Rome the French seized Ancona and entered Rome. This was followed by the annexation (May 1809) of the papal states to the French empire. The pope in June retaliated by excommunicating the robbers of the Holy See. He was next removed to Grenoble, and finally to Fontainebleau, where he was forced to sign a new concordat and sanction the annexation. The fall of Napoleon (1814) allowed him to return to Rome, and the Congress of Vienna restored him his territory. Brigandage was suppressed, as well as secret societies; while the Jesuits were restored. See Life by Mary H. Allies (1872 and 1897).

Pius IX, named **Giovanni Maria Mastai Ferretti** (1792–1878) born at Sinigaglia, took deacon's orders in 1818, in 1827 was made Archbishop of Spoleto, and in 1832 Bishop of Imola. In 1840 he became a cardinal, and on the death of Gregory XVI in 1846 was elected pope. He entered at once on a course of reforms. He granted an amnesty to all political prisoners and exiles, removed most of the disabilities of the Jews, authorized railways, projected a council of state, and in March 1848 published his *Statuto Fondamentale*, a scheme for the temporal government of the papal states by two chambers, one nominated by the pope, the other (with the power of taxation) elected by the people. At first the new pope was the idol of the populace. But the revolutionary fever of 1848 spread too fast for a reforming pope, and his refusal to make war upon the Austrians finally forfeited the affections of the Romans. On November 15, 1848, his first minister, Count Rossi, was murdered, and two days later a mob assembled in the square of the Quirinal. On the 24th the pope escaped to Gaeta, and a republic was proclaimed in Rome. In April 1849 a French expedition was sent to Civita Vecchia; in July General Oudinot took Rome, after a siege of thirty days; and henceforward the papal government was re-established. Pio Nono proved an unyielding Conservative and ultramontane, closely allied with the Jesuits. The war of the French and Sardinians against Austria in 1859 and the popular vote of 1860 incorporated a great part of papal territory with the Sardinian (Italian) kingdom; but Pius always refused to recognize the fact. He re-established the hierarchy in England, sanctioned a Catholic university in Ireland, and condemned the Queen's Colleges. He concluded a reactionary concordat with Austria. By the bull 'Ineffabilis Deus' (1854) he decreed the Immaculate Conception; his famous encyclical 'Quanta Cura' and the Syllabus of errors appeared in 1864. The Vatican Council (1869–70) proclaimed the infallibility of the pope. For the last ten years the pope's temporal power had been only maintained by the French garrison; on its withdrawal in 1870 the soldiers of Victor Emmanuel entered Rome. For the rest of his days the pope lived a voluntary 'prisoner' within the Vatican.

Pius X, named **Giuseppe Sarto** (1835–1914), born at Riese near Venice, and ordained in 1858, became Bishop of Mantua in 1884, in 1893 Cardinal and Patriarch of Venice and in 1903 was elected pope. The separation of church and state in France and Portugal, toleration in Spain, and Pius's attacks on modernism led to strained relations and embarrassments.

Pius XI, named **Achille Ratti** (1857–1939), born at Desio near Milan, was ordained in 1879. Linguist, scholar, alpinist, he was librarian of the Ambrosian (Milan) and Vatican libraries, papal nuncio to Poland, Archbishop of Lepanto, Cardinal Archbishop of Milan in 1921 and pope in 1922. He became sovereign of the Vatican State in 1929.

Pius XII, named **Eugenio Pacelli** (1876–1958), born in Rome, distinguished himself in the Papal diplomatic service and as secretary of state to the Holy See before succeeding Pius XI. He was elected pope in 1939 and during World War II under his leadership the Vatican did much humanitarian work, notably for prisoners of war and refugees. There has been continuing controversy, however, over his attitude to the treatment of the Jews in Nazi Germany, critics arguing that he could have used his influence with Catholic Germany to prevent the massacres, others that any attempt to do so would have proved futile and might possibly have worsened the situation. In the postwar years the plight of the persecuted churchmen in the Communist countries, and the fate of Catholicism there, became the Pope's personal concern. Pius XII was widely respected both in the Catholic and non-Catholic world as a distinguished scholar and as a man of immense moral authority.

PIZARRO, *pee-thar'ō*, (1) **Francisco** (*c.* 1478–1541), **born at Trujillo, served under Gonsalvo di Cordova in Italy.** In 1509 he was at Darien, and he served under Balboa when he discovered the Pacific. In 1526 Pizarro and Almagro sailed for Peru; and, after many misadventures and delays, they reached its port of Tumbes, and collected full information respecting the empire of the Incas. Pizarro repaired to Spain for authority to undertake the conquest, which he got in 1529, he being made captain-general and Almagro marshal. He sailed again from Panamá in December 1531, with 183 men and 37 horses; Almagro was to follow with reinforcements. Landing at Tumbes, the Spaniards commenced the march inland in May 1532, and in November entered Cajamarca. Near this Pizarro captured the Inca Atahualpa by treachery, and after extorting an enormous ransom, amounting to £3,500,000, put him to death, August 29, 1533. Pizarro then marched to Cuzco, set up the young Inca Manco as nominal sovereign, and was himself created a marquis by the Emperor Charles V. Almagro undertook the conquest of Chile, Pizarro was busy founding Lima and other cities on the coast, and his brothers were at Cuzco, when an Indian insurrection broke out. Both Cuzco and Lima were besieged, and Juan Pizarro was killed, but in the spring of 1537 Almagro returned from Chile, raised the siege of Cuzco, and took possession of the city. Pizarro had no intention of allowing his rival to retain Cuzco. Too old to take the field himself, he entrusted the command of his forces to his brothers, who defeated Almagro, April 26, 1538, and beheaded him soon afterwards. One of Almagro's followers, named Juan de Rada, matured a conspiracy for the assassination of Pizarro. The conspirators attacked his house in Lima, and murdered the old conqueror. His brother, Hernando Pizarro, for having beheaded Almagro at Cuzco, was imprisoned until 1560 on his return to Spain. He died in 1578. See Lives by A. Helps (1869) and Towle (1878).

(2) **Gonzalo** (*c.* 1506–48), half-brother of (1), whom he accompanied in the conquest of Peru, and did good service when the Indians besieged Cuzco, and in the conquest of Charcas. In 1539 he undertook an expedition to the eastward of Quito, and endured fearful hardships. One of his lieutenants, Francisco de Orellana, sent in advance for supplies, deserted his starving comrades, discovered the whole course of the Amazon, and returned to Spain. Only 90 out of 350

Spaniards returned with Gonzalo in June 1542. On his brother's assassination Gonzalo retired to Charcas. In 1544 the new viceroy, Vela, arrived in Peru to enforce the 'New Laws'. The Spaniards, dismayed, entreated Gonzalo to protect their interests. He mustered 400 men, entered Lima in October 1544, and was declared governor of Peru; the viceroy Vela was defeated and killed in battle (1546). When news of this revolt reached Spain, Pedro de la Gasca, an able ecclesiastic, was sent to Peru as president to restore order, and landed at Tumbes in June 1547. Gonzalo Pizarro defeated a force sent against him, and met Gasca near Cuzco in April 1548. But his forces deserting him, he gave himself up, and was beheaded at the age of forty-two. See C. R. Markham's *History of Peru* (1892).

PIZZETTI, Ildebrando, *pits-et'ee* (1880–1968), Italian composer, born in Parma. The son of a piano teacher, he studied at Parma Conservatoire, and in 1908 became professor of Harmony and Counterpoint at the Instituto Musicale, Florence. He was director there from 1917 to 1924, when he became director of the Guiseppe Verdi Conservatory, Milan. He won a high reputation as an opera composer with *Fedra* (1912) and *Debora e Jaele* (1923), and in 1936 he succeeded Respighi as professor of Composition at the Accademia di Sancta Cecilia, Rome. He composed extensively in all forms. See Life by G. M. Gatti (1951).

PLACE, Francis (1771–1854), English reformer, born in London, a self-educated London tailor, champion of radicalism and the right of combination, he contrived the repeal of the Combination Laws in 1824 and was a leading figure in the agitation which brought about the passing of the Reform Bill in 1832. Drafter of the People's Charter, and a pioneer of birth-control study, he wrote *The Principle of Population* (1822; ed. Himes, 1930). See Life by Wallas (1898; n.e. 1918).

PLANCHÉ, James Robinson, *plã-shay* (1796–1880), English playwright, antiquary and herald, born, of Huguenot descent, in London. He wrote books on the history of dress, *Regal Records* (1838), *The Pursuivant of Arms* (1852; 3rd ed. 1874), innumerable dramas, burlesques and extravaganzas and his *Recollections and Reflections* (2 vols. 1872). He was made Rouge Croix in 1845 and Somerset herald in 1866.

PLANCK, Max Karl Ernst (1858–1947), German theoretical physicist, the formulator of the quantum theory which revolutionized physics, born April 23 at Kiel, studied at Munich and under Kirchhoff and Helmholtz at Berlin where he succeeded the former in the professorship (1889–1926) and became secretary of the Prussian Academy of Sciences (1912–43) and president of the Kaiser Wilhelm Society (1930–37). His work on the law of thermodynamics and black body radiation led him to abandon classical dynamical principles and formulate the quantum theory (1900), which assumed energy changes to take place in violently abrupt instalments or quanta. This successfully accounted for and predicted certain phenomena inexplicable in the Newtonian theory. Einstein's application of the quantum theory to light (1905) led to the theories of relativity and in 1913 Niels Bohr successfully applied it to the problems of sub-atomic physics. He was awarded the Nobel prize (1918) and in 1926 was elected a foreign member of the Royal Society. One of Planck's sons, **Erwin,** was executed in 1944 for plotting against Hitler.

PLANQUETTE, Robert, *plã-ket* (1850–1903), French composer, born in Paris, and educated at the Conservatoire there, composed *Paul Jones* (1889), and other light operas.

PLANTAGENET, a surname applied to the Angevin family which in 1154 succeeded to the throne of England in the person of Henry II and reigned till Richard III's death. *Plante-geneste* was the nickname of Geoffrey, Count of Anjou, husband of Matilda, daughter of Henry I—possibly from the sprig of broom (*planta genista*) which he wore in his cap, possibly because he used a broom-switch in penance, possibly from the village of Le Genest in Maine. The first to use *Plantaginet* (*sic*) as his family name, was Richard, Duke of York, in 1460, in laying claim to the crown. But the sovereigns called Plantagenet kings are Henry II, Richard I, John, Henry III, Edward I–III, Richard II, Henry IV–VI, Edward IV–V and Richard III. See study by J. Harvey (1948).

PLANTÉ, Gaston, *plã-tay* (1834–89), French physicist, born at Orthy, followed up Ritter's discovery of the secondary cell and constructed the first practical storage battery (1860).

PLANTIN, Christophe, *plã-tĩ* (1514–89), French printer, born at St Avertin near Tours, settled as bookbinder at Antwerp in 1549; six years later he began to print. His *Biblia Polyglotta* (1569–73), his Latin, Hebrew and Dutch Bibles, and his editions of the classics are all famous. His printing-houses in Antwerp, Leyden and Paris were carried on by his sons-in-law. His office in Antwerp, bought by the city in 1876, is now the 'Musée Plantin'. See French works by M. Rooses (2nd ed. 1892), A. de Backer and C. Ruelens (1866), L. Degeorge (3rd ed. 1886), C. Clair (1960), and Plantin's *Correspondence* (1884–86).

PLANUDES, Maximus, *pla-nyoo'deez* (*c.* 1260–1310), a monk of Constantinople, sent as ambassador to Venice in 1296. His tasteless Anthology of poetry (Florence 1494), from that of Cephalas (10th century), was the only one known in the West until 1606. See his Letters, edited by Treu (Breslau 1890).

PLASKETT, John Stanley (1865–1941), Canadian astronomer, born at Woodstock, Ontario, was a graduate of Toronto University. At the Dominion Observatory, Ottawa, his work included research in spectroscopy and improvements in the design of the spectrograph. In 1918 the Dominion astrophysical observatory was built at Victoria to accommodate a huge telescope with a 72-inch reflector which he had designed. He was director here until he retired in 1935. During these years important investigations were carried out into motion and matter in interstellar space and results included the discovery of the largest known star which was named Plaskett's star.

PLATEAU, Joseph Antoine Ferdinand, *plah-tō* (1801–83), Belgian physicist, born in Brussels, became professor of Physics at Ghent (1835). In his study of optics he damaged his own eyesight by looking into the sun for twenty seconds in order to find out the effect on the eye. By 1840 he was blind, but continued his scientific work with the help of others. He was the discoverer of the tiny second drop, named after him, which always follows the main drop of a liquid falling from a surface.

PLATO (*c.* 427–*c.* 347 B.C.), Athenian philosopher, one of the supremely great philosophical geniuses of all time, born possibly in Athens, of an aristocratic family, but little is known of his early life. He saw military service in the Peloponnesian war, became a disciple of Socrates (q.v.), attended the latter's trial at the hands of the Democrats (399) and immortalized the latter's attitude and manner of death in three of his dialogues: *Apology*, or defence of his tutor; *Crito* on Socrates' willingness to die; and *Phaedo* on immortality. Socrates appears in most of Plato's 35 dialogues, but increasingly he becomes the spokesman not of Socratic but of Platonic doctrines. Plato spent some time at Megara in company with the Eleatic philosopher, Euclides, and from 390 possibly visited Egypt, was certainly at Cyrene with Theodorus, the mathematician, toured the Greek cities in Southern Italy, where he imbibed Pythagorean doctrines and at Syracuse converted Dion, son-in-law of the tyrant Dionysus I, to his ideology of the philosopher-king. In 388 Plato founded his own school, the original 'Academy' in the western suburbs of Athens in which mathematical and political studies were carried on. In 368 he returned to Syracuse at Dion's request to convert the fickle Dionysus II, but they soon quarrelled and Plato, after a second visit, gave it up. He died, in his eighty-first year, at a wedding feast. The chronology of the dialogues is a vexed subject, but stylistic considerations allow the following approximate groupings: (1) The early, truly Socratic (' what is it? ') dialogues in which the main interest is definition as, for example, of self-knowledge in *Charmides*, courage in *Laches*, piety in *Euthyphro*, virtue equated with knowledge in *Protagoras* and which include the above mentioned. (2) The middle dialogues in which Plato increasingly outlines his own characteristic doctrines, including the *Meno*, possibly the *Timaeus*, outlining Plato's Pythagorean cosmology with time as ' the moving image of eternity ' and the celebrated *Republic.* This, the first blueprint Utopia in history, examines the nature of justice, which eludes the tripartite division of the soul (wisdom, spiritedness or courage, and restrained passions) and which Plato's Socrates hopes to find ' in the larger letters of the state '. For, to this division conveniently correspond the three principal classes of the ideal state, the guardians, the military and the workers. Justice results when all these work in harmony. Plato's ideal state is static, a closed society without class mobility achieved by the propagation of convenient myths. The guardians, however, must be carefully trained and brought up to live in a Spartan communism, in which women share all the men's tasks for which they are fitted, marriages take place on certain festival days and are arranged ostensibly by lot, but rigged on eugenic principles, the offspring brought up anonymously by the state. This aristocracy may decline, first, into timocracy or government of honour by the military, then oligarchy or government of wealth, followed inevitably after the revolution of the poverty-stricken masses by democracy, the least desirable form of government barring tyranny, which necessarily follows. The education of the guardians brings Plato to his famous theory of ideas, or forms. He distinguishes sharply between the sphere of transient, finite, fickle particulars or objects of sense impressions, fit data only for opinion and belief, and that of the timeless, unchanging universal exemplars of the former, the forms, which are the true objects of knowledge. The unphilosophical man, at the mercy only of his sense-impressions is like a prisoner in a cave, who mistakes the shadows on the wall for reality. True knowledge is the apprehension of the universal forms. There is, for example, a universal form, ' table ', which subsumes all the particular tables to be found in the world of sense impressions. Since art is essentially imitation of particulars it is therefore twice removed from reality and therefore doubly misleading. Artists are to be given applause but must be instantly deported from the Republic. (3) The later dialogues are remarkable for Plato's rigorously philosophical self-criticism unequalled among philosophers with the possible exception of Wittgenstein. The theory of forms, except in the *Phaedrus* on sexual love, becomes less prominent and undergoes devastating criticism in the *Parmenides*. It is modified to a theory of types, the relationship of ' participation ' between forms and particulars is examined, but the logical problem of predication inherent in all this and unsuccessfully attempted in the *Sophist* awaits Aristotle. The *Theaetetus* examines perception, the *Laws*, considerably modify the political doctrines of the *Republic*, and the *Symposium* on love, reveals Plato, the poet. But all the dialogues are equally works of literature and philosophy. From the former standpoint, the translations by B. Jowett (new ed. 1925) are best, from the latter, F. M. Cornford's translations of *Theaetetus* and *Sophist* entitled *Plato's Theory of Knowledge* (1933), of *Timaeus*, entitled *Plato's Cosmology* (1937), of *Parmenides*, entitled *Plato and Parmenides* (1939), and the *Republic* (trans. 1941), are preferable. Of the *Epistles*, 6th, 7th, 8th are now generally regarded as authentic. Plato's influence is universal. It extends first through his great disciple and critic Aristotle, through the Stoics into Christian theology via Philo Judaeus (q.v.), was repeatedly revived beginning with the rediscovery of Plato's works (except for the *Timaeus* never lost) at the Renaissance when Aristotelian scholasticism was under attack, and by various Platonist and Neo-Platonist movements since. Rationalist and Idealist schools owe much to Plato, who successfully merged two opposing strands of Greek philosophy, the logical 'one' of Parmenides and the 'flux' ('the many') of Heraclitus into one comprehensive metaphysical thesis. See biographical studies by A. E. Taylor (1929) and G. C. Field (1930), studies of the *Republic* by N. R. Murphy (1951), R. L. Nettleship, ed. Benson (1955), on the *Phaedrus* by R. Hackforth (1952), on the *Phaedo*, by R. S. Bluck (1955), on the theory of ideas by Sir W. D. Ross (1951), ethics (1928), education (1947), art (1953), by R. C. Lodge, and general studies by E. Zeller (trans. 1888), J. Burnet, *Greek Philosophy* (1914), G. M. A. Grube (1935), W. W. Jaeger, *Paideia* (trans. 1944), D. J. Allan (1952), W. L. Robinson (1953), R. B. Levinson (1953), R. C. Lodge (1956), R. E. Cushman (1958), P. Friedländer (trans. 1958), also critical works, Cherniss, *Aristotle's Criticisms of the Academy*, K. R. Popper, vol. i, *The Open Society and Its Enemies* (1945), and R. H. S. Crossman, *Plato Today* (new ed. 1959).

PLATOV, Matvei Ivanovich, Count (1757–1818), born at Azov, served in the Turkish campaign of 1770–71, and in 1801 was named by Alexander I 'Hetman of the Cossacks of the Don'. He took part in the campaigns against the French (1805–07), and hung on their retreat from Moscow with pitiless pertinacity (1813), defeating Lefebvre at Altenburg, gaining a victory at Laon, and making his name memorable by the devastations of his hordes of semi-savages.

PLAUTUS, Titus Maccius (wrongly *M. Accius*) (*c*. 250–184 B.C.), the chief comic poet of Rome, was born at Sarsina in Umbria. It is probable that he went to Rome while still young, and acquired there his mastery of the most idiomatic Latin. At Rome he found employment in connection with the stage, and saved money enough to enable him to leave Rome and start in business on his own account in foreign trade. His plays evince close familiarity with seafaring life and adventure, and an intimate knowledge of all the details of buying and selling and book-keeping. He failed, however, in business, and returned to Rome in such poverty that he had to earn his livelihood in the service of a baker by turning a handmill. While in this humble calling he wrote three plays which he sold to the managers of the public games. The price paid him enabled him to leave the mill, and he spent the rest of his life at Rome. Probably he commenced to write about 224 B.C., and, until his death, he continued to produce comedies with wonderful fecundity. His plays appear to have been left in the hands of the actors, who probably interpolated and omitted passages to suit them for the stage. Almost all the prologues were written after his death. About 130 plays were attributed to him in the time of Gellius, who held most of them to be the work of earlier dramatists revised and improved by Plautus. Roman critics considered most of them spurious. Varro limited the genuine comedies to twenty-one; and these so-called 'Varronian comedies' are the same which we now possess, the *Vidularia* being fragmentary. Plautus's plays were immensely popular, and were acted, as Arnobius tells us, in the time of Diocletian, five centuries later. Plautus borrowed his plots to a large extent from the New Attic Comedy, which dealt with social life to the exclusion of politics. But he infused a new and robuster life, which was typically Roman. His perfect spontaneity, vivacity and vigour of language, and the comic power of his dialogues, are his own. The charm of Plautus, lying in his genuine humour and powerful grasp of character, goes deep down to the roots of human nature. Shakespeare adapted the *Menaechmi* as *The Comedy of Errors*. Molière's *L'Avare* is borrowed from the *Aulularia*. English translations are by Thornton and Warner (1767–74), H. T. Riley (1880), Sugden (1895), Sir R. Allison (5 plays, 1914). Ritschl restored the very corrupt text (2nd ed. 1871); Goetz and Schoell completed his work (1892–96). The Loeb Library edition (5 vols. 1916 *et seq.*) has a trans. by Nixon.

PLAYFAIR, (1) John (1748–1819), Scottish mathematician and geologist, born at Benvie near Dundee, studied at St Andrews, and in 1773 became minister of Liff and Benvie. In 1785 he became joint professor of Mathematics at Edinburgh, but he exchanged his chair for that of Natural Philosophy in 1805. He was a strenuous supporter of the Huttonian theory in geology, and travelled much to make observations. Besides his famous *Illustrations of the Huttonian Theory* (1802), he wrote *Elements of Geometry* (1795) and *Outlines of Natural Philosophy* (1812–16).

(2) **Lyon, 1st Baron Playfair** (1819–98), British scientist, born at Meerut, studied at St Andrews, Glasgow, London and Giessen, was manager of textile-printing works at Clitheroe 1840–43, Edinburgh Chemistry professor 1858–68, Liberal M.P. from 1868, postmaster-general 1873–74, vice-president of council 1886. He was created a peer in 1829. He wrote on chemistry and political economy.

(3) **Sir Nigel Ross** (1874–1934), English actor-manager and producer, was born in London. First a barrister, he went on the stage and from 1902 to 1918 was a successful character actor. Becoming in 1919 manager of the Lyric Theatre, Hammersmith, he was responsible for a long series of successful productions, many of which were drawn from 18th-century comedy. Outstanding of these was *The Beggar's Opera*, produced with an original artistry, and others included *The Duenna* and *The Rivals*. He wrote *The Story of the Lyric Theatre, Hammersmith* (1925) and *Hammersmith Hoy* (1930). See G. Playfair, *My Father's Son* (1937).

(4) **William Henry** (1789–1857), Scottish architect, born in London, nephew of (1), designed Donaldson's Hospital, the National Monument, National Gallery, and many other Edinburgh buildings.

PLEKHANOV, Georgi Valentinovich, *ple-kah'nof* (1857–1918), Russian Marxist revolutionary, born in Tambov province, joined the Narodnist Populist movement as a student and in 1876 led the first popular demonstration in St Petersburg. In 1883 he helped to found the League for the Emancipation of Labour and spent the years 1883–1917 in exile in Geneva. From 1889 to 1904 he was Russian delegate to the Second International.

With Lenin, whose revolutionary mentor he was, he edited the journal *Spark* (1900). After the Bolshevik-Menshevik break, he supported the latter faction, returning to Russia in 1917, where he edited a paper. He died in Finland. His commentaries on Marxist theory fill 26 volumes.

PLETHON, Georgios Gemistos, *plee'thon* (*c.* 1355–1450), Greek scholar, probably a native of Constantinople, was counsellor in the Peloponnesus to Manuel and Theodore Palaeologus, and was sent to the Council of Florence in 1439. Here, if he did little for the union of the Churches, he did much to spread a taste for Plato.

PLEVEN, René Jean, *ple-vã* (1901–), French statesman, born in Brittany, studied law and became managing director of the International Cable Company. During World War II he served with the Free French air force and in the French National Committee in London. In French governments after 1944 he was successively minister of finances, minister of defence and he was prime minister July 1950-Feb. 1951 and Aug. 1951-Jan. 1952.

PLEYEL, Ignaz Joseph, *plī'el* (1757–1831), Austrian composer, born near Vienna, in 1783 became *kapellmeister* of Strasbourg Cathedral. In 1791 he visited London, in 1795 opened a music shop in Paris and in 1807 added a pianoforte manufactory. His forgotten compositions include quartets, concertos and sonatas.

PLIMSOLL, Samuel (1824–98), English social reformer, known as 'the sailors' friend', was born at Bristol, and in 1854 started business in the coal trade in London. Shortly afterwards he began to interest himself in the dangers affecting the mercantile marine. He accumulated a mass of facts proving that the gravest evils resulted from the employment of unseaworthy ships, from overloading, undermanning, bad stowage and over-insurance. He entered parliament for Derby in 1868; but it was not until he had published *Our Seamen* (1873) and had made an appeal to the public that the Merchant Shipping Act (1876) was passed, by which, *inter alia*, every owner was ordered to mark upon his ship a circular disc (the 'Plimsoll Mark'), with a horizontal line drawn through its centre, down to which the vessel might be loaded. He retired from parliamentary life in 1880. In 1890 he published *Cattle-ships*, exposing the cruelties and dangers of cattle-shipping. See Japp, *Good Men and True* (1890).

PLINY, (1) **Gaius Plinius Secundus** (A.D. 23–79), the Elder, came of a North Italian stock possessing estates at Novum Comum (*Como*), where he was born. He was educated in Rome, and when about twenty-three entered the army and served in Germany. He became colonel of his regiment (a cavalry one), and while attentive enough to his military duties to write a treatise on the throwing of missiles from horseback and to compile a history of the Germanic wars, he made a series of scientific tours in the region between the Ems, Elbe and Weser, and the sources of the Danube. Returning to Rome in 52, he studied for the bar, but withdrew to Como, and devoted himself to readnig and authorship. Apparently for the guidance of his nephew, he wrote his *Studiosus*, a treatise defining the culture necessary for the orator, and the grammatical work, *Dubius Sermo*. By Nero he was appointed procurator in Spain, and through his brother-in-law's death (71) he became guardian of his sister's son, Pliny the Younger, whom he adopted. Vespasian, whom he had known in Germany, was now emperor, and was henceforth his most intimate friend; but court favour did not wean him from study, and he brought down to his own time the history of Rome by Aufidius Bassus. A model student, amid metropolitan distraction he worked assiduously, and by lifelong application filled the 160 volumes of manuscript which, after using them for his *Historia Naturalis* (77), he bequeathed to his nephew. In 79 he was in command of the Roman fleet stationed off Misenum when the great eruption of Vesuvius was at its height. Eager to witness the phenomenon as closely as possible, he landed at Stabiae (*Castellamare*), but had not gone far when he succumbed to the stifling vapours rolling down the hill. His *Historia Naturalis* alone of his many writings survives. Under that title the ancients classified everything of natural or non-artificial origin. Pliny adds digressions on human inventions and institutions, devoting two books to a history of fine art, and dedicates the whole to Titus. His observations, made at second-hand, show no discrimination between the true and the false, between the probable and the marvellous, and his style is inartistic, sometimes obscure. But he supplies us with information on an immense variety of subjects as to which, but for him, we should have remained in the dark.

(2) **Gaius Plinius Caecilius Secundus** (A.D. 62–*c.* 114), the Younger, was born at Novum Comum. He wrote a Greek tragedy in his fourteenth year, and made such progress under Quintilian that he became noted as one of the most accomplished men of his time. His proficiency as an orator enabled him at eighteen to plead in the Forum, and brought him much practice. Then he served as military tribune in Syria, where he frequented the schools of the Stoic Euphrates and of Artemidorus; at twenty-five, the earliest possible age, he was *quaestor Caesaris*, then praetor, and afterwards consul in 100 A.D., in which year he wrote his laboured panegyric of Trajan. In 103–5 he was propraetor of the Provincia Pontica, and, among other offices, held that of curator of the Tiber, chiefly for the prevention of floods. He married twice; his second wife, Calpurnia, is fondly referred to in one of his most charming letters for the many gifts and accomplishments with which she sweetened his rather invalid life. He died without issue about 114. It is to his letters that Pliny owes his assured place in literature as a master of the epistolatory style. His meaning, though never obscure, is generally fuller than his expression; and, reading between the lines, we discern the features of a truly lovable man, much given to hospitality, and always pleased to help a less favoured brother, such as Suetonius or Martial. We derive from

him many of our most distinct impressions of the life of the upper class in the 1st century; above all, it is from his correspondence with Trajan that we get our clearest knowledge of how even the most enlightened Romans regarded the then obscure sect of the Christians and their 'depraved and extravagant superstition'. Keil's text of the *Epistles* and *Panegyricus* (1853) is the best; a useful selection with a good commentary was published by Church and Brodribb (1871). Melmoth's translation of the Letters (1746), revised by W. M. L. Hutchinson, is given with the text in the Loeb Classical Library (1915).

PLOMER, William Charles Franklin (1903–), British writer, born at Pietersburg, Transvaal, educated at Rugby, was a farmer and trader in South Africa before turning author, and also lived a while in Greece and Japan. With Roy Campbell (q.v.) he ran a South African literary review, and in World War II he served at the Admiralty. His works include the novels *Turbott Wolfe* (1926), *Sado* (1931) and *Ali the Lion* (1936); collections of short stories *I Speak of Africa* (1928) and *Paper Houses* (1929); and *Collected Poems* (1960). He edited the diaries of Francis Kilvert (q.v.). See his autobiographical *Double Lives* (1943).

PLOTINUS, *plo-tī'-* (205–270), one of the first and most original of Neoplatonic philosophers, born possibly at Lycopolis in Egypt, in 242 joined Gordianus's expedition to Persia, in order to study philosophy there and in India, but after the emperor's assassination in Mesopotamia, barely escaped to Antioch. In 244 he settled in Rome and became a popular lecturer in Neopythagorean and Neoplatonic doctrines, advocating asceticism and the charms of a contemplative life. Many of his wealthy patrons gave away their wealth to the poor, and freed slaves in response to his appeal of ascetic piety. When sixty years old, he attempted to found with the help of the emperor Gallienus a platonic 'Republic' in Campania, but died at Minturnae. His fifty-four works were edited by his pupil Porphyry, or Malchus, who arranged them in six groups of nine books or *Enneads*. Plotinus's system combines the various pre-Socratic schools of Greek philosophy, Aristotelian metaphysics, Platonism and Stoicism with an oriental theory of Emanation. He postulates a trinity, with The One, or God at the top, Spirit or intellectual principle second and lastly the soul, or author of all living things. The last is subdivided into an inner and an outer, the first intent upwards on spirit, the second facing down to the degenerte world of matter. He greatly influenced early Christian theology and some German Idealist schools of philosophy. See translations by S. MacKenna (1917), study by W. R. Inge (1918) and F. Copleston's *History of Philosophy*, vol. i (1947).

PLOWDEN, Edmund (1518–85), English Catholic lawyer, was born in Shropshire and educated at Cambridge. He sat in parliament in the reign of Queen Mary, retiring with thirty-nine other members over the question of heresy laws. One of the ablest lawyers of his day, from 1561 to 1571 he was treasurer of the Middle Temple. His excellent commentaries were first published in 1571. A fine monument was erected to him in Temple church.

PLÜCKER, Julius (1801–68), German mathematical physicist, born at Elberfeld, was professor of Mathematics at Bonn (1836) and of Physics (1847). He investigated diamagnetism, originated the idea of spectrum analysis, and in 1859 discovered cathode rays, produced by electrical discharges in gases at low pressures.

PLUME, Thomas (1630–1704), English divine, born at Maldon, educated at Chelmsford and Christ's College, Cambridge, was vicar of Greenwich from 1658 and Archdeacon of Rochester from 1679. He endowed an observatory and the Plumian chair of astronomy and experimental philosophy at Cambridge, and bequeathed his extensive library to the town of Maldon, where it still exists intact. See Deed and Francis, *Catalogue of the Plume Library* (1959).

PLUMER, Herbert Charles Onslow, 1st Baron (1857–1932), British soldier and administrator, served in Sudan (1884), led the Rhodesian relief force to Mafeking (1900), and greatly distinguished himself as commander of the 2nd army, B.E.F. (1915–18), notably at the great attack on Messines, and G.O.C. Italian Expeditionary Force (1917–1918). He was made a field-marshal in 1919, was governor of Malta 1919–24, and high commissioner for Palestine 1925–28. See Life by C. Harington (1935).

PLUMPTRE, Edward Hayes, D.D. (1821–91), English divine, born in London, took a double first in 1844 from University College, Oxford, and was elected a fellow of Brasenose. He became a professor at King's College, London (1853), a prebendary of St Paul's (1863), principal of Queen's College, Harley Street (1875), and Dean of Wells (1881). He wrote on theology, and made verse translations of Sophocles, Aeschylus and Dante, as well as original verse.

PLUNKET, William Conyngham, 1st Baron Plunket (1764–1854), Irish lawyer, born at Enniskillen, opposed the Union (1798), prosecuted Emmett (1803), and rose to be lord chancellor of Ireland (1830–41).

PLUNKETT, Sir Horace Curzon (1854–1932), Irish agricultural reformer, third son of Lord Dunsany, after Eton and Oxford was for ten years on a cattle ranch, and from 1889 promoted agricultural cooperation in Ireland, being the founder in 1894 of the Irish Agricultural Organization Society. He was M.P. for Dublin Co. (S.) 1892–1900, vice-president of the Irish Department of Agriculture 1899–1907, and chairman of the Irish Convention 1917–18. He was a senator of the Irish Free State 1922–23. See Life by Digby (1950).

PLUTARCH, Gr. Ploutarchos (*c.* A.D. 46–*c.* 120), Greek historian, biographer and philosopher, was born at Chaeroneia in Boeotia. His higher education was commenced at Athens in 66. He paid more than one visit to Rome—once as *chargé d'affaires* of his native town—and there gave public lectures in philosophy. He spent all his mature life at his native place. His extant writings comprise his historical works, and those which are grouped under the general head of *Opera Moralia.* To the former belong his *Parallel Lives*—the work by which he is best known. These contain a gallery of forty-six portraits of the great characters of the ages preceding his own. They were published in successive books, each pair forming one book, and a Greek and Roman, with some resemblance between their respective careers, being chosen for the subject of each. The sequels which come after most of the Lives, giving a detailed comparison of each warrior, statesman, legislator or hero, are regarded as spurious by some critics. Plutarch's *Biographies* are monuments of great literary value for the precious materials which they contain, based as they are on lost records. The author adheres throughout to his professed purpose —portraiture of character; he either omits or briefly touches upon the most famous actions or events which distinguish the career of each subject of his biography, holding that these do not show a man's virtues or failings so well as some trifling incident, word or jest. The other and less known half of his writings —the *Morals*—are a collection of short treatises, sixty or more (though certainly not all from Plutarch's hand), upon various subjects—*Ethics, Politics, History, Health, Facetiae, Love-stories, Philosophy* and *Isis and Osiris.* Some of the essays breathe quite a Christian spirit, although the writer probably never heard of Christianity. The nine books of his *Symposiaca* or Table-talk exhibit him as the most amiable and genial of boon companions; while his dialogue *Gryllus* reveals a remarkable sense of humour. Though not a profound thinker, Plutarch was a man of rare gifts, and occupies a unique place in literature as the encyclopaedist of antiquity. There are translations of the *Lives* by the brothers Langhorne and one sponsored by Dryden (re-ed. Clough, 1859)— neither so scholarly as the French of Jacques Amyot (1559), from which Sir Thomas North (q.v.) made his version (1579). See Oakesmith's *Religion of Plutarch* (1902), Dill's *Roman Society* (1905), Mahaffy's *Silver Age of the Greek World* (1911).

POBEDONOSTSEV, Constantin Petrovich, *-nost'sef* (1827–1907), Russian jurist, son of a Moscow professor, became himself a professor of Civil Law there in 1858 and favoured liberal reforms in the law. Later he reacted against this, becoming strongly opposed to any westernization of Russia, and as procurator of the Holy Synod (from 1880) was the most uncompromising champion of the autocracy and of the supremacy of the orthodox church.

POCAHONTAS (1595–1617), Indian princess, daughter of an Indian chief, Powhatan, twice saved the life of Captain John Smith (q.v.). Cajoled to Jamestown in 1612, she embraced Christianity, was baptised Rebecca, married an Englishman, John Rolfe (1585–1622), in 1613, and came to England with him in 1616. Having embarked for Virginia, she died off Gravesend in March 1617. She left one son, and several Virginia families claim descent from her. See John Smith, *Travels and Works* (2 vols. 1910).

PO CHÜ-I, *paw-jü-ee* (772–846), Chinese poet under the T'ang dynasty, was born in Honan, of which he became governor in 831. He was so noted as a lyric poet that his poems were collected by imperial order and engraved on stone tablets.

POCOCKE, (1) Edward (1604–91), English orientalist, born at Oxford, was elected a fellow of Corpus in 1628. He sailed for Aleppo in 1630 as chaplain to the English factory, but in 1636 became Oxford professor of Arabic, and in 1643 rector of Childrey. He was appointed to the chair of Hebrew in 1648. His main writings were *Specimen Historiae Arabum* (1649) and an edition of Abulfaraj's History (1663).

(2) **Richard** (1704–65), English traveller, born at Southampton, studied at Corpus, Oxford. Precentor successively of Lismore and Waterford, then Archdeacon of Dublin (1745), in 1756 he became Bishop of Ossory, and had just been translated to Meath when he died. His travels, which took up nearly nine years of his life, are described in two folios, dealing with his four years' wanderings in Syria, Egypt and Mesopotamia (1743–45), in a volume on his tours in Scotland (Scot. Hist. Soc., 1887), in two on England (Camden Soc., 1888–89) and in one on Ireland (ed. 1891)—books that are as dull as they are valuable. Pococke was the pioneer of Alpine travel; in 1741 he led a dozen Englishmen to the valley of Chamonix.

PODIEBRAD, George of, *pod'ye-brat* (1420–1471), Bohemian king, born at Podiebrad, became an adherent of the moderate Hussites. When the Catholic barons (1438) carried the election of the Emperor Albert II to the Bohemian crown, Podiebrad allied himself with the Utraquists in Tabor, who offered it to Casimir, king of Poland. After forcing Albert to raise the siege of Tabor and retire to Prague, Podiebrad became leader of the Utraquists, seized Prague (1448), and had himself made regent (1453–57) for the young King Ladislaus. On Ladislaus's death, Podiebrad was crowned his successor in 1458. He succeeded for a while in allaying the bitternesses of religious zeal. In 1462 he decided to uphold the terms of the *compactata* of Prague (1433); this angered Pius II, but the emperor restrained him from excommunicating Podiebrad. The next pope, however, Paul II, excommunicated him in 1466. Matthias Corvinus of Hungary took the field to enforce the ban; but Podiebrad forced him into a truce at Wilamow (1469). Nevertheless Matthias was crowned king by the Catholic barons. Podiebrad left the succession to Bohemia to a Polish prince. See German works by Jordan (1861) and Bachmann (1878), and a French one by Denis (1891).

POE, Edgar Allan (1809–49), American poet and story writer, born at Boston, Mass., and orphaned in his third year, was adopted by John Allan, a wealthy and childless merchant. In 1815–20 the family were in England, and the boy went to school at Stoke Newington. The year 1826 was spent at the University of Virginia; but, offended by his dissipation and gambling debts, his patron removed him to the counting-room, whence he absconded to Boston. He published *Tamerlane and other*

Poems (1827), enlisted that same year, and rose to be sergeant-major in 1829. Mr Allan procured his discharge and after a year's delay his admission to West Point Military Academy (July 1830), but the next March he was dismissed for deliberate neglect of duty. Now he was thrown on his own resources. A third edition of his *Poems* (1831) contained 'Israfel', his earliest poem of value, and 'To Helen'. Of his life in Baltimore during the next two years few records remain. Nearly the first earnings of his pen was the $100 prize won in 1833 by 'A MS. found in a Bottle'. From this time he lived with his aunt, Mrs Clemm, and wrote for the *Saturday Visitor*. His connection with the *Southern Literary Messenger* began with his tale *Berenice* in March 1835; a few months later he went to Richmond as its assistant editor. In May 1836 he married his cousin Virginia. For more than a year he worked hard on the *Messenger*. But he was 'irregular, eccentric and querulous'. He left Richmond in 1837, and after a year or less in New York, of which the chief fruit was *The Narrative of Arthur Gordon Pym*, in 1838 established himself in Philadelphia. Here he published *Tales of the Grotesque and Arabesque* (1840), was connected with Burton's *Gentleman's Magazine* (1839), and for a year (1842–43) edited *Graham's Magazine*. A second prize of $100 was won in 1843 by his wonderful story 'The Gold Bug'. In 1844 he removed to New York, and in *The Evening Mirror* (January 29, 1845) published 'The Raven', which won immediate fame. On January 30, 1847, his wife died. 'The Bells', 'The Domain of Arnheim', the wild 'prose poem' *Eureka* (1848), and a few minor pieces, belong to the brief remainder of his life. He attempted suicide in November 1848, and had an attack of *delirium tremens* in June 1849. Recovering, he spent over two months in Richmond, lecturing there and at Norfolk. He became engaged to a lady of means, and in September went to wind up his affairs in the north. On October 3 he was found in a wretched condition in Baltimore, and died in the hospital. Weird, wild, fantastic, dwelling by choice on the horrible, Poe's genius was yet great and genuine. His short stories show great originality, and from some of them, e.g. 'The Murders in the Rue Morgue', Poe emerges as a pioneer of the modern detective story. The chief charm of his poems is exquisite melody. He deeply impressed Baudelaire and the 'Decadents'. See studies by Lauvrière (Paris 1911), Ransome (1915), Mauclair (1925), Pope-Hennessy (1934), Quinn (1941), Lindsay (1953), Bittner (1963), and Wagenknecht (1963).

POERIO, *pō-ay'ree-ō*, name of two Italian patriots:

(1) **Carlo** (1803–67), born in Naples, in 1848 became director of police, minister of public instruction and deputy for Naples. In July 1849 Ferdinand II had him arrested, and sentenced to twenty-four years in irons; but in 1858 shipped him with other prisoners to America. They persuaded the captain to land them at Cork, and Poerio returned to Turin, where he became a member of parliament, and in 1861 its vice-president.

(2) **Alessandro** (1802–48), brother of (1), devoted himself to poetry, and fell in battle for the liberation of Venice. He was the author of the patriotic poem *Il Risorgimento*.

POGGENDORFF, Johann Christian (1796–1877), German physicist and chemist, became professor of Chemistry at Berlin from 1834. He made discoveries in connection with electricity and galvanism, and invented a multiplying galvanometer. He was the founder of the journal *Annalen der Physik und Chemie* in 1824 and its editor until 1874.

POGGIO, later self-styled **Bracciolini**, *pod-jō* (1380–1459), Florentine humanist, in 1403 became a secretary to the Roman curia. At the Council of Constance (1414–18) he explored the Swiss and Swabian convents for MSS. He recovered MSS. of Quintilian, Ammianus Marcellinus, Lucretius, Silius Italicus, Vitruvius and others. In 1453 he retired to Florence, and became chancellor and historiographer to the republic. His writings include letters, moral essays, a rhetorical Latin *History of Florence*, a series of invectives against contemporaries, and—his most famous book—the *Liber Facetiarum*, a collection of humorous stories, mainly against monks and secular clergy. See Life and Letters by E. Walser (Leipzig 1916), J. A. Symonds, *Renaissance in Italy* (1875), and J. E. Sandys, *History of Classical Scholarship* (1908).

POINCARÉ, *pwĭ-kar-ay*, (1) **Jules Henri** (1854–1912), French mathematician, born at Nancy, Academician (1908), was a savant eminent in mathematics, physics, mechanics and astronomy. His special study was of the theory of functions in which he made important advances. As a philosopher he wrote *Science et hypothèse* (1903) and *Science et méthode* (1908), both of which have English translations. See study by Dantzig (1954).

(2) **Raymond Nicolas Landry** (1860–1934), French statesman, cousin of (1), born at Bar-le-Duc, studied law, became a deputy in 1887, senator 1903, minister of public instruction 1893, 1895, of finance 1894, 1906, premier 1911–13, 1922–24 and 1926–29. He was elected president of the Republic in 1913, remaining in office until 1920. He occupied the Ruhr 1923, and his National Union ministry averted ruin in 1926. Member of the Académie française (1909), he wrote on literature and politics, *Memoirs* (trans. 1925), and *How France is Governed* (1913).

POINSOT, Louis, *pwĭ-sō* (1777–1859), French mathematician, born in Paris, in 1804 became professor of Mathematics at the Lycée Bonaparte. From 1813 an Academician, he wrote *Éléments de la statique* (1803), which was an account of his work on the theory of couples.

POISSON, Siméon Denis, *pwa-sõ* (1781–1840), French mathematician, born at Pithiviers, studied medicine but turned to applied mathematics and became first professor of Mechanics at the Sorbonne. Famous for his researches in mathematical physics, he was made a peer of France in 1837.

POITIERS. See DIANE DE POITIERS.

POLANYI, Michael (1891–), Hungarian

physical chemist and social philosopher born in Budapest, studied there and at Karlsruhe, lectured at Berlin, but emigrated to Britain after Hitler's rise to power and was professor of Physical Chemistry (1933–1948) and of Social Studies (1948–58) at Manchester. He did notable work on reaction kinetics and crystal structure, published *Atomic Reactions* (1932) and wrote much on the freedom of scientific thought, philosophy of science and latterly social science, including *Personal Knowledge* (1958) and *The Study of Man* (1959). He was elected F.R.S. in 1944, and awarded the American Le Comte du Nouy award (1959) for his books on the compatibility of science and religion.

POLE, de la, a family descended from a Hull merchant, whose son Michael (*c.* 1330-89) in 1383 became chancellor, in 1385 was made Earl of Suffolk, and died an exile in France. His grandson, William (1396–1450), was in 1449 raised to be Duke of Suffolk, having since 1445 been practically prime minister. His administration was disastrous; and he was on his way to a five years' banishment in Flanders when he was intercepted off Dover and beheaded. John de la Pole, second Duke (1442–91), married Elizabeth, sister to Edward IV and Richard III and from this marriage sprang John, Earl of Lincoln (*c.* 1464–87), Edmund, Earl of Suffolk (*c.* 1472–1513, executed by Henry VIII), two churchmen, four daughters, and Richard, on whose death at the battle of Pavia (1525) the line became extinct.

POLE, (1) Reginald (1500–58), Archbishop of Canterbury, born at Stourton Castle near Stourbridge, was the son of Sir Richard Pole and Margaret, Countess of Salisbury (1473–1541), daughter of the Duke of Clarence and niece of Edward IV. At nineteen he went to Italy to finish his studies. He returned in 1527, and was then high in Henry VIII's favour. When the question of the divorce was raised, Pole seemed at first disposed to take the king's side; but later expressed disapproval, refused the archbishopric of York, and, going to Italy in 1532, formed intimate friendships with many eminent men eager for an internal reformation of the church. In 1535 he entered into a political correspondence with Charles V, and was now compelled by Henry to declare himself, which he did in a violent letter to the king, afterwards expanded into the treatise *Pro Unitatis Ecclesiasticæ Defensione*. The king withdrew Pole's pension and preferments. Paul III made him a cardinal (1536), and sent him as legate to the Low Countries to confer with the English malcontents. Henry retaliated by setting a price on his head and beheading his mother and other relatives. Pole's several attempts to procure the invasion of England were not successful. In 1541–42 he was governor of the 'Patrimony of St Peter'; and at the Council of Trent (1545) he was one of the presidents. In 1549 he was on the point of being elected pope; after the election of Julius III he lived in retirement until the death of Edward VI, when he was commissioned to Queen Mary as legate *a latere*. Pole was still only in deacon's orders, and cherished the idea of marrying the queen; but Charles V carried the match with his son, Philip of Spain. Pole arrived in London in November 1554, with powers to allow the owners of confiscated church property to retain their possessions. He absolved parliament and country from their schism, and reconciled the Church of England to Rome. As long as Cranmer lived, Pole would not accept the archbishopric of Canterbury, but Pole was ordained priest March 1556, and consecrated archbishop after Cranmer was burnt. Pope Paul IV, indignant at the concessions made by authority of his predecessor to the holders of church property, revived the accusations of heresy formerly brought against Pole. Paul IV was, moreover, now at war with Spain, and could not tolerate Pole as his ambassador at the court of Mary. So his legation was cancelled, and he was summoned before the Inquisition. Mary angrily protested, and the pope relented, but would not reinstate Pole. When the queen died, November 17, 1558, Pole was dangerously ill; he died on the same day. It has been disputed how far he was responsible for Mary's persecution of Protestants; certainly when Pole became the queen's supreme adviser the persecution increased in violence. See his letters, with Life (1744), and other Lives by Beccatelli (trans. 1690 and 1766), Phillipps (1764–67), Hook (*Archbishops of Canterbury*), Zimmermann (1893), Haile (1910), Schenk (1950).

(2) **William** (1814–1900), English engineer and musician, was born at Birmingham. He became professor of Engineering at Bombay (1844–47), at University College, London (1859–67), and (1871–83) was consulting engineer in London for the imperial railways in Japan. He was a high authority on music and whist.

POLIGNAC, *-leen-yak*, an ancient French family to which belonged **Cardinal Melchior de Polignac** (1661–1742), plenipotentiary of Louis XIV at Utrecht (1712) and French minister at Rome. **A Duchesse de Polignac** (1749–93) who died at Vienna, and her husband (died at St Petersburg, 1817), grand-nephew of the cardinal, were among the worst, but unhappily most favoured, advisers of Marie Antoinette, and were largely responsible for the shameful extravagance of the court. Their son, **Auguste Jules Armand Marie, Prince de Polignac** (1780–1847), born at Versailles, at the Restoration returned to France and became intimate with the Comte d'Artois, afterwards Charles X. In 1820 he was made a prince by the pope, appointed ambassador at the English court in 1823, and in 1829 became head of the last Bourbon ministry, which promulgated the fatal ordinances that cost Charles X his throne. He was condemned to imprisonment for life in the castle of Ham, but was set at liberty by the amnesty of 1836. He took up residence in England, but died in Paris.

POLITIAN, Angelo Ambrogini (1454–94), Italian humanist, born at Montepulciano in Tuscany, and called *Poliziano* from the Italian name of his birthplace, at ten was sent to Florence, and made incredible progress in the ancient languages. By his sixteenth year he had written brilliant Latin and Greek epigrams, at seventeen he began the translation of the *Iliad* into Latin hexameters and, having secured the friendship of the all-powerful Lorenzo de' Medici (whose sons he taught), he was soon recognized as the prince of Italian scholars. At thirty he became professor of Greek and Latin at Florence. Lorenzo's death in 1492 was a serious blow, and he mourned his death in a remarkable Latin elegy. He himself died in Florence, during the temporary supremacy of Savonarola, whose religious zeal was directed against every principle of that pagan revival which it had been the life work of Lorenzo and Politian to forward. Politian was vicious in life, but was a scholar of the first rank and a poet of high merit. Among his works were Latin translations of a long series of Greek authors, and an excellent edition of the *Pandects* of Justinian. His original works in Latin fill a thick quarto, half of which is made up of letters; the rest with miscellanies in prose and verse. His *Orfeo* was the first secular drama in Italian. See J. A. Symonds's *Renaissance in Italy*.

POLK, (1) James Knox (1795–1849), eleventh President of the United States, was born in Mecklenburg county, N.C. He was admitted to the bar in 1820, and in 1823 was elected a member of the legislature of Tennessee, and in 1825 returned to congress as a Democrat. For five years he was Speaker of the House of Representatives. He was in 1839 elected governor of Tennessee, and in 1844 elected president over Henry Clay, mainly because of his 'firm' attitude with regard to the annexation of Texas. In December 1845 Texas was admitted to the Union, and jurisdiction was extended to the disputed territory. The president next forced on hostilities by advancing the American army to the Rio Grande; the capital was taken in September; and by the terms of peace the United States acquired California and New Mexico. The Oregon boundary was settled by a compromise with England. Polk condemned the antislavery agitation, and he was devoted to the Democratic principles of Jefferson and Jackson—state rights, a revenue tariff, independent treasury, and strict construction of the constitution. See Life by Jenkins (1850) and Chase's History of his administration (1850).

(2) **Leonidas** (1806–64), American soldier, was born at Raleigh, N.C. Graduating at West Point in 1827, he held a commission in the artillery, but in 1831 received Holy Orders in the Episcopal Church. In 1838 he was consecrated a missionary bishop of Arkansas, and from 1841 till his death was Bishop of Louisiana, even when at the head of an army corps. In the Civil War he was made major-general by Jefferson Davis. At Belmont, in November 1861, he was driven from his camp by Grant, but finally forced him to retire. At Shiloh and Corinth he commanded the first corps; promoted lieutenant-general, he conducted the retreat from Kentucky. After Chickamauga, where he commanded the right wing, he was relieved of his command; reappointed (December 1863), he opposed Sherman's march. He was killed reconnoitring on Pine Mountain See W. M. Polk's *L. Polk, Bishop and Genera* (1915 ed.).

POLLAIUOLO, Antonio, *pol-lī-wo'lō* (1429–1498), Florentine goldsmith, medallist, metal-caster and painter, cast sepulchral monuments in St Peter's at Rome for Popes Sixtus IV and Innocent VIII. His pictures are distinguished for life and vigour. He was one of the first painters to study anatomy and apply it to his art, and was skilled in suggesting movement. His brother, **Pietro** (1443–1496), was associated with him in his work.

POLLARD, (1) Albert Frederick (1869–1948), English historian, born at Ryde, who, after graduating at Oxford, was assistant editor of *The Dictionary of National Biography*, becoming professor of Constitutional History at London University from 1903 to 1931, founding in 1920 its Institute of Historical Research. From 1908 to 1936 he was a fellow of All Souls, Oxford. Among his many historical works are lives of *Henry VIII* (1902), *Thomas Cranmer* (1904) and *Wolsey* (1929), *A Short History of the Great War* (1920) and *Factors in American History* (1925). The Historical Association was founded by him in 1906 and he was editor of *History* from 1916 to 1922.

(2) **Alfred William** (1859–1944), English scholar and bibliographer, born in London, a graduate of Oxford, was an assistant in the department of printed books at the British Museum and keeper from 1919 to 1924. In 1915 he was appointed reader in Bibliography at Cambridge and professor of English Bibliography at London from 1919 to 1932. An authority on Chaucer and Shakespeare, his contributions to Shakespearean criticism have been invaluable in such scholarly studies as his *Shakespeare Folios and Quartos* (1909) and *Shakespeare's Fight with the Pirates* (1917). Important earlier work on Chaucer had produced *A Chaucer Primer* (1893) and his edition of the Globe *Chaucer* (1898). In 1926 was completed the *Short Title Catalogue of English Books, 1475–1640*, for which he was largely responsible.

POLLIO, Gaius Asinius (76 B.C.–A.D. 4), Roman orator, poet and soldier, sided with Caesar in the civil war, commanded in Spain, and, appointed by Antony to settle the veterans on the lands assigned them, saved Virgil's property from confiscation. He founded the first public library at Rome, and was the patron of Virgil and Horace. His orations, tragedies and history have perished save for a few fragments.

POLLITT, Harry (1890–1960), British Communist politician, was born at Droylesden, Lancs, entered a cotton mill at twelve and joined the I.L.P. at sixteen. Later he became a boilermaker and was a shop steward by the age of twenty-one. He was secretary of the National Minority Movement from 1924 to 1929, when he became secretary of the Communist party of Great Britain. A stormy demagogue, he frequently clashed with authority, being imprisoned for seditious libel in 1925 and being deported from Belfast in 1933. During the Spanish War he helped to found the British battalion of the International Brigade. In 1956 he resigned the secretaryship of the party and became its chairman. See his autobiographical *Serving My Time* (1940).

POLLOCK, (1) an illustrious English family descended from David Pollock, saddler to George III, of which the following, arranged chronologically, were distinguished members.—(1) **Sir David** (1780–1847), eldest son of the saddler, chief-justice of Bombay. (2) **Sir Jonathan Frederick** (1783–1870), brother of (1), passed from St Paul's to Trinity College, Cambridge, and graduated in 1806 as senior wrangler. Next year he was elected a fellow and called to the bar. In 1827 he became K.C.; in 1831 was returned as a Tory for Huntingdon; and was successively attorney-general and chief baron of the Exchequer. He was knighted in 1834, and in 1866 made a baronet. See Life by Lord Hanworth (1929). (3) **Sir George** (1786–1872), field-marshal, third son of the saddler, entered the East India Company's army in 1803. He was engaged at the siege of Bhartpur (1805) and in other operations against Holkar, saw service in the Nepal (Gurkha) campaigns of 1814–16, and in the first Burmese war (1824–26) won his colonelcy. In 1838 he became major-general. After the massacre of General Elphinstone in Afghanistan the Indian government sent him to the relief of Sir Robert Sale in Jelalabad. In April 1842 he forced the Khyber Pass and reached Sir Robert Sale, pushed on to Kabul, defeated Akbar Khan, and recovered 135 British prisoners. Then, joined by Nott, he conducted the united armies back to India, and was rewarded with a G.C.B. and a political appointment at Lucknow. He returned to England in 1846, was director of the East India Company 1854–56, was created a field-marshal in 1870 and a baronet in 1872, and in 1871 was appointed constable of the Tower. See Life by Low (1873). (4) **Sir William Frederick** (1815–88), eldest son of (2), educated at St Paul's and Trinity, in 1838 was called to the bar. He was appointed a master of the Court of Exchequer (1846) and Queen's Remembrancer (1874); in 1876 became senior master of the Supreme Court of Judicature; in 1886 resigned his offices. He published a blank verse translation of Dante (1854) and *Personal Remembrances* (1887). (5) **Sir Charles Edward** (1823–97), fourth son of the first baronet, was a baron of Exchequer, and from 1875 justice of the High Court. (6) **Sir Frederick,** P.C., K.C. (1845–1937), eldest son of (4), third baronet, born in London, was educated at Eton and Trinity, and in 1868 obtained a fellowship. He was called to the bar in 1871, became professor of Jurisprudence at University College, London (1882), Corpus professor of Jurisprudence at Oxford (1883), professor of Common Law in the Inns of Court (1884–90), editor of the Law Reports (1895), judge of Admiralty Court of Cinque Ports (1914). Besides his *Spinoza* (1880), he published *Principles of Contract* (1875), *Digest of the Law of Partnership* (1877), *Law of Torts* (1887), all of which had many editions, *Oxford Lectures* (1891), *History of English Law before Edward I* (with Dr. F. W. Maitland, 1895), *The Etchingham Letters* (with Mrs Fuller-Maitland, 1899), and reminiscences, *For My Grandson* (1933). (7) **Walter Herries** (1850–1926), younger son of (4), was called to the bar in 1874, edited the *Saturday Review* 1884–94, and published *Lectures on French Poets, Verses of Two Tongues, A Nine Men's Morrice, King Zub,* &c. (7) **Sir Charles Edward** (1823–97), fourth son of the first baronet, was a baron of Exchequer, and from 1875 justice of the High Court.

(2) **Jackson** (1912–56), American artist, born in Cody, Wyoming, was the first exponent of tachism or action painting in America. His art developed from surrealism to abstract art and the first drip paintings of 1947. This technique he continued with increasing violence and often on huge canvases as in *One* which is seventeen feet long. Other striking works include *No. 32,* the black and white *Echo* and *Blue Poles.* He was killed in a motor accident.

POLLOK, Robert (1798–1827), Scottish poet, born at Muirhouse, Eaglesham, Renfrewshire, studied at Glasgow for the Secession Church, and in 1824–25 wrote feeble *Tales of the Covenanters,* in 1827 *The Course of Time,* a poetical description of the spiritual life of man. Meantime, seized with consumption, he set out for Italy, but died near Southampton. See Memoir (1843).

POLO, Marco (1254–1324), Venetian traveller, was born of a noble family at Venice, while his father and uncle had gone on a mercantile expedition by Constantinople and the Crimea to Bokhara and to Cathay (China), where they were well received by the great Kublai Khan. The Mongol prince commissioned them as envoys to the pope, requesting him to send 100 Europeans learned in the sciences and arts—a commission they tried in vain to carry out in Italy (1269). The Polos started again in 1271, taking with them young Marco, and arrived at the court of Kublai Khan in 1275, after travelling by Mosul, Baghdad, Khorassan, the Pamír, Kashgar, Yarkand and Khotan, Lob Nor, and across the desert of Gobi, to Tangut and Shangtu. The khan took special notice of Marco, and soon sent him as envoy to Yunnan, northern Burma, Karakorum, Cochin-China and Southern India. For three years he served as governor of Yang Chow, and helped to reduce the city of Saianfu. The khan long refused to think of the Polos leaving his court; but at length, in the train of a Mongol princess, they sailed by Sumatra and Southern India to Persia, finally reaching Venice in 1295. They brought with them great wealth in precious stones. In 1298 Marco was in command of a galley at the battle of Curzola, where the Venetians were defeated by the Genoese, and he was a prisoner for a year at Genoa. Here it was once thought that he dictated to another captive, one Rusticiano of Pisa, an account of his travels. It is now believed that he had his notes which he had written for Kublai sent to him from Venice and that Rusticiano helped to make a record from them. After his liberation he returned to Venice, where he died. Marco Polo's book consists of: (1) a Prologue the only part containing persona narrative; and (2) a long series of chapters descriptive of notable sights, manners of different states of Asia, especially that of Kublai Khan, ending with a dull chronicle of the internecine wars of the house of Genghis during the second half of the 13th century. Nothing disturbs the even tenor of his narrative. His invaluable work contains not a few too marvellous tales (such as those of the Land of Darkness, the Great Roc, &c.). Ramusio (1485–1557) assumed that it was written in Latin, Marsden supposed in the Venetian dialect, Baldelli-Boni showed (1827) that it was French. There exists an old French text, published in 1824, which Yule believed the nearest approach to Marco's own oral narrative. See Yule's edition (1871; new ed. 1921), containing a faithful English translation from an eclectic text, an exhaustive introduction, and notes; also Latham's *Travels of Marco Polo* (Penguin 1958).

POLYBIUS, *-lib'* (*c.* 205–*c.* 123 B.C.), Greek historian, born at Megalopolis, was one of the 1000 noble Achaeans who, after the conquest of Macedonia in 168, were sent to Rome and detained in honourable captivity. Polybius was the guest of Aemilius Paulus himself, and became the close friend of his son, Scipio Aemilianus, who helped him to collect materials for his great historical work. In 151 the exiles were permitted to return to Greece; Polybius, however, soon rejoined Scipio, followed him in his African campaign, and was present at the destruction of Carthage in 146. The war between the Achaeans and Romans called him back to Greece, and, after the taking of Corinth, he used all his influence to procure favourable terms for the vanquished. In furtherance of his historical labours he undertook journeys to Asia Minor, Egypt, upper Italy, southern France and even Spain. His history, the design of which was to show how and why it was that all the civilized countries of the world fell under the dominion of Rome, covers the period 221–146 B.C. The greater part has perished; of forty books only the first five are preserved complete, but the plan of the whole is fully known. The merits of Polybius are the care with which he collected his materials, his love of truth, his breadth of view, and his sound judgment; but his tone is didactic and dull. See Mahaffy, *The Greek World under Roman Sway* (1890), Laqueur's *Polybius* (1913), and commentary by Walbank (1956).

POLYCARP (*c.* 69–*c.* 155), one of the 'Apostolic Fathers', was Bishop of Smyrna during the earlier half of the 2nd century. He bridges the little-known period between the age of his master the Apostle John and that of his own disciple Irenaeus. His parentage was probably Christian. Ephesus had become the new home of the faith, and there Polycarp was 'taught by apostles', John above all, and 'lived in familiar intercourse with many who had seen Christ'. He was intimate with Papias and Ignatius. At the close of his life Polycarp visited Rome to discuss the vexed question of the time or keeping the Easter festival; and he returned to Smyrna, only to win the martyr's crown in a persecution which broke out during a great pagan festival. The fire, it was said, arched itself about the martyr, and he had to be dispatched with a dagger (A.D. 155 or 156). The graphic *Letter of the Smyrnaeans* tells the story of the martyrdom. The only writing of Polycarp extant is the *Epistle to the Philippians*, incomplete in the original Greek, but complete in a Latin translation. Somewhat commonplace in itself, it is of great value for questions of the canon, the origin of the Roman Church, and the Ignatian epistles. See Gebhardt's *Patrum Apostol. Opera* (1876) and Lightfoot's *Apostolic Fathers*, part ii (2nd ed. 1889).

POLYCLITUS, *-klī'* (5th cent. B.C.), Greek sculptor from Samos, contemporary with Phidias. He was highly thought of by Pliny, especially for his bronze *Doryphorus*, which he deemed perfect sculpture. See Gardner's *Six Greek Sculptors* (1910).

POLYCRATES, *po-lik'ra-teez*, 'tyrant' of Samos *c.* 536–522 B.C., conquered several islands and towns on the Asiatic mainland and made alliance with Amasis, king of Egypt. According to Herodotus, Amasis, thinking him too fortunate, wrote advising him to throw away his most valuable possession, and so avert the spleen of the gods. Polycrates cast a precious signet-ring into the sea, but next day a fisherman brought him a fish with the ring in its belly. It was quite clear to Amasis now that Polycrates was a doomed man, and he broke off the alliance. Polycrates yet successfully defied an attack from Spartans, Corinthians, and disaffected Samians, but was enticed to Magnesia by a Persian satrap, seized, and crucified.

POLYDORE VERGIL. See VERGIL.

POLYGNOTUS (5th cent. B.C.), a Greek painter born in the isle of Thasos, was the first to give life and character to painting. His principal works were at Athens, Delphi and Plataea.

POMBAL, Sebastião José de Carvalho e Mello, Marquês de (1699–1782), Portuguese statesman, was born near Coimbra. In 1739 he was sent as ambassador to London and to Vienna. Appointed secretary for foreign affairs (1750), he reattached many crown domains unjustly alienated; at the great Lisbon earthquake (1755) he showed great calmness and resource, and next year was made prime minister. He sought to subvert the tyranny of the church, opposed the intrigues of nobles and Jesuits, and in 1759 banished the Jesuits. He established elementary schools, reorganized the army, introduced fresh colonists into the Portuguese settlements and established East India and Brazil companies. The tyranny of the Inquisition was broken. Agriculture, commerce and finance were improved. In 1758 he was made Count of Oeyras, in 1770 Marquis of Pombal. On the accession of Maria I (1777), who was under clerical influence, the 'Great Marquis' lost his offices. See books by G. Moore (1819), John Smith (1843), Carnota (trans. 1871) and M. Cheke (1938).

POMPADOUR, Jeanne Antoinette Poisson, Marquise de (1721–64), mistress of Louis XV, was born in Paris, and was supposed to be the child of Le Normant de Tournehem, a wealthy *fermier-général*. She grew up a woman of remarkable grace, beauty and wit. In 1741 she was married to Le Normant's nephew, Le Normant d'Étoiles, became a queen of fashion, attracted the eye of the king at a ball, was installed at Versailles, and ennobled as Marquise de Pompadour. She assumed the entire control of public affairs, for twenty years swayed the whole policy of the state, and lavished its treasures on her own ambitions. She reversed the traditional policy of France because Frederick the Great lampooned her, filled all public offices with her nominees, and made her own creatures ministers of France. Her policy was disastrous, her wars unfortunate—the ministry of Choiseul was the only fairly creditable portion of the reign. She founded the École Militaire and the royal factory at Sèvres. A lavish patroness of the arts, she heaped her bounty upon poets and painters. She held her difficult position to the end, and retained the king's favour by relieving him of all business, by diverting him with private theatricals, and at last by countenancing his debaucheries. The *Mémoires* (1766) are not genuine. See Studies by Capefigue (1858), Campardon (1867), Goncourt (new ed. 1927), H. N. Williams (1902), P. de Nolhac (1904, 1913), Tinayre (1925), Trouncer (1937), N. Mitford (1958); Beaujoint's *Secret Memoirs* (1885); but esp. her *Correspondance*, ed. Malassis (1878), ed. Bonhomme (1880).

POMPEY, Gnaeus Pompeius Magnus (106–48 B.C.), at seventeen fought in the Social War against Marius and Cinna. He supported Sulla, and destroyed the remains of the Marian faction in Africa and Sicily. He next drove the followers of Lepidus out of Italy, extinguished the Marian party in Spain under Sertorius (76–71), and annihilated the remnants of the army of Spartacus. He was now the idol of the people, and was elected consul for the year 70. Hitherto Pompey had belonged to the aristocratic party, but latterly he had been looked upon with suspicion, and he now espoused the people's cause and carried a law restoring the tribunician power to the people. He cleared the Mediterranean of pirates; conquered Mithridates of Pontus, Tigranes of Armenia, and Antiochus of Syria, subdued the Jews and captured Jerusalem, and entered Rome in triumph for the third time in 61. But now his star began to wane. Henceforward he was distrusted by the aristocracy, and second to Caesar in popular favour. When the senate declined to accede to his wish that his acts in Asia should be ratified he formed a close intimacy with Caesar, and the pair, with the plutocrat Crassus, formed the all-powerful 'First Triumvirate'. Pompey's acts in Asia were ratified, and his promises to his troops fulfilled; Caesar's designs were gained; and Caesar's daughter, Julia, was given in marriage to Pompey. Next year Caesar repaired to Gaul, and for nine years carried on a career of conquest, while Pompey was wasting his time at Rome. Jealousies arose between the two, and Julia died in 54. Pompey now returned to the aristocratic party. Caesar was ordered to lay down his office, which he consented to do if Pompey would do the same. The senate insisted on unconditional resignation, otherwise he would be declared a public enemy. But crossing the Rubicon, Caesar defied the senate and its armies. The story of the war is recorded at CAESAR. After his final defeat at Pharsalia in 48, Pompey fled to Egypt, where he was murdered. His younger son, Sextus, secured a fleet, manned largely by slaves and exiles, and, occupying Sicily, ravaged the coasts of Italy. But in 36 he was defeated at sea by Agrippa, and in 37 slain at Mitylene.

PONCE DE LEÓN, *pon'thay* THay *lay-on'*, (1) **Juan** (1460–1521), Spanish explorer, born at San Servas in Spain, was a court page, served against the Moors, and became governor, first of part of Hispaniola, then (1510–12) of Porto Rico. On a quest for the fountain of perpetual youth, he discovered Florida in March 1512, and was made governor, but failed to conquer his new subjects, retired to Cuba, and died there from the wound of a poisoned arrow. See Life by A. Bell (1925).

(2) **Luis** (1527–91), Spanish monk, scholar and poet, born at Granada, in 1544 entered the Augustinian order, and became professor of Theology at Salamanca in 1561. In 1572–76 he was imprisoned by the Inquisition for his translation and interpretation of the Song of Solomon; but shortly before his death he became general of his order. His poetical remains, published in 1631, comprise translations from Virgil, Horace and the Psalms; his few original poems are lyrical masterpieces. See German monographs by Wilkens (1866) and Reusch (1873); also a Spanish Life by Blanco García (1904).

PONCELET, Jean Victor, *pō-sė-lay* (1788–1867), French engineer-officer and geometrician, was born at Metz. His *Traité des propriétés projectives des figures* (1822) gives him an important place in the development of projective geometry. He became professor of Mechanics at Metz and Paris.

PONCHIELLI, Amilcare, *pon-kyel'lee* (1834–1886), Italian composer, born at Paderno Fasolare near Cremona, wrote *La Gioconda* (1876) and other operas.

POND, John (1767–1836), English astronomer-royal from 1811, improved methods and instruments of observation at Greenwich. His work was notable for its extreme accuracy.

PONIATOWSKI, *pon-ya-tof'skee*, name of a princely family of Poland:

(1) **Joseph Antony** (1762–1813), nephew of (3), was born in Warsaw and trained in the Austrian army. In 1789 the Polish Assembly appointed him commander of the army of the south, with which he gained brilliant victories over the Russians (1792); and he commanded under Kosciusko (1794). When the duchy of Warsaw was constituted (1807), he was appointed minister of war and commander-in-chief. In 1809, during the war between Austria and France, he invaded Galicia. Three years later with a large body of Poles he joined Napoleon in his invasion of Russia, and distinguished himself at Smolensk at Borodino, and at Leipzig, where, in covering the French retreat, he was drowned in the Elster.

(2) **Stanislas** (1677–1762), father of (3), joined Charles XII of Sweden in supporting Stanislas Leszczynski and later under Augustus II and III was appointed to several administrative posts in Lithuania and Poland.

(3) **Stanislas Augustus** (1732–98), son of (2), last king of Poland, in St Petersburg in 1755 while in the suite of the British ambassador became much favoured by the Empress Catherine. Largely through her influence he was elected king in 1764, though not fitted to rule the country at such a crisis. Frederick the Great, who had gained the consent of Austria to a partition of Poland, made a like proposal to Russia, and the first partition was effected in 1772. The diet tried, too late, to introduce reforms. The intrigues of discontented nobles led again to Russian and Prussian intervention, and a second fruitless resistance was followed in 1793 by a second partition. The Poles now became desperate; a general rising took place (1794), the Prussians were driven out, and the Russians were several times routed. But Austria now appeared on the scene, Kosciusko was defeated, Warsaw was taken, and the Polish monarchy was at an end. Stanislas resigned his crown (1795), and died at St Petersburg.

PONSONBY, Sarah. See BUTLER (3).

PONT, Timothy (*c.* 1560–1630), Scottish cartographer, graduated at St Andrews in 1584, became minister of Dunnet (1601), and in 1609 subscribed for 2000 acres of forfeited lands in Ulster. He first projected a Scottish atlas, and surveyed all the counties and isles of the kingdom. His collections were rescued from destruction by Sir John Scot of Scotstarvet, and his maps, revised by Robert Gordon of Straloch, appeared in Blaeu's *Theatrum Orbis Terrarum* (1654). See Dobie's *Cunninghame Topographised by Pont* (1876).

PONTIAC (*c.* 1720?–69), Chief of the Ottawa Indians, in 1763 organized a conspiracy against the English garrisons, and for five months besieged Detroit. He was murdered by an Illinois Indian in 1769. See F. Parkman, *History of the Conspiracy of Pontiac* (1851).

PONTOPPIDAN, (1) **Erik** (1698–1764), Danish theologian, born at Aarhus, professor of Theology at Copenhagen (1738), Bishop of Bergen (1747), wrote *Annales Ecclesiae Danicae Diplomaticae*, a Danish topography, a Norwegian glossary, and *Norges Naturlige Historie* (trans. 1755), describing the Kraken (sea-serpent), &c.

(2) **Henrik** (1857–1944), Danish novelist, born a pastor's son at Fredericia, trained as an engineer but turned to writing. Among his novels were *Land of Promise* (1891–95), *Lykke-Per* (1898–1904) and *The Realm of the Dead* (1912–16). He was a Nobel prizeman (1917). See his memoirs *Back to Myself* (1941).

PONTORMO, Jacopo da (1494–1552), Florentine painter, whose family name was Carucci. He was a pupil of Leonardo da Vinci, Piero di Cosimo and Andrea del Sarto. His works included frescoes, notably of the Passion (1522–25), in the Certosa near Florence. The *Deposition* (*c.* 1525), which forms the altarpiece in a chapel in Sta Felicità, Florence, is possibly his masterpiece. This and much of his later work shows the influence of Michelangelo. He also painted portraits and the Medici villa at Poggio a Caiano was partly decorated by him.

POOLE, (1) **Paul Falconer** (1807–79), English painter, born at Bristol, was self-taught and his work, mainly of historical subjects, was very popular during his life. He was elected an A.R.A. in 1846, an R.A. in 1861.

(2) **Reginald Stuart** (1832–95), English archaeologist, born in London, lived in Cairo from 1842 to 1849, becoming an eminent Egyptologist. He was keeper of coins at the British Museum from 1870. He was a nephew of E. W. Lane (q.v.).

(3) **William Frederick** (1821–94), American librarian, born at Salem, Mass., graduated at Yale in 1849. There in 1848 he published an *Index of Periodical Literature*, to which supplements were later added. In 1856–69 he was librarian of the Boston Athenaeum, and from 1888 of the Newberry Library at Chicago.

POPE, (1) **Alexander** (1688–1744), English poet, was the son of a London linen-draper who retired in the year the poet was born and finally settled at Binfield in Windsor Forest, which is as much associated with the poet's name as Twickenham in later years. The family was Catholic, which meant that Pope was denied a formal education. He made up for it by his reading, chiefly of the English poets, but he also insisted on going to London at fifteen to be taught Italian and French and was therefore fairly well equipped for his literary career. In London, he was patronized by the elderly wits Wycherley and Walsh, who passed on his precocious verse, chiefly pastorals and modernizations of Chaucer, after the example of Dryden's *Fables*, to the fashionable wits Congreve, Garth and 'Granville the polite', so that when his first fruits appeared in Tonson's *Miscellany* (1709), that is, his four pastorals and one of his Chaucer adaptations, there was a friendly audience of 'the great' to welcome them. Here at the very entrance to his career begins the literary vendetta which poisoned his existence. The *Miscellany* also contained Ambrose Philips' much inferior pastorals which Addison or one of his whiggish henchmen was to praise in the *Guardian* at the expense of Pope. Politics bedevilled everything then, especially when the question of the succession loomed ahead. Meanwhile Pope moved between London, where he cut a dash, and the Forest, where he was familiar with the Catholic gentry, above all with the Blounts, Teresa and Martha. His spirits then can be judged by the lovely poem he wrote for Teresa on her leaving London after George I's coronation, though Martha turned out to be his 'real flame' and life-long companion. Pope's next publication was *An Essay on Criticism* (1711), in which he contrived to express the dull matter of neo-classic art in witty and quotable couplets. Unfortunately he introduced a sneer at the formidable old critic and playwright John Dennis, and this started a new vendetta in which Pope could not hope to be victor for Dennis stooped to abuse of his deformed person—a mortal blow to the poet. Addison's appreciation of the *Essay on Criticism*, conveyed in a paper in *The Spectator*, despite his disapproval of the attack on Dennis, was no doubt balm to Pope's hurt mind, but politics were soon to bedevil what was a genuine regard on both sides when Pope embarked on his friendship with the Tories, Swift, Oxford and Bolingbroke. *Windsor Forest* (1713) is a fine descriptive poem perhaps marred by its periphrastic jargon. *The Rape of the Lock*, satirizing the quarrel between two eminent families over the stealing of a lock of hair, appeared in Tonson's *Miscellanies* in 1712. This first version of the poem, in two cantos, was enlarged into mock-epical form in the five-canto version of 1714. Wit and gaiety never shone brighter and the susceptibilities aroused by it in the lady were much exaggerated. Pope now turned to translation to settle his finances. In 1715 he started on the *Iliad* and followed up by the inferior *Odyssey*, much of it the work of hacks. Altogether he made nine thousand pounds by his labours which assisted him to build and lay out his villa at Twickenham (1718). Thanks to Homer, he 'could thrive/Indebted to no prince or peer alive'. The translation, however, was the cause of more hostility between Pope and Addison because the latter openly preferred the translation of the Whig, Thomas Tickle, which appeared two days after the first book of Pope's Iliad. This was the last straw. Pope now intermittently worked at the great satirical lines on 'Atticus', to which he gave final and deadly form in the *Epistle to Doctor Arbuthnot*, first published in 1734. If any of his poems could persuade us that Pope was a romantic diverted to satire by the rage of enemies it is the *Epistle of Eloisa to Abelard* and the *Elegy to the Memory of an Unfortunate Lady* which appeared in his *Works* (1717), which also contained the final form of *The Rape of the Lock*, with the added speech of Clarissa. The romantic setting of *Eloisa to Abelard* and the genuine expression of passion are less successfully repeated in *The Elegy*, the close of which is neoclassic poetizing, but the poem is moving too, though the actual occasion on which it was based misled the author. In 1717 his father died and Pope moved with his mother to Twickenham, where his new villa engaged him, on a miniature scale, in all the delights of 18th-century artificial gardening. It was destined to become an occasional meeting place for the Tory lords who now began to revive in spirit after their defeat in 1714. The wits also frequented the poet; though Swift was in Ireland, there were still Dr Arbuthnot and Gay. Whilst he was working on his translations he ignored the attacks of the Grub Street critics. Thereafter he was free to settle accounts with those who concentrated on his lack of Greek when they were not abusing his person. He then published an edition of Shakespeare (1725), but the noted Shakespearian scholar, Lewis Theobald, exposed Pope's errors in a pamphlet, *Shakespeare Restored* (1726), and so qualified for the place of hero in the first version of *The Dunciad*, a satire on dullness in which he mocked such critics as Dennis, Colley Cibber, &c. The latter, then poet laureate, replaced Theobald as hero in the final version because of his attempts at retaliation. Beside personal pique there was the awareness, which he shared with Swift, of a catastrophic decline in standards. Both these great writers were humanists of the older type who regarded the new science and talk about progress and enlightenment as barbarous. *The Dunciad* (1726) is indeed a devastating attack on scientific humanism. The fourth part of it, which was added in 1742, is one of the most brilliant satires on pedantry and social fads ever written. It is also capital fun, though the splendid close is no laughing matter. In 1732 appeared the first part of the philosophical *Essay on Man* together with the first of his four moral essays, viz. *Of the Knowledge and Characters of Men*; *Of the Characters of Women*; and two *Of the Uses of Riches*. The *Essay on Man* has been rather unfairly censured for its second-hand philosophy, but Pope only did what Tennyson did for his day; he popularized learned notions and attitudes and gave to them brilliant expression. The two poems *Of the Uses of Riches* are concerned with contemporary taste in laying out great seats. *Of the Characters of Women* contains the terrible attacks on the Duchess of Marlborough and Lady Mary Wortley Montagu who willingly joined with Lord Hervey in the sport of Pope-baiting. He now gathered himself together for his supreme work which makes nonsense of the view that he was a romantic at heart. Bolingbroke is said to have directed him to the adaptation of the Satires and Epistles of Horace, whose situation vis-à-vis the dunces resembled Pope's own. In 1733 he modernized the first epistle of the second book, then he proceeded to the second of the same book and finished his imitations of Horace with two of the satires. Later, to make a book of it, he added two of Donne's satires (unfortunately not the splendid third) and for a prologue chose the glorious *Epistle to Arbuthnot*, which is at once an apologia and a summing-up of themes in the satires. For an epilogue he employed two political dialogues, *One Thousand Seven Hundred & Thirty Eight*, which reflected the growing hopes of the Tory party with its patriotic slogans. *The Satires and Epistles of Horace Imitated* in its final form is the greatest work of our greatest verse satirist. Pope had much to depress him in these years—ill-health, rancorous abuse, the death or absence of his friends. His beloved Gay died in 1732, his mother and his intimate Arbuthnot the following year. Bolingbroke left England for a second exile in 1735, Swift was in Ireland. The affection he expresses for these and other friends relieves the acrimony of his personal satire. The story of his publication of his Letters is both comic and scandalous. He employed the usual complaint of piracy (Curll had produced an edition in 1735) to excuse the unusual course of publishing his own letters in 1737, collected from all his correspondents but shamefully manipulated. Two years later he completed the work by including the letters to Swift which he secured by the usual subterfuges. It is clear that he wanted to present himself to posterity in the most favourable light, as he had done in the *Epistle to Arbuthnot*. The standard edition of the poems was that by Elwin and Courthope (1887–89) but now superseded by the Twickenham edition, general editor John Butt, six vols. (1932 *et seq.*), *Prose Works*, ed. Norman Ault (1936 *et seq.*). The Elwin and Courthope edition provided a Life, but much more understanding and detailed is Professor G. Sherburn's *The Early Career of Alexander Pope* (1934) and his later work on the poet. Dame Edith Sitwell's study is more intuitive than critical. G. Tillotson attempted a revaluation of Pope (1938), and has written several other studies. See also works by Ault (1949), Rogers (1955), Brower (1959), Edwards (1963). Dobrée's *Alexander Pope* (1951) is the best short study of Pope.

(2) **John** (1822–92), American army commander, born in Louisville, Ky., graduated at West Point in 1842, and served with the engineers in Florida (1842–44) and in the Mexican war. He was exploring and surveying in the west till the Civil War, when as brigadier-general in 1861 he drove the guerillas out of Missouri. As major-general he commanded the Army of the Mississippi (1862) and then that of Virginia, but was defeated at the second battle of Bull Run. He was transferred to Minnesota, where he kept the Indians in check, and held commands until 1886, when he retired.

POPHAM, Sir John (*c.* 1531–1607), English lawyer, born at Huntworth near Bridgwater, became speaker in 1580 and lord chief-justice in 1592. He presided at the trial of Guy Fawkes.

POPOV, Aleksandr Stepanovich (1859–1905), Russian physicist, claimed by his countrymen to be the inventor of wireless telegraphy, was the first to use a suspended wire as an aerial.

POPPER, Sir Karl Raimund (1902–), Austrian philosopher, born in Vienna, studied at the university there and published for the 'Vienna Circle' of logical positivists, of which he was not a member, even in some ways an opponent, the greatest modern work in scientific methodology, *Die Logik der Forschung* (1934) 'The Logic of Scientific Discovery' (trans. with postscript, 1958), in which he refuted the long-established Baconian principles of scientific method and argued that testing hypotheses by selective experimentation rather than proof was the essence of scientific induction. For Popper, to be scientific, a theory must in principle be falsifiable, not verifiable in the logical positivist sense, and this criterion marks off a genuine science, such as physics, from what he calls the 'pseudo-sciences', such as Marxian economics and Freudian psychology which instead of challenging falsification impose a rigid finality from the outset. Popper left Vienna shortly before Hitler's *Ansch uss*, lectured at Canterbury College, New Zealand (1937–45), when he became first reader in Logic (1945–48) then professor of Logic and Scientific Method at the London School of Economics. Philosophical attempts to reduce history to a predetermined pattern he exposed in articles in *Economica* (1945–48), republished under the title *The Poverty of Historicism* (1957), and in the brilliant philosophical polemic, *The Open Society and Its Enemies* (1945), written in the heat of the second World War, in which he ruthlessly examines all the great philosophical systems with totalitarian implications in political theory from Plato to Karl Marx. More recent publications include *The Logic of Scientific Discovery* (1959) and *Conjectures and Refutations* (1963). He was knighted in 1965. See his philosophical autobiography in *British Philosophy in the Mid-Century*, ed. C. A. Mace (1957).

POPSKI. See PENIAKOFF.

PORDAGE, John. See BOEHME.

PORDENONE, Il, *por-day-nō'nay* (1483–1539), the name given to the Italian religious painter, Giovanni Antonio Licinio, who was born at Corticelli near Pordenone. In 1535 he settled at Venice, and in 1538 was summoned by the duke to Ferrara. He painted frescoes in the cathedral at Cremona and in Sta Maria da Campagna at Piacenza.

PORPHYRY (*c.* A.D. 233–304), Neoplatonist, born at Tyre or Batanea, is said, improbably, to have been originally a Christian. He studied at Athens under Longinus, and about 263 at Rome under Plotinus. In Sicily he wrote his once celebrated treatise against the Christians, now lost. He then returned to Rome to teach. His philosophy keeps close to life and practical duties, its object the salvation of the soul, to be effected by the extinction of impure desires through strict asceticism and knowledge of God. His chief writings are the Lives of Plotinus and Pythagoras, *Sententiae*, *De Abstinentia*, and the *Epistola ad Marcellam*, addressed to his wife. See monograph by Bouillet (1864) and Alice Zimmern's translation of *Porphyry to his Wife Marcella* (1896).

PORPORA, Niccola Antonio (1686–1766), Italian composer and teacher of singing, born in Naples, established a school for singing, from which came many famous singers. During 1725–55 he was in Dresden, Venice, London (1734–36) and Vienna (where he taught Haydn), composing operas and teaching. He figures in George Sand's *Consuelo*.

PORSCHE, Ferdinand (1875–1951), German automobile designer, born at Hafersdorf, Bohemia, designed cars for Daimler and Auto Union, but set up his own independent studio in 1931 and in 1934 produced the plans for a revolutionary type of cheap car with engine in the rear, to which the Nazis gave the name *Volkswagen* ('People's car') and which they promised to mass-produce for the German worker. After World War II it proved a record-breaking commodity in the export market.

PORSON, Richard (1759–1808), English scholar, was born at East Ruston in Norfolk, son of the parish clerk, in 1778 entered Trinity College, Cambridge, was elected a scholar, won the Craven Scholarship and the first chancellor's medal, and in 1782 was elected a fellow. He now began to contribute to reviews; his *Notae breves ad Toupii*

Emendationes in Suidam (1790) carried his name beyond England. In 1787 appeared in the *Gentleman's Magazine* his three sarcastic letters on Hawkins's *Life of Johnson*; and during 1788–89 his far more famous letters on the Spurious Verse 1 John v, 7, which brought him no little odium. In 1792 his fellowship ceased to be tenable by a layman, and friends raised for him a fund of £100 a year; he was also appointed to the regius professorship of Greek at Cambridge, an office worth £40 a year. In 1795 he edited Aeschylus, and in 1797–1801 four plays of Euripides. He married in 1796, but his wife died five months later. In 1806 he was appointed librarian of the London Institution, but neglected his duties. Two years later he died of apoplexy. Porson possessed a stupendous memory, unwearied industry, great acuteness, fearless honesty, and masculine sense, but was hindered all his life by poverty, ill-health, dilatoriness and fits of intemperance. He achieved little, besides the works already named, but a few *bons mots*, some brilliant emendations, and the posthumous *Adversaria* (1812), notes on Aristophanes (1820), the lexicon of Photius (1822), Pausanias (1820) and Suidas (1834). His *Tracts and Criticisms* were collected by Kidd (1815). See Lives by Watson (1861), Clarke (1937), and his *Correspondence* edited by Luard (1867).

PORTA, (1) **Baccio della.** See BARTOLOMMEO.

(2) **Carlo** (1776–1821), Italian poet, was born in Milan. Writing in the dialect of Milan, he showed his insight into human character in narrative poems which are satirical and grimly realistic. These include *La Nomina del Capellan, La Guerra di Pret* and *I Disgrazzi di Giovannin Bongee.*

(3) **Giacomo della** (1541–1604), Italian architect, a pupil of Vignola, is best known for the cupola of St Peter's and his work on the Palazzo Farnese, left unfinished by Michelangelo. He was also responsible for some of the fountains of Rome.

(4) **Giovanni Battista della** (1543–1615), Neapolitan physicist and philosopher, wrote on physiognomy, natural magic, gardening, &c., besides several comedies.

(5) **Guglielmo della** (*c.* 1510–77), Italian sculptor, whose main work was the tomb of Pope Paul III in the choir of St Peter's.

PORTALIS, Jean Étienne Marie (1745–1807), French jurist and statesman, practised law in Paris, was imprisoned during the Revolution, but under Napoleon compiled the *Code Civil.* See Life by Lavollée (1869).

PORTEOUS, John (d. 1736), Scottish soldier, the ne'er-do-well son of an Edinburgh tailor, enlisted and served in Holland, and soon after 1715 became captain of the Edinburgh town guard. On April 14, 1736, he was in charge at the execution of one Wilson, a smuggler who had robbed the Pittenweem custom-house. There was some stone-throwing; whereupon Porteous made his men fire on the mob, wounding twenty persons and killing five or six. For this he was tried and condemned to death (July 20), but reprieved by Queen Caroline. But on the night of September 7 an orderly mob burst open the Tolbooth, dragged Porteous to the Grassmarket, and hanged him from a dyer's pole. See Scott's notes to *The Heart of Midlothian* and the *Trial of Capt. Porteous*, ed. by W. Roughead (1909).

PORTER, (1) **Anna Maria** (1780–1832), English novelist, younger sister of (8), born in Durham, blossomed precociously into *Artless Tales* (1793–95), followed by a long series of works, among which were *Octavia* (1798), *The Lake of Killarney* (1804), *The Hungarian Brothers* (1807), *The Recluse of Norway* (1814), *The Fast of St Magdalen* (1818) and *Honor O'Hara* (1826).

(2) **Cole** (1891?–1964), American composer, born at Peru, Indiana, studied law at Harvard before deciding upon a musical career and entering the Schola Cantorum in Paris. Attracted to musical comedy, he composed lyrics and music for many stage successes, culminating, in 1948, in *Kiss me Kate* and, in 1953, with *Can-Can.* His highly personal style and dramatic sense is illustrated by such popular songs as 'Night and Day' and 'Begin the Beguine'. See Life by G. Eells (1967).

(3) **David** (1780–1843), American sailor, born at Boston, Mass., son of a naval officer, entered the navy in 1798, became captain in 1812 and captured the first British war ship taken in the war. In 1813 he nearly destroyed the English whale fishery in the Pacific, and took possession of the Marquesas Islands; but in March 1814 his frigate was destroyed by the British at Valparaiso. He afterwards commanded an expedition against pirates in the West Indies. He resigned in 1826, and for a time commanded the Mexican navy. In 1829 the United States appointed him consul-general to the Barbary States, and then minister at Constantinople, where he died. See the Life (1875) by his son.

(4) **David Dixon** (1813–91), son of (3), born at Chester, Penn., accompanied his father against the pirates and in the Mexican service. In the Civil War, as commander of the mortar flotilla, in April 1862 he bombarded the New Orleans forts. In September, with the Mississippi squadron, he passed the batteries of Vicksburg, and bombarded the city; in December 1864 he silenced Fort Fisher, taken next month. Superintendent till 1869 of Annapolis naval academy, he was in 1870 made admiral of the navy. He wrote three romances, *Incidents of the Civil War* (1885), and *History of the Navy During the War of the Rebellion* (1887).

(5) **Eleanor Hodgman** (1868–1920), American novelist, was born at Littleton, New Hampshire, and studied music at the New England Conservatory. Her first novels included *Cross Currents* (1907) and *Miss Billy* (1911). In 1913 *Pollyanna* appeared; this was an immediate success and has retained its popularity ever since. A sequel, *Pollyanna Grows Up*, was published in 1915 and two volumes of short stories, *The Tangled Threads* and *Across the Years* appeared posthumously in 1924.

(6) **Endymion** (1587–1649), English royalist, servant to James VI and I, was groom of the bedchamber to Charles I, and fought for him in the Great Rebellion. He wrote verses and was painted by Van Dyck. See *Life and*

Letters by D. Townshend (1897) and study by G. Huxley (1959).

(7) **Gene,** *née* **Stratton** (1868–1924), American novelist, was born on a farm in Wabash Co., Ind., married in 1886 Charles D. Porter, and as Gene Stratton Porter attained great popularity by *A Girl of the Limberlost* (1909) and other stories full of sentiment and nature study.

(8) **Jane** (1776–1850), English writer, born at Durham, the daughter of an army surgeon, made a great reputation in 1803 by her high-flown romance, *Thaddeus of Warsaw*, and had even more success in 1810 with *The Scottish Chiefs*, its hero a most stilted and preposterous Wallace. Other books were *The Pastors' Fireside* (1815), *Duke Christian of Lüneburg* (1824), *Tales Round a Winter's Hearth* (with her sister Anna Maria, 1824), and *The Field of Forty Footsteps* (1828); *Sir Edward Seaward's Shipwreck* (1831), a clever fiction, edited by her, was almost certainly written by her eldest brother, Dr William Ogilvie Porter (1774–1850).

(9) **Katherine Anne** (1894–), American writer of short stories, was born at Indian Creek, Texas. She started writing at a very early age but allowed nothing to be published until she was thirty. Among her collections of stories is *Pale Horse, Pale Rider* (1939). *Ships of Fools* (1962) is an immense allegorical novel analysing the German state of mind in the 1930s. A volume of essays, *The Days Before*, appeared in 1952.

(10) **Noah** (1811–92), American clergyman, born at Farmington, Conn., studied at Yale, was a Congregational pastor 1836–46, then became professor of Moral Philosophy at Yale, and in 1871–86 was president of the college. Among his numerous works are *The Human Intellect* (1868), *Books and Reading* (1870), *Moral Science* (1885). See *Memorial*, ed. by Merriam (1893).

(11) **Robert Ker** (1775–1842), English painter, brother of (8), a clever battle painter, visited Russia in 1804, where he was historical painter to the tsar. He accompanied Sir John Moore's expedition in 1808, becoming K.C.H. in 1832. He was afterwards British consul in Venezuela, and published books of travel in Russia, Sweden, Spain, Portugal, Georgia, Persia and Armenia.

(12) **William S.** See Henry, O.

PORTLAND, Duke of. See Bentinck.

PORTO-RICHE, Georges de, *por-tō-reesh* (1849–1930), French dramatist, was born at Bordeaux. He wrote several successful psychological plays, including *L'Amoureuse* (1891), *Le Vieil homme* (1911) and *Le Marchand d'Estampes* (1917).

PORTSMOUTH, Louise de Kéroualle, Duchess of (1649–1734), mistress of Charles II of England, born in Brittany, came to England in 1670 in the train of Henrietta, Charles II's cherished sister, ostensibly as a lady in waiting, but secretly charged to influence the king in favour of the French alliance. The political influence wielded by the ' baby-faced Breton ' was negligible, but Charles was sufficiently responsive to her charms to make her his mistress and ennoble her (1673) and her son, who became Duke of Richmond. Rapacious and haughty, ' Madame Carwell ' was universally detested. See *inter alia* works by Bryant (1931) and Drinkwater (1936).

PORUS. See Alexander the Great.

POSIDONIUS (*c.* 135–51 B.C.), stoic philosopher, born at Apamea in Syria, studied at Athens, and settled at Rhodes, whence in 86 he was sent as envoy to Rome; there, the friend of Cicero and Pompey, he died, leaving works on philosophy, astronomy and history, of which only fragments are extant.

POTEMKIN, properly **Potyomkin, Grigori Aleksandrovich,** *pot-yom'kin* (1739–91), was born near Smolensk, of a noble but impoverished Polish family. He entered the Russian army, attracted the notice of Catharine II by his handsome face and figure, in 1774 became her recognized favourite, and directed Russian policy. There is good reason to believe they were secretly married. In charge of the new lands in the south acquired by conquest, he made an able administrator. In 1787 Catharine paid a visit to his government in the south, but the story of his setting her route with stage villages and hired villagers is not now believed. In the war with the Turks Potemkin was placed at the head of the army, and reaped the credit of Suvorov's victories (1791). He died in the same year. Licentious, astute and unscrupulous, in spite of his lavish extravagance he heaped up an immense fortune. He gained for Russia the Crimea and the north coast of the Black Sea, and he founded Sevastopol, Nikolaev and Ekaterinoslav (Dnepropetrovsk). See *Memoirs* (1812), Lives by his secretary Saint-Jean (German; new ed. 1888), and Soloveytchik (English 1938).

POTT, (1) August Friedrich (1802–87), German philologist, born at Nettelrede in Hanover, became in 1833 professor of the Science of Language at Halle. The foundation of Pott's reputation was laid by his *Etymologische Forschungen* (1833–36); and his article on the Indo-Germanic stock in Ersch and Gruber's *Encyklopädie* is a masterpiece.

(2) **Percival(l)** (1714–88), English surgeon, born in London, who became, after a period of training under Edward Nourse, assistant and then senior surgeon at St Bartholomew's Hospital, where his lectures became very popular with both students and visitors. His writings were many, the most important being *Fractures and Dislocations* (1765), in which he described a compound leg fracture suffered by himself and which is now known as ' Pott's fracture ', and his account of a disease of the spine, ' Pott's disease ', in *Remarks on That Kind of Palsy of the Lower Limbs which is Frequently Found to Accompany a Curvature of the Spine* (1779). He became a fellow of the Royal Society in 1764.

POTTER, (1) Beatrix (1866–1943), English authoress, born in London, lived in Kensington and the Lake District and wrote many books for children which she illustrated herself. The best known are the stories of *Peter Rabbit, Jemima Puddleduck, Mrs Tiggy-Winkle* and *Squirrel Nutkin.* She married William Heelis in 1913. See *The Tale of Beatrix Potter* by M. Lane (1946).

(2) **John** (*c.* 1674–1747), Eniglsh scholar

and divine, born at Wakefield, became regius professor of Divinity at Oxford in 1707, Bishop of Oxford in 1715, and in 1737 Archbishop of Canterbury. He published *Archaeologia Graeca, or Antiquities of Greece* (1697–99), &c.

(3) **Paul** (1625–54), Dutch painter and etcher, was born a painter's son at Enkhuizen, and died at Amsterdam. His best pictures are small pastoral scenes with animal figures. He also painted large pictures, the life size *Young Bull* (1647, at The Hague) being especially celebrated. The Rijksmuseum at Amsterdam possesses the *Bear-hunt*. See Cundall's *Landscape Painters of Holland* (1891).

(4) **Stephen** (1900–69), English writer and radio producer, joined the B.B.C. in 1938, and is best known in radio as co-author with Joyce Grenfell of the *How* series. His books include a novel, *The Young Man* (1929), an educational study, *The Muse in Chains* (1937), the comic *Gamesmanship* (1947), *Lifemanship* (1950) and *One-Upmanship* (1952), in which he humorously delineated the gentle art of demoralizing opposition, *Potter on America* (1956) and *Supermanship* (1958). See his *Steps to Immaturity* (1959).

POUISHNOFF, Leff Nicholas (1891–1959), Russian pianist, born in Odessa, left Russia at the outbreak of the revolution. Settling in Britain in 1920, he gave concerts and soon was hailed as one of the greatest modern pianists. He excelled in playing Chopin, Liszt and the Russian composers.

POUJADE, Pierre, *poo-zhad* (1920–), French political leader, born in Saint Céré. After serving in World War II, he became a publisher and bookseller. In 1951 he was elected a member of the Saint Céré municipal council, and in 1954 he organized his Poujadist movement (union for the defence of tradesmen and artisans) as a protest against the French tax system. His party had successes in the 1956 elections to the National Assembly. He published his manifesto, *J'ai choisi le combat*, in 1956.

POULENC, Francis, *poo-lãk* (1899–1963), French composer, born in Paris, fought in World War I, studied composition under Koechlin, came under the influence of Satie (q.v.), and as a member of 'Les Six' was prominent in the reaction against Debussy-esque impressionism. He wrote a good deal of chamber music in a cool, limpid style, often for unusual combinations of instruments, and is also known for some excellent ballet and *opera bouffe*, especially *Les Biches* and *Les Mamelles de Tirésias*. His cantata *Figure humaine* (1945) has as its theme the occupation of France. But perhaps his major contribution to music is his considerable output of songs, more romantic in outlook than his other compositions; they include *Poèmes de Ronsard* (1924), *Fêtes Galantes* (1943), &c.

POULSEN, Valdemar, *powl'sen* (1869–1942), Danish electrical engineer, born in Copenhagen, became associated with the Telephone Company there. He invented an arc generator for use in wireless telegraphy.

POUND, (1) **(Alfred) Dudley Pickman Rogers** (1877–1943), British sailor, became a captain in 1914, commanded with distinction the battleship *Colossus* at the battle of Jutland (1916) and for the remaining two years of World War I directed operations at the Admiralty. Promoted to the rank of rear-admiral, he from 1936 to 1939 was commander-in-chief, Mediterranean fleet, becoming in 1939 admiral of the fleet. In the same year he was appointed first sea lord and this post he held through the most difficult years of the war. He was awarded the Order of Merit in 1943, the year of his death.

(2) **Ezra Loomis** (1885–1972), American poet, was born at Hailey, Idaho. Graduating M.A. at Pennsylvania University in 1906, he became an instructor in Wabash College, but after four months left for Europe, travelling widely in Spain, Italy and Provence. He was co-editor of *Blast* (1914–15), and London editor of the Chicago *Little Review* (1917–19), and in 1920 became Paris correspondent for *The Dial*. From 1924 he made his home in Italy. He became infected with fascist ideas and stirred up much resentment by antidemocracy broadcasts in the early stages of the war. In 1945 he was escorted back to the U.S. and indicted for treason. The trial did not proceed, however, as he was adjudged insane, and placed in an asylum. In 1958 he was certified sane and released. Throughout his career he was a stormy petrel, and critical opinion is sharply divided on his merits as a writer. In addition to his poetry he wrote books on literature, music, art and economics, and translated much from Italian, French, Chinese and Japanese. As a poet, of the Imagist school at the outset of his career, he was a thoroughgoing experimenter, deploying much curious learning in his illustrative imagery and in the development of his themes. T. S. Eliot regarded him as the motivating force behind 'modern' poetry, the poet who created a climate in which English and American poets could understand and appreciate each other. *Homage to Sextus Propertius* (1919) and *Hugh Selwyn Mauberley* (1920) are among his most important early poems. His *Cantos*, a loosely-knit series of poems, appeared first in 1917, continuing in many instalments, via the *Pisan Cantos* (1948) to *Thrones: Cantos 96–109* (1959). His work in the Classics and Chinese poetry are discernible in their form. Apart from his life work in poetry, significant collections are *Translations of Ezra Pound* (1933) and *Literary Essays* (1954). See T. S. Eliot, *Ezra Pound* (1917), studies of his poetry by H. Kenner (1951), G. S. Fraser (1960), D. Davie (1965), his *Letters* (ed. D. Page, 1951), Life by N. Stock (1970), *Discretions* (1971) by his daughter, M. de Rachewiltz, and further details in the *Autobiography* of W. C. Williams (1951).

(3) **Roscoe** (1870–1964), American jurist, born at Lincoln, Nebraska, was educated at Nebraska University and the Harvard Law School. Among his appointments were those as commissioner of appeals of the supreme court of Nebraska (1901–03), assistant professor of Law at Nebraska University (1899–1903), and successively professor of Law at Northwestern University, Chicago University, Harvard Law School,

and in 1936 at the University of Harvard. An able and influential teacher, especially of jurisprudence, his theories, with the emphasis on the importance of social interests in connection with the law, have had a universal effect. His legal writings were many and include *Readings on the History and System of the Common Law* (1904), *Introduction to the Philosophy of Law* (1922), *Law and Morals* (1924) and *Criminal Justice in America* (1930). An authority also on botany, he was largely responsible for the botanical survey of Nebraska, and on this subject, in collaboration with Dr F. E. Clements, wrote *Phytogeography of Nebraska* (1898).

POUNDS, John (1766–1839), English cripple shoemaker, born at Portsmouth, became unpaid teacher of poor children, regarded as the founder of ragged schools.

POUSSIN, *poo-sī,* (1) **Gaspar** (1613–75), French painter, whose real name was Gaspar Dughet, was the brother-in-law and pupil of (2). He worked in Rome and became well known as a landscapist. His popularity in the 18th century was high, though many paintings attributed to him may not have been his work.

(2) **Nicolas** (1594–1665), French painter, born at Les Andelys in Normandy, went at eighteen to Paris to study, and by 1623 had attained the means of visiting Rome. He received important commissions from Cardinal Barberini, and soon acquired fame and fortune. Among the masterpieces of this period was the *Golden Calf*, now in the National Gallery. After sixteen years he returned to Paris and was introduced by Richelieu to Louis XIII, who appointed him painter-in-ordinary. But the altar pieces and mural decorations which he was required to paint were unsuited to his genius, and for this reason, and being annoyed by intrigues, he in 1643 returned to Rome. There, besides classical and religious works which became increasingly geometric in design, he began to paint landscapes on classical lines. His style is a combination of classical ideals and Renaissance tendencies. See works by Bouchitte (1858), Poillon (2nd ed. 1875), Magne (1914) and Friedlaender (1914).

POWELL, (1) **Baden.** See BADEN-POWELL.

(2) **Cecil Frank** (1903–69), English physicist, born at Tonbridge, Kent, professor of Physics at Bristol (1948–63), director of the Wills Physics Laboratory, Bristol, from 1964, known for his work on the photography of nuclear processes. He received the Nobel physics prize for 1950.

(3) **Frederick York** (1850–1904), English historian and Icelandic scholar, born in London, was educated at Rugby and Christ Church, Oxford. In 1894 with Professor Vigfússon he worked on the records and ancient poetry of Scandinavia and compiled with him *Icelandic Prose Reader* (1879). He became at Oxford regius professor of Modern History. He helped to found the *English Historical Review* (1885).

(4) **John Wesley** (1834–1902), American geologist, born at Mount Morris, New York, lost his right arm in the Civil War, and became a professor of Geology, surveyor (1868–72) of the Colorado River and its tributaries, and director of the Bureau of Ethnology and of the U.S. Geological Survey. He wrote on the arid region, the Uinta Mountains, the Colorado River and its canyons, and on Indian languages.

(5) **Mary.** See MILTON.

POWERS, Hiram (1805–73), American sculptor, was born a farmer's son at Woodstock, Vermont, became apprentice to a clockmaker in Cincinnati, and was taught to model in clay by a German sculptor. Employed for seven years making wax figures for the Cincinnati museum, in 1835 he went to Washington, where he executed busts, and in 1837 to Florence in Italy, where he resided till his death. There he produced his *Eve*, and in 1843 the still more popular *Greek Slave*. Among his other works were busts of Washington, Calhoun and Daniel Webster.

POWHATTAN. See POCAHONTAS.

POWYS, *pō-is,* name of three brothers, English writers, of Welsh descent:

(1) **John Cowper** (1872–1964), poet, essayist, novelist, born in Shirley, Derbyshire, best known of the three. For a time he taught German at Brighton, and later lectured. Books of verse include *Mandragora* (1917) and *Samphire* (1922). His novels are *A Glastonbury Romance* (1932), *Owen Glendower* (1940), *Porius* (1951), *All or Nothing* (1960), &c. Essays are concerned with questions of philosophy and literary criticism. See his *Autobiography* (1934).

(2) **Llewelyn** (1884–1939), essayist and novelist, brother of (1), born in Dorchester, suffered from recurrent tuberculosis which caused him to spend some years in Switzerland and in Kenya, and from which he finally died. From 1920 to 1925 he was a journalist in New York. Works include *Ebony and Ivory* (1922), *Apples be Ripe* (1930) and the biographical *Confessions of Two Brothers* (with (1), 1916), *Skin for Skin* (1925) and *The Verdict of Bridlegoose* (1926). See Life by Elwin (1953).

(3) **Theodore Francis** (1875–1953), novelist and short story writer, brother of (1) and (2), born in Shirley, lived in seclusion and wrote original and eccentric novels of which the best known is *Mr Weston's Good Wine* (1927). See also *Mr Tasker's Gods* (1925), *Captain Patch* (1935) and *Goat Green* (1937). See study by H. Coombes (1960).

POYNINGS, Sir Edward (1459–1521), English soldier and diplomat, took part in a rebellion against Richard III, escaped to the Continent and joined the Earl of Richmond (Henry VII), with whom he later returned to England. In 1493 he was governor of Calais, and in 1494 went to Ireland as deputy-governor for Prince Henry (Henry VIII). His aim was to anglicize the government of Ireland. This he accomplished by means of the Statutes of Drogheda, known as Poynings' Law, to the effect that all Irish legislature had to be confirmed by the English privy council. This was not repealed until 1782. He was often abroad on diplomatic missions. In 1520 he was present at the Field of the Cloth of Gold, which he had taken an active part in arranging.

POYNTER, Sir Edward John (1836–1919), English painter, was born of Huguenot ancestry in Paris, the son of the architect, Ambrose Poynter (1796–1886). Educated at Westminster and Ipswich, he studied 1853–1854 at Rome and 1856–60 in Paris and elsewhere. He made designs for stained glass, and drawings on wood for *Once a Week* and other periodicals, and for Dalziel's projected illustrated Bible. This led to studies in Egyptian art, which resulted in his *Israel in Egypt* (1867). His watercolours are numerous. He was elected R.A. in 1876. In 1871 he became Slade professor in University College, London, in 1876–81 director for art at South Kensington, in 1894–1905 director of the National Gallery and in 1896 was made president of the Royal Academy. Among his works are *The Ides of March* (1883), *The Visit of the Queen of Sheba to Solomon* (1891), and *Nausicaa and her Maidens*, painted (1872–79) for the Earl of Wharncliffe at Wortley Hall. In 1869–70 he designed the cartoons for a mosaic of St George in the Houses of Parliament.

POYNTING, John Henry (1852–1914), English physicist, born at Monton, Lancs, educated at Manchester and Cambridge, became professor of Physics at Birmingham (1880) and F.R.S. (1888). He wrote on electrical phenomena and on radiation, and determined the constant of gravitation by a torsion experiment. He also did important work on the measurement of the earth's density and on this subject wrote *On the Mean Density of the Earth* (1893) and *The Earth* (1913). With J. J. Thomson he wrote a *Textbook of Physics* (1899–1914).

POZZO, Andrea, *pot'sō* (1642–1709), Italian Jesuit artist, was born in the north of Italy, becoming a Jesuit lay brother in 1665. In Rome from 1681, his main work was the decoration of the church of S. Ignazio, the ceiling of which he painted in the perspective style known as *sotto in sù.* In Vienna from 1702, his work in the Liechtenstein palace is all that survives. His treatise *Perspectiva pictorum . . .* (1693–98, English trans. 1693) had considerable influence on 18th century artists.

POZZO DI BORGO, Carlo Andrea, Count, *pot'sō dee bor'gō* (1764–1842), Corsican-born Russian diplomatist, born at Alala, practised as an advocate in Ajaccio, in 1790 joined the party of Paoli, who made him president of the Corsican council and secretary of state, but in 1796 was obliged to seek safety from the Bonapartes in London. In 1798 he went to Vienna and effected an alliance of Austria and Russia against France. In 1803 he entered the Russian diplomatic service. He laboured strenuously to unite Napoleon's enemies against him, seduced Bernadotte (q.v.) from the Napoleonic cause and urged the allies to march on Paris. He represented Russia at Paris, the Congress of Vienna, the Congress of Verona, and was ambassador to London from 1834 to 1839, when he settled in Paris, where he died. See his Correspondence (Paris 1890) and a French monograph by Maggiolo (1890).

PRAED, Winthrop Mackworth, *prayd* (1802–1839), English man of letters, born in London, at Eton was one of the most brilliant contributors to the *Etonian.* In 1821 he entered Trinity College, Cambridge, distinguishing himself in Greek and Latin verse, and cultivating the lighter letters in Charles Knight's *Quarterly Magazine.* In 1829 he was called to the bar, in 1830 entered parliament as a Conservative, and in 1834–35 was secretary to the Board of Control. Praed excelled in *vers de société*—his note individual, his rhythm brilliant, and his wit bright. But he is also admirable in a kind of metrical genre painting—e.g., 'The Vicar'; while in 'The Red Fisherman' and 'Sir Nicholas' he not unskilfully emulates Hood. His Poems appeared in 1864, with a memoir by Derwent Coleridge; in 1887 his prose essays; in 1888 his political poems. See Saintsbury's *Essays in English Literature* (1890) and study by D. Hudson (1939).

PRASAD, Rajendra (1884–1963), Indian statesman, left legal practice to become a follower of Gandhi. A member of the Working Committee of the All-India Congress in 1922, he was president of the Congress several times between 1934 and 1948. In 1946 he was appointed minister for food and agriculture in the government of India and president of the Indian Constituent Assembly. He was the first president of the Republic of India from 1950 to 1962. He wrote several books, including *India Divided At the Feet of Mahatma Gandhi* and an autobiography *Atma Katha* (1958).

PRATI, Giovanni (1815–84), Italian lyric and narrative poet, was born near Trento, and died in Rome. Court poet to the House of Savoy, he became a deputy to the Italian parliament (1862) and a senator (1876). His lyrics, which fill several volumes, were published as *Canti lirici, Canti del popolo,* &c. See A. Ottolini, *Giovanni Prati* (1911).

PRAXITELES, *prax-it'ē-leez* (fl. 4th cent. B.C.), one of the greatest of Greek sculptors, was a citizen of Athens. His works have almost all perished, though his *Hermes carrying the boy Dionysus* was found at Olympia in 1877.

PREECE, Sir William Henry (1834–1913), British electrical engineer, born of Welsh parents in Carnarvon, was instructed in electrical engineering by Michael Faraday (q.v.) at the Royal Institution. With the Electric and International Telegraph Company from 1853 and the Channel Islands Telegraph Company from 1858 to 1862, he in 1870 was attached to the Post Office, of which he became electrician-in-chief, engineer-in-chief and finally consulting engineer. A pioneer of wireless telegraphy and telephony, he also improved the system of railway signalling and introduced the first telephone receivers. He wrote several books, including *Telegraphy* (1876) with J. Sivewright and *A Manual of Telephony* (1893) with A. J. Stubbs.

PREGL, Fritz, *prayg'l'* (1869–1930), Austrian chemist, born in Laibach, Yugoslavia, became professor of Applied Medical Chemistry at Innsbruck and later at Graz. He was specially noted for the microchemical methods of analysis which gained him a Nobel prize in 1923.

PREMPEH (d. 1931), last King (1888–96) of Ashanti, was deposed by the British, imprisoned at Elmina, and exiled to the Seychelles. He was allowed to return in 1924, with chief's rank from 1926.

PRÉS. See DES PRÉS.

PRESCOTT, William Hickling (1796–1859), American historian, was born at Salem, Mass., the son of a lawyer. He studied at Harvard (where a piece of bread playfully thrown blinded his left eye, and greatly weakened his right one), travelled in England, France and Italy, married in 1820, and, abandoning law for literature, devoted himself to severe study, and, in spite of his grievous disabilities, formed splendid literary projects. His first studies were in Italian literature, but by 1826 he had found his life's work in Spanish history. His *History of Ferdinand and Isabella* (1838) quickly carried his name to the Old World, and was translated into French, Spanish and German. The *History of the Conquest of Mexico* (1843), followed by the *Conquest of Peru* (1847), confirmed his reputation; he was chosen a corresponding member of the French Institute. In 1855–58 he published three volumes of his *History of Philip II*, but died in New York before completing it. Prescott's scholarly but vivid style alone would have assured him popularity. See Life by George Ticknor (1864), and D. Levin, *History as a Romantic Art* (1960).

PRESSENSÉ, *pres-sã-say*, (1) **Edmond Dehaut de** (1824–91), French Protestant theologian, studied at Paris, Lausanne, Berlin and Halle, and in 1847 became a pastor at Paris. He was deputy to the National Assembly for the Seine (1871–76), and elected a life senator in 1883. He was made D.D. by Breslau in 1869 and Edinburgh in 1884. A vigorous writer as well as eloquent preacher, Pressensé took a leading part in the great theological and ecclesiastical controversies of the day. Among his works are *L'Église et la Révolution* (1864; trans. 1869) and *Les Origines* (1882; trans. 1883). See Life by Rousset (1894).

(2) **Francis de** (1853–1914), born in Paris, son of (1), was a notable Socialist and journalist, and a defender of Dreyfus.

PRESTWICH, Sir Joseph (1812–96), English geologist, born at Pensbury, Clapham, was a wine merchant till sixty, but in 1874 became Oxford professor of Geology, and in 1896 was knighted. His work on the water-bearing strata round London (1851) was a standard authority. See Life by his wife (1899).

PRETORIUS, *pre-tō'ri-us*, (1) **Andries Wilhelmus Jacobus** (1799–1853), Boer leader, was born in the Cape Colony. A prosperous farmer, he joined the Great Trek of 1835 into Natal, where he was chosen commandant-general. He took revenge on the Zulus for earlier atrocities, and at first resisting, later accepted British rule, but, after differences with the governor, he trekked again, this time across the Vaal. Eventually the British recognized the Transvaal Republic, later the South African Republic, whose new capital was named Pretoria after him.

(2) **Marthinus Wessels** (1819–1901), son of (1), whom he succeeded as commandant-general in 1853, in 1854 led a punitive expedition against the Kaffirs. He was elected president of the South African Republic in 1857, and of the Orange Free State in 1859. Failing in his ambition to unite the two republics, he resigned the presidency of the Orange Free State in 1863. The discovery of gold in Bechuanaland and diamonds in the Vaal led to difficulties with the *Volksraad*, and he resigned the presidency of the South African Republic in 1871. He fought against the British again in 1877, until the independence of the Republic was recognized. He lived to see it extinguished in 1901.

PRÉVOST, *pray-vō*, (1) **Abbé (Antoine François Prévost d'Exiles)** (1697–1763), French novelist, born in Artois, was educated by the Jesuits. At sixteen he enlisted, but soon returned to the Jesuits, and had almost joined the order when he was again tempted to the soldier's life. In 1720, following an unhappy love affair, he joined the Benedictines of St Maur, and spent the next seven years in religious duties and in study. But about 1727 he fled for six years, first to London, where he started to write *Histoire de Cleveland*, and then to Holland (1729–31). He issued vols. i-iv of *Mémoires d'un homme de qualité* in 1728, vols. v–vii in 1731, *Manon Lescaut* forming vol. vii. He employed himself in additional novels—*Cleveland*; *Le Doyen de Killerine* and in translations. In London again after another affair, he started *Le Pour et contre* (1733–40), a periodical review of life and letters, modelled on the *Spectator*. In France by 1735, he was appointed honorary chaplain to the Prince de Conti, and compiled over a hundred volumes more. He died suddenly at Chantilly. Prévost lives securely by *Manon Lescaut*. It remains fresh, charming and perennial, from its perfect simplicity, the stamp of reality and truth throughout, and a style so flowing and natural that the reader forgets it altogether in the pathetic interest of the story. See French monographs by Harrisse (1896), Schroeder (1899).

(2) **Eugène Marcel** (1862–1941), French novelist, born in Paris, till 1891 was engineer in a tobacco factory. From the age of twenty-five he wrote in his leisure hours, and in 1909 was elected to the Académie. Of his clever novels and plays many have been translated—*Cousin Laura*, *Frédérique*, *Léa*, &c.

(3) **Pierre** (1751–1839), Swiss physician, classicist and philosopher, born at Geneva, occupied chairs of philosophy and physics at Berlin and Geneva. He formulated the theory of exchanges in connection with the laws of radiation. His writings and translations covered many subjects.

PRÉVOST-PARADOL, Lucien Anatole (1829–70), French journalist and diplomat, born in Paris, after a year at Aix as professor of French Literature became in 1856 a journalist in Paris, and from time to time published collections of essays, the best his *Essais sur les moralistes français* (1864). In 1865 he was elected to the Academy, in 1868 visited England. Opposed as a moderate Liberal to the empire, he accepted the post of envoy to the United States under Ollivier

January 1870. His mind unhinged by republican attacks and the struggle with Germany, he committed suicide at Washington just after the outbreak of the Franco-Prussian War.

PRICE, Richard (1723–91), Welsh moral and political philosopher, born at Tynton, Glamorganshire, went to a Dissenting academy in London, was preacher at Newington Green and Hackney, and established a reputation by his *Review of the Principal Questions in Morals* (1758) and *Importance of Christianity* (1766). In 1769 he was made D.D. by Glasgow, and published the celebrated *Northampton Mortality Tables*, &c. In 1771 appeared his *Appeal on the National Debt*; in 1776 his *Observations on Civil Liberty and the War with America*, which brought him an invitation from congress to assist in regulating its finances. In his great treatise on morals he held that right and wrong are simple ideas incapable of analysis, and received immediately by the intuitive power of the reason. In 1791 he became an original member of the Unitarian Society. See Lives by W. Morgan (1815), and R. Thomas (1924) and book by Cone (1952).

PRICHARD, James Cowles (1786–1848), English ethnologist, born in Herefordshire, son of a Quaker merchant, studied medicine, and from 1810 practised in Bristol. In 1813 appeared his *Researches into the Physical History of Mankind* (4th ed. 1841–51), which secured him a high standing. In *The Eastern Origin of the Celtic Nations* (1831) he established the close affinity of the Celtic with the Sanskrit, Greek, Latin and Teutonic languages. Besides several medical works, he published an *Analysis of Egyptian Mythology* (1819) and *The Natural History of Man* (1843). He was president of the Ethnological Society, and in 1845 became a commissioner of lunacy. He died in London.

PRIDE, Thomas (d. 1658), Parliamentarian, born perhaps near Glastonbury, had been a London drayman or brewer, when at the beginning of the Civil War he became parliamentary captain, and quickly rose to be colonel. He commanded a brigade in Scotland, and when the House of Commons betrayed a disposition to effect a settlement with the king, was appointed to expel its Presbyterian royalist members. By 'Pride's Purge' over a hundred were excluded, and the House, reduced to about eighty members, proceeded to bring Charles to justice. Pride sat among his judges, and signed the death warrant. He was present at the battles of Dunbar (1650) and Worcester (1651); opposed to Cromwell becoming 'king', he played little additional part in protectorate politics.

PRIDEAUX, Humphrey, *pri'dō* (1648–1724), English Orientalist, born at Padstow, from Westminster passed to Christ Church, Oxford. His *Marmora Oxoniensia* (1676), an account of the Arundel Marbles, procured for him the friendship of Heneage Finch (q.v.) and ecclesiastical appointments. His chief work, *The Old and New Testament connected in the History of the Jews* (1715–17) ran to many editions. See his *Letters to John Ellis* (Camden Soc. 1875).

PRIESTLEY, (1) John Boynton (1894–), English novelist, playwright and critic, born at Bradford, was educated there and at Trinity Hall, Cambridge. He had already made a reputation by critical writings such as *The English Comic Characters* (1925), *The English Novel* (1927), *English Humour* (1928), and books on Meredith (1926) and Peacock (1927) in 'The English Men of Letters' series when the geniality of his novel *The Good Companions* (1929) gained him a wide popularity. It was followed by other humorous novels, though not all of equal merit, including *Angel Pavement* (1930), *Let the People Sing* (1939), *Jenny Villiers* (1947), *The Magicians* (1954). His reputation as a dramatist was established by *Dangerous Corner* (1932), *Time and the Conways* (1937), and other plays on space-time themes, as well as popular comedies, such as *Laburnum Grove* (1933). Best known as a writer of novels, Priestley is also master of the essay form. He is an astute, original and controversial commentator on contemporary society—*Journey Down the Rainbow* (1955), written with his wife Jacquetta Hawkes (b. 1910; younger daughter of Sir Frederick Gowland Hopkins and a noted archaeologist and writer), is a jovial indictment of American life; in serious vein, his collected essays *Thoughts in the Wilderness* (1957) deal with both present and future social problems. See studies by Hughes (1958) and Evans (1964).

(2) **Joseph** (1733–1804), English Presbyterian minister and chemist, was born, a cloth-dresser's son, at Fieldhead in Birstall Parish, Leeds. After four years at a Dissenting academy at Daventry, in 1755 he became minister at Needham Market, and wrote *The Scripture Doctrine of Remission.* In 1758 he went to Nantwich, and in 1761 became a tutor at Warrington Academy. In visits to London he met Franklin, who supplied him with books for his *History of Electricity* (1767). In 1764 he was made LL.D. of Edinburgh, and in 1766 F.R.S. In 1767 he became minister of a chapel at Mill Hill, Leeds, where he took up the study of chemistry. In 1774, as literary companion, he accompanied Lord Shelburne on a continental tour and published *Letters to a Philosophical Unbeliever.* But at home he was branded as an atheist in spite of his *Disquisition relating to Matter and Spirit* (1777), affirming from revelation our hope of resurrection. He was elected to the French Academy of Sciences in 1772 and to the St Petersburg Academy in 1780. He became in that year minister of a chapel in Birmingham. His *History of Early Opinions concerning Jesus Christ* (1786) occasioned renewed controversy. His reply to Burke's *Reflections on the French Revolution* led a Birmingham mob to break into his house and destroy its contents (1791). He now settled at Hackney, and in 1794 removed to America, where he was well received; at Northumberland, Pa., he died, believing himself to hold the doctrines of the primitive Christians, and looking for the second coming of Christ. Priestley was a pioneer in the chemistry of gases, and one of the discoverers of oxygen (see SCHEELE).

See his *Works*, ed. Ruff (1831–32), including Autobiographical Memoir; and Life by Anne Holt (1931).

PRIM (Y PRATS), Juan, *preem* (1814–70), Spanish general, born at Reus, so distinguished himself in war and statesmanship as to be made general, marshal and marquis. As progressist he opposed Espartero. Failing in an insurrectionary attempt in 1866, he fled to England and Brussels, but here he guided the movement that in 1868 overthrew Isabella. He was war minister under Serrano, but soon became virtually dictator. Prim secured the election of Amadeus (q.v.) as king, and was later shot by an assassin.

PRIMATICCIO, Francesco, *pree-ma-teet'chō* (1504–*c.* 1570), Italian painter, born at Bologna, came to France in 1531 at the invitation of Francis I, to help in the decoration of the palace of Fontainebleau. A collection of drawings is in the Louvre.

PRIMO DE RIVERA, Miguel, Marqués de Estella (1870–1930), Spanish general, born at Jerez de la Frontera, during the Spanish-American war served in Cuba and the Philippines and from 1909 to 1913 he was in Morocco, in 1915 becoming military governor of Cadiz and in 1922 of Barcelona. He effected a military *coup d'état* in 1923, and ruled Spain as dictator until he retired in 1929.

PRINCE, (1) **Henry James** (1811–99), English divine, born at Bath, studied medicine, but took Anglican orders, and in 1849 at Spaxton near Bridgwater founded the ' Agapemone ', a community of religious visionaries. See Hepworth Dixon's *Spiritual Wives* (1868).

(2) **John** (1643–1723), a Devon clergyman, author of *The Worthies of Devon* (1701).

PRINGLE, Thomas (1789–1834), Scottish writer, born at Blakelaw, Roxburghshire, studied at Edinburgh University, and in 1817 started the *Edinburgh Monthly Magazine*, the parent of *Blackwood*. In 1820 he sailed for Cape Colony, and for three years was government librarian at Capetown. He started a Whig paper, but it was suppressed by the governor, and returning to London in 1826, he became secretary of the Anti-Slavery Society. His *Ephemerides* (1828) was a collection of graceful verse. See Life and Works by W. Hay (1912).

PRINGSHEIM, *-hīm,* (1) **Ernst** (1859–1917), German physicist, noted for his work with Otto Lummer on black-body radiation. His results influenced Planck (q.v.) in his development of the quantum theory.

(2) **Nathanael** (1823–94), German biologist, born in Wziesko in Silesia, noted for his research on the fertilization of plants, was professor at Jena for a short time but for the most part worked privately. He was the first scientist to observe and demonstrate sexual reproduction in algae. He died in Berlin.

PRINSEP, (1) **Henry Thoby** (1793–1878), English civil servant in India, born at Thoby Priory, Essex, was a member 1858–74 of the Indian Council, and wrote a history of India under the Marquis of Hastings (1823).

(2) **Valentine Cameron** (1838–1904), second son of (1), born at Calcutta, painted many Indian pictures, including one of Lord Lytton's Indian durbar at Delhi, and wrote *Imperial India, an Artist's Journal* (1879), and novels. In 1894 he was elected R.A.

PRINTEMPS, Yvonne, *prī-tã* (1894–), French actress, born in Ermont, Seine-et-Oise, made her first appearance at the Théâtre Cigale, Paris in 1908, and appeared regularly in revue and musical comedy until 1916, when she began to work with Sacha Guitry, whom she subsequently married. She appeared in London and New York, but did not undertake English parts until 1934, when she played in Noel Coward's *Conversation Piece.* In 1937 she returned to Paris as manager of the Théâtre de la Michodière.

PRIOR, Matthew (1664–1721), English diplomatist and poet, was the son of a joiner of Wimborne, Dorset, but under the patronage of Lord Dorset he was sent to Westminster School and thence with a scholarship from the Duchess of Somerset to St John's College, Cambridge. He was first employed as secretary to the ambassador to The Hague. In Queen Anne's time he turned Tory and was instrumental in bringing about the treaty of Utrecht (1713), for which dubious service he was imprisoned for two years, after the queen's death. His Tory friends recouped his fortunes by subscribing handsomely to a folio edition of his works (1719). He also received a gift of £4000 from Lord Harley to purchase Down Hall in Essex. Prior was a master of what Addison called ' the easie way of writing ', that is neat, colloquial and epigrammatic verse. His first work, in collaboration with Charles Montagu (Lord Halifax), was *The Hind and the Panther Transvers'd*, a witty satire on Dryden's *Hind and the Panther*. His long poem, *Alma or The Progress of the Mind* (1718), written in the manner of *Hudibras*, despite its surface glitter, tends to pall. The long soliloquy in couplet form *Solomon on the Vanity of the World* is definitely tedious. His political verse, with the exception of his brilliant burlesque of Boileau's *Épître au roi—An English Ballad on the Taking of Namur*, is now of historical interest only. The Prior who survives and is the delight of the anthologist is the poet of light occasional verse—mock-lyrics such as *A Better Answer* (*to Chloe Jealous*) or charming addresses to noble children (*A Letter to the Lady Margaret Cavendish when a Child*) and, in serious vein, *Lines Written in the Beginning of Mézeray's History of France*, a favourite with Scott. His most witty trifle is *The Secretary*, but perhaps the poet who comes closest to our affections is the author of *Jinny the Just*. The folio of 1719 was by no means inclusive. A. R. Waller's 2-vol. edition (1905–07) added greatly to it and included the four prose *Dialogues of the Dead*. See study by L. G. Wickham Legg (1921) and *The Literary Works of Matthew Prior*, ed. H. B. Wright and M. K. Spears, 2 vols. (1959).

PRISCIAN, Lat. **Priscianus** (fl. *c.* A.D. 500) of Caesarea, first of Latin grammarians, in the beginning of the 6th century taught Latin at Constantinople. Besides his *Institutiones Grammaticae*, which was very highly thought of in the middle ages, he wrote six smaller grammatical treatises and two hexameter poems.

PRISCILLIAN (*c.* 340–385), Bishop of Ávila, was excommunicated by a synod at Saragossa in 380, then tolerated, but ultimately executed —the first case of capital punishment for heresy in the history of the Church. His doctrine, said to have been brought to Spain from Egypt, contained Gnostic and Manichaean elements, and was based on dualism. The Priscillianists were ascetics, eschewed marriage and animal food, and were said to hold strict truth obligatory only between themselves. See *Priscillian et le Priscillianisme*, by E. C. Babut (Paris 1909).

PRITCHARD, Charles (1808–93), English schoolmaster, clergyman and astronomer, was from 1870 Savilian professor at Oxford, where he established an observatory. He wrote on stellar photometry in *Uranometria Nova Oxoniensis* (1885). See Memoirs (1896).

PROBUS, (1) **Marcus Aurelius** (d. 282), Roman emperor, born at Sirmium in Pannonia, greatly distinguished himself under Valerian on the Danube and in Africa, Egypt, Asia, Germany and Gaul, was by Tacitus appointed governor of Asia, and by his soldiers, on Tacitus's death, was forced to assume the purple (A.D. 276). The Germans were driven out of Gaul and the Barbarians from the frontier, while Persia was forced to a humiliating peace. Probus next devoted himself to developing the internal resources of the empire. But fearing that the army would deteriorate with inactivity, he employed the soldiers on public works. Such occupations, deemed degrading, excited discontent; and a body of troops engaged in draining the swamps about Sirmium murdered him in 282.

(2) **Marcus Valerius** (fl. late 1st cent. A.D.), Latin grammarian from Syria, wrote a biography of Persius and prepared annotated editions of classical authors, including Horace, Terence and Lucretius.

PROCLUS (*c.* A.D. 412–485), Greek Neoplatonist philosopher, born in Constantinople, studied at Alexandria and Athens. His vivid imagination convinced him, when all the influences of the mysteries were brought to bear upon him, of his direct intercommunion with the gods. The Orphic Poems, the writings of Hermes, and all the mystical literature of that occult age were to him the only source of true philosophy. Of an impulsive piety, and eager to win disciples from Christianity itself, he made himself obnoxious to the Christian authorities in Athens, who banished him. Allowed to return, he acted with more prudence. His Neoplatonism based on Plotinus combined all the most important strands of Greek philosophy, the traditions of the Roman, Syrian and Alexandrian schools into one comprehensive theological metaphysic. Euclid, Plato and Pythagoras are all grist to his mill. Hegel's dialectic originated in Proclus' triadic law of development. See edition of some of his works by V. Cousin (1820–25), *Elements of Theology* (trans. E. R. Dodds 1932), W. B. Frankland, *The First Book of Euclid's Elements based upon that of Proclus* (1933).

PROCOP, Andrew (*c.* 1380–1434), Bohemian Hussite leader, from a monk became one of Žižka's followers, and on Žižka's death commander of the Taborites. Under him the fearful raids into Silesia, Saxony and Franconia were carried out, and he repeatedly defeated German armies. He and his colleague, Procop the Younger, headed the internal conflict of the Taborites with the more moderate Calixtines; both fell at Lipan near Böhmischbrod.

PROCOPIUS (*c.* A.D. 499–565), Byzantine historian, born at Caesarea in Palestine, studied law, and accompanied Belisarius against the Persians (526), the Vandals in Africa (533) and the Ostrogoths in Italy (536). He was highly honoured by Justinian, and seems to have been appointed prefect of Constantinople in 562. His principal works are his *Historiae* (on the Persian, Vandal and Gothic wars), *De Aedificiis*, and *Anecdota* or *Historia Arcana*, a sort of *chronique scandaleuse* of the court of Justinian. There are editions by Haury (1905 *et seq.*), and in the Loeb Lib. with trans. by H. B. Dewing (1914–40). See THEODORA; and works by Dahn (1865) and Haury (1891).

PROCTER, (1) **Adelaide Ann** (1825–64), English minor poet, daughter of (2), was born and died in London and in 1851 turned Roman Catholic. By her *Legends and Lyrics* (1858–60), some of which were written for *Household Words*, she won poetical renown. Her verse includes *The Lost Chord*, which was set to music by Sir Arthur Sullivan.

(2) **Bryan Waller**, pseud. **Barry Cornwall** (1787–1874), born at Leeds, and educated at Harrow with Byron and Peel for schoolfellows, became a solicitor, came to London and in 1815 began to contribute poetry to the *Literary Gazette*. In 1823 he married Basil Montagu's step-daughter, Anne Benson Skepper (1799–1888). He had meanwhile published poems and produced a tragedy at Covent Garden, whose success was largely due to the acting of Macready and Kemble. He was called to the bar in 1831, and in 1832–61 was a metropolitan commissioner of lunacy. His works comprise *Dramatic Scenes* (1819), *Marcian Colonna* (1820), *The Flood of Thessaly* (1823), and *English Songs* (1832), besides memoirs of Kean (1835) and Charles Lamb (1866). The last is always worth reading; but his poems are rarely more than studied if graceful exercises. Yet 'Barry Cornwall' was a man beloved by many of the greatest of his time. See *Autobiographical Fragment*, ed. by Coventry Patmore (1877).

PROCTOR, Richard Anthony (1837–88), English astronomer, born at Chelsea, graduated from St John's, Cambridge, in 1860. Devoting himself from 1863 to astronomy, in 1866 he was elected F.R.A.S. His name is associated with the determination of the rotation of Mars, the theory of the solar corona, and stellar distribution. He charted the 324,198 stars contained in Argelander's great catalogue. Very popular as a lecturer and writer, he founded his magazine *Knowledge* in 1881, in which year he settled in the States.

PRODICUS (fl. 5th cent. B.C.), born at Iulis

in Ceos, a Greek sophist of the time of Socrates, was author of the story, 'The Choice of Hercules'.

PROKHOROV, Alexander (1916–), Russian physicist, professor at Lebedev Physics Inst., Moscow. He won the Nobel prize for physics in 1964 with Basov and Townes for work on development of laser beams.

PROKOFIEV, Sergei Sergeevitch, *pro-kof'yef* (1891–1955), Russian composer, was born at Sontsovka, Ukraine. Taught the piano by his mother, he began to compose at five and had started his first opera at the age of nine. He studied at the St Petersburg Conservatory under Rimsky-Korsakov and Liadov, composing prolifically and winning a reputation as a virtuoso pianist. During World War I Prokofiev lived in London, and at its close he moved to the United States until in 1934 he returned to Russia. Induced to do so by the Soviet Government, he simplified his style, producing a large number of occasional works for official celebrations in addition to his later Symphonies and popular pieces like *Peter and the Wolf.* His works range from the glittering romanticism of his early days to the mellow lyricism of his second Russian period, and in all spheres from opera to film music he was a consummate artist combining acute imagination with a precise technique. See *Autobiography* (1960).

PROKOP. See PROCOP.

PROKOPOVICH, Feofan, *-pō'-* (1681–1736), Russian prelate, educated at Kiev Orthodox Academy, where in 1711 he was appointed rector, and Rome. In St Petersburg in 1716 his sermons and theories for church reforms brought him to the notice of Peter the Great, who made him his adviser, Bishop of Pskov and in 1724 Archbishop of Novgorod. He was responsible for setting up a Holy Synod instead of the existing patriarchate, whereby the respective powers of church and state were established.

PROPERTIUS, Sextus (*c.* 48–*c.* 15 B.C.), the most impassioned of the Roman elegiac poets, was born probably at Asisium (the modern Assisi). He had a portion of his patrimony confiscated after Philippi by the Triumvirs, to reward their veterans, but retained means enough to proceed to Rome for education and to make poetry the business of his life. He won the favour of Maecenas, to whom he dedicated a book of his poems, and even ingratiated himself with Augustus, whose achievements he duly celebrated. But the central figure of his inspiration was his mistress Cynthia. Propertius left Rome apparently only once, on a visit to Athens. Of his poems only the first book, devoted to Cynthia, was published during his lifetime; certainly the last of the four was given to the light by his friends. Later criticism shows increasing admiration for his native force, his eye for dramatic situation, and his power over the reader's sympathies. But he is often rough to harshness and obscure from defect of finish. There are texts by Postgate, Phillimore, Richmond (1928), Butler and Barber (1933). There are translations by Phillimore (1906) and Butler (1913).

PROSPER OF AQUITAINE (*c.* 390–*c.* 463), the champion of Augustinian doctrine against the Semi-Pelagians, born in Aquitaine, was a prominent theologian in southern Gaul in 428–434, and then settled in Rome. Besides letters, *Responsiones* and pamphlets on grace and freewill, he wrote a chronicle, coming down to 455, a hexameter poem against the Pelagians, and *Epigrammata ex sententiis Sancti Augustini,* compiled from Augustine.

PROTAGORAS, *-tag'-* (*c.* 485–411 B.C.), the earliest Greek sophist, born at Abdera, taught in Athens, Sicily, &c. a system of practical wisdom fitted to train men for citizens' duties, and based on the doctrine that 'man is the measure of all things'. All his works are lost except a fragment of his *On the Gods.* He perished at sea.

PROTHERO. See ERNLE.

PROTOGENES, *-toj'ė-neez* (fl. late 4th cent. B.C.), Greek painter, born at Caunus in Caria, lived in Rhodes, where he worked steadily on through the siege of 305–304 B.C.

PROUDHON, Pierre Joseph, *proo-dõ* (1809–1865), French socialist, born at Besançon, contrived as a compositor to complete and extend his education. He became partner (1837) in the development of a new typographical process, contributed to an edition of the Bible notes on the Hebrew language, and in 1838 published an *Essai de grammaire générale.* He subsequently contributed to an *Encyclopédie catholique.* In 1840 he issued *Qu'est-ce que la propriété?* affirming the bold paradox 'Property is Theft', as appropriating the labour of others in the form of rent. In 1842 he was tried for his revolutionary opinions, but acquitted. In 1846 he published his greatest work, the *Système des contradictions économiques.* During the Revolution of 1848 he was elected for the Seine department, and published several newspapers advocating the most advanced theories. He attempted also to establish a bank which should pave the way for a socialist transformation by giving gratuitous credit, but failed utterly. The violence of his utterances at last resulted in a sentence of three years' imprisonment, and in March 1849 he fled to Geneva, but returned to Paris in June and gave himself up. While in prison he published *Confessions d'un révolutionnaire* (1849), *Actes de la Révolution* (1849), *Gratuité du crédit* (1850) and *La Révolution sociale démontrée par le coup d'état* (1852). In June 1852 he was liberated, but in 1858 was again condemned to three years' imprisonment, and retired to Belgium. Amnestied in 1860, he died near Paris. A forerunner of Marx, his theories emphasized liberty, equality and justice, and one of his main themes was that as man becomes morally mature the artificial restrictions of law and government can be dispensed with. See Lives by Sainte-Beuve (1872) and Woodcock (1956); and A. Gray, *The Socialist Tradition* (1946).

PROUST, *proost,* (1) **Joseph Louis** (1754–1826), French chemist, born at Angers, was director of the royal laboratory in Madrid (1789–1808). He returned to France after the fall of Charles IV, his patron, and the destruction of the laboratory by the French. He stated the law of constant proportion, known as *Proust's Law,* in a controversy with Berthollet lasting about eight years and was the first to isolate and identify grape sugar. He died at Angers.

(2) **Marcel** (1871–1922), French novelist, born at Auteuil, Paris, was a semi-invalid all his life. He was cosseted by his mother, and her death in 1905, when he was thirty-four years old, robbed him of desire to continue his hitherto 'social butterfly' existence. Instead he withdrew from society, immured himself in a sound-proof flat and gave himself over entirely to introspection. Out of this delving into the self below the levels of superficial consciousness, he set himself to transform into art the realities of experience as known to the inner emotional life. Despite the seemingly dilettante approach to life prior to his start on his novel, *À la recherche du temps perdu* (13 vols.), it is evident from the various volumes that make up this title that no detail ever escaped the amazingly observant eye of this artist in transcription, who subjected experience to searching analysis to divine in it beauties and complexities that escape the superficial response of ordinary intelligence. Thinking around the philosophy of Henri Bergson on the subconscious, his distinctions between the various aspects of time, and insistence on the truths perceived by involuntary memory, Proust evolved a mode of communication by image, evocation and analogy for displaying his characters—not as a realist would see them, superficially, from the outside—but in terms of their concealed emotional life, evolving on a plane that has nothing to do with temporal limitations. Consequently he comes incredibly close to the mainsprings of human action. *The Quest* started off with *Du côté de chez Swann* (1913), and, after delay caused by the war, *À l'ombre des jeunes filles en fleur*, which won the Prix Goncourt in 1919. *Le Côté de Guermantes* (1920–21; 2 vols.) followed and *Sodome et Gomorrhe* (1922; 3 vols.). These achieved an international reputation for Proust and an eager public awaited the posthumously-published titles, *La Prisonnière*, *Albertine disparue*, and *Le Temps retrouvé*, each of two volumes. Apart from his masterpiece, there has also been posthumous publication of an early novel, *Jean Santeuil* (1957) and a book of critical credo—*Contre Sainte-Beuve*, trans. by S. Townsend Warner (1958). See *Comment travaillait Proust*, with bibliography, by L. Pierre-Quint (Paris 1928), and studies by E. Seillière (Paris 1931), H. March (1948), F. C. Green (1949), Maurois (1950), G. Painter vol. i (1959), R. Barker (1959) and Moss (1963).

PROUT (1) **Ebenezer** (1835–1909), English composer and writer on musical theory, edited Handel's Messiah, for which he provided additional accompaniments. In 1894 he became professor of Music at Dublin.

(2) **Father.** See MAHONY.

(3) **Samuel** (1783–1852), English watercolourist, born at Plymouth, in 1815 was elected to the Watercolour Society, and in 1818 went to Rouen. Architecture thenceforward was the feature of his works. Prout's numerous elementary drawing-books influenced many. See Memoir by Ruskin in *Art Journal* (1852), and his *Notes on the Drawings by Prout and Hunt* (1879–80).

(4) **William** (1785–1850), English chemist and physiologist, was born at Horton near Chipping Sodbury. A graduate of Edinburgh, he practised in London from 1812. He is noteworthy for his discovery of the presence of hydrochloric acid in the stomach and for his 'Hypothesis' (1815), which, rejected at first, is now looked upon as a modification of the Atomic Theory.

PRUDENTIUS, **Marcus Aurelius Clemens** (348–*c.* 410), a Latin Christian poet, was born in the north of Spain. He practised as a pleader, acted as civil and criminal judge and afterwards received a high office at the imperial court. A Christian all his life, he devoted himself in his later years to the composition of religious poetry. The year of his death is uncertain. Of his poems the chief are *Cathemerinon Liber*, a series of twelve hortatory hymns (Eng. trans. 1845); *Peristephanon*, fourteen lyrical poems in honour of martyrs; *Apotheosis*, a defence of the Trinity; *Hamartigeneia*, on the Origin of Evil; *Psychomachia*, on the Christian Graces; *Contra Symmachum*, against the heathen gods; *Diptychon*, on scriptural incidents. He is the best of the early Christian versemakers. His works have been edited by J. Bergman (1936). See F. St John Thackeray's *Translations from Prudentius* (1890).

PRUD'HON, **Pierre Paul,** *prü-dõ* (1758–1823), French painter, born at Cluny, studied in Dijon, trained with engravers in Paris and having won the Rome prize, went to Italy. He did little work there, returning to Paris to draw and paint in a refined style not in accord with revolutionary Paris. Patronized, however, by the empresses of Napoleon, he was made court painter, and among his best work is a portrait of the empress Josephine. Many of his paintings had mythological and allegorical subjects and were commissioned for public buildings. He also designed furniture and interiors on classical lines. Unhappily married at the age of nineteen, he formed a liaison with his pupil, Constance Mayer, which ended tragically with her suicide in 1821. See works by Clément (3rd ed. 1880), Gauthiez (1886), Guiffrey (1924).

PRUS, **Boleslaw,** pseud. of **Aleksander Głowacki,** *proos* (1847–1912), Polish novelist, born at Hrubieszów, who belonged to the period of realism in literature which followed the unsuccessful revolt against Russian domination in 1863–64. His novels and short stories are written mainly about the people, the social novel being characteristic of the writing of this time, and include *The Blunder*, *The Outpost* (1884), *The Doll* (1887), considered to be his masterpiece, a vivid and sympathetic picture of Warsaw, and *Emancipated Women* (1893).

PRYDE, **James.** See NICHOLSON (8).

PRYNNE, **William** (1600–69), English pamphleteer, born at Swanswick near Bath, graduated from Oriel College, Oxford, in 1621. He was called to the bar, but was early drawn into controversy, and during 1627–30 published *The Unloveliness of Love-lockes*, *Healthes Sicknesse* (against drinking of healths), and three other Puritan diatribes. In 1633 appeared his *Histrio-Mastix: the*

Players Scourge, for which, on account of a supposed reflection on the virtue of Henrietta Maria, he was in 1634 sentenced to have his book burnt by the hangman, pay a fine of £5000, be expelled from Oxford and Lincoln's Inn, lose both ears in the pillory, and suffer perpetual imprisonment. Three years later, for assailing Laud and the hierarchy in two more pamphlets, a fresh fine of £5000 was imposed; he was again pilloried, and was branded on both cheeks with *S. L.* (' seditious libeller '; rather ' stigmata Laudis ' by Prynne's own interpretation). He remained a prisoner till in 1640 he was released by a warrant of the House of Commons. He acted as Laud's bitter prosecutor (1644), and in 1647 became recorder of Bath, in 1648 member for Newport in Cornwall. But, opposing the Independents and Charles I's execution, he was one of those of whom the House was ' purged ', and was even imprisoned 1650–52. On Cromwell's death he returned to parliament as a royalist; and after the Restoration Charles II made him keeper of the Tower records. Prynne was a great compiler of constitutional history, his best works the *Calendar of Parliamentary Writs* and his *Records*. See *Documents relating to Prynne*, ed. Gardiner (1877); Life by Kirby (1931).

PRZHEVALSKI, Nikolai Mikhailovich (1839–1888), Russian traveller, born near Smolensk, from 1867 to his death at Karakol (Przhevalsk) made important journeys in Mongolia, Turkestan and Tibet, reaching to within 160 miles of Lhasa. He explored the upper Hwang-ho, reaching as far as Kiachta. He amassed a valuable collection of plants and animals, including a wild camel and a wild horse.

PRZYBYSZEWSKI, Stanislaw, *pshi-bi-shef'-ski* (1868–1927), Polish novelist, dramatist and critic, educated in Germany, lived from 1898 in Cracow, where he became editor of *Life* and a leader of the new literary ' Young Poland ' movement. His work, reflecting his ' naturalist ' ideas, includes *Homo Sapiens* (1901), *Matka* (1903) and the drama *Śnieg* (*Snow*), which was translated into English in 1920.

PSALMANAZAR, George (*c.* 1679–1763), ' the Formosan ', real name unknown, was born probably in Languedoc. Educated by monks and Jesuits, he at sixteen turned vagabond, and wandered through France, Germany and the Low Countries, by turns an ' Irish pilgrim ', a ' Japanese convert ', a waiter, a ' heathen Formosan ' and a soldier. At Sluys in 1703 he found an accomplice in one Innes, chaplain to a Scottish regiment, who baptized him ' George Lauder ', and brought him to London. For Bishop Compton he translated the Church Catechism into the ' Formosan ' language; and to him he dedicated his *Historical and Geographical Description of Formosa* (1704), which found many believers in spite of its patent absurdities. Later he was the alleged importer of a white ' Formosan ' enamel, a tutor, a regimental clerk (1715–17), a fan-painter and, lastly, for years a diligent hack-writer. The *Universal History* was largely of his compiling; and his, too, a popular *Essay on Miracles*. But in all his strange life there is nothing stranger than the esteem expressed for him by Samuel Johnson as ' the best man he ever knew '. See his autobiographical *Memoirs* (1764) and Farrer's *Literary Forgeries* (1907).

PSELLUS, Michael (11th cent.), a Byzantine politician and teacher of philosophy, wrote *Synopsis in Aristotelis logicam* and *Chronographia*, valuable both historically and autobiographically. He had considerable influence during the reigns of Constantine Monomachus (who appointed him head of the new faculty of philosophy at the university of Constantinople), Isaac Comnenus and Constantine Ducas, whose son was his pupil.

PTOLEMY, name of the Macedonian kings who ruled Egypt for three hundred years. **Ptolemy (I) Soter** (d. 283 B.C.), a son of Lagos, was one of the greatest of the generals of Alexander the Great, upon whose death he obtained Egypt (323 B.C.). Nominally subject to Macedonia, Ptolemy occupied the first half of his reign in warding off outside attacks and consolidating his government. In 306 he was defeated by Demetrius in a sea-fight off Salamis in Cyprus. Notwithstanding this, he assumed the title of king of Egypt, and defended his dominions against Antigonus and Demetrius. In 305 he defended the Rhodians against Demetrius, and received from them his title Soter (Saviour). Alexandria, his capital, became the centre of commerce and Greek culture. He abdicated in 285 and was succeeded by his son **Ptolemy (II) Philadelphus** (d. 247), under whom the power of Egypt attained its greatest height. He was successful in his external wars, founded the Museum and Library of Alexandria, purchased the most valuable manuscripts, engaged the most celebrated professors, and had made for him the Septuagint translation of the Hebrew Scriptures and the Egyptian history of Manetho. **Ptolemy (III) Euergetes**, his son, pushed the southern limits of the empire to Axum. **Ptolemy (IV) Philopator** (221–204), his son, began his reign by murdering his mother, Berenice. He abandoned himself to luxury, and the decadence of the Egyptian empire set in. He warred with Antiochus, persecuted the Jews, and encouraged learning. He was succeeded by his infant son **Ptolemy (V) Epiphanes** (204–180). The kings of Syria and Macedonia wrested from Egypt her provinces, and the king's ministers called in the aid of Rome, whose influence in Egypt after this was supreme. The successors of Epiphanes were worthless as rulers down to the time of the celebrated Cleopatra (q.v.), after which Egypt became a Roman province. See Mahaffy, *Empire of the Ptolemies* (1896) and Bevan, *Egypt under the Ptolemies* (1927).

PTOLEMY, or **Claudius Ptolemaeus** (*c.* A.D. 90–168), astronomer and geographer, was a native of Egypt, and flourished in Alexandria. His ' great compendium of astronomy ' seems to have been denominated by the Greeks *megistē*, ' the greatest ', whence was derived the Arab name *Almagest*, by which it is generally known. With his *Tetrabiblos Syntaxis* is combined another work called *Karpos* or *Centiloquium*, because it contains a hundred aphorisms—both treat of astrological subjects, so have been held by some to be of doubtful genuineness. Then there is a treatise on the fixed stars or a species of almanac, the *Geographia*, with other works dealing with map making, the musical scale and chronology. Ptolemy, as astronomer and geographer, held supreme sway over the minds of scientific men down to the 16th–17th century; but he seems to have been not so much an independent investigator as a corrector and improver of the work of his predecessors. In astronomy he depended almost entirely on Hipparchus. But, as his works form the only remaining authority on ancient astronomy, the system they expound is called the *Ptolemaic System*, which, the system of Plato and Aristotle, was an attempt to reduce to scientific form the common notions of the motions of the heavenly bodies. The Ptolemaic astronomy, handed on by Byzantines and Arabs, assumed that the earth is the centre of the universe, and that the heavenly bodies revolve round it. Beyond and in the ether surrounding the earth's atmosphere were eight concentric spherical shells, to seven of which one heavenly body was attached, the fixed stars occupying the eighth. The apparent irregularity of their motions was explained by a complicated theory of epicycles. As a geographer Ptolemy is the corrector of a predecessor, Marinus of Tyre. His geography (ed. by Müller, Paris 1883) contains a catalogue of places, with latitude and longitude; general descriptions; details regarding his mode of noting the position of places—by latitude and longitude, with the calculation of the size of the earth. He constructed a map of the world and other maps. See works edited by Heiberg (1898–1907).

PUBLIUS SYRUS. See SYRUS.

PUCCINI, Giacomo Antonio Domenico Michele Secondo Maria, *poo-chee'nee* (1858–1924), Italian composer, born in Lucca, where, at nineteen, he was an organist and choirmaster, his first extant compositions being written for use in the church. Poverty prevented his undertaking regular studies until a grant from the queen in 1880 enabled him to attend the Milan Conservatory. His first opera, *Le Villi*, failed to secure a prize in the competition for which it was composed, but impressed Ricordi, the publisher, sufficiently to induce him to commission a second work, *Edgar*, which failed at its first performance in 1889. *Manon Lescaut* (1893) was his first great success, but it was eclipsed by *La Bohème* (1896). *Tosca* and *Madame Butterfly* (both 1900) have also remained popular favourites. His last opera, *Turandot*, was left unfinished at his death, and was completed by his friend Alfano. Puccini was, perhaps, the last great representative of the Italian operatic tradition, which absorbed almost all his energies throughout his mature working life. See *Letters*, ed. Adami (1931), Life by R. Specht (1933) and a study by M. Carner (1958).

PÜCKLER-MUSKAU, Hermann Ludwig, Fürst von, *pük'lėr-moos'cow* (1785–1871), German traveller, author and horticulturist. See Life by Assing (1873), and *Regency Visitor* (1957), ed. Butler.

PUFFENDORF, or Pufendorf, Samuel, Freiherr von (1632–94), German writer on jurisprudence, born near Chemnitz, studied at Leipzig and at Jena. He was tutor to the sons of the Swedish ambassador at Copenhagen when war broke out between Denmark and Sweden, and he was imprisoned. There he thought out his *Elementa Jurisprudentiae Universalis*, dedicated to the Elector Palatine, who made him professor of the Law of Nations at Heidelberg (1661). As ' Severinus de Monzambano ' he exposed absurdities of the constitution of the Germanic empire in *De Statu Imperii Germanici* (1667). In 1670 he became professor at Lund, and wrote his great *De Jure Naturae et Gentium* (1672), based upon Grotius (q.v.), with features from Hobbes. Appointed Swedish historiographer, he published a history of Sweden from the wars of Gustavus Adolphus to the death of Queen Christina. In 1688 the Elector of Brandenburg invited him to Berlin to write the history of the Great Elector.

PUGACHEV, Emelian, *poo-ga-chof'* (*c.* 1744–1775), Russian Cossack soldier and pretender, fought in the Seven Years' War and in the war against Turkey (1769–74), before retiring to a lawless life in the south of Russia. In 1773 proclaiming himself Peter III, Catharine II's dead husband, he began a reign of organized rebellion in the south, gathering to him the discontented masses out of which he created a military force. Promising to his followers freedom and possessions, he besieged fortresses and towns and his power by 1774 had spread alarmingly. Catharine made half-hearted attempts to curb Pugachev with a weak and badly led force, but finally sent her general Mikhelson against him, and in a battle near Tsaritsyn he was defeated, captured and conveyed in an iron cage to Moscow, where he was executed. There was not another rebellion of this magnitude in Russia until the beginning of the 20th-century revolution.

PUGET, Pierre, *pü-zhay* (1622–94), French sculptor and painter, born in Marseilles, where later he did most of his work. Examples of his sculpture may be seen in the Louvre (Hercules, Milo of Crotona, Alexander and Diogenes, &c.). See Life by Ginoux (1894).

PUGIN, *pü-zhī*, (1) **Augustus Welby** (1812–52), English architect, was born in London, the son of a French architect, Auguste Pugin (1762–1832), in whose office, after schooling at Christ's Hospital, he was trained, chiefly by making drawings for his father's books on Gothic buildings. While working with Sir C. Barry he designed and modelled a large part of the decorations and sculpture for the new Houses of Parliament (1836–37). He became about 1833 a convert to Catholicism; and most of his plans were made for churches within that faith, for example the Roman Catholic cathedral at Birmingham. He did much to revive Gothic architecture in England. He died insane at Ramsgate. He wrote *Contrasts between the Architecture of the 15th and 19th Centuries* (1836), *Chancel Screens* (1851) and *True Principles of Christian Architecture* (1841). See Ferrey's *Recollec-*

tions of Pugin and his Father (1861) and M. Trappes-Lomax, *Pugin: a Mediaeval Victorian* (1932).

(2) **Edward Welby** (1834–75), son of (1), completed much of his father's work and designed many Catholic churches, including the cathedral at Cóbh, Eire.

PUŁASKI, Kazimierz (1748–79), Polish count and military leader, fought against Russia, and was outlawed at the partition of Poland (1772). In 1777 he went to America, and for his conduct at Brandywine was given a brigade of cavalry. In 1778 he organized 'Pulaski's legion', in May 1779 entered Charleston, and held it until it was relieved. He was mortally wounded at the siege of Savannah.

PULCI, *pool'chee,* the name of two Florentine poets, brothers:

(1) **Bernardo** (1438-88), wrote an elegy on the death of Simonetta, mistress of Julian de' Medici, and the first translation of Virgil's *Eclogues.*

(2) **Luigi** (1432–84), wrote *Il Morgante Maggiore* ('Morgante the Giant', 1481), a burlesque epic with Roland for hero, one of the most valuable specimens of the early Tuscan dialect. He also produced a comic novel and several humorous sonnets.

PULITZER, Joseph (1847–1911), American newspaper proprietor was born at Makó, Hungary, of Magyar-Jewish and Austro-German parentage, but emigrated to join the American army. Discharged in 1865, he came penniless to St Louis. He became a reporter, was elected to the State legislature and began to acquire and revitalize old newspapers. The *New York World* (1883), sealed his success. He endowed the Columbia University School of Journalism, and in his will established annual Pulitzer prizes for literature, drama, music and journalism. See Life by D. C. Seitz (1924), and study by A. Ireland (1914).

PULLMAN, George Mortimer (1831–97), American inventor, born at Brocton, in New York state, in 1859 made his first sleeping-cars, and in 1863 the first on the present lines. He also introduced dining-cars. The Pullman Palace Car Company was formed in 1867. In 1880 he founded 'Pullman City', since absorbed by Chicago.

PULSZKY, Francis Aurelius, *pool'ski* (1814–1897), Hungarian politician and author, born at Eperies, studied law, travelled and published (1837) a successful book on England. In 1848 he became Esterházy's factotum, but, having joined the revolution, fled to London, where he became a journalist. When Kossuth came to England Pulszky became his companion, and went with him to America. His wife, **Theresa** (1815–66), wrote *Memoirs of a Hungarian Lady* (1850) and *Tales and Traditions of Hungary* (1851). Pulszky was condemned to death in 1852, but after living in Italy 1852–66, and being imprisoned in Naples as a Garibaldian, was pardoned in 1867. He returned to Hungary, sat in parliament, and was director of museums. See his Autobiography (1879–82; Ger. trans. 1883), and F. W. Newman's *Reminiscences of Two Exiles* (1889).

PULTENEY, William, Earl of Bath (1684–1764), English politician, the son of a London knight, was educated at Westminster and Christ Church, Oxford. He became Whig member for Heydo⁻ in 1705, and was an eloquent speaker. Disgusted with Walpole's indifference to his claim⁻, in 1728 he headed a group of malcontent 'patriots', and was henceforth Walpole's bitterest opponent. He was Bolingbroke's chief assistant in the *Craftsman,* which involved him in many political controversies, and called forth some of his finest pamphlets. On Walpole's resignation Pulteney was sworn into the privy council, and in 1742 created Earl of Bath. Horace Walpole places him amongst his *Royal and Noble Authors.*

PURBACH, or **Peuerbach, Georg von,** *poor'-bakh* (1423–61), Austrian astronomer and mathematician, the first great modern astronomer, Regiomontanus's master, was a professor at Vienna. Thought to be the first to introduce sines into trigonometry, he compiled a sines table. See German monograph by Schubert (1828).

PURCELL, (1) **Edward Mills** (1912–), American physicist, born at Taylorville, Ill., has held posts at Massachusetts Institute of Technology and Harvard University, where he was appointed professor of Physics in 1949 and Gerhard Gade professor in 1960. He was Nobel prize-winner in 1952 (with Bloch, q.v.) for his work on the magnetic moments of atomic particles.

(2) **Henry** (1659–95), English composer, born probably in Westminster, the son of Thomas Purcell, a court musician and Chapel Royal chorister, was himself one of the 'children of the chapel' from about 1669 until 1673, when, his voice having broken, he was apprenticed to the keeper of the king's keyboard and wind instruments, whom he ultimately succeeded in 1683. In the meantime he had followed Locke (q.v.) as 'composer for the king's violins' (1677), and had been appointed organist of Westminster Abbey (1679) and of the Chapel Royal (1682). It is known that he began to compose when very young, though some early pieces ascribed to him are probably the work of his uncle Henry, also a professional musician. About 1680 he began writing incidental music for the Duke of York's Theatre, and thenceforward until his early death his output was prolific. Though his harpsichord pieces and his well-known set of trio-sonatas for violins and continuo have retained their popularity, his greatest masterpieces are among his vocal and choral works. In his official capacity he produced a number of fine 'odes' in celebration of royal birthdays, St Cecilia's Day, and other occasions, also many anthems and services, but had he never written these, his incidental songs such as 'Nymphs and Shepherds' (Shadwell's *The Libertine*), 'I Attempt from Love's Sickness' (*The Indian Queen*), and 'Arise, ye Subterranean Winds' (*The Tempest*), would ensure his immortality. Purcell is credited with six operas, but of these only the first, *Dido and Aeneas* written to a libretto by Nahum Tate (q.v.) in 1689 for performance at a Chelsea girls' school, is opera in the true sense. The others—

Dioclesian (1690; adapted from Beaumont and Fletcher), *King Arthur* (1691; Dryden), *The Fairy Queen* (1692; adapted from *A Midsummer Night's Dream*), *The Tempest* (1695; Shadwell's adaptation) and *The Indian Queen* (1695; Dryden and Howard) consist essentially of spoken dialogue between the main characters interspersed with masques and other musical items supplied by nymphs, shepherds, allegorical figures and the like. Purcell was writing at the time when the new Italian influence was first beginning to be felt in England, and his music includes superb examples in both this and the traditional English style, as well as in the French style exemplified by Lully (q.v.). John Blow's fine ode on his untimely end and tributes by other contemporary musicians show that he was recognized in his own time, as now, as the greatest English composer of the age. His brother **Daniel** (*c.* 1663–1718) was also a distinguished composer, for some time organist of Magdalen College, Oxford. See Lives by J. F. Runciman (1909), Arundell (1928), Holland (1932), Westrup (1937), essays, *Henry Purcell (1659–1695)*, ed. Holst (1959) and an analytical catalogue of his music by Zimmerman (1963).

PURCHAS, Samuel (1577–1626), English compiler of travel books, born at Thaxted, studied at St John's College, Cambridge, and became vicar of Eastwood in 1604, and in 1614 rector of St Martin's, Ludgate. His great works were *Purchas his Pilgrimage, or Relations of the World in all Ages* (1613; 4th ed. enlarged, 1626), and *Hakluytus Posthumus, or Purchas his Pilgrimes* (1625), based on the papers of Hakluyt (q.v.) and archives of the East India Company. Another work is *Purchas his Pilgrim: Microcosmus, or the History of Man* (1619).

PURKINJE, Jan Evangelista (also Purkyne), *poor'kin-yay* (1787–1869), Czech physiologist, born at Libochowitz, was professor at Breslau (1823) and Prague (1850). He did research on the eye, the brain, muscles, embryology, digestion and sweat glands. 'Purkinje's figure' is an effect by which one can see in one's own eye the shadows of the retinal blood vessels. 'Purkinje's cells' are situated in the middle layer of the cerebellar cortex.

PUSEY, Edward Bouverie (1800–82), English theologian, was born at Pusey in Berkshire. His father, the youngest son of the first Viscount Folkestone, had assumed the name Pusey when he inherited the Pusey estates. He was educated at Eton and Christ Church, Oxford, in 1823 was elected a fellow of Oriel, and in 1825–27 in Germany made himself acquainted with German theological teaching. In 1828 he was ordained deacon and priest and appointed regius professor of Hebrew at Oxford, a position which he retained until his death. His first work was an essay on the causes of Rationalism in recent German theology, which was criticized as being itself rationalistic. The aim of his life was to prevent the spread of Rationalism in England. Hence, when in 1833 Newman began the issue of the *Tracts for the Times*, Pusey very soon joined him; and they, with Keble, were the leaders of the movement. They endeavoured to make the church live again before the eyes and minds of men as it had lived in times past. With this aim Pusey wrote his contributions to the *Tracts*, especially those on Baptism and the Holy Eucharist; and commenced in 1836 the *Oxford Library of the Fathers*, to which his chief contributions were translations of Augustine's Confessions and works of Tertullian. But Newman's celebrated Tract 90 was condemned in 1841, and in 1843 Pusey was suspended for two years from preaching in Oxford for a university sermon on the Holy Eucharist; at the first opportunity he reiterated his teaching, and was left unmolested. But before his suspension was over Newman, with several of his leading disciples, had joined the Roman communion. With Keble, Pusey at once set himself to reassure those who were distressed by this development. But soon another band of distinguished men, including Archdeacon (Cardinal) Manning and Archdeacon Wilberforce, departed to the Roman Church. Still Pusey loyally laboured on. His numerous writings during this period included a letter on the practice of confession (1850), a general defence of his own position in *A Letter to the Bishop of London* (1851), *The Doctrine of the Real Presence* (1856–57), and the series of three *Eirenicons* (1865–69), clear the way for reunion between the Church of England and that of Rome. The reform of Oxford University, which destroyed the intimate bond between the university and the church, greatly occupied Pusey's mind. His evidence before the commission, his remarkable pamphlet on *Collegiate and Professorial Teaching*, and his assiduous work on the Hebdomadal Council are proofs of the interest he took in the university. By 1860 the tide had turned. The teaching for which the Tractarians had laboured was beginning to be recognized. But the fruits of the intolerance and persecution of which Oxford had been the scene were also ripening into religious indifference and Rationalism. Against such teaching Pusey contended for the rest of his life. In private life Pusey was an ascetic, deeply religious man of warm affection, widely known for his gentleness, sincerity and humility, and was constantly sought as a spiritual guide by persons of every station. He spent large sums in helping to provide churches in East London and Leeds, and in founding sisterhoods. He married in 1828 Maria Catherine Barker, who died of consumption in 1839; his only son, Philip Edward (1830–80), also predeceased him. He himself died at Ascot Priory, Berks, and was buried in Oxford Cathedral. See Life by Canon Liddon and the Revs. J. O. Johnston and R. J. Wilson (4 vols. 1893–97, with vol. v, *Spiritual Letters*, 1898) and Prestige (1933).

PUSHKIN, Alexandr Sergeevich, *poosh'kin* (1799–1837), Russian poet, was born at Moscow. In 1817 he entered the service of the government, but for his Liberalism was in 1820 exiled to Southern Russia, and in 1824 dismissed and confined to his estate near Pskov, not returning to Moscow until after the accession of Nicholas I. His marriage to Natalia Goncharova proved unhappy and led to his early death in a duel. Hailed in Russia as her greatest poet, his first success was the romantic poem, *Ruslan and Lyudmila* (1820), followed by the *Prisoner of the Caucasus* (1822), *Fountain of Bakhchisarai* (1826), *Tzigani* (1827) and the masterly *Eugene Onegin* (1828), a novel in verse somewhat after the style of Byron's *Beppo*; *Poltava* (1829) has Mazeppa for its hero. *Boris Godunov* is his finest tragedy. He wrote also many graceful lyrical poems, a *History of the Revolt of Pugachev*, several tales and essays, and was appointed Russian historiographer. His *Eugene Onegin* was translated in verse by Spalding (1881), and by O. Elton (1938); and there are translations of his *Daughter of the Commandant* (1891), *Prose Tales* (1894) and *Poems*, with introduction and notes by Panin (N.Y. 1889). Later translations are by Morison (poems) (1945), V. de S. Pinto and H. W. Marshall (tragedies) (1946). See Lives by Mirsky (1926), Simmons (1937) and Magarshack (1967).

PUTNAM, (1) **George Palmer** (1814–72), American publisher, born in Brunswick, Maine, grand-nephew of (2), went to London and in 1840 became partner in a New York book firm. In 1848 he started business alone, establishing in 1866 the firm of G. P. Putnam & Sons (now G. P. Putnam's Sons). In 1852 he founded *Putnam's Magazine*. See Life (1912) by his son, **George Haven Putnam** (1844–1930), who also wrote *Memories of a Publisher* (1913), &c.

(2) **Israel** (1718–90), American general, born at Danvers, Mass., became a farmer, but in 1755 helped as a captain to repel a French invasion of New York, and was present at the battle of Lake George. In 1758 he was captured by the savages, tortured and about to be burnt when a French officer rescued him. In 1759 he was given command of a regiment, in 1762 went on the West India campaign, and in 1764 helped to relieve Detroit, then besieged by Pontiac (q.v.). In 1775, after Concord, he was given command of the forces of Connecticut, was at Bunker Hill, and held the command at New York and in August 1776 at Brooklyn Heights, where he was defeated by Howe. In 1777 he was appointed to the defence of the Highlands of the Hudson. See Life by Tarbox (1876).

(3) **Rufus** (1738–1824), cousin of (2), served against the French in 1757–60, and then settled as a farmer and millwright. In the war he rendered good service as an engineer, commanded a regiment, and in 1783 became brigadier-general. In 1788 he founded Marietta, Ohio; in 1789 he was appointed a judge of the supreme court of the Northwest Territory; and in 1793–1803 was surveyor-general of the United States.

PUVIS DE CHAVANNES, Pierre, *pü-vee dė shav-an* (1824–98), French decorative, symbolic painter, born at Lyons. Murals by him of the life of St Geneviève may be seen in the Panthéon, Paris, and large allegorical works such as 'Work' and 'Peace' on the staircase of the Musée de Picardie, Amiens. See works by Vachon (1895) Michel (1913), Mauclair (1928).

PU-YI, personal name of **Hsuan T'ung** (1906–1967), last emperor of China (1908–12) and the first of Manchukuo (from 1934 until it ceased to exist in 1945). After the revolution of 1912 the young emperor was given a pension and a summer palace near Peking. He became known as Henry Pu-yi, but in 1932 he was called from private life to be provincial dictator of Manchukuo and from 1934 to 1945 he was emperor under the name of **Kang Teh.** After then he lived as a private citizen in Peking until his death. See his *From Emperor to Citizen* (1964).

PYAT, Félix, *pyah* (1810–89), French journalist and communist, in 1831 was admitted to the bar, but chiefly wrote articles, feuilletons and plays. He signed Ledru-Rollin's appeal to the masses to arm in 1849, escaped to Switzerland, Brussels and London, and was a member of the 'European revolutionary committee'. Returning to Paris on amnesty in 1870, he was a leader of the communards, and again escaped to London. He was condemned to death, in absence, in 1873, but pardoned in 1880.

PYE, Henry James (1745–1813), English poet, born in London, studied at Magdalen College, Oxford. He held a commission in the Berkshire militia, in 1784 became member for that county, in 1790 succeeded Warton as laureate, and in 1792 was appointed a London police magistrate. He died at Pinner near Harrow. The works of 'poetical Pye' number nearly twenty, and include *Alfred: an Epic* (1801), with numerous birthday and New-Year odes, all extremely loyal and extremely dull.

PYM, John, *pim* (1584–1643), English politician, born at Brymore near Bridgwater, entered Broadgates Hall (now Pembroke College), Oxford, in 1599, as a gentleman-commoner, but left in 1602 without taking a degree, and then became a student of the Middle Temple. In 1614 he was returned to parliament for Calne, exchanging that seat in 1625 for Tavistock. He attached himself to the Country party, and made war against monopolies, papistry, the Spanish match and absolutism with a vigour that brought him 3 months' imprisonment. In 1626 he took a prominent part in the impeachment of Buckingham. In the parliament of 1628 he stood second only to Sir John Eliot in supporting the Petition of Right, but he opposed him on tonnage and poundage. In the Short Parliament (1640) he 'brake the ice by a two hours' discourse, in which he summed up shortly and sharply all that most reflected upon the prudence and justice of the government, that they might see how much work they had to do to satisfy their country'. And in the Long Parliament, having meanwhile joined with the Scots, and ridden with Hampden through England, urging the voters to their duty, Pym on November 11 named Strafford, twelve years earlier his friend and ally, as the 'principal author and promoter of all those counsels which had exposed the kingdom to so much ruin'. In the impeachment of Strafford which followed, resulting in his execution, Pym took the leading part. In the proceedings against Laud, Pym was also conspicuous, as in the carrying of the Grand Remonstrance and in every other crisis up to the time when war became inevitable; he was the one of the 'Five Members' whom Charles singled out by name. On the breaking out of hostilities he remained in London, and there in the executive rendered services to the cause not less essential than those of a general in the field. He died a month after being appointed Lieutenant of the Ordnance. 'The most popular man', says Clarendon, 'and the most able to do hurt that hath lived in any time.' He was neither revolutionist nor precisian; his intellect was 'intensely conservative', in Gardiner's phrase; he was a champion of what he believed to be the ancient constitution. See Forster's *Eminent British Statesmen* (1837), Goldwin Smith's *Three English Statesmen* (1867), C. E. Wade's *John Pym* (1912), and works cited at CHARLES I, ELIOT and STRAFFORD.

PYNE, William Henry, *pīn* (1769–1843), English artist, born in London, became popular for his landscapes filled with humorous characters. Some of these were 'Travelling Comedians', 'Bartholomew Fair' and 'Anglers'. He was one of the early members of the Old Watercolour Society. Later he concentrated on writing on art, and his books include *Microcosm, or a Picturesque Delineation of the Arts, Agriculture and Manufactures of Great Britain . . .* (1806), *The Costume of Great Britain* (1808), *The History of the Royal Residences of Windsor Castle, St James's Palace . . .* (1829), and under the pseudonym 'Ephraim Hardcastle', *Wine and Walnuts, or After-dinner Chit-chat* (1823), a series of art anecdotes.

PYNSON, Richard (d. 1530), printer of Norman birth, studied at the University of Paris, learned printing in Normandy, and practised his trade in England. In 1497 appeared his edition of Terence, the first classic to be printed in London. He became printer to King Henry VIII (1508), and introduced roman type in England (1509).

PYRRHO, *pir'ō* (*c.* 360–270 B.C.), Greek philosopher, born at Elis, whose opinions we know not from his own writings but from his pupil Timon. He taught that we can know nothing of the nature of things, but that the best attitude of mind is suspense of judgment, which brings with it calmness of mind. Pyrrhonism is often regarded as the *ne plus ultra* of (philosophical) scepticism: consistent Pyrrhonists were said even to doubt that they doubted.

PYRRHUS (*c.* 318–272 B.C.), became king of Epirus when Cassander lost it (307), was driven out again, but restored by help of Ptolemy Soter, and extended his dominions by the addition of western Macedonia. In 281 the Tarentines, a Greek colony in Lower Italy, invited him to help them against the Romans, and in 280 he sailed for Tarentum with 25,000 men and a number of elephants. The first battle, on the river Siris, was long and bloody, but Pyrrhus won it by help of his elephants, till then unknown to the Romans. 'Another such victory,' he said (now or after Asculum), 'and I must return to Epirus alone'—hence the proverbial expression 'a Pyrrhic victory'. Many of the Italian nations now joined Pyrrhus, and he marched northward, came dangerously near Rome, but found it too well prepared, and withdrew to Tarentum, where he wintered. In 279 the Romans were again defeated (at Asculum); but Pyrrhus himself lost so heavily that he had again to withdraw to Tarentum. Here a truce was agreed to, and Pyrrhus crossed over to Sicily to assist the Sicilian Greeks against the Carthaginians in 278. His first exploits in that island were brilliant; but his repulse at Lilybaeum broke the spell; he became involved in misunderstandings with the Greeks, and in 275 quitted the island to renew his war with Rome. While he was crossing over, the Carthaginians attacked him and destroyed seventy of his ships. In 274 he was utterly defeated by the Roman consul Curius Dentatus near Beneventum. He was now forced to abandon Italy and return to Epirus, where he engaged in war with Antigonus Gonatas, king of Macedonia. His success was complete; but in less than a year he was at war with the Spartans, by whom he was repulsed in all his attempts on their city. He then marched against Argos, where he was killed by a tile hurled at him from a roof by a woman. The principal ancient authority for the life of Pyrrhus is Plutarch. See also German Life by R. Schubert (1894).

PYTHAGORAS, *pī-thag'o-ras* (fl. 6th cent. B.C.), Greek philosopher and mathematician, born in Samos, became acquainted with the teachings of the early Ionic philosophers, and, through his travels, with those of the Egyptian priests and other foreigners. About 530 he settled at Crotona in Magna Graecia, where he founded a moral and religious school. Pythagoreanism was first a way of life, not a philosophy, a life of moral abstinence and purification, reactionary against the popular and poetic religions, but yet sympathetic towards the old (Doric) aristocratic forms and institutions. All that can be certainly attributed to Pythagoras is the doctrine of the transmigration of souls, the institution of certain religious and ethical regulations, the beginning of those investigations into the relations of numbers which made the school famous, and astronomical attainments beyond their contemporaries. How much of the mysticism called Neopythagorean (and akin to Neoplatonism) was directly derived from him is hard to say. The Pythagoreans as an aristocratic party became unpopular after the defeat of the Sybarites by the Crotoniates in 510, and at first were instrumental in putting down the democratic party in Lower Italy; but the tables were afterwards turned, and they had to flee from persecution. See a German monograph by Rothenbücher (1867), a French one by Chaignet (2nd ed. 1875), and B. Russell, *History of Western Philosophy* (1946).

PYTHEAS (fl. 4th cent. B.C.), of Massilia (Marseilles), a Greek mariner, about 330 B.C. sailed to Thule (?Iceland), past Spain, Gaul and the east coast of Britain.

PYTHIAS. See DAMON.

Q

Q. See Couch (Quiller); Queensberry.

QUAIN, (1) **Sir John Richard** (1817–76), English lawyer, born at Mallow, became judge of the Queen's Bench in 1871, and justice of the High Court of Judicature in 1875. Along with H. Holroyd he published *New System of Common Law Procedure* (1852).

(2) **Jones** (1796–1865), half-brother of (1), born at Mallow, studied medicine at Dublin and Paris, and in 1831–35 was professor of Anatomy in London University. He wrote the text book, Quain's *Elements of Anatomy* (1828, 10th ed. 1890–96).

(3) **Richard,** F.R.S. (1800–87), brother of (2), born at Fermoy, was professor of Clinical Surgery in University College, London (1848–1866), surgeon-extraordinary to the Queen, and president of the College of Surgeons (1868). He left £75,000 to University College for 'education in modern languages (especially English) and natural science'.

(4) **Sir Richard** (1816–98), cousin of (2), born at Mallow, was the Lumleian lecturer at the College of Physicians in 1872, and Harveian orator in 1885, and was made physician-extraordinary to the Queen, LL.D. of Edinburgh in 1889, president of the General Medical Council in 1891, and a baronet in 1891. He edited the *Dictionary of Medicine* (1882; 2nd ed. 1894).

QUANTZ, Johann Joachim, *kvants* (1697–1773), German flautist and composer, born near Göttingen, spent many years in the service of the King of Saxony, toured extensively in Italy, France and England, and became teacher of Frederick the Great and later his court composer. Author of a treatise on flute-playing, Quantz composed some three hundred concertos for one or two flutes as well as a vast quantity of other music for this instrument.

QUARLES, Francis (1592–1644), English poet, was born at the manor house of Stewards near Romford. He studied at Christ's College, Cambridge, and at Lincoln's Inn, and was successively cup-bearer to the Princess Elizabeth (1613), secretary to Archbishop Ussher (*c.* 1629), and chronologer to the City of London (1639). He married in 1618 a wife who bore him eighteen children and prefixed a touching memoir to his *Solomon's Recantation* (1645). Quarles was a royalist and churchman who suffered in the cause by having his books and manuscripts destroyed. He wrote abundantly in prose and verse. His *Emblems,* in spite of many imperfections, shows wealth of fancy, excellent sense, felicity of expression, and occasionally a flash of poetic fire. Other poetical works include *A Feast of Wormes* (1620), *Argalus and Parthenia* (1629), *Divine Poems* (1630), *The Historie of Samson* (1631), *Divine Fancies* (1632). The prose includes *Enchyridion* (1640) and *The Profest Royalist* (1645). See *Works* edited by Grosart (3 vols. 1880–81) and M. Praz, *Studies in Seventeenth-Century Imagery* (1939).

QUASIMODO, Salvatore (1901–68), Italian poet, born in Syracuse, Sicily, a student of engineering, became a travelling inspector for the Italian state power board before taking up a career in literature and music. A professor of Literature at the Conservatory of Music in Milan, he has written since 1942 five volumes of spirited poetry. These reflect above all his deep interest in the fate of Italy, and his language is made particularly striking by the use simultaneously of both Christian and mythological allusions. In 1959, for his lyrical poetry, he received the Nobel prize for literature, becoming the fourth Italian to gain this award. His works include *Ed e Subito Sera,* 'And suddenly it is Evening' (1942), *La Vita non e sogno,* 'Life is not a Dream' (1949) and *La Terra impareggiabile,* 'The Matchless Earth' (1958).

QUATREFAGES DE BRÉAU, Jean Louis Armand de, *kahtr-fahzh-dė-bray-ō* (1810–92), French naturalist and ethnologist, born at Berthezème (Gard), in 1850 was elected professor in the *Lycée Napoléon* and in 1855 at the Natural History Museum. His chief works are *Souvenirs d'un naturaliste* (1854; trans. 1857), *L'Espèce humaine* (1877; Eng. trans. 1879), *Crania Ethnica* (1875–82), *Les Pygmées* (1887; trans. 1895) and *Darwin et ses précurseurs français* (1892).

QUATREMÈRE, (1) **Antoine Chrysostome,** *kahtr'-mayr* (1755–1849), French archaeologist and politician, was condemned to death during the Terror but later acquitted. He was a member of the Council of Five Hundred. He edited a dictionary of architecture.

(2) **Étienne Marc** (1782–1857), French orientalist, born in Paris, in 1807 entered the MS. department of the Imperial Library, and in 1809 became professor of Greek at Rouen, in 1819 of Ancient Oriental Languages at Paris, in 1827 of Persian. Although a man of vast knowledge, he had little critical insight or originality. He wrote on the language of ancient Egypt, the Mameluke sultans and the Mongols of Persia, &c.

QUEEN, Ellery, pseud. of **Frederic Dannay** (1905–) and his cousin **Manfred B. Lee** (1905–71), American writers of crime fiction, both born in Brooklyn. As business men they entered for and won with *The Roman Hat Mystery* (1929) a detective-story competition and thereafter concentrated on detective fiction, using Ellery Queen both as pseudonym and as the name of their detective. Others of their very popular stories are *The French Powder Mystery* (1930), *The Greek Coffin Mystery* (1932), *The Tragedy of X* (1940), *Double, Double* (1950) and *The Glass Village* (1954). They have also written under the pseudonym Barnaby Ross.

QUEENSBERRY, (1) **William Douglas, Duke** of (1724–1810), 'Old Q', succeeded his father as Earl of March, his mother as Earl of Ruglen, and his cousin in 1778 as fourth Duke of Queensberry. From 1760 to 1789 he was lord of the bedchamber to George III.

He was famous as a patron of the turf, and infamous for his shameless debaucheries. He died unmarried, worth over a million sterling. See Lives by Robinson (1895) and Melville (1927).

(2) **Sir John Sholto Douglas, 8th Marquis of** (1844–1900), an enthusiastic supporter of Bradlaugh and a keen patron of boxing, supervised the formulation in 1867 of new rules to govern that sport, since known as the 'Queensberry rules'. In 1895 he was tried and acquitted for publishing a defamatory libel on Oscar Wilde (q.v.) of whose friendship with his son, Lord Alfred Douglas (q.v.), he disapproved. This led to the trial and imprisonment of Wilde.

QUEIPO DE LLANO, Gonzalo, Marquis of Queipo de Llano y Sevilla, *kay'i-pō* THay *lyah'nō*, (1875–1951), Spanish general, born at Valladolid. After military service in Cuba and Morocco, he was promoted to the rank of major-general in the Republican Army, but went over to the rebel side at the beginning of the Spanish Civil War. In July 1936 he led the forces which captured Seville, and became commander-in-chief of the Southern Army. In one of his many propaganda broadcasts from Seville he originated the phrase 'fifth column', using it to describe the rebel supporters inside Madrid, who were expected to add their strength to that of the four columns attacking from outside. In April 1950 he was given the title of Marquis.

QUENNELL, Peter Courtney (1905–), English biographer, son of **Marjorie Quennell** (1884–1972), the illustrator, was born in London and educated at Berkhamsted and Balliol College, Oxford. Professor of English at Tokyo in 1930, he wrote *A Superficial Journey through Tokio and Pekin* (1932). Author of several books of verse and a novel and editor of *The Cornhill Magazine* (1944–51), he is best known for his biographical studies of Byron (1935; 1941), Queen Caroline (1939), John Ruskin (1949), Shakespeare (1963), as well as those of Boswell, Gibbon, Sterne and Wilkes in *Four Portraits* (1945) and *Hogarth's Progress* (1955).

QUENTAL, Anthero de, *kān-tahl'* (1842–91), Portuguese poet, born in Ponta Delgada, in the Azores. He studied at Lisbon and Coimbra, publishing his first collection of sonnets in 1861 and his *Odes Modernas* in 1865; he followed the latter with a pamphlet, *Good Sense and Good Taste*, which propounded the view that poetry depends upon richness and vitality of ideas rather than upon technical skill with words. Quental lived in Paris and America from 1866 to 1871, and on his return to Portugal became a leading socialist until, after a severe nervous illness, he committed suicide.

QUERCIA, Jacopo Della, *kwer'cha* (*c.* 1367–1438), Italian sculptor, born in Quercia Grossa, Sienna, went to Lucca, where one fine example of his work is the beautiful tomb of Ilaria del Carretto in the cathedral. In direct contrast are the strongly dramatic reliefs for the doorway of the church of San Petronio at Bologna which he left unfinished at his death.

QUEROUAILLE or Kéroualle. See PORTSMOUTH.

QUESADA, Gonzalo Jiménez de, *kay-sah'*THa (*c.* 1497–1579), Spanish conqueror, was born at Córdoba or Granada. Appointed magistrate at Santa Marta in what is now Colombia, he in 1536 headed an expedition and after many hardships and loss of men conquered the rich territory of the Chibchas in the east. This he called New Granada and its chief town Santa Fé de Bogotá. In 1569, during a later expedition in search of El Dorado, he reached the river Guaviare not far from the point where it meets the Orinoco. His history *Los tres ratos de Suesca* has been lost. See *The Conquest of New Granada* by Sir C. Markham (1912) and by R. B. Cunninghame Graham (1922).

QUESNAY, François, *ke-nay* (1694–1774), French physician and economist, born at Mérey, Seine-et-Oise, studied medicine at Paris, and at his death was first physician to the king. But the fame of the 'European Confucius' depends on his essays in political economy. Around him and his friend, M. de Gournay, gathered the famous group of the *Économistes*, also called the Physiocratic School. Quesnay's views were set forth in *Tableaux économiques*. Only a few copies were printed (1758), and these are lost; yet Quesnay's principles are well known from his contributions to the *Encyclopédie*, and from his *Maximes du gouvernement économique*, *Le Droit naturel*, &c.—collected in Oncken's edition of his *Oeuvres* (1888). See H. Higgs, *The Physiocrats* (1897).

QUESNEL, Pasquier, *ke-nel* (1634–1719), French Jansenist theologian, born in Paris, studied at the Sorbonne, became in 1662 director of the Paris Oratory, and here wrote *Réflexions morales sur le Nouveau Testament*. In 1675 he published the works of Leo the Great, which, for Gallicanism in the notes, was placed on the *Index*. Having refused to condemn Jansenism in 1684, he fled to Brussels, where his *Réflexions* were published (1687–94). The Jesuits were unceasing in their hostility, and Quesnel was flung into prison (1703), but escaped to Amsterdam. His book was condemned in the bull *Unigenitus* (1713). See his Letters (1721–23).

QUESNOY, François du, *ke-nwa* (1594–1646), sculptor, was born at Brussels, lived much at Rome, and died at Leghorn, poisoned perhaps by his jealous brother, **Jérome** (1612–1654), a sculptor too, who was burnt for unnatural crimes.

QUÉTELET, Lambert Adolphe Jacques, *kayt-lay* (1796–1874), Belgian statistician and astronomer, born at Ghent, became in 1819 professor of Mathematics at the Brussels Athenaeum, in 1828 director of the new Royal Observatory, in 1836 professor of Astronomy at the Military School, and in 1834 perpetual secretary of the Belgian Royal Academy. In his greatest book, *Sur l'homme* (1835), as in *L'Anthropométrie* (1871), &c., he shows the use that may be made of the theory of probabilities, as applied to the 'average man'.

QUEVEDO Y VILLEGAS, Francisco Gómez de, *ke-vay'*THō *ee veel-yay'gas* (1580–1645), Spanish writer, was born at Madrid. His father was secretary to the queen, and his mother a lady-in-waiting. He quitted the

University of Alcalá with a reputation for varied scholarship. The fatal issue of a duel drove him in 1611 to the court of the Duke of Ossuna, viceroy of Sicily; he made him his right-hand man, and, when promoted to the viceroyalty of Naples, chose him for minister of finance. Quevedo was involved in Ossuna's fall in 1619, and put in prison, but allowed to retire to the Sierra Morena. He returned to Madrid in 1623 and became *persona grata* at the court of Philip IV. In his *Política de Dios* (1626) he appealed to the king to be a king, not in name only, but in fact; in 1628 he followed up this attack on government by favourites with an apologue, *Hell Reformed*. He remained, however, on friendly terms with Olivares and accepted the honorary title of royal secretary. In 1639 a memorial in verse to the king, imploring him to look to the miserable condition of his kingdom, was one day placed in Philip's napkin. Quevedo was denounced as the author, arrested and imprisoned in a convent at Leon, where he was struck down by an illness, from which he never recovered. In 1643 Olivares fell from power, and Quevedo was free to return to Madrid. He died two years later. Quevedo was one of the most prolific Spanish poets, but his verses were all written for his friends or for himself, and, except those in the *Flores* of Espinosa (1605), the few pieces published in his lifetime were printed without his consent. His poetry is therefore for the most part of an occasional character; sonnets, serious and satirical, form a large portion of it, and light humorous ballads and songs a still larger. About a dozen of his interludes are extant, but of his comedies almost nothing is known. His prose is even more multifarious than his verse. His first book (1620) was a Life of St Thomas de Villanueva, and his last (1644) one of St Paul; and most of his prose is devotional. Of his political works the *Política de Dios* is the chief. His brilliant picaresque novel, the *Vida del Buscón Pablos* (1626), or, as it was called after his death, the *Gran Tacaño*, at once took its place beside *Guzmán de Alfarache*. His five *Visions* were printed in 1627; to obtain a licence they were barbarously mutilated; and it is in this mangled shape that they have been printed since 1631. The fullest edition of his works is that in the *Biblioteca de Autores Españoles*. The earliest translations from Quevedo were into French, and from them most of the English versions have been made—e.g.: *Visions; or Hel's Kingdome*, by R. Croshawe (1640); *Hell Reformed*, by E. M. (1641); *Buscon, the Witty Spaniard*, by J. Davies (1657); and the *Visions*, by Sir R. L'Estrange (1667). Captain John Stevens in 1697–1707 produced a translation from the original of *Fortuna con Seso*, the *Vida del Buscón*, &c.; his translations, with L'Estrange's *Visions*, were published in 1798 as *Quevedo's Works*. See Eng. trans. by Duff (1926); also work by E. Mérimée (1886).

QUEZON, Manuel Luis, *kay'son* (1878–1944), first Philippine president, born at Baler, Luzon, studied at Manila, served with Aguinaldo during the insurrection of 1898 and in 1905 became governor of Tayabas. In 1909 he went to Washington as one of the resident Philippine commissioners and began to work for his country's independence. President of the Philippine senate (1916–35), he was elected first president of the Philippine Commonwealth (1935). He established a highly centralized government verging on 'one-man' rule and displayed great courage during the Japanese onslaught on General MacArthur's defences in December 1941, refusing to evacuate to the United States until appealed to by President Roosevelt. He died at Saranac, U.S.A. The new capital of the Philippines on the island of Luzon is named after him.

QUICK, Robert Hebert (1831–91), English educationist, born in London, and educated at Harrow and Trinity College, Cambridge, was a curate in Whitechapel and Marylebone, a schoolmaster, and vicar of Sedbergh 1883–87. The great interest of his life was education. To the discussion of its theories he brought wide study, independent thought, and ripe wisdom. His main work was *Essays on Educational Reformers* (1868).

QUILLER-COUCH. See COUCH.

QUILTER, Roger (1877–1953), English composer, born in Brighton. He studied in Germany and lived entirely by composition, holding no official posts and making few public appearances. His works include an opera, *Julia*, a radio opera, *The Blue Boar*, and the *Children's Overture*, based c nursery tunes, but he is best known for his songs.

QUIN, (1) **James** (1693–1766), Irish actor, born in London, made his début at Dublin in 1714. At Drury Lane in 1716 the sudden illness of a leading actor led to Quin's being called on to play Bajazet in *Tamerlane*. His success was marked. At Lincoln's Inn Fields (1718–32) and at Drury Lane (1734–41) he was by universal consent the first actor in England; then Garrick largely eclipsed him. Retiring in 1751, Quin died at Bath. See anonymous Lives (1766, 1887).

(2) **Wyndham-.** See DUNRAVEN, EARL OF.

QUINAULT, Philippe, *kee-nō* (1635–88), French poet and dramatist, born in Paris, was valet to the poet Tristan L'Hermite, qualified as an *avocat*, and wrote comedies and libretti for the operas of Lully (q.v.).

QUINCEY. See DE QUINCEY.

QUINCY, Josiah (1772–1864), American statesman, was born at Boston, Mass., the son of the lawyer, Josiah Quincy (1744–75). He graduated at Harvard, was called to the bar in 1793, was a leading member of the Federal party, and elected in 1804 to congress, distinguished himself as an orator. He denounced slavery, and in one most remarkable speech declared that the admission of Louisiana would be a sufficient cause for the dissolution of the union. Disgusted with the triumph of the Democrats and the war of 1812, he declined re-election to congress, and devoted his attention to agriculture; but he was a member of the Massachusetts legislature, served as mayor of Boston 1823–28, and in 1829–45 was president of Harvard. He died at Quincy, Mass. Among his works are Memoirs of his father (1825) and J. Q. Adams (1858), histories of Harvard (1840), the Boston Athenaeum (1851), and Boston (1852).

His *Speeches* were edited (1874) by his son, Edmund Quincy (1808–77), who was secretary of the American Anti-Slavery Society.

QUINE, Willard Van Orman (1908–), American mathematical logician, born at Akron, Ohio, from 1948 professor of Philosophy at Harvard, carried on Russellian studies in symbolic logic, and with Carnap and Tarski held that modal logic is a branch of semantics. He adapted Russell's Theory of Descriptions as a means of determining what on purely logical grounds is entitled to 'existence'. See his *Mathematical Logic* (1940), *Methods of Logic* (1950), *From a Logical Point of View* (1953) and *Set Theory and its Logic* (1963).

QUINET, Edgar, *kee-nay* (1803–75), French writer and politician, born at Bourg, studied at Strasbourg, Geneva, Paris and Heidelberg. The remarkable Introduction to his translation of Herder's *Philosophy of History* (1825) won him the friendship of Cousin and Michelet; a government mission to Greece bore fruit in *La Grèce moderne* (1830). *Ahasvérus* (1833), a kind of spiritual imitation of the ancient mysteries, was followed by the less successful poems, 'Napoléon' (1836) and 'Prométhée' (1838); in his *Examen de la vie de Jésus* (1838) he shows that Strauss is too analytic, and that religion is the very substance of humanity. Appointed in 1839 professor of Foreign Literature at Lyons, he began those lectures which formed his brilliant *Du génie des religions* (1842); then recalled to the Collège de France at Paris, he joined Michelet in attacking the Jesuits. His lectures caused so much excitement that the government suppressed them in 1846. At the Revolution Quinet took his place on the barricades, and in the National Assembly voted in the Extreme Left. After the *coup d'état* he was exiled to Brussels, whence in 1857 he emigrated to Switzerland. At Brussels he produced *Les Esclaves* (1853), and in Switzerland *Merlin l'Enchanteur* (1860). Other works were *La Révolution religieuse au XIXe siècle* (1857), *Histoire de mes idées* (1858), *Histoire de la campagne de 1815* (1862), and *La Révolution* (1865). After the downfall of Napoleon III he returned to Paris, and during the siege strove to keep patriotism aglow. He sat in the National Assemblies at Bordeaux and Versailles, and aroused great enthusiasm by his orations. Quinet's latest books were *La Création* (1870), *La République* (1872), *L'Esprit nouveau* (1874), and *Le Livre de l'exilé* (1875). His wife published in 1870 *Mémoires d'exil*; his *Correspondance inédite* followed in 1877, *Lettres d'exil à Michelet* in 1884–86. His *Oeuvres complètes* (30 vols. 1857–79) include a Life by Chassin. See also *Edgar Quinet avant et depuis l'exil* (1887–89) and *Cinquante ans d'amitié* (1900), by his second wife; books by Heath (1881), and Tronchon (1937).

QUINTANA, Manuel José, *keen-tah'-na* (1772–1857), Spanish poet and advocate, born in Madrid, whose house became a resort of advanced Liberals. Besides his classic *Vidas de los Españoles célebres* (1807–1834), he published tragedies and poetry written in a classical style, the best of which are his odes, ardently patriotic but yet restrained. On the restoration of Ferdinand VII he was imprisoned 1814–20; but he recanted, and by 1833 had become tutor to Queen Isabella. In 1835 he was nominated senator.

QUINTERO, Serafín Álvarez, *keen-tay'rō* (1871–1938) and **Joaquín Álvarez** (1873–1944), brothers, born at Utrera, Seville, wrote many plays in collaboration, usually depicting Andalusian life. These include comedies and shorter pieces such as *El Patio*, *Las de Caín* and *Malvaloca* all written with delightful insight into Spanish life and character. Translations have been made by H. and H. Granville-Barker, e.g. *Pueblo de las mujeres* (The Women have their Way), *El Centenario* (A Hundred Years Old).

QUINTILIAN, Marcus Fabius Quintilianus (*c.* A.D. 35–100) was born at Calagurris (*Calahorra*) in Spain, studied oratory at Rome, returned there in 68 in the train of Galba, and became eminent as a pleader and still more as a teacher of the oratorical art. His pupils included Pliny the Younger and the two grand-nephews of Domitian. The emperor named him consul and gave him a pension. His reputation rests securely on his great work, *De Institutione Oratoria*, a complete system of rhetoric, remarkable for its sound critical judgments, purity of taste, admirable form and the perfect familiarity it exhibits with the literature of oratory. Quintilian's own style is excellent, though not free from the florid ornament and poetic metaphor characteristic of his age.

QUINTUS CURTIUS. See CURTIUS (4).

QUISLING, Vidkun, *kwiz'-* (1887–1945), Norwegian diplomat and Fascist leader, born in Fyresdal, was an army major, League of Nations official, had the care of British interests in Russia 1927–29, was defence minister in Norway 1931–33, and in 1933 founded the *Nasjonal Samlung* (National Party) in imitation of the German National Socialist Party. As puppet prime minister in occupied Norway he has given his name to all who play a like traitorous part. He gave himself up in May 1945, was tried and executed. See study by Hewins (1965).

R

RAAB, Julius (1891–1964), Austrian politician, born at St Pölten, became an engineer and was a Christian Socialist member of the Austrian Diet (1927–34), federal minister of Trade and Transport (1938), retired from politics during the Nazi régime and in 1945 was one of the founders of the People's party, chairman of the party (1951–60), minister of economic reconstruction and in 1953 was elected chancellor of Austria.

RAABE, Wilhelm, pseud. **Jakob Corvinus**, *rah'bė* (1831–1910), German novelist, was born at Eschershausen in Brunswick, and in 1870 settled in Brunswick. Reacting against 19th-century progress, he wrote novels which were often grim, tragic and pessimistic. Some of these are *Der Hungerpastor* (1864), *Des Reiches Krone* (1870) and *Meister Autor* (1871), &c.

RABANUS MAURUS. See HRABANUS MAURUS.

RABELAIS, François, *rab-ė-lay* (1494?–1553?), French satirist, said to have been born at a farmhouse near Chinon, or possibly in the town of Chinon, where his father was an advocate. At nine he was sent to the Benedictine abbey of Seuilly, and thence to the Franciscan house of La Baumette near Angers. He became a novice of the Franciscan order, and entered the monastery of Fontenay le Comte, where he had access to a large library, learned Greek, Hebrew and Arabic, and studied all the Latin and old French authors within his reach, medicine, astronomy, botany and mathematics. In Fontenay Rabelais found a friend, André Tiraqueau, lawyer and scholar; his patron, the Bishop of Maillezais, lived close by; and he corresponded with Budaeus. But Franciscan jealousy of the old learning was transformed into jealousy of the new. His books were taken from Rabelais; he conceived a loathing for the convent, and he fled to a Benedictine house near Orleans. He seems to have sought the protection of his friend the bishop, and through him obtained the pope's permission (1524) to pass from the Franciscan to the Benedictine order; but he remained with the bishop for at least three years. In September 1530 he entered the university of Montpellier as a student of medicine. He left the university in 1532, went to Lyons, where he remained as physician to the hospital. At this time Lyons was a great intellectual centre, and round its great printer Gryphius was gathered a company of scholars and poets, men of broad thought and advanced opinions. It was at Lyons that Rabelais began the famous series of books by which he will for ever be remembered. In 1532 there appeared at Lyons fair a popular book, *The Great and Inestimable Chronicles of the Grand and Enormous Giant Gargantua.* It was almost certainly not by Rabelais, but to this book he wrote, in the same year, a sequel, *Pantagruel*, in which serious ideas are set forth side by side with overwhelming nonsense. In 1534 he supplied a first book of his own, a new *Gargantua*, fuller of sense and wisdom than *Pantagruel.* Both books (published under the name of Alcofri bas Nasier, an anagram of François Rabelais) had a prodigious success. Meanwhile he had begun his almanacs or *Pantagrueline Prognostications*, which he continued for a number of years; few of them survive. In 1533 he accompanied Jean du Bellay, Bishop of Paris, to Rome; in 1536 he was in Italy again with Du Bellay, the latter now a cardinal. There he amused himself with collecting plants and curiosities—to Rabelais France owes the melon, artichoke and carnation. He also received permission to go into any Benedictine house which would receive him, and was enabled to hold ecclesiastical offices and to practise medicine. From 1537 (when he took his doctorate) to 1538 he taught at Montpellier. From 1540 to 1543 he was in the service of the cardinal's brother, Guillaume du Bellay, sometimes in Turin (where Guillaume was governor), sometimes in France. Guillaume died in 1543, in which year Rabelais was appointed one of the *maîtres des requêtes.* For some years his movements are uncertain, but in 1546 he published his third book, this time under his own name. The Sorbonne condemned it—as it had done its predecessors—and Rabelais fled to Metz, where he practised medicine. In 1547 Francis I died; Henry II sent the French cardinals to Rome; and thither Du Bellay summoned Rabelais as his physician (1548). In Rome till 1549, he thereafter stayed near Paris; he received two livings from the Cardinal in January 1551–52, and resigned them two years later. He is said to have died April 9, 1553, certainly before May 1, 1554. A ' partial edition ' of a fourth book had appeared in 1548, the complete book in January 1552–53 (to be banned by the theologians); and a professed fifth book, *L'Isle sonante*, perhaps founded on scraps and notes by Rabelais, in 1562. The riotous licence of his mirth has made Rabelais as many enemies as his wisdom has made him friends, yet his works remain the most astonishing treasury of wit, wisdom, commonsense and satire that the world has ever seen. Of the many modern editions of Rabelais may be named those by Ch. Marty-Laveaux (6 vols. 1868–1902), Plattard (5 vols. 1929), and Abel Lefranc (director; 5 vols. 1912–31). See Eng. trans. by Urquhart and Motteux (1653–94; often reprinted), and W. F. Smith (1893); also works by Fleury (1877), W. Besant (1879, 1881), Stapfer (1889), Heulhard, Millet (1891), Bertrand (1894), A. Tilley (1907), Brémond (1877–1901), W. F. Smith (1917), Plattard (1910, 1927, 1929), Anatole France (trans. 1929), Putnam (1930), Powys (1948), Screech (1958).

RABI, Isidor Isaac (1898–), American physicist, born in Rymanow, Austria, which he left in childhood, was a graduate of

Cornell and Columbia University, where he became professor of Physics in 1937. An authority on nuclear physics and quantum mechanics, in 1944 he was awarded a Nobel prize for his precision work on neutrons.

RABUTIN. See BUSSY-RABUTIN.

RACAN, Honorat de Bueil, Marquis de, *ra-kã* (1589–1670), French poet, a disciple of Malherbe, wrote *Bergeries* (a pastoral play) and other verse, and was an original member of the Académie. See Life by Arnould (1901).

RACHEL, Élisa, properly **Élisa Félix,** *rah-shel* (1821–58), tragic actress, was born at Mumpf in Aargau, the daughter of Alsatian-Jewish pedlars. Brought to Paris about 1830, she received lessons in singing and declamation, made her début in *La Vendéenne* in 1837 with moderate success, but in June 1838 appeared as Camille in *Horace* at the Théâtre Français. From this time she shone without a rival in classical rôles, scoring her greatest triumph as Phèdre. In *Adrienne Lecouvreur*, written for her by Legouvé and Scribe, she had immense success. She visited London (Charlotte Brontë saw her there), Brussels, Berlin and St Petersburg, everywhere meeting with enthusiastic applause. In 1855, in America, her health gave way. She died of consumption at Cannet. As an artist Rachel has left a tradition never quite equalled. See Lives by F. Gribble (1911), J. Agate (1928) and J. Lucas Dubreton (1936).

RACHMANINOV or **Rakhmaninov, Sergius Vassilievich,** *-man'-* (1873–1943), Russian composer and pianist, born at Nijni-Novgorod, studied at St Petersburg Conservatoire and later at Moscow, where he won the gold medal for composition. A brilliant performer, he travelled all over Europe on concert tours, visiting London in 1899. Having fled from the Russian revolution he settled in the U.S.A. in 1918 and died in California. An accomplished composer, he wrote with ease operas, orchestral works and songs, but is best known for his piano music, which includes four concertos, the first three of which achieved enormous popularity, and the inveterate *Prelude in C Sharp Minor*, the demand for which at his own concerts nauseated even the composer himself. His style, devoid of national characteristics, epitomizes the lush romanticism of the later 19th century, which is still manifest in his last major composition, *Rhapsody on a Theme of Paganini* (1934) for piano and orchestra, a work of great craftsmanship which has remained a concert favourite. See Lives by W. Lyle (1939) and J. Culshaw (1949).

RACINE, Jean, *ra-seen* (1639–99), French dramatic poet, was born, a solicitor's son, at La Ferté-Milon (dep. Aisne), and was sent to the college of Beauvais, whence he went to Port Royal in 1655. Here he studied hard, and early discovered a faculty for verse-making and a liking for romance that caused his teachers no little uneasiness. At nineteen when he went to study philosophy at the Collège d'Harcourt, he appears to some extent to have exchanged the severity of his Jansenist upbringing for libertinism and the life of letters. He wrote an ode, *La Nymphe de la Seine*, on the marriage of Louis XIV, finished one piece and began another for the theatre, made the acquaintance of La Fontaine, Chapelain and other men of letters, and assisted a cousin who was a secretary to the Duc de Luynes. In 1661 he went to Uzès in Languedoc, hoping in vain to get a benefice from his uncle, the vicar-general of the diocese. Again in Paris, he obtained in 1664 a gift from the king for a congratulatory ode. Another ode, *La Renommée aux muses*, gained him the lifelong friendship of Boileau; and now began the famous friendship of ' the four '—Boileau, La Fontaine, Molière and Racine. His earliest play, *La Thébaïde ou Les Frères ennemis*, was acted by Molière's company at the Palais Royal (1664); his second, *Alexandre le grand* (1665), was after its sixth performance played by the rival actors at the Hotel de Bourgogne, which led to a rupture with Molière. Racine showed himself as hostile to Corneille. Stung by one of Nicole's *Lettres visionnaires* (1666) condemning in accordance with Port Royal ethics the romancer or dramatist as an ' empoisonneur public ', he published a clever letter to the author, full of indecent personalities. During the following ten years Racine produced his greatest works—*Andromaque* (1667); *Les Plaideurs* (1668), satirizing lawyers; *Britannicus* (1669); *Bérénice* (1670); *Bajazet* (1672); *Mithridate* (1673), produced almost at the moment of his admission to the Academy; *Iphigénie* (1675), a masterpiece of pathos; and *Phèdre* (1677), a marvellous representation of human agony. Now the *troupe du roi* introduced an opposition *Phèdre*, by Pradon, which was supported by a powerful party. Whether from mortification or from alleged conversion, Racine turned from dramatic work, made his peace with Port Royal, married in June 1677, and settled down to twenty years of domestic happiness. His wife brought him money (as well as two sons and five daughters); and he had found ample profit in the drama, besides enjoying an annual *gratification* that grew to 2000 livres, at least one benefice, and from 1677, jointly with Boileau, the office of historiographer-royal. In 1689 he wrote *Esther* for Madame de Maintenon's schoolgirls at Saint-Cyr; *Athalie* followed in 1691. Four *cantiques spirituelles* and an admirable *Histoire abrégée de Port Royal* make up Racine's literary work. In his later years he somehow lost the favour of the king. In France Racine is regarded as the greatest of all masters of tragic pathos; this estimate does not greatly exceed the truth. He took the conventional French tragedy from the stronger hands of Corneille, and added to it all the grace of which it was capable, perfecting exquisitely its versification, and harmoniously subordinating the whole action to the central idea of the one dominant passion. But he was a far greater poet even than dramatist, fascinating by the tender sweetness of his rhythm, the finished perfection and flexibility of his cadence. A biography was written by his son Louis (1692–1763), also a poet. The *Distressed Mother* was translated by Ambrose Philips (1712); *Phaedra* by Edmund Smith (staged 1707); and there is a complete metrical version by Boswell (1889–90). See works by Lemaître (1908), Mauriac (1930), Giraudoux (1930), Jasinski (1958), Mauran (1958); in English: Duclaux (1925), Clark (1940), Orgel (1948), Turnell (1948) and E. Vinaver (trans. P. Mansell Jones, 1955).

RACKHAM, Arthur (1867–1939), English artist, studied at Lambeth School of Art. A fellow of the Royal Society of Painters in Watercolours, he excelled in illustrating fairy tales and the like. See Life by Derek Hudson (1960).

RACOCZY. See RÁKÓCZI.

RADCLIFFE, (1) *née* **Ward, Ann** (1764–1823), English romantic novelist, was born in London. At twenty-three, at Bath, she married William Radcliffe, a graduate of Oxford and student of law, who became proprietor and editor of the weekly *English Chronicle*. In 1789 she published *The Castles of Athlin and Dunbayne*, followed by *A Sicilian Romance* (1790), *The Romance of the Forest* (1791), *The Mysteries of Udolpho* (1794), and *The Italian* (1797). For the last she received £800; for its predecessor, £500. She travelled much, and her journal shows how keen an eye she had for natural scenery and ruins. A sixth romance, *Gaston de Blondeville*, with a metrical tale, 'St Alban's Abbey', and a short Life, was published in 1826. Her contemporary reputation was considerable. She was praised by Scott, and influenced writers such as Byron, Shelley and Charlotte Brontë. Her particular brand of 'gothick romance' found many imitators, most of them unfortunately inferior to herself. Their work drew forth Jane Austen's satire *Northanger Abbey*. See studies by C. F. McIntyre (1921) and J. M. S. Tompkins (1932).

(2) **Cyril John, Viscount** (1899–), British lawyer, was educated at Haileybury and New College, Oxford. From 1941 to 1945 he was director-general of the Ministry of Information. In 1949 he was created a lord-of-appeal-in-ordinary and a life peer and in 1962 he was created Viscount. In 1956, as Constitutional Commissioner, Cyprus, he drew up a constitution for the future of the island.

(3 **Sir George** (1593–1657), English politician, born at Thornhill near Dewsbury, studied at University College, Oxford, was called to the bar, from 1627 managed the affairs of Strafford (q.v.), shared his imprisonment, and died in exile at Flushing. See Whitaker's edition of his Correspondence (1810).

(4) **John** (1650–1714), English physician, born at Wakefield, studied at University College, Oxford, became a fellow of Lincoln, took his M.B. in 1675 and his M.D. in 1682. In 1684 he removed to London, where he soon became the most popular physician of his time, original, capricious, not too temperate. A Jacobite, he yet attended William III and Queen Mary; in 1713 he was elected M.P. for Buckingham. He bequeathed the bulk of his large property to the Radcliffe Library, Infirmary and Observatory, and University College at Oxford, and St Bartholomew's Hospital, London. See Life by Hone (1950).

RADCLIFFE-BROWN, Alfred Reginald (1881–1955), British anthropologist, studied at Cambridge and was professor at Kapstadt, Sydney, Chicago and from 1937 at Oxford. By his field studies of *The Andaman Islanders* (1922), which served as a basis for his more theoretical *Structures and Function in Primitive Society* (1952), he established himself with Malinowski (q.v.) as one of the founders of modern social anthropology. He stressed the need for comparative rather than merely descriptive studies of primitive institutions and distinguished the concept of social structure from that of culture.

RADCLYFFE, James. See DERWENTWATER.

RADEK, Karl, *rah'-*, originally **Sobelsohn** (1885–?1939), Russian politician, born of Jewish parentage in Lwów, studied at Cracow and Bern. A member of the Polish Social Democratic party, he wrote for Polish and German newspapers and during World War I published propaganda literature from Switzerland. He crossed Germany with Lenin after the outbreak of the Russian revolution (1917) and took part in the Brest-Litovsk peace negotiations. He organized the German Communists during their revolution (1918) and was imprisoned (1919). Returning to the Soviet Union, he became a leading member of the Communist International, but lost standing with his growing distrust of extremist tactics. Nevertheless he became editor of *Pravda* and rector of the Sun Yat-Sen Chinese university in Moscow. He was charged as a Trotsky supporter and expelled from the party (1927–30) but readmitted only to fall victim to one of Stalin's 'trials' in 1937 when he was sentenced to ten years' imprisonment but probably soon died.

RADETZKY, Johann Joseph, Count (1766–1858), Austrian soldier, born at Trebnitz near Tabor in Bohemia, fought against the Turks in 1788–89 and in nearly all the wars between the Austrians and the French. Commander-in-chief in Lombardy from 1831, in 1848 Field-marshal Radetzky was driven out of Milan by the insurgents, but held Verona and Mantua for the Hapsburgs. Defeated at Goito, he won a victory at Custozza, and re-entered Milan. In March 1849 he almost destroyed the Sardinian army at Novara, forced Venice to surrender, and till 1857 again ruled the Lombardo-Venetian territories with an iron hand. He died at Milan. See his *Denkwürdigkeiten* (1887) and *Briefe an seine Tochter* (1892). See also work by E. Schmahl (1938).

RADHAKRISHNAN, Sir Sarvepalli (1888–), Indian philosopher and statesman, born in Tiruttani, Madras, was educated at Madras Christian College. He has been professor at the universities of Mysore, Calcutta and Oxford, where he gave the Upton lectures at Manchester College in 1926 and 1929, and in 1936 he became Spalding professor of Eastern Religions and Ethics at Oxford. He also lectured abroad, in America in 1926 and 1944 and in China in 1944. He was knighted in 1931. From 1931 to 1939 he attended the League of Nations at Geneva as a member of the Committee of Intellectual Cooperation. In 1946 he was chief Indian delegate to Unesco, becoming chairman of Unesco in 1949. A member of the Indian Assembly in 1947, he was appointed first Indian ambassador to Russia in 1949 and in 1952 became vice-president of India. He was awarded the O.M. in 1963. He has written many scholarly philosophic works including *Indian Philosophy* (1927), his Hibbert lectures of 1929 published as *An Idealist View of Life* (1932), which is often thought to be his greatest work, and *Eastern Religion and Western Thought* (2nd ed. 1939).

RADOWITZ, Joseph von (1797–1853), Prussian general, born at Blankenburg in the Harz, in 1813 entered the Westphalian army, in 1823 the Prussian, and in 1830 became chief of the artillery staff. Connected by marriage with the Prussian aristocracy, he headed the anti-revolutionary party, and was Frederick-William IV's adviser. After 1848 the Prussian scheme of a German constitution by means of the alliance of the three kings was largely his work. He wrote political treatises.

RAE, John (1813–93), Arctic traveller, born near Stromness in Orkney, studied medicine at Edinburgh, and in 1833 became doctor to the Hudson Bay Company. In 1846–47 he made two exploring expeditions, and in 1848 he accompanied Richardson on a Franklin search voyage. In 1853–54 he commanded an expedition to King William's Land. It was on this journey that he met the Eskimos who gave him definite news of Franklin's expedition and its probable fate. In 1860 he surveyed a telegraph line to America by the Faroes and Iceland, and visited Greenland, and in 1864 made a telegraph survey from Winnipeg over the Rockies. He died in London.

RAEBURN, Sir Henry (1756–1823), Scottish portrait painter, born at Stockbridge, Edinburgh, was apprenticed to a goldsmith, but took to art, producing first watercolour miniatures and then oils. At twenty-two he married the widow of Count Leslie, a lady of means, studied two years in Rome (1785–87), then settled in Edinburgh, and soon attained pre-eminence among Scottish artists. In 1814 he was elected A.R.A., in 1815 R.A.; he was knighted by George IV in 1822, and appointed king's limner for Scotland a few days before his death. His style was to some extent founded on that of Reynolds, to which a positiveness was added by his bold brushwork and use of contrasting colours. Among his sitters were Scott, Hume, Boswell, 'Christopher North', Lord Melville, Sir David Baird, Henry Mackenzie, Principal Robertson, Lord Jeffrey and Lord Cockburn. *The Macnab*, considered his best work, fetched £25,400 in 1917. See Life by his great-grandson, W. R. Andrew (1886); and studies by W. E. Henley (1890), Sir W. Armstrong (1901), J. Greig (1911).

RAEDER, Erich, *ray'dėr* (1876–1960), former German grand admiral, entered the Navy in 1894 and during World War I was chief of staff to Admiral von Hipper. In 1928 he was promoted admiral and became C.-in-C. of the Navy. In 1939 Hitler made him a grand admiral, and in 1943 he became head of an anti-invasion force. At the Nuremberg Trials in 1946 he was sentenced to life imprisonment for having helped to prepare a war of aggression. He was released in September 1955. See his Memoirs, translated by E. Fitzgerald (1959).

RAEMAEKERS, Louis, *rah'mah-kers* (1869–1956), Dutch artist, born at Roermond, attained worldwide fame in 1915 by his striking anti-German war cartoons.

RAFF, Joachim (1822–82), Swiss composer, born at Lachen on the Lake of Zürich, in 1850–56 lived near Liszt in Weimar, taught music at Wiesbaden until 1877, and then was director of the conservatory at Frankfurt-am-Main. Among his compositions are the symphonies *Lenore* and *Im Walde* and violin and piano works. In support of Wagner he wrote *Die Wagner-Frage* (1854).

RAFFAELLO. See RAPHAEL.

RAFFLES, Sir Thomas Stamford (1781–1826), English colonial administrator, was born a sea-captain's son, off Port Morant in Jamaica. In 1795 he was appointed to a clerkship in the East India House, and in 1805 secretary to an establishment at Penang. In 1811 he accompanied the expedition against Java as secretary to Lord Minto; and on its capture, as lieutenant-governor, completely reformed the internal administration. In 1816 ill-health brought him home to England, where he wrote his *History of Java* (1817), and was knighted. Lieutenant-governor of Benkoelen (1818), he formed, without authority, a settlement at Singapore, but in 1824 had again to return to England. His ship took fire off Sumatra, and his natural history collections, East Indian vocabularies, &c., were lost. He founded the London Zoo and was its first president. See Lives by his widow (1830), R. Coupland (1934), C. Wurtzburg (1954), N. Epton (1956).

RAFN, Karl Christian (1795–1864), Danish philologist, became sub-librarian of Copenhagen University in 1821, a professor in 1826, and founded (1825) the Northern Antiquities Society. His works include a Danish translation of Norse sagas (1821–26) and *Antiquitates Americanae* (1837), on the Norse discovery of America in the 10th century.

RAGLAN, Fitzroy James Henry Somerset, 1st Baron (1788–1855), British general, the youngest son of the fifth Duke of Beaufort, entered the army in 1804, graduating from regimental duty to service on Wellington's staff. He was present at Waterloo, losing his sword arm. Thereafter, he sat in parliament as M.P. for Truro, and spent many years at the War Office, being appointed master-general of the ordnance and elevated to the peerage in 1852. In 1854 he was promoted field-marshal and nominated to head a grossly ill-prepared expeditionary force against the Russians, in the Crimea, in alliance with the French. Swift pursuit after Raglan's victory at the Alma might well have ended the campaign by Sevastopol's immediate capture. But the French 'dragged their feet', as they continued to do, unreproached, throughout the ensuing weary months of siege warfare. In effect, Raglan's intended conduct of operations was sacrificed to the preservation of a queasy alliance, with the commander-in-chief an unprotesting scapegoat for cabinet unpreparedness and inefficiency. He died in harness on June 28, 1855, and 'never was there a nobler or more self-denying public servant' (Fortescue). See Fortescue, *A Gallant Company* (1927), and Vulliamy, *Crimea* (*passim*) (1939).

RAHBEK, Knud Lyne (1760–1830), Danish poet, critic and editor, was born in Copenhagen. He became professor of Aesthetics at Copenhagen University, edited several literary journals, notably *Den Danske Tilskuer* (the Danish *Spectator*). Besides poetry, he wrote many plays and songs and works on the drama.

RAHEL (Rahel Antonie Frederike Levin) (1771–1833), born a Jewess at Berlin, in 1814 turned Christian and married Varnhagen von Ense (q.v.). Her house in Berlin was a gathering-place for philosophers, poets and artists, and she encouraged the genius of Jean Paul, Tieck, Fouqué, Fichte, Hegel, Heine, Thiers, Benjamin Constant, and especially the Romanticists. Into the patriotic struggle against Napoleon she threw herself heart and soul. See her Correspondence (11 vols. 1833–75), and works by Jennings (1876), Ellen Key (trans. 1913), L. Feist (1927).

RAHERE (d. 1144), English churchman of Frankish descent who on a pilgrimage to Rome suffered an attack of malarial fever. During his convalescence, he made a vow to build a hospital and on his return to London he was granted the site at Smithfield by Henry I. In 1123 the building of St Bartholomew's hospital and St Bartholomew's Church was begun. In charge of the hospital until 1137, he retired in that year to the priory.

RAHN, Johann Heinrich (d. 1676), Swiss mathematician, town treasurer of Zürich (where he was born), in 1659 was the first to use the division sign ÷. His book *Teutsche Algebra* was translated into English.

RAIBOLINI, Francesco. See FRANCIA.

RAIKES, Robert (1735–1811), English philanthropist, born at Gloucester, in 1757 succeeded his father as proprietor of the *Gloucester Journal.* His pity for the misery and ignorance of many children in his native city led him in 1780 to start a Sunday School where they might learn to read and to repeat the Catechism. He lived to see such schools spread over England. See Lives by Gregory (1877), Eastman (1880), and study by Kendall (1939).

RAIMONDI. See MARCANTONIO.

RAINIER III, properly **Rainier Louis Henri Maxence Bertrand de Grimaldi,** *ray-nyay* (1923–), prince of Monaco, born at Monaco, succeeded his grandfather, Louis II, in 1950, as 26th ruling prince of the House of Grimaldi, which dates from 1297. In 1956 he married Grace Patricia Kelly, an American film actress, and now has two daughters, the Princesses Caroline Louise Marguerite, born 1957, and Stephanie Marie Elisabeth, born 1965, and a son, Prince Albert Alexander Louis Pierre, born in 1958, heir-presumptive to the throne.

RAINY, Robert (1826–1906), Scottish divine, studied at Glasgow and at New College in Edinburgh, and after being minister of the Free Church in Huntly and Edinburgh, was from 1862 to 1900 professor of Church History in the New (Free Church) College in Edinburgh, becoming its principal (1874). Rainy carried the union (1900) of the Free and United Presbyterian Churches as the United Free Church, of which he became the first moderator. See Life by P. C. Simpson (1909).

RAIT, Sir Robert Sangster (1874–1936), Scottish historian, born in Narborough, Leicestershire, was professor of Scottish History at Glasgow University (1913–29), its principal and vice-chancellor from 1929, and was historiographer-royal for Scotland (1919–29). He was knighted in 1933.

RÁKÓCZI, *ra-kō'tsi,* a princely family of Hungary and Transylvania that became extinct in 1780. The most important member was the popular **Francis II** (1676–1735), who in 1703 led a Hungarian revolt against Austria. He had little success but was hailed by his countrymen as a patriot and a hero. His later years were spent as a Carmelite monk first in France and then in Turkey, where he died.

RALEIGH, (1) Sir Walter (1552–1618), English courtier, navigator and author, was born of an ancient but decayed family at the Devon manor house of Hayes Barton near Sidmouth. He entered Oriel College, Oxford, in 1566, but left, probably in 1569, to volunteer in the Huguenot cause in France, and fought at Jarnac and Moncontour. In 1578 he joined the profitless expedition of his half-brother, Sir Humphrey Gilbert; in 1580 he went to Ireland with one hundred foot to act against the rebels, and quickly attracted notice by his dash and daring. Returning to England in 1581, he now entered the court as a protégé of Leicester, whom in 1582 he accompanied to the Netherlands; and after his return he became prime favourite of the queen. She heaped favours upon him—estates, the 'farm of wines', and a licence to export woollen broadcloths. In 1584 he was knighted, in 1585 appointed lord warden of the Stannaries and vice-admiral of Devon and Cornwall; that same year he entered parliament for Devon. A fleet sent out by him in 1584 to explore the American coast north of Florida took possession of a district to which Elizabeth gave the name Virginia. In 1585–87 he fitted out two more expeditions, but the colonists either returned or perished; the only results were the introduction of potatoes and tobacco into England. It is supposed that Raleigh spent £40,000 over these attempts to colonize Virginia. In 1587 the appearance at court of the handsome young Earl of Essex endangered Raleigh's place in the queen's favour, and repairing to Ireland, where he had received 42,000 acres in Munster, he set about repeopling this tract with English settlers. He became a close friend of the poet Spenser, visiting him at his estate at Kilcolman, and reading him his poem of *The Ocean's Love to Cynthia* (Elizabeth). In his Youghal garden Raleigh planted tobacco and potatoes. He quickly recovered his influence at court, and busied himself with further schemes for reprisals on the Spaniards. His famous tract on the fight of the *Revenge,* which inspired Tennyson's noblest ballad, appeared anonymously in 1591. Early in

1592 Raleigh prepared a new expedition to seize the Spanish treasure ships, but his doting mistress forbade him to sail with the fleet, which he entrusted to Frobisher and Burgh. Hardly had he got back to London when Elizabeth discovered his intrigue with Bessy Throckmorton, one of her maids-of-honour. In July he was committed to the Tower, and for more than four years after this was excluded from the queen's presence. Meantime Burgh had captured the *Madre de Dios*, and brought her into Dartmouth. So great was the excitement that none but Raleigh could control the tumult, and he was sent down to Dartmouth with a keeper. He now married Bessy Throckmorton and for the next two years lived with her in quiet happiness at Sherborne. About 1593 his imagination was fired by the descriptions of Guiana, with its vast city of Manoa and its El Dorado; and in 1595, with five ships, he explored the coasts of Trinidad, and sailed up the Orinoco. Early in 1596 he published *The Discovery of Guiana* (Hakluyt Soc. 1848, 1929). In June he sailed with Howard and Essex to Cadiz, and it was his advice that governed that splendid triumph; his *Relation of Cadiz Action* remains the best history of the exploit. It was 1597 before Raleigh was allowed to resume his place as Captain of the Guard. Essex was glad of his support in a new expedition against Spain, which, in July 1597, sailed from Plymouth. A desperate storm compelled many of the ships to put back, but Raleigh met Essex off the island of Flores. They agreed to attack Fayal, but Raleigh reached the harbour first, and carried the town by storm, to the great mortification of Essex. In 1600 Raleigh became governor of Jersey, and in three years did much to foster its trade. In the dark intrigues at the close of Elizabeth's reign he took little part, while Cecil and others got the ear of James, and poisoned his mind against Raleigh. Before long the latter was stripped of all his offices. Possibly he may have in haste spoken, or at least listened to, words expressing a preference for Arabella Stuart. But the only witness against him was the miserable Lord Cobham, and he made and retracted eight separate charges with facility. Raleigh was arrested on July 17, 1603, and in his first despair tried to kill himself. His defence on his trial at Winchester was splendid; all his popularity came back to him from that hour. Yet he was condemned to death, and only on the scaffold was his sentence commuted to perpetual imprisonment. Within the Tower Raleigh employed himself with study and chemical experiments and with writing his excellent *History of the World* (1614), whose first and only volume (in 1300 folio pages) comes down to the second Roman war with Macedon. It was at first suppressed as 'too saucy in censuring the acts of kings', but its merit was quickly realized and many editions appeared within the century. Other writings of Raleigh's captivity were *The Prerogative of Parliaments* (written 1615, published in 1628); *The Cabinet Council*, published by Milton in 1658; and *A Discourse of War*, one of his most perfect pieces of writing. On January 30, 1616, Raleigh was released from the Tower to make an expedition to the Orinoco in search of a gold-mine. He engaged not to molest the dominions of the king of Spain. In April 1617 he sailed; but storms, desertion, disease and death followed the expedition from the first, and before they reached the mouth of the river Raleigh himself was stricken down by sickness and compelled to stay behind with the ships, and to entrust the command to Keymis. The adventurers burned a new Spanish town, San Thomé, but never reached the mine. In the fight young Walter Raleigh was struck down; Keymis killed himself; and Raleigh in June 1618 arrived at Plymouth with his ship, the *Destiny*, alone and utterly cast down. Arrested by his false cousin, Sir Lewis Stukeley, at Salisbury he penned his touching *Apology for the Voyage to Guiana*; but he was beheaded at Whitehall, under the old Winchester sentence. See Lives by Cayley (1805), Tytler (1833), Kingsley (*Miscellanies*, 1859), Edwards (1868), Gosse (1886), Stebbing (1892), Hume (1897), De Sélincourt (1908), Waldman (1928), Strathmann (1951), Wallace (1960); Harlow, *Raleghs Last Voyage* (1932) and Irwin, *That Great Lucifer* (1960); also Brushfield's Bibliography (1908).

(2) **Sir Walter Alexander** (1861–1922), English scholar, critic and essayist, born in London, was professor of English Literature at Liverpool, Glasgow and at Oxford from 1904. Among his writings are *The English Novel* (1894), *Milton* (1900), *Wordsworth* (1903) and *Shakespeare* (1907). Chosen to compile the official history of the war in the air (1914–18), he died while collecting material for it. His *Letters* were edited by his wife in 1926.

RALSTON, William Ralston Shedden (1828–1889), Russian scholar and folklorist, his surname originally Shedden, was born in London. He was trained for the bar but in 1853–75 held a post in the British Museum library. He wrote on Russian folksongs and tales, besides a translation of Turgenev's *Liza* (1869), and *Kriloff and his Fables* (1869).

RAMAN, Sir Chandrasekhara Venkata (1888–1970), Indian physicist, born at Trichinopoly and educated at Madras University, became professor of Physics at Calcutta (1917–33) and then director of the Indian Institute of Science at Bangalore. In 1929 he was knighted, and in 1930 awarded the Nobel prize for physics, for important discoveries in connection with the diffusion of light (the Raman effect). He also worked on the theory of musical instruments.

RAMBAUD, Alfred Nicolas, *rã-bō* (1842–1905), French historian, born at Besançon, in 1896–98 was minister of public instruction. From 1870 he wrote on Russia, French civilization, colonial France, &c., and edited the *Histoire générale, du IVe siècle à nos jours* (12 vols. 1892–99).

RAMBOUILLET, Catherine de Vivonne, Marquise de, *rã-boo-yay* (1588–1665), French noblewoman, born at Rome, the daughter of Jean de Vivonne, Marquis of Pisani, at twelve was married to the son of the Marquis de Rambouillet, who succeeded to the title in 1611. From the beginning she disliked both the morals and manners of the French court. Virtuous and spirituelle, she gathered together in the famous Hôtel Rambouillet for fifty years the talent and wit of France culled from both the nobility and the literary world. See Livet's *Précieux et Précieuses* (4th ed. 1896) and Brunetière's *Nouvelles Études* (2nd ed. 1886).

RAMEAU, Jean Philippe, *rah-mō* (1683–1764), French composer, born at Dijon, had been organist, when he settled in Paris (1721) and wrote his *Traité de l'harmonie* (1722), a work of fundamental importance in the history of musical style. In 1732 he produced his first opera, *Hippolyte et Aricie*, which created a great sensation; his best was *Castor et Pollux* (1737). By 1760 he had composed twenty-one operas and ballets, besides harpsichord pieces. Louis XV ennobled him. See studies by Pougin (1876), La Laurencie (1908), Laloy (1908), Masson (1927) and Girdlestone (1957). Rameau's nephew, who gave the title to a singular work by Diderot (q.v.), was Louis Sébastien Mercier (1740–1814), author of the *Tableau de Paris*.

RAMÉE, De la. See RAMUS and OUIDA.

RAMENGHI. See BAGNACAVALLO.

RAMESES, *ram'seez*, the name of twelve monarchs of the 19th Egyptian dynasty (*c.* 1350–1115 B.C.). Only the second and third of the name were of importance.

Rameses II, usually called the Great, defeated the Hittites at Kadesh, then formed a peace with them, and married a Hittite princess. During his long reign (1292–1225 B.C.) he built magnificent monuments, temples, &c., completing the mortuary temple of Seti I at Luxor and the colonnaded hall of the Karnak temple, and building the rock temple of Abu Simbel.

Rameses III (1198–1167 B.C.), warred with the Philistines and maritime tribes of Greece and Asia Minor, and repeated the conquest of Ethiopia. Tradition identifies the warrior king Rameses II with the Pharaoh of the oppression, and Merenptah or Rameses III with the Pharaoh of the Exodus; the identification is doubtful. The mummy of Rameses II was found at Deir-el-Bahari in 1881, that of Rameses III at Bulak in 1886.

RAMMOHUN ROY, or **Rájá Rám Mohán Rái** (1774–1833), Indian religious reformer, born at Burdwan in Bengal of high Brahman ancestry, came early to question his ancestral faith, and studied Buddhism in Tibet. Revenue collector for some years in Rangpur, in 1811 he succeeded to affluence on his brother's death. He published various works in Persian, Arabic and Sanskrit, with the aim of uprooting idolatry; and he helped in the abolition of suttee. He issued an English abridgment of the *Vedanta*, giving a digest of the Vedas. In 1820 he published *The Precepts of Jesus*, accepting the morality preached by Christ, but rejecting His deity and miracles; and he wrote other pamphlets hostile both to Hinduism and to Christian Trinitarianism. In 1828 he began the Brahma Samaj association, and in 1830 the emperor of Delhi bestowed on him the title of raja. In 1831 he visited England, where he gave valuable evidence before the Board of Control on the condition of India, and died at Bristol. His English works were edited by Jogendra Chunder Ghose (1888).

RAMÓN Y CAJAL, Santiago, *ra-mon' ee ka-hal'* (1852–1934), Spanish histologist, born at Petilla de Aragon, a graduate of Saragossa University, he was professor of Anatomy at Valencia (1881–86), of Histology at Barcelona (1886–92) and at Madrid (1892–1922). In 1906 he shared with Golgi (q.v.) the Nobel prize for medicine. He was specially noted for his work on the brain and nerves. He wrote much on medical subjects, and also published his *Recollections* (trans. Craigie, 1937).

RAMSAY, (1). See DALHOUSIE.

(2) **Sir Alexander** (d. 1342), a Scottish patriot, famed for his deeds of bravery, who was captured and starved to death at Hermitage Castle in 1342 by William Douglas, the 'flower of chivalry'.

(3) **Allan** (*c.* 1685–1758), Scottish poet, was born at Leadhills, Lanarkshire. His father was manager of Lord Hopetoun's mines there, and his mother, Alice Bower, was the daughter of a Derbyshire mining expert. In 1704 he was apprenticed for five years to a wigmaker in Edinburgh. By 1718 he had become known as a poet, having issued several short humorous satires printed as broadsides; he had also written (1716–18) two additional cantos to the old Scots poem of *Christ's Kirk on the Green*, felicitous pictures of rustic life and broad humour. Ramsay now commenced business as bookseller, later adding a circulating library—apparently the first in Great Britain. 'Honest Allan's' career was eminently prosperous though the theatre he built in Edinburgh at his own expense (1736) was soon shut up by the magistrates. In 1740 he built himself a quaint house (the 'goose-pie') on the Castle Hill where he spent his last years in retirement. Among his works are: *Tartana, or the Plaid* (1718); *Poems*, collected edition published by subscription in 1721, by which it is said he realised 400 guineas—other editions, 1720, 1727, 1728; *Fables and Tales* (1722); *Fair Assembly* (1723); *Health, a Poem* (1724); *The Tea-table Miscellany*, a collection of songs (4 vols. 1724–37); *The Evergreen*, 'being a collection of Scots Poems wrote by the Ingenious before 1660' (1724); *The Gentle Shepherd, a Pastoral Comedy* (1725), his best and most popular work; and *Thirty Fables* (1730). See Mackail in *Essays and Studies*, x (Engl. Assoc. 1924); Gibson, *New Light on Allan Ramsay* (1927); Martin, *Allan Ramsay* (1931), and *Bibliography of Allan Ramsay* (1932).

(4) **Allan** (1713–84), eldest son of (3), was a distinguished portrait painter, who trained in Italy, worked first in Edinburgh, but in 1762 settled in London, and in 1767 was appointed portrait painter to George III. In his best works his painting is simple and delicate and he excels in portraits of women, notably that of his wife. He delighted in convers on and was acquainted with many of the writers of his day, including Samuel Johnson; he also corresponded with such men as Rousseau and Voltaire. See study by Smart (1952).

(5) **Sir Andrew Crombie** (1814–91), Scottish geologist, was born at Glasgow. In 1841 he joined the geological survey and in 1871 became director-general, retiring in 1881 with a knighthood. He died at Beaumaris. See Life by Sir Archibald Geikie (1895).

(6) **Andrew Michael (André Michel)** (1686–1743), the 'Chevalier de Ramsay', French writer, of Scottish parentage, was born at Ayr, the son of a baker. He served in the Low Countries, in 1710 was converted by Fénelon to Catholicism, and lived with him for five years. In 1724–25 he was tutor to Prince Charles Edward in Rome and in 1730 he visited England, and was made F.R.S. and D.C.L. of Oxford. He died at St Germain. He wrote *Vie de Fénelon* (1723), *Les Voyages de Cyrus* (1727), &c.

(7) **Edward Bannerman Burnett** (1793–1872), Scottish divine, was born in Aberdeen, the son of Alexander Burnett, sheriff of Kincardineshire, who in 1806 succeeded to his uncle Sir Alexander Ramsay's estates, took the surname Ramsay, and was created a baronet. Young Ramsay was educated at Durham and St John's College, Cambridge, held two Somerset curacies 1816–24, and then removed to Edinburgh. In 1830 he became incumbent of St John's, and in 1846 also dean of the diocese. He wrote various religious works, and the delightful *Reminiscences of Scottish Life and Character* (1857; 22nd ed. with Memoir by Cosmo Innes, 1874).

(8) **Sir William** (1852–1916), Scottish chemist, was born at Glasgow. Professor of Chemistry at Bristol (1880–87), at University College, London (1887–1912), in conjunction with Lord Rayleigh he discovered argon in 1894. Later he obtained helium, neon, krypton and xenon, and won a Nobel prize (1904). His writings on his subject include *The Gases of the Atmosphere* and *Elements and Electrons*. See Life by M. Travers (1956).

(9) **Sir William Mitchell** (1851–1939), Scottish archaeologist, born in Glasgow, was professor of Humanities at Aberdeen, 1886–1911. An authority on Asia Minor, he wrote a *Historical Geography of Asia Minor* (1890), and on the history of early Christian times published several works, the best known being *The Church in the Roman Empire before A.D. 170* (1893).

RAMSDEN, Jesse (1735–1800), F.R.S. (1786), English instrument-maker, born near Halifax, improved optical and survey instruments and devised the mural circle.

RAMSEY, (1) **Arthur Michael** (1904–), Archbishop of Canterbury from 1961, educated at Repton and Cambridge, where he was president of the Union (1926) and regius professor of Divinity (1950–52), became Bishop of Durham in 1952 and Archbishop of York in 1956.

(2) **Frank Plumpton** (1903–30), English philosopher, was a colleague of Wittgenstein at Cambridge and an early critic of his *Tractatus*. He maintained, in opposition to Wittgenstein, that the propositions of mathematics are tautologies, not equations, continued the Russellian quest of deriving mathematics exclusively from non-empirical propositions and in inductive logic veered towards pragmatism. He rejected the suggestion that there may be metaphysical truths inaccessible to the limitations of language by the famous remark: 'What we can't say we can't say and we can't whistle it either'. His early death prevented a major philosophical work, but his brilliant philosophical papers were published under the title, *The Foundation of Mathematics*, ed. R. B. Braithwaite (1931).

RAMUS, Petrus, or Pierre de la Ramée, *ra-mü* (1515–72), French humanist, born at Cuth near Soissons, became servant to a rich scholar at the Collège de Navarre, and by studying at night made rapid progress in learning. The dominant philosophy dissatisfied him, and he put higher value on 'reason' than on 'authority'. Graduating at twenty-three, he had great success as lecturer on the Greek and Latin authors, and undertook to reform the science of logic. His attempts excited much hostility among the Aristotelians and his *Dialectic* (1543) was fiercely assailed by the doctors of the Sorbonne, who had it suppressed. But Cardinals de Bourbon and Lorraine in 1545 had him appointed principal of the Collège de Presles; and Lorraine in 1551 instituted a chair for him at the Collège Royal. He mingled largely in the literary and scholastic disputes of the time, and ultimately turned Protestant. He had to flee from Paris, and travelled in Germany and Switzerland; but returning to France in 1571, he perished in the massacre of St Bartholomew. He wrote treatises on arithmetic, geometry and algebra, and was an early adherent of the Copernican system. His theories had no small influence after his death, and all over Europe the Ramist system of logic was adopted and taught. See studies by Waddington-Kastus (1855), Desmaze (1864), Lobstein (1878), Graus (1912).

RAMUZ, Charles Ferdinand, *ra-müz* (1878–1947), Swiss writer, was born at Cully near Lausanne. He wrote in French, mainly about life in his native canton of Vaud. His first book, *Le Petit Village*, appeared in 1903, and thereafter he wrote prolifically. His pure prose style and fine descriptive power won him wide admiration and repute, his European popularity being somewhat tempered in Britain, though he has been translated into English—*Beauté sur la terre* (1927; trans. *Beauty on Earth*) and *Présence de la mort* (1922; trans. *The Triumph of Death*). Other writings include *Jean Luc persécuté* (1909), *La Guérison de maladies* (1917), *Adam et Ève* (1932) and *Besoin de grandeur* (1937). See studies by P. Claudel (1947), A. Tissot (1948) and W. Günther (1948).

RANCÉ, Armand Jean le Bouthillier de, *rã-say* (1626–1700), French monk, founder of the Trappists, was an accomplished but worldly priest, to whom fell the Cistercian abbey of La Trappe (dep. Orne). Affected by the tragic deaths of two of his friends, he underwent a conversion, in 1662 undertook a reform of his monastery (becoming abbot), and finally established what was practically a new religious order, its principles perpetual prayer and austere self-denial. Intellectual work was forbidden; only manual labour was allowed to the monks. He wrote of his order in *Traité de la sainteté et des devoirs de* *la vie monastique* (1683), a book the contents of which caused much controversy on the place of study in monastic life. See Bremond's *L'Abbé Tempête* (1929) and its answer, Luddy's *The Real Rancé* (1931).

RANDALL, (1) **James Ryder** (1839–1908), American poet, born in Baltimore, was first a teacher, then a journalist. His lyrics, which in the Civil War gave powerful aid to the Southern cause, include 'Maryland, my Maryland' (1861), 'Stonewall Jackson' and 'There's life in the old land yet'.

(2) **Sir John Turton** (1905–), English physicist, professor at King's College, University of London, in 1940 along with Boot designed a cavity magnetron valve for use in radar. For this he received a government award of £12,000 (1949). He was knighted in 1962.

(3) **Samuel Jackson** (1828–90), American Democratic statesman, born in Philadelphia, was a member of the House of Representatives (1863–90). As speaker (1876–81), he codified the rules of the House and considerably strengthened the speaker's power.

RANDEGGER, Cavaliere Alberto (1832–1911), Italian composer, conductor and singing master, born at Trieste. He settled in London in 1854, and became in 1868 professor of Singing at the Royal Academy of Music, and afterwards a conductor of the Carl Rosa Opera Company (1879–85).

RANDOLPH, (1) **Edmund Jennings** (1753–1813), American statesman, born at Williamsburg, Va., studied at William and Mary College, and in 1786–88 was governor of Virginia, in 1787 a member of the convention which framed the U.S. constitution. He was working at a codification of the state laws of Virginia when Washington appointed him attorney-general (1789). In 1794 he was made secretary of state, but, falsely charged with bribery, resigned (1795), and was practically ruined. He resumed law practice at Richmond, Va., and was chief counsel for Aaron Burr (q.v.) at his treason trial. See Life by M. D. Conway (1888).

(2) **John** (1773–1833), 'of Roanoke', American statesman, born at Cawsons, Va., a second cousin of (1), in 1799 entered congress, where he became distinguished for his eloquence, wit, sarcasm and eccentricity. He was the Democratic leader of the House of Representatives, but quarrelled with Jefferson and opposed the war of 1812; he opposed also the Missouri Compromise and Nullification. In 1825–27 he sat in the senate, in 1830 was appointed minister to Russia. By his will he manumitted his slaves. See Lives by Garland (1850), Adams (1882), Bruce (1922).

(3) **Sir Thomas** (d. 1332), Scottish soldier and statesman, the nephew and from 1308 the comrade of Bruce, who created him Earl of Moray. He recaptured Edinburgh Castle from the English (1314), commanded a division at Bannockburn, took Berwick (1318), won the victory of Mitton (1319), reinvaded England (1320, 1327), and was regent from Bruce's death (1329) till his own at Musselburgh.

(4) **Sir Thomas** (1523–90), English political agent and ambassador, a zealous Protestant, lived abroad during Mary's reign, and by Elizabeth was employed on diplomatic missions in Germany, Russia, France and specially Scotland, where off and on during 1559–86 he played his mistress's cards. He was twice shot at there, and in 1581 had to flee for his life. From 1585 he was chancellor of the Exchequer in England.

(5) **Thomas** (1605–35), English poet and dramatist, born at Newnham near Daventry, and educated at Westminster and Trinity College, Cambridge, was elected a fellow, began early to write, gained the friendship of Ben Jonson, and led a boisterous life. He died and was buried at Blatherwick near Oundle. Randolph left a number of bright, fanciful, sometimes too glowing poems, and six plays: *Aristippus, or the Jovial Philosopher*; *The Conceited Peddler*; *The Jealous Lovers*; *The Muses' Looking-glass*; *Amyntas, or the Impossible Dowry*; and *Hey for Honesty*. See editions by W. Carew Hazlitt (1875) and Thorn-Drury (1929).

RANJIT SINGH (1780–1839), the 'Lion of the Punjab', at twelve succeeded his father, a Sikh chief, as ruler of Lahore, and directed all his energies to founding a kingdom which should unite all the Sikh provinces. With the help of an army trained by Western soldiers, including Generals Ventura and Allard, he became the most powerful ruler in India. He was a firm ally of the British, the boundary between their territories having been amicably fixed at the river Sutlej. In 1813 he procured from an Afghan prince, as the price of assistance in war, the Koh-i-noor diamond. See Life by Sir L. Griffin (1892).

RANJITSINHJI, Prince (1872–1933), the 'Black Prince of Cricketers', born in Kathiawar state, studied at Cambridge, succeeded as Jam Sahib of Nawanagar in 1906, and was made a maharaja in 1918. He wrote a book on cricket (1897). For a description of him as a cricketer see Neville Cardus, *The Summer Game* (1929).

RANK, Joseph Arthur, 1st Baron Rank (1888–1972), British film magnate, born in Hull, chairman of many film companies, including Gaumont-British and Cinema-Television. He did much to promote the British film industry at a time when Hollywood and the American companies seemed to have the monopoly. A staunch and active supporter of the Methodist church, he was keenly interested in social problems. He was raised to the peerage in 1957.

RANKE, Leopold von (1795–1886), German historian, was born at Wiehe in Thuringia, studied at Halle and Berlin, and in 1818 became a schoolmaster at Frankfurt an der Oder, but his heart was set on the study of history. A work on the Romance and Teutonic peoples in the Reformation period, and another criticizing contemporary historians, procured his call to Berlin as professor of History (1825–72). In 1827–31 he was sent to examine the archives of Vienna, Venice, Rome and Florence. The fruits of his labours were a work on South Europe in the 16th and 17th centuries (1827), books on Serbia and Venice, and *History of the Popes in the 16th and 17th Centuries* (1834–37; trans. by Sarah Austin, 1846), perhaps his greatest achievement. Then he turned his attention to central and northern Europe, and wrote on German Reformation history, Prussian history (1847–48), French history in the 16th and 17th centuries (1852–61), and English history in the 17th century (1859–67; trans. 1875). Other books were on the origin of the Seven Years' War (1871), the German Powers and the Confederation (1871), the revolutionary wars of 1791–92 (1875), Venetian history (1878), a universal history (1881–88), and the history of Germany and France in the 19th century (1887), besides monographs on Wallenstein (1869), Hardenberg (1877–78), and Frederick the Great and Frederick-William IV (1878). Ranke was ennobled in 1865, and died in Berlin. His standpoint was that of the statesman; and he fails to give due prominence to the social side of national development. See his autobiographical *Zur eigenen Lebensgeschichte* (1890), and monographs by Winckler (1885), Von Giesebrecht, Guglia, Ritter (1895), Oncken (1922).

RANKINE, William John Macquorn (1820–1872), Scottish engineer and scientist, born at Edinburgh, was appointed in 1855 to the chair of Engineering at Glasgow. Elected a fellow of the Royal Society in 1853, his works on the steam engine, machinery, shipbuilding, applied mechanics, &c., became standard textbooks; and he did much for the new science of thermodynamics and the theories of elasticity and of waves. He wrote humorous and patriotic *Songs and Fables* (1874). See Life by Tait prefixed to his *Miscellaneous Papers* (1880).

RANSOME, (1) Arthur Mitchell (1884–1967), English writer, born in Leeds, wrote studies of Edgar Allan Poe (1910), Oscar Wilde (1912), and impressions of Russia, before making his name with books for young readers. His works for them are carefully written and rank high among their kind. They include *Swallows and Amazons* (1931), *We didn't mean to go to Sea* (1938), *The Big Six* (1940) and *Great Northern?* (1947).

(2) **Robert** (1753–1830), English agricultural implement maker, born at Wells in Norfolk, in 1789 founded at Ipswich the great Orwell Works for agricultural implements.

RAOULT, François Marie, *ra-ool* (1830–1901), French chemist, born at Fournes (Nord), was educated at Paris and in 1870 became professor of Chemistry at Grenoble. He discovered the law (named after him) which relates the vapour pressure of a solution to the number of molecules of solute dissolved in it.

RAPHAEL, properly **Raffaello Santi** or **Sanzio,** *raf'a-el, raf-a-el'lō* (1483–1520), Italian painter, was born at Urbino, the son of the poet-painter, Giovanni Santi (d. 1494). He seems to have studied under Timoteo Viti, and then from about 1500 at Perugia under Perugino, becoming such a clever imitator of his style that to this day the early pictures of the disciple are confounded with those of his master. Among his earliest paintings were the *Crucifixion* (1502–03, Dudley collection), an *Assumption of the Virgin* (Vatican), and a *Marriage of the Virgin* (1504, Milan). Probably about 1504 Raphael began to discern the advantage of greater independence, yet for some time longer he showed Peruginesque influence. In 1505 he went to Siena, where he assisted Pinturicchio, and next to Florence; but before starting he probably took commissions, which produced the *Madonna Ansidei* (National Gallery), the *Madonna of Sant' Antonio* and the *Madonna of Terranuova* (Berlin Museum). Raphael, who now had painting-rooms at Florence and at Perugia, resolved to acquire and assimilate some of the boldness of Michelangelo and the sweetness of Leonardo. In portraiture more than elsewhere da Vinci's influence is visible, and the likeness of *Maddalena Doni* (Florence) is inspired by the *Mona Lisa.* Of special interest is the *St George,* sent by the Duke of Urbino to Henry VII of England; while attractive in other ways are the painter's own likeness (Uffizi) and the *Madonnas* of Orleans, of the Palm, of St Petersburg and of Canigiani in which Raphael finally appears as a pure Tuscan. The Borghese *Entombment* (1507) is an embodiment of all the new principles which Raphael acquired at Florence and of colour such as only Raphael could give. He became attracted by the style of Fra Bartolommeo; and, under the influence of that master, finished the *Madonna del Baldacchino* at Florence. Some of the best work of his Florentine period was now produced—the small *Holy Family* (Madrid), the *St Catharine* (Louvre), the *Bridgewater* and *Colonna Madonnas,* the *Virgin and Sleeping Infant* (Milan), the large *Cowper Madonna,* the *Belle Jardinière,* and the *Esterhazy Madonna.* In 1508 Raphael went to Rome at the instigation of his relative Bramante, then in high favour with Julius II, who had laid the foundation of the new cathedral of St Peter, and who caused the papal chambers to be decorated afresh because he disliked the frescoes of the older masters. The date of Raphael's engagement to paint the *Camere* of the Vatican is now fixed as 1509. In the ceiling of the chamber 'of the Signature' the space is divided into fields, in which the Temptation, the Judgment of Solomon, the Creation of the Planets, and Marsyas and Apollo were inserted side by side with medallions enclosing allegories of Theology, Philosophy, Justice and Poetry. On the walls of the *camera* Raphael began the *Disputa,* in which he represented the Eternal, Christ, Mary and the apostles and angels presiding in heaven over the Trinitarian controversy. The *School of Athens,* the Parnassus, and the allegory of Prudence followed. Subordinate pictures are the pope accepting the Decretals (1511), Justinian receiving the Pandects, and Augustus saving the manuscripts of Virgil. Raphael divided his time between the labours of the Vatican and easel pictures. The portraits of Julius II and the Virgin of the Popolo were now executed, drawings were furnished to the copperplate-engraver Marcantonio for the Massacre of the Innocents, and Madonnas and Holy Families were composed; while on the ceiling of the chamber of Heliodorus at the Vatican he finished the picture in which the Eternal appears to Noah, Abraham's Sacrifice, Jacob's Dream and the Burning Bush. The pontiff is introduced into the Expulsion of Heliodorus and the Mass of Bolsena. The death of Julius in 1513 but slightly interrupted the labours of the painter, who gave a noble rendering of Leo X and his suite in the Defeat of Attila. The Deliverance of Peter completed the decorations. The constant employment of disciples enabled Raphael in the three years 1511–14 also to finish the *Madonna di Foligno*, the *Isaiah of St Agostino*, the *Galatea of the Farnesina*, the *Sibyls of the Pace*, and the mosaics of the Popolo ordered by Agostino Chigi. He painted, too, the *Madonna of the Fish* (Madrid) and *Madonna della Sedia* (Florence), while in portraits such as *Altoviti* (Munich) and *Inghirami* (Florence) he rises to the perfect rendering of features and expression which finds its greatest triumph in the *Leo* X (Florence). Leo selected Raphael to succeed Bramante as architect of St Peter's in 1514, and secured from him for the Vatican chambers the frescoes of the Camera dell' Incendio, which all illustrate scenes from the lives of Leonine popes. But much of Raphael's attention was taken up with the cartoons (Kensington) executed, with help from assistants, for the tapestries of the Sistine Chapel. The first was completed in December 1516, the second woven at Brussels in 1519. His portraits of the Duke of Urbino, Castiglione, Bembo and Navagero, and his decoration of Cardinal Bibiena's rooms at the Vatican, tell of the company which Raphael now frequented. When Leo X succumbed to Francis I, Raphael followed the pontiff to Florence and Bologna, and found there new patrons for whom he executed the *Sistine Madonna*, the *St Cecilia* of Bologna, and the *Ezechiel* of the Pitti. The labours subsequently completed were immense, including the *Spasimo* (Madrid), the *Holy Family* and *St Michael*, which the pope sent to the king of France in 1518, the likeness of the vice-queen of Aragon, and the *Violin-player* (Sciarra collection at Rome). In wall-painting he produced, with help, the cycle of the Psyche legend at the Farnesina, the gospel scenes of the Loggie of the Vatican, and the frescoes of the Hall of Constantine. His last work, the *Transfiguration*, was nearly finished when Raphael died. See the great work on him by Crowe and Cavalcaselle (1882); H. Strachey's monograph (1900), Oppé's (1909), Holmes's (1933), Pittaluga's (1956); French works by Passavant (1860; trans. 1872), Gruyer (1863–81), Müntz (1881–96); German by Grimm (trans. 1889), Springer (3rd ed. 1896), Lübke (1881), Von Lützow (1890). Von Seidlitz (1891), Knackfuss (trans. 1899).

RAPIN, Paul de, *ra-pī* (1661–1725), French historian, born at Castres in Languedoc, the son of the Seigneur de Thoyras, studied at the Protestant college of Saumur, and passed as advocate in 1679. After the revocation of the Edict of Nantes (1685) he went to Holland, enlisted in a Huguenot volunteer corps, followed the Prince of Orange to England in 1688, was made ensign in 1689, and distinguished himself at the Boyne and at Limerick. For some years he travelled as tutor with the Earl of Portland's son, then settled at Wesel where he devoted his remaining years to the composition of his great *Histoire d'Angleterre* (1724), undoubtedly the best work on English history that had until then appeared. It was continued from William III's accession to his death by David Durant (1734), and was translated into English by Tindal (1726–31).

RAPP, (1) George (1770–1847), religious leader, founder of the Harmonists, was born in Württemberg, and emigrated with his followers to Western Pennsylvania in 1803, establishing a settlement named Harmony. After migrating to New Harmony in Indiana (1815), they returned in 1824 to Pennsylvania and built Economy on the Ohio, 15 miles NW of Pittsburgh. Looking for the speedy second coming of Christ, the community sought to amass wealth for the Lord's use, practised rigid economy, self-denial and celibacy, all things being held in common, and, diminished in number, owned farms, dairies and vineyards, and railway and bank shares worth millions of dollars. See German monograph by Knortz (1892).

(2) **Jean, Comte de** (1772–1821), French soldier, born at Colmar, entered the French army in 1788, distinguished himself in Germany and Egypt, and became aide-de-camp to Napoleon. For his brilliant charge at Austerlitz he was made general of division (1805); in 1809 he became a Count of the Empire. He accompanied the emperor on the Russian expedition, defended Danzig for nearly a year, on its surrender was sent prisoner to Russia, and did not return till 1814. During the Hundred Days he supported Napoleon, but after the Restoration he was made a peer. See his Memoirs (1823; new ed. 1895).

RASCHIG, Friedrich August, *rash-iKH* (1863–1928), German chemist and industrialist, born in Brandenburg, discovered nitramide and chloramine, and new production methods for hydrazine and phenol. He died at Duisburg.

RASHDALL, Hastings (1858–1924), English moral philosopher and theologian, born in London, was educated at Harrow and Oxford. He was elected a fellow of Hertford College, Oxford, in 1888, divinity tutor and chaplain at Balliol, and from 1895 to 1917 was tutor in philosophy at New College. Given a canonry at Hereford in 1909, he in 1917 became dean of Carlisle. Among his writings are the scholarly *Universities of Europe in the Middle Ages* (3 vols., new ed. 1936), and *Theory of Good and Evil* (2 vols. 1917), containing his nonhedonistic 'ideal utilitarian' system of ethics in which right and wrong are judged by the ideal and which may, but not of necessity, be pleasurable. *Idea of Atonement in Christian Theology* (1919) includes his Bampton lectures given in 1915. See Life by P. E. Matheson (1928).

RASK, Rasmus Christian (1787–1832), Danish philologist, born in Fünen, in 1819–23 travelled to India and Ceylon. He returned to Copenhagen, and in 1825 became professor of Literary History, in 1828 of Oriental Languages, and in 1831 of Icelandic. His study of Icelandic (1818), with Bopp's and Grimm's works opened up the science of comparative philology. See Lives by Rönning and Wimmer (1887), and study by Jespersen (1918).

RASMUSSEN, Knud Johan Victor (1879–1933), Danish explorer and ethnologist, was born at Jacobshavn, Greenland, of Danish and Eskimo parents. From 1902 onwards he directed several expeditions to Greenland in support of the theory that the Eskimos and the North American Indians were both descended from migratory tribes from Asia. In 1910 he established Thule base on Cape York, and in 1921–24 crossed from Greenland to the Bering Strait. English translations of his books include *Greenland by the Polar Sea* (1921), *Myths and Legends from Greenland* (1921–25), and *Across Arctic America* (1927).

RASPAIL, François Vincent, *ras-pah'y'* (1794–1878), French chemist, doctor, deputy, and advocate of universal suffrage, as a revolutionist was banished from France in 1848 but allowed to return in 1859. His camphor system (1845) was a forerunner of antiseptic surgery. See monograph by Saint-Martin (1877).

RASPE. See MÜNCHHAUSEN.

RASPUTIN, Grigoriy Efimovich (1871?–1916), Russian peasant monk, born at Pokrovskoye in Tobolsk province, wielded a malign, magnetic and mystic power over the Tsarina and others at the Russian court, causing the dismissal of ministers, including the prime minister Kokovtsev. He was assassinated at the Yusupov Palace by a party of noblemen led by the Grand-Duke Dimitry Pavlovich and Prince Yusupov. See studies by M. Rodzyanko (1927) and R. Fülop-Miller (1928).

RASSAM, Hormuzd (1826–1910), Turkish Assyriologist, born at Mosul, the son of Chaldaean Christians. He assisted Layard at Nineveh in 1845–47 and 1849–51, and succeeded him, until 1854, as British agent for Assyrian excavations, finding the palace of Assurbani-Pal (Sardanapalus). After holding political offices at Aden and Muscat, he was sent (1864) to Abyssinia, where King Theodore cast him into prison till 1868, when he was released by Sir Robert Napier. In 1876–82 he made explorations in Mesopotamia for the British Museum. He wrote on his Abyssinian experiences (1869), and did much work for the *Academy*, &c.

RASTELL, (1) **John** (1475–1536), English printer, lawyer and dramatist, born in Coventry, was called to the bar and in 1510 set up his own printing press. Married to the sister of Sir Thomas More (q.v.), he printed More's *Life of Pico*, a grammar by Linacre, the only copy of Medwall's play *Fulgens and Lucres* and many law books. Himself a dramatist, his plays, printed on his own press, include *Nature of the Four Elements* (1519), *Of Gentylness and Nobylyte . . .* (*c.* 1527) and *Calisto and Meleboea* (*c.* 1527). An ingenious deviser of pageants, he presented several of them at court. His expedition to found a settlement in the 'New Found Lands' in 1517 came to nothing through mutiny on his ship.

(2) **William** (1508–65), English printer and lawyer, son of (1) and nephew of Sir Thomas More (q.v.), worked until 1529 with his father. He then set up his own printing press and during the next five years printed many of More's works, Fabyan's *Chronicle*, Henry Medwall's *Nature*, plays by his brother-in-law, John Heywood, as well as many law books. Abandoning printing for law when More fell from favour with the king, he was by 1549 treasurer of Lincoln's Inn. His kinship with More and his relationship through marriage with a daughter of More's protégé, John Clement, drove him with the Clements into exile at Louvain. With him went letters and other works written by More in the Tower. These, edited and printed by him, were to appear in More's *English Works* (1557). Exiled again during the reign of Elizabeth, he died abroad.

RATHAUS, Karol, *rat'hows* (1895–1954), Polish composer, who came to England in 1934 after studying in Vienna and teaching in Berlin. He later settled in the United States. His main works are a piano concerto, three symphonies and string quartets.

RATHENAU, Walther, *rah'tĕnow* (1867–1922), German electrotechnician and industrialist, born in Berlin of Jewish family, organized the Allgemeine Elektrizitäts Gesellschaft, founded by his father, and German war industries during World War I. In 1921 as minister of reconstruction he dealt with reparations. He wrote *Von kommenden Dingen*, &c. He was murdered soon after becoming foreign minister. See study by H. Graf Kessler (1928).

RATHKE, Martin Heinrich, *raht'kĕ* (1793–1860), German biologist, born in Danzig, became professor of Physiology at Dorpat (1829) and Königsberg (1835), in 1829 discovered gill-slits and gill-arches in embryo birds and mammals. 'Rathke's pocket' is the name given to the small pit on the dorsal side of the oral cavity of developing Vertebrates.

RATICH, or Ratke, Wolfgang, *rah'tiKH* (1571–1635), German educationist, born in Holstein, based a new system of education on Bacon's *Advancement*, which he put into practice at Köthen in 1618. A second trial at Magdeburg in 1620 also ended in failure, and after some years of ineffectual wanderings he died at Erfurt. Though his ideas on education and methods of teaching were unsuccessful and unpopular in his lifetime, they had some influence on later reformers, especially Comenius. See monographs by Krause (1872), Störl (1876), Schumann (1876), Vogt (1894), and Seiler (1931); and Quick's *Essays on Educational Reformers* (1868; new ed. 1890).

RATTAZZI, Urbano, *rat-tat'see* (1808–73), Italian statesman, born at Alessandria, practised as advocate at Casale, and in 1848 entered the Second Chamber at Turin, becoming minister of the interior and later of justice till after Novara. In 1853 he took the portfolio of justice under Cavour; but, accused of weakness in suppressing the Mazzinian movement, retired in 1858. In 1859 he was minister of the interior, but retired because of the cession of Savoy and Nice (1860). Twice prime minister for a few months (1862, 1867), he twice had to resign because of his opposition to Garibaldi. See

Life by Morelli (1874) and his widow's *Rattazzi et son temps* (1881–87).

RATTIGAN, Terence Mervyn (1911–), English playwright, born in London, educated at Harrow and Oxford, scored a considerable success with his comedy *French Without Tears* (1936). Since then, most of his works, with the possible exception of *Adventure Story* (1949), a play about Alexander the Great, have been internationally acclaimed; and reveal not only a wide range of imagination but a deepening psychological knowledge. Best known are *The Winslow Boy* (1946), based on the Archer Shee case, *The Browning Version* (1948), *The Deep Blue Sea* (1952), *Separate Tables* (1954) and *Ross* (1960), a fictional treatment of T. E. Lawrence. He has been responsible for several successful films made from his own and other works.

RAUCH, Christian Daniel, *row*KH (1777–1857), German sculptor, born at Arolsen, practised sculpture while still valet to Frederick-William of Prussia, and in 1804 went to Rome. In 1811–15 he chiselled the recumbent effigy for the tomb of Queen Louisa at Charlottenburg. His works included statues of Blücher, Dürer, Goethe, Schiller and Schleiermacher; his masterpiece was the Frederick the Great (1851) in Berlin. See Life by Eggers (1873–90; Eng. trans. Boston 1893).

RAUMER, *row'mėr*, (1) **Friedrich Ludwig Georg von** (1781–1873), German historian, born at Wörlitz near Dessau, entered the Prussian state service in 1801; in 1811 became professor of History at Breslau; in 1819–53 filled the chair of Political Science at Berlin; and was secretary of the Berlin Academy. In 1848 he went to Paris as German ambassador. His chief works are a history of the Hohenstaufen emperors (1823–1825) and a history of Europe from the 16th century (1832–50). See his *Autobiography and Correspondence* (1861).

(2) **Karl Georg** (1783–1865), brother of (1), born at Wörlitz, became professor of Mineralogy at Breslau in 1811, and at Halle in 1819, of Natural History in 1827 at Erlangen. He wrote books on physiography, geography, Palestine, geognosy and crystallography, a great history of pedagogics (1843–1851), and an Autobiography (1866).

(3) **Rudolf** (1815–76), son of (2), Teutonic philologist, from 1846 was a professor at Erlangen and wrote, among other works, *Geschichte des germanischen Philologie* (1870).

RAUSCHER, Joseph Othmar von, *row'shėr* (1797–1875), Austrian cardinal, from 1853 prince-archbishop of Vienna, opposed, but ended by accepting, the infallibility dogma.

RAVAILLAC, François, *rav-ī-yak* (1578–1610), French bankrupt schoolmaster, who, after long imprisonment and a brief service in the Order of Feuillants, was moved by Catholic fanaticism to stab Henry IV (q.v.) of France. He was torn to pieces by horses. See works by Loiseleur (1873), Tharaud (1913).

RAVEL, Maurice (1875–1937), French composer, born at Ciboure in the Basque country, entered the Paris Conservatoire as a piano student in 1889. He eschewed the formal type of study and practice, and was something of a rebel; his early compositions met with considerable disapproval from the authorities, but after joining Gabriel Fauré's composition class in 1898 he developed considerably, though his first orchestral piece, the overture to *Schéhérazade*, an opera which never saw the light of day, had a hostile reception on its first performance in 1899. In the same year, however, he won recognition with his *Pavane pour une infante défunte*, slender compared with later work, but strongly redolent of his Basque background. In 1901 he was runner-up for the Prix de Rome with his cantata *Myrrha*, and his *Jeux d'eau* for piano won a popular success. He made two more fruitless attempts at the Prix de Rome and was intending to try a fourth time, but was barred from entering. He himself was indifferent, but the case was seized upon by the press as an example of personal prejudice in high quarters. Significantly, all Ravel's successful rivals were consigned to oblivion by posterity within a half-century. Now at the height of his powers, Ravel wrote his *Sonatina* (1905), *Miroirs* (1905), *Ma Mère l'Oye* (1908) and *Gaspard de la nuit* (1908) for piano; and in 1909 he began the music for the Diaghilev ballet *Daphnis et Chloé*, which was first performed in 1912. His comic opera *L'Heure espagnole* was completed in 1907 and produced in 1911. When war broke out he was forty, but he joined the army and saw active service; his *Tombeau de Couperin* (1917), a piano suite on the 18th-century pattern, which he later orchestrated, was dedicated to friends killed in action. The opera *L'Enfant et les sortilèges*, written to a libretto by Colette, was performed with great success in 1925, and the ' choreographic poem ' *La Valse*, epitomizing the spirit of Vienna, had been staged in 1920. These two works, both begun in 1917, were Ravel's last major contributions. The *Boléro* (1928), despite its popularity in Promenade concerts and elsewhere, is of smaller stature and was intended as a miniature ballet. The composer visited England in 1928 and received an honorary doctorate at Oxford. In 1933 his mental faculties began to fail, and it was found that he had a tumour on the brain. He composed no more but remained fairly active physically, and was able to tour Spain before he died, December 27, 1937. Ravel's music is scintillating and dynamic; he defied the established rules of harmony with his unresolved sevenths and ninths and other devices, his syncopation and strange sonorities, and he made the piano sound as it had never sounded before. His orchestrations are brilliant, especially in their masterly use of wind instruments and unusual percussion effects, often characteristically French, sometimes with a Spanish flavour stemming from his Basque background. It is interesting to note that his only work written purely for orchestra is *Rapsodie espagnole* (1907); everything else orchestral is either opera, ballet, or orchestrated piano pieces. See Lives by Demuth (1948), Myers (1960).

RAVENSCROFT, Thomas (1592–1640), English composer and author of *Pammelia* (1609), *Melismata* (1611) and *The Whole Book* *of Psalms* (1621). *Pammelia*, a collection of rounds and catches, was the first book of its kind in England. Some well-known tunes, such as St Davids and Bangor, are by him.

RAWLINSON, (1) **George** (1812–1902), English orientalist, brother of (2), born at Chadlington, Chipping Norton, in 1861 became Camden professor of Ancient History, in 1872 a canon of Canterbury, and in 1888 rector of All Hallows, Lombard Street. His annotated translation of Herodotus (1858–60) was followed by *The Five Great Eastern Monarchies* (1862–67), *History of Ancient Egypt* (1881), and theological works.

(2) **Sir Henry Creswicke** (1810–95), English diplomat and Assyriologist, brother of (1), born at Chadlington, entered the East India Company's army in 1827. In 1833–39 he helped to reorganize the Persian army, studying the while the cuneiform inscriptions, and translating Darius's Behistun inscription. He was political agent at Kandahar 1840–42, at Baghdad from 1843, later consul also, and made excavations and collections. A director of the East India Company in 1856, in 1859–60 he was British minister in Persia, in 1858, 1865–68, a Conservative M.P., and in 1858–59, 1868–95 a member of the Council of India. He wrote books on cuneiform inscriptions, the Russian question, *History of Assyria* (1852), &c. See Life by his brother, G. Rawlinson (1898).

(3) **Henry Seymour, 1st Baron Rawlinson** (1864–1925), eldest son of (2), served in Burma, Sudan and S. Africa, commanded the 4th Army in France in 1918, and broke the Hindenburg line, winning fame, a peerage in 1919 and a grant of £30,000. He was commander-in-chief in India (1920). See Life by Maurice (1928).

RAWSTHORNE, **Alan** (1905–71), English composer, born in Haslingden, Lancs, first studied dentistry, but turned to music at the age of twenty and studied at the Royal Manchester College of Music. From 1932 to 1934 he taught at Dartington Hall, but settled in London in 1935. His works, forthright, and polished in style, include symphonies, *Symphonic Studies*, for orchestra, concertos for piano and for violin, and various pieces of choral and chamber music.

RAY, (1) **John** (1627–1705), English naturalist, born, a blacksmith's son, at Black-Notley near Braintree, in 1649 became a fellow of Trinity College, Cambridge. At the Restoration he accepted Episcopal ordination, but was ejected by the 'Bartholomew Act' (1662). With a pupil, Francis Willughby (q.v.), Ray travelled (1662–66) over England and Wales, the Low Countries, Germany, Italy and France, studying botany and zoology. In 1667 he was elected F.R.S., and he contributed valuable papers to the *Transactions*. Ray's classification of plants was the foundation of the 'Natural System'; his zoological works were called by Cuvier the basis of all modern zoology. He wrote *Methodus Plantarum Nova* (1682), *Catalogus Plantarum Angliae* (1670), *Historia Plantarum* (1686–1704), and *Synopsis Methodica Animalium* (1693), besides three volumes on Birds, Fishes and Insects, &c. Lankester edited *Memorials of Ray* (1846) and his *Correspondence* (1848) for the Ray Society, founded in 1844, and Gunther edited *Further Correspondence* (1928). See Life by Raven (1942).

(2) **Martha.** See HACKMAN.

RAYLEIGH, (1) **John William Strutt, 3rd Baron** (1842–1919), English physicist, born near Maldon in Essex, graduated in 1865 from Trinity College, Cambridge, as senior wrangler and Smith's prizeman, and was elected a fellow (1866). He succeeded his father as third baron in 1873; was Cambridge professor of Experimental Physics 1879–84, in 1888–1905 of Natural Philosophy at the Royal Institution; and president of the Royal Society (1905–08). He became chancellor of Cambridge University (1908), O.M. (1902), and Nobel prizewinner (1904). His work included valuable studies and research on vibratory motion, the theory of sound and the wave theory of light. With Sir W. Ramsay he was the discoverer of argon (1894). Interested in psychical problems, he was a member, and president in 1901, of the Society for Psychical Research. His writings include *The Theory of Sound* (1877–1878; 2nd ed. 1894–96) and *Scientific Papers* (1899–1900). See study by his son (1924).

(2) **Robert John Strutt, 4th Baron** (1875–1947), English physicist, son of (1), born at Terling Place, Essex, became professor of Physics at the Imperial College of Science from 1908 to 1919. Notable for his work on rock radioactivity, he became a fellow of the Royal Society in 1905 and a Rumford medallist. His writings include two excellent biographies, one of his father, the other of Sir J. J. Thomson (q.v.).

RAYNOUARD, **François Juste Marie**, *ray-nwar* (1761–1836), French poet and philologist, born at Brignoles in Provence, was a prosperous Paris advocate, in 1791 entered the legislative assembly, joined the Girondins, and was imprisoned. His poems and tragedies were successful, and in 1807 he was elected to the Academy, of which he became perpetual secretary in 1817. He was elected to the imperial legislative body in 1806 and 1811. After 1816 he wrote on the Provençal language and literature, notably his *Lexique Roman* (1838–44).

READ, **Sir Herbert** (1893–1968), English poet and art critic, born near Kirby Moorside, Yorkshire. He was an assistant keeper at the Victoria and Albert Museum, London, and from 1931 to 1933 was professor of Fine Art at Edinburgh University. He was editor of the *Burlington Magazine* from 1933 to 1939, and held academic posts at Cambridge, Liverpool, London and Harvard Universities, having achieved fame as a poet and a writer on aesthetics. His publications include *The Meaning of Art* (1931), *Art Now* (1933), *Collected Poems* (1946), the autobiographical *Annals of Innocence and Experience* (1940), &c. He was knighted in 1953, and received the Dutch Erasmus prize in 1966 for contributions to European culture.

READE, **Charles** (1814–84), English novelist and playwright, was born at Ipsden House, Oxfordshire, the youngest of eleven. After five years (all flogging) at Iffley, and six under two milder private tutors, in 1831 he gained a demyship at Magdalen College, Oxford, and in 1835, having taken third-class honours, was duly elected to a lay fellowship. Next year he entered Lincoln's Inn, and in 1843 was called to the bar. In 1850 he first put pen seriously to paper, 'writing first for the stage—about thirteen dramas, which nobody would play'. Through one of these dramas he formed his platonic friendship with Mrs Seymour, a warmhearted actress, who from 1854 till her death (1879) kept house for him. His life after 1852 is a succession of plays, by which he lost money, and novels that won profit and fame. These novels illustrate social injustice and cruelty in one form or another and his writing is realistic and vivid. They include *Peg Woffington* (1852), *Hard Cash* (1863), *Foul Play* (1869, with Dion Boucicault), *A Terrible Temptation* (1871), and *A Woman-hater* (1877). His masterpiece was his long, historical novel of the 15th century, *The Cloister and the Hearth* (1861). He was not one of the great novelists of the century, but of the second order he is perhaps the best. *Charles Reade* (1887), by his brother and a nephew, is a poor biography. See Swinburne's *Miscellanies* (1886), and studies by Coleman (1903) and Elwin (1931).

READING, Rufus Daniel Isaacs, 1st Marquess of (1860–1935), English lawyer and statesman, born in London, was educated there and in Brussels and Hanover. In parliament as Liberal member for Reading in 1904, he also began to gain a reputation as an eminent advocate. In 1910 he was appointed solicitor-general and later attorney-general and as such in 1912 was the first to become a member of the cabinet. Lord chief justice in 1913, during World War I he was special envoy to the United States in negotiating financial plans. He was British ambassador in Washington from 1918 to 1921, and thereafter viceroy of India until 1926. Created marquess on his return, he took charge of many business concerns, including the chairmanship of United Newspapers Ltd. and the presidency of Imperial Chemical Industries. In 1931 he was for a short time foreign secretary in the National government.

RÉAUMUR, René Antoine Ferchault de, *ray-ō-mür* (1683–1757), French physicist, born at La Rochelle, became in 1708 a member of the Academy of Sciences, and superintended an official *Description des arts et métiers.* He made researches in natural history, as to woods, rivers and mines, and in metallurgy and glassmaking. His thermometer (with spirit instead of mercury) has eighty degrees between the freezing- and boiling-points.

RÉCAMIER, Madame (*née* **Jeanne Françoise Julie Adélaïde Bernard**), *ray-kam-yay* (1777–1849), French beauty, born at Lyons, in 1793 married a rich banker thrice her own age. Her salon was soon filled with the brightest wits of the day, but her temperament prevented any hint of scandal. When her husband was financially ruined she visited Madame de Staël at Coppet (1806). Here she met Prince August of Prussia. A marriage was arranged, provided M. Récamier would consent to a divorce. He consented to this, but Madame could not desert him in adversity. The most distinguished friend of her later years was Chateaubriand. See her *Souvenirs et correspondence* (1859), and Lives by E. Herriot (trans. 1906) and Trouncer (1949).

RECLUS, Jean Jacques Élisée, *rė-klü* (1830–1905), French geographer, born at Ste-Foix-la-Grande (Gironde), was educated at Montauban and Berlin. An extreme Democrat, he left France after the *coup d'état* of 1851, and spent seven years in England, Ireland and America. He returned in 1858, and published *Voyage à la Sierra Nevada de Ste Marthe* (1861), &c. For his share in the Commune (1871) he was banished. In Switzerland he began his masterpiece, *Nouvelle Géographie universelle* (19 vols. 1876–94; Eng. trans. by Ravenstein and A. H. Keane). He also wrote a physical geography, *La Terre* (1867–68; trans. 1871 and 1887), *Histoire d'une montagne* (1880; trans. 1881), &c. In 1893 he became a professor at Brussels.

RECORDE, Robert (*c.* 1510–58), English mathematician, born at Tenby, studied at Oxford, in 1545 took his M.D. at Cambridge, became physician to Edward VI and Queen Mary, but died in debtors' prison. His works include *The Grounde of Artes* (1540), on arithmetic; *Pathwaye to Knowledge* (1551), an abridged Euclid; *Castle of Knowledge* (1551), on astronomy; and *Whetstone of Wit* (1557), an important treatise on algebra. He was first to use the sign =.

REDGRAVE, (1) **Sir Michael Scudamore** (1908–), British stage and film actor, born at Bristol, son of actor parents and grandfather, educated at Clifton College and Magdalene College, Cambridge, was first a modern-language teacher at Cranleigh school, began his acting career with Liverpool Repertory Company (1934–36). His sensitive, intellectual approach to acting has been most successful in classical rôles, such as the title parts of *Hamlet* (Old Vic and Elsinore, 1949–50) and *Uncle Vanya* (Chichester and National Theatre, 1963–64). Modern plays in which he has appeared include *Tiger at the Gates* (1955) and his own adaptation of *The Aspern Papers* (1959), &c. He has also acted in many films since his début in *The Lady Vanishes* (1938), including *The Way to the Stars* (1945) and the outstanding *The Browning Version* (1951). Created C.B.E. (1952) and knighted (1959), he became director of the Yvonne Arnaud Theatre at Guildford in 1962. See Life by Findlater (1956). He married the actress **Rachel Kempson** (1910–) in 1935, and their three children are all actors: **Vanessa** (1937–), won acclaim with the Royal Shakespeare Company, particularly as 'Rosalind' in *As You Like It* (1961), and has also appeared successfully in films; **Corin** (1939–) acts on stage and television; and **Lynn** (1944–) is also a stage and film acress, gaining particular notice in the film *Georgy Girl* (1967).

(2) **Richard** (1804–88), English subject painter, A.R.A. (1840), R.A. (1851), from 1857 was inspector-general of art schools. He wrote, with his brother, **Samuel** (1802–76), *A Century of English Painters* (1866) and *Dictionary of Artists of the English School* (1874).

REDI, Francesco, *ray'dee* (1626–97), Italian

physician and poet, born at Arezzo, studied at Florence and Pisa, and became physician to the dukes of Tuscany. He wrote a book on animal parasites and proved by a series of experiments that maggots cannot form on meat which has been covered. He also wrote the dithyrambic *Bacco in Toscana* (1685).

REDMOND, John Edward (1856–1918), Irish politician, born in Dublin, the son of a Wexford M.P., was called to the bar at Gray's Inn 1886, and entered parliament 1881. A champion of Home Rule, he became chairman of the Nationalist party in 1900. He declined a seat in Asquith's coalition ministry (1915), but supported the war, deplored the Irish rebellion, and opposed Sinn Fein. See Life by D. Gwynn (1932).

REDON, Odilon, *rė-dõ* (1840–1916), French artist, born at Bordeaux, is usually regarded as a pioneer surrealist, owing to his use of dream images in his work. He made many charcoal drawings and lithographs of extraordinary imaginative power, but after 1900 he painted, especially in pastel, pictures of flowers and portraits in intense colour. He was also a brilliant writer; his diaries (1867–1915) were published as *À soi-même* (1922), and his *Lettres* in 1923. See also Life by M. and A. Leblond (1941).

REDPATH, Anne (1895–1965), Scottish painter, born at Galashiels, was one of the most important modern Scottish artists, her paintings in oil and watercolour showing great richness of colour and vigorous technique. She was elected to the R.S.A. in 1952, and was awarded the O.B.E. in 1955. Examples of her work have been acquired for the permanent collections of Edinburgh, Manchester, Vancouver, &c.

REED, (1) **Sir Carol** (1906–), English film director, born at Putney, educated at King's School, Canterbury, took to the stage (1924) and acted and produced for Edgar Wallace until 1930. He produced or directed such memorable films as *Kipps* (1941), *The Young Mr Pitt* (1942), *The Way Ahead* (1944), the Allied War Documentary *The True Glory* (1945), *The Fallen Idol* (1948), but is best remembered for his Cannes Film Prize-winning version of Graham Greene's novel, *The Third Man* (1949), depicting the sinister underworld of postwar, partitioned Vienna. *Outcasts of the Islands* (1952) based on a Conrad novel, was another triumph of location work in the East, and *Our Man in Havana* (1959) marked a return to his postwar brilliance. He was knighted in 1952.

(2) **Sir Edward James** (1830–1906), English naval engineer, born at Sheerness, was chief constructor of the navy (1863–70) and designed battleships for both the British and foreign navies. Created K.C.B. in 1880, he was Liberal M.P. for Cardiff until 1895, becoming lord of the Treasury in 1886. He wrote *The Stability of Ships* (1884), &c.

(3) **Isaac** (1742–1807), English editor of Shakespeare, born in London, was an unenthusiastic conveyancer with considerable interest in archaeology and literature. A meticulous commentator and editor, he is best known for his revisions of Dr Johnson's and George Steevens' 'variorum' edition of Shakespeare.

(4) **Talbot Baines** (1852–93), English author of books for boys, was born in London, the son of **Sir Charles Reed** (1819–81), chairman of the London School Board. He became head of his father's firm of typefounders and wrote books on the history of printing (see his *History of the Old English Letter-foundries* (1887)). His robust, moral, but entertaining school stories first appeared in the *Boy's Own Paper*. They include *The Fifth Form at St Dominic's* (1881), *The Master of the Shell* (1887), and *Cockhouse at Fellsgarth* (1891).

(5) **Walter** (1851–1902), American army doctor, born in Belroi, Virginia, was in the medical corps from 1875 and was appointed professor of Bacteriology in the Army Medical College, Washington, in 1893. Investigations carried out by him in 1900 proved that transmission of yellow fever was by mosquitoes and his researches led to the eventual eradication of this disease from Cuba.

REEVE, Clara (1729–1807), English novelist of the 'Gothic' school, born at Ipswich, the daughter of the rector of Freston, translated Barclay's *Argenis* (1772), and wrote *The Champion of Virtue, a Gothic Story* (1777), renamed *The Old English Baron*, which was avowedly an imitation of Walpole's *Castle of Otranto*. She wrote four other novels and *The Progress of Romance* (1785).

REEVES, John Sims (1818–1900), English singer, born at Shooter's Hill, appeared as a baritone at Newcastle in 1839, and acquired fresh fame as a tenor. He studied at Paris (1843), sang at Milan, and was recognized as the first English tenor. Leaving the stage in 1860, he sang at concerts and in oratorio. See Life by Sutherland Edwards (1881) and his own *My Jubilee* (1889).

REGENER, Erich, *ray'gen-er* (1881–1955), German physicist, professor of Physics at Berlin and Stuttgart, was dismissed for political reasons in 1937, and reinstated in 1946. He is known for his pioneer work on cosmic rays and for his researches on the stratosphere.

REGER, Max, *ray'ger* (1873–1916), German composer, born at Brand, Bavaria, taught music at Wiesbaden and Munich, became director of Music in Leipzig University (1907), and professor (1908). He composed organ music, piano concertos, choral works and songs.

REGIOMONTANUS (1436–76), the name given to **Johannes Müller,** German mathematician and astronomer, from his Franconian birthplace, Königsberg (*Mons Regius*). He studied at Vienna, and in 1461 accompanied Cardinal Bessarion to Italy to learn Greek. In 1471 he settled in Nuremberg, where the patrician Bernhard Walther subsidized him. The two laboured at the *Alphonsine Tables*, and published *Ephemerides 1475-1506* (1473), of which Columbus made much use. He established the study of algebra and trigonometry in Germany, and wrote on waterworks, burning-glasses, weights and measures, the quadrature of the circle, &c. He was summoned to Rome in 1474 by Sixtus IV to help to reform the calendar, and died there.

REGNARD, Jean François, *rė-nyahr* (1655–1709), French comic dramatist, born in

Paris, a rich shopkeeper's son, found himself at twenty master of a considerable fortune, and set out on his travels. In his autobiographical romance, *La Provençale*, we read of his and his Provençal mistress's capture and sale as slaves by Algerian corsairs, their bondage at Constantinople, and their ransom. After wanderings as far as Lapland, he found his vocation in the success of *Le Divorce* at the Théâtre-Italien in 1688. *Le Joueur* (1696), a hit at the Théâtre-Français, was followed by *Le Distrait* (1697), *Le Retour imprévu* (1700), *Les Folies amoureuses* (1704), and his masterpiece *Le Légataire universel* (1708). There are editions by Didot (1820), Michiels (1854), Fournier (1875) and Moland (1893). See studies by Mahrenholtz (1887), Hallays (1929), and *Bibliographie* by Marchéville (1877).

REGNAULT, *rė-nyō*, (1) **Alexandre Georges Henri** (1843–71), French painter of mythological, Spanish and Moorish subjects, was born in Paris, and gained the Prix de Rome in 1866. In 1869 he painted his equestrian portrait of Prim, in 1870 his *Salome* and *Moorish Execution*. In the Franco-Prussian war he volunteered as a private soldier, and fell at Buzenval. See Lives by Cazalis (1872) and Marx (1887), and his *Correspondance* (1873).

(2) **Henri Victor** (1810–78), French chemist and physicist, father of (1), born at Aix-la-Chapelle, was a shop assistant in Paris and a professor at Lyons, whence, in 1840, he was recalled to Paris as a member of the Academy of Sciences. Having filled chairs in the École Polytechnique and the Collège de France, he became in 1854 director of the Sèvres porcelain factory. He investigated gases, latent heat, steam-engines, &c., and published a *Cours élémentaire de chimie* (14th ed. 1871). See *Éloge* by Dumas (1881).

RÉGNIER, *ray-nyay*, (1) **Henri François Joseph de** (1864–1936), French Symbolist poet, novelist and critic, born at Honfleur, studied law in Paris, turned to letters, and was elected to the Academy in 1911. His *Poèmes anciens et romanesques* (1890) revealed him as a Symbolist, though later he returned to more traditional versification. In both poetry and prose his style and mood were admirably suited to evocation of the past, and expressive of a melancholy disillusion induced by the passage of time. Poetical works include *La Sandale ailée* (1906), *Vestigia flammae* (1921) and *Flamma tenax* (1928). His novels were mainly concerned with France and Italy in the 17th and 18th centuries. Two of these are *La Double Maîtresse* (1900) and *Le Bon Plaisir* (1902). See studies in French by Berton (1910), Honnert (1923) and Parmée (1939).

(2) **Mathurin** (1573–1613), French satirist, born at Chartres, was tonsured at nine, but grew up dissipated and idle, obtained a canonry at Chartres, and enjoyed the favour of Henry IV. His whole work hardly exceeds 7000 lines—sixteen satires, three epistles, five elegies, and some odes, songs and epigrams, yet it places him high among French poets. He is greatest in his satires, admirably polished, but vigorous and original and giving a lively picture of the Paris of his day. Editions are by Poitevin (1860), Barthélemy (1862), and Courbet (1875). See Cherrier's *Bibliographie* (1889), and Life by Vianey (1896).

REGULUS, Marcus Atilius (d. *c.* 250 B.C.), obtained a triumph as Roman consul in 267 B.C. Consul again (256), he defeated the Carthaginian fleet, then landed in Africa, and, at first victorious, at last suffered a total defeat and was taken prisoner (255). He remained five years in captivity, until, reverses inducing the Carthaginians to sue for peace, he was released on parole and sent to Rome with the Punic envoys. He successfully dissuaded the senate from agreeing to their proposals, then, according to legend, returned to Carthage, and was put to death with horrible tortures.

REGULUS, or Rule, St (4th cent. A.D.), according to legend a monk of Constantinople or bishop of Patras, who in A.D. 347 came to Muckross or Kilrimont (afterwards St Andrews), bringing relics of St Andrew from the East. For the possible identification of him with an Irish St Riagail of the 6th century, see Skene's *Celtic Scotland* (1877).

REICH, Ferdinand (1799–1882), German physicist, professor at the Freiberg School of Mines, codiscoverer with Richter of the element indium (1863).

REICHENBACH, *rī'KHėn-baKH*, (1) **Hans** (1891–1953), German philosopher, born in Hamburg, was professor at Berlin (1926–33), Istanbul (1933–38) and from 1938 at California. An early associate of the 'Vienna Circle' of logical positivists, he was best known for his frequencies probability logic, in which the two truth values are replaced by the multivalued concept 'weight', set out in *Warscheinlichkeitslehre*, 'Theory of Probability' (1935; trans. 1949). Other works include *Experience and Prediction* (1938) and the posthumous papers, *Modern Philosophy of Science*, ed. M. Reichenbach (1959).

(2) **Heinrich Gottlieb Ludwig** (1793–1879), German botanist and zoologist, from 1820 professor at Dresden. His writings include *Iconographia Botanica seu Plantae Criticae* (1823–32) and *Handbuch des Natürlichen Pflanzensystems* (1837).

(3) **Heinrich Gustav** (1824–89), German botanist, son of (2), was a Hamburg professor from 1862. He wrote on orchids, and from 1864 was director of the Hamburg botanical gardens.

(4) **Karl, Baron von** (1788–1869), German natural philosopher and industrialist, born at Stuttgart, in 1821–34 made a fortune as a manufacturer at Blansko in Moravia. He worked at the compound products of the distillation of organic substances, and discovered paraffin (1830) and creosote (1833). Studying animal magnetism, he discovered, as he thought, a new force, which he called Od, intermediate between electricity, magnetism, heat and light, and recognizable only by the nerves of sensitive persons. He wrote on the geology of Moravia, on magnetism and several works on 'odic force' (1852–58). See Lives by Schrötter (1869) and Fechner (1876).

REICHSTADT, Duke of. See NAPOLEON II

REICHSTEIN, Tadeusz, *rīKH'shtīn* (1897–), Swiss chemist, born in Poland, has done outstanding work on the adrenal hormones and received (with Kendall and Hench) the Nobel award for medicine in 1950.

REID, (1) Sir George (1841–1913), Scottish painter, born at Aberdeen, A.R.S.A. (1870), R.S.A. (1877), from 1891 (when he was knighted) to 1902 was P.R.S.A. Best known by his portraits, he also produced admirable landscapes and book illustrations.

(2) or **Robertson, John** (1721–1807), Scottish soldier and musician, of Perthshire stock, entered the army in 1745, rose to be general, was a flute-player and composer, and left £50,000 to found a chair of music at Edinburgh.

(3) **Sir Robert Threshie.** See LOREBURN.

(4) **Thomas** (1710–96), head of the Scottish school of Philosophy, was born at Strachan manse, Kincardineshire, took his M.A. at Marischal College, Aberdeen, in 1726, and was college librarian 1733–36. He then visited Oxford, Cambridge and London, and in 1737 became minister of New Machar in Aberdeenshire. In 1739 appeared Hume's *Treatise on Human Nature*, which determined Reid to seek a new foundation for the common notions as to a material world; and he became the chief of a school whose aim was to deliver philosophy from scepticism, by resting finally on principles of intuitive or *a priori* origin. In 1752 he became professor of Philosophy in King's College, Aberdeen, in 1763 of Moral Philosophy at Glasgow; and in 1764 he published his *Inquiry into the Human Mind.* He retired from the duties of his chair in 1780. In 1785 the *Philosophy of the Intellectual Powers* appeared, in 1788 the *Active Powers.* See Life by Dugald Stewart in Reid's works (1803), the edition by Sir W. Hamilton (1853), sketch by A. C. Fraser (1899), and study by O. M. Jones (1927).

(5) **Thomas Mayne** (1818–83), Irish writer of boys' stories, born at Ballyroney, Co. Down, in 1840 emigrated to New Orleans, and served in the U.S. army during the Mexican war (1847). Returning to England in 1849, he settled down to a literary life in London, Bucks and Herefordshire. His vigorous style and profusion of hairbreadth escapes delighted his readers. Among his books were the *Rifle Rangers* (1850), *Scalp Hunters* (1851), *Boy Hunters* (1853), *War Trail* (1857), *Boy Tar* (1859), and *Headless Horseman* (1866). See *Captain Mayne Reid* by his widow, E. Reid (1900).

(6) **Sir Thomas Wemyss** (1842–1905), Scottish journalist and biographer, born at Newcastle, edited the *Leeds Mercury* 1870–87, then was manager to Messrs Cassell, and in 1890–99 editor of the *Speaker.* He was knighted in 1894. He wrote Lives of Charlotte Brontë and Lord Houghton, a book about Tunis and several novels.

(7) **Sir William** (1791–1858), Scottish meteorologist, soldier and administrator, writer on winds and storms, born at Kinglassie, Fife, served with high distinction in the Peninsular war, and was governor of Bermuda, the Windwards and Malta.

REIMARUS, Hermann Samuel, *rī-mah'roos* (1694–1768), German philosopher, born in Hamburg, from 1728 held an Oriental chair in his native city. His famous *Wolfenbüttelsche Fragmente eines Ungenannten*, first published by Lessing in 1774–78, denied the supernatural origin of Christianity. He wrote also on natural religion in his *Vornehmste Wahrheiten der natürlichen Religion.* See studies by Strauss (trans. 1879), Engert (1908 and 1916).

REINECKE, Karl, *rī'nekė* (1824–1910), German pianist and composer, born at Altona, from 1860 to 1895 was leader of the Leipzig Gewandhaus orchestra. In his day he was considered unrivalled as an interpreter of Mozart.

REINHARDT, Max, *rīn'hart* (1873–1943), Austrian theatre manager, born at Baden near Vienna, did much to reorganize the art and technique of production. His most notable success was *The Miracle* (London 1911). Other productions were *Everyman* and *Faust* for the Salzburg festivals of 1920 ff. He left Hitler's Germany in 1933 and died in New York.

REITH, John Charles Walsham, 1st Baron Reith of Stonehaven, *reeth* (1889–1971), British statesman and engineer, born in Stonehaven. He was educated at Glasgow Academy and Gresham's School, Holt, and served an engineering apprenticeship in Glasgow. Later entering the field of radio communication, he became the first general manager of the British Broadcasting Corporation in 1922 and its director-general from 1927 to 1938. He was M.P. for Southampton in 1940, and minister of works and buildings from 1940 to 1942. Created baron in 1940, he was chairman of the Commonwealth Telecommunications Board from 1946 to 1950. See his autobiographical *Into the Wind* (1949) and *Wearing Spurs* (1966). The B.B.C. inaugurated the Reith Lectures in 1948 in honour of his influence on broadcasting.

REIZENSTEIN, Franz, *rī'zėn-shtīn* (1911–), German composer and pianist, studied under Hindemith and in 1934 came to England, where he was a pupil of Vaughan Williams. Among his compositions are cello, piano and violin concertos, the cantata *Voices by Night*, two radio operas, and chamber and piano music.

RÉJANE, Gabrielle, *ray-zhan* (1856–1920), French actress, born in Paris, was noted for her playing of such parts as 'Zaza' and 'Madame Sans-Gêne'. Equally gifted in both tragic and comic rôles, she was regarded in France almost as highly as Bernhardt and was also popular in England and the U.S.A.

REMAK, Robert (1815–65), German physician, born in Posen, from 1859 a Berlin professor, studied pathology, embryology, and was a pioneer in electrotherapy.

REMARQUE, Erich Maria, *re-mahrk'* (1898–1970), German novelist, born in Osnabrück, went to the United States in 1939 and became a naturalized American. He wrote *All Quiet on the Western Front* (1929), *The Road Back* (1931), *The Black Obelisk* (1957), &c.

REMBRANDT, in full **Rembrandt Harmensz van Rijn** (1606–69), Dutch painter, born at Leyden, the son of a prosperous miller called Harmen Gerritsz van Rijn. From his twelfth or thirteenth year he studied painting under various masters, particularly Pieter Lastmann in Amsterdam, who possibly influenced his early work by introducing him to Italian art and especially the art of Caravaggio. He began his career as an etcher early, and etched beggars and picturesque heads, including his own; also *Christ presented in the Temple*. Other works of this early period include his *Philosopher* (National Gallery) and *Supper at Emmaus* (Paris). In 1631 he settled in Amsterdam, where he set up a studio and took pupils, still finding time to paint portraits and biblical subjects and to etch forty plates in the same year. *The Anatomical Lesson* dates from 1632, and with it his reputation as a portrait painter was assured. In 1634 he married Saskia van Ulenburgh (1613–42), whom we know by the portraits her husband made of her. The year of her death produced the famous *Night Watch*. Commissioned by an officers' guild, Rembrandt produced his artistic masterpiece at the expense of his popularity. His subjects, but for two in the foreground, are in shadow and this first flouting of the conventions was followed by other financial failures. He was bankrupt now and unfashionable, but he did not relax his diligence. He continued to work with undiminished energy and power. His portraits, no longer of the wealthy burghers, became less elaborate, more arresting and displayed a deep insight into the characters of his sitters. He reached the height of his greatness with his self-portrait (National Gallery) and with the portraits of Hendrickje Stoffels (with whom he lived after the death of his wife). In his landscapes his use of light, as in all his work, was effective and often dramatic. To religious painting he brought a simplicity without detracting from the mystical significance of the subjects. His works (preserved) total over 650 oil paintings, 2000 drawings and studies, and 300 etchings. He was not blind to the merits of Italian art, but his own practice was founded on the direct study of nature, both in human life and landscape. His chiaroscuro is always conducive to his purpose. No artist ever combined more delicate skill with more energy and power. His treatment of mankind is full of human sympathy; his special study was old age. See Lives by Vosmaer (2nd ed. 1877), Michel (trans. 1893), Rosenburg (1949), de Beaufort (1959); books by M. Bell (1907), Baldwin Brown (1907), Bode (1897–1908); on the etchings by Hamerton (1894), A. M. Hind (1912); C. H. de Groot's *Catalogue raisonné* of 17th-century Dutch painters (vol. vi; trans. 1916). See also *Drawings*, ed. Benesch (6 vols. 1958).

REMIGIUS, St. See REMY.

REMINGTON, Philo (1816–89), American inventor, born at Litchfield, N.Y., entered his father's small-arms factory, and for twenty-five years superintended the mechanical department. The perfecting of the Remington breech-loading rifles and the Remington typewriter was largely due to him.

REMIZOV, Alexei Mikhailovich (1877–1957), Russian writer, born in Moscow, lived in St Petersburg, but left Russia at the revolution, going first to Berlin and finally settling in Paris. His writing is full of national pride and a deep love of old Russian traditions and folklore; it contains realism, fantasy and humour. His main works are the novels, *The Pond*, *The Clock*, *Fifth Pestilence* and *Sisters of the Cross*, legends, plays and short stories.

RÉMUSAT, *ray-mü-za*, (1) **Charles François Marie, Comte de** (1797–1875), was born at Paris, son of the Comte de Rémusat (1762–1823), who was chamberlain to Napoleon. He early developed liberal ideas, and took to journalism. He signed the journalists' protest which brought about the July Revolution, was elected deputy for Toulouse, in 1836 became under-secretary of state for the Interior and in 1840 minister of the Interior. Exiled after the *coup d'état*, he devoted himself to literary and philosophical studies, till, in 1871, Thiers called him to the portfolio of Foreign Affairs, which he retained until 1873. Among his writings are *Essais de philosophie* (1842); *Abélard* (1845); *L'Angleterre au XVIIIe siècle* (1856); studies on *St Anselm* (1853), *Bacon* (1857), *Channing* (1857), *John Wesley* (1870) and *Lord Herbert of Cherbury* (1874); *Histoire de la philosophie en Angleterre de Bacon à Locke* (1875); and two philosophical dramas, *Abélard* (1877) and *La Saint Barthélemy* (1878). See his *Correspondance* (1883–86). The *Mémoires* (1879–80) and *Lettres* (1881) of his mother, **Claire, Comtesse de Rémusat** (1780–1821), *dame du palais* to Josephine, both translated into English, throw a flood of light on the society of the First Empire and the character of Napoleon.

(2) **Jean Pierre Abel** (1788–1832), French physician and Chinese scholar, born at Paris, took his diploma in medicine in 1813, but in 1811 had published an essay on Chinese literature. In 1814 he was made professor of Chinese in the Collège de France. Among his numerous works are one on the Tartar tongues (1820) and his great *Grammaire chinoise* (1822). He wrote also on Chinese writing (1827), medicine, topography and history, and *Mélanges* (1843). In 1822 he founded the Société Asiatique, and in 1824 became curator of the oriental department in the Bibliothèque Royale.

REMY, St (*c.* 438–533), Bishop of Rheims, according to Gregory of Tours baptized Clovis, king of the Franks, in the Christian faith. He was known as the Apostle of the Franks.

RENAN, Ernest, *rê-nã* (1823–92), French philologist and historian, born at Tréguier in Brittany, till his sixteenth year was trained for the church there, wholly under clerical influences. He was one of the youths chosen in 1836 by the Abbé Dupanloup for the Catholic seminary of St Nicolas du Chardonnet in Paris, whence, after three years, he was transferred to St Sulpice and its branch at Issy. As the result of the study of Hebrew and of German criticism, traditional Christianity became impossible for him; in 1845 he quitted St Sulpice and abandoned all thoughts of the church as a profession. With his elder sister Henriette's assistance and counsel he was enabled to follow out his purpose, a life of study untrammelled by creeds or formularies. In 1850 he obtained a post in the Bibliothèque Nationale, and having become known through *mémoires* on Oriental studies, in 1860 he was one of a commission sent by the government to study the remains of Phoenician civilization. In 1861 he was chosen professor of Hebrew in the Collège de France; but the emperor, inspired by the clerical party, refused to ratify the appointment; and it was not until 1870 that he was established in the chair. In 1878 he was elected to the Academy. His work as author began with a paper (1847), developed into his *Histoire générale des langues sémitiques* (1854). *Averroès et l'Averroïsme* (1852) proved his familiarity with the life and thought of the Middle Ages. And he wrote frequent essays, afterwards collected in his *Études d'histoire religieuse* (1856); and *Essais de morale et de critique* (1859). But his European reputation dates from the publication of the *Vie de Jésus* (1863), first in the series which its author regarded as his special work, the *Histoire des origines du Christianisme*. In the *Vie de Jésus* the combined weakness and strength of Renan's method were exaggerated to caricature. Of the volumes that followed, those on St Paul (1869) and Marcus Aurelius (1882) are specially noteworthy. In completion of his life's task Renan undertook a history of the people of Israel (5 vols., 1887–94). Other works include books on Job (1858), the Song of Solomon (1860), Ecclesiastes (1882), *Questions contemporaines*, *Dialogues philosophiques*, *Drames philosophiques*, *Souvenirs d'enfance* (1883), *L'Abesse de Jouarre* (1888), and *Ma Soeur Henriette* (1895; trans. as *Brother and Sister*, 1896). Madame Renan (1838–94), whom he married in 1856, was a niece of Ary Scheffer. In London he delivered the Hibbert Lectures (1880), *The Influence of Rome on Christianity*. See Life by Mme Darmesteter (1897), and books by Monod (1893), Barry (1905), Guérard (1913), Mott (1921), Pommier (1923); Girard and Moncel, *Bibliographie* (1923), J. Psichari (1925), H. Psichari (1947) and J. H. Chadbourne (1958).

RENAUDOT, Théophraste, *rè-nō-dō* (1586–1653), French Protestant doctor, born at Loudun, settled in Paris in 1624. In 1631 he founded the first French newspaper, the *Gazette de France*, also started the earliest Mont-de-Piété (1637), and advocated gratis dispensaries. See Life by Bonnefont (1893).

RENÉ I, 'the Good' (1409–80), Duke of Anjou, Count of Provence and Piedmont, failed in his efforts (1438–42) to make good his claim to the crown of Naples, married his daughter to Henry VI of England (1445), and ultimately devoted himself to Provençal poetry and agriculture at Aix. See Life by Lecoy de la Marche (Paris 1875).

RENI, GUIDO, *ray'nee* (1575–1642), Italian painter, born near Bologna, studied under Calvaert and Ludovico Caracci, and went to Rome in 1599 and again in 1605. *Aurora and the Hours* there is usually regarded as his masterpiece, but some critics rank even higher the unfinished *Nativity* in San Martino at Naples. Because of a quarrel with Cardinal Spinola regarding an altar piece for St Peter's he left Rome and settled at Bologna, where he died. He was a prolific painter, and his works are in all the chief European galleries. He also produced some vigorous etchings. See study by M. v. Boehn (1925).

RENNELL, (1) **James** (1742–1830), English geographer, served in the navy, became a major in the East India Company's army, and surveyor-general of Bengal. His *Bengal Atlas* was published in 1779 and in 1781 he was elected a fellow of the Royal Society. Interested in hydrography, ancient geography and oceanography, he was the author of a *Treatise on the Comparative Geography of Western Asia* (posthumously 1831). See Life by C. R. Markham (1895).

(2) **James Rennell Rodd, 1st Baron** (1858–1941), English poet, historian, diplomatist, born in London, was educated at Haileybury and Balliol. His principal diplomatic service was in Italy, where he was ambassador (1908–19). He wrote many books, including the volume of poetry *Ballads of the Fleet* (1897), and the scholarly works *Rome of the Renaissance and Today* (1932) and *Homer's Ithaca* (1927). His *Social and Diplomatic Memories* were published in 3 vols. (1922–25).

RENNER, Karl (1870–1950), Austrian statesman who became first chancellor of the Austrian republic (1918–20), was imprisoned as a Socialist leader in 1934, and was chancellor again (1945). He wrote political works, and a national song. From 1946 until his death he was president of Austria.

RENNIE, (1) **George** (1791–1866), Scottish engineer, eldest son of (2), born in London, was superintendent of the machinery of the Mint, and aided his father. With his brother John he carried on an immense business—shipbuilding, railways, bridges, harbours, docks, machinery and marine engines.

(2) **John** (1761–1821), Scottish civil engineer, born at Phantassie farm, East Linton, after working as a millwright with Andrew Meikle studied at Edinburgh University (1780–83). In 1784 he entered the employment of Messrs Boulton & Watt; in 1791 he set up in London as an engineer, and soon became famous as a bridge-builder—building Kelso (1803), Leeds, Musselburgh, Newton-Stewart, Boston, New Galloway, and the old Southwark and Waterloo Bridges, and planning London Bridge. He made many important canals; drained fens; designed the London Docks, and others at Blackwall, Hull, Liverpool, Dublin, Greenock and Leith; and improved harbours and dockyards at Portsmouth, Chatham, Sheerness and Plymouth, where he constructed the celebrated breakwater (1811–41). See Smiles's *Lives of the Engineers* (1874).

(3) **John** (1794–1874), Scottish engineer, second son of (2), born in London, was knighted in 1831 on his completion of London Bridge. He was engineer to the Admiralty and wrote on harbours. See his *Autobiography* (1875).

RENOIR, (1) **Jean,** *rè-nwahr* (1894–), French film director, son of (2), born in Paris, won the Croix de Guerre in World War I, and from script-writing turned to film-making. His version of Zola's *Nana* (1926), his anti-war masterpiece, *La Grande Illusion*

(1937), *La Bête humaine* (1939), *The Golden Coach* (1953) and *Le Déjeuner sur l'herbe* (1959), are among the masterpieces of the cinema. He left France in 1941 during the invasion and became a naturalized American.

(2) **Pierre Auguste** (1841–1919), French Impressionist artist, father of (1), was born at Limoges. He began as a painter on porcelain; in this trade, and then as a painter of fans, he made his first acquaintance with the work of Watteau and Boucher which was to influence his choice of subject matter as deeply as Impressionism was to influence his style. He entered the studio of Gleyre in 1862 and began to paint in the open air about 1864. From the year 1870 onwards he obtained a number of commissions for portraits. In the years 1874–79 and in 1882 he exhibited with the Impressionists, his important, controversial picture of sunlight filtering through leaves—the *Moulin de la Galette* (in the Louvre) dating from 1876. He visited Italy in 1880 and during the next few years painted a series of *Bathers* in a more cold and classical style influenced by Ingres and Raphael. He then returned to hot reds, orange, and gold to portray nudes in sunlight, a style which he continued to develop to the end, although his hands were crippled by arthritis in later years. He is represented in the Louvre, the Tate Gallery, and in many public galleries in the United States. See monographs by G. Besson (1932) and M. Drucker (1944), and *Renoir, My Father* (1962) by (1).

RENOUF, Sir Peter Le Page, *rė-noof* (1822–1897), British Egyptologist, born in Guernsey, studied at Oxford and turned Catholic in 1842. He was professor of Ancient History and Oriental Languages in Dublin 1855–64, a school inspector 1864–85, and keeper of Egyptian and Assyrian antiquities at the British Museum 1885–91. He wrote on ancient Egypt, notably a translation of *The Book of the Dead,* and gave the Hibbert Lectures on Egyptian religion in 1879.

RENOUVIER, Charles Bernard, *rė-noo-vyay* (1815–1903), French idealist philosopher, born at Montpellier, was a modified Kantian and founder of the movement known as Neocriticism. His works include *Essai de critique générale* (4 vols. 1859–64), *Psychologie rationelle* (3 vols. 1875), *Histoire et solutions des problèmes métaphysiques* (1901) and *Le Personnalisme* (1903). See books by Séailles (1905) and Arnal (1908).

RENWICK, *ren'ik,* (1) **James** (1662–88), Scottish Covenanter, born at Moniaive, studied at Edinburgh University, joined the Cameronians, proclaimed the Lanark Declaration (1682), and was sent to complete his studies in Holland. In 1683 he preached his first sermon at Darmead Moss near Cambusnethan; in 1684 he was outlawed for his *Apologetic Declaration.* On James VII's accession he published at Sanquhar a declaration rejecting him. A reward was offered for his capture; and at last he was taken in Edinburgh, and executed. See Life by Simpson (1843).

(2) **James** (1790–1863), physicist, born at Liverpool of Scottish-American parents, was professor at Columbia College, N.Y., and wrote books on mechanics. His son **James** (1818–95) designed Grace Church and St Patrick's Cathedral, New York, the Smithsonian Institution and the Bank of the State of New York.

REPSOLD, Johann Georg (1770–1830), German instrument-maker, designed a special pendulum, named after him, for the accurate determination of 'g'. Chief of the Hamburg fire brigade, he was killed when a wall collapsed during a fire.

REPTON, Humphrey (1752–1818), English landscape-gardener, was born at Bury St Edmunds. He completed the change from the formal gardens of the early 18th century to the 'picturesque' types favoured later.

RESNAIS, Alain (1922–), French film director, born at Vannes, Brittany, studied at l'Institut des hautes études cinématographiques in Paris, made a series of outstanding and prizewinning short documentaries, e.g., *Van Gogh* (1948, Oscar award), *Guernica* (1950) and *Nuit et Bruillard* (1955), a haunting evocation of the horror of Nazi concentration camps. His first feature film, *Hiroshima mon amour* (1959), intermingles the nightmare World War II past of its heroine with her unhappy love for a Japanese against the tragic background of present-day Hiroshima. His next film, *L'Année dernière à Marienbad* (1961), illustrates his interest in the merging of past, present and future to the point of ambiguity, being hailed as a surrealistic and dreamlike masterpiece by some, as a confused and tedious failure by others. *Muriel* (1963) and *La Guerre est finie* (1967) had similarly mixed receptions.

RESPIGHI, Ottorino, *res-pee'gee* (1879–1936), Italian composer, was born at Bologna. A pupil of Bruch and of Rimski-Korsakov, his works include nine operas, the symphonic poems, *Fontane di Roma* and *Pini di Roma,* and the ballet *La Boutique fantasque.*

RESTIF (Rétif) de la Bretonne, Nicolas Edme, *res-teef* or *ray-teef* (1734–1806), French writer, was born at Sacy, Yonne. His many voluminous and licentious novels, such as *Le Pied de Fanchette, Le Paysan perverti* and *Mémoires d'un homme de qualité,* give a vividly truthful picture of 18th-century French life, and entitle him to be considered as a forerunner of realism. His own not unsullied life he described in the 16-volume *Monsieur Nicolas* (1794–97). He also wrote on social reform.

RESZKE, *resh'kė,* Polish family of singers, born in Warsaw:

(1) **Edouard de** (1856–1917), operatic bass, successful throughout Europe in a wide range of parts. He and his brother Jean frequently appeared together.

(2) **Jean de** (1850–1925), operatic tenor, brother of (1), began his career as a baritone, and after his début as a tenor in 1879, he succeeded in most of the leading French and Italian operatic rôles, adding Wagnerian parts after 1885. Originally criticised for his acting, he developed into an artist of convincing authority. See study by C. Leiser (1933).

(3) **Joséphine de** (1855–91), operatic soprano, sister of (1) and (2), sang at the Paris Opéra but withdrew from the stage on her marriage with Baron von Kronenburg.

RETHEL, Alfred, *ray'tel* (1816–59), German historical painter, born at Diepenbend near Aachen, decorated the imperial hall of the Römer, Frankfurt-am-Main, the Council House of Aachen with frescoes of the Life of Charlemagne, and executed a series of fantastic designs (1842–44; Dresden) on the theme of Hannibal's crossing of the Alps. His later drawings and woodcuts bear witness to his advancing mental derangement.

RETZ, (1) **Rais, or Raiz, Gilles de Laval, Baron de** (1404–40), a Breton of high rank who fought by the side of the Maid at Orleans, became marshal of France at twenty-five, but soon retired to his estates, where for over ten years he is alleged to have indulged in the most infamous orgies, kidnapping 150 children, who were sacrificed to his lusts or sorceries. He was hanged and burned at Nantes, after a trial closed by his own confession. See works by Bossard (1886), Baring-Gould (1865), Vizetelly (1902), Vincent and Binns (1926).

(2) **Jean Paul de Gondi, Cardinal de** (1614–1679), French churchman, born at Montmirail, was bred for the church in spite of amours, duels and political intrigues. He became in 1643 coadjutor to his uncle, the Archbishop of Paris, plotted against Mazarin, and instigated the outbreak of the Fronde in 1648. He received a cardinal's hat, but in 1652 was flung into prison. After two years he made his escape, wandered in Spain and England, appeared at Rome, and in 1662 made his peace with Louis XIV by resigning his claim to the archbishopric in exchange for the abbacy of St Denis and restoration to his other benefices. His debts (four million francs!) he provided for in 1675 by making over to his creditors his entire income save 20,000 livres. Retz figures pleasingly in the letters of Madame de Sévigné. His own masterly *Mémoires* (1655; best ed. in ' Les Grands Écrivains ', 10 vols. 1872–90) throw much light on the Fronde. See works by Curnier (1863), Topin (3rd ed. 1872), Chantelauze (1878–79), Gazier (1876), Ogg (1912), Batiffol (1927, 1930), Dyssard (1938).

RETZSCH, Friedrich August Moritz (1779–1857), German painter and engraver, born in Dresden, became a professor there in 1824. He acquired great celebrity by his etchings in outline of Schiller, Goethe, Fouqué and Shakespeare. His masterpiece is ' The Chess-players '.

REUCHLIN, Johann, *roykh'lin* (1455–1522), German humanist and Hebraist, born at Pforzheim, as travelling companion to a prince of Baden visited Paris, where he studied Greek, at Basel wrote his Latin dictionary (1476), made a second sojourn in France, and in 1481 set up as lecturer at Tübingen. In 1482, 1490 and 1498 he was in Italy on state business; in 1492 we find him studying Hebrew under a learned Jewish court physician. In 1496 Reuchlin went to Heidelberg, where he became the main promoter of Greek studies in Germany; in 1500 he received a judicial appointment at Stuttgart. In 1506 appeared his *Rudimenta Linguae Hebraicae.* In 1510 Pfefferkorn, a Jewish renegade, urged the emperor to burn all Jewish books except the Old Testament; and Reuchlin's contention that no Jewish books should be destroyed except those directly written against Christianity drew on him the enmity of the Dominicans of Cologne, especially of the inquisitor Hoogstraten; but all the independent thinkers in Germany (see HUTTEN) were on his side; and the Duke of Bavaria appointed him in 1519 professor at Ingolstadt. Reuchlin edited various Greek texts, published a Greek grammar, a whole series of polemical pamphlets, and a satirical drama (against the Obscurantists), and in *De Verbo Mirifico* and *De Arte Cabbalistica* shows a theosophico-cabbalistic tendency. See books on him by Geiger (1871), Horawitz (1877) and Holstein (1888).

REUTER, *roy'tėr,* (1) **Fritz** (1810–74), Plattdeutsch humorist, born at Stavenhagen in Mecklenburg-Schwerin, studied law at Rostock and Jena. In 1833 he was condemned to death—with other Jena students he had indulged in wild talk about the fatherland—a sentence commuted to thirty years' imprisonment. Released in 1840, with his career spoilt and his health ruined, he tried to resume his legal studies, learned farming, and taught pupils. His rough Plattdeutsch verse setting of the jokes and merry tales of the countryside, *Läuschen un Rimels* (1853), became at once a great favourite; another humorous poem, *Reis' nah Belligen* (1855), was equally successful, followed by a second volume of *Läuschen un Rimels* (1858) and the tragic poem *Kein Hüsung* (1858). The rest of his best works, except the poem *Hanne Nüte* (1860), were all written in Low German prose. *Ut de Franzosentid* (1860; Eng. trans. as *The Year '13,* 1873), *Ut mine Festungstid* (1862), and *Ut mine Stromtid* (1862–64) made him famous throughout all Germany. He lived at Eisenach from 1863, and there he died. See Wilbrandt's biography in the *Werke* (15 vols. 1863–75), and works by Glagau (2nd ed. 1875), Ebert (1874), Gaedertz (1890 and 1900), Römer (1895), Raatz (1895), Brandes (1899), Dohse (1910).

(2) **Paul Julius, Freiherr von** (1816–99), born at Cassel, in 1849 formed at Aachen an organization for transmitting commercial news by telegraph. In 1851 he fixed his headquarters in London; and gradually his system spread to the remotest regions. In 1865 he converted his business into a limited liability company, and in 1871 was made a baron by the Duke of Saxe-Coburg-Gotha. See G. Storey, *Reuters' Century* (1951) and R. Jones, *A Life in Reuters* (1951).

REUTHER, Walter Philip, *roy'tėr* (1907–70), American trade-union leader, president of the American Auto Workers' Union, in 1935 began to organize the automobile workers into what later became the largest union in the world, and fought against Communist influence in trade unionism.

REVERE, Paul, *rė-veer'* (1735–1818), American patriot, hero of a poem by Longfellow, was born in Boston, Mass., and after serving as lieutenant of artillery (1756), followed the trade of goldsmith and copperplate printer. He was one of the party that destroyed the tea in Boston harbour, and he was at the head of a secret society formed to watch the British. On April 18, 1775, the night before

Lexington and Concord, he rode from Charleston to Lexington and Lincoln, rousing the minutemen as he went. In the war he became lieutenant-colonel of artillery. In 1801 he founded the Revere Copper Company at Canton, Mass. See Lives by Goss (2 vols. 1892) and Taylor (1930).

RÉVILLE, Albert, *ray-veel* (1826–1906), French Protestant theologian of the advanced school, born at Dieppe, was pastor of the Walloon Church at Rotterdam 1851–72, lectured at Leyden, and in 1880 became professor of the History of Religions in the Collège de France. His works include a comparative history of philosophy and religion (1859; trans. 1864).

REYBAUD, Louis, *ray-bō* (1799–1879), French journalist and politician, born at Marseilles, travelled in the Levant and India, and returning to Paris in 1829, wrote for the Radical papers and edited a history of the French expedition to Egypt (1830–36), &c. His *Réformateurs ou Socialistes modernes* (1840–43) popularized the word ' Socialism '. He also wrote satirical novels, ridiculing the manners and institutions of his time.

REYMONT, Władysław Stanislaw, *ray'mont* (1867–1925), Polish novelist, born at Kobiele Wielke, author of the tetralogy, *The Peasants* (1904–09), was awarded a Nobel prize in 1924. Other books are *The Comédienne* (1896; trans. 1920) and *The Year 1794* (1913–18).

REYNAUD, Paul, *ray-nō* (1878–1966), French statesman, born at Barcelonnette, originally a barrister, held many French government posts, being premier during the fall of France in 1940. He was imprisoned by the Germans during World War II. Afterwards he re-entered politics, until losing his seat in 1962, and was a delegate to the Council of Europe (1949). Among several works are *La France a sauvé l'Europe* (1947), *Au Coeur de la mêlée 1930–45* (trans. 1955), and his *Mémoires* (1960, 1963).

REYNOLDS, (1) **George William MacArthur** (1814–79), English journalist, Chartist, and blood-and-thunder novelist, born at Sandwich. In 1850 he started *Reynolds's Weekly*.

(2) **John Fulton** (1820–63), American army officer, born at Lancaster, Pa., was commandant at West Point in 1859, fought at Mechanicsville and Gaines's Mills, and was taken prisoner at Glendale, but exchanged in August 1862. At the second battle of Bull Run his brigade prevented a total rout. In 1863 he commanded a corps at Fredericksburg, and fell at Gettysburg.

(3) **John Hamilton** (1794–1852), English minor poet and lawyer, born at Shrewsbury and educated at Christ's Hospital, friend of Leigh Hunt, Keats and Hood.

(4) **Sir Joshua** (1723–92), English portrait painter, was born at Plympton Earls near Plymouth, the seventh son of a clergyman and schoolmaster. Sent in 1740 to London to study art, in 1747 he settled at Plymouth Dock, now Devonport. At Rome (1749–52) he studied Raphael and Michelangelo, and in the Vatican caught a chill which permanently affected his hearing. He then established himself in London, and by 1760 was at the height of his fame. In 1764 he founded the literary club of which Dr Johnson, Garrick, Burke, Goldsmith, Boswell and Sheridan were members. He was one of the earliest members of the Incorporated Society of Artists, and on the establishment of the Royal Academy (1768) was elected its first president; in 1769 he was knighted. In that year he delivered the first of his Discourses to the students of the Academy, which, along with his papers on art in the *Idler*, his annotations to Du Fresnoy's *Art of Painting*, and his *Notes on the Art of the Low Countries* (the result of a visit in 1781), show a cultivated literary style. In 1784 he became painter to the king, and finished his Mrs Siddons as the *Tragic Muse*, a work existing in several versions. In 1789 his sight became affected, and he ceased to paint. The following year was embittered by a dispute with the Academy, which led to his resignation of the presidency, a resolution he afterwards rescinded. He was buried in St Paul's. It is in virtue of his portraits that Reynolds ranks as the head of the English school. They are notable for the power and expressiveness of their handling, and the beauty of their colouring. His pictures of children have an especial tenderness and beauty a in *The Strawberry Girl*, *Simplicity*, &c. His works number from two to three thousand; and from these 700 engravings have been executed. See *Memoirs* by Northcote (1813), *The Literary Works* (with memoir, &c., by Beechy, 1835), Life by Leslie and Tom Taylor (1865), *Catalogue raisonné* of the engravings by E. Hamilton (2nd ed. 1884), *Reynolds and Gainsborough* by Sir W. M. Conway (1885), and Lives by C. Phillips (1894), Graves and Cronin (1900) and D. Hudson (1958).

(5) **Osborne** (1842–1912), British engineer, born in Belfast, became the first professor of Engineering at Manchester (1868) and a Royal Society gold medallist (1888). He greatly improved centrifugal pumps. The ' Reynolds number ', a dimensionless ratio characterizing the dynamic state of a fluid, takes its name from him.

(6) **Samuel William** (1773–1835), English engineer, born in London, was an accomplished mezzotinter, and produced many engravings after portraits of Sir Joshua Reynolds, Turner, Lawrence and Opie.

(7) **Walter** (d. 1327), English churchman, the son of a Windsor baker, was made by Edward II treasurer (1307) and Bishop of Worcester (1308), chancellor (1310), and Archbishop of Canterbury (1314). He later declared for Edward III, whom he crowned.

RHAZES, or **Räzi,** *ray'zeez* (fl. 925), Persian physician and alchemist of Baghdad. He wrote many medical works, some of which were translated into Latin and had considerable influence on medical science in the Middle Ages. See A. Castiglioni, *History of Medicine* (1947).

RHEE, Syngman (1875–1965), Korean statesman, was born near Kaesong. Imprisoned from 1897 to 1904 for campaigning for reform and a constitutional monarchy, he went soon after his release to America, where he was influenced by Wilson, the apostle of self-determination. In 1910 he returned to Japanese-annexed Korea, and after the unsuccesful rising of 1919 he became president of the exiled Korean Provisional Government. On Japan's surrender in 1945 he returned to Korea, and in 1948 was elected president of the Republic of South Korea. He opposed the Korean truce of 1953, calling Korea's continued partition 'appeasement of the Communists'. Re-elected for a fourth term as president in March 1960, he was obliged to resign in April after large-scale riots and the resignation of his cabinet. A man of inflexible and often bellicose patriotism, his immense personal authority was derived from a lifetime of resistance and exile. His publications include *Japan Inside Out* (1941).

RHEGIUS, Urbanus (1489–1541), German reformer, preached Lutheran doctrines at Augsburg and later lived at Celle.

RHEINBERGER, Joseph, *rīn'berg-ėr* (1839–1901), German composer, born at Vaduz in Liechtenstein, held musical posts at Munich (1855–94). His works include operas and organ sonatas.

RHETICUS, real name **Georg Joachim von Lauchen** (1514–76), German astronomer and mathematician, born at Feldkirch in Austria, became professor of Mathematics at Wittenberg (1537). He is noted for his trigonometrical tables (1596) and his table of sines to fifteen decimal places (1613). For a time he worked with Copernicus, whose *De Revolutionibus Orbium Coelestium* he was instrumental in publishing. His own *Narratio prima de libris revolutionum Copernici* (1540) was the first account of the Copernican theory. He died at Cassovia in Hungary.

RHIGAS, Konstantinos, *ree'gas* (1760–98), Greek poet, organized the anti-Turkish revolutionary movement at Vienna, but was betrayed and shot.

RHIJN, Pieter Johannes van, *rīn* (1886–1960), Dutch astrophysicist, born at Gouda, educated at Groningen, became the assistant, collaborator and successor of Kapteyn (q.v.).

RHIND, Alexander Henry (1833–63), Scottish antiquary, born at Wick, founded the Rhind Lectures in archaeology, delivered at Edinburgh.

RHINE, Joseph Banks (1895–), American psychologist, pioneer of parapsychology, born at Waterloo, Pennsylvania, studied at Chicago and Harvard and in 1937 became professor of Psychology at Duke University. His laboratory-devised experiments involving packs of specially designed cards established the phenomena of extrasensory perception and of telepathy on a statistical basis, since some guessers achieved considerably better results than the average chance successes. See his respectably scientific works *New Frontiers of the Mind* (1937), *Extrasensory Perception* (1940), *Reach of Mind* (1948) and with J. G. Pratt, *Parapsychology* (1958).

RHODES, Cecil John (1853–1902), South African statesman, was born at Bishop's Stortford, where his father was vicar. He was sent for his health to Natal, and subsequently made a fortune at the Kimberley diamond diggings and succeeded in amalgamating the several diamond companies to form the De Beers Consolidated Mines Company in 1888. (In that year he sent £10,000 to Parnell to forward the cause of Irish Home Rule.) He came back to England, entered Oriel College, Oxford, and although his residence was cut short by ill-health, he ultimately took his degree. He entered the Cape House of Assembly as member for Barkly. In 1884 General Gordon asked him to go with him to Khartoum as secretary; but Rhodes declined, having just taken office in the Cape ministry. In 1890 he became prime minister of Cape Colony; but even before this he had become a ruling spirit in the extension of British territory in securing first Bechuanaland as a protectorate (1884) and later (1889) the charter for the British South Africa Co., of which till 1896 he was managing director, and whose territory was later to be known as Rhodesia. His policy was the ultimate establishment of a federal South African dominion under the British flag. In 1895 he was made a member of the privy council. In 1896 he resigned the Cape premiership in consequence of complications arising from the 'unauthorized' raid into the Transvaal of Dr Jameson (q.v.), the Chartered Company's administrator, in aid of the Uitlanders' claims. His action was condemned by the South Africa Commission and by the British government. In the same year he succeeded in quelling the Matabele rebellion by personal negotiations with the chiefs. In 1899 he was capped D.C.L. at Oxford. He was a conspicuous figure during the war of 1899–1902, when he organized the defences of Kimberley during the siege. He left a remarkable will which, besides making great benefactions to Cape Colony, founded scholarships at Oxford for Americans, Germans and colonials. See Lives by Williams (1921), McDonald (1927), Millin (1933) and Gross (1956), and study by Lockhart and Woodhouse (1963).

RHYS, *rees,* (1) **Ernest Percival** (1859–1946), Anglo-Welsh editor and poet, born in London, spent much of his youth in Carmarthen and became a mining engineer. Abandoning this for a writing career in 1886, he was first a freelance, then on the staff of Walter Scott's publishing house, for whom he edited the Camelot Classics series. He is perhaps best known as editor of the Everyman Library of classics. He wrote volumes of romantic verse including *A London Rose* (1891), *Rhymes for Everyman* (1933) and *Song of the Sun* (1937). Also a notable literary critic, he wrote *English Lyric Poetry* (1913). *Everyman Remembers* (1931) and *Wales England Wed* (1941) are volumes of reminiscences.

(2) **Sir John** (1840–1915), Welsh philologist, born in Cardiganshire, taught in Anglesea until 1865, when he entered Jesus College Oxford, and continued his studies in France and Germany. From 1871 an inspector of schools in Wales, in 1877 he became professor of Celtic at Oxford, in 1881 a fellow of Jesus, and in 1895 its principal. He was a distinguished authority on Celtic philology, author of *Celtic Britain* (1882), *Celtic Heathendom* (Hibbert Lectures, 1888), &c.

RHYS-DAVIDS. See DAVIDS.

RIBALTA, Francisco de (1550–1628), Spanish

painter, born in Castellón de la Plana, studied at Rome, and settled at Valencia. Noted as a painter of historical subjects and for his use of chiaroscuro, his works include *The Last Supper* and his *Christ* in Madrid. His sons, **José** (1588–1656) and **Juan** (1597–1628), were also Valencian painters.

RIBBENTROP, Joachim von (1893–1946), German politician, was a wine merchant who became a member of the National Socialist party in 1932. Finally Hitler's adviser in foreign affairs, he was responsible in 1935 for the Anglo-German naval pact, becoming the following year ambassador to Britain and foreign minister (1938–45). He was taken by the British in 1945 and condemned to death and executed at Nuremberg.

RIBERA, Jusepe de (1588–1656), called **Lo Spagnoletto** (' The Little Spaniard '), Spanish painter and etcher, born at Játiva, settled in Naples, and became court painter. He delighted in the horrible, choosing often such subjects as the martyrdom of the saints and painting them with a bold, unsympathetic power. Later works were calmer and more subtle and include *The Immaculate Conception* and paintings of the Passion.

RIBOT, *ree-bō*, (1) **Alexandre** (1842–1923), French statesman, was born at St Omer and became premier in 1892, 1895, 1917, foreign minister 1890–93, finance minister 1914–17. An academician in 1906, he wrote *Letters to a Friend*, which were translated in 1925.

(2) **Théodule Armand** (1839–1916), French psychologist, born at Guingamp, was from 1888 a Collège de France professor. A pioneer in experimental psychology, he wrote many works including *English Psychology* (1873), *Heredity* (1875) and *Diseases of the Will* (1884).

RICARDO, David (1772–1823), English political economist, born in London, was brought up by his father, a Jewish stockbroker, to the same business. In 1793 he married Priscilla Ann Wilkinson, a Quakeress, and turned Christian; then, starting for himself, he made a large fortune by 1814. In 1799 his interest in political economy was awakened by Smith's *Wealth of Nations*. His pamphlet, *The High Price of Bullion, a Proof of the Depreciation of Banknotes* (1809), was an argument in favour of a metallic basis. In 1817 appeared the work on which his reputation chiefly rests, *Principles of Political Economy and Taxation*, a discussion of value, wages, rent, &c. In 1819 he became Radical M.P. for Portarlington. He died at his Gloucestershire seat, Gatcombe Park. His collected works were edited, with a Life, by McCulloch (1846); his letters to Malthus, to McCulloch, and to H. Trower and others were edited by Bonar and Hollander (1887–1899). See study by Hollander (1910).

RICASOLI, Baron Bettino (1809–80), Italian statesman, born at Florence, was a leading agriculturist, and for ten years worked successfully at draining the Tuscan Maremma. In 1859 he opposed the grand-duke, on whose flight he was made dictator of Tuscany. A strong advocate of the unification of Italy, he supported Cavour (q.v.) in the struggle to join Piedmont with Tuscany. He was head of the ministry in 1861–62 and 1866–67. See his *Lettere e documenti* (1886–94), and Lives by Gotti (1894) and Hancock (1926).

RICCI, Matteo, *reet'chee* (1552–1610), Italian missionary, founder of the Jesuit missions in China, was born at Macerata, studied at Rome, and lived at Nanking and at Peking. He so mastered Chinese as to write dialogues, &c., which received much commendation from the Chinese literati, and he met with extraordinary success as a missionary although his methods aroused much controversy.

RICCIO. See RIZZIO.

RICE, (1) **Edmund Ignatius** (1762–1844), Irish philanthropist, born near Callan, was originally a Waterford provision merchant. In 1802-20 he founded the Irish Christian Brothers for the education of the poor. He was superior-general of the order till 1838.

(2) **Elmer** (1892–1967), American dramatist, born Elmer Reizenstein in New York, studied law and took to writing plays. His prolific output includes *The Adding Machine* (1923), *Street Scene* (1929), which won a Pulitzer prize, *The Left Bank* (1931), *Two on an Island* (1940), *Cue for Passion* (1958), &c.

(3) **James** (1843–82), English novelist, from 1872 *collaborateur* with Sir Walter Besant (q.v.), was born at Northampton, studied at Queen's College, Cambridge, drifted from law into literature, and was proprietor and editor of *Once a Week* 1868–72.

RICH, (1) **Barnabe** (*c.* 1540–1620), English pamphleteer and romance writer, was born in Essex, and under the patronage of Sir Christopher Hatton served as a soldier in France, the Low Countries and Ireland. His *Apolonius and Silla* (contained in *Riche, his Farewell to the Military Profession*, 1581) was used by Shakespeare as a source for the plot of *Twelfth Night*.

(2) **Edmund.** See EDMUND (ST).

(3) **Penelope.** See SIDNEY, SIR PHILIP.

RICHARD, name of three kings of England:

Richard I (1157–99), **Coeur de Lion,** third son of Henry II, was born at Oxford, and while still a child was invested with the duchy of Aquitaine, his mother Eleanor's patrimony. Richard did not spend in all his life a full year in England; it may reasonably be doubted whether he could speak English. He was induced by his mother to join his brothers Henry and Geoffrey in their rebellion (1173) against their father (see HENRY II); and in 1189 he was again in arms against his father and in league with Philip Augustus of France. Richard became King of England, Duke of Normandy and Count of Anjou on July 5, 1189. But he had already taken the crusader's vows; and to raise the necessary funds he sold whatever he could. In 1190 he and Philip set out for Palestine. Both spent the winter in Sicily, whose throne had just been seized by the Norman Tancred. The latter made his peace by giving up to Richard his sister Johanna, the widowed queen, and her possessions, and by betrothing his daughter to Arthur, Richard's nephew and heir. In 1191 part of Richard's fleet was wrecked on Cyprus, and the crews were most inhospitably treated by the sovereign, Isaac Comnenus. Richard sailed back from Rhodes, routed Isaac, deposed him, and gave his crown to Guy de Lusignan. In Cyprus he married Berengaria of Navarre, and on June 8 landed near Acre, which surrendered. Richard's exploits—his march to Joppa, his two advances on Jerusalem (the city he never beheld), his capture of the fortresses in the south of Palestine, and his relief of Joppa—excited the admiration of Christendom. In September he concluded a three years' peace with Saladin, and started off home alone. He was shipwrecked in the Adriatic, and in disguise made his way through the dominions of his bitter enemy, Leopold, Duke of Austria, but was recognized, seized and handed over to the Emperor Henry VI (1193), who demanded a heavy ransom. Richard's loyal subjects raised the money, and he returned home (March 1194). Although his brother John used his utmost endeavours to prevent his return, Richard generously forgave him; and, proceeding to France, spent the rest of his life warring against Philip. He was killed while besieging the castle of Chaluz, and was buried at Fontevrault. See BLONDEL; Stubbs's *Const. Hist.* (vol. i), and books by K. Norgate (1903, 1924), Ramsay (1903) and P. Henderson (1958).

Richard II (1367–1400), son of Edward the Black Prince, was born at Bordeaux, and succeeded his grandfather, Edward III, June 21, 1377. The government was entrusted to a council of twelve, but John of Gaunt (q.v.) gained control of it. The war going on with France and the extravagance of the court cost money; and more was wasted by the government, for which John of Gaunt was held to be mainly responsible. The poll tax of 1380 provoked popular risings; the men of Essex and Kent, 100,000 strong, marched upon London. The Essex men consented to return home when Richard at Mile End (June 14, 1381) assured them he would liberate the villeins and commute their personal service into money rent. The men of Kent, after destroying the Savoy (Gaunt's palace), burning Temple Bar, opening the prisons, breaking into the Tower, and slaying the Archbishop of Canterbury, met the king at Smithfield (15th), where, during the negotiations, William Walworth, mayor of London, struck down Wat Tyler, their leader. The king at once rode amongst them, exclaiming he would be their leader, and granted them the concessions demanded. From this time John of Gaunt kept much in the background, until in 1386 he retired to the Continent. In 1385 Richard invaded Scotland and burned Edinburgh. About the same time another coalition of the baronial party, headed by the Duke of Gloucester, began to oppose the king. They impeached several of his friends in 1388, and secured convictions and executions. But on May 3, 1389, Richard suddenly declared himself of age; for eight years he ruled as a moderate constitutional monarch, and the country was fairly prosperous. But in 1394 Richard's first wife, Anne of Bohemia, died; in 1396 he married Isabella (1389–1409), daughter of Charles VI of France, and seems to have adopted French tastes, manners, and ideas, and to have asserted the pretensions of an absolute monarch. He had Gloucester, Arundel and Warwick arrested for conspiracy. Arundel was beheaded; Gloucester was sent a prisoner to Calais, and died in prison, probably murdered; Warwick was banished, and so was the Archbishop of Canterbury. In 1398 the Duke of Norfolk and the Duke of Hereford (Henry, John of Gaunt's son) were accused of treason; Norfolk was banished for life and Hereford for ten years. In 1399 John of Gaunt died, and Hereford succeeded him as Duke of Lancaster. Richard in May went over to Ireland, and Henry of Lancaster landed on July 4. Richard hurried back, submitted to his cousin at Flint (August 19), and was put in the Tower. On September 29 he resigned the crown, and next day was deposed by parliament, which chose Henry as his successor. Richard seems to have been murdered at Pontefract Castle early in 1400. See study by A. Steel (1941).

Richard III (1452–85), youngest brother of Edward IV, was born at Fotheringhay Castle. After the defeat and death of his father, the Duke of York, in 1460, he was sent to Utrecht for safety, but returned to England after Edward had won the crown (1461), and was created Duke of Gloucester. In the final struggle between York and Lancaster he took an active share, and is believed to have had a hand in the murder of Prince Edward, Henry VI's son, after Tewkesbury, and of Henry himself. In 1472 he married Anne, younger daughter of Warwick the Kingmaker. This alliance was resented by his brother, the Duke of Clarence, who had married the elder sister, and wished to keep Warwick's vast possessions to himself. Clarence was impeached and put to death in the Tower, February 18, 1478. Of this judicial murder Gloucester is likewise accused; but the evidence is slight. In 1482 he commanded the army that invaded Scotland and captured Berwick. In 1483, while still in Yorkshire, he heard of King Edward's death (April 9), and learned that he himself was guardian of his son and heir, Edward V, then thirteen. On his way south the Protector arrested Earl Rivers and Lord Richard Grey, the uncle and stepbrother of the young king, and rallied to himself the old nobility. On June 13 he suddenly accused Lord Hastings, a leading member of the council, of treason, and had him beheaded. On June 16 the queen-dowager was induced to give up her other son, the little Duke of York, and he was put into the Tower to keep his brother, the king, company. The parliament desired Richard to assume the crown, and on July 6 he was crowned, Rivers and Grey having been executed on June 25. Richard's principal supporter all through had been the Duke of Buckingham; but he soon after Richard's coronation entered into a plot with the friends of Henry Tudor, Earl of Richmond (afterwards Henry VII), the chief representative of the House of Lancaster, to effect Richard's overthrow and proclaim Henry king. The attempted rising collapsed, and Buckingham was executed on November 2. It seems to have been shortly before this that Richard is believed to have had his nephews murdered in the Tower. The deed was done so secretly that the nation did not know of it until some time after, and Richard has never been conclusively proved guilty. Henry landed at Milford Haven on August 7, 1485; Richard met him at Bosworth on the 22nd, and there lost his kingdom and his life. Had Richard succeeded to the throne peacefully, he would probably have been a great king, for he was a very capable ruler. See Sir T. More's *History of King Richard III* (1513), H. Walpole's *Historic Doubts* (1768), Jesse's *Memoirs of Richard III* (1862), Legge's *The Unpopular King* (1885), Gairdner's *Life and Reign of Richard III* (3rd ed. 1898), Markham (1907), and Life by Kendall (1955, and ed. by him, *The Great Debate* (1965)).

RICHARD, (1) of Bury. See AUNGERVILLE.

(2) of Cirencester (*c.* 1335–1401), English chronicler, was in 1355 a Benedictine monk at Westminster. His only extant work is a poor compilation, the *Speculum Historiale de Gestis Regum Angliae 447–1066*, edited by Prof. Mayor (Rolls series, 1863–69). But Richard's name is best known as the alleged author of the *De Situ Britanniae*, long accepted as an authoritative work on Roman Britain, and first printed in 1758 by its ingenious compiler, Charles Julius Bertram (1723–65), English teacher at Copenhagen, who professed to have discovered it in the Royal Library there. An English translation forms one of the 'Six Old English Chronicles' in Bohn's 'Antiquarian Library' (1848). Stukeley, Gibbon and Lingard cited it with respect; but its authenticity received its deathblow from Mr B. B. Woodward in the *Gentleman's Magazine* (1866–67). See Prof. Mayor's preface.

(3) of Cornwall (1209–72), born at Winchester, second son of King John, in 1225–26 with his uncle, William of Salisbury, commanded an expedition which recovered Gascony. Married to a daughter of the Earl of Pembroke, he for some years acted with the English barons. But in 1240–41 he was away on a crusade; in 1244 he married Sanchia of Provence, sister of Queen Eleanor; and in 1257 he was elected titular king of the Romans, and crowned at Aix-la-Chapelle. In the struggle between Henry III and the barons Richard at first acted as peacemaker, but soon he sided with his brother against Simon de Montfort. He was taken prisoner at Lewes (1264), and imprisoned until Evesham (1265) set him free.

(4) of Wallingford (1292–1335), studied mathematics and astronomy, and in 1326 became abbot of St Albans. He is regarded as the father of English trigonometry.

RICHARDS, (1) Dickinson W. (1895–), American surgeon, born at Orange, N.J., educated at Yale, specialized in cardiac surgery, which he taught at Columbia University (1928–61), becoming professor of Medicine there in 1947. He was awarded jointly with Cournand and Forssmann the Nobel prize for medicine and physiology in 1956 for developing operational techniques.

(2) Frank, properly **Charles Hamilton** (1875–1961), English author of the 'Tom Merry', 'Billy Bunter' and other school-story series, wrote for boys' papers, and particularly for *The Gem* (1906–39) and *The Magnet* (1908–40). After World War II he published school stories in book and play form, and his *Autobiography* (1952).

(3) Sir Gordon (1904–), English jockey, born at Oakengates, Shropshire, the son of a miner, was champion jockey many times from 1925, and by 1952 had established the world record of winning rides (over 4500). He was knighted in 1953, and retired in 1954, thereafter concentrating on training.

(4) Henry Brinley (1819–85), Welsh pianist and composer, born at Carmarthen, the son of an organist, composed songs, piano pieces and choruses, among them 'God Bless the Prince of Wales'.

(5) Ivor A. See OGDEN.

(6) Theodore William (1868–1928), American chemist, born in Germantown, Pennsylvania, became professor at Harvard in 1901 and won the Nobel prize in 1914. Best known for his work on atomic weights, he also carried out important investigations in thermochemistry and thermodynamics.

RICHARDSON, (1) Sir Albert Edward (1880–1964), English architect, born in London. He studied at London University, was professor of Architecture there from 1919 to 1946, and in 1947 became professor in the Royal Academy Schools. He was president of the Royal Academy from 1954 to 1956. His publications include *Design in Civil Architecture* (1948) and *Georgian Architecture* (1949). He was elected to the Royal Academy in 1944 and was knighted in 1956.

(2) Charles (1775–1865), English lexicographer, born at Tulse Hill, Norwood, studied law, kept school till 1827 at Clapham, published *Illustrations of English Philology* (1815), but is remembered for his *New English Dictionary* (2 vols. 1835–37). A later work was *On the Study of Language* (1854).

(3) Dorothy Miller (1873–1957), English novelist, born at Abingdon, was an early exponent of the 'stream of consciousness' style. She wrote a dozen novels of this type, collected under the title *Pilgrimage*.

(4) Henry Handel, pen-name of **Ethel Florence Lindesay** (1870–1946), Australian novelist, was born in Melbourne, travelled and studied on the Continent, and after her marriage in 1895 lived in Strasbourg, in 1904 settling in England. Her first novel was *Maurice Guest* (1908), but she attained distinction only with the third part of the somewhat ponderous trilogy *The Fortunes of Richard Mahony* in 1929. See her unfinished posthumous autobiography *Myself When Young* (1948), study ed. Purdie and Roncoroni (1958) and Life by Buckley (1962).

(5) Henry Hobson (1838–86), an American architect, his specialty was Romanesque, and his chief work Trinity Church, Boston (1877).

(6) Sir John (1787–1865), Scottish naturalist, born at Dumfries, in 1807 became a navy-surgeon, served in the Artic expeditions of Parry and Franklin (1819–22, 1825–27), and the Franklin search expedition of 1848–1849. Knighted in 1846, he wrote *Fauna Boreali-Americana* (1829–37), *Ichthyology of the Voyage of H.M.S. Erebus and Terror* (1844–48), &c. See Life by McIlraith (1868).

(7) Jonathan (1665–1745), a London portrait painter and writer on art.

(8) **Sir Owen Willans** (1879–1959), English physicist, was born in Dewsbury, Yorks, and educated at Cambridge, where at the Cavendish Laboratory he began his famous work on *thermionics*, a term he himself coined to describe the phenomena of the emission of electricity from hot bodies; for this work he was awarded the 1928 Nobel prize for physics. He was appointed professor of Physics at Princeton in 1906, at King's College, London, in 1914, and from 1924 to 1944 was Yarrow research professor of the Royal Society. Elected F.R.S. in 1913, he was knighted in 1939.

(9) **Sir Ralph** (1902–), English actor, was born in Cheltenham. He made his London début in 1926 at the Haymarket, and played leading parts (including the title rôles of Maugham's *Sheppey* and Priestley's *Johnson over Jordan*) with the Old Vic Company (1930–32 and 1938). After war service he became codirector of the Old Vic, played with the Stratford-on-Avon company in 1952, and toured Australia and New Zealand in 1955. Other stage appearances include *Home at Seven*, *The White Carnation* and *A Day at the Sea*, and his films include *The Shape of Things to Come*, *Anna Karenina* and *The Heiress*. He was knighted in 1947. See biography by H. Hobson (1958).

(10) **Samuel** (1689–1761), English novelist, was born in Derbyshire, where his father, a London joiner, had apparently taken refuge after the Monmouth rebellion. He may have gone to Merchant Taylors' School. He was apprenticed to a printer, married his master's daughter and set up in business for himself in Salisbury Court, where in the heyday of his fame (and in much enlarged premises) he received Dr. Johnson, Young and the bluestockings. His wife does not seem to have elevated herself for such company. He was represented as the model parent and champion of women, but his three daughters seem to have had a repressed upbringing. In an autobiographic letter he says that as a boy he wrote their love letters for a group of young women and this may have been the origin of his epistolary novels. In (1741) he published *Letters Written to and for Particular Friends*, generally referred to as *Familiar Letters*, which gave advice on ' How to think and act justly and prudently in the common concerns of human life '. *Pamela* (1741), his first novel, is also ' a series of familiar letters now first published in order to cultivate the Principles of Virtue and Religion ', and this was the aim of all his works. The virtue taught was of the prudential sort and the manners mean and bourgeois and, as is well known, Fielding started his career with his parody, *Joseph Andrews*, in reaction against the printer's stuffy moralism. After holding out for conditions against her brutal employer, Pamela, in the sequel, plays the Lady Bountiful and mingles easily in genteel life. Whether we dislike more Richardson's morality or his obsequiousness to ' the quality ' is a moot point. In his second novel, *Clarissa, Or the History of a Young Lady*, we are in high life, of which Richardson confessed he knew little. Clarissa Harlowe in the toils of Lovelace is the main theme but parental repression is also to be corrected. With all her charm Clarissa is too much the victim of her pride for her tragedy to be truly moving and Lovelace is too ambiguous a character to be credible. Nevertheless, our ancestors wallowed through the seven volumes issued in 1748. Richardson was now famous, flattered by society as he took the cure at Tunbridge Wells or was visited at his fine new house, Northend. He corresponded with several society women, including Lady Bradshaigh, Mrs Chapone, &c. Fine ladies and gentlemen like Lady Mary Wortley Montagu, Horace Walpole and Lord Chesterfield might ' hesitate dislike ', the middle orders were enthusiastic. Richardson's third novel, *Sir Charles Grandison*, 1754, designed to portray the perfect gentleman, turns on the question of divided love; Sir Charles having engaged himself to an aristocratic Italian girl is not free to marry Harriet, whom he had rescued from the vicious Sir Hargrave Pollexfen. Love finds a way and in the end Clementina Porretta decides that she cannot marry a heretic. The Italian scene is quite beyond Richardson's experience and Sir Charles has always been voted a prig. Even Lady Bradshaigh protested. Still, if one can find time to get through one or other of these ' large still books ' one may understand why not only English bluestockings but Continental writers raved about them. Diderot's eulogy in *Le Journal étranger*, though extravagant, is sincere—his *La Religieuse* is modelled on Richardson—and Rousseau's *La Nouvelle Héloïse* confesses his discipleship. Apart from its technical advantages (and disadvantages), the epistolary method was a means to suggest authenticity at a time when mere fiction was frowned upon. Thus Richardson called himself the editor not author of his works. He was a redoubtable correspondent. Mrs Barbauld's edition of the correspondence, with biography, did not exhaust it, nor has it been finally collected. See studies by Clara Thomson (1900) based on Mrs Barbauld but with use of the Forster collection of letters. More recent studies are by A. D. McKillop and W. M. Sale, both 1936. Saintsbury's *Letters from Sir Charles Grandison* (1895) is useful to the student as it interweaves a synopsis of the narrative with the letters selected.

RICHELIEU, **Armand Jean Duplessis, Cardinal, Duc de**, *ree-shê-lyœ* (1585–1642), was born into a noble but impoverished family, of Richelieu near Chinon, and was baptized in Paris. He abandoned the military profession for the clerical in order to keep in the family the bishopric of Luçon, to which he was consecrated at twenty-two. In 1616 he rose to be secretary at war and for foreign affairs, but next year was sent back to his diocese. In 1622 he was named cardinal, in 1624 minister of state to Louis XIII. His first important measure was the blow to Spain of an alliance with England, cemented by the marriage (1625) of the king's sister Henrietta with Charles I. His next great task was to destroy the political power of the Huguenots. La Rochelle was starved into submission (1628); and he destroyed

Montauban, the last refuge of Huguenot independence. From 1629 he was chief minister and actual ruler of France. In 1630 he entered Italy with a splendid army, and reduced Savoy. Meanwhile he plunged into tortuous intrigues with the Italian princes, the pope and the Protestants of the North against the House of Austria. He promised a large subsidy to Gustavus Adolphus, and succeeded in persuading Ferdinand to dismiss Wallenstein. The first treaty of Cherasco (April 1631) ended the Italian war; the second gave France the strategic position of Pinerolo. Just before this final triumph Richelieu successfully surmounted a great combination formed for his downfall by the queen-mother, the House of Guise and others. He now was made duke, and governor of Brittany. Further intrigues and attempted rebellions were crushed with merciless severity. In July 1632 Richelieu had seized the duchy of Lorraine. He continued his intrigues with the Protestants against Ferdinand, subsidizing them with his gold, but till 1635 took no open part in the war. In that year, after completing his preparations and concluding an alliance with Victor Amadeus of Savoy, Bernard of Saxe-Weimar and the Dutch, he declared war on Spain. His first efforts were unsuccessful; Piccolomini entered Picardy and threatened Paris. But Richelieu rose to the height of his genius; with 30,000 foot and 12,000 horse he swept the enemy out of Picardy while Bernard drove them across the Rhine, and in 1638 destroyed the imperial army at Rheinfelden. His policy soon led to the disorganization of the power of Spain, the victories of Wolfenbüttel and Kempten over the Imperialist forces in Germany, and at length in 1641 in Savoy, also the ascendency of the French party. But the hatred of the great French nobles continued, and his safety lay in the king's helplessness without him. The last conspiracy against him was that of Cinq-Mars (q.v.), whose intrigues with the Duke of Bouillon and the Spanish court were soon revealed to the cardinal, the centre of a network of espionage which covered the whole of France. Cinq-Mars and De Thou were arrested and executed. But the great minister died December 4, 1642. While overwhelming the citizens with taxation, he had built up the power of the French crown, achieved for France a preponderance in Europe, destroyed the local liberties of France, and crushed every element of constitutional government. He never sacrificed to personal ambition what he thought the interests of his country, but he often forgot in his methods the laws of morality and humanity. The weakest point in Richelieu's character was his literary ambition. His plays sleep in safe oblivion, but his *Mémoires* are still read with interest. Other works include *Instruction du chrétien* (1619) and *Traité de la perfection du chrétien* (1646). He founded the French Academy. See his Correspondence and State Papers (8 vols. 1853–77), and books by Dussieux (1885), D'Avenel (1884–90), Fagniez (1893–94), Lodge (1896), Belloc (1937), Burckhardt (Eng. trans. 1940) and C. V. Wedgwood 1949).

RICHEPIN, Jean, *reesh-pī* (1849–1926), French poet, playwright and novelist, was humbly born at Medeah, Algeria, and prior to the appearance of his first romance in 1872 had been franc-tireur, sailor, actor. His revolutionary book of poems, *La Chanson des Gueux* (1876), led to a fine and his imprisonment.

RICHET, Charles Robert, *ree-shay* (1850–1935), French physiologist, was born and educated in Paris, where he was professor from 1887 to 1927. For his work on the phenomenon of anaphylaxis he was awarded the 1913 Nobel prize for medicine. He also did research on serum therapy.

RICHMOND, (1) **George** (1809–96), English portrait painter, was born, a miniaturist's son, at Brompton; came under Blake's influence; made a Gretna Green marriage (1831); studied in Paris, Italy, and Germany; was made A.R.A. 1857 and R.A. 1866.

(2) **Legh** (1772–1827), English clergyman, born at Liverpool. He wrote the *Dairyman's Daughter*, *Negro Servant*, and *Young Cottager*, three famous evangelical tracts, collected as *Annals of the Poor* (1814). See Mundy and Wright's *Turvey and Legh Richmond* (2nd ed. 1894).

(3) **Sir William Blake** (1843–1921), English portrait and mythological painter, son of (1), born in London, studied in Italy, was Oxford Slade professor 1878–83, and was made A.R.A. 1888, R.A. 1896, K.C.B. 1897. The St Paul's mosaics are his work.

RICHTER, (1) **Hans** (1843–1916), Hungarian conductor, born at Raab, had conducted in Munich, Budapest and Vienna, when in 1879 he began the Orchestral Concerts in London. In 1893 he became first court *kapellmeister* at Vienna, in 1900–11 was conductor of the Hallé orchestra. He was an authority on the music of Wagner, with whom he was closely associated in the Bayreuth festival.

(2) **Hieronymus Theodor** (1824–98), **German** chemist, born in Dresden, at the age of nineteen, with Reich, discovered by spectroscopic analysis the element *indium* in zincblende. He became director of the Freiburg School of Mines.

(3) **Jeremias Benjamin** (1762–1807), German chemist, was born in Silesia, studied under Kant at Königsberg, and discovered the law of equivalent proportions.

(4) **Johann Paul Friedrich,** often known as **Jean Paul** (1763–1825), German novelist and humorist, was born at Wunsiedel in N. Bavaria, and was sent in 1781 to Leipzig to study theology; but literature had stronger charm for him. He got into debt, and in 1784 fled from Leipzig, to hide in the poverty-stricken home of his widowed mother at Hof. His first literary ' children ' were satires which no one would publish, until in 1783 Voss of Berlin gave him forty louis d'or for *The Greenland Law-suits*. The book was a failure, and for three years Jean Paul struggled on at home. In 1787 he began to teach, and during his nine years of tutorship produced the satirical *Extracts from the Devil's Papers* (1789), &c., the beautiful idylls *Dominie Wuz* (1793), *Quintus Fixlein* (1796; trans. by Carlyle, 1827), and the *Parson's Jubilee* (1797); grand romances, e.g., *The Invisible Lodge* (1793), *Campanerthal* (1797) on the immor-

tality of the soul; and the prose idyll, *My Prospective Autobiography* (1799). *The Invisible Lodge* was his first literary success; *Hesperus* (1795) made him famous. For a few years Jean Paul was the object of extravagant idolatry on the part of the women of Germany. In 1801 he married and three years later settled at Bayreuth, where he died. The principal works of his married life were the romances, *Titan* (1800–03) and *Wild Oats* (1804–05), the former accounted by himself his masterpiece; *Schmeltzle's Journey to Flätz* (1809; trans. by Carlyle, 1827) and *Dr. Katzenberger's Trip to the Spa* (1809), the best of his satirico-humorous writings; the idyll *Fibel's Life* (1812); the fragment of another grand romance, *Nicholas Markgraf*, or *The Comet* (1820–22); reflections on literature (*Vorschule der Aesthetik*; improved ed. 1812); another series on education (*Levana*, 1807), a book that ranks with Rousseau's *Émile*; various patriotic writings (1808–12); and an unfinished *Autobiography* (1826). Jean Paul stands by himself in German literature. All his great qualities of imagination and intellect were made ministers to his humour, which had the widest range, moving from the petty follies of individual men and the absurdities of social custom up to the paradoxes rooted in the universe. But of all great writers he is one of the most difficult to understand. See Lives by Nerrlich (1889), Harich (1925), Burschell (1926); Carlyle's *Miscellaneous Essays*; an English Life, with Autobiography (1845); and Lady Chatterton's translated extracts (1859).

(5) **Sviatoslav Teofilovitch** (1914–), Russian pianist, born at Zhitomir, studied at the Moscow Conservatoire (1942–47). He has made extensive concert tours, with a repertoire ranging from Bach to 20th-century composers. He was awarded the Stalin prize in 1949.

RICHTHOFEN, *rikHt'hōf-en*, (1) **Ferdinand, Baron von** (1833–1905), German geographer and traveller, born at Karlsruhe in Silesia, in 1860 accompanied a Prussian expedition to eastern Asia, then during the next twelve years travelled in Java, Siam, Burma, California, the Sierra Nevada, and China and Japan (1868–72). After his return (1872) he became president of the Berlin Geographical Society (1873–78), professor of Geology at Bonn (1875), and of Geography at Leipzig (1883), at Berlin (1886). His reputation rests upon his great work on *China* (1877–1912), *Aufgaben der Geographie* (1883), &c.

(2) **Manfred, Baron von** (1882–1918), German airman, born in Schweidnitz. At first in the cavalry, he later joined the German air force, and during World War I, as commander of the 11th Chasing Squadron (' Richthofen's Flying Circus '), was noted for his high number (80) of aerial victories. He was shot down behind the British lines. See Life by Gibbons (1930) and Nowarra and Brown, *The Flying Circus* (1959).

RICKMAN, Thomas (1776–1841), English architect, born at Maidenhead, was in succession chemist, grocer, doctor, cornfactor, insurance agent at Liverpool, before becoming in 1820 architect at Birmingham. He designed a number of churches in the revived Gothic style; also the New Court at St John's College, Cambridge. He wrote *Styles of Architecture in England* (1817).

RIDDELL, (1) George Allardice Riddell, 1st Baron (1865–1934), British lawyer and newspaper proprietor, born at Duns, Berwickshire. Educated in London, he rose from boy clerk to solicitor, and through one of his clients, the Cardiff *Western Mail*, became further involved in the newspaper world, at first as legal adviser to the *News of the World*, later as its chairman; he became chairman also of George Newnes, Ltd. Knighted in 1909, he represented the British press at the Paris peace conference in 1919, and the following year was raised to the peerage. See his *Diaries* (1933) from 1908 to 1923.

(2) **Henry Scott** (1798–1870), minor Scottish poet, born, a shepherd's son, at Ewes, Dumfriesshire, from 1831 was a minister at Teviothead. See memoir by Dr Brydon prefixed to *Poems* (1871).

RIDDING, George (1828–1905), born at Winchester, and educated there and at Balliol, became a fellow of Exeter in 1851, head of Winchester in 1868, as such making widespread improvements in the amenities and standard of education of the school. He became first Bishop of Southwell in 1884.

RIDEAL, Sir Eric Keightley, *ri-deel'* (1890–), English chemist, educated at Cambridge and Bonn, held chairs at Cambridge (1930–46), the Royal Institution, London (1946–49), and London University (1950–55). He worked on colloids and catalysis, and devised the Rideal-Walker test for the germicidal power of a disinfectant. He was elected F.R.S. in 1930 and knighted in 1951.

RIDGE, William Pett (1857–1930), English writer, born at Chartham, Kent, is best known as an exponent of cockney humour (*A Clever Wife, Mord Em'ly*, &c.).

RIDGWAY, (1) Matthew Bunker (1895–), American general, commanded airborne troops in World War II, headed the U.N. Command in the Far East 1951–52, succeeded Eisenhower as supreme allied commander in Europe, was army chief of staff from 1953 until 1955, in which year he was awarded the Hon. K.C.B.

(2) **Robert** (1850–1929), American ornithologist, born in Mount Carmel, Illinois, wrote *The Birds of Middle and North America* (8 vols. 1901–19), &c.

RIDING, Laura (1901–), American poet and critic, born in New York, came to England in 1925 and remained in Europe until the outbreak of World War II. Her works include *A Survey of Modernist Poetry* (with Robert Graves, 1927), *Contemporaries and Snobs* (1928), *Collected Poems* (1938).

RIDLEY, Nicholas (*c.* 1500–55), English Protestant martyr, born at Unthank Hall near Haltwhistle, was elected in 1524 a fellow of Pembroke, Cambridge, studied at Paris and Louvain 1527–30, and became proctor at Cambridge in 1534, domestic chaplain to Cranmer and Henry VIII, master of Pembroke in 1540, canon, first of Canterbury, then of Westminster, rector of Soham, and in 1547 Bishop of Rochester. An ardent and outspoken Reformer, he was in 1550, on the deprivation of Bonner, Bishop of London, made his successor. In this high position he distinguished himself by his moderation, learning and munificence, and assisted Cranmer in the preparation of the Articles. On the death of Edward VI he espoused the cause of Lady Jane Grey, and was stripped of his dignities and sent to the Tower. In 1554 he was tried at Oxford, with Latimer and Cranmer, by a committee of Convocation; all three were adjudged obstinate heretics and condemned. Ridley lay in jail for eighteen months, and after a second trial was burnt, along with Latimer, in front of Balliol College. His writings were collected in the Parker Society series (1841). See Foxe's *Actes*, the memoir prefixed to Moule's edition of Ridley's *Declaration of the Lord's Supper* (1895) and Life by Ridley (1957).

RIDPATH, George (*c.* 1717–72), Scottish historian, born at Ladykirk manse in Berwickshire, and minister from 1742 of Stitchell, wrote a *Border History* (1776).

RIEGGER, Wallingford, *ree'gėr* (1885–1961), American composer, born in Albany, Georgia, studied at Cornell University, the Institute of Musical Art, New York, and in Berlin, returning to America when the United States entered the first World War. He held posts at Drake University and Ithaca Conservatory, New York. His works, which show the influence of Schoenberg's 'twelve note' system and his German training, received little attention until the performance of his third Symphony in 1948, since when his work has been increasingly recognized. He wrote extensively for orchestra and for chamber music combinations.

RIEL, Louis, *ree-el'* (1844–85), Canadian insurgent, born at St Boniface, Manitoba, succeeded his father as a leader of the Métis or French half-breeds, and headed the Red River rebellion in 1869–70. In 1885 he again established a rebel government in Manitoba, and on November 16, the rising having been quelled, he was executed.

RIEMANN, *ree'-*, (1) **Georg Friedrich Bernhard** (1826–66), German mathematician, born September 17 at Breselenz, Hanover, studied at Göttingen under Gauss and at Berlin and in 1851 became professor at the former. His early work was an outstanding contribution to the theory of functions, but he is best remembered for his development of the conceptions of Bolyai and Lobachevsky which resulted in a fully-fledged non-Euclidian geometry, dealing with 'manifolds' and curvatures on the assumption of poly-dimensional, finite and unbounded space. This was set out in a paper (1854; trans. *Nature*, vol. 8) 'On the hypotheses which form the foundation of Geometry'. He was elected F.R.S. in 1866.

(2) **Hugo** (1849–1919), German musicologist, author of many works on history and theory of music, was born at Sondershausen and died at Leipzig, where he was professor from 1901.

RIEMENSCHNEIDER, Tilman, *reė'mėn-shnī-dėr* (1460–1531), German sculptor, born at Osterode, spent his life after 1483 at Würzburg, where he rose to become burgomaster, but was imprisoned for participating in the peasants' revolt of 1525. The greatest carver of his period, he executed many fine sepulchral monuments and church decorations. See studies by Knapp (1935), Demmler (1939) and K. H. Stein (1944).

RIENZI, or **Rienzo, Cola di,** *ryent'see* (*c.* 1313–1354), Italian patriot, born humbly at Rome, was in 1343 spokesman of a deputation sent in vain to Avignon to beseech Clement VI to return to Rome. In May 1347 he incited the citizens to rise against the rule of the nobles. The senators were driven out, and Rienzi was invested with practically dictatorial power. At his request the Italian states sent deputies to Rome to devise measures for unification and common good, and Rienzi was crowned tribune. But the nobles were still bitterly hostile. The papal authority was turned against him; and, his seven months' reign over, he fled to Naples. After two years of religious meditation Rienzi resumed his life as political reformer, but was taken prisoner by the emperor and sent to Clement VI at Avignon. A new pope, Innocent VI, sent him to Rome to crush the power of the nobles, but after accomplishing this Rienzi aimed at re-establishing himself in supreme authority. In August 1354, having raised a small body of soldiers, he made a sort of triumphal entry into Rome. But his conduct now was such that the Romans murdered him, October 8. Wagner's opera on his story was produced in 1842. See books by Rodocanachi (1888), Cosenza (1913), Origo (1938), and Life (ed. Ghisalberti 1928).

RIESENER, Jean Paul, *rėe'zė-ner*; Fr. *reez-nayr* (1734–1806), cabinetmaker, born in München-Gladbach, Prussia, worked in Paris, was a master, favoured by Louis XVI's court, of marquetry and ebony work.

RIETSCHEL, Ernst, *ree'chėl* (1804–61), German sculptor, of the Dresden school, executed the Goethe and Schiller monument at Weimar, the Luther memorial at Worms and many other monuments and portrait busts. There is a Rietschel museum at Dresden.

RIGAUD, Hyacinthe, *ree-gō* (1659–1743), French portrait painter, born at Perpignan, settled in Paris in 1681. His portrait of Louis XIV (1701) is in the Louvre.

RIISAGER, Knudåge (1897–), Danish composer, was born at Port Kunda, Russia, and by 1900 had returned with his parents to Denmark. He took a political economy degree at Copenhagen University, then went to Paris, where, giving rein to his early musical ambitions, he studied under Paul le Flem and Albert Roussel, and was also influenced by other French composers of the time. On his return to Denmark he shocked conventional musical circles there by his revolutionary compositions and writings. Polytonality, polyrhythm and unique syncopations abound in his works, which include the overtures *Erasmus Montanus* and *Klods Hans*, four symphonies, ballets, including the well-known *Quarrtsiluni*, and a piano sonata (1931).

RILEY, James Whitcomb (1849–1916), American poet, known as the 'Hoosier poet', born at Greenfield, Indiana. His poems about children, including 'Little Orfant Annie', are well known. See Life by M. Dickey (1922).

RILKE, Rainer Maria, *-kė* (1875–1926), Austrian lyric poet, born at Prague, deserted a military academy to study art history at Prague, Munich and Berlin. The spiritual melancholy of his early verse turns into a mystical quest for the deity in such works as *Geschichten vom lieben Gott* (1900) and *Das Stundenbuch* (1905), written after two journeys to Russia (1899–1900), where he met Tolstoy and was deeply influenced by Russian pietism. In 1901 he married Klara Westhoff, a pupil of Rodin, whose secretary Rilke became in Paris, publishing *Das Rodin-Buch* (1907). Mysticism was abandoned for the aesthetic ideal in *Gedichte* (1907, 1908). *Die Aufzeichnungen des Malte Laurids Brigge* (1910) portrays the anxious loneliness of an imaginary poet. In 1923 he wrote two masterpieces, *Die Sonnette an Orpheus* and *Duineser Elegien,* in which he exalts the poet as the mediator between crude nature and pure form. His work greatly extended the range of expression and subtlety of the German language. See *Poems 1906 to 1926* trans. and intro. J. B. Leishman (1957), *Ewald Tragy* (trans. 1958), *Letters* (trans. 1958), Selected Works (trans. by Leishman, 2 vols., 1960–61), E. Heller, *The Disinherited Mind* (1952), and studies by E. M. Butler (1941), Heerikhuizen (trans. 1951), Holthusen (1952), Belmore (1954) and F. Wood (1958).

RIMBAUD, (Jean Nicolas) Arthur, *rī-bō* (1854–91), Belgian poet, was born at Charleville, Ardennes, the son of an army captain and his stern, disciplinarian wife. After a brilliant academic career at the Collège de Charleville, he published in 1870 his first book of poems, and the same year ran away to Paris, the first stage in his life of wandering. He soon returned to Charleville, where he wrote, while leading a life of idling, drinking and bawdy conversation, *Le Bateau ivre,* which, with its verbal eccentricities, daring imagery and evocative language, is perhaps his most popular work. Soon after its publication in August 1871 Verlaine invited Rimbaud to Paris, where they began together a life of debauchery and ill-repute, with periods in London. In Brussels in July 1873 Rimbaud threatened to terminate the friendship, and was thereupon shot at and wounded by Verlaine, who was imprisoned for attempted murder. The relationship had, however, given Rimbaud some measure of stability, and from its height, the summer of 1872, date many of *Les Illuminations,* the work which most clearly states his poetic doctrine. These prose and verse poems, as it were flashes of sensation, show Rimbaud as a precursor of symbolism, with his use of childhood, dream and mystical images to express dissatisfaction with the material world and a longing for the spiritual. In 1873 Rimbaud published the prose volume *Une Saison en enfer,* which symbolized his struggle to break with his past—his ' enfer ', was bitterly disappointed at its cold reception by the literary critics, burned all his manuscripts, and at the age of nineteen bade a farewell to literature. Then began years of varied and colourful wandering in Europe and the East—in Germany, Sweden, Aden, Cyprus and Harar, as soldier, trader, explorer and gun-runner. During these years, in 1886, Verlaine published *Les Illuminations* as by the ' late Arthur Rimbaud ', but the author ignored, rather than was ignorant of, the sensation they caused and the reputation they were making for him. In April 1891 troubled by a leg infection, he left Harar and sailed to Marseilles, where his leg was amputated, and where, after a brief return to Belgium, he died, November 10, 1891. See studies by E. Starkie (1937, 1947), Fowlie (1946, 1966) and Hackett (1957).

RIMINI. See FRANCESCA DA RIMINI.

RIMSKY-KORSAKOV, Nikolai Andreievich (1844–1908), Russian composer, was born at Tikhvin, Novgorod. His early musical education was perfunctory until 1859, when he took some lessons from the pianist Canille, a musician of some repute but no method, and developed a taste for composition, making arrangements of the operatic tunes of Glinka (q.v.), whom he greatly admired. In 1861 he was introduced to Balakirev (q.v.), who became his friend and mentor, and to Moussorgsky (q.v.), then young and struggling. Encouraged by his new companions, he started a callow symphony, said to be the first by a Russian, in E♭ minor (later transposed, not surprisingly, into the more manageable key of E minor). Following a family tradition, he was destined for the sea, and his musical activities were interrupted when he became a naval cadet, passed out in 1862, and went on a routine cruise which took in England and America. His interest in music had meantime subsided, but was revived when he met Balakirev again and became a member of his circle, which included Moussorgsky and Borodin (q.v.). He finished his symphony, which was performed with some local success, wrote some songs, and became interested in folk music. His knowledge of the tools of the composer's trade was still extremely limited when, in 1867, he wrote his first version of the fairy-tale fantasy *Sadko* and began his opera *The Maid of Pskov* in 1868. In 1871 he was offered a professorship at the St Petersburg Conservatoire which, conscious of his technical shortcomings, he hesitated to accept, but eventually he took the plunge and by assiduous study caught up on his academic deficiencies, though his music went through a temporary phase of stuffiness on this account. He was helped much at this time by Nadezhda Purgold, a brilliant musician and a composer in her own right, who became his wife in 1872. In 1877 he published a collection of Russian folk songs, and he spent a good deal of time studying instrumentation with his friend Borodin, after whose death he and Glazunov (q.v.) completed the unfinished *Prince Igor.* In 1887–88 he produced his three great orchestral masterpieces—*Capriccio Espagnol, Easter Festival* and *Scheherazade*—but thereafter turned to opera, which occupied his attention, apart from revisions of earlier works, for the rest of his life. Among his best in this *genre* are *The Snow Maiden* (1882), *The Tsar Saltan* (1900), *The Invisible City of Kitesh* (1906) and

The Golden Cockerel, begun in 1906, his last work, based on a satire against autocracy by Pushkin and therefore banned at first from the Russian stage. A revised version of *Sadko* appeared in 1898, and *The Maid of Pskov* reappeared, staged by Diaghilev as *Ivan the Terrible*, in 1908. Since 1892 Rimsky-Korsakov had suffered with cerebro-spinal neurasthenia, and his life was saddened by the loss of two children in 1891 and 1893. He died at Lyubensk on June 21, 1908. His music is notable for its brilliance and native vitality, and for the colour engendered by his great flair for orchestration. Ever conscious of his bygone technical shortcomings, he rewrote almost all his early work. Stravinsky (q.v.) was his pupil. See his *My Musical Life* (trans. Joffe 1942), and Lives by Montagu-Nathan (1916) and G. Abraham (1945).

RINGAN, St. See NINIAN.

RINUCCINI, Ottavio, *ree-noot-chee'nee* (1562–1621), Italian poet, wrote *Dafne* (1594), the first Italian melodrama, based on the Greek recitative. See PERI.

RIOPELLE, Jean Paul, *ree-ō-pel* (1924–), Canadian painter, born in Montreal, one of the leading colourists among the abstract 'action painters'.

RIPLEY, George (1802–80), American social reformer and literary critic, born at Greenfield, Mass., graduated at Harvard, and until 1841 was pastor in Boston. He joined in the Transcendental movement, and on leaving the pulpit he started the Brook Farm experiment. In 1849 he engaged in literary work at New York. He was joint-editor of Appleton's *New American Cyclopaedia.* See Life by Frothingham (1882).

RIPON, (1) **Frederick John Robinson, Earl of** (1782–1859), English statesman, second son of the second Lord Grantham, was educated at Harrow and St John's College, Cambridge. In 1806 he entered parliament as a moderate Tory, and had successively been under-secretary for the colonies, vice-president of the Board of Trade, and chancellor of the Exchequer, when, as Viscount Goderich, in 1827 he became head of a brief administration. He was later colonial secretary, lord privy seal, and president of the Board of Trade, and in 1833 was created Earl of Ripon. See Jones, *Prosperity Robinson* (1968).

(2) **George Frederick Samuel Robinson, Marquis of** (1827–1900), son of (1), English statesman, succeeded his father as Earl of Ripon and his uncle as Earl de Grey. Since 1852 he had sat in parliament as a Liberal, and he became successively under-secretary for war (1859), under-secretary for India (1861), secretary for war (1863), secretary for India (1866), lord president of the Council (1868), grand master of the Freemasons (1870, which office he resigned in 1874 on his conversion to Catholicism), Marquis of Ripon (1871), and viceroy of India (1880–84). He was first lord of the Admiralty in 1886, colonial secretary in 1892–95, and lord privy seal in 1905–08. See book on his viceroyalty, by S. Gopal (1953).

RIPPERDA, Johann Wilhelm, Baron de, *rip'-* (1680–1737), Dutch political adventurer who, born at Groningen, played an amazing part at the Spanish court, turned first Catholic and then Moslem, and died at Tetuan, after commanding against Spain. See French monograph by Syveton (1896).

RISHANGER, William (*c.* 1250–1312), a monk of St Albans, who wrote a number of short contemporary chronicles in continuation of the historical work of Matthew Paris, but probably did not write the *Chronica Wilhelmi Rishanger* (1259–1306).

RISTORI, Adelaide, *ree-stō'ree* (1822–1906), Italian tragédienne, born at Cividale in Friuli, rapidly became the leading Italian actress. In 1847 her marriage with the Marquis del Grillo (died 1861) temporarily interrupted her dramatic career. She won a complete triumph before a French audience in 1855, when Rachel was at the height of her fame; and gained fresh laurels in nearly every country of Europe, in the United States (1866, 1875, 1884–85), and in South America. See her *Memoirs and Artistic Studies* (trans. 1907).

RITCHIE, Anne Isabella, Lady (1837–1919), English writer, the daughter of William Makepeace Thackeray, was born in London. A close companion of her father, and well acquainted with his friends of literary and artistic note, she contributed valuable personal reminiscences to an 1898–99 edition of his works, and also wrote memoirs of their contemporaries, such as Tennyson and Ruskin. Her novels include *The Village on the Cliff* (1867) and *Old Kensington* (1873).

RITSCHL, *rich'ĕl*, (1) **Albrecht** (1822–89), Protestant theologian, born at Berlin, became professor of Theology at Bonn (1851), Göttingen (1864). His principal work is on the doctrine of justification and reconciliation (1870–74; 4th ed. 1896). Other works were on Christian perfection (1874), conscience (1876), Pietism (1880–86), theology and metaphysics (1881), &c. The distinguishing feature of the Ritschlian theology is the prominence it gives to the practical, ethical, social side of Christianity. See Life by his son, Otto (2 vols. 1892–96); and works on Ritschlianism by Pfleiderer (1891), Garvie (1899), Swing (1901), Orr (1903), Edghill (1910) and Mackintosh (1915).

(2) **Friedrich Wilhelm** (1806–76), German scholar, born near Erfurt, received classical chairs at Breslau (1834), Bonn (1839) and Leipzig (1865). His great edition of Plautus (1848–54; new ed. 1881–87) was preceded by *Parerga Plautina et Terentiana* (1845). His *Priscae Latinitatis Monumenta Epigraphica* (1864) was the forerunner of the *Corpus Inscriptionum.* See Life by Ribbeck (1879–81).

RITSON, Joseph (1752–1803), English antiquary, born at Stockton-on-Tees, came to London in 1775, and practised as a conveyancer, but was enabled to give most of his time to antiquarian studies. He was as notorious for his vegetarianism, whimsical spelling and irreverence as for his attacks on bigger men than himself. His first important work was an onslaught on Warton's *History of English Poetry* (1782). He assailed (1783) Johnson and Steevens for their text of Shakespeare, and Bishop Percy in *Ancient Songs* (1790); in 1792 appeared his *Cursory Criticisms* on Malone's Shakespeare. Other works were *English Songs* (1783); *Ancient Popular Poetry* (1791); *Scottish Songs* (1794); *Poems . . . by*

Laurence Minot (1795); *Robin Hood Ballads* (1795); and *Ancient English Metrical Romances* (1802). See his Letters edited, with Life, by Sir H. Nicolas (1833), and the studies by Burd (1916) and Bronson (1938).

RITTER, (1) **Johann Wilhelm** (1776–1810), German physicist, was born in Silesia, and while working in Jena discovered in 1802 the ultraviolet rays in the spectrum (see W. H. WOLLASTON). He also worked on electricity.

(2) **Karl** (1779–1859), German geographer, born at Quedlinburg, became professor of Geography at Berlin (1829), academician, and director of studies of the Military School. He laid the foundations of modern scientific geography, his most important work, *Die Erkunde* . . . (1817), stressing the relation between man and his natural environment. He also wrote a comparative geography (Eng. ed. 1865). See Life by Gage (1867).

RIVAROL, Antoine, *ree-va-rol* (1753–1801), French writer, born at Bagnols in Languedoc, came to Paris in 1780, and in 1788 set the whole city laughing at the sarcasms in his *Petit Almanach de nos grands hommes.* Emigrating in 1792, and supported by royalist pensions, he wrote pamphlets in Brussels, London, Hamburg and Berlin. See Lives by Le Breton (1895) and L. Latzarus (1926).

RIVAS, Angel de Saavedra, Duque de, *ree'vas* (1791–1865), Spanish politician and writer, was born in Córdoba and educated in Madrid. He served in the Civil War, lived in exile (1823–1834), became minister of the interior in 1835, and was soon exiled again. In 1837 he returned, became prime minister, and later was ambassador in Naples, Paris (1856) and Florence (1860). Alongside his political life, Rivas led his literary one, as an early exponent of Spanish romanticism. His works include the epics *Florinda* (1826) and *El Moro expósito* (1834), the dramatic poems, *Romances históricos* (1841), and several dramas, including *Don Alvaro* or *La Fuerza del Sino* (1835), on which Verdi based his opera *La Forza del Destino*. See study by Peers (1923).

RIVERA, Diego, *ri-vay'ra* (1886–1957), Mexican painter, born at Guanajuato, in 1921 began a series of murals in public buildings depicting the life and history (particularly the popular uprisings) of the Mexican people. From 1930 to 1934 he executed a number of frescoes in the U.S., mainly of industrial life. His art is a curious blend of the rhetorical realism of folk art and revolutionary propaganda, with overtones of Byzantine and Aztec symbolism. See his books *Portrait of America* (1934) and *Portrait of Mexico* (1938), and Life by Wolfe (1939).

RIVERS, (1) **Anthony Woodville, 2nd Earl** (1442?–83), son of (3), stuck closely to Edward IV, who made him captain-general of the forces. After Edward's death he was put to death by Richard III.

(2) **Augustus Pitt-.** See PITT-RIVERS.

(3) **Richard Woodville, 1st Earl** (d. 1469), English soldier, was esquire to Henry V, and during his son's reign was made governor of the Tower (1424) and knighted (1425). He fought in France and for the Lancastrians in the Wars of the Roses. He married Jacquetta of Luxembourg, widow of the Duke of Bedford, and it was their daughter Elizabeth whom Edward IV married. This led him to go over to the Yorkists, and Edward made him Constable of England, Baron Rivers (1448) and Earl Rivers (1466). But the favour shown to the Rivers family offended the old nobility, and their avarice aroused popular enmity, and in 1469 Earl Rivers was beheaded at Northampton.

(4) **William Halse Rivers** (1864–1922), English anthropologist and psychologist, lectured at Cambridge, applied his genealogical method in the Torres Straits and among the Todas, wrote important books on *Kinship* (1914) and on *The History of Melanesian Society* (1915), drawing the story of a long-past migration from the linkage of elements in a culture. In *Instinct and the Unconscious* (1920) and *Conflict and Dream* (1923) he is a modified Freudian.

RIVIÈRE, (1) **Briton,** *rē-veer'* (1840–1920), English artist, born of Huguenot ancestry in London, the son of a drawing-master, graduated at Oxford in 1867, was elected R.A. in 1881, and excelled in paintings of wild animals.

(2) **Jacques,** *ree-vyayr* (1886–1925), French writer and critic, born in Bordeaux, in 1919 became first editor of the *Nouvelle revue française*, as such playing a prominent part in the cultural life of postwar France. His writings include novels, essays and a justification of the Christian conception of God, *À la trace de Dieu* (1925). See his correspondence with Claudel (1925) and Fournier (1926–28), and the Life by B. Cook (1958).

RIVINGTON, Charles (1688–1742), English publisher, born at Chesterfield, Derbyshire, went to London, where he founded in 1711 the Rivington publishing firm which remained under family direction until absorbed by Longmans in 1890. In 1889 Septimus Rivington was a cofounder of the firm of Percival and Co., which in 1893 became Rivington, Percival and Co., and, after 1897, Rivington & Co. See S. Rivington, *The House of Rivington* (1894).

RIZAL, José, *ree-sal'* (1861–96), Filipino patriot and writer, born at Calamba, Luzon, studied medicine at Madrid, and on his return to the Philippines published a political novel, *Noli me tangere* (1886), whose anti-Spanish tone led to his exile. He practised in Hong Kong, where he wrote *El Filibusterismo* (1891), a continuation of his first novel. Returning to the Philippines, he arrived simultaneously with an anti-Spanish revolt, which he was accused of instigating, and was shot. See study by C. E. Russell and E. B. Rodriguez (1923).

RIZZIO, or **Riccio, David,** *rit'si-o, reech'-* (1533?–66), Italian courtier and musician, entered the service of Mary, Queen of Scots in 1561, and rapidly becoming her favourite, was appointed private foreign secretary in 1564. He negotiated Mary's marriage (1565) with Darnley, with whom he was at first on friendliest terms, but the queen's husband soon became jealous of his influence over Mary and of his strong political power, and entered with other nobles into a plot to kill him. Rizzio was dragged from the queen's presence and brutally murdered at the palace of Holyrood, March 9, 1566.

ROBBE-GRILLET, Alain (1922–), French novelist, born in Brest and educated in Paris, worked for some time as an agronomist and then in a publishing house. His first novel, *Les Gommes* (*The Erasers*, 1953), aroused much controversy and with the appearance of his later ones (*Dans le labyrinthe*, 1959, &c.) he emerged as a leader of the *nouveau roman* group. He uses an unorthodox narrative structure and concentrates on external reality, believing this to be the only one. He has also written film scenarios, e.g., *L'Année dernière à Marienbad* and essays, *Pour un nouveau roman* (1963).

ROBBIA, DELLA, the name of a family of Florentine sculptors, including:

(1) **Andrea** (1435–1525), nephew of (3), who worked at reliefs and whose bambini medallions are on the Ospedale degli Innocenti, Florence.

(2) **Giovanni** (1469–1529?), son of (1), whose frieze *Seven Works of Mercy* is at Pistoia.

(3) **Luca** (*c.* 1400–82), who executed between 1431 and 1440 ten unequalled panels of angels and dancing boys for the cathedral, for whose sacristy he also made (1448–67) a bronze door with ten panels of figures in relief. In marble he sculptured, in 1457–58, the tomb of the Bishop of Fiesole. He is almost equally famous for his figures in terra-cotta, including medallions and reliefs, white or coloured. See works by Cruttwell (1902) and Marquand (various, 1912–28).

ROBERT. Name of three kings of Scotland:

(1) **Robert I.** See BRUCE Family (7).

(2) **Robert II** (1316–90), born March 2, was the son of Walter Stewart (q.v.) and of Marjory, only daughter of Robert the Bruce. Throughout the disastrous reign of his uncle, David II, he was one of the most prominent nobles of Scotland, and twice acted as regent. On David's death (1371) he obtained the crown, founding the Stewart dynasty. His powerful and intractable barons shaped the policy of the country very much according to their pleasure. The misery inflicted by their raids and the reprisals of the English wardens was frightful; the great events were the invasions of Scotland by English forces in 1384 and in 1385, and the retaliatory expedition of the Scots in 1388, ending with Otterburn. He married (1384) his mistress, Elizabeth Mure of Rowallan, and (1355) a daughter of the Earl of Ross; he had over a dozen children.

(3) **Robert III** (*c.* 1340–1406), son of (2), was originally called John. His incapacity threw the government into the hands of his ambitious brother, in 1398 created Duke of Albany. In 1400 Henry IV of England invaded Scotland and penetrated as far as Edinburgh; the Scots retaliated in 1402 by the expedition which ended in the disaster at Homildon Hill. Robert had two sons, the elder of whom was David, Duke of Rothesay (1378–1402), a clever but very licentious youth. Albany receiecd orders from the king to act as his guardian, and after a short time starved him to death at Falkland. Robert, anxious for the safety of his younger son, James, sent him to France; and died when news came that the vessel in which James sailed had been captured by an English ship.

ROBERT, Duke of Normandy. See HENRY I, of England.

ROBERT-FLEURY, *ro-bayr-flœ-ree*, (1) **Joseph** Nicolas (1797–1890), French historical painter, born in Cologne, was a pupil of Gros. He is notable for his historical accuracy of subject matter and use of contemporaneous techniques.

(2) **Tony** (1837–1911), French historical painter, son of (1), born in Paris, was a pupil of Delaroche.

ROBERT OF ANJOU, *ã-zhoo* (1275–1343), king of Naples and Sicily, succeeded his father, Charles II, in 1309. He supported the Guelph cause, and was a notable patron of literature and the arts. See Baddeley's *Robert the Wise* (1897).

ROBERT OF BRUNNE, the name by which Robert Manning, or Mannyng, is usually designated from his birthplace Bourn, in Lincolnshire, 6 miles from the Gilbertine monastery of Sempringham that he entered in 1288. He died about 1338. His chief work is his *Handlyng Synne* (1303), a free and amplified translation into English verse of William of Wadington's *Manuel des Pechiez*, with such judicious omissions and additions as made his version much more entertaining than the original. It is one of the best landmarks in the transition from early to later Middle English. He also made a new version in octosyllabic rhyme of Wace's *Brut d'Angleterre*, and added to it a translation of the French rhyming chronicle of Peter Langtoft.

ROBERT OF GLOUCESTER (fl. 1260–1300), author of a metrical English chronicle to 1135, edited by Wright (Rolls series, 1887).

ROBERT OF JUMIÈGES (fl. 1037–52), a Norman abbot of Jumièges from 1037, came to England in 1043 with Edward the Confessor, who made him Bishop of London (1044) and Archbishop of Canterbury (1050). He was the head of the anti-English party which in 1051 banished Earl Godwin and his sons. Their return next year drove him to Normandy. The Witan stripped him of his archbishopric, and he died at Jumièges.

ROBERT OF MELUN, *me-lã* (d. 1167), English theologian, taught in Paris and Melun, and was elected Bishop of Hereford in 1163. He acted as a mediator between Becket and Henry II, latterly, however, giving his support to Becket.

ROBERTI, Ercole de' (*c.* 1455–96), Italian painter, born in Ferrara. His *Madonna* in the Brera Gallery, Milan, and *Pietà*, in the Walker Art Gallery, Liverpool, are characteristic of his work, which is less austere than that of Cossa and Tura (qq.v.), his contemporaries of the Ferrarese school. See B. Nicolson, *The Painters of Ferrara* (1950).

ROBERTS, (1) **Sir Charles George Douglas** (1860–1943), Canadian naturalist, writer and poet, born in New Brunswick, graduated at Fredericton in 1879, was professor in King's College, Nova Scotia (1885–95), and settled in New York as an editor, joining the Canadian army at the outbreak of World War I. He wrote *Orion*, *In Divers Tones*, and other verse, a history of Canada, *Canada in Flanders* (1918), and nature studies, in which he particularly excelled, including *The Feet of the Furtive* (1912) and *Eyes of the Wilderness* (1933). He was knighted in 1935.

(2) **David** (1796–1864), Scottish painter, born at Edinburgh, October 24, as a scene-painter at Drury Lane attracted attention with pictures of Rouen and Amiens cathedrals at the Royal Academy. Among his pictures, the fruit of his wide travels, were *Departure of the Israelites from Egypt* (1829), *Jerusalem* (1845), *Rome* (1855) and *Grand Canal at Venice* (1856). He was elected R.A. in 1841. See Life by J. Ballantine (1866).

(3) **Frederick Sleigh Roberts, Earl, of Kandahar, Pretoria, and Waterford** (1832–1914), was born at Cawnpore. He was educated at Clifton, Eton, Sandhurst and Addiscombe; entered the Bengal Artillery in 1851; was at the siege of Delhi; and took an active part in the subsequent operations down to the relief of Lucknow, winning the V.C. in 1858. He was assistant quartermaster general in the Abyssinian (1868) and Lushai (1871–72) expeditions. In the Afghan war in 1878, now major-general, he forced the Afghan position on Peiwar Kotul, and was made K.C.B. (1879). After the murder of Cavagnari and his escort at Kabul, he defeated the Afghans at Charásia, took possession of Kabul, and assumed the government. Yákúb Khan was sent a prisoner to India, but Abdul Rahman was proclaimed amir, General Burrows was crushingly defeated at Maiwand, and the British Kandahar garrison was besieged. On August 9, 1880, he set out with 10,000 men on his memorable march through Afghanistan to the relief of Kandahar; three weeks later he reached it, and routed Ayub Khan. In 1881, now a baronet, he was appointed commander-in-chief of the Madras army, and in 1885–93 he was commander-in-chief in India. Created Lord Roberts of Kandahar and Waterford in 1892, he became field marshal and commander-in-chief in Ireland in 1895. He published *The Rise of Wellington* (1895) and *Forty-One Years in India* (1895). After the first checks of the Boer war he was sent out to assume the chief command, relieved Kimberley and made the great advance to Pretoria, and came home in 1901 to be commander-in-chief. Created earl in 1901, he retired in 1904, and died while visiting troops in the field in France. See Lives by Forest (1914), de Watteville (1938) and James (1954).

(4) **Morley** (1857–1942), English writer, born in London, was educated at Bedford and Owens College, served before the mast, on Australian sheep-runs, on Texan ranches, on Californian railways, and British Columbian sawmills, and multiplied his experiences in the South Seas, the Transvaal, Rhodesia and Corsica. From 1887 onwards he published a long series of works, mostly novels, including *The Purification of Dolores Silva* (1894), *The Colossus*, *A Son of Empire*, *Immortal Youth*, *Lady Penelope* (1904) and *Sea Dogs* (1910). See Life by Jameson (1961).

(5) **William Patrick** (1895–), English artist, born in London, was associated with Roger Fry, Wyndham Lewis (as a Vorticist) and with the London Group, and in both World Wars was an official war artist. His art is now devoted to the portrayal of Cockney characters in a very formal cubist, or rather cylindrical, style, with a certain satirical emphasis. He is represented in the Tate Gallery and became an A.R.A. in 1958

ROBERTS-AUSTEN, Sir William Chandler (1843–1902), English metallurgist, was born at Kennington, London. Elected F.R.S. in 1875, he was in 1880 appointed professor at the Royal School of Mines, two years later becoming chemist and assayer at the Mint. A pioneer of alloy research, he demonstrated the possibility of diffusion occurring between a sheet of gold and a block of lead.

ROBERTSON, (1) Brain Hubert, 1st Baron of Oakridge (1896–), British general, won the D.S.O. and M.C. in World War I, and, retiring from the army, became managing director of the South African section of Dunlop (1935). In World War II he was General Alexander's administrative officer during the Italian campaign (1944–45), was deputy (1945), then military governor (1947), and finally high commissioner (1949–50) of the British Zone in Germany. From 1953–61 he was chairman of the British Transport Commission. He succeeded his father as 2nd baronet of Welbourn in 1919, and became a peer in 1961.

(2) **Frederick William** (1816–53), English clergyman, born in London, was educated for the army at Tours and Edinburgh, but devoting himself to the church, studied at Oxford (1837–40), and in 1847 became incumbent of Trinity Chapel, Brighton, where his earnestness, originality and sympathies for revolutionary ideals arrested attention, but provoked suspicion. He resigned in June 1853 because his vicar had refused to confirm his nomination of a curate. He published but one sermon—the five series (1855, 1855, 1857, 1859–63, 1880) so well known over the English-speaking world are really recollections, sometimes dictated and sometimes written out. See his *Life and Letters*, by the Rev. Brooke (1865).

(3) **George Croom** (1842–92), Scottish philosopher, born at Aberdeen, in 1866 became professor of Mental Philosophy and Logic at University College, London. He wrote on Hobbes, founded (1876) and edited *Mind*. See memoir by Prof. Bain prefixed to his *Philosophical Remains* (1894).

(4) **James Logie.** See HALIBURTON (1).

(5) **Joseph** (1810–66), Scottish antiquary, born and educated at Aberdeen, became historical curator at the Edinburgh Register House. He was an originator of the Aberdeen Spalding Club (1839–70), and contributed much to Chambers's *Encyclopaedia*. Among his works are *The Book of Bon-Accord* (1839) and *Concilia Scotiae: Ecclesiae Scoticanae Statuta, 1225–1559* (1866).

(6) **Madge.** See KENDAL.

(7) **Thomas William** (1829–71), English dramatist, brother of (6), was born at Newark-on-Trent, of an old actor family. Coming up to London in 1848, he was actor, prompter and stage manager, wrote unsuccessful plays, contributed to newspapers and magazines, translated French plays, &c. His first notable success as a dramatist was with

David Garrick (1864) and *Society* (1865), and his next comedy, *Ours* (1866), established his fame. *Caste* (1867), *Play* (1868), *School* (1869), *M.P.* (1870)—all brought out by the Bancrofts at the Prince of Wales Theatre—and *Home* (1869) and *Dreams* (1869) were all equally successful. See his *Principal Dramatic Works*, with memoir by his son (1889), and Life by Pemberton (1893).

(8) **William** (1721–93), Scottish historian, born at the manse of Borthwick in Midlothian, studied at Edinburgh, and at twenty-two was ordained minister of Gladsmuir. He volunteered for the defence of Edinburgh against the rebels in 1745, from 1751 took a prominent part in the General Assembly, and soon became leader of the 'Moderates'. From 1761 till his death he was joint minister with Dr Erskine of Greyfriars, Edinburgh. In 1761 he became a royal chaplain, in 1762 principal of Edinburgh University, and in 1764 king's historiographer. His *History of Scotland 1542–1603* (1759) was a splendid success. Next followed the *History of Charles V* (1769), his most valuable work, highly praised by Voltaire and Gibbon. The *History of America* appeared in 1777, and a disquisition on *The Knowledge which the Ancients had of India* in 1791. See Lives by Stewart (1801) and Gleig (1812).

(9) **Sir William Robert** (1860–1933), English soldier, enlisted as private in 1877 and rose to be field-marshal in 1920. Chief of the Imperial General Staff from 1915 to 1918, he became a baronet in 1919. See his autobiographical *From Private to Field-Marshal* (1921).

ROBERVAL, Gilles Personne de (1602–75), French mathematician, was born at Roberval near Beauvais, and in 1632 was appointed professor of Mathematics at the Collège de France. He devised a method of drawing tangents and invented the balance now called after him.

ROBESON, Paul Le Roy, *rōb'sėn* (1898–), American Negro singer and actor, born in Princeton, N.J., was admitted to the American bar before embarking on a stage career in New York in 1921, appearing in Britain in 1922. Success as an actor was matched by popularity as a singer, and he appeared in works ranging from *Show Boat* to plays by O'Neill and Shakespeare's *Othello*, a part which he first played in London in 1930 and in which he scored a triumphant American success ten years later. He gave song recitals, notably of Negro spirituals, throughout the world, and appeared in numerous films. From the end of World War II his racial and political sympathies somewhat embittered his relationship with the United States, and from 1958 to 1963, when he retired and returned to the U.S., he lived in England. See his autobiographical *Here I Stand* (1958) and Life by Seton (1958).

ROBESPIERRE, Maximilien Marie Isidore de, *rō-bės-pyayr* (1758–94), French revolutionary, was born, of Irish origin, at Arras, May 6, 1758. He was admitted *avocat* in 1781, and was elected to the States General in 1789 by Artois. He attached himself to the extreme Left, and soon commanded attention. His influence grew daily, and the mob frantically admired his earnest cant and his boasted incorruptibility. In 1791 he carried the motion that no member of the present Assembly should be eligible for the next, and was appointed public accuser. Next followed the flight to Varennes (June 21), Lafayette's last effort to control the right of insurrection on the Champ-de-Mars (July 17), the abject terror of Robespierre, his hysterical appeal to the Club, the theatrical oath taken by every member to defend his life, and his conduct home in triumph by the mob at the close of the Constituent Assembly (September 30). The Girondist leaders in the new Legislative Assembly were eager for war. Robespierre offered a strenuous opposition in the Jacobin Club. In April 1792 he resigned his post of public accuser. In August he presented to the Legislative Assembly a petition for a Revolutionary Tribunal and a new Convention. It does not appear that he was responsible for the September massacres. He was elected first deputy for Paris to the National Convention, where the bitter attacks upon him by the Girondists threw him into closer union with Danton. Robespierre vigorously opposed the Girondist idea of a special appeal to the people on the king's death, and Louis's execution (January 21, 1793) opened up the final stage of the struggle, which ended in a complete triumph for the Jacobins on June 2. The first Committee of Public Safety was decreed in April 1793, and Robespierre, elected in July, was now one of the actual rulers of France; but it is doubtful whether henceforth he was not merely the stalking-horse for the more resolute party within the Twelve. Next came the dark intrigues and desperate struggles that sent Hébert and his friends to the scaffold in March 1794, and Danton and Camille Desmoulins in April. The next three months Robespierre reigned supreme. He nominated all the members of the Government Committees, placed his creatures in all places of influence in the commune of Paris, and assumed complete control of the Revolutionary Tribunal. But as his power increased his popularity waned. On May 7 Robespierre, who had previously condemned the cult of Reason, advocated a new state religion and recommended the Convention to acknowledge the existence of God; on June 8 the inaugural festival of the Supreme Being took place. Meantime the pace of the guillotine grew faster; public finance and government generally drifted to ruin, and Saint-Just demanded the creation of a dictatorship in the person of Robespierre. On July 26 the dictator delivered a long harangue complaining that he was being accused of crimes unjustly. The Convention, after at first obediently passing his decrees, next rescinded them and referred his proposals to the committees. That night at the Jacobin Club his party again triumphed. Next day at the Convention Saint-Just could not obtain a hearing, and Robespierre was vehemently attacked. A deputy proposed his arrest; at the fatal word Robespierre's power crumbled to ruin. He flew to the Common Hall, whereupon the Convention declared him an outlaw. The National Guard under Barras turned out to protect the Convention, and Robespierre had his lower jaw broken by a shot fired by a gendarme. Next day (July 28; 10th Thermidor 1794) he was sent to the guillotine with Saint-Just, Couthon, and nineteen others. See histories of the Revolution by Lamartine, Michelet, Blanc, Carlyle, Von Sybel, Morse Stephens, Taine, de Tocqueville, and Machar; the Lives by G. H. Lewes (1849) and Thompson (1939); Hamel's eulogistic *Vie de Robespierre* (1865–1867), also his *Thermidor* (1891); works by Hilaire Belloc (1902), Mathiez (trans. 1927) and J. Eagan (1938).

ROBEY, Sir George (1869–1954), English comedian, born at Herne Hill, first appeared on the stage in 1891, changed his name from Wade to Robey, made a name for himself in musical shows such as *The Bing Boys* (1916), and later emerged as a Shakespearean actor in the part of Falstaff. Dubbed the 'Prime Minister of Mirth', he was famous for his robust, often Rabelaisian humour, his bowler hat, long black collarless frockcoat, hooked stick and thickly painted eyebrows. He was knighted in 1954. See his *Looking Back on Life* (1933), and A. E. Wilson's *Prime Minister of Mirth* (1956).

ROBIN HOOD, the hero of a group of old English ballads, the gallant and generous outlaw of Sherwood Forest, where he spent his time gaily under the greenwood tree with Little John, Scarlet, Friar Tuck, and his merry men all. Unrivalled with bow and quarter-staff, he waged war on proud abbots and rich knights, helping himself to riches but giving generously to the poor and needy. The 'rymes of Robyn Hood' are named in *Piers Plowman* (*c.* 1377) and the plays of Robin Hood in the *Paston Letters* (1473). Tradition made the outlaw into a political personage, a dispossessed Earl of Huntingdon and other characters, and in Scott's *Ivanhoe* he is a Saxon holding out against the Normans. But there is no evidence that he was anything but the creation of popular imagination, a yeoman counterpart to the knightly King Arthur. There are about forty Robin Hood ballads, some eight of them of the first rank. See Gutch, *Lytell Geste of Robin Hode* (1847), Hales's Introduction to the *Percy Folio* (1867), especially Child's *Ballads* (part v. 1888), and the Bibliography by J. H. Gable (1939).

ROBINS, Benjamin (1707–51), English mathematician and father of the art of gunnery, was born, of Quaker family, at Bath. He set up as teacher of mathematics in London, published several treatises, commenced his experiments on the resisting force of the air to projectiles, studied fortification, and invented the ballistic pendulum. In 1735 he demolished, in a treatise on *Newton's Methods of Fluxions*, Berkeley's objections. His *New Principles of Gunnery* appeared in 1742. Engineer to the East India Company (1749), he died at Madras. His works were collected in 1761.

ROBINSON, (1) Anastasia. See PETERBOROUGH.

(2) **Edward** (1794–1863), American scholar, born at Southington, Conn., studied in Germany, and in 1830 became a professor of Theology at Andover, in 1837 at New York. His survey of Palestine (1838) resulted in *Biblical Researches in Palestine and Adjacent Countries* (1841); and a second visit in 1852 produced a second edition (1856). See Life by Smith and Hitchcock (1863). He married in 1828 **Therese Albertine Louise von Jakob** (1797–1869), daughter of a Halle professor; under the acronym of her initials, 'Talvj', she wrote *Psyche* (1825), and translated Scott's *Black Dwarf* and *Old Mortality*, and *Volkslieder der Serben* (1825–26).

(3) **Edwin Arlington** (1869–1935), American poet, of the traditional school, was born at Head Tide, Maine, and educated at Harvard. His publications include *Captain Craig* (1902), *The Town down the River* (1910), *The Man against the Sky*, which made his name, and *King Jasper* (1935) and he was three times a Pulitzer prizewinner, for his *Collected Poems* (1922), *The Man Who Died Twice* (1925) and *Tristram* (1928), one of his several modern renderings of Arthurian legends. See studies by E. Neff (1949) and E. Barnard (1952).

(4) **(Esmé Stuart) Lennox** (1886–1958), Irish dramatist, born at Douglas, Co. Cork. His first play, *The Clancy Game*, was produced in 1908 at the Abbey Theatre, Dublin, of which he was appointed manager in 1910 and then director from 1923 to 1956. Other plays include *The Cross Roads* (1909), *The Dreamers* (1915) and *The White-Headed Boy* (1920); he also compiled volumes of Irish verse, including the Irish *Golden Treasury* (1925), and edited Lady Gregory's *Journals* (1946). See his autobiographical *Three Homes* (1938) and *Curtain Up* (1941).

(5) **Frederick John.** See RIPON (1).

(6) **George Frederick Samuel.** See RIPON (2).

(7) **Henry Crabb** (1775–1867), English lawyer and diarist, born at Bury St Edmunds, was articled to a Colchester attorney 1790–95. From 1800 he studied for five years at German universities, making friends of the great German writers of the day, and during 1807–1809 was engaged on *The Times* in Spain—the first war correspondent. In 1813 he was called to the bar, from which he retired in 1828. A Dissenter and a Liberal, he was one of the founders of London University (1828). See the selections edited by Sadler (1869) and by Edith Morley (1922–29). See Life by Edith Morley (1935).

(8) **Hercules George Robert, Lord Rosmead** (1824–97), English colonial governor, brother of (13), second son of Admiral Hercules Robinson (1789–1864), became governor of Hong Kong (1859, with a knighthood), Ceylon (1865), New South Wales (1872), New Zealand (1878), and Cape Colony, perhaps the scene of his ablest administration (1880 and again 1895); he retired in 1897. In 1875 he was created a G.C.M.G., in 1890 a baronet, and in 1896 Lord Rosmead.

(9) **John** (*c.* 1576–1625), English clergyman, pastor of the Pilgrim Fathers, was born in Lincolnshire, studied at Cambridge, held a curacy at Norwich, became a Puritan and in 1608 escaped to Leyden, where he established a church in 1609. In 1620, after a memorable sermon, he saw part of his flock set sail in the *Speedwell* for Plymouth where they joined the *Mayflower*. He died at

Leyden. See Lives by Davis (1903), Ashton (in the *Works*, 1851), Powicke (1920), and Dr J. Brown's *Pilgrim Fathers* (1895).

(10) **Mary**, known as 'Perdita' (1758–1800), English actress, born at Bristol, played Perdita and other Shakespearian parts at Drury Lane 1776–80, and became mistress in 1779 to the future George IV, who gave her a bond (never paid) for £20,000. She wrote poems, plays and novels; in 1783 she received a pension of £500, but died poor and ill. See her Memoirs, edited by her daughter (1801; 2nd ed. 1895).

(11) **Mary.** See DARMESTETER.

(12) **Sir Robert** (1886–), English chemist, was born in Chesterfield and educated at Manchester University. He held chairs at Sydney, Liverpool, St Andrews, Manchester, London and Oxford, where he was Waynflete professor from 1930 to 1955. He is particularly noted for his work on plant pigments, alkaloids and other natural products, and aided in the development of penicillin. From 1945 to 1950 he was president of the Royal Society, and was Nobel prizewinner for Chemistry in 1947. He was knighted in 1939, and awarded the O.M. in 1949.

(13) **Sir William Cleaver Francis** (1834–97), brother of (8), from 1874 was three times governor of Western Australia, and was created G.C.M.G. in 1887.

(14) **William Heath** (1872–1944), English artist, cartoonist and book-illustrator, was born in Hornsey Rise, London. He attended the Islington School of Art and the Royal Academy Schools, and in 1897 appeared an edition of *Don Quixote*, the first of many works to be illustrated by him; others include editions of *Arabian Nights* (1899), *Twelfth Night* (1908) and *Water Babies* (1915). But his fame, rests mainly on his humorous drawings—in his ability to poke fun, in colour and in black and white of superb draughtsmanship, at the machine age with countless 'Heath Robinson contraptions' of absurd and complicated design and with highly practical and simple aims, such as the raising of one's hat, the shuffling and dealing of cards, or the recovering of a collar-stud which has slipped down the back. See his autobiographical *My Line of Life* (1938) and the study by L. Day (1947).

ROB ROY, Gaelic for 'Red Robert' (1671–1734), Scottish freebooter, was the second son of Lieut.-Col. Donald Macgregor of Glengyle. Till 1661 the 'wicked clan Gregor' had for a century been pursued with fire and sword; the very name was proscribed. But from that year until the Revolution the severe laws against them were somewhat relaxed, and Rob Roy lived quietly enough as a grazier at Balquhidder. His herds were so often plundered by the outlaws from the north that he had to maintain a band of armed followers to protect both himself and such of his neighbours as paid him blackmail. And so with those followers espousing in 1691 the Jacobite cause, he did a little plundering for himself, and, two or three years later having purchased from his nephew the lands of Craigroyston and Inversnaid, laid claim to be chief of the clan. Suffering losses (1712) in cattle speculations, for which he had borrowed money from the Duke of Montrose, his lands were seized, his houses plundered, and his wife turned adrift with her children in midwinter. Rob now gathered his clansmen and made open war on the duke. This was in 1716, the year after the Jacobite rebellion, in which at Sheriffmuir, Rob Roy had stood watch for the booty. Marvellous stories were current round Loch Katrine and Loch Lomond of his hairbreadth escapes, of his evasions when captured, and of his generosity to the poor, whose wants he supplied at the expense of the rich. They in return warned him of the designs of his arch-foes, the Dukes of Montrose and Atholl, and of the redcoats; besides, Rob enjoyed the protection of the Duke of Argyll, having assumed his mother's name—Campbell. Late in life he is said to have turned Catholic, but in the list of subscribers to the Episcopalian church history of Bishop Keith (1734) occurs the name 'Robert Macgregor *alias* Rob Roy'. On December 28, 1734, Rob Roy died in his own house at Balquhidder. He left five sons, two of whom died in 1754—James, the notorious outlaw James Mohr, in Paris; and Robin, the youngest, on the gallows at Edinburgh for abduction. See the introduction and notes to Scott's *Rob Roy* (1817); Dorothy Wordsworth's *Tour in Scotland in 1803*, with her brother's poem; and the Lives of Rob Roy by K. Macleay (1818; new ed. 1881) and A. H. Millar (1883).

ROBSART, Amy. See LEICESTER, EARL OF.

ROBSON, Dame Flora (1902–), English actress, born at South Shields, first appeared in 1921 and gained fame mainly in historical rôles in plays and films, as Queen Elizabeth in *Fire over England* (1931), Thérèse Raquin in *Guilty* (1944), &c. She was made D.B.E. in 1960. See Life by Dunbar (1960).

ROCHAMBEAU, Jean Baptiste Donatien de Vimeur, Comte de, *ro-shā-bō* (1725–1807), French soldier, born at Vendôme, entered the French army in 1742, was at the siege of Maestricht, and distinguished himself at Minorca in 1756. In 1780 he was sent out with 6000 men to support the Americans, and in 1781 rendered effective help at Yorktown. He became marshal in 1791, and in 1804 Napoleon made him a grand officer of the Legion of Honour. See his *Mémoires* (1809; Eng. trans. 1838).

ROCHE, St (*c.* 1295–1327), patron of the plague-smitten, was born at Montpellier. His festival is celebrated on August 16.

ROCHEFORT, Victor Henri, Marquis de Rochefort-Luçay, *rosh-for* (1832–1913), French journalist and politician, born in Paris, became a clerk in the hôtel-de-ville, but was dismissed in 1859 for neglecting his duties. He took to journalism, in 1868 starting *La Lanterne*, which was quickly suppressed. He fled to Brussels, but returning in 1869 on his election to the Chamber of Deputies, started the *Marseillaise*, in which he renewed his attacks on the imperial régime. On the cowardly murder of his contributor, Victor Noir, by Prince Pierre Bonaparte, the paper was suppressed and its editor imprisoned. The fall of the empire opened up a rôle for him. In 1871 he was elected to the National Assembly, and soon sided with the Communards in *Le Mot d'ordre*. He escaped from Paris, but the Prussians caught him and sent him to Versailles; sentenced to life imprisonment, he escaped from New Caledonia in 1874, and returned to France after the amnesty of 1880. His *L'Intransigeant* showed him intractable as ever. He sat in the National Assembly (1885–86), buried his influence in Boulangism, fled in 1889 to London, returned to Paris in 1895, and was an active anti-Dreyfusard. See his *Adventures of my Life* (trans. 1896).

ROCHEFOUCAULD. See LA ROCHEFOUCAULD.

ROCHEJACQUELEIN. See LAROCHEJACQUELEIN.

ROCHESTER, John Wilmot, Earl of (1647–1680), English courtier and poet, was born at Ditchley, Oxfordshire, and was educated at Burford school and Wadham College, Oxford. He travelled in France and Italy, and then repaired to court, where his handsome person and lively wit made him a prominent figure. In 1665 he showed conspicuous courage against the Dutch. He is said to have been a patron of the actress Elizabeth Barry (q.v.), and of several poets. With his friend Windham, he had engaged that, 'if either of them died, he should appear and give the other notice of the future state, if there was any'. Windham was killed, but did not disturb the rest of his friend, who now plunged into a life of the grossest debauchery and buffoonery, yet wrote excellent letters, satires and bacchanalian and amatory songs and verses. At the last he was moved to repentance by Bishop Burnet (see Burnet's *Passages of the Life and Death of John, Earl of Rochester*, 1680). Among the best of his poems are imitations of Horace and Boileau, *Verses to Lord Mulgrave*, and *Verses upon Nothing*. See Hayward's edition of his *Works* (1926), and studies by Prinz (Leipzig, 1927) and Williams (1935), and *The Rochester-Saville Letters* (ed. Wilson 1941).

ROCHESTER, Viscount. See OVERBURY.

ROCKEFELLER, John Davison (1839–1937), American millionaire monopolist and philanthropist, born at Richford, New York, in 1857 was clerk in a commission house and then in a small oil refinery at Cleveland, Ohio, and after 1875, by his Standard Oil Company founded with his brother **William** (1841–1922), secured control of the oil trade of America. He gave over 500 million dollars in aid of medical research, universities, Baptist churches, the Rockefeller Foundation being established in 1913 'to promote the well-being of mankind. See study by W. H. Allen (1930). His son **John Davison, 2nd** (1874–1960), was chairman of the Rockefeller Institute of Medical Research. Of his sons, **John Davison, 3rd** (1906–), became chairman of the Rockefeller Foundation in 1952; **Nelson Aldrich** (1908–), elected Republican governor of New York State in 1958, was re-elected in 1962, and again in 1966; and **Winthrop** (1912–73), a racial moderate, became Republican governor of Arkansas in 1966. See book by J. Abels (1967).

ROCKINGHAM, Charles Watson Wentworth, Marquis of (1730–82), English statesman, in 1750 was created Earl of Malton and succeeded his father as second Marquis. In 1751 he was made K.G.; but, opposing the policy of Bute, was dismissed from his appointments in 1762. As leader of the Whig Opposition, he was in 1765 called on to form his first ministry. He repealed the Stamp Act, and would have done more for progress but for court intrigues and the defection of the Duke of Grafton. He resigned in 1766, and opposed Lord North and his ruinous American policy. He again became premier in March 1782, but died four months later. See *Memoirs* by the Earl of Albemarle (1852).

ROCKSTRO, William Smith (1823–95), English organist, composer and authority on old music, was born at North Cheam, Surrey. He composed songs, madrigals and piano works, and wrote a Life of Handel, histories of music, and textbooks on harmony and counterpoint.

ROD, Édouard, *rod* (1857–1910), Swiss writer, born at Nyon in Vaud, studied at Lausanne, Bonn and Berlin, was professor at Geneva, and settled in Paris. Among his thirty works are *La Chute de Miss Topsy* (1882), *La Course à la mort* (1885), *Le Sens de la vie* (1889), *Le Dernier Refuge* (1896) and *Les Unis* (1909).

RODBERTUS, Johann Karl (1805–75), German economist, founder of scientific socialism, was the son of a Greifswald professor, held law appointments under the Prussian government, but in 1836 settled down on his estate. In 1848 he entered the Prussian National Assembly, and for a fortnight was minister of education; in 1849 he carried the Frankfurt constitution. He held that the socialistic ideal will work itself out gradually according to the natural laws of change and progress. The state will then own all land and capital, and superintend the distribution of all products of labour. See studies by E. Gonner (1899) and Thier, Lassalle and Wagner (1930).

RODD, Sir James Rennell. See RENNELL OF RODD.

RODERIC, the last Visigoth king of Spain, was defeated by the Moors beside the Guadalete, July 711, was killed in or drowned after the battle (if there was such a battle), or escaped and survived till 713.

RODGERS, (1) **John** (1771–1838), American sailor, born in Maryland, in 1798 entered the U.S. navy, and in 1805 he extorted treaties from Tripoli and Tunis, and in the war with Britain took twenty-three prizes.

(2) **John** (1812–82), American sailor, son of (1), in 1863 captured the Confederate ironclad *Atlanta*, and became rear-admiral and (1877) superintendent of the U.S. naval observatory. See Memoir by Prof. J. Russell (1882).

(3) **Richard.** See HAMMERSTEIN (2).

RODIN, (François) Auguste (René), *rō-dī* (1840–1917), French sculptor, was born in Paris, November 12, 1840, the son of a clerk. After three unsuccessful attempts to enter the École des Beaux-Arts, from 1864 (the year in which he produced his first great work, *L'Homme au nez cassé*) until 1875 he worked in Paris and Brussels under the sculptors Barye, Carrier-Belleuse and Van Rasbourg, collaborating with the latter in some of the decorations for the Brussels Bourse. In 1875 he travelled in Italy, studying the work of Donatello, Michelangelo and others, and in 1877 made a tour of the French cathedrals; much later, in 1914, he published *Les Cathédrales de la France*. The Italian masters and the Gothic cathedrals both influenced Rodin's work considerably, as did his interest in the ancient Greeks, but the greatest influence on him was the current trend of Romanticism. This prolific Impressionist sculptor, who said of his work that it glorified 'the latent heroism of all natural movement', found his expression in the varying surfaces and degree of finish of his works, thus producing in sculpture of the most dramatic and imaginative conception the Impressionist painter's effects of light and shade. In 1877 Rodin exhibited anonymously at the Paris Salon the highly controversial *L'Âge d'airain*, the sculptor of which was accused of taking the cast from a living man, and in 1879 he exhibited the more highly developed *Saint Jean Baptiste*. The great *Porte de l'enfer*, inspired by Dante's *Inferno*, was commissioned for the Musée des arts décoratifs in 1880, and during the next thirty years Rodin was primarily engaged on the 186 figures for these bronze doors. Many of his works were originally conceived as part of the design of the doors, among them *Le Baiser* (1898) and *Ugolin*, both in the Luxembourg, and *Le Penseur* (1904), in front of the Panthéon in Paris. From 1886 to 1895 he worked on *Les Bourgeois de Calais*, there being replicas in London, at the Victoria Tower Gardens and in Paris of the original monument in Calais. His statues include those of Victor Hugo (1897) and Balzac (1898), the latter being refused recognition by the Societé des gens de lettres who had commissioned it; and among his portrait busts are those of Madame Rodin, Bastien-Lepage, Puvis de Chavannes, Victor Hugo and Bernard Shaw. His works are represented in the Musée Rodin, Paris, in the Rodin Museum, Philadelphia, and in the Victoria and Albert Museum, London, where there is a collection of his bronzes which he presented to the British nation in 1914. He died at Meudon near Paris, November 17, 1917. See works by Bourdelle (1937), S. Story (new ed. 1951) J. Cladel (new ed. 1953), Elsen (1964).

RODNEY, George Brydges Rodney, 1st Baron (1719–92), English sailor, born in London of an old Somersetshire family, entered the navy in 1732, was made lieutenant in 1739, in 1742 post-captain, and in 1747 had a brilliant share in Hawke's victory of October 14. Governor of Newfoundland 1748–52, in 1757 he served under Hawke in the futile expedition against Rochefort, and in 1758 under Boscawen at Louisburg. In 1759 as rear-admiral he commanded the squadron which bombarded Havre and destroyed the flotilla for the invasion of England. In 1761 he was appointed commander-in-chief on the Leeward Islands station, where in 1762 he captured Martinique, St Lucia and Grenada. A vice-admiral (1763) and baronet (1764), he was in 1765 appointed governor of Greenwich Hospital, but in 1771 was recalled to active service, and sent out as commander-in-chief at Jamaica. In 1774 he returned to England, and was on half-pay till 1779, when, again commander-in-chief at the Leeward Islands, he put to sea with a powerful squadron for the relief of Gibraltar. In January 1780 he captured a Spanish convoy off Cape Finisterre. Passing Cape St Vincent on the 16th he met the Spanish squadron, and took seven ships out of eleven. In February he sailed for the West Indies, and in April and May fought three indecisive engagements with a French fleet. Now a K.B., in January 1781 he seized the Dutch settlements. In December he again sailed for the West Indies, off Dominica sighted the French fleet under de Grasse, and on April 12, 1782, captured seven ships and de Grasse himself, a victory of which the full extent was not realized by the new administration in England until after Admiral Pigot had been sent out to supersede Rodney. On his return to England, however, Rodney was raised to the peerage and received the thanks of parliament and a pension of £2000. He thereafter lived in retirement until his death in Hanover Square, May 24, 1792. See Lives by Mundy (1830) and Hannay (1891).

RODÓ, José Enrique, *ro-*THŌ*'* (1872–1917), Uruguayan writer and critic, born at Montevideo, wrote in Spanish *Ariel*, in which he stresses the importance of spiritual as compared with materialistic values, and other philosophical essays, such as *Motivos de Proteo* and *El Mirador del Prospero*.

ROE, (1) Edward Payson (1838–88), American clergyman and novelist, born in New Windsor, N.Y., became chaplain in the volunteer service (1862–65), and afterwards pastor of a Presbyterian church at Highland Falls. The Chicago fire of 1871 furnished him with a subject for his first novel, *Barriers Burned Away* (1872), whose success led him to resign his pastorate in 1874. See memoirs and reminiscences by his sister (1899).

(2) **Sir Thomas** (*c.* 1580–1644), English diplomat, born at Low Leyton, near Wanstead, studied at Magdalen, Oxford, and, after holding court appointments, was knighted in 1605, and sent as a political agent to the West Indies, Guiana and Brazil. M.P. for Tamworth (1614), in 1615–19 he was ambassador to the Great Mogul Jahangir at Agra, to the Porte in 1621–28, and afterwards to Germany. See the journal of his mission to Agra (new ed. 1921).

ROEBUCK, (1) John (1718–94), English inventor, grandfather of (2), was born in Sheffield, studied at Edinburgh, and graduated M.D. at Leyden. He gave up his practice in Birmingham to return to chemistry research, which led to improvements in methods of refining precious metals and in the production of chemicals. In 1759 he founded in Stirlingshire the Carron ironworks, and later was a friend and patron of James Watt (q.v.).

(2) **John Arthur** (1802–79), British politician, grandson of (1), was born at Madras but brought up in Canada. Coming to England in 1824, and called to the bar in 1831, in 1832 he became Radical member for Bath. He

represented Sheffield 1849–68, and again from 1874 till his death at Westminster. His motion for inquiring into the state of the army before Sebastopol overthrew the Aberdeen administration (1855). He supported Beaconsfield's policy during the Eastern crisis in 1877–78, and in 1879 was made a privy councillor. He wrote *Colonies of England* (1849) and *History of the Whig Ministry of 1830* (1852). See Leader's edition of his *Life and Letters* (1897).

ROEMER, Olaus, *rœ'mer* (1644–1710), Danish astronomer, was born at Aarhus, Jutland, and became professor of Astronomy at Copenhagen. He discovered the finite velocity of light, which he measured by observing the time variations in the eclipses of Jupiter's satellites. He erected the earliest practical transit instrument.

ROGER, *ro'jèr*, Fr. *ro-zhay*, name of two Norman counts of Sicily, one of whom became king:

Roger I (1031–1101), joined his famous brother, Robert Guiscard (q.v.), in South Italy, and helped him to conquer Calabria. In 1060 he was invited to Sicily to fight against the Saracens, and took Messina. Everywhere the Normans were welcomed as deliverers from the Moslem yoke; in 1071 the Saracen capital, Palermo, was captured, and Robert made Roger Count of Sicily. After Robert's death (1085) Roger succeeded to his Italian possessions, and became the head of the Norman power in southern Europe.

Roger II (1095–1154), second son of (1), became Count of Sicily, his mother at first acting as regent. On the death (1127) of the Duke of Apulia, grandson of Robert Guiscard, his duchy passed to Roger, who thereupon welded Sicily and South Italy into a strong Norman kingdom, of which he was crowned king by Anacletus the antipope in 1130. He next added to his dominions Capua (1136), Naples and the Abruzzi (1140). In 1139 he took prisoner Pope Innocent II, with whom he concluded a bargain, Innocent recognizing him as King of Sicily, whilst Roger acknowledged Innocent and held his kingdom as a fief of the Holy See. The Byzantine Emperor Manuel having insulted his ambassador, Roger's admiral, George of Antioch, ravaged the coasts of Dalmatia and Epirus, took Corfu, and plundered Corinth and Athens (1146). He carried off silk-workers, and introduced that industry into Sicily. Finally (1147), Roger won Tripoli, Tunis and Algeria. His court was one of the most magnificent in Europe, and his government was firm and enlightened.

ROGER-DUCASSE, Jean Jules Aimable, *ro-zhay-dü-kas* (1873–1954), French composer, was born and died in Bordeaux. He studied under Fauré, in 1909 was appointed inspector of singing to Paris schools, and in 1935 succeeded Dukas at the Paris Conservatoire. His works include piano pieces, an opera, *Cantegril* (1931), choral works, and orchestral pieces. See French study by L. Ceillier (Paris 1920).

ROGER OF HOVEDON, English chronicler, was probably born at Howden in Yorkshire, and died about 1201, with which year his Latin *Chronicle* ends. It was edited by Stubbs (Rolls Series, 1868–71) and translated by Riley (1853).

ROGER OF WENDOVER (d. 1236), prior of the Benedictine monastery of St Albans, revised and carried on the abbey chronicle, enlarged later by Matthew Paris (q.v.).

ROGERS, (1) **Bernard** (1893–), American composer, born in New York. He studied under Ernest Bloch and Nadia Boulanger, and lived for a time in England, before becoming a professor of Composition at the Eastman School of Music. An amateur painter, much of his music is pictorial in intention, and he composes mainly for orchestra in classical forms. His works include operas, symphonies, an oratorio, *The Passion* (1941–42), and cantatas on Biblical subjects.

(2) **Claude** (1907–), English artist, born in London, studied and lectured at the Slade School, professor of Fine Art at Reading Univ. from 1963, and president of the London group from 1952 until 1965. With Victor Pasmore and William Coldstream he founded the Euston Road School in 1937. His work is represented in the Tate Gallery, Ashmolean Museum, &c.

(3) **James Edwin Thorold** (1823–90), English economist, born at West Meon, Hampshire, became professor of Political Economy at Oxford 1862–67, but made so many enemies by his outspoken zeal for reforms that he was not re-elected till 1888. An advanced Liberal, he represented Southwark 1880–85, and Bermondsey 1885–86. He wrote many works on economics.

(4) **John** (*c.* 1500–55), English Marian protomartyr, born near Birmingham, was a London rector 1532–34, and at Antwerp and Wittenberg embraced the Reformed doctrines. He helped to prepare the revised translation called 'Matthew's Bible' in 1537, and, having married and returned to England in 1548, preached at St Paul's Cross in 1553, just after Mary's accession, against Romanism, and was burned. See Life by J. L. Chester (1861).

(5) **Randolph** (1825–92), U.S. sculptor, lived in Rome, was born at Waterloo, N.Y. His statues include *Ruth* (Metropolitan Museum, N.Y.) and *Lincoln* (Philadelphia).

(6) **Samuel** (1763–1855), English poet, born at Stoke-Newington, at sixteen or seventeen entered his father's bank, in 1784 was taken into partnership, and in 1793 became head of the firm. In 1781 he contributed essays to the *Gentleman's Magazine*, next year wrote a comic opera, and in 1786 published *An Ode to Superstition*. In 1792 appeared *The Pleasures of Memory*, on which his poetical fame was chiefly based (19th ed. 1816). There followed *An Epistle to a Friend* (Richard Sharp, 1798), the fragmentary *Voyage of Columbus* (1812), *Jacqueline* (1814, bound up with Byron's *Lara*), and the inimitable *Italy* (1822–28). The last, in blank verse, proved a monetary failure; but the loss was recouped by the splendid edition of it and his earlier poems, brought out at a cost of £15,000 (1830–34), with 114 illustrations by Turner and Stothard. In 1803, with £5000 a year, he withdrew from the bank as a sleeping partner, and settled down to bachelor life at 22 St James's Place, to cultivate his muse and

caustic wit, to raise breakfast-giving to a fine art, to make little tours at home and on the Continent, and to gather an art collection which sold at his death for £50,000. He made a good use of his riches, for he was quietly generous to Moore and Campbell, as well as to some unknown writers. But with the kindest heart he had so unkind a tongue that 'melodious Rogers' is better remembered today by a few ill-natured sayings than by his poetry. See Dyce's *Table-talk of Samuel Rogers* (1856); *Recollections by Rogers*, edited by his nephew William Sharpe (1859); works by Clayden (1887, 1889) and Roberts (1910); the *Reminiscences and Table-talk*, ed. Powell (1903) and C. P. Barbier, *Samuel Rogers and William Gilpin* (1959).

(7) **Woodes** (d. 1732), **English navigator**, led a privateering expedition against the Spanish (1708–11) which took off Alexander Selkirk (q.v.) from Juan Fernández island and on his successful return wrote *Voyage round the World* (1712). As governor of the Bahamas (1718–21, 1729–32) he suppressed piracy, founded a House of Assembly and resisted Spanish attacks.

ROGET, Peter Mark, *ro-zhay* (1779–1869), English scholar and physician, son of a Huguenot minister, became physician to the Manchester Infirmary in 1804; physician to the Northern Dispensary, London, in 1808, F.R.S. (1815), and its secretary 1827–49; Fullerian professor of Physiology at the Royal Institution 1833–36; and an original member of senate of London University. He wrote *On Animal and Vegetable Physiology* (Bridgewater Treatise, 1834); and his *Thesaurus of English Words and Phrases* (1852) reached a 28th edition in his lifetime.

ROGIER VAN DER WEYDEN. See WEYDEN.

ROHAN-GIÉ, Henri, Duc de, *rō-ã-zhee-ay* (1579–1638), Prince of Léon, born at the Château of Blain in Brittany, was a favourite of Henry IV, and in 1605 married the daughter of Sully. After the king's murder he became a Huguenot leader. On the surrender of La Rochelle (1628) a price was set on his head, and he made his way to Venice, but soon after was summoned by Richelieu to serve his king in the Valtelline, out of which he drove Imperialists and Spaniards. He next served under Bernard of Saxe-Weimar, but died in 1638 of a wound received at Rheinfelden. See his *Mémoires* (1630 and 1738), and works by Fauvelet du Toc (1667), Schybergson (1880), Lagarde (1884), Laugel (1889), and Veraguth (German, 1894), and the *Edinburgh Review* for April 1890.

ROHAN-GUÉMÉNÉE, Louis René Édouard, Prince de, *rō-ã-gay-may-nay* (1734–1803), French cardinal, embraced the clerical life in spite of dissolute morals, and became coadjutor to his uncle the Bishop of Strasbourg. In 1772 he was sent as minister to Vienna, but injured himself at the French court by slanderous gossip about Marie Antoinette, and was recalled in 1774. In 1778 he received a cardinal's hat, and in 1779 became Bishop of Strasbourg. His eagerness to recover his footing at court made him an easy prey to Cagliostro and the Comtesse de La Motte, who tricked him into believing that the queen, who knew nothing of the affair, wished him to stand security for her purchase by instalments of a priceless diamond necklace. The adventurers collected the necklace from the jewellers supposedly to give it to the queen, but left Paris in order to sell the diamonds for their own gain. When the plot was discovered Rohan Guéménée was sent to the Bastille, but was acquitted by the *parlement* of Paris, 1786. He was elected to the States-General in 1789, but refused to take the oath to the constitution in 1791, retiring to the German part of his diocese, where he died. See works cited at LA MOTTE (2).

ROHLFS, Gerhard, *rōlfs* (1831–96), German explorer, born at Vegesack near Bremen, studied medicine, and joined (1855) the Foreign Legion in Algeria. He travelled through Morocco (1861–62), and was plundered and left for dead in the Sahara. From 1864 he travelled widely in North Africa, the Sahara and Nigeria, and, commissioned by the German emperor, undertook expeditions to Wadai (1878) and Abyssinia (1885). He wrote books about his travels, including *Drei Monate in der Libyschen Wüste* (1875) and *Quid novi ex Africa?* (1886).

RÖHM, Ernst, *rœm* (1887–1934), German soldier, politician and Nazi leader, early a supporter of Hitler, was organizer and commander of the stormtroopers, and as such was executed on Hitler's orders in June 1934. See his Memoirs (1934).

ROHMER, Sax, pseud. of **Arthur Sarsfield Ward**, *rō'mėr* (1886–1959), English author of mystery stories, was born in Birmingham. Early interested in things Egyptian, he found literary fame with his sinister, sardonic, Oriental villain, Fu Manchu, whose doings were told in many spine-chilling tales of the East, including *Dr Fu Manchu* (1913), *The Yellow Claw* (1915), *Moon of Madness* (1927) and *Re-enter Fu Manchu* (1957).

ROKITANSKY, Karl, Baron von (1804–78), Austrian physician, born in Königgrätz, professor 1834–75 of Pathological Anatomy at Vienna, wrote the great *Handbuch der pathologischen Anatomie* (1842–46; trans. 1849–52).

ROKOSSOVSKY, Konstantin, *-sof'ski* (1896–1968), Russian soldier, born in Warsaw of Polish descent, served in the first World War in the tsarist army, and joined the Red Guards in 1917. In the second World War he was one of the defenders of Moscow, played a leading part in the battle of Stalingrad, recaptured Orel and Warsaw, and led the Russian race for Berlin. In 1944 he was promoted marshal of the Soviet Union, and at the end of the war Field-Marshal Montgomery presented him with the Order of the Bath (K.C.B.). In 1949 he was appointed Polish minister of defence, a post he was made to resign when Gomulka became premier in November 1956. He then became a deputy-minister of defence of the Soviet Union, and in 1957 he was appointed to a military command in Transcaucasia.

ROLAND, *ro-lã* (acc. to tradition d. 778), hero of the *Chanson de Roland* (11th century) and most celebrated of the Paladins of Charlemagne, was the nephew of Charlemagne, and the ideal of a Christian knight. The only evidence for his historical existence is one (doubtfully genuine) passage in Einhard's *Life of Charlemagne*, which refers to Roland as having fallen at Roncesvalles. Boiardo's *Orlando Innamorato* and Ariosto's *Orlando Furioso* depart widely from the old traditions.

ROLAND DE LA PLATIÈRE, Jean Marie, *ro-lã dė la pla-tyayr* (1734–93), French statesman, born near Villefranche-sur-Saône, February 18, 1734, had risen to be inspector of manufactures at Amiens, when in 1775 he made the acquaintance of **Marie Jeanne Phlipon** (1754–93), the daughter of an engraver, whom he married in February 1780. In 1791 Roland was sent to Paris by Lyons to watch the interests of the municipality; and there Madame Roland became the queen of a coterie of young and eloquent enthusiasts that included all the leaders of the Gironde, such as Brissot, Pétion and François Buzot (1760–94). In March 1792 Roland became minister of the interior, but was dismissed three months later for a remonstrance to the king. He was recalled after the king's removal to the Temple, made himself hateful to the Jacobins by his protests against the September massacres, and took part in the last struggle of the Girondists. It was then that the friendship between Madame Roland and Buzot grew into love, but she sacrificed passion to duty. On May 31, 1793, the Twenty-two were proscribed. Roland had been arrested, but escaped and fled to Rouen; Buzot and others fled to Caen to organize insurrection, but in vain; next day Madame Roland was carried to the Abbaye. Set at liberty two days later, she was arrested anew and taken to Sainte-Pélagie. During her five months in prison she wrote her unfinished *Mémoires*, in which we have a serene and delightful revelation of her youth, though she is best and most natural in her letters. On November 8, 1793, she was guillotined. Two days later her husband committed suicide by his sword near Rouen. See book by U. Pope-Hennessy (1917).

ROLLAND, Romain, *ro-lã* (1866–1944), French author, born in Clamecy, Nièvre, studied in Paris and at the French School in Rome, and in 1895 gained his doctorate of letters with a thesis on early opera, *L'Histoire de l'opéra en Europe avant Lulli et Scarlatti*; a number of dramatic works written at this time won comparatively little success. In 1910 he became professor of the History of Music at the Sorbonne, and in the same year published *Beethoven*, the first of many biographical works including lives of Michelangelo (1906), Handel (1910), Tolstoy (1911) and Gandhi (1924). His ten-volume novel *Jean-Christophe*, the hero of which is a musician, was written between 1904 and 1912, and in 1915 he was awarded the Nobel prize for literature. During the first World War he aroused unpopularity by his writings, out of Switzerland, showing a pacifist attitude; these were published in 1915 as *Au dessus de la mêlée*. He lived in Switzerland until 1938, completing a series of plays upon the French Revolution, several novels, and a further study of Beethoven, as well as numerous pieces of music criticism. On his return to France he became a mouthpiece of the opposition to Fascism and Naziism, and his later works contain much political and social writing. See books by S. Zweig (1921), M. Descotes (Paris 1948) and R. Arcos (Paris 1950).

ROLLE, Richard. See HAMPOLE.

ROLLESTON, George, *rōl'stėn* (1829–81), English physician, born near Rotherham, elected Linacre professor of Anatomy and Physiology at Oxford in 1860, is known for his *Forms of Animal Life* (1876) and for his dissertation on craniology in Greenwell's *British Barrows* (1877).

ROLLIN, *ro-lĩ*, (1) **Charles** (1661–1741), French historian, born in Paris, was author of *Traité des études* (1726–31), *Histoire ancienne* (1730–38) and *Histoire romaine* (1738–48). He lost the rectorship of Paris University (1720) and other academic posts because of his Jansenist sympathies.

(2) **Ledru.** See LEDRU-ROLLIN.

ROLLO, or **Rou** (*c.* 860–*c.* 932), leader of a band of Northmen, secured from Charles the Simple in 912 a large district on condition of being baptized and becoming Charles's vassal. This grant was the nucleus of the duchy of Normandy. William the Conqueror's ancestor, Rollo is probably the same as Rolf the Ganger, a Norwegian chief outlawed by Harold Haarfager about 872.

ROLLOCK, Robert, *rol'ėk* (*c.* 1555–99), born at Powis near Stirling, in 1583 became first regent, in 1585 first principal, of Edinburgh University. He wrote Latin commentaries. See Masson's *Edinburgh Sketches* (1892).

ROLLS, Charles Stewart, *rōlz* (1877–1910), automobilist and aeronaut, was born in London, the third son of the 1st Baron Llangattock. Educated at Eton and Cambridge, from 1895 he experimented with the earliest motor cars and combined with F. H. Royce (q.v.) for their production. In 1906 he crossed the English Channel by balloon, and in 1910 made a double crossing by aeroplane. He lost his life in a crash soon afterwards. See H. F. Morriss, *Two Brave Brothers* (1929), and study by L. Meynell (1955).

RÖLVAAG, Ole Edvart, *rol'vahg* (1876–1931), American author, born at Dönna, Norway, emigrated to America, becoming an American citizen in 1910. Writing in Norwegian, he published in 1912 his *Letters from America*, and his best-known novel, translated as *Giants in the Earth* (1927), dealing with the life of Norwegian settlers in South Dakota in the 1870s, was followed by *Peder Victorious* (1929) and *Their Fathers' God* (1931). See biography by Jorgenson and Solum (1939).

ROMAINS, Jules, *ro-mĩ*, pseud. of **Louis Farigoule** (1885–1972), French writer, born at Saint-Julien Chapteuil, after graduating in both science and literature at the École normale supérieure, taught in various lycées. In 1908 his poems, *La Vie unanime*, established his name and, along with his *Manuel de déification* (1910), the Unanimist school. He remained prominent in French literature, and was from 1936 to 1941 president of the International P.E.N. Club. His works include the books of poems *Odes et prières* (1913), *Chants des dix années 1914–1924* (1928), *L'Homme blanc* (1937), the dramas

L'Armée dans la ville (1911), *Knock ou le triomphe de la médecine* (1923), his most successful play, and the novels *Mort de quelqu'un* (1910), *Les Copains* (1913), and the great cycle *Les Hommes de bonne volonté* in 27 volumes (1932–46), covering the early 20th-century era of French life. See his autobiographical *Souvenirs et confidences d'un écrivain* (1958).

ROMAN, Johan Helmich, *roo'man* (1694–1758), Swedish composer of the baroque era, twice visited England, where he met Handel, Geminiani and other leading figures in contemporary music, travelled in France and Italy, and in 1745 was appointed *intendent* of music to the Swedish court. His compositions, which include symphonies, concerti grossi, trio sonatas, a Swedish Mass, settings in the vernacular of the Psalms, and occasional music, show the influence of the Italian style and, less markedly, of Handel and the French and North German schools.

ROMANES, George John, *rō-mah'neez* (1848–1894), British naturalist, born at Kingston, Canada. While at Cambridge University he formed a friendship with Darwin, and he powerfully reinforced his master's arguments in his Croonian, Fullerian and other lectures, and in his various works—*Animal Intelligence* (1881), *Scientific Evidences of Organic Evolution* (1881), &c. He was elected an F.R.S. in 1879, married in that year, removed in 1890 to Oxford, and died there in 1894. Originally a defiant agnostic or sceptic, he was latterly a devout, if not wholly orthodox, Christian. See Life by his wife (1896).

ROMANINO, Girolamo (1485–1566), Italian religious painter, was born and died at Brescia, and worked in Padua, Venice and Cremona. See Pater's *Miscellaneous Studies* (1895).

ROMANO, Giulio. See GIULIO.

ROMANOV, *ro-ma'nof*, a family that originally emigrated from (Slavonic) Prussia to the principality of Moscow. Its head, Michael, was elected tsar by the other Russian boyars in 1613, and the tsardom became hereditary in his house till in 1762, on the death of the Tsaritsa Elizabeth, the Duke of Holstein-Gottorp, son of Peter the Great's daughter, succeeded as Peter III. Later tsars (till the 1917 revolution) were descended from him and his wife, Catharine II.

ROMILLY, Sir Samuel (1757–1818), English lawyer and law reformer, was born in London, the son of a watchmaker of Huguenot descent. At twenty-one he entered Gray's Inn, and found his chief employment in Chancery practice. In 1790 he published an able pamphlet on the French Revolution. Appointed solicitor-general in 1806, and knighted, he entered parliament and pertinaciously set himself to mitigate the severity of the criminal law. He shared in the anti-slavery agitation, and opposed the suspension of the Habeas Corpus Act and the spy system. He committed suicide three days after his wife's death. See his *Speeches* (1820), *Memoirs* (1840), and a book by C. G. Oakes (1935). His second son, **John, Baron Romilly** (1802–74), was solicitor-general in 1848, attorney-general in 1850, master of the rolls in 1851, and a baron in 1866.

ROMMEL, Erwin (1891–1944), German field-marshal, born at Heidenheim, educated at Tübingen, distinguished himself in World War I. An instructor at the Dresden Military Academy, Rommel was an early Nazi sympathizer. He commanded Hitler's headquarters guard during the Austrian, Sudetenland and Czech occupations and throughout the Polish campaign. Leading a Panzer Division during the 1940 invasion of France, he displayed such drive and initiative that he was promoted to command the Afrika Korps, where his spectacular successes against the attenuated 8th Army earned him the sobriquet of the 'Desert Fox' and the unstinted admiration of his opponents. *Rusé* and brilliantly opportunist, and with a talent for improvisation extremely rare in the German, his chief defect was a tendency to desert his headquarters in action for 'up forward', and thus lose control of the battle. Eventually driven into retreat by a strongly reinforced 8th Army, he was withdrawn—a sick man—from North Africa at Mussolini's insistence, the Duce believing that 'the Italian generals do better' (Goebbels Diaries). Hitler consoled him with the award of the Knight's Cross with diamonds, subsequently appointing him to an Army Corps command in France. Returning home wounded in 1944, his condoning of the plot against the Fuehrer's life brought him the choice between court martial and the firing squad, and suicide. He chose to die by self-administered poison, thus preserving his estate for his family. See *Rommel*, Young (1950), *The Rommel Papers* (1953).

ROMNEY, George, *rom'ni* or *rum'ni* (1734–1802), English painter, born at Dalton-in-Furness, Lancashire, worked for ten years at his father's trade of cabinetmaker. In 1755 he was articled to a 'Count' Steele at Kendal to be taught 'the art or science of a painter'; in 1756 married Mary Abbot of Kirkland; in 1757 set up as a portrait painter; and in 1762 came up to London, leaving behind wife, boy and baby girl, because, it is said, Sir Joshua Reynolds had told him that art and marriage do not mix. Of Romney's next thirty-five years there is little to record beyond his two visits to France (1764; 1790) and his two years' residence in Italy (1773–75), after which, for twenty-two years, he lived in Cavendish Square, and slaved at his art, which so far rewarded him that in 1786 he made by portrait painting 3500 guineas. Lady Hamilton (q.v.) he painted in fully thirty characters. *Sensibility*, Miss Sneyd as *Serena*, and *The Parson's Daughter* are also well known. In 1799, nearly mad and quite desolate, Romney returned to Kendal to his wife, who received him charitably and nursed him with devotion until his death in 1802. See, besides the Memoirs by Hayley (1809) and his son, the Rev. John Romney (1830), the Lives by Ward and Roberts (1904), and Henderson (1922); also works by Gower (1882, 1904), Chamberlain (1911) and Lloyd (1917).

ROMULUS, *rom'yoo-lus*, legendary founder and first king of Rome, according to tradition the son by Mars of Rhea Silvia, the daughter of King Numitor of Alba Longa, with his twin brother Remus exposed by a usurping uncle, but suckled by a she-wolf. In 753 B.C. he founded his city on the Tiber, and in 716 was said to have been carried up to heaven in a chariot of fire.

ROMULUS AUGUSTUS. See AUGUSTULUS.

RONALD, orig. **Russell, Sir Landon** (1873–1938), English conductor, composer and pianist, was a son of Henry Russell, the songwriter. He toured with Melba, conducted the New Symphony Orchestra, notably in Elgar, Strauss and Tchaikovsky, was principal of the Guildhall School of Music (1910–37), wrote many songs, including 'Down in the Forest Something Stirred', and was knighted in 1922. See his autobiographical *Variations on a Personal Theme* (1922) and *Myself and Others* (1931).

RONALDS, Sir Francis (1788–1873), English inventor, a London merchant's son, in 1816 fitted up in his garden at Hammersmith an electric telegraph. His offer of the invention to the Admiralty was refused; he published a description of it in 1823. He also invented (1845) a system of automatic photographic registration for meteorological instruments. He was made superintendent of the Meteorological Observatory at Kew in 1843, F.R.S. in 1844, and knighted in 1871.

RONDELET, Guillaume, *rõ-dė-lay* (1507–66), French naturalist and physician, was born at Montpellier, where he became in 1545 professor of Medicine, and published two important works (1544 and 1555) on aquatic animals of the Mediterranean.

RONSARD, Pierre de, *rõ-sahr* (1524–85), French poet, born at the Château de la Possonnière in Vendôme, September 11, served the dauphin and the Duc d'Orléans as page, and accompanied James V with his bride, Marie de Lorraine, to Scotland, where he stayed three years. Becoming deaf, he abandoned arms for letters, and studied under the great humanist Jean Dorat, at first with his future fellow member of the Pléiade, Jean Antoine de Baïf, at the house of his father the scholar and diplomat Lazare de Baïf, and later at the Collège de Coqueret, where du Bellay and Belleau (qq.v.) joined them. His seven years of study bore its first fruit in the *Odes* (1550), which excited violent opposition from the older national school. In 1552 appeared his *Amours*, a collection of Petrarchian sonnets, followed by his *Bocage* (1554), his *Hymnes* (1555), the conclusion of his *Amours* (1556), and the first collected edition of his poetry (1560). He subsequently wrote two bitter reflections on the political and economic state of the country—*Discours des misères de ce temps* (1560–69) and *Remonstrance au peuple de France* (1563), and in 1572, following the massacre of St Bartholomew, *La Françiade*, an unfinished epic. Charles IX, like his predecessors, heaped favours on the poet, who, despite recurrent illness, spent his later years in comfort at the abbey of Croix-Val in Vendôme. He died at his priory of St Cosme-les-Tours. The most important poet of 16th-century France, Ronsard was the chief exemplar of the doctrines of the Pléiade, which aimed at raising the status of French as a literary language and ousting the formal classicism inherited from the Middle Ages. Despite the great success of Ronsard's poems in his lifetime, the classicists regained the upper hand after his death, and his fame suffered an eclipse until the 19th century, when the Romantic movement brought recognition of his true worth. See Lives by Binet (1586) and Bishop (1940), and studies by Franchet (1922), Cohen (1923), Gadoffre (1960), and Desonay (3 vols., 1952, 1954, 1961).

RÖNTGEN, Wilhelm Konrad von, *rœnt'gėn* (1845–1923), German physicist, was born at Lennep in Prussia, studied at Zürich, and was professor at Strasbourg, Giessen, Würzburg, and (1899–1919) Munich. At Würzburg in 1895 he discovered the electric-magnetic rays which he called X-rays (known also as Röntgen rays), and for his work on them he was awarded in 1896, jointly with Lenard (q.v.), the Rumford medal, and in 1901 the Nobel prize for physics. He also did important work on the heat conductivity of crystals, the specific heat of gases, and the electromagnetic rotation of polarized light. See study by O. Glasser (new ed. 1958).

ROOKE, Sir George (1650–1709), English admiral, born near Canterbury, became at thirty post-captain, and in 1689 rear-admiral. In 1692 he did splendid service at Cape La Hogue, and was knighted. In 1702 he commanded the expedition against Cadiz, and destroyed the plate-fleet at Vigo. With Sir Cloudesley Shovel he captured Gibraltar (1704), and then engaged off Málaga a much heavier French fleet. See his *Journal* (1897).

ROON, Albrecht Theodor Emil, Graf von, *rõn* (1803–79), Prussian war minister from 1859, effectively reorganized the army and wrote on military subjects.

ROOSEVELT, *rōz'ė-velt,* (1) **Anna Eleanor** (1884–1962), niece of (3), wife of (2), whom she married in 1905, took up extensive political work during her husband's eight years' illness and proved herself an invaluable social adviser to him when he became president. In 1941 she became assistant director of the office of civilian defence; after her husband's death in 1945 she extended the scope of her activities, and was a delegate to the U.N. Assembly in 1946, chairman of the U.N. Human Rights Commission (1947–51) and U.S. representative at the General Assembly (1946–52). She was also chairman of the American U.N. Association. Her publications include *The Lady of the White House* (1938), *India and the Awakening East* (1953), *On My Own* (1959), and her Autobiography (1962).

(2) **Franklin Delano** (1884–1945), thirty-second president of the United States, a distant cousin of (3), was born near Poughkeepsie, N.Y. He became a barrister (1907), a New York state senator (1910–13), assistant secretary of the navy (1913–20), and was Democratic candidate for the vice-presidency in 1920. Stricken (1921–24) by paralysis, he was governor of New York (1928–32). In the presidential election of 1932 he defeated Hoover, repeal of prohibition being made a vital party issue, and at once in 1933 met an economic crisis with his 'New Deal' for national recovery. He was elected for a second term in 1936, a third (a new thing in American

history) in 1940, a fourth in 1944. He strove in vain to ward off war, modified America's neutrality to favour the Allies (as by the Lend-Lease plan), and was brought in by Japan's action at Pearl Harbour (1941). A conference with Churchill at sea produced the 'Atlantic Charter', a statement of peace aims; and there were other notable meetings, as with Churchill and Stalin at Tehran and Yalta. He died at Warm Springs, Georgia, where he had long gone for treatment, three weeks before the Nazi surrender. See studies by Lindley (1932, 1933 and 1937), Perkins (1947), Sherwood, *Roosevelt and Hopkins*, Schlesinger, *The Age of Roosevelt* (3 vols., 1957, 1959, 1961), and Leuchtenburg, *F.D.R. and the New Deal* (1963).

(3) **Theodore** (1858–1919), twenty-sixth president of the United States, was born, of Dutch and Scottish descent, in New York, studied at Harvard, was leader of the New York legislature in 1884, and president of the New York police board in 1895–97. He was assistant secretary of the navy when in 1898 he raised and commanded 'Roosevelt's Roughriders' in the Cuban war, and came back to be governor of New York State (1898–1900). Appointed (Republican) vice-president (1901), he became president on the death (by assassination) of McKinley (1901), and was re-elected in 1905. An 'expansionist', he insisted on a strong navy, the purification of the civil service, and the regulation of trusts and monopolies. He returned from a great hunting tour in Central Africa in time to take active part in the elections of 1910, and helped to split the Republican party, those with whom he acted forming the 'progressive' section. As Progressive candidate for the presidency in 1912 he was defeated by Wilson. After exploring the Rio Duvida, or Teodoro, in Brazil (1914), he worked vigorously during World War I. He wrote on American ideals, ranching, hunting, zoology. See his *Autobiography* (1913), G. E. Mowry, *The Era of Theodore Roosevelt* (1958), and Lives by Pringle (1932) and Putnam (1959).

ROOT, Elihu (1845–1937), American statesman, born at Clinton, N.Y., was U.S. secretary of war 1899–1904, of state 1905–09, and was awarded a Nobel peace prize in 1912 for his promotion of international arbitration.

ROOZEBOOM, Hendrik Willem Bakhuis, *rō'zē-bōm* (1854–1907), Dutch physical chemist, born at Alkmaar, became professor of Chemistry at Amsterdam. He demonstrated the practical application of Gibbs's phase rule.

ROPER, Margaret. See MORE (3).

ROPS, Felicien (1833–98), Belgian artist, born at Namur, known for his lithographs and etchings, which often had satirical or social significance, and for his illustrations of the works of Baudelaire.

RORSCHACH, Hermann (1884–1922), Swiss psychiatrist and neurologist, born at Zürich, devised a diagnostic procedure for mental disorders based upon the patients' interpretation of a series of standardized ink blots. See Klopfer and Kelly, *Rorschach Technique* (1946).

ROSA, *rō'za,* **(1) orig. Rose, Carl August Nicolas** (1842–89), German impresario and violinist, born at Hamburg, became *konzertmeister* there in 1863, appeared in London as a soloist in 1866, and in 1873 founded the Carl Rosa Opera Company, giving a great impulse to 'English opera'—opera sung in English, and also operas by English composers.

(2) **Salvator** (1615–73), Italian painter, was born near Naples. At Rome his talents as painter, improvisatore, actor and poet brought him fame, but he made powerful enemies by his satires, and withdrew to Florence for nine years. After that he returned to Rome, where he died. Salvator owes his reputation mainly to his landscapes of wild and savage scenes. He executed numerous etchings. His *Satires* were published in 1719. A theory that he was also a composer has now been disproved. See Lives by Baldinucci (new ed. 1830), Cantu (1844) and Cattaneo (1929).

ROSAMOND. See ALBOIN; CLIFFORD Family.

ROSAS, Juan Manuel de (1793–1877), Argentine dictator, born in Buenos Aires, became commander-in-chief in 1826, and was governor of the province in 1829–32. Disappointed of re-election, he headed a revolt, and from 1835 to 1852 governed as dictator. His rule was one of terror and bloodshed. In 1849 Rosas secured for Buenos Aires the entire navigation of the Plate, the Uruguay and the Paraná. This roused the other river provinces, and Urquiza, governor of Entre Ríos, supported by Brazil, in February 1852 routed him at Monte Caseros near Buenos Aires. Rosas escaped to England, where he lived till his death.

ROSCELLINUS, Johannes, *ros-ė-lī'nus* (*c.* 1050–after 1120), French scholar, born probably at Compiègne and studied at Soissons. He defended Nominalism, of which he is considered the founder, against attacks by Abelard. In 1092 the council of Soissons condemned his teaching as implicitly involving the negation of the doctrine of the Trinity.

ROSCIUS, Quintus (*c.* 134–62 B.C.), a slave by birth, became the greatest comic actor in Rome, reckoned the dictator Sulla and Cicero among his patrons, and gave Cicero lessons in elocution. He wrote a treatise on eloquence and acting. On his being sued at law for 50,000 sesterces, Cicero defended him in his extant oration, *Pro Q. Roscio Comoedo.* —For the 'Young Roscius', see BETTY.

ROSCOE, (1) Sir Henry Enfield (1833–1915), English chemist, grandson of (2), was born in London and educated at Liverpool High School, University College, London, and Heidelberg, where with Bunsen he did research on quantitative photochemistry. From 1857 to 1886 he was professor of Chemistry at Manchester, and worked on the preparation and properties of pure vanadium. Elected F.R.S. in 1863 and knighted in 1884, he was Liberal M.P. for South Manchester 1885–95, vice-chancellor of London University 1896–1902. His works include *Spectrum Analysis* (1868), the great *Treatise on Chemistry* (with Schorlemmer; 6 vols. 1878–89), a book on Dalton, and his own *Life and Experiences* (1906). See short Life by Thorpe (1916).

(2) **William** (1753–1831), English historian, grandfather of (1), born at Liverpool, in 1769 was articled to an attorney, and began to practise in 1774. In 1777 he published a poem, *Mount Pleasant*, and in 1787 *The Wrongs of Africa*, a protest against the slave trade. But it was his *Life of Lorenzo de' Medici* (1796) that established his literary reputation. His second great book, *Life of Leo X* (1805), like the former, was translated into German, French and Italian. He had retired from business in 1796, but in 1799 became partner in a Liverpool bank, which involved him (1816–20) in pecuniary embarrassment. He also wrote poems, of which the best known is the *Butterfly's Ball* (1807); an edition of Pope; and a monograph on Monandrian plants. See Life by his son, Henry (1833), and Espinasse's *Lancashire Worthies* (2nd series, 1877).

ROSE, (1) **George** (1744–1818), English statesman, father of (5), a supporter of Pitt, born near Brechin, died near Lyndhurst. See his *Diaries* (1859).

(2) **Hugh.** See STRATHNAIRN.

(3) **Hugh James** (1795–1838), English theologian, born at Little Horsted, Sussex, studied at Trinity, Cambridge. At his Suffolk rectory was held in 1833 the 'Hadleigh conference' that preceded the Tractarian movement. See Burgon's *Twelve Good Men* (1888).

(4) **John Holland** (1855–1942), English historian, born at Bedford, was professor of Naval History at Cambridge (1919–33) and an authority on Napoleon.

(5) **William Stewart** (1775–1843), English poet and translator, son of (1), rendered Casti's *Animali Parlanti* (1819) and the *Orlando Furioso* of Ariosto (8 vols. 1823–31) into English verse.

ROSEBERY, Archibald Philip Primrose, 5th Earl of (1847–1929), British statesman, born in London, and educated at Eton and Christ Church, succeeded his grandfather in 1868. In 1874 he was president of the Social Science Congress, and in 1878 lord rector of Aberdeen University, in 1880 of Edinburgh, in 1899 of Glasgow, in 1881–83 under-secretary for the Home Department, and in 1884 became first commissioner of works. In July 1886, and again in 1892–94, he was secretary for foreign affairs in the Gladstone administration. Cambridge gave him the degree of LL.D. in 1888. In 1889–90 and 1892 he was chairman of the London County Council. On the retirement of Gladstone he became Liberal premier (March 1894); and after his government had been defeated at the general election (1895) remained leader of the Liberal Opposition till 1896, when he resigned the leadership. A spokesman for imperial federation, he was imperialist during the Boer war, and as head of the Liberal League from 1902 represented a policy, first set forth in a famous speech at Chesterfield, but not accepted by official Liberals. His attitude in 1909–10 was Independent or Conservative. In 1911 he was created Earl of Midlothian. He died May 21, 1929. Lord Rosebery published books on Pitt (1891), Peel (1899), the 'last phase' of Napoleon's career (1900), Chatham (1910), and *Miscellanies* (2 vols. 1921). In 1878 he married Hannah (1851–90), the only daughter of Baron Meyer de Rothschild. He won the Derby thrice (1894, 1895, 1905). See Lives by the Marquis of Crewe (1931) and James (1963).

ROSECRANS, William Starke, *rōz'krans* (1819–98), American general, born at Kingston, Ohio, in 1861 became aide to McClellan, whom he succeeded, and kept Lee out of Western Virginia. In 1862 he commanded a division at the siege of Corinth, and after its capture commanded the army of the Mississippi; in September he defeated Price at Iuka, and in October defended Corinth against Price and Van Dorn. In the battles at Stone River (December 1862 and January 1863), against Bragg, he converted what had nearly been a defeat into a victory; but at Chickamauga, September 19–20, 1863, he was defeated by Bragg, although he held Chattanooga. He was superseded by Grant, but in 1864 repelled Price's invasion of Missouri. In 1868–69 he was minister to Mexico, in 1881–85 congressman, and then registrar of the U.S. treasury (1885–93).

ROSEGGER, Peter, known until 1894 as **P. K. (Petri Kettenfeier),** *rōz'ėg-gėr* (1843–1918), Austrian poet and novelist, was born of peasant parents near Krieglach, Styria. In 1870 he published *Zither und Hackbrett*, a volume of poems in his native dialect, and followed this with autobiographical works such as *Waldheimat* (1897) and later *Mein Himmelreich* (1901), and novels, including *Die Schriften des Waldschulmeisters* (1875), *Der Gottsucher* (1883) and *Jakob der Letzte* (1888), vividly portraying his native district and its people. See study by F. Pock (1943) and his biography and letters by O. Janda (1948).

ROSENBERG, *rō'-*, (1) **Alfred** (1893–1946), German politician, was born in Estonia. An avid supporter of National Socialism, he joined the party in 1920, edited Nazi journals, for a time (1933) directed the Party's foreign policy, and in 1934 was given control of its cultural and political education policy. In his *The Myth of the 20th Century* (1930) he expounded the extreme Nazi doctrines which he later put into practice in eastern Europe, for which crime he was hanged at Nuremberg in 1946.

(2) **Julius** (1917–53), and his wife **Ethel** (1916–53), American Communists, were part of a transatlantic spy ring uncovered after the trial of Klaus Fuchs (q.v.) in Britain. The husband was employed by the American army, and the wife's brother, David Greenglass, at the nuclear research station at Los Alamos. They were convicted of passing on atomic secrets through an intermediary to the Soviet vice-consul. Greenglass turned witness for the prosecution and saved his life. The Rosenbergs were sentenced to death in April 1951 and, despite numerous appeals from many West European countries and three stays of execution, were executed on June 19, 1953, at Sing Sing prison, New York.

ROSENFELD. See KAMENEV.

ROSENKRANZ, Karl (1805–79), German

philosopher, born at Magdeburg, in 1833 became professor of Philosophy at Königsberg. His works include an encyclopaedia of theology, criticisms of Schleiermacher and Strauss, and books on poetry, education, Diderot and Goethe; but he is best known by his works on the Hegelian system (1840–1856) and his Life of Hegel (1844). See his unfinished autobiography (1873) and Life by Quäbicker (1879).

ROSENKREUTZ, Christian, *rō'zĕn-kroyts*, the alleged founder in 1459 of the Rosicrucians. See ANDREÄ, and Waite's *Real History of the Rosicrucians* (1887).

ROSMEAD, Lord. See ROBINSON (8).

ROSMINI (-SERBATI), Antonio, *roz-mee'nee* (1797–1855), Italian philosopher, was born at Rovereto in the Italian Tirol, studied for the priesthood at Padua and was ordained in 1821. Master of an ample fortune, he worked out a philosophical system for the truths of revelation, while he planned a new institution for the training of teachers and priests. In 1826–28 he lived mostly in Milan, thought out the rule of his new order, visited Rome, gained the approval of Pius VIII, and published his *New Essay on the Origin of Ideas* (1830), his most important work. After a few years at Trent he settled in 1837 at Stresa on Lago Maggiore, and in 1839 received from Gregory XVI the formal approval of his Institute but incurred the hostility of the Jesuits. His dream in politics, as expressed in his *Constitution according to Social Justice* (1848), was a confederation of the states of Italy under the pope as perpetual president. For seven weeks he was envoy of Piedmont at the papal court, and followed Pius IX to Gaeta, but found his mind poisoned against him by Antonelli and the reactionary party. When his *Constitution* and *The Five Wounds of Holy Church* (1848) were prohibited by the Congregation of the Index, he returned to Stresa to spend the rest of his life in devotion and the development of his philosophy. After a scrutiny (1851–54) the Congregation had declared Rosmini's writings to be entirely free from censure, when he died July 1, 1855 In 1888 forty propositions from his posthumous works were condemned by the Holy Office. The 'Institute of the Fathers of Charity' survived. Other works are *Psychology* (1846–48, trans. 1884–88), *Maxims of Christian Perfection* (trans. 1949) and *Theosophy* (1859–74), left unfinished at his death. His *Sketch of Modern Philosophies* was translated by Father Lockhart (1882; 3rd ed. 1891). A Bibliography, with a Life is prefixed by Thomas Davidson to his trans. (1882) of the *Sistema Filosophico* (1845). See Lives by Paoli (1880–84), Lockhart (2nd ed. 1886).

ROSNY, *rō-nee*, **Joseph Henri,** joint pseudonym of the brothers **Joseph Henri** (1856–1940) and **Séraphin Justin François** (1859–1948) **Boëx,** *bō-eks'*, French novelists, born in Brussels. Their vast output of social novels, naturalistic in character, includes *L'Immolation* (1887) and *L'Impérieuse Bonté* (1905), signed jointly, and after 1908, when they separated, Rosny aîné's *L'Appel au bonheur* (1919) and *La Vie amoureuse de Balzac* (1930), and *La Courtesane passionée* (1925) and *La Pantine* (1929) by Rosny jeune. See study by Poinsot (1907).

ROSS, (1) **Alexander** (1590/1–1654), a voluminous Scottish author, remembered solely from a couplet on *Hudibras*, was born at Aberdeen, and became a schoolmaster and clergyman at Southampton.

(2) **Sir James Clark** (1800–62), English explorer, nephew of (3), accompanied Sir John on his first and second polar voyages, and in the interval between was with Parry on his expeditions. He discovered the north magnetic pole in 1831. After being employed in a magnetic survey of the British Isles, he commanded the *Erebus* and *Terror* in an expedition to the Antarctic seas (1839). He was knighted in 1843, and in 1847 published his *Voyage of Discovery*. In 1848–49 he made a voyage to Baffin Bay in search of Franklin. He died at Aylesbury. Ross Barrier, Sea and Island are named after him.

(3) **Sir John** (1777–1856), Scottish Arctic explorer, born at Inch manse in Wigtownshire, served with distinction in the French wars. In 1818 he went to explore Baffin Bay and attempt a Northwest Passage. Another expedition (1829–33), fitted out by Sir Felix Booth, discovered the peninsula of 'Boothia Felix'. He made an unsuccessful attempt to find Sir John Franklin in 1850. He wrote on his voyages (1819, 1835) and a Life of Lord de Saumarez (1838).

(4) **Martin.** See MARTIN (9).

(5) **Sir Ronald** (1857–1932), British physician, discoverer (1895–98) of the malaria parasite and of its life history, was born at Almora in India. He studied medicine at St Bartholomew's. In 1881–99 he was in the Indian Medical Service and later was professor of Tropical Medicine at Liverpool. Nobel prizewinner for medicine (1902), he was the author of poems, romances and *Memoirs* (1923), besides writings on malaria. See Life by Mégroz (1931).

ROSSE, William Parsons, 3rd Earl of (1800–1867), Irish astronomer, born in York, graduated from Magdalen College, Oxford, with a first in Mathematics (1822). During his father's lifetime he sat in parliament for King's County as Lord Oxmantown from 1821 to 1834; in 1841 he succeeded as third earl. He experimented in fluid lenses, and made great improvements in casting specula for the reflecting telescope. In 1842–45 he constructed his great reflecting telescope, 58 feet long, in the park at Birr Castle, his Irish home, at a cost of £30,000; in 1848–54 he was P.R.S. Sir Charles Parsons (1854–1931). the inventor and engineer, was his son.

ROSSETER, Philip, *ros'e-tĕr* (1568–1623), English lutenist and composer, was a musician at the court of James I when he published his *Ayres* (1601). His *Lessons for Consort* appeared in 1609, and thereafter he was active in court theatricals.

ROSSETTI, (1) **Christina** (1830–94), English poet, was born in London, the daughter of (3) and sister of (2), to whose early poetry she owed much. A devout Anglican, she denied herself the fulfilment of marriage and exercised her genuine talent on religious poetry. Her estrangement from her fiancé accounts in part for the melancholy and unhappiness in much of her poetry. In her verse, which is characterized by depth of feeling and simplicity of theme and style, she displayed to perfection the pre-Raphaelite manner from which she never deviated. Submission to God's will as in 'Passing Away' and 'Arise, Come Away, My Love, My Sister, My Spouse' strikes the devotional note, while 'Spring Quiet', 'Winter Rain' and 'Child's Talk in April' illustrate her vein of pure lyricism. See her *Goblin Market and Other Poems* (1862), *The Prince's Progress* (1866), *A Pageant and Other Poems* (1881), and *New Poems* (1896), also, in prose, *Commonplace and Other Stories* (1870), and Lives by Bell (1898) and Stuart (1930).

(2) **Dante Gabriel** (1828–82), English poet and painter, was born in London and in 1846 entered the Antique School of the Royal Academy. About 1850 he formed with Millais, Holman Hunt, Thomas Woolner and others, the pre-Raphaelite Brotherhood, whose object, as explained in *The Germ*—four numbers, 1850—was to resist modern art conventions by a return to pre-Renaissance art forms involving vivid colour and detail. Without religious belief he exploited religious feeling in paintings such as *The Girlhood of Mary Virgin* (1849), *The Annunciation* (1850) and the triptych in Llandaff Cathedral, *The Infant Christ adored by a Shepherd and a King.* His later manner became more pagan as the sense of human beauty, divorced from religion, grew in him. In both painting and poetry his development was from religious simplicity based on significant detail to a more complicated and ornate manner. *The Blessed Damozel* and the painting he made of it illustrate the earlier manner and therefore can be quoted as typical of pre-Raphaelite art. *My Sister's Sleep* and *The Portrait* are also typical of the manner but with a greater infusion of thought. In 1860 Rossetti married Elizabeth Siddal, the model in so many of his pictures, but her tragic death two years later from an overdose of laudanum affected him so strongly that he enclosed the MSS. of his poems in her coffin. They were retrieved seven years later and published in 1870. Robert Buchanan's attack on the poems, *The Fleshly School of Poetry* (1871), following upon his wife's tragedy and his enslavement to chloral turned the poet into a moody recluse. His next published work, *Ballads and Sonnets* (1881), however, includes some of his most outstanding work. He had attempted the artificial ballad in his previous volume—'Stratton Water' is his only imitation of the simple mediaeval ballad—and in 'Sister Helen' had achieved something of a masterpiece. Perhaps 'The Bride's Tragedy', and 'Rose Mary' of the later volume should be called rather mediaeval romances and 'The White Ship' and 'The King's Tragedy' historical lays. The sonnet sequence, *The House of Life*, the sumptuous expression of Rossetti's cult of love and beauty, describes love's pilgrimage from birth to death. Passion is restrained by the dialectic of love which he had learned from the early Italian poets (see his *Early Italian Poets*, 1861). See the *Family Letters*, with Memoir of the poet, by W. M. Rossetti (1895–1905), R. D. Waller's *The Rosetti Family* (1932), G. Pedrick's *Life with Rosetti* (1964), and studies by Hall Caine (1882, 1928), Hueffer (1902), Marillier (3rd ed., 1904), Waugh (1928), Gaunt (1942), Doughty (new ed., 1960).

(3) **Gabriele** (1783–1854), Italian poet and writer, father of (1), (2) and (4), sometime curator of ancient bronzes in the Museum of Bronzes at Naples, was a member of the provisional government set up by Murat in Rome, 1813. After the restoration of Ferdinand to Naples, he joined the Carbonari and saluted the constitution extorted by the patriots in 1820 in a famous ode. On the overthrow of the constitution he withdrew to London (1824), where he became professor of Italian at the new University of London. Besides writing poetry he was a close student of Dante whose *Inferno* he maintained was chiefly political and anti-papal. See book by Vincent (1936).

(4) **William Michael** (1829–1919), son of (3) and brother of (1) and (2), was an Inland Revenue official as well as a man of letters and one of the seven pre-Raphaelite 'brothers', editor of their manifesto *The Germ* (1850). Like all his family he was devoted to the study of Dante, whose *Inferno* he translated. He was equally devoted to his family, as his memoirs of his brother (1895) and his sister Christina (1904) witness.

ROSSI, *rōs'see*, (1) **Bruno** (1905–), Italian-American physicist, born in Venice, became professor of Physics at Cornell University in 1940. He has done much work, including the identification of photons, on cosmic rays.

(2) **Giovanni Battista de** (1494–1541), Italian religious painter, born in Florence, and summoned to France in 1530, committed suicide.

(3) **Giovanni Battista de** (1822–94), Italian archaeologist, born at Rome, known for his researches on the Christian catacombs there.

(4) **Pellegrino, Count** (1787–1848), Italian statesman and economist, born at Carrara, became professor of Law at Bologna at twenty-five. Exiled after the fall of Murat, he obtained a chair at Geneva, and there wrote his *Traité de droit pénal.* In 1833 Louis-Philippe made him professor of Political Economy at the Collège de France. He was sent to Rome as French ambassador in 1845. Called to the ministry by Pius IX, Rossi, by opposing the Savoy party and striving for an Italian confederation with the pope as president, roused the hatred of the Romans, and was assassinated.

ROSSINI, Gioacchino Antonio, *ros-see'nee* (1792–1868), Italian composer, was born at Pesaro, the son of a strolling horn player and a baker's daughter turned singer. He was taught to sing and play at an early age in order to help the family, and in 1806 began to study composition at the Liceo in Bologna, where in 1808 he won the prize for counterpoint with a cantata. Tiring of the stern academic routine he wrote several slender comic operas, among them *La Scala di seta* (1812), whose lively overture is popular today although the opera itself was a failure. At Milan in the same year *La Pietra del Paragone* made a great impression; in 1813 at Venice *Tancredi* and *L'Italiana in Algeri* were a success, though *Sigismondo* (1815) failed, possibly because it was an *opera seria* and Rossini's talents were more scintillating in the lighter vein; *Elisabetta*, a version of the Amy Robsart story, succeeded at Naples in the same year but gained little favour elsewhere. The name part in the latter was taken by the beautiful Spanish singer, Isabella Colbran, who became Rossini's wife in 1821. In 1816 his masterpiece, *Il Barbiere di Seviglia*, was received in Rome with enthusiasm despite a disastrous opening night. *Otello* (1816) marked an advance, but the libretto was weakened by pandering to the whims of the audience and it has justly been eclipsed by Verdi's masterpiece. *La Cenerentola* was favourably received at Rome, *La Gazza Ladra* (*The Thieving Magpie*) at Milan in 1817, and these were followed at Naples by *Armida* and *Mosè in Egitto* (1818), *La Donna del Lago* (1819) and *Maometto Secondo* (1820). *Semiramide* (1823), the most advanced of his works, had only a lukewarm reception from the Venetians. Meantime Rossini and his wife had won fresh laurels at Vienna and in London, and he was invited to become director of the Italian Theatre in Paris, where he adapted several of his works to French taste: *Maometto* (as *Le Siège de Corinth*), *Moïse* and *Le Comte Ory*. Here appeared in August 1829 his greatest work *Guillaume Tell*, conceived and written in a much nobler style than his Italian operas; its success was immense but not lasting. In 1837 he separated from La Colbran, whose extravagance and selfishness had become insupportable, and in 1847 he married Olympe Pelissier, who had been nurse to his children. From this period he produced little but the *Stabat Mater* (1841), which, despite its popularity, is too baroque for some tastes. In 1836 he retired to Bologna and took charge of the Liceo, which he raised from an almost moribund state to a high position in the world of music. The revolutionary disturbances in 1847 drove him to Florence in a condition of deep depression, but he recovered and returned to Paris in 1855, where he died. Rossini has been criticized for immoderate use of long crescendos and other devices in his overtures but he was in this a superb craftsman using the tools of his trade quite legitimately to create an atmosphere of excitement and expectancy in his audience, and the sheer sparkle and vivacity of his music, enlivened as it is by flashes of the puckish sense of humour for which he was renowned, are sufficient to ensure its immortality. See Stendhal's fascinating but innaccurate contemporary Memoir (1824); also books by Toye (1834) and Lord Derwent (1934).

ROSTAND, Edmond, *ro-stã* (1868–1918), French poet and dramatist, born at Marseilles, published *Les Musardises*, a volume of verse, in 1890, rose to fame with *Cyrano de Bergerac* (1897), *L'Aiglon* (1900), *Chantecler* (1910), and other plays in verse, in 1902 being elected to the Académie française. See studies by Grieve (1931) and Gérard (1935).

ROSTOPCHINE, Feodor Vassilievich, Count, *ros-top-cheen'* (1763–1826), Russian general, won great influence over the Emperor Paul, and in 1812 became, under Alexander, governor of Moscow. It was he who planned, or at least had a share in, the burning of Moscow. His works include historical memoirs and two comedies, &c., in Russian and French. See Life by Ségur (1872).

ROSTROPOVICH, Mstislav Leopoldovitch (1927–), Russian cellist and composer, born at Baku, studied at the Moscow Conservatoire (1937–48), where he has been professor since 1960. He was awarded the Lenin prize in 1964.

ROSWITHA. See HROSWITHA.

ROTHENSTEIN, *rō'then-stīn*, (1) **Sir John Knewstub Maurice** (1901–), English art historian, was born in London, the son of (2), and studied at Worcester College, Oxford, and University College, London. From 1927 to 1929 he taught in the United States, and was director of Leeds and Sheffield city art galleries between 1932 and 1938, when he was appointed director and keeper of the Tate Gallery, retiring in 1964. He was knighted in 1952. His many works on art include *Modern English Painters* (1952–56), and his Autobiography (2 vols., 1965, 1966). See study by R. Speaight (1962).

(2) **Sir William** (1872–1945), English artist, born at Bradford, studied at the Slade School and in Paris, won fame as a portrait painter, and was principal of the Royal College of Art, South Kensington (1920–35). See his *Men and Memories* (1931–32), *Since Fifty* (1939).

ROTHERMERE, Viscount. See HARMSWORTH (3).

ROTHSCHILD, Meyer Amschel, Ger. *rōt' shilt*; Eng. *roths'chīld* (1743–1812), German financier, named from the 'Red Shield', signboard of his father's house, born at Frankfurt, was educated as a Jewish rabbi, but founded a business as a moneylender and became the financial adviser of the Landgrave of Hesse. The house got a heavy commission for transmitting money from the English government to Wellington in Spain, paid the British subsidies to Continental princes, and negotiated loans for Denmark between 1804 and 1812. At his death, the founder left five sons, all of whom were made barons of the Austrian empire in 1822. **Anselm Meyer** (1773–1855), eldest son, succeeded as head of the firm at Frankfurt; **Solomon** (1774–1855) established a branch at Vienna; **Nathan Meyer** (1777–1836), one in 1798 at London; **Charles** (1788–1855), one at Naples (discontinued about 1861); and **James** (1792–1868), one at Paris. They negotiated many of the great government loans of the 19th century, and Nathan raised the house to be first amongst the banking houses of the world. He staked his fortunes on the success of Britain in her duel with Napoleon, and, receiving the first news of Waterloo, sold and bought stock which brought him a million of profit. His son **Lionel** (1808–79) did much for the civil and political emancipation of the Jews in Great Britain. Lionel's son, **Nathan** (1840–1915), succeeded (1876) to his uncle Anthony's baronetcy (1846), and was made Baron Rothschild in 1885. His son, **Lionel** (1868–1937), second Baron set up a valuable zoological museum at Tring. See books by Reeves (1887), Balla (1913), Corti (trans. 1928), Roth (1939) and Morton (1962).

ROTHWELL, Evelyn. See Barbirolli.

ROTROU, Jean de, *ro-troo* (1609–50), French playwright, born at Dreux, went early to Paris, qualified as a lawyer, and turned to writing plays, as well as becoming one of the five poets who worked into dramatic form the ideas of Richelieu. His first pieces were in the Spanish romantic style. Next followed a classical period, culminating in three masterpieces, *Saint-Genest*, a tragedy of Christian martyrdom, *Don Bertrand* and *Venceslas*. He died of the plague. Thirty-five of his plays are still extant. A complete edition was edited by Viollet-le-Duc (1820–1822). See works by Jarry (1868), Steffens (1891), and Stiefel (1891).

ROU. See Rollo.

ROUAULT, Georges, *roo-ō* (1871–1958), French painter and engraver, was born in Paris. He was apprenticed to a stained-glass designer in 1885, and in all his work he retained the characteristic glowing colours, outlined with black, to achieve a concise statement of his feelings about the clowns, prostitutes and Biblical characters whom he chose as his subjects. He studied under Gustave Moreau, and in 1898 was made curator of the Moreau Museum. About 1904 he joined the Fauves (Matisse, Derain and others), and in 1910 held his first one-man show. Many of his works were acquired by Vollard, who commissioned the series of large religious engravings, finally published after Vollard's death as *Miserere* (Eng. ed. 1951). See also Lives by Venturi (N.Y. 1940, new ed. 1959) and Soby (N.Y. 1947).

ROUBILLAC, Louis François, *roo-bee-yak* (1702 or 1705–62), sculptor, born at Lyons, studied at Paris, and before 1738 settled in London, where he spelt his name Roubiliac. His statue of Handel for Vauxhall Gardens in 1738 first made him popular. His other most famous statues are those of Newton (1755) at Cambridge, of Shakespeare (1758), now in the British Museum, and another of Handel in Westminster Abbey. See *Life and Works* by Esdaile (1929), Dobson's *Eighteenth Century Vignettes* (1894).

ROUGET DE LISLE, Claude Joseph, *roo-zhay dė leel* (1760–1836), French army officer, born at Lons-le-Saunier, wrote and composed the *Marseillaise* when stationed in 1792 as captain of engineers at Strasbourg. Wounded at Quiberon (1795), he quitted the army, and published in 1796 a volume of *Essais en vers et en prose*. The *Marseillaise*, by its author called *Chant de l'armée du Rhin*, was made known in Paris by troops from Marseilles. See Life by Tiersot (1892, 1915).

ROUHER, Eugène, *roo-ayr* (1814–84), French statesman, born at Riom, in 1848 was returned to the Constituent Assembly, and until 1869 held various offices in the government. He negotiated the treaty of commerce with England in 1860 and with Italy in 1863. In 1870 he was appointed president of the Senate. A staunch Napoleonist, after the fall of the empire he fled abroad. Later he represented Corsica in the National Assembly.

ROUMANILLE, Joseph, *roo-ma-nee'y'* (1818–1891), French writer, was born at Saint-Rémy, Bouches-du-Rhône. He taught at Avignon, his pupils including Frédéric Mistral (q.v.), and in 1847 he published *Li Margarideto*, a book of his own poems, in 1852 a volume of Provençal poems, and thereafter many volumes of verse and prose in Provençal dialect. With Mistral and others he founded the 'Soci dou Félibrige' for the revival of Provençal literature. See biography by Mariéton (1903).

ROUS, (1) Francis, *rows* (1579–1659), English Presbyterian, born at Dittisham, Devon, and educated at Oxford, was a member of the Long Parliament, sat in the Westminster Assembly of Divines, and in 1644 was made provost of Eton. His writings were collected in 1657. His metrical version of the Psalms was recommended by the House of Commons to the Westminster Assembly, and is still substantially the Presbyterian psalter.

(2) **Francis Peyton** (1879–1970), U.S. scientist, born in Baltimore, educated at Johns Hopkins University and Medical School. He became assistant 1909–10, associate 1910–12, associate member 1912–20 and member 1920–45 of the Rockefeller Institute for Medical Research. In 1910 he discovered a virus to induce malignant tumours in hens, the outstanding importance of which has become apparent over the years. In 1962 he received the U.N. prize for cancer research, and in 1966 shared the Nobel prize for medicine with Huggins (1).

ROUSSEAU, (1) Henri, known as Le Douanier *roo-sō, lė dwa-nyay* (1844–1910), French primitive painter, born at Laval, joined the army at about eighteen, but most of his life was spent as a minor customs official, hence his nickname. He retired in 1885 and spent his time painting and copying at the Louvre. From 1886 to 1898 he exhibited at the Salon des Indépendants and again from 1901 to 1910. He met Gauguin, Pissarro and later Picasso, but his painting remained unaffected. Despite its denial of conventional perspective and colour, it has a fierce reality more surrealist than primitive. He produced painstaking portraits, and painted dreams, e.g., the *Sleeping Gipsy* (1897) in the Museum of Modern Art, N.Y., and exotic, imaginary landscapes with trees and plants which he had seen in the Jardin des Plantes. See studies by A. Basler (Paris 1927) and G. F. Hartlaub (1956).

(2) **Jean Baptiste** (1671–1741), French poet, born in Paris, a shoemaker's son, wrote for the theatre, and by lampoons on the literary frequenters of the Café Laurent raised feuds which led to recriminations, lawsuits and a sentence of banishment (1712). Henceforth he lived abroad, in Switzerland, Vienna (with Prince Eugene) and Brussels, where he died. Rousseau's sacred odes and *cantates* are splendidly elaborate, frigid and artificial; his epigrams are bright, vigorous and unerring in their aim. See his *Life and Works* by H. A. Grubbs (1941).

(3) **Jean Jacques,** *roo-sō* (1712–78), Genevan political philosopher, educationist and essayist, was born June 28 at Geneva, his mother dying at his birth. In 1722 his father,

involved in a brawl, left him to the care of his relations. Without any formal education except his own reading of Plutarch's *Lives* and a collection of Calvinist sermons, he was employed first by a notary who found him incompetent and then by an engraver who maltreated him so that in 1728 he ran away. Feigning enthusiasm for Catholicism, he was sent to Madame de Warens who, separated from her husband, became a convert to Catholicism and assisted other converts. She sent him to Turin to be baptized and there he eventually found employment with a shopkeeper's wife, whose lover he became until her husband's return. After short spells as footman and secretary, he returned to Annecy, to Madame de Warens. He became her general factotum and lover, joined the local choir school to complete his education and picked up a fair knowledge of Italian music. On an unauthorized visit to Lyons with the music master, he meanly deserted the latter during an epileptic fit. Eventually supplanted in his mistress's affections by a wigmaker, he made for Paris in 1741 with a new musical notation, which the Academy of Sciences pronounced 'neither useful nor original'. With secretarial work and musical copying for a livelihood, he began his association, which was to be lifelong, with a maid at his hostelry, Thérèse Le Vasseur, who was neither good-looking nor literate and by whom he boasted he had five children, whom, despite his much-vaunted sensibility and regard for the innocence of childhood, he consigned, in turn, to the foundling hospital. He composed an opera *Les Muses galantes* which led to a correspondence with Voltaire and eventually acquaintance with Diderot and the *encyclopédistes*. On a visit to Diderot in prison, he discovered in a periodical the prize essay competition by the academy of Dijon on whether the arts and sciences had a purifying effect upon morals. This he won in 1750 by maintaining that they did not, having seduced man from his natural and noble estate, decreasing his freedom. He was lionized by the Parisians and further triumphed with his opera *Le Devin du village* (1752). In 1754 he wrote *Discours sur l'origine de l'inégalité parmi les hommes* (1755), which re-emphasized the natural goodness of man and the corrupting influences of institutionalized life. He returned to Geneva and Calvinism, where he began his novel in letter form, *La Nouvelle Héloïse* (1761). In *Lettre sur les spectacles* (1758) he argued against the establishment of a theatre at Geneva on puritan grounds. Back in Paris, a reformed man, who was trying hard to live up to his newly-found natural estate, he accepted a cottage for himself, Thérèse and her mother at Montmorency from an admirer, Mme d'Épinay, but quarrelling with her over her sister, he set up in 1757 in Luxembourg. The year 1762 saw his masterpiece, *Contrat social*, 'Social Contract' which attempted to solve the problem posed by its opening sentence: 'Man is born free; and everywhere he is in chains', by postulating a social contract by which the citizen surrenders his rights and possessions to the 'general will' which, thus undivided by sectarian and private interests, must necessarily aim at the impartial good. Thus if a man acts against the 'general will' or sovereign, he must in Rousseau's curious phrase 'be forced to be free'. With its slogan 'Liberty, Equality, Fraternity', it became the bible of the French revolution. Its doctrines, favourably interpreted, greatly influenced Kant, but they were easily perverted by Hegel into his philosophy of right, which gave birth to the modern totalitarian theories of the state. The same year he published his great work on education, *Émile*, in novel form, which greatly influenced such educationists as Froebel and Pestalozzi. Its views on monarchy and governmental institutions outraged the powers that be and those on natural religion, unorthodox to both Catholics and Protestants, which he placed into the mouth of the confessing Savoyard Vicar, forced him to flee to Môtiers in Neuchâtel under the protection of Frederick the Great. There he botanized, wrote *Lettres de la montagne* and accepted David Hume's generous invitation to settle in England, at Wootton Hall near Ashbourne (1766–67), where he wrote most of his *Confessions* (1781), a work remarkable for a frankness unsurpassed at that time. Persecution mania and hypersensitivity soured his relations with his English friends and a cruel practical joke by Horace Walpole who published a forged letter, convinced Rousseau that the British government through Hume were seeking his life. He fled, unjustly accusing Hume, and took shelter with the Marquis de Mirabeau and the Prince de Conti. In 1770 he was back in Paris, eking out a living as a copyist, and wrote the half-insane dialogues, justifying to himself his past actions, *Rousseau, juge de Jean Jacques*, followed by the contrastingly calm, sane *Rêveries* (1782), in parts beautifully composed as a continuation to the *Confessions*. Seeking shelter in a hospital, he eventually died insane in a cottage at Ermenonville, July 2, 1778, from a sudden attack of thrombosis, which long aroused suspicions of suicide. He was buried there until in 1794 his remains were placed with Voltaire's in the Panthéon, Paris. His writings ushered in the age of romanticism and found their echo in German and English idealism. See Lives by J. H. Fuessli (1767), de Staël (trans. 1789), J. Morley (1873), *Annales de la société Jean Jacques Rousseau* (1905) and studies by Collins (1908), Ducros (1908–12), Babbitt (1919), Wright (1929), C. E. Vulliamy (1931), Cobban (1934), Mowat (1938), Osborne (1940), Cassirer (trans. 1945), Green (1950).

(4) **Theodore** (1812–67), French landscape painter, born in Paris, studied the old masters in the Louvre, and by 1833 had begun sketching in the Forest of Fontainebleau. He first exhibited in the Salon of 1831; and in 1834 his *Forest of Compiègne* was bought by the Duc d'Orléans. Some twelve years of discouragement followed, but in 1849 he resumed exhibiting, and was thenceforward prominent. He was an exceedingly prolific, if a somewhat unequal, painter. See study by Sensier (1872); and D. C. Thomson, *The Barbizon School* (1890). His brother,

Philippe (1816–87), animal and still-life painter, was born and died in Acquigny (Eure).

ROUSSEL, *roo-sel,* (1) **Albert** (1869–1937), French composer, born in Tourcoing, educated for the navy, at the age of twenty-five resigned his commission to study with Gigout, in 1896 joining the Schola Cantorum under Vincent d'Indy. His works, after his period of study, are adventurous in harmony and texture, reconciling modern experimental styles with the conservative tradition of his teachers. A voyage to India and the Far East gave him an interest in Oriental music which inspired the choral *Évocations* (1912) and the opera *Padmâvati,* begun in 1914 and completed after World War I. Service in the war ruined Roussel's health, and after his demobilization he largely retired into seclusion, devoting his time entirely to composition. His works include ballets (the best-known of which are *Bacchus and Ariane* and *Le Festin de l'araignée*), four symphonies and numerous choral and orchestral works. See studies by Norman Demuth (1947), Robert Bernard (Paris 1948) and M. Pincherle (1957).

(2) **Ker Xavier** (1867–1944), French artist, born at Lorry-les-Metz, was a member of the Nabis, and associated with Bonnard, Vuillard and Denis. He is best known for his classical subjects portrayed in typical French landscapes, using the Impressionist palette.

ROUTH, *rowth,* (1) **Edward John** (1831–1907), British mathematician, born at Quebec, and educated at University College, London, and Peterhouse, Cambridge, became a mathematical coach, and by 1888, when he retired, had turned out twenty-seven senior wranglers. He wrote on dynamics and analytical statics.

(2) **Martin Joseph** (1755–1854), English patristic scholar, born at St Margaret's, South Elmham, Suffolk, from Beccles went up in 1770 to Queen's College, Oxford. In 1771 he was elected a demy, in 1775 a fellow, and in 1791 president of Magdalen; in 1810 he became rector of Tylehurst near Reading. He died at Magdalen, December 22, 1854, in his hundredth year. A little shrunken figure, with 'such a wig as one only sees in old pictures', he had grown very deaf, but till well after ninety retained his eyesight and marvellous memory and capacity for work. Newman and Bancroft were among his later friends; the earlier had included Dr Parr, Samuel Johnson and Porson. He was a great patristic scholar when patristic scholars were few, a Caroline churchman, a liberal Tory, a lover of animals, fond of jokes, a mighty book-buyer—his 16,000 volumes he bequeathed to Durham University. Throughout seventy years he published only six works; two of these are editions of Burnet ('I know the man to be a liar, and I am determined to prove him so'). He will be remembered by his *Reliquiae Sacrae* (1814–48) a collection of fragments of early Christian writings, but still more for his sage advice, 'Always verify your references, sir'. See Life by R. D. Middleton (1938).

ROUTLEDGE, George, *rut'lej* (1812–88), English publisher, born at Brampton, Cumberland, went to London in 1833, and started up as a bookseller in 1836, and as a publisher in 1843. In 1848, the year in which he founded his 'Railway Library' of cheap reprints, and 1851 respectively he took his two brothers-in-law, W. H. and Frederick Warne into partnership. In 1947 the firm acquired the undertaking of Kegan Paul, Trench, Trubner and Co. Ltd. See Mumby's *The House of Routledge, 1834-1934* (1934).

ROUX, *roo,* (1) **Pierre Émile** (1853–1933), French bacteriologist, born at Confolens (Charente), studied at Clermont-Ferrand, and became assistant to Pasteur, and in 1905–18 was his successor. With Yersin he discovered (1894) the antitoxic method of treating diphtheria, and he also worked on cholera and tuberculosis.

(2) **Wilhelm** (1850–1924), German anatomist and physiologist, born at Jena, became a professor at Innsbruck in 1889, at Halle in 1895. On his extensive practical and theoretical work on experimental embryology (his *Entwicklungsmechanik,* or developmental mechanics) he wrote many books, including *Entwicklungsmechanik der Organismen* (2 vols. 1895).

ROW, *roo,* (1) **John** (*c.* 1525–80), Scottish Reformer, educated at Stirling and St Andrews, in 1550 was sent by the archbishop to Rome. In 1558 he returned to Scotland, and next year turned Protestant. He aided in compiling the *Confession of Faith* (1560) and *First Book of Discipline* (1561), became minister of Perth, and sat in the first General Assembly. He was four times moderator and took a share in preparing the *Second Book of Discipline.*

(2) **John** (1568–1646), eldest son of (1), minister from 1592 of Carnock near Dunfermline, wrote a prolix but reliable *History of the Kirk of Scotland* from 1558 to 1637, continued to 1639 by his second son (edited for the Wodrow and Maitland Clubs by David Laing, 1842). He was strongly opposed to the introduction of episcopacy into Scotland.

(3) **John** (*c.* 1598–1672), son of (2), successively rector of Perth grammar school, minister at Aberdeen, moderator of the Assembly there in 1644, and principal of King's College in 1651. Like his father and grandfather he was a learned Hebraist.

ROWAN, Archibald Hamilton, *rō'an* (1751–1834), Irish nationalist, was born in London, the son of Gawin Hamilton and on his maternal grandfather's death took his name of Rowan. Educated at Cambridge, he went to Ireland in 1784, in 1791 joined the United Irishmen, and three years later was imprisoned for sedition. He escaped to France, went to America, obtained pardon and returned to Ireland, where he supported the cause of Catholic emancipation.

ROWE, Nicholas, *rō* (1674–1718), **English** poet and dramatist, born at Little Barford, Bedfordshire, and educated at Westminster, was called to the bar, but from 1692 devoted himself to literature. Between 1700 and 1715 he produced eight plays of which three (ed. Sutherland, 1929) were long popular—*Tamerlane* (1702), *The Fair Penitent* (1703) and *Jane Shore* (1714). Lothario in *The Fair Penitent* was the prototype of Lovelace in

Richardson's *Clarissa* and the name is still the synonym for a fashionable rake. Rowe translated Lucan's *Pharsalia*, and his work, says Dr Johnson, 'deserves more notice than it obtains'. His edition of Shakespeare (1709–10) at least contributed to the popularity of his author. In 1709–11 Rowe was under-secretary to the Duke of Queensberry; in 1715 he was appointed poet laureate and a surveyor of customs to the port of London; the Prince of Wales made him clerk of his Council, and Lord Chancellor Parker clerk of presentations in chancery.

ROWLAND, Henry Augustus, *rō'land* (1848–1901), American physicist, born at Honesdale, Pennsylvania, from 1875 to 1901 was first professor of Physics at Johns Hopkins University. He invented the concave diffraction grating used in spectroscopy, discovered the magnetic effect of electric convection, and improved on Joule's work on the mechanical equivalent of heat.

ROWLANDSON, Thomas, *rō'land-sėn* (1756–1827), English caricaturist, born in London, and sent at fifteen to Paris, there studied art and gained a taste for the pleasures of the town. The £7000 left him by a French aunt he gambled away, yet he hated debt, and maintained his uprightness of character. He travelled over England and Wales, and enjoyed to the full tavern life and the company of friends like Morland, Gillray and Bunbury. Rowlandson possessed rare dexterity of touch and fertility of imagination; and his work, though even for his time often crude and vulgar, is alive and vigorous. He was a relentless hater of Napoleon, belittling his greatness by countless travesties. Some of his best-known works are his *Imitations of Modern Drawings* (1784–88), and his illustrations to *Syntax's Three Tours*, the *Dance of Death*, Sterne's *Sentimental Journey*, *Peter Pindar*, the *Bath Guide*, *Munchausen*, &c. See studies by Oppé (1923), Wolf (1946) and Roe (1947).

ROWLEY, *rō-li,* (1) **Thomas.** See CHATTERTON.

(2) **William** (*c.* 1585–*c.* 1642), English actor and playwright, of whose life little is known, save that he collaborated with Dekker, Middleton, Heywood, Webster, Massinger and Ford. Four plays published with his name are extant: *A New Wonder, a Woman Never Vext* (1632); *All's Lost by Lust*, a tragedy (1633); *A Match at Midnight* (1633); and *A Shoomaker a Gentleman* (1638).

ROWNTREE, *rown'tree,* (1) **(Benjamin) Seebohm** (1871–1954), English manufacturer and philanthropist, son of (2), born at York, was chairman of the family firm (1925–41), devoted his life to the study of social problems and welfare and wrote many books, including the austere factual study of *Poverty* (1900), *Poverty and Progress*, *English Life and Leisure*, &c. See study by A. Briggs (1961).

(2) **Joseph** (1836–1925) Quaker industrialist, social and industrial reformer, father of (1), born at York, promoted with his brother, **Henry Isaac** (d. 1883), the cocoa-manufacturing business acquired by the latter in 1862.

ROWSE, Alfred Leslie (1903–), English historian, born at St Austell, educated at Oxford, became a Fellow of All Souls and wrote many works on English history including *Tudor Cornwall* (1941), *The Use of History* (1946), *The England of Elizabeth* (1950). He has also written some poetry, much of it on Cornwall, several works on aspects of Shakespeare, a Life of Marlowe (1964), and his own autobiography *A Cornishman at Oxford* (1965).

ROWTON, Montagu William Lowry-Corry, 1st Baron, *row'-* (1838–1903), English politician and philanthropist, born in London. Called to the bar in 1863, he became private secretary to Disraeli (1866–1868, 1874–80). He was created baron in 1880. Later he devoted his time and money to the provision of decent cheap accommodation for working men, and six Rowton houses were built in London, with total accommodation for five thousand. Although Rowton's motives were entirely philanthropic, his houses in fact made a profit.

ROXBURGHE, Duke of. See KERR.

ROY. See RAMMOHUN ROY.

ROY, William (1726–90), British military surveyor, born at Miltonhead, Carluke, Lanarkshire, in 1747 was engaged on the survey of Scotland, in 1755 held an army commission, was elected F.R.S. in 1767, and rose to be major-general in 1781. In 1784, in connection with the triangulation of the southeastern counties, he measured with great accuracy a base line of $5\frac{1}{8}$ miles on Hounslow Heath. For this he received the Royal Society's Copley medal. In 1764 Roy studied the Roman remains in Scotland, and his *Military Antiquities of the Romans in Britain* was published in 1793 by the Society of Antiquaries. See G. Macdonald, *Roy and his Military Antiquities* (1917).

ROYCE, (1) Sir (Frederick) Henry (1863–1933), English engineer, born near Peterborough. He was apprenticed to the G.N.R., but, becoming interested in electricity and motor engineering, he founded (1884) at Manchester the firm of Royce, Ltd., mechanical and electrical engineers. He made his first car in 1904, and his meeting with C. S. Rolls (q.v.) in that year led to the formation (1906) of the famous business of Rolls-Royce, Ltd., motor-car and aero-engine builders, of Derby and London. He was created a baronet in 1930. See Life by M. Pemberton (1935).

(2) **Josiah** (1855–1916), American philosopher, born in Grass Valley, California, was professor at Harvard from 1892. Much influenced by Hegel, he developed a philosophy of idealism, avoiding the pitfalls of both realism and mysticism, and stressed the importance of the individual in his loyalty to the community. He published *The Spirit of Modern Philosophy* (1892), *Essays upon Problems of Philosophy and of Life* (1898), *The World and the Individual* (Gifford Lectures, 1900–01) and *The Problem of Christianity* (1913).

ROYDEN, Agnes Maud (1876–1956), English social worker and preacher, was born in Liverpool, educated at Lady Margaret Hall, Oxford, was prominent in the women's suffrage movement, from 1917 to 1920 was assistant at the City Temple, and published

Woman and the Sovereign State, The Church and Woman, Modern Sex Ideals, &c. She was made C.H. in 1930.

ROYER-COLLARD, Pierre Paul, *rwa-yay ko-lar* (1763–1845), French philosopher and politician, born at Sompuis in Champagne, began as an advocate, on the outbreak of the Revolution was elected member of the municipality of Paris. In 1792 he fled from the Jacobins to his birthplace, and in 1797 served for a few months on the Council of Five Hundred. Professor of Philosophy in Paris from 1810, he exercised an immense influence on French philosophy, rejecting the purely sensuous system of Condillac, and giving special prominence to the principles of the Scottish School of Reid and Stewart. Strongly 'spiritualist' as opposed to materialist, he originated the 'Doctrinaire' school of Jouffroy and Cousin. In 1815–20 he was president of the Commission of Public Instruction, in 1815 was returned as deputy for Marne, and in 1827 entered the French Academy. He became president in 1828 of the Chamber of Representatives, and presented the address of March 1830, which the king refused to hear read.

ROZANOV, Vasili Vasilievich, *roz'-* (1856–1919), Russian writer, thinker and critic, was born at Vetluga, Kostroma, and became a teacher in provincial schools. His literary studies include that of Dostoievsky's *Grand Inquisitor*, which, published in 1894, first brought him into prominence. Though a Christian, in his prolific writings he criticized from a Nietzschian standpoint the contemporary standards in morals, religion, education, and particularly the too-strict attitude towards sex, which was for him the very soul of man. Much of his work is highly introspective and his literary reputation is firmly grounded on the two books of fragments and essays, *Solitaria* (1912; trans. 1927) and *Fallen Leaves* (1913, 1915; trans. 1929).

RUBBRA, Edmund (1901–), English composer and music critic, was born in Northampton. While working as a railway clerk, he had piano lessons from Cyril Scott, and in 1919 won a composition scholarship to Reading University. There he studied under Howard Jones and Holst, and won a scholarship to the Royal College of Music, where he was a pupil of Vaughan Williams and, most influentially, of R. O. Morris (q.v.). An interest in the polyphonic music of the 16th and 17th centuries is reflected in Rubbra's characteristic contrapuntal style of composition, which he uses not only in works such as his Spenser sonnets (1935), his madrigals and his Masses (1945 and 1949), but also in his larger symphonic canvases. In these he has progressed from a relentless prosecution of polyphonic principles in the first two to a more flexible interpretation of them in his later symphonies. As well as his seven symphonies he has written chamber, choral and orchestral music, songs and works for various solo instruments. In 1947 he was appointed lecturer in Music at Oxford, and fellow of Worcester College in 1963.

RUBENS, Peter Paul, *roo'benz* (1577–1640), Flemish painter, was born June 29, 1577, at Siegen in Westphalia, where his father, an Antwerp lawyer and religious exile in Cologne, was then imprisoned for a liaison with the wife of William the Silent. On the death of her husband at Cologne in 1587, his mother returned to Antwerp, where the boy was educated in the Jesuits' college. He was for a short time in the service of Margaret de Ligne, widow of the Count of Lanaing, and was intended for the law; but at thirteen he began to study art. In 1600 he went to Italy, and in Venice studied the works of Titian and Veronese. He next entered the service of Vincenzo Gonzaga, Duke of Mantua; and in 1605 was dispatched on a mission to Philip III of Spain, thus beginning the career as a diplomatist, for which his keen intellect, polished urbanity and linguistic attainments qualified him. While at Madrid he executed many portraits, as well as several historical subjects. On his return from Spain he travelled in Italy, copying celebrated works for the Duke of Mantua. His paintings of this Italian period are much influenced by the Italian Renaissance, and already show the Rubens characteristics of vigorous composition and brilliant colouring—for example, the altarpieces for the church of Santa Croce in Gerusalemme (now in Grasse), the *Baptism of Christ* (Antwerp) and the *Circumcision* (Genoa). In 1608 he returned home, and, settling in Antwerp, was appointed in 1609 court painter to the Archduke Albert, and soon afterwards married his first wife, Isabella Brant, whom he often portrayed; a famous full-length portrait of her and her husband is in the Old Pinakothek, Munich. Through the less successful *Adoration of the Kings* (Prado) and the *Elevation of the Cross* (Antwerp Cathedral) Rubens was now approaching his artistic maturity, and his triptych *Descent from the Cross* (1611–14) in Antwerp Cathedral is usually regarded as his masterpiece. By this time he was famous, and pupils and commissions came in a steady stream to the master's studio, from which issued vast numbers of works, witnesses to the extraordinary energy and ability of the prolific Rubens. In 1620 he was invited to France by Marie de' Medici, the queen mother, who was then engaged in decorating the palace of the Luxembourg; and he undertook for her twenty-one large subjects on her life and regency—works, exemplifying the typical collaboration of Rubens and his pupils, which were completed in 1625 and are now in the Louvre. To this period also belong an *Adoration of the Magi* (Madrid), one of many Rubens painted on this subject, a St Ildefonso triptych in the Vienna Museum, and *The Assumption of the Virgin* (Antwerp Cathedral). In 1628 he was dispatched by the Infanta Isabella on a diplomatic mission to Philip IV of Spain. In Madrid he made the acquaintance of Velazquez, and executed some forty works, including five portraits of the Spanish monarch. In 1629 he was appointed envoy to Charles I of England, to treat for peace; and, while he conducted a delicate negotiation with tact and success, he painted the *Peace and War* (National Gallery) and the portrait of the king and his queen in the *St George* at Buckingham Palace, and also made sketches for the Apotheosis of James I for the banqueting hall at Whitehall, completing the pictures on his return to Antwerp. He was knighted by Charles I, and received a similar honour from Philip IV. His first wife having died in 1626, Rubens married in 1630 Helena Fourment, and retired to his estate at Steen, where his landscape painting, direct from nature, attained the high standard of his other works. In 1635 he designed the decorations which celebrated the entry of the Cardinal Infant Ferdinand into Antwerp as governor of the Netherlands; and, having completed *The Crucifixion o St Peter* for the church of that saint in Cologne, he died at Antwerp, May 30, 1640. A successful diplomat, a distinguished humanist, a man of wide erudition and culture, Rubens was outstanding for versatility even in his time, and the main characteristics of his productions—their power, spirit and vivacity, their sense of energy, of exuberant life—may be largely attributed to the comprehensive qualities of the man himself. He produced more than twelve hundred works, many of his finest being at Antwerp; the Old Pinakothek at Munich contains many examples of his work, including the *Battle of the Amazons*, and he is well represented in the Prado, Madrid, and the Vienna Kunsthistorisches Museum. Among his works in the National Gallery, London, are *The Rape of the Sabines* (1635), *The Birth of Venus*, *The Castle of Steen*, and a painting of the Holy Family. See *The Letters of Peter Paul Rubens*, trans. and ed. by R. S. Magurn (1955), and works by Sainsbury (1859), Bertram (1928), Cammaerts (1932), H. G. Evers (1943), Leo van Puyvelde (trans. 1947 by E. Winkworth), E. Larsen (Antwerp 1952) and J. S. Held (1954 and 1959).

RUBINSTEIN, *roo'bin-stīn*, (1) **Anton** (1829–1894), Russian pianist and composer, was born in Moldavia, studied in Berlin and Vienna, and in 1848 settled in St Petersburg, where he taught music and took a part in founding the conservatoire, of which he was for a time director. He made concert tours in Europe and, in 1872–73, the United States, gaining widespread acclaim and lasting distinction for his mastery of technique and musical sensitivity. Once also highly esteemed were his compositions, including operas, oratorios and piano concertos, but, apart from some songs and melodious piano pieces, they have not stood the test of time. His brother **Nikolai** (1835–81) founded Moscow Conservatoire. See Anton's *Autobiography* (trans. 1891).

(2) **Artur** (1888–), American pianist, born in Łódź, Poland. At the age of twelve he appeared successfully in Berlin, and after further study with Paderewski, began his career as a virtuoso, appearing in Paris and London in 1905 and visiting the United States in 1906. After the second World War he lived in America, making frequent extensive concert tours. See study by B. Gavoty (1956).

RUBRUQUIS, William de, *rü-brü-kee'* (fl. 13th cent.), French traveller, born probably at Rubrouck near St Omer, entered the Franciscan order, and was sent from Acre in 1253 by Louis IX to Sartak, the son of the Mongol prince, Batû Khan, a supposed Christian. Friar William travelled across the Black Sea and the Crimea to the Volga, by Sartak was referred to his father, and by him was sent forward to the Mongol emperor, Mangû Khan, whom he found on December 27, about ten days' journey south of Karakorum in Mongolia. With him he remained until July 1254, then returned to the Volga, and by way of the Caucasus, Armenia, Persia and Asia Minor, arrived at Tripoli in August 1255. Louis had returned to France, and Friar William wrote him an account of his journey, edited by D'Avezac in *Recueil de voyages* (Paris Geog. Soc. 1839). He was still living in 1293, when Marco Polo was returning from the East.

RUCCELLAI, *roo-chel-lah'ee*, (1) **Bernardo** (1449–1514), Florentine scholar and diplomatist, father of (2).

(2) **Giovanni** (1475–1525), Italian poet, who lived much in Rome and took orders. His works, including *Le Api*, an instructive poem based on book 4 of Virgil's *Georgics*, were edited by Mazzoni, with Life (1887).

RÜCKERT, Friedrich (1788–1866), German poet, born at Schweinfurt, studied law, philology and philosophy at Würzburg, and during the Napoleonic wars stirred up German patriotism with his *Deutsche Gedichte* (1814). After the wars he studied Oriental languages, of which he became professor at Erlangen (1826–41) and Berlin (1841–48), and recast in German verse many famous books of countries of the Orient. His original work includes the lyrical *Liebesfrühling* (1923), the reflective poems *Die Weisheit des Brahmanen* (1836–39), and the personal *Kindertotenlieder*, posthumously published in 1872 and set to music by Mahler in 1902. See studies by Reuter (1891), Magon (1914) and Golfing (1935).

RUDBECK, Olof, *rood'bek* (1630–1702), Swedish zoologist and botanist, discoverer of the lymphatic glands. His name was given to the botanical genus *Rudbeckia*, and he published (1675–98) *Atlantikan.*

RUDDIMAN, Thomas (1674–1757), Scottish classical grammarian and philologist, born at Boyndie, Banffshire, studied at Aberdeen University, in 1700 was appointed assistant keeper of the Advocates' Library, Edinburgh, in 1707 starting up business also as a book auctioneer and in 1715 as a printer, and became in 1730 principal keeper of the Advocates' Library. He edited Latin works of Volusenus and Arthur Johnston (qq.v.), published in 1715 his great edition of Buchanan's works, with its controversial introduction, and produced his own *Rudiments of the Latin Tongue* (1714) and the impressive *Grammaticae Latinae Institutiones* (1725–32) on which his philological reputation mainly rests. He was an ardent Jacobite. See Life by Chalmers (1794).

RUDE, François (1784–1855), French sculptor, originally a smith, was born at Dijon, and died in Paris. His most famous work is the relief group *Le Départ* (1836) on the Arc de Triomphe in Paris. See Life by Calmette (1920).

RUDOLF. Name of three kings of Burgundy:

Rudolf I (d. 912), was king of Transjuranic Burgundy from 888.

Rudolf II (d. 937), son of the above, whom he succeeded.

Rudolf III (d. 1032), grandson of the above, ruled from 993 to 1032.

RUDOLF. Name of two German rulers:

Rudolf I (1218–91), founder of the Hapsburg imperial dynasty, was born at Schloss Limburg in the Breisgau, and, becoming a warm partisan of Frederick II, increased his possessions by inheritance and marriage, until he was the most powerful prince in Swabia. In 1273 the electors chose him German king; never having been crowned by the pope, he was not entitled to be called kaiser or emperor. Ottocar of Bohemia refused to tender his allegiance, and in 1278 was defeated and slain at Marchfeld. Rudolf did much to suppress the robber knights. He died at Speyer. His son Albert, to whom (and his brother Rudolf) Austria, Styria and Carniola had been given in 1278, succeeded him as German king. See works by Hirn (1874), Kaltenbrunner (1890) and Redlich (1903).

Rudolf II (1552–1612), born at Vienna, eldest son of the emperor Maximilian II, became King of Hungary in 1572; King of Bohemia, with the title King of the Romans, in 1575; and emperor on his father's death in 1576. Gloomy, taciturn, bigoted and indolent, he put himself in the hands of the Jesuits and low favourites, and left the empire to govern itself. His taste for astrology and the occult sciences made him extend his patronage to Kepler and Tycho Brahe; and their *Rudolphine Tables* were called after him. Meanwhile the Protestants were bitterly persecuted; the Turks invaded Hungary and defeated the Archduke Maximilian (1596); Transylvania and Hungary revolted; and at last Rudolf's brother Matthias wrested from him Hungary, Bohemia, Austria and Moravia. See works by Gindely (1865), von Bezold (1885) and Moritz (1895).

RUDOLF, Prince. See FRANCIS-JOSEPH.

RUDOLF VON EMS (d. 1254), Middle High German poet, of noble family, wrote in the style of Hartmann von Aue and Gottfried (qq.v.) the religious *Der gute Gerhard* and *Barlaam und Josaphat* and an incomplete *Weltchronik*. See study by G. Ehrismann (1919).

RUE. See DE LA RUE.

RUEDA, Lope de, *rway'THa* (*c.* 1510–65), Spanish dramatist, born in Seville, became manager of a group of strolling players. A pioneer of Spanish drama, he wrote comedies in the Italian style, short humorous pastoral dialogues, and ten burlesques (forerunners of interludes). See study by G. Salazar (Santiago de Cuba 1911).

RUFF, William (1801–56), London sporting reporter, in 1842 started his *Guide to the Turf*.

RUFFINI, Giovanni Domenico, *roof-fee'nee* (1807–81), Italian writer, born at Genoa, in 1833 joined Young Italy, and in 1836 had to flee to England. From 1875 he lived at Taggia in the Riviera. He wrote *Lorenzo Benoni: Passages in the Life of an Italian* (1853), *Dr Antonio* (1855), *Vincenzo* (1863), &c.

RUFINUS, *roo-fī'nus* (*c.* 345–410), Italian theologian, was the friend and later the opponent of St Jerome, the orthodoxy of Origen being their subject of dispute.

RUGE, Arnold, *roo'gė* (1802–80), German writer and political thinker, born at Bergen in Rügen, in 1837 helped to found the *Hallesche* (later *Deutsche*) *Jahrbücher*, the organ of Young Germany. Its liberal tendencies were condemned, and Ruge withdrew to Paris and Switzerland. He published in 1848 the democratic *Reform*, entered the Frankfurt parliament for Breslau, and took part in the disturbances at Leipzig in 1849. In 1850 he fled to England, where with Mazzini and Ledru-Rollin he organized the Democratic Committee. He settled at Brighton, and lived by teaching, writing and translating.

RUGGLES-BRISE, Sir Evelyn John, *-brīs* (1857–1935), British penal reformer, was born at Finchingfield, Essex. A civil servant, he was in 1895 appointed chairman of the Prison Commission, a position which he held for twenty-six years. Amongst the many reforms by which he humanized penal treatment, the Borstal system, introduced under the Children Act, 1908, is the best known. He was knighted in 1902. See the memoir by S. Leslie (1938).

RUHMKORFF, Heinrich Daniel, *room'korf* (1803–77), German instrument-maker, born at Hanover, settled (1839) in Paris, and invented (1855) his induction coil.

RUÏSDAEL. See RUYSDAEL.

RULE, St. See REGULUS, ST.

RUMFORD, Benjamin Thompson, Count (1753–1814), Anglo-American administrator and scientist, born at Woburn, Mass., March 26, 1753, was assistant in a store and a school teacher, but in 1771 married a wealthy Mrs Rolfe (1739–92). He was made major in a New Hampshire regiment, but left wife and baby daughter, and fled to England (1776), possibly because he was politically suspect. He gave valuable information to the government as to the state of America, and received an appointment in the Colonial Office. In England he experimented largely with gunpowder, and was elected F.R.S. (1779). In 1782 he was back in America, with a lieutenant-colonel's commission. After the peace he was knighted, and in 1784 entered the service of Bavaria In this new sphere he reformed the army, drained the marshes round Mannheim, established a cannon foundry and military academy, and planned a poor-law system, spread the cultivation of the potato, disseminated a knowledge of nutrition and domestic economy, improved the breeds of horses and cattle, and laid out the English Garden in Munich. For these services he was made head of the Bavarian war department and count of the Holy Roman Empire. During a visit to England (1795–96) he endowed the two Rumford medals of the Royal Society, and also two of the American Academy, for researches in light and heat. Back in Munich, he found it threatened by both French and Austrians. The Elector fled, leaving Count Rumford president of the Council of Regency and generalissimo. Out of his supervision of the arsenal at Munich, where he was impressed by the amount of heat generated in cannon boring, arose his experiments proving the motion, as opposed to the caloric, theory of heat. In 1799 he quitted the Bavarian service, returned to London, and founded the Royal Institution: in 1802 he removed to Paris, and, marrying Lavoisier's widow in 1804, lived at her villa at Auteuil, where he died. He also invented the Rumford shadow photometer. See Memoir by Ellis accompanying his *Works*; Life by Renwick (Boston 1845), German one by Bauernfeind (1889), Prof. Tyndall's *New Fragments* (1892), and E. Larsen, *An American in Europe* (1953).

RUMSEY, James (1743–92), American engineer whose steamboat, propelled by the ejection of water from the stern and exhibited on the Potomac in 1787, was one of the earliest constructed. He died in London while preparing a second version for exhibition on the Thames.

RUNDSTEDT, Karl Rudolf Gero von, *roont'shtet* (1875–1953), German field-marshal, was born in the Old Mark of Brandenburg. He served in World War I, rising to chief of staff of the First Army Corps. In the early 'thirties he was military commander of Berlin and in 1938 commanded occupation troops in the Sudetenland, but was ' purged ' for his outspokenness about Hitler. Recalled in 1939, he directed the *Blitzkriege* in Poland and France. Checked in the Ukraine in 1941, he was relieved of his command, but in 1942 was appointed to a command stretching from Holland to the Italian frontier. On the success of the Allied invasion of France in 1944 he was again relieved of his command, but returned as c.-in-c. in September, his last great action being the Ardennes offensive. Once more he lost his command and in May 1945 was captured by the Americans in Munich. War crimes proceedings against him were dropped on the grounds of his ill-health and he was a prisoner in Britain (1946–1948). See study by Blumentritt (1952).

RUNEBERG, Johan Ludvig, *roo'nĕ-ber-y'* (1804–77), Finnish poet, writing in Swedish, was born at Jakobstad in Finland, taught at Helsingfors from 1830, and at Borga 1837–57. Among his works are *Lyric Poems* (1830), *The Elk Hunters* (1832), *Nadeschda* (1841), a third volume of *Poems* (1843), *King Fjala* (1844), narrative poems, one of which, ' Our Land ', became Finland's national anthem, a comedy *Can't* (1862), and *The Kings in Salamis* (1863), a tragedy. In 1857 Runeberg edited for the Lutheran Church of Finland a *Psalm Book*, in which were included above sixty pieces of his own. See Söderhjelm's study (1904–07); Gosse's criticism and translations in *Studies in the Literature of Northern Europe* (1879); also Magnússon and Palmer's translation (1878).

RUNGE, Friedlieb Ferdinand, *roong'ĕ* (1795–1867), German chemist, born at Hamburg, discovered carbolic acid and aniline in coal tar (1834).

RUNYON, (Alfred) Damon, *run'-* (1884–1946), American author and journalist, was born in Manhattan, Kansas, and after service in the Spanish-American war (1898) turned to newspaper reporting, then to feature-writing. His first publications were volumes of verse, *Tents of Trouble* (1911) and *Rhymes of the Firing Line* (1912), but it was his short stories, written in a characteristic racy, present-tense style, with liberal use of American slang and jargon, and depicting life in underworld New York and on Broadway, which won for him his great popularity. One collection, *Guys and Dolls* (1932), was adopted for a musical revue (1950); other books include *Blue Plate Special* (1934) and *Take it Easy* (1939), and the play, with Howard Lindsay, *A Slight Case of Murder* (1935). From 1941 he worked as a film producer.

RUPERT, Prince (1619–82), third son of the Elector Palatine Frederick V and Elizabeth, daughter of James I of England, was born at Prague, December 18, 1619. After a year and a half at the English court, he served in 1637–38, during the Thirty Years' War, against the Imperialists, until at Lemgo he was taken prisoner, and confined for nearly three years at Linz. In 1642 he returned to England, and for the next three years the ' Mad Cavalier ' was the life and soul of the Royalist cause, winning many a battle by his resistless charges, to lose it as often by a too headlong pursuit. He had fought at Worcester, Edgehill, Brentford, Chalgrove, Newbury, Bolton, Marston Moor, Newbury again, and Naseby, when in August 1645 his surrender of Bristol so irritated Charles, who in 1644 had created him Duke of Cumberland and generalissimo, that he dismissed him. A court martial, however, cleared him, and he resumed his duties, only to surrender at Oxford to Fairfax in June 1646. He now took service with France, but in 1648 accepting the command of that portion of the English fleet which had espoused the king's cause, acquitted himself with all his old daring and somewhat more caution. But in 1650 Blake attacked his squadron, and burned or sank most of his vessels. With the remnant the prince escaped to the West Indies, where with his brother, Prince Maurice (1620–52), till the loss of the latter in a hurricane, he maintained himself by seizing English and other merchantmen. In 1653 he was back in France, where and in Germany he chiefly resided till the Restoration. Thereafter he served under the Duke of York, and in concert with the Duke of Albemarle, in naval operations against the Dutch. He took part in founding the Hudson's Bay Company, which was granted its charter in 1670. He held various offices and dignities being a privy councillor, governor of Windsor, F.R.S., &c. His last years were spent in chemical, physical and mechanical researches. Though he was not the inventor of mezzotint, he improved the processes of the art, which he described to the Royal Society in 1662; and he invented an improved gunpowder and ' Prince's metal '. See Lives by Warburton (1849), Gower (1890), Scott (1899) and Erskine (1910).

RUSH, (1) Benjamin (1745–1813), American politician and physician, born at Byberry, Pa., studied medicine at Edinburgh and Paris, and in 1769 became professor of Chemistry at Philadelphia. Elected a member of the Continental Congress, he signed the Declaration of Independence (1776). In 1777 he was appointed surgeon-general, and later physician-general, of the Continental army. In 1778 he resigned his post because he could not prevent frauds upon soldiers in the hospital stores, and resumed his professorship. In 1799 he became treasurer of the U.S. Mint. He wrote *Medical Inquiries* (1789–93), *Diseases of the Mind* (1821), &c. See Life by Goodman (1934).

(2) **Richard** (1780–1859), American lawyer and statesman, son of (1), was minister to England (1817–25), where he negotiated the Fisheries and Northeastern Boundary Treaties, and was secretary of the Treasury (1825–29).

RUSHWORTH, John (*c.* 1612–90), English historian, born at Acklington Park, Warkworth, studied at Oxford, and settled in London as a barrister. When the Long Parliament met in 1640 he was appointed clerk-assistant to the House of Commons; he represented Berwick 1657–60, 1679, and 1681; and he was secretary to Fairfax 1645–1650, and in 1677 to the lord keeper. In 1684 he was flung into the King's Bench for debt, and there he died. Rushworth's *Historical Collections* (8 vols. 1659–1701) cover the period 1618–48, and are valuable on the Great Rebellion.

RUSK, Dean (1909–), American politician, born in Cherokee County, Ga., educated at Davidson College, N.C., and at Oxford, and in 1934 was appointed associate professor of Government and dean of the Faculty in Mills College. After service in the army in World War II, he held various governmental posts, including that of special assistant to the secretary of war (1946–47), assistant secretary of state for U.N. affairs, deputy under-secretary of state and assistant secretary for Far Eastern Affairs (1950–51). In 1952 he was appointed president of the Rockefeller Foundation and from 1961 was secretary of state, in which capacity he played a major role in handling the Cuban crisis of 1962. He retained the post under the Johnson administration.

RUSKIN, John (1819–1900), English author and art critic, was the son of a prosperous wine merchant in London who was interested in the arts though, like his wife, narrowly evangelical. Private tutoring took the place of schooling so that when he went up to Christ Church, Oxford, in 1836, he was not versed in the ways of men and this lack clung to him throughout life. At Oxford he won the Newdigate prize and fancied himself as a poet till shortly after graduating he met Turner and discovered that his immediate task was to rescue the great painter from obscurity and neglect. *Modern Painters* (1843–60) was the result of this championship which may well have embarrassed the painter. It was more than that, of course, as it developed into a spiritual history of Europe with sidelooks into every phase of morals and taste. For this task he had the advantage of frequent visits to the Continent in company with his parents. His marriage in 1848 to the lady who afterwards became Millais' wife was legally annulled about the time he began his crusade on behalf of a new set of obscure or vilified painters, the pre-Raphaelite brotherhood, with which Millais was associated. *Modern Painters* and the outlying splinters of that great work, viz., *The Seven Lamps of Architecture* (1848) and *The Stones of Venice* (1851–53), with its great chapter 3 ' On the Nature of the Gothic ', made him the critic of the day and something more than that, for the moral and social criticism in those works erected him into a moral guide or prophet. Oxford made him its first Slade professor of Fine Art in 1870, an office he held, with one interruption, till 1884, though latterly his crotchets and eccentricities drew more curious than interested hearers. Following on the publication of the completed *Modern Painters* he transferred his interest in art to the social question which had been implicit in much pre-Raphaelite painting. Carlyle's attacks on utilitarianism no doubt helped, but Ruskin's resentment against the social injustice and squalor resulting from unbridled capitalism led him to a sort of Christian Communism for which he was denigrated. *Unto This Last* (1860), a protest against the law of supply and demand, was discontinued on its first appearance in *Cornhill Magazine* by Thackeray and as it approved the mediaeval injunction against interest we can understand the outcry, but most of the specific reforms proposed have been carried out. The contemptuous rejection of his social economics in this work and in *Munera Pulveris* which followed was almost mortal to Ruskin; in *Sesame and Lilies* (1864–69), addressed to privileged young ladies and admonishing them on their duties, he likened his temper to that of Dean Swift. His appointment to the Slade professorship temporarily reassured him and now his incomparable vitality showed in the publication of various Slade lectures but more memorably in *Fors Clavigera*, a series of papers addressed ' To the Workmen and Labourers of Great Britain ' (1871–84), in which his social philosophy is fully discussed. The announcement ' I simply cannot paint nor read . . . because of the misery that I know of ' links him with Tolstoy, and though he did not, like Tolstoy, denounce middle-class culture he postponed it till the social misery was a thing of the past. The response from the workers and labourers was nil. Meanwhile he began to divest himself of his fortune in such individual enterprises as the St George's Guild, a non-profit-making shop in Paddington Street, the John Ruskin school at Camberwell, and the Whitelands College at Chelsea. His last regret was that he had not, like St Francis, denuded himself of all wealth. In his last work, the singularly beautiful *Praeterita*, also published in numbers (1886–88), he discoursed quietly on his memories, all passion spent save for a final jab at the railways which disturbed rural beauty. His last years were spent at Brantwood, Coniston, his solitude being consoled by the affection of his cousin Mrs Arthur Severn and her family. We do not take our bearings in art from *Modern Painters*—the moralism is too intrusive and ' Select nothing and neglect nothing ' cannot apply to Turner's brilliant impressionism. Nor do we take our bearings in economics from *Unto This Last*, which assumes a primitive society. But apart from his splendid descriptive writing, we value Ruskin as one of the great Victorians who roused England to a sense of responsibility for the squalor in which commercial competition had involved the country. See his *Letters from Venice* (ed. Bradley, 1955); Diaries (ed. Evans and Whitehead, 1956–58) and studies by Wilenski (1955) and Quennell (1956).

RUSSEL, Alexander (1814–76), Scottish journalist, editor of *The Scotsman* from 1848, was born and died in Edinburgh. A Liberal and an antagonist of the Corn Laws, he was a caustic wit and great angler.

RUSSELL, a great Whig house whose origin has been traced back to Thor. Less fancifully, it goes back to one Henry Russell, a Weymouth M.P. and merchant in the Bordeaux wine trade, who lived at the beginning of the 15th century. Among his descendants have been the Earls and Dukes of Bedford, the Earls Russell, Sir William, Baron Russell of Thornhaugh, Edward, Earl of Orford, and William, Lord Russell, described hereafter in that order. See J. H. Wiffen, *Historical Memoirs of the House of Russell* (1833); Froude, *Cheneys and the House of Russell* (1884); G. Scott-Thomson, *Two Centuries of Family History* (1930), *Life in a Noble Household* (1937), *The Russells of Bloomsbury* (1940), and *Family Background* (1947); also *Silver-plated Spoon* (1959) by the Duke of Bedford.

John, 1st Earl of Bedford (*c.* 1486–1555), great-grandson of the above-mentioned Henry, became a gentleman usher to the king, was entrusted with several diplomatic missions and later held many court appointments, including those of comptroller of the household and lord privy seal. Among the rich possessions which he amassed were the abbeys of Woburn and Tavistock, and the London properties of Covent Garden and Long Acre. Created earl in 1550, he led the mission to Spain in 1554 which escorted back Philip to marry Mary Tudor.

Francis, 2nd Earl (1527–85), son of the above, was involved in the Lady Jane Grey affair and fled the country until Elizabeth's accession, when he returned and held several offices, among them that of lord president of Wales.

Francis, 4th Earl (1593–1641), son of Sir William, Baron Russell (see below), with the help of Inigo Jones (q.v.) developed Covent Garden and built the mansion of Woburn; he also continued the fen drainage scheme initiated by his father and known as the Bedford Level.

William, 5th Earl and 1st Duke (1613–1700), was created Marquess of Tavistock and 1st Duke in 1694. He fought with Cromwell at Edgehill (1642), turned royalist in the following year, but after the battle of Newbury changed his coat yet again for parliament. He completed the Bedford Level.

John, 4th Duke (1710–71), a member of the anti-Walpole group, was first lord of the admiralty under Pelham; lord-lieutenant of Ireland (1755–61) and ambassador to France (1762–63).

Francis, 5th Duke (1765–1802), a friend of 'Prinny', built Russell and Tavistock Squares in London and employed Henry Holland (q.v.) to make additions to Woburn.

Herbrand, 11th Duke (1858–1940), declined political office, preferring to preside autocratically over his landed estates. Elected F.R.S. for his services to zoology, president of the Zoological Society from 1899, he established the collections of rare animals at Woburn, including the Prjevalsky wild horses and the Père David deer. His duchess, **Mary du Caurroy** (1865–1937), from 1898 kept a model hospital at Woburn, in which she later worked as a radiographer, took up flying at the age of sixty and participated in record-breaking flights to India and Africa before being lost off the east coast of England while flying solo in 1937.

William, 12th Duke (1888–1953), son of the above, acquired a reputation for his collection of parrots and homing budgerigars and for his adherence to pacifism, Buchmanism and near-fascism which nearly landed him in difficulties during World War II. He was killed in a shooting accident.

John Robert, 13th Duke (1917–), was estranged from his family at an early age and lived for a while on a slender pittance in a Bloomsbury boarding house until, having been invalided out of the Coldstream Guards in 1940, he became in turn house agent, journalist and South African farmer. After succeeding to the title he became famous for his energetic and successful efforts to keep Woburn Abbey for the family by running it commercially as a show place with popular amenities and amusements.

John, 1st Earl Russell (1792–1878), British statesman, born in London, August 18, 1792, the third son of the sixth Duke of Bedford, studied at the University of Edinburgh, and in 1813 was returned for Tavistock. His strenuous efforts in favour of reform won many seats for the Liberals at the 1830 election; the 'Great Duke' was driven from office; and in Earl Grey's ministry Lord John became paymaster of the forces. He was one of the four members of the government entrusted with the task of framing the first Reform Bill (1832), and on him devolved the honour of proposing it. In November 1834 Lord John left office with Melbourne; the carrying of his motion (1835) for applying the surplus revenues of the Irish Church to education caused the downfall of Peel and the return of Melbourne to power, with Lord John as home (from 1839 colonial) secretary and leader of the Lower House. In the general election of 1841 he was returned for the City, which he represented until his elevation to the Upper House. In November 1845 he wrote a letter to his constituents announcing his conversion to the repeal of the Corn Laws. This led to Peel's resignation; and Lord John was commissioned to form an administration. He failed, owing to Lord Grey's antipathy to Palmerston, so Peel was forced back to office, and carried the repeal. On the very day the bill passed the Lords Peel was defeated by a coalition of Whigs and Protectionists; whereupon a Whig ministry succeeded, with Lord John as prime minister (1846–52). In Lord Aberdeen's Coalition of 1852 he was foreign secretary and leader in the Commons. His inopportune Reform Bill (1854), the Crimean mismanagement, his resignation (January 1855) and his bungling at the Vienna Conference, all combined to render him unpopular; and for four years he remained out of office. But in June 1859, in the second Palmerston administration, he became foreign secretary, in 1861 was created Earl Russell, and K.G. in 1862. Though he did much for Italian unity, non-intervention was his leading principle, e.g., during the American Civil War and the Schleswig-Holstein difficulty. On Palmerston's death in 1865 Earl Russell again became prime minister, but was defeated in June on his new Reform Bill and resigned. He continued busy with tongue and pen till his death at his residence, Pembroke Lodge, Richmond Park, May 28, 1878. Earl Russell was twice married, and by his second wife, daughter of the Earl of Minto, was the father of **John, Viscount Amberley** (1842–76), author of the posthumous *Analysis of Religious Belief*. His sons succeeded as second and third earl respectively. Earl Russell's works include a tale and two tragedies, a *Life of William Lord Russell* (1819), *Memoirs of the Affairs of Europe* (1824), *The Correspondence of John, fourth Duke of Bedford* (1842–46), and Memoirs of Fox and Moore. See his *Speeches and Despatches* (1870), his *Recollections and Suggestions* (1875), *Early Correspondence* (1913), and Lives by Walpole (1889), Reid (1893), and Tilby (1930). His nephew, **George William Erskine Russell** (1853–1919), was a Liberal under-secretary and miscellaneous author.

John Francis Stanley, 2nd Earl Russell (1865–1931), brother of the 3rd Earl, held secretaryships in the second Labour administration. An American divorce and marriage led to three months' imprisonment for bigamy (1901). For his third wife, see ARNIM (1).

Bertrand Arthur William, 3rd Earl Russell (1872–1970), English philosopher, mathematician and controversialist, one of the greatest logicians of all time, was born May 18 at Ravenscroft near Trelleck, Monmouthshire, son of Viscount Amberley and brother of the 2nd Earl, was educated privately and at Trinity College, Cambridge, where he graduated with first-class honours in mathematics (1893) and moral sciences (1894). After a few months as a British Embassy attaché in Paris, he went to Berlin to study economics, wrote his first book, *German Social Democracy* (1896), and married Alys Pearsall Smith. Elected fellow of Trinity (1895), his early infatuation with the Hegelian idealism of McTaggart was dispelled by his researches into the symbolic logic of Peano and Frege, his own brilliant study of Leibniz (1900) and the antimetaphysical common sense of a junior colleague, G. E. Moore (q.v.). The problem he posed himself was that first raised by Kant—how to defend the objectivity of mathematics. Frege and Peano had already attempted to derive, by means of symbolic logic, the whole of mathematics from certain logical constants. Russell wrote to the former (1902), pointing out a contradiction in his system, the famous antinomy of the class of all classes which is not a member of itself. This Frege with immense disappointment courageously acknowledged in a postscript to his work. Meanwhile Russell published his own bold *Principles of Mathematics* (1903) and with A. N. Whitehead (q.v.) carried on the Fregeian endeavour to its conclusion in the monumental *Principia Mathematica* (1910–13). In this he made strenuous attempts to resolve Frege's contradictions by the famous Russellian theory of types, or classes. Another epoch-making philosophical achievement was his famous theory of descriptions set out in an article in *Mind* (1905), 'On Denoting', which first differentiated between the logical and grammatical subject of a proposition. This successfully countered Meinong's extraordinary theory of objects which had it that every subject of a proposition, be it fictitious or otherwise, must be credited with some sort of 'existence'. Russell dissected this inflated ontology, using Occam's razor, preserving meaningfulness, if falseness, of propositions containing fictitious entities such as 'round square', 'the present king of France' as subjects. On this account 'Socrates', for example, is a disguised description and not a logically proper name. The theory of descriptions provided a masterly solution of longstanding logical problems and if it later came under attack from linguistic considerations that does not detract from Russell's permanent achievement. Russellian methods were fully deployed by his brilliant student Wittgenstein, who was at Cambridge (1912–13), in a rigorously logical and ostensibly 'anti-metaphysical' system, which eventually matured into the famous *Tractatus* (1922) for the English version of which Russell wrote the introduction. Wittgenstein's earliest views Russell entitled 'logical atomism', and believing Wittgenstein to have been killed in the war, lectured on them with generous acknowledgments in the United States and published them in *The Monist* (1919). His own last great work on the subject *Introduction to Mathematical Philosophy* (1919) was written in prison. His approach, frequently modified in later works, to general philosophical problems is set out in such works as *Some Problems in Philosophy* (1912), a minor classic, *Our Knowledge of the External World* (1914), *The Analysis of Mind* (1927), *An Enquiry into Meaning and Truth* (1940), with an excellent account of probability, and *Human Knowledge* (1948). Russell, like his 'secular' godfather, John Stuart Mill, an ardent feminist, in 1907 offered himself as a Liberal candidate but was turned down for his 'free-thinking'. In 1916 his pacificism deprived him of his Trinity fellowship and in 1918 he was imprisoned. Henceforth the controversialist, who had to make a living by lecturing and journalism took charge of Russell, the philosopher. A visit to the Soviet Union, where he met Lenin, Trotsky and Gorky, sobered his early enthusiasm and resulted in the critical *Theory and Practice of Bolshevism* (1919). He was professor at Peking (1920–21), was divorced by his wife and married Dora Winifred

Black, a fellow of Girton College, Cambridge. With her he ran a progressive school near Petersfield (1927) and set out his educationist theories in *On Education* (1926) and *Education and the Social Order* (1932). His second divorce (1934) made his book *Marriage and Morals* (1932) highly controversial, although much of its advocacy was no more startling than the matrimonial reforms in More's *Utopia*. Nevertheless, his lectureship at the City College of New York was terminated in 1940 after protests from clergy and ratepayers against this 'enemy of religion and morality'. But he won an action against the Barnes Foundation which broke a lecture contract. In 1936 he married Helen Patricia Spence, his research assistant for *Freedom and Organisation, 1814-1914* (1934). The evils of fascism analysed in *In Praise of Idleness* (1936), he renounced pacificism in 1939 and went so far in the early postwar period as to advocate atomic bombardment of Russia, while the United States still had the nuclear monopoly. After 1949 he became a champion of nuclear disarmament, engaging in unprecedented correspondence with various world leaders, as at the time of the Cuban crisis in 1963, and protesting against U.S. involvement in Vietnam. In 1952, having divorced his third wife, he married an American fellow-novelist, Edith Finch. His fellowship at Trinity was restored in 1944 and he gave the first B.B.C. Reith Lectures, *Authority and the Individual* (1949). A controversial public figure, an 18th-century rationalist who had strayed into the 20th, who wrote his own jesting obituary notice for *The Times*, he will be remembered as the greatest logician since Aristotle. He succeeded to his brother's title in 1931, was elected F.R.S. (1908), awarded its Sylvester medal (1934), O.M. (1949) and Nobel prize for literature (1950). See also his popular expositions, *ABC of Atoms* (1923), *ABC of Relativity* (1925; revised 1958), *Why I am not a Christian* (1957), collections of his best philosophical papers, *Mysticism and Logic* (1910), *Logic and Knowledge*, ed. R. C. Marsh (1956), his edition of his parents' letters and diaries, *The Amberley Papers* (1937), his biting literary outlines of leading contemporaries, *Portraits from Memory* (1956), the autobiographical note and critical studies by fellow-philosophers in *The Philosophy of B. Russell*, ed. P. A. Schilpp (1944), *My Philosophical Development* (1959), and his *Autobiography* (Vol. 1, 1967, Vol. 2, 1968); also studies by Fritz (1952) on his satire, ed. Egner (1958), and Lives by Leggett (1949) and Wood, *The Passionate Sceptic* (1957).

Sir William, Baron Russell (cr. 1603) of **Thornhaugh** (*c.* 1558–1613), son of the 2nd Earl of Bedford, was governor of Flushing (1587–88) and lord deputy of Ireland (1594–1597). His experience of lowland drainage methods while in the former post led him to initiate reclamation work in the Cambridgeshire fens.

Edward, Earl of Orford (1683–1727), nephew of the 1st Duke of Bedford, English admiral, was a supporter of William of Orange, and is remembered as the commander of a combined British and Dutch fleet in the victory over the French at La Hogue (1692). He was created an earl in the same year.

William, Lord Russell (1639–83), born September 29, 1639, third son of the fifth Earl of Bedford, studied at Cambridge, made the Grand Tour, and at the Restoration was elected M.P. for Tavistock. He was 'drawn by the court into some disorders' (debts and duelling), from which he was rescued by his marriage (1669) with Lady Rachel Wriothesley (1636–1723), second daughter and co-heiress of the Earl of Southampton and widow of Lord Vaughan. In 1674 he spoke against the actions of the Cabal, and thenceforth was an active adherent of the Country Party. He dallied unwisely with France, but took no bribe; he shared honestly in the delusion of the Popish Plot; he presented the Duke of York as a recusant; and he carried the Exclusion Bill up to the House of Lords. He was arrested with Essex and Sidney for participation in the Ryehouse Plot, was arraigned of high treason, and, infamous witnesses easily satisfying a packed jury, was found guilty, and beheaded on July 21, 1683. The pity of his judicial murder, the pathos of Burnet's story of his end, and the exquisite letters of his noble wife, who at his trial appeared in court as his secretary, have secured him a place in history. See Life by Lord John Russell (1819; 4th ed. 1853); Letters of Lady Russell (1773; 14th ed. 1853); and Lives of her by Miss Berry (1819), Lord John Russell (1820), Guizot (Eng. trans. 1855) and Lady Stepney (1899).

RUSSELL, (1) Anna, stage name of **Claudia Anna Russell-Brown** (1911–), English singer and musical satirist, born in London, studied singing, and began an orthodox operatic career before realizing the possibilities of satire offered by opera and concert singing, and appearing as a concert debunker of musical fads in New York in 1948, since when she has achieved universal fame in this medium.

(2) **Bertrand.** See RUSSELL, 3RD EARL, under RUSSELL Family.

(3) **Charles Taze** (1852–1916), 'Pastor Russell', born at Pittsburgh, was a travelling preacher, and founded the International Bible Students' Association (Jehovah's Witnesses), a sect with peculiar views of prophecy and eschatology.

(4) **George** (1857–1951), English horticulturist, born at Stillington, Yorkshire. After twenty-five years of research and experiment he succeeded in producing lupins of greatly improved strains and of over sixty different colours. For this achievement he was awarded a Veitch Memorial Medal by the Royal Horticultural Society in 1937 and the M.B.E. in 1951.

(5) **George William**, pseud. Æ (1867–1935), Irish poet, writer and economist, was born at Lurgan, Co. Armagh. In 1877 the family went to Dublin, where at the Metropolitan School of Art Russell met W. B. Yeats, and, already something of a mystic, through him became interested in theosophy; this led him to give up painting, except as a hobby. Having worked first in a brewery, then as a draper's clerk, Russell published in 1894 his first book, *Homeward: Songs by the Way*,

and thereafter became a recognized figure in the Irish literary renaissance. Of nationalistic sympathies, he was editor of the *Irish Homestead* from 1906 to 1923, when it amalgamated with the *Irish Statesman*, and as editor of the latter from 1923 to 1930, he aimed at expressing balanced Irish opinion of the 1920's. His writings include books on economics, *The Candle of Vision* (1918), which is an expression of his religious philosophy, books of essays, many volumes of verse, all expressing his mysticism, among them *The Divine Vision* (1903) and *Midsummer Eve* (1928), and a play, *Deirdre* (1907). See Memoir by John Eglinton (1937).

(6) **Henry.** See (11).

(7) **Henry Norris** (1877–1957), American astronomer, was born at Oyster Bay, N.Y., was educated at Princeton and Cambridge, and became professor of Astronomy at Princeton in 1911. He developed a theory of stellar evolution, from dwarf to giant stars, which has now been superseded.

(8) **Jack,** properly **John** (1795–1883), English 'sporting parson', born at Dartmouth, and educated at Oxford, was perpetual curate of Swymbridge near Barnstaple (1832–1880), and withal master of foxhounds and sportsman generally. A breed of terrier found in the West Country was named after him. See Memoir (new ed. 1883).

(9) **John** (1745–1806), English portrait painter and Methodist enthusiast, was born at Guildford, and elected R.A. in 1788. See Life by Williamson (1894).

(10) **John Scott** (1808–82), Scottish engineer, inventor of the 'wave system' of shipbuilding, was born near Glasgow, and died at Ventnor.

(11) **William Clark** (1844–1911), born in New York, was son of the vocalist **Henry Russell** (1812–1900), who, born at Sheerness, was composer of 'Cheer, Boys, Cheer', 'A Life on the Ocean Wave' and other popular songs. Clark Russell served an apprenticeship at sea, and from 1874 devoted himself to writing a long succession of sea stories. See also RONALD.

(12) **Sir William Howard** (1821–1907), British special correspondent, born near Tallaght, County Dublin, joined *The Times* in 1843, and was called to the bar in 1850. From the Crimea he wrote those famous letters (published in book form 1856) which opened the eyes of Englishmen to the sufferings of the soldiers during the winter of 1854–55. He next witnessed the events of the Indian Mutiny. He established the *Army and Navy Gazette* in 1860; and in 1861 the Civil War drew him to America, which he soon made too hot for him by a candid account of the Federal defeat at Bull Run. He accompanied the Austrians during the war with Prussia (1866), and the Prussians during the war with France (1870–71); visited Egypt and the East (1874) and India (1877) as private secretary to the Prince of Wales; and went with Wolseley to South Africa in 1879. He was knighted in 1895. Among his books are a novel, *The Adventures of Dr Brady* (1868), *Hesperothen* (1882) and *A Visit to Chile* (1890). See R. Furneaux, *The First War Correspondent* (1945).

RUSSELL OF KILLOWEN, Charles Russell, 1st Baron (1832–1900), British lawyer, born at Newry, studied at Trinity College, Dublin, was called to the English bar in 1859. He became a Q.C. (1872), a Liberal M.P. (1880), attorney-general (1886, 1892–94), a knight (1886), lord chief justice (1894), and a life peer. A supporter of Irish home rule, he was leading counsel for Parnell in the tribunal of 1888–89. See Life by O'Brien (1901).

RUTEBEUF (*c.* 1230–86), French trouvère, Champenois in origin but Parisian by adoption, was author of the semi-liturgical drama *Miracle de Théophile* (*c.* 1260, a prototype of the Faust story), the *Dit de l'Herberie*, a monologue by a quack doctor, full of comic charlatanesque rhetoric, and also several typical *fabliaux*. See studies by Clédat (1891) and Leo (1922).

RUTH, George Herman (Babe) (1895–1948), U.S. baseball player, born in Baltimore, began his career with the Baltimore Orioles before joining the Boston Red Sox, then the New York Yankees, with whom he played till his retirement in 1934. He was the holder of innumerable records and took part in more World series matches than any other player. *The Babe Ruth Story* was filmed in 1948.

RUTHERFORD, *ruTH'-*, (1) **Alison.** See COCKBURN (2).

(2) **Daniel** (1749–1819), Scottish physician and botanist, stepbrother of Sir Walter Scott's mother, was born in Edinburgh, where he became professor of Botany in 1786. In 1772 he published his discovery of the distinction between 'noxious air' (nitrogen) and carbon dioxide.

(3) **Ernest Rutherford, 1st Baron Rutherford of Nelson** (1871–1937), New Zealand-born British physicist, one of the greatest pioneers of subatomic physics, was born August 30 at Spring Grove (later Brightwater) near Nelson, New Zealand, the fourth of twelve children of a wheelwright and flaxmiller. Educated at local state schools, he won scholarships to Nelson College and Canterbury College, Christchurch. His first research projects were on magnetization of iron by high-frequency discharges (1894) and magnetic viscosity (1896). In 1895 he was admitted to the Cavendish Laboratory and Trinity College, Cambridge, on an 1851 Exhibition scholarship. There he made the first successful wireless transmissions over two miles. Under the brilliant direction of J. J. Thomson (q.v.), Rutherford discovered the three types of uranium radiations. In 1898 he became professor of Physics at McGill university, Canada, where, with Soddy, he formulated the theory of atomic disintegration to account for the tremendous heat energy radiated by uranium, thus overthrowing the classical law of conservation of matter. In 1907 he became professor at Manchester and there established that alpha particles were doubly ionized helium ions by counting the number given off with a Geiger counter. This led to a revolutionary conception of the atom as a miniature universe in which the mass is concentrated in the nucleus surrounded by planetary electrons. His assistant, Niels Bohr (q.v.), applied to this the quantum theory (1913) and the concept of the 'Rutherford-Bohr atom' of nuclear

physics was born. During World War I, Rutherford did research on submarine detection for the admiralty. In 1919, in a series of brilliant experiments, he discovered that alpha-ray bombardments induced atomic transformation in atmospheric nitrogen, liberating hydrogen nuclei. The same year he succeeded J. J. Thomson to the Cavendish professorship at Cambridge and reorganized the laboratory, the world's centre for the study of *The Newer Alchemy* (1937). In 1920 he predicted the existence of the neutron, later discovered by his colleague, Chadwick, in 1932. He was elected F.R.S. in 1903, was awarded its Rumford (1904) and Copley (1922) medals, the Nobel prize for chemistry (1908) and the O.M. (1925), was knighted (1914) and made a peer (1931), was president of the British Association (1923), of the Royal Society (1925–30) and was chairman of the advisory council of D.S.I.R. (1930–37). He published nearly 150 original papers, and his books include *Radioactivity* (1904), *Radioactive Transformations* (1906) and *Radioactive Substances* (1930). He died at Cambridge, October 19, 1937, and was buried in Westminster Abbey. See biographical studies by A. S. Eve (1939), N. Feather (1940) and J. Rowland (1955).

(4) **Dame Margaret** (1892–1972), British theatre and film actress, born in London, made her first stage appearance in 1925 at the Old Vic theatre, and her film début in 1936. She gradually gained fame as a character actress and comedienne, her gallery of eccentrics including such notable rôles as 'Miss Prism' in *The Importance of Being Earnest* (stage 1939, film 1952), 'Madame Arcati' in *Blithe Spirit* (stage 1941, film 1945), and 'Miss Whitchurch' in *The Happiest Days of Your Life* (stage 1948, film 1950). She also scored a success as Agatha Christie's 'Miss Marple' in a series of films from 1962, appearing with her husband, the actor **Stringer Davis** (1899–), whom she married in 1945. She was created O.B.E. in 1961, D.B.E. in 1967, and won an Oscar as Best Supporting Actress for her part in *The V.I.P.s* in 1964.

(5) **Mark.** See WHITE (9).

(6) **Samuel** (*c.* 1600–61), Scottish theologian and preacher, born at Nisbet near Jedburgh, took his M.A. at Edinburgh in 1621. In 1623 he was appointed professor of Humanity; he was dismissed in 1626, having 'fallen in fornication'; but next year he was settled as minister of Anwoth. Here he began that correspondence with his godly friends which has been called 'the most seraphic book in our literature'. *Exercitationes pro divina Gratia* (1636) was against the Arminians, and brought him an invitation to a Divinity chair in Holland and a summons before the High Commission Court in July 1636, when he was forbidden to preach, and banished to Aberdeen (till 1638). He became professor of Divinity at St Andrews in 1639, and in 1647 principal of the New College; in 1643 he was sent to the Westminster Assembly. His *Due Right of Presbyteries* (1644), *Lex Rex* (1644), &c., belong to this period. *Lex Rex* was burned by the hangman in Edinburgh in 1661, and its author deposed and summoned for high treason; but he received the citation when on his deathbed. See Lives by Murray (1828) and Thomson (1884), Bonar's edition of the *Letters*, and Dr A. Whyte's *Samuel Rutherford and his Correspondents* (1894).

RUTHVEN, *riv'ĕn*, (1) **John** (*c.* 1578–1600), second son of (2), succeeded a brother as 3rd Earl in 1588, and travelled in Italy, Switzerland and France. Soon after his arrival back in Scotland he was killed with a brother in his house at Perth in the 'Gowrie Conspiracy'—controversially an alleged attempt to murder or kidnap James VI. See Barbé's *Tragedy of Gowrie House* (1887) and Roughead's *The Riddle of the Ruthvens* (1919).

(2) **William** (*c.* 1541–84), created Earl of Gowrie in 1581, carried off the boy king, James VI, to Castle Ruthven near Perth—the 'Raid of Ruthven'—was first pardoned, then ordered to leave the country, but was beheaded at Stirling for his part in a conspiracy to take Stirling Castle.

RUTLAND, John James Robert Manners, 7th Duke of (1818–1906), English politician, born at Belvoir Castle, entered parliament in 1841, succeeded to the dukedom in 1888, and held office in the various Conservative ministries between 1852 and 1892. A member of the Young England party (1842–45), he wrote poems, descriptions of tours and a yachting cruise, ballads, &c. See study by C. Whibley (1925).

RUYSBROEK, Johannes, *roys'brook* (1293–1381), Flemish mystic, born at Ruysbroek near Brussels, was vicar of St Gudule's in Brussels, but in 1353 withdrew to the Augustinian monastery of Groenendael near Waterloo, of which he became prior. His mysticism is expressed in his *Book of Supreme Truth*, &c. See Lives of the *Doctor ecstaticus* by Engelhardt (1838) and Otterloo (1874), and books by Maeterlinck (Eng. trans. 1894) and Evelyn Underhill (1915).

RUYSDAEL, or Ruïsdael, Jacob van, *roys'dahl* (*c.* 1628–82), one of the greatest landscape painters of the Dutch school, was born in Haarlem. Perhaps a pupil of his uncle **Salomon van Ruysdael** (*c.* 1600–70), a Haarlem landscape painter, he became a member of the Haarlem painters' guild in 1648, about 1655 moved to Amsterdam, thereafter travelling in Holland and Germany. He died in an almshouse in Haarlem. His best works are country landscapes, and he also excelled in cloud effects, particularly in his seascapes. He was not highly regarded by his contemporaries, but modern appreciation of him has prevailed in spite of an unpleasant darkening through time of the green of his landscapes. He is represented in the National Gallery, London (*Holland's Deep* and *Landscape with Ruins*), Glasgow Art Gallery (*View of Katwijk*), the Louvre (*Le Coup de Soleil*), &c. See study by Rosenberg (1928).

RUYTER, Michiel Adrianszoon de, *roy'tėr* (1607–76), Dutch sailor, born at Flushing, went to sea as a cabin boy, but by 1635 had become a captain in the Dutch navy. In the war with England in 1652 he repelled an attack off the Lizard, and with de Witt had to retire after attacking Blake off the mouth of the Thames; but two months later they defeated Blake off Dover. In 1653 he repeatedly fought with Blake, Monk and Deane, and was at the battle off the Texel (July 29), where his superior, Tromp, was killed and the Dutch fleet defeated. After 1654 he blockaded the coasts of Portugal, and then those of Sweden; and after the Dano-Swedish war was ennobled by the king of Denmark. The years 1661–63 were principally occupied with the Barbary corsairs. In the next English war (1664) he took Gorée and some Guinea forts; in 1665 he preyed upon English merchant vessels in the West Indies; in 1666, now admiral-in-chief, he held his own for four days (June 1–4) against Monk and Prince Rupert off Dunkirk; in July he was driven back to Holland by Monk. In 1667 he sailed up the Medway to Rochester, burned some of the English ships, and next sailed up the Thames to Gravesend, besides attacking Harwich. In a third war (1672) against England and France combined, he attacked the English and French fleets under the Duke of York, the Earl of Sandwich, and Count d'Estrées in Solebay (May 28, 1672); and defeated Prince Rupert and d'Estrées in June 1673, and again in August. In 1675 de Ruyter sailed for the Mediterranean to help the Spaniards against the French. He encountered the French fleet near the Lipari Islands about the New Year, and again in the Bay of Catania. In the second fight the Dutch-Spanish fleet was routed and de Ruyter wounded. He died April 29, in Syracuse. See Lives by Brandt (1698), Richer (1783) and Blok (trans. 1933).

RUŽIČKA, Leopold, *roo'zheech-ka* (1887–), Swiss chemist, born at Vukovar, Yugoslavia, became professor of Chemistry at Utrecht in 1926 and at Zürich in 1929. He made the earliest synthesis of musk, worked on higher terpenes and steroids, and was the first to synthesize sex hormones, for which he was awarded with Butenandt the 1939 Nobel prize for chemistry.

RUZZANTE, real name **Angelo Beolco**, *root-tsan'tay* (1502–42), Italian dramatist and actor, born in Padua, wrote mainly comedies of rural life. See study by Cataldo (1933).

RYDBERG, *rüd'ber-y'*, (1) **Abraham Viktor** (1828–95), Swedish author, born in Jönköping, was on the staff of a Göteborg newspaper, later a professor in Stockholm. Among his works are several novels of the highest merit, including *Fribrytaren på Östersjön* (1857). He also wrote Biblical criticism.

(2) **Johannes Robert** (1854–1919), Swedish physicist, born at Halmstad, was professor at Lund from 1901 to 1919, developed a formula for spectral lines, incorporating the constant known by his name.

RYDER, *rī'dėr*, (1) **Albert Pinkham** (1847–1917), American painter, born in New Bedford, Mass., excelled in figures and landscapes, executed in a romantic style.

(2) **Samuel** (1859–1936), English businessman, donor (1927) of the Ryder Cup, competed for by British and American professional golfers. Ryder, the son of a Cheshire nurseryman, built up, mainly by his scheme of selling penny packets of seeds, a prosperous business at St Albans.

RYLANDS, John, *rī'lėndz* (1801–88), English textile manufacturer and merchant, born at St Helens. In 1899 his widow established the John Rylands Library in Manchester.

RYLE, *rīl*, (1) **Gilbert** (1900–), English philosopher, educated at Brighton College and Queen's College, Oxford, served in the Welsh Guards from 1939 until 1945, when he became Waynflete professor of Metaphysical Philosophy at Oxford. In 1931 he became a convert to the view that 'philosophy is the detection of the sources of linguistic idioms of recurrent misconstructions and absurd theories'. His *Concept of Mind* (1949) displays brilliant linguistic detective work in exorcizing 'the ghost in the machine' or the philosophical remains of Cartesian dualism. In 1947 he became editor of *Mind*. Other works include *Dilemmas* (1954) and *Plato's Progress* (1966). He edited *Revolution in Philosophy* (1957).

(2) **Herbert Edward** (1856–1925), second son of (3), born in London, Bishop of Exeter (1900–03), Bishop of Winchester (1903–10), Dean of Westminster (1910), K.C.V.O. (1921), wrote on the Old Testament canon, Genesis, Philo, &c. See Fitzgerald's Memoir (1928).

(3) **John Charles** (1816–1900), Bishop of Liverpool (1880–1900), was born at Macclesfield. A prominent Evangelical, he wrote countless popular tracts and books. See Life by M. L. Loane (1953).

(4) **Martin** (1918–), English radio-astronomer, educated at Bradfield and Christ Church, Oxford, worked at the Cavendish Laboratory, Cambridge (1945–48), and subsequently became a fellow of Trinity, lecturer in Physics (1948–59), and professor of Radio-astronomy from 1959. Using the Cambridge radio-telescope to plot the intensity-distribution curve of stars up to 3000 million and more light years distant, he obtained controversial data which led him in 1961 to throw doubt on the generally accepted 'steady state' theory of the universe.

RYMER, Thomas, *rī'mėr* (1641–1713), English critic and historian, born at Yafforth Hall, Northallerton, Yorks, the son of a Roundhead gentleman who was hanged at York in 1664, studied at Sidney Sussex, Cambridge, and entered Gray's Inn in 1666. He published translations, critical discussions on poetry, dramas and works on history, and in 1692 was appointed historiographer royal. His principal critical work is *The Tragedies of the Last Age Considered* (1678); but he is chiefly remembered as the compiler of the collection of historical materials known as the *Foedera* (1704–35). Hardy's *Syllabus* of the whole was published in 1869–85.

RYMOUR. See THOMAS THE RHYMER.

RYSBRACK, (John) Michael, *rīs'brak* (*c.* 1693–1770), Flemish sculptor, born perhaps at Antwerp, settled in London in 1720. Among his works are the monument to Sir Isaac Newton in Westminster Abbey (1731), statues of William III, Queen Anne, George II, and busts of Gay, Rowe, Pope, Sir R. Walpole, &c. See study by Webb (1954).

RYVES, Mrs. See OLIVE, PRINCESS.

S

SAADI. See SÁDI.

SAARINEN, **Eero** (1910–61), Finnish-American architect, born in Finland, accompanied his father, **Gottlieb Eliel Saarinen** (1873–1950), to the U.S. in 1923. After studying sculpture in Paris and architecture at Yale University he worked with his father, designing many public buildings in U.S.A. and in Europe, including the Columbia Broadcasting System H.Q., N.Y., and the U.S. chancelleries in Oslo and London. He claimed an almost religious rôle for architecture. See *Eero Saarinen on his Work* (1963).

SABATIER, *sa-ba-tyay*, (1) **Louis Auguste** (1839–1901), French Protestant theologian, born at Vallon (Ardèche), wrote the very influential *Esquisse d'une philosophie de la religion* (1897, trans. 1897).

(2) **Paul** (1858–1928), French Protestant theologian, brother of (1), was a vicar in Strasbourg until expelled by the Germans in 1889, became professor at Strasbourg in 1919, and after a *Life* in 1893 wrote much on St Francis of Assisi.

(3) **Paul** (1854–1941), French chemist, was born at Carcassonne, and in 1882 became professor at Toulouse. He did notable work in catalysis, discovering with Senderens (q.v.) a process for the catalytic hydrogenation of oils, and shared with Grignard (q.v.) the 1912 Nobel prize for chemistry.

SABATINI, **Rafael**, *sa-ba-tee'nee* (1875–1950), novelist, was born of Italian and British parentage at Jesi, Italy. Writing in English, he first made his name as an author of historical romances with *The Tavern Knight* (1904), which he followed after he settled in England in 1905 with many other such tales, including *The Sea Hawk* (1915) and *Scaramouche* (1921), historical biographies, and a study of *Torquemada* (1913).

SABBATAI Z'VI, *sa-bat'ay-ī tsė-vee'* (1626–1675), a messiah, who, born in Smyrna, gained a great following, but latterly embraced Islam. See Life by Kastein (1931).

SABINE, **Sir Edward**, *sa'bin* (1788–1883), British astronomer, physicist and soldier, born in Dublin, accompanied Ross and Parry as astronomer in 1818–20. But his reputation rests on his valuable pendulum experiments and labours in terrestrial magnetism. He was elected F.R.S. in 1818, was P.R.S. 1861–71, was knighted in 1869 and became a general in 1870.

SACCHETTI, **Franco**, *sak-ket'tee* (*c.* 1330–1400), Italian novelist, a follower of Boccaccio, was born in Florence, and held several diplomatic offices. Of his 258 *Novelle*, first printed in 1724, ten are translated in Roscoe's *Italian Novelists* (1825). Gigli edited his *Opere* (1857–61) and *Novelle* (1886); Morpurgo his *Rime* (1892), with a Life.

SACCHI, **Andrea**, *sak'kee* (*c.* 1599–1661), Italian painter, was born at Netturo near Rome. He upheld the classical tradition in Roman painting, and is represented by the *Vision of St Romuald* and *Miracle of Saint Gregory*, painted for Pope Urban VIII, and by religious works in many Roman churches.

SACCHINI, **Antonio Maria Gasparo**, *sak-kee'nee* (1734–86), Italian composer, born at Pozzuoli, travelled in Italy and Germany, lived in London (1772–82). He wrote operas and church and chamber music.

SACCO, **Nicola** (1891–1927), and **Vanzetti Bartolomeo** (1888–1927), chief figures in an American *cause célèbre* which had world-wide reverberations. Accused of a payroll murder and robbery in 1920, they were found guilty, and seven years later were executed in spite of conflicting and circumstantial evidence, and the confession of another man to the crime. Both had been extreme left-wing labour agitators, and the suspicion that this had provoked deliberate injustice aroused an outcry in all parts of the world.

SACHARISSA. See WALLER (2).

SACHER-MASOCH, **Leopold von**, *zahKH'ėr-mah'zoKH* (1836–95), Austrian lawyer and writer, born in Lemberg, wrote many short stories and novels, including *Der Don Juan von Kolomea* (1866), depicting the life of smalltown Polish Jews. The term 'masochism' has been coined to describe the form of eroticism detailed in his later works.

SACHEVERELL, *sa-shev'ėr-ėl*, (1) **Henry** (*c.* 1674–1724), English political preacher, was born at Marlborough, the son of a High Church rector, and went in 1689 to Magdalen College, Oxford, where he shared rooms with Addison, who dedicated to his 'dearest Henry' *An Account of the Greatest English Poets* (1694). Gaining his doctorate in 1708, he had held the Staffordshire vicarage of Cannock, when in 1709 he delivered the two sermons—one at Derby assizes, the other at St Paul's—which have given him a place in history. The rancour with which he assailed the Revolution Settlement and the Act of Toleration, while asserting the doctrine of nonresistance, roused the wrath of the Whig government, and he was impeached (1710) before the House of Lords. Ardent crowds, shouting 'High Church and Sacheverell!' and now and then wrecking a meeting house, attended him to Westminster. He was found guilty, and suspended from preaching for three years. The Godolphin ministry fell that same summer, and in 1713 Sacheverell was selected by the House of Commons to preach the Restoration sermon. He was presented to the rich rectory of St Andrew's, Holborn, after which little is heard of him save that he squabbled with his parishioners, and was suspected of complicity in a Jacobite plot. See F. Madan's *Bibliography of Dr Sacheverell* (1887).

(2) **William** (1638–91), English politician, sometimes called the 'First Whig', studied law, entered the House of Commons as member for Derbyshire in 1670, and rapidly became one of the leaders of the anti-Court party, instrumental in framing the Test Act, which overthrew Charles II's 'cabal'

ministry. He was prominent amongst those later demanding the resignation of Lord Danby and a keen supporter of the Exclusion Bill. Fined by Judge Jeffreys in 1682 for opposing the king's remodelled charter for Nottingham, and defeated in the 1685 election, he sat in the Convention parliament of 1689 which offered the throne to William. Throughout his career of 'opposition' Sacheverell was distinguished for his powers of parliamentary oratory.

SACHS, *zahks*, (1) **Hans** (1494–1576), German poet and dramatist, born November 5, 1494, at Nuremberg, the son of a tailor, was bred a shoemaker, and early learnt verse-making from a weaver. On finishing his apprenticeship in 1511 he travelled through Germany, practising his craft in various cities, and frequenting the schools of the *Meistersinger*. On his return to Nuremberg in 1516 he commenced business as a shoemaker, becoming a master of his guild in the following year; and, after a long and prosperous life, died January 19 (or 25), 1576. Sachs' literary career, which resulted in the tremendous output of more than 6300 pieces, falls into two periods. In the first he celebrated the Reformation and sang Luther's praises in an allegorical tale (1523) entitled *Die Wittenbergisch Nachtigall*, while his poetical flysheets, numbering about 200, furthered in no small measure the Protestant cause. In his second period his poetry deals more with common life and manners, and is distinguished by its vigorous language, good sense, homely morality and fresh humour. It is, however, deficient in high imagination and brilliant fancy, and contains much prosaic and insipid verse. His best works are *Schwänke*, or Merry Tales, the humour of which is sometimes unsurpassable; serious tales; allegorical and spiritual songs; and Lenten dramas. His *Complete Works* were edited by Goetze and Von Keller (1870–1908). See the studies by Genée (1902), Geiger (1904), Landau (1924) and Röttinger (1927).

(2) **Julius von** (1832–97), German botanist, born at Breslau, in 1867 became professor of Botany at Freiburg, in 1868 at Würzburg. There he carried on important experiments, especially on the influence of light and heat upon plants, and the organic activities of vegetable growth. See study by E. C. Pringsheim (1932).

(3) **Nelly** (1891–1970), Swedish writer, born in Berlin of Jewish descent, fled from Germany in 1940, settled in Stockholm and took Swedish nationality. Her first book *Legends and Tales* (1921) was followed by numerous lyrical and dramatic works and anthologies. She was awarded the Nobel prize for literature in 1966, jointly with Agnon.

SACKVILLE, (1) **Charles, 6th Earl of Dorset** (1638–1706), succeeded to the earldom in 1677, having two years before been made Earl of Middlesex. He was returned by East Grinstead to the first parliament of Charles II, and became an especial favourite of the king, and notorious for his boisterous and indecorous frolics. He served under the Duke of York at sea, but could not endure the tyranny of James II and ardently supported the cause of William His later years were honoured by a generous patronage of Prior, Wycherley, Dryden. He died at Bath, January 19, 1706. He wrote lyrics (as 'To all you Ladies now at Land') and satirical pieces.

(2) **Lord George** (1716–85), youngest son of the first Duke of Dorset, was wounded at Fontenoy (1745), and dismissed the service for not charging at Minden (1759). Colonial secretary 1775–82, in 1770 he took the surname Germain, and in 1782 was created Viscount Sackville. See L. Marlowe, *Sackville of Drayton* (1948).

(3) **Thomas, 1st Earl of Dorset** (1536–1608), English poet and statesman, was born at Buckhurst in Sussex, the only son of Sir Richard Sackville, chancellor of the Exchequer. In 1555 he married, and in 1558 was in parliament. With Thomas Norton he produced the blank-verse tragedy of *Ferrex and Porrex* (afterwards called *Gorboduc*) which in 1560–61 was acted before Queen Elizabeth, Sackville's second cousin. This work, after the style of Seneca, claims notice as the earliest tragedy in English. Dramatic energy it has none, but the style is pure and stately, evincing eloquence and power of thought. *The Induction* and *Buckingham*, contributed to *A Myrrovre for Magistrates* (1563), are noble poetry. His prodigality brought Sackville into disgrace, and he travelled in France and Italy (*c.* 1563–66), was imprisoned in Rome as a suspected spy, received Knole as a gift from the queen (1566), and in 1567 was knighted and created Lord Buckhurst. He was then employed as a diplomatist in France and the Low Countries, in 1586 announced her death sentence to Mary, Queen of Scots, and in 1589 was made K.G., in 1599 lord high treasurer, and in 1604 Earl of Dorset. He died April 19, 1608. See Works, ed. Sackville-West (1859), *Induction* and *Buckingham*, ed. M. Hearsey (1936, from the author's MS., with Life); Sackville-West, *Knole and the Sackvilles* (1947).

SACKVILLE-WEST, Victoria Mary (1892–1962), English poet and novelist, born at Knole House, Kent, the daughter of the 3rd Baron Sackville. In her *Orchard and Vineyard* (1921) and her long poem *The Land*, which won the 1927 Hawthornden prize, her close sympathy with the life of the soil of her native county is expressed. Her prose works include the novels *The Edwardians* (1930), *All Passion Spent* (1931), *Knole and the Sackvilles* (1947) and studies of Andrew Marvell and Joan of Arc. In 1913 she married Harold Nicolson (q.v.). *Passenger to Teheran* (1926) records their years in Persia. She was made C.H. in 1948.

SACROBOSCO, Johannes de (or **John Holywood**), English mathematician, seems to have been born at Halifax, to have studied at Oxford, and to have been professor of Mathematics at Paris, where he died in 1244 or 1256. He was one of the first to use the astronomical writings of the Arabians. His treatise, *De Sphaera Mundi*, a paraphrase of part of Ptolemy's *Almagest*, passed during 1472–1647 through forty editions.

SACY, *sa-see*, (1) **Antoine Isaac, Baron Silvestre de** (1758–1838), French Arabist, born in Paris, became in 1795 professor of Arabic in the Institute of Oriental Languages, in 1806 also of Persian. He was perpetual secretary of the Academy of Inscriptions, founder and member of the Asiatic Society, and member of the Chamber of Peers.

(2) **Samuel Ustazade Silvestre de** (1801–79), son of (1), long one of the leading writers on the *Journal des débats* from 1855 a member of the Academy, edited (1861–64) the letters of Madame de Sévigné.

SADE, Donatien Alphonse François, Marquis de, *sahd* (1740–1814), French writer, born in Paris, fought in the Seven Years' War, and was in 1772 condemned to death at Aix for his cruel sexual vices. He made his escape, but was afterwards imprisoned at Vincennes and in the Bastille, where he wrote his fantastically scandalous romances, *Justine* (1791), *La Philosophie dans le boudoir* (1793), *Juliette* (1798) and *Les Crimes de l'amour* (1800). He died mad at Charenton. The word 'sadism', derived from his name, is used to describe the type of unnatural sexual perversion from which he suffered. See study by Gorer (1934).

SÁ DE MIRANDA, Francisco, *sa-THė-mee-rãn'da* (*c.* 1485–1558), Portuguese poet, founder of the Petrarchan school, born at Coimbra, spent some years in Italy, wrote sonnets, eclogues, prose comedies and interesting verse epistles.

SÁDI, Saadi, or **Sa'adi,** the assumed name of **Sheikh Muslih Addin** (*c.* 1184–?1292), Persian poet, highly regarded in his native land, was a descendant of Ali, Mohammed's son-in-law. He studied at Bagdad, travelled much, and near Jerusalem was taken prisoner by the Crusaders, but was ransomed by a merchant of Aleppo, who gave him his daughter in marriage. The catalogue of his works comprises twenty-two different kinds of writings in prose and verse, in Arabic and Persian, of which odes and dirges form the predominant part. The most celebrated of his works, however, is the *Gulistan*, or Flower Garden, a kind of moral work in prose and verse, intermixed with stories, maxims, philosophical sentences, puns and the like. Next comes the *Bostan*, or Tree Garden, in verse, and more religious than the *Gulistan.* Third stands the *Pend-Nameh*, or Book of Instructions. The *Gulistan* has been translated into English by Gladwin, Ross, Eastwick and Platts. The *Bostan* was translated by H. W. Clarke (1879). See the French essay by H. Massi (1919).

SADLEIR, Michael, *sad'lėr* (1888–1957), English author and publisher, born at Oxford, a son of **Sir Michael Ernest Sadler** (1861–1943), educationist and great-grand-nephew of M. T. Sadler (q.v.), he reverted to an older form of the name to avoid confusion. Educated at Rugby and Oxford, he joined the publishing firm of Constable, becoming a director in 1920. As well as numerous bibliographical works—he was Sandars reader in Bibliography at Cambridge in 1937—he published novels, including *Hyssop* (1915), *These Foolish Things* (1937) and *Fanny by Gaslight* (1940), and biographies, of which *Michael Ernest Sadler: a memoir by his son* (1949) and *Anthony Trollope* (1927) are noteworthy.

SADLER, (1) Sir Michael Ernest. See SADLEIR.

(2) **Michael Thomas** (1780-1835), English social reformer, born at Snelston, Derbyshire, became a linen manufacturer, sat in parliament (1829–32), wrote on Irish social questions, and did much to reduce the monstrous hours of children in factories, introducing in 1831 the first Ten-hour Bill. He died at Belfast. See memoir by Seeley (1842).

(3) **Sir Ralph** (1507–87), English diplomat, born at Hackney, from 1537 was employed in diplomacy with Scotland. He was left one of the twelve councillors of Edward VI's minority, fought at Pinkie, sat in the commission on Queen Mary at York, was her jailer at Tutbury, and was perhaps sent with the news of her execution to her son. His *Papers*, valuable for Border and Scottish history, were edited by Arthur Clifford, with historical notes by Sir Walter Scott (1809).

SADOLETO, Jacopo, *sa-dō-lay'tō* (1477–1547), Italian churchman, born at Modena, went to Rome in 1502, and took orders. Leo X made him apostolical secretary, an appointment he retained under Clement VII and Paul III. By Leo he was made Bishop of Carpentras in 1517, and by Paul in 1536 a cardinal. In 1544 he was legate to Francis I. Sadoleto ranks as one of the great churchmen of his age. He corresponded with many Protestant leaders, and sought to find a basis for reunion. There is a French study by Joly (1856).

ŠAFAŘIK, Pavel Josef, *sha'far-zheek* (1795–1861), Czech author of important works on Slavonic literature and antiquities, was from 1848 professor at Prague University.

SAGAN, Françoise, *sah-gã*, pen-name of **Françoise Quoirez** (1936–), French novelist, born in Paris and educated at a convent and private schools, at eighteen wrote the best-selling *Bonjour tristesse* (1954; filmed 1958), followed by *Un Certain Sourire* (1956; filmed 1958), both remarkably direct testaments of wealthy adolescence, written with the economy of a remarkable literary style. Irony creeps into her third, *Dans un mois, dans un an* (1957), but moral consciousness takes over in her later novels, such as *Aimez-vous Brahms . . .* (1959; filmed 1961 as *Goodbye Again*), *La Chamade* (1966). A ballet to which she gave the central idea, *Le Rendez-vous manqué*, enjoyed a temporary *succès de scandale* in Paris and London in 1958. Her later work, including several plays, e.g., *Château en Suède* (1960) and *Les Violons, parfois . . .* (1961), has had a mixed critical reception.

SAGASTA, Práxedes Mateo, *-gas'-* (1827–1903), Spanish Liberal leader from 1875, born at Torrecilla, took part in insurrections in 1856 and 1866, and had twice to flee to France. Several times premier, he introduced universal male suffrage and trial by jury.

SA'ID, Nuri Es. See ES-SA'ID.

SA'ID PASHA, *sa-eed'* (1822–63), viceroy of Egypt from 1854, gave the concession for the Suez Canal.

SAINT AMANT, Antoine Girard de, *sĩt a-mã* (1594–1661), French poet, was born in Rouen. An early exponent of French burlesque poetry, he also wrote the heroic idyll, *Moyse sauvé*, and an ode, *À la solitude.*

SAINT ARNAUD, Jacques Leroy de, *sĩt ar-nō* (1796–1854), French soldier, born at Bordeaux, fought for the Greeks (1822–26), but made his reputation in Algeria, and in 1851 carried on a bloody but successful warfare with the Kabyles. Louis Napoleon recalled him; and as war minister he took an active part in the *coup d'état* of December 2. He was rewarded with the marshal's baton. In the Crimean war he commanded the French forces, and co-operated with Lord Raglan at the Alma, but nine days afterwards died on his way home to France. See his *Lettres* (1864) and work by Cabrol (1895).

SAINTE-BEUVE, Charles Augustin, *sĩt-bœv* (1804–69), French writer, the greatest literary critic of his time, was born at Boulogne-sur-Mer, December 23, 1804, son of a commissioner of taxes, who died three months before the birth of his son, leaving his wife in straitened circumstances. Till his fourteenth year Sainte-Beuve attended school in Boulogne, then went to the Collège Charlemagne in Paris, and next (1824–27) followed a course of medical study. M. Dubois, one of his teachers at the Collège Charlemagne, founded a literary and political paper called the *Globe*, and to it, along with Jouffroy, Rémusat, Ampère and Mérimée, Sainte-Beuve became a contributor. For three years he wrote the short articles collected as *Premiers Lundis*. In 1827 a eulogistic review of the *Odes et Ballades* of Victor Hugo led to the closest relations between the poet and his critic, which lasted until broken in 1834 by Sainte-Beuve's liaison with Madame Hugo. For a time Sainte-Beuve was the zealous advocate of the romantic movement. In 1828 he published *Tableau de la poésie française au seizième siècle*; in 1829 and 1830 *Vie et Poésies de Joseph Delorme* and *Les Consolations*, poems fraught with morbid feeling. In 1829 in the *Revue de Paris* he began the *Causeries* or longer critical articles on French literature. After the Revolution of July 1830 he again wrote for the *Globe*, now in the hands of the Saint-Simoniens; but his new colleagues soon passed the limits of his sympathy, and for the next three years he was on the staff of Carrel's *National*, the organ of extreme republicanism. In 1830–36 he became a sympathetic listener of Lamennais; but with the ultra-democratic opinions of Lamennais after his breach with Rome he had no sympathy. His solitary novel, *Volupté* (1835), belongs to this period. In 1837 he lectured on the history of Port Royal at Lausanne; in book form these lectures contain some of his finest work. At Lausanne he produced his last volume of poetry, *Pensées d'août*. A journey into Italy closes the first period of his life. In 1840 he was appointed keeper of the Mazarin Library. During the next eight years he wrote mainly for the *Revue des deux mondes*, in 1845 he was elected to the French Academy. The political confusions of 1848 led him to become professor of French Literature at Liège, where he lectured on *Chateaubriand et son groupe*. In 1849 he returned to Paris, and began to write for the *Constitutionnel* an article on some literary subject, to appear on the Monday of every week. In 1861 these *Causeries du lundi* were transferred to the *Moniteur*, in 1867 back to the *Constitutionnel*, and finally in 1869 to the *Temps*. In 1854, on his appointment by the emperor as professor of Latin Poetry at the Collège de France, the students refused to listen to his lectures, and he was forced to demit the office; the undelivered lectures contained his critical estimate of Virgil. Nominated a senator in 1865, he regained popularity by his spirited speeches in favour of that liberty of thought which the government was doing its utmost to suppress. He died in Paris, October 13, 1869. It was his special instruction that he should be buried without religious ceremony. It is by the amount and variety of his work, and the ranges of qualities it displays, that Sainte-Beuve holds such a place among literary critics. He is unapproachable in his faculty of educing the interest and significance of the most various types of human character and the most various forms of creative effort. His work marks an epoch in the intellectual history of Europe. By its delicacy, subtlety and precision it extended the limits of the study of human character and of the products of human intelligence. Besides the writings mentioned above he published many other literary works, including *Critiques et portraits littéraires* (1836–39), *Portraits de femmes* (1844), and, posthumously, *M. de Talleyrand* and *Souvenirs et indiscrétions*. See Sainte-Beuve's own 'Ma Biographie' in *Nouveaux Lundis*, vol. xiii; the strongly prejudiced book of the Vicomte d'Haussonville, *C. A. Sainte-Beuve, sa vie et ses oeuvres* (1875); and the *Souvenirs* of his last secretary, M. Troubat (1890). See works by Levallois (1872), Morand (1895), Michaut (1921), Mott (1925) and Bellesort (1927).

SAINTE-CLAIRE DEVILLE, Henri Étienne, *sĩt-klayr dė-veel* (1818–81), born in St Thomas, West Indies, in 1851 became professor of Chemistry in the École normale at Paris, and shortly afterwards in the Sorbonne. It was he who first produced aluminium (1855) and platinum in commercial quantities, and demonstrated the general theory of the dissociation of chemical compounds at a high temperature. He also examined the forms of boron and silicon, and produced artificially sapphire, aluminium, &c. Besides many papers, he published *De l'aluminium* (1859) and *Métallurgie du platine* (1863). See French Life by Gay (1889).

SAINT-ÉVREMOND, Charles Marguetel de Saint Denis, Seigneur de, *sĩt-ay-vrė-mõ* (1610–1703), French writer and wit, born at St Denis le Guast near Coutances, fought at Rocroi, Freiburg and Nördlingen, was steadily loyal throughout the Fronde, but in 1661 fled by way of Holland to England on the discovery of his witty and sarcastic letter to Créqui on the Peace of the Pyrenees. He was warmly received by Charles II, and in London he spent almost all the rest of his days, delighting the world with his wit. His satire, *La Comédie des académistes* (1644), is masterly, and his letters to and from Ninon de Lenclos charming. Des Maizeaux collected his writings with Life (1705). See studies by W. M. Daniels (1907) and K. Spalatin (1934).

SAINT-EXUPÉRY, Antoine de, *sĩt-eg-zü-pay-ree* (1900–44), French airman and author, was born in Lyon, and became a commercial airline pilot and wartime reconnaissance pilot. His philosophy of 'heroic action', based on the framework of his experiences as a pilot, is expressed in his sensitive and imaginative *Courier sud* (1929), *Vol de nuit* (1931) and *Pilote de guerre* (1942). He was declared missing after a flight in the second World War. See studies by A. Gide (1951) and J. Bruce (1953), and M. A. Smith's *Knight of the Air* (1959).

SAINT-GAUDENS, Augustus, *saynt-gawd'ènz* (1848–1907), born in Dublin, a French shoemaker's son, was taken to America as a baby, trained as a cameo-cutter, studied sculpture in Paris and in Rome, where he was influenced by the Italian renaissance and returned to America, where he became the foremost sculptor of his time. See his *Reminiscences* (1913) and study by Hind (1908).

SAINT-GELAIS, Mellin de, *sĩ-zhė-lay* (1491–1558), French poet, a contemporary and imitator of Clement Marot (q.v.).

SAINT-HILAIRE. See BARTHÉLEMY and GEOFFROY.

SAINTINE, or Boniface, Joseph Xavier, *sĩ-teen* (1798–1865), a Frenchman, the author of plays, poems and tales without number, the best known being the sentimental *Picciola, the Story of a Prison Flower* (1836).

ST JOHN, Henry. See BOLINGBROKE (2).

SAINT-JOHN PERSE, pen-name of **Marie René Auguste Alexis Saint-Léger Léger** (1887–), French poet and diplomat, born at St Léger des Feuilles, an island near Guadeloupe, studied at Bordeaux and after adventurous travels in New Guinea and a voyage in a skiff along the China coast, entered in 1904 the French foreign ministry. Secretary-general in 1933, he was dismissed in 1940 and fled to the United States, where he became an adviser to Roosevelt on French affairs. The Vichy government burnt his writings and deprived him of French citizenship, restored in 1945. His blank verse utilizes an exotic vocabulary of little-used words. The panoramic sweep of his landscape imagery, heightened by liturgical metres, gives his poetry a visionary quality. The best known of his earlier works, which include *Images à Crusoë* (1909), *Éloges* (1910), *Amitié du prince* (1924), is the long poem *Anabase* (1924; trans. T. S. Eliot, 1930). Later works include *Exil* (1942), *Pluies* (1944), *Amers* (1957) and *Chroniques* (1960). Hammarskjöld (q.v.) was his Swedish translator. He was awarded the Nobel prize in 1960. See study by R. Caillois (1954).

SAINT-JUST, Louis Antoine Léon Florelle de, *sĩ-zhüst* (1767–94), French revolutionary, was born at Decize near Nevers, and educated by the Oratorians at Soissons, studied law at Rheims, but early gave himself to letters. At nineteen he set off for Paris, with some of his mother's valuables, and was, at her request, imprisoned for selling them. He published (1789) a poor poem, *L'Organt*, and in 1791 an essay of a different promise, *L'Esprit de la révolution.* Returned for Aisne to the Convention (1792) he attracted notice by his fierce tirades against the king; and as a devoted follower of Robespierre was sent on missions to the armies of the Rhine and the Moselle. He made bombastic speeches before the Convention, and began the attacks on Hébert which sent him and Danton to their doom. In 1794 he laid before the Convention a comprehensive report on the police, and soon after proposed, along with other fanciful schemes of like Spartan character, Robespierre's preposterous civil institutions, by which boys were to be taken from their parents at seven and brought up for the state. Saint-Just fell with Robespierre by the guillotine, July 28, 1794. See Fleury, *Saint-Just et la Terreur* (1851), and studies by D. C. Bineau (1936) and R. Korngold (1937).

ST LAURENT, Louis Stephen, *sĩ-lō-rã* (1882–1973), Canadian politician, was born in Compton, Quebec, trained as a lawyer in Quebec, and entered the Dominion parliament in 1941 as a Liberal. He was minister of justice and attorney-general (1941–46) and minister of external affairs (1946–48), and in 1948 became leader of the Liberal party and prime minister of Canada. He resigned the latter office on the defeat of his party in the 1957 General Election, and in 1958 was succeeded as leader of the party by Lester Pearson (q.v.).

ST LEGER, *sel'in-jėr* or (the race always) *saynt lej'ėr*, (1) **Sir Anthony** (*c.* 1496–1559), English statesman, was in 1540 appointed lord deputy of Ireland, where he was at first highly successful in his treatment of the fractious clans, who, however, later rebelled. Accused of fraud, he died during the investigation.

(2) **Barry** (1737–89), British army colonel, fought in the American revolution, and founded in 1776 his horse-racing stakes at Doncaster.

SAINT-LÉGER, Alexis. See SAINT-JOHN PERSE.

SAINT-MARC GIRARDIN. See GIRARDIN (3).

SAINT-MARTIN, Louis Claude de, *sĩ-mar-tĩ* (1743–1803), French philosopher ('le Philosophe inconnu'), a vigorous opponent of sensationalism and materialism, was born at Amboise. See Life by Waite (1901 and 1922).

SAINT-PIERRE, *sĩ-pyayr*, (1) **Charles Irénée Castel, Abbé de** (1658–1743), French writer, published an optimistic *Projet de la paix perpétuelle* (1713), was expelled from the Academy in 1718 for his *Discours sur la polysynodie*, and wrote on political economy and philosophy, in which his principles were those of the physiocratic school. See study by Drouet (1912).

(2) **Jacques Henri Bernardin de** (1737–1814), French author, was born at Havre, January 19, 1737, and after a voyage to Martinique served some time in the Engineers, but quarrelled with his chiefs and was dismissed, and next year was sent to Malta, with the same result. His head was turned by the writings of Rousseau, and he made public employment impossible by the innumerable utopian criticisms with which he deluged the ministers. With dreams of a new state to be founded on the shores of the Sea of Aral, he

travelled to Russia, and returned in dejection to Warsaw. He abandoned a government expedition to Madagascar at the Île de France (Mauritius), to spend there almost three years of melancholy and observation. His *Voyage à l'Île de France* (1778) gave a distinctly new element to literature in its close portraiture of nature. His *Études de la nature* (3 vols. 1784) showed the strong influence of Rousseau; a fourth volume (1788) contained the popular *Paul et Virginie*, the story, to modern readers over-sentimental and over-didactic, of the growth of love between two young people, untainted by civilization, in the natural surroundings of Mauritius. His next works were *Voeux d'un solitaire* (1789) and the novel, *La Chaumière indienne* (1791). His *Harmonies de la nature* (1796) was but a pale repetition of the *Études*. Besides these *Le Café de Surate* and the *Essai sur J.-J. Rousseau* alone merit mention. A member of the Institute from its foundation in 1795, he was admitted to the Academy in 1803. Napoleon heaped favours upon him, and he lived comfortably till his death at Eragny near Pontoise, January 21, 1814. His *Oeuvres complètes* (1813–20) and *Correspondance* (1826) were edited by Aimé Martin. See the extravagant Life by the latter (1820), with others works by Mornet (1907), Roule (1930) and d'Alméras (1937).

SAINT-RÉAL, César Vichard, Abbé de, *sĩ-ray-al* (1631–92), French historian, born at Chambéry, visited London, and in 1679 returned to his birthplace as historiographer to the Duke of Savoy. He wrote *Dom Carlos* (1672) and *La Conjuration que les Espagnols formèrent en 1618 contre Venise* (1674), early examples of the serious French historical novel. See study by Dulong (1921).

SAINT-SAËNS, (Charles) Camille, *sĩ-sãs* (1835–1921), French composer and music critic, was born in Paris on October 9, 1835. He entered the Paris Conservatoire in 1848, was a pupil of Benoist and Halévy, and at the age of sixteen had begun his long and prolific career of composition with his prizewinning *Ode à Sainte Cécile* (1852), followed shortly afterwards by his first symphony (performed 1853, published 1855). He was a distinguished pianist, and from 1858 to 1877 won considerable renown as organist of the Madeleine in Paris, giving recitals also in London, Russia and Austria. Although himself conservative as a composer, he was a founder in 1871 of the Société Nationale de Musique, and as such was influential in encouraging the performance of works by young contemporary French composers, for whose style he was also an impeccable model of directness, clarity and technical skill. He wrote four further symphonies, thirteen operas, including his best-known, *Samson et Dalila* (1877), four symphonic poems, *Le Rouet d'Omphale* (1871), *Phaëton* (1873), *Danse macabre* (1874) and*La Jeunesse d'Hercule* (1877), five piano, three violin and two cello concertos, *Carnaval des animaux* (1886) for two pianos and orchestra, church music, including his *Messe solennelle* (1856), and chamber music and songs. He was a sound music critic, although latterly somewhat prejudiced, because of his own temporarily declining reputation against his younger contemporaries; his writings include *Harmonie et mélodie* (1885), *Portraits et souvenirs* (1899) and *Au courant de la vie* (1914). Saint-Saëns died at Algiers. See studies by A. Hervey (1921), W. Lyle (1923), A. Dandelot (1930) and J. Chantavoine (1947).

SAINTSBURY, George Edward Bateman (1845–1933), English literary critic, was born at Southampton and educated at King's College School, London, and Merton College, Oxford. In 1868–76 he was a schoolmaster at Manchester, Guernsey and Elgin, but soon after established himself as one of the most active critics of the day; in 1895–1915 he was professor of English Literature at Edinburgh. All his work is characterized by clearness of thought, fullness of knowledge and force, if not always grace of style. He contributed to the greater magazines (he edited *Macmillan's*), and to encyclopaedias. Among his books are histories of literature, both French and English; books on Dryden, Marlborough, Scott, Matthew Arnold, Thackeray, the early renaissance, minor Caroline poets; histories of criticism (3 vols. 1900–04), English prosody (1906–10), prose rhythm (1912), and a novel (1912); and after his retirement came *The Peace of the Augustans* (1916), *A History of the French Novel* (1917–19), *Notes on a Cellar-book* (1920) and *Scrapbooks* (1922–1924).

SAINT-SIMON, *sĩ-see-mõ*, (1) **Claude Henri, Comte de** (1760–1825), founder of French socialism, was born of the ducal line in Paris, October 17. He served in the American War of Independence; during the French Revolution he was imprisoned as an aristocrat, but made a small fortune by speculating in confiscated lands. His marriage (1801) was terminated by a divorce; and his lavish expenditure reduced him to utter poverty. Beginning to be in straits, he published his *Lettres d'un habitant de Genève à ses contemporains* (1803); but the first enunciations of socialism occurred in *L'Industrie* (1817), followed by *L'Organisateur* (1819), *Du système industriel* (1821), *Catéchisme des industriels* (1823), and his last and most important work, *Nouveau christianisme* (1825). But for the kindness of friends and a small pension allowed him by his family in 1812 he would have died of starvation. In 1823 he tried to shoot himself, and lost an eye in the attempt; he died in Paris May 19, 1825. Saint-Simon's works are wanting in judgment and system; but notwithstanding all his vagaries, the man who originated Comtism and French socialism must be regarded as a seminal thinker of high rank. In opposition to the destructive spirit of the Revolution, he sought after a positive reorganization of society. He desired that the feudal and military system should be superseded by an industrial order controlled by industrial chiefs, and that the spiritual direction of society should pass from the church to the men of science. See monographs by A. J. Booth (1871), Charléty (1896), Bouglé (1925), Butler (1926) and N. Mitford (1958).

(2) **Louis de Rouvroy, Duc de** (1675–1755), was born at Paris, January 16, son of a page and favourite of Louis XIII who became

duke in 1636, but soon after fell from favour. He entered the army at sixteen but left dissatisfied in 1702, and repaired to Versailles, without for some years enjoying any measure of the royal favour. He embroiled himself in endless disputes about precedence and privilege, but recovered the king's favour by his efforts to bring his friend Orleans to a more reputable life. The king's death in 1714 opened up a bitter struggle between Orleans and the Duc de Maine, eldest of the king's bastards, in which Saint-Simon supported his friend with warmth and boldness. His influence decreased as that of Dubois rose; but he was sent to Spain in 1721 to demand the hand of the Infanta for the young king, Louis XV. After the death of Orleans in 1723, he retired to his château of La Ferté Vidame near Chartres. He died, utterly bankrupt, March 2, 1755. He seems to have begun his journal before 1699, and to have prepared the *Mémoires* (1752) in their final form. This precious manuscript, with his impressions and descriptions, sometimes lively, sometimes cumbersome, but always diverse, imaginative and convincingly detailed of court life as he saw and experienced it between 1695 and 1723, was impounded in 1761 by the Duc de Choiseul for the French foreign office. A volume of garbled extracts appeared in 1780; in 1830 the first authentic edition appeared. The first adequate edition was by Chéruel in 1856–58. But the final edition is that in *Les Grands Écrivains*, by M. A. de Boislisle (43 vols. 1879–1930). There is an abridged English translation by F. Arkwright (1915 *et seq.*), and selections by L. Norton, *Saint-Simon at Versailles*, were published in 1958. See monographs by Chéruel (1865), Collins (1880), Cannan (1885), Pilastre (1905, 1909) and Doumic (1919).

ST VINCENT, John Jervis, Earl (1735–1823), English admiral, born at Meaford Hall, Stone, Staffordshire, January 9, entered the navy in 1749, became a lieutenant in 1755, and so distinguished himself in the Quebec expedition in 1759 that he was made commander. In 1778 he fought in the action of Brest, and in 1782 captured the *Pégase* of 74 guns, whereupon he was made a K.B. In 1793 he commanded the naval part of the successful expedition against the French West India Islands. In 1795, now admiral, he received the command of the Mediterranean fleet. On February 14, 1797, with fifteen sail, he fell in, off Cape St Vincent, with the Spanish fleet of twenty-seven. Jervis completely defeated the enemy, and captured four ships. The genius of Nelson contributed greatly to the success of the day. Jervis was created Earl St Vincent, and parliament granted him a pension of £3000. After repressing a mutiny off Cadiz, he was compelled by ill-health to return home. As commander of the Channel fleet he subdued the spirit of sedition, and as first lord of the Admiralty in 1801–04 reformed innumerable abuses. He resumed the Channel command 1806–07, and died March 13, 1823. See poor Life by Brenton (1838), good ones by Tucker (1844) and Anson (1913); and *Letters, 1801–04* (1927).

SAKI. See MUNRO (2).

SALA, George Augustus Henry (1828–95), English journalist and novelist, born in London of Italian ancestry, studied art and did book illustrations, but in 1851 became a contributor to *Household Words*, as afterwards to the *Welcome Guest*, *Temple Bar* (which he founded and edited 1860–66), the *Illustrated London News* and *Cornhill*. As special correspondent of the *Daily Telegraph* he was in the United States during the Civil War, in Italy with Garibaldi, in France in 1870–71, in Russia in 1876, and in Australia in 1885. *Twice Round the Clock* (1859) is a social satire, and he also wrote novels, many books of travel and the autobiographical *Life and Adventures* (1895).

SALADIN, in full **Salah-ed-din Yussuf ibn Ayub**, *sal'-* (1137–93), sultan of Egypt and Syria and founder of a dynasty, was born at Tekrit, on the Tigris, of which his father Ayub, a Kurd, was governor under the Seljuks. He entered the service of Nur-eddin, emir of Syria, held command in the expeditions to Egypt (1167–68), and was made grand vizier of the Fatimite calif, whom in 1171 he overthrew, constituting himself sovereign of Egypt. On Nur-eddin's death (1174) he further proclaimed himself sultan of Egypt and Syria, reduced Mesopotamia, and received the homage of the Seljuk princes of Asia Minor. His remaining years were occupied in wars with the Christians and in the consolidation of his extensive dominions. In 1187 the Christian army suffered a terrible defeat near Tiberias; then Jerusalem was stormed (October 3), and almost every fortified place on the Syrian coast was taken. Thereupon a great army of crusaders, headed by the kings of France and England, captured Acre in 1191; Richard Cœur-de-Lion defeated Saladin, took Caesarea and Jaffa, and obtained a three years' treaty. Saladin died at Damascus. His wise administration left traces for centuries in citadels, roads and canals. His opponents recognized his chivalry, good faith, piety, justice and greatness of soul. See Lives by Reinaud (1874) and Stanley Lane-Poole (1926).

SALANDRA, Antonio (1853–1931), Italian statesman, professor of Administrative Science at Rome, was premier (1914–16) when Italy entered the first World War. Though at first an opponent of Fascism, he became a senator under Mussolini in 1928.

SALAZAR, António de Oliviera, *-zahr'* (1889–1970), Portuguese dictator, born near Coimbra, studied and became professor of Economics there. In 1928 he was made minister of finance by Carmona with extensive powers to deal with the widespread economic chaos. Having been elected prime minister in 1932, he gradually converted Portugal into a corporate state by virtue of his considerable financial skill. His tenure of the ministries of war (1936–44) and of foreign affairs (1936–47) included the delicate period of the Spanish Civil War. He further curtailed political opposition, which in any case was only permitted during the brief election periods, after his opponent polled relatively well in 1959. He retired in 1968.

SALDANHA, João Carlos, Duke of, *sal-dan'ya* (1790–1876), Portuguese statesman and marshal, born at Arinhaga, fought at Busaco (1810), helped Brazil against Montevideo (1817–22), sided with Dom Pedro against Dom Miguel as a moderate constitutionalist, and during 1846–56 was alternately head of the government and in armed opposition. Created a duke in 1846, he was twice ambassador at Rome, prime minister in 1870, and ambassador at London from 1871.

SALE, (1) **George** (*c.* 1697–1736), English oriental scholar, was born in Kent, educated at King's School Canterbury, and bred to the law. He is best known by his translation of the Koran (1734; new ed. 1882–86).

(2) **Sir Robert Henry** (1782–1845), British soldier, was commissioned in 1795, fought at Seringapatam (1799), the capture of Mauritius (1810), and throughout the Burmese war (1824–25). In the Afghan war of 1838 he distinguished himself at Ghazni. In Jalalabad he was besieged for six months (1841–42), until relieved by Pollock. He was killed at Mudki, fighting against the Sikhs, December 18, 1845. See Gleig, *Sale's Brigade in Afghanistan* (1846). Lady Sale, whom he married in 1809, and who was captured by the Afghans and kept prisoner until Pollock's arrival, wrote a *Journal of the Disasters in Afghanistan* (1843).

SALES, Francis of. See FRANCIS (SAINTS) (3).

SALIERI, Antonio, *sa-lyay'ree* (1750–1825), Italian composer, was born in Verona and died in Vienna, having worked there for fifty years. A teacher of Beethoven and Schubert, he was bitterly antipathetic towards Mozart, whom he did not, however, contrary to a once prevalent tale, poison. He wrote over forty operas, an oratorio and masses.

SALINGER, Jerome David (1919–), American author, born in New York, educated there at Pennsylvania military academy, served with the army in World War II. He began writing at an early age but his fame rests mainly on his novel *Catcher in the Rye* (1951), written in the first person in the idiom of a New York 16-year-old and portraying with acute observation and sympathetic insight the motivation of a ' mixed-up ' teenager who has run away from school. Other books, generally made up of stories of novella length, include *For Esmé, with Love and Squalor* (1953) and *Franny and Zooey* (1962); many of the stories portray his highly intelligent and temperamental Glass family. See *Personal Portrait*, ed. Grunwald (1964).

SALISBURY, Earls and Marquises of. See CECIL.

SALISBURY, *sawlz'bėr-i,* (1) **Frank Owen** (1874–1962), British artist, executed a large number of pictures, many of them official, and portraits of members of the British royal family and of notable Americans. See his book *Sarum Chase* (1953). He was created C.V.O. in 1938.

(2) **John of.** See JOHN OF SALISBURY.

(3) **William** (*c.* 1520–*c.* 1600), Welsh lexicographer, published a Welsh and English Dictionary (1547), and translated the New Testament into Welsh (1567).

SALK, Jonas Edward (1914–), American virologist, discoverer of the anti-poliomyelitis vaccine in 1953, was born of Polish-Jewish immigrant parents in New York. He worked as a research fellow on an influenza vaccine at Michigan (1942–44), where he was appointed assistant professor and transferred to Pittsburgh as director of virus research (1947–49) and research professor (1949–54). There in 1953–54 he prepared the vaccine which, after stringest tests, he tried out successfully on his family. A huge publicity campaign (1955) in which, unknown to him, vaccine was used which had not been as stringently tested, resulted in over 200 cases of polio, 11 of them fatal. But an improved vaccine has fully vindicated his achievement. He has since been engaged on cancer research.

SALLUST, Lat. **Gaius Sallustius Crispus,** *sal'ust* (86–34 B.C.), Roman historian, was born of Plebeian family at Amiternum in the Sabine country. He had risen to be tribune in 52 when he helped to avenge the murder of Clodius upon Milo and his party. Such was the scandal of his licentious life that he was expelled in 50 from the senate—though his attachment to Caesar's party doubtless strengthened the reasons for his expulsion. In 47 he was made praetor and restored to senatorial rank. He served in the African campaign, and was left as governor of Numidia. His administration was sullied by oppression and extortion, but the charges brought against him failed before the partial tribunal of Caesar. With the fruit of his extortion he laid out famous gardens on the Quirinal and the splendid mansion which became an imperial residence of Nerva, Vespasian and Aurelian. In this retirement he wrote his famous histories, the *Catilina*, the *Jugurtha* and the *Historiarum Libri Quinque* (78–67 B.C.), of which latter but a few fragments survive. He was one of the first Roman writers to look directly for a model to Greek literature. There are translations by Pollard (1882) and Rolfe (1921).

SALMASIUS, Claudius, or **Claude de Saumaise** (1588–1653), French scholar, born at Semur in Burgundy, studied philosophy at Paris and law at Heidelberg (1606), where he professed Protestantism. In 1629 appeared his chief work, *Plinianae Exercitationes in Solinum* (1629), after whose publication he mastered Hebrew, Arabic and Coptic. In 1631 he was called to Leyden to occupy Joseph Scaliger's chair. Unavailing efforts were made (1635–40) to induce him to return to France. He was probably the most famous scholar of his day in Europe. In England Salmasius is best known through his controversy with Milton. At the request of Charles II, Salmasius published (1649), his *Defensio Regio pro Carolo I*, answered in 1651 by Milton in his *Pro Populo Anglicano Defensio.* See the *Vita* prefixed to his letters (1656).

SALOME, *sa-lō'may* (*c.* A.D. 14–before A.D. 62), traditional name of the daughter of Herodias—see HEROD (2). She danced before Herod and, at her mother's instigation, asked for as a reward, and received, the head of John the Baptist.

SALOMON, Johann Peter (1745–1815), German violinist, impresario and composer, born at Bonn served Prince Henry of Prussia

1765–80, and then settled in London. At his philharmonic concerts (1791–94) were produced the twelve 'Salomon' or 'London' symphonies commissioned from Haydn.

SALOTE, *sa-lō'tay* (1900–65), Queen of Tonga, educated in New Zealand, succeeded her father, King George Tupou II, in 1918. Her prosperous and happy reign saw in 1924 the reunion, for which she was mainly responsible, of the Tongan Free Church majority with the Wesleyan Church. Queen Salote is remembered in Britain for her colourful and engaging presence during her visit in 1953 for the coronation of Queen Elizabeth.

SALT, Sir Titus (1803–76), English manufacturer and benefactor, born at Morley near Leeds, was a wool stapler at Bradford, started wool-spinning in 1834, and was the first to manufacture alpaca fabrics in England. Round his factories in a pleasant valley, 3 miles from Bradford, on the Aire, rose the model village of Saltaire (1853). Mayor of Bradford in 1848, and its Liberal M.P. in 1859–61, he was created a baronet in 1869. See Life by Balgarnie (1877).

SALTEN, Felix (1869–1945), Austrian novelist and essayist, born at Budapest, known especially for his animal stories, including *Bambi* (1929), and *Bambi's Children* (1940), which, in translation, achieved great popularity in America and Britain.

SALTYKOV, Michail Evgrafovich, pseud. of **N. Shchedrin,** *sal-ti-kof'* (1826–89), Russian writer, born in Tver, was exiled (1848–56) because of his satirical story *Contradictions* (1847), but later became a provincial vice-governor. He edited with Nekrasov the radical *Notes of the Fatherland*, and of his many, mainly melancholy, books *The Golovlyov Family* and the *Fables* are among those translated.

SALVATOR ROSA. See ROSA (2).

SALVIATI, Antonio (1816–90), born at Vicenza, and died at Venice, revived in 1860 the glass factories of Murano and the art of mosaic.

SALVINI, Tommaso, *sal-vee'nee* (1830–1915), Italian actor, born at Milan, first became well known as a member of Ristori's company. In Paris he played in Racine and in London he enjoyed immense popularity in Shakespearean rôles, especially as Othello and Hamlet. He played also in comedies such as those of Goldoni, but won fame mainly as a tragedian. The part which he played in fighting in the revolutionary war of 1848 added to his popularity. In 1884 he retired. See his *Autobiography* (1893) and *Ricordi* (1895).

SAMAIN, Albert Victor, *sa-mi* (1858–1900), French poet, born at Lille, was a clerk in the Prefecture of the Seine. His symbolist poetry, though not original in subject, is delicate, fresh and musical and was well received in his lifetime. Among his collections of verse are *Au jardin de l'infante* (1893), *Aux flancs de la vase* (1898) and *Le Chariot d'or*, published posthumously. See L. Bocquet, *Albert Samain* (1905), and E. Gosse, *French Profiles* (1905).

SAMBOURNE, Edward Linley (1844–1910), English cartoonist, born in London, was at sixteen apprenticed to marine engineer works at Greenwich, but in April 1867 began his lifelong connection with *Punch*. He illustrated Kingsley's *Water Babies*, Andersen's *Fairy Tales*, &c.

SAMSON, (1) the last of the twelve judges in the Book of Judges. His life as recounted in the Bible, however, represents him not as a leader but as an individual whose deeds on behalf of Israel made him a popular hero. His exploits suggested to Goldziher (*Hebrew Mythology*, Eng. trans. 1877) the improbable idea that elements of solar mythology may have come into his story.

(2) (*c.* 480–565), a Welsh saint, who died Bishop of Dol in Brittany.

(3) (1135–1211), in 1182 became abbot of Bury St Edmunds. See JOCELIN.

SAMUEL (Heb. *Shemû'el*, probably 'name of God', 11th cent. B.C.), last of the judges, first of the prophets, and next to Moses the greatest personality in the early history of Israel, was an Ephraimite, native of Ramathaim or Ramah in Mount Ephraim. As a child he was dedicated to the presthood. The story of 1 Sam. vii–xvi combines two widely different accounts of his career. According to one of these, Israel lay under the Philistine yoke for twenty years, when a national convention was summoned to Mizpah by Samuel. The Philistines came upon them, but only to sustain a decisive repulse. The prophet thenceforward ruled peacefully and prosperously as judge over Israel till age compelled him to associate his sons with him in the government. Dissatisfaction with their ways gave the elders a pretext for asking for a king such as every other nation had. Although seeing the folly of this, equivalent to a rejection of Yahweh, he, after some remonstrance, granted their prayer, and at Mizpah Saul was chosen. The older account makes him a 'man of God', a man 'held in honour', and a seer whose every word 'cometh surely to pass', but occupying a position hardly so prominent as that of judge of Israel. Saul was divinely made known to him as God's instrument to deliver Israel, and the seer secretly annointed him. A month later Saul's relief of Jabesh-Gilead resulted in his being chosen king. The accounts of Samuel's conduct during Saul's reign are also discrepant.

SAMUEL, Herbert Louis, 1st Viscount Samuel (1870–1963), British Liberal statesman and philosophical writer, born into a Jewish banking family, was educated at University College School and Balliol, Oxford. Entering parliament in 1902, he held various offices, including that of chancellor of the Duchy of Lancaster (1909), postmaster-general (1910 and 1915), home secretary (1916; 1931–32) and was high commissioner for Palestine (1920–25). His philosophical works include *Practical Ethics* (1935), *Belief and Action* (1937) and *In Search of Reality* (1957). He was president of the Royal Statistical Society (1918–20), was created viscount (1937) and was awarded the O.M. (1958). See Life by J. Bowle (1957).

SANCHEZ, Thomas, *san-cheth* (1550–1610), Jesuit moral theologian and casuist, became master of novices at Granada. His *Disputationes de Sancto Matrimonii Sacramento*

(1592) deals with the legal, moral and religious questions that arise out of marriage.

SANCROFT, William (1617–93), Archbishop of Canterbury, born at Fressingfield, Suffolk, was elected fellow of Emmanuel, Cambridge, in 1642, but in 1651 was expelled from his fellowship or refusing to take the 'Engagement', and in 1657 crossed over to Holland. After the Restoration his advancement was rapid—king's chaplain and rector of Houghton-le-Spring (1661), prebendary of Durham and master of Emmanuel (1662), Dean first of York and next of St Paul's (1664), as such having a principal hand in the rebuilding of the cathedral, Archdeacon of Canterbury (1668), and Archbishop (1678). A Tory and High Churchman, Sancroft refused to sit in James II's Ecclesiastical Commission (1686), and in 1688 was sent to the Tower as one of the Seven Bishops. But after the Revolution, having taken the oath of allegiance to James, he would not take it to William and Mary, so was suspended (1689), and retired to his native village where he died. The *Fur Praedestinatus* (1651), an attack on Calvinism by an unknown author, has been ascribed to him. See Life by D'Oyly (1821) and Miss Strickland's *Lives of the Seven Bishops* (1866).

SANCTORIUS (Santorio Santorio) (1561–1636), Italian physician, born in Capodistria, studied at Padua and in 1611 became professor of Theoretical Medicine there. He invented the clinical thermometer, a pulsimeter, a hygrometer and other instruments. But he is best known for his investigations into the fluctuations in the body's weight under different conditions due to 'insensible perspiration'. His experiments were conducted on a balance made by himself. See A. Castiglioni, *History of Medicine* (1947).

SAND, (1) George, the pseud. of **Amandine Aurore Lucie Dupin, 'Baronne' Dudevant,** *sã* (1804–76), French novelist, born in Paris. Aurore's father died when she was very young, and she lived principally at Nohant in Berri with her grandmother, Madame Dupin, on whose death the property descended to her. At eighteen she was married to Casimir, Baron Dudevant, and had two children, and after nine years left her husband and went to Paris to make her living by literature in the Bohemian society of the period (1831). For the best part of twenty years her life was spent in the company and partly under the influence of various more or less distinguished men. At first her interests were with poets and artists, the most famous being Alfred de Musset (q.v.), with whom she travelled in Italy, and Chopin (q.v.), who was her companion for several years. In the second decade her attention shifted to philosophers and politicians, such as Lamennais, the socialist Pierre Leroux (qq.v.), and the republican Michel de Bourges. After 1848 she settled down as the quiet 'châtelaine of Nohant', where she spent the rest of her life in outstanding literary activity, varied by travel. In her work some have marked three, others four periods. When she first went to Paris, and with her companion Jules Sandeau (q.v.), from the first half of whose name her pseudonym was taken, settled to novel-writing, her books—*Indiana* (1832), *Valentine* (1832), *Lelia* (1833) and *Jacques*—partook of the Romantic extravagance of the time, informed by a polemic against marriage. In the next her philosophical and political teachers engendered the socialistic rhapsodies of *Spiridion* (1838), *Consuelo* (1842–44) and the *Comtesse de Rudolstadt* (1843–45). Between the two groups came the fine novel *Mauprat* (1837). Then she began to turn towards the studies of rustic life—*La Petite Fadette, François le Champi, La Mare au diable* (1846)—which some constitute a third division and are, by modern standards, her best works. A fourth group would comprise the miscellaneous works of her last twenty years—some of them, such as *Les Beaux Messieurs de Bois Doré, Le Marquis de Villemer, Mlle la Quintinie,* of high merit. Her complete works (over 100 vols.), besides novels, plays, &c., include the charming *Histoire de ma vie, Hiver à Majorque, Elle et lui* (on her relations with de Musset), and delightful letters, published after her death. See monographs by Rocheblave (1905), Gribble (1907), Séché and Bertaut (1909), R. Doumic (trans. 1910), Karénine (1899–1927); Maurras, *Les Amants de Venise* (new ed. 1917); M. L'Hôpital, *La Notion d'artiste chez George Sand* (1946); M. Toesca, *The Other George Sand* (1947).

(2) **Karl Ludwig** (1795–1820), Jena theological student and member of the Burschenschaft, was beheaded for stabbing Kotzebue (q.v.).

SANDAY, William (1843–1920), English biblical critic, born at Holme Pierrepont, Nottingham, was principal of Hatfield's Hall, Durham (1876–82), Ireland professor of Exegesis at Oxford (1882–95), and then Lady Margaret professor of Divinity and canon of Christ Church. He wrote many critical works, including *The Authorship and Historical Character of the Fourth Gospel* (1872), *The Early History and Origin of the Doctrine of Biblical Inspiration* (1893) and perhaps the most important, in collaboration with A. C. Headlam, *Commentary on the Epistle to the Romans* (1895). He did much to promote modern methods of biblical study.

SANDBURG, Carl (1878–1967), American poet, born at Galesburg, Ill., of Swedish stock, after trying various jobs, fighting in the Spanish-American war and studying at Lombard College, became a journalist and started to write for *Poetry*. His verse, realistic and robust but often also delicately sensitive, reflects industrial America. Among his volumes of poetry are *Cornhuskers* (1918), *Smoke and Steel* (1920), *Slabs of the Sunburnt West* (1922) and *Good Morning, America* (1928). His *Complete Poems* gained him the Pulitzer prize in 1950. Interested in American folksongs and ballads, he published a collection in *The American Songbag* (1927). He also wrote a vast *Life of Abraham Lincoln.* See *Selected Poems*, ed. Rebecca West (1926), and F. B. Millett, *Contemporary American Authors* (1940).

SANDBY, (1) Paul (1725–1809), English painter born in Nottingham, has been called the father of the watercolour school. His career began as a draughtsman, but later, living at Windsor with his brother, he made seventy-six drawings of Windsor and Eton. His watercolours, outlined with the pen, and only finished with colour, take, however, the purely monochrome drawing of this school one step forward. He was an original member of the Royal Academy.

(2) **Thomas** (1721–98), deputy-ranger of Windsor Park from 1746, was brother of (1). He also became an R.A. and first professor of Architecture to the Royal Academy. See W. Sandby, *Thomas and Paul Sandby* (1892), and A. R. Oppé, *The Drawings of Paul and Thomas Sandby at Windsor Castle* (1947).

SANDEAU, Jules, *sã-dō* (1811–83), French author, born at Aubusson, went early to Paris to study law, but soon gave himself to letters. He was associated with George Sand in *Rose et Blanche* (1831). His first independent novel was *Madame de Sommerville* (1834) and his first hit *Marianna* (1840). His books give an accurate picture of the social conflicts of the France of his day and he was a master of the *roman de mœurs.* He became keeper of the Mazarin Library in 1853, an Academician in 1858, and librarian at St Cloud in 1859. See Life by Claretie (1883), and Saintsbury's *Essays on French Novelists* (1891).

SANDEMAN, Robert. See GLAS (2).

SANDERS, or **Saunder, Nicholas** (*c.* 1530–81), Roman Catholic historian and controversialist, born near Reigate, was educated at Winchester and New College, Oxford. A fellow in 1548, he lectured on Canon Law in 1558, in 1559 he went abroad; at Rome was created D.D. and ordained priest, and in 1561 accompanied Cardinal Hosius to the Council of Trent. He had been theological professor at Louvain for thirteen years, and had twice visited Spain (1573–77). As a papal agent in 1579 he landed in Ireland where he later died. His best known works are *De Visibili Monarchia Ecclesiae* (1571) and *De Origine ac Progressu Schismatis Anglicani* (completed by Rishton, 1585; trans. 1877).

SANDERSON, Robert (1587–1663), greatest of English casuists, born in Yorkshire, graduated at Lincoln College, Oxford, of which he became a fellow (1606–19), reader of logic (1608) and thrice subrector (1613–16). Regius professor of Divinity (1642–48), he was deprived of his professorship during the Civil War but was reinstated and became Bishop of Lincoln in 1660. To him are due the second preface to the Prayer Book and perhaps the General Thanksgiving, as well as works on casuistry. See Life by Izaak Walton (1678).

SANDOW, Eugene, *san'dō* (1867–1925), German 'strong man' and exponent of physical culture, was born in Königsberg of Russian parents. After a successful career as a strong man and as an artist's model, he opened an Institute of Health in St James's Street.

SANDRART, Joachim von (1606–88), German painter, copper-engraver and historian of art, was born at Frankfurt, and died at Nuremberg.

SANDWICH, (1) Edward Montagu, 1st Earl of (1625–72), English admiral, fought for the parliament at Marston Moor, sat in parliament 1645–48, shared the command of the fleet with Blake from 1653. For helping to forward the Restoration, he was given an earldom. Ambassador to Spain 1666–69, he was blown up in a sea-fight with the Dutch. See Life by Harris (1912).

(2) **John Montagu, 4th Earl of** (1718–92), corrupt politician, remembered as the inventor of *sandwiches,* to eat at the gaming-table.

SANDYS, *sands,* (1) **Duncan** (1908–), British Conservative politician, educated at Eton and Oxford, in the Diplomatic Service from 1930 to 1933, he became in 1935 M.P. for Norwood, London. In 1951 he was made minister of supply in the Churchill government, in 1954 became minister of housing, and as minister of defence (1957) inaugurated a controversial programme of cutting costs and streamlining the Forces. When the Conservatives were returned in 1959 he was minister of aviation (1959–60), secretary of state for commonwealth relations (1960-64), and for the colonies (1962–64). In opposition after 1964 his strongly right-wing views made him a controversial figure. In 1935 he married Diana, daughter of Winston Churchill (q.v.).

(2) **George** (1578–1644), English traveller and translator, born at Bishopthorpe, Yorkshire, son of the Archbishop of York, wrote *Relation of a Journey Begun An. Dom. 1610,* an account of his travels in Europe and the Near East. In America (1621–31) he acted as treasurer of the colony of Virginia and made a verse translation of Ovid's *Metamorphoses.* He was much admired by Dryden as a versifier. He also wrote poetic versions of the Psalms and the Song of Solomon and a tragedy, *Christ's Passion* (1640). See study by R. B. Davies (1955).

SANGER, (1) **John** (1816–89), and his brother **George** (1825–1911), English showmen, both calling themselves 'Lord', became famous first with their travelling circuses in the provinces and then in London. See George Sanger's *Seventy Years a Showman.*

(2) **Margaret** (1883–1966), American leader of the birth control movement, was born in New York and educated at Claverack College. Her interest in contraception being excited by the tragedies which she encountered as a nurse, she risked charges of obscenity by stressing the need for birth control in her magazine *Woman Rebel.* In 1914 she left the U.S., having been charged for founding the National Birth Control League, and visited the Jacobs Birth Control Clinics in Holland. In 1916 she was imprisoned for starting such a clinic in Brooklyn but gradually she overcame prejudice. She visited many other countries and launched the birth control movement in India.

SANKEY, Ira David. See MOODY (1).

SAN MARTÍN, José de (1778–1850), S. American patriot, born at Yapeyu, Argentina, played a great part in winning independence for his native land, Chile and Peru. In January 1817 he led an army across the Andes into Chile. In 1821 he became protector of Peru but resigned in 1822 and died an exile in Boulogne. See book by Schoelkopf (1924), and Pilling, *The Emancipation of South America* (1893).

SANNAZARO, Jacopo, *-zah'rō* (*c.* 1458–1530), Italian poet, born at Naples, attached himself to the court there. His *Arcadia* (1485), a medley of prose and verse, is full of beauty and had a direct influence on Sydney's *Arcadia.* It went through many editions. Other works are *Sonetti e Canzoni* and *De Partu Virginis.* See *Arcadia*, ed. E. Carrara (1926).

SANSON, a family of Paris executioners. 'M. de Paris', Charles Henri Sanson, executed Louis XVI. See *Memoirs of the Sansons* (1875).

SANSOVINO, *san-sō-vee'nō*, (1) or properly **Andrea Contucci** (1460–1529), Italian religious sculptor, born at Monte Sansovino, from which he took his name. He worked in Florence, Portugal, at the court of John II and in Rome. Some of his work survives, including, at S. Maria del Popolo, a monument of Cardinal Sforza.

(2) properly **Jacopo Tatti** (1486–1570), sculptor and architect, born at Florence, was a pupil of (1) and took his name. He lived from 1527 in Venice, where he did his best work. As an architect his most noteworthy works are the Libreria Vecchia, the Palazzo della Zecca and the Palazzo Corner, and as a sculptor, the two giants on the steps of the ducal palace. See L. Pittoni, *I Sansovino* (1909).

SANT, James (1820–1916), English subject and portrait painter (R.A. 1870, painter-in-ordinary to Queen Victoria 1871, C.V.O. 1914), was born at Croydon.

SANTA ANNA, Antonio López de (1797–1876), Mexican president, born at Jalapa, in 1821 joined Iturbide, but in 1822 overthrew him, and in 1833 himself became president of Mexico. His reactionary policy in 1836 cost the country Texas. He invaded the revolted province, but was routed by Houston, and imprisoned for eight months. In 1838 he lost a leg in the gallant defence of Vera Cruz against the French. From 1841 to 1844 he was either president or the president's master, and was recalled from exile in 1846 to be president during the unlucky war with the United States, in which he was twice defeated in the field. He was recalled from Jamaica by a revolution in 1853, and appointed president for life, but in 1855 he was driven from the country. Under Maximilian he intrigued industriously, and ultimately had to flee. In 1867, after the emperor's death, he tried to effect a landing, was captured, and sentenced to death, but allowed to retire to New York. He returned at the amnesty in 1872. See Lives by F. C. Hanighen (1934), W. H. Calcott (1936) and R. F. Muñoz (1936).

SANTAYANA, George (1863–1952), Spanish-born American philosopher, poet and novelist, was born in Madrid and educated in America. He became professor at Harvard (1907–12) but retained his Spanish nationality. His writing career began as a poet with *Sonnets and other Verses* (1894), but later philosophy became his chief interest. His reputation as a stylist, however, rather than his importance as a philosopher proved the more lasting. He held that the given was no more than appearance and that 'animal faith' alone led to the belief in substance. His major philosophical works were *The Life of Reason* (1905–06), *Scepticism and Animal Faith* (1923), &c.; *The Last Puritan* (1935) was a witty and very successful novel. See studies of his work edited by P. A. Schilpp (1940) and of his aesthetics, I. Singer (1957).

SANTERRE, Antoine Joseph, *sã-ter* (1752–1809), wealthy French brewer, received a command in the National Guard in 1789, took part in the storming of the Bastille and was in charge at the king's execution. Appointed general of division (1793), he marched against the Vendéan royalists, but, miserably beaten, was recalled and imprisoned. See Life by Carro (1847).

SANTILLANA, Iñigo López de Mendoza, Marqués de (1398–1458), Spanish scholar and poet, influenced by the poetry of Dante and Petrarch, introduced their style and methods into Spanish literature. His shorter poems, especially his *serranillas*, are among his best work and he was the first Spanish poet to write sonnets. His principal prose work, *Carta Proemio*, is a discourse on European literature of his day.

SANTLEY, Sir Charles (1834–1922), English baritone singer, was born in Liverpool and trained partly in Milan (1855–57). He made his début in Haydn's *Creation* in 1857, and from 1862 devoted himself to Italian opera. Latterly he again became better known at concerts and in oratorio. He was knighted in 1907. See his *Reminiscences* (1909).

SANTOS-DUMONT, Alberto (1873–1932), Brazilian aeronaut, born in São Paolo, in 1898 built and flew a cylindrical balloon having a gasoline engine. In 1901 he did the same with an airship in which he made the first flight from St Cloud round the Eiffel Tower and back. Two years later he built the first airship station, at Neuilly. He then experimented with heavier-than-air machines, and eventually flew 715 feet in a plane constructed on the principle of the box-kite. In 1909 he succeeded in building a light monoplane, a forerunner of modern light aircraft. See study by Wykeham (1962).

SAPPHO (born *c.* 650 B.C.), Greek poetess, born in Lesbos, fled about 596 B.C. from Mitylene to Sicily, but after some years was again at Mitylene. Her famous plunge into the sea from the Leucadian rock, because Phaon did not return her love, seems to have no historical foundation. Tradition represents her as exceptionally immoral, a view first disputed by Welcker (1816). The greatest poetess of antiquity, she wrote lyrics unsurpassed for depth of feeling, passion and grace. Only two of her odes are extant in full, but many fragments have been found in Egypt. See H. T. Wharton's edition, with Life, translation, bibliography, &c. (4th ed. 1898), and H. J. Rose, *Handbook of Greek Literature* (1934).

SARASATE, Martin Meliton, *sah-ra-sah'tay* (1844–1908), Spanish violinist, born of Basque parentage at Pampeluna, studied at Paris, and in 1857 began to give concerts. A skilled performer in concertos, he perhaps played best the Spanish dance music he composed himself.

SARDANAPALUS (669–640 B.C.), the Greek form of **Assur-bani-pal**, king of Assyria, eldest son of Esar-Haddon, and grandson of Sennacherib, with all the ambition but without the genius of his father, was a generous patron of art and letters, and his reign marks the zenith of Assyrian splendour. He extended his sway from Elam to Egypt, but the revolt of Babylon shook the empire.

SARDOU, Victorien (1831–1908), French dramatist, was born at Paris. His first efforts were failures, but through his marriage with the actress Brécourt, who nursed him when sick and in want, he became acquainted with Déjazet, for whom he wrote successfully *Monsieur Garat* and *Les Prés Saint-Gervais* (1860). Soon he had amassed a fortune and had become the most successful playwright of his day, not only in France but in Europe, and his popularity was immense in America. Pieces like *Les Pattes de monde* (1860), *Nos intimes* (1861), *La Famille Benoîton* (1865), *Divorçons* (1880), *Odette* (1882), and *Marquise* (1889) are fair samples of his work. For Sarah Bernhardt he wrote *Fédora* (1883), *La Tosca* (1887), &c., and with Moreau *Madame Sans-Gene*; for Irving, *Robespierre* (1899), *Dante* (1903). He attempted the higher historical play in *La Patrie* (1869). Today his plays appear over-technical and over-theatrical and the plots and characters shallow and rather obvious. Sardou was elected to the Academy in 1877. See study by J. Hart (1913).

SARGENT, (1) Sir (Harold) Malcolm (Watts) (1895–1967), English conductor, born at Stamford, trained originally as an organist. He first appeared as a conductor when his *Rhapsody on a Windy Day* was performed at a Promenade Concert in 1921. He was conductor of the Royal Choral Society from 1928, was in charge of the Liverpool Philharmonic Orchestra (1942–48), and of the B.B.C. Symphony Orchestra (1950–57). Sargent's outstanding skill in choral music, his sense of occasion and unfailing panache won him enormous popularity at home and abroad. He was knighted in 1947.

(2) **John Singer** (1856–1925), American painter, born at Florence, the son of a physician, studied painting there and in Paris, where he first gained recognition. Most of his work was, however, done in England, where he became the most fashionable portrait painter of his age. He was elected an R.A. in 1897. His early painting shows the influence of France, but Spain had a more lasting effect and *Carmencita* is perhaps the best example of this. He travelled much to America, where as well as portraits he worked on series of decorative paintings for public buildings, including the *Evolution of Religion* for Boston library. He also, especially in later life, painted landscapes, often in watercolour, but it was as a painter of elegant and lively portraits that he will always be best known.

SARMIENTO. See DARÍO.

SAROYAN, William, *-roy'-* (1908–), American playwright and novelist, was born in Fresno, California. His first work, *The Daring Young Man on the Flying Trapeze* (1934), a volume of short stories, was followed by a number of highly original novels and plays. One of his plays, *The Time of Your Life* (1939), was awarded the Pulitzer prize. A later work was an autobiography, *The Bicycle Rider in Beverley Hills* (1952).

SARPI, Pietro, or Fra Paolo (1552–1623), born at Venice, from 1575 was professor of Philosophy in the Servite monastery there. He studied Oriental languages, mathematics, astronomy, medical and physiological sciences, &c. In the dispute between Venice and Paul V about clerical immunities Sarpi became the champion of the republic and of freedom of thought. On the repeal (1607) of the edict of excommunication launched against Venice, he was summoned to Rome to account for his conduct. He refused to obey, was excommunicated and was seriously wounded by assassins. He afterwards busied himself with writing his great *Istoria del Concilio Tridentino* (London 1619). He tended to favour the Protestants and was also interested in the new developments in Science. His collected works were published at Naples (24 vols. 1789–90). See Lives by Campbell (1869), Bianchi-Giovini (1836), Pascolato (1893) and A. Robertson (1894), and T. A. Trollope's *Paul the Pope and Paul the Friar* (1861). A new edition of the *Istoria* (3 vols.) by G. Gambarin appeared in 1935.

SARRAIL, Maurice Paul Emmanuel, *sar-rah'y'* (1856–1929), French general, born at Carcassonne, led the 3rd army at the battle of the Marne in 1914, commanded the Allied forces in the East (Salonica) 1915–17, and as high commissioner in Syria (1924–25) was recalled after the bombardment of Damascus during a rising.

SARSFIELD, Patrick, Earl of Lucan (1645?–1693), Irish soldier, born at Lucan near Dublin, had fought abroad under Monmouth, and at Sedgemoor against him, when in 1688 he was defeated at Wincanton, and crossed over to Ireland. Created Earl of Lucan by James II, he drove the English out of Sligo, was present at the Boyne and Aghrim, defended Limerick, and on its capitulation (1691) entered the French service. He fought at Steenkirk (1692), and was mortally wounded at Neerwinden. See Life by Todhunter (1895).

SARTI, Guiseppe (1729–1802), composer, born at Faenza, held posts at Copenhagen, Venice, Milan and St Petersburg, and died at Berlin. He composed a dozen operas, masses, sonatas, &c. Cherubini was one of his pupils.

SARTO, Andrea del (1486–1531), Florentine painter, whose real name was **Vannucchi,** ' del Sarto ' being an allusion to his father's trade of tailor. In 1509–14 he was engaged by the Servites in Florence to paint for their church of the Annunciation a series of frescoes and a second series was next painted for the Recollets. In 1518, on the invitation of Francis I, he went to Paris, returned next year to Italy, with a commission to purchase works of art, but squandered the money and dared not return to France. He died of the plague at Florence. Many of Andrea's most celebrated pictures are at Florence. He was a rapid worker and accurate draughtsman, displaying a refined feeling for harmonies of colour, but lacked the elevation and spiritual imagination of the greatest masters. See studies by H. Guinness (1899), F. Knapp (1908) and A. J. Rucconi (1935).

SARTORIS, Adelaide. See KEMBLE (1).

SARTRE, Jean-Paul, *sahr'tr'* (1905–), French philosopher, dramatist and novelist, with Heidegger the most prominent exponent of atheistic existentialism, born in Paris, taught philosophy at Le Havre, Paris and Berlin (1934–35), joined the French army in 1939, was a prisoner in Germany (1941), and after his release became an active member of the resistance in Paris. In 1945 he emerged as the leading light of the left-wing, left-bank intellectual life of Paris, with the Café de Flore as its hub, but he eventually broke with the Communists. In 1946 he became editor of the avant-garde monthly *Les Temps modernes.* A disciple of Heidegger, he developed his own characteristic existentialist doctrines, derived from an early anarchistic tendency, which found full expression in his autobiographical novel *La Nausée* (1938) and in *Le Mur* (1938), a collection of short stories. The Nazi occupation provided the grim background to such plays as *Les Mouches*, a modern version of the Orestes theme, and *Huis clos*, 'Vicious Circle' (both 1943). *Les Mains sales* (1952), the inept title of the film and English version of which was *Crime passionel*, movingly portrayed the tragic consequences of a choice to join an extremist party. Choice is at the core of Sartre's existentialism. Existence is prior to essence. Man is nothing at birth and throughout his life he is no more than the sum of his past commitments. To believe in anything outside his own will is to be guilty of 'bad faith'. Existentialist despair and anguish is the acknowledgment that man is condemned to freedom. There is no God, so man must rely upon his own fallible will and moral insight. He cannot escape choosing. His doctrines are outlined in *L'Existentialisme est un humanisme* (1946; trans. and intro. P. Mairet 1948) and fully worked out in *L'Être et le néant* (1943), 'Being and Nothingness' (trans. and intro. H. E. Barnes, 1957). Its cumbersome Hegelian terminology defies analysis, except on its own terms. Other notable works include *Les Chemins de la liberté* (1945), and the play *Les Séquestrés d'Altona* (1959). In 1964 he was awarded, but declined to accept, the Nobel prize for literature. See works by his disciple, Simone de Beauvoir, and studies in French by R. Troisfontaines (1945), G. Varet (1948), and in English by P. Dempsey (1950), I. Murdoch (1953), W. Desani (1954), A. Ussher (1955), P. Thody (1960) and M. Cranston (1962).

SASSOFERRATO, or Giovanni Battista Salvi (1605–85), Italian religious painter, was born at Sassoferrato in the March of Ancona, and worked at Rome. Very popular in the 19th century, his paintings are now regarded as over-sentimental though very fine in colouring. See E. K. Waterhouse, *Baroque Painting in Rome* (1937).

SASSOON, Siegfried Lorraine, *-soon'* (1886–1967), English poet and novelist, was born in Kent. World War I, in which he served, engendered in him a hatred of war, fiercely expressed in his *Counterattack* (1918) and *Satirical Poems* (1926). A semifictitious autobiography, *The Complete Memoirs of George Sherston* (1937), was begun with *Memoirs of a Fox-Hunting Man* (1928; Hawthornden prize 1929), and continued in *Memoirs of an Infantry Officer* (1930) and *Sherston's Progress* (1936). Truly autobiographical are *The Old Century* (1938), *The Weald of Youth* (1942) and *Siegfried's Journey 1916–20* (1945). He was created C.B.E. in 1951 and became a Roman Catholic in 1957. See study by M. Thorpe (1966) and S. Jackson *The Sassoons* (1968).

SATIE, Erik Alfred Leslie, *sa-tee* (1866–1925), composer, born at Honfleur of French-Scottish parents, after work as a café composer studied under D'Indy and Roussel. In his own work (ballets, lyric dramas, whimsical pieces) he was in violent revolt against Wagnerism and orthodoxy in general, and had some influence on Debussy, Ravel and others. See study by Myers (1948).

SAUD IBN. See IBN SAUD.

SAUL, *sawl* (11th cent. B.C.), son of Kish, the first king elected by the Israelites, conquered the Philistines, Ammonites and Amalekites, became madly jealous of David, his son-in-law, and was ultimately at feud with the priestly class. At length Samuel secretly anointed David king. Saul fell in battle with the Philistines on Mount Gilboa.

SAUMAREZ, James, 1st Baron de, *sō'ma-rez* (1757–1836), British naval commander, born in Guernsey, served in the navy during the American war (1774–82). Now a commander, he distinguished himself in the fight between Rodney and De Grasse (April 12, 1782), and for his capture (1793) of the frigate *La Réunion* was knighted. He fought at L'Orient (1795) and Cape St Vincent (1797), and was second in command at the Nile. In 1801, a baronet and vice-admiral, he fought his greatest action, off Cadiz (July 12), defeating fourteen French-Spanish ships with six, and was made K.C.B. He commanded the British Baltic fleet sent (1809) to assist the Swedes. He was promoted to the rank of admiral in 1814 and created a peer in 1831. See Sir John Ross, *Memoirs and Correspondence of Admiral Lord de Saumarez* (1838), and Mahan, *Types of Naval Officers* (1902).

SAUNDER, Nicholas. See SANDERS.

SAUNDERSON, Nicholas (1682–1739), English blind mathematician, born at Thurlstone near Penistone, lost his eyesight from smallpox when a year old. At Cambridge he lectured on the Newtonian philosophy, optics, &c., and in 1711 became Lucasian professor of Mathematics. A Life is prefixed to his *Algebra* (1740); another treatise by him is on *Fluxions* (1756).

SAUSSURE, *sō-sür,* (1) **Horace Benédict de** (1740–99), Swiss physicist and geologist, born at Conches near Geneva, was professor of Physics and Philosophy at Geneva (1762–1788). He travelled in Germany, Italy and England, and traversed the Alps by several routes. He was the first traveller (not a guide) to ascend Mont Blanc (1787). A pioneer in the study of mineralogy, botany, geology and meteorology, his invaluable observations are recorded in his *Voyages dans les Alpes* (1779–96). He devised the hair hygrometer and other instruments and published an *Essai sur l'hygrométrie* (1783).

The mineral saussurite is named after him and it was he who introduced the word *geology* into scientific nomenclature. See Lives by Senebier (1801) and D. W. Freshfield (1920).

(2) **Nicolas Théodore** (1767–1845), son of (1), botanist, wrote *Recherches chimiques sur la végétation* (1804), which contains valuable discoveries about the growth of plants.

SAUVAGE, Frédéric, *sō-vahzh* (1785–1857), Boulogne shipbuilder, is by the French regarded as the inventor of the screw-propeller, in virtue of his having in 1832 improved the pattern in use.

SAVAGE, Richard (1697?–1743), English poet, claimed to be the illegitimate child of Richard Savage, fourth and last Earl Rivers, and the Countess of Macclesfield. In the dedication to his comedy *Love in a Veil* (1718) he asserted the parentage, but in Curll's *Poetical Register* (1719) the story is for the first time fully given. Aaron Hill befriended him, and in 1724 published in *The Plain Dealer* an outline of his story which brought subscribers for his *Miscellanies* (1726). In 1727 he killed a gentleman in a tavern brawl, and narrowly escaped the gallows. His attacks upon his alleged mother (now Mrs Brett), became louder and more bitter in his poem *The Bastard* (1728). *The Wanderer* (1729) was dedicated to Lord Tyrconnel, nephew of Mrs Brett, who had befriended him. Savage's disreputable habits brought misery and hunger, and the queen's pension (1732) of £50 for a birthday ode was dissipated in a week's debauchery. On Queen Caroline's death (1737) Pope tried to help him, but after about a year he went to Bristol, was flung into jail for debt, and died there. Savage owes his reputation solely to Samuel Johnson, who knew him in his own years of hunger in London, and, moved by pity to partiality, wrote what is perhaps the most perfect shorter Life in English literature. That the story contains improbabilities and falsehoods was proved by Moy Thomas in *N. & Q.* (1858). See Makower, *Richard Savage: A Mystery in Biography* (1909).

SAVARIN. See BRILLAT-SAVARIN.

SAVART, Felix, *sa-vahr* (1791–1841), French physician and physicist, was born at Mézières in Ardennes. He taught physics in Paris, and invented *Savart's wheel* for measuring tonal vibrations, and the *Savart quartz plate* for studying the polarization of light. With Biot he discovered the law (named after them) governing the force in a magnetic field round a long straight current. He died in Paris.

SAVARY, Anne Jean Marie René, Duc de Rovigo, *sav-a-ree* (1774–1833), French soldier, born at Marcq in Ardennes. Napoleon employed him in diplomatic affairs. In 1804 he presided at the execution of the Duc d'Enghien, and in the wars of 1806–08 acquired high reputation. Now Duke of Rovigo (1808), he was sent to Spain, and negotiated the kidnapping of the Spanish king and his son. In 1810 he became minister of police. After Napoleon's fall he wished to accompany him to St Helena, but was confined at Malta. He escaped and (1819) was reinstated in his honours. In 1831–33 he was commander-in-chief in Algeria. His *Mémoires* (1828) are unreliable.

SAVIGNY, Friedrich Karl von, *sa-veen-yee* (1779–1861), German jurist, born of Alsatian family at Frankfurt, in 1803 became a Law professor at Marburg, and published a treatise on the Roman law of property (Eng. trans. 1849) that won him European fame. In 1808 he was called to Landshut and in 1810 to Berlin, where he was also in 1810–42 member of the commission for revising the code of Prussia, &c. He resigned office in 1848. His greatest books were his *Roman Law in the Middle Ages* (1815–31; trans. 1829) and *System of Roman Law* (1840–49), with its continuation on *Obligations* (1851–1853). See books by Arndt (1861), Rudorff (1862), Bethmann-Hollweg (1867) and Landsberg (1890).

SAVILE, (1). See HALIFAX (4).

(2) **Sir Henry,** *sav'il* (1549–1622), scholar, born at Bradley near Halifax, became fellow of Merton College, Oxford, travelled on the Continent (1578), was Queen Elizabeth's tutor in Greek and mathematics, became warden of Merton in 1585, and provost of Eton in 1596, and was knighted in 1604. In 1619 he founded chairs of Geometry and Astronomy at Oxford. His principal works are *Rerum Anglicarum Scriptores* (1596), containing the works of William of Malmesbury, Henry of Huntingdon, Roger Hoveden, and 'Ingulph' (q.v.); *Commentaries concerning Roman Warfare* (1598); *Fower Bookes of the Histories* and the *Agricola* of Tacitus (1581); and a magnificent edition of St Chrysostom (1610–13).

SAVONAROLA, Girolamo (1452–98), Italian religious and political reformer, was born of noble family at Ferrara and in 1474 entered the Dominican order at Bologna. He seems to have preached in 1482 at Florence; but his first trial was a failure. In a convent at Brescia his zeal won attention, and in 1489 he was recalled to Florence. His second appearance in the pulpit of San Marco—on the sinfulness and apostasy of the time—was a great popular triumph; and by some he was hailed as an inspired prophet. Under Lorenzo the Magnificent art and literature had felt the humanist revival of the 15th century, whose spirit was utterly at variance with Savonarola's conception of spirituality and Christian morality. To the adherents of the Medici therefore, Savonarola early became an object of suspicion but till the death of Lorenzo (1492) his relations with the church were at least not antagonistic and when, in 1493, a reform of the Dominican order in Tuscany was proposed under his auspices, it was approved by the pope, and Savonarola was named the first vicar-general. But now his preaching began to point plainly to a political revolution as the divinely-ordained means for the regeneration of religion and morality, and he predicted the advent of the French under Charles VIII, whom soon after he welcomed to Florence. Soon, however, the French were compelled to leave Florence, and a republic was established, of which Savonarola became the guiding spirit, his party ('the Weepers') being completely in the ascendant. Now the Puritan of Catholicism displayed to the full his extraordinary genius and the extravagance of his theories. The republic of Florence was to be a Christian commonwealth, of which God was the sole sovereign, and His Gospel the law; the most stringent enactments were made for the repression of vice and frivolity; gambling was prohibited; the vanities of dress were restrained by sumptuary laws. Even the women flocked to the public square to fling down their costliest ornaments, and Savonarola's followers made a huge 'bonfire of vanities'. Meanwhile his rigorism and his claim to the gift of prophecy led to his being cited in 1495 to answer a charge of heresy at Rome and on his failing to appear he was forbidden to preach. Savonarola disregarded the order, but his difficulties at home increased. The new system proved impracticable and although the conspiracy for the recall of the Medici failed, and five of the conspirators were executed, yet this very rigour hastened the reaction. In 1497 came a sentence of excommunication from Rome; and thus precluded from administering the sacred offices, Savonarola zealously tended the sick monks during the plague. A second 'bonfire of vanities' in 1498 led to riots; and at the new elections the Medici party came into power. Savonarola was again ordered to desist from preaching, and was fiercely denounced by a Franciscan preacher, Francesco da Puglia. Dominicans and Franciscans appealed to the interposition of divine providence by the ordeal of fire. But when the trial was to have come off (April 1498) difficulties and debates arose, destroying Savonarola's prestige and producing a complete revulsion of public feeling. He was brought to trial for falsely claiming to have seen visions and uttered prophecies, for religious er[illegible], and for sedition. Under torture he made avowals which he afterwards withdrew. He was declared guilty and the sentence was confirmed by Rome. On May 23, 1498, this extraordinary man and two Dominican disciples were hanged and burned, still professing their adherence to the Catholic Church. In morals and religion, not in theology, Savonarola may be regarded as a forerunner of the Reformation. His works are mainly sermons, theological treatises, the chief *The Triumph of the Cross*, an apology of orthodox Catholicism, some poems, and a discourse on the government of Florence. An edition appeared in 1633–40; Ferrari edited *Prediche e Scritti* (1930), Ridolfi his *Lettere* (1933). The great Life of him is by Prof. Villari (2 vols. 1859–61; Eng. trans. 1863). See English works by R. Madden (1853), W. R. Clark (1878), Herbert Lucas, S.J. (1899), P. Villari (1918) and R. Ridolfi (trans. 1959); Mrs Oliphant, *Makers of Florence*; George Eliot, *Romola* and M. de la Bedoyère, *The Meddlesome Friar* (1958).

SAWTREY, William (?–1401), a Lollard burnt at Smithfield, February 26, 1401, the first victim in England.

SAXE, (1) John Godfrey (1816–87), American poet, born at Highgate, Vt., was by turns lawyer, journalist, politician, lecturer and journalist again. His numerous poems are mostly humorous and satirical.

(2) Maurice, Comte de (1696–1750), usually called **Marshal de Saxe,** natural son of Augustus II, Elector of Saxony and king of Poland, and Countess Aurora von Königsmark, was born at Goslar. At twelve he ran off to join the army of Marlborough in Flanders, and next the Russo-Polish army before Stralsund (1711). He fought against the Turks in Hungary under Prince Eugene, and studied the art of war in France. In 1726, elected Duke of Courland, he maintained himself against Russians and Poles, but was compelled to retire in 1729. He took a brilliant part in the siege of Philippsburg (1734); and in the war of the Austrian succession he invaded Bohemia and took Prague by storm. In 1744, now marshal of France, he commanded the French army in Flanders, showed splendid tactical skill, and took several fortresses. In 1745 he defeated the Duke of Cumberland at Fontenoy. In 1746 he gained the victory of Raucoux, and was made marshal-general. For the third time, at Laffeld (July 2, 1747), he defeated Cumberland and captured Bergen-op-Zoom. He then retired to his estate of Chambord, and died November 30, 1750. His work on the art of war, *Mes Rêveries*, was published in 1751. See Carlyle's *Frederick the Great*, Lives by Karl von Weber (2nd ed. 1870), Saint-René Taillandier (1865), Vitzthum von Eckstädt (1867), the Duc de Broglie (1891), Brandenburg (1897), J. M. White (1962) and J. Colin, *Les Campagnes du Maréchal de Saxe* (3 vols. 1901–06).

SAXE-COBURG-GOTHA, Alfred Ernest Albert, Prince of (1844–1900), second son of Queen Victoria, was born at Windsor Castle and studied at Bonn and Edinburgh before entering the royal navy in 1858. He was elected King of Greece in 1862, but declined the dignity. In 1866 he was created Duke of Edinburgh and in 1874 married the Russian Grand Duchess Marie Alexandrovna (1853–1920). In 1893 he succeeded his uncle as reigning Duke of Saxe-Coburg-Gotha.

SAXO GRAMMATICUS, 'the Scholar' (*c.* 1140–1206), Danish chronicler and a Zealander by birth, was secretary to Archbishop Absalom of Roskilde, at whose request he wrote the *Gesta Danorum* in 16 books. This fine example of medieval literature, partly legendary (bks. i–ix) and partly historical, is written after the style of Valerius Maximus. He is said to have died at Roskilde. See O. Elton's translation of Books i–ix (1894) and Weibull, *Saxo* (1915).

SAY, Jean Baptiste (1767–1832), French political economist, born at Lyons, passed part of his youth in England. On the outbreak of the Revolution he worked for Mirabeau on the *Courrier de Provence*, and was secretary to the minister of finance. In 1794–1800 he edited *La Décade*, and in it expounded the views of Adam Smith. A member of the tribunate in 1799, as a protest against the arbitrary tendencies of the consular government he resigned (1804). In 1803 he issued his *Traité d'économie politique* (8th ed. 1876). In 1814 the government sent him to England to study its economics; he laid down the results in *De l'Angleterre et des Anglais* (1816). From 1819 he lectured on political economy, and in 1831 became professor at the Collège de France. He also wrote *Catéchisme d'économie politique* (1815) and *Mélanges et correspondance* (1833). As a disciple of Adam Smith and through his own writings his influence on French economics of the first half of the 19th century was of the greatest importance. His grandson, **Léon** (1826–96), was a journalist, statesman and political economist.

SAYCE, Archibald Henry (1845–1933), English philologist, born at Shirehampton near Bristol, took a classical first from Oxford in 1869, and became a professor of Assyriology (1891–1919). A member of the Old Testament Revision Company, he wrote on biblical criticism and Assyriology.

SAYERS, (1) **Dorothy Leigh** (1893–1957), English writer, born in Oxford. Perhaps the most celebrated detective-story writer since Conan Doyle. Her novels are distinguished by a taste and style unequalled at the time when they were written. Beginning with *Clouds of Witness* (1926), she related the adventures of her hero Lord Peter Wimsey in various accurately observed milieux—such as advertising in *Murder Must Advertise* (1933) or campanology in *The Nine Tailors* (1934)—until, in *Gaudy Night* (1935) and *Busman's Honeymoon* (1937), her characters started to walk out of their frames and she wrote no more about them. She next earned a reputation as a leading Christian apologist with two successful plays, *The Zeal of Thy House* (1937) and *The Devil to Pay* (1939), a cycle for broadcasting, *The Man Born to be King* (1943) and a closely reasoned essay *The Mind of the Maker* (1941). A translation of Dante's *Inferno* appeared in 1949 and of *Purgatorio* in 1955. The *Paradiso* was left unfinished at her death.

(2) **James** (1912–), British physicist, a member of the British team associated with the atomic bomb project, became professor of Electron Physics at Birmingham (1946). In 1949 he was given a government award for his work on the cavity magnetron valve, of much importance in the development of radar.

(3) **Tom** (1826–65), pugilist, was born in Pimlico, and became a bricklayer. From 1849, his first fight, he was beaten only once, though under the average of middleweight champions. His last and most famous contest with Heenan, the Benicia Boy, in 1860, lasted for 2 hours and 6 minutes and ended after 37 rounds in a draw. A subscription of £3000 was raised for Sayers. See account of the Sayers-Heenan fight in *My Confidences* by F. Locker-Lampson (1896).

SCALA, Della. See SCALIGER.

SCALIGER, *skal'i-jėr,* (1) **Joseph Justus** (1540–1609), third son of (2), was born at Agen. After studying at Bordeaux, with his father and in Paris, acquired a surpassing mastery of the classics and eventually boasted that he spoke 13 languages, ancient and modern. While in Paris he became a Calvinist and later visited Italy, England and Scotland, only the last of which seems to have appealed to him, especially through the beauty of its ballads. In 1570 Scaliger settled at Valence and for two years studied under the jurist Cujacius. From 1572 to 1574 he was professor in Calvin's College at Geneva. He then spent twenty years in France and there produced works which placed him at the head of European scholars. Among them are his editions of Catullus, Tibullus, Propertius and Eusebius. By his edition of Manilius and his *De Emendatione Temporum* (1583) he founded modern chronology. From 1593 he held a chair at Leyden and to his inspiration Holland owes her long line of scholars. His last years were embittered by controversy, especially with the Jesuits, who charged him with atheism and profligacy. By his combined knowledge, sagacity and actual achievement he holds the first place among the scholars of his time. See his *Autobiography* (trans. 1927), Life by Bernays (1855), works by Nizard (1852) and Tamizey de Larroque (1881), and Mark Pattison's *Essays* (1889).

(2) **Julius Caesar** (1484–1558), father of (1), according to the highly doubtful story of his famous son, was the second son of Benedetto della Scala, descendant of a princely family of Verona and was brought up a soldier under his kinsman the Emperor Maximilian, gaining marvellous distinction in the French armies attempting the conquest of Italy. Despite these activities, he is said to have gained a knowledge of medicine and Greek. But it seems more probable that he was the son of a signpainter, Benedetto Bordone, and that he graduated in medicine at Padua. He became a French citizen in 1528 and settled at Agen, where he produced learned works on the Latin cases, on Theophrastus, Aristotle and Hippocrates. His poems of invective, as in his attack on Erasmus, were considerable. See books by Nisard (1860) and Magen (1880).

SCANDERBEG. See SKANDERBEG.

SCARLATTI, (1) **Alessandro** (1659–1725), Italian composer, born at Palermo, Sicily. His musical career began in Rome, where in 1680 he produced his first opera. This gained him the patronage of Queen Christina of Sweden, whose *maestro di cappella* he became. A few years later he went to Naples, where he was musical director at the court (1693–1703) and conducted the conservatoire there. He was the founder of the Neapolitan school of opera. He wrote nearly 120 operas; 35 of these survive, the most famous being *Tigrane* (1715). He also wrote 200 masses, 10 oratorios, 500 cantatas and many motets and madrigals. See study by E. J. Dent (new ed. 1960).

(2) **Guiseppe Domenico** (1685–1757), son of (1), also a musician, born at Naples, held many court appointments. In Rome (1709) he was official composer to the Queen of Poland, for whom he composed several operas. In Lisbon (1720) he served the king, taught the Infanta Barbara, and in 1729 went to the Spanish Court in Madrid. He was also (1714–19) choirmaster of St Peter's, Rome, and wrote much church music. He was a skilled performer on the harpsichord and it is as a writer of brilliant sonatas for this instrument that he is best remembered. He wrote over 600, and his work had an important effect on the development of the sonata form. See S. Sitwell,

A Background for Domenico Scarlatti (1935).

SCARLETT, (1) **James, Baron Abinger** (1769–1844), born in Jamaica, studied at Trinity, Cambridge, took silk in 1816, and in 1819 became Whig M.P. for Peterborough. Canning made him attorney-general, with a knighthood, in 1827; and in 1834, now lord chief baron of the Exchequer, he was created Baron Abinger.

(2) **Sir James Yorke** (1799–1871), British general, second son of (1), was educated at Eton and Trinity. He commanded the 5th Dragoon Guards (1840–53), and on October 25, 1854, led the heavy-cavalry charge at Balaclava. He subsequently commanded all the cavalry in the Crimea, and in 1865–70 commanded at Aldershot.

(3) **Robert** (*c.* 1499–1594), the Peterborough sexton who buried Catharine of Aragon and Mary, Queen of Scots.

SCARRON, Paul, *ska-rõ* (1610–60), French writer, born at Paris, the son of a lawyer, became an *abbé*, and gave himself up to pleasure. About 1634 he paid a long visit to Italy, and in 1638 began to suffer from a malady which ultimately left him paralysed. He obtained a prebend in Mans (1643), tried physicians in vain, and, giving up all hope of remedy, returned to Paris in 1646 to depend upon letters for a living. From this time he began to pour forth endless sonnets, madrigals, songs, epistles and satires. In 1644 he published *Typhon, ou la gigantomachie*; and made a still greater hit with his metrical comedy, *Jodelet, ou le maître valet* (1645), followed by *Les Trois Dorothées* and *Les Boutades du Capitan Matamore* (the plots taken from the Spanish). In 1648 appeared his *Virgile travesti* (part i) and the popular comedy, *L'Héritier ridicule*. One of the bitterest satires against Mazarin which he wrote for the *Fronde* probably lost him his pensions. The burlesque predominates in most of his writing, but it is as the creator of the realistic novel that he will always be remembered. *Le Roman comique* (1651–57) was a reaction against the euphuistic and interminable novels of Mlle de Scudéry and Honoré d'Urfé. The work of Le Sage, Defoe, Fielding and Smollett owes much to him. In 1652 he married Françoise d'Aubigné, afterwards Madame de Maintenon (q.v.), who brought an unknown decorum into his household and writings. See books by Christian (1841), Morillot (1888), Boislisle (1894), Chardon (1904); Magne, *Scarron et son milieu* (1924), *Roman comique*, ed. Magne (1938); and Jusserand's introduction to Tom Brown's *Comical Works of Scarron* (1892).

SCÈVE, Maurice, *sayv* (1510–64), French renaissance poet, born at Lyons, a leader of the *école lyonnaise*, which paved the way for the *Pléiade* (see RONSARD).

SCHACHT, Hjalmar Horace Greely, *shah*KHt (1877–1970), German financier, born of Danish descent at Tinglev, North Schleswig, in 1923 became president of the Reichsbank, and founded a new currency which ended the inflation of the mark. He resigned in 1929, was called back by the Nazis in 1933, and the following year, as minister of economics, he restored the German trade balance by unorthodox methods and by undertaking an expansionist credit policy. He resigned his post as minister of economics in 1937, and in 1939 was dismissed from his office as president of the Reichsbank because of his disagreement with Hitler over the latter's rearmament expenditure. Charged with high treason and interned by the Nazis, in 1945 he was acquitted by the Allies at Nuremberg of crimes against humanity, and was finally cleared by the German de-Nazification courts in 1948. In 1952 he advised Dr Mossadeq on Persia's economic problems, and in 1953 set up his own bank in Düsseldorf. Schacht, while deploring the excesses of the Nazi régime, helped to give it in its formative years financial stability and efficiency. See his autobiographical *My First Seventy-six Years* (1955).

SCHADOW, *shah'dō*, name of a family of Prussian artists:

(1) **Friedrich Wilhelm,** changed surname to **Schadow-Godenhaus** (1789–1862), son of (2), was a painter of the Overbeck school, from 1819 professor at Berlin, and in 1826–59 head of the Düsseldorf Academy. See Hübner, *Schadow und seine Schule* (1869).

(2) **Johann Gottfried** (1764–1850), father of (1) and (3), born at Berlin, became court sculptor and director of the Academy of Arts.

(3) **Rudolf** (1786–1822), son of (2), also a sculptor, executed *Spinning Girl* and the *Daughters of Leucippos* at Chatsworth. His works include the quadriga on the Brandenburg Gate at Berlin.

SCHAFER, Sir Edward Sharpey-. See SHARPEY-SCHAFER.

SCHAFF, Philip, *shaf* (1819–93), Swiss-born American Presbyterian theologian, born at Coire in Switzerland, was *privat-dozent* in Berlin, when in 1844 he was called to a chair at the German Reformed seminary at Mercersburg, Penn. In 1870 he became professor in the Union Seminary, New York. A founder of the American branch of the Evangelical Alliance, he was president of the American Old Testament Revision Committee. Among his works are a *History of the Christian Church* (1883–93), *The Creeds of Christendom* (1877), &c.

SCHALL, Johann Adam von (1591–1669), German Jesuit, born at Cologne, was sent out to China as a missionary in 1622, and at Pekin was entrusted with the reformation of the calendar and the direction of the mathematical school. By favour of the Manchu emperor the Jesuits obtained liberty to build churches (1644), and in fourteen years they are said to have made 100,000 converts. But in the next reign Schall was thrown into prison, and died there. A large MS. collection of his Chinese writings is preserved in the Vatican. In Latin he wrote a history of the China Mission (1655).

SCHAMYL. See SHAMYL.

SCHARF, Sir George, *shahrf* (1820–95), British illustrator, son of a Bavarian lithographer, George Scharf (1788–1860), who settled in London in 1816, became a draughtsman, painted a few oil pictures, travelled in Lycia, lectured on art, and was the first secretary of the National Portrait Gallery (from 1857).

SCHARNHORST, Gerhard Johann David von, *shahrn'horst* (1755–1813), German general, son of a Hanoverian farmer, fought in Flanders (1793–95). He directed the training-school for Prussian officers (1801). Wounded at Auerstädt and taken prisoner at Lübeck, he was present at Eylau; from 1807 he reorganized the Prussian army, introduced the short-service system, restored the morale of the Prussian army, so making it possible to defeat Napoleon at Leipzig (1813). But before that he died at Prague of a wound received at Grossgörschen. See Lives by Klippel (1869–71) and Lehmann (1886–87).

SCHARWENKA, Xaver, *shahr-veng'ka* (1850–1924), German-Polish pianist and composer, born at Samter near Posen, in 1881 started a music school in Berlin, and in 1891–98 was in New York. He composed symphonies, piano concertos and Polish dances. See his autobiography (1922).

SCHAUDINN, Fritz Richard, *show'din* (1871–1906), German zoologist, born at Röseningken, in East Prussia, became director of the department of protozoological research, Institute for Tropical Diseases, Hamburg. He demonstrated the amoebic nature of tropical dysentery, and with Hoffmann discovered the *spirochaeta pallida* which causes syphilis (1905).

SCHAUKAL, Richard, *show'kahl* (1874–1942), Austrian symbolist poet, born at Brünn in 1874, was in the Austrian civil service, and like Hofmannsthal turned away from the decadence of the declining Austrian empire to seek perfection in lyrical expression of poetic dreams in *Verse* (1896), *Tage und Träume* (1899), *Sehnsucht* (1900), &c., and *Spätlese* (1943).

SCHEELE, Carl Wilhelm, *skay'lė* (1742–86), Swedish chemist, born at Stralsund (then Swedish), was apprenticed to a chemist at Gothenburg, and was afterwards chemist at Malmö, Stockholm, Uppsala and Köping. He discovered hydrofluoric, tartaric, benzoic, arsenious, molybdic, lactic, critic, malic, oxalic, gallic, and other acids, and separated chlorine (1774), baryta, oxygen, glycerine (1783), and sulphuretted hydrogen. He first described the pigment called Scheele's green, or arsenite of copper, and scheelite or tungsten. He showed in 1777, independently of Priestley, that the atmosphere consists chiefly of two gases, one supporting combustion, the other preventing it. In 1783 he described prussic acid. His papers were translated by Dobbin (1931) See Life by O. Zekert (1931).

SCHEEMAKERS, Pieter, *skay'mah-kėrs* (1691–1770), Belgian sculptor, Nollekens' master, was born and died at Antwerp, lived in London (1735–69), and executed several monuments and portrait busts, including those of Mead and Dryden in Westminster Abbey.

SCHEER, Reinhard (1863–1928), German admiral, born in Hesse-Nassau, commanded the German High Seas Fleet in 1916–18 and was in charge at the battle of Jutland.

SCHEFFEL, Joseph Viktor von, *shef'fel* (1826–86), German poet and novelist, born at Karlsruhe, was bred for the law at Heidelberg, Munich and Berlin, but in 1852 went to Italy to write. His best book is *Der Trompeter von Säckingen* (1854), a romantic and humorous tale in verse. Other works include a novel, *Ekkehard* (1857), a collection of songs, *Gaudeamus* (1867), the romances, *Hugideo* (1884) and *Juniperus* (1863) and poems. He settled at Karlsruhe in 1864. See Lives by Prölss (1902), Sallwürk (1920).

SCHEFFER, Ary (1795–1858), French painter, born at Dordrecht, Holland, of a German father, studied under Guérin, and became known for his subject pictures and portraits in the romantic style. Puvis de Chavannes (q.v.) was his pupil.

SCHEFFLER, Johann. See ANGELUS.

SCHEIDEMANN, Philipp, *shī'dė-* (1865–1939), German socialist political leader, was minister of finance and colonies in the provisional government of 1918, and first chancellor of the republic in 1919.

SCHELLING, Friedrich Wilhelm Joseph von (1775–1854), German philosopher, born at Leonberg in Württemberg, studied at Tübingen and Leipzig, and from 1798 lectured on philosophy at Jena as successor to Fichte. In 1803–08 he was professor at Würzburg; then until 1820 secretary of the Royal Academy of Arts at Munich; again professor at Erlangen until 1827, when he returned to Munich; and finally from 1841 at Berlin. His works may be grouped into three periods, in the first of which (1797–1800), embracing the *Philosophy of Nature* (1799) and *Transcendental Philosophy* (1800), he was under the influence of Fichte; the second (1801–03) culminates in the 'Philosophy of Identity', Schelling's lights being Spinoza and Boehme; the third and least valuable represents the growth of his Positive (in opposition to the previous Critical or Negative) Philosophy. He began as an adherent of Fichte's principle of the Ego as the supreme principle of philosophy, and developed the pantheism characteristic of the idealism of Fichte and Hegel. In the *Philosophy of Nature* writings and in *The World-Soul* (1797–99) he supplements the Fichtian Ego or Absolute Ego by showing that the whole of Nature may be regarded as an embodiment of a process by which Spirit tends to rise to a consciousness of itself. The *Transcendental Idealism* (1800) speaks of the two fundamental and complementary sciences, Transcendental Philosophy and Speculative Physics. The promised Positive Philosophy which was to advance beyond merely negative or critical philosophy came to be simply the philosophy of Mythology and Revelation. His son edited his works (1856–1861; new ed. 1927–28). See books by Noack (1859), Plitt (Life, 1870), Becker (1875), Watson (1883), Groos (1889), Metzger (1911), H. Knittermeyer (1929).

SCHENKEL, Daniel, *shen-kel* (1813–85), German Protestant theologian, born at Dägerlen in Zürich, was professor of Theology at Heidelberg from 1851. His *Charakterbild Jesu* (1864) is an attempt to construct the human character of Jesus and entirely eliminate the supernatural.

SCHIAPARELLI, Giovanni Virginio, *skyah' pah-rel'li* (1835–1910), Italian astronomer, born at Savigliano, Piedmont, worked under F. G. W. Struve (q.v.) at Pulkova, was head of Brera observatory, Milan, studied meteors and double stars, and discovered the 'canals' of Mars (1877) and the asteroid Hesperia (1861).

SCHICKELE, René, *shik'e-lè* (1883–1940), German Alsatian writer, born at Oberehnheim, wrote poems, novels, including the trilogy *Das Erbe am Rhein* (1925–31), and plays.

SCHIEFNER, Franz Anton von, SHee- (1817–1879), Russian philologist of Ostiak and other Siberian tongues.

SCHILLER, (1) Ferdinand Canning Scott (1864–1937), British pragmatist philosopher, tutor at Corpus Christi College, Oxford, and professor of Philosophy (1929) at Los Angeles, wrote *Humanism* (1903), his name for pragmatism, *Logic for Use* (1929), &c. See study by Abel (1955).

(2) **Johann Christoph Friedrich von** (1759–1805), German master of the historical drama, poet and historian, was born November 10, the son of an army surgeon, in the service of the Duke of Württemberg at Marbach on the Neckar. He was educated at the grammar school at Ludwigsburg, and intended for the church, but at thirteen, at the personal behest of the duke, was obliged to attend the latter's military academy, studying the law instead of theology, but finally qualified as a surgeon (1780) and was posted to a regiment in Stuttgart. Although outwardly conforming well, he found an outlet for his true feelings in the reading and eventually writing of *Sturm und Drang* verse and plays. His first play, *Die Räuber* (1781), published at his own expense, was, on account of its seemingly anarchical and revolutionary appeal, an instant success when it reached the stage at Mannheim the following year. But its noble revolutionary hero, Karl Moor, does finally recognize the social order in the memorable words 'Two such men as I would destroy the entire moral structure of the world'. Schiller played truant from his regiment to attend the performance, was arrested but, forbidden to write anything but medical works in the future, fled and, in hiding at Bauerbach, finished the plays, *Fiesko* and *Kabale und Liebe* (1783). For a few months he was dramatist to the Mannheim theatre. He next issued a theatrical journal, *Die rheinische Thalia*, begun in 1784, in which were first printed most of his *Don Carlos*, many of his best poems, and the stories *Verbrecher aus verlorener Ehre* and *Der Geisterseher*. In 1785 he went by invitation to Leipzig; and at Dresden, where Körner was living, he found rest from emotional excitement and pecuniary worries. Here he finished *Don Carlos* (1787), written in blank verse, not prose, his first mature play, though it suffers artistically from excessive length and lack of unity. Amongst the finest fruits of his discussions with Körner and his circle are the poems *An die Freude*, later magnificently set to music by Beethoven in his choral symphony, and *Die Künstler*. After two years in Dresden and an unhappy love affair (not the first) he went to Weimar, where he studied Kant, met his future wife, Charlotte von Lengefeld, and began his history of the revolt of the Netherlands. In 1788 he was appointed honorary professor of History at Jena, and married, but his health broke down with overwork from writing a history of the Thirty Years' War, the letters on aesthetic education (1795) and the famous *Über naive und sentimentalische Dichtung* (1795–96), in which he differentiates ancient from modern poetry by their different approaches to nature. His short-lived literary magazine, *Die Horen* (1795–97), was followed by the celebrated *Xenien* (1797), a collection of satirical epigrams against philistinism and mediocrity in the arts, in which the newly found friendship between Goethe and Schiller found mutual expression. This inspired the great ballads (1797–98), *Der Taucher, Der Ring des Polykrates, Die Kranische des Ibykus*, the famous *Lied von der Glocke*, 'Song of the Bell', completed in 1799 and, under Shakespeare's spell, the dramatic trilogy, *Wallenstein* (1796–99), comprising *Wallensteins Lager, Die Piccolomini*, and *Wallensteins Tod*, the greatest historical drama in the German language. This was followed by *Maria Stuart* (1800; trans. S. Spender 1957), a remarkable psychological study of the two queens, Elizabeth and Mary, in which the latter by her death gains a moral victory. Schiller the historian is here at odds with Schiller the dramatist. Again, in *Die Jungfrau von Orleans* (1801) St Joan dies on the battlefield and is resurrected; no doubt in the interests of dráma. *Die Braut von Messina* (1803) portrays the relentless feud between two hostile brothers and the half-legend of *Wilhelm Tell* (1804) is made by Schiller a dramatic manifesto for political freedom. There is a fragment of *Demetrius*, his unfinished work. He was ennobled (1802), fell ill (1804) and died May 9, 1805, at Weimar. See collected works, intro. C. G. Körner (1812–15), Lives by Thomas Carlyle (1825), R. Weltrich (1855–99), J. Sime (1882), H. W. Nevinson (1889), K. Berger (1905–09), F. Strich (1927), H. Cysarz (1934), E. Tonnelat (1934), A. Buchenwald (1937), and studies by L. Bettermann (3rd ed. 1905), J. G. Robertson (1905), T. Rea (1906), V. Basch (1911), K. Berger (1939), H. Hefele (1940), E. Spranger (1941), E. L. Stahl (1954).

SCHILLING, Johannes (1828–1910), German sculptor, born at Mittweida in Saxony, professor of Art at Dresden (1868–1906), executed the four groups of the *Seasons* for Dresden; the Niederwald monument of Germania (1883) opposite Bingen; and he also executed monuments of Schiller for Vienna, the Emperor Maximilian for Trieste, &c.

SCHIMMELPENNINCK, *née* **Galton, Mary Anne** (1778–1856), English author, born at Birmingham, a Quaker, in 1818 joined the Moravian communion. Her nine works (1813–60) include two on Port Royal, a *Theory of Beauty, Sacred Musings*, and an *Autobiography*.

SCHIMPER, Andreas Franz Wilhelm (1856–1901), German botanist, son of Wilhelm Philipp (1808–80), the authority on mosses, born at Strasbourg, became an extraordinary professor at Bonn. He prepared the first map of plant distribution (1898), studied the development of starch grains and introduced the term *chloroplast*. His father's uncle, **Karl Friedrich** (1803–67), made important contributions to plant morphology.

SCHINKEL, Karl Friedrich (1781–1841), German architect, born at Neuruppin in Brandenburg, in 1820 became professor at the Berlin Royal Academy, designed military buildings, Berlin, in classical style, museums, churches, &c. He also attained distinction as a painter and illustrator. See monograph by F. Stahl (1912).

SCHIRACH, Baldur von, *sheer'a*KH (1907–), German Nazi politician, born in Berlin, became a party member in 1925, a member of the Reichstag in 1932, and in 1933 founded and organized the Hitler Youth, of which he was leader until his appointment as Gauleiter of Vienna in 1940. Captured in Austria in 1945 and tried before the Nuremberg Tribunal, he was found guilty of participating in the mass deportation of Jews, and was sentenced to 20 years' imprisonment. He was released from Spandau prison in 1966. See *The Price of Glory* by his wife (1960).

SCHLAF, Johannes, *shlahf* (1862–1941), German novelist and dramatist, born at Querfurt, studied at Berlin and with Holz wrote *Papa Hamlet* (1889), a volume of short-stories, *Die Familie Selicke* (1890), a social drama, *Peter Boies Freite* (1902), &c.

SCHLAGINTWEIT, *shlah'gint-vīt,* the name of five brothers, born in Munich, distinguished as travellers and scientific writers on geography:

(1) **Adolf von** (1829–57), worked closely together with **Hermann** (1826–82) and **Robert** (1833–85). Hermann and Adolf published two books (1850–54) on the physical geography of the Alps (1850, 1854). Wilhelm von Humboldt then had them recommended to the British East India Company, which sent the three brothers to India to make observations on terrestrial magnetism, altitudes in the Deccan, the Himalayas, Tibet, Assam, &c. Hermann was the first European to cross the Kunlun mountains. Adolf was put to death by the emir of East Turkestan. Robert became professor of Geography at Giessen in 1863, travelled to the United States and wrote on the Pacific railway (1870), California (1871) and the Mormons (1874). See their *Results of a Scientific Mission to India and High Asia* (1860–69).

(2) **Eduard von** (1831–66), a fourth brother, took part in the Spanish invasion of Morocco (1859–60), wrote an account of it and fell at Kissingen fighting for Bavaria against the Prussians.

(3) **Emil von** (1835–1904), the fifth brother, became a lawyer, but wrote *Buddhism in Tibet* (London 1860), *Die Könige von Tibet* (1865), *Indien in Wort und Bild* (1880–81), &c.

(4) **Hermann von.** See under (1).

(5) **Robert von.** See under (1).

SCHLEGEL, *shlay-gel,* (1) **August Wilhelm von** (1767–1845), German poet and critic, brother of (2), born at Hanover, studied theology at Göttingen, but soon turned to literature. In 1795 he settled in Jena, and in 1796 married a widow, Caroline Böhmer (1763–1809), who separated from him in 1803 and married Schelling. In 1798 he became professor of Literature and Fine Art at Jena, and in 1801–04 he lectured at Berlin. Most of the next fourteen years he spent in the house of Madame de Staël at Coppet, though he lectured on *Dramatic Art and Literature* (Eng. trans. 1815) at Vienna in 1808, and was secretary to the crown prince of Sweden, 1813–14. From 1818 till his death (May 12, 1845) he was professor of Literature at Bonn. He is famous for his translations of 17 plays of Shakespeare, revised, and the remaining plays translated by D. Tieck and W. Baudissin, which versions are still regarded as the best. He also translated works by Dante, Calderón, Cervantes and Camoens, and edited the *Bhagavad-Gita* and the *Ramayana.* A leading figure of the romantic movement, he severely criticized Schiller, Wieland and Kotzebue, although his own poetry was lifeless. His lectures, essays and history of fine arts are still valued. See A. Sidgwick, *Caroline Schlegel and her Friends* (1889), and study by O. Brandt (1919).

(2) **Karl Wilhelm Friedrich von** (1772–1829), the greatest critic produced by the German romantic movement, brother of (1), was born at Hanover, March 10, and educated at Göttingen and Leipzig. He abducted in 1798 Dorothea (1763–1839), daughter of Moses Mendelssohn, wife of the Jewish merchant Veit, and mother of Veit the religious painter, and next year utilized his experiences in a notorious romance, *Lucinde.* He then joined his brother at Jena, and with him wrote and edited the journal *Das Athenaeum,* in the interests of Romanticism. The *Charakteristiken und Kritiken* (1801) contain some of both brothers' best writing. From 1808 down to his death at Dresden, Friedrich, who had become a devout Roman Catholic, was employed in the public service of Austria; it was he who penned the Austrian proclamations against Napoleon in 1809. His best-known books are lectures on the *Philosophy of History* (Eng. trans. 1835) and *History of Literature* (trans. 1859). There are also English versions of his *Philosophy of Life* (1847) and *Lectures on Modern History* (1849). *Über die Sprache und Weisheit der Indier* (1808) was a pioneer for the study of Sanskrit in Europe. See his Letters to his brother (1890), and studies by C. Enders (1913), F. Imle (1927) and B. von Wiese (1927).

SCHLEICHER, *shlī'*KH*er,* (1) **August** (1821–1868), German philologist, in 1850 became professor of Slavonic Languages at Prague, and in 1857 honorary professor at Jena, compiled the *Comparative Grammar of the Indo-Germanic Languages* (4th ed. 1876; Eng. trans. 1874–77). See Memoir by Lefmann (1870).

(2) **Kurt von** (1882–1934), German general and politician, born at Brandenburg, was on the general staff during World War I. Minister of war in von Papen's government of 1932, he succeeded him as chancellor, but his failure to obtain dictatorial control provided Hitler with his opportunity to seize power in 1933. Schleicher and his wife were

executed by the Nazis on a trumped-up charge of treason. See study by K. von (Reibnitz (1932).

SCHLEIDEN, Matthias Jakob, *shlī'den* (1804-1881), German botanist, born at Hamburg, in 1839 became professor of Botany at Jena, and in 1863 at Dorpat. He did much to establish the cell theory.

SCHLEIERMACHER, Friedrich Ernst Daniel, *shlī'ėr-mah-KHer* (1768–1834), German theologian and philosopher, born at Breslau, having broken from the dogmatic narrowness of the Moravians, studied philosophy and theology at Halle. From 1796, then a preacher in Berlin, he was closely allied with the devotees of Romanticism. In his *Reden über die Religion* (1799), *Monologen* (1800), and *Grundlinien einer Kritik der bisherigen Sittenlehre* (1803) he expounded that hostility to the traditional moral philosophy and the Kantian ethic to which he had already (1801) given expression in the 'Confidential Letters on Schlegel's *Lucinde*'. The translation of Plato, begun by him and Schlegel, was carried through in 1804–10 by Schleiermacher alone. He was professor at Halle (1804–06) and Berlin (1810). He was equally eminent as a preacher, and was the soul of the movement which led to the union in 1817 of the Lutheran and Reformed Churches in Prussia. He produced *Die Weihnachtsfeier* (1806; Eng trans. *Christmas Eve*, 1889); a critical treatise on the first epistle to Timothy (1807); and his most important work, *Der christliche Glaube* (1821–22; 6th ed. 1884). Afterwards appeared a work on Christian ethics, a Life of Jesus, sermons and letters (partly trans. by Frederica Rowan, 1860). He taught that religion, philosophy and science do not contradict one another, but that religion needed to be purged of metaphysical and dogmatic reflections. See his Correspondence (1852–87); Lives by Schenkel (1868), Dilthey (1870; new ed. 1922); essays by K. Barth in *From Rousseau to Ritschl* (trans. 1959) and *Theology and Church* (trans. 1962); R. R. Niebuhr, *Schleiermacher: On Christ and Religion* (1965).

SCHLICK, Moritz (1882–1936), German philosopher, one of the leaders of the 'Vienna Circle' of logical positivists, born in Berlin, was professor in Rostock, Kiel and from 1922 in Vienna. He was an early exponent of Einstein's relativity theories and in *Allgemeine Erkenntnislehre* (1918) foreshadowed some of the doctrines of Wittgenstein's *Tractatus*. Other important works include *Problems of Ethics* (1930; trans. 1939) and the collected essays (1938). He was shot down on the steps of the university by a student whose thesis he had rejected. See A. J. Ayer, *Logical Positivism* (1960).

SCHLIEFFEN, Alfred, Count von, *shleef'ėn* (1833–1913), Prussian field-marshal, born in Berlin, who advocated the plan which bears his name (1895) on which German tactics were unsuccessfully based in World War I. In the event of a German war on two fronts, he envisaged a German breakthrough in Belgium and the defeat of France within six weeks by a colossal right-wheel flanking movement through Holland and then southwards, cutting off Paris from the sea, holding off the Russians meanwhile with secondary forces. See study by Ritter (trans. 1958).

SCHLIEMANN, Heinrich, *shlee'mahn*)1822–1890), German archaeologist, the excavator of the sites of Mycenae and with Dörpfeld (q.v.) of Troy, born at Neubuckow, went into business at home, in Amsterdam (1842–46) and in St Petersburg (1846–63), acquiring a large fortune and a knowledge of the principal modern and ancient European languages. He retired early in order to realize his ambition, set out in his *Ithaka, der Peloponnes und Troja* (1869), of vindicating Homer by excavating the mound of Hissarlik, the traditional site of Troy, which city current Homeric criticism held to be part of the Homeric myth. Official delays overcome, excavations were begun in 1872 and his first publication *Trojanische Althertümer* (1874) sceptically received. Assisted by the professional Dörpfeld, he discovered nine superimposed city sites, one of which contained a considerable treasure, which he overhastily identified as Priam's, although part of an earlier pre-Homeric site. The Trojan findings he presented to the German nation in violation of his agreement with the Turkish government, and after compensation was paid, they were housed in the Ethnological Museum in Berlin (1882). He also excavated the site of Mycenae (1876), the treasure of which is in the Athens Polytechnic, in Ithaca (1869 and 1878), at Orchomenos (1881–82) and at Tiryns (1884–85), and his reports were published and translated under these names. An amateur who had the courage to keep his own counsel in the face of expert opinion, he was responsible for some of the most spectacular archaeological discoveries of modern times. See his autobiography (1891), study by Schuchhardt (trans. 1891), Lives by Emil Ludwig (1931), L. and G. Poole (1967), Cottrell, *The Bull of Minos* (1953) and R. Payne *The Gold of Troy* (1960).

SCHMELZER, Johann Heinrich (1623–80), Austrian composer, son of a soldier, was trained as a musician in the emperor's service and won fame throughout Europe as a violinist. In 1679 he became *kapellmeister* to Leopold I, but next year died of the plague in Prague, whence the court had fled from the great epidemic in Vienna. The first to adapt the tunes of the Viennese street musicians and Tyrolean peasants to the more sophisticated instrumental styles of the court, he is often regarded as the true father of the Viennese waltz.

SCHMIDT, (1) **Bernhard** (1879–1935), German astronomer of Swedish-German origin, born at Nargen, Estonia, studied optics in Sweden and made a precarious living grinding reflectors at Jena with his left hand, as his right had been lost in early youth. In 1926 he became associated with the Bergedorf observatory near Hamburg. In 1932 he devised a method to overcome aberration of the image in spherical mirrors and lenses, by the introduction of a correcting plate at the centre of curvature. This was utilized in the Palomar Schmidt telescope.

(2) **Johann Friedrich Julius** (1825–84), German astronomer, born at Eutin, became in 1858 director of the national observatory

in Athens. An eminent selenographer, he suggested that the moon's surface is still changing slightly. He also published a map of the moon (1875).

(3) **Johannes** (1877–1933), Danish biologist, born at Jägerspris, solved the problem of the European eel's life history, by his discovery of the breeding-ground on the ocean bed near Bermuda in 1904.

SCHNABEL, Artur, *shnah'bėl* (1882–1951), Austrian pianist and composer, born in Lipnik, studied under Leschetizky and made his début at the age of eight. He taught in Berlin, making frequent concert appearances throughout Europe and America, and with the advent of the Nazi government, settled first in Switzerland, then in America from 1939. He was an authoritative player of a small range of German classics—notably Beethoven, Mozart and Schubert; his compositions include a piano concerto, chamber music and piano works. See Life by C. Saerchinger (1957).

SCHNITZER, Eduard. See EMIN PASHA.

SCHNITZLER, Arthur (1862–1931), Austrian dramatist and novelist of Jewish origin, born in Vienna, was a physician before he turned playwright. His highly psychological, often strongly erotic short plays and novels, executed with great technical skill, frequently underline some social problem, mostly against the familiar easy-going Viennese background, as in *Anatol* (1893) and *Reigen* (1900), which are cycles of one-act plays linked with one another by the overlapping of one of the characters until the chain is completed by a character of the last meeting one from the first, as in the film *La Ronde* (1950). Other notable works include *Der grüne Kakadu* (1899), *Liebelei* (1895), *Der Weg ins Freie* (1908), *Professor Bernhardi* (1912), on anti-Semitism, and *Flucht in die Finsternis* (1931). Several have been translated into English.

SCHNORR VON CAROLSFELD, Baron Julius (1794–1872), German historical and landscape painter, born at Leipzig, became associated with the school of Cornelius and Overbeck, who went back for their inspiration to Raphael's predecessors. He was professor of Historical Painting at Munich (1827), and painted frescoes of the *Nibelungenlied*, Charlemagne, Barbarossa, &c. In 1846 he became professor at Dresden and director of the gallery. He illustrated the *Nibelungen*, designed stained-glass windows, &c.

SCHÖFFER, Peter (*c.* 1425–1502), German printer in Mainz, the partner of Gutenberg and Fust, whose son-in-law he was and with whom he printed most probably the Mazarin Bible before 1456, although this work is also claimed for Gutenberg, by whose name it is also known. In 1457 they issued the *Mainz Psalter*, the first work on which the name of the printer and date of publication appears. After the death of Gutenberg and Fust, Schöffer claimed to be the inventor of printing. See work by Roth (1892).

SCHOFIELD, John McAllister, *skō'-* (1831–1906), American general, born in Chautauqua county, New York, in the Civil War distinguished himself at Franklin (1864) and Wilmington (1865), was secretary of war 1868–69, and was commander-in-chief 1888–1895.

SCHOLES, Percy Alfred, *skōlz* (1877–1958), English musicologist, born at Leeds, graduated at Oxford in 1908, and as university extension lecturer there, at Manchester, London and Cambridge, as music critic to the *Observer* (1920–25), as the first music adviser to the B.B.C., and as the editor of *The Oxford Companion to Music* (1938), widely fostered musical appreciation and knowledge. But it is as the author of *The Puritans and Music* (1934) and *The Life of Dr Burney* (1948) that his reputation as musicologist rests. He was awarded the O.B.E. in 1957.

SCHOMBERG, (1) **Frederick Hermann, 1st Duke of** (1615–90), general in French and British service, born at Heidelberg of a German father and English mother, fought against the Imperialists in the Thirty Years' War. He was captain in the Scottish Guards in the French army (1652–54), fought at the battle of the Dunes (1658), and, though a Protestant, obtained a marshal's baton in 1675. After the revocation of the Edict of Nantes (1685), he retired to Portugal and afterwards took service under the Elector of Brandenburg. He commanded under William of Orange in the English expedition (1688), was made K.G. and created Duke of Schomberg (1689) and was commander-in-chief in Ireland. He conducted the Ulster campaign, but was killed at the Boyne.

(2) **Meinhard, 1st Duke of Leinster and 3rd Duke of Schomberg** (1641–1719), British soldier, son of (1), after serving under the French and the Elector of Brandenburg, commanded the right wing in the battle of the Boyne (1690) and fought in the Spanish Succession War.

SCHOMBURGK, Sir Robert Hermann, *-boork* (1804–65), Prussian-born British traveller and official, surveyed (1831) in the Virgin Islands, where he was a merchant, and was sent by the Royal Geographical Society to explore British Guiana (1831–35). In ascending the Berbice River he discovered the magnificent Victoria Regia lily, described in his *British Guiana* (London 1840) and magnificent *Views in the Interior of Guiana* (folio, 1841). In 1841–43 he was employed by government in Guiana to draw the long-controverted 'Schomburgk-line' as a provisional boundary with Venezuela and Brazil, and in 1844 was knighted. He was accompanied by his brother **Richard** (1811–90), who wrote *Reisen in Britisch Guiana, 1840–44* (Leipzig 1847–48). In 1848 Sir Robert published a *History of Barbadoes*. In 1848–57 he was British consul in San Domingo, in 1857–64 in Siam.

SCHÖNBEIN, Christian Friedrich, *shœn'bīn* (1799–1868), German chemist, born at Metzingen, Württemberg, from 1828 professor at Basel, discovered ozone, gun-cotton and collodion, and experimented on oxygen. See Life by Hagenbach (1869).

SCHÖNBERG, Arnold, *shœn'-* (1874–1951), Austrian composer, born in Vienna, learned the violin as a boy, but, apart from lessons in counterpoint, he was entirely self-taught. In his twenties he earned his living by orchestrating operettas while composing such early works as the string sextet *Verklärt*

Nacht (1899) and the mammoth *Gurrelieder* (1900), and from 1901 until 1903, when he returned to Vienna, he was in Berlin as conductor of a cabaret orchestra and teacher. His search for a personal musical style began to show in such works as his first *Chamber Symphony*, which caused a riot at its first performance in 1907 through its abandonment of the traditional concept of tonality, and Schönberg's works up to the time of his military service in the first World War are written in the style that has come to be known as 'atonal'. From this position, he evolved the discipline known today as 'twelve-note' or 'serial' music. At the end of the first World War he taught in Vienna, visited Amsterdam, and then became a professor at the Prussian Academy of Arts until he was exiled by the Nazi government in 1933 and settled in America. A teacher of unusual authority and integrity, Schönberg avoided any sort of propaganda for his own music and theories both in the lecture hall and in his textbooks, and his later works such as the Third String Quartet have shown that despite the originality and complexity of his style, it can become a vehicle for deeply moving and profound works. See books by Wellesz (1925), Leibowitz (1949), Stuckenschmidt (1960), and *Letters* (ed. Stein; trans. 1964).

SCHONGAUER, or **Schön, Martin,** *shōn'-gow-ėr* (1450–91), German painter and engraver, was born at Colmar. His famous *Madonna of the Rose Garden* altar piece at Colmar, one of the most exquisite of early representations of the Virgin, shows Flemish influence, probably that of Rogier van der Weyden. Other religious paintings attributed to Schongauer have not been authenticated, but well over 100 of his engraved plates have survived, including *The Passion*, *The Wise and Foolish Virgins*, *Adoration of the Magi*, and other religious subjects, executed with a delicacy of line and a feeling for modelling and composition unequalled among 15th-century German engravers. See studies by H. Wendland (1907) and E. Buchner (1941).

SCHOOLCRAFT, Henry Rowe (1793–1864), American ethnologist, born in Albany county, N.Y., in 1820 went with General Cass to Lake Superior as geologist. In 1822 he became Indian agent for the tribes round the lakes, and in 1823 married a wife of Indian blood. In 1832 he commanded an expedition which discovered the sources of the Mississippi (*Narrative*, 1834). While superintendent for the Indians, he negotiated treaties by which the government acquired 16,000,000 acres. In 1845 he collected the statistics of the Six Nations (*Notes on the Iroquois*, 1848). For the government he prepared his *Information respecting the Indian Tribes of the U.S.* (6 vols. 1851–57).

SCHOPENHAUER, Artur, *shō'pen-how-er* (1788–1860), German pessimist philosopher, born February 22 at Danzig. His father was a banker, his mother a novelist who in her later life kept a literary salon at Weimar. He was educated at Gotha, Weimar, Göttingen and Berlin, graduated from Jena with his first book, *On the Fourfold Root of the Principle of Sufficient Reason* (trans. 1888), and in 1819 became *privat-dozent* in Berlin. He boldly held his lectures at the same times as Hegel, but without success. In 1821 he finally retired to Frankfurt-am-Main, a lonely, violent and unbefriended man, who shared his bachelor's existence with a poodle, named 'Atma', or 'world soul'. In him feeling and reason were in perpetual conflict; his disposition was severe, distrustful and suspicious. Lastly, he believed that he had founded a philosophy which made him the successor of Socrates, yet saw himself and his thinking passed over, and what he regarded as the fatuous ravings of Hegel, Schelling and Fichte praised as the highest wisdom. The cardinal articles of his philosophical creed were: first, Subjective Idealism—i.e., that the world is my idea, a mere phantasmagoria of my brain, and therefore in itself nothing; secondly, that the possibility of knowledge of the 'thing-in-itself' was demolished for ever by Kant; and thirdly, that to the intuition of genius the ideas of Art are accessible—the only knowledge not subservient to the Will and to the needs of practical life. Finally, Will, the active side of our nature, or Impulse, is the key to the one thing we know directly from the inside—i.e., the self, and therefore the key to the understanding of all things. Will is the creative, primary, while Idea is the secondary, receptive factor in things. His chief work, *The World as Will and Idea* (1819; trans. Haldane and Kemp, 8th ed. 1937) expounds the logic, metaphysics, aesthetics and ethics of this view. *Seeing and Colours* (1816) contains practically Goethe's entire theory of colour, and *Parerga and Paralipomena* (1851) Schopenhauer's occasional papers. The doctrine of the will reappears in the philosophies of Nietzsche, Bergson, James and Dewey, but his influence has been greater in the world of literature, not least upon Thomas Mann. Frauenstädt edited his complete works (1876). See also *Selected Essays* by E. B. Bax (1891) and W. Jekyll, *The Wisdom of Schopenhauer* (1911), German Lives by W. von Gwinner (1862) and J. Volkelt (5th ed. 1923), English Lives by H. Zimmern (1876); rev. ed. 1932), E. Wallace (1890) and T. Whittaker (1909), and studies by G. Simmel (1907), C. Gebhardt (1913), H. Masse (1926), K. Pfeiffer (1932), Thomas Mann (1938; trans. 1939) and F. Copleston (1946).

SCHOUVALOFF. See SHUVALOV.

SCHRADER, Eberhard, *shrah'dėr* (1836–1908), German oriental scholar, born at Brunswick, professor of Theology at Zürich, Giessen, and Jena, and of Oriental Languages at Berlin (1875), pioneered the study of Assyriology in Germany.

SCHREIBER, *née* **Bertie, Lady Charlotte Elizabeth,** *shrī'bėr* (1812–95), Welsh scholar, born at Stamford, a daughter of the Earl of Lindsey, married in 1833 Sir Josiah John Guest, and in 1855 Charles Schreiber, M.P. She is best known for her translation (1838–1849) of the *Mabinogion*, but was also an authority on fans and playing-cards. She bequeathed her collections of these to the British Museum.

SCHREINER, Olive, *shrī'ner* (1855–1920), South African author, born in Basutoland, the daughter of a Methodist missionary of German origin, grew up largely self-educated and became a governess. She lived in England (1881–89), where her novel, *The Story of a South African Farm* (1883), the first sustained, imaginative work to come from Africa, was published under the pseudonym Ralph Iron. The manuscript had been rejected by three publishers but was accepted by the fourth, whose reader was George Meredith. She had a fiery, rebellious temperament, a lifelong hatred of her mother and in her later works the creative artist gave way to the passionate propagandist for women's rights, pro-Boer loyalty and pacificism. These include *Trooper Peter Halket* (1897), *Woman and Labour* (1911), *From Man to Man* (1926). In 1894 she married S. P. Cronwright, who took her name, wrote a Life of her (1924) and edited her letters (1926). See also A. Le B. Chapin, *Their Trackless Way* (1931), and books by O. L. Hobman (1955) and L. Gregg (1957). Her brother, **William Philip** (1857–1919), was prime minister of the Cape Colony (1898–1900) and high commissioner for South Africa from 1914.

SCHRÖDINGER, Erwin, *shrœ'-* (1887–1961), Austrian physicist, born and educated in Vienna, became professor at Stuttgart, Breslau, Zürich, Berlin, fellow of Magdalen College, Oxford (1933–38), professor at the Dublin Institute for Advanced Studies (1940) and returned to Vienna as professor in 1956. He originated the study of wave mechanics as part of the quantum theory with his celebrated wave equation for which he shared with Dirac the Nobel prize in 1933, and also made contributions to the field theory. In 1949 he became a foreign member of the Royal Society and was awarded the German O.M. See his *Collected Papers* (1928), *What is Life?* (1946) and *Science and Man* (1958), &c.

SCHRÖTER, Johann Hieronymus (1745–1816), German astronomer, born at Erfurt, studied at Göttingen and in 1778 became chief magistrate of Lilienthal near Bremen, where he built an observatory and studied the surface of the moon, measuring the heights of many of its mountains.

SCHUBART, Christian Friedrich Daniel (1739–91), German poet, born at Obersontheim in Swabia, wrote satirical and religious poems. He was imprisoned at Hohenasperg (1777–87) by the Duke of Württemberg, whom he had irritated by an epigram. He is largely remembered for his influence on Schiller (q.v.). See his Autobiography (1791–93), and monographs by D. F. Strauss (1849), Hauff (1885) and Nagele (1888).

SCHUBERT, (1) **Franz** (1808–78), German violinist and composer of Dresden, who felt insulted when the publishers attributed to him works by his great Viennese contemporary (2).

(2) **Franz Peter** (1797–1828), Austrian composer, born January 31 in Vienna, the son of a schoolmaster, received early instruction in the violin and piano, at eleven entered the *Stadtkonvikt*, a choristers' school attached to the court chapel. During the five austere years he spent there, he tried his hand at almost every kind of musical composition, including a symphony in D (1813). In 1814 he became assistant master at his father's school, composed an opera, the Mass in F and that masterpiece of song, *Gretchen am Spinnrade*, from Goethe's *Faust*. Another, equally famous, the *Erlkönig*, followed in 1815, but was not performed until 1819. From 1817 he lived on his wits and on his Bohemian friends, who included amateur artists and poets and the operatic baritone, Vogl, with whom he was to found the new Viennese entertainment, the 'Schubertiads', private and public accompanied recitals of his songs, which made them known throughout Vienna. In 1818, and again in 1824, he stayed at Zseliz as the tutor of Count Esterházy's three daughters. The famous 'Trout' piano quintet in A major was written after a walking tour with Vogl in 1819. Schubert's veneration of Beethoven made him frequent the same coffee house, but he was too awestruck ever to approach the great man, except when the latter was sick, when he sent him his compositions; in 1822 a set of variations for a piano duet dedicated to Beethoven, and in 1827 a collection of his songs, which the dying Beethoven greatly admired. The year 1822 saw the Unfinished Symphony (No. 8), the 'Wanderer' fantasia for piano and the spiritual conflicts in the composer that came with the knowledge that he had contracted syphilis. The song cycle, *Die schöne Müllerin*, which includes the well-known refrain, *Das Wandern*, and the incidental music to *Rosamunde* followed in 1823, the string Quartets in A and D minor in 1824. Schubert sent Goethe in 1825 a number of settings of his poems, but the latter returned them ungraciously without acknowledgment. In 1826 Schubert applied unsuccessfully for the post of assistant musical director to the court, wrote the *Winterreise* cycle of songs, the string quartets in G major and D minor and the songs *Who is Sylvia?* and *Hark, Hark the Lark*, which, however, contrary to popular belief, he did not hurriedly scribble on the back of a menu or bill. Before he died of typhus on November 19, 1828, he had written the great C major symphony (No. 9), the fantasy in F minor for four hands and the posthumously published songs, the *Schwanengesang*, or 'Swan-song'. He was buried as near as possible to Beethoven's grave under Grillparzer's well-meant but unjust epitaph: 'Music has here entombed a rich treasure, but still fairer hopes'. For Schubert's works are sufficient to preserve his place among the great masters, not least for his infectiously lyrical spontaneity, his lavish musical inventiveness and as the originator and greatest exponent of the art of the German Lieder See Schubert's *Letters and Other Writings* (1928), study by R. Capell (1928) and *Symposium*, ed. G. Abraham (1947), and Lives by N. Flower (1928), A. Hutchings (1945), O. E. Deutsch (1946), M. J. E. Brown (1958), and *Memoirs by his Friends*, ed. O. E. Deutsch (1958).

SCHUCHARDT, Hugo, *shooKH'-* (1842–1927), German philologist, born at Gotha, professor of Philology at Halle and Gotha, chiefly known for his studies in Romance philology which concentrated on linguistic rather than social or historical phenomena, and which include *Der Vokalismus des Vulgärlateins* (1866–68) and *Baskische Studien* (1893). See Life by L. Spitzer (2nd ed. 1928).

SCHULENBURG, Countess Ehrengard Melusina von der (1667–1743), German mistress of George I, nicknamed 'the Maypole' because of her lean figure, was created Duchess of Kendal in 1719.

SCHULZE-DELITZSCH, Hermann, *shoolt'zė day'leech* (1808–83), German cooperative politician and economist, born at Delitzsch in Prussian Saxony, advocated constitutional and social reform on the basis of self-help in the National Assembly in Berlin. He started the first 'people's bank' at Delitzsch, on a cooperative basis. Other branches were founded and joined in 1864 under one organization which eventually spread over middle Europe. He wrote on banks and cooperation. See Life by Bernstein (1879).

SCHUMACHER, Kurt Ernst Karl, *shoo'ma*KH*ėr* (1895–1952), German statesman, born at Kulm, Prussia, studied law and political science at the universities of Leipzig and Berlin, and from 1930 to 1933 was a member of the Reichstag and of the executive of the Social Democratic parliamentary group. An outspoken opponent of National Socialism, he spent ten years from 1933 in Nazi concentration camps, where he showed outstanding courage. He became in 1946 chairman of the Social Democratic party and of the parliamentary group of the Bundestag, Bonn. He strongly opposed the German government's policy of armed integration with Western Europe.

SCHUMAN, (1) Robert (1886–1963), French statesman, born in Luxemburg, a member of the Resistance during World War II, prime minister in 1947 and 1948, propounded (1950), the 'Schuman plan' for pooling the coal and steel resources of Western Europe, was elected president of the Strasbourg European Assembly in 1958 and awarded the Charlemagne prize. He survived de Gaulle's electoral reforms, being re-elected to the National Assembly in November 1958.

(2) **William Howard** (1910–), American composer, born in New York, studied under Roy Harris and at Salzburg, winning in 1943 the first Pulitzer prize to be awarded to a composer. In 1945 he became president of the Juilliard School of Music in New York. His work ranges from the gay (e.g., his opera, *The Mighty Casey*) to the austere and grim. He composed eight symphonies, concertos for piano and violin and several ballets as well as choral and orchestral works.

SCHUMANN, (1) Clara Josephine, *née* **Wieck** (1819–96), German pianist and composer, wife of (3) and daughter of the Leipzig pianoforte teacher, Wieck, who turned her into one of the most brilliant concert pianists of her day. She gave her first *Gewandhaus* concert when only eleven and the following year four of her Polonaises were published. After their marriage in 1840, the Schumanns made concert tours to Hamburg and she alone to Copenhagen (1842) and to Russia. From 1856 she very often played for the Philharmonic Society in London, fostering her husband's work wherever she went. Her own compositions include a Trio in G minor, a set of three Preludes and fugues and lighter pieces such as the *Soirées musicales*, many of which were taken over by her husband for his Impromptus, the 'Davidsbundlertänze' &c. From 1878 she was principal pianoforte teacher in the Frankfurt-am-Main Conservatoire. See Life by B. Litzmann (trans. 1913) and under (3).

(2) **Elisabeth** (1889–1952), German-born operatic soprano and lieder singer, born at Merseburg, was in 1919 engaged by Richard Strauss for the Vienna State Opera and sang in his and Mozart's operas all over the world, making her London début in 1924. Latterly she concentrated more on Lieder by such composers as Schubert, Wolf and Richard Strauss. She left Austria in 1936 and in 1938 became a citizen of the United States. See Puritz, *The Teaching of Elisabeth Schumann* (1956).

(3) **Robert Alexander** (1810–56), German composer, husband of (1), born at Zwickau, spent his boyhood browsing in his father's bookshop, and began at twenty-one a desultory course of legal studies at Leipzig and Heidelberg. After hearing Rossini's operas performed in Italy and Paganini playing at Frankfurt-am-Main, he persuaded his parents to allow him to change over to the pianoforte, under the formidable teacher Wieck of Leipzig. The latter, however, was mostly away on his daughter's concert tours and Schumann, left to his own devices, studied Bach's *Well-tempered Clavier*, wrote a prophetic newspaper article on the talents of the young Chopin, and broke a finger of his right hand on a finger-strengthening contraption (1832), thus ruining for good his prospects as a performer. The deaths of a brother and a sister-in-law and an obsessive fear of insanity drove him to attempt suicide. Fortunately, his first compositions, the Toccata, Paganini studies, and Intermezzi, were published in 1833 and in 1834 he founded and edited (for ten years) the biweekly *Neue Leipzige Zeitschrift für Musik*, his best contributions to which were translated under the title, *Music and Musicians* (1877–80). In these, he championed romanticism, and in 1853 contributed another prescient essay, this time on the young Brahms. In 1835 he met Chopin, Moscheles and Mendelssohn, who had become director of the Leipzig *Gewandhaus*. The F sharp minor sonata was begun and another in C major, written post-haste for the Beethoven commemorations, but not published until 1839. His attachment to Clara Wieck did not escape the disapproving father, who whisked her away on concert tours as much as possible. That they were secretly engaged, however, he did not know. Clara dutifully repudiated Schumann, who retaliated by a brief encounter with the Scottish pianist, Robina Laidlaw, to whom he dedicated his *Fantasiestücke*. In 1839, the former lovers were reconciled and after a long legal wrangle to obtain permission to marry without her father's consent, they married in September 1840, after Schumann had written his first songs, the Fool's Song in

Twelfth Night, and aptly, the Chamisso songs *Frauenliebe und Leben*, or 'Woman's Love and Life'. Clara immediately brought pressure on her bridegroom to attempt some major orchestral composition, and her efforts were rewarded by the first symphony in B flat major, which was performed under Mendelssohn's direction at the *Gewandhaus*. Then followed the A Minor piano concerto the Piano Quintet, the choral *Paradise and the Peri*, and his best work in that medium, the scenes from *Faust*, completed in 1848, the 'Spring' Symphony in B flat, &c. In 1843 he was appointed professor of the new Leipzig Conservatoire. The Schumanns' Russian concert tour, during which Clara played before Nicholas I (1844), inspired Robert to write five poems on the Kremlin. Recurring symptoms of mental illness prompted the move from Leipzig to the less exciting Dresden. The Symphony in C major was completed in 1847 and the death of his great friend prompted him to write *Reminiscences of Mendelssohn-Bartholdy*, first published in 1947. Revolution broke out in Dresden in 1849 when Prussian troops confronted republican revolutionaries, among them Wagner. The Schumanns fled, but Robert wrote some stirring marches. His mental state allowed him one final productive phase in which he composed pianoforte pieces, many songs and the incidental music to Byron's *Manfred*. His appointment as musical director at Düsseldorf in 1850 only worsened his condition, of which he was fully aware. He heard alternatively sublime and hellish music, took to table-turning, and in 1854 threw himself into the Rhine, only to be rescued by fishermen. He died in an asylum two years later. Schumann was primarily the composer for the pianoforte. His early works show a tremendous fertility of musical and extra-musical ideas, to which the names of many of them, '*Abegg*' variations (after a dancing partner), *Carnaval*, *Kreisleriana*, *Papillons*, &c., testify. His operatic and many of his orchestral compositions were not successful because of their repetitive character. But his music comprises the best in German romanticism. See Lives by J. W. von Wasielewski (1858; trans. 1878), H. Bedford (1925), F. Niecks (1925), A. W. Patterson (1934), J. Chissell (1948; new ed. 1956), O. Wheeler (1949), P. M. Young (1961) and *A Symposium*, ed. G. Abraham (1952).

SCHURZ, Carl, *shoorts* (1829–1906), German-American statesman and journalist, born near Cologne, joined the revolutionary movement of 1849. In America from 1852 he was politician, lecturer, lawyer, major-general in the Civil War, journalist, senator 1869–75, secretary of the interior 1877–1881. He wrote Lives of Henry Clay and Lincoln, and *Reminiscences* (1909).

SCHUSCHNIGG, Kurt von (1897–), Austrian statesman, born at Riva, South Tirol, served and was decorated in the first World War and then practised law. He was elected a Christian Socialist deputy in 1927, became minister of justice (1932) and education (1933). After the murder of Dollfuss in 1934, he succeeded as chancellor until March 1938, when Hitler occupied Austria. Imprisoned by the Nazis, he was liberated by American troops in 1945. He was professor of Political Science at St Louis in the United States (1948–67). See his *Farewell Austria* (1938) and *Austrian Requiem* (trans. 1947).

SCHUSTER, Sir Arthur (1851–1934), British physicist, born in Frankfurt of Jewish parents, studied at Heidelberg and Cambridge and became professor of Applied Mathematics (1881) and Physics (1888–1907) at Manchester. He carried out important pioneer work in spectroscopy and terrestrial magnetism. The Schuster-Smith magnetometer is the standard instrument for measuring the earth's magnetic force. He led the eclipse expedition to Siam in 1875, was president of the British Association in 1915 and was knighted in 1920.

SCHÜTZ, Heinrich, also known by the Latin form **Sagittarius** (1585–1672), German composer, was born at Köstritz near Gera, and in 1608 went to Marburg to study law. Going in 1609 to Venice to study music, he became a pupil of Gabrieli (q.v.), and published in 1611 a book of five-part madrigals, showing the Italian influence. He returned to Germany in 1613, continued his law studies at Leipzig, and in 1617 was appointed *Hofkapellmeister* in Dresden, where he introduced Italian-type music and styles of performance—madrigals, the use of continuo, and instrumentally-accompanied choral compositions, for example his *Psalms of David* (1619)—and he may thus be regarded as the founder of the Baroque school of German music. A visit to Italy in 1628 acquainted him with the more recent developments effected by Monteverdi in Italian music, and from 1633 until his return to Dresden in 1641 he travelled between various courts, including those at Copenhagen and Hanover, everywhere preaching his gospel of Italianism. Creatively Schütz lies between the polyphony of Palestrina and the more elaborate orchestration of such composers as Bach and Handel, his compositions including much church music—psalms, motets, passions ('The Seven Words on the Cross' and 'The Resurrection'), a German requiem, and the first German opera, *Dafne*, produced in Torgau in 1627. See studies by A. Einstein (1928), H. Hoffmann (1940) and H. J. Moser (1959).

SCHUYLER, Philip John, *skī'ler* (1733–1804), a leader of the American Revolution, born at Albany, raised a company and fought at Lake George in 1755. He was a member of the colonial assembly from 1768, and delegate to the Continental congress of 1775, which appointed him one of the first four major-generals. Washington gave him the northern department of New York, and he was preparing to invade Canada when ill-health compelled him to tender his resignation. He still retained a general direction of affairs from Albany, but jealousies rendered his work both hard and disagreeable, and in 1779 he finally resigned. Besides acting as commissioner for Indian affairs and making treaties with the Six Nations, he sat in congress 1777–81, and was state senator for thirteen years between 1780 and 1797, U.S. senator 1789–91 and 1797–98, and surveyor-general of the state from 1782. With Hamilton and John Jay he shared the leadership of the Federal party in New York; and he aided in preparing the state's code of laws. See Lives by Lossing (enlarged ed. 1872), G. W. Schuyler (1888), B. Tuckerman (1905).

SCHWABE, Heinrich Samuel, *shvah'bė* (1789–1875), German astronomer, born at Dessau, discovered (1843) a ten-year sunspot cycle (later found to be rather more than eleven years).

SCHWANN, Theodor, *shvahn* (1810–82) German physiologist, born at Neuss, in 1838 became professor at Louvain, in 1848 at Liège. He discovered the enzyme pepsin, investigated muscle contraction, demonstrated the rôle of micro-organisms in putrefaction and brilliantly extended the cell theory, previously applied to plants, to animal tissues. See Life by Henle (1882).

SCHWANTHALER, Ludwig von, *shvahn'tahlėr* (1802–48), Munich sculptor, executed for King Louis of Bavaria bas-reliefs and figures for public buildings, and in 1835 became professor at Munich Academy. Among his works are the colossal statue of Bavaria, statues of Goethe, Jean Paul Richter, Mozart, &c.

SCHWARZ, Berthold, *shvahrts* (fl. 1320), German Franciscan monk of Freiburg (or Dortmund), whose real name was Konstantin Anklitzen, Schwarz ('black') being a nickname due to his chemical experiments. He it was who about 1320 brought gunpowder (or guns) into practical use. See monograph by Hansjakob (1891).

SCHWARZENBERG, *shvarts'ėn-*, (1) **Adam, Count von** (1584–1641), was (1619) prime minister of George William, Elector of Brandenburg, and was all-powerful during the Thirty Years' War.

(2) **Felix Ludwig Johann Friedrich** (1800–1852), Austrian statesman, nephew of (3), sent on a mission to London in 1826, became involved in the Ellenborough divorce suit, was Austrian ambassador at Naples 1846–48, then distinguished himself in the Italian campaign, as prime minister called in the aid of the Russians against Hungary, and pursued a bold absolutist policy. See Lives by Berger (1853), E. Heller (1932) and A. Schwarzenberg (1946).

(3) **Karl Philipp, Prince of** (1771–1820), Austrian field-marshal, uncle of (2), served against the Turks and the French republic. He was ambassador to Russia in 1808, fought at Wagram (1809), conducted the negotiations for the marriage between Napoleon and Maria Louisa, and as ambassador at Paris gained the esteem of Napoleon, who demanded him as general of the Austrian contingent in the invasion of Russia in 1812. In 1813 he was generalissimo of the united armies which won the battles of Dresden and Leipzig. In 1814 he helped to occupy Paris. See Life by Kerchnawe and Veltze (1913).

SCHWARZKOPF, Elisabeth, *shvahrts'-* (1915–), German soprano, born at Jarotschin, studied at the Berlin High School for Music and sang in the Vienna State Opera (1944–48) and Royal Opera, Covent Garden (1949–52), at first specializing in coloratura rôles and only later appearing as a lyric soprano. See monograph by B. Gavoty (1958).

SCHWATKA, Frederick (1849–92), American Arctic explorer, born at Galena, Ill., was lieutenant of cavalry on the frontier till 1877, meanwhile being admitted to the Nebraska bar and taking a medical degree in New York. In 1878–80 he commanded an expedition which discovered the skeletons of several of Franklin's party, and filled up all gaps in the narratives of Rae and M'Clintock, besides performing a sledge-journey of 3251 miles. In 1883 he explored the course of the Yukon, in 1886 led the *New York Times* Alaskan expedition, and in Alaska in 1891 opened up 700 miles of new country. See his *Along Alaska's Great River* (1885), and book by W. H. Gilder (1881).

SCHWEIGGER, Johann Salomo Christoph, *shvī'gėr* (1779–1857), German physicist, born at Erlangen, invented the string galvanometer.

SCHWEINFURTH, Georg August, *shvīn'foort* (1836–1925), German explorer, born at Riga, in 1864 made a journey up the Nile and along the Red Sea to Abyssinia. In 1869 from Khartoum he passed through the country of the Dinka, Niam-Niam and Monbuttu, and discovered the Welle. Between 1874 and 1883 he made botanical expeditions in Egypt and Arabia, and in Eritrea (1891–94). See his *Heart of Africa* (new ed. 1918).

SCHWEITZER, Albert, *shvī'-* (1875–1965), Alsatian medical missionary, theologian, musician and philosopher, in terms of intellectual achievement and practical morality the noblest figure of the 20th century, born January 14 at Kaysersberg in Alsace and brought up at Günsbach in the Münster valley, where he attended the local *realgymnasium*, learnt the organ eventually under Widor in Paris, studied theology and philosophy at Strasbourg, Paris and Berlin, and in 1896 made his famous decision that he would live for science and art until he was thirty and then devote his life to serving humanity. In 1899 he obtained his doctorate on Kant's philosophy of religion, became curate at St Nicholas Church, Strasbourg, in 1902 *privat-dozent* at the university, and in 1903 principal of the theological college. In 1905 he published his authoritative study, ***J. S. Bach, le musicien-poète*** (1905), translated by Ernest Newman (1911), followed in 1906 by a notable essay on organ-design. Schweitzer was all for the preservation of old organs, many of which he considered had a better tone than modern factory-built ones. The same year appeared the enlargement of his theological thesis (1901), ***Von Reimarus zu Wrede***, re-issued in 1913 as ***Geschichte der Leben-Jesu Forschung***, 'The Quest of the Historical Jesus' (trans. 1910), a thoroughgoing demolition of Liberal theology which had emphasized the rôle of Christ as ethical teacher, in favour of an eschatological interpretation, i.e., Christ as the herald of God's Kingdom at hand, in which the ethical teaching, which would only serve a short interim period, is correspondingly devalued. It marked a revolution in New Testament criticism. To these his Pauline studies *Geschichte der Paulinischen Forschung* (1911; trans. 1912) and ***Die Mystik des Apostels***

Paulus (1930; trans. 1931) were intended as companion volumes. True to his vow, despite his international reputation as musicologist, theologian and organist, he began to study medicine (1905), resigned as principal of the theological college (1906) and, duly qualified (1913), set out with his newly-married wife to set up a hospital to fight leprosy and sleeping sickness at Lambaréné, a deserted mission station on the Ogowe river in the heart of French Equatorial Africa. Except for his internment by the French (1917–18) as a German and periodic visits to Europe to raise funds for his mission by organ recitals, he made his self-built hospital the centre of his paternalistic service to Africans, in a spirit 'not of benevolence but of atonement'. His newly discovered ethical principle 'reverence for Life' was fully worked out in relation to the defects of European civilization in *Verfall und Wiederaufbau der Kultur* (1923), 'The Decay and Restoration of Civilization' (trans. 1923) and philosophically in *Kultur und Ethik* (1923; trans. 1923). He was Hibbert lecturer at Oxford and London (1934) and Gifford Lecturer at Edinburgh (1934–35). He was awarded the Nobel peace prize (1952) and an honorary O.M. (1955). See his *On the Edge of the Primeval Forest* (trans. 1922), *More from the Primeval Forest* (trans. 1931), *Out of My Life and Thought* (1931; postscript 1949), *From My African Notebook* (1938), theological studies by E. N. Mozley (1950) and G. Seaver (rev. ed. 1955), musical studies, ed. C. R. Joy (1953), philosophical study by J. M. Murry (1948), biographical studies by C. E. B. Russell (1944), O. Kraus (1944), G. Seaver (1948), H. Hagedorn (1954), F. Franck (1959), McKnight (1964), and pictorial study (1955) and film (1957) by Anderson.

SCHWENKFELD, Kaspar von, *shvengk'-* (*c.* 1490–1561), German reformer, founder of a Protestant sect, born at Ossig near Liegnitz, served at various German courts, and about 1525 turned Protestant, though he differed widely from Luther. His doctrines resembled those of the Quakers, and brought him banishment and persecution; but he everywhere gained disciples. He died at Ulm. Most of his ninety works were burned by both Protestants and Catholics. Some of his persecuted followers (most numerous in Silesia and Swabia) emigrated to Holland. In 1734 forty families emigrated to England, and thence to Pennsylvania, where, as Schwenkfeldians, they maintained a distinct existence, numbering some 300 members. See monographs by Kadelbach (1861), F. Hoffmann (1897), Hartrauft, Ellsworth and Johnson (1907 ff.).

SCHWINGER, Julian (1918–), American scientist, professor at Harvard, shared the 1965 Nobel prize for physics with Feynman and Tomonaga, for work in quantum electrodynamics.

SCIOPPIUS, or Schoppe, Kaspar (1576–1649), German classical scholar controversialist, born at Neumarkt, at Prague in 1598 abjured Protestantism and attacked his former coreligionists, together with Scaliger and James I of England. He devoted himself at Milan to philological studies and theological warfare (1617–30), and died at Padua. A great scholar, he wrote *Grammatica Philosophica* (1628); *Verisimilium Libri Quatuor* (1596), *Suspectae Lectiones* (1597), &c.

SCIPIO, Publius Cornelius, Africanus Major (237–183 B.C.), Roman general, fought against the Carthaginians at the Trebia and at Cannae. In 210 he was sent as a general extraordinary to Spain. By a sudden march he captured (209) Nova Carthago, stronghold of the Carthaginians, checked Hasdrubal, and soon held the whole of Spain. He was consul in 205, and in 204 sailed with 30,000 men to carry on the war in Africa. His successes compelled the Carthaginians to recall Hannibal from Italy, and the great struggle between Rome and Carthage was terminated by the Roman victory at Zama in 202. Peace was concluded in 201. The surname of Africanus was conferred on Scipio, and popular gratitude proposed to make him consul and dictator for life—honours Scipio refused. In 190 he served as legate under his brother Lucius in the war with Antiochus, whose power they crushed in the victory of Magnesia. But on their return the brothers were charged with having been bribed by Antiochus, the excuse being the too lenient terms granted. Popular enthusiasm supported Scipio against the ill-will of the senatorial oligarchy; but he soon retired to his country-seat at Liternum in Campania. He daughter was Cornelia, mother of the Gracchi. He is regarded as the greatest Roman general before Julius Caesar. See B. H. L. Hart, *A Greater than Napoleon* (1926), and study by Scullard (1930).

SCIPIO ÆMILIANUS, Publius Cornelius, Africanus Minor (185–129 B.C.), Roman statesman and general, was a younger son of Lucius Aemilius Paulus who conquered Macedon, but was adopted by his kinsman Publius Scipio, son of the great Scipio Africanus. He accompanied his father against Macedon, and fought at Pydna (168). In 151 he went to Spain under Lucius Lucullus, and in 149 the third and last Punic war began. The incapacity of the consuls, Manilius and Calpurnius Piso (149–148), and the brilliant manner in which their subordinate rectified their blunders, drew all eyes to him. In 147 he was elected consul and invested with supreme command. The story of the siege of Carthage, the despairing heroism of its inhabitants, the determined resolution of Scipio, belongs to history. The city was finally taken in the spring of 146, and by orders of the senate levelled to the ground. Scipio was now sent to Egypt and Asia on a special embassy; but affairs meanwhile were going badly in Spain, where the Roman armies had suffered the most shameful defeats. At last in 134 Scipio, re-elected consul, went to Spain, and after an eight months' siege forced the Numantines to surrender, and utterly destroyed their city. He then returned to Rome, where he took part in political affairs as one of the leaders of the aristocratic party, and although a brother-in-law of Tiberius Gracchus (q.v.), disclaimed any sympathy with his aims. The Latins, whose lands were being seized under the Sempronian law, appealed to

Scipio, and he succeeded (129) in getting the execution suspended. But his action caused the most furious indignation, and shortly after Scipio was found dead in his bed, doubtless murdered by an adherent of the Gracchi.

SCOGAN, John (fl. 1480–1500), English jester at the court of Edward IV whose *Jests* are said to have been compiled by Andrew Boorde (q.v.).

SCOPAS (fl. 395–350 B.C.), Greek sculptor, founder, with Praxiteles, of the later Attic school, was a native of Paros, and settled in Athens. See Gardner, *Six Greek Sculptors* (1910).

SCORESBY, William (1789–1857), English Arctic explorer, born near Whitby, went as a boy with his father, a whaling captain, to the Greenland seas, and himself made several voyages to the whaling grounds. He attended Edinburgh University, and published *The Arctic Regions* (1820), the first scientific accounts of the Arctic seas and lands. In 1822 he surveyed 400 miles of the east coast of Greenland. Having studied at Cambridge, and been ordained (1825), he held various charges at Exeter, and Bradford. He was elected F.R.S. in 1824. See Life by his nephew (1861).

SCOT, (1) Michael. See SCOTT (18).

(2) or **Scott, Reginald** (*c.* 1538–99), English author, was a younger son of Sir John Scot of Smeeth in Kent. He studied at Hart Hall, Oxford, was collector of subsidies for the lathe of Shepway in 1586–87 and was M.P. (1588–89). He is credited with the introduction of hop-growing into England, and his *Perfect Platform of a Hop-garden* (1574) was the first manual on hop culture in the country. His famous *Discoverie of Witchcraft* (1584), is an admirable exposure of the childish absurdities which formed the basis of the witchcraft craze, and excited the antipathy of King James, who wrote his *Daemonologie* (1597) 'chiefly against the damnable opinions of Wierus and Scot', and had Scot's book burnt by the hangman. Answers and refutations were also written by Meric Casaubon and other divines.

SCOTT, name of a great Scottish Border family which has been traced back, somewhat dubiously, to one Uchtred Filius Scoti, or Fitz-Scot, a witness to David I's charter to Holyrood Abbey (1128), and thereafter to Richard Scot of Murthockston in Lanarkshire (1294), the cradle, however, of the race having been Scotstoun and Kirkurd in Peeblesshire. We find them possessors of Buccleuch in Selkirkshire in 1415, and of Branxholm near Hawick, from 1420–46 onwards. The then Sir Walter Scott fought for James II at Arkinholm against the Douglases (1455), and received a large share of the forfeited Douglas estates; his descendants acquired Liddesdale, Eskdale, Dalkeith, &c., with the titles Lord Scott of Buccleuch (1606) and Earl of Buccleuch (1619). Among them were two Sir Walters, one of whom (*c.* 1490–1552) fought at Flodden (1513), Melrose (1526), Ancrum (1544) and Pinkie (1547), and in 1552 was slain in a street fray at Edinburgh by Kerr of Cessford, while the other Sir Walter, 1st Baron Scott of Buccleuch (1565–1611), was the rescuer of Kinmont Willie from Carlisle Castle (1596). Francis, second earl (1626—51), left two daughters—Mary (1647—61), who married the future Earl of Tarras, and Anna (1651–1732), who married James, Duke of Monmouth, who took the surname Scott and was created Duke of Buccleuch. After his execution (1685) his duchess, who had borne him four sons and two daughters, retained her title and estates, and in 1688 married Lord Cornwallis. Her grandson Francis succeeded her as second duke, and through his marriage in 1720 with a daughter of the Duke of Queensberry that title and estates in Dumfriesshire devolved in 1810 on Henry, third Duke of Buccleuch (1746–1812), a great agriculturist. Walter Francis, fifth duke (1806–84), was the builder of the pier and breakwater at Granton. The Harden branch (represented by Lord Polwarth) separated from the main stem in 1346; and from this sprang the Scotts of Raeburn, ancestors of Sir Walter. See works by Sir William Fraser (1879), J. R. Oliver (1887), K. S. M. Scott (1923) and Jean Dunlop (1957).

SCOTT, (1) Alexander (*c.* 1525–84), a Scottish lyrical poet of the school of Dunbar, who lived near Edinburgh, wrote thirty-six short poems (Scot. Text Soc. 1895) rather in the style of the love lyrics in *Tottel's Miscellany*, though more terse and strong. He was essentially of the pre-Reformation period in Scottish literature.

(2) **Charles Prestwich** (1846–1932), one of the great modern English newspaper editors, born in Bath, was educated at Corpus Christi College, Oxford, became at twenty-six editor of the *Manchester Guardian*, which he raised into a serious Liberal rival of *The Times* by highly independent and often controversial editorial policies, such as opposition to the Boer war, and by his high literary standards. He was Liberal M.P. (1895–1906). See Life by J. L. Hammond (1934). He was succeeded in 1929 by his son, **Edward Taylor** (1883–1932), who was accidentally drowned in Lake Windermere the year his father died.

(3) **Cyril Meir** (1879–1970), English composer, born in Oxton, Cheshire, as a child studied the piano in Frankfurt-am-Main, returning there to study composition in early manhood. His works won a hearing in London at the turn of the century, and in 1913 he was able to introduce his works to Vienna; his opera, *The Alchemist*, had its first performance in Essen in 1925. Scott has composed three symphonies, piano, violin and cello concertos, and numerous choral and orchestral works, but is best known for his piano pieces and songs. He has also written poems, studies of music and occultism, &c. See his *My Years of Indiscretion* (1924).

(4) **David** (1806–49), Scottish historical painter, born in Edinburgh, was apprenticed to his father as a line-engraver, and in 1829 was admitted R.S.A. In 1831 he designed his twenty-five 'Illustrations to the *Ancient Mariner*' (1837). In 1832–33 he visited Italy, and painted *The Vintager*, now in the National Gallery; many historical paintings followed. The main value of his works lies in their Blake-like power and originality. See Memoir (1850) by his brother, **William Bell**

(1811–90), also a painter, and monograph by J. M. Gray (1884).

(5) **Dred** (1795?–1858), American Negro slave whose claim (1852–57) to be free as having long lived in the free state of Illinois was negatived by the Supreme Court. The case was of great importance in the slavery controversy as it involved constitutional issues. See book by Hopkins (1951).

(6) **Duncan Campbell** (1862–1947), Canadian poet, born at Ottawa, rose in the Canadian civil service to deputy superintendent-general for Indian affairs, wrote *The Magic House* (1893), *Labour and the Angel* (1898), *New World Lyrics and Ballads* (1905) and other collections of verse reflecting romantically his love for the Canadian Rockies and Prairies. His prose sketches include *In the Village of Viger* (1896).

(7) **Dukinfield Henry** (1854–1934), British botanist, son of (9), studied at Oxford, became assistant professor at the Royal College of Science and in 1892 keeper of Jodrell Laboratory, Kew. He collaborated with W. E. Williamson in a number of brilliant studies of fossil plants and established in 1904 the class Pteridospermeae.

(8) **Francis George** (1880–1958), Scottish composer, born in Hawick, studied at the universities of Edinburgh and Durham, and in Paris under Roger-Ducasse. From 1925 until 1946 he was lecturer in Music at Jordanhill Training College for Teachers, Glasgow. His *Scottish Lyrics* (five vols. 1921–39) comprise original settings of songs by Dunbar, Burns and other poets, and exemplify Scott's aim of embodying in music the true spirit of Scotland. Primarily a song composer, Scott also wrote the orchestral suite *The Seven Deadly Sins* (after Dunbar's poem) and other orchestral works. See essay by Hugh McDiarmid (1955).

(9) **Sir George Gilbert** (1811–78), English architect, grandson of (24), grandfather of (10) and father of (7), was born, July 13, at Gawcott, Bucks. Aroused by the Cambridge Camden Society and an article of Pugin's (1840–41), he became the leading practical architect in the Gothic revival, and, as such, the building or restoration of most of the public buildings, ecclesiastical or civil, was in his hands. The Martyrs Memorial at Oxford (1841), St Nicholas at Hamburg (1844), St George's at Doncaster, the new India office (exceptionally, owing to pressure by Lord Palmerston, in the style of the Italian Renaissance), the Home and Colonial Offices (from 1858), the somewhat notorious Albert Memorial (1862–63), St Pancras Station and hotel in London (1865), Glasgow University (1865), the chapels of Exeter and St John's Colleges, Oxford, and the Episcopal Cathedral at Edinburgh are examples of his work. He was elected A.R.A. (1855), R.A. (1861), P.R.I.B.A. (1873–76); he was professor of Architecture at the Royal Academy (1868); and he was knighted (1872). The establishment of the Society for Protection of Ancient Buildings (1877) was due to his inspiration. He died March 27, 1878, and was buried in Westminster Abbey. He wrote works on English mediaeval Church architecture. See his *Recollections* (1879).

(10) **Sir Giles Gilbert** (1880–1960), English architect, grandson of (9), was educated at Beaumont College, Old Windsor. He was the architect, pre-eminently, of the great Anglican Cathedral at Liverpool, and also designed, among many other public buildings, the new nave at Downside Abbey, the new buildings at Clare College and the new library at Cambridge. He planned the new Waterloo bridge and was responsible for the rebuilding of the House of Commons after World War II. Elected R.A. (1922), he was knighted (1924) and received the O.M. (1944).

(11) **Hew** (1791–1872), Scottish divine, born at Haddington and educated at Aberdeen, was, from 1839, minister of Wester Anstruther, compiled *Fasti Ecclesiae Scoticanae* (1866–71; new ed. 1915–28).

(12) **Hugh Stowell.** See MERRIMAN (1).

(13) **John.** See ELDON.

(14) **John** (1783–1821), Scottish journalist, born and educated at Aberdeen, became first editor of the *London Magazine* in 1820, and was shot in a duel with Jonathan Christie, whose friend, Lockhart, he had attacked in the magazine.

(15) **John** (1794–1871), English horse-trainer, born at Chippenham and brought up in West Australia, trained six Derby winners, including West Australian, which won the three great racing events in 1853, the Two Thousand Guineas, the Derby and the St Leger.

(16) **Lady John.** See SPOTTISWOODE (1).

(17) **Michael** (*c.* 1175–*c.* 1230), Scottish scholar and astrologer, the 'wondrous wizard', who studied at Oxford and on the Continent, was tutor and astrologer at Palermo to Frederick II, settled at Toledo 1209–20 and translated Arabic versions of Aristotle's works and Averrhoës' commentaries. Returning to the Imperial court at Palermo, he refused the proffered archbishopric of Cashel (1223). His translation of Aristotle was seemingly used by Albertus Magnus, and was one of the two familiar to Dante. Dante alludes to him in the *Inferno* (canto xx, 115–117) in a way which proves that his fame as a magician had already spread over Europe; and he is also referred to by Albertus Magnus and Vincent of Beauvais. In Border folklore he is credited with having in Scott's words (*Lay of the Last Minstrel*, C. III, xiii), 'cleft the Eildon Hills in three and bridled the Tweed with a curb of stone'; and his grave is shown in Melrose Abbey. See Life by J. Wood Brown (1897).

(18) **Michael** (1789–1835), Scottish author, born at Cowlairs, Glasgow, after four years (1801–06) at the university went to seek his fortune in Jamaica. He spent a few years in the W. Indies, but in 1822 settled in Glasgow. His vivid, amusing stories, *Tom Cringle's Log* (1829–33), *The Cruise of the Midge* (1834–35), &c., first appeared in *Blackwood's*.

(19) **Michael** (1902–), English Anglican missionary and agitator, was educated at King's College, Taunton, and St Paul's College, Grahamstown, served in a London East End parish and as chaplain in India (1935–39), where he collaborated with the Communists. Invalided out of the R.A.F. in 1941, he served (1943–50) in various

missions in South Africa. No longer associating with Communists, he exposed the atrocities in the Bethal farming area and in the Transvaal, defended the Basutos against wrongful arrest, and brought the case of the dispossessed Herero tribe before the United Nations. He became *persona non grata* in the Union and in the Central African Federation. He founded the London Africa Bureau in 1952. In 1958 he suffered a short imprisonment for his part in nuclear disarmament demonstrations. He was expelled from Nagaland in 1966. See his autobiography, *A Time to Speak* (1958).

(20) **Sir Percy Moreton, 1st bart. (1853–1924), English sailor and gunnery expert, was born in London, entered the Navy and served (1873–1900) in Ashanti, Egypt, S. Africa and China. Retiring in 1909, he returned to active service as gunnery adviser to the fleet; and in September 1915 was placed in charge of the anti-aircraft gun defences of London. . See his *Fifty Years in the Royal Navy* (1919).**

(21) **Sir Peter Markham** (1909–), English artist, ornithologist and broadcaster, born in London, the son of (23), began to exhibit his characteristic paintings of bird scenes and his portraits in 1933. He represented Britain (single-handed dinghy sailing) at the 1936 Olympic Games, served with distinction with the Royal Navy in World War II, founded the Severn Wild Fowl Trust in 1948, explored in the Canadian Arctic in 1949, and was leader of several ornithological expeditions (Iceland, 1951 and 1953; Australasia and the Pacific, 1956–57). Through television he has helped to popularize natural history, and his writings include *Morning Flight* (1935), *Wild Chorus* (1938), *The Battle of the Narrow Seas* (1945) and *Wild Geese and Eskimos* (1951). He was created C.B.E. in 1953, and was rector of Aberdeen University, 1960–63. He was knighted 1973. See his autobiographical *The Eye of the Wind* (1961).

(22) **Robert.** See LIDDELL.

(23) **Robert Falcon** (1868–1912), English Antarctic explorer, father of (21), born near Devonport, entered the navy in 1881 and in the *Discovery* commanded the National Antarctic Expedition (1900–04) which explored the Ross Sea area, and discovered King Edward VII Land. Scott was promoted captain in 1906, and in 1910 embarked upon his second expedition in the *Terra Nova* and with a sledge party which consisted of Wilson, Oates, Bowers, Evans and himself reached the South Pole on January 17, 1912, only to discover that the Norwegian expedition under Amundsen had beaten them by a month. Delayed by blizzards and the sickness of Evans, who died, and Oates, who gallantly left the tent in a blizzard, the remainder eventually perished in the tantalizing vicinity of One Ton Depot at the end of March, where their bodies and diaries were found by a search party eight months later. Scott was posthumously knighted and the statue of him by his wife, Kathleen, Lady Scott, the sculptress, stands in Waterloo Place, London. The Scott Polar Research Institute at Cambridge was founded in his memory. See his *Voyage of the Discovery* (1905) and diary published as *Scott's Last Expedition*, ed. L. Huxley (1913), accounts of the expeditions by A. B. Armitage (1905), G. Taylor (1916), E. R. Evans (1921), A. Cherry-Garrard (1922), and Lives by S. Gwynn (1929) and G. Seaver (1940).

(24) **Thomas** (1747–1821), English divine, grandfather of (9), born at Braytoft, Lincolnshire, began as a surgeon but is best remembered by his *Bible, with Explanatory Notes* (1788–92). See Life (1822) by his son.

(25) **Walter** (*c.* 1614–94), of Satchells, Scottish soldier and genealogist, served in Holland and at home 1629–86, and then wrote his doggerel *History of the Scotts* (1688; 5th ed. 1894).

(26) **Sir Walter** (1771–1832), Scottish novelist and poet, was born at Edinburgh, son of a writer to the Signet and of Anne Rutherford, a daughter of the professor of Medicine at the University. When young he was sent to his grandfather's farm at Sandyknowe and thus early came to know the Border country which is perhaps the main scene in his creative work. Neither at the High School, Edinburgh, nor at the University did he show much promise. His real education came from people and from books—Fielding and Smollett, Walpole's *Castle of Otranto*, Spenser and Ariosto and, above all, Percy's *Reliques* and German ballad poetry. He did better in his father's office as a law clerk and was admitted advocate in 1792. His first incursion into the Highlands, which were to be second only to the Borders as an inspiration for his work, occurred when, as a law clerk, he was directing an eviction. The young advocate made his first raid on Liddesdale, which also was to figure in his novels, in 1792. His first publication was rhymed versions of ballads by Bürger, 1796. The year following we find him an ardent volunteer in the yeomanry and on one of his 'raids' he met at Gilsland spa a Mlle Charpentier, daughter of a French émigré, whom he married at Carlisle on Christmas Eve, 1797. Two years later he was appointed sheriff of Selkirkshire. The ballad meanwhile absorbed all his literary interest. *Glenfinlas* and *The Eve of St John* were followed by a translation of Goethe's *Goetz von Berlichingen*. His prenticeship in the ballad led to the publication by James Ballantyne, a printer in Kelso, of Scott's first major work, *The Border Minstrelsy* (vols. 1 & 2, 1802, vol. 3, 1803). The *Lay of the Last Minstrel* (1805) made him the most popular author of the day. The other romances which followed, *Marmion* (1808), and *The Lady of the Lake* (1810), enhanced his fame, but the lukewarm reception of *Rokeby* (1811), despite its superior human interest, and of *Lord of the Isles* (1815) warned him that this vein was exhausted. The calculation was fortunate, for modern taste rejects a great deal of this verse romance outpouring, while the novel which replaces it is permanent in the affections of readers everywhere. The business troubles which darkened his later career began with the setting up of James Ballantyne and his brother John as publishers in the Canongate. All went well at first, but with expanding business came

expanding ambitions, and when Constable with his London connections entered the scene, Scott lost all control over the financial side of the vast programme of publication, much of it hack publication, on which he now embarked. Hence the bankruptcy in mid-stream of his great career as a novelist (1826). The Waverley novels fall into three groups—first from *Waverley* (1814) to *Bride of Lammermoor* and *Legend of Montrose* (1819); next from *Ivanhoe* to *The Talisman* (1825), the year before his bankruptcy; *Woodstock* opens the last period, which closes with *Castle Dangerous* and *Count Robert of Paris* (1832), in the year of his death. The first period established the historical novel based, in Scott's case, on religious dissension and the clash of races English and Scottish, Highland and Lowland, his aim being to illustrate manners but also to soften animosities. In *Guy Mannering* first appear his great character creations of the humorous sort, but *Heart of Midlothian* and *Old Mortality* divide the honours. *The Bride of Lammermoor* has the stark outlines of the ballad. His Scottish vein exhausted, he turned to the Middle Ages in *Ivanhoe*, the scene of which is now England. With *The Monastery* and *The Abbot* he moved to Reformation times, where he showed a respect for what was venerable in the ancient church which might have been predicted from his harshness to the covenanters in *Old Mortality*. This group is distinguished by its portrait gallery of queens and princes. The highlights in the last period are *Woodstock* (1826), not quite successful, and *The Fair Maid of Perth* (1828), where again the ballad motif appears. Modern taste may reject much in the verse romances (not however the introductions to *Marmion* with their playful charm or patriotic ardour), but it does not reject the fine lyrics scattered throughout the novels. Here also he worked best on a traditional or ballad theme, as in *Proud Maisie*, but Highland themes, as in *The Pibroch* and *The Coronach*, equally called forth his lyric powers. There are also his immense labours for the publishers, much of which was simply hack work—the editions of Dryden (1808); of Swift (1814); the *Life of Napoleon* (1827), &c. The *Tales of a Grandfather* (1828–30), however, keeps its charm, and his three letters 'from Malachi Malagrowther' (1826), are remembered for their patriotic assertion of Scottish interests. Scott has been criticized on the grounds of style and also for his lack of ideas. The language of his verse romances is often trite, due partly to haste of composition, and the more romantic or manufactured material in his novels is too often tinged with tushery. In dialogue his gentlefolk (especially in love scenes) tend to be affected, but there are many shades here—nobody, for example, would charge the talk in the noble last scenes of *Redgauntlet* with affectation, and all are agreed that the talk of his more humble characters is in character. As for lack of ideas (E. M. Forster's complaint), Scott's acceptance of his world and its conventions ruled that out. The charge that he patronized his peasants and fisherfolk hardly holds. Cuddie Headrigg may be too much of a bumpkin and his mother Mause too strident, but the episode of the Mucklebakkits in *The Antiquary* shows a rare sympathy with working folk. Having regard to the esteem in which Scott as man and writer has been held we may take as his epitaph 'Scott is greater than anything he wrote'. Lockhart's great Life (1837–38) is a classic, but as the publication of the *Letters* by Grierson (1932–1937) showed, dealt too tenderly with certain episodes. Grierson's own *Life* (1938) puts these in better perspective. This had been preceded by John Buchan's admirable Life (1932). See also Scott's *Journal*, ed. Tait (1939, &c.). O. Elton's study, *A Survey of English Literature, 1780-1830*, chap. xi, is excellent. Georg Brandes, *Main Currents in 19th-Century Literature* (trans. 1905) started a school of denigration (which E. M. Forster encouraged).

(27) **William.** See STOWELL.

(28) **William Bell.** See SCOTT (4).

(29) **Winfield** (1786–1866), American soldier, born near Petersburg, Virginia, was admitted to the bar in 1807, but obtained a commission as artillery captain in 1808. As major-general, he framed the 'General Regulations' and introduced French tactics and helped (1839) to settle the disputed boundary line of Maine and New Brunswick. He succeeded to the chief command of the army in 1841. He took Vera Cruz, March 26, 1847, put Santa Anna to flight, and entered the Mexican capital in triumph, September 14. Unsuccessful Whig candidate for the presidency (1852), he retained nominal command of the army until October 1861. See his Memoirs (1864) and the Life by M. J. Wright (1894).

SCOTT-MONCRIEFF, (1) Charles Kenneth Michael (1889–1930), British translator into English of Proust, Stendhal, Pirandello, &c., was educated at Winchester and Edinburgh University, and was on the staff of *The Times* (1921–23).

(2) **Sir Colin Campbell,** K.C.S.I., K.C.M.G. (1836–1916), Scottish engineer and administrator, had a great hand in Egyptian irrigation, and in 1892–1902 was under-secretary for Scotland. See Life by M. A. Hollings (1917).

SCOTUS. See DUNS, ERIGENA, MARIANUS.

SCRIABIN, Alexander, *skryah'byin* (1872–1915), Russian composer and pianist, born at Moscow, studied at the conservatoire with Rachmaninov and Medtner and was professor of the Pianoforte (1898–1904). His compositions include three symphonies, two tone poems, ten sonatas, studies and preludes. His piano music is technically highly original, but he increasingly relied on extramusical factors and applied religion, occultism (and even light) in *Prometheus* and other tone poems. See study by A. E. Hull (1916).

SCRIBE, Augustin Eugène, *skreeb* (1791–1861), French dramatist, born in Paris, was intended for the law. After 1816 his productions became so popular that he established a type of theatre workshop in which numerous *collaborateurs* worked under his supervision turning out plays by 'mass-production' methods. His plots are interesting and his dialogue light and sparkling, if in modern eyes highly artificial. The best known are *Le Verre d'eau* (1840), *Adrienne Lecouvreur* (1848), *Bataille des dames* (1851), &c. Scribe also wrote novels and composed the *libretti* for sixty operas, including *Masaniello, Fra Diavolo, Robert le Diable, Les Huguenots, Le Prophète*, &c. See Life by Legouvé (1874), and study by N. C. Arvin (1924).

SCRIBLERUS. See ARBUTHNOT.

SCRIBNER, Charles (1821–71), American publisher, born in New York, graduated at Princeton in 1840, and in 1846 founded with Isaac Baker the New York publishing firm bearing his name. *Scribner's Magazine* dates from 1887. His three sons continued the business.

SCRIPPS. Family of American newspaper publishers: **James Edmund** (1835–1906), born in London, was the founder of the *Detroit Evening News*. He was associated with his half-brother, **Edward Wyllis** (1854–1926), in the foundation of many newspapers, notably at St Louis and Cleveland. His sister, **Ellen Browning** (1836–1932), born in London, served on many of the family newspapers. The family interest passed to **Robert Paine** (1895–1938), Edward's son. The Scripps were first in the field of syndicated material with the Newspaper Enterprises Association (1902).

SCROGGS, Sir William (1623–83), English judge, born at Deddington, Oxfordshire, chief justice of the King's Bench from 1678, was notorious for cruelty and partiality during the 'Popish Plot' trials (see OATES). In 1680 he was impeached, but removed from office by the king on a pension.

SCROPE, *skroop*, a north of England family that produced Richard le Scrope, chancellor in 1378 and 1381–82; Richard le Scrope (*c.* 1350–1405), Archbishop of York, beheaded for conspiracy against Henry IV; and Henry Lord Scrope, warden of the West Marches under Queen Elizabeth.

SCUDDER, (1) **Horace Elisha** (1862–1902), American storyteller, biographer, historian, editor, &c., was born at Boston, Mass.

(2) **Janet** (1875–1968), American sculptor, known for her statues of children and her sculptured fountains.

(3) **Samuel Hubbard** (1837–1911), American entomologist, an authority on fossil insects, also wrote on the Orthoptera and Lepidoptera.

SCUDÉRY, *skü-day-ree*, (1) **Georges de** (1601–1667), French writer, brother of (2), born at Le Havre, after a brief military career wrote a number of plays, which achieved some success. In 1637 his *Observations sur le Cid* led to a controversy with Corneille. He later wrote novels and had some small share in his sister's works, which first appeared under his name.

(2) **Madeleine de** (1608–1701), French novelist, sister of (1), was left an orphan at six, came to Paris *c.* 1630 and with her brother was accepted into the literary society of Mme de Rambouillet's *salon*. From 1644 to 1647 she was in Marseilles with her brother. She had begun her literary career with the romance *Ibrahim ou l'illustre Bassa* (1641), but her most famous work was the ten-volume *Artamène ou le Grand Cyrus* (1649–1659), followed by *Clélie* (1654–60). These highly artificial, ill-constructed pieces, overladen with pointless dialogue, were popular at the court because of their sketches of and skits on public personages. See Lives by MacDougall (1938) and Mongrédien (1946).

SEABORG, Glenn Theodore (1912–), American nuclear chemist and physicist, professor of Chemistry at Berkeley, California, since 1945, helped to discover the transuranic elements plutonium (1940), americium and curium (1944). By bombarding the last two with alpha rays he produced the elements berkelium and californium in 1950. He was awarded the Nobel prize in 1951.

SEABURY, Samuel (1729–96), American divine, born at Groton, Conn., graduated at Yale in 1748, studied medicine at Edinburgh, and received orders in England in 1753. Three years a missionary of the S.P.G., in 1757 he became rector of Jamaica, Long Island, and in 1767 of Westchester, New York. Despite imprisonment for his loyalty to Britain which he maintained through the War of American Independence as a royalist army chaplain, he was elected first bishop of Connecticut in 1783. The Church of England refusing to consecrate him because he could not take the Oath of Allegiance, three bishops of the Scottish Episcopal Church performed the ceremony at Aberdeen (1784). See *Memoir* by W. J. Seabury (1909).

SEAMAN, Sir Owen, 1st Bart. (1861–1936), was educated at Shrewsbury and Clare College, Cambridge, became professor of Literature at Newcastle (1890), was *Punch* editor (1906–32). His parodies and *vers de société*, which include *Paulopostprandials* (1883), *In Cap and Bells* (1889), *From the Home Front* (1918), &c., rank him with Calverley.

SEARLE, *serl*, (1) **Humphrey** (1915–), English composer, born in Oxford, studied at the Royal College of Music and in Vienna, became musical adviser to Sadler's Wells Ballet in 1951. He has written *Twentieth Century Counterpoint*, and a study of the music of Liszt. An exponent of the 'twelve note system', he has composed several symphonies, a piano concerto and a trilogy of works for speaker and orchestra to words by Edith Sitwell and James Joyce.

(2) **Ronald William Fordham** (1920–), English artist, born in Cambridge. He served in World War II with the Royal Engineers and the drawings he made during his three years' imprisonment by the Japanese helped to establish his reputation as a serious artist. After the war he soon became widely known as the creator of the macabre schoolgirls of 'St Trinians'. He joined the staff of *Punch* in 1956.

SEBASTIAN, St (d. 288), was a native of Narbonne, a captain of the praetorian guard, and secretly a Christian. Diocletian, hearing that he favoured Christians, ordered him to be slain. But the archers did not quite kill him; a woman named Irene nursed him back to life. When he upbraided the tyrant for his cruelty, Diocletian had him beaten to death with rods.

SEBASTIAN (1554–78), king of Portugal, a grandson of the Emperor Charles V, fell in battle against the Moors at Alcazar in Algeria; but soon doubt was thrown upon his death, and impostors began to crop up—first in 1584 a son of a potter; then Matheus Alvares, a sort of brigand-insurgent; in 1594 a Spanish cook; then one Catizzone, a Calabrian, hanged in 1603. The popular belief that Sebastian would come again revived in 1807–08 during the French occupation, and again in 1838 in Brazil. See Life by A. Figueiredo (1925).

SÉBASTIANI, François Horace Bastien, Count, *say-bast-ya-nee* (1772–1851), French soldier and diplomat, born near Bastia in Corsica, became one of Napoleon's most devoted partisans. He fought at Marengo, was wounded at Austerlitz, twice undertook missions to Turkey (1802–06), commanded an army corps in Spain, and distinguished himself in the Russian campaign (1812) and at Leipzig. He joined Napoleon on his return from Elba, but after 1830 was twice in the ministry, and was ambassador at Naples and London. He was made marshal of France in 1840.

SEBASTIANO DEL PIOMBO. See PIOMBO.

SÉBILLOT, Paul, *say-bee-yō* (1843–1918), French folklorist, born at Matignon, Côtes-du-Nord, abandoned law for painting, and from 1870 to 1883 exhibited in the Salon. He then held a post in the ministry of public works, became Chevalier of the *Légion d'honneur* 1889, and devoting himself to the study of Breton folk tales, published the standard work *Le Folklore de France* (1907), &c.

SECCHI, Angelo, *sek-kee* (1818–78), Italian astronomer, born at Reggio and trained as a Jesuit, became professor of Physics at Washington, U.S., and in 1849 director of the observatory at the Collegio Romano. He originated classification of stars by spectrum analysis.

SECKENDORFF, (1) Friedrich Heinrich (1673–1763), Austrian soldier and diplomat, nephew of (2), defeated the French at Klausen (1735) and fought in the Bavarian army during the War of the Austrian Succession.

(2) **Veit Ludwig von** (1626–92), German statesman, uncle of (1), served the princes of Saxony and Brandenburg, was chancellor of the University of Halle, and wrote a Latin compendium of church history (1664) and a work *De Lutheranismo* (1688).

SEDGWICK, (1) Adam (1785–1873), English geologist, born at Dent, fifth wrangler at Trinity College, Cambridge, in 1808, became a fellow in 1810, Woodwardian professor of Geology in 1818, a canon of Norwich in 1834, and vice-master of Trinity in 1847. His best work was on *British Palaeozoic Fossils* (1854); with Murchison he studied the Alps and the Lake District. He strongly opposed Darwin's *Origin of Species*. See his *Life and Letters* by Clark and Hughes (1890).

(2) **Anne Douglas** (1873–1935), American novelist, born at Englewood, New Jersey, studied painting in Paris and, influenced by Henry James, wrote *Tante* (1911), *The Encounter* (1914), *Dark Hester* (1929), &c., and volumes of short stories. See her autobiographical *Portrait in Letters*, ed. by her husband, B. de Selincourt (1936).

SEDLEY, Sir Charles (1639–1701), English courtier and poet, born probably in London, was notorious at court for debauchery and wit. He joined William III at the Revolution, out of *gratitude* to James, who had seduced his daughter and made her Countess of Dorchester. 'Since his Majesty has made my daughter a countess' said he, 'it is fit I should do all I can to make his daughter a queen.' He is remembered less for his plays—*The Mulberry Garden, Antony and Cleopatra, Bellamira*—than for a few songs and *vers de société*. See study (1927) by V. de Sola Pinto, who also edited the *Works* (1928).

SEEBOHM, Frederic (1833–1912), English historian, was called to the bar in 1856, but became partner in a bank at Hitchin. He was author of *The Oxford Reformers of 1498* (1867), *The English Village Community* (1883), &c. His brother, **Henry** (1832–95), was ornithologist and traveller in Greece, Asia Minor, Norway, Siberia, &c.

SEEFRIED, Irmgard, *zay'freet* (1919–), Austrian soprano, born in Köngetried, Germany, famed for her performances with Vienna State Opera, especially in the operas of Mozart and Richard Strauss.

SEELEY, Sir John Robert (1834–95), English historian, third son of the publisher, Robert Benton Seeley (1798–1886). He was educated at City of London School and at Cambridge. In 1863 he became professor of Latin in University College, London, in 1869 of Modern History at Cambridge. His *Ecce Homo* (1865), a popular Life of Christ, caused much controversy in religious circles. Other works include the authoritative *Life and Times of Stein* (1874) and *The Expansion of England* (1883). He was knighted in 1894. See memoir by Prothero prefixed to Seeley's *Growth of British Policy* (1895).

SEELIGER, Hugo, *zay'-* (1849–1924), German astronomer, born at Bielitz, professor of Astronomy at Munich, is best known for his work on star distribution and for his theory for the birth of a nova.

SEFERIADES, George (pseud. Seferis) (1900–1971), Greek poet and diplomat, born in Smyrna, educated at Athens and the Sorbonne. Ambassador to the Lebanon (1953–1957) and the U.K. (1957–62), he wrote lyrical poetry, collected in *The Turning Point* (1931), *Mythistorema* (1935), &c. He translated T. S. Eliot's *Waste Land* into Greek. In 1963 he was awarded the Nobel prize for literature.

SEFSTRÖM, Nils Gabriel (1787–1854), Swedish physician and chemist, in 1831 discovered the element vanadium in a specimen of soft iron.

SEGONZAC, André Dunoyer de, *sè-gō-zac* (1884–), French painter and engraver, born at Boussy-Saint-Antoine. He was influenced by Courbet and Corot, and produced many delicate watercolour landscapes, etchings and illustrations. His series of engravings of *Beaches* was published in 1935, and his work is represented in the Musée d'art moderne, Paris.

SEGOVIA, Andres, *se-gō'vee-a* (1894–), Spanish guitarist, born in Limares. Influenced by the Spanish nationalist composers, he has evolved a revolutionary guitar technique permitting the performance of a wide range of music, and many modern composers have composed works for him. See monograph by Gavoty (1956).

SEGRAVE, Sir Henry O'Neal de Hane, *see'-* (1896–1930), British racing driver, born of Irish parentage at Baltimore, U.S.A., was educated at Eton and Sandhurst, served in the Royal Flying Corps and was wounded in 1916, when he became technical secretary to the air minister. A leading postwar racing driver, he helped to design the Sunbeam car, in which he broke the land speed record with a speed of 203·9 m.p.h., raising this to 231 in 1929, when he was knighted. He was killed in his boat *Miss England* on Lake Windermere, June 13, 1930, when on a trial run, during which he had surpassed the world motorboat speed record.

SEGRÈ, Emilio, *seg'ray* (1905–), Italian-American physicist, a pupil of Fermi (q.v.), fled from the Mussolini régime to the U.S.A. and took American nationality in 1944, having already been on the staff of the University of California for several years. He shared the 1959 Nobel prize with Owen Chamberlain for researches on the antiproton.

SEGUIER, William, *seg-yay* (1771–1843), English artist, born in London of Huguenot descent, studied under George Morland, but abandoned painting for the art of the restorer and connoisseur, and helped George IV to gather together the Royal Collection. When the National Gallery was inaugurated, he became its first keeper. As superintendent of the British Institution, he was succeeded at his death by his brother **John** (1785–1856), also a painter and his partner in the picture-restoring business.

SÉGUR, *say-gür,* a French family, distinguished in arms and letters, some of whose members were Huguenots.

(1) **Henri François,** Comte de Ségur (1689–1751), was a general in the War of the Austrian Succession.

(2) **Philippe Henri,** Marquis de Ségur-Ponchat (1724–1801), son of (1), fought in the Seven Years' War, and became marshal in 1783.

(3) **Louis Philippe,** Comte de Ségur d'Aguesseau (1753–1820), son of (2), ambassador at St Petersburg, was a great favourite with Catharine II, served in the American War of Independence, and hailed the French revolution. Among his writings (33 vols.) are *La Politique de tous les cabinets de l'Europe* (1793), &c.

(4) **Philippe Paul** (1780–1873), son of (3), was a general of the first empire, and wrote a history (1824) of the Russian campaign of 1812, *Histoire de Russie et de Pierre le Grand* (1829), &c. See Life by Taillandier (1875) and his Reminiscences (Eng. trans. 1895).

(5) **Pierre** (1853–1916), French historian.

(6) **Sophie Rostopchine,** Comtesse de Ségur (1799–1874), author of *Les Mémoires d'un âne* and many other writings for the young.

SEIBER, Mátyás, *zī'-* (1905–60), Hungarian-born British composer, born at Budapest, studied there under Kodály, and was a private music teacher (1925) and professor of Jazz (1928–33) at Hoch's Conservatory at Frankfurt-am-Main. He settled in Britain in 1935 and in 1942 became a tutor at Morley College, London. He gained only belated recognition as a composer, with strong musical affinities to Bartok and Schönberg. His compositions include three string quartets, of which the second (1935) is the best known, other chamber works, piano music and songs and the *Ulysses* cantata (1946–47) based on Joyce's novel. He was killed in a motor accident in South Africa.

SEJANUS. See TIBERIUS.

SELBORNE, (1) **Roundell Palmer, 1st Earl of** (1812–95), English jurist and hymnologist, father of (2), born at Mixbury, Oxfordshire, was solicitor-general (1861), attorney-general (1863–66), but his dislike of Gladstone's Irish Church policy delayed his promotion to lord chancellor (1872–74, 1880–85). He reformed the judicators and wrote hymnological and liturgical studies. See his *Memorials* (1898).

(2) **William Waldegrave Palmer, 2nd Earl of** (1859–1942), English politician, son of (1), was under-secretary for the Colonies (1895–1900) first lord of the Admiralty (1900–05), high commissioner for S. Africa (1905–10), president of the Board of Agriculture (1915–1916), warden of Winchester (1920–25).

(3) **Roundell Cecil Palmer, 3rd Earl of** (1887–), son of (2), was minister of works (1940–42) and minister of economic warfare (1942–45).

SELBY-BIGGE, Sir John. See BIGGE.

SELDEN, John (1584–1654), English historian and antiquary, born near Worthing, studied at Oxford and London, where he acquired wealth, yet found time for profound and wide study. In 1610 appeared his *Duello*, or *Single Combat*; his *Titles of Honour* (1614) is still an authority. *Analecton Anglo-Britannicon* (1615) dealt with the civil government of Britain previous to the Norman Conquest. In 1617 appeared his erudite work on the Syrian gods, *De Diis Syriis*. His *History of Tithes* (1618), demolishing their divine right, brought upon his head the fulminations of the clergy, and was suppressed by the privy council. In 1621 Selden was imprisoned for advising the parliament to repudiate King James's doctrine that their privileges were originally royal grants, in 1623 he was elected member for Lancaster. In 1628 he helped to draw up the Petition of Right, and the year after he was committed to the Tower with Eliot, Holles and the rest. In 1635 he dedicated to the king his *Mare Clausum* (an answer to the *Mare Liberum* of Grotius). In 1640 he entered the Long Parliament for Oxford University, and opposed the policy that led to the expulsion of the bishops from the House of Lords and finally to the abolition of Episcopacy. He took no direct part in the impeachment of Strafford and voted against the Attainder Bill, and had no share in Laud's prosecution. He sat as a lay member in the Westminster Assembly (1643), and was appointed keeper of the records in the Tower and (1644) an Admiralty commissioner. In 1646 he subscribed the Covenant. In 1647 he was appointed a university visitor, and sought to moderate the fanaticism of his colleagues. After the execution of Charles I, of which he disapproved, he took little share in public matters. He was buried in the Temple Church. He had also written in Latin books on the Arundel Marbles (1624) and on Hebrew law (1634–50), besides posthumous tracts and treatises, of which the most valuable is his *Table Talk* (1689). See Singer's biographical preface to his works (1726), Aikin's *Lives of Selden and Usher* (1811), G. W. Johnson's *Memoir* (1835), and S. H. Reynolds's introduction to his edition of the *Table Talk* (Oxford 1892).

SELEUCUS, the name of six kings of the Seleucidae, the dynasty to whom fell that portion of Alexander the Great's Asiatic conquests which included Syria, part of Asia Minor, Persia, Bactria, &c. See ANTIOCHUS.

Seleucus I, surnamed Nicator (*c.* 358–280 B.C.), Macedonian general under Alexander the Great, obtained Babylonia, to which he added Susiana, Media and Asia Minor, but was assassinated in 280 B.C. He founded Greek and Macedonian colonies, and also built Antioch, Seleucia on the Tigris, &c.

Seleucus II, surnamed Callinicus (*c.* 247–226 B.C.), son of Antiochus II, was beset by Ptolemy of Egypt, his own half-brother, and the Parthians, and lost Asia Minor and Parthia.

SELFRIDGE, Harry Gordon (1858?–1947), British merchant, born at Ripon, Wisconsin. Educated privately, he joined a trading firm in Chicago, brought into the business new ideas and great organizing ability, and in 1892 was made a junior partner. While visiting London in 1906 he bought a site in Oxford Street, and built upon it the large store, opened in March 1909, which bears his name. He took British nationality in 1937. See Life by R. Pound (1960).

SELIM. The name of three sultans of Turkey:

Selim I (1467–1520), in 1512 dethroned his father, Bajazet II, and caused him, his own brothers, and nephews to be put to death. In 1514 he declared war against Persia, and took Diarbekir and Kurdistan. He conquered in 1517 Egypt, Syria and the Hejaz, with Medina and Mecca; won from the Abbasid calif at Cairo the headship of the Mohammedan world; chastized the insolence of the Janizaries; sought to improve the condition of the peoples he had conquered; and cultivated the poetic art. He was succeeded by his son, Soliman the Magnificent.

Selim II (1524–74), a degraded sot, succeeded his father, Soliman, in 1566; he owed whatever renown belongs to his reign to his father's old statesmen and generals. Arabia was conquered in 1570, Cyprus in 1571, but the Turkish fleet was annihilated by Don John of Austria in 1571 off Lepanto. During this reign occurred the first collision of Turks with Russians; three-fourths of the Turkish army were lost in the Astrakhan expedition.

Selim III (1761–1807), succeeding his brother in 1789, prosecuted the war with Russia; but the Austrians joined the Russians, and Belgrade surrendered to them, while the Russians took Bucharest, Bender, Akerman and Ismail. Numerous reforms were projected; but the people were hardly prepared for them, and Selim's projects cost him his throne and life.

SELKIRK, (1) Alexander or Alexander Selcraig (1676–1721), Scottish sailor, whose story is supposed to have suggested the Robinson Crusoe of Defoe, was a native of Largo in Fife. After getting into several scrapes at home, in his twenty-eighth year he joined the South Sea buccaneers. In 1704 he quarrelled with his captain, and at his own request was put ashore on Juan Fernández. Having lived alone here four years and four months, he was at last taken off by Thomas Dover (q.v.). He returned to Largo in 1712, and at his death was a lieutenant on a man-of-war. See Life by Howell (1829).

(2) **J. B.**, pseud. of **James Brown** (1832–1904), Scottish poet, born in Galashiels but a lifelong dweller in Selkirk. Besides poems (1869, &c.) he published two prose volumes.

(3) **Thomas Douglas, 5th Earl of** (1771–1820), Scottish colonizer, settled emigrants from the Scottish Highlands in Prince Edward Island (1803) and in the Red River Valley, Manitoba, although twice evicted by the Northwest Fur Company (1815–16). See his *Diary*, 1803–04 (Toronto 1958), and account of his work by C. Martin (1916).

SELLAR, William Young (1825–90), born near Golspie, was educated at Edinburgh Academy, Glasgow University and Balliol, graduating with a classical first. He filled for four years (1859–63) the Greek chair at St Andrews, and was then elected to the Latin chair at Edinburgh. He made his name widely known by his brilliant *Roman Poets of the Republic* (1863; enlarged 1881), which was followed by *The Roman Poets of the Augustan Age—Virgil* (1877) and *Horace and the Elegiac Poets* (1892), the latter edited by his nephew, Andrew Lang, with memoir.

SELLON, Priscilla Lydia (1821–76), English founder in 1849 at Plymouth of the second Anglican sisterhood, its spiritual director Dr Pusey. See Life by T. J. Williams (1950).

SELOUS, Frederick Courtenay, *se-loos'* (1851–1917), English explorer and big-game hunter, born in London, first visited South Africa in 1871. He wrote *A Hunter's Wanderings in Africa* (1881), *Travel and Adventure in South-east Africa*, &c., fought in Matabeleland (1893, 1895), and in 1916 won the D.S.O. and fell in action in East Africa. See Life by J. G. Millais (1918).

SELWYN, (1) George (1719–91), English wit, was educated at Eton and Hertford College, Oxford, whence, after making the Grand Tour, he was expelled (1745) for a blasphemous travesty of the Eucharist. He entered parliament in 1747, and sided generally with the Court party. At Paris he had the *entrée* of the best society, while among his intimates were the Duke of Queensberry, Horace Walpole and 'Gilly' Williams. He died penitent. See Lives by H. J. Jesse (1843) and S. P. Kerr (1909).

(2) **George Augustus** (1809–78), English divine, born at Hampstead, was educated at Eton and St John's College, Cambridge, where he rowed in the first university boat-race (1829), and graduated in 1831. In 1841,

he was consecrated first and only Bishop of New Zealand and Melanesia of whose church he played a large part in settling the constitution. In 1867 he was appointed Bishop of Lichfield, where upon his initiative the first Diocesan Conference in which the laity were duly represented met in 1868. Selwyn College, Cambridge, was founded (1882) in his memory. See Lives by Tucker (2 vols. 1879) and Creighton (1923). His son, **John Richardson** (1844–98), was Bishop of Melanesia 1877, and master of Selwyn College, Cambridge.

SEMENOV, Nikolai, *sem-yo'nof* (1896–), Russian scientist, born at Saratov, graduated at Petrograd in 1917 and after a spell on the staff of Leningrad Physical Technical Institute (1920–31) joined the Institute of Chemical Physics of the Soviet Academy of Sciences, later being made its director. An expert in molecular physics, he carried out important research on chain-reactions, for which he was awarded the Nobel prize, jointly with Hinshelwood, in 1956.

SEMIRAMIS, *-mir'-* (9th cent. B.C.), wife of Ninus, with whom she is supposed to have founded Nineveh. The historical germ of the story seems to be the three years' regency of Sammu-ramat (811–808 B.C.), widow of Shamshi-Adad V, but the details are legendary, derived from Ctesias and the Greek historians, with elements of the Astarte myth. See Lenormant, *La Légende de Sémiramis* (1873).

SEMLER, Johann Salomo (1725–91), German theologian, born at Saalfeld, in 1753 became professor of Theology at Halle. He exercised a profound influence as pioneer of the historical method in biblical criticism. He was distinctively a rationalist, but he sincerely believed in revelation. In insisting on the distinction of the Jewish and Pauline types of Christianity he anticipated the Tübingen school. See his Autobiography (1781–82) and W. Nigg, *Die Kirchengeschichtsschreibung* (1934).

SEMMELWEISS, Ignaz Philipp, *zem'ĕl-vīs* (1818–65), Hungarian obstetrician, born at Budapest, studied there and at Vienna. Appalled by the heavy death-rate in the Vienna maternity hospital where he worked, he introduced antiseptics. The death-rate fell from 12% to 1¼%, but his superiors would not accept his conclusions and he was compelled to leave Vienna and return to Pest. He contracted septicaemia in a finger and died in a mental hospital near Vienna from the disease he had spent his life in combating. See Life by W. J. Sinclair (1909), and F. G. Slaughter, *Immortal Magyar* (1950).

SEMMES, Raphael, *sems* (1809–77), American sailor, commander of the Confederate States cruiser *Alabama*, entered the U.S. navy in 1826, but was called to the bar. He served again during the Mexican war, and in 1858 was made secretary to the Lighthouse Board. On the outbreak of the Civil War he first commanded the *Sumter*; then, taking over the *Alabama* at the Azores (August 24, 1862), proceeded to capture 65 vessels, nearly all of which were sunk or burned, and to destroy property estimated at $6,000,000. But it was by the heavy insurance for war risks, and still more by the difficulty in getting freights, that the *Alabama's* career caused almost incalculable injury to the U.S. marine. On June 19, 1864, the *Alabama* was sunk in action off Cherbourg by the U.S. cruiser *Kearsarge*; but its commander escaped. Later he edited a paper, was a professor, and practised law in Mobile. He wrote several books on service afloat. See Arthur Sinclair *Two Years on the Alabama* (1896).

SEMPER, (1) Gottfried (1803–73), German architect, born in Hamburg, deserted law for architecture and travelled in France, Italy and Greece. In 1834 he was appointed professor at Dresden, but his part in the revolution of 1848 compelled him to flee to England, where he designed the Victoria and Albert Museum. He eventually settled in Vienna, where the Burgtheater, the imperial palace and two museums, as well as the art gallery and railway station at Dresden, testify to his adaptation of the Italian renaissance style. See *Monograph* by C. Lipsius (1880).

(2) **Karl** (1832–93), German naturalist, born at Altona, studied at Kiel, Hanover and Würzburg, and, after travelling in the Philippines and South Sea Islands, became in 1868 professor of Zoology at Würzburg. He wrote on the Philippines, on several problems of comparative anatomy, and *The Natural Conditions of Existence as they affect Animal Life* (trans. 1880).

SEMPILL, (1) Francis (1616?–1682), Scottish minor poet, son of (3), author of *The Banishment of Povertie*.

(2) **Robert** (1530?–1595), Scottish author of witty ballads full of coarse vigour, e.g., *The Legend of a Lymaris Life* and *Sege of the Castel of Edinburgh*. He was an enemy of Queen Mary and wrote satirical Reformation broadsides, such as the *Life of the Tulchene Bishop of St Andrews*.

(3) **Robert** (1595?–1665?), father of (1). He revived the methods of the Scottish *Makaris* and set the fashion for future vernacular elegies. He wrote *Habbie Simson*, *The Blythesome Bridal* (also attributed to (1)), and, possibly, *Maggie Lauder*.

SEN, Keshub Chunder (1838–84), Indian religious reformer, a native of Bengal, about 1858 was attracted by the Brahma Samâj (see RAMMOHUN ROY), and in 1866 founded the more liberal 'Brahma Samâj of India' He visited England in 1870. In 1878 a schism broke out in his church, caused largely by his autocratic temper; and his last years brought disappointment. See Max-Müller's *Biographical Essays* (1884).

SÉNANCOUR, Étienne Pivert de, *say-nã-koor* (1770–1846), French author, born in Paris. After nine years in Switzerland, he returned to Paris about 1798. His fame rests securely on three books: *Rêveries sur la nature primitive de l'homme* (1799), *Obermann* (1804) and *Libres Méditations d'un solitaire inconnu*. In the first we see the student of Rousseau weighed down by the dogma of necessity. In *Obermann* the atheism and dogmatic fatalism of the *Rêveries* have given place to universal doubt no less overwhelming. Nowhere is the desolating 'mal du siècle' more effectively expressed than in this book, which is yet completely original in its delicate feeling for nature, and its melancholy eloquence. The influence of Goethe's

Werther is persistent in his work. Sénancour, neglected in his day, found fit audience in George Sand, Sainte-Beuve and Matthew Arnold.

SENDERENS, Jean Baptiste (1856–1937), French chemist, born at Barbachen, Hautes-Pyrénées, with Sabatier discovered the hydrogenation of oils by catalysis in 1899.

SENEBIER, Jean, *sè-nè-byay* (1742–1809), Swiss pastor, chemist and librarian in Geneva, in 1782 first demonstrated the basic principle of photosynthesis.

SENECA, *sen'e-ka,* **(1) Lucius (or Marcus) Annaeus,** called **'the Elder'** (*c.* 55 B.C.–*c.* A.D. 40), Roman rhetorician, father of (2), born at Cordova, Spain. Besides a history of Rome, now lost, he wrote *Oratorum et Rhetorum Sententiae, Divisiones, Colores Controversiae* (partly lost) and *Suasoriae.* His other sons were M. Annaeus Novatus and by adoption L. Iunius Gallio (of the Acts xviii. 12); also M. Annaeus Mela, father of Lucan, the poet.

(2) **Lucius Annaeus,** called **'the Younger'** (*c.* 5 B.C.–A.D. 65), Roman philosopher and statesman, son of (1), born in Cordova, Spain, and educated for the bar in Rome. After years of devotion to philosophy and rhetoric, he entered the Curia, but in A.D. 41 lost the favour he had won with Claudius by getting involved in a state trial and was banished to Corsica, whence he returned after eight years. Entrusted by Agrippina with the education of her son Nero, he acquired over the youth a strong and salutary influence, and by Nero (now emperor) was made consul in A.D. 57. His high moral aims gradually incurred the aversion of the emperor, and he withdrew from public life. An attempt by Nero to poison him having failed, he was drawn into the Pisonian conspiracy, accused, and condemned. Left free to choose his mode of death, he elected to open his veins, A.D. 65. In philosophy he inclined to the Stoic system, with Epicurean modifications. He employed an epigrammatic style, which despite his moralizing lacked depth. His writings include *De Ira, De Consolatione, De Providentia, De Animi Tranquillitate, De Constantia Sapientis, De Clementia, De Brevitate Vitae, De Vita Beata, De Otio aut Secessu Sapientis, De Beneficiis, Epistolae ad Lucilium, Apocolocyntosis* (a scathing satire on the Emperor Claudius) and *Quaestiones Naturales.* Seneca was also a poet, if we may accept as his the epigrams and the eight tragedies (*Hercules Furens, Thyestes, Phaedra, Oedipus, Troades, Medea, Agamemnon, Hercules Oetaeus,* and part of a *Thebais*) usually comprised among his *opera omnia.* The publication of the *Tenne Tragedies* in 1581 was important in the evolution of Elizabethan drama, which took from it the five-act division, as well as the horrors and the rhetoric. See C. W. Barlow, *Seneca's Correspondence with St Paul* (1938) and T. S. Eliot, *Selected Essays* (1932).

SENEFELDER, Aloys, *zay'nè-fel-der* (1771–1834), Bavarian inventor, born in Prague, and successively actor, author and printer, about 1796 invented lithography, and after various trials in 1806 opened an establishment of his own in Munich, where he died.

SENIOR, Nassau William (1790–1864), English economist and 'prince of interviewers', born at Compton Beauchamp, Berks, was educated at Eton and Magdalen College, Oxford. In 1819 he was called to the bar; in 1825–30, and again in 1847–62, was professor of Political Economy at Oxford; in 1832 was appointed a Poor-law commissioner; and in 1836–53 was a master in chancery. He stressed the importance of the last hour's work in the cotton factories and opposed the trade unions. His publications include *On the Cost of Obtaining Money* (1830), *Value of Money* (1840), as well as many biographical and critical essays. See study by S. L. Levy (1928).

SENNACHERIB, *-nak'-* (d. 681 B.C.), king of Assyria, succeeded his father, Sargon, in 705 B.C. He invaded Judaea and besieged Hezekiah in Jerusalem. His great achievement was the rebuilding of Nineveh, and the making of the embankment of the Tigris, canals, water-courses, &c. He was slain by one of his sons.

SENUSRIT. See SESOSTRIS.

SEPÚLVEDA, Juan Ginés de (1490–1574), Spanish historian, born near Córdoba, became historiographer to Charles V, preceptor to the future Philip II, and a canon of Salamanca. He was a champion of humanism. His Latin works include histories of Charles V and Philip II, a Life of Albornoz, and a History of Spain in the New World.

SÉQUARD. See BROWN-SÉQUARD.

SEQUOYAH, *se-kwoy'è* or **George Guess** (*c.* 1770–1843), American half-Cherokee scholar, who in 1826 invented a Cherokee syllabary of eighty-five characters. His name was given to a genus of giant coniferous trees (*Sequoia*) and to a national park. See Life by G. E. Foster (1886).

SERAO, Matilde, *say-rah'ō* (1856–1927), Italian novelist, was born at Patras in Greece, the daughter of an Italian political refugee and a Greek, and in 1880 she married Edoardo Scarfoglio, editor of a Neapolitan paper. Her tales, mostly of Neapolitan life, include *Cuore Infermo, Fantasia, Le Leggende Napolitane, Riccardo Joanna, All' Erta Sentinella, Il Paese di Cuccagna.* See Life by R. Garzia (1916).

SERF, St, a Scottish saint who founded the church of Culross between 697 and 706, but who yet figures in the legend of St Kentigern (q.v.).

SERGEYEV-TSENSKY, Sergey (1875–1958), Russian novelist, born in Tambov province, from a Dostoevskian passion for morbid characterization, as in *The Tundra* (1902), developed greater simplicity of style and social sense in the massive ten-volume novel sequence, *Transfiguration* (1914–40), which won him the Stalin prize in 1942.

SERRANO, Francisco, Duke de la Torre, *ser-rah'nō* (1810–85), Spanish statesman, fought against the Carlists and, nominally a liberal, favoured by Isabella, played a conspicuous part in various ministries. Banished in 1866, he in 1868 drove out the queen, and was regent until the accession of Amadeus of Savoy (1870). He waged successful war against the Carlists in 1872 and 1874; and again regent (1874), resigned the power into the hands of Alfonso XII. See Life by Marqués de Villa-Urrutia (1932).

SERRES, Olivia. See OLIVE (PRINCESS).

SERTORIUS, Quintus (123–72 B.C.), Roman soldier, born in Nursia in the Sabine country, fought with Marius in Gaul (102 B.C.), supported him against Sulla, then led an adventurous life in Spain, where he headed a successful rising of natives and Roman refugees, holding out against Sulla's commanders for eight years till he was assassinated. See Life by A. Schulten (1926).

SERTÜRNER, Friedrich Wilhelm Adam (1783–1841), German chemist, born at Neuhaus near Paderborn, in 1805 isolated morphine from opium and proved that organic bases contained nitrogen.

SERVETUS, Michael, *-vay'-* (1511–53), Spanish theologian and physician, born at Tudela, worked largely in France and Switzerland. In *De Trinitatis Erroribus* (1531) and *Christianismi Restitutio* (1553) he denied the Trinity and the divinity of Christ; he escaped the Inquisition but was burnt by Calvin at Geneva for heresy. He studied medicine at Paris and discovered the pulmonary circulation of the blood. See Life by W. Osler (1910), and E. M. Wilson, *A History of Unitarianism* (1945).

SERVICE, Robert William (1874–1958), English-born Canadian poet, born at Preston, went to Canada, travelled as a reporter for the *Toronto Star*, served as ambulance driver in World War I and wrote popular verse, such as *Rhymes of a Rolling Stone* (1912) and *The Shooting of Dangerous Dan McGrew.* He also wrote novels, of which *Ploughman of the Moon* (1945) and *Harper of Heaven* (1948) are autobiographical.

SERVIUS TULLIUS (578–534 B.C.), 6th king of Rome, distributed all freeholders (for military purposes primarily) into tribes, classes and centuries, making property, not birth, the standard of citizenship. His reforms provoked patrician jealousy, and he was assassinated.

SESOSTRIS, or Senusrit, according to Greek legend an Egyptian monarch who invaded Libya, Arabia, Thrace and Scythia, subdued Ethiopia, placed a fleet on the Red Sea, and extended his dominions to India, but was possibly Sesostris I (*c.* 1980–1935 B.C.), II (*c.* 1906–1887 B.C.) and III (*c.* 1887–1849 B.C.) compounded into one heroic figure.

SESSIONS, Roger (1896–), American composer, born in Brooklyn, New York, studied under Ernest Bloch. From 1925 to 1933 he was in Europe, but later taught in the United States, becoming professor of Music at California University in 1945 and professor at Princeton University (1953–65). His compositions include five symphonies, a violin concerto, piano and chamber music, a one-act opera of Brecht's *The Trial of Lucellus* and a three-act opera, *Montezuma* (1959–63).

SETTLE, Elkanah (1648–1724), English dramatist, born at Dunstable, went from Oxford to London to make a living by his pen. In 1671 he made a hit by his tragedy of *Cambyses.* To annoy Dryden, Rochester got his *Empress of Morocco* played at Whitehall by the court lords and ladies. In *Absalam and Achitophel* Dryden scourged 'Doeg' with his scorn, and Settle speedily relapsed into obscurity.

SEURAT, Georges Pierre, *sæ-rah* (1859–91), French artist, born in Paris. He studied at the École des Beaux-Arts. In 1883 he painted *Une Baignade* (in the Tate Gallery, London) and in 1885–86 the famous *Un Dimanche d'été à la Grande Jatte* (at Chicago). All his works were painted according to his divisionist method, called by the critics pointillist, the entire picture being composed of tiny rectangles of pure colour, which merge together when viewed from a distance. The composition was also constructed architecturally according to scientific principles. His colour theories influenced Signac, Pissarro, Degas and Renoir, but his principal achievement was the marrying of an impressionist palette to classical composition. See studies by G. Seligmann (1947) and J. Rewald (1947), his *Paintings and Drawings,* edited by D. C. Rich (1958), and C. M. de Hauke: *Seurat et son œuvre* (1963).

SEVERINI, Gino, *say-vè-ree'nee* (1883–1966), Italian artist, born at Cortona. He studied in Rome and Paris and signed the first Futurist manifesto in 1910, associating with Balla and Boccioni, with whom he exhibited in Paris and London. After 1914 he reverted to a more representational style, which he used in fresco and mosaic work, particularly in a number of Swiss and Italian churches. From 1940 onwards he adopted a decorative cubist manner. His many publications include *Du cubisme au classicisme* (1921) and an autobiography *Tutta la vita di un pittore* (1946). See the monographs by J. Maritain (1930) and P. Courthion (1941).

SEVERN, Joseph (1793–1879), portrait and subject painter, the son of a Hoxton music master, about 1816 befriended Keats, whom he accompanied on his last journey to Rome in 1820. He was British consul in Rome (1861–1872). See books by William Sharp (1892), Lady Birkenhead (1943). His son, **Joseph Arthur Palliser** (1841–1931), who married Ruskin's cousin, was also an artist.

SEVERUS, (1) Lucius Septimius (146–211), Roman emperor, born near Leptis Magna in Africa, rose to be praetor in 178, and commander of the army in Pannonia and Illyria. After the murder of Pertinax (193) he was proclaimed emperor, marched upon Rome, utterly defeated his two rivals in 195 and 197, and between these dates made a glorious campaign in the East, and took Byzantium. In 198 he met with the most brilliant success in his campaign against the Parthians. He replaced the praetorian guard by a new guard drawn from the legions. At Rome in 202 he gave shows of unparalleled magnificence, and distributed extravagant largess. A rebellion in Britain drew him thither in 208, when he marched, it is said, to the extreme north of the island. To shield south Britain from the Meatae and Caledonians, he repaired Hadrian's wall and died soon after at Eboracum (York), February 4, 211. See also ALEXANDER SEVERUS.

(2) **Sulpicius.** See SULPICIUS.

SÉVIGNÉ, Madame de, *née* **Marie de Rabutin-Chantal,** *say-veen-yay* (1626–96), French writer, born at Paris, was early left an orphan and was carefully brought up by an uncle, the Abbé de Coulanges. She married the dissolute Marquis Henri de Sévigné (1644); but he was killed in a duel (1651). Henceforward, in the most brilliant court in the world, her thoughts were centred on her children Françoise Marguerite (b. 1646) and Charles (b. 1648). On the marriage of the former to the Comte de Grignan in 1669, she began the series of letters to her daughter which grew sadder as friend after friend passed away. She died at Grignan of smallpox, after nursing her daughter through a tedious illness. Madame de Sévigné's twenty-five years of letters reveal the inner history of the time in wonderful detail, but the most interesting thing in the whole 1600 (one-third letters to her from others) remains herself. She was religious without superstition; she had read widely and gained much from conversation. She possessed a solid understanding and strong good sense. But it needed the warm touch of affection to give her letters the freedom, the rapidity, the life of spoken words. See edition of her *Letters* ed. Hammersley (1955), and Lives by Miss Thackeray (1881), G. Boissier (1887; trans. 1882), E. Faguet (1910), M. Duclaux (1914), A. Hallays (1920), A. Tilley (1936).

SEWARD, (1) **Anna** (1747–1809), English poet, known as the 'Swan of Lichfield', born at Eyam Rectory, Derby, lived from ten at Lichfield, where her father, himself a poet, became a canon. He died in 1790, but she lived on in the bishop's palace, and wrote romantic poetry. Her 'Elegy on Captain Cook' (1780) was commended by Dr Johnson. Scott edited her works (1810). See Lives of 'the Swan' by E. V. Lucas (1909), M. Ashmun (1931) and H. Pearson (1936).

(2) **William Henry** (1801–72), American statesman, born at Florida, N.Y., May 16, graduated at Union College in 1820, and was admitted to the bar at Utica in 1822. In 1830 he was elected to the state senate, where he led the Whig opposition to the dominant democratic party. In 1838 and 1840 he was governor of New York State; in 1849 he was elected to the U.S. senate, and re-elected in 1855. In 1850, while urging the admission of California to the Union, he declared that the national domain was devoted to liberty by 'a higher law than the constitution'. He opposed the Compromise Bill of 1850, separated himself from those Whigs who followed President Fillmore in his pro-slavery policy, and on the formation of the Republican party became one of its leaders. In 1860 he was a candidate for the presidential nomination, but, failing, became Lincoln's secretary of state (1861–69). The Civil War rendered the foreign relations of the United States unusually delicate, especially in view of the attitude of France and Britain. In the '*Trent* affair' during the Civil War he advised that the Confederate envoys should be given up to England. He protested against the fitting out of the *Alabama* and similar vessels in British ports, and declared that the United States would claim indemnities. He supported President Johnson's reconstruction policy, thereby incurring much censure from his own party. In 1870–71 he made a tour round the world. See his Autobiography (1877), Life by his son (1895), Memoir by Baker in his *Works* (5 vols. 1853–84), and Welles, *Lincoln and Seward* (N.Y. 1874).

SEWELL, Anna (1820–78), British novelist, born in Yarmouth, was an invalid for most of her life. Her *Black Beauty* (1877), the story of a horse, written as a plea for the more humane treatment of animals, is perhaps the most famous fictional work about horses. See study by M. J. Baker (1956).

SEXTUS EMPIRICUS (fl. A.D. 200–250), Greek physician and philosophical sceptic, who lived at Alexandria and Athens, as physician was a representative of the Empirics, as philosopher the chief exponent of scepticism. In his two extant works—the *Hypotyposes* and *Adversus Mathematicos*—he left a prodigious battery of arguments against dogmatism in grammar, rhetoric, geometry, arithmetic, music, astrology, logic, physics, ethics. See Loeb Library edition, trans. R. G. Bury (1933–36).

SEYDLITZ, Friedrich Wilhelm, Baron von, *zīd'-* (1721–73), Prussian cavalry general, born at Kalkar, Cleve, served in the Silesian wars and so distinguished himself at Kolin (1757) that at Rossbach (1757) Frederick the Great promoted him over the heads of two generals to take charge of the cavalry, which under Seydlitz's brilliant charges won the battle practically without infantry. Seydlitz was wounded but won another victory at Zorndorf (1758) and covered the Prussian retreat at Hochkirch. Severely wounded at the defeat of Kunersdorf (1758), he did not return to the front until 1761, when, in command of both cavalry and infantry groups, he won the battle of Freyburg (1762).

SEYMOUR, an historic family, originally from St Maur in Normandy (hence the name), who obtained lands in Monmouthshire in the 13th century, and in the 14th at Hatch Beauchamp, Somerset, by marriage with an heiress of the Beauchamps. Important members are:

(1) **Algernon, 7th Duke of Somerset** (1684–1750), son of (2), who, in 1749, was created Earl of Northumberland, with remainder to his son-in-law, Sir Hugh Smithson, the ancestor of the present Percy line.

(2) **Charles, 6th Duke of Somerset** (1662–1748), known as the 'proud Duke of Somerset', held high posts under Charles II, William III and Anne. He married the heiress of the Percies.

(3) **Edward** (*c.* 1506–52), eldest son of (10), was successively created Viscount Beauchamp, Earl of Hertford, and Duke of Somerset, and, as Protector, played the leading part in the first half of the reign of Edward VI (q.v.). He defeated a Scottish army at Pinkie 1547, but was indicted by Warwick (Northumberland) and executed.

(4) **Edward** (1539–1621), son of (3), by a second marriage, created Earl of Hertford by Elizabeth, married the Lady Catherine Grey, sister of Lady Jane Grey—a marriage which cost him nine years' imprisonment and a fine of £15,000.

(5) **Sir Edward** (1695–1757), became 8th

Duke of Somerset on the death of (1); he was a descendant of (3) by his first marriage.

(6) **Francis, 3rd Marquis of Hertford** (1777–1842), grandson of (7), was the prototype of Thackeray's Marquis of Steyne.

(7) **Francis Seymour-Conway** (1719–94), cousin of (5), was, when the earldom became extinct, created Earl of Hertford in 1750, Marquis in 1793.

(8) **Frederick Beauchamp Paget.** See ALCESTER.

(9) **Jane** (*c.* 1509–37), became the third queen of Henry VIII and mother of Edward VI. Holbein painted her picture. She was daughter of (10).

(10) **Sir John** (*c.* 1476–1536), father of Jane Seymour, helped to suppress the Cornish insurrection in 1497, and accompanied Henry VIII to France.

(11) **Thomas** (*c.* 1508–49), fourth son of (10), created Lord Seymour of Sudeley, became lord high admiral of England and the second husband of Henry's widow (Catherine Parr). On her death, he wished to marry the Princess Elizabeth, but was arrested and executed for treason.

(12) **William** (1588–1660), grandson of (4), in 1621 became Earl of Hertford, secretly married Lady Arabella Stuart (1610), a cousin of James I; and subsequently played a conspicuous part in the Royalist cause (he defeated Waller at Lansdown and took Bristol in 1643), obtained a reversal of the Protector's attainder, and at the Restoration took his seat in the House of Lords as 3rd Duke of Somerset.

SEYSS-INQUART, Artur von, *sis-* (1892–1946), Austrian 'Quisling', was born in the Sudetenland, practised as a lawyer in Vienna and saw much of Schuschnigg. When the latter became chancellor in 1938, he took office under him, informing Hitler of every detail in Schuschnigg's life, in the hope of becoming Nazi chancellor of Austria after the 'Anschluss'. Instead, he was appointed commissioner for the Netherlands in 1940, where he ruthlessly recruited slave labour. In 1945, he was captured by the Canadians, tried at Nuremberg and executed for war crimes.

SFORZA, name of a celebrated Italian family founded by a peasant of the Romagna called Muzio Attendolo (1369–1424), who became a great *condottiere* or soldier of fortune, and received the name of Sforza ('Stormer'—i.e., of cities). Its most noteworthy members were:

(1) **Francesco** (1401–66), natural son of the above and father of (2) and (3), sold his sword to the highest bidder, fighting for or against the pope, Milan, Venice and Florence. From the Duke of Milan he obtained his daughter's hand and the succession to the duchy; and before his death had extended his power over Ancona, Pesaro, all Lombardy and Genoa. See C. M. Ady, *History of Milan under the Sforza* (1907).

(2) **Galeazzo Maria** (1444–76), son of (1), a competent ruler, although notorious for his debauchery and prodigality, was assassinated.

(3) **Ludovico,** called **Il Moro,** 'the Moor' (1451–1508), from 1480 became the real ruler of Milan, his nephew **Gian Galeazzo** (1476–1494), the rightful ruler, being reduced to a constitutional puppet. But, fearing an insurrection from the latter's friends, Ludovico called in the aid of the French (1494), who in 1499 drove him out, and he died a prisoner in France. He was a sound administrator and is best remembered as the patron of Leonardo da Vinci. See F. Malaguzzi-Valeri, *La Corte di Lodovico Il Moro* (1913–1923).

SFORZA, Carlo, Count (1873–1952), Italian statesman, born at Lucca, became minister of foreign affairs (1920–21) and negotiated the Rapallo treaty. A senator (1919–26) he became leader of the anti-Fascist opposition and from 1922 lived in Belgium and the United States (1940). See his *European Dictatorships* (1931), &c.

SGAMBATI, Giovanni (1841–1914), Italian composer and pianist, born in Rome, was a friend of Liszt. His compositions include two symphonies, a requiem and chamber and piano music.

SHACKLETON, Sir Ernest Henry (1874–1922), British explorer, born at Kilkee, Ireland. He was educated at Dulwich College, apprenticed in the Merchant Navy, and became a junior officer under Captain Robert Scott, on the *Discovery*, in the National Antarctic Expedition, 1901–03. In 1909, in command of another expedition, he reached a point 97 miles from the South Pole—at that time a southern record. While on another expedition, in 1915, his ship *Endeavour* was crushed in the ice. By sledges and boats Shackleton and his men reached Elephant Island, from where Shackleton and five others made a perilous voyage of 800 miles to South Georgia and organized relief for those on Elephant Island. He died at South Georgia while on a fourth Antarctic expedition, begun in 1920. He was knighted in 1909. See his own *The Heart of the Antarctic* (1909) and *South* (1919), and the biography by M. and J. Fisher (1957).

SHADWELL, Thomas (*c.* 1642–92), English dramatist, born at Broomhill House, Brandon, made a hit with the first of his thirteen comedies, *The Sullen Lovers* (1668). He also wrote three tragedies. Dryden, grossly assailed by him in the *Medal of John Bayes,* heaped deathless ridicule upon him in *MacFlecknoe* ('Shadwell never deviates into sense'), and as 'Og' in the second part of *Absalom and Achitophel.* His works (ed. in 5 vols. by Montague Summers, 1927) exhibit talent and comic force. He succeeded Dryden as laureate in 1689. See *Works,* ed. M. Summers (1927), and study by A. S. Borgman (1930).

SHAFTESBURY, (1) **Anthony Ashley Cooper, 1st Earl of** (1621–83), was born July 22, 1621, at Wimborne St Giles, Dorset, the seat of his mother's father, Sir Anthony Ashley (1551–1628), a clerk of the privy council. He was the elder son of John Cooper of Rockborne in Hampshire, who next year (1622) was created a baronet. As a gentleman commoner at Exeter College, Oxford, he 'not only obtained the good-will of the wiser and elder sort, but became the leader even of all the rough young men'. He left without a degree, and in 1639 married Margaret, daughter of the lord keeper Coventry. She died in 1649; and nine months later he married Lady Frances Cecil, the Earl of Exeter's sister, who died in 1654. In 1655 he married the pious Margaret Spencer, the Earl of Sunderland's sister, who survived him till 1693. By all three marriages he largely strengthened his family connections. Meanwhile in 1640 he had entered the Short Parliament for Tewkesbury, but he had not a seat in the Long. A Royalist colonel (1643) after ten months' service he went over to the parliament, and commanded their forces in Dorsetshire, then from 1645 to 1652 lived as a great country gentleman. In 1653 he entered the Barebones Parliament, and was appointed one of Cromwell's council of state, but from 1655 he was in opposition. He was one of the twelve commissioners sent to Breda to invite Charles II home, and a carriage accident on the way thither caused him that chronic internal abscess which in 1666 secured him a lifelong attendant and friend in Locke. He was made a privy councillor (1660), and next year Baron Ashley and chancellor of the Exchequer. He served on the trial of the regicides; supported the war with Holland; and after Clarendon's fall (1667) sided with Buckingham, with whom he formed one of the infamous Cabal, and like whom he was fooled as to the Catholic clauses in the secret treaty of Dover (1669–70). He seems to have opposed the 'stop of the exchequer' (1672), which yet he justified; that same year was made Earl of Shaftesbury and lord chancellor (he proved a most upright judge); but in 1673, espousing the popular Protestantism, supported the Test Bill, which broke up the Cabal. In October the Great Seal was demanded of him, and he ranged himself as a champion of toleration (for Dissenters only) and of national liberties. He opposed Danby's nonresistance Test Bill (1675), and in 1677, for his protest against a fifteen months' prorogation, was sent to the Tower, whence he was only released a year later on making a full submission. Though the 'Popish Plot' was not of his forging, he used that two years' terror (1678–80) with ruthless dexterity. Not even the Habeas Corpus Act, long known as Shaftesbury's Act, is a set-off against the judicial murder of Lord Stafford, his personal enemy. The fall of Danby was followed by his appointment as president of Temple's new privy council of thirty members (1679), and an attempt to exclude James from the succession, in favour of Shaftesbury's puppet, the bastard Monmouth. Shaftesbury now received his congé from the king, and driven to more extreme opposition, indicted James as a recusant (1680), and brought armed followers to the Oxford parliament (1681). In July 1681 he was again sent to the Tower for high treason, but the Middlesex Whig grand jury threw out the bill. Monmouth and Russell hung back from the open rebellion to which he urged them, and he fled to Holland in December 1682. On January 22, 1683, he died at Amsterdam. Transcendently clever, eloquent and winning, he yet stands condemned by the many talents committed to him; self was the dominant principle to which alone he was true. He was the author of party government, ever ready to make capital out of religious animosities, 'atrocities', perjuries, forgeries, anything. It is doubtful whether he was the pure, highminded and great statesman that Christie would make him, or, what Charles pronounced him, 'the wickedest dog in England'. See Dryden's *Absalom and Achitophel* and *Medal* (1681), part iii of Butler's *Hudibras* (1678), Life by L. F. Brown (1933) and other works cited at LOCKE and CHARLES II.

(2) **Anthony Ashley Cooper, 3rd Earl of** (1671–1713), English philosopher, grandson of (1), was born in London. Locke superintended his early education at Clapham; he spent three years at Winchester and three more in travel. He sat as a Whig for Poole in 1695–98, but ill-health drove him from politics to literature. On his two visits to Holland (1698–99 and 1703–04) he formed friendships with Beyle and Le Clerc. He succeeded to the earldom in 1699 and in 1711 removed to Naples, where he died. His somewhat overfine writings were all, with one exception, published after 1708, and were collected as *Characteristics of Men, Manners, Opinions, Times* (1711, enlarged 1714). Here he expounded the system immortalized in the *Essay on Man*, and argued that ridicule is the test of truth, that man possesses a moral sense, and that everything in the world is for the best. He found a follower in Hutcheson (q.v.). While at home he was attacked as a deist; abroad he attracted the attention of Leibnitz, Voltaire, Diderot, Lessing and Herder. See Lives by Rand (1900) and R. L. Brett (1951), study by T. Fowler (1882), and J. Bonar, *Moral Sense* (1930); also his *Letters*.

(3) **Anthony Ashley Cooper, 7th Earl of** (1801–85), English factory reformer and philanthropist, born in London, educated at Harrow and Christ Church, Oxford, entered parliament in 1826. He succeeded to the peerage in 1851. As Lord Ashley, he undertook the leadership of the factory reform movement in 1832 and piloted successive factory acts (1847, 1850) through the House, regulating conditions in the coal-mines and the provision of lodging-houses for the poor (1851). His Coal Mines Act (1842) prohibited underground employment of women and of children under thirteen. He was chairman of the Ragged Schools Union for 40 years, assisted Florence Nightingale in her schemes for army welfare and took an interest in missionary work. Strongly evangelical, he opposed radicalism although he worked with the trade unions for factory reforms. See study by J. L. and L. B. Hammond (1939).

SHAGALL. See CHAGALL.

SHAH JAHAN (1592–1666), 5th of the Mogul Emperors of Delhi, was from 1624 in revolt against his father, Jehangir, but on his death (1627) succeeded him. The chief events of his reign were a war in the Deccan, ending in the destruction of the kingdom of Ahmadnagar (1636) and the subjugation (1636) of Bijapur and Golconda; an attack on the Uzbegs of Balkh (1645–47); unsuccessful attempts to recover Kandahar from the Persians (1637, 1647–53); and a second successful war in the Deccan (1655). In 1658 the emperor fell ill, and was held prisoner by his son Aurungzebe till his death. He was a just and an able ruler; the magnificence of his court was unequalled; and he left buildings such as the Taj Mahal, the tomb of his beloved Mumtaz Mahal and the 'pearl mosque' in the Red Fort at Agra and the palace and great mosque at Delhi. See Life by B. P. Sakasena (1932).

SHAHN, Ben (1898–1969), American painter, born in Kaunas, Lithuania, emigrated with his parents to New York, and studied painting in night school. In 1922 he visited the European art centres and came under the influence of Rouault. His didactic pictorial commentaries on contemporary events such as his 23 satirical gouache paintings on the trial of Sacco and Vanzetti (1932) and the 15 paintings on Tom Mooney, the Labour leader (1933), *Death of a Miner* (1947) and the precarious world situation caught in the frightening confidence of a team of trick cyclists in *Epoch* (1950; Philadelphia) earned him the title of 'American Hogarth'. He was the first painter to deliver the Charles Eliot Norton Lectures at Harvard, published as *The Shape of Content* (1958). See study by Soby (1947).

SHAIRP, John Campbell (1819–85), Scottish poet, born at Houston House, West Lothian. He became deputy professor (1857), professor of Latin (1861) and principal (1868) of St Andrews, and in 1877 and 1882 he was appointed professor of Poetry at Oxford. Strong poetic instincts and a keen and kindly critical faculty appear in his writings, which include *Kilmahoe and Other Poems* (1864), *Studies in Poetry and Philosophy* (1868) and *Burns* (1879). See Knight's *Shairp and his Friends* (1888).

SHAKESPEARE, William (1564–1616), English dramatist and poet, was born at Stratford-on-Avon in April 1564, the son of John Shakespeare, a glover, and of his wife, Mary Arden, who came of prosperous farming stock. William was the eldest of three sons; there were four daughters, only one of whom survived the poet. Modern scholarship has uncovered a good deal more about his upbringing and life than was known even to so late a biographer as Sidney Lee, whose revised Life of Shakespeare appeared in 1915. The first *Life*, by Nicholas Rowe, was prefixed to his edition of the works (1709); this was followed by Aubrey's account of Shakespeare in his *Brief Lives* (written in the 17th century, but not printed till 1813). Between them Rowe and Aubrey gave currency to various rumours somewhat damaging to Shakespeare's start in life. Rowe was the more culpable for he underrated the position of John Shakespeare in Stratford—he was really a man of some civic consequence and not a butcher—set going the legend that the boy was removed from the 'Free-school' at a tender age and so 'had no knowledge of the writings of the ancient poets' (which then meant total ignorance) and that after an early marriage he 'fell into ill company'. The deer-stealing episode follows, with Shakespeare's flight to London to avoid prosecution. Aubrey repeated some of this, but corrected the story in one important point, viz., he had heard from a Mr Beeston that the poet had enough education to become a schoolmaster. The classical allusions and quotations in the early plays would seem to support this notion, which was developed by Dr J. S. Smart in his *Shakespeare Truth and Tradition* (1928) and has since then been regarded as at least plausible. Aubrey's guess that Shakespeare came to London in 1585 is also plausible. His wife, Anne Hathaway, of good farming stock, had borne him a daughter, Susanna, in 1583, and the twins Hamnet and Judith two years later. The poet may well have sought the city for a livelihood. Since the first published reference to him (Greene's attack in *A Groat's-worth of Witte*) is in 1592, there is a gap variously filled in by scholars, the most conjectural view being that of Professor Peter Alexander (*A Shakespeare Primer*, 1951), viz., that having certainly written the third part of *Henry VI*, Shakespeare may be credited with having written also the first two parts of that trilogy and perhaps the early comedies, *Two Gentlemen of Verona* and the *Comedy of Errors*. *Love's Labour's Lost*, however, cannot be earlier than 1592. The traditional view that 1591 is the start of his dramatic career is, however, still held by critics of the standing of E. K. Chambers, Dover Wilson and others. During the years 1592–94, when the theatres were closed for the plague, Shakespeare wrote his erotic poems 'Venus and Adonis' and 'The Rape of Lucrece', 1593 and 1594 respectively, both dedicated to the Earl of Southampton, the ideal Renaissance man, soldier and scholar, who may figure as the friend in the 'drama' of the sonnets. They illustrate the pagan side of the Renaissance with its sensual mythological imagery. The sonnets present an intractable problem. They were not published till 1609, but were known by 1598, when Francis Meres talks of 'his sugred sonnets among his private friends'. There are two main groups of sonnets—1 to 126 addressed to a fair young man, and 127 to 154 addressed to a 'dark lady' who holds both the young man and the poet in thrall. The young man's suit is preferred (there is also a rival poet), hence self-loathing on the part of the poet. Who these people are—we cannot dismiss them as fictitious—has provided an exercise in detection for numerous critics. The favourite guess is that the young man ('Mr W. H.' in the dedication) is Henry Wriothesley, Earl of Southampton, to whom the poems were dedicated; but it may be William Herbert, Earl of Pembroke, the lover of Mary Fitton who is not the 'Dark Lady of the Sonnets', since she was fair. It is the poetry of the sequence which enchants us, the eloquent discourse and unfailing verbal melody, the amazing variety of tone from serene acceptance to towering passion, and the lovely imagery. The themes are those current at the Renaissance—the idea of Beauty, the eternizing power of the poet, the theme of Identity. But Shakespeare makes them his own. The first evidence of Shakespeare's association with the stage is the Treasurer's order to pay three leading members of the Chamberlain's company of players—William Kemp, William Shakespeare and Richard Burbage—for two performances in the Christmas week, 1594. The Chamberlain's men had previously acted as the servants of Lord Strange. Shakespeare had apparently been associated with a rival company, Lord Pembroke's men, for four of his early plays, printed in garbled versions in 1594–95, profess to have been acted by that company. On the failure of Pembroke's men (owing to the enforced idleness of the plague years) he transferred to the Chamberlain's company, later 'the King's men', taking with him the doubtful *Titus Andronicus*, *The Taming of the Shrew* and an early reputed version of *Hamlet*. Their playhouse was the Theatre (built and owned by the father of the tragic actor Richard Burbage) down to 1597, when the expiry of the lease forced them to seek new quarters. The expense of building the new structure on the south bank of the river, the famous Globe, probably induced the Burbages to take in as partners five of the company, of whom Shakespeare was one. He was now on the way not only to fame but to the financial rewards which do not always go with fame. He lived modestly at the house of a Huguenot refugee in Silver Street from about 1602 to 1606 and then shifted to the south side near the Globe. Dr Leslie Hotson disclosed two facts which enhance our view of the poet in London society—the Thos. Russell, Esq., who acted as executor to his will was familiar with the great world, and William Johnson who witnessed a mortgage for Shakespeare was the host of the Mermaid. Slender facts to build on, but they indicate what we expect on other grounds—that he was known to scholars and soldiers and was equally at home among the wits of the Mermaid. His preparations for retirement to Stratford—purchasing arable land and buying up tithes—show that he was the successful manager anxious to figure as a man of consequence in his native place. Russell was near him there and the well-known physician, Dr Hall, married his elder daughter Susanna. It is interesting to note that he entertained Ben Jonson and Drayton at New Place, his Stratford house. Families could not count then on generations. Susanna, the poet's heir, had a daughter, Elizabeth, who survived to 1670, but Judith's three daughters died childless. The only living descendants must trace their lineage through Joan Hart, the poet's married sister. The only reference to his wife, Anne Hathaway, after the christening of the twins in 1595, is as a beneficiary of his will (' my second-best bed with the furniture ') which good Shakespearians will not take as derisory. An enormous amount of investigation on the authorship, text and chronology of the plays marks the modern era of Shakespeare scholarship. In addition, works like Dover Wilson's *Life in Shakespeare's England* (1911) and the tercentenary *Shakespeare's England* (1916) greatly extend our knowledge of the age or of particular aspects of it. Intimate study of the Elizabethan stage, including audience reaction, the players' companies, &c., has also yielded valuable results. Authorship is still a controversial subject in respect of certain plays such as *Titus Andronicus*, *Two Noble Kinsmen*, *Henry VI*, part I, and of Shakespeare's part in *Timan of Athens*, *Pericles* and *Henry VIII* The question of text is one of great difficulty, involving, for example, such differences as exist between the first and second Quarto editions of *Hamlet* and between these and the Folio version of 1623. This has entailed among other things an examination of the complicated business of publication in that era. In a series of studies from 1909 onwards A. W. Pollard, employing the test of ' good ' and ' bad ' quartos, assigned prior authority to the quartos. His *Shakespeare's Fight with the Pirates* (1917) became a classic. His example was followed by Dover Wilson in his editing of the New Cambridge Shakespeare. The authority of the Folio of 1623 was thus weakened because its editors, Heminge and Condell, had inveighed against ' diverse stolne and surreptitious copies ', claiming that they had direct access to Shakespeare's MSS., whereas they retained the text of certain ' good ' quartos unchanged. They also included plays which Shakespeare certainly did not write. The whole matter is too complicated for discussion here, but we can say that to the pioneers of ' scientific ' textual criticism—to W. W. Greg (*Principles of Emendation*, 1918); to A. W. Pollard for the work referred to above and for the series which he edited with Dover Wilson, *Shakespeare Problems*; to Professor Peter Alexander for the third volume of that series in which he proved Shakespeare's authorship of 2 and 3 *Henry VI*, we owe a vastly improved text. The most outstanding disciple of these pioneers is Prof. George Duthie with his *The Bad Quarto of Hamlet* (1941) and his *King Lear* (1949). With regard to appreciations of Shakespeare's work, Dr Johnson's famous preface, Morgann's essay on Falstaff, Coleridge's lectures on Shakespeare and A.C. Bradley's *Shakespearian Tragedy* were early highlights. But of more modern interpretation there has been a great deal, most of it controversial. The main difference is between the idealists or traditionalists who write as if Shakespeare could not go wrong and who gloss over his contradictions, and the realists who explain his inconsistencies of fact and characterization by the conditions in which he worked. The American critic Prof. Stoll and the German Prof. Lewin Schücking were the disruptive influences here, but their work was a salutary check to the 'idealism' of which Alexander's admirable *A Shakespeare Primer* is not free and of which Dover Wilson's *What Happened in Hamlet*—a best seller in literary detective work—is a notable example. Another important method of interpretation, of which G. Wilson Knight's *Wheel of Fire* and *The Imperial Theme* (1931) are eloquent examples, proceeds by an examination of the imagery and symbolism of the plays. This method gives rather much scope for fancy, but Knight's work adds another dimension to Shakespearean study. A word on the chronology of the plays. We have long since rejected Dowden's sentimental categories (*Shakespeare's Mind and Art*, 1883), but we recognize phases in Shakespeare's development. His earliest period closes in 1594 when we may assume he had written the *Henry VI* trilogy, *Titus Andronicus* (if it was his), *The Taming of the Shrew*, and perhaps an early *Hamlet*. Garbled versions of these (except for *Titus Andronicus* which is a 'good' text) appeared in the Stationers' registers (1594–95). We may also conjecture that to this period belong the comedies *Two Gentlemen of Verona*, *Comedy of Errors* and *Love's Labour's Lost*. Francis Mere's *Palladis Tamia* (1598) lists six comedies and six tragedies and gives a clue (apart from other evidence) to the plays of the second period, that is 1594–99. In default of genuine tragedies (*Romeo and Juliet* is here however), Meres ekes out with four histories, Richard II, Richard III, Henry IV and King John. For comedy he lists '*Gentlemen of Verona*, his *Errors*, his *Love's Labour's Lost*, his *Midsummer's Night Dreame* and his *Merchant of Venice*'. We may assign *Richard II* and *Merchant of Venice* to 1595; *Romeo and Juliet* and *Midsummer Night's Dream* to 1596 and the two parts of *Henry IV* and *Merry Wives of Windsor* to 1597; *Much Ado About Nothing* and *As You Like it* to 1598 and *Henry V* to 1599. The third period, 1599–1608, opens with *Julius Caesar* (1599), and includes a final *Hamlet*, *Othello*, *Lear*, *Macbeth*, *Antony and Cleopatra*, *Timon of Athens* and the 'dark' comedies— *All's Well that Ends Well*, *Measure for Measure* and *Troilus and Cressida*. *Cymbeline*, *A Winter's Tale* and *The Tempest* and his part in *Henry VIII* are the work of his last period, 1609–13. If we did not realize that these plays represent the highest flight of genius, we might think the list tedious. To give some slight idea of their contents—the histories were his prentice work in tragedy. The earlier cycle, *Henry VI* to *Richard III* followed the line of history which is rarely conclusive in the way tragedy should be. These histories are therefore episodic and relieved only by the patriotism and comic matter which his audience came to expect. They are, however, a textbook of political, often cynical, wisdom. In the second cycle, from *Richard II* onward, history begins to provide a background for the conflict in the mind of the 'hero', but the two Richards being weak or vicious characters, those plays resemble more the 'falls of princes' than true tragedies. The theme of 'This England', however, appears in Gaunt's speech in *Richard II*, culminates in *Henry V*, and has its final echo in Cranmer's speech over Elizabeth's cradle in *Henry VIII*, which is almost Shakespeare's last word to the world. In the *Henry IV-Henry V* trilogy he often displays a ruthlessness to certain characters—the rejection of Falstaff is the classic instance—which also appears in the comedies along with a complacency towards evil-doers at the close and this is not altogether to be excused by the story he worked on. The early comedies show a tiro's preference for symmetry in character and situation resulting in a certain lifelessness. *Midsummer Night's Dream* is a beautiful fantasy relieved by the fun of the rustics and enchantingly lyrical in tone. Equally lyrical and pictorial, *As You Like It* has a deeper vein of thought—the theme being the contrast between the corrupt court and country innocence—not so innocent after all. In Jaques we have the type (fashionable just then) Malcontent of which Hamlet is the splendid realization. The 'dark' comedies—*All's Well*, *Measure for Measure* and *Troilus*—prepare us for the great tragedies but with this difference that the ugly cynicism of the former gives place to the serenity of high tragedy which plumbs the depths but also purges the soul. We should resist the temptation to explain the sombre nature of these comedies by reference to personal loss or frustration on Shakespeare's part, the collapse of Essex's party to which the poet may have been sympathetic, or the supposed betrayal of his passion in the drama of the sonnets. Better, perhaps, refer it to the *zeitgeist* and the example of his contemporaries Ben Jonson and Middleton. In the great tragedies every stop of the mighty organ is out. All the passions which destroy men and empires are explored. Stoll thought it a mistake to impose the Aristotelian formula for tragedy on Shakespeare—that is the grave flaw in a hero having tragic consequences. The formula fits Othello well enough, but Hamlet leaves us puzzled; no explanation of his conduct is convincing—hence T. S. Eliot's denigration. The 'flaw' in *Lear*, as shown in the first two scenes, is ludicrously insufficient to bear the tremendous passion which develops. In the Roman plays—*Julius Caesar*, *Antony and Cleopatra*, *Coriolanus*—the human passions are involved in the ruin of the world. The first two are panoramic in the scope of the scene. Perhaps the strict adherence to the unities of time and place in *The Tempest* is Shakespeare's reply to Jonson's ridicule of such romantic extravagance. That he returned to Romance in his last period has been taken as a sign of world weariness, which calls for forgiveness and reconciliation. That is too simple. Prospero's breaking of his magic wand and the ensuing reconciliations do not dispose of evil in the heart of man. On the contrary, *The Tempest* has inspired such meditations on the human situation as Browning's 'Caliban upon Setebos' and W. H. Auden's 'The Sea and the Mirror'. But one must not think of Shakespeare after 1600 as having quite divested himself of his native gaiety. *Twelfth Night* belongs to the same year as *Hamlet*, that is 1601. For Bacon and other anti-Stratford theories see R. C. Churchill, *Shakespeare and His Betters* (1958). If Shakespeare took little interest in the publication of his plays, posterity has made up for it. Curiously the 17th century contented itself with reprints of the great Folio of 1623 (1632, 1663–64 and 1685). The 18th century has nine new editions to its credit and scholarship begins to appear with Rowe's edition (with a Life) in 1709. Between that and Malone's critical edition (1790), which first discussed the chronology on modern lines, we have Pope's edition (1726), with its happy guesses at difficult passages; Theobald's improved text; and Dr Johnson's edition (1765), with its monumental preface. Variorum editions, involving a closer scrutiny of the text, culminated in Furness's great Variorum edition from 1871 onwards. Various one-volume and school texts heralded a new era of publication—Sir Sidney Lee's Caxton Shakespeare and the old Arden Shakespeare, with its agreeable format, were gradually ousted by the New (Cambridge) edition edited by Quiller-Couch and J. Dover Wilson (begun 1921) and this, now completed, has a friendly rival in the new Arden edition begun after the war and edited by Ellis-Fermor. The standard Life is by E. K. Chambers (1930, revised 1951); but see also Dr J. S. Smart's *Shakespeare Truth and Tradition* (1928), and P. Alexander's *Shakespeare's Life and Art* (1939). For sources see *Narrative and Dramatic Sources* (ed. Bullough, 1957). For criticism Nichol Smith, *Eighteenth Century Essays on Shakespeare*; Granville-Barker, *Prefaces to Shakespeare's Plays*; and C. H. Herford's *A Sketch of Recent Shakespearian Investigation* (1923). For the stage see Chambers, *Elizabethan Stage* (1923). See also other works by the above-mentioned authors, as well as various books on aspects of Shakespeare by F. S. Boas, Ivor Brown, J. R. Brown, L. B. Campbell, L. C. Knights, K. Muir, A. L. Rowse, E. M. Tillyard and P. A. Traversi.

SHALIAPIN. See CHALIAPIN.

SHAMYL, i.e., **Samuel** (1797–1871), leader of the tribes in the Caucasus in their thirty years' struggle against Russia, became a Sufi mullah or priest, and strove to end the tribal feuds. He was one of the foremost in the defence of Himry against the Russians in 1831, in 1834 was chosen head of the Lesghians, and by abandoning open warfare for surprises, ambuscades, &c., secured numerous successes for the mountaineers. In 1839, and again in 1849, he escaped from the stronghold of Achulgo after the Russians had made themselves masters of it, to continue preaching a holy war against the infidels. The Russians were completely baffled, their armies sometimes disastrously beaten, though Shamyl began to lose ground. During the Crimean war the allies supplied him with money and arms, but after peace was signed the Russians compelled the submission of the Caucasus. On April 12, 1859, Shamyl's chief stronghold, Weden, was taken. For several months he was hunted till surprised, and after a desperate resistance captured.

SHAPLEY, Harlow (1885–1972), American astrophysicist, born at Nashville, Tenn., worked at the Mount Wilson observatory from 1914 and was director of Harvard Univ. Observatory (1921–52). He demonstrated that the Milky Way is much larger than had been supposed, and that the Solar System is located on the Galaxy's edge, not at its centre. He has done notable work on photometry and spectroscopy and his writings include *Star Clusters* (1930), *Galaxies* (1943), *Climatic Changes* (1954) and *The Vew from a Distant Star* (1963).

SHARP, (1) **Abraham** (1653–1742), English astronomer, in 1684–91 assisted Flamsteed at Greenwich Observatory in constructing the large mural arc, &c. He published tables of logarithms and *Geometry Improved* (1717). See life by Ludworth (1889).

(2) **Cecil James** (1859–1924), English collector of folk songs (of which he published numerous collections) and folk dances, was born in London, and was principal of the Hampstead Conservatoire in 1896–1905. His work is commemorated by Cecil Sharp House, the headquarters of the English Folk Dance (founded by him in 1911) and Song Societies. See Life by A. H. Fox-Strangways (1933).

(3) **Granville** (1735–1813), English abolitionist, born at Durham, was apprenticed to a London linen-draper, in 1758 got a post in the Ordnance department, but resigned in 1776 through sympathy with America. He wrote many philological, legal, political and theological pamphlets; but his principal labours were for the Negro. He defended the Negro James Sommersett or Somerset, securing the decision (1772) that as soon as a slave touches English soil he becomes free; and worked with Clarkson for the abolition of Negro slavery. His idea of a colony for freed slaves at Sierra Leone was put into practice in 1787. He was also active in many religious associations, including the British and Foreign Bible Society (1804), and wrote on New Testament scholarship. See Memoirs by P. Hoare (1820), and study by E. C. P. Lascelles (1928).

(4) **James** (1613–79), Scottish divine, born at Banff, May 4, studied for the church at King's College, Aberdeen (1633–1637). In 1651–52 he was taken prisoner to London with some other ministers; and in 1657 he was chosen by the more moderate party in the church to plead their cause before Cromwell. Sent by Monk to Breda, he had several interviews with Charles II (1660). His correspondence for some months after his return from Holland is full of apprehensions of Prelacy; but its perfidy stands revealed in his letter of May 21, 1661, to Middleton, which proves that he was then in hearty co-operation with Clarendon and the English bishops for the re-establishment of Episcopacy in Scotland. The bribe was a great one, for in December he was consecrated Archbishop of St Andrews. The dexterous tool of Middleton or Lauderdale, an oppressor of those he had betrayed, he soon became an object of popular detestation and of contempt to his employers. On May 3, 1679, twelve Covenanters (see JOHN BALFOUR and HACKSTON) dragged him from his coach on Magus Muir and hacked him to death. See Life by T. Stephen and O. Airy, Lauderdale Papers (1884).

(5) **William** (1749–1824), English engraver, born in London, a businessman in the City, executed plates after Guido, West, Trumbull and Reynolds. He was a friend of Thomas Paine and Horne Tooke. See Life by W. S. Baker (1875).

(6) **William** (1855–1905), Scottish writer, born at Paisley, settled in London 1879, and published *Earth's Voices* (1884). He wrote books on contemporary English, French and German poets, but is chiefly remembered as the author of the remarkable series of Celtic —or neo-Celtic—tales and romances by ' Fiona Macleod '—a pseudonym he systematically refused to acknowledge. They include

Pharais (1894), *The Mountain Lovers* and *The Sin-Eater* (1895), *The Immortal Hour* (1900), &c. The latter, a verse play set to music, had a great success in London during the 1920s. See Memoir by his wife (1910).

SHARPE, Charles Kirkpatrick (1781–1851), Scottish antiquarian, born at Hoddam Castle, Dumfries, contributed two original ballads to Scott's *Minstrelsy*, and edited club books, but is chiefly remembered by his correspondence (2 vols. 1888).

SHARPEY-SCHAFER, Sir Edward (1850–1935), English physiologist, born at Hornsey, educated at University College, London, was professor there (1883–99) and at Edinburgh (1899–1933). Known especially for his researches on muscular contraction, he devised the prone-pressure method of artificial respiration.

SHASTRI, Lal Bahadour (1904–66), Indian politician, born in Benares, the son of a clerk in Nehru's father's law office, joined Gandhi's independence movement at 16 and was seven times imprisoned by the British. He excelled as a Congress Party official and politician in the United Provinces and joined Nehru's cabinet in 1952 as minister for the railways, becoming minister of transport (1957) and of commerce (1958) and home secretary (1960). Under the Kamaraj plan to invigorate the Congress Party at ' grass roots ' level he resigned with other cabinet ministers in 1963 but was recalled by Nehru in 1964, after the latter's stroke, as minister without portfolio, and succeeded him as prime minister in 1964. He died suddenly of a heart attack in 1966 while in Tashkent, U.S.S.R., for discussions on the India-Pakistan dispute.

SHAW, (1) George Bernard (1856–1950), Irish dramatist, essayist, critic and pamphleteer, was born of Irish Protestant parents in Dublin. His mother established herself as a singing-teacher both in Dublin and later in London, and from her he inherited strength of character and the great love and knowledge of music so influential in his life and work. After short and unhappy periods at various schools, he entered in 1871 a firm of land-agents, disliked office routine, and left Ireland for good to follow his mother and sister Lucy, a musical-comedy actress, to London. His literary life had already begun in 1875 with a letter to the press (henceforth one of his favourite means of expression), shrewdly analysing the effect on individuals of sudden conversion by the American evangelists, Moody and Sankey. In London his early years were a long period of struggle and impoverishment, and of the five novels he wrote between 1879 and 1883, the best of which are probably *Love Among the Artists* and *Cashel Byron's Profession*, all were rejected by the more reputable publishers. But in them is already to be found, besides some striking character studies and much originality of thought, glimmerings of the supple and virile Shavian style to be more fully developed after several years of experience. An encounter (1882) with Henry George and the reading of Karl Marx turned his thoughts towards Socialism, and while any direct propagation of it is absent from his plays, his faith in it and a ' kindly dislike ' (if not dread) of capitalist society form the backbone of all his work. Political and economic understanding stood him in good stead as a local government councillor in Saint Pancras (1897–1903) and also on the executive committee of the small but influential Fabian Society, to which he devoted himself selflessly for many years (1884–1911) and for which he edited *Fabian Essays* (1889) and wrote many well-known socialist tracts. Journalism provided another lively platform for him, and it was as ' Corno di Bassetto ', music critic for the new *Star* newspaper (1888–90), that he made his first indelible impact on the intellectual and social consciousness of his time. In this and in his later music criticism for *The World* (1890–94) and, above all, in his dramatic criticism for Frank Harris's *Saturday Review* (1895–98), he was in fact attempting, as De Quincey said of Wordsworth, to create the taste by which he was to be appreciated. To this period also belong *The Quintessence of Ibsenism* (1891) and *The Perfect Wagnerite* (1898), tributes to fellow ' artist-philosophers ' who, together with Bunyan, Dickens, Samuel Butler and Mozart, had acknowledged influence on his work. The rest of Shaw's life, especially after his marriage (1898) to the Irish heiress Charlotte Payne-Townshend, is mainly the history of his plays. His first, *Widowers' Houses*, was begun in 1885 in collaboration with his friend William Archer, but was finished independently in 1892 as the result of the challenge he felt to produce the newer drama of ideas he had been advocating. Into the earliest plays, which also include *Mrs Warren's Profession*, *Arms and the Man* and *Candida* (one of the first in a long series of remarkable female portraiture), comes already the favourite Shavian theme of conversion—from dead system and outworn morality towards a more creatively vital approach to life—and this is further developed in *Three Plays for Puritans*: *The Devil's Disciple*, *Caesar and Cleopatra*, and *Captain Brassbound's Conversion*. His long correspondence with the famous Lyceum actress, Ellen Terry, was also at its peak during these years. At last Shaw was becoming more widely known, first of all in the United States and on the Continent, and then, with the important advent of the playwright-producer-actor, Harley Granville-Barker, in England itself, especially after the epoch-making Vedrenne-Barker Court Theatre season of 1904–07. This had been preceded by one of Shaw's greatest philosophical comedies, *Man and Superman* (1902), in which, in quest of a purer religious approach to life, Shaw advocated through his Don Juan the importance of man's unceasing creative evolutionary urge for world-betterment as well as for his own self-improvement. Other notable plays from the early part of the century are *John Bull's Other Island* (1904), *Major Barbara* (1905), *The Doctor's Dilemma* (1906), and two uniquely Shavian discussion plays, *Getting Married* (1908) and *Misalliance* (1910). They further display Shaw's increasing control of his medium and the wide range of his subject matter (from politics and statecraft to family life, prostitution and vaccination). Before the Joint Committee on Stage Censorship in 1909 he proudly proclaimed himself as 'immoralist and heretic', and insisted on the civilized necessity for toleration and complete freedom of thought. Just before World War I came two of his most delightful plays: *Androcles and the Lion*, a 'religious pantomime', and *Pygmalion*, an 'anti-romantic' comedy of phonetics (adapted as a highly successful musical play, *My Fair Lady* (1956), filmed in 1964). During the war, though he later toured the Front at official invitation, he called forth controversy and recrimination with his *Common Sense About the War*, one of the most provocative and fearless documents ever written. After the war followed three of his very greatest dramas in near succession: *Heartbreak House* (1919), an attempt to analyse in an English Chehovian social environment the causes of present moral and political discontents; *Back to Methuselah* (1921), five plays in one, in which Shaw conducted a not altogether successful dramatic excursion from the Garden of Eden to 'As Far as Thought Can Reach'; and *Saint Joan* (1923), in which Shaw's essentially religious nature, his genius for characterization (above all of saintly but very human women), and his powers of dramatic argument are most abundantly revealed. In 1925 Shaw was awarded the Nobel prize for literature, but donated the money to inaugurate the Anglo-Swedish Literary Foundation. In 1931 he visited Russia, and during the 30's made other long tours, including a world one with Mrs Shaw in 1932, during which he gave a memorable address on Political Economy in the Metropolitan Opera House, New York. Greater perhaps than any of the plays written during the last years of his life are the two prose works: *The Intelligent Woman's Guide to Socialism and Capitalism* (1928), one of the most lucid introductions to its subjects, and *The Black Girl in Search of God* (1932), a modern *Pilgrim's Progress*. The later plays, except for *The Apple Cart* (1929), have scarcely received adequate public stage presentation, but they continue to preach the stern yet invigorating Shavian morality of individual responsibility, self-discipline, heroic effort without thought of reward or 'atonement', and the utmost integrity. Plays such as *Too True to Be Good* (1932) and *The Simpleton of the Unexpected Isles* (1934) also show signs of sounding a newer and even more experimental dramatic note altogether. Shaw died at the age of 94 on November 2, 1950. In spite of some decline in his personal popularity in Britain after his death, the interest in his work now seems to be increasing and universal. His plays, prefaces and essays, as published in the Standard Edition of his work (Constable & Co. Ltd.), take up 35 substantial volumes, and the number of books about him is considerable—see those by G. K. Chesterton (1910, new ed. 1935), A. Henderson (1911), H. Pearson (1942), E. R. Bentley (1947, new ed. 1967), C. E. M. Joad (1949), D. McCarthy (1951) and St John Ervine (1956).

(2) **Henry Wheeler.** See BILLINGS (1).

(3) **Jack** (1780–1815), English pugilist of prodigious strength who, serving in the Life Guards, fell at Waterloo, first killing ten cuirassiers.

(4) **Martin** (1876–1958), English composer, born in London, studied under Stanford at the Royal College of Music, composed the ballad opera, *Mr Pepys* (1926), with Clifford Bax, set T. S. Eliot's poems to music, but is best known for his songs and as co-editor with his brother, **Geoffrey Turton** (1879–1943), the church musician, of national song-books, and with Vaughan Williams of *Songs of Praise* and the *Oxford Carol Book*. See his autobiography, *Up to Now* (1929).

(5) **Richard Norman** (1831–1912), English architect in London, born in Edinburgh, was a leader of the trend away from Victorian styles back to traditional Georgian designs, as in Swan House, Chelsea, New Scotland Yard (1888), the Gaiety Theatre, Aldwych (1902; now demolished), and the Piccadilly Hotel (1905). See Life by R. Blomfield (1940).

(6) **Sir William Napier** (1854–1945), English meteorologist, born in Birmingham, was 16th wrangler at Cambridge in 1876 and in 1877 was elected fellow of Emmanuel College and became assistant director of the Cavendish Laboratory. He was director of the Meteorological office, London (1907–20), and from 1918 scientific adviser to the government. He became professor of the Royal College of Science in 1920. In his *Life History of Surface Air Currents* (1906) he established with Lempfert the 'polar front' theory of cyclones propounded by Bjerknes (q.v.). In 1915 he was knighted and received the Royal Medal of the Royal Society (1923). His *Manual of Meteorology* (1919–31) became a standard work.

SHAW-LEFEVRE, *-le-fee'ver*, (1) **Charles, 1st Viscount Eversley** (1794–1888), English Liberal politician, was called to the bar in 1819, in 1830 entered parliament, and was speaker 1839–57, being then made a peer.

(2) **George John, Baron Eversley** (1832–1928), English Liberal politician, born in London, served in Liberal ministries (1881–1884, 1892–95), formed with Grote, Stephen and John Stuart Mill in 1866 the Commons Preservation Society to protect common lands from the encroaching builder, as P.M.G. (1883–84) introduced sixpenny telegrams, as commissioner of works (1880–83, 1892–94) threw open Hampton Court park and Kew Palace, served on the London County Council from 1897 and in 1906 was created baron.

SHAWCROSS, Sir Hartley William, Baron Shawcross (1902–), English lawyer, born in Giessen, Germany, was educated at Dulwich College, called to the bar at Gray's Inn in 1925 and was senior lecturer in Law at Liverpool (1927–34). After service in World War II, he was attorney-general (1945–51) and president of the Board of Trade (1951) in the Labour government. He established an international legal reputation for himself as chief British prosecutor at the Nuremberg Trials (1945–46), led the investigations of the Lynskey Tribunal (1948) and prosecuted in the Fuchs atom spy case

(1950). Finding the narrow opposition tactics of the Labour Party irksome, he resigned his parliamentary seat in 1958. He was knighted in 1945 and created a life peer in 1959.

SHAYS, Daniel (1747–1825), American leader of the rebellion in Western Massachusetts (1786–87) which bears his name, served against the British at Bunker's Hill, Ticonderoga, &c., and was commissioned. He led the insurrection by the farmers against the U.S. government, which was imposing heavy taxation and mortgages. After raiding the arsenal at Springfield, Mass., the insurrectionists were routed at Petersham (1787) and Shays was condemned to death, but pardoned (1788).

SHEE, Sir Martin Archer (1769–1850), Anglo-Irish painter, born in Dublin, in 1788 settled in London, and became R.A. in 1800 and P.R.A. 1830, when he was knighted. His *Captain John Wolmore* at Trinity House shows the influence of Lawrence. He also dabbled in literature. See Life by his son (1860).

SHEEPSHANKS, (1) John (1787–1863), English art-collector, born in Leeds, who in 1857 presented his collection (233 oil paintings and 103 drawings) to the nation. They are now at South Kensington.

(2) **Richard** (1794–1855), English astronomer, brother of (1), instrumental in the adoption of a standard of length (1855).

SHEFFIELD, John, 1st Duke of Buckingham and Normanby (1648–1721), English political leader and poet, succeeded his father as third Earl of Mulgrave in 1658, served in both navy and army, and was lord chamberlain to James II and a cabinet councillor under William III, who in 1694 made him Marquis of Normanby. Anne made him Duke of (the county of) Buckingham (1703); but for his opposition to Godolphin and Marlborough he was deprived of the Seal (1705). After 1710, under the Tories, he was lord steward and lord president till the death of Anne, when he lost all power, and intrigued for the restoration of the Stuarts. Patron of Dryden and friend of Pope, he wrote two tragedies, a metrical *Essay on Satire*, an *Essay on Poetry*, &c.

SHEIL, Richard Lalor, *sheel* (1791–1851), Irish dramatist and politician, born at Drumdowney, Kilkenny, wrote a series of plays, aided O'Connell in forming the New Catholic Association (1825), and supported the cause by impassioned speeches. He was M.P. and in 1839 under Melbourne became vice-president of the Board of Trade, and a privy councillor—the first Catholic to gain that honour. In 1846 he was appointed master of the Mint. See *Memoir* by McCullagh (1855) and his *Speeches* (1845–55).

SHELBURNE, William Petty, 2nd Earl of (1737–1805), English statesman, great-grandson of Sir William Petty (q.v.), was born in Dublin, studied at Christ Church, Oxford, served in the army, entered parliament, succeeded his father to the earldom in 1761, and in 1763 was appointed president of the Board of Trade, and in Chatham's second administration (1766) secretary of state. Upon the fall of Lord North's ministry in 1782 Shelburne declined to form a government, but became secretary of state under Rockingham. Upon the latter's death the same year, the king offered Shelburne the Treasury. Fox resigned, and Shelburne introduced William Pitt into office as his chancellor of the Exchequer. This ministry resigned when outvoted by the coalition between Fox and North (February 1783). Shelburne was in 1784 made Marquis of Lansdowne, and at Lansdowne House and Bowood, Wilts, he collected a splendid gallery of pictures and a fine library. See Lives by Lord Edmond Fitzmaurice (1912) and C. W. Alvord (1925).

SHELDON, Gilbert (1598–1677), English prelate, chaplain to Charles I, warden of All Souls College, Oxford, and from 1663 Archbishop of Canterbury, built the Sheldonian Theatre at Oxford (1669).

SHELLEY, (1) Mary Wollstonecraft (1797–1851), English writer, was the daughter of William Godwin and Mary Wollstonecraft (qq.v.). Her life from 1814 to 1822 was bound up with that of Shelley. Her first and most impressive novel was *Frankenstein* (1818), her second *Valperga* (1823). In 1823 she returned to England with her son. Her husband's father, in granting her an allowance, insisted on the suppression of the volume of Shelley's *Posthumous Poems*, edited by her. *The Last Man* (1826), a romance of the ruin of human society by pestilence, fails to attain sublimity. In *Lodore* (1835) the story is told of Shelley's alienation from his first wife. Her last novel, *Falkner*, appeared in 1837. Of her occasional pieces of verse the most remarkable is *The Choice*. Her *Journal of a Six Weeks' Tour* (partly by Shelley) tells of the excursion to Switzerland in 1814; *Rambles in Germany and Italy* (1844) describes tours in 1840–43; Garnett collected her *Tales* in 1890. Koszul edited two unpublished mythological dramas, *Proserpine* and *Midas*, in 1922. See Lives by F. A. Marshall (1889), R. Church (1928), R. G. Grylls (1938), and H. N. Brailsford, *Shelley, Godwin and their Circle* (2nd ed. 1951).

(2) **Percy Bysshe** (1792–1822), was born at Field Place, Horsham, Sussex. After two years at Sion House School, Isleworth, where he acquired a taste for natural science, but where he was bullied, he entered Eton in 1804. Here, besides the classics, he imbibed sceptical and revolutionary ideas. In 1810 he became an undergraduate at University College, Oxford. His chief friend there, Thomas Jefferson Hogg, has described his career at Oxford, which was terminated after only a year by expulsion for issuing a pamphlet, *The Necessity of Atheism*. Hogg shared in this undergraduate revolt and was sent down at the same time. Left to himself in London the poet formed a connection with Harriet Westbrook, daughter af a retired coffee-house keeper, whose unhappy home circumstances induced Shelley to make a runaway marriage at Edinburgh (August 1811). The rights and wrongs of this unfortunate union have never been satisfactorily decided—Shelley never reproached himself for Harriet's tragedy—but no doubt the aim

he now set himself of 'reforming the world' under the direction of the teaching of the philosopher, William Godwin, explains almost everything. This aim led for a time to an itinerant mission to, among other places, Dublin and Lynmouth where he commenced his long poem *Queen Mab*—the first of his poems, which might be called 'Godwin versified'. Of Harriet's unhappy life during the three years (1811–14) they more or less lived together, little is known. Possibly her insistence on a Church re-marriage in 1814 led to the final breach and left Shelley free to cultivate the friendship of Godwin's daughter Mary. Such was his notion of marital fidelity—free love was part of the Godwinian ideology—we find him after the breach inviting Harriet to join him and Mary Godwin in a visit to Switzerland. The year before, Harriet had borne him a daughter Ianthe and now, January 1816, Mary bore him a son, William, out of wedlock. A few months later Harriet was found drowned in the Serpentine. By arrangement with his father Shelley now had settled on him out of his grandfather's estate £1000 a year and so was free to marry Mary Godwin and travel abroad. A lawsuit over the custody of Harriet's children Ianthe and Charles (1814–26) was decided by Lord Eldon against him on the ground of his atheistic opinions, a verdict which further embittered him against the 'Establishment'. In 1818 he set out for Italy accompanied by Mary, his son William and daughter Clara, and Miss Clairmont, Mary's half-sister, and her daughter Allegra, child of an amour with Byron. This family of free-lovers was now to travel round Italy from Venice (where Shelley met Byron) to Rome, to Naples, back to Rome (where he wrote the last two acts of *Prometheus Unbound*), to Leghorn and Florence and finally to the lonely house on the bay of Spezia where 'The Triumph of Life' was written and whence he set out for Leghorn to meet Leigh Hunt and his family, a journey from which he was not to return, his small boat having foundered in a storm on the way home. The seriousness with which Shelley (unlike the libertine Byron) held his heretical doctrines is best indicated by the immense liberation the Italian scene effected on his spirits and his poetry. Hitherto, apart from the doctrinal poems, *Queen Mab* and *The Revolt of Islam*, he had only *Alastor* (1816), a study of the egocentric romantic, himself, which has been much overpraised, the *Hymn to Intellectual Beauty* and *Mont Blanc* to his credit. Now in *Lines Written in the Euganean Hills* the theme of Italian liberty is worked out in octosyllables of striking force and brevity of diction. In *Julian and Maddalo* also, which belongs to his 'Venetian' period he found another medium for his conversation with Byron, who is Maddalo, viz., a finely modulated conversational form of the heroic couplet, which he later used for both humorous and romantic purposes in his *Letter to Maria Gisborne* (1820). These two poems along with his satire on Wordsworth, *Peter Bell the Third*, are the answer to those critics who think of him as a poet of moonshine and cloud shapes. He further displayed technical versatility in his esoteric drama *The Cenci* which owes something to the Jacobean school of Webster and Tourneur. It is a study of absolute evil and he had a story to work on, in which the dreadful and the heroic mingle. The poetry is kept to a minimum here and there is no humour. If we are to think of the 'uncommitted' Shelley, reference must also be made to that brilliant poem, the finest of all his fantasies, *The Witch of Atlas*, which gathers up all the gaieties of classical mythology—a rainbow fabric of pure vision, which recalls Renaissance virtuosity at its best. *Prometheus Unbound*, completed at Rome, 1820, is a study of the revolt of man against law and custom which oppress him. This is Godwinian doctrine removed to the realm of mythology, but now quickened by the more genial spirit of Plato, whose Symposium he had translated in 1818. Christianity is dethroned, but it is by the spirit of Christ. The assertion of the Godwinian doctrine of free love, modified by the Platonic notion of intellectual love, appears in *Epipsychidion* (1821) in the most seductive guise. To the same year belongs *Adonais*, which fittingly celebrates Keats and crowns his own career as poet and 'legislator'. He had the machinery of classical pastoral elegy to work on, but he etherealizes it and performs the feat of employing the Spenserian stanza for a heroic purpose. It is enshrined in the hearts of all lovers of the two poets. In 1822 he returned to the theme of liberty. !*Hellas* sings prophetically of the delivery of Greece from the Turk. It contains his greatest impersonal lyric 'The world's great age begins anew'. His last (unfinished) poem, *The Triumph of Life*, is a Petrarchian pageant, a vision of the world to be, marred only by the intrusion of Rousseau. He has not quite mastered Dante's terza rima, but the strict form imposes some restraint on him. The theme is again that of *The Revolt of Islam*—the true conquerors are those who resist 'royal anarchs'. Shelley is still the rebel and the anarchist, as he was when he wrote *The Masque of Anarchy* to denounce 'Peterloo'. Saintsbury remarked on his immediate mastery of every poetical form he attempted. This is certainly true of his lyrics, which are as perfect in his early as in his latest period. This lyricism, effortless as breathing, pervades all his poetry. Of the longer sort of lyric or ode 'To a Skylark', 'Ode to the West Wind', 'The Cloud' and 'The Sensitive Plant' register with consummate artistry the whole range of his feeling. The shorter love lyrics—'I arise from dreams of thee', 'To Constantia singing', 'Rarely, rarely comest thou', 'Swifter far than summer's flight', &c., rank with the greatest of their kind. Shelley was also a skilful master of the art of prose writing. His prose work includes the uncompleted *A Defence of Poetry* (1822), stating the eternal problem of art in its bearing on conduct. He asserts the Platonic notion that the poet is divinely inspired and therefore may be, in some sense, a 'legislator' to mankind. The modern edition of the *Collected Works* is by Ingpen and Peck (10 vols. 1926–30), but H. Buxton Forman, whose *Complete Works* (8 vols.

1876–80) it displaced, did invaluable work for the text and bibliography. The two-volume edition of the *Poems* by C. D. Locock (1911) has a valuable introduction by A. Clutton Brock, who also wrote *Shelley, the Man and the Poet* (1909). The *Letters*, ed. R. Ingpen (1909) are indispensible. Peck's Life (1927), followed by R. Bailey's study (1934) and E. Blunden's *Shelley, a Life Story* (1946), displaced Dowden's standard Life (1886). Other studies are Brailsford's *Shelley, Godwin and their Circle* (2nd ed. 1951), *Shelley and his Circle* (ed. by K. N. Cameron, 1961); Campbells' *Shelley and the Unromantics* (1924), Maurois' *Ariel* (1924, trans. 1961), and King-Hele's *Shelley, his Thought and Work* (1960). See also Life of Harriet by L. S. Boas (1962).

SHENSTONE, William (1714–63), English poet, born at Halesowen, studied at Pembroke College, Oxford, published in 1741 *The Judgment of Hercules* and the following year *The Schoolmistress*, which, written in imitation of Spenser, foreshadowed the mood of Gray's *Elegy*. *Pastoral Ballad* (1755) was commended by Gray and Johnson. In later life he suffered many financial embarrassments due to his elegant mode of life on his estate of the Leasowes. See *Letters*, ed. Williams (1939), and Lives by E. M. Purkis (1931), M. Williams (1935) and A. R. Humphreys (1937).

SHEPILOV, Dmitri Trofimovitch (1905–), Soviet politician, was born at Ashkhabad and was educated at Moscow University. From 1926 to 1931 he was a public prosecutor in Siberia and later became a lecturer in political economy. In 1952 he became chief editor of *Pravda*; in 1954 a member of the Supreme Soviet; and in 1956 foreign minister. He was 'purged' by the party leadership in 1957 and banished to a distant teaching post.

SHEPPARD, (1) Hugh Richard Lawrie, known as **'Dick'** (1880–1937), Anglican divine and pacifist, born at Windsor, a popular preacher with distinctly modern views on the Christian life and a pioneer of religious broadcasting, was vicar of London's St Martin-in-the-Fields (1914–27), published *The Human Parson* (1924) and *The Impatience of a Parson* (1927), became dean of Canterbury (1929–31) and canon of St Paul's Cathedral (1934–37). He was an ardent pacifist and founded the Peace Pledge Union in 1936. He was appointed C.H. in 1927. See Lives by R. E. Roberts (1941) and Matthews (1948).

(2) **Jack** (1702–24), English robber, born at Stepney, committed the first of many robberies in July 1720, and in 1724 was five times caught, and four times escaped. He was hanged at Tyburn in the presence of 200,000 spectators. He was the subject of many plays and ballads, tracts by Defoe and a novel by Ainsworth. See book ed. Bleakley and Ellis (1933).

SHERATON, Thomas (1751–1806), English cabinetmaker, born at Stockton-on-Tees, settled in London about 1790, wrote a *Cabinetmaker's Book* (1794). His neo-classical designs had a wide influence on contemporary taste in furniture. See studies, ed. R. Edwards (1945).

SHERBROOKE, Robert Lowe, 1st Viscount (1811–92), English politician, born at Bingham, Notts, from Winchester went in 1829 to University College, Oxford. Called to the bar in 1842, he emigrated the same year to Australia, soon attained a lucrative practice, and also took a leading part in politics. Home again in 1850, and returned to parliament (1852), he took office under Aberdeen and Palmerston. During 1859–64 he was vice-president of the Education Board, and introduced the Revised Code of 1862 with its 'payment by results'. In 1868 his feud with the Liberals was forgotten in his strenuous aid towards disestablishing the Irish Church, and Gladstone made him chancellor of the Exchequer. In 1873 he became home secretary; in 1880 went to the Upper House as Viscount Sherbrooke. He opposed the exclusive study of the classics. See Life by A. Patchett Martin (1893).

SHERE ALI, *shayr ah'lee* (1825–79), Amir of Afghanistan, a younger son of Dost Mohammed, succeeded as amir in 1863. Disagreements with his half-brothers soon arose, which kept Afghanistan in anarchy; Shere Ali fled to Kandahar; but in 1868 regained possession of Kabul, with assistance from the viceroy of India, Sir John Lawrence. In 1870 his eldest son, Yakub Khan, rebelled, but was captured and imprisoned. Shere Ali's refusal to receive a British mission (1878) led to war; and, after severe fighting, he fled to Turkestan, there to die. Yakub Khan succeeded.

SHERIDAN, (1) Philip Henry (1831–88), American soldier, born in Albany, N.Y., March 6, of Irish parentage, in 1848 entered West Point, and graduated in 1853. In 1861 he was an infantry captain, but in 1862 was given a cavalry regiment, and rose rapidly to command a division. He distinguished himself at Perryville and at Stone River, fought at Chickamauga, and was engaged in all the subsequent operations of the Civil War, gaining credit for the gallantry with which his division drove the enemy over Missionary Ridge. In 1864 he was given command of the cavalry of the Army of the Potomac, took part in the Battle of the Wilderness, made a notable raid on Confederate communications with Richmond, and led the advance to Cold Harbor. In August Grant placed him in command of the Army of the Shenandoah with instructions to make the valley 'a barren waste'. In September he attacked the enemy under Early, drove him beyond Winchester, again dislodged him from Fisher's Hill, and pursued him through Harrisonburg and Staunton, but Early, reinforced by Lee, again appeared in the Shenandoah Valley, and on October 19 surprised the Northern army and drove it back in confusion. Sheridan, who was at Winchester, twenty miles away, galloped to the field and turned defeat into victory. He was promoted major-general and received the thanks of congress. Defeating the enemy at Five Forks on April 1, he had an active share in the final battles which led to Lee's surrender at Appomattox Court-house, April 9, 1865. A lieutenant-general in 1870, he was with Moltke at Gravelotte and other battles. In 1883 he succeeded Sherman as general-in-chief. He died at Nonquitt, Mass., August 5. Sheridan never lost a battle. Among the Northern generals he ranks next to Grant and Sherman. See his *Personal Memoirs* (1888) and Life by Davies (1895).

(2) **Richard Brinsley** (1751–1816), British dramatist, born in Dublin, October 30, was grandson of Swift's friend, Thomas Sheridan, D.D. (1687–1738), and son of Thomas Sheridan (1719–88), a teacher of elocution, actor and author of a *Life of Swift*. His mother, Frances Sheridan, *née* Chamberlaine (1724–66), was the author of a novel called *Sidney Biddulph* and of one or two plays. Richard Sheridan was educated at Harrow, and after leaving school, with a school-friend named Halhed wrote a three-act farce called *Jupiter* and tried a verse translation of the *Epistles of Aristoenetus*. After a romantic courtship, Richard married Elizabeth Linley in 1773. The young couple settled in London to a life much beyond their means. Sheridan now made more serious efforts at dramatic composition. On January 17, 1775, *The Rivals* was produced at Covent Garden, and after a slight alteration in the cast met with universal approval. In the same year appeared the poor farce called *St Patrick's Day* and also *The Duenna*. In 1776 Sheridan, with the aid of Linley and another friend, bought half the patent of Drury Lane Theatre for £35,000 from Garrick, and in 1778 the remaining share for £45,000. His first production was a purified edition of Vanbrugh's *Relapse*, under the title of *A Trip to Scarborough*. Three months later (1777) appeared his greatest work, *The School for Scandal*. *The Critic* (1779), teeming with sparkling wit, was Sheridan's last dramatic effort, with the exception of a poor tragedy, *Pizarro*. On the dissolution of parliament in 1780 Sheridan was elected for Stafford, and in 1782 became under-secretary for foreign affairs under Rockingham, afterwards secretary to the treasury in the coalition ministry (1783). His parliamentary reputation dates from his great speeches in the impeachment of Warren Hastings. In 1794 he again electrified the House by a magnificent oration in reply to Lord Mornington's denunciation of the French Revolution. He remained the devoted friend and adherent of Fox till Fox's death, and was also the defender and mouthpiece of the prince regent. In 1806 he was appointed receiver of the Duchy of Cornwall, and in 1806 treasurer to the navy. In 1812 he was defeated at Westminster, and his parliamentary career came to an end. In 1792 his first wife died, and three years later he married Esther Ogle, the silly and extravagant daughter of the Dean of Winchester, who survived him. The affairs of the theatre had gone badly. The old building had to be closed as unfit to hold large audiences, and a new one, opened in 1794, was burned in 1809. This last calamity put the finishing touch to Sheridan's pecuniary difficulties, which had long been serious. He died July 7, 1816, in great poverty, but was given a magnificent funeral in Westminster Abbey. See Memoirs in editions of his works by Leigh Hunt (1840), and Rhodes (1928); *Memoirs of Mrs Frances Sheridan*, by her granddaughter, Alicia Le Fanu (1824); Lives by Fraser Rae (2 vols. 1896) and W. Sichel (2 vols. 1909), Rhodes (1933), Darlington (1933); also the articles DUFFERIN and NORTON.

SHERIFF, Lawrence (d. 1567), London grocer, born at Rugby, founded its great public school (1567).

SHERLOCK, (1) Thomas (1678–1761), English prelate, son of (2), bishop successively of Bangor (1728), Salisbury (1734) and London (1748), opposed Bishop Hoadly (q.v.) in the Bangorian controversy and temporarily lost influence at court. See Life by E. F. Carpenter (1936).

(2) **William** (1641–1707), English prelate, father of (1), born at Southwark, became master of the Temple in 1685 and Dean of St Paul's in 1691. He was a nonjuror, but took the oaths in 1690. The most controversial of his 60 works were *Vindication of the Doctrines of the Trinity and of the Incarnation* (1690), which made South charge him with Tritheism, and *Case of Allegiance* (1691).

SHERMAN, (1) Henry Clapp (1875–1955), American biochemist. Educated at Maryland and Columbia, Sherman became professor of Organic Chemistry (1907), of Nutritional Chemistry (1911) and of Chemistry (1924) at the latter university. He did important quantitative work on vitamins.

(2) **John** (1823–1900), American statesman, brother of (4), born at Lancaster, Ohio, was in turn chairman of financial committees in both houses of Congress. He was largely author of the bills for the reconstruction of the seceded states and for the resumption of specie payment in 1879. He was appointed in 1877 secretary of the Treasury, and in 1878 had prepared a redemption fund in gold that raised the legal tender notes to par value. In 1881 and 1887 he was again returned to the senate, was its president, and afterwards chairman of the committee on foreign relations. In 1897 he was made secretary of state, but retired on the war with Spain in 1898. The Sherman Act (1890; repealed 1893) sanctioned large purchases of silver by the Treasury. See Life by Bronson (2nd ed. 1888), *Selected Speeches* (1879), *Sherman Letters*, between the brothers (1894), his *Recollections of Forty Years* (N.Y. 1896).

(3) **Roger** (1721–93), American statesman and patriot, born at Newton, Mass., lived in Connecticut from 1743. First elected to the state assembly in 1755, he became a judge of the superior court (1766–89) and mayor of New Haven (1784–93). A signatory of the Declaration of Independence, as a delegate to the Convention of 1787 he took a prominent part in the debates on the Constitution. See Life by Boutell (1896).

(4) **William Tecumseh** (1820–91), American soldier, brother of (2), born at Lancaster, Ohio, graduated at West Point in 1840. After serving in Florida and California, he became a banker in San Francisco. In May 1861 he was commissioned colonel of the Thirteenth Infantry; at Bull Run he won his promotion to brigadier-general of volunteers. In August he was sent to Kentucky, at first under Anderson, but when he asked for 200,000 men to put an end to the war there, he was deprived of his command. But soon

in command of a division, he took a distinguished part in the battle of Shiloh (April 1862) and was made major-general. In Grant's various movements against Vicksburg Sherman was most active. In July 1863, promoted brigadier, he drove General Johnston out of Jackson, Miss. In November he joined Grant at Chattanooga, and rendered excellent service in the victory of the 25th; soon after, he relieved Burnside, besieged at Knoxville. In March 1864 he was appointed by Grant to the command of the southwest. In April he commenced his campaign against Atlanta. He first encountered Johnston at Dalton, May 14, and drove him beyond the Etowah, and finally to Atlanta, which was evacuated on September 1. After giving his army a rest Sherman commenced his famous march to the sea, with 65,000 men. Meeting with little serious opposition, he reached Savannah on December 10. The works were soon carried, and on the 20th the city was evacuated. In February he left Savannah for the north, and by the 17th, compelling the evacuation of Charleston, had reached Columbia. Thence he moved on Goldsboro', fighting two battles on the way. On April 9 Lee surrendered, and Johnston made terms with Sherman (disapproved as too lenient by Secretary Stanton). For four years Sherman commanded the Mississippi division; when Grant became president he was made head of the army. In 1874, at his own request, to make room for Sheridan, he was retired on full pay. He died in New York, February 14. See his own Memoirs (1875; revised 1891), his Letters, ed. Thorndike (1894), and Lives by E. Robins (1905), B. Liddell Hart (1930) and A. H. Burne (1939).

SHERRIFF, Robert Cedric (1896–), British playwright, novelist and scriptwriter, born at Kingston-upon-Thames, achieved an international reputation with his first play, *Journey's End* (1929), based on his experiences in the trenches during the first World War. In 1931 he turned student at Oxford and in 1933 went to Hollywood. His later plays did not match up to his first, but he wrote the scripts for such films as *The Invisible Man* (1933), *Goodbye Mr Chips* (1936), *The Four Feathers* (1938), *Lady Hamilton* (1941) and *The Dambusters* (1955).

SHERRINGTON, Sir Charles Scott (1857–1952), English physiologist, born in London, passed through Caius College, Cambridge, was professor of Physiology at Liverpool (1895–1913) and Oxford (1913–35). His researches on reflex action and especially on *The Integrative Action of the Nervous System* (1906) constitute a landmark in modern physiology. His poetry is worthy of note. In 1920–25 he was P.R.S., in 1922 president of the British Association; he was awarded the O.M. in 1924, and a Nobel prize for medicine in 1932. See Life by Lord Cohen (1958).

SHERWOOD, (1) Mary Martha (1775–1851), English writer of children's books, daughter of Dr Butt, chaplain to George III, was born at Stanford, Worcs. In 1803 she sailed for India. Her 77 works include *Little Henry and his Bearer*, and the long-popular *History of the Fairchild Family*. See her own *Life* (ed. Darton, 1910), and one by her daughter, Mrs Kelly (1854).

(2) **Robert Emmet** (1896–1955), American playwright and author, born in New Rochelle, New York. He wrote his first play, *Barnum Was Right*, while at Harvard, and after service in the first World War became editor (1924–28) of *Life*. He won four Pulitzer prizes, the first three for drama (*Idiot's Delight*, 1936; *Abe Lincoln in Illinois*, 1939; and *There Shall be No Night*, 1941), and the last (1949) for his biographical *Roosevelt and Hopkins*.

SHEVCHENKO, Taras (1814–61), Ukrainian poet and prose writer, born a serf at Kirilovka (Kiev), was freed and became professor at Kiev (1845), founded an organization for radical social reforms, was exiled to Siberia for ten years, and published collections of poems in the Ukrainian language.

SHIELD, William (1748–1829), English viola player and composer, born at Swalwell in Durham, was apprenticed to a boatbuilder, and, encouraged by Giardini, studied music, composed anthems that were sung in Durham cathedral, and conducted at Scarborough. He published a comic opera, *The Flitch of Bacon*, in 1778, and, as composer to Covent Garden (1778–97), produced others. Some of his songs are still known. In 1792 he travelled in Italy. From 1817 he was master of the King's Musicians. See *Memorial* (1891).

SHIH HUANG TI (259–210 B.C.), Chinese emperor from 246, and 4th monarch of the Chin dynasty. Assuming the title of 'the first emperor', he greatly extended the empire and built the Great Wall, completed in 204, to keep out barbarians. He had all historical documents burnt in 212 to maintain himself and his successors in power.

SHILLABER, Benjamin Penhallow (1814–90), American humorist, author of *Sayings of Mrs Partington* (1854).

SHILLIBEER, George (1797–1866), British pioneer of London omnibuses, born in London, established a coachbuilding business in Paris and from 1829 ran the first London omnibus coach service from the City to Paddington.

SHINWELL, Emanuel (1884–), British Labour politician, born in Spitalfields, London, began work as an errand boy in Glasgow at the age of twelve. An early student of public library and street-corner Socialism, he was elected to Glasgow Trades Council in 1911 and, one of the 'wild men of Clydeside', served a five months' prison sentence for incitement to riot in 1921. M.P. in 1931 and secretary to the Department of Mines (1924, 1930–31), in 1935 he defeated Ramsay MacDonald at Seaham Harbour, Durham, in one of the most bitterly contested election battles of modern times. From 1942 he was chairman of the Labour Party committee which drafted the manifesto 'Let Us face the Future', on which Labour won the 1945 election. As minister of fuel and power he nationalized the mines (1946), and the following year, when he was said to be a scapegoat for the February fuel crisis, he became secretary of state for war.

From 1950 to 1951 he was minister of defence. In these last two offices, 'Manny's' considerable administrative ability outshone his prickly party political belligerence and earned him the respect of such discerning critics in defence matters as Churchill and Montgomery. In his later years he mellowed into a back-bench 'elder statesman'. He became Labour Party chairman in 1964, was created C.H. in 1965 and awarded a life peerage in 1970. See his autobiographical *Conflict without Malice* (1955).

SHIPTON, (1) Eric Earle (1907–), British mountaineer. He gained his early mountaineering experience during five expeditions to the mountains of East and Central Africa, climbing Kamet (25,447 ft.) in 1931. He obtained much of his knowledge of the East during his terms as consul-general in Kashgar (1940–42 and 1946–48) and in Kunming (1949–51). Between 1933 and 1951 he either led or was member of five expeditions to Mount Everest. He probably did more than any other man to pave the way for the successful Hunt-Hillary expedition of 1953. He was made a C.B.E. in 1955. See his *Upon that Mountain* (1948), *Mount Everest Reconnaissance Expedition* (1951).

(2) **Mother** (1488–*c.* 1560), English witch, born near Knaresborough, and baptized as Ursula Southiel, at twenty-four married Tony Shipton, a builder, and died at over seventy years of age—according to S. Baker, who edited her 'prophecies' (1797). A book (1684) by Richard Head tells how she was carried off by the devil, bore him an imp, &c. A small British moth, with wing-markings, resembling a witch's face, is named after her. See book by W. H. Harrison (1881).

SHIRLEY, (1) Sir Anthony (1565–*c.* 1635), English adventurer. After following Essex from 1597, he was knighted by the king of France without the assent of Queen Elizabeth, who had him imprisoned until he renounced the title, which is therefore nominal only. His voyage to America and Jamaica (1595) is recorded by Hakluyt. In 1599 he went to Persia on a trade mission, and returned as the Shah's envoy in an unsuccessful attempt to form an alliance against the Turks. His account of this adventure was published in 1613. Proscribed from entering Britain, he wandered in Europe and died at Madrid.

(2) **James** (1596–1666), English late Elizabethan dramatist, born in London, September 18, from Merchant Taylors' passed in 1612 to St John's, Oxford, but migrated to Catharine Hall, Cambridge. He took orders, and held a living at St Albans. Turning Catholic, he taught (1623–24) in the grammar school there, but soon went to London and became playwright. The suppression of stage plays in 1642 ended his livelihood, and he took to teaching again. The Restoration revived his plays, but brought him no better fortunes. His death was a result of the Great Fire of London. Beaumont and Fletcher and Ben Jonson were his models, but he has little of the grand Elizabethan manner. Most of his plays are tragi-comedies. His chief works are *Eccho* (1618), a poem on the Narcissus subject; comedies, *The Witty Fair One* (1628); *The Wedding* (1628); *The Grateful Servant* (1629); *The Example* (1634); *The Opportunity* (1634); *The Lady of Pleasure*, the most brilliant of his comedies (1635); tragedies, *The Cardinal*, to the author himself 'the best of his flock' (1641); *The Traytor* (1631), a great drama. As a masque writer he is second only to Jonson; among his best masques are *The Triumph of Peace* (1633) and *The Contention of Ajax and Ulysses* (1659, including 'The glories of our blood and state'). His thirty-five plays were edited by Gifford and Dyce (1833), his *Poems* by R. L. Armstrong (1941). See studies by Schipper (1911), Forsythe (1915) and Nason (1915).

(3) **John** (1366?–1456), English traveller and transcriber of Chaucer and Lydgate.

(4) **Lawrence.** See FERRERS.

(5) **Robert** (1581?–1628), brother of (1), accompanied him to Persia and remained there. He made two journeys to European courts as envoy of the Shah of Persia (1608, 1615), being accepted by James I of England for three years (1624–27), when he returned to Persia and died out of favour.

SHIRREFF, (1) Emily Anne Eliza (1814–97), English pioneer of women's education, was mistress of Girton College from 1870. She published works on Kindergartens and the Fröbel system.

(2) **Patrick** (1791–1876), Scottish farmer in East Lothian, born near Haddington, was the pioneer of cereal hybridizing, and produced many varieties of wheat and oats.

SHOLOKHOV, Mikhail (1905–), Russian novelist, born near Veshenskaya, wrote *Quiet Flows the Don* (trans. 1935) and other novels of Cossack life, *The Upturned Soil* (1940) on the effects of the new régime on farm life, and short stories. He won the Stalin prize in 1941, and the Nobel prize for literature in 1965.

SHORE, (1) Jane (d. *c.* 1527), born in London, early married William Shore, a goldsmith. After her intrigue with Edward IV began, about 1470, her husband abandoned her, but she lived till Edward's death in luxury, enjoying great power, yet 'never abusing it', as More tells us, 'to any man's hurt, but to many a man's comfort and relief'. After the king's death she lived under the protection of Hastings, and on his death, it is said, of the Marquis of Dorset; but Richard III, to make his brother's life odious, relieved her of over two thousand marks, and caused the Bishop of London to make her walk in open penance, taper in hand, dressed only in her kirtle. She forms the subject of a tragedy by Rowe (1714).

(2) **John, 1st Baron Teignmouth** (1751–1834), English governor-general of India (1793–98), originated the Bengal *zamindari* system and many of Cornwallis's reforms. He supported Hastings at the latter's trial (1797) and settled the Oude succession. He was first president of the British and Foreign Bible Society and was created an Irish peer (1798).

SHORT, Sir Frank (1857–1945), English engraver, known especially for etchings and mezzotints, including the plates for Turner's *Liber Studiorum*.

SHORTER, Clement King (1858–1926),

English journalist and critic, born in London, edited the *Illustrated London News* (1891–1900), founded and edited the *Sketch*, and from 1900 was editor of the *Sphere*. He wrote on the Brontës, on Victorian literature, on Borrow and Boswell. His first wife was **Dora Sigerson** (d. 1918), Irish author of *Verses* (1894), *The Fairy Changeling* (1897), &c.

SHORTHOUSE, Joseph Henry (1834–1903), English novelist, born at Birmingham, became a chemical manufacturer there. In 1881 his romance, *John Inglesant*, revealed a subtle and sympathetic insight into old-world phases of the spiritual mind. It was followed by *The Little Schoolmaster Mark* (1883–84), *Sir Percival* (1886), *A Teacher of the Violin* (1888), *The Countess Eve* (1888), and *Blanche, Lady Falaise* (1891). See his Life by his wife (1905).

SHOSTAKOVICH, Dmitri, *-ko'-* (1906–), Russian composer, was born in St Petersburg (now Leningrad), where he entered the Conservatoire in 1919. His First Symphony, composed in 1925, the year his studies ended, attracted considerable attention. His music, in which he attempted to support Soviet principles, was at first highly successful, but the development of a more conservative attitude on the part of the Soviet Government, coinciding with his own development of a more experimental outlook, led to official criticism of his opera *The Nose*, his Second (' October ') Symphony, and a second opera, *A Lady Macbeth of Mtensk*, which had to be withdrawn after violent press attacks on its decadence and its failure to observe the principles of ' Soviet realism '. Shostakovich was reinstated by his Fifth Symphony (1938). He has composed prolifically in all forms, and his Seventh (' Leningrad ') Symphony, his Tenth Symphony, and his Violin Concerto have won considerable popularity outside Russia. His Eleventh Symphony, for which he was awarded a Lenin prize in 1958, is based upon the events of the October Revolution of 1905. See study by Rabinovich (1960).

SHOVEL, Sir Cloudesley (1650–1707), English sailor, served against the Dutch and in the Mediterranean, burned four corsair galleys at Tripoli (1676), commanded a ship at the battle in Bantry Bay (1689), and was knighted. In 1690 he took part in the battle off Beachy Head; in 1692 he supported Russell at La Hogue, and burned twenty of the enemy's ships. He served under Rooke in the Mediterranean, and with him took Gibraltar in 1704. In 1705 he was made rear-admiral of England. That year he took part with Peterborough in the capture of Barcelona, but failed in his attack on Toulon in 1707. On the voyage home his ship (and others) struck a rock off the Scilly Isles on the foggy night of October 22, 1707, and went down. His body was washed up, and buried in Westminster Abbey.

SHRAPNEL, Henry (1761–1842), English artillery officer, retired from active service as a lieutenant-general in 1825. In about 1793 he invented the shrapnel shell.

SHREWSBURY. See TALBOT Family.

SHUTE, (1) John. See BARRINGTON (3).

(2) **Nevil**, pen-name of **Nevil Shute Norway** (1899–1960), English writer, born in Ealing, emigrated to Australia. He served in the 1914–18 war and immediately afterwards began an aeronautical career. He was chief calculator to the Airship Guarantee Company during the construction of the airship R100 and flew the Atlantic twice in her. He founded Airspeed Ltd., aircraft constructors, and became its managing director. His novels include *The Pied Piper* (1942), *Most Secret* (1945), *The Chequerboard* (1947), *No Highway* (1948), *A Town Like Alice* (1949), *Round the Bend* (1951), *Requiem for a Wren* (1955), *Beyond the Black Stump* (1956) and *On the Beach* (1957). His success was largely due to his brisk style and his ability to make technical language and procedure understandable to a lay public.

SHUVALOV, *shoo-vah'lof*, (1) **Count Paul** (1830–1908), Russian general, brother of (2), fought at Sebastopol and Inkermann, and helped to organize the liberation of the Russian serfs (1861). He fought in Turkey (1878), was ambassador to Germany (1885) and governor of Warsaw (1895).

(2) **Count Petr Andreyevich** (1827–89), Russian diplomatist, brother of (1), became head of the secret police in 1866; in 1873 sent on a secret mission to London, he arranged the marriage between the Duke of Edinburgh and the only daughter of Alexander II. In 1878 he was one of the Russian representatives at the Congress of Berlin.

SIBBALD, Sir Robert (1641–1722), Scottish naturalist and physician, born at Edinburgh, became a physician there, but gave much time to botany and zoology. He helped to establish a botanic garden, and was virtual founder of the Royal College of Physicians of Edinburgh. He was knighted in 1682 and appointed professor of Medicine and Scottish geographer royal. He wrote *History of Fife* (1710), pamphlets on medical subjects, natural history and antiquities, and *Autobiography* (1833; 1932).

SIBELIUS, Jean, *si-bay'li-oos* (1865–1957), Finnish composer, born in Tavastehus. The son of a surgeon, he studied the piano as a child, but was sent to Helsinki University to study law. He abandoned a legal career for full-time musical study in 1885, leaving Helsinki Conservatory in 1889 with a state grant which enabled him to continue his studies in Berlin and Vienna. A passionate nationalist, on his return to Finland he began the series of symphonic poems (including the well-known *Swan of Tuonela*) based on episodes in the Finnish epic *Kalevala*, and his first great success came with *En Saga* (1892). From 1897 until his death a state grant enabled him to devote himself entirely to composition, and his symphonies, symphonic poems—notably *Finlandia* (1899)—and violin concerto won great popularity, in Britain and America as well as in Finland, for their originality of form and idiom. After his Seventh Symphony (1924–25) and *Tapiola* (1926), he released no more music for performance or publication. See studies by C. Gray (1935), Neville Cardus (1945), H. E. Johnson (1960), and of his symphonies by S. Parmet (trans. 1959).

SIBLEY, Henry Hastings (1811–91), American statesman, first governor and 'Father of Minnesota', born at Detroit, put down the Sioux outbreak of 1862.

SIBOUR, Marie Dominique Auguste (1792–1857), French prelate, from 1848 Archbishop of Paris, was murdered during mass by an excommunicated priest. See Life by Poujoulat (2nd ed. 1863).

SICKERT, Walter Richard (1860–1942), British artist, was born at Munich. After three years on the English stage (an interest reflected in many pictures of music halls) he studied at the Slade School, and under Whistler. While working in Paris, he was much influenced by Degas. He had many studios in London, paying regular visits to France, and he used Degas' technique to illustrate London low life. Sickert was a member of the New English Art Club, and about 1910 the Camden Town Group (later the London Group) was formed under his leadership. His famous interior *Ennui* (in the Tate Gallery) belongs to this period. Both his painting and his writings on art have had great influence on later English painters; see his autobiography *A Free House!* (1947), the *Life and Opinions* edited by R. Emmons (1941), and study by L. Browse (1960).

SICKINGEN, Franz von, *zik'-* (1481–1523), German knight, born at Ebernburg near Kreuznach, fought in 1508 against the Venetians for the Emperor Maximilian, but in peace led the life of a freelance. During 1513–19 he warred against Worms, Metz, Philip of Hesse and Württemberg. Ulrich von Hutten from 1520 was his constant guest, and won him over to the cause of the Reformation. In 1521 he assisted the emperor in his French campaign; in 1522 he opened a Protestant war against the Archbishop of Trier. That war miscarried; and, put to the ban of the empire and besieged in his castle of Landstuhl, he was killed.

SIDDAL, Elizabeth Eleanor. See ROSSETTI (2).

SIDDONS, Sarah (1755–1831), English actress, was born at Brecon, July 5, the eldest child of Roger Kemble (q.v.), manager of a small travelling theatrical company, of which Sarah was a member from her earliest childhood. In 1773 she married at Coventry her fellow-actor, William Siddons. Her first appearance at Drury Lane in December 1775 as Portia met with no great success. But her reputation grew so fast in the provinces that in 1782 she returned to Drury Lane, and made her reappearance in October as Isabella in Garrick's adaptation of Southerne's *Fatal Marriage*. Her success was immediate, and from this time she was the unquestioned queen of the stage. In 1803 she followed her brother, John Philip Kemble, to Covent Garden, where she continued till her formal farewell to the stage as Lady Macbeth, June 29, 1812. Thereafter she appeared occasionally, but only for special benefits, and she sometimes gave public readings. Endowed with a gloriously expressive and beautiful face, a queenly figure, and a voice of richest power and flexibility, she worked assiduously to cultivate her gifts until as a tragic actress she reached a height of perfection probably unsurpassed by any player of any age or country. In comedy she was less successful. See Lives by Boaden (1827; new ed. 1893), Thomas Campbell (1834), N. H. Kennard (1886), F. M. Parsons (1909), A. Maurois (1927) and N. G. R. Smith (1933).

SIDGWICK, (1) Henry (1838–1900), English moral philosopher, born at Skipton, was educated at Rugby and Trinity College, Cambridge, of which he was fellow (1859–69), praelector of Moral Philosophy (1875–83) and then Knightsbridge professor. He is best known for his analytical examination of the various schools in moral philosophy in *Methods of Ethics* (1874), in which he attempts to restate the philosophically unsatisfactory arguments of J. S. Mill's *Utilitarianism* by relating it to intuitionism. Other works include *Outlines of the History of Ethics* (1886), the *Principles of Political Economy* (1883) and *Practical Ethics* (1898). He was an active member of the Psychical Research Society. See Life (1906) by his brother, the Greek scholar, **Arthur Sidgwick** (1840–1920) and his widow, **Eleanor Mildred Balfour** (1845–1936), sister of A. J. Balfour and principal of Newnham College (1892–1910). See also C. D. Broad, *Ethics and the History of Philosophy* (1952).

(2) **Nevil Vincent** (1873–1952), English chemist, professor at Oxford, known for his work on molecular structure and his formulation of a theory of valency. See his *The Electronic Theory of Valency* (1927). He was elected F.R.S. in 1922 and awarded the Royal Society's Royal Medal in 1937.

SIDI MOHAMMED BEN YOUSSEF (1911–61), sultan of Morocco from 1927, was born in Meknès, a scion of the Alouite dynasty. Exercising both spiritual and temporal power, he privily supported the nationalist Istaqlal party and constantly obstructed French hegemony. Tribal hostility to him gave the French the chance to depose him in 1953, but he was restored in 1955, and when Morocco attained independence in 1957 he became King Mohammed V. He died suddenly after a minor operation and was succeeded by his eldest son, **Prince Moulay Hassan**, who had already emerged as the spokesman of chauvinistic Moroccan youth. His eldest daughter, **Princess Lalla Ayesha** repudiated the *yasmak* and became a leader of the women's emancipation movement.

SIDMOUTH, Henry Addington, 1st Viscount (1757–1844), English statesman, the son of Lord Chatham's physician, **Anthony** (1713–1790), was educated at Winchester and Brasenose College, Oxford, quitted the bar for politics, and in 1783 was returned for Devizes. He was speaker 1789–1801, when, upon Pitt's resignation, he was invited to form a ministry. His undistinguished administration, whose one great event was the Peace of Amiens (1802), came to an end in 1804. Next year he was created Viscount Sidmouth, and thereafter was thrice president of the Council, once lord privy seal, and from 1812 to 1821 home secretary, as such being unpopular for his coercive measures.

He retired from the Cabinet in 1824. He was a sincere Tory. See Life by L. G. Pellew (1847) and E. M. G. Belfield, *Annals of the Addington Family* (1960).

SIDNEY, (1) **Algernon** (1622?–83), English politician, grandnephew of Sir Philip, and second son of the second Earl of Leicester, was born probably at Penshurst, Kent, and in 1622. He accompanied his father on his embassy in 1632 to Denmark, and in 1636 to France. In 1641–43 he commanded a troop of horse in Ireland, of which country his father was (nominally) lord-lieutenant. Declaring for the parliament, he was wounded at Marston Moor (1644); in 1645 was appointed governor of Chichester, and returned by Cardiff to parliament; in 1646 attended his brother, Viscount Lisle, now lord-lieutenant, to Ireland as lieutenant-general of horse and governor of Dublin; and in 1647, after receiving the thanks of the House of Commons, was appointed governor of Dover. In 1649, though nominated a commissioner, he took no part in the king's trial, which however he justified on abstract grounds. An extreme republican, he resented Cromwell's usurpation of power, and retired to Penshurst (1653–59). Then, made one of the Council of State, he undertook a political mission to Denmark and Sweden. After the Restoration he lived on the Continent, but in 1677 was pardoned and returned to England. In 1679 he twice stood unsuccessfully for parliament, and an attempt was made to involve him in the sham Meal-tub Plot. The attempt miscarried; still, he deemed it prudent to retire to France, and, to detach Louis XIV from Charles, entered into negotiations with him through Barillon. That prior to this he had taken monies from the French ambassador, either for himself or (more likely) for the republican cause, is admitted by Hallam and Macaulay, but disputed by Ewald. The next year he was back in England, and possibly helped Penn with the Pennsylvanian constitution, features of which were the ballot, universal suffrage, the abolition of a property qualification, religious equality, prison reform, and the abolition of capital punishment save for murder and treason. In June 1683, when the Rye House Plot was announced, the chance was seized to get rid of men felt to be dangerous, and, with Lords Russell, Essex and Howard, Sidney was sent to the Tower. In November he was tried for high treason before Jeffreys, and, on no evidence but the traitor Lord Howard's and his own unpublished *Discourses concerning Government* (1698), was beheaded December 7. His attainder was reversed in 1689. See R. C. Sidney's *Brief Memoir* of the trial (1685), Blencowe's *Sidney Papers* (1813), and Lives by Meadley (1813) and Ewald (1873).

(2) **Dorothea.** See WALLER (2).

(3) **Sir Henry** (1529–86), English administrator, father of (4), lord deputy of Ireland (1565–71; 1575–78), crushed Shane O'Neill in Ulster (1566–67), failed to establish English settlers, but organized a system of presidency councils. He served also as president of the council of Wales (1559–86).

(4) **Sir Philip** (1554–86), English poet, son of (3), born November 30 at Penshurst, Kent. Philip went up about 1568 from Shrewsbury to Christ Church, Oxford, and in 1572–75 travelled in France, Germany and Italy. At first a favourite of the queen, he was sent in 1577 as ambassador to the Emperor Rudolf and then to the Prince of Orange. Elizabeth displayed her ingratitude towards his father for his exertions as lord deputy in Ireland, and Philip wrote in his defence; he also addressed the queen against her projected match with the Duke of Anjou. Elizabeth was displeased; and his mother's brother, the once-powerful Leicester, fell into disfavour. Sidney retired (1580) to his sister Mary, now Lady Pembroke, at Wilton, where, probably, most of his *Arcadia* was written. In 1583 he was knighted, and married Frances, daughter of Sir F. Walsingham. His arrangement (1585) to accompany Drake on one of his buccaneer expeditions was defeated by Elizabeth's caprice and Drake's treachery. It was poor amends that Sidney was ordered to accompany Leicester, chosen by the queen to carry her half-hearted support to the Netherlanders in their struggle against Spain. After one small brilliant exploit, he received, September 22, 1586, his death wound under the walls of Zutphen, dying like a hero and a Christian on October 17. His work in literature we may place between 1578 and 1582. Widely celebrated as it was in his lifetime, nothing was published till after his death. His brilliant character, his connections, his generous patronage of men of letters, with the report of those to whom his writings were communicated, united to give him his pre-eminent contemporary fame. This was, however, amply supported when the *Arcadia* (written probably 1578–80, but never finished) appeared, imperfectly in 1590, completely in 1598. This book long retained a vast popularity, though now it is almost unread. It is a pastoral romance, founded upon the *Arcadia* (1504) of Sannazaro, being an intricate love story, intermixed with poems and written in melodious but elaborate prose, not free from the artificial 'conceits', the euphuism, of that age. But here Englishmen found their earliest model for sweet, continuous, rhythmical prose. To about 1580 may be assigned Sidney's *Apologie for Poetrie* (1591, afterwards named *Defence of Poesie*), written in clear, manly English in reply to an abusive Puritan pamphlet. In 1575 Sidney had met Penelope Devereux (*c.* 1562–1607), daughter of the first Earl of Essex; but it was only in 1581, the year following her marriage to the Puritan Lord Rich, who afterwards divorced her, that Sidney awoke too late to love for her, and to find also that she might have loved him. The 108 sonnets and 11 songs of *Astrophel and Stella* (1591) offer a marvellous picture of passionate love. That Sidney's fame falls far below his deserts is due in part to that inequality of his workmanship which he shares with other supreme writers of sonnet sequences; nor did life allow him to acquire their finished art. See the *Complete Works*, ed. by Feuillerat (4 vols. 1912–26); Lives by Fulke Greville (1652; 1907), Symonds (1886), Wallace (1915), M. Wilson

(1931); and studies by S. Goldman (1934), Myrick (1935), Boas (1955), Howell (1968).

SIDONIUS APOLLINARIS (*c.* 430–*c.* 483), French Latin author, born at Lyons, held high civil offices at Rome, and in 472 became Bishop of Clermont. His letters are modelled on Pliny's; his poems comprise panegyrics on three emperors, and two epithalamia. See study by Stevens (1933).

SIEBOLD, *zee'bolt,* **(1) Karl Theodor Ernst** (1804–65), German anatomist, brother of (2), was professor at Munich, and wrote on the Invertebrata (trans. 1857), parthenogenesis, salamanders, and the freshwater fish of central Europe. See Life by Siebold (1896).

(2) **Philipp Franz von** (1796–1866), German physician and botanist, brother of (1), born at Würzburg, became sanitary officer to the Dutch in Batavia, and, accompanying the Dutch embassy to Japan, made Japan known to the Western world by his writings.

SIEGBAHN, Karl Manne Georg (1886–), Swedish physicist, born at Örebro, professor at Lund (1920), at Uppsala (1923) and professor of the Royal Academy of Sciences and director of the Nobel Institute for Physics at Stockholm from 1937, discovered the M series in X-ray spectroscopy for which he was awarded the Nobel prize for 1924. He also constructed a vacuum spectrograph.

SIEGEN, Ludwig von, *zee'gen* (1609–*c.* 1675), German engraver, in 1642 invented the mezzotint process, which he disclosed to Prince Rupert at Brussels in 1654.

SIEGFRIED, André, *zeeg'freed* (1875–1959), French economist, historian and Academician, was specially noted for his studies of Canada, the States and Latin America. See his *Les États-unis d'aujourd'hui* (1927, trans. *America comes of Age*), *Le Canada, Puissance internationale* (1937), *Suez and Panama* (trans. 1940) and *America in Mid-century* (1955).

SIEGMUND. See SIGISMUND.

SIELMANN, Heinz, *zeel'-* (1917–), German naturalist and photographer specializing in nature films; born at Königsberg. Interested in animal photography from boyhood, he started making films in 1938 and won the German Oscar for documentary films three years running (1953–55). He evolved techniques enabling him to take films of happenings inside the lairs of animals and inaccessible types of birds' nests (e.g., the woodpecker), which have revolutionized the study of animal behaviour. See his *My Year with the Woodpeckers* (trans. 1959).

SIEMENS, *zee'-*, name of a German family of electrical engineers and industrialists, of whom the following are especially noteworthy:

(1) **Ernst Werner von** (1816–92), German engineer and founder of the firm, brother of (2), born at Lenthe, Hanover, in 1834 entered the Prussian artillery, and in 1844 took charge of the artillery workshops at Berlin. He developed the telegraphic system in Prussia, discovered the insulating property of gutta-percha, and devoted himself to making telegraphic and electrical apparatus. In 1847 was established at Berlin the firm since 1867 called Siemens Brothers, with branches elsewhere. Besides devising numerous forms of galvanometer and other electrical instruments, Siemens was one of the discoverers of the self-acting dynamo. He determined the electrical resistance of different substances, the Siemens Unit being called after him. In 1886 he endowed a technological institute; in 1888 he was ennobled. See his *Personal Recollections* (trans. 1893), and Life by J. O. Scott (1958). One of his sons, **Wilhelm** (1855–1919), was one of the pioneers of the incandescent lamp.

(2) **Sir William (Karl Wilhelm)** (1823–83) German-born British electrical engineer, brother of (1), born at Lenthe, in 1843 visited England, introduced a process for electro-gilding invented by Werner and himself, in 1844 patented his differential governor, and was naturalized in 1859. F.R.S. from 1862, he received many distinctions for his inventions in metallurgy, was president of the British Association (1882), was knighted in April 1883, and died in London. As manager in England of the firm of Siemens Brothers, he was actively engaged in the construction of telegraphs, designed the steamship *Faraday* for cable-laying, promoted electric lighting, and constructed the Portrush Electric Tramway (1883). The principle of his regenerative furnace was largely utilized, notably by himself in the manufacture of steel. Other inventions were a water-meter, pyrometer and bathometer. See Lives by Pole (1888) and J. D. Scott (1958). He was assisted in England by another brother, **Friedrich** (1826–1904), who invented a regenerative smelting oven (1856) extensively used in glassmaking.

SIENKIEWICZ, Henryk, *sheng-kyay'vich* (1846–1916), Polish novelist, born near Łuków, lived in America from 1876 to 1878, and after a hunting expedition in East Africa (1892) wrote the children's story *Desert and Wilderness.* Most of his works, however, are strongly realistic; many have been translated, among them *With Fire and Sword* (1884), *The Deluge* (1886), *Children of the Soil* (1893) and *Quo Vadis* (1896). He was awarded the Nobel prize in 1905. See *Letters*, ed. C. Morley (1960).

SIERRA. See MARTÍNEZ SIERRA.

SIEYÈS, Emmanuel Joseph Comte, *syay-yes* (1748–1836), French statesman, generally called the Abbé Sieyès, born at Fréjus, May 3, studied theology and became canon at Tréguier (1775), then chancellor and vicar-general of Chartres, and as such was sent to the assembly of the clergy of France. His three pamphlets carried his name over France: *Vues sur les moyens d'exécution* (1788), *Essai sur les privilèges* (1788), and, the most famous of all, *Qu'est-ce que le tiers-état?* (1789). He was elected deputy for Paris, and had much to do with the formation of the National Assembly. He gained great influence, and the division of France into departments was mainly his work. He took part in the declaration of the Rights of Man (August 26, 1789), and opposed the royal veto. He was elected to the Legislative Assembly, sat in the centre, and also voted for the king's death; but as the Revolution grew, he lapsed into 'philosophic silence'. He opposed the new constitution of Year III

(1795), and declined a seat on the Directory named by the new *corps législatif*, but had a share in the *coup d'état* of September 3, 1797. In 1798 he went on a mission to Berlin, in 1799 was elected to the Directory. Bonaparte returned from Egypt in October, and together they plotted the Revolution of 18th Brumaire (November 9, 1799), the result of which was the institution of the Consulate of Sieyès, Bonaparte and Roger Ducos. Sieyès drew up a constitution, a masterpiece of complexity, its aim to break the force of democracy by dividing it. Finding himself deceived by Bonaparte, he threw up his consulship, but received the title of count, 600,000 francs, and the estate of Crosne. Exiled at the Restoration, he lived in Belgium for fifteen years, returned in 1830, and died June 20, 1836. See works by Mignet (1836), Beauverger (1858), Bigeon (1894), Clapham (1912), Van Deusen (1932) and P. Bastid (1939).

SIGISMUND (1368–1437), Holy Roman emperor (1411–37), son of Charles IV, in 1396 as king of Hungary was heavily defeated by the Turks at Nicopolis, but later conquered Bosnia, Herzegovina and Serbia. As Holy Roman emperor, he induced Pope John XXIII to summon the Council of Constance to end the Hussite schism, supported the party of reform, but made no effort to uphold the safe conduct he had granted to Huss, and permitted him to be burned. In consequence his succession to the throne of Bohemia was opposed by the Hussites. See a book by Main (1903).

SIGISMUND, the name of three kings of Poland:

Sigismund I (1466–1548), king from 1506, father of (II). His court was filled with factions fomented by his wife, the daughter of the Duke of Milan, and the Reformation raised new troubles. In a war with Russia he lost Smolensk, but was partly compensated with the overlordship of Moldavia. In 1537 occurred the first rebellion of the nobility against the kingly authority, and Sigismund was obliged to make concessions.

Sigismund II (1520–72), king from 1548, son of (I), uncle of (III). During his reign the Reformation spread rapidly. In 1569 Lithuania was joined to Poland, and Poland acquired Livonia.

Sigismund III, Sigismund Vasa (1566–1632), elected king of Poland in 1587, from 1592 to 1604 was also at least nominal king of Sweden. Constant disputes took place between him and the Diet, and he was a great persecutor of the Protestants. He supported the false Demetrius (q.v.). The Poles took Moscow and caused his son, **Ladislaus**, to be crowned tsar, but in 1618 he finally resigned his claims.

SIGNAC, Paul, *see-nyak* (1863–1935), French artist, born in Paris. He exhibited in 1884 with the Impressionists and was later associated with Henri Edmond Cross (1856–1910), and Seurat (q.v.) in the neo-Impressionist movement. Signac, however, used mosaiclike patches of pure colour (as compared with Seurat's pointillist dots), mainly in seascapes, for he sailed to most French ports and was particularly fond of St Tropez. He published *D'Eugène Delacroix à néo-impressionisme*, in which he sought to establish a scientific basis for his 'divisionist' theories (1899), and a study of *Jongkind* (1927).

SIGNORELLI, Luca, *seen-yo-rel'lee* (*c.* 1441–1523), Italian painter, born at Cortona, worked, especially in frescoes, at Loreto, Rome, Florence, Siena, Cortona and Orvieto, where the cathedral contains his greatest work, the frescoes of *The Preaching of Anti-Christ* and *Last Judgment* (1500–04) which display his great technical skill in the drawing of male nudes. He was one of the painters summoned by Pope Julius II in 1508 to adorn the Vatican, and dismissed to make way for Raphael. See studies by M. Crutwell (1899), G. Mancini (1903) and A. Venturi (1922).

SIGURDSSON, Jón, *si'gurths-son* (1811–79), Icelandic scholar and politician, was educated at Copenhagen University. He published editions of the Icelandic classics as well as authoritative works on the history and laws of Iceland. He became the revered leader of the movement to secure greater political autonomy and freedom of trade for Iceland—a movement which culminated in 1874 in the grant of a constitution by Denmark.

SIKORSKI, Władysław (1881–1943), Polish statesman and soldier, born in Galicia, studied engineering at Cracow and Łwów universities, joined the underground movement for Polish freedom from Tsarist rule, served under General Piłsudski as head of the war department, but after the treaty of Brest-Litovsk was imprisoned by the Austrians. In 1919 he commanded a Polish Infantry Division at Vilna during the Russian-Polish war and in 1920 defended Warsaw. In 1921 he became commander-in-chief and in 1922 was elected premier. After Piłsudski's *coup d'état* (1926) he retired and wrote military history in Paris. He returned to Poland in 1938, advocated a strong alliance with Britain and France, but was treated with suspicion and refused a command when Poland was invaded. He fled, fought in France, became c.-in-c. of the Free Polish forces and premier of the Polish government in exile from June 1940 in London. He signed a treaty with the Soviet Union in 1941 which annulled the Russo-German partition of Poland in 1939. But the discovery of Polish officers' graves at Katyn (1943) led to the breaking off of diplomatic relations between the two countries. He was killed in an air-crash over Gibraltar, July 4, 1943.

SIKORSKY, Igor Ivan, *-kor'-* (1889–1972), Russian-born American aeronautical engineer, born in Kiev, built and flew the first four-engined aeroplane (1913). emigrated to Paris (1918) and to the United States (1919) and founded the Sikorsky Aero Engineering Corporation (1923), which later was merged into the United States Aircraft Corporation. He built several flying-boats and the first successful helicopter in the western hemisphere (1939). He was awarded the Presidential Certificate of Merit (1948) and the Silver Medal of the British Royal Aeronautical Society (1949).

SILESIUS. See ANGELUS.

SILHOUETTE, Étienne de, *sil-oo-et* (1709–1767), the parsimonious French minister of finance in 1759 whose name was applied to cheap blacked-in shadow outlines.

SILIUS ITALICUS, Gaius (A.D. 25–101), minor Latin poet, became a prominent forensic orator, was consul in 68, and then proconsul in Asia. Having contracted an incurable disease, he starved himself to death. His epic poem, *Punica* is unoriginal. See study by Nicol (1936).

SILLANPÄÄ, Frans Eemil (1888–1964), Finnish writer, born at Hämeenkyrö, author of short stories and novels, in which realism and idealism are fused with remarkable psychological insight. Two of his masterpieces, *The Maid Silja* (1931) and *Meek Heritage* (1938), have been translated into English. He was awarded the Nobel prize for literature in 1939.

SILLIMAN, (1) Benjamin (1779–1864), American chemist, father of (2), born at Trumbull, Conn., was admitted to the bar in 1802, but became professor of Chemistry at Yale and studied this subject at Philadelphia, Edinburgh and London, specializing in electrolysis. He was founder (1818) and editor of the *American Journal of Science.* See Lives by G. P. Fisher (1866) and E. H. Thomson (1947).

(2) **Benjamin** (1816–85), American chemist, son of (1), born in New York, became professor at Yale, assisted his father in his editorial work and showed that petroleum was a mixture of hydrocarbons, different in character from vegetable and oils, and could be separated by fractional distillation.

SILVA, Antonio José da (1705–39), Portuguese playwright and Offenbachian librettist, who was born at Rio de Janeiro, studied law at Coimbra, and was burnt with wife and mother by the Inquisition at Lisbon as a relapsed Jew.

SILVESTER. See SYLVESTER.

SIMENON, Georges, *see-mè-nõ* (1903–), Belgian-born master of the detective story, born at Liège, in Paris became one of the most prolific authors of his day, writing under a variety of pseudonyms. He revolutionized detective fiction by his tough, morbidly psychological Inspector Maigret series (1930 ff.), in which the ordinary, everyday person assumes importance only as a victim of an exceptionally violent crime. Gide once described him as 'the best novelist in French literature today'.

SIMEON, Charles (1759–1836), English evangelical preacher, born at Reading, fellow of King's College, Cambridge, led the evangelical revival in the Church of England. See *Memoirs* by Carus (1857), and studies by Moule (1892) and C. H. Smyth (1940).

SIMEON OF DURHAM (d. before 1138), monkish chronicler, wrote *Historia Ecclesiae Dunelmensis, Historia Regum Anglorum et Dacorum.* Arnold edited his *Opera* (Rolls Series, 1882–85).

SIMEON STYLITES, St, *stī-lī'teez* (A.D. 387–459), earliest of the Christian ascetic Pillar-saints, after living nine years in his Syrian monastery without leaving his cell, at Telanessa near Antioch established himself on the top of a pillar 72 feet high. Here he spent thirty years, preaching to crowds.

SIMMS, William Gilmore (1806–70), American novelist, born at Charleston, where he edited the *City Gazette* and published *Lyrical and other Poems* (1827), *The Vision of Cortes* (1829), *The Tricolour* (1830), *Atalantis* (1832), *The Yemassee* (1835), *The Partisan* (1835), *Charlemont* (1856), and many other works. He was an apologist for slavery and the South. See Lives by Cable (1888) and Trent (1892).

SIMNEL, Lambert (*c.* 1477–*c.* 1534), English impostor, a baker's son, in 1487 was set up in Ireland as, first, a son of Edward IV, and then as the Duke of Clarence's son, Edward, Earl of Warwick (1475–99), then imprisoned in the Tower, and afterwards beheaded, by Henry VII. Backed by Margaret of Burgundy, his suppositious aunt, Simnel had some success in Ireland and was crowned at Dublin as Edward VI, but, landing in Lancashire with 2000 German mercenaries, he was defeated at Stoke Field, Notts (June 16), and subsequently became a royal scullion and falconer.

SIMON, (1) Sir John (1816–1904), English pathologist, was surgeon at St Thomas's Hospital, London, and first medical officer of health for London. He was responsible for many sanitary reforms. See study by R. Lambert (1963).

(2) **John Allsebrook Simon, 1st Viscount** (1873–1954), English statesman and lawyer, born at Bath, educated at Fettes College, Edinburgh, and Wadham, Oxford, was junior counsel for the British government in the Alaska boundary arbitration. He became Liberal M.P. in 1906, took silk in 1908 and was knighted in 1910 when he became solicitor-general. He was attorney-general (1913–15), home secretary (1915–16), resigned from the Cabinet for his opposition to conscription, served at the front (1917–18) and returned to become one of the wealthiest members of the legal profession. As chairman of the Indian statutory commission (1927–30) he proved in advance of Conservative opinion of the time. Deserting the Liberals, he fully supported MacDonald's coalition governments and became foreign secretary (1931) and leader of the National Liberals. He attempted a middle-of-the-road policy in European affairs but without much success, proposing the 'Eastern Locarno' pact. He was home secretary again (1935–1937), was chancellor of the Exchequer (1937–40) and lord chancellor in Churchill's wartime coalition government (1940–45). His second wife, **Kathleen Harvey,** was a well-known anti-slavery crusader. He was created viscount in 1940. He wrote a standard legal work on income tax (1956). See his autobiographical *Retrospect* (1952).

(3) **Jules François,** *see-mõ* (1814–96), French statesman and philosopher, a philosophy lecturer at the Sorbonne in 1839, became a deputy in 1848 and, refusing the oath of allegiance, established himself as a leader of the left-wing republicans in 1873, when he resigned as minister of public instruction because his educational reforms were severely attacked. He directed the *Siècle* newspaper from 1874, became prime minister in 1876, but resigned following a

dispute with President Macmahon. He edited the French rationalists Descartes, Malebranche and Arnauld, and wrote a number of works on political philosophy and biographical studies. See Life by Séché (1878).

(4) **Richard** (1638–1712), French biblical critic, born at Dieppe, entered the Oratory in 1659, lectured on philosophy, and catalogued the oriental MSS. in the library of the order at Paris. His criticisms upon Arnauld caused great displeasure among the Port-Royalists, and the scandal caused by the liberalism of his *Histoire critique du Vieux Testament* (1678) in which he denied that Moses was the author of the Pentateuch, led to his expulsion from the order and retirement to Belleville as *curé*. In 1682 he resigned his parish, and lived thereafter in literary retirement. Few writers of his age played a more prominent part in polemics. His *Histoire critique* (Eng. trans. 1682), suppressed through Bossuet's and the Jansenists' influence, often anticipates the later German rationalists, and is the first work which treats the Bible as a literary product.

SIMONIDES OF AMARGOS, *sī-mon'i-deez* (fl. 660 B.C.), Greek iambic poet, native of Samos, founded a colony on the island of Amargos.

SIMONIDES OF CEOS, *see'os* (556–468 B.C.), Greek lyric poet, born in the island of Ceos, lived many years at Athens. From the Persian invasion of Greece he devoted his powers to celebrating the heroes and the battles of that struggle in elegies, epigrams, odes and dirges. He won fifty-six times in poetical contests, and carried off the prize from Æschylus by an elegy on the heroes who fell at Marathon. He spent his last years at the court of Hiero of Syracuse.

SIMON MAGUS ('Simon the Magician') appears about A.D. 37 as having become a commanding personality in Samaria through his sorceries. With Peter's reply to his offer to buy the gift of the Holy Ghost, and Simon's submission, the narrative of the Acts (viii. 9–24) leaves him. Later Christian authors bring him to Rome, and make him the author of heresies.

SIMONOV, Konstantin Mikhailovich (1915–), Russian writer, achieved a considerable reputation by his historical poem about Alexander Nevski, his poems of the second World War, *Days and Nights*, a novel about the defence of Stalingrad, and the play *The Russians*. He was awarded the Stalin prize three times.

SIMPSON, (1) **Sir George** (1792–1860), Canadian explorer, born in Scotland, was administrator (1821–56) of the Hudson's Bay Company's territory. In 1828 he made an overland journey round the world. Simpson's Falls and Cape George Simpson are named after him.

(2) **Sir George Clarke** (1878–1965), English meteorologist, was born at Derby and became a lecturer at Manchester University (1905). He was Scott's meteorologist on the Antarctic expedition (1910), investigated the causes of lightning, and was elected president of the Royal Meteorological Society (1940–1942).

(3) **Sir James Young, 1st Bart.** (1811–70), Scottish obstetrician, born at Bathgate, studied medicine at Edinburgh, where he became professor of Midwifery in 1840. He originated the use of ether as anaesthetic in childbirth, January 19, 1847, and experimenting on himself in the search for a better anaesthetic, discovered the required properties in chloroform, November 4, 1847, and championed its use against medical and religious opposition until its employment at the birth of Prince Leopold (1853) signalized general acceptance. He founded gynaecology by his sound tests, championed hospital reform, and in 1847 became physician to the Queen in Scotland. An enthusiastic archaeologist, he was created a baronet in 1866. See Lives by Duns (1873), H. L. Gordon (1898), and J. D. Comrie, *History of Scottish Medicine* (II, 1932).

(4) **Thomas** (1710–61), English mathematician, 'the oracle of Nuneaton', where he was born, educated himself, became professor of Mathematics at Woolwich (1743) and was elected F.R.S. in 1746. He published a long series of works (1737–57) on fluxions, chance, annuities, algebra, trigonometry, &c. See Life by Hutton prefixed to Davis's edition of the *Fluxions* (1805).

SIMROCK, Karl Joseph (1802–76), German poet and scholar, born at Bonn, entered the Prussian state service. He translated the *Nibelungenlied* (1827), edited German mediaeval poets and legends, wrote on Shakespeare's sources (1831), &c. He was professor of Old German at Bonn from 1850. See monograph by Hocker (1877).

SIMS, George Robert (1847–1922), English author, born in London, contributed his 'Dagonet' ballads and other articles to the *Referee*. He wrote plays, including *The Lights o' London* (1881), and novels. He was made a Swedish knight of St Olaf in 1905. See *My Life* (1916).

SIMSON, Robert (1687–1768), Scottish mathematician, became professor of Mathematics at Glasgow (1711). His great work was his restoration of Euclid's lost treatise on *Porisms* (1776). He published *Sectiones Conicae* (1735) and a restoration of Apollonius's *Loci Plani* (1749); his *Elements of Euclid* (1756) was the basis of nearly all editions for over a century. See a volume of *Reliqua* (1776) and Memoir by Trail (1812).

SINATRA, Francis Albert (Frank) (1917–), American singer and film actor, born in New Jersey, started his long and highly-successful career as recording artist singing with bands and on radio, and as one of the most-publicized teenage idols. He made his film début in musicals in 1943, but later successfully switched to dramatic rôles, most notably in *From Here to Eternity* (1953, Oscar as Best Supporting Actor). See study by A. Shaw (1968).

SINCLAIR, or St Clair, the name of the Earls of Orkney (1379–1471) and afterwards of Caithness. They were hereditary grand-master masons of Scotland 1455–1736. Roslin Castle near Edinburgh was the seat of the St Clairs.

SINCLAIR, (1) **Sir Archibald Henry MacDonald, 1st Viscount Thurso** (1890–1970), Scottish Liberal politician, descendant of (2), educated at Eton and Sandhurst, served in the army (1910–21), entered parliament in

1922, became chief whip (1930–31) and leader of the Liberals (1935–45), and was secretary of state for Air in the Churchill administration (1940–45).

(2) **Sir John, 1st Bart.** (1754–1835), Scottish politician and agriculturalist, born at Thurso Castle, studied at Edinburgh, Glasgow and Oxford, was admitted to both the Scottish and English bars (1775–82), and sat in parliament (1780–1811). In 1784 he published a *History of the Revenue of the British Empire*; and in 1786 was created a baronet. He established the Board of Agriculture in 1793, and compiled a *Statistical Account of Scotland* (1791–99), comprising a description of every parish in Scotland, mainly by help of the parish ministers. See Correspondence (1831) and Life (1837). His daughter, **Catherine** (1800–64), wrote children's books, &c.

(3) **May** (1865?–1946), British novelist, born at Rock Ferry, Cheshire, and educated at Cheltenham, wrote *The Divine Fire* (1904), *The Creators* (1910), *The Dark Night* (1924), *Anne Severn*, &c. She also wrote books on philosophical idealism.

(4) **Upton Beall** (1878–1968), American novelist, born at Baltimore, horrified the world with his exposure of meat-packing conditions in Chicago in his novel *The Jungle* (1906). Later novels such as *Metropolis* (1908), *King Coal* (1917), *Oil* (1927) are more and more moulded by his socialist beliefs. He was for many years prominent in Californian politics and attempted to found a communistic colony at Englewood, New Jersey. His *Dragon's Teeth* (1942) won the Pulitzer prize. See his autobiographical works (1932, 1962) and *A World to Win* (1946).

SINDHIA, the title of the Mahratta princes of Gwalior. Their founder was **Ranaji Sindhia**, who rose to high rank in the bodyguard of the Peshwa, and had a grant of half the province of Mala. His most noteworthy successors in chronological order, were: (1) **Mádhava Ráo Sindhia** (d. 1794), illegitimate son of the above, joined the Mahratta confederation, and was crippled for life at Panipat (1761). In 1770, along with the Peshwa and Holkar, he aided the Moghul to expel the Sikhs and became virtually supreme in Hindustan. He came into collision with the British in 1779, and was thoroughly beaten by Hastings, but by the treaty of Salbai (1783) was confirmed in all his possessions. In 1784 he captured Gwalior, in 1785 marched on Delhi, and subsequently seized Agra, Alighur and nearly the whole of the Doab. He raised and drilled an army in European fashion, neglecting the cavalry, and won Akbar and crushed Jodhpur, Udaipur and Jaipur, three Rajput states, and Holkar remained his ally. He died, or was murdered, at Poona. See Keene's *Mádhava Ráo Sindhia* (1892). (2) **Daulat Rao Sindhia** (1779–1827), grandnephew of (1), ravaged Indore and Poona, but was routed by Holkar (1802), and next year brought upon himself the vengeance of the East India Company. The Mahrattas were routed at Assaye and Argaum by Sir Arthur Wellesley, and were scattered at Laswari by Lord Lake. Thereupon Sindhia ceded all his possessions in the Doab and along the right bank of the Jumna to the British. Gwalior was restored in 1805. (3) **Baji Rao** (d. 1886), who during the Mutiny took the field against the rebels; but most of his troops deserted him, and he fled to Agra. He was reinstated, and was succeeded by his adopted son.

SINDING, Christian (1856–1941), Norwegian composer, born at Kongsberg, studied in Germany. He wrote two violin and a piano concerto, and three symphonies, as well as chamber music and songs. His brother, **Otto** (1842–1909), was a painter. Another, **Stephan** (1846–1922), a sculptor.

SINGER, Isaac Merritt (1811–75), American inventor and manufacturer of sewing-machines, born at Pittstown, New York, patented a rock drill (1839), a carving machine (1849) and at Boston (1852) an improved single-thread, chain-stitch sewing-machine, and although he had to pay **Elias Howe** (1819–67) compensation for his use of the Howe needle, the success of his Singer Manufacturing Company was assured. He died at Torquay, England.

SIQUEIROS, David Alfaro, *si-kay'ros* (1898–   ), Mexican mural painter, born at Chihuahua. With Rivera and Orozco, he launched the review *El Machete* in Mexico City in 1922, and in 1930 he was imprisoned for revolutionary activities. He was later expelled from the U.S.A., and during the 'thirties he worked in South America. He is one of the principal figures in 20th-century Mexican mural painting, and notable for his experiments in the use of modern synthetic materials. He exhibited at the Venice Biennale of 1950.

SISLEY, Alfred, *sees-lay* (1839–99), French Impressionist painter and etcher, born in Paris, of English ancestry. He joined Monet and Renoir in Gleyre's studio and was also influenced by Corot. He painted landscapes almost exclusively, particularly in the valleys of the Seine, the Loing and the Thames, and was noted for his subtle treatment of skies.

SISMONDI, Jean Charles Léonard Simonde de, *-mon'-* (1773–1842), Swiss historian and economist of Italian descent, was born at Geneva. The French Revolution drove his family into exile, but in 1800 Sismondi himself went back to Geneva, and obtained a municipal office. His *Histoire des républiques italiennes du moyen âge* (1807–18), a pioneer work, contributed greatly to the Italian Liberal tradition. In 1813 appeared his *Littérature du midi de l'Europe* (Eng. by Roscoe), and in 1819 he began his *Histoire des Français*. His *Richesse commerciale* (1803) is written from the standpoint of the *Wealth of Nations*; but his *Nouveaux Principes d'économie politique* (1819) inclines to socialism. See *Lettres inédites* (1863), and Life by J. R. De Salis (1932).

SITTER, Willem de (1872–1934), Dutch astronomer, became director and professor of Astronomy at Leyden (1908). He computed the size of the universe as two thousand million light years in radius, containing about 80,000 million galaxies. As opposed to Einstein's static conception, he visualized the universe as an expanding space-time continuum with motion and no matter (dynamic).

SITTING BULL (1834–90), American Indian warrior, chief of the Dakota Sioux, was a leader in the Sioux War of 1876–77, after which he escaped to Canada but surrendered in 1881. Still rebellious, he was killed while attempting to evade the police in the 'ghost dance' uprising of 1890.

SITWELL, (1) **Edith** (1887–1964), English poet, sister of (2) and (3), daughter of Sir George Sitwell of Renishaw, Derbyshire, and Lady Ida Sitwell, daughter of Lord Londesborough, born at Scarborough. In his *The Scarlet Tree* her brother Sir Osbert Sitwell has described the isolation and frustration experienced by the young girl till her governess introduced her to music and literature. She first attracted notice by her editorship of an anthology on new poetry entitled *Wheels* (1916–21). This was the *avant garde* of a poetry which repudiated the flaccid quietism of Georgian verse, but Miss Sitwell's shock tactics were not fully displayed till *Façade* appeared in 1922, when, with William Walton's music, it was given a stormy public reading in London. *Façade* was succeeded by *Bucolic Comedies*, which is for the most part in the same fantastic vein, but the elegiac romantic begins to appear and this vein is fully exploited in *The Sleeping Beauty* (1924), and finally worked out in the amazing *Elegy for Dead Fashion* (1926), with its profusion of riches which perhaps tire the imagination in the end. The short poems of this romantic period, 'Colonel Fantock', 'Daphne', 'The Strawberry' and above all 'The Little Ghost who died for Love' are probably the tenderest, most beautiful things she ever wrote. At the close of this period Miss Sitwell suddenly flamed into indignation over the evil in society—in *Gold Coast Customs* (1929) the gaiety of *Façade* is replaced by the horror underlying civilization. In the 'thirties she turned to prose work. *Alexander Pope* (1930) rather mothers the poet, but contributed to the modern revival of his fame by close analysis of the beauty of his texture. Perhaps she chose Swift also as the subject of her novel *I Live Under a Black Sun* because of the madness which threatens those too finely constituted to bear the horrors of life in a grim age. During World War II Miss Sitwell denounced with great vehemence the cruelty of man. The brittle artifice of *Façade* would not suit the vatic utterance of *Street Songs* (1942) or *Green Song* (1944), *The Song of the Cold* (1945) and *The Shadow of Cain* (1947). Direct statement does not, however, chill her imagerial faculty though the symbolism is less esoteric. Christian symbolism now triumphs, though mingled with that of the oriental mystics and even the anthropologists. Horror and compassion inspire poems like 'Still falls the Rain', 'An Old Woman', and 'Invocation' (from *Green Song*). Opinions differ as to whether she is a greater poet in her early or her late work. She set out to refresh the exhausted rhythms of traditional poetry by introducing the rhythms of jazz and other dance music and also by free association in expression and the transference of the bodily senses (light 'creaked' and the rain 'squawks down . . . grey as a guinea-fowl')—with the result that sense was sacrificed to the evocation of states of feeling. In her late verse these gay vanities disappear, but one detects a certain lack of control in her poems on the age of the atom bomb—*Dirge for the New Sunrise*, *The Shadow of Cain* and *The Canticle of the Rose* (1949). Other works include *The English Eccentrics* (1933), *Victoria of England* (1936), *Fanfare for Elizabeth* (1946), *The Outcasts* (verse; 1962), *The Queens and the Hive* (on Elizabeth and Mary; 1962). She was created D.B.E. in 1954. See her autobiography *Taken Care Of*, published posthumously, (1965) and critical studies by R. L. Mégroz, *The Three Sitwells* (1927), D. Powell, C. M. Bowra (1947), also *Celebrations for Edith Sitwell*, ed. J. G. Villa (1948).

(2) **Sir Osbert** (1892–1969), English author, brother of (1), was born in London and educated at Eton. His youth was spent mainly at Renishaw with occasional visits to Scarborough, which figures a good deal in his own satiric work, and in that of Edith Sitwell, as a symbol of Victorian decrepitude. He served in the Brigade of Guards in World War I, and in 1916 was invalided home. This provided him with the leisure to set up as a satirist of war and the types which ingloriously prosper at home. Many of his satirical poems were published in the *Nation* and collected in *Argonaut and Juggernaut* (1919) and *Out of the Flame* (1923). After the war he narrowed his literary acquaintance to the *habitués*, i.e., his sister and brother, Ezra Pound, T. S. Eliot and Wyndham Lewis. The object of the group was the regeneration of arts and letters, and in this pursuit the Sitwells acquired notoriety, Sir Osbert not least by his novel *Before the Bombardment* (1927), which anatomized the grandees of Scarborough and by implication the social orders in general. Neither this nor his other novel, *Miracle on Sinai* (1933), was successful, and he has always done better in the short story, especially in those, like the collection *Dumb Animal* (1930), where his delicacy of observation and natural compassion are more in evidence than is satire. The paternalism of the aristocracy is expressed in *England Reclaimed, a Book of Eclogues* (1927). When he came to collect his short stories and his verse, the same volume offers this contrast between mordant satire and human kindliness—the satiric sharpness of *Triple Fugue* (1924) with the humanity of the stories in *Dumb Animal* parallels the resentment of the early verse with the acceptance of rural manners in the *Eclogues*. His aristocratic bent took the form of travel in the grand manner in the 'thirties. He had published *Discursions on Travel, Art and Life* in 1925, but now *Winters of Content* (1932) displayed mature descriptive powers. *Brighton* (1935, in collaboration with Miss Margaret Barton) anticipated the vogue of 18th- and early 19th-century architecture and at the close of the 'thirties *Escape with Me*, describing a journey to China, proved his most charming book of travel. All these elements enter into the great autobiography he was planning. The first volume of *Left Hand: Right Hand*

appeared in 1944, to be followed by *The Scarlet Tree* (1946), *Great Morning* (1947) and *Laughter in the Next Room* (1948). *Noble Essences* (1950) completed this great work, which must rank with the finest of its kind in any language. Other collections of essays and stories include *Penny Foolish* (1935), *Sing High, Sing Low* (1944), *Alive-Alive Oh* (1947) and *Pound Wise* (1963). He succeeded to the baronetcy in 1942. See study by Fulford (1951), Mégroz, *Five Novelists of Today* (1933), Joyce, *Triad of Genius* (1943).

(3) **Sacheverell** (1897–), English poet and art critic, younger brother of (2), went through the same preparatory stages as Sir Osbert—the same private school, Eton, officer in a Guards regiment and unlimited travel abroad. After the war of 1914 the brothers toured Spain and Italy. Italy became their second country, the fruit of which in Sacheverell's case was *Southern Baroque Art*, a remarkable achievement for a man in his twenties. *The Gothick North* followed in 1929, and this with his *German Baroque Art* completed his study of European art. The popularity of the baroque today owes much to his persistent praise of this mode. Poetry went hand in hand with the sister muse. The critics so far have not accepted Dame Edith's assurance that he is one of the greatest poets of the last one hundred and fifty years. His verse is much more traditional than his sister's, indeed at his best, and it can be very good, he is an imitator of past modes, playing quite lovely variations on Pope and others in which the note is a sumptuous melancholy. His descriptions of paintings in *Canons of Giant Art* are interesting, but his ambitious study of good and evil, *Dr Donne and Gargantua*, seems to get bogged down in philosophical subtleties. His poems include, beside the works mentioned, *Hortus Conclusus*, *The People's Palace*, *The Hundred and One Harlequins*, *The Thirteenth Caesar* and *The Cyder Feast*. The life can best be disengaged from the various volumes of Sir Osbert's *Left Hand: Right Hand*, but see also Mégroz, *The Three Sitwells* (1927) and Sacheverell's *Journey to the Ends of Time* (Vol. I, 1959).

SIVERTSEN. See ADELAER.

SIXTUS, the name of five popes.—The first was beheaded *c.* A.D. 125; the second was martyred in 258; the third was pope (432–440) when St Patrick began his mission in Ireland:

Sixtus IV, or Francesco della Rovere (1414–84), pope from 1471, was a famous Franciscan preacher. His nepotism led to many abuses, and he is said to have connived at the Pazzi conspiracy against the Medici at Florence; it was certainly engineered by his nephew. He fostered learning, built the Sistine chapel and the Sistine bridge, enriched the Vatican library, and was a patron of painters; but he lowered the moral authority of the Papacy. In 1482 he entered into an alliance with the Venetians which led to a general Italian war. His private life seems to have been blameless. See Pastor's *Popes from the Close of the Middle Ages* (trans. 1895).

Sixtus V (Felice Peretti) (1521–90), pope from 1585, was also a great Franciscan preacher and a professor of Theology Created a cardinal (Montalto) in 1570, his assumed feebleness procured him election to the Papacy in succession to Gregory XIII in 1585. But his rule was marked by vigorous measures of improvement. He repressed licence and disorder, reformed the administration of the law and the disposal of patronage, carried on many public enterprises, and having found an empty treasury, secured a surplus of five million crowns. To the Jews he extended liberty. The great aim of his foreign policy was to combat Protestantism and uphold the balance of the Catholic powers. He fixed the number of cardinals at seventy. Under his authority were published new editions of the Septuagint and Vulgate—the latter very inaccurate.

SKANDERBEG, i.e., **Iskander** or **Alexander Bey**, also known as **George Castriota** (1403–1468), Albanian patriot, was born of Serb descent. Carried away by Turks when seven, brought up a Moslem, he was a favourite commander of Sultan Murad II. In 1443 he changed sides, renounced Islam, and drove the Turks from Albania, where he valiantly defeated every force sent against him. For 20 years he maintained the independence of Albania with only occasional support from Naples, Venice and the pope. After his death Albanian opposition to the Turk collapsed. See Paganel's *Histoire du Scanderbeg* (1855).

SKEAT, Walter William (1835–1912), English philologist, born in London, and educated at King's College School and Christ's College, Cambridge, graduated as fourteenth wrangler in 1858, and became a fellow in 1860, and in 1878 professor of Anglo-Saxon. He was the first director of the Dialect Society (established 1873), and he contributed more than any scholar of his time to a sound knowledge of Middle English and English philology generally. He edited important texts, especially for the Early English Text Society. Other works are *A Moeso-Gothic Glossary* (1868), his admirable *Etymological English Dictionary* (new ed. 1910) and its abridgment (1911); *Principles of English Etymology* (1887–91); his great *Chaucer* (6 vols. 1894–95); the *Student's Chaucer* (1895); *A Student's Pastime* (1896); *Chaucerian and other Pieces* (1897); *The Chaucer Canon* (1900); *Glossary of Tudor and Stuart Words* (1914); and papers on place names.

SKELTON, (1) John (*c.* 1460–1529), English satirical poet, studied at Cambridge, perhaps also at Oxford, was created 'poet laureate' by both, was tutor to Prince Henry, and became rector of Diss, but seems later to have been suspended for having a concubine or wife. He had produced some translations and elegies in 1489, but began to strike an original vein of satirical vernacular poetry, overflowing with grotesque words and images and unrestrained jocularity, as in *The Bowge of Courte*, *Colyn Cloute* and *Why come ye nat to Courte*. Of these, the first is an allegorical poem; the second an unsparing attack on the corruptions of the church; and the last a sustained invective against Wolsey for which Skelton had to take sanctuary at Westminster. Other poems include *Garlande of Laurell* and *Magnyfycence*, his one surviving morality. See Dyce's edition (1843), books by Lloyd (1938), Gordon (1943).

(2) **Sir John** (1831–97), Scottish lawyer and writer, born in Edinburgh, wrote a defence of Mary Stuart (1876), sumptuous Lives of her (1893) and Charles I (1898), besides *Maitland of Lethington* (1887), *Table Talk of Shirley* (1895–96), &c.

SKENE, *skeen,* (1) **Sir John, Lord Curriehill** (*c.* 1543–1617), Scottish advocate, regent of St Mary's College, St Andrews, lived in Scandinavia, was ambassador, lord advocate, lord clerk-register and lord of session. He edited and translated into Scots a collection of old laws, *Regiam Majestatem* (1609).

(2) **William Forbes** (1809–92), Scottish historian, born at Inverie, a close friend of Scott. In 1881 succeeded Hill Burton as Scottish historiographer. Among his works are *The Highlanders of Scotland* (1837), *Celtic Scotland* (1876–80), &c.

SKINNER, (1) **James** (1778–1841), Indian soldier of Eurasian origin, joined the Indian army at fifteen, was promoted to lieutenant for gallantry, but dismissed by General Perron in 1803 because of his mixed origin. Under General Lord Lake, he formed Skinner's Horse, one of the most famous regiments in India. His rank of lieutenant-colonel was not recognized in London until 1827, when he was also made a Companion of the Bath. With these honours, the fabulous wealth of thirty years' looting, and several wives, he settled down to the life of a rich Mogul in his town house at Delhi and his country seat near by. Always inclined to scholarship and philanthropy, he now wrote books in flawless Persian, with decorations and numerous paintings by local artists, on the princes, castes and tribes of Hindustan; and built a mosque, a temple and the Church of St James in Delhi. Of his burial there it has been said that 'None of the Emperors of Hindustan was ever brought into Delhi in such state as Sikander Sahib'—the name associates his military genius with Alexander (Sikander) the Great. See Life by J. B. Fraser (1851).

(2) **John** (1721–1807), Scottish historian and songwriter, born at Birse, Aberdeenshire, became an Episcopalian minister at Longside near Peterhead. Although no Jacobite, his house was pillaged and his chapel burnt in 1746. He wrote *The Ecclesiastical History of Scotland* (1788) and several songs, of which 'The Ewie wi' the crookit horn' and 'Tullochgorum' are the best known. See Life by Walker (1883). His son, **John** (1744–1816), was Bishop of Aberdeen.

SKOBELEFF, Mikhail Dmitrievich, *sko'byi-lyef* (1843–82), Russian soldier, fought against the Polish insurgents (1863), and in 1871–75 was at the conquest of Khiva and Khokand. In the Russo-Turkish war of 1877–78 he bore a conspicuous part at Plevna, in the Shipka pass, and at Adrianople; in 1881 he stormed the Turkoman stronghold Göktepe. He was an ardent Panslavist.

SKORZENY, Otto (1908–), Austrian colonel, born in Vienna, was personally chosen by Hitler to kidnap Mussolini from co-belligerent internment in a mountain hotel on the Gran Sasso range. In September 1943 he succeeded in landing with a detachment of men in gliders on the short inclined slope in front of the hotel and after a short engagement whisking the dictator off in a small aeroplane, and so to Hitler's headquarters in East Prussia. In September 1944 he daringly infiltrated into the Citadel of Budapest and forcibly prevented Horthy from making a separate peace with Stalin, thus endangering German troops, and during the Ardennes offensive in December of that year carried out widespread sabotage behind Allied lines, for which he was tried as a war criminal but acquitted. See his memoirs, *Skorzeny's Special Missions* (trans. 1959).

SKRIABIN. See SCRIABIN.

SLADE, Felix, *slayd* (1790–1868), English antiquary and art collector of Halsteads, Yorkshire, bequeathed to the British Museum his engravings and Venetian glass, and founded art professorships at Oxford, Cambridge, and University College, London.

SLATER, Oscar (1873–1948), supposed murderer. A German Jew, he was convicted of the murder of Marion Gilchrist in Glasgow in 1909. Three witnesses identified him as the man seen leaving the scene of the crime, although their descriptions varied considerably and at least one of them was thought to have seen Slater's photograph before identifying him. After the trial, at which he was not called to give evidence, he was sentenced to death but this was commuted to life imprisonment. Because of protests of injustice by Conan Doyle and others, he was released after nineteen years and received £6000 in compensation.

SLATIN, Baron Rudolf Carl von, *slah'teen* (1857–1932), Austrian-born soldier in the British service, born near Vienna, in 1878 took service under Gordon in the Sudan. Governor of Darfur (1881), on the defeat of Hicks Pasha he surrendered (1883) to the Mahdi, escaped in 1895, and wrote a vivid description of his experiences, *Fire and Sword in the Soudan* (trans. 1896). As colonel he served in the Dongola and Omdurman expeditions (1896–98). He was inspector-general of the Sudan in 1900–14; and in World War II president of the Austrian Red Cross.

SLEIDANUS, properly **Philippi, Johannes** (1506–56), German historian, born at Schleiden, in 1537 entered the service of Francis I of France; but turning Protestant, was dismissed (1541), and served as ambassador of the Protestant princes of Germany. He wrote a Latin history of Charles V (1555). See Life by Baumgarten (1876).

SLESSOR, (1) **Sir John Cotesworth** (1897–), British air-marshal, born at Rhanikhet, India, educated at Haileybury, served in the Royal Flying Corps in World War I and was awarded the M.C. He was instructor at the R.A.F. Staff College (1924–25) and at Camberley (1931–34). His part in the Waziristan operations (1936–37) earned him the D.S.O. During World War II he was c.-in-c. of Coastal Command (1943) and of the Mediterranean theatre (1944–45). Promoted marshal in 1940, he was chief of the Air Staff (1950–52). His often original, penetrating and unorthodox views on nuclear strategy are expressed in *Strategy for the West* (1954) and *The Great Deterrent* (1957). He was knighted in 1943.

(2) **Mary** (1848–1915), Scottish missionary, born at Dundee, worked in a factory from childhood but, conceiving a burning ambition to become a missionary, got herself accepted by the United Presbyterian Church for teaching in Calabar, Nigeria, where she spent many years of devoted work among the natives. See Life by Livingstone (1931).

SLEVOGT, Max, *slay'fōKHt* (1868–1932), German Impressionist painter and engraver, born at Landshut. He studied in Munich and Berlin (where he later taught at the Academy), and worked with the Impressionist Corinth. His works comprise murals of historical scenes and swiftly executed landscapes and portraits.

SLEZER, John (d. 1714), Dutch engraver employed by Charles II and the Duke of York to make engravings of Scottish buildings. His *Theatrum Scotiae* (1693) was reprinted, with memoir, in 1874.

SLIM, William Joseph, 1st Viscount (1891–1970), British field-marshal, educated at King Edward's School, Birmingham. During World War I he served in Gallipoli, France and Mesopotamia. Transferring to the Gurkha Rifles, a succession of command and staff appointments brought him to high command in World War II. His greatest achievement was to restore morale in Burma and lead his reorganized forces, the famous 14th 'forgotten' army to victory over the Japanese. He was chief of the Imperial General Staff 1948–52, and governor-general of Australia 1953–60. He was created K.C.B. in 1944 and viscount in 1960. See his *Defeat into Victory* (1956) and memoirs, *Unofficial History* (1959).

SLOANE, Sir Hans, 1st Bart. (1660–1753), British physician, born at Killyleagh, County Down, the son of an Ulster Scot, studied in London and in France, and settled in London as a physician. Already F.R.S., he spent over a year (1685–86) in Jamaica, collecting a herbarium of 800 species. He was secretary to the Royal Society (1693–1713), president (1727), and, a baronet from 1710, was physician-general to the army (1716) and royal physician. His museum and library of 50,000 volumes and 3560 MSS. formed the nucleus of the British Museum. His great work was the *Natural History of Jamaica* (1707–25). See study by G. de Beer (1953).

SLOCUM, Joshua, *slō'kėm* (1844–*c.* 1910), American mariner, born at Wilmot Township, Nova Scotia, went early to sea as a ship's cook and in 1869 captained a trading vessel off the Californian coast. In 1886 he set off with his second wife and two sons on a converted bark, *Aquidneck*, for South America, was wrecked on a Brazilian sandbar, but from the wreckage built a canoe which took them all back to New York. In 1895 he set out from Boston without capital on the sloop *Spray* for the first solo cruise around the world, arriving back at Newport in 1898, having supported himself by lecturing on the way. In November 1909 he set out once more, but was not heard of again. See his *Sailing Alone Around the World* (1900), and Life by W. M. Teller (1959).

SŁOWACKI, Juljusz, *slo-vat'ski* (1809–49), Polish poet, born at Krzemieniec, settled in Paris in 1831. He belonged to the Romantic school, the influence of Byron, among others being perceptible in his work, which includes the historical drama *Marie Stuart* (1830), the dramatized legend *Balladyna* (1834), *Lilla Weneda* (1840), perhaps the most famous Polish tragedy, and *Mazeppa* (1839), which was translated into English.

SLUTER, Claus (*c.* 1350–1405/6), Flemish sculptor, born probably at Haarlem, went to Dijon under the patronage of Philip the Bold of Burgundy, and died there. His chief works are the porch sculptures of the Carthusian house of Champmol near Dijon, and the tomb of Philip the Bold. See study by Troescher (1932).

SMART, (1) **Christopher** (1722–71), English poet, born at Shipbourne near Tonbridge, was elected fellow of Pembroke College, Cambridge, in 1745. Improvidence, wit and a secret marriage upset his academic career and he settled to a precarious living in London. He died insane. Samuel Johnson assisted him in his monthly *Universal Visitor*. Smart's works include epigrams, birthday odes and occasional poems; the *Hilliad*, a heavy satire; and several translations from the Bible and the classics. His one real poem, *A Song to David* (first printed 1763; ed. Blunden, 1924), though marred by repetitions and defects of rhythm, shows a genuine spark of inspiration. See Browning's *Parleyings* and Gosse's *Gossip in a Library* (1892), and Lives by Mackenzie (1925) and Ainsworth and Noyes (1943).

(2) **Sir George Thomas** (1776–1867), English musician, uncle of (3), friend of Haydn and Weber, visited Beethoven and promoted Mendelssohn's music in England. He composed anthems, chants and glees.

(3) **Henry Thomas** (1813–79), English composer, nephew of (2), was organist to the Chapel Royal and composed an *Ave Maria* and part-songs, &c. See Life by Sparks (1880).

SMEATON, John (1724–94), English engineer, born at Austhorp near Leeds, gave up law and about 1750 removed to London as a mathematical-instrument maker. Elected F.R.S. in 1753, he won the Copley Medal for his mathematical and experimental researches into the mechanics of waterwheels and windmills and established his reputation with his novel design for the third Eddystone lighthouse (1756–59), which remained in use till 1877, and was re-erected on Plymouth Hoe as a memorial. His other chief engineering works include Ramsgate Harbour (1774), the Forth and Clyde Canal, &c. See Smiles's *Lives of the Engineers* (1905).

SMECTYMNUUS, a composite pseudonym used by Stephen Marshal, Edward Calamy, Thomas Young, Matthew Newcomen, and William Spurstow, who published in 1641 a pamphlet attacking Episcopacy which was answered by Hall and defended by Milton.

SMETANA, Bedřich, *smet'-* (1824–84), Czech composer, born in Litomyšl. He studied in Prague, and in 1884 opened a music school with the financial support of Liszt, who recommended his music to the German publisher Kistner. From 1856 to 1859 and again in 1860 he was conductor of the Philharmonic Orchestra in Göteborg, Sweden, but after his return to Prague he opened a new music school, and in 1866 became conductor of the new National Theatre, for which his operas were composed. Overwork destroyed his health, and in 1874 he became totally deaf, though he continued to compose until his mental breakdown in 1883. His compositions, intensely national in character, include nine operas (one unfinished), of which the best known are *The Bartered Bride*, *Dalibor* and *The Kiss*; his many orchestral and chamber works include the series of symphonic poems entitled *Má Vlast* (My Country) and the string quartet *Aus meinem Leben* (From My Life), both composed when he was deaf. See study by Bartoš (trans. 1953).

SMILES, Samuel (1812–1904), Scottish author and social reformer, was born at Haddington, took his Edinburgh M.D. at twenty, and published *Physical Education* (1838). He practised in Haddington, and then settled as a surgeon in Leeds, but became editor of the *Leeds Times*, secretary of the Leeds and Thirsk Railway in 1845, and in 1854 secretary of the Southeastern Railway, retiring in 1866. While at Leeds he met George Stephenson, and undertook a Life of him (1857). His famous *Self-Help* (1859; n.e. intro. A. Briggs 1958), with its short Lives of great men and the admonition ' Do thou likewise ', was the ideal Victorian school-prize. An *Autobiography* (published 1905) completed a long series of works, including *Lives of the Engineers* (3 vols. 1861–62; rev. eds. 1874, 1904, 5 vols.; reprinted 1969), *Character* (1871), *Thrift* (1875), *Duty* (1880), &c. See Life by A. Smiles (1956).

SMILLIE, Robert, *smī'li* (1857–1940), Scottish Labour politician, born of Scottish parents in Belfast, was president of the Scottish Miners' Federation 1894–1918, and again from 1921; and from 1912 to 1921 president of the Miners' Federation of Great Britain. He was Labour M.P. for Morpeth (1923-29).

SMIRKE, Sir Robert (1781–1867), English architect, son of Robert Smirke (1752–1845), painter and book-illustrator, was born in London. He became R.A. in 1811, was architect to the Board of Works and was knighted in 1831. Smirke's public buildings are usually classical, his domestic architecture Gothic. Covent Garden Theatre (1809) was his first great undertaking; the British Museum (1823–47) his best known. His brother, **Sydney** (1799–1877), completed the west wing of the museum and the reading room (1854), and rebuilt the Carlton Club (1857). He was elected R.A. in 1859.

SMITH, (1) Adam (1723–90), Scottish economist and philosopher, whose *Wealth of Nations* is the first masterpiece in political economy, born June 5 at Kirkcaldy, the posthumous son of the comptroller of customs, studied at Glasgow and Balliol College, Oxford. From 1748 he became one of the brilliant circle in Edinburgh which included David Hume, John Home, Hugh Blair, Lord Hailes and Principal Robertson. In 1751 he became professor of Logic at Glasgow, but exchanged the professorship for that of Moral Philosophy the following year. In 1759 he published his *Theory of Moral Sentiments*, based on Humeian doctrines. The essence of moral sentiments was sympathy, but a specialized conscience-stricken sympathy which Smith defined as that of an impartial and well-informed spectator. He met Quesnay, Turgot, Necker and others in Paris, when he was travelling tutor to the Duke of Buccleuch. He watched over the illness and death of his illustrious friend Hume, edited his noncontroversial papers and wrote a moving account of the latter's end to a Mr Strahan of London, which became controversial since respectability resented a prominent atheist dying with such dignity. Shortly afterwards (1776) Smith removed himself to London, where he became a member of the club to which Reynolds, Garrick and Johnson belonged. The same year he published a volume in five chapters intended as the first of a complete theory of society in the tradition of Scottish ' Moral Philosophy ', i.e., comprising natural theology, ethics, politics and law. This one volume, entitled *Inquiry into the Nature and Causes of the Wealth of Nations*, his magnum opus, examined in detail the consequences of economic freedom such as division of labour, the function of markets and mediums of exchange and the international implications. He attacked mediaeval mercantile monopolies and the theories of the French physiocrats, who made land the economic basis of wealth. But his doctrines were not yet those of full-blooded *laissez faire* for which the 19th-century utilitarians were responsible, for Smith wanted his economics to implement his earlier work on moral sentiments. Few works have had such influence. At a public dinner at Wimbledon, Pitt asked Smith to be seated first because prophetically in his words ' we are all your scholars '. His appointment as commissioner of customs (1778) brought him back to Edinburgh, where he died July 17, 1790, and was buried in the Canongate churchyard. He was elected F.R.S. (1767) and in 1787 lord rector of Glasgow University. Other works include essays on the formation of languages, the history of astronomy, classical physics and logic and the arts. His works were edited by Dugald Stewart (1811–12), who contributed a biography. Smith's Glasgow *Lectures on Justice, Police, Revenue, Arms* were edited from notes by a student in 1896. See Lives by Haldane (1887), Macpherson (1899), Hirst (1904), Scott (1937) and Fay (1956).

(2) **Alexander** (1829–67), Scottish poet, born at Kilmarnock, became a pattern-designer in Glasgow, sending occasional poems to the *Glasgow Citizen*. His *Life Drama* (1851) was highly successful at first but was strongly satirized by Aytoun in *Firmilian, a Spasmodic Tragedy*, and the adjective has stuck to Smith's poetry ever since. Immature and extravagant the poem was certainly, and its unconscious echoes of

Keats and Tennyson gave colour to the charge of plagiarism; still, Smith has a richness and originality of imagery that more than atone for all defects of taste and knowledge. In 1854 he was appointed secretary to Edinburgh University, and next year produced *Sonnets on the War* with Sydney Dobell, his brother poet of the 'Spasmodic' school. *City Poems* (1857) and *Edwin of Deira* (1861) were followed by essays, collected under the title *Dreamthorp* (1863), and novels. See Memoir by P. P. Alexander prefixed to his *Last Leaves* (1869), and Life by T. Brisbane (1869).

(3) **Alfred Emanuel** (1873–1944), American Democrat politician, born in New York, rose from newsboy to be governor of N.Y. State (1919–20, 1923–28). 'Al' Smith was beaten as Democratic candidate for the U.S. presidentship in 1928.

(4) **Augustus John** (1804–72), English lessee or 'king' from 1834 of the Scilly Islands, was M.P. for Truro from 1857.

(5) **Bernard** (1630–1708), English organ-builder, called 'Father Smith'. See HARRIS, RENATUS.

(6) **Mrs Burnett.** See SWAN, ANNIE.

(7) **Dodie**, pseud. until 1935 **C. L. Anthony** ( ), English playwright, novelist, and theatre producer, started as an actress but took up a business career. Her first play, *Autumn Crocus* (1930), was an instant success and enabled her to devote all her time to writing. Other plays include *Dear Octopus* (1938), *Letter from Paris* (adapted from *The Reverberator* by Henry James, 1952) and *I Capture the Castle* (adapted from her own novel, 1952). Other works include the children's book *The Hundred and One Dalmations* (1956).

(8) **Lady Eleanor Furneaux** (1902–45), English novelist, born in Birkenhead, a daughter of the 1st Earl of Birkenhead. She possessed a lively imagination and an intimate knowledge of Romany and circus life, and her novels, which include *Red Wagon* (1930), *Flamenco* (1931) and *Man in Grey* (1941), were, if rather sentimental, colourful and romantic. See her autobiographical *Life's a Circus* (1939), and Life by Birkenhead (1953).

(9) **Eli** (1801–57), American Congregational missionary from 1829 in Syria, born at Northford, Conn., died at Beirut, translated the Bible into Arabic. His son, **Benjamin Eli** (1857–1913), edited *The Century Dictionary, Atlas*, &c.

(10) **Sir Francis Pettit** (1808–74), English inventor, born at Hythe, was first with Ericsson in building screw-propelled ships (1834–1836). He also built the first screw steamship, the *Rattler* (1841–43). In 1860 was appointed curator of the Patent Office Museum, South Kensington, and in 1871 was knighted.

(11) **Frederick Edwin.** See BIRKENHEAD.

(12) **George** (1840–76), English Assyriologist, born in London, was a banknote engraver who studied cuneiform inscriptions in the British Museum, and in 1867 became an assistant there. He helped Sir H. Rawlinson with his *Cuneiform Inscriptions* (1870), furnished (1871) the key to the Cypriote character, and deciphered from Layard's tablets in 1872 the Chaldaean account of the Deluge. In 1873 he was dispatched to Nineveh to find the missing fragment of the tablet. It and other results of his excavations were presented to the British Museum, which itself sent him out again next year. While on a homeward journey from his third expedition, he died at Aleppo. See his *Assyrian Discoveries* (1875), &c.

(13) **George** (1824–1901), English publisher, joined his father's firm of Smith & Elder in 1838, becoming head in 1846. He founded the *Pall Mall Gazette* in 1865, in 1882 began the *Dictionary of National Biography*, and published the works of George Eliot, the Brownings, Mrs Gaskell, Trollope, &c.

(14) **Sir George Adam** (1856–1942) Scottish Biblical scholar, born in Calcutta, was a minister in Aberdeen (1882–92) and at the same time professor of Hebrew at Glasgow, wrote studies on Isaiah and the minor prophets. In 1909 he became principal of Aberdeen University, was knighted in 1916 and made moderator. See Life by L. A. Smith (1943).

(15) **George Joseph** (1872–1915), British murderer, born in London, drowned his three 'brides in the bath', Beatrice Williams, Alice Burnham and Margaret Lofty, for the total gain of £3500, the first and last in London (1912, 1914), the second in Blackpool (1913). See trial account, ed. Watson (1949).

(16) **Gerrit** (1797–1874), American philanthropist, active in these and and other reform movements such as dress, prison, women's suffrage, &c., aided John Brown (q.v.). See Life by Frothingham (1878).

(17) **Sir Grafton Elliot** (1871–1937), Australian anatomist and ethnologist, authority on brain anatomy and human evolution, born at Grafton, N.S.W., was professor in Cairo School of Medicine, Manchester and London. His books, *Migrations of Early Culture* (1915), *The Evolution of the Dragon* (1919), *The Diffusion of Culture* (1933), &c., explain similarities in culture all over the world by diffusion from Egypt.

(18) **Sir Harry George Wakelyn, 1st Bart.** (1788–1860), English soldier, born at Whittlesey, fought in the Peninsular, Waterloo, Kaffir and Sikh campaigns, by his strategy winning the battle of Aliwal (1846), and, as Cape governor, all but brought the Kaffir war to a successful issue.

(19) **Henry John Stephen** (1826–83), Irish mathematician, born in Dublin, and educated at Rugby and Balliol College, Oxford, of which he was elected a fellow. In 1861 he became Savilian professor of Geometry. He was the greatest authority of his day on the theory of numbers, and also wrote on elliptic functions and modern geometry. See biographical sketches in his *Mathematical Papers* (ed. by Glaisher, 1897).

(20) **Horace** or **Horatio.** See (23).

(21) **Ian Douglas** (1919–), Rhodesian politician, born at Selukwe, educated in Rhodesia and at Rhodes University, S. Africa. He was a fighter pilot in World War II and became an M.P. in 1948. From 1953 he was a member of the United Federal Party, resigning in 1961 to become a founder of the Rhodesian Front, dedicated to immediate independence without African majority rule.

He was minister of the treasury (1962–64), and prime minister from April 1964, and of external affairs (to Aug. 1964), of defence (to May 1965). With an overwhelming majority, despite lengthy talks and strenuous attempts to avert it, he unilaterally declared independence in Nov. 1965. Britain declared his government rebels and, supported by many other countries, applied increasingly severe economic sanctions. His meetings (1966 and 1968) with Harold Wilson, the British prime minister, aboard H.M.S. *Tiger* and H.M.S. *Fearless* off Gibraltar failed to resolve the situation.

(22) **James** (1789–1850), Scottish agricultural engineer, of Deanston, Perthshire, manager of the cotton mills there from 1807, the inventor of 'thorough drainage' by means of a subsoil plough. He was a philanthropist.

(23) **James** (1775–1839) and **Horace** (1779–1849), English authors of *The Rejected Addresses*, were educated at Chigwell, Essex. James succeeded his father as solicitor to the Board of Ordnance; Horace made a fortune as a stockbroker. Both wrote for magazines. When a prize was advertised for an address to be spoken at the opening of the new Drury Lane Theatre in 1812, the brothers produced a series of supposed 'Rejected Addresses', James furnishing imitations of Wordsworth, Southey and Coleridge; Horace those of Scott, Byron, 'Monk' Lewis and Moore. James also wrote Charles Mathews' entertainments; and Horace the *Tin Trumpet* (1836) and more than a score of novels. Of Horace's *Poems* (1846) the best known is the 'Ode to an Egyptian Mummy'. See Beavan, *James and Horace Smith* (1899).

(24) **Sir James Edward** (1759–1828), English botanist, born at Norwich, was founder and first president (1788) of the Linnean Society. He compiled *English Botany* (36 vols. 1790–1814).

(25) **John** (1580–1631), English adventurer, born at Willoughby, Lincolnshire, was apprenticed to a Lynn merchant, but went to France, and saw some soldiering under Henry IV. Next he served with distinction against the Turks in Hungary, but was captured and sold as a slave. In 1605 he joined an expedition to colonize Virginia; and he was saved from death by Princess Pocahontas (q.v.). His energy and tact in dealing with the Indians were useful to the colonists and he was elected president of the colony in 1608, but returned to England in 1609. During 1610–17 he was again in North Virginia. His works, reprinted in 1910, include *A Description of New England* (1616) and *History of Virginia* (1624). See Lives by Scheibler (1782), Warner (1881), Bradley (1905), Johnson (1915), Syme (1954), and Barbour (1964).

(26) **John** (1790–1824), British missionary in Demerara, who was sentenced to death by the governor for refusing to help in suppressing a Negro uprising. Public protests at home, led by Wilberforce, caused the government to override the governor, but instructions arrived after Smith had perished in an insanitary jail. His fate hastened the passing of the Emancipation Act (1833). See Life by D. Chamberlin (1823).

(27) **John Raphael** (1750–1812), English miniaturist, portrait painter and especially mezzotinter, son of **Thomas Smith** (*c.* 1709–1767), Derby landscapist. Many of his plates are from the works of Reynolds, Romney, &c.

(28) **John Stafford** (1750–1836), English composer. The tune of *The Star-spangled Banner* has been attributed to him.

(29) **Joseph** (1805–44), founder of the Mormons, was born at Sharon, Vt., December 23, received his first 'call' as a prophet at Manchester, N.Y., in 1820. In 1823 an angel told him of a hidden gospel on golden plates, with two stones which should help to translate it from the 'Reformed Egyptian'; and on the night of September 22, 1827, the sacred records were delivered into his hands. The *Book of Mormon* (1830) contained a fanciful history of America from its colonization at the time of the confusion of tongues to the 5th century of the Christian era, and claimed to have been written by a prophet named Mormon. Despite ridicule and hostility, and sometimes open violence, the new 'Church of the Latter-day Saints' rapidly gained converts. In 1831 it established its headquarters at Kirtland, Ohio, and built Zion in Missouri. Things culminated in 1838 in a general uprising in Missouri against the Mormons; and Smith was often arrested. In Illinois, near Commerce, was founded Nauvoo (1840), and within three years the Mormons in Illinois numbered 20,000, Smith meanwhile starting 'spiritual wives'. But on June 27, 1844, 150 masked men broke into Carthage jail, where Smith and his brother Hyrum were imprisoned, and shot them dead. See YOUNG (BRIGHAM), and Kennedy's *Early Days of Mormonism* (N.Y. 1888).

(30) **Logan Pearsall** (1865–1946), American writer, born at Millville, N.J., took British nationality in 1913. He is remembered for his delightful essays, collected in *All Trivia* (1933), his short stories, critical writings, and works on the English language.

(31) **Madeleine Hamilton** (1835–1928), Scottish defendant in the most baffling murder trial of modern times, the daughter of a Glasgow architect, stood trial in Edinburgh (1857) for the alleged murder by arsenic poisoning of her former lover Pierre Emile L'Angelier, a clerk and native of Jersey. Her uninhibited love letters to him, published during the trial, stirred up much Victorian resentment against her. But although she had sufficient motive for ridding herself of L'Angelier, after her engagement to a more congenial suitor, and although she had purchased arsenic on three occasions, evidence was lacking of any meeting between them on the last days or nights prior to his last violent illness. She was brilliantly defended by John Inglis (q.v.), Dean of Faculty, and the verdict was 'Not Proven'. In 1861 she married a London artist-publisher George Wardle, an associate of William Morris, and after a normal family life in Bloomsbury, separated from her husband and eventually emigrated to America, resisting Hollywood's endeavours to make her take part in a film of her life by threatening to have her deported. She died in 1928, the widow of

her second husband, an American, Sheehy. See account of the trial, ed. F. Tennyson Jesse (1927), and books by G. L. Butler (1935), P. Hunt (1950) and N. Norland (1957).

(32) **Sir Matthew Arnold Bracy** (1879–1959), English artist, born at Halifax, studied at the Slade School, and first went to Paris in 1910, when he met Matisse and the Fauves. In 1915 he exhibited with the London Group and he later painted much in Provence. His flowers, nudes and landscapes are modelled with a full brush in rich glowing colour, e.g., *Gladioli in a Yellow Jug* (1938) in the Tate Gallery, London. See the monograph by P. Hendy (1944).

(33) **Norman Kemp** (1872–1958), Scottish philosopher, born at Dundee, lectured at Glasgow (1879–1906). He was then appointed professor of Psychology (1906) and of Philosophy (1914) at Princeton. After war work in London (1916–18) he became professor of Logic and Metaphysics at Edinburgh (1919–45) and achieved an enduring reputation with his remarkable *Studies* (1902) and *New Studies* (1952) in, and selected translations (1953) of, Descartes' philosophical writings, his book on Hume (1941) and especially with his monumental *Commentary to Kant's Critique of Pure Reason* (1918), in which he advocated the 'patchwork' theory to solve many problems of interpretation of that difficult work, which he also translated (1929) into such unambiguous English that even German students preferred to tackle Kant via Kemp Smith's translation.

(34) **Robert** (1689–1768), English mathematician, Plumian professor of Astronomy at Cambridge from 1716, and master of Trinity from 1742, published works on optics, sound and hydrostatics and discovered a theorem on the *n*th roots of unity.

(35) **Rodney** (1860–1947), English evangelist, known as 'Gipsy Smith', born of nomadic gipsy parents near Epping Forest, was converted at a Primitive Methodist meeting in 1876, soon afterwards joined William Booth (q.v.) and became one of the first officers in the newly formed Salvation Army, which he left in 1882 to carry on his evangelism under the auspices of the Free Church, preaching forcefully in America, Australia and elsewhere as well as in Britain. See Murray, *Sixty Years an Evangelist* (1937).

(36) **Sydney** (1771–1845), English journalist, clergyman and wit, born at Woodford, Essex, was educated at Winchester and New College, Oxford, of which he became a fellow. He was ordained (1794) and served at Netheravon near Amesbury, and Edinburgh. There he married, and in 1802, with Jeffrey, Horner and Brougham, started the *Edinburgh Review*. He next lived six years in London, and soon made his mark as a preacher, a lecturer at the Royal Institution on moral philosophy (1804–06), and a brilliant talker; but in 1809 was 'transported' to the living of Foston in Yorkshire. In 1828 Lord Lyndhurst presented him to a prebend of Bristol, and next year enabled him to exchange Foston for Combe-Florey rectory, Somerset. In 1831 Earl Grey appointed him a canon of St Paul's. His writings include sixty-five articles, collected in 1839 from the *Edinburgh Review; Peter Plymley's Letters* (1807–08) in favour of Catholic emancipation; *Three Letters on the Ecclesiastical Commission* (1837–39); and other letters and pamphlets on the ballot, American repudiation, the game laws, prison abuses, &c. Their author is chiefly remembered as the creator of 'Mrs Partington', the kindly, sensible humorist who stands immeasurably above Theodore Hook, if a good way below Charles Lamb. See *Selected Writings*, ed. Auden (1957), Lives by Holland (1855), Russell (1905), Pearson (1934), and study by Chevrilon (1894).

(37) **Sir Sydney Alfred** (1883–1969), New Zealand-born medico-legal expert, father of (38), born at Roxburgh, N.Z., was educated at Victoria College, Wellington, and Edinburgh University, was Medical Officer of Health for New Zealand, professor of Forensic Medicine at Cairo and from 1917 principal medico-legal expert for the Egyptian government, particularly in the case of the assassination of Sir Lee Stack Pasha, the commander-in-chief in 1924. He was regius professor of Forensic Medicine at Edinburgh (1928–53) and dean of the Medical Faculty from 1931 and played a foremost part in the medical and even ballistic aspects of crime detection, not least in the Merrett (1926) and Ruxton (1936) murder cases, often effectively opposing his brilliant English colleague, Spilsbury (q.v.). He wrote a *Text-Book of Forensic Medicine* (1925) and edited Taylor's *Principles and Practices of Medical Jurisprudence*, was knighted (1949) and elected rector of Edinburgh University (1954). See his autobiographical, *Mostly Murder* (1959).

(38) **Sydney Goodsir** (1915–), Scottish poet, born in Wellington, N.Z., son of (37), studied at Oriel College, Oxford, and with such works as *Skail Wind* (1941), *The Deevil's Waltz* (1946), *Under the Eildon Tree* (1948), a great modern love poem, spiced with a satirical sketch of the Edinburgh bohemian, *Orpheus and Eurydice* (1955), *Figs and Thistles* (1959) has established a reputation as the best modern Lallans poet after MacDiarmid. His first play, *The Wallace*, was commissioned for the Edinburgh Festival for 1960.

(39) **Sir Thomas** (1514–77), English statesman and Greek scholar, author of *De Republica Anglorum*, born at Saffron Walden, became a fellow of Queen's College, Cambridge, and was knighted in 1548. He negotiated the peace of Troyes (1564).

(40) **Thomas.** See (27).

(41) **Thomas Southwood** (1788–1861), English sanitary reformer, born at Martock, Somerset, took charge of a Unitarian chapel in Edinburgh in 1812 and at the same time studied medicine. In 1824 he became physician at the London Fever Hospital, publishing in 1830 his *Treatise on Fever*. Bentham left him his body for dissection and Smith kept the skeleton fully clothed until it was transferred to University College, London. He served on the Poor Law and Children's Employment Commissions, &c. See Life by C. L. Lewis (1894).

(42) **Walter Chalmers** (1824–1908), Scottish poet, born in Aberdeen, studied at Aberdeen

and Edinburgh, and from 1876 to 1894 was a Free Church minister in Edinburgh, and was moderator (1893). He wrote *The Bishop's Walk*, by 'Orwell' (1861); *Olrig Grange*, by 'Hermann Kunst' (1872); *North-Country Folk* (1883); *Kildrostan, a Dramatic Poem* (1884); *A Heretic* (1890), &c. A collected edition appeared in 1902.

(43) **William** (1769–1839), the father of English geology, was born at Churchill, Oxfordshire, and in 1794, appointed engineer to the Somerset Coal Canal, began his study of the strata of England, introducing the law of strata identified by fossils. His epoch-making Geological Map of England (1815) was followed by twenty-one geologically-coloured maps of English counties (1819–24), in which he was assisted by his nephew, John Phillips (q.v.). He was awarded the first Wollaston medal (1831) and was an expert on irrigation. See study by T. Sheppard (1920).

(44) **Sir William** (1813–93), English lexicographer, born in London, in 1840 edited parts of Plato and Tacitus. His great *Dictionary of Greek and Roman Antiquities* (1840–42; 3rd ed. 1891), was followed by the *Dictionary of Greek and Roman Biography and Mythology* (1843–49) and *Dictionary of Greek and Roman Geography* (1853–57). His Gibbon appeared in 1854. Another famous series comprises the *Dictionary of the Bible* (1860–63; new ed. 1893), *Dictionary of Christian Antiquities* (with Archdeacon Cheetham, 1875–80) and *Dictionary of Christian Biography and Doctrines* (with Dr Wace, 1877–87). Editor of the *Quarterly* from 1867, a D.C.L. of Oxford (1870), &c., Smith was knighted in 1892.

(45) **William Henry** (1792–1865), father of (46) entered the newsagent's business of his father in the Strand, London, in 1812 and aided by his brother, **Henry Edward**, expanded it into the largest in Britain by making extensive use of railways and fast carts for country deliveries.

(46) **William Henry** (1825–91), English newsagent, bookseller and statesman, son of (45), born in London, became his father's partner in 1846 and later assumed full control. The business steadily expanded, and in 1849 secured the privilege of selling books and newspapers at railway stations. Smith entered parliament in 1868, was financial secretary of the Treasury (1874–77), first lord of the Admiralty (1877–80), secretary for War (1885); in the second Salisbury ministry he was first lord of the Treasury and leader of the Commons till his death, October 6, 1891. See Life by Sir Herbert Maxwell (1893).

(47) **William Robertson** (1846–94), Scottish theologian and orientalist, born at Keig, Aberdeenshire, studied at Aberdeen, Edinburgh, Bonn and Göttingen, and in 1870 became professor of Hebrew and Old Testament Exegesis in the Free Church College, Aberdeen. His *Encyclopaedia Britannica* article 'Bible' (1875) was strongly attacked for heterodoxy, but he was acquitted of heresy (1880). He was deprived of his professorship (1881) for another article on 'Hebrew Language and Literature'. In 1883 he became Lord Almoner's professor of Arabic at Cambridge, in 1886 university librarian and Adams professor of Arabic (1889). In 1887 he became chief editor of the *Encyclopaedia Britannica.* His chief works are: *The Old Testament in the Jewish Church* (1881), *The Religion of the Semites* (1889), &c. See Life by J. S. Black and G. Chrystal (1902).

(48) **Sir William Sidney** (1764–1840), English sailor, born at Westminster, entered the navy, and in 1780 was promoted lieutenant for his bravery at Cape St Vincent. He became captain in 1782, was knighted in 1792, and aided Hood in burning the ships and arsenal at Toulon in 1793. He next watched the Channel for French privateers, but was taken prisoner in 1796, escaped in 1798, and was sent as plenipotentiary to Constantinople, whence he hastened to St Jean d'Acre on hearing of Bonaparte's threatened attack. On March 16, 1709, he captured the enemy's vessels, and held the town heroically until the siege was raised, May 20. For this he received the thanks of parliament and a pension. He aided Abercromby in Egypt, destroyed the Turkish fleet off Abydos (1807), blockaded the Tagus, became vice-admiral of the blue in 1810, a K.C.B. in 1815, and admiral in 1821. He died at Paris, May 26, 1840. See Life by Barrow (1848).

SMITHSON, James Macie (1765–1829), English founder of the Smithsonian Institution, a natural son of the first Duke of Northumberland (see PERCY), devoted himself to chemistry and mineralogy, and died at Genoa. In a fit of pique at the Royal Society's rejection of a paper by him in 1826, bequeathed the reversion of £105,000 to found an institution at Washington 'for the increase and diffusion of knowledge among men'. See two works by W. R. Rhees (1879–80), and *The Smithsonian Institution*, by Goode (1898).

SMOLLETT, Tobias George (1721–71), Scottish novelist, was born in Dunbartonshire, grandson of Sir James Smollett. He was educated at Glasgow University, but leaving without means, sailed as surgeon's mate in the expedition to Carthagena in 1741. Three years later he settled in London, practising as a surgeon, but literature in the form of novel writing was his real interest. His first efforts succeeded—*Roderick Random* (1748) and *Peregrine Pickle* (1751), a picaresque novel—despite the ill-humoured attacks of Fielding in the *Covent Garden Journal.* The former is modelled on Le Sage's *Gil Blas* and besides describing episodes in the life of the unprincipled hero utilizes Smollett's experiences in the Carthagena expedition. *Peregrine Pickle* pursues the hero's amatory and military adventures throughout Europe. There is also the amusing episode of Commodore Trunnion and his man Pipes and the novel closes with much vitriolic satire on English literary and social coteries. *Ferdinand, Count Fathom* (1753) is the story of another heartless villain, whom an easy repentance saves from the gallows. Cervantes now succeeded Le Sage as a model—Smollett's translation of *Don Quixote* (1755) is still current—but his imitation of the master, *Sir Launcelote Greaves*, is crude work. In 1753 he was settled at Chelsea editing the new *Critical Review*—which led to his imprisonment for libel in 1760—and writing his *History of England*, which is not now current. Ordered abroad for his health, he visited France and Italy and saw little to please him there. His ill-natured record, *Travels in France and Italy* (1766), earned for him Sterne's nickname of 'Smelfungus'. His next publication was a coarse satire on public affairs, *The Adventures of an Atom* (1769). Fortunately he was still to write *Humphrey Clinker* (1771), which is much more kindly in tone and is still a favourite. A series of letters from and to members of a party touring round England and 'North Britain', it amuses us with the humours of various eccentrics, including Lieutenant Lismahago, a needy but proud Scot who wins the heart of the termagant sister of Matthew Bramble, the valetudinarian who arranges the tour. Smollett died at Leghorn in 1771. Saintsbury edited the Works (12 vols. 1925); Noyes the Letters in 1926. See also studies by Buck (1925–27), Martz (1943) and Kahrl (1945).

SMUTS, Jan Christiaan (1870–1950), South African statesman, was born at Malmesbury, Cape Colony, and educated at Christ's College, Cambridge. Late in the Boer War he took the field with de la Rey; entered the House of Assembly in 1907 and held several cabinet offices, subsequently succeeding Botha as the premier of the Union of South Africa (1919). Entrusted during World War I with minor operations in German East Africa, as a political gesture he was made a member of the Imperial War Cabinet. As minister of justice under Hertzog, his coalition with the Nationalists in 1934 produced the United Party, of which he became prime minister. Despite numerous wild utterances—he informed a 1939 Royal Institute of National Affairs audience that 'the expectation of war tomorrow or in the near future is sheer nonsense'—he acquired a reputation as a political oracle, his counsel being freely sought by the War Cabinet during World War II. In the immediate postwar years he proclaimed his readiness to see Russia 'bestride Europe like a colossus'. He was created field-marshal 1941, O.M. 1947. See Armstrong, *Grey Steel* (1937), and Lives by Smuts (1952) and Hancock (2 vols. 1962, 1968).

SMYTH, Dame Ethel (1858–1944), English composer and suffragette, born in London, studied at Leipzig, composed a Mass in D, symphonies, choral works, the operas *Der Wald* (1901), *The Wreckers* (1906), &c., contended for women's suffrage—in 1911 she was imprisoned for 3 months—was created D.B.E. in 1922, and wrote reminiscences. See Life by C. St John (1959).

SMYTHE, (1) **Francis Sydney** (1900–49), British mountaineer, was born at Maidstone. He was member of three Everest expeditions, 1933, 1936 and 1938, and he shared the world's altitude climbing record with Norton, Harris and Wager. In 1930 he was a member of the Swiss Kanchenjunga expedition and was the first to climb the Himalayan peak Kamet in 1931. During World War II, he commanded the Commando Mountain Warfare School. His many books, beautifully illustrated by his fine mountain photography, include *Kamet Conquered* (1932), *Camp Six* (1937), *Adventures of a Mountaineer* (1940), *Over Welsh Hills* (1941), &c.

(2) **George Augustus,** &c. See STRANGFORD.

SNELL, (1) **John** (1629–79), Scottish philanthropist, born at Colmonell, Ayrshire, founded the Snell exhibitions at Balliol College, Oxford. See W. J. Addison, *The Snell Exhibitions* (1901).

(2) **Willebrod van Roijen, Lat. Snellius** (1591–1626), Dutch mathematician, was professor of Mathematics at Leyden (1613) and discovered the law of refraction known as Snell's law, based on a constant known as the refractive index. He attempted to use triangulation in a survey of the earth (1617).

SNIDER, Jacob (1820–66), American inventor, a Philadelphia wine merchant, who devised *inter alia* a system of converting muzzle-loading rifles into breechloaders.

SNORRI STURLASON (1179–1241), Icelandic historian, in 1215 was elected supreme judge of the island, but, meddling with the domestic troubles of Norway, incurred the ill-will of King Haakon, who had him murdered. Snorri was a poet of no mean order, and composed the Younger or Prose *Edda* (trans. by Brodeur, 1916) and the *Heimskringla*, a series of sagas of the Norwegian kings down to 1177 (trans. and ed. Monsen, 1932). See Lives by W. Morris (1905), E. Monsen (1932), and study by W. P. Ker (1906).

SNOW, Charles Percy, 1st Baron (1905–), English novelist and physicist, born at Leicester, was educated at Leicester and Cambridge and was a fellow of Christ's College (1930–50) and a tutor there (1935–45). During World War II he was chief of scientific personnel for the ministry of labour. He was editor of *Discovery* (1938–40) and the author of a cycle of successful novels portraying English life from 1920 onwards. The continuity is maintained by means of the character Lewis Eliot, through whose eyes the dilemmas of the age are focused, starting with *Strangers and Brothers* (1940), the general title of the series. *Time of Hope* (1949) and *Homecomings* (1956) deal with Eliot's personal life. *The Masters* (1951) stages the conflict aroused by the election of a new master in a Cambridge college. *The New Men* (1954) poses the dilemma of the scientists in the face of the potentials of nuclear fission. Other volumes are *The Light and the Dark* (1947), *The Conscience of the Rich* (1958), *The Affair* (1960), *Corridors of Power* (1964), and *The Sleep of Reason* (1968). Several have been adapted for theatre and TV. Though the chief characters of his cycle are rather supine, being manipulated to exhibit the expressed problems, mostly of power and prestige in all their facets, his work shows a keen appreciation of moral issues in a science-dominated epoch. His controversial *Two Cultures* (Rede lecture, 1959) discussed the dichotomy between science and literature and his belief in closer contact between them. He was made a C.B.E. in

1943, knighted in 1957 and created a life peer in 1964. He was parliamentary secretary at the ministry of technology (1964–66), and lord rector of St Andrews University (1961–64). In 1950 he married another outstanding novelist, **Pamela Hansford Johnson** (1912–), best known for her sensitive portrayal of her native London postwar, stripped of its wartime poise and a prey to the second rate in mind and heart. Her works include *An Avenue of Stone* (1947), its sequel *A Summer to Decide* (1948), the tragi-comical *The Un-Speakable Skipton* (1958), her study of I. Compton Burnett (1953), and *Six Proust Reconstructions* (1958).

SNOWDEN, Philip Snowden, 1st Viscount (1864–1937), English Labour statesman, born near Keighley, was crippled in a cycling accident and forced to leave the civil service. He was chairman of the I.L.P. (1903–06), Socialist M.P. from 1906, opposed conscription (1915) and as chancellor of the Exchequer in the Labour governments of 1924 and 1929 maintained orthodox policies and aggravated the financial crises. As a free trader he resigned from the national government in 1932, having been created viscount in 1931. See his *Autobiography* (1934) and Life by Cross (1966).

SNYDERS, Frans (1579–1657), Dutch painter of Antwerp, specialized in still life and animals, often assisting Rubens and other painters in the latter field. He was court painter to the governor of the Low Countries.

SOANE, Sir John (1753–1837), English architect, son of a mason, Swan, near Reading, gained the travelling scholarship of the Royal Academy, and spent 1777–80 in Italy. He designed the Bank of England and held various official appointments. He bequeathed to the nation his house in Lincoln's Inn Fields. See books by Britton (1834) and Birnstingl (1925).

SOBIESKI. See JOHN III (of Poland); and for the 'SOBIESKI-STUARTS', see ALBANIE.

SOBRERO, Ascanio, *sob-ray'rō* (1812–88), Italian chemist, was the discoverer of nitroglycerine (1847).

SOCINUS, *so-sī'noos*, (1) **Faustus** (1539–1604), nephew of (2), one of the founders of the sect of Socinians, was born at Siena, December 5, studied theology at Basel (1575), and in 1579 went to Poland, teaching that Luther and Calvin had not gone far enough, and that human reason was the only solid basis of Protestantism. Driven from Cracow, he combated, at the Synod of Bresz in 1588, all the chief Christian dogmas—the divinity of Christ, propitiatory sacrifice, original sin, human depravity, the doctrine of necessity, and justification by faith. In 1594, on the publication of his *De Jesu Christo Servatore*, he was nearly murdered, and sought refuge in the village of Łucławice, where he died, March 3, 1604. See Life by Wallace (1850), and E. M. Wilbur, *History of Unitarianism* (1945).

(2) **Lælius,** or **Lelio Sozzini** (1525–62), born at Siena, was, with (1), a founder of the sect of Socinians. Driven from Siena he travelled widely in Europe and finally settled at Zürich. See the *Vita* by Illgen (1814).

SOCRATES, *sok'ra-teez* (before 469–399 B.C.), Athenian philosopher, was the son of Sophroniscus, a sculptor, and Phaenaretē, a midwife. He received the usual education of an Athenian youth, and also learned geometry and astronomy. The most important influence on his mental development was his intercourse with the sophists who frequented Athens. He took part in three campaigns at Potidaea (432–29), Delium (424) and Amphipolis (422), and distinguished himself by his bravery, extraordinary physical vigour, and indifference to fatigue or cold or heat. He was a good citizen, but the only political office he ever held was when in 406 he was one of the senate of Five Hundred. He held aloof from politics because of a call to philosophy. The Delphic Oracle declared him the wisest man in the world, but he wrote no books. Out of his wide circles of acquaintances some came to be attached to him more closely by ties of affection and admiration; yet there was no formal bond of discipleship. From two of these friends, Xenophon and Plato, we learn all we can know with certainty about his personality and his way of thinking. Yet, while Plato often makes Socrates the mouthpiece of ideas that in all likelihood were not held by him, Xenophon, a soldier and by no means a philosopher, makes Socrates a very much more commonplace person than he must have been. Despite this, we can accept the picture Plato gives us of the habits and conversation of Socrates. Socrates was ugly, snubnosed, with a paunch. His wife, Xanthippe, was supposed to have had a shrewish temper which Socrates bore patiently. There has been much diversity of opinion about the 'divine sign', of which Socrates used to speak, a supernatural voice that stopped him doing wrong; certainly to the average Athenian there was something blasphemous in his attitude towards religion and his aristocratic connections did not improve matters when the democracy was restored. He was charged in 399 as 'an evil doer and a curious person, searching into things under the earth and above the heaven; and making the worse appear the better cause, and teaching all this to others'. The substance of Socrates' magnificent defence appears in Plato's *Apology*. He was condemned by only a majority of six in a jury numbering possibly five hundred. His refusal at first even to contemplate the alternative to death, a fine, was interpreted as insolence by the judges, who then voted for the death penalty. Thirty days elapsed because of a sacred mission to Delos. Socrates' friends planned his escape, but he refused to break the law. Having spent his last days conversing with his friends as described in Plato's *Phaedo*, although possibly the views expressed on the immortality of the soul are those of Plato, Socrates drank the hemlock. For Socrates, virtue was knowledge, and knowledge was to be elicited by the dialectical technique which he derived from Zeno. Feigning total ignorance before the opinionated, he would with celebrated Socratic irony pose a simple question such as 'What is courage?' From the replies given he would construct contradictory consequences and so start again. His aim was to act as a midwife to those in labour for knowledge. He exposed the mere sophist. Apart from his overwhelming influence upon his celebrated pupil, Plato, who made him the chief spokesman in most of his dialogues, his unwritten philosophy was the starting-point of the Megaric, Cynic and Cyrenaic schools. See Xenophon, *Memorabilia* and *Symposium*, Plato, *Apology*, *Crito*, *Phaedo* and *Symposium*, Aristophanes' caricature in *The Clouds*, and studies by E. Zeller (1877), J. Burnet, *Greek Philosophy* (1914), F. Cornford (1932), A. E. Taylor (1933), Sir R. W. Livingstone (1938), W. Jaeger, *Paideia*, vol. 2 (trans. 1944), L. Nelson (trans. 1949) and the critical biographical study by A. J. Chroust (1957).

SODDY, Frederick (1877–1956), British radiochemist, born at Eastbourne, studied at the University College of Wales and Merton College, Oxford, and became professor of Chemistry at Glasgow, Aberdeen and Oxford. He collaborated with Lord Rutherford and in 1904 with Ramsay discovered the transformation of radium emanation into helium. In 1913 he gave the name *isotope* to forms of the same element having identical chemical qualities but different atomic weights; and his discovery of this phenomenon earned him the Nobel prize in 1921 and in 1955 the Albert medal. He was elected F.R.S. in 1910. See Life by M. Howorth (1959).

SÖDERBLOM, Nathan (1866–1931), Swedish theologian, born at Trönö near Söderhamm, studied at Uppsala and was ordained in 1893. He became Archbishop of Uppsala and primate of the Swedish Lutheran Church in 1914, after a period as minister of the Swedish Church in Paris and twelve years as professor of Theology at Uppsala from 1901 to 1914. A leader in the ecumenical movement, author of theological books, and a great worker for peace, he was awarded the Nobel peace prize in 1930. See Lives by Herklots (1948) and Katz (1949).

SODOMA, Il, *sod'-*, the sobriquet of **Giovanni Antonio Bazzi** (1477–1549), Italian religious and historical painter. He was born a Lombard at Vercelli, painted frescoes in Monte Oliveto Maggiore near Siena, before being called to the Vatican in 1508, where he was, however, superseded by Raphael, but where he painted the frescoes of *Alexander and Roxana* in the Villa Farnesina. His masterpieces date from his second Siena period and include *Christ at the Column*, *St Sebastian* (Uffizi, Florence) and *Ecstasy of St Catherine*. The influence of Michelangelo is apparent in his work, which often shows great insight into the portrayal of religious feeling, if sometimes lacking finality. See works by Hobart Cust (1960) and Le Gielly (1911).

SOEKARNO. See SUKARNO.

SOFFICI, Ardengo, *sof'fi-chee* (1878–1964), Italian artist and author, born at Rignano, lived in Paris (1900–08). In his painting early experiments in Futurism were followed by a return to a more representational style founded on a study of the techniques of early Italian masters. Among his writings are *Giornale di bordo* (1915), *Estetica futurista* (1920) and *Diario di Borghi* (1933).

SOLARIO, Antonio, *so-lah'ryō* (c. 1382–1455), Neapolitan painter, born at Civita in the Abruzzi, and nicknamed 'Lo Zingaro', originally a blacksmith, painted frescoes in the Benedictine monastery at Naples.

SOLIMAN. See SULAIMAN.

SOLIS, Juan Díaz de, *so-lees'* (c. 1470–1516), Spanish navigator, sailed with Pinzón, and, himself sent out to find a passage to the E. Indies via America, discovered the Río de la Plata, but was killed by the natives (1516). See Life by Medina (1897).

SOLIS Y RIBADENEYRA, Antonio de (1610–86), Spanish author, wrote poems and dramas and *Historia de la Conquista de Mexico* (1684), &c.

SOLOGUB, Fedor, pseud. of **Fedor Kuzmich Teternikov** (1863–1927), Russian novelist, wrote *The Little Demon* (trans. 1916), and many short stories, fables, fairy tales and poems.

SOLOMON (c. 1015–977 B.C.), king of Israel, was the second son of David and Bathsheba. His reign was outwardly splendid. The kingdom attained its widest limit; the temple and royal palaces were built on a scale of magnificence heretofore unknown. But the taxation entailed by the luxury of the court bred the discontent that led in the next reign to the disruption of the kingdom; and the king's alliance with heathen courts and his idolatrous queens and concubines provoked the discontent of the prophetic party. Solomon was credited with transcendent wisdom; in later Jewish and Mohammedan literature he was believed to control the spirits of the invisible world. There is no reason to suppose that he had anything to do with any of the works to which his name has been attached—Proverbs, Ecclesiastes, Song of Solomon, and, in the Apocrypha, the Wisdom of Solomon. See studies by M. D. Conway (1900) and Thieberger (1947).

SOLOMON, (1) professional name of **Solomon Cutner** (1902–), English pianist, born in London; after appearing with enormous success as a child prodigy, he retired for some years' further study, and has won a high reputation as a performer of the works of Beethoven, Brahms and some of the modern composers, though he has not toured so extensively as most players of his rank.

(2) **Solomon Joseph** (1860–1927), English portrait and mural painter, born in London, served in World War I and initiated the use of camouflage in the British army. He was elected R.A. in 1906, P.R.B.A. in 1918.

SOLON (c. 640 or 638–c. 559 B.C.), Athenian lawgiver, a merchant and a poet, archon in 594 (or 591), in a time of economic distress, he was appointed to reform the constitution. He set free all people who had been enslaved for debt (Seisachtheia), reformed the currency, and admitted a fourth class (Thetes) to the Ecclesia, so that they elected the magistrates, and to the Heliaea, so that they judged them. Thus he laid the foundations for the Athenian democracy; but he was a moderate and kept many privileges of the wealthy. After ten years' voluntary exile, he returned (580), and, in a poem, stirred up the Athenians to capture 'lovely Salamis' (c. 569). He died soon after the usurpation of Pisistratus, the story of his connection with Croesus being legendary. See Lives by K. Freeman (1926) and W. J. Woodhouse (1938).

SOLOVIEV, Vladimir, *sol'ė-vyof* (1853–1900), the 'first Russian philosopher', was born at Moscow, son of Sergei Soloviev (1820–79), historian of Russia. He wrote *Justification of Good* (trans. 1918), &c. See studies by Séverac (1912), D'Herbigny (1918) and Muckermann (1946).

SOLVAY, Ernest (1838–1922), Belgian chemist, born at Rebecq, Brussels, devised a process for the production of sodium carbonate (1863). Later this was replaced by the Leblanc process.

SOMBART, Werner (1863–1941), German economist, born at Ermsleben, studied under Schmoller, and became professor at Breslau in 1890 and at Berlin in 1914. One of the founders of modern social science, he reacted against the Marxism which he had early supported, but was not a believer in National Socialism. Among his best works are *Sozialismus und soziale Bewegung* (1911), *Der moderne Kapitalismus* (1902–28), *Die Juden und das Wirtschaftsleben* (1911) and *Deutscher Sozialismus* (1934). Several have been translated, notably *New Social Philosophy* (1937).

SOMERS, *sum'-*, **(1) Sir George** (1554–1610), whose shipwreck on the Bermudas led to their colonization from Virginia by him in 1610. They were known as the Somers Islands during their early history.

(2) **John, 1st Baron** (1651–1716), English Whig statesman, was born at Worcester, an attorney's son, studied at Trinity College, Oxford, and was called to the bar in 1676. Associated with the 'country party', he was one of the counsel for the Seven Bishops (1688) and presided over the drafting of the Declaration of Rights; and after the Revolution was successively solicitor-general, attorney-general, and lord keeper of the Great Seal, until in 1697 he became lord chancellor and Baron Somers of Evesham. He was William's most trusted minister, and was the object of frequent attacks, one of which in 1700 resulted in his being deprived of the seal, and another in 1701 in an impeachment by the Commons, rejected by the Lords. He was president of the council (1708–10). The *Somers Tracts* (1748), state papers from his library, were re-edited by Sir Walter Scott (1809–15).

SOMERSET, Dukes of. See SEYMOUR.

SOMERSET, (1) Edward. See WORCESTER (1).

(2) **Henry.** See BEAUFORT.

(3) **James.** See SHARP (3).

SOMERVELL, Sir Arthur (1863–1937), English composer, known for the cantata *The Forsaken Merman*, *Thalassa*, a symphony, children's operettas and for his collection of English folksongs.

SOMERVILLE, (1) Edith Oenone. See MARTIN (9).

(2) **Sir James Fownes** (1882–1949), English sailor, saw service in the Dardanelles (1915), was c.-in-c. in the West Indies (1938–39), and, recalled from retirement as vice-admiral in the Mediterranean, sank the French ships at Oran (1940), shelled Genoa (1941), helped in the sinking of the *Bismarck* (1941), took part in the Malta convoy battle (1941), and after the entry of the Japanese into the war, became c.-in-c. of the British fleet in the Indian ocean. In 1945 he was promoted admiral of the Fleet.

(3) *née* **Fairfax, Mary** (1780–1872), Scottish mathematician and scientific writer, born at Jedburgh, the daughter of Admiral Sir William Fairfax, wrote *Celestial Mechanism* (1830), a popular version of Laplace's work, &c. Somerville College at Oxford is named after her. See her Autobiography (1873).

(4) **William** (1675–1742), English poet, squire of Edstone, Warwickshire, was born at Wolseley in Staffordshire. He wrote *The Chase* (1735) and other poetry.

SOMMERFELD, Arnold (1868–1951), German physicist, born at Königsberg, professor of Mathematics at Clausthal (1897), of Physics at Aachen (1900) and at Munich (1906), with Klein developed the theory of the gyroscope, researched into wave spreading in wireless telegraphy, applied the quantum theory to spectral lines and the Bohr atomic model and evolved a theory of the electron in the metallic state.

SONNINO, Baron Sidney (1847–1922), Italian statesman, born at Pisa—his mother was English—entered parliament in 1880, was finance minister 1893–96, premier 1906 and 1909–10, and as foreign minister (1914–20) denounced the Triple Alliance and brought Italy into the European war (May 1915).

SOONG, name of an influential Chinese family:

(1) **Charles Jones** (d. 1927), Chinese merchant and Methodist missionary, father of (2), (3) and (4), born on Hainan Island, went to U.S.A., was converted to Christianity and educated at Vanderbilt University. He returned to Shanghai, founded the first Y.M.C.A. there and set up as Bible publisher and salesman.

(2) **Ching Ling.** See SUN YAT-SEN.

(3) **Mayling.** See CHIANG KAI-SHEK.

(4) **Tse-ven,** abbreviated T.V. (1891–1971), Chinese financier, son of (1), studied at Harvard and Columbia, became finance minister of the Nationalist Government, Canton (1925–27), and at Nanking (1928–33), westernizing Chinese finances.

SOPER, Donald Oliver, 1st Baron (1903–), English Methodist minister, born at Wandsworth. Widely-known for his open-air speaking on London's Tower Hill, he became superintendent of the West London Mission in 1936, and has written many books on Christianity and social questions, and particularly on international issues from the pacifist angle. He was president of the Methodist Conference in 1953, and was created a life peer in 1965.

SOPHIA (1630–1714), electress of Hanover, youngest daughter of Elizabeth (q.v.), queen of Bohemia, in 1658 married Ernest Augustus, Duke of Brunswick-Lüneburg, afterwards elector of Hanover, and was the mother of George I. See her Memoirs, and a book by Sir A. W. Ward (2nd ed. 1909). For the wife of George I (q.v.), see KÖNIGSMARK.

SOPHOCLES, *sof'ō-kleez* (*c.* 496–*c.* 405 B.C.), Athenian tragedian, one of the great figures of

Greek drama, born at Colonus Hippius, an Athenian suburb, had to forgo his ambitions for the stage on account of a weak voice. He wrote well over a hundred items, most of them conventional satyr plays of which only the *Ichneutae* survives, as well as seven major plays, still extant, all written after his victory over Aeschylus in a dramatic contest in 468. He won first prize at the Great Dionysia 18 times. The problem of burial is prominent in both the *Ajax* and *Antigone* (possibly *c.* 441), in the first an Olympian directive that hatred should not pursue a noble adversary beyond the grave, in the second as a clash between sisterly compassion for a dead traitor brother and the stately proprieties of King Creon. Aeschylus, Euripides and Sophocles each wrote versions of *Electra*, the gruesome matricide by Orestes in revenge for his father's death at the hands of his mother's paramour. The great Sophoclean masterpiece, however, is *Oedipus Tyrannus*, on which Aristotle based his aesthetic theory of drama in the *Poetica* and from which Freud derived the name and function of the Oedipus complex King Oedipus proclaims sentence on the unknown murderer of his father Laius, whose presence is thought to be the cause of a plague at Thebes. By a gradual unfolding of incidents. he learns that he was the assassin and that Jocasta his wife is also his mother. He blinds himself, goes into exile and Jocasta commits suicide. The dramatic characteristics are the gradual reversal in fortune of an estimable, conventionally good person, through some untoward discovery in personal relationships, but also linked to some seemingly minor defect in character, in Oedipus' case, pride. This combination of a minor defect with the external cruel machinations of *atē*, or personal destiny abetted by the gods, constitutes, according to Aristotle, the famous 'tragic flaw which arouses the tragic emotions of pity and fear in the spectator and allows their purgation in a harmless manner This is in sharp contrast to Aeschylean tragedy, which is essentially static. There is no development in the plot the hero is doomed from the beginning. The *Trachiniae* explores the ruinous love of Heracles and Deianira. The *Philoctetes* (produced in 409) and *Oedipus Coloneus* would hardly be called tragic, except for the grave circumstances which attend the achievement of glory. See editions and translations by L. Campbell (1871–81), R. C. Jebb (1883–1908), F. Storr (1919) and A. C. Pearson (1924), and studies by Earp (1944), Bowra (1944), Whitman (Harvard 1951), Waldock (1951), Letters (1953), Kitto (1958), and also the latter's studies in Greek drama (1939 and 1956), and Lattimore. *The Poetry of Greek Tragedy* (1958).

SOPHONISBA, *sof-ō-niz'ba* (d. *c.* 204 B.C.), daughter of the Carthaginian general Hasdrubal, was betrothed to the Numidian prince Masinissa but married for reasons of state his rival Syphax, whom the former however defeated in battle, recapturing his one-time betrothed and marrying her The Romans objected to this marriage and Masinissa gave her up but sent her poison to prevent her falling into Roman hands. Corneille, Voltaire and Alfieri have written tragedies around this theme.

SOPWITH, Sir Thomas Octave Murdoch (1888–), British aircraft designer and sportsman, won the Baron de Forest prize in 1910 for flying across the English Channel; founded the Sopwith Aviation Company at Kingston-on-Thames (1912), where he designed and built many of the aircraft used in World War I. He was chairman of the Hawker Siddeley Group from 1935, president from 1963, and chairman of the Society of British Aircraft Constructors (1925–27). A keen yachtsman, he competed for the America cup in 1934. He was made C.B.E. in 1918 and knighted in 1953.

SORAYA, properly **Princess Soraya Esfandiari Bakhtiari** (1932–), ex-Queen of Persia, born at Isfahan of Persian and German parents. She was educated at Isfahan, and later in England and Switzerland, and became Queen of Persia on her marriage in 1951 to His Majesty Mohammad Reza Shah Pahlavi. The marriage was dissolved in 1958. See Life by Krause (trans. 1956).

SORBON, Robert de (1201–74), Louis IX's confessor, founded the college of the Sorbonne (1253).

SORBY, Henry Clifton (1826–1908), English chemist and geologist, born at Woodbourne, Sheffield; elected F.R.S. in 1857, he devised a method of examining metals by treating polished surfaces with etching materials under the microscope. He wrote on biology architecture and Egyptian hieroglyphics.

SORDELLO (d. *c.* 1270), Italian troubadour named by Dante, was born at Mantua. His poems (mostly in the ballad form) in the Provençal language alone survive Palazzi edited his poems (Venice 1887).

SOREL, (1) **Agnes** (*c.* 1422–50), Frenchwoman, mistress from 1444 of Charles VII of France, was born at Fromenteau, Touraine. Her influence may have been partly beneficial. See study by Champion (1931).

(2) **Albert** (1842–1906), French historian, born at Honfleur, elected to the Academy in 1894, wrote *L'Europe et la révolution française* (8 vols. 1885–1904).

(3) **Georges** (1847–1922), French syndicalist philosopher, a road engineer who in middle age turned to politics and became the champion of Dreyfus. Influenced by Nietzsche, Marx and Bergson, he formulated a political theory set down in his *Refléxions sur la violence* (1908: trans. T E. Hulme. 1915) by which he showed that true Socialism could only come by violent revolution at the hands of a disciplined proletariat. educated through trade union organizations. Theoretically extreme, he compromised nevertheless with his political opponents and had little effect on the French trade unions His emphasis on the 'social myth as a means to collective action, however, impressed Mussolini and foreshadowed the hideous Nazi concept of the *Herrenvolk* See his *Matériaux pour une théorie du prolétariat* (1919). studies by A. Lanzillo (1910) and P Perrin (1925), and Lives by G Pirou (1927), P Lasserre (1928) and V Sartre (1937)

SÖRENSEN, Sören Peter Lauritz (1868–1939) Danish biochemist. director of Chemistry at the Carlsberg Laboratory, did pioneer work on hydrogen-ion concentration, devising the symbol pH for the negative logarithm of the hydrogen-ion concentration.

SORGE, Reinhard Johannes, *zor'gė* (1892–1916), German poet, born at Rixdorf, pioneered dramatic expressionism with his play *Der Bettler* (1912). At first a believer in the Nietzschean doctrine, he was converted to Catholicism in 1913, and thereafter his work tended to be tinged with mysticism. His poems include *Mutter der Himmel* (1918). He was killed in the battle of the Somme.

SOROKIN, Pitirim Alexandrovich (1889–1968), Russian sociologist, lived in the United States after 1923, was born in Turia, Russia, became after a varied career as factoryhand, journalist, tutor, cabinet minister (1917), professor of Sociology at Leningrad (1919–1922), specializing in the study of the social structure of rural communities. Banished by the Soviet government in 1922, he became professor at Minnesota and then (1931-64) at Harvard. His works include *Sociology of Revolution* (1925), *Principles of Rural-Urban Sociology* (1929), *Crisis of our Age* (1941), *Russia and the United States* (1944), *Altruistic Love* (1950), *Fads and Foibles of Modern Sociology* (1956), &c.

SOROLLA Y BASTIDA, Joaquín, *so-rol'ya ee bas-tee'*THA (1863–1923), Spanish painter, born at Valencia, became one of the leading Spanish Impressionists, known especially for his sunlight effects, as in *Swimmers*, *Beaching the Boat* (Metropolitan, New York), &c.

SOTHEBY, John, *su*TH'- (1740–1807), English auctioneer and antiquarian, nephew of **Samuel Baker** (d. 1778) who founded at York Street, Covent Garden, in 1744 the first sale room in Britain exclusively for books, manuscripts and prints. John became a director of the firm (1780–1800) which became known as Leigh and Sotheby. In 1803 it was transferred to the Strand. His nephew, **Samuel** (1771–1842), and grand-nephew, **Samuel Leigh** (1806–61), an authority on cataloguing and early printing, continued the business.

SOTHERN, Edward Askew, *su*TH'- (1826–81), English comic actor, born at Liverpool, in 1849 joined a company of players in Jersey, and soon afterwards the stock company at Birmingham. From 1852 he appeared in the United States, with small success, until in 1858 he made his name as Lord Dundreary in Taylor's *Our American Cousin*. See *Memoir* by T. E. Pemberton (1890), and *The Melancholy Tale of Me* (1916) by his son, **Edward Hugh** (1859–1933), also an actor.

SOTO, Ferdinando de. See DE SOTO.

SOUBISE, Charles de Rohan, Prince de, *soo-beez* (1715–87), French general, was defeated by Frederick the Great at Rossbach (1757); next year he gained victories at Sondershausen and Lützelburg.

SOUFFLOT, Jacques Germain, *soof-lō* (1709–1780), French architect, born at Irancy, designed the Panthéon and the École de Droit in Paris.

SOULAGES, Pierre, *soo-lahzh* (1919–), French artist, born at Rodez. He is one of the most original of the established non-figurative painters, and has designed décors for the theatre and ballet. In 1952 he exhibited at the Venice Biennale.

SOULT, Nicolas Jean de Dieu, *soolt* (1769–1851), French marshal, born at Saint-Amans-la-Bastide, Tarn, March 29, enlisted in 1785, and in 1794 became general of brigade. Masséna made him general of division (April 1799), and owed to him much of the glory of his Swiss and Italian campaigns. In 1804 Soult was appointed by Napoleon marshal of France. He led the right wing in the campaign closed at Austerlitz, did good service in the Prussian and Russian campaigns (1806–07), and after the peace of Tilsit was created Duke of Dalmatia. In Spain he pursued the retreating British, and, though repulsed at Coruña, forced them to evacuate the country. He then conquered Portugal, and governed it till the arrival of Wellesley at Coimbra made him retreat to Galicia. In 1809–10, as commander-in-chief in Spain, he gained a brilliant victory at Ocaña and overran Andalusia. In attempting to succour Badajos he was defeated by Beresford at Albuera (1811). After Salamanca and the advance of the British on Madrid, Soult, vexed at the obstinacy of Joseph Bonaparte and the rejection of his plans, demanded his recall; but Napoleon, after Vitoria, sent him back to Spain. By brilliant tactics he neutralized the strategy of Wellington, but was defeated at Orthez and Toulouse. He turned a royalist after Napoleon's abdication, but joined him again on his return from Elba and was made chief of staff. After Waterloo he rallied the wreck of the army at Laon, but agreed with Carnot as to the uselessness of further resistance. He was banished and not recalled till 1819, but was gradually restored to all his honours and was minister of war (1830–34). He died at Soultberg, his château near his birthplace, November 26. See Soult's *Mémoires* (1854), and works by Salle (1834) and Clerc (1893).

SOUSA, John Philip, *soo'za* (1854–1932), American composer and bandmaster, born in Washington, D.C. His early training as a conductor was gained with theatre orchestras, and in 1880 he became conductor of the United States Marine Band. His own band, formed twelve years later, won an international reputation. As well as more than a hundred popular marches, Sousa composed ten comic operas, the most successful of which was *El Capitan*. See his *Marching Along* (1928).

SOUTAR, William, *soo'*- (1898–1943), Scottish poet, born at Perth, was educated at Perth Academy and, after active service with the Royal Navy (1916–18), at Edinburgh University. Extreme osteoarthritis (1923) confined him to bed for the last fourteen years of his life, but in the words of his best-loved poem 'Gang doun wi' a sang, gang doun'. The best examples of his output in English are *In the Time of Tyrants* (1939) and the collection *The Expectant Silence* (1944). His *Poems in Scots* (1935), containing the remarkable 'Auld Tree', and the four last lyrics included in the posthumous collection, ed. MacDiarmid (1948), as well as the earlier collection of bairn-rhymes, *Seeds in the Wind* (1933), give him a permanent place in the Scottish literary revival. See his remarkable *Diaries of a Dying Man*, ed. A. Scott (1954), and the latter's biography, *Still Life* (1958).

SOUTH, (1) Sir James (1785–1867), English astronomer, born at Southwark, practised medicine and discovered 160 compound stars. In 1829 he was elected president of the Astronomical Society, and was knighted the following year.

(2) **Robert** (1634–1716), English high-church theologian and preacher, born at Hackney; from Westminster passed as a student to Christ Church in 1651. He was for a time in sympathy with Presbyterianism, but in 1658 he received orders secretly and in 1660 was appointed public orator of Oxford. His vigorous sermons, full of mockery of the Puritans, delighted the restored Royalists. He became domestic chaplain to Clarendon, prebendary of Westminster in 1663, canon of Christ Church in 1670, rector of Islip in 1678, but his outspokenness prevented any further preferment. He 'aquiesced in' the Revolution, but strongly opposed the scheme of Comprehension. In 1693 began his great controversy with Sherlock, Dean of St Paul's, who had defended the Trinity against the Socinians. South scorned mysticism and extravagance, but was a stern apologist for the Stuart theories of divine right. See his *Sermons on Several Occasions* (new ed. 1878), &c.

SOUTHAMPTON, Earls of, (1) Sir Thomas Wriothesley, 1st Earl, *riz'li* (1505–50), English statesman, son of William Wriothesley the York Herald, held various state offices under Thomas Cromwell, with whom he actively participated in the iconoclastic measures associated with the Dissolution, and in 1538 was ambassador to the Netherlands. Having avoided sharing Cromwell's fate only by turning evidence against him and through his own erstwhile opposition to Anne of Cleves as a wife for Henry VIII, he again came into favour, and as the author of the defensive treaty with Spain was created a baron. Lord chancellor in 1544–47, he won an unenviable reputation for brutality, especially towards reformers; he is said to have personally racked Anne Askew (q.v.). He was created an earl on the accession of Edward VI, but soon after was deprived of the Great Seal for dereliction of duty.

(2) **Henry Wriothesley, 2nd Earl** (1545–81), son of the above, turned Catholic and became involved in intrigues for the advancement of Mary, Queen of Scots, for which activity he was imprisoned in the Tower.

(3) **Henry Wriothesley, 3rd Earl** (1573–1624), son of the above, soldier and patron of poets, particularly of Shakespeare, who dedicated to him his *Venus and Adonis* (1593) and *The Rape of Lucrece* (1594), graduated from Cambridge in 1589, accompanied Essex to the Azores (1597), incurred Elizabeth's displeasure by marrying Essex's cousin, took part in Essex's rebellion, reviving *Richard II* in order to arouse antimonarchic feeling, and was sentenced to death (afterwards commuted to life imprisonment) but was released by James I. He helped the expedition to Virginia (1605), was imprisoned in 1621 on charges of intrigue, and died of fever at Bergen-op-Zoom while in charge of the English volunteer contingent helping the Dutch against Spain. See Life by Stopes (1922).

(4) **Thomas Wriothesley, 4th Earl** (1607–67), son of the above, educated at Eton and Magdalen, sided with the Commons on certain aspects of royal privilege, but became one of Charles I's foremost advisers. Owing perhaps to his moderate views, he was leniently treated by Cromwell, and at the Restoration was made lord high treasurer.

SOUTHCOTT, Joanna (*c.* 1750–1814), English fanatic, a farmer's daughter in Devon, about 1792 declared herself to be the woman of Rev. xii. She came to London on the invitation of William Sharp the engraver, and published *A Warning* (1803), *The Book of Wonders* (1813–14), &c. At length she announced that she was to give birth on October 19, 1814, to a second Prince of Peace. Her followers received this announcement with devout reverence. But she merely fell into a trance, and died December 27. Her followers, who believed that she would rise again, still numbered over 200 in 1851, and were not yet extinct at the beginning of the 20th century. See Life by C. Lane (1912).

SOUTHERNE, Thomas (1660–1746), British dramatist, born at Oxmantown, Co. Dublin, from Trinity College, Dublin, passed to the Middle Temple, London, and in 1682 began his career with a compliment to the Duke of York in *The Loyal Brother*. Dryden wrote the prologue and epilogue, and Southerne finished Dryden's *Cleomenes* (1692). He served a short time under the Duke of Berwick and at his request, wrote the *Spartan Dame*. His best plays were *The Fatal Marriage* (1694) and *Oroonoko* (before 1696), based on Aphra Behn. His comedies are thin, but made him fat. See Life by J. W. Dodds (1933).

SOUTHEY, Robert (1774–1843), English poet and writer, was born at Bristol. His father died early, and an uncle sent him to Westminster, whence he was expelled for applying his Jacobin principles to a school magazine. He was at Balliol in 1793, where he was infected with Coleridge's dream of a 'pantisocracy', and in 1795 he married Edith Fricker, whose elder sister Sara married Coleridge. He made two trips to Lisbon (1795 and 1800), and then, after studying law, settled at Great Hall, Keswick (where Coleridge and his wife and sister-in-law were already); and there he remained. He had only £160 a year from his school friend Wynn on which to live, until the government gave him a similar amount. By this time his political views had mellowed and Southey had become something of a Tory; and Peel raised the pension by £300 in 1835—he had been poet laureate since 1813. He had joined the *Quarterly Review* in 1809 and remained a contributor under Gifford and Lockhart. Essentially a family man, he sustained a great shock when his wife died insane in 1837; and, though he married Catherine Anne Bowles, the poetess, in 1839, she became little more than a nurse, and on March 21, 1843, he died of softening of the brain. No poet so well known by name is so little known by his poetry, yet some of his ballads—the 'Holly Tree', 'Battle of Blenheim', 'Old Woman of Berkeley'—had an influence at the time; and in them there is evidence that he appreciated the ballad principle of 'anapaestic equivalents' at least as early as Coleridge. His fanciful epics, in which he used a rimeless metre not blank verse, have little appeal, but his prose, written in the middle style, has clearness and ease, and no mannerisms. His *Nelson* belongs to universal literature. Yet even here he wrote too much and his subjects in history are often too large. His works include *Joan of Arc* (1795), *The Curse of Kehama* (1810), *Roderick* (1814), Lives of *Nelson* (1813), *Wesley* (1820) and *Bunyan* (1830), *A Vision of Judgment* (1821), *Book of the Church* (1824), *Colloquies on Society* (1829), *Naval History* (1833–40) and *The Doctor* (1834–47), a miscellany, in which appears the nursery classic, *The Three Bears*. He was a voluminous letter writer, as illustrated in his *Life and Correspondence* (1849–1850), by his younger son, the Rev. **Cuthbert Southey** (1819–89); and there is his *Commonplace Book* (1849–51), his *Correspondence with Caroline Bowles* (1881), and his *Journal of a Tour of Scotland in 1819* (1929). See also books by Dowden (1880), Dennis (new ed. 1895), S. R. Thompson (1888), the *Early Life* by Wm. Hather (1917), J. Simmons (1945) and G. Carnall (1960).

SOUTHWELL, Robert, *suTH'él* (1561?–95), English poet and Jesuit martyr, was born at Horsham, Norwich. He was educated at Douai and Rome, being received into the Society of Jesus in 1578. He was appointed prefect of the English College, was ordained priest in 1584, and two years later, arriving in England with Garnet (q.v.), was first sheltered by Lord Vaux, and next became chaplain to the Countess of Arundel, when he wrote his *Consolation for Catholics* and most of his poems. In 1592 he was betrayed, tortured and thrown into the Tower, and on February 21, 1595, he was hanged and quartered at Tyburn for high treason. He was beatified in 1929. His longest poem is *Saint Peter's Complaint*; his most famous, *The Burning Babe*, an exquisite little piece of sanctified fancy. See a book by Mrs Hood (1926) and study by P. Janelle (1935).

SOUTINE, Chaim, *soo-teen'* (1893–1943), Lithuanian artist, born at Smilovich, studied at Vilna and went to Paris in 1911. He is best known for his paintings of carcases, his series of *Choirboys* (1927) and the magnificent psychological study, *The Old Actress* (1924; Moltzau collection, Norway). After his death his vivid colours and passionate handling of paint gained him recognition as one of the foremost Expressionist painters. See Life by M. Wheeler (1950).

SOUZA, Madame de (1761–1836), French novelist, born Adélaïde Marie Émilie Filleul at the Norman château of Longpré, married the Comte de Flahaut (1727–93). At the Revolution she found refuge with her only son in Germany and England, and here learned of her husband's execution at Arras. She turned to writing, her first book the delightful *Adèle de Sénange* (1794). In 1802 she married the Marquis de Souza-Botelho (1758–1825), Portuguese minister at Paris. Later novels include *Émilie et Alphonse* (1799) and *Charles et Marie* (1801).

SOWERBY, (1) James (1757–1822), English illustrator, born at Lambeth, commenced as portraitist and miniaturist, but is remembered by his illustrated *English Botany* (1792–1807, the text by Sir J. E. Smith; new ed. 1863–86). Three sons followed in his footsteps: **James de Carle** (1787–1871), **George Brettingham** (1788–1854) and **Charles Edward** (1795–1842); as did a son of the second, **George Brettingham** (1812–84), and of the third, **John Edward** (1825–70).

(2) **Leo** (1895–), American composer and organist, born at Grand Rapids, Mich., studied in Chicago and Rome. His music employs a traditional European style in works often evocative of American scenes, such as *Prairie*, an orchestral tone poem, and the suite *From the Northland*.

SOYER, Alexis, *swa-yay* (1809–58), born at Meaux, was destined for the church, but became the most famous cook of his time. He fled to London in 1830, and was chef in the Reform Club 1837–50. He went to Ireland during the famine (1847), and in 1855 to reform the food system in the Crimea, where he introduced the 'Soyer Stove'. He wrote, amongst other works, *Culinary Campaign in the Crimea* (1857). See Memoirs by Volant and Warren (1858), and H. Morris, *Portrait of a Chef* (1938).

SPAAK, Paul Henri (1899–1972), Belgian statesman, was born in Brussels, where he began to practise law in 1922. A Socialist deputy for Brussels in 1932, he rose to become, in 1938, the first Socialist premier of Belgium, but resigned the following year. He was foreign minister with the government-in-exile in London during World War II, and in 1946 was elected president of the first General Assembly of the United Nations. Prime minister again in 1946 and from 1947 to 1949, as president of the consultative assembly of the Council of Europe (1949–51) he was in the forefront of the movement for European unity. He was again foreign minister 1954–1957, secretary-general of N.A.T.O. 1957–61, and foreign minister from 1961 until his resignation from parliament in 1966.

SPAGNOLETTO. See RIBERA.

SPAHLINGER, Henry (1882–1965), Swiss bacteriologist, was educated at Geneva. In 1912, he discovered a serum for the treatment of tuberculosis, and also did research on endocrine glands and on cancer.

SPALDING, John (*c.* 1609–70), Aberdeen diarist, royalist and commissary clerk, after whom was named a book club (1839–70; revived 1887).

SPALLANZANI, Lazaro, *spal-lan-tsah'nee* (1729–99), Italian biologist, born at Scandiano in Modena, held chairs at Reggio, Modena and Pavia, disposed of the doctrine of spontaneous generation. In 1780 he demonstrated the true nature of digestion and the functions of spermatozoa and ovum and discovered artificial insemination.

SPARK, Muriel (1918–), British novelist and poet, born in Edinburgh, educated at James Gillespie's High School, editor of *Poetry*

Review (1947–49), has published poetry, short stories, and critical biographies. She is best known, however, for her distinctive novels, written in a highly formal and ironic style, witty and fantastic in content. Her works include *The Comforters* (1957), *Memento Mori* (1959), a tragi-comic study of old age, *The Bachelors* (1960), *The Prime of Miss Jean Brodie* (1961) and *The Mandelbaum Gate* (1965). She was made an O.B.E. in 1967. See study by D. Stanford (1963).

SPARKS, Jared (1789–1866), American biographer, was tutor at Harvard and, for a time, a Unitarian minister at Baltimore, and chaplain to congress (1821). He edited the *North American Review* (1824–31) and in 1832 began his *Library of American Biography*. At Harvard, he was McLean professor of History (1839–49) and president (1849–53). He wrote, among other works, Lives of John Ledyard (1828) and Gouverneur Morris (1832), and edited works of Washington and Franklin. See Life by Adams (1892).

SPARTACUS (d. 71 B.C.), Roman rebel, a Thracian shepherd who became a robber and was captured and sold to a trainer of gladiators at Capua. In 73 B.C. he escaped, with about seventy others, to Vesuvius, where he was joined by many runaway slaves. He repulsed C. Claudius Pulcher, defeated several Roman armies and laid waste much of Italy. He was defeated and killed by Crassus near the river Silarus in 71.

SPEAIGHT, Robert William (1904–), English actor and author, son of **Frederick William** (1869–1942) the architect, played most of the major Shakespearean rôles for the Old Vic from 1930, played Becket in Eliot's *Murder in the Cathedral* at the Canterbury Festival (1935), wrote many biographies including *Hilaire Belloc* (1956), edited the latter's correspondence (1958) and published works on drama.

SPEAR, Ruskin (1911–), English artist, born in London, studied at the Royal College of Art, was elected to the London Group in 1942, and was its president in 1949–50. His paintings of London life are in the Sickert tradition and have had considerable influence through his teaching at the Royal College of Art and the St Martin's School of Art.

SPECKBACHER, Joseph, *-bakH-ėr* (1767–1820), Tirolese patriot, known as 'Der Mann vom Rinn', who, like Hofer (q.v.), fought with distinction in 1809 against the French. See Lives by Mayr (1851) and Knauth (1868).

SPEDDING, James (1808–81), English scholar, born at Mirehouse near Bassenthwaite, entered the colonial service, served as secretary to Lord Ashburton's mission to the U.S.A. (1842) and to the newly founded civil service commission (1855), was a fellow of Trinity, Cambridge, and the editor and vindicator of Bacon (q.v.). He published his *Life and Letters* (1861–74) and *Evenings with a Reviewer* (1848), a refutation of Macaulay's *Essay* on Bacon. See brief Memoir by G. S. Venables prefixed to last and also Edward FitzGerald's *Letters* (1889).

SPEE, Count Maximilian von, *shpay* (1861–1914), German admiral, born in Copenhagen, entered the Imperial German Navy in 1878. In 1908 he became chief of staff of the North Sea Command. In late 1914 he was in command of a commerce-raiding force in the Pacific. Off Coronel he encountered a British squadron of inferior speed and gun power, which he punished severely, sinking H.M.S. *Good Hope* and *Monmouth*. A powerful armament was sent out to deal with him, and off the Falkland Islands exacted a grim vengeance, sinking six out of eight enemy vessels. Von Spee went down with his flagship. See Life by Pochhammer (1933).

SPEED, John (1542–1629), English antiquary and cartographer, born in Cheshire, worked most of his days in London as a tailor. His extraordinary historical learning gained him the acquaintance of Sir Fulke Greville and Spelman, and opened up the door for the publication of his fifty-four *Maps of England and Wales* (1608–10; incorporated into *The Theatre of Great Britain*, 1611) and *History of Great Britain* (1611).

SPEIDEL, Hans, *shpī'del* (1897–), German general, born in Metzingen, Württemberg, served in World War I and in 1939 was senior staff officer. From 1940 to 1942 he was chief of staff to the German commander in occupied France. In July 1944, when he was chief of staff to Rommel during the Allied invasion of Europe, he was imprisoned after the anti-Hitler bomb plot. In 1951 he became military adviser to the West German government. His N.A.T.O. appointment as c.-in-c. land forces, Central Europe (1957–63), aroused wide controversy. He became president of the Institution of Science and Politics in 1964. See his *Invasion 1944*, and *The Destiny of Rommel and the Reich* (1949).

SPEKE, John Hanning (1827–64), British explorer, born at Jordans, Ilminster, in the Indian army saw service in the Punjab. In 1854 he joined Burton in a hazardous expedition to Somaliland; in 1857 the Royal Geographical Society sent out the two to search for the equatorial lakes of Africa. Speke, while travelling alone, discovered the Victoria Nyanza, and saw in it the headwaters of the Nile. In 1860 he returned with Captain J. A. Grant, explored the lake, and tracked the Nile flowing out of it. He was about to defend the identification against Burton's doubts at the British Association meeting at Bath, September 15, 1864, when, that very morning, he accidentally shot himself while partridge-shooting. He wrote *Journal of the Discovery of the Source of the Nile* (1863) and *What led to the Discovery of the Source of the Nile* (1864).

SPELMAN, Sir Henry (1562–1641), English antiquary, born at Congham, Lynn, passed from Trinity College, Cambridge, to Lincoln's Inn. He was high sheriff of Norfolk in 1604, was employed in public affairs at home and in Ireland, and was knighted. In 1612 he settled in London to pursue his studies. His ponderous *Glossarium Archaiologicum* (1626–1664) was completed by his son and Dugdale; his *Concilia Ecclesiastica Orbis Britannici* (1639–64) he also left incomplete. *Reliquiae Spelmannianae* was edited, with a Life, by (Bishop) Edmund Gibson (1698). His son, **Sir John** (1594–1643), is remembered for his Life of King Alfred.

SPEMANN, Hans (1869–1941), German zoologist, educated in Stuttgart and Heidelberg, was director of the Institute of Biology at Rostock (1914) and professor at Freiburg (1919). He worked on embryonic development, discovering the 'organizer function' of certain tissues. For this he received a Nobel prize in 1935.

SPENCE, (1) Sir Basil Unwin (1907–), Scottish architect, born in India of Scots parents, educated at George Watson's College, Edinburgh, and London and Edinburgh Schools of Architecture, assisted Lutyens (q.v.) with the drawings of the viceregal buildings at Delhi. He was twice mentioned in dispatches during World War II, and gradually emerged as the leading postwar British architect with his fresh approach to new university buildings and conversions at Queen's College, Cambridge, Southampton, Sussex, &c., Universities; his pavilions for the Festival of Britain (1951); and his prizewinning designs for housing estates at Sunbury-on-Thames (1951) and the fishermen's houses in a traditional setting at Dunbar (1952) and Newhaven, Edinburgh (1960), &c. But best known by far is his prize design for the new Coventry Cathedral (1951) which boldly merged new and traditional structural methods, and the controversial design for Hampstead's new civic centre (1958). He was professor of Architecture at Leeds (1955–56) and at the Royal Academy from 1961, and president of the R.I.B.A. (1958–60). His crusading zeal in the interests of modern architecture have earned him the nickname 'St Basil' and he was awarded the O.B.E. (1948), a knighthood (1960), and the O.M. (1962). See his *Phoenix at Coventry* (1962).

(2) **(James) Lewis (Thomas Chalmers)** (1874–1955), Scottish anthropologist, author and poet, born at Broughty Ferry, studied at Edinburgh, was subeditor on *The Scotsman* and subsequently edited various magazines. He ranks first as an authority on the mythology and customs of ancient Mexico, South America, the Middle East as well as Celtic Britain, having written numerous books including *Mythologies of Mexico and Peru* (1907), *Dictionary of Mythology* (1913), *Encyclopaedia of Occultism* (1920), &c., and secondly as a poet whose researches into the style and language of the Makars, subtly exploited in such collections as *The Phoenix* (1924) and *Weirds and Vanities* (1927), can be said to have given the cue to the Scottish literary renaissance. He was a fellow of the Royal Anthropological Institute.

(3) **Joseph** (1699–1768), English anecdotist, educated at Winchester and New College, Oxford, where he became professor of Poetry (1727), is remembered for his *Essay on Pope's Odyssey* (1727) and his anecdotes of Pope and other celebrities.

SPENCER, Earls, a family founded by the Hon. John Spencer, youngest son of the 3rd Earl of Sunderland by Anne, daughter of the great Duke of Marlborough (his brother became 3rd duke). His only son, **John** (1734–83), was created Earl Spencer in 1765. Noteworthy members were:

(1) **George John Spencer, 2nd Earl** (1758–1834), son of the above, who, as Pitt's First Lord of the Admiralty (1794–1801), improved naval administration, put down mutinies at the Nore and Spithead, and sent out Nelson to the Eastern Mediterranean. He was a famous collector of books and first president of the Roxburgh Club.

(2) **John Charles Spencer, 3rd Earl** (1782–1845), son of the above, who was educated at Harrow and Trinity College, Cambridge. Known under his courtesy title of Lord Althorp, he became Whig chancellor of the Exchequer and leader of the House of Commons, and was mainly responsible for carrying through the Reform Bill of 1832, and the bill for reforming the Irish Church. He resigned on account of the Irish Coercion Bill, but resumed office in the Melbourne administration. On succeeding as earl in 1834 he passed to the House of Lords. See a memoir by D. Le Marchant (1876); Bagehot, *Biographical Studies* (1881); and Life by Myres (1890).

(3) **John Poyntz Spencer, 5th Earl** (1835–1910), was lord-lieutenant of Ireland in 1868–74 and 1882–85. In 1880 he became lord president of the Council, and again in 1886, having embraced Gladstone's Home Rule policy. He was first lord of the Admiralty in 1892–95.

SPENCER, (1) Gilbert (1892–), English artist, brother of (3), born at Cookham. He has executed many watercolours (e.g., the *Tolpuddle Martyrs* in the Tate Gallery) and murals. From 1932–48 he was professor of Painting at the Royal College of Art, and was head of the department of Painting and Drawing at the Glasgow School of Art from 1948–50, and held a similar post at the Camberwell School of Art 1950–57.

(2) **Herbert** (1820–1903), English evolutionary philosopher, born at Derby, became a railway engineer in 1837 but engaged extensively in journalism. Subeditor of *The Economist* (1848–53), he wrote a defence of *laissez faire* economics in *Social Statics* (1851), later modified in *Man Versus the State* (1884). A firm believer in evolution before Darwin, he propounded evolutionary *Principles of Psychology* (1855), and when *The Origin of Species* appeared four years later, regarded it merely as a special application of his own *a priori* principles. In his *System of Synthetic Philosophy* (1862–93) he argued that the ultimate scientific principles are unknowable and, agnostically, that the Unknowable must be a power, or God. The function of philosophy is as a science of the sciences, unifying their only partial unity. He applied evolution to biology and sociology and worked out evolutionary *Principles of Ethics* (1879–93). Darwin confessed that he could not understand Spencer's philosophy and Bradley pungently said of his agnosticism that he was taking something for God, because he did not know 'what the devil it can be'. Deeply enmeshed in the scientific outlook of his day, his philosophy has dated. See his *Autobiography* (1904), Lives by D. Duncan (1908), W. H. Hudson (1908) and E. Compayré (trans. 1908), and studies by A. D. White (1897), H. Macpherson (1900), J. Royce (1904), J. A. Thomson (1906) and H. S. R. Elliot (1917).

(3) **Sir Stanley** (1891–1959), English artist, brother of (1), born at Cookham, where he mainly lived and worked. He studied at the Slade School. From 1926 to 1933 he executed murals (utilizing his war experiences) in the Oratory of All Souls, Burghclere. He produced many purely realistic landscapes, but his main works interpret the Bible in terms of everyday life (e.g., the *Christ Carrying the Cross* and the two paintings of the *Resurrection* in the Tate Gallery, London), using bold distortion of the figures. During World War II he painted a series of panels depicting *Shipbuilding on the Clyde*. He was elected R.A. in 1950 and knighted in 1959. See monographs by Rothenstein (1945) and Newton (1947), and Lives by (1), and by Collis (1962).

(4) **Sir Walter Baldwin** (1860–1929), British ethnologist, born at Stretford, Lancashire, crossed Australia from south to north with F. J. Gillen, and jointly with him wrote standard works on the aborigines.

SPENDER, (1) **Edward Harold** (1864–1926), English journalist, biographer and novelist, son of (3) and father of (4), wrote *One Man Returns* (1914), and biographies of Asquith, Botha and Lloyd George. See his autobiographical *Fire of Life* (1926).

(2) **John Alfred** (1862–1942), English journalist and biographer, son of (3), born at Bath, became editor of the Liberal *Westminster Gazette* (1896–1922) and one of the leading journalists of the day. A member of Lord Milner's special mission to Egypt (1919–20), he wrote a number of political books and biographies of Campbell-Bannerman, Asquith, &c. See his *Life* (1926).

(3) **Lilian** (1835–95), English novelist, married John Kent Spender in 1858 and became mother of (1) and (2). Her novels include *Lady Hazleton's Confession* (1890).

(4) **Stephen** (1909–), English poet and critic, son of (1), born in London. Educated at University College, Oxford, he was in the 'thirties one of the 'modern poets', left-wing in outlook, who set themselves the task of recharging the impulses of poetry both in style and subject matter. In his thought he is essentially a Liberal, despite his earlier flirtings with Communism. He translated Schiller, Toller, Rilke and Lorca, among others, besides writing much penetrating literary criticism. From his beginnings in 1930 with *Twenty Poems* to 1957—*Engaged in Writing* (a nouvelle), he relived his experiences in his work. *Poems from Spain* (1939) link up with his service in the Spanish Civil War. In World War II he served as a fireman in the London blitz, and volumes of poems, *Runes and Visions* (1941), *Poems of Dedication* (1941), *The Edge of Darkness* (1949), carry on his self-analysis. Alongside these are critical evaluations such as *The Destructive Element* (1936), *Life and the Poet* (1942), *The Creative Element* (1944), and his first autobiography, *World within World* (1951). From 1939 to 1941 he was co-editor, with Cyril Connolly, of the brilliant monthly, *Horizon*, and in 1953 was co-editor of *Encounter*.

SPENER, Philipp Jakob, *shpay'ner* (1635–1705), German theologian, 'the Father of Pietism', born in Alsace. At Strasbourg and Frankfurt he tried to reawaken the dormant Christianity of the day. His *Pia Desideria* (1675) spread the movement far beyond the range of his personal influence, but not without enmity. See Lives by Hossbach (1828; 3rd ed. 1861), Wildenhalm (1842–47; trans. 1881) and Grünberg (1893–1906).

SPENGLER, Oswald (1880–1936), German historicist writer, born at Blankenburg, Harz, studied at Halle, Munich and Berlin and taught mathematics (1908) in Hamburg before devoting himself entirely to the compilation of the morbidly prophetic *Untergang des Abendlandes* (Vol. I, 1918; Vol. II, 1922) 'Decline of the West', trans. C. F. Atkinson (1926–29), in which he argues by analogy, in the historicist manner of Hegel and Marx, that all civilizations or cultures are subject to the same cycle of growth and decay in accordance with predetermined 'historical destiny'. The soul of Western civilization is dead. The age of soulless expansionist Caesarism is upon us. It is better for Western man, therefore, to be engineer rather than poet, soldier rather than artist, politician rather than philosopher. Unlike Toynbee, whom he influenced, he was concerned with the present and future rather than with the origins of civilizations. His verdict, achieved by his specious method, greatly encouraged the Nazis although he never became one himself. Another work attempted the identification of Prussianism with Socialism (1920). See study by M. Schroeter (1922), E. Heller, *The Disinherited Mind* (1952), and K. R. Popper, *The Poverty of Historicism* (1957).

SPENSER, Edmund (1552?–99), English poet, was born in London, the son of a gentleman tradesman who was connected with the Spencers of Althorp. He was educated at Merchant Taylors' School and Pembroke Hall, Cambridge. His juvenilia, partly written at Cambridge, include the *Visions* of Petrarch and some sonnets of Du Bellay translated. Shortly after leaving Cambridge (1576) he obtained a place in Leicester's household and this led to a friendship with Sir Philip Sidney and a circle of wits, called the Areopagus. His first original work, *The Shepheards Calendar* (1579), dedicated to Sydney, was the first clear note of Elizabethan poetry and no doubt assisted in his career as a courtier. In 1580 he was appointed secretary to Lord Grey de Wilton, lord deputy in Ireland, whose assignment was to crush native rebellion, and Spenser was drawn into the tragic business. His reward for his work as one of the 'undertakers' for the settlement of Munster was Kilcolman Castle in the county of Cork, where he settled in 1586 and where he hoped to have leisure to write his *Faerie Queene* and other courtly works, written with an eye to the court no less than as a brilliant presentation of the art and thought of the Renaissance. In 1589 he visited London in company with Sir Walter Raleigh, who had seen the first three books of *The Faerie Queene* at Kilcolman and now carried him off to lay them at Elizabeth's feet. Published in 1590, they were an immediate success, but a previous misdemeanour, viz., the attack in *Mother*

Hubberd's Tale on the proposed match between Elizabeth and the Duc d'Alençon, was not forgotten and the poet returned to Ireland in 1591 a disappointed man. The charming *Colin Clout's Come Home Again* commemorates the visit. *Complaints*, published the same year, contains, beside his juvenilia, the brilliantly coloured but enigmatic *Muiopotmos*; *Mother Hubberd's Tale*, which is now provided with a bitter satire on Court favour; *The Early Tears of the Muses*, which lamented the lack of patronage; and his pastoral elegy for Sydney which is so frigid as to make us question their intimacy. In 1594 Spenser married again, celebrating his wooing of Elizabeth Boyle in the sonnet sequence *Amoretti* and his wedding in the supreme marriage poem *Epithalamion*. He revisited London in 1596, with three more books of *The Faerie Queene*, which were published along with the *Four Hymns*. These consisted of the early *Hymns in Honour of Love and Beauty* and two new ones of *Heavenly Love and Beauty* in which his early Platonism is overlaid by Christian feeling. This was a year of unwonted activity. Under the roof of Lord Essex he wrote *Prothalamion*, which is sufficiently praised when we say it rivals *Epithalamion*, and his prose *View of the Present State of Ireland*, which, taken with the fifth book of *The Faerie Queene*, is probably the first explicit statement of the imperialism which is now discredited. *The Faerie Queene* is designed to show the ideal gentleman or courtier in action—a favourite Renaissance theme, of which Castiglione's *Il Cortigiano* (from which Spenser drew extensively) is the exemplar. The charming Book I is evangelical and has been transposed as a coloured tract. Book II on the Aristotelian virtue of Temperance (which Spenser misconceived) shows the puritan in him at odds with the artist in the provocative scenes in Acrasia's bower. Book III is a tribute to the Virgin Queen, but also demonstrates that marriage is the end of love, *amour courtois* being a false species. Book IV, of friendship, is a tangle of romantic episodes. Book V treats of England's wars on behalf of Protestantism and dominion. Here Lord Grey, as Sir Arthegal, is the maligned hero pursued by the Blatant Beast, i.e., Scandal, which it is Caledore's assignment to destroy in Book VI. This last book however, of the specific virtue of the gentleman, i.e., courtesy, is largely taken up with devising tests for the hero's courtesy. The Blatant Beast looks in from time to time but Spenser's experience had taught him that scandal can never be destroyed. This summary gives no idea of the qualities which make Spenser the ' poet's poet '—the lulling harmonies of the verse, the brilliant artistry specially in chiaroscuro, the poetic diction which, though avoided today, was probably salutary at that stage of English poetry if ever it was to vie with Continental poetry. Modern editions are by de Selincourt and Smith (1924 and 1952); Renwick's edition (1928–34), discontinued at the fourth volume (*View of the State of Ireland*), probably on the appearance of the sumptuous Columbia edition, ed. Greenlaw and others (10 vols. 1952–57). See also Kate Warren's ed. of *The Faerie Queen* (1913); there are studies by Renwick (a valuable treatment of Spenser as the Renaissance poet), Legouis (1926), Davis (1933) and Atkinson (1937).

SPERANSKI, Mikhail, Count, *spyay-rahns' kyee* (1772–1839), Russian statesman and reformer, became Tsar Alexander I's adviser and in 1809 produced a plan for the reorganization of the Russian structure of government on the Napoleonic model, but was dismissed when Napoleon invaded Russia (1812). Under Nicholas I he was restored to power and was responsible for the trial and conviction of the Decembrist conspirators of 1825. See Life by M. Raeff (The Hague 1958), and Tolstoy's *War and Peace*.

SPERRY, Elmer Ambrose (1860–1930), American inventor, born at Cartland, invented a new-type dynamo, arc-light and searchlight, the gyroscopic compass (1911) and stabilizer for ships and devised an electrolytic process for obtaining pure caustic soda from salt. He also founded several companies for the manufacture of these inventions.

SPEUSIPPUS, *spyoo-sip'us* (*c.* 394–336 B.C.), Athenian philosopher, nephew of Plato, accompanied the latter to Sicily and in 361 succeeded him as head of the Academy. Only one fragment, on Pythagorean numbers, of his works is still extant.

SPIELHAGEN, Friedrich, *speel'hah-gėn* (1829–1911), German novelist, was born at Magdeburg. His works include (besides poems, plays, books of travel, &c.) *Durch Nacht zum Licht* (1861), *Die von Hohenstein* (1863), *In Reih und Glied* (1866), *Susi* (1895). See his Autobiography (1890), and study by M. Geller (1917).

SPILSBURY, Sir Bernard Henry (1877–1947), British pathologist, born in Leamington, studied physiology at Magdalen College, Oxford, then entered the medical school of St Mary's Hospital, Paddington, and specialized in what was at that time the new science of pathology. He made his name at the trial of Crippen (1910), where his expert evidence was delivered with the imperturbable objectivity and serenity he was invariably to show under cross-examination. Appointed pathologist to the Home Office, his abilities were recognized by a knighthood (1923). As expert witness for the Crown, Sir Bernard was involved in many notable murder trials, such as those of Mahon (1924), Thorne (1925) and Rouse (1931). His last important case was the murder of de Antiquis (1947). By then his strength was failing and on December 17, 1947, he died by his own hand. He has been described as the ideal scientific witness. See study by Browne and Tullett (1951).

SPINELLO ARETINO (*c.* 1330–1410), Italian painter, spent nearly all his life between Arezzo (his birthplace) and Florence. His principal frescoes were done for San Miniato, at Florence, for the *campo santo* of Pisa, and for the municipal buildings of Siena.

SPINOLA, Ambrogio, Marquis of Los Balbases (1569–1630), Italian soldier in Spanish service, was born at Genoa. In 1602 he raised and maintained at his own cost 9000 troops and served under Mendoza in the Netherlands. In 1603 he succeeded to the marquisate on the death of his brother Federigo in a naval battle against the Dutch. Spinola was meanwhile besieging Ostend, which fell in 1604 after a three years' siege. War continued largely as a duel between Spinola and Maurice of Nassau; but the former saw the necessity for peace and was one of the plenipotentiaries at the Hague Conference, which made the twelve-year truce in 1609. Early in the Thirty Years' War, Spinola was in Germany, subduing the Lower Palatinate. But he was recalled to the Netherlands to fight once more against his old opponent. Maurice, however, died of fever while attempting to relieve Breda, which fell to Spinola in 1625. Shortly afterwards, ill-health forced him to resign. His long service found little reward, but in 1629 he was in Italy, acting as governor of Milan; and in the same year, while besieging Casale, he died. See French Life by Siret (1851).

SPINOZA, Baruch, *Lat.* **Benedict, de,** *spi-nō'za* (1632–77), Dutch-Jewish philosopher and theologian, born November 24 at Amsterdam into one of the many Jewish émigré families from Spain and Portugal who had been compelled to profess Christianity but secretly kept loyal to their faith. His deep interest in optics, the new astronomy and Cartesian philosophy made him unpopular at the synagogue, and at the age of twenty-four he was formally excommunicated from the only society to which he naturally belonged. He made a living grinding and polishing lenses from 1656, and became the leader of a small philosophical circle. In 1660 he settled in Rijnsburg near Leyden, and wrote his *Short Treatise on God, Man and his Well-being* and *Tractatus de Intellectus Emendatione* (1677), 'Short Treatise on the Correction of the Understanding'. In the beautiful opening passage he outlines his aim of discovering 'a true good, capable of imparting itself, by which alone the mind could be affected to the exclusion of all else . . . a joy continuous and supreme to all eternity'. He also wrote most of his commentary on Cartesian geometry (1663), the first part of his masterpiece *Ethica*, and carried on a correspondence with Oldenburg, the secretary of the English Royal Society, Huygens and Boyle. In 1663 he moved to Voorburg, near The Hague, and began the *Tractatus Theologica politicus*, published in 1670, which despite its anonymity made him famous. In 1671 he sent to Leibniz a tract on optics and in 1676 the latter stayed at The Hague and they met. The details of their conversations are unfortunately not preserved, possibly because the socially ambitious Leibniz, so utterly opposed in temperament and ambition to the otherworldly Spinoza, did not wish to publicize any debt to a thinker, such as the latter, commonly thought subversive of religion. *Ethica* (posthumously 1677), despite its title, is a thoroughgoing metaphysical system, developed in Euclidian fashion from axioms, theorems and definitions. The basic substance is *deus sive natura*, 'God or nature'. Thought and extension are merely two of the infinite attributes of God, applicable to human beings. Minds and bodies are mere modes, or aspects, termed *natura naturata* of the divine being, *natura naturans*. This pantheistic activist monism resolves the Cartesian dualism of mind and matter. Finite things are defined by their boundaries, by negation. Only God is infinite. Everything happens according to a 'logical' necessity. There is nothing which corresponds to ordinary notions of free will. We are limited in so far as our passions make us subject to outside causes, and 'free' in so far as we act in accordance with God. Wrong action is synonymous with rational error. It is 'logically' impossible that events should be other than they are. In 1672 Spinoza risked his life protesting against the murder of the de Witt brothers by the mob. In 1673 he refused the professorship of Philosophy at Heidelberg, offered by the Elector Palatine, in order to keep his independence. In the last years of his life he worked on the unfinished *Tractatus Politicus*, a popular exposition of his political philosophy, which derived from Hobbes but differed in Spinoza's advocacy of democracy. He died February 21, 1677, at Amsterdam of phthisis, aggravated by the glass dust in his lungs. Van Vloten and Land edited Spinoza's works (The Hague 1883). See J. A. Froude, *Short Studies* (1867), Matthew Arnold, *Essays in Criticism* (1865), and studies by Sir F. Pollock (1880 and 1935), J. Martineau (1882), J. Caird (1888), H. H. Joachim (1901 and 1940), R. A. Duff (1903), R. McKeon (1928), L. Roth (1929), H. F. Hallett (1930, 1949 and 1957), S. Hampshire (1951), R. L. Saw (1951), G. H. R. Parkinson (1954), and A. G. Wernham, *Political Works* (1958).

SPITTELER, Karl Friedrich Georg (1845–1924), Swiss poet and novelist, born at Liestal (Basel), studied law and theology at Basel, Zürich and Heidelberg, was a tutor in Russia, teacher and journalist in Switzerland, and retired to Lucerne in 1892. *Der Olympische Frühling* (1900–03) is a great mythological epic, but perhaps his most mature work is *Prometheus der Dulder* (1924). Besides poetry he wrote tales (*Konrad der Leutnant*, &c.), essays (*Lachende Wahrheiten*) and reminiscences. He was awarded the Nobel prize in 1919.

SPODE, Josiah (1754–1827), English potter, born at Stoke-on-Trent, learnt his trade in his father's workshops, and in 1800 began to use bone as well as felspar in the paste, which resulted in porcelain of a special transparency and beauty. He did much to popularize the willow pattern and he became the foremost china manufacturer of his time. He was appointed potter to George III in 1806. See W. B. Honey, *English Pottery and Porcelain* (1947).

SPOFFORTH, Frederick Robert (1853–1926), Australian cricketer, known as 'the demon', the greatest bowler in the history of the game, was born at Balmain, Sydney. On May 27, 1878, he took 11 wickets for 20 runs against the M.C.C., and during 1884 he took 218 wickets in first-class cricket with a bowling average of 12·53.

SPOHR, Ludwig (1784–1859), German composer, violinist and conductor, born at

Brunswick, was *kapellmeister* at the court of Hesse-Kassel in 1822–57. Remembered chiefly as a composer for the violin, for which he wrote 17 concertos, he also composed operas, oratorios, symphonies, &c. See his Autobiography (trans. 1864), Lives by Malibran (1860) and Schletterer (1881), and D. M. Mayer, *The Forgotten Master* (1959).

SPONTINI, Gasparo Luigi Pacifico, *spon-tee′nee* (1774–1851), Italian composer, born near Ancona, went to Paris in 1803. His operas *La Vestale* (1807) and *Ferdinand Cortez* (1809) were greeted with enthusiasm. In Berlin (1820–42) only court influence supported him against the public and the press. *Hohenstaufen* (1829) is his greatest work. Spontini was dismissed by Frederick-William IV in 1842. See Life by Robert (1883).

SPOONER, William Archibald (1844–1930), Anglican clergyman and educationalist, dean (1876–89) and warden (1903–24) of New College, Oxford. As an albino he suffered all his life from weak eyesight, but surmounted his disabilities with heroism and earned a reputation for kindness and hospitality. His life was bound up with his college and his popularity was not lessened by his occasional scathing comments. His name is forever associated with his own nervous tendency to transpose initial letters or syllables—as in the 'spoonerism' 'a half-warmed fish' for 'a half-formed wish'.

SPOTTISWOODE, (1) Alicia Ann, Lady John Scott (1811–1900), Scottish composer and author of *Annie Laurie* and other songs.

(2) **John** (1565–1639), Scottish churchman, educated at Glasgow University, at first a Presbyterian, he later became Episcopalian. He was Archbishop of Glasgow (1610) and of St Andrews (1615). He promoted Episcopal government, and forced the Perth Assembly (1618) to sanction the Perth Articles. He officiated at the coronation of Charles I at Holyrood in 1633, and in 1635 was appointed chancellor of Scotland. He reluctantly entered into the king's liturgical scheme, and so made himself hateful to the Covenanters. The king compelled him to resign the chancellorship in 1683, and he was deposed and excommunicated. He died in London. His chief work is the *History of the Church of Scotland* (1655).

(3) **William** (1825–83), English mathematician, physicist and publisher, born in London, was educated at Harrow and Balliol, where he lectured in Mathematics. In 1846, he succeeded his father as head of the printing house of Eyre and Spottiswoode and did original work in polarization of light, electrical discharge in rarefied gases and wrote a mathematical treatise on determinants. He was elected F.R.S. in 1853 and was president of the British Association.

SPRENGEL, (1) Christian Konrad (1750–1816), German botanist, born at Brandenburg, became rector of Spandau, but neglected his duties for his original observations of pollination in plants and the rôle of insects, which aroused Darwin's interest. His nephew, **Kurt** (1766–1833), wrote histories of medicine (1803) and botany (1818).

(2) **Hermann Johann Philipp** (1834–1906), German-born British chemist, born near Hanover, came from Göttingen and Heidelberg for research in Oxford and London and remained in Britain. He invented a new type of vacuum pump (1865) and devised the U-tube method for comparing liquid densities.

SPRENGER, (1) Aloys (1813–93), Austrian orientalist, was born at Nassereut in Tyrol, studied at Vienna, came to London, in 1843 sailed to Calcutta, worked as interpreter, librarian, and translator, and in 1857 became Oriental professor at Bern. In 1881 he settled at Heidelberg. He wrote a great *Leben und Lehre des Mohammed* (1861–65) and books on the ancient geography of Arabia, Babylonia, &c.

(2) **Jacob,** German theologian, Dominican and professor of Theology in Cologne, and **Henricus Institor** (Latinized form of Krämer), compiled the famous *Malleus Maleficarum* (1489), which first formulated the doctrine of witchcraft, and formed a text-book of procedure for witch trials. They were appointed inquisitors by Innocent VIII in 1484.

SPRING, Howard (1889–1965), British novelist, born in Cardiff, from errand boy became newspaper reporter and literary critic and established himself as a writer with his best-selling *Oh Absalom* (1938), renamed *My Son, My Son.* Other novels include *Fame is the Spur* (1940), *Dunkerleys* (1946), *These Lovers Fled Away* (1955), *Time and the Hour* (1957), as well as three autobiographical works (1939, 1942 and 1946).

SPRUNER VON MERTZ, Karl (1803–92), German cartographer and Bavarian general, whose name is associated with a great historical *Handatlas* (1837–52; 3rd ed. by Menko, 1862–79).

SPURGEON, Charles Haddon (1834–92), English Baptist preacher, born at Kelvedon, Essex, became in 1854 pastor of the New Park Street Chapel, London. The Metropolitan Tabernacle, seating 6000, was erected for him in 1859–61 (burnt April 1898). In 1887 he withdrew from the Baptist Union because no action was taken against persons charged with fundamental errors. Apart from sermons, he wrote *John Ploughman's Talk* (1869) and many other works. See *Letters* (ed. by his son, 1924), Lives by Shindler (1892), Fullerton (1920), and the Autobiography, compiled by his wife and J. Harrald (1897–1900).

SPURR, Josiah Edward (1870–1950), American geologist, was mining engineer to the Sultan of Turkey (1901), geologist in the U.S. Geological Survey (1902) and eventually professor of Geology at Rollins College (1930–32). As a result of his work, the age of the Tertiary period has been estimated as 45 to 60 million years. His exploration in Alaska in 1896 and 1898 was commemorated by the name Mt Spurr. Among other works, he wrote *Geology Applied to Mining* (1904).

SPURZHEIM, Johann (Christoph) Caspar, *spoorts′hīm* (1776–1832), German phrenologist, born near Trier, studied medicine in Vienna and became the disciple of Gall (q.v.) the phrenologist, and, lecturing in Britain, gained a powerful adherent in George Combe (q.v.). See Memoir by Carmichael (1833).

SQUARCIONE, Francesco, *skwahr-chō'nay* (1394–1474), Italian painter, Mantegna's master, founded the Paduan school of painters.

SQUIER, *skwīr*, (1) **Ephraim George** (1821–1888), American archaeologist, born at Bethlehem, N.H., in 1841–48 was a newspaper editor, latterly in Ohio. He explored the antiquities of the Mississippi Valley, and then of New York, and in 1849 was appointed *chargé d'affaires* to Central America, in 1863 U.S. commissioner to Peru. Among his works are *Nicaragua* (1852), *Serpent Symbols* (1852), *Waikau* (1855), *Central America* (1857) and *Peru* (1877).

(2) **George Owen** (1865–1934), American military and electrical engineer, chief signals officer in the U.S. army (1917), invented the polarizing chronophotograph sine-wave system of cable telegraphy and multiline radio systems, &c.

SQUIRE, Sir John Collings (1884–1958), English author, born at Plymouth, educated at Blundell's and St John's College, Cambridge, and was literary editor of *The New Statesman* and (1919–34) *The London Mercury*. He leant towards the lighter side of verse and to parody, as in *Steps to Parnassus* (1913) and *Tricks of the Trade* (1917), and in anthologies was a friend to the minor poet. He was knighted in 1933. His writings also include criticisms and short stories. See his autobiographical *Water Music* (1939), &c.

SSU-MA CH'IEN, *soo-mah chi-yen* (*c.* 145–87 B.C.), Chinese historian, born at Lungmen, succeeded his father in 110 B.C. as grand astrologer, but incurred the emperor's wrath for taking the part of a friend who, in command of a military expedition, had surrendered to the enemy. Ssu-ma Ch'ien was imprisoned for three years and castrated, but was gradually restored to favour. He is chiefly remembered for the *Shih Chi*, the first history of China compiled as dynastic histories in which annals of the principal events are supplemented by princely and other biographies and notes on economic and institutional history. It had been begun by his father, **Ssu-ma T'an.** See Life by B. Watson (1958).

SSU-MA HSIANG-JU, *-shi-ang-yoo* (d. 117 B.C.), Chinese poet, born in Ch'engtu, Sezechwan province, wrote the *Tzu Hsu Fu*, a series of poems describing and denouncing the pleasures of the hunt and which hold an important place in Chinese literary history.

STAAL, Marguerite Jeanne, Baronne de, *stahl* (1684–1750), French writer of memoirs, born the daughter of a poor Parisian painter, Cordier, whose name she dropped for that of her mother, Delaunay. Her devotion to the interests of her employer, the Duchesse de Maine, brought her two years in the Bastille, where she had a love affair with the Chevalier de Menil. In 1735 she married the Baron de Staal. Her *Mémoires* (1755; trans. 1892) describe the world of the regency with intellect, observation and a subtle irony, and are written in a clear, firm and individual style. Her *Œuvres complètes* appeared in 1821. See study by Frary (1863).

STACPOOLE, Henry de Vere (1863–1951) British physician and writer, born in Kingstown (Dun Laoghaire), Ireland. He was the author of many popular novels, including *The Blue Lagoon* (1909), *The Pearl Fishers* (1915) and *Green Coral* (1935). See his autobiographical *Men and Mice* (1942 and 1945).

STAËL, (1) **Anne Louise Germaine Necker, Madame de (Baronne de Staël-Holstein)** (1766–1817), the greatest of French women writers, the only child of Necker (q.v.), was born in Paris, April 22. In her girlhood she wrote romantic comedies, tragedies, novels, essays and *Lettres sur Rousseau* (1789). She married in 1786 the Baron de Staël-Holstein (1742–1802), the bankrupt Swedish ambassador. She bore him two sons (1790 and 1792) and a daughter (1797), but to protect her fortune separated formally from him in 1798. Her vast enthusiasms and the passionate intensity of her affections gave force and colour to her rich and versatile character, and combined to form a personality whose influence was irresistible. Her brilliant *salon* became the centre of political discussion, but the Revolution opened up new horizons for France; Necker's fall only hastened the dénouement of the tragedy; and she quitted Paris for Coppet in September 1792. From Coppet she went to England, where at Mickleham in Surrey she was surrounded by Talleyrand and others of the French *émigrés*. She joined her husband at Coppet in May 1793, and published her *Réflexions sur le procès de la reine* in the vain hope of saving Marie Antoinette. In 1795 she returned to Paris, where her husband had re-established himself as ambassador. She prepared for a political rôle by her *Réflexions sur la paix intérieure* (1795), but was advised to return to Coppet. Her *Influence des passions* appeared in 1796. Bonaparte allowed her to return to Paris in 1797, but received her friendly advances with such studied coldness that admiration soon turned to hatred. In 1800 she published her famous *Littérature et ses rapports avec les institutions sociales.* She was again back in Paris in 1802, when her *salon* was more brilliant than ever, and published *Delphine*, a novel. At length the epigrams of Constant, her friendship with disaffected men like Moreau and Bernadotte, and the appearance of Necker's *Dernières vues* exhausted the patience of Napoleon, and in the autumn of 1803 she received orders to keep forty leagues from Paris. Her husband had died, and in December 1803 she set out with her children for Weimar, where she dazzled the whole court, and met Schiller and Goethe. At Berlin she made acquaintance with August Schlegel. She next turned her steps towards Vienna, but learned of her father's death, and returned to Coppet, writing the touching eulogy, *Du caractère de M. Necker.* Then she set out for Italy with Schlegel, Wilhelm von Humboldt, and Bonstetten, but returned to Coppet, where, as usual, a brilliant circle assembled, in June 1805 to write *Corinne* (1807), a romance, which at once brought her European fame. She revisited Germany at the end of 1807, and began to turn for consolation to religion—she was a Protestant. Her famous *De l'Allemagne* was finished in 1810, passed by the censor, and partly printed, when the whole impression was seized and destroyed, and herself ordered from Paris to Coppet. The work was published by John Murray at London in 1813. But her exile had now become a bitter reality; she found herself encompassed with spies. She escaped secretly to Bern, and thence made her way to St Petersburg, Stockholm and (1813) London. In England admiration reached its climax on the publication of *De l'Allemagne*, the most finished of all her works. It revealed Germany to the French and made Romanticism—she was the first to use the word—acceptable to the Latin peoples. Louis XVIII welcomed her to Paris in 1814, and the two millions which Necker had left in the Treasury was honourably paid to her. The return of Napoleon drove her from Paris, and she spent the winter in Italy for the sake of the health of Albert de Rocca, an Italian officer in the French service, whom she had married secretly in 1811. She died in Paris, July 14, 1817. Her surviving son and daughter published her unfinished *Considérations sur la Revolution française* (1818), esteemed by Sainte-Beuve her masterpiece, the *Dix Années d'exil* (1821), and her complete works (1820–21). See Lives by Stevens (1880), Blennerhassett (Berlin 1887–89; trans. 1889), Wilson (1931), studies by Duffy (1887), Sorel (trans. 1892), Cléron (1925), Larg (trans. 1926), de Pange (1938), *Mistress to an Age* by Hérold (1959), and her *Lettres à Ribbing* (ed. by Balayé, 1961).

(2) **Nicolas de** (1914–55), French painter, born in St Petersburg. He studied in Brussels, travelled in Spain and Italy, and worked in Paris. His paintings were mainly abstract, and he made inspired use of rectangular patches of colour; his later pictures were more representational and in subdued colours. See monograph by Duthuit (1950), and study by Cooper (1962).

STAFFORD, William Howard, 1st Viscount Stafford (1614–80), English Catholic nobleman, beheaded on Tower Hill as a victim of the perjuries of Oates (q.v.). His attainder was reversed in 1824.

STAHL, (1) **Friedrich Julius** (1802–61), German philosopher and politician, born of Jewish parents at Munich, turned Protestant, studied law, and published *Die Philosophie des Rechts* (1830–37; rev. 1878). In 1840 he became professor of Philosophy of Law at Berlin, and was a leader of the reactionary party in the First Chamber. Among his other works was *Der christliche Staat* (1847), in which he advocated a sovereign despotism based on divine right.

(2) **Georg Ernest** (1660–1734), German chemist, born at Ansbach, became professor of Medicine (1694) at Halle, body physician (1714) to the king of Prussia and expounded the phlogiston theory and animism.

STÅHLBERG, Kaarlo Juho (1865–1952), Finnish lawyer, was professor of Law at Helsingfors and first president (1919–25) of Finland. Kidnapped in 1930, he was narrowly defeated in 1931.

STAINER, (1) **Jakob,** *shtī'nėr* (1621–83), Austrian violinmaker born at Absam near Hall in Tirol, made violins at Innsbruck, and died in a Benedictine monastery. See two works by Ruf (1872–92).

(2) **Sir John,** *stay'-* (1840–1901), English composer, born in London, became organist of Magdalen College, Oxford, in 1860, and of St Paul's (1872), and Oxford professor of Music (1889). He was knighted in 1888. He wrote cantatas and church music, notably *The Crucifixion* (1887), also a *Treatise on Harmony*, a *Dictionary of Musical Terms* (with W. A. Barrett), &c.

STAIR, a Scottish title derived from an Ayrshire village by the Dalrymple family, one of whom was among the Lollards of Kyle summoned before James IV; his great-grandson embraced the Reformed doctrines. See also DALRYMPLE, HAILES, and J. Murray Graham's *Stair Annals* (1875). Its most noteworthy members, in chronological order, were:

(1) **James Dalrymple, 1st Viscount, new line** (1619–95), Scottish jurist, father of (2), studied at Glasgow University, served in the army, acted as Regent in Philosophy at Glasgow, joined the bar (1648), and was recommended by Monk to Cromwell for the office of a lord of session. He advised the former to call a free parliament (1600). He was confirmed in office and created a Nova Scotia baronet in 1664. The luckless marriage in 1669 of his daughter Janet to Baldoon suggested to Scott *The Bride of Lammermoor*. In 1670 Dalrymple was made president of the Court of Session and member of the privy council; but when the Duke of York came to govern at Edinburgh in 1679 he retired to the country, and prepared his famous *Institutes of the Law of Scotland*. His wife and his tenants were devoted to the Covenant, and he was soon involved in a fierce dispute with Claverhouse. He fled in 1682 to Holland, returned with the Prince of Orange, and, restored to the presidency, was created in 1690 Viscount Stair. See Memoir by J. G. Mackay (1873), and study by A. H. Campbell (1954).

(2) **Sir John Dalrymple, 1st Earl of** (1648–1707), Scottish judge and politician, son of (1), studied law, and was knighted in 1667. He came into violent collision with Claverhouse, and was flung into prison in Edinburgh and heavily fined, but early in 1686 became king's advocate, and in 1688 lord justice-clerk. Under William III he was lord advocate, and as secretary of state from 1691 had the chief management of Scottish affairs. On his shoulders, therefore, with Breadalbane and the king, mainly rests the infamy of the massacre of Glencoe. He was accused of exceeding his instructions and resigned (1695). In 1703 he was created an earl. He took an active part in the debates and intrigues that led to the Treaty of Union, and died suddenly, January 8, 1707. See Omond, *Lord Advocates of Scotland* (1883), Sir John Dalrymple, *Memoirs of Great Britain* (1788).

(3) **John Dalrymple, 2nd Earl** (1673–1747), Scottish soldier, was born at Edinburgh. At eight he shot his elder brother dead by accident, so was exiled by his parents to Holland, studied at Leyden, fought under the Prince

of Orange at Steenkerk, and by 1701 was lieutenant-colonel in the Scots Footguards, in 1706 colonel of the Cameronians. He was aide-de-camp to Marlborough in 1703, commanded an infantry brigade at Ramillies, was made colonel of the Scots Greys in 1706 and in 1708 secretly married Viscountess Primrose. He distinguished himself greatly at Oudenarde (1708) and Malplaquet. General in 1712, he retired to Edinburgh to intrigue for the Hanoverian succession. Under George I he was ambassador to Paris, and checkmated the Pretender and Alberoni. Recalled in 1720, he devoted himself to agriculture, growing turnips and cabbages. Made field-marshal (1742), he was governor of Minorca and fought at Dettingen.

STAKHANOV, Aleksei Grigorievich, *stĕ-KHah'nof*, Russian coalminer, who started an incentive scheme (1935) for exceptional output and efficiency by individual steel workers, coalminers, &c. Such prize workers were called Stakhanovites.

STALIN, Joseph, properly **Iosif Vissarionovich Dzhugashvili** (1879–1953), Russian leader, born in Georgia, was educated at the Tiflis Theological Seminary, from which he was expelled for 'propagating Marxism'. Joining the Bolshevik 'underground', he was arrested and transported to Siberia, whence he escaped in 1904. The ensuing years witnessed his closer identification with revolutionary Marxism, his many escapes from captivity, his growing intimacy with Lenin and Bukharin, his early disparagement of Trotsky, and his co-option, in 1912, to the illicit Bolshevik Central Committee. With the 1917 Revolution and the forcible replacement of the feeble Kerensky government by Lenin and his supporters, Stalin was appointed commissar for nationalities and a member of the Politbureau, although his activities throughout the counter-revolution and the war with Poland were confined to organizing a Red 'terror' in Tsaritsin—subsequently renamed Stalingrad. With his appointment as general secretary to the Central Committee in 1922, Stalin began stealthily to build up the power that would ensure his control of the situation after Lenin's death. When this occurred in 1924, he took over the reins, putting his overriding authority to successful test in 1928 by engineering Trotsky's degradation and banishment. Stalin's reorganization of the Soviets' resources, with its successive Five Year Plans, suffered many industrial setbacks and encountered consistently stubborn resistance in the field of agriculture, where the *kulaks*, or peasant proprietors, steadfastly refused to accept the principle of 'collectivization'. The measures taken by the dictator to 'discipline' those who opposed his will involved the death by execution or famine of up to 10 million peasantry (1932–33). The blood bath which eliminated the 'Old Bolsheviks' and the alleged right-wing 'intelligentsia', and the carefully staged 'engineers' trial', were followed by a drastic purge of some thousands of the Officer corps, including Marshal Tuchachevsky, Stalin professing to believe them guilty of pro-German sympathies. Red Army forces and material went to the support of the Spanish Communist government in 1936, although Stalin was careful not to commit himself too deeply. After the Munich crisis Franco-British negotiations for Russian support in the event of war were guilefully protracted until they ended in the *volte face* of a non-aggression pact with Hitler, which gained Stalin the time to prepare for the German invasion he sensed to be inevitable. In 1941 the prosperity of the Nazis' initial thrust into Russia could be accounted for in part by the disposal of the Red Army on the frontiers, ready to invade rather than repel invasion. Thereafter, Stalin's strategy followed the traditional Muscovite pattern of plugging gaps in the defences with more and more bodies and trading space for time in which the attrition begotten of impossible climatic conditions could whittle away the opponents' strength. Sustained by many millions of pounds' worth of war material furnished by Britain and America, the Red Army obediently responded to Stalin's astutely phrased call to defend not the principles of Marx and Engels, but 'Mother Russia'; although the Red dictator lost no time in demanding a 'Second Front' in Europe to relieve the strain on his unnumbered forces. Quick to exploit the unwarranted Anglo-American fear that Russia might 'go out of the war', Stalin easily outwitted the allied leaders at the Teheran and Yalta conferences. Seeming to acquiesce in decisions he had no intention of implementing, he never deviated an inch from the path he had marked out for himself. With the Red Army's invasion of German soil, Soviet bayonets were encouraged to penetrate far beyond the point where they had last been employed. Thus Stalin's domination of the Potsdam conference, followed by the premature break-up of the Anglo-American forces, left the Red dictator with actual possessions enlarged by 182,480 square miles which, with 'satellites' increased the Soviet sphere of influence by 763,940 square miles, bearing alien but submissive populations totalling 134,188,000. While Stalin consolidated his gains an 'iron curtain' was dropped to cut off Soviet Russia and her satellites from the outside world. At the same time the 'Hozyain' inaugurated a 'cold war' against all non-Communist countries—which included the blockade of Berlin—prosecuting it with all the ruthlessness, resource and illimitable Oriental cunning at his command. An entirely unscrupulous *arrivist*, Stalin consistently manipulated Communist imperialism for the greater glory of Soviet Russia and the strengthening of his own autocratic sway as its satrap. He died, in somewhat mysterious circumstances, in 1953. See works by Souvarine (n.d.), Deutscher (1949), Basseches (1952), and E. H. Carr, *Socialism in One Country* (3 vols., 1958–64); Stalin's *Works* (trans. 13 vols., 1953–55); and *Twenty Letters to a Friend* (1967), by his daughter, Svetlana, published after her much-publicized departure from Russia to America in 1967.

STAMBOLOV, Stephan Nikolov (1854–95), Bulgarian statesman, born at Trnova, took part in the rising of 1875–76. Chief of the

Russophobe regency (1886) and premier (1887–94), he ruled with a strong hand. Forced then to retire, he was assassinated (1895). See Life by Beaman (1895).

STAMITZ, (1) **Carl Philipp** (1746–1801), German composer and violinist, son of (2), studied under the latter and became a travelling instrumentalist in Paris, London, St Petersburg, Prague and Nuremberg. He wrote 80 symphonies, one of which was for a double orchestra, and concertos for violin, viola, 'cello, flute, oboe, clarinet and harpsichord. His brother, **Anton Johann Baptista** (1754–?1809), was also a musician.

(2) **Johann** (1717–57), Bohemian violinist and composer, father of (1), founder of the Mannheim school, was born at Havlickuv Brod. He first attracted attention at the coronation celebrations in Prague (1741) and was engaged by the Mannheim court, where he became a highly salaried court musician and concert master. He visited Paris (1754–1755). His compositions include 74 symphonies, concertos for harpsichord, violin, oboe, flute and clarinet (the last possibly the first of its kind), chamber music and a mass. He developed the sonata form, introduced sharp contrasts into symphonic movements and wrote some of the finest concerto music of the 18th century.

STAMP, Josiah Charles, 1st Baron Stamp of Shortlands (1880–1941), British economist, born in London, served on the Dawes Committee on German reparations, was chairman of the L.M.S. railway, director of Nobel Industries, and on the outbreak of World War II was made economic adviser to the government. An expert on taxation, he wrote on this and other financial subjects. He was killed in an air-raid.

STANDISH, Myles (*c.* 1584–1656), English colonist, born probably at Ormskirk, served in the Netherlands, and sailed with the *Mayflower* in 1620. He was military head of Massachusetts (against the Indians), and long its treasurer. Longfellow and Lowell wrote about his exploits against the Indians. See R. G. Usher, *The Pilgrims and their History* (1918), and Life by Porteus (1920).

STANFIELD, Clarkson (1794–1867), Irish marine painter, born of Irish Catholic parentage at Sunderland, left the navy for scene painting. He painted *Market-boats on the Scheldt* (1826), and *The Battle of Trafalgar* (1836).

STANFORD, (1) **Sir Charles Villiers** (1852–1924), Irish composer, was born at Dublin, studied at Cambridge, Leipzig and Berlin, and became organist at Trinity College (1872–93), professor in the Royal College of Music (1882), and Cambridge professor of Music (1887). He was knighted in 1901. Among his works are choral settings of Tennyson's *Revenge* (1886) and *Voyage of Maeldune* (1889); the oratorios *The Three Holy Children* (1885) and *Eden* (1891); the operas *The Veiled Prophet of Khorassan* (1881), *Savonarola*, *The Canterbury Pilgrims* (1884), *Shamus O'Brien* (1896), *Much Ado About Nothing* (1901), *The Critic* (1916); and he set a high standard in English church music. See his *Pages from an Unwritten Diary* (1914) and Life by Greene (1935).

(2) **Leland** (1824–93), American railway magnate, born at Watervliet, N.Y., in 1856 settled in San Francisco, became president of the Central Pacific Company, superintended the construction of the line, and was governor of California 1861–63, and U.S. senator from 1885. In memory of their only child, he and his wife founded and endowed a university at Palo Alto (1891). See Life by G. T. Clark (1932).

STANHOPE, an English family descended from the first Earl of Chesterfield. Its most noteworthy members, in chronological order, were:

(1) **James, 1st Earl Stanhope** (1675–1721), an eminent soldier and favourite minister of George I. See Life by B. Williams (1932).

(2) **Charles, 3rd Earl Stanhope** (1753–1816), English scientist and politician, father of (3), born in London, educated at Eton and Geneva, became an M.P. and married the sister of the younger Pitt, and his continued enthusiasm for the French Revolution made him the 'minority of one' in advocating non-interference in French affairs (1794) and peace with Napoleon (1800). Neglecting his wives and children, he invented a cylindrical biconvex lens to eliminate spherical aberration, calculating machines, the first iron hand printing press and a method of stereotyping adopted by the Clarendon press (1805). See Life by G. Stanhope and Gooch (1914).

(3) **Lady Hester Lucy** (1776–1839), eldest daughter of (2), went in 1803 to reside with her uncle, William Pitt, and as mistress of his establishment and his most trusted confidante, had full scope for her queenly instincts. On Pitt's death (1806) the king gave her a pension of £1200. The change from the excitements of public life was irksome to her; in 1809 she was grieved by the death at Coruña of her brother Major Stanhope, and of Sir John Moore, whom she had loved; and in 1810 she left England, wandered in the Levant, went to Jerusalem, camped with Bedouins in Palmyra, and in 1814 settled on Mount Lebanon. She adopted Eastern manners, interfered in Eastern politics, and obtained a wonderful ascendency over the tribes around her, who regarded her as a sort of prophetess; her last years were poverty-stricken on account of her reckless liberality. See her *Memoirs* by C. L. Meryon (1845), *Life and Letters* (1913) by the Duchess of Cleveland, books by Hamel (1913), J. Haslip (1934).

(4) **Philip Dormer.** See CHESTERFIELD.

(5) **Philip Henry, 5th Earl Stanhope** (1805–1875), English historian, born at Walmer, studied at Oxford, entered parliament in 1830, was instrumental in passing the Copyright Act (1842), and was foreign under-secretary under Peel (1834–35), and secretary to the Indian Board of Control (1845–46). He edited Peel's memoirs. He was known as Lord Mahon till in 1855 he succeeded to the earldom. His principal work was *A History of England, 1713–83* (1836–54); and his other works include Lives of Belisarius, Condé and Pitt; *War of the Succession in Spain*, *History of Spain under Charles II*, *Essays* and *Miscellanies*. He was president of the Society of Antiquaries

(1846) and lord rector of Aberdeen University (1858). He helped to secure the appointment of the Historical MSS. Commission and the foundation of the National Portrait Gallery.

(6) **Edward Stanhope** (1840–93), English politician, second son of (5), became Conservative colonial secretary (1886) and as secretary for War (1887–92) reformed army administration, established the Army Service Corps and adopted the magazine rifle.

(7) **James Richard, 7th Earl Stanhope** (1880–1967), English politician, grandson of (5), served in the Boer War (1902) and in World War I, winning the M.C. (1916) and the D.S.O. (1917), became the first commissioner of works (1936), first lord of the Admiralty (1938–39) and lord president of the Council (1939–40).

STANISLAUS LESZCZYŃSKI, *lesh-chin'y' skee* (1677–1766), born at Lemberg, was elected king of Poland in 1704, but in 1709 was driven out by Peter the Great to make room for Augustus II (q.v.). He formally abdicated in 1736, receiving the duchies of Lorraine and Bar; and he died of a burning accident at Lunéville. See also PONIATOWSKI.

STANISLAVSKY, professional name of **Konstantin Sergeivitch Alexeyev** (1865–1938), Russian actor, producer and teacher, born in Moscow. His first notable production was in 1891, Tolstoi's *Fruits of Enlightenment*, ana when he joined the Moscow Arts Theatre in 1898 he was able to develop his theories to the full. These were: to present an illusion of reality by means of a highly stylized combination of acting, setting and production, based on an exhaustive examination of the background and psychology of the characters. His 'method' was most successful in Chehov, Gorky, Maeterlinck and Andreyev. A superb actor, he gave up acting because of illness, but his influence on the theatre remains enormous. See his autobiographical *My Life in Art* (1924), his posthumous *Stanislavsky rehearses Othello* (1948), study by D. Magarshack (1951), and *Stanislavsky's Legacy*, ed. and trans. E. R. Hapgood (1959).

TANLEY, (1). See DERBY (EARL OF).

(2) **Arthur Penrhyn** (1815–81), English divine, born at Alderley, Cheshire, educated at Rugby under Arnold, whose *Life* he wrote (1844), and at Balliol, won the Ireland and Newdigate prizes, and in 1838 was elected fellow of University College and took orders. He travelled in the East, accompanied the Prince of Wales to the Holy Land, in 1851 became a canon of Canterbury, in 1856 professor of Ecclesiastical History at Oxford and in 1864 Dean of Westminster. For all his large tolerance, charity and sympathy, High Church Anglicans could never forgive him for championing Colenso and for preaching in Scottish Presbyterian pulpits. He was pre-eminently representative of the broadest theology of the Church of England. He cared little for systematic theology and not at all for the pretensions of the priesthood; while he regarded as 'infinitely little' the controversies about postures, lights, vestments and the like. His works include *Memorials of Canterbury* (1854), *Sinai and Palestine* (1856), *Christian Institutions* (1881). See Lives by G. G. Bradley (1883), R. E. Prothero (1893), and *A Victorian Dean*, ed. A. V. Baillie and H· Bolitho (1930).

(3) **Sir Henry Morton** (1841–1904), British explorer and journalist, was born of unmarried parents at Denbigh, Wales, and at first bore the name of John Rowlands. In 1859 he went as cabin boy to New Orleans, where he was adopted by a merchant named Stanley. He served in the Confederate army and U.S. navy, contributed to several journals, and in 1867 joined the *New York Herald*. As its special correspo aent he accompanied Lord Napier's Abyssinian expedition; and the first news of the fall of Magdala was conveyed to Britain by the *New York Herald*. Stanley next went to Spain for his paper, and in October 1869 recieved from Mr Gordon Bennett the laconic instruction, 'Find Livingstone'. But first he visited Egypt for the opening of the Suez Canal, and travelled through Palestine, Turkey, Persia and India. In March 1871, he left Zanzibar for Tanganyika and on November 10 he 'found' Livingstone at Ujiji. The two explored the north end of Lake Tanganyika, and settled that it had no connection with the Nile basin. In 1872, he returned alone and published *How I found Livingstone*. An expedition under Stanley, who had followed the Ashanti campaign for the *New York Herald*, was fitted out jointly by the *Herald* and the *Daily Telegraph* to complete Livingstone's work, and in August 1874 he left England for Bagamoyo. Thence he made for the Victoria Nyanza, circumnavigated the lake, formed a close friendship with King Mtesa of Uganda, next determined the shape of Lake Tanganyika, passed down the Lualaba to Nyangwé, and traced the Congo to the sea. Having published *Through the Dark Continent* (1878), in 1879 he again went out to found, under the auspices of the king of the Belgians, the Congo Free State, having been refused help in England. He took part in the Congo Congress at Berlin in 1884–85. In March 1886 his expedition for the relief of Emin Pasha (q.v.) landed at the mouth of the Congo. In June he left a part of his 650 men under Major Barttelot on the Aruwimi, and with 388 men marched into the forest. Disaster overtook the rear column but Emin and Stanley met in April 1888 on the shores of Lake Albert. After relieving the rearguard he returned with Emin overland to the east coast, and Bagamoyo was reached in December 1889. He had discovered Lake Edward and Mount Ruwenzori. In 1890 he married the artist, Miss Dorothy Tennant. He was naturalized as a British subject in 1892, and sat as a Unionist for Lambeth (1895–1900). Other works include a novel, *My Kalulu* (1873), *Coomassie and Magdala* (1874), *The Congo* (1885), *My Early Travels in America and Asia* (1895). See his Autobiography (1909), Wassermann, *Bula Mataria* (1932), Life by Anstruther (1956), B. Farwell, *The Man who Presumed* (1958), and T. Sterling, *Stanley's Way* (1960).

(4) **John** (1713–86), English composer, born in London, was blind from the age of two, having fallen on a stone hearth while holding a china bowl, but his musical talent

was such that he became organist at All Hallows, Bread Street, at the age of eleven. Later he held posts at St Andrew's, Holborn, and at the Inner Temple. His compositions, which include oratorios (*Zimri* and *The Fall of Egypt*), cantatas, organ voluntaries, concerti grossi and instrumental sonatas, have won increasing recognition, and Stanley is today regarded as one of the greatest of 18th-century English composers.

(5) **Thomas** (1625–78), English author, born at Cumberlow, Herts, studied at Pembroke Hall, Cambridge, practised law, and published translations from the Greek, Latin, French, Spanish and Italian poets; but his great works were the *History of Philosophy* (1655–62) based on Diogenes Laertius, and an edition of Aeschylus, with Latin translation and commentary (1663–64). See the *Poems*, ed. Brydges (1814–15, with Life); *Original Lyrics*, ed. Guiney (1907).

(6) **Venetia.** See DIGBY (1).

(7) **Wendell Meredith** (1904–), American biochemist, educated at Earlham College and Illinois University, professor of Molecular Biology and of Biochemistry at California University from 1948, did important work on the chemical nature of viruses. He isolated and crystallized the tobacco mosaic virus and worked on sterols and stereoisomerism. He shared the Nobel prize for chemistry in 1946 with Northrop and Sumner.

(8) **William** (1858–1916), American electrical engineer, after working for Maxim, set up on his own and invented the transformer. His work also included a long-range transmission system for alternating current.

STANSGATE, William Wedgwood Benn, 1st Viscount (1877–1960), English politician, was a Liberal M.P. from 1906 until 1927, when he joined the Labour Party and was next year elected for N. Aberdeen. In 1929–31 he was secretary for India and in 1945–46 secretary for Air. He won the D.S.O. and D.F.C. in World War I, served in the R.A.F. in World War II, and was created a viscount in 1941. His son **Anthony** (b. 1925), a Labour M.P. (1950–60), was debarred from the Commons on succeeding to the title, but was able to renounce it in 1963, and was re-elected to parliament the same year. He was postmaster-general from 1964 to 1966, when he became minister of technology.

STANTON, Edwin McMasters (1814–69), American lawyer and statesman, was born at Steubenville. He rose to legal prominence when he successfully opposed the plan for bridging the Ohio at Wheeling on the grounds of interference with navigation. He was secretary of war under Lincoln, was suspended by Johnson (1867) and reinstated by the Senate. When Johnson's impeachment failed, Stanton resigned (1868).

STAPELDON, Walter de (1261–1326), Bishop of Exeter 1308–26, and founder of Exeter College, Oxford, was born at Annery in Devon, was favoured by Edward II, and for this reason was beheaded by the insurgent Londoners.

STAPLETON, Thomas (1535–98), English controversial theologian, born at Henfield, Sussex, educated at Winchester and New College, Oxford, became prebendary of Chichester, but was deprived of his prebend in 1563, went in 1569 to Douai, became a professor there and in 1590 at Louvain. A learned Catholic controversialist in Latin, he is remembered for his fine Elizabethan English prose translations of Bede (Antwerp 1565; ed. Hereford, 1930), and his careful Latin life of Sir Thomas More (Douai 1588).

STARK, (1) **Johannes** (1874–1957), German physicist, was educated at Munich and became professor at Würzburg. He discovered the Stark effect concerning the splitting of spectrum lines by subjecting the light source to a strong electrostatic field, and also the Doppler effect in canal rays. He was awarded a Nobel prize in 1919.

(2) **John** (1728–1822), American general, saw much service against the Indians, by whom he was captured (1752). He served at Bunker's Hill, and won a victory at Bennington (1777). He was a member of the court martial which condemned André.

STARLEY, James (1831–81), English inventor, born at Albourne, Sussex, worked in Coventry, invented a sewing-machine and the 'Coventry' tricycle and the 'Ariel' geared bicycle and set up as a manufacturer of these.

STARLING, Ernest Henry (1866–1927), English physiologist, born in London, was lecturer in Physiology at Guy's Hospital and later professor at University College. He introduced the term *hormones* for the internal secretions of the ductless glands and, with Bayliss, discovered the intestinal hormone *secretin* (1902). He wrote *Principles of Human Physiology* (1912).

STAS, Jean Servais (1813–91), Belgian chemist, born at Louvain, was professor of Chemistry at Brussels. He developed more up-to-date methods for determination of atomic weights and analysis. He apparently disproved Prout's hypothesis.

STASSEN, Harold Edward (1907–), American politician, born at West St Paul, Minnesota. He studied law at the University of Minnesota, and became at thirty-one the youngest governor in Minnesota history. He served in the navy in World War II, failed in 1948 and 1952 to secure the Republican presidential nomination, and became administrator of foreign aid under Eisenhower. He represented the U.S. at the London disarmament conference in 1957. He resigned in 1958 following disagreements with John Foster Dulles (q.v.). He wrote *Where I Stand* (1947).

STATIUS, Publius Papinius (*c.* A.D. 45–96), Latin poet, born at Naples, flourished as a court poet and a brilliant improviser in the favour of Domitian till 94, when he retired to Naples. His *Thebaïs*, an epic on the struggle between the brothers Eteocles and Polynices of Thebes, is tedious as a whole, marred by over-alliteration and allusiveness, but redeemed by exquisite passages. Of another epic, the *Achilleïs*, only a fragment remains. His *Silvae*, or occasional verses, have freshness and vigour. Dante (*Purgatorio* xxii, 89) refers to him.

STAUDINGER, Hermann, *shtow'-* (1881–1965), German chemist, born at Worms, was professor of Organic Chemistry at Freiburg (1926–51) and was awarded the Nobel prize for chemistry in 1953 for his research in macro-molecular chemistry.

STAUFFENBURG, Count Berthold von, *shtow'fĕn-boorg* (1907–44), German soldier, born in Bavaria, was a colonel on the General Staff in 1944. One of the ringleaders, he placed the bomb in the unsuccessful attempt to assassinate Adolf Hitler on July 20, 1944. He was shot next day.

STAUNTON, Howard (1810–74), English Shakespearean scholar and chess player, studied at Oxford, and settled down to journalism in London. His victory in 1843 over M. St Amand made him the champion chess player of his day. He wrote *The Chess-player's Handbook* (1847), &c. His Shakespeare (1858–60) contained excellent textual emendations.

STAVISKY, Serge Alexandre (1886?–1934), French swindler, born in Kiev. He came to Paris in 1900 and became naturalized in 1914. He floated fraudulent companies, liquidating the debts of one by the profits of its successor until, in 1933, he was discovered to be handling bonds to the value of more than five hundred millions francs on behalf of the municipal pawnshop in Bayonne. Stavisky fled to Chamonix and probably committed suicide; but in th· meantime the affair had revealed widespread corruption in the government and ultimately caused the downfall of two ministries. Stavisky was found guilty during a trial that ended in 1936 with the conviction of nine other persons.

STEAD, William Thomas (1849–1912), English journalist, born at Embleton, Alnwick, and educated at Wakefield, was a Darlington editor 1871–80, and then on the *Pall Mall* till 1889, from 1883 as editor. He got three months over the 'Maiden Tribute' (1885), founded his *Review of Reviews*, and worked for peace, spiritualism, the 'civic church', and friendship with Russia. Although pro-Boer, admired Cecil Rhodes. He was drowned in the *Titanic* disaster, April 15, 1912. See Lives by his daughter (1913), Whyte (1925).

STEDMAN, (1) Charles (1753–1812), American historian, born at Philadelphia, Pa., wrote a standard history (with valuable maps) of the American War of Independence from the British point of view (1794).

(2) **Edmund Clarence** (1833–1908), American poet and critic, born at Hartford, Conn., studied at Yale, was war correspondent of the *New York World* 1861–63, and then became a New York stockbroker and banker. He published *Poems* (1860), *Victorian Poets* (1875), *Edgar Allan Poe* (1880), *Poets of America* (1886), *Nature of Poetry* (1892), *Victorian Anthology* (1896), &c. See Stedman and Gould, *Life and Letters*.

STEED, Henry Wickham (1871–1956), English journalist and author, born in Long Melford. In 1896, as correspondent in Berlin, he began his long association with *The Times*, later becoming correspondent in Rome and Vienna, foreign editor during World War I, when he directed much Allied propaganda, and editor from 1919 until his resignation in 1922. From 1923 to 1930 he was proprietor and editor of *The Review of Reviews*. He wrote many authoritative books on European history and affairs, and lectured on Central European history at King's College, London, from 1925 to 1938.

STEELE, Sir Richard (1672–1729), English essayist, dramatist and politician, was born in Dublin and educated at Charterhouse, where Addison was a contemporary, and Merton College, Oxford, whence he entered the army as a cadet in the Life Guards. Reacting against the 'irregularity' of military life, he wrote *The Christian Hero* (1701), to show that the gentlemanly virtues can be practised only on a Christian basis. He next wrote three comedies, *The Funeral, or Grief à la mode* (1702), *The Tender Husband* (1703) and *The Lying Lover* (1704). In 1706 he became gentleman waiter to Princ George of Denmark, and in 1707 Harley appointed him gazetteer. Steele's first venture in periodical literature, *The Tatler*, ran from April 1709 to January 1711 and was published on Tuesdays, Thursdays and Saturdays to suit the outgoing post-coaches. It had a predecessor in Defoe's *Review*, and like the *Review* included items of current news, but after No. 83 it concentrated on the social and moral essay, with occasional articles on literature, usually from the pen of Addison who had joined forces with Steele at the eighteenth issue. The chief fare, however, was social comedy, which covered the affectations and vices of society. These were exposed by humorous raillery, with the aim of putting the Christian at ease in society. Christianity was to become fashionable and to this end—for formal preaching was unpalatable—a wealth of concrete social situations and types was created, including coffee-house politicians, 'pretty fellows', pedants and bores at every level of society. The coffee houses and chocolate houses provided most of these types, but society women and the family were the theme of many of the articles, for Steele's plea in *The Christian Hero* for a more chivalrous attitude to women implied the correction of female frivolity in high places and the insistence on the family as the source of genuine happiness. Types which satisfy the moralist's notion of good-breeding allied to virtue—Sophronius, the true gentleman (No. 21), Paulo, the generous merchant (No. 25), Aspasia, the ideal woman, &c.—offset the satirical portraits. Aspasia, identified as Lady Elizabeth Hastings, evoked Steele's famous tribute 'to behold her is an immediate check to loose behaviour; and to love her is a liberal education'. Steele is perhaps at his best in scenes of domestic felicity (cf. Nos. 95, 104 and 150), and here we note the intrusion of bourgeois sentiment and morality which is to be the mark of the age, in contrast to the aristocratic ethos of the Restoration. The beginnings of the domestic novel are here, not only in the relations between the pseudonymous editor, Isaac Bickerstaff, and his half-sister Jennie, but in numerous conversation pieces and in the social context provided by the Trumpet Club, forerunner of the more famous Spectator Club which Steele first outlined in No. 2 of that periodical, though Addison wrote most of the articles. In 1713 Steele entered parliament, but was expelled the following year on account of a pamphlet, *The Crisis*, written in favour of the house of Hanover, a cause to which his periodical *The Englishman* was also devoted. He was rewarded on the succession of George I with the appointment of supervisor of Drury Lane theatre, and a knighthood followed. In 1718 a difference on constitutional procedure led to an estrangement from Addison, who was in the ministry, and loss of his office. In 1722 financial troubles made him retire to Wales, where he died in 1729. His letters to his wife ('dearest Prue'), whom he married in 1707, attest the sincerity of his preachments on married love. The standard Life is by G. A. Aitken (2 vols. 1889), but see also *Sir Richard Steele* by Willard Connely (1934). *The Tatler* was published in full, 4 vols. by G. A. Aitken (1898–99); the Correspondence by R. Blanchard (1941).

STEELL, Sir John (1804–91), Scottish sculptor, born at Aberdeen, was educated as an artist at Edinburgh and Rome. Most of his chief works are in Edinburgh, including the equestrian statue of the Duke of Wellington (1852), and that of Prince Albert (1876), for which Steell was knighted.

STEEN, Jan, *stayn* (1626–79), Dutch painter, born at Leyden, the son of a brewer, joined the Leyden guild of painters in 1648 and next year went to The Hague until 1654, afterwards following his father's trade at Delft. He spent his last years as an innkeeper at Leyden. His best works were genre pictures of social and domestic scenes depicting the everyday life of ordinary folk with rare insight and subtle humour, as in *The Music Lesson* (Nat. Gall.), *The Christening Feast* (Wallace Coll.), *Tavern Company*, *The Doctor's Visit*, &c.

STEENSEN, Niels. See STENSEN.

STEENSTRUP, (1) **Johannes** (1844–1935), Norwegian antiquarian, son of (2), was professor of Northern Antiquities at Copenhagen (1877) and wrote *Normannerne* (1876–82), a book about Viking times, &c.

(2) **Johannes Iapetus Smith** (1813–97), zoologist, father of (1), born at Vang in Norway, was professor of Zoology at Copenhagen (1845–85). His books treat of hermaphroditism, alternation of generations, flounders' eyes, and Cephalopods; and he explored the kitchen middens of Denmark for prehistoric relics.

STEENWIJK, Hendrik van, *stayn'vīk* (*c.* 1550–1603), Dutch painter of architectural interiors, settled at Frankfurt in 1579. His son **Hendrik** (1580–1649), also a painter, came to London on Van Dyck's advice in 1629.

STEER, Philip Wilson (1860–1942), English painter, was born at Birkenhead and studied at Paris. He began as an exponent of Impressionism and to this added a traditionally English touch. A founder and faithful member of the New English Art Club, he taught at the Slade. He excelled, too, as a figure painter, as shown in the Pitti *Self-Portrait*, *The Music Room* (Tate), and the *Portrait of Mrs Hammersley*, painted in the style of Gainsborough. He was awarded the O.M. in 1931. See Life by D. S. MacColl (1945) and study by R. Ironside (Phaidon 1943).

STEEVENS, George (1736–1800), English Shakespearean commentator, called by Gifford 'the Puck of commentators', born at Stepney, was educated at Eton and King's College, Cambridge. His reprint from the original quartos of *Twenty Plays of Shakespeare* (1766) brought him employment as Johnson's collaborator in his edition (1773). Jealous of Malone (q.v.), Steevens issued a doctored text using his own emendations (1793–1803), which held authority till Boswell's publication of Malone's *Variorum Shakespeare* (1821). See I. D'Israeli, 'On Puck the Commentator' in *Curiosities of Literature* (1817).

STEFAN, Joseph (1835–93), Austrian physicist, born near Klagenfurt, became professor at Vienna in 1863. He proposed Stefan's law (or the Stefan–Boltzmann law), that the amount of energy radiated per second from a black body is proportional to the fourth power of the absolute temperature.

STEFÁNSSON, Vilhjálmur (1879–1962), Canadian Arctic explorer, born of Icelandic parents at Arnes, Manitoba, explored Arctic America and wrote on the Eskimos. See his *Unsolved Mysteries of the Arctic* (1939), *Greenland* (1943), &c.

STEFFANI, Agostino (1654–1728), Italian priest, operatic composer, diplomatist, friend of Handel, born at Castelfranco, in 1688 settled at Hanover court. He wrote a fine *Stabat Mater*, several operas and vocal duets.

STEIN, *stīn*, (1) **Sir Aurel** (1862–1943), British archaeologist, born at Budapest, held educational and archaeological posts under the Indian government, for which from 1900 he made important explorations in Chinese Turkestan and Central Asia.

(2) **Charlotte von** (1742–1827), the friend of Goethe, married in 1764 the Duke of Saxe-Weimar's Master of the Horse. Her friendship with Goethe was broken suddenly (1788), but renewed before her death. Goethe's Letters to her were published in 1848–51. See works by Düntzer (1874), Bode (1910), Calvert (1877).

(3) **Gertrude** (1874–1946), American writer, born in Allegheny, Pa. She studied psychology under William James, and medicine at Johns Hopkins; but settled in Paris, where she was absorbed into the world of experimental art and letters. She sometimes attempted to apply the theories of abstract painting to her own writing, which led to a magnified reputation for obscurity and meaningless repetition. Her first book, *Three Lives* (1908), reveals a sensitive ear for speech rhythms, and by far the larger part of her work is immediately comprehensible. Her influence on contemporary artists—particularly Picasso—is probably less than she imagined, though her collection of pictures was representative of the best of its era. Her main works include *Tender Buttons* (1914), *The Making of Americans* (1925), *The Autobiography of Alice B. Toklas* (1933), *Four Saints in Three Acts* (1934) and *Everybody's Autobiography* (1937). See Life by E. Sprigge (1957), study by Sutherland (1951), and J. M. Brinnin, *The Third Rose* (1960).

(4) **Heinrich Friedrich Carl, Baron vom**

(1757–1831), Prussian Liberal statesman and German nationalist, born at Nassau, entered the service of Prussia in 1780, and became president of the Westphalian chambers (1796). His tenure as secretary for trade (1804–07) was unfruitful and he resigned, only to be recalled after the treaty of Tilsit, when he abolished the last relics of serfdom, created peasant proprietors, extirpated monopolies and hindrances to free trade, promoted municipal government, and supported Scharnhorst in his schemes of army reform. Napoleon insisted upon his dismissal, and Stein withdrew (1808) to Austria, but not before issuing his *Political Testament.* In 1812 he went to St Petersburg and built up the coalition against Napoleon. From the battle of Leipzig to the Congress of Vienna he was the ruling spirit of the opposition to French imperialism. Stein liberalized the Prussian state, but at the same time fostered the dangerous myth of German destiny and aggressive nationalism, not least by founding the *Monumenta Germaniae Historica* in 1815. See Lives by J. R. Seeley (1878), F. Schnabel (1931) and G. Ritter (Stuttgart 1958).

STEINBECK, John Ernest, *stīn'bek* (1902–68), American novelist, born at Salinas, California. *Tortilla Flat* (1935), his first novel of repute, is a faithful picture of the shifting *paisanos* of California, foreshadowing the solidarity which characterizes his major work, *The Grapes of Wrath* (1939), a study of the poor in the face of disaster and threatened disintegration. His journalistic grasp of significant detail and pictorial essence make this book a powerful plea for consideration of human values and common justice. It led, like *Uncle Tom's Cabin,* to much-needed reform, and won for Steinbeck the 1940 Pulitzer prize. His other works include *Of Mice and Men* (1937), *The Moon is Down* (1942), *East of Eden* (1952), *Winter of our Discontent* (1961), as well as the light-hearted and humorous *Cannery Row* (1945), *The Wayward Bus* (1942) and *The Short Reign of Pippin IV* (1957). He received the Nobel prize for literature in 1962. See *Writers in Crisis,* by M. Geismar (1942).

STEINER, *shtī'nėr,* (1) **Jakob** (1796–1863), German-Swiss geometrician, born at Utzendorf, from 1834 was professor at Berlin, pioneered 'synthetic' geometry, particularly the properties of geometrical constructions, ranges and curves. His collected works were edited by Weierstrass (Berlin 1881–1882).

(2) **Rudolf** (1861–1925), Austrian social philosopher, founder of 'anthroposophy', born at Kraljevec, studied science and mathematics and edited Goethe's scientific papers at Weimar (1890–97) before coming temporarily under the spell of Annie Besant (q.v.) and the Theosophists. In 1912, however, he propounded his own 'science' of spirituality and established the 'Goetheanum', a centre at Dornach near Basel where he applied his theories for research. He claimed that in modern times, the psychologically valuable, play-acting, myth-making and artistic activities had become isolated from the practical activities of life and aimed at reuniting them for therapeutic and especially for educational purposes, advocating the art of eurhythmy. Steiner schools for maladjusted children have since been established in Europe and the U.S.A. See his *Philosophy of Spiritual Activity*, *Knowledge of the Higher Worlds* and *Outline of Occult Science* (all in trans.), and studies by Weisshaar (1928), Edmunds (1955) and Freeman (1956).

STEINITZ, William, *shtīn'its* (1836–1900), Czech chess champion of the world (1862–1894), was born at Prague.

STEINLEN, Théophile Alexandre, *shtīn'len* (1859–1923), Swiss painter and illustrator, born at Lausanne, settled in Paris, made his name as a poster-designer and by his work in French illustrated papers.

STEINMETZ, *shtīn'mets,* (1) **Carl Friedrich von** (1796–1877), Prussian general, born at Eisenach, fought through the campaign of 1813–14, and in 1866 routed three Austrian corps at Náchod and Skalitz. In 1870 he commanded the right wing of the German advance; but he proved unequal to the task, and after Gravelotte was appointed governor-general of Posen and Silesia.

(2) **Charles Proteus** (1865–1923), American electrical engineer, born in Breslau, educated at the Technical High School, Berlin, emigrated to America, discovered magnetic hysteresis, a simple notation for calculating alternating current circuits, &c.

STEINTHAL, Heymann, *shtīn'tahl* (1823–99), German philologist, born at Gröbzig in Anhalt, in 1850 became lecturer on Philology at Berlin, and in 1863 extra-ordinary professor. He wrote *The Origin of Language* (1851), &c.

STEINWAY, Heinrich Engelhard, *stīn'-,* orig. **Steinweg,** *-vekh* (1797–1871), German-born American piano-maker, established a piano factory in Brunswick, but in 1850 transferred the business to New York, leaving his son, Theodor, to carry on the German branch. The latter was eventually handed over to the Grotian family and Theodor joined his father in America.

STENDHAL, pseud. of Marie Henri Beyle (1783–1842), French writer, born in Grenoble. He was a soldier under Napoleon and served through the disastrous Russian campaign of 1812. In 1821 he settled in Paris. After the Revolution of 1830 he was appointed consul at Trieste and then at Civitavecchia. He wrote biographies of Haydn (1814), Rossini (1824) and others, a history of Italian painting (1817), and the very popular novels for which he is best known, *Le Rouge et le noir* (1831) and *La Chartreuse de Parme* (1839). Unappreciated in his own time, his works had considerable vogue from 1880 onwards, when his influence on the later realists became felt. See studies by Mélia (1910), Green (1939), Martineau (1945), Bardèche (1947). See the autobiographical *Life of Henry Brulard,* trans. J. Stewart and C. J. G. Knight (1958).

STENSEN, or Steenson or Steno, Niels (1638–1686), Danish anatomist, geologist and theologian, born at Copenhagen. Brought up a strict Lutheran, he settled in Florence, turned Catholic and became bishop and in 1677 vicar-apostolic to North Germany. He was the first to point out the true origin of fossil animals (1669), explain the structure of the earth's crust and differentiate between stratified and volcanic rocks. As a physician to the grand-duke of Florence, he gained a considerable reputation, discovered Steno's duct of the parotid gland and explained the function of the ovaries.

STEPHAN, Heinrich von (1831–97), German administrator, was the chief promoter of the International Postal Union (1874).

STEPHANUS BYZANTIUS, a Greek geographical writer of the 5th century A.D., lived at Constantinople, wrote a geographical dictionary.

STEPHEN, St, one of the seven chosen to manage the finance and alms of the early church. Tried by the Sanhedrin for blasphemy, he was stoned to death—the first Christian martyr.

STEPHEN, the name of ten popes, of whom the following are noteworthy:

Stephen I, saint, martyr and pope (254–257), maintained against Cyprian that heretics baptized by heretics need not be rebaptized.

Stephen II died two days after his election (752), and so is often not reckoned as a pope.

Stephen II or III, pope (752–757), when Rome was threatened by the Lombards, turned to Pepin, King of the Franks, who forced the Lombards to withdraw, and gave the pope the exarchate of Ravenna, the real foundation of the temporal power.

STEPHEN (1097?–1154), king of England, was the third son of Stephen, Count of Blois, by Adela, daughter of William the Conqueror (q.v.). He was sent in 1114 to the court of his uncle, Henry I, received from him the countship of Mortain in Normandy, and acquired that of Boulogne by marriage. When Henry I resolved to settle the crown on his daughter Matilda or Maud, Empress of Germany, and afterwards wife of Geoffrey Plantagenet, Stephen with the rest swore fealty to her, but on Henry's death (December 1, 1135), he hurried over from Normandy, was enthusiastically received, and was crowned on the 22nd. He attempted to strengthen his position with the help of Fleming mercenaries, and he made more enemies than friends by the favours he heaped on some of the great lords. King David of Scotland invaded the north on Matilda's behalf, was defeated near Northallerton (1138), but retained Cumberland. The first powerful enemy that the king made was Robert, Earl of Gloucester, an illegitimate son of Henry I; next he arrayed against himself the clergy, by his quarrel with the justiciar, Bishop Roger of Salisbury. The realm now fell into sheer anarchy; the barons plundered and burned at their pleasure. In 1139 Matilda landed at Arundel, in 1141 took Stephen prisoner at Lincoln, and was acknowledged queen, but her harshness and greed soon disgusted Englishmen. The men of London rose, and she fled to Winchester. In November 1141 Stephen regained his liberty, and 1142 saw him again in the ascendant. In 1148 Matilda finally left England, but her son Henry (see HENRY II) in 1153 crossed over to England, and forced Stephen to acknowledge him as his successor. Stephen died at Dover, October 24, 1154. See study by R. H. C. Davis (1967).

STEPHEN, the name of five kings of Hungary:

Stephen I, Saint (*c.* 975–1038), first king of Hungary from 997, was baptized about 985, formed Pannonia and Dacia, inhabited by semi-independent Magyar chiefs, into a regular kingdom, organized Christianity, and laid the foundation of many institutions surviving to this day. He received from Pope Sylvester III the title of 'Apostolic King', and was canonized in 1083. See B. Hóman, *Szent István* (1938).

STEPHEN (1533–86), king of Poland, uncle of Elizabeth Bathori (q.v.), succeeded to the throne in 1576. A born ruler and soldier, he won campaigns against Ivan the Terrible (1579–81), but his plans for Hungary's liberation from Turkish rule were cut short by his early death.

STEPHEN, (1) James (1758–1832), English lawyer, grandfather of (2) and (3), born at Poole, first a parliamentary reporter, then a colonial official at St Kitts in the West Indies, which experience turned him into a slavery abolitionist. He married Wilberforce's sister (1800), entered parliament (1808) and became colonial under-secretary. He was the author of *The Slavery of the British West Indies* (1824–30).

(2) **Sir James Fitzjames, 1st Bart.** (1829–1894), British jurist, grandson of (1), born at Kensington, was a legal member of the Viceregal Council (1869–72), professor of Common Law at the Inns of Court (1875–79) and a judge of the High Court (1879–91). Holding in the main a retributive theory of punishment, he wrote a standard *History of the Criminal Law* (1883) and was responsible for the Indian Evidence Act. See Lives by his brother (3) and L. Radzinowicz (1958).

(3) **Sir Leslie** (1832–1904), English critic, biographer, mountaineer and philosopher, brother of (2), born at Kensington, educated at Eton and King's College, London, and at Trinity Hall, Cambridge, where he became fellow and tutor until reading the works of Mill, Kant and Comte made him openly reject Christianity, and he was (1875) obliged to give up his tutorship (1864) and relinquished his orders. He later became president of Ethical Societies in London, greatly popularized the term 'agnostic', coined by Huxley in 1870, and published his collected addresses to these societies under the title *Essays on Free Thinking and Plain Speaking* (1873) and *An Agnostic's Apology* (1893). A distinguished athlete, he once walked fifty miles to London in twelve hours and was president of the Alpine Club (1865–68). He became editor of the *Cornhill* in 1871 and of the first 26 volumes of the new *Dictionary of National Biography* (1885–91), from 1890, conjointly wit Sir Sidney Lee (q.v.). He also wrote studies of Samuel Johnson (1878), Pope (1880), Swift (1882) and George Eliot

(1902). *The Science of Ethics* (1882), which combined utilitarianism with a modified evolutionary ethics, his edition of J. R. Green's Letters (1903) and his study on Hobbes (1904) are his principal philosophical works. He died of cancer. In 1905, the Leslie Stephen Lectureship at Cambridge was founded by his friends. His first wife was a daughter of Thackeray. His two daughters were Virginia Woolf (q.v.) and Vanessa (see Clive Bell). See Lives by Maitland (1906) and Annan (1951).

STEPHEN DUSHAN, *doo'shan* (*c.* 1308–1355), Serbia's greatest tsar (1336–55), the subjugator of Bulgaria, Macedonia and Albania.

STEPHENS (French **Éstienne** or **Étienne**), a Provençal family renowned as printers. See works by Renouard (1843), Bernard (1856), Clément (1899), and Mark Pattison, *Essays* (1889). Its prominent members were:

(1) **Antoine** (1592–1674), grandson of (4), printed in Paris.

(2) **Charles** (1504–64), son of (3), took charge of his brother's business in Paris when he withdrew to Geneva, and wrote and printed an encyclopaedic work *Dictionarium Historicum ac Poeticum* (1553), *Praedium Rusticum* (1554), &c.

(3) **Henri** (*c.* 1460–1520), established the business in Paris.

(4) **Henri** (1528–98), son of (5), a classical scholar, travelled in Italy, England and the Netherlands, collating MSS. In 1556 he set up a press in Geneva, and issued many ancient Greek authors, including some twenty 'first editions', as also his own Greek dictionary (1572). He wrote also, in French, the semi-satirical *Apologie pour Hérodote* (1566). His son, **Paul** (1566–1627), continued the family printing business in Paris.

(5) **Robert** (1503–59), son of (3), succeeded his father, and was in 1539 and 1540 appointed printer to the king in Latin, Greek and Hebrew. He early became a Protestant, more than once got into difficulties with the University of Paris, and in 1550 retired to Geneva, where he printed several of Calvin's works. A scholar as well as a printer, he published (1532) a famous Latin dictionary (*Thesaurus Linguae Latinae*). His Latin New Testament (1523), Latin Bible (1528) and Greek New Testament (1550) deserve mention. He also printed classic authors and Latin grammars.

STEPHENS, (1) **Alexander Hamilton** (1812–1883). American politician, born near Crawfordsville, Ga., was admitted to the bar in 1834, and sat in congress 1843–59. He advocated the annexation of Texas in 1838, in 1854 defended the Kansas-Nebraska act, at first opposed secession, but in 1861 became Confederate vice-president. He sat in congress again 1874–83, in 1882 was elected governor of Georgia, and wrote *War between the States* (1867–70). See Life by R. von Abele (1946).

(2) **George** (1813–95), English archaeologist, born in Liverpool, and educated at University College London, settled at Stockholm in 1833, and became in 1855 professor of English at Copenhagen. His great works are his *Old Northern Runic Monuments* (1866–68–84), &c.

(3) **James** (1824–1901), Fenian agitator, born at Kilkenny, became an active agent of the Young Ireland party. Slightly wounded at Ballingarry (1848), he hid for three months in the mountains, and then escaped to France. In 1853 he journeyed over Ireland, preparing for the Fenian conspiracy; as its 'Head Centre' he exercised an enormous influence. He started the *Irish People* to urge armed rebellion, visited America in 1864, was arrested in Dublin November 11, 1865, but easily escaped. He found his way to New York, was deposed by the Fenians and with the decline in his political importance was allowed to return to Ireland in 1891. See O'Leary's *Recollections of Fenianism* (1896).

(4) **James** (1882–1950), Irish poet, born and died at Dublin, came into notice with *Insurrections* (1909), *The Crock of Gold* (1912, a story), followed by *Songs from the Clay* (1914), *The Demi-Gods* (1914), *Reincarnation* (1917), *Deirdre* (1923), &c.

(5) **John Lloyd** (1805–52), American traveller and archaeologist, born at Shrewsbury, N.J., wrote two books of Levant travel, and on the archaeology of Central America, where he was U.S. minister.

(6) **Joseph Rayner** (1805–79), Scottish social reformer, born in Edinburgh, was expelled from his Methodist ministry in 1834 for supporting church disestablishment. He made himself a name as a factory reformer, opened three independent chapels at Ashton-under-Lyne, and took an active part in the anti-poor-law demonstrations (1836–37) and the Chartist movement, of which, however, he refused actual membership. He was imprisoned for his struggle for the Ten Hours Act (1847). See Life by G. J. Holyoake (1881), and G. D. H. Cole, *Chartist Portraits* (1941).

STEPHENSON, (1) **George** (1781–1848), English inventor of the locomotive, son of a colliery enginekeeper, father of (2), was born at Wylam near Newcastle, June 9. He rose to be fireman in a colliery, and contrived meanwhile to pay for a rudimentary education at night school. In 1815 he invented, contemporaneously with Davy, a colliery safety lamp, the 'Geordie', for which he received a public testimonial of £1000. In 1812 he had become enginewright at Killingworth Colliery, and here in 1814 he constructed his first locomotive. 'My Lord', running 6 miles an hour, for the colliery tram roads; his invention next year of the steam-blast made it an ultimate success. In 1821 Stephenson was appointed engineer for the construction of the Stockton and Darlington mineral railway (opened September 27, 1825), and in 1826 for the Liverpool and Manchester Railway, which, after inconceivable difficulties, was opened September 15, 1830. The October before had seen the memorable competition of engines, resulting in the triumph of Stephenson's 'Rocket', running 30 miles an hour. In 1834–37 he was engineer on the North Midland, York and North Midland, Manchester and Leeds, Birmingham and Derby.

and Sheffield and Rotherham Railways; and during the railway mania his offices in London were crowded. In 1845 he visited Belgium and Spain. He died at his country seat of Tapton near Chesterfield, August 12, 1848. See Lives by Smiles (1857; vol. iii of *Lives of the Engineers*), Rowland (1954) and Rolt (1960).

(2) **Robert** (1803–59), English engineer, son of (1), born at Willington Quay, was apprenticed to a coalviewer at Killingworth. In 1822 his father sent him for six months to Edinburgh University. In 1823 he assisted his father in surveying the Stockton and Darlington Railway; and after three years in Colombia, he became manager of his father's locomotive engine-works at Newcastle. He attained independent fame by his Britannia Tubular Bridge (1850), those at Conway (1848) and Montreal (1859), the High Level Bridge at Newcastle (1849), the Border Bridge at Berwick (1850), &c. He was M.P. for many years from 1847 and was buried in Westminster Abbey. See Smiles's *Lives of the Engineers* (vol. iii), and Jeaffreson's Life (1864); also book on George and Robert by L. T. C. Rolt (1960).

STEPINAC, Aloysius (1898–1960), Yugoslav cardinal, Primate of Hungary, born at Krasić near Zagreb, was imprisoned by Tito (1946–1951) for alleged wartime collaboration and with failing health, released, but lived the remainder of his life under house arrest.

STEPNYAK, ' Son of the Steppe ', *nom de guerre* of **Sergius Mikhailovich Kravchinsky** (1852–95), Russian revolutionary, was an artillery officer, but becoming obnoxious to government as an apostle of freedom, he was arrested, and subsequently kept under such surveillance that he left Russia and settled (1876) in Geneva, and then (1885) in London. He was, however, held to be the assassin of General Mesentzeff, head of the St Petersburg police (1878). He was run over by a train in a London suburb. Among his works were *La Russia Sotteranea* (Milan 1881; Eng. trans *Underground Russia*, 1883), studies of the Nihilist movement; *Russia under the Tsars* (trans. 1885); *The Career of a Nihilist*, a novel (1889).

STERLING, John (1806–44), British writer, was born at Kames Castle, Bute, where his father, Edward Sterling (1773–1847), an ex-army officer, was farming, but later settled in London, and became a noted contributor to *The Times*. John went to Glasgow University and to Cambridge, where he distinguished himself at the Union; he left without a degree in 1827, and soon was busy on the *Athenaeum*. Influenced by Coleridge, and liberal in sympathies, he nearly sailed on the expedition to Spain which ended in the execution at Málaga of his friend General Torrijos and his own cousin Boyd. He married in November 1830, but soon fell dangerously ill, and spent fifteen months in St Vincent. In 1833 he took orders, and served eight months as Julius Hare's curate at Herstmonceux. His health again giving way, he resigned. He contributed to *Blackwood's* and the *Westminster*. In August 1838 he founded the (later) Sterling Club, among whose members were Carlyle, Allan Cunningham, G. C. Lewis, Maiden, Mill, Milnes, Spedding, Tennyson, Thirlwall, W. H. Thompson and Venables. See Julius Hare's edition of his *Essays and Tales* (1848) with a memoir, and Carlyle's *Life* (1857).

STERN, (1) Daniel. See AGOULT.

(2) **Otto** (1888–1969), German-American physicist, born at Sohrau, was educated at Breslau and worked at Zürich, Frankfurt, Rostock and Hamburg, before becoming research professor of Physics at the Carnegie Technical Institute (1933–45). He worked on the quantum theory and the kinetic theory of gases; and, for his work on the magnetic moment of the proton and for his development of the molecular-ray method of studying atomic particles, he was awarded a Nobel prize in 1943.

STERNE, Laurence (1713–68), English novelist, was born at Clonmel, November 24, 1713. His father, Roger, was an infantry ensign, and Laurence's early youth was a struggle. In 1724, he was sent to Halifax Grammar School, and, seven years later, to Jesus College, Cambridge. In 1738, he was ordained, and appointed to the living of Sutton-on-the-Forest and made a prebendary of York, where his great-grandfather had been archbishop. In 1741 he made an unsuccessful marriage with Elizabeth Lumley. Of their two daughters, only Lydia survived. In 1759 he wrote the first two volumes of *The Life and Opinions of Tristram Shandy*, first published at York, but published anew at London in 1760. The public welcomed it; and in April Dodsley brought out a second edition. This was followed by *Sermons* of the ' Rev. Mr Yorick '. In January 1761, vols. III and IV of *Tristram* came out, Sterne having meanwhile moved to Coxwold, thenceforward his infrequent home. Between 1761 and 1767 the rest of *Tristram* appeared; Sterne, whose health was now failing, spending much of the time in France and Italy. *A Sentimental Journey through France and Italy* appeared in 1768; and the author, succumbing to pleurisy, died in London on March 18. Few writers of any age or country have displayed such mastery over every form of humour both in situation and in character, a humour at times coming near to that of his acknowledged master Cervantes. Yet it is impossible to overlook the imperfections of his art, alike in conception and in execution. The wild eccentricity of his manner and arrangement—a deliberate and usually successful bid for laughter—was also the convenient cloak for what some, such as Goldsmith, might call a singularly slipshod literary style. His indecencies, less gross than those of Swift or Rabelais, are all too prurient. He was unscrupulous in his borrowings. His pathos too often takes the form of overstrained sentimentalism. Yet this very sentimentalism was also his strength. For Sterne's great contribution to the development of the novel was to widen its scope and loosen its structure; and in his hands it became the channel for the utterance of the writer's own sentiments. See his *Letters from Yorick to Eliza* (1775–79); also Lives by J. Ferriar (1798), P. Stapfer (1870), F. Fitzgerald (1896), H. D. Traill (1882),

Sichel (1910), Lewis Melville (1911), W. L. Cross (1909, rev. ed 1929), editor of the *Works* (12 vols. 1904), who first printed his *Journal to Eliza* (Mrs Draper his 'Bramine' and inspirer), and his *Letter Book* (1925), and reprinted (1914) his *Political Romance* (1759), and Jefferson (1954); and studies by L. P. Curtis (1929), J. B. Priestley, *English Comic Characters* (1925), P. Quennell, *Four Portraits* (1945) and H. Fluchère (1961).

STERNHOLD, Thomas (1500–49), joint-author of the English version of psalms formerly attached to the Prayer Book, was born near Blakeney in Gloucestershire, or, according to Fuller and Wood, in Hampshire. He was Groom of the Robes to Henry VIII and Edward VI. The first edition (undated) contains only nineteen psalms; the second (1549), thirty-seven. A third edition, by Whitchurch (1551), contains seven more by J. H. (John Hopkins) (d. 1570). The complete book of psalms, which appeared in 1562, formed for nearly two centuries almost the whole hymnody of the Church of England and was known as the 'Old Version' after the rival version of Tate and Brady appeared (1696). Forty psalms bore the name of Sternhold. See J. Julian's *Dict. of Hymnology* (new ed. 1907).

STESICHORUS, *-sik'-* (*c.* 630–556 B.C.), greatest of the old Dorian lyric poets, was born at Himera in Sicily, and died in Catania. Only some thirty short fragments of his works remain.

STEUBEN, Frederic William Augustus, Baron, *shtoy'ben* (1730–94), German soldier in the American revolutionary army, born at Magdeburg, at fourteen served at the siege of Prague, and in 1762 was on the staff of Frederick the Great. While at Paris in 1777 he was induced to go to America, and his services were joyfully accepted by congress and Washington. He was appointed inspector-general, prepared a manual of tactics for the army, remodelled its organization, and improved its discipline. In 1780 he received a command in Virginia, and took part in the siege of Yorktown. Congress in 1790 voted him an annuity of 2400 dollars and land near Utica, N.Y. See Life by F. Kapp (1860).

STEVENS, (1) Alfred (1818–75), English artist and sculptor, born at Blandford, Dorset, studied in Italy and became assistant to Thorvaldsen (q.v.) in Rome and, returning home, became teacher of architectural design at Somerset House, London (1845–47). During the next ten years he decorated and designed household furniture, fireplaces, porcelain, including plans for the dining-room and salon at Dorchester House, the mantelpiece of the former being preserved in the Tate Gallery. His portrait of Mrs Collman (1854) is in the National Gallery. From 1856 he worked on the Wellington monument (completed after his death by John Tweed) and the mosaics under the dome of St Paul's Cathedral. See study by H. Stannus (1891) and Life by K. R. Towndrow (1939).

(2) **Richard John Samuel** (1757–1837), English organist and composer, born in London, composed harpsichord sonatas and glees, mostly to Shakespeare's songs.

(3) **Thaddeus** (1792–1868), American statesman, born at Danville, Vt., in 1816 settled as a lawyer at Gettysburg, Pa., was member of congress (1849–53), a Republican leader, and chairman at the trial of President Johnson (1868).

(4) **Wallace** (1879–1955), American poet, born in Reading, Pa., educated at Harvard, practised journalism, law and then joined a Hartford insurance company, of which he became vice-president. For many years he wrote impressionist and highly intellectual verse relying for effect upon rhythmic and tonal imagery, but he was over forty when his first volume, *Harmonium* (1923), was published, followed by *Ideas of Order* (1936), *Owl's Clover* (1936), &c. His *Collected Poems* (1954) won him his second National Book Award, and he won the Pultizer prize in 1955. See studies by Pack (1958), Kermode (1960), and *Selected Letters* (ed. Stevens, 1967).

STEVENSON, (1) Adlai Ewing (1900–65), American Democrat politician and lawyer, the grandson of another A. E. Stevenson (1835–1914) who was vice-president under Cleveland (1893–97). He was born in Los Angeles, studied at Princeton, spent two years editing a family newspaper and then took up law practice in Chicago. From 1943 he took part in several European missions for the State Department and from 1945 served on the American delegations to the foundation conferences of the U.N.O. In 1948 he was elected governor of Illinois, where his administration was exceptional for efficiency and lack of corruption. He stood against Eisenhower as Democratic presidential candidate in 1952 and 1956, but each time his urbane 'egg-headed' campaign speeches, published under the titles *Call to Greatness* (1954) and *What I Think* (1956), had more appeal abroad than at home. See his *Friends and Enemies* (1959), Life by N. F. Busch (1952) and studies by K. S. Davis and J. H. Muller (1968).

(2) **Robert** (1772–1850), Scottish engineer, born at Glasgow, lost his father in infancy; and his mother in 1786 married Thomas Smith, first engineer of the Lighthouse Board. Stevenson then took to engineering, and in 1796 succeeded his stepfather. During his forty-seven years' tenure of office he planned or constructed twenty-three Scottish lighthouses, employing the catoptric system of illumination, and his own invention of 'intermittent' and 'flashing' lights. He also acted as a consulting engineer for roads, bridges, harbours, canals and railways. See Life by his son, David Stevenson (1878). Another son, **Alan** (1807–65), built the Skerryvore Lighthouse (1844).

(3) **Robert Louis Balfour** (1850–94), Scottish author, son of Thomas Stevenson, engineer to the Board of Northern Lighthouses, was born in Edinburgh. At the University of Edinburgh he studied engineering for a session (1867) with a view to the family calling, but transferred to law, becoming an advocate in 1875. His true bent, however, was for letters. For the next few years he travelled chiefly in France. His *Inland Voyage* (1878) describes a canoe tour in Belgium and northern France, and his

Travels with a Donkey in the Cevennes a tour undertaken in the same year. In 1876 he was at Fontainebleau (which he made the subject of travel sketches), and it was at the neighbouring Barbizon that he met the divorcée, Fanny Osbourne, whom he followed to America and married in 1880. His return to Europe with his wife and stepson Lloyd Osbourne marked the beginning of a struggle against tuberculosis which his natural gaiety as a writer conceals. His wife and stepson have described the inconvenience and *ennui* experienced at makeshift homes—Davos, Pitlochry and elsewhere—but in those difficult circumstances he was 'making himself' not only as a writer of travel sketches but of essays and short stories which found their way into the magazines. *Thrawn Janet*, in the vernacular, his first venture in fiction, appeared in *Cornhill Magazine* (1881) and *The Merry Men* serially the following year, in which year also appeared *The New Arabian Nights*. *Treasure Island*, the perfect romantic thriller, brought him fame in 1883 and entered him on a course of romantic fiction which still endears him to young and old alike. *Kidnapped* (1886) is probably the high water mark here if pure adventure is in question, but *Catriona* (1893), introducing the love element, has its passionate adherents. *The Master of Ballantrae* (1889) is a study in evil of a sort not uncommon in Scottish fiction, but here also are the wildest adventures. *Dr Jekyll and Mr Hyde* is not a romance, but it further illustrates Stevenson's metaphysical interest in evil. *The Black Arrow* (1888) shows declining powers, but *Weir of Hermiston*, though unfinished, is acclaimed his masterpiece and it may be, for the canvas is larger, the issues involved more serious and the touch as sure as ever in delineating the types of character he knew at first hand. *St Ives*, which was also left unfinished, was completed by A. Quiller-Couch in 1897. Stevenson's work as an essayist is seen at its best in *Virginibus Puerisque* (1881) and *Familiar Studies of Men and Books* (1882). If in these we sometimes see the 'sedulous ape' at work—Hazlitt and Montaigne imitation particularly—he is always readable. The verse in those years is another matter. Though *A Child's Garden of Verses* (1885) is not poetry in the adult sense, it is one of the best recollections of childhood in verse. *Underwoods* (1887) illustrates the Scot's predilection for preaching in prose or verse and is the poetry of the good talker rather than the singer and the tone is usually nostalgic. Only occasionally, as in *The Woodman*, does he touch on metaphysical problems, but vernacular poems such as *A Loudon Sabbath Morn* subtly describe the Calvinism whose moorings he had dropped but which intrigued him to the end. In 1888 Stevenson settled in Samoa and there with his devoted wife and stepson he passed the last five years of his life on his estate of Vailima, which gives its name to the incomparable series of letters which he wrote chiefly to friends in Britain. It was in no derogatory sense that Desmond MacCarthy called Stevenson 'a little master'. Nobody knew better than MacCarthy how much toil it takes to make a little master and how much delight he may convey to posterity. See Lives by G. Balfour (1901), S. Colvin (1924) and J. Steuart (1924); also studies by D. Daiches (1947), M. Elwin (1950), and E. N. Caldwell (1960); also Furnas's *Voyage to Windward* (1950).

(4) **William** (d. 1575), English scholar, entered Christ's College, Cambridge, in 1546, and became a fellow. He was probably the author of *Gammer Gurtons Nedle* (1575), sometimes attributed to John Still or John Bridges.

STEVINUS, Simon (1548–1620), Flemish mathematician and physicist, born at Bruges, held offices under Prince Maurice of Orange. He wrote on fortification, book-keeping and decimals; and invented a system of sluices and a carriage propelled by sails.

STEWART, House of, a Scottish family, from whom came the royal line of the Kings of Scotland, and, later, of Great Britain and Ireland, was descended from a Breton, **Alan Fitzflaald** (d. *c.* 1114), who received the lands of Oswestry in Shropshire from Henry I. His elder son, **William Fitzalan** (*c.* 1105–60),was the ancestor of the Earls of Arundel. Members in chronological order were:

(1) **Walter** (d. 1177), second son of the above, coming to Scotland, received from David I large possessions in Renfrewshire, Teviotdale, Lauderdale, &c., along with the hereditary dignity of Steward of Scotland, which gave his descendants the surname of Stewart, by some branches modified to Steuart or the French form Stuart.

(2) **Walter**, grandson of (1), was also justiciary of Scotland.

(3) **Alexander** (1214–83), fourth Steward, was regent of Scotland in Alexander III's minority and commanded at the battle of Largs (1263). From his second son's marriage with the heiress of Bonkyl sprang the Stewarts of Darnley, Lennox and Aubigny.

(4) **James** (1243–1309), fifth Steward, was one of the six regents of Scotland after the death of Alexander III.

(5) **Walter** (1293–1326), sixth Steward, did good service at Bannockburn, and defended Berwick against Edward II. His marriage in 1315 with Marjory, Bruce's daughter, brought the crown of Scotland to his family.

(6) **Robert** (1316–90), seventh Steward, son of (5), on the death of David II in 1371, ascended the throne as Robert II. He was twice married—first (1349) to Elizabeth, daughter of Sir Adam Mure of Rowallan, and secondly (1355) to Euphemia, Countess of Moray, daughter of Hugh, Earl of Ross. Elizabeth Mure was related to him within the prohibited degrees, so in 1347 he obtained a papal dispensation (only discovered in the Vatican in 1789) for the marriage, legitimizing the children already born.

(7) **John, Earl of Carrick** (*c.* 1337–1406), eldest son of (6), succeeded him as Robert III.

(8) **Robert** (*c.* 1339–1420), third son of (6), was in 1398 created Duke of Albany.

(9) **Alexander, Earl of Buchan** (*c.* 1343–*c.* 1405), fourth son of (6), and overlord of Badenoch, received the earldom on his

marriage (1382). His continued attacks on the bishopric of Moray earned him the title of the 'Wolf of Badenoch'.

(10) **John** (*c.* 1381–1424), nephew of (9), leading a Scottish force, defeated the English at Baugé (1421). He became constable of France but fell fighting at Verneuil. Between 1371 and 1714, fourteen Stewarts sat upon the Scottish, and six of these also on the English, throne, and these, listed below, have separate entries:

ROBERT II (1316–90)
ROBERT III (*c.* 1340–1406)
JAMES I (1394–1437)
JAMES II (1430–60)
JAMES III (1451–88)
JAMES IV (1473–1513)
JAMES V (1512–42)
MARY (1542–87)
JAMES VI and I (1566–1625)
CHARLES I (1600–49)
CHARLES II (1630–85)
JAMES VII and II (1633–1701)
MARY (1662–94)
ANNE (1665–1714).

(11) **James Francis Edward** (1688–1766), known as the 'Old Pretender', only son of James VII and II and his second wife, Mary of Modena, and father of (12), was born at St James's Palace, June 10, by many falsely believed to have been introduced in a warming-pan. Six months later, he was conveyed by his fugitive mother to St Germain, where, on his father's death in 1701, he was proclaimed his successor. On an attempt (1708) to make a descent upon Scotland, the young 'Chevalier de St George' was not allowed to land; after his return he served with the French in the Low Countries, distinguishing himself at Malplaquet. But in Mar's ill-conducted rebellion, he landed at Peterhead (December 1715), only to sneak away six weeks afterwards from Montrose. France was now closed to him by the treaty of Utrecht, and almost all the rest of his life was passed at Rome, where he died, January 1, 1766. In 1719 he had married Princess Clementina Sobieski (1702–35), who bore him two sons. See Lives by M. Haile (1907), Shield and Lang (1907) and A. and H. Tayler (1934).

(12) **Charles Edward Louis Philip Casimir** (1720–88), known variously as the 'Young Pretender', the 'Young Chevalier', and 'Bonny Prince Charlie', elder son of (11), was born in Rome, December 31, and educated there and became the centre of Jacobite hopes. He first saw service at the siege of Gaeta (1734); fought bravely at Dettingen (1743); and next year repaired to France, to head Marshal Saxe's projected invasion of England. But the squadron which was to have convoyed the transports with 15,000 troops to Kent fled before the British fleet; the transports themselves were scattered by a tempest; and for a year and a half Charles was kept hanging on in France, until at last, sailing from Nantes, he landed with seven followers at Eriskay in the Hebrides on July 23, 1745, and on August 19 raised his father's standard in Glenfinnan. The clansmen flocked in; on September 17 Edinburgh surrendered, though the castle held out; and Charles kept court at Holyrood, the palace of his ancestors. There followed the victory over Sir John Cope at Prestonpans (September 21), and on November 1 he left for London at the head of 6500 men. He took Carlisle and advanced as far as Derby. Londoners became alarmed, especially since the cream of the British army was engaged on the Continent. Eventually the Duke of Cumberland was dispatched against the insurgents. Charles meanwhile had been unwillingly argued into a withdrawal by his commanders and the Highlanders turned back, winning one last victory against the government forces at Falkirk, January 17, 1746, before suffering a crushing defeat at the hands of Cumberland's troops at Culloden Moor, April 16. The rising was ruthlessly suppressed by the duke, who earned the name 'Butcher Cumberland', and Charles was hunted in the highlands and islands for five months with a price of £30,000 on his head, but no one betrayed him. He was helped by Flora Macdonald (q.v.) when he crossed from Benbecula to Portree in June 1746, disguised as 'Betty Burke', her maid. He landed in Brittany, September 29, and was given hospitality at the French court until the peace of Aix-la-Chapelle (1748) caused his forcible expulsion from France, although he spent a while at Avignon until the English found out and protested, and afterwards lived secretly in Paris with his mistress, Clementina Walkinshaw. He made two or three secret visits to London between 1750 and 1760, even declaring himself a protestant. He assumed the title of Charles III of Great Britain and retired to Florence, where he married in 1772 the Countess of Albany (q.v.), but the marriage was later dissolved. His natural daughter, Charlotte (1753–89) by his mistress Walkinshaw, he had created Duchess of Albany. He died in Rome, January 31, was buried at Frascati, later at St Peter's. See Lives by A. C. Ewald (1875), A. Lang (1903), W. D. Norrie (1903–04), Wilkinson (1932), Dumont-Wilden (1934), H. Tayler (1945) and under MACDONALD, Flora.

(13) **Henry Benedict Maria Clement, Duke of York** (1725–1807), Scottish cardinal, brother of (12), was born in Rome. After the failure of the '45 he became in 1747 a cardinal and priest, and in 1761 Bishop of Frascati. He enjoyed, through the favour of the French court, the revenues of two rich abbeys, as well as a Spanish pension. The French Revolution stripped him of his fortune, and he had to take refuge in Venice for three years. In 1800 George III granted him a pension of £4000; he died, the last of the Stuarts, July 13, 1807. The crown jewels, carried off by James II, were bequeathed by him to George IV, then Prince of Wales, who in 1819 gave fifty guineas towards Canova's monument in St Peter's to 'James III, Charles III, and Henry IX'. See H. M. Vaughan, *Last of the Royal Stuarts* (1906); and Lives by A. Shield (1908) and B. Fothergill (1958).

Next to the exiled Stuarts came the descendants of Henrietta (q.v.), Charles I's youngest daughter, who in 1661 was married to the Duke of Orleans. From this marriage sprang Anne Mary (1669–1728), who married Victor Amadeus, Duke of Savoy and King of Sardinia; their son Charles Emmanuel III (1701–73), King of Sardinia; his son, Victor Amadeus III (1726–96), King of Sardinia; his son, Victor Emmanuel I (1759–1824), King of Sardinia; his daughter, Mary (1792–1840), who married Francis, Duke of Modena; their son, Ferdinand (1821–49), who married Elizabeth of Austria; and their daughter, Maria Teresa (1849–1919), who in 1868 married Prince (from 1913 to 1918 King) Louis of Bavaria, and whom, as 'Mary III and IV', the 'Legitimist Jacobites' of 1891 put forward as the 'representative of the Royal House of these realms'. Rupert, her son, was ninth in descent from Charles I; he represented Bavaria at Queen Victoria's Diamond Jubilee, June 1897, and early in World War I took command of a German army group in France. The branch of the family which the Act of Settlement (1701) called to the throne on the death of Anne were the descendants of the Electress Sophia of Hanover, granddaughter of James VI and I by her mother the Princess Elizabeth (q.v.), Electress Palatine and Queen of Bohemia. By that act the above-mentioned descendants of Henrietta of Orleans were excluded, and also the Roman Catholic descendants of the Princess Elizabeth's sons. Queen Elizabeth II is 26th in descent from Walter Fitzalan, 20th from Robert II and 12th from James VI and I.

Arabella (1575–1615), was the daughter of the Earl of Lennox, Darnley's younger brother, and so a great-great-granddaughter of Henry VII, a third cousin to Queen Elizabeth, and a first cousin to James VI and I. At twenty-seven she was suspected of having a lover in the boy William Seymour, who had Tudor blood in his veins; but on James's accession (1603) she was restored to favour, only, however, to contract a secret marriage in 1610 with him. Both were imprisoned, and both escaped—Seymour successfully to Ostend, but she was retaken, and died, insane, in the Tower. See Lives by M. E. Bradley (1889), M. Lefuse (1913), B. C. Hardy (1913).

The cadets of the house of Stewart are: (1) descendants of Robert II; (2) descendants of natural sons of his descendants; (3) descendants of natural sons of Stewart kings; and (4) legitimate branches of the Stewarts before their accession to the throne. To the first belong the Stuarts of Castle-Stewart, descended from Robert, Duke of Albany, Robert II's third son, through the Lords Avondale and Ochiltree. They received the titles of Lord Stuart of Castle-Stewart in the peerage of Ireland (1619), Viscount Castle-Stewart (1793), and Earl (1809). To the second class belong the Stuart Earls of Traquair (1633–1861), descended from a natural son of James Stewart, Earl of Buchan. To the third class belong the Regent Moray, the Marquis of Bute, and the Shaw-Stewarts; and to the fourth belong the Earls of Galloway (from a brother of the fifth High Steward), the Lords Blantyre, the Stewarts of Fort-Stewart, and the Stewarts of Grandtully (from the fourth High Steward; the last baronet died in 1890).

See, besides works cited in the articles on the several Stewart sovereigns and in Marshall's *Genealogist's Guide* (new ed. 1903), Stewart genealogies, &c., by Symson (1712), Hay of Drumboote (1722), Duncan Stewart (1739), Noble (1795), Andrew Stuart of Castlemilk (1798), A. G. Stuart (Castle-Stewart branch, 1854), Sir W. Fraser (Grandtully branch, 1868), W. A. Lindsay (1888); William Townend, *Descendants of the Stuarts* (1858); the Marchesa Campana de Cavelli, *Les Derniers Stuarts* (1871); books by Gibb and Skelton (1890), F. W. Head (1901), J. J. Foster (1902), S. Cowan (1908), T. F. Henderson (1914); M. Stewart and J. Balfour, *Scottish Family Histories* (1930), and *Study of the Kings* by J. P. Kenyon (1958).

STEWART, (1) Alexander Turney (1803–76), American merchant, born near Belfast, who acquired great wealth in America in the retail store business. His body was stolen in 1878, and restored to his widow three years after on payment of $20,000 through a lawyer.

(2) **Balfour** (1828–87), Scottish physicist, born at Edinburgh, studied at St Andrews and Edinburgh, and became assistant to Forbes at Edinburgh and afterwards director of Kew Observatory (1859), and professor of Physics at Owens College, Manchester (1870). He made his reputation by his work on radiant heat (1858), was one of the founders of spectrum analysis and wrote papers on terrestrial magnetism and sunspots.

(3) **Sir Charles.** See CASTLEREAGH.

(4) **Dugald** (1753–1828), Scottish philosopher, son of Matthew Stewart the mathematician (1717–85), born November 22 at Edinburgh, studied there and under Reid at Glasgow, became assistant in Mathematics at Edinburgh under his father (1775) and joint-professor in 1775. He succeeded Ferguson to the chair of Moral Philosophy (1785–1810) and in 1806 was awarded a Whig sinecure. A disciple of the 'common sense' philosophy of Reid, he systematized the doctrines of the Scottish school and allowed psychological considerations their full share in a philosophy of mind. See his *Elements of the Philosophy of the Human Mind* (vol. I, 1792; vols. II and III, 1814-17), *Outlines of Moral Philosophy* (1793), *Philosophical Essays* (1810), *Philosophy of the Active and Moral Powers* (1828) and his Life and edition of Adam Smith's works (1811–12). He died in Edinburgh, June 11, 1828. See Veitch's *Life* in Sir William Hamilton's edition of his works (1954–58), and J. McCosh, *Scottish Philosophy* (1874).

(5) **Frances Teresa, Duchess of Richmond and Lennox** (1647–1702), the granddaughter of Lord Blantyre, was appointed maid of honour to Catherine of Braganza. Described by Pepys as 'the greatest beauty' he ever saw in his life, her charms made a deep impression on the susceptible Charles II. Despite contemporary whispers to the contrary, she resisted his proposals; although consenting to pose as the effigy of Britannia

on the coinage. In 1667 'la belle Stewart' married the oafish 3rd Duke of Richmond, and fled the Court. In later years she was restored to the King's favour. See works by Bryant (1931) and Grammont (1903).

(6) **(Robert) Michael (Maitland)** (1906–), British Labour politician, born in London, educated at Christ's Hospital and St John's College, Oxford. A schoolmaster before World War II, he stood unsuccessfully for parliament in 1931 and 1935. M.P. for Fulham since 1945, he has had a varied ministerial career. Secretary of state for war (1947–51), for education and science (1964–65), he came to the fore as foreign minister (1965–66), as minister for economic affairs (1966–67) and as first secretary of state from 1966. He replaced George Brown as foreign minister on the latter's resignation in March 1968.

STEYN, Martinus Theunis, *stayn* (1857–1916), South African statesman, born in Winburg, Orange Free State, of which he was president (from 1896), joined the Transvaal in the war (1899–1902). He promoted the Union of 1910, but later encouraged Boer extremists and their rebellion of 1914. His son, **Colin Fraser** (1887–1959), mediated between Generals Botha and de Wet, and was minister of justice in the Smuts government (1939–45) and of labour (1945–48).

STIFTER, Adalbert (1805–68), Austrian novelist and painter, born at Oberplan, Bohemia, studied at Vienna and as private tutor to various aristocratic families had several unhappy love affairs. Deeply disturbed by the Revolution of 1848, he settled in Linz and became an official in the ministry of education. Unhappiness and illness terminated in suicide. His humanism, his love of traditional values, his belief in the greatness of life pervade the *Bildungroman*, *Der Nachsommer* (1857), *Witiko* (1865–67), a heroic tale set in 12th-century Bohemia, and the short stories *Der Condor* (1840), &c. He was also a considerable painter of city views. See also *Studien* (1844–50) and *Bunte Steine* (1853), complete works, ed. A. Sauer (1901–1928), study by A. von Grotman (1926), and Lives by Blackall (1948) and Steffen (1955).

STIGAND (d. 1072), English ecclesiastic, was made his chaplain by Edward the Confessor, Bishop of Elmham (1044), Bishop of Winchester (1047), and, uncanonically, Archbishop of Canterbury (1052). On the death of Harold, whom, possibly, he had crowned, Stigand supported Edgar Atheling. Hence he was deprived by William I, whom he had helped to crown, of Canterbury and Winchester (1070), and he died a prisoner at Winchester.

STILICHO, Flavius, *stil'i-kō* (*c.* A.D. 359–408), Roman general, by blood a Vandal, was sent as ambassador to Persia in 384, and rewarded with the hand of Serena, niece of the Emperor Theodosius. In 394 he departed from Constantinople for Rome in charge of the youthful Honorius, placed him on the throne of the Western empire, and administered in his name the affairs of state. On the death of Theodosius (394) Stilicho's rival, Rufinus, instigated Alaric to invade Greece. Stilicho marched against Alaric, blocked him up in the Peloponnesus, but permitted him to escape with captives and booty. In 398 his daughter became the wife of Honorius. Alaric invaded Northern Italy, but was signally defeated by Stilicho at Pollentia (403) and Verona. When Radagaisus, at the head of 200,000 to 400,000 Goths, ravaged the country as far as Florence (406), Stilicho routed the invaders and saved the Western empire a second time. Next Vandals, Alans and Suevi invaded Gaul; Stilicho's proposed alliance with Alaric against them was interpreted as treachery and he was credited with aiming at the imperial dignity. A Roman army mutinied, and Stilicho fled to Ravenna, where he was murdered. Three months later Alaric was at the gates of Rome.

STILL, William Grant (1895–), American Negro composer, born in Woodville, Mississippi, worked as an arranger of popular music and played in theatre and night-club orchestras while studying under Varèse. His music shows the influence of this work and of racial and European styles. It includes five operas, four symphonies, one of which is a study of the modern American Negro, three ballets, chamber and choral music and orchestral pieces.

STILLING. See JUNG (2).

STILLINGFLEET, (1) Benjamin (1702–71), English author and botanist, grandson of (2), born in Norfolk, studied at Trinity College, Cambridge, published essays on music and the art of conversation, but is best known for his preface 'Observation on Grasses' to his own translation (1759) from the Latin of six of Linnaeus's botanical essays. The term 'blue stocking' originated from those he habitually wore at the fashionable, mixed 'evening assemblies without card playing' at Mrs Vesey's of Bath, to which he contributed erudite conversation.

(2) **Edward** (1635–99), English divine, grandfather of (1), born at Cranborne in Dorset, became in 1653 fellow of St John's College, Cambridge, later vicar of Sutton, Bedfordshire. His *Irenicum* (1659) advocated union between the Episcopalians and the Presbyterians. His *Origines Sacrae* (1662) and *Rational Account of the Grounds of the Protestant Religion* (1664), defending the Church of England's breach with Rome, led to preferment. He became chaplain to Charles II, Dean of St Paul's (1678) and after the deposition of James II Bishop of Worcester. In three letters or pamphlets (1696–1697) he defended the doctrine of the Trinity against the consequences of what he understood to be Locke's denial of substance in the latter's *Essay*, but Locke merely denied that one can have a genuine idea of 'pure substance in general' and give it a significant content. See Life by R. Bentley, prefaced to the Collected Works (1710).

STILWELL, Joseph, nicknamed 'Vinegar Joe' (1883–1946), American soldier, was born in Florida, graduated at West Point in 1904, and rose to lt.-col. in the first World War. An authority on Chinese life and an expert Chinese speaker, he was military attaché to the U.S. Embassy in Peking from 1932 to 1939. In 1941 he became U.S. military representative in China and in 1942 commander of the 5th and 6th Chinese Armies in Burma. In the Burma counter-offensive in 1943 he was commanding general of the U.S. Forces in China, Burma and India, but was recalled to America following a dispute with Chiang Kai-shek. See *The Stilwell Papers* (posthumous, 1949).

STINFALICO. See MARCELLO.

STIRLING, (1) **James Hutchison** (1820–1909), Scottish idealist philosopher, born at Glasgow, studied both arts and medicine at Glasgow and philosophy at Heidelberg. His *Secret of Hegel* (1865) introduced that philosopher's system into Britain and was a masterly exposition despite the unkind critic's remark that the secret had been well kept. He also wrote a *Complete Textbook to Kant* (1881) and three attacks, one on *Sir William Hamilton; being the Philosophy of Perception* (1865), another on Huxley's biology, entitled *As Regards Protoplasm* (1869), a third on *Darwinianism* (1894). He delivered the first Gifford lectures at Edinburgh in 1890. See Life by his daughter, A. H. Stirling (1912), and J. H. Muirhead, *The Platonic Tradition in Anglo-Saxon Philosophy* (1931).

(2) **Mary Ann,** *née* **Kehl** (1816–95), English actress, born in Mayfair, London, was educated in France, made her début in 1833, and played till 1886, her finest parts 'Peg Woffington' and the Nurse in *Romeo and Juliet*. She married early the Drury Lane stage manager, Edward Stirling, and in 1894 Sir Charles Hutton Gregory.

(3) **William Alexander, 1st Earl of** (*c.* 1567–1640), minor Scottish poet, born at Alva. Knighted by 1609, in 1613 he was attached to the household of Prince Charles; in 1614 he published part i of his huge poem *Doomesday* (part ii 1637). He received in 1621 the grant of 'Nova Scotia'—a vast tract in N. America soon rendered valueless by French expansion; in 1631 he was made sole printer of King James's version of the Psalms. From 1626 till his death he was the (unpopular) secretary of state for Scotland. He was created Viscount (1630) and Earl of Stirling (1633), also Earl of Dovan (1639), but he died insolvent in London. His tragedies—*Darius* (1603), *Croesus* (1604), *The Alexandrean Tragedy* (1605), *Julius Caesar* (1607)— are of French Senecan type; their quatrains are graceful. The songs, sonnets, elegies, madrigals of *Aurora* (1604) are marred by conceits, yet show fancy and ingenuity. See Kastner and Charlton's edition of his poems (1921–29); *Memorials* by Rogers (1877).

STIRLING-MAXWELL, Sir William, Bart. (1818–78), Scottish historian and art critic, born in Glasgow, added the name of Maxwell to his own on succeeding to the estates of his uncle, Sir John Maxwell, in 1866. He travelled in Italy and Spain, was the first British collector to buy Spanish paintings of the 16th and 17th centuries, and wrote *Annals of the Artists of Spain* (1848), *Cloister Life of Charles V* (1852), *Velazquez* (1855), &c. His second wife (1877) was the Hon. Mrs Norton (q.v.).

STIRNER, Max, pseud. of **Kaspar Schmidt** (1806–56), German anarchistic writer, who was born at Bayreuth, and taught in a girls' school in Berlin, wrote *Der Einziger und das Eigentum* (1845, trans. 1912). See works by R. Engert (1921) and H. Schultheiss (1932).

STITNY, Thomas (*c.* 1325–1404), a Bohemian philosophical writer, a predecessor of Huss.

STOBAEUS, Johannes (fl. A.D. 500), Greek anthologist, born at Stobi in Macedonia, compiled about A.D. 500 an anthology from 500 Greek poets and prose-writers. It has preserved fragments from many lost works.

STOCKHAUSEN, Karlheinz (1928–), German composer, born at Mödrath, near Cologne, educated at Cologne and Bonn Universities, studied under Frank Martin and Messaien, employed the twelve-tone system, but advanced further, joined the *Musique Concrète* group in Paris and experimented with compositions based on electronic sounds. He has written orchestral, choral and instrumental works, including some which combine electronic and normal sonorities; also some effective piano pieces in an advanced idiom.

STOCKMAR, Christian Friedrich, Baron (1787–1863), German diplomat, born of Swedish descent at Coburg, became physician and adviser to Prince Leopold (q.v.) of Coburg, the husband first of the Princess Charlotte and then king of the Belgians. He was made a baron in 1831. In 1836 he became the mentor of Prince Albert, and was the trusted friend of the young queen of England. See his *Denkwürdigkeiten* (Eng. trans. *Notabilia*, 1872), Juste, *Le Baron Stockmar* (1873), and Sir T. Martin, *Monographs* (1923).

STOCKTON, (1) **Francis Richard** (1834–1902), American humorist and engraver, born at Philadelphia, became assistant editor of *St Nicholas*. He first attracted notice by his stories for children, but is best known as author of *Rudder Grange* (1879). Later works are *The Lady, or the Tiger?* (1884), *Mrs Cliff's Yacht* (1896), *The Great Stone of Sardis* (1897), *The Girl at Cobhurst* (1898), &c.

(2) **Robert Field** (1795–1866), American naval officer, conquered California with Frémont (1846–47) and organized a government.

STODDARD, Richard Henry (1825–1903), American poet, was born at Hingham, Massachusetts. His poems include *Songs in Summer* (1857), *The King's Bell* (1862), *The Book of the East* (1867), *Lion's Cub* (1891). *Under the Evening Lamp* (1893) and *Recollections* (1903) contain literary studies. His wife, **Elizabeth Drew,** *née* **Barstow** (1823–1902), was also a novelist and poet.

STODDART, Thomas Tod (1810–80), Scottish angler poet, lived at Kelso from 1836. His *Death-Wake, or Lunacy* (1830), was reprinted in 1895, with an introduction by Andrew Lang, and his *Songs of the Seasons* (2nd ed. 1881) contains an autobiography.

STOKER, Bram, properly **Abraham** (1847–1912), Irish writer, born in Dublin, educated at Trinity College there, studied law and science, partnered Henry Irving in running the Lyceum Theatre from 1878 and wrote, among other books, the classic horror tale *Dracula* (1897) and *Personal Reminiscences of Henry Irving* (1906). See study by H. Ludlam (1962).

STOKES, (1) **Sir George Gabriel, Bart.** (1819–

1903), British mathematician and physicist, born at Skreen, Sligo, graduated in 1841 as senior wrangler from Pembroke College, Cambridge, and in 1849 became Lucasian professor of Mathematics. In 1851 he was made fellow, and in 1854–85 was secretary, of the Royal Society, in 1885–92 president. In 1887–92 he was Conservative M.P. for Cambridge University, in 1889 was created a baronet. He first used spectroscopy as a means of determining the chemical compositions of the sun and stars, published a valuable paper on diffraction (1849), identified X-rays as electromagnetic waves produced by sudden obstruction of cathode rays and formulated the law which bears his name, in terms of a formula for the force opposing a small sphere in its passage through a viscous fluid. See his *Memoir* (1907).

(2) **Whitley** (1830–1909), Irish jurist, son of William Stokes, regius professor of Medicine at Dublin, studied law at Trinity College, Dublin, went to India in 1862, and was in 1879 president of the Indian law commission and draughtsman of the law and criminal codes. He wrote many legal works and edited Irish and other Celtic texts.

STOKESLEY, John (1475?–1539), English divine, born at Collyweston, Northamptonshire, Bishop of London, was chaplain to Henry VIII and wrote in favour of the divorce (1531). He condemned John Frith (q.v.) and other Protestants, but opposed the translation of the Bible into English and was in opposition to Cromwell.

STOKOWSKI, Leopold, *sto-kof'skée* (1882–), American conductor of Polish origin, born in London, studied at the Royal College of Music there and built up an international reputation as conductor of the Philadelphia Symphony Orchestra (1912–36), the New York Philharmonic (1946–50) and the Houston Symphony Orchestra (1955–60). He appeared with Deanna Durbin in the film *A Hundred Men and a Girl* (1937) and in Walt Disney's *Fantasia* (1940). In 1962 he founded and has since conducted the American Symphony Orchestra in New York.

STOLBERG, (1) **Christian, Count of** (1748–1821), German poet, one of the Göttingen poet band, born at Hamburg, was in the public service of Holstein (1777–1800). Besides writing poems, he translated Sophocles.

(2) **Friedrich Leopold, Count of** (1750–1819), German poet, brother of (1), also of the Göttingen school, was in the Danish service (1789–1800). Then turning Catholic, he published a history of Christianity. He produced poems, dramas, translations from the Greek, &c. See works by Menge (1862), Janssen (3rd ed. 1882) and Keiper (1893).

STONE, (1) **Lucy** (1818–93), American feminist, born in Massachusetts, became active *c.* 1847 in anti-slavery and suffragist movements, and founded (1855) the *Woman's Journal.* She married **Henry Brown Blackwell,** the abolitionist, in the same year.

(2) **Nicholas, the elder** (1586–1647), English mason and architect, carried out designs of Inigo Jones (q.v.) and completed the tombs of Bodley and Donne. His sons, **Nicholas, John** and **Henry,** were also sculptors.

STONEY, George Johnstone (1826–1911), Irish mathematical physicist, became professor of Natural Philosophy at Queen's College (1852), and was elected F.R.S. in 1861. He calculated an approximate value for the charge of an electron (1874).

STOPES, Marie Carmichael (1880–1958), English pioneer advocate of birth control, suffragette, and palaeontologist, born near Dorking, Surrey, studied at University College, London, and at Munich and in 1904 became the first female science lecturer at Manchester, specializing in fossil plants and coalmining. In 1907 she lectured at Tokio and with Professor Sakurai wrote a book on the Japanese *No* plays (1913). Alarmed at the unscientific manner in which men and women embark upon married life, after the unhappiness of her first marriage she wrote a number of books on the subject, of which *Married Love* (1918), in which birth control is mentioned, caused a storm of controversy. With her second husband, **Humphrey Verdon Roe** (1878–1949), the aircraft manufacturer, she founded the first birth control clinic in North London in 1921. Her seventy books also include studies of the sex cycle, a play, *Our Ostriches* (1923), and poetry.

STORACE, *sto-rah'chay,* (1) **Anna Selina** (1766–1817), English singer and actress of Italian descent, sister of (2), sang at Florence and La Scala, Milan, and in London. She was the original Susanna in Mozart's *Nozze di Figaro,* in Vienna (1786) and partnered John Braham (q.v.) on the continent.

(2) **Stephen** (1763–96), English composer of *The Haunted Tower* (1789) and other operas, brother of (1), was born in London.

STORM, Theodor Woldsen (1817–88), German poet and storywriter, born at Husum in Schleswig-Holstein, was a magistrate and judge (1864–80), wrote one volume of poems (1857) and a number of tales, characterized by a vivid, often eerie descriptive power. See his correspondence with Keller (1904) and Lives by G. Storm (1912), P Schütze (1925), and study by F. Stuckert (1940).

STÖRMER, Carl Fredrik Mülertz (1874–1957), Norwegian mathematician and geophysicist, was educated at Oslo and became professor there (1903). He carried out research on cosmic rays and discovered the 'forbidden' directions lying within the Störmer cone. He gave his name to the unit of momentum at which a particle can circle around the equator.

STORR, Paul (1771–1844), English goldsmith, began his career in partnership with William Frisbee in 1792, establishing his firm in Dean Street, Soho, in 1807. He produced much domestic silver and monumental work from the designs of John Flaxman (q.v.) for the royal collection at Windsor Castle. See study by Penzer (1954).

STORY, (1) **John** (1510?–71), English jurist, first regius professor of Civil Law (1544) at Oxford, opposed the Act of Uniformity (1548) and went into exile at Louvain, whence he returned during Mary's reign to become a persecutor of Protestants and proctor at Cranmer's trial (1555). Pardoned by Elizabeth, he soon fell foul of the authorities again, fled to Spain but was kidnapped and executed at Tyburn.

(2) **Joseph** (1779–1845), American jurist, father of (3), born at Marblehead, Mass., graduated at Harvard in 1798, was admitted to the bar in 1801, elected to the state legislature in 1805, and became a leader of the Republican (Democratic) party. In 1808 he entered congress, in 1811–45 was a justice of the Supreme Court, and also professor of Law at Harvard from 1829. His works include *Commentaries on the Constitution of the U.S.* (1833), *The Conflict of Laws* (1834), and *Equity Jurisprudence* (1835–36). See Life by his son (1851), who also edited his *Miscellaneous Writings* (1851).

(3) **William Wetmore** (1819–95), American poet and sculptor, son of (2), was born at Salem, Mass., and was admitted to the bar, but went to Italy (1848) and became a sculptor as well as a poet. His writings include *Poems* (1847–56–86), *Roba di Roma* (1862), *Castle of St Angelo* (1877), *He and She* (1883), *Fiametta* (1885), *Excursions* (1891) and *A Poet's Portfolio* (1894). See Life by Henry James (1903).

STORY-MASKELYNE. See MASKELYNE (2).

STOSS, or **Stozz, Veit,** *shtōs* (1447–1533), German woodcarver and sculptor, born probably in Nuremberg. Except for a period in 1486 when he worked in the church of St Sebald in Nuremberg, he was from 1477 to 1496 in Cracow, where he carved the high altar of the Marienkirche. He returned to Nuremberg, and for the next thirty years worked in various churches there, including St Lorenz's, where is his *Annunciation.* Despite the great size of many of his works, they all show great delicacy of sculpture. See German monographs by H. Wilm (1935) and E. Lutze (1938).

STOTHARD, Thomas (1755–1834), English painter and engraver, born in London, was apprenticed to a pattern-drawer. A series of designs for the *Town and Country Magazine* was followed by illustrations for Bell's *Poets* and the *Novelist's Library.* His earliest pictures exhibited at the Academy were *The Holy Family* and *Ajax defending the Body of Patroclus.* In 1794 he became R.A. and in 1813 Academy librarian. Some 3000 of his designs were engraved, including those to Boydell's *Shakespeare*, *The Pilgrim's Progress*, *Robinson Crusoe* and Rogers's *Poems.* His *Canterbury Pilgrims* and *Flitch of Bacon* are well known by engravings. See Life (1851) by Mrs Bray (q.v.), widow of his son, **Charles Alfred Stothard** (1786–1821), antiquarian draughtsman; and another by A. C. Coxhead (1907).

STOUT, George Frederick (1860–1944), English philosopher and psychologist, born at South Shields, studied at St John's College, Cambridge, was elected fellow (1884) and after lecturing at Cambridge, where his students included Moore and Russell, at Aberdeen and Oxford, was appointed professor of Logic and Metaphysics at St Andrews (1903–36), and was a distinguished editor of the philosophical journal *Mind* (1891–1920). His *Analytic Psychology* (1896) ranks high among the classic contributions to the philosophy of mind. *Manual of Psychology* (1899) was long the English textbook. His Gifford lectures (1919–21) became the basis of his formidable treatment of the problems of perception, in which psychological considerations weighed heavily and which ultimately tended towards idealistic metaphysics. The first volume, *Mind and Matter*, appeared in 1931 and was somewhat clarified by *God and Nature* (1952). This also contains a memoir by J. A. Passmore. See also his collected *Studies in Philosophy and Psychology* (1930). He was elected F.B.A. in 1903.

STOW, (1) **David** (1793–1864), Scottish pioneer of coeducation, born at Paisley, founder of Glasgow Normal school, advocated the mixing of the sexes and the abolition of prizes and corporal punishment in schools.

(2) **John** (1525–1605), English chronicler, was a tailor in Cornhill, but about his fortieth year devoted himself to antiquarian pursuits. His principal works, which, for his time, are accurate and businesslike, are his *Summary of English Chronicles* (1565); *Annals, or a General Chronicle of England* (1580); and the noted *Survey of London and Westminster* (1598), an account of their history, antiquities, and government for six centuries. Stow also assisted in the continuation of Holinshed's Chronicle, Speght's Chaucer, &c. See the *Survey*, ed. Kingsford (1908), and Everyman edition (1955).

STOWE, Harriet Elizabeth Beecher (1811–96), American novelist, daughter of Lyman Beecher (q.v.), born at Litchfield, Connecticut, was brought up with puritanical strictness and joined her sister Catherine (q.v.) at her seminary at Hartford. In 1836 she married the Rev. C. E. Stowe, a theological professor at Lane Seminary, with whom she settled at Brunswick, Maine. She became famous through her *Uncle Tom's Cabin* (1852), which immediately focused anti-slavery sentiment in the North. Her second anti-slavery novel, *Dred* (1856), had a record sale in England, but she lost her English popularity with *Lady Byron Vindicated* (1870), although the charges made therein against Byron were later proven. Her best books deal with New England life, such as *The Minister's Wooing* (1859), *Old Town Folks* (1869), &c. See Life by F. Wilson (1941).

STOWELL, William Scott, 1st Baron (1745–1836), English judge, eldest brother of Lord Eldon (q.v.), born at Heyworth, went up to Corpus, Oxford, in 1761, was a college tutor (1765–77), and in 1780 was called to the bar. In 1788 he was made a judge and privy councillor, and knighted. Both as an ecclesiastical and admiralty judge he won high distinction, and he was the highest English authority on the law of nations. He sat for Oxford 1801–21, when he was made Baron Stowell; in 1828 he retired. See Lives by Surtees (1846), E. S. Roscoe (1916).

STRABO (*c.* 60 B.C.–post A.D. 21), Greek geographer, born at Amasia in Pontus, was of Greek descent on his mother's side. *Strabo* means 'squint-eyed'. He seems to have spent his life in travel and study, was at Corinth in 29 B.C., ascended the Nile in 24, seems to have been settled at Rome after A.D. 14, and died sometime after A.D. 21. Of Strabo's great historical work in forty-seven books—from the fifth a continuation to his own time of Polybius—we have only a few fragments; but his *Geographica* in seventeen books has come down to us almost complete. It is a work of great value in those parts especially which record the results of his own extensive observation. He makes copious use of his predecessors, Eratosthenes, Polybius, Aristotle, Thucydides, and many writers now lost to us, but he depreciates Herodotus and quotes few Roman writers.

STRACHAN, Douglas, *strawn* (1875–1950), Scottish artist, born in Aberdeen, after being political cartoonist for the *Manchester Chronicle* (1895–97) and a portrait painter in London, found his true medium in stained glass work. His first great opportunity was the window group which Britain contributed to the Palace of Peace at The Hague. He designed the windows for the shrine of the Scottish National War Memorial. Other examples of his work may be seen in King's College Chapel, Aberdeen, the University Chapel, Glasgow, and the church of St Thomas, Winchelsea. As an artist Strachan never wholly identified himself with any movement. His work glows with rich colour schemes and his subjects are treated with originality and imagination.

STRACHEY, *stray-chi,* (1) **(Evelyn) John St Loe** (1901–63), English Labour politician, educated at Eton and Magdalen College, Oxford, was Labour M.P. from 1929 until 1931, when he resigned from the Labour Party and gave his support to extremist political organizations. He served in the R.A.F. during World War II and in 1945 became Labour under-secretary for air. His controversial period as minister of food (1946–50) included the food crisis (1947), the unpopular prolongation of rationing, and the abortive Tanganyika ground-nuts and Gambia egg schemes (1947–49). As secretary of state for war (1950–51) he had to contend with the Korean war and the Communist insurrection in Malaya. His numerous books include *The Menace of Fascism* (1933), *The Theory and Practice of Socialism* (1936), *Contemporary Capitalism* (1956), *The Strangled Cry* (1962), &c.

(2) **(Giles) Lytton** (1880–1932), English biographer, was born in London. Educated at Cambridge, he began his writing career as a critic with *Landmarks in French Literature* (1912), which shows clearly his affinities with Sainte-Beuve and his francophile sympathies. *Eminent Victorians* (1918) was a literary bombshell, constituting, as it did, a vigorous, impertinent challenge to Victorian smug self-assurance. The irony, the mordant wit, the ruthless pinpointing of foible that was his method of evoking character, the entire battery of his gifts brought into action to demolish stuffed legendary figures, all combined to make this book a turning-point in the art of biography. After him, pedestrian accumulation of fact (the product of conscientious hacks) could no longer be the accepted thing. Through Strachey, biography had become a literary genre. He followed up his success with *Queen Victoria* (1921), *Books and Characters* (1922), *Elizabeth and Essex* (1928), *Portraits in Miniature* (1931) and *Characters and Commentaries* (1933). Appreciation of his generosity and catholicity of taste has restored Strachey's reputation, which after his death suffered belittlement. See studies by M. Beerbohm (1943), R. A. Scott-James (1955), C. R. Sanders (1958) and M. Holroyd (2 vols. 1967–68), and J. K. Johnstone, *The Bloomsbury Group* (1954).

STRADELLA, Alessandro (*c.* 1645–81), Italian composer, born in Naples (or Venice). His *San Giovanni Battista* influenced Purcell and Scarlatti. Legend has it that he eloped from Venice to Turin with the mistress of one of the Contarini, who sent assassins to murder him. He was wounded, but recovered. Or, as some say, his would-be murderers found him conducting one of his oratorios, and, touched by the music, allowed him to escape. He was, however, eventually murdered in Genoa. He did not compose *Pietà, Signore.* His legend has furnished the story for operas and Marion Crawford used it for his novel *Stradella* (1909).

STRADIVARI, or **Stradivarius, Antonio** (*c.* 1644–1737), famous Italian violin maker of Cremona, pupil of Niccolo Amati (q.v.), experimented with the design of string instruments and perfected the Cremona type of violin. His two sons, of two marriages, **Francesco** (1671–1743) and **Omobono** (1679–1742), assisted him. Estimates suggest that he made over a thousand violins, violas and violoncellos in the years 1666–1737. See monographs by H. Petherick (1900) and W. H., A. F. and A. E. Mill (1909).

STRAFFORD, Thomas Wentworth, 1st Earl of (1593–1641), English statesman, was born in London, April 13, of a Yorkshire family with royal connections, studied at St John's College, Cambridge; in 1611 was knighted and married; and having travelled in France and Italy, in 1614 became member for Yorkshire, and succeeded his father in the baronetcy. In 1615 he was appointed *custos rotulorum* for the West Riding, a post from which Buckingham sought two years later to oust him. During James I's reign he was a generally silent member in three brief parliaments, and a frequent attendant at the Court of the Star Chamber. His first wife, a daughter of the Earl of Cumberland, died in 1622, and in 1625 he married a daughter of Lord Clare. Conscious of his own abilities, with no great belief in parliamentary wisdom, loyal in his devotion to crown and church, an eager advocate of domestic reforms, Wentworth in Charles's first parliament (1625) acted with the Opposition; from the second he was excluded by his appointment as sheriff of Yorkshire. In July of that year (1626) he was curtly dismissed from the keepership of the rolls, and for refusing to pay the forced loan was imprisoned. So in the third parliament (1628) he headed the onslaught on the king's ministers. From its meeting in March until May he was the leader of the Lower House; on July 7 the Petition of Right, superseding a similar measure of his own, became law; and on the 22nd he was created Baron Wentworth, in December Viscount Wentworth and President of the North. As such at York he set himself to strengthen government with an efficient militia and ample revenue, and to 'comply with that public and common protection which good kings afford their good people'. Towards these ends he used on occasion high-handed methods, which embroiled him, however, chiefly with the gentry. His second wife died in 1631, leaving a son, William, second Earl of Strafford (1626–95, died *s.p.*), and two daughters; and within a year he married privately the daughter of Sir George Rhodes. In January 1632 he was appointed lord deputy of Ireland, but it was not till July 1633 that he landed at Dublin. He straightway proceeded to coerce Ireland into a state of obedience and well-being, introducing the flax industry, reducing piracy and reconstituting the army. The aim of his policy (he and Laud called it 'Thorough') was to make his master 'the most absolute prince in Christendom'. Not till 1639 did Wentworth become the king's principal adviser, when he was made Earl of Strafford and lord-lieutenant of Ireland (January 1640). In May 1640 he offered to lead an Irish army against Scotland. It was too late. The rebellion, provoked in Scotland by Charles's unwisdom, was spreading to England; and Pym and his followers judged rightly that Strafford was the one obstacle to their triumph. Strafford was impeached and lodged in the Tower. In the great trial by his peers, which opened in Westminster Hall on March 22, 1641, he defended himself with a fortitude, patience and ability that moved and alarmed his accusers. The twenty-eight charges amounted at most to 'cumulative treason'; the gravest of them, his having counselled the king that 'he had an army in Ireland which he could employ to reduce *this kingdom*' (query England or Scotland), was supported by only one witness, his personal enemy, Vane. Despairing of a conviction by the Lords, the 'inflexibles' dropped the impeachment for a bill of attainder. It passed a third reading in both Houses; on May 10 it received the royal assent; and Strafford was executed on Tower Hill, May 12, 1641: he is buried at Wentworth-Woodhouse. See Knowler's edition of his *Letters and Correspondence* (1739), with the short Life by Sir George Radcliffe (q.v.); and Lives by W. A. H. C. Gardner (1931), C. V. Wedgwood (1935) and Lord Birkenhead (1938), and study by H. F. Kearney (1959).

STRANG, William (1859–1921), Scottish painter and illustrator, born at Dumbarton, studied at the Slade under Legros and lived all his life in London. His etchings are realistic, but his book illustrations are strongly imaginative. In painting, he was influenced sometimes by the Venetian colourists and sometimes, as in *Bank Holiday* (1912), by Manet. His son **Ian** (1886–1952) was also a well-known etcher and engraver.

STRANGE, orig. **Strang, Sir Robert** (1721–92), Scottish line-engraver, was born at Kirkwall, July 14, 1721. He fought on the Stewart side at Prestonpans, Falkirk and Culloden, and in 1747 married a Jacobite, Isabella Lumisden. He studied in Paris and settled in London (1750). He had a European reputation as a historical line-engraver, in opposition to the stippling of his rival, Bartolozzi (q.v.). On a second visit to the Continent (1760–65) he was made a member of the Academies of Rome, Paris, Florence, Bologna and Parma. He was eventually president of the Academy and was knighted by George III (1787). See his Life by Dennistoun (1855) and that by Woodward prefixed to *Twenty Masterpieces of Strange* (1874).

STRANGFORD, (1) **George Augustus Frederick Percy Sydney Smythe, 7th Viscount** (1818–57), English politician, brother of (3), was one of Disraeli's 'New England' party. He was member for Canterbury (1841–52), but after 1846 abstained from debate. In 1852, he fought what is said to have been the last duel in England. He wrote articles for the press and *Historic Fancies* (1844).

(2) **Percy Clinton Sydney Smythe, 6th Viscount** (1780–1855), English politician, succeeded in 1801. He was secretary of legation at Lisbon, and ambassador to Portugal, Sweden, Turkey and Russia. He was made Baron Penshurst in 1825. His smooth translation of the *Rimas* of Camoens was published in 1803.

(3) **Percy Ellen Frederick William Smythe, 8th Viscount** (1826–69), English philologist, brother of (1), born at St Petersburg, educated at Harrow and Merton College, Oxford, entered the diplomatic service, early acquired an unexampled command of eastern languages, and was Oriental secretary during the Crimean war. In 1857 he succeeded as eighth and last viscount, thereafter living mostly in London, immersed in philological studies, but wrote little more than a few brilliant *Saturday*, *Pall Mall* and *Quarterly* articles. His *Selected Writings* (1869) and his *Letters and Papers* (1878) were published by his widow. See family history by E. B. de Fonblanque (1877).

STRAPAROLA, Giovan Francesco, *-rō'-* (d. *c.* 1557), Italian 'novelist', born at Caravaggio, published in 1550–54 *Piacevoli notti*, a collection of seventy-four stories in the style of the *Decameron.* See Eng. trans. by W. G. Waters (1894).

STRATFORD, John de (d. 1348), English statesman and divine, was Bishop of Winchester (1323). He was closely connected with the deposition of Edward II and was chancellor and principal adviser to Edward III for ten years. He was made Archbishop of Canterbury in 1333.

STRATFORD DE REDCLIFFE, Stratford Canning, 1st Viscount (1786–1880), English diplomat, born in London, was educated at Eton and King's College, Cambridge. In 1807 he became précis writer to his cousin, George Canning, at the Foreign Office; in 1808 first secretary to the Constantinople embassy; and in 1810 minister-plenipotentiary. His duty was to counteract French influence at the Porte, and he negotiated the treaty of Bucharest (1812) between Russia and Turkey. He was minister in Switzerland 1814–17, commissioner at the Vienna Congress of 1815, minister to the United States 1819–23. In 1824 he was sent on a mission to Vienna and St Petersburg, and in 1825 went to Constantinople as ambassador, where he mediated on behalf of Greek independence, but his efforts were frustrated by the battle of Navarino (1827). He resigned in 1828, and was made G.C.B.; in 1831 he was again sent to Constantinople to delimit Greece. When in 1833, after a mission to Portugal, he was gazetted ambassador to St Petersburg the tsar declined to receive him. During the intervals in his diplomatic career he sat in parliament. As ambassador at Constantinople 1842–58 he built up that extraordinary influence which gained him the name of the 'Great Elchi'. He induced the sultan to inaugurate reforms. His peace efforts failed owing to the obstinacy of Nicholas and the weakness of Lord Aberdeen's government. His alleged responsibility for the Crimean war rests on his known determination not to accept Russian protectorate over the Orthodox Christians, and his clear realization that if this could be prevented in no other way, then it was necessary to prepare for war. Created a viscount in 1852, he returned home in 1858, and in 1869 was made K.G. See Lives by S. Lane-Poole (1888), E. F. Malcolm-Smith (1933), and H. W. V. Temperley, *The Crimea* (1936).

STRATHCONA, Donald Alexander Smith, 1st Baron (1820–1914), Canadian statesman, born at Forres, emigrated to Canada and rose from clerk (1838) to governor (1889) of the Hudson's Bay Company. Chief promoter of the Canadian Pacific Railway (completed 1855), he became high commissioner for Canada in London in 1896, and a peer in 1897. See Life by B. Willson (1915), O. D. Stetton, *The Railway Builders* (1916), and J. McAvity, *Lord Strathcona's Horse* (1947).

STRATHNAIRN, Hugh Rose, 1st Baron (1801–85), British soldier, son of the diplomatist Sir George Rose, was born at Berlin. Military attaché to the Turkish army in 1840, he was consul-general for Syria 1841–48, secretary to Lord Stratford de Redcliffe and *chargé d'affaires* at Constantinople in 1852–1854. On the arrival of Menshikoff in 1853, he precipitated a crisis by sending for the British fleet. He was commissioner at French headquarters during the Crimean war. Sent to India in 1857, he virtually reconquered Central India. In 1860 he succeeded Lord Clyde as commander-in-chief in India, held the same post in Ireland 1865–1870, and was made a peer in 1866, a field-marshal in 1877. See Sir O. T. Burne's *Clyde and Strathnairn* (1891).

STRATTON, Charles Sherwood (1838–83), 'General Tom Thumb', a dwarf 31 inches high, was born at Bridgeport, Conn.

STRATTON-PORTER. See PORTER (7).

STRAUS, Oskar, *shtrows* (1870–1954), Austrian composer, born in Vienna but from 1939 a naturalized French citizen. A pupil of Bruch, he is best known for his many operettas and comic operas, such as *Waltz Dream* (1907) and *The Chocolate Soldier* (1908, from Shaw's *Arms and the Man*). He was the composer of the music for the film *La Ronde*. See Life by Grun (1955).

STRAUSS, *shtrows,* (1) **David Friedrich** (1808–74), German theologian, born at Ludwigsburg in Württemberg, studied for the church at Tübingen, where in 1832 he became *repetent* in the theological seminary, lecturing also on philosophy in the university as a disciple of Hegel. In his *Leben Jesu* (1835; trans. by George Eliot, 1846) he sought to prove the gospel history to be a collection of myths, and by an analytical dissection of each separate narrative to detect a nucleus of historical truth free from every trace of supernaturalism. The book marks an epoch in New Testament criticism and raised a storm of controversy. Strauss, dismissed from his post at Tübingen, in 1839 was called to be professor of Dogmatics and Church History at Zürich; but the appointment provoked such opposition that it had to be dropped. His second great work followed, *Die christliche Glaubenslehre*, a review of Christian dogma (1840–41). A new *Life of Jesus, composed for the German People* (1864; trans. 1865), attempts to reconstruct a positive life of Christ. In *Der alte und der neue Glaube* (1872) Strauss endeavours to prove that Christianity as a system of religious belief is dead, and that a new faith must be built up out of art and the scientific knowledge of nature. He also wrote several biographies, notably that of Ulrich von Hutten (trans. 1874) and lectures on Voltaire (1870). He separated from his wife, the opera singer Agnese Schebest (1813–70). See Life by Zeller (trans. 1874), and works by Hausrath (1878), Eck, Harräus and Ziegler (1909), and an appreciation of his critical work by A. Schweitzer in *The Quest of the Historical Jesus* (1910).

(2) **Johann, 'the elder'** (1804–49), Viennese violinist and conductor, as were his sons **Eduard** (1835–1916) and **Josef** (1827–70). founded with Lanner (in whose quartet he played for a while) the Viennese Waltz tradition, a development from Schubert. He toured extensively in Europe with his own orchestra, played during Queen Victoria's coronation festivities (1838) in London, composed the *Radetzky March* (1848) in honour of the general, and numerous waltzes including the *Lorelei* and the *Donaulieder*, but was eclipsed by his son (3).

(3) **Johann, 'the younger'** (1825–99), Viennese violinist, conductor and composer, born October 25, son of (2), who made him take up law, began to flout his father's wishes from 1844 when he appeared as a young conductor and composer of promise. He toured with his own orchestra and appeared in London in 1869 and visited the United States in 1872. His waltzes, which number over 400, are more full-blooded, more melodious and tasteful than his father's, and although they often seem to be written purely for the violin, Strauss showed in his introduction to *Wine, Women and Song* (1869) and in *Perpetuum Mobile* that the art of orchestration was not by any means beyond him. The best known include that symbol of romantic Vienna, *The Blue Danube*, *Artist's Life* (both 1867), *Tales from the Vienna Woods* (1868), *Voices of Spring* (1882) and *The Emperor* (1888). He also wrote a number of operettas, including *Die Fledermaus* (1874) and *A Night in Venice* (1883). He died in Vienna June 3, 1899. See study by H. E. Jacob (1940).

(4) **Richard** (1864–1949), German composer, son of the first horn player in the court

opera in Munich, where he was born. He began to compose at the age of six, and his first publications date from his eleventh year. In 1882 he entered Munich University, but began musical studies in Berlin in the following year, and shortly afterwards became assistant conductor to von Bülow at Meiningen. There he was converted from the school of Brahms, under whose influence his early compositions had been written, to that of Wagner and Liszt, composing his first symphonic poems and succeeding von Bülow in 1885. After a period (1886–89) as assistant conductor at the Munich opera he moved to Weimar, and was invited by Cosima Wagner to conduct at Bayreuth in 1891. His first opera, *Guntram*, was produced at Weimar in 1894 and in the same year Strauss became conductor of the Berlin Philharmonic Orchestra. *Salome*, his opera upon a German translation of Oscar Wilde's play, produced in 1905, led to his concentration upon opera, and *Elektra* (1909) began the collaboration with the dramatic poet Hugo v. Hofmannsthal which produced much of Strauss's best work for the theatre, including the popular *Der Rosenkavalier* (1911) and *Ariadne auf Naxos* (1912). His work with Stefan Zweig upon *Die schweigsame Frau* led him into difficulties with the Nazi government, which had previously appointed him president of the Reichsmusikkammer, a post which he resigned; his commanding position at the head of German musical life protected him from serious political persecution, and, active to the end of his life, he worked on two operas with Josef Gregor. After the completion of *Capriccio*, his final opera, he ended his career with a series of small-scale orchestral works. See Life by W. S. Mann (1954), and studies by Newman (1908), Blom (1930), Armstrong (1931) and Del Mar (1962).

STRAVINSKY, Igor Fedorovich, *-vin'-* (1882–1971), Russian composer, born at Oranienbaum near St Petersburg, June 18, studied law but soon turned to musical composition under Rimsky-Korsakov, whose influence pervades his first symphony in E flat (1907). But it was with the Diaghilev ballet that Stravinsky leapt to fame with the glittering and enchanting music for *The Firebird* (1910). A second ballet, *Petrushka* (1911), consolidated his international reputation. Originally it was intended as a purely orchestral piece, characterized by harmonic warfare between solo pianoforte and the orchestra, but on Diaghilev's suggestion Stravinsky made it into a ballet of puppet drama. His masterful handling of the eternal triangle theme has had a greater influence on modern music than his deliberately violent, chaotic musical protrayal of the primitive *The Rite of Spring* (1913), which infringes every canon of harmony, yet somehow achieves a strange integration. The Hans Andersen opera, *The Nightingale* (1914), was followed by the wartime 'shoe-string' entertainments, *Renard* (1917) and *The Soldier's Tale* (1918), which aptly illustrate Stravinsky's adaptability. Essentially an experimenter, he then plunged headlong into neoclassicism. The ballets *Pulcinella* (1920) based on Pergolesi, *Apollo Musagetes* (1928), *The Card Game* (1937), *Orpheus* (1948) and the austere *Agon* (1957), using Schönberg's 12-tone system, exemplify this trend, no less than the opera-oratorio *Oedipus Rex* (1927) based on a Jean Cocteau version but translated into Latin for greater dignity, and the magnificent choral *Symphony of Psalms* (1930) 'composed to the glory of God'. Stravinsky settled in France (1934) and finally in the U.S. (1945). Other characteristic and outstanding works include the *Symphonies of Wind Instruments*, dedicated to Debussy (1921), the *Symphony in C major* (1940), the opera *The Rake's Progress* (1951) for which Auden helped to write the libretto, and the serial-music *In Memoriam Dylan Thomas* (1954), for voice, string quartet and four trombones, *The Flood* (1962), a musical play, *Elegy for J. F. K.* (1964), for voice and clarinets, *Variations* (1965) for orchestra in memory of Aldous Huxley, and *Requiem Canticles* (1966), for voice and orchestra. In 1939, he was Charles Eliot Norton professor of Poetry at Harvard and in 1954 was awarded the gold medal of the Royal Philharmonic Society. See his *Chronicles of My Life* (1936) and *The Poetics of Music*, and studies, ed. M. Armitage (N.Y. 1946), E. W. White (1947), ed. Corle (N.Y. 1949), Lederman (ed.), *Stravinsky in the Theatre* (1951), Life by Vlad (trans. 1960), *Conversations*, I. Stravinsky and R. Craft (3 vols. 1959–62), and White, *The Composer and His Works* (1966). His son, **Sviatoslav Soulima** (1910–), is also pianist, composer and teacher.

STRAWSON, Peter Frederick (1919–), English philosopher, fellow of University College, Oxford (1948–68), and of Magdalen College from 1968. He became Waynflete professor of Metaphysical Philosophy at Oxford in 1968. Strawson applied Wittgensteinian doctrines in his standard work, *Introduction to Logical Theory* (1952), in which he demonstrated the impossibility of justifying induction and in which he ably defended 'informal' logic against Quine and Russell, whose theory of description he attacked in an article in *Mind* (1950) 'On Referring', showing that whereas a sentence could be meaningless or significant, only a statement could be classified as true or false. His *Individuals* (1959) tackles the conceptual problems involved in these the fundamentals of human thought. *The Bounds of Sense* appeared in 1966.

STREET, George Edmund (1824–81), British architect, born at Woodford, Essex; an assistant of Sir George Gilbert Scott (q.v.), he restored Christ Church in Dublin, designed the London Law Courts, and wrote *Architecture of N. Italy* (1855) and *Gothic Architecture in Spain* (1865). See Memoirs by his son (1888), by G. G. King (1917).

STREICHER, Julius, *strīKH'ėr* (1885–1946), German journalist and politician, born in Bavaria. He was associated with Hitler in the early days of the National Socialist party, taking part in the 1923 putsch. A ruthless persecutor of the Jews, he incited anti-Semitism through the newspaper *Der Stürmer*, which he founded and edited, and of which copies were widely displayed in prominent red boxes throughout the Reich.

He was hanged at Nuremberg as a war criminal.

STRESEMANN, Gustav, *shtray'zė-man* (1878–1929), German statesman, born in Berlin. Entering the Reichstag in 1907 as a National Liberal, he rose to become leader of that party, and after the first World War founded and led its successor, the German People's party. He was chancellor of the new German (Weimar) Republic for a few months in 1923, when, and as minister of foreign affairs (1923–29), he pursued a policy of conciliation, and in 1925 negotiated the Locarno Pact of mutual security with Aristide Briand and Austen Chamberlain. He secured the entry of Germany into the League of Nations in 1926, and shared with Briand the Nobel peace prize for that year. See the biography by A. Vallentin (trans. E. Sutton, 1931) and study by Gatzke (1954).

STREUVELS, Stijn, *stræ'-* (1871–), pen-name of **Frank Lateur,** Flemish writer, until 1905 a baker near Courtrai. His novels of peasant life are masterpieces of Flemish literature. See his *Path of Life* (trans. 1915).

STRIJDOM, Johannes Gerhardus, *strī'dom* (1893–1958), South African statesman, born at Willowmore, Cape Province. He was educated at Stellenbosch and Pretoria, and after a start as a farmer, took up law practice in the Transvaal. Elected M.P. for Waterberg in 1929 he became leader of the extremists in the National party. His two main political ends were native apartheid and the setting up of an Afrikaner Republic outside the Commonwealth. He was prime minister of South Africa from 1954 until shortly before his death.

STRINDBERG, Johan August (1849–1912), Swedish dramatist, born at Stockholm, studied at Uppsala University and settled in Stockholm as a writer. His own unstable personality, three unsuccessful marriages and the critical society around him are reflected in his subjective works against the background of whatever 'ism' was momentarily holding his attention, for he ranged through realism, naturalism, mysticism, romanticism, and even a hint of expressionism. Novels, plays, critical essays, scientific preoccupations, painting, all laid claim to his time. From his first play, the historical *Mäster Olof* (1872), and in works such as *Hemsöborna* (1887) 'The People of Hemsö' (trans. 1959), one of the classic novels of Swedish literature, he poured out his views on the social problems of his time. Particularly was he obsessed by a hatred of the idea of emancipation for women and much of his work is vitiated by his misogynist bias, as also by his exasperated sensibilities exploding into violent diatribe or sinking into profoundly mournful brooding. He first achieved fame with his novel *Röda Rummet* (1879), a satire on the art circles of Stockholm, and he followed this up with the plays *Gillets Hemlighet* (1880), *Lycko-Pers Resa* (1882) and *Herr Bengts Hustru* (1882). He sojourned in France, Switzerland and Denmark and published his *Giftas I* and *II* (1884–86), collections of short stories, which led to his recall to Sweden (1884) to stand trial for alleged blasphemy. He next set to work on his autobiography—*Tjänstekvinnans son* (1886) 'The Son of a Servant' (trans. 1913), a piece of self-revelation of audacious candour. He continued to write short stories, but his ideas began to take shape in play form again and *Fadren* (1887) and *Fröken Julie* (1888) brought him to the forefront as the exponent of naturalistic drama. Further reminiscences *Inferno* (1897) and *Legender* (1898), carry on his autobiography. In 1901 appeared *Dödsdansen* 'The Dance of Death' (trans 1929), followed by historical dramas, miracle plays and 'fairy' pieces which led him finally to what he called 'chamber plays' written for his *Intimate Theatre,* which he founded in 1907. His work suffers from his own self-contradictions, which obscured the social problems he was dramatizing. Nevertheless, in terms of imaginative power he ranks high after Ibsen, a major figure in west European literature. See Collected Works (55 vols. 1912–20), and studies by N. Erdmann (Stockholm 1920), K. Jaspers (1922), V. J. McGill (1930), A. Jolivet (Paris 1931), E. M. S. Sprigge (1949) and B. M. E. Mortensen and B. W. Downs (1949).

STRODE, (1) **Ralph** (fl. 14th cent.), English scholastic philosopher, was fellow of Merton College, Oxford (*c.* 1360), and a colleague of John Wycliffe, whose doctrine of predestination he attacked. Chaucer dedicated to him and to the poet John Gower, his *Troylus and Cryseyde.* Of his works, *Logica* has been lost but *Consequentiae* and *Obligationes* are extant.

(2) **William** (1602–45), English poet and divine, born at Plympton, educated at Westminster and Christ Church College, Oxford, where he became canon and public orator. He is best known for his elegies and lyric verse which were rediscovered by Dobell in 1907 and for his tragi-comedy, *The Floating Island,* acted by the students of Christ Church before Charles I in 1636.

STROHEIM, Erich von, *-hīm* (1886–1957), Austrian film director and actor, born in Vienna, served in the Austrian army and in 1916 appeared in the American film, *Intolerance.* His first success as film director was with *Blind Husbands* (1919), which was followed by the classic film *Greed* (1923), the war film *The Wedding March* (1927), &c. Later he returned to film acting as 'Rommel' in *Desert Fox.* See monograph by J. M. Finler (1967).

STROMEYER, Friedrich (1776–1835), German chemist, born in Göttingen, and professor of Chemistry there, was the discoverer of cadmium in 1817.

STRONG, Leonard Alfred George (1896–1958), British novelist and poet, of Irish extraction on his mother's side, born at Plymouth, was educated at Brighton College and Wadham College, Oxford, took up school teaching until he established a reputation as a lyric poet and author of *Dewer Rides* (1929), a macabre novel set in Dartmoor. The element of cruelty survived in *The Brothers* (1932). His collected poems appeared under *The Body's Imperfections* (1957). He also wrote a study of James Joyce (1950) and a Life of the singer John McCormack (1949). His collection of short stories, *Travellers*, won the James Tait Black memorial prize (1945). See his autobiographical *Green Memory* (1960).

STRONGBOW, name by which **Richard de Clare, 2nd Earl of Pembroke** (*c.* 1130–1176), was known. He succeeded to estates in Normandy and Wales and in 1170 crossed to Ireland by permission of Henry II to give military help to Dermot, King of Leinster, whose daughter he married. He offered his Irish conquests to Henry to appease the latter's jealousy of his success.

STROUD, William, *strowd* (1860–1938), English physicist and inventor, born in Bristol. From 1885 to 1909 he was Cavendish professor of Physics at Leeds, where began his long association with Archibald Barr (q.v.).

STROZZI, *strot'see*, a noble Italian family which figured prominently in the Florentine renaissance. Important members include:

(1) **Filippo the Elder** (1428–91), having been deprived by the Medici, was exiled to Sicily but returned in 1466. He began building the famous Palazzo Strozzi in 1489.

(2) **Filippo the Younger** (1489–1538), was prominent in the revolt which overthrew the Medici in 1527, but the republic then established lasted only three years. The restored Medici, Alessandro, having been assassinated in 1537, Filippo judged the time opportune to launch an attack on his successor Cosimo, but was captured and executed.

(3) **Palla** (1372–1462), promoted Greek studies in Florence and founded the first public library there.

(4) **Pietro** (d. 1558), Italian soldier, fought the Medici, escaped to France and was made a marshal of France by Henry II in 1556 after campaigns in Italy. He found out the weaknesses of the defences of Calais before its capture by Guise in 1558, and was killed at the siege of Thionville.

STRUENSEE, Johann Friedrich, Count, *shtrün'zay* (1737–72), German-born Danish statesman, son of a Halle pastor, in 1768 became physician to Christian VII of Denmark. He soon gained the confidence of the weak young king and of his consort, Caroline Matilda (1751–75), George III's sister, and, with her monopolizing all power, sought to free Denmark from Russian influence and to find an ally in Sweden. His reforms and retrenchments were unpopular; but it was solely by a court intrigue that in January 1772 the queen and her new-made count were arrested. From both a confession of criminal intimacy was extorted; and Struensee, found guilty of treason, was beheaded. Queen Caroline's marriage was dissolved; she was conveyed by a British frigate to Hanover, and died at Zell (Celle). See *Memoirs* (1849) of Sir R. M. Keith, British envoy; Wraxall's *Life of Queen Caroline* (1864); and Wilkins, *A Queen of Tears* (1903).

STRUTHER, Jan, pseud. of **Mrs Joyce Anstruther Piaczek** (1901–53), English writer, born in London. Her most successful creation was Mrs Miniver, whose activities, first narrated in articles to *The Times*, became the subject of one of the best films of World War II. Miss Struther's writings were varied in character and included hymns, verse, short stories and novels, all exhibiting considerable talent but little originality. Her books of verse include *Betsinda Dances* (1931) and *The Glassblower* (1940).

STRUTT, (1) **Jedediah** (1726–97), English cotton spinner and inventor, born at Blackwell, Derbyshire. With his brother-in-law, William Woollatt, he patented (1758–59) a machine which, fixed to a stocking-frame, made possible the manufacture of ribbed goods. In 1771 he was joined in partnership by Richard Arkwright (q.v.). See R. S. Fitton and A. P. Wadsworth, *The Strutts and the Arkwrights, 1758–1830* (1959).

(2) **John William.** See RAYLEIGH (1).

(3) **Joseph** (1742–1802), English antiquary and engraver, born at Springfield in Essex, at fourteen was apprenticed to an engraver, studied at the Royal Academy, and from 1771 devoted himself to research at the British Museum. He published *Regal and Ecclesiastical Antiquities of England* (1773); *Chronicle of England*, down to the Conquest (1777–78); *Dictionary of Engravers* (1785–1786); *Dresses of the People of England* (1796–99); and, his best-known work, *Sports and Pastimes of the People of England* (1801; enlarged 1903). See Life by Miller-Christy (1898).

STRUVE, *shtroo'vė*, (1) **Friedrich Georg Wilhelm** (1793–1864), German astronomer, father of (2), grandfather of (3), born at Altona, became director of the Dorpat observatory in 1817, and in 1839 of Pulkova near St Petersburg, which was constructed to his specifications through the patronage of Tsar Nicholas. He made important observations of double stars, carried out one of the first determinations of stellar distance and several geodetic operations.

(2) **Otto Wilhelm** (1819–1905), German astronomer, son of (1), born at Dorpat, succeeded his father at Pulkova, discovered 500 double stars and in 1847 a satellite of Uranus, and studied the rings of Saturn. His son **Hermann** (1854–1920) was director of the Berlin observatory (1904) and superintended its transfer to Babelsberg. He made micrometric observations of the satellites of Mars, Neptune and Saturn. Another son, **Ludwig** (1858–1920), was professor of Astronomy at Kharkov and investigated the proper motion of the solar system. Ludwig's son **Otto** (1897–1963) became a U.S. citizen and director of the Yerkes and McDonald observatories (1932).

(3) **Peter Berngardovich** (1870–1944), Russian political economist, grandson of (1), born in Perm, as a leading Marxist wrote *Critical Observations on the Problem of Russia's Economic Development* (1894), which Lenin attacked for its 'revisionism'. He edited several political magazines with Liberal tendencies, was professor at the St Petersburg Polytechnic (1907–17), was closely connected with the 'White' movement in South Russia, after the revolution and after 1925 lived in exile in Belgrade and Paris, where he died during the Nazi occupation. Perhaps the greatest Russian economist, his principal work is *Economy and Price* (1913–1916). See S. Hoare, *The Fourth Seal* (1930),

and Bernard Pares, *My Russian Memoirs* (1931).

STRYDOM. See STRIJDOM.

STRYPE, John (1643–1737), English ecclesiastical historian, born in London, was educated at St Paul's School and Cambridge, and became curate of Low Leyton, Essex. His prolix and reliable, if ill-arranged, works (19 vols., Clar. Press edn., 1812–24) include *Memorials of Cranmer* (1694); Lives of Bishop Aylmer (1701), Sir John Cheke (1705), Archbishop Grindal (1710), Archbishop Parker (1711), and Archbishop Whitgift (1718); *Annals of the Reformation* (1709–31); *Ecclesiastical Memorials, 1513–58* (1721). He also completely re-edited and enlarged Stow's *Survey of London* (1720).

STUART (noble family). See STEWART and ALBANIE.

STUART, (1) Gilbert Charles (1755–1828), American painter, born at Narragansett, Rhode Island, in 1772 came to Edinburgh with a Scottish painter, Cosmo Alexander, but on the latter's death worked his passage home, and began to paint portraits at Newport. In 1775 he made his way to London, where he endured much hardship till in 1778 his talent was recognized by West, and he became a fashionable portrait painter in the manner of Reynolds. In 1792 he returned to America, and painted portraits of Washington, Jefferson, Madison and John Adams. He died at Boston. He is well represented in the National Portrait Gallery, London. See Lives by G. C. Mason (1879), L. Park (1926) and J. H. Morgan (1936).

(2) **James** (1713–88), English architect, born in London, known as the 'Athenian Stuart' for his drawings and measurements with Nicholas Revett of the *Antiquities of Athens* (1762–1814). He also rebuilt the interior of the chapel of Greenwich Hospital (1779), &c.

(3) **John McDouall** (1815–66), Scottish-born Australian explorer, born at Dysart, Fife, accompanied Captain Sturt's expedition (1844–45), made six expeditions into the interior (1858–62), and in 1860 traversed Australia from south to north. Mount Stuart is named after him. See Life by M. S. Webster (1959).

(4) **Lady Louisa** (1757–1851), Sir Walter Scott's witty correspondent, the Earl of Bute's youngest daughter. See Life by S. Buchan (1932).

(5) **Marie Pauline Rose.** See BLAZE DE BURY.

(6) **Moses** (1780–1852), American theologian, born at Wilton, Conn., studied at Yale, was professor of Sacred Literature at Andover (1810–48). He published Hebrew grammars, commentaries on the Old Testament, &c.

STUBBES, (1) John (*c.* 1541–91), English Puritan pamphleteer, kinsman of (2), educated at Cambridge and Lincoln's Inn, wrote an answer to Cardinal Allen's *Defence of the English Catholics* and *The Discoverie of a Gaping Gulf* (1579), against the marriage of Elizabeth with the Duke of Anjou, for which he and his printer had their right hands struck off. He died in France.

(2) **Philip** (d. 1593), English Puritan pamphleteer, kinsman of (1), was author of the *Anatomie of Abuses* (1583), a vehement denunciation of the luxury of the times. The work was reprinted by Turnbull in 1836, and by Furnivall (1879–82).

STUBBS, (1) George (1724–1806), English anatomist, painter of animals, and engraver, born at Liverpool. He studied and taught anatomy at York Hospital, and in 1754 travelled in Italy and Morocco. In 1766 he published his monumental *Anatomy of the Horse*, illustrated by his own engravings. He was best known for his sporting pictures, and excelled in painting horses. One of his noted works is his picture of *The Grosvenor Hunt*. In 1780 he was elected A.R.A., and R.A. in 1781. See Life by Gilbey (1898), and Memoir by Mayer (1876). His son, **George Townley** (1756–1815), was also an engraver.

(2) **William** (1825–1901), English historian, born at Knaresborough, studied at Ripon and Christ Church, Oxford. He became a fellow of Trinity, vicar of Navestock, Essex (1850), diocesan inspector of schools (1860), Oxford regius professor of Modern History (1866), rector of Cholderton, Wilts (1875), a canon of St Paul's (1879), and Bishop of Chester (1884), of Oxford (1889). His chief works are *Registrum Sacrum Anglicanum*, on the Episcopal succession in England (1858); Mosheim's *Institutes*, revised (1863); *Select Charters*, from the earliest period to the reign of Edward I (1870); the monumental three-volume *Constitutional History of England*, down to 1485 (1874–78), which put the study of English constitutional origins on a firm basis; *The Early Plantagenets* (1876); and a number of volumes for the 'Rolls Series'. With Haddan, he began a collection of *British Councils and Ecclesiastical Documents* (1869–78). See his *Letters* (1904).

STUCKENBERG, Viggo (1863–1905), Danish poet, born at Copenhagen, was an important figure in the lyrical revival of the 1890s. His works include *Fagre Ord* (1895), *Flyvende Sommer* (1898), &c.

STUKELEY, William, the 'Archdruid' (1687–1765), British antiquarian, was born at Holbeach. M.B. and M.D. (Cantab.), in 1729 took orders, and in 1747 became a London rector. His twenty works (1720–26) include records of his valuable and objective fieldwork at Stonehenge and Avebury, but are marred by his later fantastic speculations. He was the dupe of the brilliant 'Richard of Cirencester' forgeries. See his *Diary and Correspondence* (Surtees Soc. 1884–87), and Life by Piggott (1950).

STURDEE, Sir Frederick Charles Doveton, 1st Bart. (1859–1925), British sailor, entered the navy in 1871, commanded the squadron which wiped out the German squadron under von Spee off the Falkland Islands, December 8, 1914, was created baronet, served at the battle of Jutland and was promoted admiral of the fleet (1921).

STURE, *stoo'rė*, name of a Swedish family which during 1470–1520, when Sweden was nominally united with Denmark, gave it three wise and patriotic regents—Sten Sture the Elder (d. 1503); his nephew, Svante Nilsson

Sture (d. 1512); and his son, Sten Sture the Younger (d. 1520).

STURGE, Joseph (1794–1859), English Quaker philanthropist and Radical, born at Elberton, became a corn merchant in Birmingham and a prominent campaigner against slavery, the Corn Laws, the Crimean war and for Chartism, adult suffrage, &c. See Lives by H. Richard (1864) and S. Hobhouse (1919).

STURGEON, William (1783–1850), English scientist, born at Whittington, North Lancashire, became a shoemaker's apprentice and in 1825 constructed the first practical electromagnet, the first moving-coil galvanometer (1836) and various electromagnetic machines. His *Annals of Electricity* (1836) was the first journal of its kind in Britain.

STURLASON. See SNORRI.

STURM, (1) Jacques Charles François, *stürm* (1803–55), French mathematician, born at Geneva, died, an Academician, in Paris. He discovered the theorem named after him concerning the real roots of an equation. With Colladon, in 1826, he measured the velocity of sound in water by means of a bell submerged in Lake Geneva.

(2) **Johannes,** *shtoorm* (1507–89), German educationist, born at Schleiden near Aix-la-Chapelle, from the Liège school of the Brethren of the Common Life went to Louvain University, and at Paris in 1530 lectured on Cicero. He favoured the Reformation, and in 1536 was invited by Strasbourg to reorganize the education of the town. Both in religion and politics Sturm took a prominent part, siding with Zwingli against Luther; and he was sent on missions to France, England and Denmark. Through his efforts, Strasbourg became a great educational centre. In 1538 a gymnasium was established, with Sturm as its rector, and in 1564 an academy, the two together supplying a complete course of instruction. In 1581 he was driven from Strasbourg by Lutheran intolerance, but was ultimately permitted to return. See French monograph by Charles Schmidt (Strasbourg 1855), and German works by Laas (1872), Kückelhahn (1872), Heil (1888) and Schnud (1889).

STURT, Charles (1795–1869), British explorer, went as an army captain to Australia, and during 1828–45 headed three important expeditions, discovered the Darling (1828), the lower Murray (1830). Blinded by hardship and exposure, he received in 1851 a pension from the first South Australian parliament. He wrote two narratives of his explorations (1833–48), and died at Cheltenham, England. See Life by N. G. Sturt (1899).

STUYVESANT, Peter, *stī'-* (1592–1672), Dutch administrator, born in Holland, became governor of Curaçao and lost a leg in the attack on St Martin in 1644. As director from 1646 of New Netherland colony (later New York), he proved a vigorous but arbitrary ruler, a rigid sabbatarian, and an opponent of political and religious freedom. Yet he did much for the commercial prosperity of New Amsterdam (later New York city) until his reluctant surrender to the English in 1664. See Life by B. Tuckerman (N.Y. 1893).

STYLITES. See SIMEON STYLITES.

SUAREZ, Francisco de, *swah'reth* (1584–1617), Spanish-Jewish Jesuit theologian and scholastic philosopher, born at Granada, taught theology at Segovia, Valladolid, Rome, Alcala, Salamanca and Coimbra. A Molinist in his views of grace, he foreshadowed in his *Tractatus de Legibus* (1612) the modern doctrine of international law, and wrote the *Defensio Fidei* (1613), a treatise condemning the extravagant divine-right theories of James I of England. See Lives by Deschamps (1671), Werner (1861) and Fichter (1940).

SUCHET, Louis Gabriel, Duc d'Albufera, *sü-shay* (1770–1826), French soldier, born at Lyons, fought in Italy and Egypt and was made a general. He checked an Austrian invasion of the south of France (1800), took part in the campaigns against Austria (1805) and Prussia (1806), and as generalissimo of the French army in Aragon reduced the province to submission, defeating Blake outside Saragossa and again at Belchite, and securing a marshal's baton. He captured Tortosa in 1811, in 1812 destroyed Blake's army at Sagunto, and by his capture of Valencia earned the title of Duc d Albufera. He was created a peer of France by Louis XVIII, but joined Napoleon on his return from Elba. Deprived of his peerage after Waterloo, he did not return to court till 1819. See his *Mémoires sur les campagnes en Espagne* (1829–34), and Life by Barault-Roullon (1954).

SUCRE, Antonio José de, *soo'kray* (1793–1830), South American soldier-patriot, born in Cumana, Venezuela, was Bolivar's lieutenant and first president (1826) of Bolivia, which he freed. He resigned in 1828, took service with Colombia, winning the battle of Giron (1829) and was assassinated on his way home from the Colombian Congress, of which he had been president. See Life by G. A. Sherwell (1924).

SUDERMANN, Hermann, *soo'-* (1857–1928), German dramatist and novelist, born at Matzicken, East Prussia, wrote a succession of skilful, if superficial, realist plays, *Die Ehre* (1889), *Sodoms Ende* (1891), *Heimat* (1893; English version, *Magda*), &c., and equally successful novels, including *Frau Sorge* (1887), *Der Katzensteg* (1890), *Es war* (1894), &c.

SUE, (Marie Joseph) Eugène, *sü* (1804–57), French novelist, born in Paris, served as surgeon in Spain (1823) and at Navarino Bay (1827) and wrote a vast number of Byronic novels, many of which were dramatized, idealizing the poor to the point of melodramatic absurdity, but nevertheless highly successful at the time and a profound influence upon Victor Hugo, whose *Les Misérables* has much in common with Sue's *Les Mystères de Paris* (1843). Other novels include *Le Juif errant* (1845), *Les Sept Péchés capitaux* (1849) and *Les Mystères du peuple* (1849), the last condemned as immoral and seditious. A republican deputy, he was driven into exile in 1851 and died at Annecy. See Life by E. de Mirecourt (1858), and study by N. Atkinson (1929).

SUESS, Eduard, *züs* (1831–1914), Austrian geologist, founder of the 'new geology', was born in London, became professor of

Geology at Vienna 1857–1901. Of his works, *Das Antlitz der Erde* (1885–1909; trans. as *The Face of the Earth*, 1904–10) was the most important. He was a Radical politician, an economist, an educationist, a geographer, and sat in the Austrian Lower House.

SUETONIUS, Gaius Suetonius Tranquillus (A.D. 75–160), Roman biographer and antiquarian, became Hadrian's secretary, a post he held till about fifty, when, compromised in a court intrigue, he forfeited it. His best-known work is *The Lives of the First Twelve Caesars*, remarkable for terseness, elegance and impartiality. Other works were *De Illustribus Grammaticis* (of which a complete copy existed in the 15th century), *De Claris Rhetoribus*, and fragmentary lives of Terence, Horace, Persius, Lucan, Juvenal and Pliny, a friend of his.

SUETONIUS PAULINUS. See BOADICEA.

SUFFOLK. See BRANDON and POLE (1).

SUFFREN SAINT TROPEZ, Pierre André de, *süf-frã sĩ trō-pay* (1729–88), French sailor, a younger son of a Provençal noble, entered the French navy, fought in the action with the English off Toulon (1744) and in the vain attempt to retake Cape Breton (1746), was captured by Hawke next year, and served six years in Malta amongst the Knights Hospitallers. He was again captured in Boscawen's destruction of the Toulon fleet (1759), took part in the bombardment of Sallee (1765), was again four years in Malta, and returned to France as captain in 1772. In 1777 he sailed to America, and fought at Grenada in 1779. After an action at the Cape Verde Islands, he fought a series of engagements with the English off Madras and Ceylon, and captured Trincomalee. Returning to Paris in 1784, he was received with great honours. See Laughton's *Naval Studies* (1887).

SUGDEN, Samuel (1892–1950), English chemist, born at Leeds, was professor at Birkbeck College (1932) and University College London (1937). He did original work on molecular volumes and surface tension and introduced the *parachor*.

SUGER, *sü-zhay* (*c.* 1081–1151), French prelate, abbot of St Denis from 1122, carried out substantial reforms and rebuilt its church in the Gothic style, the first building to be so done. Louis VI and Louis VII employed him on a number of missions, and during the latter's absence on the second crusade, Suger was one of the regents. His Life of Louis VI (ed H. Waquet, 1929) is valuable for the view it affords of the time. See his writings on the church of St Denis and its art treasures, trans. Panofsky (1946).

SUGGIA, Guilhermina, *sood'ja* (1888–1950), Portuguese cellist, born in Oporto. She was a member of the Oporto City Orchestra at the age of twelve, and aided by a royal grant, she subsequently studied at Leipzig and under Casals, whom she married in 1906. After extensive concert tours she settled in England in 1914, last appearing in public at the 1949 Edinburgh Festival.

SUHRAWARDY, Husein Shaheed (1893–1963), Pakistani politician, born in East Bengal and educated at Oxford. In 1921 he became a member of the Bengal Assembly. He was Pakistan's minister of law (1954–55) and prime minister (1956–57).

SUIDAS, *swee'das*, the reputed author of an encyclopaedic Greek *Lexicon*, about whom nothing is known, although he is placed about A.D. 975.

SUK, Joseph, *sook* (1875–1935), Czech composer and violinist, studied in Prague under Dvořák, whose daughter he married, and carried on the master's romantic tradition by his violin *Fantaisie* (1903), the symphonic poem *Prague* and particularly by his deeply-felt second symphony, *Asrael* (1905), in which he mourned the deaths of his master and of his wife. He was for forty years a member of the Czech Quartet and in 1922 became professor of Composition in the Prague Conservatoire.

SUKARNO, Achmad (1902–70), Indonesian statesman, born in Surabaya, Eastern Java, was early identified with the movement for independence, forming the Partai National Indonesia in 1927. He was freed by the Japanese and became the first president of the Indonesian Republic in 1945. The tremendous popularity of 'Bung Karno' with the people was gradually eroded as Indonesia suffered increasing internal chaos and poverty, while Sukarno and his government laid themselves open to charges of corruption. His protestations of political 'neutralism' were offset by his increasingly virulent anti-Western foreign policy. The abortive Communist *coup* of 1965 led to student riots and Congress criticism of Sukarno's alleged part in it, and the army eventually took over. Sukarno's absolute powers were gradually weakened until finally in 1967 General Suharto took complete control, Sukarno remaining president in name only. See studies by Gerbrandy (1950), Woodman (1955) and Hughes (1968).

SULAIMAN, *sü-lay-man'*, name of three sultans of Turkey:

Sulaiman I (d. 1411), eldest son of Bajazet I, ruled in Adrianople from 1403.

Sulaiman I or II, 'the Magnificent' (1494–1566), sultan from 1520, son of Sultan Selim I, added to his dominions by conquest Belgrade, Budapest, Rhodes, Tabriz, Baghdad, Aden and Algiers. He fought a war with Venice, and his fleets dominated the Mediterranean, although he failed to capture Malta. He died during the siege of Szigeth in his war with Austria. His system of laws regulating land tenure earned him the name, *Kanuni*, the lawgiver. He was devoted to 'Roxelana', his Russian consort, was a great patron of arts, wrote poetry and employed Selim Sinan to build such architectural masterpieces as the four mosques to himself and to members of his family in Constantinople. He was the greatest of the sultans. See histories of the Ottoman Empire by H. A. Gibbons (1916), W. Miller (1927).

Sulaiman II or III (1641–91), sultan from 1687, was defeated by the Austrians, but through Mustafa Kuprili introduced many liberal reforms.

SULEIMAN PASHA, *soo-lī'man* (1838–92), Turkish general, entered the army in 1854, fought in Montenegro, Crete and Yemen, and in peace taught in the Military Academy at Constantinople, of which he became director. He distinguished himself against the Serbians in 1876. When the Russians declared war (1877) Suleiman checked them at Eski Zagra, but destroyed his army in heroic attempts to force them from the Shipka Pass. In October he became commander-in-chief of the army of the Danube, but suffered defeat near Philippopolis (January 1878). Court-martialled, he was condemned to fifteen years' imprisonment, but the sultan pardoned him.

SULLA (inaccurately **Sylla**), **Lucius Cornelius**, by himself surnamed **Felix** (138–78 B.C.), Roman general and statesman, was a scion of the illustrious house of the Cornelii. As quaestor in 107 under Marius in Africa he had first secured the line of retreat from Mauretania and then induced the Mauritanian king to surrender Jugurtha (106). The war of the Cimbri and Teutones (104–101) saw Sulla again serving under the jealous Marius. In 93 he was praetor and in 92 propraetor in Cilicia, where, on his own responsibility, he raised an army and restored Ariobarzanes to the throne of Cappadocia, from which Mithradates had expelled him. The private hatred of Marius and Sulla became political, as Sulla took the aristocratic side more strongly; but the breaking out of the Social War put an end to all private quarrels for the time. Marius was aggrieved when the senate bestowed on Sulla, after his consulship in 88, supreme command in the Mithradatic war; and Marius rushed into treason and civil strife. Then followed the expulsion of Sulla, his triumphant return to Rome at the head of six legions, the overthrow of the Marian party, and the first proscription. By the beginning of 87 Sulla was able to embark for the East. During his four years there he won the victories of Chaeronea (86) and Orchomenus. Next he crossed the Hellespont, crushed the army sent out by the Marian party (which, in his absence, had again got the upper hand in Italy), forced Mithradates to sue for peace, then landed in Italy in 83. Marius was dead and had no worthy successors, and the victory over the Samnites and Lucanians at the Colline Gate brought the struggle to a close (82), and left Sulla master of Italy. Then followed his dictatorship, and the proscriptions (81)—a virtual reign of terror. During the next two years he made several important constitutional changes, mostly reactionary, tending to increase the authority of the senate—nearly all were rescinded within ten years—and he effected a permanent reform of the criminal courts. In 79 Sulla rather unexpectedly resigned the dictatorship and retired to his estate at Puteoli, where he ended his life in thorough dissipation. See Life by P. Baker (1927), and French study by J. Carcopina (1931).

SULLIVAN, (1) **Sir Arthur Seymour** (1842–1900), English composer, best known for his partnership with the librettist, Sir William Schwenck Gilbert (q.v.) in the 'Gilbert and Sullivan' light operas; born in London, May 13, studied music under Sterndale Bennett and at the Leipzig *Gewandhaus*. Together with his friend Sir George Grove (q.v.) he discovered the lost *Rosamunde* music by Schubert. His association with the theatre, begun with his music to Morton's *Box and Cox*, was consolidated by his eighteen years' partnership with Gilbert, which after *Thespis* in 1871 produced thirteen other comic operas; *Trial by Jury* (1875), *The Sorcerer* (1877), *H.M.S. Pinafore* (1878), *The Pirates of Penzance* (1880), *Patience* (1881), *Iolanthe* (1882), *Princess Ida* (1884), *The Mikado* (1885), *Ruddigore* (1887), *The Yeoman of the Guard* (1888), *The Gondoliers* (1889), *Utopia Limited* (1893) and *The Grand Duke* (1896). Sullivan also composed an opera, cantatas, ballads, a *Te Deum*, and hymn-tunes, became first principal of the National Training College (1871), later the Royal College of Music, and was knighted in 1883. He was buried in St Paul's Cathedral. See Life by H. Sullivan and N. Flower (1950), joint Lives by I. Goldberg (1929) and H. Pearson (1935), G. E. Dunn, *Gilbert and Sullivan Dictionary* (1936), and study by G. Hughes (1960).

(2) **John** (1740–95), American general, served in Canada (1776) and at Trenton and Brandywine. He fought against the Six Nations in 1779 and won the battle of Newtown.

(3) **John Lawrence** (1858–1918), American boxer, born in Boston, world heavyweight champion from 1882, when he beat Paddy Ryan. His famous fight with Jake Kilrain in 1889 was the subject of a poem by Vachel Lindsay. See Life by Fleischer.

(4) **Louis Henri** (1856–1924), American architect, born in Boston, studied in Paris and won the New Exposition building contract (1886) with Dankmar Adler. His experimental, functional skeleton constructions of skyscrapers and office blocks, particularly the Gage building and stock exchange, Chicago, earned him the title 'Father of Modernism' and greatly influenced Frank Lloyd Wright (q.v.) and others.

SULLY, **Maximilien de Béthune, Duc de**, *sül-lee* (1560–1641), French financier, Henry IV's great minister, the second son of the Huguenot Baron de Rosny, was born at the château of Rosny near Mantes, December 13. He accompanied Henry of Navarre in his flight from the French court (1576), took an active part in the war, and helped materially to decide the victory of Coutras (1587). At Ivry he captured the standard of Mayenne. He approved of the king's politic conversion, but refused himself to become a Roman Catholic, and throughout the reign remained a trusted counsellor. His first task was the restoration of the economy after 30 years of civil war. Before his time the whole administration was an organized system of pillage; but Rosny made a tour through the provinces, examined the accounts, reduced exemptions from taxation and amassed 110 million livres revenue in the Bastille. The arsenals and fleet were put into good order. In 1606 he was created Duc de Sully. After Henry's assassination he had to resign the superintendence of finance, but was presented by Marie de' Médicis with 300,000 livres. He retired to his estates, Rosny and Villebon, and died December 22, 1641. His Memoirs (1634; critical ed. S. R. Lefèvre 1942), if not rigidly historical, are of priceless value for the reign of Henry IV. They contain the famous grouping of Europe, except Russia and Turkey, into a Christian republic of fifteen states, balanced by an international Amphictyonic Assembly. See books by H. Carré (1932) and H. Pourrat (1942).

SULLY-PRUDHOMME, René François Armand, *prü-dom* (1839–1907), French poet, born at Paris, studied science and developed an interest in philosophy which underlies most of his poetical works. His early *Stances et poèmes* (1865) gained the praises of Sainte-Beuve; later volumes, *Les Épreuves, Croquis italiens, Les Solitudes, Impressions de la guerre, Les Destins, Les Vaines Tendresses, La France, La Révolte des fleurs*, extended his fame as a poet. His finest poems are steeped in a serene but penetrating melancholy. Masterpieces of subtlety are his didactic poems *La Justice* (1878) and *Le Bonheur* (1888). Other works are a metrical translation of book i of Lucretius (new ed. 1886); in prose—*L'Expression dans les beaux arts, Réflexions sur l'art des vers* (1892), *Testament poétique* (1901), *La Vraie Religion selon Pascal* (1905). His *Œuvres complètes* appeared in 1883–1908. Elected to the Academy in 1881, he was awarded the Nobel prize in 1901. He died in Paris. See studies by Zyromski and P. Fons (1907), and Life by E. Estève (1925).

SULPICIUS SEVERUS (*c.* 365–425), French monkish historian, born in Aquitania, wrote a *Chronica*, from the Creation to A.D. 403, and a Life of St Martin of Tours. See study by P. Monceaux (trans. 1928).

SUMMERS, Alphonsus Joseph-Mary Augustus Montague (1880–1948), English priest and man of letters. He wrote brilliantly on the theatre and drama of the Restoration and on other literary subjects, but his most important works are two major reference books on witchcraft, *The History of Witchcraft and Demonology* (1926) and *The Geography of Witchcraft* (1927).

SUMNER, (1) **Charles** (1811–74), American statesman, born in Boston, January 6, graduated at Harvard in 1830, and in 1834 was admitted to the bar and also studied jurisprudence in Europe (1837–40). He took little interest in politics until the threatened extensions of Negro slavery over newly-acquired territory. In 1848 he joined with others to form the Free Soil party. Nominated for congress, he was defeated by the Whig candidate, but in 1851 was elected to the national senate by the combined Free Soil and Democratic votes of the Massachusetts legislature. This post he held for life. At the outset, through abiding by the terms of the Constitution, he stood alone in the senate as the uncompromising opponent of slavery; in 1856, in the senate chamber, he was struck on the head by Preston S. Brooks, a South Carolina member of congress, and incapacitated for public life for nearly four years. In 1860 he delivered a speech on the admission of Kansas as a free state, published as *The Barbarism of Slavery*. The secession of the southern states left the Republican party in full control of both houses of congress, and in 1861 Sumner was elected chairman of the senate committee on foreign affairs. He supported the impeachment of President Johnson, and opposed President Grant's project for the acquisition of San Domingo. His continuous and acrimonious censures on Grant's administration brought about a rupture with the leading Republican politicians, which was rendered complete by his support of Greeley as candidate for the presidency in 1872.

(2) **James Batcheller** (1887–1955), American biochemist, born at Canton, Mass., was educated at Harvard and became professor of Biochemistry at Cornell in 1929. He is noted for his research on enzymes and proteins and shared the Nobel prize for chemistry in 1946 with Northrop and Stanley.

(3) **John Bird** (1780–1862), English theologian, born at Kenilworth, educated at Eton and King's Coll., Cambridge, became rector of Mapledurham, Oxon. (1818), Bishop of Chester (1828), and Archbishop of Canterbury (1848). An Evangelical but conciliatory and moderate, he wrote *Apostolical Preaching* (1815) and *Evidences of Christianity* (1824).

SUMTER, Thomas (1734–1832), American general in the War of Independence, opposed the British under Tarleton in South Carolina. He was defeated at Fishing Creek but gained a victory at Blackstock Hill (1780).

SUNDERLAND, name of an earldom, granted with that of Spencer (q.v.) and the dukedom of Marlborough (q.v.) to members of the English family of Spencer, originating from Robert Despenser, steward to William the Conqueror, and from the Hugh Despensers, favourites of Edward II. **Henry Spencer, 3rd Baron Spencer** (1620–43), was created 1st Earl of Sunderland (1643) and fell in the Civil War at the first battle of Newbury, fighting for the king. His noteworthy descendants and successors, in chronological order, were:

(1) **Robert Spencer, 2nd Earl of** (1641–1702), English politician, son of the above, father of (2), born in Paris, became in 1679 secretary of state for the Northern Department and united with Essex and Halifax in opposing Shaftesbury, who wished to set Monmouth on the throne. He encouraged Charles II to persevere in the French alliance, and, with the Duchess of Portsmouth, negotiated a treaty by which, for a French pension, Charles agreed to assemble no parliament for three years. Before the year was out a new triumvirate, consisting of himself, Hyde and Godolphin, succeeded to the confidence of Charles. The French treaty was broken off, and Sunderland, now afraid of the Whigs, engaged the king in an alliance with Spain. After the dissolution of the last exclusion parliament he lost his office; but in 1682 he was, 'upon great submission made to the Duke [of York], restored to be secretary'. Under James II his influence grew greater than ever, and in 1685 he became principal secretary of state. He alone was entrusted with a knowledge of the king's intention to establish Catholicism, and he openly professed his own conversion. Yet we find him in correspondence with William of Orange. When William came over, Sunderland went to Amsterdam, but in 1691 he was allowed to return to England, and in 1695 William spent a week at his seat, Althorp, then a

rallying-point for the Whigs. He was made lord chamberlain, allegedly for services to William in James II's reign, but resigned in 1697. See Life by J. P. Kenyon (1958).

(2) **Charles Spencer, 3rd Earl of** (1675–1722), English statesman, son of (1), became secretary of state in 1706 and under George I rose to be all-powerful, but was forced to resign in 1721 through public indignation at his part in the South Sea Bubble. His grandson, **John** (1734–83), was created 1st Earl Spencer (q.v.) in 1765.

(3) **Charles Spencer, 3rd Duke of Marlborough, 5th Earl of Sunderland** (1706–58), English soldier, second son of (2), succeeded his brother to the earldom (1729) and in 1733 to the honours of his maternal grandfather, John Churchill, the dukedom of Marlborough. He fought at Dettingen (1743) and in the expedition against St Malo (1758).

SUN YAT-SEN, or **Sun Wen**, *soon* (1866–1925), Chinese revolutionary, born November 12 at Tsuiheng near Canton, brought up by his elder brother in Hawaii, graduated in medicine at Hong Kong in 1892, practising at Macao and Canton. He visited Honolulu in 1894 and founded his first political organization there, the *Hsin Chung Hui* (New China Party). After his first abortive uprising against the Manchus in Canton in 1895, he lived abroad in Japan, America and Britain, studying Western politics and canvassing the support of the Chinese in these countries for his cause. While in London in 1896, he was kidnapped and imprisoned in the Chinese legation and was saved from certain death by the intervention of Sir Edward Cantlie, the surgeon, his former tutor, to whom he smuggled out a letter and who enlisted the help of the British Foreign Office to get him released. After ten unsuccessful uprisings, engineered by Sun from abroad, he was at last victorious in the revolution of 1911. In February 1912 China was proclaimed a republic with Sun as its provisional president. Sun, however, made way for the Northern general, Yüan Shih-kai (q.v.) who had forced the emperor's abdication, but as president (1913–16) sought to make himself dictator. Sun opposing him from the South, was defeated and found himself again in exile. In 1923 he was back in Canton and elected president of the southern republic. With expert help from the Russians, Sun reorganized the Kuomintang and established the Whampoa Military Academy under Chiang Kai-shek (q.v.), who three years after Sun's death achieved the unification of China under a government inspired by Sun's *San Min Chu I* (1927) or *The Three Principles of the People*, in short nationalism, democracy and livelihood. While at a conciliatory conference with other Chinese political leaders he died of cancer in Peking, March 12, 1925. Acknowledged by all political factions as the father of the Chinese Republic, he was reinterred in a mausoleum built in his honour in Nanking in 1928. Sun was essentially empirical in his political teachings and rejected the Communist dogma of the class war. See Lives by J. Cantlie (1912), L. S. Sharman (1934), Buck (1954), and B. Martin, *Strange Vigour* (1944), and studies by F. W. Price (1929), P. M. A. Linebarger (1937) and N. Gangulee (1945). His second wife, **Ching Ling Soong** (1890–   ), one of the Soong family (q.v.), was educated in the United States, became Sun's secretary and in 1916 married him. After his death, she lived in Moscow (1927–31) and became a bitter left-wing opponent of her brother-in-law, Chiang Kai-shek, returning to China from Hong Kong during the Japanese war in 1937. In 1950 she was one of the three non-Communist vice-chairmen of the new Chinese Communist Republic.

SUPERVIELLE, Jules, *sü-per-vyel* (1884–1960), French-Uruguayan writer, born at Montevideo, wrote many volumes of poems (including the notable *Poèmes de la France malheureuse*, 1939-41), novels, tales (*L'Enfant de la haute mer*, 1931; *L'Arche de Noé*, 1938), plays (*La Belle au bois*, 1932; *Shéhérazade*, 1949), and *Bolivar*, an opera with music by Milhaud, 1950. See studies by C. Sénéchal (Paris 1939), L. Specker (Zürich 1942), and D. S. Blair (1960).

SUPPÉ, Franz von, *soop-pay* (1820–95), Viennese composer of operettas, songs, masses, &c., was born at Spalato of Germano-Belgo-Italian origin. His *Light Cavalry* and *Poet and Peasant* overtures are still firm favourites.

SURAJA DOWLAH, Siraj-ud-Dowla, in the *Gentleman's Magazine* of the time **Sir Roger Dowler** (d. 1757), the young Nawab of Bengal, having captured Fort William, the fort of the English factory at Calcutta (1756), confined his 146 prisoners in the military prison, the ' Black Hole ' (300 sq. ft.). In the morning there were twenty-three survivors. Clive (q.v.) at Plassey (*Palási*) on June 23, 1757, inflicted a crushing defeat on Suraja Dowlah, who fled and was slain. See Holwell's *Narrative of the Black Hole* (1758).

SURCOUF, Robert, *sür-koof* (1773–1827), French privateer, was born and died at St Malo. He preyed on the English shipping in the Indian seas during the war, his greatest exploits being the capture of the *Triton* (1785) and *Kent* (1800). See Sir J. K. Laughton's *Studies in Naval History* (1887).

SURREY, Henry Howard, Earl of (*c.* 1517–47), English courtier and poet, was the eldest son of Thomas Howard (q.v.), who in 1524 succeeded as third Duke of Norfolk. In 1532 he accompanied Henry VIII to France; in 1542 he was made a Knight of the Garter, but was sent to the Fleet prison for issuing a challenge; and next year he was again committed for breaking windows in the streets at night. Soon released, he served in the camp near Boulogne, distinguished himself at Montreuil in 1544, and in 1545 held command at Guisnes and Boulogne, but, defeated by a superior French force, was superseded by the Earl of Hertford. For his bitter speeches against Hertford, Surrey was imprisoned at Windsor in July, and in December was, like his father, committed to the Tower on a charge of high treason. His offence was merely that he had assumed the arms of his ancestor Edward the Confessor in conjunction with his own; but he was found guilty, condemned to death, and beheaded, January 21, 1547. He was, almost as much as Sir Philip Sidney, the type of perfect knight and his love poems are a late manifestation of the courtly love of the Middle Ages. He was much under the influence of Petrarch. His poems were first printed, with poems by Wyatt and others, in *Tottel's Miscellany* (1557). They consist of sonnets, lyrics, elegies, translations, paraphrases of the Psalms and Ecclesiastes, besides translations in good blank verse—the first in English—of books ii and iv of Virgil's *Aeneid.* He was among the first in English to employ the sonnet, using not the Petrarchan form but that used by most of the Elizabethans. See Lives by Nott in his edition (1815 and 1866), and Casady (1938); H. W. Chapman, *Two Tudor Portraits* (1960).

SURTEES, (1) **Robert** (1779–1834), English antiquary and topographer, born at Durham, studied at Christ Church, Oxford, and the Middle Temple, and in 1802 inherited Mainsforth near Bishop Auckland. Here he compiled his *History of the County of Durham* (1816–23), to vol. iv of which (ed. by Raine, 1840) a memoir by George Taylor is prefixed. To Scott's *Minstrelsy* Surtees contributed two 'ancient' ballads he himself had made—*Barthram's Dirge* and *The Death of Featherstonhaugh.* The Surtees Society was founded in 1834 to publish unedited MSS. relating chiefly to the northern counties.

(2) **Robert Smith** (1803–64), English sporting writer, of Hamsterley Hall, Durham, wrote anonymously a series of inimitable sporting novels, introducing Mr Jorrocks, grocer and sportsman. Among the best known are *Handley Cross* (1843, 1854) and *Mr Facey Romford's Hounds* (1865)—illustrated by John Leech and 'Phiz'. See memoirs by himself and Cuming (1924), F. Watson (1933), and *Hunting Scenes from Surtees,* ed. Gough (1953).

SUSO, or **Seuse, Heinrich** (*c.* 1295–1366), German mystic, born at Ueberlingen, Baden, was a Dominican monk and a disciple of Eckhart. His *Das Büchlein der ewigen Weisheit* (1328) achieved great popularity. See his own *Life* (trans. 1952).

SUTHERLAND, Graham Vivian (1903–), English artist, born in London. He studied at Goldsmiths' College of Art, and worked mainly as an etcher till 1930. During the next ten years he made his reputation as a painter of romantic, mainly abstract landscapes, with superb, if arbitrary, colouring. From 1941 to 1945 he was an official war artist. In 1946 he was commissioned to paint a *Crucifixion* for St Matthew's Church, Northampton, and he has since produced several memorable portraits, including *Somerset Maugham* (1949) and *Sir Winston Churchill* (1955). He has also designed ceramics, posters and textiles: his large tapestry, *Christ in Majesty,* was hung in the new Coventry Cathedral in 1962. His work is represented in the Tate Gallery, London, the Musée d'Art Moderne, Paris, and the Museum of Modern Art, New York. He was awarded the O.M. in 1960. See the studies by Sackville-West (1955) and Cooper (1961).

SUTRO, Alfred (1863–1933), English dramatist, born in London, gave up a successful business, translated Maeterlinck, and from 1900 wrote a series of successful plays—*The Foolish Virgins* (1904), *The Walls of Jericho* (1906), *John Glayde's Honour* (1907), *The Perplexed Husband* (1913), *Freedom,* &c. See his autobiographical *Celebrities and Simple Souls* (1933).

SUTTNER, Bertha von, *née* **Kinsky** (1843–1914), Austrian writer and pacifist, born at Prague, spread anti-war sentiment by her *Die Waffen nieder* ('Lay Down your Arms', 1899), which was translated into many European languages, and other pacifist books. She was awarded the Nobel peace prize in 1905. See her *Memoirs* (1909), and Life by Ellen Key (1919).

SUTTON, Thomas (1552–1611), a London merchant, founder of the Charterhouse, obtained a lease of rich coal lands in Durham and made an enormous fortune.

SUVOROV, or Suwarrow, Count Aleksandr Vasilyevich (1729–1800), Russian general, born at Moscow, had won fame in the Seven Years, War, and in Poland and Turkey, when in 1799 he was sent to Italy to assist the Austrians against the French. He defeated Moreau on the Adda, Macdonald at Trebbia, and Joubert at Novi. Then he was directed to join Korsakov to sweep the French out of Switzerland. After a terrible march over the Alps he found that Masséna had defeated Korsakov, and, too weak to attack, he barely escaped over the mountains into Austria. He died at St Petersburg. See Lives by Spalding (1890) and Blease (1920).

SVEDBERG, Theodor, *svay-ber'y'* (1884–1971), Swedish chemist, born at Valbo, Gävleborg, invented the ultracentrifuge for the study of colloidal particles. He won a Nobel prize in 1926.

SVENDSEN, Johan Severin (1840–1911), Norwegian composer, born at Christiania, after wide travels, became court *kapellmeister* at Copenhagen (1883). He wrote two symphonies and a violin concerto. His best-known work is his *Carnival at Paris.*

SVERDRUP, Otto, *svayr-droop* (1855–1930), Norwegian explorer, born in Sogndal, led many expeditions to the Arctic.

SVETCHINE. See SWETCHINE.

SVEVO, Italo, pen-name of **Ettore Schmitz,** *zvay'vō* (1861–1928), Italian novelist, born at Trieste. A friend of James Joyce, who encouraged his talent, he had a considerable success with *La Coscienza di Zeno* ('The Confessions of Zeno'), a psychological study of the inner tensions and conflicts of an average man. His work is concerned largely with the human unconscious, and shows the influence of Zola. See *A History of Italian Literature* by Ernest Hatch Wilkins (1954).

SWAMMERDAM, Jan (1637–80), Dutch naturalist, born at Amsterdam. His system for classifying insects laid the foundations of entomology. His *Biblia Naturae* (1737–38) are the finest one-man collection of microscopical observations. He first observed red blood corpuscles (1658) and discovered the valves in the lymph vessels and the glands in Amphibia named after him. He finally succumbed to the mystic influences of Bourignon (q.v.) and abandoned science.

SWAN, (1) **Annie S(hepherd)** (1860–1943), Scottish novelist, born near Gorebridge, wife of Dr J. Burnett-Smith, contributed to *The Woman at Home* and the *People's Friend*, and wrote *Aldersyde* (1883) and many other popular stories, and reminiscences. See her autobiography, *My Life* (1934).

(2) **Sir Joseph Wilson** (1828–1914), English physicist and chemist, born at Sunderland, became a manufacturing chemist, patented the carbon process for photographic printing in 1864, invented the dry plate (1871) and bromide paper (1879). In 1860 he invented an electric lamp which anticipated Edison's by twenty years, and in 1897 demonstrated a lamp which improved considerably on Edison's patent model. He first produced practicable artificial silk. He was knighted in 1904.

SWEDENBORG, Emanuel (1688–1772), Swedish mystic, born January 29 in Stockholm, son of Jesper Svedberg, later Bishop of Skara, studied at Uppsala and travelled widely in Europe and on his return was appointed assessor in the college of mines and military engineer. The family was ennobled in 1719 and the name changed to Swedenborg. He wrote books on algebra and the differential calculus, on navigation, astronomy, on docks and sluices and on chemistry considered as atomic geometry. He declined a professorship of Mathematics (1724) because he preferred practical subjects. In 1734 he published at Leipzig, at the expense of the Duke of Brunswick, his monumental *Opera Philosophica et Mineralia* (1734), a mixture of metallurgy and metaphysical speculation on the creation of the world, carried further in *Philosophical Argument on the Infinite* (1734) and concluded by anatomical and physiological studies, *Economy of the Animal Kingdom* (1741) and *Animal Kingdom* (1744–1745). Curious dreams during 1743–44 convinced him that he had direct access to the spiritual world. He resigned his assessorship, communicated his spiritual explorations in *Heavenly Arcana* (1749–56) and spent the rest of his life in Amsterdam, Stockholm and London, expounding his mystical doctrines, based on the law of correspondences, which reveals that there are three heavens and three hells, that creation is dead, except through the intervention of God, who invests man with apparent life, but only himself really lives. He has been regarded, falsely, as a spiritualist 'medium', but he denied that spirits can enter the material world, and his works are too reasoned and matter-of-fact to be called mystical. His other works (all first published in Latin) are *Heaven and Hell*, *The New Jerusalem*, *Divine Love and the Divine Wisdom*, *Divine Providence*, *The Apocalypse Revealed* and *Conjugal Love*. His translated theological works number forty volumes. He died in London, March 29, 1772, was buried first in St George's of the East in London and in 1908 reinterred at Stockholm. He made no attempt to establish a sect; his followers, who call themselves 'the New Church signified by the New Jerusalem in the Revelation', were organized as a distinct denomination in 1787 by some Wesleyan preachers; there are branches throughout the world. Kant, who somewhat admired Swedenborg the mystic, demolished Swedenborg the metaphysician in *Dreams of a Ghost Seer* (1776). See Lives by J. G. Wilkinson (1849), W. White (1867), G. Trobridge (1907), S. Toksvig (1949), and studies by S.M. Warren (1885) and E. A. G. Kleen (1917–20).

SWEELINCK, Jan Pieterszoon, *sway'-* (1562–1611), Dutch composer, organist and harpsichordist, born at Deventer or Amsterdam, studied in Venice and composed mainly church music and organ works, and developed the fugue. He founded the distinctive North German school which later included Buxtehude and the young Johann Sebastian Bach.

SWEET, Henry (1845–1912), English philologist, pioneer of Anglo-Saxon philological studies, born in London, became reader in Phonetics at Oxford. His works include Old and Middle English texts, primers, and dictionaries, a historical English grammar, *A History of English Sounds* (1874), and *A History of Language* (1900). He constructed a 'Romaic' phonetic alphabet. Professor Higgins of Bernard Shaw's *Pygmalion* was based on him.

SWETCHINE, Madame, *née* **Anne Sophie Soymanov** (1782–1857), Russian author, born at Moscow, married in 1799 General Swetchine, joined the Roman Catholic communion in 1815, and settled finally in Paris in 1818, where she maintained a famous salon. See Life by de Falloux (1858); his edition of her Letters (1861); and work by Naville (1863).

SWETTENHAM, *swet'nėm*, (1) **Sir Alexander** (1846–1933), Colonial administrator. He began his career in 1868 as a clerk in the Ceylon civil service, and rose through various posts in Cyprus, Singapore, British Guiana, and the Straits Settlement to become captain-general and governor-in-chief in Jamaica from 1904 to 1907. He was created K.C.M.G. in 1898.

(2) **Sir Frank Athelstane** (1850–1946), brother of (1). He was British resident in Selangor (1882) and Perak (1889–95), and later resident-general in the Federated Malay States (1896–1901). He was governor and commander-in-chief of the Straits Settlement from 1901 to 1904 and became an authority on Malay language and history, writing a number of books on the subject. He was created K.C.M.G. in 1897. Port Swettenham, Selangor, is named after him.

SWEYN, *svay'in*, name of three kings of Denmark:

Sweyn I, known as **Sweyn Forkbeard** (d. 1014), was father of Canute (q.v.) and son of Harold Blaatand, whom he defeated and killed, making himself king (986). He led many plundering expeditions to Britain and defeated and killed the Norwegian Olaf, the Victorious. He died at Gainsborough.

Sweyn II (d. 1075), born in England, became king in 1047, carried on a war with Harold III of Norway until 1064, attempted twice to conquer England, but was driven away by Canute. Five of his sons were kings of Denmark.

Sweyn III (d. 1157), was king of part of Denmark from 1147 and waged civil war against Canute V, whom he killed. He was himself assassinated by Waldemar I.

SWIFT, Jonathan (1667–1745), English satirist,

was born in Dublin, the son of English parents. He was educated at Kilkenny Grammar School and Trinity College, Dublin, where he obtained his degree only by 'special grace' in 1685. Family connections helped him to embark on a career as secretary to the renowned diplomat, Sir William Temple, then resident at Moor Park, Farnham. Here Swift obtained his first acquaintance with the great world, but his relations with Temple were sometimes strained. However, he supported his patron on the side of the Ancients in the 'Querelle des Anciens et des Modernes' which had spread here from France. Swift's contribution was the mock-epic *Battle of the Books* which was published along with the much more powerful satire on religious dissension, *A Tale of a Tub*, in 1704. At Moor Park he first met Esther Johnson, then a child of eight, who henceforward as pupil and lover or friend was to be intertwined with his life and to survive for posterity in Swift's verse tributes and the *Journal to Stella*. When Swift was presented to the living of Laracor near Dublin, Stella accompanied him, but the precautions he took precluded scandal. It is uncertain if he ever married her. In 1708 during one of his numerous visits to London he met Esther Vanhomrigh, who insisted on being near him in Ireland with fatal consequences to herself. She is the Vanessa of Swift's too clever poem *Cadenus and Vanessa*, a tribute to the lady but also a manœuvre of disengagement. His visits to London were largely political, but friendship with the great, literary and aristocratic, bulked largely in them. For the first time the literary world met on equal terms with statesmen. Having been introduced to the political world by Temple, he supported the Whigs, but, his first care being the English Church, he gradually veered to the Tory party. The friendship of Harley, later Earl of Oxford, assisted the change which was decisively made in 1710 when Harley returned to power. His *Four Last Years of the Queen* described the ferment of intrigue and pamphleteering during that period. The chief aims of the Tory party were to make the Establishment secure and to bring the war with France to a close. The latter object was powerfully aided by his *On the Conduct of the Allies* (1713), one of the greatest pieces of pamphleteering. The death of the Queen disappointed all the hopes of Swift and his friends of the 'Scriblerus Club', founded in 1713. Swift accepted his 'exile' to the Deanery of St Patrick's, Dublin, and henceforth, except for two visits in 1726 and 1727, correspondence alone kept him in touch with London. Despite his loathing for Ireland he threw himself into a strenuous campaign for Irish liberties, denied by the Whig government. The *Drapier's Letters* is only the most famous of these activities which were concerned with England's restrictions on Irish trade, particularly the exclusion of Irish wool and cattle. This campaign and his charitable efforts for Dublin's poor greatly retrieved his name. On his first visit to London after the Tory debacle of 1714 he published the world-famous satire *Gulliver's Travels* (1726). The completion of this work seems to have released the talent for light verse which he had displayed so happily for the amusement of the ladies of the viceregal Lodge in earlier days. His poems of this sort now range from the diverting *The Grand Question Debated* (1729) to the *Verses on His Own Death*, which, with its mingling of pathos and humour, ranks with the great satirical poems in the lighter manner. He himself considered his *On Poetry; a Rhapsody* his best verse satire. An attack on Grub Street, it corresponds in some way to Pope's *Dunciad*. There is also of this period a group of odious satires on women which in a writer of his cloth almost hint at derangement. As a relief we note his constant preoccupation with the speech and manners of the servant class and equally with the banality of fashionable society. The ironical *Directions to Servants* and *A Complete Collection of Genteel and Ingenious Conversation* (in hand in 1731) are examples of both. The satire in the first part of *Gulliver's Travels* is directed at political parties and religious dissension. The second part can be equally enjoyed for the ingenious adventures and the detailed verisimilitude which, as in Defoe, is part of the manner. But there is deepening misanthropy culminating in the King's description of mankind as 'the most pernicious race of little odious vermin that Nature ever suffered to crawl upon the surface of the earth'. The third part, a satire on inventors, is good fun though less plausible. The last part, in the country of the Houyhnhnms, a race of horses governed only by reason, is a savage attack on man which points to the author's final mental collapse. Politics apart, Swift's influence, like that of the 'Scriblerus Club' generally and Pope in particular, was directed powerfully against the vogue of deistic science and modern invention and in favour of orthodoxy and good manners. His religion, as we see from his sermons, was apparently sincere, but as he exalted reason above emotion, there is little Christian warmth in it. The Temple Scott edition of the works (1897–1910) replaced the old edition by Sir Walter Scott (1814). H. Davis edited the *Prose Works* (1939 *et seq.*); Birkbeck Hill, *Unpublished Letters* (1899); and F. E. Ball the *Correspondence* (1910–14). Important studies are by Churton Collins (1893); Stephen Gwynn (1933); R. Quintana (1936); Life by B. Acworth (1948), and I. Ehrenpreis, *The Personality of Jonathan Swift* (1958), and study by K. Williams (1959).

SWINBURNE, (1) **Algernon Charles** (1837–1909), English poet and critic, was born in London, the eldest son of Admiral and Lady Jane Swinburne. He was educated partly in France, passed from Eton to Balliol, left without taking a degree, travelled on the Continent, where he came under the spell of Victor Hugo. He visited Landor in Florence (1864), and on his return became associated with D. G. Rossetti and William Morris. After a breakdown due to intemperate living, he submitted to the care of his friend Watts-Dunton, in whose house, No. 2, The Pines, he continued to live in semiseclusion for the rest of his life. His first publication, the two plays *The Queen Mother* and *Rosamond* (1860), attracted little attention, but *Atalanta in Calydon* (1865), a drama in the Greek form but modern in its spirit of revolt against religious acquiescence in the will of Heaven, proved that a new artist with an exquisite lyrical gift had arisen. He returned to Greek myth with his noble lyric drama *Erectheus* (1876). It was, however, the first of the series of *Poems and Ballads* (1865) which took the public by storm. The exciting or languorous rhythms of *Hesperia*, *Itylus*, *The Garden of Proserpine*, *The Triumph of Time* were intoxicating to English ears, but the uninhibited tone of certain passages affronted English puritanism. The second series of *Poems and Ballads* hardly maintained the excitement and the third series (1889) witnessed his waning vogue in this kind. Meanwhile he found scope for his detestation of kings and priests in the struggle for Italian liberty. *Songs before Sunrise* (1871) best expresses his fervent republicanism. He had been working at a trilogy of Mary, Queen of Scots, since before 1865 when his *Chastelard* appeared. The second play of the series, *Bothwell, a Tragedy*, appeared in 1874 and *Mary Stuart* completed the trilogy in 1881. The year following, *Tristram of Lyonesse*, an Arthurian romance in rhymed couplets, achieved a real success and must be considered among the best of Victorian dealings with the mediaeval cycle. He had resented Tennyson's moralistic treatment of the theme in *The Idylls of the King*. *Tristram* is intense and passionate and has some great descriptive passages. When he returned to mediaeval romance in *A Tale of Balen* (1896), there was obvious lack of power. His dramas are all closet-plays and except for some high passages in the *Mary Stuart* trilogy are forgotten. Swinburne represented the last phase of the Romantic movement—with a little posthumous life in the early Yeats. His absorption in romantic themes which he treated with a wealth of rhetoric hardly experienced in previous poetry and an excess of neologisms and archaisms has caused his reputation to diminish, but this fact cannot entirely negate his genuine and lasting contribution to the poetic scene. His novel, *Love's Cross Currents* (1877), is a curiosity, but his critical works, above all his work on Shakespeare and his contemporaries, are stimulating. His *Essays and Studies* (1875) and *Studies in Prose and Poetry* (1894) are his chief contribution to criticism. Five volumes of the *Collected Poems* appeared in 1917 and twenty volumes of the *Complete Works* from 1926 onwards. A new edition of his *Correspondence*, ed C. Y. Lang, appeared in 1960. Gosse wrote the standard Life in 1917. Studies by Mackail (1909), Nicholson (1926) and Lafourcade (1932) are important. Max Beerbohm's essay *No. 2, the Pines* is a masterly ironic picture of Swinburne's life with Watts-Dunton.

(2) **Sir James, 9th Baronet** (1858–1958), British scientist, ' the father of British plastics ', was a pioneer in that industry and the founder of Bakelite, Ltd. His research on phenolic resins resulted in a process for producing synthetic resin, but his patent for this was anticipated by one day, by the Belgian chemist Baekeland. He lived to be a centenarian.

SWINTON, Sir Ernest Dunlop (1868–1951), British soldier, writer and inventor, born in Bangalore, India. One of the originators of the tank, Swinton was responsible for the use of the word ' tank ' to describe armoured fighting vehicles. Under his pseudonym **Ole Luk-Oie** he wrote *The Green Curve* (1909), *A Year Ago* (1916), and translations. He was professor of Military History at Oxford (1925–39).

SWITHIN, or Swithun (d. 862), English saint and divine, was adviser to Egbert (q.v.) and was made Bishop of Winchester (852) by Ethelwulf. When in 971 the monks exhumed his body to bury it in the rebuilt cathedral, the removal, which was to have taken place on July 15, is said to have been delayed by violent rains. Hence the current belief that if it rains on July 15 it will rain for forty days more.

SYBEL, Heinrich von, *zee'bėl* (1817–95), German historian, born at Düsseldorf, studied at Berlin under Ranke; became professor of History at Bonn (1844), Marburg (1845), Munich (1856) and Bonn again (1861); and in 1875 was made director of the state archives at Berlin. He published the political correspondence of Frederick the Great, shared in issuing the *Monumenta Germaniae Historica*, and founded and edited the *Historische Zeitschrift*. His history of the First Crusade (1841) often ran counter to the accepted opinions of centuries; his next work was on the title ' German king ' (1844). Then came his masterpiece, *Geschichte der Revolutionszeit, 1789–95* (1853–58; 4th ed. to 1800, 1882), a history of the French Revolution based upon official documentary evidence. He also wrote a history of the founding of the German empire (1889–94; trans. 1891–92), marred by its Prussian bias. He was a member of the Prussian Diet.

SYDENHAM, (1) Floyer (1710–87), English scholar, educated at Wadham College, Oxford, in his fiftieth year began the publication of an excellent translation of Plato's *Dialogues* (1759–80). It had no market, neither had his dissertation on Heraclitus (1775) or his *Onomasticon Theologicum* (1784). Arrested for unpaid meals, he died in prison. The Literary Fund was founded as a consequence of his death to help deserving authors.

(2) **Thomas** (1624–89), English physician, ' the English Hippocrates ', born September 10 at Wynford Eagle, Dorset, left Magdalene Hall, Oxford, to fight as captain of horse for the Parliamentarians. He returned to Oxford in 1647, read medicine at Wadham College and was awarded the degree of M.B. (1648) without any previous examinations and was elected fellow of All Souls. In 1651 he was severely wounded at Worcester. From 1655 he practised in London, but although he became a licentiate of the Royal College of Physicians and took an Oxford M.D. (1676) he was never elected a fellow of the Royal College. A great friend of such empiricists as Boyle and Locke, he stressed the importance of observation in clinical medicine. He wrote a masterly account of

gout (1683), a disease from which he himself suffered, distinguished the symptoms of venereal disease (1675), recognized hysteria as a distinct disease and gave his name to the mild convulsions of children, 'Sydenham's chorea', and to the use of liquid opium, 'Sydenham's laudanum'. He remained in London except when the plague was at its peak (1665). Some of his epidemiological theories on the fevers of London are supported today, although he failed to stress the rôles of contagion and infection. One of his quainter 'remedies' for senile decrepitude was to put the patient to bed with a young vital person. In England he suffered professional opposition, but on the Continent his fame was immediate. Boerhaave (q.v.) is said never to have referred to him without raising his hat. See W. A. Greenhill's edition (1844; trans. R. G. Latham 1848) for the Sydenham Society of *Opera Omnia* (1705); *Selections*, ed. J. D. Comrie (1922); Life by J. F. Payne (1900); and C. E. A. Winslow, *The Conquest of Epidemic Disease* (1944).

SYDNEY, Algernon. See SIDNEY (1).

SYLLA. See SULLA.

SYLVESTER, the name of three popes:

Sylvester I (pope 314-335), is falsely claimed to have baptized and cured of leprosy Constantine the Great, and to have received from him the famous Donation, now considered apocryphal. Under him the Council of Nicaea (325) defined the articles of the Christian faith. He was canonized.

Sylvester II (*c.* 940–1003), pope from 999, was born Gerbert at Aurillac in Auvergne, and from his attainments in chemistry, mathematics and philosophy acquired the reputation of being in league with the Devil. He made a large collection of classical manuscripts and is said to have introduced Arabic numerals and to have invented clocks. He became Abbot of Bobbio (982) and Archbishop of Ravenna (988). He upheld the primacy of Rome against the separatist tendencies of the French church. See French works by Olleris (1876), and German by Werner (1878) and Schultess (1891–93).

Sylvester III, was antipope 1044–46 to Benedict IX and was Bishop of Sabina.

SYLVESTER, (1) James Joseph (1814–97), English mathematician, born in London, studied at St John's College, Cambridge (where, as a Jew, though he was second wrangler (1837), he was disqualified from a degree), and was professor at University College, London, at the University of Virginia, at Woolwich, at the Johns Hopkins University in Baltimore, and at Oxford (1883–94). He made important contributions to the theories of invariants, numbers and equations, and took up and graduated in Law. See his *Collected Mathematical Papers* (4 vols. 1904–12).

(2) **Joshua** (1563–1618), English translator, achieved success neither as merchant nor as poet. His own works are forgotten; his chief literary work was his translation of *Divine Weeks and Works* of Du Bartas (q.v.). Grosart reprinted his *Works* (1878).

SYLVIUS, (1) Franciscus, or Franz de la Boë (1614–72), German physician, born at Hanau, Prussia, became professor of Medicine at Leyden (1658). He first treated the pancreatic, saliva and other body juices chemically, described the relationship between the tubercle and phthisis and founded the iatrochemical school. He died in Leyden.

(2) properly **Jacques Dubois** (1478–1555), French physician, born at Amiens, became professor of Medicine at the Collège de France. He discovered the fissure in the brain, described many anatomical structures and systematized anatomical terms. He wrote commentaries on Galen and Hippocrates. See C. Singer, *Evolution of Anatomy* (1925).

SYME, James, *sīm* (1799–1870), Scottish surgeon, born in Edinburgh, studied under Robert Liston (q.v.) at the university there and at Paris and in Germany. In 1818, he announced a method of waterproofing, afterwards patented by Macintosh (q.v.). In 1823–33 he lectured on Clinical Surgery. In 1831 appeared his treatise on *The Excision of Diseased Joints*; in 1832 his *Principles of Surgery*. In 1833 he became professor of Clinical Surgery. His life abounded in controversies. Syme, who had no superior either as operator or as teacher, wrote further on pathology, stricture, fistula, incised wounds, &c. See *Memoir* by Paterson (1874).

SYMEON OF DURHAM. See SIMEON OF DURHAM.

SYMINGTON, William (1763–1831), Scottish engineer and inventor, born at Leadhills, became a mechanic at the Wanlockhead mines. In 1787 he patented an engine for road locomotion and, in 1788, he constructed for Patrick Miller (q.v.) a similar engine on a boat 25 feet long, having twin hulls with paddle-wheels between, which was launched on Dalswinton Loch. In 1802 he completed at Grangemouth the *Charlotte Dundas*, the first workable steamboat ever built. It was intended as a tug, but vested interests prevented its use, asserting that the wash would injure the sides of the Forth and Clyde Canal. Symington died in London, in poverty.

SYMMACHUS, (1) Coelius, pope 498–514.

(2) **Quintus Aurelius** (*c.* A.D. 345–410), Roman orator, became prefect of Rome in 384 and consul in 391 under Theodosius. He was devoted to the old religion, and showed the highest nobility of character. His extant writings, edited by Kroll in 1893, consist of letters, three panegyrics on Valentinian I and Gratian, and fragments of six orations. See Morin's *Étude* (1847) and Kroll's *De Symmacho* (1891).

SYMONDS, John Addington, *sim'-* (1840–93), English author, born at Bristol, was educated at Harrow and Balliol, won the Newdigate, and was elected a fellow of Magdalen in 1862. His *Introduction to the Study of Dante* (1872) was followed by *Studies of the Greek Poets* (1873–76), his great *Renaissance in Italy* (6 vols. 1875–86), and *Shakespeare's Predecessors in the English Drama* (1884). He wrote also sketches of travel in Italy and elsewhere; monographs on *Shelley*, *Sidney*, and *Ben Jonson*; fine translations of the *Sonnets of Michelangelo and Campanella* (1878), of Benvenuto Cellini's autobiography, and of 12th-century students' Latin songs (1884); a *Life of Michelangelo* (1892); some verse; and an account of his residence (for health) at Davos (1892). See Life (1895) by H. F. Brown, who edited his *Letters and Papers* (1923); and biographical studies by Brooks (1914) and Grosskurth (1964).

SYMONS, *sim'-*, (1) **Arthur** (1865–1945), British critic and poet, born of Cornish stock in Wales, did much to familiarize the British with the literature of France and Italy—he translated d'Annunzio (1902) and Baudelaire (1925). He also wrote on *The Symbolist Movement in Literature* (1899) and *The Romantic Movement in English Poetry* (1909).

(2) George James (1838–1900), English meteorologist, born in London, served as clerk in the meteorological department of the Board of Trade, founded the British Rainfall Organization for collecting rainfall data with the cooperation of the general public. The Royal Society appointed him to investigate the Krakatoa eruption (1883). Fellow of the Royal Society, he was secretary and twice president of the Royal Meteorological Society, the highest award of which, the Symons Memorial Gold Medal, bears his name.

SYNESIUS (*c.* A.D. 375–413), Greek philosopher and poet, Bishop of Ptolemais, born at Cyrene, studied at Alexandria under Hypatia (q.v.) and at Athens, and then returned to the Pentapolis, resolved to spend his life in study and in the pursuits of a country gentleman. About 399 he was appointed a delegate from Cyrene to the emperor at Constantinople, where he remained three years, and wrote an allegory *Concerning Providence.* After his return, he married and wrote *Concerning Dreams, The Praise of Baldness, Dion or Self-discipline,* and *Hymns.* When Libyan nomads made raids upon the fertile Pentapolis, Synesius organized the defence of Cyrene. About 401 he turned Christian; and *c.* 410 the people of Ptolemais begged him to become their bishop. Finally he yielded, and was consecrated at Alexandria. His 156 letters reveal a man of high spirit, passionately fond of intellectual pursuits and of sport. His *Hymns* show him as the poet of Neoplatonism. See books by Druon (1859), Volkmann (1869), Gardner (1886), Crawford (1901), Grützmacher (1913); Fitzgerald's translation (1926–30).

SYNGE, John Millington, *sing* (1871–1909), Irish dramatist, born near Dublin, studied at Trinity College, Dublin, and then spent several years in Paris until, on the advice of Yeats, he settled among the people of the Aran Islands who provided the material for his plays, *In the Shadow of the Glen* (1903), *Riders to the Sea* (1904), *The Well of the Saints* (1905), and his humorous masterpiece *The Playboy of the Western World* (1907) followed by *The Tinker's Wedding* (1909). He had a profound influence on the next generation of Irish playwrights and was a director of the Abbey Theatre from 1904. See biographical study by D. H. Greene and E. M. Stephens (1959).

SZENT-GYÖRGYI, Albert von Nagyrapolt, *sent-dyur'dyi* (1893–), Hungarian biochemist, born at Budapest, lectured at Groningen, Cambridge, &c., was professor at Szeged (1931–45) and at Budapest (1945–47), then became director of the Institute of Muscle Research in Massachusetts, U.S. He isolated Vitamin C and was awarded the Nobel prize in 1937. He made important studies of biological combustion, muscular contraction and cellular oxidation.

SZÖNYI, Stephen (1894–1960), Hungarian artist, born at Ujpest. He studied at Budapest, and his paintings, particularly those of nudes, gained him a large following among the younger Hungarian artists.

SZYMANOWSKI, Karol, *shim-an-of'skee* (1883–1937), Polish composer, born at Tymoszowska, in the Ukraine, eventually became director of the State Conservatoire in Warsaw. Reckoned by many to be the greatest Polish composer since Chopin, he wrote operas, incidental music, symphonies, concertos, chamber music and many songs.

T

TAAFFE, Eduard Franz Josef, Graf von, *tah'fè* (1833–95), 11th Viscount Taaffe and Baron of Ballymote in the Irish peerage, Austrian statesman, was born in Vienna, and became minister of the interior (1867) and chief minister (1869–70, 1879–93). He showed great tact in an attempt to unite the various nationalities of the Empire into a consolidated whole. See *Memoirs of the Family of Taaffe* (1856).

TÁBARI, Abu Jafar Mohammed Ben Jariral- (839–923), Arab historian, born in Persia, travelled in Syria, Egypt, &c., wrote in Arabic invaluable Moslem annals (ed. De Goeje and others, 1878–91), and died at Baghdad.

TABLEY, John Byrne Leicester Warren, 3rd Baron de (1835–95), English poet, educated at Eton and Christ Church, Oxford, was called to the bar at Lincoln's Inn in 1859, and succeeded his father as third baron in 1887. He was author of nine volumes of poetry, mostly written anonymously or under a pseudonym, some plays and novels, and a *Guide to Book Plates* (1880). See Memoir by Sir M. Grant Duff prefixed to his *Flora of Cheshire* (1899) and *Selected Poems*, ed. J. Drinkwater (1924).

TACITUS, Publius or Gaius Cornelius, *tas'i-toos* (*c.* 55–120), Roman historian, was born perhaps at Rome, where he studied rhetoric, rose to eminence as a pleader at the Roman bar, and in 77 married the daughter of Agricola, the conqueror of Britain. By 88 he was already praetor and a member of one of the priestly colleges. Next year he left Rome for Germany; and he did not return till 93. He was an eye witness to Domitian's reign of terror, and we have his own testimony as to the relief wrought by the accession of Nerva and Trajan. Under Nerva he became consul suffrectus, succeeding Virginius Rufus. We may assume that he saw the close of Trajan's reign, if not the opening of Hadrian's. The high reputation he enjoyed is attested by the eulogistic mention of him in Pliny's letters of which there are eleven addressed to him. The earliest work generally attributed to him, the *Dialogus de Oratoribus*, treats of the decline of eloquence under the empire. It is doubtful whether the *Agricola* is a funeral *éloge* or a panegyric for political ends. As biography it has grave defects, partly due to his admiration for his father-in-law; but it will always be read for its elevation of style, its dramatic force, invective and pathos. The third work, the *Germania*, is a monograph of great value on the ethnography of Germany. Fourth in order comes the *Historiae*, or the history of the empire from the accession of Galba in A.D. 68 to the assassination of Domitian in 96. Of the twelve books originally composing it only the first four and a fragment of the fifth are extant. Tacitus is at his strongest here, and his material was drawn from contemporary experience. His last work, the so-called *Annales*, is a history of the Julian line from Tiberius to Nero (A.D. 14 to 68); of probably eighteen books only eight have come down to us entire, four are fragmentary, and the others lost. His statuesque style is often obscure from condensation. He copied much from earlier historians and was biased in his republican ideals and hatreds. See studies by G. Boissier (1908), R. V. Pöhlmann (1913), R. Syme (1958) and C. W. Mendell (1958).

TADEMA. See ALMA-TADEMA.

TAFT, (1) **Robert Alfonso** (1889–1953), American Republican senator and lawyer, son of (2), born at Cincinnati, Ohio, studied law at Yale and Harvard and in 1917 became counsellor to the American Food Administration in Europe under Hoover. Elected Senator in 1938, he co-sponsored the Taft-Hartley act (1947) directed against the power of the trade unions and the 'closed shop'. A prominent isolationist, Taft failed three times (1940, 1948, 1952) to secure Republican nomination for the presidency. He died of cancer.

(2) **William Howard** (1857–1930), 27th president of the United States, father of (1), was born at Cincinnati, the son of President Grant's secretary of war and attorney-general; and having studied at Yale and qualified as a barrister at Cincinnati, held numerous appointments in Ohio, and in 1890 became solicitor-general for the United States. In 1900 he was made president of the Philippine Commission, and in 1901 first civil governor of the islands. In 1904–08 he was secretary of war for the United States, in 1906 provisional governor of Cuba, in 1909–1913 Republican president of the United States. He secured an agreement with Canada that meant relatively free trade. From 1913 he was professor of Law at Yale and from 1921 chief justice of the United States. See Lives by Duffy (1930), H. F. Pringle (1939) and Hicks (1945).

TAGLIACOZZI, Gasparo, *tahl-yah-kot'see* (1546–99), Italian surgeon, born at Bologna, was professor there of Surgery and of Anatomy, famous for repairing injured noses by transplanting skin from the arm.

TAGLIONI, Maria, *tahl-yō'nee* (1804–84), Italian *danseuse*, born at Stockholm of an Italian ballet master and a Swedish mother. Badly formed and plain, she danced with astonishing grace and after some initial setbacks triumphed with her creation of *La Sylphide* in 1832 which marked the great romantic era in ballet. She may have introduced *sur les pointes* dancing in ballet. She married Count de Voisins in 1832 and ended her career teaching deportment to the British royal children. She died in poverty. Her brother **Paul** (1808–84) and his daughter were also famous dancers.

TAGORE, Sir Rabindranath (1861–1941), Indian poet and philosopher, born in Calcutta. He studied in England and, for seventeen years, managed his family estates at Shileida, where he collected the legends and tales he afterwards used in his work. His first book was a novel, *Karuna*, followed by a drama, *The Tragedy of Rudachandra*. In 1901 he founded near Bolpur the Santiniketan, a communal school to blend Eastern and Western philosophical and educational systems. He received the Nobel prize for literature in 1913, the first Asiatic to do so, and was knighted in 1915—an honour which he resigned in 1919 as a protest against British policy in the Punjab. He was openly critical of Gandhi's noncooperation as well as of the Government attitude in Bengal. His work includes *Gitanjali* (1913), *Chitra* (1914) his finest play, and *The Religion of Man* (1931). See *My Reminiscences* (1917) and *My Boyhood Days*; also Lives by Rhys (1915), Thompson (1928), and studies by the latter (1926), Sen (1929), H. l'A. Fausset, *Poets and Pundits* (1947), and A. Bose (1958).

TAILLEFER, *tah-y'-fer* (d. 1066), Norman minstrel, sang war songs at the battle of Hastings, in which he was killed.

TAILLEFERRE, Germaine (1892-), French pianist and composer, one of 'les Six'. Her works include chamber music, a ballet, *Le Marchand d'oiseaux*, a piano concerto and songs.

TAINE, Hippolyte Adolphe, *ten* (1828–93), French critic, historian and philosopher, born at Vouziers in Ardennes, April 21, studied a year at Paris before turning author. He made a reputation by his critical analysis of La Fontaine's *Fables* (1853), followed by the *Voyage aux eaux des Pyrénées* (1855). His positivism was forcefully expressed in his critical *Les Philosophes français du dix-neuvième siècle* (1857) and also coloured his *Philosophie de l'art* (1881) and *De l'intelligence* (1870), in which moral qualities and artistic excellence are explained in purely descriptive, quasi-scientific terms. Taine's greatest work, *Les Origines de la France contemporaine* (1875-94) constitutes the strongest attack yet made on the men and the motives of the Revolution. Taine died March 5. *Derniers Essais* appeared in 1895, and *Carnets de voyage* in 1897. His *Notes sur l'Angleterre* (1871) are too ambitious in scope on the basis of only ten weeks' stay in England. See his *Life and Letters* (trans. 1902–08) and French studies by V. Giraud (1901) and A. Chevrillon (1932).

TAIT, (1) **Archibald Campbell** (1811–82), Scottish Anglican divine, born at Edinburgh, December 22, was educated at the Edinburgh Academy, Glasgow University and Balliol College, Oxford. A fellow and tutor, he was one of the four who in 1841 protested against Newman's Tract 90; in 1842 he became headmaster of Rugby, in 1849 Dean of Carlisle, and in 1856 Bishop of London. He showed firmness and broad-mindedness, as well as tact in dealing with controversies over church ritual; he condemned the *Essays and Reviews* and Colenso's teaching, but intervened to secure fair play. As Archbishop of Canterbury (1869), he helped to compose the strifes raised by Irish disestablishment, but was less successful with the Public Worship Regulation Act and the Burials Bill. He did much to extend and improve the organization of the church in the colonies; and the Lambeth Conference of 1878 met under his auspices. See Life by Davidson and Benham (1891).

(2) **Peter Guthrie** (1831–1901), Scottish mathematician and golf enthusiast, born at Dalkeith, was educated at the Edinburgh Academy and University and at Cambridge, where he graduated senior wrangler. Professor of Mathematics at Belfast (1854), of Natural Philosophy at Edinburgh (1860–1900) and secretary of the Royal Society of Edinburgh from 1879, he wrote on quaternions, experimented in thermoelectricity and collaborated with Kelvin in a *Treatise on Natural Philosophy*. He played on one occasion a round of golf with phosphorescent balls after nightfall. His mathematical theory of golfing dynamics led to the conclusion (which did not account for spin) that it was impossible to drive a ball more than 190 yards on a calm day. His son, **Freddie** (1870–1900), who lowered the St Andrews record to 72, and twice won the Amateur championship (1896 and 1898), appeared to falsify this result by a tremendous carry of 250 yards at St Andrews in 1893. Freddie was killed in action near Koodoosberg during the Boer war. See Life by C. G. Knott (1911).

(3) **William** (1792–1864), Scottish publisher, was the founder of *Tait's Edinburgh Magazine* (1832–64), a literary and radical political monthly to which De Quincey, John Stuart Mill, Cobden and Bright contributed.

TALBOT, name of an English family, descended from **Richard de Talbot**, named in the *Domesday* book, and from **Gilbert** (d. 1346), the first baron. The Earl of Shrewsbury and Talbot is the premier earl on the Rolls of England and Ireland and hereditary lord high steward of Ireland. The Lords Talbot de Malahide represent a family in Ireland which settled there in 1167. The former's most noteworthy members, in chronological order, were:

(1) **Sir John, 4th Baron,** and **1st Earl of Shrewsbury** (*c.* 1390–1453), twice lord-lieutenant of Ireland (1414 and 1445), was the famous champion of English arms in France in Henry VI's reign. Successful in many engagements, he was finally checked at Orleans by Joan of Arc (1429), and taken prisoner at Patay (1429), remaining a captive till 1431. Created Earl of Salop (1422), Earl of Shrewsbury (1442) and Earl of Waterford (1455), he fell at Castillon, after taking Bordeaux.

(2) **John, 2nd Earl of Shrewsbury** (*c.* 1413–1460), son of (1), fell at Northampton, fighting for the Lancastrians.

(3) **George, 4th Earl of Shrewsbury** (*c.* 1528–1590), fourth husband of Elizabeth (' Bess of Hardwick ') (1518–1608), long held Mary of Scotland a prisoner at Tutbury, Chatsworth and Sheffield Castle (1569–84).

(4) **Charles, 12th Earl** and only **Duke of Shrewsbury** (1660–1718), though serving under Charles II and James II, gave money to William of Orange and did much to bring about the Revolution of 1688. Twice secretary of state (1689 and 1694), he withdrew from public affairs in 1700, and went to Rome. In 1710 he helped to bring about the fall of the Whigs and was made lord chamberlain. In 1712 he was ambassador to France, and then lord-lieutenant of Ireland. At the crisis on the death of Anne (1714), as treasurer and lord justice, he acted with courage and decision and did much to secure the peaceful succession of the Hanoverians. He was created Duke of Shrewsbury in 1694, but the dukedom died with him. See Life by Nicholson and Turberville (1930).

(5) **Bertram Arthur, 17th Earl** (1832–56), died without issue, when the title passed to **John Chetwynd, 3rd Earl Talbot** (1803–68), of a 15th-century branch.

TALBOT, (1) **Mary Anne** (1778–1808), the ' British Amazon ', served as a drummer boy in Flanders (1792) and as a cabin boy at the battle of June 1, 1794.

(2) **William Henry Fox** (1800–77), English pioneer of photography, born at Melbury House, Evershot, educated at Harrow and Trinity, Cambridge, sat in the reformed parliament (1833–34) and in 1838 succeeded in making photographic prints on silver chloride paper, for which he was awarded the Royal Society medal (1838) and the Rumford medal (1842). He published works on astronomy and mathematics, and helped to decipher the Ninevite cuneiform inscriptions. His *Pencil of Nature* (1844) was the first photographically illustrated book.

TALFOURD, Sir Thomas Noon (1795–1854) English lawyer and author, born at Reading, which he represented in parliament, had his tragedy *Ion* (1835) produced by Macready at Covent Garden, wrote on Charles Lamb and is best known for his Copyright Act (1842). See his *Letters* (1837).

TALIACOTIUS. See TAGLIACOZZI.

TALIESIN, *tal-i-ay'sin* (fl. *c.* 550), Welsh bard, possibly mythical, to whom are ascribed many admirable poems, not older in language than the 12th century, however. See book by D. W. Nash (1858).

TALLARD, Comte Camille de, Duc d' Hostun, *tah-lahr* (1652–1728), French soldier, created marshal of France, was defeated and taken prisoner by Marlborough at Blenheim (1704).

TALLEMANT DES RÉAUX, Gédéon, *tal-mã day ray-ō* (*c.* 1619–1700), French man of letters, born at La Rochelle, married his cousin Élisabeth Rambouillet, whose fortune enabled him to give himself to letters and society. His famous *Historiettes* (written 1657–59; published 1834–40), 376 in number, are illustrative anecdotes rather than biographies. The most finished group is that of the famous circle of the Hôtel de Rambouillet. He was admitted to the Academy in 1666. See studies by E. Magne (1921 and 1922) and E. Gosse (1925).

TALLEYRAND - PÉRIGORD, Charles Maurice de, Prince of Benevento, *tal-ay-rã* (1754–1838), French statesman, was born at Paris, February 13, son of the Comte Talleyrand de Périgord (1734–88) who fought in the Seven Years' War. He was educated for the church, made himself a fair scholar, and cultivated the character of a rake and a cynical wit. Abbot of St Denis (1775) and *agent-général* to the French clergy (1780), he was by Louis XVI nominated Bishop of Autun in 1788. Next year the clergy of his diocese elected him to the States General, and he was one of the members of the Assembly selected to draw up the Declaration of Rights. He took a cynical delight in attacking the calling to which he still nominally belonged, and proposed the measure confiscating the landed property of the church. In February 1790 he was elected president of the Assembly. In 1791 he consecrated two new bishops, declaring at the same time his attachment to the Holy See, but, excommunicated by the pope, he gave up his clerical career. Early in 1792 Talleyrand was sent to London, but failed to conciliate Pitt; in December he was placed on the list of *émigrés*. He was again in London, an exile, till January 1794, when the Alien Act drove him to the United States. After the fall of Robespierre he returned to Paris (1796), attached himself to Barras, and in 1797 was made foreign minister under the Directory; he was for a time the first man in France. He had already recognized the genius of Bonaparte and established intimate relations with him. For a time he was in disgrace for his willingness to sell his services towards a treaty between Great Britain and the United States. But under the Consulate he was restored to his post, and was privy to the kidnapping and murder (March 1804) of the Duc d'Enghien. He was greatly instrumental in consolidating the power of Napoleon as consul for life (1802) and as emperor (1804). When in 1805 Great Britain formed a European coalition against France, it was partially broken up by Talleyrand. To him as much as to Napoleon was owing the organization (1806) of the Confederation of the Rhine. After being created Prince de Bénévent, he withdrew from the ministry. His voice was on the whole for a policy of wisdom during the later years of the first empire. He was opposed to the invasion of Russia; and this gives some justification for his desertion of Napoleon in 1814. As far back as Tilsit (1807) he seems to have been in communication with Britain; at Erfurt (1808), he had revealed state secrets to Russia; and he had mortally offended Napoleon, after the disasters in Spain, by making, with Fouché (q.v.), tentative arrangements for the succession. Now, he became the leader of the anti-Napoleonic faction; and through him communications were opened with the allies and the Bourbons. He dictated to the Senate the terms of Napoleon's deposition, and he became minister of foreign affairs under Louis XVIII. He negotiated the treaties by which the allies left France in possession of the boundaries of 1792, and at the Congress of Vienna he established her right to be heard. He had not calculated on the Hundred Days, and offered no help to Louis; being taken back after the second restoration, he became, through pressure of the allies, prime minister for a short time, but he was not *persona grata* with the king, and was disliked by all parties in France. Under Louis XVIII and Charles X he was little better than a discontented senator; but he was Louis-Philippe's chief adviser at the July revolution, for which he was partly responsible, went to London as ambassador and reconciled the British ministry and court to France. He retired into private life in 1834, and died May 17, 1838. See his *Mémoires*, edited by the Duc de Broglie (1891; Eng. trans. 1891–92), his *Correspondance*, ed. Pallain (1887–91), and Lives by G. Lacour-Gayet (1930–31), A. Duff Cooper (1932) and J. Vivent (1940).

TALLIEN, Jean Lambert, *tal-yĩ* (1769–1820), French revolutionary, born in Paris, made himself famous in 1791 by his Jacobin broadsheets, *L'Ami des citoyens*. He was conspicuous in the attack on the Tuileries, and in the September massacres, was elected to the Convention (1792), voted for the death of the king, was elected to the Committee of General Safety, and played a part in the downfall of the Girondists. On his mission to Bordeaux he quenched all opposition with the guillotine. Comtesse Thérèse de Fontenay, born Jeanne Marie Ignace Thérésa Cabarrus (1773–1835), whom he married in 1794 after saving her from death on the guillotine, also became famous for her harsh and dissolute conduct. He was recalled to Paris, and in March 1794 was chosen president of the Convention. But Robespierre hated him, and Tallien, recognizing his danger, led the successful attack of 9th Thermidor. He helped to suppress the Revolutionary Tribunal and the Jacobin Club, and drew up the accusations against Carrier, Le Bon and other Terrorists; but his importance ended with the Convention, though he accompanied Napoleon to Egypt and edited the *Décade égyptienne* at Cairo. On the voyage home he was captured by an English cruiser, and in England was made a hero by the Whigs (1801). Consul at Alicante (1805), he lost an eye there by yellow fever, and died in Paris in poverty.

TALLIS, Thomas (*c.* 1505–85), English musician, 'the father of English cathedral music', was organist of Waltham Abbey at the dissolution in 1540, when it is conjectured he became 'a gentleman of the Chapel Royal'. Elizabeth gave him, with Byrd (q.v.), a monopoly of music printing. In Day's Psalter (1560) there are eight tunes by him, one of which, known as Tallis's Canon, is now used for Ken's Evening Hymn. The *Cantiones* (1575) contained eighteen motets by Byrd and sixteen by Tallis. He was one of the greatest contrapuntists of the English School; an adaptation of his plainsong responses, and his setting of the Canticles in D Minor, are still in use. He wrote much church music, among it a motet in forty parts.

TALMA, François Joseph (1763–1826), French tragedian, was born and died in Paris, and made his début in 1787. Hitherto actors had worn the garb of their own time and country; Talma made a point of accuracy in costume. He achieved his greatest success in 1789 as Charles IX in Chénier's play. See his *Mémoires* (ed. by A. Dumas, 1849–50).

TAMAYO, Rufino (1899–), Mexican artist whose style combines the ancient art of his own country with the art of modern Europe. Among his works are frescoes in the National Conservatory of Music and in Smith College Library.

TAMERLANE (i.e., **Timur-i-Leng,** 'Lame Timur') (1336–1405), Tatar conqueror, was born at Kesh, S. of Samarkand, his father being a Mongol chief. In 1369 he ascended the throne of Samarkand. He subdued nearly all Persia, Georgia and the Tatar empire, conquered (1398) all the states between the Indus and the lower Ganges, and returned to Samarkand with a fabulous booty. Having set out against the Turks of Asia Minor, he turned aside to win Damascus and Syria from the Mameluke sovereigns of Egypt. At length on the plains of Angora the Mongol and Turkish hosts met, and Sultan Bajazet was routed and taken prisoner. The conqueror died on the march towards China. See Marlowe's tragedy (1590), Howorth's *History of the Mongols* (1876–88), and Life by H. Hookham (1962).

TANCRED (1078–1112), Norman crusader, son of the Palgrave Otho the Good, joined his cousin, Bohemund of Tarentum, Guiscard's son, in the first Crusade, and distinguished himself in the sieges of Nicaea, Tarsus, Antioch, Jerusalem, and at Ascalon. His reward was the principality of Tiberias. For some time he ruled Bohemund's state of Antioch, and shortly before his death was invested with the principality of Edessa. He is the hero of Tasso's *Gerusalemme Liberata*.

TANDY, James Napper (1740–1803), Irish agitator, born in Dublin, became a prosperous merchant there. A Presbyterian, he took an active part in corporation politics, and was the first secretary to the Dublin United Irishmen. In 1792 he challenged the solicitor-general for his abusive language, and was arrested. In 1793 he was to have stood trial on the minor charge of distributing a 'seditious' pamphlet against the Beresfords, when the government learned that he had taken the oath of the Defenders, a treasonable offence. He fled to America, crossed to France in 1798, shared in the ill-fated invasion of Ireland, by landing on Rutland Island, and at Hamburg was handed over to the English government. In February 1800 he was acquitted at Dublin. Again put on trial (April 1801) at Lifford for the treasonable landing on Rutland Island, he was sentenced to death, but permitted to escape to France, and died at Bordeaux. See Madden's *United Irishmen* (1846).

TANEY, Roger Brooke, *taw'ni* (1777–1864), American jurist, born in Calvert County, Md., and admitted to the bar in 1799, was elected to the Maryland senate in 1816. In 1824 he passed from the Federal to the Democratic party, and supported Andrew Jackson, who in 1831 made him attorney-general, and in 1833 secretary of the Treasury. The senate, after rejecting his appointment as chief justice in 1835, confirmed it in 1836. His early decisions were strongly in favour of state sovereignty, but his most famous decision was in the Dred Scott case, when he ruled that the Missouri compromise over the colour question was unconstitutional and that no Negro could claim state citizenship for legal purposes. Although an early opponent of slavery, Taney wished to put an end to anti-slavery agitation. See Life by C. B. Swisher (1938).

TANEYEV, Sergei Ivanovich, *tan-yay-yef* (1856–1915), Russian composer and pianist, was born in Vladimir, studied at the Conservatory, Moscow, and was professor there. A pupil of Tchaikovsky, he wrote music of all kinds, including two cantatas, *John of Damascus* and *After the Reading of a Psalm*, and six symphonies. Well known as a teacher, among his pupils were Scriabin and Rachmaninov.

TANFUCIO, Neri. See FUCINI.

TANGUY, Yves, *tã-gee* (1900–55), American artist, born in Paris. He was mainly self-taught, and began to paint in 1922, joining the surrealists in 1926. In 1930 he travelled in Africa, and went to the U.S.A. in 1939, becoming an American citizen in 1948. All his pictures are at the same time surrealist and nonfigurative, being peopled with numerous small objects or organisms, whose meaning and identity, as in the landscape of another planet, is unknown. See Life by J. T. Soby (1955).

TANNAHILL, Robert (1774–1810), Scottish poet, was born at Paisley, the son of a handloom weaver, and composed many of his best songs to the music of his shuttle. His *Poems and Songs* (1807) proved popular, the best-known being *Gloomy Winter's noo awa*, *Jessie the Flower o' Dunblane*, *The Braes o' Gleniffer*, *Loudon's Bonnie Woods and Braes* and *The Wood o' Craigielea*. But after a publisher declined a revised edition his body was found in a canal near Paisley. See Life in Semple's edition of his poems (1876) and Brown's *Paisley Poets* (vol. i 1889).

TANNER, Thomas (1674–1735), English antiquary, born at Market Lavington vicarage, Wiltshire, became a fellow of All Souls (1696), archdeacon of Norwich (1710), canon of Christ Church, Oxford (1724), and Bishop of St Asaph (1732). An enlarged edition of his *Notitia Monastica* (1695) appeared in 1744. Not less valuable is his biographical and bibliographical *Bibliotheca Britannico-Hibernica* (1748).

TANSLEY, Sir Arthur George (1871–1955), British botanist, born in London, Sherardian professor at Oxford (1927–37), founded the precursor (1904) of the Ecological Society (1914), the *New Phytologist* (1902) which he edited for 30 years, published textbooks on botany and contributed to anatomical and morphological botany and to psychology. He was elected F.R.S. in 1915 and received the Linnean Society gold medal in 1921.

TANTIA TOPEE (d. 1859), Brahman soldier from Gwalior, was Nana Sahib's lieutenant in the Indian Mutiny. With the Rani of Jhansi he occupied Gwalior and then held the field after his chief had fled. He was captured April 7, 1859, and executed.

TARKINGTON, (Newton) Booth (1869–1946), American author, born in Indianapolis. Many of his novels have an Indiana setting, including *The Gentleman from Indiana*, which is concerned with political corruption; but he is best known to English readers as the author of *Monsieur Beaucaire* (1900) and his 'Penrod' books—*Penrod* (1914) and *Seventeen* (1916). His other works include a trilogy, *Growth* (1927), including *The Magnificent Ambersons* (1918), which won the Pulitzer prize, *Alice Adams* (1921, Pulitzer prize), and a book of reminiscences, *The World does Move* (1928).

TARLETON, Sir Banastre, 1st Bart. (1754–1833), English soldier, born in Liverpool, educated at Oxford, served under Clinton and Cornwallis in America. He held Gloucester till it capitulated (1782), and then returned to England. Member for Liverpool (1790–1806; 1807–12), he was created baronet in 1815. See his *History of the Campaigns of 1780 and 1781* (1781).

TARLTON, Richard (d. 1588), English comedian, a man of 'happy unhappy answers', was introduced to Elizabeth through the Earl of Leicester and became one of the Queen's players (1583). He died in poverty, and on him was fathered *Tarlton's Jests* (1592?–1611?), in three parts.

TARQUINIUS, an Etruscan family, named after the city of Tarquinii, to which two of the kings of Rome belonged:

(1) **Lucius Tarquinius Priscus**, originally **Lucumo**, arrived a stranger in Rome with a favourable omen, and is said to have reigned 616–578 B.C., to have modified the constitution, and to have begun the Servian agger and the Circus Maximus. He was murdered.

(2) **Lucius Tarquinius Superbus**, king (534–510 B.C.), seventh and last King of Rome, extended his dominion more than any of his predecessors, and by establishing colonies founded Rome's greatness. But his tyranny, especially in the matter of Lucretia (q.v.), excited the discontent of both patricians and plebeians, and in consequence of a rising under his nephew, Brutus, he and all his family were banished. He took refuge with Lars Porsena at Clusium and, with him, levied successful war against Rome. He was later defeated at Lake Regillus (498 B.C.) and died a fugitive.

TARSKI, Alfred (1902–), Polish logician, born in Warsaw, was professor there (1925–1939), at Harvard, New York and Princeton, and since 1942 at Berkeley, California. He modified Carnap's extreme positivism, pioneered semantics, but for English tastes took too lightly the distinction between questions of logic and questions of fact. Quine (q.v.) is his prominent disciple. His chief works are *Introduction to Logic and the Methodology of Deductive Sciences* (1936; trans. 1941), *Undecidable Theories* with Mostowski and Robinson (1953), *Logic, Semantics and Metamathematics* (1956) and *Logic, Methodology and Philosophy of Science* (ed. with Nagel and Suppers, 1962).

TARTINI, Giuseppe, *tar-tee'nee* (1692–1770), Italian composer, born at Pirano in Istria, gave up the church and the law for music and fencing. Having secretly married the niece of the Archbishop of Padua, he fled to Assisi, but, after living in Venice, Ancona and Prague, returned before 1728 to Padua. Tartini 'was one of the greatest violinists of all time, an eminent composer, and a scientific writer on musical physics'. His best-known work is the *Trillo del Diavolo*.

TASMAN, Abel Janszoon (1603–*c.* 1659), Dutch navigator, was born in Lutjegast near Groningen. In 1642 he discovered Tasmania —named Van Diemen's Land—and New Zealand, in 1643 Tonga and Fiji, having been dispatched in quest of the 'Great South Land' by Antony Van Diemen (1593–1645), governor-general of Batavia. He made a second voyage (1644) to the Gulf of Carpentaria and the N.W. coast of Australia. See *Journal*, with trans. and Life by Heeres (Amsterdam 1898).

TASSIE, James (1735–99), Scottish modeller, born at Pollokshaws, Glasgow, in 1766 settled in London, and used a 'white enamel composition' in his well-known reproductions of the most famous gems. He also executed many cameo portraits of his contemporaries, and the plaster reproductions of the Portland Vase. His nephew, **William Tassie** (1777–1860), succeeded him. See Life by J. M. Gray (1895).

TASSO, (1) **Bernardo** (1493–1569), Italian poet, father of (2), was born at Venice of an illustrious family of Bergamo. After suffering poverty and exile owing to the outlawry by Charles V (1547) of his patron, the Duke of Salerno, he took service with the Duke of Mantua. His *Amadigi*, an epic on Amadis of Gaul, is a melodious imitation of Ariosto's manner, but exaggerated in sentiment. He began another epic, *Floridante* (1587), finished by his son, and wrote numerous lyrics (1749). See *Lettere di Bernardo Tasso* (ed. Campori, 1869) and his *Lettere inedite* (ed. Portioli, 1871).

(2) **Torquato** (1544–95), Italian poet, son of (1), was born at Sorrento, March 11, and shared his exiled father's wandering life, but in 1560 he was sent to study law and philosophy at Padua, where he published his first work, a romantic poem, *Rinaldo*. In the service of Cardinal Luigi d'Este he was introduced to the court of the Duke of Ferrara; and there, encouraged by the sisters of the duke, he began his great epic poem and masterpiece, *Gerusalemme Liberata.* In 1571 he accompanied Cardinal d'Este to France, and on his return to Italy

in 1572 became attached to the service of Duke Alfonso at Ferrara. For the court theatre he wrote his beautiful pastoral play, *Aminta* (1581). Tasso completed his great epic in 1575, and submitted it before publication to the critics of the day. Their fault-finding and Tasso's replies are recorded in his correspondence and in his *Apologia*. In 1576 he showed the first signs of mental disorder; he became suspicious and melancholy, and obsessed with fears of assassination. He was confined at Ferrara, but escaped, and eventually made his way to Naples, Rome and Turin, where he was welcomed by the Duke of Savoy. Returning to Ferrara in 1579, he met with a cold reception, and wounded by some real or imagined slight, broke into furious invectives against the duke, his courtiers, all the world. He was confined at Ferrara by order of the duke as insane (not, as is often alleged, for his love for the Princess Leonora, a story on which Byron based his *Lament of Tasso*); and in his seven years' confinement wrote many noble verses and philosophical dialogues and a vigorous defence of his *Jerusalem*, published without his leave and with many errors. The cruel contrast between his fate and the daily growing fame of his great poem had excited popular interest, and in July 1586 he was liberated on the intercession of Prince Vincenzo Gonzaga. He followed his new patron to Mantua, where he wrote his only tragedy, *Torrismondo*. Broken in health and spirits, he began again his restless wanderings, spending, however, most of these later years in Rome and Naples, helped and protected by many kind friends and patrons. He busied himself in rewriting his great epic, according to the modifications proposed by his numerous critics. The result, a poor simulacrum of his masterpiece, was published under the name *Gerusalemme Conquistata* (1593). Summoned to Rome by Pope Clement VIII to be crowned on the Capitol as poet laureate, he took ill on arrival and died in the monastery of Sant' Onofrio on the Janiculum, April 25. His *Jerusalem*, an idealized story of the first Crusade, is a typical product of his time, its blind idolatry of classic forms conflicting with newly-revived religious superstition. See his letters and prose writings (ed. Guasti, 1853–75), and Lives by W. Boulting (1907), E. Donadoni (1921), L. Tonelli (1935) and C. Previtera (1936).

TATA, Jamsetji Nasarwanji (1839–1904), Indian industrialist, born in Gujerat, built cotton mills at Nagpur (1877) and at Cooria near Bombay. He did much to promote scientific education in Indian schools. See Life by F. R. Harris (1958). His son, **Sir Dorabji** (1859–1932), developed the Indian iron-ore industry, applied hydroelectricity to the Cooria cotton mills and founded a commercial airline.

TATE, (1) Sir Henry, 1st Bart. (1819–99), English sugar magnate, art patron and philanthropist, born at Chorley, Lancashire, patented a method for cutting sugar cubes in 1872 and attained great wealth as a Liverpool sugar refiner. He founded the University Library at Liverpool and gave the nation the 'Tate Gallery', Millbank, London, which was opened in 1897, and contained his own valuable private collection. He was made a baronet in 1898.

(2) **Nahum** (1652–1715), Irish poet and dramatist, born in Dublin, studied at Trinity College there and saw his first play staged in London in 1678. With Johnson's approval, he wrote a number of 'improved' versions of Shakespeare's tragedies, substituting happy endings to suit the popular taste. With Dryden's help he wrote a second part to the poet's *Absalom and Achitophel* (1682) and with Brady compiled a metrical version of the psalms. 'While Shepherds watched their Flocks by Night' is attributed to him, and he wrote the libretto of Purcell's *Dido and Aeneas* (1689). He became poet laureate in 1692. His best-known work is *Panacea or a Poem on Tea* (1700). See E. K. Broadus, *The Laureateship* (1921).

TATI, Jacques, *tah-tee*, pseud. of **Jacques Tatischeff** (1908–), French actor, author and film producer, born in Pecq (S. et O.). His first appearance before English audiences was as the ghost in *Sylvie et le Fantôme*, but it was not until he appeared in *Jour de Fête* (1951), directed and written by himself, that he made his reputation as the greatest film comedian of the postwar period. This was enhanced by *M. Hulot's Holiday* (1954) and *Mon Oncle* (1958), satirizing the tyranny of luxurious, labour-saving gadgetry, which won a Cannes Festival prize (1958) and the American 'Oscar' and was hailed as a worthy successor to Chaplin's *Modern Times*.

TATIAN (2nd cent.), Christian apologist, born in Assyria, studied Greek philosophy, but was converted to Christianity by the martyr Justin at Rome in whose lifetime he wrote his *Oratio ad Graecos* (ed. by Schwartz, 1888), a glowing exposure of heathenism as compared with the new 'barbarian philosophy'. After Justin's death (166) Tatian fell into evil repute for heresies, and he retired to Mesopotamia, probably Edessa, writing treatise after treatise, all of which have perished. The notions of his which gave most offence were his excessive asceticism, his rejection of marriage and animal food, and certain Gnostic doctrines about a demiurge and the aeons. He was assailed in turn by Irenaeus, Tertullian, Hippolytus, Clement of Alexandria and Origen. He died, perhaps at Edessa, about 180. Of his writings one maintained a place of importance in the Syrian Church for two centuries. This was the *Diatessaron*, a kind of patchwork gospel freely constructed out of our four gospels. See German works by Zahn, Sellin, Gebhardt and Harnack; English ones by Hemphill (1888), R. Harris (1890), and J. H. Hill (1893).

TATIUS, Achilles (fl. *c.* A.D. 500), Greek romancer, was a rhetorician at Alexandria. He wrote *Leucippe and Cleitophon*.

TATTERSALL, Richard (1724–95), English auctioneer, born at Hurstwood, Lancashire, came early to London. He entered the Duke of Kingston's service, became an auctioneer, and in 1776 set up auction rooms at Hyde Park Corner, which became a celebrated mart of thoroughbred horses and a great racing centre. They were transferred to Knightsbridge in 1867. See *Memories of Hurstwood* by Tattersall Wilkinson and J. F. Tattersall (1889).

TAUBER, Richard, *tow'bėr* (1891–1948), Austrian-born British tenor, born at Linz, established himself as one of Germany's leading tenors, particularly in Mozartian opera, until 1925 when he increasingly appeared in light opera, notably Lehár's *Land of Smiles,* which he brought to London in 1931. This won him great popularity, repeated by his part in his own *Old Chelsea* (1943), but at the expense of the finer qualities of his voice. He appeared at Covent Garden in 1938, became a British subject and died in Sydney, Australia. See Life by his wife (1959).

TAUBMAN-GOLDIE, Sir George Dashwood (1846–1925), Manx traveller and administrator, son of Colonel Goldie Taubman, speaker of the House of Keys, was born in the Isle of Man, travelled in Africa, and as founder and governor of the Royal Niger Company greatly extended English commerce and influence.

TAUCHNITZ, Karl Christoph Traugott, *towKH'nits* (1761–1836), German publisher, born near Grimma, set up in 1796 a small printing business in Leipzig, to which he added publishing and typefounding. In 1809 he began to issue his cheap editions of the classics. He introduced stereotyping into Germany (1816). His nephew, **Christian Bernhard, Baron von Tauchnitz** (1816–95), also founded in 1837 a printing and publishing house in Leipzig famous for its collection of 'British and American Authors', begun in 1841.

TAULER, Johann, *tow'ler* (*c.* 1300–61), German mystic, was born at Strasbourg, and became a Dominican (*c.* 1318). Driven from Strasbourg by a feud between the city and his order, he settled at twenty-four at Basel, and associated with the devout 'Friends of God', having before then been a disciple of Meister Eckhart (q.v.). His fame as a preacher spread far and wide, and he became the centre of the quickened religious life in the middle Rhine valley. He died at Strasbourg. See English Life by S. Winkworth (1857), and German books by Karl Schmidt (1841–75) and Siedl (1911).

TAUNTON, Lord. See LABOUCHÈRE (1).

TAUSSIG, Frank William, *tow'sig* (1859–1940), American economist, born at St Louis, Mo., became professor at Harvard (1892–1935) and was best known for his *Principles of Economics* (1911).

TAVERNER, (1) **John** (*c.* 1495–1545), English musician, organist at Boston and Christ Church, Oxford, composed notable motets and masses. Accused of heresy, he was imprisoned by Wolsey, but released, 'being but a musitian'. He died at Boston.

(2) **Richard** (*c.* 1505–75), English author, was patronized by Wolsey and Cromwell, for whom he compiled Taverner's Bible (1539), which was really a revision o Matthew's Bible (1537). On the fall of Cromwell, he was imprisoned but soon released and was M.P. for Liverpool (1545).

TAVERNIER, Jean Baptiste, Baron d'Aubonne, *ta-ver'nyay* (1605–89), French traveller, was born at Paris, the son of a Protestant engraver from Antwerp. His first journey to the East (1631–33) was by way of Constantinople to Persia, thence by Aleppo and Malta to Italy. The second journey (1638–43) was across Syria to Ispahan, Agra and Golconda; the third (1643–49), through Ispahan, much of Hindustan, Batavia and Bantam, thence to Holland by the Cape; and the fourth (1651–55), fifth (1657–62) and sixth (1663–68) to many districts of Persia and India. Tavernier travelled as a dealer in precious stones. Louis XIV, gave him 'letters of nobility' in 1669, and next year he bought the barony of Aubonne near Geneva. In 1684 he started for Berlin to advise the Elector of Brandenburg in his projects for eastern trade. In 1689 he went to Russia, and died at Moscow. His famous *Six Voyages* was published in 1676; the complementary *Recueil* in 1679. See *Travels in India,* trans. by Dr V. Ball (1890), and a French work by Joret (1886).

TAWNEY, Richard Henry (1880–1962), English economic historian, born in Calcutta, was educated at Rugby and Balliol College, Oxford, of which he was elected fellow in 1918. After a spell of social work at Toynbee Hall in the East End of London, he became tutor, executive (1905–47) and president (1928–44) of the Workers' Educational Association. As a sergeant in the Manchester Regiment, he was severely wounded during the battle of the Somme (1916). A socialist in the non-Marxist Keir Hardie tradition and a Christian, he wrote a number of studies in English economic history, particularly of the Tudor and Stuart periods, of which the best known are *The Acquisitive Society* (1926), *Religion and the Rise of Capitalism* (1926), *Equality* (1931) and *Business and Politics under James I* (1958). He was professor of Economic History at London (1931–49) and was elected F.B.A. in 1935. He married a sister, Annette Jeanie (d. 1958), of Lord Beveridge in 1909.

TAYLOR, (1) **Alfred Edward** (1869–1945), English scholar and philosopher, born at Oundle, Northamptonshire, became professor of Logic at McGill University (1903–08) and of Moral Philosophy at St Andrews (1908–24) and Edinburgh (1924–41). An authority on Plato, he wrote *Plato, The Man and his Work* (1926), *A Commentary on Plato's Timaeus* (1928), and translated his *Laws* (1934). Other notable works are *The Problem of Conduct* (1901), *Elements of Metaphysics* (1903), the Gifford lectures which he gave at St Andrews on *The Faith of a Moralist,* and studies of St Thomas Aquinas (1924) and Socrates (1932).

(2) **Alfred Swaine** (1806–80), English medical jurist, born at Northfleet, for forty-six years was professor of Medical Jurisprudence at Guy's Hospital. Elected F.R.S. (1845), he wrote two standard works on medical jurisprudence (1844 and 1865) and one on poisons (1848).

(3) **Bayard** (1825–78), American traveller and author, was born in Chester county, Penn., and apprenticed to a printer, wrote a volume of poems (1844), visited Europe, published *Views Afoot* (1846), and obtained

a post on the *New York Tribune.* As its correspondent he made extensive travels in California and Mexico, up the Nile, in Asia Minor and Syria, across Asia to India, China and Japan—recorded in a great number of travel books which he published. In 1862–63 he was secretary of legation at St Petersburg; in 1878 became ambassador at Berlin, where he died. His poetical works include *Rhymes of Travel* (1848), *Poems of the Orient* (1854), *Poems of Home and Travel* (1855), *Prince Deukalion* (1878), a play, but he was best known for his translation of Goethe's *Faust* (1870–71). Among his novels is *Hannah Thurston* (1863). See his *Life and Letters* (1884) by M. Hansen-Taylor and H. E. Scudder.

(4) **Brook** (1685–1731), English mathematician, born at Edmonton, studied at St John's College, Cambridge, and in 1715 published his *Methodus*, the foundation of the Calculus of Finite Differences, containing 'Taylor's Theorem'. In 1714–18 he was secretary to the Royal Society. His *Contemplatio Philosophica* (1719) was edited with a Life by Sir W. Young (1793).

(5) **Sir Henry** (1800–86), English poet, was born, the son of a gentleman farmer, at Bishop-Middleham, in Durham, and was a clerk in the colonial office (1824–72). D.C.L. (1862) and K.C.M.G. (1869), he died at Bournemouth. He wrote four tragedies, *Isaac Comnenus* (1827), a remarkable study in character, *Philip van Artefelde* (1834), *Edwin the Fair* (1842) and *St Clement's Eve* (1862). A romantic comedy, *The Virgin Widow* (1850), was afterwards entitled *A Sicilian Summer.* In 1845 he published a volume of lyrical poetry, and in 1847 *The Eve of the Conquest.* His prose included *The Statesman* (1836) and *Autobiography* (1885).

(6) **Isaac** (1787–1865), Anglo-Jewish author, was born at Lavenham, son of the London engraver **Isaac** (1759–1829) and father of (7). After a course of study he settled down to a literary life at Ongar, and among his chief books were *Natural History of Enthusiasm* (1829), *Natural History of Fanaticism* (1833), *Spiritual Despotism* (1835), *Physical Theory of Another Life* (1836), and *Ultimate Civilisation* (1860).

(7) **Isaac** (1829–1901), English philologist, son of (6), born at Stanford Rivers, studied at Trinity College, Cambridge, and became in 1875 rector of Settrington and canon of York in 1885. His *Words and Places* (1864) made him known, while *The Alphabet* (1883) brought him a wide reputation. Other publications include *Etruscan Researches* (1874), *The Origin of the Aryans* (1890) and *Names and their Histories* (1896). See his family history of the Taylors (1867).

(8) **Jeremy** (1613–67), English divine, the third son of a Cambridge barber, entered Caius College, and became a fellow of All Souls, Oxford (1636), chaplain to Archbishop Laud, and in 1638 rector of Uppingham. *The Sacred Order and Offices of Episcopacy* (1642) gained him his D.D. During the Civil War he is said to have accompanied the royal army as a chaplain and was taken prisoner at Cardigan Castle (1645). After the downfall of the cause he sought shelter in Wales, kept a school, and found a patron in the Earl of Carbery, then living at Golden Grove, Llandilo, immortalized in the title of Taylor's still popular manual of devotion (1655). During the last thirteen years (1647–60) of Taylor's enforced seclusion appeared all his great works, some of them the most enduring monuments of sacred eloquence in the English language. The first was *The Liberty of Prophesying* (1646), a noble and comprehensive plea for toleration and freedom of opinion. *The Life of Christ, or the Great Exemplar* (1649) is an arrangement of the facts in historical order, interspersed with prayers and discourses. *The Rule and Exercises of Holy Living* (1650) and *The Rule and Exercises of Holy Dying* (1651) together form the choicest classic of English devotion. The fifty-two *Sermons* (1651–53), with the discourses in the *Life of Christ* and many passages in the *Holy Living* and *Dying*, contain the richest examples of their author's characteristically gorgeous eloquence. The more formal treatises were *An Apology for Authorised and Set Forms of Liturgy* (1646); *Clerus Dominio* (on the ministerial office, 1651); *The Real Presence in the Blessed Sacrament* (1654); *Unum Necessarium* (on repentance, 1655), which brought on him the charge of Pelagianism; *The Worthy Communicant* (1660); *The Rite of Confirmation* (1663); *The Dissuasive from Popery* (1664); and the famous *Ductor Dubitantium* (1660), the most learned and subtle of all his works, intended as a handbook of Christian casuistry and ethics. During the Civil War Taylor was thrice imprisoned, once for the preface to the *Golden Grove*; the last time in the Tower for an 'idolatrous' print of Christ in the attitude of prayer in his *Collection of Offices* (1658). In 1658 he got a lectureship at Lisburn, at the Restoration the bishopric of Down and Connor, with next year the administration of Dromore; and became vice-chancellor of Dublin University and a member of the Irish privy council. In his first visitation (in spite of his *Liberty of Prophesying*) he ejected thirty-six Presbyterian ministers, but neither severity nor gentleness could prevail to force a form of religion upon an unwilling people. He died at Lisburn, August 13, and was buried in the cathedral of Dromore. See Heber's edition of his works, with Life (1820–22; revised 1847–54), and Lives by E. Gosse (1904), W. J. Brown (1925) and Stranks (1952).

(9) **John** (1580–1653), English poet, the 'Water-poet', born at Gloucester, became a Thames waterman, but, pressed into the navy, served at the siege of Cadiz. At the outbreak of the Civil War (1642) he kept a public house in Oxford, gave it up for another in London, and there hawked his own doggerel poems, which yet are not destitute of natural humour and low, jingling wit. The chief event of his life was his journey afoot from London to Edinburgh (1618), described in his *Penniless Pilgrimage* (1618); similar books were his *Travels in Germanie* (1617) and *The Praise of Hempseed*, a story of a voyage in a brown paper boat from London to Queenborough (1618).

(10) **John Edward** (1791–1844), English

journalist, born at Ilminster, son of a Unitarian minister, was the founder in 1821 of the liberal *Manchester Guardian.*

(11) **John Henry** (1871–1963), English golfer, born at Northam in Devon, was the winner of the British Open Championship in 1894. This triumph was repeated in 1895, 1900, 1909 and 1913. Twice he won the French Open Championship, in 1908 and 1909, and once the German Open Championship, in 1912. A brilliant player, he was specially known for his skill with the mashie. He wrote the very popular *Taylor on Golf* (1902).

(12) **Nathaniel William** (1786–1858), American theologian, born at New Milford, Conn., became in 1822 professor of Theology at Yale. His 'New Haven theology', long assailed as heretical, was a softening of the traditional Calvinism of New England, maintained the doctrine of natural ability, and denied total depravity; sin is a voluntary action of the sinner, but there is, derived from Adam, a bias to sin, which is not itself sinful. Porter edited his works in 1858–59.

(13) **Rowland** (d. 1555), English Protestant martyr, born at Rothbury, became rector of Hadleigh (1544), Archdeacon of Exeter (1551), and a canon of Rochester. Under Mary he was imprisoned as a heretic, and on February 8, 1555, was burned near Hadleigh.

(14) **Thomas** (1758–1835), English scholar, 'the Platonist', a Londoner educated at St Paul's School, entered Lubbock's bank as a clerk. His fifty works include translations of the Orphic Hymns, parts of Plotinus, Proclus, Pausanias, Apuleius, Iamblichus, Porphyry, &c., Plato (nine of the Dialogues by Floyer Sydenham, 1804), and Aristotle (1806–12). *The Spirit of All Religions* (1790) expresses his strange polytheistic creed. See sketch by Axon (1890).

(15) **Tom** (1817–80), Scottish dramatist and editor, born at Sunderland, studied at Glasgow and Trinity College, Cambridge, and was elected a fellow. Professor for two years of English at University College, London, and called to the bar in 1845, he was secretary to the Board of Health 1850–72, and then to the Local Government Act Office. From 1846 he wrote or adapted over a hundred pieces for the stage, among them *Our American Cousin, Still Waters Run Deep* (1855), *The Ticket of Leave Man* (1863), and *'Twixt Axe and Crown.* He edited the autobiographies of Haydon and Leslie, completed the latter's *Life and Times of Reynolds*, translated *Ballads and Songs of Brittany* (1865), and in 1874 became editor of *Punch. The Times* art critic, he appeared as a witness for Ruskin in the libel action brought against him by Whistler in 1878.

(16) **William** (1765–1836), English author, 'of Norwich', son of a Unitarian merchant, entered his father's counting-house in 1779 and, travelling extensively on the Continent introduced the works of Lessing, Goethe &c., to English readers, mainly through, criticisms and translations, collected in his *Historic Survey of German Poetry* (1828–30). Borrow's *Lavengro* describes his scepticism and inveterate smoking. See Life by Robberds (1843).

(17) **Zachary** (1784–1850), American soldier and 12th president of the United States, born in Orange County, Va., entered the army in 1808. In 1812 he held Fort Harrison on the Wabash against Indians, and in 1832 fought with Black Hawk. In 1836, now colonel, he was ordered to Florida, and in 1837 defeated the Seminoles at Okeechobee Swamp, and won the brevet of brigadier-general. In 1840 he was placed in command of the army in the southwest. When Texas was annexed in 1845 he gathered 4000 regulars at Corpus Christi in March 1846, marched to the Rio Grande, and erected Fort Brown opposite Matamoros. The Mexicans crossed the Rio Grande to drive him out. But the battles of Palo Alto and Resaca de la Palma on May 8 and 9 repulsed them, and Taylor seized Matamoros. In September he captured Monterey. After seven weeks' vain waiting for reinforcements the march was resumed. Victoria was occupied, but the line of communication was too long for the meagre force, while Polk's Democratic administration, fearing the rising fame of Taylor, who was a Whig, crippled him by withholding reinforcements. Taylor was falling back to Monterey when his regulars were taken from him to form part of a new expedition under General Scott. Santa Ana, the Mexican general, overtook his 5000 volunteers near the pass of Buena Vista; but Taylor, on February 22, 1847, repulsed the 21,000 Mexicans with a loss thrice as great as his own. In 1848 the Whigs selected Taylor as their candidate for the presidency. He was elected in November and inaugurated next March. The struggle over the extension of slavery had begun. The Democratic congress opposed the admission of California as a free state, while the president favoured it. To avert the threatened danger to the Union Henry Clay introduced his famous compromise. Taylor remained firm and impartial though his son-in-law, Jefferson Davis, headed the extreme proslavery faction. Before a decision was reached President Taylor died, July 9, 1850. See Life by Gen. O. O. Howard (1892).

TCHAIKOVSKY, Piotr Ilyich, *chī-kof'skee* (1840–93), Russian composer, was born May 7 at Kamsko-Votinsk, where his father was inspector of government mines. His early musical talents were encouraged, but on the family's moving to St Petersburg he entered the school of jurisprudence and started his life as a minor civil servant. In 1862 he enrolled at the recently opened conservatoire, but after three years he was engaged by his previous orchestration teacher, Nicholas Rubinstein, to teach harmony at the latter's own conservatoire at Moscow. His operas and 2nd symphony brought him into the public eye, and in 1875 his piano concerto in B flat minor had its première in Moscow. Temperamentally unsuited to marriage, he left his bride Antonina Ivanovna Miliukova a month after the wedding (1877) in a state of nervous collapse. After recuperation abroad he resigned from the conservatoire and retired to the country to devote himself entirely to composition. He made occasional trips abroad and in 1893 was made an honorary Mus.D. of Cambridge University. Soon after his return to Russia from England and after the first performance of his 6th ('Pathétique') symphony, he took cholera and died at St Petersburg. Three years earlier his correspondence, dating back to 1876, with Nadezhda von Meck, widow of a wealthy engineer, had come to a stop. Though they never met, her artistic, moral and financial support played a very important part in his career. Though acquainted with Balakirev, Rimsky-Korsakov and other members of the group of late 19th-century composers known as the 'Five', he was not in sympathy with their avowedly nationalistic aspirations and their use of folk material, and was himself regarded by them as something of a renegade cosmopolitan. The melodiousness, colourful orchestration, and deeply expressive content of his music brought him and still brings him an enthusiastic following exceeding that of any other Russian composer. His introspective and melancholy nature is reflected in some of his symphonies and orchestral pieces, but not in his ballet music—*Swan Lake*, *The Sleeping Beauty* and *Nutcracker*—which are by common consent masterpieces of their kind. In such cases his weakness in large-scale structural organization was concealed. His works include 6 symphonies, of which the last three are best known, 2 piano concertos (a third was left uncompleted), a violin concerto, a number of tone poems, including *Romeo and Juliet* and *Italian Capriccio*, songs and piano pieces. Of his 11 operas, *Eugene Onegin* and *The Queen of Spades* have successfully survived. See studies by E. Blom (1927), E. Evans (1935), Weinstock (1943) and G. Abraham (1946); also *Life and Letters* (1906), ed. M. Tschaikovsky, and his *Diaries* (1945).

TCHEKHOV. See CHEHOV.

TCHEREPNIN, Nikolai Nikolaievich, *che-rep-neen'* (1873–1945), Russian composer, born in St Petersburg. He was trained as a lawyer, but abandoned this profession to study under Rimsky-Korsakov, and first appeared as a pianist. In 1901 he became conductor of the Belaiev Concerts and took charge of opera at the Maryinsky Theatre. From 1908 to 1914 Tcherepnin worked with Diaghilev, conducting ballet and opera throughout Europe. In 1914 he went to Petrograd, leaving there four years later to become director of the Tiflis Conservatory. He settled in Paris in 1921. Works include two operas, a number of ballets, much orchestral music, and piano pieces.

TEBALDI, Renata, *-bal'-* (1922–), Italian operatic soprano, born in Pesaro. She studied at Parma Conservatory, made her début at Rovigo in 1944, and was invited by Toscanini to appear at the re-opening of La Scala, Milan, in 1946. She has appeared in England, France, Spain, South America and at the Metropolitan, New York, and San Francisco.

TECUMSEH (*c.* 1768–1813), American Indian chief of the Shawnees, joined his brother, 'The Prophet', in a rising against the whites suppressed at Tippecanoe by Harrison in 1811, and passing into the English service, commanded the Indian allies in the war of 1812–13 as brigadier-general. He fell fighting at the Thames in Canada (1813). See Lives by Eggleston (1878) and Raymond (1915).

TEDDER, Arthur William, 1st Baron Tedder of Glenguin (1890–1967), marshal of the R.A.F., born at Glenguin, Stirlingshire, was in the Colonial Service when war broke out in 1914. By 1916 he had transferred to the R.F.C. Remaining in the service, at the outbreak of World War II he was director-general of research and development, Air Ministry. From 1940 he organized the Middle East Air Force with great success, moving on to the Mediterranean theatre and later becoming deputy supreme commander under Eisenhower. His services were recognized in his appointment as marshal of the R.A.F. (1945). Created a baron in 1946, in 1950 he became chancellor of the University of Cambridge and also a governor of the B.B.C. See his *Air Power in the War* (1948) and autobiography, *With Prejudice* (1966).

TEGETMEIER, William Bernhard, *teg'et-mī-ėr* (1816–1912), Anglo-German ornithologist, was born at Colnbrook, S. Bucks. He assisted Darwin in his work and for many years edited *The Field*.

TEGETTHOFF, Baron Wilhelm von (1827–1871), Austrian admiral, born at Marburg, defeated the Danes off Heligoland (1864) and an Italian fleet under Persano near Lissa (1866), the first battle between ironclads.

TEGNÉR, Esaias, *teng-nayr* (1782–1846), Swedish poet, born at Krykerud in Värmland, the son of a pastor, graduated in 1802 at Lund University, and was appointed a lecturer in 1803. His stirring *War-song for the Militia of Scania* (1808) made his name known, and *Svea* (1811) made it famous. In 1812 he became professor of Greek. His best poems all belong to eight years—*Song to the Sun* (1817); *Degree Day at Lund* (1820); *Axel*, a romance of the days of Charles XII (1821); and his masterpiece, *Frithiof's Saga* (1825). He became Bishop of Vexiö (1824). See Life by Böttiger prefixed to his collected works (1847–51); also works by Brandes (Stockholm 1878), Kippenberg (Leipzig 1884), and Christensen (3rd ed. Leipzig 1890).

TEILHARD DE CHARDIN, Pierre, *tay-yahr dė shahr-dī* (1881–1955), French geologist, palaeontologist, Jesuit priest and philosopher, the son of an Auvergne landowner, was educated at a Jesuit school, lectured in pure science at the Jesuit College in Cairo and in 1918 became professor of Geology at the Institut Catholique in Paris. In 1923 he undertook palaeontological expeditions in China, and later in central Asia, but increasingly his researches did not conform to Jesuit orthodoxy and he was forbidden by his religious superiors to teach and publish, and in 1948 was not allowed to stand for a professorship at the Sorbonne in succession to the Abbé Breuil (q.v.). Nevertheless, his work in Cenozoic geology and palaeontology became known and he was awarded academic distinctions, including the Legion of Honour (1946). From 1951 he lived in America. Posthumously published, his philosophical speculations, based on his scientific work, trace the evolution of animate matter to two basic principles: nonfinality and complexification. By the concept of *involution* he explains why *homo sapiens* is the only species which in spreading over the globe has resisted intense division into further species. This leads on to transcendental speculations, which allow him original, if theologically unorthodox, proofs for the existence of God. This work, *The Phenomenon of Man* (trans. 1959; intro. Sir Julian Huxley), is complementary to *Le Milieu divin* (trans. 1960). See Lives by N. Corte (trans. 1960) and C. Cuénot (1965).

TEISSERENC DE BORT, Léon Philippe, *tes-rã dė bor* (1855–1913), French meteorologist, born in Paris, became chief meteorologist at the Bureau Central Météorologique in Paris. He discovered and named the stratosphere as distinct from the troposphere, in the upper atmosphere. He was awarded the Symons Gold Medal by the Royal Meteorological Society in 1908.

TEIXEIRA, Pedro, *tay-shay'ra* (*c.* 1575–1640), Portuguese soldier, in 1614 fought against the French in Brazil. He helped to found Pará in 1615, of which he was governor (1620 and 1640). He led an important expedition up the Amazon (1637–39) and across the mountains to Quito, returning by the same route.

TELEKI, Count Paul, *tel'e-kee* (1879–1941), Hungarian statesman, born in Budapest, where he became professor of Geography at the university in 1919. Combining politics with an academic career, he was also in that year appointed foreign minister and, from 1920 to 1921, premier. Founder of the Christian National League and chief of Hungary's boy scouts, he was minister of education in 1938 and again premier in 1939. He was fully aware of the German threat to his country, but all measures to avert it, including a pact with Yugoslavia, were unavailing through lack of support. When Germany marched against Yugoslavia through Hungary, he took his own life.

TELEMANN, Georg Philipp, *tay'lė-mahn* (1681–1767), German composer, born in Magdeburg, the son of a clergyman, was largely self-taught. He gained his musical knowledge by learning to play a host of instruments (including the violin, recorder and zither, and later the shawm, oboe, flute and bass trombone) and by studying the scores of the masters. In 1700 he was a student of languages and science at Leipzig University and in 1704 was appointed organist of the New Church and *kapellmeister* to Prince Promnitz at Sorau. In 1709 he was *kapellmeister* at Eisenach, from 1712 to 1721 *kapellmeister* to the Prince of Bayreuth and in 1721 was appointed music director of the Johanneum at Hamburg, a post which he held until his death. One of the most prolific composers, Telemann's works include church music, forty-four passions, forty operas, oratorios, including *Der Tag des Gerichts* and *Die Tageszeiten*, countless songs and a large body of instrumental music. In his lifetime ranked above his friend J. S. Bach and admired by Handel, who borrowed from his music, he lost popularity after his death and not until the 1930s were his musical gifts rediscovered. Though his masterly grasp of the techniques of all forms of musical composition was always recognized, especially his skill as a contrapuntist, critics regarded him as unoriginal and condemned his easily turned out works as lacking in depth and sincerity. But through his study of and admiration for the French composers, notably Lully, a new grace and richness was introduced into German music. Much of the liveliness and gaiety in his work sprang from his sense of humour and also from an interest in folk music aroused at Sorau where he heard the tunes of the Polish and Moravian dances. He wrote three autobiographies, the last of which was published in 1739. See works by H. Hörner (1931), K. Schäfer (1931), and a Life by E. Valentin (1931).

TELFORD, Thomas (1757–1834), Scottish engineer, was born, a shepherd's son, at Westerkirk, Langholm, August 9, 1757, at fourteen was apprenticed to a stonemason, in 1780 went to Edinburgh, and in 1782 to London. In 1784 he got work at Portsmouth dockyard; in 1787 became surveyor of public works for Shropshire; and his two bridges over the Severn at Montford and Buildwas gained him the planning of the Ellesmere Canal (1793–1805). In 1801 he was commissioned by government to report on the public works required for Scotland; and he constructed the Caledonian Canal (1803–23), more than 1000 miles of road, and 1200 bridges, besides churches, manses, harbours, &c. Other works by him were the road from London to Holyhead, with the Menai Suspension Bridge (1825), the Dean Bridge, Edinburgh (1832), and the St Katharine's Docks (1826–28) in London; he was also responsible for draining large tracts of the Fen country. He was elected F.R.S. in 1827 and was the first president of the Institution of Civil Engineers. He was buried in Westminster Abbey. See Lives by himself (1838), Sir Alexander Gibb (1935) and L. T. C. Rolt (1958).

TELL, William, Swiss patriot of Bürglen in Uri, reputed the saviour of his native district from the tyranny of Austria. Johannes von Müller tells at length, in his History of Switzerland (1786), how Albert II of Austria strove to annex the Forest Cantons; how in 1307 his tyrannical steward Gessler compelled the Swiss to do reverence to the ducal hat erected on a pole in Altorf; how Tell, a famous marksman, was for noncompliance condemned to shoot an apple off his own son's head; and how afterwards Tell slew the tyrant, and so initiated the movement which secured the independence of Switzerland. Von Müller had no doubt of the truth of the story; but the tale of the 'master shot' is found in Aryan, Samoyede and Turkish folklore. Tell's very existence is disputed; his name first occurs in a ballad of 1470, and the full story in Tschudi's *Swiss Chronicle* (1572). Albert II was a just, if severe, ruler; and Gessler's name is never once mentioned till 1513. See French studies by Albert Rilliot (1868) and H. Naef (1942) and German ones by Kopp (1851) and K. Meyer, *Der Ursprung der Eidgenossenschaft* (1941).

TELLER, Edward (1908–), Hungarian-born American nuclear physicist, born at Budapest, graduated in chemical engineering at Karlsruhe, studied theoretical physics at Munich, Göttingen and under Niels Bohr at Copenhagen. He left Germany in 1933, lectured in London and Washington (1935) and contributed profoundly to the modern explanation of solar energy, anticipating thereby the theory behind thermonuclear explosions. He worked on the atomic bomb project (1941–46), joined Oppenheimer's theoretical study group at Berkeley, California, where, after his appointment to a professorship at Chicago (1946), he was (1952–53) consultant at and (1958–60) director of the new nuclear laboratories at Livermore. From 1953 he was professor of Physics at California University, and chairman of the department of Applied Science there from 1963. He repudiated as scientist any moral implications of his work, stating that, but for Oppenheimer's moral qualms, the U.S. might have had hydrogen bombs in 1947. After Russia's first atomic test (1949) he was one of the architects of Truman's crash programme to build and test (1952) the world's first hydrogen bomb. See his *Our Nuclear Future* (1958; with A. Latter).

TÉLLEZ. See TIRSO DE MOLINA.

TEMPLE, (1) Frederick (1821–1902), English divine, father of (4), born at Santa Maura in the Ionian islands, educated at Blundell's School and Balliol College, Oxford, of which he became a Mathematics lecturer and fellow. He was principal of Kneller Hall Training College (1858–69), inspector of schools and headmaster of Rugby (1857–69), wrote the first of the allegedly heterodox *Essays and Reviews* (1860) which almost prevented his appointment to the bishopric of Exeter in 1869, and supported the disestablishment of the Irish Church. In 1885 he became Bishop of London and in 1897 Archbishop of Canterbury. He was responsible with Archbishop MacLagen of York for the 'Lambeth Opinions' (1889) which attempted to solve some ritual controversies.

(2) **Richard Grenville, 1st Earl** (1711–79), English statesman, elder brother of George Grenville (q.v.), in 1756–61 held office as first lord of the admiralty and lord privy seal under the elder Pitt, who had married his sister. He bitterly opposed Bute and broke with Pitt (Chatham) on the Stamp Act in 1766.

(3) **Sir William** (1628–99), English diplomatist and essay writer, born in London, studied at Emmanuel College, Cambridge, but at nineteen went abroad, after falling in love with Dorothy Osborne (1627–95). Their seven years of separation gave opportunity for Dorothy's delightful letters and they were married in 1655. His diplomatic career, begun in 1655, was crowned by his part in the Triple Alliance (1668) of England, Holland and Sweden against France. Temple also took part in the Congress of Aix-la-Chapelle (1668), and was ambassador at The Hague—a post to which he returned (1674) after the war between England and Holland. In 1677 he helped to bring about the marriage of the Prince of Orange with the Princess Mary. He suggested the scheme of a reformed privy council of thirty, and for a short while formed with Halifax, Essex and Sunderland an inner council of four. After the revolution he declined a secretaryship of state to devote himself to literature in retirement at Moor Park in Surrey, where Swift was his secretary. An outstanding essayist, he was one of the reformers of English style, showing a development in rhythmical finish and avoiding unnecessary quotations and long parentheses. See his *Miscellanea* (1679, 1692), a collection of essays, including the famous essay 'Upon the Ancient and Modern Learning', his Correspondence, ed. Moore-Smith (1928), study by Marburg (1932), and Life by Woodbridge (1940); for Dorothy Osborne see Cecil's *Two Quiet Lives* (1948).

(4) **William** (1881–1944), English ecclesiastic, son of (1), born at Exeter, was educated at Rugby and Oxford, where he was a fellow of Queen's College (1904–10). He took orders in 1908, was headmaster of Repton School (1910–14) and became a canon of Westminster in 1919. In 1921 he became Bishop of Manchester, in 1929 Archbishop of York and in 1942 Archbishop of Canterbury. With interests as broad as his humanity, he united solid learning and great administrative ability. As Primate, he was one of the greatest moral forces of his time. An outspoken advocate of social reform, he made as his main task the application to current problems of his conception of the Christian philosophy of life, crusading against usury, slums, dishonesty, and the aberrations of the profit motive. Temple's leadership was also seen in his chairmanship of the Doctrinal Commission of the Church of England and in his work for the Ecumenical Movement of Christian Union. His publications include *Church and Nation* (1915), *Christianity and the State* (1928) and *Christianity and the Social Order* (1942). See the study by F. A. Iremonger (1948) and essays, ed. Baker (1958).

TEMPLER, Sir Gerald (1898–), British general, was educated at Wellington College and the R.M.C., Sandhurst. Commissioned in the Royal Irish Fusiliers, he served with them in World War I, becoming a brevet lieut.-col. World War II eventually brought him command of the 6th Armoured Division. He was vice-chief of the Imperial General Staff (1948–50), and C.I.G.S. (1955–58). As high commissioner and c.-in-c. Malaya (1952–54) his military firmness and resourceful support for the loyal elements of the population went far to frustrate the Communist guerillas' offensive. He was created K.B.E. in 1949, G.C.M.G. in 1953, G.C.B. in 1955, and K.G. in 1963.

TEMPLEWOOD, Sir Samuel John Gurney Hoare, 1st Viscount (1880–1959), British Conservative politician, was educated at Harrow and Oxford. He entered politics in 1905 as assistant private secretary to the colonial secretary and in 1910 became M.P. for Chelsea, a seat he held till he received a peerage in 1944. He was secretary of state for Air (1922–29), and as secretary of state for India (1931–35) he piloted the India Act through the Commons against the opposition of Winston Churchill. In 1935, as foreign secretary, he was criticized for his part in the discussions which led to the abortive Hoare-Laval pact over the Italian invasion of Ethiopia. He resigned, and in 1936 was appointed first lord of the Admiralty. Home secretary (1937–39), he was a strong advocate of penal reform. His Criminal Justice Bill (1938) never became law because of the outbreak of war, but much of it was embodied in the Act of 1948. From 1940 to 1944 he was ambassador on special mission to Madrid. In his later years he continued as an apologist for the National Government, whose 'appeasement' policy towards the dictators he helped to direct, and as a determined opponent of capital punishment. His publications include *The Shadow of the Gallows* (1951) and *Nine Troubled Years* (1954).

TEN BRINK. See BRINK.

TENCIN, Claudine Alexandrine Guérin de, *tã-sĩ* (1681–1749), French beauty and writer, born at Grenoble, entered the religious life, but in 1714 came to Paris, where her wit and beauty attracted a crowd of lovers, among them the Regent and Cardinal Dubois. She had much political influence, enriched herself, and helped the fortunes of her brother, Cardinal Pierre Guérin de Tencin (1680–1758). But her importance died with the regent and the cardinal in 1723. In 1726 she lay a short time in the Bastille, after one of her lovers had shot himself in her house. Her later life was more decorous, and her *salon* one of the most popular in Paris. Fontenelle was one of her oldest lovers; D'Alembert one of her children. Her romances include *Mémoires du Comte de Comminges* (1735), *Le Siège de Calais* (1739) and *Les Malheurs de l'amour* (1747). See her letters to her brother (1790) and the Duc de Richelieu (1806), and books by Nicolaus (1908), Masson (1909) and de Coynart (1910).

TENIERS, *ten-eers'*, **(1) David, the elder** (1582–1649), Flemish genre painter, father of (2), born and died at Antwerp. His subjects are generally homely tavern scenes, rustic games, weddings, &c. His *Temptation of St Anthony* is well known.

(2) David, the younger (1610–90), Flemish genre painter, son of (1), quickly gained distinction, enjoying the favour and friendship of the Austrian archduke, the Prince of Orange, and the Bishop of Ghent. In 1647 he took up his abode at Brussels. His seven hundred pictures possess, in superlative degree, the qualities that mark his father's work. None has realized more richly the charm of joyous open-air life. His scriptural subjects alone are unsatisfactory. See Life by G. Eekhoud (1926).

TENISON, Thomas (1636–1715), English divine, born at Cottenham in Cambridgeshire, studied at Corpus Christi, Cambridge, and was made Bishop of Lincoln by William III in 1691, and Archbishop of Canterbury in 1694. He was a favourite at court, crowned Queen Anne and George I, and strongly supported the Hanoverian succession. His works comprise antipapal tracts, sermons, and a criticism of Hobbes. See Life by E. Carpenter (1948).

TENNANT, (1) Smithson (1761–1815), English chemist, born at Selby, was educated at Edinburgh and Cambridge. He discovered osmium and iridium (1804) and proved that diamond is pure carbon. Professor of Chemistry at Cambridge (1814), he was killed in a riding accident.

(2) William (1784–1848), Scottish poet, born at Anstruther, studied at St Andrews, and, a lifelong cripple, became in 1813 schoolmaster of Dunino. His mock-heroic poem *Anster Fair* (1812) was the first attempt to naturalize the Italian *ottava rima*—soon after adopted with splendid success by Hookham Frere and by Byron. He was teacher from 1816 at Lasswade, from 1819 at Dollar Academy, and from 1835 professor of Oriental Languages at St Andrews. Other poems were the *Thane of Fife* (1822) and *Papistry Stormed* (1827); dramas were *Cardinal Beaton* (1823) and *John Baliol* (1825). See memoir by M. F. Conolly (1861).

TENNIEL, Sir John, *ten'yel* (1820–1914), English caricaturist, born in London, son of a celebrated dancing-master. A self-trained artist, he was selected in 1845 to paint one of the frescoes—Dryden's 'St Cecilia'—in the Houses of Parliament. He is better known as a book illustrator, and best as the cartoonist of *Punch*, the staff of which he joined in 1851, his best-known cartoon being *Dropping the Pilot* (1890). His illustrations to *Alice in Wonderland* and *Through the Looking-glass* (see DODGSON) are remarkable for their delicacy and finish; earlier book illustrations were to *Aesop's Fables*, Moore's *Lalla Rookh*, the *Ingoldsby Legends*, *Once a Week*, &c. He was knighted in 1893. See Life by F. Sarjano (1948).

TENNYSON, Alfred, 1st Baron Tennyson (1809–92), English poet, was born at Somersby rectory, Lincolnshire, the fourth son of the rector. His elder brothers, Frederick and Charles, were both poets and were the subject of a memoir by H. Nicolson (*Tennyson's Two Brothers*, 1947). The father died young, but the family was allowed to stay on at the rectory and Tennyson was somehow enabled to go to Trinity College, Cambridge, where he became a member of an ardent group of young men, including Arthur Hallam, whose early death was to be mourned in that great elegiac poem *In Memoriam.* His early ventures in verse, viz., *Poems Chiefly Lyrical* (1830) and *Poems* (1833) were slighted by the critics as being namby-pamby, and this we can understand for the first volume is largely 'album verse' and the second is not free from an enervating sentimentality. But the critics ought to have detected the great poet in the first version of 'The Lady of Shalott', 'Oenone', 'The Lotus-eaters' and other poems in the 1833 volume. Nine years of revising these poems and adding fresh material resulted in the volume of 1842, which established his fame. He had been engaged since 1833 in writing the series of loosely connected lyrics or elegies which as *In Memoriam* crowned his fame in 1850, the year he succeeded Wordsworth as poet laureate and the year of his marriage to Emily Sarah Sellwood, a lady from his own county. The long Victorian afternoon followed with shifts of residence to Farringdon in the Isle of Wight and Aldworth in Sussex and sunned by the homage of the entire nation from the Queen downward, so truly and flatteringly did his poetry reflect that world. With his wife he made short tours but rarely left his Victorian England behind him. His poetry has declined in popularity as that insular England has receded, but there should be no doubt that the volume of 1842 and *In Memoriam* contain some of the most finished artistry in English poetry, in which the mood of the poem is perfectly reflected in rhythm and language. After 1850 he devoted himself to the fashionable verse novelette—*Maud; a Monodrama* (1855), *Enoch Arden* (1864), *Locksley Hall Sixty Years After* (1886). Incredibly, for we are inclined to think that *Maud*, apart from the lyrics, verges on the vulgar, Tennyson regarded it as his best poem. The public, however, was waiting for what was to be the crowning triumph. The first instalment of *Idylls of the King* (1859), seemed to the Victorians to be just that, but here again, in *Geraint and Enid* and *Lancelote and Elaine* we are in the domain of the verse novelette and throughout the whole series (completed in 1885) Victorian morality imposed on the old chivalric matter stifles the poetry save in the descriptive passages where Tennyson's hand is as sure as ever. In the 1870s he tried his hand at drama. Irving gave *Becket* a considerable run, but *Harold*, *Queen Mary*, &c., are dead matter. He had a late flowering in his seventies when he wrote the perfect poem *To Virgil*, *Tiresias*, and the powerful *Rizpah*, but the conflict between science and the Faith, discoursed optimistically in *In Memoriam*, now becomes an obsession—hence the 'double shadow', viz., 'Astronomy and Geology, terrible muses'. He retained to the end the gift of felicitous occasional verse of which the verse letter to F. D. Maurice and *To Virgil* are examples. Perhaps his own estimate of his powers, in a remark to Carlyle, is not far out—'I don't think that since Shakespeare there has been such a master of the English language as I—to be sure, I have nothing to say'. Contemporaries thought he had plenty to say, but it was all occasioned by the topics of the day. *The Princess*, for example (1847), gave him a chance to 'say something', but the subject of woman's education is treated in serio-comic fashion, which we find trying and the image of John Bull he projects in the poem is offensive to modern taste. To be sure there are the lovely lyrics and none disputes his eminence in the lyric any more than in the wonderful pre-Raphaelite and classical poetry in the volume of 1842, the sustained elegiac note of *In Memoriam*, and his felicity in occasional verse. These after all make a considerable body of work. The peerage bestowed on him in 1884 probably was intended to honour the author of *Idylls of the King* (completed in that year), the perfect mirror of the Victorian era. His son Hallam, 2nd Lord Tennyson, issued the authoritative Life in 1897. This was preceded by several studies, the best of which are those by Churton Collins (1891), and Van Dyke (1896). Since then there have been studies by A. C. Benson (1904), Fausset (1922), Harold Nicolson (1923) and ed. J. Killham (1960). See also T. J. Wise's Bibliography (1897), with a supplement by F. L. Lucas (1957).

TENTERDEN, Charles Abbott, 1st Baron (1762–1832), English lawyer, born a barber's son at Canterbury, became a fellow and tutor of Corpus Christi, Oxford, was called to the bar and in 1801 became recorder of Oxford. Lacking in eloquence, he made his reputation by his revision and novel treatment in terms of principle rather than precedent of the *Law relative to Merchant Ships and Seamen* (1802). In 1816 he became puisne judge in the Court of Common Pleas, in 1818 he was knighted and became chief justice of the King's Bench, and, raised to the peerage in 1827, strongly opposed the Catholic Relief and Reform Bills.

TENZING NORGAY (1914–), Nepalese mountaineer, born at Tsa-chu near Makalu, made his first climb as a porter with a British expedition to Everest in 1935. In the years following he climbed many of the Himalayan peaks and on two later attempts on the ascent of Everest he reached 23,000 ft. in 1938 and 28,215 ft. in 1952. In 1953 on Col. John Hunt's expedition, he, with Edmund Hillary (q.v.), succeeded in reaching the summit of Everest and for this triumph he was awarded the George Medal. In 1954 he studied at a mountaineering school in Switzerland, and on his return to Darjeeling, was appointed head of the Institute of Mountaineering. He also became president of the Sherpa Association. See Sir John Hunt's *Ascent of Everest* (1953), Y. Malartie's *Tenzing of Everest* (1954), and his autobiography, *Man of Everest*, written for him by J. R. Ullman (1955).

TERBORCH, or Terburg, Gerard, *ter-bor*KH (*c.* 1617–81), Dutch painter, born at Zwolle, studied under Pieter Molijn at Haarlem and visited England, Italy, Germany, painting the conference of 'The Peace of Munster' (1648; National Gallery, London), and Velásquez in Spain. From 1654 to his death he lived at Deventer, where he became burgomaster. He worked mostly on a small scale, producing genre pictures and fashionable portraits characterized by an almost incredible skill in the rendering of textures.

TERBRUGGHEN, Hendrik (1588–1629), Dutch painter, born at Deventer, studied under Bloemaert, was until 1616 in Italy and came under the influence of Caravaggio. Like the latter he excelled in chiaroscuro effects and in the faithful representation of physiognomical details and drapery. His *Jacob and Laban* (1627) is in the National Gallery, London. His works are represented in Edinburgh, Amsterdam, Metropolitan, New York, Ashmolean, Oxford, &c. See study by B. Nicolson (1958).

TERENCE (Publius Terentius Afer) (*c.* 190–159 B.C.), Roman comic poet, born at Carthage, became the slave of the Roman senator P. Terentius Lucanus, who brought him to Rome, educated him, and manumitted him. His first play was the *Andria* (166); its success introduced Terence to the most refined society of Rome. His chief patrons were Laelius and the younger Scipio. After spending some years in Rome he went to Greece, and died there. We have six of his comedies—*Andria*, *Eunuchus*, *Heauton Timoroumenos*, *Phormio*, *Hecyra* and *Adelphi*. Terence has no claim to creative originality, his plays, Greek in origin and Greek in scene, being directly based on Menander. But he wrote in singularly pure and perfect Latin. Many of his conventions and plot constructions were later used by Sheridan, Molière, &c. See study by G. Norwood (1923).

TERESA, or **Theresa, Saint** (1515–82), Spanish saint and mystic, born of a noble family at Ávila in Old Castile, March 28, 1515, in 1533 entered a Carmelite convent there. About 1555 her religious exercises reached an extraordinary height of asceticism, she was favoured with ecstasies, and the fame of her sanctity spread far and wide. She obtained permission from the Holy See to remove to a humble house in Ávila, where she re-established (1562) the ancient Carmelite rule, with additional observances. In 1567 the general of the Carmelite order urged on her the duty of extending her reforms; in 1579 the Carmelites of the stricter observance were united into a distinct association; and within her own lifetime seventeen convents of women and sixteen of men accepted her reforms. She died October 4, 1582, and was canonized in 1622. The most famous of her many works are her autobiography, *The Way of Perfection*, *The Book of the Foundations* (trans. by Dalton, 1853), which describes the journeys she made and the convents she founded or reformed, and *The Interior Castle* (trans. by Dalton, 1852). English Lives are by Dalton (1851), Cardinal Manning (1864), Father Coleridge (3 vols. 1881–88), G. Cunninghame-Graham (1894), A. Whyte (1897), E. A. Peers (1954), E. Hamilton (1960).

TERMAN, Lewis Madison (1877–1956), American psychologist, born at Johnson County, Indiana, became professor at Stanford in 1916 and introduced the Binet-Simon and Terman Group Intelligence Tests into the U.S. army in 1920.

TERNAUX-COMPANS, Henri, *ter-nō-kō-pā* (1807–64), French bibliographer and historian, born in Paris, collected books on America, compiled *Bibliothèque américaine* (1836), and a French translation of voyages of American discovery (1836–40).

TERRY, (1) **Daniel** (*c.* 1780–1829), English actor and playwright, born in Bath, after an architectural apprenticeship joined a theatrical company under the elder Macready at Sheffield probably in 1805, making his London début in 1812. He played in many dramatizations of Sir Walter Scott's novels, became an intimate friend of the latter, copying him even to the point of calligraphy. He also played the major Shakespearean rôles, and in Sheridan, &c., at Covent Garden and Drury Lane, London.

(2) **Edward O'Connor** (1844–1912), English comedian, born in London, made his début at Christchurch in 1863, and, after four years in the provinces, played in London 1867. He opened Terry's Theatre in 1887.

(3) **Dame Ellen Alice** (1848–1928), English actress, sister of (4), born at Coventry, the daughter of a provincial actor, was apprenticed to the stage from infancy, and at eight appeared as Mammilius in *The Winter's Tale* at the Prince's Theatre, London. From 1862 she played in Bristol and after a short-lived marriage with the painter, Watts (1864), and a second retirement from the stage (1868–74) during which her two children, Edith and Edward Gordon Craig (q.v.), were born, she established herself as the leading Shakespearean actress in London and from 1878 to 1902 dominated in partnership with Henry Irving (q.v.) the English and American theatre. Her natural gentleness and vivacity made her excel, particularly as Portia and Ophelia, and she would have made an ideal Rosalind, but Irving's professional jealousy withheld such an opportunity at the Lyceum. In 1903 she went herself into theatre management and engaged her son to produce Ibsen's *Vikings*. Barrie and Shaw wrote parts especially for her, e.g., Lady Cicely Waynflete in the latter's *Captain Brassbound's Conversion* (1905). She married Charles Kelly (Wardell) in 1876 and in 1907 the American actor, James Carew. She received the G.B.E. in 1925. See her correspondence with Shaw (1929), her *Memoirs* ed. by Craig and St John (1932), Steen's *A Pride of Terrys* (1962), and Life by R. Manvell (1968).

(4) **Fred** (1863–1933), English actor, brother of (3), born in London, played in the companies of Tree, Forbes Robertson and Irving and established a reputation as a romantic actor as Sir Percy Blakeney in *The Scarlet Pimpernel* (1905). His sisters, **Kate** (1844–1924), Marion and Florence were also actresses, as was his wife Julia Neilson (q.v.).

TERTULLIAN, properly **Quintus Septimius Florens Tertullianus** (*c.* A.D. 160–220), Carthaginian theologian, of the fathers of the Latin Church, was born at Carthage. He lived for some time at Rome, was converted (*c.* 196) and then returned to Carthage. That he was married is shown by his two books *Ad Uxorem*, in which he argues against second marriages. His opposition to worldliness in the church culminated in his becoming a leader of the Montanist sect about 207. He had the heart of a Christian with the intellect of an advocate. His style is most vivid, vigorous and concise, abounding in harsh and obscure expressions, abrupt turns and impetuous transitions, with here and there bursts of glowing eloquence. He was the creator of ecclesiastical Latinity, and many of his sentences have become proverbial, e.g., 'The blood of the martyrs is the seed of the church' and 'The unity of heretics is schism'. His works are divided into three classes: (1) controversial writings against heathens and Jews, as in *Apologeticum*, *Ad Nationes*, *Adversus Judaeos*; (2) against heretics, as in *De Praescriptione Haereticorum*, *Adversus Valentinianos*, *De Anima*, *De Carne Christi* (against Docetism), *De Resurrectione Carnis*, *Adversus Marcionem*, *Adversus Praxean*; (3) practical and ascetic treatises, in which we can trace his increasing hostility to the church and his adoption of Montanist views. Hence the division of these treatises into Pre-Montanist and Montanist, of which *De Virginibus Velandis* marks the transitional stage. Tertullian had a greater influence on the Latin Church than any theologian between Paul and Augustine. His Montanism, indeed, prevented its direct exercise, but Cyprian was the interpreter who gave currency to his views. See translations of his works in Ante-Nicene Library (1868–70), German study by H. Hoppe (1903) and French study by A. d'Alès (1905).

TESLA, Nikola (1856–1943), Yugoslav-born American inventor, born at Smiljan, Croatia, studied at Graz, Prague and Paris, emigrating to the United States in 1884. He left the Edison Works at Menlo Park to concentrate on his own inventions, which include improved dynamos, transformers and electric bulbs and the high-frequency coil which bears his name.

TETRAZZINI, Luisa, *tet-ra-tzee'nee* (1871–1940), Italian coloratura soprano singer, born at Florence, made her début in 1895 in Meyerbeer's *L'Africaine.* She appeared mostly in Italian opera of the older school, one of her most notable successes being in *Lucia di Lammermoor.* She sang in London and in America and was in 1913–14 a member of the Chicago Opera Company. See *My Life of Song* (1921).

TETZEL, Johann (*c.* 1465–1519), German monk, born at Leipzig, entered the Dominican order in 1489. A famous preacher, he was appointed in 1516 to preach an indulgence in favour of contributors to the building fund of St Peter's at Rome. This he did with great ostentation, thereby provoking the Wittenberg theses of Luther (q.v.). In reply, he published counter-theses, written for him by Conrad Wimpina, but was rebuked by the papal delegate for his literary extravagance.

TEWFIK PASHA, Mohammed, *too-feek'* (1852–92), khedive of Egypt, eldest son of Ismail Pasha (q.v.), succeeded on his abdication in 1879. The chief events of his reign were Arabi's insurrection (1882), the British intervention, the war with the Mahdi (1884–1885), the pacification of the Sudan frontiers, and the improvement of Egypt under British administration. He was succeeded by his son Abbas Hilmi (q.v.).

TEY, Josephine. See MACKINTOSH (2).

THACKERAY, William Makepeace (1811–63), English novelist, was born at Calcutta, where his father was in the service of the East India Company. The father having died in 1816 and his mother marrying again, the boy was sent home. He went to Charterhouse (1822) and Trinity Hall, Cambridge (1829), but left without taking a degree. His first venture in print was a parody of Tennyson's prize poem *Timbuctoo.* After dissipating much of his patrimony in travel abroad, he decided to repair his fortunes by journalism, though art equally attracted him. A short stay in Paris as an art student came to a close through lack of funds and it was then (1835) he made his application to illustrate *Pickwick.* He had now married (1836), but financial worry, due to the bankruptcy of his stepfather, finally determined him to earn a living in London journalism. We find him contributing regularly to *The Times,* the *New Monthly* and *Fraser's Magazine.* Domestic trouble now engulfed him. The birth of his third daughter affected Mrs Thackeray's mind, the home was broken up and the children sent to their grandmother in Paris. His first publications, starting with *The Paris Sketch-book* (1840), and written under various pseudonyms (Wagstaff, Titmarsh, Fitz-Boodle, Yellowplush, Snob, &c.) were a comparative failure although they included *The Yellowplush Papers, The Great Hoggarty Diamond* and *The Luck of Barry Lyndon,* all contributed to *Fraser's* (1841–44). It was his work on *Punch* from 1842 onwards which attracted attention by exploiting the view of society as seen by the butler ('Jeames's Diary') and the great theme of English snobbery. The great novels that were to follow—*Vanity Fair* (1847–48), *Pendennis* (1848), *Henry Esmond* (1852) and *The Newcomes* (1853–55), all monthly serials, established his fame. *Vanity Fair* is the first novel to give a conspectus of London society with its mingling of rich parvenus and decadent upper class through both of which the social climber, Becky Sharp, threads her way. The novel is a little marred by the sentimentality of Amelia Sedley and Captain Dobbin, but Thackeray's art moves between the extremes of sentimentality and cynicism. The great historical novel, *Esmond,* shows Thackeray's consuming love of the 18th century. Its sequel, *The Virginians* (1857–59), is not reckoned a success. *The Newcomes* shows young love at the mercy of scheming relatives and mean-spirited rival suitors. Colonel Newcome's portrait has been taken as that of the ideal gentleman, but is also marred by the author's sentimentality. Thackeray retired from *Punch* in 1854 and became the editor of the *Cornhill,* where much of his later work appeared—ballads, novels, &c., now largely unreadable. Mention should be made of the lecturing tours which he undertook in this country and America, the fruit of which, apart from *The Virginians,* was *The English Humorists of the 18th century* (1853) and *The Four Georges* (1860). Trollope's Life is readable but needs to be supplemented by Lewis Melville's 2-vol. Life (1910), and the studies by Whibley (1903) and Ray (1955–58). Best of all perhaps is Saintsbury's Thackeray (1909), and his prefaces to the novels. Thackeray's daughter, Anne Isabella, Lady Ritchie (q.v.), contributed valuable introductions to an edition (1898–99) of his novels.

THAIS, *thay'is* (fl. *c.* 330 B.C.), an Athenian courtesan, famous for wit and beauty, who, according to a doubtful legend, induced Alexander the Great to fire Persepolis. She had several children by Ptolemy Lagus. See opera by Massenet.

THALBERG, Sigismond, *tahl'berg* (1812–71), Swiss-German pianist, was born at Geneva, the natural son of a prince, studied music at Vienna under Hummel and from 1830 made extensive tours in Europe and North America, settling near Naples in 1858. His compositions comprise fantasias and variations, a piano concerto and operas.

THALES, *thay'leez* (fl. 580 B.C.), Greek natural philosopher, one of the Ionian school, the earliest known in Greek philosophy, was born at Miletus. His mercantile journeys took him to Egypt and Babylon, where he acquired land-surveying and astronomical techniques, but is said to have invented geometry by refining these by deductive reasoning. He is supposed to have predicted the solar eclipse in 585 B.C. Aristotle attributes to him the doctrine that water is the original substance and all things derive from and resolve into water. See B. Farrington, *Greek Science* (1949), and J. Burnet, *Greek Philosophy, Thales to Plato* (new ed. 1955).

THANT, U (1909–), Burmese diplomat, born at Pantanaw, became a schoolmaster under Thakin Nu, the future prime minister, whom he later succeeded as headmaster of Pantanaw National High School. When Burma became independent in 1948 he took up government work and after holding several appointments he became permanent U.N. representative for Burma in 1957. In 1961 he was elected acting secretary-general of the U.N. after the death of Hammarskjöld (q.v.), and became permanent secretary-general in 1962. He played a major diplomatic rôle during the Cuban crisis and headed a mission to the Cuban leader (1962). He formulated a plan for the ending of the Congolese civil war (1962) which ended the Katanga secession (1963) and mobilized a U.N. peace-keeping force containing British troops for Cyprus in 1964. He resigned 1971.

THEBAW, *thee'-* (1858–1916), last king of Burma from 1878, in 1885 was deposed by the British, and sent as a prisoner to India.

THEED, William (1804–91), English sculptor, born at Trentham, the son of the sculptor **William Theed** (1764–1817), studied under Thorvaldsen and executed the Africa group on the Albert Memorial.

THEILER, Max, *tī'ler* (1899–1972), South African bacteriologist, born at Pretoria, settled in the U.S.A. in 1922, was awarded the Nobel prize for medicine in 1951 for his work in connection with yellow fever, for which he discovered the vaccine 17D in 1939.

THELLUSSON, Peter (1737–97), a naturalized British merchant, born in Paris, the Genevan ambassador's son, became a London merchant in 1762. After bequeathing fortunes to his family, he left the residue to trustees, to accumulate for his great-grandsons. The will was held valid by Lord Loughborough (1799) and affirmed in the House of Lords in 1805; though the Thellusson Act (1800) thenceforth restrained testators from devising their property for accumulation for more than twenty-one years.

THELWALL, John (1764–1834), English reformer and elocutionist, born in London, was a tailor's apprentice and studied law. He supported Horne Tooke (q.v.), with whom he was arrested (1794) for his revolutionary views. He wrote poems (1787 and 1795) and *Treatment of Cases of Defective Utterance* (1814). See Life by C. Cestre (1906), and Hobhouse's *Liberalism* (1911).

THEMISTOCLES, *the-mis'to-kleez* (*c.* 523–*c.* 458 B.C.), Athenian general and statesman, as archon in 493 convinced his countrymen that a powerful fleet was necessary for their welfare. Against the Persians he commanded the Athenian squadron (200 of the 324 Greek vessels), but agreed to serve under the Spartan Eurybiades; on the eve of Salamis (480) it required all his energy to induce his timid superior to await the attack of the enemy. In his eagerness to precipitate a collision he sent a messenger to urge the Persian generals to make an immediate attack, as the Greeks had resolved on retreat. A great victory was won and Themistocles became a national hero. The rebuilding of the walls of Athens by his advice on a vastly larger scale aroused uneasiness at Sparta, but Themistocles cajoled the ephors till the walls were high. So the Spartan faction in Athens plotted his ruin, and in 470 he was ostracized. Argos was his first retreat, but the Spartans secured his expulsion (467), and he fled to Corcyra and thence to Asia; Artaxerxes received him with great favour, and listened to his schemes for the subjugation of Greece; and at Magnesia he lived securely till his death. His patriotism seems at times to have been merely a larger kind of selfishness, but he was convinced that only he could realize the dream of a great Athenian empire. See Life by Bauer (1881).

THÉNARD, Louis Jacques, *tay-nahr* (1777–1857), French chemist, born at Louptière, a peasant's son, studied pharmacy at Paris and became professor at the Collège de France and was made a baron in 1825 and chancellor of the University of Paris. He discovered sodium and potassium peroxides, Thénard's blue, which is used for colouring porcelain, and which made him wealthy, and proved that caustic soda and potash contain hydrogen. He was closely associated with Gay-Lussac (q.v.) and wrote a once-standard work on chemistry.

THEOBALD, *thee'o-bawld* or *tib'ėld,* (1) or **Tebaldus** (d. 1161), English ecclesiastic, was a monk at Bec, abbot (1137) and in 1138 became Archbishop of Canterbury. He crowned Stephen in Canterbury, and after the latter's death refused to regard Stephen's son as his successor and eventually crowned Henry II (1154). He advanced his archdeacon, Thomas à Becket, to the chancellorship, introduced the study of civil law into England and resisted all attempts by the monasteries to throw off episcopal jurisdiction. See Life by Saltman (1956).

(2) **Lewis,** *tib-bold* (1688–1744), English Shakespearean critic, born at Sittingbourne, studied law but took to literature. He published translations of the Greek classics, thirty papers in *Mist's Journal* (1715), and started the *Censor*, a tri-weekly paper. His pamphlet *Shakespeare Restored* (1726) was directed against Pope's edition, and Pope took revenge by making him, unfairly, the hero of the *Dunciad*, though he incorporated many of his corrections in the second edition. Theobald's edition of Shakespeare (1734), however, surpassed that of his rival. See study by R. F. Jones (1919).

THEOCRITUS, *thee-ok'-* (*c.* 310–250 B.C.), the pastoral poet of Greece, was born probably at Syracuse, was brought up in Cos where he came under the influence of Philetas, lived for a time at the court of Ptolemy Philadelphus in Alexandria, returning later to Cos. In his pastoral poems he struck out an entirely new form of literature, which is for ever fresh. The authenticity of some of the thirty poems of his which we have has been disputed. They fall into three classes—half-epic, mimic and idyllic. Probably the half-epic poems were the earliest. He wrote a series of poems dealing with heroic legend, especially that of Heracles. Theocritus's famous 15th Idyll, *The Ladies of Syracuse*, said to be copied from Sophron, describes delightfully the visit of a Syracusan lady and her friend, both living in Alexandria, to the festival of Adonis. Theocritus raised the rude pastoral poetry of the Doric race in Sicily into a new and perfect form of literature. His short poems dealing with pastoral subjects, and representing a single scene, came to be called Idylls (*eidullia*). His countrymen are genuine, typical of peasants everywhere. He combined realism with romanticism, and every touch is natural. Virgil imitates him closely in his *Eclogues*; Tennyson was deeply influenced by him, as were the pastoral poets of the Renaissance.

THEODORA (*c.* 500–547), Byzantine empress, consort of Justinian I, the daughter of Aracius the Cypriot, had, according to Procopius, already been actress, dancer and courtesan when she won the heart of the austere and ambitious Justinian, to become in succession his mistress, his wife and the sharer of his throne (527). As Justinian's trustiest counsellor she bore a chief share in the work of government, and saved the throne by her high courage at the crisis of the Nika riots (532). She lavished her bounty on the poor, especially the unfortunate of her own sex. Her character descended to history unspotted until the appearance (1623) of the *Secret History* of Procopius (q.v.), who in the full favour of the court had in his other writings extolled Justinian and Theodora. There is not a word of her profligacy in Evagrius or Zonaras. See works by Débidour (1885), Houssaye (1890) and Holmes (1905–1907), Mallet in *Eng. Hist. Rev.* (1887), Diehl, *Byzantine Portraits* (trans. 1927).

THEODORE, (1) or **Kassai** (1816–68), King of Abyssinia, nephew of the governor of Kuara, in 1853 crushed the vice-regent Ras Ali, and, in 1855 overthrowing the prince of Tigré, had himself crowned negus of Abyssinia as Theodore II. At first he was guided by two Englishmen, Plowden and Bell; but after they were killed in a rebellion (1860) his rule became tyrannical. He had made several vain attempts to procure the alliance of England and France against his Mohammedan neighbours, and he now began to entertain hatred towards Europeans. A letter sent to Queen Victoria in 1862 went somehow unnoticed, and a fancied slight was also received from Napoleon III. Thereupon Theodore imprisoned the consuls along with other Europeans. Negotiations failed, and a British military expedition under General Napier landed in Abyssinia in the spring of 1868, and on April 9 reached Magdala. On the 10th an Abyssinian attack was repulsed. Theodore sued for peace and released the prisoners, but, as he declined to surrender, the fort was stormed on the 13th. Theodore shot himself.

(2) **'King of Corsica'**, otherwise **Baron von Neuhoff** (1686–1756), German adventurer, son of a Westphalian noble, was born at Metz, served in the French army, the Swedish diplomatic service, became chargé d'affaires to the Emperor Charles VI and, in 1736, led a Corsican rising against the Genoese, supported by the Turks and the Bey of Tunis. He was elected king, solemnly crowned and raised money by selling knighthoods. He left after seven months to procure foreign aid, but his attempts to return in 1738 and in 1743 were frustrated. He settled in London in 1749, was imprisoned for debt but was set free by a subscription raised by Horace Walpole. In Spain he had married an Irish lady, daughter of the Earl of Kilmallock. His only son by her, known as **Colonel Frederick** (*c.* 1725–97), wrote a book on Corsica, and shot himself in the porch of Westminster Abbey. See V. Pirie, *His Majesty of Corsica* (1939).

THEODORE OF MOPSUESTIA (*c.* 350–428), Greek theologian, born at Antioch, became first a monk, then a deacon there, and in 392 Bishop of Mopsuestia in Cilicia. The teacher of Nestorius, he was, perhaps, the real founder of Nestorianism. He wrote commentaries on almost all the books of Scripture, of which remain, in the Greek, only that on the Minor Prophets; in Latin translations, those on the Epistles of Paul (ed. by Swete, Camb. 1880–82), besides many fragments. As an exegete he eschews the allegorical method, adopts the literal meaning, considers the historical and literary circumstances, and assumes varying degrees of inspiration. Already suspected, as he was, of leaning towards the 'Pelagians', when the Nestorian controversy broke out, he was attacked in his polemical writings, which were condemned by Justinian (544). The fifth ecumenical council (553) confirmed the condemnation. See a book by L. Patterson (1927), Sellers, *Two Ancient Christologies* (1940) and study by Norris (1963).

THEODORE OF TARSUS, St (*c.* 602–690), Archbishop of Canterbury, born at Tarsus and educated at Athens, was sent in 668 by Pope Vitalian to Canterbury, where he established a Greek school. Stubbs described him as the 'real organizer of the administrative system of the English Church'. See study by Reany (1944).

THEODORET, *thee-od'-* (*c.* 393–458), Greek theologian and Church historian, born at Antioch, entered a monastery, and in 423 became Bishop of Cyrrhus, a city of Syria. As a foremost representative of the school of Antioch he became deeply involved in the Nestorian and Eutychian controversies, and was deposed, in his absence, by the 'Robber Council' of Ephesus in 449. He was restored by the general Council of Chalcedon in 451. His works (edited by Schulze and Nösselt, 1769–74) consist of commentaries on Canticles, the Prophets, Psalms and St Paul's Epistles; a *History of the Church*, from A.D. 325 to 429; *Religious History*, being the lives of the so-called Fathers of the Desert; the *Eranistes*, a dialogue against Eutychianism; *A Concise History of Heresies*, together with orations and nearly 200 letters. See works by Roos (Latin, 1883), Bertram (Latin, 1883), Güldenpenning (German, 1889) and Räder (Latin, 1900).

THEODORIC, the name of two kings of the Visigoths:

Theodoric I (d. 451), was chosen king by the Visigoths in 418. Alternately an ally and an enemy of Rome, in 421 (or 422) he treacherously joined the Vandals and attacked the Roman troops from behind. In 435, he attacked the Romans in Gaul and besieged Narbonne. Forced to retreat to Toulouse, he there defeated a Roman army (439). On the invasion of Attila (q.v.) in 451, he joined the Romans, under Aetius, and at Troyes commanded the right wing. He drove back the Huns under Attila but was killed.

Theodoric II (d. 466), son of the first Theodoric, rebelled against Thorismund, had him assassinated and ascended the throne in 453. His policy at first was to spread Gothic dominion in Spain and Gaul through the Roman alliance. On the murder of the Emperor Maximus, he supported Avitus in his bid for the Empire, and marched with him into Italy, where he was proclaimed emperor. On his abdication in 456, Theodoric broke the friendship with Rome and besieged Arles, but was forced by Majorian to make peace. In 462, he made another attempt in Gaul, but was defeated near Orléans (464). He was murdered in 466 by his brother Euric, who succeeded him.

THEODORIC, or **Theoderic,** surnamed **the Great** (A.D. 455–526), king of the Ostrogoths and founder of the Ostrogothic monarchy. Shortly before he became king (475) the Ostrogoths had overrun Macedonia. After fourteen years of petty warfare, sometimes as the ally, sometimes as the enemy, of the Romans. Theodoric obtained from the Emperor Zeno permission to wrest Italy from Odoacer (q.v.). With 250,000 Ostrogoths he completed the conquest after a five years' war, and Odoacer was soon after murdered by Theodoric's own hand. His thirty-three years' reign secured for Italy tranquillity and prosperity. The Goths and the Romans continued distinct nations, each with its own tribunals and laws. Catholics and Jews enjoyed full liberty of worship, and protection from all encroachment on their civil rights (Theodoric was an Arian). His official letters show his unwearied energy and enlightened zeal for his subjects' welfare. His last three years are tarnished by the judicial murders of Boethius and Symmachus, and by acts of oppression against the Catholic church. To the Germans he is Dietrich von Bern, and one of the great heroes of legend, figuring in the *Nibelungenlied*. See Hodgkin, *Theodoric the Goth* (1891; new ed. 1923), and R. Latouche, *Les Grandes Invasions* (1946).

THEODORUS OF SAMOS, *-do'-* (*c.* 550 B.C.), Greek artist, worked in metal, inventing several kinds of tools for use in casting. He is said to have made, with Telecles, the Pythian Apollo at Samos.

THEODOSIUS, (1) surnamed **the Elder** (d. 376), Roman general, father of Theodosius the Great, by birth a Spaniard, campaigned in Britain against the Caledonians, naming a reconquered district *Valentia* after the emperors. After a victorious campaign on the Upper Danube he quelled a revolt in Africa, but was executed at Carthage on some trumped-up charge.

(2) **Theodosius I,** surnamed **the Great** (*c.* 346–395), Roman emperor, son of Theodosius the Elder (q.v.), was born at Cauca in northwest Spain, won fame by his exploits in Moesia and Thrace, but retiring, on his father's death, to his native farm, was summoned thence by Gratian to become his colleague and emperior in the East (379). It was a critical time. The Goths, flushed with victory, were roaming the country at will. Theodosius made Thessalonica his headquarters, and within four years broke up the vast Gothic army, attached many of its members as allies, and restored tranquillity south of the Danube. A serious illness in 380 led to his baptism as a Trinitarian and to edicts against Arianism. He summoned the second general council (at Constantinople, 381). The murder of Gratian at Lyons, the advance towards Italy of Maximus, proclaimed emperor in Britain, and the arrival of Valentinian II begging for help led to Theodosius's victory at Aquileia (388) and to the restoration of his youthful colleague. For some years Theodosius lived at Milan in friendship with St Ambrose. He had cancelled the severe measures meted out to Antioch after a riot (387); but in 390, when the governor of Thessalonica was lynched by a circus mob, Theodosius invited the citizens into the circus, and had 7000 of them massacred. Ambrose wrote upbraiding them with the deed, and even withstood his attempt to enter the church at Milan until after eight months' retirement and public penance. In 392 Valentinian II was murdered, and in 394 Theodosius marched against the Franks and their puppet emperor Eugenius. After a stubborn fight he gained a complete victory, and for four months ruled as sole Roman emperor. He died in Ambrose's arms. See German Life by Güldenpenning and Ifland (1878). His grandson, **Theodosius II** (401–450), succeeded his father Arcadius in 408 as Eastern emperor. He allowed affairs to be managed by his sister Pulcheria and his empress Eudocia.

(3) **of Tripolis,** a Greek mathematician and astronomer, born in Bithynia in the 1st or 2nd century B.C., wrote a book on spherical geometry.

THEOGNIS, *-og'-* (fl. 544–541 B.C.), Greek elegiac poet, was a Dorian noble of Megara. During the confusion which followed the overthrow of the tyrant Theagenes, he was driven from Megara, and visited Euboea and Sicily. Under his name survive 1389 elegiac verses, social, political and gnomic, showing shrewd sense and oligarchical principles—perhaps only partly his. See E. Harrison's *Studies in Theognis* (1903), works by T. Hudson Williams (1910) and F. Jacoby (1931).

THEON. See HYPATIA.

THEOPHILUS, *-of'-*, (1) patriarch of Alexandria from 385 till his death in 412, destroyed the pagan temple of Serapis, drove out the Originist monks of Nitria and defended his actions before a synod at Constantinople called by the emperor Arcadius and St John Chrysostom (q.v.). He made peace with the monks but used his influence with the empress to have St John banished to Armenia.

(2) (fl. 2nd cent.), Bishop of Antioch (169) 177), wrote an important Apology of Christiantity (*c.* 180).

THEOPHRASTUS, *-fras'-* (*c.* 372–286 B.C.), Greek philosopher, born at Eresus in Lesbos, repaired to Athens, where he heard Plato and Aristotle; of the latter he became the intimate friend and successor. He inherited the whole Aristotelian library, including the philosopher's manuscripts. As head of the peripatetic school he displayed great versatility, was the reputed author of 227 works, and was long a paramount authority. His writings are in great part lost; but we still possess his books on plants (important in botanical history), on stones, on fire, on winds and weather signs, and on the senses. His *Characters*, a masterly delineation of moral types, which, however, some scholars deem a later compilation from a more discursive original of Theophrastus, has had much influence in modern literature.

THEOPHYLACT (*c.* 1078–*c.* 1107), Greek ecclesiastic, born at Euripus in Euboea, became Archbishop of Achrida in Bulgaria in 1078. He wrote Bible commentaries, printed in Venice (1754–58), and *The Education of a Prince* for the son of the emperior Michael VII, to whom he had been tutor.

THEOPOMPUS OF CHIOS, *kīos* (*c.* 378–*c.* 300 B.C.), Greek historian and rhetorician, studied under Isocrates (q.v.). He was twice exiled from Chios and wrote a history of Greece (411–394), &c. Only fragments remain.

THEORELL, Axel Hugo Theodor (1903–), Swedish biochemist, born at Linköping, was assistant professor at Uppsala (1930) and then director of the Nobel Institute of Biochemistry at Stockholm (1937). He worked on myoglobin and was (1955) awarded a Nobel prize for his work on oxidation enzymes.

THEOTOCOPOULI. See GRECO (EL).

THERAMENES, *the-ram'i-neez* (fl. 411–403 B.C.), Athenian statesman, made himself unpopular by a policy of compromise between oligarchy and democracy, and while a member of the government of the Thirty Tyrants, incurred the hatred of the most notorious of them all, Critias (q.v.), whose health he drank in the hemlock cup.

THERESA, St. See TERESA.

THESIGER. See CHELMSFORD.

THESEUS, *thee'si-oos*, semi-legendary hero of Athens, the son of Aegeus, king of Athens, by Aethra, daughter of Pittheus, King of Troezen, at whose court he grew up. His perilous journey back to Athens, to succeed his father, according to legend, was a succession of Herculean feats against powerful adversaries, including Procrustes, who fitted everyone he caught into his bed, either by stretching the victim or cutting him down to size, the grey sow of Crommyon and the rebellious Pallantidae, his uncles, at Athens. He was then sent as part of the annual human tribute of six youths and six maidens exacted by Minos of Crete, who had defeated the Athenians, to the Minotaur's labyrinth on Crete, but was saved by the help of Minos's daughter, Ariadne, who provided him with a sword to slay the Minotaur and a thread to find his way out of the labyrinth. He forgot to change the black sails of his boat to white ones, signalizing success, on his return to Athens, and Aegeus, expecting the worst, drowned himself. Theseus as ruler continued his legendary exploits, such as his defeat of the Amazons, but his unification of the various Attican communities into one state, his exile and death on the island of Scyros are historical facts. His supposed remains were later reinterred in Athens. See Life in Plutarch and novels by Renault, *The King must Die* (1958) and *The Bull from the Sea* (1962).

THESPIS (fl. 534 B.C.), Greek poet, reputed founder at Athens of drama.

THEURIET, André, *tœr-yay* (1833–1907), French poet and novelist, born at Marly-le-Roi, Seine-et-Oise, received in 1857 a post under the finance minister. His collections of verse include *Le Chemin des bois* (1867), the so-called epic *Les Paysans de l'Argonne, 1792* (1871) and *Le Bleu et le Noir* (1872). But he is best known by his novels *Le Mariage de Gérard* (1875), *Raymonde* (1877), *Sauvageonne* (1880), &c. In 1897 he became an Academician. See study by Besson (1890).

THÉVENOT, Jean de, *tay-vè-nō* (1633–77), French traveller, born in Paris, travelled over Europe, the Levant, Mesopotamia and India, and died on his way to Tabriz. See *Collected Voyages* (1689).

THIARD, Pontus de. See TYARD.

THIBAUD, Jacques, *tee-bō* (1880–1953), French violinist, born at Bordeaux in 1880, studied with Marsick and played with Cortot and Casals. He died in an air crash.

THIBAULT, Jacques. See FRANCE (ANATOLE).

THIERRY, Augustin, *tyer-ree* (1795–1856), French historian, born at Blois, joined the Paris Liberals in 1814, and published *De la réorganisation de la société européenne*, inspired by Saint-Simon, whose secretary Thierry became. In 1817, however, they disagreed, and Thierry attached himself to Comte. In 1825 he published his masterpiece, the *Norman Conquest of England*, followed in 1827 by *Lettres sur l'histoire de France*. In 1835 he became librarian at the Palais Royal, and published his *Dix Ans d'études historiques*. His last work was on the *Tiers État* (1853). He resurrected historical studies, used original documents, where possible, but overdramatized. See monograph by Aubineau (1879) and study by A. A. Thierry (1922). His brother, **Amédée Simon Dominique** (1797–1873), was also a historian.

THIERS, Louis Adolphe, *tyer* (1797–1877), French statesman and historian, born at Marseilles, April 16, was sent in 1815 to study law at Aix, where he made the acquaintance of Mignet, and cultivated literature rather than the law. At twenty-three he was called to the bar; and his articles in the Liberal *Constitutionnel* gained him the entry to the most influential *salons* of the Opposition. Meanwhile he was rapidly preparing his *Histoire de la révolution française* (10 vols. 1823–27), which though untrustworthy and inaccurate gave him a prominent place among politicians and men of letters. In January 1830, along with Carrel and Mignet, he started the *National*, and waged relentless war on the Polignac administration. Its attempted suppression brought about the July Revolution; and Thiers entered on an active career as a politician. He was elected deputy for Aix, was appointed secretary-general to the minister of finance, and became one of the most formidable of parliamentary speakers. Radical though he was as compared with Guizot, he in 1832 became minister of the interior, and of commerce and public affairs, and then foreign minister; his 'spirited foreign policy' is now seen to have been a great mistake. In 1836 he was appointed president of the council, but in August he resigned, and led the Opposition. Again president of the council and foreign minister (1840), he for six months was a terror to the peace of Europe. He refused Palmerston's invitation to enter into an alliance with Britain, Austria and Prussia for the preservation of the integrity of the Ottoman Empire, aiming like Napoleon at French supremacy in the Levant. Irritation at the isolation of France led to his resignation. *L'Histoire du consulat et de l'empire* (20 vols. 1845–62), the most ambitious of all Thiers's literary enterprises, is a large rather than a great work; that it is inaccurate and unfair has been admitted even by French critics. Thiers would have hindered the revolution of 1848, and, though he accepted the Republic, was arrested and banished at the *coup d'état* of 1851, being allowed, however, to return the next year. He re-entered the Chamber in 1863, and his speeches were filled with taunts at the second Empire on account of its loss of prestige. After the collapse of the Empire Thiers declined to become a member of the Government of National Defence, but voluntarily undertook (unsuccessful) diplomatic journeys to Great Britain, Russia, Austria and Italy. Twenty constituencies elected him to the National Assembly, and he became head of the provisional government. With great difficulty he persuaded the Assembly to agree to peace on terms practically dictated by Germany (1871). The Commune he suppressed with characteristic energy. In August he was elected president of the Republic. He was mainly instrumental in securing the withdrawal of the Germans, in paying the war indemnity and in placing the army and the civil service on a more satisfactory footing. He was detested by the extreme Left, and, Reactionaries and Radicals combining to harass him, in 1872 he tendered his resignation. It was not accepted. What he interpreted as a vote of no confidence was carried May 24, 1873, and he resigned. In 1877 he took an active part in bringing about the fall of the de Broglie ministry. He died of apoplexy at St Germain-en-Laye, September 3, 1877. Thiers was not a great statesman or a great historian. But he was a man of indomitable courage, and his patriotism, if narrow and chauvinistic, was deep and genuine. He became a member of the Academy in 1834. His *Discours parlementaires* fill 16 vols. (1879–89). See works by Jules Simon (1878–85), Mazade (1884), Rémusat (1889; trans. 1892), Poincaré (1913), Reclus (1929), Allison (1932) and H. Malo (1932).

THIRKELL, Angela. See MACKAIL.

THIRLWALL, Connop (1797–1875), English divine and historian, born at Stepney, from Charterhouse passed in 1814 to Trinity College, Cambridge, and was elected a fellow. He was called to the bar in 1825, but in 1827 took orders, having two years before translated Schleiermacher's *Essay on St Luke*. Returning to Cambridge, he translated Niebuhr's *Rome* (1828) with Julius Hare; and their *Philological Museum* (1831–33) contained some remarkable papers, among them Thirlwall's 'On the Irony of Sophocles'. He petitioned and wrote (1834) in favour of the admission of Dissenters to degrees and was forced to resign his university appointments. Almost immediately he was presented by Brougham to the Yorkshire living of Kirby-Underdale. Here he wrote for *Lardner's Cyclopaedia* his *History of Greece* (1835–44; improved ed. 1847–52). In 1840 Lord Melbourne raised him to the see of St David's. For thirty-four years he laboured with the utmost diligence in his diocese, building churches, parsonages and schools, and augmenting poor livings. His eleven Charges remain an enduring monument of breadth of view—the first a catholic apology for the Tractarians. He joined in censuring *Essays and Reviews*, but was one of the four bishops who refused to inhibit Colenso. He supported the Maynooth grant, the admission of Jews to parliament, and alone amongst the bishops the disestablishment of the Irish Church. He resigned his see in May 1874, died at Bath, July 27, 1875, and was buried in Westminster Abbey, in the same grave as Grote. Perowne edited his *Remains, Literary and Theological* (1877–78); Perowne and Stokes his *Letters, Literary and Theological* (1881); and Dean Stanley the series of *Letters to a Friend* (1881). See Life by J. C. Thirlwall (1936).

THISTLEWOOD, Arthur (1770–1820), English conspirator, born near Lincoln, served in the army, but having imbibed revolutionary ideas in America and France, organized a mutiny at Spa Fields (1816) and in 1820 the Cato Street Conspiracy to murder Castlereagh and other ministers at Lord Harrowby's. The conspirators were arrested in a stable in Cato (Homer) Street, Edgware Road, and Thistlewood with four others was convicted of high treason and hanged.

THOM, (1) John Nichols. See COURTENAY.

(2) **William** (1799–1848), Scottish minor poet, author of *The Mitherless Bairn* and other poems, was born at Aberdeen, worked as a handloom weaver there and at Inverurie, and died at Hawkhill, Dundee.

THOMA, *tō-mah*, (1) **Hans** (1839–1924), German painter and lithographer, born in Bernau in the Black Forest, was a leader of the modern German school, known especially for his landscapes, genre scenes and religious and allegorical works. His early style was influenced by Courbet. His paintings include *At Lake of Garda*, *Solitude* and *Scenes from the Life of Christ*.

(2) **Wilhelm von** (1891–1948), German general, served in World War I, commanded the German tank forces in the Spanish Civil War, served under Guderian in France at the beginning of World War II, and was captured in Tunisia with remnants of the Afrika Korps in November 1942.

THOMAS, St, called **Didymus**, one of the Twelve Apostles, who according to John xx, 24–29, doubted until he had seen proof of Jesus's resurrection. One tradition has it that he founded the church in Parthia and was buried in Edessa. Another, that he preached in India. The Christians of St Thomas claim him as their founder. He is patron saint of Portugal and his feast day is on December 21.

THOMAS, (1) *tom'as*, Fr. *tō-mah* (fl. 12th cent.), Anglo-Norman poet, author of the earliest extant text (*c.* 1155–70) of the legend of Tristan and Iseult, a fragment of 3144 lines covering the final episodes including the death of the lovers. Though he has greater pretensions to a literary style, Thomas lacks the impressive primitive simplicity of Béroul, author of the slightly later and fuller of the two early versions, both of which appear to be based on an earlier poem now lost. Thomas is sometimes confused with Thomas the Rhymer (q.v.).

(2) **Albert** (1878–1932), French politician, born at Champigny-sur-Marne, was a Socialist member of the Chamber from 1910 to 1921, when he became director of the International Labour Office of the League of Nations.

(3) **(Charles Louis) Ambroise** (1811–96), French composer, born at Metz, studied at the Paris Conservatoire (1828–32). He wrote many light operas, of which *Mignon* (1866) is the best known, for the Opéra Comique and the Grand Opéra, and innumerable cantatas, part-songs and choral pieces. He became a member of the Institute (1851), professor of Composition (1852), director of the Conservatoire (1871).

(4) **Arthur Goring** (1850–92), English composer, born near Eastbourne, wrote the operas *Esmeralda* (1883) and *Nadeshda* (1885), the cantata *Sun-worshippers* (1881), and many songs. He died insane.

(5) **Brandon** (1849–1914), English actor and playwright, born in Liverpool. He first appeared as a comedy actor in 1879, and wrote a number of successful light plays, one of which, *Charley's Aunt* (1892), has retained enormous popularity.

(6) **Dylan Marlais** (1914–53), Welsh poet, born in Swansea. The son of a schoolmaster, he worked for a time as a reporter on the *South Wales Evening Post* and established himself with the publication of *Eighteen Poems* in 1934. He married Caitlin Macnamara in 1936 and published *Twenty-Five Poems* the same year. His other works include *The Map of Love* (1939), *Portrait of the Artist as a Young Dog*. (1940), *The World I Breathe* (1940), *Deaths and Entrances* (1946) and a scenario, *The Doctor and the Devils*. His *Collected Poems, 1934–1952*, were published in 1952 and he then turned to larger dramatic works. From 1944 he worked intermittently on a radio script about a Welsh seaside village and in its first form it was called *Quite Early One Morning*. Thomas expanded it into *Under Milk Wood* (published 1954). Until the appearance of this work, he had enjoyed a *succès d'estime*. Edith Sitwell had eulogized his poetry and other critics had praised his striking rhythms, his original imagery and his technical ingenuities—such as the seventy-two variations of line endings in *I in My Intricate Image*—but he could in no sense be called a popular writer. *Under Milk Wood* was immediately comprehensible, Rabelaisianly funny, had moments of lyric tenderness, fresh yet recognizable similes, and it presented most of the non-intellectual English concepts of Welsh thought and behaviour. It had a second success as a stage play. In 1955 *Adventures in the Skin Trade* was published, an unfinished novel described by the author as ' a mixture of Oliver Twist, Little Dorrit, Kafka, Beachcomber and good old three-adjectives-a-penny, belly-churning Thomas, the Rimbaud of Cwmdonkin Drive '. This description might apply to all his prose works, including *A Prospect by the Sea*, ed. D. Jones (1955). See studies by D. Stanford (1953), E. Olson (1954), H. Treece (1956), J. Brinnin (1956), Caitlin Thomas, *Leftover Life to Kill* (1957), Heppenstall, *Four Absentees* (1960), and his *Selected Letters* (ed. by Fitzgibbon, 1966).

(7) **Edward.** See (13).

(8) **Freeman Freeman-.** See WILLINGDON.

(9) **George Henry** (1816–70), American soldier, born in Virginia, graduated at West Point, entered the artillery in 1840, gained three brevets for gallantry and in the Civil War, in 1861, was appointed brigadier-general of volunteers, and in January 1862 won the battle of Mill Springs. Major-general in command of the centre of Rosencrans's army, he saved the battle of Stone River; and at Chickamauga again rendered the victory a barren one for the Confederates. In October 1863 he was given the command of the Army of the Cumberland, and in November captured Mission Ridge. In 1864 he commanded the centre in Sherman's advance on Atlanta, was sent to oppose Hood in Tennessee in December and won the battle of Nashville. He afterwards commanded the military division of the Pacific. See Lives by Van Horne (1882), Coppée (1893) and Piatt (1893).

(10) **George John** (*c.* 1756–1802), Irish adventurer, born at Tipperary, deserted in India from the navy in 1781, and as general to the Begum Somru performed feats of arms against the Sikhs, and became the independent ruler of extensive Sikh territories, until driven out in 1802. See Compton's *European Adventurers of Hindustan* (1892).

(11) **Hugh Owen** (1833–91), Welsh orthopaedic surgeon, born in Anglesey, studied medicine at University College, London, Edinburgh University and in Paris, and

practised surgery at Liverpool. He pioneered orthopaedic surgery, constructing many appliances which are still used, especially Thomas's splints for the hip and the knee. See Lives by Watson (1935) and Vay (1956).

(12) **James Henry** (1874–1949), British Labour politician, born at Newport, Mon.; an enthusiastic trade unionist, he was elected M.P. for Derby in 1910. As assistant secretary of the Amalgamated Society of Railway Servants he helped to organize the strike of 1911 and the merger of smaller unions in 1913 which formed the National Union of Railwaymen, of which he ultimately became general secretary (1917). He led the successful railway strike of 1919. When Labour came to power in 1924 he was appointed colonial secretary, and in Ramsay MacDonald's 1929 Cabinet he was lord privy seal, subsequently becoming dominions secretary (1930–35). His adherence to the 1931 National Government aroused the hostility of his former Labour colleagues; and the ensuing bitterness clouded the last few years of his political career, which came to an untimely end when, as colonial secretary (1935–36), he was found guilty by a judicial tribunal of divulging budget secrets. See his *My Story* (1937) and Life by Blaxland (1964).

(13) **Philip Edward** (1878–1917), English critic and poet, born in London, educated at St Paul's school and Lincoln College, Oxford, became a hack writer of reviews, critical studies and topographical works. Not until 1914, encouraged by Robert Frost, did he realize his potential as a poet, writing most of his poetry during active service between 1915 and his death at Arras in 1917. His impressive poetry, though rooted in the English tradition of nature poetry, broke with the Georgian tradition in its lack of rhetoric and formality and in its emphasis on the austerity of Nature and solitariness of man. See his *Collected Poems* (1920), some of which appeared under the pseudonym of Edward Eastaway, and study by Farjeon (1958).

(14) **Ronald Stuart** (1913–), Welsh priest and poet, educated at the University of Wales and St Michael's College, Llandaff, was ordained in 1937 and has been vicar at Eglwysfach since 1954. His deceptively simple poetry, published in collections such as *Song at the Year's Turning* (1955), *Poetry for Supper* (1958) and *The Bread of Truth* (1963), conveys his love of Wales and its people, particularly evoked by his use of nature imagery.

(15) **Sidney Gilchrist** (1850–85), English metallurgist, born in London; a police-court clerk, he studied at Birkbeck College and discovered a method of separating the phosphorus impurities from iron in the Bessemer converter.

THOMAS THE RHYMER, or Thomas Rymour of Erceldoune (*c.* 1220–*c.* 1297), Scottish seer and poet, lived at Erceldoune (now Earlston, Berwickshire), and in 1286 is said to have predicted the death of Alexander III and the battle of Bannockburn, becoming known as 'True Thomas'; Boece calls him Thomas Learmont. Legend relates that he was carried off to Elfland, and after three years allowed to revisit the earth, but ultimately returned to his mistress, the fairy queen. In a charter of Petrus de Haga of Bemersyde *c.* 1260–70 the Rhymer appears as a witness; and in another of 1294 Thomas of Erceldoune, 'son and heir of Thomas Rymour of Erceldoune', conveys lands to the hospice of Soutra. The Rhymer's 'prophecies' were collected and published in 1603. Sir Walter Scott believed him to be the author of the poem of *Sir Tristrem* (as did McNeill), which was founded on a 12th-century French poem by another Thomas, a poet of genius, almost certainly an Englishman. See *The Romances and Prophecies of Thomas of Erceldoune*, edited by Sir J. A. H. Murray (Early English Text Soc. 1875); Brandl's *Thomas of Erceldoune* (Berlin 1880); *Sir Tristrem*, edited by Scott (1804), by Kölbing (1882), and by McNeill (Scot. Text Soc. 1886); Child's *Popular Ballads* (part ii, 1884); and Burnham's study (1908).

THOMAS À BECKET. See BECKET.

THOMAS À KEMPIS. See KEMPIS.

THOMAS AQUINAS. See AQUINAS.

THOMAS OF CELANO. See CELANO.

THOMAS OF HEREFORD, St. See CANTELUPE.

THOMAS OF WOODSTOCK (1355–97), youngest son of Edward III, born at Woodstock, was created Duke of Gloucester in 1385. He led the opposition of the lords appellant to Richard II, was arrested in 1397 and imprisoned at Calais, where he died.

THOMASIUS, Christian (1655–1728), German rationalist, philosopher and international jurist, born at Leipzig, lectured on law there and at Berlin, and at Halle became professor of Jurisprudence. He was the first to lecture not in Latin but German, broke away from pedantry and mediaeval terminology, and was a courageous opponent of trial for witchcraft and torture. See his *Gedanken und Erinnerungen* (1723–26), and works by Landsberg (1894), Fleischmann (1931).

THOMASON, (1) George (d. 1666), English bookseller and publisher who made a complete and valuable collection of tracts and pamphlets printed in England during the years of the Civil War and the Restoration. These were given to the British Museum by George III in 1762. See *Thomason Collection, Catalogue, 1640–1661*, ed. Fortescue (1908).

(2) **James** (1804–53), English administrator in India, as lieutenant-governor of the Northwest Provinces (1843-53) did admirable work in land settlement, education, &c.

THOMPSON, (1) Benjamin. See RUMFORD.

(2) **Sir D'Arcy Wentworth** (1860–1948), Scottish zoologist, born in Edinburgh and educated at Edinburgh Academy and Trinity College, Cambridge, in 1897 became professor of Biology at Dundee and later at St Andrews. His study *On Growth and Form* (1917) has literary as well as scientific merit. Other works include papers on fishery and oceanography, *Glossary of Greek Birds* (1895) and *Glossary of Greek Fishes* (1945). See Life by his daughter (1958).

(3) **David** (1770–1857), Canadian explorer, born in Westminster, went to Canada in 1784, and explored much of the west, including the Columbia River (1807–11).

(4) **Edith** (d. 1923), English murderess, with her accomplice Frederick Bywaters was tried in December 1922 for stabbing her husband two months previously on the way home from a London theatre. The trial at the Old Bailey provided much sensation; the couple were found guilty, and in spite of many petitions for reprieve were executed. See F. Young's study (1951).

(5) **Elizabeth Southerden.** See BUTLER (16).

(6) **Francis** (1859–1907), English poet, born at Preston, Lancs, was brought up in the Catholic faith and studied for the priesthood. By temperament unsuited for this, he turned to medicine at Owens College, Manchester, but failed to graduate. He moved to London, where extreme poverty and ill-health drove him to become an opium addict. From this he was rescued by Wilfrid and Alice Meynell, to whom he had sent some poems for Meynell's magazine *Merry England.* His health was restored at a monastery in Sussex, where he wrote several poems, including the well-known *Hound of Heaven.* Thereafter he was succoured by the Meynells until his death from tuberculosis. His works include *Poems* (1893), *Sister Songs* (1895, written for the Meynell girls) and *New Poems* (1897). His notable *Essay on Shelley* (1909) appeared posthumously, as did his *Life of St Ignatius Loyola* (1909). His poems, mainly religious in theme, are rich in imagery and poetic vision. See the *Works* (1913, ed. E. Meynell), *Poems of Francis Thompson* (1946), studies by Delattre (1909), Mégroz (1927), Olivers (Eng. trans. 1938) and Lives by Meynell (1913), Reid (1959) and Thomson (1961).

(7) **Sir Henry** (1820–1904), English surgeon, born at Framlingham, studied medicine at University College, London, and became professor of Surgery there and at the Royal College of Surgeons. Knighted (1867) and made a baronet (1899), he wrote on the urethra, lithotomy and calculus, and advocated cremation. A collector of Nankin china, and an astronomer, he exhibited at the Royal Academy.

(8) **Sir John Sparrow David** (1844–94), Canadian statesman, born at Halifax, entered the Nova Scotia Legislature in 1877, became premier of Nova Scotia (1881) and of Canada in 1892. He was knighted in 1888 and died at Windsor, on a visit to England.

(9) **John Taliaferro** (1860–1940), American soldier and inventor, was born in Newport, Kentucky, and graduated in 1882 at the Military Academy. In 1920 he invented the submachine gun known as the 'Tommy' gun, which was a ·45 calibre gun weighing 10 lb. It was first used for military purposes by the U.S. Marines in Nicaragua in 1925. A modification was adopted for use by the Allies in World War II. He retired in 1914, but was recalled during World War I as Chief of the Small Arms Division of the U.S. Ordnance Department.

(10) **John Vaughan** (1779–1847), English zoologist, after seeing service as an army surgeon studied marine zoology, distinguishing himself by his publications on barnacles and the common crab.

(11) **Randall** (1899–), American composer, born in New York, studied under Ernest Bloch, and from 1922 to 1925 was a fellow of the American Academy at Rome, subsequently teaching at Harvard, Princeton and California. His music assimilates romantic and popular American idioms, and includes three symphonies, an oratorio *The Peaceable Kingdom, The Testament of Freedom,* a setting of passages from the writings of Thomas Jefferson, chamber, piano, orchestral and theatre music.

(12) **Silvanus Phillips** (1851–1916), English physicist, born at York, professor of Physics and principal of the City and Guilds Technical College, Finsbury, wrote on electricity, light and magnetism and a witty, effective little book called *Calculus made Easy* (1910).

(13) **William** (*c.* 1785–1833), Irish landowner and writer on economics, was a follower of Bentham. One of the early socialists, his works include *An Inquiry into the Principles of the Distribution of Wealth most Conducive to Human Happiness* (1824), *An Appeal of one half of the Human Race* (1825), and *Practical Directions for the Speedy and Economical Establishment of Communities on the Principle of Mutual Co-operation* (1830).

(14) **William Hepworth** (1810–86), English Greek scholar, born at York, studied at Trinity College, Cambridge, became regius professor of Greek in 1853, and in 1866 master of Trinity. He edited Plato's *Phaedrus* and *Gorgias,* and is chiefly remembered by a few incomparable sarcasms.

THOMS, William John (1803–85), English antiquary and bibliographer, born in Westminster, after twenty years as a clerk in Chelsea Hospital became a clerk to the House of Lords, and its deputy librarian (1863–82). He founded (1849) and edited (till 1872) *Notes and Queries,* devised the word 'folklore', and edited *Early Prose Romances* (1828).

THOMSEN, Vilhelm (1842–1927), Danish philologist, born at Copenhagen, professor there from 1875, wrote *The Relations between Ancient Russia and Scandinavia* (1878) and deciphered the Orkhon inscriptions (1893).

THOMSON, (1) Sir Charles Wyville (1830–1882), Scottish zoologist, born at Bonsyde, Linlithgow, studied at Edinburgh and held professorships in Natural History at Cork, Belfast and Edinburgh. He was famous for his deep-sea researches, described in *The Depths of the Oceans* (1872), and in 1872 was appointed scientific head of the *Challenger* Expedition (1872–76). He was elected F.R.S. in 1869. See his *The Voyage of the Challenger* (1877), and Sir W. A. Herdman, *Founders of Oceanography* (1923).

(2) **Elihu** (1853–1937), English-born American inventor, born in Manchester, emigrated to the United States and was educated in Philadelphia, becoming a chemistry teacher. He cooperated in his 700 patented electrical inventions, which include the three-phase alternating-current generator and arc lighting, with Edward James Houston (q.v.), founding the Thomson-Houston Electric Company (1883), which merged with Edison's in 1892 to form the General Electric Company.

(3) **George** (1757–1851), collector of Scottish music, friend of Burns, born at

Limekilns, was clerk to the Board of Trustees in Edinburgh for sixty years. Burns, Scott and Campbell contributed to his *Collection of Scottish Songs and Airs* (5 vols. 1799–1818). See his Correspondence (ed. Hadden, 1898).

(4) **Sir George Paget** (1892–), English physicist, son of (10), born and educated at Cambridge, where he became a fellow of Trinity College, served in the Royal Flying Corps in World War I, was professor of Physics at Aberdeen (1922), Imperial College, London (1930), and master of Corpus Christi (1952–62). He was elected F.R.S. (1930), and awarded its Hughes (1939) and Royal (1949) medals. In 1937 he shared the Nobel prize with Davisson for their discovery, separately and by different methods, of electron diffraction by crystals. He was knighted (1943), and scientific adviser to the U.N. Security Council (1946–47). In 1960 for his contributions to electrical science he was awarded the Faraday medal by the Institution of Electrical Engineers. See his *The Atom* (1937) and *Theory and Practice of Electron Diffraction* (1939).

(5) **James** (1700–48), Scottish poet, born at Ednam manse, Kelso, educated at Jedburgh School and Edinburgh University for the ministry, abandoned his studies and went to seek his fortune as a writer in London. He published *Winter* (1726), a short poem in blank verse, *Summer* (1727), *Spring* (1728), and *Autumn* appeared with the other three under the collective title *The Seasons* (1730). In 1729 his *Sophonisba* was produced. One luckless line, ' O Sophonisba, Sophonisba O ', is still remembered for the parody, ' O Jemmy Thomson, Jemmy Thomson O ', which killed what little life the piece possessed. His other tragedies were *Agamemnon* (1738), *Edward and Eleonora* (1739), *Tancred and Sigismunda* (1745) and *Coriolanus* (1748). The poem *Liberty* (1735–1736) was inspired by the Grand Tour which he undertook as tutor to Lord Chancellor Talbot's son in 1731, and was dedicated to the Prince of Wales, who awarded him a pension. 'A Poem sacred to the Memory of Isaac Newton ' (1727) and ' Britannia ' (1729), which criticized Walpole's foreign policy, secured him further patronage and the sinecure of surveyor-general of the Leeward Isles (1744). *Alfred, a Masque* (1740) contains the song ' Rule Britannia ', also claimed for Mallet (q.v.). The Spenserian *The Castle of Indolence* (1748) is considered his masterpiece. Thomson stood on the threshold of the Romantic Age. The proper study of mankind was to be no longer man but nature, with science unravelling ever greater harmonies. Despite the pleasing melody of much of his verse, he often substitutes verbosity for feeling. See Lives by L. Morel (1896), W. Bayne (1898) and G. C. Macaulay (1908), and studies by A. D. McKillop (1942) and D. Grant (1951).

(6) **James** (1822–92), Scottish engineer, elder brother of Lord Kelvin (q.v.), born at Belfast, was professor of Engineering at Belfast (1851) and Glasgow (1873–89). He was an authority on hydraulics, invented a turbine, discovered the effect of pressure upon the freezing-point of water, and wrote papers on elastic fatigue, under-currents and trade winds.

(7) **James** (1834–82), British poet, was born, a sailor's son, at Port Glasgow, and educated in an orphan asylum. He was trained as an army schoolmaster, but through his friend Bradlaugh contributed (1860–75) to the *National Reformer*, in which appeared many of his sombre, sonorous poems, including *The City of Dreadful Night* (1874), his greatest work. He became a lawyer's clerk in 1862, went to America as a mining agent (1872), was war correspondent with the Carlists (1873), and from 1875 onwards depended largely on contributions to a tobacconists' trade monthly. Ill-health and melancholia drove him to narcotics and stimulants, and he died in University College Hospital. *The City of Dreadful Night and other Poems* (1880; ed. E. Blunden, 1932) was followed by *Vane's Story* (1881), *Essays and Phantasies* (1881), *A Voice from the Nile* (1884, with memoir by Bertram Dobell), *Shelley, a Poem* (1885), and *Biographical and Critical Studies* (1896). His pseudonym B.V., Bysshe Vanolis, was partly from Shelley's second name, partly from an anagram of Novalis. See Salt's *Life of James Thomson, ' B.V.'* (1889; revised ed. 1914).

(8) **John** (1778–1840), Scottish painter, born at Dailly manse, Ayrshire, was from 1800 the minister of Dailly and from 1805 of Duddingston. He was one of the first landscape painters of Scotland. See Lives by Baird (1895), Napier (1919).

(9) **Joseph** (1858–95), Scottish explorer, born at Penpont, Dumfriesshire, studied at Edinburgh, went (1878–79) to Lake Tanganyika, and in 1883–84 passed through the Masai country. For the Niger Company he visited Sokoto (1885), and for the Geographical Society he explored southern Morocco (1888). He wrote *To the Central African Lakes and Back* (1881), *Through Masai Land* (1885), *Travels in the Atlas* (1889), a Life of Mungo Park (1890), &c. See Life by his brother, J. B. Thomson (1896).

(10) **Sir Joseph John** (1856–1940), British mathematical physicist, one of the outstanding pioneers of nuclear physics, father of (4), was born at Cheetham Hill near Manchester, December 18, the son of a Scottish bookseller. He entered Owen's College, Manchester, at fourteen with the intention of becoming a railway engineer, but a scholarship took him to Trinity College, Cambridge, where he graduated second wrangler. In 1884 at the age of twenty-seven he succeeded Lord Rayleigh as Cavendish professor of Experimental Physics, and in 1919 was himself succeeded by his great student, later Lord Rutherford (q.v.). Thomson's early theoretical work was concerned with the extension of Clerk-Maxwell's electromagnetic theories. This led on to the study of gaseous conductors of electricity and in particular the nature of cathode rays. Using Röntgen's discovery of X-rays (1895), he showed that cathode rays were rapidly-moving particles and by measuring their speed and specific charge, the latter by two independent methods, he deduced that these ' corpuscles ' (electrons) must be nearly

two thousand times smaller in mass than the lightest known atomic particle, the hydrogen ion. This, the greatest revolution in physics since Newton, was inaugurated by his lecture to the Royal Institution, April 30, 1897, and published in October in the *Philosophical Magazine*. Before the outbreak of World War I, Thomson had successfully studied the nature of positive rays (1911), and this work was crowned by the discovery of the isotope. He also formulated a theory for the calculations on the scattering of X-rays by electrons in atoms. During the war he was engaged in admiralty research and helped to found the Department of Scientific and Industrial Research. 'J. J.' made the Cavendish Laboratory the greatest research institution in the world. Although simplicity of apparatus was carried to 'string and sealing wax' extremes, seven of his research assistants subsequently won the Nobel prize. He was the first man of science to become master of Trinity College (1918–1940). Thomson was awarded the Nobel prize (1906), knighted (1908), O.M. (1912), was president of the British Association (1909) and of the Royal Society (1915–20). He was buried near Newton in the nave of Westminster Abbey. See his *Recollections and Reflections* (1936), Lives by Lord Rayleigh (1942) and his son G. P. Thomson (1964), and *History of the Cavendish Laboratory* (1910).

(11) **Roy Herbert, 1st Baron Thomson of Fleet** (1894–), Canadian-born British newspaper and television magnate, son of a Scottish barber, was born at Toronto. Successively clerk, salesman, farmer, stenographer and book-keeper, he gained a commission in the Canadian militia during World War I. He became prosperous when, as a radio salesman, he set up his own commercial transmitter at North Bay (1931) in an area of poor reception, thus boosting sales and founding what later became the N.B.C. network. He started more radio stations and acquired 28 Canadian and 6 American newspapers, which he turned over to his son in 1953. In that year he settled in Edinburgh on acquiring his first British paper, *The Scotsman*, and associated publications. In 1957 he obtained a licence for commercial television in Scotland and in 1959 he became one of Britain's leading newspaper proprietors with the acquisition of the Kemsley newspapers. Unlike his predecessors, he did not impose a policy on his editors. In 1966 he took over *The Times*. He was created a peer in 1964.

(12) **Virgil** (1896–), American composer and critic, was born at Kansas City and educated at Harvard and Paris. He set some of the writings of Gertrude Stein (q.v.) to music, and wrote operas, *Four Saints in Three Acts* (1934), first performed by a cast of Negroes, and *The Mother of Us All* (1947), besides symphonies, ballets, choral, chamber and film music. His work is notable for its simplicity of style. He was music critic of the *New York Herald Tribune* (1940–54). See study by Hoover and Cage (1959).

(13) **Sir William.** See KELVIN (LORD).

THOREAU, Henry David, *thor'ō* (1817–62), American essayist and poet, the 'hermit of Walden', born of Jersey stock at Concord, Mass., July 12, 1817, graduated at Harvard in 1837, became a teacher at Concord, and lectured. He soon gave up teaching, and joined his father in making lead pencils, but about 1839 began his walks and studies of nature as the serious occupation of his life. In 1839 he made the voyage described in his *Week on the Concord and Merrimack Rivers* (1849). Thoreau early made the acquaintance of Emerson, and in 1841–43 and in 1847 was a member of his household. In 1845 he built himself a shanty in the woods by Walden Pond, where he wrote much of the *Week*, his essay on Carlyle, and the American classic, *Walden, or Life in the Woods* (1854). After the Walden episode he supported himself by whitewashing, gardening, fence building and land surveying. He also lectured now and then, and wrote for magazines. He made three trips to the Maine woods in 1846, 1853 and 1857, described in papers collected after his death (1864). In 1850 he made a trip to Canada, which produced *A Yankee in Canada* (1866). Thoreau began in 1835 to keep a daily journal of his walks and observations, from whose thirty volumes were published *Early Spring in Massachusetts* (1881), *Summer* (1884) and *Winter* (1887). Other publications are *Excursions in Field and Forest*, with memoir by Emerson (1863), *Cape Cod* (1865), *Letters to Various Persons*, with nine poems (1865), *Familiar Letters* (1894) and *Poems of Nature* (1896). See *Collected Poems* (ed. by Bode, 1943, rev. ed. 1964), Correspondence, ed. Harding and Bode (1959), Lives by W. E. Channing (1873), H. S. Salt (1890–96), H. S. Canby (1939), and E. Seybold (1951), and studies by M. van Doren (1916), Krutch (1949) and Keyes (1955).

THORNDIKE, (1) Edward Lee (1874–1949), American psychologist, born at Williamsburg, Mass., studied at Wesleyan University and afterwards, under William James (q.v.), at Harvard. As professor at Columbia (1904–1940), he formulated important theories of educational psychology. He devised intelligence tests and stressed the effect of chance associations in educational processes. His works include *The Principles of Teaching* (1905), *Psychology of Learning* (1914), *Psychology of Arithmetic* (1922) and *of Algebra* (1923), and *The Measurement of Intelligence* (1926).

(2) **Dame Sybil** (1882–), English actress, born in Gainsborough, trained as a pianist but turned, despite considerable discouragement, to the stage. She made her first stage appearance with Greet's Pastoral Players in *The Merry Wives of Windsor* in 1904. After four years spent touring the United States in Shakespearean repertory, she became a prominent member of Miss Horniman's Repertory Company in Manchester, and worked from 1914 to 1919 at the Old Vic, subsequently collaborating with her husband, **Sir Lewis Casson**, whom she married in 1908, in a biography of Lilian Baylis. In 1924 she played the title rôle in the first English performance of Shaw's *Saint Joan*, and, during World War II, was a notable member of the Old Vic Company,

playing at the New Theatre, London. She was created D.B.E. in 1931. See Life by Trewin (1955).

THORNEYCROFT, (George Edward) Peter, Baron (1909–), English politician, educated at Eton and the R.M.A. Woolwich, served as a regular artillery officer (1930–33), left the army to become a barrister, and entered parliament in 1938. President of the Board of Trade in 1951-57, he was appointed chancellor of the Exchequer in 1957, but, disagreeing with government financial policy, resigned after a year in office. Minister of aviation (1960–62), of defence (1962–64), and secretary of state for defence (1964), he lost his parliamentary seat in the 1966 election. In 1967 he was created a life peer.

THORNHILL, Sir James (1675–1734), English painter, born at Melcombe Regis, Dorset, executed paintings for the dome of St Paul's, Blenheim, Hampton Court and Greenwich Hospital. He painted some portraits, including those of Codrington, the criminal Jack Sheppard and a self-portrait; and of his easel paintings the best known is that of the House of Commons (1730). He founded a drawing school and Hogarth (q.v.), who became his son-in-law, was one of his pupils. He was knighted by George I in 1720 and was appointed serjeant-painter, becoming in 1728 history painter to the king. From 1722 he was M.P. for Melcombe Regis.

THORNTON, Henry (1760–1815), English banker and economist, born in London, became in 1782 a member of parliament and gave considerable support to the aims and schemes of his friend Wilberforce. He became known in the government as an astute financier, this reputation being confirmed by his excellent *An Enquiry into the Nature and Effects of the Paper Credit of Great Britain* (1802). He was a member of the bullion committee (1810), a director and governor of the Bank of England, and a great part of his personal fortune he gave to charitable causes.

THORNYCROFT, Sir William Hamo (1850–1925), English sculptor, was born in London. *Artemis* (1880), his first success, was followed by *The Mower* (1884), and statues of General Gordon in Trafalgar Square (1885), John Bright at Rochdale (1892), and Cromwell at Westminster (1899). He was elected R.A. (1888), and was knighted (1917). His grandfather, **John Francis** (1780–1861); his mother, **Mary** (1814–95); and his father, **Thomas** (1815–85), were all sculptors. His brother, **Sir John Isaac** (1843–1928), knighted in 1902, was a naval architect, engineer, and F.R.S.

THORPE, Benjamin (1782–1870), English philologist, edited numerous Anglo-Saxon texts, and wrote *Northern Mythology* (1852).

THORVALDSEN, Bertel (1770–1844), Danish sculptor, born probably at Copenhagen, was the son of an Icelandic woodcarver. He studied at Copenhagen, and from 1797 at Rome, where his model for a 'Jason' was highly admired by Canova, but remained unsold till in 1803 he received from 'Anastasius' Hope a commission for its production in marble. Now famous, he in 1819 made a triumphal return to Denmark. He again lived in Rome 1820–38 and 1841–44. In the latter year, having revisited Copenhagen to complete some of his works, he died suddenly in the theatre, March 24. All the works in his possession he bequeathed, with the bulk of his fortune, to his country. Among his works are *Christ and the Twelve Apostles*, the reliefs *Night* and *Morning*, the *Dying Lion* at Lucerne and the Cambridge statue of Byron. See Danish Lives by Thiele (1831–50; Eng. abridgment by Barnard, 1865) and Sigurd Müller (1893), French Life by E. Plon (1830; trans. C. Hoey 1874), and Life by S. Trier (1903).

THOTHMES, or **Thutmose**, the name of four Egyptian pharaohs of the 18th Dynasty:

(1) **Thothmes I and II.** See HATSHEPSUT.

(2) **Thothmes III** (pharaoh 1479–47 B.C.), one of the greatest of Egyptian rulers, son of Thothmes I and father of Amenhotep II, reigned jointly at first with his wife and half-sister, Queen Hatshepsut (q.v.), from *c.* 1501. He invaded Syria, extended his territories to Carchemish on the Euphrates and made several invasions into Asia. He built the great temple of Amen at Karnak, restored those at Memphis, Heliopolis and Abydos, and erected obelisks, including 'Cleopatra's Needle', now in London.

(3) **Thothmes IV** (pharaoh *c.* 1420–11 B.C.), son of Amenhotep II and father of Amenhotep III (qq.v.), fought campaigns in Syria and Nubia.

THOU, Jacques Auguste de (Latinized **Thuanus**), *too* (1553–1617), French historian and statesman, born at Paris of a great legal family, was intended for the church, but turned to law, became president of the *parlement* of Paris, and was a distinguished diplomat under Henry III and Henry IV. His great Latin history of his own time (5 vols. 1604–20; ed. by S. Buckley, London 1733) was placed on the Index. At his death, he left also commentaries on his own life and some Latin verse. See Collinson's *Life of Thuanus* (1807), monographs by P. Chasles (1824) and H. Harrisse (1905), and Stirling-Maxwell's *Miscellaneous Essays* (1891).

THRALE. See PIOZZI.

THRASYBULUS, *-si-boo'-* (d. 388 B.C.), Athenian general, was a strenuous supporter of the democracy. In 411 B.C. he helped to overthrow the Four Hundred, and was responsible for the recall of Alcibiades (q.v.). He was banished by the Thirty Tyrants, but restored the democracy in 403. He conquered Lesbos and defended Rhodes, but was slain in 388 at Aspendus. Nepos has a Life of him.

THRING, Edward (1821–87), English schoolmaster, born at Alford House, Somerset, from Eton passed to King's College, Cambridge, and was elected a fellow. He was curate at Gloucester and elsewhere, but in 1853 found the work of his life as headmaster of Uppingham, which he made one of the best public schools of England, raising its numbers from 25 to 330. His works include volumes of school songs, an English grammar, *Theory and Practice of Teaching* (1883), and *Uppingham Sermons* (1886). See Life by Dr G. R. Parkin (2 vols. 1898), and study by Hoyland (1946).

THROCKMORTON, or **Throgmorton**, name

of an English family of the 15th and 16th centuries. Its important members were:

(1) **Francis** (1554–84), English conspirator, son of (3), was apprehended in the act of writing in cipher to Mary, Queen of Scots, confessed under torture and was executed at Tyburn.

(2) **Sir John** (d. 1445), was a clerk in the treasury who became chamberlain of the exchequer and under-treasurer to Henry VI.

(3) **Sir John** (d. 1580), English judge, father of (1) and brother of (4), with whom he was involved in Wyatt's rebellion (1554), but was acquitted and made chief justice of Chester.

(4) **Sir Nicholas** (1515–71), English diplomatist, fought bravely at Pinkie (1547), was ambassador to France, where he was imprisoned for siding with the Huguenots, and was repeatedly ambassador to Scotland during 1561–67. In 1569 he was sent to the Tower for promoting the scheme for marrying Mary, Queen of Scots, to the Duke of Norfolk. His daughter, **Elizabeth**, married Sir Walter Raleigh.

THUANUS. See THOU.

THUCYDIDES, *thoo-sid'i-deez* (*c.* 460–*c.* 400 B.C.), Greek historian of the Peloponnesian war, son of Olorus, was born near Athens. He suffered in the Athenian plague (430) but recovered. He commanded an Athenian squadron of seven ships at Thasos (424), when he failed to relieve Amphipolis; and, condemned therefore to death as a traitor, took refuge in exile, and retired to his Thracian estates. He lived in exile twenty years (possibly visiting Sicily), and probably returned to Athens in 404. He did not live long enough to revise book viii or to bring his history down to the end of the war. Thucydides wrote in a difficult style, his matter often based on speeches made by prominent politicians and analysed according to his own rationalist principles of historical criticism, which aimed at impartiality. He admired Pericles and clearly understood the causes of Greece's future decline. See studies by G. B. Grundy (1911 and 1948), J. H. Finley (1942) and A. W. Gomme (1945).

THUMB, Tom. See STRATTON.

THURBER, James Grover (1894–1961), American journalist, writer and playwright, born in Ohio. He was a member of the staff of *The New Yorker* from 1927, where his reputation was made. See his *Years with Ross* (1959). His drawings first appeared in his book *Is Sex Necessary?* (1929). They have been described as being 'like what everyone thinks he can do himself', but their crazy yet conventionalized inconsequence has a markedly individual technique. His comic and satirical books, illustrated by himself, include *The Seal in the Bedroom* (1931), *The Owl in the Attic* (1932), *My Life and Hard Times* (1933), with Elliott Nugent, *The Male Animal* (1940), a play, *Fables for Our Times* (1941 and 1951). There are also several anthologies of his work, such as *The Thurber Album* (1952), *Thurber's Dogs* (1955) and the posthumous *Vintage Thurber* (1963).

THURLOE, John (1616–68), English parliamentarian politician, was secretary of the council of state (1652), a member of Oliver Cromwell's second council (1657) and supported Richard Cromwell. He was accused of high treason at the Restoration, but was eventually set free. His correspondence (1742) is an important source for the history of the Protectorate. See *Cromwell's Master Spy* by D. L. Hobman (1961).

THURLOW, Edward, 1st Baron (1731–1806), English politician, born at Bracon-Ash, Norfolk, was as insolent and insubordinate at Caius College, Cambridge, as at King's School, Canterbury, and was sent down. He was called to the bar in 1754 and as King's Counsel in the Douglas peerage case (1769) made his reputation, entered parliament as a loyal supporter of Lord North, became solicitor-general (1770) and attorney-general (1771) and won George III's favour by upholding the latter's American policy. In 1778 he became lord chancellor and while retaining office under the Rockingham administration, opposed all its measures. Under Fox and North he was compelled to retire (1783), but was restored by Pitt and presided at the trial of Warren Hastings (1788). He was finally removed by Pitt in 1792 with the King's approval. He was vulgar, arrogant, profane and immoral, but 'No man' said Fox, 'was so wise as Thurlow looked'. See Life by R. G. Brown (1953).

THUROT, François, *tü-rō* (1726–60), French privateer, born at Nuits in Côte-d'Or, served first on a privateer. Captured and imprisoned for a year at Dover, he escaped by seizing a small boat and crossed the Channel. By 1748 he was able to fit out a merchant ship. He spent a few years in England, dividing his time between music, mathematics and dissipation, varied by smuggling and possibly piracy. At the outbreak of war (1755) he was given the command of a squadron with which he scoured the east coast of Britain, and engaged two frigates off the Forth. In October 1759 he sailed for Lough Foyle with a squadron carrying 1200 soldiers. High gales made it impossible to enter; and three British frigates appearing, Thurot fought till he was struck down.

THURSTAN (d. 1140), English divine, was a native of Bayeux and made Archbishop of York 1114. As archbishop, he struggled for primacy with Canterbury. On the invasion of David of Scotland (1137), he first persuaded him to accept a truce, and then collected forces at York and beat him at the Battle of the Standard (1138). He did much to help the growth of monasticism in the North and was concerned in the foundation of Fountains Abbey (1132). He entered the Cluniac order and died at Pontefract Priory.

THURSTON, (1) **Ernest Charles Temple** (1879–1933), English novelist and playwright, first wrote a volume of poems when he was sixteen. His sentimental novels were popular in his lifetime and include *The Apple of Eden* (1904), *The City of Beautiful Nonsense* (1909), *The Passionate Crime* (1920) and *A Hank of Hair* (1932). Of his plays, *The Wandering Jew* (1920) was the best known.

(2) **Katherine Cecil** (1875–1911), novelist, wife of (1), whom she divorced in 1910, was born in Cork. Her first book, *The Circle* (1903), was followed by several popular novels, the best of which was *John Chilcote*

M.P. (1904), with its theme of impersonation. This was dramatized by her husband as *The Masquerader* (1905).

THURTELL, John (1794–1824), English murderer, son of a Norwich alderman, was hanged at Hertford for the brutal murder, in Gill's Hill Lane, of a fellow-swindler, Weare. He appears in Borrow's *Lavengro*.

THUTMOSE. See THOTHMES.

TIBERIANUS, a 4th-century Latin poet of the African school, author of *Amnis ibat inter arva*.

TIBERIUS (Tiberius Claudius Nero) (42 B.C.–A.D. 37), second emperor of Rome, son of Ti. Claudius Nero and of Livia, was born November 16, three years before her complaisant husband yielded Livia to the triumvir Octavianus. He was nine when his father's death transferred him to the tutelage of his stepfather. Almost the whole of his first twenty years of manhood were spent in the camp—in Spain, Armenia, Gaul, Pannonia and Germany. He brought back the standards lost with Crassus; in 15 B.C. he cooperated with his brother Drusus in subduing the Rhaeti and Vindelici; warred with the Pannonians (12–9), and traversed Germany. Tiberius was compelled (12 B.C.) by Augustus to divorce his wife, Vipsania Agrippina, daughter of Agrippa by his former wife Pomponia, in order to marry Agrippa's widow Julia, the profligate daughter of Augustus. He was then sent to crush a revolt in Dalmatia and Pannonia; and for his wars in Germany received a full triumph (9 B.C.). But he retired to Rhodes (6 B.C.) where he gave himself to study and to astrology. Before his return (A.D. 2) the infamous Julia was banished to Pandataria (2 B.C.), and the deaths of the young princes Lucius and Gaius led Augustus to adopt Tiberius (A.D. 4) as heir to the imperial dignity. He spent the next seven years in active service in north Germany, in quelling insurrections in Pannonia and Dalmatia, and in taking vengeance upon the enemy who had annihilated the army of Varus in A.D. 9. Along with Germanicus he made two marches into the heart of Germany (9–10), returning to enjoy a splendid triumph (12). Tiberius succeeded Augustus in 14. According to Tacitus, the first eight years of his reign were marked by just government, frugality and care for the interests of the provincials. During this period only twelve state trials for high treason are recorded; during 23–28 the number rose to twenty. His minister Sejanus secured vast influence by playing on the morbid suspicions of his master; and in a six years' reign of terror 100 people perished, mostly by direct mandate of the prince who though not vindictive himself lived in terror of assassination. In 26 Tiberius left Rome for Campania, and the year after took up his abode in Capreae, where according to Suetonius he wallowed in brutish sensualities. He had left the whole control of government to Sejanus, but, awakened at length to his ambitious designs, struck him down without hesitation (31). Macro, the successor of Sejanus, had all his vices without his talents. The murder of Agrippa Postumus in 14, the mysterious death of Germanicus in the East (19), the poisoning of Tiberius's own son Drusus by Sejanus (23), the banishment of Agrippina and the death of her young sons Nero and Drusus (31 and 33) were some of the dark tragedies that befell the house of Augustus. In his last years, the emperor's mind was darkened by gloom, superstition, perhaps insanity. On March 16, 37, he died at Misenum. Tacitus (Annals, Bks 1–6) is factually accurate but is hardly fair to Tiberius. More charitable are the modern studies by F. B. Marsh (1931), R. S. Rogers (1937), D. M. Pippede (1944) and Maranon (trans. Wells, 1956). See also *Claudius* novels by Robert Graves.

TIBULLUS, Albius (*c.* 54–19 B.C.), Roman poet, was born, it is believed, at Gabii. He acquired the friendship of the poet-statesman, M. Valerius Messala, and went on his staff, when Augustus commissioned him (30 B.C.) to crush a revolt in Aquitania. But though he distinguished himself in the campaign, he disliked a soldier's life as much as he enjoyed Roman society; and though again he started with Messala on a mission to Asia, he sickened on the voyage, and turned back at Corcyra. His tender, elegiac love poems to living inamoratas, by their limpid clearness and unaffected finish, still justify Quintilian in placing Tibullus at the head of Roman elegiac poets. The heroine of his first book was the wife of an officer absent on service in Cilicia; of his second, a fashionable courtesan. The third book can hardly be his, while the fourth is also by another hand. See studies by M. Schuster (1930) and N. Salanitro (1938).

TICHBORNE, a pre-Conquest Catholic family of Hampshire, who received a baronetcy in 1626. After the death of Sir Alfred Joseph Tichborne (1839–66), eleventh baronet, a butcher from Wagga-Wagga in New South Wales, Thomas Castro, otherwise Arthur Orton of Wapping, came forward to personate an elder brother, Roger Charles Tichborne (1829–54), who had been lost at sea off America. His case collapsed on March 6, 1872, the 103rd day of a trial to assert his claims. The 'Claimant', committed for perjury, on February 28, 1874, the 188th day of his new trial, the cost of which was £55,315, got fourteen years' hard labour. Released 1884, in 1895 he confessed the imposture, and died April 1, 1898. See Sir Alex. Cockburn's *Charge* (2 vols. 1875), and studies by J. B. Atlay (1916) and D. Woodruff (1957).

TICKELL, Thomas (1686–1740), English poet, born at Bridekirk, Carlisle, was a fellow of Queen's, Oxford (1710–26). His complimentary verses on *Rosamond* (1709) gained him the favour, and his own virtues the friendship, of Addison, who, on becoming in 1717 secretary of state, made him his under-secretary; from 1725 he was secretary to the lords justices of Ireland. He was skilful in occasional poetry, and was favourably reviewed in the *Spectator*. His translation of book i of the *Iliad* appeared in 1715, about the same time as Pope's. Pope professed to believe it the work of Addison himself, designed to eclipse his version, and wrote the famous satire on Atticus. But though

Addison corrected it, the translation was doubtless by Tickell. His longest poem is *Kensington Gardens*; his most popular, *Colin and Lucy*; his finest, the exquisite elegy prefixed to his edition of Addison's Works (1721). See R. E. Tickell's study (1931).

TICKNOR, (1) **George** (1791–1871), American author, born in Boston, Mass., gave up his legal practice in order to study and travel in Europe, recounted in his interesting *Letters and Journals* (1876). He was professor of French and Spanish and Belles Lettres at Harvard (1819–35) and then spent three more years in Europe, collecting materials for his great *History of Spanish Literature* (1849). See Life by G. W. H. Milburn (1893).

(2) **William Davis** (1810–64), American publisher, born in Lebanon, N.H., became a publisher in Boston in 1832, at first with John Allen, and then with James T. Fields. As Ticknor & Fields they published the *Atlantic Monthly* and the *North American Review*, and their office was the resort of Emerson, Longfellow, Hawthorne, Holmes, Lowell and Whittier. Ticknor was one of the first Americans to remunerate foreign authors. See C. Ticknor, *Hawthorne and his Publisher* (1913).

TIECK, Johann Ludwig, *teek* (1773–1853), German critic and poet of the Romantic school, born in Berlin, lived the life of a man of letters, at Berlin, Dresden and near Frankfurt an der Oder. After two or three immature romances, he struck out a new line in clever dramatized versions of Puss in Boots, Blue Beard, &c. He followed up this first success (1797) by a tragedy, a comedy (1804) and *Phantasus* (1812–17), a collection of traditional lore in story and drama. Besides superintending the completion of A. W. Schlegel's translation of Shakespeare, he edited the doubtful plays and wrote a series of essays (*Shakespeares Vorschule*, 1823–29). *Don Quixote* he himself translated in 1799–1804. He holds an honourable place among Germany's dramatic and literary critics, in virtue of his *Dramaturgische Blätter* (2nd ed. 1852) and *Kritische Schriften* (1848). Some of his fairy tales and novels were translated into English by Carlyle and Thirlwall. See Lives by Köpke (1855), Friesen (1871) and Klee (1894); Carlyle's *Essays*, vol. i, and studies by H. Lüdeke (1922) and R. Minder (1935).

TIEPOLO, Giovanni Battista, *tyay'pō-lō* (1696–1770), Italian artist, the last of the great Venetian painters, was a productive artist, elegant, rich in colour, though inaccurate in representation, as for example his *The Finding of Moses* (in 17th-century costume) in the National Gallery, Edinburgh. In his ceiling paintings in the Würzburg and Madrid palaces he spreads imaginary skies filled with floating, gesticulating baroque figures, apparently unbounded by the structure of the buildings. See monograph by A. Morassi (1955).

TIERNEY, George (1761–1830), a sarcastic Whig politician, born at Gibraltar, fought a bloodless duel with Pitt (1798), and held office under Addington, Grenville, Canning and Goderich. See Life by Olphin (1934).

TIETJENS. See TITIENS.

TIGHE, Mary, *née* **Blachford,** *tī* (1772–1810), Irish poetess of Wicklow, whose Spenserian *Cupid and Psyche* (1805) influenced Keats.

TIGLATH-PILESER, name of three kings of Assyria, of whom the most noteworthy were:

(1) **Tiglath-Pileser I,** king (*c.* 1115–*c.* 1093 B.C.), extended his dominions to the upper Euphrates, and defeated the king of Babylonia.

(2) **Tiglath-Pileser III,** known also as **Pulu,** king (745–727 B.C.), a great empire-builder, conquered the cities of north Syria and Phoenicia, including Damascus and Babylon.

TIGRANES I, the Great (d. after 56 B.C.), king of Armenia, was set on the throne by Parthian troops (*c.* 94 B.C.). In alliance with Mithridates, he was a threat to Rome, to remove which Sulla (q.v.) was sent to the East (92). Left undisturbed owing to a Roman agreement with the Parthians, he made many conquests and founded Tigranocerta. In 69, Lucullus was sent out from Rome, and captured the new capital; and eventually Tigranes surrendered to Pompey (q.v.) (66), ruling henceforward over Armenia only.

TILDEN, (1) **Samuel Jones** (1814–86), American statesman, born, a farmer's son, at New Lebanon, N.Y., was admitted to the bar, and secured a large railway practice. By 1868 he had become leader of the Democrats in the state, and he attacked and destroyed Tweed and Tammany. In 1874 he became governor of New York; in 1876 he was the unsuccessful Democratic candidate for the presidency, after a special tribunal controlled by his opponents had vetted the votes cast. He left much of his fortune to found a free library in New York City. See Life by T. P. Cook (1876), and his Writings and Speeches, edited by John Bigelow (1835).

(2) **Sir William Augustus** (1842–1926), English chemist, born at St Pancras, London, professor at the Royal College of Science, London, made possible the manufacture of artificial rubber by his synthetic preparation of isoprene.

(3) **William Tatem** (1893–1953), American lawn-tennis player and writer, was born in Germantown, Pa. Seven times American champion and three times world champion, he was one of the greatest tennis players of the United States. He was for a time a journalist, a film actor, the publisher and editor of *Racquet Magazine* as well as the author of many books on tennis, including *The Art of Lawn Tennis* (1920), *The Phantom Drive* (1924) and a novel, *Glory's Net*.

TILLEMONT, Louis Sébastien le Nain de, *tee-y'-mō̃* (1637–98), French ecclesiastical historian, was born in Paris, and educated by the Port Royalists. He entered the priesthood in 1676, and after the dispersion of the Solitaires in 1679 lived mostly on his estate at Tillemont near Paris. His chief works are the laborious and solid *Histoire ecclésiastique des six premiers siècles* (1693–1712) and *Histoire des empereurs* (1691–1738).

TILLETT, Benjamin (1860–1943), English trade-union leader, born at Bristol, worked as brickmaker, bootmaker, sailor, and Labour M.P. (1917–24, 1929–31). He was notable as organizer of the Dockers' Union in London and leader of the great dockers' strike in 1889, and of the London transport workers' strike, 1911. He was expelled from Hamburg and from Antwerp (1896) for supporting dock strikes.

TILLEY, Vesta, professional name of **Lady de Frece**, *née* **Matilda Alice Powles** (1864–1952), English comedienne, born in Worcester. She first appeared as The Great Little Tilley, aged four, in Nottingham, and did her first male impersonation the following year. She soon adopted the name of Vesta Tilley and became, through her charm, vivacity and attention to sartorial detail, the most celebrated of all male impersonators. Of the many popular songs 'made' by her, *Burlington Bertie, Following in Father's Footsteps, Sweetheart May* and *Jolly Good Luck to the Girl who loves a Soldier* are still familiar. See her *Recollections of Vesta Tilley* (1934).

TILLICH, Paul Johannes (1886–1965), German Protestant theologian, born at Starzeddel, Prussia, was a Lutheran pastor (1912) and served as chaplain in the German army during World War I. He lectured at Berlin and subsequently held professorships in Theology at Marburg, Dresden, Leipzig, in Philosophy at Frankfurt, and, having been dismissed from this post by the Nazis in 1933, in Philosophy and Theology at the Union Theological Seminary, New York (1933–55), at Harvard Divinity School (1955–1962), and at Chicago Divinity School from 1962. His theology allowed for scientific method, philosophical scepticism and psychoanalysis, and was characterized by a realistic concern for the problems of contemporary society. God is the unconditional fulfilment intended in every ambiguous fulfilment in history. His works include *The Interpretation of History* (1936), *The Protestant Era* (1948), *The Courage to Be* (1952), his *magnum opus, Systematic Theology* (3 vols., 1953–63), essays, *Theology of Culture* (1959), &c. He took American nationality (1940) and was Gifford lecturer at Edinburgh (1953). See theological essays contributed by Marcel, Bultmann, Barth and others in his honour, *Religion and Culture* (1959).

TILLOTSON, John (1630–94), Archbishop of Canterbury, born at Sowerby, Yorkshire, studied at Clare Hall, Cambridge, becoming a fellow in 1651. Although with the Presbyterians at the Savoy conference, he submitted to the Act of Uniformity (1662) and henceforth received preferment, becoming dean of Canterbury in 1672 and archbishop, in place of the deposed nonjuror Sancroft, in 1691. He advocated the Zwinglian doctrine of the eucharist. According to Burnet 'he was not only the best preacher of the age, but seemed to have brought preaching to perfection'. In 1664 he married a niece of Oliver Cromwell. See his complete works, with a Life by Birch (1707–12).

TILLY, (1) **Comte Alexandre de** (1761–1816), French courtier and libertine, wrote his *Mémoires* in exile. See translation by Mme Delisle (1933).

(2) **Jan Tserklaes, Count of** (1559–1632), Flemish soldier, born at the castle of Tilly in Brabant, and brought up by the Jesuits, learned the art of war under Parma, fought in Hungary against the Turks, and was appointed in 1610 by Duke Maximilian of Bavaria to reorganize his army. He was given the command of the Catholic army at the oubreak of the Thirty Years' War, and by his decisive victories at Weisser Berg and Prague (both 1620) dissipated the dreams of the Elector Palatine. He separated the armies of Mansfeld and of the Margrave of Baden, beat the latter at Wimpfen (1622), and expelled Christian of Brunswick from the Palatinate, defeating him in two battles. Created a count of the empire, he defeated the king of Denmark at Lutter (1626), and with Wallenstein compelled him to sign the Treaty of Lübeck (1629). Next year he succeeded Wallenstein as commander-in-chief of the imperial forces, and stormed Magdeburg (May 20, 1631), when the atrocities he allowed his Croats and Walloons to perpetrate cast a foul stain upon his reputation. Gustavus Adolphus at Breitenfeld (September 17) drove him to retreat behind the Lech, and forced the passage of the river (April 5, 1632), after a desperate conflict in which Tilly received his death-wound.

TIMBS, John (1801–75), English antiquarian and miscellanist, born in London, wrote over 150 volumes on interesting facts gathered on a varied number of subjects and places, often antiquarian, such as *Curiosities of London* (1855), *Romance of London* (1865), *Abbeys, Castles, and Ancient Halls of England and Wales* (1869), &c. He was elected a fellow of the Society of Antiquaries (1854) and died in poverty.

TIMOLEON, *ti-mō'lee-on* (d. *c.* 337 B.C.), Greek statesman and general of Corinth, overthrew the tyranny of his brother and retired from public life. But when Dionysius II and others tried to establish themselves in Syracuse, he was prevailed upon to return to public life. He manœuvred Dionysius II into abdication and fought the Carthaginians, who were supporting the other tyrants, defeating them at the Crimessus in 341. He then promptly retired again, having taken measures to stabilize the economy of Greek Sicily. See Lives by Plutarch and Diodorus Siculus, and study by Westlake (1952).

TIMON, (1) **the Misanthrope of Athens**, a contemporary of Socrates. According to the comic writers who attacked him, he was disgusted with mankind on account of the ingratitude of his early friends, and lived a life of almost total seclusion. Lucian made him the subject of a dialogue; Shakespeare's play is based on the story as told in Painter's *Palace of Pleasure*.

(2) **the Sillographer** (*c.* 320–*c.* 230 B.C.), Greek poet and philosopher, lectured at Chalcedon and spent his last years at Athens. He wrote *Silloi*, sarcastic hexameters upon Greek philosophers.

TIMOSHENKO, Semyon Konstantinovich (1895–1970), Russian general, born in Bessarabia of peasant stock, in 1915 was conscripted into the tsarist army. In the revolution he took part in the defence of Tsaritsin. In 1940 he headed 27 divisions to smash the resistance of 3½ Finnish divisions—a Naysmith hammer to crack a walnut. With the German blitz of 1941 Timoshenko replaced Budenny in the Ukraine, ' Russia's breadbasket '; but his attempt to stem the 1942 Nazi drive on the Crimea resulted in no more than a Pyrrhic victory. From 1940–41 he served as People's Commissar of Defence, and commanded the Byelo-Russian district from 1956 to his retiral in 1960. See *Behind the Steel Wall*, Fredborg (1944).

TIMUR. See TAMERLANE.

TINDAL, Matthew (1655–1733), English deistical writer, born at Beer-Ferris rectory, S. Devon, was elected a fellow of All Souls College, Oxford. A Roman Catholic under James II, he reverted to Protestantism of a somewhat freethinking type, and wrote *An Essay of Obedience to the Supreme Powers* (1693), and *Rights of the Christian Church asserted against the Romish and all other Priests* (1706). The latter raised a storm of opposition; but even a prosecution failed to prevent a fourth edition in 1709. In 1730 Tindal published his *Christianity as old as the Creation*, which was soon known as ' the Deist's Bible '; its aim is to eliminate the supernatural element from religion, and to prove that its morality is its only claim to the reverence of mankind. Answers were issued by Waterland, Foster, Conybeare, Leland, &c.

TINDALE, William. See TYNDALE.

TINTORETTO, properly Jacopo Robusti (1518–94), the greatest of the late Venetian painters, was born probably in Venice, the son of a dyer or *tintore*. Little is known of his life. He is supposed to have studied under Titian, but only for a short time as the master was jealous of the boy's genius. Tintoretto claims to have set up independently, practically untaught, by 1539, but it is likely that he had some supervision, possibly from Bonifazio. He married (1550), and three of his seven children also became painters. Except for visits to Mantua (1580, 1590–93), he lived all his life in Venice. With an insatiable appetite for creative opportunities rather than for wealth, he often contented himself with little more than the cost price of a painting and went to any length to undercut his fellow-painters. When a work was to be entrusted to Veronese, for example, he undertook to paint it, and actually did, in the style of that artist for a smaller fee. Tintoretto pioneered the way from the classical to the baroque. Already, in his early work, *The Miracle of the Slave* (1548; Accademia, Venice), in which he consciously set out to combine Titian's colours with Michelangelo's sculptural draughtsmanship, there is a tendency towards a dynamic interrelationship of the groups of figures in respect of the central character depicted, rather than the individual self-sufficiency of every detail as in classical composition. His early work, however, is still undecided and experimental, e.g., *The Miracle of St Agnes* (1550; Madonna dell' Orto) and the two votive pictures, *St Louis and St George with the Princess* (1552) and *SS. Andrew and Jerome* (1552; both in the Accademia, Venice). His mastery in depicting the female nude is apparent in the three *Susanna* paintings (*c.* 1555, Louvre, particularly 1556–60, Vienna, and 1560, Prado, Madrid) and there are a number of significant portraits of this period, e.g., *Portrait of a Venetian* (National Gallery, Edinburgh). After 1556 Tintoretto seems to have found himself. *The Last Judgment*, *The Golden Calf* (both *c.* 1560, Madonna dell' Orto, Venice) and *The Marriage of Cana* (1561, Santa Maria della Salute, Venice) were followed by two masterpieces of perspective and lighting effects, both *c.* 1562, *The Finding* (Brera, Milan) and *The Removal of the Body of St Mark* (Accademia, Venice). From 1564 Tintoretto was employed in decorating the Albergo, and the Halls of the Scuola of San Rocco and its church. The Scuola contains probably the largest collection of works by one artist in a single building, prearranged in a vast iconographical scheme from the Old and New Testaments. These include the dynamic rendering of the *Crucifixion* (1565), teeming with incident, *The Annunciation* and *Massacre of the Innocents* (both 1583–87). Other notable late works are *The Origin of the Milky Way* (after 1570; Nat. Gall., London), the *Paradiso*, famous for its colossal size (1588; Ducal Palace, Venice), his last version of *The Last Supper* (1592–94), no longer an exclusive gathering but set among maids and attendants and fully expressing the religious fervour of the counter-Reformation, and *Entombment* (1594; both San Giorgio Maggiore, Venice). The ' painter of dark turbulence ' left an unrivalled number of paintings. See the contemporary account of his life and work in C. Ridolf's *Le Maraviglie dell' Arte*, vol. ii, ed. D. F. von Hadeln (1924), J. Ruskin, *Stones of Venice* (1863), B. Berenson, *Italian Pictures of the Renaissance* (1932), and monographs by E. M. Phillipps (1911), F. P. B. Osmaston (1915; on the *Paradiso*, 1910), E. von der Bercken (Munich 1942), H. Tietze (1948) and E. Newton (1952).

TINWORTH, George (1843–1913), English artist in terracotta, born in London, the son of a poor wheelwright, in 1864 entered the Royal Academy schools, and in 1867 obtained an appointment in the Doulton art pottery. The works which made him famous were mainly terracotta panels with groups of figures in high relief illustrating scenes from sacred history.

TIPPETT, Sir Michael (1905–), English composer, born in London. He studied at the Royal College of Music and became conductor of educational organizations under the London County Council and 1940–51 director of Music at Morley College. He first attracted attention with his chamber music and Concerto for Double String Orchestra (1939), but his oratorio, *A Child of our Time* (1941), reflecting the political and spiritual problems of the 1930s and 1940s, won him wide recognition. A convinced pacifist, Tippett went to prison for three months as a conscientious objector during World War II. He scored a considerable success with the operas, *The Midsummer Marriage* (1952) and *King Priam* (1961). His other works include three symphonies (1934, later withdrawn, 1945, 1958) and a piano concerto (1957). He was created C.B.E. in 1959, and was knighted in 1966.

TIPPOO ṢAHIB, or Tipú Sultán (1749–99),

sultan of Mysore, son of Haidar Ali (q.v.), during his father's wars with the British completely routed Bailey(1780 and 1782) and Braithwaite (1782). In 1782 he succeeded his father as sultan of Mysore. In 1783 he captured and put to death most of the garrison of Bednur, but after the conclusion of peace between France and Britain he agreed to a treaty (1784) stipulating for the *status quo* before the war. He sent ambassadors in 1787 to France to stir up a war with Britain, and, failing in this, invaded (1789) the protected state of Travancore. In the ensuing war (1790–92) the British, under Stuart and Cornwallis, were aided by the Mahrattas and the Nizam, and Tippoo was compelled (1792) to resign one-half of his dominions, pay an indemnity of 3030 lakhs of rupees, restore all prisoners, and give his two sons as hostages. Resuming his intrigues, he sent another embassy to the French. Hostilities began in March 1799, and Tippoo was driven from the open field, attacked in Seringapatam, and after a month's siege slain at the storming, by General Harris, of the fort (May 4). See L. B. Bowring's *Haidar Ali and Tipú Sultán* (1893) and *Select Letters of Tipú Sultán* (ed. Kirkpatrick, 1881).

TIRABOSCHI, Girolamo, *teer-a-bos'kee* (1731–94), Italian scholar, born at Bergamo, became professor of Rhetoric at Milan, and in 1770 librarian to the Duke of Modena. His *Storia della Letteratura Italiana* (1772–81) is an accurate survey down to 1700.

TIRPITZ, Alfred P. Friedrich von (1849–1930), Prussian sailor, born at Küstrin, entered the Prussian navy in 1865, was ennobled in 1900, and rose to be lord high admiral (1911). As secretary of state for the Imperial Navy (1897–1916), he piloted the German navy laws (1900, &c.) and raised a fleet to challenge British supremacy of the seas. An upholder of unrestricted submarine warfare, he commanded the German navy from August 1914 to March 1916 and wrote *Memoirs* (1919).

TIRSO DE MOLINA, pseud. of **Gabriel Téllez** (*c.* 1571–1648), Spanish playwright, born at Madrid, was prior of the monastery of Soria. Lacking his great contemporary Lope's lyrical gifts, he wrote *Comedias*, partly Interludes, and *Autos Sacramentales* (originally about 300), excelling in the portrayal of character, particularly of spirited women, and in his treatment of the Don Juan legend in his masterpiece *Burlador de Sevilla*. See Rios de Lampérez, *Enigma Biográfico* (1929).

TISCHENDORF, Lobegott Friedrich Konstantin von, *tish'en-dorf* (1815–74), German biblical scholar, born at Lengenfeld in Saxony, in 1839 became a lecturer, in 1845 a professor, at Leipzig. His search for MSS. of the New Testament resulted in the discovery of the 4th-century Sinaitic Codex at the monastery on Mount Sinai; he described his journeys in *Reise in den Orient* (1846; trans. 1847) and *Aus dem Heiligen Lande* (1862). Among his works are the editions of the Sinaitic (1862; in facsimile, 1863) and many other MSS., the *Editio VIII* of the New Testament (1864–72), an edition of the Septuagint, and the *Monumenta Sacra Inedita* (1846–71). *When were our Gospels Written?* was translated in 1866.

TISELIUS, Arne Wilhelm Kaurin (1902–), Swedish chemist, born at Stockholm, became professor of Biochemistry at Uppsala (1938), investigated serum proteins by electrophoretic analysis, and in chromatography evolved new methods for the analysis of colourless substances. He won the Nobel prize in 1948, and was president of the Nobel Foundation (1960–64).

TISSANDIER, Gaston, *tee-sã-dyay* (1835–1899), French aeronaut, invented (1883) a navigable balloon.

TISSAPHERNES, *tis-a-fer'neez* (d. 395 B.C.), Persian satrap from 413, notorious for his duplicity in the conflicts between Athens and Sparta. Deprived of a province in favour of Cyrus, he denounced him to King Artaxerxes, for whom he fought and won the battle of Cunaxa (401 B.C.), after which he murdered the leaders of the Greeks, including Cyrus, leaving the ten thousand Greek mercenaries to find their way back. But he was himself defeated in the war with Sparta and executed for the murder of Cyrus.

TISSOT, James Joseph Jacques, *tee-sō* (1836–1902), French painter, was born in Nantes and settled in London. He travelled to Palestine in 1886 and as a result produced his best-known work, a series of the life of Christ in watercolour. Other examples of his work are paintings of life in Victorian times, now in the Tate gallery.

TISZA, *ti'so,* (1) **Kalman** (1830–1902), Hungarian statesman, father of (2), was premier and virtually dictator from 1875 to 1890.

(2) **Count Stephen** (1861–1918), son of (1), also Liberal leader, a chauvinistic Magyar, premier of Hungary 1903–05, 1913–17, supported Germany, and was assassinated on October 31, the first day of the Hungarian Revolution.

TITCHENER, Edward Bradford (1867–1927), English psychologist, born at Chichester, studied at Oxford and Leipzig before going to America to Cornell University. A follower of Wundt (q.v.), under whose influence he had come in Leipzig, he became the great exponent of experimental psychology in America, founding the 'experimental psychologists' group. He wrote many scholarly works on this subject, including *Psychology of Feeling and Attention* (1908) and *Experimental Psychology of the Thought Processes* (1909).

TITE, Sir William (1798–1873), English architect, born in London, rebuilt the Royal Exchange (1844), was knighted in 1869 and was elected F.R.S. in 1835. He opposed the neo-Gothic revival.

TITIAN, *ti'shèn,* properly **Tiziano Vecelli** (d. 1576), one of the greatest of the Venetian painters, was born at Pieve di Cadore in the Friulian Alps. His year of birth is a matter of controversy, but *c.* 1490 is more probable than *c.* 1477 as indicated by Titian's own statements. He lived from the age of ten with an uncle in Venice and studied under Zuccato, a mosaicist, Gentile and Giovanni Bellini (q.v.) and assisted Giorgione (q.v.). Giovanni's influence is apparent in such early works as *Bishop Pesaro before St Peter* (*c.* 1506; Antwerp). Titian assisted Giorgione with the paintings for the Fondaco dei Tedeschi (1508) and completed many of the latter's works, e.g., *Noli me tangere* (*c.* 1510; National Gallery, London) and the *Sleeping Venus* (*c.* 1510; Dresden), which was to serve as a model for Titian's more naturalistic *Venus of Urbino* (1538; Uffizi, Florence). The first works definitely attributable to Titian alone are the three frescoes of scenes in the life of St Anthony at Padua (1511), but Giorgione's influence predominates in these, the pastoral setting of *The Three Ages of Man* (*c.* 1515; National Gallery Edinburgh) and the masterly fusion of romantic realism and classical idealism achieved in the *poesa*, *Sacred and Profane Love* (*c.* 1515; Borghese, Rome), a masterpiece of Renaissance art. After 1516 restrained postures and colouring give way to dynamic compositions in which bright colours are contrasted and the classical intellectual approach gives way to sensuous, full-blooded treatment. *Assumption of the Virgin* (1516–18), *Madonna of the Pesaro Family* (1519–26), both in the Frari, Venice, and *St Peter Martyr* (destroyed 1867) exemplify the beginnings of Titian's own revolutionary style. For the Duke of Ferrara he painted three great mythological subjects, *Feast of Venus* (*c.* 1515–18), *Bacchanal* (*c.* 1518; both in the Prado, Madrid) and the richly coloured. exuberant masterpiece *Bacchus and Ariadne* (1523; Nat. Gallery, London). In sharp contrast is the finely-modelled historical picture, *Presentation of the Virgin* (1534–38; Accademia, Venice). In 1530 he met the Emperor Charles V, of whom he painted many portraits, including the striking equestrian *Charles V at the Battle of Mühlberg* (1548; Prado, Madrid), also the portraits of many notables assembled for the Augsburg peace conference, and was ennobled. To this period also belongs *Ecce Homo* (1543; Vienna), portraits of the Farnese family including *Pope Paul III and his nephews* (1545–46; Naples) painted on Titian's first visit to Rome. The impact of the art collections there is reflected in a new sculptural treatment of the *Danae* (1545; Naples, also 1554; Prado, Madrid). For King Philip of Spain, he executed a remarkable series of *poesies* on mythological scenes, to which belong *Diana and Actaeon* (1559) and *Diana and Callistro* (1559; both National Gallery, Edinburgh) and *Perseus and Andromeda* (*c.* 1556; Wallace, London). To the poignant religious and mythological subjects of his last years belong *The Fall of Man* (*c.* 1570), *The Entombment* (1565; both Prado, Madrid), *Christ Crowned with Thorns* (*c.* 1570; Munich), *Madonna Suckling the Child* (1570–1576; Nat. Gallery, London), *Lucrezia and Tarquinius* (*c.* 1570; Fitzwilliam, Cambridge) and the unfinished *Pietà* (1573–76; Accademia, Venice). Titian was fortunate in his patrons, despite his negligence and delays and a polished courtier's love of pensions, privileges and sinecures. He died August 27 during a plague epidemic, but not of the plague, and was ceremoniously buried in the church of S. Maria dei Frari, Venice. Colour rather than imaginative conception is the touchstone of his art, which greatly influenced Tintoretto, Rubens, Velasquez, Poussin, Van Dyck and Watteau. See books by G. Gronau (1904), Sir C. Phillips (1906), O. Fischel (1911), especially H. Tietze (1937 and 1950), E. K. Waterhouse, *Titian's Diana and Actaeon* (1952), and F. Fosca (1955).

TITIENS, or **Tietjens, Teresa** (1831–77), Hungarian soprano, born at Hamburg, achieved an international reputation in operatic rôles. During a performance of Weber's *Oberon* in Dublin in 1868, she replied to the tumultuous applause which greeted the *Ocean* song with *The Last Rose of Summer*, before the opera was resumed.

TITO, Marshal, the name adopted by **Josip Broz** (1892–), Yugoslav leader, born near Klanjec. In World War I he served with the Austro-Hungarian Army, and, taken prisoner by the Russians, he adopted Communism and took part in the 1917 Revolution. In 1928 he was imprisoned in Yugoslavia for conspiring against the régime. In mid-1941 he organized partisan forces to harry the Axis conquerors of his country and his efforts were sufficiently effective to pin down about thirty enemy divisions, and to have the price of 100,000 gold marks set on his head. With exceptional guile he contrived to discredit utterly the rival partisan leader Mihailovich in Anglo-American eyes and win support, in arms and material, solely for himself. Following the Axis defeat, and with a ' popular ' franchise constituted to elect the future government, Tito's list of candidates was the only one published, although a small dummy opposition was erected by way of a democratic façade. Established in 1945 as Yugoslavia's first Communist prime minister, in 1953 Tito consolidated his position of supreme power by assuming the office of president. His breach with the Cominform in 1948, however, served notice on the Kremlin of his intention to emulate Kipling's cat and ' walk by himself '. Since then he has successfully ' played the middle against both ends ', alternating his profitable coquetting with those Western powers that can bolster up his shaky economy, with conciliatory gestures to Moscow. Yugoslavia's strategic geographical position, plus Tito's possession of a standing army of 300,000, with ample reserves, encourages the Marshal to exploit his canny sense of opportunism, reinforced by a resolute spirit of independence. See Maclean, *Eastern Approaches* (1949), Clissold, *Whirlwind* (1949), Halperin, *The Triumphant Heretic* (1958), Djilas, *Land without Justice* (1958), and study by Neal (1958).

TITUS, a companion of the apostle Paul, was a Greek, and remained uncircumcised. Ecclesiastical tradition makes Titus ' bishop ' of Crete.

TITUS, Flavius Sabinus Vespasianus (A.D. 39–81), eleventh of the twelve Caesars, was eldest son of Vespasian. He early served with credit in Germany and Britain, and in Judaea under his father. On Vespasian's elevation to the throne Titus brought the Jewish war to a close by the capture of Jerusalem (70). For a time he gave himself up to pleasure, conducting a liaison with Berenice, sister of Herod Agrippa. But when he assumed undivided power (79) his character changed. He put a stop to prosecutions for *laesa majestas*, and decreed heavy punishments against informers. He completed the Colosseum, built the baths which bear his name, and lavished his beneficence upon the sufferers from the eruption of Vesuvius (79), the three days' fire at Rome, and the pestilence. He was now the idol of his subjects, but he died suddenly, not without suspicion of his having been poisoned by his brother Domitian.

TIZARD, Sir Henry Thomas (1885–1959), English scientific administrator, educated at Westminster school and Magdalen College, Oxford, of which he was elected president in 1942, the first scientist to hold such an office in an Oxford College. He served in the R.A.F. during World War I and was assistant comptroller of aeronautical research (1918–1919). He was secretary to the D.S.I.R. (1927–29), chairman of the Aeronautical Research Committee (1933–43), from 1947 chairman of the Defence Research Policy Committee and president of the British Association in 1948. He was elected F.R.S. in 1926 and knighted in 1937.

TOCQUEVILLE, Alexis Charles Henri Clérel de, *tok-veel* (1805–59), French historian, born at Verneuil of an aristocratic Norman family, was called to the bar in 1825 and became assistant-magistrate at Versailles. Sent in 1831 to the United States to report on the prison system, he returned to publish a penetrating political study, *De la démocratie en Amerique* (1835), which gave him a European reputation and in which he came to certain general conclusions, for example, that greater equality requires greater centralization and therefore diminishes liberty. Before publication, then still relatively unknown, he paid, in 1833, his first visit to England, married a Miss Mottley and kept an extensive diary of his *Journeys to England and Ireland* (ed. J. P. Mayer and trans. 1958), in which his abiding impression, confirmed by a later visit in 1857, of the English was of underlying national solidarity, despite political dissensions. In 1839 he was returned to the Chamber of Deputies by the Norman farmers. After 1848 he was the most formidable opponent of the Socialists and extreme Republicans, and as strenuously opposed Louis Napoleon; but he became in 1849 vice-president of the Assembly, and from June to October was minister of foreign affairs. After the *coup d'état* he retired to his Norman estate, Tocqueville, and agricultural pursuits, and there wrote the first volume of *L'Ancien Régime et la Révolution* (1856), in which he argued with masterful objectivity that the Revolution did not constitute a break with, but merely accelerated a trend of, the past, namely centralization of government. See studies by Marcel (1910), Mayer (1939), and introduction to *Democracy in America* by Commager (1947).

TODD, (1) Alexander Robertus, 1st Baron of Trumpington, (1907–), Scottish chemist, born in Glasgow, professor at Manchester (1938) and Cambridge (1944), fellow and master since 1963 of Christ's College, Cambridge, and first chancellor of the new University of Strathclyde. He was awarded the Nobel prize in 1957 for his researches on vitamins B_1 and E, was elected F.R.S. in 1942, knighted in 1954 and made a life peer in 1962.

(2) **Mike** (1909–58), American showman, born Avrom Hirsch Goldbogen, the son of a poor rabbi in Minneapolis, started life as a fairground attendant at nine, but was already making his first fortune at fourteen in sales promotion. In 1927 he went to Hollywood as a soundproofing expert, staged a real 'Flame Dance' spectacle at the Chicago World Fair in 1933, followed through the years by plays, musical comedies and films, including a jazz version of Gilbert and Sullivan, *The Hot Mikado* (1939), and an up-to-date *Hamlet* (1945). He perfected with Lowell Thomas the three-dimensional film and sponsored 'TODD-AO' wide-screen process, by which his greatest film, Jules Verne's *Around the World in Eighty Days*, which won him the Academy Award (1956), was made and presented. He married his third wife, the film actress Elizabeth Taylor, in 1957 and was killed in an aircrash over New Mexico. See Life by A. Cohn (1959).

TODHUNTER, Isaac (1820–84), English mathematician, born at Rye, studied at University College, London, and St John's, Cambridge, where in 1848 he graduated senior wrangler and Smith's prizeman. Elected fellow of St John's, he became its mathematical lecturer, and wrote textbooks. See Memoir by Mayer (1884).

TODI, Jacopone da (*c.* 1230–1306), Italian religious poet, born at Todi in the duchy of Spoleto, practised as an advocate, was converted in 1268 and became a Franciscan in 1278, and was imprisoned (1298–1303) for satirizing Boniface VIII. To him is ascribed the authorship of the *Stabat Mater*, and other Latin hymns; and he wrote *laude*, which became important in the development of Italian drama. See works by D'Acona (1884 ed.) and Underhill (1928).

TODLEBEN, or Totleben, Eduard Ivanovitch, *tōt-lay'ben* (1818–84), Russian soldier and military engineer, was born of German descent at Mitau in Courland. He served in the Caucasus, and in the Danubian Principalities in 1853. Till he was severely wounded (June 1855) he conducted with skill and energy the defence of Sevastopol; thereafter he completed the fortification of Nikolaieff and Cronstadt. During the Turkish war of 1877–78 he was called to besiege Plevna, which he took after a brilliant defence. See Life by Brialmont (1884).

TODT, Fritz, *tōt* (1891–1942), German engineer, born at Pforzheim, as Hitler's inspector of German roads (1933) was responsible for the construction of the *Reichsautobahnen*. The 'Todt Organization' was also responsible for the construction of the Siegfried Line (1937). Nazi minister for armaments (1940), fuel and power (1941), he was killed in an aircrash.

TOGO, Count Heihachiro (1847–1934), Japanese admiral, was born at Kagoshima and trained at Greenwich. He served against China (1894) and was commander-in-chief during the Russian war (1904–05). He bombarded Port Arthur, and defeated the Russian fleet at Tsushima on May 29, 1905.

He was awarded the English O.M. (1906) and created count (1907).

TOJO, Hideki, *tō-jō* (1885–1948), Japanese soldier, born in Tokyo, attended military college and in 1919 was appointed military attaché in Germany. He served with the Kwantung army in Manchuria as chief of the secret police and chief of staff from 1937 to 1940. He became minister of war (1940–41) and from 1941 he was premier and dictator of Japan, resigning in 1944. Arrested, he attempted and failed to commit suicide. He was sentenced to death in 1948.

TOLAND, John (1670–1722), Irish deistical writer, born of Catholic parents near Redcastle, Londonderry, entered Glasgow University in 1687, took his M.A. at Edinburgh in 1690, and studied theology at Leyden and Oxford. In *Christianity not Mysterious* (1696) he adopted a rationalistic attitude, and his work was burnt by the hangman in Ireland. In *Amyntor* (1699) and other works he debated the comparative evidence for the canonical and apocryphal scriptures. He took refuge in England and his Hanoverian pamphlet *Anglia Libera* secured him the favour of the Princess Sophia when he accompanied the ambassador to Hanover. His later life as literary adventurer is set forth in D'Israeli's *Calamities of Authors*. He also wrote a Life of Milton (1698). See Life by Des Maizeaux prefixed to his miscellaneous works (1747).

TOLKIEN, John Ronald (1892–1973), English philologist and author, born in Bloemfontein, educated at King Edward VII School, Birmingham, and Oxford, where he became professor of Anglo-Saxon (1925–45) and of English Language and Literature (1945–59). His scholarly publications include an edition of Sir Gawain and the Green Knight (1925), and studies on Chaucer (1934) and Beowulf (1936). His interest in language and saga and his fascination for the land of Faerie prompted him to write tales of a world of his own invention peopled by strange beings with their own carefully constructed language and mythology. These include *The Hobbit* (1937), a fascinating tale of the perilous journey of Bilbo Baggins and the dwarfs to recover treasure from Smaug, the dragon, and the more complex sequel, *The Lord of the Rings* (3 vols., 1954–55) in which Bilbo's nephew, Frodo, sets out to destroy a powerful but dangerous ring in Mordor, the land of darkness and evil. Later works include *The Adventures of Tom Bombadil* (1962) and *Smith of Wootton Major* (1967).

TOLLENS, (1) Bernhard Christian Gottfried (1841–1918), German chemist, with Fittig, synthesized toluene in 1864.

(2) **Hendrik** (1780–1856), Dutch poet, born at Rotterdam, was the author of the Dutch national hymn, *Wien Neerlandsch Bloed*. He also wrote comedies and a tragedy, romances and ballads.

TOLLER, Ernst (1893–1939), German-Jewish poet and playwright, born at Samotschin, was imprisoned (1919–24) in Germany as a revolutionary. He was elected to the Bavarian diet 1924, escaped from Nazi rule, and committed suicide in New York in 1939. His expressionist plays include *Masse Mensch* (trans. 1923), *Die Maschinenstürmer* (trans. 1923), &c.; he also wrote poetry and the autobiographical *Eine Jugend in Deutschland* (1933).

TOLSTOY, or **Tolstoi,** name of a family of Russian nobles. **Count Peter** (1645–1729) was a trusted agent of Peter the Great. **Count Peter Alexandrovich** (1761–1844) was one of Suvorov's generals and under Nicholas I head of a government department. **Count Dmitri Andreievich** (1823–89) was a reactionary minister of Education, champion of Russian orthodoxy and a 'russifier' of the Poles. His *Romanism in Russia* was translated in 1874. The most noteworthy members of the family were:

(1) **Count Alexey Konstantinovich** (1817–1875), Russian dramatist, lyrical poet and novelist, born at St Petersburg, wrote a historical trilogy in verse, *The Death of Ivan the Terrible* (1867), *Tsar Fyodor Ioannovich* (1868) and *Tsar Boris* (1870), nonsense verse and the historical novel, *Prince Serebrenni* (trans. 1874).

(2) **Count Alexey Nikolayevich** (1882–1945), Russian writer, joined the White Army after the 1917 Revolution which he portrayed vividly in *The Road to Calvary* (trans. 1945), emigrated but returned to Russia in 1922. Other novels include *The Lame Squire*, &c.

(3) **Count Leo Nikolayevich** (1828–1910), Russian writer aesthetic philosopher, moralist and mystic, one of the greatest of European novelists, was born on August 28 on the family estate of Yasnaya Polyana in Tula province. He was educated privately and at Kazan University, where he read law and oriental languages but did not graduate. He led a gay and dissolute life in town, played the gentleman farmer, and finally, in 1851 accompanied his elder brother Nicholay to the Caucasus, where he joined an artillery regiment and there began his literary career. *An Account of Yesterday* (1851) was followed by the autobiographical trilogy, *Childhood* (1852), *Boyhood* (1854) and *Youth* (1856). Commissioned at the outbreak of the Crimean War (1854), he commanded a battery during the defence of Sevastopol (1854–55). After the war, the horrors of which inspired *Tales of Army Life* and the *Sketches of Sevastopol*, he left the army, was lionized by the St Petersburg *literati* (1856), travelled abroad, visiting Britain, and in 1862 married Sophie Andreyevna Behrs, who bore him 13 children. He settled on his Volga estate and combined the duties of a progressive landlord, with the six years' literary toil which produced *War and Peace* (1863–69), by many considered the greatest novel ever written. This is at once a domestic tale, depicting the fortunes of two notable families, the Rostovs and the Bolkonskis, and a national epic of Russia's struggle, defeat and victory over Napoleon. The whole gamut of experience, finds expression somewhere in its pages. The characters grow up naturally with time, and the Bohemian exuberance of youth is superbly recorded. The proud, shy duty-conscious Prince Andrew and the direct, friendly, pleasure-loving but introspective, morally questing Pierre reflect the dualism in Tolstoy's own character. On his vivid description of

military life Tolstoy mounts his conception of history, which demotes 'great men' to mere creatures of circumstance and ascribes victory in battle to the confused, chance events which make up the unpredictable fortunes of war. In Pierre's association with freemasonry, Tolstoy expressed his criticism of the established autocratic order. His second great work, *Anna Karenina* (1874–76), carries with it the seeds of Tolstoy's personal crisis between the claims of the creative novelist and the moralizing, 'committed' propagator of his own ethical code, which culminated in *A Confession* (1879–82) and the dialectical pamphlets and stories such as *The Death of Ivan Ilyitch* (1886), *The Kreutzer Sonata* (1889), *What I Believe*, &c., in which Christianity is purged of its mysticism and transformed into a severe asceticism based on the doctrine of nonresistance to evil. *The Kingdom of God is within You* (1893), *Master and Man* (1894), the play *The Fruits of Enlightenment* (1891) and *Resurrection* (1899–1900) strayed so far from orthodoxy that the Holy Synod excommunicated him (1901) and he denounced the worship of Jesus as blasphemy. In *What is Art?* he argued that only simple works, such as the parables of the Bible, constitute great art. Everything sophisticated, stylized and detailed, such as his own great novels, he condemned as worthless. He made over his fortune to his wife and lived poorly as a peasant under her roof. Domestic quarrels made him leave home clandestinely one October night, accompanied only by a daughter and his personal physician. He caught a chill and died November 7 in a siding of Astapovo railway station, refusing to see his waiting wife to the last. His doctrines founded a sect and Yasnaya Polyana became a place of pilgrimage. Gandhi, who had corresponded with him, adopted the doctrine of nonresistance. But to posterity he is best known as the consummate master of the 'psychological' novel, a blend of Dickens and Stendhal. Boris Pasternak's father, **Leonid,** illustrated Tolstoy's works. See his *Diaries and Journals* (trans. 1917, 1927), his son's *Reminiscences* (trans. 1917), his wife's diary (trans. 1928) and autobiography (trans. 1933), his love letters (trans. 1923), the personal recollections of M. Gorky (trans. 1923) and T. Kuzminskaya (1948), Lives by his friend and translator, Aylmer Maude (1930), E. J. Simmons (1949), and biographical studies by Rolland (trans. 1911), Noyes (1919), Nazarov (1930), Abraham (1935), Leon (1944), Lavrin (rev. 1945), Redpath (1960) and Troyat (1968).

TOMBAUGH, Clyde William (1906–), American astronomer, was born at Streator, Ill., and educated at Kansas. He worked at the Lowell Observatory, Arizona State College and then at California as professor. He is the discoverer (1930) of Pluto, the existence of which had been predicted by Lowell, and of galactic star clusters. In 1946 he became astronomer at the Aberdeen Ballistics Laboratories in New Mexico, and was astronomer (1955–59), associate professor (1961–65) and professor from 1965, at N.M. State University.

TOMKINS, Thomas (1572–1656), English composer and organist, born in St David's where his father was organist, one of five brothers who were all accomplished musicians. Tomkins studied under Byrd, and in his early twenties, became organist of Worcester Cathedral, where most of his life was spent. In 1621 he became one of the organists of the Chapel Royal, and composed music for the coronation of Charles I five years later. His compositions include a vast amount of church music, madrigals, part-songs and instrumental works. See Life by Denis Stevens (1957).

TOMLINSON, Henry Major (1873–1958), English author, born in London, wrote *The Sea and the Jungle* (1912), *Tidemarks* (1924) and other travel books as well as novels such as *Gallions Reach* (1927) and a Life of Norman Douglas (1931).

TOMONAGA, Shinichiro (1906–), Japanese scientist, born and educated at Kyoto, professor of Physics at Tokyo University. He was awarded the Nobel prize for physics in 1965 together with Feynman and Schwinger for work in quantum electrodynamics.

TONE, Theobald Wolfe (1763–98), Irish nationalist, was born a coachmaker's son in Dublin, studied at Trinity College, was called to the bar in 1789, acted as secretary of the Catholic Committee, helped to organize the United Irishmen, and had to flee to America and to France (1795). He laboured incessantly to induce the Republican government to invade Ireland, and held a command in Hoche's expedition. In 1798 he again embarked in a small French squadron, which after a fierce fight was captured. Tone was taken to Dublin, tried, and condemned to be hanged as a traitor, but cut his throat in prison. See his *Autobiography* (1826) and Life by F. MacDermot (1939).

TONKS, Henry (1862–1937), English artist, born at Solihull. After becoming a fellow of the Royal College of Surgeons, he gave up medicine for art, joined the New English Art Club, and was associated with Sickert and Steer. From 1917 to 1930 he was Slade Professor of Fine Art in the University of London, where he taught many artists who were later to become famous.

TONSON, Jacob (1656–1736), London bookseller, published for Otway, Dryden and Pope, Addison and Steele. He was one of the founders of the Kit Cat club.

TONTI, Lorenzo (fl. *c.* 1653), a Paris banker, born at Naples, who proposed the tontine or latest-survivor system of life insurance.

TOOKE, John Horne (1736–1812), English politician, born June 25, in Westminster, the son of John Horne, a poulterer, studied at Eton and St John's, Cambridge. He entered the Middle Temple, but in 1760, to please his father, accepted the living of New Brentford. Travelling as a tutor (1763–65), he met John Wilkes at Paris, and conceived the strongest admiration for him, defending him, on his return, in *The Petition of an Englishman* (1765); they afterwards fell out, and in 1771 had a rasping epistolary controversy. Horne, who in 1770 had composed the famous (unspoken) speech of Lord Mayor Beckford to the king, encountered, not without success, the formidable 'Junius'. In 1773 he resigned his living, and resumed the study of law. About this time his spirited opposition to an enclosure bill procured him the favour (plus £8000) of the rich Mr Tooke of Purley in Surrey. To this were due both his assumption in 1782 of the surname Tooke and the subtitle of his *Epea Pteroenta, or the Diversions of Purley* (1786–1805), that witty medley of etymology, grammar, metaphysics and politics which he began writing in prison for promoting a subscription for the Americans 'barbarously murdered at Lexington in 1775'. In 1779 he was refused admission to the bar as a clergyman. He supported Pitt against Fox in *Two Pair of Portraits* (1790). In 1790 and 1797 he stood unsuccessfully for Westminster; in 1794 was tried for high treason, but acquitted; and in 1801 obtained a seat for Old Sarum, but was excluded by special act from the next Parliament. See Lives by A. Stephens (1813), M. C. Yarborough (1927).

TOOLE, John Lawrence (1832–1906), English comedian, born in London, went to the City of London School, and in 1853 gave up his desk in a wine merchant's to become an actor. He first played at Ipswich and in London at the St James's Theatre in 1854. In 1874–75 he played in the United States, and in 1890 in Australia. In 1879 he became lessee of the Folly Theatre, which he enlarged, changing the name to 'Toole's Theatre'. See his *Reminiscences*, chronicled by Joseph Hatton (1888).

TOPELIUS, Zachris (1818–98), Swedish poet and novelist, was born at Nykarleby, Finland, and studied at Helsinki, where he edited the *Helsingfors Tidningar* (1842–61). He was professor of Finnish History at Helsinki (1854–78), in the last three years being rector of the university. He wrote four collections of lyrics and several plays. His six novels, describing life in Sweden and Finland in the 17th and 18th centuries, were published as *The Surgeon's Stories* (1872–74).

TÖPFFER, Rodolphe (1799–1846), Swiss artist and novelist, born at Geneva, founded a boarding-school in 1825, which he conducted till his death, and in 1832 became professor of Rhetoric at Geneva Academy. He wrote the humorous *La Bibliothèque de mon oncle* (1832), *Nouvelles genevoises* (1841), *Rosa et Gertrude* (1846), &c. His own drawings in his *Voyages en zig-zag* (1843–53) are almost better than the text. See Lives by Relave (1886), Blondel Mirabaud (1887), Glöckner (1891) and P. Chaponnière (Lausanne 1930).

TOPINARD, Paul, *top-ee-nahr* (1830–1911), French anthropologist, born at Isle-Adam (Seine-et-Loire), took a degree in medicine in Paris and urged by his master Broca (q.v.) he devoted himself after 1870 to anthropology, becoming assistant director and conservator of the anthropological laboratory. His works include *L'Anthropologie* (1876), *Éléments d'anthropologie générale* (1885) and *L'Homme dans la nature* (1891).

TOPLADY, Augustus Montague (1740–78), English hymnwriter, born at Farnham, and educated at Westminster and Trinity College, Dublin, in 1768 became vicar of Broad Hembury, Devon, and in 1775 preacher in a chapel near Leicester Fields, London. A strenuous defender of Calvinism, he was a bitter controversialist. His *Church of England vindicated from Arminianism* (1769) is forgotten; but no hymn is better known than 'Rock of Ages'. In 1759 he published *Poems on Sacred Subjects*; his *Psalms and Hymns* (1776) was a collection with but few of his own. See Life by T. Wright (1912).

TOPOLSKI, Feliks (1907–), British painter, draughtsman and illustrator, born in Poland. He studied at Warsaw, and in Italy and Paris, and came to England in 1935. From 1940 to 1945 he was an official war artist, and he was naturalized in 1947. Lively and sensitive drawings by him, depicting everyday life, have appeared in many periodicals, and he has also designed for the theatre. His works are represented in the British Museum and the Tate Gallery, London, and his publications include *Britain in Peace and War* (1941), *88 Pictures* (1951) and *Topolski's Chronicle* (1953–).

TORQUEMADA, Tomas de, *tor-kay-mah'da* (1420–98), first inquisitor-general of Spain, born at Valladolid, entered the Dominican order and became prior at Segovia. He persuaded Ferdinand and Isabella to ask the pope to sanction the institution of the 'Holy Office' of the Inquisition, with himself as inquisitor-general from 1483. In this office he displayed pitiless cruelty.

TORRICELLI, Evangelista, *tor-ree-chel'lee* (1608–47), Italian physicist and mathematician, born probably at Faenza, went in 1627 to Rome, where he devoted himself to mathematical studies. His *Trattato del Moto* (1641) led to his being invited by Galileo to become his amanuensis; on Galileo's death he was appointed mathematician to the grand-duke and professor to the Florentine Academy. He discovered that, because of atmospheric pressure, water will not rise above 33 feet in a suction pump. To him we owe the fundamental principles of hydromechanics, and in a letter to Ricci (1644) the first description of a barometer or 'torricellian tube'. He greatly improved both telescopes and microscopes, and made several mathematical discoveries.

TORRIGIANO, Pietro, *tor-ree-jah'no* (*c.* 1472–1522), Florentine sculptor, was forced to leave his native city after he had broken the nose of his fellow-pupil Michelangelo in a quarrel. After working in Bologna, Siena, Rome and in the Netherlands, he came to England, where he introduced Italian Renaissance art. He executed the tombs of Margaret Beaufort in Westminster Abbey, of Henry VII and his queen and of Dr Young (now in the Record Office) in 1516. The unfinished sarcophagus for Henry VIII's tomb was later used for that of Nelson. He settled in Spain and died in the prisons of the Inquisition.

TORRINGTON, Viscount. See BYNG.

TORSTENSSON, Lennard, Count of Ortala (1603–51), Swedish general, born at Torstena, accompanied Gustavus Adolphus to Germany in 1630, and in 1641 was appointed to the command of the Swedish army in Germany. He invaded Silesia, and, when driven back by the imperialists, turned and defeated them at Breitenfeld (November 2, 1641). Next winter he swept the Danes out of Holstein, and then drove the Austrians back into Bohemia. In 1645 he advanced to the walls of Vienna; in 1646 he returned in ill-health to Sweden.

TORU DUTT (1856–77), Indian authoress, a precocious Christian Hindu girl, born at Calcutta, spent 1869–73 in England and France, published a critical essay on Leconte de Lisle, and translated portions of the *Vishnupurana* into English blank verse. In 1876 appeared her *Sheaf gleaned in French Fields*; in 1879 a romance, *Le Journal de Mdlle d'Arvers*. See Gosse's Memoir in her *Ancient Ballads of Hindustan* (1882) and Life by Das (1921).

TOSCANINI, Arturo, *tos-kah-nee'nee* (1867–1957), Italian conductor, born at Parma, the son of a tailor, won a scholarship at the Parma conservatory at the age of nine and studied the 'cello and composition. While on tour with an Italian opera company, presenting *Aïda* in Rio de Janeiro in 1886, the audience hooted at the conductor and in the crisis the orchestra prevailed upon Toscanini to take the rostrum. His impeccable musical memory made it a triumphant performance. In 1891 he opened the season at the Carlo Felice in Genoa and by 1898 he had reached La Scala, Milan, where he remained until 1908, returning (1920–29). He conducted at the Metropolitan Opera House, New York (1908–15), the New York Philharmonic (1926–36), at Bayreuth (1930–31) and Salzburg (1934–37) festivals, and brought into being the National Broadcasting Orchestra of America (1937–53). As late as 1952 he conducted at the Festival Hall, London. Toscanini was scornful of any need for 'interpreting' a work. His fanatical concern for musical values made him the enemy of exhibitionism, the unremitting slave of every detail of the musical score and possibly the most tyrannical, yet self-effacing, and certainly the greatest conductor of his time. See books by Chotzinoff (1956) and R. C. March (1956).

TOSTI, Sir Francesco Paolo (1846–1916), Italian composer, born at Ortona (Abruzzi), became a naturalized British subject, taught the British royal family and was knighted in 1908. He was the composer of many popular drawing-room songs, including *Good-bye* and *Mattinata*.

TOSTIG. See HAROLD II.

TOTLEBEN. See TODLEBEN.

TOTNES, Earl of. See CAREW (2).

TOTTEL, Richard (d. 1594), London printer, an original member of the Stationers' Company, founded 1557, published from his shop at the Star in Hand in Fleet Street a notable anthology of Elizabethan poetry (1557), including Surrey's and Wyatt's. See *Tottel's Miscellany*, ed. H. E. Rollins (1928–1930).

TOULOUSE-LAUTREC (-MONFA), Henri (Marie Raymond) de, *too-looz-lō-trek* (1864–1901), French painter and lithographer, was born November 24 into a wealthy aristocratic family at Albi. Physically frail, he was encouraged to engage in the traditional field sports, but at the age of fourteen broke both his legs, which then ceased to grow. From 1882 he studied under Bonnat and Cormon in Paris and in 1884 settled in Montmartre, which his paintings and posters were to make famous. Degas was the decisive influence upon him, but whereas Degas painted the world of ballet from a ballet-lover's theatrical point of view, Lautrec's studies of the cabaret stars, the prostitutes, the barmaids, the clowns and actors of Montmartre betrayed an unfailing if detached interest in the individuality of the human being behind the purely professional function. Hence his dislike of models, his concentration on the human form caught in a characteristic posture which his superb draughtsmanship facilitated to the neglect of chiaroscuro and background effects. Often his studies verge on caricature as in *Dolly the English Barmaid* (1899), which recalls Hogarth's *Shrimp Girl*, and more tellingly in the haunting study of a tired, lifeless cabaret star, *Jane Avril Leaving the Moulin Rouge* (*c.* 1892; Courtauld Institute, London), after a performance. His revolutionary poster designs influenced by Japanese woodcuts which flatten and simplify the subject matter also served to sharpen his gifts for caricature, as in the posters of the music-hall star Aristide Bruant (1892) and Yvette Guilbert (1894). No one has portrayed so effectively the clientèle of these establishments as Lautrec in *Monsieur Boileau at the Café* (1892; Cleveland), *The Bar* (1898; Zürich) and the *Moulin Rouge* paintings (1894; Chicago, Prague, &c.). In 1895 he visited London, in 1896 Spain and in 1897 Holland. His alcoholism brought on a complete breakdown, forcing him to go into a sanatorium; he recovered to resume his hectic life until his death on September 9, 1901, from a paralytic stroke brought on by venereal disease. His works also depict fashionable society, *At the Races* (1899), &c., and he executed remarkable portraits of his mother (1887), of Van Gogh in pastel (1887; Amsterdam) and of Oscar Wilde, a drawing (1899). His life has been the subject of many novels and a film, *Moulin Rouge*. Over 600 of his works are in the Musée Lautrec at Albi, including the above-mentioned works, if not otherwise stated. See works by M. Joyant (Paris 1926–27), G. Mack (1938), J. Lassaigne (1939), D. Cooper (1955), P. H. Wilenski (1955), L. and E. M. Hanson (1956), H. Landholt (N.Y. 1956) and H. Tietze (1958).

TOURGUENIEFF. See TURGENEV.

TOURNEFORT, Joseph Pitton de, *toorn-for* (1656–1708), French botanist, born in Aix, travelled in Greece, &c., and died professor in the Collège de France. His system of grouping plants maintained its ground till the time of Linnaeus.

TOURNEUR, Cyril, *toor-nœr* (*c.* 1575–1626), English dramatist, served in the Low Countries, and died in Ireland. In 1600 he published his *Transformed Metamorphosis* (discovered in 1872), a satirical poem, marred by pedantic affectations; in 1609 a *Funeral Poem* on Sir Francis Vere; in 1613 an *Elegy* on Prince Henry. His fame rests on two plays, *The Revenger's Tragedy* (assigned by some critics to Webster or Middleton), printed in

1607, and the poorer *The Atheist's Tragedy*, printed in 1611. *The Revenger's Tragedy*, a tangled web of lust and blood, shows tragic intensity, extreme bitterness of mood and fiery strength of phrase. See edition of his works by Allardyce Nicoll (1930), and T. S. Eliot, *Selected Essays* (1932).

TOURVILLE, Anne Hilarion de Cotentin, Comte de, *toor-veel* (1642–1701), French sailor, born at the Château Tourville, near Coutances. In the year 1690 he inflicted a disastrous defeat on the English and Dutch off Beachy Head, and cast anchor in Torbay. In 1692, Louis XIV having resolved to invade England on behalf of James II, Tourville sailed from Brest with forty-two ships of the line. The English and Dutch, eighty-two ships strong, under Admiral Russell, completely defeated him off Cape La Hogue (May 19). In 1693, he defeated an Anglo-Dutch fleet off Cape St Vincent, and a month later (June 27), he defeated Rooke in the Bay of Lagos, capturing or destroying a large part of the Smyrna fleet. Tourville, made a marshal of France, inflicted enormous damage on English shipping (1694). See E. de Broglie's *Tourville* (1908).

TOUSSAINT L'OUVERTURE, Pierre Dominique, *too-sĩ loo-ver-tür* (1746–1803), Negro revolutionary leader (the surname from his bravery in once making a *breach* in the ranks of the enemy), was born a slave in Haiti. In 1791, he joined the Negro insurgents and in 1797 was made by the French Convention commander-in-chief in the island. He drove out British and Spaniards, restored order and prosperity, and about 1800 began to aim at independence. Bonaparte proclaimed the re-establishment of slavery, but Toussaint declined to obey. He was eventually arrested and died in a prison in France. See his *Mémoires* (1853), James, *The Black Jacobins* (1938), and Leyburn, *The Haitian People* (1941).

TOUT, Thomas Frederick (1855–1929), English historian, born in London, was educated at St Olave's School, Southwark, and Balliol College, Oxford. Professor at Manchester (1890–1925), he wrote *Chapters in the Administrative History of Mediaeval England* (1920–33), in which he first used household and wardrobe accounts in the public record office, so becoming the leading authority on English mediaeval history. See his *Collected Papers* (1932 *et seq.*).

TOVEY, (1) Sir Donald Francis (1873–1940), English pianist, composer and writer on music, was born at Eton. He studied under Parratt at Windsor and Parry at Balliol; and he was influenced by Joachim and by a schoolmistress to whom Tovey owed his musical education until he was nineteen. He made his professional début as a pianist in 1900, but his reputation stood higher on the Continent than in England, where his musical erudition annoyed the critics. In 1914 he became professor of Music at Edinburgh, where he built up the Reid Symphony Orchestra. He was knighted in 1935. He composed an opera, *The Bride of Dionysus*, in 1907–08, a symphony, a piano concerto (1903), a 'cello concerto (for Casals; 1937), and chamber music. But his fame rests largely on his writings, remarkable for great musical perception and learning: *Companion to the Art of Fugue* (1931), *Essays on Musical Analysis* (1935–39), and his articles on music in the *Encyclopaedia Britannica*. He edited Beethoven's sonatas and edited and completed J. S. Bach's *Art of Fugue*. See Life by Mary Grierson (1952).

(2) **John Cronyn, 1st Baron Tovey** (1885–1971), British admiral, a destroyer captain in the First World War, as c.-in-c. of the Home Fleet (1941–43) was responsible for the operations leading to the sinking of the German battleship *Bismarck*. He became admiral of the fleet and G.C.B. in 1943, and was created baron in 1946.

TOWNE, Francis (*c.* 1739–1816), English painter, born probably in London, a landscapist little known until the 20th century, when his gift for painting simple but graphic watercolours was recognized. Works done in Italy, which he visited in 1780, are now in the British Museum.

TOWNES, Charles Hard (1915–), American physicist, professor of Physics at Massachusetts Institute of Technology (1961–67), then professor-at-large at California University. He was joint winner of the Nobel prize for physics with Basov and Prokhorov in 1964 for his work on the development of laser beams.

TOWNSEND, Sir John Sealy Edward (1868–1957), Irish physicist, born at Galway, became a demonstrator at the Cavendish Laboratory, Cambridge, under Sir J. J. Thomson (q.v.) before becoming professor of Physics at Oxford (1900). He was elected F.R.S. in 1903, contributed to the theory of ionization of gases by collision and calculated in 1897 the charge on a single gaseous ion.

TOWNSHEND, (1) Charles, 2nd Viscount Townshend (1674–1738), English statesman, born at Raynham Hall, Norfolk, was educated at Eton and King's College, Cambridge. In 1687, he succeeded his father, Sir Horatio, who, though a Presbyterian, had zealously supported the Restoration and been made baron (1661) and viscount (1682). Charles entered public life as a Tory, but soon, as a disciple of Lord Somers (q.v.), cooperated with the Whigs. He was one of the commissioners for the Union with Scotland (1707), was joint-plenipotentiary with Marlborough at The Hague, and negotiated the Barrier Treaty with the States-General. Dismissed in 1712 on the formation of the Harley ministry, Townshend obtained the confidence of the Elector of Hanover, who, on his succession as George I, made him secretary of state. With Stanhope, he formed a Whig ministry, which had Walpole, his brother-in-law, for chancellor of the Exchequer and which passed the Septennial Act (1716). He was lord-lieutenant of Ireland (1717) and became president of the Council and secretary for the Northern Department. His reputation unsullied by the South Sea scandal, he became secretary of state in 1721, but retired in 1730 to Raynham, to grow turnips and improve the rotation of crops.

(2) **Charles** (1725–67), English statesman, grandson of (1), entered the House of Commons in 1747. Bute gained him over from

Pitt by the offer of the post of secretary at war; but on Bute's resignation in 1763 he was appointed first lord of trade and the plantations. In the Chatham ministry of 1766 he became chancellor of the Exchequer and leader of the Lower House. Chatham relaxing his grip of affairs, Townshend carried those taxation measures that led to the separation of the American colonies. He was about to form a ministry when he died. A brilliant speaker, by his witty irrelevancies he was able to intoxicate the House of Commons, as in his famous 'champagne speech' (1767). He was, according to Earl Russell, 'a man utterly without principle, whose brilliant talents only made more prominent his want of truth, honour and consistency'. See Life by Fitzgerald (1886).

(3) **Sir Charles Vere Ferrers** (1861–1924), British soldier, great-great-grandson of (4), whose *Military Life* (1901) he wrote, joined the Indian army and held Chitral Fort for 46 days (1895). As major-general in 1915, in conjunction with naval forces up the Tigris, he took Amara. Defeated at Ctesiphon, he fell back upon Kut, where he held out for a month before surrendering. He was M.P. from 1920. See his *My Campaign in Mesopotamia* (1920).

(4) **George, 4th Viscount and 1st Marquess** (1724–1807), English soldier, brother of (2), was educated at St John's College, Cambridge. He fought at Culloden, but retired owing to a difference with the Duke of Cumberland (q.v.). He was brigadier-general under Wolfe at Quebec, and, after Wolfe's death, assumed the command. As lord-lieutenant of Ireland (1767–72), he tried to break down the government by 'undertakers', but his habits became dissipated and he was recalled. He was created marquess (1786). See *Military Life* by (3) (1901).

TOYNBEE, (1) **Arnold** (1852–83), English economic historian and social reformer, uncle of (2), born in London, lectured in Economic History at Balliol College, Oxford, and to numerous workers' adult education classes, and undertook social work in the East End of London with Samuel Barnett (q.v.). He is best known as the coiner of the phrase and author of *The Industrial Revolution in England* (1884). Toynbee Hall, a university settlement in Whitechapel, London, was founded in his memory in 1885. See Lives by F. C. Montague (1889) and Viscount Milner (1895). His brother, Paget (1855–1932), was a biographer and authority on the works of Dante.

(2) **Arnold Joseph** (1889–), English historian, nephew of (1), born in London, educated at Winchester and Balliol College, Oxford, of which he became a fellow, married in 1913 a daughter of Gilbert Murray (divorced 1946), served in the Foreign Office in both World Wars and attended the Paris peace conferences (1919 and 1946). He was Koraes professor of Modern Greek and Byzantine History at London (1919–24) and director and research professor of the Royal Institute of International Affairs, London (1925–55). Profound scholarship in the histories of world civilizations combined with the wide sweep of a near metaphysical turn of mind produced the brilliant, if later unfashionable, historical writing and synthesis on the grand scale, the monumental, ten-volume *History of the World* (1934–54), echoes of which reverberated through his stimulating and controversial B.B.C. Reith Lectures, *The World and the West* (1952). His numerous works include *Greek Historical Thought* (1924), *War and Civilization* (1951), &c. He was made a C.H. in 1956. One of his sons, **(Theodore) Philip** (1916–), is a well-known novelist and journalist (with *The Observer* since 1950). His works include *The Savage Days* (1937), *Comparing Notes* (with his father, 1963) and *Two Brothers* (1964).

TRADESCANT, John (1608–62), English naturalist, born at Meopham, Kent, the son of Charles I's Dutch gardener, whom he succeeded, gave his collection of specimens from Virginia to Elias Ashmole (q.v.). See *The Tradescants* by M. Allen (1964).

TRAHERNE, Thomas, *trė-hœrn'* (*c.* 1636–74), English poet, a Hereford shoemaker's son, studied at Brasenose College, Oxford, became rector of Credenhill and in 1667 chaplain to the lord keeper of the great seal, Sir Orlando Bridgeman. He wrote *Centuries* of religious meditations in prose, as well as poetry, full of the strikingly original imagery of the mystic, yet a mystic who as a 'Christian Epicurean' was prepared to give *Thanksgiving for the Body.* See critical biography by G. I. Wade (1944), study by G. E. Willet and a complete collection of his works, ed. H. M. Margoliouth (1958).

TRAILL, Henry Duff (1842–1900), English journalist and man of letters, was born at Blackheath and educated at St John's College, Cambridge. He wrote *The New Lucian* (1884, 1899) and several biographies. He was editor of *The Observer* (1889–91) and of *Social England* (1893–97).

TRAJAN, Marcus Ulpius Trajanus, *tray'jėn* (*c.* 53–117), Roman emperor, was born near Seville. Gaining distinction in the Parthian and German campaigns, he was made praetor and consul (91), was adopted (97) by Nerva as his colleague and successor, and became sole ruler in 98. In 101 Trajan set out on his campaign against the Dacians. The struggle was long and fierce; but the Romans at last gained a decisive superiority, and in a second campaign (105) completely subdued their opponents, whose country became the Roman province of Dacia. In 113 the emperor left Italy for his great expedition in the East, directed mainly against the Parthians. He made Armenia and Mesopotamia into Roman provinces, but met with some defeats, as at Ctesiphon which he captured (115). Meanwhile the Jews rose in Cyprus and Cyrene; other enemies took advantage of the emperor's absence; and Trajan, already in failing health, set sail for Italy, but died at Selinus in Cilicia, August 117. Though most of Trajan's reign was spent in the field, the internal administration was excellent. Informers were severely punished and peculating governors of provinces prosecuted. The empire was traversed in all directions by new military routes; canals, bridges, and harbours were constructed, new towns built, the Pontine Marshes partially drained, and the magnificent 'Forum Trajani' erected. Trajan's mildness and moderation were proverbial, though he persecuted Christianity as subversive of the state. See works by Francke (2nd ed. 1840), Dierauer (1868), de la Berge (1877), and chaps. 8–12 of B. W. Henderson's *Five Roman Emperors* (1927).

TRAPASSI, Pietro. See METASTASIO.

TRAUBE, *trow'bė,* (1) **Ludwig** (1818–76), German pathologist, brother of (2), born at Ratibor, became professor at the Friedrich-Wilhelm Institute (1853) and at the university (1872), both at Berlin. He pioneered the study of experimental pathology in Germany.

(2) **Moritz** (1826–94), German chemist, brother of (1), born at Ratibor, at Breslau made artificial semipermeable membranes and so made possible the determination of osmotic pressures.

TRAVERS, (1) **Ben** (1886–), English dramatist and novelist, born at Hendon, educated at Charterhouse, served in the R.A.F. in both world wars and was awarded the Air Force Cross (1920). A master of light farce, he wrote to suit the highly individual comic talents of Ralph Lynn, Robertson Hare and Tom Walls in such pieces as *A Cuckoo in the Nest* (1925), *Rookery Nook* (1926), *Thark* (1927), *Plunder* (1928), &c., which played in the Aldwych Theatre, London, for many years.

(2) **Morris William** (1872–1961), English chemist, born at London and educated at Blundells, London, and Nancy, was an authority on glass technology. Professor at Bristol (1904–37), he was technical consultant to the Ministry of Supply (1940–45). He discovered, with Ramsay, the inert gases krypton, xenon and neon (1894–1908), and investigated the phenomena of low temperatures. He wrote *The Discovery of the Rare Gases* (1928) and a *Life of Sir William Ramsay* (1956).

TREDGOLD, Thomas (1788–1829), English engineer and cabinetmaker, born at Brandon (Durham), became a carpenter and studied building construction and science in London. His *Elementary Principles of Carpentry* (1820) was the first serious manual on the subject. He also wrote manuals on cast iron (1821), *The Steam Engine* (1827), &c.

TREE, Sir Herbert Beerbohm (1853–1917), English actor-manager, half-brother of Sir Max Beerbohm (q.v.), born in London. After a commercial education in Germany, he took to the stage and scored his first success as Spalding in *The Private Secretary*. In 1887 he took over the Haymarket theatre until in 1897, with the box-office success of *Trilby*, he built His Majesty's theatre, where he rivalled, by his mastery of stagecraft, the Shakespearean productions of Irving at the Lyceum. A great character actor, Svengali, Falstaff, Hamlet, Fagin, Shylock, Malvolio, Micawber were all grist to his mill. He scored a tremendous success when he first produced Shaw's *Pygmalion* in 1914. See his *Memoirs*, ed. Sir Max Beerbohm (1920), and Life by Hesketh Pearson (1956). His wife **Helen Maud** (1864–1937), whom he married in 1883, excelled in such comic rôles as Mrs Quickly, Mrs Malaprop and Lady Teazle. She directed Wyndham's theatre from 1902 and made her last professional appearance in the film *The Private Life of Henry VIII* (1936).

TREGELLES, Samuel Prideaux, *-gel'is* (1813–1875), English biblical scholar, born of Quaker parentage at Falmouth, wrote a critical edition of the Greek New Testament (1857–72).

TREITSCHKE, Heinrich von, *trītsh'kė* (1834–1896), German historian, born at Dresden, studied at Bonn, Leipzig, Tübingen and Heidelberg, and became a professor at Freiburg-im-Breisgau (1863), Kiel (1866), Heidelberg (1867) and Berlin (1874). He succeeded Ranke in 1886 as Prussian historiographer. A member of the Reichstag 1871–1888, he died at Berlin. His chief work *History of Germany in the Nineteenth Century* (1879–94; trans. 1915–18), though written from the dogmatic Prussian viewpoint, is of great literary and historical value, and his method, scope and treatment of the subject have been compared to those of Macaulay in his *History of England*. An ardent believer in a powerful Germany with a powerful empire, and in the necessity of war to achieve and maintain this, his writings had a strong influence before World War I. See his *Politics* (trans. 1916); Adolf Hausrath *Treitschke: his Life and Work* (trans. 1914); and H. W. C. Davies on his *Political Thought* (1914).

TRELAWNY, (1) **Edward John** (1792–1881), English author and adventurer, born of a famous Cornish family, entered the navy at eleven but deserted, and lived a life of desperate enterprise in Eastern seas. In 1821 he made the acquaintance of Shelley at Pisa, and helped to burn the drowned poet's body. Next year he accompanied Byron to Greece, and remained there some time after Byron's death. He travelled in America, lived a while in Italy, eloped about 1841 with Lady Goring, and spent his last years in Monmouthshire or Sussex. His *Adventures of a Younger Son* (1830; new ed. 1890) was based on his own youth; his *Recollections of Shelley and Byron* (1858) was recast in 1878. See his *Letters* (1911), and Life by H. J. Massingham (1930).

(2) **Sir Jonathan, 3rd Baronet** (1650–1721), English divine, became bishop in turn of Bristol (1685), Exeter (1688) and Winchester (1707). Though intensely loyal to the crown, he was one of the seven bishops tried under James II, and is the hero of R. S. Hawker's ballad, 'And shall Trelawny die?'

TRENCH, (1) **Frederick Herbert** (1865–1923), Irish poet, dramatist and producer, born at Avoncore, County Cork, educated at Haileybury and Keble College, Oxford, wrote volumes of verse, *Deirdre Wed* (1900) and *New Poems* (1907), &c., and was artistic director of the Haymarket theatre (1909–11). See French study by A. Chevalley (1925).

(2) **Richard Chenevix** (1807–86), Irish divine, philologist and poet, was born at Dublin. Educated at Harrow and Trinity College, Cambridge, he became curate in 1841 to Samuel Wilberforce. During 1835–1846 he published six volumes of poetry,

reissued in 1865. In 1845 he became rector of Itchenstoke; in 1847 professor of Theology in King's College, London; in 1856 Dean of Westminster; and from 1864 to 1884 he was Archbishop of Dublin. He was buried in Westminster Abbey. In philology he contrived to fascinate his readers with the 'fossil poetry and fossil history imbedded in language', and the *Oxford English Dictionary* was begun at his suggestion. His principal works are *Notes on the Parables* (1841), *Notes on the Miracles* (1846), *The Study of Words* (1851), *Lessons in Proverbs* (1853), *New Testament Synonyms* (1854), *Life and Genius of Calderón* (1856), *Select Glossary of English Words* (1859), *Studies on the Gospels* (1867), &c. See his *Letters and Memorials* (1888).

TRENCHARD, Hugh Montague, 1st Viscount Trenchard (1873–1956), British service chief, marshal of the R.A.F., entered the Forces in 1893, serving on the N.W. Frontier, in South Africa, and with the West African Frontier Force. His early interest in aviation led to his appointment as assistant commandant, Central Flying School (1913–14), and to his posting as the first general officer commanding the R.F.C. in the field. Chief of the Air Staff between 1919 and 1929, his subsequent work as commissioner of the metropolitan police did nothing to obscure his fame as the 'Father of the R.A.F.', though he carried out a number of far-reaching reforms, including the establishment of the Police College at Hendon. He was raised to the peerage in 1930 and awarded the O.M. in 1951.

TRENCK, (1) Franz, Baron, or Freiherr von der (1711–49), Austrian adventurer, was born at Reggio in Calabria, where his father was an Austrian general. At sixteen he entered the army, but soon had to leave it, as likewise the service of Russia. In the Austrian War of Succession he raised (1741) at his own cost a body of Pandours, who were even more distinguished for cruelty than for daring. On September 7, 1742, he attacked and destroyed Cham, in the Palatinate, and in 1745 he offered to capture Frederick the Great, and did secure the king's tent and much booty. He was suspected, however, of treachery, and imprisoned, escaped, but was recaptured, and condemned to lifelong imprisonment on the Spielberg at Brünn, where he poisoned himself. See his Autobiography (1748; new ed. 1807), and Life by J. O. Teichman (1927).

(2) **Friedrich, Baron** (1726–94), German adventurer, a cousin of (1), born at Königsberg, the son of a Prussian major-general, in 1742 entered the army, and two years afterwards attempted an intrigue with the Princess Amalie. The discovery of a correspondence with his Austrian cousin led to his imprisonment at Glatz, whence in 1746 he escaped to take service with Russia and Austria. Having returned to Prussia on family business, he was imprisoned at Magdeburg by Frederick the Great (1754), and on his attempting to escape was put in irons. He was released in 1763, and settled at Aix-la-Chapelle as a wine merchant. Having ventured to Paris in 1791, he was guillotined by Robespierre as a political agent. See his autobiography (1787), abridged by Murray (1927).

TRENT. See BOOT.

TREVELYAN, *-vel'-*, **(1) Sir Charles Edward, 1st Bart.** (1807–86), English administrator, father of (4), educated at Charterhouse and Haileybury, became a writer in the Bengal civil service, assistant-secretary to the Treasury (1840–59), governor of Madras (1859–60) and Indian finance minister (1862–1865), when he carried out great social reforms and a public works programme. He had married Hannah Moore, Macaulay's sister, in 1834. He was created a baronet in 1874 and wrote on Indian education (1838), &c.

(2) **Sir Charles Philips, 3rd Bart.** (1870–1958), English politician, son of (4) and brother of (3) and (5), was educated at Harrow and Trinity College, Cambridge, entered Parliament in 1899 and in 1908 became Liberal parliamentary secretary to the Board of Education. He resigned in 1914, disapproving of war with Germany. From 1922 he sat as a Labour M.P. and became president of the Board of Education (1924, 1929–31), but resigned when his School Attendance Bill was rejected. He was lord lieutenant of Northumberland (1930–49).

(3) **George Macaulay** (1876–1962), English historian, son of (4), born at Stratford-on-Avon, was educated at Harrow and Trinity College, Cambridge, of which he was elected master (1940–51). He served in the First World War and was regius professor of Modern History at Cambridge (1927–40). He is probably best known for his *English Social History* (1944), in which his considerable literary gifts find full expression; it is a companion volume to his *History of England* (1926). Other works include studies of Garibaldi (1907, 1909, 1911), Lives of John Bright (1913) and his father, G. O. Trevelyan (1932), *British History in the Nineteenth Century* (1922), &c., and several volumes of lectures and essays, including an autobiography (1949). He was awarded the O.M. in 1930 and elected F.R.S. in 1950. See study by Plumb (1951).

(4) **Sir George Otto, 2nd Bart.** (1838–1928), English statesman, son of (1) and father of (2), (3) and (5), born at Rothley Temple, Leicestershire, and educated at Harrow and Trinity College, Cambridge. He entered parliament in 1865 as a Liberal and became a lord of the Admiralty (1868–70), parliamentary secretary to the same (1880–82), chief secretary for Ireland (1882–84) and a secretary for Scotland (1886, 1892–95). He wrote a number of historical works, among them a Life of his uncle, Macaulay (1876–1908), a Life of Fox (1880), and the *American Revolution* (1909), &c. He was awarded the O.M. in 1911. See Life by his son (3) (1932).

(5) **Robert Calverley** (1872–1951), English poet and playwright, son of (4), educated at Harrow and Trinity College, Cambridge, wrote volumes of verse, *Mallow and Asphodel* (1898), *The Bride of Dionysus* (1912), set to music by Tovey (q.v.), &c., translations from Leopardi and *Windfalls* (1944) a collection of essays.

TREVES, Sir Frederick, *treevz* (1853–1923)

English surgeon, born at Dorchester, was educated in London, became professor at the Royal College of Surgeons. He was a founder of the British Red Cross Society and made improvements in operations for appendicitis.

TREVIRANUS, *-rah'-*, (1) **Gottfried Reinhold** (1776–1837), German biologist and anatomist, brother of (2), born at Bremen, wrote an important work on biology (1802–22) and made histological and anatomical studies of Vertebrates.

(2) **Ludolf Christian** (1779–1864), German naturalist, brother of (1), was born at Bremen and was professor at Bremen, Rostock, Breslau and Bonn. He is known for his discovery of intercellular spaces.

TREVISA. See JOHN OF TREVISA.

TREVITHICK, Richard (1771–1833), English engineer and inventor, born at Illogan, Redruth, became a mining engineer at Penzance, and in 1796–1801 invented a steam carriage, which ran between Camborne and Tuckingmill at from four to nine miles an hour, and which in 1803 was run from Leather Lane to Paddington by Oxford Street. He was in Peru and Costa Rica 1816–27, where his engines were introduced into the silver mines. The development of the high-pressure engine was largely due to him. See Life by his son (1872), study by Dickinson and Titley (1934).

TREVOR, Sir John (*c.* 1637–1717), English politician, was in 1685 elected Speaker, and made master of the Rolls. Though a minion of Judge Jeffreys, he was again Speaker (1690–95). For accepting a bribe as first commissioner of the court of Chancery, he was expelled from parliament in 1695; he still, however, retained the mastership of the Rolls.

TRIBONIANUS (d. *c.* A.D. 544), Roman jurist, born, probably, in Pamphylia, held various offices under the Emperor Justinian, and is famous through his labours on Justinian's Code and the Pandects.

TRICOUPIS, Spyridon, *tri-koo'pees* (1788–1873), Greek statesman and writer, born at Missolonghi, was private secretary to Lord Guilford in the Ionian Isles, studied in Rome, Paris and London, and joined the patriots on the outbreak of the War of Independence (1821). He was thrice envoy-extraordinary to London, was minister of foreign affairs and of public instruction (1843), vice-president of the Senate (1844–49), and envoy-extraordinary to Paris (1850). His *Speeches* appeared in 1836; his *History of the Greek Revolution* in 1853–57. His son, **Charilaos** (1832–96), was foreign minister (1866) and premier repeatedly in 1875–95.

TRIDUANA, St (4th c.), is said to have come to Scotland with St Rule (q.v.). Legend relates that, troubled by the attentions of the local king and learning of his admiration for her eyes, she plucked them out and sent them to him. She retired to Restalrig, where there is a well once famous as a cure for eye diseases.

TRILLING, Lionel (1905–), American author and critic, was educated at Columbia University, where he was professor of English from 1948. He wrote literary studies on Matthew Arnold (1939), Forster (1948), *The Liberal Imagination* (1950), *The Opposing Sel* (1955) and *A Gathering of Fugitives* (1957).

TRIVET, or Trevet, Nicholas (fl. 1300), an English Dominican friar, who wrote *Annales Sex Regum Angliae*, covering the period 1136–1307.

TROCHU, Louis Jules, *tro-shü* (1815–96), French soldier, born at Palais (Morbihan), who, after a distinguished military career in the Crimea and elsewhere, entered the ministry of war. But the unpalatable truths contained in his *L'Armée française en 1867* set the court against him. In 1870 he received a command at Toulouse, on August 17 was made governor of Paris, and under the republic became chief of the national defence. Regarded as overcautious and timid, he probably saw only too well the hopelessness of his task. He resigned the governorship in January 1871, but remained president of the national defence until 1872. Works by him in his own defence are *Pour la vérité et pour la justice* (1873) and *La Politique et le siège de Paris* (1874).

TROLLOPE, (1) Anthony (1815–82), English novelist, was born in London. His *Autobiography* tells the story of family misfortunes through the mismanagement of the father but relieved by the mother's industry as a novelist. His career can be divided into two periods—the year of his admission to the Post Office (1834), which entailed service in Ireland, to the publication of *The Warden*, the first of the Barsetshire series, in 1855; and thenceforward as the novelist and clubman who still retains his enthusiasm for his official work. His devotion to hunting is reflected in many of his novels. He married a Miss Heseltine in 1844 and was eminently happy in his family. His first two novels, *The Macdermots of Ballycloran* (1847) and *The Kellys and the O'Kellys* (1848), were not successful, though in character-drawing and episodes they foreshadow the great series to come. The simple story of Hiram's Hospital in *The Warden* gave Trollope the chance to introduce some of his great fictional characters—Mr Harding, who appears in all the Barchester series; Archdeacon Grantly, a study in ecclesiastical politics; and old Bishop Proudie who appears prominently in *Barchester Towers* with his redoubtable wife and finishes greatly in the superb duel with her in *The Last Chronicle*, though this is as much Mr Crawley's book as Mrs Proudie's or the bishop's. The six novels of the series—*The Warden*, *Barchester Towers*, *Framley Parsonage*, *Doctor Thorne*, *Last Chronicle of Barchester*—include also *The Small House at Allington* which, however, does not 'breathe Barchester air' but which introduces two characters who are to be very important in the political series which followed. *The Eustace Diamonds* and *Can You Forgive Her?* are usually included in this series, but more generally, it comprises *Phineas Finn*, *Phineas Redux*, *The Prime Minister* and *The Duke's Children*. In these fine novels Plantagenet Palliser, heir to the Duke of Omnium, and Lady Glencora emerge as Trollope's finest creations—so he thought himself—and figure much more prominently than in their first minor appearance in *The Small House*. These political novels occupy Trollope's middle period from *Phineas Finn* (1869) to *The Duke's Children* (1880), though we should perhaps date this era from his meeting with Thackeray, which resulted in the serial appearance of *Framley Parsonage* in *Cornhill* in 1864. Trollope employed the political novels to express his views on public questions, and he brilliantly evokes the atmosphere of Westminster and well describes the great political houses and clubs. But the hero of the first two, Phineas Finn, is poor stuff and the questions broached chiefly Church reform, are rather nebulous. It is in *The Prime Minister* and *The Duke's Children* that Palliser and Lady Glencora emerge as finished studies of rectitude in high places. Michael Sadleir has done something to correct the notion that the latest novels are of no account. *The Way We Live Now* (1875), *Dr Wortle's School* (1881), *Mr Scarborough's Family* (1883), his 'troubled' novels, show new range and new interests, and *Ayala's Angel*, published a year before his death, returns to the charming manner of the Barsetshire series with a wealth of new characterization. Michael Sadleir's *Trollope: a Commentary* (1928, revised 1945) is the definitive work on Trollope. See also *Letters*, ed. Brook-Booth (1951), *Autobiography* (World's Classics, 1936), and studies by Escott (1913), Morgan (1946), Page (1950) and Brown (1950); also studies by two novelists, Hugh Walpole (1928) and Elizabeth Bowen (1946), and by B. A. Booth (1958).

(2) **Frances** (1780–1863), *née* **Milton**, English novelist, mother of (1) and (4), was born at Stapleton near Bristol. In 1809 she married Thomas Anthony Trollope (1774–1835), a barrister and fellow of New College, Oxford. In 1827 he fell into dire financial distress, which was not relieved by a removal to Cincinnati. During her three years in the States, Mrs Trollope amassed the material for her *Domestic Manners of the Americans* (1832), a book much resented in America. Left a widow in 1835, she eventually settled in Florence (1843), where she died. Of her novels, the most successful were *The Vicar of Wrexhill* (1837), *The Widow Barnaby* (1839), with its sequel, *The Widow Married* (1840). In all she wrote 115 volumes, now mostly forgotten.

(3) **Sir Henry** (1756–1839), English sailor, in 1796 with the *Glatton* defeated seven French vessels off Helvoetsluys, and next year brought information to Duncan that led to the victory of Camperdown. Long troubled by gout, he blew out his brains.

(4) **Thomas Adolphus** (1810–92), English author, son of (2) and brother of (1), was educated at Winchester and Oxford. In 1841 he settled at Florence, where his house was a meeting-place for many writers, English and foreign. In 1890 he returned to England, and died at Clifton. He wrote works on Italian subjects, including a *Life of Pius IX*, and many novels, such as *Marietta* and *The Garstangs*.

TROMP, (1) **Cornelis** (1629–91), Dutch sailor, the son of (2), shared the glory of de Ruyter's four days' fight (June 1 to 4, 1666) off the Downs, and won fame in the battles against the combined English and French fleets, June 7 and 14, 1673. On a visit to England in 1675 he was created baron by Charles II and was appointed lieutenant-governor of the United Provinces (1676).

(2) **Maarten Harpertszoon** (1597–1653), Dutch admiral, father of (1), born at Briel, went to sea as a child with his father, was captured by an English cruiser, and compelled to serve two years as a cabin boy. In 1624 he was in command of a frigate; lieutenant-admiral, he defeated a superior Spanish fleet off Gravelines in 1639. The same year he defeated another fleet off the Downs, and captured thirteen richly-laden galleons. On May 19, 1652, he was worsted by an English fleet under Blake. In November he again encountered Blake in the Strait of Dover, this time successfully, but whether Tromp actually sailed up the Channel with a broom at his masthead, to denote that he had swept the enemy from the seas, is uncertain. On February 18, 1653, Blake, with Monk and Deane, defeated Tromp off Portland, after an obstinate three days' contest. On June 2 and 3 another terrific battle between Tromp and Deane took place off the North Foreland, the Dutch being defeated. In the final battle with Monk, July 31, 1653, off the coast of Holland, the Dutch lost thirty men-of-war, but their greatest loss was Tromp, who died in the battle, shot through the heart. See *Tromp's Journal of 1639*, ed. C. R. Boxer (1930).

TROTSKY, Leon, alias of **Lev Davidovich Bronstein** (1879–1940), Russian Jewish revolutionary, born in Yanovka in the Ukraine and educated in Odessa. At the age of nineteen he was arrested as a member of a Marxist group and was sent to Siberia. He escaped in 1902, joined Lenin in London, and in the abortive 1905 revolution became president of the first Soviet in St Petersburg. Escaping from a further exile period in Siberia, he became a revolutionary journalist among Russian émigrés in the West. After the March 1917 revolution he returned to Russia, joined the Bolshevik party and with Lenin was mainly responsible for organizing the November Revolution. As commissar for foreign affairs he conducted negotiations with the Germans for the peace treaty of Brest-Litovsk. In the civil war Trotsky as commissar for war brought the Red Army of 5,000,000 men into being from a nucleus of 7000 men. On Lenin's death in 1924 Trotsky's influence began to decline. Within two years Stalin had ousted him from the Politbureau and in 1927 he was exiled to Central Asia. His repetition of Lenin's warnings against Stalin, and his condemnation of Stalin's autocratic ambitions, led to Trotsky's expulsion from Russia in 1929. He continued to agitate and intrigue as an exile in several countries. In 1937, having been sentenced to death in his absence by a Soviet court, he found asylum in Mexico City. There he was assassinated in 1940 by Ramon del Rio (alias Jacques Mornard). Ruthless, energetic, a superb orator and messianic visionary, Trotsky inspired as much confidence in Lenin as he awakened mistrust in the still wilier Stalin. In his later years he was the focus of those Communists, Russian and otherwise, who opposed the endless opportunism of Stalin. He was the revolutionary 'pur sang'—and a writer of power, wit and venom. His publications include *History of the Russian Revolution* (1932) *The Revolution Betrayed* (1937), *Stalin* (1948) and *Diary in Exile* (trans. 1959). See I. Deutscher, *The Prophet Armed* (1954) and *The Prophet Unarmed* (1959) and also *The Trotsky Papers*, vol. I, 1917–22, ed. J. M. Meijer (1964).

TROTZENDORF. See FRIEDLAND.

TROYON, Constant, *trwah-yõ* (1810–65), French painter of landscapes and particularly of animals, born at Sèvres. Many of his paintings are in the Louvre and two are in the Wallace Collection, London.

TRÜBNER, Nicholas (1817–88), German publisher, born at Heidelberg, came to London in 1843, started up his business in 1852 and developed a business connection in the United States. An oriental scholar, he published a series of oriental texts as well as works for the Early English Text Society. The business was merged in 1889 to become Kegan Paul, Trench, Trübner & Co.

TRUMAN, Harry S. (1884–1972), 33rd president of the United States, was born at Lamar, Missouri, and was educated at Independence, Mo. After World War I, in which he served as an artillery captain on the Western Front, he returned to his farm and later went into partnership in a men's clothing store in Kansas City which failed. In 1922 he became judge for the Eastern District of Jackson County, Mo., and in 1926 presiding judge, a post he held till 1934 when Missouri elected him to the U.S. senate. He was re-elected in 1940 and was chairman of the special committee investigating defence which was said to have saved the U.S. more than 1,000,000,000 dollars. He was elected vice-president in 1944 and became president in April 1945 on the death of President Franklin D. Roosevelt. He was re-elected in November 1948 in a surprise victory over Thomas E. Dewey, which made nonsense of Dr Gallup's forecasts. As the 'everyday American' who became president, Truman astonished his earlier critics. Few presidents have had to take so many historically important decisions—dropping the first atom bomb on Japan; pushing through congress a huge postwar loan to Britain; making a major change in U.S. policy towards Russia, signalized by the 'Truman doctrine'; sending U.S. troops on behalf of the U.N. to withstand the Communist invasion of South Korea; dismissing General Douglas MacArthur from all his commands in 1951. For seven crucial years President Truman, who called himself 'the hired man of 150,000,000 people', held the American people together while new alignments were taking shape. He did not stand for re-election in 1952 and retired to Independence. Later he became a strong critic of the Eisenhower Republican administration. See his autobiography (2 vols. 1955–56), *The Man of Independence* by J. Daniels, *Mr President*, by W. Hillman (1957) and study by C. Phillips (1966).

TRUMBULL, (1) James Hammond (1821–97), American philologist and historian, born at Stonington, Conn., was an authority on the languages of the North American Indians, on which he wrote several works.

(2) **John** (1750–1831), American lawyer and poet, wrote a satire on educational methods, *The Progress of Dullness* (1772–73), and a revolutionary satire, *McFingal* (1775–1782), in imitation of Butler's *Hudibras.* See Life by A. Cowie (1936).

(3) **John** (1756–1843), American historical painter, son of (4), born at Lebanon, Conn., served in the Revolutionary War as colonel and deputy adjutant-general. The war inspired him to paint many historical pieces. See his Autobiography (1841).

(4) **Jonathan** (1710–85), American patriot, father of (3), born at Lebanon, Conn., was judge, deputy-governor, and governor of Connecticut, and took a prominent part in the War of Independence. 'Brother Jonathan', the personification of the United States, was once thought, but erroneously, to refer to him. See Life by J. Trumbull (1919).

TRYON, Sir George (1832–93), English sailor, born at Bulwick Park, Northants, became an admiral in 1884 and commander-in-chief in the Mediterranean in 1891. By his mistaken order during manœuvres, his ship, the iron-clad *Victoria* was rammed and sunk. He and most of the crew perished. See Life by C. C. P. Fitzgerald (1897), and R. Hough's *Admirals in Collision* (1959).

TSAI LUN, *tsī loon* (? A.D.50–?), Chinese alleged inventor (105) of paper made from tree bark and rags, was a eunuch at the Han court.

TSCHAIKOWSKY. See TCHAIKOVSKY.

TSCHUDI, *choo-dee*, (1) **Aegidius,** or **Gilg** (1505–72), Swiss historian, was born at Glarus and was active on the Catholic side during the Reformation in the Swiss canton of Glarus. His *Schweizerchronik* (1734–36) was long the standard Swiss history.

(2) **Johann Jacob von** (1818–89), Swiss naturalist, born at Glarus, investigated the natural history and ethnography of South America. He was ambassador to Brazil (1860) and Austria (1866–83). He wrote on the batrachians, *Fauna Peruana* (1844–46), the Quichua language, Peruvian antiquities, &c.

TSO CH'IU MING (*c.* 6th cent. B.C.), Chinese author, mentioned by Confucius in his *Analects*, wrote the *Tso Chuan*, a commentary on the *Ch'un Ch'iu*, one of the five classics. Modern scholars also ascribe to him the *Kuo Yü* and these two works comprise the most important historical sources of the period. The simplicity of his style served as a model to later writers.

TSWETT or **Tsvett, Mikhail Semenovich** (1872–1919), Russian botanist, devised a percolation method of separating plant pigments in 1906, thus making the first chromatographic analysis.

TUCKER, (1) Charlotte Marie (1821–93), English author, born at Barnet, under the pseudonym **ALOE** (a Lady of England) wrote many stories from 1854, and died at Amritsar, in India, where she was a missionary.

(2) **Josiah** (1712–99), English economist

and divine, became Dean of Gloucester (1758). He wrote on economics, as well as on politics and religion, and anticipated some of Adam Smith's arguments against monopolies.

TUDOR, Owen. See HENRY VII.

TU FU, *doo foo* (712–770), Chinese lyric poet of the T'ang dynasty, born in Shensi province.

TUKE, (1) **Henry Scott** (1858–1929), English painter, great-grandson of (2), studied at the Slade and painted chiefly nudes against sea backgrounds. His *August Blue* (1894; Tate) caused considerable controversy.

(2) **William** (1732–1822), English Quaker philanthropist, founded a home for the mentally sick, and contemporaneously with Pinel in France pioneered new methods of treatment and care of the insane.

TULASNE, Louis René, *tü-lahn* (1815–85), and his brother **Charles** (1816–84), French mycologists, made important researches in the structure and development of fungi. See their *Selecta Fungorum Carpologia* (3 vols. 1861–65; Eng. trans. with intro. 1931).

TULL, Jethro (1674–1741), English agriculturist, born at Basildon in Berkshire, and educated at St John's College, Oxford, invented a drill, introduced new farming methods in his native county, his chief innovation being the planting of seeds in rows. He wrote *The Horse-Hoing Husbandry* (1733; suppl. 1740).

TULLOCH, John (1823–86), Scottish theologian, born at Bridge of Earn, after holding charges in Forfarshire was in 1854 appointed principal and professor of Divinity in St Mary's College, St Andrews. He was a founder of the Scottish liberal church party (1878) and wrote many religious and philosophical works and an address to young men, *Beginning Life* (1862). See Memoir by Mrs Oliphant (1888).

TULLY. See CICERO.

TULSI DAS, *tool-see dahs* (1532–1623), Indian poet, born a Brahman, possibly at Rajpur in Sarwariya, dedicated himself, at the instigation of his wife, to Rama. Inspired to write as well as preach, his great *Rāmāyan, Rām-Charit-Mānas* (The Lake of Rama's Deeds), composed in the language of ordinary people, is one of the masterpieces of Hindu poetry. Venerated still, it is the Bible of the Hindus of northern India. He wrote several lesser works to the glory of Rama before retiring to Benares, where he died aged 91.

TUNSTALL, Cuthbert (1474–1559), English divine, born at Hackforth, Yorkshire, brother of Sir Brian Tunstall who fell at Flodden, became rector of Stanhope, archdeacon of Chester, rector of Harrow-on-the-Hill, master of the Rolls, dean of Salisbury (1519), bishop of London (1522) and of Durham (1530). In 1516–30 he went repeatedly on embassies to the emperor (making friends with Erasmus) and to France. He accepted the royal supremacy, but took alarm at the sweeping reforms under Edward VI, and was in 1552 deprived. The accession of Mary restored him. Under his mild rule not a single victim died for heresy throughout the diocese. On Elizabeth's accession he refused to take the oath of supremacy and was again deprived See memoir by G. H. Ross-Lewin (1909).

TUPPER, Martin Farquhar (1810–89), English poet and inventor, born at Marylebone, studied at Charterhouse and at Christ Church, Oxford. He was called to the bar (1835), but soon turned to writing. Of his works, forty in number, only *Proverbial Philosophy* (1838–67), brought him and his publisher considerable profit. His inventions, safety horseshoes, steam vessels with the paddles inside, &c., were less successful. See *My Life as Author* (1886) and Life by D. Hudson (1949).

TURA, Cosimo, *too'ra* (*c.* 1430–95), Italian artist, was born at Ferrara. The leader, with Cossa (q.v.), of the Ferrarese school, he studied under Squarcione at Padua, and his metallic, tortured forms and unusual colours give a strange power to his pictures, e.g., the *Pietà* in the Louvre and the *S. Jerome* in the National Gallery, London. See study by Eberhard Ruhmer (1958) and B. Nicolson, *The Painters of Ferrara* (1950).

TURBERVILE, George (*c.* 1540–*c.* 1610), English poet, and secretary to Sir Thomas Randolph, born at Whitchurch, Dorset, was educated at Winchester and New College, Oxford. He wrote epigrams, songs, sonnets, *The Booke of Falconrie* (1575), *The Noble Art of Venerie* (1576), and translated Ovid (ed. Boas, 1928), the Italian poets and others. He was a pioneer in the use of blank verse.

TURENNE, Henri de la Tour d'Auvergne, Vicomte de (1611–75), French soldier, the second son of the Duke of Bouillon and Elizabeth of Nassau, William the Silent's daughter, was born at Sedan, September 11. Brought up in the Reformed faith, he learned the art of war under his uncle, Prince Maurice, and in 1630 received a commission from Richelieu. During the alliance of France with the Protestants in the Thirty Years' War he fought with distinction, and in 1641 was entrusted with the supreme command. For the conquest of Roussillon from the Spaniards in 1642 he was in 1644 made marshal of France, and received the chief command on the Rhine. For a time he was superseded by Condé; and his restoration to supreme command was followed by his rout by the Imperialists at Marienthal (May 5, 1645). But on August 3 this disgrace was avenged by Condé at Nördlingen; and Turenne concluded France's share in the war by the conquest of Trèves electorate and of Bavaria (with the Swedes, 1646–47), and by a successful campaign in Flanders. In the civil wars of the Fronde, Turenne joined the *frondeurs*, and after being defeated at Rethel (1650) he withdrew to Flanders. On Mazarin's return Turenne joined his party, while Condé deserted to the *frondeurs*. Turenne twice triumphed over his former chief (1652), and forced him to retire from France; afterwards he subdued the disaffected cities, conquered much of the Spanish Netherlands, and defeated Condé at the Dunes (1658). In 1660 he was created marshal-general of France, and in 1668 turned Catholic. His next campaign in Holland was triumphant (1672), and in 1673 he held his ground against both the Imperialist Montecuculi and the Elector of Brandenburg. In 1674 he crossed the Rhine, mercilessly ravaged the Palatinate, crushed Brandenburg at Colmar, laid waste Alsace, and then advanced into Germany again to meet Montecuculi. Here he was killed reconnoitring at Sasbach, July 27, 1675. See Turenne's *Mémoires* (new ed. 1909–14); Lives by Ramsay (1733), Raguenet (1738), Duruy (5th ed. 1889), T. Longueville (London 1907), Weygand (trans. 1930); works by Neuber (1869), Roy (1884), Choppin (1875–1888), Legrand-Girarde (1910).

TURGENEV, Ivan Sergeevich, *toor-gyay'nyef* (1818–83), Russian novelist, born in the province of Orel. Child of landed gentry, he had an unsatisfactory childhood through the cruelty of his mother, whose great inherited wealth made her a petty tyrant in the home. After graduating from St Petersburg University he broke away by going to study philosophy in Berlin and there mingled with the radical thinkers of the day. With Alexander Herzen, in particular, he became firm friends. He returned to Russia in 1841 to enter the civil service, but in 1843 abandoned this to take up literature. His mother strongly disapproved and his infatuation for a singer, Pauline Garcia (Mme Viardot), also displeased her. She stopped his allowance and until her death in 1850, when he came into his inheritance, he had to support himself by his pen. He began with verse, *Parasha* (1843) showing strong Pushkin influence, but Turgenev early recognized prose as his medium and in 1847 produced *Khor and Khalynich,* his first sketch of peasant life, which appeared again in *Sportsman's Sketches* (1852). This book, sympathetic studies of the peasantry, made his reputation, but earned governmental ill-favour, as it was interpreted as an attack on serfdom. A laudatory notice of Gogol, on his death in 1852, exacerbated the ill-feeling and resulted in a two years' banishment to his country estates. After his exile he spent much time in Europe, writing nostalgically of life in Russia. *Rudkin* appeared in 1856, *The Nest of Gentlefolk* in 1859, *On the Eve* in 1860, all faithful delineations of Russian liberalism, with its attendant weaknesses and limitations. In his greatest novel, *Fathers and Children* (1862), he portrayed the new generation with its reliance on the practical and materialistic, its faith in science and lack of respect for tradition and authority, in short the Nihilists. But the hero, Bazarov, pleased nobody in Russia. The revolutionaries thought the portrait a libel and the reactionaries thought it a glorification of iconoclasm. Turgenev's popularity slumped in Russia but rose abroad, particularly in England, where the book was recognized as a major contribution to literature. Successive novels, *Smoke* (1867) and *Virgin Soil* (1877), dealt respectively with the Slavophile-Western controversy (he dismisses as nebulous Russian intellectual life) and the underground revolutionary movement. Turgenev returned to the short story, producing powerful pieces like *A Lear of the Steppes,* and tales of the supernatural to which his increasing melancholy of spirit drew him. A passive resignation, lyrically expressed, is his abiding quality. His style, graceful and controlled in emotion, lacks colour and pulsating life. But he is a balanced and objective commentator, sensitive, intelligent, and dedicated to the highest claims of art. His work lives for its universal qualities of understanding and devotion to aesthetic standards. See studies by E. Garnett (1917), A. Yarmolinsky (1926), J. A. T. Lloyd (1943), R. Freeborn (1960), and *Literary Reminiscences and Autobiographical Fragments,* trans. D. Magarshack (1959).

TURGOT, (1) (d. 1115), a Saxon monk of Durham, where he became an archdeacon, and helped to found the new cathedral, was Bishop of St Andrews 1109–15, and confessor to St Margaret (q.v.) of whose *Life* he was the probable author.

(2) **Anne Robert Jacques,** *tür-gō'* (1727–81), French economist and statesman, born of old Norman stock in Paris, May 10, was destined for the church, but adopted the legal profession, and joined the *Philosophes.* Appointed intendant of Limoges in 1761, he found the people poor, degraded, immoral and superstitious. He introduced a better administration of imposts, and abolished compulsory labour on roads and bridges, securing the support of the central government and of the rural priests. Soon after the accession of Louis XVI (1774) he was appointed comptroller-general of finance, and at once entered upon a comprehensive scheme of reform, reducing the expenditure and augmenting the public revenue without imposing new taxes. He sought to break down the immunity from taxation enjoyed by the privileged classes. He established free trade in grain throughout the interior of France, and removed the fiscal barriers which prevented free intercourse between the provinces. He abolished the exclusive privileges of trade corporations. But these efforts towards a more economical, efficient and equitable administration moved the privileged orders to combine for his overthrow. Louis XVI was too weak to resist such pressure, Turgot was dismissed after holding office for twenty months, and France drifted rapidly into the great catastrophe of 1789. The fallen minister occupied himself with literature and science till his death in Paris, March 8, 1781. His chief work, *Réflexions sur la formation et la distribution des richesses* (1766), was the best outcome of the Physiocratic school, and largely anticipated Adam Smith. See Lives by Condorcet (1786), L. Say (trans. 1888), Stephens (1895) and F. Alengry (1942), and studies by D. Dakin (1939) and F. Alengry (1942).

TURINA, Joaquín, *too-ree'na* (1882–1949), Spanish composer and pianist, born in Seville. His early promise was guided by the organist of Seville Cathedral, and at the age of fifteen he made his first appearance as a pianist. By the time he went to Madrid, in 1902, and came under the influence of de Falla and the Spanish Nationalist composers, he had a large number of compositions, including his first opera, to his credit. In 1905 he went to Paris to study at the Schola Cantorum, and became an important figure, both as a pianist and as a composer, in French musical life. Returning to Madrid in 1914, Turina became immensely active as composer, pianist and critic until the Spanish Civil War, in which he was an ardent supporter of General Franco, curtailed his activities. When peace was restored, Turina found himself regarded as the leader of Spanish music, but he is best known for those of his works, which include four operas, orchestral and chamber works as well as piano pieces, that like *Canto a Sevilla*, the orchestral *La Procesión del Rocio* and the string quartet *La Oración del Torero* combine strong local colour and idiom with traditional forms.

TURLE, James (1800–82), English composer of church music and organist of Westminster Abbey for over fifty years. His son, **Henry Frederick** (1835–83), was editor of *Notes and Queries* from 1878.

TURNEBUS (1512–65), the latinized surname of **Adrien Turnèbe**, French classical scholar, born at Rouen, who attained a European reputation as professor of Greek and Philosophy in the Collège Royal in Paris.

TURNER, (1) Charles (1773–1857), English engraver, mezzotinter after Turner, Reynolds, Raeburn, &c., was born at Woodstock, and died in London. He did the engravings for J. M. W. Turner's *Liber Studiorum.*

(2) **Charles Tennyson** (1808–79), English poet, born at Somersby, an elder brother of Alfred Tennyson (q.v.), graduated from Trinity, Cambridge, in 1832, and was for many years vicar of Grasby, Lincolnshire. He took the name Turner under the will of a relation. Besides collaborating with his brother in *Poems by Two Brothers* (1827), he wrote 341 sonnets (collected, with introductory essay by Spedding, 1880).

(3) **Joseph Mallord William** (1775–1851), English painter, one of the great masters of landscape art and of watercolour, was born April 23 at 26 Maiden Lane, Covent Garden, London, a barber's son. He was brought up by an uncle at Brentford and had some schooling, but throughout his life he remained almost illiterate. However, at fourteen he entered the Royal Academy and in the following year was already exhibiting. His early work was mostly adaptations of engravings. He also worked for architects, coloured prints for engravers, gave lessons and made sketches for sale in his father's shop. At eighteen he began wandering about England and Wales in search of material and made architectural drawings in the cathedral cities. For three years in the mid-nineties, he joined forces with Thomas Girtin (q.v.), the latter drawing the outlines and Turner washing in the colour. Between them they raised the art of watercolour to new heights of delicacy and charm. Turner remarked after his colleague's death, 'If Tom Girtin had lived, I should have starved'. From 1796 he gradually abandoned his niche as a topographical watercolourist and, strongly influenced by Wilson and Claude, took to oils in *Millbank Moonlight* (1797; Tate). In 1802 he visited the Louvre collections, swollen with Napoleon's loot, and was greatly attracted by Titian and Poussin, although he himself struck out for romanticism in *Calais Pier* (1803). His work led to a battle royal among the critics. More and more he became preoccupied with the delicate rendering of shifting gradations of light on such diverse forms as waves, shipwrecks, fantastic architecture and towering mountain ranges, conveying a generalized mood or impression of a scene, sometimes accentuated by a theatrically arbitrary choice of vivid colour. *Frosty Morning* (1813), *The Shipwreck* and *Crossing the Brook* (1815) embody Turner's trend. For one who defined painting as 'a rum thing', he found it easier to defend himself against the critics by producing a collection of engravings, *Liber Studiorum* (1807–19), which remained uncompleted and failed because he underpaid the engravers. In 1819 he paid his first visit to Italy and at first his inspiration gave way to literary influences, although *Ulysses deriding Polyphemus* (1829) is generally regarded as one of his masterpieces. His illustrations, however, for T. D. Whitaker's *History of Richmondshire* (1823), the *Rivers of England* (1824), *The Provincial Antiquities of Scotland* (1827–38) and *The Rivers of France* (1834) contain his best achievements in watercolour. His second visit to Italy (1829) marked his last great artistic period, which included the famous pictures of Venice, *The Fighting Téméraire* (1839) and *Rain, Steam and Speed* (1844). The above-mentioned pictures, unless otherwise stated, are in the National Gallery, London. Turner led a secretive private life. He never married and when not staying with his patron Lord Egremont at Petworth, he lived in London taverns such as the 'Ship and Bladebone' at Limehouse Reach. He died December 19, 1851, in a temporary lodging at Chelsea under the assumed name of Booth. His will was subjected to litigation, and a relation whom Turner had left out benefited at the expense of the hostelry for impoverished artists which Turner had envisaged. But 300 of his paintings and 20,000 watercolours and drawings were bequeathed to the nation. Turner's revolution in art foreshadowed Impressionism and found a timely champion in John Ruskin, whose *Modern Painters* (Vol. I 1843) helped to turn the critical tide in Turner's favour. Turner was elected R.A. at twenty-eight and professor of Perspective (1808). See biographical studies by Thornbury (1862, 1897), Monkhouse (1879), Swinburne (1902), Armstrong (1903), Finberg (1939, 1963) and Clare (1951).

(4) **Sir Tomkyns Hilgrove** (*c.* 1766–1843), English soldier, fought at Aboukir Bay and Alexandria, whence he brought to Britain from French custody the Rosetta stone (1801–02).

(5) **Walter James Redfern** (1889–1946), Australian poet, novelist and critic, was born in Melbourne and educated there and at Munich and Vienna. He published *The Dark Fire* (1918), *The Landscape of Cytherea* (1923) and other volumes of poetry. His other writings include studies of Beethoven, Mozart and Wagner, a play *The Man Who Ate the Popomack* (1922), and novels such as *The Aesthetes* (1927) and *The Duchess of Popocatepetl* (1939).

(6) **William** (*c.* 1520–68), English physician,

botanist and dean of Wells, born at Morpeth, fellow of Pembroke Hall, Cambridge, travelled extensively abroad and under the influence of Gesner (q.v.) introduced scientific botany into Britain, through his *New Herball* (1551). He named many plants, including *goatsbeard, hawkweed*, &c.

TURPIN, (1) or **Tilpinus** (d. *c.* 794), French ecclesiastic, became archbishop of Reims (*c.* 753), and was the supposititious author of the *Historia Karoli Magni et Rotholandi*, really written after 1131 by a French monk of Compostela, and continued about 1220.

(2) **Dick** (1705–39), English robber, born at Hempstead, Essex, was, successively or simultaneously, butcher's apprentice, cattle-lifter, smuggler, housebreaker, highwayman and horse-thief. He entered into partnership with Tom King and, going north, was hanged at York, April 10, 1739, for the murder of an Epping keeper. His ride to York belongs, if to any one, to 'Swift John Nevison', who in 1676 is said to have robbed a sailor at Gadshill at 4 a.m., and to have established an 'alibi' by reaching York at 7.45 p.m. See account of his trial by T. Kylls (1739).

TURRETIN, *tür-tĭ*, (1) **François** (1623–87) Swiss theologian, father of (2), was pastor to the Italian congregation at Geneva, and from 1653 professor of Theology. He took a principal part in originating the Helvetic Consensus, and wrote an *Institutio Theologiae Elencticae* (1679–85; Edinburgh 1847–48). See Life by E. de Budé (1880).

(2) **Jean Alphonse** (1671–1737), Swiss theologian, son of (1), became pastor of the Italian congregation, in 1697 professor of Church History, in 1705 of Theology. He laboured to promote a union of the Reformed and Lutheran Churches, and succeeded in abolishing the Helvetic Consensus in 1725. His famous *Discourse concerning the Fundamental Articles in Religion* was translated in 1720. His *Cogitationes et Dissertationes Theologicae* appeared in 1737. See Life by E. de Budé (1880).

TUSSAUD, Marie, *née* **Grosholtz**, *tü-sō* (1760–1850), Swiss modeller in wax, born in Berne, was early apprenticed to her uncle, Dr Curtius, in Paris and inherited his wax museums after his death. After the revolution, she had to attend the guillotine to take death masks from the severed heads. After a short imprisonment, she married a French soldier, Tussaud, but separated from him in 1800 and came over to England with her two children. She toured Britain with her life-size portrait waxworks, a gallery of heroes and rogues, and in 1835 set up a permanent exhibition in Baker Street, London, which was burnt down in 1925 and re-opened in Marylebone Road in 1928. The exhibition still contains Madame Tussaud's own handiwork, notably of Marie Antoinette, Napoleon, Sir Walter Scott, and Burke and Hare in the Chamber of Horrors, the last two having been joined by a succession of notable murderers, including Christie and his kitchen sink. See Life by L. Cottrell (1951).

TUSSER, Thomas (*c.* 1520–*c.* 1580), English writer on agriculture, in Fuller's phrase 'successively a musician, schoolmaster, serving-man, husbandman, grazier, poet, more skilful in all than thriving in any vocation', was born at Rivenhall, Essex. For a time a chorister at St Paul's, he was educated at Eton and Trinity Hall, Cambridge; and after a residence at court as musician to Lord Paget he married and settled as a farmer at Cattawade in Suffolk, where he compiled his famous work, *A Hundreth Good Pointes of Husbandrie* (1557). Tottel published (1573) an enlarged edition, *Five Hundreth Pointes of Good Husbandrie*, with a curious metrical autobiography. Editions are by Mavor (1812), Arber (1873), and the English Dialect Society (1879; reprod. 1931).

TUT-ANKH-AMEN, *toot-ahnk-ah'men*, Egyptian pharaoh of 18th dynasty, the son-in-law of Akhnaton (q.v.), became king at the age of twelve and died at eighteen in *c.* 1340 B.C. His magnificent tomb at Thebes was discovered in 1922 by Lord Carnarvon and Howard Carter. See archaeological studies by the latter and A. C. Mace (1923–33), T. E. Peet, C. L. Woolley, &c. (1923–39) and P. Fox (1951).

TWAIN, Mark, pseud. of **Samuel Langhorne Clemens** (1835–1910), American writer, born at Florida, Mo. A printer first, and afterwards a Mississippi pilot, he adopted his pen-name from a well-known call of the man sounding the river in shallow places ('mark twain' meaning 'by the mark two fathoms'). In 1861 he went to Nevada as secretary to his brother, who was in the service of the governor, and while there tried goldmining without success. He next edited for two years the Virginia City *Enterprise*; in 1864 he moved to San Francisco, and in 1867 he visited France, Italy and Palestine, gathering material for his *Innocents Abroad* (1869), which established his reputation as a humorist. He was afterwards editor of a newspaper at Buffalo, where he married the wealthy Olivia Langdon. Later he moved to Hartford, Conn., and joined a publishing firm which failed, but largely recouped his losses by lecturing and writing. *Roughing It* (1872) is a humorous account of his Nevada experiences, while *The Gilded Age* (1873), a novel which was later dramatized, takes the lid off the readjustment period after the Civil War. His two greatest masterpieces, *Tom Sawyer* (1876) and *Huckleberry Finn* (1884), drawn from his own boyhood experiences, are firmly established among the world's classics; other favourites are *A Tramp Abroad* (1880) and *A Connecticut Yankee in King Arthur's Court* (1889). Mark Twain pokes fun at entrenched institutions and traditions, but his 'debunking' is mostly without malice and his satire is free from bitterness, except in his later work, when fate had been unkind to him. In places his subject-matter is inclined to date, but his best work is not only classic humorous writing but a graphic picture of the 19th-century American scene. See his autobiography (ed. Neider, 1960), and Lives by Paine (1912) and Grant (1962).

TWEED, (1) **John** (1869–1933), Scottish sculptor, was born at Glasgow. Among his principal works are the Cecil Rhodes memorial at Bulawayo, the completion of Stevens's *Duke of Wellington* at St Paul's and *Clive* in Whitehall. See Life by his daughter Lendal Tweed and F. Watson (1936).

(2) **William Marcy** (1823–78), American criminal and politician, one of the most notorious ' bosses ' of the Tammany Society, born in New York, trained as a chair-maker. He became an alderman (1852–53), sat in congress (1853–55), and was repeatedly in the state senate. In 1870 he was made commissioner of public works for the city; and, as head of the ' Tweed Ring ', he controlled its finances. His gigantic frauds exposed in 1871, he was convicted, and, after escaping to Cuba and Spain (1875–76), died in New York jail while suits were pending against him for recovery of $6,000,000. See Life by Lynch (1927).

TWEEDMOUTH, Edward Marjoribanks, 2nd Baron (1849–1909), English Liberal politician, who as first lord of the Admiralty, speeded up British naval construction to keep pace with rival German increases, but was censured for an alleged disclosure of British naval estimates (1908) and resigned.

TWEEDSMUIR. See BUCHAN.

TWISS, Sir Travers (1809–97), English jurist, born in Westminster, became professor of International Law at King's College, London (1852–55), and then of Civil Law at Oxford. In 1867 he became Queen's advocate-general and was knighted. He resigned all his offices in 1872. In 1884 he drew up a constitution for the Congo Free State and in 1885 was legal adviser to the African Conference at Berlin. His *Law of Nations* (1861–63) was long a standard work.

TWORT, Frederick William (1877–1950), English bacteriologist, born at Camberley, Surrey, became professor of Bacteriology in the University of London. He studied Jöhne's disease and methods for the culture of acid-fast leprosy; and in 1915 he discovered the bacteriophage, a virus for attacking certain bacteria.

TWYSDEN, Sir Roger, 2nd Bart. (1597–1672), English antiquary, represented Kent in the Short Parliament but was imprisoned (1643–50) as a royalist, though, having refused to pay ship money, he was not *persona grata* with the court. He wrote the pioneering *Historia Anglicanae Scriptores Decem* (1652).

TYANA, Apollonius of. See APOLLONIUS.

TYARD, or Thiard, Pontus de, *tyahr* (1521–1605), French poet, born at Bissy-sur-Fleys (Saône-et-Loire), belonged to the group of Lyons poets who took Petrarch for their master. Influenced, however, by the work of Ronsard (q.v.), his verse bridges the gap between the Petrarchan style and that of the Pléiade poets. Volumes of poetry include *Erreurs amoureuses* (1549–55), *Le Livre des vers lyriques* (1555) and *Oeuvres poétiques* (1573). He was bishop of Chalon-sur-Saône and wrote also theological and philosophical works, including *Discours philosophiques* (1587).

TYCHO. See BRAHE.

TYE, Christopher (*c.* 1500–73), English musician, musical instructor to Edward VI, received his Mus.D. from Cambridge and Oxford in 1545–48. Under Elizabeth he was organist to the Chapel Royal, and wrote some notable church music.

TYLER, (1) John (1790–1862), tenth president of the United States, was born in Charles City Co., Virginia, and in 1809 was admitted to the bar. Having sat in the state legislature 1811–16, he entered congress. In 1825 he was elected governor of Virginia, and in December 1826 U.S. senator. In the case of the United States Bank he resented the despotic methods by which Jackson overthrew it, supported Clay's motion to censure the president, and, declining to vote for expunging this motion from the minutes, in 1836 resigned his seat. In 1840 he was elected vice-president. President Harrison died in 1841, a month after his inauguration, and Tyler became president. The Whig majority, headed by Clay, regarded his election as a victory for them and for the project of a re-established national bank, but the president's firmness destroyed the project. The Ashburton Treaty and the annexation of Texas in 1845 marked his administration. Adhering to the Confederate cause, he was a member of the Confederate congress until his death, January 18, 1862. See Life by O. P. Chitwood (1939).

(2) **Wat** (d. 1381), English leader of the Peasants' Revolt of 1381. According to the most probable account, the commons of Kent after taking Rochester Castle, chose Wat Tyler of Maidstone as their captain. Under him they moved to Canterbury, Blackheath and London. At the Smithfield conference with Richard II (q.v.) blows were exchanged; William Walworth, mayor of London, wounded Wat, and finding he had been removed to St Bartholomew's Hospital, had him dragged out and beheaded (June 15).

TYLOR, Sir Edward Burnet (1832–1917), English anthropologist, born at Camberwell, travelled with Henry Christy to Mexico. Keeper of the University Museum, Oxford, and reader in Anthropology, he was first professor (1895–1909) of Anthropology. He was knighted in 1912. His chief works are *Primitive Culture* (1871) and *Anthropology* (1881). See Life by R. R. Marett (1936).

TYNAN, Katherine (1861–1931), Irish poet and novelist, born at Clondalkin, County Dublin, friend of Parnell, the Meynells and the Rossettis and a leading author of the Celtic literary revival. She married in 1893 H. A. Hinkson, and wrote volumes of tender, gentle verse, over a hundred novels and five autobiographical works, the last of which was *Memories* (1924). See also Yeats' Letters to her, ed. McHugh (1955).

TYNDALE, Tindale, or Hutchins, William (d. 1536), English translator of the Bible, born probably at Slymbridge in Gloucestershire, was educated at Magdalen Hall, Oxford (1510–15). After a spell at Cambridge he became chaplain and tutor in a household at Little Sodbury in Gloucestershire. His sympathy with the New Learning aroused suspicion and, already a competent Greek scholar, in 1523 he went up to London. Bishop Tunstall having refused support for his translation of the Bible, he went in 1524 to Hamburg, to Wittenberg, where he visited Luther, and in 1525 to Cologne, where he began that year with Quentel the printing of his English New Testament. This had not proceeded beyond the gospels of Matthew and Mark when the intrigues of Cochlaeus forced Tyndale to flee to Worms, where Peter Schoeffer printed for him 3000 New Testaments in small octavo. The translation owed much to Luther and Erasmus, much to his own scholarship and literary skill. Tunstall and Warham denounced the book; hundreds of copies were burned; but it made its way. In 1527 he removed to Marburg to the protection of Philip the Magnanimous; in 1529 he was shipwrecked on the way to Hamburg, where he met Coverdale; in 1531 he went to Antwerp. There probably (ostensibly at Marburg) was published his Pentateuch (1530–31; reprinted 1885), where the marginal glosses, almost all original, contain violent attacks on the pope and the bishops. Here he leans heavily on Luther. In 1531 appeared his version of Jonah, with a prologue (facsimile, 1863). An unauthorized revision of Tyndale's New Testament was made at Antwerp in August 1534, and in November Tyndale himself issued there a revised version. One copy of this work was struck off on vellum for presentation to Anne Boleyn, under whose favour apparently was printed in 1536 by T. Godfray a reprint of Tyndale's revised New Testament—the first volume of Holy Scripture printed in England. Tyndale revised his Testament in 1535, this time without the marginal notes. The emissaries of Henry VIII had often tried to get hold of him, when in 1535 he was seized at Antwerp through the treachery of Henry Philips, a Roman Catholic zealot, imprisoned in the Castle of Vilvorde, tried (1536), and on October 6 was first strangled, then burned. His chief original works were *A Parable of the Wicked Mammon* (1528); *Obedience of a Christian Man*, his most elaborate book (1528); and *Practyse of Prelates* (1530), a pungent polemic. His *Works* were published, with those of Frith and Barnes, in 1573. See Lives by Demaus (revised ed. by Richard Lovett, 1886), J. F. Mozley (1937), and studies by Bone and Greenslade (1938) and W. E. Campbell (1949).

TYNDALL, John (1820–93), Irish physicist, born at Leighlin-Bridge, County Carlow, and largely self-educated, he was employed on the ordnance survey and as a railway engineer, before studying physics in England and in Germany under Bunsen. Elected F.R.S. in 1852, he became professor at the Royal Institution in 1854. In 1856 he and T. H. Huxley (q.v.) visited the Alps and collaborated in *The Glaciers of the Alps* (1860), when he made the first ascent of the Weisshorn. In 1859 he began his researches on heat radiation, followed by the acoustic properties of the atmosphere and the blue colour of the sky, which he suggested was due to the scattering of light by small particles of water. His presidential address to the British Association in 1874 in Belfast was denounced as materialistic. He was a prolific writer on scientific subjects. He died from accidental poisoning with chloral. See Life by Eve and Creasy (1945).

TYRCONNEL, Richard Talbot, 1st Earl of (1630–91), Irish Jacobite leader, came at the Restoration to London, and soon gained the favour of the royal family by a readiness for dirty work. James II created him Earl of Tyrconnel, with command of the troops in Ireland, and in 1687 appointed him lord-deputy of Ireland. He strove to undo the Protestant ascendency, but the Revolution brought his schemes to nought; and he tried in vain to intrigue with William. After the Battle of the Boyne Tyrconnel retired to France till 1691, when he returned as lord-lieutenant, dying of apoplexy soon after the Battle of Aughim. He was created earl (1685) and made titular duke (1689) by the deposed James II.

TYRONE. See O'NEILL (2).

TYRRELL, (1) George (1861–1909), Irish theologian, born in Dublin, became a Roman Catholic in 1879, and a Jesuit in 1880. His 'modernism' led to his expulsion from the Society (1906) and the minor excommunication. His works include *Christianity at the Crossroads* (1909) and *Essays on Faith and Immortality* (1914). See his *Autobiography* (1912) and *Letters* (1920).

(2) **Sir Walter.** See WILLIAM II.

TYRTAEUS, *tær-tee'us* (fl. *c.* 685–668 B.C.), Greek elegiac poet, probably born in Sparta, whose warsongs inspired the Spartans during the second Messenian War. See C. M. Bowra's *Early Greek Elegists* (1938).

TYRWHITT, Thomas, *tir'it* (1730–86), English classical commentator, born in London, was educated at Eton and Queen's College, Oxford, and in 1762 became clerk of the House of Commons, resigning in 1768. He published an edition of the *Canterbury Tales* (2 vols. 1775) and commentaries on classical texts, notably Aristotle's *Poetics* (1794).

TYSON, Edward (1651–1708), English physician, born at Bristol, studied at Magdalen Hall, Oxford, and set up practice in London, lectured in anatomy and was a physician to Bridewell and Bethlehem Hospitals. His papers on comparative anatomy, on the porpoise which he classified as both fish and mammal, on the respiratory and genital organs of the rattlesnake and, with William Cowper, on the female and male opossum, as well as his work on the classification of the male pygmy (1699), marked important advances. See Life by M. F. Ashley Montagu (1943) and F. J. Cole, *History of Comparative Anatomy* (1944).

TYTLER, (1) Alexander Fraser (1747–1813), Scottish historian, son of (3), became in 1780 professor of Universal History at Edinburgh. He was judge advocate of Scotland (1790) and a judge of session (1802) as Lord Woodhouselee.

(2) **Patrick Fraser** (1791–1849), Scottish historian, son of (1), published a critical *History of Scotland 1249–1603* (1828–43), still valuable. See Life by Dean Burgon (1859).

(3) **William,** of Woodhouselee (1711–92), Scottish historian, father of (1), an Edinburgh Writer to the Signet, published an exculpatory *Inquiry into the Evidence against Mary, Queen*

of Scots (1759; 4th ed. 1790), and edited the *Poetical Remains of James I of Scotland* (1783).

TYUCHEV, Fyodor Ivanovich (1803–73), Russian lyric poet, of a noble landowning family, spent 20 years abroad in the diplomatic service and then worked in the censorship department. His first collection of poems appeared in 1854 and was hailed with enthusiasm. A metaphysical romantic, he reached full recognition with the advent of symbolism. The tragic love poems of his later period are outstanding in Russian literature. See D. S. Mirsky, *History of Russian Literature* (1927) and D. Stremooukhov, *La Poésie et l'idéologie de Tiouttchev* (1937).

TZETZES, Johannes, *tset'seez* (*c.* 1120–83), Byzantine author, wrote *Iliaca*; *Biblos Istorike*, or *Chiliades*, a review of Greek literature and learning, a collection (in worthless verse) of over 600 stories; and commentaries.

TZU-HSI, *tsoo-shee'* (1834–1908), empress-dowager of China, became regent for her nephew Kwang-sü in 1875, and was largely responsible for the antiforeign agitation which culminated in the Boxer rising of 1900.

U

UBALDINI, Petruccio, *oo-bal-dee'nee* (*c.* 1524–88), Florentine illuminator on vellum, came to England in 1549, and wrote an Italian version of Boece's Description of Scotland (1588), Lives of English and Scottish Ladies (1591), &c.

UCCELLO, Paolo, *oo-chel'lō* (1397–1475), the name given to the Florentine painter, di Dono, who trained as a goldsmith, applied the principles of perspective to his paintings, sometimes pedantically insisting on vanishing points. In his best-known work, the *Deluge*, his use of perspective and foreshortening gives a sternly realistic effect which becomes modified and more decoratively imaginative in later works such as the three battle paintings in the Uffizi, Florence, the National Gallery and the Louvre. See studies by J. Pope-Hennessy (1950) and P. D'Ancona (1960).

UDALL or Uvedale, *yoo'dėl, oov'dayl*, (1) **John** (1560–92), English Puritan divine, educated at Cambridge, was one of the authors of the Martin Marprelate tracts, was arrested in 1590 and sentenced to death, but pardoned. He was author of a well-known Hebrew grammar (1593) and several volumes of sermons.

(2) **Nicholas** (1504–56), English dramatist, born in Hampshire and educated at Winchester and Corpus Christi College, Oxford, became (*c.* 1534) headmaster of Eton. He published a selection from Terence, *Flowers of Latin Speaking*, for his pupils, who soon learnt of his predilection for corporal punishment. His dismissal in 1541 for indecent offences did not affect his standing at the court. Edward VI appointed him prebendary of Windsor, and despite his great enthusiasm for the Reformation, he survived the reign of Queen Mary without disfavour. He translated Erasmus, selections from the Great Bible and Latin commentaries on the latter, but is chiefly remembered as the author of the rollicking comedy, *Ralph Roister Doister*, written *c.* 1553 but not published until 1567, which, inspired by his favourite classical writers, Plautus and Terence, was to influence later English writers of comedies.

UDET, Ernst, *oo'det* (1896–1941), German airman, born at Frankfurt-am-Main, was a leading German air ace in World War I, and from 1935 worked in the German air ministry. A *Luftwaffe* quartermaster-general in World War II, he committed suicide by an air crash, having fallen foul of the Gestapo. The authorities described his death as an accident while testing a new air weapon. Zuckmayer's play, *The Devil's General*, is based on his life.

UEXKÜLL, Jakob Johann von, *üks'kül* (1864–1944), German biologist, born at Gut Keblas in Estonia in 1864, studied at Dorpat, and became in 1905 professor at Hamburg. From physiological research he developed a vitalistic philosophy in *Theoretische Biologie* (rev. 1928) and other books.

UGOLINO, Count, *oo-gō-lee'nō* (d. 1289), Pisan partisan leader, member of the great Ghibelline house of Gherardesca, with Giovanni Visconti, head of the Guelphic party, laid a plot to secure arbitrary power. The plot was discovered, and they were banished; but Ugolino, allying himself with the Florentines and Lucchese, forced the Pisans in 1276 to restore to him his territories. During the war with the Genoese, in the battle at Malora (1284), Ugolino, by treacherously abandoning the Pisans, occasioned the annihilation of their fleet, with a loss of 11,000 prisoners; but when Florentines and other enemies of the republic gathered together to destroy it, the Pisans had no resource but to throw themselves into his arms. Ugolino now gave free scope to his despotic nature, persecuting and banishing all who were obnoxious to him, till at length a conspiracy was formed against him. Dragged from his palace, July 1, 1288, he was starved to death in the tower of Gualandi, with his two sons and two grandsons. His fate is treated by Dante (*Inferno*, xxxiii).

UHLAND, Johann Ludwig, *oo'lant* (1787–1862), German lyric poet, the leader of the 'Swabian School', was born at Tübingen, where he studied law. He published poems from an early age and gradually added to his *Gedichte* (1815), which contain such popular songs as 'Der gute Kamerad'. He also wrote a number of admirable literary essays. He was a Liberal deputy for Tübingen at the assemblies of Württemberg (1819) and Frankfurt (1848). See Lives by his widow (1874) and H. Schneider (1920).

ULANOVA, Galina, *oo-lahn'ō-va* (1910–), Russian ballerina, studied at the Maryinski Theatre School, and made her début in *Les Sylphides* at the Kirov Theatre in Leningrad in 1928. She became the leading ballerina of the Soviet Union and was four times a Stalin prizewinner. She visited London in 1956 with the Bolshoi Ballet, when she gave a memorable performance in *Giselle*. She has appeared in several films made by the Moscow State Ballet Company and in 1957 was awarded the Lenin prize. See study by Beresovsky, trans. S. Garry and J. Lawson (1952).

ULBRICHT, Walter, *ool'brikht* (1893–1973), East German Communist politician, born in Leipzig. In 1928, after some years in Russia, he became Communist deputy for Potsdam. He left Germany on Hitler's advent in 1933. He went first to Paris and was in Spain during the civil war, but spent the greater part of his exile in Russia. As Marshal Zhukov's political adviser and head of the German Communist party, he came back in 1945, and by 1950 had become deputy premier of the German Democratic Republic. The same year he was made secretary-general of the Party, and was largely responsible for the 'sovietization' of E. Germany. He survived a workers' uprising in 1953 and went on to establish his position. He will be remembered chiefly for building the Berlin wall in 1961. He retired in 1971.

ULFILAS, or **Wulfila,** *ool'fee-las* (*c.* 311–383), Gothic translator of the Bible, was born among the Goths north of the Danube. Consecrated a missionary bishop to his fellow-countrymen by Eusebius of Nicomedia in 341, after seven years' labour he was forced to migrate with his converts across the Danube. For over thirty years he laboured in Lower Moesia, visiting Constantinople in 360 in the interest of the Arian party, and again in 383, only to die a few days after his arrival. See Lives by Waitz (1840), Bessel (1860) and Balg (N.Y. 1891).

ULIANOV. See Lenin.

ULLOA, Antonio de, *ool-yō'a* (1716–95), Spanish statesman and mathematician, born at Seville, twice visited America, and in 1746, having been brought a prisoner to England, was elected F.R.S.

ULPIANUS, Domitius (*c.* A.D. 170–228), Roman jurist, born at Tyre, held judicial offices under Septimius Severus and Caracalla, and, on the accession of Alexander Severus (222), became his principal adviser and *praefectus praetorio*. He was murdered by his own soldiery. He was a voluminous writer. In Justinian's *Digest* there are 2462 excerpts from Ulpian; the originals are almost wholly lost. See Abdy and Walker, *The Commentaries of Gaius and the Rules of Ulpian* (3rd ed. 1885).

ULUGH-BEG, *oo'loog-* (fl. *c.* 1430), grandson of Tamerlane, succeeded in 1447 to the throne. He was a successful warrior, but was defeated and slain (1449) by his rebellious son. He founded the observatory at Samarkand, and was a diligent observer. His astronomical works were partly translated into Latin by Greaves (1650) and Hyde (1665).

ULYANOV. See Lenin.

UMBERTO. See Humbert.

UNAMUNO, Miguel de, *oo-na-moo'nō* (1864–1936), Spanish philosopher and author, born at Bilbao, of Basque parentage, was professor of Greek at Salamanca from 1892. He wrote mystic philosophy, historical studies, brilliant essays, books on travel, and austere poetry. Among his most important works are *Vida de Don Quijote y Sancho* (1905), his novel *Niebla* (1914), *Del sentimiento trágico de la vida* (1913) and a volume of religious poetry, *El Cristo de Velázquez* (1920). From 1924 to 1930 he was exiled as a republican to the island of Fuerteventura, reinstated at Salamanca on the founding of the republic in 1931. But always a rebel and an individualist though with the deepest faith in and interest of his country at heart, he was soon at variance with the Socialist régime. The Civil War for him was a nationalist struggle and he denounced foreign interference. See study by Barea (1952).

UNDERHILL, Evelyn (1875–1941), English poet and mystic, was born in Wolverhampton, educated at King's College, London, married in 1907 Herbert Stuart Moore, a barrister, and became in 1921 lecturer on the Philosophy of Religion at Manchester College, Oxford. A friend and disciple of Hügel (q.v.), she found her way intellectually from agnosticism to Christianity, wrote numerous books on mysticism, including *The Life of the Spirit* (1922), volumes of verse and four novels. Her *Mysticism* (1911) became a standard work. See Life by M. Cropper (1958).

UNDSET, Sigrid, *oon'set* (1882–1949), Norwegian novelist, born in Kalundborg, Denmark. She was the daughter of a noted Norwegian archaeologist, **Ingvald Undset,** from whom she inherited much of her interest in the Middle Ages in Norway. From 1899 she worked in an office, where her experiences and her concern for the problem of young middle-class women were the basis of her early novels, including *Jenny* (1911). Between 1920 and 1922 she produced her masterpiece *Kristin Lavransdatter*, a 14th-century trilogy, which gives a graphic and authentic picture of the period, followed by the series *Olav Audunssön* (four vols. 1925–27). She became a Roman Catholic in 1924, a circumstance that influenced her subsequent work. Most of this had contemporary settings. She was awarded the Nobel prize for literature in 1928. See study by H. A. Larsen, and Life by Winsnes, trans. Foole (1958).

UNGARETTI, Giuseppe, *oong-gar-ret'ti* (1888–1970), Italian poet, born at Alexandria, studied at Paris, was professor of Italian Literature at São Paulo, Brazil (1936–42) and at Rome (1942–58). He is the author of 'hermetic' poems characterized by their symbolism, compressed imagery and modern verse structure.

UNRUH, Fritz von, *oon'roo* (1885–1970), German playwright and novelist, born at Koblenz, served in World War I as a cavalry officer. An ardent pacifist, the ideal of a new humanity underlies all his Expressionist works, particularly the novel *Opfergang* (1916), and the two parts of an unfinished dramatic trilogy, *Ein Geschlecht* (1916) and *Platz* (1920). He left Germany in 1932 and went to the U.S., where he wrote *The End is not Yet* (1947) and *The Saint* (1950). He returned to Germany in 1952.

U NU, *oo-noo* (1907–), Burmese politician and writer, born at Wakema, studied at Rangoon, became a schoolmaster although his real ambition was to be a dramatist. He joined the Thakin Party and founded the Red Dragon Book Society. Imprisoned by the British (1940), he was released by the Japanese and served in Ba Maw's puppet administration but retained the confidence of the anti-Japanese resistance. In 1946 he was elected president of the Burmese Constituent Assembly. After the assassination of the cabinet in July 1947, U Nu became the first prime minister of the now independent Burmese Republic. Splits in his own party, the Anti-Fascist People's Freedom League, were followed by his resignation (1956), re-election (1957), defeat at the polls by General Ne Win, who set up a military government (1958), and victory of his right-wing faction and his return to the premiership (1960). He was overthrown by a military *coup* in 1962, declared a rebel and imprisoned but released in 1966. See autobiographical introduction to his novel, *Man, the Wolf of Man.*

UNVERDORBEN, Otto, *oon-fer-dor'ben* (1806–73), German chemist, born at Dahme, prepared aniline by the distillation of indigo (1826).

UNWIN, (1) Mary. See COWPER, WILLIAM.

(2) Sir Stanley (1884–1968), English publisher, chairman of the firm of George Allen and Unwin, founded in 1914, studied the book-trade in Germany. An international figure in publishing, he was president of the Publishers Association of Great Britain (1933–35) and president of the International Publishers Association (1936–1938, 1946–54). His books include *The Truth about Publishing* (1926; rev. ed. 1960), *Publishing in Peace and War* (1944) and *The Truth about a Publisher* (autobiography; 1960).

URBAIN, Georges, *ür-bī* (1872–1938), French chemist, born in Paris, became professor of Inorganic Chemistry at the Sorbonne (1908), discovered the rare earth lutecium (1907), the law of optimum phosphorescence of binary systems, and showed that several elements which were hitherto considered pure were in fact mixtures.

URBAN, the name of eight popes; the most noteworthy are:

Urban I, bishop of Rome (222–230), said to have been a martyr.

Urban II (1042–99), pope from 1088, born at Châtillon-sur-Marne, France, became cardinal-bishop of Ostia (1078), was elected pope during the schismatical pontificate of Guibert, styled Clement III. He laid Henry IV of Germany under the ban and drove him out of Italy, triumphed by the same means over Philip I of France, and aroused the crusading spirit by his eloquence at the council he held at Piacenza and Clermont (1095).

Urban IV (d. 1264), pope from 1261, born Jacques Pantaléon, the son of a cobbler of Troyes, was bishop of Verdun and patriarch of Jerusalem. He instituted the feast of Corpus Christi (1264).

Urban V (1309–70), pope from 1362, born Guillaume de Grimoard at Grisac, France. He was abbot of St Victor at Marseilles, was elected at Avignon, but set out for Rome in 1367, only to return a few months before his death.

Urban VI (1318–89), pope from 1378, born Bartolomeo Prignano at Naples, became Archbishop of Bari (1377). The French cardinals set up against him the Bishop of Cambray as the antipope Clement VII, beginning the Great Schism in the West.

Urban VIII (1568–1644), pope from 1623, born Maffeo Barberini, in Florence, supported Richelieu's policy against the Hapsburgs, condemned Galileo, canonized Loyola and Philip Neri, and wrote sacred poetry. He carried out much ecclesiastical reform and established his own family in the Roman aristocracy.

URE, Andrew, *yoor* (1778–1857), Scottish chemist, born at Glasgow, studied at the university, became professor of Chemistry and Natural Philosophy in Anderson's College, astronomer in the city observatory, and in 1834 analytical chemist to the Board of Customs in London. F.R.S. in 1822, he produced a *Dictionary of Chemistry* (1821), and other works.

UREY, Harold Clayton (1893–), American chemist, born at Walkerton, Indiana, educated at Montana, California, and Copenhagen, became professor of Chemistry at Columbia (1934) and at Chicago (1945–52). He was director of war research, Atomic Bomb Project, Columbia (1940–45). In 1932 he isolated heavy water and discovered the heavy hydrogen isotope, deuterium, which was of great importance in the development of nuclear fission. He also investigated entropy of gases, absorption spectra and isotopes. He was awarded the Nobel prize in 1934 and the Davy medal of the Royal Society (1940), of which he was elected foreign member (1947).

URFÉ, Honoré d', *ür-fay* (1568–1625), French writer, born at Marseilles, fought in the religious wars of France and later settled in Savoy. He was the author of the pastoral romance, *Astrée* (1610–27), which is regarded as the first French novel. He was killed at Villefranche-sur-mer during the war between Savoy and Genoa.

URQUHART, *ær'kērt,* **(1) David** (1805–77), Scottish diplomatist, born in Cromarty, served in the Greek navy during the Greek War of Independence and received his first diplomatic appointment in 1831, when he went to Constantinople with Sir Stratford Canning. His anti-Russian policy caused his recall from Turkey in 1837 and he was member of parliament for Stafford from 1847 to 1852. A strong opponent of Palmerston's policy, he believed Turkey was capable of dealing with Russia without European intervention. He founded the *Free Press*, afterwards called the *Diplomatic Review*, in which these views were expressed. He retired in 1864. Among his many writings were *The*

Pillars of Hercules (1850), in which he suggested the introduction of Turkish baths into Britain, and *The Lebanon* (1860).

(2) **Sir Thomas** (*c.* 1611–60), Scottish author, born in Cromarty, studied at King's College, Aberdeen, and travelled in France, Spain and Italy. On his return he took up arms against the Covenanting party in the north but was worsted and forced to flee to England. Becoming attached to the court, he was knighted in 1641. The same year he published his *Epigrams Divine and Moral.* On succeeding his father he went abroad. At Cromarty, though much troubled by his creditors, he produced his *Trissotetras; or a most exquisite Table for resolving Triangles, &c.* (1645). In 1649 his library was seized and sold. He again took up arms in the royal cause, and was present at Worcester, where he lost most of his MSS. At London, through Cromwell's influence, he was allowed considerable liberty, and in 1652 published *The Pedigree* and *The Jewel.* The first was an exact account of the Urquhart family, in which they are traced back to Adam; the second is chiefly a panegyric on the Scots nation. In 1653 he issued his *Introduction to the Universal Language* and the first two books of that English classic, his brilliant translation of *Rabelais* (q.v.). The third was not issued till after his death, which is said to have occurred abroad, in a fit of mirth on hearing of the Restoration. His learning was vast, his scholarship defective. Crazy with conceit, he yet evinces a true appreciation of all that is noble, and has many passages of great power. See his *Works* in the Maitland Club series (1834); Willcock's *Sir Thomas Urquhart* (1899); Whibley's Introduction to the *Rabelais* ('Tudor Trans.' 1900); and study by H. Brown (1933).

URSULA, St, a legendary saint and martyr, especially honoured at Cologne, where she is said to have been slain with her 11,000 virgins by a horde of Huns on her journey home from a pilgrimage to Rome. She became the patron saint of many educational institutes, particularly the teaching order of the Ursulines. Her feast day is October 21.

USHER, or **Ussher, James** (1581–1656), Irish divine, was born in Dublin, son of a gentleman of good estate; his uncle, Henry Usher (*c.* 1550–1631), was his predecessor as archbishop of Armagh. He was a scholar (1594) and fellow (1599–1605) of Trinity College, Dublin. About 1606 he became chancellor of St Patrick's, in 1607 professor of Divinity, in 1620 Bishop of Meath, in 1623 privy councillor for Ireland, and in 1625 Archbishop of Armagh. He left Ireland for England in 1640, continued to live in England, declined to sit in the Westminster Assembly, and for about eight years was preacher at Lincoln's Inn. He was constant in his loyalty to the throne, yet was treated with favour by Cromwell, and was buried in Westminster Abbey. He was distinguished not only by his learning but also by his charity and sweetness of temper. He was Calvinistic in theology and moderate in his ideas of church government. Of his numerous writings, the greatest is the *Annales Veteris et Novi Testamenti* (1650–54), which gave us the long-accepted chronology of Scripture, the Creation being fixed at 4004 B.C. Amongst his other works, the *De Graeca Septuaginta Interpretum Versione Syntagma* (1655) was the first attempt at a real examination of the Septuagint. His complete writings were edited by Elrington and Todd (17 vols. 1841–64). See the Life prefixed thereto by Carr (1895), and W. Ball Wright's *The Ussher Memoirs* (1889).

USPENSKI, Gleb Ivanovich, *oo-spyen'skee* (*c.* 1840–1902), Russian author of novels of peasant life, such as *Power of the Soil* (1882), notable for their realism as opposed to the prevalent romantic conception of the agricultural worker. He died insane. See D. S. Mirsky, *History of Soviet Literature* (1927).

USTINOV, Peter Alexander, *yoo'stin-of* (1921–), English actor and dramatist, born in London. The son of White Russian parents, Ustinov first appeared on the stage in 1938, and had established himself as an accomplished artist both in revues and legitimate drama by 1942, when four years' army service interrupted his career. His subsequent work for films as actor, writer and producer, and in broadcasting as a satirical comedian, has enhanced his reputation. A prolific playwright, his works—most successful amongst which are *The Love of Four Colonels* (1951) and *Romanoff and Juliet* (1956)—are marked by a serious approach to human problems often presented with an acute sense of comedy and a mastery of unconventional stagecraft.

UTRILLO, Maurice, *oo-tree'lo* (1883–1955), French painter, born in Montmartre, Paris, the son of the painter Suzanne Valadon (q.v.), was adopted by the Spanish writer Miguel Utrillo. He began to paint at Montmagny in 1902, but it was the streets of Paris, particularly old Montmartre, and village scenes which were to provide him with most of his subjects. Despite acute alcoholism, and consequent sojourns in various nursing-homes, his productivity was astonishing, and by 1925 he was famous. His 'White Period' paintings of about 1908–14 are much sought after, for their subtle colouring and sensitive feeling for atmosphere. He signed his work 'Maurice Utrillo V', incorporating the initial of his mother's family name. See studies by G. Charenson (1929), F. Jourdan (1948), G. Ribemont-Dessaignes (1948) and W. George (1960).

V

VACHELL, Horace Annesley, *vay'chĕl* (1861–1955), English novelist, great-grandson of the first Lord Lyttelton (q.v.), born at Sydenham, was educated at Harrow and Sandhurst and from 1883 until the death of his American wife in 1899 lived in the United States. He is best known for his school story about Harrow, *The Hill* (1905), and *Quinneys* (1914). He also wrote plays, three autobiographical works, of which the last was his *Methuselah* memoirs (1951) and a volume of essays, *Quests* (1945).

VACHEROT, Étienne, *vash-rō* (1809–97), French philosopher, born at Langres, was appointed professor of Philosophy at the Sorbonne in 1839, but was dismissed in 1852 when he refused to sign the oath of allegiance to the Empire. His anti-clericalism and the publication of his book, *La Démocratie*, caused his imprisonment in 1859. In 1871 he was elected to the Assembly. Other writings include *La Métaphysique et la Science* (1858) and *La Religion* (1868).

VAIHINGER, Hans, *fī'-* (1852–1933), German philosopher, born in Württemberg, professor at Halle (1884–1906), wrote a remarkable commentary to Kant's *Critique of Pure Reason* (1881–92) and developed the idealist positivism of Lange in *The Philosophy of 'As If'* (1911; trans. C. K. Ogden, 1924). See his autobiography in *Philosophie in Selbstdarstellungen*, Vol. 2 (1921).

VALADON, Suzanne, *va-la-dõ* (1869–1938), French painter, mother of Utrillo (q.v.), became an artist's model after an accident ended her career as an acrobat, modelling for Renoir and others. With the encouragement of Toulouse-Lautrec, Degas and Cézanne, she took up painting herself and excelled in her realistic treatment of nudes, portraits and figure studies, her work having some affinity with that of Degas. Two of her flower pieces are in the Luxembourg. See Life by J. Storm (1959).

VALBERT, G. See CHERBULIEZ.

VALDÉS, *vahl'days,* **(1) Armando Palacio** (1853–1938), Spanish novelist, born at Entralgo in Asturias. Some of his novels were translated as *The Marquis of Peñalba*, *Maximina*, *Sister Saint Sulpice*, *Froth* and *The Grandee*.

(2) **Juan de** (1500–41), Spanish religious reformer, born in Cuenca, became an object of suspicion to the Inquisition, and lived in Naples from 1534. But he sought the regeneration of the Church from within, and never inclined to Lutheranism. Among his works are *The Christian Alphabet* (1536) and Commentaries, some of them translated into English (1865–83). See monographs by Stern (1869) and Carrasco (1880), and Life by Wiffen prefixed to his translation of Valdés' *CX Considerations* (1865).

VALDIVIA, Pedro de, *vahl-dee'vya* (*c.* 1510–1559), Spanish soldier, born near La Serena, Estremadura, went to Venezuela (*c.* 1534) and then to Peru, where he became Pizarro's (q.v.) lieutenant. He won renown at Las Salinas (1538), and was in real command of the expedition to Chile. He founded Santiago (1541) and other cities. In 1559, attempting, with a small force, to relieve Tucapel, which was besieged by the Araucanians, he was captured and killed by the Indians. See study by R. B. Cunninghame Graham (1926).

VALENTINIAN, the name of three Roman Emperors:

Valentinian I (321–375), born at Cibalis in Pannonia, rose rapidly in rank under Constantius and Julian, and on the death of Jovian was chosen as his successor (364). He resigned the East to his brother Valens, and himself governed the West with watchful care until his death.

Valentinian II, his second son (372–392), received from his elder brother, Gratianus (q.v.), the provinces of Italy, Illyricum and Africa. During his minority the Empress Justina administered the government; about three years after her death Valentinian was murdered, probably by Arbogastes, commander-in-chief of his army.

Valentinian III (*c.* 419–455), grand-nephew of II, the son of Constantius III, was given the Western empire by Theodosius II, emperor of the East, in 425. A weak and contemptible prince, he never really ruled during his thirty years' reign; his mother, Placidia, governed till her death (450), and then the eunuch, Heraclius. Valentinian's treatment of Bonifacius made him throw himself into the arms of the Vandal, Genseric (q.v.), and thus lost Africa to the empire. He stabbed Aetius (q.v.) to death (454), but next year was himself slain by Maximus, whose wife he had ravished.

VALENTINO, Rudolph, *-tee'-* (1895–1926), Italian-born American film actor, born Rodolpho Alphonso Guglielmi di Valentina d'Antonguolla at Castellaneta, studied agriculture but emigrated to the United States and first appeared on the stage as a dancer. In 1919 he made his screen début as Julio in *The Four Horsemen of the Apocalypse*, and his subsequent performances in *The Sheikh* (1921), *Blood and Sand* (1922), *The Young Rajah* (1922), *Monsieur Beaucaire* (1924), *The Eagle* (1925) and *The Son of the Sheikh* (1926) established him as the leading 'screen lover' of the 'twenties. He died suddenly at the height of his adoration in New York and his funeral resembled that of a popular ruler. Besides good looks and athletic bearing he had considerable dramatic gifts. He wrote *Daydreams* (1923), a book of poems. See Lives by his second wife, N. Rambova (1927), and S. G. Ullman (1927).

VALERA, (1). See DE VALERA.

(2) **Don Juan,** *vah-lay'ra* (1824–1905), Spanish novelist and critic, born at Cabra in Córdoba, held diplomatic posts in Europe and U.S.A., and was a deputy, minister of commerce, minister of public instruction, councillor of state, senator, and member of

the Spanish Academy. His literary studies (1864) and essays (1882) brought him reputation; but his fame depends on his romances, *Pepita Jiménez* (1874; trans. 1891), *Las ilusiones del Doctor Faustino* (1876), *El comendador Mendoza* (1877; trans. 1893), *Doña Luz* (1878; trans. 1892) and *La buena fama* (1895).

VALERIANUS, Publius Licinius (*c.* 193–260), was proclaimed Roman emperor by the legions in Rhaetia after the murder of Gallus (253), and assumed as colleague his eldest son, Gallienus. Throughout his reign trouble hovered on every frontier of the empire; and marching against the Persians, he was completely defeated at Edessa (260). He was seized by King Sapor, and, imprisoned until his death, suffered every oriental cruelty.

VALERIUS FLACCUS. See FLACCUS.

VALERIUS MAXIMUS (fl. A.D. 14–30), Roman historian, wrote *c.* A.D. 29 historical anecdotes, biased in favour of the emperor Tiberius.

VALÉRY, Paul Ambroise, *va-lay-ree* (1871–1945), French poet and writer, born at Cette, settled in Paris in 1892 and after publishing some remarkable Mallarméesque verse, he relapsed into a twenty years' silence, taken up with mathematics and philosophical speculations. He emerged in 1917 with a new poetic outlook and technique in *La Jeune Parque* (1917), a poem full of difficult symbolism, because of the dualism it enveloped—emotion against reason, life against death, being against doing, consciousness against the world of facts and things. This was followed by a remarkable collection, *Charmes* (1922), containing *Le Cimetière marin*, recalling in treatment and metre Gray's *Elegy*, *L'Ébauche d'un serpent*, *Au platane*, &c., remarkable for the poetic shorthand, the compression and conciseness of his imagery and ideas. His prose works comprise *Soirée avec M. Teste* (1895), in which intelligence personified by M. Teste watches itself at work, records its 'inner' experience and several aesthetic studies, as the dialogue *Eupalinos* (1924), in which architecture and music are compared, and *L'Âme et la danse* (1924). A late, short play, *Le Solitaire*, foreshadows Samuel Beckett. See studies by A. R. Chisholm (1938), Sewell (1952), Suckling (1954), H. Mondor (Paris 1957), and introduction by T. S. Eliot to Vol. VII of the *Collected Works*, trans. by D. Folliot (1959).

VALETTE, Jean Parisot de la (1494–1568), French knight of St John, nobly born at Toulouse, became Grand Master in 1557. His exploits against the Turks culminated in his successful defence of Malta, from May 18 till September 8, 1565. He founded the city of Valetta.

VALLA, Laurentius (*c.* 1405–57), Italian humanist, born at Rome, taught the classics at Pavia, Milan and Naples, incurred many enmities, but in 1435 found a protector at Naples in Alfonso V. He was expelled from Rome for attacking the temporal power in his *De Donatione Constantini Magni*, was prosecuted by the Inquisition in Naples, but in 1448 was again in Rome as apostolic secretary to Nicholas V. His Latin versions of Xenophon, Herodotus and Thucydides were admirable; and he greatly advanced New Testament criticism by his comparison of the Vulgate with the Greek original. His *De Elegantia Latinae Linguae* was long a textbook. See works by Mancini (1891), Wolff (1893) and Schwabe (1896).

VALLE-INCLÁN, Ramón María del, *val'yay-eeng-klahn* (1869–1936), Spanish novelist, dramatist and poet, was born at Puebla de Caramiñal. Among his works are four *Sonatas* on the seasons (1902–07), written in fine prose in the form of novels, a graphic but erroneous history *La guerra carlista* and the masterly *Águila de blasón* (1907) and *Romance de Lobos* (1908), set in a vivid mediaeval background. Many of his novels and plays are collected in *Esperpentos* and among several volumes of fine verse is his *Cara de Plata* (1923).

VALLIÈRE. See LA VALLIÈRE.

VALLISNIERI, Antonio, *val-lees-nyay'ree* (1661–1730), Italian naturalist, born at Modena, became professor of Medicine at Padua, made important studies of the reproductive systems of insects, and wrote treatises on the ostrich (1712) and the chameleon (1715). The waterweed *Vallisneria spiralis* is named after him.

VALLOTTON, Felix, *va-lō-tõ* (1865–1925), Swiss painter, born at Lausanne, studied the graphic arts in Paris and excelled in the woodcut, but later took to painting. At first a member of the 'Nabis', the symbolist movement, he later pioneered an extreme expressionist realism, inspired by his woodcuts and transferred to his oil painting.

VALOIS, Dame Ninette de, *val-wah*, stage-name of **Edris Stannus** (1898–), British ballerina, born in Ireland. She studied under Cecchetti, and first appeared, in 1914, in the pantomime at the Lyceum Theatre; she subsequently appeared with the Beecham Opera Company and at Covent Garden. After a European tour with Diaghilev (1923–1925), she partnered Anton Dolin in England, and became director of Ballet at the Abbey Theatre, Dublin. In 1931 she founded the Sadler's Wells Ballet School and became artistic director of the company. In 1935 she married Dr A. B. Connell. She organized the National Ballet school of Turkey (1947) and was created D.B.E. in 1951. She wrote *Invitation to the Ballet* (1937) and her autobiography, *Come Dance with Me* (1957). Her choreographic works include *The Rake's Progress*, *Checkmate* and *Don Quixote*.

VÁMBÉRY, Arminius, *vam'bay-ree* (1832–1913), Hungarian traveller and philologist, born at Duna-Szerdahely, Hungary, at twelve was apprenticed to a ladies' dressmaker, but afterwards took to teaching, and struggled to support himself. A desire for Eastern travel led him to Constantinople, where he taught French in the house of a minister, and in 1858 issued a German-Turkish dictionary. Having travelled in 1862–64 in the disguise of a dervish through the deserts of the Oxus to Khiva and Samarkand, he wrote *Travels and Adventures in Central Asia* (1864). In his writings and lectures Vámbéry supported the claim that

Britain's rule in the East was most beneficent. Professor of Oriental Languages in Budapest till 1905, he published works on the Eastern Turkish and Tatar languages, the ethnography of the Turks, the origin of the Magyars, and on many other oriental subjects. See his autobiography (1883) and *Story of My Struggles* (1904).

VANBRUGH, *van'brœ*, (1) **Dame Irene** (1872–1949), English actress, sister of (3), born in Exeter, was trained by Sarah Thorne and made her first appearance at Margate as Phoebe in *As You Like It* (1888). She married Dion Boucicault the younger, in 1901, and acted with Tree, Alexander, Hare and Frohman, winning a reputation as an interpreter of Pinero and Barrie heroines. She was created D.B.E. in 1941. She shared with her sister the family height, dark expressive eyes, magnificent presence and tremendous charm.

(2) **Sir John** (1664–1726), English playwright and baroque architect, the grandson of a Protestant refugee from Ghent, was educated in France, commissioned into Lord Huntingdon's regiment and suffered imprisonment in the Bastille (1690–92). A staunch Whig, he became a leading spirit in society life and scored a success with his first comedy, *The Relapse* (1696), followed, again with applause, by *The Provok'd Wife* (1697). *The Confederacy* (1705) was put on in the Haymarket, where Congreve and Vanbrugh joined together as theatre managers. A natural playwright of the uninhibited Restoration comedy of manners period, Vanbrugh also achieved success as architect of Castle Howard (1702) and in 1705 was commissioned to design Blenheim Palace at Woodstock. The immense baroque structure aroused the ridicule of Swift and Pope, and the Duchess of Marlborough disliked the plans and especially its enormous cost so much that she long refused to pay Vanbrugh. He was made comptroller of royal works in 1714, was knighted and was Clarencieux king-of-arms (1705–25). See *Complete Works*, ed. B. Dobrée and C. Webb (1928), and study by L. Whistler (1938).

(3) **Violet Augusta Mary** (1867–1942), English actress, sister of (1), born in Exeter. She first appeared in burlesque in 1886 and two years later played Ophelia at Margate, where she had been trained by Sarah Thorne. She then joined the Kendals for their American tour and on her return played Ann Boleyn in Irving's production of *Henry VIII*, also understudying Ellen Terry. She married Arthur Bourchier in 1894 and enhanced many of his successes with her elegance and ability.

VAN—those not listed below may be found under their respective surnames.

VAN BUREN, Martin (1782–1862), eighth president of the United States, born at Kinderhook, N.Y., was called to the bar in 1803. In 1812 and 1816 he was elected to the state senate, and in 1816–19 was state attorney-general. In 1821 he entered the U.S. senate as a Republican and was elected governor of New York in 1828. He supported Jackson for the presidency, and in 1829 became secretary of state. In 1832 he was elected vice-president, and in 1836 president, but by a popular majority of less than 25,000, largely owing to his opposition to the 'slightest interference' with slavery. His four years of office were darkened by financial panic; but he did what he could to lighten it by forcing a measure for a treasury independent of private banks. He was strictly neutral during the Canadian rebellion of 1837. In 1840 his party were overwhelmingly defeated by the Whigs. See Lives by W. L. Mackenzie (1846), E. M. Shepard (1888), G. Bancroft (1889), D. T. Lynch (1929).

VANCOUVER, George (*c.* 1758–98), English navigator and explorer, sailed with Cook (q.v.) on his second and third voyages and, promoted captain (1794), did survey work in Australia, New Zealand and the West coast of N. America, sailing round Vancouver Island (1795). See his *Voyage* (1798), and Life by G. Godwin (1930).

VANDAMME, Dominique Joseph, *-dahm* (1770–1830), French soldier, born at Cassel in Nord, in 1799 fought at Austerlitz, in 1806–07 reduced Silesia, but was defeated and taken prisoner at Kulm in 1813. He held a command during the Hundred Days, after the second Restoration was exiled, but returned from America in 1824. See Life by Du Casse (1870).

VANDENBERG, Arthur Hendrick (1884–1951), United States Republican senator, born in Grand Rapids, Michigan, studied at the university there and was elected to the senate (1928). An isolationist before World War II, he strongly supported the formation of U.N.O., was delegate to the San Francisco conference and to the U.N. Assembly from 1946.

VANDERBILT, Cornelius (1794–1877), American financier, born on Staten Island, New York, at sixteen bought a boat and ferried passengers and goods. By forty he had become the owner of steamers running to Boston and up the Hudson; in 1849, during the gold rush, he established a route by Lake Nicaragua to California, and during the Crimean war a line of steamships to Havre. At seventy he entered on a great career of railroad financing, gradually obtaining a controlling interest in a large number of roads. He gave $1,000,000 to found Vanderbilt University at Nashville. **William Henry** (1821–85), his eldest son, greatly extended the Vanderbilt system of railways. **Cornelius** (1843–99), left some £25,000,000. See Croffut, *The Vanderbilts* (1886), and Life by A. D. Howden Smith (1928).

VAN DER GOES, Hugo, KH*oos* (*c.* 1440–82), Flemish painter, born probably at Ghent, was dean of the painters' guild at Ghent (1473–75) and died insane in a Soignies monastery. His large and dramatic *Portinari Altarpiece* is in the Uffizi and the Stuart triptych has been ascribed to him.

VAN DE VELDE, *-vel'dė*, (1) **Henri** (1863–1957), Belgian architect, born at Antwerp, began as a painter before pioneering the modern functional style of architecture. He established the famous Weimar School of Arts and Crafts (1906) from which the *Bauhaus* sprang. Gropius (q.v.) was his pupil. See his *Vom Neuen Stil* (1907) and *Le Nouveau* (1929).

(2) **Willem, the Elder** (*c.* 1611–93), Dutch marine painter, father of (3), born at Leyden, came in 1657 to England and painted large pictures of sea battles in indian ink and black paint for Charles II and James II.

(3) **Willem, the Younger** (1633–1707), the greatest of Dutch marine painters, son of (2), born at Leyden, followed his father to England and became court painter to Charles II in 1674. Smith catalogues 330 of his paintings. His brother, **Adriaen** (1636–1672), was a landscape painter. See E. Michel's family study (1892) and introduction to a catalogue of their drawings compiled by M. S. Robinson (1958).

VAN DIEMEN. See TASMAN.

VAN DOREN, (1) **Carl Clinton** (1885–1950), American critic and biographer, brother of (2), born at Hope, Illinois, studied at the state university and at Columbia, where he lectured in English Literature (1911–30). He was literary editor of the *Nation* (1919–22), of the *Century Magazine* (1922–25) and of the *Cambridge History of American Literature* (1917–21). He was also a distinguished biographer of Thomas Love Peacock (1911), Cabell (1925), Swift (1930), Sinclair Lewis (1933) and Benjamin Franklin (1938), which last work won the Pulitzer prize (1939). He edited Franklin's *Letters and Papers* (1947), and critical studies include *The American Novel* (1921) and with (2), *American and British Literature since 1890* (1925). He also wrote *The Ninth Wave* (1926), a novel, and his autobiography, *Three Worlds* (1936). His first wife (divorced), **Irita Bradford** (1891–1967), was also an editor.

(2) **Mark Albert** (1894–), American poet and critic, brother of (1), was born at Hope, Illinois, studied at the state university and at Columbia, where he became professor of English. He served in the army during World War I, succeeded (1) to the editorship of the *Nation* (1924–28) and was awarded the Pulitzer prize (1940) for his *Collected Poems* (1939) chosen from such volumes of verse as *Spring Thunder* (1924), *Now the Sky* (1928), &c. Later volumes include *The Mayfield Deer* (1941), *The Country Year* (1946), *New Poems* (1948) and *Spring Birth* (1953). He collaborated with (1) in *American and British Literature Since 1890* (1925), edited the *Oxford Book of American Prose*, wrote critical studies of Thoreau (1916), Dryden (1920), Shakespeare (1939) and Hawthorne (1949), and the novels *Transients* (1935) and *Windless Cabins* (1940). His wife, **Dorothy Graffe** (1896–), was also novelist and editor.

VAN DYCK, Sir Anthony, *-dik* (1599–1641), Flemish painter, one of the great masters of portraiture of the 17th century, was born March 22 at Antwerp, the son of a cloth manufacturer. He studied painting under H. van Balen and Rubens, and many of his early paintings have been attributed to the latter, who greatly influenced his style. In 1618 he was admitted a master of the Guild of St Luke at Antwerp and in 1620 commissioned to paint the Lady Arundel (Pinakothek, Munich). He visited England, and records show that he also executed a full-length portrait of James I at Windsor. From 1621 he was in Italy. At Genoa he painted a number of portraits, two of which, that of the *Lomellini* family and the *Knight in Black Armour*, are in the National Gallery, Edinburgh. In Rome, he painted religious subjects including an *Ascension* and an *Adoration of the Magi* for the pope, but in this field he did not rival his Italian contemporaries. By 1627 he was back in Antwerp, where he painted the *Ecstasy of St Augustine* for the monastery there, *Christ Crucified between Thieves* for the church of the Récollets at Mechlin, later transferred to the cathedral, and the portraits of Philippe Le Roy and his wife (Wallace, London). His fine draughtsmanship is apparent in the heads he etched for his *Iconographia* (1641; British Museum). At The Hague he painted the Prince of Orange and his family. In 1632 he came to London, was knighted by Charles I, who made him a painter-in-ordinary with a pension of £200 to induce him to stay. Back in Holland on leave (1634–35), he painted Ferdinand of Austria (Madrid) and *The Deposition* (Antwerp). His flair for, and psychological accuracy in, rendering the character of his sitters, always with a hint of flattery and in the most favourable settings, greatly influenced the great British school of portraiture in the next century and imparted to posterity a thoroughly romantic glimpse of the Stuart monarchy. Among the best of these portraits are the large group of Charles I, Queen Henrietta Maria and the two royal children, the equestrian portrait of the king, the three aspects of the king (1637) to serve as a model for Bernini's sculpture (all at Windsor) and the magnificent *Le Roi à la chasse* (Louvre). There is a remarkable self-portrait in the Uffizi, Florence, a full-length of Henrietta Maria (Hermitage, Stalingrad) and portraits of most of the notables of the time, including Strafford and Archbishop Laud. In 1639 he married Mary Ruthven, a granddaughter of the Earl of Gowrie. His scheme for decorating the banqueting hall in Whitehall with scenes from the history of the Order of the Garter was turned down and he failed to obtain the commission for the decoration of the gallery of the Louvre, which went to Poussin. An amorous, extravagant courtier, he died in his studio at Blackfriars, December 9, 1641, and was buried in Old St Paul's. See studies by L. Cust (1900 and 1902), on the etchings F. Newbolt (1906), E. Schaeffer (1909), A. M. Hind (1923), H. Knackfuss (1923), A. L. Mayer (1923) and G. Glück (1931).

VAN DYKE, Henry (1852–1933), American clergyman and writer, born at Germantown, Pa., studied theology at Princeton and Berlin and was a prominent pastor of the Brick Presbyterian Church, New York (1883–1890). He was professor of English Literature at Princeton (1900–23), and under Woodrow Wilson, American minister to the Netherlands (1913–16). He was awarded the Legion of Honour for his services as naval chaplain in World War I. His many writings include poems, essays and short stories, mostly on religious themes, such as the Christmas tale *The Story of the other Wise Man, The Ruling Passion* (1901), *The Blue Flower* (1902), *The Unknown Quantity* (1912) and *Collected Poems* (1911). His brother **Paul** (1859–1933) was professor of History at Princeton (1898–1928).

VANE, Sir Henry (1613–62), English statesman, was born at Hadlow, Kent. His father 'Old Sir Henry' (1589–1654), was a bustling and time-serving statesman, who rose to be principal secretary of state, but who, having, with his son, been a chief agent in Strafford's destruction, was deprived of his offices, and sided thereafter with the triumphant party. Passing in 1628 from Westminster to Magdalen Hall, Oxford, 'Young Sir Henry' seems there to have embraced those republican principles for which he afterwards became so famous. His travels to Vienna and Geneva (1631) confirmed his aversion to the Church of England, and in 1635 he sailed for New England. He was chosen governor of Massachusetts; but his advocacy of toleration, and bias to the Antinomian views of Anne Hutchinson (q.v.), soon robbed him of his popularity, and in 1637 he returned to England. In 1640 he entered parliament for Hull, was made joint treasurer of the navy, and was knighted (1640). When the Civil War broke out no man was more conspicuous in military and theological politics than Vane, the close friend of Pym and Hampden. He relinquished the profits of his office (equivalent now to £30,000 per annum); he carried to the Upper House the articles of impeachment against Laud; he was a 'great promoter of the Solemn League and Covenant' (though in his heart he abhorred both it and presbytery, and used them solely to attain his ends); with Cromwell he engineered the Self-denying Ordinance and the New Model (1644–45); and through the ten years 1643–53 he was unmistakably the civil leader—'that in the state', said his enemy Baxter, 'which Cromwell was in the field'. But he had no share in the execution of the king, and, though a close friend of Cromwell, he did not view with satisfaction the growing power of Cromwell and the army. On the establishment of the Commonwealth he was appointed one of the Council of State; but it was largely Cromwell's dislike of his redistribution bill (1653) that prompted the dissolution of the 'Rump'. Retiring to his Durham seat, Raby Castle, he wrote his *Healing Question* (1656), whose hostility to the protectorate brought him four months' imprisonment in Carisbrooke Castle. On Cromwell's death he returned to public life, but in the July following the Restoration was arrested and sent to the Tower. Thence he was taken to the Scilly Islands, brought back to be tried for high treason, and on June 14, 1662, beheaded upon Tower Hill. His youngest son was raised to the peerage by William III. Vane was a singular compound of high-minded, far-seeing statesman and fanatical Fifth Monarchist. See Lives by Sikes (1662), Upham (1835), Forster (1840), Hosmer, Ireland (1907), Willcock (1913).

VAN GOGH, Vincent Willem, *go*KH (1853–1890), Dutch post-Impressionist painter, born March 30 at Groot-Zundert, the son of a Lutheran pastor. At sixteen he became an assistant (1869–76) with Goupil and Co., the international firm of art-dealers in their shops in The Hague, London and Paris. An unrequited love affair with an English schoolmistress accentuated his inferiority complex and religious passion. He became an assistant master at Ramsgate and Isleworth (1876) and there trained unsuccessfully to become a Methodist preacher. His family rescued him from despair as a bookshop assistant at Dortrecht and provided him with tuition for the university entrance examination (1877–78), which he finally never sat. He became instead an evangelist for a religious society requiring no academic qualifications at the Belgian coalmining centre of Le Borinage (1878–80), where, first as a resident, later as an itinerant preacher, he practised the Christian virtues with such zeal, sleeping on the floor of a derelict hut and giving away his possessions, that his society became alarmed at his lack of dignity, the mine-owners at his support for strikers, and the miners mocked him for his confessions in public. In April 1881 he at last set off for Brussels to study art, but another unfortunate love affair, this time with a cousin, threw him off balance and he eventually settled at The Hague, where he lived with his model Christien or 'Sien', a prostitute, whom he chivalrously insisted on marrying when he found her to be pregnant by another man. She appears in the drawing *Sorrow* (1882; Stedelijk, Amsterdam) and *Sien Posing* (1883; Kröller-Müller, Otterlo), but proved a worthless wife. Convalescing at Drenthe from malnutrition and general neglect, Van Gogh became the object of love of another woman, whom he rejected and who tried to commit suicide. In his father's new parish at Nuenen he painted that dark, haunting, domestic scene of peasant poverty, *The Potato Eaters* (1885), his first masterpiece, and *Boots*, both in the Stedelijk, Amsterdam. His devoted brother, Théo, now an art dealer, made it possible to continue his studies in Paris (1886–88) under Cormon, and there he met Gauguin, Toulouse-Lautrec, Seurat and the famous art-collector Tanguy, who is the subject, surrounded by Japanese woodcuts, of one of Van Gogh's remarkable portraits (1887–88; Rodin, Paris). These new influences brightened his palette and on Lautrec's advice he left Paris in February 1888 to seek the intense colours of the Provençal landscape at Arles, the subject of many of his best works. There also he painted *Sunflowers* (1888; Tate, London), *The Bridge* (1888; Cologne), *The Chair and the Pipe* (1888; Tate, London) and invited Gauguin to found a community of artists. Gauguin's stay ended in a tragic quarrel in which Van Gogh in remorse for having threatened the other with a razor, cut off his own ear and was placed in an asylum at St Rémy (1889–90). There he painted the grounds, the *Ravine* (1889; Kröller-Müller Hoenderlo) with increasingly frantic brushstrokes, the keeper and the physician. In May 1890 he went to live at Auvers-sur-Oise near Paris, under the supervision of a physician, *Dr Paul Gachet* (1890; N.Y.), himself an amateur painter and engraver. That year an exhaustive article appeared by A. Aurier which at last brought Van Gogh some recognition. But on July 27, 1890, Van Gogh shot himself at the scene of his last painting, the foreboding *Cornfields with Flight of Birds* (Stedelijk, Amsterdam), and died two days later. Théo, deeply shocked at the news, followed his brother to the grave within six months. Van Gogh was one of the pioneers of Expressionism. He used colour primarily for its emotive appeal and profoundly influenced the Fauves and other experimenters of 20th-century art. See his *Complete Letters* (1958), E. du Q. Van Gogh, *Personal Recollections* (trans. 1913), Lives by J. Meier-Graefe (trans. 1927), P. Burra (trans. 1934), C. Nordenfalk (1953), L. and E. Hanson (1955), studies by J. de Laprade (1953), D. Cooper (1955), F. Elgar (1958), and I. Stone, *Lust for Life*, the popular novel (1935) and film (1957).

VAN GOYEN, Jan Josephszoon (1596–1656), Dutch painter, was born at Leyden. He produced many sea and river pieces in soft browns and greys, and, unusually for his time, omitted small details and developed a broad atmospheric effect. Jan Steen, who became his son-in-law, was one of his pupils. His *River Scene* (*c.* 1645) is in the National Gallery, London.

VANHOMRIGH, Esther. See SWIFT.

VANINI, Lucilio, *van-ee'nee* (1585–1619), Italian freethinker, born at Taurisano, studied the new learning and science at Naples and Padua, and took orders, but his 'Naturalist' views soon brought him into collision with the church. Having taught in France, Switzerland and the Low Countries, he had to flee in 1614 to England, where he was again imprisoned. Finally, at Toulouse, having first had his tongue cut out, he was strangled and burned. From his *Amphitheatrum Aeternae Providentiae* (1615) and his *De Admirandis Naturae Arcanis* (1616) it is plain that, if not an atheist, he taught pantheism of an extreme type. He was more notable for vanity and audacity than for learning or originality. See monographs by Fuhrmann (Leipzig 1800), Vaisse (Paris 1871), and Palumbo (Naples 1878), and John Owen, *Skeptics of the Italian Renaissance* (1893).

VANLOO, *-lō'*, (1) **Jean Baptiste** (1684–1745), French painter, brother of (2), born at Aix-en-Provence of Flemish parentage, studied in Rome and became a fashionable portrait painter in Paris, being admitted a member of the Academy (1731) and appointed professor of Painting (1735). In 1737 he visited England, where he painted the actor Colley Cibber, the Prince and Princess of Wales and Sir Robert Walpole.

(2) **Charles André** (1705–65), French painter, brother of (1), born at Nice, likewise studied at Rome and settled as portrait painter in Paris but executed also some sculpture. He became chief painter to Louis XV and member of the Academy (1735). His vigorous, colourful majestic style gave rise to a new French verb 'vanlooter'. He painted Diderot, Helvétius and most of the celebrities of his day.

VAN LOON, Hendrik Willem, *lōn* (1882–1944), Dutch-born American popular historian, born in Rotterdam, emigrated to the United States in 1903 as a journalist and history teacher and in 1922 published the best selling, illustrated *Story of Mankind*, and from then onwards produced a number of popular histories.

VAN MEEGEREN, Han or Henricus, *may'gėr-ėn* (1889–1947), Dutch artist and forger, was born at Deventer. In 1945 he was accused of selling art treasures to the Germans. To clear himself, he confessed to having forged the pictures, and also the famous *Supper at Emmaus*, 'discovered' in 1937, and accepted by the majority of experts as by Vermeer. His fakes were subjected to a detailed scientific examination, and in 1947 their maker was sentenced to twelve months' imprisonment for forgery. He died a few weeks later. He was an extremely skilful craftsman, and was reputed to have made about £600,000 by the sale of his fakes. See studies by Coremans (1949) and Lord Kilbracken (1968), Decoen's *Back to the Truth* (1951), and *Vermeer Forgeries* by Baesjou (1956).

VANNUCCI. See PERUGINO.

VAN RENSSELAER, Stephen, *ren'sel-ler* (1765–1839), American statesman, eighth 'patroon' of the vast estate near Albany, born in New York, was a leader of the Federalists in his state, and served in congress (1823–29). In the war of 1812 he held command on the northern frontier, and captured Queenston Heights; but the refusal of his militia to cross the Niagara enabled the British to recover the place, and he resigned. He promoted the construction of the Erie and Champlain canals and founded the Rensselaer Technical Institute (1826).

VANSITTART, *-sit'-*, (1) **Nicholas, 1st Baron Bexley** (1766–1851), English statesman, son of **Henry** (1732–70), a governor of Bengal of Dutch extraction, became a Tory chancellor of the Exchequer (1812–23) and in 1823 was raised to the peerage.

(2) **Robert Gilbert, 1st Baron Vansittart of Denham** (1881–1957), British diplomat, descended from **Henry** (see (1)), educated at Eton, joined the diplomatic service in 1902 and served successively in Paris, Teheran, Cairo and Stockholm with intervals at the Foreign Office. From 1920 to 1924 he was private secretary to Lord Curzon and in 1930 became permanent under-secretary for foreign affairs. He visited Germany in 1936, talked with Hitler and his henchmen and became the uncompromising opponent of Nazi Germany. His warnings of coming catastrophe unless Britain armed to meet the German menace—warnings expressed with undiplomatic pungency—put him at variance in 1937 with Neville Chamberlain. On January 1, 1938, he was steered into a backwater as 'chief diplomatic adviser to the Government'. He retired in 1941, and was raised to the peerage. He threw himself into parliamentary work, authorship and journalism, fiercely denouncing Nazidom and ridiculing the 'myth' of the 'two Germanys' (good and bad). After the war he was no less active in exposing Communist methods, lashing out at injustice and illuminating the shortcomings of statesmen. See his *The Singing Caravan* (poems, 1933); *Black*

Record (1941); *Lessons of My Life* (1943); and his autobiography, *The Mist Procession* (1958).

VAN'T HOFF. See HOFF.

VAN TIEGHEM, Philippe, *tyay-gem'* (1839–1914), French botanist and biologist, well known for his studies of myxomycetes, bacteria, &c., and a new classification of plants.

VAN VEEN, Otto, *vayn* (*c.* 1556–1634), Dutch painter, born at Leyden, settled first at Brussels, later at Antwerp, where Rubens was his pupil. The name Van Veen is also sometimes given to the Haarlem painter, **Martin van Heemskerk** (1498–1574), whose *Ecce Homo* and *Holy Family* are at Haarlem. Hampton Court Palace also has examples of his work.

VANZETTI. See SACCO.

VARDON, Harry (1870–1937), British golfer, born at Grouville in Jersey, first won the British Open Championship in 1896, a success which was repeated five times in 1898, 1899, 1903, 1911 and 1914. Winner of the American championship in 1900, he became a professional in 1903, and other triumphs included the winning of the German Open in 1911 and the *News of the World* Tournament in 1912. His graceful style had a lasting influence and he is remembered also for the grip, which though not original, was popularized by him and is still known as the 'Vardon grip'. He was the author of *The Complete Golfer* (1905), *How to Play Golf* (1912) and *My Golfing Life* (1933).

VARÈSE, Edgar (1885–1965), American composer of Italo-French parentage, born in Paris, studied under Roussel, D'Indy and Widor in Paris, and later under Busoni. Until World War I, Varèse was active in movements to bring music to the French people, and after two years' service in the French Army, he settled in New York, where in 1919 he founded the New Symphony Orchestra to further the cause of modern music, and in 1921 organized the International Composers' Guild, which has become the leading organ of progressive musicians. Varèse's work is almost entirely orchestral, often using unconventional percussion instruments, and its abstract nature is demonstrated by such titles as *Metal, Ionisation* and *Hyperprism.*

VARGAS, Getulio Dornelles (1883–1954), president of Brazil, born at São Borja in southern Brazil, was elected Federal deputy for his native province in 1923. In 1930 he seized power by revolution. From 1937, when he dissolved congress and suppressed all political parties and trade unions, he governed as dictator. In 1945 he was ousted by popular clamour for a new and democratic constitution, but under this in 1950 was voted back to office. Four years later, believed to be planning a new *coup d'état*, he was compelled to resign. He then shot himself. See K. Loewenstein, *Brazil under Vargas.*

VARLEY, a versatile English family of engineers and artists. Of this family:

(1) **Cornelius** (1781–1873), watercolour painter, invented the graphic telescope, experimented in electricity, and exhibited at the Academy and Watercolour Society.

(2) **Cromwell Fleetwood** (1828–83), the son of (1), was an electrical engineer, who invented a double-current key and relay used in telegraphy, and helped to renew the transatlantic cable (1858).

(3) **John** (1778–1842), a watercolourist, the brother of (1) and (4), was born at Hackney. He was a highly successful teacher, exhibited at the R.A., and was a founder member of the Watercolour Society. A friend of William Blake, he was also interested in astrology and wrote on perspective. See Life by Bury (1946).

(4) **William Fleetwood** (1785–1856), younger brother of (1) and (3), was also a watercolourist, and wrote on *Colouring* (1820).

VARNHAGEN, Francisco Adolpho de, Viscount de Porto Seguro, *farn'hah-gên* (1816–1878), Brazilian historian, born at São João de Ypanema, São Paulo, spent his youth in Portugal but took Brazilian nationality in 1841, afterwards holding several diplomatic posts. Amongst his works are a *History of Brazil* (1854–57) and monographs on Amerigo Vespucci.

VARNHAGEN VON ENSE, Karl August, *en'zè* (1785–1858), German writer, born at Düsseldorf, in 1809 joined the Austrian army and was wounded at Wagram. In 1813, he passed over to the Russian service, and went to Paris as adjutant. Here he was called to the Prussian diplomatic service, and accompanied Hardenberg to the Congress of Vienna (1814) and to Paris, becoming next resident minister at Karlsruhe (till 1819). He had married in 1814 the Jewess Rahel (q.v.). He wrote Lives of Goethe (1823), Marshal Keith (1844), Gen. von Bülow (1853), &c.; *Biographische Denkmäler* (1824–1830), and *Denkwürdigkeiten* (1843–59). His Correspondence and Diaries fill 22 vols. (1860–70). See Life by Misch (1926), and letters to him by Humboldt (1860) and Carlyle (1892).

VARRO, (1) Marcus Terentius (116–27 B.C.), Roman scholar and author, born at Reate, studied at Athens, saw service under Pompey, and in the Civil War was legate in Spain. He awaited the result of Pharsalia with Cicero and Cato at Dyrrachium, and was kindly treated by the conqueror, who appointed him librarian. Under the second triumvirate Antony plundered his villa, burned his books, and placed his name on the list of the proscribed. But he was soon exempted, and Augustus restored his property. A man of upright and honourable character, he survived till 27 B.C. His total works amounted to 620 books. Of the poems we know nothing but the names. But of the 150 books of the *Saturae Menippeae*, a medley of prose and verse, fragments (ed. Bücheler, 1882) remain. His prose writings embraced oratory, history, jurisprudence, grammar, philosophy, geography and husbandry. The chief were *Antiquitates Rerum Humanarum et Divinarum*; *De Lingua Latina*, of whose twenty-five books only v–x are extant (ed. Goetz and Schoell, Leipzig 1910); and *Rerum Rusticarum Libri III*, almost entire (ed. Goetz, 1912). His *Disciplinarum Libri IX* was an encyclopaedia of the liberal arts; his *Imagines*, or *Hebdomades*, a series of 700

Greek and Roman biographies. His works are translated in the Loeb edition (1912).

(2) **Publius Terentius** (*c.* 82–37 B.C.), Roman author, called Atacinus from his birth at Atax in Narbonensian Gaul, wrote satires and an epic on Caesar's Gallic wars. His *Argonautica* was an adaptation of Apollonius Rhodius; his erotic elegies pleased Propertius.

VARUS, Publius Quintilius (d. A.D. 9), Roman official, consul in 13 B.C., as governor of Syria suppressed the revolt of Judaea, and in A.D. 9 was sent by Augustus to command in Germany. Utterly routed by Arminius (q.v.), he killed himself.

VASA. See GUSTAVUS I.

VASARI, Giorgio, *va-zah'ree* (1511–74), Italian art historian, born at Arezzo, studied under Michelangelo, and lived mostly at Florence and Rome. He was a greater architect than painter; but today his fame rests on his *Vite de' più eccellenti Pittori, Scultori, e Architettori* (1550; Eng. trans. by G. de Vere, 10 vols. 1912–15). In spite of inaccuracies in the earlier biographies, it remains a model of art criticism and biography. See Life by Carden (1910).

VASCO DA GAMA. See GAMA.

VASCONCELOS, Caroline Michaelis De, *vash-kōn-se'loosh* (1851–1925), Portuguese scholar and writer, born in Berlin, studied and wrote on romance, philology and literature. An honorary professor of Hamburg University, she lived, after her marriage, in 1876, in Oporto, where she did much scholarly research on the Portuguese language, its literature, and especially its folk literature. Most noteworthy is her edition of the late 13th or early 14th century *Cancioneiro da Ajuda.* Other writings include *Notas Vicentinas* (1912), an edition of the poetry of Sá de Miranda, and essays, studies and correspondence with other Portuguese scholars.

VATTEL, Emmerich de, *fah'tèl* (1714–67), Swiss jurist, born at Couret in Neuchâtel, entered the diplomatic service of Saxony, and was Saxon representative at Bern (1746–64). His *Droits des gens* (1758; trans. 1834) systematized the doctrines of Grotius, Puffendorf and Wolf.

VAUBAN, Sébastien le Prestre de, *vō-bã* (1633–1707), French military engineer, born at Saint Léger near Avallon, May 1, enlisted under Condé, and followed him into the service of Spain. Taken prisoner in 1653, he was persuaded by Mazarin to enter the French king's service; by 1658 he was chief engineer under Turenne; and eight years of peace he devoted to works at Dunkirk and elsewhere. In 1667 he helped to reduce Lille; in 1672–78 in the Netherlands he took part in seventeen sieges and one defence. He introduced the method of approach by parallels at the siege of Maestricht (1673) with great effect; notable also were his defence of Oudenarde and the sieges of Valenciennes and Cambrai. During 1678–88 he surrounded the kingdom with a cordon of fortresses; and he planned the magnificent aqueduct of Maintenon. He invented the socket bayonet (1687). In 1703 he became marshal of France. He conducted the sieges of Philippsburg (1688)—introducing here his invention of ricochet-batteries—Mannheim, Mons (1691), Namur (1692), Charleroi (1693), Ath (1697) and Breisach (1704), and constructed the entrenched camp near Dunkirk (1706). After the peace of Ryswick in 1697 he had applied himself to study the faults in the government of France. His *Dîme royale* (1707), in which he discussed the question of taxation and anticipated the doctrines which eighty years later overthrew the French monarchy, was condemned and prohibited. He died March 30, 1707. See *Lettres intimes inédites* (1924), and Lives by G. Michel (1879) and R. Blomfield (1938).

VAUGELAS, Claude Favre de, *vōzh-la* (1585–1650), French grammarian, author of *Remarques sur la langue française* (1647), was a founder of the French Academy.

VAUGHAN, *vawn,* (1) **Benjamin** (1751–1835), British diplomat, born in Jamaica, promoted unofficially the Anglo-American peace negotiations (1782), settled in Maine, carried out agricultural research and corresponded with the first six presidents. Parts of his library he left to Harvard and Bowdoin.

(2) **Charles John** (1816–97), English divine, born in Leicester, elected fellow of Trinity College, Cambridge, he was vicar of St Martin's Leicester (1841–44); headmaster of Harrow (1844–59); vicar of Doncaster (1860–1869); master of the Temple (1869–94); and Dean of Llandaff from 1879. An eloquent preacher of the Liberal evangelical school, he prepared in his home a large number of men for ordination, popularly known as 'Vaughan's Doves'.

(3) **Henry** (1622–95), Welsh religious poet, the self styled 'Silurist' as a native of South Wales, the land of the old Silures, was born at Newton-by-Usk, Llansaintfraed, Breconshire, twin-brother of the alchemist Thomas Vaughan (1622–66). He entered Jesus College, Oxford, in 1638, and in 1646 published *Poems, with the tenth Satyre of Juvenal Englished.* He took his M.D., and practised first at, then near, Brecon. The collection of poems entitled *Olor Iscanus* was published by his brother without authority in 1651. In 1650–55 he printed his *Silex Scintillans,* pious meditations, and in 1652 *The Mount of Olives,* devotions in prose, and the *Flores Solitudinis,* also in prose. *Thalia Rediviva: the Pastimes and Diversions of a Country Muse,* a collection of elegies, translations, religious pieces, &c., was also published without authority (1678) by a friend. He died at his birthplace, April 23, 1695. Vaughan's poetry is very unequal; at his best he reaches an exquisite fantasy of expression beyond the reach of George Herbert. See Life by F. E. Hutchinson (1947) and studies by E. Blunden (1927), E. Holmes (1932), R. Garner (1960), and H. R. Ashton, *The Swan of Usk* (1940).

(4) **Herbert** (1832–1903), English Roman Catholic divine, born at Gloucester, was educated at Stonyhurst and at Rome, entered the priesthood in 1854, and in 1872 was consecrated Bishop of Salford. In 1892 he succeeded Manning as Archbishop of Westminster, next year was raised to the cardinalate, and died June 19, 1903. He was founder of St Joseph's College for foreign

missions at Mill Hill, was responsible for the building of Westminster Cathedral, and proprietor of the *Tablet* and the *Dublin Review*. See Life by J. G. Snead-Cox (1910). His brother, **Roger William Bede** (1834–83), Archbishop of Sydney from 1877, wrote a Life of Aquinas (1871–72). Another brother, **Bernard** (1847–1922), was a notable preacher.

(5) **Keith** (1912–), English artist, was born at Selsey Bill. He was associated with the younger Romantic artists influenced by Graham Sutherland. In 1951 he executed a large mural in the Festival of Britain Dome of Discovery, and he illustrated several books. His works (mainly of figures and landscape) are represented in the Tate Gallery, London, and the Museum of Modern Art, New York.

(6) **Robert** (1795–1868), British divine and historian, born in Wales, was Independent minister at Worcester and Kensington, professor of History in London University (1830–43), and president of the Independent College at Manchester (1843–57). He founded the *British Quarterly* in 1845, and edited it till 1867. Among his books are *Life of Wycliffe* (1828), *History of England under the Stuarts* (1840) and *Revolutions in History* (1859–63).

(7) **William** (1577–1641), British poet and colonizer, born in S. Wales, graduated at Jesus College, Oxford (1597), and bought an interest in Newfoundland, where he sent out settlers in 1617. He wrote an allegory *The Golden Fleece* (1626) and other works.

VAUGHAN WILLIAMS, Ralph (1872–1958), English composer, was born October 12 at Down Ampney, Gloucestershire. His early aptitude for music was encouraged by his parents and at Charterhouse School. He subsequently worked under Stanford at the Royal College of Music, under Max Bruch in Berlin and under Ravel in Paris. The essentially English character of all Vaughan Williams' music, unaffected by the European influence which still clung to the work of Stanford and Parry, makes him the first fundamentally national composer since the 16th century. In touch from the start with the English choral tradition, his first success was the choral *Sea Symphony* (1910), set to words of Walt Whitman, in which traditional choral styles were married to a vigorously contemporary outlook. Under the influence of Gustav Holst, Vaughan Williams became an enthusiastic leader in the English folksong movement, adding this tradition to the number of influences—Tudor church music, the choral and orchestral styles of Parry and the refinement gained from Ravel's teaching—that were assimilated in his own work. Of his early orchestral music his *Fantasia on a Theme of Tallis* (1909) for strings is noteworthy and is the work performed most regularly by orchestras outside Britain. Between the *London Symphony* (1914) and the *Pastoral Symphony* (1922), came a large number of works in all forms, vigorous and exploratory in style and including the ballad opera *Hugh the Drover* (1911–14). The ballet *Job* (1930) opened a new chapter in the composer's career, notable for its obvious concern with the moral issues of contemporary life, and it was followed by seven further symphonies (with their varied interests ranging from prophecy in the *Fourth, Fifth and Sixth*, to sheer delight in experimental sonorities in the *Eighth* and *Ninth*), the opera *The Pilgrim's Progress* (1948–49) and numerous choral works. The wide range, exploratory vigour and innate honesty of Vaughan Williams' work was illustrated by his ability to provide music of equal excellence for hymns, for the stage (as for Aristophanes' *The Wasps* (1909), and for films such as *49th Parallel* and *Scott of the Antarctic*. During World War I he served with the R.A.M.C. and with the Artillery; from 1905 onwards he was director of the Leith Hill Festival and in 1935 he was awarded the O.M. His artistic credo is contained in his books *National Music* (1934) and *Beethoven's Choral Symphony and Other Papers*. See studies by H. J. Foss (1950), F. Howes (1954) and S. Pakenham (1957) and Life by his wife, with study (1964).

VAUQUELIN, Louis Nicolas, *vōk-lī* (1763–1829), French chemist, was born and died at St André d'Hébertot, rose from laboratory assistant to be professor of Chemistry at Paris (1809). In 1798 he discovered chromium and its compounds, later beryllium compounds and asparagine.

VAUVENARGUES, Luc de Clapiers, Marquis de, *vōv-narg* (1715–47), French moralist, born at Aix, entered the army in 1733, fought at Dettingen, but retired in impaired health in 1743 to settle at Paris. In 1746 he published, anonymously, his *Introduction à la connaissance de l'esprit humain*, with *Réflexions et maximes* appended. In these he singles out the love of fame, courage and energy as noble virtues, tempered by humane sympathies for one's fellow men. To scientific and social progress, he remained curiously indifferent. See Lives by M. Wallas (1928), G. Lanson (1930) and F. Vial (1938).

VAVILOV, (1) **Nikolai Ivanovich** (1887–1943), Russian plant geneticist, brother of (2), was appointed to direct Soviet agricultural research by Lenin in 1930. He established 400 research institutes and built up a collection of 26,000 species and varieties of wheat. This enabled him to formulate the principle of diversity, which postulates that, geographically, the centre of greatest diversity represents the origin of a plant. Vavilov's international reputation was challenged by the politico-scientific 'theories' of Lysenko (q.v.), who denounced him at a Genetics Conference (1937) and gradually usurped Vavilov's position. The latter died in disgrace, allegedly in a Siberian concentration camp. He was made a foreign member of the Royal Society (1942).

(2) **Sergei** (1891–1951), Russian physicist, brother of (1), was born in Moscow, studied physics at the University there and researched into luminescent materials. He was president of the Soviet Academy of Sciences from 1945, chief editor of the Soviet Encyclopaedia and was twice awarded the Stalin prize.

VAZOV, Ivan (1850–1921), Bulgarian national poet, born at Sopot, wrote a collection of poems and songs under the title *Sorrows of Bulgaria* and *Under the Yoke* and other novels. He was twice exiled from his native land for his nationalist sympathies, but became minister of education in 1897.

VEBLEN, Thorsten (1857–1929), American sociologist, born at Cato, Wis., lectured in Economics in Chicago, Stanford, Missouri and New York and is best known for his *The Theory of the Leisure Class* (1899), *The Theory of Business Enterprise* (1904), *Engineers and the Price System* (1921), &c. See Life by J. A. Hobson (1936).

VECELLIO. See TITIAN.

VEDDER, (1) **David** (1790–1854), Scottish poet, sailor and custom-house officer, was born at Deerness, Orkney, and died in Edinburgh.

(2) **Elihu** (1836–1923), American painter, born at New York, studied at Paris and in Italy, settling in Rome. He executed *Minerva* and other murals in the Library of Congress, Washington, and illustrated the Rubáiyát of Omar Khayyám.

VEEN. See VAN VEEN.

VEGA. See GARCILASO DE LA VEGA.

VEGA CARPIO, Lope Félix de, *vay'gah kahr'pyō* (1562–1635), Spanish dramatist and poet, born at Madrid, November 25, lost his parents early; was a student and graduate of Alcalá; served in the Portuguese campaign of 1580 and in the Armada; was secretary to the Duke of Alva, Marquis of Malpica, and Marquis of Sarria; had many amours, was twice married, and begot at least six children, three of them illegitimate; was banished from Madrid because of a quarrel, and lived two years at Valencia; took orders, became an officer of the Inquisition; and died August 27, 1635, a victim to hypochondria. He died poor, for his large income from his dramas and other sources was all but wholly devoted to charity and church purposes. The mere list of Lope's works presents a picture of unparalleled mental activity. His first work of any length was a poem, the *Angelica*, written at sea in 1588, but not printed till 1602. The *Arcadia*, the story, in a pompous, pastoral setting, of the prenuptial vagaries of the Duke of Alva, was written before the duke's marriage, July 1590, but it was kept back till 1598. The *Dragontea*, a shout of exultation in ten cantos over the death of the Dragon (Drake) appeared the same year, and was Lope's first publication under his name. But it was as a ballad-writer that he first made his mark. The more notable of his miscellaneous works are the *Rimas* (1602); *Peregrino en su Patria* (1604), a romance; *Jerusalén Conquistada* (1609), an epic in competition with Tasso; *Pastores de Belén* (1612), a religious pastoral; *Filomena* and *Circe* (1621–24), miscellanies in emulation of Cervantes; *Corona Trágica* (1627), an epic on Mary Stuart; *Laurel de Apolo* (1630); *Rimas de Tomé de Burguillos* (1634), a collection of lighter verse, with the *Gatomaquia*, a mock-heroic. *Dorotea* (1632), in form a prose drama, is obviously the story of his own early love adventures. All these works show the hand, not of a great artist, but of a consummate artificer. Lope was a master of easy, flowing, musical, graceful verse; but he rarely passes the frontier line into true poetry. Though he had written plays, he did not become a writer for the stage until after 1588. He gave the public what it wanted—excitement pure and simple; with a boundless invention, he could string striking situations and ingenious complications one after another without stop or stay, and keep the audience breathless and the stage in a bustle for three long acts, all without sign of effort. Imagination and creative power were not among his gifts; his *dramatis personae* have seldom more individuality than a batch of puppets. Lope's plays may be roughly divided into the historical or quasi-historical and those that deal with everyday life. Of the latter the most characteristic are the 'cloak and sword plays'. The *Noche de San Juan*, one of his very last plays; the *Maestro de Danzar*, one of his first; and the *Azero de Madrid*, the source clearly of Molière's *Médecin malgré lui*, are excellent specimens. His peculiarities and excellences may be studied with advantage in such plays as the *Perro del hortelano*, *Desprecio agradecido*, *Esclava de su Galán*, *Premio del bien hablar*; and no student of Calderón should overlook the *Alcalde de Zalamea*, a bold vigorous outline which was filled in in Calderón's famous play. The number of Lope's plays seems to have been 1500, exclusive of 400 *autos*. Of these the very names of all but between 600 and 700 have been lost, and often nothing but the name survives. We have about 440 plays and 40 *autos* in print or MS. See Life by H. A. Rennert (1904), studies by K. Vossler (1933) and M. Romera-Navarro (1935), and chronology of his works, ed. Morley and Bruerton (1940).

VEGETIUS (Flavius Vegetius Renatus), *ve-jee' shus*, Latin writer, produced after A.D. 375 the *Epitome Institutionum Rei Militaris*, mainly extracted from other authors, which during the Middle Ages was a supreme authority on warfare.

VEIT, Philipp, *fīt* (1793–1877), German painter, was born at Berlin. His mother, daughter of Moses Mendelssohn, had for her second husband Friedrich Schlegel, and Veit embraced the ideas of his stepfather. Like him he turned Catholic, and, settling at Rome in 1815, became conspicuous among the young German painters who sought to infuse into modern art the earnestness of mediaeval times. His first famous work was the *Seven Years of Plenty* for the Villa Bartholdy. In 1830 he became director of the Art Institute at Frankfurt-am-Main. Here he painted the large fresco, *Christianity bringing the Fine Arts to Germany*. See Life by M. Spahn (1901).

VEITCH, *veech*, (1) **John** (1829–94), Scottish author, born at Peebles, studied at Edinburgh, and became professor of Logic and Rhetoric at St Andrews (1860), and then at Glasgow (1864). His works include Lives of Dugald Stewart (1857) and Sir W. Hamilton (1869), *Tweed and other Poems* (1875), *History and Poetry of the Scottish Border* (1877; new ed. 1893), *Feeling for Nature in Scottish Poetry* (1887), *Merlin and other Poems* (1889), *Dualism and Monism* (1895) and *Border Essays* (1896). See his Life by Mary Bryce (1896).

(2) **William** (1794–1885), Scottish classical

scholar, born at Spittal near Jedburgh, qualified for the Scottish ministry, but devoted himself to a life of scholarship at Edinburgh, his chief work the invaluable *Greek Verbs Irregular and Defective* (1848; 4th ed. 1878). He revised Liddell and Scott's *Greek Lexicon*, Smith's *Latin Dictionary*, &c.

VELASQUEZ, Diego de Silva y, *vay-las'keth* (1599–1660), one of the great Spanish masters, was born at Seville. He may have studied under Herrera, but in 1613 he did become the pupil of Francisco Pacheco, an indifferent painter but considerable art historian, whose daughter he married in 1618 and who in his *Art of Painting* provides an account of the young Velasquez. In 1618 Velasquez set up his own studio. His early works were *bodegónes*, characteristically Spanish domestic genre pieces, of which *Old Woman Cooking Eggs* (1618; National Gallery, Edinburgh) is a typical example. In 1622 he tried his luck at court in Madrid and persuaded Góngora (Boston) the poet to sit for him. The following year he achieved lifelong court patronage with his equestrian portrait, since lost, of Philip IV, who had all other portraits of himself withdrawn. The other court artists accused Velasquez of being incapable of painting anything but heads. The king ordered a competition on an historical subject, which Velasquez won with his *Expulsion of the Moriscos by Philip III*, now lost. In 1628 Rubens visited Madrid and befriended him. His advice and the palace collection of Italian art encouraged Velasquez's visit to Italy (1629–31). His sombre, austere, naturalistic style was transformed into the lightly modelled, more colourful styles of Titian and Tintoretto, as is apparent in his *Forge of Vulcan* (*c.* 1630) and *Joseph's Coat* (1630; Escorial, Madrid) and in the new type of portrait which Velasquez improvised, of the king (*c.* 1634) or his brother, or son in hunting costume with dog and landscape. One of the most striking of his many portraits of his royal master is full-length (*c.* 1632; National Gallery, London). The only surviving historical painting is his baroque *Surrender of Breda* (*c.* 1634). There are also many portraits of the royal children, particularly *Infante Baltasar Carlos on Horseback* (1635–36), the *Infanta Margarita* (1653–54, 1656, 1659; Vienna) and the *Infanta Maria Theresa* (1652–53; Vienna), and of the court dwarfs (1644, 1655) and jester, nicknamed *Don Juan de Austria* (1652–59). In 1650 he was again in Rome to obtain art treasures for the king and there painted the portrait of *Pope Innocent X* (Doria, Rome) and the two impressionistic *Views from Villa Medici*. On his return he captured the pathetic facial expression of the new queen, the young Maria Anne of Austria, in his best feminine full-length portrait (1552). But he is best remembered for his three late masterpieces, *Las Meniñas*, ' Maids of Honour ' (1656), in which the Infanta Margarita, her dwarf and attendants and the artist himself with easel are grouped around a canvas in a large palace room, hung with paintings, *Las Hilanderas*, 'The Tapestry Weavers' (*c.* 1657), and the famous *Venus and Cupid*, known as the 'Rokeby Venus' (*c.* 1658; National Gallery, London), one of the few nudes in Spanish painting. Velasquez was appointed usher to the king's chamber (1627), superintendent of works (1643), palace chamberlain (1652) and was made a knight of the Order of Santiago (1658), the highest court award. His painting is distinguished for its unflattering realism, in which nothing is imaginatively embellished or otherwise falsified, a remarkable achievement for a court painter. Goya carried on his tradition a century later and Whistler, Manet and the French Impressionists acknowledged his influence. All his abovementioned works, unless otherwise indicated, are in the Prado, Madrid. See studies by J. Justi (trans. 1889), R. A. M. Stevenson (1895, ed. Crombie 1962), A. de Beruete (trans. 1906), J. Allende-Salazar (trans. 1925), A. L. Mayer (trans. 1936), E. Lafuente-Ferrari (1960) and J. López-Rey (1963).

VELLEIUS PATERCULUS. See PATERCULUS.

VENANTIUS FORTUNATUS, Honorius Clementainus, St (d. *c.* 600), Latin poet, born at Ceneda, Italy, became Bishop of Poitiers and wrote *Pange lingua*, *Vexilla regis prodeunt*, and many other hymns. Feast day, December 14.

VENDÔME, Louis Joseph, Duc de, *vã-dõm* (1654–1712), French soldier, born at Paris, saw his first service in the Dutch campaign of 1672. He next served with distinction under Turenne in Germany and Alsace, again in the Low Countries under Luxembourg, and in Italy under Catinat; in 1695 he received the command of the army in Catalonia. He crowned a series of brilliant successes by the capture of Barcelona (1697). After five years of sloth and sensuality he superseded Villeroi in Italy. He fought an undecided battle with Prince Eugene at Luzzara (August 15), then burst into Tirol, returning to Italy to check the united Savoyards and Austrians. On August 16, 1705, he fought a second indecisive battle with Prince Eugene at Cassano, and at Calcinato he crushed the Austrians (April 19, 1706). That summer he was recalled to supersede Villeroi in the Low Countries. The defeat at Oudenarde (July 11, 1708) cost him his command, but in 1710 he was sent to Spain to aid Philip V. His appearance turned the tide of disaster; he brought the king back to Madrid, and defeated the English at Brihuega, and next day the Austrians at Villaviciosa. After a month of gluttony beyond even his wont, he died at Vinaroz in Castellón de la Plana, June 11, 1712.

VENIZELOS, Eleutherios, *vay-nyee-zay'los* (1864–1936), Greek statesman, born near Canea, Crete, studied law in Athens, led the Liberal party in the Cretan chamber of deputies and took a prominent part in the Cretan rising against the Turks in 1896. When Prince George became governor of Crete, Venizelos first served under him as minister of justice, then opposed him from the mountains at Therisso with guerilla warfare. In 1909 he was invited to Athens, became prime minister (1910–15), restored law and order but excluded the Cretan deputies from the new parliament and promoted the Balkan League, against Turkey (1912) and Bulgaria (1913) and so extended the Greek kingdom. His sympathies with France and Britain at the outbreak of World War I clashed with those of King Constantine and caused Venizelos to establish a provisional rival government at Salonika and in 1917 forced the king's abdication. He secured further territories from Turkey at the Versailles Peace Conference, but his prestige began to wane with his failure to colonize Turkish Asia Minor and he was heavily defeated in the general elections (1920) which brought the royalists and King Constantine back to power. He was prime minister again (1924, 1928–32 and 1933) and regained his ascendancy by his public works programmes and treaties with Italy and Yugoslavia. His friend General Plastiras tried unsuccessfully to establish a dictatorship during the general elections (1933) in which the Venizelists were doing badly, but Venizelos gained public sympathy once again after an unsuccessful attempt on his life, in which his wife was wounded. In 1935 he came out of retirement to support another Cretan revolt staged by his sympathizers, but it failed and he fled eventually to Paris, where he died. See his *Vindication of Greek National Policy* (1910), Lives by C. Kerofilas (1915), E. B. Chester (1921) and study by W. H. C. Price (1917).

VENN, (1) **Henry** (1725–97), English divine, father of (2), born at Barnes, vicar of Huddersfield (1759), took a prominent part with Lady Huntingdon and Whitefield in the Evangelical revival. He wrote *The Compleat Duty of Man* (1763) and other sermons.

(2) **John** (1759–1813), English divine, son of (1), born in Clapham, in 1792 became vicar there and a prominent member of the wealthy group of families with their distinctive religious and social ideals, known as the Clapham sect. In 1799 he founded the Church Missionary Society, of which his son, **Henry** (1796–1873), was secretary from 1841 until his death. See Life of John by M. Hennell (1958).

(3) **John** (1834–1923), English logician, developed Bode's symbolic logic and in his *Logic of Chance* (1866) the 'frequency' theory of probability.

VERBOECKHOVEN, Eugen Joseph, *ver' book-hō-ven* (1798–1881), Brussels animal-painter and etcher, noted for landscapes with sheep.

VERCINGETORIX. See CAESAR.

VERDAGUER, Mosen Jacinto, *ver'THah-ger* (1845–1902), Catalan poet, born at Folgarolas, became a priest with a vast popular following. He wrote *L'Atlántida*, and *Lo Canigó*, two epic poems of great beauty, and on the first of these Manuel de Falla based his choral work *Atlántida*. His *Idilis y Cants Mistichs* (1870), also set to music, have been embodied in the music of the Catalan church.

VERDI, Giuseppe (Fortunino Francesco), *ver'dee* (1813–1901), Italian composer. Of humble rural origin—his father kept an inn and grocer's store at Le Roncole near Busseto—much of his early musical education came from Provesi, organist of Busseto cathedral. Subsidized by local admirers of his talent, he was sent to Milan, but was rejected by the conservatoire as over age. Instead he studied profitably under Lavigna, *maestro al cembalo* at La Scala. On returning home he failed in his ambition of succeeding Provesi as cathedral organist, but was given a grant by the Philharmonic Society. Three years later he married the daughter of his friend and patron Barezzi, but wife and both children died in 1839–40. By this time his first opera, *Oberto*, had already been produced at La Scala, but it was with *Nabucco* (1842) that he achieved his first major success. Thereafter his career was one of almost continuous triumph. Although few of his pre-1850 operas apart from *Macbeth* and *Luisa Miller* remain in the normal repertory, *Rigoletto* (1851), *Il Trovatore* (1853) and *La Traviata* (1853) established unshakably his position as the leading Italian operatic composer of the day. These three works and their successors like *Un Ballo in Maschera* (1859) and *La Forza del Destino* (1862) were products of his maturity. This phase came to an end with the spectacular *Aïda*, commissioned for the new opera house in Cairo, built in celebration of the Suez Canal. Its première was in fact delayed until 1871 because of the Franco-Prussian war. Apart from the *Requiem* (1873) written in commemoration of Manzoni, there was then a lull in output until, in his old age, goaded and inspired by his brilliant literary collaborator Boito, he produced two masterpieces, *Otello* (1887) and *Falstaff* (1893). Both had their premières at La Scala, so ending nearly twenty years of feud with that theatre. Apart from some sacred choral pieces, Verdi wrote no more before his death. Though his reputation was worldwide, he stayed at heart a countryman, preferring above all to cultivate his property at Busseto in the intervals of composition. His long association with the former operatic soprano Giuseppina Strepponi, who became his wife in 1859, ensured a happy domestic context for his work. In his young days he had been an enthusiastic nationalist; some of his choruses were freely construed by patriots as being anti-Austrian, and were liable to lead to demonstrations. However, active participation in politics was not to his taste, and he soon resigned his deputyship in the first Italian parliament (1860). Later in life he became a senator. Though rich and greatly esteemed, Verdi led a simple life, and took almost as much pride in his estate management and in the founding of a home for aged musicians in Milan as in his creative work. Verdi dominated Italian opera between the Bellini-Donizetti era and that of Puccini. Over the years his methods changed from the robust melodramatic effectiveness of his youthful production to the extraordinary subtlety and sophistication of his last two operas. But at the root of his genius was his superb sense of theatre and his reservoir of unforgettable tunes. See studies by Bonavia (1934), Hussey (1940), Werfel (1942), Sheean (1959) and Life by Walker (1962).

VERE, Aubrey Thomas de. See DE VERE.

VERE, (1) Edward de, 17th Earl of Oxford

(1550–1604), English court poet, was a cousin of (2), (3) and (4). He was an Italianate Englishman, violent and a spendthrift, but one of the best of the Elizabethan courtier-poets. Of his lyrics, published in various collections, *What cunning can expresse* is perhaps the best.

(2) **Sir Francis** (*c.* 1560–1609), English soldier, grandson of the 15th Earl of Oxford, obtained a company in the Bergen-op-Zoom garrison in 1586, and won his first laurels in the defence of Sluys, being knighted by Lord Willoughby, whom he succeeded in 1589 in the chief command in the Netherlands. His skill and energy at Breda, Deventer and a hundred fights carried his fame far beyond the Netherlands. He shared the glory of the Cadiz expedition (1596), and next year the failure of the Island Voyage. Again in Holland, he governed Brill, and helped Maurice to victory at Turnhout (1597) and Nieuwpoort (1600), as well as in the heroic defence of Ostend. He wrote commentaries on his campaigns (1657).

(3) **Sir Horace, 1st Baron** (1565–1635), brother of (2), took a hero's share in all his brother's battles. Knighted for his courage at Cadiz, he succeeded his brother as governor of Brill, and, sent in the Thirty Years' War to defend the Palatinate, was shut in at Mannheim and forced to surrender to Tilly (1623). He was created baron in 1625.

(4) **Robert** (d. 1595), another brother, died in the Netherlands on the battlefield. See Sir Clements R. Markham, *The Fighting Veres* (1888).

VERENDRYE, Pierre Gaultier de Varennes, Sieur de la, *vay-rã-dree* (1685–1749), French explorer, born at Three Rivers, Quebec, served with the French army, and being wounded at Malplaquet, returned to Canada to become a trader with his base at Nipigon on Lake Superior. Fired by Indian tales, he and his three sons travelled over much of unexplored Canada, discovering Rainy Lake, the Lake of the Woods, and Lake Winnipeg. On later expeditions he and hi remaining two sons (the eldest having been killed by the Sioux) reached the Mandan country south of the Assiniboine river, upper Missouri, Manitoba and Dakota. Finally, before his death one of his sons traced the Saskatchewan river to its junction. See his journals and letters, edited by L. J. Burpee (1927).

VERESHCHAGIN, Vasili, *vye-ryesh-chah'-gyin* (1842–1904), Russian painter of battles and executions, born at Tcherepovets in Novgorod, entered the navy in 1859, but studied art under Gérôme at Paris. He was with Kauffmann in the Turkoman campaigns (1867), visited India (1874), saw the Russo-Turkish war (1877), and in 1884 went to India, Syria and Palestine and portrayed what he saw in gruesomely realistic pictures of plunder, mutilated corpses and executions of mutinous sepoys, with Tolstoy's aim of fostering revulsion against war. He was blown up with Admiral Makarov's flagship off Port Arthur on April 13, 1904. See his travel sketches (trans. 1887) and study by Zabel (1900).

VERGA, Giovanni, *vayr'gah* (1840–1922), Italian novelist, born at Catania in Sicily, wrote numerous violent short stories describing the hopeless, miserable life of Sicilian peasantry, including *La vita de' campi* (1880) and *Cavalleria rusticana* (1884), which was made into an opera by Mascagni. The same Zolaesque theme prevails in his novels, *I Malavoglia* (1881) and *Mastro Don Gesualdo* (1888), &c. D. H. Lawrence translated some of his works. See Life by L. Russo (Bari 1941) and study by E. De Michelis (Florence 1941).

VERGENNES, Charles Gravier, *ver-zhen* (1717–87), French statesman, Louis XVI's foreign minister, sought to humble England by promoting the independence of the United States. He negotiated the Peace of Paris (1783) and Pitt's commercial treaty (1786). See Life by C. de Chambrun (1944).

VERGIL. See VIRGIL.

VERGIL, Polydore (*c.* 1470–*c.* 1555), Italian historian, otherwise named De Castello, was born at Urbino, and educated at Bologna and Padua. His first work was *Proverbiorum Libellus* (1498); his second, *De Inventoribus Rerum* (1499), also the earliest book of its kind, was translated into English, Spanish and Italian. He was sent by the pope to England in 1501 as deputy-collector of Peter's pence, and was presented to the Leicestershire living of Church Langton in 1503. In 1507 he became a prebendary of Lincoln, in 1508 archdeacon of Wells, and in 1513 a prebendary of St Paul's, having been naturalized in 1510. In 1515 he was imprisoned for slandering Wolsey. In 1525 he published the first genuine edition of Gildas, in 1526 the treatise *De Prodigiis.* His great *Historiae Anglicae Libri XXVI* appeared at Basel in 1534; a 27th book (to 1538) was added in the third edition (1555). About 1550 he returned to Italy. See Camden Soc. works by Sir H. Ellis (1844–46), and study by Hay (1952).

VERGNIAUD, Pierre Victurnien, *vern-yō* (1753–93), French politician, born at Limoges, settled as an advocate at Bordeaux in 1781, and was sent to the National Assembly in 1791. His eloquence made him the leader of the Girondists. In the Convention he voted for the king's death, and as president announced the result. When the Girondists clashed with the rival revolutionary faction, known as the Mountain, composed mainly of Parisians who had borne the brunt of the revolution and wanted to retain power by dictatorial means, Vergniaud and his party were arrested and guillotined on October 31. See Life by Bowers (N.Y. 1950).

VERHAEREN, Emile, *-hahr'-* (1855–1916), Belgian poet, born at St Amand near Termonde, studied law, but took to literature. His poetry hovers between powerful sensuality as in *Les Flamandes* (1883) and the harrowing despair of *Les Débâcles* (1888); the affirmation of the life force and the revulsion against modern industrial conditions. His best work is possibly *La Multiple Splendeur* (1906). He died in a train accident at Rouen. See study by S. Zweig (trans. 1914) and P. M. Jones (1926).

VERHEIDEN, Jakob, *-hī'-*, Dutch publisher at The Hague in 1602 of the *Effigies et Elogia* of the leading Reformers, the portraits (including the well-known one of John Knox based on that in Beza's *Icones*) being engraved by Hondius.

VERLAINE, Paul, *-layn* (1844–96), French poet, born at Metz on March 30, was educated at the Lycée Condorcet and entered the civil service. Already an aspiring poet, he mixed with the leading Parnassian poets and writers in the cafés, and especially at the salon of Nina de Callias and under their romantic battle cry 'Art for art's sake', against the formless sentimentalizing of the romantic school, gained some recognition by his contribution of articles and poems to their *avant garde* literary magazines, especially the short-lived *Le Parnasse contemporain.* The youthful morbidity of his first volume of poems, *Poèmes saturniens* (1867), was criticized by Sainte-Beuve as trying vainly to outdo Baudelaire. The evocation of a past age, the 18th century of the paintings of Watteau, provided the theme of his second beginning, *Fêtes galantes* (1869), by many considered his finest poetical achievement. His love for the sixteen-year-old Mathilde Mauté during an engagement prolonged by the doubts of the girl's father was sublimated in *La Bonne Chanson* (1870). During the Franco-Prussian war Verlaine did guard duty in Paris and then served as press-officer for the Communards. The birth of a son did nothing to heal the incompatibilities of his married life, from which he escaped (1872) on travels in Flanders, Belgium and England in Bohemian intimacy with the fledgling poe Rimbaud (q.v.), ten years his junior. Their friendship ended in Brussels (1873), when Verlaine, drunk and desolate at Rimbaud's intention to leave him, shot him in the wrist. Verlaine's overpowering remorse made it psychologically impossible for Rimbaud to leave, so he staged an incident in the street and had Verlaine arrested. He did not foresee that the police would in searching for a motive suspect immorality. Verlaine was convicted and sentenced to two years' hard labour and his past associations with the Communards disqualified him from any intercession by the French ambassador. *Romances sans paroles* (1874) were written in Mons prison, where he studied Shakespeare in the original, and after his wife had left him, he turned Catholic (1874). He unsuccessfully attempted to enter a monastery on release, taught French at Stickney, Lincolnshire, and St Aloysius' College, Bournemouth (1875), where he completed his second masterpiece *Sagesse* (1881), full of the spirit of penitence and self-confession that appeared again in *Parallèlement* (1889). In 1877 he returned to France to teach English at the Collège of Notre Dame at Rethel, adopted a favourite pupil, Lucien Létinois, for whom he acquired a farm at Coulommes and whose death of typhus (1883) occasioned *Amour* (1888). *Poètes maudits* (1884), comprising critical studies, were followed by short stories *Louis Leclerc* and *Le Poteau* (1886), sacred and profane verse *Liturgies intimes* (1892) and *Élégies* (1893). The consummate master of a poetry which sacrificed all for sound, in which the commonplace expressions take on a magic freshness, he lived during his last years in Parisian garret poverty, relieved by frequent spells in hospitals and finally by a grand lecture tour in Belgium, Holland and England (1893), the last sponsored in part by William Rothenstein (q.v.), who drew several portraits of him. He died in Paris, January 8, 1896. See the autobiographical *Mes hôpitaux* (1892), *Mes prisons* (1893) and *Confessions* (1895), *Œuvres poétiques complètes*, ed. Y. G. Le Dantec (1938), and books by E. Lepelletier (1907), E. Delahaye (1919), H. Nicolson (1921), P. Martino (1924), M. Coulson (1929), A. Adam (1936), P. Valéry (1937), C. E. B. Roberts (1937), F. Porché (1937), A. Fontaine (1937), V. P. Underwood (Paris 1958) and L. and E. Hanson (1958).

VERMEER, *ver-mayr,* (1) **Jan,** of Haarlem (1628–91), was a notable Dutch landscape painter. His son, **Jan** the Younger (1656–1705), was also a painter.

(2) **Jan** (1632–75), Dutch painter, born in Delft, the son of an art dealer, inherited his father's business and painted purely for pleasure. His life was obscure, possibly because he was a Catholic in a Protestant country. He may have studied under Carel Fabritius. His work shows some Neapolitan influence as well as that of the genre painting of Pieter de Hooch. In 1653 he married Caterina Bolones, who was to bear him eleven children, and the same year he was admitted master painter to the guild of St Luke, which he served as headman (1662–63; 1670–71). He gained some recognition in his lifetime in Holland and his work was sought by collectors, but he made little effort to sell. After his death his baker held two pictures for outstanding bills, and Vermeer's wife, declared a bankrupt, could not retrieve them. His art was forgotten until the researches of Thoré (1866) and Havard (1883) re-established and enhanced his reputation. Apart from a few portraits, *The Allegory of Faith* (Metropolitan, N.Y.), *The Procuress* (1656; Dresden), *Christ in the House of Martha and Mary* (National Gallery, Edinburgh) and two views of Delft (one in The Hague), he confined himself to the domestic interiors of his own house, spiced with an art dealer's furnishings and trappings, every scene perfectly arranged so that everything, material or human, should obtain equal prominence and meticulous attention. His detachment, acute appreciation of perspective, unrivalled paintwork, which shows no trace of the brush and effects a translucent purity and richness of colour (particularly his blues and yellows), and above all his masterly treatment of the manifold tones of daylight, impart to each painting the quality of a still-life. A trivial subject becomes a work of art. Forty of his paintings are known. These include three music-making scenes (two, National Gallery, London; one, Royal Collection, Windsor), the *Allegory of Painting* (Vienna), two *Woman reading a Letter* (Amsterdam and Dresden) and other domestic scenes. During World War II, forged Vermeers were produced by Van Meegeren (q.v.) who for some time deceived the experts. See monograph by J. Chantavoine (1936) and studies by T. Bodkin (1939), de Vries (1961), L.

Gowing (1952), of the Van Meegeren forgeries, J. Baesjou (1956) and L. Goldschneider (1958).

VERMIGLI. See PETER MARTYR.

VERMUYDEN, Sir Cornelius, *-mī'-* (*c.* 1595–*c.* 1683), Dutch drainage engineer, born on the island of Tholen, Zeeland, in 1621 was commissioned to repair the breach of the Thames at Dagenham and drained the Bedford Level (1634–52). See Life by J. K. Altes (1925) and study by L. E. Harris (1953).

VERNE, Jules (1828–1905), French novelist, born at Nantes, studied law, from 1848 wrote opera libretti until in 1863, with the publication of *Cinq Semaines en ballon*, he struck a new vein in fiction—exaggerating and often anticipating the possibilities of science and giving ingenious verisimilitude to adventures carried out by means of scientific inventions in exotic places. He greatly influenced the early science fiction of H. G. Wells. His best-known books, all of which have been translated, are *Voyage au centre de`la terre* (1864), *Vingt mille lieues sous les mers* (1870) and *Le Tour du monde en quatre-vingts jours* (1873). Film versions of the last two achieved an astonishing popularity as late as the nineteen-fifties. See Lives by M. A. de la Füye (1928), K. Allott (1940), G. H. Waltz (1943) and I. O. Evans (1956).

VERNET, *ver-nay,* name of a notable family of French painters, of whom the most important members were:

(1) **Antoine Charles Horace** (1758–1835), known as 'Carle', son of (2) and father of (3), born at Bordeaux, showed early promise and went to Italy, where he decided to become a monk. Back in Paris, however, he took to painting horses again and the vast battle pieces of Marengo and Austerlitz (now at Versailles) for which Napoleon awarded him the Légion d'honneur, and *The Race* (Louvre), which earned him the order of St Michael from Louis XVIII.

(2) **Claude Joseph** (1714–89), landscape and marine painter, father of (1), was born at Avignon. His voyage to Rome gave him a fascination for the sea and he became primarily known for his seascapes and the paintings in the Louvre of France's 16 chief seaports, commissioned by the king.

(3) **Emile Jean Horace** (1789–1863), known as 'Horace', son of (1), born in Paris, became one of the great French military painters. He decorated the vast Constantine room at Versailles with battle scenes from Valmy, Wagram, Bouvines and *Napoleon at Friedland.* His *Painter's Studio* depicts him as he loved to be, surrounded by groups of people, boxing, playing instruments and leading horses. His paintings lack composition, but are treated vigorously and with an impromptu brilliance. There are five paintings in the National Gallery, London. See study by Rees (1880).

VERNEY, the name of an English family in Buckinghamshire, among whose members was **Ralph Verney**, lord mayor of London in 1465. Other important members in chronological order were:

(1) **Sir Edmund** (1590–1642), a royalist standard-bearer, who fell at Edgehill.

(2) **Sir Ralph** (1613–96), son of (1), fought for the parliament, but refused the covenant, and in exile at Blois was created a baronet in 1661. His descendants held the titles of Baron Verney, Viscount Fermanagh and Earl Verney, the second and last earl dying in 1791.

(3) **Sir Edmund** (1616–49), son of (1), fought for the king in the Civil War, but did not survive the massacre of Drogheda.

(4) **Frances, Parthenope** (d. 1890), elder sister of Florence Nightingale, married in 1858 **Sir Harry** (1801–94). She wrote novels and the first half of *Memoirs of the Verney Family* (4 vols. 1892–99).

VERNIER, Pierre, *vern-yay* (*c.* 1580–1637), French mathematician, born at Ornans near Besançon, spent most of his life serving the king of Spain in the Low Countries and in 1631 invented the famous auxiliary scale to facilitate an accurate reading of a subdivision of an ordinary scale.

VERNON, (1) **Edward** (1684–1757), British admiral, entered the Royal Navy in 1700. He was present at the capture of Gibraltar in 1704, and fought in the great battle off Málaga. A captain at twenty-one and a rear-admiral at twenty-four, he sat in parliament as M.P. for Penhryn and then Portsmouth, from 1727 to 1741. In 1739 he was sent to harry the Spaniards in the Antilles, and his capture of Portobello transformed him into a national hero. Against his urgent and reasoned advice, he was sent to reduce Cartagena; but the failure of the attempt owed much to the ineptitude of his military coadjutor. Recalled by the Government, at the time of the '45 Jacobite rebellion his masterly dispositions in the Channel successfully pinned the standby Gallic reinforcements to their ports. But Vernon was too cantankerous, too outspoken, and also too often right in his judgments, for the Cabinet to stomach, and he was jockeyed into resigning his command. He continued to be a thorn in the administration's side until his death in 1757. He was nicknamed 'Old Grog', from his grogram coat, and in 1740 ordered the dilution of navy rum with water, the mixture being thenceforward known as 'grog'. See Lives by Ford (1907) and Hughes Hartmann (1953), and Beatson's *Naval and Military Memoirs* (1804).

(2) **Robert** (1774–1849), English breeder of horses, in 1847 gave to the nation the Vernon Gallery.

VERNON-HARCOURT, Augustus George (1834–1919), English chemist, born in London, graduated at Oxford, where he became reader in Chemistry. He invented a standard lamp of ten candle power, using pentane as fuel.

VERONESE, Paolo, *vay-ro-nay'zay* (1525–88), the name by which Paolo Cagliari, the greatest of the Venetian decorative painters, is known. He was born a sculptor's son, at Verona, and after some work there and in Mantua, in 1555 settled in Venice, where he soon made both wealth and fame, ranking with Titian and Tintoretto. The church of San Sebastiano in Venice contains many pictures of the period before his visit to Rome (1560). The influence of the Roman school on his style was marked. new dignity, grace of pose, and ease of movement being added to his rich Venetian colouring. In 1563 he painted the *Marriage Feast at Cana* (Louvre), possibly the greatest of his works. Other subjects include *The Family of Darius before Alexander* (*c.* 1570), *The Adoration of the Magi* (1573), both in the London National Gallery, and *Feast in the House of the Levi* (1753) in the Venice Academy. This last-mentioned painting brought him before the Inquisition for trivializing religious subjects by the introduction of nonhistorical accessories such as dwarfs, jesters and the like. Veronese was incapable of deep emotion, but was an exquisite colourist stamped in the aristocratic milieu of his time. He used architectural detail to heighten the sense of occasion and the rhetorical nature of his work is especially evident in such decorative pieces as the ceiling of the council chamber of the ducal palace at Venice, the *Apotheosis of Venice* (1585). See books by G. Fiocco (1928) and P. H. Osmond (1928).

VERONICA, saint, according to legend, met Christ and offered him her veil to wipe the sweat from his brow, when the divine features were miraculously imprinted upon the cloth. This veil is said to have been preserved in Rome from about 700, and was exhibited in St Peter's in 1933. Possibly *Veronica* is merely a corruption of *vera icon*, ' the true image ' (i.e., of Christ). See Karl Pearson's German monograph (1887).

VERRES, Gaius (d. 43 B.C.), Roman official, was quaestor in 84, and then attached himself to Sulla. He went to Cilicia in 80 under Dolabella, and after helping to plunder the provincials, gave evidence against his chief in 78. He was praetor in 74, owing to bribery, and governor of Sicily (73–70), where he trampled on the rights of Roman and provincial alike. On his return, he was summoned before a senatorial court, and Cicero, for the prosecution, amassed such strong evidence that Verres fled before the trial. He seemed to have lived at Massilia, but perished under Antony's proscription.

VERRIO, Antonio (*c.* 1640–1707), Italian decorative painter, born in Lecce, Southern Italy, was brought to London by Charles II and decorated Windsor Castle, Hampton Court, &c., and executed an equestrian portrait of the king, now in Chelsea Hospital.

VERROCCHIO, Andrea del, *ver-rok'kee-ō* (1435–88), the name by which Cione, Florentine sculptor, painter and goldsmith is known. Of the paintings ascribed to him only the *Baptism* in the Uffizi can be so with certainty, and this was completed by Leonardo da Vinci. He executed several bronze figures for the Medici tombs in San Lorenzo and is best known for his magnificent equestrian statue of Colleoni at Venice. See monographs by M. Cruttwell (1904) and M. Reymond (1906).

VERTUE, George (1684–1756), English engraver and antiquary, born in London, made his name with a fine line-engraving of Lord Somers. Horace Walpole made use of his MSS. (valuable to the art historian) in *Anecdotes of Painting*.

VERWOERD, Hendrik Freusch, *fer-vœrt'* (1901–66), South African politician, born in Amsterdam, was a professor at Stellenbosch (1927–37). He edited the nationalist *Die Transvaler* (1938–48) and opposed South Africa's entry into World War II. Exponent of the strict racial segregation policy of *apartheid*, Verwoerd became vice-chairman of the National Party of the Transvaal in 1946, was elected senator in 1948 and minister of native affairs in 1950. In 1958 he was elected national leader by the Nationalist party parliamentary caucus and as 6th prime minister of South Africa he dedicated himself to the founding of a South African republic. After strong opposition to his policy of *apartheid* and an attempt on his life in 1960, South Africa broke from the commonwealth on becoming a republic in 1962, after which Verwoerd pursued a strict *apartheid* policy. He was assassinated in 1966.

VERY, *veer'i,* **(1) Edward Wilson** (1847–1910), American ordnance expert and inventor. He served in the American Navy from 1867 to 1885, became an admiral, and in 1877 invented chemical flares (' Very Lights ') for signalling at night.

(2) **Frank Washington** (1852–1927), American astronomer, born at Salem, Mass., estimated lunar temperatures, designed a method for measuring the Fraunhofer lines, proved that white nebulae are galaxies and that the Martian atmosphere contains oxygen and water vapour. He became director of the Westwood Astrophysical observatory in 1906.

(3) **Jones** (1813–80), American mystic, was born and died at Salem, Mass. He wrote sonnets of mystical inspiration contained in *Essays and Poems* (1839). See Life by W. I. Bartlett (1942).

VESALIUS, Andreas, *ve-zay'lyus* (1514–1564), Belgian anatomist, born in Brussels, became professor at Padua, Bologna and Basle. In 1538 he published his six anatomical tables, still largely Galenian, and in 1541 edited Galen's works. His own great work, however, the celebrated *De Humani Corporis Fabrica* (1543), greatly advanced the science of biology with its excellent description of bones and the nervous system, supplemented by the magnificent drawings of muscle dissections by Jan Stephen van Calcar, a pupil of Titian. It was condemned by the Galenists and he was sentenced to death by the Inquisition for ' body snatching ' and for dissecting the human body. The sentence however was commuted to a pilgrimage to Jerusalem, which he undertook, but died on the return journey on the island of Zante. He was court physician to Charles V and Philip II. He was the first to challenge the Aristotelian doctrine that the heart was the physical correlative of personality, in favour of the brain and the nervous system. See Life by M. Roth (1892), H. Cushing, *Bio-bibliography* (1943), and C. Singer, *A Prelude to Modern Science* (1946).

VESPASIAN, Titus Flavius Vespasianus, *-spay'zhėn* (A.D. 9–79), Roman emperor, born near Reate, served as tribune in Thrace, and as quaestor in Crete and Cyrene. In the reign of Claudius he commanded a legion in Germany and in Britain; was consul in 51, and next proconsul of Africa; and in

67 was sent by Nero to reduce the Jews to subjection. When the struggle began between Otho and Vitellius he was proclaimed imperator by the legions in the East and on the death of Vitellius was appointed emperor. Leaving the war in Judaea to his son Titus, he reached Rome in 70, and soon restored the government and finances to order, besides showing an admirable example to a corrupt age by the simplicity of his life. He embarked however on an ambitious building programme in Rome, began the Colosseum, and extended and consolidated Roman conquests in Britain and Germany. See study by Langford (1928).

VESPUCCI, Amerigo, *ves-poot'chee* (1451–1512), Florentine explorer, born at Florence, was a provision contractor at Seville in 1495–1498. He contracted for one (or two) of the expeditions of Columbus. He had some knowledge of cosmography, but was not a practical navigator (still less a pilot) when, at fifty, he promoted a voyage to the New World in the track of Columbus, sailed with its commander Hojeda (1499), and explored the coast of Venezuela. In 1505 he was naturalized in Spain, and from 1508 till his death was pilot-major of the kingdom. His name was absurdly given to two continents (America) through an inaccurate account of his travels published at St Dié in Lorraine in 1507, in which he is represented as having discovered and reached the mainland in 1497. This account was based on Vespucci's own letters, in which he claims to have made four voyages. Sir Clements Markham in his introduction to a translation of the letters (Hakluyt Society, 1894) proved one of these to be a pure fabrication, the others quite unsupported. But see also books by Coote (1894), H. Vignaud (1918), Pohl (1945), and the Princeton Vespucci Texts and Studies (1916).

VESTRIS, Lucia Elizabeth (1797–1856), English actress, *née* **Bartolozzi,** a granddaughter of the engraver, was born in London. At sixteen she married the dancer Armand Vestris (1787–1825), member of an originally Florentine family that gave to France a series of distinguished chefs, actors and ballet-dancers. In 1815 they separated and she went on the stage in Paris. She appeared at Drury Lane in 1820, became famous in *The Haunted Tower,* was even more popular as Phoebe in *Paul Pry,* and in light comedy and burlesque was equally successful. She had been nine years lessee of the Olympic when in 1838 she married Charles James Mathews (q.v.). She afterwards undertook the management of Covent Garden and the Lyceum. See Life by C. E. Pearce (1923).

VEUILLOT, Louis François, *vœ-yō* (1813–1883), French Ultramontane editor of the Paris *L'Univers,* was born at Boynes, Loiret. He wrote novels, poems, polemical essays, &c. See Lives by E. Veuillot (1883), Tavernier (1913) and E. J. M. Gauthier (1939).

VEZIN, Hermann (1829–1910), American actor, born at Philadelphia, made his début at York in 1850 and acted in London from 1852. Among his leading rôles were Hamlet, Jacques and Ford.

VIAN, Sir Philip, *vī'ėn* (1894–1968), British sailor, educated at Dartmouth. In 1940, in command of the destroyer *Cossack,* Captain Vian penetrated Norwegian territorial waters to rescue 300 British prisoners from the German supply ship *Altmark;* subsequently being sunk in the *Afridi* while covering the withdrawal from Namsos. In 1942 his skill and courage in beating off enemy interception enabled a vital convoy to reach Malta. Subsequently, he was deeply engaged in the Normandy invasion. Service as fifth sea lord was followed by the command of the Home Fleet. He was created K.B.E. in 1944.

VIARDOT-GARCÍA. See GARCÍA (4).

VIAU, Théophile de, *vee-ō* (1590–1626), French poet, born at Clairac, wrote the tragedy *Pyramé et Thisbé* (1621) and much love poetry distinguished by its naturalness. He was condemned to the stake (1623) for the impiety and obscenity of his poems contributed to *Le Parnasse satyrique* but his sentence was commuted to exile for life.

VIAUD, Louis Marie Julien, *vee-ō* (1850–1923), French novelist who wrote under the pseudonym of 'Pierre Loti', was born at Rochefort. His voyages as a sailor and as a traveller provide the scenes for most of his writings, and from the native women of the South Sea Islands he gained his pseudonym Loti, Flower of the Pacific. *Aziyadé* (1879), his first novel, was a series of pictures of life on the Bosporus and it was followed by the very successful *Rarahu* (1880), published in 1882 as *Le Mariage de Loti.* Semi-autobiographical, this story set among the coral seas, of the love of an Englishman for a Tahiti girl, immediately captured the imagination. Of his novels, the best known is *Pêcheur d'Islande* (1886), a descriptive study of Breton fisher life. All his writing is subjective; there is a simplicity yet an intensity of sensuous impressions, a sympathy with nature and a deeply felt melancholy at the transitoriness of human life. Other works include *Le Roman d'un Spahi* (1881), *Mon Frère Yves* (1883), *Madame Chrysanthème* (1887), and *Vers Ispahan* (1904).

VICENTE, Gil, *vee-sen'tay* (*c.* 1470–*c.* 1537), the father of Portuguese drama. His *Belém monstrance* is in the Lisbon museum. He wrote 44 plays, 16 in Portuguese, 11 in Spanish and 17 using both languages. His early plays were religious, but gradually social criticism was added. His farces *Inês Pereira, Juiz da Beira* and the three *autos das barcas* (*Inferno, Purgatório and Glória*) are his best. He displays great psychological insight, superb lyricism and a predominantly comical spirit. See Lives by Freire and Pratt (1931).

VICKY (1913–66), professional name of **Victor Weisz,** British political cartoonist of Hungarian-Jewish extraction, born in Berlin. He emigrated to Britain in 1935, worked with the *News Chronicle,* the *Daily Mirror,* the *New Statesman* and the *Evening Standard,* establishing himself as the most outstanding left-wing political cartoonist of the period. He published collections of his work, including *Vicky's World* (1959), *Home and Abroad* (1964).

VICO, Giovanni Battista, *vee-kō* (1668–1744), Italian philosopher, born at Naples, studied law, but devoted himself to literature, history and philosophy and became in 1697 professor of Rhetoric at Naples. In his *Scienza Nuova* (1725; recast 1730) he argued that the historical method is no less exact than the scientific, and postulated evolutionary cycles in civilizations, corresponding to mental development. His historicism influenced the German Romantics. See his *Autobiography*, intro. Fisch and Bergin (1944), and works by Flint (1884), Croce, trans. R. G. Collingwood (1913), Gentile (1927) and Adams (1935).

VICTOR, Claude Perrin, Duc de Belluno (1764–1841), French soldier, born at La Marche. Napoleon made him marshal on the field of Friedland (1807), and later Duke of Belluno. In 1808–12 he commanded in Spain, and, after initial successes, lost the battles of Talavera and Barrosa; in the Russian campaign he covered the crossing of the Berezina. He fought at Dresden and Leipzig, lost the emperor's favour by neglecting to occupy the bridge of Montereau-sur-Yonne, and was wounded at Craonne. Louis XVIII gave him high command and the presidency of the commission for trying his old companions who had deserted to Napoleon during the 'Hundred Days'. He was minister of war (1821–23). See his *Mémoires* (1846).

VICTOR AMADEUS II (1666–1732), succeeded his father as Duke of Savoy in 1675, and was saved from the clutches of France by the military genius of Price Eugene (q.v.), a distant cousin, who routed the French before Turin in 1706. By the Treaty of Utrecht (1713) he gained the principality of Montferrat and the kingdom of Sicily. Seven years later the Emperor of Austria forced him to exchange the crown of Sicily for that of Sardinia. He abdicated in 1730.

VICTOR EMMANUEL, the name of three kings of Sardinia, of whom two were also kings of Italy:

Victor Emmanuel I (1759–1824), was king of Sardinia (1802–21). His oppression of liberalism led to a rising in 1821, when he abdicated in favour of his brother Charles Felix.

Victor Emmanuel II (1820–78), first king of Italy, son of Charles Albert (q.v.) of Sardinia, was born March 14, in 1848–49 displayed great gallantry at Goito and Novara. Charles Albert abdicating in his favour, he ascended the throne of Sardinia, March 23, 1849; and in August peace was concluded between Sardinia and Austria. Perhaps the most important act of his rule was the appointment (1852) of Cavour (q.v.) as his chief minister. In January 1855 Sardinia joined the allies against Russia, and a contingent of 10,000 men landed in the Crimea. At the Congress of Paris (March 1856) the Sardinian envoys urged upon the attention of France and England the oppressive government of the states of Italy. In 1857 diplomatic relations were broken off with Austria. In 1859 Austria demanded the disarmament of Sardinia; this was refused, and next day the Austrians crossed the Ticino. A French army advanced to aid the Sardinians, and the Austrians were defeated at Montebello (May 20), Magenta (June 4) and Solferino (June 24). By the Treaty of Villafranca, Lombardy was ceded to Sardinia. In 1860 Modena, Parma, the Romagna and Tuscany were peacefully annexed to Sardinia. Sicily and Naples were added by Garibaldi, while Savoy and Nice were ceded to France. The papal territories were saved from annexation only by the presence of a French force of occupation. In February 1861 Victor Emmanuel was proclaimed king of Italy at Turin, whence the capital of Italy was transferred to Florence. In 1866 the Austro-Prussian war, in which Italy took part as the ally of Prussia, added Venetia to the Italian kingdom. In the same year the French withdrew from Rome, but owing to an incursion by Garibaldi they returned. After the fall of the Empire in 1870 the French occupation of Rome was at an end, the king entered Rome, and the province was added to his kingdom. The 'honest king' reigned as a strictly constitutional monarch. He was succeeded by his eldest son, Humbert I. See Life by C. S. Forester (1927).

Victor Emmanuel III (1869–1947), king of Italy (1900–46), son of Humbert I (q.v.), was born at Naples. He generally ruled as a constitutional monarch with Giolitti as premier but defied parliamentary majorities in bringing Italy into World War I on the side of the Allies in 1915 and in 1922 when he offered Mussolini the premiership. The latter reduced the king to a constitutional façade, conferring on him in May 1936 the title of emperor of Abyssinia. The king, however, supported the dictator until the latter's fall in June 1944. Victor Emmanuel then retired from public life, leaving his son Humbert as lieutenant-general of the realm, and abdicated in May 1946. See HUMBERT II.

VICTORIA, in full **Alexandrina Victoria** (1819–1901), Queen of the United Kingdom of Great Britain and Ireland, and (in 1876) Empress of India, only child of George III's fourth son, Edward, Duke of Kent, and Victoria Maria Louisa of Saxe-Coburg, sister of Leopold, king of the Belgians, was born at Kensington Palace on May 24, 1819. Called to the British throne on the death of her uncle, William IV, June 20, 1837, the provisions of Salic Law excluded her from dominion over Hanover, which passed to another uncle, Ernest, Duke of Cumberland. Crowned at Westminster, June 28, 1838, she speedily demonstrated that clear grasp of constitutional principles and the scope of her own prerogative in which she had been so painstakingly instructed in the many tutelary letters from her uncle, Leopold of Belgium, who remained her constant correspondent. Companioned in girlhood almost exclusively by older folk, her precocious maturity and surprising firmness of will were speedily demonstrated. For with the fall of Melbourne's government in 1839 she resolutely exercised her prerogative by setting aside the precedent which decreed dismissal of the current ladies of the bedchamber. Peel thereupon resigned, and the Melbourne administration, which she personally preferred, was prolonged till 1841. Throughout the early formative years of her reign Melbourne was both her prime minister and her trusted friend and mentor. His ripe experience and thoroughly English outlook served as a useful counter-balance to that more 'Continental' line of policy of which 'Uncle Leopold' was the untiring and far from unprejudiced advocate. On reaching marriageable age the Queen became deeply enamoured of Prince Albert of Saxe-Coburg and Gotha, to whom she was wed on February 10, 1840. Four sons and five daughters were born: Victoria, the Princess Royal, who married Frederick III (q.v.) of Germany; Albert Edward, afterwards Edward VII (q.v.); Alice (q.v.), who married the Duke of Hesse; Alfred, Duke of Edinburgh and of Saxe-Coburg-Gotha (q.v.); Helena, who married Prince Christian of Schleswig-Holstein (see MARIE LOUISE); Louise, who married the Marquis of Lorne (see ARGYLL); Arthur, Duke of Connaught (q.v.); Leopold, Duke of Albany (q.v.), and Beatrice, who married Prince Henry of Battenberg. Strongly influenced by her husband with whom she worked in closest harmony, after his death the stricken queen went into lengthy seclusion, which brought her temporary unpopularity. But with the adventurous Disraeli administration vindicated by the queen's recognition as Empress of India, Victoria rose high in her subjects' favour. Her experience, shrewdness and innate political flair brought powerful influence to bear on the conduct of foreign affairs, as did the response to the country's policy made by her innumerable relatives amongst the European Royal Houses. Unswerving in her preference for ministers of conservative principles, such as Melbourne and Disraeli, rather than for counsellors of more radical persuasion, such as Palmerston and Gladstone, in the long run the Queen's judgment of men and events was rarely to be faulted; although her partiality for all things German had the effect of throwing her heir almost too eagerly into the arms of France. Her *Letters* (ed. Benson, 1908, re-issued ed. Buckle, 1926–32), although prolix and pedestrian in style, bear witness to her unwearying industry, her remarkable practicality, and her high sense of mission. See also her *Leaves from the Journal of our Life in the Highlands* (1869), *More Leaves* (1884), and books by Duke of Argyll (1901), Sir Sidney Lee (1902), Sir Theodor Martin (1908), J. Holland Rose (1909), Mrs Jerrold (1912–16), Visc. Esher (1912–14), Lytton Strachey (1921), H. Bolitho (1949), R. Fulford (1951) and E. Longford (1964).

VICTORIA, Tomás Luis De, or Vittoria, Tommaso Ludovico da (*c.* 1535–1611), Spanish composer, born at Avila, was sent as a priest to Rome by Philip II, to study music. At Loyola's Collegium Germanicum he was appointed chaplain in 1566 and in 1571 choirmaster. In 1576 he became chaplain to the widowed Empress Maria, sister of Philip, returning with her to Madrid in 1583 to the convent of the Descalzas Reales, where he remained as choirmaster until his death. Deeply devout, Victoria wrote only religious music and all of equal excellence. Often compared with his contemporary Palestrina (q.v.), his music, though similar, is more individualistic. Often flavoured with Spanish melody, it is passionate but restrained, exalted but serene. Among his 180 works are the *Officium Hebdonadae Sanctae* (1585), books of motets and masses and his last work, the masterly *Requiem Mass*, composed at the death of the Empress Maria in 1603 and published in 1605. See studies by H. Collet (1914) and F. Pedrell (1918).

VIDA, Marco Girolamo, 'the Christian Virgil' (*c.* 1480–1566), Italian Latin poet, born at Cremona, was made Bishop of Alba in 1532. He wrote Latin orations and dialogues, a religious epic, *Christias* (1535), *De Arte Poetica* (1537), and poems on silk-culture and chess (1527).

VIDAL, Pierre, *vee-dahl* (fl. *c.* 1200), Provençal troubadour, was a professional court minstrel who accompanied Richard Cœur de Lion to Cyprus (1190).

VIDOCQ, Eugène François, *vee-dok* (1775–1857), French criminal, 'the detective', was the son of an Arras baker, whose till he often robbed. After a spell in prison, he was an acrobat, then served in the army till disabled by a wound, and in 1796 was sentenced for forgery to eight years in the galleys. Escaping, he joined a band of highwaymen, whom he betrayed to the authorities. In 1808 he offered his services as a spy on the criminal classes. In 1812 a 'Brigade de Sûreté' was organized, with Vidocq as chief; its efficiency was marvellous, but suspicions grew rife that Vidocq himself originated many of the burglaries that he showed such skill in detecting, and in 1825 he was superseded. His *Mémoires* (1828) are untrustworthy. See Life by Hodgetts (1929).

VIEBIG, Clara, *vee'-* (1860–1952), German novelist, born at Trier, married F. Cohn in 1896 and wrote Zolaesque novels and short stories, including *Kinder der Eifel* (1897), *Das Weiberdorf* (1900), *Das schlafende Heer* (1904), &c. See German study by G. Scheuffler (1927).

VIEIRA, Antonio, *vyay-ee-ra* (1608–97), Portuguese ecclesiastic and missionary, born in Lisbon, was chaplain to John IV and from 1653 to 1661 was in Brazil, where he converted and emancipated the Indians. Unpopular with the colonists, who forced him to return to Portugal, he was imprisoned for two years (1665–67) by the Inquisition. In 1681, with the support of Pope Clement X, he returned to Brazil, became superior in Bahia, where he remained until his death. Of his writings, his *Sermons* are noteworthy and his *Letters* give a clear picture of his time.

VIELÉ-GRIFFIN, Francis, *vee-lay-gri-fī* (1864–1937), French symbolist poet, the son of the American general Egbert Louis Vielé (1825–1902), born at Norfolk, Virginia, made his home in Touraine, France, and became a leading exponent of *vers libre*. His poems collected under the titles *Cueille d'avril* (1886), *Poèmes et Poésies* (1895), *Sapho* (1911), *La Sagesse d'Ulysse* (1925), &c., are of high lyrical quality, tending towards musical impressionism and embody a serene outlook on life. He was elected to the Belgian academy. His American brother,

Herman Knickerbocker Vielé (1856–1908), was a painter and novelist.

VIERGE, Daniel, *vee-er'hay* (1851–1904), Spanish artist, born at Madrid, worked largely in black-and-white. At Paris, he was employed on *Le Monde Illustré* and *La Vie Moderne*, and he illustrated Hugo (1874–82). His pen-and-ink work shows perfect modelling of figures and artistic rendering of architecture, as in Quevedo's *Don Pablo de Segovia* (1882). See work by Marthold (1905).

VIETA, Franciscus, *vyay-tah*, or **François Viète** (1540–1603), French mathematician, born at Fontenay-le-Comte, became a privy councillor to Henry VI and solved an important Spanish cypher. His *Artem Analyticam Isagoge* (1591) is probably the earliest work on symbolic algebra, and he devised methods for solving algebraic equations to the fourth degree. He also wrote on trigonometry and geometry and obtained the value of π as an infinite product. Descartes expressly denied having borrowed from Vieta's work.

VIEUXTEMPS, Henri, *vyœ-tã* (1820–81), Belgian violinist and composer of six violin concertos, born at Verviers, in 1870 became a teacher in the Brussels conservatoire. See Life by Radoux (1893).

VIGÉE LEBRUN. See LE BRUN (2).

VIGFÚSSON, Gudbrandur, *veeg'foos-son* (1827–89), Scandinavian scholar, born at Breidafjord, Iceland, studied and lived at Copenhagen (1849–64). He edited a long series of sagas, completed the *Icelandic Dictionary* (1873) undertaken by Cleasby (q.v.), and, with York Powell, compiled the magnificent *Corpus poeticum boreale* (1883). He went to London in 1864 and thence to Oxford, where in 1884 he was appointed lector in Icelandic.

VIGNEAUD, Vincent du, *veen-yō* (1901–), American biochemist, born in Chicago, professor at Cornell from 1938, synthesized penicillin and oxytocin, discovered the structure of biotin, and won the 1955 Nobel prize for work on hormone synthesis.

VIGNOLA, Giacomo Barozzi da, *vee-nyo'lah* (1507–73), Italian architect, born at Vignola, studied at Bologna. He designed the Villa di Papa Giulio for Pope Julius III and the church of the Gesù, which with its cruciform plan, side chapels, &c., had a great influence on French and Italian church architecture.

VIGNY, Alfred Victor, Comte de, *veen-yee* (1797–1863), French romantic writer, born at Loches, Indre-et-Loire, March 27, served in the Royal Guards (1814–28), retiring with a captaincy. His experiences provided the material for *Servitude et grandeur militaires* (1835), a candid commentary on the boredom and irresponsibility, yet desire for devotion and self-sacrifice induced by peacetime soldiering. He married an Englishwoman, Lydia Bunbury (1828). He had already published anonymously a volume of verse (1822) followed by *Eloa* (1824), the fallen angel condemned for self-pity, and *Poèmes antiques et modernes* (1826; expanded 1829), which includes his grand poetic conception of Moses, as the hopelessly overburdened servant of God. Vigny's life, marred by domestic unhappiness, his failure to enter parliament (1848–49), was that of a congenital misfit who bears his loneliness with dignity. This is reflected in his work, especially in that masterpiece of romantic drama, *Chatterton* (1835), written for his love, the actress Marie Dorval, as well as the volume of exhortatory tales, *Stello*, describing the tragic fates of the young poets, Chatterton, Gilbert and Chénier, concluded in the posthumous sequel *Daphné* (1912). These exemplify Vigny's pessimism, his exaltation of the poet as a godlike outsider, whose knowledge is yet necessary for society, his aristocratic stoicism alleviated unexpectedly by a tinge of Saint-Simonism. Other notable works include the historical novel *Cinq Mars* (1826), the plays *Othello* (1829) and *La Maréchale d'Ancre* (1831), the philosophical poems glorifying social order and discipline, *Les Destinées* (posthumous, 1864), and the biographical notes, *Journal* (1867). He was elected to the Academy (1845) and died in Paris, September 17, 1863. See *Oeuvres complètes* (1921–25), Lives by A. France (1868), E. Dupuy (1910–12), F. Baldensperger (1933), A. Whitridge (1933), A. Pravial (1934) and E. Lauvrière (Paris 1948).

VILLA-LOBOS, Heitor, *vee'la-lō'boosh* (1887–1959), Brazilian composer and conductor, born in Rio de Janeiro. His first published composition was *Salon Waltz* (1908), and a set of *Country Songs* (1910) show his interest in Brazilian folk music and folklore. After taking part in a scientific expedition up the Amazon studying folk music in 1915, he composed five symphonies, five operas and a number of large-scale symphonic poems on Brazilian subjects. He was also responsible for several ballets. A meeting with Milhaud in 1918 aroused his interest in modern music and led him to spend several years in Paris, where his music was first heard in 1923. Abandoning symphonic forms, he composed several *Chôros*, in popular Brazilian styles, and he followed these works with the four suites *Bachianas Brasileiras*, in which he treats Brazilian-style melodies in the manner of Bach. In 1932 Villa-Lobos became director of Musical Education for Brazil.

VILLANI, Giovanni (*c.* 1275–1348), Florentine historian, wrote the *Cronica Universale* (1559), valuable for its vivid portrayal of Florence at the beginning of its prosperity. The chronicle was continued by his brother Matteo and his nephew Filippo. See *Selections*, ed. by Selfe and Wicksteed (1906).

VILLARI, Pasquale, *veel'lah-ree* (1827–1917), Italian historian, born at Naples, took part in the Neapolitan revolution of 1848 and was professor of History at Florence (1866–1909). He was made a senator in 1884 and was minister of Education (1891–92). His works, of which *Machiavelli* (1877–82; trans. 1888) was the best, were all translated by his English wife, Linda White.

VILLARS, Claude Louis Hector, Duc de, *vee-lahr* (1653–1734), French soldier, was born at Moulins. He distinguished himself in the wars of the Low Countries, on the Rhine, and in Hungary, fighting against the Turks. From 1699 till 1701 he represented France at Vienna. In 1702, sent to succour the Elector of Bavaria, he crossed the Rhine defeated the Markgraf of Baden at Friedlingen, and was made a Marshal of France; next year he again crossed the Rhine, but his scheme for advancing upon Vienna was defeated by the obstinacy of the Elector. He was next commissioned to put down the Camisards. He defended the northeastern frontier against Marlborough; in 1708 he defeated the attempts of Prince Eugene to penetrate into France. In 1709 he was sent to oppose Marlborough in the north, but at Malplaquet was severely wounded. In 1711 he headed the last army France could raise, and with it fell upon the British and Dutch under Albemarle, who were entrenched at Denain (July 24, 1712), carried their entrenchments, and turning upon Prince Eugene, drove him under the walls of Brussels; then as plenipotentiary he signed the peace of Rastatt (1714). He became the principal adviser on military affairs and on foreign policy, was a strong opponent of Law's financial measures, and for a time lost favour at court. But the war of 1732-34 in Italy showed that the weight of years had left his military genius untouched. He died at Turin, June 17, 1734. See his *Mémoires* (ed. by De Vogüé, 1884–1904), and Lives by Anquetil (1784), Giraud (1881) and De Vogüé (1888).

VILLEHARDOUIN, Geoffroi de, *veel-ahr-dwĩ* (*c.* 1160–1213), first of the French historians, was born at the castle of Villehardouin in Aube, took part in the Fourth Crusade, and became marshal of 'Romania'. His *Conqueste de Constantinople*—he was present at the capture—describing the events from 1198 to 1207, is of even greater value as literature than as history.

VILLEMAIN, Abel François, *veel-mĩ* (1790–1870), French author and politician, born at Paris, became professor of Rhetoric at the Lycée Charlemagne, the École Normale, and the Sorbonne (1816–26), was made a peer in 1831, and was minister of Public Instruction under Guizot. He was long perpetual secretary of the French Academy. He wrote on the history of French literature, studies of Pindar and Chateaubriand, *Histoire de Cromwell* (1819), *Lascaris, ou les Grecs du XV*^ème^ *siècle* (1825), &c. See study by E. G. Atkin (Wisconsin 1924).

VILLENEUVE, Pierre Charles Jean Baptiste Sylvestre de, *veel-nœv* (1763–1806), French sailor, was born at Valensoles (Basses Alpes), December 31. As rear-admiral, he commanded the rear division of the French navy at the battle of the Nile, and saved his vessel and four others. In 1805 he took command of the Toulon squadron. At Cadiz he was joined by the Spanish fleet, and in order to lure the British fleet from the coasts of Europe bore away to the West Indies. A month later he sailed back, still pursued by Nelson. Off Finisterre he fought an undecided battle with Sir Robert Calder, and, returning to Cadiz, was there blockaded by Nelson. This ruined Napoleon's scheme for the invasion of England, and Villeneuve, about to be superseded, determined to fight before his successor could reach Cadiz. In the battle of Trafalgar (October 21) Villeneuve's flagship, the *Bucentaure*, was dismasted and forced to strike. The admiral lay a prisoner in England till April 1806. On the journey to Paris he stopped at Rennes to learn how the emperor would receive him; and on April 22 he was found in bed, having stabbed himself to death.

VILLEROI, François de Neuville, Duc de, *veel-rwah* (1644–1730), French soldier, was educated with Louis XIV at court, where he was the glass of fashion, but was banished on account of a love affair. In 1680 he returned to court, and in 1693 became a marshal, having distinguished himself at Neerwinden. As commander in the Netherlands (1695–96) he showed great incapacity; and in Italy in 1701 he was defeated and taken prisoner by Prince Eugene at Cremona (1702). Again in command in the Netherlands, he was defeated by Marlborough at Ramillies (1706). Madame de Maintenon had him made guardian to Louis XV. Orleans sent him to live on his estate in 1722 because of his intrigues; but he was subsequently governor of Lyons.

VILLIERS, (1). See BUCKINGHAM, CLARENDON (2) and CLEVELAND (1).

(2) **Charles Pelham** (1802–98), English statesman and Corn-Law reformer, a younger brother of the fourth Earl of Clarendon. He was educated at Haileybury and St John's College, Cambridge, and was called to the bar in 1827. He was returned for Wolverhampton as a Free Trader in 1835, and continued its member for upwards of sixty years, latterly as a Liberal Unionist, becoming the 'Father of the House of Commons'. He made his first motion in favour of Free Trade in 1838, moving a resolution against the Corn Laws each year till they were repealed in 1846. In 1859–66 he sat with Cabinet rank as president of the Poor-Law Board.

VILLIERS DE L'ISLE ADAM, Auguste, Comte de, *veel-yay dė leel a-dã* (1838–89), French writer, pioneer of the symbolist movement, a Breton count who claimed descent from the Knights of Malta, was born at St Brieuc. He dedicated his *Premières Poésies* (1856–58) to de Vigny, but developed into a considerable stylist in prose. His famous short stories, *Contes cruels* (1883) and *Nouveaux Contes cruels* (1888), are in the manner of Poe. Hegelian idealism and Wagnerian romanticism inform his highly didactic novels and plays. The former include *Isis* (1862) on the Ideal and *L'Ève future* (1886) a satire on the materialism of modern science. The latter include his masterpiece, *Axel* (1885). A pronounced Catholic aristocrat, he lived for a while with the monks of Solesmes and died of cancer in a Paris hospital. See Lives by R. de Heussey (1893; trans 1904) and de Rougemont (1910), P. Quennell, *Baudelaire and the Symbolists* (1929), and E. Wilson, *Axel's Castle* (1931).

VILLON, *vee-yõ*, (1) **François** (1431–?), one of France's greatest poets, was born in Paris. His name was de Montcorbier or de Logos, but took that of his guardian, Guillaume de Villon, a priest and a close relative. The latter enabled François to study at university, to graduate (1449) and to become

M.A. (1452). While a student, he fell into bad company and in 1455 had to flee from Paris after fatally wounding a priest in a street brawl. He joined a criminal organization, the 'Brotherhood of the Coquille', which had its own secret jargon in which Villon was to write some of his ballades. Pardoned in 1456, he returned to Paris and there wrote the *Petit Testament*, took part in the organized robbery of the funds of the Collège of Navarre, and fled to the court of the duke of Orleans at Blois. There he was sentenced to death for another unknown crime, but released as an act of grace on a public holiday. The same happened again at Meung-sur-Loire (1461), the year of the *Grand Testament*. In 1462–63 he was in trouble again for theft and brawling. Sentence of death was commuted to banishment in January 1463. He left Paris and nothing further is known of him. The first printed edition of his works was published in 1489. The *Petit Testament* comprises 40 octosyllabic octaves, the *Grand*, 172 bridged by sixteen ballades and other verse forms. Six of the Coquille jargon ballades have been definitely attributed to him. Villon's artistry is in the vitality with which he imbued the outworn mediaeval verse forms such as the ballade and the rondeau and the stark realism with which he dispassionately observes himself and life around him, whether the subject is the fat old courtesan Margot or the grim 'Ballade of the Hanged' or even the 'Ballade made by Villon at his mother's request as a Prayer to Our Lady', one of the masterpieces of religious poetry. With Chaucer he shares a flair for penetrating, unsentimental, often ironic comment, with Verlaine a longing for forgiveness. See biographical and literary studies by Longnon (1877), G. Paris (1901), M. Schwob (1912), P. Champion (1913), H. de Vere Stacpoole (1916), D. B. Wyndham Lewis (1928) and C. Mackworth (1948).

(2) **Jacques,** pseud. of **Gaston Duchamp** (1875–1963), French artist and engraver, born at Damville. From 1891 to 1930 he drew for various periodicals, and made many etchings and lithographs. In 1912 he organized the Section d'Or exhibition in Paris with Léger, Juan Gris, &c. His paintings, many of which are abstract, transmute nature into crystalline forms reminiscent of Cézanne, using clear, bright colour. In 1950 he exhibited at the Venice Biennale and also won the first prize at the Pittsburgh International with his painting *The Thresher*. See study by P. Eluard and René-Jean (1948).

VINCENT, St (d. 304), Spanish protomartyr, born at Saragossa and according to St Augustine became a deacon. Under Diocletian's persecutions, he was imprisoned and tortured at Valencia, where he died. His feast is on January 22.

VINCENT, (1) **Sir Charles Edward Howard** (1849–1908), English politician, born at Slinfold, in Sussex, was first director of C.I.D., Scotland Yard. He wrote on criminal law and police code (1882), the law of Extradition (1881), and was knighted (1896). See Life by Jeyes and How (1912).

(2) **William** (1739–1815), English scholar, born in Westminster, was headmaster of Westminster (1788–1802), canon (1801) and then Dean of Westminster (1802). He wrote on education (1801) and ancient geography (1807). See Life by Nares (1817).

VINCENT DE BEAUVAIS (Latinized *Vincentius Bellovacensius*), *vī-sã* (*c.* 1190–1264), French Dominican and encyclopaedist, gathered together, under the patronage of Loius IX, the entire knowledge of the middle ages in his *Speculum Majus*, in three parts, *Naturale*, *Doctrinale et Historiale* (1473) to which *Speculum Morale* was added anonymously. See Life by Bourgeat (1856).

VINCENT DE PAUL, St (*c.* 1580–1660), French priest and philanthropist, born at Pouy in Gascony, April 24, and admitted to priest's orders in 1600. On a voyage from Marseilles to Narbonne in 1605 he was captured by corsairs and was sold into slavery at Tunis. His master, a renegade Savoyard, was persuaded by Vincent to return to the Christian faith; so, escaping, they landed in France in 1607. Having gone to Rome, he was entrusted with a mission to the French court in 1608, and became almoner of Henry IV's queen. He formed assocations for helping the sick, and in 1619 was appointed almoner-general of the galleys. Meanwhile he had laid the foundation of the Congregation of Priests of the Missions, sanctioned by Urban VIII in 1632, and called Lazarists from their priory of St Lazare in Paris. The Paris Foundling Hospital, the Sisterhood of Charity (1634) and associated lay nursing organizations were of his founding. He died September 27, 1660, and was canonized 1737. His feast day is on July 19. See Lives by E. K. Sanders (1913), P. Coste (1932; trans. 1935) and Giraud (trans. 1955). See OZANAM.

VINCENTIUS LERINENSIS (d. *c.* 450), was a monk of the island of Lerna (Lérins), who defined the three marks of Catholicity—'Quod ubique, quod semper, quod ab omnibus'. Canon Heurtley translated his *Commonitorium* (1895).

VINCI. See LEONARDO DA VINCI.

VINET, Alexandre Rodolphe, *vee-nay* (1797–1847), Swiss Protestant theologian and critic, born at Ouchy near Lausanne, was ordained in 1819, became in 1835 professor of French Language and Literature at Basel and in 1837 of Practical Theology at Lausanne. He was forced to resign when he led a secession from the Swiss church in 1845. He published studies of French literature of the 16th-19th centuries, defended freedom of conscience and the disestablishment of the church. See Lives by Lane (1890) and studies by Rambert (1875) and Molines (1890).

VINJE, Aasmund Olavson, *vin'yė* (1816–70), Norwegian poet and critic, born at Vinje, was in turn teacher, journalist, student and employed in a lawyer's office, before gaining recognition. Intermittently between 1858 and 1866, he brought out a weekly journal *Dōlen*, written entirely by himself. He visited England in 1862 and wrote his critical *A Norseman's View of Britain and the British* (in English) (1863). Back in Norway, he indulged in adverse political criticism which led to his dismissal from an official post at Christiania. Best known for his poetry, Vinje was one of the leading writers in the *landsmål* (the language of the people) movement which was rapidly gaining ground. His works include *En Ballade om Kongen* (1853), *Storegut* (1866) and *Blandkorn* (1867).

VINOGRADOFF, Sir Paul, *vee-nō-grah'doff* (1854–1925), Russian social historian, born at Kostroma, studied at Moscow, became professor of History there. He settled in England and in 1903 he was appointed professor of Jurisprudence at Oxford. Knighted in 1917, he was an authority on mediaeval England, and among his writings are *Villeinage in England* (1892), *Growth of the Manor* (1905) and *English Society in the Eleventh Century* (1908).

VIOLLET-LE-DUC, Eugène, *vyō-lay-lė-dük* (1814–79), French architect and archaeologist, born in Paris, in 1840 became director of the restoration of the Sainte Chapelle, and from this time on was the great restorer of ancient buildings in France including the cathedrals of Notre Dame at Paris, Amiens, Laon, and the Château de Pierrefonds. He served as engineer in the defence of Paris, and was an advanced republican politician. His best-known work was his great dictionary of French Architecture (1853–69). See Lives by Sauvageot (1880), Saint-Paul (2nd ed. 1881), Gout (1914).

VIOTTI, Giovanni Battista, *vyot'tee* (1753–1824), Italian violinist and composer of a number of violin and piano concertos, born at Fontanetto, lived mostly in Paris, where he was director of the Italian Opera and from 1792 was a wine merchant in London. He was one of the leading violinists of his day.

VIRCHOW, Rudolf, *feer-*KHŌ (1821–1902), German pathologist, born at Schivelbein, Pomerania, became professor of Pathological Anatomy at Würzburg (1849) and at Berlin (1856). His *Cellularpathologie* (1858) established that every morbid structure contained cells derived from previous cells. He contributed to the study of tumours, leukaemia, hygiene and sanitation, and as a Liberal member of the *Reichstag* (1880–93) strenuously opposed Bismarck. See studies by Becher (1891) and Pagel (1906).

VIRET, Pierre, *vee-ray* (1511–71), Swiss reformer, born at Orbe in Vaud, converted Lausanne to the Protestant faith (1536). See monograph by Godet (1893).

VIRGIL, (Publius Vergilius Maro) (70–19 B.C.), greatest of Latin poets, was born at Andes near Mantua, October 15. His father owned a small property; the boy was sent to school at Cremona and Milan, and at sixteen went to Rome and studied rhetoric and philosophy. In 41 B.C. the victorious triumvirs were settling disbanded soldiers on confiscated lands throughout Italy. Virgil's farm was part of the confiscated territory; but by advice of the governor of the district, Asinius Pollio, he went to Rome, with special recommendations to Octavianus; and though his own property was not restored to him, he obtained ample compensation from the government, and became one of the endowed court poets who gathered round the prime minister Maecenas. In 37 B.C. his *Eclogues*, ten pastorals modelled on those of Theocritus, were received with unexampled enthusiasm. Soon afterwards Virgil withdrew from Rome to Campania. The munificence of Maecenas had placed him in affluent circumstances. He had a villa at Naples and a country-house near Nola. The *Georgics*, or *Art of Husbandry*, in four books, dealing with tillage and pasturage, the vine and olive, horses, cattle, and bees appeared in 30 B.C., and confirmed Virgil's position as the foremost poet of the age. The remaining eleven years of his life were devoted to a larger task, undertaken at the urgent request of the emperor, the composition of a great national epic on the story of Aeneas the Trojan, legendary founder of the Roman nation and of the Julian family, from the fall of Troy to his arrival in Italy, his wars and alliances with the native Italian races, and his final establishment in his new kingdom. By 19 B.C. the *Aeneid* was practically completed, and in that year Virgil left Italy to travel in Greece and Asia; but at Athens he fell ill, and returned only to die at Brundisium, September 21. At his own wish he was buried at Naples, on the road to Pozzuoli, his tomb, for many hundreds of years after, being worshipped as a sacred place. His sincerity and sweetness of temper won the warm praise of Horace, and the fastidious purity of his life in an age of very lax morality gained him the same name of 'the lady' by which Milton was known at Cambridge. A few juvenile pieces of more or less probable authenticity are extant under his name. These are the *Culex* and the *Moretum*, both in hexameter verse; the *Copa*, a short elegiac piece; and fourteen little poems in various metres, some serious, others trivial. The *Ciris* is now agreed to be by a contemporary imitator. The supremacy of Virgil in Latin poetry was immediate and almost unquestioned; in the *Eclogues* the Latin tongue assumed a richness, harmony, and sweetness till then unknown. The promise shown in the *Eclogues* was more than fulfilled in the *Georgics*. The workmanship of the *Aeneid* is more unequal; but in its great passages there is the same beauty, with an even fuller strength and range. Virgil's works were established classics even in his lifetime, and soon after his death had become, as they still remain, the textbooks of western Europe. By the 3rd century his poems ranked as sacred books, and were regularly used for purposes of divination. In the Dark Ages his fabled powers as a magician almost eclipsed his real fame as a poet; but with the revival of learning he resumed his old place. Dante chose him as his guide in the *Divine Comedy*. The standard English edition is still that of Conington and Nettleship (4th ed. 1881–83). See works on the poet by W. Y. Sellar (1897), T. R. Glover (1915), T. Frank (1922), E. K. Rand (1931), W. F. J. Knight (1944) and Haarhoff (1949), on the *Aeneid* by M. M. Crump (1920) and D. L. Drew (1924), on the *Eclogues* by R. S. Conway (1907) and H. J. Rose (1942) and C. M. Bowra, *From Virgil to Milton* (1945).

VIRGIL, Polydore. See VERGIL.

VIRGINIA. See CLAUDIUS (APPIUS).

VIRIATHUS, *-ah'toos* (d. 139), a Lusitanian herdsman, headed a rising against the

Romans, and from 151 to 141 B.C. repeatedly defeated Roman armies. He was murdered by the Romans.

VIRTANEN, Artturi Ilmari (1895–), Finnish biochemist, born at Helsinki, became professor of Biochemistry there in 1939. He elucidated the processes by which plants obtain nitrogen and complex organic substances from the soil. He showed that silage can be preserved by dilute hydrochloric acid, and studied nutrition and the development of food resources, for which he was awarded the Nobel prize for chemistry (1945).

VISCHER, Peter, *fish'ėr* (1455–1529), German sculptor in bronze, was born and died at Nürnberg. He was responsible for the *King Arthur* statue at Innsbruck, the tomb of Archbishop Ernst at Magdeburg and the basic structure of that of St Sebald at Nürnberg. His sons **Hans** (1489–1550), **Hermann** (1486–1517) and **Peter,** the younger (1487–1528), were also distinguished sculptors. See monograph by C. Headlam (1901).

VISCONTI, the name, taken from the hereditary office of viscount, of a Milanese family of Ghibelline nobility which rose to prominence when **Ottone Visconti** (d. 1295) became archbishop of Milan in 1262 and his nephew **Matteo** (1255–1322) captain of the people. Its most important members in chronological order, were:

(1) **Giovanni** (d. 1354) archbishop and lord of Milan from 1349, brought Genoa and Bologna under his jurisdiction.

(2) **Gian Galeazzo** (1351–1402), Milanese statesman, grandnephew of (1), succeeded his father, Galeazzo II, as joint ruler (1378–85) with his uncle Bernabo, whom he had executed (1385). As duke (1385) he made himself master of the northern half of Italy, bringing many independent cities into one state, arranged marriage alliances with England, France, Austria and Bavaria, and was a great patron of the arts. See Life by D. M. Bueno de Mesquita (1941).

(3) **Filippo Maria** (1392–1447), Milanese statesman, son of (2), restored the unity of his father's dominions, but died without issue. The duchy passed to the Sforza family (q.v.). See D. Muir, *A History of Milan under the Visconti* (1924).

VISCONTI, name of an Italian family of archaeologists and architects:

(1) **Ennio Quirino** (1751–1818), son of (2), father of (3), was keeper of the Capitoline Museum from 1787. During the Roman Republic of 1798 he was one of the five consuls, then fled to Paris, where he became curator at the Louvre and professor of Archaeology. In 1817 he came to England to examine the Elgin marbles. He wrote *Iconographie grecque* (1801) and *romaine* (1817).

(2) **Giovanni Battista Antonio** (1722–84), father of (1), succeeded Winckelmann as prefect of antiquities at Rome (1768), reorganized the Museo Pio-Clementino in the Vatican and with his son edited the catalogue of the museum's engravings. He supervised the excavations which led to the discovery of Scipio's tomb.

(3) **Lodovico Tullio Gioacchino** (1791–1853), son of (1), was a Parisian architect (from 1799). He built Napoleon's mausoleum and was responsible for the scheme joining the Louvre and the Tuileries. His nephew, **Pietro Ercole** (1802–80), was commissioner of antiquities at Rome and curator of the Vatican art collections.

VISSCHER, Cornelis, *vis'ėr* (*c.* 1629–58), a Dutch copperplate engraver, famous for his portraits and for engravings after Guido Reni, Brouwer and Ostade.—His brother, **Jan** (1634–92), was similarly distinguished.

VIT, Vincenzo de (1811–91), Italian scholar, born in Padua, was editor of Forcellini's *Lexicon Totius Latinitatis* (1858–79). A canon of Rovigo and town librarian, in 1850 he joined the brotherhood of Rosmini (q.v.). His unfinished *Onomasticon* was to contain all proper names down to the 5th century.

VITELLIUS, Aulus, *-tel'-* (A.D. 15–69), Roman emperor, was a favourite of Tiberius, Caligula, Claudius and Nero. Appointed by Galba to the command of the legions on the Lower Rhine, he was proclaimed emperor at Colonia Agrippinensis (Cologne) at the beginning of 69; and his generals put an end to the reign of Otho by the victory of Bedriacum. Vitellius, during his brief reign, gave himself up to pleasure and debauchery. Many of his soldiers deserted when Vespasian was proclaimed emperor in Alexandria. Vitellius was defeated in two battles by his rival, dragged through the streets of Rome and murdered, December 21.

VITORIA. See ESPARTERO.

VITRUVIUS POLLIO, Marcus, *-troo'vee-oos* (1st cent. A.D.), Roman architect and military engineer, a North Italian in the service of Augustus, wrote *De Architectura* (before A.D. 27), which is the only Roman treatise on architecture still extant. See edition by F. Granger (1931).

VITRY, Jacques de, *vee-tree* (d. 1240), a French cardinal legate, who died at Rome, is known by his *Historia Orientalis,* a valuable source book, letters and sermons.

VITTORINO DA FELTRE, *veet-to-ree'nō da fel-trė* (*c.* 1378–1446), Italian educationist, was summoned to Mantua as tutor to the children of the Marchese Gonzaga (1423) and founded a school for both rich and poor children (1425), in which he applied his own methods of instruction. See study by W. H. Woodward (1897).

VITUS, St, *vī-* (early 4th cent.), is said to have been the son of a Sicilian pagan and converted by his nurse Crescentia and her husband Modestus, with whom he suffered martyrdom under Diocletian. He was invoked against sudden death, hydrophobia and chorea or St Vitus' Dance, and is sometimes regarded as the patron of comedians and actors. His feast day is June 15.

VIVALDI, Antonio, *-vahl'-* (1678–1741), Venetian violinist and composer, known as 'the Red Priest', on account of his red hair, born at Venice, took orders (1703), but gave up officiating and was attached to the hospital of the Pietà at Venice (1703–40), dying at Vienna. The twelve concertos of *L'Estro Armonico* (1712) gave him a European reputation; *The Seasons* (1725), an early example of programme music, proved highly popular; and he wrote many operas and some sacred music. Though he really consolidated and developed the solo concerto, he was forgotten after his death. Bach transcribed many of his concertos for the keyboard and from the 19th century they were increasingly played. See Life by Mario Rinaldi (Milan 1943) and Italian study by M. Pincherle (1948; abridged and trans. 1958).

VIVARINI, *vee-vah-ree'-nee*, name of a family of Venetian painters of the 15th century, including:

(1) **Antonio** (active *c.* 1440–*c.* 1476/84), first worked in partnership with his brother-in-law Giovanni d'Alemagna and later with his brother (2). His paintings, often of Madonnas and saints, are modelled first on Gentile da Fabriano and then on Mantegna and Giovanni Bellini (q.v.).

(2) **Bartolommeo** (active 1450–99), brother of (1), worked under the same influences, but his painting shows a step forward towards the renaissance style.

(3) **Luigi or Alvise** (active 1457–*c.* 1503/5), son of (1), was possibly a pupil of both his father and uncle. Influenced by Antonello da Messina and Bellini, his works include portrait busts and altarpieces, especially a *Madonna and six Saints* (1480) in the Academy, Venice.

VIVES, Juan Luis, generally known as **Ludovicus Vives,** *vee-vays* (1492–1540), Spanish philosopher and humanist, born at Valencia, studied philosophy at Paris, but, disgusted with the empty quibblings of scholasticism there, went to Louvain in 1519, where, as professor of Humanities, he edited St Augustine's *Civitas Dei.* He dedicated it to Henry VIII, who summoned him to England in 1523 as tutor to Princess Mary. He also taught at Oxford and became a fellow of Corpus Christi. He was imprisoned in 1527 for opposing Henry VIII's divorce from Catharine of Aragon and after 1528 lived mostly at Bruges. His commentary on Aristotle's *De Anima* foreshadowed Bacon in his emphasis on inductive methods. He also wrote a remarkable treatise on education, *De Disciplinis* (1531).

VIVIANI, René, *vee-vyah'nee* (1862–1925), French statesman, born at Sidi-bel-Abbès, Algeria, was prime minister at the outbreak of World War I and in order to demonstrate France's peaceful intentions withdrew French forces from the German frontier. He was minister of justice (1915) and French representative at the League of Nations (1920).

VIVIN, Louis, *vee-vĩ* (1861–1936), French primitive painter, born at Hadol, was a Post Office employee until he retired in 1922. He painted mainly still-lifes and views of Paris and its parks. His naïve and charmingly coloured pictures are meticulous in every detail.

VIZETELLY, Henry Richard, *viz-ė-tel'i* (1820–1894), English publisher of Italian descent, was born in London. As an engraver he early contibuted to the newly founded *Illustrated London News* and in 1843 set up in competition his own *Pictorial Times.* He became a foreign correspondent to the *Illustrated London News* in Paris (1865–72) and in Berlin (1872). He witnessed the siege of Paris and with his son, Ernest, wrote *Paris in Peril* (1867). As a publisher in later life, he produced translations of French and Russian authors, notably of the works of Zola, which involved him in two legal actions for obscene libel. In 1893 his memoirs were published as *Glances Back Through Seventy Years.* His brother, **Frank** (1830–83), also a foreign correspondent for the *Illustrated London News*, was killed in the Sudan. His sons, **Edward Henry** (1847–1903) and **Ernest Alfred** (1853–1922), were also journalists, while **Frank Horace** (1864–1938) was a notable lexicographer on the staff of the Funk and Wagnall Company in New York.

VLADIMIR, *vla-dee'-meer*, the name of two notable Russian rulers:

Vladimir I, known as Saint Vladimir, or 'the Great' (*c.* 956–1015), ruled from 980 as the first Christian sovereign of Russia, extending its dominions into Lithuania, Galicia and Livonia, with Kiev as his capital.

Vladimir II, surnamed **Monomachus** (1053–1125), became by popular demand Grand Prince of Kiev in 1113 instead of the prior claimants of the Sviatoslav and Iziaslav families, thus founding the Monomakhovichi dynasty. A popular, powerful, enlightened and peaceful ruler, he colonized, built new towns, dethroned unruly princes and introduced laws against usury. He left careful instructions to his son and cousin in the manuals *Puchenie* and *Poslanie.*

VLAMINCK, Maurice de, *vla-mĩk* (1876–1958), French artist, born in Paris. He was largely self-taught, and for a time was a racing cyclist. About 1900 he began to work with Derain. At this time he was much influenced by Van Gogh, and by 1905 he was one of the leaders of the Fauves, using typically brilliant colour. From 1908 to 1914, however, he painted more realistic landscapes under the influence of Cézanne. After 1915 his palette was more sombre, and his style more romantic than Cézannesque, though still with an expressionist zest. He mainly lived in the country as a farmer, and this may have given him his consistent sensitivity to the nuances of landscape and atmosphere. Also a talented violinist, he wrote several books, including *Communications* (1921). See Lives by K. G. Perls (1941) and R. Queneau (1949).

VODNIK, Valentin (1758–1819), Slovene poet and teacher, born at Zgornja Šiška near Ljubljana, who by his writings helped to revive Slovene nationalism. He wrote poetry, educational and school books in the language of the peasantry and this became established as the literary language of Yugoslavia.

VOELCKER, Augustus, *fœl'kėr* (1822–84), German agricultural chemist and writer, was born at Frankfurt-am-Main. After studying at Göttingen and Utrecht, he worked in Edinburgh under the auspices of the Highland and Agricultural Society of Scotland, was appointed professor of Agriculture at the Royal Agricultural College, Cirencester, in 1849, and in 1857 was attached to the Royal Agricultural Society of England as consulting chemist. Agricultural chemistry was greatly advanced by Voelcker's work and writings on farm feeding stuffs, on soil research and on artificial manures. In 1870 he was elected a fellow of the Royal Society and in 1875 chairman of the Farmers' Club.

VOGEL, (1) **Hermann Carl** (1841–1907), German astronomer, born at Leipzig, became assistant and later director of the observatory at Potsdam (1882). He discovered spectroscopic binaries.

(2) **Hermann Wilhelm** (1834–98), German chemist, born at Dobrilugk, Brandenburg, taught at Berlin, and invented the orthochromatic photographic plate (1873), studied spectroscopic photography and designed a photometer.

(3) **Sir Julius** (1835–99), New Zealand statesman, born in London, edited and founded newspapers in Australia and New Zealand, where he was elected colonial treasurer in 1869. He established a government public trust office (1872), improved immigration facilities and planned the introduction of trunk railways, borrowing £10,000,000 for his public works programme. He formed a government in 1872 and was premier (1873–75). His resolution (1874) foreshadowed the abolition of the provinces. He resigned in 1875 to devote himself to business, but was again treasurer during the economic crisis in 1884.

(4) **Vladimir** (1896–), Russian composer, born at Moscow, studied in Moscow and under Busoni in Berlin. He composed orchestral works and chamber music and secular oratorios, including *Wagadu Destroyed* (1935) with saxophone accompaniment.

VOGLER, Georg Joseph, *fōg'lėr* (1749–1814), German composer, styled Abt Vogler, was born at Würzburg, the son of a violin maker, was ordained priest at Rome in 1773, and made Knight of the Golden Spur and chamberlain to the pope. At Mannheim he established his first school of music; his second was at Stockholm. After years of wandering and brilliant successes in London and Europe as a player on his 'orchestrion' (a modified organ), he settled as *kapellmeister* at Darmstadt, and opened his third school, having as pupils Weber and Meyerbeer. His compositions and his theories of music are now forgotten; but his name survives in Robert Browning's poem. See study by Schafhäutl (1887).

VOGÜÉ, *-gü-ay,* (1) **Charles Jean Melchior, Marquis de** (1829–1916), French archaeologist and diplomatist, born in Paris, travelled in Syria (1853–54 and 1861), was ambassador at Constantinople (1871–75) and at Vienna (1875–79). Elected to the Académie (1901), he wrote on the churches of Palestine (1860 and 1865).

(2) **Eugène Marie Melchior, Vicomte de** (1848–1910), French historian, cousin of (1), was born at Nice. He was secretary at St Petersburg (1876–82) and was admitted to the Académie (1888). He wrote *Le Roman russe* (1886), a valuable study of the Russian novels of Tolstoy and Dostoevsky, *Les Morts qui parlent* (1899) and works on Syria and Egypt.

VOITURE, Vincent, *vwah-tür* (1598–1648), French poet and letter-writer, born at Amiens, was an original member of the Académie, and enjoyed the favour of Gaston d'Orléans, Richelieu, Mazarin and Louis XIII. His brilliant sonnets and *vers de société* were the delight of the Hôtel Rambouillet, but were not published till 1650. See Sainte-Beuve's *Causeries* and study by E. Magne (1911).

VOLNEY, Constantin François Chassebœuf, Comte de (1757–1820), French scholar and author, born at Craon in Mayenne, studied at Paris medicine, history and the Oriental languages, adopted the name of Volney, and travelled in Egypt and Syria (1783–87), publishing his valuable *Voyage* (1787). A zealous reformer, he was elected to the Constituent Assembly in 1789, but later was thrown into prison till the downfall of Robespierre. His reputation chiefly rests on his famous work *Les Ruines, ou Méditations sur les révolutions des empires* (1791). Professor of History at the short-lived École Normale, he collected in the United States (1795–98) materials for his *Tableau du climat et du sol* (1803), and was admitted to the Academy. Napoleon made him senator, count and commander of the Légion d'honneur; Louis XVIII made him a peer. See Life by L. Séché (1899) and Sainte-Beuve's *Causeries*.

VOLSTEAD, Andrew J. (1860–1947), American politician, born in Goodhue Co., Minnesota, practised law and entered congress as a Republican in 1903. He was the author of the Farmers' Cooperative Marketing Act, but is best known for the Prohibition Act of 1919, named after him, which forbade the manufacture and sale of intoxicant liquors. This act, passed over President Wilson's veto, was in force until 1933.

VOLTA, Alessandro, Count, *vol'tah* (1745–1827), Italian physicist, born at Como, in 1774–1804 was professor of Natural Philosophy at Pavia. He retired to his native town, but was summoned to show his discoveries to Napoleon, and received medals and titles at home and abroad, including the Copley medal (1791). He developed the theory of current electricity, discovered the electric decomposition of water; invented an electric battery, the electrophorus, an electroscope and made investigations on heat and gases. His name is given to the unit of electric pressure, the volt. See monographs by Bianchi and Mochetti (1829–32), and by Volta (1875).

VOLTAIRE, François Marie Arouet de, *voltayr* (1694–1778), French author, the embodiment of the 18th-century 'enlightenment', was born November 24 in Paris, where his father, François Arouet, held a post in the Chambre des comptes. In his ninth year he entered the Collège Louis-le-Grand, the chief French seminary of the Jesuits. Leaving college at seventeen, he was destined for the bar, but law disgusted him. Alarmed by the dissipated life which he was leading, his father gladly saw him admitted into the suite of his godfather's brother, the Marquis de Châteauneuf, French ambassador to Holland; but in consequence of an undiplomatic love affair with a French Protestant *émigrée* at The Hague, he was sent home. He again entered an attorney's office, but his stay in it was short, and he soon obtained notoriety as the author of a satire on his successful rival in the poetic competition for an Academy prize. In 1716, on suspicion of lampooning the regent, the Duc d'Orléans, he was banished for several months from Paris; and in 1717–18, a savage lampoon, accusing the regent of all manner of crimes, resulted in his eleven months' imprisonment in the Bastille, where he rewrote his tragedy *Œdipe*, began a poem on Henry IV and assumed the name Voltaire, supposed to be an anagram of Arouet l(e) j(eune). *Œdipe* was performed in 1718, and was triumphantly successful. His next dramatic attempts were almost failures, and he devoted himself to his poem on Henry IV. But the authorities refusing to sanction its publication on account of its championship of Protestantism and of religious toleration, Voltaire had the epic poem surreptitiously printed at Rouen (1723) and smuggled into Paris, as *La Ligue ou Henri le grand*. Famous and a favourite at court, he was denounced by the Chevalier de Rohan-Chabot as a parvenu. Voltaire retorted with spirit, and circulated caustic epigrams on the Chevalier, whose revenge was to have Voltaire beaten by his hirelings. Voltaire challenged the author of the outrage, and was once more thrown into the Bastille, and liberated only on the condition that he would proceed at once to England, where he landed in May 1726. Here Bolingbroke made him known to Pope and his circle. He made the acquaintance of Peterborough, Chesterfield, the Herveys and the Duchess of Marlborough, and became intimate with Young, Thomson and Gay. He acquired some knowledge of Shakespeare and Milton, Dryden and Butler, Pope's works, Addison's *Cato*, and the Restoration dramatists. He was strongly attracted to Locke's philosophy, and he mastered the elements of Newton's astronomical physics. The English Deists furnished weapons or at least a stalking-horse (Bolingbroke). Queen Caroline accepted his dedication to her of the *Henriade*, the new form of *La Ligue*; and when permitted to return to France in 1729 he took with him his *History of Charles XII* and the materials for his *Letters on the English*. He laid the foundation of his great wealth by purchasing shares in a government lottery and by speculations in the corn trade, ultimately increased by the profits from large army contracts. He formed an intimacy with Madame du Châtelet (q.v.), and made her husband's château of Cirey in Champagne their headquarters (1734). Here he wrote dramas (*Mahomet* (1741) and *Mérope* (1743) among them), poetry, his *Treatise on Metaphysics*, much of his *Siècle de Louis Quatorze* (1751) and *Les Mœurs et l'esprit des nations*, with his *Elements of the Philosophy of Newton* (1738). Apart from Madame du Châtelet, his correspondence (1640–50) testifies to a love affair with his niece, the widowed Madame Denis. Since the appearance of his *Letters on the English* he had been out of favour at court. But his *Princesse de Navarre*, performed on the occasion of the Dauphin's marriage (February 1745), pleased Louis XV by its adroit adulation. This and the patronage of Madame de Pompadour procured him the appointments of royal historiographer and of gentleman-in-ordinary to the king, as well as his election to the French Academy. In 1747 an imprudent speech at a court card-party drove him to take refuge with the Duchesse de Maine, for whose amusement he now wrote *Zadig* and others of the Oriental tales. When he was allowed to reappear at court, some injudicious flattery of Madame de Pompadour excited the indignation of the queen, and Voltaire had again to migrate. The death (September 1749) of Madame du Châtelet allowed him at last to accept the repeated invitation of Frederick the Great. In July 1750 Voltaire found himself at Berlin as king's chamberlain, with a pension of 20,000 francs and board in one of the royal palaces. But he entered into some questionable financial operations with a Berlin Jew; Frederick was still more gravely offended by his satirical criticisms on Maupertuis; and in March 1753 Frederick and Voltaire parted, never to meet again. In Prussia Voltaire had published his *Siècle de Louis Quatorze* (1751). On his way home he was arrested at Frankfurt, through Frederick's representative there, instructed to recover from Voltaire a volume of the king's poems. Voltaire avenged himself by writing a malicious sketch of Frederick's character and account of his habits, first printed after the writer's death. Voltaire settled in 1755 near Geneva—after 1758 at Ferney, four miles from Geneva. In 1756–59 appeared his *Mœurs et l'Esprit des nations*, his pessimistic poem on the earthquake of Lisbon and that satirical masterpiece, the short story, *Candide* which attacked what Voltaire understood by the Leibnizian optimistic theology that 'all is for the best in this best of all possible worlds'. The suspension of the *Encyclopédie* by the French government, and the condemnation by the parliament of Paris of a harmless poem of his own on natural religion, impelled Voltaire to declare war by word and deed against the bigoted, 'L'Infâme'. In 1762 appeared the first of his antireligious writings which were to include didactic tragedies, biased histories, pamphlets and the *Dictionnaire philosophique* (1764). The judicial murder (1762) of Jean Calas (q.v.), falsely accused of having, from Protestant zeal, killed one of his sons to keep him from turning a Catholic, aroused Voltaire to exert himself successfully to get his innocence established and to rescue members of the Calas family from punishment. This and similar efforts on behalf of victims of French fanaticism, for whom he provided a refuge at Ferney, won widespread admiration. The Genevan government prevented Voltaire from staging plays and from establishing a theatre at Geneva. Rousseau's support for the Swiss government terminated Voltaire's friendship with the philosopher (1758). In 1778, in his eighty-fourth year, he was given a 'royal' welcome in Paris, when he arrived to put on his last tragedy, *Irène*. The excitement brought on illness and death on May 30, 1778. After the Revolution, which his works and ideas helped to foster, his remains were fitly reinterred in the Panthéon, Paris. See his *Correspondence with Frederick the Great* (trans. 1927), his *Love Letters to His Niece* (ed. and trans. T. Besterman, 1958); Lives by G. Desnoiresterres (1867–76), Viscount Morley (1872), L. Crouslé (1899), C. E. Vulliamy (1930), H. N. Brailsford (1935), A. Noyes (1936), R. Naves (1942), A. Maurois (1952); and political and philosophical studies by G. Pellissier (1908), A. Bellescort (1925), C. Rowe (1955) and P. Gay (1959).

VOLTERRA, (1) **Daniele da** (*c.* 1509–66), Italian artist, born at Volterra, was Michelangelo's assistant. He painted the *Descent from the Cross* in the Trinità dei Monti at Rome.

(2) **Vito** (1860–1940), Italian mathematician, born at Ancona, professor at Pisa, Turin and Rome, contributed to modern mathematical analysis and theory of equations. He became a foreign member of the Royal Society in 1902.

VOLUSENUS, Florentius-Florence Wilson, or **Wolsey**, *vol-oo-say'noos* (1504–46), Scottish humanist, born near Elgin, went to the University of Paris, and attained a mastery of Latin which ranks him with the first scholars of his time. After acting as tutor to a reputed son of Cardinal Wolsey, he became principal of a school at Carpentras near Avignon; and died at Vienne in Dauphiné. His chief work is his *De Animi Tranquillitate*. See Hume Brown, *Surveys of Scottish History* (1919).

VONDEL, Joost van den (1587–1679), the greatest of the Dutch poets, born at Cologne of Dutch immigrant parents, became a prosperous hosier in Amsterdam and devoted his leisure to the penning of satirical verse, himself turning from Anabaptism through Armenianism to Roman Catholicism. Having acquired a wide knowledge of the classics, Vondel turned to Sophoclean drama and produced *Jephtha* (1659) and *Lucifer* (1654), a masterpiece of lyrical religious drama, which brings to mind Milton's *Paradise Lost* (*c.* 1660–63) and greatly influenced the German poetical revival after the Thirty Years' War. See his complete *Werken*, ed. with Life by J. F. M. Sterck (1927–40) and study by A. J. Barnouw (1926).

VON WRIGHT, Georg Hendrik (1916–), Finnish logician and philosopher, born in Helsinki, took part in the discussions of the Vienna Circle of logical positivists and studied under and succeeded Wittgenstein (q.v.) at Cambridge (1948–51). He was professor of Philosophy at Helsinki (1946–61), visiting professor at Cornell (1954, 1958), California (1963) and Pittsburgh (1966) universities, and professor at large at Cornell since 1965. He was Gifford Lecturer (1959–1960) on *Norms and Values* at St Andrews. Von Wright formalized the traditional, vain attempts at justifying induction in *The Logical Problem of Induction* (1941; rev. ed. 1957) and *A Treatise on Induction and Probability* (1951), and has greatly contributed to metalogic with *Form and Content in Logic* (1941), *An Essay in Modal Logic* (1951), *Logical Studies* (1957), and in 1963 *The Varieties of Goodness*, *The Logic of Preference* and *Norm and Action*. He wrote a memorable introduction to *Ludwig Wittgenstein—A Memoir* by N. Malcolm (1958).

VON DER DECKEN. See DECKEN.

VORAGINE, Jacobus de, *vo-raj'ee-nay* (1230–98), Italian hagiologist, a Dominican, born at Viareggio near Genoa, became Archbishop of Genoa. He wrote the *Golden Legend*, a famous collection of lives of the saints, translated by Caxton in 1483. He is also said to have produced the first Italian translation of the Bible.

VORONOFF, Serge (1866–1951), Russian physiologist, born at Voronezh and educated in Paris, became director of experimental surgery at the Collège de France. He specialized in grafting animal glands into the human body and wrote on his theory connecting gland secretions with senility.

VOROSHILOV, Klimenti Efremovich, *vor-ė-shee'lĕf* (1881–1969), president of the Soviet Union from Stalin's death (1953) to 1960, was born near Dniepropetrovsk in the Ukraine. He joined the Communist Party in 1903 and political agitation soon brought about his exile to Siberia. He remained a fugitive right up to 1914, and took a military rather than a political rôle in the 1917 Revolution. From 1925 to 1940 he was commissar for defence and so mainly responsible for the modernization of the Red Army and its success in defeating Hitler's invasion of 1941. His long friendship with Stalin, dating from 1906, possibly excused some of his later mistakes.

VÖRÖSMARTY, Michael, *vœ'rœsh-mort-y'* (1800–55), Hungarian poet, born at Szekesfehervar, was an advocate and in 1848 a member of the National Assembly. He wrote the national song, *Szozat* (1840), lyric and epic poetry and eleven plays, of which *Csongor es Tünde* (1831) is his masterpiece. He also translated Shakespearean tragedies.

VORTIGERN (fl. 450), the prince of south-east Britain, reported by Bede, Nennius and Geoffrey of Monmouth to have invited the Saxons into Britain to help him against the Picts, and to have married Rowena, daughter of Hengist.

VOS, Cornelis de (1585–1651), Antwerp painter of portraits and religious and mythological pieces, worked occasionally for Rubens. His brother, **Paul** (1590–1678), painted animals and hunting scenes.

VOSS, *fos*, (1) **Johann Heinrich** (1751–1826), German poet and translator, born at Sommersdorf in Mecklenburg, studied at Göttingen, and in 1778 went from editing the *Musenalmanach* at Wandsbeck to be schoolmaster at Otterndorf. Here he translated the *Odyssey*. In 1782 he became rector of a school at Eutin, whence in 1789 he issued his translation of Virgil's *Georgics*. In 1802 he settled in Jena, in 1805 was appointed professor at Heidelberg, where he translated Horace, Hesiod, Theocritus, Bion, Moschus, Tibullus and Propertius; other translations were of Aristophanes and (with the aid of his two sons) Shakespeare—a work far inferior to Schlegel's. *Luise* (1795), an idyll, is his best original poem. See Lives by Paulus (1826) and by Herbst (1876).

(2) **Richard** (1851–1918), German writer, born at Neugrape in Pomerania, published a long series of poems, dramas and romances.

VOSSIUS, (1) **Gerard Jan** (1577–1649), Dutch scholar, father of (2), born near Heidelberg, studied at Leyden, and became in 1600 rector of the school at Dort and in 1615 of the theological college of Leyden. His *Historia Pelagiana* (1618), with its Arminian leanings, brought down upon him the wrath of the orthodox. Laud made him a prebend in Canterbury. In his *De Historicis Latinis* (1627) he made a prudent recantation. In 1632 he became professor of History in the Athenaeum at Amsterdam. His chief works are *Commentaria Rhetorica* (1606), *De Historicis Graecis* (1624) and *Aristarchus* (1635).

(2) **Isaak** (1618–88), Dutch scholar, son of (1), born in Leyden, travelled in England, France and Italy, collecting many valuable manuscripts, and was at the court of Queen Christina of Sweden, but returned to Holland in 1658. In 1670 he settled in England, and, although a libertine, was appointed by Charles II a canon of Windsor. He edited the epistles of Ignatius (1646), Justin, Pomponius Mela and Catullus, and wrote on chronology.

VOUET, Simon, *voo-ay* (1590–1649), French painter, born in Paris, after fourteen years in Italy, returned to France, where his religious and allegorical paintings and decorations in the baroque style became very popular. A contemporary of Poussin, who criticized him but was not a serious rival during his lifetime, his pupils included Lebrun and Le Sueur. There are paintings by him in galleries throughout Europe, including the Louvre, the Uffizi and the National Gallery, London.

VOWELL, John. See HOOKER (4).

VOYNICH, E. L. See BOOLE.

VOYSEY, Charles (1828–1912), English theist, born in London, studied at St Edmund's Hall, Oxford, was transferred from his curacy at St Mark's, Whitechapel, in 1863, to the living of Healaugh near Tadcaster, for preaching against the doctrine of perpetual punishment. His sermons and writings on inspiration led to the deprivation of his living in 1871. He then became founder and pastor of a Theistic church in London, and wrote on *The Mystery of Pain, Death and Sin* and on *Theism*.

VRCHLICKÝ, Jaroslav, *værKH'lits-ki* (1853–1912), pseud. of **Emil Frida**, Czech lyric and epic poet and translator of the classics of European poetry, born at Laun, was a pupil of Victor Hugo who inspired the *Fragments of the Epic of Humanity*. His best ballads, *Legend of St Procopius* (1879), *Peasant Ballads* (1886), are on nationalistic and patriotic themes. His early lyric poetry on love and the pleasures of life gave way to reflections upon suffering and misfortune. In 1893, at the height of his reputation, he was appointed professor of European literature at Prague.

VRIES. See DE VRIES.

VUILLARD, Jean Edouard, *vwee-yahr'* (1868–1940), French artist, born at Cuiseaux, died at La Baule. One of the later Impressionists, he shared a studio with Bonnard, and was strongly influenced by Gauguin and by the vogue for Japanese painting. Although his outlook was limited and mainly devoted to flower pieces and to simple and intimate interiors, these are painted with an exquisite sense of light and colour. See Life by C. Roger-Marx (1948), and studies by same (Paris 1945) and Jacques Mercanton (Paris 1948).

VULPIUS, Christiane. See GOETHE.

VYSHINSKY, Andrei, *vee-shins'kee* (1883–1954), Soviet jurist and politician, born of Polish origin in Odessa, studied law at Moscow University but was debarred from a lecturership on account of his Menshevik revolutionary activities until 1921, when he left the Red Army. He became professor of Criminal Law and simultaneously attorney-general (1923–25) and was rector of Moscow University (1925–28). He was notoriously the public prosecutor at the Metropolitan-Vickers trial (1933) and the subsequent state trials (1936–38) which removed Stalin's rivals, Bukharin, Radek, Zinoviev, Kamenev and Sokolnikov. He was promoted deputy foreign minister under Molotov (1940) and was permanent Soviet delegate to the United Nations (1945–49, 1953–54), succeeding Molotov as foreign minister in 1949 until the death of Stalin (1953). He was the cynically brilliant advocate of the disruptive and negative Stalin-Molotov foreign policies, the author of many textbooks on Soviet Law and the recipient of the Order of Lenin and Stalin prize in 1947.

W

WAAGE, Peter, *vaw'gė* (1833–1900), Norwegian chemist, became (1862) professor in Christiania, and established (1864) with Guldberg (q.v.) the law of mass action.

WAAGEN, Gustav Friedrich, *vah'gen* (1794–1868), German art critic, appointed (1844) Art History professor at Berlin university. One of his best-known books is *The Treasures of Art in Great Britain* (3 vols. 1854).

WAALS, Johannes Diderik van der, *vals* (1837–1923), Dutch physicist, professor at Amsterdam University (1877–1908), famed for the discovery (1873) of van der Waals' equation, defining the physical state of a gas or liquid, and investigator of the weak attractive forces (van der Waals' forces) between molecules. He was awarded a Nobel prize in 1910.

WACE, Robert (?), *ways* (*c.* 1115–*c.* 1183), Anglo-Norman poet, born in Jersey, studied in Paris, and was a canon of Bayeux between 1160 and 1170. He wrote several verse lives of the saints, a free Norman-French version of Geoffrey of Monmouth's *Historia Regum Britanniae* entitled *Roman de Brut* (1155), used by Layamon and Brunne (qq.v.), also the *Roman de Rou*, an epic of the exploits of the Dukes of Normandy. See studies by Payne-Payne (1916) and Philpot (1926).

WACKENRODER, Wilhelm Heinrich, *vak'ėn-rō-dėr* (1773–98), German writer, an early exponent of Romanticism and a close friend of Tieck (q.v.), with whom he collaborated in *Herzensergiessungen eines kunstliebenden Klosterbruders* (1797) and *Phantasien über die Kunst* (1799).

WADDELL, Helen (1889–1965), English mediaevalist and writer, born in Tokyo, published *Lyrics from the Chinese* (1913), *Mediaeval Latin Lyrics* (1929), *The Wandering Scholars* (1927), *Peter Abelard* (1933), *The Desert Fathers* (1936), &c.

WADDING, Luke (1588–1657), Irish theologian, born at Waterford, in 1607 entered the Franciscan order, in 1617 became president of an Irish college in Salamanca, was founder in 1625 of another college in Rome, famed for his *Annales Ordinis Minorum* (1625–54; the history of the Franciscans), *Scriptores Ordinis Minorum* (1650), and his edition (1639) of Duns Scotus. See Life by J. A. O'Shea (1885) and study by G. Cleary (1925).

WADDINGTON, William Henry, Fr. *vad-ī-tõ* (1826–94), French statesman and archaeologist, born in Paris, the son of an Englishman, who became a French subject. He was educated chiefly in England, devoted himself to study and travel in Asia Minor, Syria and Cyprus, and was ambassador at London from 1883 till 1892.

WADE, (1) George (1673–1748), British field-marshal, born probably in Westmeath, entered the army in 1690, after the Jacobite rebellion of 1715 judiciously pacifying and disarming the clans in the Scottish highlands, where he constructed (1726–37) a system of metalled military roads, with forty stone ('Wade') bridges. Wade became a privy councillor and a lieutenant-general in 1742, and a field-marshal in 1743. Unsuccessful in engagements in the Netherlands in 1744, he was evaded, as commander-in-chief of George II's forces in England, by Prince Charles Edward's army, both on the latter's advance into, and on its retreat from, that country in 1745.

(2) **Sir Thomas Francis** (1818–95), British diplomatist and scholar, ambassador at Peking (1871–83), professor of Chinese at Cambridge University (1889–95), inventor of the Wade system of transliterating Chinese.

WADSWORTH, Edward (1889–1949), English artist, born in Yorkshire. He studied engineering in Munich, attended the Slade School in 1910, and was associated with Wyndham Lewis, Roger Fry, Unit One, and the London Group. His still-lifes and seascapes with marine objects, painted in tempera with dreamlike clarity and precision, made him internationally known.

WAGNER, *vahg'ner,* **(1) Adolph** (1835–1917), German economist, son of (2), born at Erlangen, was professor at Vienna, Hamburg, Dorpat, Freiburg and Berlin. In his numerous works he represented the historical school and supported state socialism.

(2) **Rudolf** (1805–64), German anatomist and physiologist, father of (1), born at Bayreuth, professor (1832–40) at Erlangen and (1840–64) Göttingen, from whose works were translated (1839) *System of Physiology* and (1844) *Comparative Anatomy.*

(3) **(Wilhelm) Richard** (1813–83), German composer, father of (4), born at Leipzig, was educated chiefly at Dresden. His musical training was perfunctory until he was accepted as a pupil by Weinlig of the Thomasschule in 1830 after notice had been taken of a formidable but abortive concert overture which Dorn (q.v.), a friend of the family and conductor at the new Leipzig Court Theatre, had been cajoled into performing. Some immature efforts were followed by his first opera *Die Feen* (1833), adapted from Gozzi's *Donna Serpente* and owing much to Weber's *Oberon.* It was not performed during the composer's lifetime. His next effort, *Das Liebesverbot* (1834), flopped deservedly after one performance at Magdeburg, where he had obtained the post of conductor at the opera house, and where he met Minna Planer, a member of the company, who was to become his wife in 1836. The Magdeburg opera soon went bankrupt, as did the theatre at Königsberg, where Wagner found his next post. Riga, where Dorn was now teaching, seemed more promising, but Wagner resolved to try his luck in Paris with his new partially-finished opera based on Bulwer-Lytton's romance *Rienzi.* There, in spite of Meyerbeer's help, he barely made a living by journalism and doing hack operatic arrangements. He left Paris in 1842 with *Rienzi,* which he had finished in a debtors' prison, still unperformed but now accepted for presentation at Dresden, where it scored a resounding success. *Der fliegende Holländer* (1843) was not so well received, but Wagner was shortly appointed *kapellmeister* at Dresden. *Tannhäuser* (1845) also failed through too stringent economies in production and poor interpretation by the cast; when restaged at a later date it succeeded. *Lohengrin* was finished in 1848, but by this time Wagner was deeply implicated in the revolutionary movement and barely escaped arrest by fleeing from Saxony. Declining an offer of asylum by Liszt at Weimar, he went first to Paris and later to Zürich. *Lohengrin* was eventually produced at Weimar by Liszt in 1850. During his exile he again had to make a living by writing, among other things, *Art of the Future* (1849), the anti-Semitic *Judaism in Music* (1850), *Opera and Drama* (1851), and the autobiographical *Communication to my Friends* (1851–52). The poem of the *Ring* cycle was finished in 1852, and in 1853 he began the music of *Das Rheingold,* followed by *Die Walkure* (1856) and Part I of *Siegfried* (1857). In 1857–59 he was at work on *Tristan und Isolde,* based on the old German version of the legend by Gottfried von Strassburg, and the opera is often claimed

to have been inspired by his current love affair with Mathilde, wife of his friend and patron Otto Wesendonck. Once again he sought to gain favour in Paris, and eventually Napoleon called for a command performance of *Tannhäuser*, but the opera failed. In 1861 he was allowed to return to Germany, but he still had a hard battle for recognition. *Tristan* was accepted at Vienna but abandoned as impracticable before it could be performed, and, now aged fifty, pursued by creditors and vilified by critics, the composer was on the point of giving up in despair when the tide turned with dramatic suddenness. The eccentric young king of Bavaria, Ludwig II, impressed by the pageantry of *Lohengrin*, read Wagner's *Ring* poem with its pessimistic preface. At once he summoned the composer to his court, where every facility was offered and no expense spared. *Tristan* was staged with brilliant success at Munich in 1865, but Wagner's extravagance, political meddling, and preferential treatment aroused so much hostility that he was obliged to withdraw temporarily to Switzerland. Cosima, wife of the musical director, von Bülow, and daughter of Liszt, left her husband and joined him, eventually marrying him in 1868 after being divorced, Minna having died in 1866. In Switzerland he finished *Die Meistersinger*, his only nontragic piece, which scored a success in 1868. But his greatest ambition, a complete performance of the *Ring*, was as yet unfulfilled. A tentative production of *Das Rheingold* in 1869 was a fiasco, the reception of *Die Walküre* in 1870 was lukewarm, and Ludwig had given up his project for a special Wagnerian opera house in Munich. Determined to fulfil his wish, Wagner set about raising funds himself, and on a fraction of the required total plus a large amount of credit he started the now famous theatre at Bayreuth, which opened in 1876 with a first complete programme of the *Ring* cycle. *Parsifal*, his last and perhaps greatest opera, was staged in 1882, a year before his sudden death from a heart attack. Wagner reformed the whole structure of opera. The one canon was to be dramatic fitness, and to this end he abandoned the classical tradition of recitative and aria, replacing it with an ever-changing dramatic line linked with the emotional colour of the story and accentuated skilfully by use of the *leitmotiv*, which he was the first to adopt with a definite purpose. His works show a progressive development. *Rienzi* is in the grand opera style of Meyerbeer and Spontini; *Der fliegende Holländer* strikes out in a new style, followed up in *Tannhäuser* and reaching perfection in *Lohengrin*. From this time dates the music drama, of which *Tristan* is the most uncompromising type. The *Ring* (*Walküre, Siegfried, Gotterdämmerung*, with the *Rheingold* as introduction) is full of Wagner's most characteristic writing and orchestration. It is loosely based on the old Teutonic legend of the Nibelungen, but the symbolism and the purport of the story is purely Wagnerian, while the ideology stems largely from Nietzsche and Schopenhauer. *Parsifal*, from Wolfram von Eschenbach's version of the Grail legend with its mysticism, stands by itself. Wagner's music, life and writings are apt to arouse either blind adulation or violent antipathy, but seldom indifference. Supremely egotistical and unable to sense when he was wrong, he was capable of somersaults of opinion and conduct which mystified and sometimes antagonized his friends, as with Meyerbeer, his erstwhile Good Samaritan, whom he mercilessly insulted in *Judaism in Music*, and his one-time admirer Nietzsche, for whom Siegfried had once appeared as the prototype of his Superman, but who later came to see in the composer the embodiment of decadence. In his own time Wagner was set up with Liszt as the deity of the Romantic faction in opposition to the followers of Brahms and Schumann, and for many years clashes between the rival partisans were the bane of concert-promoters and conductors all over Europe. The bibliography of Wagner is very much split up into 'pro' and 'anti', the most objective Life being perhaps Ernest Newman's great work (1933–47). See also Lives by C. F. Glasenapp (6 vols. 1894–1911, trans. Ellis, 1901 *et seq.*), Hadow (1934), Jacobs (1935); also F. Praeger, *Wagner as I Knew Him* (1892), Shaw, *The Perfect Wagnerite* (1898).

(4) **Siegfried** (1869–1930), son of (3), born near Lucerne, was trained as an architect but later turned to music. He was director of the Bayreuth Festspielhaus from 1909 and died at Bayreuth.

(5) **Wieland** (1917–66), son of (4), born at Bayreuth, took over the directorship of the Festspielhaus at his father's death and revolutionized the production of the operas, stressing their universality as opposed to their purely German significance. He died at Munich.

WAGNER-JAUREGG, or **Wagner von Jauregg, Julius**, *yow'rek* (1857–1940), Austrian neurologist and psychiatrist, born in Wels, won the Nobel prize (1927) for his discovery in 1917 of a treatment for general paralysis by infection with malaria.

WAIN, John Barrington (1925–), English critic and novelist, born at Stoke-on-Trent, studied at and was elected fellow of St John's College, Oxford, and lectured in English Literature at Reading University (1947–55) before turning freelance author. His first four novels, *Hurry on Down* (1953), *Living in the Present* (1955), *The Contenders* (1958) and *Travelling Woman* (1959), tilt at postwar British, particularly London, social values as viewed by a provincial. His debunking vigour and humour has affinities with that of Kingsley Amis (q.v.). He has also written poetry such as *Weep Before God* (1961), edited literary magazines and produced a notable collection of *Preliminary Essays* (1957) in literary criticism. See his autobiographical *Sprightly Running* (1962).

WAINEWRIGHT, Thomas Griffiths (1794–1847), English art critic, painter, forger and probably poisoner, was born at Chiswick. He took to writing (as 'Janus Weathercock', &c.) art criticisms and miscellaneous articles for the periodicals. He married, and, soon outrunning his means, committed forgery (1822, 1824), and almost certainly poisoned with strychnine his half-sister-in-law (1830), probably also his uncle (1828), mother-in-law (1830) and possibly others. The sister-in-law had been fraudulently insured for £16,000, but two actions to enforce payment failed; and Wainewright, venturing back from France in 1837, was sentenced to life transportation for his old forgery. In Van Diemen's Land (Tasmania) he painted portraits, ate opium, and died in Hobart hospital. He is the 'Varney' of Lytton's *Lucretia* (1846) and the 'Slinkton' of Dickens's *Hunted Down* (1860). See his *Essays and Criticisms*, edited, with a memoir, by W. C. Hazlitt (1880); B. W. Procter's *Autobiography* (1877), Oscar Wilde's *Intentions* (1891), J. Curling, *Janus Weathercock* (1938), and R. Crossland, *Wainewright in Tasmania* (1954).

WAINWRIGHT, Jonathan Mayhew (1883–1953), American general, born at Walla-Walla, commanded the epic retreat in the Bataan peninsula after MacArthur's departure during the Philippines campaign in 1942. Taken prisoner, he was released in 1945 and awarded the Congressional Medal of Honour.

WAITZ, *vīts,* (1) **Georg** (1813–86), German historian, born at Flensburg, professor from 1849 till 1875 at Göttingen, where he formed the Göttingen historical school, editor of (1875–86) and contributor to the *Monumenta Germaniae Historica,* he wrote the great *Deutsche Verfassungsgeschichte* (1844–78) and works on Schleswig-Holstein and Ulfilas. See books by Steindorff (1886) and E. Waitz (1913), his son.

(2) **Theodor** (1821–64), German anthropological psychologist, born at Gotha, professor of Philosophy at Marburg from 1848, author of *Anthropologie der Naturvölker* (1859–71) and works on psychology and pedagogics.

WAKE, William (1657–1737), English churchman, born at Blandford, became Bishop of Lincoln (1705), Archbishop of Canterbury (1716). His writings include *State of the Church and Clergy of England* (1703), &c. He worked for union between the Anglican and Nonconformist churches.

WAKEFIELD, (1) **Edward Gibbon** (1796–1862), British colonial statesman, born in London, sentenced for abduction in 1827, wrote in prison *A Letter from Sydney* (1829), which outlined his theory of colonization, expanded in *England and America* (anon. 1833) and *A View of the Art of Colonization* (1849). He influenced the South Australian Association (which founded South Australia in 1836) and, as a secretary (1838) to Lord Durham (q.v.), the Durham Report, formed (1837) the New Zealand Association and forced the British government to annex (1839) New Zealand. With Lyttelton and Godley he founded (1850) the Anglican colony of Canterbury. See Lives by R. Garnett (1898), A. J. Harrop (1928), I. O'Connor (1929).

(2) **Gilbert** (1756–1801), English scholar and controversialist, born at Nottingham, became fellow of Jesus College, Cambridge, renounced his Anglican orders and became classical tutor in dissenting colleges at Warrington and Hackney. He was opposed to slave trade, field sports, war and public worship, and was a critic of civil and ecclesiastical government and of Pitt, Richard Watson's defence of the latter evoking Wakefield's libellous 'Reply', for which he was imprisoned for two years (1799–1801) in Dorchester. His works include editions of Greek and Roman poets, notably Lucretius (1796–99), and *Silva Critica* (1789–95), illustrating the Scriptures from profane learning. See his *Memoirs* (2nd ed. 1804) and his *Correspondence with Fox* (1813).

WAKLEY, Thomas, *wak'li* (1795–1862), English surgeon, born at Membury, Devonshire, founder (1823) and first editor of the *Lancet,* through which he denounced abuses in medical practice and made exposures which led to the Adulteration of Food and Drink Act (1860). He was M.P. for Finsbury from 1835 till 1852, and coroner from 1839, procuring reforms for coroners' courts. See Life by Sprigge (1897).

WAKSMAN, Selman Abraham (1888–), American biologist, born at Priluka in the Ukraine, took U.S. nationality in 1915, graduating the same year at Rutgers university, where he ultimately became professor of Microbiology in 1930. His researches into the breaking down of organic substances by micro-organisms and into antibiotics led to his discovery of streptomycin, for which he was awarded the Nobel prize for medicine in 1952. He wrote *Enzymes* (1926), *Principles of Soil Microbiology* (1938), &c., and the autobiographical *My Life with the Microbes* (1954).

WALBURG, Walburga. See WALPURGA.

WALDEN, Paul, *val'den* (1863–1957), Russian chemist, born at Wenden, Latvia, discovered, and gave his name to, a type of optical isomerism (Walden inversion).

WALDO, or Valdes, Peter (fl. 1175), French merchant, born in Lyons, became a preacher, founded, and gave name to, the Waldenses.

WALDORF. See ASTOR.

WALDSEEMÜLLER, Martin, *valt'zay-mül-ėr* (*c.* 1480–*c.* 1521), German cartographer, born at Radolfzell, at St Dié made use of an account of the travels of Vespucci (q.v.) to publish (1507) the map and globe on which the new world was said to have first been called America.

WALDTEUFEL, Émile, *valt'toy-fėl* or *-tœ-* (1837–1915), French composer, born in Strasbourg. He studied at the Paris Conservatory and joined a piano manufacturer's until he was appointed pianist to the Empress Eugénie. A prolific composer of dance music, several of his waltzes, notably *The Skaters* and *Estudiantina,* remain popular.

WALEWSKA, Marie, *va-lef'-* (1789–1817), Polish countess, Bonaparte's mistress, whose son by him became Count Walewski.

WALEWSKI, Alexandre Florian Joseph Colonna, Count (1810–68), French diplomat, natural son of Napoleon I, held various appointments, including that of ambassador to Britain (1851), and was foreign minister (1855–60) and minister of state (1860–63).

WALKER, *waw'kėr,* (1) **Frederick** (1840–75), English artist, born in London, designed for wood-engravers, his illustrations appearing in *Once a Week, Cornhill,* and other periodicals. His works, once popular, include watercolours and oils. He was made an A.R.A. in 1871. See Lives by J. G. Marks (1896) and C. Phillips (1897).

(2) **George** (1618–90), hero of the siege of Londonderry, born of English parents, allegedly in Tyrone, attended Glasgow University, and became rector of Donaghmore, helped to garrison Londonderry for its successful resistance to the siege in 1689 by James II's forces, during which, as joint-governor, he led sallies against the enemy and exhorted the citizens by rousing sermons. For this he received the thanks of king and commons, degrees from Oxford and Cambridge, and was nominated Bishop of Derry. He fell at the Battle of the Boyne and is commemorated by the Walker Monument (1828) in Londonderry. He wrote *A True Account of the Siege of Londonderry* (1689), reprinted in P. Dwyer's *Siege of Derry* (1893).

(3) **Sir James** (1863–1935), Scottish chemist, born in Dundee, professor there (1894–1908) and (1908–28) in Edinburgh. Known for his work on hydrolysis, ionization, and amphoteric electrolytes, he was elected F.R.S. in 1900 and knighted in 1921.

(4) **John** (1674–1747), English ecclesiastical historian, born in Exeter, noted for his account (1714), called forth by the writings of Calamy (q.v.) on the ejected Nonconformists, of the sufferings of the clergy in the Revolution (1689). See G. B. Tatham, *Dr John Walker and the Sufferings of the Clergy* (1910).

(5) **John** (1732–1807), English dictionary-maker, born at Colney Hatch, was by turns actor, schoolmaster and peripatetic teacher of elocution. His dictionary for rhyming (1775) has run to many editions (*Rhyming Dictionary of the English Language*, 1957), as did his *Critical Pronouncing Dictionary* (1791).

(6) **John** (1770–1831), English antiquary, born in London, whose works included *Curia Oxoniensis, Oxoniana, Curious Articles from the Gentleman's Magazine* (all 1809), *Letters Written by Eminent Persons* (1813).

(7) **John** (*c*. 1781–1859), English inventor, born at Stockton-on-Tees, where, in 1827, as a chemist, he made the first friction matches, called by him 'Congreves' (alluding to Congreve's rocket), later named lucifers and matches by others.

(8) **Thomas** (1784–1836), English author, born at Chorlton-cum-Hardy near Manchester. He was an authority on pauperism, and from May till December 1835, published weekly *The Original*, a general magazine containing well-known articles on gastronomy, and since reappearing in editions and selections under other titles (e.g., *The Art of Dining*, 1928).

(9) **William** (1824–60), American filibuster, born at Nashville, Tennessee, studied medicine at Edinburgh and Heidelberg, which he practised in U.S., as well as law and journalism. He landed (1853) with a force in the Mexican state of Lower California, declaring (1854) it, with the neighbouring Sonora, an independent republic, but was soon forced to withdraw to U.S. territory. He next invaded (1855) Nicaragua, took Granada, and was elected president; his government, recognized (1856) by U.S., restored slavery. He published *The War in Nicaragua* (1860). Twice expelled (1857) from Nicaragua, he entered (1860) Honduras, taking Trujillo, but was apprehended by the captain of a British sloop-of-war and given up to the Honduran authorities, who had him shot. See C. W. Doubleday, *Reminiscences* (1886) and W. O. Scroggs, *Filibusters and Financiers* (1916).

(10) **William Sidney** (1795–1846), English critic, born at Pembroke, of whose invaluable studies some appeared posthumously as *Shakespeare's Versification* (1854), *A Critical Examination of the Text of Shakespeare* (1859) and *Poetical Remains* (1852).

WALKINSHAW, Clementina. See STEWART, HOUSE OF (12).

WALKLEY, Arthur Bingham, *wawk'li* (1855–1926), English dramatic critic, born at Bristol, contributed to the *Star*, *The Times* and other newspapers and periodicals. See his *Dramatic Criticism* (1903).

WALLACE, *wol'is,* (1) **Alfred Russel** (1823–1913), British naturalist, born at Usk, in Monmouthshire, travelled and collected (1848–52) in the Amazon basin, for a time with H. W. Bates, and (1854–1862) in the Malay Archipelago. His memoir, sent to C. R. Darwin (q.v.) in 1858 from the Moluccas, formed an important part of the Linnaean Society paper which first promulgated the theory of natural selection, modifying the nature, and hastening the publication, of Darwin's *The Origin of Species*, a work amplified by Wallace's *Contributions to the Theory of Natural Selection* (1870) and *Darwinism* (1889). Excluding man from the unaided operation of natural selection, he wrote *On Miracles and Modern Spiritualism* (1881). In his great *Geographical Distribution of Animals* (1876), *Island Life* (1880), and earlier work, Wallace contributed much (including 'Wallace's Line' between faunas) to the scientific foundations of zoogeography. Other works include *Travels on the Amazon and Rio Negro* (1853), *Palm Trees of the Amazon* (1853), *The Malay Archipelago* (1869), *Tropical Nature* (1878), *Australasia* (1879), *Land Nationalization* (an advocation, 1882), *Vaccination, a Delusion* (1898), *The Wonderful Century* (1898), *Man's Place in the Universe* (1903), *My Life, an Autobiography* (1905), *The World of Life* (1910). He was elected F.R.S. in 1893 and awarded the O.M. in 1910. See J. Marchant, *Alfred Russel Wallace* (1916), Life by L. T. Hogben (1918), and B. Petronijevic, *Charles Darwin and A. R. Wallace* (1925).

(2) **Sir Donald Mackenzie** (1841–1919), Scottish author and journalist, born in Dunbartonshire, became foreign correspondent of *The Times*, and after spending six years in Russia wrote his highly successful *Russia* (1877). He was private secretary to two viceroys of India.

(3) **Edgar** (1875–1932), English writer, was found abandoned in Greenwich when nine days' old and brought up by a Billingsgate fish-porter. He served in the army in South Africa, where he later (1899) became a journalist, and in 1905 he published his first success, the adventure story *The Four Just*

Men. Another early series in a different vein was set in West Africa and included *Sanders of the River* (1911), *Bones* (1915), &c. From then on he wrote prolifically—his output numbering over 170 novels and plays—being best remembered for his crime novels, such as *The Clue of the Twisted Candle* and *The Melody of Death*, and plays, including *The Ringer* and *The Squeaker*. See his autobiography, *People* (1926) and Life by M. Lane (1938; rev. 1964).

(4) **Henry** (1836–1916), American agricultural leader, father of (6), born in Pennsylvania, trained for the church but turned to farming and agricultural journalism, founding in 1895 the successful periodical *Wallace's Farmer*.

(5) **Henry Agard** (1888–1965), American agriculturalist and statesman, son of (6), born in Adair County, Iowa, edited *Wallace's Farmer* from 1933 until 1940, when he was nominated vice-president to Roosevelt, whose 'new deal' policy he supported. He was chairman of the Board of Economic Warfare (1941–45) and secretary of commerce (1945–46). He failed to obtain renomination as vice-president in 1944, and unsuccessfully stood for president in 1948.

(6) **Henry Cantwell** (1866-1924), American agriculturist, son of (4), helped his father to found *Wallace's Farmer*, which he edited from 1916. Long secretary of the Corn Belt Meat Producers' Association, he was appointed secretary of agriculture in 1921.

(7) **Lewis**, pop. **Lew** (1827–1905), American author and soldier, born at Brookville, Ind., was governor of Utah (1878–81) and minister to Turkey (1881). He was author of the remarkably successful religious novel *Ben Hur* (1880), which has twice formed the subject of a spectacular film. See his *Autobiography* (1906).

(8) **Sir Richard, Bart.** (1818–90), English art collector and philanthropist, born in London, inherited from his putative father, the marquis of Hertford, the paintings and objets d'art later bequeathed (1897) by his widow to the nation. These now comprise the Wallace Collection, housed in Hertford House, London, once his residence. During the siege of Paris (1870–71) Wallace equipped ambulances and founded a British hospital there.

(9) also **Walays or Wallensis** (' Welshman ') **Sir William** (*c.* 1274–1305), Scottish patriot, chief champion of Scotland's independence, was reputedly the second of the three sons of Sir Malcolm Wallace of Elderslie, near Paisley. According to Fordun, he got his early education from an uncle, the priest of Dunipace, and Blind Harry (see HARRY) associates the hero's boyhood with Dundee and his youthful manhood with Ayrshire. Wallace's presence at the burning of the English garrison in the 'Barns of Ayr', the date of that event, and its being the start of the War of Independence, are matters for conjecture. In 1297 Wallace, at the head of a small band, burnt Lanark, slew Hazelrig, the English sheriff, to avenge, asserts Wyntoun, the murder of the young wife of the patriot, who later retired with a large company into the forest of Selkirk. On September 11 of the same year Wallace, fighting Edward I's army under Warenne, Earl of Surrey, won the great battle of Stirling Bridge. From positions at the base of the Abbey Craig, on which now stands his national monument, he routed that part of the English army which had crossed the narrow wooden bridge over the Forth to the northeast of Stirling, the remainder fleeing before the Scots. In consequence of this and other actions, the English were expelled from Scotland and a devastating raid was carried out on the north of England; on his return Wallace was elected governor of Scotland. In 1298 Edward invaded Scotland with 88,000 men. Wallace was forced to give battle at Falkirk on July 22, where, deserted by the cavalry, his infantry were shot down by the English archers and routed. Wallace visited France (*c.* 1299), possibly to seek aid, his whereabouts thereafter being unknown until his arrest, allegedly near Glasgow, by Menteith, sheriff of Dumbarton, about August 3, 1305. He was taken to London, tried in Westminster Hall, condemned, and hanged, drawn, beheaded, and quartered, the quarters being sent to Newcastle, Berwick, Stirling and Perth. See J. Stevenson, *Documents illustrative of Sir William Wallace* (Maitland Club, 1841), the Marquis of Bute, *Early Days of Sir William Wallace* (1876) and *Burning of the Barns of Ayr* (1878), A. Brunton, *Sir William Wallace* (1881), H. Gough, *Scotland in 1298* (1888), J. Moir, *Wallace* (1888), A. F. Murison, *Sir William Wallace* (1898), J. Fergusson, *Wallace* (1938), with bibliography and play by Sydney Goodsir Smith (1960).

(10) **William** (1844–97), Scottish philosopher, born in Cupar, wrote works on Hegel, a life of Schopenhauer, *Epicureanism* (1880), &c.

(11) **William** (1860–1940), Scottish composer, born in Greenock, wrote a symphony, symphonic poems, songs, and works on music.

(12) **(William) Vincent** (1813–65), Irish operatic composer, born at Waterford, emigrated to Australia, well-known for the first of his operas, *Maritana* (1845), and, formerly, for *Lurline* (1860).

WALLACH, Otto, *val'aKH* (1847–1931), German organic chemist, born at Königsberg, a Nobel prizewinner in 1910 for his work on the essential oils and terpenes.

WALLAS, Graham (1858–1932), English socialist political psychologist, born at Monkwearmouth, Sunderland, was educated at Shrewsbury and Corpus Christi College, Oxford, and after a spell of schoolmastering and university extension lecturing, became a lecturer in the London School of Economics, which he, a Fabian, had helped to found, and was professor of Political Science there (1914–23). His influential teaching and writings in social psychology, *Human Nature in Politics* (1908), *The Great Society* (1914), &c., emphasized the rôle of irrational forces which determine public opinion and political attitudes.

WALLENSTEIN, or Waldstein, Albrecht Wenzel Eusebius von, *wol'en-stīn,* Ger. *val'en-shtīn, valt'shtīn* (1583–1634), duke of

Friedland and of Mecklenburg, prince of Sagan, born near Jaroměř, in Bohemia. When his father, a Czech Protestant noble, died, a Catholic uncle entrusted the boy's education to the Jesuits. He married a Bohemian widow, whose vast estates he inherited in 1614. In 1617 he personally commanded a force, chiefly of cavalry, which he supplied to Archduke Ferdinand (later Ferdinand II, q.v.) for use against Venice. At the outset of the Thirty Years' War he assisted in the crushing of the Bohemian revolt (1618–20) under Frederick V (q.v.), thereafter acquiring numerous confiscated estates, and consolidating them into Friedland, of which he became (1623) duke. In 1625, for raising an army for Ferdinand II, he was appointed commander-in-chief of all the Imperial forces, and at Dessau bridge defeated the army of Mansfeld (q.v.). Establishing peace in Hungary by a truce imposed on the combined forces of Mansfeld and Bethlen Gabor (q.v.), he subdued (1627) Silesia, acquiring the dukedom of Sagan, joined Tilly against Christian IV, was invested (1628) with the duchies of Mecklenburg, which he had overrun, but encountered resistance in garrisoning the Hanse towns, notably at his unsuccessful siege (1628) of Stralsund, consequently failing to remove the threat of Protestant invasion by sea. This materialized in 1630, following Ferdinand II's Edict of Restitution, when Gustavus Adolphus and his forces invaded northern Germany. Enmity of the Catholic princes, aroused by Wallenstein's ambition, forced Ferdinand to dismiss him (1630) and appoint Tilly commander-in-chief. After Tilly's defeat at Breitenfeld and death on the Lech, Wallenstein was reinstated. His new army, in repulsing the attempt by Gustavus Adolphus's forces to storm his entrenched camp near Nuremberg, prevented the Swedish king from advancing on Ferdinand in Vienna. Wallenstein was defeated (1632) by Gustavus Adolphus at Lützen, where, however, the latter fell. In the interests of a united Germany with himself as its supreme authority, Wallenstein now intrigued with Protestants and Catholics. At length his enemies persuaded the emperor to depose him again and denounce him. Threatened in Pilsen by Piccolomini (q.v.) and others, he went to Eger, hoping for support from Bernhard, Duke of Weimar; there traitors in his train, notably the Irishman, Butler, and the Scotsmen, Gordon and Leslie, killed his faithful adherents, while the first's compatriot, Devereux, slew Wallenstein on the evening of February 25, 1634. He had been throughout a firm believer in astrology. The Wallenstein trilogy by Schiller (q.v.) is based on Wallenstein's career. See Lives by Ranke (5th ed. 1895), Förster (1834), Aretin (1846), Hunter (1855); monographs by Irmer (1888–89), Hildebrand (1885), Huch (1919), Wiegler (1920) and Tritsch (1936); Schmid's *Wallenstein—Litteratur* (1878).

WALLER, *wol'ĕr*, (1) **Augustus Volney** (1816–1870), English physiologist, born near Faversham, discovered and gave name to Wallerian degeneration of, and the related Wallerian method of tracing, nerve fibres.

(2) **Edmund** (1606–87), English poet, born at Coleshill near Amersham, Herts (now Bucks), was educated at Eton and King's College, Cambridge. Thought to have represented Amersham in 1621, he was returned for Ilchester in 1624, Chipping Wycombe in 1625 and Amersham in 1627. In 1631 he married a London heiress, who died in 1634, and from about 1635 to 1638 he unsuccessfully courted Lady Dorothy Sidney, eldest daughter of the Earl of Leicester, whom he commemorated in verse as 'Sacharissa'. Returned to the Long Parliament in 1640, he opened the proceedings in 1641 against Crawley, impeached for his judgments in the king's favour. In 1643 Waller plunged into a conspiracy ('Waller's plot') against Parliament, was arrested, and expelled from the House. He avoided execution, unlike his fellow conspirators, by abject confession and the payment of a £10,000 fine, and was banished the realm. He lived mostly in France, entertaining impoverished exiles in Paris, his own banishment being revoked in 1651, after which he returned to England. His collected poems, reviving the heroic couplet and including 'Go, lovely Rose', had been published in 1645 and were followed by *A Panegyric to my Lord Protector* (1655) and *To the King upon his Majesty's Happy Return* (1660) addressed to Cromwell and Charles II respectively. See his *Poems* (critical ed. by G. Thorn-Drury, 1893), also *Sacharissa* (1892) by Julia Cartwright.

(3) **Sir William** (*c.* 1597–1668), English parliamentary general, a member of the Long Parliament, fought in 1643 in the west country, at Oxford and Newbury in 1644, and at Taunton in February 1645. He suggested reforms on which the New Model Army was to be based, but in April 1645 was removed from command by the Self-denying Ordinance. By June 1647 he was levying troops against the army, from 1648 to 1651 he was imprisoned for royalist sympathies, and in 1659 he plotted for a royalist rising and was again imprisoned. In 1660 he became a member of the Convention Parliament, but was unrewarded at the Restoration.

WALLIS, John (1616–1703), English mathematician, born at Ashford, Kent, was trained at Cambridge, and took orders, but in 1649 became Savilian professor of Geometry at Oxford. He sided with the parliament, was secretary in 1644 to the Westminster Assembly, but favoured the Restoration. Besides the *Arithmetica Infinitorum*, in which was presaged the calculus and the binomial theorem and a value given for π, he wrote on proportion, mechanics, the quadrature of the circle (against Hobbes), grammar, logic, theology, and the teaching of the deaf and dumb, was an expert on deciphering, and edited some of the Greek mathematicians. He was a founder of the Royal Society. His collected works appeared in 1791. See J. F. Scott, *The Mathematical Work of John Wallis*.

WALPOLE, (1) Horace, 4th Earl of Orford (1717–97), youngest son of (3), was born September 24 in London. At Eton and at King's College, Cambrigge, he had Gray the poet as a friend; and while still at the university was appointed by his father to lucrative government sinecures. Gray and he started on the Grand Tour, but quarrelled and separated at Reggio, where Walpole fell ill. He returned to England (1741) to take his seat for Callington in Cornwall. Although he interested himself in cases like the Byng trial of 1757, his function in politics was that of the chronicling spectator rather than the earnest actor. He exchanged his Cornish seat in 1754 for the family borough of Castle Rising, which he vacated in 1757 for the other family borough of King's Lynn. In 1745 his father died, leaving him with ample means. In 1747 he purchased, near Twickenham, the former coachman's cottage which he gradually ' gothicized ' (1753–76) into the stuccoed and battlemented pseudo-castle of Strawberry Hill, which, mildly ridiculous though it may seem, helped in its way to reverse the fashion for classical and Italianate design. This transformation, correspondence and authorship, visits to Paris, and the establishment of a private press on which some of his own works as well as Lucan's *Pharsalia* with Bentley's notes, and Gray's *Progress of Poesy* and *The Bard*, were printed, constituted the occupations of his life. He inherited his brother's title in 1791 and died March 2, 1797. His essays in Moore's *World* exhibit a light hand, and he had gifts as a verse-writer. In such squibs as the *Letter from Xo Ho to his friend Lien Chi at Pekin* (1757) he is at his best. His *Castle of Otranto* (1764) set the fashion of supernatural romance. His tragedy of *The Mysterious Mother* (1768) is strong but gruesome. Other works are *Catalogue of Royal and Noble Authors* (1758), *Fugitive Pieces in Verse and Prose* (1758), *Anecdotes of Painting in England* (1761–71), *Catalogue of Engravers* (1763), *Historic Doubts on Richard III* (1768), *Essay on Modern Gardening* (1785), &c. Walpole's literary reputation rests chiefly upon his letters, which deal, in the most vivacious way, with party politics, foreign affairs, literature, art and gossip. His firsthand accounts in them of such events as the Jacobite trials after the '45, and the Gordon Riots, are invaluable. Two of his chief correspondents were Sir Horace Mann and Madame du Deffand; with the latter he exchanged more than 1600 letters. See also the *Memoirs* edited by Eliot Warburton (1852), and Life by Austin Dobson (1890; rev. P. Toynbee, 1927), books by Yvon (1924), D. M. Stuart (1927), Gwynn (1932), Cremer (1946), and bibliography by Hazen (1948).

(2) **Sir Hugh Seymour** (1884–1941), English novelist, born in Auckland, N.Z., son of the Rev. G. H. S. Walpole who subsequently became Bishop of Edinburgh, was educated in England and graduated from Emmanuel College, Cambridge, in 1906. He was intended for the church but turned first schoolmaster and then author. Widely read in English literature, he wrote prolifically and was said to have the knack of making the most of a moderate talent; nevertheless his books, which were enormously popular during his lifetime, display a straightforward, easy-flowing style, great descriptive power, and a genius for evoking atmosphere which he unfortunately overworked at times, as for example in *The Cathedral*, whose down-town scenes with their unnatural aura of malevolence have been a target for the parodist. Many authors have paid tribute to Walpole's kindness and integrity, and he was knighted for his services to literature in 1937. His novels include *Mr Perrin and Mr Traill* (1911), *Fortitude* (1913), *The Dark Forest* (1916), *The Secret City* (1919, Tait Black Memorial Prize), *The Cathedral* (1922), which owes much to Trollope, one of Walpole's favourite authors, and *The Herries Chronicle* (1930–33). See Life by R. Hart-Davis (1952).

(3) **Sir Robert, Earl of Orford** (1676–1745), English statesman, born at Houghton in Norfolk. Educated at Eton and King's College, Cambridge, he was returned to parliament in 1701 for Castle Rising, in 1702 for King's Lynn, quickly winning a high position in the Whig Party. In 1708 he became secretary-at-war and in 1710 treasurer of the navy. Following upon his support of Godolphin in the impeachment of Sacheverell, Walpole was expelled the House and sent to the Tower (1712) for alleged corruption. Restored to fortune on the accession of George I, he was made a privy councillor. He conducted the impeachment of Bolingbroke and others, and became in 1715 chancellor of the Exchequer and first lord of the Treasury. In 1717 he resigned, after introducing the first general sinking fund. Out of office he has been charged with somewhat unscrupulous opposition. He brought about the rejection of the peerage bill (1718) and was given (1720) the post of paymaster-general by Sunderland. After the collapse of the South Sea Scheme, the public looked to Walpole to restore order in their affairs; in 1721 he again became first lord of the Treasury and chancellor of the Exchequer and from this time was responsible for the country's government. Under him there was a transfer of power to the House of Commons and Walpole was involved in the rôle of Britain's first prime minister. By bribery he secured a Whig House of Commons. His first successful trial of strength (1724) was with Carteret (q.v.); later he held his own against Bolingbroke (q.v.) and Pulteney (q.v.); forced on the breach with Townshend (q.v.), who retired (1730); and quarrelled with Chesterfield (q.v.). His failure to secure the passage of an excise bill (1733) against smuggling and fraud weakened his position, which deteriorated further as a result of his unpopular foreign policy. He resigned on February 2, 1742, and was created Earl of Orford, with a pension of £4000 a year. A committee appointed by the House of Commons gave a report against him on the charge of bribery, unsupported by evidence, and proceedings were ultimately dropped. He withdrew to Houghton, and died at Arlington St, London, on March 18. See W. Coxe, Memoirs of *Sir Robert Walpole* (1798), monographs by A. C. Ewald (1877) and J. Morley (1889), F. S. Oliver, *The Endless Adventure* (1930–35), some of the works cited at (1), and a Life by J. H. Plumb 1956–61).

(4) **Sir Spencer** (1839–1907), British historian, born in London, educated at Eton. In the course of his civil service, he was (1882–93) lieutenant-governor of the Isle of Man. His principal work is the *History of England from 1815* (1878–86) continued in his *History of Twenty-Five Years* (1904–08). He wrote Lives of Perceval (1874; his grandfather) and Lord John Russell (1889).

WALPURGA, Walpurgis or **Walburga, St,** *val-poor'ga* (*c.* 710–*c.* 777), with her brother Willibald, companion of St Boniface (q.v.), went from England to Germany, and was abbess of Heidenheim, where she died, her bones being translated (*c.* 870) to Eichstatt. Walpurgis night (April 30) is so called from a confusion of the saint's day, May 1, and the popular superstitions regarding the flight of witches on that night.

WALSINGHAM, *wawl'sing-am*, (1) **Sir Francis** (*c.* 1530–90), English statesman, born at Chislehurst, Kent, studied at King's College, Cambridge. Burghley sent him on an embassy to France in 1570–73; and having discharged his diplomatic duties with consummate skill, he was appointed one of the principal secretaries of state to Elizabeth, sworn of the privy council, and knighted. In 1578 he was sent on an embassy to the Netherlands, in 1581 to France, and in 1583 to Scotland. He contrived a most corrupt system of espionage at home and abroad, enabling him to reveal the Babington (q.v.) plot, which implicated Mary, Queen of Scots (q.v.) in treason, and to obtain in 1587 details of some plans for the Spanish armada. He was one of the commissioners to try Mary at Fotheringhay. His personal integrity and disinterested patriotism are undoubted. He favoured the Puritan party, and in his later days gave himself up to religious meditation. Elizabeth acknowledged his genius and important services, yet she kept him poor and without honours; and he died in poverty and debt. His daughter Frances became successively the wife of Sir Philip Sidney, of the Earl of Essex, and of Richard de Burgh, fourth Earl of Clanricarde. See Stählin, *Walsingham und seine Zeit* (1908); Conyers Read, *Mr Secretary Walsingham* (1925).

(2) **Thomas** (d. *c.* 1422), English chronicler, associated chiefly with St Albans abbey but for a time prior of Wymondham, an authority for English history from 1377 until 1422, noted for his *Historia Anglicana, 1272–1422* (1863–64) and other works.

WALTER, *val'tėr*, (1) properly **Schlesigner, Bruno** (1876–1962), German-American conductor, born in Berlin. He first conducted at Cologne while still in his teens, and work with Mahler in Hamburg and Vienna followed, profoundly influencing his musical outlook. He was in charge of Munich Opera 1913–22, and from 1919 was chief conductor of the Berlin Philharmonic. International tours won him a great British and American reputation, and driven from both Germany and Austria by the Nazis, he settled in the U.S.A., where he became chief conductor of the New York Philharmonic in 1951. Perhaps the last great exponent of the German romantic tradition, he was most famous for his performances of Haydn, Mozart and Mahler.

(2) **Hubert** (d. 1205), English statesman and prelate, became a judge in 1185, Dean of York in 1189 and Bishop of Salisbury in the same year. He went crusading with Richard I, after whose capture by the Saracens he negotiated the ransom, and on whose recommendation he was made Archbishop of Canterbury (1193). As chief justiciar he played a major part in the suppression of John's rebellion, and during Richard's absence was virtual ruler of England until the pope made him resign political office. On the accession of John (1199) he became chancellor, and was instrumental in avoiding war with France.

(3) **John** (1739–1812), English printer and newspaper publisher, born in London, initially an unsuccessful underwriter at Lloyds, in 1784 acquired a printing office in Blackfriars, London, nucleus of the later Printing House Square buildings, in 1785 founded *The Daily Universal Register* newspaper. which in 1788 was renamed *The Times.*

(4) **John** (1776–1847), son of (3), became manager and editor of *The Times* in 1803; under him the newspaper attained its great status. He obtained news, especially from abroad, often more rapidly transmitted than official reports and from sources independent of them. In 1814 Walter adopted, for the printing of *The Times*, the double-cylinder steam-driven press invented by Friedrich König (q.v.).

(5) **John** (1818–94), son of (4), proprietor of *The Times*, under whom was introduced (1869) the important cylindrical Walter press, in which, for the first time, curved stereotyped plates and reels of newsprint were used.

Of the other members of the family, **Arthur Fraser** (1846–1910), under whom the fortunes of *The Times* were impaired by the publication (1887) of articles on C. S. Parnell (q.v.) by R. Pigott (q.v.), was proprietor until 1908, when the controlling interest was acquired by A. Harmsworth (q.v.). A. F. Walter's son, **John** (1873–1968), was chairman from 1910 till 1923, sharing control (after Harmsworth's death in 1922) with J. J. Astor (q.v.). See *The History of 'The Times'* (4 vols. 1935–52).

(6) **Lucy** (1630–58), born probably in Pembrokeshire, was the 'brown, beautiful, bold but insipid' mistress of Charles II, to whom she bore James, Duke of Monmouth.

WALTHER VON DER VOGELWEIDE, *vahl'ter fon der fōg'el-vī-dė* (*c.* 1170–1230), greatest of the German minnesinger, was born probably in Tirol. In 1180–98 he was in high favour at the court of Austria; later he was at Mainz and Magdeburg; in 1204 he outshone his rivals in the great contest at the Wartburg. He first sided with the Guelphs, but made friends with the victorious Hohenstaufen, Frederick II, who gave him a small estate. See monographs by Uhland (1822), Wustmann (1913), Schönbach (1923), and Halbach (1927).

WALTON, (1) **Brian** (*c.* 1600–61), English divine, editor of the *London Polyglott Bible*, was born at Seymour, Yorkshire, studied at

Cambridge, and held cures in London and Essex. Sequestered in 1641, he found refuge in Oxford, and then in London devoted himself to his great bible (6v ols. 1653–57), in which he had aid from Usher, Lightfoot, Pocock and other scholars. He was consecrated Bishop of Chester in 1660. Nine languages are used in the Polyglott—Hebrew, Chaldee, Samaritan, Syriac, Arabic, Persian, Ethiopic, Greek and Latin. Other works were an *Introductio* to Oriental languages (1654) and *Considerator Considered* (1659), a defence of the *Polyglott*. See Life by H. J. Todd (1821).

(2) **Ernest Thomas Sinton** (1903–), Irish physicist, born in Dungarvan, Waterford, became professor of Natural and Experimental Philosophy at Trinity College, Dublin, in 1946. With (Sir) John Cockcroft (q.v.) in 1932 he disintegrated lithium by proton bombardment, for which work they were jointly awarded the 1951 Nobel prize for physics.

(3) **Izaak** (1593–1683), English writer, was born at Stafford, August 9. In 1621 he was settled in London as an ironmonger or a linen-draper, and about 1644 he retired with a modest competence. In 1626 he married a great-grandniece of Cranmer, and in 1647 Ann Ken, a half-sister of Thomas Ken (q.v.). He spent most of his time ' in the families of the eminent clergymen of England '; lived latterly much at Winchester; and died there, December 15, 1683. The first edition of *The Compleat Angler, or the Contemplative Man's Recreation*, appeared in 1653; the fifth, grown from thirteen chapters to twenty-one, in 1676. The latter contained also a treatise by Charles Cotton (q.v.). The discourse of fishes, of English rivers, of fishponds, and of rods and lines is interspersed with scraps of dialogue, moral reflections, quaint old verses, songs, and sayings, and idyllic glimpses of country life and is a book of perennial charm. The anonymous *Arte of Angling* (1577), discovered in 1957, has been found to be one of his chief sources. Not less exquisite are his *Lives*—of Donne (1640), Wotton (1651), Hooker (1665), Herbert (1670) and Sanderson (1678). Editions include those by (Sir) John Hawkins (1760), Major (1824, &c.), Sir Harris Nicolas (1836), Bethune (New York 1847), Jesse and Bohn (1856), Dowling (1857) and A. Lang (1897). See S. Martin, *Walton and his Friends* (1903).

(4) **Sir William Turner** (1902–), English composer, born at Oldham, received his earliest musical training as a cathedral chorister at Christ Church, Oxford, whence he passed to university as a student in 1918 and in the same year wrote his first major work, a piano quartet, which was performed at the Salzburg festival of contemporary music in 1923. His *Façade* (1923), originally an extravaganza accompanying declamatory verses by Edith Sitwell (q.v.), created quite a sensation and subsequently reappeared *sans* orator as a pair of suites and as ballet music. Scored for an unusual instrumental combination containing saxophone, glockenspiel and varied percussion, it caricatures in lively manner conventional song and dance forms. The *Sinfonia Concertante* (1927) for piano and orchestra, and the viola concerto (1929) are more serious efforts; *Belshazzar's Feast* (1931), a biblical cantata with libretto by Osbert Sitwell, is a powerful and vital work in which exciting instrumentation for an augmented orchestra is contrasted with moving unaccompanied choral passages. The *Symphony* (1932–35) is characterized by use of the pedal-point bass to preserve orientation in the midst of advanced harmonies and cross-rhythms. Some of Walton's subsequent compositions make more concessions to melody and his ballet music for *The Wise Virgins* (1940), based on pieces by Bach, contains a concert favourite in his orchestral arrangement of the aria *Sheep May Safely Graze*. During World War II he began composing incidental music for films and emerged as the supreme exponent of this art, with a masterly flair for building up tension and atmosphere, as in Shakespeare's *Henry V*, *Hamlet* and *Richard III*. Later works include the opera *Troilus and Cressida* (1954), a 'cello concerto (1956), a second symphony (1960) and a comic opera, *The Bear* (1967). He was knighted in 1951, and awarded the O.M. in 1967.

WANG WEI, *way* (699–759), Chinese poet and painter of the T'ang dynasty, an ardent Buddhist, founded a monochrome school of painting.

WARBECK, Perkin (*c.* 1474–99), Flemish impostor, pretender to the English throne, born in Tournai, appeared in 1490 at the court of the Duchess of Burgundy, sister of Edward IV of England, and professed to be Richard, Duke of York, younger of the two sons of Edward IV murdered in the Tower. In 1491 he was welcomed at Cork, in 1492 at the court of Charles VIII of France; and from Burgundy he made an ineffectual landing in Kent (July 1495). In Scotland, James IV gave him his kinswoman, Catherine Gordon, a daughter of the Earl of Huntly, in marriage. In 1498 he attempted to besiege Exeter, then went on to Taunton, but ran away to the sanctuary at Beaulieu in Hampshire, surrendered on promise of pardon, and was imprisoned. On a charge of endeavouring to escape, he was thrown into the Tower, and executed in November 1499. See J. Gairdner, *Richard the Third, and the Story of Perkin Warbeck* (1898).

WARBURG, Otto Heinrich, *vahr'boorg* (1883–1970), German physiological chemist, born at Freiburg Baden, was educated at Berlin and Heidelberg, won the *Pour le Mérite*, the German V.C., during World War I and became director of the physiological department of the Max Planck Institute, Berlin. Engaged on cancer research, he won the Nobel prize (1931) for medicine for his work on enzymes and was elected a foreign member of the Royal Society (1934).

WARBURTON, (1) Eliot, fully **Bartholomew Elliott George** (1810–52), Irish novelist, was born at Tullamore, Co. Offaly. He was called to the bar, but soon devoted himself to literature. His eight works include *The Crescent and the Cross* (1844), *Memoirs of Prince Rupert* (1849) and *Darien* (1851).

Sailing to Panamá, he was lost in the *Amazon* off Land's End.

(2) **William** (1698–1779), English divine, born at Newark, the town clerk's son, practised as attorney until he took deacon's orders in 1723. He was ordained priest in 1727 and became rector of Brant Broughton in Lincolnshire in 1728, and for eighteen years immersed himself in study. His *Alliance between Church and State* (1736) first called attention to his powers, but *The Divine Legation of Moses* (1737–41; and some posthumously in Hurd's edition of his works) formed the sure foundation of his fame. The work displays no profundity of thought, but vigour in verbal logic, much, if inaccurate, reading, dogmatism, and extreme arrogance. In 1739 he defended the orthodoxy of Pope's *Essay on Man*, became his friend and literary executor, and secured influential patrons. Successively preacher of Lincoln's Inn (1746), prebendary of Gloucester (1753), king's chaplain (1754), prebendary of Durham (1755), Dean of Bristol (1757) and Bishop of Gloucester (1759), he wore out his days in endless warfare with Hume, Jortin, the Deists, Voltaire, Lowth and Wesley. In his early years he had aided Theobald in his Shakespeare, and in 1747 he himself issued an edition which brought him no credit. Other works were *Julian* (1750) and *The Principles of Natural and Revealed Religion* (1753–67). A sumptuous edition of his works was published in 1788 by Bishop Hurd; another in 1811. See Lives by F. Kilvert (1860), J. S. Watson (1863), and a book by A. W. Evans (1932).

WARD, (1) **Sir Adolphus William** (1837–1924), English historian, born at Hampstead, became in 1860 a fellow of Peterhouse, Cambridge. In 1866 he was appointed professor of History and English Literature at Owens College, Manchester, of which he was principal in 1890, and he played a major part in the establishment of the independent University of Manchester. In 1900 he became master of Peterhouse, and was knighted in 1913. Notable is his translation (1868–73) of Curtius's *History of Greece*, and he also wrote *Great Britain and Hanover* (1899), *The Electress Sophia* (1903), *Germany 1815–1890* (1916 *et seq.*), an invaluable *History of English Dramatic Literature* (1875), &c. See A. T. Bartholomew's *Bibliography* (1926), with a Memoir by T. F. Tout.

(2) **Artemus**. See BROWNE (1).

(3) **Arthur Sarsfield**. See ROHMER, SAX.

(4) **Edward**, called **Ned** (1667–1731), English 'Grubstreet' writer, born in Oxfordshire, became a London innkeeper, wrote coarse satirical and humorous verse, and was pilloried for attacking the Whigs in his *Hudibras Redivivus* (1705). His chief work was the *London Spy*, published in monthly parts from 1698. See study by H. W. Troyer (1947).

(5) **Edward Matthew** (1816–79), English painter, father of (12), born in London, studied at the Royal Academy, and in Rome and Munich, becoming R.A. in 1855. He is noted for his historical paintings of 17th- and 18th-century scenes, including *The Escape of Charles II with Jane Lane*, *Charlotte Corday*, *The Last Sleep of Argyll* and *A Scene in Lord Chesterfield's Ante-room*. See Life by Dafforne (1879) and his widow's *Reminiscences* (1911).

(6) **F. Kingdon-**. See KINGDON-WARD.

(7) **Dame Geneviève** (1837–1922), American prima donna and actress, born in New York, a great singer in youth, a great tragedienne in maturity, still acted at 83. She was created D.B.E. in 1921. See *Both Sides of the Curtain* (1918) by herself and Richard Whiteing.

(8) **Harry Marshall**. See KINGDON-WARD.

(9) **Mrs Humphry**, *née* **Mary** Augusta **Arnold** (1851–1920), English novelist, born in Hobart, Tasmania, a granddaughter of Dr Arnold of Rugby. The family returned to Britain in 1856 and, after attendance at boarding schools, Mary joined them in Oxford in 1867. In 1872 she married **Thomas Humphry Ward** (1845–1926), born in Hull, fellow and tutor of Brasenose College, member of the staff of *The Times*, and editor of *The English Poets* (5 vols., 1880–1918). Mrs Ward contributed to *Macmillan's*, and, a student of Spanish literature, lives of early Spanish ecclesiastics to Smith's *Dictionary of Christian Biography*. A child's story, *Milly and Olly* (1881), *Miss Bretherton* (1884), a slight novel, and a translation (1885) of Amiel's *Journal intime* preceded her greatest success, the spiritual romance *Robert Elsmere* (1888) which inspired the philanthropist Passmore Edwards to found a settlement for the London poor in 1897 in Tavistock Square, now known by her name. Of the many novels which followed, most notable is *The Case of Richard Meynell* (1911). Mrs Ward was also an enthusiastic social worker and anti-suffragette. See her *A Writer's Recollections* (1918), and the Life by her daughter, J. P. Trevelyan, wife of G. M. Trevelyan (1923).

(10) **James** (1843–1925), English psychologist and philosopher, born at Hull, was a Congregational minister until he entered Cambridge in 1872, becoming a fellow of Trinity in 1875. He first made his name as a psychologist, particularly by his articles in the *Encyclopaedia Britannica*, in which he severely criticized the British associationist tradition and put forward his own theory of experience. These articles represented Ward's psychological standpoint until the publication in 1918 of his *Psychological Principles*. In 1897 he was appointed professor of Mental Philosophy at Cambridge, and propounded his philosophy in two sets of Gifford lectures, published as *Naturalism and Agnosticism* (1899), a refutation of naturalism, and *The Realm of Ends* (1911), an exposition of pluralism. His *Study of Kant* appeared in 1922. See O. W. Campbell's *Memoir* in Ward's *Essays in Philosophy* (1927).

(11) **Sir Joseph George** (1856–1930), New Zealand statesman, born in Melbourne, entered parliament in 1887 and was Liberal prime minister in 1906–12, 1928–30.

(12) **Sir Leslie** (1851–1922), English caricaturist, son of (5), was 'Spy' of *Vanity Fair* (1873–1909). He was knighted in 1918. See his *Forty Years of 'Spy'* (1915).

(13) **Mary** (1585–1645), English founder in 1609 of a Catholic society for women, modelled on the Society of Jesus. She and her devotees founded schools and taught in

them, gave up the cloistered existence and the habit of nuns. Although their work was not questioned, these innovations were and Pope Urban VIII at last called her to Rome and suppressed her society in 1630. She was allowed to return to England in 1639. Her institute was fully restored, with papal permission, in 1877 and became the model for modern Catholic women's institutes. See Life by M. Oliver (1960).

(14) **Mary Augusta.** See (9).

(15) **Nathaniel** (1578–1652), English divine, born at Haverhill, Suffolk, studied at Emmanuel College, Cambridge, was pastor of Agawam, now Ipswich, in Massachusetts till 1645, when he returned to England. He helped to frame the first legal code in New England (enacted 1641), and wrote the controversial *The Simple Cobbler of Agawam* (1647).

(16) **Nathaniel Bagshaw** (1791–1868), English botanist, born in London, invented the Wardian case for the transport of plants.

(17) **Seth** (1617–89), English astronomer and divine, was born in Hertfordshire. He was educated at Sidney Sussex College, Cambridge, was Savilian professor of Astronomy at Oxford from 1649 to 1660, propounded (1653) a theory of planetary motion, and took part with John Wallis (q.v.) in the latter's controversy with Hobbes. He was Bishop of Exeter from 1662 to 1667, when he became Bishop of Salisbury.

(18) **William George** (1812–82), English theologian, born in London, was educated at Winchester and Christ Church, Oxford, and became fellow and tutor of Balliol. A strong Tractarian, he published in 1844 *The Ideal of a Christian Church*, for which he was deprived of his degree and had to leave the university. He joined the Roman Catholic church and became editor of the *Dublin Review*. See studies (1889; 1893) by his son **Wilfrid** (1856–1916), Catholic apologist and biographer.

WARDLAW, (1) **Elizabeth, Lady** (1677–1727), Scottish poetess, daughter of Sir Charles Halket of Pitfirrane, Fife, married in 1696 Sir Henry Wardlaw, is the reputed author of the ballad *Hardyknute* (1719; see Percy's *Reliques*, 1767 ed.), and, doubtfully, of *Sir Patrick Spens*, which she more probably amended, along with other ballads.

(2) **Henry** (fl. 1378, d. 1440), Scottish divine, studied and lived for some years in France, in 1403 became bishop of St Andrews, and played a prominent part in the foundation (1411) of St Andrews University.

WARHAM, William, *waw'rĕm* (*c.* 1450–1532), English prelate, born near Basingstoke, took orders, but practised law, and became advocate in the Court of Arches. His diplomatic services to Henry VII obtained for him rapid preferment—master of the Rolls (1494), lord chancellor (1503), Bishop of London (1503) and Archbishop of Canterbury (1503). In 1515 he had to resign the great seal to Wolsey. He was a close friend of the New Learning and its apostles, but had no stomach for fundamental reform, though he agreed to recognize the king's supremacy. See vol. vi of Hook's *Lives of the Archbishops* (1868).

WARLOCK, Peter, pseud. of **Philip Arnold Heseltine** (1894–1930), English musicologist and composer, born in London. In 1910 he met Delius and in 1916 Bernard van Dieren, both of whom had a profound musical influence on him, and his friendship with D. H. Lawrence is also reflected in his music. In 1920 he founded *The Sackbut*, a spirited musical periodical, and his works include the song cycle *The Curlew* (1920–22), *Serenade* (1923) to Delius, the orchestral suite *Capriol* (1926), many songs, often in the Elizabethan manner, and choral works. He edited much Elizabethan and Jacobean music, wrote *Frederick Delius* (1923; under his own name) and *The English Ayre* (1926). See a Memoir (1934) by Cecil Gray.

WARMING, Johannes Eugenius Bülow, *var'ming* (1841–1924), Danish botanist, born in the North Frisian island of Manö, was professor at Stockholm (1882–85) and Copenhagen (1885–1911). He wrote important works on systematic botany (1879) and ecology (1895), being regarded as a founder of the latter.

WARNER, (1) **Charles Dudley** (1829–1900), American writer, born at Plainfield, Mass., practised law in Chicago till 1860, then settled as an editor at Hartford. In 1884 he became co-editor of *Harper's Magazine*, in which his papers on the South, Mexico and the Great West appeared. In 1873 he wrote with Mark Twain *The Gilded Age*. Other works are *My Summer in a Garden* (1871), *Back-log Studies* (1873), *Being a Boy* (1878), *Washington Irving* (1881), *Captain John Smith* (1881), books of travel, such as *In the Levant* (1876), &c.

(2) **Sir Pelham,** nicknamed **'Plum'** (1873–1963), English cricketer, born in Trinidad, educated at Rugby and Oriel College, Oxford, won his cricket blue, played for Middlesex, and captained the victorious English team in the Australian tour of 1903. He also led the team in South Africa in 1905 and again in Australia in 1911. He was secretary of the M.C.C. in 1939–45, president in 1950, and was knighted in 1937. Editor of the periodical *Cricket*, his many books on the game include *The Fight for the Ashes*, and *Lord's 1787–1945*. See his *My Cricketing Life* (1921) and *Long Innings* (1951).

(3) **Rex** (1905–), English author, born in Birmingham. A specialist in classical literature, he was a teacher before turning to writing. Pre-eminently a novelist of ideas, his distinction lies in the original, imaginative handling of conflicting ideologies. *The Wild Goose Chase* (1937), *The Professor* (1938) and *The Aerodrome* (1941) established his reputation as a writer concerned with the problems of the individual involved with authority. *Men of Stones* (1949) explores the nature of totalitarianism, but it and *Why was I Killed?* (1944), are less successful than his other works. He is perhaps best known for his later historical novels such as *The Young Caesar* (1958), *Imperial Caesar* (1960) and *Pericles the Athenian* (1963). He is a poet of sensuous quality (*Poems*, 1931, and *Poems and Contradictions*, 1945), and also a translator of Greek classics.

(4) **Susan Bogert** (1819–85), American novelist, born at New York, published under

the pen-name of **Elizabeth Wetherell** *The Wide, Wide World* (1851), next to *Uncle Tom's Cabin* the most succesful American story of its day. There followed *Queechy* (1852), and other sentimental and emotional tales. See Life (1910) by her sister and collaborator, **Anna Bartlett** (1827–1915), who, as Amy Lothrop, wrote popular stories, and the study by O. E. P. Stokes (1926).

(5) **William** (*c.* 1558–1609), English poet, born in London, practised as an attorney, wrote *Pan his Syrinx* (1585), translated Plautus (*Menæchmi*, 1595), and gained a high contemporary reputation with his *Albion's England* (1586-1606), a long metrical history in fourteen-syllable verse.

WARREN, (1) Sir Charles (1840–1927), British general and archaeologist, born at Bangor, Wales, entered the Royal Engineers in 1857. He played a conspicuous part during the last quarter of the 19th century as a commander of British forces in South Africa, where he helped to delimit Griqualand West, and served also elsewhere. He is, however, chiefly remembered for his work in connection with the archaeological exploration of Palestine, especially Jerusalem, and for his writings arising from it: *Underground Jerusalem* (1876), *Temple and Tomb* (1880), *Jerusalem* (with Conder, 1884). He also wrote on ancient weights and measures. See Life by W. W. Williams (1941).

(2) **John Byrne Leicester.** See TABLEY.

(3) **Robert Penn** (1905–), American novelist and poet, born at Guthrie, Kentucky, was educated at Vanderbilt, Berkeley and Yale universities, and was a Rhodes scholar at Oxford. Professor of English at Louisiana (1934–42), at Minnesota (1942–50), he was professor of Drama (1951–56), and of English from 1961 at Yale. Recipient of two Pulitzer prizes (Fiction, 1947; Poetry, 1958), he established an international reputation by his novel, *All the King's Men* (1943; filmed 1949), in which the demagogue Willie Stark closely resembles Governor Huey Long (q.v.). Other works include *John Brown* (1929), *Night Rider* (1939), *The Cave* (1959), *Wilderness* (1961) and some volumes of short stories and verse, including *Selected Poems, Old and New, 1923–66* (1966).

(4) **Samuel** (1807–77), British novelist, born near Wrexham, studied medicine and law, was called to the bar, and made a Q.C. (1851). He is chiefly remembered by his *Passages from the Diary of a Late Physician* (1838) and *Ten Thousand a Year* (1841). Other works were *Now and Then* (1847), *The Lily and the Bee* (1851), and several lawbooks.

WARTON, (1) Joseph (1722–1800), English critic, born at Dunsfold, Surrey, was the son of the Rev. Thomas Warton (1688–1745), vicar of Basingstoke and Oxford professor of Poetry. In 1740 he passed from Winchester to Oriel, and, rector of Winslade from 1748, returned to Winchester in 1755, and was its head 1766–93. His preferments were a prebend of St Paul's, the living of Thorley, a prebend of Winchester, and the rectories of Wickham, Easton and Upham. His *Odes* (1746) marked a reaction from Pope. An edition of Virgil (1753), with translation of the *Eclogues* and *Georgics* gained him a high reputation. He and his brother Thomas associated with Johnson in the Literary club. In 1757 appeared vol. i of his *Essay on Pope* (vol. ii in 1782), with its distinction between the poetry of reason and the poetry of fancy. Later works were editions of Pope (1797) and Dryden (completed by his son, 1811). See the panegyrical *Memoirs* by J. Wooll (1806).

(2) **Thomas** (1728–90), brother of (1), born at Basingstoke, became in 1751 a fellow of Trinity, Oxford, and in 1757 professor of Poetry. He also held two livings. His *Observations on the Faerie Queene* (1754) established his reputation; but he is remembered by his *History of English Poetry* (1774–1781; ed. by W. C. Hazlitt, 1871). In 1785 he became poet laureate and Camden professor of History. His miscellaneous writings included burlesque poetry and prose, genial satires on Oxford, an edition of Theocritus (1770), *Inquiry into the Authenticity of the Rowley Poems*, &c. See Life by Clarissa Rinaker (Illinois, 1916), and Dennis's *Studies in English Literature* (1876).

WARWICK, Richard Neville, Earl of, *wor'ik* (1428–71), 'the Kingmaker', English soldier and statesman, eldest son of Richard, Earl of Salisbury, married as a boy the daughter of the Earl of Warwick, and so at twenty-one got the earldom. The Wars of the Roses began with the battle of St Albans (1455), gained for the Yorkists chiefly by Warwick's help. He was rewarded with the captaincy of Calais, and scoured the Channel at his pleasure. In the campaign of 1459 the Yorkists failed owing to their inactivity. The leaders, including Warwick, fled to the coast of Devon, and thence to Calais. Warwick was in England again in 1460, and in July at Northampton the Yorkists gained a complete victory, taking Henry VI prisoner. Up to this time Warwick's conception of the war was merely the natural struggle of the one party with the other for power; and when the Duke of York made his claim to the throne, Warwick prevailed upon him to waive it till the death of the king. In December 1460 the duke was defeated and slain at Wakefield, and early in 1461 Warwick himself was defeated in the second battle of St Albans. But, with Edward, the Duke of York's son, he marched on London, and proclaimed him as Edward IV. Soon after, the Yorkists gained a complete victory at Towton (1461), the Lancastrian cause was lost, and Henry was captured by Warwick and lodged in the Tower. But now Edward, jealous of Warwick, drove him into open revolt, but was himself compelled to flee to Holland, while the Kingmaker placed Henry once more upon the throne. But soon Edward returned, and at Barnet routed Warwick, who was surrounded and slain, April 14, 1471. See C. W. C. Oman's study (1891), J. Gairdner, *The Houses of Lancaster and York* (1874), Sir J. Ramsay, *Lancaster and York* (1892), and Life by P. M. Kendall (1957).

WASHINGTON, (1) Booker Taliaferro (1856–1915), American educationist, born a Mulatto slave at Hales Ford, Va., educated at Hampton Institute, became a teacher, writer and speaker on Negro problems, and in 1881 principal of the Tuskegee Institute for coloured persons, Alabama. See his *Up from Slavery* (1901), and a study by Stowe and Scott (1916).

(2) George (1732–99), commander of American forces and first president of the U.S., born February 22, at Bridges Creek, Westmoreland county, Virginia, of English stock from Northamptonshire. In 1658 his great-grandfather, John Washington, appeared in Virginia, and soon acquired wealth and position. His grandson, Augustine, died while his son George was still a boy, leaving a large family and inadequate means. George seems to have been a good, healthy boy, with a sober-mindedness beyond his years, although the incident of cherry tree and hatchet is probably the invention of his biographer, Mason Weems. In 1747 he went to Mount Vernon, the residence of his eldest half-brother, Lawrence, who had received the better part of the Washington property. Here the boy had access to books, and came to know the Fairfaxes, the family of his brother's wife; in 1748 Lord Fairfax employed him to survey his property. Surveying alternated for a while with hunting; he learned, too, the use of arms, and studied the art of war. In 1751 he accompanied his half-brother, who was dying of consumption, to the Barbados, and at his death next year was left guardian of his only daughter and heir to his estates in the event of her death without issue. The French were at this time connecting their settlements on the Great Lakes with those on the Mississippi by a chain of posts on the Ohio, within the sphere of English influence. Governor Dinwiddie of Virginia determined to warn the intruders off, and his second messenger was Washington. The French, however, paid no attention to these warnings; and an expedition was sent against them, of which Washington was (by the death of his superior early in the campaign) in command. Washington was driven back, shut up in a little fort, and forced to surrender. He served on the personal staff of Braddock (q.v.), and saved the remnant of the van of Braddock's army in 1755. He was then placed at the head of the Virginia forces (1756). In 1759 he married a rich young widow, Martha Custis (1732–1802). His niece was now dead, and the conjoint estates of Mount Vernon and of the widow Custis made him one of the richest men in the land. He kept open house, entertained liberally, led the hunting, and farmed successfully. He represented his county in the House of Burgesses. On the quarrel with the mother country (1765–70) he favoured peaceful measures first, and was thus one of the leaders in the anti-importation movements; but he soon became convinced that nothing save force would secure to his countrymen their rights. He represented Virginia in the first (1744) and second (1775) Continental Congresses, and at once took a leading part. He was neither orator nor writer, but in rude common sense and in the management of affairs he excelled. He was the one American soldier of national reputation, and was the inevitable commander-in-chief. He had remarkable powers as a strategist and tactician, but was pre-eminent as a leader of men. It was this dignified, well-dressed gentleman who took command of the New England farmers and mechanics assembled at Cambridge in the summer of 1775. It seems scarcely credible that these half-disciplined, half-armed men should have held cooped up in Boston a thoroughly-disciplined and well-equipped British army and forced their evacuation (1776); the retreat from Concord and the slaughter at Bunker Hill were largely due to the incompetence of the English commander. The only really able English commander was Cornwallis, and he was hampered by the stupidity of his superior. Following reverses in the New York area, Washington made a remarkable retreat through New Jersey, inflicting notable defeats on the enemy at Trenton and Princeton (1777). He suffered defeats at Brandywine and Germantown but held his army together through the winter of 1777–78 at Valley Forge. After the alliance with France (1778) and with the assistance of Rochambeau, Washington forced the defeat and surrender of Cornwallis (q.v.), at Yorktown in 1781, which virtually ended the War of Independence. Washington retired to Mount Vernon, and sought to secure a strong government by constitutional means. In 1787 he presided over the convention of delegates from twelve states at Philadelphia which formulated the constitution; and the government under this constitution began in 1789 with Washington as first chief-magistrate or president. Unlike the old, the new administration was a strong consolidated government. Parties were formed, led by Washington's two most trusted advisers, Jefferson and Hamilton. At the outset Washington sought to enlist on the side of the new government the ablest men in the country, whether they had approved or disapproved that precise form of the constitution. As time went on, however, it became evident that those desiring greater liberty for the individual would no longer be content with passive opposition. A strong party sprang into life, and began a campaign which has never been surpassed for personal abuse and virulence. Stung by their taunts, Washington lost his faith in American institutions, went over heart and soul to the Federalist party, and even doubted whether Republicans should be admitted into the army. He retired from the presidency in 1797 and died (childless) at Mount Vernon on the Potomac, December 14, 1799. The federal capital of the U.S., in the planning of which he associated, bears his name. See books by J. Marshall (1804–07), Washington Irving (1855–59), A. Bancroft (new ed. 1851), H. C. Lodge (1889), Woodrow Wilson (1897; new ed. 1927), Frederic Harrison (1901), N. Hapgood (1902), J. A. Harrison (1906), F. T. Hill (1914), J. O'Boyle (1915), Rupert Hughes (1926–30), N. W. Stephenson and W. H. Dunn (1940), D. S. Freeman (1949–55), and its continuation by J. A. Carroll and H. W. Ashworth (1958), M. Cunliffe (1959) and B. Knollenberg (1965); and his *Writings*, ed. W. C. Ford (14 vols. 1889–93), ed. Fitzpatrick (26 vols. 1931–38).

WASSERMANN, *vas'ĕr-man*, (1) **August von** (1866–1925), German bacteriologist, born at Bamberg, worked at bacteriology and chemotherapy in Berlin, discovered (1906), and gave his name to, a blood-serum test for syphilis.

(2) **Jakob** (1873–1933), German novelist, born, a Jew, at Fürth in Bavaria, lived at Vienna and in Styria. His impressive novel *Die Juden von Zirndorf* (1897) was followed by a succession culminating in the trilogy completed just before his death: *Der Fall Maurizius* (1928), *Etzel Andergast* (1931), *Joseph Kerkhovens dritte Existenz* (1934). He wrote also short stories, lives of Columbus and H. M. Stanley, and an autobiography (1921).

WATERHOUSE, (1) **Alfred** (1830–1905), English architect, was born at Liverpool, and became R.A. in 1885, designed Manchester town hall and assize courts, Owens College, Manchester, Girton College, Cambridge, St Paul's School, Hammersmith, &c.

(2) **John William** (1847–1917), English painter, born in Rome, became R.A. in 1895. Among his pictures are *Ulysses and the Sirens* (1892) and *The Lady of Shalott* (1894).

WATERLAND, Daniel (1683–1740), English theologian, born at Walesby, Lincolnshire, a fellow of Magdalene, Cambridge (1704), canon of Windsor (1727), archdeacon of Middlesex and vicar of Twickenham (1730), controversially opposed the views of Samuel Clarke and Daniel Whitby (qq.v.). Van Mildert edited his works, with Memoir (11 vols. 1823–28).

WATERTON, Charles (1782–1865), British naturalist, born at Walton Hall near Wakefield, and educated at Stonyhurst, was much in America (South and North) in 1804–24. Besides his *Wanderings in South America* (1825; 6th ed. 1866) he published *Essays on Natural History* (1838–57; with Life by Moore, 1879). See P. Gosse, *The Squire of Walton Hall* (1940).

WATSON, (1) **James Dewey** (1928–), U.S. scientist, born in Chicago, where he graduated at the university. He came to England and worked with Crick and Wilkins (3) on the structure of DNA before becoming professor of Biology at Harvard (1961). He was awarded the Nobel prize for medicine and physiology with Crick and Wilkins in 1962. See his *The Double Helix* (1968).

(2) **John.** See MACLAREN (2).

(3) **John Broadus** (1878–1958), American psychologist, born in Greenville, S.C., a leading exponent of behaviourism. His most important work is *Behavior—An Introduction to Comparative Psychology* (1914).

(4) **Richard** (1737–1816), English divine, born at Heversham, educated at Trinity College, Cambridge, where he later became professor of Chemistry (1764) and regius professor of Divinity (1771), and Bishop of Llandaff (1782), published a famous *Apology for Christianity* (1776) in reply to Gibbon, and an *Apology for the Bible* (1796) in reply to Paine. He gave much time to agriculture at his estate on Windermere, and introduced the larch to that district. See his egotistical *Anecdotes of the Life of R. W.* (1817).

(5) **Robert** (1746–1838), Scottish adventurer, born at Elgin, fought for American independence, took his M.D. in Scotland, and was Lord George Gordon's secretary, president of the revolutionary Corresponding Society, state prisoner for two years in Newgate, Napoleon's tutor in English, and president of the Scots College at Paris. He unearthed the Stuart papers at Rome, and ended by strangling himself in London.

(6) **Thomas** (*c.* 1557–92), English lyric poet, was a Londoner who studied at Oxford. Coming to Marlowe's help in a street fight, he killed a man in 1589. He excelled in Latin verse, but he is best known for his English 'sonnets' in *Hecatompathia* (1582) and *Tears of Fancie* (1593).

(7) **Sir William** (1715–87), English scientist, born in London, was one of the earliest experimenters on electricity, being first to investigate the passage of electricity through a rarefied gas. He did much to introduce the Linnaean system to Britain.

(8) **Sir William** (1858–1935), English poet, born at Burley-in-Wharfedale, Yorks, first attracted notice with *Wordsworth's Grave* (1890). *Odes and other Poems* followed in 1894, *The Father of the Forest* in 1895, *For England* (1903), *Sable and Purple* (1910), *Heralds of the Dawn* (1912), *The Man who Saw* (1917), *The Superhuman Antagonists* (1919), *Poems, Brief and New* (1925), &c. He was knighted in 1917.

WATSON-WATT, Sir Robert Alexander (1892–1973), Scottish physicist, born at Brechin, educated at Dundee and St Andrews, worked in the Meteorological Office, the D.S.I.R., and the National Physical Laboratory before becoming scientific adviser to the Air Ministry in 1940. He played a major rôle in the development and introduction of radar, for which he was knighted in 1942. See his *Three Steps to Victory* (1958).

WATT, (1) **James** (1736–1819), Scottish inventor, born at Greenock, January 19, son of a merchant and town councillor, went to Glasgow in 1754 to learn the trade of a mathematical-instrument maker, and there, after a year in London, he set up in business. The hammermen's guild put difficulties in his way, but the university made him its mathematical-instrument maker (1757–63). He was employed on surveys for the Forth and Clyde canal (1767), the Caledonian and other canals; in the improvement of the harbours of Ayr, Port Glasgow and Greenock; and in the deepening of the Forth, Clyde and other rivers. As early as 1759 his attention had been directed to steam as a motive force. In 1763–64 a working model of the Newcomen engine from a college classroom was sent for repair. He easily put it into order, and, seeing the defects of the machine, hit upon the expedient of the separate condenser. Other improvements were the air pump, steam jacket for cylinder, double-acting engine, &c. He entered into a partnership with Matthew Boulton of Soho near Birmingham in 1774, when (under a patent of 1769) the manufacture of the new engine was commenced at the Soho Engineering Works. Watt's soon superseded Newcomen's machine as a pumping-engine; and between 1781 and 1785 he obtained patents for the sun and planet motion, the expansion principle, the double engine, the parallel motion, a smokeless furnace, and the governor. He described a steam locomotive in one of his patents (1784). He also invented a letter-copying press, a machine for copying sculpture, &c. The composition of water was discovered, not by Watt, but by Henry Cavendish (q.v.). The watt, a unit of power, is named after him, and the term horsepower, another unit, was first used by him. He retired in 1800, and died at Heathfield Hall, his seat near Birmingham, August 19. See Lives by Jacks (1901), Dickinson and Jenkins (1927), and study by I. B. Hart (1958).

(2) **Robert** (1774–1819), Scottish bibliographer, born near Stewarton in Ayrshire, became a distinguished physician, known for his great *Bibliotheca Britannica* (1819–24).

WATTEAU, Jean Antoine, *va-tō* (1684–1721), French painter, born at Valenciennes, studied under the local artist Gérin, but in 1702 ran away to Paris and worked as a scene painter at the Opera, as a copyist, and as assistant to Claude Gillot and Claude Audran. The latter was keeper of the Luxembourg, and it was here that Watteau found the opportunity to study the work of Rubens, which influenced him considerably, and to paint from nature the palace-garden landscapes which form the typical backcloth to many of his pictures. After 1712 he enjoyed the patronage of the collector Crozat, who introduced him to the paintings of Veronese, an influence visible in the colouring and style of his later work. His early canvases were mostly military scenes, but it was the mythological *Embarquement pour Cythère* which won him membership of the Academy in 1717. While staying at the castle of Montmorency with Crozat he painted his *Fêtes galantes*, quasi-pastoral idylls in court dress which became fashionable in high society. A lifelong sufferer from tuberculosis, he visited London in 1720 to consult the celebrated Dr Mead (q.v.), but his health was rapidly deteriorating, and on his return he painted his last great work, depicting the interior of the shop of his art-dealer friend Gersaint, drawn from nature and intended as a signboard, but in fact the most classical and most perfectly composed of his paintings, rivalled only by the *Embarquement*. Essentially aristocratic in conception, Watteau's paintings fell into disfavour at the Revolution, and it was not until the end of the 19th century that, aided by de Goncourt's *Catalogue raisonnée* (1875), they regained popularity. Watteau is now regarded as one of the leading French masters, a pioneer in the study of nature, and a forerunner of the Impressionists in his handling of colour. He influenced and was imitated by many later artists, notably Fragonard and Boucher (qq.v.). See studies by Cellier (1867), Mollet (1883), Sir C. Phillips (1902), C. Mauclair (trans. 1906), S. Sitwell (1925) and K. T. Parker (1931).

WATTS, (1) **Alaric Alexander** (1797–1864), English journalist and poet, born in London, founded the *United Services Gazette* (1833) and the annual *Literary Souvenir* (1824–37), and published two volumes of poetry, but is now remembered chiefly for his alliterative alphabetical *jeu d'esprit* 'An Austrian army awfully arrayed'. See Life by his son A. A. Watts (1884).

(2) **George Frederick** (1817–1904), English painter, born in London, formed his style after the Venetian masters and first attracted notice by his cartoon of *Caractacus* (1843) in the competition for murals for the new Houses of Parliament. He became known for his penetrating portraits of notabilities, 150 of which he presented to the National Portrait Gallery in 1904, and in these his best work is to be seen; but in his lifetime his somewhat sickly subject pieces enjoyed enormous popularity, and monochrome reproductions of *Paolo and Francesca, Sir Galahad, Love Triumphant*, &c., adorned the walls of countless late Victorian middle-class homes. He also executed some sculpture, including *Physical Energy* (Kensington Gardens). In 1864 he married Ellen Terry (q.v.), but parted from her within a year. He declined a baronetcy in 1885 and was awarded the O.M. in 1902. See books by H. Macmillan (1903), Pantini (1904), G. K. Chesterton (1904), Mrs R. Barrington (1905), Mrs M. Watts, his widow (1912), E. H. Short (1925) and R. Chapman (1945).

(3) **Henry** (1815–84), English chemist, born in London, best known by his *Dictionary of Chemistry* (1863–68; supplements, 1872–75–1881; revised by Muir and Morley, 1889–94), based on Ure's.

(4) **Isaac** (1674–1748), English hymnwriter, born at Southampton, in 1702 succeeded an Independent minister in Mark Lane, London, becoming eminent as a preacher. His hymns and psalms are contained in *Horae Lyricae* (1706), *Hymns and Spiritual Songs* (1707–09) and *Psalms of David Imitated* (1719), and include 'Jesus shall reign where'er the sun', 'When I survey the wondrous cross', and 'O God, our help in ages past'. See Lives by Dr Gibbons, Dr Johnson, Southey, T. Milner (1834), T. Hood (1875), E. P. Wright (1914) and H. Escott (1962).

(5) **James Winston** (1904–), American neurosurgeon, born at Lynchburg, Va., famous for his brain surgery, with W. Freeman (q.v.) developed the operation known as prefrontal lobotomy.

WATTS-DUNTON, Walter Theodore (1832–1914), English poet and critic, was born at St Ives, Huntingdonshire. To the name Watts he added his mother's name, Dunton, in 1896. In London he became the centre of a very remarkable literary and artistic company, and the intimate friend of Rossetti, William Morris, Swinburne, and afterwards Tennyson. He wrote enough to fill many volumes—in the *Athenaeum* (1876–98) and elsewhere. In *The Coming of Love* (1897) he gave a selection of his poems. In 1898 appeared *Aylwin*. *Old Familiar Faces* (1915) contains recollections of Borrow, Rossetti, Morris, &c., from the *Athenaeum*. See works cited at ROSSETTI, and Life and Letters by T. Hake and A. Compton-Rickett (2 vols. 1916).

WAUGH, *wokH*, (1) **Alec,** in full **Alexander Raban** (1898–), English novelist and traveller, elder brother of (3), was born in London and educated at Sherborne and Sandhurst. His first novel, a classic of school life, was *The Loom of Youth* (1917), and there followed other novels, including *Wheels within Wheels* (1933), *Where the Clock Chimes Twice* (1952), *Island in the Sun* (1956; filmed 1957), travel books, such as *The Sunlit Caribbean* (1948), and short stories. See his *The Early Years of Alec Waugh* (1962) and *My Brother Evelyn and Other Profiles* (1967).

(2) **Edwin** (1817–90), English dialect writer, the 'Lancashire poet', was born at Rochdale. Among his numerous prose writings are the *Besom Ben Stories* (1892), and the admirable descriptions of natural scenery in *Tufts of Heather* and *Rambles in the Lake Country* (1862). His songs in periodicals were published as *Poems and Lancashire Songs* (1860). There is an edition of his works, with memoir, by G. Milner (8 vols. 1892–93).

(3) **Evelyn Arthur St John** (1903–66), English author, was born in London. Son of the critic and publisher, Arthur Waugh (1866–1943), and younger brother of (1), he turned naturally to writing when he left Oxford. Novels such as *Decline and Fall* (1928), *Vile Bodies* (1930), *Black Mischief* (1932) and *Scoop* (1938) found an eager public, compounded as they are of light-hearted banter and witty conversation pieces at the expense of the follies of social life in the 1920s and onwards. His later books, on the whole, exhibit a more serious attitude and the bantering tone is replaced by a sardonic wit, with occasional rasping undertones. Notable titles are *Put Out More Flags* (1942), *Brideshead Revisited* (1945), *Scott-King's Modern Europe* (1946), *The Loved One* (1948), *Men at Arms* (1952), *Love Among the Ruins* (1953), *Officers and Gentlemen* (1955), *Unconditional Surrender* (1961), and a self-portrait, *Gilbert Pinfold* (1957). *Men at Arms* won the James Tait Black prize, and a Life of Edmund Campion the Hawthornden prize in 1936. See his autobiography *A Little Learning* (1964) and study by F. J. Stopp (1958).

WAUTERS, Emile, *wow'ters* (1846–1933), Belgian historical and portrait painter, born at Brussels. His well-known *Mary of Burgundy before the Magistrates* is in Liège museum.

WAVELL, Archibald Percival Wavell, 1st Earl (1883–1950), British field-marshal, born at Winchester, educated at Winchester and R.M.C. Sandhurst, was commissioned in the Black Watch 1901, and served in South Africa and India. Wounded in 1916, he lost the sight of one eye. Posted to the General Staff, his admiration for Allenby's methods of command and his high commissionership in Egypt was reflected in two books which are models of succinct prose. Between the wars he was entrusted with command and staff appointments of steadily rising importance. In 1939 he was given the Middle East Command. With dangerously slender resources he speedily found himself fighting eight separate campaigns, five of them simultaneously; a task which made heavy demands on his outstanding quality of 'robustness'. His defeat of a numerically superior Italian army, with the capture of 130,000 prisoners, was as notable as his adroit conquest of Abyssinia. Thereafter, lacking means, his military fortunes declined. Widely read, his love of verse was reflected in his anthology *Other Men's Flowers* (1944). His own masterly little work *Generals and Generalship* (1941), was invariably included in the field kit of his most formidable enemy, Erwin Rommel. From 1943 to 1947, during the difficult years which preceded the transfer of power, he was viceroy of India. He became field-marshal and viscount (1943), earl (1947), constable of the Tower (1948), lord-lieutenant of London (1949). See works by Rowan-Robinson and R. J. Collins (1948) and Life by J. Connell (1964).

WAVERLEY, John Anderson, 1st Viscount (1882-1958), British administrator and politician, was born at Eskbank, Midlothian. Educated at Edinburgh and Leipzig, he entered the Colonial Office in 1905, was chairman of the Board of Inland Revenue (1919-22), and permanent under-secretary at the Home Office from 1922 until his appointment as governor of Bengal in 1932. He was home secretary and minister of Home Security from 1939 to 1940—the Anderson air-raid shelter being named after him—became in 1940 lord president of the Council, and chancellor of the Exchequer in 1943, when he introduced the pay-as-you-earn system of income-tax collection devised by his predecessor Sir Kinglsey Wood. He was created viscount in 1952 and awarded the O.M. (1958). See Life by J. Wheeler-Bennett (1962).

WAYNE, Anthony (1745-96), 'mad Anthony', American soldier, born at Easttown (now Waynesboro), Pa., raised in 1776 a volunteer regiment, and in Canada covered the retreat of the provincial forces at Three Rivers. He commanded at Ticonderoga until 1777, when he joined Washington in New Jersey. He fought bravely at Brandywine; led the attack at Germantown; captured supplies for the army at Valley Forge; carried Stony Point; and saved Lafayette in Virginia (1781). In 1793 he led an expedition against the Indians. See Life by J. R. Spears (1903).

WAYNFLETE. See WILLIAM OF WAYNFLETE.

WEBB, (1) Sir Aston (1849–1930), English architect, born in London, R.A. 1903, P.R.A. 1919-24, designed the new front of Buckingham Palace, the Admiralty Arch, Imperial College of Science, and many other London buildings.

(2) **Beatrice.** See (6).

(3) **Daniel** (*c.* 1719–98), Irish critic of poetry, painting and music, a precursor of the romantics, born at Maidstown (Limerick), lived at Bath. See Life by H. Hecht (1920).

(4) **Mary Gladys,** *née* **Meredith** (1881–1927), English writer, born at Leighton, near the Wrekin, married (1912) H. B. L. Webb, lived mostly in Shropshire, market-gardening and novel-writing, and latterly in London. *Precious Bane* (1924) won her a belated fame as a writer of English and a novelist of Shropshire soil, Shropshire dialect, Shropshire superstition, and 'the continuity of country life'. Her other works are *The Golden Arrow* (1916), *Gone to Earth* (1917), *The House in Dormer Forest* (1920), *Seven for a Secret* (1922) and the unfinished *Armour*

Wherein he Trusted (1929)—novels; *The Spring of Joy* (1917)—nature essays; and poems. See studies by W. R. Chappell (1930), H. Addison (1931), T. Moult (1935) and W. B. Jones (1948).

(5) **Matthew** (1848-83), English swimmer, born at Dawley, Salop, was the first man to swim the English Channel. Starting from Dover, August 25, 1875, he reached Calais in 21¾ hours. He was drowned attempting to swim the Niagara rapids.

(6) **Sidney James, Baron Passfield** (1859–1947) and **(Martha) Beatrice**, *née* **Potter** (1858–1943), English social reformers, social historians and economists, married in 1892. Sidney was born in London, the son of an accountant, and in 1885 graduated LL.B. at London University. In the same year he was introduced by Bernard Shaw to the newly-founded Fabian Society, of which he became one of the most powerful members, writing the tracts *Facts for Socialists* (1887), *Facts for Londoners* (1889) and contributing to *Fabian Essays* (1889). He became a Progressive member of the L.C.C. in 1892. Beatrice was born near Gloucester, the daughter of an industrial magnate. Through her friendship with Herbert Spencer (q.v.) and through rent-collecting she became interested in the social problems of the time, and assisted Charles Booth (q.v.) in research for the survey *Life and Labour of the People in London*. In 1891 she published *The Co-operative Movement in Great Britain*. After their marriage the Webbs began a joint life of service to socialism and trade unionism, publishing in 1894 their classic *History of Trade Unionism* based on a sound personal knowledge of the movement. They also collaborated in *Industrial Democracy* (1897), the invaluable *English Local Government* (9 vols. 1906-29), *The Truth about Russia* (1942), &c. They started the *New Statesman* (1913), and participated in establishing the London School of Economics (1895). Labour M.P. for Seaham (1922–29), Sidney Webb was made president of the Board of Trade in 1924, and in 1929 was raised, much against his inclination, to the peerage, becoming dominions and colonial secretary (1929-30) and colonial secretary (1930-31). In 1931 the Webbs visited Russia, where they accumulated material for several books on Soviet Communism. See Beatrice's *My Apprenticeship* (1926), and *Our Partnership* (1948); also Lives by M. A. Hamilton (1933) and K. Muggeridge and R. Adam (1967).

WEBER, *vay'ber*, (1) **Carl Maria Friedrich Ernst von** (1786–1826), German composer and pianist, was born of a noble but impoverished Austrian family, at Eutin near Lübeck. Soon after, his father with his wife (a singer) and boy began to wander from town to town at the head of a small dramatic company. As soon as he could sit at the piano the boy was plied with music lessons; but his serious training began in 1796. His second opera, *Das Waldmädchen* (1800), produced at Freiberg before he was fourteen, he afterwards remodelled in *Silvana*. At Vienna in 1803 he was warmly welcomed as a pupil by Abt Vogler (q.v.), who obtained for him the conductorship of the opera at Breslau, where he gave evidence of rare talent for organization. In 1806 he became secretary to a brother of the king of Württemberg, ran into debt and dissipation, was through his thriftless old father's fault charged with embezzlement, and with his father ordered to quit the country (1810). The next twelve months he spent at Mannheim and Darmstadt, composing the operetta *Abu Hassan*; at Munich in 1811 he was writing concertos. In 1813 he settled at Prague as opera *kapellmeister*, and about this time composed ten patriotic songs and the cantata *Kampf und Sieg*. In 1816 he was invited by the king of Saxony to direct the German opera at Dresden, superseding Italian opera. In 1817 he married Carolina Brandt, the famous singer. In 1818 he wrote his Mass in E flat and the Jubel cantata and overture, in 1819 the Mass in G for the royal golden wedding. *Der Freischütz* was completed in May 1820, and produced with great success at Berlin (1821). His next opera, *Euryanthe*, was produced at Vienna in 1823. His final masterpiece, *Oberon*, was undertaken at the request of Charles Kemble for Covent Garden Theatre. March 1826 saw Weber in London, and the first performance of *Oberon* was the crowning triumph of his life. During the next few weeks he conducted frequently at the theatre and played at many concerts. Such labour proved too much for his exhausted body. He died June 4, and was buried at St Mary's, Moorfields, whence in 1844 his remains were removed to Dresden. As founder of German romantic opera, Weber was the forerunner of Wagner. Other works include the music to *Preciosa*, the overture, *Der Beherrscher der Geister*, two symphonies, three concertos, sonatas, &c., as well as scenas, cantatas and songs. See Spitta in Grove's *Dictionary*, J. Benedict (1881), and German works by F. W. Jähns (1871–73), J. Kapp (1922), K. Tetzel (1926) and W. Saunders (1939).

(2) **Ernst Heinrich** (1795–1878), German scientist, born in Wittenberg, from 1818 professor of Anatomy, and from 1840 of Physiology at Leipzig, devised a method of determining the sensitivity of the skin, enunciated in 1834, and gave name to the Weber-Fechner Law of the increase of stimuli.

(3) **Max** (1864–1920), German economist, born at Erfurt, professor at Berlin (1893), Freiburg (1894), Heidelberg (1897) and Munich (1919), noted for his work on the relation between the spirit of capitalism and protestant ethics. See studies by H. Robertson (1935) and R. Bendix (1961).

(4) **Max** (1881–1961), Russian-born American painter, studied under Matisse in Paris and was one of the pioneer abstractionist painters in New York. He later abandoned this extreme form for a distorted naturalism. His works include *The Two Musicians* (1917; Modern Art, N.Y.), *Tranquillity* (1928), *Latest News* (*c.* 1940), *Three Literary Gentlemen* (1945).

(5) **Wilhelm Eduard** (1804-91), German scientist, brother of (2), from 1831 professor of Physics at Göttingen, deposed in 1837; from 1843 professor at Leipzig, associated

with Gauss in his researches on electricity and magnetism, inventor of the electro-dynamometer, first to apply the mirror and scale method of reading deflections, and author, with (2), of a notable treatise on waves.

WEBERN, Anton von (1883–1945), Austrian composer, born in Vienna, studied under Schönberg and became one of his first musical disciples, even surpassing his master in the extreme application of the latter's twelve-tone techniques. Fragmentation of melody to achieve fleeting, impressionistic effects (*Klangfarbenmelodien*) make the maximum demands on the listener, and performances of his works at first always invited hostile demonstrations. For a while he conducted the Vienna Workers' Symphony Orchestra, founded a choir called the *Kunstelle*, but lived most of his life in retirement at Mödling. The Nazis banned his music and he worked as a proofreader during World War II. He was accidentally shot dead by a U.S. soldier near Salzburg, September 15, 1945. His works include a symphony, three cantatas, *Four Pieces for Violin and Pianoforte* (1910), *Five Pieces for Orchestra* (1911–13), a concerto for nine instruments and songs, including several settings of Stefan George's poems (1908–1909).

WEBSTER, (1) Daniel (1782–1852), American orator, lawyer and statesman, born at Salisbury, N.H., studied at Dartmouth, Salisbury and Boston, was admitted to the bar in 1805, and was sent to congress in 1813. Settling in Boston as an advocate in 1816, he distinguished himself in the Dartmouth College case, and as an orator became famous by his oration on the bicentenary of the landing of the Pilgrim Fathers. Returning to congress in December 1823 as a Massachusetts representative he found new rivals there; in 1827 he was transferred to the senate. He had favoured free trade, but in 1828 defended the new protective tariff. His whole career was marked by a deep reverence for established institutions and accomplished facts, and for the principle of nationality. His 'Bunker Hill' oration was made in 1825 and another, on the supremacy of the Union, in 1830. The Whig party triumphed in 1840, and Webster was called into Harrison's Cabinet as secretary of state; under Tyler he negotiated the Ashburton treaty with Great Britain, but resigned in May 1843. In 1844 he refused his party's nomination for president and supported Clay. He opposed the war with Mexico. In 1850 he said that he abhorred slavery, but was unwilling to break up the Union to abolish it. Under Fillmore he was called to his former post as secretary of state to settle differences with England. On October 24 he died at Marshfield, his Massachusetts home. Daniel Webster was unquestionably the greatest of American orators. His speeches were published in 1851; his *Private Correspondence* in 1857. See Lives by G. T. Curtis (1870), H. C. Lodge (1883), Brooks (1893) J. B. McMaster (1902) and C. M. Fuess (1930), and Fisher's *True Daniel Webster* (1912).

(2) John (*c.* 1580–*c.* 1625), English dramatist, supposed to have been at one time clerk of St Andrews, Holborn. In *Lady Jane* and *The Two Harpies* (both lost) he was the collaborator of Dekker, Drayton, Chettle and others. In 1604 he made some additions to *The Malcontent* of Marston. In 1607 were printed the *Famous History of Sir Thomas Wyat*, a tragedy, and two comedies, *Westward Hoe* and *Northward Hoe*, all three the joint work of Webster and Dekker. *The White Divil* (1612) first revealed his powers. *The Dutchesse of Malfi* (1623) is a yet greater achievement. *Appius and Virginia* (first published 1654) may be Heywood's (or partly); *The Devil's Law Case* (1623) is largely disagreeable and sordid. A poem on the death of Prince Henry, and other fragments of verse, survive, with some doubtful works. The tragedy, *A Late Murder of the Son upon the Mother* (1624), unpublished and lost, although licensed, was written by Ford and Webster. Not popular in his own day, Webster was first recognized by Charles Lamb. Webster's works were edited by A. Dyce (1830), W. C. Hazlitt (1857–58), F. L. Lucas (1927). See Rupert Brooke's monograph (1916), and E. E. Stoll, *John Webster* (1905).

(3) Noah (1758–1843), American lexicographer, born in Hartford, Conn., graduated at Yale in 1778, and, after a spell as teacher, was admitted to the bar in 1781. But he soon resumed teaching, and made a great hit with the first part (1783; later known as 'Webster's Spelling-Book') of *A Grammatical Institute of the English Language*. Political articles and pamphlets, lecturing, a few years of law and journalism occupied him till 1798, when he retired to a life of literary labour at New Haven. He published an English grammar (1807) and the famous *American Dictionary of the English Language* (1828; latest ed. *Webster's New International Dictionary of the English Language*). See Life by E. Scudder (1882).

WEDDELL, James (1787–1834), English navigator, born at Ostend. In his principal voyage (1822–24) he penetrated to the point 74° 15′ S. by 34° 17′ W. in that part of Antarctica which later took his name (Weddell Sea; Weddell Quadrant), as did a type of seal taken by him in the area.

WEDDERBURN, Alexander, 1st Baron (1780) **Loughborough, 1st Earl** (1801) **of Rosslyn** (1733–1805), Lord Chancellor, born in Edinburgh, son of a Scottish judge, in 1757 abruptly left the Scottish bar for the English, entered parliament in 1762, and distinguished himself in the Douglas cause (1771).

WEDEKIND, Frank, *vay'dĕ-kint* (1864–1918), German dramatist, born in Hanover, won fame with *Erdgeist* (1895), *Frühlings Erwachen* (1891; first performed 1906), *Die Büchse der Pandora* (1903; first performed 1918), and other unconventional tragedies. See studies by P. Fechter (1920) and A. Kutscher (1922–31).

WEDGWOOD, (1) Dame Cicely Veronica (1910–), English historian, born at Stocksfield, Northumberland, and studied at Lady Margaret Hall, Oxford. A specialist in 17th-century history, her publications include biographies of *Strafford* (1935), *Oliver Cromwell* (1939), *William the Silent* (James Tait Black Memorial prize, 1944) and *Montrose* (1955), *The Thirty Years' War* (1938); also *The King's Peace* (1955), *The King's War* (1958) and *The Trial of Charles I* (1964). She was created D.B.E. in 1968 and awarded the O.M. in 1969.

(2) **Josiah** (1730–95), English potter, born at Burslem of a family notable in the industry, patented (1763) a beautiful cream-coloured ware (Queen's Ware). He emulated antique models, producing the unglazed blue Jasper ware, with its raised designs in white, the black basalt ware, and, in 1769, named his new works, near Hanley, 'Etruria'. His products, and their imitations, were named after him (Wedgwood ware). He associated with the potters T. Whieldon and T. Bentley, and employed J. Flaxman (q.v.), from 1775, to furnish designs. See Life by A. Kelly (1963) and books on the family by L. Jewitt (1865), J. C. Wedgwood (1908); on Josiah by E. Meteyard (1865–66), J. Wedgwood (1915), W. Burton (1922) and C. V. Wedgwood (1951); his *Correspondence* (1903–06), and W. Mankowitz, *Wedgwood* (1953).

WEED, Thurlow (1797–1882), American journalist, born at Cairo, N.Y., in 1830 founded the Albany *Evening Journal*, which he controlled for thirty-five years; in 1867–68 he edited the New York *Commercial Advertiser*. See his *Autobiography* (1884).

WEELKES, Thomas (*c.* 1575–1623), one of the greatest of English madrigal composers, was organist at Winchester College (1597) and Chichester Cathedral (1602). He graduated B.Mus. at New College, Oxford, in 1602. A friend of Thomas Morley (q.v.), he contributed to the *Triumphes of Oriana*.

WEENIX, *vay'-*, (1) **Jan** (1640–1719), Dutch painter, born at Amsterdam, son of (2), known for hunting scenes, animal subjects and still-life paintings featuring dead game-birds, hares, &c.

(2) **Jan Baptist** (1621–60), Dutch painter, father of (1), specialized in landscapes and seaport subjects.

WEEVER, John (1576–1632), English poet and antiquary, born in Lancashire; his works include *Epigrammes in the Oldest Cut and Newest Fashion* (1599; ed. R. B. McKerrow, 1922), and *Ancient Funerall Monuments* (1621; 3rd ed. by Tooke, 1767).

WEGENER, Alfred Lothar, *vay'gė-ner* (1880–1930), German explorer and geophysicist, born in Berlin, professor of Meteorology at Hamburg (1919), of Geophysics and Meteorology at Graz (1924). His theory of continental drift is named after him (Wegener Hypothesis), and is the subject of his chief work (1915; trans. 1924 as *Origin of Continents and Oceans*). He died in Greenland on his fourth expedition there.

WEIERSTRASS, Karl, *vī'ėr-shtras* (1815–97), German mathematician, born at Ostenfelde, became professor of Mathematics at Berlin, noted for his work on the theory of functions. He proposed coordinates, and devised a curve, with related function, all of which are named from him.

WEIGEL. See Brecht.

WEIL, *vīl,* (1) **Gustav** (1808–89), German orientalist, professor of Oriental Languages at Heidelberg, wrote on Mohammedan history, and translated the *Arabian Nights* (1837–41).

(2) **Simone** (1903–43), French philosophical writer, born in Paris, taught philosophy in schools at Le Puy, Bourges and St Quentin, but interspersed this with periods of hard manual labour on farms and at the Renault works in order to experience the working-class life. In 1936 she served in the Republican forces in the Spanish Civil War. In 1941 she settled in Marseilles, where she befriended the Dominican, Father Perrin, who introduced her to Gustave Thibon and their joint influence was the crucial experience of her short life. A deep mystical feeling for the Catholic faith, yet a profound reluctance to join an organized religion is at the heart of most of her writing which, posthumously published, includes *La Pesanteur et la Grâce* (1947; trans. 1952), *Attente de Dieu* (1950; trans. 1951), *The Notebooks* (1952–55; trans. 1956), and *Oppression and Liberty* (trans. 1959). She escaped to the United States in 1942 and worked for the Free French in London, before her death at Ashford, Kent. See Memoir by J. M. Perrin and G. Thibon (1952; trans. 1953), and studies by Davy (trans. 1951), Tomlin (1954), Rees (1958), and Cabaud (1967).

WEILL, Kurt, *vīl* (1900–50), German composer, born in Dessau. He studied under Humperdinck and Busoni, worked with Brecht, achieved fame with *Die Dreigroschenoper*, a modernization of Gay's *Beggar's Opera*, in 1928. A refugee from the Nazis, he settled in the U.S.A. in 1934. In all his works, Weill was influenced by the idioms of jazz, but his later operas and musical comedies, all of which contain an element of social criticism, did not repeat the success of the first.

WEIMAR, Marguerite Josephine. See George, Mlle.

WEINBERGER, Jaromir, *vīn'ber-gėr* (1896–1967), Czech composer, born in Prague, studied under Reger, was professor of Composition at Ithaca Conservatory, New York (1922–26), settling in the U.S.A. in 1939. He wrote theatre music, orchestral works, and four operas, the most famous of which is *Schwanda the Bagpiper* (1927).

WEINGARTNER, (Paul) Felix (1863–1942), Austrian conductor and composer, born in Zara, Dalmatia, studied under Liszt, succeeded Mahler (1908) as conductor of the Vienna Court Opera, and later toured extensively in Britain and America. His works include operas, symphonies, and *Über das Dirigieren* (1895). See his autobiographical *Lebenserinnerungen* (trans. 1937 'Buffets and Rewards').

WEISMANN, August, *vīs'man* (1834–1914), German biologist, born at Frankfurt-am-Main, in 1867 became professor of Zoology at Freiburg. One of his first works was on the development of the Diptera. In 1868–76 appeared a series of papers, translated in 1882 as *Studies in the Theory of Descent.* His theory of germ-plasm (Weismannism—a form of neo-Darwinism), expressed in a series of essays (trans. as *Essays upon Heredity and*

Kindred Biological Problems, 1889–92), raised opposition in Britain. He wrote other works on evolution.

WEISZ, Victor. See VICKY.

WEIZMANN, Chaim, *vīts'man* (1874–1952), Jewish statesman, born near Pinsk, studied in Germany and lectured on Chemistry at Geneva and Manchester. His complete and articulate faith in Zionism played a large part in securing the Balfour Declaration of 1917, by which the Jews were promised a national home in Palestine. He was president of the Zionist Organization (1920–30, 1935–1946), and of the Jewish Agency (from 1929). When the state of Israel came into being in 1948, he became its first president. See Life by Berlin (1958), and *A Biography by Several Hands* (ed. Weisgal and Carmichael, 1962).

WEIZSÄCKER, *vīts'ek-ėr,* (1) **Julius** (1828–1889), German historian, born at Oehringen near Heilbronn, professor at Tübingen, Strasbourg, Göttingen and Berlin, edited vols. 1-6 of the *Deutsche Reichstagsakten.*

(2) **Karl Heinrich** (1822–99), German Protestant theologian, brother of (1), born at Oehringen, became professor at Tübingen. His most notable work was translated as *The Apostolic Age* (1894–95).

WELCH, John. See WELSH (2).

WELCKER, *vel'ker,* (1) **Friedrich Gottlieb** (1784–1868), German philologist and archaeologist, born at Grünberg (Hessen), professor at Giessen, Göttingen and Bonn, was notable for his works on Greek history and literature. See Life (1880) by Kekule.

(2) **Karl Theodor** (1790–1869), German publicist and politician, brother of (1), born at Öberofleiden (Hessen), was professor at Kiel, Heidelberg, Bonn and Freiburg.

WELENSKY, Sir Roy (1907–), Rhodesian politician, born at Salisbury, S. Rhodesia, the son of a Lithuanian-Jew. He was elected to the Legislative Council of N. Rhodesia in 1938, in 1940 became a member of the Executive Council, was knighted in 1953, and from 1956 to its break-up in 1963 was prime minister of the Federation of Rhodesia and Nyasaland, of which he was a most energetic advocate and architect. His handling of the constitutional crisis in 1959 aroused much controversy. See D. Taylor, *The Rhodesian.*

WELLES, (George) Orson (1915–), American director and actor, born in Kenosha, Wisconsin. He appeared at the Gate Theatre, Dublin, in 1931, returned to America, became a radio producer in 1934, and founded the Mercury Theatre in 1937. In 1938 his radio production of Wells's *War of the Worlds* was so realistic that it caused panic in the U.S. In 1941, he wrote, produced, directed and acted in the film *Citizen Kane,* a revolutionary landmark in cinema technique, and in 1942 produced and directed a screen version of Booth Tarkington's *The Magnificent Ambersons,* a masterly evocation of a vanished way of American life. His later work, giving ample rein to his varied and unpredictable talents, although never equalling his two masterpieces, includes his individual film versions of *Macbeth* (1948), *Othello* (1951), Kafka's *The Trial* (1962) and *Chimes at Midnight* (based on Shakespeare's Falstaff character, 1965); and a variety of memorable stage and film rôles, the most celebrated being that of 'Harry Lime' in *The Third Man* (1949). See studies by P. Noble (1956) and P. Cowie (1965).

WELLESLEY, *welz'li,* (1) **Arthur.** See WELLINGTON.

(2) **Richard Colley Wellesley, 1st Marquis** (1760–1842), British administrator, brother of (1), born in Co. Meath, became (1781) Earl of Mornington on the death of his father, and was returned to parliament in Westminster in 1784. He supported Pitt's foreign policy and Wilberforce's efforts to abolish the slave trade, and in 1786 became a lord of the treasury. In 1797 he was raised to the English peerage as Baron Wellesley and made governor-general of India. Under his outstanding administration (1797–1805) British rule became supreme in India; the influence of France there was extinguished with the disarming of its forces in Hyderabad, the power of the princes much reduced by the crushing (1799) of Tippoo Sahib at Seringapatam by General Harris, and (1803) of the Marathas, with the help of (1), and the revenue of the East India Company was more than doubled. In 1799 he was given the rank of marquis in the Irish peerage. In 1805 he returned to England and in 1809 went as ambassador to Madrid. On his return he was made foreign minister (1809–12), and later (in 1821 and 1833) lord-lieutenant of Ireland. See M. Martin, *Despatches of the Marquess Wellesley* (1840); *Wellesley Papers: Life and Correspondence* (1914); and a Life by G. B. Malleson (1889).

WELLESZ, Egon Joseph, *vel'es* (1885–), Austrian composer and musicologist, born in Vienna, studied under Schoenberg and subsequently became professor of Musical History at Vienna, specializing in Byzantine, Renaissance and modern music. Exiled from Austria by the Nazis, he became a research fellow at Oxford in 1938, and was lecturer in Music there from 1944 to 1948. His works include five operas and a quantity of choral and chamber music.

WELLHAUSEN, Julius, *vel'how-zėn* (1844–1918), biblical scholar, born at Hameln, professor at Greifswald (1872), Halle (1882), Marburg (1885) and Göttingen (1892), known for his investigations into Old Testament history and source criticism of the Pentateuch, was the author of several works, notably the *Prolegomena zur Geschichte Israels* (1883; trans. as *History of Israel,* 1885).

WELLINGTON, Arthur Wellesley, 1st Duke of (1769–1852), third of the four surviving sons of the 1st Earl of Mornington, was born in Ireland on April 29, 1769. Desultory study at Chelsea, Eton, Brussels and a military school at Angers led, in 1787, to an ensign's Commission in the 73rd Foot. Something of a dilettante, he transferred to the 76th Foot, thence to the 41st, 12th Light Dragoons and then to the 58th Foot, which brought him to Captain's rank. As A.D.C. to two lords-lieutenant of Ireland and member for Trim in the Irish Parliament, his lack of means forbade immediate marriage with Lady Katherine Pakenham. Securing a majority in the 33rd Foot, Wellesley set himself seriously 'to learn the business of a regimental officer', in his retrospective view the foundation of all successful soldiering. His brother's generosity purchased him command of the 33rd; and in the 1794 retreat of the British forces on the Ems he displayed great coolness and capacity when his regiment formed part of the rearguard. He had 'learned how things should not be done', and he carefully took note of the lesson. His disillusioned resolve to seek civil employment was reversed by his regiment's dispatch to India in 1797, where his brother arrived as governor-general within a year. With Napoleon gaining victories in Egypt, Wellesley was dispatched to deal with Tippoo Sahib of Mysore, who was speedily cured of giving aid to the French. As brigade commander under General Harris Wellesley did admirable work throughout the Seringapatam expedition and as subsequent administrator of the conquered territory. His campaigns against Holkar and Scindhia saw the enemy capital of Poona subjected in 1803, Mahratta power broken at Ahmednagar and hard-fought Assaye, and final victory achieved at Argaum. Created K.B. for his services, Sir Arthur's Indian fighting had taught him caution and the paramount importance of sound 'logistics'—lessons that were to prove advantageous to him. Returning home in 1805, in 1806 he married 'Kitty' Pakenham—who bore him three sons and three daughters—and was returned M.P. for Rye; becoming Irish Secretary in 1807. The same year he accompanied the Copenhagen expedition, defeating the Danes at Sjaelland. In 1808 the 'Sepoy General', as his detractors termed him, was sent to the aid of the Portuguese against the French. Defeating Junot at Roliça his victory at Vimeiro was stultified by his last-minute supersession by General Burrard; at the latter's behest he consented to the Convention of Cintra which spared the French unconditional surrender. Wellesley resumed his secretaryship; but Moore's retreat on Coruña sent him back, in 1809, to assume chief command in the Peninsula. His aim was to maintain a tactical defensive within a strategical offensive until his opponents, uncooperative and ill-nourished over long and vulnerable supply lines, would be so disrupted and worn down that they could be assailed in detail with complete confidence. Talavera (July 1809) was nearly a blunder, but it was speedily retrieved and the overall plan tenaciously pursued. Salamanca (July 1812) unequivocally demonstrated the superior fighting qualities of the British and their Portuguese and German allies; and although there were minor setbacks, ultimately the French were driven out of Spain and brought to submission at Toulouse in 1814. Wellesley was created G.C.B., and by 1814 had become Field-Marshal the Duke of Wellington, K.G., Duke of Ciudad Rodrigo, Magnate of Portugal, Spanish Grandee of the First Class, and the recipient of the most distinguished foreign orders, including the Golden Fleece. A committee of the assembly presented the thanks of the House of Commons which awarded him £400,000. With Napoleon's escape from Elba Wellington hastened from the Congress of Vienna to take command of the scratch force—'an infamous army', he termed it—mustered to oppose the Corsican. Blücher's supporting forces having been defeated at Ligny, Wellington took up position on the well-reconnoitred field of Waterloo, where the French were totally routed on June 18, 1815. Rewarded with the Hampshire estate of Strathfieldsaye, in 1818 the Duke joined the Liverpool administration as master-general of the Ordnance. In 1826 he was made constable of the Tower, and in 1827 commander-in-chief, an office in which he was confirmed for life in 1842. In 1829 he materially assisted in Peel's reorganization of the Metropolitan Police. In general, Wellington's political policy was to refrain from weakening established authority and to avoid foreign entanglements, since Britain never possessed a sufficient army to enforce her will. When Canning intervened to bind Britain, France and Russia to impose recognition of Greek autonomy on Turkey, he resigned; but with Canning's death in 1827 and the collapse of the nebulous Goderich administration, the Duke became prime minister. His reluctance to oppose the Test and Corporation Acts cost him the allegiance of Huskisson and the Liberals; while his support of Catholic emancipation culminated in a bloodless duel with the Earl of Winchilsea. His non-intervention in the East after Navarino offended the majority of his party; while his opposition to the indiscriminate enlargement of the franchise brought widespread unpopularity—and broken windows at Apsley House on the anniversary of Waterloo. In the political crisis of 1834 Wellington again formed a government; in Peel's temporary absence abroad he acted for all the secretaries of state. Chosen chancellor of the University of Oxford in 1834, with Peel's return to power in 1841 Wellington joined his cabinet, but without portfolio. He retired from public life in 1846. Made lord high constable of England, in 1848 he organized the military in London against the Chartists. He was in the procession for the opening of the Great Exhibition of 1851; retiring thereafter, as lord warden of the Cinque Ports, to Walmer Castle, where he passed peacefully away on September 14, 1852. He was buried in St Paul's Cathedral with the ceremony befitting a brilliant soldier and a great servant of the state. See Lives by Gleig, Stocqueler, Brialmont, W. H. Fitchett (1911), Sir H. Maxwell (1899, new ed. 1914), Fortescue (1925), Guedalla (1931), M. Wellesley (1937), R. Aldington (1946); his dispatches (ed. Gurwood and by his son, 1852–67), Greville's, Stanhope's, Croker's, Creevy's and Mrs Arbuthnot's Memoirs, and works cited at NAPOLEON.

WELLS, (1) **Charles Jeremiah** (*c.* 1800–79), English poet, was born in London, and educated at Edmonton. His *Stories after Nature* (1822) were followed in 1824 by the biblical drama, *Joseph and his Brethren*, which remained unknown until Swinburne praised it in the *Fortnightly* (1875).

(2) **Herbert George** (1866–1946), English author, born in London of lower middle-class

extraction, was initially apprenticed to a draper, but quickly abandoned this for teaching and very shortly made his mark in journalism and thereafter in literature. As biologist, journalist, writer and prophet, he played a vital part in disseminating the ideas which characterized the first quarter of the 20th century. He had a Dickensian exuberance which spilled over into all sorts of activities, and, though much of his writing is dated now, there can be no doubt that as a generative force in literature he pushed back the frontiers of ignorance for a large proportion of his readers. His scientific romances are immensely readable and some of his short stories have real impact and lasting beauty. *Country of the Blind* (1911) and *Collected Short Stories* (1927) contain some of his best writing; while *The Time Machine* (1895), *War of the Worlds* (1898) and *The Shape of Things to Come* (1933) show his fecund imagination at full strength. In his early novels, Wells, as spokesman for the urban worker, creates such unforgettable characters as Kipps, Mr Polly and Bert Smallways, types of the eternal 'little man', pathetic, sturdy, comic and heroic. Other novels deal with social questions and *Ann Veronica* (1909), *Tono-Bungay* (1909), and *Marriage* (1912) affected the public opinion of his day as radically as did the plays of Bernard Shaw. Wells's preoccupation with Utopian ideals—a belief that the millennium was coincident with the onward march of science—led to scintillating dissertations such as *The Work, Wealth and Happiness of Mankind* (1932), but as he began to see that science could work for evil as well as for good, his faith deserted him, and he declined into pessimism. His compendiums of knowledge, *The Outline of History* (1920) and *Science of Life* (1929–30), written in collaboration with his son and Julian Huxley, are immense achievements. See his Autobiography (1934), and studies by Nicholson (1950), Brome (1951) and Meyer (1956).

(3) **Horace** (1815–48), American dentist, born at Hartford, Vt., foresaw the value of nitrous oxide as an anaesthetic but his attempt to demonstrate it at Harvard in 1845 was a failure and he later committed suicide.

(4) **Sir Thomas Spencer** (1818–97), English surgeon, born in St Albans, the first to practise ovariotomy successfully, author of *Diseases of the Ovaries* (1865).

WELSH, (1) **Jane.** See CARLYLE (3).

(2) **John** (*c.* 1568–1622), Presbyterian divine born at Colliston, Dumfriesshire, imprisoned and banished by James VI, and ancestor of (1). See Life by J. Young (1866).

WELTE, Benedikt. See WETZER.

WEMYSS, Francis Wemyss Charteris Douglas, Earl of, *weemz* (1818–1914), British politician, born in Edinburgh, promoter of the volunteer movement (1859 onwards), and of the National Rifle Association.

WENCESLAUS, St (*c.* 903–935), duke and patron of Bohemia, 'good king Wenceslas', received a Christian education and after the death of his father encouraged Christianity in Bohemia, against the wishes of his mother. Probably at her instigation, and because of the fact that he had put his duchy under the protection of Germany, he was murdered by his brother Boleslaw.

WENCESLAUS (1361–1419), son of Charles IV, was crowned king of Bohemia 1363, king of the Romans 1376 (deposed 1400).

WENTWORTH, (1) **Charles Watson.** See ROCKINGHAM.

(2) **Thomas.** See STRAFFORD.

(3) **William Charles** (1793–1872), Australian statesman, born on Norfolk Island, took part in the expedition which explored the Blue Mountains in 1813 before he went to England to study at Cambridge. When called to the bar in 1822 he had already published his classic *Statistical Account of the British Settlements in Australasia* (1819). A staunch protagonist of self-government, which he made the policy of his newspaper *The Australian* (established 1824), he founded Sydney University in 1852.

WERFEL, Franz, *ver'fel* (1890–1945), Austrian-Jewish author, born at Prague, lived in Vienna until 1938, when he moved to France, whence he fled from the Nazi occupation in 1940 to the U.S.A. His early poems and plays were expressionistic; he is best known for his novels, including *The Song of Bernadette* (1941).

WERGELAND, Henrik Arnold, *ver'ge-lan* (1808–45), Norwegian poet, dramatist and patriot, now remembered more for his lyrics than for his efforts in the cause of Norwegian nationalism.

WERNER, (1) **Abraham Gottlob** (1750–1817), German geologist, born at Wehrau in Silesia, teacher at Freiburg in Saxony from 1775, one of the first to frame a classification of rocks, gave his name to the Wernerian or Neptunian theory of deposition, which he advocated in controversy with J. Hutton (q.v.).

(2) **Alfred** (1866–1919), Swiss chemist, born at Mülhausen, Alsace, professor in Zürich from 1893, was notable for his researches on isomerism and the complex salts, and was awarded a Nobel prize in 1913.

(3) **(Friedrich Ludwig) Zacharias** (1768–1823), German romantic dramatist, born at Königsberg. His chief works are *Die Söhne des Thals* (1803), *Das Kreuz an der Ostsee* (1804) and *Martin Luther* (1806). A convert to Catholicism, he died a priest at Vienna. See Carlyle's *Miscellanies*; also studies by Hankamer (1926), Carow (1933), and his diaries, ed. Floeck (1939–40).

WESKER, Arnold (1932–), British dramatist, born in London's East End, of Russian-Jewish parentage, he left school at fourteen. His intimate Jewish family background and his varied attempts at earning a living are important ingredients of his plays. The Kahn family trilogy, *Chicken Soup with Barley*, *Roots* and *I'm talking about Jerusalem* (1959–60), echo the march of events, pre- and post-World War II, in the aspirations and disappointments of the members of a left-wing family. *Roots* is an eloquent manifesto of Wesker's socialism: an aesthetic recipe for all which he attempted to put into practice by taking art to the workers through his Centre–42 (1961). Other plays are *The Kitchen* (1959), *Chips With Everything* (1962), *The Four Seasons* (1966), &c.

WESLEY, (1) **Charles** (1707–88), English hymnwriter and evangelist, brother of (2), born at Epworth, Lincs, studied at Christ Church, Oxford, where he formed (1729) a small group known as the Oxford Methodists, later joined by (2). Ordained in 1735, he accompanied (2) to Georgia as secretary to Oglethorpe, returning to England in 1736. He was the indefatigable lieutenant of his more famous brother; after his conversion on May 21, 1738, he wrote over 5500 hymns, including 'Jesu, Lover of my soul' and 'Love divine, all loves excelling'. He married Sarah Gwynne in 1749. See *Representative Verse* (ed. F. Baker, 1962); and Lives by T. Jackson (1841–49), J. Telford (1886) and F. L. Wiseman (1933).

(2) **John** (1703–91), English evangelist and founder of Methodism, was born June 17, son of the rector of Epworth. In 1720 he passed from the Charterhouse to Christ Church, Oxford. He was ordained deacon in 1725, priest in 1728, and in 1726 became a fellow of Lincoln and Greek lecturer. In 1727 he left Oxford to assist his father, but returned as tutor in 1729. At this time he was much influenced by the spiritual writings of William Law (q.v.). He became leader of a small dedicated group which had gathered round his brother Charles (q.v.), called derisively the Holy Club or Methodists, a name later adopted by John for the adherents of the great evangelical movement which was its outgrowth. The members of the Club, who in 1730 were joined by James Hervey and George Whitefield (q.v.), practised their religion with a then extraordinary degree of devotion, in strict accordance with the rubrics. On his father's death (1735), accompanied by Charles, John went as a missionary to Georgia, where his lack of experience led him to make many mistakes and aroused the hostility of the colonists. After an unfortunate love-affair with a Miss Hopkey, he returned to England (1738). He had been influenced by Moravians on the voyage out, and now he met Peter Böhler, and attended society meetings, at one of which, held in Aldersgate Street (May 24), during the reading of Luther's preface to the Epistle to the Romans, he experienced an assurance of salvation which convinced him that he must bring the same assurance to others. But his unwonted zeal alarmed and angered most of the parish clergy, who closed their pulpits against him; this intolerance, Whitefield's example, and the needs of the masses drove him into the open air at Bristol (1739). There he founded the first Methodist chapel. He preached in, and bought, the ruinous Foundry in Moorfields, London, Methodist anniversaries sometimes being reckoned from this event; the Foundry was for long the headquarters of Methodism in the capital. During his itinerary of half a century, 10,000 to 30,000 people would wait patiently for hours to hear him. He gave his strength to working-class neighbourhoods; hence the mass of his converts were colliers, miners, foundrymen, weavers, and day-labourers in towns. His life was frequently in danger, but he outlived all persecution, and the itineraries of his old age were triumphal processions from one end of the country to the other. During his unparalleled apostolate he travelled 250,000 miles and preached 40,000 sermons. Yet he managed to do a prodigious amount of literary work, and produced grammars, extracts from the classics, histories, abridged biographies, collections of psalms, hymns and tunes, his own sermons and journals, and a magazine. His works were so popular that he made £30,000 which he distributed in charity during his life. He founded charitable institutions at Newcastle and London and Kingswood School in Bristol. Wesley broke with the Moravians in 1745, and his acceptance of what was then known as an Arminian theology led to divergences with Whitefield in 1741, a separate organization of Calvinistic methodists under the Countess of Huntingdon (q.v.), and to an acute controversy (1769–78) with Toplady. Wesley was determined to remain loyal to the Church of England and urged his followers to do the same; but increasing pressures were brought to bear on him and in 1784 he himself ordained one of his assistants for work in America (much to his brother's distress), a practice which he later extended. However, he always regarded Methodism as a movement within the Church and it remained so during his lifetime. In 1751 he married the widow Mary Vazeille, who deserted him in 1776. He died March 2, 1791. His *Journal* was edited (8 vols. 1909–1916) by N. Curnock. See Lives by R. Southey (1820), J. Wedgwood (1870), J. Telford (1886; new ed. 1953), L. Tyerman (6th ed. 1890), J. H. Overton (1891), W. H. Fitchett (1906), C. T. Winchester (1906), J. S. Simon (1921–34), V. H. H. Green (1964); his *Letters* (1931); and a book on the family by G. J. Stevenson (1876).

(3) **Samuel** (1766–1837), English organist and composer, born in Bristol, son of (1). One of the most famous organists of his day, he was an early and ardent enthusiast of J. S. Bach. Though a Roman Catholic (to the displeasure of his father and uncle), he wrote also for the Anglican liturgy, leaving a number of fine motets and anthems, including *In Exitu Israel.* His natural son **Samuel Sebastian** (1810–76), born in London, was a brilliant cathedral organist.

WESSEL, *ves'el,* (1) **Horst** (1907–30), German national socialist, born at Bielefeld, composer of the Nazi anthem 'Die Fahne Hoch', known as the Horst Wessel song.

(2) **Johan,** or **Wessel Harmens Gansfort** (1420–89), Dutch pre-Reformation reformer and theologian, born at Groningen.

WESSON, Daniel Baird (1825–1906), American gunsmith, devised a new type of repeating mechanism for small-arms in 1854 and founded the firm of Smith and Wesson at Springfield, Mass., in 1857.

WEST, (1) **Benjamin** (1738–1820), English painter, born in America at Springfield, Pa., showed early promise, was sent on a sponsored visit to Italy, and on his return journey was induced to settle in London (1763). George III was his patron for 40 years. The representation of modern instead of classical costume in his best-known picture *The Death of General Wolfe* was an innovation in

English historical painting. See Life by H. E. Jackson (Philadelphia 1900).

(2) **Mae** (1892–), American film actress, born in Brooklyn, specialized in flamboyant rôles, and gave her name to an airman's pneumatic life-jacket which, when inflated, was considered to give the wearer the generous bosom for which she herself was noted.

(3) **Dame Rebecca,** pen-name (from Ibsen's *Rosmersholm*) of **Mrs H. M. Andrews,** *née* **Cicily Isabel Fairfield** (1892–), British novelist and critic. Born in Kerry, educated in Edinburgh, she was for a short time on the stage but turned to journalism. Her alert observation, style and wit made her work notable, as in *Black Lamb and Grey Falcon* (1942), an account of Yugoslavia in 1937. Novels include *The Judge* (1922), *The Thinking Reed* (1936), *The Fountain Overflows* (1957) and *The Birds Fall Down* (1966). Studies arising from the Nuremberg war trials were *The Meaning of Treason* (1947) and *A Train of Powder* (1955). She was created D.B.E. in 1959.

WESTBURY, Richard Bethell, Baron (1800–1873), English judge, was born at Bradford-on-Avon. In 1823 called to the bar, he became solicitor-general in 1852, attorney-general in 1856, and in 1861 lord chancellor, with the title of Baron Westbury. He promoted measures of law reform, but failed to carry his schemes for codifying the statutes and for combining law and equity. He was noted for his sarcastic wit. See Lives by Nash (1888) and by his son Arthur (1903).

WESTCOTT, Brooke Foss (1825–1901), English scholar, born near Birmingham, was a canon of Peterborough, regius professor of Divinity at Cambridge in 1870, Canon of Westminster in 1883, and in 1890 Bishop of Durham. He helped to prepare the revised version (1881) of the New Testament and, with F. J. A. Hort, *The New Testament in the Original Greek* (1881). See Lives by A. Westcott (1903) and J. Clayton (1906).

WESTERMARCK, Edvard Alexander, *ves'tėr-mark* (1862–1939), Finnish social philosopher, born at Helsinki, was lecturer on Sociology there, professor of Sociology in London, wrote a *History of Human Marriage* (5th ed. 1925), *The Origin and Development of the Moral Ideas* (1906–08), *Christianity and Morals* (1939), books on Morocco, and an Autobiography (trans. from Swedish 1929).

WESTINGHOUSE, George (1846–1914), American engineer, born at Central Bridge, N.Y., gave name to an air-brake for railways, which he invented (1868), and a company (now a corporation), which he founded for the manufacture of this, and other appliances. He was a pioneer in the use of alternating current for distributing electric power. See Life by H. G. Prout (1922).

WESTMACOTT, (1) Sir Richard (1775–1856), English sculptor and sculptor's son, born in London, studied at Rome, in 1816 was elected R.A., and was knighted in 1837. In 1827 he became professor of Sculpture at the Royal Academy.

(2) **Richard** (1799–1872), son of (1), also a sculptor, studied in Italy 1820–26, became F.R.S. and R.A., and succeeded his father as professor of Sculpture. He wrote a *Handbook of Ancient and Modern Sculpture* (1864).

WETHERELL, Elizabeth. See WARNER (4).

WETSTEIN, or **Wettstein, Johann Jakob,** *vet'shtīn* (1693–1754), Swiss scholar, was born in Basel. Charged with heresy in the preparation of his famous text, *Novum Testamentum Graecum* (1751–52), and his *Prolegomena* (1730) he left Basel, and was appointed (1733) to the chair of Church History in the Remonstrants' College at Amsterdam. See Life by C. L. Hulbert-Powell (1938).

WETTACH, Adrien. See GROCK.

WETTE. See DE WETTE.

WETZER, Heinrich Josef, *vets'ėr* (1801–53), German scholar, born at Anzefahr, Hesse, editor with Benedikt Welte of the great Roman Catholic theological encyclopaedia (12 vols. 1846–60; revised ed. 1882–1903), became professor of Oriental Philology at Tübingen in 1830.

WEYDEN, Rogier van der, *vī'den* (1400–64), Flemish religious painter, was born at Tournai, and by 1436 was official painter to the city of Brussels. Influenced, and possibly taught, by the Van Eycks, he himself was the teacher of Hans Memling. See studies by Friedlander (1924) and Destrée (Paris 1930).

WEYER. See WIER.

WEYGAND, Maxime, *vay-gã* (1867–1965), French soldier, born in Brussels, trained at St Cyr and became a cavalry officer and instructor. As chief of staff to Foch (1914–1923), he rendered admirable service, but as chief of staff of the army (1931–35) he was gravely handicapped by his lack of experience as a field commander. In 1940 his employment of an outmoded linear defence to hold a penetration in depth completed the rout of the French army. A prisoner of the Germans, and later of the French provisional government, he was allowed to retire into obscurity. See his memoirs, *Recalled to Service* (1952).

WEYL, Hermann, *vīl* (1885–), German-born mathematician, born at Elmshorn, Schleswig-Holstein, was professor of Mathematics at Zürich (1913), Göttingen (1930–33) and from 1933 at Princeton, N.J. He made important mathematical contributions to relativity physics and the philosophy of mathematics.

WEYMAN, Stanley John, *wī'mėn* (1855–1928), English novelist, born at Ludlow, studied at Oxford, and became a barrister. He made himself popular with *A Gentleman of France* (1893), *Under the Red Robe* (1894) and other historical romances.

WHALLEY, Edward (d. 1675?), English regicide, fought at Marston Moor and Naseby, a member of the court which tried Charles I, was a signatory of the death warrant. In 1660 he fled to New England with his son-in-law William Goffe (q.v.) and remained in hiding till his death.

WHARNCLIFFE, James Archibald Stuart Wortley Mackenzie, 1st Baron (1776–1845), British statesman, grandson of the 3rd Earl of Bute, served in the army, entered parliament in 1797, and was made a peer in 1826. A Tory, he opposed Catholic emancipation, but helped to pass the Reform Bill; he opposed Peel's free-trade policy. In 1841 he was president of the council.

WHARTON, (1) Edith, ***née*** **Jones** (1861?–1937), American analytical novelist, born in New York, married in 1885 and was divorced in 1912. She published her first stories, *The Greater Inclination*, in 1899. Of her novels, *The House of Mirth* (1905), *Ethan Frome* (1911) and *The Custom of the Country* (1913) are regarded as her greatest. *The Age of Innocence* (1920) and *Old New York* (1924) were each awarded the Pulitzer prize. See her *A Backward Glance* (1934), and Lives by M. J. Lyde (1960), G. Kellogg (1966) and M. Bell (1966).

Philip, Duke of Wharton (1698–1731), son of (3), was given an Irish dukedom in 1718 for his support of the government in the Irish House of Peers, but in England set up an opposition political paper, the *True Briton* (1723–24). While travelling in Europe he accepted the Garter from the Pretender at Rome, assumed the title of Duke of Northumberland, and fought for Spain, for which he was convicted of high treason in his absence and deprived of his estates. See Life by L. Melville (1913).

(3) **Thomas, 1st Marquis of Wharton** (1648–1714), father of (2), Whig statesman, lord-lieutenant of Ireland (1708–10), was created earl in 1706 and marquis in 1714. He is remembered as author of the satirical anti-Catholic ballad *Lilliburlero*.

WHATELY, Richard (1787–1863), English Archbishop of Dublin, born in London, in 1805 entered Oriel College, Oxford, and in 1811 was elected a fellow. He became a college tutor and rector of Halesworth, and for the *Encylopaedia Metropolitana* wrote what he afterwards expanded into treatises on Logic (1826) and Rhetoric (1828). In 1825 he was appointed principal of St Alban's Hall, in 1829 professor of Political Economy and in 1831 Archbishop of Dublin. A founder of the Broad Church party, he opposed the Tractarian movement, supported Catholic emancipation, and worked for unsectarian religious instruction. His caustic wit and outspokenness made him unpopular. See the rambling *Memoirs* by Fitzpatrick (1864) and the Life by Whately (1866).

WHEATLEY, Henry Benjamin (1838–1917), English bibliographer and scholar, born at Chelsea, became clerk to the Royal Society (1861–79) and assistant secretary (1879–1908) to the Society of Arts. He was one of the founders of the Early English Text Society.

WHEATON, Henry (1785–1848), American jurist, born at Providence, R.I., in 1812–15 edited the *National Advocate* in New York, where for four years he was a justice of the Marine Court, and from 1816 to 1827 reporter for the Supreme Court. In 1827–35 he was *chargé d'affaires* at Copenhagen, and in 1835–46 minister at Berlin. His most important work was *Elements of International Law* (1836, with many later editions).

WHEATSTONE, Sir Charles (1802–75), English physicist, born in Gloucester, first became known as a result of experiments on sound. He invented the concertina (1829). He became professor of Experimental Philosophy at King's College, London (1834), and F.R.S. (1836). In 1837 he and W. F. Cooke took out a patent for an electric telegraph. In 1838, in a paper to the Royal Society, he explained the principle of the stereoscope (see BREWSTER). He invented a sound magnifier for which he introduced the term *microphone*. Wheatstone's Bridge, a device for the comparison of electrical resistances, was brought to notice (though not invented) by him. He was knighted in 1868.

WHEELER, (1) Sir Charles (1892–), English sculptor, born at Codsall, Staffordshire, studied at the Wolverhampton Art School and the Royal College of Art, and is noted for his portrait sculpture and his decorative sculptures on monuments and buildings, e.g., South Africa House and the Jellicoe Memorial Fountain in Trafalgar Square, London. Elected R.A. in 1940, he was created C.B.E. in 1948, knighted in 1958, K.B.E. in 1966, and from 1956 to 1966 was president of the Royal Academy. See the autobiographical *High Relief* (1968).

(2) **Sir Robert Eric Mortimer** (1890–), British archaeologist, was born in Glasgow. In 1924 he became director of the National Museum of Wales. In 1926 he was appointed keeper and secretary of the London Museum where he remained until 1944. In 1945 he led the Government mission from India to Iran and Afghanistan. On his return he became professor of the Archaeology of the Roman Provinces at the University of London, and secretary of the British Academy. He was made C.H. in 1967. His works include *Archaeology from the Earth* (1954), and the autobiographical *Still Digging* (1955).

WHEWELL, William (1794–1866), English scholar, born, a joiner's son, at Lancaster, became a fellow and tutor of Trinity. In 1820 he was elected F.R.S., in 1828–32 was professor of Mineralogy, and in 1838–55 professor of Moral Theology. In 1841 he became master of Trinity, and in 1855 vice-chancellor. His works include *History of the Inductive Sciences* (1837), *Elements of Morality* (1855), and other writings on the tides, electricity and magnetism, besides translations of Goethe's *Hermann and Dorothea*, Grotius's *Rights of Peace and War* and Plato. See Life by Todhunter (1876); Life and Correspondence by Stair Douglas (1881).

WHICHCOTE, Benjamin (1609–83), English philosopher and theologian, a Cambridge Platonist, born at Stoke in Shropshire, became in 1644 provost of King's, but lost this office at the Restoration. He wrote *Discourses* (1701–07) and *Moral and Religious Aphorisms*, collected from his MSS. (1703).

WHIPPLE, George Hoyt (1878–), American pathologist, a graduate of Yale and Johns Hopkins, in 1921 became professor of Pathology at Rochester. In 1934 he shared with Minot and Murphy the Nobel prize for medicine, as a result of their researches on the liver treatment of anaemia.

WHISTLER, (1) James Abbott McNeill (1834–1903), American artist, born at Lowell, Mass., spent five years of his boyhood in St Petersburg, where his father, an engineer, was engaged on a railway project for the tsar. Returning home, he studied first for the army at West Point but failed his exams, and after a fruitless year with the Coast Survey he left

America, never to return, and went to study art in Paris. His teacher, Gleyre, had little influence on his subsequent work, but he was deeply impressed by Courbet and later by the newly-discovered Hokusai (q.v.), and he exhibited at the *Salon des réfusés*. He began spending more and more time in London; when his mother came over from the U.S.A. in 1863 it became the centre of his activities, and he became celebrated as a portraitist. Ruskin's vitriolic criticism of his contributions to the Grosvenor Gallery exhibition of 1877, accusing him of 'flinging a pot of paint in the public's face', provoked the famous lawsuit in which Whistler was awarded a farthing damages. His feelings on the subject are embodied in his *Gentle Art of Making Enemies* (1890), a witty and diverting piece of prose writing. A recalcitrant rebel at a time when the sentimental Victorian subject picture was still *de rigueur*, Whistler conceived his paintings, even the portraits, as experiments in colour harmony and tonal effect; the famous portrait of his mother, now in the Louvre, was originally exhibited at the Royal Academy as *An Arrangement in Grey and Black*, and evening scenes such as the well-known impression of Battersea Bridge (Tate Gallery) were called 'nocturnes'. If there was little emphasis on draughtsmanship in his painting technique, the reverse is true of his etchings, especially his 'Thames' set, which succeed in imparting beauty to some unpromising parts of the London riverside. Witty, argumentative, quick to take offence, and theatrical in his manner, he often dressed like the cartoonist's stock artist-type. His individual style of painting did not evoke wide imitation and cannot be said to have initiated or belonged to any particular school, but his etchings were emulated by a host of followers, none of whom succeeded in capturing his spontaneity and charm. See studies by Laver (1938), Lane (N.Y. 1942) and Pearson (1952).

(2) **Rex** (1905–44), English artist. He studied at the Slade School, and excelled in the rendering of eighteenth-century life, ornament and architecture, particularly in book illustration (e.g., a fine edition of *Gulliver's Travels* in 1930), murals (e.g., in the Tate Gallery) and designs for the theatre and ballet. See the Life (1948) by his brother Laurence, the poet and designer; also study by L. Whistler and R. Fuller (1960)

WHISTON, William (1667–1752), English clergyman and mathematician, born at Norton rectory in Leicestershire, became in 1693 a fellow of Clare College, Cambridge, chaplain to the Bishop of Norwich in 1696, and in 1698 rector of Lowestoft. His *Theory of the Earth* (1696) attracted attention, and in 1703 he became Lucasian professor at Cambridge. For Arianism he was in 1710 expelled from the university and in 1747 joined the Baptists. He spent the remainder of his life in London, engaged in one controversy after another. His translation of Josephus was his best-known work. See his whimsical Memoirs (1749–50).

WHITAKER, Joseph (1820–95), English bookseller and publisher, was born in London, the son of a silversmith. He started the *Educational Register*, *Whitaker's Clergyman's Diary*, *The Bookseller* in 1858, and in 1868 *Whitaker's Almanac.*

WHITBREAD, Samuel (1758–1815), English politician, son of **Samuel** (1720–96), founder of the famous brewing firm, from Eton passed to Oxford, and in 1790 entered parliament. The intimate friend of Fox, under Pitt he was leader of the Opposition, and in 1805 headed the attack on Melville.

WHITBY, Daniel (1638–1726), English divine, born at Rushden near Higham Ferrers, became in 1664 a fellow of Trinity College, Oxford, prebendary of Salisbury in 1668, and rector of St Edmund's there in 1669. After attacking popery he tried from 1682 to find a basis of union with the Dissenters; his *Protestant Reconciler* (1682) was publicly burned at Oxford. His *Last Thoughts* appeared in 1727.

WHITE, (1) **Ethelbert** (1891–1972), English artist, born at Isleworth, painted many watercolours of the English scene, and also engraved for book illustration.

(2) **Sir George Stuart** (1835–1912), British soldier, field-marshal (1903), O.M. (1905), received the Victoria Cross in the Afghan campaign of 1879–80. Commander-in-chief in India in 1893–98, he defended Ladysmith in 1899–1900, and was governor of Gibraltar (1900–04). See Life by Durand (1915).

(3) **Gilbert** (1720–93), English clergyman and naturalist, born at Selborne in Hampshire, in 1744 obtained a fellowship at Oriel College, Oxford, in 1747 took orders, in 1752 became junior proctor, and in 1758 obtained the sinecure college living of Moreton Pinkney, Northants. From 1755 he lived uneventfully at Selborne as curate of that or a neighbouring parish. His charming *Natural History and Antiquities of Selborne* (1789) has become an English classic. Among its countless editions are those by Jesse (1851), Buckland (1875), Bell (1877), Jefferies (1887), Burroughs (1895), Bowdler Sharpe (1901). See his *Life and Letters* (1901) by R. Holt-White, *Journals* ed. Johnson (1931), and Life by W. S. Scott (1950).

(4) **Henry Kirke** (1785–1806), English poet, born in Nottingham, in 1803 published *Clifton Grove*, which brought him the friendship of Southey and the Rev. Charles Simeon, through whom he became a sizar of St John's College, Cambridge. Southey edited his *Remains* (1807).

(5) **Joseph Blanco** (1775–1841), theological writer, was born at Seville of an Irish Catholic family. Ordained a priest in 1800, he lost his faith, and, coming in 1810 to London, edited a monthly Spanish paper 1810–14, then received an English pension of £250, was tutor to Lord Holland's son 1815–16, and was admitted to Anglican orders. He was tutor in Whately's (q.v.) family at Dublin (1832–35), but fled to Liverpool on adopting Unitarian views. He contributed to the *Quarterly* and *Westminster*, edited the short-lived *London Review*, wrote *Letters from Spain* (1822), *Evidence against Catholicism* (1825), &c., and one notable sonnet, 'Night and Death'. See his Autobiography (1845).

(6) **Patrick** (1912–), London-born Australian author, educated at Cheltenham

College and King's College, Cambridge. He wrote *Happy Valley* (1939), *The Living and the Dead* (1941), *The Aunt's Story* (1946), before achieving international success with *The Tree of Man* (1954). In this symbolic novel about a small community in the Australian Bush, he attempts to portray every aspect of human life and to find the secret that makes it bearable. As the Parker family gradually fail to understand each other we are impressed by the terrible isolation of man, which White stresses even in his early novels. In 1957 appeared *Voss*, an allegorical account, in religious terms, of a gruelling attempt to cross the Australian continent. This was followed by *Riders in the Chariot* (1961) and *The Solid Mandala* (1966). He has also published *The Burnt Ones* (1964) and *Four Plays* (1965). See study by B. Argyle (1968).

(7) **Pearl** (1892–1938), American cinema actress, born in Glen Ridge, Mo., began her film career in 1910, and as the heroine of *The Perils of Pauline* (1914), *The Exploits of Elaine*, &c., made an enormous reputation as the exponent *par excellence* of the type of serial film popularly called 'cliff-hanger'.

(8) **Richard Grant** (1821–85), American Shakespearean scholar, born in New York, after studying medicine and law, became a journalist. His Shakespearean studies include criticisms on J. Payne Collier's folio MS. emendations (1852) and two editions (1857–1865, 1883) of the works. Other works are *Words and their Uses* (1870), *Everyday English* (1881), and *England Without and Within* (1881). His son, **Stanford** (1853–1906), was an eminent architect who designed a number of public buildings in New York.

(9) **William Hale, pseud. Mark Rutherford** (1831–1913), English writer, was born at Bedford, the son of William White (1797–1882), bookseller, and doorkeeper (1850–80) to the House of Commons (see his *Inner Life of the House of Commons*, 1897). In 1848–51 Hale White qualified at Cheshunt and New College for the Congregational ministry, but, expelled for his views on inspiration, became a journalist and miscellaneous writer. His translation of Spinoza's *Ethica* (1883; new ed. 1894) was published under his own name but he owed his literary eminence to the series of novels, *The Autobiography of Mark Rutherford* (1881), *Mark Rutherford's Deliverance* (1885), and *The Revolution in Tanner's Lane* (1887), 'edited by Reuben Shapcott'. See studies by Maclean (1955), Stock (1956).

WHITEFIELD, George (1714–70), English evangelist, one of the founders of Methodism, was born in the Bell Inn, Gloucester. At eighteen he entered as servitor Pembroke College, Oxford. The Wesleys had already laid the foundations of Methodism at Oxford, and Whitefield became an enthusiastic evangelist. He took deacon's orders in 1736, and preached his first sermon in the Crypt Church, Gloucester. In 1738 he followed Wesley to Georgia, returning to be admitted to priest's orders, and to collect funds for an orphanage. The religious level of the age was low, and Whitefield was actively opposed by his fellow churchmen. But when the parish pulpits were denied him he preached in the open air, the first time with great effect, on Kingswood Hill near Bristol. His life was then spent in constant travel and preaching. About 1741 differences on predestination led to his separation as a rigid Calvinist from John Wesley as an Arminian. His supporters now built him a chapel in Bristol and a 'Tabernacle' in London; and his preaching gathered immense audiences. But he founded no distinct sect, many of his adherents following the Countess of Huntingdon (q.v.) in Wales, and ultimately helping to form the Calvinistic Methodists. The Countess appointed him her chaplain, and built and endowed many chapels for him. He made seven evangelistic visits to America, and spent the rest of his life in preaching tours through England, Scotland and Wales. One of the most famous of these missionary journeys was that which he made to Scotland in 1741. In that year he married a Welsh widow, Mrs James. He set out for America for the last time in 1769, and died near Boston. His writings (sermons, journals, and letters), with the *Memoirs* by Dr Gillies, fill 7 vols. (1771–72). See Lives by J. P. Gledstone (1871 and 1900), Tyerman (1876) and Belden (1955).

WHITEHEAD, (1) Alfred North (1861–1947), English mathematician and Idealist philosopher, born in London, was educated at Sherborne and Trinity College, Cambridge, where he was senior lecturer in Mathematics until 1911. He became professor of Applied Mathematics at Imperial College, London (1914–24), and of Philosophy at Harvard (1924–37). Extending the Booleian symbolic logic in a highly original *Treatise on Universal Algebra* (1898), he contributed a remarkable memoir to the Royal Society, 'Mathematical Concepts of the Material World' (1905). Profoundly influenced by Peano (q.v.), he collaborated with his former pupil at Trinity, Bertrand Russell (q.v.), in the *Principia Mathematica* (1910–13), the greatest single contribution to logic since Aristotle. In his Edinburgh Gifford Lectures, *Process and Reality* (1929), he attempted a metaphysics comprising psychological as well as physical experience, with events as the ultimate components of reality. Other more popular works include *Adventures of Ideas* (1933) and *Modes of Thought* (1938). He was elected F.R.S. (1903), was awarded the first James Scott prize (1922) of the Royal Society of Edinburgh, and in 1947 the O.M. See an anthology of his works by F. S. C. Northrop and M. W. Gross (1953), B. Russell, 'Whitehead and Principia Mathematica' (*Mind* 1948) and studies by D. Emmet (1932), ed., P. A. Schilpp (1941), A. H. Johnston (1950, 1952), I. Leclerc (1958), W. Mays (1959).

(2) **Charles** (1804–62), English poet and novelist, was born in London, the son of a wine merchant. He devoted himself to letters after publishing *The Solitary* (1831), a poem of reflection. His *Autobiography of Jack Ketch* (1834) showed humour, but when Chapman & Hall asked him for a popular book in instalments he declined, recommending young Dickens, who thus began the *Pickwick Papers*. His novel, *Richard Savage*

(1842), earned the praises of Dickens and Rossetti. Whitehead went out to Melbourne in 1857, but died miserably, leaving unfinished the *Spanish Marriage*, a drama. See *A Forgotten Genius*, Mackenzie Bell (1884).

(3) **Paul** (1710–74), English satirist, 'a small poet' in Johnson's phrase, was born, a tailor's son, in Holborn, was apprenticed to a mercer, married a short-lived imbecile with a fortune of £10,000, lay some years in the Fleet for the nonpayment of a sum for which he had stood security, became active in politics, was one of the infamous 'monks' of Medmenham Abbey, and became deputy treasurer of the Chamber. Among his satires are *State Dunces* (1733), inscribed to Pope, and *Manners* (1739), for which Dodsley the publisher was brought before the House of Lords. His *Collected Works*, edited by E. Thompson, appeared in 1777.

(4) **Robert** (1823–1905), English inventor, born at Bolton-le-Moors, trained as an engineer in Manchester, settled (1856) at Fiume where he invented the first self-propelling torpedo (1866).

(5) **William** (1715–85), English poet, a Cambridge baker's son, educated at Winchester and Clare Hall, a fellow in 1742, travelled as tutor to Lord Jersey's son, became in 1755 secretary of the Order of the Bath, and in 1757 poet laureate. He wrote tragedies (*The Romén Father*, in imitation of Corneille's *Horace*, 1750; *Creusa*, 1754), farces (*School for Lovers*, 1762), epistles, &c.

WHITELEY, William (1831–1907), English merchant, born at Wakefield, opened in 1863 what became London's first department store, applied to himself the name of 'Universal Provider', and was murdered. See Lambert, *The Universal Provider* (1938).

WHITELOCKE, Bulstrode (1605–76), English lawyer and statesman, born in London, the son of a judge, studied law, sat in the Long Parliament for Great Marlow, and took a half-hearted part on the popular side in the Civil War. He was appointed a commissioner of the Great Seal (1648), but would not act in the king's trial, and was sent as ambassador to Sweden (1653). Although nominated by Richard Cromwell keeper of the Great Seal he was later included in the Act of Oblivion. He died at Chilton in Wiltshire. Whitelocke's *Memorials* was first published in 1682 in a falsified form; better in 1732. His *Journal of the Embassy to Sweden* was edited by Reeve (1855). See *Memoirs* by Whitelocke (1860).

WHITEMAN, Paul (1891–1967), American bandleader, born in Denver, Colorado. He became famous in the 1920s as a pioneer of 'sweet style', as opposed to the traditional 'classical' style jazz. His band employed such brilliant exponents of true jazz as Bix Beiderbecke, the trumpeter, and Whiteman became popularly regarded as the 'inventor' of jazz itself rather than of a deviation from true jazz style. He was responsible for Gershwin's experiments in 'symphonic' jazz, commissioning the *Rhapsody in Blue* for a concert in New York in 1924. See *Jazz*, by Paul Whiteman and Mary McBride.

WHITGIFT, John (*c.* 1530–1604), English prelate, Archbishop of Canterbury, born at Grimsby, in 1555 was elected fellow of Peterhouse, Cambridge, took orders in 1560, and rose to be Dean of Lincoln (1571), Bishop of Worcester (1577), Archbishop of Canterbury (1583), and privy councillor (1586). He was a great pluralist. He attended Queen Elizabeth in her last moments, and crowned James I. With a Calvinistic bias, Whitgift yet was a champion of conformity, and vindicated the Anglican position against the Puritans. His ninety-four writings were edited for the Parker Society (1851–53). See vol. v of Hook's *Archbishops of Canterbury* (1875), and Clayton's *Whitgift and his Times* (1911).

WHITING, John (1917–63), English playwright, educated at Taunton School, studied at the Royal Academy of Dramatic Art (1935–37). After serving in the Royal Artillery in World War II he resumed his acting career before emerging as a dramatist. *Saint's Day* (1951), depicting the sense of hopelessness, failure and self-destruction of the Southman ménage, gained recognition for his talent although it was not a popular success. It was followed by *A Penny for a Song* (1951), a gay comedy, and *Marching Song* (1954), a play of ideas with little action or dramatic situation whose plot deals with the decision facing General Rupert Forster: to stand trial as a scapegoat for his country's failure or to commit suicide. After *Gates of Summer* (1956) he was commissioned by the Royal Shakespeare Company to dramatize Huxley's *The Devils of Loudon*, as *The Devils* (1961), which achieved great success, despite harrowing scenes such as the torture of Grandier.

WHITLEY, John Henry (1866–1935), English politician, born at Halifax, educated at Clifton and London University, was Liberal M.P. for Halifax 1900–28, speaker 1921–28 during the difficult period which culminated in the general strike, and presided over the committee that proposed (1917) Whitley Councils for joint consultation between employers and employees.

WHITMAN, Walt (1819–91), American poet, born at West Hills, Long Island, N.Y., served first in a lawyer's and then in a doctor's office, and finally in a printer's. He next became an itinerant teacher in country schools. He returned shortly to printing, and in 1846 became editor of the *Brooklyn Eagle*. This and his other numerous press engagements were only of short duration. He seemed unable to find free expression for his emotions until he hit upon the curious, irregular, recitative measures of *Leaves of Grass* (1855), originally a small folio of 95 pages, which grew in the eight succeeding editions to nearly 440 pages. This, with his prose book, *Specimen Days and Collect*, constitutes his main life-work as a writer. Summoned to tend his brother, wounded in the war against the South, he became a volunteer nurse in the hospitals of the Northern army. The exertion, exposure, and strain of those few years left Whitman a shattered and almost aged man. About the close of the war he received a government clerkship; was dismissed by Secretary Harlan as the author of 'an indecent book'; but almost immediately obtained a similar post.

In 1873 he left Washington for Camden, N.J., where he spent the remainder of his life. Partially paralysed, he would have fallen into absolute poverty but for the help of trans-Atlantic admirers. Later on several wealthy American citizens liberally provided for his simple wants. Whitman set himself the task of uplifting into the sphere of poetry the whole of modern life and man. Hence the inclusion of subjects at that time tabooed. He was in fact an idealist who bound himself to be a thoroughgoing realist. A selection from Whitman by W. M. Rossetti appeared in 1868 (new ed. 1910), his *Complete Writings* in 1902, *Uncollected Poetry and Prose* (2 vols.), ed. Holloway, in 1922. See books by J. A. Symonds (1893), John Burroughs, Kennedy (1896), Binns (1905), B. de Selincourt (1914), Fausset (1941), Canby (1943), R. V. Chase (1956) and R. Asselineau (1961).

WHITNEY, (1) **Eli** (1765–1825), American inventor, born at Westborough, Mass., was educated at Yale, went to Georgia as a teacher, but finding a patron in the widow of General Greene, resided on her estate, read law and set to work to make a cotton-gin. Reports of his success prompted rogues to break into his workshop and steal and copy his machine; he went to Connecticut to carry out his invention; but lawsuits in defence of his rights carried off all his profits and $50,000 voted him by the state of South Carolina. In 1798 he got a government contract for the manufacture of firearms, and made a fortune in this business.

(2) **Josiah Dwight** (1819–96), American geologist, born at Northampton, Mass., graduated at Yale, and in 1840 joined the New Hampshire survey. He explored the geology of the Lake Superior region, Iowa, the upper Missouri, and California, and in 1855 was made professor at Iowa University, in 1860 state geologist of California, and in 1865 professor at Harvard. Mount Whitney, S. Cal., the highest mountain in the U.S., is named after him

(3) **William Dwight** (1827–94), American philologist, brother of (2), studied at Williams and Yale, and in Germany with Roth prepared an edition of the *Atharva Veda Sanhita* (1856). In 1854 he became professor of Sanskrit at Yale, in 1870 also of Comparative Philology. He was an office-bearer of the American Oriental Society, edited numerous Sanskrit texts, and contributed to the great Sanskrit dictionary of Böhtlingk and Roth (1853–67). He waged war with Max-Müller on fundamental questions of the science of language. Among his works were *Material and Form in Language* (1872), *Life and Growth of Language* (1876), *Essentials of English Grammar* (1877) and *Mixture in Language* (1881). He was editor of the 1864 edition of Webster's Dictionary and editor-in-chief of the *Century Dictionary* (1889–91).

WHITTIER, John Greenleaf (1807–92), American Quaker poet and abolitionist, was born near Haverhill, Mass., the son of a poor farmer, and obtained education with difficulty. In 1829 he embarked on an editorial career; in 1831 appeared *Legends of New England*, a collection of poems and stories. In 1840, he settled at Amesbury, a village near his birthplace. He devoted himself to the cause of emancipation, but his anti-slavery poems have, like his prose writings, mostly served their purpose. His collection *In War Time* (1864) contains the well-known ballad *Barbara Frietchie*. A final edition of Whittier's poems revised by himself appeared in 1888–89. *At Sundown* was published in 1892. In his day he was considered second only to Longfellow. See monographs by G. K. Lewis (1913), A. Mordell (1933).

WHITTINGTON, Richard (*c.* 1358–1423), English merchant, is supposed to have been the youngest son of Sir William Whittington of Pauntley in Gloucestershire, on whose death he set out at thirteen for London, and apprenticed himself to Sir John Fitz-Warren, a prosperous mercer, whose daughter he afterwards married. We find him a member of the Mercers' Company in 1392, in 1393 an alderman and sheriff, in 1397 (on the mayor's death), 1398, 1406, 1419 mayor of London, in 1416 member of parliament. Childless, he left all his great wealth to charity. The legend of his cat is an accepted part of English folklore. See Lyson's *Model Merchant of the Middle Ages* (1860) and Besant and Rice's *Sir Richard Whittington* (1881).

WHITTLE, Sir Frank (1907–), English inventor, from Cambridge joined the R.A.F. and began research on the problems of jet propulsion. He successfully developed the jet engine for aircraft (1941) and became government technical adviser on engine design (1946–48). His many honours include F.R.S. (1947) and K.B.E. (1948). See his *Jet* (1953).

WHITWORTH, Sir Joseph (1803–87), English engineer and inventor, born at Stockport, at the Exhibition in 1851 exhibited many tools and machines. In 1859 he invented a gun of compressed steel, with spiral polygonal bore. Created a baronet in 1869, he founded Whitworth scholarships for encouraging engineering science. He was responsible for the standard screw-thread named after him.

WHYMPER, Edward (1840–1911), English wood-engraver and mountaineer, born in London, was trained as an artist on wood, but became even more famous for his mountaineering than for his book illustrations. In 1860–69 he conquered several hitherto unscaled peaks of the Alps, including the Matterhorn. In 1867 and 1872 he made many geological discoveries in N. Greenland. His travels in the Andes (including ascents of Chimborazo) took place in 1879–80. See his own *Scrambles amongst the Alps* (1871, 1893), *Zermatt and the Matterhorn* (1897) and F. S. Smythe, *Edward Whymper* (1940).

WHYTE-MELVILLE, George John (1821–1878), British writer and authority on field sports, born at Mount-Melville, St Andrews, served in the Crimean war, and wrote novels on fox-hunting, steeplechasing, &c.

WICLIFFE. See Wycliffe.

WIDOR, Charles Marie (1845–1937), French composer, born at Lyons, organist of St Sulpice, Paris, was professor of Organ and Composition at the Paris Conservatoire (1891) and secretary of the Académie des Beaux-Arts from 1914 until his death. He composed ten symphonies for the organ, as well as a ballet, chamber music and other orchestral works. See his *La Technique de l'orchestre moderne* (1904).

WIECHERT, Ernst, *vee'KHĕrt* (1887–1950), German writer, born at Kleinort in East Prussia, published novels dealing with psychological problems such as postwar readjustment, among them *Der Wald* (1922), *Der Totenwolf* (1924), *Der silberne Wagen* (1928), *Die Majorin* (1934) and *Das einfache Leben* (1939), the last-named probably his masterpiece. *Wälder und Menschen* (1936) is autobiographical, as is *Der Totenwald* (1946), which describes his six months confinement in Buchenwald concentration camp.

WIECK, Clara. See SCHUMANN.

WIELAND, *vee'lant,* (1) **Christoph Martin** (1733–1813), German writer, born near Biberach, the son of a pietist pastor, in 1760 became an official there. Bodmer invited him (1752) to Zürich, and inspired him to write *Der geprüfte Abraham* and other books full of sentimentality and religious mysticism. But Wieland's bent was in the opposite direction, and in 1760–70, besides making the first German translation of Shakespeare (1762–66), he wrote the romances *Agathon* and *Don Silvio von Rosalva, Die Grazien* and other tales, the didactic poem *Musarion,* &c. Their elegance, grace and lightness made Wieland popular with fashionable society. After holding for three years a professorship at Erfurt, he was called to Weimar to train the grand-duchess's sons, and there he spent most of the rest of his life, the friend of Goethe and Herder. The Weimar period produced his heroic poem *Oberon,* by which he is best remembered, and various other works; he also edited several magazines. See Lives by Gruber (1827–28) and Loebel (1858); books about him by Funck (1882), Keil (1885), Hirzel (1891), Michel (1938); Wieland's Correspondence (1815–20); and Stadler, *Wieland's Shakespeare* (1910).

(2) **Heinrich Otto** (1877–1957), German organic chemist, born at Pforzheim, studied at Munich, Berlin and Stuttgart before returning to Munich as professor of Organic Chemistry at the Technische Hochschule (1917). In 1921 he went to Freiburg and in 1925 again became a professor at Munich. In 1927 he was awarded the Nobel prize for chemistry, in recognition of his research on the bile acids, organic radicals, nitrogen compounds, &c.

WIEN, *veen,* (1) **Max Carl** (1866–1938), German physicist, cousin of (2), born at Königsberg, Röntgen's assistant (1892–95) and professor at Jena (1911–35), carried out research on high-frequency waves and discovered a method of measuring alternating current.

(2) **Wilhelm** (1864–1928), German physicist, cousin of (1), born at Gaffken in East Prussia, became professor at Aachen, Giessen, Würzburg and finally Munich (1920). In 1911 he was awarded the Nobel prize for physics, for his work on the radiation of energy from black bodies. His researches also covered X-rays, hydrodynamics, &c.

WIENER, Norbert, *wee'-* (1894–1964), American mathematical logician, founder of cybernetics, born in Columbia, pursued postgraduate studies at Harvard, Cornell, under Bertrand Russell at Cambridge and at Göttingen, and in 1932 became professor of Mathematics at the Massachusetts Institute of Technology, where he had lectured from 1919. During World War II he worked on predictors and guided missiles and his study of the handling of information by electronic devices, based on the feedback principle, encouraged comparison between these and analogous mental processes in *Cybernetics* (1948) and other works. He won the American Design Award (1933) and was vice-president of the American Mathematical Society (1935–37). See *I am a Mathematician* (1956).

WIENIAWSKI, Henri, *vye-nyaf'skee* (1835–1880), Polish composer of concertos, études, &c., for the violin, born at Lublin, was for twelve years solo violinist to the tsar, and taught at the Brussels Conservatoire. His brother, **Joseph** (1837–1912), pianist, taught in the Moscow Conservatoire, and was a conductor at Warsaw 1871–77.

WIER, or Weyer, Johann, *vī'ėr* (1516–88), Belgian physician, one of the first opponents of the witchcraft superstition, born at Grave in North Brabant, studied medicine at Paris and Orleans, and settled about 1545 as a physician at Arnheim, whence he was called to Düsseldorf to be physician to the Duke of Jülich. To him he dedicated his famous *De Praestigiis Daemonum et Incantationibus ac Veneficiis* (1563), a plea against the folly and cruelty of the witchcraft trials. The book roused the fury of the clergy; but the duke protected Wier till his death. His great treatise was followed by other works. See study by Binz (1885).

WIERTZ, Anton Joseph, *veerts* (1806–65), Belgian painter, born at Dinant, in 1836 settled in Liège, and in 1848 at Brussels. His original aim was to combine the excellences of Michelangelo and Rubens; but about 1848–50 he began to paint speculative and mystical pieces, dreams, visions, and the products of a morbid imagination. In 1850 the state built him a studio which became the Musée Wiertz.

WIGGIN, Kate Douglas, *née* **Smith** (1856–1953), American novelist, born in Philadelphia, wrote novels for both adults and children, but was more successful with the latter. *Rebecca of Sunnybrook Farm* (1903) is probably her best-known book, although the *Penelope* exploits, *The Birds' Christmas Carol* (1888) and *Mother Carey's Chickens* (1911) were all firm favourites. See *My garden of memory* (1923), and the biography by her sister, N. Smith.

WIGNER, Eugene Paul (1902–), Hungarian-born physicist, a native of Budapest, educated at Berlin Technische Hochschule, professor of Mathematical Physics at Princeton from 1938, known for his many contributions to the theory of nuclear physics, especially the Breit-Wigner formula for resonant nuclear reactions and the Wigner theorem concerning the conservation of the angular momentum of electron spin. His name is also given to the most important class of mirror nuclides (Wigner nuclides), and to a number of other physical phenomena. His calculations were used by Fermi (q.v.) in building the first reactor in Chicago. He received the Fermi award in 1958, the Atom for Peace award in 1959, and the Nobel physics prize for 1963.

WILAMOWITZ-MOELLENDORFF, Ulrich von, *vil-a-mō'vits mœ'lėn-dorf* (1848–1931), German classical scholar, born at Markowitz, Posen, studied at Bonn and Berlin, and became professor at Greifswald (1876), Göttingen (1883), and Berlin (1897–1922). He was Mommsen's son-in-law. His works on Greek literature and editions of Greek classics were numerous and valuable. See his *Erinnerungen* (1928; trans. 1930).

WILBERFORCE, (1) **Henry William** (1807–1873), youngest son of (4), educated at Oriel College, Oxford, took Anglican orders in 1834, but joined the Church of Rome in 1850. He then became a journalist as proprietor and editor of *The Catholic Standard* (1854–63).

(2) **Robert Isaac** (1802–57), second son of (4), a fellow of Oriel and prebendary of York, joined the Catholic church in 1854 and died on his way to become a priest at Rome. He collaborated with (3) in writing a Life of his father.

(3) **Samuel** (1805–73), English prelate, third son of (4), was born at Clapham, September 7. In 1826 he graduated from Oriel, Oxford, and was ordained in 1828. In 1830 he became rector of Brightstone, I.O.W., in 1840 rector of Alverstoke, canon of Winchester and chaplain to the Prince Consort, in 1845 Dean of Westminster and Bishop of Oxford. He took part in the controversies of the Hampden, Gorham, *Essays and Reviews,* and Colenso cases. Instrumental in reviving Convocation (1852), he instituted Cuddesdon theological college (1854). The charm of his many-sided personality, his administrative capacity, his social and oratorical gifts, were apt to be forgotten in the versatile ecclesiastic, nicknamed 'Soapy Sam'. He edited *Letters and Journals of Henry Martyn* (1837), wrote along with (2) the Life of his father (1838), and himself wrote *Agathos* (1839), *Rocky Island* (1840) and *History of the American Church* (1844). Bishop of Winchester from 1869, he was killed by a fall from his horse. See Life by his eldest son R. G. Wilberforce (1905). Of his two younger sons, **Ernest Roland** (1840–1908) became first Bishop of Newcastle (1882) and Bishop of Chichester (1895); **Albert Basil Orme** (1841–1916) became Archdeacon of Westminster (1900), chaplain to the Speaker, and an eloquent advocate of temperance.

(4) **William** (1759–1833), English philanthropist, born at Hull, son of a wealthy merchant, father of (1), (2) and (3). Educated at St John's, Cambridge, in 1780 he was returned for Hull, in 1784 for Yorkshire, and was a close friend of Pitt, though he remained independent of party. In 1784–85, during a tour on the Continent with Dean Milner, he came under the latter's strong evangelical influence; and in 1787 he founded an association for the reformation of manners. In 1788, supported by Clarkson and the Quakers, he entered on his nineteen years' struggle for the abolition of the slave trade, crowned with victory in 1807. He next sought to secure the abolition of the slave trade abroad and the total abolition of slavery itself; but declining health compelled him in 1825 to retire from parliament. He was for long a central figure in the 'Clapham sect' of Evangelicals. He was buried in Westminster Abbey. He wrote a *Practical View of Christianity* (1797), helped to found the *Christian Observer* (1801), and promoted many schemes for the welfare of the community. See the Life by his sons (1838), his *Private Papers,* edited by Mrs A. M. Wilberforce (1898), and study by R. Coupland (1923).

WILBYE, John (1574–1638), one of the greatest of English madrigal composers, was born at Diss in Norfolk, was a household musician at Hengrave Hall, 1593–1628, and after that at Colchester. His madrigals are marked by sensitive beauty and excellent workmanship.

WILCOX, Ella, *née* **Wheeler** (1850–1919), American writer, prolific producer of verse, born at Johnstown Center, Wis., had completed a novel before she was ten, and later wrote at least two poems a day. The first of her many volumes of verse was *Drops of Water* (1872); the most successful was *Poems of Passion* (1883). Her *Story of a Literary Career* (1905) and *The Worlds and I* (1918) were autobiographical.

WILD, Jonathan (*c.* 1682–1725), English criminal, born at Wolverhampton, served an apprenticeship to a Birmingham bucklemaker. About 1706 he deserted his wife, came up to London, was imprisoned for debt, consorted with criminals, turned a receiver of stolen goods and a betrayer of such thieves as would not share with him, until for theft and receiving he was hanged at Tyburn. His story suggested the theme of Fielding's satire *Jonathan Wild.*

WILDE, (1) **Jane Francisca Speranza, Lady** (1826–96), daughter of Archdeacon Elgee, in 1851 married Sir W. R. W. Wilde (1799–1869), a distinguished surgeon, antiquarian, and president of the Irish Academy. As 'Speranza' she published *Poems* (1864), and in her own name many other works. For years her *salon* was the most famous in Dublin.

(2) **Oscar Fingall O'Flahertie Wills** (1854–1900), Irish poet, wit and dramatist, son of (1), studied at Magdalen College, Oxford, and in 1878 won the Newdigate prize for his *Ravenna.* In 1881 he published *Poems*; in 1891 a novel, *Dorian Gray*; in 1893 the plays *Lady Windermere's Fan,* and (in French) *Salomé*; in 1894 *A Woman of No Importance*; in 1895 *An Ideal Husband*; in 1899 *The Importance of being Earnest. The Ballad of Reading Gaol* (1898) and *De Profundis* (1905) bear the impress of two years' hard labour for homosexual practices revealed during his abortive libel action (1895) against the Marquis of Queensberry, who had objected to Wilde's association with his son Lord Alfred Douglas (q.v.). He died an exile in Paris, having adopted the name of **Sebastian Melmoth.** While Wilde was alive his controversial 'art for art's sake' personality and the notoriety of his trial made difficult an impartial assessment of his work. He was strongest as a dramatist, his brilliant epigrams lending distinction to his writing and making

a penetrating commentary on the society of his time. See *Complete Works* (4 vols. 1936), studies by Symons (1930), Renier (1933), Woodcock (1949), and H. Pearson, *The Life of Oscar Wilde* (1946); trial proceedings ed. Hyde (1948); *Letters* ed. R. Hart-Davis (1962).

WILDENBRUCH, Ernst von, *vil'dėn-broo*KH (1845–1909), German romantic novelist, poet and dramatist, born at Beirut, served in the army and Foreign Office. His strongly-expressed patriotism made him the national dramatist of Prussia during the empire of the Hohenzollerns, to whom he was related.

WILDER, Thornton Niven (1897–), American author and playwright, born in Madison, Wisconsin. He was educated at Yale and served in both wars, becoming a lieutenant-colonel in 1944. His first novel, *The Cabala*, appeared in 1926. Set in contemporary Rome, it established the cool atmosphere of sophistication and detached irony that was to permeate all his books. These include *The Bridge of San Luis Rey* (1927), a best-seller and winner of the Pulitzer prize, *The Woman of Andros* (1930), *Heaven's My Destination* (1935) and *The Ides of March* (1948). His first plays—*The Trumpet Shall Sound* (1926), *The Angel That Troubled the Waters* (1928) and *The Long Christmas Dinner* (1931)—were literary rather than dramatic; but in 1938 he produced *Our Town*, a successful play that evokes without scenery or costumes a universal flavour of provincial life. This was followed in 1942 by *The Skin of Our Teeth*, an amusing yet profound fable of humanity's struggle to survive. Both these plays were awarded the Pulitzer prize. His later plays include *The Matchmaker* (1954) and *A Life in the Sun* (1955). See Bibliography by J. M. Edelstein (1959).

WILDGANS, Anton, *vilt'-* (1881–1932), Austrian poet and dramatist, born in Vienna. His plays include *Dies Irae* (1918) and the biblical tragedy *Kain* (1920). The epic poem *Kirbisch* appeared in 1927. From 1921 to 1923 he was director of the Vienna Burgtheater.

WILENSKI, Reginald Howard (1887–), English art critic and art historian, born in London. In 1929 and 1930 he was special lecturer in Art at Bristol University, and from 1933 to 1946 at Manchester University. His analysis of the aims and achievements of modern artists, *The Modern Movement in Art* (1927 and later editions), has had considerable influence. His other publications include *English Painting* (1933) and *Modern French Painters* (1940).

WILFRID, or Wilfrith, St (634–709), Bishop of York, born in Northumbria, and trained at Lindisfarne, upheld the Roman views which triumphed at the Synod of Whitby (664). Bishop of York (*c.* 665), he improved the minster of York, built a splendid church at Hexham, and raised a new minster at Ripon. Theodore divided Northumbria into four sees, and Wilfrid appealed to Rome. On the journey he was driven by a storm to the coast of Friesland, where he baptized thousands of pagans. Pope Agatho decided in his favour, but King Ecgfrid flung him into prison. He escaped to Sussex, was allowed to return by the new king, Alfdrid, in 686, and was finally allowed to keep the sees of Ripon and Hexham, but not York. See Eddius's *Vita Wilfridi*, edited by Raine (1879); Browne, *Theodore and Wilfrith* (1897), and historical works by Poole (1934) and Levison (1946).

WILHELMINA (Helena Pauline Maria of Orange-Nassau) (1880–1962), Queen of the Netherlands (1890–1948), succeeded her father William III at a very early age and until 1898 her mother Queen Emma acted as regent. Queen Wilhelmina fully upheld the principles of constitutional monarchy, especially winning the admiration of her people during World War II. Though compelled to seek refuge in Britain, she steadfastly encouraged Dutch resistance to the German occupation. In 1948, in view of the length of her reign, she abdicated in favour of her daughter **Juliana** (q.v.) and assumed the title of Princess of the Netherlands. See her *Lonely but not Alone* (1960).

WILHELMINE, Princess. See ANSPACH.

WILKES, (1) Captain Charles (1798–1877), American naval officer, in 1839–40 explored various Pacific island groups and sailed along the coast of what is now known as Wilkes Land; in 1861 intercepted at sea the British mail-steamer *Trent*, and took off two Confederate commissioners accredited to France, thereby raising a risk of war with Britain.

(2) **John** (1727–97), English politician, born at Clerkenwell, the son of a distiller, studied at Leyden, and became a man of fashion and profligate. To please his parents, he married at twenty-two the daughter of the eminent and wealthy physician, Dr Mead. She was ten years his senior, and after a daughter had been born to them the ill-matched pair separated. One of the infamous 'Monks of Medmenham', Wilkes took up politics as a supporter of Pitt, was returned for Aylesbury in 1757, and was also high-sheriff for Bucks and colonel of the Bucks Militia. Lord Bute having declined to appoint him ambassador to Constantinople or governor of Quebec, he attacked the ministry in the *North Briton* (1762–63), a weekly journal he had founded. Before the twenty-seventh number appeared he was threatened with prosecution, and had to fight a duel with Lord Talbot. In the forty-fifth number some strong comments were made upon the king's speech on opening parliament. Lord Halifax as secretary of state issued a general warrant for the apprehension of all concerned in the article. Wilkes was seized and committed to the Tower. Lord chief justice Pratt ordered his release on the ground of privilege as M.P.; and it was then determined that general warrants were unconstitutional. He obtained large damages at law, and became the hero of the hour. The Earl of Sandwich read extracts in the House of Lords from the purloined copy of Wilkes's verse 'Essay on Woman', printed at his private press, which was declared to be an 'obscene libel'; and the House of Commons expelled him on January 19, 1764, as author of No. 45 of the *North Briton*. Before this he was wounded in a duel with Mr Martin. He was tried and found guilty during his absence from England for publishing the 'Essay on Woman' (1763) and was outlawed for non-appearance

Returning to England in 1768, he stood unsuccessfully for the City of London, but was triumphantly returned for Middlesex. His outlawry was reversed on a purely technical point, and he was sentenced to twenty-two months' imprisonment and a fine of £1000. In prison he penned a charge against the secretary of state of instigating the massacre in St George's Fields, and this was made the pretext for his expulsion from parliament. He had been four times re-elected, when the house declared him ineligible. In 1771 he was elected sheriff for London and Middlesex; in 1774 he became lord mayor, and re-entered parliament as M.P. for Middlesex. In 1780 he lost some popularity by his part in suppressing the Gordon riots. In 1782 the resolutions invalidating his previous elections were expunged. He became chamberlain of the City in 1779, and retired from parliament in 1790. The present liberty of the press owes much to his efforts. See J. S. Watson, *Biographies of John Wilkes and William Cobbett* (1870); Thorold Rogers, *Historical Gleanings* (1870); Daly, *Dawn of Radicalism* (1886); Fraser Rae, *Wilkes, Sheridan, Fox* (1873); Nobbe, *The North Briton* (1939); Lives by Percy Fitzgerald (1888), Bleackley (1917), Sherrard (1930), Postgate (1930).

WILKIE, Sir David (1785–1841), Scottish painter, born at Cults manse in Fife, in 1799 was sent to study in the Trustees' Academy at Edinburgh, and returning home in 1804, painted his *Pitlessie Fair*. The great success of *The Village Politicians* (1806) caused him to settle in London. In 1809 he was elected A.R.A., and in 1811 R.A. In 1817 he visited Scott at Abbotsford, and painted the family group now in the Scottish National Gallery. His fame mainly rests on such genre pictures as the *Card Players, Village Festival, Reading the Will*, &c. Later he changed his style, sought to emulate the depth and richness of colouring of the old masters, and chose more elevated subjects, to the height of which he could never raise himself. He also painted portraits, and was successful as an etcher. In 1830 he was made painter-in-ordinary to the king, and in 1836 knighted. In 1840, for his health, he visited Syria, Palestine and Egypt, but died on his voyage home. See books on him by Allan Cunningham (1843), J. W. Mollett (1881) and Lord R. Sutherland-Gower (1902).

WILKINS, (1) Sir George Hubert (1888–1958), Australian polar explorer, born at Mt Bryan East, first went to the Arctic in 1913. In 1919 he flew from England to Australia, 1920–22 he spent in the Antarctic, and after that collected material in Central Australia on behalf of the British Museum. In 1926 he returned to the Arctic, and in 1928 was knighted for a pioneer flight from Alaska to Spitsbergen, over polar ice. In 1931 he was again exploring in the Arctic, this time with the submarine *Nautilus*, but an attempt to reach the North pole under the ice was unsuccessful. After his death his ashes were conveyed to the pole, where they were scattered into the wind. See his books *Flying the Arctic* (1928), *Undiscovered Australia* (1928), *Under the North Pole* (1931).

(2) **John** (1614–72), English churchman and scientist, Bishop of Chester, born near Daventry, graduated B.A. from Magdalen Hall in 1631. As domestic chaplain he studied mathematics and mechanics, and was one of the founders of the Royal Society. In the Civil War he sided with parliament, and was appointed warden of Wadham. In 1656 he married a widowed sister of Oliver Cromwell, and in 1659 was appointed by Richard Cromwell master of Trinity College, Cambridge. Dispossessed at the Restoration, he soon recovered court favour, and became preacher at Gray's Inn, rector of St Lawrence Jewry, Dean of Ripon and Bishop of Chester (1668). In his *Discovery of a World in the Moon* (1628) he discusses the possibility of communication by a flying-machine with the moon and its supposed inhabitants; the *Discourse concerning a New Planet* (1640) argues that the earth is one of the planets; *Mercury, or the Secret and Swift Messenger*, shows how a man may communicate with a friend at any distance; *Mathematical Magic* dates from 1648; the *Essay towards a Real Character and a Philosophical Language* (1668) is founded on Dalgarno's treatise.

(3) **Maurice Hugh Frederick** (1916–), British chemist, born in New Zealand, educated at King Edward's School, Birmingham, and St John's College, Cambridge, did research on uranium isotope separation at the University of California in 1944. He joined the Medical Research Council's Biophysics Research Unit at King's College, London, in 1946, becoming deputy-director in 1955. With Crick and Watson (1) he was awarded the Nobel prize for medicine and physiology in 1962 for work on the structure of DNA.

WILKINSON, (1) Ellen Cicely (1891–1947), English feminist and Labour politician, born in Manchester, was an early member of the Independent Labour Party and an active campaigner for women's suffrage. In 1920 she joined the Communist party, but left it by 1924, when she became M.P. for Middlesbrough East. Losing this seat in 1931, she re-entered parliament in 1935 as member for Jarrow. In 1940 she became parliamentary secretary to the ministry of home security, in 1945 minister of education, the first woman to hold such an appointment.

(2) **Sir John Gardner** (1797–1875), English traveller and Egyptologist, born at Hardendale in Westmorland, and educated at Harrow and Exeter College, Oxford, in 1821–1833 made a complete survey of Egypt, publishing *Materia Hieroglyphica* (1828), *Survey of Thebes* (1830), *Topography of Thebes* (1835), and his famous *Manners and Customs of the Ancient Egyptians* (1837–41). Knighted in 1839, he visited Egypt again several times. He presented his antiquities to Harrow.

WILLARD, Frances Elizabeth (1839–98), American worker for temperance and the enfranchisement of women, was born at Churchville, New York. She studied at the Northwestern University, Evanston, Ill., was professor of Aesthetics there, in 1874 became secretary of the Women's Christian Temperance Union, and edited the Chicago

Daily Post. She helped to found the International Council of Women. Her books include many on temperance, &c., and *My Happy Half-Century* (autobiographical, 1894). She died at New York. See Lives by Florence White (1899), Strachey (1912).

WILLCOCKS, Sir William (1852–1932), British engineer, born in India, planned and carried out great irrigation works for Egypt (Aswan), South Africa and Mesopotamia (Hindiya).

WILLETT, William (1856–1915), English builder, born at Farnham, is chiefly remembered for his campaign for ' daylight saving '. A Bill was promoted in parliament in 1908, but opposition was strong and the measure was not adopted until a year after his death.

WILLIAM, name of four kings of England:

William I (1027–87), ' the Conqueror ', was born at Falaise, the bastard son of Robert III, Duke of Normandy, by Arlette, a tanner's daughter. On his father's death in 1035, the nobles accepted him as duke; but his youth was passed in difficulty and danger. In 1047 the lords of the western part of the duchy rebelled, but Henry I of France came to his help, and the rebels were defeated at Val-ès-dunes. In 1051 he visited his cousin, Edward the Confessor, and received the promise of the English succession. He married Matilda, daughter of Baldwin V, Count of Flanders, in 1053. In the next ten years William repulsed two French invasions, and in 1063 conquered Maine. Probably in 1064 Harold (q.v.) was at his court, and swore to help him to gain the English crown on Edward's death. When, however, Edward died, in 1066, Harold became king. William laid his claim before the pope and Western Christendom. The pope approved his claim, and on October 14 William defeated Harold at the battle of Hastings or Senlac. Harold was slain, and William was crowned on December 25. The west and north of England were subdued in 1068; but next year the north revolted, and William devastated the country between York and Durham. The constitution under William assumed a feudal aspect, the old national assembly becoming a council of the king's tenants-in-chief, and all title to land being derived from his grant. Domesday Book contains the land settlement. He brought the English Church into closer relations with Rome. The Conqueror's rule was stern and orderly. In 1070 there was a rebellion in the Fen Country, and under the leadership of Hereward the rebels for some time held out in the Isle of Ely. English exiles were sheltered by the Scottish king, Malcolm, who plundered the northern shires; but William in 1072 compelled Malcolm to do him homage at Abernethy. In 1073 he reconquered Maine. He made a successful expedition into South Wales. His eldest son, Robert, rebelled against him in Normandy in 1079; and, having entered on a war with Philip I of France in 1087, William burned Mantes. As he rode through the burning town his horse stumbled, and he received an injury, of which he died at Rouen on September 9. He left Normandy to his son Robert, and England to William. See Freeman's *Norman Conquest*, ii, iii, iv, and his *William the Conqueror*; studies by F. M. Stenton (1908), P. Russell (1934), G. Slocombe (1959) and D. C. Douglas (1964); the histories of Palgrave, iii, Stubbs, i, Gneist, i.

William II (reigned 1087–1100), called **Rufus**, third, and second surviving, son of William the Conqueror, was born before 1066. On his father's death in 1087 he was crowned king. The next year many of the Norman nobles in England rebelled against him in favour of his eldest brother Robert, Duke of Normandy. Rufus appealed to the English people for help, promising them good government and a relaxation of the forest laws and of fiscal burdens. The rebellion was suppressed, but he did not keep his promises. Treating ecclesiastical benefices like lay fiefs, Rufus sold them, and kept them vacant, seizing their revenues during vacancy. The see of Canterbury had been vacant four years when, in 1093, he fell sick, repented, and appointed Anselm as archbishop. When he recovered he quarrelled with Anselm for maintaining the liberties of the church. Rufus warred with Robert in Normandy, but peace was made in 1091; and in 1096 the duchy was mortgaged to him. In 1098 he reconquered Maine, but failed to hold the whole of it. Malcolm, king of Scotland, invaded Northumberland in 1093, and was slain at Alnwick. Rufus thrice invaded Wales, twice with little success. As he was hunting in the New Forest on August 2, 1100, he was killed by an arrow, probably shot by Walter Tirel although this was never established. He was buried in Winchester Cathedral. See Freeman's *Reign of William Rufus* (2 vols. 1882) and G. Slocombe, *Sons of the Conqueror* (1960).

William III (1650–1702), posthumous son of William II of Orange (1626–50) by Mary (1631–60), eldest daughter of Charles I of England, was born at The Hague. On the murder of De Witt in 1672 he was chosen Stadthouder of the United Provinces. The republic was at this time carrying on an apparently hopeless contest with Louis XIV of France; but by the valour and wisdom of William the war was in 1678 terminated by the advantageous treaty of Nimeguen (Nijmegen). In 1677 William had married his cousin, the Princess Mary (born April 30, 1662), daughter of James II by Anne Hyde. When James's tyranny had estranged the affections of his subjects, eyes were turned towards the Stadthouder as their only hope; and on the day that the Seven Bishops were acquitted William was invited to come over and redress grievances. On November 5, 1688, he landed at Torbay with an English and Dutch army of 15,000. Men of all parties quickly came over to him; James fled; the Convention Parliament declared the throne vacant; and on February 13, 1689, William and Mary were proclaimed king and queen. The Scottish Convention did the same, April 4 to 11. James's adherents held out in Scotland and Ireland, but the fall of Dundee at Killiecrankie (July 1689) and the surrender of Limerick (October 1691) virtually ended resistance. William thus was left free for his Continental campaigns, in which he was outmatched by the Duke of Luxembourg. The latter's death in 1695 was a turning-point in the war, which was ended by the peace of Ryswick (1697). In spite of his sterling qualities, and of the debt that they owed him, he and his subjects were never in sympathy; his foreign birth, his reserve, his ill-health, were against him. The death (December 28, 1694) of his wife materially injured his position. His schemes were thwarted by parliament; continual plots for his assassination were hatched by James's adherents; and the death in 1700 of Charles II of Spain, and the succession of Philip of Anjou, was another blow to his policy. He pursued it, however, with unflagging vigour till his death, caused by the stumbling of his horse over a molehill. He left no children, and the crown passed to Anne, Mary's sister. During his reign the National Debt was commenced, the Bank of England established, the modern system of finance introduced, ministerial responsibility recognized, the standing army transferred to the control of parliament, the liberty of the press secured, and the British constitution established on a firm basis. See Histories of Burnet, Macaulay and Lodge; the *Memoirs* of Queen Mary, ed. by Doebner (1885); Traill's *William III* (1888); *Mary II*, by M. F. Sandars (1913), by H. Chapman (1953); and studies of William by Trevelyan (1930) and Renier (1939).

William IV (1765–1837), the 'sailor king', third son of George III, was born at Buckingham Palace. He entered the navy in 1779, and saw some service in America and the West Indies. In 1789 he was created Duke of Clarence and St Andrews and Earl of Munster, with an allowance of £12,000 a year. He was formally promoted through the successive ranks to that of admiral of the Fleet (1811), and in 1827–28 he held the revived office of lord high admiral. From 1790 to 1811 he lived with the actress Mrs Jordan (q.v.), who bore him ten children; on July 13, 1818, he married Adelaide (1792–1849), eldest daughter of the Duke of Saxe-Meiningen. The two daughters born (1819 and 1820) of this marriage died in infancy. By the Duke of York's death in 1827 the Duke of Clarence became heir-presumptive to the throne, to which he succeeded at the death of his eldest brother, George IV, June 26, 1830. A Whig up to his accession, he then turned Tory, and did much to obstruct the passing of the first Reform Act (1832). The abolition of colonial slavery (1833), the reform of the poor laws (1834), and the Municipal Reform Act (1835) were results of that great constitutional change. William died June 20, 1837, and was succeeded by his niece, Victoria. See, besides the articles on his premiers, GREY, MELBOURNE and PEEL, the Duke of Buckingham's *Courts and Cabinets of William IV and Victoria* (1861), the *Greville Memoirs*, Percy Fitzgerald's *Life and Times of William IV* (1884), J. F. Molloy's *The Sailor King* (1903), and study by W. G. Allen (1960).

WILLIAM, German **Wilhelm**, name of two German emperors:

William I (1797–1888), seventh king of Prussia and first German emperor, second son of Frederick-William III, was born at Berlin, March 22. In 1814 he received his 'baptism of fire' on French territory at Bar-sur-Aube, and entered Paris with the allies. During the king's absence in Russia he directed Prussian military affairs. In 1829 he married Princess Augusta of Saxe-Weimar (1811–90). On the accession of his brother, Frederick-William IV, in 1840, he became heir-presumptive. In 1844 he visited England and formed a friendship with Queen Victoria and the Prince Consort. During the revolution of 1848 his attitude towards the people made him very unpopular. He was obliged to quit Prussia, and took up his quarters at the Prussian Legation in London. In two months, however, he received his recall. In 1849 he subdued the disaffection in Baden. He was appointed regent (1858) in consequence of the prolonged ill-health of the king, on whose death, January 2, 1861, he succeeded as William I. He soon made plain his intention of consolidating the throne and strengthening the army. A few months after his accession he narrowly escaped assassination. Prince Bismarck was placed at the head of the ministry, with Roon, the author of the new army system, as war minister. The scheme was very unpalatable to the parliament, but the minister-president forced it upon the nation, with the necessary increased expenditure, by overriding the constitution. In 1864 the Schleswig-Holstein difficulty led to a war with Denmark, in which the Prussian and Austrian troops were victorious; but in 1866 the allies quarrelled over the spoils, and struggled for the supremacy over the German states. Austria was crushed at Sadowa, and Prussia gained in territory and prestige. The affair of the Duchy of Luxemburg nearly led to a war between France and Prussia in 1867, but the difficulty was adjusted by the treaty of London. In 1870 the inevitable struggle between France and Prussia was precipitated. The Spanish throne having become vacant, Prince Leopold, son of the Prince of Hohenzollern-Sigmaringen, was put forward as a candidate. As King William was the head of the House of Hohenzollern, this gave great umbrage to France. Although the candidature was withdrawn, Napoleon III forced a quarrel on Prussia, by making impossible demands. William took the field on July 31, and in the deadly struggle which ensued, the French forces were defeated almost everywhere; Napoleon capitulated at Sedan; and by the end of September Paris was invested. At Versailles on January 18, 1871, William was proclaimed German emperor. Peace was signed on February 26. An Austro-German alliance of 1871 was strengthened in 1873 by the adhesion of the tsar. The rapid rise of Socialism in Germany led to severe repressive measures, and in 1878 the emperor's life was twice attempted by Socialists, as again in 1883. William I, though holding tenaciously to the prerogatives of his kingly office, was of a simple and unassuming personal character. See Lives by A. Forbes (1889) and Barnett Smith (1887); Simon (trans. from French, 1886); German Lives by Schmidt and Otto, and

Oncken; Whitman's *Imperial Germany* (1892); and books cited at BISMARCK.

William II (1859–1941), third German emperor (1888–1918), and ninth king of Prussia, the eldest son of Prince Frederick, later Frederick III (q.v.) and of Victoria, the daughter of Britain's Queen Victoria, was born at Potsdam, Berlin, January 27. He received a strict military and academic education at the Kassel gymnasium and the University of Bonn, taking part in military exercises despite a deformed left arm. Early estranged from his mother, he put her under arrest after his accession (1888). A passion for military splendour, a deep conviction of the divine right of the Hohenzollerns, a quick intelligence but an uncertain temperament characterized the young ruler. He quarrelled with and dismissed (1890) the elder statesman Bismarck, who disapproved of William's projected overtures to capture working-class support and who had forbidden any minister to see the emperor except in his, Bismarck's, presence. A long spell of personal rule followed, helped out by political favourites such as Holstein and Von Bülow. William's speeches had as their constant theme German imperialism. In 1896 he sent a telegram to President Kruger of South Africa congratulating him on the suppression of the Jameson raid. He paid state visits to the Arab countries of the Middle East (1898), adopted an anti-British attitude at the start of the Boer war, but after several visits to Queen Victoria at Windsor was for a while seriously, if clumsily, concerned with Anglo-German reconciliation. But despite such temporary goodwill, he backed von Tirpitz's plans for a large German navy to match the British and in 1911 without provocation dispatched the warship *Panther* to the closed Moroccan port of Agadir, but withdrew it after Lloyd George's instant reaction. He supported immoderate demands on Serbia after the assassination of the Archduke Franz Ferdinand at Sarajevo (1914), but made strenuous efforts to preserve the peace once he realized that a world war was imminent. But political power passed from him to the generals and during the war he became a mere figurehead far removed from the great warlord of popular imagination. With the collapse of the German armies and a revolution in progress, William was forced to abdicate, November 9, 1918, and flee the country. He and his family settled first at Amerongen, then at Doorn near Arnheim, where he wrote his *Memoirs 1878–1918* (trans. 1922), felled trees and ignored the Nazi 'Liberation' (1940) of Holland. He married Princess Augusta Victoria of Schleswig-Holstein in 1881, by whom he had six sons and one daughter, and after her death in 1921, Princess Hermine of Reuss. See also *My Early Life* (1926), Speeches, *Reden Kaiser Wilhelms* (*1888–1912*), and biographical studies by E. Ludwig (1926), D. V. Beseler (1932), E. Eyck (1948) and J. von Kürenberg (trans. 1954).

WILLIAM OF CHAMPEAUX (1070–1121), French scholastic philosopher, the head of a famous school of logic in Paris, was the founder of scholastic Realism. He was a teacher and rival of Abelard.

WILLIAM OF JUMIÈGES (d. *c.* 1090), Norman Benedictine monk who compiled a history of the Dukes of Normandy from Rollo to 1071, of value for the story of the Conquest.

WILLIAM OF MALMESBURY (*c.* 1090–1143), English chronicler, became a monk in the monastery at Malmesbury, and in due time librarian and precentor. He took part in the council at Winchester against Stephen in 1141. His *Gesta Regum Anglorum* gives the history of the kings of England from the Saxon invasion to 1126; the *Historia Novella* brings down the narrative to 1142. The *Gesta Pontificum* gives an account of the bishops and chief monasteries of England to 1123. Other works are an account of the church at Glastonbury and Lives of St Dunstan and St Wulfstan.

WILLIAM OF NEWBURGH (*c.* 1135–*c.* 1200), English chronicler, was perhaps a native of Bridlington, a monk of Newburgh Priory (Coxwold). His *Historia Rerum Anglicarum* (ed. Hamilton, 1856; Howlett, 1884–85), is one of the chief authorities for the reign of Henry II.

WILLIAM OF NORWICH, St (1132?–44), English martyr, apparently the prototype of the Christian boys reported to have been crucified by Jews (see HUGH OF LINCOLN). *The Life and Miracles of St William of Norwich*, edited in 1897 by Jessopp and James, is a story from a 12th-century MS. of a boy said to have been martyred March 22, 1144 or 1145.

WILLIAM OF TYRE (*c.* 1130–85), churchman and historian, probably of Italian birth, became Archdeacon of Tyre in 1167, and Archbishop in 1175. He was tutor to Baldwin, son of King Amalric, and one of the six bishops representing the Latin Church of the East at the Lateran Council (1179). His *Historia Rerum in Partibus Transmarinis Gestarum* deals with the affairs of the East in 1095–1184; a 13th-century French translation was edited by P. Paris (1880). English ones were made by William Caxton (ed. Colvin for the Early English Text Society, 1893); and by Krey and Babington (1942). Another work was *Historia de Orientalibus Principibus*, a history of the successors of Mohammed, now lost.

WILLIAM OF WAYNFLETE (1395–1486), English prelate, educated probably at New College, Oxford, became provost of Eton in 1443, Bishop of Winchester in 1447, and in 1448 founded Magdalen College, Oxford. He was involved in the negotiations which ended Jack Cade's rebellion in 1450, and as a Lancastrian played an important rôle as adviser to Henry VI in the Wars of the Roses. He was lord chancellor (1456–60).

WILLIAM OF WYKEHAM (1324–1404), English churchman and statesman, born at Wickham, near Fareham, was sent to school at Winchester, and by Edward III appointed surveyor of Windsor and other royal castles in 1356–59. He built Queensborough Castle in 1361, was keeper of the privy seal and secretary to the king in 1364, became Bishop of Winchester 1367 and chancellor of England 1367–71 and 1389–91. In 1379 he founded New College, Oxford, and in 1382

Winchester School. In 1394 he undertook the transformation of the nave of Winchester Cathedral, and personally supervised the work. The money he laid out on building would represent half a million. In 1404 he endowed a magnificent chantry at Winchester and, dying the same year, was buried in it. Wykeham was not an ardent theologian; he founded his colleges 'first for the glory of God and the promotion of divine service, and secondarily for scholarship'. He has been called the 'father of the public school system'; and he established (though he did not invent) the Perpendicular architecture. See Lives by Lowth (new ed. 1777), Chandler (1842), Moberly (new ed. 1893); *Winchester College 1393–1893* by Old Wykehamists (1894); and *Winchester College* by A. F. Leach (1899).

WILLIAM THE LYON (1143–1214), King of Scotland, was the grandson of David I, and brother of Malcolm IV, whom he succeeded in 1165. Whence he derived his designation is one of the mysteries of history. His predecessors had long contested with England the sovereignty of Northumberland; but under Malcolm these claims were virtually abandoned, and the king of Scots received, as an equivalent, the earldom of Huntingdon and other estates, holding from the English crown. William attended Henry of England in his Continental wars, and is supposed to have pressed for a portion of the old disputed districts. In his disappointment he invaded them, and on July 13, 1174, fell into the hands of an English party near Alnwick Castle. He was conveyed to Normandy, and there, by the treaty of Falaise, consented, as the price of his liberation, to perform homage for his kingdom. The treaty was revoked in 1189 by Richard I of England in consideration of a payment of 10,000 marks. William had disputes with the church, but founded in 1178 the Abbey of Arbroath, where later he was buried.

WILLIAM THE SILENT (1533–84), Prince of Orange, was born, the Count of Nassau's son, at the castle of Dillenburg in Nassau. He inherited from his cousin René the independent principality of Orange (near Avignon) and the family estates in Holland; and by Charles V before his abdication he was made commander-in-chief in the Netherlands and Stadthouder of Holland, Zeeland and Utrecht, though only twenty-two years of age. He opposed the oppressive policy of Philip II, and resigned his offices (1567). Proclaimed a traitor by Alva and put under the ban by Philip, he professed Protestantism, was chosen by the Netherlanders commander by sea and land, and was the soul of the successful rising against Spanish tyranny. Till the capture of Briel by the Gueux (1572), the Spaniards were absolute masters of the Netherlands; the union of the northern provinces was accomplished in 1579; and in 1584 the free Netherlands had renounced for ever their allegiance to Philip or to Spain. But on July 10, 1584, William was shot at Delft by Balthasar Gérard. He was called 'the Silent' because of his ability to keep a state secret (specifically, Henry II's scheme to massacre all the Protestants of France and the Netherlands, confided to him when he was a hostage in France in 1559), not for lack of affability. See Motley's Histories; Lives by Barrett (1883), Putnam (1895), F. Harrison (1897), J. C. Squire (1912), C. V. Wedgwood (1944); in French by Juste (1883), in German by Klose (1864), Kolligs (1885), Rachfahl (1906–24).

WILLIAMS, (1) **Emlyn** (1905–), Welsh playwright and actor, born in Flintshire. The son of an ironmonger, he won a scholarship to Oxford, where he entered Christ Church College. In 1927, attracted by the stage, he joined J. B. Fagan's repertory company. His first real success as a dramatist was with *A Murder has been Arranged* (1930). He then adapted a French play by René Fauchois—*The Late Christopher Bean* (1933)—and continued his success with the terrifying psychological thriller *Night Must Fall* (1935). He was not limited to light entertainment, and a seriousness of purpose characterizes most of his other work. Other successes have been *The Corn is Green* (1938), *The Light of Heart* (1940), *The Wind of Heaven* (1945), *Trespass* (1947), *Accolade* (1951). He has generally played the lead in his own and has acted in other dramatists' plays, besides appearing at the Old Vic and at Stratford, and featuring in films. His solo performance as Charles Dickens giving his celebrated readings from his works was a *tour de force*, but a like endeavour as Dylan Thomas did not meet with such success. See his autobiographical *George* (1961).

(2) **Sir George** (1821–1905), English social reformer, born at Dulverton, became a partner in the London drapery firm of Hitchcock, Williams & Co., made a hobby of temperance work, lay preaching, and teaching in ragged schools, and founded in 1844 the Y.M.C.A. He was knighted in 1894, the jubilee year of the association. See Life by J. E. Hodder Williams (1906).

(3) **Isaac** (1802–65), Welsh clergyman and tractarian, born near Aberystwyth, ordained in 1831, wrote religious poetry, but is best remembered as the author of Tract 80, on 'Reserve in Religious Teaching'. See *Autobiography* (1892).

(4) **John** (1796–1839), English missionary the martyr of Erromango, was born at Tottenham, and, sent by the London Missionary Society in 1817 to the Society Islands, laboured in Raïatéa with marvellous success. Going in 1823 to Raratonga, he christianized the whole Hervey group, and during the next four years visited many of the South Sea Islands, including Samoa. In 1834 he returned to England, superintended the printing of his Raratongan New Testament, and raised £4000 to equip a missionary-ship. In 1838 he visited many of his stations, and sailed for the New Hebrides, where he was killed and eaten by the natives of Erromango. He published his *Narrative of Missionary Enterprises* in 1837. See Lives by B. Mathews (1915) and Prater (1947).

(5) **Sir Monier Monier-** (1819–99), English Sanskrit scholar, was born at Bombay, took his B.A. at Oxford in 1844, and was professor of Sanskrit at Haileybury 1844–58, master at Cheltenham 1858–60, and then Boden

professor of Sanskrit at Oxford. He was knighted in 1886 at the opening of the Indian Institute, established mainly through his energy, and completed in 1896. His books include Sanskrit grammars (1846 and 1860) and dictionaries (1854 and 1872), editions of the *Sákuntalá* (1853) and other Sanskrit texts, books on India, and *Reminiscences of Old Haileybury* (1894). He died at Cannes.

(6) **Roger** (*c.* 1604–83), apostle of toleration and founder of Rhode Island, was originally thought to have been born in Wales, but later research makes this London. Educated at the Charterhouse and Pembroke College, Cambridge, he took Anglican orders, became an extreme Puritan, and emigrated to New England in 1630. He refused to join the congregation at Boston because it would not make public repentance for having been in communion with the Church of England; he therefore went to Salem, but was soon in trouble for denying the right of magistrates to punish Sabbath-breaking. For his opposition to the New England theocracy he was driven from Salem, and took refuge at Plymouth. Two years later he returned to Salem, only to meet renewed persecution and banishment (1635). He escaped to the shores of Narragansett Bay, where he purchased lands of the Indians, founded the city of Providence (1636), and established a pure democracy. Having adopted the tenet of adult baptism, he established (1639) the first Baptist church in America. In 1643 and 1651 he came to England to procure a charter for his colony, and published a *Key into the Language of America* (1643), *The Bloudy Tenent of Persecution for Cause of Conscience* (1644), *The Bloudy Tenent yet more bloudy by Mr Cotton's Endeavour to wash it White in the Blood of the Lamb* (1652), &c. He returned to Rhode Island in 1654, and was president of the colony till 1658. He refused to persecute the Quakers, but had a famous controversy with them—recorded in *George Fox digged out of his Burrowes* (1676). See Memoirs by Elton (1853), Dexter (1876), Straus (1894), Easton (1930), Ernst (1932), E. Winslow (1958); his Letters ed. Bartlett (1882); his Works (Narragansett Club, 1866–74).

(7) **Rowland** (1817–70), English scholar and Liberal theologian, born at Halkyn in Flintshire, and educated at Eton, became fellow and tutor of King's College, Cambridge, in 1850 vice-principal and Hebrew professor at Lampeter College, and in 1859 vicar of Broad-Chalke near Salisbury; hither he retired in 1862 after the storm caused by his contribution, 'Bunsen's Biblical Researches', to *Essays and Reviews*. His chief books are *Christianity and Hinduism* (1856), *The Hebrew Prophets* (1868–71), *Psalms and Litanies* (1872). See Life by his widow (1874).

(8) **Tennessee**, pseud. of **Thomas Lanier Williams** (1912–), American playwright, born at Columbus, Miss., educated at Missouri, Iowa and Washington universities. His work is characterized by fluent dialogue and searching analysis of the psychological deficiencies of his characters. His plays, almost all set in the Deep South against a background of decadence and degradation, include *The Glass Menagerie* (1944), *A Streetcar Named Desire* (1947), awarded the 1948 Pulitzer prize, *Cat on a Hot Tin Roof* (1955), awarded the 1955 Pulitzer prize, *Orpheus Descending* (1957), *Suddenly Last Summer* (1958), and *Night of the Iguana* (1961).

(9) **Sir William Fenwick** (1800–83), British army officer, born at Halifax, Nova Scotia, the hero of Kars, had, as colonel of engineers, been engaged in defining the Turco-Persian boundary when in 1854, during the Crimean war, he was appointed British Military Commissioner with the Turkish army in Asia. He reached Kars in September, and found the Turks utterly demoralized; but with indomitable energy he corrected abuses, got rid of corrupt officials, and became idolized by the Turkish army. In June 1855 the Russians appeared before Kars. After a most heroic defence, Williams had to surrender on November 25. He was detained prisoner in Russia till the peace, when he was given a baronetcy and an annuity of £1000. See works on the siege by Sandwith (1856) and Oliphant (1856).

WILLIAMSON, (1) Alexander William (1824–1904), English chemist, studied medicine at Heidelberg and chemistry at Giessen. From 1849 to 1887 he was professor of Chemistry at University College, London. F.R.S. in 1855, he was president of the British Association in 1873. His researches on etherification had great importance. He published a *Chemistry for Students*.

(2) **Henry** (1895–), English author, born in Bedfordshire, after service in World War I became a journalist, but turned to farming in Norfolk. He wrote several novels, semi-autobiographical, including his long series *A Chronicle of Ancient Sunlight* on the life story of his hero Phillip Maddison. He is best known, however, for his classic nature stories *Tarka the Otter* (1927, Hawthornden prize), and *Salar the Salmon* (1935).

(3) **William Crawford** (1816–95), English botanist, born in Scarborough, trained in medicine and became professor of Natural History and later of Botany at Owens College, Manchester (1851–92). He was the first to point out the importance of the plant life forms in coal. At the time, however, the full significance of his work in fossil botany was not appreciated. See his *Reminiscences of a Yorkshire Naturalist* (1896).

WILLIBALD (700–786), a Northumbrian, and brother of St Walpurga (q.v.), made the pilgrimage to Palestine, settled as monk at Monte Cassino, became the companion of St Boniface, and died Bishop of Eichstätt.

WILLIBROD, or **Wilbrord, St** (*c.* 658–739), English missionary, born in Northumbria, became a Benedictine, and, sent about 690 as missionary to Friesland, was made Bishop of Utrecht, and laboured with the utmost zeal and success. See Lives by Thijm (1863), Verbist (1939), and W. Levison's *England and the Continent in the 8th Century* (1946).

WILLINGDON, Freeman Freeman-Thomas, 1st Marquis of (1866–1941), British administrator. Educated at Eton and Cambridge, he was Liberal M.P. for Hastings (1900–06) and for Bodmin (1906–10), governor of Bombay (1913–19) and of Madras (1919–24).

From 1926 to 1931 he was governor-general of Canada. As viceroy of India (1931–36) he persuaded Gandhi to come to London to the second Round Table Conference, helped to shape the Government of India Bill, and started the new machine of government in India. An administrator of great tact and brilliance, he was one of the few commoners to be rewarded with a marquisate (1936).

WILLIS, (1) Nathaniel Parker (1806–67), American editor and writer, born at Portland, Me., issued several volumes of poetry, established the *American Monthly Magazine*, in 1831 visited Europe, and contributed to the *New York Mirror* his *Pencillings by the Way*. Appointed *attaché* to the American legation at Paris, he visited Greece and Turkey, and returned to England in 1837. He contributed to the London *New Monthly* his *Inklings of Adventure* (collected 1836), and published *Letters from under a Bridge* (1840). In 1844 he engaged in editing the *Daily Mirror*, revisited Europe, and published *Dashes at Life with a Free Pencil* (1845). He returned to New York in 1846, and established the *Home Journal*, in which much of his work first appeared. See Life (1885) by H. A. Beers. His sister, **Sara Payson Willis**, 'Fanny Fern' (1811–72), was a popular writer. See her Life (1873) by her husband, James Parton (q.v.).

(2) **Thomas** (1621–73), English physician, was for a time Sedleian professor of Natural Philosophy at Oxford, but became famous as a physician in Westminster. He was one of the first fellows of the Royal Society, and was a pioneer in the anatomy of the brain. He wrote on the plague.

WILLKIE, Wendell (1892–1944), American politician, born at Elwood, Ind., became first a lawyer, later an industrialist. Having removed his support from the Democrat to the Republican cause in 1940, he was nominated as presidential candidate by the party and narrowly defeated in the election of that year. In 1941–42 he travelled the world representing the president. An opponent of Isolationism, he was leader of the left-wing element in his party.

WILLOUGHBY, Sir Hugh (d. 1554), English explorer, of whom little is known save his unfortunate fate. In 1553 an expedition was fitted out by the merchants of London 'for the discovery of regions, dominions, islands, and places unknown', and Willoughby was appointed its commander. On May 10 he sailed from Deptford with three vessels, one commanded by Richard Chancellor (q.v.). They crossed the North Sea in company, and sighted the coast of Norway. In September Chancellor's ship parted company in a storm with the two others, which reached Russian Lapland. Here Sir Hugh determined to pass the winter, but here with his sixty-two companions he perished of scurvy. Next year Russian fishermen found the ships with the dead bodies and the commander's journal (published in Hakluyt; new edition by Hakluyt Society, 1903).

WILLS, (1) William Gorman (1828–91), Irish playwright and poet, born in Kilkenny Co., studied at Trinity College, Dublin, and started as an artist. His *Man o' Airlie* (1866) was followed by *Charles I* (1872), *Jane Shore* (1876), *Olivia*, *Claudian* (1885), &c. He also wrote novels. His ballads include *I'll sing thee Songs of Araby*. See Life by F. Wills (1898).

(2) **William John** (1834–61), Australian explorer, studied medicine, became a surveyor of crown lands in Victoria and was third in command of R. O. Burke's (q.v.) ill-fated expedition to the north, on which he perished.

WILLSTÄTTER, Richard, *vil'shtet-ėr* (1872–1942), German chemist, born at Karlsruhe, studied at Munich and became professor at Zürich, Berlin, and finally Munich in 1917. His researches included alkaloids and their derivatives, and the work on plant pigments for which in 1915 he was awarded the Nobel prize for chemistry. In 1925 he resigned his professorship at Munich, and in 1939 left Germany for Switzerland, where he died.

WILLUGHBY, Francis (1635–72), English naturalist, born at Middleton, Warwickshire, the son of Sir Francis Willughby, studied at Cambridge and Oxford, and then started on a Continental tour (1663–64) with John Ray (q.v.), collecting zoological specimens. Ray edited and translated his *Ornithologia* (1676–1678) and edited his *Historia Piscium* (1686).

WILLUMSEN, Jens Ferdinand, *vil'oom-sen* (1863–1958), Danish painter and sculptor, born at Copenhagen. His best-known painting, *After the Storm* (1905), is in the Oslo National Gallery. As a sculptor his masterpiece is the *Great Relief*, in coloured marbles and bronze. He bequeathed his works and his art collection to form a Willumsen museum in Frederikssund.

WILMOT. See ROCHESTER (EARL OF).

WILSON, (1) Alexander (1766–1813), Scottish ornithologist of N. America, born at Paisley, travelled as a pedlar, and published poems (1790) and *Watty and Meg* (1792). Prosecuted for a lampoon, he sailed for America in 1794. He got work in Philadelphia, travelled as a pedlar in New Jersey, and was a schoolteacher in Pennsylvania. His skill in drawing birds led him to make a collection of all the birds of America. In October 1804 he set out on his first excursion, and wrote *The Foresters, a Poem*. In 1806 he was employed on the American edition of *Rees's Cyclopaedia*. He soon prevailed upon the publisher to undertake an American Ornithology, and in 1808–13 he brought out seven volumes. In 1811 he made a canoe voyage down the Ohio, and travelled overland through the Lower Mississippi Valley from Nashville to New Orleans. Vols. viii and ix of the Ornithology were completed after his death by Ord, his assistant. The work was continued by C. L. Bonaparte (1828–33).

(2) **Angus Frank Johnstone** (1913–), British writer, educated at Westminster and Merton College, Oxford, began writing in 1946 and rapidly established a reputation with his brilliant collection of short stories, *The Wrong Set* (1949), satirizing the more aimless sections of pre-war middle-class society. *Such Darling Dodos* (1950), *For Whom the Cloche Tolls* (1953) and *A Bit off the Map* (1957) added to his prestige, and in 1955 he gave up his office of deputy-superintendent of the British Museum reading room to

devote himself solely to writing. The novels *Hemlock and After* (1952), *Anglo-Saxon Attitudes* (1956), &c., and the play *The Mulberry Bush* (1955) were still good but perhaps less successful than his short stories, but *No Laughing Matter* (1967), an ambitious family chronicle of the egocentric Matthews family spanning the 20th century, was hailed as an outstanding work.

(3) **Sir Arthur Knyvet** (1842–1921), G.C.B., G.C.V.O., O.M. (1912), British admiral, served in the Crimea (1854), China (1865), Egypt (1882) and Sudan (1884), where he won the V.C., and was commander-in-chief of the Home and Channel Fleets 1903–07, admiral of the Fleet 1907, and first sea lord 1909–12.

(4) **Charles Thomson Rees** (1869–1959), Scottish pioneer of atomic and nuclear physics, born at Glencorse near Edinburgh, was educated at Manchester and at Cambridge, where later he became professor of Natural Philosophy (1925–34). He was noted for his study of atmospheric electricity, one by-product of which was the successful protection from lightning of Britain's wartime barrage balloons. His greatest achievement was to devise the cloud chamber method of marking the track of alpha-particles and electrons. The movement and interaction of atoms could thus be followed and photographed. In 1927 he shared with Compton the Nobel prize for physics, and in 1937 received the Copley medal.

(5) **Sir Daniel** (1816–92), Scottish archaeologist, born in Edinburgh, educated at the university there, had been secretary to the Scottish Society of Antiquaries when in 1853 he became professor of History and English Literature at Toronto. President of the university from 1881, he was knighted in 1888. His numerous works include *Edinburgh in the Olden Time* (1847; new ed. 1892), *Prehistoric Annals of Scotland* (1851; 2nd ed. 1863), *Chatterton* (1869), *Left-handedness* (1891) and *The Lost Atlantis* (1892).

(6) **Edmund** (1895–1972), American literary and social critic, born at Red Bank, New Jersey, studied at Princeton and became journalist, associate editor of the *New Republic* (1926–31) and book critic of the *New Yorker*. His outstanding critical works include *Axel's Castle* (1931) on the symbolist movement, *The Wound and the Bow* (1941) and on social questions, *The American Earthquake* (1958), &c. He also wrote verse, a number of plays including *This Room and This Gin and These Sandwiches* (1937), historical works such as *The Scrolls of the Dead Sea* (1955) and books on travel. He was married four times, his third wife being Mary McCarthy (q.v.).

(7) **Edmund Beecher** (1856–1939), American zoologist, born at Geneva, Illinois, studied at Yale and Johns Hopkins universities, and after several teaching posts became Da Costa professor of Zoology at Columbia University, New York. He contributed greatly to cytology and embryology. See his *The Cell in Development and Heredity* (1925).

(8) **Edward Adrian** (1872-1912), British physician, naturalist and explorer, born at Cheltenham, in 1901 went to the Antarctic with Scott in the *Discovery*. Back in England he did research on grouse diseases and made use of his skill as a watercolourist in preparing illustrations for books on birds and mammals. In 1910 he returned to the Antarctic with Scott in the *Terra Nova*, acting as chief of the expedition's scientific staff. One of the ill-fated polar party, he perished with his companions on the return journey from the pole in 1912. See G. Seaver, *Edward Wilson of the Antarctic* (1933).

(9) **Sir Erasmus** (1809–84), British surgeon, born in London, was a skilful dissector at the College of Surgeons in London, but was best known as a specialist on skin diseases. He published *Anatomist's Vademecum*, *Book of Diseases of the Skin*, *Report on Leprosy*, and *Egypt of the Past*. The great wealth he acquired by his practice he bestowed largely in benefactions to the poor and to science, and in promoting Egyptian research. He brought Cleopatra's Needle to London in 1878 at a cost of £10,000. President of the College of Surgeons, he was knighted in 1881.

(10) **Florence.** See VOLUSENUS.

(11) **(James) Harold** (1916–), British Labour politician, was born in Huddersfield and educated there, in Cheshire and at Oxford, where he became a lecturer in Economics in 1937. From 1943 to 1944 he was director of economics and statistics at the ministry of fuel and power. Becoming M.P. for Ormskirk in 1945, he was appointed parliamentary secretary to the ministry of works. In 1947 he became successively secretary for overseas trade and president of the Board of Trade till his resignation on the tide of Bevanism in April 1951. In 1951 and 1955 he was re-elected M.P. for Huyton, the division he had represented since 1950. The youngest Cabinet minister since Pitt, after 1956, when he headed the voting for the Labour 'shadow' Cabinet, he became the principal Opposition spokesman on economic affairs. An able and hard-hitting debater, in 1963 he succeeded Gaitskell as leader of the Labour party, becoming prime minister in October 1964 with a precariously small majority and being re-elected in April 1966 with comfortably large support. His government's economic plans were badly affected by the balance of payments crisis, leading to severe restrictive measures; while abroad he was faced with the Rhodesian problem (increasingly severe economic sanctions being applied), continued intransigence from de Gaulle over Britain's proposed entry into the Common Market, and the important question of Britain's new status in world politics as a lesser power. His party lost power in the 1970 general election and he became leader of the opposition. See Life by Smith (1967).

(12) **Harriette, *née* Dubochet** (1786–1855), English demi-mondaine, was born in Mayfair, London, of French descent. Her long career as a genteel courtesan began at the age of fifteen with the Earl of Craven; subsequent paramours included the Duke of Argyll, the Duke of Wellington, the Marquis of Worcester and a host of others. All these figured in her lively but libellous *Memoirs*, brought out in parts from 1825 to the accompaniment of a barrage of suggestive advance publicity aimed

at blackmail of the victims, most of whom echoed the celebrated outburst of Wellington on the occasion—' Publish and be damned!' See Life by A. Thirkell (1936), and L. Blanch, *The Game of Hearts* (1957).

(13) **Henry** (1812–73), American politician, vice-president of the United States, was the son of a farm-labourer at Farmington, N.H. Born Jeremiah Jones Colbath, he changed his name when he came of age, worked as a shoemaker, became prominent as an Abolitionist in the 'thirties, and was elected to the Massachusetts legislature and state senate. He was an active leader of the Free-soilers, assisted in forming the new Republican party, sat in the U.S. senate 1855–73, and then became vice-president of the United States. In the Civil War he was chairman of the military committee. He wrote *Rise and Fall of the Slave Power in America* (1872–1875). See Life by Russell and Nason (1872).

(14) **Sir Henry Hughes** (1864–1922), G.C.B., D.S.O., British field-marshal (1919), born at Edgeworthstown, Ireland, served in Burma, S. Africa, &c., and won fame in World War I, starting (1914) as director of Military Operations, and ending (1918) as chief of the Imperial General Staff. He received a baronetcy and a £10,000 grant in 1919. He was shot in London by two Irishmen on June 22, 1922, for having assisted the government of Northern Ireland. See Life by B. Collier (1961).

(15) **Henry Maitland, 1st Baron Wilson** (1881–1964), British field-marshal, was educated at Eton and commissioned in the ' Greenjackets '. He fought in South Africa and in World War I, and by 1937 was G.O.C. 2nd Division, Aldershot. On the outbreak of World War II he was appointed G.O.C.-in-C., Egypt, and after leading successfully the initial British advance in Libya and capturing Bardia, Tobruk and Benghazi, he was given command of the short and ill-fated Greek campaign. In 1943 he was appointed c.-in-c. Middle East, and in 1944 he became Supreme Allied Commander in what had become the relatively subordinate Mediterranean theatre. He headed the British Joint Staff Mission in Washington (1945–47) and in 1955 became constable of the Tower. He was raised to the peerage in 1946.

(16) **Horace Hayman** (1786–1860), English Orientalist, born in London, in 1808 went to India as assistant surgeon, and in the Calcutta mint became Leyden's assistant. In 1833 he became Boden professor of Sanskrit in Oxford, and soon after librarian at the East India House. His dictionary (1819) and grammar (1841) of Sanskrit, together with his other works, helped to lay the foundations of Indian philology in Europe.

(17) **James** (1805–60), British economist, born at Hawick, settled in business in London, and became an authority on the Corn Laws and the currency, founded the *Economist*, entered parliament as a Liberal in 1847, and was financial secretary to the Treasury, vice-president of the Board of Trade, and member of the council of India. See the *Economist* centenary volume (1943).

(18) **John**, pseud. **Christopher North** (1785–1854), Scottish journalist, was born at Paisley, attended Glasgow and Oxford Universities, becoming famous for his intellectual gifts and as an athlete. In 1807 he settled in Westmorland, where he purchased Elleray, overlooking Windermere, and associated with Wordsworth, Southey, Coleridge, De Quincey and their friends. In May 1811 he married and devoted himself to poetry, in 1812 publishing his *Isle of Palms*, and in 1816 *The City of Plague*. In 1815 the loss of his patrimony through an uncle's unjust stewardship obliged him to give up living constantly at Elleray and settle at his mother's house in Edinburgh. He was called to the Scottish bar, but on the starting in 1817 of *Blackwood's Magazine* he proffered his services; and he and Lockhart were the soul of ' Maga's ' success. Lockhart was withdrawn in 1826 to London; and Wilson was, not formally but practically, editor. In 1820 he was elected to the Edinburgh chair of Moral Philosophy. His works (ed. his nephew and son-in-law, Ferrier, 1855-58), include *Lights and Shadows of Scottish Life* (1822), *The Trials of Margaret Lyndsay* (1823) and *The Foresters* (1825), as well as thirty-nine out of seventy of the ' Noctes Ambrosianae ', which appeared in *Blackwood* (1822–35), and enjoyed an amazing vogue. See the Memoir by his daughter, Mrs Gordon (1862); a study by E. Swann (1934); Watts-Dunton's article in the *Athenaeum* (July 8, 1876); Saintsbury's *Essays* (1891); Mrs Oliphant's work on the Blackwoods (1897); and Sir G. Douglas's *Blackwood Group* (1897).

(19) **John** (1800–49), Scottish singer, born in Edinburgh, was first a compositor, then a precentor, and for years a favourite operatic tenor in London; and finally gave entertainments in Britain and America as an unsurpassed singer of Scots songs.

(20) **John Dover** (1881–1969), English Shakespearean scholar, was born in London and educated at Cambridge. After some years as teacher, lecturer and H.M. Inspector of adult education, he became professor first of Education at King's College, London (1924–35), then of Rhetoric and English Literature at the University of Edinburgh (1935–45). Made C.H. in 1936, he is best known for his Shakespearean studies, the result of penetrating and impartial research over many years, particularly on the problems in *Hamlet*. From 1921 till 1966 he was editor of the New Shakespeare series. Works include *Life in Shakespeare's England* (1911), *The Essential Shakespeare* (1932), *The Fortunes of Falstaff* (1943), *What Happens in Hamlet* (1935) and *Shakespeare's Sonnets—An Introduction for Historians and Others* (1963).

(21) **John** (1804–75), Scottish missionary, born, a farmer's son, near Lauder, and educated at Edinburgh University, ministered in Bombay from 1828 until his death, and was much consulted by government, especially during the crisis of 1857. He was twice president of the Bombay branch of the Asiatic Society, and was vice-chancellor of Bombay University. His chief writings were *The Parsi Religion* (1843) and *Lands of the Bible* (1847). See Life by Dr George Smith (1878). His son, **Andrew** (1830–81), edited

the *China Mail* and later the *Bombay Gazette*, but is best known for his account of Gordon's *Ever-Victorious Army* (1868) and his book on the Himalayas, *The Abode of Snow* (1875).

(22) **John Mackay** (1804–35), Scottish writer and editor, born in Tweedmouth, known for his *Tales of the Borders* (6 vols. 1834–40), originally issued in weekly numbers, and continued after his death for his widow with Alexander Leighton (1800–74) as editor.

(23) **Richard** (1714–82), British landscape-painter, born at Penegoes rectory, Montgomeryshire, after a visit to Italy (1749–56), gave up portrait-painting for landscape and anticipated Gainsborough and Constable in forsaking strait-laced classicism for a lyrical freedom of style. In London in 1760 he exhibited his *Niobe*, and became one of the leading painters of his time. Famous also was his *View of Rome from the Villa Madama*. In 1776 he became librarian to the Royal Academy. Works may be seen in the National Gallery and in the National Museum of Wales. See study by W. G. Constable (1953).

(24) **Sir Robert Thomas** (1777–1849), British soldier, born in London, having served in Belgium, against the Irish rebels (1798), and in the campaign of the Helder, commanded Abercromby's cavalry in Egypt, helped to conquer the Cape of Good Hope in 1806, and went with a mission to Prussia. In the Peninsula he helped to train the Portuguese army, and commanded a Spanish brigade at Talavera. He was attached in 1812 to the Russian army, in Germany and France was in the camp of the allies, and at Lützen commanded the Prussian reserve. Involved in Queen Caroline's affairs, he was dismissed from the army, but reinstated. In 1841 he became general, in 1842–49 was governor of Gibraltar, and in 1818–31 sat as a Liberal for Southwark. He wrote several works on military history. See his *Private Diary* (1861) and the Life by Randolph (1863).

(25) **Thomas** (1663–1755), English churchman, born at Burton in Cheshire, became Bishop of Sodor and Man in 1698. His *Principles of Christianity*, or 'the Manx Catechism' (1707), and *Instruction for the Indians* were combined to form *The Knowledge of Christianity made Easy* (1755). Better known are *Short Instructions for the Lord's Supper* (1733) and *Sacra Privata* (1781).

(26) **Thomas Woodrow** (1856–1924), American statesman, twenty-eighth president of the United States, born at Staunton, Virginia, studied at Princeton and Johns Hopkins, practised law at Atlanta, lectured at Bryn Mawr and Princeton, became president of Princeton in 1902, and governor of New Jersey in 1911, and in 1912 and 1916, as Democratic candidate, was elected president of the United States. Wilson's administration, ending in tragic failure and physical breakdown, is memorable for the prohibition and women's suffrage amendments of the constitution, trouble with Mexico, America's participation in the Great War, his part in the peace conference, his 'fourteen points' and championship of the League of Nations, and the Senate's rejection of the Treaty of Versailles. He wrote a *History of the American People* (1902), &c. See Life by R. S. Baker (1928–39), studies by Link (1947), Hugh-Jones (1947), H. Hoover (1958) and Latham (1959).

WILTON, Marie. See BANCROFT (4).

WINCHILSEA, Anne Finch, Countess of (1661–1720), English poetess, born at Sidmonton, was daughter of Sir William Kingsmill, and wife of Heneage Finch, 4th Earl of Winchilsea. Her longest poem, *The Spleen*, in Cowley's manner, was printed in 1701; her *Miscellany Poems* in 1713. She was a friend of Pope. See *Select Poems*, ed. J. M. Murry (1928), and E. Gosse, *Gossip in a Library* (1891).

WINCKELMANN, Johann Joachim (1717–1768), German archaeologist, was born at Stendal in Prussian Saxony. He studied the history of art, published a treatise on the imitation of the antique (1754), and was librarian to a cardinal at Rome (1755). In 1758 he examined the remains of Herculaneum, Pompeii, and Paestum, and went to Florence. He wrote a treatise on ancient architecture (1762), the epoch-making *Geschichte der Kunst des Alterthums* (1764), and *Monumenti Antichi Inediti* (1766). In 1763 he was made superintendent of Roman antiquities. He was murdered at Trieste. See Life by Justi (new ed. 1923) and study by Curtius (1941).

WINDAUS, Adolf, *vind'ows* (1876–1959), German chemist, educated at Freiburg and Berlin, was professor of Applied Medical Chemistry at Innsbruck and Göttingen. In 1928 he was awarded the Nobel prize for chemistry for his work on sterols, in particular for his discovery that ultraviolet light activates ergosterol and gives vitamin D_2. He was also an authority on cardiac poisons.

WINDHAM, William (1750–1810), English statesman, born at London, studied at Eton, Glasgow and Oxford, opposed Lord North (1778), and in 1784 was returned for Norwich. In 1783 he was principal secretary to Lord Northington, lord-lieutenant of Ireland. He followed Burke in his view of the French Revolution, and in 1794 became secretary-at-war under Pitt. He went out with Pitt in 1801, and eloquently denounced Addington's peace of Amiens (1801). This lost him his seat for Norwich, but he was elected for St Mawes in Cornwall, and on the return of the Grenville party to power (January 1806) became war and colonial secretary. He helped Cobbett to start his *Political Register* (1802), carried a scheme for limited service in the army (1806), and in 1806 was returned by New Romney, and in 1807 by Higham Ferrers. He went out when the Portland administration was formed. Windham was a member of the famous Literary Club, and stood by Johnson's deathbed. His brilliant talents were neutralized by an intellectual timidity, a morbid self-consciousness, and a fondness for paradox. See his speeches (1806, with Life by Amyot); his *Diary 1784–1810*, ed. Mrs Baring (1866); and the *Windham Papers* (1913).

WINDISCHGRÄTZ, Prince Alfred, *vind'ish-grets* (1787–1862), Austrian field-marshal, suppressed the revolution of 1848–49 at

Prague and Vienna, and defeated the Hungarians repeatedly, but was superseded after his defeat by them at Gödöllö.

WINDSOR, Duke and Duchess of. See EDWARD VIII.

WINDTHORST, Ludwig (1812–91), German Catholic politician, was born near Osnabrück, and became distinguished as advocate and politician in Hanover. After the absorption of Hanover by Prussia, he became leader of the Ultramontanes in the German parliament and chief opponent of Bismarck during the Kulturkampf.

WINER, Johann Georg Benedikt, *vee'nėr* (1789–1858), German New Testament scholar, born at Leipzig, became a professor of Theology there, at Erlangen in 1823, and at Leipzig again in 1832. The most important of his many works is his *Grammar of New Testament Greek* (1822, trans. Moulton 1882).

WINFRIED. See BONIFACE.

WINGATE, (1) Orde Charles (1903–44), British general, was educated at Charterhouse and R.M.A., joining the R.A. in 1922. With the Sudan Defence Force from 1928 to 1933, he later saw service in Palestine and Transjordan. In the Burma theatre in 1942, realizing that the only answer to penetration is counter-penetration, he obtained sanction to organize the Chindits—specially trained jungle-fighters. Supplied by air, they thrust far behind the enemy lines, gravely disrupting the entire supply system. Wingate was killed in a plane crash in Burma, in March 1944. See Halley, *With Wingate in Burma* (1946), Mosley, *Gideon Goes to War* (1955), and Life by C. Sykes (1959).

(2) **Sir Reginald, Bart.** (1861–1953), British general, entered the R.A. in 1880. Duty in India and Aden preceded his posting to the Egyptian Army. Service in Evelyn Wood's Nile Expedition and the Dongola campaign lead to his appointment as Sirdar. As governor-general of the Sudan from 1899 to 1916 he left his mark on a territory that owed its security and increasing prosperity to his lifelong devotion to its interests. He retired in 1922 after service as High Commissioner of Egypt. G.C.B. 1914, G.C.V.O. 1912, G.B.E. 1918, K.C.M.G. 1898. See his memoirs, *Wingate of the Sudan* (1955).

WINIFRED, St, legendary 7th-century Welsh saint, a noble British maiden, beheaded by Prince Caradog for repelling his unholy proposals. The legend relates that her head rolled down a hill, and where it stopped a spring gushed forth—famous still as a place of pilgrimage, Holywell in Flintshire. Her head was replaced by St Beuno.

WINKELRIED, Arnold von, *vin'kel-reet* (d. 1386), Swiss patriot, knight of Unterwalden, at the battle of Sempach (July 9, 1386), when the Swiss failed to break the compact line of Austrian spears, is said to have grasped as many pikes as he could reach, buried them in his bosom, and borne them by his weight to the earth. His comrades rushed into the breach, slaughtered the Austrians like sheep, and gained a decisive victory.

WINKLER, Clemens Alexander, *vink'lėr* (1838–1904), German chemist, born and educated at Freiberg, where he became professor of Chemistry, in 1886 discovered the element germanium. He also made important contributions to the study of the analysis of gases. He died at Dresden.

WINSLOW, (1) Edward (1595–1655), one of the Pilgrim Fathers, born at Droitwich, sailed in the *Mayflower*, and from 1624 was assistant governor or governor of the Plymouth colony, which he described and defended in *Good Newes from New England* (1624), *Hypocrisie Unmasked* (1646) and *New England's Salamander* (1647). Sent by Cromwell against the West Indies, he died at sea. His son, **Josiah** (1629–80), was assistant governor 1657–73, and then governor. In 1675 he was chosen general-in-chief of the United Colonies. His grandson, **John** (1702–1774), carried out the removal of the Acadians and **John Ancrum** (1811–73), descendant of one of Edward Winslow's brothers, commanded the *Kearsarge* in her action with the *Alabama*.

(2) **Forbes Benignus** (1810–74), London physician and specialist in mental illnesses, was a pioneer in the humane treatment of the insane. He was instrumental in gaining acceptance for the plea of insanity in criminal cases.

WINSOR, Justin (1831–97), American librarian and historian, born at Boston, Mass., studied at Harvard and Heidelberg; was librarian at Boston 1868–77, and then at Harvard; and published bibliographical works, *Memorial History of Boston* (1880–81), *Narrative History of America* (1884–90) and a Life of Columbus (1891).

WINSTANLEY, Henry (d. 1703), English architect and engraver, perished with his (the first) Eddystone Lighthouse in 1703, when it was swept away in a gale.

WINT, Peter de (1784–1849), English watercolourist, was born, of Dutch descent, at Stone, Staffordshire. His fame rests on his watercolour illustrations of English landscape, English architecture, and English country life. Among them are *The Cricketers*, *The Hay Harvest*, *Nottingham*, *Richmond Hill* and *Cows in Water*. Many of his works are in Lincoln Art Gallery. His watercolours are well represented in the Victoria and Albert Museum, which also owns the oils *A Cornfield* and *A Woody Landscape*. See Memoir by Armstrong (1888) and Redgrave's *David Cox and Peter de Wint* (1891).

WINTER, Jan Willem de (1750–1812), Dutch admiral from 1795, born on the island of Texel, was defeated by Duncan at Camperdown in 1797. He was ambassador to France 1798–1802.

WINTERHALTER, Franz Xaver (1805–73), German painter, made a successful portrait of Grand Duke Leopold of Baden and was appointed his court painter. In 1834 he went to Paris, with Queen Marie Amélie as his patron. One of his many royal sitters was Queen Victoria, and Winterhalter became the fashionable artist of the day. Some of his works are at Versailles, and he is represented in the British royal collection.

WINTHROP, (1) John (1588–1649), English colonist, father of (2), born at Groton in Suffolk, was bred to the law, and in 1629 was appointed governor of Massachusetts colony. He was re-elected governor, with brief intervals, during his life, and had more influence probably than any other man in forming the political institutions of the northern states of America. The first part of his *Journal* was published in 1790, and the whole in 1825–26 (later ed. with additions, 1853). See *Life and Letters*, by R. C. Winthrop (1864–67).

(2) **John** (1606–76), son of (1), governor of Connecticut, went to America in 1631, became a magistrate in Massachusetts, in 1635 went to Connecticut, and founded New London in 1646. In 1657 he was elected governor, and, except for one year, held that post till his death. He obtained from Charles II a charter uniting the colonies of Connecticut and New Haven, and was named first governor under it; and was the father of paper currency in America.

(3) **John**, known as **Fitz-John** (1639–1707), son of (2), served under Monk and in the Indian wars, was agent in London for Connecticut (1693–97), and governor of the colony from 1698. See *Winthrop Papers* (Mass. Hist. Soc. 1889).

(4) **John** (1714–79), physicist, descendant of (1), was born at Boston, and in 1738 became professor of Mathematics and Natural Philosophy at Harvard. In 1740 he observed the transit of Mercury. He published papers on earthquakes, comets, &c.

(5) **Robert Charles** (1809–94), orator descendant of (1), was admitted to the bar in 1831, and was in the state legislature 1834–40, then in congress, and in 1847–49 its speaker. In 1850–51 he was senator from Massachusetts. He published *Addresses and Speeches* (1852–86); a Life of the first John Winthrop; and *Washington, Bowdoin, and Franklin* (1876). See Memoir by son (1897).

(6) **Theodore** (1828–61), descendant of (1), born at New Haven, studied at Yale, was admitted to the bar (1855), but, volunteering in the Civil War, fell in battle at Great Bethel. His novels include *Cecil Dreeme* (1861), *John Brent* (1861) and *Edwin Brothertoft* (1862).

WINTON, Will McClain (1884–), American geologist from Florida, in 1930 became professor of Geology at Texas. He evolved a method of deciding the age of layers of sediments by studying the annual growth rings of bivalve shells buried in them.

WINZET, Ninian, *win'yet* (1518–92), Scottish churchman, born at Renfrew, and ordained priest in 1540, about 1552 became schoolmaster at Linlithgow, then provost of the collegiate church there. At the Reformation (1561) he was deprived of his office, came to Edinburgh, and as a Catholic wrote his *Tractatis* (1562). Forced to quit Scotland in 1563, he held office in the University of Paris. In 1574 he removed to the English College of Douai, and in 1577 became abbot at Ratisbon. See Hewison's edition of his works (Scottish Text Soc. 1891).

WISDOM, Arthur John Terence Dibber (1904–), English philosopher, professor of Philosophy at Cambridge from 1952, was profoundly influenced by Wittgenstein, but worked out his own characteristic, if elusive methods of dealing with philosophical paradoxes, which he showed need not always be written off as mere linguistic confusion, but may be invoked to point out unexpected similarities and dissimilarities in the use of sentences. See his collected philosophical papers, *Other Minds* (1952), *Philosophy and Psychoanalysis* (1953) and *Paradox and Discovery* (1965). He was president of the Aristotelian Society (1950–51). His cousin, **John Oulton Wisdom,** is professor of Philosophy at the London School of Economics.

WISE, Thomas James (1859–1937), English bibliophile and literary forger, born at Gravesend, began collecting books in his youth and built up a library of rare editions of the English poets and other works, including a collection of pamphlets and MSS., especially of the 19th-century romantics and the literary wing of the pre-Raphaelite movement. In 1934 certain pamphlets which he had sold to dealers and others for high prices were alleged to be faked and a sensational literary scandal ensued which was only checked by his death. His collection (the Ashley Library) was sold to the British Museum. See his *Letters to J. H. Wrenn* (1944); Carter and Pollard, *An Enquiry into the Nature of Certain 19th Century Pamphlets* (1934); W. Partington, *Forging Ahead* (1939); D. F. Foxon, *T. J. W. and the Pre-Restoration Drama* (1959), and studies ed. W. B. Todd (1960).

WISEMAN, (1) Nicholas Patrick Stephen (1802–65), cardinal, was born at Seville, of an Irish family settled in Spain. He was brought up at Waterford and Ushaw, entered the English College at Rome, received holy orders in 1825, and became rector of the college (1828). He established the *Dublin Review* (1836), and in 1840 was named Coadjutor Vicar-apostolic and president of St Mary's College at Oscott. In 1847 he was transferred to the London district. His appointment by the pope to be Roman Catholic Archbishop of Westminster and Cardinal in 1850 called forth a storm of religious excitement, which led to the passing of the Ecclesiastical Titles Assumption Act, when he published his conciliatory *Appeal on the Catholic Hierarchy*. One of his best known works was *Fabiola* (1854). See Memoir by G. White (1865), Lives by D. Gwynn (1929) and B. Fothergill (1963), J. J. O'Connor, *The Catholic Revival* (1942), and I. F. Reynolds, *Three Cardinals* (1958).

(2) **Richard** (d. 1679), surgeon to Charles II, was called 'the father of English surgery', and wrote *Seven Chirurgical Treatises*. See monograph by Sir T. Longmore (1892).

WISHART, George (*c*. 1513–46), Scottish reformer and martyr, belonged to a Kincardineshire family, his eldest brother King's Advocate. In 1538 he was schoolmaster in Montrose, where he incurred a charge of heresy for teaching the Greek New Testament. In 1539 he was in Bristol, and had to abjure heresy again. The next few years he spent on the Continent, and translated the Swiss *Confession of Faith*. In 1543 he accompanied a commission sent to Scotland by Henry VII in connection with the marriage of his son Edward and Mary Stuart; and he preached the Lutheran doctrine of justification by faith at Dundee and Montrose, in

Ayrshire and East Lothian. At Cardinal Beaton's instance he was arrested on January 16, 1546, and burned at St Andrews on March 1. Knox was first inspired by Wishart. It is doubtful whether he was or was not a Scotsman of the name who was concerned in a proposal made to Henry VIII for the assassination of Beaton. See David Laing, *Works of John Knox* (vols. i and vi); Lorimer's *Precursors of the Reformation*; C. Rogers's *Life of Wishart* (1876); and Maxwell's *Old Dundee* (1891).

WISLICENUS, Johannes Adolf (1835–1902), German chemist, born near Querfurt in Prussian Saxony, went to America as a young man, taught chemistry at Cambridge (U.S.), New York, Zürich and Würzburg, and in 1885 became professor at Leipzig. He had done important work, particularly on the lactic acids, and had edited a handbook of chemistry (1874–77).

WISTER, Owen (1860–1938), American author, born in Philadelphia, took a music degree at Harvard and intended to be a composer but won fame with his novel of cowboy life in Wyoming, *The Virginian* (1902). He wrote several less successful stories and a life of Theodore Roosevelt (1930).

WITHER, George (1588–1667), English poet, born at Bentworth, Hampshire, studied at Magdalen, Oxford (1604–06), and entered Lincoln's Inn in 1615. For his *Abuses Stript and Whipt* (1613) he was imprisoned. It is supposed that his satire addressed to the king (1614), together with the Earl of Pembroke's intercession, procured his release. In 1618 appeared *The Motto*, a curious piece of self-confession. His finest poem, *Fair Virtue, or the Mistress of Philarete* (1622), though often uneven, shows exquisite fancy. There followed his *Hymns and Songs of the Church* (1623), *Psalms of David translated* (1631), *Emblems* (1634), and *Hallelujah* (1641). Now a fiery Puritan, in 1642 he sold his estate to raise a troop of horse for parliament, but was taken prisoner. Later Cromwell made him major-general in Surrey and Master of the Statute Office. At the Restoration he lost his position and property, and, on suspicion of having written the *Vox Vulgi*, a satire on the parliament of 1661, was imprisoned. He was released in 1663. His poetry fell into almost complete oblivion, but the praises of Southey, Sir Egerton Brydges, Hallam, and especially Charles Lamb revived interest in his work. His *Juvenilia* (1622) were reprinted by the Spenser Society (1870–72). See Massingham, *Seventeenth Century English Verse* (1919).

WITHERING, William (1741–99), English physician, born at Wellington in Shropshire and educated at Edinburgh, wrote a *British Flora* and *An Account of the Foxglove* (1785), introducing digitalis as a drug for cardiac disease. He was the first to see the connection between dropsy and heart disease.

WITHERSPOON, John (1723–94), Scottish theologian, born at Yester near Haddington, was minister at Beith and Paisley, and in 1768 emigrated to America and became president of the college and pastor at Princeton. He was a representative of New Jersey to the Continental Congress, and was one of the signatories of the Declaration of Independence. His writings include *Ecclesiastic Characteristics* (1753), against the Moderates; *Serious Enquiry into the Nature and Effects of the Stage* (1757); and two on *Justification* (1756) and *Regeneration* (1764).

WITSIUS, Hermann (1636–1708), Dutch Calvinist theologian, became in 1675 a professor at Franeker, in 1680 at Utrecht, and in 1698 at Leyden. His great work is *De Oeconomia Foederum Dei cum hominibus* (trans. 1763). Other writings translated are *Antinomians and Neonomians* (1807), *The Creed* (1823), and *The Lord's Prayer* (1839).

WITT, De. See De Witt, Guizot.

WITTGENSTEIN, Ludwig Josef Johann, *vit'gen-shtīn* (1889–1951), Austrian philosopher, was born April 26 in Vienna, the son of a wealthy Jewish engineer, and was baptized a Roman Catholic. Educated privately until fourteen, he studied engineering at Berlin and Manchester (1908–11), where he designed a jet reaction propeller, became seriously interested in mathematics and finally mathematical logic, which he studied, on Frege's advice, under Russell at Cambridge (1912–13). Moore and Russell soon regarded Wittgenstein as a friend and colleague rather than as a student. Wittgenstein extended Russell's doctrines into a full-blown scheme for a logically perfect language, a perfect instrument for assertion and foolproof against philosophical nonsense. Inheriting considerable wealth, he gave it away to support the poets Trakl and Rilke. He served as an Austrian artillery officer during World War I, was captured by the Italians and ended the war in a P.O.W. camp near Monte Cassino, where he completed the *Tractatus Logico-philosophicus* (1921, Leipzig) which was published as a parallel English-German text (1922, London) with a masterly introduction by Russell, of which, however, Wittgenstein strongly disapproved. According to the *Tractatus*, all significant assertion can be analysed into compound propositions containing logical constants and are 'truth functions' of 'elementary propositions' which do not. An 'elementary proposition' (one kind of fact) symbolizes a real or 'atomic fact' or possibility (*Sachverhalt*). But how can one kind of fact symbolize another, how does language symbolize the world? Wittgenstein's fundamental thesis is that this correspondence can only be shown or 'pictured' in language, but not stated, for this would require an extra-linguistic and extra-worldly medium for expression and 'whereof one cannot speak, thereof one must be silent'. All speculative philosophy, ethics and aesthetics as well as the *Tractatus* (in showing this fallacy by the use of language) attempt to utter the unspeakable. The last, a merely elucidatory aid to seeing the world rightly, must also be discarded. Philosophy becomes merely a corrective activity. Wittgenstein, true to his doctrines, gave up philosophy, became an elementary village schoolmaster in Austria (1920–26), served for a time as a monastery gardener's assistant, designed on the functional lines of Loos a mansion for his sister (1926–28), turned to sculpture and was only reluctantly induced to return to philosophy at Cambridge by his English friends, having for some time corresponded with the 'Vienna Circle' of logical positivists. He was a fellow of Trinity College, Cambridge (1930–36), and professor (1939–47), interrupting his duties to become a wartime porter in Guy's Hospital and in a laboratory at Newcastle. *The Blue and Brown Books* (posthumously, 1958) are notes taken by his pupils (1933–35) and form the beginnings of the *Philosophical Investigations* (posthumously, English-German parallel text, 1953), an album of arguments compiled in a solitary hut on the Galway coast in Ireland in 1948. These repudiate some of the characteristic *Tractatus* doctrines, particularly the reduction of ordinary language to a logically perfect instrument of assertion. By means of 'language games', he examined the varieties of linguistic usage of certain philosophically important expressions, as a means of curing philosophically perplexity. He found that the varieties of linguistic usages of a word in many cases pointed to a 'family resemblance' between them rather than to one single essential meaning. Philosophy was for him still a therapeutic activity, even if the methods had changed. He became a naturalized British subject in 1938. His austere mode of living, his distaste for any form of pretence, made him an exacting companion, even for his friends. In the first half of the 20th century he was the dominating philosophical figure of the English-speaking world. He died of cancer in Cambridge, April 29, 1951. See also *Philosophical Remarks on the Foundations of Mathematics* (1956), memoir by N. Malcolm and G. H. von Wright (1958), studies on the *Tractatus* by E. Stenius (1959) and G. E. M. Anscombe (1959), the later philosophy by D. Pole (1958) and polemically critical works by G. R. G. Mure, *Retreat from Truth* (1958), and E. Gellner, *Words and Things* (1959).

WODEHOUSE, Pelham Grenville (1881–), novelist, English by birth, since 1955 an American citizen, started work in a London bank but gave this up in favour of free-lancing. To begin with he wrote school stories, in one of which the popular Psmith made his first appearance (see the later *Psmith in the City*, *Leave it to Psmith*, &c.). In 1918 the novel *Piccadilly Jim* was a great success, and Wodehouse was established as a humorous writer. With the creation of Bertie Wooster and his 'gentleman's gentleman' Jeeves (*The Inimitable Jeeves*, 1924, &c.), his position was assured as the greatest humorous novelist of his time. A prolific writer, he produced a succession of sparkling novels, short stories, sketches and librettos (with Guy Bolton he collaborated in many musical comedies). In 1939 he was living in France, where he was overtaken by the Germans. During the war years he incurred criticism for his Nazi-controlled broadcasts. Subsequently he has lived in the U.S.A., of which he is now a citizen. See the autobiographical *Performing Flea* (1953) and *Over Seventy* (1957). See study by R. Usborne (1961).

WODROW, Robert (1679–1734), Scottish church historian, born at Glasgow, studied theology under his father, who was professor of Divinity there; in 1703 he became minister of Eastwood. His *History of the Sufferings of the Church of Scotland 1660–88* (1721–22) was dedicated to George I. Posthumous works include *Lives of the Scottish Reformers* (1834–45), *Analecta, or a History of Remarkable Providences* (1842–43), &c.

WOFFINGTON, Margaret ('Peg') (1720–1760), Irish actress, was a Dublin bricklayer's daughter. From seventeen to twenty she played on the Dublin stage, and in 1740 appeared at Covent Garden as Sylvia in *The Recruiting Officer*. Her beauty and vivacity carried all hearts by storm. David Garrick was one of her admirers. On May 3, 1757, she broke down, and left the stage never to return. Her last days were given to charity and good works. See Lives by Daly (1888) and Molloy (1884), and the novel *Peg Woffington* by Charles Reade (1853).

WÖHLER, Friedrich, *vœl'ėr* (1800–82), German chemist, born near Frankfurt, educated at Heidelberg, became professor at Göttingen in 1836. He isolated aluminium (1827) and beryllium (1828), and discovered calcium carbide, from which he obtained acetylene. His synthesis of urea from ammonium cyanate in 1828 revolutionized organic chemistry.

WOHLGEMUTH. See WOLGEMUT.

WOLCOT, John, pseud. **Peter Pindar** (1738–1819), English satirist, born at Dodbrooke, Devon, studied medicine for seven years, took his M.D. at Aberdeen (1767), and, going to Jamaica, became physician-general of the island. He returned to England to take orders, but soon started medical practice at Truro. Here he discovered the talents of young Opie, and with him in 1780 removed to London, to devote himself to writing audacious squibs and satires in verse. His sixty or seventy poetical pamphlets (1778–1818) include *The Lousiad*, *The Apple-dumplings and a King*, *Whitbread's Brewery visited by their Majesties*, *Bozzy and Piozzi*, and *Lyrical Odes* on the Royal Academy Exhibitions. Although witty and fluent, his works were coarse and ephemeral. See *Blackwood's Magazine* for July 1868, and H. Walker, *English Satire and Satirists* (1925).

WOLF, (1) Friedrich August (1759–1824), German classical scholar, born at Hagewrode, went to Göttingen in 1777. In 1779, while teacher at Ilfeld, he established his fame by an edition of Plato's *Symposium*, and in 1783 he became professor at Halle. He edited Demosthenes' *Oratio adversus Leptinem* (1789), and in his *Prolegomena ad Homerum* (1795) he unfolded his bold theory that the *Odyssey* and *Iliad* are composed of ballads by different minstrels, strung together by later editors—a view defended in his spirited *Briefe an Heyne* (1797). In 1801 Wolf cast doubts upon the genuineness of some orations of Cicero. After 1806 he became a member of the Academy of Sciences at Berlin, helped to re-organize the university, and became a professor. The *Darstellung der Alterthumswissenschaft* (1807) is his most finished work. See Mark Pattison's *Essays* (i 1889), and Sandys's *Classical Scholarship* (iii 1908).

(2) **Hugo** (1860–1903), Austrian composer, chiefly of songs, born at Windischgraz in Styria, was destined for the family leather business, but early turned to music. For a time he studied without satisfaction at the Vienna Conservatoire, then earned a meagre living by teaching and conducting. From 1884 to 1888 he was music critic of the *Wiener Salonblatt*, violently attacking Brahms and extolling Wagner. All this time he was composing, but his best work came from 1888 onwards. It includes the Mörike set of 53 songs (1888), settings of poems by Goethe (1888–89), the *Italienisches Leiderbuch* of Heyse and Geibel (1889–90), and three sonnets of Michelangelo (1897). He also wrote an opera, *Der Corregidor* (1895), and other works. He was at his best in his treatment of short lyrical poems, to many of which he gave new significance by means of the sensitive commentary of his settings. For the most part he lived in poverty. In 1897 he became insane. After a brief period of recovery he was confined from 1898 onwards in the asylum at Steinhof near Vienna, where he died. See books by Decsey (1919), Newman (1907) and F. Walker (1951).

(3) or **Wolff, Johann Christian von** (1679–1754), German philosopher, born at Breslau, studied at Jena, lectured at Leipzig, and became professor at Halle. His system of philosophy quickly spread; but attacked by pietistic colleagues and ordered in 1723 to quit Prussia, he got a chair at Marburg. Frederick the Great recalled him (1740) to be professor of the Law of Nations, and he became in 1743 chancellor of the university, and was made Baron of the Empire by the Elector of Bavaria. Wolf systematized and popularized the philosophy of Leibniz. His *Theologia Naturalis* (1737) gave a great impulse to rationalism. See his Autobiography, ed. Wuttke (1841), and German works by Frauendienst (1927) and Joesten (1931).

(4) **Maximilian Franz Joseph Cornelius** (1863–1932), German astronomer, educated at Heidelberg, where he was born, and Stockholm, became professor of Astronomy at Heidelberg (1896) and director of the Königstuhl astrophysical observatory there. He invented the photographic method of discovering asteroids, and with Barnard was the first to appreciate ' dark ' nebulae in the sky.

WOLFE, (1) **Charles** (1791–1823), Irish poet, born at Dublin, went to Winchester, and in 1814 took his B.A. at Dublin. He is remembered for his poem *The Burial of Sir John Moore*, which appeared anonymously in 1817 and at once caught the admiration of the public. Wolfe in 1817 became curate of Ballyclog in Tyrone, and then rector of Donoughmore. His *Remains* were published in 1825 by Russell, and his poems by Litton Falkiner in 1903 (each with a memoir).

(2) **Humbert** (1885–1940), English poet and critic, born in Milan, was educated at Bradford and at Wadham College, Oxford. In 1908 he entered the Civil Service, becoming in 1938 deputy secretary to the Ministry of Labour. He was created C.B.E. in 1918 and C.B. in 1925. He published *London Sonnets* (1919), *Lampoons* (1925), *Requiem* (1927), and several other collections of verse, all marked by deep feeling and meticulous craftsmanship. His critical writings include *Notes on English Verse Satire* (1929) and studies of Tennyson, Herrick, Shelley and George Moore. See his autobiographical *Now A Stranger* (1933) and *The Upward Anguish* (1938).

(3) **James** (1727–59), British soldier, was born at Westerham vicarage, Kent, the eldest son of General Edward Wolfe (1685–1759). In 1742 he received an ensign's commission, in 1743 fought at Dettingen, in 1745–46 served against the Scottish Jacobites at Falkirk and Culloden, and in 1747 was wounded at Lawfeldt. In 1749–57 he was engaged in garrison duty in Scotland and England. In the mismanaged expedition against Rochefort (1757) he was quartermaster-general; in 1758, with the rank of colonel, he received from Pitt the command of a brigade in the expedition against Cape Breton under General Amherst; and to him was mainly due the capture of Louisburg. Pitt was now organizing his grand scheme for expelling the French from Canada, and the expedition for the capture of Quebec he entrusted to Wolfe's command. As major-general, and commanding 9000 men, Wolfe sailed from England in February 1759, and on June 26 landed below Quebec. The attack on Montcalm's strong position proved one of stupendous difficulty, and Wolfe was completely foiled. But at last, scaling the cliffs at a point insufficiently guarded, at dawn on September 13 he found himself on the Plains of Abraham. After a short struggle the French were routed; Montcalm (q.v.) was killed; Quebec capitulated; and its fall decided the fate of Canada. Wolfe died in the hour of victory. His body was buried in Greenwich church. See Lives by Wright (1864), Bradley (1895), Willson (1909), Waugh (1929), Grinell-Milne (1963), and studies by Parkman (1884), Findlay (1928).

(4) **Thomas Clayton** (1900–38), American novelist, born at Asheville, N.C., studied in the ' 47 workshop ' at Harvard. His *Look Homeward, Angel* (1929) and *Of Time and the River* (1935), first of a projected series of six related novels, enjoyed a great success. *The Web and the Rock* (1939) and *You Can't Go Home Again* (1941) were brought out after his early death from pneumonia. See study by P. H. Johnson (1947).

WOLFENDEN, Sir John Frederick (1906–), British governmental adviser on social questions, born at Halifax, was fellow and tutor in Philosophy at Magdalen College, Oxford (1929–34), headmaster of Uppingham School (1934–44) and Shrewsbury (1944–50), and vice-chancellor of Reading University from 1950. He is best known as the chairman of the Royal Commission on homosexuality and prostitution, the report of which (1957) is known by his name. He was also chairman of another royal commission (1960) on sport.

WOLFF, (1) **G. W.** See HARLAND.

(2) **Sir Henry Drummond** (1830–1908), son of (3), English diplomat, was educated at Rugby, and after holding several Foreign Office appointments, entered parliament in 1874, becoming one of the 'Fourth Party'. In 1892 he was made ambassador to Spain.

(3) **Joseph** (1795–1862), father of (2), a German Jew who turned Roman Catholic in 1812, but came to England and entered the Anglican Church in 1819, becoming a missionary to the Jews in the East. His adventurous journey to Bokhara (1843), to inquire into the fate of Conolly and Stoddart, is described in *Mission to Bokhara* (1845) and *Travels and Adventures* (1860). He died vicar of Ile-Brewers, Somerset.

(4) **Kaspar Friedrich** (1733–94), German anatomist and physiologist, founder of embryology, was born at Berlin, was a surgeon in the Seven Years' War, and died a member of the Academy at St Petersburg.

WOLF-FERRARI, Ermanno, *volf-fer-ahr'ee* (1876–1948), Italo-German composer, born in Venice. Sent to Rome to study painting, he turned to music and became a pupil of Rheinberger, in Munich. In 1899 he returned to Venice, where his first opera was unsuccessfully produced in the following year. His later operas were equally successful in both Italy and Germany. From 1902 to 1912 he was director of the Liceo Benedetto Marcello, in Venice. Wolf-Ferrari composed choral and chamber works, and music for organ and piano as well as the operas, notably *Susanna's Secret* (1909), *The Jewels of the Madonna* (1911) and *School for Fathers* (1906).

WOLFIT, Sir Donald (1902–68), English actor-manager, born in Newark-on-Trent. He began his stage career in 1920, and made his first London appearance in 1924 in *The Wandering Jew*. With his own company, formed in 1937, he played Shakespeare in the provinces, and during World War II he instituted the first London season of 'lunchtime Shakespeare' during the Battle of Britain. Known especially for his portrayal of Shakespearean heroes and of Jonson's Volpone, he was created C.B.E. in 1950 and knighted in 1957. He also appeared in several films and on television. His autobiography, *First Interval*, appeared in 1954.

WOLFRAM VON ESCHENBACH (fl. beginning of 13th cent.), German poet, born near Anspach in Bavaria, lived some time in the Wartburg near Eisenach, at the court of the Count of Thuringia, where he met Walther von der Vogelweide. Besides *Parzival* he left seven *Love Songs*, a short epic, *Willehalm*, and two fragments called *Titurel*. The *Parzival* is an epic, having for its main theme the history of the Grail, and is one of the most notable poems of the Middle Ages. From it Wagner derived the libretto of his *Parsifal*. See study by Richey (1958).

WOLGEMUT, Michael, *vōl'ge-moot* (1435–1519), German painter and engraver, born at Nuremberg, the son of Valentin Wolgemut, also an engraver, was the master of Albrecht Dürer (q.v.), who did a portrait of him. His altarpieces show some Flemish influence. See study by Stadler (1913).

WOLLASTON, *wool'-*, (1) **William** (1659–1724), English philosophical writer, author of the *Religion of Nature*, born at Coton near Stafford, studied at Sidney Sussex, Cambridge, took orders in 1681, and in 1682 became assistant master at Birmingham, but in 1688 inherited an ample estate. His one notable work was printed in 1722 for private circulation, but soon reached an issue of over 10,000 copies. See Life prefixed to 6th ed. (1738).

(2) **William Hyde** (1766–1828), English chemist and natural philosopher, was born at East Dereham, Norfolk, the second son of the Rev. Francis Wollaston (1731–1815), who was the grandson of (1), rector of Chiselhurst, and an astronomer. He went to Caius College, Cambridge, took his M.D. in 1793, and gained a fellowship. Starting practice as a physician at Bury St Edmunds in 1789, he soon removed to London; but being beaten in a competition for the post of physician to St George's Hospital in 1800, he vowed to devote himself to scientific research. His researches were extremely fruitful both in chemistry and in optics. He discovered new compounds connected with the production of gouty and urinary concretions; and in the ore of platinum distinguished two new metals, palladium (1804) and rhodium (1805). By his method of rendering platinum ductile he made £30,000; and other practical discoveries were also highly lucrative. Among his contributions to optics were the reflecting goniometer, the camera lucida, the discovery of the dark lines in the solar spectrum and of the invisible rays beyond the violet. He did much to establish the theory of definite proportions, and demonstrated the identity of galvanism and electricity. He was elected F.R.S. (1793), its second secretary (1806), and F.R.A.S. (1828). See his thirty-nine memoirs in the *Philosophical Trans.* for 1809–29, and George Wilson's *Religio Chemici* (1862).

WOLLSTONECRAFT, Mary. See GODWIN.

WOLSELEY, Garnet Joseph, Viscount, *woolz'li* (1833–1913), British soldier, was born of an old Staffordshire line at Golden Bridge House, County Dublin, June 4, and entered the army in 1852. He served in the Burmese war of 1852–53, and was dangerously wounded; in the Crimea he lost the use of one eye, and received the cross of the *Légion d'honneur*. He was in India during the Mutiny, and in the Chinese war of 1860. Next year he went to Canada, and in 1870 put down the Red River rebellion under Riel without losing a man. On the outbreak of the Ashanti war Wolseley, now K.C.M.G., was appointed to the command, and on his return received the thanks of parliament and a grant of £25,000. In 1875, now a major-general, he was dispatched to Natal; in 1876 he was nominated a member of the Indian Council. In 1878 he was made high commissioner in Cyprus, and in 1879 held supreme civil and military command in Natal and the Transvaal. He was commander-in-chief of the expedition to Egypt in 1882, received the thanks of parliament, was gazetted Baron Wolseley of Cairo and of Wolseley in Stafford and received a large money grant. He was made general in the same year, viscount after the Sudan campaigns of 1884–85, and field-marshal in 1894. In 1890–95 he was commander-in-chief in Ireland, and in 1895–1900 commander-in-chief of the entire army. Besides his *Story of a Soldier's Life* (1903–04), he wrote *Narrative of the War with China in 1860* (1862), the *Soldier's Pocket Book*, *Field Manœuvres* (1872), a novel (*Marley Castle*, 1877), a Life of Marlborough (2 vols. 1894),

The Decline and Fall of Napoleon (1895), and several essays. See his *Story of a Soldier's Life* (1903) and the Lives by Maurice and Arthur (1934) and J. H. Lehmann (1964).

WOLSEY, Thomas (*c.* 1475–1530), English cardinal, was born at Ipswich, the son of a prosperous butcher and grazier. He took early and fruitful advantage of the educational facilities offered by Magdalen College, Oxford, succeeding to a fellowship and obtaining a post as master in the seminary attached to the foundation. After nineteen years at Oxford, the powerful Dorset interest secured him the living at Lymington in Somerset. Influence also brought him the post of secretary and domestic chaplain to the Archbishop of Canterbury. With the primate's death in 1502 Wolsey was endowed with the chaplaincy of Calais, where the ability with which he discharged his duties brought him to the notice of Henry VII. Appointed a chaplain to the king (1507), he was careful to cultivate the favour of Bishop Fox, the lord privy seal, and that of the treasurer of the royal household, Sir Thomas Lovel. Entrusted with the transaction of much of the sovereign's private business, the skill in negotiation he exhibited in his embassies to Scotland and the Low Countries brought him the lucrative deanery of Lincoln. With the accession of Henry VIII, Wolsey sedulously strove to render himself indispensable. From almoner to royal councillor, from the registrarship of the Order of the Garter to a Windsor canonry, his progress to the deanery of York was steady and encouraging for a pluralist whose growing need for money was only matched by his increasing arrogance. In 1513 Wolsey accompanied the king to the seat of war in France; and with the English monarch ready to come to terms with Francis I, Wolsey's conduct of the negotiations brought him the bishopric of Lincoln, the archbishopric of York (1514) and a cardinate (1515), and the promise of Gallic support for further claims to preferment. In the same year, he was made lord chancellor and his very considerable estates were augmented by Henry's award of the administration of the see of Bath and Wells and the temporalities of the wealthy abbey of St Alban's. Wolsey even hazarded a breach of the Statute of Praemunire by accepting the appointment of papal legate from Leo X. Deep in the King's confidence, the Cardinal had attained a position more powerful than that enjoyed by any minister of the Crown since Becket. As the controller of England's foreign policy he lent support to France and Germany alternately, serving his own interests, but also seeking a powerful position for England in Europe. His aim in England was absolute monarchy with himself behind the throne. He established Cardinal (Christ Church) College at Oxford and a grammar school at Ipswich. Wolsey's downfall originated in his prevarication and evasiveness over the question of Henry's divorce from Catherine of Aragon. This not only provoked the king's angry impatience but aroused the bitter enmity of the Boleyn faction and of many other enemies, outraged by the Cardinal's haughtiness, his parvenu display, and his punishing fiscal exactions. In effect, Wolsey's outmoded assertion of the ecclesiastical right to dominate secular policy had proved entirely unacceptable to the upstart but powerful aristocracy of the counting-house bred by the new spirit of mercantilism. Prosecuted under the Statute of Praemunire in 1529, the Cardinal had to surrender the Great Seal and retire to Winchester. Impeachment by the House of Lords was followed by the forfeiture of all his property to the Crown. Arrested again on a charge of high treason, he died—on November 29, 1530—while journeying from his York diocese to London. See works by Brewer (1884), Froude (1891), Innes (1905), Pollard (1929), Belloc (1930), C. Ferguson, *Naked to Mine Enemies* (1958), and the earliest Life of Wolsey, by George Cavendish, his gentleman usher ed. R. S. Sylvester (1959)

WOLVERHAMPTON, Henry Hartley Fowler, 1st Viscount (1830–1911), English Liberal politician, born at Sunderland, mayor of Wolverhampton 1863, its M.P. 1880, was under-secretary in the Home Office (1884), financial secretary to the Treasury (1886), president of the Local Government Board (1892), secretary for India (1894), and chancellor of the Duchy of Lancaster (1895), and lord president of the Council (1908–10). He was created viscount in 1908.

WOMBWELL, George (1788–1850), a London bootmaker, became a noted menagerie proprietor.

WOOD, (1) **Sir Andrew** (*c.* 1455–1539), Scottish naval commander, belonged to Largo and was associated with James IV in his efforts to build up a Scottish navy. He was specially successful against English vessels raiding in the Firth of Forth.

(2) or **À Wood, Anthony** (1632–95), English antiquary, born at Oxford, studied at Merton College 1647–52, and being of independent means, devoted himself to heraldry and antiquarian studies. The delegates of the university press had translated his History of Oxford into Latin as *Historia et Antiquitates Universitatis Oxoniensis* (1674). Wood was ill-satisfied with the translation, and made a new copy of his English MS., which was not published until 1786–96. His great *Athenae Oxonienses; an Exact history of all the Writers and Bishops who had their Education in Oxford from 1500 to 1690, to which are added the Fasti or Annals for the said time* was published in 1691–92. Other works were *The Ancient and Present State of the City of Oxford* (1773) and the ill-natured *Modius Salium, a Collection of Pieces of Humour* (1751). A third volume of the *Athenae* is included in the second edition (1721). The Autobiography (1848) is included in *The Life and Times of Wood* (Oxford Hist. Soc., 5 vols., 1891–1900), ed. by Andrew Clark, and abridged by L. Powys (1932).

(3) **Sir Charles.** See HALIFAX (2).

(4) **Christopher** (1901–30), English artist, born at Knowsley. Between 1920 and 1924 he wandered over most of Europe, and painted in various styles, but it was in his landscapes of Cornwall and Brittany that

he found himself as an artist. They are simple and apparently childlike in conception, but they show a fine sensitivity to colour, light, and atmosphere. See monograph by Eric Newton (1959).

(5) **Edward Frederick Lindley.** See HALIFAX (3).

(6) **Haydn** (1882–1959), English composer and violinist, was born in Slaithwaite, Yorkshire. He studied at the Royal College of Music and was selected to play at the opening of the College's Concert Hall. He worked for a time in music halls with his wife, Dorothy Court, for whom he wrote a large number of ballads, but withdrew from these activities as his serious compositions attracted attention after his Fantasy String Quartet won the second prize in the first Cobbett Chamber Music Competition. Wood composed very prolifically for orchestra, brass band, chamber music groups and voices. Of his ballads, the best known is 'Roses of Picardy'.

(7) **Mrs Henry,** *née* **Ellen Price** (1814–87), English novelist, born at Worcester, married Henry Wood, a ship agent living in France, and after his death settled in London, and wrote for magazines. *East Lynne* (1861) had an almost unexampled success. She never rose above the commonplace in her many novels, but showed some power in the analysis of character in her anonymous *Johnny Ludlow* stories (1874–80). In 1867 she acquired the monthly *Argosy*, and her novels went on appearing in it long after her death. See *Memorials* of her by her son (1895).

(8) **Sir Henry Evelyn** (1838–1919), British soldier, born at Cressing vicarage, Braintree, entered the navy in 1852, and served in the Crimea in the Naval Brigade. As cavalry officer and brigade-major he fought in the Indian Mutiny, receiving the Victoria Cross and the thanks of the Indian government. As lieutenant-colonel he was with Wolseley during the Ashanti war. He was called to the bar in 1874, but commanded a column through the Zulu war. Created K.C.B. in 1879, he had a share in the Transvaal war (1880–81). As G.C.M.G. he received the thanks of parliament for his services in Egypt in 1882, and in the same year became commander-in-chief of the Egyptian army. From 1886 onwards he held home appointments. In 1897 he was made adjutant-general of the army, in 1903 field-marshal. He wrote *The Crimea in 1854–94*, on Cavalry, *From Midshipman to Field-marshal* (1906), and *Winnowed Memories* (1917).

(9) **Sir Henry Joseph** (1869–1944), English conductor, born in London, with Robert Newman founded the Promenade Concerts which he conducted annually from 1895 until his death. As 'Paul Klenovsky' he arranged Bach's Organ Toccata and Fugue in D minor as an orchestral work. He composed operettas and an oratorio, *Saint Dorothea* (1889), but his international reputation was gained as conductor of the Queen's Hall symphony and promenade concerts. He was knighted in 1911. See *My Life of Music* (1938), and book by J. Wood (1954).

(10) **John** (*c.* 1705–54), English architect, 'of Bath', was responsible for many of the best-known streets and buildings of Bath, such as the North and South Parades, Prior Park and other houses. His son **John** (d.1782) designed the Crescent, the Assembly Rooms, &c.

(11) **Sir Kingsley** (1881–1943), English statesman, born in London, was trained as a solicitor, entered parliament in 1918 as Conservative member for Woolwich West, was knighted in 1919, and after holding several junior ministerial offices became postmaster-general (1931–35), minister of health (1935–38), secretary of state for air (1938–40), and chancellor of the exchequer (1940–43), in which capacity he devised the pay-as-you-earn income-tax system.

(12) **Robert Williams** (1868–1955), American physicist, born at Concord, Mass., educated at Harvard, Chicago and Berlin, was professor of Experimental Physics at the Johns Hopkins University (1901–38). He carried out researches on optics, atomic and molecular radiation, sound waves, &c.; wrote *Physical Optics* (1905), some fiction, and illustrated nonsense verse, *How to Tell the Birds from the Flowers* (1907).

(13) **William** (1671–1744), a London ironfounder, to whom was granted a share of the profits from coining 'Wood's Halfpence' for Ireland. Swift's Drapier's Letters (1724) denounced the job with such effect that the patent was cancelled and Wood was compensated with a pension.

WOODFALL, Henry Sampson (1739–1805), English printer and journalist, published the anonymous letters of 'Junius' in the *Public Advertiser* (1769–72) and in book form (1772 and later editions). Associated with him were his brother, **William** (1746–1803), and his son and successor, **George** (1767–1844).

WOODS, Margaret Louisa (1856–1945), English writer, daughter of Dr Bradley, dean of Westminster, was born at Rugby, and in 1879 was married to the Rev. Henry George Woods, from 1887 till his resignation in 1897 president of Trinity College, Oxford. She published novels such as *A Village Tragedy* (1887), *The Invader* (1907, rev. 1922), *A Poet's Youth* (1924), and verse such as *Lyrics and Ballads* (1889), *Collected Poems* (1913).

WOODVILLE, (1) **Elizabeth** (*c.* 1437–92), eldest of the thirteen children of Sir Richard Woodville (afterwards Lord and Earl Rivers) and the Dowager Duchess of Bedford, married first Sir John Grey, who fell at St Albans (1461), and next, in 1464, Edward IV. She died in the abbey of Bermondsey. Her eldest daughter, **Elizabeth** (1465–1503), in 1486 married Henry VII.

(2) **Richard.** See RIVERS.

WOODWARD, (1) **Sir Arthur Smith** (1864–1944), British geologist, born at Macclesfield, was keeper of geology at the British Museum (1901–24) when he was knighted. He did notable work on fossil fishes, but is chiefly remembered for his part in the controversy over the Piltdown Man. He was the one to whom Charles Dawson (q.v.) gave the skull for identification, and his firm conviction that the remains were human was a main reason for the success of the hoax. See his *Outlines of Vertebrate Palaeontology* (1898).

(2) **Robert Burns** (1917–), U.S. chemist,

born at Boston, Mass., professor of Science at Harvard University since 1950 and director of the Woodward Research Institute at Basel since 1963. He was awarded the Nobel prize for chemistry in 1965 for work on organic synthesis, including his synthesis of chlorophyll in 1961.

WOOLF, (1) **Leonard Sidney** (1880–1969), English publicist, born in London, educated at St Paul's and Cambridge, was in the Ceylon Civil Service (1904–11), and his early writings, *The Village and the Jungle* (1913), &c., have Ceylon as a background. In 1912 he married Virginia Stephen (see below). In 1916 he joined the Fabian Society and in 1917 along with his wife he founded the Hogarth Press. His works include *Socialism and Co-operation* (1921), *After the Deluge* (1931, 1939) and *Principia Politica* (1953). See his autobiography in 4 vols. (1960–67).

(2) **Virginia** (1882–1941), English novelist, born in London, daughter of Sir Leslie Stephen, married (1) in 1912, and from 1915 published novels (*The Voyage Out, Mrs Dalloway, To the Lighthouse, Orlando, The Waves*, &c.) and essays (*A Room of One's Own, The Common Reader*, &c.). Her style is evasive and impressionistic, a development of the stream-of-consciousness technique, which, allied to psychological penetration, gives her prose a quality more usually found in poetry. Under the strain of World War II she ended her life by drowning. *A Writer's Diary* (1953) contains extracts from her journal, and two vols. of her *Collected Essays* (ed. by (1)) appeared in 1966. See studies by Holtby (1932), Forster (1942), Daiches (1945), Chambers (1948) and Bibliography (1957) by Kirkpatrick.

WOOLLETT, William (1735–85), English line-engraver, born at Maidstone, was one of the greatest of his kind. His first important plate, from Richard Wilson's *Niobe*, was published by Boydell in 1761. In 1775 he was appointed engraver to George III. See L. Fagan's *Catalogue Raisonné* of his 123 engraved works (1885).

WOOLLEY, Sir (Charles) Leonard (1880–1960), English archaeologist, born in London, was educated at St John's School, Leatherhead, and New College, Oxford. He was assistant keeper of the Ashmolean Museum, Oxford, from 1905 to 1907. He carried out excavations at Carchemish (1912–14) and in Sinai, and directed the important excavations (1922–34) at Ur in Mesopotamia, which included the royal cemetery discoveries. He was knighted in 1935, and from 1943 to 1946 was archaeological adviser to the War Office. His publications include *Digging up the Past* (1930), *Ur Excavations* (1934), works on Carchemish, and *Alalakh* (1955).

WOOLMAN, John (1720–72), American Quaker preacher, was born at Northampton, N.J., a farmer's son, and was for some time a tailor. He spoke and wrote against slavery, and published several religious works. His *Journal* (1774, often reprinted) was a favourite book with Lamb. He died at York on a visit to England. See Life by Shore (1913), and study by J. Whitney (1943).

WOOLNER, Thomas (1826–92), English poet-sculptor, was born at Hadleigh, and studied at the Royal Academy from 1842. In 1843 his first major work, *Eleanor sucking the Poison from Prince Edward's Wound*, attracted much attention. As a conspicuous member of the pre-Raphaelite Brotherhood (see ROSSETTI) he contributed poems to *The Germ*, which with others were published in a volume as *My Beautiful Lady* (1863). In 1852–54 he was in Australia. He executed statues or portrait busts of most of his famous contemporaries (his bust of Tennyson is in Westminster Abbey). Made A.R.A. in 1871 and R.A. in 1874, he was professor of Sculpture to the Academy 1877–79. See Life by his daughter, Amy Woolner (1917).

WOOLSEY, (1) **Sarah Chauncey.** See COOLIDGE, SUSAN.

(2) **Theodore Dwight** (1801–89), American scholar, born at New York, was professor of Greek at Yale 1831–46, and then its president till 1871. He was president of the American New Testament revisers. Besides editions of Greek plays, &c., he wrote an *Introduction to International Law* (1860), *Divorce Legislation* (1869) and *Political Science* (1877).

WOOLSTON, Thomas (1670–1731), English Deist, born at Northampton, became a fellow of Sidney Sussex, Cambridge, and took orders. In 1705 he published the *Old Apology for the Truth of the Christian Religion Revived*, affirming that the Old Testament was allegorical only. In 1721 his college deprived him of his fellowship. He joined the Deist controversy with *The Moderator between an Infidel and an Apostate* (1725). In his famous six *Discourses on the Miracles of Our Saviour* (1727–29, with two *Defences*) he maintained that the gospel narratives, taken literally, were a tissue of absurdities. Sixty answers were made to the *Discourses*; and an indictment for blasphemy was brought against him. Fined and sent to prison, he died there. His works were collected in 1733 with a Life.

WOOLTON, Frederick James Marquis, 1st Baron (1883–1964), Conservative politician and businessman, was born in Liverpool. He attended Manchester Grammar School and Manchester University, and then taught mathematics at Burnley Grammar School. During a spell as warden of Liverpool University Settlement, in the dock area, he ran the David Lewis Club and this brought him to the attention of Lewis, the managing director of the Manchester store, who took him into the business. He rose rapidly in Lewis's, where he revolutionized the merchandising side, and became chairman in 1935. He was made a baron in 1939. At the beginning of the war, he went to the Ministry of Supply, but made his name at the Ministry of Food, where from 1940 he had the responsibility of seeing that the entire nation was well-nourished. In 1946 he became chairman of the Conservative party, and is credited with much of the success in rebuilding the party's organization which led it to victory in 1951. Woolton became lord president of the Council, but ill-health later led him to take on the less onerous office of chancellor of the Duchy of Lancaster. See his *Memoirs* (1959).

WOOLWORTH, Frank Winfield (1852–1919),

American merchant, was born in Rodman, Jefferson County, N.Y. He attended country schools, and was a farm worker until becoming a shop-assistant in 1873. His employers backed Woolworth's scheme to open in 1879 in Utica a store for five-cent goods only; this failed, but later the same year a second store, in Lancaster, Pennsylvania, selling also ten-cent goods, was successful. In partnership with his employers, his brother, and cousin, Woolworth began building a large chain of similar stores, and at the time of his death the F. W. Woolworth company controlled over a thousand stores from their headquarters in the Woolworth Building, N.Y., for a time the world's tallest building (792 feet). Woolworth's stores came to Britain in 1910, but their main development outside America was after the death of the founder.

WOOTTON, Barbara Frances, Baroness Wootton of Abinger (1897–), English social scientist, born at Cambridge, the daughter of a don, studied and lectured (1920–22) at Girton College in Economics. She was a research worker for the Labour Party (1922–25), principal of Morley College, London (1926–1927), director of studies (1927–44) and professor in Social Studies (1948–52) at London. A frequent royal commissioner and London magistrate, she is best known for her work, *Testament for Social Science* (1950), in which she attempted to assimilate social to the natural sciences. Another work was *Social Science and Pathology* (1959). She was created a life peeress in 1958.

WORCESTER, *woos'tėr*, (1) **Edward Somerset, Marquis of** (*c.* 1601–67), inventor of a steam engine, was probably born in London, About 1628 we find him engaged in mechanical pursuits with Caspar Kaltoff, his lifelong assistant. At the Rebellion he sided with the king, in 1642 was made General of South Wales, in 1644 was created Earl of Glamorgan, and in 1645 was sent to Ireland to raise troops for the king. His mission failed. Charles disowned him, and he was imprisoned for a short time. In 1646 he succeeded his father, and in 1648 went into exile in France. In 1652, venturing back to England, he was sent to the Tower, but in 1654 was let out on bail, and at the Restoration recovered a portion of his vast estates—he claimed to have disbursed £918,000 'for king and country'. His *Century of Inventions* (written 1655; printed 1663) gives a brief account of a hundred inventions—ciphers, signals, automata, mechanical appliances, &c. No. 68 deals with a steam apparatus which could raise a column of water 40 feet, and which seems to have been at work at Vauxhall (1663–70)—probably an improved form (with two chambers) of Della Porta's contrivance, forcing steam into a chamber containing water, with an opening below the water. See Life by Dircks prefixed to his reprint of the *Century* (1863).

(2) **Joseph Emerson** (1784–1865), American lexicographer, born at Bedford, N.H., taught at Salem, Mass., and then turned author. All his works were laborious—gazetteers, manuals of geography and history, &c. He edited Chalmers's abridgment of Todd's Johnson's Dictionary, with Walker's Pronouncing Dictionary (1828), abridged Webster (1829), and printed his own *English Dictionary* (1830; enlarged ed. 1855), *Critical Dictionary* (1846), and great quarto *Dictionary of the English Language* (1860).

(3) **Sir Thomas Percy, Earl of** (1344–1403), English soldier, son of Sir Henry, 3rd Baron Percy, fought in France, accompanied Chaucer on a diplomatic mission to Flanders in 1377, was made an admiral by Richard II and commanded in several expeditions, notably those of John of Gaunt to Spain (1386) and of the Earl of Arundel to La Rochelle (1388). He was created an earl in 1397. Having joined Northumberland's rebellion in 1403 he was captured at Shrewsbury and executed.

WORDE, Wynkyn de (d. 1535?), printer, born in Holland or in Alsace, was a pupil of Caxton, and in 1491 succeeded to his stock-in-trade. He made great improvements in printing and typecutting, printed many books, and was still living in 1535. See study by H. R. Plomer (1925).

WORDSWORTH, (1) **Charles** (1806–92), English Episcopal clergyman in Scotland, second son of (2), educated at Christ Church, Oxford, became a tutor, Manning and Gladstone being among his pupils. After being a master at Winchester he became the first Warden of Glenalmond School in Perthshire (1846) and thereafter Bishop of St Andrews, in which capacity he ardently sought the reunion of the churches. His *Annals of my Life* (1891–93) is curious reading on that and kindred topics of the day.

(2) **Christopher** (1774–1846), English clergyman, youngest brother of (7), was elected a fellow of Trinity College, Cambridge, in 1798 and after occupying various livings became master of Trinity (1820–21). His *Ecclesiastical Biography* (1809) is a good selection of lives, and his *Christian Institutes* (1836) of the writings of the great English divines. He engaged in the *Eikon Basilike* controversy without much success.

(3) **Christopher** (1807–85), youngest son of (2), had an unsuccessful career as headmaster of Harrow (1836–44), and became Bishop of Lincoln (1869). In 1851 he produced a memoir of his uncle the poet, to whom he was literary executor. His edition of the correspondence of Bentley is a sound work as also is his *Theocritus* (1884). See Life by his daughter **Elizabeth** (1840–1932), who became first principal of Lady Margaret Hall, Oxford (1868–1908).

(4) **Dorothy** (1771–1855), only sister of (7), was his companion through life, both before and after his marriage, and on tours to Scotland, the Isle of Man and abroad, the records of which are to be found in her *Journals*. The *Journals* show that Dorothy's keen observation and sensibility provided a good deal of poetical imagery for both her brother and his friend Coleridge—more than that, they regarded her as the embodiment of that joy in Nature which it was their object to depict. In 1829 she suffered a breakdown from which she never fully recovered. Her *Tour made in Scotland* (1874) is a classic. See also *Letters of William and Dorothy*

Wordsworth (ed. De Selincourt, 1935–39), and by De Selincourt (1933).

(5) **John** (1805–39), eldest son of (2), became a fellow of Trinity in 1830, took orders in 1837, and at his death was preparing an edition of Aeschylus and a classical dictionary.

(6) **John** (1843–1911), eldest son of (3), a graduate of New College, Oxford, proceeded in the family path through college preferment and various lectureships (Grinfield, 1876; Bampton, 1881) to the Oriel professorship of Interpretation of the Scriptures (1883) and the see of Salisbury (1885). His studies in the Latin biblical texts, particularly his critical edition of the Vulgate New Testament (1889 *et seq.*) form a landmark in scriptural scholarship.

(7) **William** (1770–1850), English poet, was born at Cockermouth, where his father was an attorney. Having lost both parents at an early age he was sent to Hawkshead in the Lake District for board and education. This, as we learn from *The Prelude*, was one of the formative periods of his life. His guardian sent him to Cambridge (1787–91), where he was troubled in mind by the agnostic and revolutionary ideas he had already picked up. A walking tour through France and Switzerland in his second long vacation (1790) showed him France *en fête* for the earlier stage of the Revolution before disillusionment had set in. Two immature poems belong to this period—*An Evening Walk* and *Descriptive Sketches*, both published in 1793. Leaving Cambridge without a profession, he stayed for a little over a year at Blois, and there, as Legouis and Harper first disclosed, had an affair with Annette Vallon, the result of which was an illegitimate daughter, Ann Caroline. The incident is reflected in *Vaudracour and Julia*. Pitt's declaration of war with France (January 1793) drove the poet back to England, but the depressing poem *Guilt and Sorrow*, which dates from this period, shows that he was not yet cured of his passion for social justice. For a time he fell under the spell of Godwin's philosophic anarchism, but the unreadable *Borderers* shows that by 1795 he was turning his back both on the Revolution and on Godwinism, and with the help of his sister Dorothy, with whom he set up house at Racedown in Dorset, and of Coleridge, who had renounced his revolutionary ardour somewhat earlier, he discovered his true vocation, that of the poet exploring the lives of humble folk living in contact with Divine Nature and untouched by the rebellious spirit of the times. When the Wordsworths settled at Alfoxden in Somerset with Coleridge three miles away at Nether Stowey (1797), there began a close association which resulted in *Lyrical Ballads* (1798), the first manifesto of the new poetry, which opened with Coleridge's *Ancient Mariner* and concluded with Wordsworth's *Tintern Abbey*. The poems between, mostly Wordsworth's, were not all silly sooth, but enough of them were such to make them the object of parody, a weapon to which Wordsworth, except in his exalted mood, was peculiarly vulnerable. The removal of the Wordsworths to Grasmere after a visit to Germany in Coleridge's company, and the marriage of the poet to Mary Hutchinson (1802) closes this first stormy period with Wordsworth set on his proper task and modestly provided for by a legacy of £900. Now followed a long spell of routine work and relative happiness broken only by family misfortunes—the death of his sailor brother John (1805), which may have inspired the *Ode to Duty*, and Dorothy's mental breakdown (1832). Meanwhile Napoleon's ambitions had completely weaned the poet from revolutionary sympathies, as the patriotic sonnets sent to the *Morning Post* at about the time of the Peace of Amiens (1802–03) and after bear witness. Apart from the sonnets, this was his most inspired period. The additions to the third edition of *Lyrical Ballads* (1801) contained the grave pastoral *Michael*, *Ruth* and four of the exquisite *Lucy* poems, while the first of his tours in Scotland (1803), of which Dorothy wrote the perfect tour journal, yielded some fine poems, including *The Solitary Reaper*. The great poem he was now contemplating—*The Recluse*—was never finished, but *The Prelude*, the record of the poet's mind, was read to Coleridge in 1805. It remained unpublished till after his death, when it appeared with all the tamperings of a lifetime but substantially in its form of 1805, which fortunately has survived. Two volumes of poems appeared in 1807, the fruit of five years of intense activity. The ode *Intimations of Immortality* is only the loftiest of a number of masterpieces, including the patriotic sonnets, the *Affliction of Margaret*, the *Memorials of a Tour in Scotland*, the *Ode to Duty*, &c. Critics are inclined to mark the decline of his powers after this remarkable outpouring. Jeffrey was not altogether wrong in saying of *The Excursion* (1814) 'This will never do', and the 'Memorials' of various tours he now undertook and the *Ecclesiastical Sonnets* are decidedly below form. Only in two directions does he recall the poet he had been—the classical vein shown in *Laodamia* and *Dion* is impressive, and in the *Duddon* series the lifelong lover of nature reappears, although shorn of the mysticism. Wordsworth resented being called a pantheist, but pantheist he was until the horror of the times drove him to seek the comfort of revealed religion. In his *Ode to Dejection* Coleridge effectively disposed of Wordsworth's nature worship and in his *Biographia Literaria* (1819) he indicated the limitations of his theory about poetic diction, which now seems to be only a protest against the inflated idiom of descriptive poetry. None of these factors, however, detract from Wordsworth's greatness as a poet. Wordsworth succeeded Southey as poet laureate in 1843. He died at Rydal Mount (his home since 1813), April 23, 1850, and was buried at Grasmere. See Works, together with Dorothy's *Journals*, ed. W. Knight (1896), Works, ed. De Selincourt (1940 *et seq.*), *Letters*, ed. De Selincourt (1935–39); Lives by C. Wordsworth (1851), W. Knight (1889) and G. M. Harper (1916); Legouis, *La Jeunesse de Wordsworth* (new ed. 1921) and *Annette Vallon* (1922); also studies by

Coleridge (*Biographia Literaria*), Matthew Arnold, W. Pater, Raleigh (1908), Garrod (1924), Fausset (1923), Smith (1944), Bateson (1954) and Clarke (1962).

(8) **William Brocklesby** (1908–), English composer, a descendant of (2), was born in London. He studied under Sir Donald Tovey, and achieved prominence when his second symphony won the first award in the Edinburgh International Festival Competition in 1950. He has composed four symphonies, a piano concerto, songs and a quantity of chamber music.

WORK, Henry Clay (1832–84), American songwriter, born at Middletown, Conn., a printer by trade, attracted notice during the Civil War by his 'Marching through Georgia'.

WORNUM, Ralph Nicholson (1812–77), English art critic, was born at Thornton, Northumberland, and was from 1853 keeper and secretary of the National Gallery. The first effective holder of this post, he rearranged and catalogued the collections, and vigorously campaigned for better accommodation for the art treasures of the nation.

WORSAAE, Jens Jacob Asmussen, *vor'saw-ė* (1821–85), Danish archaeologist, in 1838–43 was assistant in the Copenhagen Museum of Northern Antiquities. Between 1842 and 1854 he made repeated visits to other Scandinavian lands, to Great Britain, Germany and France, which bore fruit in numerous works, two of which have been translated as *Primeval Antiquities of England and Denmark* (1849) and *The Danes and Norwegians in England* (1852). He opposed the spread of German tendencies in the duchies, as in *Jylland's Danskhed* (1850). He was minister of education 1874–75.

WORTH, Charles Frederick (1825–95), Anglo-French costumier, born at Bourn in Lincolnshire, went to Paris in 1846, and achieved such success as a fashion designer that he gained the patronage of the empress Eugénie, and his establishment in the Rue de la Paix became the centre of the fashion world.

WOTTON, Sir Henry (1568–1639), English traveller, diplomatist, scholar and poet, was born of ancient family at Boughton Malherbe in Kent. He was educated at Winchester and Oxford, then set out for a seven years' sojourn in Bavaria, Austria, Italy, Switzerland and France. On his return he became the confidant of the Earl of Essex. On his friend's downfall he betook himself to France, then to Italy, and was sent by Ferdinand, Duke of Florence, on a secret mission to James VI of Scotland. James on his succession to the throne of England knighted him and sent him as ambassador to Venice (1604), where he was intermittently employed for nearly twenty years, being next sent to the German princes and the Emperor Ferdinand II, returning to England a poor man in 1624. He was made provost of Eton, and took orders. His tracts, letters, &c., were collected as *Reliquiae Wottonianae* (1651), prefaced by Izaak Walton's exquisite little Life. One of his few poems is 'The Character of a Happy Life'. It was Wotton who described an ambassador as an honest man sent abroad to lie for the good of his country. See Lives by A. W. Ward (1898) and L. P. Smith (1907).

WOUTERS, Rik, *vow'-* (1882-1916), Belgian painter, born at Mechlin, came under the influence of Cézanne and was the leading exponent of Fauvism in Belgium.

WOUWERMAN, Philip, *vow'vėr-man* (1619–1668), Dutch painter of battle and hunting pieces, born at Haarlem, passed his entire life there in the assiduous practice of his art. His pictures are mostly small landscapes, with plenty of figures in energetic action. His cavalry skirmishes, with a white horse generally in the foreground, were specially characteristic and popular. He had two brothers, also painters, **Peter** (1623–82) and **Jan** (1629–66), who chose similar subjects.

WRANGEL, *vrang'gėl,* (1) **Ferdinand Petrovitch, Baron von** (1794–1870), Russian vice-admiral and explorer, was born in Livonia, voyaged much in Arctic waters and on Siberian coasts, and made valuable surveys and observations. The island he nearly reached in 1821 was sighted by Sir H. Kellett in 1849, and named after Wrangel by Long in 1867. See his *Polar Expedition* (trans. 1840).

(2) **Friedrich Heinrich Ernst** (1784–1877), Prussian field-marshal and count, born at Stettin, distinguished himself in the campaigns of 1807, 1813, and 1814, and in 1848 commanded the Federal troops in Schleswig-Holstein. He crushed the insurrection in Berlin (1848); in 1856 became field-marshal; in 1864 had supreme command over Prussian and Austrian troops in the Danish war; and, ennobled in 1866, served that year against the Austrians. See Lives by Brunckow (1876), Meerheimb (1877) and Maltitz (1884).

WRAXALL, Sir Nathanael William (1751–1831), English writer of memoirs, born at Bristol, was for three years in the East India Company's service, travelled over Europe (1772–79), and had a confidential mission from Queen Caroline-Matilda of Denmark to her brother George III. He published his *Cursory Remarks made in a Tour* in 1775, his *Memoirs of the Valois Kings* in 1777, entered parliament in 1780 as a follower of Lord North, but went over to Pitt, and was made a baronet in 1813. His next books were the *History of France from Henry III to Louis XIV* (1795); *Memoirs of the Courts of Berlin, Dresden, Warsaw, and Vienna* (1799); and the famous *Historical Memoirs of my own Time, 1772–84* (1815). For a libel here on Count Woronzov, Russian envoy to England, he was fined £500 and sentenced to six months' imprisonment. Violent attacks on his veracity were made by the reviews, but Wraxall's *Answers* were accounted on the whole satisfactory. A continuation of *Memoirs* (1784–90) was published in 1836. See Wheatley's edition of the whole work (5 vols. 1884).

WREDE, Karl Philipp, *vray'dė* (1767–1838), Bavarian soldier, born at Heidelberg, shared in the campaigns of 1799 and 1800, as commander of the Bavarians invaded Tyrol, fought at Wagram along with the French, and was made a count by Napoleon. He led the Bavarians under Napoleon to Russia in 1812; then commanded a united Bavarian and Austrian army against the French, by whom he was defeated at Hanau. He was, however, victorious in several battles in France in 1814, and was made field-marshal and prince. He represented Bavaria at the Vienna Congress (1814).

WREN, Sir Christopher (1632–1723), English architect, born at East Knoyle in Wiltshire, October 20, was the son of Dr Christopher Wren, dean of Windsor, and the nephew of Dr Matthew Wren (1585–1667), the High Church bishop successively of Hereford, Norwich and Ely. He passed from Westminster to Wadham College, Oxford, became a fellow of All Souls, distinguished himself in mathematics and physics, and helped to perfect the barometer. In 1657 he became professor of Astronomy at Gresham College in London, but in 1661 returned to Oxford as Savilian professor of Astronomy. Before leaving London, Wren had, with Boyle, Wilkins and others, laid the foundation of the Royal Society. In 1663 he was engaged by the Dean and Chapter of St Paul's to make a survey of the cathedral, with a view to repairs. The first work built from a design by Wren was the chapel at Pembroke College, Cambridge, in 1663; and in 1663–66 he designed the Sheldonian Theatre at Oxford and the Library, &c., of Trinity College, Cambridge. In 1665 Wren visited Paris. The Great Fire of London (1666) opened a wide field for his genius. He drew designs for the rebuilding of the whole city, embracing wide streets and magnificent quays but, thwarted by vested interests, the scheme was never implemented. In 1669 he was appointed surveyor-general and was chosen architect for the new St Paul's (1675–1710) and for more than fifty other churches in place of those destroyed by the Great Fire. Other works by him were the Royal Exchange, Custom House, Temple Bar, the College of Physicians, Greenwich Observatory, Chelsea Hospital, the Ashmolean Museum at Oxford, Hampton Court, Greenwich Hospital, Buckingham House, Marlborough House, and the western towers and north transept of Westminster Abbey. In 1672 Wren was knighted, in 1680 made president of the Royal Society, in 1684 comptroller of the works at Windsor Castle, and in 1698 surveyor-general of Westminster Abbey. He was returned for Windsor in 1689, but unseated on petition. Wren was buried in St Paul's. See Lives by Elmes (1852), Weaver (1923), Webb (1937), Briggs (1953), Summerson (1953), Bolton (1956), and the Wren Society publications.

WRIGHT, (1) Sir Almroth Edward (1861–1947), English bacteriologist, born in Yorkshire, educated at Dublin, Leipzig, Strasbourg and Marburg, became professor of Experimental Pathology in the University of London. He was known specially for his work on the parasitic diseases, and for his research on the protective power of blood against bacteria. He introduced a system of antityphoid inoculation.

(2) **Fanny.** See DARUSMONT.

(3) **Frank Lloyd** (1869–1959), American architect, born in Richland Center, Wis., studied civil engineering at the University of Wisconsin, where the collapse of a newly-built wing led to his determination to apply engineering principles to architecture. Having set up in practice, he became known for his low-built prairie-style residences, but soon launched out into more daring and controversial designs, and is regarded as the outstanding designer of modern private dwellings, planned in conformity with the natural features of the land. Among his larger works are the earthquake-proof Imperial Hotel at Tokyo and the Guggenheim Museum of Art in New York, in which the exhibits line the walls of a continuous spiral ramp. He was an innovator in the field of open planning. See his Autobiography (N.Y. 1932) and study by Gutheim (N.Y. 1941).

(4) **Georg von.** See VON WRIGHT.

(5) **Joseph** (1734–97), English genre and portrait painter, called 'Wright of Derby', passed his whole life in his native town, save a few years spent in London, in Italy and at Bath. His portrait groups often show odd light effects. See Bemrose's folio (1886).

(6) **Joseph** (1855–1930), English philologist, D.C.L., professor of Comparative Philology at Oxford, editor of the *Dialect Dictionary*, and author of many philological works, was born at Bradford and as a boy worked in a wool mill. See Life by his widow and collaborator (1932).

(7) **Orville** (1871–1948), born at Dayton, Ohio, and his brother **Wilbur** (1867–1912), born near Millville, Ind., American airplane pioneers, were the first to fly in a heavier-than-air machine, December 17, 1903, at Kitty Hawk, N.C. Encouraged by this, they abandoned their cycle business and formed an aircraft production company (1909), of which Wilbur was president until his death. In 1915 Orville sold his interests in it in order to devote himself to research.

(8) **Thomas** (1810–87), English antiquary, born of Quaker parentage near Ludlow, graduated from Trinity, Cambridge, was elected F.S.A. in 1837, and helped to found the Camden Society, Archaeological Association, and Percy and Shakespeare Societies. From 1836 he published eighty-four works, including *Biographia Britannica Literaria* (1842–46); *England in the Middle Ages* (1846); *Dictionary of Obsolete and Provincial English* (1857); *Political Poems, 1327–1485* (1859–61); and *Anglo-Latin Twelfth Century Satirical Poets* (1877).

(9) **William Aldis** (1836–1914), English man of letters, born at Beccles, became librarian, and in 1888 vice-master, of Trinity College, Cambridge. He edited the Cambridge and Globe Shakespeares (with W. G. Clark), *Generydes*, Robert of Gloucester, Edward FitzGerald's Letters, &c., and was well known by his *Bible Word-Book* (1866).

WRÓBLEWSKI, Zygmunt Florenty von, *vroo-blef'ski* (1845–88), Polish physicist, born at Grodno, was professor of Physics at Cracow University and noted for his work on the liquefaction of gases. He was the first to liquefy air on a large scale. Working with Olszewski at Cracow he liquefied oxygen, nitrogen and carbon monoxide. He died at Cracow.

WU CHENG-EN, *woo chung-un* (fl. 16th cent.

A.D.), Chinese author of *Monkey* (trans. A. Waley, 1942), based on the pilgrimage of Hsuang Chuang (q.v.).

WULSTAN, or **Wulfstan**, name of several churchmen in Anglo-Saxon England, notably:

(1) (fl. *c.* 1000), a monk of Winchester, author of a Life of Bishop Ethelwold and a poem on St Swithin's Miracles.

(2) (d. 1023), Archbishop of York from *c.* 1002, author of Anglo-Saxon homilies (see Napier's German monograph, 1882).

(3) (*c.* 1009–95), Bishop of Worcester and saint, reputed author of part of the Anglo-Saxon Chronicle, submitted to William the Conqueror and supported William Rufus. By his preaching at Bristol he is understood to have put an end to the slave trade practised there. He was canonized in 1203. See his Life, Latin trans. by William of Malmesbury, ed. Darlington (1929), English trans. by Peile (1934).

WUNDERLICH, Carl August, *voon'dėr-lee*KH (1815–77), German physician, born at Sulz-on-Neckar, professor of Medicine at Leipzig, was the first to introduce temperature charts into hospitals, in accordance with his contention that fever is a symptom and not a disease. The clinical thermometer used by him was a foot long and took twenty minutes to register the temperature. He died at Leipzig.

WUNDT, Wilhelm Max, *voont* (1832–1920), German physiologist and psychologist, born at Neckarau, Baden, in 1875 became professor of Physiology at Leipzig. A distinguished experimental psychologist, he wrote on the nerves and the senses, the relations of physiology and psychology, logic, &c. His *Human and Animal Psychology* and *Outlines of Psychology* were translated in 1896, *Ethics* in 1901, *Folk Psychology* in 1916.

WURTZ, Charles Adolphe, *vürts* (1817–84), French chemist, born at Strasbourg, wrote numerous works, of which *The Atomic Theory* (1880), *Modern Chemistry* (4th ed. 1885), &c., have been translated. From 1875 he was professor of Chemistry at the Sorbonne. He was the discoverer of glycol (1856). See Life by Gautier (1884).

WYATT, (1) **James** (1746–1813), English architect, born in Staffordshire, succeeded Sir W. Chambers in 1796 as surveyor to the Board of Works. He built Fonthill Abbey for Beckford, and was killed in a carriage accident. See study by Dale (1956). His son, **Matthew Cotes** (1777–1862), was a sculptor.

(2) **Sir Mathew Digby** (1820–77), English architect, was born at Rowde near Devizes, the son of a London police magistrate, a member of a family that produced many architects and sculptors, including (1) and (3). He was secretary to the royal commissioners for the 1851 exhibition, and ı 1869 was knighted and made Slade professor of Fine Arts at Cambridge. He wrote *Metal Work and its Artistic Design* (1852), *Industrial Arts of the Nineteenth Century* (1853), *Art Treasures of the United Kingdom* (1857), *Fine Art* (1870), and *Architect's Handbook in Spain* (1872). See study by Pevsner (1950).

(3) **Richard** (1795–1850), English classical and poetical sculptor, of the same family as (1) and (2), born in London, studied at Paris and Rome, where he died.

(4) **Sir Thomas** (1503–42), English courtier and poet, was born at Allington Castle in Kent, son of Sir Henry Wyatt, and studied at St John's College, Cambridge. He was warmly received at court, in 1536 knighted, and in 1537 made high sheriff of Kent. He contrived to retain the king's favour, and was employed on missions to Spain and the imperial court. In 1541 he got a grant of lands at Lambeth, and in 1542 was named high steward of the king's manor at Maidstone. In 1557 his poems, with Surrey's, were published in *Tottel's Miscellany* (ed. Rollins 1928 *et seq.*). Some of the shorter pieces are models of grace, and the satires possess merit. His poems were edited by Dr Nott (1815–16), Prof. Simonds (1889), and Miss Foxwell (complete variorum edit., 1913). Simonds seeks to show that Anne Boleyn was the object of Wyatt's love. See studies by Alscher (Vienna 1886), Tillyard (1929), E. K. Chambers (1933).

(5) **Sir Thomas, the Younger** (1520?–54), son of (4), fought bravely at the siege of Landrecies (1544), and continued in service on the Continent till 1550. In 1554, with Lady Jane Grey's father, he led the Kentish men to Southwark; and failing to capture Ludgate, was taken prisoner, and executed.

WYCHERLEY, William, *wich'-* (*c.* 1640–1716), English dramatist, born at Clive near Shrewsbury, in early youth was sent to France, left Queen's College, Oxford, without a degree, and entered the Middle Temple. For some years he lived as a man about town and a courtier, but took early to work as a dramatist. *Love in a Wood, or St James's Park*, a brisk comedy founded on Sedley's *Mulberry Garden*, was acted with much applause in 1671. Buckingham gave him a commission in a regiment, and King Charles made him a present of £500. He served for a short time in the fleet, and was present at a sea fight—probably one of the drawn battles fought between Rupert and De Ruyter in 1673. *The Gentleman Dancing-master* (1672) was a clever farcical comedy of intrigue. *The Country Wife* (1675), Wycherley's coarsest but strongest play, partly founded on Molière's *École des Femmes*, was followed in 1677 by *The Plain Dealer*, founded partly on Molière's *Misanthrope*. A little after 1679 Wycherley married the young widowed Countess of Drogheda, with whom he lived unhappily. At her death a few years later she left him all her fortune, a bequest which involved him in a lawsuit whereby he was reduced to poverty and cast into the Fleet prison for some years. At last James II, having seen a representation of *The Plain Dealer*, paid his debts and gave him a pension of £200 a year. At sixty-four Wycherley made the acquaintance of Pope, then a youth of sixteen, to whom he entrusted the revision of a number of his verses, the result being a quarrel. Wycherley's money troubles continued to the end of his days. At seventy-five he married a young woman in order to balk the hopes of his nephew; and he died eleven days after his marriage; according to Pope, in the Roman Catholic faith. In literary brilliance Congreve infinitely outshines him, but Wycherley is a far more dexterous playwright. See Ward's *Wycherley* (' Mermaid ', 1893); Churchill's edition of *The Country Wife* and *The Plain Dealer* (1924); Summers's edition of the *Complete Works* (4 vols. 1924); Nicoll's *Restoration Comedy* (1923); a French study by Perromat (1921); Dobrée's *Restoration Comedy* (1924); and Wilcox, *The Relation of Molière to Restoration Comedy* (1938).

WYCLIFFE, John, *wik'lif* (*c.* 1329–84), English reformer, is believed to have sprung from a family which held the manor of Wycliffe on Tees, and to have been born at Hipswell near Richmond in Yorkshire. He distinguished himself at Oxford, where he was a popular teacher. In 1360 he was master of Balliol College, but resigned soon afterwards on taking the college living of Fillingham, which he exchanged in 1368 for Ludgershall, Buckinghamshire. He was possibly warden for a time of Canterbury Hall. He also held some office at court, where he was consulted by government and employed as a pamphleteer. In 1374 he became rector of Lutterworth, and the same year was sent (doubtless as a recognized opponent of papal intrusion) to Bruges to treat with ambassadors from the pope concerning ecclesiastical abuses. His strenuous activity gained him support among the nobles and the London citizens. But his maintenance of a right in the secular power to control the clergy was offensive to the bishops, who summoned him before the archbishop in St Paul's in 1377; but the council was broken up by an unseemly quarrel between the Bishop of London and the Duke of Lancaster. The pope now addressed bulls to the king, bishops and University of Oxford, bidding them to imprison Wycliffe and make him answer before the archbishop and the pope. When at last proceedings were undertaken, the prosecution had little effect upon Wycliffe's position. The whole fabric of the church was now (1378) shaken by the election of an antipope. Hitherto Wycliffe had attacked the manifest abuses in the church, but now he began to strike at its constitution, and declared it would be better without pope or prelates. He denied the priestly power of absolution, and the whole system of enforced confession, of penances, and indulgence. Up to this time his works had been written in Latin; he now appealed to the people in their own language, and by issuing popular tracts became a leading English prose writer. He organized a body of itinerant preachers, his ' poor priests ', who spread his doctrines widely through the country, and began his translation of the Bible, of which as yet there was no complete English version. The work was carried through rapidly, and widely circulated. He entered upon more dangerous ground when in 1380 he assailed the central dogma of transubstantiation. A convocation of doctors at Oxford condemned his theses; he appealed without success to the king. In 1382 Archbishop Courtenay convoked a council and condemned Wycliffite opinions. Wycliffe's followers were arrested, and all compelled to recant; but for some unknown reason he himself was not judged. He withdrew from Oxford to Lutterworth, where he continued his incessant literary activity. His work in the next two years, uncompromising in tone, is astonishing in quantity, and shows no falling off in power. The characteristic of his teaching was its insistence on inward religion in opposition to the formalism of the time; as a rule he attacked the established practices of the church only so far as he thought they had degenerated into mere mechanical uses. The influence of his teaching was widespread in England, and, though persecution suppressed it, continued to work up to the Reformation. Huss (q.v.) was avowedly his disciple; and there were ' Lollards ' or Wycliffites in Ayrshire down to the Reformation. Thirty years after Wycliffe's death forty-five articles extracted from his writings were condemned as heretical by the Council of Constance, which ordered his bones to be dug up and burned and cast into the Swift—a sentence executed in 1428. See Lives by Lewis (1723) and Vaughan (1828); Lechler, *Wycliffe and his English Precursors* (trans. 1884); Poole, *Wycliffe* (1889); Loserth, *Wyclif and Hus* (1884); studies by Workman (1926) and MacFarlane (1953); Trevelyan, *Age of Wycliffe* (1899).

WYKEHAM, WILLIAM OF. See WILLIAM OF WYKEHAM.

WYLIE, Elinor Hoyt (1885–1928), American authoress, was born at Somerville, N.J. Her first volume of poetry, *Nets to Catch the Wind*, which won the Julia Ellsworth Ford prize in 1921, was followed by several more collections and by four highly individual novels, *Jennifer Lorn* (1923), *The Venetian Glass Nephew* (1925), *The Orphan Angel* (1927) and *Mr Hodge and Mr Hazard* (1928). See studies by H. W. Benét (1932), and N. Hoyt (1934).

WYNANTS, or Wijnants, Jan, *wī'-* (*c.* 1620–1679), Amsterdam landscape painter, was born at Haarlem.

WYNDHAM, Sir Charles (1837–1919), British actor-manager, born at Liverpool, and trained as a doctor, first appeared on the stage at New York in 1861, and made his début in London in 1866. Among the parts he played were those of Charles Surface and David Garrick. In 1899 he opened Wyndham's Theatre. He was knighted in 1902.

WYNKYN DE WORDE. See WORDE.

WYNTOUN, Andrew of (1350?–1420?), a Scottish rhyming chronicler, was a canon regular of St Andrews, who about 1395 became prior of the monastery of St Serf on Loch Leven, and wrote *The Orygynale Cronykil of Scotland*, specially valuable as a specimen of old Scots. It is brought down to 1406, and of its nine books the first five give a fragmentary outline of the histor and geography of the ancient world.

WYON, a family of noteworthy English medallists and seal-engravers:

(1) **Benjamin** (1802–58), son of (4), was chief engraver of seals to William IV, for whom he designed the great seal and a number of medals.

(2) **Joseph Shepherd** (1836–73), son of (1), succeeded his father as chief engraver of

seals and designed many medals and the great seal of Canada.

(3) **Leonard Charles** (1826–91), eldest son of (6), designed contemporary coinage and military medals, including the South African, Indian, and Albert medals.

(4) **Thomas** (1767–1830), father of (1) and (5), was chief engraver of the seals from 1816.

(5) **Thomas** (1792–1817), son of (4), became chief engraver at the mint at the age of 23. He designed the new silver coinage in 1816 and the Waterloo medal.

(6) **William** (1795–1851), father of (3), born in Birmingham, became chief engraver to the mint in 1828. He designed much of the new British and colonial coinage of George III and IV, and was in 1838 the first medallist to be elected R.A.

WYSPIANSKI, Stanislaw, *vis-pyan'skee* (1869–1907), Polish poet and painter, born at Cracow, was a leader of the Polish neo-Romantics. Besides portraits and genre pictures he executed window designs for the cathedral and the Franciscan church at Cracow before the loss of an arm obliged him to abandon art for poetry and drama, some of which is based on Greek mythology.

WYSS, Johann Rudolf, *vees* (1781–1830), Swiss writer, born at Bern, famous for his connection with *The Swiss Family Robinson.* He completed and edited the MS. originally written by his father, **Johann David Wyss.** He was professor of Philosophy at Bern from 1806. His lectures on the supreme good (1811) and Swiss tales (1815–30) would hardly have preserved his name; but *Der Schweizerische Robinson* (1812–13) has been frequently translated—into English in 1820.

WYSZYNSKI, Stepan, *vi-shin'ski* (1901–), Polish cardinal, was born at Zuzela, near Warsaw, and educated at Włocławek seminary and Lublin Catholic university. During the second World War he was associated with the resistance movement. In 1945 he became rector of Włocławek seminary, in 1946 Bishop of Lublin and in 1948 Archbishop of Warsaw and Gniezno and primate of Poland. In October 1953, following his indictment of the Communist campaign against the Church, he was suspended from his ecclesiastical functions and arrested. He was freed after the ' bloodless revolution ' of October 1956 and agreed to a reconciliation between Church and State under the ' liberalizing ' Gomulka régime.

WYTHER, George. See WITHER.

WYTTENBACH, Daniel (1746–1820), Swiss scholar, born at Bern, became professor of Greek at Amsterdam in 1771, of Philosophy in 1779, and in 1799 of Rhetoric. He retired in 1816. He edited Plutarch's *Moralia* (1795–1830), and wrote on logic, a Life of Ruhnken, &c. See Latin Life by Mahne (1823). His wife, **Johanna Gallien** (d. 1830), whom he married at seventy-two, lived after his death at Paris, was given the doctorate of philosophy by Marburg in 1827, and wrote *Théagène* (1815), *Das Gastmahl des Leomis* (1821) and *Alexis* (1823).

X

XANTHIPPE. See SOCRATES.

XAVIER, Saint Francis. See FRANCIS (SAINTS, 4).

XENOCRATES, *zen-ok'ra-teez* (396–314 B.C.), Greek philosopher, born at Chalcedon, from 339 presided over the Platonic Academy as successor to Speusippus, himself the successor of Plato. He wrote numerous treatises, of which only the titles have been preserved; and he introduced into the Academy the mystic Pythagorean doctrine of numbers.

XENOPHANES, *zen-of'an-eez* (fl. 540–500 B.C.), Greek philosopher, founder of the Eleatic School, emigrated from Colophon to Elea in southern Italy about 536 B.C. He held that a supreme intelligence or deity was identical with the world.

XENOPHON, *zen'o-fon* (*c.* 435–354 B.C.), Greek historian, essayist, and military commander, the son of Gryllus, an Athenian knight, came under Socrates' influence during the thirty-five years he spent at Athens. In 401 he accepted the invitation of Proxenus of Boeotia, a commander of Greek mercenaries, to join him at Sardis and take service under the Persian prince, Cyrus, ostensibly against the Pisidians, but really against Cyrus's own brother, King Artaxerxes Mnemon. After the failure of this bold scheme, and the death of the rebel prince at Cunaxa (401), Xenophon succeeded Proxenus in the command of the Ten Thousand Greeks. He became the life and soul of the army in its march of 1500 miles, as they fought their way against the ferocious mountain tribes through the highlands of Armenia and the ice and snow of an inclement winter; and with such skill did he lead them that in five months they reached Trapezus (Trebizond), a Greek colony on the Black Sea, and ultimately Chrysopolis (Scutari), opposite Byzantium (399). After serving a while under a Thracian chief, he got his soldiers permanent service in the Lacedaemonian army engaged to fight against the Persians. Sentence of banishment from Athens for thus taking service with Sparta was passed against him. Forming in 396 the closest friendship with the Spartan king, Agesilaus, he accompanied him in his eastern campaign; was in his suite when he returned to Greece to conduct the war against the anti-Spartan league of Athens, Corinth, and Thebes (394); and witnessed the battle of Coronea. He went back with the king to Sparta, where he resided on and off until the Spartans presented him with an estate at Scillus, a town taken from Elis. Hither in 387 he went with his wife Philesia and his two sons, Gryllus and Diodorus; and here he spent some twenty years of his life, indulging his taste for literary work and the pursuits of a country gentleman. But the break-up of Spartan ascendency after the battle of Leuctra (371) drove him from his retreat. The Athenians, who had now joined the Spartans against Thebes, repealed the sentence of banishment against him. But he settled and died at Corinth. His writings give us the idea of having been written with great singleness of purpose, modesty, and love of truth. They may be distributed into four groups: (1) historical—the *Hellenics* (the history of Greece for forty-nine years), *Anabasis* (the story of the expedition with Cyrus) and *Encomium of Agesilaus*; (2) technical and didactic—on *Horsemanship*, the *Hipparchicus* (' guide for a cavalry commander ') and the *Cynegeticus* (' guide to hunting '); (3) politico-philosophical—*The Lacedaemonian Polity*, *The Cyropaedeia* (' the education of Cyrus ', rather a historical romance) and *Athenian Finance*; (4) ethico-philosophical—*Memorials of Socrates* (sketches and dialogues illustrating the life and character of his master), *Symposion*, *Oeconomicus*, *Hieron* and *Apology of Socrates*. The *Polity of Athens* is probably an anonymous work written about 415 B.C. Xenophon's style and language are unaffected, simple and clear, without any attempt at ornamentation. The *editio princeps* of the Greek text was that of Boninus (1516), followed by the Aldine in 1525. Later editions of the whole or part of his works are by Hutchinson, Weiske, Fischer, Schneider, Bornemann, Breitenbach, Krüger, Kühner, Sauppe, Dindorf, Schenkl, Hertlein, Cobet, O. Keller, Hug and Holden. See books by Roquette (1884), Croiset (1873), Lange (1900); Bury's *Greek Historians* (1909), and the *Penguin Classics* (in translation).

XERXES I, *zerks'eez* (519?–465 B.C.), king of Persia in 485–465 B.C., succeeded when his father, Darius, died preparing for a third expedition against Greece. He first subdued the rebellious Egyptians, then started with a vast army drawn from all parts of the empire, and an enormous fleet furnished by the Phoenicians. A bridge, consisting of a double line of boats, was built across the Hellespont, and a canal cut through Mount Athos. In the autumn of 481 B.C. Xerxes arrived at Sardis. Next year the army began its march towards the Hellespont; it took seven days and nights to pass the bridge of boats. Herodotus puts the number of fighting men at 2,641,610, and the ships-of-war at 1207, besides 3000 smaller vessels. When this immense force reached Thermopylae, it was brought to a stand by Leonidas and his 300 Spartans. After these had been slain Xerxes marched on to Athens (480), and, finding it deserted, destroyed temples and houses alike. Meantime the fleet had sailed round from Euboea. Xerxes witnessed the fight in the strait between Salamis and Attica. Confounded at the result, he fled to the Hellespont; and his hopes of conquest died with the fall of his general, Mardonius, on the fatal field of Plataea (479 B.C.). Xerxes, possibly the Ahasuerus of Ezra iv. 6 and Esther i.–x., was later murdered by Artabanus.

XIMENES, Cardinal, in full Francisco Jiménez de Cisneros, *hee-may'neth* (1436–1517), Spanish churchman and statesman, was born of an ancient family, at Torrelaguna in Castile, and was educated at Alcalá, Salamanca and Rome, where he obtained from the pope a nomination to the archpriestship of Uzeda in 1473. The archbishop refused to admit him, and for six years imprisoned him. On his release in 1479 he was named vicar-general of Cardinal Mendoza, but gave this up to enter a Franciscan monastery at Toledo (1482). Queen Isabella chose him for her confessor in 1492, and in 1495 made him Archbishop of Toledo. As archbishop he maintained the austerity of the monk and carried out extensive reforms in several monastic orders. As the queen's spiritual counsellor he was the guiding spirit of Spanish affairs; and on her death in 1504 he held the balance between the parties of Ferdinand and Philip of Burgundy, husband of Joanna, the mad heiress to the crown. Appointed regent in 1506, he conducted the affairs of the kingdom through a critical time with consummate skill. In 1507 he was created cardinal, and next year organized at his own expense and commanded the expedition for the conquest of Oran and extirpation of piracy. Ferdinand on his deathbed (1516) named Ximenes regent of Spain till the arrival of his grandson Charles; and the aged cardinal quickly overawed the hostile grandees into submission, and quelled a revolt in Navarre. He died, possibly of poison, at Roa on his way to greet Charles, just arriving in Spain. Ximenes was fanatical in his hatred of heresy, and as grand inquisitor caused the death of 2500 persons. The revolution he effected in breaking down the feudal power of the nobles has often been compared with the change wrought in France by Richelieu. He was a munificent patron of religion and learning and founded out of his private income the University of Alcalá de Henares. He also published the famous Complutensian Polyglot Bible. See Latin Life by Gómez de Castro (1569), English Life by Lyell (1917), and Merton, *Ximenes and the Making of Spain* (1934).

Y

YALE, (1) **Elihu** (1649-1721), English official in India and benefactor to America, born at Boston, Mass., of British parents. They returned to Britain in 1652, and he was educated in London; in 1672 he went out to India in the service of the East India Company, becoming governor of Madras in 1687. He was resident in England from 1699, and, through the sale in America of some of his effects, donated money to the collegiate school established (1701) at Saybrook, Connecticut, which afterwards moved to New Haven. There in 1718 it took the name of Yale College in honour of its benefactor, and in 1887 the much-expanded institution become Yale University, the third oldest in the United States.

(2) **Linus** (1821–68), American inventor and manufacturer, born at Salisbury, N.Y. He invented various types of locks, including the small cylinder locks by which his name is known.

YAMAGATA, Prince Aritomo (1838–1922), Japanese general and politician, born at Hagi, became adviser to the emperor, and was appointed war minister (1873) and chief of staff (1878), in which capacity his modernization of the military system led to the emergence of Japan as a significant force in world politics. He was twice prime minister (1889–93, 1898), chief of staff in the Russo-Japanese war (1904), and president of the privy council (1905). See J. Morris, *Makers of Modern Japan* (1906).

YAMASHITA, Tomoyuki (1885–1946), Japanese general, commanded the forces which overran Singapore in 1942 and then took over the Philippines campaign, capturing Bataan and Corregidor. Still in charge when MacArthur turned the tables in 1944–45, he was captured and hanged at Manila for atrocities perpetrated by his troops.

YANG, Chen Ning (1922–), Chinese physicist, born in Hofei, the son of a professor of Mathematics, gained a scholarship to Chicago in 1945, was professor at the Institute for Advanced Studies, Princeton (1955–65), and from 1965 was professor of Science at New York State University Centre. With Tsung-Dao Lee, who had been his fellow-student at Chicago, he disproved the established physical principle known as the parity law, and for this the two were awarded the Nobel prize for 1957.

YARMOUTH, Sophia von Walmoden, Countess of (d. 1765), already known to George II in Hanover, on Queen Caroline's death (1737) was brought to England as the king's mistress, and created a countess.

YATES, (1) **Dornford,** pseud. of **Cecil William Mercer** (1885–1960), English novelist, born in London, educated at Harrow and Oxford, achieved great popularity with an entertaining series of fanciful escapist adventure fiction—*Berry and Co* (1921), *Jonah and Co* (1922), &c.

(2) **Edmund** (1831–94), British journalist and novelist, born at Edinburgh, the son of the actor-manager Frederick Henry Yates (1797–1842). From 1854 he published over a score of novels and other works; was editor of *Temple Bar*, *Tinsley's* and other periodicals; and in 1874 founded, with Grenville Murray, a successful 'society' weekly, *The World*, which, for a libel on Lord Lonsdale, involved him in 1884 in two months' imprisonment. See his *Recollections* (1884).

YEAMES, William Frederick (1835–1918). British historical and subject painter, born at Taganrog, studied in London, Florence and Rome, and became A.R.A. in 1866, R.A. in 1878. His best-known work is *When did you last see your Father?*

YEATS, *yayts*, (1) **Jack Butler** (1871–1957), Irish artist and writer, born in London, the brother of (2). Both in his painting and his writing he portrayed life in Ireland with romantic bravura. His publications include *The Amaranthers* (1936) and several plays, and he is represented in many art galleries.

(2) **William Butler** (1865–1939), Irish poet and dramatist, born near Dublin, son of the distinguished artist, **John Butler Yeats** (1839–1922). He was educated in London and Dublin and became an art student. He developed an interest in occultism and theosophy, and in his early twenties turned from painting to writing. His first publication was a play, *Mosada* (1886), and two years later he began, with *The Wanderings of Oisin*, a series of ballads and poems that established his reputation. *The Celtic Twilight*, a book of peasant legends, appeared in 1893. Its title was used to label a school of writing that attempted a renaissance of ancient Irish culture. With the help of Lady Gregory Yeats he turned to the formation of an Irish National Theatre. His three most popular plays, *The Countess Kathleen*, *The Land of Heart's Desire* and *Kathleen ni Houlihan*, appeared respectively in 1892, 1894 and 1903. For the Abbey Theatre he wrote *Shadowy Waters*, *The King's Threshold*, *Deirdre* and *The Golden Helmet*. Later, in addition to several volumes of fine poetry, he wrote *Four Plays for Dancers*, *Resurrection* and *A Vision* (a philosophical treatise); and, in 1938, two plays, *The Herne's Egg* and *Purgatory*. His autobiography is contained in three volumes: *Reveries over Childhood*, *The Trembling of the Veil* (both 1926) and *Dramatis Personae* (1936). He was awarded the Nobel prize in 1923, and his collected poems appeared in 1933. Yeats died near Roquebrune in the south of France, and in 1948 was re-interred near Sligo, Ireland. See the Lives by Hone (1942) and Jeffares (1949), studies by MacNeice (1941) and Rajan (1965), F. A. C. Wilson, *W. B. Yeats and Tradition* (1957), Stallworthy, *Between the Lines* (1963), and Bibliography by Wade (1951).

YENDYS, Sydney. See DOBELL (2).

YERKES, Charles Tyson (1837–1905), American railway financier, endowed in 1892 the

Yerkes Observatory in connection with the University of Chicago, but 45 miles N.W. of the city.

YERSIN, Alexandre Émile John, *yer-sī* (1863–1943), Swiss-French bacteriologist, born at Rougemont and educated at Lausanne, Marburg and Paris, did research at the Pasteur Institute in Paris, working along with Roux on diphtheria antitoxin. In Hong Kong in 1894 he discovered the plague bacillus at the same time as Kitasato. He developed a serum against it, and founded two Pasteur Institutes in China. He introduced the rubber tree into Indo-China.

YONGE, Charlotte Mary, *yung* (1823–1901), English novelist, only daughter of W. C. Yonge of Otterbourne, Hants, achieved great popular success with her *Heir of Redclyffe* (1853) and its successors, publishing some 120 volumes of fiction, High Church in tone. Part of the profits of the *Heir of Redclyffe* was devoted to fitting out the missionary schooner *Southern Cross* for Bishop Selwyn; and those of the *Daisy Chain* (£2000) she gave to build a missionary college in New Zealand. She also published historical works, a book on *Christian Names* (1863), a *Life of Bishop Patteson* (1873), and a sketch of *Hannah More* (1888), besides translating much and editing the *Monthly Packet*. See Life by Georgina Battiscombe (1943), and *Victorian Best-seller* by Mare and Percival (1948).

YORCK VON WARTENBURG, Hans David Ludwig (1759–1830), Prussian soldier, was the son of a Pomeranian captain, Von Yorck, York or Jarck, claiming English descent. He entered the army in 1772, was cashiered for insubordination, and served in the Dutch East Indies, but rejoining the Prussian service, gained glory in the wars of 1794, 1806, 1812 and 1813–14. Ennobled in 1814, he was made a field-marshal in 1821.

YORK, Cardinal. See STEWART Family (13).

YORK, Duke of: the title normally reserved for the second son of the English monarch. Edward III's son, **Edmund of Langley,** founded that House of York that fought the Wars of the Roses. Charles II's brother **James** bore the title until his accession in 1685; George I conferred it on his brother **Ernest Augustus; Frederick** (1763–1827), George III's second son, was trained for a military career in Germany; marrying Fredericka, the Princess Royal of Prussia, in 1791. In 1793 he commanded the small British contingent in the Coalition armies confronting the French revolutionary forces in the Netherlands. His personal success at the siege of Valenciennes and Beaumont was not properly exploited, and the campaign collapsed. No better fortune attended the expedition to the Helder of 1799. The duke had been appointed commander-in-chief in Great Britain in 1798, and his steady, knowledgeable and thoroughgoing reform of the army was of lasting benefit, and gave Wellington (q.v.) the first-class fighting material with which he defeated the French. Although exonerated from complicity in the traffic in Commissions carried on by his mistress, Mary Anne Clarke (q.v.), he resigned his office. Reinstated in 1811, he continued to justify his honourable sobriquet of 'the soldier's friend' until his death, still in harness, in 1827. **George V** (q.v.) bore the title until created Prince of Wales in 1901; as did **George VI** (q.v.) prior to his accession on the abdication of **Edward VIII.**

YORKE, Philip, Earl of Hardwicke (1690–1764), English judge, a Dover attorney's son, in 1737 became lord chancellor, supported Walpole, and held office under the Duke of Newcastle. He presided at the trial of the rebel lords in 1745, and promoted the laws that proscribed tartan and abolished heritable jurisdiction in Scotland. His Marriage Act of 1754 abolished Fleet marriages. His son, **Philip,** second Earl (1720–90), held public offices, wrote *Athenian Letters* and edited *Walpoliana.*

YOSHIDA, Shigeru (1878–1967), Japanese politician, was born in Tokyo and educated at Tokyo Imperial University. He entered diplomacy in 1906 and after service in several capitals was vice-minister for foreign affairs. From 1930 to 1932 he was ambassador to Italy and from 1936 to 1938 ambassador in London. In October 1945 he became foreign minister and in May 1946, as first chairman of the Liberal party, he formed the Government which inaugurated the new constitution. He was re-elected in 1950 and resigned in 1954. See his *Memoirs* (1961).

YOUNG, (1) **Andrew** (1807–89), Scottish minor poet, an Edinburgh and St Andrews schoolmaster, wrote 'There is a happy Land'.

(2) **Andrew John** (1885–1971), British clergyman and poet, born in Elgin, canon of Chichester Cathedral since 1948, has written nature poems (*Winter Harvest*, 1933, *The White Blackbird*, 1935, &c.), a verse play (*Nicodemus*, 1937), and botanical essays (*A Prospect of Flowers*, 1945, and *A Retrospect of Flowers*, 1950). In 1952 he was awarded the Queen's Medal for Poetry.

(3) **Arthur** (1741–1820), English writer on agriculture, was born at Whitehall, but spent his boyhood, as indeed most of his life, at Bradfield near Bury St Edmunds, his father being rector and a prebendary of Canterbury. In 1763 he rented a small farm of his mother's, on which he made 3000 unsuccessful experiments; during 1766–71 held a good-sized farm in Essex (ruin the result); from 1776 to 1778 was in Ireland; resumed farming at Bradfield; and in 1793 was appointed secretary to the Board of Agriculture, with a salary of £400. Blind from 1811, he died in London, and was buried at Bradfield. Young, in his writings, was one of the first to elevate agriculture to a science. They include *A Tour through the Southern Counties* (1768), *A Tour through the North of England* (1771), *The Farmer's Tour through the East of England* (1770–71), *Tour in Ireland* (1780), *Travels in France during 1787–88–89–90* (a valuable account of the state of France just before the Revolution, 1792–94), *The Farmer's Kalendar* (215th ed. 1862), and 'Agricultural Surveys' of eight English counties, besides many papers in *The Annals of Agriculture*, which he edited. See A. W. Hutton's edition of the *Tour in Ireland*, with bibliography (1892), and C. Maxwell's (1925); M. Betham-

Edwards's edition of the *Travels in France* (1890) and her edition of his Autobiography (1898); and Life by Defries (1938).

(4) **Brigham** (1801–77), American Mormon leader, born at Whitingham, Vt., was a carpenter, painter, and glazier in Mendon, N.Y. He first saw the 'Book of Mormon' in 1830, and in 1832, converted by a brother of Joseph Smith (q.v.), was baptized and began to preach near Mendon. Next he went to Kirtland, Ohio, was made an elder, and preached in Canada 1832–33. In 1835 he was appointed one of the twelve apostles of the church, in 1844 president; and the Mormons, when driven from Nauvoo, were led by him to Utah in 1847. In 1840 he visited England and made 2000 proselytes. In 1847 the great body of Mormons arrived at Utah, and founded Salt Lake City; and in 1850 President Fillmore appointed Brigham Young governor. In 1858 a new governor, Cumming, was sent with a force of United States troops. The determination of the United States to abolish polygamy, and the appointment in 1869 of another 'Gentile' governor, reduced Young's authority. Practical and far-seeing (though a fanatic), he encouraged agriculture and manufactures, made roads and bridges, and carried through a contract for 100 miles of the Union Pacific Railroad. He died leaving $2,500,000 to seventeen wives and fifty-six children.

(5) **Charles Mayne** (1777–1856), English tragedian, son of a rascally London surgeon, was driven from home with his mother and two brothers, and had for a while been a clerk in a West India house, when in 1798 he made his début at Liverpool; in 1807 he appeared in London as 'Hamlet'. He was a really original actor, second only, in some parts superior, to Kean himself. In 1832 he retired with a fortune of £60,000. In 1805 he had married a brilliant young actress, Julia Anne Grimani (1785–1806). Their son, **Julian Charles Young** (1806–73), was rector of Southwick in Sussex (1844–50), and then of Ilmington, Worcestershire; he published a most amusing *Memoir of Charles Mayne Young* (1871), four-fifths of it his own Journal, and supplemented in 1875 by *Last Leaves* from that same Journal.

(6) **Douglas** (1913–), Scottish poet and scholar, born at Tayport, Fife, was educated at Merchiston Castle, St Andrews and Oxford, and became a lecturer in Classics at Aberdeen and St Andrews. His collections of verse include *Auntran Blads* (1943) and *A Braird o' Thristles* (1947). He is best known for *The Puddocks* (1958) and *The Burdies* (1959), translations into Lallans of Aristophanes' plays. He was gaoled for refusing war service except in an independent Scotland's army and his attitude split the Scottish National Party, of which he was controversially elected chairman (1942). After the war he became a Labour parliamentary candidate.

(7) **Edward** (1683–1765), English poet, author of *Night Thoughts*, was born at Upham rectory near Bishop's Waltham, the son of a future dean of Salisbury, and in 1708 received a law fellowship of All Souls, Oxford. He came before the world as a poet in 1712 with an *Epistle* to George Granville on being created Lord Lansdowne. In 1719 he produced a tragedy, *Busiris*, at Drury Lane; in 1716 he was in Ireland in attendance on the dissolute young Marquis (afterwards Duke) of Wharton; and he was tutor in the family of the Marquis of Exeter. His second tragedy, *The Revenge*, was produced in 1721; his third and last, *The Brothers*, in 1753. His satires, *The Love of Fame, the Universal Passion* (1725–28), brought money as well as fame; and for *The Instalment* (1726), a poem addressed to Sir Robert Walpole, he got a pension of £200. In 1724 Young took orders; in 1727 he was appointed a royal chaplain; in 1730 he became rector of Welwyn. Next year he married Lady Elizabeth Lee, daughter of the Earl of Lichfield and widow of Colonel Lee. The *Night Thoughts* (1742–44) occasioned by her death and other sorrows, has much fustian sublimity and artificial melancholy, but many of its sententious lines have passed into proverbial use; some parts are real poetry. See his *Life and Letters* by H. C. Shelley (1914); Life by Croft in Johnson's *Poets* (1782); George Eliot's *Essays*; Thomas's *Le Poète E. Young* (1901), J. W. Mackail's *Studies of English Poets* (1926).

(8) **Emily Hilda** (Mrs Daniell) (1880–1949), English writer, born in Northumberland, wrote *Miss Mole* (1930, Tait Black Memorial prize) and other novels of the school of Jane Austen.

(9) **Francis Brett** (1884–1954), English novelist, born at Halesowen, Worcs. Established first as a physician, with a period as ship's doctor, he achieved celebrity as a writer with *Portrait of Clare* (1927), which won the Tait Black Memorial prize. From then on he wrote a succession of acceptable novels of leisurely charm, characterized by a deep love of his native country. Noteworthy titles are *My Brother Jonathan* (1928), *Far Forest* (1936), *Dr. Bradley Remembers* (1935), *A Man about the House* (1942) and *Portrait of a Village* (1951). In 1944 he essayed a long epic poem, *The Island*, cast in lyric, ballad, elegiac and narrative forms, as well as in dialogue. An ambitious undertaking, it remains, however, a story-teller's poem rather than the great work of a poet. *In South Africa* (1952) was his last book, and he died in Cape Town.

(10) **James** (1811–83), Scottish industrial chemist, born in Glasgow, was a joiner, and studied chemistry, &c., at Anderson's College. He became Thomas Graham's assistant there (1832) and (1837) in University College, London. As manager of chemical works near Liverpool (1839) and near Manchester (1843), he discovered cheaper methods of producing sodium stannate and potassium chlorate; and it was his experiments (1847–1850) that led to the manufacture of paraffin oil and solid paraffin on a large scale.

(11) **Thomas** (1587–1655), Scottish Puritan divine, born in Perthshire, studied at St Andrews, was Milton's tutor till 1622, and afterwards held charges at Hamburg and in Essex. He was the chief author in 1641 of an *Answer* to Bishop Hall by 'Smectymnuus', a name compounded of the initials of Stephen

Marshall, Edmund Calamy, Thomas Young, Matthew Newcomen and William Spurstow.

(12) **Thomas** (1773–1829), English physicist, physician and Egyptologist, born at Milverton, Somerset, studied medicine at London, Edinburgh, Göttingen and Cambridge, and started as doctor in London in 1800, but devoted himself to scientific research, and in 1801 became professor of Natural Philosophy to the Royal Institution. His *Lectures* (1807) expounded the doctrine of interference, which established the undulatory theory of light. He did valuable work in insurance, haemodynamics and Egyptology, and made a fundamental contribution to the deciphering of the inscriptions on the Rosetta Stone. See Life by Peacock (1855) and Prof. Tyndall's *New Fragments* (1892).

YOUNGHUSBAND, Sir Francis (1863–1942), British explorer, born at Murree in India, explored Manchuria in 1886 and on the way back discovered the route from Kashgar into India via the Mustagh Pass. In 1902 he went on the expedition which opened up Tibet to the Western world. British resident in Kashmir (1906–09), he wrote much on India and Central Asia. Deeply religious, he founded the World Congress of Faiths in 1936.

YOURIEFFSKAIA, Princess. See DOLGORUKOVA.

YOUSEF, Sidi Mohammed ben. See SIDI MOHAMMED.

YPRES, Earl of. See FRENCH.

YPSILANTI, *ip-si-lan'tee*, distinguished Greek Phanariot family, claiming descent from the Comneni:

(1) **Alexander** (1725–1805), father of (3), became hospodar of Wallachia, but was put to death on suspicion of fostering Greek ambitions.

(2) **Alexander** (1783–1828), eldest son of (3), served with distinction in the Russian army in 1812–13, and was chosen by the Greek 'Hetairists' as their chief in 1820. He headed a Rouman movement, but, defeated by the Turks, took refuge in Austria, where he died.

(3) **Constantine** (d. 1816), son of (1), became also hospodar of Moldavia and Wallachia. Deposed in 1805, he came back with some thousands of Russian soldiers, stirred up the Serbs to rebellion, and made another plan for restoring Greece, but had to flee to Russia.

(4) **Demetrius** (1793–1832), younger son of (3), also served in the Russian army, and aided his brother's schemes for emancipating the Christian population of Turkey. In Greece he took part in the capture of Tripolita (October 1820). His gallant defence of Argos stopped the victorious march of the Turks, and in 1828–30 he was Greek commander-in-chief. He died in Vienna.

YRIARTE, Charles, *ee-ri-art* (1832–98), French man of letters, born in Paris, of Spanish ancestry, studied architecture but from 1861 devoted himself to literature. He was editor-in-chief of *Le Monde Illustré*. Specially interested in the Italian Renaissance period, he wrote histories of Venice (1877) and Florence (1880), as well as biographies of Francesca da Rimini (1882) and Caesar Borgia (1889).

YSAYE, Eugène (1858–1931), Belgian violinist, one of the greatest of his time, born at Brussels, made many tours in Europe and America. First teacher of the violin at the Brussels Conservatoire (1886–98), he composed violin concertos, sonatas, &c.

YUAN SHIH-KAI, *-shee-kī* (1859–1916), Chinese dictator, born in Honan province, served in the army and became imperial adviser, minister in Korea (1885–94), governor of Shantung (1900), but was banished after the death of Emperor Kuang Hsü (1908). He participated in the revolution of 1911 and became first president of China (1912–16), Sun Yat-Sen (q.v.) standing down for him, but was opposed by the latter from the south when he tried to make himself emperor. His manner of death is unknown.

YUKAWA, Hideki (1907–), Japanese physicist, predicted (1935) the existence of the meson, a particle hundreds of times heavier than the electron. For his work on quantum-theory and nuclear physics he was awarded the Nobel prize for physics in 1949, the first Japanese so honoured. Professor of Physics at Kyoto University (1939–50) and director of Kyoto Research Institute from 1953, he was visiting professor at Princeton and Columbia Universities (1948–53).

YULE, Sir Henry (1820–89), British orientalist, born at Inveresk, served in the Bengal Engineers (1840–62), sat on the Indian Council (1875–89), and wrote *Cathay and the Way Thither* (1866) and *The Book of Ser Marco Polo* (1871). He was created K.C.S.I. in 1889.

Z

ZACCARIA, Antonio (1502–39), Italian religious, founded the Barnabite preaching order (1530), and was canonized in 1897.

ZACHARIAS, Saint (d. 752), a Greek by descent, born in Calabria, was pope from 741 to 752, and recognized Pepin the Short as king of France (752).

ZADKIEL, pseud. of **Richard James Morrison** (1794–1874), who in 1830 started a best selling astrological almanac.

ZADKINE, Ossip (1890–), Russian sculptor, born at Sindensk, developed an individual style, making effective use of the play of light on concave surfaces, as in *The Three Musicians* (1926), *Orpheus* (1940), and *Destroyed City* (1952). See monograph by Jianou (1965).

ZAHAROFF, Sir Basil, orig. **Basileios Zacharias** (1850–1936), armaments magnate and financier, born in Anatolia, Turkey, of Greek parents, entered the munitions industry and became a shadowy but immensely influential figure in international politics and finance, amassing a huge fortune in arms deals, oil, shipping and banking. Knighted (1918) for his services to the allies in World War I, he donated large sums of money to universities and other institutions, but was suspected by many of using his influence to intrigue for his own profit. See study by Lewinsohn (1934).

ZAHN, Theodor von (1838–1933), German Biblical scholar, born at Mörs, professor in several universities, including Göttingen and Leipzig, known for his series on the New Testament Canon (1881–93), including *Tatian's Diatessaron* and an introduction to the New Testament (1897). With Gebhardt and Harnack he edited the *Patres Apostoli* (1876–78).

ZAMENHOF, Lazarus Ludwig (1859–1917), a Jewish Warsaw oculist, born at Bialystok, invented Esperanto. See Life by M. Boulton (1960).

ZANGWILL, Israel (1864-1926), Jewish writer, born in London, went to school at Plymouth and Bristol, but was mainly self-taught, graduated with honours at London University, and, after teaching, became a journalist. A leading Zionist, he wrote poems, plays, novels, and essays, and became widely known by his Jewish tales—*Children of the Ghetto* (1892), *Ghetto Tragedies* (1894), &c. Other works are *The Master*, *Without Prejudice* (essays), *A Revolted Daughter*, *The Melting Pot* (1908), *We Moderns* (1925).

ZANUCK, Darryl Francis, *za'nuk* (1902–), American film producer, born in Wahoo, Neb. He worked with Joseph Schenck, Warner Brothers and Twentieth-Century Pictures, becoming vice-president of that company and, after its merger with Fox Films in 1935, of Twentieth-Century Fox Films Corporation. Among his many successful films are *Little Caesar*, *The Jazz Singer*, *How Green was My Valley*, *The Grapes of Wrath*, *The Snake Pit* and *All About Eve*.

ZAPOLYA, a powerful Hungarian family which included:

(1) **John** (1487–1540), prince of Transylvania, who was proclaimed king of Hungary in 1526, despite the superior claim of Ferdinand of Hapsburg, who drove him out in 1527 but was defeated by Suleiman the Magnificent, who reinstated John as puppet ruler.

(2) **John Sigismund** (1540–71), son of (1), succeeded his father, but, Suleiman having made Hungary a Turkish province, he had to content himself with the voivodship of Transylvania.

(3) **Stephen** (d. 1499), father of (1), gained renown as a military leader under Matthias Corvinus (q.v.) by his defeat of the Turks and his conquest of Austria, of which he was made governor (1485).

ZATOPEK, Emil, *zat'-* (1922–), Czech athlete, born in Moravia. After many successes in Czechoslovak track events, he won the 10,000 metres title at the Olympic Games in London in 1948. In the succeeding four years he showed himself to be the greatest long-distance runner of his time by breaking thirteen world records, and by further successes, including the 5000 metres and the Marathon, at the 1952 Olympics.

ZECHARIAH, minor prophet, born in Babylonia during the captivity, went back with the first band of exiles to Judaea. Of the Book of Zechariah only the first eight chapters are by him.

ZEEMAN, Pieter (1865–1943), Dutch physicist, born at Zonnemaire, Zeeland, lecturer at Leyden (1897), professor at Amsterdam (1900), was an authority on magneto-optics. While at Leyden he discovered the *Zeeman effect*, i.e., when a ray of light from a source placed in a magnetic field is examined spectroscopically the spectral line is widened or occasionally doubled. In 1902 he shared with Lorentz the Nobel prize for physics. In 1922 he was awarded the Rumford medal of the Royal Society.

ZEFFIRELLI, Franco (1923–), Italian stage, opera and film director, born and educated in Florence, began his career as actor and theatre-set and costume designer (1945–51). His first opera production, *La Cenerentola* (1953) at La Scala, was followed by a brilliant series of productions in Italy and abroad, culminating in *Lucia di Lammermoor*, *Cavelleria Rusticana* and *I Pagliacci* at Covent Garden in 1959 and an outstanding *Falstaff* at the New York Metropolitan Opera House in 1964. His stage productions include *Romeo and Juliet* at the Old Vic (1960), almost universally acclaimed for its originality, modern relevance and realistic setting in a recognizable Verona, and *Who's Afraid of Virginia Woolf* (Paris 1964, Milan 1965). He has also filmed zestful and spectacular versions of *The Taming of the Shrew* (1966) and *Romeo and Juliet* (1968).

ZEISS, Carl, *tsis* (1816-88), German optician, established at Jena (1846) the factory which became noted for the production of lenses, microscopes, field glasses, &c. His business was organized on a system whereby the workers had a share in the profits.

ZELLER, Eduard (1814–1908), German philosopher and theologian, born at Kleinbottwar in Württemberg, studied at Tübingen and Berlin, and settled at Tübingen in 1840 as *privatdozent* in Theology. In 1847 he became professor of Theology at Bern, and in 1849 at Marburg, whence he was called to the chair of Philosophy at Heidelberg in 1862, at Berlin in 1872. He forsook theology and his early Hegelianism for historical work, carried on in an impartial and eclectic spirit. He published Platonic studies in 1839, a trenchant work on the Acts of the Apostles (on Baur's lines, 1854; trans. 1876), books on Zwingli (1853), D. F. Strauss (1874), and Frederick the Great (1886); a history of German philosophy since Leibniz (1872), and a manual of Greek philosophy (1883; trans. 1886); and his masterly work, *Die Geschichte der Griechischen Philosophie* (1844–52).

ZENO (426–491), emperor of the East (474-491), was a weak ruler, and during his reign internal distractions and foreign troubles greatly increased. His *Henoticon* (482), designed to bring about union in the Church only occasioned a new schism.

ZENO OF CITIUM (342–270 B.C.), founder of the Stoic philosophy, a native of Citium, Cyprus, possibly a Phoenician, in 320 went to Athens, where he did the rounds of the philosophical schools, and finally opened his own at the 'Painted Porch' (*Stoa Poikilē*). He taught that virtue is necessarily good, that most things in life are morally indifferent, e.g., most objects of desire such as goods, honours, children, wife, and that these are at best only relatively good. He wrote eighteen books, including the anarchical *Republic*. In extreme old age he committed suicide. See works on Stoicism by E. Zeller (1870), R. D. Hicks (1911), E. V. Arnold (1911; new ed. 1958), M. Pohlenz (1948–49), and S. Sambursky on the Physics (1959).

ZENO OF ELEA (fl. 5th cent. B.C.), Greek philosopher, a native of Elea, a Greek colony in Lucana, Italy. A favourite disciple of Parmenides (q.v.), he went with him to Athens and on his return to Elea joined an unsuccessful conspiracy against the tyrant Nearchus. He defended Parmenidian monism against Pythagorean pluralism, by taking a Pythagorean postulate such as 'things are a many' and working out from it a pair of contradictory conclusions. Best known of all are his four arguments against motion, which is a necessary consequence of pluralism. They are 'Achilles and the Tortoise', 'The Flying Arrow', 'The Stadium' and 'The Row of Solids'. They were refuted by Aristotle, but reinstated by Lewis Carroll, Bergson and Bertrand Russell in their different ways. Only fragments of his works remain. He appears in Plato's dialogue, *Parmenides*, as instructor to Socrates. See E. Zeller, *Presocratic Philosophy* (trans. 1881), B. Russell, *Mysticism and Logic* (1918), J. Burnet, *Early Greek Philosophy* (4th ed. 1930), G. S. Kirk and J. E. Raven, *The Presocratic Philosophers* (1957).

ZENO OF SIDON (1st cent. B.C.), Epicurean philosopher, taught at Athens to 78 B.C.

ZENO OF TARSUS (3rd cent. B.C.), succeeded Chrysippus as head of the Stoic school.

ZENOBIA, *-nō'-* (3rd cent. A.D.), queen of Palmyra, born there probably of Arab descent, became the wife of the Bedouin Odenathus, lord of the city, who in A.D. 264 was recognized by Gallienus as governor of the East. On her husband's murder (*c.* 271) nearly the whole of the eastern provinces submitted to her sway. When Aurelian assumed the purple, he marched against her, defeated her in several battles, besieged her in Palmyra, and ultimately captured her as she was attempting flight (272). She saved her life by imputing the blame of the war to her secretary, Longinus (q.v.); he was beheaded and Palmyra destroyed. Zenobia, decked with jewels, was led in triumphal procession at Rome, and presented by her conqueror with large possessions near Tivoli, where, with her two sons, she passed the rest of her life in comfort and even splendour. Strikingly beautiful and of high spirit, she governed with prudence, justice, and liberality. See W. Wright, *Palmyra and Zenobia* (1895).

ZEPHANIAH, *zef-ė-nī'a* (fl. 7th cent. B.C.), Hebrew prophet of the Old Testament whose account of a coming Day of Wrath inspired the mediaeval Latin hymn *Dies Irae*.

ZEPPELIN, Count Ferdinand von (1838–1917), German army officer, born at Constance, Baden, served in the Franco-German war, and in 1897–1900 constructed his first airship or dirigible balloon of rigid type, named a *zeppelin*, after its inventor, who set up a works for their construction at Friedrichshafen.

ZERNIKE, Frits (1888–1966), Dutch physicist, born at Amsterdam, professor of Physics at Groningen (1910–58), developed the phase-contrast principle used in microscopy. He was awarded the Nobel physics prize in 1953.

ZEROMSKI, Stefan, *zhe-rom'ski* (1864–1925), Polish novelist, born at Strawczyn, wrote *The Homeless* (1900), *The Ashes* (1904, English edition 1928), *The Fight with Satan* (trilogy, 1916–18), &c., pessimistic, patriotic, lyrical in tone.

ZEUSS, Johann Kaspar, *tsoys* (1806–56), German founder of Celtic philology, became professor in the Lyceum at Bamberg in 1847. He edited *Grammatica Celtica* (1853).

ZEUXIS, *zook'sis* (fl. late 5th cent. B.C.), Greek painter, born at Heraclea, excelled in the representation of natural objects. According to legend, his painting of a bunch of grapes was so realistic that birds tried to eat the fruit.

ZHUKOV, Georgi Konstantinovich (1896–), Russian soldier, was born of peasant parents at Strelkovka, Kaluga region, worked in Moscow as an apprentice furrier, and was conscripted into the Tsarist Army, and in 1918 joined the Red Army. In 1939 he commanded the Soviet tanks in Outer Mongolia, and in 1941, as general, became Army chief of staff. In December 1941 he lifted the siege of Moscow, and in February 1943 his counter-offensive was successful at Stalingrad. In command of the First Byelo-Russian Army in 1944–45, he captured Warsaw and conquered Berlin. On May 8, 1945, on behalf of the Soviet High Command, he accepted the German surrender. After the war he became c.-in-c. of the Russian zone of Germany, in 1955 becoming minister of defence, and in 1957 supported Khrushchev against the Malenkov-Molotov faction. He was later dismissed by Khrushchev, and in 1958 was attacked for his 'revisionist' policy and for his alleged 'political mistakes' in the administration of the forces. He published several war studies and holds the Lenin prize for journalism, being foreign editor of *Pravda* 1952–57, &c.

ZHUKOVSKY, Vasily Andreyevich (1783–1852), Russian poet, born in the government of Tula, known chiefly for his translations into Russian of English, French and German poetry.

ZIEGFELD, Florenz, *zig'feld* (1869–1932), American theatre manager, born in Chicago, the son of the president of Chicago Musical College. He was the deviser and perfector of the American revue spectacle, based on the *Folies Bergères*, and his *Follies of 1907* was the first of an annual series that continued until 1931 and made his name synonymous with extravagant theatrical production. He produced other musical shows, such as *The Red Feather*, *Kid Boots*, *Sally*, *Show Boat*, and the American production of *Bitter Sweet*

ZIEGLER, Karl (1898–1973), German chemist, born at Helsa (Oberhessen), taught at

Marburg from 1920, at Heidelberg from 1936, and in 1943 was appointed director of the Max Planck Carbon Research Institute at Mulheim. With Giulio Natta he was awarded the Nobel prize in 1963 for researches on long-chain polymers leading to new developments in industrial materials.

ZIETEN, or **Ziethen, Hans Joachim von,** *tzee'tĕn* (1699–1786), Prussian cavalry general, born at Wustrau (Brandenburg), was dismissed from the Prussian cavalry for insubordination in 1727, but in 1730 rehabilitated. As colonel of hussars (1741) he increased the efficiency of the Prussian light cavalry. In 1744 he burst into Bohemia, then executed a dexterous retreat; in the Seven Years' War he covered himself with glory at Prague, Collin, Leuthen, Liegnitz and Torgau. 'Old Father Zieten' thereafter lived in retirement at Berlin, in high favour with Frederick the Great. See Life by Winter (1886).

ZIMBALIST, Efrem (1889–), violinist and composer, was born in Rostov, Russia, and later took American nationality, becoming director of the Curtis Institute of Music in Philadelphia. He has composed for both violin and orchestra.

ZIMISCES, John, *zi-mis'eez* (925–76), Byzantine emperor in 969–976, fought stoutly against Saracens, Bulgars and Russians. See study of his time by Schlumberger (*L'Épopée Byzantine*, 1897).

ZIMMERMANN, *tzim'-*, (1) **Arthur** (1864–1940), German politician, was born in East Prussia. After diplomatic service in China he directed from 1904 the Eastern Division of the German Foreign Office and was foreign secretary (November 1916–August 1917). In January 1917 he sent the famous 'Zimmermann telegram' to the German minister in Mexico with the terms of an alliance between Mexico and Germany, by which Mexico was to attack the United States with German and Japanese assistance in return for the American states of New Mexico, Texas and Arizona. This telegram finally brought the hesitant U.S. government into the war against Germany. See Tuchman, *The Zimmermann Telegram* (1959).

(2) **Dominikus** (1685–1766), German architect, born at Wessobrunn, a leading exponent of the Rococo style in southern Germany, as seen in his churches at Wies, Buxheim, Gunzberg, &c.

(3) **Johann Georg, Ritter von** (1728–95), Swiss doctor and writer, born at Brugg, studied medicine at Göttingen, and became town physician at Brugg, where he published his sentimental book *On Solitude* (1755; rewritten 1785), which was translated from the German into almost every European language. He also wrote on 'national pride' and on medical subjects. In 1768 he went to Hanover with the title of physician to George III, and was summoned to Berlin to the last illness of Frederick the Great. See books by Bodemann (1878) and Ischer (1893).

(4) **Robert** (1824–98), Austrian Herbartian philosopher and writer on aesthetics, an opponent of Hegel.

ZINOVIEV, Grigoriy, *zin-ov'yef* (1883–1936), Russian politician, born at Elisavetgrad, Ukraine, was in 1917–26 a leading member of the Soviet government, but then suffered expulsion, in 1936 death. The so-called 'Zinoviev Letter' influenced the British general election of 1924.

ZINSSER, Hans (1878–1940), American bacteriologist, born in New York, professor at Columbia (1913–23), then at Harvard Medical School. In 1915 he was one of the Red Cross Commission to Serbia for the purpose of investigating typhus. In 1923 he was a League of Nations commissioner in Russia, studying cholera. With others he developed immunization methods against typhus (1930).

ZINZENDORF, Nicolaus Ludwig, Graf von (1700–60), German religious leader, refounder of the Moravian Brethren, was born at Dresden, studied at Wittenburg, and held a government post at Dresden. He invited the persecuted Moravians to his Lusatian estates, and there founded for them the colony of Herrnhut ('the Lord's keeping'). His zeal led to troubles with the government, and in 1736–48 he was exiled. He visited England, and in 1741 went to America. During his exile from Saxony he was ordained at Tübingen, and became Bishop of the Moravian Brethren. He died at Herrnhut, having written over a hundred books. His emphasis on feeling in religion influenced German theology. See Life by Weinlick (1956).

ZISKA, or **Žižka, John,** *zhish'ka* (*c.* 1370–1424), Bohemian Hussite leader, nobly born at Trocznov, was brought up as page to King Wenceslas. He fought for the Teutonic Knights against the Poles, for the Austrians against the Turks, and for the English at Agincourt (1415). In Bohemia soon after the murder of Huss he became chamberlain to King Wenceslas, joined the extremist party of hatred against Rome and lost an eye in the civil wars. After the outbreak at Prague (July 30, 1419), Ziska was chosen leader of the popular party, with 4000 men defeated the Emperor Sigismund's 40,000, captured Prague (1421), and erected the fortress of Tabor, whence his party were called Taborites. In 1421 he lost his remaining eye at the siege of Raby, but continued to lead on his troops to a succession of twelve unexampled victories, with but one defeat, compelling Sigismund to offer the Hussites religious liberty. But he died of plague at the siege of Przibislav before the war was over, and was buried ultimately at Caslav. See study by Heymann (1955).

ZITTEL, Karl Alfred von (1839–1904), German geologist and palaeontologist, born at Bahlingen, Baden, a distinguished authority on his subjects and their history, taught at Vienna, Karlsruhe and Munich, and were president of the Bavarian Academy. His *Textbook of Palaeontology* appeared in English translation 1900–02 (ed. Eastman). It was later revised by Woodward (1925).

ZOË (980–1050), daughter of the Byzantine emperor Constantine VIII, caused the murder of her husband, Romanus III, made her paramour emperor as Michael IV (1034), and after his exile (1042) married Constantine IX.

ZOFFANY, John (1733–1810), R.A. (1769), a London portrait painter, of German origin. After studying art in Rome, in 1758 he settled in London. Securing royal patronage, he painted many portraits and conversation pieces. 1772–79 he spent in Florence; 1783–90 in India. See study by Manners and Williamson (1920).

ZOG I, orig. **Ahmed Bey Zogu**, *zōg* (1895–1961), king of Albania, was born the son of a highland tribal chieftain, and was educated in Istanbul. He became head of the clan at the age of twelve, growing up in an atmosphere of tribal feuds, and in 1912, when Albania declared her independence, Zog took a blood oath to defend it. As the outstanding nationalist leader, in 1922 he formed a republican government and was its premier, president and commander-in-chief; in 1928 he proclaimed himself king. After Albania was overrun by the Italians Zog came to Britain, and in 1946 took up residence in Egypt, in 1955 on the French Riviera.

ZOILUS (fl. 3rd cent. B.C.), Greek rhetorician, born at Amphipolis, became known as *Homeromastix* (scourge of Homer), from the bitterness with which he attacked Homer. His name became proverbial for a malignant critic.

ZOLA, Émile (1840–1902), French novelist, was born in Paris, the son of an Italian engineer. He entered the publishing house of Hachette as a clerk, but soon became an active journalist. His work in criticism, politics and drama was almost uniformly unfortunate. His true forte for short stories showed itself in the charming *Contes à Ninon* (1864), *Nouveaux Contes à Ninon* (1874), the collections entitled *Le Capitaine Burle* and *Naïs Micoulin*, and the splendid *Attaque du Moulin* (1880). In the later years of the Empire he had formed with Flaubert, Daudet, the Goncourts, and Turgenev a sort of informal society, out of which grew the 'Naturalist school'. In this direction *Thérèse Raquin* (1867) is a very powerful picture of remorse. But it was not until after the war that he began the great series of novels with a purpose called *Les Rougon-Macquart*; it comprises a score of volumes, all connected by the appearance of the same or different members of the family. The two 'mother ideas' of Zola's naturalism were heredity and a certain cerebral infirmity; and in order to apply his theory to the study of *le document humain*, he mastered the technical details of most professions, occupations and crafts, as well as the history of recent events in France. He began with a sort of general sketch called *La Fortune des Rougon*. *La Curée* and *Son Excellence Eugène Rougon* deal with the society of the later days of the Second Empire. *La Faute de l'Abbé Mouret* is an attack upon celibacy, and is, like *La Conquête de Plassans*, a vivid study of provincial life. *Le Ventre de Paris* deals with the lowest strata of the Parisian population. *L'Assommoir* depicts drunkenness; *Pot-Bouille* the lower *bourgeoisie* and their servants; *Au Bonheur des dames* 'universal providers'. *Une Page d'amour* and *La Joie de vivre* are more generally human. *Nana* is devoted to the cult of the goddess Lubricity. *L'Oeuvre* deals with art and literature. *La Terre* is an appallingly repulsive study of the French peasant, and *Germinal* of the miner; *La Bête humaine* contains minute information as to the working of railways; *Le Rêve* displays a remarkable acquaintance with the details of church ritual; *L'Argent* exploits financial crashes; and *La Débâcle* recounts the great disaster of 1870. *Dr Pascal* (1893) is a sort of feeble summing-up. *Lourdes* (1894), dealing with faith-healing, is hardly a novel, any more than is *Rome* (1896), a critical study of the Papal Curia, or *Paris* (1898). *Fécondité* (1899), *Travail* (1901), and *Vérité* (1903) form part of 'Les Quatre Évangiles'. Zola espoused the cause of Dreyfus (q.v.), impeached the military authorities, and was sentenced to imprisonment (1898), but escaped for a year to England. He died in Paris, accidentally suffocated by charcoal fumes. See his *Correspondance* (1907–08), works by Sherard (1893), Vizetelly (1904), Josephson (1928), Barbusse (trans. 1932), and (in French) Lepelletier (1908), Seillière (1923), D. Le Blond-Zola (his daughter; 1931), Hemmings (1953) and Laroux (1955).

ZORN, Anders Leonhard (1860–1920), Swedish etcher, sculptor and painter, born at Utmeland, near Mora. His bronze statue of Gustavus Vasa is in his native town of Mora. His paintings deal mainly with Swedish peasant life. He achieved European fame as an etcher, with studies of Verlaine, Proust, Rodin, &c., and a series of nudes executed with unique skill. See a monograph by E. M. Lang (1924).

ZOROASTER, Grecized form of **Zarathushtra**, mod. **Zaradusht**, Iranian prophet, the founder or reformer of the ancient Parsee religion, appears as an historical person only in the earliest portion of the Avesta. His family name was Spitama. As the centre of a group of chieftains, one of whom was King Vîshtâspa, he carried on a political, military, and theological struggle for the defence or wider establishment of a holy agricultural state against Turanian and Vedic aggressors. He lived in N.W. Persia perhaps in the 6th century B.C. Some put him as early as *c.* 1000 B.C. The keynote of his system is that the world and history exhibit the struggle between Ormuzd and Ahriman (the creator or good spirit, and the evil principle, the devil), in which at the end evil will be banished and the good reign supreme. See studies by Jackson (1898), Dhalla (1938), Herzfeld (1947) and Guillemin (1949).

ZORRILLA Y MORAL, José (1817–93), a fluent Spanish poet, born at Valladolid, wrote many plays based on national legend. He died poor in Madrid, but his play *Don Juan Tenorio* (1844) is performed annually on All Saints' Day in Spanish-speaking countries.

ZOSIMUS, (1) (5th cent. A.D.), a pagan Greek historian, who held office at Constantinople under Theodosius II (408–450). His *Historia Nova* deals with the Roman emperors to A.D. 410.

(2) Pope (417–418), involved in the Pelagian controversy. See PELAGIUS.

ZSCHOKKE, Johann Heinrich Daniel, *chok'e* (1771–1848), German writer, born at Magdeburg, was a strolling playwright, then a student at Frankfurt, lectured there and adapted plays, and finally opened a boarding-school at Reichenau in the Grisons. In 1799 he settled at Aarau, where he became a member of the Great Council. His books include histories of Bavaria and Switzerland, and a long series of tales—*Der Creole*, *Jonathan Frock*, *Clementine*, *Oswald*, *Meister Jordan*, &c. The most popular of all was the *Stunden der Andacht* (1809–16; trans. as *Hours of Meditation*, 1843)—a Sunday periodical, expounding rationalism with eloquence and zeal. His collected writings fill 35 vols. (1851–54). See his autobiographical *Selbstschau* (trans. 1847).

ZSIGMONDY, Richard Adolf, *zhig'mon-di* (1865–1929), Austrian chemist, born in Vienna, from 1907 a professor at Göttingen, was a pioneer of colloid chemistry, gaining the Nobel prize for 1925. In 1903 he introduced the ultramicroscope.

ZUCCARO, Taddeo, *tsook'ka-rō* (1529–66), Italian painter in Rome, born at S. Angelo in Vado, near Urbino, left some pretentious but not valuable frescoes and easel pieces of no especial merit. He did much work for the Farnese family, and examples may be seen in the Palazzo Farnese, Rome and Caparola. His brother, **Federigo** (1543–1609), during his travels painted portraits (Queen Elizabeth, Mary Stuart, &c.), but devoted most of his time to unsatisfactory frescoes at Florence, Venice, the Escorial, &c. He founded at Rome the Academy of St Luke (1595).

ZUCCHI, Antonio Pietro, *tsook'kee* (1726–95), Italian painter, was brought to England in about 1766 by the Adam brothers (q.v.), for whom he executed many excellent ceiling medallions and wall paintings (Kenwood, Harewood House, Osterley Park, &c.). Also working for the brothers was Angelica Kauffmann (q.v.), whom he married in 1781. He was elected an A.R.A. in 1770.

ZUCKMAYER, Carl (1896–), German dramatist, born at Nackenheim, Rhineland, lived in Austria, but after that country's annexation, emigrated to the U.S.A. His best-known plays are *Der Hauptmann von Köpenick* (1931) and *Des Teufels General* (1942–45), both filmed.

ZUKERTORT, Johann Hermann (1842–88), Polish chess master, born at Lublin, studied medicine at Breslau, but from 1867 devoted himself to chess. Settling in England in 1872, he founded and edited the *Chess Monthly*, won tournaments in Paris and London, was defeated by Steinitz in America in 1885, and died in London. He published two German chess manuals (1869–73).

ZULOAGA, Ignacio, *thoo-lo-ah'ga* (1870–1945), Spanish painter, born, the son of a metalworker, at Eibar in the Basque country, studied painting at Rome and Paris, and won recognition abroad and then at home as the reviver of the national tradition in Spanish painting. Works may be seen in the Luxembourg, Paris, and in galleries at Ghent and Leipzig.

ZUMALACÁRREGUY, Tomás, *thoo-mah-la-kar'ray-gee* (1788–1835), greatest of Spanish Carlist generals, was born at Ormáiztegui in the Basque province of Guipúzcoa. He fought against Napoleon, on the re-establishment of absolutism was made governor of Ferrol, but in 1832, with other Carlists, was dismissed the army. Head of the Basque Carlist insurrection (1833), he kept his opponents at bay, and gained a series of victories over the Cristino generals. This turned the weak head of Don Carlos, and led him to interfere with the plans of his general, who was anxious to strike for Madrid, but who, ordered to lay siege to Bilbao, was mortally wounded by a musketball. See Henningsen's *Twelve Months' Campaign* (1836) and *Cornhill* for January 1871.

ZÚÑIGA. See ERCILLA Y ZÚÑIGA.

ŽUPANČIĆ, Oton, *zhoo'pan-chit-y'* (1878–1949), Slovene poet, the translator of Shakespeare into Slovene.

ZURBARÁN, Francisco, *thoor-ba-rahn'* (1598–1662), Spanish religious painter, born at Fuente de Cantos in Andalusia, the son of a labourer, spent most of his laborious life at Seville. His masterpiece, an altarpiece, is in the museum there. Apart from a few portraits and still-life studies, his main subjects were monastic and historical, and he came to be called the ' Spanish Caravaggio '.

ZWEIG, *tsvīg*, (1) **Arnold** (1887–1968), German-Jewish author, was born at Glogau. His writing is socialistic in outlook and is also coloured by the interest in Zionism which led him to seek refuge in Palestine when exiled by the Nazis in 1934. His works include the novels *Claudia* (1912), *Der Streit um den Sergeanten Grischa* (1928), *Junge Frau von 1914* (1931) and *De Vriendt kehrt heim* (1932), all of which have appeared in English translation; also the play *Die Umkehr* (1927) and some penetrating essays.

(2) **Stefan** (1881–1942), Austrian writer, born in Vienna of Jewish parentage, was first known as poet and translator (of Ben Jonson, &c.), then as biographer (Balzac, Dickens, Marie Antoinette, &c.), short-story writer (e.g., *Kaleidoscope*, 1934) and novelist (*Beware of Pity*, 1939, &c.). A feature of all his work is its deep psychological insight. From 1934 to 1940 he lived in London, and acquired British nationality. He later went to U.S.A. and Brazil. It was in Petropolis, Brazil, that he died by his own hand in 1942. See his autobiographical *The World of Yesterday* (published posthumously, 1943).

ZWICKY, Fritz (1898–), American physicist, born in Bulgaria, educated at Zürich, joined the staff of the California Institute of Technology in 1927, becoming professor of Astrophysics there in 1942. He is known for his research on novae, cosmic rays and slow electrons.

ZWINGLI, Huldreich, *tsving'lee*, **Lat. Ulricus Zuinglius** (1484–1531), Swiss reformer, was born at Wildhaus in St Gall, studied at Bern, Vienna and Basel, and became priest at Glarus in 1506. Here he taught himself Greek, and twice (1513, 1515) as field-chaplain accompanied the Glarus mercenaries. Transferred in 1516 to Einsiedeln, whose Black Virgin was a great resort of pilgrims, he made no secret of his contempt for such superstition. In 1518 elected preacher in the Zürich minster, he roused the council not to admit within the city gates Bernhardin Samson, a seller of indulgences.

He preached the gospel boldly, and in 1521 succeeded in keeping Zürich from joining the other cantons in their alliance with France. The Bishop of Constance sent his vicar-general, who was quickly silenced in debate with Zwingli (1523), in presence of the council and six hundred; whereupon the city adopted the Reformed doctrines as set forth in Zwingli's sixty-seven theses. A second disputation followed (1523), with the result that images and the mass were swept away. Zwingli married Anna Meyer (*née* Reinhard), a widow of forty-three, in 1524; on Easter Sunday 1525 he dispensed the sacrament in both kinds; and the Reformation spread widely over Switzerland. Zwingli first made public his views on the Lord's Supper in 1524; and the first stage of the controversy with Luther, destined to rend the Protestant Church, closed with the fruitless conference at Marburg (1529). He rejected every form of local or corporeal presence, whether by transubstantiation or consubstantiation. Meantime the progress of the Reformation had aroused bitter hatred in the Forest Cantons. Five of them formed in 1528 an alliance, to which the Archduke Ferdinand of Austria was admitted. Zürich declared war in 1529 on account of the burning alive of a Protestant pastor seized on neutral territory, but bloodshed was averted for a time by the first treaty of Cappel (1529). But the Forest Cantons made a sudden dash on Zürich with 8000 men, and were met at Cappel by 2000, including Zwingli. The men of Zürich made a desperate resistance, but were completely defeated, and Zwingli was among the dead. Zwingli preached substantially the Reformed doctrines as early as 1516, the year before the appearance of Luther's theses. Original sin he regarded as a moral disease rather than as punishable sin or guilt. He maintained the salvation of unbaptized infants, and he believed in the salvation of such virtuous heathens as Socrates, Plato, Pindar, Numa, Scipio and Seneca. On predestination he was as Calvinistic as Calvin or Augustine. With less of fire and power than Luther, he was the most open-minded and liberal of the Reformers. Zwingli's *Opera* fill four folios (1545); later editions are by Schuler and Schulthess (1828–42; supp. 1861); Egli and others (1905 *et seq.*). The chief is the *Commentarius de vera et falsa religione* (1525); the rest are mainly occupied with the exposition of Scripture and controversies on the Eucharist, &c. There are old Lives by Myconius and Bullinger; later studies by Finsler (1897; a bibliography), and Farner (1952). See also numerous works by Köhler, and publications of the Zwingli Society.

ZWORYKIN, Vladimir Kosma (1889–), Russian-born physicist, educated at Petrograd Technical Institute and the University of Pittsburgh, took U.S. nationality in 1924, joined the Radio Corporation in 1929, in 1934 was appointed director of electronic research, and in 1947 vice-president and technical consultant. Known for his work in the fields of photoelectricity and television, he invented the iconoscope and was a pioneer in the development of the electron microscope.

SUBJECT INDEX

Entries refer to the relevant articles. Self-explanatory and relatively obscure or insignificant titles and subjects have not been included.

ART AND ARCHITECTURE

CINEMA

EXPLORATION AND GEOGRAPHY

HISTORY

LITERATURE AND DRAMA

Black Mischief → Waugh (3)
Black Obelisk, The → Remarque
Black Swan, The → Brown (18)
Black Tulip, The → Dumas (1)
Bleak House → Dickens
Blessed Damozel, The → Rossetti (2)
Blind Beggar of Bethnal Green, The → Dodsley
Bliss → Mansfield
Blithe Spirit → Coward
Blocus, Le → Erckmann-Chatrian
Blood and Sand → Ibáñez
Bloomsbury Circle → Bell (5), Forster (1), Fry (2), Keynes, Moore (6), Woolf (1) and (2)
Blue Lagoon, The → Stacpoole
Boat, The → Hartley (2)
Bold Stroke for a Wife, A → Centlivre
Bon Gaultier Ballads → Aytoun
Bones → Wallace (3)
Bonjour Tristesse → Sagan
Book of Nonsense → Lear
Book of the Duchess → Chaucer
Book of Thel → Blake (3)
Boris Godunov → Pushkin
Borough, The → Crabbe
Borstal Boy → Behan
Bosnian Story → Andrić
Bostonians, The → James (4)
Boule de suif → Maupassant
Bourgeois Gentilhomme, Le → Molière
Bouvard et Pecuchet → Flaubert
Box and Cox → Morton (4)
Boxiana → Egan (2)
Boy stood on the burning deck, The → Hemans
Boy with a Cart, The → Fry (2)
Boy's Will, A → Frost (2)
Bracebridge Hall → Irving (3)
Braes of Yarrow, The → Hamilton (14) Logan (2)
Bragelonne → Dumas (1)
Brand → Ibsen
Brave New World → Huxley (1)
Breakfast at Tiffany's → Capote
Bridal Canopy → Agnon
Bride of Corinth → Byron
Bride of Lammermoor → Scott (26)
Brideshead Revisited → Waugh (3)
Bridge of San Luis Rey, The → Wilder
Bridge of Sighs → Hood (5)
Bridge on the Drina, The → Andrić
Brief Encounter → Coward
Brigadier Gerard → Doyle (1)
Bright Shawl The → Hergesheimer
Brighton Rock → Greene (1)
Britannia → Camden (2)
Britannia's Pastorals → Browne (11)
Broad Highway, The → Farnol
Brod und Wein → Hölderlin
Brook Evans → Glaspell
Brook Kerith, The → Moore (5)
Brothers, The → Strong
Brothers Karamazov, The → Dostoevsky
Brown Decades, The → Mumford
Brown Jug, The → Fawkes (1)
Browning Version, The → Rattigan
Brus, The → Barbour
Brut → Layamon Wace
Buddenbrooks → Mann (4)
Burgraves, Les → Hugo
Burial of Sir John Moore → Wolfe (1)
Burlader de Sevilla → Tirso de Molina
Burning Glass, The → Morgan (2)
Bush Ballads and Galloping Rhymes → Gordon (1)
Bussy d'Ambois → Chapman (1)
Busybody, The → Centlivre
By Love Possessed → Cozzens

Cabala, The → Wilder
Cabbages and Kings → Henry (3
Cabin, The → Ibáñez
Cadenus and Vanessa → Swift
Caesar and Cleopatra → Shaw (1)
Cahier Rouge, Le → Coppée
Cakes and Ale → Maugham
Caligula → Camus
Call of the Wild, The → London
Caller Herrin' → Nairne
Calligrammes → Apollinaire
Cambyses → Settle
Camilla → Burney (2)
Candida → Shaw (1)
Candide → Voltaire
Cannery Row → Steinbeck
Canterbury Tales → Chaucer
Captain Brassbound's Conversion → Shaw (1)
Captain Kettle stories → Hyne
Captain Singleton → Defoe
Card, The → Bennett (1)
Caretaker, The → Pinter
Carnival → Mackenzie (4)
Carthusian, The → Eötvös
Casa Guidi Windows → Browning (1)
Cass Timberlane → Lewis (7)
Caste → Robertson (7)
Castle, The → Kafka
Castle of Indolence, The → Thomson (5)
Castle of Otranto → Walpole (1)
Castle Rackrent → Edgeworth (3)
Catcher in the Rye → Salinger
Cathedral, The → Walpole (2)
Catilina → Crébillon (2)
Cat on a Hot Tin Roof → Williams (8)
Catriona → Stevenson (3)
Causeries du lundi → Sainte-Beuve
Cautionary Tales → Belloc
Cavalcade → Coward
Cave, The → Warren (3)
Celtic Twilight, The → Yeats (2)
Cenci, The → Shelley (2)
Chairs, The → Ionesco
Chance → Conrad
Chandos Letters → Hofmannsthal
Changeling, The → Middleton (3)
Chansons des rues et des bois, Les → Hugo
Chants du crépuscule → Hugo
Charivari → Jasmin
Charles O'Malley → Lever (1)
Charley's Aunt → Thomas (5)
Charlie Chan detective novels → Biggers
Charmed Circle → Ertz
Chartreuse de Parme, La → Stendhal
Châtiments, Les → Hugo
Chatte, La → Colette
Chatterton → Vigny
Chéri → Colette
Chérie → Goncourt
Cherrie and the Slae, The → Montgomerie (2)
Cherry Orchard, The → Chehov
Cherry Ripe → Herrick
Chicken Soup with Barley → Wesker
Childe Harold's Pilgrimage → Byron
Childermass, The → Lewis (8)
Children of the Ghetto → Zangwill
Child's Garden of Verse, A → Stevenson (3)
Chips with Everything → Wesker
Choir Invisible, The → Allen (5)
Christabel → Coleridge (3)
Christian Hero, The → Steele
Christmas Carol, A → Dickens
Chronicles of Clovis → Munro (2)
Chu Chin Chow → Asche
Chute d'un ange, La → Lamartine
Cid, Le → Corneille (1)
Cimetière marin, Le → Valéry
Cinq Mars → Vigny
Citadel, The → Cronin
Città morta, La → D'Annunzio
City of Dreadful Night, The → Thomson (7)
Civilisation → Duhamel
Clandestine Marriage, The → Colman (1)
Clarissa → Richardson (10)
Claude Gueux → Hugo
Claudia → Zweig (1)
Claudius the God → Graves (3)
Clayhanger series → Bennett (1)
Clélie → Scudéry (2)
Cléopatre captive → Jodelle
Clerihew → Bentley (1)
Clochemerle → Chevallier
Clockmaker, The → Haliburton (2)
Cloister and the Hearth, The → Reade

MADAME GERVAISAIS → Concourt
MADEMOISELLE DE MAUPIN → Gautier
MADRAS HOUSE, THE → Granville-Barker
MADWOMAN OF CHAILLOT, THE → Giraudoux
MAGIC MOUNTAIN, THE → Mann (4)
MAGNETIC MOUNTAIN, THE → Day-Lewis
MAGNOLIA STREET → Golding (1)
MAGNUS MERRIMAN → Linklater
MAID SILJA, THE → Sillanpää
MAID'S TRAGEDY, THE → Beaumont (2), Fletcher (3)
MAIGRET STORIES → Simenon
MAIN STREET → Lewis (7)
MAJOR BARBARA → Shaw (1)
MAKAMAT → Hariri
MALADE IMAGINAIRE, LE → Molière
MALCONTENT THE → Marston (1)
MALENTENDU, LE → Camus
MALTESE FALCON, THE → Hammett
MAN AGAINST THE SKY, THE → Robinson (3)
MAN AND SUPERMAN → Shaw (1)
MAN BORN TO BE KING, THE → Sayers (1)
MAN IN DRESS CLOTHES, THE → Hicks (1)
MAN IN GREY → Smith (8)
MAN IN THE MOON → Godwin (1)
MAN IN THE ZOO, A → Garnett (1)
MAN OF MODE, OR SIR FOPLING FLUTTER → Etherege
MAN OF PROPERTY, THE → Galsworthy
MAN WHO CAME TO DINNER, THE → Kaufman
MAN WITH THE BLUE GUITAR → Stevens (4)
MANCHESTER GUARDIAN → Taylor (10)
MANDARINS, LES → De Beauvoir
MANON LESCAUT → Prévost (1)
MANSFIELD PARK → Austen
MANY CARGOES → Jacobs (2)
MANY INVENTIONS → Kipling
MANYOSHU → Akahito
MARCHING SONG → Whiting
MARE AU DIABLE, LA → Sand
MARÉCHALE D'ANCRE, LA → Vigny
MARGARET CATCHPOLE → Cobbold
MARIA STUART → Schiller (2)
MARIAGE DE FIGARO, LE → Beaumarchais
MARIAGE DE GÉRARD, LE → Theuriet
MARIE CLAIRE → Audoux
MARIE TUDOR → Hugo
MARION DELORME → Hugo
MARIUS THE EPICUREAN → Pater (2)
MARMION → Scott (26)
MARRIAGE OF HARLEQUIN, THE → Frankau (2)
MARRIAGE OF HEAVEN AND HELL, THE → Blake (3)
MARTIAN, THE → Du Maurier (1)
MARTIN ARROWSMITH → Lewis (7)
MARTIN CHUZZLEWIT → Dickens
MARTIN FIERRO → Hernández
MARY BARTON → Gaskell
MARY HAD A LITTLE LAMB → Hale (5)
MARY ROSE → Barrie
MARY STUART → Drinkwater (2)
MASCHERA E IL VOLTA, LA → Chiarelli
MASTER-BUILDER, THE → Ibsen
MASTER OF BALLANTRAE, THE → Stevenson (3)
MÄSTER OLAF → Strindberg
MASTERMAN READY → Marryat
MASTERS, THE → Snow
MATCHMAKER, THE → Wilder
MATEO FALCONE → Mérimée
MAUD → Tennyson
MAX CARRADOS → Bramah (1)
MAYOR OF CASTERBRIDGE, THE → Hardy (5)
MEASURE FOR MEASURE → Shakespeare
MEDAL, THE → Dryden
MEDAL OF JOHN BAYES → Shadwell
MEDEA → Euripides
MÉDECIN MALGRÉ LUI, LE → Molière
MEEK HERITAGE → Sillanpää
MEMBER OF THE WEDDING, THE → McCullers
MÉMOIRES D'OUTRE-TOMBE → Chateaubriand
MEMOIRS OF A FOX-HUNTING MAN → Sassoon
MEMOIRS OF A MIDGET → De La Mare
MEMOIRS OF AN INFANTRY OFFICER → Sassoon
MEMOIRS OF MARTINUS SCRIBLERUS → Arbuthnot
MEMORY HOLD-THE-DOOR → Buchan (3)
MENDIANT, LE → Chénier
MENTEUR, LE → Corneille (1)
MERCHANT OF VENICE, THE → Shakespeare
MERLIN → Geoffrey of Monmouth
MERRY MUSE, THE → Linklater
MERRY WIVES OF WINDSOR, THE → Shakespeare
METAMORPHOSES → Ovid
MIDDLEMARCH → Eliot (2)
MIDSUMMER NIGHT'S DREAM, A → Shakespeare
MILESTONES → Bennett (1)
MILL ON THE FLOSS, THE → Eliot (2)
MINNA VON BARNHELM → Lessing
MINT, THE → Lawrence (7)
MIROIR DE MARIAGE → Deschamps
MISANTHROPE, LE → Molière
MISÉRABLES, LES → Hugo
MISS JULIE → Strindberg
MISS MARPLE DETECTIVE STORIES → Christie (2)
MISS MOLE → Young (8)
MISS SARA SAMPSON → Lessing
MISTER JOHNSON → Cary (2)
MOBY DICK → Melville (4)
MODERN PAINTERS → Ruskin
MOLL FLANDERS → Defoe
MOLLUSC, THE → Davies (4)
MON FRÈRE YVES → Viaud
MONASTERY, THE → Scott (26)
MONK OF FIFE, THE → Lang (1)
MONKEY'S PAW, THE → Jacobs (2)
MONSIEUR ALPHONSE → Dumas (2)
MONSIEUR BEAUCAIRE → Tarkington
MONSIEUR LECOQ → Gaboriau
MONTE CRISTO → Dumas (1)
MOON AND SIXPENCE, THE → Maugham
MOON IS DOWN, THE → Steinbeck
MOONRAKER → Jesse (2)
MOONSTONE, THE → Collins (8)
MORGUE → Benn (2)
MORT DE POMPÉE, LA → Corneille (2)
MORTE D'ARTHUR → Malory
MOTHER AND SON → Compton-Burnett
MOTHER INDIA → Mayo (2)
MOTTKE THE THIEF → Asch
MOUCHES, LES → Sartre
MOUNTAIN BARD, THE → Hogg (1)
MOURNING BECOMES ELECTRA → O'Neill (1)
MOUSETRAP, THE → Christie (2)
MR BOLFRY → Bridie
MR MIDSHIPMAN EASY → Marryat
MR NORRIS CHANGES TRAINS → Isherwood
MR PERRIN AND MR TRAILL → Walpole (2)
MR PIM PASSES BY → Milne (1)
MR WESTON'S GOOD WINE → Powys (3)
MRS CAUDLE'S CURTAIN LECTURES → Jerrold
MRS DALLOWAY → Woolf (2)
MRS MINIVER → Struther
MRS WARREN'S PROFESSION → Shaw (1)
MS FOUND IN A BOTTLE → Poe
MUCH ADO ABOUT NOTHING → Shakespeare
MULBERRY BUSH, THE → Knoblock
MÜNCHHAUSEN → Immermann
MUR, LE → Sartre
MURDER IN THE CATHEDRAL → Eliot (6)
MURDERS IN THE RUE MORGUE → Poe
MY BROTHER JONATHAN → Young (9)
MY COUSIN RACHEL → Du Maurier (3)
MY FAMILY AND OTHER ANIMALS → See under DURRELL
MY LIFE AND HARD TIMES → Thurber
MY MIND TO ME A KINGDOM IS → Dyer (1)
MY SON, MY SON → Spring
MYSTÈRES DE PARIS, LES → Sue
MYSTERIES OF UDOLPHO, THE → Radcliffe (1)
MYSTERY OF EDWIN DROOD, THE → Dickens
MYSTERY OF A HANSOM CAB, THE → Hume (4)

NANA → Zola
NAPOLÉON LE PETIT → Hugo
NAPOLEON OF NOTTING HILL, THE → Chesterton
NATURAL HISTORY OF SELBORNE → White (3)
NATURALISM → Daudet (1), Flaubert, Goncourt Turgenev, Zola
NEEDY KNIFE-GRINDER, THE → Frere (2)
NEVEU DE RAMEAU, LE → Diderot
NEW ARABIAN NIGHTS → Stevenson (3)
NEW BATS IN OLD BELFRIES → Betjeman
NEW GRUB STREET → Gissing
NEW WAY TO PAY OLD DEBTS, A → Massinger

MUSIC

Swan of Tuonela → Sibelius
Swanee river → Foster (5)
Symphonie cévenole → Indy
Symphonie fantastique → Berlioz
Symphony of Psalms → Stravinsky

Tales from the Vienna Woods → Strauss (3)
Tales of Hoffmann → Barbier (2), Offenbach
Tancredi → Rossini
Tannhäuser → Wagner (3)
Testament of Freedom → Thompson (11)
Thaïs → Massenet
These Things Shall be → Ireland (2)
Thieving Magpie, The (La Gazza Ladra) → Rossini
Three Bears → Coates (1)
Three-cornered Hat → Falla
Three Elizabeths, The → Coates (1)
Threepenny Opera → Weill
Thunderbolt P. 47 → Martinu
Tintagel → Bax
Tom Bowling → Dibdin (1)
Tom Jones → German
Tombeau de Couperin → Ravel
Tonic Solfa → Curwen, Guido d'Arezzo
Tosca → Giacosa, Puccini, Sardou
Tower of Voivod, The → Dohnanyi
Tragic Overture → Brahms
Traviata, La → Verdi
Trial by Jury → Sullivan (1)
Tristan und Isolde → Wagner (3)
Triumphes of Oriana, The → Morley (5)
Trout quintet → Schubert (2)
Trovatore, Il → Verdi
Troyens, Les → Berlioz
Trumpet Voluntary → Clarke (9)
Turandot → Puccini
Turn of the Screw, The → Britten
Twelve-tone system → Schönberg, Searle (1), Webern

Ulysses → Seiber
Under the Greenwood Tree → Arne
Unfinished Symphony → Schubert (2)

Variations on a Nursery Theme → Dohnanyi
Variations on a Theme of Haydn → Brahms
Venus and Adonis → Blow
Verklärte Nacht → Schönberg
Vestale, La → Spontini
Vida Breve, La → Falla
Village Romeo and Juliet, A → Delius (1)
Vingt Regards sur l'enfant Jésus → Messiaen
Voices by Night → Reizenstein
Voices of Spring → Strauss (3)

Wae's me for Prince Charlie → Glen
Walküre, Die → Wagner (3)
Waltz Dream → Straus
Waltzing Matilda → Paterson (1)
Wanderer fantasy → Schubert (2)
Wandern Das → Schubert (2)
Wat Tyler → Bush
Water-Carrier, The → Cherubini
Water Music → Handel
Well-tempered Clavier, The → Bach (4)
Welsh Rhapsody → German
Werther → Massenet
West Side Story → Bernstein (3)
When I Survey the Wondrous Cross → Watts (4)
Who is Sylvia? → Schubert (2)
Wien Neerlandsch Bloed → Tollens
Winterreise → Schubert (2)
Woodland sketches → Macdowell
Wozzeck → Berg, Büchner (1)
Wreckers, The → Smyth

Yattendon Hymnal → Bridges
Ye Mariners of England → Campbell (15)
Yeoman of the Guard, The → Sullivan (1)
Young Person's Guide to the Orchestra, The → Britten

Zampa → Hérold
Zigeunerlieder → Brahms

NICKNAMES AND PERSONALITIES

Abyssinian, The → Bruce (3)
Aldiborontiphoscophornio → Ballantyne (1)
American Hogarth → Shahn
Angelic Doctor → Aquinas
Ape → Pellegrini
Apostate, The → Julian
Apostle of Free Trade → Cobden
Apostle of Germany → Boniface, St
Apostle of Greenland → Egede
Apostle of Ireland → Patrick, St
Apostle of the Alps → Bernard of Menthon, St
Apostle of the Franks → Remy, St
Apostle of the Gentiles → Paul
Apostle of the Indians → Las Casas
Apostle of the Indies → Francis (4)
Archdruid → Stukeley
Atticus → Addison (2)

Bab → Gilbert (10)
Baby-faced Breton → Portsmouth
Balafré, Le → Guise (4)
Bastard of Orleans → Dunois
Beauclerc → Henry I of England
Beauty of Holiness → Hurd
Belle Cordière, La → Labé
Bell-the-Cat → Douglas, 5th Ea of Angus
Beloved Physician → Luke (1)
Blind Jack of Knaresborough → Metcalf
Blind Traveller → Holman
Bloody Mary → Mary I
Bobbing Joan/John → Mar
Bomba → Ferdinand II
Bonny Prince Charlie → Stewart, House of (12)
Bossu d'Arras, Le → Halle
British Amazon → Talbot (1)
Brown Bomber → Louis

Cambridge Platonist → More (2)
Caro Sassone → Handel
Chagarlab → Háfiz
Christian Virgil → Vida
Citizen King → Louis-Philippe
Clarinda → Maclehose
Cocher de l'Europe, Le → Choiseul-Amboise
Copernicus of the Mind → Freud (3)
Corn Law Rhymer → Elliott (1)
Cornish Metaphysician → Drew (2)

Defender of the Faith → Henry VIII
Dighenis → Grivas
Dockers' K.C. → Bevin
Doctor Christianissimus → Gerson
Doctor Profundus → Bradwardine
Doctor Resolutissimus → Durandus (2)
Doctor Seraphicus → Bonaventura, St
Doctor Subtilis → Duns Scotus
Doctor Universalis → Albertus Magnus

Égalité → Orléans (4)
Éminence grise → Joseph
English Hippocrates → Sydenham (2)
English Hobbema → Nasmyth (3)
Enlightened Doctor → Lully (2)
Ettrick Shepherd → Hogg (1)
Euphuist → Lyly
Ever-memorable → Hales (2)

Fa Presto → Giordano
Fair Maid of Kent → Edward the Black Prince
Father Prout → Mahony
First Gentleman in Europe → George IV
First Grenadier of France → La Tour D'Auvergne
Formosan, The → Psalmanazar
French Fenimore Cooper → Aimard
Fulmen Galliae → Biron (3)

Gandhi of Sicily → Dolci (2)

GÉNÉRAL BAÏONETTE → Ghassé
GENERAL TOM THUMB → Stratton
GENTLEMAN JIM → Corbett
GERMAN LENIN → Ulbricht
GLOOMY DEAN → Inge
GOLDEN FARMER → Davis (8)
GRANDE MADEMOISELLE, LA → Montpensier
GREAT ELCHI → Stratford de Radcliffe
GREAT PROFILE, THE → Barrymore (2)
GREY EMINENCE → Joseph

HAMMER OF THE MONKS → Cromwell (3)
HAMMER OF THE SCOTS → Edward I
HERMIT OF WALDEN → Thoreau
HIGHLAND MARY → Burns (4)
HOMEROMASTIX → Zoilus
HONEST KING → Victor Emmanuel II
HOOSIER POET → Riley
HUCKSTER KING → Henry VII
HYAENA OF BRESCIA → Haynau

ILLUMINATOR, THE → Gregory, St
INDIAN APOSTLE → Eliot (4)
INSECTS' HOMER → Fabre (2)
IRON CHANCELLOR → Bismarck

JERSEY LILY → Langtry
JINGLING GEORDIE → Heriot
JUNIUS → Francis (3), Woodfall
JUPP → Goebbels

KINGMAKER → Warwick
KING OF ICELAND → Jörgensen (2)
KING OF PAINTERS AND PAINTER OF KINGS → Gérard (2)

LANDLORD OF NEW YORK → Astor (5)
LAST OF THE DANDIES → D'Orsay
LAUREATE OF THE SOUTH → Hayne
LAWGIVER OF PARNASSUS → Boileau
LETHINGTON → Maitland (2)
LIBERATOR → O'Connell
LITTLE SPANIARD → Ribera
LORD HAW-HAW → Joyce (2)
LUCERNA JURIS → Irnerius

MADAME CARWELL → Portsmouth
MAGUS OF THE NORTH → Hamann
MAID OF KENT → Barton (5)
MAIDS OF LLANGOLLEN → Butler (3), Ponsonby
MANN VOM RINN, DER → Speckbacher
'MARSHAL FORWARDS' → Blücher
MASTER OF FLÉMALLE → Campin
MASTER OF SENTENCES → Lombard
MASTER OF THE 'DEATH OF THE VIRGIN' → Cleve (3)
MAYPOLE → Schulenburg
MELLIFLUOUS DOCTOR → Bernard of Clairvaux, St
MILL-BOY OF THE SLASHES → Clay
MISANTHROPE OF ATHENS → Timon (1)
MOB'S HERO → Granby
MONSIEUR DE PARIS → Sanson
MORLEY, MRS → Anne
MORO, IL → Sforza (3)
MUSCOVY GENERAL → Dalyell
MUSE OF CUMBERLAND → Blamire

NESTOR OF GOLF → Morris (6)

OLD BULLION → Benton
OLD DREADNOUGHT → Boscawen
OLD GEORGE → Monk (1)
OLD GROG → Vernon (1)
OLD HICKORY → Jackson (1)
OLD PRETENDER → Stewart, House of (11)
OLD Q. → Queensberry (1)
ONZE JAN → Hofmeyr
ORACLE OF NUNEATON → Simpson (4)

PATER PATRIAE → Medici (1)
PEARL OF YORK → Clitherow
PERDITA → Robinson (10)
PÈRE DUCHESNE → Hébert
PESARESE, IL → Cantarini
PET MARJORIE → Fleming (4)
PHILOSOPHE INCONNU, LE → Saint-Martin
PLATONIST,THE → Taylor (14)
PLOTTER, THE → Ferguson (5)
POPE OF THE HUGUENOTS → Mornay
PORTUGUESE HORACE → Ferreira
PORTUGUESE PINDAR → Diniz da Cruz e Silva
PRIME MINISTER OF MIRTH → Robey
PRINCE OF INTERVIEWERS → Senior
PRINCES IN THE TOWER → Edward V
PRISONER OF CHILLON → Bonivard
PROPHET OF ROMANTICISM → Novalis
PUCK OF COMMENTATORS → Steevens

RED DEAN → Johnson (4)
RED PRIEST → Vivaldi
RED PRINCE → Frederick-Charles
RIGDUMFUNNIDOS → Ballantyne (1)
ROI DES RIMES → Banville
ROI SOLEIL, LE → Louis XIV
ROSCIUS → Burbage
ROYAL SAINT → Henry VI
RUPERT OF DEBATE → Derby (2)

SAGE DE LA GRANDE ARMÉE, LE → Drouot
SAGE OF CHELSEA → Carlyle (3)
SAILOR KING → William IV
SAIR SANCT FOR THE CROWN → David I
SASSONE, IL → Hasse
SATCHMO → Armstrong (6)
SCOTORUM MALLEUS → Edward I
SCOTT OF PAINTING → Gilbert (6)
SCOTTISH VAN DYCK → Jamesone
SCOURGE OF GOD → Attila
SILLOGRAPHER → Timon (2)
SILLY BILLY → Gloucester (11)
SOLDIER'S FRIEND → York
SPANISH CARAVAGGIO → Zurbarán
SPANISH HORACES → Argensola
STEENIE → Buckingham (1)
SWAN OF LICHFIELD → Seward (1)
SWEDISH NIGHTINGALE → Lind (2)
SWEET SINGER OF ISRAEL → David

THUNDERBOLT OF ITALY → Foix
TIGER → Clemenceau
TOOM TABARD → Baliol (2)
TOUCH DOCTOR → Greatrakes

VINEGAR JOE → Stilwell
VIRGIN QUEEN → Elizabeth I
VOICE OF NEW ENGLAND → Frost (2)

WATER-POET → Taylor (9)
WEEPING PHILOSOPHER → Heraclitus
WHITE KING → Charles I
WINTER KING → Frederick V
WINTER QUEEN → Elizabeth of Bohemia
WOLF OF BADENOCH → Stewart, House of (9)

YOUNG CHEVALIER → Stewart, House of (12)
YOUNG PRETENDER → Stewart, House of (12)
YOUNG ROSCIUS → Betty

ZINGARO, LO → Solario

PHILOSOPHY AND THEOLOGY

ACADEMY → Plato
ACHILLES AND THE TORTOISE → Zeno of Elea
ADVANCEMENT OF LEARNING, THE → Bacon (2)
ADVENTURES OF IDEAS → Whitehead (1)
AGNOSTICISM → Huxley (6), Spencer (2)
ANALYTICS, PRIOR AND POSTERIOR → Aristotle
ANOMOEANS → Eunomius
APPEARANCE AND REALITY → Bradley (3)
AUGUSTINUS → Jansen (1)
AURORA → Boehme

BANGORIAN CONTROVERSY → Hoadly

SCIENCE AND INDUSTRY

Star clusters → Herschel (2)
Static electricity → Gray (5)
Steamboat → Bell (9), Fitch (1), Fulton, Miller (5), Rumsey, Symington
——, turbine → Parsons (2)
Steam-carriage → Cugnot, Trevithick
Steam digester → Papin
Steam-engine → Newcomen, Watt (1), Worcester (1)
——, high pressure → Evans (8)
Steam hammer → Nasmyth (2)
Steam-jet → Gurney (1)
Steam locomotive → Stephenson (1), Trevithick
—— pile-driver → Nasmyth (2)
Steam-plough → Fowler (4)
Steam turbine → Laval (1), Parsons (2)
Stearin → Chevreul
Steel, manganese → Hadfield
——, rails → Brown (15)
——, silicon → Hadfield
——, smelting → Bessemer, Siemens
——, stainless → Hadfield, Haynes
Stereo-camera, single lens → Clark (4)
Stereophonic sound → Baird (2)
Stereoscope → Brewster, Lyons (2), Wheatstone
Stereotyping → Ged, Stanhope (2)
Sterols → Windaus
Stethoscope → Laënnec
Stratosphere → Piccard (2), Teisserenc de Bort
——, ionized layer → Heaviside
Streptomycin → Waksman
Strontium → Davy (1)
Strychnine → Caventou, Pelletier
Submachine gun → Thompson (9)
Submarine telegraphy → Crampton, Gooch (1)
Suez Canal → Lesseps
Sugar, beet → Achard, Marggraf
——, synthetic → Fischer (1)
Sulfapyridine → Ewins
Sulphanilamide → Domagk
Sulphuretted hydrogen → Scheele
Sun-and planet wheels → Watt (1)
Sun, dark spectrum lines → Fraunhofer
Sunspots → Fabricius (3), Galilei, Schwabe
Surveying chain → Gunter
Suture, surgical → Carrel

Tables, mathematical → Briggs, Napier (3), Regiomontanus, Rheticus
Tangents → Finck (2), Girard (1), Roberval
Tantalum → Ekeberg
Tartaric acid → Scheele
Tay Bridge → Bouch
Telegony → Ewart (1)
Telegraph key, double-current → Varley (2)
Telegraph typewriter → Hughes (2)
Telegraphy → Edison, Gray (3), Morse, Ronalds, Siemans (2), Wheatstone
Telepathy → Barrett (1), Rhine
Telephone → Bell (1)
Telephotography → Fournier D'Albe
Telescope, achromatic → Dollond, Hall (6)
——, reflecting → Amici, Foucault, Gregory (3), Herschel (2), Hooke
——, refracting → Galilei, Jansen (2)
Television → Baird, De Forest
Tellurium → Kitaibel, Klaproth (2), Müller (2)
Terpenes → Ružička
Tesla transformer → Elster, Geitel
Tetanus → Behring, Kitasato
Thallium → Crookes
Thames Tunnel → Brunel (1) and (2)
Thermite process → Goldschmidt (1)
Thermodynamics → Bridgman (3), Clausius, Hoff, Kelvin, Mayer, Nernst
Thermometer → Allbutt, Boulliau, Fahrenheit, Galilei, Réaumur
——, centigrade → Celsius
——, clinical → Sanctorius
——, differential → Leslie (5)
Thermopile → Nobili
Thermos flask → Dewar
Thiophene → Meyer (4)
Thorium → Berzelius
Thyroxine → Harington (1), Kendall
Titanium in ilmenite → Gregor
Tobacco mosaic virus → Stanley (7)
Toluene → Fahlberg
Torpedo → Whitehead (4)
Torsion balance → Boys, Coulomb, Michell
Tourniquet → Petit (2)
Transformer → Elster, Geitel, Stanley (8)
Transit instrument → Roemer
Treadmill → Cubitt (2)
Trigonometry → Albuzjani, Fourier (2), Girard (1), Gunter, Hipparchus, Vieta
Tropism → Sachs (2)
Tsetse fly → Bruce (2)
Tube, radio → De Forest, Fleming (3)
Tuberculosis → Calmette, Spahlinger
Tungsten → Scheele
Tuning fork → Koenig
Turbine → Thomson (6)
Typhus → Fleming (1), Jenner (2), Leishman, Nicolle
Tyrothricin → Du Bos (2)

Ultracentrifuge → Svedberg
Ultramicroscope → Zsigmondy
Ultraviolet rays → Ritter
Uranium → Klaproth (2), Rutherford (3)
Uranus → Herschel (2), Struve (2)
Urea, synthetic → Wöhler
U-tube → Sprengel (2)

Vaccination → Jenner (1)
Vacuum flask → Dewar
Vacuum pump → Sprengel (2)
Vacuum tube → Crookes
Valve, radar → Randall (2), Sayers (2)
——, Radio → De Forest, Fleming (3)
Vanadium → Del Rio, Roscoe (1), Sefström
Variable stars → Goodricke
Velocipede → Edgeworth (4)
Venus → Fontana (3)
Veronal → Fischer (1)
Veterinary school, first in Europe → Bourgelat
Virtual velocities → Galilei
Vitamins → Eijkman, Funk (1), Hopkins (2), Kuhn (2), Sherman (1)
——, A → Heilbron, Karrer, Mendel (2)
——, B → Karrer, Lipmann, Todd (1)
——, C → Haworth, Mendel (2), Szent-Györgyi
——, D → Heilbron, Windaus
——, E → Karrer, Todd (1)
——, H (biotin) → Vigeaud
——, K → Dam, Karrer
Volkswagen → Porsche
Vulcanized rubber → Goodyear

Water brake → Chatelier
Water-meter → Siemens (2)
Wave theory → Huygens, Schrödinger
Weather forecasting → Bjerknes, Henry (1)
Welder, electric → Thomson (2)
Welding → Goldschmidt (1)
Wheat → Biffen
Whooping cough → Bordet
Winds → Halley
Wireless telegraphy → Appleton (2), De Forest, Duddell, Heaviside, Lodge (3), Marconi, Popov, Rutherford (3)
Wolframite → Elhuyar

X-rays → Barkla, Compton (1), Moseley, Röntgen, Siegbahn, Stokes (1)
Xenon → Ramsay (8), Travers (2)
Xylonite → Parkes (1)

Yeast → Buchner (1)
Yellow fever → Carroll (1), Gorgas

Zinc and copper alloy → Pinchbeck (1)
Zirconium → Klaproth (2)
Zodiacal light → Cassini (3)

MISCELLANEOUS

CHAMBERS
biographical dictionary

Chambers
Paperback
Reference
Books

CHAMBERS

biographical dictionary

VOLUME TWO
Jewett–Zworykin

chambers
EDINBURGH

First published in *Chambers Paperback Reference Books* 1975

Edited by J. O. Thorne MA and T. C. Collocott MA

ISBN 0 550 18002 8 volume one
ISBN 0 550 18003 6 volume two

Printed in Great Britain by Hazell, Watson and Viney Ltd, Aylesbury, Bucks